Eastern Europe and the Commonwealth of Independent States 1994

Eastern Europe and the Commonwealth of Independent States 1994

SECOND EDITION

EUROPA PUBLICATIONS LIMITED

Second Edition 1994

18 Bedford Square, London, WC1B 3JN, England

Australia and New Zealand
James Bennett (Collaroy) Pty Ltd, 4 Collaroy Street, Collaroy, NSW 2097, Australia

Japan
Maruzen Co Ltd, POB 5050, Tokyo International 100-31

ISBN 0-946653-95-X
ISSN 0962-1040

Printed in England by
Staples Printers Rochester Limited
Neptune Close, Medway City Estate, Frindsbury, Rochester, Kent ME2 4LT.

Bound by Hartnolls Ltd,
Bodmin, Cornwall.

FOREWORD

The second edition of EASTERN EUROPE AND THE COMMONWEALTH OF INDEPENDENT STATES examines 27 countries in central and eastern Europe, the Caucasus and Central Asia. The region consists of what was the USSR (12 countries which are members of the Commonwealth of Independent States and the three Baltic republics) and the old Communist bloc of 'Eastern Europe'. The area continues to be defined more by its political experience than its geography. The countries of the region still remain distinct from a Western Europe which has so far made few concessions to the aspirations of the East to be included in a 'common European home'.

Thirty specialist writers have contributed to this comprehensive description and analysis of the countries of the region, placing them in their international and historical context. The extensively restructured introduction, Part One, consists of 12 essays providing a general background and assessment of a range of regional issues. There is also an essay on the former Soviet state and there are a number of general maps of the region.

In Part Two there are chapters on each of the 27 countries of the region. Only five of these countries existed in their current form before 1991. The potential for further fracturing remains. Thus, the section of the directory which covers local government in each country also embraces the 89 members of the Russian Federation (pp. 587–602) and the two constituent republics of the Federal Republic of Yugoslavia (pp. 748–54), as well as a number of polities with varying degrees of official recognition. The detailed, augmented and extensively updated statistical and directory sections also include information on major companies, other financial and business organizations, government and state institutions, religion, the media, environmental organizations and culture, to list but a few. These sections are preceded by information on the country, its people, its history, its politics and its economy: a geography and map is followed by a chronology and then two essays, one a political narrative, the other an examination of the economy. Each chapter concludes with a bibliography.

Part Three is an up-to-date Political Profiles section, expanded to include more than 200 biographical outlines of men and women prominent in the political life of the region.

The Editor is grateful to all the contributors for their articles and help and to the numerous governments and organizations which have returned questionnaires and provided statistical and other information.

April 1994

ACKNOWLEDGEMENTS

The editors gratefully acknowledge the co-operation, interest and advice of all the authors who contributed to this volume. We are also indebted to many organizations connected with the region, particularly the national statistical offices and the ministries of information, whose help is greatly appreciated. We are especially grateful to David Lewis and to a number of chambers of commerce and ministries of local government. In addition, we are grateful to Edward Oliver, who prepared the maps which are included in this volume.

We are most grateful for permission to make extensive use of material from the following sources: the United Nations' *Demographic Yearbook, Statistical Yearbook, Yearbook of Industrial Statistics* and *Yearbook of National Accounts Statistics*; the Food and Agriculture Organization of the UN's *Yearbook of Fishery Statistics, Production Yearbook* and *Yearbook of Forestry Products*; UNESCO's *Statistical Yearbook*; the International Monetary Fund's *International Financial Statistics* and *Supplement on Countries of the former Soviet Union*; and *The Military Balance, 1993–94*, published by the International Institute for Strategic Studies, 23 Tavistock Street, London WC2E 7NQ, United Kingdom.

The following publications have been of special use in providing regular coverage of the affairs of the region: *Summary of World Broadcasts: Part 1, Former USSR* and *Summary of World Broadcasts: Part 2, Eastern Europe*, from the BBC, Reading; and *RFE/RL Research Report*, from Radio Free Europe/Radio Liberty Research Institute, Oettingenstraße 67, W-8000 Munich 22, Germany. Notable among its many publications, the International Monetary Fund's *Economic Reviews* of the countries of the former USSR have been most helpful.

EXPLANATORY NOTE ON THE DIRECTORY SECTION

The Directory section of each chapter is arranged under the following headings, where they apply:

THE CONSTITUTION

THE GOVERNMENT
- HEAD OF STATE
- CABINET/COUNCIL OF MINISTERS
- MINISTRIES

LEGISLATURE

LOCAL GOVERNMENT

POLITICAL ORGANIZATIONS

DIPLOMATIC REPRESENTATION

JUDICIAL SYSTEM

RELIGION

THE PRESS

PUBLISHERS

RADIO AND TELEVISION

FINANCE
- CENTRAL BANK
- STATE BANKS
- DEVELOPMENT BANKS
- COMMERCIAL BANKS
- FOREIGN BANKS
- STOCK EXCHANGE
- INSURANCE

TRADE AND INDUSTRY
- PUBLIC CORPORATIONS
- CHAMBERS OF COMMERCE AND INDUSTRY
- COMMERCIAL AND INDUSTRIAL ORGANIZATIONS
- EMPLOYERS' ORGANIZATIONS
- TRADE UNIONS
- CO-OPERATIVES
- MAJOR INDUSTRIAL COMPANIES

TRANSPORT
- RAILWAYS
- ROADS
- INLAND WATERWAYS
- SHIPPING
- CIVIL AVIATION

TOURISM

CULTURE
- NATIONAL ORGANIZATIONS
- CULTURAL HERITAGE
- SPORTING ORGANIZATIONS
- PERFORMING ARTS
- ASSOCIATIONS

EDUCATION
- UNIVERSITIES

SOCIAL WELFARE
- NATIONAL AGENCIES
- HEALTH AND WELFARE ORGANIZATIONS

ENVIRONMENT
- GOVERNMENT ORGANIZATIONS
- ACADEMIC INSTITUTIONS
- NON-GOVERNMENTAL ORGANIZATIONS
- REGIONAL ORGANIZATIONS

DEFENCE

CONTENTS

CONTENTS

List of Maps

THE CONTRIBUTORS

Shirin Akiner. School of Oriental and African Studies, University of London.

John B. Allcock. University of Bradford.

Richard Ross Berry. University of Glasgow.

Rev. Canon Michael Bourdeaux. Keston College.

Cathie Carmichael. Middlesex University.

Richard J. Crampton. Professor at St Edmund Hall, University of Oxford.

Bob Deacon. Leeds Metropolitan University.

David Dyker. University of Sussex.

Jonathan Eyal. Director of Studies at Royal United Services Institute.

Tom Gallagher. University of Bradford.

Kestutis Girnius. Radio Free Europe/Radio Liberty.

Philip Hanson. Professor at University of Birmingham.

Raymond Hutchings. Freelance writer.

Adam Jolly. Eastern European Initiative, Confederation of British Industry.

Charles King. New College, University of Oxford.

Margot Light. London School of Economics, University of London.

David Norris. University of Nottingham.

Martyn Rady. University of London.

Angus Roxburgh. Journalist and broadcaster.

Peter Rutland. Professor at Wesleyan University, Connecticut, USA.

Andrew Ryder. University of Portsmouth.

Michael Sheehan. University of Aberdeen.

Alan Smith. University of London.

Keith Sword. University of London.

Marcus Tanner. Journalist.

Miranda Vickers. Freelance writer.

Rachel Walker. University of Essex.

Gordon Wightman. University of Liverpool.

Andrew Wilson. London School of Economics, University of London.

John Wright. School of Oriental and African Studies, University of London.

ABBREVIATIONS

Acad.	Academician; Academy
Adm.	Admiral
admin.	administration
a.i.	ad interim
AID	(US) Agency for International Development
AIDS	Acquired Immunodeficiency Syndrome
Al.	Aleja (Alley, Avenue)
Alt.	Alternate
AM	Amplitude Modulation
amalg.	amalgamated
AO	Autonomous Oblast
AOk	Autonomous Okrug
approx.	approximately
ASEAN	Association of South East Asian Nations
asscn	association
assoc.	associate
ASSR	Autonomous Soviet Socialist Republic
asst	assistant
Aug.	August
auth.	authorized
Ave	Avenue
b.	born
Bd	Board
Bd.	Bulevardi
b/d	barrels per day
Bldg	Building
br.(s)	branch(es)
Brig.	Brigadier
bul.	bulvar (boulevard)
C	Centigrade
c.	circa; child, children
cap.	capital
Capt.	Captain
Cdre	Commodore
CEI	Central European Initiative
Cen.	Central
CEO	Chief Executive Officer
CFE	Conventional Forces in Europe
Chair.	Chairman/woman
c.i.f.	cost, insurance and freight
CIS	Commonwealth of Independent States
C-in-C	Commander-in-Chief
circ.	circulation
cm	centimetre(s)
CMEA	Council for Mutual Economic Assistance
c/o	care of
Co	Company; County
Col	Colonel
Commdr	Commander
Commdt	Commandant
Commr	Commissioner
Corpn	Corporation
CP	Communist Party
CPSU	Communist Party of the Soviet Union
CSCE	Conference on Security and Co-operation in Europe
Cttee	Committee
cu	cubic
cwt	hundredweight
d.	daughter(s)
d.d.	dioničko društvo (Joint-Stock Company)
DDR	Deutsche Democratische Republik (German Democratic Republic)
Dec.	December
Dep.	Deputy
dep.	deposits
Dept	Department
devt	development
Dir	Director
DM	Deutsche Mark
Dr	Doctor
dwt	dead weight tons
E	East; Eastern
EBRD	European Bank for Reconstruction and Development
EC	European Communities
ECE	(United Nations) Economic Commission for Europe
ECO	Economic Co-operation Organization
Econ.	Economist; Economics
ECOSOC	(United Nations) Economic and Social Council
ECU	European Currency Unit
Ed.	Editor
edn	edition
EEC	European Economic Community
EFTA	European Free Trade Association
e.g.	exempli gratia (for example)
eKv	electron kilovolt
eMv	electron megavolt
Eng.	Engineer; Engineering
est.	established; estimate; estimated
et al.	et alii (and others)
etc.	etcetera
EU	European Union
excl.	excluding
exec.	executive
F	Fahrenheit
f.	founded
FAO	Food and Agriculture Organization
Feb.	February
FM	frequency modulation
fmrly	formerly
f.o.b.	free on board
Fr	Father
FRG	Federal Republic of Germany
Fri.	Friday
FRY	Federal Republic of Yugoslavia
ft	foot (feet)
g	gram(s)
GATT	General Agreement on Tariffs and Trade
GDP	gross domestic product
GDR	German Democratic Republic
Gen.	General
GNP	gross national product
Gov.	Governor
Govt	Government
grt	gross registered tons
GWh	gigawatt hours
ha	hectares
HE	His (or Her) Eminence; His (or Her) Excellency
hl	hectolitre(s)
HM	His (or Her) Majesty
Hon.	Honorary (or Honourable)
hp	horsepower
HQ	Headquarters
HRH	His (or Her) Royal Highness
IAEA	International Atomic Energy Agency
IBRD	International Bank for Reconstruction and Development (World Bank)
ICC	International Chamber of Commerce
ICFTU	International Confederation of Free Trade Unions
ICRC	International Committee of the Red Cross
IDA	International Development Association
i.e.	id est (that is to say)
ILO	International Labour Organisation/Office
IMF	International Monetary Fund
in (ins)	inch (inches)
Inc, Incorp., Incd	Incorporated
incl.	including
Ind.	Independent
INF	Intermediate-range Nuclear Forces
Ing.	Engineer
Insp.	Inspector
Int.	International
IRF	International Road Federation
irreg.	irregular
Is	Islands

IUCN	International Union for the Conservation of Nature and Natural Reserves
Jan.	January
JNA	Jugoslavenska Narodna Armïja (Yugoslav People's Army)
Jr	Junior
Jt	Joint
kg	kilogram(s)
kHz	kilohertz
km	kilometre(s)
kv.	kvartira (apartment)
kW	kilowatt(s)
kWh	kilowatt hours
lb	pound(s)
LCY	League of Communists of Yugoslavia
Lt, Lieut	Lieutenant
Ltd	Limited
m	metre(s)
m.	married; million
Maj.	Major
Man.	Manager; managing
mem.	member
MEV	mega electron volts
mfrs	manufacturers
Mgr	Monseigneur; Monsignor
MHz	megahertz
Mil.	Military
mm	millimetre(s)
Mon.	Monday
MP	Member of Parliament
MSS	Manuscripts
MW	megawatt(s); medium wave
MWh	megawatt hour(s)
N	North; Northern
n.a.	not available
nab.	naberezhnaya (embankment, quai)
nám.	náměští (square)
Nat.	National
NATO	North Atlantic Treaty Organisation
NCO	Non-Commissioned Officer
NMP	net material product
no.	number
Nov.	November
nr	near
nrt	net registered tons
Obl.	Oblast (region)
Oct.	October
OECD	Organisation for Economic Co-operation and Development
OIC	Organization of the Islamic Conference
Ok	okrug (district)
OPEC	Organization of Petroleum Exporting Countries
opp.	opposite
Org.	Organization
p.	page
p.a.	per annum
Parl.	Parliament(ary)
per.	pereulok (lane, alley)
Perm. Rep.	Permanent Representative
pl.	ploshchad (square)
PLC	Public Limited Company
PLO	Palestine Liberation Organization
POB	Post Office Box
pr.	prospekt, praspekt (avenue)
Pres.	President
Prin.	Principal
Prof.	Professor
Pte	Private
p.u.	paid up
publ.	publication; published
Publr	Publisher
q.v.	quod vide (to which refer)
Rd	Road
reg., regd	register; registered
reorg.	reorganized
res	reserve(s)
retd	retired
Rev.	Reverend
RSFSR	Russian Soviet Federative Socialist Republic
s.	son(s)
S	South; Southern; San
SAR	Serbian Autonomous Region
SDR(s)	Special Drawing Right(s)
Sec.	Secretary
Secr.	Secretariat
Sen.	Senior
Sept.	September
SFRY	Socialist Federal Republic of Yugoslavia
Soc.	Society
Sq.	Square
sq	square (in measurements)
SSR	Soviet Socialist Republic
St	Saint; Street
START	Strategic Arms' Reduction Treaty
Str.	Strada (street)
Sun.	Sunday
Supt	Superintendent
tech., techn.	technical
tel.	telephone
Thurs.	Thursday
Tř	třída (avenue)
Treas.	Treasurer
Tues.	Tuesday
TV	television
u.	utca (street)
u/a	unit of account
UK	United Kingdom
ul.	ulitsa, ulica (street)
UN	United Nations
UNCTAD	United Nations Conference on Trade and Development
UNDP	United Nations Development Programme
UNESCO	United Nations Educational, Scientific and Cultural Organization
UNHCR	United Nations High Commissioner for Refugees
Univ.	University
UNPA	United Nations Protected Area
UNPROFOR	United Nations Protection Force in Yugoslavia
USA	United States of America
USAID	United States Agency for International Development
USSR	Union of Soviet Socialist Republics
VAT	Value Added Tax
Ven.	Venerable
VHF	Very High Frequency
viz.	videlicet (namely)
vol.(s)	volume(s)
Vul.	vulitsa (street)
W	West; Western
WCL	World Confederation of Labour
Wed.	Wednesday
WFTU	World Federation of Trade Unions
WHO	World Health Organization
yr	year

LATE INFORMATION

ALBANIA (p. 124)

Government Change

On 17 January 1994 TRITAN SHEHU was replaced, by an independent:

Minister of Health and Environmental Protection: MAKSIM CIKULI.

AZERBAIJAN (pp. 157–8)

Government Changes
(April 1994)

On 12 January 1994 LALA SHOVKET HAJIYEVA was dismissed as Secretary of State and it was reported that the office might be abolished.

On 4 April the Supreme Majlis of Nakhichevan elected NATIG HASANOV as its Chairman.

BELARUS (p. 176)

On 26 January 1994 the Chairman of the Supreme Soivet (head of state), STANISLAU SHUSHKEVICH, was dismissed by parliament. On 28 January MYACHESLAU HRYB (Myachyslav Gryb) was elected by the Supreme Soviet as its new Chairman.

The Supreme Soviet adopted a new Constitution on 15 March 1994 and the Chairman of the Supreme Soviet signed it on 28 March. The Constitution provided for a democratic, presidential republic. Presidential elections were scheduled for 23 June 1994.

Government changes in February and April 1994 resulted in the following new appointments:

Deputy Chairman of the Council of Ministers and Minister of Finance: SIARHEY S. LINH (formerly the Chairman of the State Committee for the Economy and Planning).

Minister of Internal Affairs: ULADZIMIER ANTONAVICH DANKO.

Minister of Culture and the Press: ANATOLIY BUTEVICH (formerly Minister of Information).

Minister of Natural Resources and Environmental Protection: ANATOLIY M. DOROVEYEV (formerly Chairman of the State Committee for Ecology).

Chairman of the State Committee for Television and Radio: ALEKSANDR G. STOLYAROV.

BOSNIA AND HERZEGOVINA (pp. 191–2)

A Constituent Assembly, dominated by the Bosnian Muslim (Bosniak) and Croat deputies of the old Assembly of the Republic of Bosnia and Herzegovina, declared a Federation of Bosnia and Herzegovina on 31 March 1994. This followed an agreement signed in Washington, DC (USA). A new President and Governmment were to be elected by the Assembly in April.

As part of the internationally mediated peace process, the European Union (formerly known as the European Community) proposed a German politician and former mayor as the administrator of the city of Mostar in April 1994:

Administrator of Mostar: HANS KOSCHNICK (designate).

'Herzeg-Bosna'

On 8 February 1994 MATE BOBAN resigned as President of Herzeg-Bosna and an 11-member Presidential Council was elected to carry out his duties (as Herzeg-Bosna was a party to the creation of the Federation of Bosnia and Herzegovina, its separate state institutions were likely to cease functioning in April):

Presidential Council: KRESIMIR KUBAK (President), IVAN BENDER (also elected Chairman of the Chamber of Deputies), PERO MARKOVIĆ, IVO ŠIVKOVIĆ, BRANIMIR HUTERER, JADRANKO PRLIĆ, JOZO MARTINOVIĆ, VALENTIN CORIĆ, MILE AKMADŽIĆ, ANTE ROSO, IVO LOZANCIĆ.

'Serbian Republic'

The Prime Minister of the Serbian Republic of Bosnia and Herzegovina (which refused participation in the new Federation), VLADIMIR LUKIĆ, announced his resignation on 28 March 1994, in order to allow a reorganization of government.

BULGARIA (p. 216)

Government Change

On 16 January 1994 the Minister of the Interior, Col VIKTOR MIKHAILOV, was dismissed.

CROATIA (p. 245)

'Republic of Serbian Krajina'
(April 1994)

On 12 February 1994 the newly elected Assemly chose its speaker (Chairman). On 20 March the Prime Minister, DJORDJE BJEGOVIĆ, announced his resignation, although he was to continue in office until the premier designated by the President had agreed a new coalition administration:

Chairman of the Assembly: BRANKO VOJNIĆ (Serbian Radical Party).

Prime Minister: BORISLAV MIKELIĆ (designate).

GEORGIA (p. 318)

Presidential Elections
(March 1994)

Deputy Prime Ministers: AVTANDIL MARGIANI (responsible for agriculture and food production), TEMUR BASILIA, TAMAZ NADAREISHVILI.

Minister of Finance and Economic Reform: DAVIT IAKOBIDZE.

YUGOSLAVIA (p. 748)

Montenegrin Government Changes
(April 1994)

Minister of Labour, Social Welfare and the Protection of Veterans and Disabled Persons: BRANIMIR BOJANIĆ.

Minister of Environmental Protection: ANA MISUROVIĆ.

Minister of Maritime Affairs and Transport: VOJISLAV MICUNOVIĆ.

Minister of Planning: NIKSIĆ RADOVAN BAKIĆ.

PART ONE
Introductory Essays

POLITICAL PERSPECTIVES ON EASTERN EUROPE

JONATHAN EYAL

In the final decade of the 20th century, Europe saw a century which began with a political assassination in Sarajevo draw to a close with mass murder in the same city of Bosnia and Herzegovina. From Sarajevo to Sarajevo: the years which followed the end of the Cold War were taking their toll.

'Europe whole and free is calling for a new beginning. We invite our peoples to join in this great endeavour.' Almost every sentiment in this declaration, adopted with great pomp by the leaders of the member countries of the Conference on Security and Co-operation in Europe (CSCE) at a special Paris summit, in November 1990, was thwarted within a few years. The lesson of Yugoslavia was that, far from being 'whole', Europe remained divided, paralysed by a maddening competition between institutions. The European Community (from November 1993 a part of the new European Union, which, under the Treaty of Maastricht, enhanced the non-economic aspects of the association of 12 Western European states), the North Atlantic Treaty Organisation (NATO), the CSCE, the Western European Union (WEU) and the UN: all were supposed to solve the continent's problems, but were all found wanting, for they still worked according to priorities devised for a world order which no longer existed. For Eastern Europe (the former Communist countries of central Europe and the Balkans), 1993 appeared to mark the beginning of the decline. After the elation of liberation came the reality of economic and political reform. Instead of collective security and peace, the Eastern Europeans witnessed the dismemberment of Yugoslavia and Western Governments proclaiming principles they had no intention of upholding, while eschewing direct involvement in the problems of the area. After the disaster in Yugoslavia the peaceful dissolution of Czechoslovakia, as 1993 began, was actually received with relief. And, after the rule of idealistic intellectuals, came the return of the hardened politicians, in the shape of Poland's former Communists. However, to be more positive, although Western Europe proved to be woefully inadequate at handling the problems of the East, the crises in Eastern Europe also shattered the West's own illusions. Whether it would wish it or not, the West was inextricably linked to Eastern Europe; either the problems were to be solved together, or all the institutions which ensured Europe's co-operation and stability after the end of the Second World War would fall apart.

It may be tempting to place the blame for the political paralysis which engulfed the West in the face of the crises in the East on incompetent leaders, bereft of what former US President George Bush called the 'vision thing'. However, the true causes of the malaise were more profound, for they were rooted in a fundamental misunderstanding of the consequences of the demise of Communism. The decades of the Cold War conditioned generations of Western politicians into believing that, confronted by the threat of the USSR, all other conflicts were of little significance. On the fault lines between the ideological blocs, in South-East Asia, the Middle East and Africa, wars did erupt. Yet they were often just testing exercises by one 'superpower' or another. Europe, where the slightest move across the divide would have triggered a nuclear cataclysm, remained frozen in a state of outward calm.

Many Europeans genuinely believed that, with the demise of Communism, there was no need for either large armies or coherent security policies. The West had triumphed and all that the Eastern Europeans needed to do was to become 'people like us': to reform their economies and restructure their societies. Western constitutional experts descended on the East (throughout the former USSR, as well as the old Eastern European bloc in central Europe and in the Balkans) in order to teach the natives 'democracy'. Furthermore, everyone advocated the virtues of the market economy, at a time when the very meaning of this concept was still being debated in the West. By the mid-1990s what results there were were fairly haphazard: most of Eastern Europe still had constitutions imposed from above, intended to teach people democracy, rather than genuine constitutional contracts demanded from below by people persuaded of democracy's virtues. There was also a market economy, but alongside a vast and loss-making state sector. Much of this was unavoidable, given the region's history. Yet much of the pain of transformation was far too severe, mainly because the Western part of Europe was never seriously persuaded that the East's problems were also its own. What went wrong?

In essence, the West's understanding of Europe's challenges was at fault. For the previous 40 years the Western Europeans had spoken of a united continent when, in fact, it was known that Europe's division into ideological blocs could not be reversed. So, the West proceeded to create institutions which answered its own needs. Thus, the European Community (EC) co-ordinated economic policy and NATO, with its US contribution, protected the West from a sudden Soviet attack. Meanwhile, market economies ensured a steadily rising standard of living. In the process, many of the conflicts which previously drove the continent into war were settled. The border between France and Germany was no longer questioned and, with the end of the Spanish, Portuguese and Greek dictatorships, human rights became fundamental values which all Western Europeans shared. The West forgot that Eastern Europe's problems were essentially similar and that they were never settled. Borders, minorities, economies and security: all these were questions which confronted the West too in 1945. The solution to any of these problems could only come through international co-operation, yet, after the end of the Cold War, nothing of the kind was on offer. In at least this respect, therefore, the war in Yugoslavia was entirely unsurprising.

MINORITIES AND FRONTIERS

The basis of Eastern Europe's ethnic and territorial problems was clearly historic. In the West the formation of states was lengthy and ancient; in the East it was sudden and fairly recent. In the West states were created by the gradual enlargement of central authority to the provinces; in the East countries were born out of the collapse of central authority. At the beginning of the 20th century the Eastern Europeans were citizens of three multi-ethnic empires: the Ottoman, the Habsburg and the Russian. All three Empires collapsed in 1918 and the results remained present at the end of the 20th century, as did the historic memories.

More than anywhere else in the world, current frontiers in Eastern Europe do not coincide with the pattern of ethnic distribution. Furthermore, many of the frontiers were imposed by the USSR at the end of the Second World War. The results of this experience were very similar throughout Eastern Europe. All states were acutely sensitive of their own national unity: all try to claim—despite all the evidence to the contrary—that they are homogeneous nation-states. Thus, no Eastern European country could contemplate emulating Spain after the death of Franco and accommodate different nationalities in a federal structure allowing a great deal of local autonomy. For the Eastern European leaders, even if democratically elected, decentralization was equated with weakness and disintegration. Furthermore, since the reality was that none of the Eastern European states were ethnically homogeneous, leaders were trying to fit realities into fiction, by ignoring or oppressing their minorities. The predominantly Serb policy of 'ethnic cleansing' (the forcible expulsion of one ethnic group by another, to create a homogeneous population) in Bosnia and Herzegovina is the most perfect example of what happens if the belief in the 'homogeneous' nation-state is taken to its logical conclusion.

Furthermore, the Eastern Europeans were not simply engaged in a process of economic and political reform. In essence, they were recreating their states. Everything was being questioned, everything needed change. The West believed that with the advent of democracy most of these issues, although painful, would be solved. Yet democracy is not only a system of government, but, ultimately, a way of life. Clearly, democracy depends on free elections, an independent press and judiciary, parliaments and a proper division of powers. However, these are the mere formal trappings, for, fundamentally, durable democracies depend on a sense of tolerance for diversity. The British, the Portuguese and the French, for example, all have different systems of government, but all blend tolerance into their own local traditions. It is precisely this ingredient which was missing in the East; tolerance for people that are different is not something which can be taught quickly.

Indeed, in the 1990s the lack of a democratic political education remained the biggest handicap. Throughout the region, former Communist officials were nationalists. They were succeeding in attracting support, mainly because people had been been educated to believe instinctively in easy answers: thus, if they were out of work, it must be the fault of the 'international Jews'; or, if they cannot succeed in a market economy, it must be because ethnic Hungarians have taken all the jobs. Eradicating this mentality was a process which would take decades and which would be constantly hampered by local leaders seeking an easy political advantage. Indeed, Eastern Europe was not suffering from only one, but two, nationalist trends. The first was sponsored by the local governments; the second was sponsored by opposition parties wishing to gain power. In an area where people avoid ideologies, nationalism was the only concept with popular appeal.

Furthermore, to make matters worse, every state in Eastern Europe was both a supporter and a challenger of the existing territorial *status quo*. Thus, the Romanians claimed that their border with Hungary could not change, but still wanted to regain the lands of Moldova (Moldavia), incorporated into the USSR in 1944. The Serbs occupied territory in Croatia and Bosnia and Herzegovina, supposedly in order to protect ethnic Serbs in these republics. However, they also refused to surrender their control over the province of Kosovo (Kosovo-Metohija), which was overwhelmingly populated by ethnic Albanians.

The West responded to these problems with two principles: borders should not change; and minorities should be protected in their states of residence. The concepts are clearly correct, but, in the absence of any indication how they might be applied, they remained irrelevant. No less than 40% of all ethnic Hungarians lived outside the borders of Hungary, in significant numbers in Romania (2m.), Slovakia (600,000), Serbia (400,000—mainly in the Vojvodina) and Ukraine (up to 300,000). With the exception of Ukraine, ethnic Hungarians were discriminated against in each of these states. The Hungarian Government was powerless to help them, but, also, could not ignore their fate. The result was both frustration and rising tensions.

In practice, the West proclaimed a set of principles, but did nothing in order to see them applied. Far from punishing the resort to violence, the war in Yugoslavia indicated that frontiers were still changed only by force. Croatia and Slovenia achieved their independence not because the West wanted them to, but because they were prepared to fight for their freedom. Bosnia and Herzegovina virtually disappeared during 1993 only because it lost a similar fight.

There was much that could be done in order to prevent the violence of Yugoslavia from spreading. First, the proportions must be borne in mind. Despite the tragedy in Yugoslavia, it is only fair to say that this Balkan state was a special case. The three countries which disintegrated after the end of Communism (Czechoslovakia, the USSR and Yugoslavia) were precisely the three countries in which the very identity of the state was always questioned. Countries such as Bulgaria, Romania and Slovakia might have their ethnic minority problems, and they might even be acute, but they were unlikely to disintegrate. Eastern Europe was not threatened by the creation of 'city states' as some Western politicians claimed. Thus, the problems of ethnic minorities and borders were both confinable and not nearly as intractable as those in the former Yugoslavia. To deal with these problems required a proper understanding of the very nature of nationalism. Nationalism is not a disease and, therefore, there is no miraculous cure. Promising a radiant future on the basis of a glorious (and often fabricated) past, nationalism can be used by any politician or any ideology. Europe had nationalism of the left and nationalism of the right, religious nationalism and nationalism opposed to religion. In practice, it was merely a framework for other political ideologies and it is that which makes it so durable.

Yet, although not amenable to a quick solution, nationalist violence can be tackled by establishing a new relationship between ethnic minorities and majorities. Minorities should be loyal to their state of residence, but the authorities of that state should also accord them special group rights, in order to safeguard their existence. Officially, all Eastern European countries accepted this principle. Yet, in the absence of an international system of supervision, such minority rights are usually ignored. It was this particular international system which needed to be implemented urgently.

Most people do not engage in politics and most of the problems which inflame nationalist passions usually start with trivial events, such as the renaming of a street or the closure of a minority school in a remote village. A supervision system should, therefore, be detailed enough to tackle such issues, but also bold enough to address wider and more widespread tensions. Such an international legal regime would be particularly effective ensuring that ethnic questions did not become entangled with territorial disputes, that minorities could remain within their states of residence, while at the same time being able to protect their distinct cultural identity.

The main problem always was that no Western government was prepared to consider the implementation of an international system for ethnic minority protection, because none wanted to acquire new obligations. Decrying the fate of ethnic Hungarians or Russians was easier than devising a system which would protect everyone, including Corsicans, Basques or Northern Irish Roman Catholics. France, Spain and the United Kingdom constantly opposed the establishment of any European-wide system of ethnic minority protection. So, while the West told the Eastern Europeans what they must do in order to deal with their problems, it also refused to accept its own recommendations.

By September 1993, however, the first indications appeared that, after the bloody experience of Yugoslavia, the West was finally prepared to do something. The Council of Europe held its first ever summit meeting, in Vienna (Austria), on the subject of protecting ethnic minorities and, despite the fact that no minorities protection system was put in place, all states were pressured to make new recommendations urgently. Meanwhile, the CSCE's High Commissioner for Ethnic Minorities completed his first year in operating what might well emerge as the beginning of Europe's new policy for handling ethnic disputes. Whether the continent had the political will to use the powers of these institutions then became the main question.

Prompted by its experience in the presidency of the EC at the height of the Yugoslav war in 1991, it was the Netherlands that urged the creation of a High Commissioner for Minorities. The Dutch proposal sought, from the start, to compromise between the fear of states about outside intervention, in what were still considered (at least in practice, if not legally) internal affairs, and the principle that minority rights were the concern of an entire continent. Thus, the High Commissioner was to operate in relative secrecy, in order to avoid embarrassment to any country. As a further reassurance to apprehensive states, the High Commissioner was precluded from directly entertaining complaints from individuals. Nevertheless, the High Commissioner was entitled: to collect information and study the fate of any minority (with the possible help of specially appointed experts); to visit any CSCE country for this purpose; and to engage in written communication with non-governmental institutions and local authorities in areas where minorities resided. After more than one year of intensive diplomatic discussions the CSCE adopted a compromise version, in 1992, which reduced the High Commissioner's powers even further. The High Commissioner, responsible to the CSCE's main officials, needed the specific approval of both the Governments concerned and of the CSCE officials before undertaking an investigation in any state. Furthermore, the High Commissioner could not investigate any ethnic dispute which resulted in 'terrorism' (a flexible concept allowing any state the justification to refuse his involvement) and, finally, he could do little more than compile a report on any ethnic dispute.

It could be suggested that governments had no need for a commissioner to inform them of the dangers inherent in neglecting the issue of the Hungarians in central Europe, the 25m. ethnic Russians in former Soviet countries, the Turks in Bulgaria, the Kurds in Turkey and Roma (Gypsies) everywhere. Nevertheless, and despite all limitations, the creation of a High Commissioner for Minorities was a huge advance. First, the High Commissioner was part of a wider system of early-warning and conflict-prevention measures. The High Commissioners's reports might provide an impetus for the CSCE's involvement in wider mediation efforts or peace-keeping activities. Secondly, accurate information is precisely one of the most important ingredients in handling any ethnic conflict. Also, without the pressures of publicity, the High Commissioner might be able to persuade governments to compromise in order to avoid greater tension.

More than one year after its establishment, towards the end of 1993, the office of High Commissioner had performed better than anyone expected. Much of this was owing to the personality of the High Commissioner, Max van der Stoel, a Dutch politician. Despite his originally restricted mandate, van der Stoel interpreted his powers widely. He mediated in the problem of the ethnic Russians in the Baltic states and the ethnic Hungarians in Slovakia. Furthermore, he also patiently persuaded the Greek Governments to allow him to intervene in the Greek–Albanian dispute. He presented recommendations to all the governments concerned. Many of these problems remained unresolved. Yet, as long as they did not escalate into open violence, van der Stoel's achievement, performed privately and with great tact and moderation, remained immense. He was, however, still handicapped by suspicious governments. The very same states which constantly advocate the prevention of violence in the East allocated to the office of the High Commissioner a budget of a mere US $100,000 per year. Had it not been for the readiness of the Dutch Government to underwrite many of his expenses, van der Stoel would not have been able to operate even the modest office he had in The Hague (Netherlands).

Furthermore, the achievements of the High Commissioner would be limited unless a system of minority protection also existed. A minority-protection system should not only enumerate rights, but also ensure that their supervision is removed from the politicians as far as possible and separated from territorial disputes. Such a mechanism existed: the Council of Europe remained the institution which, throughout the decades after the Second World War, promoted respect for human rights in the West. The Council had all the instruments at its disposal, including the European Court of Human Rights. The Council's legal documents, however, did not prove adequate at safeguarding minority rights up to the early 1990s for one simple reason: they were designed to protect individual human rights, while the requirement was for the protection of minorities as groups. Nevertheless, as a condition of full membership of the Council, every Eastern European state was required to safeguard the rights of minorities. Despite institutional disputes, the CSCE High Commissioner for Minorities and the Council of Europe co-ordinated their activities closely.

In essence, the two institutions were complementary. Through his office, van der Stoel could ensure that minority disputes were dealt with as soon as possible. If he failed, the states concerned could be held accountable before the Council of Europe for their activities. At its Vienna summit of September 1993, the Council of Europe agreed to simplify its operations and to adopt new procedures clarifying minority rights. If ultimately successful, a proper division of responsibilities between the CSCE High Commissioner for Minorities and the Council of Europe would benefit both institutions as well as Europe's stability. Success was by no means guaranteed: 1994 would be a year of intense negotiations as to which minority rights should be safeguarded and how this would be best performed. Nevertheless, after four years of indecision Europe had finally created the basis of a system which could avoid ethnically based violence.

INTERNAL CHANGES, REFORM OF THE ECONOMY AND PRIVATIZATION

Former Communist 'Eastern Europe' was always a loose concept rather than a political reality, and it masked some major differences. On one extreme there was Poland, a country where 'shock-therapy' economic reform was first launched, but where Governments were replaced with bewildering regularity. In the middle ground there was the Czech Republic, where economic reform was slower to start with, but where there was considerable progress during 1993. Hungary, on the other hand, continued to enjoy great political stability, but relied on its reformist credentials, to find itself relatively slower in its pace of economic reform by the end of 1993. Then there were the Balkan countries of Romania or Bulgaria, where rulers were still challenged less for what they did and more because of who they were. In both these states the process of economic reform basically halted in the early 1990s; administrations described as 'technocratic' were, in fact, staffed by former Communists who never relinquished power and had no immediate intention of doing so. The countries of central Europe always believed that the Balkans were a special case, but, in 1993, years after the collapse of Communism, the former ruling party was returned to power, through democratic means, in Poland. Although the victory of the former Communists in the September elections in Poland could serve as a warning for the entire region, extrapolating from that result to the rest of Eastern Europe was neither necessary nor particularly helpful.

It was true that Communists everywhere in Eastern Europe (and, often, in the countries of the former USSR) remained well-organized (partly because they were initially treated as political pariahs). It was also obvious that, after years of economic reforms which promised prosperity but, by necessity, started with delivering further misery, some of the electorate of the region would be attracted to the remembered certainties of the old regime and the Communist message of social justice. Despite some excitement for new political freedoms, many more remained more interested in their own basic needs. The populist slogans of the past, the instinctive beliefs that there was a median line (the so-called 'third way') between the market and the command economy and that, somehow, one might have both Western-style prosperity and Eastern-style full employment were appealing concepts everywhere (including, incidentally, in the West). However, it was also clear that the return of the Communists in Poland was owing to some specific circumstances, not easily repeated in other Eastern European states.

There were several factors important among the many leading to the restoration of the former Communists to government in Poland. There was a split Solidarność (Solidarity) movement which, although it had been extremely effective in its opposition to the former Communist regime, was less successful in promoting a cohesive platform of reform. The President of the country was better at criticizing his Governments than at promoting a stable political agenda (apart from a party which promoted President Lech Wałęsa himself, but failed to elicit much support among the electorate). The main social problem affecting the situation was the division between the towns and the countryside. The urban population tended to gain from the economic reforms, while the countryside, and particularly the peasantry, were deprived of investment and, therefore, had no vested interest in the reforms. Institutionally, the constitutional arrangements allowed 29 fragmented political parties to be elected to parliament, thereby discrediting the democratic process from the start. Furthermore, the parliamentary process paralysed decision-making and so created a curious dual process: a sharp economic decline, without any political accountability. The result was that, apart from the Communists (who had been isolated from the ruling coalitions), every other politician was seen as guilty for the economic situation, and no one was able to offer any clear policy of cohesive change.

The economic problems expected to follow the ending of the federation with the Czech Republic might also, in time, produce a similar phenomenon in Slovakia as well. However, in both the Czech Republic and in Hungary, democrats appeared to be firmly in control. Poland's ultimate problem was that it did not nurture a viable opposition alternative to its first post-Communist political élite: the electorate had a simple choice between supporting the Government, widely regarded as responsible for the economic misery, and the former Communists. In the Czech Republic, towards the end of 1993, the Government continued to be popular, while in Hungary, a non-Communist, credible alternative to the existing Government did exist. The return of the Communists (at least in much of central Europe) was by no means inevitable and, in any case, the modern parties were much reformed and adapted. Furthermore, economic and political reform had dispersed the concentration of power to such an extent that it seemed unlikely that any leader would be able to recreate a dictatorship. Eastern Europe's main danger, therefore, was not from the old system. Rather, it could arise from limited economic reform, a process in which an unproductive state sector might continue as a financial and structural restraint on a private sector which might, otherwise, be flourishing.

In all former Communist states of Eastern Europe, privatization was not only seen as the most important ingredient in economic reform, but also a political tool of prime importance. For the post-Communist leaders, ending state controls over the economy remained a political imperative. Thus, it was instructive, for instance, that, just as Russian President Boris Yeltsin was increasingly beleaguered by conservatives in the parliament and the bureaucracy, so the Government's privatization programme accelerated. The same could not be said about Hungary, where a relatively relaxed approach to privatization was not replaced by speedier process until the last year of József Antall's administration.

Every Eastern European government had a set of choices, which were becoming immutable to a process of privatization. The first option was to sell enterprises to national investors, at whatever price the market will bear. By far the simplest and least contentious, this alternative was also the least realistic. Capital accumulation in Eastern Europe was in its infancy and, where the approach was attempted, it was usually the old Communist oligarchy (the people who always had access to money and connections) which benefited. Since the aim of most governments was to disperse power rather than to vest it in the old political class, this approach was usually not favoured by many.

A second option was to sell state enterprises at a fixed price, to both internal and external investors. Quite apart from having all the disadvantages of the previous choice, this approach also imposed heavy responsibilities on local government. The 'true' worth of companies was difficult to estimate; problems of land ownership and original claims to property had to be settled; and local investors, usually less versed in the workings of the market and with inferior capital resources, were most likely to be outmanoeuvred by more astute foreign investors (who were often *émigrés* from Eastern Europe, settled in the West for many years).

A third approach was to offer enterprises for foreign purchase, either at a fixed price, or to the highest bidder. Ostensibly, this alternative allowed an Eastern European state to exploit theoretically unlimited resources of Western investment, expertise and potential markets. The problem—as the Hungarian Government, which followed this approach, quickly discovered—was that the scheme was haphazard: foreign investors might or might not be interested enough to attend an auction; might or might not bid for businesses; and were more likely than not to concentrate in a particular sector to the neglect of others. More importantly, the scheme was politically unacceptable, since most Eastern Europeans rightly assumed that foreign investors would only invest in the viable businesses, leaving behind the other enterprises dependent on depleted treasuries. Moreover, given the exchange rates, coupled with the governments' inability to price their assets adequately, there was plenty of opportunity for speculation and political corruption. Hungary discovered, for instance, that a large share of its media business was soon purchased by Western conglomerates, as was a significant part of the larger retail sector. When it came to much of the industrial legacy of Communism, such as the steel industry, foreign investors were few.

It was, therefore, not surprising that most Eastern European states opted for a middle way: the 'voucher' privatization. The scheme, subjected to many permutations, introduced an element of social fairness, since all the citizens of a state were theoretically entitled to a share of the national assets. Through various auction schemes, it was also possible to arrive at the highest price the market would bear. Furthermore, since the entire operation was operated by governments, both the less attractive and the potentially profitable parts of the state sector could be privatized at the same time, in what was usually known as a 'mass privatization'. Finally, the implementation of voucher privatization did not preclude exploiting Western capital markets. Problems remained: the schemes were usually bureaucratic and took some time to implement; they were relatively expensive in administrative terms (although official Western aid was usually made available); and they were not guaranteed to provide newly privatized enterprises with either the expertise which they needed nor the array of responsible, active shareholders which they desired (a recipient of the vouchers might either dispose of their equity immediately, in order to pay daily bills, or hoard the shares for years to come, but was unlikely to attend shareholders' meetings).

Resolving the conflicting problems and advantages of all these options was a principal issue for each former Communist state. In addition to a number of former Soviet Republics, the Czech Republic, Poland, Romania, Slovakia and Slovenia all instituted some permutations of the voucher scheme. Yet, despite all the plans (and much voucher-printing), the country to proceed furthest was Czechoslovakia (from the beginning of 1993 the Czech Republic and Slovakia). Before it split into two countries, Czechoslovakia managed to dispose of more than one-half of its enterprises' book value, by including some fairly large concerns.

Czechoslovakia

Czechoslovakia's (Czechoslovakia to the end of 1992, then, from the beginning of 1993, two separate countries of the Czech Republic and Slovakia) highly socialized agriculture was privatized through the return to the original owners of or the heirs to land expropriated under the Communists. The remaining land and assets were divided among collective-farm members or used to form new, private co-operatives. Even in Slovakia, where the pace of restructuring was slower, a great many of the formerly state-owned small shops were sold, mainly through auction procedures.

The Czechoslovak experiment with industrial privatization entailed large auctions, in which all citizens could either bid with their vouchers directly, or participate through the multiplicity of investment funds (over 400 were operating by 1993, many making unlikely claims about their assets and viability). Furthermore, a certain stake in equity was reserved for foreign participation, although this varied from enterprise to enterprise. It was up to each enterprise to prepare itself for privatization, although the federal authorities always retained a say over the final sale price and the suitability of any enterprise for disposal. Yet, despite a not inconsiderable scepticism, the scheme was a great success, with advertising by investment funds provoking much enthusiasm and interest (1,500 companies were up for sale, vying for the favour of 8.4m. voucher-holding citizens). Many of the manifestations resembled a great state lottery rather than an orderly mass privatization. However, the result was a vast distribution of ownership, which was virtually irreversible, regardless of which political party might enter government in the future.

One major problem was that, at least in the initial stage, the Government underestimated the importance of the investment funds in the privatization process. It introduced regulations for their operations only after millions of Czechs and Slovaks (72% of the total) were enticed to place their vouchers with the funds on the basis of profit promises which could not be realized. In fact, the concentration was even higher, for the 10 leading funds held over one-half of the voucher 'points' assigned to them. Originally, fund managers were not required to reveal how many vouchers or investors they had and management fees varied widely. In the last days of the country's federal parliament, in December 1992, a law was enacted regulating the activities of such funds more closely. They were required to diversify their assets and hold no more than 20% in any one company. Stock exchanges opened in Prague and Bratislava. Foreign investors were limited to 30% in both, under current legislation. Yet the appearance of strong investment funds would not prevent a much bigger problem. The funds were 'closed-end' investments, which could not buy back their own shares; if many of the investors chose to take advantage of the promised 'quick profit', the Czech and Slovak Governments feared that there was the potential for a collapse of their nascent equity markets. Privatization could do little to spur capital accumulation in the first year and this might also mean that many investors would wish to dispose of their newly acquired assets as quickly as possible.

There remained three questions about Czechoslovakia's privatization which could still not be answered by the end of 1993. First, many funds invested in companies with both Czech and Slovak interests. Indeed, since most investors knew that Czech firms had a better chance of surviving and of market prospects, many funds in Slovakia had disproportionate stakes in Czech industries. As long as the federation remained, such considerations did not matter. From the beginning of 1993, however, the introduction of separate currencies and taxation systems was likely to affect dividend payments and the ability to trade in equity. Moreover, ownership patterns might be affected should either of the two countries chose to treat the other as simply foreign. Second, the appearance of vast investment funds might do nothing to increase shareholders' responsibility in companies. Although there was some evidence that funds were taking an interest in the management of enterprises in which they had invested, it was still far too early to suggest that this might translate into a traditional pattern of relations between shareholders and enterprises, as in the West. Third, the entire scheme did not, of course, solve a crucial problem behind any privatization in Eastern Europe: how many of the newly private enterprises were actually viable? The answer to this, however, was bound to be found during the mid-1990s, especially once company legislation was completed in both the successor states of the former Czechoslovakia.

Poland

Throughout 1992 Governments struggled to gather support for the relaunch of Poland's economic reforms, without much evident success. The privatization law, adopted in June 1991, had not been implemented that year, although some 80% of the retail sector was already privately owned, as were almost all the enterprises in the construction and road-transport sectors. The number of private firms totalled more than 50,000, in 1992, four times the number in existence when the Communists agreed to share power with the democratic opposition in 1989. More remarkably, the private sector accounted for almost one-half of Poland's gross domestic product (GDP), according to official estimates.

On 19 August 1992 the Government announced a renewed attempt to effect its mass privatization plan. The Polish voucher scheme, started later than the Czechoslovak experiment, claimed to benefit from any supposed shortcomings in the neighbouring state. Unlike Czechoslovakia, Poland relied on the creation of holding companies, which would act as financial intermediaries, with the intention of performing an active role in the management of the enterprise in which they were to have a stake (limited usually to 30% of the equity in each concern). Each Polish citizen was to receive a share in a holding company and, after an allotted period, the shares were to be tradable, either between holding companies or for shares in individual firms.

The scheme appeared simple, obviating many of the bureaucratic problems which beset Czechoslovakia's administrators. Yet, towards the end of 1993, the scheme was being revised by the country's new Government (dominated by the former Communists) and, although many of its features would remain intact, those allowing foreigners to manage many of the privatized assets were likely to change.

Hungary

Alone in Eastern Europe, the Hungarian Government did not initially adopt any voucher schemes. Its privatization plans ultimately depended on foreign participation. Hungary wanted to raise foreign ownership, from 4% of assets in 1993 to 30% by 1995, and pursued policies to encourage foreign investment, including tax incentives, liberal foreign investment rules (allowing full repatriation of profits) and policies of political and financial stability. Most privatization revenues came from sales to foreigners. Several factors encouraged this policy. Hungary continued to be one of the main Eastern European choices for foreign investors, attracting some US $1,600m. in 1991 alone, and an even higher amount during 1992. As many joint ventures were formed in 1991—over 5,600—as in all of 1977–90. Unfettered by fears of supposed German domination or a desire to balance EC investment with US involvement, the Hungarian Government, at the end of 1993, continued to provide the most welcoming environment to foreign financial interests.

Furthermore, the Hungarian Government believed that it had practically invented privatization in Eastern Europe. Indeed, Hungary's relatively liberal Communist regime began to privatize some state firms in 1988, nearly one year before the collapse of Communism elsewhere. According to the original privatization plans, the country was meant to convert to capitalism steadily but slowly, with the sale of one-half of all state assets by 1994. Despite a series of subsequent programmes, however, the pace of privatization was disappointingly slow. The entire process experienced all the problems inherent in other privatization methods: popular concern that the former Communist officials would benefit unduly, inadequate state regulation, difficulties in determining asset valuation and property rights, as well as inadequate capital markets.

Officially, Hungary had 2,244 state-owned large firms to sell. By the end of 1992, the Government claimed to have completed the privatization of 17% of the book value of state-owned assets. This exaggerated the amount of property transferred to private ownership, because the state remained a majority shareholder in many firms. Nevertheless, lease rights to many small shops had already been auctioned and the Government hoped to sell 10,000 retail outlets by 1994. There, again, it might find its expectations disappointed, as long as local authorities continued to refuse to sell the shops outright, offering instead merely fixed exploitation rights.

Concerned with the slow pace of privatization, the central Government drastically revised its privatization strategy. During 1992 Prime Minister Antall appointed a close political confidant, Tamás Szabó, as Minister without Portfolio, with responsibility for privatization. New legislative proposals on privatization presented to the National Assembly modified the privatization strategy by decentralizing the process and by creating a state assets holding agency, which was to retain from privatization as much as one-third of all assets (particularly useful for assets with no obvious buyer).

The Government tactic seemed to be to concentrate on the sale of shares in larger enterprises through the Stock Exchange. During 1992 the Government received 70,000m. forint (equivalent to some US $875m.) from the sale of state-owned assets. During 1993–94 it expected receipts of 47,000m. forint (about $588m.). Furthermore, a method of voucher privatization was also intended to raise public interest in the entire project, on the eve of the parliamentary elections due in early 1994. This would be attractive, partly because capital accumulation in the country had advanced much more than elsewhere in the region and partly because there appeared to be a public demand for such an approach.

Romania

The Romanians have been accused of excelling at offering appearances rather than realities. Two elections in as many years failed to remove the old Communist élite from power; no less than 75 legislative acts dealt with economic reform, but the economy still remained largely in state ownership. The victory of President Ion Iliescu at the September 1992 elections slowed down economic reform even further. The Government of Prime Minister Nicolae Vacaroiu (a tax expert with little political experience) promised a 'comprehensive' economic plan. One year later, by the last quarter of 1993, nothing of substance had been tabled before parliament and the Government had reverted to the old ways, by reimposing price controls, in an attempt to halt an inexorable rise in the rate of inflation. There were many promises, but little was accomplished.

The consequences were not surprising: Romania's industrial production (at least as far as official figures from before 1989 can be believed), at the end of 1993, was barely one-half that registered in 1989, the last year of official Communist rule, while the inflation rate exceeded 270% per year and was rising. While many retail stores were leased or sold to private operators, the privatization of the industrial sector had yet to get properly under way in Romania. In August 1991 legislation was enacted to allow the National Agency for Privatization (established in August 1990) to begin privatization of the thousands of large state enterprises, except public utilities. However, implementation moved slowly because of the Government's limited resources, political instability and concern about growing unemployment. By the end of 1992 the authorities had sold only 236 of 4,837 state assets and usually according to imprecise criteria. According to official statistics, the urban private sector employed only 4% of the labour force by the end of 1992, despite the registration of over 70,000 private enterprises, most of which were nothing but a company name, set up in order to benefit from tax-free status and to process profits gained elsewhere.

In early 1992, after a long and inexplicable delay, the Romanian Government started issuing privatization 'certificates' (vouchers) to the entire population. In practice, the process had still not been completed by the end of 1993 (the authorities claimed to have had no printing capacity, for instance) and the mass privatization, promised to resemble the one designed for Poland, was a long way off. The agricultural sector also suffered from delays in implementing the Land Reform Act. Farmers, unsure of whether they would own their crops, reduced plantings, so that the food surpluses needed to spur the development of exports and private markets did not materialize. The lack of credits for agriculture (a problem throughout the region) compounded Romania's economic disaster. A country which had no foreign debt in 1989, had contracted some US $4,000m.-worth of debt by the end of 1993. A Government which had barely begun to deal with privatization seriously, already had an unemployment rate of over 10% of the labour force.

Bulgaria

Competing privatization legislative proposals were submitted by the Government and by trade-union sympathizers, and the parliamentary debate continued for more than a year. Nevertheless, external pressure—including the World Bank's delay of the second US $100m. instalment of its structural adjustment loan—encouraged the legislature to enact a compromise law in April 1992. Under the law, all or a portion of the shares of about 1,000 joint stock companies (formed in 1991 when 130 of the largest state-owned firms were dismembered) were to be sold to domestic and foreign investors. Small businesses with capital valued up to about US $550,000 were to be auctioned, while large firms were to be privatized over a period of five to 10 years. The Government, restructured in May 1992, quickly began to prepare plans to begin implementation of the privatization law. However, perennial problems reappeared: because of the peculiar combination of restitution and sale of state assets at the same time, ownership rights were constantly challenged, bankruptcy procedures were impeded and the entire process moved very slowly. By the end of 1992 only 92 enterprises were identified as candidates for privatization, with the petrochemical industries and banking sector still exempt from privatization proposals. Then, in December 1992, when the Government of the ruling Union of Democratic Forces finally collapsed, most of the privatization projects were simply forgotten.

Nevertheless, laws that returned property rights to owners of small shops virtually annihilated the state-controlled retail sector and spurred the creation of a buoyant real-estate market in the large cities. A government decision of 5 November 1992 restored the property rights of corporate bodies as they existed before the 1949 nationalization, leaving the Consistory of Jews, for instance, with a fairly significant amount of real estate, but not many Bulgarians of the Jewish faith who could benefit from the proceeds. At the same time, the Government reversed the decrees relating to immovable property implemented in 1944–47, thereby allowing all original owners, even those living overseas or incorporated overseas, to resume their original property rights.

By the end of 1993, in all the countries of Eastern Europe, the hardest part of the privatization process was only beginning. Even in the countries which had done most to implement a coherent procedure, the real test would be the viability of existing enterprises and the legal regime governing their operations. In many more states privatization was still a question of promise rather than reality. Nevertheless, as Ukraine and Romania discovered, in 1992 and 1993, slowing down the process of privatization did not achieve a balance of benefits from both the free market and the command economy. Instead, it generated both unemployment and rampant inflation, with no glimmer of economic prosperity either. Despite the difficulties, the economies of Poland and the Czech Republic were already growing in 1993, and Eastern Europe had successfully redirected its foreign trade away from the former USSR and towards the West. Proceeding with reforms, even if hesitantly and with many mistakes, seems to be the choice for all former Communist states. Yet, to succeed, Eastern Europe needed the support of the two institutions which mattered most in the Europe of the early 1990s: the EC and NATO. On the ability of these two institutions, which successfully guaranteed economic prosperity and military security for the Western part of Europe for decades, the future stability of an entire continent depended. The initial indications, as Europe entered the mid-1990s, however, were that Western governments were still not prepared to accept the eastward expansion of their institutions.

REFUGEES AND ASYLUM SEEKERS

Despite the protests of liberal opinion, Western governments basically decided to try and seal the Western part of Europe from the impending large flows of refugees likely to come from Eastern Europe and the former Soviet empire. Even refugees from Bosnia and Herzegovina, even those who might have been in concentration camps reportedly run by Croats and Serbs, were admitted in only exceptional circumstances. Thus, France decided to make its immigration rules stricter and the Germans amended their Constitution in order to achieve the same result. Even in November 1993 there were further reports that high officials of the EC (or, rather, the European Union) were attempting to plan against a renewed winter influx of refugees from the former Yugoslavia.

The 1951 Geneva Convention defined refugees as individuals with a 'genuine fear' of persecution on account of ethnic origin, religious or political beliefs. For decades such loosely defined concepts mattered little. Most of the world's refugees would have difficulty travelling to Europe and the few Eastern Europeans and Soviet citizens who managed to escape from Communism had no problems getting asylum. However, after the fall of Communism most European states registered a 10-fold increase in the number of asylum applications. All former Communist states were granting passports on demand. Furthermore, by the 1980s and 1990s, travel from outside the European continent had become relatively cheap and readily available. European states always maintained a distinction between 'genuine' refugees and 'economic migrants', the latter being people who would claim asylum as a way of escaping wretched conditions in their home countries. In reality, the distinction between 'economic' and 'real' refugees was more apparent than real. For, as the case of the Communist regimes indicated, dictatorships generate both poverty and political persecution. Irish labourers and Russian Jews fled both ills during the 19th century, just as, for instance, Vietnamese and Eastern Europeans were doing in the 20th century.

However, there is no question that the issue assumed great political importance: by the early 1990s tightening border controls was politically respectable in the West, despite persistent advocacy of a European Union. Warnings about 'hordes' of immigrants was, previously, the preserve of right-wing extremists. By the final decade of the 20th century many of those extremists had acquired significant popular support in many countries of Western Europe and even politicians in more established parties likely to form a government found that capitalizing on anti-foreigner sentiment was not without its benefits. All seemed to suggest that refugees were indistinguishable from immigrants and that, once admitted, refugees were likely to settle in their new countries for good.

Clearly, asylum procedures had been abused and needed to be amended. Yet, in the process, Western Europe was in danger of extinguishing the concept of refugee status altogether. There was no question that the German Government could not tolerate for long an inflow exceeding 500,000 arrivals per year. However, the first group of people marked for deportation from Germany included Romanian Roma, precisely the ethnic minority which was not only the poorest in Eastern Europe, but also the most persecuted. The Roma had no powerful lobby or nation-state; they could, therefore, be deported with impunity. Similarly, many considered the actions of the United Kingdom reprehensible when confronted with a real refugee problem in the former Yugoslavia.

Furthermore, behind the scenes, it was claimed that a much more cynical policy was being developed. A refugee cannot choose a country of residence: the first port of call is often also the last. Western European governments knew that most of the people eager to leave the former USSR would travel overland, through Eastern Europe. The moment they did so, they would no longer have a legal claim for refugee status in the West. Eastern Europe, impoverished as it was, was, therefore, to become a 'buffer zone' for the unwanted of Europe; during 1993 Germany even offered Poland and the Czech Republic financial assistance in order to take more of those who had already made it to the West.

Whether they had originally had reservations or not, the Eastern European countries became resigned to their status as the continent's human buffer zone. Some signed treaties accepting back people refused entry in the West and, in turn, trying to return them further East. Western states, knowing that population movements were just beginning, would be loath to devise any new principles or elaborate a joint strategy with former Communist states. Yet, ultimately, they would have to come to terms with realities. In essence, a large movement of people cannot be prevented, almost regardless of how strict admission procedures are. Precisely because of this, the United Kingdom, naturally defended from mainland Europe by the English Channel, refused to lift its passport-control procedures at its frontiers, as it was required to do under new EC regulations of the early 1990s. Likewise France, which castigated the British Government for this, eventually resolved on the same course: the premier, Edouard Balladur, decided to delay the implementation of the Schengen Agreement, which would have opened all the frontiers between France, Belgium, Germany, Italy, Luxembourg, the Netherlands and Spain at the end of 1993. Europe's frontier controls would, therefore, not be ended and, so, the movement of people would never be totally free. Furthermore, as long as border controls remained, the temptation to use them for economic purposes (export paperwork, protective duties, etc.), would always be there. The impending flow of refugees was basically redefining a new European arrangement, which might not be that similar to the one envisaged in the 'honeymoon' period which preceded the end of the Cold War. Moreover, since no Eastern European state was any more anxious to receive their neighbours' unwanted people, the borders in the East were also, paradoxically, being reinforced.

THE EUROPEAN COMMUNITY

After decades of dispute, uncertainty and indecision the Maastricht Treaty for European Union finally came into effect on 1 November 1993. However, the dispute about the Community's future, particularly the process of ratification in many countries, had seriously wounded all the EC structures. Everything, from the future of monetary union to the Franco-German alliance which dominated EC affairs, was put in question. As long as these issues were unresolved, Eastern Europe would remain a side issue. France was often accused of being a principal contributor to this myopic attitude. Its fears were that based on the idea that the end of the Cold War had ended the usefulness of its policy of balancing East against West, while Germany's reunification threatened the entire Western European arrangement. The conclusion, therefore, seemed to be that delaying the consequences of an historic process was preferable to any alternative: Eastern Europe could be dealt with only after the Maastricht process enchained the German giant.

In the early 1990s former Communist economies, still largely state owned and short of financial resources, were hardly in a position to sustain competition from highly developed industrial countries. Bulgaria, Czechoslovakia, Hungary, Poland and Romania were, therefore, offered association treaties designed to manage their transition to EC membership (or, at least, the creation of a free-trade area) perhaps by the end of the century. Establishing such targets, it was suggested, would actually encourage democratic transformations and real reforms. Association treaties with Czechoslovakia (the terms of which were succeeded to by the Czech Republic and Slovakia in 1993), Hungary and Poland were signed in December 1991, subsequently with Bulgaria and Romania.

This argument was dangerous, precisely because it appeared so compelling. In order to join the EC at anything approaching the economic convergence criteria in force at the beginning of the 1990s, the countries of Eastern Europe would need to double their gross national product by the end of the 20th century. However, because much of the capital stock which they possessed was effectively worthless, any sustained growth to the average levels of the EC would require estimated foreign investment of at least US $100,000m. each year for the rest of the 1990s. Nothing on this scale was likely: Hungary, the most successful Eastern European investment proposition, managed to attract only $1,600m. in 1992 and, with the recession worsening in the West, even less during 1993. It was widely acknowledged that the prospect of economic convergence was unlikely, not only between the East and West, but even within the West, yet no government was willing to accept this.

The Eastern Europeans, nevertheless, realized that they were not in a strong negotiating position and accepted the association agreements. However, instead of magnanimity, they were confronted by the full force of the Community's protectionist interests. In the short term, agricultural products represented Eastern Europe's best export opportunities: Poland's grain output was second only to France in Europe; its potato crop was equal to that of all the EC countries together; and Hungary was an efficient producer of meat. The EC though, the Common Agricultural Policy of which still absorbed about one-half of its budget despite promised reforms, had no intention of allowing Eastern

Europe offer cheaper produce to its consumers. At one point during the negotiations for association treaties the French delegation vetoed a compromise proposal which would have allowed Hungary to export an additional 550 metric tons of beef to the Community. The vision of a single Europe was reduced to banalities as the West imposed restrictive trade quotas. Furthermore, even after the treaties of association did come into effect (the ratification of Bulgaria's treaty was delayed for a longer period), the Commission of the EC sought to find other excuses for not opening markets, by applying 'emergency' procedures against the 'dumping' of Eastern European steel or 'health requirements' on Eastern European meat. However, it then appeared that the EC had miscalculated: far from accepting the situation, the Eastern Europeans retaliated during 1993, by imposing their own punitive tariffs against EC products. The EC eventually relented, because it was likely to lose much more in such a trade war. At their Copenhagen (Denmark) summit meeting, in June 1993, EC leaders, agreed to accelerate the implementation of their promise of opening EC markets to free trade with the East. Nevertheless, they still insisted that Eastern European economies would have to 'converge' much more before they could be considered candidates for full membership of the EC. This can be viewed as the major fallacy of EC policy towards the East.

From its foundation the EC worked on the premise that close economic ties would gradually lead to growing political co-operation, thereby avoiding future European wars. In dealing with the problems of Eastern Europe, however, the two issues were inseparable and urgently needed to be addressed. The first generation of post-Communist leaders, with some exceptions, genuinely believed in Europe's mission, just as much as Jean Monnet and others who inspired the ideal of the EC ever did. Their efforts had little effect and they were replaced by less idealistic politicians. A Community, or, rather, from November 1993, a Union, which described itself as 'European', still represented only the Western part of the continent. Moreover, it had every intention of keeping it this way for some time into the future. Whatever plans the Western leaders, including President Mitterrand of France and Chancellor Helmut Kohl of Germany, might have had or might have been evolving, no eastward expansion was envisaged.

THE NORTH ATLANTIC TREATY ORGANISATION

For far too long into the 1990s the main arguments for NATO's existence were based on past achievements. The mighty alliance claimed that it could do nothing to stop the Serbs in the Balkans, but its generals remained interested in recounting yesterday's feats, fact and fiction. Despite its undoubted achievements, NATO never actually sought to liberate Eastern Europe from Communism; its main aim was to prevent the Western tip of the continent from succumbing to the Soviet system. Maintaining the 'Iron Curtain', therefore, was NATO's main activity. When the Eastern Europeans themselves dismantled Communism in 1989, it was NATO which claimed the credit. However, the NATO officials did not consider that victory bore liabilities. NATO was surprised by the collapse of one Iron Curtain, and so sought to recreate Europe's division under a different guise.

First there were the supposedly technical justifications. The old Warsaw Treaty Organization (WTO or Warsaw Pact), NATO urged, should be preserved as an institution dedicated to managing arms-control agreements. The Warsaw Pact was a Soviet-imposed military structure which had the dubious distinction of having taken action twice in its history—on both occasions against its own member states. Not surprisingly, the Eastern European countries were not persuaded of NATO's argument and proceeded to dismantle the Warsaw Pact (while being careful not to alarm the USSR), although formal dissolution was not agreed until mid-1991.

And so the great era of 'visions' began. The Eastern Europeans were invited to join in the 'construction' of a 'new continent'. There was the spectacle of Western leaders nodding sagely as Mikhail Gorbachev, the last Soviet leader, repeated talk of a 'Common European Home'. It was still argued that NATO could be preserved for only part of the continent, but the Eastern Europeans were offered other ersatz institutions. The CSCE, which hitherto had been of little substance, was to be Eastern Europe's salvation. There was also mention of the WEU, another organization which continued to be a set of principles and ideas with few concrete institutions. However, after a long period of indecision, NATO did establish the North Atlantic Co-operation Council (NACC). The NACC held an inaugural meeting in December 1991 and, before mid-1992, all the former Communist countries, including all the successor states to the USSR, had joined. The NACC, then defined by a US ambassador as a 'temporary measure for dealing with former adversaries' remained a negotiating board with no permanent staff or specialist advisers. There ensued a plethora of security structures proposed by different Western governments, for various reasons, and others suggested a 'European architecture' of interlocking institutions. The tragedy of Yugoslavia, however, indicated that, far from interlocking institutions, Europe was afflicted by conflicting structures, all of which attempted to resolve the problems of Yugoslavia. Yugoslavia had no less than four peace-keeping operations, but no peace to keep. Two organizations provided naval patrols in the Adriatic Sea, neither of them with authority to interdict Serbian or Montenegrin shipping on the high seas. It was not until the latter part of 1993, after four years of political manoeuvres, that the West finally accepted a debate on what should have been discussed from the start: should the Eastern Europeans be included in Western structures or not?

Those who opposed NATO's enlargement claimed that Eastern Europeans should first prove that they were 'durable democracies' before being allowed to join. Yet it can be argued that both 'durability' and 'democracy' are inherently nebulous concepts, while Eastern Europeans democratic credentials seem better than those of Gen. Franco's Spain or Salazar's Portugal when they were founding members of the Alliance. Opponents of enlargement also claimed that, even if the Czech Republic, Hungary, Poland and Slovakia might be acceptable partners, it would be 'impossible' to favour them and ignore the others. However, discrimination in membership is probably inherent in any durable institution. NATO's problem was that it had no desire to elaborate viable criteria for such discrimination. There would seem to be a strong case for the Eastern Europeans to be incorporated into NATO. Including the Russian Federation in NATO, however, would serve no purpose: a country with interests from Norway to Japan was simply too large to articulate its policy within one alliance.

Yet although many NATO officials accepted this distinction, they also asserted that it was precisely because of this that the Alliance's enlargement could not be contemplated. The organization's eastward expansion, even if stopping short of those countries of the former USSR, would be fiercely resisted by Russian conservatives, they argued, and would, therefore, complicate President Boris Yeltsin's fight for 'democracy' within Russia. However, Russia was the only former Communist state which still possessed ample means for its own self-defence, even though it was Russia's security concerns that the West was claiming to be so keen to accommodate. The claim that NATO could be regarded as a direct threat to Russian interests was untenable: apart from a tiny border strip on the Baltic Sea, Russia did not actually have a frontier with any central European country. Accommodating such a claim, therefore, would amount to a double appeasement: an acceptance that Russia should have a crucial interest in the borders of former Soviet republics with central Europe, as well as a continuing interest in an 'Eastern Europe' sphere of influence. Furthermore, it would be an appeasement which, once accepted, would be exceedingly difficult to discard: if Boris Yeltsin, a fairly pro-Western leader, was opposed to NATO's eastward expansion, what future Russian leader was likely to accept this with equanimity? Finally, the West had already persuaded Russia (or, rather, the then USSR, which did have borders with central Europe and direct strategic interests in the former Communist bloc) to abandon its objections to the most sensitive subject of all: Germany's unification took place within NATO's structures within a matter of months.

More importantly, once undertaken, the policy of accommodating Russia's 'concerns' would be unending, as events in the latter part of 1993 demonstrated. One of the last actions of the Polish Government which lost power to the former Communists was to obtain from President Yeltsin an official undertaking that Russia would not oppose Poland's membership of NATO. Yet, within days, Yeltsin was claiming to have been misquoted. He circulated a secret letter to his major Western partners which suggested that, instead of enlarging NATO, the West should join Russia is 'guaranteeing' Eastern Europe's security. This plea, however, contained three implicit problems. First, having just liberated themselves from Soviet control, the Eastern Europeans were unlikely to contemplate Russian security guarantees. Furthermore, Russia's offer only made sense if it included Ukraine as well (Russia could hardly concentrate on Eastern Europe alone and ignore this intervening state). Finally, the Russians argued that the treaty governing Germany's unification in 1990 already precluded NATO's eastward expansion. In reality, Yeltsin was pleading for recreating the Yalta Agreement of 1945 and its division of Europe, not for a new security partnership. With the political balance in Russia so finely placed, despite the ominous bombardment of the parliamentary building in Moscow on behalf of the nascent Russian 'democracy' (October 1993), no Western leader rejected Yeltsin's arguments outright. All, therefore, continued to hope that the Eastern Europeans' demands for security guarantees could be silenced without annoying Russia. This, in essence, was the European security dilemma at the end of 1993.

However, the situation had to be resolved soon. NATO no longer had an option between remaining within its present borders or enlarging its membership; the survival of the Alliance depended on its eastward expansion, for a very simple reason. France and the United Kingdom could afford to waste many years debating the merits of one co-operation structure or another, but Germany could not allow the unsettled situation on its eastern frontiers to remain. NATO had either to treat the problems of the Eastern Europeans in unison or Germany would, ultimately, have to conclude that NATO no longer served its interests. Even with NATO's 'Partnership for Peace' proposals, made in January 1994, although the problems were addressed, too many questions were left unanswered. Moreover, at the same time, the West seemed to be accepting Russia's reassertion of its influence in its former territories, despite the resurgent nationalism in the country and the revival of pan-Orthodox alignment in the Balkans.

The practical difficulties of enlarging either the EC or NATO were considerable, but what was the alternative? Historic experience would seem to indicate that if Eastern Europe was left in a limbo, it would only become a buffer zone between a chaotic Russia and a relatively stable West, a permanent threat to the security of an entire continent. Thus, expanding the two fundamental institutions was really in the interests of everyone, including Russia. If the West missed the opportunity of the early 1990s, not only Eastern Europe would unravel, but the arrangements which ensured stability in the West could go as well. Help for the Eastern Europeans could, therefore, be seen as a strategic imperative. Europe had all the necessary co-operation structures and all the reforming ideas it could possibly require. The real question of the mid-1990s was whether Western Europe's leaders could understand that they had to rule in extraordinary times.

RELIGION IN THE REGION

Rev. Canon MICHAEL BOURDEAUX

Wherever one looks in the tangled aftermath of Communism, it is clear that religion, especially where it combined with the forces of nationalism, played a role in the collapse of the old system. The precise nature of this contribution varied from country to country. It could be said to have been part of a subliminal stirring in the hearts of people who had long since been deprived of the basic right even to worship God (such as Albania). More tangibly, organized religion could provide a secure environment where human rights could be discussed (German Democratic Republic) or there could be an explosive alliance of religion and nationalism (Lithuania, Poland).

It has often been asked why Communism so resolutely selected religion as the object of special persecution? Ultimately, history showed that its leaders, in their own terms, were 'right' to do so: belief in God, religious commitment, could eventually activate men and women to political engagement long after the relevant institutions had lost their temporal power.

Soviet anti-religious policy originated with Lenin (Vladimir Ilych Ulyanov). His hostility went far beyond anything to be found in the writings of Karl Marx and Friedrich Engels, the progenitors of Communism. In a letter to Maxim Gorky (1913), Lenin wrote, 'Every religious idea, every idea of God, even every flirtation with this idea of God, is unutterable vileness'. Starting with his Decree on the Separation of Church and State, in January 1918, Lenin proceeded to turn his philosophical thoughts on religion into practical policy. Stalin (Iosif V. Dzhugashvili) soon proved his faithful disciple. By 1941, when German forces invaded the USSR, the Russian Orthodox Church had virtually ceased to exist as an institution. However, when the war against Hitler seemed lost, Stalin had asked the leaders of the Church for their moral support in defence of the homeland. In return, they were to receive the right to repossess church buildings, to reinstate 'loyal' clergy into parishes and even to reopen a small number of theological seminaries.

In the vast new territories which the Red Army gained by conquest at the end of the Second World War, religion, especially the Roman Catholic Church, was strong almost everywhere. It is an irony of history that Stalin had spent so much energy on reducing the Church at home, during the 1930s, but then, in the last year of the War, acquired Christianity in a particularly vigorous form. Soviet policy was to break the power of the Church. Only in those parts of the USSR which had been newly incorporated, following the conquests of the Red Army (Soviet Moldavia or Moldova, Western Ukraine, Western Belarus and the Baltic Republics), were the same repressive policies to apply as in Poland, Czechoslovakia and other recently subjugated countries. The years 1948–56 are the last about which it is possible to speak of a general Communist policy towards religion.

From the time of Khrushchev's denunciation of Stalin, in 1956, each regime in the region followed its own policies on religion. These varied from the Polish attempts to reach a compromise to the Albanian savage campaign of elimination, exceeding even Soviet policy of the 1930s. While these variations in the different countries are, perhaps, even stronger in post-Communist Europe, it is, nevertheless, instructive to examine the diversity of the situations by looking at each major religion and denomination, rather than dealing with the subject on a narrower, geographical basis.

THE ROMAN CATHOLIC CHURCH

Roman Catholics (of both Western—'Latin'—and Eastern—'Byzantine'—rites) played an important part in the overthrow of Communism in Eastern Europe and, indeed, in the eventual toppling of the USSR itself. It is, therefore, appropriate first to consider the role of the Vatican and its many followers in the region.

From the outset, it was clear that the Stalinist policy of brutal oppression was doomed to failure in Poland, short of the incarceration of much of the population. The country contained perhaps the most powerful national Roman Catholic Church, and one of the most homogeneous populations, in the world. In fact, by the end of 1953 (the year of Stalin's death), Cardinal Wyszyński, eight other bishops, 900 priests and about 1,000 lay activists were in prison. Even this formidable total, however, formed no more than a few empty rows in the multitude of church-goers and served to harden the resolve of the millions of faithful who remained at liberty.

Upon his release, in 1956, Cardinal Wyszyński proclaimed a Novena, a nine-year programme of re-educating the people in the faith, to compensate for the 10 years lost under the Communists. Gradually, but consistently, the Church regained lost ground, though the state never completely stopped interfering in Church affairs.

In October 1978 a conclave of the Roman Catholic Church's College of Cardinals elected Karol Wojtyła of Kraków as the first Slav Pope. It was clearly seeking spiritual strength from where the Church had its greatest reserves; what the cardinals did not envisage was that they were also contributing to the beginning of a process which would, in barely more than one decade, overthrow Communism itself. Christians throughout the region, even some Protestant groups in Siberia, could draw inspiration from this unprecedented event. Wojtyła's first visit to Poland, as Pope John Paul II, in mid-1979, stimulated massive popular demonstrations. This was followed by widespread labour unrest, in 1980, and the foundation of Solidarność (Solidarity), the first anti-Communist, and specifically Christian, trade union in the bloc. Its repression and the imposition of martial law, in December 1981, did no more than harden the opposition. In April–May 1989 the Church, or at least its 'political wing', in the form of Solidarność, was strong enough to bring about a 'round-table' conference between government and opposition. This introduced a limited democratic process and the eventual representation of anti-Communist forces in government. By the end of 1990 a Roman Catholic Prime Minister (Tadeusz Mazowiecki) and a Roman Catholic President (Lech Wałęsa) had been elected. The virtually bloodless collapse of Communism was complete.

Polish Church leaders, after decades in the forefront of the political struggle, wished then to withdraw quietly to the huge work of social and moral reconstruction. Although the decay of traditional morality was not perceived to have eaten as deeply as in other Communist countries, the years since 1948 had had some effect (the controversy over abortion indicates the conflict between religious and secular values). The Church wished to counter this and became involved in the massive undertaking of rebuilding Christian educational and social institutions. The style of Cardinal Glemp, primate since the death of Cardinal Wyszyński, in 1981, was not to seek publicity and he had a further task of resisting the inevitable inroads of secularism into the life of the Church following the years of its political glory. Toleration for minorities, which was urged by Pope John Paul II during his visit of June 1991, is also not a trait which comes entirely naturally to the Polish Catholic.

Poland is far from being the only country where the Roman Catholic Church has played a major political role in the region. It was prominent in the abortive counter-revolution in Hungary, in 1956. Cardinal József Mindszenty was one of the best known and, from the moral point of view, most vigorously defended of all the hierarchs who suffered indignities under Stalin. When the Hungarians briefly regained their freedom he was released from prison and his words, broadcast over the radio, became a classic Christian defence against Communism. Not even implied criticism later on, or his removal from office by the Vatican itself (while he was, from 1956 to 1974, a refugee in the US legation in Budapest and the Church authorities were pursuing an accord with the Government) could ever eradicate his example. This was demonstrated by the crowds who attended the reinterment of his remains at Esztergom, in 1991.

The Roman Catholic Church in Hungary is not monolithic, as it is in Poland. The total population of Hungary is some 10m., of whom an estimated 63% were baptized Roman Catholics at the beginning of 1989, but there is much nominalism and the Church receives solid support only in some country areas.

As Hungarian society moved away from the repressions following the 1956 uprising, criticism of the Church leadership by their followers became more insistent. The Vatican, too, had appointed new bishops after the secular authorities had agreed the names. As a counterweight, however, 'base communities' were quietly encouraged and they developed into a strong movement. At its peak there were some 5,000 groups and 100,000 members. In the late 1970s and early 1980s, however, the Base Communities proved to be a source of tension within the Church as they clashed with the bishops; the movement threatened the relationship with the secular authorities by their pacifism and challenge to Communism.

No single Christian leader emerged to galvanize believers as democracy became more of a real possibility. From 1988, however, the Roman Catholic bishops became increasingly insistent in their questioning of the political leadership. The Prime Minister, Károly Grósz, heard from Cardinal Paskai that youth work was increasing. Grósz replied: 'We agree that only a Church that is capable of functioning can fruitfully assist the realization of our social objectives.' But the days when the Church could help any Hungarian government achieve social, in the sense of Marxist, objectives were now numbered. On 23 January 1990, with a majority of 304 to 1, the democratic National Assembly enacted a law guaranteeing complete freedom of religion.

Vatican *Ostpolitik* for decades planned for a very long period when the Church would not be free. The appointment of bishops approved by the state was a price that had to be paid in return for the promise of freedom of worship and some rights in education. The suddenness of the collapse of Communism found the Church (not only the Roman Catholics) in many places considerably less than ready to take best advantage of the new freedoms. The rebuilding of Roman Catholicism in Hungary was not, therefore, destined to be a speedy undertaking.

Christians in the former Czechoslovakia were much more openly engaged in an active struggle for freedom. The policy of the regime virtually ensured that this would be so, because it remained repressive during the 1970s and 1980s while, in nearby Hungary, the Government was gradually relaxing restrictions. After the 'Prague Spring' and the Soviet invasion of 1968, Christian activists, Protestants as well as Roman Catholics, were systematically removed from the professions and forced to take menial jobs. They did not succeed in eventually moving back into their former work, so their reinstatement was all the more dramatic when it did occur, after the events of late 1989. The churches lost nearly two-thirds of their members under Communism, but the remainder (for the Roman Catholics, over 3m.) were a substantial minority. Gradually they regained their self-confidence, following the trauma of 1968. For example, the human-rights movement, Charter 77, contained Christian activists from its foundation.

The Roman Catholic Church, as an international organization, enjoyed the benefits of foreign contacts, stronger and more public even than the links of the Czechoslovak Protestants. Perhaps most influential of all was the way in which the aged Roman Catholic primate, František Tomá šek (from 1978 the Archbishop of Prague), became more outspoken and seemingly tougher with his declining years. He was already in his mid-70s when he became a cardinal, in 1976 (the appointment was not announced immediately), and he fiercely opposed the 'peace priests' of the Pacem in Terris organization, a group which the state had persuaded to endorse its political propaganda. Later, after the decline in their influence, his public statements became a rallying call; he acted as though his venerable years rendered him inviolable.

Cardinal Tomášek lived to see the collapse of Communism, in 1989, and retired at the age of 91. He died on 4 August 1992. His successor, Miloslav Vlk (who was made a cardinal in May 1991), was a man with a double doctorate, who had nevertheless spent many years as a window cleaner. No other of the new Eastern European democracies saw quite such dramatic transformations (as happened with President Havel himself); dozens of other demoted churchmen found themselves, often overnight, back in leading roles.

The Roman Catholic Church in Czechoslovakia remained surprisingly silent during the approach to the division of their country into two, as of 1 January 1993. It was predictable that the Church's role was to be different in the two new states of the Czech Republic and Slovakia. Indeed, religious differences contributed to the reasons for the dissolution of the federation. The Czech Lands (Bohemia and Moravia) continued to be among the most secularized of the formerly Communist territories. Conversely, Slovakia exhibited a traditional piety and Roman Catholicism engaged the loyalty of the majority of the population. Slovakia became one of Europe's most Christian countries, comparable to its northern neighbour, Poland. However, of the Slovak Roman Catholics, a large number in Eastern Slovakia (around Prešov and Košice) were the dispossessed Catholics of the Eastern Rite ('Greek Catholics', as they call themselves; often known as Uniates). Communist policy banned this Church, in 1948, with all its property passing to the less numerically significant Orthodox Christians. This political act by the regime repeated the fate of the Ukrainian Greek Catholics immediately to the east (see below). Although the Slovak Eastern-Rite faith regained legal status during the Prague Spring of 1968 no property was returned. The collapse of Communism, therefore, saw the opportunity for the Eastern-Rite Roman Catholics to reclaim their property from the Orthodox, a group now wedged into a narrower corner than their numbers deserved. The majority, Latin-Rite Roman Catholics coexisted in considerable numbers with the Greek Catholics in eastern Slovakia and dominated the west of the country, so the picture remained unsettled.

In the former USSR the Roman Catholic Church (of both Western and Oriental rites) was involved in action less well known but, perhaps, ultimately, no less decisive than in Poland.

The Roman Catholic Church in Lithuania bound together a small nation, the very existence of which was threatened by rule from the Kremlin in Moscow. Mikhail Gorbachev (Soviet leader, 1985–91) failed to realize how powerful were the forces with which he was dealing. *Perestroika*, the policy of 'restructuring' the Communist state, allowed the release of repressed nationalist feelings and the churches were deeply involved as the nation reclaimed its heritage, leading to the independence declaration of March 1990. The outrage caused by shootings in Vilnius, in January 1991, whether sanctioned by Gorbachev or not, led to international condemnation of the Soviet regime and unquestionably contributed to the dissolution of the USSR later in the year.

The Roman Catholic Church was no less involved in Ukrainian events. There, originally, nationalism seemed to be the motivator of a minority of intellectuals, and this remained so for decades. However, it was taken up by the banned Ukrainian Greek Catholic Church (forcibly merged with the Orthodox, upon Stalin's orders, in 1946), as it more insistently began to demand legal recognition in the 1980s.

That 'nationalist' Western Ukraine secured the secession vote in 1991, over the more populous and russified (and less 'religious') east remains one of the more surprising events in the drama of that year. Without the Ukrainian separatist vote, some form of 'USSR' would probably have remained in existence. That referendum could not conceivably have taken a nation of 50 million people out of the Union without the background of dissatisfaction of some 5m. people in the west of the Republic, dispossessed of their Catholic heritage and allowed to regain it only when Pope John Paul II received Gorbachev in the Vatican, on 1 December 1989.

In Romania, too, the Eastern-Rite Catholics re-emerged, following their abolition and incorporation into the Romanian Orthodox Church, in 1948. In May 1991 their leader, Archbishop Todea, was made a cardinal. As the Orthodox Church had acquiesced in the suppression of the Uniates, relations between the two were strained. The fact that most of the 1.3m. Latin-Rite Roman Catholics were of the minority ethnic Hungarian and German communities was a further source of tension. Most of the Latin dioceses were also without bishops during the Communist regime.

The most dramatic instance of Roman Catholic revival in Eastern Europe occurred in Albania. In 1967 Enver Hoxha's regime went further than any other Communist state in banning religion totally. Even the People's Republic of China, which provided Albania's ideological model, retained a nominal church leadership during the Cultural Revolution of that time. At the beginning of the 1990s, of this country of 3m. people, it was estimated that about 70% were Muslims, 20% Eastern Orthodox Christian (mostly in the south, adjacent to Greece) and 10% Roman Catholics (in the north). Although the smallest of the main groups, from the late 19th century Roman Catholicism was strongly linked with Albanian nationalism. After the ban, not only was every place of worship closed, but many of the buildings were destroyed and all the most active clergy removed to prison camps. There was evidence for the clandestine observance of religious practices, such as fasting in Lent and the celebration of Easter. The authorities campaigned relentlessly against religion. Even after Hoxha's death, in 1985, the ideological structure of the state seemed to remain intact. Albania's imperviousness to the fall of Communism in 1989, however, was to be only apparent. The northern city of Shkodër became the first focus for riots of growing intensity, beginning in January 1990. Some of the activists were Roman Catholics. On 8 May 1990 the Government announced that the ban on religious propaganda was ended. Now clearly on the defensive, the Government permitted public Easter celebrations, with the Roman Catholic service in Tirana attended by the best-known Albanian of all, Mother Teresa, on her first visit. In Shkodër the cathedral was reopened. In mid-1991 the Pope and the Albanian premier agreed that diplomatic relations should be established between the Holy See and Albania. In April 1993 the Pope made the first ever papal visit to Albania. With the devastation of all religious institutions, it is not easy to forecast how easily believers will begin to play a significant role in public life again. Religious education had to begin from a void and will take decades to rebuild.

THE EASTERN ORTHODOX CHURCH

With its age-old tradition of political passivity and collaboration with the secular state, going back to Eastern Roman (Byzantine) times, the role of the Orthodox Church was far less dramatic in its heartland than that of the Roman Catholic Church. For decades Russian Orthodoxy claimed that it had sufficient breathing space to perform its own functions under an atheist regime. Many considered this to be an unreal facade and this opinion was confirmed with the advent of Gorbachev's *glasnost* ('openness').

The end of Soviet Communism also sharply reduced the ability of the Moscow Patriarchate to influence events in the former Union Republics where Orthodoxy was strong: Moldova, Ukraine, Belarus, Georgia. In the last, for example, although the Georgian Orthodox Church is older and theoretically an entirely separate institution from its Russian counterpart, the Soviet regime permitted no theological seminaries there, thus forcibly russifying Georgian religion. The advent of Georgian independence sharply reversed this trend.

As early as 1988 Gorbachev appeared to realize that his *perestroika* programme was in trouble. Like Stalin in 1944, Gorbachev decided to use the Church. On 29 April 1988 he summoned a group of leading Russian Orthodox bishops to tell them that the rebuilding of Soviet society was as much their responsibility as that of the Communists. He had already released most of the religious prisoners. Doubtless mindful of the fact that well over one-third of the population still counted themselves as having religious belief, Gorbachev referred to the building of socialism as 'our common cause'. He criticized the rigid state controls of the past as a deformation of Marx's original ideals. He acknowledged the existing laws to be unjust and promised that there would be new legislation. Against opposition, however, this took years. However, in the meantime, the Church acted as if it had formally gained its freedom. The Russian Orthodox Church had access to the media for the first time during its millenium celebrations of June 1988. Thereafter, religious programmes became a feature of Soviet television. Hospitals, psychiatric clinics, orphanages and even prisons opened their doors to the ministrations of teams of Christians of all denominations. They were originally intended to compensate for the deficiencies of the system, carrying out the most menial tasks. Soon they were more prominent in these institutions and even openly preaching the Gospel. At one time children of families which had the reputation of being religious zealots were being removed to state institutions; now directors of these sometimes sought Christian families who would adopt institutionalized children. Most controversial of all, head teachers began to invite clergy to speak about their faith and teach moral precepts to children. According to the statute book, this was still an offence carrying a long prison sentence. In the autumn of 1990 both the all-Union and the Russian legislatures enacted new laws on religious freedom, the latter being the more liberal. It was, of course, the Russian law which survived the coup attempt of August 1991 and the subsequent dissolution of the USSR.

The Russian leader, President Boris Yeltsin, frequently made known his sympathy for the Church, both in proclaiming that any democratic society must enjoy religious liberty and in publicly attending worship at the great festivals (his critics claimed the latter was a gesture to ensure he retained the popular vote). However, in 1993 the Russian Supreme Soviet or parliament made a controversial move to introduce more restrictive legislation. First it established an 'Experts Consultative Council', which seemed to be a successor to the old KGB-dominated instrument of oppression, the Council for Religious Affairs. Then, in July 1993, new legislation came before the Russian legislature. It was widely believed that the Moscow Patriarchate had covertly used its considerable influence with the leaders of the old order, who dominated the Supreme Soviet, to help achieve its stated aim to restrict and control 'foreign' (that is, mainly Roman Catholic and Protestant) religious activity.

The Romanian Orthodox Church, similarly, used resurgent nationalism and the opportunity for new freedoms to reinforce its own position in national life. Nothing could prevent the passing of new legislation allowing Protestants greater rights, especially in education, and the Eastern-Rite Catholics the right to exist. Nevertheless, religion—not least the Orthodox Church—did play a role in the development of civic consciousness, in a country where the suppression of opposition was widespread and effective. The Romanian Orthodox Church claimed at least 17m. adherents (some 75% of the population), lulled into political quiescence by its bishops, who had long since become active or passive supporters of the regime. The Church remained the state religion after 1945, co-operated with the Communist regime and became dependent upon the Moscow Patriarchate. It did not, however, entirely escape persecution or harassment. Despite the compliance of the bishops, there were individuals still prepared to speak out. In the mid-1970s a Christian Committee for the Defence of Religious Freedom and Freedom of Conscience emerged, in which a few Orthodox and Baptists joined forces. The state neutralized this by forcing the leading activists to emigrate. Then Fr Gheorghe Calciu-Dumitreasa attracted the ire of the regime and of his own hierarchy by teaching courses critical of socialism at the Bucharest Theological Academy. His imprisonment, in 1979, caused international protests, as did the Romanian leader Nicolae Ceaușescu's plans for building his palace and for replacing old villages by apartment blocks, both of which entailed considerable destruction of church properties. None of this, however, elicited any official protest from the Romanian Orthodox Church. Patriarch Teoctist was supporting the regime in public virtually up to the day Ceaușescu died. He did resign shortly after, only to be reinstated because his fellow bishops took the view that there was no one yet spiritually ready to succeed him.

In Bulgaria individual churchmen emerged to play an important part in the progress of democratization. The most influential was the Bulgarian Orthodox monk (and Moscow-trained former scientist) Hristofor Subev, who established an Independent Association for the Defence of Human Rights in Bulgaria, in January 1988. Its membership included representatives of both the Muslim and the Protestant minorities. Persecuted by the state and pressurized by his own Church, Fr Subev nevertheless supported Muslim cultural and religious rights when protests and hunger strikes began in May 1989. His imprisonment for about 10 weeks, in mid-1989, only served to harden the opposition. Up to this time the Orthodox Church (2m. of the 9m. population, with many more baptized, but inactive, members) had been among the most passive of all within the Communist bloc. It had endured a widespread campaign of persecution and intimidation during the 1950s, but enjoyed the benefits of being a national church. As an organization it was not critical of the regime and discouraged its priests, like Fr Subev, from being so. In December 1989, however, agitating with the support of other emerging human-rights groups, the Independent Committee was granted legal status. In July 1990 the Holy Synod of the Bulgarian Orthodox Church made public an act of repentance, in which they declared they were in error to have criticized Fr Subev in the way they did. In the early 1990s Subev became involved in a schism in the Bulgarian Orthodox Church. He and two of the 11 Metropolitans (incidentally, the two considered the most compromised with the Communist regime) set up an alternative synod, in opposition to the Bulgarian Patriarchy. This schism had not been resolved in mid-1993.

The Orthodox Church in the countries of the former Communist bloc as a whole enjoyed major influence in many of them. It would be a fair summary of its situation generally that it was spiritually unprepared for the major new opportunities, which arose after 1989, and in the early 1990s it continued in its failure to play a 'prophetic' role in the creation of a new society.

THE PROTESTANT CHURCHES

Of all the countries of the formerly Communist bloc of 'Eastern Europe' and the USSR, only in the former German Democratic Republic (GDR—'East Germany') and in Estonia and Latvia were the Protestant Churches the major religious grouping. Lutherans emerged in each of these to stimulate pluralism and the hastening of the democratic process.

The territory of the GDR was the heartland of the Reformation, Martin Luther's land, but the Evangelische Kirche (EKD), under the Communist regime, declined to probably not more than 3m. members, out of a population of 17m. The psychology of the country, after the defeat of the Second World War, was different from that of other Eastern European countries: there was never a purge of the Church leadership, such as occurred elsewhere in the socialist bloc. The clergy never compromised with the political system under duress. Nor did the Church leaders adopt an anti-Communist stance, as in Poland; rather, they described themselves as 'the Church in Socialism' and reserved the right to criticize if the regime clearly contradicted Christian morality or did something opposed to the interests of the Church.

In the 1980s, however, this gradually began to change. Young people began to challenge Marxism more openly. The Church, often literally, provided space and protection for them. Political opposition began to congregate in and around Protestant churches. In a dilemma, the leadership took a principled stand and decided it could not expel these people from church premises. The state, fearful of causing a scandal, treated them as though they had gained the medieval right of sanctuary. In April 1989 a state official warned an ecumenical conference in Dresden to end the protection, but this served only to harden their determination.

On Monday evenings, in St Nicholas Church, Leipzig, there had been prayer services for peace since 1982. Increasingly these began to accommodate young activists who had an agenda other than a purely Christian one. In mid-1989 the state security service (Staatssicherheitsdienst or, colloquially, the Stasi) planned to arrest some 1,500 clergy and activists, and remove them to remote castles in Thuringia. Their resolve, however, failed before they proceeded. In September and early October some 6,000 people were attending the meetings and three times as many again were marching around the city at night, chanting slogans. By now the clergy were powerless to restrain the demonstrations. It seemed as though a bloody confrontation was inevitable. Yet, once again, the Stasi failed to intervene. The huge crowd would sing Luther's hymn, *Ein' feste Burg*. The political events acquired their own momentum, which resulted in the breaching of the Berlin Wall, on 9 November 1989. The leading role of the Church, however, was indicated by four of the 23 ministers in the new Government being clergy, with several others being Christian laymen. The demise of the German Democratic Republic as an independent state, therefore, brought to an end a remarkable chapter in 20th-century church history.

In Romania, too, the Protestant Church triggered the anti-Communist revolution, in December 1989. László Tőkés was a member of the large Hungarian-speaking minority in Transylvania and an outspoken pastor of the Hungarian Reformed Church. The authorities, with the support of the bishop, attempted to evict him from his parish house in Timişoara. His resistance inspired street protests there, bringing opposition into the open, and stimulated riots elsewhere in the country. After the fall of Ceauşescu, Tőkés became a bishop and enjoyed regional and international authority. However, he is still treated as a highly suspect Hungarian nationalist by the authorities in Bucharest.

In Estonia and Latvia the Lutheran Churches for many years were mainly passive towards the Soviet regime, but in the late 1980s emerged to play a role in the democratic process which eventually led to independence.

Baptists, spread throughout the former USSR, were for decades the object of special persecution. Their self-defence provided a notable chapter in the evolution of the struggle for civil rights. After the collapse of Communism they received considerable support from outside the country, but avoid publicity while developing their evangelistic and educational work. The small Pentecostal and Adventist Churches also made considerable progress in this direction.

JUDAISM

Free emigration to Israel, even from the then USSR, largely removed the 'Jewish question' from the international agenda and reduced the number of Jews everywhere. However, Russia and Ukraine, particularly, never entirely rid themselves of anti-Semitism (strongly present and often encouraged under the Communist regime). This did not change with the passing of the old regimes and was considered likely to remain a problem into the 1990s.

The traditional anti-Semitism in Romanian society was exacerbated by the extreme nationalism associated with the Ceauşescu regime. Subsequent to this, it was alleged, it was being used for political purposes, despite the negligible size of the Jewish community. The Chief Rabbi, Moses Rosen, criticized anti-Semitic publications and nationalist attempts to minimize the genocidal massacres of Jews during the Second World War. In June 1991 Rosen threatened the mass emigration of the remaining Jewish population from Romania to Israel and criticized the authorities. He was, nevertheless, still heckled by anti-Semitic revisionists at a memorial service later that month.

ISLAM

The rise of Islam in many parts of the region was certainly the most important new factor on the religious scene after the collapse of Communism. For some considerable time previously, the beginnings of this could be observed, but the removal of the constraints imposed by Communism accelerated the process. The religious status quo of the region could alter significantly.

During the Soviet period Muslims in the five Central Asian Republics, perhaps numbering as many as 40m. believers, were overtly quiescent. They were isolated from contact with mainstream Islam, in the Arab countries, Iran and Pakistan; they could not develop their own institutions because of the dominance of Soviet atheism. This constantly claimed success in its modernization programme for the region, particularly the liberation of women. Beneath the surface, however, there was an enduring culture, with extensive devotion to domestic ritual. The ministration of wandering mullahs and the survival of secret Sufi brotherhoods ensured that Islam was more than dormant.

With the evaporation of the restraints one might expect a massive resurgence of Islam. Each of these newly independent Muslim countries was seeking its own identity and culture, while geography still does not facilitate ready contact with Islamic centres outside the region. In the early years of independence there seemed still to be tolerance towards non-Muslim (i.e. Slavophone) minorities. However, political conflict in the region, such as in in Tajikistan, where there was serious bloodshed, could begin to alter this balance.

The worst conflict in the former USSR was that between Armenia and neighbouring Azerbaijan. The Turkish persecution at the beginning of the 20th century of a people proud of and loyal to one of Christendom's most ancient religions, the Armenian Apostolic Church, left a scar which never healed. In the late 1980s the Shi'ite Azeris renewed Armenian sensitivities to this, in a conflict focusing particularly on whether an ethnic Armenian enclave inside Azerbaijan (Nagorny Karabakh) should have the right to become part of Armenia itself. There was clearly a religious as well as an ethnic element in this conflict, but the two are impossible to disentangle.

In Bulgaria the Muslim minority benefited considerably from the ending of Communist rule. It had virtually lost all rights under the old regime and had even suffered the 'bulgarization' of personal and family names. With the advent of democracy, a period of consolidation could begin.

In Albania Muslims were in the majority (approximately 70% of the population) before Communism. With the ethnic Albanian (and also predominantly Muslim) population under threat in neighbouring Serbian Kosovo, from the late 1980s and into the 1990s, there was considerable volatility in a country which is strongly nationalistic, but is without balancing democratic institutions. Furthermore, the continuing persecution of the Bosnian Muslims (Bosniaks) is an ominous warning of religious instability throughout the former Communist bloc, particularly in the Balkans.

BIBLIOGRAPHY

Beeson, T. *Discretion and Valour: Religious Conditions in Russia and Eastern Europe*. London, Fontana, 1974.

Bourdeaux, M. *Gorbachev, Glasnost and the Gospel*. London, Hodder and Stoughton, 1990.

Land of Crosses: The struggle for religious freedom in Lithuania, 1939–78. Chulmleigh, Devon, Augustine Publishing House, 1979.

Corley, F., and Eibner, J. *In the Eye of the Romanian Storm: the heroic story of Pastor László Tőkés*. New Jersey, Fleming H. Revell Co, 1990.

Ellis, J. *The Russian Orthodox Church: A Contemporary History*. Beckenham, Kent, Croom Helm, 1986.

Frontier. Two-monthly magazine. Oxford, Keston Research.

Religion, State and Society: the Keston Journal. Quarterly academic journal. Oxford, Keston Research.

Sawatsky, W. *Soviet Evangelicals since World War II*. Ontario, Herald Press, 1981.

Sikorska, G. *Light and Life*. London, Fount Paperbacks, 1989.

Walters, P. (Ed.). *Eastern Europe: World Christianity Series*. California, Marc Europe International and World Vision International, 1988.

Weigel, G. *The Final Revolution*. Oxford, Oxford University Press, 1992.

Appendix: The Religions of the Region

There is a vast range of religions, denominations and sects in the region, from the many Christian churches, through Islam to the religions of Asia, such as Buddhism. A brief survey of the main groups follows.

CHRISTIANITY

The Christian religion is a monotheistic faith, which evolved from Judaism in the first century AD. Christianity is based on a belief in the divinity and teachings of Jesus Christ, the Messiah or Son of God, through whom salvation (life after death) can be obtained. His followers established the institution of a single Church, originally based on the four leading cities of the Roman Empire: Antioch, Alexandria, Rome itself and Constantinople (from AD 330, the capital). Four distinct traditions emerged: the Syrian or Jacobite Church was based on Antioch; the Coptic Church was based on Alexandria; the western, or Latin, Church was based on Rome and became known as the Roman Catholic Church (the Protestants sprang from this tradition too); and the eastern, or Greek, Orthodox Church became centred on Constantinople (this is the tradition of most of the region's Orthodox Churches). Later divisions resulted in the emergence of the Armenian (Gregorian) Church and the Nestorian Church.

The Church also established the Christian era (a calendar of years denoted by *Anno Domini*), a reckoning which is now the most widely-used international system and is in official use throughout Eastern Europe and the former USSR. Likewise, it was the Church that preserved the use of the ancient Roman, Julian calendar, which was used in the Russian Empire until the Revolution. In 1582 a reformed Gregorian calendar (in normal use now) was first introduced, but by Pope Gregory XIII, so its adoption was initially resisted by non-Roman Catholic countries. For religious purposes the Eastern Orthodox Church still uses a version of the old Julian calendar. (The Muslims and Buddhists use a lunar calendar, which is about 10 days shorter than the solar calendar of the Gregorian reckoning. Islam dates its years from the date of the *Hijra*, so the year 1415 AH (*Anno Hegirae*) begins on AD 10 June 1994. The Buddhist era is usually dated from the death of Gautama Buddha, reckoned to be 544 BC, with AD 1994 approximately conterminous with 2537.

The Eastern Orthodox Church

In 1054 the split (schism) in the Church that had become established in the old Roman Empire became formal. The bishops of what had been the Latin-speaking West supported the authority of the Pope, the Roman patriarch, and the insertion of the *filioque* clause into the standard Nicene Creed. (This claimed that the Holy Spirit, a constituent part of the triune deity, was a product of both the Father and the Son—*Logos*—not merely of the Father.) The bishops of the Greek-speaking Eastern Roman Empire, dominated by the Byzantine Patriarch of Constantinople (today still regarded as the Ecumenical Patriarch), rejected this and so formalized a division of Europe into East and West. The Eastern, or Greek, Orthodox Church continued to use the Greek alphabet, but had also added to the success of its missionary work among the 'barbarian' peoples, on the Byzantine borders, by the introduction of the Cyrillic alphabet and a Slavonic liturgy. This powerful formative influence of the Church, particularly on culture, education and national identity, is still most relevant today. The Romanian Orthodox are unique among the Orthodox in the use of the Latin alphabet (in Soviet Moldavia—now Moldova—the authorities forced the adoption of a Cyrillic alphabet to replace the traditional Latin one, although this was reversed after independence). The other Orthodox churches use the Cyrillic alphabet, the invention of which is attributed to the Byzantine missionaries, St Cyril (Constantine) and St Methodius, in the ninth century.

The Eastern Orthodox churches have a membership of some 200m., most of them in Eastern Europe and the Russian Federation. They are not formally linked save in acknowledging the pre-eminence of the Ecumenical Patriarch (Bartholomeo I of Constantinople), who did convene a meeting of 12 of the highest Eastern Orthodox patriarchs, in the Turkish city of Istanbul (formerly Constantinople). There are some Greek Orthodox in southern Albania, who fall under the jurisdiction of the Greek Church. The Russian Orthodox Church is the largest denomination and also assumed jurisdiction over the Orthodox of Soviet Moldavia, Trans-Carpathian Ukraine and Galicia. After the collapse of the USSR, however, it increasingly devolved power from the Moscow Patriarchy, in an attempt to retain the local Church's position in the more nationalist-charged atmosphere. The main autocephalous (autonomous) Orthodox churches of Eastern Europe are in Bulgaria, Romania and Yugoslavia (the Serbian Orthodox Church). The separate existence of the Macedonian Orthodox Church is not acknowledged by the others. All the countries of the region have at least some Orthodox Christians.

Within the former USSR, there are missions of the Eastern Orthodox Patriarchs of Antioch and Alexandria, but the other main Orthodox Church is the Georgian. The Primate of the Georgian Orthodox Church, the Catholicos-Patriarch, also enjoys jurisdiction over several Russian and Greek communities, but, under the Communists, the Church was restricted by the lack of its own seminary and instruction in Georgian devotional literature and liturgical traditions. After independence, this position was reversed.

With the liberalization of religion, such groups increasingly demanded greater autonomy and a reversal of russification, as with the Ukrainian Autocephalous Orthodox Church or the Gagauz Turkish-speaking Orthodox. There was also the return of those Orthodox who went into exile after the Communists came to power, and often formed rival hierarchies abroad, and the secession of the Uniates who were forcibly amalgamated with the Orthodox. Even within the established Church, the end of a Communist-imposed monopoly created strains; thus, in the early 1990s, the Bulgarian Church was in schism.

The Roman Catholic Church

The western, or Roman Catholic Church, was the Church of Poland and the Baltic peoples, and the peoples of the central European empires of the Germans, Austrians and Hungarians (though, after the Reformation, a significant number became Protestant). The importance of this original divide was important in the disintegration of the former Yugoslavia and the continuing tensions in the area: the Slovenes are Roman Catholic; so too are the Croats, who speak the same language as the Serbs, but write it in the Latin script. The Roman Catholics were distinguished by their use of a liturgy in Latin, which is still referred to as the Latin rite, although most services are now conducted in the vernacular.

The Latin rite is not used by the adherents of the 'Greek Catholic' or 'Uniate' Church. This denomination is part of the Roman Catholic Church, but uses the Eastern or 'Byzantine' rite; their Orthodox predecessors had acknowledged the primacy of the Roman pontiff, the Pope (also the existence of Purgatory, the doctrine of the *filioque* and the use of unleavened bread for communion), but retained their traditional liturgies and ecclesiastical organization. This first occurred in the late 15th century, as an attempt to consolidate Polish (Roman Catholic) power, in a traditionally Orthodox area. A similar process took place in Transylvania, at the end of the 17th century. Not all Uniates use the Byzantine rite; there are some from non-Orthodox traditions. In the region there are the Armenian Catholics and some Chaldean (Nestorian) Catholics, who also retain their Oriental customs and rites (the remaining Uniates are the Maronites, the Syrian Catholics and the Coptic Catholics).

Protestant Churches

In the Reformation period of the 16th and 17th centuries some of the western, or Catholic, Christians protested against the authority of the Roman pontiff, the Pope, and formed separate ('Protestant') sects. Most of these groups relied more on the authority of the Bible and rejected the episcopal organization of the Church (the Lutherans and some others retain bishops in the hierarchy, but reject the 'apostolic' nature of their authority). The main denominations are Lutheran Evangelical (who define their faith by the Augsburg Confession of 1530); the more fundamentalist Calvinists and Presbyterians (the Reformed Church of Hungary, etc.); Baptists; Pentecostalists; and Unitarians. There are also communities of Seventh-day Adventists (distinguished among Christians by their observance of the Sabbath on Saturday), Methodists, Mennonites (mainly of German descent, combine characteristics of the Baptists and the Society of Friends—Quakers), Molokans (pacifist fundamentalists in the Caucasus) and many others.

Other Christian Churches

The Armenian Apostolic, or Gregorian, Church is one of the Monophysite churches, like the Coptic and Syrian Jacobite Churches. It separated from the rest of the Church when it rejected the authority of the Council of Chalcedon, in 451. (The Monophysites maintain that there is a single, divine nature in the person of the incarnate Christ, whereas Chalcedon decreed that Christ had two natures, both human and divine.) There are significant Armenian communities in the region and abroad, apart from in Armenia itself. Another ancient Christian sect which differed from the orthodox on the nature of Christ, were the Nestorians (followers of a fifth-century Patriarch of Constantinople), some communities of whom live in the countries that once formed the USSR.

The major split in the western Church was the Protestant defection from Rome. However there were some precursors of this movement in the 15th century, notably the Hussites of Bohemia and Moravia, who adapted the teachings of English Lollardy. Several sects which sprang from the Hussite factions still exist, mainly in the former Czechoslovakia: the Hussite Church and the Brethren churches, notably the Moravian Church, which has a significant worldwide presence, owing to its extensive missionary activity.

Both the Roman Catholic and the Orthodox Churches lost some members when they underwent reformation. There are Old Catholic communities in many of the countries of Eastern Europe (formed in the 19th century). The Old Believers (Raskolniki) of the Russian Orthodox tradition, who rejected reforms of the 18th century, have long had an eminent role in Russian cultural and spiritual life. The main Old Believer group, those of the Belokrinitsky Concord, elected their own patriarch, the Metropolitan of Moscow and All-Russia, in 1991.

ISLAM

Islam means 'submission' or surrender to God. It is the preferred name for the monotheistic religion founded by Muhammed, the Prophet (AD 570–632), in Arabia. The unparalleled spread of the religion in its first centuries can be attributed to the concept of holy war (*jihad*).

The Five Pillars of the practice of Islam are: the Witness that 'there is no god but God' (*Allah*) and that 'Muhammed is His Prophet'; Prayer, which takes place five times daily and includes prostration in the direction of the holy city of Mecca and recitation of set verses, and is also performed in congregational worship at a mosque on Fridays, the Muslim holy day; Almsgiving; Fasting, which must take place during the hours of daylight for the whole of the ninth month of Ramadan (some exceptions are allowed); finally, the Pilgrimage (*hajj*) to Mecca, which is incumbent at least once in the lifetime of a Muslim. The heart of Islam is contained in the Koran, which is considered above criticism as the very Word of God as uttered to his Prophet. This authority is supplemented by various traditions (*hadith*). To interpret the application of Islamic law (*shari'a*) into normal activity, four main schools of thought emerged, the main one in the region being the Hanafi. An ideal of the Islamic community (*umma*) is that the brotherhood of Muslims is its basis and that the religion is international and beyond tribal division. However there has not been an unchallenged Muslim leader since the Prophet, and the last of the caliphs (*khalifas* or 'successors' of Muhammed), who resided in Constantinople (Istanbul), had his office abolished by the Turkish Government in 1924.

Uzbekistan has the largest Muslim population in the region, although the other states in Central Asia and Azerbaijan are also predominantly Muslim. There are significant minorities of Turkish Muslims throughout the Balkan countries. The Caucasus is another important Muslim region, and there are small Tatar communities in Poland and Lithuania. In central Russia and Siberia there are large numbers of Volga Tatars, Chuvash and Bashkirs. In the former Communist bloc of Eastern Europe the main Muslim groups are either Albanian or Slavic Muslims, the latter mainly being the Bosnian Muslims (Bosniaks) of Bosnia and Herzegovina, the Sandjak Muslims of Yugoslavia and the Pomaks of Bulgaria. There are a large number of Muslim Roma (Gypsies), mainly in Central Asia, some Chinese Muslims (Dungans) and a small number of Muslim Semites (most unusually in Uzbekistan, with the Arabs of Samarkand and the Chalas, Bukharan Jews who converted to Islam, but remained Jewish secretly).

Sunni Muslims

Some 80% of the world's Muslims are Sunni or followers of 'the path' or customary way. They acknowledge the first four Caliphs as successors of Muhammed—Abu Bakr, 'Umar (Omar), 'Uthman (Othman) and 'Ali—and follow one of the four main schools of law. Other Muslims differ only in the interpretation of the true tradition (*sunna*). Except in the Iranian (Persian) influenced area of Azerbaijan, most of the region's Muslims are Sunni and of the Hanafi sect. The so-called Wahhabi sect (with no known links to the Saudi Arabian group) are an ascetic, fundamentalist movement based mainly in Uzbekistan. Although small in numbers, they were of increasing influence.

Shi'a Muslims

The Shi'a, or 'followers' of 'Ali (cousin of Muhammed and husband of Fatima, the Prophet's daughter), reject the first three Caliphs of Sunni Islam, and assert that the fourth Caliph was the rightful successor. 'Ali's son, Husain, is the great Shi'ite martyr. 'Ali's name is added after Muhammed's in the confession of faith, otherwise their beliefs are similar to the Sunnis. They instituted an *imam*, rather than a caliph, as their spiritual 'leader'. Most Shi'ites are 'Twelvers' and recognize a succession of 12 Imams, the last disappearing in AD 878; this occluded or hidden Imam, it is believed, will return as the *Mahdi* ('guided one').

Some Shi'ites, however, the Isma'ilis, are known as 'Seveners', because they believe that Isma'il, or one of his sons, was the seventh and last Imam, and disappeared in AD 765. There were political reasons for the schism, but the Isma'ilis also have a more mystical faith. There are several sects. The main group in the region is in Gorno-Badakhshon (Tajikistan), and they are Pamirs, followers of the Aga Khan (some Pamirs are Sunni).

Sufis

The Sufis are mystics, found in all branches of Islam since very early in the religion's history. Named for their woollen (*suf*), monastic robes, the Sufis tempered orthodox formalism and deism, with a quest for complete identification with the Supreme Being and annihilation of the self (the existence of the latter is known as polytheism—*shirk*), although this sometimes approached pantheism. The Sufis verged on the edge of acceptability for some time, but became an important influence. They are organized into what are loosely known as 'brotherhoods' (*turuq* or, singular, *tariqa*). In Soviet Central Asia clandestine Sufi groups were responsible for bolstering the officially tolerated Islamic institutions; they were fiercely anti-Communist. After the dissolution of the USSR their influence became more apparent, not only in Central Asia, but also in the eastern Caucasus. In Albania, a Sufi dervish sect, the liberal Bektashis, enjoyed strong support before the suppression of religion and were making a revival during the early 1990s.

BUDDHISM

The number of Buddhists in Russia is uncertain, but there have been reports of up to 1m., mostly among the Buryats and Tuvinians of Siberia. There are only small groups of Buddhist converts in Eastern Europe.

The founder of the faith, sometimes referred to as 'the Buddha', was a north Indian of the warrior caste, Siddhartha Gautama (usually ascribed the dates 563–483 BC). He renounced his privileges in the search for enlightenment, which he found under the Bo or Bodhi-tree and understood the cycle of existence, the cycle of suffering and the way to Nirvana. He had become a Buddha or 'enlightened one' and, with the support of a monastic following, taught his *Dharma* (law, virtue, right, religion or truth), which must be followed on a Middle Way between the extremes of sensuality and asceticism. Gautama taught a scheme of moral and spiritual improvement by which the endless round of existence could be escaped and Nirvana or oblivion obtained. Sometimes described as agnostic, or even atheistic, this ignores the adoration of the Buddha himself. Furthermore, northern Buddhism, as practised in Siberia, has particularly retained and developed the hosts of celestial beings who can help. There are not only many Buddhas, but countless Bodhisattvas ('beings of enlightenment'), who have deferred their own salvation. The northern Buddhists describe themselves as *Mahayana*, followers of the 'great vehicle' to salvation.

OTHER RELIGIONS

Judaism is the oldest of the major monotheistic religions, and also advocates a code of morality and civil and religious duties. Its holy book (the Old Testament of the Christian Bible) is supported by traditions, which are expounded by the rabbis, who are doctors of the law and leaders of the Jewish congregations which meet in synagogues. There are two main Jewish communities, which observe distinct rituals but have no doctrinal differences. The predominant European group is the Ashkenazim; the Sephardim of the region are mainly found in the Balkans, with some in the Caucasian and Central Asian republics. Although both Christianity and Islam claim descent from, or to be the fulfilment of, Judaism, the Jews, as a race as well as a religion, have long been the victims of prejudice. Anti-Semitism has a long history in the Christian Church and, in Islam, the more recent Arab–Israeli conflict of the 20th century bolstered the prejudice. The Jews are widespread throughout Eastern Europe and the Russian Federation. Their numbers, however, were seriously reduced during the Second World War, particularly in areas dominated by the Nazis. This holocaust of the Jewish people was the most extreme manifestation of the anti-Semitism that was endemic in central and eastern Europe and in the Russian Empire. These traditional prejudices were not completely rejected by the Communist regimes, but, after the fall of these governments, anti-Semitism re-emerged strongly in some areas, despite the often small number of Jews. Emigration, usually to Israel, also reduced numbers. Some Turkic peoples of the region, notably a small minority of ethnic Azerbaijanis, practice Judaism, surviving since the times of the Khazar (Hazar) kaganate, an empire to the north of the Caucasus which disappeared in the 11th century AD.

There are few Hindus in the region, but missionary work was conducted by one such sect, the Hare Krishna (named for their chant) or Krishna Consciousness. They worship the Hindu pantheon and advocate a harmonious lifestyle, are vegetarian, and distinguished by the orange robes of their devotees. The Communist authorities displayed an ambivalent attitude to them and, in the Russian Federation, they continued to have difficulties in the early 1990s.

Some traditional beliefs persist in Russia and other parts of the former USSR, including some shamanistic practices and ancestor-worship. There are also some small Zoroastrian communities, to the north of Iran. This ancient religion is sometimes described as dualistic, but believes in the ultimate triumph of the principle of good. It is thought to have influenced both Judaism and Christianity and was once the state religion of Persia (Iran). Some of the Kurdish people are Yazidis, most of whom live in Armenia and Georgia. They are sometimes known as 'Devil-worshippers', owing to a mistaken understanding of their belief in the redemption of Lucifer, the fallen angel or evil principle of Christian and Zoroastrian cosmology. The Yazidi beliefs are a synthesis of Zoroastrian, Nestorian Christian, Jewish and Muslim traditions. In August 1991 it was reported that they had formed a national congress, and were attempting to register as a separate ethnic group and to establish a Yazidi Ziyaret or church.

SOCIAL POLICY IN EASTERN EUROPE AND THE FORMER USSR

BOB DEACON

INTRODUCTION

As the Communist regimes across Eastern Europe were replaced by new economic and political systems more similar to those of Western Europe, and as the countries of the former USSR embarked, more uncertainly, on the path of democratization and marketization, one of the tests that future historians might use to evaluate the past and the emerging present will be the extent to which these societies met, and would in the future meet, the welfare needs of their populations. This short assessment of the situation is divided into four parts. Firstly, there will be a summary of the social policy of the old regimes and some description of the legacy of social problems which they bequeathed. This will be followed by a survey of the new social problems and the worsening social conditions, consequent upon the transfer to different economic mechanisms and policies. Thirdly, the broad social policy strategies of the new governments of Eastern Europe and the former USSR will be reviewed, in their attempts to manage both the legacy of social problems from the past and the new social problems of the present. Finally, in more detail and in terms of new social policy and provision, developments in five specific fields will be described: poverty; unemployment and social security; health and medical care; housing; and education. In conclusion there will be a few speculative comments on future developments.

THE LEGACY OF THE PAST

Despite many shortcomings, until 1989 there was a broadly coherent and, in general terms, similar system of welfare policy and provision in operation across the whole of the USSR and Eastern Europe. The old social welfare contract, between the party-state apparatus, the nomenklatura, and the people, consisted of the provision of highly subsidized prices on food, housing, transport and basic necessities, guaranteed employment, and small differentials between the wages of workers, professionals and managers, in return for the political quietude of the population. There were, of course, hidden privileges available to the nomenklatura, but the important point is that they were hidden, because they breached the essential contract.

This system had its achievements and its shortcomings. Thus the advantages of job security for the many did not counter the inadequacy, or absence, of unemployment benefit. Likewise, although workers' wages compared well with average wages, the Party and state bureaucrats benefited from hidden privileges. Health services were free (apart from bribes and 'gifts'), but inefficient and underdeveloped in the preventative approach to health; there were high mortality and morbidity rates. Working women, especially in the German Democratic Republic (GDR) and Hungary, received favourable treatment, such as three-year child-care grants and the right to resume their previous employment; however, there was an obligation on women not only to work but to remain responsible for family care, and the division of labour remained sexist. Accommodation was highly subsidized, through cheap rents and mortgages, but it tended to be the better-off who received the most generous subsidies. The state organized a comprehensive system of social security and sick pay, but there was limited index-linking of benefits and a consequent erosion by inflation. A final example: the advantages of a paternalist system involved a converse disadvantage, in the total absence of the right to autonomously articulate social needs from below.

The system of social welfare, with its achievements and shortcomings described above, was part of a total economic and political system which, in general, eschewed both market mechanisms and political democracy. The consequence was a system that was economically inefficient and insensitive to welfare and to those consumer needs, which, elsewhere, would find expression either through the ballot box or in a free market environment. The work and welfare guarantees coexisted with an egalitarianism of poverty and an inefficient provision of services.

Social Consequences

The legacy of social problems bequeathed to successor regimes was legion. These included extensive poverty among, in particular, the elderly, larger families, and those such as the Roma (Gypsies) living outside the rigid work-eligibility requirements of the system. In the case of the USSR, a 1989 estimate suggested that 7%–8% of the 285m. population were in need of help on account of poverty. In the case of Hungary, it was shown that, between 1977 and 1987, the proportion of the poor among active wage earners increased; it was about 14% of this group in 1987, according to unofficial figures. Another of the most serious of the bequeathed social problems was that of high mortality rates and excessive morbidity. In general, life expectancy within the former USSR and across Eastern Europe was far shorter than that in Western Europe; for a long period during the 1960s and 1970s, and even into the 1980s, the life expectancy of men of working age was actually declining. Hungary showed the most dramatic decline between 1960 and 1979, across all age groups.

The reasons for this were complex and associated with poor and environmentally unsound working conditions, excessive work (not helped by the prevalence of Stakhanovite economics), poor diet and excess alcohol consumption. Particularly following the anti-alcohol campaign in the USSR, there was some evidence of a localized reversal in the trend of these figures. Thus, according to unofficial figures, male life expectancy at birth, in the USSR, moved from 65.3 in 1960, to a nadir of 62.3 in 1980, before rising slowly to 62.9 in 1983 and 65.0 in 1986.

Housing provision, while cheap and increasing in availability, was still far from adequate to meet the needs in all the countries being surveyed. In Poland, during the 1980s, the average waiting time for a flat was 24 years. Furthermore, according to a 1989 estimate, in the towns 22% of houses were without bathrooms. These figures were not untypical for the other countries of the region.

In education the main problem bequeathed by the Communist regimes was that the system was geared too much to the production of academically and professionally qualified people and too little to the needs of industry. Many graduates found themselves in jobs for which they were overqualified.

In relation to the social situation of women, the double burden of having to work and care was not shifted. This was in spite of the availability of both work and the provision of welfare, in cash and kind, to facilitate child care. Gender relations remained, for the most part, unreconstructed.

As for the social situation of ethnic minorities, a more complex conclusion must be drawn. On the one hand the living conditions of the Roma people, for instance, across Eastern Europe was very poor; until very near the end of the regime, for example, Communist urban authorities in Hungary were still building segregated streets for the Roma, with no running water and no sewage systems. On the other hand, within the USSR, the Soviet concern to develop the outposts of the old empire led to the comparable improvement of the social situation of, for example, those living in Soviet Central Asia (Kyrgyzstan, Tajikistan, Turkmenistan and Uzbekistan). Life expectancy and literacy rates were higher than those in comparable countries outside the region. One recent study used average life expectancy at birth as an example: in 1979/80 it was 63.2 years for males and 69.8 for females in Soviet Central Asia (in the USSR as a whole, it was 62.2 and 72.5 respectively); in neighbouring Iran, in 1970, average life expectancy at birth was 55.8 for males and 55.0 for females; in Turkey, in 1980–85, it was 60.0 for males and 63.3 for females.

NEW SOCIAL PROBLEMS OF TRANSITION

With varying degrees of speed and conviction all the countries of Eastern Europe and, more slowly, those that had once constituted the USSR were trying to replace their centralized, command economies and their one-party political systems with economies governed by the rules of the market and by political systems that provide for a degree of democracy. This was to have an immediate, and in some cases, dramatic impact upon social conditions across the region. Unemployment was created, and continued to be, or was made explicit where previously it was hidden. Inflation, often initially very rapid, eroded living standards that were already low. The removal of subsidies resulted in a dramatic increase in rents. Previously inefficient and underprovided medical-care establishments found themselves unable to operate in the new cost-accounting frameworks imposed upon them, and many closed. Some educational institutions, particularly the Academies of Science, found themselves in a similar situation. Women's child-care support systems and other rights and entitlements (for example, to free abortion services) were under threat. Ethnic minorities, while gaining the freedom to organize autonomously, found that the same freedom gave rise to increased expression of racism and the intolerance of minorities. Foreign workers were repatriated. However, there were some examples of positive progress in cultural autonomy: Bulgarian Turks were allowed to reclaim their names back; Hungarians in Romania could be educated in their mother tongue.

Some of the indicators that measure the immediate impact on the well-being of the population (unemployment, decline in living standards, price rises consequent upon the transfer towards a free-market economic system), during the period of transition, are summarized here. Details for Albania are difficult to ascertain; in May 1991 there were between 50,000 and 90,000 people unemployed, of a total working population of some 1.5m. The subsidy of food prices was abolished in 1991, leading to generalized impoverishment and a dependence on food aid. In Bulgaria, the unemployment rate rose to 18% of the working population, in 1992; by 1991 a 30% decline in living standards was estimated for the period of transition; in January 1991 the price of bread was increased by 600% and that of other basic foods by 700%. Czechoslovakia's unemployment was only 0.7% in 1990, but, by 1992, reached 3% in the Czech Republic and some 6% in Slovakia; the new bankruptcy laws were still to take effect and this would, it was reckoned, increase unemployment in 1993 and 1994. Czechoslovakia, in the last four years before its dissolution, on 1 January 1993, witnessed a 30% decline in living standards. In Hungary unemployment reached 14% in 1992, with an estimated decline in living standards of 20% during the transition; in January 1990 food prices rose by 38%, rents by 35% and mortgages by between 50% and 100%, while in one year later, bread went up by 38% and milk by 20%. In Poland unemployment was 14% in 1992, with local unemployment of 50%; the decline in living standards was 30% during 1990; in January 1990 prices for bread rose by 38%, meat by 55% and electricity by 300%. Romanian unemployment was 8.0% by 1992 and was predicted to rise to well over 10% in 1993; a 30% fall in living standards took place during 1991; price rises of 100% occurred for some goods in November 1990 and for bread and meat in April 1991, with more rises taking place in May 1993. The situation in the former Yugoslavia was complex because of the conflict there. Slovenia escaped with relatively low unemployment and, towards the end of 1993, still enjoyed the highest standard of living of all the ex-Communist states; the other territories of the former Yugoslavia had economies severely damaged by war or the consequences of sanctions. In the Russian Federation there were massive price rises on most goods in January 1992 and living standards plummeted. Eastern Germany, formerly part of the region as the GDR, experienced local unemployment rates of up to 50%.

It should be noted that in some countries, such as Poland and Hungary, price rises and the consequent decline in living standards began with the so-called 'shock therapy' programme of reforms, early in 1990. Other countries, such as Czechoslovakia, Bulgaria and Romania, only entered this phase in 1991 (in the first of these countries, the strain contributed to the split of the federation). The countries of the former USSR only began to do so in 1992, at variable paces.

In Bulgaria, Romania and parts of the former USSR, price rises were sometimes compensated for with rises in pay and benefits, but this in turn generated inflation and strained the dwindling state budget. An overall decline in living standards, of at least 30%, and an increase in unemployment, to over 10%, appeared, in the short term, to be the price for transition from Communism to capitalism.

Emerging Social Policy Strategies

In response to the legacy of social problems of the past, and in recognition of the need to develop social policies which both facilitate the move to marketization but compensate those who are paying the highest price for this, each of the governments of Eastern Europe and the countries of the former USSR were developing initial policy responses that were broadly similar. These measures and their immediate consequences include:

An *ad hoc* approach to the development of services and benefits for the new unemployed and to the compensation of social security recipients and employees for rapid inflation; in many cases initally more generous rates of and conditions of entitlement to unemployment benefit have had to be severely cut back in 1992;

appeals to philanthropy and voluntary effort to compensate for any withdrawn state services; and reliance to alleviate poverty on the access of citizens to a range of formal and informal sources of income;

rapid removal of subsidies on many goods and services, including housing, with limited provision for the social consequences; rent arrears are a rapidly growing problem with little enforcement of eviction;

some limited privatization of some health and social care services (this may accelerate) and initial steps to develop insurance-based health services with consequent exclusion of entitlement for some;

the emergence of independent social initiatives in the sphere of social care, although there are evident differences in the capacity of citizens to participate;

desecularization of education and pluralization of control over schools and colleges with recourse to a two-tier and private system in many places;

erosion of women's rights to some child-care benefits and services and to free legal abortions (although the final outcome was not clear);

deconstruction of the state social security system in favour of fully funded social insurance funds, often differentiated by categories of worker;

many health and recreational facilities provided by enterprises, for their employees, are being abolished or converted into local community or private facilities or simply closed;

irresolution on whether to raise pension age to cut costs or encourage early retirement to cut unemployment;

ending of privileged access by the nomenklatura to special clinics and services;

increase of local community control over local social provision, but in an impoverished context; local authorities were often given the impossible task of providing a 'safety-net' social assistance system;

tension between the limitation of social citizenship rights for certain ethnic minorities (Roma everywhere, Turks in Bulgaria, Hungarians in Romania), on the one hand, and the increased autonomous articulation of ethnic minority needs on the other;

shift in the nature of social inequalities, in the use of and the access to social provision, from those based on bureaucratic or political privilege, to those based on market relations.

There were, however, some obvious differences between countries, even in the initial responses. Commitment to socialist values and the balancing of egalitarianism and efficiency, and social guarantees and autonomy, continued to apply in parts of the former USSR, Romania and Bulgaria, but not in the rest of Eastern Europe, where the old ideology was abandoned and the inequalities and efficiency of capitalism was favoured instead. In early 1994 all but three of the 15 countries of the former USSR were ruled by ex-Communists, the exceptions being Armenia, Estonia and Kyrgyzstan.

By 1993 the new and fragile civil society and the associated democratic politics appeared to prevailing in the Czech Republic and Hungary, for example. However, tendencies to authoritarian populism were much more evident in countries such as Croatia, Poland, Romania, the Russian Federation and Slovakia.

The Roman Catholic Church influenced abortion policy and contributed to voluntary social provision in Poland and, to a much lesser extent, elsewhere, whereas the Eastern Orthodox Church in Bulgaria and other places has little to say or do in these areas.

The pre-Second World War social-democratic tradition was being tapped in the Czech Republic, whereas this did not exist elsewhere.

The rapid absorption of the GDR, into the Federal Republic of Germany, led to a different pace of change.

Although, in mid-1993, it was too early to draw any firm conclusions about the longer-term direction that social policy would take in each of the countries, some initial speculation might provide a framework for thinking about and analysing events as they transpire. It was evident that the Czech Republic, Hungary, Poland, and Slovenia, for example, were likely to develop into one or other variant of the Western welfare state. Western welfare states range in type from those that provide for a minimal state entitlement and act on the subsidiarity principle (liberal welfare states like the USA), through those that conserve and reflect the inequalities of capitalism within their welfare policy by, for example, providing differentiated benefits according to status (conservative, corporatist welfare states like Germany), to social-democratic welfare states that are concerned to redistribute from richer to poorer and extend the full range of services to all social classes (such as Sweden). It seemed likely that the Czech Republic would eventually develop social-democratic policies, reflective of the social-democratic traditions from the period between the First and Second World Wars. Hungary would probably emerge as a liberal welfare regime. The extent of the influence of the Roman Catholic Church in Poland and Slovenia was hard to judge, but something more approaching a conservative, corporatist welfare regime might develop. Romania and countries of the Balkans, such as Bulgaria, Albania and the Federal Republic of Yugoslavia (Serbia and Montenegro), together with many countries of the former USSR, appear, at this stage, to be developing a new historical variant. This was distinguished by a less-than-enthusiastic rush to the capitalist market system: property changes took place more slowly; the influence of the Communist ideology of equality and protection for workers was higher; the trade unions still appeared to be playing a role; and many of the old nomenklatura wish to retain something of the past. A post-Communist corporatism may be developing, which strikes a new balance between efficiency and justice. Negotiations ensured that some price rises were being partially, or even wholly, compensated for with agreed wage rises. This was at the clear cost of less efficiency. It might be, however, that this is a temporary phase, before these countries, too, join the leading market-led countries of the region, Hungary and Poland. Some republics of the former USSR, such as Estonia and Latvia would certainly wish to move more quickly in this direction; the outcome for Russia depended in part on the resolution of the power struggles between President Boris Yeltsin, the legislature and the regions. There was much variation and local devolution within the Russian Federation in matters of social policy.

Another way of looking into the future in terms of a country's social welfare is to predict, on the basis of a time series analysis, how long it might take, if rates of change remained constant, for former Communist countries to match the West—existing OECD countries. In some respects, of course (for example, women's participation in the work-force and access to associated benefits) these societies were already in advance of OECD countries. However, one useful indicator of social progress, of the meeting of human needs, is the infant mortality rate. It was in matters of ill health and early mortality that much of Eastern Europe and the USSR fell behind the West. In the early 1990s all former Communist countries remained below the average OECD rates of infant mortality. At the rates of differential progress prevailing in 1992, it would take the former GDR only one year to catch up, Lithuania eight, Bulgaria 12, Latvia 14, Hungary and Poland 17,

Czechoslovakia 19, Romania 28, Russia 31 and Estonia 47 years. The differentials within the former USSR were, of course, striking. Whereas to reach even the threshold of OECD rates it would take Ukraine 'only' 13 years and Russia 29 years, it would take 100 years for Kazakhstan and 200 years for Tajikistan to make this progress, unless major new state policy initiatives force a more rapid pace of change.

NEW POLICY AND PROVISION

Where this information is available, the basic social policy measures taken in each field, by each country, will be summarized below. Recent social-welfare policies in the Czech Republic, Hungary, Poland and the former USSR are dealt with, in the principal fields of: unemployment benefit; retraining measures; price rise compensation measures; housing policy; medical care policy; and education policy. The information was accurate for mid-1993; policy and provision was still changing rapidly, often by the month, in some countries, during this period of transition.

The Czech Republic

Unemployment benefit was initially set at 50%–60% of the previous level of earnings, for one year, but, in 1992, it was reduced to an entitlement for six months only; small additional earnings were also allowed. Benefit appeared to be dependent upon accepting retraining (benefits were still received during retraining), and there were enterprise allowances for those hoping to start a business. Compensation for price rises was achieved through minimum wages and through a state compensation allowance initially payable to all, but subsequently restricted to families and old people. Consideration was being given to raising the pension age. A fully funded social-insurance scheme was developed. The Czech Republic, along with Slovakia, had unique social minimum legislation, which entitled all to means-tested social assistance. However, universal benefits, such as child benefits, were likely to be means-tested. Housing policy involved the gradual reduction of state subsidies, restitution of property rights, the marketization of new housing and supplementary benefits for those unable to meet new costs. The state health service was shifted to an insurance basis, from 1993, and provision for private services was made in the enabling legislation. In education, the state service continued, but with private and religious schools being allowed.

Hungary

Originally, at the beginning of the 1990s, unemployment benefit was to be paid for two years, at a level proportional to the years of previous work (75% of past earnings with 10 years of employment, 65% with two years and nothing for less), and then at a reduced rate. However, the length of entitlement was reduced to 18 months in 1992; no casual or parallel employment was permitted and disqualification followed the refusal of a job offer. Retraining schemes were being developed and there were enterprise allowances (the equivalent of two years of benefit, available in a single payment). Benefit rises were linked to inflation (an independent social security fund was established), but there was no systematic policy protecting earnings from the effects of price rises. A residual social assistance scheme was introduced, in 1993, but this did not provide for a national social minimum. Impoverished local authorities were developing varied means of dealing with the situation. Entitlement to a family support benefit was denied to women with no recent work record, thereby excluding the Roma population. In housing, the subsidy was gradually being reduced. Thus, mortgage payments were increased by 100% or 50%, depending on whether the loan originated more or less than 10 years previously; and rents could not exceed 20% of a family's income, with pensioners excluded from any rent rises. State housing was being sold to tenants. In medical-care policy, an insurance system was introduced and private facilities were being encouraged. State schooling was being diversified in form and religious schools were permitted; private schools were developing.

Poland

Immediately after the replacement of the Communist regime, benefit levels for the unemployed were initially set at 70% of past earnings for three months, 50% for the next six months and then 40%, with a maximum payment set by the average public-sector wage and a minimum by the minimum wage. However, these entitlements were severely reduced, in 1992, to a low percentage of the minimum wage. Registration for work was compulsory; benefits were forfeited if two job offers, retraining or a public-works programme were refused. Retraining was initially available with 80% of previous earnings, for six or 12 months (100% of previous earnings if redundant and 125% of the minimum wage if no previous work experience), and there were loans available for starting businesses. It fell to local authorities to ensure that the poor did not go without, but this was often assistance given in kind. Policy towards price rises was dictated by the need to prevent compensatory wage claims; pensions and benefits were linked to the falling real wage levels; there was a voluntary emergency fund. In the housing sector, the rent subsidy was gradually being reduced, with tenants having to meet the real costs by 1993, but benefits were available if rent exceeded 80% of the family income. House building was being transferred to the private sector. Initially, the state health service was retained, but cost accounting closed some facilities and there were new charges for some services and for pharmaceuticals; a private sector was beginning to emerge, in an unplanned way. The state health budget was dramatically reduced. State schooling was retained, but with private education allowed; the introduction of religious education, by Roman Catholic priests, was being contested.

The Former USSR

The pattern of social policy emerging in the countries of the former USSR was not being systematically documented. The picture was confused and changing. In the Russian Federation, presidential decrees on, for example, setting up health insurance or allowing schools to run their own budgets were not debated, not understood and only partially implemented. Regions within Russia and town councils (soviets) developed their own poverty policies. In Russia, unemployment was not officially acknowledged until 1992; no new benefits were planned, particularly as it was claimed that all redundant workers were found new employment or retrained on full wages. In April 1991 the 66% price rises were compensated for by an 85% increase in benefit levels for pensioners, students and low-earning families; pensions were set at the level of the minimum wage; wage levels that over-compensated were still being met. The pattern of partially compensating for price rises continued in 1993. Rents, before 1989 at 3% of household costs, were not systematically increased, despite cost-accounting measures, and the tenants' right to buy their homes (in Moscow) was not being implemented. In medical care, an element of cost accounting was introduced in some areas of the health service and there was a major anti-alcohol campaign. In education there was an attempt to emphasize vocational, rather than academic, training.

Regional Comparisons and Commentary

In the related fields of unemployment benefit, retraining provision, compensation for price rises consequent upon the move to marketization and the provision of a safety net of social assistance, there are several points to note. There was diversity between countries, ranging from those of the former USSR, where measures to compensate the unemployed had hardly begun, to countries like Poland, where detailed schemes were in operation, but with less generous provision than initially foreseen. Even here, though, it must be noted that the provision, for example, for labour exchanges and retraining was often only formal, as the network of offices was only just being set up and provision was erratic and underfunded. There is also a broad distinction to be drawn between two approximate categories of countries. There are places such as Bulgaria, Romania (the details for which are not described above) and the countries of the former USSR, where price rises were being systematically compensated for (in the case of both workers and welfare beneficiaries) by agreements or regulations about wages and prices promulgated at a national level. There are also those countries, such as Poland, where no such all-embracing wage compensation exists. For those dependent on state benefits (pensioners, the ill, children), the compensation situation is variable. Compensation linked to wage levels, as in Poland, means that these people share in the falling living standards. In the former Czechoslovakia, compensation, or valorization, seems to be connected to price rises. Only the Czech and Slovak Republics have a national entitlement to a means-tested social assistance scheme in operation. Elsewhere, benefit levels were not specified or responsibility had been devolved to impoverished local authorities.

Housing policy, where it was becoming clear, seemed to be taking the same direction in all of the countries, but with Bulgaria, Romania and the former USSR adopting their distinctive pace. The goal, certainly in Poland and Hungary and, to a large extent, in the Czech Republic, was the removal of state subsidy for rent and mortgages over a three-year period. This was to be replaced by specific, targeted housing, or equivalent, benefits, for those who could not afford to pay. There were differences between countries on what was to be regarded as a reasonable percentage of family income to spend on housing costs: Polish policy initially favoured 80% (including heating and lighting); Hungarians preferred 20%. In Czechoslovakia (and, initially at least, then in the Czech Republic and Slovakia) and Hungary whole categories of persons, such as pensioners, were excluded from rent rises. Another, related, policy was to privatize building and construction and to sell, to sitting tenants, the rented state sector. The development of the second of these aims would seem to depend on the capacity of the tenant to purchase. Restitution of property rights to former owners, combined with a right of the tenant to remain or to be rehoused in equivalent accommodation, was generating new social tensions.

In medical-care and education policy there was, not surprisingly, a much greater intention, at least in the short term, to retain a prominent role for the state in policy and provision. There were, however, moves towards cost accounting, which was leading to closures, and towards allowing private health and educational facilities to be developed alongside the state sector. Insurance systems in health care were more generally being introduced, with the consequence, notable in Hungary, of exclusion of categories of the poor from health-care entitlement. Religious organizations were being allowed an increased influence over both medical-care institutions' policy and educational institutions and policy. Religious education was returning, both as a separate provision and as a part of the curriculum in all schools. Roman Catholic pressure to change the previously freely available abortion provision was beginning to be experienced. The salaries of doctors and teachers were being raised everywhere.

There are important features of policy, which are not included above. There was pressure to increase the pension age in Hungary and Bulgaria; in both, in 1993, it was still 55 years old for women and 60 for men: the cost was regarded as too high. On the other hand, increasing unemployment may lead to a countervailing pressure.

The existing, often generous, provision of child-care grants and allowances for women was also under discussion. It was too early to say whether this provision would be eroded or whether, again, the countervailing pressures of reducing the unemployment total, by removing women from the figures of the unemployed, would work in the opposite direction. Certainly in Poland, when women registered for the new unemployment benefit, the law was rapidly changed to disqualify from receipt of benefit those who had not worked for at least six weeks in the previous 12 months. The likely outcome was the continuation of grants and allowances for the early years of motherhood but the removal of the right to return to work without loss of status or salary. By 1993 this had already happened in Hungary.

New services for the care of dependants, for the alleviation of the new poverty and for coping with the increasing homelessness and destitution were being developed within local areas in many of the countries. Often these were new, voluntary initiatives. They existed, however, within or alongside under-funded, ill-organized, local social-welfare or social-aid services. A large part of the social costs of transition was seemingly being placed on local agencies, which themselves were impoverished because of the new rigours of cost accounting. It was evident that, in the short term, they were often not coping.

CONCLUSION

It was uncertain whether, during this period of transition, the new governments would succeed in transferring to a market economy and whether the populations would allow this to happen with only partial compensation for their impoverishment and unemployment, owing to the existing, haphazard welfare measures. It seems likely that in some countries the process might become frozen into a new type of post-Communist regime, which has only a partially marketized economy, perhaps less efficient, but with many more of the old, 'statist' welfare policies and provisions in place. In other countries, variations on the theme of developed welfare capitalism may emerge within the mid-1990s, but with the constant danger of a slippage into a Brazilian-style non-welfare capitalism.

BIBLIOGRAPHY

Castles, M., and Deacon, B., et al. *Eastern Europe in the 1990s: Past Development in and Future Prospects for Welfare.* London, Sage Publication Ltd, 1992.

Deacon, B. 'Sociopolitics or social policy: Bulgarian welfare in transition', in *IJHS*, 17:3. 1987.

Deacon, B. (Ed.). *Social Policy, Social Justice and Citizenship in Eastern Europe.* Aldershot, Avebury, 1992.

Deacon, B., and Szalai, J. *Social Policy in the New Eastern Europe.* Aldershot, Avebury, 1990.

Esping-Anderson, G. *The Three Worlds of Welfare Capitalism.* Oxford, Polity, 1990.

McAuley, A. 'The Central Asian Economy in Comparative Perspective', in *The World Congress of Soviet and East European Studies*. Harrogate, 1990.

Mezentseva, E., and Rimachevskaya, N. 'The soviet country profile: health of the USSR population in the '70s and '80s', in *Social Science and Medicine*, 31:8.

Ringen, S., and Wallace., C. (Eds). *Societies in Transition: East Central Europe Today*, Vol. 1. Central European University, 1993.

Szalai, J. 'Poverty in Hungary during the period of economic crisis', in *Manuscript*, 1990. Budapest.

Tretyakov, V. *Philanthropy in Soviet Society*. Moscow, Novosti Press, 1989.

Welfare in a Civil Society. Vienna, European Centre for Welfare Policy and Research, 1993.

BUSINESS DEVELOPMENT IN EASTERN EUROPE

ADAM JOLLY

Eastern Europe attracted international companies for a wide variety of reasons. While there was certainly scope for adding value in almost every sector, significant operational difficulties were being encountered in establishing and developing business. On the positive side for market entrants, the commercial infrastructure was making constant improvements. However, competition was increasing greatly in many of the most attractive areas for trade and investment.

NEW CONSUMER TERRITORIES

The most immediate opportunities opened in the region were in the gaining of access to new territories for consumer goods. No gambling, for instance, was allowed under the Communists. Thus, the revolutions of late 1989 were a signal for opportunities to provide the new markets of Eastern Europe with a vast number of second-hand coin-gaming machines. In Czechoslovakia (Czech Republic and Slovakia from the beginning of 1993) this early, chaotic and unregulated market came to an end at the beginning of 1991, when a law was introduced establishing procedures for authorizing machines and specifying maximum stakes and pay-outs.

As coin-gaming machines are closely regulated in most developed markets, a new, open market was important for producers. However, Barcrest established a strong, early position in Czechoslovakia, by not using the market as a 'dumping ground', but instead emphasizing quality and developing games specifically for local consumers. Refinements were dispensed with in favour of traditional gambling features, as gamblers were as yet inexperienced compared to Western markets. This approach was well received by the many new owners of bars and restaurants, who were in the process of setting up, as a result of the small privatization process. Barcrest was also first to provide wrapped coins, a major advantage in a country handicapped by slow banking.

Other consumer products, such as toothpaste, attracted similar attention. In the estimate of Smith Kline Beecham, a major multinational pharmaceuticals company, use in Poland, in 1992, was some two-thirds that of a developed market such as the United Kingdom. Existing products tended to be simple formulations of chalk and soap. With costs of launching products nationally amongst the lowest in the world, there were nine brands of toothpaste being promoted during 1992. Smith Kline Beecham's first priority was to establish its distribution channels, before moving on to set up a manufacturing plant for its Aquafresh brand.

The stakes for establishing products throughout the region rose swiftly. While US $200,000 might have been the upper limit for an annual advertising budget in Russia in 1992, there were perhaps 10 of some $1m. in 1993, according to estimates by Gallup, the polling organization. These were primarily seeking to exploit new resources of consumer buying power. In the Russian Federation, for instance, there was a category of wealthy Russians emerging with an expectation of living to Western standards. According to Young & Rubicam estimates, these constituted 1%–2% of the population as a whole and 4%–5% in Moscow. Thus, in a city of almost 10m., that meant 400,000 discerning, prosperous consumers, and this is without taking into account the large expatriate communities. Rolls Royce, the British manufacturer of luxury cars, established a showroom in 1993 and was expecting to sell more cars in Moscow than in Manchester (United Kingdom) that year. These wealthy consumers represent only a fraction of the Russian population of course. For those on the average income of 50,000 roubles per month, 70% of expenditure was on food, compared with the European Community (EC) average of 19% (according to figures produced by the Economist Intelligence Unit in Vienna—Austria). Those on low incomes spent 85% of their earnings on food and 0%–3% on consumer products. However, before making assumptions about poverty levels, the degree to which rents and utilities, such as heating and gas, remained subsidized, should be taken into account.

The scope for building up retail operations without an initial base was borne out by Bradleys of London, a British retail and property venture designed specifically for Ukraine and Russia. It traded on the widely held respect for the quality of British goods, an opinion which was inherited from before 1917. Bradley's stocked a range of luxury consumer goods, such as clothing and confectionery, which it sold for roubles and for convertible ('hard') currency. Profits in the first year of operations amounted to some £1m. The advantage Bradleys had locally was that there was limited experience of proper distribution skills, such as electronic stock control and customer service. By applying these, it proved possible to meet unexpected surges in demand, such as for white tuxedos. Potential Western competitors initially tended to treat the Russian market as a dumping ground for end-of-line stock. Bradleys saw it as a worthwhile entity in its own right from the start.

PROFITABLE NICHE MARKETS

As the markets of Eastern Europe developed, unexploited areas of potential remained, where strong, even dominant, market positions could be achieved. TKD, a German-Hungarian venture, created a 1,000m.-forints-per-year business for hand-held, computerized translators, with a market share of 99%. According to the company's research, only 1% of Hungarians spoke a Western European language fluently. The costs of reaching potential consumers through television advertising and hiring space on every other page of the Budapest telephone directory remained low.

Video Arts, the British production company which trains managers through the humour of actors and comedians such as John Cleese, started early in the market for management training programmes. As a result it had little competition in the market and, by 1993, was achieving sales in Hungary at a higher level than in many Western European markets. Sales were mainly to Hungarian companies, at a price of 54,000 forints (some £415). The selling point was less the humour of John Cleese—Hungarians, generally, had never heard of him—but more the over-riding need to get managers to international standards.

CREATIVE PACKAGES

While there was a transparent need to improve the infrastructure and basic services, such as the health services, the funding necessary was in short supply. Devising creative packages to release finance to the Western supplier was at a premium. Adpol, a British healthcare consortium, developed a workable business proposal in Poland, through a combination of tidying Warsaw's dilapidated streets and meeting the needs of Western advertisers. It won a contract from the municipal authorities at the end of 1991 to replace all its bus and tram shelters. In return, Adpol received exclusive advertising rights for the next 20 years. The shelters were boldly designed, with illuminated advertising panels. The company also established a similar sort of mechanism with the local authority in the Greater Urals (Russian Federation).

Supplying healthcare products did not bring direct access to either the benefits of the British Export Credits Guarantee Department (ECGD—now NCM Credit Insurance Ltd) or foreign-exchange earnings. So, Adpol used a 'switch trading' mechanism to cover the cost of supplying medical equipment and expertise. Finance was generated by the sale of raw materials produced in the region, particularly aluminium and cobalt once used in the Soviet arms programme. Once revenue was paid into the consortium's escrow account, it would then proceed with shipment. The first targets for improving care agreed with the local authority were maternity and, in an area with high exposures to radiation, cancer patients. A new clinic was built and training programmes for local doctors were being conducted. These initial projects were expected to be the forerunners to a long-standing relationship with the local authority.

EXPLORING MARKETS

Exploring the markets through relatively simple trading mechanisms was the first step for many Western corporations unused to business conditions in Eastern Europe. Marks & Spencer, the British retailing chain, opened a small outlet in Hungary, on Budapest's main shopping street, in September 1992, in co-operation with a local retailer and an Austrian trading house. At 600 square feet (180 sq m) it was the smallest Marks & Spencer in the world, although it might act as a grounding for further outlets. Offering an exclusive range of ladies' wear, initial results were three times more than the expectations.

Allied Breweries was another company that decided to take time to learn about the market. In 1990 it established a John Bull bar ('pub') in the centre of Budapest, aimed mainly at expatriates and tourists. It was British in design and appearance, right down to the darts board. The first year proved successful, particularly with the local clientele. Building on this experience, Allied Breweries then began to set up 12–15 other pubs, not in attractive city centres, but in huge housing estates badly served by local amenities.

TRANSFER OF 'KNOW HOW'

Successful businesses were being built on the transfer of know how and expertise from the West. For example, granite, cobbled streets were one of the most attractive features of Eastern European towns. Replacement and maintenance costs, however, were prohibitively high. The British company Creteprint developed a technique to produce substitutes at a fraction of the cost. Within five months of attending a construction trade fair and giving a demonstration in the middle of Prague (Czech Republic), Creteprint generated £120,000 worth of orders from the Czech Republic and Slovakia, through a network of regional licences. Business in Prague proved particularly fruitful, as so much money was being made available to renovate the city. One of the side benefits was that a healthy export trade in old cobblestones, to Germany, emerged.

INDUSTRIAL EXPORTS FROM THE WEST

As Eastern European state enterprises adapted to the often harsh conditions of a market economy, they found themselves having to cope with high real interest rates and mounting 'bad debts' (debts unlikely to be repaid). The priority in these circumstances was to import value added parts, on a consignment basis, resulting in clear productivity improvements. Gone was the time when foreign trade organizations placed large, secure contracts well in advance.

This was a transition that Tucker Fasteners, producers of blind rivets, had to negotiate in Poland. Severe cash flow problems locally meant that large orders were becoming fewer and fewer by 1989. Instead, there emerged increasing numbers of relatively small, private customers, often operating assembly plants. Orders were often on a monthly or even weekly basis. This new environment also necessitated representation at a much lower level, although choosing a distributor proved a difficult experience, on the grounds that candidates were expecting extended credits. Finally, Tucker Fasteners found someone prepared to risk some of their own resources and who was successful in pursuing business all over Poland. This particular man's initial base was his grandmother's flat, in Warsaw, one bedroom acting as an office, the other as a warehouse. This example illustrates two of the most encouraging trends for the development of business: the entry of large automotive manufacturers to Poland; and the emergence of small stockists.

DEVELOPING PRODUCTION FACILITIES

Growing trade resulted in new production facilities being established. British Vita, manufacturers of polymer and foam, saw its business with the Polish furniture and bedding sectors burgeon, and identified the scope for supplying automotive manufacturers. In 1992 it bought land at auction, near Wrocław, and installed up-to-date production facilities. This phase of its business development represented a £4m. investment. Stanley Tools adopted a reverse philosophy: having a manufacturing base was the surest way of making a significant sales impact. In early 1990 it reviewed every hand-tool producer in Poland, eventually selecting a manufacturer of pliers, pincers and nippers, which complemented its existing product range. The factory was equipped with ideal assets from the West and training was given to employees both in the EC and in the USA. New products were sold into Western markets from the start of 1992. Sales in Poland were targeted at new private companies and hardware stores.

GROWTH SECTORS

Automotive industries and glass were two areas attracting major investments in central Europe in the early 1990s. The Italian car manufacturer, Fiat, took a stake in the automotive maker FSM of Poland, with a commitment to invest further. The new Cinquecento small car, produced in Poland, was being marketed throughout Europe by 1993. On a smaller scale, the British company Rover was proposing to transfer the assembly of its Maestro cars and vans to Bulgaria, to meet local demand: 7,000 vehicles per year were to be manufactured initially, rising to 46,000. Overall, the local market demanded 120,000 cars per year in the early 1990s. The first phase was scheduled to cost Rover £11m. and the second, which involved full production, some £70m.

The glass industry's two largest customers, the construction sector and the motor-vehicle industry, were likely to be vectors for economic development in the region. Sklo Union (Czech Republic), valued at US $120m., was sold to the Belgian-Japanese company Glaverbel. Also during 1993, the British company Pilkington was setting up Poland's first float-glass factory, in a deal worth some $171.5m.

VALUE ADDED

The introduction of Western expertise and processes might transform the fortunes of loss-making enterprises. In Hungary, one of the strongest food producers in the region, turkey farming was subject to cyclical variations in output. It was an industry in a serious loss-making position, despite exports to Italy, Germany and Switzerland. Bernard Matthews, the British turkey producer based in Norfolk, acquired an interest in the Sarvar poultry company and was applying the techniques of overcoming the 'boom or bust' nature of the industry pioneered in the United Kingdom. A range of value-added products and recipes, for the Hungarian market, were developed, which would find a more consistent level of demand.

Watmoughts, the printing group, espoused a similar intention in purchasing a £3m. share in the Hungarian printing company Revai Nymoda. It was a move intended to serve the growing market for prestige magazines and to regain some of the quality work which had been going to Austria. While product quality standards were high, it proved more difficult than expected to specialize, as functions like type-setting and film making, which were subcontracted in the West, had to be retained in-house. Watmoughts also found itself in competition with state enterprises not labouring under the same imperatives of cost and profit, which made it possible for them to undercut Watmoughts prices unrealistically.

By combining with a low-cost producer in Poland, Trunature captured a 45% share of a market in meat netting worth £1,500m. per year. Trunature's partner had been making sock tap elastic and was planning to diversify. Trunature wrote off two machines in the United Kingdom, supplying them as equity. The Polish partners supplied the premises, as well as the equipment. The joint venture was competing against an old-style state monopoly and was winning business by producing the netting in a more efficient and attractive manner.

IMPROVING COST BASES

While it was possible to achieve product quality close to the best international standards, wage levels in Eastern Europe were as low as 10% of EC levels. As a result, most of the textile industry in Hungary, for instance, was working on 'cut, make and trim' contracts for Western designers, including Gucci and Yves St Laurent. Overall, 80% of its textile production was being exported to Western markets.

Coats Vyella, the British manufacturer of thread, positioned itself to benefit from a trend where consumption of thread was rising as rapidly in the East as it was falling in the West. Prior to the Second World War Coats held significant market share throughout the region, with a number of production bases. After the events of 1989 it once again purchased a stake in a factory it had established on the outskirts of Budapest (Hungary) in 1927. While the twisting machines were very modern German units, the spinning ones were the original 1927 models! Coats was achieving cost advantages over its Western competitors of up to 20% and one-half of its output was going to Western markets. This had implications for its overall European strategy: over the five years from 1993 production units were likely to be reduced in the EC, with high value activities going to Budapest and commodity items being produced in countries of the Commonwealth of Independent States (CIS).

ROOM FOR EXPANSION

Littlewoods, the retail organization, after reviewing markets from Spain to central Europe, opted to set up a joint venture in St Petersburg (Russia). This was on the grounds that the Russian Federation, unlike mature, 'over-shopped' markets in the West, offered scope to pursue a diverse range of retailing projects and to establish significant market share. In the absence of any real competition, there was the opportunity to serve huge catchment areas, which went some way to offset the disadvantages of the declining standards of living. A dual strategy was being pursued: hard currency shops, stocked with imported Western goods, were servicing a new type of wealthy Russian consumer; while rouble stores, with local supplies, were catering for ordinary Russians. In 1993 the two parts of the business were roughly equal in value, but, over time, the rouble element would predominate.

The first full year's (1992) trading proved profitable and expansion in 1993 was being funded by retained earnings and limited rouble borrowings. During 1993 Littlewoods started to buy small stakes in local suppliers, as a way of acting as a catalyst for operations where the main limitation was working capital. These producers were expecting to generate a return through foreign-exchange earnings, as well as establishing Littlewoods as the privileged local customer.

LOCAL TECHNOLOGY

Russian aerospace succeeded in producing serviceable aircraft over many years for the Russian military and for the world's largest air carrier, Aeroflot. While its new generation of civil aviation jets had well designed modern airframes, they had shortcomings which would prevent their sale to international markets. Fleming's Russian Investment Corporation (FRIC) identified this as an opportunity where Western industrial expertise and capital could be matched with a source of Eastern European competitive advantage. It set up a Russian joint venture, to sell the Tupolev 204 aircraft to international markets for hard currency, in competition with the US company Boeing and the European Airbus 200 seaters. Modifications had to be made first. Tupolev's existing engines suffered from a shortage of power, combined with heavy fuel emissions. The modernized version of the plane was to use engines provided by Rolls Royce (RB 221s). Avionics were to be supplied from the USA and a British company was to put in place the sort of product and technical support in which international buyers would have confidence. All told Bravia expected to have a 30% cost advantage in the battle for sales, from 1995, when the Tu 204 should receive its European certification.

Amersham International, the British health science group, used Russia as a source for radio isotopes. Its supplies from reactors in the United Kingdom (Harwell) gradually diminished, so it became increasingly important to consolidate the links it had already established with Russia. Under the old Soviet system, however, the identity of the supplier was unknown. As the market opened, it was found that 80% of the isotopes had been coming from Mayak, Russia's largest nuclear processing plant, situated in Cherlyabinsk 65, a secret city in the Urals. The production of nuclear weapons had stopped, but uranium reprocessing was still carried out. At the start of 1991 Amersham began negotiations to establish a marketing joint venture. This would allow it to service its own needs as well as trading isotopes world-wide. Initial revenue was projected at US $15m. per year, with the potential to rise to $100m. Amersham held a 40% stake and was providing advice on the development, handling and distribution of radioactive products.

NATURAL RESOURCES

In the early 1990s Russia held 34% of the world's known natural-gas reserves and petroleum earned 70% of the country's export revenues, with total reserves estimated at 7,500m. metric tons. One of the gas fields which the MMMMs consortium was developing off Sakhalin island, in the Far East, was five times larger than any North Sea gas field. As the market became more accessible to foreign penetration, it seemed an ideal opportunity to match Russia's huge hydrocarbon reserves and its dilapidated industry with Western expertise and capital.

The intricacy of negotiating deals in Russia's volatile political and investment climate, however, militated against such expectations. As a result, many of the major multinational and Western companies sought opportunities in other CIS countries, with more clearly defined legislation and negotiating powers. In Russia, although things were likely to improve after the resolution of the conflict between executive and legislature in September–October 1993, such companies were experimenting with test projects, such as well workovers with rapid return on the initial investment. A few large projects were progressing, mainly in remote and often frozen areas where exploitation and transportation were difficult. In the Arctic Circle, Polar Lights was the first US-Russian joint venture registered to develop a new oilfield. Along with its Russian partner, a geological enterprise, the US company in the project, Conoco, was exploring and developing four fields in the frozen tundra of the Arkhangelsk (Archangel) region. The Chief Executive Officer of Conoco, Constantine Nicandros, commented that potential investors in petroleum and gas have to, 'contend with an intricate thousand-piece jigsaw puzzle—a mass of irregularly shaped pieces—the sort that could test the patience of a modern-day Job'. The first part of the Polar Lights project was to build a 37-mile (60 km) pipeline, with the first petroleum scheduled by the end of 1994.

Russia supplied some 30% of Europe's natural gas supplies, through 18 pipelines from the Arctic. The equivalent of the United Kingdom's total consumption, 60m. cubic metres per year, was consumed in pumping gas through these pipelines. In the 1970s Rolls Royce supplied 42 gas turbines for the Siberian pipeline, which were still functioning in the early 1990s. The US-led embargo following the Soviet invasion of Afghanistan put a stop to this business. However, Rolls Royce began negotiations with the newly independent Russian Government to sell 30 more engines, for use in the compressor stations, to help prevent wasteful loss of gas during transportation by pipeline, and secured US $210m. in credit insurance. Other supply opportunities were likely to become available, as Russia intended to increase its production of gas by 50% by 2010 and, in 1992, Gazprom, the national gas company, set aside $2,000m. for imports of equipment.

INFRASTRUCTURE

Building an infrastructure capable of withstanding the demands placed on it by the daily transactions of a market economy was a priority for the region as a whole. The first major road project was awarded on a concession finance basis, by the Hungarian Government. A 43-km (27-mile) stretch of motorway, completing the link between Budapest and Vienna (Austria), was to be built under a 35-year concession, by a French-Austrian-Hungarian consortium, led by Transroute, the French motorway operator. It was being built over 27 months and was scheduled to open at the end of 1995. Project costs were scheduled at £250m., 20% financed by the consortium's own equity, 40% by local debt and 40% by international funding. It was an important test case of Hungary's stated commitment to develop the infrastructure through concessions. Six new motorways, totalling 450 km, were planned, with two bridges over the Danube (Duna). Concessions might also be used in a range of smaller, local projects.

SETTING UP

The danger with developing business proposals in Eastern Europe was that companies either expend considerable financial and managerial resources in one of the capital cities, without making much progress, or, inspired by the breadth of the potential, build up quite unrealistic expectations.

There were several problems for Western interests hoping to set up business in Eastern Europe and the CIS. Planning was a painful process: market data was limited; the commercial infrastructure was still evolving; decisions rapidly assumed a political dimension; and funding was limited. Avoiding the detailed preparation work could risk the venture failing later on. The process of putting contracts together might not conform to expectations: nothing could be guaranteed until the final signature, and clauses settled earlier in the negotiating process could still emerge as subjects of debate towards the end. It was important to ensure that the thinking behind different points was clear right from the beginning, because the expectations of the Eastern parties were unlikely to be defined in terms that a Western company would immediately understand. Instead of producing an all-encompassing agreement covering each and every angle of the business, it would be better to produce something short, sharp and governed by Western norms. Negotiations were likely to be complicated by the involvement of a wide number of parties: ministries, local governments, workers' councils and all manner of other authorities. One large construction project in Prague had to get planning consent from 88 different authorities. There might indeed be fewer bureaucrats than under the Communist regime, but then, at least, it was a structured hierarchy. In the early 1990s no one was willing to take responsibility.

Even if a secure contract was achieved, there was a limited appreciation of the extent to which commercial activities were governed by law. Under the old system, when one could be deprived of rights by administrative fiat, there was no tradition of reliance placed on any contract. It was simply a formality. Also, many business activities were governed by a 'get-rich-quick' mentality, the search for a quick profit. In consumer goods, this encouraged protection rings and widespread smuggling. Moreover, in all of the economies of the region, as a private sector struggled to get established, it was often outside the boundaries of the tax system.

CONCLUSIONS

In the early 1990s it would seem that the risks of Eastern European markets suggested they only represented opportunities for large companies. However, ironically, it was the small, entrepreneurial businesses, able to adapt to market conditions, which set up profitable operations most quickly and efficiently. It was in this spirit that most German and Austrian companies entered the market, although in some of the countries they also had the advantage of a close rapport with neighbours.

The main reason for ventures failing in Eastern Europe was neither financial nor legal, but cultural. It was no surprise, therefore, that one of the key lending criteria required for applicants by international banks established in the region was proof of managerial commitment to the market.

EASTERN EUROPEAN ECONOMIES

ALAN H. SMITH

INTRODUCTION

Poor economic performance, which had reached crisis proportions by the late 1980s, played a critical role in the collapse of Communist power in Eastern Europe. Growing dissatisfaction with stagnating (or even deteriorating) living standards and the widening gap between living standards in Eastern and Western Europe contributed to popular unrest in Eastern Europe which became widespread dissent in 1989. The Eastern European economies suffered from a number of common economic problems, at the end of the 1980s, although their extent varied from country to country. Firstly, each country had experienced a continuous slowdown in economic growth since 1950, that had turned into stagnation or decline in several of the economies by 1989. Secondly, each country suffered from disequilibria in state retail markets reflected in growing shortages of consumer goods, burgeoning legal and illegal private markets for goods that could not be obtained in the state sector and growing savings, in relation to incomes and consumption, as incomes grew faster than the growth of supplies in the state retail sector. Finally, growing convertible ('hard') currency debt, which had become acute in Poland, Hungary and Bulgaria by 1989, reflected the lack of competitiveness of the many Eastern European products in Western markets and the lack of incentives to enterprises to seek export markets.

The common nature of the economic problems confronting the Eastern European economies at the end of the 1980s suggests that they had common origins. The principal causes were the imposition of the Stalinist model of industrialization, which concentrated investment in heavy industry, in each country of the bloc, with little or no regard to their natural resources or comparative advantage. Also, the Soviet model of central economic planning was imposed in each country of the bloc, as well as the enforced isolation of the Eastern European economies from world markets and technology and the forced redirection of their trade towards the USSR. These policies had been adopted by Stalin (Josef V. Dzhugashvili/Jugashvili) in the 1930s, in response to the specific conditions facing the USSR at the time. However, they were singularly inappropriate for the smaller, relatively resource-poor and trade-dependent economies of Eastern Europe in the post-Second World War era.

Although many economists in Eastern Europe were aware of the systemic nature of the problems confronting their economies, attempts at economic reform under Communism encountered major political constraints. Successive attempts to introduce elements of a market economy into a centrally planned economy not only failed to bring about a significant improvement in economic performance, but created new sets of problems, which frequently resulted in the recentralization of economic decision-making. In the early 1990s the majority of Eastern European governments had come to accept that economic recovery would involve: the transformation of centrally planned economies into market economies; the redirection of trade flows to the West and to the European Community (EC) in particular; and the adoption of a more rational structure of investment.

The post-Communist governments in central Europe (Poland, Hungary and Czechoslovakia) firmly rejected the idea of a 'Third Way' between capitalism and socialism, in favour of the relatively rapid transition to a Western type of market economy. By the end of 1992 these economies could be said to be effectively functioning as market economies (from 1993 on, this group included only the Czech Republic, while Slovakia favoured a more gradual transition to a market economy). The process of transition was proving more difficult and was likely to take considerably longer in the Balkan economies of Albania, Bulgaria and Romania.

THE ECONOMICS OF COMMUNISM

The Eastern European Economic System, 1948–89

The basic features of the Eastern European economic system were established following the Communist accession to power in 1948. This consisted of the replacement of a market economy with a Soviet-style central-planning bureaucracy. It involved the nationalization (normally without compensation) of large-, medium- and small-scale industries and services; the abolition of the majority of private retail and wholesale markets, to be replaced by state-run networks for retail trade and the administration of inter-enterprise supplies (wholesale trade); the abolition of capital and financial markets and their replacement by a single state banking (monobank) system, which involved a greatly enhanced role for the state budget in financial investment; the destruction of existing money wealth by a combination of excessive printing of money, leading to an exceptionally high rate of inflation ('hyperinflation'), and a confiscatory money reform; the establishment of a centrally administered state monopoly of foreign trade; and the collectivization of agriculture (which was reversed after the death of the Soviet leader Stalin, but reimposed in each country, except Poland, after 1957).

The critical distinguishing feature of the economic system that emerged after 1948 was the passive, accountancy function attributed to money and prices, following the destruction of the financial system. Both retail and wholesale prices were fixed by the central authorities and did not respond to changes in supply and demand. Excess demand for a product in the retail market was reflected in queues and shortages and did not evoke an increase in supply. Similarly, enterprise production decisions were largely unaffected by the prices of either inputs or outputs.

The broad range of economic decisions about who produces what, where and how, which are normally taken in a market economy by private enterprises responding to price and profit criteria, were taken by central planners. The economy was more centrally administered than centrally planned in that central planners were responsible for a large number of routine operational decisions. The process of drawing up detailed plans (plan formulation) and putting them into practice (plan implementation) necessitated the creation of a hierarchical administrative planning bureaucracy with its apex at the central planning agency and its base at the productive enterprise.

The principal intermediate agencies in the planning process were industrial ministries. These exercised operational responsibility for an entire industrial sector (such as machine tools, chemicals, electric power) and were further subdivided into departments, which exercised more detailed control over specific products. In addition 'functional' ministries were responsible for administering prices, investment, foreign trade, etc. The system was explicitly designed to ensure that economic control was exercised by people who were politically reliable (the nomenklatura) and who were responsible to the Communist Party.

The enterprise in this system was entirely a creature of the state which had no independent existence or rights. It did not control the prices of its inputs or its outputs, which were fixed by the state. It did not choose its suppliers or the users of its products, which were determined by the state. It was only entitled to receive such inputs as it had been allocated by the state and could not, legally, buy additional inputs from suppliers. Although the enterprise maintained independent accounts, profits arising from its activity belonged to the state and were returned to the state budget. Any losses from its activity (including unplanned losses) were normally underwritten by the state budget (the 'soft' budget constraint). Consequently enterprises had no incentive to use inputs efficiently. The enterprise did not own its assets and did not have the right to dispose of them. Investment in the enterprise normally took the form of a state budget grant. The enterprise could be merged or disbanded by the state.

In theory, all decisions concerning the enterprises' inputs and outputs were taken by the state planning apparatus. In practice central planners did not possess detailed information about every enterprise under their jurisdiction and were unable to send out precise instructions specifying what should be produced (and where, when and how). Information had to be aggregated according to a common denominator (normally expressed in physical units, such as tons of steel, numbers of cars, etc.), and then disaggregated as it passed up and down the planning hierarchy. Central planners drew up highly aggregated output instructions, which were then passed down to enterprises, with a greater degree of detail being added at each stage of the process. Enterprises in turn passed up information concerning production possibilities and the levels of inputs that would be required to achieve plan targets. Central planners in Eastern Europe worked with data relating to very basic economic aggregates, while a far greater degree of detail was left to the lower level authorities. In practice this gave enterprise managers a considerable degree of control over their economic environment, which they could use to ensure that they both received plans that could be relatively easily fulfilled, and that they received an adequate supply of inputs to meet plan targets.

Economic Growth and the Ratchet Principle

The Stalinist growth strategy attempted to achieve a high rate of growth of industrial output in the USSR by maintaining a high rate of growth of inputs (labour, capital and raw materials) to industry. This strategy placed more emphasis on the mobilization of resources to meet centrally determined targets and less on improving the efficiency with which inputs were used. The strategy also made widespread use of non-indigenous technology, normally by constructing new plants that replicated processes which were then in use in Europe and the USA. A high rate of growth of the capital stock was achieved by devoting a relatively large proportion of national income to investment, which was concentrated in the heavy engineering and metallurgical industries. A high rate of growth of the industrial labour force was achieved by the forced transfer of labour from agriculture and by increased female participation in the industrial labour force.

This economic strategy was transferred to Eastern Europe, in the period from the end of the Second World War to the death of Stalin (in 1953). In 1945–48 the Eastern European countries had started to create 'mixed market economies', in which some large-scale industries were nationalized, but small-scale industry, handicrafts, services and agriculture remained in private ownership. During this period the coalition governments advocated a strategy of 'balanced industrialization', involving government policies to stimulate a level of industrialization, but which took into account the comparative advantages of the countries concerned and their natural resource endowment. Following the Communist assumption of power in Eastern Europe, in 1948, each of the Eastern European countries adopted the highly centralized Soviet model of a command economy. At the same time the Communist governments accelerated plans to develop an industrial base, increasing the proportion of national income devoted to investment and concentrating a greater share of this in heavy industry. Following the outbreak of the Korean conflict, in 1950, the development of heavy industry in each Eastern European country was revised upwards, under Stalin's instructions. In the 1951–55 plan period each country was instructed to increase its investment in heavy engineering goods. The aim was to double or treble the output of producers' goods and heavy engineering products, in order to meet the Soviet demand for engineering products and weaponry, which was generated by the war in Korea.

Central planning enabled planners to direct resources towards the fulfilment of long-term economic strategies. In the 1950s Eastern European planners were principally concerned with the problem of creating an industrial base. Central direction involved the construction of large new plants (often in 'green-field' sites), together with related workers' hostels, housing and other facilities. During this period central planners could exercise a considerable degree of influence over output and growth rates simply by determining the structure of investment. According to official statistics, in the early 1950s industrial output growth in each of the Eastern European countries exceeded 10% per year. However, as new plants came into use, a greater proportion of output was determined by the production capacity of existing plants. The maintenance of high planned growth rates depended to a greater degree on expanding output from existing plants.

In response to political pressures to maintain growth rates, central planners simply 'ratcheted' aggregate plan targets upwards, from the output level that had been achieved in the previous year, in order to obtain the aggregated growth targets that had been established in the five year plan. The new output target was then passed on to industrial ministries, who similarly increased each individual enterprise's output target by the required amount, in order to arrive at the aggregate target for the industry as a whole. The desire of central authorities to generate rapid output growth also led to the preoccupation with gross output targets. Enterprise managers were rewarded for the fulfilment, or overfulfilment, of planned output targets (normally specified in gross physical units) by the payment of money bonuses, which were distributed to both management and workers. Other, non-monetary, material rewards (for example, improved social facilities at the enterprise) were also linked to the overfulfilment of gross output targets. Failure to fulfil gross output targets could also result in sanctions being taken against the manager.

The importance of gross output targets meant that enterprise managers knew that they would always have a guaranteed and rising demand for their output. The enterprise manager's problem, therefore, was the opposite of that which faced a manager in a market economy. The latter's primary problem is finding a market for production (demand constraints). The enterprise manager's problem became one of ensuring that the enterprise could obtain all the supplies necessary to meet centrally determined output instructions (supply constraints).

The 'ratchet principle' meant that enterprise managers knew that next year's plan target, and the level of inputs they would receive, depended on output and consumption in the current year. Consequently, they had an incentive to produce below their real production potential and to overindent and overconsume inputs each year. Once an enterprise had obtained an output plan that could be fulfilled easily, it had an incentive to overfulfil the plan by only a small margin, to prevent a sharp increase in subsequent plan targets. Similarly an enterprise had an incentive to accept (and hoard, consume or barter) any inputs offered to it (which were effectively costless), to ensure it would have adequate supplies for the period when plan targets were increased.

A number of critical problems resulted from the use of gross output indicators for bonus formation. Enterprises were not subject to competitive pressures and had little interest in either the quality of their output or whether the assortment of products (sizes, colours, etc.) corresponded with consumer wishes, provided it met the specifications established in plan targets. Manufactured consumer goods (for which plan targets were frequently specified in volume terms) were frequently faulty and obsolete, in comparison with products in world markets, and might even lack vital components. If output targets were specified in terms of weight, enterprises would concentrate on the production of heavier items in their production range.

The most critical problem was the bias against innovation and the diffusion of new technology at the enterprise level. Enterprises operating with a guaranteed market for their products and facing difficulties in obtaining supplies, preferred to maintain existing product ranges, rather than attempt to bring out a new product, as this was likely to incur start-up problems (particularly if it required altering the input mix), which would jeopardize the fulfilment of plan targets and bonuses. The system effectively punished innovation at the enterprise level. Similarly, the absence of competitive pressures meant that new products and processes were diffused through the economy far more slowly than in a market economy.

A Hungarian economist argued that these phenomena result principally from the 'soft' budget constraint (Kornai, 1980). Enterprises in a capitalist market economy face 'hard' budget constraints. If they fail to cover their costs, fail to modernize production or make poor investment decisions, they risk the ultimate prospect of either bankruptcy or take-over. Eastern European enterprises, however, traditionally had a soft budget constraint. Managers were aware that cost over-runs would be met by state budget subsidies, and, consequently, had no incentive either to produce goods demanded by the markets, or to reduce their costs of production. Similarly, workers who had guaranteed employment at their workplace had no fear of unemployment resulting from poor or shoddy work.

The CMEA and the Redirection of Eastern European Trade

The rapid development of heavy industry increased Eastern European demand for energy and raw materials in general, and for iron ore, coal and coking coal, ferrous and non-ferrous metals and crude petroleum in particular. The Eastern European countries are not well-endowed with raw materials and energy. Poland has major deposits of coal, while Romania was a substantial net exporter of petroleum at the end of the Second World War (and continued to be a net petroleum exporter until 1977) and also possesses rapidly depleting reserves of natural gas. The other major Eastern European sources of primary energy consist of brown coals and lignites, which are low in calorific content, but are extremely high in pollutants. Although the Eastern European countries have some mineral deposits (including rich deposits of uranium in the former Czechoslovakia), the majority were not sufficiently rich to justify commercial exploitation. Nearly 90% of reserves of fossil fuels, and nearly all of the economically viable deposits of iron ore in the Council for Mutual Economic Assistance (CMEA—sometimes known as Comecon) countries were located in the USSR.

The imposition of Stalinist industrial priorities in Eastern Europe resulted in growing Eastern European dependence on Soviet energy and raw materials. Meanwhile the excessive development of heavy industry exceeded European demands for these products. Eastern European industry was therefore forced into long-term dependence upon the Soviet market.

The foundation of the CMEA, in January 1949, formalized the division of Europe into two separate trade blocs. Between the World Wars the Eastern European economies had been largely dependent upon trade with Germany and other Western European countries and had conducted a relatively small volume of trade with the USSR. The start of the 'Cold War', in the 1940s, led to Stalin's veto on Eastern European participation in the US-financed European Reconstruction Programme ('Marshall Plan') and the establishment of Western restrictions on the export of strategic goods to Communist countries (administered by COCOM—the Co-ordinating Committee for Multilateral Export Controls).

The overexpansion of heavy industry in Eastern Europe placed considerable strain on the Soviet ability to meet Eastern European demands for energy and raw materials. The major Soviet sources of energy and raw materials were located in the distant terrains of Siberia, which involved a higher marginal cost of development and transportation to Eastern Europe than alternative sources of supply from world markets. Despite this, until 1990 the USSR supplied energy to Eastern Europe on terms that were more favourable to Eastern Europe than the latter could have obtained from trading in world markets. At least until 1986, when there was a dramatic fall in world petroleum prices, the USSR exported petroleum and gas to Eastern Europe at prices that were substantially below world market prices. The USSR imported manufactured goods from Eastern Europe at prices which were closer to the world market price for equivalent goods, but which did not reflect their inferior quality. Some authors have argued that this pricing arrangement represented a deliberate Soviet subsidy to Eastern Europe which reached a maximum of US $18,600m., in 1981 (Marrese and Vanous, 1983). In exchange, the USSR received the security benefits offered by the ability to station troops in Eastern Europe and the allegiance of the Eastern European governments.

Eastern European dependence upon Soviet energy continued to grow through the 1970s and 1980s. By 1987 31% of Eastern European energy consumption was met by imports from the USSR: Bulgaria was dependent on the USSR for 68% of its consumption; Hungary for 46%; and Czechoslovakia for 40%. Following the collapse of world petroleum prices, in 1986, the USSR came under increasing economic pressure to reduce energy exports to Eastern Europe in order to increase supplies to Western Europe to maintain hard-currency earnings. During 1989 and 1990 the USSR experienced major difficulties in meeting contracted delivery schedules to Eastern Europe, resulting in further economic dislocation in the region. In December 1989 the Soviet prime minister announced that, from January 1991, trade between the USSR and Eastern Europe would be conducted in convertible currency. This move contributed to the halving of intra-CMEA trade in the first quarter of 1991, resulting in major economic difficulties for the Eastern European economies.

The CMEA was formally dissolved in June 1991, but it was the collapse of the Soviet economy and the eventual dissolution of the USSR which were more important factors in rupturing trade links between Eastern Europe and the former Soviet republics. This indicates that it would be exceedingly difficult to restore these trade links, even if the Eastern European economies wished to do so.

Intra-CMEA trade resembled a series of spokes radiating from the USSR to the individual economies of Eastern Europe. At the same time the Eastern European economies failed to develop a rational pattern of trade between themselves. Economic integration in Eastern Europe itself was hampered by the failure to develop a properly functioning financial and monetary system, which, in turn, reflected the underdeveloped role of money and price relations in the domestic economies. The absence of an adequate means of payments for settling international accounts had two principal consequences. The individual Eastern European countries were reluctant to incur surpluses in their trade with one another. Also, trade relations between the Eastern European countries were reduced to a series of cumbersome bilateral barter arrangements.

East–West Trade under Communism

The Eastern European economies were also required to adopt the Soviet foreign-trade system which incorporated a state monopoly of foreign trade. The essential features of this system (in its purest form) were that all foreign-trade relations were conducted by a ministry of foreign trade (or its subordinate bodies) and that enterprises and individuals were not permitted to engage directly in import or export activities. The domestic price system was separated from world market prices, while the domestic currency was nominally linked to world market currencies by an arbitrary, and highly overvalued, official exchange rate. Eastern European currencies were inconvertible, in the sense that the currencies were not traded in international financial markets, residents could not convert the domestic currency into foreign currencies and foreigners could not purchase the currency for purposes of trade or investment. Special arrangements and exchange rates were introduced to cover the currency needs of visitors to and from the countries.

Eastern European enterprises were protected from foreign competition by the state monopoly of foreign trade and, as they were provided with guaranteed markets in the domestic economy and the CMEA, had no incentive to export to the more competitive Western markets. The Eastern European economies found themselves increasingly isolated from international technical developments. This was particularly the case as they had isolated themselves from the investment, marketing and production activities of multinational corporations. These had become both a major source of technology transfer and a means of integration into the world economy for medium-developed countries since the 1960s.

In the mid-1960s the majority of the Eastern European economies made limited attempts to expand trade links with the West. The more radical reformers in Czechoslovakia and Hungary had envisaged opening their economies to foreign competition as part of a complete reform package designed to stimulate efficiency. However the strategies pursued by the Eastern European economies in the late 1960s and early 1970s were largely seen as a substitute for radical domestic reform. This strategy involved attempts to establish trade relations and co-operation ventures with Western multinational corporations and was intended to enable the Eastern European partner to acquire Western technology. The aim was to modernize industry, but neither to allow the foreign partner to exercise genuine ownership or control over the resulting operation nor to have direct access to the Eastern European market. It was initially hoped that Western corporations would be interested in a number of forms of joint production ventures (whereby the Western partner would supply physical capital, in exchange for repayment in products) and joint ventures, in which the Western partner could have minority participation. However the low degree of control offered to potential Western partners (particularly when compared with establishing wholly owned subsidiaries in newly industrializing economies in South-East Asia) meant that they were unenthusiastic about this form of co-operation. Consequently the Eastern European economies were forced into greater reliance on direct purchases of Western licences, of Western plant and equipment and of complete installations (turnkey projects), chiefly paid for by credits denominated in convertible currency. It was intended that the Eastern European countries would export a significant proportion of the production of the new plants to Western markets, earning the convertible currency both to service debt (that is, to pay the interest on the loan) and, eventually, to repay the credits. However the Eastern European economies were unable to generate a large enough volume of 'hard' currency exports to both service debt and repay credits.

This problem has been largely attributed to the failure of the Eastern European governments to adopt the systemic reforms that would have been necessary to make Eastern European goods competitive in Western markets. It has been argued (Poznanski, 1986) that Eastern European exports of manufactured goods were no more sophisticated than those emanating from the newly industrializing economies of South-East Asia, while less sophisticated Eastern European goods were not competitive with exports from these countries, on grounds of price or quality. As a result, the newly industrializing economies' share of markets for manufactured goods in Western industrialized countries rose, from 2.8% in 1970 to 8.6% in 1983, while the share of Eastern European products actually fell, from 1.2% to 1.1% over the same period.

Furthermore, the maintenance and operation of imported equipment necessitated a constant supply of imported components, spare parts and raw materials, placing further strain on the balance of payments. In Poland the problem was further aggravated by the policy of the Gierek Government, which imported consumer goods to increase living standards, following popular unrest in 1968 and 1971. This, in turn, generated popular expectations about the growth of consumption that could not be sustained in the long term. A major debt crisis emerged in the late 1970s.

Eastern European convertible-currency debt continued to grow throughout the 1970s and reached a peak of US $67,000m., in 1981. Of this, Poland accounted for $25,000m. and Romania $10,000m. In 1981 and 1982 Poland and Romania, respectively, were forced to reschedule their debts. This contributed to a major re-evaluation by Western banks of the risks involved in lending to Eastern Europe, which, in turn, resulted in the virtual withdrawal of credit facilities. In the early 1980s the Eastern European economies were forced to reduce convertible-currency imports, being unable to expand exports in order to reduce their convertible-currency debt. The major impact of the reduction was on imports of machinery and equipment and food, as the Eastern European economies attempted to sustain imports of industrial components and materials to keep industrial plant in operation. In the 1986–90 period import restraint could not be sustained, as the Eastern European economies attempted to re-expand their economies. By the end of 1989 three Eastern European countries, Poland, Hungary and Bulgaria, had acute problems of external indebtedness. Poland's gross convertible-currency debt had grown to $41,400m. (or $38,000m. net, that is excluding Polish assets at Western banks), equivalent to some 550% of the annual value of exports. Hungary's gross debt of $20,700m. ($19,300m. net) represented the highest debt per head of population in the bloc (just under $2,000 per head). Bulgarian gross debt had increased threefold, from comparatively safe levels in 1985, to $9,500m. ($8,500m. net) at the end of 1989. The level of convertible-currency debt was of less concern in Czechoslovakia, the German Democratic Republic (GDR—'East Germany') and Romania. However the foreign trade relations of these countries still displayed signs of systemic weakness. Romania had succeeded in eliminating its external debt entirely, but only by imposing draconian restrictions on household consumption of energy and foodstuffs, to the extent that living standards were the lowest in Europe, with the exception of Albania.

The Economic Crisis of the 1980s

In the 1980s the countries of Eastern Europe experienced a combination of stagnating output, deteriorating real terms of trade with the USSR and the attempt to maintain trade surpluses in convertible currency to repay debt. This resulted in a decline in the volume of resources available to satisfy domestic demand for investment and consumption. Western estimates (Alton, 1989) show that the levels of investment in the majority of Eastern European economies, in the mid- and late-1980s, were substantially below the levels recorded in the late 1970s. Reductions in levels of investment were most pronounced in the industrial sector and with 'unproductive investment' in transport, communications, education, housing and health. Cuts in investment in industry and infrastructure resulted in a failure to modernize and even repair industrial plant and equipment. This contributed to increasing product obsolescence and to growing backwardness in transport and telecommunications, which further damaged the long-term competitiveness of Eastern European products in world markets. Reductions in investment in health care were reflected in a decline in life expectancy, high rates of infant mortality and a high incidence of cardio-vascular disease (Eberstadt, 1990).

Although the Eastern European authorities attempted to protect the consumer from the full effects of economic stagnation, personal consumption grew very slowly, if at all, during the 1980s. At the same time wages and money incomes grew faster than the available supply of consumer goods. Basic staple goods, including food, housing and transport, were heavily subsidized by the state as part of a deliberate social policy to keep prices 'pro-poor'. Prices in the state retail networks were fixed centrally and in many cases were unchanged for several years. In state retail markets of virtually all the Eastern European economies this resulted in a rising proportion of the state budget devoted to subsidies, which led to growing budget deficits and to an excess of money demand over the available supply of consumer goods. As prices could not rise in response to excess money demand and the supply of deficit goods was unaltered, this led to growing queues for, and shortages of, basic staple goods and the problems of suppressed inflation. This latter grew more acute towards the end of the 1980s.

An indicator of suppressed inflation (or 'inflationary overhang') is the growth of deposits in state savings banks which, in part, represented involuntary savings arising from frustrated purchases. The value of total deposits in state savings banks (excluding cash) grew, on average, by approximately 66%, between 1980 and 1988, in all Eastern European countries, except Poland, which permitted price increases. Here, savings deposits increased eightfold, but prices also grew ninefold. As these savings were entirely uncapitalized they purely reflected unsatisfied or deferred demand for consumer goods. Excess demand, however, also seeped through into the legal and illegal private markets, where prices were substantially higher than those on state markets, creating new sources of private income and wealth.

Economic Reforms in Eastern Europe

The majority of the Eastern European countries made a serious attempt to introduce economic reforms in the mid-1960s. This was mainly a response to an initial reduction in the rates of growth, which was most marked in the more industrialized economies. Here labour shortages were making it increasingly difficult to secure economic growth by the traditional 'extensive' method (increasing inputs to industry), implying a greater importance for the efficient use of resources. This involved the need for the use of more labour-saving technology and the modernization of machinery and equipment at existing plant, as well as the closure of obsolete plant, which would permit the relocation of labour to modern enterprises. This, in turn, implied sacrificing the goal of job security and accepting open unemployment.

Reforms to the system of industrial management in Bulgaria, the GDR, Poland and Romania left the essential features of the traditional economic system intact. Enterprises continued to receive compulsory output targets (frequently specified in gross outputs) from central authorities and had little genuine autonomy. Changes in enterprise indicators were primarily intended to provide enterprises with an incentive to economize on the use of resources. Enterprise profits remained the property of the state, and the level of profits to be paid to the state budget, or to be retained by the enterprise (for money bonuses or decentralized investment), was negotiated on a case-by-case basis, not according to fixed rules. Prices remained centrally determined, money remained passive and the state monopoly of foreign trade remained intact. Poland attempted to introduce more radical reforms in the 1980s, under stricter political controls, including martial law.

More far reaching reforms were launched in Czechoslovakia and Hungary. The Hungarian New Economic Mechanism (NEM) was introduced in January 1968. Central planning was reduced to establishing long-term (upwards of five years) macroeconomic targets and to controlling investment in key sectors. Enterprises no longer received detailed annual plans, but drew up their own output targets after considering the general proposals of the five-year plan. The central administration of inter-enterprise supplies was abandoned and enterprises were expected to find their own sources of supply. Planners guided enterprises towards long-term targets by the use of financial instruments, including prices, exchange rates, bank credits and rules on wage determination (Marer, 1986). In principle, enterprises were instructed to maximize profits, which could be used to pay wage increases, to finance new investment, and to establish reserves. The central authorities attempted to influence the use of profits by differentiating taxes according to the use to which profits were put and by charging punitive taxes on wage increases above a centrally determined norm. A comprehensive price reform was introduced, which linked prices to production costs.

Reforms were confined to the economic arena and were not allowed to challenge the authority of the Communist party. A major recentralization of economic administration took place in 1972–79, although this did not amount to the formal abandoning of the NEM. This partly reflected the authorities' desire to protect loss-making industries, following the increase in world petroleum prices in 1973, but also revealed anxiety at the widening of income differentials and the growing importance of private-sector activity. The period from 1979 to 1990 saw a reaffirmation of the principles of the NEM. This involved an extension of the use of financial and market levers, to such a degree that it represented a major departure from the traditional economic system.

The principal changes introduced in Hungary between 1979 and 1990 included the dismantling of large enterprises and new rules to encourage the development of small enterprises in the state, co-operative and private sectors. This was intended to increase competition and provide a greater incentive to innovation and the development of new products (Hare, 1987). Other reforms included: an easing of the restrictions on private-sector activity and increased scope for the private sector, such that, by 1989, any private individual or organization could employ up to 500 workers; price reforms, including the gradual abolition of subsidies, which brought domestic relative prices closer to world market prices; the break-up of the monobank system, in 1985, and the development of a Western-type, two-tier banking system, based on a central bank and a series of commercial banks (which became independent in 1987); the establishment of a bond market, whereby local authorities (in 1981) and then enterprises (in 1983) could issue and buy bonds, with the right to buy bonds extended to individuals in 1983; the development of a share market and the reopening of the Budapest Stock Exchange, in 1989, with the possibility of foreign ownership of shares; the decentralization of foreign trade and, in particular, of export rights to all enterprises (1989) and the introduction of a single, unified exchange rate; changes to and experiments with the system of enterprise management and employee relations, including the establishment of workers' councils and the formation of workers' co-operatives and associations within the enterprise, and the election of managers by workers; and, finally, in 1988, the introduction of a non-discriminatory, *ex ante* tax system based on corporation tax, value added tax (sales tax) and a progressive income-tax system (Hare, 1987; Marer, 1986; Richet, 1990). These reforms represented a radical departure from the old system and laid the foundations for the introduction of a market economy after the collapse of Communism. However, the reforms had not reached that critical mass whereby they could be described as irreversible under Communist rule.

The Czechoslovak reforms of 1967–69 were more radical in conception than the Hungarian NEM. They explicitly regarded economic and political reforms as interdependent. Czechoslovak reformers (Sik, 1967) openly stated that worker alienation created by the political system was a major factor contributing to poor economic performance in the 1960s. However, they argued that the political system itself could not be changed unless central planning was replaced by a market system. Unlike the NEM, market and financial criteria were not considered to be subordinate to plan criteria, but were to become the major determinant of economic activity (Kohoutec, 1968). Enterprises were to become self-managed, with elected workers' councils responsible for major decisions. Enterprises could choose suppliers and markets, and could elect to merge with other enterprises if they wished. Prices, eventually, would be determined by supply and demand. Enterprises would not receive compulsory plan targets, but would attempt to maximize net income, which would be divided between wage payments, investment, social investment, etc. Enterprise taxes were to be differentiated, according to the uses to which enterprise income was to be put. The economy was to be opened to foreign competition. The state would determine long-term economic policy largely through influencing strategic investment decisions, through the medium of an interventionist state banking system. These reforms were abandoned after the Soviet-led invasion of Czechoslovakia, in 1968.

POST-COMMUNIST ECONOMIC POLICIES

Strategies for the Transition to a Market Economy

Eastern and Western economists advising the new post-Communist governments argued that the economic problems which had contributed to the collapse of Communist authority in 1989 could not be overcome by further attempts to streamline the existing system. They urged the necessity of transforming the centrally planned economies into market economies with a substantial private sector. The rapid deterioration of the Soviet economy, culminating in the dissolution of the USSR, also resulted in the progressive reduction of trade with the USSR and its successor states. This accelerated the need to establish new markets in the Western industrialized economies.

The majority of governments in Eastern Europe accepted that a number of measures were essential for a successful transition to a market economy. These policies, derived from the experience of economic stabilization programmes implemented in Latin America in the 1980s, under the supervision of the International Monetary Fund (IMF), were initially adapted for Poland by the Harvard economist Jeffrey Sachs. They included: macroeconomic stabilization, which was required to eliminate the inflationary overhang inherited from Communism and to ensure subsequent balance between money incomes and the supply of consumer goods and services; economic liberalization, which involved the removal of the majority of government restrictions on economic activity, including restrictions on wholesale and retail prices and wages and incomes; privatization, including the spontaneous development of a private sector and the transfer in ownership of existing state enterprises, and other interim measures to improve the supply-side performance of the economy by introducing greater competition, including the dissolution of monopolies; and measures to open the economy to foreign trade and investment and to encourage domestic enterprises to seek foreign markets. It was hoped that this programme would be supplemented by Western help and co-operation. This was to involve not just financial assistance, but also technical assistance, including advice, education and training. An inflow of private investment and improved access to Western markets was envisaged.

In the majority of Eastern European countries these measures had to be preceded by parliamentary legislation. A legal framework for the operation of a market-orientated financial system had to be created, and legislation to define and regulate the activities of the newly created commercial and private sectors was necessary. There were various stages, such as the creation of stock and commodity exchanges and the replacement of the monobank system by a conventional two-tier banking system incorporating a central bank and private commercial banks, subject to supervision and regulation by the central bank. There was legislation to determine property rights and to facilitate the privatization and demonopolization of industry and services (this process would range from the development of a private sector *ab initio* in services and small-scale production and the privatization of small-scale state industry and services, to the eventual privatization and dismantling of large-scale state industry). Further legislation codified and regulated the activity of the new commercial sector, including contract law, safety legislation, etc. A tax system had to be introduced, based largely on income taxes and value added taxes (VAT); it was to be established according to predetermined rules, in place of the arbitrary expropriation of state-enterprise profits as the major source of budget revenue. A social welfare system had to be established, to replace the distribution of welfare through the enterprise. Other measures opened the economy to international competition, made the currency convertible and stimulated foreign investment (by attracting direct investment from multinational corporations and by opening domestic capital markets to foreign investors).

Fundamental problems and disagreements arose over the speed and sequencing of the reform proposals. There were further technical questions of how to implement the proposals, the size of the economic and human costs that would be incurred during the transition and whether and how the reform proposals should be adapted in light of specific problems facing individual countries. It was generally accepted that macroeconomic stabilization to ensure at least a reasonable degree of price stability was an essential condition for the efficient operation of a market economy; this must precede, or at the very least accompany, measures for structural transformation. The need for macroeconomic stabilization was most urgent in those countries with high levels of inflationary overhang (suppressed inflation), which were at risk of hyperinflation once price controls were lifted. This would have to be followed by tight fiscal and monetary policies and, possibly, controls over wages, to prevent the re-emergence of inflationary pressures after the initial stabilization.

Major differences of opinion arose (in both the East and the West) over how to implement reform. Some advocated 'shock therapy', the rapid transition to a market economy, with a minimum of government intervention. Others, gradualists, supported an approach that would be sequenced to the specific circumstances in each country and would involve a slower pace of structural adjustment, less austere macroeconomic policies and a greater role for the government in economic policy.

Economists who supported a rapid transition to a market economy (shock-therapists) stressed four major points. Firstly, rapid transformation reduced the period over which inconsistent or incompatible elements of centralized controls and spontaneous market forces co-existed (such as the continuation of subsidies and price controls in the state sector combined with free secondary markets). Centralized pricing and subsidy resulted in economic distortions (e.g. by perpetuating shortages at controlled prices), which increased the rewards for arbitraging activities in place of productive activities in unregulated markets and stimulated economic crime and black-market activity. Secondly it was argued that removing the source of economic distortions as quickly as possible would weaken the power of conservative elements in the economic bureaucracy (nomenklatura), who controlled prices and supplies and could manipulate shortages to their own advantage—they frequently opposed reform because this power was threatened. Thirdly it was argued that rapid reform strengthened the credibility and consistency of the reforms; it provided enterprise managers with a clear sign that 'old practices' should be discontinued in favour of a more consumer-orientated and cost-conscious approach. Fourthly it was argued that public support for essential, but painful, measures would be greatest in the period immediately following the collapse of Communism, when the problems could be blamed on the old system, not the transition itself.

A number of counter-arguments can be made in favour of a gradual approach to reform. Firstly, it was argued that if prices were liberalized before the implementation of structural reforms designed to break the monopoly power of enterprises, enterprises and wholesale agencies would respond to price liberalization by increasing prices and reducing output. The counterargument to this was that the monopoly power of enterprises could be best overcome by exposing them to competition from imports. This however raised the problem that enterprises that might be viable in the long term would be unable to withstand foreign competition in the short term and would need time to adjust to new prices and new technologies. It was also argued that administrators and bankers (trained under Communism) did not possess either the expertise or the appropriate financial data to decide which enterprises would be viable in the long term and which should close. Gradualists argued that decisions concerning the long-term future of enterprises needed to be delayed until a proper system of economic appraisal could be conducted.

The privatization of existing state-owned industries (which were responsible for a substantial proportion of industrial output in each country) proved to be of major concern for the speed of structural transformation. This raised major technical questions of identification of property rights and evaluation of assets as well as questions concerning efficiency and equity. Consequently the privatization of state industry on a wide scale could not be implemented in the early stages of the transition. This indicated that there was a need for a minimum level of sequencing of reform proposals. It did not, however, indicate that shock therapy was impossible. Advocates of shock therapy accepted that the process of transition would be a long and difficult process. However, they proposed that it was still advisable to proceed as quickly as possible, in as many areas as possible, to achieve the point at which the economy could be described as a market economy in the shortest possible time.

The Process of Transition in Eastern Europe

Poland, where the economic problems inherited from Communism were amongst the most severe in Eastern Europe, was the first economy to attempt the rapid transition to a market economy. This became the standard against which other reform programmes in Eastern Europe tend to be assessed. The Government was confronted by the immediate problem of hyperinflationary pressures, following the removal of retail price controls on a large number of goods by the outgoing Communist Government. This did have the advantage that the previous Government had removed much of the inflationary overhang and had borne much of the unpopularity for this measure. On the positive side, agriculture was largely in private hands and markets for food functioned more efficiently than elsewhere in Eastern Europe. The 'Balcerowicz Plan' (named after the academic who was responsible for implementing it as Minister of Finance) came into effect in January 1990. It consisted of an austere macroeconomic stabilization programme, combined with the use of price levers (rather than quantitative controls) to regulate the economy, and the formulation of institutional measures for the creation of a market economy (Rosati, 1991).

The stabilization plan was drawn up with IMF support and largely following IMF guidelines. It consisted of the removal of the majority of remaining price controls, in order to draw out any remaining repressed inflation, combined with a strict monetary policy, involving an attempt to balance the budget (in practice, a surplus was achieved in the first half of 1990) to prevent the re-emergence of inflationary pressures. Budgetary balance was mainly achieved by the withdrawal and elimination of subsidies on basic staple goods (including food and energy) and subsidies to enterprises. In practice, this was combined with the introduction of positive real interest rates (that is, interest rates higher than the rate of inflation) which also discouraged the expansion of inter-enterprise credit. Wages were regulated and kept below the growth of inflation by the imposition of progressive tax penalties on enterprises that paid wage increases higher than norms, which were set at proportions of the official inflation rate.

A critical feature was that the economy was exposed to foreign competition by the removal of the majority of restrictions on import and export activity and by the introduction of a single, fixed (but highly depreciated) exchange rate, which incorporated 'resident' convertibility. The latter enabled residents to exchange the domestic currency freely into convertible currencies, for the purchase of imported goods. This exposed domestic producers to competition from imports and provided a ceiling to domestic price increases, while the depreciated exchange rate offered an incentive to potential exporters and afforded some protection to domestic producers, through prices, instead of quantitative restrictions on imports.

The immediate results of the Balcerowicz Plan were largely positive. After an immediate increase in open inflation, which rose to a monthly rate of 79.6%, in January 1990, it was reduced to 1.8% by the following August. The economy was transformed from one of supply constraints to one of demand constraints in a very short period of time. In the retail sector, street trading grew rapidly and developed into a more sophisticated shop-based economy, following the privatization of a large number of state retail outlets. The growth of the private sector, which contributed to 31% of industrial sales in 1992 and to 44% of employment outside agriculture, was impressive. In 1990 exports to convertible-currency markets grew by 43.4%, leading to a convertible-currency trade surplus, and by a further 17.5% in 1991 and 10% in 1992. However, a 46.9% growth of convertible-currency imports, in 1991, caused the trade balance to return to deficit.

On the negative side, gross domestic product (GDP) fell by 11.6% in 1990 and by a further 7% in 1991. Industrial production fell by roughly 35% to the end of 1991. However, in 1992 Poland became the first country in Eastern Europe to record positive growth of both industrial output and GDP. Although inflation had been reduced from an annual average rate of 586% in 1990 to 70% by 1991, it remained at 43% in 1992 and stayed at that level during the first half of 1993. This necessitated further depreciations of the złoty to preserve the competitiveness of exports and to curtail the growth of imports.

The policy also entailed major social costs. The purchasing power of wages (in terms of wages to retail prices) fell by 24% in 1990, while the removal of subsidies on energy and food badly affected poorer members of the community. Although total incomes grew at roughly the same rate as prices in 1991 and 1992, the distribution of income had become less equal. Open unemployment grew from virtually nothing to 7% of the employed labour force, in 1990, and reached 15% by the end of 1992. Social tensions contributed to strikes, while parliamentary problems resulted in difficulties in implementing government programmes for the privatization of state industry. This background and the consequent desire to alleviate the effects of shock therapy contributed to the electoral gains of the former Communists in the parliamentary elections of September 1993.

The other extreme example of shock-therapy treatment was the case of the former GDR, which ceased to exist as an independent state in October 1990, following the accession of its states (Länder) to the Federal Republic of Germany. This involved monetary and economic union, the adoption of the Deutschmark as the common currency, while the wealthier west of the country (the original Federal Republic—'West Germany') effectively became responsible for the financial costs of macroeconomic stabilization (including welfare payments and the loss of tax revenues resulting from transitional policies) and for the foreign debt of the former GDR (much of which was owed to German banks). West Germany also provided the personnel and expertise for the privatization programme. Furthermore, reunification entailed the absorption of the former GDR into Western Europe and the EC without a transitional period.

The scale of the problems encountered in the transition, resulting from the uncompetitiveness of East German industry and the size of the financial transfers required from West to East to prevent an economic disaster, exceeded all but the most pessimistic estimates. By the end of 1991 industrial output on the territory of the former GDR had fallen to between one-half and one-third of its 1989 level and over 40% of the work-force was either unemployed or on substantially reduced hours of work. The attempt to reduce the inflationary impact of the federal budget deficits (which were a direct result of reunification) by borrowing from international capital markets resulted in high interest rates throughout Western Europe. This was a major contributor to Western recession in the early 1990s.

The Czech and Slovak Federative Republic (CSFR—Czechoslovakia) implemented a form of shock-therapy programme in 1991, after discussions which lasted a year and were affected by political disagreements and nationality problems. In September 1990 the Czechoslovak parliament approved a radical reform programme, drawn up by the market-orientated Minister of Finance, Václav Klaus. It resulted in the introduction of price liberalization on 1 January 1991. Some price controls were retained and currency depreciation was less severe than that of Poland. The extent and pace of macroeconomic stabilization and structural transformation in the CSFR in 1991–92 was such that, by the middle of 1992, it appeared to have overtaken Poland as the most advanced in the transition to a market economy. At this stage irreconcilable disagreements over the pace of the transition were a major factor contributing to the dissolution of the federation into two separate republics, from the beginning of 1993. Elections in June 1992 brought to office a Czech Government under Václav Klaus, committed to an austere macroeconomic stabilization programme and rapid structural reform. In Slovakia (which had inherited more severe structural adjustment problems as a result of its overdeveloped metallurgical and armaments industries and where the unemployment rate was four times higher than the rate in the Czech Republic) the elections resulted in a Government headed by Vladimír Mečiar, which was committed to a slower pace of reform and a relaxation of austere macroeconomic policies.

In 1993 the two new countries established a customs union involving duty-free trade in goods and services and a common external tariff. Monetary union proved to be impractical and short-lived. Moves to establish separate currencies with clearing accounts between the central banks of the two republics were agreed by the parliaments of both countries in February 1993. Although the separation created new problems of defining property rights, citizenship and labour mobility which slowed the pace of structural reform, the Czech Republic continued to pursue relatively rapid reforms in 1993, including a voucher scheme for privatization and a bankruptcy law. Slovakia pursued a slower path of structural reform, involving privatization by more orthodox methods, including direct sales and managerial buy-outs. Ironically, the loss of transfers from the former federal budget to Slovakia, combined with shortages of foreign exchange, were likely to necessitate the adoption of a more austere stabilization programme than would have been the case if the federation had been maintained.

In Hungary progress towards the introduction of market principles was most advanced under socialism and several of the institutions of a market economy had been created in embryonic form. This enabled Hungary to pursue a more gradual approach to structural reform than Poland or the Czech Republic, with more emphasis on the development of a 'social market'. However, the pace of change in Hungary was still dynamic and bore more resemblance to the rapid reformers of central Europe than to the rate of reform in either the Balkan economies or the former Soviet countries. By the end of 1992 Hungary had been the most successful Eastern European economy in attracting foreign investment, which had reached US $4,500m. since 1989, although there were some indications that this was slowing down in early 1993.

The slower pace of reform in Bulgaria and Romania in part reflects the less-favourable location of the Balkan economies as trade partners for the EC and also the impact on their trade of the conflicts in the former Yugoslavia. Bulgaria further suffered from the fact that it was the most heavily dependent on trade with the USSR. The collapse of the Soviet economy (and of the USSR itself) and the CMEA had a far greater impact on Bulgaria's economy and affected its precarious energy supplies. Furthermore, the loss of the Soviet market for its industrial output left Bulgaria with a higher proportion of insolvent enterprises, which complicated macroeconomic stabilization. Bulgaria was also unable to service the high level of foreign debt it inherited from the Communist regime and suspended payments in March 1990. This made it virtually impossible to attract new commercial credits.

Despite the many political and economic differences between Romania and Bulgaria, the slow progress of reform largely reflected the greater political uncertainty and the weaker power base of those committed to reform in both countries. In mid-1993 the Governments in both countries were comprised of coalitions which included technocrats, former Communists and ethnic-based parties. The administrations were headed by technocrats who favoured a gradual transition to a market economy. In Bulgaria the former Communist Party (the Bulgarian Socialist Party) was the strongest in the region and exercised considerable intellectual as well as political influence. In Romania greater power lay with the presidency, and President Ion Iliescu, a former Communist, favoured the gradual implementation of reforms. In both countries the nomenklatura still exercised considerable power at the local and enterprise level. As a result, the transition strategy was implemented with less credibility and certainty than in central Europe. This was reflected in a slower pace of structural transformation, including privatization of state industry and a slower growth of the private sector *ab initio*, and greater difficulties in introducing fiscal reforms and implementing a strict macroeconomic stabilization programme. In both countries, however, the shortage of foreign exchange required the Governments to comply with IMF policies, which was likely to act as a stimulus to reform.

Economic Recovery and the Progress of Stabilization

One of the most remarkable positive features of the early stage of the transition throughout Eastern Europe was the rapid and spontaneous growth of a private sector, initially in retail trade and services, but subsequently extending into manufacturing. This contributed to an improvement in the supply of goods and services on the domestic market and also contributed to the growth of exports.

On the negative side there was a major reduction in reported industrial output and real GDP in each of the former Communist economies. In practice, official statistics tend to overstate the loss of both output and welfare, as reported output under Communism was overstated by enterprises and ministries, to secure bonuses linked to reported output. Even where output fell, this partly reflected the elimination of 'wasteful' production or production of producers' goods which did little or nothing to satisfy consumer welfare. Finally, official statistics after the fall of Communism frequently did not fully reflect the growth of the private sector, as a result of both methodological problems and the under-reporting of output to avoid taxation. Despite these problems, it was apparent that there was a real fall in output and official statistics remained the only guide available.

According to official statistics, between 1989 and the end of 1992 real GDP fell by 23% in the CSFR, by 18% in Hungary and Poland, but by 33% in Romania and Bulgaria. In the same period industrial output fell by approximately one-third in Poland, Hungary and the CSFR, but by over one-half in Romania and Bulgaria. Industrial output grew by 4% in Poland, in 1992, and industrial output and GDP both recorded a small growth in the CSFR and Hungary towards the end of 1992, although falling for the year as a whole. It appeared that the more rapid reformers, Poland and the Czech Republic, had reached the nadir of the transformation programme and would achieve positive growth in 1993, as the growth of private-sector output exceeded the decline in output from state enterprises. The Hungarian Government anticipated that GDP would stabilize in 1993 and grow in 1994. There were fewer grounds for optimism in Romania, Bulgaria and, possibly, Slovakia. Industrial output continued to fall, by 22.5% in Romania and 11% in Bulgaria in 1992, and GDP was expected to fall further in 1993, with economic recovery delayed into the mid- to late-1990s.

The transformation was also associated with the growth of open unemployment, which was a new phenomenon in Eastern Europe, where industrial workers were accustomed to job security under the Communist system. Unemployment grew steadily throughout the region, reaching some 15% in Poland and Bulgaria, 12% in Hungary and 10% in Romania and Slovakia by the end of 1992, but only 2.6% in the Czech Republic, where the growth of the private sector absorbed a significant volume of labour. In general, unemployment was concentrated among women and young workers under 30 years of age who experienced difficulty in securing their first employment. The decline in industrial employment, however, was slower than the decline in reported output throughout the region, implying a fall in labour productivity and the continuation of 'hidden unemployment'. The growth of the private sector (on which economic growth and employment would depend in the long term) was expected to offer fewer opportunities for employment than the fall in employment in the state sector, as unviable enterprises were closed and viable enterprises reduced their work-forces. As a result of this, unemployment was expected to rise for a considerable period after economic growth resumed.

Nearly all of the Eastern European economies encountered major difficulties in reducing central-government budget deficits below the targets established as part of agreements for financial assistance from the IMF. Poorly developed capital markets in the majority of Eastern European economies severely limited the ability of government to borrow from the public to finance government deficits during the transition period. As a result, budget deficits tended to be financed largely by the inflationary process of printing money. Reducing and eventually eliminating budget deficits proved difficult to achieve against the background of falling tax revenues. This was largely a result of the change to a new tax system, based on income taxes and VAT (which require detailed administration and are easier to avoid the payment of), in place of the direct expropriation of enterprise profits. At the same time growing pressure for unemployment benefits and expenditure to protect living standards affected by the transition made it difficult to limit government expenditure.

Despite these problems consumer-price inflation in Hungary was kept down to 23% in 1992; it was reduced from 58% in 1991 to 11% in 1992 in the CSFR, where the Government had the greatest success in containing budget deficits. Romania and Bulgaria experienced the greatest difficulties in controlling inflation. The annual average rise in consumer prices in Romania was 161% in 1991, rose to 224% in 1992 and showed no signs of falling in the first half of 1993. In Bulgaria inflation reached 334% in 1991, but was reduced to 90% in 1992. However, it showed signs of increasing above that level in 1993, following an easing of monetary and fiscal policy as the reform process slowed, and certainly had not fallen below that level in the first half of 1993.

The control of inflation in Romania was complicated by the phased introduction of price increases. This series of increases led to the general expectation among the populace that prices would continue to rise. This made it difficult to control wages and industrial costs; it also required a continuous exchange-rate depreciation, to preserve international competitiveness. An apparently tight monetary policy was further undermined in Romania by the inability to control inter-enterprise debt, which was eventually underwritten by bank credits.

The major area of success throughout the region (with the exception of Romania) was the growth of exports to the Western industrialized nations and to the EC in particular. According to Western data (which were more reliable than Eastern European trade statistics, as the new Governments had difficulties in implementing new recording systems), the dollar (US $) value of imports, by the industrialized West, from Czechoslovakia grew by 121%, from Bulgaria by 94% (although Bulgarian data show a fall), from Poland by 83% and from Hungary by 63%; however, the value of imports to the West from Romania fell by 40%. These figures included the redesignation of imports by the GDR as German imports from 1991, which is significant in the case of Czechoslovakia and Poland. However, there was evidence that the real volume of Czechoslovak and Polish exports to the industrialized West grew by more than 50%, and from Hungary by nearly 50%, between 1989 and 1992. In the case of Poland this offset the contraction in intra-CMEA trade. A significant proportion of this growth came from the private sector.

The growth of exports was a major factor preventing a further contraction of demand in the region, without which the fall in output and the growth of unemployment would have been far more severe. The EC accounted for 77% of Eastern European exports to the industrialized West in 1992, a figure that was explained by the high proportion of Eastern European exports with a high ratio of transport costs to value. Nearly 50% of these goods (including agricultural exports) were composed of products which the EC considers to be 'sensitive', from the perspective of employment in the EC. Similarly, 75% of Eastern European imports from the industrialized West originated in the EC and approximately doubled in value between 1989 and 1992. The expansion of Eastern European convertible-currency exports, between 1989 and 1992, was the most important factor in facilitating the growth of Eastern European imports from the West (and the EC in particular), which should enable the growth of imports of capital goods for economic reconstruction in the long term. Continued access to EC markets (which was covered by association agreements with the EC, allowing for a phased reduction of EC tariffs on imports of manufactured goods from Eastern Europe) was consequently of vital importance to continued economic development in Eastern Europe and of greater long-term significance than Western financial assistance.

CONCLUSION

The transition to a market economy was more rapid and accompanied by a smaller reduction in output in central Europe than in the Balkans, although it was not without economic and human costs that created political and social tensions. It also appeared that these countries would be the first to emerge from recession. There was considerable evidence to suggest that, despite the difficulties, those economies that successfully implemented a strict macroeconomic stabilization programme made more progress towards the introduction of a market economy and to economic recovery than those that failed to stabilize the economy. Furthermore the stabilizing economies were also far more successful in increasing their hard-currency exports, which would help to facilitate a long-term growth in imports and stimulate recovery. Eastern European critics, however, sometimes argue that the stabilization programmes, although correct in principle, were too austere and involved too great a reduction in output and loss of welfare. There was also a real danger that these countries would experience major difficulties in reducing unemployment to socially acceptable levels without incurring accelerating inflation. The Balkan countries made far slower progress towards creating a market economy, in reversing economic decline and in replacing the CMEA market by exports to the West. By the second half of 1993 it was becoming questionable whether they would be able to achieve these goals without considerable assistance from the West.

BIBLIOGRAPHY

Alton, T. P. 'East European GNPs, Domestic Final Uses of Gross Product, Rates of Growth, and International Comparisons', in *Pressures for Reform in the East European Economies*, Vol. 1, pp. 77–97. Washington, DC, USGPO (Joint Economic Committee of the US Congress), 1989.

Brus, W. 'The Peak of Stalinism', in Kaser, M. (Ed.). *The Economic History of Eastern Europe 1919–1975*. Oxford, Clarendon Press, 1986.

Clague, C., and Rausser, G. C. (Eds). *The Emergence of Market Economies in Eastern Europe*. Oxford, Basil Blackwell, 1992.

Dietz, R. 'Advantages and Disadvantages in Soviet Trade with Eastern Europe: The Pricing Dimension', in *Eastern European Economies: Slow Growth in the 1980s*, Vol. 2. Washington, DC, USGPO (Joint Economic Committee of the US Congress), 1986.

Eberstadt, N. 'Health and Mortality in Eastern Europe 1965–85', in *Communist Economies*, 3, pp. 347-372. 1990.

Economic Commission for Europe. *Economic Bulletin for Europe*, Vol. 44. New York, United Nations, 1993.

Hare, P. 'Hungary: Internal Economic Developments', in *The Economies of Eastern Europe and Their Foreign Economic Relations*. Brussels, NATO, 1987.

'From Central Planning to the Market Economy: Some Microeconomic Issues', in *The Economic Journal*, 1990.

Holzman, F. D. 'Comecon: A 'Trade-Destroying' Customs Union?', in *Journal of Comparative Economics*, 1985 (pp. 410–423).

Kaser, M. C. 'The Technology of Decontrol: Some Macroeconomic Issues', in *The Economic Journal*, 1990.

Kolodko, G. W. 'Economic Reform and Inflation in Socialism: Determinants, Mutual Relationships and Prospects', in *Communist Economies*, 2, pp. 167–182. 1989.

Kohoutec. 'On Problems of the Plan and Market', in *Czechoslovak Economic Papers*, 1968.

Kornai, J. ''Hard' and 'Soft' Budget Constraint', in *Acta Oeconomica*, Vol. 25, pp. 231–245. 1980.

Koves, A. *Central and East European Economies in Transition*. San Francisco, California, Westview Press, 1992.

Marer, P. 'Economic Reform in Hungary: From Central Planning to Regulated Market', in *Eastern European Economies: Slow Growth in the 1980s*, Vol. 2, pp. 223–98. Washington, DC, USGPO (Joint Economic Committee of the US Congress), 1986.

Marrese, M., and Vanous, J. *Soviet Subsidisation of Trade with Eastern Europe: A Soviet Perspective*. Berkeley, California, University of California Press, 1983.

Nuti, M. 'The Polish Crisis: Economic Factors and Constraints', in Drewnowski, J. (Ed.). *Crisis in the East European Economy*, pp. 18–64. London, Croom Helm, 1982.

OECD. *Economic Outlook*, Dec. 1992 and June 1993.

Poznanski, K. 'Competition Between Eastern Europe and Developing Countries in the Western Markets for Manufactured Goods', in *Eastern European Economies: Slow Growth in the 1980s*, Vol. 2, pp. 62–89. Washington, DC, USGPO (Joint Economic Committee of the US Congress), 1986.

Richet, X. 'Hungary: Reform and Transition towards a Market Economy', in *Communist Economies*, 4, pp. 509–24. 1990.

Rosati, D. K. 'The Polish Road to Capitalism: A Critical Appraisal of the Balcerowicz Plan', in *Thames Papers in Political Economy*, 2. 1991.

Smith, A. H. *The Planned Economies of Eastern Europe*. London, Croom Helm, 1983.

Winiecki, J. *Post-Soviet-type Economies in Transition*. Aldershot, Avebury, 1993.

THE ECONOMIES OF THE FORMER USSR: AN OVERVIEW

Prof. PHILIP HANSON

After 1991 there were 15 sovereign states in the territory once occupied by the Union of Soviet Socialist Republics (USSR). Relations between them were neither uniform across the vast former Soviet empire nor stable over time. They nonetheless had a great deal in common. It is true that their designation as 'Soviet successor states' was problematic in international law. So far as their economies were concerned, however, they were clearly successors of the former USSR. Their economic structures, and their problems, reflected their common inheritance from the Soviet era.

Their level of development had always been hard to assess. The attempts, in most of them, at political and economic liberalization did not make it any easier. Both the structure of economic activity and the structure of prices remained very different from those of the Western world, even though both relative outputs and relative prices were changing dramatically. Across most former Soviet territory, in 1993, direct and indirect price regulation and subsidies were still extensive. Currency inconvertibility remained the norm. State control of foreign trade was much reduced, but still significant. Several of the states began to use Western-style national income accounting, but in none of them was the statistical system fully adapted to internationally acceptable levels of reporting. In short, the old problems of comparison of economic data were still present.

At the same time the beginnings of economic transformation brought new difficulties for statisticians. The decline in economic activity in 1989–92 appeared to be enormous, but was exaggerated in the available data. The new private sector was inadequately covered by statistical reporting. Part of officially reported output in the past had been a statistical mirage, which disappeared along with producers' needs to exaggerate their output to qualify for plan-fulfilment bonuses. Another part of the officially reported output decline was real enough, but consisted of a loss of wasteful economic activity under the old system. Another part of the officially recorded 'slump' was a loss of arms production, of no value to consumers. Meanwhile, some economic activity that was of the greatest value to households, such as subsistence food production, was substantial, but had never been properly covered in the statistics. This activity probably did not fall at all.

The living standards of households in the former USSR were, therefore, exceptionally hard to measure to begin with; and the decline in general economic conditions after 1989 was, at the same time, exaggerated by the available figures. It can be estimated from the official statistics of the 15 states that net material product (NMP—the old-style Soviet measure of total output, which excludes most services) in the former USSR fell by about 30% between 1989 and 1992. One Russian estimate for the first quarter of 1993 put total gross domestic product (GDP—the more usual, Western measure of total output, including services and depreciation), for the then 10 members of the Commonwealth of Independent States (CIS), at 73% of the first quarter of 1989. The two figures are roughly compatible.

If, as the US Central Intelligence Agency estimated in the late 1980s, the average Soviet consumption level was on a par with that of Portugal or Mexico, a fall of 30% in production, accompanied, as it was, by a decrease in foreign trade, would seem to entail the most severe economic decline for some segments of the population, particularly low-income families with large numbers of children and some pensioners not supported by other members of an extended family. However, the decline experienced by most households, for the reasons given above, was considerably less than the official percentage falls would suggest. One additional reason, not cited above, was that investment fell dramatically; this was damaging for the future of the Soviet successor states, but not for the welfare of the inhabitants of the former USSR in the short term. The extreme economic turbulence following the formal dissolution of the USSR, in December 1991, continued an earlier unravelling which began in about 1988. That, in turn, could be seen as an outcome of destabilizing efforts to reverse the long-term deterioration in Soviet economic performance.

Between the 1920s and the early 1970s the Soviet economy had, on the whole, grown relatively fast. One result was that, on most assessments, the difference between GDP per head in the USSR and in the USA was tending to decline. Thus, the famous Leninist-Stalinist objective of 'catching up and overtaking' the developed capitalist countries was, for a long time, something that Soviet socialism was indeed achieving.

From the late 1950s, however, the growth of Soviet output and productivity slowed remorselessly. By the early 1970s, on official Soviet measurements, the difference between the USSR and the USA was no longer being reduced. For the long-term survival of a regime with ideological claims to economic superiority, this was an ominous development. For a military 'superpower', the prospect of gradually comparing more and more unfavourably with other world economies was even more ominous. However, no serious attempt was made to tackle the problem until the mid-1980s. While Leonid Brezhnev was Party leader (1964–82), there was an early attempt at economic reforms, but, thereafter, the main impulse in policy making was not to disturb the *status quo*.

In 1983, under Yuri Andropov, and from March 1985 to the USSR's collapse in December 1991, under Mikhail Gorbachev, there were serious and increasingly radical attempts by the policy-makers to improve Soviet economic performance. At first there was little agreement on the causes of the slowing of growth, so that remedial efforts were constantly being redirected. Among the causes suggested, with some degree of plausibility: were major economic policy errors (such as in the choice of investment priorities); an excessive military burden; semi-isolation from Western trade and technology; and an erosion of discipline in an economic and political system that relied heavily on authority to function.

In 1987, however, when Gorbachev's early efforts at change began to seem ineffectual, a consensus developed among policy-makers that it was above all the centrally administered economic system that was responsible for the relative economic decline. It followed that a shift from 'planning' to 'the market' was needed. What that meant, however, was not clear to politicians and economists who had grown up in the traditional system. For some time

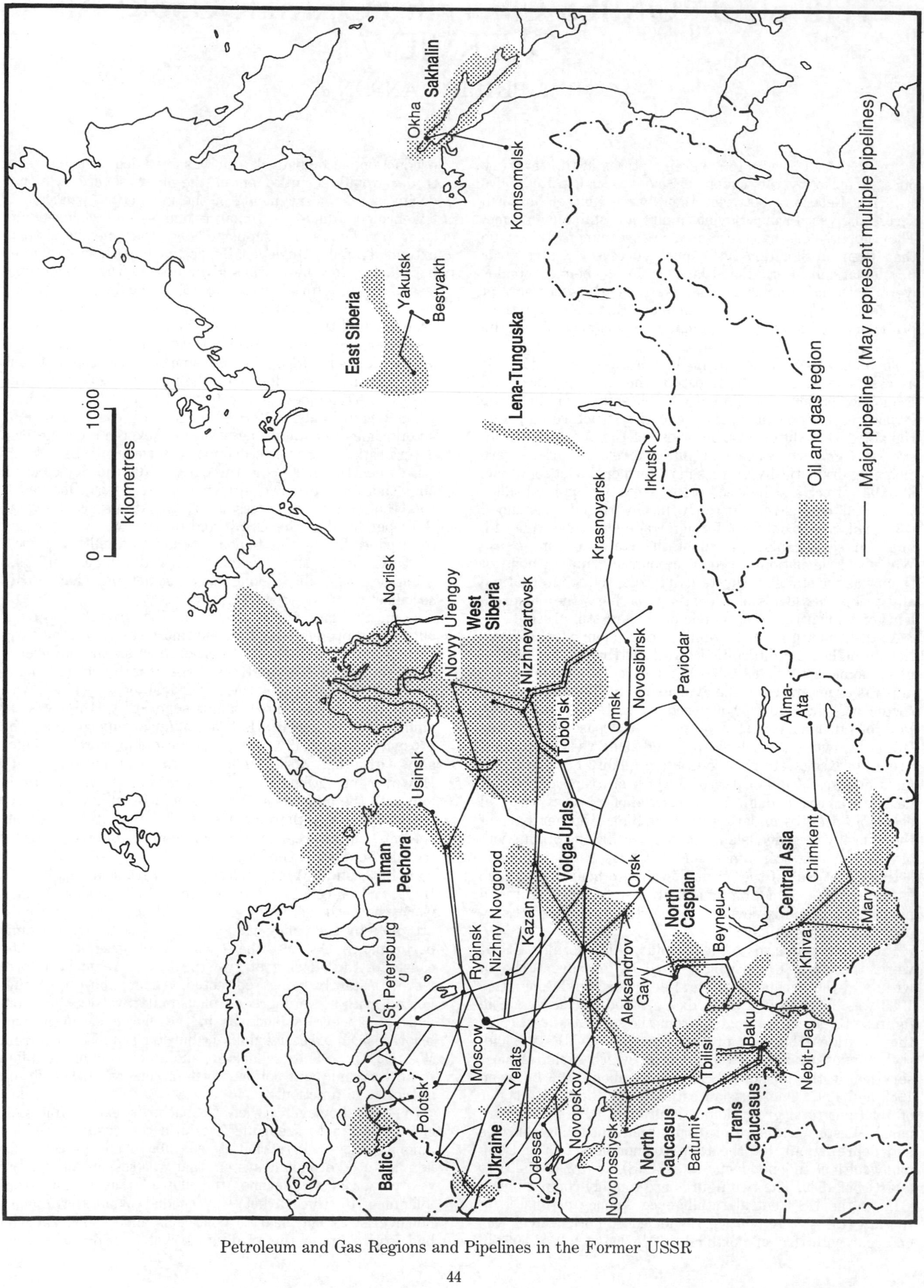

Petroleum and Gas Regions and Pipelines in the Former USSR

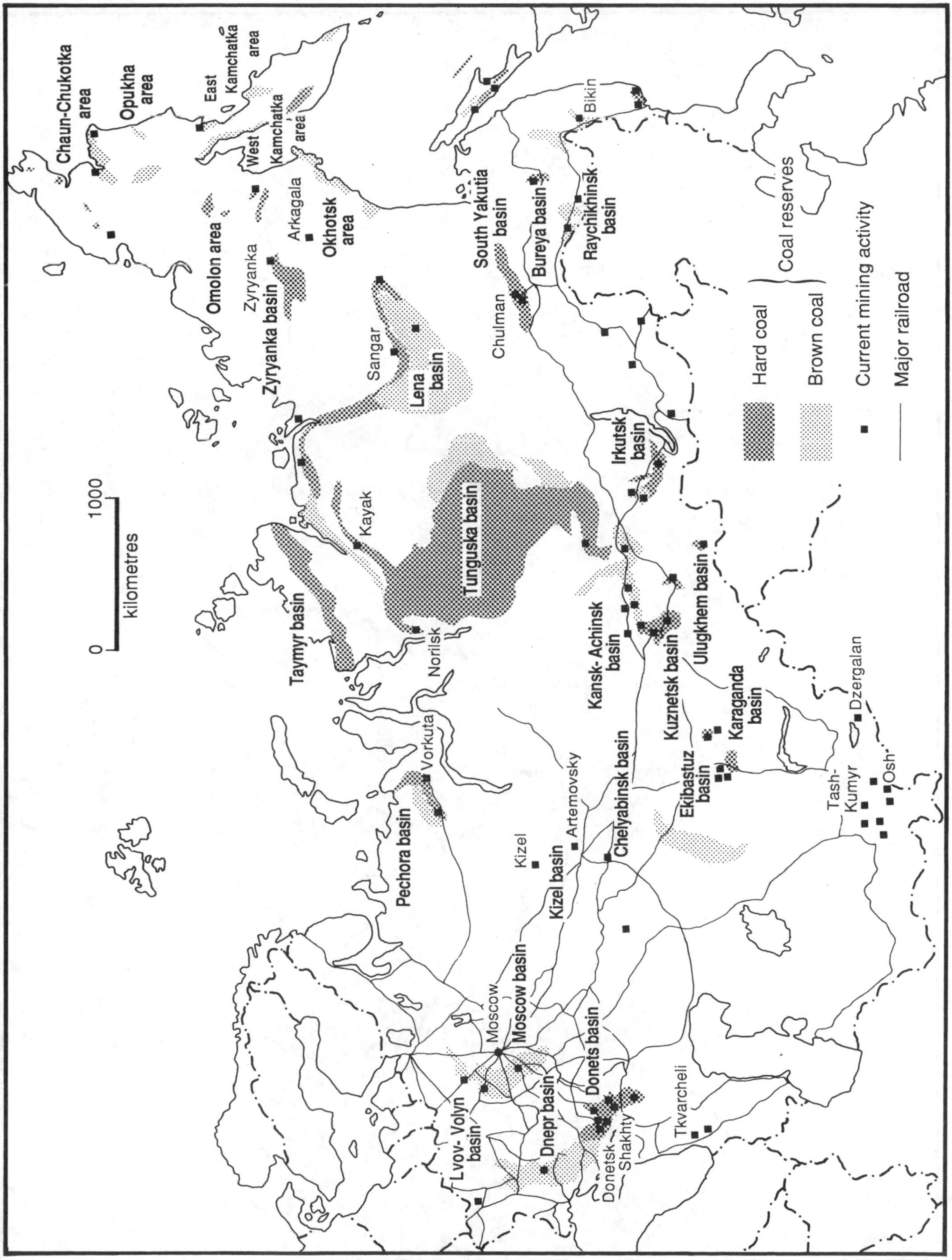
Chaun-Chukotka area
Opukha area
East Kamchatka area
West Kamchatka area
Omolon area
Zyryanka
Arkagala
Okhotsk area
Zyryanka basin
Sangar
Lena basin
South Yakutia basin
Chulman
Bureya basin
Bikin
Raychikhinsk basin
Hard coal
Brown coal
Coal reserves
Current mining activity
Major railroad
0
1000
kilometres
Taymyr basin
Kayak
Tunguska basin
Norilsk
Irkutsk basin
Kansk- Achinsk basin
Ulugkhem basin
Kuznetsk basin
Karaganda basin
Dzergalan
Vorkuta
Pechora basin
Kizel
Artemovsky
Kizel basin
Chelyabinsk basin
Ekibastuz basin
Tash-Kumyr
Osh
Moscow
Moscow basin
Donets basin
Lvov- Volyn basin
Dnepr basin
Donetsk
Shakhty
Tkvarcheli

Mining and Railways in the Former USSR

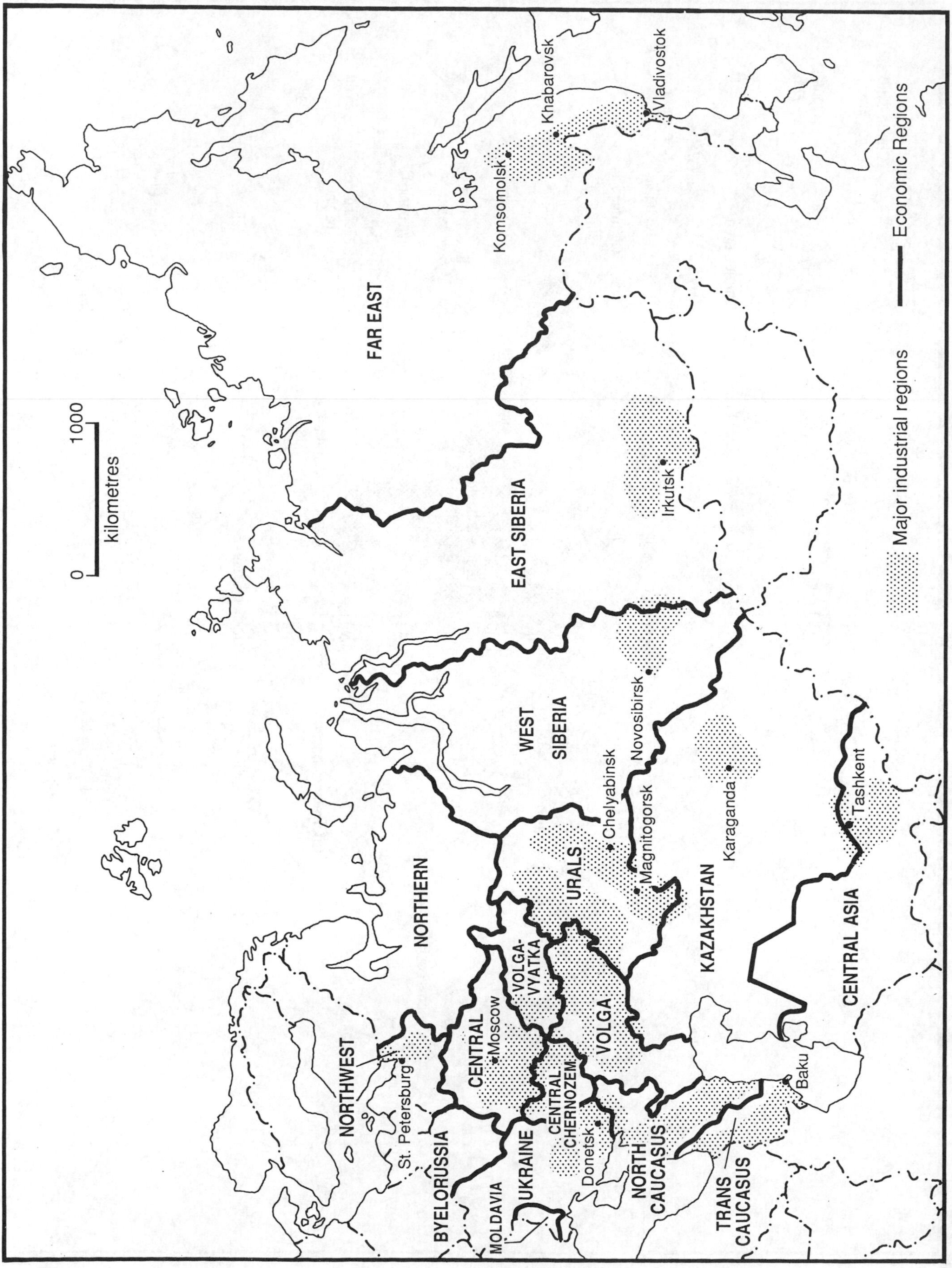

Economic and Industrial Regions of the Former USSR

they aimed to establish a 'half-way house' economy, in which there would be markets for products, but state ownership of nearly all farms and factories would continue. That meant product markets without land or capital markets. Experience in Poland and, especially, Hungary, where such semi-market reforms had been tried, supported the view of some Western economists that a 'Third Way' of this sort was not, in fact, viable.

In Moscow, from about 1989, the idea of a transformation to a Western type of private-enterprise economy began increasingly to be accepted. This remarkable shift in thinking was reflected in a large volume of legislation designed to create the legal framework of a full market economy, with various forms of private enterprise, commercial banks, stock markets, anti-monopoly rules, a convertible currency, and so on. Such a deliberate transformation of an entire economic system in peacetime was unprecedented. It was not surprising that it proved to be a turbulent process. In the four years that followed it was hard to identify clear gains amidst the general upheaval. In principle, a successful transformation of the economic system was a change from which, in the long run, all were likely to benefit. In practice, and in the short run, there were many people whose position would deteriorate, and there was greater uncertainty for everyone about jobs and prices. Moreover, the political liberalization that accompanied the economic changes released hitherto suppressed separatist tendencies and ethnic animosities among the peoples of the USSR. In 1990–91, amidst increasing economic disarray, inter-ethnic and national separatist tensions increased. The failed *putsch* attempt by traditionalists in the Soviet leadership, in August 1991, precipitated a final dissolution. Most of the 15 republics increased their pressure for greater powers at the expense of the centre. Within weeks of the suppression of the coup attempt, the three Baltic states regained the independent status they had enjoyed in 1918–40. In December the Russian leadership, under its President, Boris Yeltsin, effectively signalled that an end to the USSR was now decided.

Turmoil and liberalization both continued across most of the former USSR during 1992 and 1993. The CIS, initially with 11 members (the 15 former Union Republics less Georgia and the Baltic states of Estonia, Latvia and Lithuania), was not a federation or confederation. It was not even a coherent economic community or a functioning military alliance. For much of that period such issues and balances were still being resolved, while there were civil wars underway in Georgia, Moldova and Tajikistan and a war between Armenia and Azerbaijan over the disputed territory of Nagorny Karabakh. Towards the end of 1993 all the former Union Republics had joined, or rejoined, the CIS, excluding the three Baltic countries, which had virtually completed their withdrawal from the USSR before its dissolution. In September Azerbaijan (which had effectively withdrawn in October 1992) rejoined the CIS and, in October, the Georgian Government of Eduard Shevardnadze (shortly after suffering defeat from Abkhazian separatists) conceded that the country should also become a member of the Commonwealth.

The 10 CIS member states in early 1993, however, accounted for about 93% of the USSR's all-Union 1990 GDP. The five successor states outside the CIS accounted for only about 7% of the total. For all the weaknesses of the official statistics, the variation those statistics show in economic fortunes amongst the successor states provides at least some guidance to the degree of difficulty they were in. The greatest output declines occurred in Armenia and Tajikistan, within the CIS, and in Georgia and Lithuania of the 'outsiders'. The least damaged, according to the official statistics, were Turkmenistan, Uzbekistan and Belarus.

The pattern that emerges from these admittedly poor quality statistics makes sense. The large output falls in Armenia, Georgia and Tajikistan reflect the effects of extensive and prolonged conflict on their territories. The large fall in Lithuanian output is attributable to a combination of a chaotic and destabilizing economic policy, under President Vytautas Landsbergis, and particularly poor relations with Russia, which led to significant disruptions to fuel deliveries from the CIS. For much of 1992 and early 1993 Lithuanian industry and housing were subject to prolonged periods without fuel and energy. The ex-Soviet states that exhibited the most modest falls in output—Turkmenistan, Uzbekistan and Belarus—had one thing in common: they had done very little to change their economic systems. Their relatively stable rates of output, therefore, were signs of atrophy rather than health. In these economies the necessary liberalization of prices, stabilization of the price level, privatization of ownership, opening to the world economy and restructuring of economic activity had been deferred. This was not the result of an explicit adoption of the old, Communist ideological stance by their leadership. The situation, broadly, was that policy-making was dominated by traditionalists from the old élite, who spoke of the need to proceed cautiously with reform but did not openly repudiate reform in general. Market reform had become the new orthodoxy. The real division amongst policy-makers was between those who were serious about it and those who were unenthusiastic and nervous about their chances of keeping power if they embarked on substantial change.

Rapid inflation was a common experience for all but two of the ex-Soviet republics. Estonia and Latvia carried out successful monetary reforms, introducing new currencies whose exchange rates they succeeded in stabilizing. In the case of Estonia, this was the kroon (crown), introduced as the sole legal tender in June 1992; in the case of Latvia there was first a transitional currency, the rublis or Latvian rouble, and then, in 1993, the lat was introduced. In the first half of 1993 officially measured consumer-price inflation in both countries was down to annual rates of 20% or less and exchange rates against major Western currencies had held steady for about one year. In the other former Soviet states inflation was typically around 2,000%–2,500%, in 1992, and 500%–1,000%, at an annual rate, in mid-1993.

Despite the apparent collapse of output, officially recorded unemployment remained low. In Russia, in the first quarter of 1993, registered unemployment was only 1% of the labour force. This was a typical figure for most of the former USSR. Even in Latvia and Estonia, where tough monetary and fiscal policies had been in effect, registered unemployment remained below 5%. As with so much of the official statistical information, however, these numbers were misleading. Many people were on short-time working, or on enforced vacations from work-places that had no work for them; others had recently been made redundant but did not yet qualify for unemployment benefit for the maximum period allowed, or had, in any case, withdrawn from the labour force, discouraged about the chances of finding work.

At the same time, the low official unemployment figures did not entirely misrepresent the situation across most of the former USSR. State enterprises were not being closed down. Nor were they being forced to make mass redundancies. With the exception of Estonia and Latvia, monetary policies generally remained soft, and budget subsidies continued to support many state enterprises. In other words, progress in the restructuring of the successor state economies was limited.

GROSS DOMESTIC PRODUCT

The statement that restructuring was limited is based on casual observation rather than a secure statistical picture. The structure of economic activity in the former USSR as a whole could not be depicted with any precision for the first few years after the fragmentation into 15 different countries. Data from some successor states were lacking; in others, divergences in statistical concepts and measures were reducing comparability between the different countries; even if these problems had not existed, variations amongst the states in the extent and pattern of price liberalization would have made any compilation of the numbers unreliable.

In 1990 the composition of Soviet GDP, at current prices, was: industry 32%, agriculture 18%, construction 10%, transport and communications 6%, retail and wholesale trade 12%, other services 22%. At that time the farm sector's share was probable under-stated. Some very rough calculations, for Russia and Ukraine combined, give some idea of what the official figures for some of these sectoral shares might be in 1992 for the former USSR. Between them, Russia and Ukraine accounted, in 1990, for 75% of Soviet GDP, 82% of gross industrial output and 69% of gross agricultural output. Combining Russian and Ukrainian official data indicates that the share of industry in total output, in 1992, was about the same as in 1990. Official measures of both industry and GDP had fallen, but, in the two countries together, they had fallen in about the same proportion. The farm sector's share of the total had risen very slightly: that is, farm output fell somewhat less than GDP.

The reality was probably somewhat different from the story told by these official figures. The industrial output figures were probably upward-biased, relative to the other figures, so more reliable measurements would probably show a slight decline in industry's share of total economic activity. The official data imply that there had been little change in the share of the services sector. That is almost certainly misleading. The new private sector was heavily concentrated in services, including business services, and the growth of that sector was underestimated in the official data.

The composition of Soviet GDP, by end-use, in 1990, according to official sources, was: household consumption 50.2%; public-sector consumption 19.7%; gross fixed investment 23.0%; and changes in inventories 7.1%.

The one thing that is certain about subsequent changes in the relative importance of those final spending categories across the successor states is that the fixed investment share fell sharply in the following two years. Where investment figures were available, they all showed a marked decline. Indeed, it is clear that in many sectors gross investment was less than retirements of capital assets, so that the capital stock was shrinking. One effect was to reduce capacity in some branches of production. Another was to reduce technological change, since much new technology would have been embodied in new machinery.

The share of household consumption in total final expenditure appeared to have increased. This does not automatically follow from the relative fall in investment, since other final end-use categories exist, but it was implied by the evidence both of a relatively modest decline in farm output and a lesser decline in the output of manufactured consumer goods than of manufacturing in total. A more complete and accurate picture than that provided by the official data could be expected to strengthen this conclusion. Under-recorded activities, in other words, tended to be related to consumption.

DIFFERENT TENDENCIES AMONGST THE SUCCESSOR STATES

The economies of individual Soviet successor states are discussed in the relevant chapters in Part Two. The broad picture shows rather little uniformity amongst them, beyond their common heritage. The dissolution of the USSR was widely expected to cause very great damage for all the Republics except the Russian Federation. The poorer countries, especially those in Central Asia, benefited from budget transfers from the all-Union Government under the old order. They had to endure severe budgetary problems when those transfers ceased, weakening their chances of maintaining a politically viable minimum of social services or of avoiding highly inflationary budget deficits—or both.

All the former Soviet countries had generally had, according to official figures, a deficit in the deliveries of merchandise between Russia and themselves if the goods in question were valued at world prices. This was not obviously the case when these flows were measured in Soviet rouble prices; the main source of this discrepancy was the underpricing in roubles of petroleum and gas, of which Russia was the dominant supplier. This assessment, however, was always problematic.

To begin with, all Soviet prices were distorted in a variety of ways, not easily captured in the world-price valuations that the statisticians in Moscow were using.

The flows of services, as distinct from goods, were neglected. In several cases, such as Ukrainian and Baltic-state provision of transit and port services, these could be the source of substantial net earnings for the states in question under a liberalized regime.

More fundamentally, there was no reason to suppose that the previous pattern of flows of goods, set by the Soviet planners, would have much justification under a new, reforming, economic order. Some of the desirable adjustment involved, however, could only occur as the structure of production capacities changed. That, in turn, would require investment and would not, therefore, occur immediately.

A third expected source of difficulty for most of the former Soviet Republics was their transactions with the outside world. With a few exceptions, notably Russia, they generated only small export flows to the outside world, compared with the imports allocated to them by Soviet planners. And no republic could be expected to inherit useful reserves of gold and hard currency net of foreign debt, since the USSR as a whole was widely understood, from the available data, to have bequeathed net liabilities to its successor states (Russia subsequently negotiated implementation of the 'zero option' with many of the successor states, whereby it assumed responsibility for their share of the Soviet debt in exchange for their renunciation of any claim to Soviet assets).

In the event, the varying economic fortunes of the 15 countries, in 1991–92, could not be explained by the dissolution of the USSR. All showed a severe decline in economic activity. However, the variations amongst them in the depth of that decline did not coincide with projections of their degree of 'dependency' on Russia or the rest of the former USSR. Small states with large budget transfers from Moscow in the past, and very large shares of output dependent on transactions with the rest of the USSR, did not necessarily fare worse than the others.

One reason for this was that failures in supplies of materials and components occurred between production units within each successor state, and by no means only in cross-border flows. At the same time other internal factors, specific to each of the 15 states, rather than the links between them, had powerful effects on the course of economic events in each case.

Particularly important were: war and civil war and the presence of reformist or traditionalist leaderships. Countries engulfed in fighting suffered both from the direct effects of war on economic activity and from an inability to put efforts into economic reorganization. The most systematic reformers succeeded in cutting inflation, but at the cost of substantial declines in economic activity. States that embarked on reform but failed in stabilization had high inflation but slightly less of a decline in output. The most unreconstructed of the successor states exhibited somewhat lower inflation than the would-be reformers, and substantially less of an output decline than any of the other states. Finally, there were some special instances, where factors unique to a particular state played a role.

The main economic casualties of war were mentioned earlier. They were Armenia, Georgia and Tajikistan. In Armenia and Georgia, officially recorded output in 1992 was one-half or less of the 1989 level. Moldova, where fighting had been localized and was brought to at least a temporary halt, showed less severe decline. Both Armenia and Georgia, with traditionally entrepreneurial cultures and, in the case of the former, a large and wealthy diaspora, had more potential for economic modernization than the rest of the former USSR. In both cases, land and housing privatization, requiring less elaborate policy-making than industrial privatization, were developing relatively well, despite the disruptions of war. However, both suffered not only from the direct effects of war but from having supply routes from the outside world blocked for reasons to do with the fighting.

Tajikistan, like Turkmenistan and Uzbekistan, was, furthermore, a slow reformer, as was Moldova. The much higher rates of inflation in Moldova than in Central Asia seemed to reflect its greater intertwining with the Russian and Ukrainian economies. Thus, inflation was much the same in Moldova as in the two larger states.

In Kazakhstan and Kyrgyzstan, price liberalization was more cautious than in Russia, but reform policy, in the sense of privatization, was quite active. Policy-makers in Kazakhstan, where there was a well-endowed natural-resource base, were able to convince some major Western energy companies that the country was politically more stable and better-administered than Russia, and began to attract some significant foreign direct investment.

So far as price and trade liberalization and macroeconomic stabilization were concerned, Estonia and Latvia were well in advance of the other former Soviet countries. As was mentioned above, in 1992–93 both succeeded in achieving control over the money supply and inflation, thus creating an economic environment favourable to the development of a market economy. Like Lithuania, they had the special advantage of being able to claim back modest stocks of gold, which had been held in the West for the pre-Second World War independent Baltic regimes. In Lithuania, however, although privatization made progress, particularly poor financial relations with Russia, combined with considerable disorder in economic management in 1991–92, produced rapid inflation. There was also an officially reported output fall as severe as that experienced by Georgia or Armenia.

The Russian Federation, with about one-half the population of the old USSR and perhaps three-fifths of Soviet GDP, naturally had a large influence on all the other former Soviet states. Its leadership approached reform more seriously than any of the others, except Estonia and Latvia, but encountered powerful domestic resistance to liberalization and stabilization (progress was more likely after the October suppression of the conservative parliament, which had often impeded implementation of the Yeltsin Government's reform proposals). In general, Russia fared slightly worse than the ex-Soviet average, if the official data for inflation and output decline were any guide. Ukraine and Belarus adhered to moderately traditionalist policies, and exhibited smaller falls in output than Russia. Belarus, however, appeared to do rather better than Ukraine at suppressing inflation by price controls. Early Ukrainian experiments with a separate national currency were particularly ill-conceived and damaging to stability. Its economic crisis was compounded through 1993 by the continuing failure to resolve the conflict of powers between a conservative parliament and a reformist Government—an exacerbating factor in Ukraine, unlike Russia, was that, ultimately, the President was unwilling to back his premier.

In general, the developments in the Soviet successor-state economies reflected a multitude of influences, and the range of outcomes was quite wide.

ECONOMIC RELATIONS BETWEEN THE SUCCESSOR STATES

In late 1991, as the USSR was in the last stages of disintegration, strenuous efforts were made to establish an economic union. Grigory Yavlinsky, the economic official who led the negotiations on behalf of the Soviet Government, said at the time that some sort of economic community was the most that could, by then, be negotiated; mistrust and mutual animosities precluded, in his view, the salvaging of even a loose political confederation. What he and his allies—including, at this stage, the International Monetary Fund (IMF)—hoped for, was the maintenance of a 'single economic space': essentially, a single currency and an area in which goods, labour and capital could move freely. The project failed.

To keep a single currency and also stabilize it (that is, reduce inflation to a low level) required close co-ordination of monetary and budgetary policies. It also required that those policies be kept restrictive. If co-ordination was lacking, growing budget deficits and credit creation in some of the states would have inflationary effects on all of them. Indeed, the temptation for each state to pursue inflationary fiscal policies was strong, since the inflationary consequences of its deficits would be spread across the whole currency area. Only Russia was so large a part of the ex-Soviet economy that its policy-makers could reasonably identify their national inflationary tendencies with those of the whole region.

Yavlinsky and others at this stage drew up plans for an inter-state bank, under which rouble monetary policy would be controlled for the whole 'rouble zone'. On the analogy of the US Federal Reserve system, this would have been a central bank, jointly controlled by the Soviet Republics.

There were three fundamental difficulties with this project. First, there were suspicions and animosities between many of the states and a widespread reclaiming of national identity, which made co-operation politically hard to achieve. Second, the differences in development level and location relative to other, non-Soviet states were very great. Output per head in Tajikistan was perhaps one-third that of Estonia and well under one-half that of Russia. The gravitational pull of trade with 'outside' partners would, in the long run, be very different for different successor states: for Kazakhstan, with China and the countries of South and South-East Asia; for Ukraine, with Poland and central Europe, and so on. Finally, the position of Russia was such as to create particular difficulties. For nationalist leaders in many of the successor states, Russia represented the imperial power against which they were asserting their identity; and it was, in addition, such a large part of the total that it was bound to dominate any 'Commonwealth' or 'economic union'.

When the 15 states embarked on their separate national existences, the rouble remained the common currency of all of them. Links between producers and customers in different successor states were close and well-established. The Kreenholm Textile Works, in Narva (Estonia), for example, was processing Uzbekistani cotton, and selling fabrics and clothes to many other Republics, including Ukraine.

There was, moreover, a high degree of monopoly, because of the traditional Leninist obsession with economies of scale, the central planners' need to deal with as small a number of production units as possible, and the absence of a monopoly pricing problem in a centrally administered economy. Almost all better-quality school exercise books were produced at a paper mill in Kaunas (Lithuania), for example, and there was only one producer of tractor-feed computer-printer paper in the USSR.

The scope for rapid adjustment of the pattern of production and supply was, therefore, limited. It was not as limited as it might at first appear to have been, however, for two reasons. First, many Soviet enterprises produced for their own use a great many items which were outside their official 'profile' components (specialized machinery and even food for their own work-force). Second, much of what was produced was wasted, or not wanted at all, and the transport of many supplies was also unnecessarily indirect and costly. Therefore, some adjustment of the pattern of output and deliveries was already occurring in 1991 and continued to develop in 1992–93 without additional investment being needed to support a restructuring of capacity.

In the long run, with market economies established, production capacities reshaped, and a reorientation of trade relationships allowed, it was likely that trade amongst the former Soviet Republics would fall and trade with the outside world expand. Two independent projections of the effects of such changes, made in 1992, suggested a broadly similar picture: in the long run, with market economies and a general opening to world trade, the trade between the former Soviet Republics would be likely to be some 20%–40% of its 1987 level and trade with the outside world correspondingly larger.

Even so, inter-republic trade could usefully continue at relatively high levels for a time. The adjustments to a new environment would take several years. The changes in trade patterns which could be made in the short run were limited by the inherited structure and location of capacity. Given those limitations, the maintenance of open trading amongst the successor states, and above all an effective system of payments, was desirable. Moreover, fragmentation into different currencies would put a great strain on the skills and institutions available to operate 15 different monetary systems. Such expertise as there was, was mainly to be found in Moscow. The IMF's initial support for a single rouble currency zone was understandable. However, the necessary co-ordination of monetary policies was, for political reasons, not feasible.

The successor states began 1992 with a common rouble currency. The Russian central banking authorities in Moscow retained the sole right to issue rouble notes and coins. Credit expansion, however, was in the hands of the new central banks in the other 14 states. Budgetary policy, likewise, was in the hands of their governments and parliaments. Goods deliveries were largely at the discretion of individual enterprises, but state and, often, local authorities took control of some of the output of enterprises on their territory and traded it themselves, or tried to impose control on enterprise transactions by licensing. Meanwhile, border controls at the new inter-state boundaries were rare and, where they did exist, of an improvised character.

All the states tried to impose some sort of control on cross-border flows, mainly on exports of food, consumer goods and key raw materials. In conditions of shortage and sellers' markets, the governments concerned were trying to raise apparent domestic availability of these items, regardless of the damage done to each country's gains from trade.

Russia first introduced export licences for deliveries outside the former USSR, and then extended the licensing system to exports to other former Soviet Republics. For some products, this may have worked. For many others, the customs controls were inadequate. Large quantities of metals showed up in Estonian exports, for example. Some of this was scrap recycled from inside Estonia, but much of it came from Russia.

Many trade agreements were signed between the various states. The implementation of them, however, was low. The governments mostly had insufficient control over production and distribution on their own territories to be able to deliver what they promised.

Prices in inter-republic trade were mostly, in 1992–93, not world market prices; settlement was initially in roubles. By mid-1992, however, the Russian administration had come to view the 'rouble zone' as a threat to its own efforts to control inflation. Poorly controlled credit expansion in other states allowed their enterprises to buy supplies from Russia with rouble settlement through the banking system. On the Russian side, at least in early 1992, a serious attempt was being made to control credit. Thus, most of the other former Soviet states were operating trade deficits with Russia, and rouble bank accounts were being established in Russia from the credit expansion in Russia's partners. The Russian authorities moved to curb this by requiring all cross-border rouble payments to go through correspondent accounts at the Russian Central Bank and by imposing upper limits on the imbalance that could be accumulated in these correspondent accounts. The idea of the limits was to limit the growth of Russia's money supply through the import of excess money creation in the other states. Accordingly, the limits were made adjustable, in the light of each partner's monetary behaviour. If one of the other states was willing to allow its money supply to be controlled, in effect, by Moscow, the limit could be raised, if not, it would be lowered. The third possibility was that the other country might introduce its own currency; if it did so, settlement with Russia might still be carried out through the correspondent account, but the other state would be under pressure to introduce its own currency in such a way as to keep the inflationary effect on Russia to a minimum—for example, by withdrawing its cash roubles from circulation and handing them over to the Russian Central Bank, rather than letting them flood into Russia as they ceased to be legal tender in the other state.

The rouble thus ceased to be a common currency, freely exchangeable across the whole of what had been a single rouble zone. Some of the ex-Soviet states were, in any case, introducing their own currencies. In 1992 there were two types of new currency: those that had been introduced as the sole legal tender and those that had been introduced as a parallel currency to circulate alongside the rouble. The two successful examples of the first type, the Estonian kroon and the Latvian rublis (later, the lat) have already been described. The Lithuanian talon (replaced by the litas in mid-1993), the Ukrainian karbovanet, and several others, were less successful currencies (or, rather, coupons—temporary currencies, which did not fully comply with IMF, etc., requirements), representing no improvement over the rouble.

From mid-1992, even those states outside Russia still mainly using currency known as 'roubles' were, in reality, outside a single rouble currency area. It remained open to all ex-Soviet states, however, with or without new currencies, to continue to trade with Russia on the basis of rouble settlement. Their correspondent accounts with the Russian Central Bank would then be their reserves, supporting trade with Russia and with each other. This option was akin to the sterling area of 1931–68, although the pound sterling in the last years of the sterling area was a convertible currency, while the rouble was not.

The other main options were the use of US dollars for inter-state settlement, the revival of the rouble zone, and the establishment of a payments union, under which net balances outstanding would be periodically settled in a mixture of convertible ('hard') currency and credit. The restoration of the rouble zone would require the establishment of a joint, inter-state bank. That proved impossible to agree during 1993. Dollar settlement would need quantities of dollars that would be impossible for some of the states to provide. The clearing-union scheme would need less hard currency, but would call for a degree of co-operation and appropriate expertise to operate it.

In the course of 1992–93, payments arrangements were a shifting mixture of rouble zone, rouble area and dollar settlement. Arrangements varied over time, amongst different groups of states and across different types of transaction. In addition, many transactions across the new state borders were carried out on a barter basis or with the use of cash roubles.

A combination of real economic contraction, some reorientation of trade towards the outside world, the abandonment of wasteful and unwanted transactions and the disintegration of the rouble zone led to a fall in the volume of trade amongst the former Soviet Republics, in 1992–93. The dimensions of this decline could not be reliably measured. Official data for Russia, which might be misleading even for Russia's trade alone, indicated declines in the volume of deliveries of particular products, between 1990 and 1992, as large as 76%. Of the 13 products for which such data was published, only one—natural gas—showed an increase in deliveries to the rest of the former USSR. The largest fall, the 76% decline mentioned, was for passenger cars. Deliveries of steel fell 61%, of fuel oil 40%, and so on.

The fall in this intra-republican trade was probably greater than the decline in production. For Russia, deliveries to the rest of the former USSR fell more than output for 11 out of the 13 products. The exceptions were crude petroleum and natural gas.

The extent to which trade fell varied greatly between the different states. Early on, Russia sought to make the terms of its trade less attractive for non-CIS members than for its CIS partners. The main lever, so far as these terms were concerned, was the threat to shift to 'world prices' and hard-currency settlement. For most of 1992, however, Russian energy prices, even to the Baltic states, were below world market levels. Subsequently, dollar payment began to be demanded. Estonia, for example, arranged, in June 1993, to pay US $6m. arrears owing for Russian gas. Lithuania continued to default on payment for Russian energy supplies and suffered accordingly.

Increasingly, in late 1992 and 1993, pressure also began to be put on other ex-Soviet states, whose formal relations with Russia were closer than those of the Baltic states. A CIS Oil and Gas Council, meeting in Surgut, West Siberia, was established, in March 1993, to co-ordinate petroleum and natural gas distribution. Lithuania, despite not being a CIS member, was represented. Estonia and Latvia were not. Around this time, Ukraine, at least, was being asked to pay world prices for Russian gas supplies, and was retaliating by asking a transit fee of $2.20 per thousand cubic metres of gas crossing Ukrainian territory to Western European markets. Demands were also made of Belarus later in the year. It was calculated that if Belarus were to pay in hard currency and at world prices for its energy supplies from Russia, it would cost some 250% of the value of the country's hard-currency export earnings.

By the beginning of June 1993, arrears of payment for Russian petroleum and gas delivered to other republics were 400,000m. roubles. Belarus, one of Russia's closest allies, was being offered deliveries of only 0.3m. tons of petroleum products in the third quarter of 1993, about 10% of what the Belarusians claimed they needed.

Russia began, in mid-1993, to demand that its CIS partners pay for accumulated arrears, either by the transfer of state assets or in hard currency, and then to provide hard-currency deposits as security against future Russian credits. Deposits of the order of $5,000m. were mentioned. Five thousand million dollars from each of 14 states, at the then-current rouble exchange rate, would have been a capital sum equivalent to almost one-half the estimated 1993 Russian GDP.

The deals actually reached were, in most cases, nothing like these opening Russian bids. Belarus had payment arrears of 177,000m. roubles converted to a formal inter-state credit, with a seven-year grace period and no interest. Unless the nominal value of the credit was indexed to the rouble price level or rouble inflation was brought quickly under control, this was tantamount to eliminating the debt. Kazakhstan, on the other hand, reportedly agreed to make a US-dollar deposit, but only of $3m.

In general, a pattern rather reminiscent of the old Council of Mutual Economic Assistance (CMEA) was emerging. The Soviet authorities in the 1970s, on a steeply rising energy market, complained about the costs of supplying Eastern Europe (that is, the Communist bloc of central Europe and the Balkans) on preferential terms, but, nonetheless, continued to do so, raising the energy price to its CMEA partners but still keeping it well below world levels and not insisting on hard-currency payment. It was only when real energy prices on world markets fell, in the 1980s, that this gap began to be closed. The other former Soviet states, or at least those that entered and remained in the CIS, similarly received better-than-world-market terms for Russian energy. Even those, like Ukraine, with which Russia had poor relations, were not simply required to pay world prices and settle debts in convertible currency.

The common elements in the CMEA and CIS relationships were the relative weakness of Russia's partners, and Russia's security and economic interests in their not collapsing.

In mid-1993, proposals of an inter-state bank or a payments union continued to circulate amongst Western experts advising the ex-Soviet states, but neither was close to being introduced. However, in July 1993, Russia precipitated a reform of the rouble-zone system by its sudden and unilateral withdrawal of pre-1993-issue roubles and its refusal to replace the notes for non-Russians. This move seemed to be an attempt to bring the money supply under Russian control and to make those countries still using the rouble come to a decision about whether to introduce their own national currency or to remain in the rouble zone on Russian terms. It was estimated that other countries additionally printed 'substitute roubles' (i.e. local currencies or coupons) equivalent of up to 15% of Russia's rouble output.

At the time of the currency reform nine other countries used the rouble exclusively as their currency (Kazakhstan, Tajikistan, Turkmenistan and Uzbekistan) or in conjunction with a local currency/coupon system (Armenia, Azerbaijan, Belarus, Georgia and Moldova). The abrupt ending of the old rouble zone was reckoned to be likely to have a severe affect on economic relations between the Soviet successor states and exacerbate the recessionary situation, but was a reform that was necessary at some point. By the end of September 1993 Armenia, Belarus (which also had some policy-makers claiming that a new currency would still be introduced), Kazakhstan, Tajikistan and Uzbekistan had made bilateral arrangements with Russia setting up a new rouble zone. They effectively subordinated monetary policy to the control of the Russian Central Bank. When such arrangements were to come into force, their effectiveness and whether all the relevant parliaments would approve the measure remained uncertain. However, from the Russian economic perspective, a strict monetary policy had become more practicable, particularly with the Government's greater control over the state budget, following the end to the 'war of laws' with parliament.

The remaining countries of the former rouble zone seemed to have decided to commit themselves to dependence on their own currencies. Azerbaijan's attempt to make its manat the sole legal tender, at the beginning of September 1993, however, demonstrated the difficulties of ending the association with the rouble. Georgia announced that it intended to introduce its own currency, but the timetable was unclear and its main preoccupation in September and October was the struggle with Abkhazian separatists. Moldova planned to make the lei its national currency by the end of 1993 and Turkmenistan intended to replace the rouble with its manat before the end of the year. These proposals were effected by the end of the year and, in January 1994, only Tajikistan was in the new rouble zone, although Belarus was negotiating its entry.

FOREIGN TRADE

Before the dissolution of the USSR, the Russian Federation was the predominant source of hard-currency earnings for the whole of the country. There are considerable difficulties in identifying a meaningful Russian 'share' in Soviet merchandise exports, but one not-unreasonable Russian estimate put it at about 81% of the Soviet total in 1990, along with about a two-thirds share in Soviet gold sales, which were counted separately from exports of merchandise. Russia was not, however, so predominant in the receipt of imports. According to the same source, the Russian share of merchandise imports in 1990 was 67%. This situation, when taken in conjunction with Russia's supplying energy on generous terms to the rest of the former USSR, provided grounds for assertions that Russia was 'exploited' by the other Soviet Republics, and that the latter would find themselves in severe external financial difficulties after the USSR disintegrated.

In the event, all the Soviet successor states, with the unexpected exception of Estonia, found themselves in balance-of-payments difficulties in 1992–93. Even in Estonia there were grounds for doubting if the early accumulation of foreign reserves could be maintained.

The USSR bequeathed to its successor states low foreign-exchange reserves, modest gold reserves (by comparison with the position in 1980), debts to Western banks and governments that were moderately large by international standards, arrears of payments to many companies and outstanding credits to a number of Third World countries—credits that were reckoned to be mostly irrecoverable.

When the USSR ceased to exist, in December 1991, the best estimate of its outstanding debt to Western banks and governments was US $65,300m. There were also Soviet payments due to Eastern Europe, the valuation of which was in dispute. Offsetting this was $8,800m. in foreign currency, 240 metric tons of gold and the possibly worthless 'asset' of debt owed to the USSR by Third World countries, plus some liquid assets overseas, like embassy premises.

There was much speculation about a flight (export) of capital having taken place. So far as money banked abroad by individuals, enterprises and the Communist Party was concerned, however, the chances of its being appropriated by the successor states and used to assist debt repayment and interest payments were slight. The available evidence was that the USSR's heritage in international finances was a net liability. Getting the debt serviced (that is, the payment of interest on the debt) became a main objective of Western creditor banks and governments. In the view of many observers, this was both a lost cause and a hindrance to effective Western assistance in post-Soviet economic transformation.

In October 1991 a formula was worked out for the sharing of the debt burden amongst the ex-Soviet states. In this formula, Russia had 61% of the debt allocated to it, Ukraine 16% and Belarus and Kazakhstan about 4% each. Of the three treaties relating to the joint servicing of this debt, only nine of the 15 states signed at least one. Estonia, Latvia and Lithuania consistently declared they were not legal successors of the USSR, having been forcibly incorporated in the USSR in the first place. Ukraine and Russia, though they both signed all three treaties, were unable to reach agreement on how to manage the debt servicing. Meanwhile arrears of commercial payments to Western suppliers, which had begun to accumulate in 1990–91, continued.

Increasingly, in practice, the debt to the West came to be seen as Russia's debt. In June 1992 Russia formally proposed that it take over all the ex-Soviet debt, on condition that the other former Soviet Republics renounced all claim on Soviet foreign assets. Superficially, this so-called zero option was a most generous offer. However, the information on foreign assets was weak and mutual suspicions were strong. Most countries declined the offer, although some subsequently agreed to it.

In 1992–93 that debt was virtually not serviced, and increased steadily. By mid-1993 the gross debt to the West may have been of the order of $80,000m. Net debt—that is, the gross debt net of former Soviet official hard-currency deposits in the West—was only slightly less. Western creditors were organized in two groups, representing commercial banks and governments, for purposes of debt negotiations. Government creditors, organized in the so-called 'Paris Club', routinely rolled the Russian/Soviet debt over (that is, postponed payments due) every 90 days, and the banks followed suit. A more extended period of debt relief, or a formal rescheduling of the debt, was sought by the Russian Government. This was eventually incorporated in the 1992 and 1993 arrangements for financial assistance announced by the Group of Seven ('G7') leading Western countries.

Exports from the former USSR to the rest of the world in 1992, according to the best estimates, were only 48% of their 1990 level, and imports 43%. There were a variety of reasons for this steep decline. The fall in production reduced export supply capacity. In particular, this was the case for the staple export of crude petroleum, on which Soviet hard-currency earnings had depended so heavily in the past. The earlier dismantling of the CMEA, and the unresolved payments problems between the ex-USSR and the former Eastern European bloc countries, curtailed transactions with ex-socialist trade partners. Concern over debt servicing and over making payments for current imports induced successor-state governments to maintain control over imports and to tax export revenues. The collapse of the rouble exchange rate, from about 100 roubles to the US dollar, when the 'black market' and official rates were effectively merged in mid-1992, to close to 600 in December, and then to 1,000 by mid-1993, made imports expensive. Desperate, 'fire-sale' marketing of aluminium and other metals in the West, by factories looking for any means to raise revenue, provoked anti-dumping measures, or threats of them, in the European Community (EC) and the USA.

Even though most ex-Soviet states showed a favourable merchandise trade balance in 1992, none of them, outside the three Baltic states, with the possible exception of Kazakhstan, could avoid the most extreme external financial difficulties. There was an external financing deficit to be dealt with, especially when debt service was taken into account.

The G7 countries announced a series of measures, worth $24,000m. in aid to Russia, in April 1992. This was followed by $43,000m. announced in 1993. These seemed to be substantial amounts, capable of delivering real assistance to the former USSR. (Assistance to Russia was considered likely, to some extent, to 'trickle down' to other former Soviet states.) Moreover, disbursement was close to, or more than, the amount pledged. The best 1993 estimates, from various sources, of assistance disbursed in 1992, ranged from about $17,000m. to over $30,000m. Economists in the IMF, in many ways the leading organization in the whole Western assistance effort, put the total disbursed at slightly above the amount pledged.

The reality, however, was much less helpful than the appearance. A large part of the sums disbursed consisted of debt relief. In other words, it was a recognition of the fact that the debt was not going to be serviced anyway. Another large part consisted of Western governments' export credits, designed primarily to promote each country's capital-goods exports, and on terms close to market terms. Very little of the aid pledged or disbursed was made up of grants; nearly all of it was loans, generating a later balance-of-payments burden. In this respect, the two packages bore no resemblance to the USA's Marshall Plan aid to Western Europe after the Second World War, which was predominantly in the form of grants. A relatively small proportion was technical assistance, ranging from guidance on macroeconomic policy to assistance with schemes of food packaging and distribution. Some of this was useful, but much of it came in for strong criticism for being delayed, misdirected and chiefly benefiting the consultants who were paid to provide it.

Some of the potentially most helpful forms of assistance—stand-by loans and currency stabilization funds to be provided by the IMF—were not disbursed to the main ex-Soviet states. In the most important case, that of Russia, this was because conditions of prior policy achievements, set by the Russian Government in agreement with the IMF, were not met. In particular, the Russian Government was unable to reduce its budget deficit and inflation rate in 1992, in the manner it had promised to do. It was hoped that this would be more achievable from late 1993 and in 1994, with the seeming stabilization of the political situation.

The Baltic states were more successful, in proportion to their size, in eliciting IMF and, subsequently, World Bank funds, because they performed better in their own stabilization efforts. They also attracted other help, especially from the Nordic countries (Scandinavia and Finland). The $944m. in multilateral financing pledged to the three Baltic states in 1992 was slightly over one-half the equivalent financing pledged to Russia, the population of which was about 19 times greater.

Official aid was by no means the only, or the most important, channel through which Western countries could contribute to the economic transformation and recovery of the ex-Soviet states. Access for those countries' exports to Western markets was of much greater consequence and, in the long run, foreign private direct investment, it was hoped, would play a major role in transforming the ex-Soviet economies. In both these areas, however, experience in 1992–93 was sobering. It is true that, even in 1992, the much-reduced merchandise exports of the former USSR amounted to a sum ($54,900m.) that was large relative to their output: large, that is, if the latter was measured at current market exchange rates. Export earnings, moreover, were at the disposal of the firms and governments of the countries which had earned them, and carried no future debt-service burden with them. But a World Bank study, published in 1993, showed that the exports to the West of the former USSR were subject to significant Western trade barriers. Moreover, these barriers seemed to be somewhat greater in the ex-Soviet states' most important Western market, the EC, than in the USA or even Japan.

Given the product composition of Soviet exports to countries of the Organisation for Economic Co-operation and Development (OECD) in 1991, the average EC tariff rate was calculated at 6.6%, against 5.2% in Japan and 5.0% in the USA. Perhaps more importantly, it was calculated that EC non-tariff barriers applied to 19% of the former Soviet countries' export categories, the same as in Japan and more than three times the US percentage. The EC's Common Agricultural Policy benefited Russia and some other former Soviet states, since they were net importers of heavily subsidized food from EC surplus stocks. However, Ukraine and the Baltic republics were likely to be penalized by the CAP protection against farm imports from outside the EC, although, in early 1993, a possible change in this situation, so far as the three Baltic states were concerned, began to seem possible. They had a free-trade arrangement with the Nordic countries, and Sweden and Finland, when negotiating for EC membership, asserted that they would insist on maintaining this arrangement with the Baltics as a condition of their EC membership.

The inflow of foreign direct investment to the former USSR remained extremely modest. Joint ventures with foreign partners, registered on the territory of the former USSR, together with the wholly-owned subsidiaries of foreign firms, were certainly numerous. However, most were small and far more were registered but not functioning than were actually operational. Reliable information on them was lacking. The broad indications, however, were that Estonia and Latvia, yet again, were beginning to attract foreign investment of some significance, in relation to the small size of their economies, and that Kazakhstan had been more successful than Russia in attracting at least some large-scale Western investment in the energy sector. A perception of political stability was considered important to attracting Western interest. This prejudice was only reinforced by the change in regime in Azerbaijan in mid-1993, which seemed to make doubtful two major deals with Western partners: one with a consortium of multinational petroleum companies and the other with Turkey on a gas pipeline deal.

PROBLEMS AND PROSPECTS

As was noted at the beginning of this article, by 1993 it had become quite difficult to generalize across the 15 Soviet successor states. They always differed substantially in development levels and cultural inheritance. In the early

1990s, with separate currencies, the scope for further divergence had greatly increased.

In all of them, the institutions and regulations of the economic system were moving in the general direction of private enterprise and the market. However, the 15 states were moving not only at different speeds but along somewhat different routes. For example, Lithuania had clearly made less progress than Estonia or Latvia in macroeconomic stabilization. On the other hand, it was considered by Estonian policy-makers that Lithuania was moving faster than they were in terms of privatization.

In some cases, at mid-1993, it did not appear that they had moved very far at all. Top–down administrative control (that is, direction from the centre and the higher bureaucracy, rather than the operation of subsidiarity) remained the norm, for example, in Uzbekistan and Belarus. The main change in more traditionalist regimes such as these, was that small-scale private enterprise was legally permitted and, indeed, encouraged.

Even in states where governments made major efforts to liberalize, such as Estonia, Latvia and Russia, property rights typically remain unclear. Sometimes there was a conflict between selling assets to the public and potential foreign investors and restoring property to pre-Communist owners. This was a problem chiefly in the Baltic states. In mid-1993, for example, it was one of the factors delaying the redevelopment of the important Latvian port of Riga. Sometimes local and national governments were in dispute over their rights to control assets, including the right to sell them and receive the proceeds. Sometimes there was considerable obscurity and conflict surrounding the rights of foreigners to acquire assets. That was particularly true of land and natural resources all over the former USSR.

In the opinion of lawyers, nevertheless, several of the successor states had, by 1993, approved an 'adequate first generation' of commercial and property law. The property-rights problems in such cases were more to do with interpretation and an underdeveloped judicial system than the legislation as it existed on paper. This unevenly developed nature of the judicial system was an example of a general and fundamental problem: completely new institutions and skills could not come into being quickly. Most commercial banks were former branches of the state bank. Most enterprises, even after they were officially privatized, had the same internal organization as before, the same management and often the same propensity to look for state subsidies when financial troubles were imminent.

The tendency of managers in privatized firms to expect state help was apparent in several of the ex-Soviet states, notably Russia. It would, in the right circumstances, only be a transitional problem. Russia designed the privatization process so that it favoured initial ownership by managers and workers of each firm. However, a strong regime of financial stringency would force even state enterprises to behave in a more cost-effective way and should, in principle, have the same effect on worker-owned firms. The difficulty was that privatization of medium-sized and large enterprises ahead of macroeconomic stabilization forced the newly privatized firms into a situation where there was little credit available. Widespread disenchantment with privatization could follow. Meanwhile, political pressures to soften financial policies would be greater than if worker-ownership were not the norm. In some of the successor states the whole process of change, at mid-1993, was a delicate, early stage. Competition was not usual; financial circumstances were uncertain; a capital market which would allow the development of effective, concentrated ownership was yet to take shape; and industrial restructuring had not yet been embarked upon.

In these circumstances, unemployment was still low. A substantial rise in the numbers out of work would be a sign, simultaneously, of progress in economic transformation and of heightened political risk. With or without tougher policies, output would be likely to continue to fall for some time.

Successor states with traditionalist regimes and not involved in wars were economically less fragile. However, they had the prospect of either long-run stagnation or a delayed exposure to the dangers already confronted by those trying to modernize. The only Soviet successor states that seemed, in mid-1993, as though they were on the verge of stabilization and recovery of output were Latvia and Estonia. Both of these, however, were vulnerable to conflicts over their large Russian-speaking minorities. In addition, their long-run prospects, as very small economies, depended heavily on their being inside a free-trade area or common market, whether Eastern or Western.

Two broad conclusions can be drawn. First, the process of economic change in the former USSR, at any rate outside the Baltic states, was bedeviled by the strong political constituencies opposed to it and by the lack of political coherence of reform movements. These impediments were larger than in Hungary, Poland or the Czech Republic. Taken in conjunction with the actual and potential ethnic conflicts in the former USSR, they made economic transformation considerably more difficult than in central Europe. Second, if the political process of reform from above was handicapped, change from below could still continue. Throughout the former USSR, household behaviour was adapting to new conditions and a new business class was emerging.

SECURITY AND INTERNATIONAL RELATIONS IN EASTERN EUROPE

Dr MICHAEL SHEEHAN

INTRODUCTION

The revolutions of 1989 in Eastern Europe marked a historical watershed in the post-Second World War history and political development of the region. They were part of a broader process of political evolution in Europe, yet contributed directly to the dramatic acceleration in the speed of that evolution. Nowhere was this more so than in the area of security and international relations. In the period 1945–89 this subject could be looked at in the context of Soviet military and political domination of the region and 'Eastern Europe' was quite clearly a political subsystem with clearly defined structures and processes. The democratic regimes that emerged in central Europe and the Balkans in 1989–90 chose to dismantle those structures and institute new processes. While the old stable pattern disappeared, too little time has passed by mid-1993 for the states completely to have defined their new foreign-policy orientation and the new security frameworks and alliance patterns were still in the process of being built. Nevertheless, certain patterns of foreign policy and networks of international co-operation had begun to emerge, both within Eastern Europe and between Eastern and Western European countries. The new regimes emerged from a pre-existing background, however, and it is necessary to review the impact of that background before going on to address the question of what patterns were likely to prevail in the future.

SOVIET DOMINANCE OF EASTERN EUROPEAN SECURITY, 1945–89

At the end of the Second World War, in 1945, the armies of the USSR occupied most of eastern and central Europe. These armies gave it the opportunity to shape the future political development of the region in such a way as to meet the perceived security needs of the USSR. That perception was dominated by the need to constrain Germany in the post-War era and to avoid a repetition of the devastating German invasions of the two World Wars. To this end Stalin (Iosif V. Dzhugashvili/Jugashvili) was determined to maintain substantial Soviet forces in the eastern part of a divided Germany. Likewise, the USSR was determined to ensure that the post-War regimes in Eastern Europe would not only pose no security threat to the USSR in themselves, but would form a pro-Soviet buffer zone between Soviet territory and that of a reviving post-War Germany. Between 1945 and 1947, however, the USSR gradually consolidated its political control over Eastern Europe. The speed and completeness of Communist consolidation varied from country to country.

As the 'Cold War' deepened, the USSR moved to consolidate its control over Eastern Europe, seeing the region as an essential buffer zone between itself and the political and military threat represented by the West. By late 1948, therefore, the dynamics of the Cold War had led to the creation of a group of states in Eastern Europe dominated by the Soviet military presence and with political and economic systems modelled upon that of their Soviet mentor.

Although the West's North Atlantic Treaty Organization (NATO) was formed in 1949, the establishment of the Warsaw Treaty Organization (Warsaw Pact or WTO) did not take place until 1955. The trigger for the formation of the Warsaw Pact was the entry of the Federal Republic of Germany ('West Germany') into NATO. The establishment of the Warsaw Pact did not really change the military or political realities in Eastern Europe, since the USSR already had bilateral treaties with Poland, Czechoslovakia, Hungary, Romania and Bulgaria, committing the signatories to providing aid in the event of an attack. However, the Warsaw Treaty provided for the establishment of a combined military command and prohibited signatories from joining other alliances whose purposes were 'incompatible' with the purposes of the Warsaw Treaty. (The Warsaw Treaty of Friendship, Co-operation and Mutual Assistance was first signed in May 1955 by the USSR and all the countries of the Eastern European Communist bloc, except for Yugoslavia: Albania—which ceased participation in 1961 and formally withdrew in 1968, Bulgaria, Czechoslovakia, Hungary, Poland, Romania and also the German Democratic Republic—GDR or 'East Germany'.) Neither the bilateral treaties of the late 1940s nor the Warsaw Treaty legitimized the Soviet military presence in Eastern Europe. This was done in 1956-57, through a second series of bilateral treaties.

The difficulty for the USSR, in the period from 1945 to 1985, was that it was trying to maintain a dynamic equilibrium which balanced conflicting pressures. Its security needs demanded a cordon of Eastern European states which were internally stable, politically orthodox and externally loyal. In order for these regimes to be internally stable they required a degree of internal legitimacy which in turn demanded that their governments be at least partially responsive to the wishes of their populations, which meant the USSR tolerating change and non-conformity.

The relationship between the USSR and Eastern Europe did not alter during the first 18 months after Mikhail Gorbachev became General-Secretary of the Communist Party of the Soviet Union (CPSU) and, hence, leader of the USSR. Indeed, Gorbachev had been in power for only one month when the Warsaw Treaty was renewed for a further 20 years, in April 1985. In February 1986, however, at the 17th Party Congress of the CPSU, Gorbachev spoke of the 'unconditional respect in international practice for the right of every people to choose the paths and forms of its development'. In this period, however, Gorbachev still appeared to have seen a stable, Soviet-dominated Eastern Europe as an essential defence, even during a period of domestic reform. He virtually reaffirmed the 'Brezhnev Doctrine' (whereby the USSR had asserted its right to intervene in any socialist—in Western terminology, Communist—state, in the interests of 'world socialism and the world revolutionary movement') during a visit to Poland in July 1986. Soviet attitudes towards Eastern Europe evolved during 1987–88. By mid-1987 Gorbachev was beginning to advocate the Soviet reform programme as a model for other Warsaw Pact states.

By 1988 the process of *perestroika* (restructuring) in the USSR began to experience serious difficulties. Gorbachev reacted by both extending the scope and accelerating the pace of reform in the USSR. He also accelerated his efforts to defuse the military confrontation in Europe, following his success in achieving the Intermediate-range Nuclear Forces (INF) Treaty of 1987. In December 1988 Gorbachev announced at the UN that the USSR would unilaterally reduce its armed forces by 500,000 men, including 50,000 men and 5,000 tanks based in Eastern Europe. Earlier that year, on a visit to Yugoslavia, Gorbachev emphasized the right of each nation to pursue independent development and declared that 'the time has passed when a handful of big states made decisions for the whole world and divided it into spheres of influence according to the law of might is right'. In July 1988 Vadim Medvedev, shortly to become the Soviet Chief of Ideology, stressed the 'unconditional' nature of the principle of sovereignty in bloc relations. He suggested that these ties should be no different than relations between states with different social systems. The Brezhnev Doctrine appeared to be defunct. The events of 1989 were to confirm that this was so.

Gorbachev told the European Parliament, in June 1989, that social change 'is the exclusive affair of the people of that country and is their choice. Any interference in domestic affairs and any attempts to restrict the sovereignty of states, both friends, allies or any other, is inadmissible'. It was within the context of this new 'doctrine' that the revolutions of 1989 took place and within the same context that the new democracies attempted to structure their foreign policies. Between 1988 and 1990 the USSR gradually ceased to define its European security needs in terms of the maintenance of a group of similarly governed states in Eastern Europe.

The sweeping political changes that took place in Eastern Europe in 1989 transformed the security situation. While to an extent they simply confirmed a process that was already underway, that is the transition from an era of confrontation to one of co-operation within Europe, they also radically altered the nature of that transition and altered also the security agenda for the new Europe. Prior to 1989, the prospects were for a continuation of the division of Europe into two blocs, but for the steady evolution of the relationship between the two blocs, in a more co-operative direction, with a dramatic reduction in the armed forces of both sides. This approach was reflected in the pattern of unilateral arms reductions in the late 1980s, in the 1987 INF Treaty and in the 1990 Conventional Forces in Europe (CFE) Treaty.

The Warsaw Pact was always an alliance based upon the needs of the USSR and to a lesser extent a shared leadership perception among the Eastern European leaders of a military-ideological threat represented by the NATO alliance. As the Communist regimes fell from power in 1989, so the *raison d'être* of the Warsaw Pact fell with them. That the Pact was not immediately dissolved was due only to the political sensitivity of the new democratic governments, who were anxious to reassure the Soviet regime that the political developments of 1989 did not represent a threat to the national security of the USSR. Nevertheless, having lived for 40 years under the strict tutelage of a hegemonic power, it was inevitable that the Eastern European states would wish to escape from the constraints represented by the Warsaw Treaty as speedily as possible.

The problem for the former Warsaw Pact states was to decide what security posture should replace Warsaw Pact membership. One possibility was swiftly made clear. For the foreseeable future membership of the NATO alliance would not be an option. NATO was quick to declare that it would not consider membership for the former Warsaw Pact states, since such an action would be unnecessarily provocative to the USSR and might undermine the domestic political position of the leaders of reform within the USSR.

The second strand of security policy related to diplomatic efforts aimed at the enhancement and institutionalization of the Conference on Security and Co-operation in Europe (CSCE) process. Czechoslovakia, for example, sought a merger of the 22-state negotiations on conventional armed forces with the 34-state CSCE talks on confidence- and security-building measures. They aimed to institutionalize a Europe-wide security infrastructure that would at one and the same time provide the essential reassurance to the USSR that it was more, not less secure after the events of 1989 and also embed Eastern European states in what would effectively become a European collective security arrangement. The aim, according to Czechoslovakia, would be to 'establish firm, all-European security structures that would be based on a low level of armaments and a high level of mutual confidence'. The search for multilateral security frameworks by the new democracies was clearly necessitated by the political realities of their security environment. The option of a completely independent defence policy, on the model of the heavily armed Swiss neutrality, was not feasible. All the pressures, domestic and international, were towards reduced defence establishments. Agreements like the CFE Treaty imposed lower numerical ceilings for equipment, while the need to release funds for socio-economic development, coupled with public disenchantment with conscription and a large visible military presence, meant that national defence effort would contract sharply. Security needs would, therefore, have to be met through bilateral and multilateral co-operation.

One of the features of the relationship between the USSR and the states of Eastern Europe between 1945 and 1989 was that it was always highly country-specific. Soviet tolerance of the rate of reform and the nature of that reform varied markedly from country to country. This attitude produced variation in the degree to which states attempted to exercise a certain independence in foreign policy. This, in turn, affected the degree to which the new democratic regimes could build upon foreign-policy traditions established by their predecessors. Romania, as the most rigidly Stalinist state before 1989, clearly believed that its ideological reliability allowed it to exercise extreme dissidence in foreign-policy terms. Ironically, once ideological conformity disappeared, it proved more cautious than the other new democracies in asserting its independence in the security field. All the Eastern European states were already engaged in a military reduction process by 1990. Every Warsaw Pact state except Romania was engaged in significant unilateral force reductions. Hungary, for example, announced cuts in the size of the armed forces and of the defence budget in January 1989.

NEW PATTERNS OF SECURITY POLICY IN EASTERN EUROPE

The security policies of the Eastern European Warsaw Pact states gradually crystallized into two dominant strategies. The first emphasized disengagement from the embrace of the USSR. It found form in efforts to loosen and eventually end the constraints imposed by membership of the Warsaw Pact and negotiations to secure the withdrawal of the Soviet garrisons in Eastern Europe. The second strategy involved reaching towards the West for security guarantees and membership of Western organizations such as NATO and the European Community (EC—from November 1993, the European Union). While pursuing these strategies the Eastern Europeans sought to encourage the development of a new security architecture for Europe which would supersede the old East–West divide and guarantee mutual security for all European states, including the USSR. The pursuit of these objectives showed up a marked difference in outlook and approach between the states of central Europe and those in the Balkans.

In practice the Eastern Europeans were able to achieve their aims in certain areas far more quickly than others. Breaking the security linkage with the USSR, paradoxically, proved easier than gaining security guarantees from the West.

Initially, the new democratic governments in Eastern Europe took a cautious attitude towards continued membership of the Warsaw Treaty Organization. This reflected their desire not to alarm the USSR unnecessarily and their awareness that Hungary's decision to leave the Warsaw Pact in 1956 had been one of the major factors prompting the Soviet intervention of that year. Nevertheless, in September 1990 the Ministers of Defence and Foreign Affairs of Poland, Czechoslovakia and Hungary met at Zakopane (Poland) to consider the role of the armed forces in the light of the political changes in Eastern Europe. Soviet representatives were not invited, the first time such an event had happened since the formation of the Warsaw Pact. However, the Soviet decision to use armed force against dissident Lithuania, in January 1991, led to a reconsideration of this attitude. The repression brought unwelcome reminders of the events of 1956 and 1968 and led several Warsaw Pact governments to fear that the Warsaw Treaty might be used as a pretext for intervention against the reformed regimes in Eastern Europe. An emergency cabinet meeting in Czechoslovakia, on 13 January 1991, produced a statement which declared that 'the use of military force . . . mars the process of the consolidation of security, peace and relaxation in Europe, and undermines confidence in the democratic changes which have been taking place in the USSR in the last few years'.

The Czechoslovak foreign minister, Jiří Dienstbier, was instructed to discuss possible joint reaction with Hungary and Poland, including a rapid withdrawal from the Warsaw Pact. Until this point, while Hungary had declared its preference for withdrawal from the Warsaw Pact, Czechoslovakia had been working for the transformation of the Warsaw Pact from a military into a primarily political organization. Both Czechoslovakia and Hungary had previously supported the efforts of the Baltic states (Estonia, Latvia and Lithuania) to regain full sovereignty. Czechoslovakia established diplomatic representation in the Lithuanian capital, Vilnius, in November 1990.

On 22 January 1991 a meeting of the Czechoslovak, Hungarian and Polish foreign ministers, held in Budapest (Hungary), led to a joint statement demanding that the military structure of the Warsaw Pact be abolished by 1 July 1991 and for the organization itself to be dissolved within one year. Géza Jeszenszky, the Hungarian Minister of Foreign Affairs, stated that the three Governments would prefer agreement with the USSR on the dissolution of the Warsaw Pact, but that if this was not forthcoming the step would be taken unilaterally. For the benefit of the sensitivities of the USSR, they argued that the Warsaw Pact had been rendered obsolete by the moves to set up a collective security system in Europe (an argument that could equally well suggest the dissolution of NATO, although this was not mentioned). The Minister expressed support for the independence of the Baltic states, but denied that there was a link between the Soviet use of force in Lithuania and their joint decision to leave the Warsaw Pact. Jeszenszky insisted that 'the Warsaw Pact should be abolished as part of an all-European process'. The three central European Governments also agreed to increase trilateral co-operation, in areas such as achieving full political independence and EC membership.

In the event, President Gorbachev surprised the three states, in early February 1991, by himself suggesting the dissolution of the military aspects of the Warsaw Treaty by April that year. A joint meeting of Czechoslovakia, Hungary and Poland, held in Visegrad (Hungary) in mid-February, reaffirmed the emergence of a trilateral approach on security and foreign-policy issues. Progress was swift. The foreign and defence ministers of the six remaining Warsaw Pact states (the GDR had left the Pact in September 1990, prior to its dissolution and incorporation into the Federal Republic) met in Budapest (Hungary) on 25 February to end the Warsaw Pact's military structure. The agreements took effect on 21 March. The meeting demonstrated continuing differences with the USSR, which wished to maintain the political structure of the Warsaw Pact for the bloc-to-bloc negotiations with NATO at the CFE and CSCE meetings. The 'trilateral group' (or 'Visegrad group') re-emphasized their desire to see the remaining functions of the Warsaw Pact ended before the end of 1991. Hungarian foreign minister Jeszenszky characterized the Warsaw Pact as 'an organization resting on mistaken fundamentals which has outlived itself'.

A crucial change of emphasis, apparent by late February 1991, was the desire for the continuation of NATO and a closer association with it, in contrast with the earlier emphasis on neutrality. The trilateral states were beginning to move towards bilateral military co-operation agreements with each other as well as attempting to strengthen their political links with NATO.

Progress was also made steadily throughout 1990–91 on the withdrawal of the Soviet forces in Eastern Europe. By July 1991 73,500 Soviet troops and their equipment had completed their withdrawal from Czechoslovakia and the 49,500-strong Soviet force in Hungary had left. Negotiations on the withdrawal of the 50,000-strong garrison in Poland had only been completed in mid-February 1991, but the first convoys were returning to the USSR by 9 April. The process of disengaging from the Soviet military embrace was a difficult one, involving much more than just the withdrawal of the troop presence. Domestic and international politico-military reforms were required, such as efforts to reduce the Soviet near-monopoly on arms supplies. Breaking the linkages between the Soviet and Eastern European officer corps was also necessary, involving the retirement or transfer of the most pro-Soviet officers, re-education of the officer corps and efforts to establish links with Western forces. Czechoslovak officers began training courses with the German army, the Bundeswehr, while Romania expressed a desire to send its officers to France, Germany, Italy and the United Kingdom for training. All the former Warsaw Pact states explored the possibility of US training. The intelligence-sharing arrangements with the USSR were also severed.

Withdrawal of weapons from Eastern Europe also took place in this period. Victor Dubinin, commander of Soviet forces in Poland, revealed that Soviet nuclear weapons had been based in Poland until 1990. He even asserted that these belonged to Poland, a charge quickly rejected by Poland, worried that it might be deemed to be in violation of the nuclear non-proliferation treaty. Hungary's former Communist leader, Károly Grósz, revealed that Soviet nuclear weapons had also been deployed in Hungary, but had been withdrawn at Grósz's request, in 1988.

While the withdrawal of Soviet forces was an entirely welcome development in terms of sovereignty, the central European administrations in particular were concerned about the emerging lack of security arrangements in Eastern Europe. The demise of the Warsaw Pact had not been followed by the creation of a new European collective security order, nor had NATO given any security guarantees to the new democracies. Hungary and Czechoslovakia, as well as strengthening the trilateral link with Poland, began to show more interest in Italy's proposal for linkages between the 'pentagonal' group of states that had formed parts of the old Austro-Hungarian Empire: Italy, Austria, Hungary, Czechoslovakia and Yugoslavia. The first meeting of the Pentagonal, held in Venice (Italy) in August 1990, produced a broad agenda similar to the CSCE, involving security, economic and human-rights issues. The Hungarian foreign minister expressed the hope that the new grouping might have a role to play in regional conflict mediation. In June 1991, when Slovenia and Croatia declared their independence from Yugoslavia, the two Western members of the Pentagonal, Italy and Austria, were quick to announce that they would not recognize the new states.

The search for a new security order was pursued in the new context created by the successful conclusion of the CFE Treaty. The Treaty was designed on a bloc-to-bloc basis to dramatically reduce the scale of the military confrontation in Europe. While it could still achieve this end, it was largely overtaken by events. Even so, the CFE Treaty, taken together with the bilateral agreements with the USSR on troop withdrawals and the CSCE agreement of November 1990, represented a tremendous gain for the security of the Eastern European states. Under the CFE Treaty, NATO and the Warsaw Pact were each required to reduce their forces in Europe to a maximum of 20,000 tanks, 3,000 armoured personnel carriers, 2,000 artillery pieces, 6,800 combat aircraft and 2,000 attack helicopters. This entailed an enormous reduction in Warsaw Pact forces, most of them Soviet: of 19,200 tanks, 16,500 armoured personnel carriers, 12,000 artillery pieces, 2,100 combat aircraft and 1,700 helicopters. All these had to be destroyed or moved east of the Ural Mountains (that is, out of Europe). Thus, the USSR was committed both to withdrawing its garrisons from Eastern Europe through bilateral agreements and to dramatically reducing its ability to successfully re-intervene, through multilateral agreements. In addition, while for political reasons NATO showed no enthusiasm for Eastern European membership of NATO, the Joint Declaration signed by NATO and the Warsaw Pact in Paris (France), in November 1990, specifically reaffirmed the right of any state either to be, or not to be a party to a treaty or an alliance.

The trilateral states, Poland, Czechoslovakia and Hungary sought, unsuccessfully, to have NATO extend its security guarantee as far as the borders of the then USSR. Poland's Minister of Foreign Affairs, Krzysztof Skubiszewski, expressed fears of a 'domino effect' of destablization, extending out from a collapsing USSR, and which could only be halted if NATO operated throughout Europe, as part of a European security system. The Eastern European states feared that even with the withdrawal of Soviet forces, Europe would remain divided between a secure West and insecure East. The East was left in a security vacuum by NATO. NATO discouraged Eastern applicants, on the grounds that it did not wish to alarm the USSR and urged the Eastern states to depend on the CSCE process for their security. On the other hand, because they felt that NATO must remain the basis of Western security and did not wish to see the CSCE emerge as a competitor, NATO states prevented the CSCE from acquiring the structures and competencies that would allow it to replace NATO. This satisfied Western objectives, but left the former Warsaw Pact states neglected, in a limbo with which their experiences in the late 1930s made them deeply dissatisfied. They had no wish to be preserved as a 'buffer' between East and West; they wished to be politically and economically 'Western', in a Europe undivided in security terms. As with EC membership, incorporation in the Western security framework would both guarantee the post-Communist countries against a reassertive USSR and would secure their new political and economic systems within a family of similar regimes. Scepticism about the value of the CSCE as an alternative increased in the early 1990s, when it failed to deter the use of force by Soviet troops in Lithuania, in January 1991, and by its ineffectiveness in mediating the Armenian–Azerbaijan disputes or being involved in the negotiations over the conflicts in the former Yugoslavia.

NATO, like the EC, regarded full membership for Eastern states as premature, but showed a willingness to begin a process of associating these states with NATO through low-level contacts and consultative arrangements, such as the North Atlantic Co-operation Council. NATO, however, wished to convince the USSR (as later, Russia) that it was not threatened by the Western alliance. It saw Eastern membership of NATO as counter-productive in that respect.

THE IMPACT OF THE END OF THE USSR

The period 1991–93 saw continuing huge changes in the security situation in Eastern Europe. The most crucial event was the collapse of Communism in the USSR, after the failure of the August 1991 coup attempt, and then the dissolution of the USSR itself, into a number of non-Communist successor states.

These two events altered the situation in Eastern Europe in a number of fundamental ways. In the first place they created a large number of new states with their own foreign policy and security concerns. Of these, only the Baltic countries of Estonia, Latvia and Lithuania had any history of previous existence as independent states on which to draw for guidance. The other states, such as Ukraine, Belarus, Moldova, Georgia and Armenia, varied dramatically in the degree to which they wished to distance themselves from Russia.

For the existing states of Eastern Europe, the end of the USSR was crucial. Prior to the end of the USSR the former Warsaw Pact states had concentrated on disengagement from the USSR. With its collapse and the emergence of a number of unstable successor states, the concern at the emergence of a 'security vacuum' in Eastern Europe was significantly heightened. This led to increased efforts to gain association with the major Western European organizations, especially NATO, the EC and the Western European Union (WEU), and deepening of the process of regional association. Indeed, in security terms, from late 1991 it becomes easier to examine the region in terms of the key sub-regional groups: the Commonwealth of Independent States (CIS); the Baltic states; the central European countries; and the Balkans.

The Commonwealth of Independent States

When the CIS was created in December 1991, it was widely assumed that its life-span would be brief. It could be viewed as a Russian attempt to maintain the USSR in another form, so the adherence of the other republics was likely to be brief and they would use it to moderate the process achieving full sovereignty. Political conflicts between the member states, notably the war between Armenia and Azerbaijan over Nagorny Karabakh and the dispute between the Russian Federation and Ukraine over the Crimea and the Black Sea fleet, reinforced the impression that the CIS would not survive long.

In the event it proved more durable than expected. There were two reasons for this. Russia adopted a less coercive attitude towards leadership of the Commonwealth and came to value the CIS as an association of states keen to maximize co-operation, rather than as a remodelled USSR. In turn, the other member states began to appreciate the advantages of belonging to the Commonwealth, particularly with Russian leadership being exercised in a more tactful and less threatening manner.

The security relationship of the CIS is defined by the so-called Tashkent Agreement, the Treaty on Collective Security signed at Tashkent (Uzbekistan) on 15 May 1992. The Russian President, Boris Yeltsin, summed up the key collective defence provision of the Treaty as, 'that in the event of aggression against any CIS state, all the other Commonwealth members will regard this as aggression against them and will take reciprocal measures'.

The Tashkent Agreement represented a highly significant development of the CIS. When the CIS was initially established, Russia expected that it would have a single, unified armed forces, that it would simply continue the armed forces of the USSR. However, less than one month after the CIS was established, the Acting Commander-in-Chief of the Armed Forces of the CIS, Marshal Yevgeny Shaposhnikov, was forced to concede that the member states of the CIS had rejected the idea, in favour of separate national forces.

Although the Russian Federation itself established a separate Russian army, Russia continued to argue that her security could not be divorced from that of the other CIS states, and that all the CIS states would be more secure as part of a collective defence system. Russia's draft military doctrine in fact described the goal of the armed forces in wartime as being to 'defend the sovereignty and territorial integrity of Russia and of its CIS allies'. Russia saw the CIS Armed Forces as being similar to the allies within the defunct Warsaw Pact; indeed, the former Warsaw Pact buildings were made the location of the Headquarters of the CIS Joint High Command (the High Command had an advisory and co-ordination function). This concern represented a contraction of the area considered of vital security significance; the main Russian interest was increasingly in maintaining the borders of the former Soviet states. However, Russia also inherited many of the security habits and prejudices of the USSR and, in September 1993, following the use of the army to enforce the dissolution of parliament, Boris Yeltsin reversed his earlier policy of not opposing Polish entry to NATO. This revealed the resurgent influence of the military and their continuing security tradition.

Only six of the 11 CIS member states signed the Treaty of Tashkent and Ukraine was a notable abstainer. Nevertheless, the Treaty represented a significant consolidation of the CIS. It provided a framework of legitimacy for Russia's continuing definition of the entire CIS region as an area of intense, justifiable Russian interest and activity. It reflected the expectation of the signatories that the CIS would continue. It also reflected an acceptance of a 'two-speed' CIS framework by Russia. Russia clearly no longer saw the CIS as a 'revived USSR', nor did it expect all CIS members to co-operate in all manners to the same degree. The Tashkent signatories indicated an inner core of CIS members, willing to integrate to a greater degree than states like Ukraine, and Russia appeared comfortable with this development. This development also made it more likely that the outer group of CIS states like Ukraine would be willing to remain members for much longer than had been originally anticipated. It was an option for CIS states to accede to the Tashkent Agreement subsequently, if they so desired. The marked policy divisions between Russia and Ukraine, which earlier appeared likely to destroy the CIS, no longer seemed so threatening. By 1993 Ukraine itself appeared more positively disposed towards the new, more flexible CIS. President Leonid Kravchuk of Ukraine spoke of the need to improve the working of the CIS, which performed valuable functions. Even the possibility of Ukraine acceding to the Tashkent Agreement at a future date was not ruled out. Similarly, although Belarus did not sign the Tashkent Treaty originally, it negotiated co-operation with the CIS military framework on a bilateral basis and, in April 1993, parliament sanctioned, with provisos, the country's accession to the Tashkent security system.

For Russia itself, the leadership role in the CIS military structure was a complicating factor. The Russian army had to develop two roles and images, one purely Russian, and one CIS. This was accepted because of the importance Russia attached to the development of a 'defensive space' within the Commonwealth. Implementation was difficult because the Russian armed forces were still enmeshed in an exceptionally complicated array of problems inherited from the end of the Warsaw Pact and the USSR itself.

Under a number of bilateral and multilateral agreements concluded after 1989, Russia, was withdrawing its forces from the territories of former Warsaw Pact allies, the three former Soviet Baltic states and many of the CIS states. At the same time, under the CFE agreement it was committed, as the main successor of the USSR, to huge reductions in the overall size of the armed forces. Russia's 2.8m.-strong forces were to fall to 1.5m. by the year 2000, with a reduction to 2.1m. scheduled for 1994/95. These changes proved extremely traumatic to implement. Lowering the numbers in the conscript forces was not too difficult, but reducing the officer corps was. There was an enormous shortage of housing for the officers being withdrawn to Russian territory. For this reason, the 1993/94 period was being devoted to construction of housing and reorganization as such. In certain territories, such as the Baltic states, the Russian officers corps refused to leave unless it had adequate housing to return to, causing major diplomatic difficulties between Russia and the 'host' nations.

Russia also had problems with a shortfall of equipment. During the Cold War Soviet forces were forward-deployed in Eastern Europe and the western military districts of the USSR. Thus, when the USSR dissolved, Russia found itself with less ex-Soviet equipment on its European territory than did Ukraine and Belarus. During the 1992 Tashkent meeting of the CIS a formula for the equitable division of this equipment was agreed, with Russia getting 54%, Ukraine 27%, Belarus 12% and the remaining 7% divided between Armenia, Azerbaijan, Georgia and Moldova.

The division of former Soviet naval forces in the Black Sea produced a major crisis between Russia and Ukraine. Russia and the CIS General Staff argued that dividing the fleet would undermine its value. The struggle between Russia and Ukraine for control of the fleet soured relations and led to a series of crises as ships attempted to 'defect' to Ukraine. Then, to complicate the situation further, on 21 May 1992 the Russian Supreme Soviet declared the 1954 transfer of the Crimea to Ukraine illegal. Negotiations on the naval issue continued throughout 1992 and led to a 14-point agreement, signed on 3 August 1992. Under the agreement the fleet was to be divided by 1995. Until that point it was to be shared equally between Russia and Ukraine. However, the issue was not completely resolved, as the occasional disputes during 1993 demonstrated. Ukraine, of course, had become a major military power in its own right, as a result of the dissolution of the USSR. Within six months some 80% of the military personnel stationed in Ukraine had taken the oath of allegiance to the new state and a huge amount of Soviet military equipment in Ukrainian territory had been nationalized. Ukraine thereby found itself with the second-largest army in Europe and with the world's third-largest array of nuclear weapons on its territory.

These forces complicated the disarmament treaties signed by the former USSR. Protocols were required to the CFE and START (Strategic Arms' Reduction Treaty) I treaties to determine the relative proportions of the 'Soviet' total that each successor state, such as Ukraine, was entitled to. The reluctance of Ukraine to ratify the START I agreement became a major irritant in Ukraine's relations with the USA, since it delayed implementation of the treaty.

Ukraine was engaged in the process of reducing the huge armed forces it inherited. At mid-1993, as the authorities were trying to minimize the social disruption involved, particularly for the Russian officers, the reduction process was proceeding fairly slowly. Nevertheless, the armed forces were due to fall from 800,000 in 1991 to 400,000 by the end of 1995, with a reduction to under 200,000 likely by the end of the century—unless relations with Russia deteriorate seriously.

The Belarus parliament voted to establish a separate army in March 1992. As with Ukraine, there was a surplus of equipment and a military establishment larger than required. A total of around 95,000 was anticipated once the process of reduction was complete. Like Ukraine, Belarus was showing sensitivity towards the plight of the huge Russian officer corps stranded in the country and was exerting no pressure for them to leave before suitable accommodation in Russia was available.

The Baltic Republics

Unlike the CIS states, the three former Soviet Baltic states were anxious to break with Russia and its allies as quickly and completely as possible. Relationships with Russia were complicated by the continuing presence of large Russian armed forces in the countries and, in the case of Estonia and Latvia, by the presence of very large Russian minorities in the state. None of the Baltic countries believed that they could create armed forces which could realistically defend them against Russia. Their diplomacy was, therefore, aimed at integration with the West and participation in wider security groupings. They wished to be associated with central Europe rather than with the other former Soviet republics.

Estonia's policy envisaged the achievement of security through a three-phase process. This would begin with collaboration with Latvia and Lithuania and broaden into a Baltic regional security zone. Finally, Estonia would seek to join a pan-European system based on an expanded NATO. In 1993 Estonia's primary security concern remained the Russian forces still deployed in Estonia. Estonia asked for the Russian personnel to be withdrawn as quickly as possible, but for the equipment to be left behind to equip the Estonian army, which, when complete, was to number around 8,000.

Latvian security concerns also focused on Russia: not only the Russian forces in Latvia, but also the danger of political instability within Russia itself. Latvia intended to maintain extremely small armed forces and shared Estonia's concerns about the loyalty of the large Russian minority population. Latvia argued that Russian personnel and their families had no more right to remain in Latvia than the Russian personnel then being withdrawn from the former GDR.

Lithuania also had concerns about instability in Russia, but was fortunate in having no significant Russian minority population. However, Lithuania wished the Russian forces on its territory to withdraw as quickly as possible and was concerned both about their presence and the fact that Russian units leaving eastern Germany, Poland and Kaliningrad (formerly Königsberg), must pass through Lithuania en route. Kaliningrad, a Russian enclave on the Baltic, was a source of concern and Lithuania suggested that it be demilitarized.

All three of the Baltic countries were concerned that Russia was reluctant to withdraw its forces, because many of them were extremely important to Russian security. Latvia, for example, was the site of the Ballistic Missile Defence facilities at Skrunda, which Russia was extremely reluctant to abandon.

Security worries remained of much importance to the Baltic countries, because of the tremendous disproportion in size and military power between them and their Russian neighbour. None of the three countries pretended that their forces could resist or deter an invasion and all shared the doctrine that the purpose of their armed forces was to make it unambiguous that aggression had occurred and define the crisis in a way that international action could restore their independence. Only eventual NATO membership would fully allay their security concerns.

Central Europe: the Visegrad Group

The dissolution of the Warsaw Pact and the CMEA and the reluctance of NATO to extend its 'zone of stability' eastwards, led groups of Eastern European states to seek to create sub-regional groupings as a first step towards integration in Western European international organizations. The most effective of these in the early 1990s was the trilateral states, or the Visegrad Group, of Poland, Hungary and Czechoslovakia (from 1993, the Czech Republic and Slovakia). This grouping began to emerge as early as January 1991, when Hungary and Czechoslovakia signed a bilateral military agreement to begin regular contacts between their armed forces in the post-Warsaw Pact era and identify confidence-building measures. This was followed by similar bilateral agreements between Poland and Czechoslovakia (27 February 1991) and Poland and Hungary (20 March 1991).

The trilateral states emphasized that these agreements were not mutual or collective defence treaties, but were designed to maximize information exchanges and military co-operation over common problems related to the reforms needed in the post-Warsaw Pact era, such as retraining, disarmament and re-equipment and relocation of forces away from the western frontiers. In the words of Polish foreign minister Skubiszewski, it was a mechanism for 'loose collaboration'. The statements that these agreements were not a formal military alliance and were not directed against any other country were designed to reassure the USSR. In this they were successful, since even prior to the Moscow coup attempt of August 1991, the USSR accepted the grouping as legitimate and non-threatening. There was an implicit assumption by the Soviet regime that the emergence of the trilateral grouping made it less likely that these countries would attempt to join NATO. After the coup and the collapse of the USSR, however, the trilateral group did initiate co-ordinated efforts to join both NATO and the EC.

The key meetings in the evolution of this grouping were a summit conference of all three states at Visegrad (Hungary—hence 'Visegrad Group'), in February 1991, and the meeting at Kraków (Poland) of October 1991. The Visegrad Summit provided evidence that the states were concerned that Eastern Europe should not be seen as a 'buffer' or neutral zone between NATO and the USSR/Russia. The Kraków Declaration emphasized that the three states sought 'full-range integration into the European political, economic and juridical, as well as security, system'. They thus sought membership of both the EC and NATO. NATO, in its London Declaration of July 1990, asserted that the security of the NATO states was 'inseparably linked to that of all other states in Europe'. This theme was stressed by the trilateral states, which declared at Kraków that they saw Europe 'as a single and indivisible territory where the security of each of the countries is indissolubly connected with the security of others'. The CSCE symbolically recognized the importance of central Europe by designating Prague (Czechoslovakia—now the Czech Republic) as the site for the CSCE Secretariat and Warsaw (Poland) as the site of the CSCE election-monitoring centre.

The period after 1991 saw an evolution in the Visegrad Group's foreign policies, with the emergence of the CIS and the Soviet successor states. Poland was the first state to recognize the independence of Ukraine, while Hungary was the first to sign a bilateral treaty. The emergence of the CIS created a buffer zone between Russia and the Visegrad countries, though the latter were keen to develop positive bilateral relations in order to promote stability in the region. The sense of Eastern Europe itself being in an indeterminate position *vis-à-vis* security issues, was not diminished by the dissolution of the USSR, however. On the contrary, with NATO maintaining its Cold War borders and Russia defining a special sphere of interest in the CIS states, central Europe and the Balkans, the former Eastern Europe Communist bloc, were thereby defined as a 'no-mans land' in between. Poland, Hungary and Czechoslovakia continued to assert that sub-regional co-operation could be of only limited value in resolving this security situation and an extension of NATO's security zone eastwards was deemed essential in the long term.

Poland saw a need to ensure security from both Russia and from Germany. During 1989 and 1990 Poland was the ally most reluctant to disband the Warsaw Pact and the last to request its Soviet garrison to leave. This was owing to a lingering concern about unified and resurgent Germany, particularly given that Poland was not convinced that Germany had fully accepted the permanence of Poland's 1945 borders. By early 1991 a combination of factors changed this stance: the new Soviet policy of repression in the Baltic republics refocused attention on the eastern frontier; the agreements of 1990 satisfied Poland that Germany had fully accepted the 1945 frontiers; and the election of Lech Wałęsa as President produced a more assertively nationalistic leadership, less sympathetic to Soviet concerns. Even so, Poland recognized that given that it bordered the secessionist Soviet Republic of Lithuania and straddled the traditional western invasion route into Russia, the USSR would be peculiarly sensitive regarding Polish security policy and membership of NATO was out of the question for the foreseeable future. This attitude changed with the collapse of the USSR in December 1991. However, Poland was not able to achieve membership of NATO, although it was a member of the North Atlantic Co-operation Council and gained associate status with the EC. By mid-1993 it seemed as if Russia had withdrawn its objections to Polish membership of NATO, but traditional antipathy to this idea was resurgent after the armed dissolution of parliament, in September.

Poland was keen to become a full member of the 'Western' group of states, and pursued its security through seeking Western ties, though it valued the regional ties of the Visegrad Group. After the dissolution of the USSR it sought to improve relations with its new eastern neighbours, Belarus and Ukraine. It encouraged Ukraine to develop links with, and consider membership of, the Visegrad Group and, indeed, Polish-Ukrainian contacts developed so well that Russia expressed dissatisfaction at it. Despite its security concerns, economic pressures and CFE obligations meant that Poland was in the process of reducing its armed forces to around 250,000 by 1995.

In the early 1990s Hungary's forces were in the process of being reduced from 100,000 to 70,000, by 1995, and were being restructured to give them a more 'defensive' character, primarily by reducing the number of tank regiments. The withdrawal of Soviet forces from Hungary was completed on schedule and Hungary's primary security concern was no longer its relationship with Russia, but rather the zone of instability on its southern borders.

Hungary had two primary concerns. The first was the position of the large Hungarian minorities in several neighbouring states, notably Slovakia, Ukraine, Romania (Transylvania) and Yugoslavia (Vojvodina in Serbia). Hungary alarmed its neighbours soon after the formation of the first post-Communist Government, when the premier, József Antall, declared that he was also premier 'in spirit' of Hungarians living in other states. This unfortunate remark gave the misleading impression that Hungary intended to interfere in the domestic politics of its neighbours. However, no such desire appeared to exist. Nevertheless, Hungary felt a clear concern for the Hungarian minorities and this was a sensitive issue in relations with Romania.

The issue overlapped the problem of the collapse of Yugoslavia. The savage wars there disturbed Hungary for many reasons, quite apart from the gross violations of human rights and of the laws of war being perpetrated. Serbia had a large Hungarian minority in the Vojvodina region and Hungary was profoundly alarmed by the 'ethnic cleansing' campaigns carried out by Serbs in Croatia and in Bosnia and Herzegovina and by the West's complicit acceptance of this. It would be difficult for Hungary to ignore such a campaign directed against the Hungarians of the Vojvodina. Moreover, as a small state, Hungary saw the West's acceptance of aggression against and partition of Bosnia and Herzegovina as an ominous signal to states like Hungary in the 'no-mans land' of Eastern Europe.

These fears made Hungary attach even more importance to its membership of the trilateral Visegrad Group and of the Central European Initiative. Hungary participated in the launching of the regional co-operation initiative involving Italy, Austria, Czechoslovakia and Yugoslavia, the so-called Pentagonal of former Habsburg countries. This became the 'Heptagonal' when Poland and Slovenia joined, but Croatia's admission led to the adoption of the title of Central European Initiative, formed at a CSCE meeting in March 1992.

Czechoslovakia expressed the strongest concern at the emergence of a security vacuum in central Europe. After the end of Communist rule the new Government attached great importance to the CSCE process, which it hoped would be 'the medium out of which a new security structure and a new system of all-European security continues to grow'. However, it soon became disillusioned with the CSCE process, particularly owing to its inability to affect the crises in the Baltic, in 1990–91, and in Bosnia and Herzegovina, in 1992–93. Czechoslovakia sought integration with NATO but was unsuccessful. In the medium-term, therefore, it turned to a policy of developing good relations with its neighbours, diversifying its diplomatic contacts, building on the trilateral group and the Central European Initiative and pursuing contacts with NATO. The defence doctrine of Czechoslovakia identified no enemies and stipulated an equal distribution of forces around the country.

On 1 January 1993 the Czechoslovak federal state divided into two new countries, the Czech Republic and Slovakia. The strategic position of the former was actually significantly improved by this development. It lost its frontiers with the unstable Balkan and east European (former USSR) regions and bordered only Austria, Germany, Poland and Slovakia. As the most westernized and Western-leaning part of the former federation, the Czech Republic should find it easier to achieve its medium-term aim of full integration into NATO and the EC. Slovakia, by contrast, inherited a more problematic situation. Its foreign-policy stance was more enthusiastic about pursuing regional co-operation, through the Visegrad Group and the Central European Initiative, and more amenable to developing relations with its countries to the east, particularly Ukraine.

The Balkans

The post-Communist Balkans became a region of grave instability, with savage conflict in the former Yugoslavia and the possibility of war between the new Federal Republic of Yugoslavia (Serbia and Montenegro) and Albania should violence erupt in the Kosovo-Metohija region. The fighting in the Yugoslav states was already the worst in Europe since 1945. The wars in Slovenia, Croatia and Bosnia and Herzegovina left over 100,000 dead and 2m. refugees. Within the borders of the old Yugoslavia alone, Serbian expansion threatened to spread the conflict to Kosovo-Metohija, Macedonia and the Vojvodina, with the possibility of a wider Balkan war.

For the Eastern Europeans the Yugoslav wars demonstrated the alarming weakness of the post-Cold War security arrangements in Europe and the inability of existing international bodies to deal with conflicts created by competing nationalisms in the successor states. It represented an alarming precedent, since most of the states of the region had been engaged in the process of dramatically reducing the size of their armed forces and restructuring them for purely defensive purposes. On the edge of the Balkans, on Romania's northern border, Moldova, for example, like the Baltic republics, argued that its armed forces were designed not with a serious hope of defending the state but 'in order to fix the act of aggression'. Parliament declared Moldova a neutral state but, in the light of Bosnia and Herzegovina's dismemberment, watched by an inactive Western world, Moldova's security could be seen as purely at the whim of its neighbours. For such reasons, the Balkan states may show more interest in Romania's 1991 proposal for an Eastern version of the WEU, in which it seemed to envisage a revival of the Warsaw Pact, without the then USSR (i.e. Russia).

CONCLUSIONS

A unifying theme of the Eastern European states was the desire to become full members of the EC at the earliest possible date, regardless of the economic and political strains being experienced during the painful transition to a market economy. This desire originated as much from political as from economic motivations. Similar considerations lay behind the successful applications of Hungary, Poland and Czechoslovakia to become members of the Council of Europe. While the Eastern Europeans wished to avoid being seriously affected by the collapse of the Soviet economy and the end of the CMEA, they wished to join the EC because, like Greece, Spain and Portugal before them, anchoring their sovereignty in the EC was seen as insurance of the survival of 'Western' political and economic values and systems. The EC was seen as the core of the 'new Europe', of which the Eastern states desperately wanted to be part. President Havel of Czechoslovakia (subsequently President of the Czech Republic) told the European Parliament, in Brussels (Belgium), in March 1991, that the political need to be integrated into the EC far outweighed the difficulties posed by the parlous state of the Czechoslovak economy. He suggested Czechoslovak involvement in the EC's discussions on political union and a common foreign and security policy as a way to overcome the disadvantages of being denied NATO membership. He also said Czechoslovakia wanted to have links with the WEU.

Whereas immediately after the collapse of Communism in Eastern Europe the new democracies placed great emphasis on a strengthened CSCE for achieving their security goals, they soon saw the CSCE as inadequate and focused their efforts on integration with NATO. Virtually none of the Eastern states believed that they could defend themselves alone and many saw their armed forces as serving a token purpose of 'registering the act of aggression'. NATO membership was, therefore, seen as crucial. NATO, however, remained reluctant to admit them, for fear of alarming Russia and because NATO feared being drawn into problems of ethnic nationalism with which it was ill-equipped to deal. The 'Partnership for Peace' proposals of January 1994 did not go far enough to satisfy all the anxieties of the East.

Although they tried to compensate for this by forming regional associations, these were not of a 'collective defence' character and were not seen as being an adequate substitute for eventual membership of NATO and the EC. Diplomatic emphasis was upon improving relations with immediate neighbours and with both NATO and the EC, as institutions and with their individual member states.

The eagerness to break with the USSR and build links with the West meant that the 1989–91 period saw a comparative neglect of relations with the USSR/Russia, but, subsequently, a start was made on correcting this and interactions with the CIS states grew. The continuing instability throughout the early 1990s in the former USSR remained a matter deep concern, given the uncertainty surrounding the control of the enormous nuclear and conventional forces of the former USSR. It was recognized that stability in Russia and the CIS was crucial to the security of Eastern Europe.

In general terms the security of Eastern European countries clearly increased as a result of the end of the Cold War and collapse of the USSR. Eastern Europe was no longer targeted by enormous numbers of NATO nuclear weapons, nor was it menaced by a heavily armed, unified Communist USSR. But the region was still not a zone of true security. The unpredictability of developments in the CIS remained a cause for serious concern and the fear that Eastern Europe would be abandoned as a buffer zone between NATO and Russia was a real one. By 1993, while the pattern of international relations and defence policy was beginning to emerge, the continuing process of state disintegration in the former Warsaw Pact area left the fear of instability and attractiveness of full NATO membership a continuing theme.

BIBLIOGRAPHY

Brown, A. (Ed.). *The Soviet–East European Relationship in the Gorbachev Era.* Boulder, Colorado, Westview, 1990.

Dawisha, K. *Eastern Europe, Gorbachev and Reform: The Great Challenge.* Cambridge, Cambridge University Press, 1988.

Dawisha, K., and Valdes, J. 'Socialist Internationalism in Eastern Europe', in *Problems of Communism*, Vol. 36, No. 2 (March/April), 1987.

de Nevers, R. 'The Soviet Union and Eastern Europe: The End of an Era', in *Adelphi Papers*, No. 249. London, Brasseys and International Institute for Strategic Studies, 1990.

European Security, Vol. I, No. 4 (Winter), 1992. Special issue on Eastern Europe.

Holden, G. *The Warsaw Pact: Soviet Security and Bloc Politics*. Oxford, Basil Blackwell, 1989.

Kittrie, N., and Volgyes, I. (Eds). *The Uncertain Future: Gorbachev's Eastern Bloc*. New York, Paragon House, 1988.

Linden, R. H. (Ed.) *Studies in East European Foreign Policy*. New York, Praeger, 1980.

Nelson, D. N. 'Europe's Unstable East', in *Foreign Policy*, No. 82 (Spring), 1991.

INTERNATIONAL RELATIONS OF RUSSIA AND THE COMMONWEALTH OF INDEPENDENT STATES

Dr MARGOT LIGHT

INTRODUCTION

Foreign policy in the traditional sense did not, at first, play a very large part in the activities of the 15 independent countries which emerged after the disintegration of the USSR. Eleven of the new states immediately founded the Commonwealth of Independent States (CIS), and all 15 concentrated, perforce, on the problems of independent statehood and on disentangling themselves from one another rather than on their relations with the world outside the former USSR.

The largest of the independent republics, the Russian Federation, was immersed in the particular identity problem of existing as a state without an empire, and in the perplexities of converting domestic policy (in other words, the relationships between the old Union Republics) into foreign policy. With regard to its relations with the outside world, the Russian Government was concerned, first, to please the West, to ensure that economic and technical assistance would be forthcoming, and, second, to distinguish its foreign policy from that of the USSR under its last President, Mikhail Gorbachev.

Apart from Estonia, Latvia and Lithuania (which, essentially, returned to the *status quo ante* 1940 and their incorporation into the USSR, and which will not be considered in this chapter), the non-Russian successor states had never before enjoyed independent statehood in the modern international system. Their primary tasks were domestic: establishing internal sovereignty and setting up the institutions to run their political and economic systems which had previously been part of a highly centralized integral whole. The symbols of external sovereignty—international recognition and individual membership of international organizations like the United Nations (UN)—were granted immediately. It was more difficult, however, to establish an active and independent foreign policy.

The urgent need to untangle the economies and military forces of countries which had always been run from Moscow, as a single highly interdependent system, soon made it clear to all the successor governments that their most acute foreign problems centred on the 'near abroad', as Russians called the territory of the former USSR. After considering in more detail the problems facing them as they attempted to consolidate their independence and establish a foreign policy, therefore, this chapter will turn to the relationships between the former Soviet republics, and the efforts to create an economic and defence alliance within the CIS.

While there are arguments both for and against the benefits of economic integration within the CIS, the large number of violent disputes within the former USSR complicated their international relations. The third section of the chapter will look at the major conflicts which have bedeviled economic recovery and peaceful development in the former USSR. Relations with the 'far abroad', in other words, the relations of the successor states to countries outside the CIS, are examined in the final section, before an assessment is made of the future prospects for the international relations of Russia and the CIS.

Unlike the USSR, Russia was not a superpower but, in terms of size, military strength and economic potential, it was certainly a great power. Moreover, it was the world's second-largest nuclear power. Russia was recognized internationally as the legal heir to the USSR and permanent membership of the Security Council of the UN was immediately, and almost automatically, transferred from the USSR to the Russian Federation. While the Russian Government denied that it aspired to dominate the CIS, there could be no doubt that the most important aspect of the foreign policies of the other successor states was their relationship with Russia. As far as the outside world was concerned, Russia received far more international diplomatic and economic attention than the other republics. Inevitably, therefore, the foreign policy of Russia will figure more prominently in this chapter than those of the other former Soviet states.

FOREIGN POLICY AND THE ESTABLISHMENT OF INDEPENDENT STATEHOOD

Of the 15 successor states to the USSR, the Russian Federation began from the most advantageous position. When the central, all-Union Government ceased to exist, the Russian Ministry of Foreign Affairs (RMFA) took over the Soviet Ministry of Foreign Affairs, including its buildings and most of its personnel. Moreover, to the chagrin of the other republics, the RMFA laid claim to Soviet embassies around the world which, with some personnel changes, immediately began to represent the interests of the Russian Federation abroad. However, Russia inherited more than the property of the former Soviet foreign ministry. The foreign ministry of the USSR had been staffed predominantly by Russians. The few diplomats who were non-Russian by nationality evinced little interest in serving the foreign ministries of their putative homelands. The RMFA, therefore, began with a large staff of highly professional people with diplomatic expertise, experience of the international system and well-established channels of communication. Moreover, as the recognized legal heir to the USSR and a permanent member of the UN Security Council, Russia immediately enjoyed prominent international status.

Few of the other successor states enjoyed any of these benefits. Although all the republics, in theory at least, possessed foreign ministries, only Ukraine and Belarus had experience of foreign representation, having had separate seats at the UN since its inception and having contributed staff to its international civil service and to the specialized UN agencies. Ukraine and Belarus also had a large intelligentsia and, therefore, a potential pool of foreign ministry employees. The size of the educated élite in the other republics was smaller and there were too few suitable people to staff the new ministries. Furthermore, in all the successor states, pay and conditions of work in the public sector were inferior to the many other opportunities which had become available to the educated élite in the new business world, making recruitment difficult.

Apart from lack of diplomatic expertise and shortages of experienced staff, there were severe material difficulties in establishing foreign representation abroad. Rental costs were prohibitive in the large industrialized states and there was a shortage of suitable accommodation at home for foreign embassies. Most of the republics also had poorly developed communications infrastructures—Moscow had previously been the hub from which the Soviet transport system and telecommunications network had radiated. The foreign representatives to many of the successor states, therefore, continued to operate from Moscow and they themselves, unlike Russia, established few embassies abroad.

However, Russia, too, had problems. Russia had always been an empire and the identity of Russian statehood had been closely associated with the idea and the fact of empire. There had never been a Russian nation-state and nor was the newly independent Russian Federation a nation-state. A multinational federation, it was invented in 1922, some argue in order to legitimize the continuation of the Russian Empire within the newly formed USSR. As a result of the association of statehood with empire, many Russians found it difficult to accept that some areas, particularly those where there were large Russian populations, were no longer part of Russia. A new identity and a new role had to be forged for Russia and there was uncertainty and disagreement about what it should be and what it would imply for Russian foreign policy, particularly with regard to the near abroad.

Moreover, Russian foreign policy expertise was little help in dealing with the CIS. Apart from the difficulty of redefining what had been domestic politics as foreign policy, there was no specialized knowledge about the other republics in the Ministry of Foreign Affairs. For a while there was talk of establishing a separate ministry, on the lines of the old British Colonial (subsequently Commonwealth) Office. In fact, however, there was very little expertise elsewhere and a separate ministry might have exacerbated the apprehension already felt in the other republics that Russia intended to re-establish the pre-revolutionary empire. With regard to the West, the Russian President, Boris Yeltsin, and his Government wanted to continue the friendly relations established by Gorbachev. At the same time, however, it was important to make a distinction between Russian foreign policy and that of the former USSR. Western aid seemed to depend both upon being able to demonstrate Russia's loyalty to Western policies and upon establishing a market economy. The economic reforms required to do this inevitably affected Russia's relations with the near abroad.

None of the other successor states were nation-states and many of them, particularly those that had not aspired to independence, also had identity problems. Unlike Russia, they did not need to distinguish their foreign policy from that of the USSR, but they faced the more basic problem of formulating a foreign policy for the first time, both in relation to Russia and the other former Soviet republics and with regard to the outside world. Moreover, all of them badly needed economic assistance and they had to dissuade the West from concentrating all its attention on Russia.

The conditions under which the successor states attempted to resolve these problems were not auspicious. Their economic conditions were catastrophic and, in many of them, the economic situation was exacerbated by domestic political turmoil. None of the inter-ethnic conflicts which had characterized the last years of the existence of the USSR had been resolved by its disintegration and new disputes appeared almost immediately. The CIS, which initially had seemed designed to facilitate the peaceful disintegration of the USSR, proved woefully inadequate for that purpose and incapable of dealing with the gamut of new problems which arose almost as soon as it was established.

THE COMMONWEALTH OF INDEPENDENT STATES

On 8 December 1991 the leaders of Belarus, Russia and Ukraine announced the creation of a Commonwealth of Independent States, open to all members of the former USSR. Although its capital was to be in Minsk (Belarus), a supra-national organization was not envisaged, since the CIS was intended to preserve the sovereignty of its members and prevent the creation of the strong centre which had characterized the USSR. On 21 December the leaders of Armenia, Azerbaijan, Kazakhstan, Kyrgyzstan, Moldova, Tajikistan, Turkmenistan and Uzbekistan joined the three Slavic states in signing the founding Commonwealth treaty. The three Baltic republics and Georgia had declared independence by then and, whereas the last sent observers to CIS meetings, the former made it clear from the outset that they had no intention of joining. The treaty was never presented to the Azerbaijani parliament for ratification and the Azerbaijani participants in CIS meetings technically remained observers until September 1993, when membership was ratified. The treaty did not prescribe the degree and extent of co-operation expected from members. They would be free to choose to participate in some activities and to abstain from others.

Many observers believed that the CIS was essentially a transitional body, the main function of which would be to ensure the orderly disintegration of the USSR and to arrange for the division of Soviet property and obligations. Although the members initially insisted that they intended to maintain joint control over nuclear weapons, to set up a united army and co-ordinate economic policy, it soon became clear that the various governments did not share the same goals. The Ukrainian Government rejected the establishment of a permanent Commonwealth infrastructure, for example, lest it simply recreate the USSR and give Russia a dominant position. Many of the Central Asian leaders, on the other hand, wanted the CIS to have a single economic system and close military integration. The Russian Government seemed to veer from hoping that the CIS would ensure the preservation of a common economic space and 'rouble zone', as well as a unified defence force, to wanting complete disintegration.

Even before the treaty founding the CIS had been ratified by its members, therefore, serious differences of opinion had begun to appear and this delayed the establishment of institutions and agreements to turn it into a functional economic and military alliance. Since many of the states wished to have their own conventional armed forces, for example, the only unified CIS forces which could be created were those in charge of nuclear weapons. However, the issue of whether Russia alone would have control over operation of the nuclear weapons, or whether the leaders of the other three countries in which there were strategic nuclear arms (Belarus, Kazakhstan and Ukraine) would have a veto, remained contentious. It took until May 1992 for a CIS collective security agreement to be tabled and it was signed by only six states: Armenia, Kazakhstan, Kyrgyzstan, Russia, Tajikistan and Uzbekistan (Belarus acceded effectively, if not formally, later)—the Treaty on Collective Security, or Tashkent Agreement, was signed on 15 May in Uzbekistan. Five of these states also agreed to set up joint peace-keeping forces, but few of them actually contributed troops. Russia became the CIS 'peace keeper', but that aroused suspicions in some republics about the ultimate intentions of the Russian Government. In May 1993 the joint CIS military command was dissolved and the idea of collective security seemed to have been replaced by reliance on bilateral defence agreements.

Similarly, Yeltsin's insistence on immediately freeing prices in Russia, without waiting until other republics were ready for this step, placed the future of economic co-operation and a retention of the rouble zone under threat. Some countries elected to replace the rouble with their own national currencies, but all suffered as Russian prices rose. Although a number of agreements were made to co-ordinate economic reform and to co-operate in various economic fields, they were rarely translated into action. Invariably the Central Asian states of Tajikistan, Uzbekistan and, particularly, Kazakhstan were the most enthusiastic proponents of economic integration, while Ukraine was the most reluctant participant in co-operative agreements. When a CIS Charter was finally formulated, in January 1993, envisaging a defence alliance, an economic co-ordination committee and an inter-state court, only seven of the 11 members agreed to present it to their parliaments for ratification. Nonetheless, and contrary to many predictions, the CIS did not disintegrate.

Most countries in the near abroad were dependent on Russia for energy and, as energy prices rose, they became increasingly indebted to Russia. By July 1993 economic necessity had persuaded Belarus, Russia and Ukraine to form an economic alliance and, in September, six states (Armenia, Belarus, Kazakhstan, Russia, Tajikistan and Uzbekistan) agreed to co-ordinate monetary, fiscal, banking and customs policies, in effect forming an economic union and recreating the rouble zone. One week later Ukraine agreed to join. It seemed doubtful, however, that this agreement would be any more effective than previous economic decisions made by the members of the CIS. In October Eduard Shevardnadze, the president of Georgia, announced that Georgia would join the CIS—with Azerbaijan having finally joined the previous month, all the former Union Republics of the USSR, with the exception of the Baltic states, were now members of the CIS.

Apart from the differences in what the CIS members envisaged from the Commonwealth and the difficulties of establishing an organization with variable membership and no infrastructure, the main obstacle to co-operation within the CIS was the fear of Russian hegemony felt by many of the other members. That apprehension was particularly strong in Ukraine and, in effect, Russian-Ukrainian bilateral relations dominated the affairs of the CIS. Apart from their diametrically opposed views of what the CIS should be and their difficult economic ties, there were three inter-related issues which divided Russia and Ukraine: the Crimea; the future of the Black Sea naval fleet; and Ukraine's nuclear status.

In 1954, in celebration of the 300th anniversary of the union between Russia and Ukraine, the then Soviet leader, Nikita Khrushchev, transferred the Crimea, which had been annexed by Russia in the 18th century, from the administrative jurisdiction of the Russian Federation to Ukraine. Since both were in the USSR, it made little difference to the local population or to Russia. Although the population of the Crimea was predominantly ethnic Russian (Stalin—Iosif V. Dzhugashvili deported the indigenous Crimean Tatars, in 1944, and they only began to return to the area after 1985), a majority of the population voted in favour of Ukrainian independence when a referendum was held in 1991. In theory, Russians in the Russian Federation supported the rights of the other republics to independence and self-determination. In practice, however, many of them found the loss of the Crimea difficult to contemplate and the Russian parliament soon began to question the legality of the 1954 transfer. In May 1992 the Crimean parliament (soviet) voted for independence from both Ukraine and Russia, but it reversed its own decision a few days later, settling for regional autonomy within Ukraine. This did not resolve the territorial dispute between Russia and Ukraine, however, because the Russian parliament renewed its demands from time to time for the return of the Crimea to Russia. More importantly, Sevastopol, the naval base of the Black Sea fleet, was situated in the Crimea and the future of the fleet and its base remained a divisive issue between the two countries. Each time they argued about the fleet, the territorial issue re-emerged.

The battle for the Black Sea fleet began almost as soon as the USSR disintegrated. Initially, the question was whether it should be under combined CIS control or whether it should be shared and, if divided, how it should be apportioned. The Black Sea coastline is shared by Russia, Ukraine and Georgia and all three countries could reasonably claim part of the fleet. Continuous civil war prevented Georgia from making a serious bid, but Russia and Ukraine were in constant dispute over its future. On some occasions the Russian and Ukrainian Presidents agreed to joint control; on others they agreed to divide the fleet, most recently on the basis of an equal share. Each time the agreement broke down. For Russians, the future of the fleet concerned not just the ships, but also the port of Sevastopol, since there were no naval facilities on the Russian section of the Black Sea coast.

To the consternation both of President Yeltsin and of the Ukrainian Government, the Russian parliament intervened in July 1993, declaring that both the fleet and Sevastopol belonged to Russia. Yeltsin disassociated himself from their declaration. In September 1993, however, he claimed that he had made a deal with President Kravchuk, at Massandra, in the Crimea: Russia would take over the Ukrainian share of the fleet, in return for forgiving Ukraine's debts to Russia, and it would also lease Sevastopol from Ukraine. This time it was President Kravchuk who disassociated himself: he may or may not have agreed to the deal, but he rapidly withdrew any commitment, on the grounds that any agreement would have to be confirmed by the Ukrainian parliament. Yeltsin also claimed that, as part of the same deal, the third contentious bilateral issue, Ukraine's nuclear status, had been resolved. President Kravchuk had, he said, agreed to turn over its 1,800 nuclear warheads to Russia for dismantling. In return, Russia would supply Ukraine with fuel for its nuclear power stations. As with the rest of the Massandra agreement, however, there was some doubt whether Kravchuk had made a firm commitment and even more whether the Ukrainian parliament would agree to the deal.

In effect, when the USSR disintegrated the Russian Federation inherited Soviet nuclear status. However, three new nuclear powers were created, simply because Soviet intercontinental weapons were based in Belarus, Kazakhstan and Ukraine, as well as in the Russian Federation. Tactical weapons were widely spread throughout the former USSR, but the expectation was that they would be transferred to Russia immediately for safe keeping and eventual destruction. Ground-based strategic missiles could not easily be moved, however, and they remained under the control of the Strategic Rocket Forces which, as mentioned above, were converted into CIS forces. The immediate problem was to associate Belarus, Kazakhstan and Ukraine to the Strategic Arms' Reduction Treaty (START), signed by the USSR in July 1991 (and inherited by the Russian Federation), in such a way that they agreed to Russia being a nuclear power, while they themselves became non-nuclear. Although all three states had insisted before the disintegration of the USSR that they wished to be non-nuclear, once independence was achieved they became ambivalent. In part this was because of the expense of destroying the weapons and of disposing of the nuclear material recovered from them. However, it was also because they began to see their inherited nuclear weapons as a means of ensuring their security.

Under the terms of the Lisbon Protocol, agreed in May 1992, in Portugal, the leaders of the three republics undertook, after the ratification of the Protocol, to eliminate all the strategic nuclear weapons on their territory and to accede to the Non-Proliferation Treaty as Non-Nuclear-Weapon States. Whereas Kazakhstan and Belarus soon ratified the Protocol, however, the Ukrainian parliament kept postponing discussion. The question of Ukrainian nuclear status became a controversial issue in Russian–Ukrainian relations, as well as in Ukraine's relations with the West. The Ukrainian Government was determined that Russia and the West should compensate Ukraine for the cost of disposing of the weapons. Since the expertise to fulfil this task did not exist in Ukraine, Ukrainians were also concerned about the implications for Ukrainian sovereignty if the weapons were destroyed on Ukrainian territory by Russians. The Ukrainian Government also demanded security guarantees from Russia and the West, against both nuclear and conventional attack.

Throughout 1992 and 1993 the nuclear issue was used as a lever in Russian–Ukrainian relations whenever tension rose about the Black Sea fleet, the future of the CIS or about economic affairs. Although the weapons continued to be under the operational control of Russia and protected by CIS forces, the Ukrainian Government claimed 'administrative' control of the weapons on its soil and, from time to time, there were rumours or threats that it was on the verge of gaining operational control. Ukraine also mooted the idea of disposing of those weapons which were subject to the terms of the START 1 treaty, but keeping the rest and delaying acceding to the Non-Proliferation Treaty. Both the West and the Russian Government were delighted, therefore, when the issue seemed to have been resolved in Massandra, in September 1993. In Kiev, however, it was far less clear that Russia and Ukraine had finally reached agreement.

Ukraine and Russia were the two largest members of the CIS and it was not surprising that little progress was possible in integrating the Commonwealth as long as their bilateral relations remained tense. However, the CIS was also put under severe strain by the violent conflicts which afflicted its members. We turn now to a brief survey of these disputes.

CONFLICT IN THE FORMER USSR

In the two years after the formation of the CIS there was violent conflict between Armenia and Azerbaijan, in Moldova and in Tajikistan, all members of the CIS. There were also three conflicts in Georgia. Despite the collective security agreement signed by some members of the CIS and the agreement to establish peace-keeping forces, the organization was unable to mediate in the conflicts or to restore peace. Russian troops, on the other hand, either on their own or in combination with other troops (but not under CIS command), were used as peace keepers, even in those areas where Russia itself was implicated in the conflict.

The long-standing and seemingly intractable conflict between Armenia and Azerbaijan, over the status of Nagorny Karabakh, a predominantly Armenian autonomous area within the state of Azerbaijan, predated the disintegration of the USSR. The conflict began in early 1988, when Nagorny Karabakh unsuccessfully requested the transfer of the area from Azerbaijani to Armenian jurisdiction. Many Armenian refugees left Azerbaijan throughout 1988 and 1989, when Azerbaijanis responded by attacking Armenians living in Azerbaijan. In January 1990 there was a large-scale massacre of Armenians, in Baku (Azerbaijan), which triggered violent clashes between the republics of Armenia and Azerbaijan which neither Soviet troops nor various efforts to mediate were able to halt.

Once the USSR disintegrated, the conflict escalated. Troops of the former Soviet army were withdrawn from the area and many of their weapons were either sold to or stolen by local forces. Both sides in the conflict accused Russia of assisting the other side. Whether or not Russian military commanders based in the area intervened in the war, official Russian policy was to try to mediate in the conflict. Several cease-fires were negotiated, some of them by Russia, but all of them were breached by one side or the other just as soon as they had been agreed.

The war caused enormous economic hardship, particularly in Armenia, since its supply route from Russia passed through Azerbaijan. It also destabilized the political situation in Azerbaijan, where successive regimes fell because they could not win the war. During 1993 Armenia captured a large swathe of territory around Nagorny Karabakh and seemed set to hold it in order to improve its negotiating position, so that it could better secure the independence of Nagorny Karabakh. In September the new Azerbaijani President, Heydar Aliyev (former member of the Soviet Politburo), offered immediate consultations with Armenian leaders, arousing hopes of a negotiated settlement.

The CIS played no part in negotiating an end to the war between Armenia and Azerbaijan and it proved equally incapable of dealing with civil war in Moldova. When the USSR disintegrated, the area east of the Dniester river ('Transdnestria'), dominated by ethnic Russians, declared itself independent, fearing that Moldova intended to unite with Romania. Fighting broke out between the central Moldovan authorities and separatist forces. After several weeks the foreign ministers of Moldova, Romania, Russia and Ukraine managed to negotiate a cease-fire, in April 1992, but it soon broke down. When the fighting resumed Russian arms were used by the Transdnestrians and soldiers from the 14th Russian army stationed in that area were accused of fighting with them. In June 1992 another cease-fire was negotiated. Although 10 members of the CIS agreed to deploy a joint peace-keeping force in Moldova, the troops which eventually arrived were Russian rather than CIS forces. They managed to keep a fragile peace and a political solution to the dispute looked more likely following the defeat of the nationalist parties in the March 1994 elections.

The conflict in Tajikistan was also, essentially, a domestic political dispute which had turned violent, but it also spilled over the border, raising the spectre of another war with Afghanistan. In the first nine months of 1992 over 1,000 people were killed in Tajikistan, as rival groups struggled to take control. When President Nabiyev was forced from power, in September, the Acting President appealed to the CIS for help to stop the fighting. Russian reinforcements were rushed in to seal the border with Afghanistan and, in October, along with troops supplied by Uzbekistan, they began to patrol the capital, Dushanbe. Despite their presence, at least 20,000 people were reported killed and 600,000 rendered homeless in one year of civil war. Some refugees crossed the border into Afghanistan, launching raids into Tajikistan from border villages.

In July 1993, when the conflict spread over the border, Kazakhstan and Kyrgyzstan responded by sending small troop contingents to join the Russian and Uzbekistani troops, which by now numbered more than 15,000. Once again the Russians were accused of taking sides, backing ex-Communists against what some called an Islamic insurgency and others maintained was simply a different clan. In the Tajikistan case, the Russian Government believed that a political solution was possible and it put pressure on the Tajikistan Government to negotiate with their opponents. It also demanded negotiations with the Afghanistan Government, to help police the border.

Russian troops, together with Georgian and South Ossetian troops, were also keeping the peace in South Ossetia, an autonomous area within Georgia, where conflict smouldered for two years when the Georgian Government ended South Ossetia's autonomy and South Ossetians opted for independence from Georgia and unification with North Ossetia (an Autonomous Republic within the Russian Federation). Here, however, there seemed to have been little effort to find a political solution to the conflict.

Russian policy in Abkhazia, the second ethnic conflict that rent Georgia, was more ambiguous than in South Ossetia. Throughout 1992 and 1993 Georgia accused Russian troops of participating in the conflict in support of Abkhazia. Under threat of economic sanctions from Russia, a cease-fire was finally negotiated in July 1993, under the terms of which the Georgian leader, Eduard Shevardnadze (previously the Soviet foreign minister), agreed to withdraw his troops from the area and both sides agreed to withdraw heavy weaponry. The UN sent an observer mission to Georgia, to monitor compliance. In September, before the full UN mission had arrived, however, the Abkhazians unexpectedly reneged on the cease-fire, capturing Sukhumi and, later, the whole area with heavy arms, which the Georgians maintained they had obtained from Russian forces. Furthermore, the Georgians argued that, as guarantor of the cease-fire, Russia should have intervened to stop the fighting. Later they adapted their complaint, accusing Russian conservative factions rather than the Russian Government of supporting the Abkhazian separatists. Moreover, in a complete reversal of previous policy, Georgia agreed to join the CIS, in October, and requested Russian assistance to defeat Zviad Gamsakhurdia, the ousted previous President (his death at the end of 1993 effectively ended the third civil conflict in Georgia).

An essential principle of international peace-keeping operations is the neutrality of the peace keepers. Russian peace keepers in the conflicts in the former USSR, by contrast, were frequently accused of taking sides and the distinction between armed intervention and sending in forces to keep warring sides apart (always a thin line) sometimes seemed blurred. Nonetheless, given the unwillingness of other CIS members to share the responsibility and of the UN to intervene, there were few alternatives to Russian peace keeping. The international community was reluctant, however, to endorse Russia's right to this role.

THE FAR ABROAD

Although the Russian Government was determined to distinguish between its foreign policy and that of the USSR, it was assumed that Russia's relations with the far abroad would, like that of the USSR under Gorbachev, be orientated towards the West. Moreover, like Soviet policy under Gorbachev, Russian policy towards the West concentrated primarily on arms control and the search for foreign aid. While President Yeltsin was far more successful than Gorbachev in soliciting aid, however, negotiating arms control proved enormously complex since, once the USSR had disintegrated, agreements had to suit not just Russia but also the other states which they would affect. Dividing the force and weapons levels agreed in the treaty on Conventional Forces in Europe (CFE—negotiated by the USSR) between the successor states located west of the Urals demonstrated just how intricate future arms agreements were likely to be.

Nonetheless, at the first summit meeting between the US President George Bush and the Russian President Boris Yeltsin, in June 1992, START 2 proposals were announced: by the year 2003 Russia and the USA would cut their nuclear arsenals to 3,000–3,500 warheads each, a reduction of two-thirds of their current level. Moreover, both sides agreed to eliminate all multiple warheads, while Russia undertook to get rid of all its heavy land-based intercontinental missiles and the USA to reduce the number of nuclear warheads on submarines to 1,750, a reduction of 50%. START 2 was signed in January 1993. However, it could not come into effect before the reductions agreed in START 1 had been completed and, as was indicated above, Ukraine, in particular, was reluctant to ratify START 1 without security guarantees from the West and Russia.

By now, moreover, it had become clear that the costs of dismantling weapons were prohibitive and that there were physical problems in disposing of the nuclear material recovered from them. The West, anxious about the cost of disarmament as well as the safety of the nuclear installations (military and civilian) of the former USSR, began to pledge technical and financial aid to assist the decommissioning process. Ukraine, however, believed that its US $175m. share of the $500m. pledged by the USA for this purpose was insufficient and that Western economic aid was unfairly biased towards Russia. The Ukrainian Government believed that Western policy, in general, was short-sighted, relegating Ukraine to a subsidiary position and neglecting the new geopolitical threats in Europe.

It was true that both bilateral and multilateral aid (via the Group of Seven—'G7'—industrialized Western nations, the International Monetary Fund, the World Bank and the European Bank for Reconstruction and Development—EBRD) was directed primarily to Russia and that this, in part, reflected Western concentration on Russia at the expense of the other successor states. It also stemmed from the fact, however, that Western aid was conditional on the implementation of particular reform policies and, of all the CIS states, Russia had gone furthest towards introducing a market economy. However, it should be stressed that far more aid was pledged to Russia than was actually disbursed, and that the pledges were frequently made at times of domestic political crisis, with implementation slowing down once the crisis was over.

With regard to Ukraine's security concerns, the West believed that guarantees were implicit in the terms of the Non-Proliferation Treaty. It was also hoped that extending membership to all the former Soviet states of the North Atlantic Co-operation Council (NACC), initially established to allay the security fears of central European and Balkan states (the old Communist bloc of 'Eastern Europe'), would serve to enhance their security. The 1994 'Partnership for Peace' proposals were another such scheme. The successor states also became members of the UN and of the Conference on Security and Co-operation in Europe (CSCE), and various CSCE and UN missions were sent to monitor conflict situations in the CIS. What the West would not do, however, was to offer explicit guarantees against future Russian expansionism, which was at the heart of Ukrainian fears. On the other hand, despite disquiet about the conflicts within the former USSR and fears that they would spread, the West responded unenthusiastically to Russian proposals for UN assistance and auspices in fulfilling peace-keeping missions in the former USSR.

It was not only the industrialized Western states which established relations with the successor states. The disintegration of the USSR created new opportunities for regional powers to develop ties with individual republics. The Muslim states of Central Asia and the Caucasus were courted by both Iran and Turkey, for example, provoking fears that either or both might intervene in the conflicts in those areas (and arousing memories of the historical struggles between the Persian, Ottoman and Russian Empires in this region). A Black Sea Co-operation Agreement was signed between 11 states bordering the Black Sea, and the four southern Central Asian countries, Azerbaijan and Afghanistan joined Pakistan, Turkey and Iran in the Economic Co-operation Organization. Progress in either was unlikely, however, unless the regional conflicts in both areas were resolved.

Over the first two years of its independent existence (1992 and 1993), it gradually became clear that the initial expectation that Russian interests would always coincide with those of the West had been unrealistic. Russian and Western governments held different views about policy towards Serbia and Bosnia and Herzegovina, for example, and US and Russian interests with regard to potential arms sales were bound to conflict. It was also soon evident that Russian foreign-policy interests extended beyond a purely Western orientation and active steps were taken to improve relations with the People's Republic of China, with the states of South-East Asia and with India. The territorial dispute over ownership of the Kurile Islands (Japanese territory captured by the USSR at the end of the Second World War) prevented complete *rapprochement* with Japan, however, and made it impossible to get as much aid from Japan as the Russian Government had hoped. It also indicated that foreign policy was an important aspect of the domestic power struggle in Russia and that certain taboos (for example, maintaining Russia's territorial integrity or supporting other Orthodox believers) could not be broken without alienating domestic public opinion.

The fact that 25m. Russians lived outside the Russian Federation also began to influence Russian foreign policy. At the same time as Russia became more active in the far abroad, it also became clear that protection of the Russians who lived in the other former Soviet countries was perceived as the most vital of Russia's national interests. That meant that, despite the growing interest in the wider world, the CIS and the near abroad would remain the most important sphere of Russian foreign policy. As long as that was so, relations with Russia would dominate the foreign policy priorities of the other successor states.

FUTURE PROSPECTS

By the end of 1993 the survival of the CIS seemed more assured than it had at any time since its inception. However, if it was to develop into an efficient organization for promoting economic integration, resolving the violent conflicts within the former USSR and preventing further conflicts from occurring, several conditions would have to be fulfilled.

First, it would require an infrastructure designed in such a way as to allay the many fears that a strong centre was being reconstructed. Second, a mechanism would be required for collective decision-making, both to prevent Russia from dominating the organization and to alleviate other countries' suspicions that this was Russia's goal. Third, Russia and Ukraine would have to find a *modus vivendi*, since as long as their bilateral relations were tense the CIS could not thrive and, if either withdrew, the organization would disintegrate. Fourth, CIS members would have to agree on an economic reform programme and implement it at the same pace. Fifth, a peace-keeping force would have to be formed which was genuinely CIS-wide and under CIS command. It would need to operate with a mediation or conciliation commission, which could resolve political solutions to existing conflicts and intercede in areas where future conflicts were likely to arise.

These were clearly difficult and demanding conditions which would require a great deal of political will. However, if they were not even attempted, the CIS would probably continue to make 'paper' agreements, which were rarely translated into action, conflicts within it would continue to break out and the economic predicament of all the countries would deteriorate further. As far as the wider world was concerned, until relations in the near abroad were stabilized, it would be difficult for any of the successor states to play a full and active role in the international system.

BIBLIOGRAPHY

Allison, R. 'Military Forces in the Soviet Successor States', in *Adelphi Papers*, No. 280. London, Brasseys and International Institute for Strategic Studies, October 1993.

Dawish, K., and Parrott, B. B. *Russia and the New States of Eurasia: The Politics of Upheaval.* Cambridge, Cambridge University Press, 1994.

MacFarlane, S. N. 'Russia, the West and European Security', in *Survival*, Vol. 35, No. 3 (Autumn), pp. 3–25. 1993.

Shearman, P. (Ed.). *Russian Foreign Policy.* Boulder, Colorado, Westview Press, 1993.

Webber, M. 'The Emergence of the Foreign Policy of the Russian Federation', in *Communist and Post-Communist Studies*, Vol. 26, No. 3 (September), pp. 243–263. 1993.

Appendix: The Commonwealth of Independent States

The Commonwealth of Independent States (CIS) was founded in December 1991, precipitating the resignation of Mikhail Gorbachev, President of the Union of Soviet Socialist Republics, which thereby was effectively dissolved. The CIS was founded by 11 of the former Union Republics, although Azerbaijan did not subsequently ratify its membership and, effectively, ceased to be a member until September 1993, when it formally joined. In the following month Georgia also joined the CIS, bringing the total number of member-states to 12 (all the successor states and former Soviet Union Republics except for the three Baltic countries). Since its inception, few of the agreements of the CIS have been effected, although the Tashkent Agreement (the Treaty on Collective Security, signed on 15 May 1992) formed the basis of bilateral military arrangements between the Russian Federation and several other republics. In 1993, however, what combined military command the CIS had was ended. Its founding documents are recited below.

Executive Secretary: IVAN KOROTCHENYA; Minsk, Belarus.

THE MINSK AGREEMENT

The Minsk Agreement establishing a Commonwealth of Independent States was signed by the heads of state of Belarus, the Russian Federation and Ukraine on 8 December 1991. The text is as follows:

Preamble

We, the Republic of Belarus, the Russian Federation and the Republic of Ukraine, as founder states of the Union of Soviet Socialist Republics (USSR), which signed the 1922 Union Treaty, further described as the high contracting parties, conclude that the USSR has ceased to exist as a subject of international law and a geopolitical reality.

Taking as our basis the historic community of our peoples and the ties which have been established between them, taking into account the bilateral treaties concluded between the high contracting parties;

striving to build democratic law-governed states; intending to develop our relations on the basis of mutual recognition and respect for state sovereignty, the inalienable right to self-determination, the principles of equality and non-interference in internal affairs, repudiation of the use of force and of economic or any other methods of coercion, settlement of contentious problems by means of mediation and other generally-recognized principles and norms of international law;

considering that further development and strengthening of relations of friendship, good-neighbourliness and mutually beneficial co-operation between our states correspond to the vital national interests of their peoples and serve the cause of peace and security;

confirming our adherence to the goals and principles of the United Nations Charter, the Helsinki Final Act and other documents of the Conference on Security and Co-operation in Europe;

and committing ourselves to observe the generally recognized internal norms on human rights and the rights of peoples, we have agreed the following:

Article 1

The high contracting parties form the Commonwealth of Independent States.

Article 2

The high contracting parties guarantee their citizens equal rights and freedoms regardless of nationality or other distinctions. Each of the high contracting parties guarantees the citizens of the other parties, and also persons without citizenship that live on its territory, civil, political, social, economic and cultural rights and freedoms in accordance with generally recognized international norms of human rights, regardless of national allegiance or other distinctions.

Article 3

The high contracting parties, desiring to promote the expression, preservation and development of the ethnic, cultural, linguistic and religious individuality of the national minorities resident on their territories, and that of the unique ethno-cultural regions that have come into being, take them under their protection.

Article 4

The high contracting parties will develop the equal and mutually beneficial co-operation of their peoples and states in the spheres of politics, the economy, culture, education, public health, protection of the environment, science and trade and in the humanitarian and other spheres, will promote the broad exchange of information and will conscientiously and unconditionally observe reciprocal obligations.

The parties consider it a necessity to conclude agreements on co-operation in the above spheres.

Article 5

The high contracting parties recognize and respect one another's territorial integrity and the inviolability of existing borders within the Commonwealth.

They guarantee openness of borders, freedom of movement for citizens and of transmission of information within the Commonwealth.

Article 6

The member-states of the Commonwealth will co-operate in safeguarding international peace and security and in implementing effective measures for reducing weapons and military spending. They seek the elimination of all nuclear weapons and universal total disarmament under strict international control.

The parties will respect one another's aspiration to attain the status of a non-nuclear zone and a neutral state.

The member-states of the community will preserve and maintain under united command a common military-strategic space, including unified control over nuclear weapons, the procedure for implementing which is regulated by a special agreement.

They also jointly guarantee the necessary conditions for the stationing and functioning of and for material and social provision for the strategic armed forces. The parties contract to pursue a harmonized policy on questions of social protection and pension provision for members of the services and their families.

Article 7

The high contracting parties recognize that within the sphere of their activities, implemented on the equal basis through the common co-ordinating institutions of the Commonwealth, will be the following:

co-operation in the sphere of foreign policy;

co-operation in forming and developing the united economic area, the common European and Eurasian markets, in the area of customs policy;

co-operation in developing transport and communication systems;

co-operation in preservation of the environment, and participation in creating a comprehensive international system of ecological safety;

migration policy issues;

and fighting organized crime.

Article 8

The parties realize the planetary character of the Chernobyl catastrophe and pledge themselves to unite and co-ordinate their efforts in minimizing and overcoming its consequences.

To these ends they have decided to conclude a special agreement which will take consider the gravity of the consequences of this catastrophe.

Article 9

The disputes regarding interpretation and application of the norms of this agreement are to be solved by way of negotiations between the appropriate bodies, and, when necessary, at the level of heads of the governments and states.

Article 10

Each of the high contracting parties reserves the right to suspend the validity of the present agreement or individual articles thereof, after informing the parties to the agreement of this a year in advance.

The clauses of the present agreement may be addended to or amended with the common consent of the high contracting parties.

Article 11

From the moment that the present agreement is signed, the norms of third states, including the former USSR, are not permitted to be implemented on the territories of the signatory states.

Article 12

The high contracting parties guarantee the fulfilment of the international obligations binding upon them from the treaties and agreements of the former USSR.

Article 13

The present agreement does not affect the obligations of the high contracting parties in regard to third states.

The present agreement is open for all member-states of the former USSR to join, and also for other states which share the goals and principles of the present agreement.

Article 14

The city of Minsk is the official location of the co-ordinating bodies of the Commonwealth.

The activities of bodies of the former USSR are discontinued on the territories of the member-states of the Commonwealth.

THE ALMATY DECLARATION

The Almaty Declaration was signed by 11 heads of state on 21 December 1991.

Preamble

The independent states:

The Republic of Armenia, the Republic of Azerbaijan, the Republic of Belarus, the Republic of Kazakhstan, the Republic of Kyrgyzstan, the Republic of Moldova, the Russian Federation, the Republic of Tajikistan, the Republic of Turkmenistan, the Republic of Ukraine and the Republic of Uzbekistan;

seeking to build democratic law-governed states, the relations between which will develop on the basis of mutual recognition and respect for state sovereignty and sovereign equality, the inalienable right to self-determination, principles of equality and non-interference in the internal affairs, the rejection of the use of force, the threat of force and economic and any other methods of pressure, a peaceful settlement of disputes, respect for human rights and freedoms, including the rights of national minorities, a conscientious fulfilment of commitments and other generally recognized principles and standards of international law;

recognizing and respecting each other's territorial integrity and the inviolability of the existing borders;

believing that the strengthening of the relations of friendship, good neighbourliness and mutually advantageous co-operation, which has deep historic roots, meets the basic interests of nations and promotes the cause of peace and security;

being aware of their responsibility for the preservation of civilian peace and inter-ethnic accord;

being loyal to the objectives and principles of the agreement on the creation of the Commonwealth of Independent States;

are making the following statement:

The Declaration

Co-operation between members of the Commonwealth will be carried out in accordance with the principle of equality through co-ordinating institutions formed on a parity basis and operating in the way established by the agreements between members of the Commonwealth, which is neither a state, nor a super-state structure.

In order to ensure international strategic stability and security, allied command of the military-strategic forces and a single control over nuclear weapons will be preserved, the sides will respect each other's desire to attain the status of a non-nuclear and (or) neutral state.

The Commonwealth of Independent States is open, with the agreement of all its participants, to the states—members of the former USSR, as well as other states—sharing the goals and principles of the Commonwealth.

The allegiance to co-operation in the formation and development of the common economic space, and all-European and Eurasian markets, is being confirmed.

With the formation of the Commonwealth of Independent States the USSR ceases to exist. Member states of the Commonwealth guarantee, in accordance with their constitutional procedures, the fulfilment of international obligations, stemming from the treaties and agreements of the former USSR.

Member states of the Commonwealth pledge to observe strictly the principles of this declaration.

AGREEMENT ON COUNCILS OF HEADS OF STATE AND GOVERNMENTS

A provisional agreement on the membership and conduct of Councils of Heads of State and Government was concluded between the members of the Commonwealth of Independent States on 30 December 1991.

Preamble

The member states of this agreement, guided by the aims and principles of the agreement on the creation of a Commonwealth of Independent States of 8 December 1991 and the protocol to the agreement of 21 December 1991, taking into consideration the desire of the Commonwealth states to pursue joint activity through the Commonwealth's common co-ordinating institutions, and deeming it essential to establish, for the consistent implementation of the provisions of the said agreement, the appropriate inter-state and inter-governmental institutions capable of ensuring effective co-ordination, and of promoting the development of equal and mutually advantageous co-operation, have agreed on the following:

Article 1

The Council of Heads of State is the supreme body, on which all the member-states of the Commonwealth are represented at the level of head of state, for discussion of fundamental issues connected with co-ordinating the activity of the Commonwealth states in the sphere of their common interests.

The Council of Heads of State is empowered to discuss issues provided for by the Minsk Agreement on the creation of a Commonwealth of Independent States and other documents for the development of the said Agreement, including the problems of legal succession, which have arisen as a result of ending the existence of the USSR and the abolition of Union structures.

The activities of the Council of Heads of State and of the Council of Heads of Government are pursued on the basis of mutual recognition of and respect for the state sovereignty and sovereign equality of the member-states of the Agreement, their inalienable right to self-determination, the principles of equality and non-interference in internal affairs, the renunciation of the use of force and the threat of force, territorial integrity and the inviolability of existing borders, the peaceful settlement of disputes, respect for human rights and liberties, including the rights of national minorities, conscientious fulfilment of obligations and other commonly accepted principles and norms of international law.

Article 2

The activities of the Council of Heads of State and the Council of Heads of Government are regulated by the Minsk Agreement on setting up the Commonwealth of Independent States, the present agreement and agreements adopted in development of them, and also by the rules of procedure of these institutes.

Each state in the council has one vote. The decisions of the council are taken by common consent.

The official languages of the Councils are the state languages of the Commonwealth states.

The working language is the Russian language.

Article 3

The Council of Heads of State and the Council of Heads of Government discuss and where necessary take decisions on the more important domestic and external issues.

Any state may declare its having no interest in a particular issue or issues.

Article 4

The Council of Heads of State convenes for meetings no less than twice a year. The decision on the time for holding and the provisional agenda of each successive meeting of the Council is taken at the routine meeting of the Council, unless the Council agrees otherwise. Extraordinary meetings of the Council of Heads of State are convened on the initiative of the majority of Commonwealth heads of state.

The heads of state chair the meetings of the Council in turn, according to the Russian alphabetical order of the names of the Commonwealth states.

Sittings of the Council of the Heads of State are generally to be held in Minsk. A sitting of the Council may be held in another of the Commonwealth states by agreement among those taking part.

Article 5

The Council of Heads of Government convenes for meetings no less frequently than once every three months. The decision concerning the scheduling of and preliminary agenda for each subsequent sitting is to be made at a routine session of the Council, unless the Council arranges otherwise.

Extraordinary sittings of the Council of Heads of Government may be convened at the initiative of a majority of heads of government of the Commonwealth states.

The heads of government chair meetings of the Council in turn, according to the Russian alphabetical order of the names of the Commonwealth states.

Sittings of the Council of Heads of Government are generally to be held in Minsk. A sitting of the Council may be held in another of the Commonwealth states by agreement among the heads of government.

Article 6

The Council of Heads of State and the Council of Heads of Government of the Commonwealth states may hold joint sittings.

Article 7

Working and auxiliary bodies may be set up on both a permanent and interim basis on the decision of the Council of the Heads of State and the Council of the Heads of Government of the Commonwealth states.

These are composed of authorized representatives of the participating states. Experts and consultants may be invited to take part in their sittings.

AGREEMENT ON STRATEGIC FORCES

The Agreement on Strategic Forces was concluded between the 11 members of the Commonwealth of Independent States on 30 December 1991.

Preamble

Guided by the necessity for a co-ordinated and organized solution to issues in the sphere of the control of the strategic forces and the single control over nuclear weapons, the Republic of Armenia, the Republic of Azerbaijan, the Republic of Belarus, the Republic of Kazakhstan, the Republic of Kyrgyzstan, the Republic of Moldova, the Russian Federation, the Republic of Tajikistan, the Republic of Turkmenistan, the Republic of Ukraine and the Republic of Uzbekistan, subsequently referred to as 'the member-states of the Commonwealth', have agreed on the following:

Article 1

The term 'strategic forces' means: groupings, formations, units, institutions, the military training institutes for the strategic missile troops, for the air force, for the navy and for the air defences; the directorates of the Space Command and of the airborne troops, and of strategic and operational intelligence, and the nuclear technical units and also the forces, equipment and other military facilities designed for the control and maintenance of the strategic forces of the former USSR (the schedule is to be determined for each state participating in the Commonwealth in a separate protocol).

Article 2

The member-states of the Commonwealth undertake to observe the international treaties of the former USSR, to pursue a co-ordinated policy in the area of international security, disarmament and arms control, and to participate in the preparation and implementation of programmes for reductions in arms and armed forces. The member-states of the Commonwealth are immediately entering into negotiations with one another and also with other states which were formerly part of the USSR, but which have not joined the commonwealth, with the aim of ensuring guarantees and developing mechanisms for implementing the aforementioned treaties.

Article 3

The member-states of the Commonwealth recognize the need for joint command of strategic forces and for maintaining unified control of nuclear weapons, and other types of weapons of mass destruction, of the armed forces of the former USSR.

Article 4

Until the complete elimination of nuclear weapons, the decision on the need for their use is taken by the president of the Russian Federation in agreement with the heads of the Republic of Belarus, the Republic of Kazakhstan and the Republic of Ukraine, and in consultation with the heads of the other member-states of the Commonwealth.

Until their destruction in full, nuclear weapons located on the territory of the Republic of Ukraine shall be under the control of the Combined Strategic Forces Command, with the aim that they not be used and be dismantled by the end of 1994, including tactical nuclear weapons by 1 July 1992.

The process of destruction of nuclear weapons located on the territory of the Republic of Belarus and the Republic of Ukraine shall take place with the participation of the Republic of Belarus, the Russian Federation and the Republic of Ukraine under the joint control of the Commonwealth states.

Article 5

The status of strategic forces and the procedure for service in them shall be defined in a special agreement.

Article 6

This agreement shall enter into force from the moment of its signing and shall be terminated by decision of the signatory states or the Council of Heads of State of the Commonwealth.

This agreement shall cease to apply to a signatory state from whose territory strategic forces or nuclear weapons are withdrawn.

AGREEMENT ON ARMED FORCES AND BORDER TROOPS

The Agreement on Armed Forces and Border Troops was concluded between the members of the Commonwealth of Independent States on 30 December 1991.

Preamble

Proceeding from the need for a mutually-acceptable settlement of matters of defence and security, including guarding the borders of the Commonwealth member-states, the member-states of the Commonwealth of Independent States have agreed the following:

The Agreement

The commonwealth member-states confirm their legitimate right to set up their own armed forces;

jointly with the Commander-in-Chief of the armed forces, to examine and settle, within two months of the date of this agreement, the issue of the procedure for controlling general purpose forces, taking account of the national legislations of the Commonwealth states and also the issue of the consistent implementation by the Commonwealth states of their right to set up their own armed forces. For the Republic of Ukraine, this will be from 3 January 1992;

to appoint I. Ya. Kalinichenko Commander-in-Chief of Border Troops;

to instruct the Commander-in-Chief of Border Troops to work out, within two months and in conjunction with the leaders of the Commonwealth member-states, a mechanism for the activity of the Border Troops, taking account of the national legislations of the Commonwealth states, with the exception of states with which a mechanism for the activity of Border Troops has already been agreed.

Note: In addition, Marshal Yevgeny Shaposhnikov was confirmed as acting Commander-in-Chief of the Armed Forces of the Commonwealth of Independent States. Shaposhnikov resigned this position in 1993, when the above arrangement was ended.

THE COUNCIL OF HEADS OF STATE

(March 1994)

Members

Armenia: Levon H. Ter-Petrosyan.

Azerbaijan: Heydar Aliyev.

Belarus: Myachyslau Hryb.

Georgia: Eduard Shevardnadze.

Kazakhstan: Nursultan A. Nazarbayev.

Kyrgyzstan: Askar Akayev.

Moldova: Mircea Ion Snegur.

Russia: Boris N. Yeltsin.

Tajikistan: Imamali S. Rahmovov.

Turkmenistan: Saparmurat A. Niyazov.

Ukraine: Leonid M. Kravchuk.

Uzbekistan: Islam A. Karimov.

THE COUNCIL OF HEADS OF GOVERNMENT

(March 1994)

Members

Armenia: Hrand Arutyunyan.

Azerbaijan: Surat Husseynov.

Belarus: Vyacheslau F. Kebich.

Georgia: Otar Patsatsia.

Kazakhstan: Sergey Tereshchenko.

Kyrgyzstan: Apas Jumagulov.

Moldova: Andrei Sangheli.

Russia: Viktor Chernomyrdin.

Tajikistan: Abdujalil Samadov.

Turkmenistan: Saparmurat A. Niyazov.

Ukraine: Yefim Zvyahilsky (acting).

Uzbekistan: Abdulkhashim Mutalov.

THE CAUCASUS REGION: AN OVERVIEW

JOHN WRIGHT

A theory gaining currency in the successor states of the USSR is that without nationalism, democracy is impossible. Such a theory is a revitalization of 19th century attitudes towards the then emerging nation states. That is to say, the binding force that nationalism brings provides the basis for a common law and hence the foundation for democratic organization. Such an analysis, when applied to the former USSR, attempts to explain the dynamics of state creation, in the aftermath of 70 years of ideological and totalitarian control. To this extent, according to the supporters of this hypothesis, there should not be undue concern at this outbreak of nationalism. For, in the same way that nationalism was necessary to produce independence, so, in time, it would aid the progress towards democratization.

In the early 1990s the Caucasus region consisted of the three independent states of Armenia, Azerbaijan and Georgia, along with the smaller ethnic groups residing in the North Caucasus, in the Russian Federation. All were trying, with, at mid-1993, as yet small success, to define and bring to existence democratic states with liberal economies within a climate of extreme ethno-nationalism.

Along with the three former Soviet Baltic states, the peoples of the Caucasus were in the vanguard of the national movements which contributed significantly to the collapse of the world's last multinational empire. For the five years from 1987 the renewed national expression in Armenia, Azerbaijan and Georgia was necessary to be able to bring the respective states towards a position of independence. However, this nationalist assertion brought forward less attractive characteristics incorporating ideas of exclusiveness. This plagued the process of state building after independence. It is this dualistic aspect of nationalism which perhaps explains the fact that the Caucasus witnessed more conflict than any other Soviet successor region.

The Caucasus, that area of land bottle-necked between the Black and Caspian Seas to the west and east, is the home to a mosaic of some 40 ethnic groups, ranging in size from the most numerous Azeris (8m.) to the least, the Ginukhs (400). In total, around 21m. people live in the region, which comprises 144,171 square miles (373,403 sq km). Politically, the region divides between the three Transcaucasian states of Armenia, Azerbaijan and Georgia, and the North Caucasus, currently administered through the Russian Federation. Chechnya (Checheniya—then part of the Chechen-Ingush Autonomous Soviet Socialist Republic—ASSR) declared itself independent in 1991, but this was not recognized through membership in the UN.

Coinciding with this period of nationalist resurgence, as in other parts of the former USSR, there was a marked upsurge in religious expression. Both Armenia and Georgia have national churches, both of which, through the centuries, helped to preserve respective traditions and cultures. The significance of the power of religion in these two states can be gauged from the example of Georgian leader Eduard Shevardnadze's baptism into the Georgian Orthodox Church. In the eastern Caucasus Islam reasserted itself as a dominant force in society, particularly the Sufi orders in Chechnya and Daghestan. Indeed, there is strong evidence to suggest that the Sufis helped to keep the Chechen leader, Jokhar Dudayev, in power.

The region, hitherto, was notable for its linguistic diversity, comprising some four distinct indigenous language families: Southern Caucasian or Kartvelian languages (of which there were four); North-Western Caucasian (four); Northern Caucasian (three); and North-Eastern Caucasian (32). Additionally, mainly to the south and the centre, are found Indo-European- and Turkic-speaking populations, the Armenians, Ossetians and Azerbaijanis, along with the smaller Turkic groups of the Karachay and the Balkars. Dispersed throughout the region are Slavic peoples, predominantly Russians, a legacy of, in total, 400 years of influence, although, more pronouncedly, from the beginning of the 18th century.

During medieval times the region was a sphere of competition between the Ottoman Turk and the Persian Empires. During the 19th and 20th centuries Russia dominated, despite a brief period of independence immediately following the First World War, during the revolutionary transformation from tsarist rule to Soviet Communism. The rapidity of Soviet collapse forced, by the end of 1991, the retreat of Russia's effective southern border. For the first time in 200 years, Russia found itself with no direct southern border with Iran and Turkey (and hence with the Middle East). Instead, the southernmost territories of Russia stretch to Georgia and Azerbaijan and, even here, there was no guarantee of stable frontiers, given the increasing desire among the peoples of the North Caucasus to gain independence.

At the same time, what were closed frontiers between the USSR and Turkey and Iran were opened completely, permitting the relatively straightforward movement of goods and people. The previous 70 years' experience of nation building in Turkey and Iran (the successor states of the Ottoman and Persian Empires, respectively) resulted in commercial and other ties being forged with different neighbours. A cursory analysis of industrial location in these states reveals industrial enterprise in Turkey on its south-western Mediterranean coastline and in Iran to the south, circumventing the Persian (Arabian) Gulf. This position tends to mitigate against any realistic desire for large-scale involvement in Transcaucasian development, despite 'popular' and, at times, governmental advances.

Apart from some covert Russian destabilization techniques in Georgia and Azerbaijan, the prospects for stability in the region and democratization rest largely with the local governments and populations. At mid-1993 the new period of independence had been characterized by the conflict of different nationalities and ethnic groups.

ETHNIC CONFLICT

After the advent of *perestroika* (restructuring) and *glasnost* (openness) four conflicts emerged in the Caucasus. These were, successively, the wars in: Nagorny Karabakh; South Ossetia; Abkhazia; and Ingushetia and Ossetia. While these conflicts escalated into significant fighting, other disputes were developing with equally violent potential.

Given the extreme nationalist overtones on each side of these various disputes, the justification of the claims to the particular piece of land tended to be then bolstered by local historians and their sympathizers further afield. Parallel arguments would be displayed, 'proving' continuous settlement or control over the region over a number of centuries, in many cases quite forgetting that the whole Caucasus was prey to successive invasion from external powers for longer periods than local control was exerted.

For 70 years the Communist theory of history was taught but, in the main, unbelieved. For people attempting to come to terms with their recent past, the absence of anything but the nationalist approach to history and the interpretation of events, backed by media and academic circles, drove the protagonists further and further apart. To this extent, without exception, however large or small the group, each would claim with great vehemence that they were totally right and justified in what they were doing, while the other side was completely wrong.

At the same time, however, in all the disputes, no side could match their apparent certainty in justification with an equal strength in military or institutional terms. Hence, as shall be examined, all the Caucasian conflicts showed few signs of easy resolution.

Nagorny Karabakh

The longest running conflict in the region was between Armenia and Azerbaijan, entering its fifth year in 1993. At the height of the *glasnost* period the Armenians demanded that the then Soviet authorities redesignate the Nagorno-Karabakh Autonomous Oblast (Nagorny Karabakh or Daglygh Karabagh) under Armenian control. Throughout the Communist era, the fact that Nagorny Karabakh had been administered by Azerbaijan, following a decision by Stalin (Iosif Vissarionovich Dzhugashvili or Jugashvili) in 1923 to grant the territory to Azerbaijan, was a contentious matter with the Armenian people. In 1988, following the earthquake in Armenia, Soviet leader Mikhail Gorbachev found, on his sudden visit to the devastated region, that all appeals were for the Karabakh to become a part of Armenia.

In essence, the small enclave of mountainous territory, Nagorny Karabakh, served to galvanize nationalist movements in both Armenia and Azerbaijan. For Armenians the drive towards independence coalesced around the question of the oblast, while in Azerbaijan the response to the Armenians' active move to control Nagorny Karabakh helped to unite and rekindle national aspirations in the apparently least nationalist of the three Transcaucasian republics.

The conflict, simply stated, revolved around who should administer the territory. To Azerbaijan the argument was clear. At the time of the disintegration of the USSR Nagorny Karabakh was part of their state and thus, in their terms, under international law, it should remain so. On the Armenian side, because the land was predominantly inhabited by Armenians and the majority of the local population wished to belong to an Armenian state, this should be granted, either by joining to the existing Armenian state or by creating an independent Karabakh. Therefore, there was what, in the post-Cold War age, was emerging as one of the predominant issues: how to resolve the territorial inviolability of states with local demands for self-determination.

During 1992–93 various attempts were made to resolve the conflict, involving the USA, Russia, Turkey, Iran, the UN and the Conference for Security and Co-operation in Europe (CSCE). As at mid-1993 nothing had effectively resulted from any of these overtures (although there had been meetings between the leaderships of Azerbaijan and the 'Republic of Nagorny Karabakh' in September 1993). Instead, characteristic of previous periods of this conflict, the Armenians had achieved notable success militarily, while Azerbaijan continued to experience state instability as a direct result of its failures on the ground. Being better organized, the Armenians achieved further advances and consolidated their position, to the extent that they controlled Nagorny Karabakh as well as the 'Lachin corridor', a strip of land linking the enclave with Armenia proper. From mid-1993, furthermore, they advanced into the territory of 'metropolitan' Azerbaijan, which earned them condemnation by the UN.

The consequences of the war upon Armenia were most marked economically. Being land-locked, good relations with neighbouring countries was crucial to the state's very survival. However, Azerbaijan enforced an effective blockade against the country. Turkey, to the west, was more or less overtly helping Azerbaijan and, combined with the traditional mutual animosity between Turkey and Armenia, little help was available from there. To the north, instability in Georgia meant that necessary gas supply routes could not be guaranteed. Armenia was becoming reliant upon Iran and Russia for its economic survival. However, in the latter part of 1993 its incursions into Azerbaijan proper were protested by Iran and, from June, its relationship with Russia was threatened by the accession of a more pro-Russian regime in Azerbaijan, which then re-entered the Commonwealth of Independent States (CIS).

For Azerbaijan, while the war obviously reduced resources available for economic development, the most striking consequence was in the political arena. Failure in the Karabakh culminated in the elected President, Abulfaz Elchibey, being ousted from office by a disgruntled former commander in Nagorny Karabakh, Surat Husseynov, during June 1993. The confusion surrounding Husseynov's march from his stronghold in Gyanja to the state capital of Baku allowed Heydar Aliyev, a former First Secretary of the republican Communist Party and member of the Soviet Politburo under Leonid Brezhnev, to return to the leadership of Azerbaijan.

These political events coincided with what should have been the final agreement with a consortium of five petroleum companies in London (United Kingdom) for exploitation of off-shore Azerbaijani crude petroleum. The ousting of the pro-Turkish Elchibey and the collapse of the petroleum agreement prompted speculation that forces in Russia had been involved in promoting the destabilization of Azerbaijan, not wishing the west Caspian petroleum reserves to fall outside Russian influence.

Ossetia

One of Eduard Shevardnadze's first achievements upon returning to take control in Georgia was the negotiation of a cease-fire and the introduction of a tripartite troop structure of Russians, Ossetians and Georgians in South Ossetia, formally an Autonomous Oblast within Georgia. This structure was still maintaining the peace in the latter part of 1993, although there was little movement towards establishing durable institutional arrangements to prevent further fighting. Refugees displaced during the conflict remained reluctant to return.

The then President of Georgia, Zviad Gamsakhurdia, decided to abolish South Ossetian autonomy in 1990. He thereby provoked fierce fighting and the loss of some 600 lives. In Georgia, the well-documented events of the night of 8–9 April 1989 (the killing, in Tbilisi, of demonstrators by the security forces) marked the crystallization of the Georgian nationalist movement towards independence, a process which produced a greater intolerance of ethnic dissension within the republic. In South Ossetia the abolition of autonomy provoked the fledgling nationalist movement, which made more urgent demands for unification with North Ossetia, within the Russian Federation.

Throughout 1993 Georgia and Russia negotiated the terms of a definitive treaty, but there were increasing difficulties because of the ethnic minority questions concerning both Ossetia and Abkhazia. While the tendency in the Georgian capital of Tbilisi was towards building a unitary state and codifying clear borders between it and Russia, this would bisect the area of Ossetian settlement. The North Ossetian parliament, in an appeal to the Russian President, Boris Yeltsin, stated the problem clearly: 'Any talks on delimiting the section of the border which divides Ossetia into two parts must take this as their starting point, together with the need to establish a special border regime which will take account of the unitary Ossetian people'.

The CSCE was active in helping conflict resolution, establishing commissions for economic development, law and order and the return of refugees. These three issues must be addressed. However, owing to the continued climate of nationalism, for stability and democracy to begin, methods for solving outstanding political questions had yet to be dealt with effectively.

Abkhazia

Far more intractable was the conflict in Abkhazia, an Autonomous Republic in the north-west of Georgia. Fighting began in August 1992, when Georgian troops were sent into the area officially to protect rail routes from Russia and to hunt for hostages taken by followers of ex-President Gamsakhurdia. Soon, however, under the command of the then defence minister, Tengiz Kitovani, troops entered the regional capital of Sukhumi and the local parliament building was stormed. Some two months earlier the Abkhazian parliament, organized on confessional lines, had voted by a simple majority for a 1925 Constitution, which effectively announced Abkhazia to be independent. This decision was revoked in Tbilisi. Abkhazian leaders were, at the time, eager to stress that what they demanded was a federal relationship with Georgia, as two sovereign states, rather than the apparent unitary model advocated by many politicians in Tbilisi.

From that time conflict continued. In September 1992 Yeltsin secured an agreement, signed in Moscow, which seemed to offer a possible mechanism for establishing a cease-fire, but both sides soon abrogated it. Similar to the other conflicts in the Caucasus the issues involved both the territorial inviolability of a state, in this case Georgia, and also the rights of minorities to self-determination. The issue became further complicated by two factors. Firstly, the Abkhazians numbered no more than 17% of the population of the Autonomous Republic. Secondly, the Abkhaz were joined by volunteers from the North Caucasus, whose leaders perceived both a common bond with the Abkhazians, as well as the possibility of gaining their own independence, through destabilizing relations between Georgia and Russia. In Tbilisi, this prompted the belief that Russia was aiding the Abkhaz. Similar claims were made by the opposing side, that Russia was helping Georgia. Following the expulsion of Georgian forces from Abkhazia, in September 1993, there were further allegations of Russian support for the separatists.

It was clear that certain parts of the Russian military and right-wing establishments were content to see Georgia unstable, as this helped to continue Russian influence in the Transcaucasus (Georgian membership of the CIS, agreed to in October 1993, it was hoped would satisfy such factions). There were still large numbers of Russian forces in Georgia. Resolution of the Abkhazia conflict would ensure the signing of a Russo-Georgian treaty, containing within it the timetable for the withdrawal of all Russian troops from the country.

The prospects remained bleak for the compromises necessary to witness an end to the fighting and the beginning of peace building. In July 1993 Shevardnadze made a dramatic appeal for assistance from the West, which resulted in the promise of sending some 50 UN observers. With the prospect of outright victory for one side or the other seeming small, Russia then succeeded in negotiating a cease-fire and the beginnings of a resolution. In September 1993, however, alleging Georgian breaches of the agreement, Abkhazian forces (supported by Russians) advanced on Sukhumi and seized it, despite the personal leadership of the Georgian defence by Shevardnadze. A major problem on the Abkhaz side had been that, in spite of being able to acquire significant quantities of weapons, their very numbers precluded their ability to retain territory (although many ethnic Georgians fled the territory in September and October). However, the Georgians were racked by military ill-discipline and a lack of coherence. This was compounded by the loss of morale after the defeat in Sukhumi and the resurgence of fighting with Gamsakhurdia supporters in western Georgia. The dismissal of Kitovani might have engendered further discipline, but Georgia had yet to create a real national army. The country remained prey to the manoeuvring of local militias, the policies and loyalties of which did not continuously coincide with that of the Government.

Politically, the demands of the Georgian side were clearer than those of the Abkhazians. To Georgia there appeared to be some scope for negotiation on everything apart from the border. The offer of autonomy for Abkhazia within Georgia was made and restated, although over 1992 and 1993 there was some debate on how Georgia was to be governed, either as a unitary state or permitting stronger local and regional government. Georgian leader Shevardnadze established a constitutional commission to report on these issues.

For the Abkhaz the settlement they wanted remained unclear. Their leader, Vladislav Ardzinba, made a precondition for negotiations the withdrawal of Georgian troops from the area. It was Georgian violations of the agreement on troops which gave the Abkhazians the justification for their advance on Sukhumi. Even before this insurrection, however, in terms of a political arrangement it was far from certain whether the Abkhaz would accept autonomy within Georgia, federation with Georgia, unification with the Russian Federation or total independence. This situation remained uncertain in the immediate aftermath of the Georgian expulsion from the area.

Without the active involvement of the West, however, the prospect for peace remained bleak, not only in the Abkhazian conflict but elsewhere. In the heightened nationalist atmosphere, resolution of such conflicts was difficult, even after a seemingly convincing military victory—thus, although the Abkhazians secured control of their territory at the end of September 1993, their limited numbers ensured the essential insecurity of their situation.

Ossetia-Ingushetia

The first outbreak of fighting in post-Communist Russia occurred in the North Caucasus region and was between the North Ossetians and the Ingush. During the regime of Stalin many of the Ingush, along with the Chechens and other groups, were deported *en masse* to Central Asia. The Chechen-Ingush ASSR was not reconstituted until 1957. As a consequence, there remained a legacy of dispute over which piece of land should belong to which ethnic group. The particular case at issue involved the rayon of Prigorodny. Before 1944 this belonged to the Ingush, but was then granted and settled by the Ossetians, although, by the beginning of the 1990s, the Ingush again formed a majority. The problem, once more, concerned control of territory. The Ingush demanded the territory as theirs, to be united with the rest of 'Ingushetia' (created by the proclamation of a Chechen Republic in most of the former ASSR), while the North Ossetians believed it should remain part of their republic, now sovereign within the Russian Federation. Fighting broke out in October 1992. The central authorities in Moscow acted quickly to quell the conflict, fearing that it could provoke a wider outbreak of hostilities in the North Caucasus, one which could even be the start of a process leading to the collapse of the Russian Federation, in the same manner as the USSR.

The effects of what seemingly was a small border conflict had wider repercussions. Galina Staravoytova was dismissed as adviser on nationalities for the Russian leadership and the head of the provisional administration, Georgy Khizha, was replaced by Sergey Shakhray, who also became chairman of the committee on nationalities for the whole Russian Federation. A commission was established to look for ways of solving the conflict, which subsided, although both sides continued to make allegations of terrorism. On 1 August 1993, however, the head of the state-of-emergency area on the borders of the two republics was murdered and the importance attached to stability in the area was indicated by the immediate attention of the highest officials in the Russian Government.

POLITICAL DEVELOPMENTS

Both Georgia and Azerbaijan demonstrated, during 1992 and 1993, the weakness of existing political institutions for creating permanent democratic states. Throughout the Caucasus there were more-or-less free and fair elections in which politicians were elected. However, combined with the problems of ethnic and minority rights, which the reawakening of nationalism brought forth, there was also a decline in respect for the rule of law. The situation was conducive to the formation of private militias and the dominance of the politics of the street.

Georgia

In December 1991 the elected President, Zviad Gamsakhurdia was ousted in a civil-military coup. He took refuge in Armenia, initially, before going on to Chechnya (where he remained until October 1993, when he returned to Georgia). Until March 1992 the country was run by a triumvirate of Tengiz Kitovani, Jaba Ioselliani and Tengiz Sigua, before the rearrival into Georgian politics of the former Soviet minister, Eduard Shevardnadze. Well known in the West as the man who facilitated the ending of the Cold War and the reunification of Germany, his stature helped belatedly to gain the new state's recognition by the world community. This was despite Georgia being the second Soviet republic (after Lithuania) to declare independence, in April 1991.

The ruling Military Council was rearranged by Shevardnadze into the State Council, drawing upon a fairly wide constituency of interests, pending elections which took place in October 1992. Following the experience under Gamsakhurdia, it was decided not to employ the position of President. This being the case, Shevardnadze, not being willing to ally himself with any one political party, was elected, unopposed, to the post of Chairman of the Supreme Soviet (that is, head of state) and was then vested with supreme executive authority. With war continuing in Abkhazia, and sporadic guerrilla warfare from the supporters of the ousted President, the Government's concerns were with the mere survival of the Georgian state. By October 1993 this was under considerable threat, and certainly Shevardnadze's position was, following the defeat in Abkhazia and the resurgence of support for Gamsakhurdia, whose supporters had secured control of much of western Georgia (Mingrelia). It was this situation which forced the Government to take Georgia into the CIS, although it was also helped by Gamsakhurdia's death, at the end of the year.

Azerbaijan

Azerbaijani politics reflected its lack of success in pursuing the war in Nagorny Karabakh. Such failures significantly contributed towards two presidents being ousted during the first two years after the dissolution of the USSR. Firstly, the hard-line Ayaz Niyazi ogly Mutalibov (a supporter of the abortive Moscow coup of August 1991) was forced to resign as President in March 1992. Three months of turmoil resulted, coinciding with significant Armenian advances in the Karabakh. In the end, Mutalibov attempted to regain power by means of an effective constitutional coup, before being finally defeated when the Popular Front of Azerbaijan (PFA) stormed the parliament building. Presidential elections were held in June 1992. There were three candidates, the winning one being PFA leader Abulfaz Elchibey, who gained 55.1% of the votes cast.

The inability of the Azerbaijan Government to organize the war effort continued to cause instability for the regime. Discretely, the pro-Turkish Elchibey was attempting to uncouple Azerbaijan from Russia. However, with reverses in the struggle over Nagorny Karabakh, continuing economic problems and allegations of widespread corruption in the administration, by June 1993 such was the weakness of both the Government and its institutions that it was possible for a disgruntled former colonel in the Azerbaijan armed forces to march unopposed from his base, in the country's second city of Gyanja, to Baku and claim a share of power in the state.

The speed of events allowed the veteran of Soviet Azerbaijani political life, Heydar Aliyev to assume the presidency. Under Brezhnev he had favoured the Union and done much to link Azerbaijan with Russia and the rest of the USSR, but, since withdrawing from all-Union and republican affairs, Aliyev had been in charge of the strategic autonomy of Nakhichevan, an enclave separated from the rest of Azerbaijan by Armenian territory. Remaining popular (as indicated by support for his New Azerbaijan party, founded in late 1992), his resumption of authority, in June 1993 (confirmed by presidential elections in October), marked the latest in a series of returns to power by former Communists throughout the territory of the former USSR.

Armenia

The only leader to retain control in Transcaucasia from independence into the mid-1990s was President Levon Ter-Petrosyan of Armenia. However, even there, from 1992, there were problems such as the replacement of the Government and continuing difficulties persisting between the roles of the radical Dashnaktsutyun party and the Armenian diaspora and the more moderate Yerevan regime. These tensions were manifested when foreign minister Raffi Hovannisyan was dismissed in September 1992. The son of one of the most prominent Armenian scholars in the West and himself a Californian lawyer, Hovannisyan had been invited into the Government to bridge the relationship between the diaspora and the new country. However, it was over Armenia's relationship with Turkey that differences began to emerge, with the diaspora concerned to revive the memories of the genocide and emphasize Turkish human-rights abuses, while the local Armenians, and Ter-Petrosyan in particular, were more concerned to follow a policy which took account of the Republic's realities.

The North Caucasus

Most notable in the attempt to rid themselves of Russian domination were the Chechens, the largest of the North Caucasian nationalities. Displaced in 1944–57, by Stalin's deportations, and with memories handed down of their defiance against Russian imperial designs on the Caucasus in the 19th century, it was perhaps not so surprising that the Chechens should be in the forefront of those trying to gain independence from the Russian Federation. From 1992 the Chechen leader Dudayev had to deal with his country being placed under an economic blockade by Russia (still in force in late 1993) and had to struggle against an attempt to oust him. Whether Chechnya would achieve its declared independence remained predicated upon Russia. It was unlikely that Russia would willingly surrender its position in the Caucasus and it feared that any recognition of Chechnya could cause the Russian Federation to disintegrate in the same way as the USSR.

An apparent force for North Caucasian unity existed in the Confederation of Mountain Peoples. As of late 1993 it remained unelected, but it was reasonable to suppose that it represented the majority of people in the region. Headed by a Kabardian, Musa Shanibov, the aim was to achieve the independence attained by its precursor at the start of the 20th century. Much of the effort of the Confederation was directed towards helping the Abkhazians in Georgia. This caused both Georgia and Russia to describe it as a terrorist grouping. However, although unable to prevent bloodshed between two of its members, the Ingush and the Ossetians, the Confederation remained the most potent force, Chechnya apart, for destabilizing the *status quo* and gaining further local control for the peoples of the North Caucasus. Whether it could survive the simmering disputes between its members remained an open question.

ECONOMICS

The general move towards creating a market-led economic system was considered desirable, but the actualities of experience proved highly problematic. Of the three Transcaucasian states, Armenia introduced more legislation in the fields of privatization and land reform. However, with an economic blockade from Azerbaijan and general difficulties with supply routes, Armenia's economy remained highly vulnerable towards the end of 1993. In Georgia continued ethnic and political struggles precluded any major economic activity and restructuring. By 1993 Georgia had already been warned by the World Bank for not proceeding fast enough with its economic reform programme. Agricultural production, intended to provide the basis of Georgian economic activity, was blighted, in the main, by the destruction of crops by anti-government forces. Equally, the prevalence of banditry made delivery to internal and external markets precarious. An indicator of the crisis in the Georgian economy was evident from the experience of introducing coupons as a sort of currency, to counter the import of rouble inflation from Russia. Some two months after its introduction, at parity with the rouble, the coupon-currency had fallen by one-fourth in value. For Azerbaijan and, to a lesser extent, Chechnya in the North Caucasus, petroleum should provide the basis for economic development. A five-company international consortium attempted to negotiate for rights to off-shore exploitation of the Azerbaijani hydrocarbon reserves. Yet again though, internal instability precluded effective economic progress.

Throughout the Caucasus, in the early 1990s, there continued the danger of hyperinflation. Incentives to work and invest did not exist. In general, the way to make a living was through short-term speculative ventures, such as by borrowing large sums of money off local banks, quickly changing the money into something convertible, trading across in neighbouring states and returning the money to the bank, having made a small profit on the buying-and-selling venture. Naturally, governments would gain very little in the way of income from taxation and, thus, public utilities and services continued to decline. Apart from petroleum development in Baku, where there was major Western interest, the continuing spiral of ethnic conflict made the region unattractive for external investment. The insecurity of the conventional economic system encouraged a parallel economy or 'black market', while the ethnic and political conflicts allow banditry—reinforcing the prejudice associating the Caucasian nationalities (especially Chechens) with the activity of organized crime in the Russian Federation.

PROSPECTS

It is difficult to feel optimistic about the future direction of the Caucasus, based upon the experiences of the peoples of the region between *de facto* independence at the end of 1991 and the end of 1993. At the outset of this article it was mentioned that nationalism was necessary for democracy. However, in the Caucasus during the period mentioned, the nationalism manifested there, which had a highly exclusive character, created the conditions within which it was almost impossible to foresee a process of genuine democratization taking place.

The very geographical position of the Caucasus, bridging the continents of Europe and Asia, affords the opportunity to act as both a north–south and a west–east transportation route, with the advantages this would bring. In the early 1990s discussions had, indeed, begun to this effect, with plans to build, for example, a major road link from the Black Sea to the Caspian, to permit the speedy transportation of goods to and from Europe to the emerging markets in the east. Equally a petroleum pipeline was planned, linking Azerbaijan to the Turkish Mediterranean coast (although the route might be changed to a link with the Black Sea, following the change in regime in mid-1993). The region taken as a whole was rich in minerals which world markets would wish to purchase, had a good agricultural base (capable of supplying its own needs and a surplus for export), a comparatively well-educated and well-trained work-force and an emerging entrepreneurial class.

However, all these resources would remain useless until the necessary features of compromise and federation started to enter the political discussion. If appropriate political structures, based on federal principles permitting local decision-making, could become generally favoured, there was no reason why the Caucasus could not regain some of the prosperity it enjoyed during parts of the Soviet era.

BIBLIOGRAPHY

Altstadt, A. L. *The Azerbaijani Turks: Power and Identity under Russian Rule.* Stanford, California, Hoover Institution Press, 1992.

Aves, J. *Post-Soviet Transcaucasia.* London, Royal Institute of International Affairs, 1993.

Bennigsen Broxup, M. (Ed.). *The North Caucasus Barrier.* London, Hurst and Co, 1992.

Bremmer, I., and Taras, R. *Nations and Politics in Soviet Successor States.* Cambridge, Cambridge University Press, 1993.

Diuk, N., and Karatnycky, A. *New Nations Rising: the Fall of the Soviets and the Challenge of Independence.*

New York, and Chichester, West Sussex, John Wiley and Sons, 1993.

Lang, D. M. *A Modern History of Georgia.* London, Weidenfeld and Nicolson, 1962.

Suny, R. G. *The Making of the Georgian Nation.* London, I. P. Tauris, 1989.

Looking Towards Ararat: Armenia in Modern History. Bloomington and Indianapolis, Indiana University Press, 1993.

Walker, C. J. *Armenia: the Survival of a Nation.* London, Routledge, 1990.

The Caucasus

Central Asia

CENTRAL ASIA: AN OVERVIEW OF KYRGYZSTAN, TAJIKISTAN, TURKMENISTAN AND UZBEKISTAN

Dr SHIRIN AKINER

INTRODUCTION

The term 'Central Asia' is used in general international usage to refer to all or any part of the vast, land-locked hinterland of Asia. In Russian, however, a clear distinction used to be made between the Asian territories which formed part of the tsarist Empire and, later, the USSR, and those further to the east, which were under Chinese rule or nominally independent, such as Mongolia. The latter region was designated 'Central Asia' (*Tsentral'naya Aziya*). The former, that which was under Russian/Soviet rule, was subdivided into two zones, the steppe region of the north (i.e. modern Kazakhstan) and so-called 'Middle-Asia' (*Srednyaya Aziya*), which encompassed the lands to the south (now Kyrgyzstan, Tajikistan, Turkmenistan and Uzbekistan).

This division was largely a reflection of the course of tsarist conquest (Kazakh lands in the north came under Russian domination some two centuries before the southern belt) and, subsequently, of the administrative structures of the imperial, and later Soviet, systems. There are many features that are common to north and south, but there are also marked geographical and cultural differences. It is, therefore, sometimes useful to distinguish between the two blocs, that is, between Kazakhstan on the one hand and Kyrgyzstan, Tajikistan, Turkmenistan and Uzbekistan on the other. After the collapse of the USSR (December 1991), there was a growing tendency within the region itself to use the term 'Central Asia' (*Tsentral'naya Aziya* or, in the Turkic tongues, *Orta Asiya*) to refer to all five of these former Soviet republics, partly in order to conform to international usage, partly to emphasize the (albeit somewhat illusory) unity of the region. In this chapter, only the southern group of countries will be considered, namely Kyrgyzstan, Tajikistan, Turkmenistan and Uzbekistan. The term 'Central Asia', when used collectively, will here be used to refer to these four states, unless specified to the contrary.

Geography

The territory covered by the four southern Central Asian countries encompassed some 1.3m. square kilometre (sq km—some 502,000 sq miles), an area somewhat larger in size than Egypt (almost 1m. sq km). The combined population of these four states (22.7m., according to the 1989 census) was, however, considerably smaller than that of Egypt (53.2m.). However, in age structure the populations were similar (in the Central Asian countries, some 50% of the population was under 16 years of age; the annual rate of natural increase in population ranges between 2.5%, in Kyrgyzstan, to 3.5%, in Tajikistan). Again like Egypt, large tracts of Central Asia are not conducive to human settlement. In the central and western areas, which constitute some two-thirds of the total territory, there are barren deserts and semi-deserts; in the east, there are the jagged mountain ranges of the Tien Shan and the Hindu Kush. The climate is sharply continental. In many places average summer (June–August) temperatures rise above 35°C (95°F), while winter temperatures of below −30°C (86°F) are not uncommon. Sand storms occur throughout the desert regions (apparently increasing in frequency since the 1970s, owing to the deteriorating ecological situation). Freezing currents of air carry strong wind-chill factor and cause abrupt falls in temperature, even in the summer. The skies are predominantly clear and there are long periods of sunshine.

The chief curb on human settlement has been the chronic shortage of water. In most areas agriculture is only viable if irrigated. After the Second World War industrialization, urbanization and the massive growth in population vastly increased water consumption, placing severe strains on already scarce resources. In the mountains of the south-east (Kyrgyzstan and Tajikistan) the problem was not so acute, since there were numerous lakes and rivers (now mostly harnessed to produce hydroelectric power) and precipitation is relatively high, being upwards of 500 mm per year. On the plains, however, water resources were extremely limited. Precipitation is very low (in the delta of the Amu-Dar'ya, approximately 800 mm per year). There were substantial reserves of ground water, but, as of the early 1990s, these had not been greatly exploited. The chief river is the Amu-Dar'ya (anciently known as the Oxus), which rises in the Pamirs, in the area where China, Afghanistan and Tajikistan converge; from there it flows down to the plains, to follow a north-westerly course between Turkmenistan and Uzbekistan towards the Aral Sea. Up to the 1970s the Amu-Dar'ya used to empty into the Aral Sea, but over-exploitation of its waters so reduced the flow that, in most years, it now dries up far short of the Sea. This was one of the chief causes of the shrinking of the Aral Sea, a development that has had grave ecological consequences for the region as a whole. The other major rivers of the southern belt, most of which flow along the periphery, include the Syr-Dar'ya (ancient Jaxartes), which crosses the eastern corner of Uzbekistan before turning northwards into Kazakhstan, and the Murgab and Tejen, which flow through southern Turkmenistan.

There are chains of oases along the river valleys and, from ancient times, these were the focus for important urban settlements (the most historic being Samarkand, Bukhara, Mary—Merv and Khwarezm—Khorezm). In the latter part of the 20th century they provided the bases for large-scale agricultural and industrial developments. During the Soviet period a vast network of reservoirs and irrigation canals was constructed to meet the region's growing demand for water. The showpiece of the system was the mighty Kara-Kum Canal, which channelled water from the Amu-Dar'ya to the deserts of central Turkmenistan. However, although these grandiose schemes were initially successful in improving water supplies and, thereby, raising agricultural and industrial productivity, the inherent technical and ecological shortcomings were such that they subsequently created as many problems as they sought to solve.

The largest of the southern republics are those on the plains: Turkmenistan (488,100 sq km), which is the westernmost, bordering the Caspian Sea in the west, Iran and Afghanistan in the south and Kazakhstan and Uzbekistan to the north; and Uzbekistan (447,400 sq km), which stretches diagonally across Central Asia, bordering four former Soviet states (Kazakhstan to the north, Kyrgyzstan and Tajikistan to the east and Turkmenistan to the south-west) and, in the south, Afghanistan. The mountain republics are considerably smaller: Kyrgyzstan (198,500 sq km), the most easterly of the four, is wedged between China to the east, Kazakhstan to the north, Uzbekistan to the west and Tajikistan to the south-west; Tajikistan (143,100 sq km), in the south-eastern corner of the region, borders Kyrgyzstan to the north-east, Uzbekistan to the north-west and China and Afghanistan to the south. Uzbekistan had by far the most numerous population. According to the 1989 census (the most reliable figures available), there was a population of 19.9m. in Uzbekistan, 5.1m. in Tajikistan (possibly reduced in the early 1990s by some 500,000, owing to the upheavals caused by the civil war), 4.3m. in Kyrgyzstan and 3.5m. in Turkmenistan. The level of urbanization in Central Asia, according to estimates for 1991 by the UN Development Programme, ranged from 31% in Tajikistan to 45% in Turkmenistan. Within each country population densities varied greatly from region to region. In Uzbekistan and Turkmenistan, the main concentrations were in the river valleys of the south, where there were average densities of 300—400 people per sq km; in Tajikistan and Kyrgyzstan, the most populous regions were in the valleys and lower foothills of the western and central areas. Elsewhere, settlements were very few and far between.

The Central Asian countries are extremely well endowed with natural resources. Turkmenistan and Uzbekistan have vast reserves of petroleum and natural gas, as well as a wide range of valuable minerals, including, in Uzbekistan, considerable deposits of gold; both were major producers of cotton (in the early 1980s Uzbekistan alone was producing almost as much as the entire USA). There was some industrial development in the region, although less than in the European parts of the former USSR. Much of it was linked to the extractive industries (petrochemical plants, iron and steel works and heavy engineering). In Tashkent (Uzbekistan) there was an important aircraft-manufacturing plant, which, during the Soviet period, was of all-Union significance. Kyrgyzstan and Tajikistan also have important deposits of petroleum and gas, but, because of their remote location, these hydrocarbon reserves were far less amenable to exploitation. The most readily accessible wealth of the mountain republics lies in their mineral reserves, which include sizeable deposits of gold, uranium, mercury and tungsten, also of rare earths valuable in the electronics industry. There were major hydroelectric installations in both countries (even before the 1990s Kyrgyzstan was already exporting hydroelectricity to China and planned to sell more in the future); Tajikistan, however, was the more heavily industrialized, with large chemical plants in the north (Khojand—Khodzhent, formerly Leninabad) and a massive aluminium works in the centre (Tursunzade). Both republics were significant producers of wool, tobacco and other agricultural produce.

HISTORICAL BACKGROUND

Central Asia is far from representing a unified cultural entity. Throughout history the region was subjected to a long succession of invasions, some of which engulfed large swathes of territory, while others affected relatively small areas. Achaemenians, Greeks, Kushans, Sasanians, Huns, a variety of Turkic peoples, Arabs, Mongols and Russians all held sway over some part of Central Asia. However, the region was only twice united under a single ruler: first (and only nominally), under the Mongols (13th century), then under tsarist/Soviet rule (19th-20th centuries). For the remainder of its history, Central Asia was characterized by disunity and internecine warfare. Up until the 19th century the chief division was between the settled peoples of the oases and the nomads of the deserts and the steppes. However, tribal conflicts and rivalries between regional leaders added further layers of potential fragmentation. Many of the tensions which surfaced in the 1990s had their roots in these ancient hostilities. Under Russian/Soviet rule they were held in check, or at least contained within certain limits. As the power of the central government weakened, however, old disputes over land and water rights re-emerged, made all the sharper by newer economic concerns such as the competition for housing and employment.

Although each wave of invaders left its own distinctive imprint, there were three that radically changed the culture of the region as a whole. The first of these was the influx of Turkic tribes which entered Central Asia over a period of approximately one millenium, from the 6th to the 16th centuries AD. They came originally from the east, from their original homeland in what is today Mongolia, later from the west, from the lands that had been conquered by the Golden Horde. The effect of this prolonged immigration was largely to submerge previous cultures (most notably, the Iranian—Persian stratum in the south) and to create of Central Asia a predominantly Turkic enclave; medieval Arab geographers were already referring to the region as Turkestan, ('land of the Turks'), a term which remained in use even in the 1990s.

The second crucial invasion was that of the Arabs, in the second half of the 7th century. Their territorial conquests were short-lived and limited to the urban centres of the south, but they succeeded in establishing the first outposts of Islam in Central Asia. The new religion spread rapidly among the settled peoples and, by the 9th century, the oasis cities of Central Asia, although physically on the periphery of the Muslim world, had become culturally and spiritually an integral part of the Caliphate. Scholars such as Avicenna, Al-Bukhari, Al-Khwarezmi and many others were born in Central Asia, but actively contributed to the mainstream of Islamic thought. From the 16th century onwards, the region became more isolated, chiefly owing to the change in trading patterns (the development of sea routes in preference to the overland 'Silk Road'). The tradition of Islamic scholarship remained strong in cities such as Bukhara and Samarkand, however, although it was marked increasingly by conservatism rather than the innovative brilliance of earlier periods.

The impact of Islam on the remoter regions and, in particular, on the nomads, was much weaker than in the urban centres. Some of the Kazakhs and Kyrgyz were only converted in the 19th century and then scarcely more than superficially. Nevertheless, even amongst these peoples, Islam was to become one of the parameters of their identity. Even at its weakest, it provided a defence mechanism: the beliefs and legal tenets of the religion may not have been well understood, but the exclusive nature of its practices (e.g. circumcision, burial rites, dietary laws) enabled the indigenous peoples to preserve an inner distance from the newcomers. During the Soviet period any form of Islamic observance was discouraged and, at times, actively suppressed, but at a notional level, as a statement of identity, Islam was to remain a constant.

The third turning point in Central Asian history was the tsarist conquest of the region. Most of the territory that constitutes Kyrgyzstan, Tajikistan, Turkmenistan and Uzbekistan came under direct Russian rule in the second half of the 19th century, although two of the khanates, those of Bukhara and Khiva, were able to retain some of their lands and to maintain a semblance of independence as Protectorates of the Russian Empire. Kokand, the third of the large khanates, was fully annexed in 1876. For the Russians, the reasons for the incorporation of Central Asia into the tsarist Empire were mainly economic and strategic.

Compared with other colonial powers, they had little missionary zeal and were content to allow most local institutions to continue to function as before. However, by virtue of the fact that the indigenous population, especially the wealthy, educated élite, were suddenly exposed to new ideas in technology, trade, finance, politics and even social conduct, some changes in outlook were inevitable. Yet it was the imposition of the superstructure of colonial administration that was to have the more profound effect, in that it introduced new levels of authority and brought about a modification of existing hierarchical structures. The maintenance of law and order, like the right to levy and collect taxes, were now no longer local matters, but subject to external authority. It was this that gradually undermined the traditional patterns of social organization and prepared the ground, albeit unintentionally, for the momentous feats of social engineering which were to be undertaken under Soviet rule. Thus, although the tsarist episode did not, in itself, cause a major transformation of the region, it played a crucial role in initiating the transition from a pre-modern society to a modern one.

THE FORMATION OF THE CENTRAL ASIAN REPUBLICS

Bolshevik (Soviet) power was established in Central Asia in 1918, although fighting with various rebel groups continued for some years, especially in the eastern-most region of Bukhara (part of Tajikistan). That same year, however, the Turkestan Autonomous Soviet Socialist Republic (ASSR) was proclaimed, as part of the Russian Federation (RSFSR); it incorporated the 'Turkestan Territory' (the designation of the former tsarist administrative unit) and had Tashkent as its capital. Six years later, in 1924, the National Delimitation of Central Asia was carried out, as a result of which the five modern republics were created, although at the time only Turkmenistan and Uzbekistan were granted the status of Soviet Socialist Republics (SSR)—constituent Union Republics in the Soviet federation. Tajikistan, originally an Autonomous Republic within Uzbekistan, was elevated to this status in 1929 (at the same time it acquired the Khojand region), while Kyrgyzstan and Kazakhstan only became Union Republics in 1936. Karakalpakstan, situated on the lower reaches of the Amu-Dar'ya, was first created an Autonomous Province within the Kazakh ASSR, but was later elevated to an ASSR and subsequently transferred to Uzbekistan. In 1993 Karakalpakstan (Kara-Kalpak Autonomous Republic) was in the ambiguous position of being an independent republic, but still within the jurisdiction of Uzbekistan.

The new republican boundaries were based upon ethnolinguistic division. In Central Asia, prior to this, clan or tribal affiliations, regional or territorial bases and, when confronted by non-Muslims, religion, were the primary factors in self-definition. The khanates of Bukhara, Khiva and Kokand, which straddled the territory of the four countries, were, from a modern perspective, multi-ethnic and multilingual. At the time, however, these distinctions were of significance only to foreign historians, ethnographers, philologists and the like. Within the region itself, neither ethnicity (whether interpreted in a cultural or a biological sense) nor language were important markers of identity. Nevertheless, there were clear cultural, dialectal and historical divisions between the different groups. These are well attested in the accounts of 19th century travellers and scholars, including those by Western Europeans and at least one US citizen. The attempt to differentiate between these groups on a 'national' basis may have been motivated primarily by Moscow's political machinations, but it was not entirely without substance. The Turkmen for example, descendants of the Oghuz-Seljuq Turks, had a distinct sense of group awareness, despite the fact that this was riven by fierce tribal hostilities. The Kyrgyz, also nomads of Turkic origin, appeared to have had a looser sense of communal identity, possibly a result of being geographically more scattered, but, nevertheless, they, too, were conscious of a sense of shared historical links within a distinct tribal confederation. The Uzbeks and Tajiks, both settled peoples, were so closely intermingled that no meaningful distinction could be made between them. The former were of Turkic origin, the latter of Iranian, but long proximity and frequent intermarriage had created a common bilinguistic affiliation, providing the basis for kinship networks amongst these sedentarized groups.

Territorially, the Central Asian 'peoples' were in fairly compact groups and, with no movement of population, in 1924 some 85%–95% of the total population of the three main ethnic groups—Uzbeks, Turkmen and Kyrgyz—were encompassed within their own titular republics (whereas previously they had been divided between the three khanates). Those who suffered most from the National Delimitation were undoubtedly the Tajiks. It was impossible to dismember at a stroke the centuries-old fusion of Turko-Iranian traditions in such a way as to satisfy both groups. The Tajiks acquired their own territory, which gave them cultural and political autonomy from the numerically superior Uzbeks, but, at the same time, they lost their historic urban centres, including Samarkand and Bukhara, and received instead rugged mountains and a scattering of rude provincial towns. Less than 65% of the total Tajik population was included within the borders of the Tajik ASSR in 1924, while 36% remained in Uzbekistan. The balance changed somewhat when the Khojand district was added to Tajikistan in 1929, but, even in the 1990s, approximately one-fifth of the Tajik population was domiciled in Uzbekistan, mostly in Samarkand and Bukhara. This was a cause of deep resentment among the Tajiks, who regarded this region as their own. Many still harboured (probably vain) hopes that it would one day be transferred to the jurisdiction of Tajikistan.

THE SOVIETIZATION AND MODERNIZATION OF CENTRAL ASIAN SOCIETY

The drawing of national boundaries was a relatively simple technical task. Far more difficult was the creation of 'modern' identities. This required the deconstruction and radical refashioning of existing self-images. It was a huge task, one that could only have been conceived and attempted by a totalitarian state. Virtually no areas of public life and few of private life were to survive unchanged. Education and mass communication were the key tools in the process of transformation. It was not merely the content of the message that was changed, but the very medium itself: the linguistic context was altered, as dialects were codified and transformed into new-minted national languages, replete with large quantities of loanwords (mostly international terms borrowed through Russian) to express unfamiliar concepts; even the visual image of language was changed as the Arabic script, which had been introduced into Central Asia, along with Islam, over 1,000 years before, was replaced first by the Latin script (*c.* 1930), then the Cyrillic (1940). (In early 1993 Turkey authorized the addition of five new characters to its version of the Latin alphabet, to accommodate the Turkic languages of Central Asia and Azerbaijan, and, in September that year, Uzbekistan officially introduced a Latin script.) The sheer quantity of information on offer was increased dramatically, as handwritten manuscripts (few printed works were available in Central Asia before the Soviet period) gave way to a vast number of mass-produced posters, newspapers and books. Novel ways of disseminating ideas were also introduced, including public performances of overtly propagandist plays. Later (from the 1930s onwards), Western-style operas, ballets and films were used to influence people's perceptions and expectations. In the post-Second World War period, television was to prove an even more effective ideological tool.

Mass education was given a high priority, partly because of the obvious social and economic benefits, but also, and very importantly, because of the potential it afforded for political indoctrination. The level of illiteracy in the southern republics in the early Soviet period was above 95%; within 50 years it had been virtually eradicated. Inevitably, there were shortcomings in the system and standards were not always as high as official statistics implied, but, nevertheless, progress was rapid and impressive and, by the 1950s, a full range of educational facilities, from primary level through to advanced research, was available in all the Central Asian republics. By the 1990s basic literacy was universal and levels of secondary and tertiary education, amongst both male and female populations, compared favourably with those in many developed countries.

Another area in which state intervention had clear political as well as social goals was the emancipation of women. The ostensible aim of this campaign was to improve the lot of women by freeing them from male domination. The deeper implications, however, were that it would facilitate the remodelling of society by altering the very nature of the relationships within the most intimate social unit, the family. This, in turn, would hasten the destruction of the old order. The main symbol of male domination, in the eyes of the would-be-reformers, was the voluminous black veil worn in public by women in the settled regions of the south. This was the most visible focus of the attack on traditional society, but many other institutions were also fundamentally transformed. A legal framework was created which gave Central Asian women rights similar to those of other Soviet citizens in such fields as marriage, inheritance, custody of children, education and employment. By the mid-1930s these measures were making a perceptible impact on society and, though some regional characteristics persisted throughout the Soviet period (for example, Central Asian girls continued to marry at a significantly younger age and to have larger families than their counterparts in the European part of the USSR), nevertheless, the old taboos were gradually broken and women, especially in urban areas, came to expect a greater degree of independence.

Alongside the drive for female emancipation, and in many ways intertwined with it, was a far broader and deeper campaign—to eradicate Islam. Similar anti-religious campaigns were carried out throughout the USSR, but the attacks on Islam in Central Asia were particularly virulent, since this religion was not only a belief system, but also a rival political philosophy, one that offered a vision of an alternative social (and in many respects, socialist) order. Moreover, to the Communist regime, Islam represented a world that was corrupt, backward and inward-looking, an ogre that had to be vanquished before modernization, Westernization and Sovietization could be initiated. However, it was the dominant culture of the region and, as such, could not be attacked immediately, for fear of alienating the indigenous population. The educational, legal and administrative infrastructure of Islam, therefore, was tolerated for the first few years of Soviet rule. Then, towards the end of the 1920s, *maktab* and *madrassa* (Islamic schools and colleges) and Islamic law courts were phased out, to be replaced by secular Soviet institutions. Large numbers of mosques were closed, religious texts destroyed and Muslim scholars subjected to all forms of persecution. The abolition of the Arabic script (the script in which the holy Koran is written and, therefore, a visual symbol of Islam for Muslims all over the world), the emancipation of women and the introduction of heavily ideologized mass education were all aspects of the campaign to undermine the power of Islam. This was also the period of the terrible Stalinist purges: in Central Asia, as elsewhere in the USSR, the flower of the intelligentsia was wiped out. The result was the creation of an atmosphere of fear and confusion and this, combined with an instinct for self-preservation, served to bring about a state of what can best be termed as voluntary amnesia, in which traditional culture, including the most basic precepts and rituals of Islam, was largely forgotten. The spiritual vacuum that this produced was readily filled by Soviet ideology.

The institutionalization of ethnicity was an integral component of the Soviet nationalities policy, the mechanism whereby national aspirations could be harnessed to serve, rather than disrupt, the Soviet entity. Arguably, it is in Central Asia that the policy, with all its cultural, political and administrative ramifications, achieved its greatest success, since there it was actively involved in shaping the very national identities which it sought to manipulate. This was a region which was more vulnerable than most to such pressures, because the physical isolation, as well as the low level of literacy, meant that the broad mass of the population had extremely limited access to alternative sources of information. Moreover, by tradition, great trust was placed in individual figures of authority, both secular and religious. When Soviet power was established, such leaders of society were, if they opposed the new system, eliminated (executed, frightened into silence or forced to flee abroad) or, if they were prepared to acquiesce, co-opted into its service. Indigenous pro-Soviet élites—political activists, artists, writers, scholars—soon emerged and, by their support, gave popular legitimacy to the regime. It was this, more perhaps than any other single factor, that helped to consolidate the foundations of the new order. At the same time, however, it enabled the Central Asians to take over the system and manipulate it, almost imperceptibly, to their own ends. On the surface, they were the most compliant and politically least ambitious of all the Soviet nationalities. Few sought high office in distant Moscow, since their power bases were, as they had always been, in their own regions. Here, beneath the façade of subservience, they succeeded in exercising a high degree of unofficial 'subsidiarity', running the collective farms, districts and even republics as though they were their private fiefdoms.

The modernization of Central Asian society was hastened by economic integration into the USSR. From the 1920s onwards the all-Union authorities devoted substantial human and material resources towards making the region more productive. Transportation and communications networks were vastly improved and there was considerable industrial development. The main thrust of economic policies, however, particularly from the 1950s onwards, was directed towards raising agricultural output, particularly of cotton, but also of rice, fruit and vegetables. In mountain areas (especially in Kyrgyzstan), sheep rearing was intensified in order to increase wool yields. These undertakings brought greater prosperity to the Central Asian republics, raised levels of technical competence and created a serviceable technical infrastructure. However, the massive onslaughts on the fragile ecological balance of the region were eventually to cause serious environmental damage (on the plains, through the overuse of agro-chemicals, as well as through ill-conceived, shoddily executed irrigation schemes which resulted in the creation of both barren dust bowls and saline swamps; in the mountains, through over-grazing, leading to severe soil erosion). Until the late 1970s–early 1980s the general perception was that the benefits of development outweighed possible disadvantages. By the 1990s the flawed nature of this legacy was all too apparent. The human and material assets which the republics gained under Soviet rule would undoubtedly help them to exploit their natural resources more effectively in the future, but, at the same time, they inherited a crippling burden of ecological problems.

A concomitant of the process of integration and modernization of Central Asia was a massive influx of immigrants into the region. The number of Slavs (Russians and Ukrainians mainly) in the area, in 1926, ranged from under 1% of the population in Tajikistan to some 18% in Kyrgyzstan. During the 1920s there was a sizeable inflow of professionals, skilled labourers and administrative, political and security personnel. During the Second World War (1941–45) a number of industries, as well as academic and cultural institutions, were uprooted from the more exposed western Union Republics and relocated to Central Asia, bringing both advanced technology and a new wave of immigrants into the region. More immigrants arrived when, on the eve of the War and in the war years, many thousands of supposedly unreliable and anti-Soviet 'nationalities' were deported *en masse* to Central Asia, adding Koreans, Greeks, Chechens, Crimean Tatars, Meskhetian Turks and many others to the increasingly mixed populations in these republics. During the 1950s there was another influx of Slavs, but, thereafter, the percentage share of these immigrants in the population as a whole began to fall. This was initially as a result of the lower birth rate amongst the Slavs, compared with that of the indigenous peoples, and later, from the end of the 1980s, as a result of out-migration. In 1959 the Russian populations in Tajikistan and Uzbekistan represented approximately 13.5% of the respective total populations, in Turkmenistan 17.3% and in Kyrgyzstan 30.2%. By the time of the 1989 census this had fallen to 7.6% in Tajikistan, 8.3% in Uzbekistan, 9.5% in Turkmenistan and 21.5% in Kyrgyzstan. In all, this was a total of some 3.3m. Russians (10% of the regional population); there were also some 337,000 Ukrainians (just over 1%) and a smaller number of Belarusians in the region.

THE ROAD TO INDEPENDENCE

During the second part of the 1980s separatist sentiments began to surface in a number of the Soviet republics. In Central Asia, however, there was still an almost total acceptance of the regime. Nevertheless, even here there were inchoate stirrings of dissatisfaction at the all-Union Government's high-handed treatment of the region. The anti-corruption campaigns, conducted with a singular lack of regard for local customs and sensitivities, were a particular source of resentment. Possibly as a result of this, there was a reawakening of interest in indigenous culture. One aspect of this was renewed curiosity about Islam. To some extent it was encouraged by state officials, since it was felt that religion might help to combat the wave of corruption which was engulfing society. The most extreme manifestation of the Islamic revival was the appearance of the so-called Wahhabis, small groups of self-taught devotees who tried to live according to Muslim precepts. They were located mainly in the Fergana valley, on the borders of Uzbekistan, Kyrgyzstan and Tajikistan. Elsewhere, there was little active support for their views, but their very existence was indicative of an incipient change of mood in Central Asia.

Concerns about the status of the national languages (which, in public life, had been largely ousted by Russian) and the level of environmental degradation were the focus for the socio-political movements which began to appear at the end of the 1980s. The first and best organized of these was Birlik (Unity), founded in Uzbekistan in 1989. Despite some initial success, however, neither this nor any of the other movements which followed in its wake were able to attract significant popular support. More ominous signs of emergent nationalism were the violent conflicts which erupted between Meskhetian Turks and Uzbeks and Kyrgyz in 1989–90. The main causes were economic competition, but there were undoubtedly elements of a traditional power struggle. As the ability of the centre to control the periphery grew weaker, so such ethnic tensions multiplied. Latent clan and tribal rivalries also became more pronounced and the 'mafia'—organized criminal networks—more blatant in their activities. Some of the Russian community began to leave, disturbed by the general air of instability. This sudden loss of skilled labour caused further problems, exacerbating an already tense situation. Meanwhile the Union itself was in a state of flux. The Central-Asian Party First Secretaries were transformed into Presidents and these Union Republics, as many others, made declarations of sovereignty during 1990. In the referendum of March 1991, however, they, nevertheless, voted by overwhelming majorities to remain within the Union. The August coup attempt against the Soviet President Mikhail Gorbachev surprised the regimes of the region and, in the aftermath, all four Central Asian countries made declarations of independence (Kyrgyzstan on 31 August, Tajikistan on 9 September, Turkmenistan on 27 October and Uzbekistan on 31 August too). This was widely seen as an attempt to distance the still Communist-dominated authorities from the struggles in Moscow (only President Askar Akayev of Kyrgyzstan had been unequivocal in condemning the coup leaders). It is doubtful whether anyone in the region had, at this stage, thought through the full implication of such declarations. By the end of the year, however, the USSR had ceased to exist and, suddenly, independence had became a reality.

In January 1992, for the first time since their creation, the Central Asian governments assumed full and sole responsibility for all the social, economic and environmental problems in their respective countries. The task was daunting and made yet more difficult by the highly volatile situation in the other former Soviet states, in particular, in the Russian Federation. Inevitably, the following months were a time of hardship, with falling standards of living and visible signs of deterioration in all areas of public service. The Central Asian countries were the most adversely affected by the economic dislocation caused by the collapse of the USSR, because standards of living here were lower than elsewhere; there was a greater dependency on inter-republican trade and subsidies from the centre had supported much of the social-welfare programme. Moreover, there were virtually no communications and transportation links with the outside world, except through Moscow. Nevertheless, some progress was made during the following two years towards consolidating their independence. A degree of economic and constitutional reform was implemented and reasonably efficient welfare networks were created to provide protection for the most vulnerable members of society.

There was an increase in social tensions in all the countries, but it was only in Tajikistan that there was a complete disintegration of law and order. This state's sudden descent into anarchy and civil war not only served to encourage the authorities in the neighbouring countries to adopt a highly authoritarian position, but it also made such an approach more acceptable to the population at large. Western-style democratic ideas had little chance of success in such a climate, but some degree of stability, however, was achieved.

In the conduct of relations with foreign countries, as in domestic affairs, the Central Asians had, hitherto, been dependent on decision-makers in the all-Union Government. After independence they had to formulate their own policies in this field, too. All four countries displayed great pragmatism and were following an 'open door' policy, avoiding the temptation to be drawn into any one ideological camp. They formed good links with the Muslim world, but also with Israel and, likewise, with many Asian countries, also with Western Europe and the USA. Turkey and Iran both made major efforts to establish 'special relationships' with the Central Asian states, with apparently equal success up to the end of 1993. Russia remained the most important trading partner and the dominant regional political influence. However, all the Central Asian republics were conscious of the need to diversify their links. Road, rail and air networks were greatly improved during 1992 and 1993 and, gradually, these new countries were becoming part of the international community.

This was very much a period of transition and what the outcome would be was far from clear. The long-term prospects for the Central Asian states were promising, but there were very considerable obstacles that would have to be overcome. The main threats to the stability and prosperity of the region included the rapidly widening poverty gap (the disparity between the wealthier and the poorer groups in society), which was causing large sections of the population to feel alienated and betrayed. There could be a serious social reaction, which might well, in some areas, take on a religious fundamentalist aspect. On a regional level, water could prove to be a major cause of conflict between all the Central Asian countries. On an international level, the greatest danger was that foreign rivalries would be projected into Central Asia, such as, for example, those between India and Pakistan, Saudi Arabia and Iran, China and Russia. It might be that the Central Asian leaders would succeed in turning such competition to their advantage. In the early 1990s, however, everything was still in flux and predictions as to the future course of events could be little more than guesswork.

THE CONFLICTS IN THE FORMER YUGOSLAVIA

MARCUS TANNER

When, in December 1988, Yugoslav leaders celebrated the 70th anniversary of Yugoslavia's foundation, few imagined that their country would collapse, bloodily, within only two years. The President of the Federal Executive Council, the country's prime minister, Ante Marković, was promoting Yugoslavia as the most advanced of the countries in the Communist bloc and well worth Western investment. There was speculation about joining the European Community (EC).

The potential for disintegration was always there. From the day of its foundation as the Kingdom of Serbs, Croats and Slovenes, Yugoslavia never enjoyed a common language, culture or religion. To the dominant Serbs, Yugoslavia was an extension of Serbia. The Croats, the second-largest nationality, resented the loss of the autonomy which had existed under Habsburg Austria-Hungary. The murder of the Croat leader, Stjepan Radić, by a Montenegrin in parliament, in 1929, increased tension between the two groups. After the suspension of parliamentary democracy and the institution of a royal dictatorship later the same year, extreme Croat nationalists, led by Ante Pavelić built up a Fascist insurrectionary movement, the Ustaša (Rebel), with support from Italian leader Benito Mussolini. The German invasion of 1941 and the ferocious civil war which followed hardened ethnic divisions. The Ustaša, in April 1941, proclaimed an Independent State of Croatia, including most of Bosnia and Herzegovina. In their short-lived regime they allegedly massacred many thousands of Serbs, Gypsies (Roma) and Jews.

By 1944 the Partisans (the National Liberation Army), dominated by the Communists led by Josip Broz (Tito), controlled most of Yugoslavia. The new Yugoslav leadership, from 1945, reunited the country with a mixture of terror and showmanship, but did not allow ethnic divisions to become a major issue. They did not attempt to restore the *ancien régime* of centralized Serb rule, they established the country as a federation and they delegated some powers to the federal units of six republics and two autonomous provinces. However, it would seem that the old hatreds and rivalries continued to fester beneath the public professions of fraternity and unity. After Tito's death, in 1980, and a severe economic crisis from 1983 onwards, all the old problems of the 1930s and 1940s returned.

The last hope for the committed Yugoslavs was Ante Marković, federal prime minister from 1989. Although a Croat, Marković was a reformed Communist and a convinced Yugoslav, determined to salvage the country's economy. This was to be done with a radical programme aimed at creating a free-market economy, reducing public spending dramatically, halting inflation and making the Yugoslav currency convertible. His appointment and economic programme came too late. In Serbia, Slobodan Milošević, a dynamic but conservative Communist, effectively sabotaged any changes which threatened the leading role of the ruling League of Communists of Yugoslavia (LCY) or the Serb-run Yugoslav People's Army (YPA—Jugoslavenska Narodna Armija), a bastion of conservatives with close ties to Milošević.

Milosević had risen to power in 1987 as a nationalist 'technocrat', with an agenda based on ending the home-rule aspirations of the almost-2m. ethnic Albanians in Serbia's impoverished Autonomous Province of Kosovo. Technically part of Serbia, Kosovo had enjoyed virtual republic status under the 1974 Constitution, a source of grievance to the Serbs. An exodus of Serbs, claiming harassment by Albanians, and a rapid increase in the number of Albanians (the official census results of March 1991 put Albanians at 77% of the provincial population and the Serbs 13%) fuelled ethnic tensions and gave Milošević a solid basis of political support.

Once in power in Serbia, Milošević began a programme of constitutional changes aimed at stripping Kosovo and the Autonomous Province of Vojvodina of their independence. There were massive public rallies throughout Serbia, to mobilize public support for the Milošević agenda and to put pressure on the leaders of the other Republics to endorse the changes. the Albanians staged street protests and industrial strikes of their own in vain. The Albanian leader in Kosovo, Azem Vlasi, lacked support from leaders of the other Republics, who opted to appease Serbia.

In March 1989 Serbia effectively ended the autonomy of Kosovo and Vojvodina through control of the Party apparatus and Milošević felt strong enough to order the arrest of Vlasi, on charges of 'counter-revolutionary nationalism and separatism'. Serbian police were sent to patrol the townships of Kosovo and impose a curfew. Over 60 Albanians were killed in street protests, but such actions only justified the authorities in tightening their grip on the region. Troops of the YPA were sent into Kosovo in February 1990 and, a few months later, a new Serbian Constitution was approved. It came into effect on 28 September, formally ending the independence of the institutions of Autonomous Provinces of Kosovo (officially renamed Kosovo and Metohija) and Vojvodina.

With the Kosovo situation under control, Milošević moved to attack opponents in Slovenia and Croatia, where resistance was strongest to the increase in Serb nationalism. In these Republics the tactics of organized public demonstrations failed to bring the leaderships into agreement with the Serbians. On 28 June 1989, at a celebration marking the 600th anniversary of the battle of Kosovo Polje ('the Field of Blackbirds'), Milošević delivered a triumphalist and aggressive speech to about 1m. enthusiastic supporters, clearly stating a nationalist agenda.

Milošević's most serious opponent was Milan Kučan, the reformist leader of the Alpine territory of Slovenia. Perceiving a threat to Slovenian autonomy, in September 1989 the Republic's parliament reaffirmed the sovereignty of Slovenia and declared its right to secede from the Yugoslav federation. Serbia retaliated, in November, by beginning a trade boycott of Slovenian goods. The escalating conflict was to end the reforming attempts at unity of Marković, whose impotence to control the flow of events in Yugoslavia became increasingly obvious.

The Slovenians and the predominantly Serb leaders of the YPA first clashed in the early 1980s, when the Slovenians demanded large reductions in the military budget and the right of Slovene soldiers to use their own language (the YPA use of Serbo-Croat was the only exception to the constitutional equality of the languages of the Yugoslav nationalities). In 1987 the YPA arrested three Slovene journalists from the student magazine, *Mladina*, and a soldier, for publishing an army contingency plan to arrest hundreds of suspect liberals. The trial of the so-called

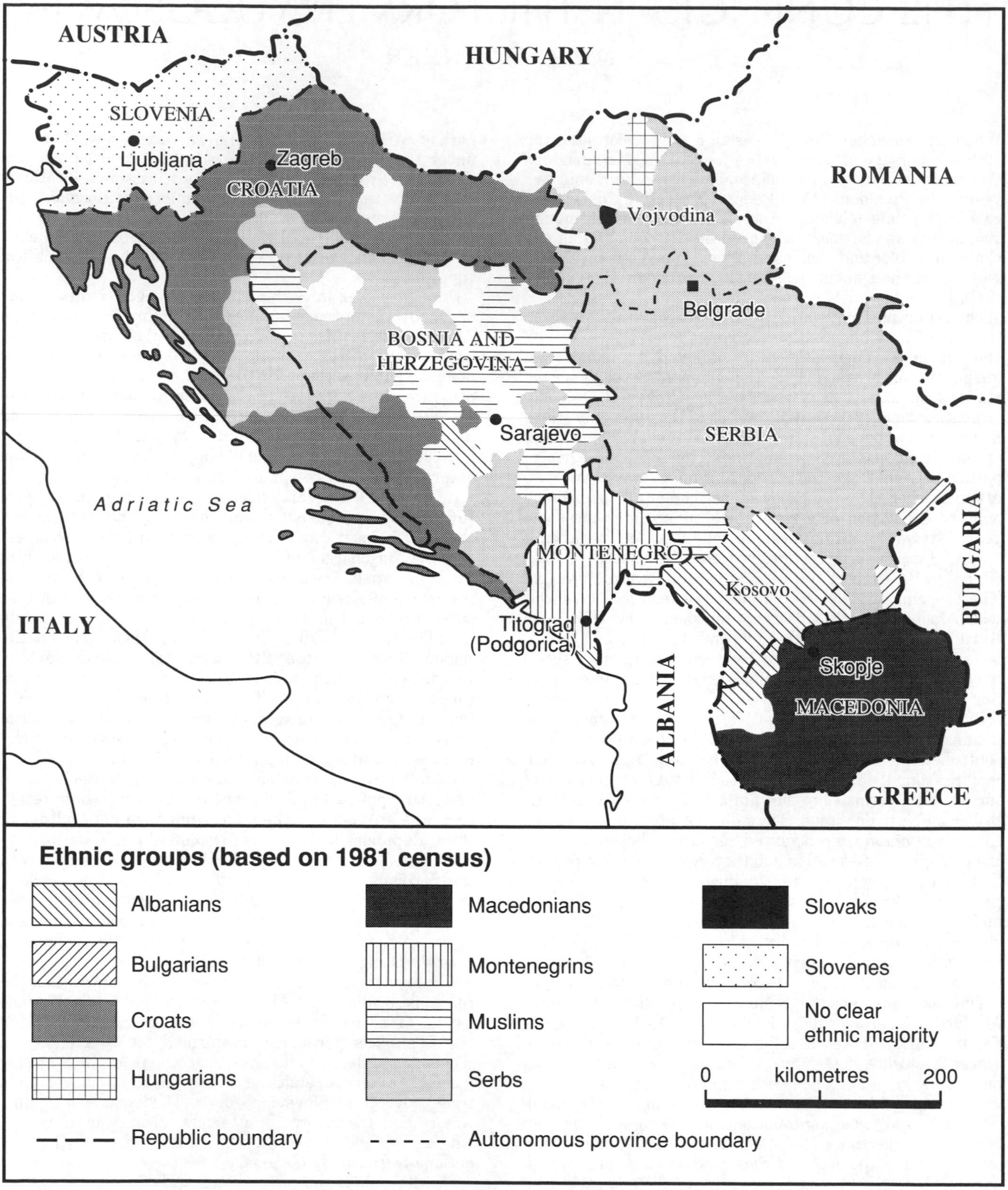
AUSTRIA
HUNGARY
SLOVENIA
Ljubljana
Zagreb
CROATIA
ROMANIA
Vojvodina
Belgrade
BOSNIA AND HERZEGOVINA
Sarajevo
SERBIA
Adriatic Sea
MONTENEGRO
Kosovo
BULGARIA
ITALY
Titograd (Podgorica)
ALBANIA
Skopje
MACEDONIA
GREECE
Ethnic groups (based on 1981 census)
Albanians
Bulgarians
Croats
Hungarians
Macedonians
Montenegrins
Muslims
Serbs
Slovaks
Slovenes
No clear ethnic majority
0 kilometres 200
Republic boundary
Autonomous province boundary

Ethnic Groups in the Former Yugoslavia

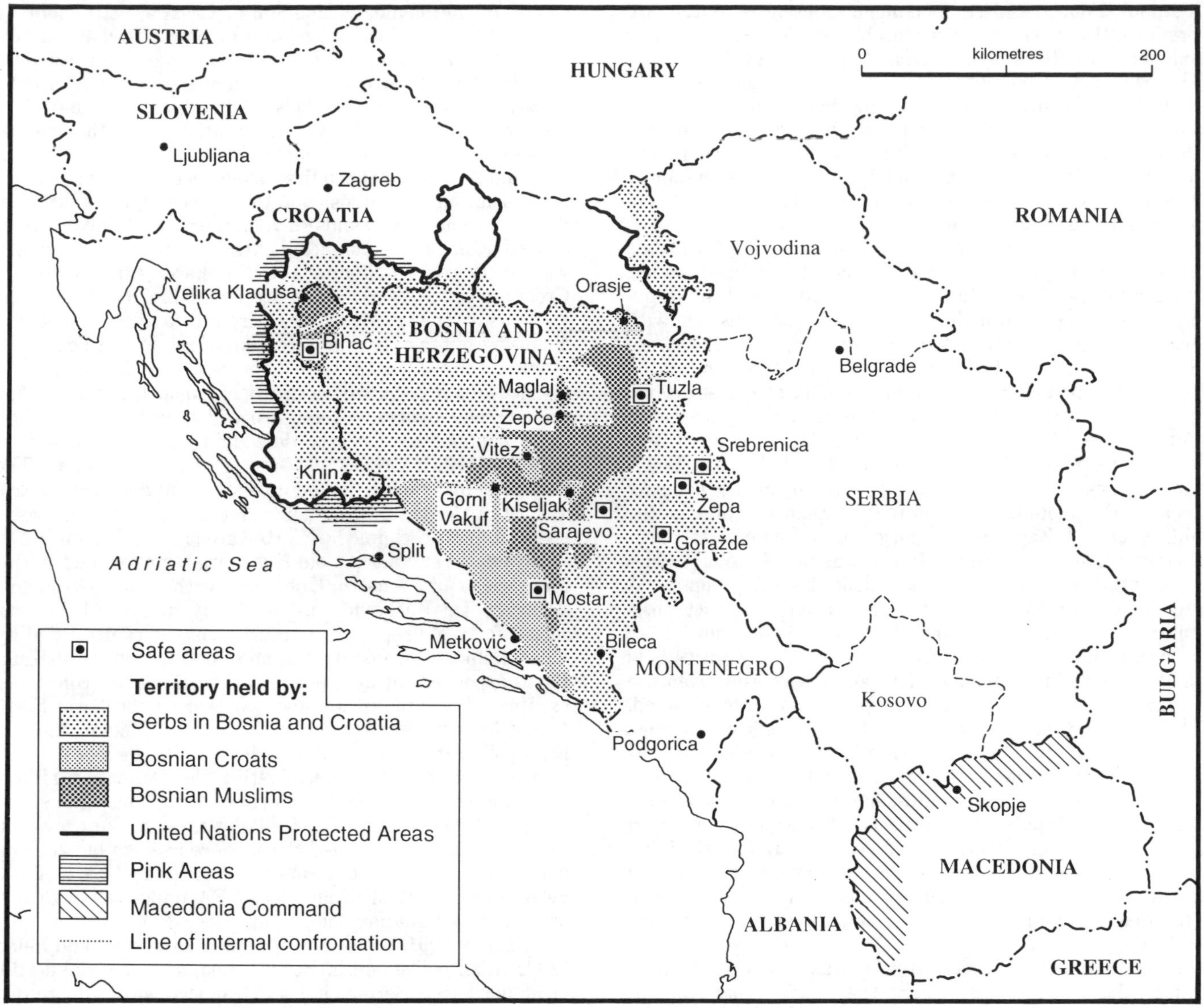

Areas of Military Occupation in the Former Yugoslavia

'Famous Four' resulted in nominal sentences, but, more significantly, revealed considerable support for greater independence from Yugoslavia, if not outright secession. The Slovenian Communists under Kučan dealt cautiously with the anti-army agitators, seeing them as useful popular allies in the worsening struggle with Serbia. In January 1989 Kučan allowed a right-wing academic, Dmitrij Rupel, to have the founding congress of an openly anti-Communist pro-independence party, the Slovenian Democratic Union, in Ljubljana's civic centre.

In Croatia the Communist rulers were edging towards a more liberal regime. However, the local Communist leader, Ivica Račan, lacked Kučan's decisive manner and the Republic's progression was impeded by ethnic tensions with local Serbs. Of Croatia's 4.7m. population, some 12% were Serbs (according to the 1991 census the Serbs constituted 12.2% of a population of 4.76m.) and, in the post-Second World War era they dominated the republican League of Communists, the police, the judiciary, the media and major state enterprises. In 11 of Croatia's 102 districts Serbs formed local majorities; these districts formed a compact area in the mountainous interior of Dalmatia and in the hills south of Zagreb. In charge of a Communist party dominated by ethnic Serbs, Račan was unable to articulate Croat nationalist aspirations and make his party popular.

Civil war in Yugoslavia first appeared a distinct possibility in January 1990, when the LCY finally split, after an acrimonious and inconclusive emergency Congress held in Belgrade. The Slovenian delegation withdrew from the Congress, because their reform proposals were rejected. The next month the League of Communists of Slovenia renounced its links with the LCY and re-formed itself as the Party of Democratic Reform. At the same time the regime announced that multi-party elections would take place in the Republic in April. These elections confirmed Kučan's canny grasp of political realities. Deftly shedding his mantle as leader of the former Communists, he emerged as the first elected President of non-Communist Slovenia. He presided over a parliament dominated by a fractious right-of-centre coalition.

Less than three weeks later it was Croatia's turn to reject the Communists. There the change was fraught. Lacking any kind of nationalist credentials, Račan's Communists were easily defeated by the Croatian Democratic Union (CDU), led by Franjo Tudjman, an elderly, combative relic of the *Maspok* era. During the campaign, Tudjman exploited Croatia's simmering ethnic tensions, even parading with Croatian flags through ethnic Serb areas. Opponents accused him of making racist remarks and, in some speeches, he appeared to lay claim to all, or parts of, Bosnia and Herzegovina. In the Dalmatian town of Benkovac, a Serb tried to shoot him. The furore undoubtedly helped him to win his party the election, but made a worrying start to Croatia's post-Communist era. These fears were confirmed during the first session of the new parliament (the Sabor or Assembly), at the end of May 1990. For Croatian nationalists it was a day of euphoria, as government ministers attended a celebratory mass in Zagreb's restored Gothic cathedral, then marched to the parliament building to proclaim Tudjman the President of Croatia. However, Serb nationalists from the newly formed Serbian Democratic Party (SDP), led by Jovan Rašković, refused to take their seats in the parliament—indicating that many Serbs were not reconciled to the new order.

In Belgrade the state-controlled media immediately began to devote its considerable influence to the situation in Croatia, rather than that in Slovenia, encouraging Serb nationalists to defy the new Government. The centre of trouble was the dusty Dalmatian town of Knin. Once the capital of the medieval kingdom of Croatia, settlement by ethnic Serbs from the 17th century onwards changed this mountain town into a Serb bastion, the chief town of the area once known as the Krajina—borderlands. In the Croatian elections Rašković's SDP easily won control of the municipal council. A confrontation with the central authorities in Zagreb was inevitable.

In mid-August 1990 the first armed clashes in the process of dissolution of Yugoslavia took place. Overnight local Serb police and thousands of volunteers erected barricades around Knin and renounced allegiance to Croatia, which was being re-formed into a Croat state. An attempt by Croatian police to regain control of Knin, by helicopter, was easily thwarted by the airforce—a signal that the Yugoslav military had no intention of remaining neutral in ethnic conflicts. On 19 August the Serbs in Knin and other districts (having formed a 'Serb National Council') defied the Zagreb Government and proceeded with a referendum on autonomy from Croatia, demanding the right to remain in Yugoslavia if Croatia seceded from the federation. The Serb militants rapidly linked up districts under their control and, with the results of their referendum in their favour, on 1 October proclaimed a 'Serb Autonomous Region (SAR) of Krajina'—reviving the old Habsburg term for the frontier territories of Austria-Hungary with the Ottomans. Although Dr Rašković was nominally in control, he was soon effectively replaced by much younger radicals, led by Milan Babić, a former dentist and now the mayor of Knin. Babić espoused an aggressive policy of seizing control of as much of Croatia as possible, whether or not it was Serb. In the local YPA commander, Col Ratko Mladić, and the Knin police chief, Milan Martić, he found close allies.

In early 1991, after consolidating the Dalmatian hinterland, the Krajina militants launched expeditions against the national park of Plitviče. In Pakrac, a market town in central Croatia, the armed Serbs were seen to be working more openly with the co-operation of the YPA. As the Serbs seized control of an area, YPA tanks would follow, preventing a Croatian counter-attack.

On 2 May 1991, when Serb gunmen ambushed and killed 12 Croatian policemen in Borovo Selo, an industrial settlement bordering Serbia, it was clear that local village disputes were escalating into a fall-scale war, in which the YPA and well-organized volunteer units from Serbia proper were playing a major role. The attacks on the eastern border region of Croatia (Western Slavonia), where Croats formed a substantial majority, emphasized that the Croats were confronted by a plan to expel them from large parts of their Republic. Shortly after the capture of Borovo Selo, Serb forces surrounded a small Croat hamlet, Celje, and set it on fire. Attacks on the villages of Dalj, Erdut and Aljmas followed. By the latter part of the year the swathe of territory in eastern Croatia under Serb control had almost isolated the large industrial town of Vukovar, soon to become the centre of a bloody three-month siege.

The worsening war in eastern Croatia, and the obvious involvement of the YPA, encouraged Croatia's leadership to opt for outright independence. On 19 May 1991, in a referendum on independence, some 85% of the electorate (93% of the votes cast) voted to quit the existing federation. This decision was no doubt encouraged by the refusal, four days before, of the 'Serbian bloc' (i.e. the members for Montenegro, Serbia, Kosovo-Metohija and Vojvodina) on the federal State Presidency to permit the expected election of the non-Communist Croatian member, Stjepan 'Stipe' Mesić, as President of the State Presidency—Yugoslavia's effective head of state.

Slovenia also made progress towards secession, suddenly conducting a referendum, on 23 December 1990, in which

94% of the electorate voted, with a decisive 89% of them in favour of independence. Then, in January 1991, anti-federation prejudices were confirmed when it was revealed that Serbia had ensured an illegal transfer from the National Bank of Yugoslavia of some 18,300m. new dinars (over US $1,700m.), to subsidize Serbia's ailing 'smokestack' industries. President Kučan concluded that the federal administration of Ante Marković was no longer in control and, in February, the Slovenian parliament authorized the start of a process leading to 'dissociation' from the rest of Yugoslavia.

An announcement that Slovenia would proclaim independence—that is, the start of its disassociation—from the Yugoslav federation from midnight on 25 June 1991 caused alarm in Croatia. It feared being isolated. Although preparations were not so advanced, Croatia announced that it would leave the federation on the same day as Slovenia. The claim provoked disbelief in Belgrade and abroad, although it was made more credible following the May crisis over the failure to elect the President of the Yugoslav State Presidency. Only days before 'independence' the US Secretary of State, James Baker, made a rapid tour of the Yugoslav Republics, advocating support for the failing Marković administration and claiming that the USA would 'never' recognize secessionist Republics.

Nevertheless, the Slovenians hoisted their new flag in the centre of Ljubljana on the evening of 25 June 1991, the parliaments of Slovenia and Croatia declaring the Republics' sovereignty and independence from 26 June. To give substance to these claims, also on 25 June, a force of 3,000 police assumed control of the frontier crossing with Croatia. The next day prime minister Marković pleaded with the Slovenians to withdraw from the border, accusing Slovenia of aggression. On the morning of 27 June Slovenians in Ljubljana found roads into their city blocked by vehicles, amid radio reports of fighting between the YPA and the Slovenian Territorial Defence forces for control of the border crossings. The drama was not of great duration but exercised a decisive effect on the whole course of events in Yugoslavia. The war destroyed the final claims of the YPA to be a multi-ethnic force of 'Southern Slavs', ultimately finished the credibility of the federal regime of Ante Marković and set a pattern for secession which was then repeated in Croatia and Bosnia and Herzegovina.

The number of casualties was surprisingly small. When the Yugoslav airforce bombed a column of lorries, they killed about 10 Turkish and Bulgarian lorry drivers. There were fears of air raids, but extensive bombing never took place. A long column of tanks, which had set out for Slovenia from Serbia, never arrived. The 30,000 Slovenian Territorials quickly established control of the entire Republic.

The Serbian nationalists under Milošević did not force Slovenia to stay in the Yugoslav federation. Instead, they forced the troublesome republic out, to strengthen their hand against Croatia. To the dismay of the Croatian leaders, the federal State Presidency and the Yugoslav General Staff agreed to the withdrawal of the YPA from Slovenia—in effect recognizing Slovenia's secession. In July 1991, at a meeting on the island of Brioni (Croatia) with a 'troika' of EC negotiators, the Serbians hastily secured consent to a plan to station EC observers in Slovenia, to oversee the army withdrawal. In return the troika obliged Slovenia to agree to suspend its dissociation from Yugoslavia for a three-month 'cooling-off' period. The Croatians only managed to obtain an unspecific pledge to station EC observers in Croatia and, as it turned out, a rather useless agreement to allow Stipe Mesić to assume the symbolic post of President of the State Presidency of Yugoslavia. For, as President, Mesić found he was powerless to influence events in favour of Croatia. The YPA, of which he was nominal commander-in-chief, continued to arm and assist Croatia's rebellious Serbs, while attacks on Croatia escalated within days of the Brioni conference and were not affected by the deployment of EC observers.

Later in July 1991 the YPA moved into the fertile Baranja region (Beli Minastir) on Croatia's north-east border with Serbia. On 25 August Serbs, who constituted one-quarter of the local population, attacked Baranja, in a campaign which lasted only a few days. Baranja fell to the Serbs by the first week in September. At the same time the Serbs seized a considerable arc of land around Okucani in central Croatia, severing the main Belgrade–Zagreb road. Fighting then erupted in the hilly Banija region, south of Zagreb, where sporadic attacks near the town of Petrinja soon escalated into full-scale warfare. Reports of Serb massacres of Croats in the villages of Zamlaca and Banska Struga spread panic among rural Croats and, on 13 September, the strategic town of Kostajnica, on the border with Bosnia and Herzegovina, fell to the Serbs. Soon after the Serbs were within 30 miles (76 km) of the Croatian capital.

After capturing Banija the Serbs concentrated their attentions again on Kordun, a hilly region to the north of Dalmatia and south of Karlovac. The area population was roughly two-thirds Croat and one-third Serb, but its position as the central link of the Krajina, between Banija and Serb-held parts of Dalmatia, made it an important target for the Serbs. Throughout September 1991 Serb attacks on isolated Croat villages increased. The local capital, Slunj, was soon isolated and fell to the Serbs in mid-October, after which western Slavonia became the principal object of the Serbs. However, the proximity to Zagreb meant that the Serbs were unable to expel the Croatian forces. Even so, from their strongholds in the Papuk hills of Slavonia, the Serbs were able to advance northwards and almost sever the road connecting Zagreb with Osijek, the chief city of eastern Croatia. On 21 September Croats were executed in the village of Vocin, but the Serbs of 'Western Slavonia' (another SAR) did not get much support from the heavily committed YPA. The Croatians were able to force them back towards Okucani. Meanwhile, in eastern Croatia, the Serbs of the 'SAR of Slavonia, Baranja and Western Srem' ('Srem' is Serb for Syrmia) were being supplied with weapons and manpower from Serbia. Here the Serb advance was relentless. On 17 November the town of Vukovar surrendured to the overwhelmingly superior forces of Serb irregulars and the YPA. There were allegations that many of the patients in the hospital were then massacred by the occupying forces and a mass grave from roughly this time was later uncovered by the UN, in the nearby village of Ovcare.

After the fall of Vukovar the war in Croatia subsided. Being in control of over one-quarter of Croatia by November 1991, the local Serbs found their resources under strain, particularly with more successful Croatian tactics of besieging army and naval bases. Abroad, Croatia's plight engaged the strong sympathy of Austria and Germany—traditional allies. In spite of fierce opposition from France and the United Kingdom, Germany and Sweden announced that they would recognize Croatia that January. On 13 January 1992, in order to preserve the facade of EC unity, all 12 EC countries recognized Croatia and Slovenia. They were preceded by Sweden and the former Soviet republics of Ukraine and the Baltic states. Angered by EC recognition of Croatia and Slovenia the federal leadership welcomed the offices of the UN special envoy, Cyrus Vance, a former US Secretary of State. The 'rump' federal authorities and the Milošević regime strongly supported the peace plan which Vance proposed for Croatia in January 1992. It aimed to 'freeze' the battle lines by deploying peace-keeping forces in the republic. The Krajina Serb radicals under Milan Babić came under heavy pressure from Belgrade to agree to the plan. Moreover, this initiative was advantageous to the Serbs because it deployed UN peace keepers along the frontline. The plan envisaged refugees returning home and setting up an ethnically mixed police force in Serb-held areas, but there was no timetable and most of the provisions proved illusory. There was no reference to Croatia's sovereignty over the disputed region and the United Nations Protection Force (UNPROFOR) achieved limited success in its demilitarization of the SARs (known as UN Protected Areas—UNPAs) and the so-called 'pink zones' (Serb-occupied territories that were not part of the SARs), which were also under UN protection. However, Croatia did gain a respite from the heavy bombardments and a chance to rebuild.

The UN chose the capital of Bosnia and Herzegovina, Sarajevo, as the base for the UNPROFOR operation, at the request of the Government of Bosnia and Herzegovina. As an ethnically mixed city of Serbs, Croats and Muslims (Bosniaks), Sarajevo seemed an ideal headquarters. In the event it was a disastrous decision. The ebbing of hostilities in Croatia overlapped the start of ethnic warfare in Bosnia and Herzegovina. In south-western Bosnia and Herzegovina Serb irregulars burned down the Croat village of Ravno. Then, at the end of March 1992, there was savage ethnic fighting between Serbs and Croats in Bosanski Brod, on the northern border with Croatia. Meanwhile, Yugoslav airforce jets attacked Listica, in south-western Bosnia and Herzegovina, in a dawn raid, killing several families.

The end of formal Communist rule in Bosnia and Herzegovina was marked by multi-party elections, conducted in three rounds in November–December 1990. The Communists were displaced by ethnic-based parties representing Muslims, Croats and Serbs. The Muslim-led Party of Democratic Action won most seats—86 of the 240 total in the new Assembly. The Serbian Democratic Party gained 72 seats and the Croatian Democratic Union of Bosnia and Herzegovina 44. At the same time there were elections to the seven-member republican Presidency, in which Fikret Abdić of the PDA won the most votes. However, the PDA leadership did not favour Abdić, a former Communist and a businessman who had been jailed for alleged fraud, as the President of the Presidency. This post went to Dr Alija Izetbegović, the leader of the PDA and a religious Muslim hardliner. Izetbegović had been jailed under the Communists in 1946, for 'pan-Islamic activity', and, again, in 1983, for 'hostile counter-revolutionary acts', meaning religious activism. The latter charge centred on the *Islamic Declaration*, which Izetbegović wrote in 1970 and which opponents alleged advocated an Islamic republic in Bosnia and Herzegovina, although he denied being a fundamentalist.

At first the three ethnic parties agreed to establish a loose coalition, dividing up government ministries and the principal offices of state. However, the secession of Slovenia and the war in Croatia put Bosnia and Herzegovina in an awkward position, with warnings of far bloodier strife than was seen even in Croatia if conflict was allowed to spread into the republic. A smaller Muslim party, led by millionaire businessman Adil Zulfika Rparsić, favoured an 'historic agreement' with Serbia, safeguarding Bosnia and Herzegovina's integrity within a Serb-dominated mini-Yugoslavia. Izetbegović favoured outright independence and most Muslims, Croats and Yugoslavs were reluctant to remain in a 'Greater Serbian' state. Majorities on both the republican Presidency and in the Assembly recommended seeking independence in October 1991 and did go so far as to declare the sovereignty, within its existing borders, of Bosnia and Herzegovina. This provoked the formation of an 'Assembly of the Serb Nation' which ordered a referendum for the Serbs of the republic, on 9–10 November, the result of which favoured remaining in the Yugoslav federation. However, on 20 December 1991, the Bosnia and Herzegovina Presidency voted, five in favour and two against, to seek independence and international recognition for the republic. 'It was independence or remaining in a 'rump' Yugoslavia, which the majority of our citizens would never accept', a Presidency spokeswoman said. It was also the first step towards war. The two votes against independence were the two Serbs.

A referendum on independence in Bosnia and Herzegovina, held on 28 February–1 March 1992, seemed to be a success for Izetbegović. Virtually all of the 63% of the electorate who participated voted in favour of independence. However, the poll revealed the strength of Serb extremists, who, on the night of 1 March put up barricades around Sarajevo in protest against the referendum. Although the Serbs claimed the actions were in retaliation for the killing of a Serb in Sarajevo's Old Town, as he left a wedding party, the action was clearly planned in advance. The siege was a formidable display of Serb military might and a portent of events to come. The barricades were dismantled on 3 March, after a night of large civilian protests in Sarajevo. The authorities wrongly concluded that the Serbs could be swayed by civic demonstrations. In fact, they were emboldened by the realization of how easy it was to paralyse the capital.

Immediately the results of the referendum were announced, President Izetbegović declared the independence of Bosnia and Herzegovina, although the Assembly did not ratify this until the following month. In the interval between the referendum and the declaration of independence by parliament, on 5 April 1992, the situation in Bosnia and Herzegovina quickly degenerated towards full-scale ethnic warfare between Muslims and Croats on one side and Serbs on the other. On 6 April, the day the EC gave recognition to the new country, the Bosnia and Herzegovina Government declared a state of emergency. This was after Serb gunmen, based inside the Holiday Inn Hotel in Sarajevo, fired shots into a crowd of some 20,000 peace demonstrators and killed a student. One day later the Serb leadership declared an independent 'Serbian Republic of Bosnia and Herzegovina', based in the former Olympic skiing resort of Pale, a suburb of Sarajevo. The siege of Sarajevo was resumed in earnest.

The leaders of Bosnia and Herzegovina declared independence without any serious military preparations. In eastern Bosnia the Serbs assumed control over large areas, encountering little or no resistance. Muslim villagers were, it was alleged, indiscriminately killed. On 9 April Zvornik, the largest town of eastern Bosnia, fell to Serb forces. Along the river Drina, the border between Bosnia and Herzegovina and Serbia, YPA units and Serb irregulars seized one town after another. At Višegrad a local Muslim commander vainly tried to slow the Serb advance by threatening to destroy a large dam. In Foča, where it was believed several thousand Muslims were massacred by Serbs in the Second World War, Muslim forces surrendered their weapons. Two small and isolated Muslim towns in the east—Srebrenica and Goražde—held out, but they were surrounded. Meanwhile, quite apart from the many Muslims killed outright in the Serb advance, there was widespread reporting of thousands more being herded into detention centres, near Brčko, in northern Bosnia, and at Omarska and Manjaca, in north-eastern Bosnia. There, many of the prisoners were mistreated and killed, prompting protests from the international community.

While the Serbs were securing control over northern and eastern Bosnia and Herzegovina, large parts of in the south and centre of the country, particularly western Herzegovina and southern Bosnia, fell more quietly to Croats. The Croat forces were organized into the Croatian Defence Council, the HVO (Hrvatsko Vijece Obrane). As well as districts with Croat majorities, the HVO assumed power in Muslim areas, without bloodshed. At the time the disorganized local Muslims feared Croat domination much less than death at the hands of the Serbs. In Mostar, the old capital of Herzegovina, a Croat-Muslim force ejected the Serbs from the eastern part of the city. However, the Muslim-Croat alliance soon disintegrated. As the Muslim-dominated official Army of Bosnia and Herzegovina was slowly built up and as the Croats moved towards establishing their own 'autonomous republic', called Herzeg-Bosna, a clash between the two forces could not be postponed for long.

While the Serbs and Croats took over most of Bosnia and Herzegovina within weeks, world attention focused on the desperate plight of Sarajevo, where intense mortar bombardment by the Serbs started on 2 May 1992. The shelling made the work of overseeing the UN peace-keeping operation in Croatia impossible and, on 16 May, most of the UN forces withdrew from the city. On 19 May the YPA announced that it was withdrawing all its units from Bosnia and Herzegovina, with the exception of those based in the Marshal Tito Barracks in Sarajevo, where the soldiers were blockaded by Muslims. On 21 May the UN High Commissioner for Refugees announced that their personnel were also being recalled from Bosnia and Herzegovina, after a series of attacks (reportedly mainly by Serbs) on relief convoys.

Reports of Serb atrocities in Muslim villages and the worsening bombardment of Sarajevo put pressure on the international community to take action over the situation in Bosnia and Herzegovina. There was some consensus that the West had failed to take sufficient action to restrain the Serbs in Croatia and that the same pattern must not be repeated in Bosnia and Herzegovina. On the other hand, the Great Powers were averse to any military intervention in the former Yugoslavia. On 26 May 1992 a massacre in central Sarajevo shocked world opinion; over 20 civilians were killed by an exploding mortar bomb as they queued for water. On 29 May the UN finally acted: the Security Council voted to implement wide-ranging sanctions on the 'rump' Yugoslavia (Serbia and Montenegro), including an embargo on petroleum, the suspension of air-traffic links and a boycott on sporting events and contacts. Milošević was defiant and declared that sanctions were, 'the price Serbia has to pay for supporting Serbs outside Serbia'.

Sanctions did not deter the Bosnian Serb commander, Gen. Ratko Mladić, who had assumed control of the Serb forces in Bosnia and Herzegovina upon the orders of Milošević, having already commanded in Croatia. The assaults on Sarajevo increased in number and intensity. The evacuation of the last YPA soldiers from the Sarajevo barracks, on 5 June 1992, was followed by the worst ever bombardment of the city. However, the more the Serbs bombed, the more the UN came under heavy pressure, especially from outraged Muslim countries, to end the Serb siege. On 7 June, amid heavy fighting in Sarajevo, the Secretary-General of the UN approved a plan to send 1,100 peace keepers to secure the airport of Sarajevo and to open an air link. On 10 June a convoy under a Canadian general, Lewis Mackenzie, set off from Belgrade for Sarajevo, to start work on reopening the airport. Heavy fighting around the city threatened to thwart the mission, but, at beginning of July, after a dramatic visit to Sarajevo by the French President, François Mitterrand, the airport opened for aid flights.

War and the imposition of sanctions interrupted but did not end the diplomatic process. On 20 August 1992 representatives of the Serbs, the Muslims and the Croats attended a conference in London (United Kingdom), chaired by the British Prime Minister, John Major. However, this was overshadowed by reports of Serb-run detention camps. Western human-rights organizations claimed that up to 170,000 Muslims and Croats were being held and that as many as 20,000 had been killed, while television footage provided pictures which shocked many around the world. In spite of the public furore, however, no explicit moves were made against Serbia by the international community. The Serbs promised to transfer control of the camps to the International Red Cross, but otherwise the London Conference achieved little change in Bosnia and Herzegovina. The Serbs proceeded to gain more land from the Croats and Muslims, securing a corridor across northern Bosnia, linking their strongholds around Banja Luka to Serbia, through Derventa, Bosanski Brod and Odžak. In central Bosnia and Herzegovina the Serbs took Jajce, symbolically important as the medieval captial of Bosnia and the town where Communist Yugoslavia was founded, in 1943.

By the end of 1992 and into early 1993, with the onset of winter, the outgunned and hungry Muslim enclaves in eastern Bosnia began to succumb one by one. The small enclaves were simply conquered. UN-negotiated surrender agreements prevented massacres of larger communities in Srebrenica and Zepa. In central and south-western Bosnia and Herzegovina the alliance between the Muslims and Croats disintegrated. There was growing pressure for the warring parties to come to an agreement dividing the republic on ethnic lines and the different groups wished to gain as much territory as possible before a final settlement was negotiated. In addition, the Croats resented the influx of vast numbers of Muslim refugees from Serb-held territories into Travnik, Bugojno and Mostar, which transformed the ethnic balance. In April 1993 simmering discontent erupted into full-scale warfare in central Bosnia and in Herzegovina (Mostar). The more numerous Muslims secured control of Travnik, Bugojno and most of central Bosnia, leaving the Croats isolated in part of the Lašva valley, in Vitez and Busovača. In Mostar, the conflict was to continue for most of the rest of that year.

In spite of these territorial gains at the expense of the Croats, pressure on Izetbegović to accept a peace deal unfavourable to the Muslims was growing. Cyrus Vance (UN envoy) and Lord Owen (EC envoy) proposed a settlement for Bosnia and Herzegovina, loosely based on ethnic divisions, splitting the republic into 10 autonomous provinces. The Muslims (43.7% of the population, according to the 1991 census) were to get three provinces and 37% of the territory. Sarajevo was to be an open city. The Serbs were to return much of the territory they had seized. Milošević, finally impressed by mounting threats of Western military intervention, pledged support for this 'Vance-Owen Plan' and said he would close the border with Bosnia and Herzegovina if the Bosnian Serbs rejected it. Nevertheless, Karadžić refused absolutely to countenance the Plan and, on 19 May 1993, a Bosnian-Serb referendum against the produced an overwhelming vote against the Vance-Owen Plan. The Serbs succeeded in outfacing international pressure. The West retreated from its threats of intervention and at the end of May, at a summit meeting in Washington, DC (USA), between the foreign ministers of the France, Russia, Spain, the United Kingdom the USA, the Vance-Owen scheme was abandoned. Instead the Western Powers pledged to safeguard six 'safe areas' for Muslims (a policy adopted, with some success, for the Kurds in Iraq, following the UN intervention of 1991), around Sarajevo, Srebrenica, Zepa, Goražde, Tuzla and Bihac.

The safe-areas scheme shattered Muslim hopes of eventual Western military intervention against the Serbs and left Izetbegović with no obvious strategy to resort to. Rivals in his own party, led by Fikret Abdić, soon opposed the President, publicly demanding peace and criticizing his war policy. The international mediators relentlessly urged him to reach an accommodation with the Serbs and the Croats and satisfy their determination to win separate polities.

In August 1993 a new plan, proposed by Lord Owen and the new UN mediator, Thorvald Stoltenberg (a former Norwegian foreign minister), conceded most Serb demands. Instead of 10 provinces, there were to be three 'republics' (in a nominal 'Union of Bosnia and Herzegovina'). The Serb republic was to retain most of the territory Serb forces had seized in the war. Instead of the 37% of Bosnia and Herzegovina which Muslims were awarded under the Vance-Owen Plan, Owen-Stoltenberg offered only 30%. The Croats were to have only 17%, reflecting the loss of much of central Bosnia to the Muslims over the previous summer months. Again the Muslims demurred.

At the end of 1993 the former Yugoslavia remained gripped by a seemingly insoluble crisis. The Serbs were firmly in control of about one-quarter of Croatia and more than two-thirds of Bosnia and Herzegovina and there was no imminent solution. The cost of the fighting and the consequences of the international sanctions had ruined the Serbian economy, which was experiencing 'hyperinflation', but had strengthened the hold on power within Serbia of Milošević's authoritarian regime. Montenegro, also suffering economically, was witnessing increasing dissatisfaction with the republic's partnership in the Serbian-dominated, 'renewed' Yugoslav federation, the Federal Republic of Yugoslavia. Warfare in Croatia, over the status of the Krajina region, could resume at any time (although a seemingly successful cease-fire agreement was signed in April 1994), while the position of 2m. ethnic Albanians in Serbia's troubled Kosovo region (Kosovo-Metohija province) remained a source of potential strife. In Macedonia too there were tensions with an Albanian minority, in addition to the instability caused by the continued failure of the Western Powers to recognize the country under the name of 'Macedonia', owing to Greek nationalist fears (Greece was in the EC—or, as it was known from November 1993, the European Union). Even without the risk of other countries becoming embroiled and although hundreds of thousands had been killed and millions of people driven from their homes in the previous two years, the bloodshed in the former Yugoslavia seemed far from over. Even the new Federation of Bosnia and Herzegovina, proclaimed on 31 March 1994, which institutionalized the Croat-Muslim alliance (revived in the USA by an agreement signed in Washington, DC), did not resolve the dispute with the Serbs. Moreover, this US involvement, together with the threat of NATO intervention (air power was used against Serb ground forces in April 1994), prompted Russia's return to Balkan politics and its indication of sympathy with the Orthodox Serbs.

THE SOVIET STATE AND ITS DEMISE

Dr RACHEL WALKER

The Union of Soviet Socialist Republics (USSR) was in existence for about 70 years, its history effectively beginning in 1917, when Lenin (Vladimir Ilych Ulyanov, 1870–1924) and the Bolsheviks took power, and ending in December 1991, when Mikhail Gorbachev finally resigned as the last President of the USSR. For about 46 of those years the USSR was one of the world's two superpowers, engaged in an 'arms race' and a struggle for global influence with the USA. By the 1970s Soviet might appeared to be assured and, even as late as 199O, no one predicted that the country could cease to exist. In the mid-1990s the world was still adjusting to the consequences of Soviet disintegration.

THE ORIGINS OF THE SOVIET STATE

The USSR formally came into existence on 30 December 1922. At that time it basically consisted of four states (or Union Republics, as they were to become known): the Soviet Socialist Republics (SSRs) of Belarus (Byelorussia) and Ukraine, the Transcaucasian Soviet Federative Socialist Republic (TSFSR) and the Russian Soviet Federative Socialist Republic (RSFSR or Russian Federation), which was by far the largest. The Union was, in principle, based on equality between the republics, but, in practice, was dominated by the RSFSR and, later, by the centralized structures of the planning system and of the Communist Party of the Soviet Union (CPSU). The number of constituent Union Republics was subsequently increased, both through territorial acquisition (Moldavia—Moldova—and the Baltic states of Estonia, Latvia and Lithuania, annexed in 1939 under the Nazi-Soviet Pact) and through the administrative redefinition of internal boundaries. Thus, TSFSR was dissolved in 1936, Armenia, Azerbaijan and Georgia each becoming full Union Republics, while the Central Asian republics of Kyrgyzstan, Tajikistan, Turkmenistan and Uzbekistan essentially emerged from the administrative dismemberment of Turkestan during the 1920s and 1930s.

The new polity was extremely weak and unstable. The six years between 1917 and 1923 were marked by war—the First World War, from which Russia withdrew at great cost in 1918), civil war (1918–21), armed foreign intervention (1918–21)—and its catastrophic consequences. By 1921 the economy had been devastated. Industrial output in the main branches of manufacture was down to one-fifth of its 1913 level. Agriculture had been similarly reduced. Quite apart from the losses sustained by the army or in the fighting, millions of people died from famine and disease. The conditions in which the Bolsheviks came to power presented it with many seemingly intractable problems. A Party dedicated to the construction of Communism—a utopian society based on classless equality, social harmony and an abundance of material goods—found itself having to manage a deficit war economy riven by civil war and lacking in almost anything. The instruments of state (civil service, police and armed forces) had largely disintegrated with the collapse of tsarism, in 1917, or their functionaries were hostile to the new regime. Large areas of the country were beyond control. Russia was internationally isolated and under threat from far more developed industrial powers which, as their intervention indicated, were inimical to the existence of a socialist regime.

These problems and the Bolshevik attempts to find solutions to them generated a series of structural tensions and contradictions which were to beset the Soviet system for the rest of its existence. The fundamental problem confronting the Party was, and remained, how to construct a highly industrialized and technologically advanced socialist society in a country which was economically backward, overwhelmingly populated by peasant farmers and internationally isolated. The commitment to the construction of socialism entailed a commitment to democratic forms and to a certain level of egalitarianism that the Party could never quite abandon, since it claimed to rule in the people's interests and justified its existence on the basis that it was bringing them nearer to Communism. On the other hand, there was the commitment to industrialize and modernize, the necessary precursor to the creation of material abundance, and there was the need to build and maintain the country's defences. Both these requirements entailed a commitment to high levels of centralized direction and managerial control, as well as insinuating a systemic imperative towards the promotion of wage and incentive differentials and the introduction of market forms of economic regulation. It was these contradictions, between democracy and control, the demands of industrialization and the demands of social welfare, the imperatives of directed growth and of the search for economic efficiency and productivity, that were to animate many of the policies and reform programmes introduced by successive Party Secretaries up to, and including, Mikhail Gorbachev himself. These contradictions were present from the outset, in the strategies adopted by the Bolsheviks to save the regime in the early years.

The last Russian Tsar, Nicholas II, abdicated in March 1917 and a Provisional Government assumed authority. The Bolsheviks seized power from this administration in a *coup d'état*, on 25 October (New Style date: 7 November) 1917. However, between 1918 and 1921, known as the period of War Communism, the Bolsheviks only succeeded in retaining their hold on power through tight internal organization and the dedicated support of the urban working class, combined with the ruthless centralization of the country's political economy and the brutal suppression of all opposition. This strategy won them the civil war and enabled them to repel the foreign invaders, but at the cost of some of the outlying districts of the Russian Empire and, more importantly, of their working-class support and of increasing dissension within the Party. By February 1921 the evident loss of working-class support (symbolized by the Kronstadt rebellion) and the fact that the economy was in dire need of reconstruction forced a change of direction.

In March 1921 Lenin and the Bolshevik leadership introduced the New Economic Policy (NEP), which established a mixed economy. The state retained control of heavy industry, banking and foreign trade, but abolished the state monopoly of small-and medium-scale manufacturing, retail trade and services. It also abandoned grain-requisitioning in favour of a much less punitive tax in kind and restored freedom of private trade. The result was fairly rapid economic regeneration, but no real extension of democratic freedom. The Party did not relinquish its grip on political power, although the repressive depredations ('the Red Terror') of the Cheka, the secret police of Felix Dzerzhinsky were reduced and culture and the arts allowed to flourish.

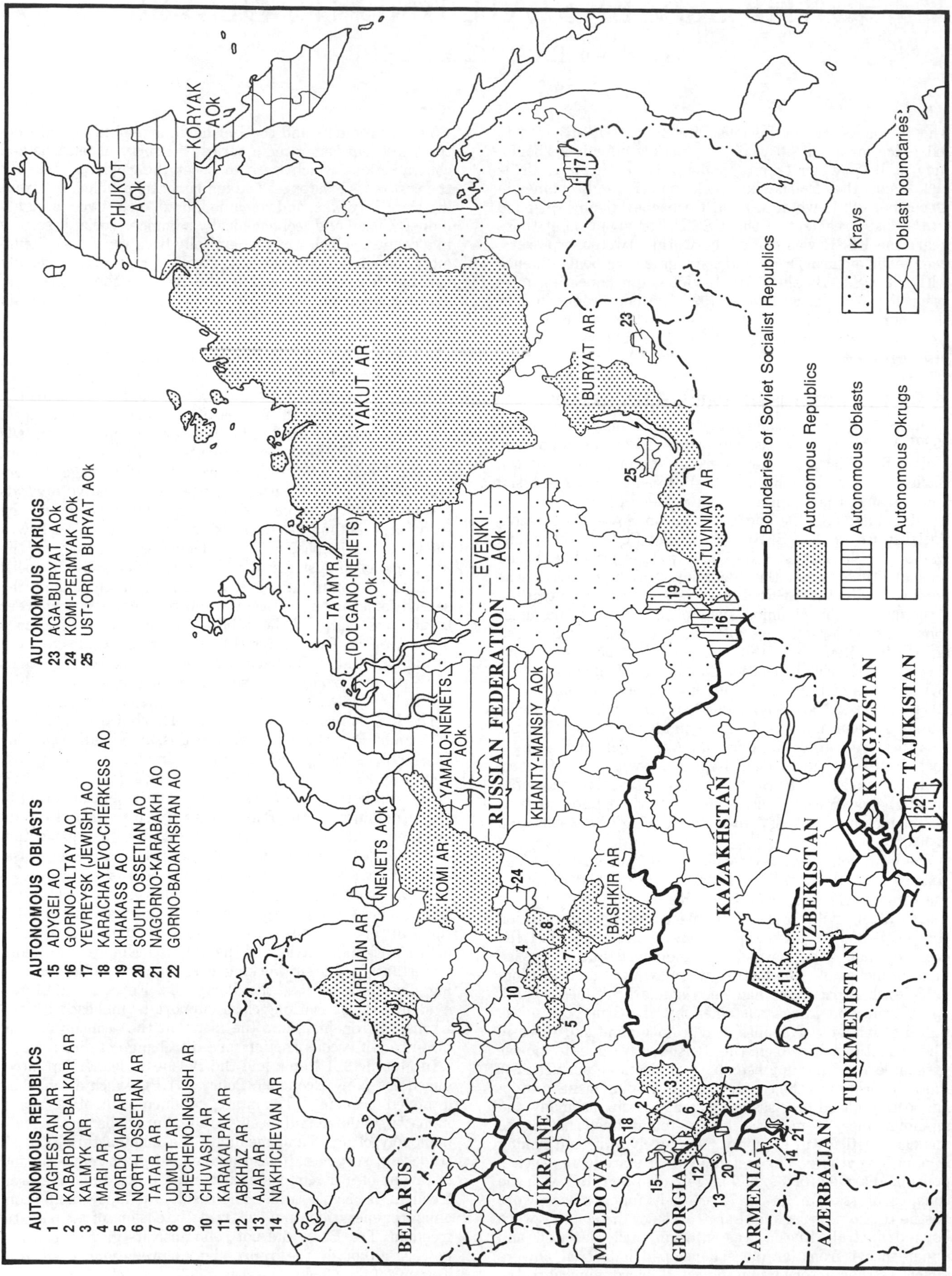
AUTONOMOUS REPUBLICS
1 DAGHESTAN AR
2 KABARDINO-BALKAR AR
3 KALMYK AR
4 MARI AR
5 MORDOVIAN AR
6 NORTH OSSETIAN AR
7 TATAR AR
8 UDMURT AR
9 CHECHENO-INGUSH AR
10 CHUVASH AR
11 KARAKALPAK AR
12 ABKHAZ AR
13 AJAR AR
14 NAKHICHEVAN AR
AUTONOMOUS OBLASTS
15 ADYGEI AO
16 GORNO-ALTAY AO
17 YEVREYSK (JEWISH) AO
18 KARACHAYEVO-CHERKESS AO
19 KHAKASS AO
20 SOUTH OSSETIAN AO
21 NAGORNO-KARABAKH AO
22 GORNO-BADAKHSHAN AO
AUTONOMOUS OKRUGS
23 AGA-BURYAT AOk
24 KOMI-PERMYAK AOk
25 UST-ORDA BURYAT AOk
CHUKOT AOk
KORYAK AOk
YAKUT AR
BURYAT AR
TUVINIAN AR
EVENKI AOk
TAYMYR (DOLGANO-NENETS) AOk
YAMALO-NENETS AOk
RUSSIAN FEDERATION
KHANTY-MANSIY AOk
NENETS AOk
KOMI AR
KARELIAN AR
BASHKIR AR
KAZAKHSTAN
UZBEKISTAN
KYRGYZSTAN
TAJIKISTAN
TURKMENISTAN
BELARUS
UKRAINE
MOLDOVA
GEORGIA
ARMENIA
AZERBAIJAN
Boundaries of Soviet Socialist Republics
Autonomous Republics
Autonomous Oblasts
Autonomous Okrugs
Krays
Oblast boundaries

Political Boundaries of the USSR (1991)

The introduction of the NEP initiated a major debate within the Party about the long-term developmental strategy of the Soviet state. On one side were those who were committed to the introduction of some form of political and industrial democracy, to the raising of general living standards and to economic policies which would maximize the support and co-operation of the peasantry with the goals of the Bolshevik regime. These people, notably Nikolay Bukharin (1888–1938), were broadly in favour of the long-term continuation of the NEP as a model for balanced growth and consensual town–country relations. Against them were those who were critical of the NEP and the burgeoning private sector, not to mention the social and economic inequalities which it rapidly gave rise to, and they were extremely suspicious of the private peasant economy. These people advocated rapid industrialization at the expense of the peasantry and at the expense of democratic forms for the foreseeable future. This argument was most clearly put forward by Leon Trotsky (1879–1940). The only thing that united all the sides in the debate was the realization that, in the absence of successful proletarian revolutions in the industrialized countries (immediate hopes ended with the Communist failures in Germany in 1923), the USSR would have to survive alone. The debate was wide-ranging and long, but inconclusive. However, its import was significantly raised by Lenin's illness and increasing incapacitation, from late 1921, and his death in January 1924.

The arguments over long-term strategy and tactics, therefore, became intertwined with the power struggle for Lenin's succession. In the end it was not so much theory or intellect that won in either struggle, but the appeals of Stalin (Iosif Vissarionovich Dzhugashvili, 1879–1953) to patriotism and common sensibilities and his superior organizational cunning. Stalin's concept of 'socialism in one country' appealed to the growing numbers of younger Party members, both because it was easy to understand and because it emphasized what had already been achieved. It stressed that the Party and the people, united in a common aim, were perfectly capable of building Soviet socialism by their own efforts. This message earned Stalin a great deal of support at the lower levels of the Party, which he was then able to manipulate to his own advantage. Stalin proved far more adept at political infighting than his opponents. He replaced Lenin as the Party's General Secretary in 1922 (a purely administrative post at the time) and, thereafter, ensured that he became a member of all the key committees. This enabled him to staff key policy-making organs with his own supporters and, thus, create an institutional bias in his favour. He had consolidated his position as Party leader by 1929. In the event, Stalin abandoned the NEP and resorted to an infinitely more extreme version of the rapid growth model advocated by Trotsky than anyone could possibly have anticipated.

STALINISM

Stalinism was justifiably known as the 'revolution from above'. It transformed Soviet society and resolved the developmental dilemmas of the Soviet state by simply, and quite literally, breaking through and attempting to eliminate all the physical, moral, social, political and economic constraints which others had regarded as limits. The essential strategy of Stalinism was intense industrialization, with massive emphasis on heavy industry and defence, and the rapid elimination of the private peasant economy through forced collectivization. Both of these policies were achieved by means of the extreme centralization of power in the state and the institutionalization of coercion and terror as instruments of rule. The costs of this developmental solution were incalculable in terms of human life and the distortions and imbalances which were built into the political economy of the country. But it did succeed, in a very short time, in creating a military-industrial base that not only enabled the USSR to survive the Second World War, but also enabled it to become the world's second superpower in the post-War years.

Stalinism can be divided into three periods, of which the first is most important, because it was then that the basic structure of the Stalinist system was established. From 1929 until 1941, when Germany invaded the USSR, was the period of 'high' Stalinism, the 'revolution from above' proper. During these years monopolistic state control was extended to cover all spheres of Soviet life. The economy as a whole was recentralized under the control of the state planning organs, eliminating virtually all private activity. Economic development was governed by successive Five-Year Plans, which operated on the teleological principle that planning can be used to escape physical and resource constraints (as opposed to 'genetic' planning, which assumes that planning aims to optimize solutions within given constraints). This philosophy was reflected in plan targets which were hopelessly optimistic. The operation of teleological planning was reinforced by coercion, fear, increasingly draconian labour laws and the use of income differentials, which gave every individual both positive and negative incentives to try and fulfil impossible plan targets, by whatever means, for fear of retribution if they did not. The aim of Soviet planning thereafter became not to achieve balanced and ordered economic development, but to maximize growth in the priority sectors and extract as much as possible from the system, at whatever cost. The costs were incalculable, in both the short and the long term, because this strategy resulted in structural inefficiency, waste, devastating environmental damage and the chronic under-resourcing of the country's infrastructure and agriculture, service and light-industry sectors.

Agriculture was transformed by forced collectivization, which began in 1930 and proceeded in successive phases until about 1936, by which time some 90% of the rural population had been collectivized. It simultaneously destroyed and restructured rural life. All the more prosperous and, therefore, more successful and efficient farmers and their families were either deported to Siberia or eliminated by famine. Accurate figures are impossible to come by, but well-informed Western estimates reckon that some 2m. families, or some 10m. individuals, were destroyed in this way. Millions more were caught up in the process of denunciations and in the famines which occurred (allegedly as the result of deliberate engineering) in Ukraine and the Volga basin in 1932 and 1933. The effects on the country's livestock were equally disastrous. The numbers of cattle, pigs, sheep and goats in the country halved between 1928 and 1933, as farmers ate what they owned to prevent expropriation. Livestock numbers were not restored to their former levels until the mid-1950s, which meant that the population as a whole suffered terrible shortages of meat and milk for the next twenty years. The only concession made to the peasantry was that they were allowed to retain small private plots on which they could farm for their own needs. In the event, the private plots proved to be the most productive sector of the agricultural economy.

Life in the towns and cities was not much better for the majority. The urban working class virtually trebled in size between 1928 and 1940, as peasants fled the countryside. The urban infrastructure, in terms of housing and sanitation especially, was totally inadequate to the demand. Wages were low and working conditions were frequently appalling. Above all, failure to conform in any detail threatened every individual with the possibility of arbitrary arrest, especially at the height of the purges, in 1936–38. In the event, the resources for industrialization were largely extracted from the expanding working class, which had to endure poor housing and social provision and was constantly expected to produce more for low rewards.

Coercive political control was increasingly exerted over education, culture, science, the arts and the media from 1930 onwards. National cultures in the non-Russian areas were 'russified' and undermined, by campaigns against religion as well as by the destruction wrought during collectivization. Above all, the purges, which began in a small way with the Shakhty (a mining area in the Donbass—some mining engineers were accused of sabotage) trial of 1928 and reached their height in 1936–38, set in train a murderous process of show trials, summary arrests and executions (or exile to the rapidly expanding GULag or Gulag—the name of the Chief Administration of Corrective Labour Camps) which eventually affected almost all sectors of the population. It is impossible to quantify the effects of the purges with any precision. They certainly destroyed large sections of the country's élite. Certainly there were few families remaining entirely unaffected. Anyone who posed a threat to Stalin, however remote, was effectively eliminated. Thus, for example, the succession struggle of the mid-1920s was completed in 1935–38. All the leading Bolsheviks of the time, including almost every member of every 'opposition' or 'fraction' which had ever existed, was arrested and executed. The qualitative effects of the purges are less difficult to estimate. Fear and the corresponding imperative to conform, at whatever cost, were imprinted on the psyche of the Soviet population for years to come. This was certainly claimed by many intellectuals after 1985, once *glasnost* ('openness' or 'publicity') enabled them to speak out. By the same token, absolute power passed to Stalin and, below him, to the internal security organs.

The new political élite was also formed during this period. There was massive and rapid upward social mobility. The processes of industrialization created an inexhaustible demand for skilled personnel. The educational system was expanded rapidly as a consequence, although the quality of education actually delivered was often very poor. The massive growth of state institutions absorbed huge numbers of people. And, needless to say, the purges opened up a variety of avenues for promotion. As a consequence, large numbers of peasants and workers, those who were adept exploiting the system, were able to better themselves very rapidly. They became known as the vydvizhentsy (or the upwardly socially mobile). They were to form the new political, administrative and technological élites for the next 40 or so years. Nikita Khrushchev (1894–1971), who replaced Stalin as Party First Secretary, in 1953, was a classic example of the peasant who prospered during the 1930s. Even as late as 1980 about one-half of the CPSU Politburo was made up of people with a vydvizhentsy background (including Leonid Brezhnev). The real generational break only came with the election of Mikhail Gorbachev (born in 1931) to the Party leadership in 1985.

In short, high Stalinism effectively created a new society, although it traumatized the various peoples of the USSR in the process. The second period, the war years from 1941 to 1945, visited new deprivations on the Soviet population. Much of what had been laboriously constructed during the previous decade was damaged or destroyed. Ukraine, Belarus and most of European Russia were devastated. Twenty-five million people were rendered homeless; the economy was gravely distorted by military production and seriously depleted; and more than 20m. people lost their lives. This was to have long-term demographic effects. Victory was finally achieved because Stalin proved adept at changing his policy in order to generate a patriotic sense of national unity. Moreover, because the central planning system was uniquely geared to the rapid mobilization of human and material resources, industry and population could be quickly evacuated eastward after the German invasion. Also, the brutality of the Nazi regime quickly persuaded many of those who had been sufficiently disaffected with the Soviet regime to welcome the Germans to change their minds, once the realities of German occupation became apparent. By the end of the Second World War the Soviet economy was in desperate need of reconstruction and the Soviet population was in desperate need of some improvement in its situation.

However, the years from 1946 to 1953 (when Stalin died) brought little relief from the hardship. All the repressive features of the Stalinist system were reimposed. Moreover, Stalinism was extended to countries that had not previously experienced it. The new territories annexed during the War—the three Baltic states, Moldova (seized from Romania in 1940) and Transcarpathian Ukraine (Carpatho-Ruthenia, annexed from Czechoslovakia in 1945) were subjected to repression and rapid restructuring along Stalinist lines. Much the same applied, over a longer period and with variations, to the countries of central Europe and the Balkans which had come into the Soviet orbit as a result of the War. From 1948 Bulgaria, Czechoslovakia, Hungary, Poland and Romania, as well as eastern Germany, were under strict Soviet control and developing political economies that mirrored the Soviet one, and laying the foundation of the 'Eastern Europe' bloc.

KHRUSHCHEV AND DESTALINIZATION

By the time of Stalin's death, in March 1953, it was becoming clear to the Soviet leadership that the system had become intolerably repressive and that some change was unavoidable. To begin with, the political élite was under threat from the internal security organs, headed by Lavrentii Beria (1899–1953). Almost the first act of the leadership after Stalin's death was Beria's summary arrest and execution and the exertion of control over the security empire. As a consequence mass terror was tacitly abandoned as an instrument of rule. Secondly, it was also clear that the system was in incipient crisis. The Gulag, by now containing about 8m. people, was becoming increasingly difficult and expensive to run and was absorbing far too many potentially productive workers, who were needed in an economy that was desperately short of able-bodied men. Agriculture was in a parlous state, as were the light-industry and service sectors. Heavy industry was perhaps the only sector which managed to register any real improvement.

Finding solutions to these enormous difficulties was not easy. The search generated considerable (and, for the times, remarkable) public debate about the direction of reform, especially in 1953–57, when Khrushchev had not fully succeeded in consolidating his power. Greater reliance on market mechanisms and material incentives, more decentralization and the promotion of private initiative within the collective system all figured (tentatively) as possible solutions. In the event, however, Khrushchev's reforms dealt with symptoms rather than causes and, consequently, failed to address the fundamental problems of Soviet centralized command planning and political control. With hindsight, the most significant thing about the Khrushchev period was the electrifying effect of his denunciation of Stalin on the younger generations—people like Gorbachev, then in his mid-20s—both in the USSR and Eastern Europe, for whom the possibility of change now became thinkable.

There was a certain logic to Khrushchev's reforms. At its centre was the critique of Stalin. This critique served two purposes. It enabled Khrushchev to outflank Stalin's closest associates, who were most closely implicated in his crimes and most resistant to change, thus allowing Khrushchev to consolidate his position by 1957. Secondly, it enabled him to distance the Party from the worst Stalinist excesses, notably the purges. However, both the critique itself and the tacit abandonment of mass terror (although not of coercion) necessitated a search for a new legitimacy, a new means of harnessing the population to the goals of the regime. This was found in a return to Lenin's more utopian formulas. Thus, the new Party Programme, presented at the 22nd Party Congress, in 1961, promised the achievement of Communism by 1980. This entailed creating the material abundance whereby everyone would receive from society according to need rather than work, which, in turn, meant paying some attention to consumption as well as production and eliminating the grosser forms of inequality which had emerged under Stalin. It also entailed the 'withering away of the state' and its replacement by 'organs of public self-government', which meant reducing the power and the size of the central party-state bureaucracies and opening them up to popular scrutiny. Most of Khrushchev's policies followed quite logically from these premises.

From the outset Khrushchev attended to all the areas that had previously been neglected. For example, investment in agriculture increased four-fold between 1953 and 1964. Restrictions on private plots were eased and collective farmers were paid much higher state procurement prices for their produce. Between 1955 and 1964 the USSR's housing stock nearly doubled. Social security benefits were greatly improved. Most of Stalin's draconian labour laws were abolished and minimum wages were raised. In education, the grosser inequalities were removed, the system was greatly expanded and standards were raised. Overall, the general standard of living and the quality of life improved quite markedly, although levels of investment, and the return on investment, were never enough to keep pace with demand. Even in the labour camps living conditions were ameliorated and a process of release and rehabilitation ensued. Between 1954 and 1958 over 2m. political prisoners were set free. Khrushchev sought, in part, to pay for these new expenditures by reducing the intensity of the Cold War, through his policy of 'peaceful coexistence', which advocated extended co-operation with the capitalist world, correspondingly reducing the level of defence expenditure and of investment in the military-industrial complex. This met with great resistance from the military and was, therefore, only partially achieved.

Khrushchev also sought to inject more dynamism into the economy, by attempting to reduce both its grotesque over-centralization and the enormous power of the great industrial ministries. However, any reliance on market-type mechanisms was rejected in favour of a rather sweeping and contradictory attempt to decentralize the system without abandoning central planning. Khrushchev's solution was to abolish the central ministries, in 1957, and replace them with 105 regional economic councils (sovnarkhozy), which were to be co-ordinated by larger republican bodies and the central planning agencies. This created enormous confusion, since it proved well-nigh impossible to plan and co-ordinate the activities of 105 regional councils. It consequently made matters worse rather than better.

Popular participation in the system was encouraged in a number of ways. The decision-making process, both at the top and lower down the system, was opened up to the participation of specialists. The powers of local soviets and trade unions were enhanced. Comrades courts were established, to encourage popular participation in the adjudication of the law at least for minor offences. Volunteer patrols (druzhiny) were created to bolster the work of the militia and people were encouraged to inform on official misbehaviour. Legal reform and the introduction of a new criminal code, in 1958, went some way to protecting the citizen against the state, by regularizing the law and removing some of the possibilities for arbitrary rule. Finally, the Party itself was reformed. Terms of office were fixed for the first time in 1961, which greatly undermined the security of long-standing Party bureaucrats. The Party's internal life was revived and regularized and the participation of ordinary Party members in the decision-making processes was encouraged. In addition, Khrushchev sought to bring the Party closer to production, by bifurcating its committees at regional and district level into 'industrial' and 'agricultural' departments, in 1962. These measures did democratize the CPSU to a very limited extent, but they also disrupted the Party's ability to function as an executive co-ordinating body within the economy, particularly in the case of the 'bifurcation' reform.

Although these reforms went a long way to improving the general prosperity of the USSR, they also generated much chaos and resistance, which was, ultimately, to lead to Khrushchev's downfall, in 1964. Matters were made worse by Khrushchev's tendency to resort to Stalinist methods, as in the 'Virgin Lands' and maize campaigns of the 1950s and his adoption of an increasingly arbitrary and wilful approach to policy-making as his plans encountered resistance. The fundamental difficulty was that the reforms did not go far enough and, therefore, combined opposing principles which worked against themselves. The central ministries were abolished in an attempt to decentralize managerial control, but central planning was retained. Popular participation was encouraged, but the Party retained its dominant role in society. The result was growing confusion and frustration and the eventual disaffection of strategic groups. By 1964 Khrushchev was deeply unpopular and his removal from office, in October, was not greatly mourned. It is an indication of how much the country had changed, however, that Khrushchev was merely voted out of office by the Central Committee and sent into quiet retirement.

THE BREZHNEV PERIOD: CONSOLIDATION OR STAGNATION?

Leonid Brezhnev (1906–82) replaced Khrushchev as First Secretary of the CPSU in October 1964. The first step of the new leadership was to reverse the more disruptive of Khrushchev's reforms. The central ministries were reinstated and the sovnarkhozy disbanded. The Party was reunited and the limit to terms of office was quickly removed. Stalin and Stalinism were quietly rehabilitated at the ideological level and Khrushchev's extravagant promises about the achievement of Communism were quietly abandoned in favour of the new concept of 'developed socialism' (which essentially promised nothing except the continued dominance of the CPSU and the state in the life of society). Not all of Khrushchev's policies were reversed, however, largely because they had now become part of the élite consensus on what needed to be done. Agriculture remained important on the political agenda and agricultural investment remained high. Khrushchev's social policies were also sustained through increasing state investment in social benefits, housing, education and health. Khrushchev's commitment to legal proceduralism was retained, as was, in general terms, the commitment to some level of popular participation in the system. There was also something of a return to Khrushchev's early foreign policy of peaceful coexistence under the guise of the new concept of *détente* emerged at the end of the 1960s.

The period of Brezhnev's rule was marked by a high level of stability. This partly reflected Brezhnev's attitude to government, which was consensual and managerial, where Khrushchev's had been confrontational. It also reflected his method of dealing with incipient policy conflict within the élite by giving in to demands rather than opposing them. This dual approach produced a type of neo-corporatist politics in which the main institutional interests were able to exert considerable influence over the making and implementation of policy, under the overall tutelage and supervision of the Party leadership. It also provided the Soviet population with 20-odd years of much needed calm after decades of upheaval. However, this was only achieved at great systemic cost. The Soviet political economy became enormously conservative, increasingly corrupt and inefficient and stiflingly conformist.

In the first place, Brezhnev was satisfying the politico-military élite's desire for strategic parity with the USA (which was achieved by 1975, roughly). There were also industrial demands for greater investment. As well as these two major demands, the USSR was sustaining high levels of expenditure on civilian consumption and social welfare, thus placing enormous burdens on the state budget, which could not be sustained by declining growth rates over the long-term. By 1985, with the growth rate at, effectively nought, the 'guns versus butter' choice was becoming inescapable (that is, the choice between military and civilian expenditure).

Secondly, the institutional interests in the system became increasingly powerful and, in many cases, operated almost autonomously of the central authorities. This was particularly the case with the massive ministerial empires in the military-industrial complex. It also applied, to a lesser extent, to republican and regional Party élites, who acquired a great deal of latitude in deciding how central policies would be implemented and were able to wield enormous power over their populations. Moreover, the total absence of any accountability meant that Party and state officials could exploit their positions for personal gain almost with impunity (subject only to retaining the favour of their superiors) and frequently did so.

Thirdly, any impulse to meaningful structural reform was lost because it was too threatening to these increasingly powerful vested interests. Efforts to make the civilian economy more responsive and efficient did not entirely cease, but they invariably foundered on bureaucratic opposition and were, in any case, always very limited in scope. As a result, with the reversal of Khrushchev's reforms, the economic system returned to its Stalinist essentials. In the context of a relatively complex and differentiated economy the net result was gradual degeneration. Productivity declined, the return on investment diminished drastically, product innovation became increasingly difficult and the planning system itself was slowly transformed. This last became a process of bargaining between different levels in which the key to getting things done was provided by the long-established and gradually expanding informal and unofficial networks of contacts between officials; these networks were based on the barter of favours, goods, and black-market access.

The Brezhnev leadership attempted to circumvent this domestic *impasse* by promoting foreign ties, in order to enable the rapid importation of technological expertise, consumer goods and credits. One of the functions of *détente* was precisely to facilitate this. It was, however, an entirely inadequate solution, since imports could not match demand and, in any case, the Soviet economy could not absorb advanced Western technology without degrading it, often quite considerably. The leadership also attempted to impose labour discipline through legal means, social pressure, exhortation and a renewed stress on social conformism. This failed too, because it dealt entirely with symptoms rather than causes.

Finally, the political and intellectual climate, at least in the public sphere, became stultifying. Adherence to the old goals of the CPSU was reduced to formulaic repetition. Selective repression was used against dissident individuals, although very few people were willing to risk themselves, for fear of the punishments that might be visited on them by their immediate superiors and their colleagues. Many sought refuge in 'internal emigration' and 'truth speaking' at home. Good work was still done in the interstices of the system, in small institutes like the Novosibirsk Institute of Economics (the base for specialists like Tatyana Zaslavskaya and Abel Aganbegyan, who were subsequently to become Gorbachev advisers), but this work did not begin to percolate into official circles until after Brezhnev's death.

By 1982 it was becoming clear to a small number of people, inside as well as outside the Party, that the system was decaying and losing the competition with the industrialized world. It was, however, to be another four years, effectively, before anything meaningful was done about this. Yury Andropov (1914–84), who replaced Brezhnev as First Secretary of the CPSU in 1982, focused almost entirely on campaigns to promote discipline in the work place and to reduce alcoholism, which did nothing to effect real change. He was, in any case, both old and dying. Konstantin Chernenko (1911–85), who replaced Andropov, died in March 1985, of emphysema, before he could have much discernable effect.

However, although the succession of Mikhail Gorbachev to be General Secretary of the CPSU, in 1985, marked the accession of a new generation in the Soviet leadership, his first two years in office largely repeated old patterns. Like his predecessors Gorbachev was greatly exercised by the problem of economic growth, efficiency and technological modernization. He initially resorted to classic methods to achieve them. The targets set by the Twelfth Five-Year Plan (1986-1990) were over-optimistic (following the classic teleological model) and placed enormous strains on the system which it could not sustain. Also, it was accompanied by campaigns against alcoholism and 'unearned incomes' which created havoc in the economy. There were some small innovations early on. *Glasnost* entered the political vocabulary and led to more openness about the Party's activities. Also, the idea of 'social justice' was promulgated as a means of attacking official corruption. However, little was done to change the system itself. Where Gorbachev was different from his predecessors, was in that he was absolutely determined to restore the system and willing to learn from his mistakes, at least insofar as he understood them.

REFORM AND REVOLUTION

The reforms that ultimately led to the demise of the USSR did not really begin to emerge until 1987–88 and certainly did not begin to take effect until 1989. The instrumental changes were: the expansion of *glasnost*; the national elections of March 1989 to the new legislature, the all-Union Congress of People's Deputies; the republican and local soviet elections of late 1989 and 1990; the emphasis on law, legal proceduralism and constitutionalism; certain aspects of economic reform, particularly the attempt to decentralize managerial control to the Union Republics; and certain elements of foreign policy ('new thinking'), notably the withdrawal of Soviet support from the Eastern European regimes and its consequences. It was these changes which turned what was effectively another 'revolution from above' in the years 1985–88 into a 'revolution from below' from 1989 onwards.

Gorbachev's overall goal in launching radical *perestroika* ('restructuring'), in 1987–88, was always an economic one: the creation of a modern, innovative industrial economy which could compete on the same terms as the Western capitalist states. He sought to achieve this by radically reducing the country's defence burden—hence the innovations in foreign policy; and by bringing intense pressure to bear on the party-state bureaucracies, both from above and from below, in order to force a real change in their behaviour. Gorbachev's reforms were, therefore, always more limited than they seemed and this was, probably, their most fundamental weakness. Gorbachev did not want to eliminate central planning, but to rationalize it. He wanted to maintain the 'leading role' of the Party in society, but also wanted to make it genuinely popular and reasonably accountable. He did not want to abandon socialism, but to give it real substance. Thus, he resurrected many of the system's old contradictions, prime among them the potential for conflict between the 'Party's will' and the 'people's will', but, unlike his predecessors, took them to their logical conclusion.

As in the case of Khrushchev's reforms, there was a certain ineluctable logic to both economic and political *perestroika*. Gorbachev moved first on the economy. He endeavoured to rationalize and make more efficient the planning system, by reducing the number of central ministries and the number of people employed by them. Ministerial staff were reduced by 46% between 1986 and 1989 and the employees of the USSR State Planning Agency (Gosplan) were reduced by more than one-half between 1986 and 1988. At the same time he also tried to encourage local initiative by decentralizing a certain amount of managerial power to the Union Republics, in July 1987, and by giving greater autonomy to enterprises generally and to private enterprise in the service sectors. He did not, however, abandon the principle of central planning or relinquish central control over such matters as pricing, finance, and so on. These changes slowly but successfully disorganized the old system without actually reforming it. The people at the centre were still obliged to oversee the implementation of the ambitious Twelfth Five-Year Plan, which necessitated continued and detailed goal-setting, but their ability to control the activities of the agencies below them, already very limited by the degeneration of the system, was further reduced by the new elements of autonomy which gradually undermined the old links in the ministerial system of command and control. The introduction of political reform made matters worse for the old Soviet system. The cohesion of the Party as an executive co-ordinating agency was undermined. Also, the constituent Republics of the Soviet federation, and the organs of local government, were given both the grounds and the means for wresting greater autonomy and control from the centre.

By mid-1990 the economic effects of this systemic disorganization were already so severe that a complete market reform appeared to be the only alternative. To begin with, there was a remarkable degree of élite consensus about the need for 'marketization' as a general principle. The consensus foundered, however, on fundamental questions concerning the means and the speed of change and, in particular, the degree of power which would have to be devolved to the Union Republics and to enterprises if a genuine market economy was to be created. By the end of that summer, before the end of 1990, Gorbachev, initially enthusiastic about the proposals contained in the market-orientated '500-day Programme' drawn up by his (and the Russian Government's) closest economic advisers, had withdrawn his support. Economic policy-making simply disintegrated thereafter.

Gorbachev's political reforms were equally partial. Their main aim was to make party-state officials genuinely accountable, and consequently more responsive and efficient, and to restore the CPSU's reputation in society by giving it some genuine democratic basis. The concepts of *glasnost*, 'the law-based state', 'pluralism of opinions' and the introduction of multi-candidate elections, were never intended to enable the possibility of genuine political choice or to effect a real change in the balance of power between Party, state and society. This was indicated by the fact that they were always prefaced by the word 'socialist' and by Gorbachev's repeated insistence that the Soviet people could not renege on the 'socialist choice' which had been made in 1917. Rather, these reforms were intended to subject individual officials to public scrutiny and public sanction, without challenging the institutions for which they worked. In the event, however, Gorbachev's attempts to combine the incompatible principles of Soviet socialism with certain aspects of Western proceduralism served to demonstrate for all to see that the party's rule was illegitimate.

The expansion of *glasnost*, from 1987, was the first of several factors precipitating the Party's loss of credibility. Partly as a result of Gorbachev's own criticisms of the past and partly as a result of his unwillingness to use repressive measures, it proved impossible to contain the flow of information or the burgeoning 'pluralism of opinions' within the bounds that the Party leadership sought to set for them. By 1990 almost nothing was forbidden in public debate.

The March 1989 elections to the new Congress of People's Deputies were the second precipitating factor. The way in which they were organized enabled the Party apparatus to dominate both the electoral process and the membership of the new Congress. At the same time the elections were sufficiently competitive, especially in the large cities, where democrats had managed to organize, to allow for the election of some 300 or so radicals (including Gorbachev's critic, Boris Yeltsin) to the Congress. Of all the many Party officials who stood for election as congressional deputies not many lost, but, where they did (as in Moscow and Leningrad—St Petersburg), they lost spectacularly. Although they did not, thereby, lose their Party positions, their lack of public support was revealed for all to see. These elections traumatized and divided the Party. They also enraged public opinion, which now began to understand that as long as the Party retained its leading role there could be no such thing as genuine democracy: they could not vote for Party officials, but they could not vote the Party out of power.

The third precipitating factor was the first session of the Congress itself (25 May–9 June 1989). As congressional deputies had parliamentary immunity, the radical deputies used this to expand *glasnost* in all directions. In addition, these debates were televised, which helped to politicize enormous numbers of people. Mass miners strikes ensued and the public demand for the abolition of the CPSU's leading role became so insistent, and followed so logically from the reform process, that Gorbachev was eventually forced to capitulate, in February 1990.

The fourth precipitating factor was the republican and local elections of 1989–90, combined with the influence of the Eastern European revolutions during 1989. These elections were much more genuinely competitive, because the Union Republics were allowed to regulate them. The result was massive defeats for republican Party organizations, particularly in the Baltic Republics, where the Communist establishment entirely lost control of the republican legislatures. Moreover, the elections permitted the emergence, for the first time, of governments with a legitimate popular mandate. These new regimes now began not only to assert their rights (as laid out in the Soviet Constitution of 1977, which described the Union Republics as 'sovereign socialist republics'), but to enforce them, by refusing to obey the central authorities in what became known as the 'war of laws' and the 'parade of sovereignties'. By the end of 1990 every Union Republic had issued a declaration of state sovereignty which gave supremacy to republican law over all-Union law and asserted the rights of the republican governments. The liberation of Eastern Europe during 1989 only made them more determined.

The consequences of these changes were fatal for the system. The Party was dismembered as local Communist organizations fought for survival by whatever means they could. The economy was dismembered because republican and local governments simply refused to implement central demands and/or imposed local protectionist measures. Even the structure of Soviet government within the Union Republics was dismembered, as local soviets assumed control in order to promote and defend local interests. Gorbachev's attempts to manage the spiralling crisis by establishing a strong executive presidency, in March 1990, and, belatedly, promising to renegotiate federal relations, simply exacerbated the situation. On the one hand he concentrated even more power in his own person, and on the other hand, promised the Union Republics too little too late. The Soviet presidency and central Soviet institutions were ineffective without the co-operation of the Republics (especially of the Russian Federation) and, by late 1990, the republican authorities had realized this. Consequently, despite Gorbachev's attempts firmly to restore order in late 1990 and early 1991, he was increasingly forced to concede what the majority of the Union Republics (that is, those that did not want to secede from the USSR altogether) now wanted. This was a new Union Treaty, which would grant them the autonomy and independence they had been demanding and which the reform process itself, logically, appeared to promise them. From April to August 1991 Gorbachev and the nine Republics still interested in maintaining a Union came very close to achieving this, but were forestalled by the doomed August coup attempt of 18–23 August.

This failed *putsch* was a last attempt to save the old Union and the old order. The conservatives in the military-industrial complex, the armed forces, the internal security organs and the CPSU apparatus, consistently outflanked by Gorbachev's manoeuvring, had been forced to endure the loss of the Eastern European empire and the loss of the Party's leading role, but they were not prepared to tolerate the loss of the Union. However, they were too late. By August 1991, with Russia's first-ever democratically elected President, Boris Yeltsin, newly installed in the Russian parliament in Moscow (in June), it was clear that the processes of disintegration could not be stopped, let alone reversed. In the event the coup simply accelerated them. The Baltic states moved swiftly to secede formally, as did Georgia. Union negotiations resumed after August but they now had a completely different character. Instead of trying to create a new federal state, the Republics concentrated on finding ways to prevent the complete collapse of what remained of the Soviet economy. However, even these negotiations were overtaken by events.

The overwhelming vote for independence in Ukraine, on 1 December 1991, marked the end of any attempt to maintain some sort of Union. Once Ukraine, the second-most powerful Republic in the Union, decided to leave it, there was nothing left to preserve. The *coup de grâce* was executed on 8 December, when the leaders of the three Slav Republics—Belarus, Russia and Ukraine—agreed to create a new Commonwealth of Independent States (CIS). On 21 December 11 of the constituent Republics of the USSR signed a founding document of the CIS and Gorbachev was left with no alternative but to resign as President of the USSR, which he did on 25th December 1991.

CONSEQUENCES

The consequences resultant upon the rapid collapse of a nuclear superpower and the last of the great multi-national empires were incalculable, but some comment can be made. None of the new states that emerged from the former USSR, with the partial exception of Russia, was viable economically, at least for the foreseeable future. The old Soviet economy generated levels of mutual interdependence and, in particular, dependence on Russian resources, which forced these states to re-establish at least some of the links that were broken. Their economies were mostly in chaos as a result of *perestroika*. As the mid-1990s approached the old centralized planning and production structures had by no means all disappeared, privatization was proving far more difficult than had been anticipated, while, at the same time, market mechanisms were scarcely established either in law or in fact. Moreover, all the countries were left with a terrible legacy of environmental destruction, which presented a real threat to public health and would take decades, enormous human and material resources and considerable inter-state co-operation to resolve. None of them was politically stable either. On the contrary, they were forced to confront political fundamentals that were completely new to many of them. Battles for power and control between legislatures and executives ensued in several states, notably Russia, but also in Ukraine, the Baltic countries and Tajikistan. There was no obvious means of resolution, because of the absence of constitutional law and the lack of consensus about the direction of change, unless force was resorted to, as had happened in Russia in September–October 1993. This lack of political stability did, of course, inhibit economic development even further. Moreover, the particular way in which the Soviet federation disintegrated left a legacy of national and regional self-awareness which threatened several states with the potential for instability and further disintegration.

Largely because of the haste with which it was created, the CIS was not able to do much to facilitate the search for solutions to the multiple crises which threatened these states. Nobody anticipated that it would last very long and it initially lacked any institutional identity. By 1993 this showed signs of changing, however, because of the overwhelming pressure of circumstances.

Finally, the disintegration of the Soviet superpower dramatically destabilized international relations. The Cold War, and the competition between the USSR and the USA which drove it, might have been costly and dangerous, but it provided a set of international rules which everyone could understand and manipulate to their own advantage. This stability finally went at the end of 1991 and international organizations, like the UN, were foundering under the attempt to establish a new form of global order. At the beginning of 1994, as a result of the USSR's collapse, the world still appeared to be more unstable than it had done at any time since the Second World War.

Note: For a Chronology of the former USSR, see below (p. 540), in the chapter on the Russian Federation.

PART TWO
Country Surveys

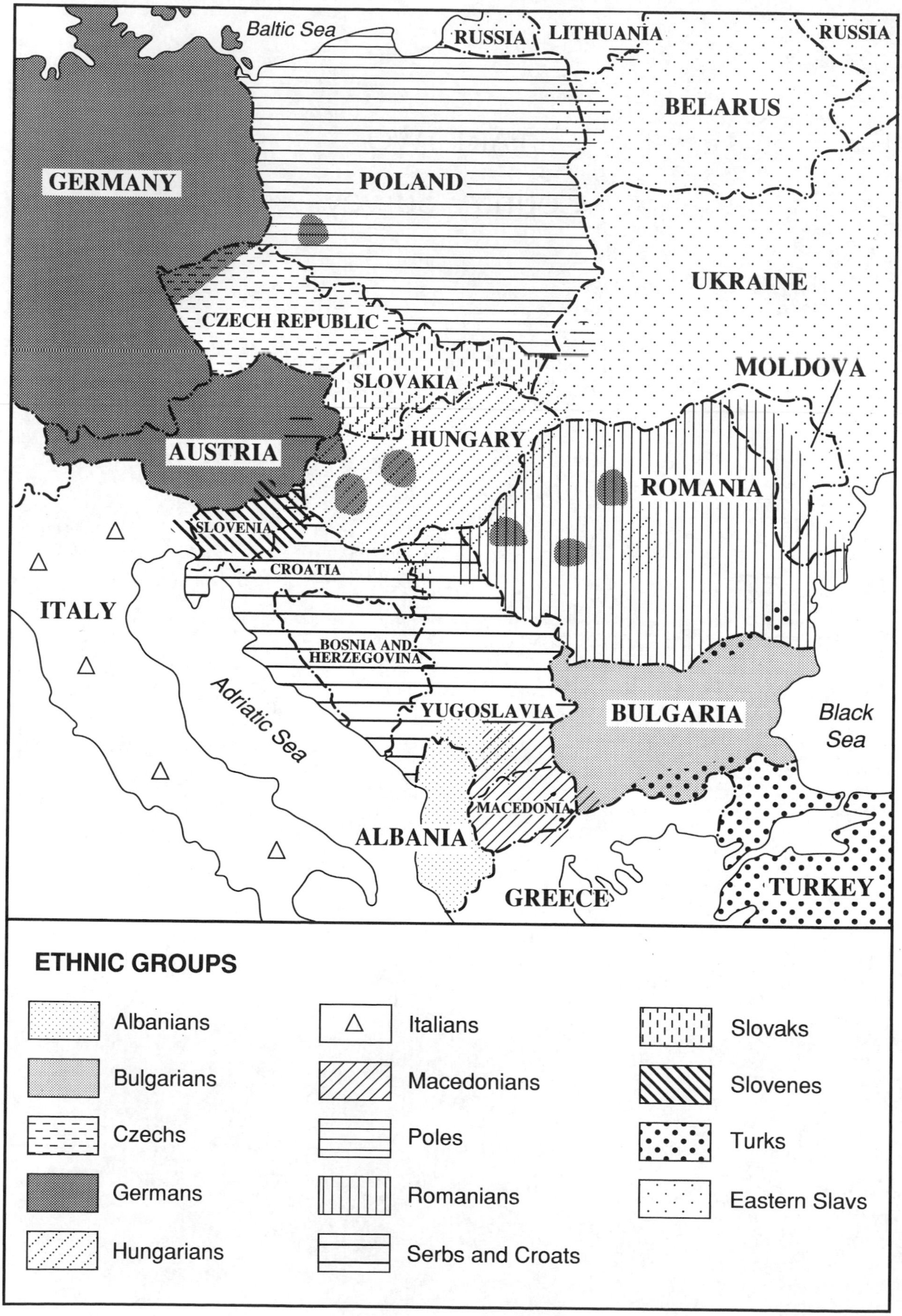

Ethnic Groups of Eastern Europe

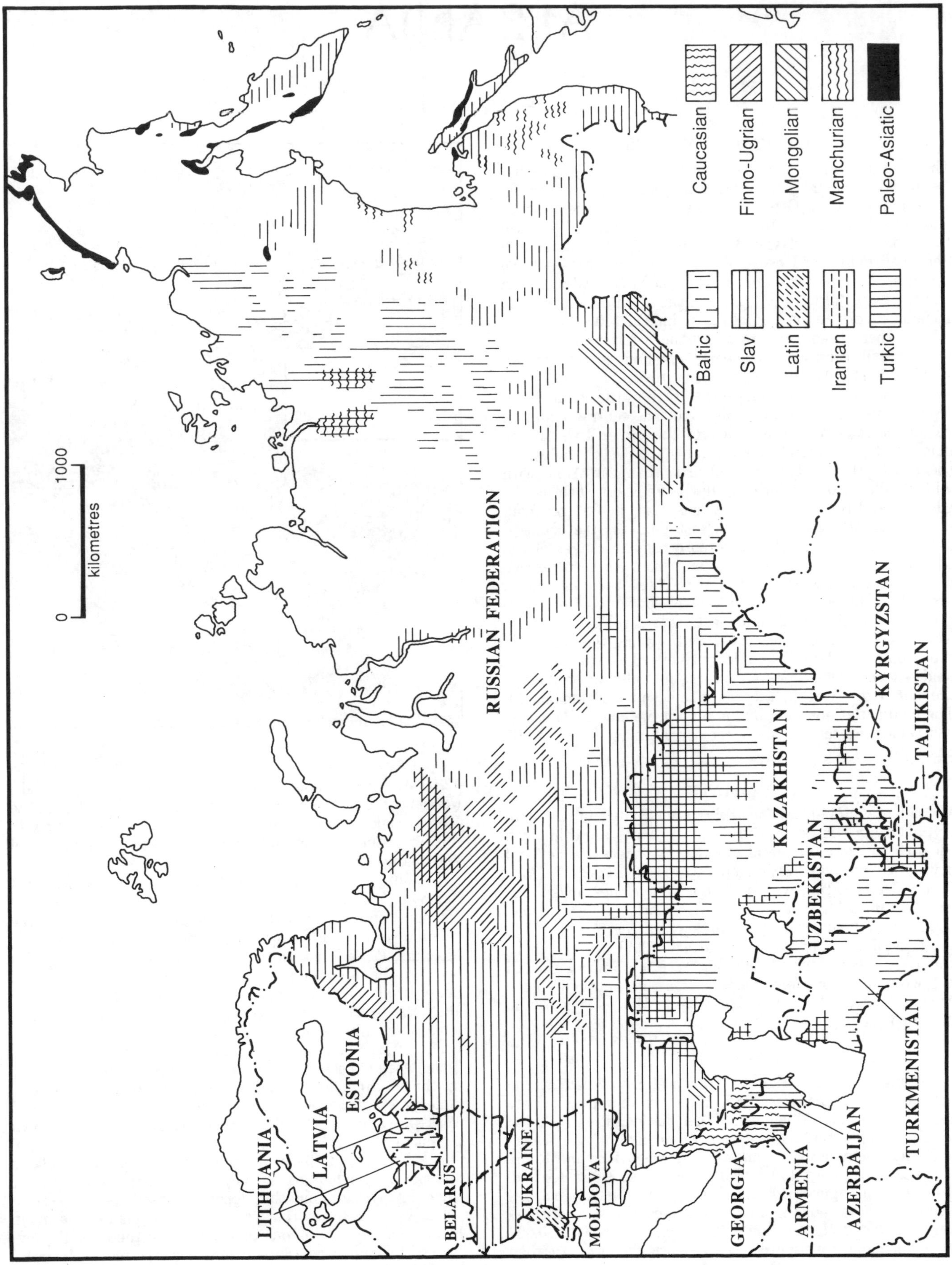

Ethnic Groups of the Former USSR

ALBANIA

Geography

PHYSICAL FEATURES

The Republic of Albania (formerly the People's Socialist Republic of Albania) is situated in south-eastern Europe. It is bordered by Greece, to the south, by the Former Yugoslav Republic of Macedonia, to the east, and the two Republics of Yugoslavia: Montenegro to the north, and Serbia (Province of Kosovo-Metohija) to the north-east. To the west there is a 420-km coastline along the Adriatic Sea and the Strait of Otranto (parts of the Mediterranean Sea). Albania covers an area of 28,748 sq km (11,100 sq miles).

More than three-quarters of Albania's territory is mountain or hill country and nearly one-half is covered by woodland. The Albanian Alps, characterized by tall forests and alpine pastures, dominate the north of the country and rise to a height of 2,693 m at Jezerce. The central mountain region lies between the valley of the River Drin in the north and the central Devoll and lower Osum valleys in the south. It is a less rugged area than the Alps, with wider valleys, dense forests, and large lakes such as the Ohrid and Prespa, but it also has high peaks, reaching 2,751 m at Mt Korabi, the highest point in the country. South of the Osum valley the more regular ranges of the southern mountain region continue into northern Greece and extend westwards to the sea. These three mountain areas surround the western coastal lowlands. Communications with the south and east, therefore, are difficult. There are, however, east-west routes along the valleys of the Shkumbin, Devoll and Drin rivers. The western lowlands extend some 200 km from the foothills of the Alps in the north to Vlorë in the south and some 50 km inland. The land is flat and marshy and extensive land reclamation has been necessary to allow previously unused areas to be cultivated.

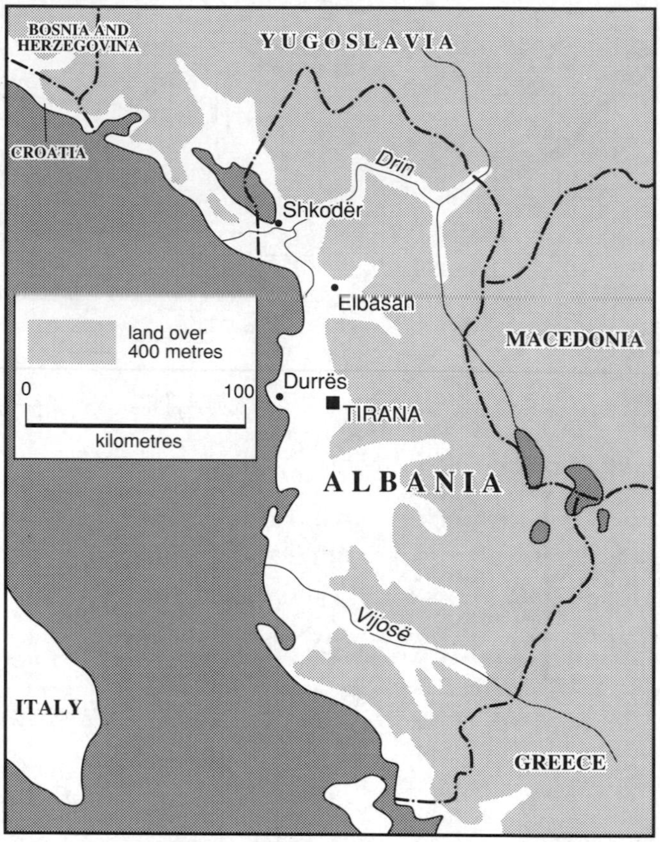

CLIMATE

The climate is Mediterranean throughout much of the country, although winters in the mountain areas are cold, with snow cover lasting several months. Summers are hot and dry, with average July temperatures of 24°–25°C (75°–77°F). During the winter frequent cyclones make the weather unstable, but it remains relatively mild in the plains, with January temperatures averaging 8°C (47°F) in the coastal town of Durrës, and 4°C (39°F) in the more northerly inland city of Shkodër. Average annual rainfall is 1,300 mm, but regional variations are pronounced; in the Alps it is over 2,000 mm, whereas in the valleys of the interior it is only 650–700 mm.

POPULATION

According to official figures, the total population at the census of April 1989 was 3,182,417, of which approximately 98% were ethnic Albanians. Other nationalities included 58,758 Greeks, the majority of whom live in the south, 4,697 Macedonians, small numbers of Bulgarians and Roma (Gypsies) and about 100 Serbs, Croats and Montenegrins. However, all figures for minority groups in Albania are disputed. Some sources assert that there are several thousand Serbs and Montenegrins in Albania and 55,000–60,000 Macedonians. Greek sources claim that there are more than 300,000 ethnic Greeks living in Albania, whereas independent estimates assert a lower figure of some 100,000–120,000. Western sources also mention some 35,000 Vlahs (descendants of the autochthonous Thracians), living in the Korçë region, and more than 5,000 Roma. According to official estimates, at mid-1991 the total population of Albania was some 3.3m.

The official ban on religious worship, which was in effect between 1967 and 1990, makes it difficult to assess the religious affiliations of the population. According to the religious census of 1945, 72.8% of the population were Muslims, 17.1% Eastern Orthodox and 10.1% Roman Catholic. Of the Muslim population, an estimated 25% were members of the liberal Bektashi sect. In late 1990 and early 1991 the small community of some 300 Albanian Jews emigrated in its entirety to Israel.

The official language is Albanian, the principal dialects being Gheg (spoken north of the River Shkumbin) and Tosk (in the south). The literary language is a fusion of the two dialects, with the phonetic and morphological structure of Tosk prevailing. Ethnic Greeks continue to use their own language.

The majority of the population live on the coastal plains and nearly one-half of the population lives outside major towns. Average population density (persons per sq km), in 1991, was 114.8, but that of the lowland plains was much higher. In 1988 the population density in the coastal province of Lushnjë was 185.7, whereas in the mountain province of Pukë, in the north, it was only 46.6. There are many ethnic Albanians living in other countries, including some

1.7m. in Yugoslavia, mainly in the Kosovo region of Serbia (Kosovar Albanians), and a further 450,000 in Macedonia. There is a small number of Albanians in northern Greece (the Çam community). The capital, Tirana (Tiranë) is situated in the centre of the country and had an estimated population of 244,200 in mid-1990. Other important towns include Durrës, Albania's largest port (85,400), Elbasan, a major industrial centre (83,300), and Shkodër (81,900).

Chronology

168 BC: Illyria (which included modern-day Albania) was annexed by the Roman Empire.

AD 395: Following a division of the administration of the Roman Empire, Illyria was ruled by the Eastern Roman ('Byzantine') Emperor in Constantinople (Istanbul).

6th–7th centuries: Slavs invaded the Balkan peninsula.

11th century: Vlachs (Wallachians) migrated into the territory still occupied by the remnants of the Thracian-Illyrian population.

1385: Ottoman (Turkish) forces reached the Albanian coast.

1443: Gjergj Kastrioti (Skënderbeu or Skenderbeg) led Albanians in a revolt against Ottoman dominance.

1468: Death of Skënderbeu.

1478: The Ottomans established full control over Albania and, under their rule, many Albanians converted to Islam.

1756: Mehemet of Bushan established an independent principality in northern Albania.

1787: Ali Pasha of Tepelenë (Janina) established an independent principality in southern Albania and neighbouring territories.

1822: Ottoman forces overthrew Ali Pasha.

1831: Mustafa Pasha, of the Bushan dynasty, was overthrown.

1878: The Congress of Berlin allotted parts of Albanian territory to Bulgaria, Montenegro, Serbia and Greece. The Albanian League for the Defence of the Rights of the Albanian Nation was established.

1881: The Albanian League was disbanded by the Ottomans.

1910: An uprising against Ottoman rule was suppressed by Turkish forces.

October 1912: The First Balkan War began; Albania was occupied by neighbouring powers.

28 November 1912: A national convention, convened in Vlorë, proclaimed the independence of Albania; Ismail Qemal was appointed President.

July 1913: The London Ambassadors' Conference recognized the principle of Albanian independence, but designated the country a protectorate, under the control of the Great Powers; Kosovo was granted to Serbia; other territories were gained by Greece.

March 1914: Prince William of Wied, who had been appointed ruler of the Albanian protectorate by the Great Powers, arrived in Albania.

August 1914: Italy and Greece occupied southern Albania at the outbreak of the First World War.

September 1914: Prince William of Wied left Albania, following local opposition to his rule.

April 1915: The secret Treaty of London was signed, which provided for much of Albania to be partitioned between Greece, Italy, Serbia and Montenegro.

January 1920: The Congress of Lushnjë reaffirmed Albania's independence and appointed a new Government; Tirana (Tiranë) was declared the capital of Albania.

August 1920: Italy agreed to withdraw its forces from Albania and recognize Albanian independence.

December 1920: Albania was admitted to the League of Nations.

10 June 1924: After an armed uprising, a Government headed by Fan Noli came to power.

24 December 1924: The Government of Fan Noli was overthrown by forces led by Ahmet Zogu.

January 1925: The Republic of Albania was proclaimed; Ahmet Zogu was appointed President.

September 1928: A monarchy was established, with Zogu proclaiming himself King Zog I.

April 1939: Italian troops invaded Albania; King Zog was forced into exile. The union of Albania and Italy under the Italian Crown was subsequently proclaimed.

November 1941: The Communist Party of Albania was founded; Enver Hoxha became its first leader.

September 1942: The National Liberation Front, a Communist-led resistance organization, was established.

September 1943: Italy surrendered to the Allies; Albania was invaded by Nazi German forces.

1943–44: Fierce fighting occurred between Nazi forces and resistance groups, and also between resistance groups of different political persuasions.

24–28 May 1944: The Congress of Përmet established, as a provisional government, the Anti-Fascist Committee for National Liberation, headed by Enver Hoxha.

29 November 1944: The National Liberation Front proclaimed the liberation of Albania.

2 December 1945: Elections with only Communist candidates took place; the Communists, as the Democratic Front, won some 90% of the votes cast.

11 January 1946: The People's Republic of Albania was proclaimed; King Zog was declared deposed.

October 1946: Two British warships were damaged in the Corfu Channel (between the Greek island of Corfu and the Albanian coast) by mines, allegedly planted by Albania.

1948: Close relations with Yugoslavia were ended after Yugoslavia was expelled from the Communist Information Bureau (Cominform). Yugoslav personnel in Albania were expelled and economic agreements between the two countries abrogated. The Albanian Communist Party was renamed the Party of Labour of Albania (PLA).

1949: Albania joined the Council for Mutual Economic Assistance (CMEA). Koci Xoxe (former Minister of the Interior) and other officials were executed as alleged pro-Yugoslav traitors.

1954: Hoxha resigned as Chairman of the Council of Ministers (head of government), but retained effective power as First Secretary of the PLA. Mehmet Shehu was appointed head of government.

1955: Albania joined the Warsaw Treaty Organization (Warsaw Pact). The Soviet *rapprochement* with Yugoslavia strained Soviet-Albanian relations.

1959: The Soviet leader, Nikita Khrushchev, visited Albania in an attempt to dissuade the Albanians from seeking an alliance with the People's Republic of China.

1961: The USSR denounced Albania and severed diplomatic relations after Hoxha announced his support for the Chinese Communist leader, Mao Zedong, in his ideological conflict with the USSR.

1962: Albania formally left the CMEA.

1967: Religious worship was outlawed and all mosques and churches were closed.

1968: Albania formally left the Warsaw Pact.

1972: Improved US–Chinese relations were denounced by Albania.

1975: Gen. Beqir Balluku, who had been dismissed as Minister of Defence in 1974, was executed as an alleged pro-Chinese traitor.

1976: A new Constitution was adopted; the country's name was changed to the People's Socialist Republic of Albania.

1978: Albania declared its support for Viet Nam, in its conflict with the People's Republic of China; China suspended all military and economic ties.

December 1981: Mehmet Shehu, head of government, died in a shooting incident. There were subsequent allegations that he had been murdered.

November 1982: Ramiz Alia replaced Haxhi Lleshi as Chairman of the Presidium of the People's Assembly (head of state).

April 1985: Death of Enver Hoxha. He was succeeded as First Secretary of the PLA by Ramiz Alia.

August 1987: In an attempt to improve relations, Greece ended the technical state of war which had existed between it and Albania since 1945.

November 1989: Some political prisoners were released as part of a general amnesty, in the first sign of reform.

December 1989: There were reports of anti-government demonstrations in the northern town of Shkodër and such activity increased throughout 1990.

17 April 1990: At the 10th Plenum of the PLA Central Committee, Alia announced some relaxation of economic controls and the intention to re-establish relations with the USSR (diplomatic relations were renewed in July 1990) and the USA (March 1991).

May 1990: The People's Assembly adopted measures to liberalize the penal code, to end the ban on religious propaganda and to relax the constitutional prohibition on foreign investment.

July 1990: Some 5,000 Albanians were eventually allowed to leave the country after seeking asylum in the embassies of foreign countries.

12 December 1990: Opposition activists announced the formation of the Democratic Party of Albania (DPA), the day after the PLA agreed to the legalization of opposition parties; it was officially registered as Albania's first opposition party since the Second World War one week later.

31 December 1990: A draft of the new Constitution, guaranteeing multi-party democracy and economic liberalization, was published, after a month of increasing, and sometimes violent, anti-government protest.

January 1991: Konstantinos Mitsotakis, the Prime Minister of Greece, visited Tirana, in an attempt to quell the exodus of ethnic Greeks from Albania. Later in the month a new Government included more reformists, such as Fatos Nano, an economist.

February 1991: Several thousand people demonstrated in Tirana; a statue of Enver Hoxha, in Skënderbeu Square, was pulled down by crowds. Ramiz Alia declared presidential rule and appointed a provisional government, under Nano, after student protests in Enver Hoxha University and demonstrations in Tirana.

March 1991: The Italian navy was ordered to prevent any more vessels landing at the Italian port of Brindisi, after some 20,000 Albanians had arrived on ships seized in Albanian ports.

31 March 1991: The PLA won over 60% of the votes cast in Albania's first multi-party election since the 1920s.

30 April 1991: Ramiz Alia was elected to the new post of President of the Republic, by the People's Assembly, which had renamed the country the Republic of Albania.

June 1991: After continuing protests throughout the country and a general strike, Ylli Bufi became head of government; he formed a Government which included the first non-Communist ministers since the Second World War. The PLA changed its name to the Socialist Party of Albania (SPA) and elected Nano its leader. Albania was finally admitted as a member of the Conference on Security and Co-operation in Europe (CSCE).

September 1991: Large demonstrations in Tirana demanded new elections, full freedom for the media and the arrest of former PLA/SPA leaders.

October 1991: The Assembly voted to recognize the 'Republic of Kosovo' (the predominantly ethnic Albanian area of neighbouring Yugoslavia), after protests at Serbian repression.

December 1991: The Bufi Government finally collapsed when the DPA withdrew from the coalition; Vilson Ahmeti was the new Chairman of the Council of Ministers. There were food riots in various parts of the country and increasing industrial unrest.

February 1992: A new electoral law prevented the Democratic Community of the Greek Minority (OMONIA), which held five seats in the Assembly, from putting forward candidates for the general election.

22 and 29 March 1992: Elections to the new Assembly were won by the DPA, which gained 62% of the votes cast in the first round (and 92 of the 140 seats), while the SPA only gained 26% (and 38 seats).

9 April 1992: Sali Berisha of the DPA was elected President of the Republic by the People's Assembly, following the resignation of Alia some days before. Berisha appointed Aleksander Meksi to lead a new coalition Government.

July 1992: The Albanian Communist Party was banned. At local elections the DPA gained the most votes (43% of the total), but the SPA improved its support, gaining 41%.

September 1992: There was a split in the DPA, when a section of the party, including Neritan Çeka and Gramoz Pashko, formed the Albanian Democratic Alliance (ADA), accusing the Berisha regime of becoming more right-wing and authoritarian. Former President Alia was arrested and charged with corruption, joining several other prominent members of the old Communist regime in detention.

April 1993: President Berisha appointed four new members of the Council of Ministers, including Petrit Kalakula, a leader of the so-called Balli Kombëter right-wing faction of the DPA.

June 1993: The Social Democratic Party began a boycott of parliament, in protest at the delay in adopting a new Constitution, and, for various reasons, was supported by the SPA and the Union of Human Rights Party (which represented the Greek community); the boycott was ended at the end of August. The Albanian authorities provoked a severe deterioration in relations with Greece by expelling a senior Greek Orthodox cleric from the country.

July 1993: Fatos Nano, the former premier, was arrested and accused of financial improprieties while in office.

August 1993: Petrit Kalakula was dismissed as Minister of Agriculture and Food, after making an allegedly pro-Fascist statement in the People's Assembly.

October 1993: Premier Meksi proposed a reorganization of the ministries, which led to the appointment of a new finance minister, Pjetër Dishnica, in the following month.

History

MIRANDA VICKERS

THE ESTABLISHMENT OF THE ALBANIAN STATE

On 28 November 1912, after more than 400 years under Ottoman (Turkish) rule, Albania declared its independence under a provisional government. The Albanians' decision to declare full independence was provoked by the fear that their lands would be divided between Greece, Serbia and Montenegro. In October of that year these states had gained important victories against the Ottoman armies, in the First Balkan War. The declaration of independence was followed by international recognition, at the London Conference of July 1913. However, the Conference also diminished the territory claimed by the Albanian state, granting the region of Kosovo to Serbia and the area known as Çamëria (Chamouria) to Greece. During the turmoil of the First World War, the armies of Greece, Italy and Austria, and, for a short period, the forces of Serbia, occupied Albanian territory. Italy continued its occupation until 1920, when it agreed to withdraw its forces and Albanian independence was re-established.

In 1920 Albania's first national Government was established at the Congress of Lushnjë, but the limitations of the weakly constructed Constitution were soon evident, as the numerous political forces struggled for power. Until 1924 the country underwent a period of great internal instability, with frequent changes of government. In 1924 there was a short experience of democracy, under Fan Noli, but, being politically inexperienced, he failed to cope with Albania's social and economic disarray.

In December 1924 Ahmet Beg Zogu, who had previously held office as Minister of Internal Affairs, overthrew the Government of Fan Noli and assumed power. In 1925 Albania was declared a republic and Zogu was elected President. Zogu quickly established an autocratic, centralized state and proclaimed himself King Zog I, in 1928. In order to consolidate his regime, Zogu accepted substantial financial subsidies from Italy. Italian economic influence was accompanied by increased political influence in Albania. Zogu's need for Italian capital and patronage led to further Italian encroachments into Albania's economy and administration until, eventually, in 1939, Mussolini, the Italian leader, demanded a formal protectorate over Albania. When Zogu objected, the Italians invaded. Although the Albanian armed forces resisted, they were soon defeated and Zogu fled into exile. Albania was united with Italy for four years, before being occupied by German forces in 1943. The Germans withdrew one year later, allowing the Communist-led National Liberation Front to take power, in November 1944.

THE ESTABLISHMENT OF COMMUNIST POWER IN ALBANIA

During the 1930s Communist cells were established within Albania, but ideological factionalism prevented the establishment of a unified Communist organization and, by 1941, there were several small Communist groups. In 1941 Tito (Josip Broz), leader of the Communist Party of Yugoslavia (CPY), sent two delegates to Albania. They brought together the Communist leaders and factions which they favoured and a unified Albanian Communist Party (ACP) was formed in November 1941. In 1942 a National Liberation Movement (NLM) was established under Yugoslav direction. Although Communists predominated in the NLM, non-Communists were also represented, including some members of Balli Kombëtar (the National Front). This latter was a resistance movement which was formed in 1942 by moderately liberal nationalists, who were opposed to the return of Zogu and favoured the re-establishment of a republic.

By the end of 1942 the NLM had sufficiently impressed representatives of the Allied Powers to be granted military aid. During 1943, however, a fundamental disagreement arose between the Communists and Ballists (members of Balli Kombëtar) over the conduct of the war and over the future of the Kosovo region of Yugoslavia, which was mainly populated by Albanians. Although, initially, they both agreed that a plebiscite should take place in the region, the Communists soon repudiated this, under strong Yugoslav pressure. As distrust intensified, military conflict began between the two groups, culminating in the Communist victory in November 1944. A provisional government was established, headed by Enver Hoxha, the leader of the ACP. In December 1945 elections took place, with a single list of candidates, all sponsored by the Communists.

ALBANIA UNDER ENVER HOXHA

After 1945 Albania was dominated by the personality of Enver Hoxha, the chief ideologist of Albanian-style socialism. He was born in Gjirokastër, in southern Albania, in 1908. During the early 1930s he studied and worked in France and Belgium. In 1936 he returned to Albania to become a teacher. He became active in the Communist movement and was elected leader of the Provisional Committee of the ACP in 1941.

Under Hoxha's rule Albania experienced four distinct phases. During the period 1944–48 Albania developed very close relations with Yugoslavia, and the ACP became virtually a branch of the CPY. Customs and monetary unions were established between the two countries and Albanian sovereignty effectively disappeared as its dependence on Yugoslavia grew. Had it not been for the rupture of relations between Tito and the Soviet leader, Stalin (Iosif V. Dzhugashvili), in 1948, Albania would probably have become the seventh Republic of Yugoslavia.

During the second phase of Hoxha's rule, from 1948 to 1961, Albania's main international ally was the USSR. After the CPY was forced to leave the Communist Information Bureau (Cominform) in 1948, accused of ideological 'revisionism', Hoxha, fearing Yugoslav expansionism, relied on the USSR for help. Yugoslav advisers in Albania were replaced by Soviet personnel and, in 1949, Albania joined the Soviet-dominated Council for Mutual Economic Assistance (CMEA). Hoxha studiously imitated the Soviet leader, Stalin, in developing his dictatorship, using widespread purges to eliminate any opposition to the ruling Party of Labour of Albania (PLA—the name was changed from the Albanian Communist Party in 1948). While ensuring political orthodoxy, the leadership also continued the transformation of the economy and social system, eliminating private ownership of industry and commerce and forcibly effecting the collectivization of agriculture. Ambitious schemes in social and health policy improved access to educational and medical facilities.

Soviet–Albanian relations began to deteriorate after Stalin's death in March 1953. Nikita Khrushchev's *rapprochement* with Tito in 1955, and his denunciation of Stalin the next year, severely strained Soviet–Albanian relations. In

1960 the Albanian leadership openly declared their support for the People's Republic of China in the escalating Sino-Soviet ideological dispute. In response, the USSR severed relations with Albania in 1961. Soviet technicians were replaced by Chinese personnel, but the country's precarious economic situation was only partly relieved by Chinese loans, credits and technical expertise. In 1962 Albania ended participation in the CMEA, causing further problems for the economy. Furthermore, in the relentless pursuit of ideological purism, in 1967 the practice of religion was prohibited, and Albania was proclaimed the world's first atheist state. Persecution intensified as Hoxha attempted to imitate the Chinese 'Cultural Revolution' in his own country. There were further purges following a decline in petroleum production in the early 1970s, when there was some questioning of economic policy, particularly regarding decentralization. Many of the leading figures in Albanian economic activity and several politicians were executed, including the Politburo members Abdyl Kellezi and Koco Theodosi and the director-general of the Albanian hydrocarbons industry, Lipe Nasho. Furthermore, from the early 1970s, relations with the People's Republic of China deteriorated. This followed the improvement in Chinese relations with the USA, in 1972, and the death of Mao Zedong, in 1976. In 1978 the People's Republic of China suspended all economic and military co-operation with Albania, after Albania had declared its support for Viet Nam in the Sino-Vietnamese dispute.

During the fourth phase of Hoxha's rule, from 1978 until 1985, Albania's isolationist policies reached their most extreme. Internal political orthodoxy was enforced with the utmost vigour. The internal security police, the Sigurimi, prevented the development of any opposition movements within Albania. Meanwhile, volume after volume of Hoxha's collected works consolidated his 'cult of personality'.

THE POST-HOXHA YEARS

Enver Hoxha died in April 1985 and was succeeded as First Secretary of the PLA by Ramiz Alia. Alia had played an important role in the development of post-1945 Albania, as Secretary for Ideology in the PLA from the 1960s onwards. His rise to the leadership began after the death of Hoxha's expected successor, Mehmet Shehu, in suspicious circumstances, in 1981. One year later Alia replaced Haxhi Lleshi as Chairman of the Presidium of the People's Assembly, the nominal head of state. As First Secretary, Alia adopted a less rigid style than his predecessor and, during the late 1980s, the Government began to distance itself gradually from the Hoxha legacy. There were cautious attempts at liberalization and decentralization and a more flexible foreign policy led to improved relations with a number of Western European countries.

Albania's relations with its immediate neighbours, Yugoslavia and Greece, improved during the 1980s, although alleged ill-treatment of the Albanian community in Yugoslavia and the ethnic Greek minority in Albania at times threatened increased co-operation. Relations with Greece were normalized in 1987, when Greece decided formally to end the technical state of war with Albania, which had been in existence since 1945, and annul Greek territorial claims to 'northern Epirus' (southern Albania). However, the status of the ethnic Greek minority in southern Albania remained a sensitive issue.

In 1988 Albania participated in the Balkan Conference of Foreign Ministers in Belgrade (Yugoslavia), the first official meeting of all six Balkan states in more than 50 years. By its involvement, Albania accomplished a goodwill gesture, reassuring its neighbours, especially Yugoslavia, of the country's willingness to help establish a general framework of co-operation in the region. Yugoslavia was one of Albania's major trading partners, and any ideological differences between them tended to be exaggerated, involving more rhetoric than reality. This was especially so in the case of the Albanian population in the Yugoslav region of Kosovo (officially known as Kosovo-Metohija from September 1991). After the violent unrest in Kosovo, in March 1989, which left at least 25 Albanians dead, Albania accused Yugoslavia of brutally oppressing the Kosovar Albanians. The Communist victory in Albania had ended any possibility of the country fighting actively for union with Kosovo, and, after 1948, the intended Yugoslav annexation of Albania became impossible. Since then Albania had offered only verbal and written encouragement to the ethnic Albanians of Kosovo.

Regardless of the geopolitical difficulties of any union between Albania and Kosovo, any attempted integration of the Kosovar Albanians would have been a reckless move, considering the strongly contrasting ideo-political systems of the two countries. The overwhelmingly Muslim Kosovars, who could openly practise their religion in Yugoslavia, would not have willingly accepted Albania's enforced atheism. Nor would Albania's agricultural collectivization have appealed to the Kosovar peasants, who owned their own land. Hoxha valued ideological purity above national unity; Albania, therefore, limited its interests in Kosovo to cultural politics.

Although the Albanian leadership often used the situation in Kosovo as a way of deflecting discontent at home, several decades of isolation accentuated the social and psychological differences separating Albanians from Kosovars. Should the two ever unite, a problem of regionalism could arise. The comparatively sophisticated Kosovars are related to Albania's northern, Gheg-speaking people; these groups are divided by cultural, linguistic and historical differences from the southern, Tosk-speaking Albanians. Although Tosk became the predominant dialect after the Second World War, it did not have the unifying affect anticipated, and, with the diffusion of central authority, regionalism was again surfacing in the early 1990s.

ALBANIA'S *PERESTROIKA*

Albania embarked on mildly reformist policies, for economic reasons, before the collapse of Communist regimes in Eastern Europe in 1989. However, the example of the 1989 revolutions, and notably the Romanian revolution of December, forced the PLA to consider more fundamental reforms. The impetus for reform initially came from within the PLA itself, particularly from its educated élite, although large and frequent student protests accelerated the pace of change in 1990.

The first signs of political liberalization appeared in November 1989, when an amnesty was announced for certain political prisoners. The pace of reform quickened throughout 1990, after a number of demonstrations and strikes in the early part of the year, notably in the northern town of Shkodër, in January, where as many as 7,000 people joined protests. In late January the Ninth Plenum of the Central Committee of the PLA approved a programme of limited reforms, which proposed greater decentralization of the economy and some democratic reform in political institutions. Addressing the Central Committee, Alia proposed bonuses for workers in important industries, pricing changes, and, most significant of all, multi-candidate elections. He also proposed some decentralization of Party authority, which would enable local organizations to appoint all but the most senior officials. Nevertheless, Alia continued to reject the idea of a multi-party system, claiming that such a system was not appropriate for Albania.

In June 1990 the People's Assembly (Albania's legislature) approved further measures of liberalization. The penal code was changed, considerably reducing the number of crimes carrying the death penalty, and religious worship was also to be tolerated. The Ministry of Justice, which had been abolished in 1965, was re-established, and enterprises were to be allowed to sell some surplus goods on the free market. Albanians were also to be granted the right to travel abroad. The announcement that the practice of religion was no longer to be an offence was a major reversal of past policy, and gradually, throughout 1991, the country's churches and mosques were reopened.

Despite increasing liberalization, there was further unrest in July 1990, when security forces violently dispersed anti-government demonstrators in Tirana. Immediately after the violence, four Albanians sought asylum in the embassy of the Federal Republic of Germany and, over the next few days, several thousand people sought refuge in foreign embassies. The refugee crisis was finally resolved when some 5,000 Albanians were allowed to leave the country, assisted by a multi-national relief operation, co-ordinated by the UN.

In foreign affairs there were significant changes, as Albania sought to escape its self-imposed isolation. In June 1990 Albania made an official request to join the Conference on Security and Co-operation in Europe (CSCE), with an agreement that Albania would adopt all the principles of the 1975 Helsinki Final Act, and, in July, the restoration of diplomatic links with the USSR was announced. In August talks began in Washington, DC (USA), on the resumption of diplomatic ties with the USA. The US Government showed some reluctance to restore diplomatic relations until multi-party elections were announced; relations were finally re-established in March 1991. Representatives from the United Kingdom and Albania also met to discuss the restoration of diplomatic relations between the two countries. Albania had always insisted on the return of gold seized by the United Kingdom at the end of the Second World War before diplomatic ties could be resumed. The United Kingdom's claim on this gold was agreed by the International Court of Justice (based in the Netherlands) as compensation for the sinking, allegedly by Albanian mines, of a British naval ship in the Corfu Channel in 1946; the gold was valued at some £20m. in 1991. However, both parties agreed that arguments over the confiscated gold should be postponed until after the resumption of diplomatic ties, which were finally restored in May 1991.

In October, as the process of change gathered momentum, the credibility of the Government's reform programme suffered a reverse when Ismail Kadare, the country's foremost author, sought asylum while in Paris. His criticism of the limitations of the reforms being implemented severely embarrassed the Albanian Government, which was hosting the Balkan Conference at the time. In response to popular pressure for more radical reform, Alia announced proposals for reforming the political system, including redefinition of the role of the PLA and a new electoral procedure, requiring the presentation of at least two candidates in every constituency.

THE INTRODUCTION OF A MULTI-PARTY SYSTEM

In early December 1990 there were student demonstrations in Tirana, demanding the introduction of a multi-party system for the elections to the People's Assembly, which had been scheduled for February 1991. On 11 December, in response to growing unrest, the Central Committee of the PLA agreed to legalize independent political parties. The formation of the Democratic Party of Albania (DPA), the first legal opposition party since before the Second World War, was announced the next day. The DPA, led by Dr Sali Berisha, a cardiologist, and Gramoz Pashko, an economist, demanded that Albania agree to the four principles of the Paris Charter (signed by members of the CSCE—all European countries except Albania—in Paris, France, in late 1990): a free-market economy, self-determination, free elections and the right to own private property. The first opposition newspaper, *Rilindja Demokratike* (Democratic Revival) was published in January 1991. By March 1991 the membership of the DPA had risen to some 60,000, as opposed to the PLA's estimated 130,000 members.

The announcement of the new party came amidst an outbreak of violent unrest in Shkodër, as people protested at the slow pace of reform. Shortages of consumer goods and the rationing of basic goods had led to bitter discontent and demands for more radical changes. The Government's response was the dismissal of more conservative officials, and an admission by Alia that the PLA must now 'deviate from many of the principles of socialism'. There was also a cautious but significant renunciation of Stalinism, when the Council of Ministers decreed that Stalin's name should be removed from state institutions and places. However, such concessions did not prevent strikes occurring in the mining and public-transport sectors in mid-January 1991, forcing the second round of government personnel changes in less than six weeks, in which Fatos Nano and Shkelqim Çani, both reformist economists, were appointed deputy premiers.

The concessions won from the PLA also failed to stop an increasing number of ethnic Greeks from attempting to leave Albania. By mid-January 1991 more than 5,000 Greeks had crossed the border into Greece. Although the majority had passports, the Greek embassy in Tirana was reluctant to issue more than a minimum of visas, fearing that Greece might be overwhelmed by large numbers of ethnic Greek Albanians. The Albanian Government estimated the officially recognized minority in the southern provinces at 50,000, but Greece long claimed a figure of 250,000 or more (all of whom would be eligible for Greek citizenship if they crossed the border). In mid-January Konstantinos Mitsotakis, the Prime Minister of Greece, was invited to Tirana to discuss the crisis. He sought to discourage further refugees by urging ethnic Greeks to remain in Albania and keep faith in the reform process.

The months of February and March 1991 were a time of political crisis in Albania, with many observers predicting military intervention to quell student demonstrations throughout the country. On 20 February several thousand people marched to the centre of Tirana and pulled down the statue of Enver Hoxha in the central Skënderbeu Square. Later the same day, in response to the growing unrest, Ramiz Alia declared presidential rule, denouncing the demonstrators as 'vandals' and announcing the formation of a new Government and the establishment of a Presidential Council. The demonstrations continued the next day, and the unrest was only ended by a combination of concessions, including the removal of Enver Hoxha's name from the University, and the increased use of force by the police and security forces. The underlying tensions, however, remained. The status of Hoxha remained the main focus of the conflict between the youth-led, anti-Communist opposition in the towns and the older, conservative Communists who controlled the security forces and were stronger in the provinces. By the end of February there were reports of serious divisions within the PLA and Alia warned for the first time that his leadership was threatened by more conservative elements in the party.

In early March 1991 a new crisis began, as thousands of Albanians attempted to emigrate to Italy. The would-be emigrants, mostly unemployed young men, commandeered ships in the port of Durrës and sailed to the Italian port of Brindisi. The Italian navy was ordered to prevent any more ships from docking and the Albanian authorities placed ports under military rule to prevent any more refugees from leaving Albania. In all, more than 20,000 people arrived in Brindisi, some of whom subsequently returned to Albania, perhaps disillusioned with the lack of aid offered them by the Italian authorities. Other refugees were moved to camps in southern Italy.

THE 1991 ELECTIONS AND THEIR AFTERMATH

Despite the unrest which preceded them, Albania's first multi-party elections for six decades took place peacefully, at the end of March 1991. The elections had originally been scheduled for 10 February, but one of the demands of the DPA had been their postponement, to allow the new parties time to campaign and thus enable a more even contest. After talks between the Government and the opposition parties, it was agreed there would be a 'no-strike policy' until 1 May, in exchange for a delaying of the elections until 31 March.

After the establishment of the DPA, in December 1990, other smaller parties were registered, including the Albanian Republican Party (ARP), the Agrarian Party, the Ecology Party, or the Albanian Green Party, and the Democratic Union of the Greek Minority (OMONIA). All of these smaller parties nominated candidates for the elections, but the main contenders were the DPA and the PLA. While the PLA offered a gradual transition away from Stalinism, the DPA campaign promised a transformation of living standards, to be brought about by membership of the European Community (EC), Western financial aid and jobs in Italian and German factories for the thousands of unemployed. They also advocated privatization of land, a policy which was attacked by the PLA, who claimed it would leave peasants landless.

The most important of the smaller parties was the Republican Party, with a manifesto similar to that of the DPA, but less radical. It advocated a gradual programme of privatization, relying on more foreign investment, in contrast to the DPA's advocacy of rapid privatization and an immediate transition to a free enterprise system. The Green Party, with its small membership, campaigned for social harmony and environmental protection rather than traditional political and economic issues. OMONIA, while supporting democratic changes, mainly campaigned on issues specific to the Greek minority. The newest of the opposition groups, the Agrarian Party, promised to raise the living standards of Albania's large rural population.

According to official figures, in the first round of elections on 31 March 1991, almost 97% of the 1.9m. people eligible to vote did so, the highest level in any multi-party election in Eastern Europe. In the first round of voting, the PLA won 162 of the 250 seats in the Assembly. The DPA won 65 seats, including 17 out of the 19 seats in Tirana, and some 40% of the votes cast. The opposition won all the urban constituencies while the rural areas, where almost 60% of the population live, voted predominantly for the PLA, attracted by their promises of improved standards of living, better housing, and increased wages. A crucial factor in the defeat of the DPA was the widespread belief that the DPA would privatize and redistribute the land, whereas the PLA had promised to protect the peasantry from privatization.

On 7 and 14 April 1991 further rounds of voting took place in the 17 electoral districts where no candidate had won an absolute majority in the first round, and in two constituencies where no contest had occurred. In these rounds the DPA won 10 seats, the PLA seven and OMONIA two. Overall, the PLA won a total of 169 of the 250 seats in the People's Assembly, just over the two-thirds majority (167 seats) required to adopt a new constitution; the DPA won 75 seats and OMONIA won five seats. The most surprising result was the failure of Alia to win a seat in the People's Assembly. He won only 36% of the votes cast in his Tirana constituency, whereas his DPA-supported opponent won 62.5%. Alia apparently misjudged the mood of the capital's population and was a victim of the urban electorate's determination to rid themselves of the PLA.

The PLA fared best in the Tosk-inhabited south, where Communist sympathies were strongest, but they also did well in Pezë, just outside Tirana, and Dibra, which borders Macedonia; both regions with a traditionally strong Communist following. The opposition lacked the transportation and communication facilities necessary to disseminate its views widely outside urban areas, something particularly difficult in Albania with its poor infrastructure. The DPA contradicted the consensus among the 260 international observers by claiming that the elections had been conducted in a 'climate of terror'. Most independent Western observers attested to the overall fairness of the elections, claiming that fraud and manipulation were minimal, although they admitted that the PLA had close control of election scrutineers in some rural areas and had dominated the media. The results of the elections were, in some respects, similar to those in other, former one-party Balkan states, where many rural voters were wary of change, while the urban population was anxious to see rapid and fundamental reform.

The PLA's victory in the election provoked protests from DPA supporters, especially among the younger urban population. On 2 April 1991, after the first election results had been announced, a demonstration took place in Shkodër, protesting against alleged incidents of fraud and manipulation during the elections. When security forces attempted to disperse the crowd, four people were killed and many injured, allegedly as a result of shots fired by the police. With the elections over, it seemed possible that conservative factions within the PLA, including the military, might attempt to arrest the process of reform. Although many senior military officers were opposed to reforms, it is probable that they were dissuaded from attempting to reverse the process by doubts concerning the loyalty of conscripts and junior officers.

Following the violence in Shkodër, Alia appealed to the DPA to participate in a 'national salvation coalition government', so as to diffuse 'unnecessary political antagonisms'. His proposal was rejected by the opposition, who insisted that those responsible for the shootings in Shkodër be brought to trial. The new People's Assembly (which first convened on 10 April) established a parliamentary commission to investigate the events of Shkodër. It reported that the police were to blame for provoking violence from initially peaceful demonstrators.

A draft constitution was presented to the Assembly in late April 1991. The draft contained many structural changes, including the establishment of political pluralism and the renaming of the country from the People's Socialist Republic of Albania to simply the Republic of Albania. However, the opposition objected to the adoption of a new constitution so soon after the elections; instead, interim legislation was adopted outlining the basic principles of the state. This transitional legislation included most of the provisions of the draft constitution. The right to private property was endorsed and the rights to strike, to demonstrate and to emigrate were guarantee. In contrast to the previous system (in which the highest organ of state power was the Presidium of the People's Assembly), there was no provision for a collective organ of government. Instead, an executive President of the country was to be elected by two-thirds of the votes cast in the People's Assembly.

On 30 April 1991 Ramiz Alia, still First Secretary of the PLA, was elected to this new post by an overwhelming majority, since all the opposition deputies abstained. After his election as President, Alia resigned as First Secretary of the PLA, which he had led for six years, in accordance with the new constitutional amendment, which prevented the President from holding office in a political party. He also resigned from the Politburo and the Central Committee of the PLA. In early May the People's Assembly approved a new Government, headed by Fatos Nano, the former deputy premier. All the new ministers were PLA members, but the programme presented to the Assembly by Nano envisaged fundamental reforms in both political and economic affairs, including extensive privatization and a rapid shift to a market-based economy. The new Government, however, faced immense problems. Nano admitted that the economy was in crisis, industrial and agricultural production having fallen markedly since 1988, while population growth remained high.

THE END OF COMMUNIST RULE

In mid-May 1991 the newly established Union of Independent Trade Unions of Albania (UITUA) organized a general strike, in which as many as 300,000 workers participated. The strikers demanded pay rises of up to 100% and a further investigation into the deaths of demonstrators in Shkodër in April. In late May miners began a hunger strike, as the Government continued to reject the unions' demands, and in Tirana several people were injured when a rally in support of the miners was dispersed by the police. The continuing unrest, and the deteriorating economic and political situation in the country forced the resignation of Nano's Government, on 4 June. The next day Ylli Bufi, previously the Minister for Food in the outgoing Government, was appointed Chairman of the Council of Ministers (Prime Minister), and a new 'Government of National Stability', with a total of 12 non-Communist ministers, was formed, thus ending nearly 50 years of exclusive Communist rule in Albania. The PLA held 12 portfolios, the DPA gained seven, and the Republican Party, the newly formed Social Democratic Party (SDP) and the Agrarian Party shared the other five between them.

Further changes were evident at the 10th Congress of the PLA, which also took place in June 1990. The PLA was renamed the Socialist Party of Albania (SPA) and Fatos Nano, former Chairman of the Council of Ministers, was elected President of a new Managing Committee, which replaced the Central Committee. The ideology of the party was also reformed; the new party manifesto stated that the SPA would be a modern, progressive party, committed to democracy, social justice and economic reform.

Despite domestic unrest, Albania continued its reintegration into international society. In June 1991 it was finally admitted to the CSCE and diplomatic relations were established with the EC. However, armed conflict in Yugoslavia did not encourage any further development of Balkan co-operation. The Albanian Government issued statements containing strong criticism of the policies of the Serbian leadership in Kosovo, and, in August, Albanian armed forces were placed on alert, after reported incidents between Yugoslav and Albanian border guards. In October the People's Assembly voted to recognize the 'Republic of Kosovo' as a 'sovereign and independent state'.

In the two months after its formation the National Stability Government introduced important legislation, notably on the privatization of land and the replacement of People's Councils (local administrative organs) by multi-party bodies. This was a belated attempt to prevent further chaos in the countryside, where some collective-farm members were reportedly seizing land on the basis of pre-collectivization boundaries, while others were left without any land to cultivate. The new legislation allowed an equal share for all collective-farm members, but this resolution of the issue was too late to guarantee a good harvest in 1991; many fields had been left untouched until final ownership was established.

In August 1991 there was a further exodus of some 10,000 migrants to Italy on ships commandeered in Albanian ports. There were also further strikes, particularly in the fuel supply industry, and opposition demonstrations in October demanded new elections and the resignation of President Alia. In late November the crisis deepened when Dr Sali Berisha, Chairman of the DPA, demanded that DPA members resign from the Government and all seven ministers left the 21-member cabinet. Berisha accused the SPA of deliberately obstructing the reform process in the countryside and instigating the rise in violent crime and the refugee crisis. However, Gramoz Pashko, Deputy Prime Minister and a leader of the DPA, opposed the dissolution of the Government, arguing that it would lead the country to anarchy and chaos. Nevertheless, on 6 December 1991, Ylli Bufi and his Government resigned. In an attempt to restore some political stability, President Alia appointed a temporary Government, composed mainly of non-party specialists, under a new Prime Minister, Vilson Ahmeti. The Government was only to hold office until new elections were held in March 1992.

In February 1992 a new electoral law was approved, which reduced the size of the People's Assembly from 250 to 140 members, 60% of which were to be elected from single-candidate constituencies and 40% by a system of proportional representation. More controversially, the new legislation did not allow candidates from ethnically based parties to stand for election, thus automatically outlawing the main party supported by ethnic Greeks, OMONIA, and causing deep dissatisfaction in the Greek community. The Greeks partly circumvented the new rule by presenting their candidates as members of a new group, the Union of Human Rights Party (UHRP), which also included members of a smaller group, Prespa, which campaigned on behalf of the small Macedonian minority in Albania.

The turn-out in the elections was again high, with 90% of eligible voters participating on 21 March 1992. This time the DPA won an overwhelming victory, gaining 62% of all votes cast in the first round of the general election, while support for the SPA fell to just 26%. On 29 March the DPA consolidated its first-round victory, by gaining a further 11 seats in areas where a second round of voting was necessary. In total, the DPA received 92 seats in the new parliament, just one short of a two-thirds majority, while the SPA was reduced to 38 seats. Seven seats were won by the SDP, two by the UHRP and one by the Republican Party.

The defeat of the SPA finally ended five decades of Communist rule, a process completed on 3 April 1992 by the resignation of President Ramiz Alia. On 9 April, Sali Berisha was elected to the presidency by a large majority in parliament. Berisha then appointed a new Government, led by Aleksander Meksi, a member of the DPA. In addition to the premiership, the DPA occupied 14 ministries in the new administration, while the SDP and the Republican Party received one portfolio each. The SPA was not represented in the new Government.

The new, youthful and inexperienced Government faced a huge range of problems. Industrial and agricultural production had fallen disastrously, and there were high levels of unemployment. In addition, the rapid dismantling of the one-party state had led to a breakdown in state authority, resulting in a sharp increase in serious crime, which acted as a major deterrent to foreign investment. In early July 1992, in yet another bid to escape the country's deepening economic crisis, some 6,000 Albanians commandeered ships in an attempt to migrate to Italy, prompted by the discontinuation of unemployment benefit for state workers. The collapse in agricultural production had left Albania's population almost entirely dependent on foreign aid, and only Operation Pelican, the Italian food distribution programme, was preventing mass starvation.

Against this background of social and economic hardship, it was not surprising that electoral support for the DPA decreased sharply at local elections in late July 1992. The DPA gained some 43% of the votes cast, significantly less than in the March general election, while the SPA's share of the vote rose to 41%. Moreover, in September 1992 serious divisions within the DPA culminated in the defection of several leading members of the party to form a new political grouping, the Albanian Democratic Alliance (ADA). Among them was Gramoz Pashko, who strongly criticized Berisha's administration for becoming more authoritarian and intolerant, and described the party's programme as 'right-wing extremism'.

On 6 April 1993 President Berisha announced four new members of the Council of Ministers, one of them, Petrit Kalakula, a prominent member of a right-wing faction in the DPA, known as Balli Kombëter, after the non-Communist resistance group in the Second World War. However, two other new ministers were independents, apparently chosen for their expertise rather than their political opinions. Political controversy was renewed in June, when deputies of the SDP began a boycott of the People's Assembly, in protest at the delay in adopting a new Constitution. They were joined by deputies from the SPA and the UHRP, the latter concerned to exert more pressure on the Government on behalf of the Greek minority, and the former, according to many observers, anxious to force a general election, which it believed it could now win. The deputies only ended their boycott at the end of August.

On 12 September 1992 former President Ramiz Alia was placed under house arrest and charged with corruption. His supporters claimed that the real cause of his arrest was a series of outspoken newspaper articles, which strongly criticized the Government for the fall in the standard of living since it came to power. His arrest followed that of other former Communist leaders, also charged with corruption and misuse of power. Among them was Nexhmije Hoxha, the widow of the former PLA leader, who was sentenced to nine years' imprisonment (later increased to 11 years) for illegal use of state funds. At the end of December five former PLA and police officials were sentenced to periods of imprisonment of up to 20 years, after being found guilty of ordering the fatal shooting of the four demonstrators in Shkodër in 1991. However, opponents of the Government accused the DPA of using the trials of former leaders, such as Hoxha, Alia and Ahmeti (the former premier) to distract public attention away from the acute social and economic problems being experienced by Albanians. Also, in late July 1993, Fatos Nano, the former Prime Minister and the leader of the SPA, was arrested and charged in connection with a financial scandal involving the supply of Italian food aid. Furthermore, Ramiz Alia was imprisoned in August, on the same charges as Nano. These further arrests of former Communists gave added credence to reports that the right wing of the Democratic Party was gaining influence over Berisha's administration, including a more forthright stance in foreign affairs.

Berisha's foreign policy, which opponents accused him of conducting largely single-handed, was marked by controversy, particularly concerning Albania's relations with Islamic countries, and with Macedonia and Greece. On 2 December 1992, on the initiative of Berisha, Albania became a member of the Organization of the Islamic Conference (OIC). The decision was strongly opposed by the SPA, which was increasingly concerned about greater activity by Muslim organizations in Albania and relatively large amounts of aid received from Islamic states. Berisha's enthusiasm for the development of close relations with Muslim countries, and above all with Turkey, reflected a need not only for economic assistance, but a desire to gain some measure of support should the conflict in Bosnia and Herzegovina spread south to Kosovo or if Albanian–Greek relations should worsen yet further.

Although relations with Greece improved markedly during the late 1980s, in 1992–93 they deteriorated rapidly, owing to alleged mistreatment of the Greek minority in southern Albania and the influx of Albanian refugees into Greece. In late June 1993 the Albanian authorities expelled Archimandrite Chrysostomos Maidans, a senior Greek Orthodox clergyman, from Albania, accusing him of advocating the secession of southern Albania to Greece. Greece retaliated by deporting some 20,000 Albanian immigrants, a small part of the more than 150,000 Albanians believed to have entered Greece since 1990, most of them illegally. Prime Minister Mitsotakis of Greece warned the Albanian Government that relations between the two countries would not improve unless Albania extended full human rights to its Greek minority. The Albanian Government responded by accusing Greece of interfering in its internal affairs. Relations between the two countries were not improved by the nationalist sentiments expressed during the Greek general election campaign and, even towards the end of 1993, the situation remained tense.

Although the position of the Greek minority improved considerably from the 1980s—they enjoyed freedom of religion and had their own Greek-language schools, newspapers, publishing houses and broadcasting facilities—there were continued allegations of ill-treatment of ethnic Greeks by Albanian security forces. There was also strong criticism of the electoral law which outlawed the Greeks' main party, OMONIA. Although there was a variety of opinion in the Greek community, many seemed to favour recognition of a separate 'Epirot' identity, leading to the gradual integration of southern Albania into the Epirus region of northern Greece.

Despite some improvement in the Albanian economy in 1992–93, Berisha's administration continued to confront considerable social and economic problems, in addition to the problems caused by the unstable international environment in the Balkans. The relative political stability which seemed to have been achieved following the DPA victory in the March 1992 elections proved to be short-lived. Albanian politics became sharply polarized in 1993. The right-wing Balli Kombëter faction of the DPA claimed about one-half of all DPA deputies in the People's Assembly by mid-1993, and remained in a position to exert considerable influence on the leadership. However, Berisha seemed to be attempting to avert a possible split in the party by refusing to support either the right-wing or the left-wing factions of the party. In August Petrit Kalakula was dismissed from office, for an allegedly pro-Fascist statement, demonstrating the limits of Berisha's tolerance of the right. Nevertheless, the shift to more nationalistic and anti-Communist policies by the DPA prompted the SDP and the Republicans to try and distance themselves from the DPA, while remaining in the Government. The SPA, meanwhile, remained politically isolated and seriously damaged by the continuing arrests and trials of its members for their actions under the Communist regime. Nevertheless, any worsening in the economic situation could bring it political benefits.

The Economy

MIRANDA VICKERS

Revised for this edition by the Editor

Albania, Europe's poorest country, remained economically undeveloped for decades. The country was, however, rich in resources, with an estimated US $50,000m.-worth of extractable minerals and $40,000m.-worth of onshore petroleum reserves. Other energy-related minerals included lignite, natural gas and asphalt. Metallic minerals included chromite (chromium ore), nickeliferous iron ore, copper ore and smaller quantities of cobalt and nickel. There were also deposits of phosphorous, bauxite, precious metals, kaolin clay, asbestos and titanomagnetite.

Until the early 1990s the system was rigidly centralized, with fixed prices, state or co-operative ownership of all means of production and planned regulation of output. The result was a shortage of skilled manpower, a decline in labour productivity owing to absenteeism, low morale, outdated, inefficient enterprises and a chronic lack of consumer goods. After Enver Hoxha's death, in 1985, in an attempt to modernize the underdeveloped economy, the leadership experimented with new schemes designed to revitalize the system, without changing its ideological basis. Following the victory of the Democratic Party of Albania (DPA) in the elections of March 1992, however, the new non-Communist Government introduced policies designed to produce a radical transformation of the economic system, including large-scale privatization and the introduction of a market economy. Such policies, though necessary, remained fraught with difficulties, as both industrial and agricultural production declined sharply, and the economy became dependent on external assistance. However, some improvement was evident in 1993, as agricultural production revived, and the standard of living was slightly improved by remittances from some 200,000 Albanians working in other countries. Nevertheless, Albania still had many problems: a young population with rising expectations; a largely obsolete industrial base; a backward agricultural sector; major infrastructure weaknesses; and political instability.

THE ALBANIAN ECONOMY AFTER 1945

Before the Second World War Albania was a largely agricultural country with very little industry. Once the Communists had seized power they nationalized most economic resources and began a programme of rapid industrialization. By 1960, according to official figures, industry accounted for 57.1% of total national income, an increase from 9.8% in 1938. New industrial enterprises included hydroelectric power stations, mineral-processing plants and industrial ventures associated with forestry and agriculture. However, this increase in industrial production in the 1950s was not matched by a corresponding improvement in agricultural production. Anxiety about this imbalance between agriculture and industry was reflected in the third Five-Year Plan (1961–65), in which the planned growth rate for agriculture was, for the first time, greater than that envisaged for industry.

The withdrawal of Soviet assistance from Albania in 1961 had severe affects on the Albanian economy throughout the early 1960s. However, by the beginning of the fourth Five-Year Plan (1966–70), partly as a result of aid and technical expertise from the People's Republic of China, Albania had largely recovered from the economic crisis of 1961–63. Living standards remained extremely low by Western standards, a position reinforced during Albania's 'Cultural Revolution' in the 1960s (a conscious imitation of the policies initiated in the People's Republic of China), when attempts were made to minimize differentials between workers in different sectors of the economy and between manual and non-manual workers. During the 1970s measures continued to narrow income differentials. Nevertheless, there was some progress in the introduction of modern technology, including the opening of Albania's first television station, in 1971, and the completion of an internal telephone system, in 1973.

According to Western estimates, annual growth of real gross national product (GNP) was estimated at 4.2% during the 1970s, and in 1979 GNP was estimated to be US $2,240m., equivalent to about $840 per head. (The lack of reliable economic date, however, made all such estimates little more than rough approximations.) The 1976 constitutional prohibition on accepting loans and credits from foreign sources severely constrained economic growth and served to keep foreign trade at the barter stage. The ban saved Albania from convertible-currency indebtedness, but also deprived the country of valuable knowledge of foreign markets. The ending of all economic agreements with the People's Republic of China, which, until 1978, accounted for about one-half of all Albania's foreign trade, also had serious consequences for Albania's international trade.

During the 1980s growth rates steadily declined and both industry and agriculture had great difficulty meeting their planned production targets. During the seventh Five-Year Plan (1981–85) net material product (NMP—a similar measure to GNP used in centrally planned economies) increased by 16% against a target of 35%–37%, an average annual growth rate of 3%, only slightly ahead of annual population growth. In November 1986, at the Ninth Congress of the PLA, Ramiz Alia, First Secretary of the PLA, admitted that economic performance during the seventh Five-Year Plan had been much poorer than expected. According to Alia, agricultural production grew by 27%, instead of the planned 36%–38%, and petroleum extraction reached only about one-half of the expected 58%–60% growth. Alia proposed some slight reforms of the system, with changes in management structures, limited decentralization of the economy, and the introduction of incentive payments in certain industries. These tentative moves away from Hoxha's strictly ideological approach to the economy, together with exhortations to the labour force to develop a more competitive spirit, were a response to dire economic necessity, but produced few results.

One of Albania's major problems was the high rate of population growth encouraged by the Communist regime. The total population rose from 1.2m. in 1950 to 3.3m. in 1990 and, at the end of the 1980s, the population was still growing at a rate of 2.1% per year, the highest rate in Europe. Almost two-thirds of the population was under the age of 26 and the annual addition to the labour force was around 40,000. This demographic boom was not matched by economic growth and contributed to the problem of mass unemployment experienced in the early 1990s.

AGRICULTURE

Agriculture remained the principal sector of the Albanian economy, employing 48.4% of the population and contributing 35.9% of NMP in 1990. In the same year the total area of arable land was 704,000 ha, nearly double the 391,000 ha in use in 1950. This increase was achieved largely through terracing, irrigation, drainage and desalination projects carried out in the 1960s and 1970s. There was considerable investment in afforestation and the construction of reservoirs and irrigation canals. In 1987 some 57% of agricultural land was irrigated, compared to only 10% of a much smaller area of agricultural land in 1938.

In 1983 there were 420 state and co-operative farms, which were the only legal forms of agricultural landholding, except for small personal allotments granted to collective-farm members. Private landholdings were merged into collective and state farms in the 1950s and early 1960s and, by 1967, collectivization was claimed to be complete. Greater use of agricultural machinery was also introduced, although draught animals remained common. By the end of the 1980s most machinery was outdated. Moreover, the general economic decline of the early 1990s made access to spare parts for machinery increasingly difficult. Some of the most productive agriculture was on peasants' private allotments, which, until 1990, were not permitted to exceed 200 sq m.

The development of livestock farming was given the highest priority for the eighth Five-Year Plan (1986–1990). This was prompted by the failure of a previous campaign to herd livestock held on private plots on to collective farms. Farmers reacted to this directive by slaughtering thousands of animals, with dramatic results on the supply of meat and dairy products. In July 1990, in a reversal of the previous policy, it was decided to allow peasants to rear cattle on their own plots; co-operatives were asked to transfer some of their stock to members for this purpose. It was also recommended that co-operatives in hilly or mountainous regions grant their members 2,000 sq m of land each, in addition to their private plots; co-operative members in lowland areas were permitted to increase their existing landholdings up to a maximum of 2,000 sq m. In a further relaxation of the existing regime, private markets were opened in July 1990, where farmers were permitted to set their own prices. In addition, state procurement prices were increased to reflect production costs. This new policy was an extension of reforms introduced in certain districts in 1989, as a result of which substantial improvements in food supplies were reported in those localities. However, the 9% increase in agricultural output in 1989 was only in comparison with very poor levels of output in 1988.

Despite the new policies, in 1990 the value of agricultural production fell by some 800m. lekë in comparison with 1989, a decrease of 7%, and in 1991 the situation continued to worsen. The need for reform of the system of co-operative and state farms was one of the main elements in the programme of the DPA, the PLA's main contender in the March 1991 general elections. The DPA proposed the privatization of land, giving smallholdings to each member of collective or state farms. Such plans were firmly opposed by the PLA. However, during April and May 1991 there were reports of collective-farm members unilaterally claiming plots of land, sometimes on the basis of pre-collectivization boundaries. The coalition Government, which took office in June, adopted legislation formally allowing private ownership of land, including rights of inheritance.

The uncertainty surrounding the ownership of land led to a sharp fall in the amount of land cultivated in 1991, as farmers refused to sow crops on land that might be taken from them in the future. In all, gross agricultural production fell by some 25% in 1991. A lack of fertilizers, insecticides and other materials, plus the lack of spare parts for largely obsolete machinery, all contributed to a crisis situation by 1992, when the urban population, and even part of the rural population, became dependent on international food aid for survival.

By September 1993 92% of collective farm land and 75% of state farm land had been distributed to private farmers, and the first positive results of privatization were evident. In the first six months of 1993 agricultural production was 17% higher than during the same period of 1992. Production of dairy and meat products was some 30% higher than in 1992, as a result of private farmers herding sheep, goats and cattle more efficiently than under the collective system. However, production requiring extensive use of machinery, fertilizers, or large landholdings (the size of the average landholding was reduced to just two hectares by the dissolution of collective farms) was slower to recover. Whereas in the 1970s and 1980s Albania was self-sufficient in wheat, production decreased by almost 60% in 1991–92, and in 1992 only 265,000 metric tons were produced, some 380,000 tons short of domestic needs. However, estimated production in 1993 was 400,000 tons, the increase partly encouraged by higher state purchasing prices for grain and also by the creation of farmers' associations, in which private farmers joined with neighbouring landholders to form farms averaging about 40 ha. Export crops were also badly affected in 1992, in particular, olives, oranges and tobacco. Tobacco had been a major earner of foreign currency, at one time being the third-most important export commodity.

INDUSTRY AND MINING

Although by 1993 agriculture was showing signs of recovery, it was not expected that Albanian industry would respond as quickly (if at all) to the introduction of a market economy. According to official figures, in 1990 industry accounted for 41.8% of NMP and employed 22.9% of the labour force. In the period 1981–85 industrial output increased by 27%, but in the following years growth rarely rose above 2%, except in 1989 when production rose by 5.6% in comparison with the previous year. In 1990, however, the value of industrial output fell by 1,400m. lekë, or 8%, compared with output in 1989. In 1991 industrial production declined even more dramatically, with a drop in the value of output of some 50%, as many factories ran out of raw materials and spare parts, and were forced to close down.

Before the changes in the early 1990s the five largest industrial sectors, measured by the value of output, were food processing, light industry, engineering, mining and construction materials. In the 1960s Albania began developing a manufacturing base which produced a fairly wide range of basic products. The light and food-processing industries provided more than 85% of domestic requirements in 1987. In the same year they accounted for 38% of gross industrial production and for 40% of the country's total exports. The production of chemicals was developed as an adjunct to mining and to benefit agriculture. The growth of engineering was several times faster than that of industry as a whole, stimulated by the need for domestic production of spare parts for the many types of foreign-made machines in the country, introduced as a result of the two major changes in Albania's alliance orientation. Production of spare parts increased by more than 25 times between 1960 and 1984.

Energy

Albania was almost self-sufficient in energy resources, largely owing to the development of hydroelectric power stations. Hydroelectric stations, such as the Vau i Dejes (250,000 kW) and the Fierzë (500,000 kW) plants, provided more than 80% of the country's total electricity production in 1988. Albania's largest power station was a 600,000-kW plant at Koman, on the River Drin. However, the reliance on hydroelectricity left Albania vulnerable to the effects of drought, as occurred in 1990, when Albania was unable to maintain exports of electricity to Yugoslavia and Greece, thus losing a valuable source of revenue. Indeed, the Government was forced to import an additional 7m. kWh of electricity, at a cost of US $2m., and 11,000 metric tons of fuel, costing $1.7m., expenditures which the economy could ill afford. In 1991 the situation improved considerably, as rainfall returned to normal levels and exports of electricity were resumed.

Albania's other energy sources were based on petroleum, natural gas and coal, most of which were extracted domestically. The country's main hydrocarbons reserves were to the south of Tirana, with the industry concentrated around the cities of Vlorë and Berat. The petroleum industry was a state monopoly under the Communist regime and remained under the control of a single company, Albpetrol, which was formed in March 1992, after democratization. The country had proven reserves of some 200m. metric tons of petroleum at existing production sites, but recoverable stocks, in 1991, were only 25m. tons. In 1970 production reached a record 1,486,000 metric tons, but, during the 1980s, output steadily declined, as extraction encountered increasing technical difficulties, reaching only 1.1m. tons in 1990 and some 0.5m. by 1992. Little was done to stabilize or increase production from active petroleum wells and there was a low extraction coefficient in new wells. At some sites only 12% of the petroleum available was extracted, whereas the introduction of modern technology would allow extraction of up to 40%. In an attempt to reverse the decline in production and begin extraction at new sites attempts were made to attract foreign investment into the industry. In 1991–92 contracts for technical assistance and exploration rights were negotiated with Denimex, a German company, with the US firms Occidental Petroleum and Chevron, and with Agip of Italy. By 1993 five concessions for offshore exploration had been granted to foreign corporations. Without foreign investment and modern technology it was unlikely that the performance of the petroleum industry would improve significantly, which, in turn, would further impede Albania's economic recovery. However, there was considerable foreign interest in the petroleum industry, which, by 1993, seemed on the point of resolving many of its difficulties and was being prepared for at least partial privatization.

Proven reserves of natural gas in Albania were estimated at 22,500m. cubic metres (cu m). During the period 1986–90 an average of 600m. cu m of natural gas was produced each year and it was planned to increase annual production to 1,100m. cu m. by 1995. However, production declined in the early 1990s, partly because of the obsolete equipment in use, and partly as a result of industrial unrest. As much as 20% of natural-gas production was reinjected, 40% was used as fertilizer feedstock and 15% was consumed in power stations.

Albania was largely self-sufficient in coal, but the coal produced was mostly low-quality lignite (brown coal of a particularly low calorific value) from small deposits scattered throughout Albania. Hence, some 300,000 metric tons of coking coal were imported annually, mainly from Greece and Bulgaria. The industry, which, by the early 1990s, was no longer economically viable, produced 2.3m. tons in 1987. The coal was used mainly to generate electricity in power stations and was a major cause of environmental pollution in Albania.

Ore Mining

Albania was well endowed with mineral resources, the most profitable of which (chromite, ferronickle and copper) were located mainly in the north of the country. However, the poor standard of equipment and techniques used hindered efforts to exploit this mineral wealth. The cost of mining and concentrating iron ore became so expensive in some places that plants were forced to close. Similar problems beset copper and nickel mining.

In the mid-1980s Albania was the world's second-largest producer of chromite (chromium ore), producing some 800,000 metric tons per year, but in 1990 unofficial estimates claimed that production had fallen to about 500,000 tons. The reduction in power supplies caused by the 1990 drought forced the closure of ferrochrome enterprises at Burrel and Elbasan. The consequent losses in exports amounted to an estimated US $1.8m. In April 1991 workers in the chromite industry went on strike, causing further losses estimated at $800,000. Owing to the poor quality of its ore, Albania lost ground to South Africa in the competition for markets. The poor reputation of Albania's chromium could largely be blamed on mismanagement, poor techniques, obsolete equipment, a lack of refining and processing plants and inadequate transport facilities. Some of the equipment used dates from the 1930s or even earlier, while a projected railway line to the main chromium mines, in the north-east, was left unfinished in the late 1980s. In 1992 production was probably as low as 300,000 tons, although exact figures were not available.

The extraction of copper ore also decreased drastically, from some 1m. tons in 1989 to just 256,000 tons in 1992. Although some improvement was expected in 1993, there was little possibility of foreign investment in modernization of the mines, since the quality of Albania's ores was poor, with only 1%–3% metal content.

TRANSPORT

In 1990 there were about 7,450 km of main roads and some 10,000 km of other roads. Road transport reached even the most inaccessible parts of the country, although many roads were of poor quality, and only one-third were hard-surfaced. In the absence of an extensive rail network, roads continued to carry most of the country's freight. Traffic grew considerably once the ownership of private cars was legalized in 1991, but bicycles and draught animals were still common. By 1993 there were an estimated 120,000 private cars in Albania. In July 1990 a protocol was signed by a group of Greek construction companies to build a 200-km motorway across southern Albania. The road was planned to extend from the Albanian–Greek border to the port of Durrës and was expected to take four years to build, at a cost of US $500m.

In 1990 Albania had 720 km of railways, mainly linking the towns in the western lowlands. The potential for foreign trade was enhanced by the opening, in September 1986, of a line from Shkodër to Titograd (now Podgorica) in Montenegro (Yugoslavia), which linked Albania with the European railway network, although the expected expansion of foreign trade was seriously undermined by the conflict in Bosnia and Herzegovina. Of great importance to Albania was a planned rail link with Greece, but its further development would depend on improved relations between the two countries. Albanian railways were standard gauge and thus easily compatible with neighbouring railway networks. No railway lines had been electrified by the early 1990s. The building of a line from Milot to Klos, in north-central Albania, and a viaduct near Bulqizë, the main centre of chromium production, designed to facilitate the transportation of minerals, remained uncompleted owing to a lack of finance.

After 1990 Albania developed air links with most major European cities and a weekly flight to the USA was inaugurated in November 1992. In March 1993 an Austrian business consortium announced that it would invest $45m. in the modernization of Rinas airport, near Tirana, to allow it to handle more international flights. A freight ferry service between Durrës and Trieste (Italy) began in 1983, and a similar service linked Sarandë with the Greek island of Corfu. A regular shipping line also began services between Ohrid in Macedonia and Pogradec in Albania.

TOURISM

Tourism in Albania was not encouraged until the late 1980s, for fear of contact between Albanians and 'alien ideological influences', but, from 1989, tourism was viewed as an important potential source of convertible currency. In 1989 and 1990 tourists visited Albania in unprecedented numbers, attracted by an unspoiled coastline and beautiful inland scenery. In 1990 there were some 30,000 foreign visitors, an increase of more than 50% on the previous year. Nevertheless, Albania did not possess the necessary infrastructure for any significant increase in tourism, and failed to attract sufficient foreign investment into development of hotels or tourist resorts. However, the European Bank for Reconstruction and Development stressed the potential for tourism in Albania and, in July 1993, provided credit worth US $22.5m. for two major hotel development projects in Tirana.

PRICES, WAGES AND RETAIL TRADE

Official figures for retail trade revealed increases in trading of 3.3% in 1987 and 2.7% in 1988, suggesting that the supply of goods was barely keeping pace with the growth of population. Interruptions and shortages in supply were constant in the state-controlled system of distribution. In July 1990, in an attempt to satisfy demand for goods not available in state shops, the Government agreed to the legalization of private handicraft and family trade businesses. These were permitted to set their own prices and find their own suppliers, but were not permitted to employ any person outside the immediate family. By December 1990 there were some 1,500 private entrepreneurs and some 7,000 service units had been privatized, including craft workshops, shops and restaurants. This minor reform of the system became a fully fledged commitment to privatization of retail trade under the DPA Government, elected in March 1992, and during 1992–93 around 20,000 state-owned shops were sold, mostly by auction to Albania's nascent class of entrepreneurs, or to the shop's employees.

Under the centrally planned system wages were extremely egalitarian for most of the population. In 1983 monthly wages ranged from approximately 400 lekë for the average worker to some 900 lekë for the manager of a large enterprise. In September 1990 it was announced that all wages below 450 lekë per month were to be increased by 10%, and by April 1991 the average wage was 650–700 lekë. A series of strikes in 1991, culminating in the general strike in May, forced the Government to raise wages for workers by up to 80%. Inevitably, these wage rises had an inflationary effect at a time of severe shortages of goods, as the amount of money in circulation was increased to finance salary increases. In July 1991 the annual rate of inflation was officially estimated to have reached more than 25%. The Government ended price controls on almost all goods in August 1992, which produced a sharp increase in inflation to an initial (and largely artificial) monthly rate of 47%, and an annual rate for 1992 of an estimated 200%. Over the next few months the Government's economic reforms succeeded in reducing inflation to 6.8% in January 1993 and just 0.9% in March of that year.

UNEMPLOYMENT

Until 1991 the existence of unemployment was not officially admitted, yet absenteeism and underemployment were widespread. In the early 1990s, however, Albanian leaders admitted that there were many unprofitable enterprises which would have to be closed, and that most other industrial plants were overstaffed. The closure of some obsolete plants and the reduction of staff in others produced very high unemployment in 1992, especially among young people, thus prompting the mass emigration to Greece and Italy seen in 1991 and 1992. According to official figures, by mid-1993 unemployment had reached 280,000, equivalent to 18.2% of the national labour force. At the same time, there were an estimated 200,000 Albanians working in other countries, of which about 150,000 were in Greece.

FOREIGN TRADE

Despite its isolationist economic policy, Albania maintained trade links with about 50 countries in the 1980s, although at a low level. The bulk of exports were fuels and minerals, notably copper, nickel, chromite and petroleum; agricultural products, including alcoholic beverages (raki, brandy), cigarettes (mostly for Eastern Europe), fruit, olives, tomatoes, sardines and anchovies; and electricity. While the value of exports remained fairly constant throughout the 1980s, the value of imports rose by 51% in 1980–90, the bulk of the increase being in 1987–90, as Albanian domestic production failed to keep pace with population growth and demand for foodstuffs and consumer goods increased. The country's dependence on imported fuel and materials was also increasing. Machinery and equipment, however, continued to form the largest proportion of imports (25.2% in 1990), followed by fuels, metals and minerals (24.5%), non-food agricultural raw materials (15.7%), foodstuffs (10.1%), chemical products (9.3%) and consumer goods (8.4%).

Much of the increase in trade was with Western Europe, rather than with Albania's traditional partners in the Communist (or former Communist) bloc. Until 1989 more than one-half of all trade went to member countries of the Council for Mutual Economic Assistance (CMEA—54.3% of exports and 50.8% of imports in 1988), but the collapse of the CMEA and Albania's need for more consumer goods and higher quality equipment led to a reorientation of trade towards regional partners, regardless of their political system. Imports from industrialized countries rose from 31.4% of total imports in 1988 to 45.7% in 1990. In 1990 imports from the West were worth an estimated US $245m., compared with about $165m. in 1989. Czechoslovakia (the Czech Republic and Slovakia since the beginning of 1993) remained the main trading partner, but Germany (both the Federal Republic and the German Democratic Republic) was increasingly important.

The collapse in Albanian industrial production in 1991 led to a fall in the volume of foreign trade of about one-half in comparison with 1990. The decline in exports led to a balance-of-payments crisis, which had already been evident in 1990, as the value of exports decreased to just 59% of that of imports (down from 94% in 1987). In that year convertible-currency earnings were some $316m. less than the economic plan had projected, and the trade deficit increased from $96m. to $254m. In 1991 Albania asked its foreign creditors for a postponement on debt repayments and was permitted a moratorium on about one-quarter of its outstanding convertible-currency obligations. In the short term Albania received economic aid from Western countries, to enable the Government to continue importing food.

Trade would continue to be constrained by Albania's limited foreign reserves and its small number of export commodities which are able to compete effectively on the international market. In its efforts to increase exports Albania was constrained by two major factors. Firstly, the move to rationalize production and increase efficiency was hampered by the shortage of technology and skilled personnel. Secondly, the pressure on Albania's export industry was compounded by the Government's commitment to channel more resources into the domestic consumer-goods sector to appease a restless population.

BANKING AND FINANCE

Traditionally, the Albanian budget was based on Soviet-type categories, although the total budget was more centralized. Personal taxes were abolished in 1970, most state revenue coming from economic production. The interim constitutional law, adopted in April 1991, contained provisions committing the state to a return to personal taxation as the main source of state revenue. National revenue fell by 1,300m. lekë in 1990, from a total of 8,558m. lekë in 1989, and in May 1991 it was admitted that the budget deficit had reached 3,200m. lekë, equivalent to some 30% of total budgeted expenditure and 28% of gross domestic product (GDP). As industrial production decreased sharply in 1991, state revenue also fell, owing to the overwhelming dependence on taxation of enterprises. Meanwhile, social expenditure was rising, as unemployment increased. The Government initially provided 80% of previous salaries as unemployment benefit, but this was sharply reduced after August 1992, on the insistence of the International Monetary Fund (IMF). Reductions in government expenditure were not matched by increases in taxation revenue, despite new taxes imposed on service industries and additional customs duties introduced in 1993. The 1992 budget deficit was an estimated 17% of GDP, while the budget agreed in March 1993 envisaged an increase to 22% of GDP.

Change was slow in the banking sector, although the role of the Albanian State Bank was enlarged to allow it to grant more short- and long-term credits to industry. Also, in 1990 the Albanian State Bank for Foreign Relations was established, to provide and direct funds for foreign trade. More commercial banks were planned and the savings-bank sector was to be restructured. In April 1991 the Iliria Bank, Albania's first private commercial bank, was opened.

The prohibition on receipt of foreign credits, which had been in the 1976 Constitution, was annulled in 1990, thus allowing Albania to receive much-needed credits from abroad. A report issued in January 1991, by the State Bank's foreign exchange and treasury department, concluded that Albania could service a debt of around US $4,000m. However, as Albania's convertible-currency earnings decreased during 1991, its ability to accommodate such debts seemed illusory. By the end of 1992 the country's foreign debts totalled some US $600m., at a time when export revenues remained low, and it was experiencing serious problems servicing its creditors. The proposed budget for 1993 envisaged receipt of some 11,700m. lekë in foreign loans, some 11% of GDP, and it was evident that only continuing external assistance could prevent a severe budgetary crisis.

PROBLEMS AND PROSPECTS

Despite the promise shown by the expansion of small-scale private enterprise and the improvements in agricultural production, the Albanian economy remained in deep crisis in the early 1990s, dependent for the foreseeable future on external aid and remittances from Albanians working abroad. Enver Hoxha's policies of economic autarky left Albanians with a devastated economy, in which most industries were inefficient and unlikely to be viable in the long-term. The privatization of large enterprises would inevitably produce yet higher levels of unemployment, a prospect that the Government could hardly consider. Yet state subsidies to loss-making industries threaten to overwhelm government expenditure.

The psychological aspects of reform were as important as structural impediments. Attempts to encourage enterprise managers to act more independently from the state revealed some serious, if not unpredictable, problems: a reluctance to take independent decisions; a tendency to exaggerate difficulties and wait for solutions from above; and a lack of self-motivation. Inertia and resistance to change proved difficult to overcome, the legacy of nearly 50 years of managerial dependence on political decisions made at the centre.

Albania's attempts to address the problems of its economy developed from the relatively small-scale reforms announced in mid-1990, to the radical programme, including privatization, developed by the DPA Government elected in March 1992. The most crucial changes came in accordance with an agreement with the IMF, in August 1992, whereby the Government adopted a strict reform programme, in exchange for a stand-by loan of US $18m. The reforms accelerated privatization (almost complete in agriculture by mid-1993), liberalized prices and reduced government expenditure. The results were a slow growth in agricultural production, the stabilization of the lek, and a reduction in inflation to around 10% per month. However, the cost of reforms, in terms of decreasing living standards, was immense, and only an estimated $1,000m.-worth of aid in 1991–92 prevented serious food shortages.

The technological modernization which Albania needed to overcome its inefficiencies and economic weakness was dependent on greater interaction with the rest of the world. Yet foreign investment was limited by the overall instability of the Balkans, the cumbersome Albanian bureaucracy and poor infrastructure. By mid-1993 only $60m. had been invested. There were, however, relatively good investment incentives and a large expatriate community, including the ethnic Albanians of Kosovo and Macedonia, which was already beginning to invest in light manufacturing, road construction and tourist development in Albania. Serbian policies in Kosovo limited the economic opportunities of the Kosovars, who were, therefore, keen to trade with Albania. There were also the psychological incentives of nationalism and a long-term interest in unification. Geographically and commercially Albania–Kosovo trade links were practical and were likely to continue to grow.

Nevertheless, Albania would require more extensive investment than could be provided by Albanians in other countries. However, years of isolation resulted in Albania having the most underdeveloped trade links of any European country. This lack of expertise in international trade and the poor quality of Albania's current exports did not allow Albania to earn the foreign currency it required to improve its infrastructure and production capacity. The future of the Albanian economy was, therefore, dependent on far-sighted Western investment and aid programmes. This, in turn, depended on the ability of Albania's leaders to create an economic environment in which such investment would succeed.

Statistical Survey

Source (unless otherwise stated): Drejtoria e Statistikës, Tirana.

Area and Population

AREA, POPULATION AND DENSITY

Area (sq km)	
Land	27,398
Inland water	1,350
Total	28,748*
Population (census results)	
January 1979	2,591,000
2 April 1989	
Males	1,638,900†
Females	1,543,500†
Total	3,182,417
Population (official estimates at mid-year)	
1989	3,199,233
1990	3,255,891
1991	3,300,000
Density (per sq km) at mid-1991	114.8

* 11,100 sq miles.

† Provisional.

Ethnic Groups (census of 2 April 1989): Albanian 3,117,601; Greek 58,758; Macedonian 4,697; Montenegrin, Serb, Croat, etc. 100; others 1,261.

DISTRICTS (mid-1990)*

	Area (sq km)	Population	Density (per sq km)
Berat	1,027	180,489	175.7
Dibër	1,568	153,775	98.1
Durrës	848	251,029	296.0
Elbasan	1,481	248,676	167.9
Fier	1,175	251,115	213.7
Gramsh	695	44,791	64.4
Gjirokastër	1,137	67,392	59.3
Kolonjë	805	25,291	31.4
Korçë	2,181	218,219	100.1
Krujë	607	109,876	181.0
Kukës	1,330	104,731	78.7
Lezhë	479	63,505	132.6
Librazhd	1,013	73,871	72.9
Lushnjë	712	137,830	193.6
Mat	1,028	78,754	76.6
Mirditë	867	51,701	59.6
Përmet	929	40,419	43.5
Pogradec	725	73,333	101.1
Pukë	1,034	50,286	48.6
Sarandë	1,097	89,459	81.5
Shkodër	2,528	47,605	18.8
Skrapar	775	241,549	311.7
Tepelenë	817	51,022	62.5
Tiranë	1,238	374,483	302.5
Tropojë	1,043	45,965	44.1
Vlorë	1,609	180,725	112.3
Total	28,748	3,255,891	113.3

Source: *Statistical Directory of Albania.*

* In mid-1991 certain changes were made to the administrative-territorial structure of the country, including the creation of the new district of Kavajë.

PRINCIPAL TOWNS (population at mid-1990)

Tiranë (Tirana, the capital)	244,200
Durrës (Durazzo)	85,400
Elbasan	83,300
Shkodër (Scutari)	81,900
Vlorë (Vlonë or Valona)	73,800
Korçë (Koritsa)	65,400
Fier	45,200
Berat	43,800
Lushnjë	31,500
Kavajë	25,700
Gjirokastër	24,900
Kuçovë*	22,300

* This town was known as Qyteti Stalin during the period of Communist rule, but has since reverted to its former name.

Source: *Statistical Directory of Albania.*

BIRTHS, MARRIAGES AND DEATHS

	Registered live births		Registered marriages		Registered deaths	
	Number	Rate (per 1,000)	Number	Rate (per 1,000)	Number	Rate (per 1,000)
1986	76,435	25.3	25,718	8.5	17,369	5.7
1987	79,696	25.9	27,370	8.9	17,119	5.6
1988	80,241	25.5	28,174	9.0	17,027	5.4
1989	78,862	24.7	27,655	8.6	18,168	5.7
1990	82,125	25.2	28,992	8.9	18,193	5.6

Average Life Expectation (1989/90): 72.2 years (Males 69.3 years, Females 75.44 years).

Source: mainly *Statistical Yearbook of the PSR of Albania* and *Statistical Yearbook of Albania.*

ECONOMICALLY ACTIVE POPULATION
(ILO estimates, '000 persons at mid-1980)

	Males	Females	Total
Agriculture, etc.	338	339	677
Industry	237	74	311
Services	144	79	223
Total	719	492	1,211

Source: ILO, *Economically Active Population Estimates and Projections, 1950–2025.*

Mid-1990 (estimates in '000): Agriculture, etc. 753; Total 1,556 (Source: FAO, *Production Yearbook*).

EMPLOYMENT IN THE 'SOCIALIZED' SECTOR
(excluding agricultural co-operatives)

	1986	1987	1990*
Industry	272,300	287,000	313,782
Construction	78,300	77,800	82,082
Agriculture	182,100	190,300	203,728
Transport and communications	38,000	39,600	41,872
Trade	55,400	56,400	54,876
Education and culture	55,800	57,600	63,161
Health service	37,200	37,700	40,685
Others	40,300	41,800	59,230
Total	759,400	788,200	859,416

* **1988:** Total: 811,000. Figures for 1989 are not available.
Source: *Statistical Directory of Albania.*

Agriculture

PRINCIPAL CROPS ('000 metric tons)

	1989	1990*	1991*
Wheat and spelt	611	450	300†
Rice (paddy)	8	6	5
Barley	40*	30	26
Maize	302	200	180
Rye	9†	7	7
Oats	30*	20	18
Sorghum	36*	28	25
Potatoes	88*	71	65
Dry beans	20*	15	12
Sunflower seed	24	18	14
Cottonseed	12†	12	12
Olives	32*	24	18
Vegetables	397	299	248
Grapes	19	19	18
Sugar beet	320*	230	205
Apples	18†	13	11
Plums	15†	10	7
Oranges	15	12	10
Tobacco (leaves)	20†	15	12
Cotton (lint)	7*	6	5

* FAO estimate(s). † Unofficial estimate.
Source: FAO, *Production Yearbook.*

LIVESTOCK ('000 head, year ending September)

	1989	1990*	1991*
Horses	101†	102	100
Mules	23*	23	23
Asses	53*	53	53
Cattle	680	700	650
Pigs	180	183	170
Sheep	1,600	1,630	1,600
Goats	1,100	1,150	1,000

Poultry (million): 6 in 1989; 6* in 1990; 5* in 1991.
* FAO estimate(s). † Unofficial estimate.
Source: FAO, *Production Yearbook.*

LIVESTOCK PRODUCTS (FAO estimates, metric tons)

	1989	1990	1991
Beef and veal	27,000	26,000	23,000
Mutton and lamb	19,000	16,000	15,000
Goats' meat	12,000	9,000	6,000
Pig meat	8,000	8,000	7,000
Poultry meat	14,000	14,000	13,000
Cows' milk	314,000	302,000	283,000
Sheep's milk	45,000	45,000	44,000
Goats' milk	40,000	38,000	35,000
Cheese	13,600	12,100	10,700
Butter	3,924	2,925	2,250
Hen eggs	14,200	10,500	8,100
Wool:			
greasy	3,800	2,800	2,200
scoured (clean)	2,280	1,700	1,300
Cattle hides	4,312	4,180	3,861
Sheep and lamb skins	2,475	2,375	2,375
Goat and kid skins	976	812	572

Source: FAO, *Production Yearbook.*

Forestry

ROUNDWOOD REMOVALS ('000 cubic metres)

	1989*	1990	1991*
Industrial wood	680	520	1,000
Fuel wood	1,608	1,556	1,556
Total	2,2028	2,076	2,556

* FAO estimates.
Source: FAO, *Yearbook of Forest Products.*

SAWNWOOD PRODUCTION ('000 cubic metres)

	1989*	1990	1991*
Coniferous (soft wood)	105	86	86
Broadleaved (hard wood)	95	296	296
Total	200	382	382

* FAO estimates.
Source: FAO, *Yearbook of Forest Products.*

Fishing

('000 metric tons, live weight)

	1987	1988	1989
Inland waters	4.9	6.7	5.4
Mediterranean Sea	8.2	7.9	6.6
Total catch	13.1	14.6	12.0

1990: Catch as in 1989 (FAO estimates).
Source: FAO, *Yearbook of Fishery Statistics.*

Mining

PRODUCTION (estimates, '000 metric tons)

	1988	1989	1990
Brown coal (incl. lignite)	2,184	2,193	2,071
Crude petroleum	1,167	1,128	1,067
Natural gas (terajoules)	186	233	243
Copper ore	1,087	1,136	931
Iron-Nickel ore	1,067	1,179	931
Chromium ore	1,109	1,200	1,011

Source: *Statistical Directory of Albania.*

Note: Figures for metallic ores refer to gross weight. The estimated metal content (in '000 metric tons) was: Copper 17 in 1988, 17 in 1989; Nickel 8 in 1988, 8 in 1989; Chromium 216 in 1988, 201 in 1989 (Source: UN, *Industrial Statistics Yearbook*).

Industry

MAIN INDUSTRIAL PRODUCTS
('000 metric tons, unless otherwise indicated)

	1988	1989	1990
Electric energy (million kWh)	3,984	4,123	3,198
Blister copper	15	15.3	12
Copper wires and cables	11.6	12.3	8.7
Carbonic ferrochrome	38.7	38.8	24
Metallurgical coke	291	290	230
Rolled wrought steel	96	93	65
Phosphatic fertilizers	165	165	141
Ammonium nitrate	96	109	93
Urea	77	92	90
Sulphuric acid	81	82	68
Caustic soda	31	33	32
Soda ash	22	26.6	23
Machinery and equipment (million lekë)	496	486	369
Spare parts (million lekë)	493	513	432
Cement	746	754	645
Bricks and tiles (million pieces)	319	327	308
Refractory bricks	30	27	26
Furniture (million lekë)	131	144	133
Heavy cloth (million metres)	11.3	11.9	8.6
Knitwear (million pieces)	12.2	11.4	9.7
Footwear ('000 pairs)	5,396	6,103	5,990
Television receivers ('000)	16.5	23.2	18.1
Radio receivers ('000)	25	30	26.4
Beer ('000 hectolitres)	237	228	187.4
Cigarettes (million)	5,310	6,184	4,947
Soap and detergent	21.5	24.8	21.4

Source: *Statistical Directory of Albania.*

1990 (FAO estimates, '000 metric tons): Wine 18; Raw sugar 15 (unofficial estimate); Olive oil 3 (Source: FAO, *Production Yearbook*).

Finance

CURRENCY AND EXCHANGE RATES

Monetary Units
100 qindarka (qintars) = 1 new lek.

Denominations
Coins: 5, 10, 20 and 50 qintars; 1 lek and 2 lekë.
Notes: 1, 3, 5, 10, 25, 50, 100 and 500 lekë.

Sterling and Dollar Equivalents (30 September 1993)
£1 sterling = 164.5 lekë;
US $1 = 110.0 lekë;
1,000 lekë = £6.079 = $9.091.

Exchange Rate
The non-commercial rate, applicable to tourism, was fixed at US $1 = 7.000 lekë between June 1979 and September 1988. A revised rate of $1 = 6.000 lekë was introduced in September 1988 and remained in force until September 1989. The rate was fixed at $1 = 15.000 lekë in November 1990. This rate was in effect until June 1991, when the lek was revalued to 10 per dollar. In September 1991 it was announced that the currency would henceforth be linked to the EC's European Currency Unit (ECU). The initial exchange rate was set at 1 ECU = 30 lekë (US $1 = 25 lekë). A revised rate of $1 = 50 lekë was introduced in February 1992. This was adjusted to $1 = 110 lekë in September 1992.

STATE BUDGET (million lekë)

Revenue	1988	1989	1990
National economy	7,669	8,412	7,326
Non-productive sector and other income from the socialist sector	889	922	967
Total revenue	8,558	9,334	8,293

Expenditure	1988	1989	1990
National economy	4,211	5,135	5,998
Socio-cultural measures	2,725	2,820	2,991
Defence	955	965	990
Administration	155	169	167
Total expenditure (incl. others)	8,552	9,309	10,869

Source: *Statistical Directory of Albania.*

NATIONAL ACCOUNTS

Net Material Product (percentages at 1986 prices)

Activities of the Material Sphere	1988	1989	1990
Industry*	46.3	44.8	41.8
Agriculture	31.5	32.3	35.9
Construction	6.5	6.5	6.4
Transport, trade, etc.	15.7	16.4	15.9
Total	100.0	100.0	100.0

* Comprising mining, manufacturing, electricity, gas and water.

External Trade

(million lekë)

	1988	1989	1990
Imports c.i.f.	3,218	3,792	3,795
Exports f.o.b.	2,549	3,029	2,273

Source: *Statistical Directory of Albania.*

PRINCIPAL COMMODITIES (%)

Imports	1988	1989	1990
Machinery and equipment	28.5	23.8	25.2
Spare parts and bearings	4.8	4.4	5.7
Fuels, minerals and metals	25.2	26.1	24.5
Chemical and rubber products	13.1	12.1	9.3
Construction materials	0.1	0.8	1.1
Raw materials of plant or animal origin	14.0	17.8	15.7
Foodstuffs	8.1	7.2	10.1
Other consumer goods	6.2	7.8	8.4
Total	100.0	100.0	100.0

Exports	1988	1989	1990
Fuels	7.9		
Electricity	7.3	54.4	46.8
Minerals and metals	39.8		
Chemical products	0.8	0.6	1.5
Construction materials	1.5	1.4	1.1
Raw materials of plant or animal origin	16.1	16.7	17.8
Processed foodstuffs	8.7	17.2	20.1
Unprocessed foodstuffs	8.2		
Other consumer goods	9.7	9.7	12.7
Total	100.0	100.0	100.0

Source: *Statistical Directory of Albania.*

PRINCIPAL TRADING PARTNERS (%)

Exports f.o.b	1988	1989	1990
Austria	5.4	4.1	4.7
Bulgaria	9.4	10.3	8.3
China, People's Republic	5.1	5.6	4.9
Cuba	1.3	1.2	1.1
Czechoslovakia	10.0	11.4	14.8
Egypt	1.2	1.1	1.7
France	1.6	1.7	1.4
German Democratic Republic	8.2	9.2	4.5
Germany, Federal Republic	4.2	4.9	5.3
Greece	1.8	3.0	2.9
Hungary	5.9	3.7	5.7
Italy	6.3	7.9	9.0
Japan	1.8	1.7	2.1
Poland	7.5	6.7	4.7
Romania	9.7	9.1	4.7
Sweden	4.6	2.9	1.8
Switzerland	2.5	4.0	6.2
Yugoslavia	7.1	4.9	6.9
Total (incl. others)	100.0	100.0	100.0

Source: *Statistical Directory of Albania.*

Imports c.i.f.	1988	1989	1990
Austria	2.6	3.8	6.0
Bulgaria	9.3	7.3	6.3
China, People's Republic	8.7	4.4	6.2
Czechoslovakia	11.3	8.7	8.6
Egypt	1.8	1.2	1.2
France	1.4	1.7	2.6
German Democratic Republic	7.3	8.5	8.7
Germany, Federal Republic	6.1	9.3	8.8
Greece	4.9	7.2	5.5
Hungary	4.6	3.4	3.8
Italy	7.2	8.7	9.8
Japan	0.1	0.2	0.1
Poland	6.9	6.1	4.4
Romania	8.1	7.0	4.8
Turkey	0.6	1.0	1.4
Yugoslavia	4.2	4.8	5.2
Total (incl. others)	100.0	100.0	100.0

Source: *Statistical Yearbook of Albania.*

Transport

RAILWAYS (traffic)*

	1988	1989	1990
Passengers carried ('000)	10,966	11,724	11,908
Passengers-km (million)	703.0	752.4	779.2
Freight carried ('000 metric tons)	7,659	8,048	6,646
Freight ton-km (million)	626.4	674.2	584.0

* Figures refer to operations by the Ministry of Transport only.

Source: *Statistical Directory of Albania.*

ROAD TRAFFIC

	1988	1989	1990
Passenger journeys ('000)	191,187	189,155	171,724
Passenger-km (million)	2,242.5	2,313.4	2,174.0
Freight carried ('000 metric tons)	76,982	82,815	75,744
Freight ton-km (million)	1,269.0	1,303.5	1,195.3

Source: *Statistical Directory of Albania.*

Motor vehicles in use ('000 at 31 December 1991): Passenger cars 16.0; Buses and coaches 1.9; Goods vehicles 30.0; Vans 1.0 (Source: International Road Federation, *World Road Statistics*).

INTERNATIONAL SEA-BORNE SHIPPING
(freight traffic, '000 metric tons)

	1987	1988	1989
Goods loaded	1,073	1,090	1,112
Goods unloaded	998	1,020	1,040

Source: UN, *Monthly Bulletin of Statistics.*

Communications Media

	1988	1989	1990
Book production:			
Titles	1,018	1,137	1,049
Copies ('000)	7,000	8,000	8,000
Newspapers:			
Number	42	42	40
Copies ('000)	62,000	65,000	63,000
Radio receivers in use	525,000	514,980	n.a.
Television receivers in use	260,000	324,905	n.a.

1991: 200 book titles.

Sources: *Statistical Yearbook of Albania* and UNESCO, *Statistical Yearbook.*

Education

(1990)

	Institutions	Teachers	Pupils
Pre-primary	3,926	5,664	130,000
Primary (8-year)	1,726	28,798	557,000
Secondary:			
general	47	2,318	68,000
vocational	466	7,390	138,000
Higher	8	1,806	27,000

Source: *Statistical Yearbook of Albania.*

Directory

The Constitution

The Constitution adopted on 28 December 1976 was declared invalid in April 1991, following the adoption of interim constitutional legislation. The People's Assembly appointed a commission to draft a new Constitution, a version of which was published in June 1993. On 30 April 1991 the People's Assembly adopted the Law on the Major Constitutional Provisions of the People's Assembly of the Republic of Albania, which was, in effect, an interim organic law. The following is a summary of the main provisions of that legislation:

THE SOCIAL ORDER

The Political Order

Articles 1–9. The Republic of Albania is a parliamentary republic. The Republic is a juridical and democratic state which observes and defends the rights and freedoms of its citizens.

The fundamental principle of state organization is the separation of legislative, executive and judicial powers. The people exercise their power through their representative organs, which are elected by free, universal, direct and secret ballot.

Legislative power belongs to the People's Assembly; the Head of State is the President of the Republic; the supreme body of executive power is the Council of Ministers; judicial power is exercised by courts, which are independent and guided only by the provisions of the law.

Albania recognizes and guarantees those fundamental rights and freedoms that are proclaimed in international law, including those of national minorities. Judicial norms must be applied equally to all state bodies, political parties and other groups and organizations. All citizens are equal under the law.

Political pluralism is a fundamental condition of democracy in Albania. Political parties are entirely separate from the State and are prohibited from activities in military bodies, state ministries, diplomatic representations abroad, judicial institutions and other state bodies.

Albania is a secular state. The State observes the freedom of religious belief and creates conditions to exercise it.

The Economic Order

Articles 10–14. The country's economy is based on diverse systems of ownership, freedom of economic activity and the regulatory role of the State. All kinds of ownership are protected by law. Foreign persons may gain the right to ownership and are guaranteed the right to carry out independent economic activity in Albania, to form joint economic ventures and to repatriate profits.

All citizens are liable for contributions to state expenditure in relation to their income.

SUPREME BODIES OF STATE POWER

The People's Assembly

Articles 15–23. The People's Assembly is the supreme body of state power and sole law-making body. It defines the main directions of the domestic and foreign policy of the State. It approves and amends the Constitution and is competent to declare war and ratify or annul international treaties. It elects its Presidency which is composed of a Chairman and two Deputy Chairmen. It also elects the President of the Republic of Albania, the Supreme Court, the Attorney-General and his or her deputies. It controls the activity of state radio and television, the state news agency and other official information media.

The People's Assembly is composed of at least 140 deputies, elected for a period of four years.

The President of the Republic of Albania

Articles 24–32. The President of the Republic is Head of State and is elected by the People's Assembly, in a secret ballot, and by a two-thirds majority of the votes of all the deputies. The term of office is five years. No person is to hold the office of President for more than two successive terms. The President may not occupy any other post while fulfilling the functions of President.

The President guarantees the observation of the Constitution and legislation adopted by the People's Assembly; he appoints the Chairman of the Council of Ministers and accepts his or her resignation; he exercises the duties of the People's Assembly when the legislature is not in session.

The President is Commander-in-Chief of the Armed Forces and Chairman of the Council of Defence. The Council of Defence is responsible for organizing the country's resources to ensure the territorial defence of the Republic. Its members are proposed by the President and approved by the People's Assembly.

The Supreme Organs of State Administration

Articles 33–41. The Council of Ministers is the supreme executive and legislative body. It directs activity for the realization of the domestic and foreign policies of the State and directs and controls the activity of ministries, other central organs of state administration and local organs of administration. It is composed of the Chairman, Vice-Chairmen, Ministers and other persons defined by law. The Chairman of the Council of Ministers is appointed by the President; Ministers are appointed by the President upon the recommendation of the Chairman. The composition of the Council of Ministers is approved by the People's Assembly. Members of the Council of Ministers may not have any other state or professional function.

The Chairman and Vice-Chairmen of the Council of Ministers constitute the Presidency of the Council of Ministers.

FINAL PROVISIONS

Articles 42–46. The creation, organization and activity of the local organs of power, administration, courts and the Attorney-General are made according to existing legal provisions, except those invalidated by the Law on Major Constitutional Provisions. Drafts for amendments to the Law on Major Constitutional Provisions may be proposed by the President of the Republic, the Council of Ministers or one-quarter of the deputies of the People's Assembly. The adoption of amendments requires a two-thirds majority of all deputies. The provisions of the Law on Major Constitutional Provisions operate until the adoption of the Constitution of the Republic of Albania, which will be drafted by the Special Commission appointed by the People's Assembly. The Constitution of the People's Socialist Republic of Albania, adopted on 28 December 1976, is invalidated.

The Government

(November 1993)

HEAD OF STATE

President of the Republic: Dr SALI BERISHA (elected 9 April 1992).

COUNCIL OF MINISTERS

A coalition of the Democratic Party of Albania (DPA), the Social Democratic Party of Albania (SDP), the Albanian Republican Party (ARP) and independents.

Chairman (Prime Minister): ALEKSANDER MEKSI (DPA).

Deputy Chairman (responsible for economic reform): BASHKIM KOPLIKU (DPA).

General Secretary: VULLNET ADEMI (SDP).

Minister of Agriculture and Food: HASAN HALILI.

Minister of Construction, Housing and Land Distribution: ILIR MANUSHI (DPA).

Minister of Culture, Youth and Sport: DHIMITËR ANAGNOSTI (DPA).

Minister of Defence: SAFET ZHULALI (DPA).

Minister of Education: XHEZAIR TELITI (Independent).

Minister of Finance: PJETËR DISHNICA (DPA).

Minister of Foreign Affairs: ALFRED SERREQI (DPA).

Minister of Health and Environmental Protection: TRITAN SHEHU (DPA).

Minister of Mining and Energy Resources: ABDYL XHAJA (Independent).

Minister of Justice: KUDRET ÇELA (Independent).

Minister of Labour, Emigration, Social Welfare and the Politically Persecuted: DASHAMIR SHEHI (DPA).

Minister of Public Order: AGRON MUSARAJ.

Minister of Tourism: EDMOND SPAHO (Independent).

Minister of Industry and Trade: SELIM BELORTAJA (DPA).

Minister of Transport and Communications: FATOS BITNICKA (ARP).

Minister without portfolio (responsible for local government): REXHED UKA (DPA).

Chairman of the Committee of Science and Technology: MAKSIM KONOMI (DPA).

Chairman of the Control Commission: BLERIM ÇELA (DPA).

MINISTRIES

Council of Ministers: Këshilli i Ministrave, Tirana; telex 4201.

Ministry of Agriculture and Food: Ministria e Bujqësisë dhe Ushqimit, Tirana; tel. (42) 26147; telex 4209.

Ministry of Construction, Housing and Land Distribution: Tirana.

Ministry of Culture, Youth and Sport: Ministria e Kulturës, Rinisë dhe Sporteve, Bulevardi Dëshmorët e Kombit, Tirana; tel. (42) 29715; fax (42) 27878.

Ministry of Defence: Ministria e Mbrojtjes, Tirana.

Ministry of Education: Ministria e Arsimit, Tirana; telex 4203.

Ministry of Finance: Ministria e Financave, Tirana; telex 4297.

Ministry of Foreign Affairs: Ministria e Punëve të Jashtme, Tirana; tel. (42) 34600; telex 2164; fax (42) 32971.

Ministry of Health and Environmental Protection: Ministria e Shendetesisë dhe Mbrojtjes së Ambjentit, Tirana; telex 4205.

Ministry of Industry and Trade: Ministria e Industrisë dhe Tregtisë, Tirana; tel. (42) 34668; telex 2152; fax (42) 34658.

Ministry of Justice: Ministria e Drejtësisë, Tirana.

Ministry of Labour, Emigration, Social Welfare and the Politically Persecuted: Ministria e Punës, Emigracionit, Ndihmës Sociale dhe të Persekutuarve Politikë, Tirana.

Ministry of Mining and Energy Resources: Ministria e Rezervave Minerale dhe Energjisë, Tirana; telex 4204.

Ministry of Public Order: Ministria e Rendit Publik, Tirana.

Ministry of Tourism: Ministria e Turizmit, Tirana; telex 4290.

Ministry of Transport and Communications: Ministria e Transporteve dhe Komunikacionit, Tirana; telex 4207.

Legislature

KUVENDI POPULLOR

(People's Assembly)

Presidency: PJETËR ARBNORI (Chair.), SHAQIR VUKAJ, TOMORR MALASI (Deputy Chair.).

General Election, 22 and 29 March 1992

Party	% of votes*	Seats
Democratic Party of Albania (DPA)	62.09	92
Socialist Party of Albania (SPA)	25.73	38
Social Democratic Party (SDP)	4.38	7
Union for Human Rights	2.90	2
Albanian Republican Party (ARP)	3.11	1
Others	1.78	—
Total	100.00	140

* Figures refer to votes cast on 22 March, when 89 of the 100 directly elective seats were won by an absolute majority. Voting in the second round, on 29 March, was to choose between the two leading candidates in each of the 11 constituencies where no candidate received 50% of the votes in the first round. The remaining 40 seats were allocated on the basis of proportional representation.

Local Government

Until mid-1991 Albania was divided into 26 districts (rrethe) and 140 communities (lokaliteteve). In July 1991 the Council of Ministers made certain changes to the administrative-territorial structure of the country, including the creation of the new district of Kavajë. Until 1991 administrative affairs in each district were the responsibility of a People's Council. In mid-1991 multi-party executive committees were established to take over the responsibilities of the People's Councils. New local councils were elected in July 1992. (For a full list of districts see Statistical Survey.)

Political Organizations

Agrarian Party (AP): Rruga Budi 6, Tirana; tel. (42) 27481; fax (42) 27481; f. 1991; Chair. LUFTER XHUVELI.

Albanian Communist Party (Partia Komuniste Shqiptare): Tirana; authorized 1991, outlawed 1992.

Albanian Democratic Alliance: Tirana; f. 1992 by former members of the DPA; Leader NERITAN ÇEKA.

Albanian Green Party (Partia e Blerte Shqiptare): f. 1990 as the Ecology Party (Partia Ekologjike); campaigns on environmental issues; Chair. NASI BOZHEGU.

Albanian Helsinki Forum (Forum Shqiptar i Helsinkit): Tirana; f. 1990; mem. International Federation of Helsinki; Chair. Prof. ARBEN PUTO.

Albanian Liberal Party (Partia Liberale Shqiptare): Tirana; f. 1991; Chair. VALTER FILE.

Albanian National Democratic Party (Partia Nacional Demokratike): Tirana; f. 1991; Chair. FATMIR ÇEKANI.

Albanian Republican Party—ARP (Partia Republikane Shqiptare): Tirana; f. 1991; Gen. Council of 54 mems, Steering Commission of 21 mems; Chair. SABRI GODO; Vice-Chair. FATMIR MEDIU; Sec. CERCIZ MINGOMATAS.

Albanian Women's Federation (Forum i Grus Shqiptare): Tirana; tel. (42) 28309; f. 1991; independent organization uniting women from various religious and cultural backgrounds; Chair. DIANA ÇULI.

Çamëria Political and Patriotic Association (Shoqata Politike-Patriotike Çamëria): Tirana; supports the rights of the Çam minority (an Albanian people) in northern Greece; f. 1991; Chair. Dr ABAZ DOJAKA.

Democratic Party of Albania—DPA (Partia Demokratike të Shqipërisë): Tirana; tel. (42) 28463; fax (42) 28463; f. 1990; committed to liberal-democratic ideals and market economics; Chair. EDUARD SELAMI; Deputy Chair. ALI SPAHIA; Sec. TOMOR DOSTI.

Democratic Prosperity Party (Partia e Prosperitetit Demokratik): Tirana; f. 1991; Chair. YZEIR FETAHU.

Democratic Union of the Greek Minority (OMONIA—Bashkimia Demokratik i Minoritet Grek): Tirana; f. 1991; electoral regulations of 1992 forbade it participating in elections, as the party of an ethnic minority; Pres. SOTIRIS KYRIAZATIS; Chair. THEODORI BEZHANI.

Democratic Unity Party (Partia e Bashkimit Demokratik): Tirana; Chair. XHEVDET LIBOHOVA.

Independent Party (Partia Indipendente): Tirana; f. 1991;Chair. EDMOND GJOKRUSHI.

Legality Movement Party (Partia Lëvizja e Legalitetit): Tirana; f. 1992; Chair. AGOSTIN SHOSHAJ.

National Committee of the War Veterans of the Albanian People (Komiteti Kombëtar i Veteranve te Luftes te Popullit Shqiptar): Tirana; Chair. PIRRO DODBIBA.

National Progress Party (Partia e Perparimit Kombetar): Tirana; f. 1991; Chair. MYRTO XHAFERRI.

Party of National Unity (Partia e Unitetit Kombëtar): Rruga Alqi Kondi, Tirana; tel. (42) 27498; fax (42) 23929; f. 1991; Chair. of Steering Cttee IDAJET BEQIRI.

People's Party (Partia Popullore): Tirana; f. 1991; aims to eradicate Communism; Chair. BASHKIM DRIZA.

People's Unity Party (Partia Bashkimi Popullor Demokristiane): Tirana; f. 1991; Chair. GJERGJ NDOJA.

Social Democratic Party of Albania—SDP (Partia Social Demokratike e Shqipërise): Tirana; f. 1991; advocates gradual economic reforms and social justice; 11-member Managing Council; Chair. Prof. Dr SKËNDER GJINUSHI; Sec. LISIEN BASHKURTI.

Social Labour Party of Albania(Partia Socialpuntore Shqiptare): Burrel; f. 1992; Pres. RAMADAN NDREKA.

Socialist Party of Albania—SPA (Partia Socialiste e Shqipërisë): Tirana; tel. (42) 27409; telex 4291; fax (42) 27417; f. 1941 as Albanian Communist Party, renamed Party of Labour of Albania (PLA) in 1948, adopted present name in 1991; until 1990 the only permitted political party in Albania; now rejects Marxism-Leninism and claims commitment to democratic socialism and a market economy; Managing Cttee of 81 mems, headed by Presidency of 15 mems; 130,000 mems and candidate mems; Pres. FATOS NANO; Vice-Pres NAMIK DOKLE, SERVET PELLUMBI.

Union for Human Rights Party—UHRP (Partia për Mbrojtjen e te Drejtave te Njeriut): Tirana; f. 1992; represents the Greek and Macedonian minorities; Chair. VASIL MELE.

Diplomatic Representation

EMBASSIES IN ALBANIA

Bulgaria: Rruga Skënderbeu 12, Tirana; tel. (42) 33155; Ambassador: STEFAN NAUMOV.

China, People's Republic: Rruga Skënderbeu 57, Tirana; tel. (42) 32077; telex 2148; Ambassador: GU MAOXUAN.

Cuba: Rruga e Durrësit 13, Tirana; tel. (42) 25176; telex 2155; Ambassador: JULIO C. CANCIO FERRER.

Czech Republic: Rruga Skënderbeu 10, Tirana; tel. (42) 32117; telex 2162.

Egypt: Rruga Skënderbeu 43, Tirana; tel. (42) 33022; telex 2156; Ambassador: AHMED NABAWY ESSA.

France: Rruga Skënderbeu 14, Tirana; tel. (42) 34250; telex 2150; Ambassador: JACQUES FAURE.

Germany: Rruga Skënderbeu 8, Tirana; tel. (42) 32050; telex 2254; fax (42) 33497; Ambassador: Dr CLAUS VOLLERS.

Greece: Rruga Frederick Shiroka 3, Tirana; tel. (42) 34290; fax (42) 34443; Ambassador: CHRISTOS TSALIKIS.

Holy See: Rruga e Durrësit 13, Tirana; tel. (42) 33516; fax (42) 32001; Apostolic Nuncio: Most Rev. IVAN DIAS, Titular Archbishop of Rusubisir.

Hungary: Rruga Skënderbeu 16, Tirana; tel. (42) 32238; telex 2257; fax (42) 33211; Ambassador: FERENC PÓKA.

Italy: Rruga Lek Dukagjini, Tirana; tel. (42) 34343; telex 2166; Ambassador: TORQUATO CARDILLI.

Korea, Democratic People's Republic: Rruga Skënderbeu 55, Tirana; tel. (42) 22258; Ambassador: KIM U-CHONG.

Libya: Rruga Donika Kastrioti 9, Tirana; tel. (42) 34106; Bureau Chief: ABDELHAMIT FARHAT.

Poland: Rruga e Durrësit 123, Tirana; tel. (42) 34190; Ambassador: JERZY ZAWALONKA.

Romania: Rruga Themistokli Gërmenji 2, Tirana; tel. (42) 32287; Ambassador: GHEORGHE MIKU.

Russia: Rruga Asim Zeneli 5, Tirana; tel. (42) 34500; telex 2121; fax (42) 32253; Ambassador: VIKTOR YEFIMOVICH NERUBAYLO.

Slovakia: Rruga Skënderbeu 10, Tirana; tel. (42) 32117; telex 2162.

Switzerland: Hotel Dajti, Tirana; tel. (42) 27860; Chargé d'affaires: CHRISTIAN HAUSWIRTH.

Turkey: Rruga Konferenca e Pezës 31, Tirana; tel. (42) 33399; Ambassador: METIN ORNEKOL.

USA: Rruga Labinoti 103, Tirana; tel. (42) 32875; Ambassador: WILLIAM E. RYERSON.

Viet Nam: Rruga Lek Dukagjini, Tirana; tel. (42) 22556; telex 2253; Ambassador: NGUYEN CHI THANH.

Yugoslavia: Rruga e Durrësit 192–196, Tirana; tel. (42) 23042; telex 2167; Ambassador: MIRKO MANOJLOVIĆ.

Judicial System

The judicial system is administered by the Ministry of Justice (re-established in 1990), which supervises the organization and functioning of the courts.

Extensive reforms of the judicial system were announced in May 1990. In addition to the re-establishment of the Ministry of Justice (the Minister being empowered to overturn court rulings), defendants were guaranteed the right to a defence lawyer. The number of capital offences was reduced from 34 to 11, women being exempt from the death penalty. Further reforms were implemented in 1991. All laws that were in contradiction to the constitutional legislation that the People's Assembly adopted in April 1991 were declared invalid. Trials are held in public. Accused persons are assured the right of defence, and the principle of presumption of innocence is sanctioned by the Code of Penal Procedure.

In April 1992 an extensive re-organization of the judicial system was implemented. The measures created a new system of courts, consisting of the Supreme Court, Appeal Courts (one for every 36 District Courts) and District Courts, as well as a newly-created Constitutional Court.

The Supreme Court may examine the judgements of both Appeal and District Courts, and cases may be brought by the Attorney-General or the Chairman of the Supreme Court or participants in the specific case.

The Chairman of the Supreme Court and his or her deputies are elected by the People's Assembly. The officials of the Appeal Courts and the District Courts are nominated by a Higher Judicial Council, which is presided over by the President of the Republic and which is composed of the Chairman of the Supreme Court, the Minister of Justice, the Attorney-General and nine members elected by the Supreme Court and the Attorney-General's Office.

The Constitutional Court comprises nine members, of whom five are elected by the People's Assembly and four are appointed by the President of the Republic. The Constitutional Court interprets the Constitution and judges the constitutional viability of proposed laws. It resolves disagreements between local and central authorities, and problems linked with the constitutionality of political parties and social organizations, whose activities it is empowered to prevent if it sees fit. It also formulates legislation concerning the election of the President of the Republic.

Military tribunals are held at the Supreme Court and at District and Appeal Courts.

Attorneys' offices are state organs that control strictly and uniformly the application of the laws from ministries and other central and local organs, from courts, organs of investigation, enterprises, institutions and citizens' organizations. The Attorney-General and his or her deputies are appointed by the People's Assembly on the recommendation of the President of the Republic.

President of the Supreme Court: NURO HOTI.

Attorney-General: ALUSH DROGOSHI.

Chairman of the Constitutional Court: RUSTEM GJATA.

Religion

All religious institutions were closed by the Government in 1967 and the practice of religion was prohibited. Many places of worship were converted into museums, sports halls, etc. In 1990, however, the prohibition on religious activities was revoked, religious services were permitted, and, from 1991, mosques and churches began to be reopened. Transitional legislation, adopted in April 1991 to replace the 1976 Constitution, states that Albania is a secular state which observes 'freedom of religious belief and creates conditions in which to exercise it'. On the basis of declared affiliation in 1945, it is estimated that some 70% of the population are of Muslim background, 20% Eastern Orthodox (mainly in the south) and some 10% Roman Catholic (in the north). During 1991 the small number of Albanians who were adherents of the Jewish faith emigrated to Israel.

CHRISTIANITY

The Roman Catholic Church

After November 1990, when 5,000 Roman Catholics in Shkodër attended the first public service since 1967, many churches were reopened. In September 1991 diplomatic relations were restored with the Holy See. Initially, the development of the church was hindered by the lack of Albanian clergymen, but by mid-1993 65 priests had been ordained. In April 1993, during a visit to Albania by the Pope, archbishops were appointed to Albania's two archdioceses of Durrës and Shkodër.

Archbishop of Shkodër: FRANO ILLIA.

Archbishop of Durrës: RROK MIRDITA.

The Orthodox Church

Kisha Ortodokse Shqiptare (Albanian Orthodox Church): Rruga Kavaja, Tirana; the Albanian Orthodox Church was proclaimed autocephalous at the Congress of Berat in 1922, and its status was approved in 1929, although the Serbian, Macedonian and Greek churches do not recognize its separate existence; during 1991 churches were reopened in at least 10 cities, and the Ecumenical Patriarchate in Istanbul (Constantinople), Turkey, appointed a Greek bishop as Exarch of the Albanian Church, because there were no longer any Albanian bishops alive; Archbishop ANASTAS JANULATOS.

ISLAM

Bashkesia Islamike Shqiptare (Albanian Islamic Community): c/o Ethem Bay Mosque, Tirana; f. 1991; Chair. HAFIZ SABRI KOCI; Grand Mufti of Albania HAFIZ SALIH TERMAT HOXHA.

Bektashi Sect

World Council of Elders of the Bektashis: Tirana; f. 1991; Chair. RESHAT BABA BARDHI.

The Press

Until 1991 the press was controlled by the Party of Labour of Albania, now the Socialist Party of Albania (SPA), and adhered to a strongly Marxist-Leninist line. In 1991–92 several newspapers were established by independent political organizations. The most influential newspapers are the SPA daily, *Zëri i Popullit*, and the publication of the Democratic Party of Albania, *Rilindja Demokratike*. The leading independent newspaper is *Koha Jonë*. Other new papers include *Republika*, the Albanian Republican Party journal, and *Progresi Agrar*, the publication of the Agrarian Party. In 1990 there were 40 newspapers in publication, with a total circulation of 63,000. There were 77 other periodicals, with a total circulation of 26,000.

PRINCIPAL DAILIES

Rilindja Demokratike (Democratic Revival): Rr. Fortuzi, Tirana; f. 1991; organ of the DPA; Editor-in-Chief BASHKIM TRENOVA; circ. 30,000.

Zëri i Popullit (The Voice of the People): Bulevardi Deshmorët e Kombit, Tirana; tel. (42) 27808; telex 4251; fax (42) 27813; f. 1942; daily, except Mon.; organ of the SPA; Editor-in-Chief THOMA GËLLÇI; circ. 50,000.

PERIODICALS

Tirana

Agrovizion: Rruga d'Istria, Tirana: tel. (42) 26147; f. 1992; twice weekly; agricultural economic policies, new technology in farming, advice for farmers; circ. 3,000.

Albania: Tirana; f. 1991; weekly; organ of the Albanian Green Party; environmental issues.

Albanian Foreign Trade: Tirana; 6 a year; Editor-in-Chief AGIM KORBI.

Alternativa SD: Tirana; f. 1991; twice weekly; organ of the Social Democratic Party.

Arbër: Tirana; f. 1992; twice monthly; social, literary and artistic review.

Bashkimi Kombëtar: Bulevardi Deshmorët e Kombit, Tirana; tel. (42) 28110; f. 1943; twice weekly; Editor-in-Chief QEMAL SAKAJEVA; circ. 30,000.

Balli i Kombit (The Head of the Nation): Tirana; f. 1991.

Çamëria—Vatra Amtare (Çamëria—Maternal Hearth): Tirana; f. 1991; weekly; organ of the Çamëria Political and Patriotic Association.

Drita (The Light): Rruga Konferenca e Pezës 4, Tirana; tel. (42) 27036; f. 1960; weekly; publ. by Union of Writers and Artists of Albania; Editor-in-Chief BRISEIDA MEMA; circ. 31,000.

Ekonomia Botërore (World Economics): Tirana; f. 1991; monthly; independent.

Fatosi (The Valiant): Tirana; tel. (42) 23024; f. 1959; fortnightly; literary and artistic magazine for children; Editor-in-Chief XHEVAT BEQARAJ; circ. 21,200.

Filmi (The Film): Tirana; f. 1992; monthly; illustrated cinema review.

Hosteni (The Goad): Tirana; f. 1945; fortnightly; political review of humour and satire; publ. by the Union of Journalists; Editor-in-Chief NIKO NIKOLLA.

Koha Jonë (Our Time): Tirana; f. 1991; independent; twice weekly; Editor-in-Chief ALEKSANDER FRANGAJ.

Kombi (The Nation): Rruga Alqi Kondi, Tirana; tel. (42) 27498; fax (42) 23929; f. 1991; 2 a week; organ of the Party of National Unity; circ. 15,000.

Kushtrim Brezash (Clarion Call of Generations): Tirana; f. 1992; weekly; organ of the National Committee of the Association of War Veterans of the Albanian People.

Luftëtari (The Fighter): Tirana; f. 1945; 2 a week; publ. by the Ministry of Defence; Editor-in-Chief DEMOKRAT ANASTASI.

Mbrojtja (The Defence): Tirana; f. 1991; monthly; publ. by the Ministry of Defence.

Mësuesi (The Teacher): Tirana; f. 1961; weekly; publ. by the Ministry of Education; Editor-in-Chief THOMA QENDRO.

Ndërtuesi (The Builder): Tirana; 4 a year.

Nëntori (November): Baboci 37z, Tirana; f. 1954; monthly; publ. by the Union of Writers and Artists of Albania; Chief Editor KIÇO BLUSHI.

Official Gazette of the Republic of Albania: Kuvendi Popullore, Tirana; tel. (42) 29385; telex 4298; f. 1945; occasional government review.

Panorama Agroushqimore (Agro-food Panorama): Rruga d'Istria, Tirana; f. 1921, publ. under several names; monthly; specialist agricultural magazine; circ. 3,000.

Pasqyra (The Mirror): Bulevardi Dëshmorët e Kombit, Tirana; f. 1991 to replace *Puna* (Labour—f. 1945); 2 a week; also 4 times a year in French; organ of the Confederation of Albanian Trade Unions; Editor-in-Chief KRISTAQ LAKA.

Patrioti (The Patriot): Tirana; f. 1992; organ of the Elez Isufi Patriotic Association; Editor-in-Chief VEDIP BRENSHI.

Përmbledhje Studimesh (Collection of Studies): Tirana; 4 a year; summaries in French; bulletin of the Ministry of Industry, Mining and Energy Resources.

Progresi Agrar (Agrarian Progress): Rruga Budi 6, Tirana; tel. (42) 27481; fax (42) 27481; f. 1991; 2 a week; organ of the Agrarian Party.

Republika: Tirana; f. 1991; 2 a week; organ of the Albanian Republican Party; Editor-in-Chief VANGJUSH GAMBETA.

Revista Pedagogjike: Naim Fracheri St 37, Tirana; fax (42) 22573; f. 1945; 4 a year; organ of the Institute of Pedagogical Studies; educational development, psychology, dialectics; Editor JUAN HAJDARAGA; circ. 10,000.

Rinia e Lire (Free Youth): Tirana; f. 1992; organ of the Albanian Free Youth Federation.

Shëndeti (Health): M. Duri 2, Tirana; tel. (42) 27803; fax (42) 27803; f. 1949; monthly; publ. by the National Directorate of Health Education; issues of health and welfare, personal health care; Editors-in-Chief KORNELIA GJATA, AGIM XHUMARI.

Shqipëria e Re (New Albania): Rruga Themistokli Germenji 6, Tirana; f. 1947; monthly in Albanian; every 2 months in English, French and Spanish; organ of the Committee for Cultural Relations with Foreign Countries; illustrated political and social magazine; Editor YMER MINXHOZI; circ. 170,000.

Shqiptarja e Re (The New Albanian Woman): Tirana; f. 1943; monthly; political and socio-cultural review; Editor-in-Chief VALENTINA LESKAJ.

Sindikalisti (Trade Unionists): Tirana; f. 1991; newspaper; organ of the Union of Independent Trade Unions of Albania; Editor-in-Chief VANGJEL KOZMAI.

Skena dhe Ekrani (Stage and Screen): Tirana; 4 a year; cultural review.

Spektër (The Spectre): Tirana; f. 1991; illustrated independent monthly; in Albanian and Italian.

Sporti (Sport): Rruga e Durrësit 23, Tirana; tel. (42) 27544; fax (42) 23577; f. 1935; weekly; publ. by the National Olympic Committee; Editor BESNIK DIZDARI; circ. 10,000.

Studenti (The Student): Tirana; f. 1967; weekly.

Tirana: Tirana; f. 1987; independent; twice weekly; publ. by Tirana District SPA.

Tregtia e Jashtme Popullore (Albanian Foreign Trade): Rruga Konferenca e Pezës 6, Tirana; tel. (42) 22934; telex 2179; f. 1961; every 2 months; in English and French; organ of the Albanian Chamber of Commerce; Editor AGIM KORBI.

Tribuna e Gazetarit (The Journalist's Tribune): Tirana; every 2 months; publ. by the Union of Journalists of Albania; Editor NAZMI QAMILI.

Ushtria dhe Koha (Army and Time): Tirana; f. 1992; monthly; publ. by the Ministry of Defence.

Zeri i Atdheut (The Voice of the Country): Tirana; f. 1992; weekly.

Zëri i Rinisë (The Voice of Youth): Tirana; f. 1942 as the newspaper of the Union of Albanian Working Youth; 2 a week; Editor-in-Chief REMZI LANI; circ. 53,000.

Other Towns

Adriatiku (Adriatic): Durrës; f. 1967; independent; 2 a week.

Dibra: Dibër; f. 1991; independent; twice weekly.

Egnatia: Berat; f. 1991; independent; twice weekly.

Korçë Demokratike (Democratic Korçë): Korça; f. 1992; independent; twice weekly.

Ore (The Clock): Shkodër; f. 1992; independent; twice weekly.

Universi Rinor (The Youth Universe): Korçë; f. 1991.

Zëri i Vlorës (The Voice of Vlorë): Vlorë; f. 1967; 2 a week; Editor-in-Chief DASHO METODASHAJ.

NEWS AGENCIES

Albanian Telegraphic Agency (ATA): Bulevardi Marcel Cachin 23, Tirana; tel. (42) 24412; telex 2142; f. 1945; domestic and foreign news; branches in provincial towns and in Vienna, Austria; Dir ILIR ZHILLA.

Foreign Bureau

Xinhua (New China) News Agency (People's Republic of China): Rruga Skënderbeu 57, Tirana; tel. (42) 33139; fax (42) 33139; Bureau Chief LI JIYU.

PRESS ASSOCIATIONS

Bashkimi i Gazetarëve të Shqipërisë (Union of Journalists of Albania): Tirana; tel. (42) 28020; f. 1949; Chair. MARASH HAJATI; Sec.-Gen. YMER MINXHOZI.

Lidhja e Gazetarëve të Shqipërisë (The League of Journalists of Albania): Tirana.

Publishers

In 1990 a total of 1,049 book titles were published. In the same year some 8m. copies were produced. In 1991 several new independent book publishers were established; however, owing to the severe economic crisis and a scarcity of paper, only 200 titles were published in that year.

Drejtoria Qëndrore e Përhapjes dhe e Propagandimit të Librit (Central Administration for the Dissemination and Propagation of the Book): Tirana; tel. (42) 27841; directed by the Ministry of Education.

Albania: Tirana; f. 1991.

Bota Sportive: Tirana; f. 1991; sports.

Botime të Akademisë së Shkencave të RSH: Tirana; publishing house of the Albanian Academy of Sciences.

Botime te Universitetit Bujqësor te Tiranës: Kamzë, Tirana; publishing house of the Agricultural University of Tirana.

Botime të Shtëpisë Botuese 8 Nëntori: Tirana; tel. (42) 28064; f. 1972; books on Albania and other countries, political and social sciences, translations of Albanian works into foreign languages, technical and scientific books, illustrated albums, etc.; Dir XHEMAL DINI.

Botime të Shtëpisë Botuese të Librit Shkollor: Tirana; tel. (42) 22331; f. 1967; educational books; Dir FEJZI KOÇI.

Dea: Tirana; f. 1991.

Dituria: Tirana; f. 1991; dictionaries, calendars, encyclopaedias.

Dora d'Istria: Tirana; f. 1991.

Fan Noli: Tirana; f. 1991; Albanian and foreign literature.

Globus: Tirana; f. 1991.

Hasan Tahsini: Tirana; f. 1991; humorous literature.

Lura: Tirana; f.1991.

Qendr e Informacionit për Bujsinë dhe Ushqimin (Information Centre for Agriculture and Food): Rruga d'Istria, Tirana; tel. (42) 26147; f. 1970; publishes various agricultural periodicals; Gen. Dir SALI ÇELA.

Shtëpia Botuese 'Libri Universitar': Rruga Dora d'Istria, Tirana; tel. (42) 25659; telex 2211; fax (42) 28304; f. 1988; publishes university textbooks on science, medicine, engineering, geography, history, literature, foreign languages, economics, etc.; Dir MUSTAFA FEZGA.

Shtëpia Botuese e Lidhjes së Shkrimtarëve: Konferenca e Pezës 4, Tirana; tel. (42) 22691; fax (42) 25912; f. 1990; artistic and documentary literature; Dir ZIJA ÇELA.

Shtëpia Botuese Naim Frashëri: Tirana; tel. (42) 27906; f. 1947; fiction, poetry, drama, criticism, children's literature, translations; Dir GAQO BUSHAKA.

Union of Writers and Artists Publishing House: Tirana; f. 1991; fiction, poetry incl. foreign literature and works by the Albanian diaspora.

WRITERS' UNIONS

Bashkimi i Shkrimtarëve te Pavarur (The Independent Union of Writers): Tirana; f. 1991; Chair. AGIM SHEHU.

Lidhja e Shkrimtarëve dhe e Artistëve të Shqipërisë (Union of Writers and Artists of Albania): Rruga Konferenca e Pezës 4, Tirana; tel. (42) 29689; f. 1945; 26 branches throughout the country; 1,750 mems; Chair. BARDHYL LONDO.

Radio and Television

In 1989 there were 514,980 radio receivers and 324,905 television receivers in use. In 1991 state broadcasting was removed from political control and made subordinate to the Parliamentary Commission for the Media.

Radiotelevisioni Shqiptar: Rruga Ismail Qemali, Tirana; tel. (42) 23239; telex 2216; f. 1944; Gen. Dir SKENDER BUÇPAPA.

RADIO

Radio Tirana: Tirana; telex 4158; broadcasts 24 hours of internal programmes daily from Tirana; regional stations in Korçë, Gjirokastër, Kukës and Shkodër; in 1991 radio broadcasts in Macedonian began in the area of Korçë; in Gjirokastër, programmes in Greek are broadcast for two hours daily.

External Service: broadcasts for 20 hours daily in eight foreign languages; Dir MICHO ZIMA.

TELEVISION

There is only one television station, in Tirana, which broadcasts for 11 hours daily; Dir of Television QEMAL SAKAJEVA.

Finance

BANKING

Central Bank

National Bank of Albania: Sheshi Skënderbeu 1, Tirana; tel. (42) 28315; telex 2153; f. 1992; 37 branches; Man. Dir ADRIAN XHYHERI.

Other Banks

Agricultural Bank: Sheshi Skenderbej 1, Tirana; tel. (42) 28275; f. 1991; Dir TEODOR GEDESHI; 34 brs.

Albanian State Bank (Bank a e Shtëtit Shqiptar): Sheshi Skenderbej 1, Tirana; tel. (42) 28421; telex 2153; fax (42) 27821; f. 1945; bank of issue; Gen. Dir DYLBER VRIONI; 7 brs.

Albanian State Bank for Foreign Relations: Tirana; f. 1990; to provide and direct funds for foreign trade.

Commercial Bank: Sheshi Skenderbej 1, Tirana; tel. (42) 33338; telex 22118; f. 1990.

Savings Bank of Albania: Rruga 4 Shkurti 6, Tirana; tel. (42) 24540; telex 2192; f. 1991; Dir EDVIN LIBOHOVA; 27 brs.

Swiss-Albanian Iliria Bank (SAI-Bank): Tirana; f. 1991 as Albania's first private commercial bank since 1945; joint venture to encourage foreign investment in construction of new projects and in renovation of existing plants.

In 1990 there were 107 savings banks in operation with 3,800 agencies. In 1987 deposits totalled 1,329m. lekë.

INSURANCE

Instituti i Sigurimeve të Shqipërisë (Insurance Institute of Albania): Bulevardi Dëshmorët e Kombit 3, Tirana; tel. (42) 26001; telex 2245; fax (42) 23838; f. 1991; Gen. Dir QEMAL DISHA; 27 brs.

Trade and Industry

CHAMBERS OF COMMERCE

Chamber of Commerce of the Republic of Albania: Rruga Konferenca e Pezës 6, Tirana; tel. (42) 27997; telex 2179; f. 1958; Pres. LIGOR DHAMO.

Durrës Chamber of Commerce: Durrës; f. 1988; promotes trade with southern Italy.

Gjirokastër Chamber of Commerce: Gjirokastër; f. 1988; promotes trade with Greek border area.

Shkodër Chamber of Commerce: Shkodër; promotes trade with Yugoslav border area.

There are also chambers of commerce in Korçë, Kukës, Peshkopi, Pogradec, Sarandë and Vlorë.

SUPERVISORY ORGANIZATION

Albkontroll: Rruga Skënderbeu 15, Durrës; tel. (52) 22354; telex 2181; fax (52) 22791; f. 1962; brs throughout Albania; independent control body for inspection of goods for import and export, means of transport, etc.; Gen. Man. STEFAN BOSHKU.

NATIONAL FOREIGN TRADE ORGANIZATIONS AND MAJOR COMPANIES

Since 1990 the National Foreign Trade Organizations have no longer been the sole institutions authorized to engage in foreign trade.

Agroeksport: Rruga 4 Shkurti 6, Tirana; tel. (42) 22533; telex 2262; fax (42) 23871; exports vegetables, fruit, canned fish, wine, tobacco, etc.; imports rice, coffee and other foodstuffs, paper products, etc.; Gen. Man. PORPARIUM RAMA.

Agrokoop: Rruga 4 Shkurti 6, Tirana; tel. (42) 23871; fax (42) 34357; telex 2248; specializes in foodstuffs and consumer goods.

Albkoop: Rruga 4 Shkurti 6, Tirana; tel. (42) 24179; telex 2187; f. 1986; import and export of consumer goods, incl. clothing, textiles, handicrafts, stationery, jewellery; Gen. Man. ISMAIL ÇELA.

Albpetrol: c/o Ministria e Reservave Minerale dhe Energjisë, Tirana; f. 1992 to take control of state petroleum industry; in 1994 it was planned to split it into three companies; state-owned but independent co; consists of 46 enterprises and several scientific instits; exploration, extraction, refining, distribution of petroleum, natural gas, etc.; 20,000 employees; Exec. Dir BAHRI SHANAY.

Alimpeks: Tirana; f. 1991; exports tobacco and foodstuffs; imports raw materials, chemicals, foodstuffs, etc.; Dir ALTIN YLLI.

Arteksportimport: Rruga 4 Shkurti 6, Tirana; tel. (42) 26417; telex 2154; fax (42) 23832; f. 1989; exports handicrafts and light industrial products; imports raw materials for chemical and textile industries; Gen. Dir TEFIK KOKONA.

Eksimagra: Rruga Gjon Muzaka, Tirana; tel. (42) 23128; telex 2111; f. 1989; exports fresh vegetables and fruit, figs, pheasants, etc.; imports meat, cereals, edible fats, packaging, etc.

Industrialimpeks: Rruga 4 Shkurti 6, Tirana; tel. (42) 26123; telex 2112; exports copper wires, furniture, kitchenware, paper, timber, wooden articles, cement, etc.; imports fabrics, cement, chemicals, paper, cardboard, school and office items, etc.; Gen. Man. FARUK BOROVA.

KESH (State Electricity Co-operative of Albania): Tirana; public utility co and major exporter of electricity; Chair. (vacant).

Makinaimpeks: Rruga 4 Shkurti 6, Tirana; tel. (42) 25220; telex 2128; imports vehicles, factory installations, machinery and parts; exports explosives; Gen. Man. AFRIM BALLKA.

Mandimpeks: Rruga Lek Dukagjini, Tirana; tel. (42) 34508; imports metals, concrete, paints and design materials; exports cement, marble and ceramics.

Mekalb: Rruga e Durrësit 83, Tirana; tel. (42) 25444; telex 2102; fax (42) 34304; f. 1990; imports machine tools, metal products, spare parts for cars and agricultural machinery, food products, etc.; Gen. Dir BASHKIM JUPI.

Minergoimpeks: Rruga Marcel Cachin, Tirana; tel. (42) 22148; telex 2238; f. 1990; exports products of the mining, metallurgical and petroleum industries; imports machinery and equipment, lubricating oils and raw materials; Gen. Man. QAZIM QAZAMI.

Transshqip (Transalbania): Rruga 4 Shkurti 6, Tirana; tel. (42) 27429; telex 2131; fax (42) 27605; f. 1960; transport and forwarding of foreign trade goods by sea, road and rail; agents in Durrës, Vlorë and at Albanian border crossings.

REGIONAL FOREIGN TRADE ORGANIZATIONS

Dibërimpeks: Peshkopi; f. 1990; handles border trade with Yugoslavia and Macedonia; minerals and agricultural products.

Durrësimpeks: Rruga Skënderbeu 177, Durrës; tel. (52) 22199; telex 2181; f. 1988; handles border trade with southern Italy (Puglia); industrial and agricultural goods; Dir TAQO KOSTA.

Gjirokastërimpeks: Rruga Kombëtare 55, Gjirokastër; tel. 707; f. 1988; handles border trade with Greece; industrial and agricultural goods.

Korçaimpeks: Korçë; handles border trade with Greece.

Kukësimpeks: Kukës; handles trade with Yugoslavia and Macedonia; Dir ASIM BARUTI.

Pogradecimpeks: Pogradec; handles border trade with Macedonia.

Sarandaimpeks: Sarandë; handles trade with Corfu and other regions of southern Greece.

Shkodërimpeks: Shkodër; handles border trade with Yugoslavia (Montenegro); industrial and agricultural goods.

Vloraimpeks: Vlorë; handles trade and economic co-operation with southern Italy; industrial and agricultural goods.

TRADE UNIONS

Until 1991 independent trade union activities were prohibited. The official trade unions were represented in every work and production centre. They were responsible for improving levels of production and ensuring implementation of the economic production plans of the PLA. They also provided some social and health facilities for their members. During 1991 independent unions were established. The most important of these was the Union of Independent Trade Unions of Albania (UITUA). Other unions were established for workers in the food industry, the defence industry, mineral processing industries and other sectors of the economy.

Confederation of Albanian Trade Unions (Konfederata e Sindikatave të Shqipërisë): Bulevardi Dëshmorët e Kombit, Tirana; f. 1991 to replace the official Central Council of Albanian Trade Unions (f. 1945); includes 17 trade union federations representing workers in different sectors of the economy; Chair. of Managing Council KASTRIOT MUÇO.

Union of Independent Trade Unions of Albania (Bashkimi i Sindikatave të Pavarura të Shqipërisë): Tirana; f. 1991; Chair. VALER XHEKA.

Other Trade Unions

Agricultural Trade Union Federation (Federata Sindikale e Bujqesise): Tirana; f. 1991; Leaders ALFRED GJOMO, NAZMI QOKU.

Autonomous Union of Public-Service Workers: Tirana; f. 1992; Chair. MINELLA KURETA.

Free and Independent Miners' Union (Sindikata e Lire dhe e Pavarur e Minatoreve): Tirana; f. 1991; Chair. SHYQRI XIBRI.

Independent Trade Union Federation of Workers in the Artistic Articles, Handicrafts, Glassware and Ceramics Industries: Tirana; f. 1991.

Independent Trade Union Federation of the Food Industry: Tirana; f. 1991.

Independent Trade Union of Dock Workers: Durrës; f. 1992.

Independent Trade Union of Radio and Television: Tirana; f. 1991; represents interests of media workers.

Trade Union Federation of Education and Science Workers: Tirana; f. 1991; represents teachers and academics.

Union of Oil Industry Workers: seceded from the Confederation of Albanian Trade Unions in 1991; represents workers in the petroleum and natural gas industry; Chair. MENPOR XHEMALI.

Transport

RAILWAYS

In 1990 there were 720 km of railway track, with lines linking Tirana-Vlorë-Durrës, Durrës-Kavajë-Rrogozhinë-Elbasan-Librazhd-Prenjas-Pogradec , Rrogozhinë-Lushnjë-Fier-Ballsh, Milot-Rrëshen, Vlorë-Laç-Lezhë-Shkodër and Selenicë-Vlorë. There are also standard-gauge lines between Fier and Selenicë and between Fier and Vlorë. A 50-km line between Shkodër and Titograd (now Podgorica), Montenegro (Yugoslavia), opened to international freight traffic in September 1986.

Drejtoria e Hekurudhave: Tirana; railways administration; Dir M. DIZDARI.

ROADS

In 1990 the road network comprised 7,450 km of main roads, of which 2,850 km were asphalted, and 4,600 km were unasphalted. There were also some 10,000 km of other roads and tracks. All regions are linked by the road network, but many roads in mountainous districts are unsuitable for motor transport. Private cars were banned in Albania until 1991, but many have since been imported (estimated at over 120,000 by the end of 1993). Bicycles and mules are widely used. Proposals to construct a 200-km motorway between Durrës and the border with Greece, in co-operation with a group of Greek companies, were agreed in 1990.

SHIPPING

Albania's merchant fleet had an estimated total displacement of 56,000 grt in 1982. The chief ports are those in Durrës, Vlorë, Sarandë and Shëngjin. Durrës harbour has been dredged to allow for bigger ships. A ferry service between the Port of Durrës and Trieste (Italy) was inaugurated in November 1983. An agreement to establish a ferry service between Sarandë and the Greek island of Corfu was confirmed in 1988 and the establishment of a service between Bari (Italy) and Durrës was agreed in June 1991. There is also a service between Vlorë and Brindisi (Italy).

Drejtoria e Agjensisë së Vaporave: Port of Durrës; shipping administration.

CIVIL AVIATION

Albania has air links with Austria, Bulgaria, France, Greece, several cities in Germany, Hungary, Italy, Romania, Slovenia and Switzerland. An occasional charter service operates from the United Kingdom. A weekly service to New York (USA) was introduced in 1992. There is a small international airport at Rinas, 28 km from Tirana. There is no regular internal air service.

Albtransport: Rruga e Durrësit 202, Tirana; tel. (42) 23026; telex 2154; air agency.

Tourism

In 1990 an estimated 30,000 tourists visited Albania, an increase of more than 50% on 1989. The main tourist centres include Tirana, Durrës, Sarandë and Shkodër. The Roman amphitheatre at Durrës is one of the largest in Europe. The ancient towns of Apollonia and Butrint are important archaeological sites and there are many other towns of historic interest. However, expansion of the tourist industry has been limited by Albania's poor infrastructure and a lack of foreign investment in the development of new facilities.

Albturist: Bulevardi Dëshmorët e Kombit 6, Tirana; tel. (42) 23860; telex 2148; fax (42) 27956; brs in main towns and all tourist centres; 28 hotels throughout the country; Gen. Man. JETON HAJDARAJ.

Culture

NATIONAL ORGANIZATIONS

Albanian Committee for Cultural Relations with Foreign Countries (Komiteti Shqiptar për Marrëdhënie Kulturore me Botën e

Jashtme): Tirana; tel. (42) 23338; telex 2164; fax (42) 23791; attached to the Ministry of Foreign Affairs; manages cultural relations with over 40 countries; Chair. JORGO MELICA.

Ministry of Culture, Youth and Sport: see section on The Government (Ministries).

CULTURAL HERITAGE

Centre for Archaeological Research (Qendra e Kërkimeve Arkeologjike): Bulevardi Dëshmorët e Kombit, Tirana; tel. (42) 26541; telex 2214; f. 1948; responsible for research into Albania's archaeological sites and for the **National Museum of Archaeology**; Dir MUZAFER KORKUTI; Curator of Museum ILIR GJIPALI.

Fine Arts Gallery: Tirana; Dir KSENOFON DILO.

Institute of National Culture: Tirana; tel. (42) 27497; f. 1960; includes historical archive of recordings and collection of instruments; responsible for the **Albanian National Culture Museum**; Dir ALI XHIKU.

National Historical Museum: Tirana; f. 1991; history of Albania since Roman times; Dir KSENOFON DILO.

National Library: Tirana; tel. (42) 23843; fax (42) 23843; f. 1922; 1m. vols; over 30,000 items on Albanology; Dir NERMIN BASHA.

SPORTING ORGANIZATIONS

Bashkimi i Kultures Fizike e Sporteve (Union of Physical Culture and Sports): Tirana; national body responsible for providing sports facilities.

National Olympic Committee of the Republic of Albania: Rruga Dervish Hima 31, Tirana; tel. (42) 28447; telex 2228; fax (42) 28447; Pres. ARBEN JORGONI; Sec.-Gen. MARIETA ZAÇE.

PERFORMING ARTS

In 1991 there were eight professional theatrical companies in Albania, 15 variety companies and 26 puppet-show groups.

Ensemble of Folk Songs and Dances: Tirana; tel. (42) 27701; f. 1957; Dir RIZO HAJRO.

National Opera and Ballet Theatre (Teatri i Operes e i Baletit): Palace of Culture, Sheshi Skënderbeu, Tirana; tel. (42) 25856; fax (42) 27495; f. 1953; opera, ballet and folk-music; Gen. Dir AGRON XOXA; Man. BESIM PETRELA.

National Theatre: Tirana; Dir ROBERT NDRENIKA.

Film Studio

New Albania Film Studio (Shqipëria e Re): Tirana; tel. (42) 32733; f. 1952; produces 40 documentaries and 12–15 feature films annually; Dir TEODOR LACO.

ASSOCIATION

Union of Writers and Artists of Albania (Lidhja e Shkrimtarëve dhe e Artistëve të Shqipërisë): Rruga Konferenca e Pezës 4, Tirana; tel. (42) 29689; f. 1945; 26 branches throughout the country; 1,750 mems; Chair. DRITËRO AGOLLI.

Education

Education is free and compulsory at primary and secondary level; students in higher education pay a fee related to the family income. Children between the ages of three and six years may attend nursery school (kopshte). Children in the age group of seven to 15 years must attend an 'eight-year school'. There are three main categories of secondary school, namely '12 year schools' (shkollat 12-vjeçare) providing 4-year general courses, secondary technical-professional schools (shkollat e mesme teknik-profesionale), which combine vocational training with a general education, and lower vocational schools (shkollat e ulte profesionale), which train workers in the fields of agriculture and industry.

There are eight institutes of higher education and an Academy of Sciences, which provides facilities for research. Reforms have taken place in education, including the cessation of compulsory military training for schoolchildren and the teaching of ideologically-orientated subjects. In May 1991 two new universities were established: the Luigj Gurakuji University of Shkodër (formerly the Luigj Gurakuji Higher Institute of Education); and the Agricultural University of Tirana (formerly the Higher Institute of Agriculture).

UNIVERSITIES

Agricultural University of Tirana (Universiteti Bujqësor i Tiranës): Kamzë, Tirana; f. 1991 to replace the Higher Institute of Agriculture; Rector BESNIK GJONGECAJ; Vice-Rector VLADIMIR SPAHO.

Luigj Gurakuji University of Shkodër: Shkodër; tel. (22) 43747; fax (22) 43747; f. 1991 to replace the Luigj Gurakuji Higher Institute of Education (f. 1957); 3 faculties; Rector Dr GJOVALIN KOLOMBI.

University of Tirana (Universiteti i Tiranës): Bulevardi Deshmorët e Kombit, Tirana; tel. (42) 28258; telex 2211; fax (42) 28258; f. 1957; in 1991 the name was changed from the Enver Hoxha University of Tirana; 8 faculties, 1,051 teachers, 12,000 students; brs in Berat, Elbasan, Korçë, Shkodër; Rector Prof. Dr NIKOLLA KONOMI.

Social Welfare

The state funds a basic range of medical services for the whole population. However, the quality of health care has declined considerably during the ealry 1990s. In 1990 the number of hospitals totalled 160 and there were 13,228 beds available. In the same year there were 5,566 doctors and dentists, the equivalent of one for every 585 persons. Women are entitled to 180 days of maternity leave, receiving 80% of their salary. There is a non-contributory state social insurance system for all workers, with 70%–100% of salary being paid during sick leave. In 1991 a system of social security payments for the unemployed was introduced; previously the existence of unemployment was not officially acknowledged. A pension system provides for the old and disabled. Men retire between the ages of 50 and 60, and women between 45 and 55.

NATIONAL AGENCIES

Ministry of Health and Environmental Protection: see section on The Government (Ministries); incl.:

National Directorate for Health Education: M. Duri 2, Tirana; tel. (42) 27106; fulfils educational role in preventative health.

Ministry of Labour, Emigration, Social Welfare and the Politically Persecuted: see section on The Government (Ministries).

Permanent Commission of the People's Assembly on Health, Protection of the Environment, and Public Services: Kuvendi Popullor, Tirana.

HEALTH AND WELFARE ORGANIZATIONS

Albanian Association for the Blind: Tirana; f. 1991.

Albanian Red Cross (Kryqi i Kuq i Shqiptar): Qamil Guranjaku St 2, Tirana; tel. (42) 25855; fax (42) 25855; f. 1921; President Prof. Dr SHYQYRI SUBASHI; Sec.-Gen. Dr PANDORA KETRI.

Albanians for Albania: Tirana; f. 1991; humanitarian assen; Chair. MARJETA LJARJA.

Association of Former Political Prisoners and Detainees: Tirana; f. 1991; social and humanitarian organization est. to help ex-political prisoners; Pres. OSMAN KAZAZI.

Forum for the Protection of Human Rights (Forumi per Mbrojtjen e të Drejtave të Njeriut dhe Lirive Themelore): Tirana; f. 1990; provides humanitarian assistance to former political prisoners; Chair. Prof. ARBEN PUTO.

The Environment

The Ecology Party (Albanian Green Party), founded in late 1990, was the first unofficial response to environmental problems in Albania. Albania does not have the same concentration of heavy industries as some parts of Eastern Europe, but, nevertheless, there is serious pollution from coal-fired power stations and obsolete factories. In July 1991 the Government of Albania signed a declaration on the ecological protection of the Adriatic Sea, implementing the Adriatic Initiative agreed with Italy, Yugoslavia and Greece in Umag, in 1989. At the same time Albania and Italy agreed to co-operate in environmental and tourist affairs.

GOVERNMENT ORGANIZATIONS

Ministry of Health and Environmental Protection: see section on The Government (Ministries); incl.:

State Sanitary Inspectorate: responsible for environmental health, pollution monitoring, research.

Permanent Commission of the People's Assembly on Health, Protection of the Environment, and Public Services: Kuvendi Popullor, Tirana.

The Ministry of Agriculture and Food is also involved in matters affecting the environment.

ACADEMIC INSTITUTES

Academy of Sciences (Akademia Shkencave): Rruga Myslim Shyri 7, Tirana; tel. (42) 26049; telex 2214; f. 1972; Pres. ALEKS BUDA.

Institute of Hydrometeorology (Instituti Hidrometeorologjik): Rruga e Durrësit, Tirana; tel. (42) 22169; f. 1962; responsible for monitoring pollution; Dir JAVER ÇOBANI.

Agricultural Research Institute (Instituti i Kërkimeve Bujqësore): Lushnjë; f. 1947; studies incl. agric. pollution control; Dir MILTO HYSO.

Faculty of Natural Sciences, University of Tirana (Fakulteti Shkencave të Natyrës, Universiteti i Tiranës): Bulevardi Deshmorët e Kombit, Tirana; tel. (42) 27669; f. 1957; Dean of Faculty of Natural Sciences Prof. Dr DRITAN SPAHIU.

Agricultural University of Tirana (Universiteti Bujqësor i Tiranës): Kamzë, Tirana; f. 1991 to replace the Higher Institute of Agriculture; research incl. water-and land-use problems and forestry; Rector BESNIK GJONGECAJ; Vice-Rector VLADIMIR SPAHO.

NON-GOVERNMENTAL ORGANIZATION

Albanian Green Party (Partia e Blerte Shqiptare): see section on Political Organizations.

Defence

In June 1992, according to Western estimates, the total strength of the armed forces was 40,000 (including 22,400 conscripts), comprising 27,000 in the Army, 11,000 in the Air Force and 2,000 in the Navy. Paramilitzry forces numbered some 16,000 (including an internal security force of 5,000 and a people's militia of 3,500). Military service is compulsory for all males and lasts for 18 months, although the system was under review in 1993. Ranks were abolished in the armed forces in the 1960s, but were reintroduced in 1991. Defence expenditure in 1991 was estimated at 950m. lekë.

Commander-in-Chief: President of the Republic.

Chief of the General Staff: Lt-Gen. ILIA VASHO.

Bibliography

Altman, F.-L. (Ed.). *Albanien im Umbruch*. Munich, Sudost-Institut, Oldenbourg, 1990.

Biberaj, E. *Albania and China: A Study of an Unequal Alliance*. Boulder, Colorado, Westview Press, 1986.

Griffith, W. E. *Albania and the Sino-Soviet Rift*. Cambridge, MA, MIT Press, 1963.

Hibbert, R. *Albania's National Liberation Struggle*. London, Pinter, 1991.

Kaser, M. 'Albania under and after Enver Hoxha' in *East European Economies*, Vol. 3. Washington, DC, USGPO (Joint Economic Committee of the US Congress), 1986.

Logoreci, A. *The Albanians: Europe's Forgotten Survivors*. Boulder, Colorado, Westview Press, 1977.

Marmallaku, R. *Albania and the Albanians*. London, C. Hurst, 1975.

Pano, N. C. *The People's Republic of Albania*. Baltimore, Maryland, Johns Hopkins Press, 1968.

Pipa, A. *Albanian Stalinism*. Colombia, East European Monographs, Columbia University Press, 1990.

Prifti, P. *Socialist Albania since 1944*. Cambridge, MA, MIT Press, 1978.

Skendi, S. *The Albanian National Awakening, 1878–1912*. Princeton, Princeton University Press, 1967.

ARMENIA

Geography

PHYSICAL FEATURES

The Republic of Armenia (formerly the Armenian Soviet Socialist Republic) is situated in south-west Transcaucasia, on the north-eastern border of Turkey. Its other borders are with Iran to the south, Azerbaijan to the east and Georgia to the north. The Nakhichevan Autonomous Republic, an Azerbaijani territory, is an enclave within Armenian territory. The Republic of Armenia, which today covers 29,800 sq km (11,506 sq miles), is the remnant of a much larger area of Armenian settlement that existed before the First World War and included many areas of eastern Turkey and other regions of the Caucasus. In mid-1993, owing to the conflict over Nagorny Karabakh (or Daglygh Karabagh), an autonomous oblast within Azerbaijan, ethnic Armenian militia controlled not only Nagorny Karabakh itself but also areas of Azerbaijani territory around the disputed enclave.

The central physical feature of Armenia is Lake Sevan, a mountainous lake at an altitude of 1,924 m (6,313 feet), which is surrounded by high mountain ranges, reaching 4,090 m (13,419 feet) at Mt Aragats. The mountains are drained by numerous streams and rivers flowing into the River Araks, which empties into the Caspian Sea. The Araks marks the south-western border of the Republic and its basin forms a fertile lowland to the south of Yerevan called the Ararat Plain.

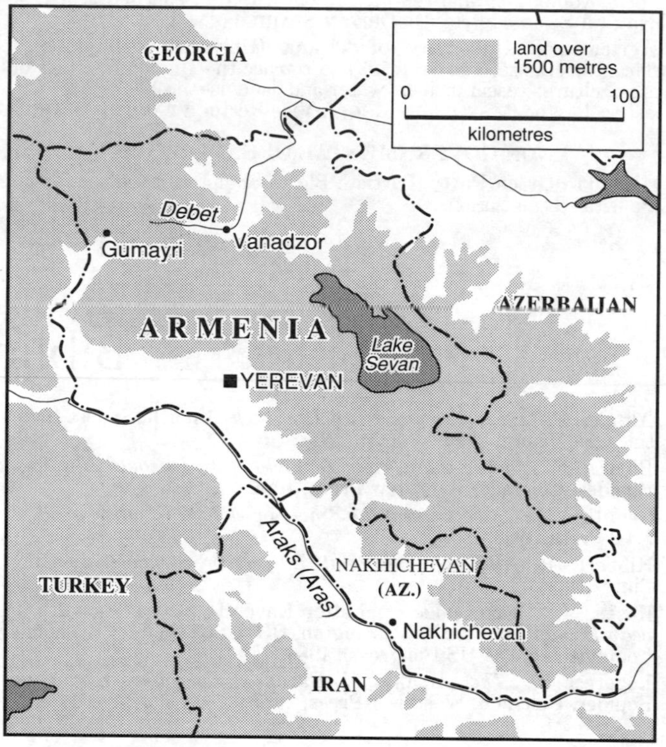

CLIMATE

The climate is typically continental: dry, with strong temperature variations. Winters are cold, the average January temperature in Yerevan being −3°C (26°F), but summers can be very warm, with August temperatures averaging 25°C (77°F), although high altitude moderates the heat in much of the country. Precipitation is low in the Yerevan area (annual average, 322 mm), but much higher in the mountains.

POPULATION

At the 1989 census, 93.3% of the total *de facto* population of 3,287,677 were Armenians, 1.7% Kurds and 1.5% Russians. Other ethnic groups included Ukrainians (8,341), Assyrians (5,963), Greeks (4,650) and Georgians (1,364). As a result of inter-ethnic tension, almost the entire Azerbaijani population (in 1989 2.6% of the total) was reported to have left Armenia after the census was conducted, and Armenian refugees entered Armenia from Azerbaijan. There are many Armenians in neighbouring states, notably in Georgia and in Azerbaijan, although numbers in the latter have fallen since the recent inter-ethnic conflict. There are also important Armenian communities abroad, particularly in the USA and France. The official language is Armenian, the sole member of a distinct Indo-European language group. It is written in the Armenian script. Most of the population are taught Russian as a second language, and Kurdish is used in broadcasting and publishing for some 56,000 Kurds living in the Republic. Most of the population are adherents of Christianity, the largest denomination being the Armenian Apostolic Church. There are also Russian Orthodox, Protestant, Islamic and Yazidi communities.

The estimated total population at 1 January 1991 was 3,354,000. The capital is Yerevan, which had an estimated population of 1,202,000 in January 1990. Other important towns include Vanadzor (formerly Kirovakan) and Gumayri (formerly Leninakan).

Chronology

c. 850 BC: Indo-European tribes, Chaldeans, occupied territory to the south of the Caucasus, destroying the ancient kingdom of Urartu (Ararat); these two peoples were the ancestors of the Armenians.

64: The Roman Empire secured its pre-eminence in the region with the final defeat of the Kingdom of Pontus, to which the Armenians had been allied; parts of Armenia eventually became a Roman province.

AD 117: The Emperor Hadrian withdrew the borders of the Roman Empire back to the River Euphrates again (i.e. still including what was known as Lesser Armenia), despite his predecessor Trajan's conquest of much territory to the east (Greater Armenia).

c. 295: St Gregory the Illuminator converted Armenia, which became the first Christian state, at a time of renewed struggle for dominance in the region, between the Empires of Rome and Persia.

451: The Fourth Council of Chalcedon condemned Monophysitism (see p. 19), isolating the Armenians from the rest of the Christian Church.

639: The first Arab raids on Armenia marked the start of Muslim influence in the area.

1071: The Seljuq Turk victory at the Battle of Manzikert (now Malazgirt) confirmed Eastern Roman ('Byzantine') expulsion from Armenia and its environs and the dominance of the Sultanate of Iconium (Konya) or Rum.

1375: Mamelukes of Egypt conquered the Armenian capital of Sis and ended the country's nominal independence.

1639: After some years of dispute, Armenia was partitioned between the Turkish Ottoman Empire (which secured the larger, western part) and the Persian Empire.

1828: Persia (now Iran) ceded Persian (Eastern) Armenia to the Russian Empire by the Treaty of Turkmenchai.

1878: Russia gained the province of Kars from the Ottomans by the Congress of Berlin.

1915: The Ottoman massacres and persecution of Armenians, increasing since the 1890s, reached its worst and was rapidly depopulating Anatolian Armenia.

April 1918: Proclamation of a Transcaucasian federation (Armenia, Azerbaijan and Georgia), following the collapse of tsarist rule and the Soviet signing of the Treaty of Brest-Litovsk.

28 May 1918: Turkish menaces caused the collapse of Transcaucasia and the proclamation of an independent Armenia, which was governed by the Armenian Revolutionary Federation (ARF—Dashnaktsutyun); Armenia was forced to cede territory around Kars to the Turks.

10 August 1920: The Treaty of Sèvres, between the Allied Powers and the Ottoman authorities, recognized an independent Armenia, but the Treaty was rejected by the new Turkish leader, Mustafa Kemal (Atatürk).

September 1920: Turkish troops invaded Armenia after the ARF Government intervened in Anatolia, concerned at the savage persecution of ethnic Armenians there.

29 November 1920: Proclamation of the Soviet Republic of Armenia, following the invasion of Bolshevik troops.

1921: A series of treaties led to the establishment of Nagorny Karabakh as a mainly ethnic Armenian enclave within, and part of, Azerbaijan; Turkey recognized its borders with Soviet Transcaucasia.

December 1922: Armenia became a member of the Transcaucasian Soviet Federative Socialist Republic (TSFSR), which itself joined the Union of Soviet Socialist Republics (USSR).

December 1936: The new Soviet Constitution dissolved the TSFSR and Armenia became a full Union Republic in its own name.

September 1987: As a result of the policies of *glasnost* of the new leader of the USSR, Mikhail Gorbachev, Soviet Armenia experienced its first public demonstrations against ecological degradation and at corruption in the local Communist Party of Armenia (CPA).

February 1988: Anti-Armenian violence occurred in Sumgait, Azerbaijan.

May 1988: The First Secretary of the CPA was dismissed, because of his failure to prevent the rise of ethnic tensions over Armenian demands for the enclave of Nagorny Karabakh to be transferred from Azerbaijan jurisdiction.

December 1988: Northern Armenia, particularly the city of Leninakan (now Gumayri), was devastated by an earthquake.

May 1989: Massive demonstrations secured the release of the leaders of the so-called Karabakh Committee, who had been in prison since December.

November 1989: The Armenian Supreme Soviet (republican legislature) declared Nagorny Karabakh to be part of a unified Armenian Republic, following the end of direct rule in the enclave by the all-Union Government (since January) and the restoration of Azerbaijan authority.

January 1990: The Armenian Supreme Soviet resolved that it had the power to veto central legislation when the all-Union Supreme Soviet declared that Armenia's November declaration had been unconstitutional.

May–July 1990: In the elections to the Armenian Supreme Soviet, the Armenian Pan-national Movement (APM), the successor to the opposition Karabakh Committee, became the largest single party, with 35% of the votes cast; the APM leader, Levon Ter-Petrosyan, was elected Chairman of the Supreme Soviet (republican head of state).

23 August 1990: The Armenian SSR declared its sovereignty and changed its name to the Republic of Armenia.

March 1991: Armenia refused to participate in the referendum on the Union, negotiations on which it had refused to join since late 1990.

21 September 1991: Armenia held a referendum on secession from the USSR; the new Soviet law on secession, involving a five-year transitional period, was expected to govern the process.

23 September 1991: The results of the referendum (94.4% of the electorate participated and, of them, 99.3% voted in favour of secession) prompted the republican Supreme Soviet to declare Armenia an independent state immediately.

16 October 1991: Ter-Petrosyan remained head of state after national elections for the post of President of the Republic.

19 October 1991: The Armenian Government signed the new Soviet Treaty of Economic Community, but continued in its resolve not to commit itself to any new political arrangements with the other Soviet Republics.

21 December 1991: Armenia signed the Almaty Declaration, by which it became a member of the Commonwealth of Independent States (CIS).

February 1992: Armenia was admitted to the Conference on Security and Co-operation in Europe (CSCE).

March 1992: Armenia became a member of the United Nations (UN).

May 1992: Armenia and Azerbaijan negotiated a cease-fire, although Armenia claimed to have no control over the Nagorny Karabakh militia, which had secured the whole enclave and a 'corridor' to Armenia; other states made it clear they would not intervene.

15 May 1992: Armenia signed the Five-Year Collective Security Agreement in Tashkent (Uzbekistan), with Kazakhstan, the Russian Federation, Tajikistan, Turkmenistan and Uzbekistan.

July 1992: The Armenian Supreme Soviet passed a resolution on the status of Nagorny Karabakh, in which it pledged consistent support for the enclave and for the rights of its population.

August 1992: Supporters of the National Union, a grouping of opposition legislators, held mass rallies in Yerevan, to protest against President Ter-Petrosyan's policies on the Nagorny Karabakh crisis and on economic reform.

December 1992: President Ter-Petrosyan declared a national emergency in Armenia.

January 1993: In Minsk (Belarus), Armenia and six other member states of the CIS committed themselves to seeking closer co-operation.

30 April 1993: The UN Security Council, under Resolution 822, demanded that all Armenian forces immediately withdraw from Azerbaijani territory and that a cease-fire be agreed upon.

24 May 1993: The Armenian Government agreed to a CSCE-negotiated peace plan for Nagorny Karabakh. Azerbaijan also signed the plan, but it was not accepted by the Nagorny Karabakh leadership until June.

29 July 1993: The immediate withdrawal of the Nagorny Karabakh militia from Agdam (a town in Azerbaijan proper, to the east of the disputed enclave) was demanded by the UN Security Council, under Resolution 853.

26 August 1993: In Moscow (Russian Federation), Armenia and five other member states of the CIS signed a resolution on military co-operation.

7 September 1993: Armenia, Belarus, Kazakhstan, the Russian Federation and Uzbekistan signed an agreement on the formation of a rouble zone. However, an Armenian currency, the dram, was introduced in November.

14 October 1993: The UN Security Council adopted Resolution 874, endorsing the CSCE's schedule for implementing Resolutions 822 and 853.

History

Although Armenia was an important power in ancient times, for much of its history it has been ruled by foreign states. In 1639 Armenia was partitioned, with the larger, western part being annexed by the Turkish Ottoman Empire and the eastern region becoming part of the Persian Empire. In 1828, after a period of Russo-Persian conflict, eastern Armenia was ceded to the Russian Empire by the Treaty of Turkmenchai and subsequently became a province of the Empire.

At the beginning of the 20th century Armenians living in western, or Anatolian, Armenia, under Ottoman rule, were subject to increasing persecution by the Turks. By the end of the First World War, as a result of brutal massacres and deportations, particularly in 1915, the Anatolian lands were largely emptied of their Armenian population. After the collapse of Russian imperial power in 1917, Russian Armenia joined the anti-Bolshevik Transcaucasian federation, which included Georgia and Azerbaijan. This collapsed when threatened by Turkish forces and, on 28 May 1918, Armenia was forced to establish an independent state. Without Russian protection, however, the newly-formed Republic was almost defenceless against Turkish expansionism and was forced to cede the province of Kars and other territories to Turkey. Armenia was recognized as an independent state by the Allied Powers, and by the Ottomans in the Treaty of Sèvres, signed on 10 August 1920. However, the rejection of the Treaty by the new Turkish ruler, Mustafa Kemal (Atatürk), left Armenia vulnerable to renewed Turkish threats.

SOVIET ARMENIA

In September 1920 Turkish troops attacked Armenia. The Turks were only prevented from establishing full control over the country by the invasion of Armenia, from the east, by Russian Bolshevik troops, and the establishment, on 29 November 1920, of a Soviet Republic of Armenia. In December 1922 the Republic became a member, together with Georgia and Azerbaijan, of the Transcaucasian Soviet Federative Socialist Republic (TSFSR), which, in turn, became a constituent republic of the USSR. In 1936 the TSFSR was dissolved and the Armenian Soviet Socialist Republic (Armenian SSR) became a full Union Republic of the USSR.

Although many Armenians suffered under Communist rule, advances were made in economic and social development. Under tsarist rule Russian Armenia had been an underdeveloped region of the Empire, with very little infrastructure. However, under Soviet rule a policy of forced modernization was carried out, which expanded communications and introduced industrial plants. Literacy and education were also improved.

Soviet leader Mikhail Gorbachev's policies of *perestroika* (restructuring) and *glasnost* (openness) had little initial impact in Armenia. The first manifestations of the new policies were campaigns against corruption in the higher echelons of the Communist Party of Armenia—CPA (renamed the Armenian Democratic Party in 1993). On a more public level, ecological problems became a focus for popular protest. The first demonstrations against ecological degradation took place in September 1987, but the demands of protesters soon began to include historical and political problems.

Among the historical and ethnic issues discussed in late 1987 and early 1988 the status of Nagorny Karabakh (or Daglygh Karabagh), an autonomous oblast within Azerbaijan, but largely populated by Armenians, was the most significant. Demands for the incorporation of Nagorny Karabakh into the Armenian Republic began within the enclave itself in early 1988. In February 1988 crowds of up to one million people took part in demonstrations in Yerevan supporting their demands. The demonstrations were organized by a group of Yerevan intellectuals, who formed a group known as the Karabakh Committee.

In response to increased unrest within Armenia, many Azerbaijanis began to leave the Republic. Rumours of ill-treatment of the refugees led to anti-Armenian riots in Sumgait (Azerbaijan) in late February 1988, in which 26 Armenians died. The inability of the local authorities to control the unrest led to the dismissal, in May, of the First Secretary of the CPA.

In December 1988 a severe earthquake struck northern Armenia. The city of Leninakan (now Gumayri) was seriously damaged and the village of Spitak was completely destroyed. Some 25,000 people were reported to have been killed. Thousands more were made homeless.

Throughout 1989 unrest continued both in Armenia and within Nagorny Karabakh, but there were other significant political developments within the Republic. *Glasnost* allowed a much fuller examination of Armenian history and culture and a number of unofficial groups, concerned with both cultural and political issues, were formed. In May the *yerakuyn*, the national flag of independent Armenia, was flown again, and 28 May, the anniversary of the establishment of independent Armenia, was declared a national day. However, all internal politics continued to be dominated by events in Nagorny Karabakh (for details of which, see chapter on Azerbaijan). Following a general strike in Azerbaijan, an economic blockade was implemented against Armenia, seriously affecting the reconstruction programme required after the 1988 earthquake.

The increasing disillusionment among Armenians with the Soviet Government (following the declaration by the all-Union Supreme Soviet in late 1989) was apparently responsible for the low turn-out in the elections to the Armenian Supreme Soviet, which took place in May–July 1990. No party achieved an overall majority, but the Armenian Pan-national Movement (APM), the successor to the Karabakh Committee, was the largest single party, with some 35% of the seats in parliament. Supported by other non-Communist groups, Levon Ter-Petrosyan, the leader of the APM, defeated Vladimir Movsisyan, the First Secretary of the CPA, in elections to the chairmanship of the Supreme Soviet. Vazgen Manyukan, also a leader of the APM, was appointed Chairman of the Council of Ministers (head of government). On 23 August 1990 the Armenian Supreme Soviet adopted a declaration of sovereignty, including the right to maintain armed forces. The Armenian SSR was renamed the Republic of Armenia. The new Government began to establish political and commercial links with the Armenian diaspora and several prominent exiles returned to the Republic. In late November the CPA, after heated debate, voted to become an independent organization within the CPSU. Stepan Pogosyan was elected First Secretary, replacing Movsisyan.

The Armenian Government refused to enter into the negotiations on a new Treaty of Union, which took place in late 1990 and early 1991. It officially boycotted the referendum on the renewal of the Union, which took place in March 1991 in nine of the other Republics. Instead, the Supreme Soviet decided to conduct a referendum on Armenian secession from the USSR on 21 September 1991. It was planned that the referendum would be carried out within the provisions of the Soviet law on seccession, adopted in April by the all-Union Supreme Soviet. This entailed a transitional period of at least five years before full independence could be achieved.

The moderate policies of the new Government, especially in developing relations with Turkey, attracted internal criticism from more extreme nationalist groups, notably the Union for National Self-determination (UNS), which continued to seek the recovery of lands lost to Turkey after the First World War. The CPA also attacked the Government for its willingness to develop relations with Turkey, as did the Armenian Revolutionary Federation (ARF—in Armenian, Dashnaktsutyun, which had formed the Government of independent Armenia in 1918–20). Nevertheless, the Government insisted that good relations with Turkey were essential to Armenia if it were to survive outside the USSR. The CPA strongly opposed the idea of secession, while the ARF advocated a more gradual process towards independence. The acceptance by the Government of the principles of the Soviet law on secession was criticized by the UNS, which campaigned for immediate secession in breach of the constitutional procedure.

INDEPENDENCE AND AFTER

The attempted coup in Moscow, and subsequent events of August 1991, forced the Government to accelerate the moves towards independence. The response of the Armenian leadership to the overthrow of Soviet President Mikhail Gorbachev on 19 August was initially cautious, with Ter-Petrosyan stressing the need for maximum restraint. He was, it seems, anxious not to provoke further action by Soviet troops in Nagorny Karabakh, or even in Armenia proper. The events of August provided further support for those who advocated complete independence for Armenia. The referendum on secession took place as scheduled, on 21 September. According to official returns, 94.4% of the electorate took part, of which 99.3% voted in favour of Armenia being 'an independent, democratic state outside the Union'. Instead of conforming to the Soviet law on secession, on 23 September the Supreme Soviet (henceforth the Supreme Council) declared Armenia to be an independent state.

The independence declaration was followed, on 16 October 1991, by elections to the post of President of the Republic. There were six candidates in the election, but it was won overwhelmingly by the incumbent head of state, Ter-Petrosyan. He continued to demand international recognition of Armenia, but also signed the Treaty of the Economic Community with other Soviet Republics on 19 October. He stressed that it did not encroach on Armenia's political sovereignty, and refused to sign a new treaty on political union. The Armenian leadership did, however, join the Commonwealth of Independent States (CIS), signing the founding Almaty Declaration, on 21 December.

In mid-August 1992 supporters of the National Union, a grouping of opposition legislators (mainly belonging to the ARF), held mass rallies in Yerevan to protest against President Ter-Petrosyan's handling of the Nagorny Karabakh crisis and on the issue of economic reform. Economic conditions in the Republic were declining as a direct result of the conflict. In mid-1992 a huge influx of refugees (an estimated 330,000, which amounted to approximately 10% of the Republic's population) arrived from Azerbaijan and Nagorny Karabakh. At the end of that year the UN established a US $6.4m. emergency relief operation for Armenia and Azerbaijan, which focused on providing refugees with food and housing for the winter. Fighting in neighbouring Georgia, Turkey's refusal to allow humanitarian aid through its border and the economic blockade by Azerbaijan, which had been in force since late 1989, were causing widespread shortages in foodstuffs and fuel. Most of the country's 450 factories had been forced to close and production had declined for the fourth consecutive year. In December 1992 Ter-Petrosyan declared a national emergency in Armenia.

The chronic shortage of fuel at home and the threat of Turkish intervention in the Nagorny Karabakh conflict, on behalf of Azerbaijan, made the Ter-Petrosyan administration anxious for a peace settlement. In May 1993 the Armenian Government agreed to a peace plan proposed by Turkey, the USA and the Russian Federation, but thousands of demonstrators in Yerevan, encouraged by the opposition ARF, which strongly opposed the Government's lenient policy towards Turkey, protested against the signing of the plan.

In September 1993, both Iran and Turkey, as a sign of protest against the continuing occupation by ethnic Armenian militia of Azerbaijani territory near the Iranian border, began to mobilize troops. In late October the Turkish leadership stated that no normalization of relations between Turkey and Armenia could occur until Armenian aggression in Azerbaijan had ceased. On 14 October the UN Security Council adopted Resolution 874, which recognized the Nagorny Karabakh Armenians as a separate party in the conflict and endorsed the schedule of the Conference on Security and Co-operation in Europe (CSCE) for implementing Resolutions 822 and 853. The Armenian Government had approved the schedule, which was proposed in early October, and accepted the UN resolution.

Armenia declared its independence in September 1991, but only achieved widespread international recognition upon the formation of the CIS and the consequent dissolution of the USSR. In February 1992 Armenia was admitted as a member of the CSCE, at the same time as Azerbaijan. It was the so-called 'Minsk Group' of nine CSCE countries (including Italy, Russia and Turkey) that led international attempts to mediate in the contentions over Nagorny Karabakh. Armenia and Azerbaijan were both admitted to the UN in March 1992. On 15 May Armenia, along with five other CIS members, Kazakhstan, the Russian Federation, Tajikistan, Turkmenistan and Uzbekistan, signed the Five-Year Collective Security Agreement. Azerbaijan withdrew from the CIS in October of that year but rejoined in September 1993. In January 1993, in Minsk (Belarus), Armenia and six other member states of the CIS signed a commonwealth charter aimed at achieving closer co-operation. On 26 August, in Moscow (Russian Federation), representatives of Armenia, the Russian Federation, Kazakhstan, Kyrgyzstan, Uzbekistan and Tajikistan approved a resolution on the improvement of CIS defences and of mutual military co-operation.

The Economy

The Armenian economy is highly dependent on trade, mainly with other states of the former USSR. Armenia developed a limited industrial base under Soviet rule and its economy remained primarily industrial. In 1991, according to International Monetary Fund (IMF) estimates, Armenia's gross domestic product (GDP), at current prices, was 15,671m. roubles, equivalent to 4,759 roubles per head. In that year net material product (NMP), measured at current prices, was estimated to be 12,329m. roubles. In 1991 NMP decreased, in real terms, by an estimated 12%, compared with the previous year. According to the IMF, the cumulative fall in GDP, in 1991–1992, was estimated at around 50%, among the steepest decreases experienced by any of the former Soviet republics. In 1992 Armenia's rate of economic reform slowed as its situation deteriorated, despite initial progress, and the consequent growth of the private sector, although the latter had yet to impinge on official statistics. As well as problems common to other successors of the Soviet economic system, Armenia, in the early 1990s had still to confront other problems unique to the country. It remained a landlocked nation, completely dependent on imported energy, and with considerable further assistance still needed to alleviate the effects of the 1988 earthquake (damage to infrastructure and property, etc). The conflict with Azerbaijan caused that country to introduce an economic blockade (first imposed in 1989), the effects of which were compounded by Turkey's closure of its border with Armenia. The war distracted scarce resources and discouraged investment. Finally, Armenia's vital trade with the rest of the former USSR was further disrupted by the unrest in its northern neighbour, Georgia.

AGRICULTURE

Agriculture contributed an estimated 26% of NMP in 1991, when approximately 4% of the working population were employed in the sector. The principal crops are potatoes, with an estimated harvest in 1991 of just over 275,000 metric tons, and other vegetables (with a harvest of 443,500 metric tons in 1991). The grain harvest in 1991 was an estimated 304,000 metric tons. Other agricultural goods include a wide variety of fruits, grapes, tobacco, industrial crops and melons. Wines and brandies are also produced, but the wine industry suffered as a result of Gorbachev's campaign against alcoholism in the mid-1980s and the decline in production levels continued into the 1990s. In general, agricultural production in Armenia rose sharply in 1991, largely owing to the effects of land privatization, which began in 1991. Private farms accounted for an estimated one-third of agricultural production. By September 1992 some 90% of arable land had been privatized.

INDUSTRY

Industry was the dominant sector in Armenia's economy. It contributed 42.3% of NMP in 1991, when an estimated 31% of the working population were employed in this sector. The principal industrial sector in Armenia was light manufacturing, especially textiles (of the value of 711m. roubles in 1991) and leather footwear (worth 484m. roubles in 1991). Other major products were electrical equipment, instruments, machinery and computers. The chemical industry and non-ferrous metallurgy were also important. In 1991 every category of industrial production showed a decline and, in most cases, the level of production was less than that for 1989. Production of electric generators, one of the country's major industrial products, fell by over 50% in 1991, following a decline of nearly one-third in 1990. According to official estimates, total industrial production in Armenia declined by more than 50% in the first nine months of 1992. The main contributory factor was the shortage of power.

Construction contributed 14.6% of NMP in 1991 and accounted for 14% of those in employment. Total construction activity, in value, amounted to 2,207.0m. roubles, in 1991, of which 1,028.0m. roubles were in the production sphere and 1,179.0m. roubles in the nonproduction sphere.

MINING AND ENERGY

Armenia has few mineral resources, although, according to the authorities, it does possess a number of coal mines, which could produce some 100m. metric tons of coal. It does have certain advantages that could contribute to the growth of a chemical industry: some 35% of the world's resources of mineral salt and large deposits of calcium oxide and carbon. Copper, molybdenum, gold, silver and iron are extracted on a small scale.

Most of Armenia's requirements for the energy sector are met through imports (hydroelectricity being the only significant domestically produced source of energy). The transportation and pipeline blockade, fully in force since 1991, and, subsequent to that, the intermittent civil disorders in Georgia, greatly limited energy imports. In 1991, 3,500m. cubic metres of natural gas were imported, and it was estimated, by the Ministry of Energy and Fuel that less than one-half that amount would be imported in 1992. Similarly, imports of other significant energy sources such as mazut (a semi-processed petroleum derivative, used mainly for fuel), benzine, coal and diesel fuel continued to decline after 1992. The country's sole nuclear power station, at Medzamor, was closed in 1988, although in October 1993 the International Atomic Energy Agency (IAEA) agreed to help Armenia restore it. The Russian Federation was also prepared to assist with the enterprise. According to preliminary studies, the power station was capable of producing 10m. kilowatt hours (kWh) of electricity per day—approximately 25% of Armenia's fuel needs. In 1992 plans were being considered to build two medium-sized hydroelectric power stations on the Dzoraget and Debet rivers with a total generation capacity of 575m. kWh per year. Another plan envisaged building 300–450 small power stations on Armenian lakes, which would generate some 1,000m. kWh per year. In April 1993 Armenia had almost concluded a US $57.4m. agreement with the European Bank for Reconstruction and Development (EBRD) to finish a 300 MW petroleum- and gas-fired electricity unit at Hrazdan, some 40 km from Yerevan. In August 1993 the Armneft fund was established in Washington, DC (USA), to finance the extraction of petroleum and natural gas on Armenian territory.

TRADE

After the dissolution of the USSR, in December 1991, Armenia not only attempted to maintain close economic links with its traditional trading partners in the former USSR, but also sought to expand economic relations with Turkey and Iran. Total trade, in 1991, was estimated to be equivalent to about 94% of GDP. In 1990 the value of total exports was estimated at approximately 3,500m. roubles, a steady decline since the 1986 figure of 5,000m. roubles. In the same year Armenia recorded a visible trade deficit of 1,345m. roubles. The principal exports were light industrial products, machinery-building and metal products and food items. The principal imports were light industrial products, industrial raw materials and energy products. During 1987–90 Armenia's foreign exports, consisting mainly of light industrial products to other Soviet Republics, were relatively few compared to its foreign imports. The deficit on inter-republican trade was estimated at 4,400m. roubles for 1992, or 6.3% of GDP. The trade deficit with other countries for 1992 was estimated at approximately US $45m.

FINANCE

In Armenia the state budget included the operations of both national and local government. Even in 1993 the timing, preparation and approval procedures for the budget, as well as policies governing the allocation of revenue and expenditure, were still decided on an *ad hoc* basis. In 1991 there was an estimated budget deficit of some 304m. roubles (equivalent to approximately 1.9% of GDP). Official estimates of the projected 1992 primary deficit on the state budget were, on an accrual basis, 13,611m. roubles (19.4% of GDP) or, on a cash basis, 9,785m. roubles (13.9% of GDP). There were several contributory factors to the deterioration in the budgetary position in 1992: the accumulation of domestic expenditure arrears and of substantial interest-payment arrears on Armenia's share of the USSR's foreign debt; a fundamental reform of the entire taxation system, causing a fall in revenue; price liberalization requiring increased expenditure. At the beginning of 1992 Armenia's total external debt was estimated to be over US $750m.

The average annual increase in consumer prices was estimated at 10.3% in 1990 and 100.3% in 1991; in the first nine months of 1992 alone, consumer prices increased by 973%. This surge reflected price liberalization in general, as well as further increases to the administered prices of foodstuffs in January and June 1992. In 1993 consumer prices continued to surge, which was partly the result of the influx of large quantities of old roubles from the former Soviet republics. On 16 November 1993 the National Bank of Armenia announced that a new Armenian currency, the dram, would be introduced by the end of the month.

Armenia became a member of the IMF, the World Bank, and the EBRD in 1992. It is likely to become a member of the IAEA. On 7 September 1993 representatives from the Armenian Government and the National Bank of Armenia, with representatives from Belarus, Kazakhstan, the Russian Federation and Uzbekistan, signed an agreement on a 'new-style' rouble zone in which the Russian rouble would be the legal means of payment. Nevertheless, in November, Armenia was obliged to introduce its own currency, the dram.

THE SOVIET LEGACY

Even before the disintegration of the USSR the Armenian economy had entered a serious decline. For several years it had registered a contraction of NMP, a fall in output and significant increases in inflation. The final collapse of the Soviet central planning system and internal trading structure only served to exacerbate Armenia's economic crisis. The effects of the earthquake of 1988, which required considerable resources for reconstruction and for humanitarian relief, and the war in Nagorny Karabakh were equally severe. In 1989 Armenia's political adversary, Azerbaijan, first imposed an economic blockade, closing both the railway link and the gas pipeline to Armenia. (Hitherto, almost 90% of Armenia's imports from other Union Republics had arrived via Azerbaijan.) The losses suffered by enterprises in 1990 as a result of the blockade were estimated at 784m. roubles (equivalent to some 5% of estimated GDP in that year). By late 1991 the volume of industrial production had declined drastically, with many enterprises inoperative, owing to widespread shortages of fuel. The gas pipeline from Azerbaijan was completely and finally closed in November 1991 and strife in Georgia further limited the import of energy. By late 1992 it was reported that most of Armenia's 450 factories had been forced to close down. Food shortages were also reported throughout the country, with a system of rationing introduced in some areas. The economic blockade also meant that Armenia's flow of exports was disrupted. The economy was further strained by the massive influx of refugees from both Nagorny Karabakh and Azerbaijan. However, in 1993 some growth in the manufacturing sector was reported. Forty-five factories (approximately 15% of industrial capacity) were reopened in April, after the natural-gas pipeline from Georgia was reconnected. Such restraints had impeded progress in the process of transferring enterprises to private ownership (a law on privatization had been enacted in mid-1992). Privatization of housing also was limited in effect, this being detrimental to new construction and growth. However, privatization in the agricultural sector had impressive results. Generally, despite the economic problems common to the former Soviet territories, and its own situation, Armenia made considerable progress in establishing a basis for a market economy during the early 1990s.

In September 1993 Armenia and the Russian Federation signed an agreement whereby the Russian Federation would assume all responsibility for Armenia's share of the USSR's foreign debt. Armenia was granted US $209,000 foreign credit and is likely to receive a further $28.7m. interest free credit from the World Bank for repairing the damage inflicted by the earthquake of 1988.

Statistical Survey

Principal sources: IMF, *Armenia, Economic Review*; World Bank, *Statistical Handbook: States of the Former USSR.*

Area and Population

AREA, POPULATION AND DENSITY

Area (sq km)	29,800*
Population (census result)	
12 January 1989†	
Males	1,619,308
Females	1,685,468
Total	3,304,776
Population (official estimates at 1 January 1991)	3,354,000
Density (per sq km) at 1 January 1991	112.6

* 11,500 sq miles.

† Population is *de jure*. The *de facto* total was 3,287,677.

PRINCIPAL TOWNS

(estimated population at 1 January 1990)

Yerevan (capital) 1,202,000; Gumayri (formerly Leninakan) 123,000.

BIRTHS, MARRIAGES AND DEATHS

	Registered live births		Registered marriages		Registered deaths	
	Number	Rate (per '000)	Number	Rate (per '000)	Number	Rate (per '000)
1987	78,492	22.8	30,259	8.8	19,727	5.7
1988	74,707	22.1	26,581	7.9	35,567	10.5
1989	75,250	22.9	27,257	8.3	20,853	6.3

Source: UN, *Demographic Yearbook*.

Agriculture

PRINCIPAL CROPS ('000 metric tons)

	1989	1990	1991
Grain*	192.1	271.0	304.0
Tobacco	3.3	1.7	1.8
Geraniums	28.0	6.5	8.5
Potatoes	266.3	212.5	275.2
Other vegetables	485.0	389.7	443.5
Garden produce	51.5	31.4	35.5
Berries	169.5	155.5	166.7
Grapes	118.8	143.6	191.2

* Cereals and pulses.

LIVESTOCK ('000 head at 1 January)

	1989	1990	1991
Cattle	742.0	478.5	428.9
Pigs	319.4	187.2	170.0
Sheep	1,450.1	812.3	686.5
Poultry	n.a.	9,067.0	6,731.2

LIVESTOCK PRODUCTS ('000 metric tons)

	1989	1990	1991
Meat (slaughter weight)	133.2	145.1	133.2
Milk	491.2	431.9	412.0
Eggs (million)	561.4	517.9	485.0
Wool (greasy)	3.3	2.8	2.4

Industry

SELECTED PRODUCTS

	1989	1990	1991
Synthetic rubber (metric tons)	39,150	1,441	10,613
Tyres ('000)	1,338	1,009	914
Cement ('000 metric tons)	1,639	1,466	1,507
Carpets ('000 sq m)	1,585	1,300	947
Leather footwear ('000 pairs)	17,952	18,740	11,340
Wine ('000 hectolitres)	580.3	419.1	433.3
Electric energy (million kWh)	12,137	10,377	9,532

Finance

CURRENCY AND EXCHANGE RATES

Monetary Units

100 kopeks = 1 rubl (ruble or rouble).

Denominations

Coins: 1, 2, 3, 5, 10, 15, 25 and 50 kopeks; 1 rouble.
Notes: 1, 3, 5, 10, 25, 50 and 100 roubles.

Sterling and Dollar Equivalents (30 September 1992)

£1 sterling = 454.3 roubles;
US $1 = 255.0 roubles;
1,000 roubles = £2.201 = $3.922.

Average Exchange Rate (roubles per US $)

1989 0.6274
1990 0.5856
1991 0.5819

Note: The figures for average exchange rates refer to official rates for the Soviet rouble. However, a multiple exchange rate system was in operation, with separate non-commercial and tourist rates. A commercial exchange rate was introduced on 1 November 1990, replacing the official rate for most transactions. The commercial rate (roubles per US dollar) was: 1.692 at 31 December 1990; 1.671 at 31 December 1991. Between November 1989 and April 1991 the tourist exchange rate valued the rouble at one-tenth of the official rate. In April 1991 this rate, renamed the 'special rate', was set at $1 = 27.6 roubles. It was subsequently adjusted. Following the dissolution of the USSR in December 1991, Russia and several other former Soviet republics retained the rouble as their monetary unit. However, on 22 November 1993, Armenia introduced its own currency, the dram, at an exchange rate of 84 roubles per dram.

STATE BUDGET (million roubles)*

Revenue†	1990	1991	1992‡
Taxation	2,171	2,471	11,662
Value added tax	—	n.a.	3,599
Excise	1,464	n.a.	919
Profits taxes	494	n.a.	4,210
Tax on fixed assets of enterprises	—	n.a.	839
Income taxes	213	n.a.	1,229
Other tax revenue	—	n.a.	867
Other receipts	1,352	1,606	119
Total	3,523	4,077	11,781

Expenditure	1992‡
Current expenditure	28,786
Wages	5,315
Subsidies on transport and milk	245
Interest on external debt	7,394
Pension contributions	1,435
Child allowances	1,190
Other purposes	13,206
Health	5,129
Education	2,543
Capital expenditure	4,000
Total	32,786

1990 (million roubles): Total expenditure 3,454 (all current).
1991 (million roubles): Total expenditure 4,381.

* Figures refer to the consolidated accounts of republican and local authorities, excluding the operations of the Pension and Employment Fund.

† Excluding transfers from the USSR budget (618 million roubles in 1990).

‡ Including projections for the fourth quarter of the year.

BALANCE OF PAYMENTS (estimates, US $ million)

	1990	1991	1992*
Merchandise exports			
Inter-republican (former USSR)	4,285.0	3,645.4	321.0
Foreign (other countries)	118.8	86.2	32.5
Merchandise imports			
Inter-republican	−4,385.0	−4,331.6	−344.5
Foreign	−1,442.5	−436.8	−77.1
Trade balance			
Inter-republican	−100.0	−686.2	−23.5
Foreign	−1,323.8	−350.6	−44.6
Services (net)			
Inter-republican	−160.3	−341.7	−20.0
Foreign	−166.4	−59.3	−50.9
Unrequited transfers (net)			
Inter-republican	568.8	376.8	—
Foreign	227.7	150.8	2.1
Current balance			
Inter-republican	308.5	−660.1	−43.5
Foreign	−1,262.4	−259.1	−93.4
Long-term capital (net)			
Inter-republican	n.a.	n.a.	2.7
Foreign	n.a.	n.a.	−138.6
Short-term capital (net)			
Inter-republican	n.a.	n.a.	—
Foreign	n.a.	n.a.	7.4
Net errors and omissions			
Inter-republican	n.a.	n.a.	15.4
Foreign	n.a.	n.a.	40.9
Overall balance			
Inter-republican	n.a.	n.a.	−25.4
Foreign	n.a.	n.a.	−183.7

* Including projections for the second half of the year.

NATIONAL ACCOUNTS

Net Material Product
(million roubles at current prices)

Activities of the material sphere	1989	1990	1991
Agriculture and forestry	993	1,205	3,166
Industry*	3,473	3,165	5,959
Construction	1,463	1,773	1,800
Transport and communications	243	287	274
Trade and catering	300	320	689
Others	443	226	440
Total	6,915	6,977	12,329

* Including turnover tax.

External Trade

PRINCIPAL COMMODITIES
(million roubles at current prices)

Imports	1988	1989	1990
Industrial products	4,661	4,692	4,361
Energy products	456	435	304
Ferrous metallurgy	277	284	210
Non-ferrous metallurgy	150	141	113
Chemical products	362	385	370
Machine-building and metal products	1,002	1,005	975
Wood and paper products	148	136	173
Building materials	87	98	83
Products of light industry	1,117	1,107	1,166
Products of food industry	843	946	754
Agricultural products (unprocessed)	212	200	290
Total (incl. others)*	4,877	4,898	4,868

* Of which imports from other Soviet Republics (in million roubles) totalled: 4,019 in 1988; 3,842 in 1989; 3,715 in 1990.

Exports	1988	1989	1990
Industrial products	3,747	3,659	3,492
Non-ferrous metallurgy	120	112	89
Chemical products	376	338	213
Machine-building and metal products	845	861	828
Products opf light industry	1,501	1,427	1,501
Products of food industry	584	641	412
Total (incl. others)*	3,767	3,691	3,523

* Of which exports to other Soviet Republics (in million roubles) totalled: 3,683 in 1988; 3,598 in 1989; 3,428 in 1990.

Education

(1990/91)

	Institutions	Students
Secondary schools	1,397	608,800
Secondary specialized institutions	70	45,900
Higher schools (incl. universities)	14	68,400

Directory

The Constitution

In late 1992 a special commission drafted a new constitution, which was expected to enter force by 1994.

The Government

(November 1993)

HEAD OF STATE

The President of the Republic is elected every five years by universal suffrage.

President: LEVON H. TER-PETROSYAN (elected 16 October 1991).

Vice-President: GAGIK G. ARUTYUNYAN.

COUNCIL OF MINISTERS

Prime Minister: HRAND BAGRATYAN.

Deputy Prime Minister: VIGEN I. CHITECHYAN.

State Ministers: GAGIK SHAHBAZYAN, S. TASHJYAN.

Minister of Foreign Affairs: VAHAN PAPAZYAN.

Minister of Culture: HAGOP HAGOPYAN.

Minister of Finance: LEVON BARKHODARYAN.

Minister of Trade: TIGRAN GRIGORYAN.

Minister of Industry: ASHOT SAFARYAN.

Minister of Internal Affairs: VANIK S. SIRADEGHYAN.

Minister of Higher Education and Science: VARDGES GNOUNI.

Minister of Construction: GAGIK MARTIROSYAN.

Minister of Lower Education: HAIK GHAZARYAN.

Minister of Nature and Environmental Protection: KAREN DANELYAN.

Minister of Defence: SERZHIK SARKISYAN.

Minister of Communications: GRIGOR POGHPATYAN.

Minister of Transport: HENRIK KOCHINYAN.

Minister of Agriculture: ASHOT VOSKANYAN.

Minister of Labour and Social Security: ASHOT YESAYAN.

Minister of Health: ARA BABLOYAN.

Minister of Justice: VAHE STEPANYAN.

Minister of Energy and Fuel: MIRON SHISHMANYAN.

Minister of Light Industry: RUDOLF TEIMURSYAN.

Minister of Industry: S. TASHJYAN.

Minister of Material Resources: VAHAN MELKONYAN.

Minister of Food and State Procurements: DAVIT ZADOYAN.

Minister of Economy: ASHOT YEGHIAZARIAN.

Minister of National Security: EDWARD SIMONYANS.

Chairmen of State Committees

Chairman of the State Committee for Planning and Construction: R. JULHAKYAN.

Chairman of the State Committee for Emergency: STEFAN BADALYAN.

Chairman of the State Commitee for Refugees: VLADIMIR MOVSESYAN.

Chairman of the State Committee for Statistics and Information Analysis: LEVON DAVITYAN.

Chairman of the State Committee for Geology: LAZR SARKISYAN.

Chairman of the State Committee for Special Programmes: LEONID PETROSYAN.

MINISTRIES

Office of the Prime Minister: 375010 Yerevan, Parliament Sq. 1, Government House.

Ministry of Agriculture: 375010 Yerevan, Republic Sq. 3; tel. (8852) 52-46-41; telex 243369; fax (8852) 52-37-93.

Ministry of Communications: 375002 Yerevan, Saryan St 22; tel. (8852) 52-66-32; telex 243311; fax (8852) 53-86-45.

Ministry of Construction: 375010 Yerevan, Republic Sq. 3; tel. (8852) 58-90-80.

Ministry of Culture: 375001 Yerevan, Tumanyan St 5; tel. (8852) 56-19-20; telex 243366; fax (8852) 52-39-22.

Ministry of Defence: 375830 Proshyan, Nairy District.

Ministry of the Economy: 375010 Yerevan, Republic Sq. 3.

Ministry of Education: 375010 Yerevan, Movses Khorenatsi St 13; tel. (8852) 52-47-49.

Ministry of Energy and Fuel: 375010 Yerevan, Republic Sq. 2.

Ministry of Finance: 375010 Yerevan, Melik-Adamyan St 1; tel. (8852) 52-70-82.

Ministry of Food and Fisheries: 375010 Yerevan, Nalbandyan St 48; tel. (8852) 52-19-64; telex 243369; fax (8852) 52-37-93.

Ministry of Foreign Affairs: 375019 Yerevan, Marshal Baghramyan St 10; tel. (8852) 52-35-31; telex 243313; fax (8852) 56-56-16.

Ministry of Health: 375001 Yerevan, Tumanyan St 8; tel. (8852) 58-24-13; telex 243347; fax (8852) 56-41-59.

Ministry of Higher Education and Science: 375010 Yerevan, Movses Khorenatsi St 13.

Ministry of Industry: 375010 Yerevan, Republic Sq. 2.

Ministry of Internal Affairs: 375025 Yerevan, Nalbandyan St 130; tel. (8852) 56-09-08; fax (8852) 57-84-40.

Ministry of Justice: 375010 Yerevan, Parliament St 8; tel. (8852) 58-21-57.

Ministry of Labour and Social Security: 375025 Yerevan, Isaahakyan St 18; tel. (8852) 56-53-21; telex 243306; fax (8852) 56-30-75.

Ministry of Light Industry: 375033 Yerevan, P. Kochar St 4; tel. (8852) 22-65-00.

Ministry of Lower Education: 375010 Yerevan, Khorenatsi St 13.

Ministry of Material Resources: 375015 Yerevan, Khorenatsi St 3.

Ministry of Protection of Nature and the Environment: 375002 Yerevan, Moskovyan St 35.

Ministry of Trade: 375009 Yerevan, Teryan St 69; tel. (8852) 56-25-91.

Ministry of Transport: 375015 Yerevan, Zakyan St 10; tel. (8852) 56-33-91; fax (8852) 52-52-68.

Legislature

GERAGUIN KHORHURT

(Supreme Council)

The supreme legislative body in the Republic is the 260-member Supreme Council. Elections to the Supreme Council were held in May–July 1990.

Chairman: BABKEN ARARKTSYAN.

Vice-Chairman: ARDASHES TUMANYAN.

Local Government

Armenia is divided into 37 administrative regions (districts), each with its own legislative and executive body.

Political Organizations

Armenian Democratic Party: Yerevan; fmrly Communist Party of Armenia, renamed 1993; dissolved Sept. 1991, re-legalized 1992; Chair. ARAM SARKISYAN.

Armenian Pan-national Movement (APM): 375019 Yerevan, Marshal Baghramyan St 14; f. 1989; Pres. LEVON H. TER-PETROSYAN; Chair. Rev. HUSIK LAZARYAN.

Armenian Revolutionary Federation—ARF (Hai Heghapokhakan Dashnaktsutyun): 375025 Yerevan, Myasnyak Ave 2; f. 1890; formed the ruling party in independent Armenia, 1918–20; prohibited under Soviet rule, but continued its activities in other countries; permitted to operate legally in Armenia from 1991; 40,000 mems; Chair. RUBEN HAKOBYAN, VAHAN HOVHANISYAN.

National Democratic Union: Yerevan; f. 1991 as a splinter party from the APM; Leader VAZGEN MANUKYAN.

Party of Democratic Freedom (Partiya Ramkavar Azatakan): 375010 Yerevan, Anrapetutyan St 47; f. 1905; Chair. of Founding Council RUBEN MIRZAKHANYAN.

Republican Party of Armenia: Yerevan; f. 1990 following a split in the Union for National Self-determination; Chair. ASHOT NAVASRDYAN.

Union for National Self-determination (UNS): Yerevan; Chair. PARUIR HAIRIKYAN.

Diplomatic Representation

EMBASSIES IN ARMENIA

Canada: Yerevan, Pionerakan St 72, Hotel 'Hrazdan'.

China, People's Republic: Yerevan, Pionerakan St 72, Hotel 'Hrazdan'.

France: Yerevan, Pionerakan St 72, Hotel 'Hrazdan', 9th Floor; tel. (8852) 53-18-96; fax (8852) 15-11-05; Ambassador: FRANCE DE HARTINGH.

Germany: Yerevan, Pionerakan St 72, Hotel 'Hrazdan'.

Greece: Yerevan, Mosgovyan St 22.

Iran: Yerevan, Pionerakan St 72, Hotel 'Hrazdan'; Ambassador: BAHRAM QASEMI.

Russian Federation: Yerevan, Pionerakan St 72, Hotel 'Hrazdan'; Ambassador: VLADIMIR STUPISHIN.

USA: 375019 Yerevan, Marshal Baghramyan St 18; tel. (8852) 15-11-44; telex 243137; fax (8852) 15-11-38; Chargé d'affaires a.c.: THOMAS L. PRICE.

Judicial System

Chairman of the Supreme Court: T. K. BARSEGYAN.

General Procurator: A. A. GEVORGYAN.

Religion

The major religion is Christianity. The Armenian Apostolic Church is the leading denomination and was widely identified with the movement for national independence. There are also Russian Orthodox and Islamic communities, although the latter have lost adherents as a result of the large numbers of Muslim Azerbaijanis who have left the Republic. However, most Kurds are also adherents of Islam, although some are Yazidis.

GOVERNMENT AGENCY

Council for the Affairs of the Armenian Church: 375001 Yerevan, Abovyan St 3; tel. (8852) 56-46-34; fax (8852) 56-41-81; Chair. LYUDVIG KHATCHATRYAN.

CHRISTIANITY

Armenian Apostolic Church: Echmiadzin; tel. 52-24-77; four dioceses in Armenia, three in other ex-Soviet Republics and 20 bishoprics in the rest of the world; 4m. members; there are 13 monasteries and one theological seminary; main following is in Armenia and Georgia; Supreme Patriarch VAZGEN I, Catholicos of All Armenians.

The Press

At 1 January 1991 there were 45 national newspapers being published in Armenia and 60 periodicals. There were also 37 local newspapers.

PRINCIPAL NEWSPAPERS

(In Armenian except where otherwise stated.)

Ankakhutiun (Independence): 375013 Yerevan, Gregory the Illuminator St 15; tel. (8852) 58-18-64, 56-28-16; daily; organ of the Union for National Self-determination; Editor PARIUR HAIRIKIAN.

Avangard: 375023 Yerevan, Arshakunyats Ave 2; f. 1923; 3 a week; organ of the Youth League of Armenia; Editor M. K. ZOHRABYAN.

Epokha (Epoch): 375023 Yerevan, Arshakunyats Ave 2; f. 1938; fmrly *Komsomolets*; weekly; Russian; organ of the Youth League of Armenia; Editor V. S. GRIGORYAN.

Golos Armenii (The Voice of Armenia): 375023 Yerevan, Arshakunyats Ave 2; tel. (8852) 52-88-38, 53-45-42; f. 1934 as *Kommunist;* 6 a week; organ of the Armenian Democratic Party (fmrly the Communist Party of Armenia); Russian; Editor B. M. MKRTCHYAN.

Grakan Tert (Literary Paper): 375019 Yerevan, Marshal Baghramyan St 3; tel. (8852) 52-05-94; f. 1932; weekly; organ of the Union of Writers; Editor F. H. MELOYAN.

Hayastan (Armenia): 375023 Yerevan, Arshakunyats Ave 2; tel. (8852) 52-84-50; f. 1920; organ of the Armenian Democratic Party (fmrly the Communist Party of Armenia); 6 a week; Editor G. ABRAMYAN.

Hayastani Hanrapetutyun (Republic of Armenia): 375023 Yerevan, Arshakunyats Ave 2; f. 1990; tel. (8852) 52-93-34; fax (8852) 52-69-74; 6 a week; organ of the Supreme Council of the Republic of Armenia; also in Russian (as *Respublika Armeniya*); Editors A. MORIKYAN (Armenian), T. AKOPYAN (Russian).

Hayk (Armenia): 375019 Yerevan, Marshal Baghramyan St 14; tel. (8852) 56-34-56; weekly; organ of the Armenian Pan-national Movement; Editor S. GUEVORKIAN; circ. 30,000.

Hazatamart (The Battle for Freedom): 375070 Yerevan, Atarbekyan 181; organ of the Armenian Revolutionary Federation; Editor M. MIKAYELYAN.

Hazg (Nation): 375010 Yerevan, Hanrapetutyan St 47; organ of the Party of Democratic Freedom; Editor AVETIS AVETIKYAN.

Hnchak Hayastani (The Bell of Armenia): 375019 Yerevan; Lord Byron St 12; weekly.

Ria Taze (New Way): Yerevan; 2 a week; Kurdish.

Yerkir (Country): 375009 Yerevan, Yeznik Koghbatsi St 50A; tel. (8852) 53-05-70, 53-78-82; daily; organ of the Armenian Revolutionary Federation.

Yerokoyan Yerevan (Evening Yerevan): 375023 Yerevan, Orjonikidze Ave 2; tel. (8852) 53-86-22, 52-83-40, 52-97-82; organ of Yerevan City Council; Editor N. YENGIBARYAN.

PRINCIPAL PERIODICALS

Aghbiur (Source): Yerevan; f. 1923, fmrly *Pioner;* monthly; for teenagers; Editor T. V. TONOYAN.

Angakhutyun: Yerevan; journal of the Union for National Self-determination.

Aroghchapakutyun (Health): 375001 Yerevan, Tumanyan St 8; f. 1956; monthly; journal of the Ministry of Health; illustrated; Editor M. A. MURADYAN.

Arvest (Art): 375001 Yerevan, Tumanyan St 5; f. 1932, fmrly *Sovetakan Arvest* (Soviet Art); monthly; publ. by the Ministry of Culture; aspects of Armenian national art; Editor G. A. AZAKELYAN.

Garun (Spring): 375015 Yerevan, Karmir Banaki St 15; tel. (8852) 56-29-56; f. 1967; monthly; independent; fiction and socio-political issues; Editor L. Z. ANANYAN.

Gitutyun ev Tekhnica (Science and Technology): Yerevan; f. 1963; monthly; journal of the Research Institute of Scientific-Technical Information and of Technological and Economic Research; illustrated.

Hayastani Ashkhatavoruhi (Working Women of Armenia): Yerevan; f. 1924; monthly; illustrated; Editor A. G. CHILINGARYAN.

Hayastani Zhoghovrdakan Tntesutyun (People's Economy of Armenia): Yerevan; f. 1957; monthly; organ of the State Committee for the Economy and the Academy of Sciences of Armenia; Editor R. H. SHAKHKULYAN.

Hayreniky Dzayn (Voice of the Motherland): Yerevan; f. 1965; weekly; organ of the Armenian Committee for Cultural Relations with Compatriots Abroad; Editor L. H. ZAKARYAN.

Literaturnaya Armeniya (Literature of Armenia): 375019 Yerevan, Marshal Baghramyan St 3; tel. (8852) 56-36-57; f. 1958; monthly; journal of the Union of Writers; fiction; Russian; Editor A. M. NALBAUDYAN.

Nork: Yerevan; f. 1934; fmrly *Sovetakan Grakanutyun* (Soviet Literature); monthly; journal of the Union of Writers; fiction; Editor R. G. HOVSEPYAN.

Veratsnvats Hayastan (Reborn Armenia): Yerevan; f. 1945 as *Sovetakan Hayastan* (Soviet Armenia); monthly; journal of the Armenian Committee for Cultural Relations with Compatriots Abroad; fiction; illustrated; Editor V. A. DAVTYAN.

Vozni (Hedgehog): Yerevan; f. 1954; 3 a month; satirical; Editor A. A. SAHAKYAN.

NEWS AGENCIES

Armenpress (Armenian Press Agency): Yerevan; state information agency; Dir G. OGANESYAN.

Hay Lur (Armenian News): Yerevan; tel. (8852) 58-77-43, fax (8852) 56-57-28; Dir TIGRAN NAGHDALYAN.

Noyan Tapan (Noah's Ark): Yerevan; fax (8852) 52-42-79; Dir TIGRAN HARUTIUNYAN.

Snark: Yerevan; tel. (8852) 52-99-42; fax (8852) 56-22-51.

Publishers

In 1989 a total of 1,003 titles (books and pamphlets) were published, of which 699 were in Armenian.

Academy of Sciences Publishing House: 375019 Yerevan, Marshal Baghramyan St 24G; Dir KH. H. BARSEGHYAN.

Anait: Yerevan; art publishing.

Arevik (Sun Publishing House): Yerevan, Isaahakyan St 28; political, scientific, fiction for children; Dir V. S. KALANTARYAN.

Hayastan (Armenia Publishing House): 375009 Yerevan, Isaahakyan St 91; tel. (8852) 52-85-20; f. 1921; political and fiction; Dir D. SARGSYAN.

Haykakan Hanragitaran (Armenian Encyclopedia): 375001 Yerevan 1, Tumanyan St 17; tel. (8852) 52-43-41; f. 1967; encyclopaedias and other reference books; Editor K. S. KHOUDAVERDYAN.

Luys (Enlightenment Publishing House): Yerevan, Kirov St 19A; textbooks; Dir S. M. MOVSISYAN.

Nairi: Yerevan, Teryana St 91; fiction; Dir H. H. FELEKHYAN.

Radio and Television

State Committee for Television and Radio Broadcasting of the Armenian Republic: 375025 Yerevan, Mravyan St 5; Chair. H. V. HOVHANNISYAN.

Radio Yerevan: 3 programmes; broadcasts inside the Republic in Armenian, Russian and Kurdish; external broadcasts in Armenian, Russian, Kurdish, Turkish, Arabic, English, French, Spanish and Persian (Farsi).

Armenian Television: broadcasts in Armenian and Russian.

Finance

(cap. = capital; dep. = deposits; m. = million; brs = branches; amounts in roubles, unless otherwise stated)

BANKING

Central Bank

National Bank of Armenia: 375010 Yerevan, Nalbandyan St 6; tel. (8852) 58-38-41; telex 243337; fax (8852) 56-04-41; Dir ISAAK I. ISAAHAKYAN.

Commercial Banks

Agricultural Bank of Armenia (Agroprombank-Armenia): Yerevan; incorporated as joint-stock co in 1992; cap. 125m. (1991); 42 brs.

Armenian State Commercial Bank (ASCB): Yerevan, Nzhdehy St 72; tel. (8852) 44-16-06; telex 243274; fax (8852) 56-27-05; incorporated as joint-stock co in 1992; corporate banking; cap. 100m. (1991); 18 brs.

Bank for Industry and Construction (Promstroibank-Armenia): Yerevan; legally separated from Soviet counterparts in 1991, incorporated as joint-stock co in 1992; largest bank in Armenia.

Export-Import Bank of Armenia (Armimpex Bank): Yerevan; f. 1991 by reorganization of the Vneshekonombank of Armenia; specializes in foreign-exchange banking transactions; dep. 650m. (and US $35m.).

Apart from these established financial institutions, there were 45 new commercial banks authorized to operate in Armenia, of which about 40 were reported to have been active during 1992.

Savings Bank

State Savings Bank of Armenia (Sberbank-Armenia): Yerevan; dep. 10,000m. (1991), with the dissolution of the USSR at the end of 1991 the bank's status and overall financial position became uncertain, reopened 1993; 47 regional brs, approx. 700 smaller brs.

COMMODITY EXCHANGE

Yerevan Commodity and Raw Materials Exchange: 375051 Yerevan, Aram Khachaturyan St 31/1; tel. (8852) 25-26-00; fax (8852) 25-09-93; f. 1991; authorized cap. 5m.; Gen. Man. ARA ARZUMANAYAN.

Trade and Industry

CHAMBER OF COMMERCE

Chamber of Commerce and Industry of the Republic of Armenia: 375010 Yerevan, Alevardyan St 39; tel. (8852) 56-54-38; telex 243322; fax (8852) 56-50-71; Chair. (vacant).

FOREIGN TRADE ORGANIZATION

Armenintorg—Armenian State Foreign Economic and Trade Association: 375012 Yerevan, H Kochar St 25; tel. (8852) 22-43-10; telex 243323; fax (8852) 22-00-34; f. 1988; import and export of all types of goods, marketing, consultancy, auditing and other services, conducts training programmes, arranges international exhibitions and trade fairs; Gen. Dir Dr A. DARBINYAN; 20 employees.

MAJOR INDUSTRIAL ENTERPRISES

Legislation to privatize state enterprises was enacted in July 1992. By September some 300 small and five large enterprises had become part of the private sector.

Airumsky Cannery: 377100 Noemberyansky, Poc. Airum; tel. 22447; produces fruit juices, canned and frozen food; Dir GEORGY MAMAJANYAN; 1,115 employees.

Armelektromash (Armenian Scientific-Production Electronic Machinery Association): 375083 Yerevan, 41 Telman St; tel. (8852) 42-45-83; Dir K. DEMIRCHYAN.

Armstroymateriali: 375009 Yerevan, 1 Jrashala St; produces building materials; Gen. Dir L. MAKARYAN.

Garun: 375023 Yerevan, 26 Brusov St; tel. (8922) 56-17-23; produces outdoor clothing; Gen. Dir G. ENOKYAN.

Haigorg: 375006 Yerevan, 9 Chimiagortseri St; tel. (8852) 44-35-27; telex 243231; fax (8922) 44-15-72; produces carpets; Gen. Dir A. HARUTUNYAN.

Luys Production Association: Yerevan; Dir BENIAMIN TUMASYAN.

Mars Production Association: 375065 Yerevan, 27–29 Babadjanyan St; tel. (8922) 77-28-25; telex 243316; fax (8922) 77-81-77; Gen. Dir S. DEMIRCHYAN.

Nairit: 375029 Yerevan, 70 Bagratunyats Ave; tel. (8922) 44-03-03; produces acids, latex, acetlyene, rubber; Gen. Dir A. SUKIASYAN.

Van: 375020 Yerevan, 21 Arshakunyants Ave; tel. (8922) 56-23-45; produces men's and women's footwear; Dir. V. KIRAKOSYAN.

Vector: 375062 Yerevan, Knunyants 8; tel. (8852) 57-03-25; clothing and textiles; Chair. KAREN GRIGORIYAN.

Yeraz (Yerevan Automobile Factory): Yerevan; Dir EDVARD BABADZHYAN; 2,000 employees.

Yerevan Cognac Factory: 375082 Yerevan, 2 Isakov St; tel. and fax (8922) 56-74-27; telex 243353; Dir A. GEROJAN.

Yerevan Jewellery Plant: 375023 Yerevan, 12 Arshkunyats Ave; tel. (8922) 52-53-21; fax (8922) 56-10-26; produces silver, gold and plastic jewellery; Dir E. GRIGORYAN.

Yerevan Milling-Machine Factory: 375014 Yerevan, 60 Komilas St; tel. (8852) 23-14-21; Dir M. LAVRENTIEV.

Zakavkazkabel: 375061 Yerevan, Tamantsineri 55; tel. (8852) 44-12-50; production of cables and wires; Gen. Dir EDUARD SASUNTS-YAN; 2,200 employees.

EMPLOYERS' ORGANIZATION

Armenian Business Forum: Yerevan; tel. (8852) 52-75-43; fax (8852) 52-43-32; f. 1991; promotes joint ventures, foreign capital investments; Pres. VAHÉ JAZMADARYAN.

TRADE UNIONS

Council of Armenian Trade Unions: 375010 Yerevan, Nalbandyan St 26; Chair. MARTIN ARUTYUNYAN.

Transport

RAILWAYS

In 1992 there were 825 km of railway track, on which Armenia Railways was operating about 100 diesel electric locomotives and 80 diesels. There were international lines to Turkey, Iran, Georgia and Azerbaijan, although all were subject to varying degrees of disruption because of the different conflicts in the region.

Armenia Railways: Yerevan.

ROADS

In 1992 there were 7,700 km of paved roads in Armenia, of which 40% were estimated to be in poor condition and in need of repair. Government vehicles (some 100,000 buses, taxis, lorries and cars) were poorly maintained and lacking spare parts, ensuring that almost one-third of the fleet was unavailable on any given day.

CIVIL AVIATION

In 1991 the Armenian Airlines Company, which was an integral part of the USSR Ministry of Civil Aviation, was restructured as the State Airlines Company of Armenia, using aircraft from the Aeroflot fleet. It operated scheduled and commercial passenger flights. A new joint-venture company was established to handle air freight. In 1993 the company returned to using the name Armenian Airlines.

Armenian Airlines Company: 375042 Yerevan; tel. (8852) 77-59-20; fax (8852) 77-04-94; f. 1993; Chair. ARSHAK G. NALBANDYAN; 2,500 EMPLOYEES.

Culture

NATIONAL ORGANIZATION

Ministry of Culture: see section on The Government (Ministries).

CULTURAL HERITAGE

Armenian State Picture Gallery: 375010 Yerevan, Spandaryan St 1; tel. (8852) 58-07-65; f. 1921; Western European, Armenian, Russian and oriental art; Dir A. TER-GABRIELYAN.

Museum of Armenian History: 375010 Yerevan, Republic Sq.; 160,000 exhibits tracing the history of the Armenian people; Dir M. S. ASRATYAN.

Matenadaran Institute of Ancient Armenian Manuscripts: Yerevan, Mashtots Ave 111; tel. (8852) 58-32-92; f. 1920; manuscripts and archival documents on Armenian history; Dir S. AREVSHATYAN.

State Library of the Republic of Armenia: 375009 Yerevan, Teryan St 72; tel. (8852) 56-58-45; f. 1921; over 6.4m. vols; Dir A. M. TIRABYAN.

PERFORMING ARTS

Alexander Spendiarov Opera and Ballet Theatre: Yerevan, Tumanyan St 36.

Tumanyan Puppet Theatre: Yerevan, Savat Novy Ave 4.

Yerevan Drama Theatre: Yerevan, Isaakyan St 28.

Yerevan Institute of Fine Arts and Theatre: 375009 Yerevan, Isaakyan St 36; tel. (8852) 56-07-26; f. 1944; training in all aspects of theatre and fine arts; Rector VAHAN MKRTOHYAN.

ASSOCIATIONS

Armenian Committee for Cultural Relations with Compatriots in Other Countries: Yerevan; develops links with the Armenian disapora.

Union of Writers of Armenia: 375019 Yerevan, Marshal Baghramyan St 3; tel. (8852) 56-38-11.

Education

Education is free and compulsory at primary and secondary levels. Until the early 1990s the general education system conformed to that of the centralized Soviet system. Extensive changes were made, with more emphasis placed on Armenian history and culture. In 1989 58% of the population over 15 years had completed secondary education and 14% had completed higher education. Most instruction is in Armenian, although Russian is widely taught as a second language. In 1988, in general day schools, 80.5% of all pupils were taught in Armenian, 15.1% in Russian and 4.4% in Azerbaijani. In addition to Yerevan State University and the newly-established State Engineering University, higher eduation was provided at seven other institutes of higher education.

UNIVERSITIES

Yerevan State University: 375049 Yerevan, Mravyan St 1; tel. (8852) 55-46-29; telex 243575; fax (8852) 55-87-29; f. 1920; languages of instruction: Armenian and Russian; 17 faculties; 1,250 teachers; 9,000 students; Rector RADICK M. MARTIROSYAN.

State Engineering University of Armenia: 375009 Yerevan, Teryan St 105; tel. (8852) 56-01-32; fax (8852) 15-10-68; f. 1991; fmrly Yerevan Polytechnic Institute (f. 1933); 13 faculties; 885 teachers; 18,650 students; brs in Goris, Gumayri and Vanadzor; Rector YURI L. SARKISYAN.

Social Welfare

Much of Armenia's expenditure on health and welfare services was directed towards the victims of the 1988 earthquake, which caused an estimated 25,000 deaths and 8,500m. roubles-worth of damage. However, the escalation in the conflict with Azerbaijan and the collapse of the USSR encouraged a large number of refugees to flee to Armenia, creating new demands of social expenditure at a time of restricted government revenue. Furthermore, the adaptation to a market economy and the economic blockade on the country also exacerbated the situation. In 1992 the Ministry of Labour and Social Security estimated that about one-seventh of the population was 'needy' (excluding refugees—estimated at some 350,000). It was attempting to control social expenditure by targeting resources, as well as encouraging private and voluntary involvement. Under the Soviet system, all medical and social services were provided by the state, so a full range of basic services remained available. In 1986/87 average life expectancy at birth was 73.9 years, considerably higher than the average for the USSR, partly perhaps because Armenia had the lowest rate of alcoholism in the USSR, with 175 recorded cases per 100,000 of the population in 1988. In that year 400,000 people were in receipt of state pensions, 75% of which were provided on account of old age. A Pension Fund was created in August 1991. It was later merged with the Employment Fund, to create the Pension and Employment Fund, which, in 1992, was the only extrabudgetary fund remaining in Armenia.

GOVERNMENT AGENCIES

Ministry of Labour and Social Security: see section on The Government (Ministries).

Pension and Employment Fund: 375025 Yerevan, Moskovyan St 35; originally a branch of the USSR Pension Fund, a separate Armenian Pension Fund was established in 1991 and then united with the Employment Fund in March 1992; largely funded by payroll contributions; Chair. Z. NUNUSHYAN.

Institute of Volunteers:375025 Yerevan, Isaakyan St 18; f. 1991 to train social workers and help Government research social-issue priorities.

The Environment

As in other Soviet Republics environmental problems were among the major political issues of the late 1980s. Yerevan experiences particularly severe pollution as a result of its high concentration of industrial enterprises and the surrounding mountains, which can confine the pollution. The conflict with Azerbaijan, with the influx of refugees and the shortage of fuel, created further environmental degradation.

NATIONAL AGENCY

Ministry of Protection of Nature and the Environment: see section on The Government (Ministries).

ACADEMIC INSTITUTES

Academy of Sciences of the Republic of Armenia: 375019 Yerevan, Marshal Baghramyan St 24; tel. (8852) 52-07-04; telex 243344; f. 1943; Pres. V. A. AMBARTSUMYAN.

Armenian Botanical Society; Yerevan; Chair. V. O. KAZARYAN.

Armenian Geographical Society: Yerevan; Chair. L. A. VALESYAN.

Council on Problems of the Biosphere: Yerevan; Chair. G. A. BAGHRAMYAN.

Defence

Following the dissolution of the USSR in December 1991, Armenia became a member of the CIS and its collective security system. The country also began to establish its own armed forces (estimated to number some 50,000 by mid-1992). Some moblization of reserves by conscription was reported. Armenia denied the participation of its forces in the conflict in Nagorny Karabakh (see History). There were approximately 23,000 Russian troops (ex-Soviet border troops) remaining on Armenian territory in mid-1992. In 1992 an estimated 2.3% of budgetary expenditure (approximately 250m. roubles) was allocated to defence.

Commander-in-Chief of the Armed Forces: President of the Republic.

Chief of General Staff of the Armed Forces: S. SARKISYAN.

Bibliography

Chahin, M. *The Kingdom of Armenia.* London, Croom Helm, 1987.

Dédéyan, G. (Ed.). *The History of the Armenians.* London, Routledge, 1989.

Garsoïan, N. *Armenia between Byzantium and the Sasanians.* London, Variorium Reprints, 1985.

Hovannisyan, R. *Armenia on the Road to Independence, 1918.* Berkeley, University of California Press, 1967.

Lang, D. *Armenia: Cradle of Civilization.* London, Allen and Unwin, 1970.

Sonyel, S. *The Ottoman Armenians: Victims of Great Power Diplomacy.* London, K. Rustem, 1987.

Suny, R. *Looking toward Ararat: Armenia in Modern History.* Bloomington, Indiana University Press, 1993.

Uras, E. *The Armenians in History and the Armenian Question.* Istanbul, Istanbul Documentary Publs, 1988.

Walker, C. *Armenia: the Survival of a Nation,* 2nd Edn. London, Routledge, 1990.

AZERBAIJAN

Geography

PHYSICAL FEATURES

The Republic of Azerbaijan (formerly the Azerbaijan Soviet Socialist Republic) is situated in eastern Transcaucasia, on the western coast of the Caspian Sea. There are international borders with Iran to the south, with Armenia to the west, with Georgia to the north-west and, to the north across the Caucasus, with the Republic of Daghestan (the Daghestan Autonomous Republic) in the Russian Federation. The Nakhichevan Autonomous Republic is part of Azerbaijan, although it is separated from the rest of Azerbaijan by Armenian territory. The enclave lies to the west of metropolitan Azerbaijan, with Iran to the south and west and Armenia to the north and east. There is a short border with Turkey at the north-western tip of the territory. Azerbaijan also includes the Nagorno-Karabakh Autonomous Oblast (Nagorny Karabakh), which lies in the south-west of the country. It is largely populated by Armenians. Armed conflict over the status of Nagorny Karabakh began in 1989 and, by October 1993, Azerbaijan had lost control of the enclave and of about one-fifth of its own territory to Armenian militia (see below). The historical region of Azerbaijan also includes northern regions of Iran, where there is a significant Azerbaijani minority. The Republic covers an area of 86,600 sq km (33,436 sq miles), 10% of which is forested. Nagorny Karabakh covers an area of 4,400 sq km.

The greater part of Azerbaijan is dominated by the lowlands around two rivers; the River Kura flows from the north-west into the Caspian Sea, and its tributary, the Araks, runs along the border with Iran. North of the Kura lies the main axis of the Greater Caucasus mountain range (Bolshoy Kavkaz), the traditional boundary between Asia and Europe. This mountain range extends along the northern border of the Republic into north-east Azerbaijan and ends in the Apsheron Peninsula, a promontory in the Caspian Sea which has significant petroleum reserves. Numerous mountain rivers flow into the Kura basin from the mountains of the Lesser Caucasus in the south-west. South of the mouth of the Kura, the Caspian littoral around the town of Lenkoran forms the Lenkoran plain, an area noted for its subtropical climate.

CLIMATE

The Kura plain has a hot, dry, temperate climate with an average July temperature of 27°C (80°F) and an average January temperature of 1°C (34°F). Average annual rainfall on the lowlands is 200–300 mm, but the Lenkoran plain normally receives between 1,000 mm and 1,750 mm.

POPULATION

According to the 1989 census, at which the total population was 7,037,867, Azerbaijanis formed the largest ethnic group (82.7% of the total population), followed by Russians and Armenians (each 5.6%) and Lezghis (2.4%). However, after the outbreak of the Nagorny Karabakh conflict, many Armenians fled the country. There were also small numbers of Avars, Ukrainians, Tatars, Jews, Talysh, Turks, Georgians, Kurds, Udins and others. Armenians predominate in Nagorny Karabakh (75.9% in 1979) and ethnic Azerbaijanis in Nakhichevan. The official language is Azerbaijani, one of the South Turkic group of languages. In 1989, while only 27% of Azerbaijanis claimed to have a good knowledge of Russian, less than 2% of Russians and less than 1% of Armenians in the Republic claimed fluency in Azerbaijani. In 1992 the parliament of Azerbaijan chose to abandon use of the Cyrillic alphabet (in use since 1939) and restore the Latin script. The Turkish version of this was adopted and, in 1993, the Turkish authorities sanctioned the introduction of five additional letters to the alphabet, specifically to accommodate Azerbaijan and the Turkic states of Central Asia. Religious adherence corresponds largely to ethnic origins: almost all ethnic Azerbaijanis are Muslims, some 70% being Shi'ite and 30% Sunni. There are also Christian communities, mainly representatives of the Russian Orthodox and Armenian Apostolic denominations.

At 1 January 1991 the total estimated population was 7,174,000. The capital is Baku, which had a population of 1,149,500 on 1 January 1990. It is located on the coast of the Caspian Sea, near the southern shore of the Apsheron Peninsula. Other major cities include Sumgait, a port on the Caspian Sea to the north of Baku, and Gyanja (formerly Kirovabad), an industrial town in the north-west of the country, in the foothills of the Lesser Caucasus.

Chronology

625–585 BC: The Medes, under their ruler Cyaxares, with his capital at Ecbatana (now Hamadan, Iran), became a major power in the territories west of the River Tigris.

550: Cyrus II of Persia (Iran) conquered the kingdom of Media (Mada) and united the Medes and the Persians.

323: After the death of Alexander III ('the Great') of Macedon, who had conquered the Persian Empire, the satrap Atropates established an independent state in northern Media.

AD 637: The Persian Empire of the Sasanians, which had ruled Atropatene Media (from which is derived the name of Azerbaijan) since the third century AD, was conquered by the Arabs, under the Caliph 'Umar (Omar); the islamicization of the area began.

11th century: The assimilation of Turkic settlers by the previous population was to produce the Azeri people, distinct from the Persic people of modern Iran.

1502: The Safawids, an Azeri dynasty, assumed control of the Persian Empire.

1728: After two centuries of rivalry between the Ottoman and Persian Empires, the Treaty of Constantinople affirmed Ottoman control; continued disputes and the decline of the two powers enabled the rise of increasingly independent khanates in Azerbaijan.

1828: By the Treaty of Turkmenchai, following years of increasing Russian influence, Persia conceded the partition of Azerbaijan; territory to the north of the River Araks (Araxes) became part of the Russian Empire.

***c.* 1900:** The province of Azerbaijan was a major producer of petroleum and this attracted increasing Slav immigration.

1911: The 'Equality' (Musavat) Muslim Democratic Party was founded; it was a left-wing, nationalist movement, similar to the 'Young Turks' of the Ottoman Empire.

1917: The Russian Revolution impelled Musavat and the Bolsheviks to assume control in Baku, although Musavat withdrew from this administration in the following month and established the Transcaucasian Commissariat.

April 1918: A Bolshevik and left-Menshevik soviet was established in Baku; proclamation of a Democratic Federal Republic of Transcaucasia (Azerbaijan with Armenia and Georgia), following the Soviet signing of the Treaty of Brest-Litovsk.

28 May 1918: The collapse of Transcaucasia forced Azerbaijan to establish its own government. Subsequently, Musavat began negotiations with the Turks; the Red Army was prevented from making an attempt to occupy Baku by a British military presence.

September 1918: The British left Baku, leaving anti-Bolshevik forces in charge, but were implicated in the execution of the Bolshevik leaders involved in the previous governments; this was accompanied by a massacre of Armenians.

November 1918: The British reoccupied Baku, but did not favour an independent Musavat regime's close links with Turkey (an ally of the Central Powers in the First World War); the United Kingdom did recognize a coalition Government in the following month.

August 1919: British forces finally left Baku, withdrawing to Persia.

28 April 1920: Following the occupation of Baku by the Red Army, on the previous day, a Soviet Republic of Azerbaijan was proclaimed.

March 1921: In a friendship treaty, the Turks and Soviet Russia agreed to guarantee that the enclave of Nakhichevan should fall under the jurisdiction of Azerbaijan.

June 1921: The arbitrating Soviet Bureau of Transcaucasian Affairs (Kavburo) voted to recommend the union of Nagorny Karabakh (a predominantly ethnic Armenian enclave within Azerbaijan) with the Soviet Republic of Armenia, but Stalin (Iosif V. Dzhugashvili) enforced the reversal of this decision; in 1923 Nagorny Karabakh was granted special status within Azerbaijan, as an autonomous oblast.

October 1921: The Treaty of Kars agreed the borders of the Soviet Republics of Azerbaijan, Armenia and Georgia with Turkey, and the status of Nagorny Karabakh and Nakhichevan as territories of Azerbaijan.

December 1922: The Soviet Socialist Republic (SSR) of Azerbaijan became a member of the Transcaucasian Soviet Federative Socialist Republic (TSFSR), which itself became a constituent member of the Union of Soviet Socialist Republics (USSR).

December 1936: The TSFSR was dissolved and the Azerbaijan SSR became a full Union Republic.

1937–38: Purges of the local Communists included Azerbaijan's leader, Sultan Mejit Efendiev.

1946: Following a protest to the UN by Iran (known as Persia until 1935), Allied pressure forced the USSR to end its attempts to integrate Iranian Azerbaijan with Soviet Azerbaijan.

1969: Heydar Aliyev became First Secretary of the Communist Party of Azerbaijan (CPA) and the Republic's leader.

October 1987: Aliyev dismissed, because of corruption in government and in the Party.

February 1988: Nagorny Karabakh attempts to be transferred to Armenian jurisdiction caused increased inter-ethnic tension, culminating in anti-Armenian riots in Sumgait, in which 32 people were killed.

January 1989: The local authorities in Nagorny Karabakh were suspended and the oblast was placed under the administration of a Special Administrative Committee (SAC), responsible to the all-Union Council of Ministers.

September 1989: A general strike secured the official recognition of the nationalist opposition movement, the Popular Front of Azerbaijan (PFA), established earlier in the year.

23 September 1989: Under increasing popular pressure, the Supreme Soviet of Azerbaijan effectively declared the Republic's sovereignty and imposed an economic blockade on Armenia (Soviet troops maintained the Baku–Yerevan rail link).

November 1989: The SAC for Nagorny Karabakh was replaced by a republican Organizing Committee dominated by ethnic Azerbaijanis.

1 December 1989: The Armenian Supreme Soviet declared Nagorny Karabakh to be part of a 'unified Armenian republic', a claim which was termed unconstitutional by the all-Union Supreme Soviet the following month.

January 1990: The PFA were prominent in attacks on government and Party buildings, on Armenians and on the border posts with Iranian Azerbaijan; PFA demonstrators also attempted to declare the secession of Nakhichevan from the USSR; Soviet troops evacuated those who were not ethnic Azerbaijanis from Baku and enforced a state of emergency amid some violence; Abdul Vezirov was replaced by Ayaz Niyaz ogly Mutalibov as First Secretary of the CPA.

September–October 1990: In the elections to the Azerbaijan Supreme Soviet (postponed from February), the CPA, now firm on the Nagorny Karabakh issue, won some 80% of the seats; the opposition PFA, which had campaigned with other groups as the Democratic Alliance, alleged irregularities in the conduct of the elections and criticized the state of emergency.

February 1991: The Supreme Soviet convened, with the opposition deputies grouped as the Democratic Bloc of Azerbaijan.

March 1991: Azerbaijan participated in the Soviet referendum on the renewal of the Union; official results were that 93.3% of those who had voted (75.1% of the electorate) favoured remaining in the USSR, although in Nakhichevan only 20% supported this; the opposition claimed that only some 20% of the electorate voted.

30 August 1991: Following the failure of the coup attempt in Moscow and large anti-government demonstrations, the

Supreme Soviet of Azerbaijan voted in favour of claiming independence.

8 September 1991: President Mutalibov won 84% of the votes cast at the presidential elections, which were boycotted by the opposition. Nagorny Karabakh declared itself a republic, but, in the same month, Russian and Kazakhstan secured agreement to peace negotiations between Armenia and Azerbaijan.

18 October 1991: The Supreme Soviet enacted legislation effecting the declaration of independence of 30 August and also voted not to sign the new Soviet Treaty of Economic Community.

10 December 1991: In a referendum, residents of Nagorny Karabakh voted overwhelmingly for independence; the Azerbaijani authorities considered the poll as irregular.

21 December 1991: Azerbaijan signed the Almaty Declaration, by which it became a member of the Commonwealth of Independent States (CIS).

January 1992: President Mutalibov declared Nagorny Karabakh to be under direct presidential rule.

February 1992: Azerbaijan was admitted to the Conference on Security and Co-operation in Europe (CSCE) and signed, with eight other countries, the Black Sea Co-operation Accord.

March 1992: President Mutalibov resigned owing to military reversals in Nagorny Karabakh. (He was replaced on an interim basis by Yagub Mamedov.) In the same month CIS troops were withdrawn from the area as Armenian forces began to achieve some success against Azerbaijan. Azerbaijan became a member of the UN.

May 1992: By the time Armenia and Azerbaijan negotiated a cease-fire, the Nagorny Karabakh militia had secured control over the whole enclave and a 'corridor' along the Lachin valley to Armenia. The Supreme Soviet voted to reinstate Mutalibov as President, but he was deposed after one day in office; this effective coup by the PFA was reinforced by the suspension of the Supreme Soviet and the transfer of its powers to the National Assembly (Milli Majlis).

7 June 1992: Abulfaz Elchibey, leader of the PFA, was elected President of Azerbaijan by direct vote. Azerbaijan launched a counter-offensive in Nagorny Karabakh.

August 1992: The Nagorny Karabakh legislature declared a state of martial law; a State Defence Committee replaced the enclave's government.

October 1992: Azerbaijan and the Russian Federation signed a treaty of friendship, co-operation and mutual security. In the same month the Milli Majlis voted overwhelmingly to withdraw Azerbaijan from the CIS.

February 1993: Col Surat Husseinov, who had successfully commanded Azerbaijani forces in the conflict over Nagorny Karabakh, withdrew to Gyanja, prompting allegations by President Elchibey that he was planning a military coup against the Government. Husseinov was subsequently dismissed from his posts and expelled from the PFA.

March 1993: The Nagorny Karabakh militia began an offensive on Azerbaijan proper.

April 1993: President Elchibey declared a three-month state of emergency in Azerbaijan. Azerbaijan withdrew from CSCE-sponsored negotiations, in protest at a large-scale Armenian offensive.

30 April 1993: The UN Security Council adopted Resolution 822 demanding an immediate cease-fire and the withdrawal of all Armenian units from Azerbaijani territory.

24 May 1993: Azerbaijan approved a peace plan formulated by the Russian Federation, Turkey and the USA and negotiated by the CSCE; it was not accepted by the Nagorny Karabakh leadership until June.

4 June 1993: President Elchibey ordered a punitive attack in Gyanja by the Azerbaijani army on 709th Brigade, a unit still loyal to their rebel leader, Surat Husseinov. Over 60 people were killed. Husseinov assumed control of the town.

16 June 1993: Heydar Aliyev, the former Communist Party leader, was elected Chairman of the Milli Majlis; Aliyev subsequently assumed the powers of the presidency, despite Husseinov's claims to lead the country, and the Milli Majlis voted to impeach Elchibey.

17–18 June 1993: President Elchibey fled to Nakhichevan.

25 June 1993: The Milli Majlis voted to impeach President Elchibey.

28 June 1993: Surat Husseinov's troops, having marched to Baku, pledged allegiance to Heydar Aliyev, the Acting President.

29 June 1993: Thousands of PFA supporters attended a rally in Baku to protest against Elchibey's impeachment.

1 July 1993: Aliyev nominated Husseinov Prime Minister and Supreme Commander.

July 1993: The CSCE mediator, Mario Raffaeli, cancelled a trip to Nagorny Karabakh, after reports that Armenian militia had seized Agdam; this was despite Nagorny Karabakh accepting the CSCE-sponsored proposals of May (see above).

29 July 1993: The UN Security Council adopted Resolution 853, demanding the immediate withdrawal of the Nagorny Karabakh militia from Agdam.

23 August 1993: Alikram Gumbatov, leader of so-called 'Talysh-Mugan Autonomous Republic' (proclaimed during the Husseinov revolt of June), based in Lenkoran, fled the city after his headquarters were stormed by PFA supporters.

24 August 1993: In Bandar Anzali (Iran) Azerbaijan formed a caviar cartel with the Russian Federation, Iran, Turkmenistan and Kazakhstan, to co-ordinate the global marketing of caviar.

1 September 1993: The Milli Majlis endorsed the results of the referendum of 29 August, in which 97.5% of participants voted in favour of President Abulfaz Elchibey's impeachment.

20 September 1993: A resolution for Azerbaijan to rejoin the CIS was adopted by the Milli Majlis; the country was officially admitted to the Commonwealth on 24 September and parliament ratified the Almaty Declaration, the Commonwealth Charter and the Tashkent Agreement on Collective Security on 29 September, despite PFA protests.

3 October 1993: Heydar Aliyev was elected President of Azerbaijan, against two other candidates, with 98.8% of the votes cast.

14 October 1993: Resolution 874, adopted by the UN Security Council, endorsed the CSCE's schedule for implementing Resolutions 822 and 853.

27 October 1993: Armenia and Azerbaijan signed a cease-fire. Armenia and Nagorny Karabakh agreed to the schedule for the withdrawal of ethnic Armenian militia from Azerbaijani territory. Azerbaijan rejected the schedule as the CSCE plan did not envisage Armenian withdrawal from the Lachin corridor. However, in the following month, a CSCE peace conference opened in Minsk (Belarus).

History

The Azerbaijanis, or Azeris, are probably descendants of the area's indigenous inhabitants, although linguistically influenced by Turkish settlers. An independent state was first established in the region in the fourth century BC by Atropates, a vassal of Alexander III of Macedon. From Atropates came the name Azerbaijan. The Persian Sasanian dynasty took control of the region in the third century AD and it remained part of their empire until the Muslim Arab conquest of the area in the seventh century. From the 11th century the Persian-speaking indigenous inhabitants began to be assimilated by the increasing numbers of Turkic settlers, who migrated to the region from the east. In the early 16th century Azerbaijan again came under Persian domination, but there were frequent incursions into the area by the Ottoman Turks and, in 1728, their control over the region was confirmed by the Treaty of Constantinople. After a short reassertion of Persian supremacy from 1735, local khanates established a degree of independence from both the Ottomans and the Persians. Meanwhile, Russia was increasing its influence in Transcaucasia and by 1805 several of the khanates had become Russian protectorates. In 1828, after a period of Russo-Persian conflict, Azerbaijan was divided, with the River Araks as the border, between Persia (which was granted southern Azerbaijan) and Russia (northern Azerbaijan) by the Treaty of Turkmenchai. During the latter half of the 19th century petroleum was discovered in Azerbaijan and, by 1900, the region had become one of the world's leading petroleum producers. Immigrant Slavs began to dominate Baku and other urban areas.

SOVIET AZERBAIJAN

After the October Revolution of 1917 in Russia, there was a short period of pro-Bolshevik rule in Baku before a nationalist Government took power and established an independent state, with Gyanja as the capital. Azerbaijan was occupied by both Allied and Central Power troops during its two years of independence; after their withdrawal Azerbaijan was invaded by the Red Army, in April 1920, and a Soviet Republic of Azerbaijan was established (28 April 1920). In December 1922 the Republic became a member of the Transcaucasian Soviet Federative Socialist Republic (TSFSR), which entered the USSR as a constituent republic on 31 December 1922. The TSFSR was disbanded in 1936 and Azerbaijan became a full Union Republic.

Following the Soviet seizure of power in 1920, many nationalist and religious leaders and their followers were persecuted or killed. Religious persecution was particularly severe in the 1930s and many mosques and religious sites were destroyed. In 1930–31 forced collectivization led to peasant uprisings which were suppressed by Soviet troops. Many members of the Communist Party of Azerbaijan (CPA) were executed or imprisoned in the purges of 1937–38, including Sultan Mejit Efendiev, the Republic's leader, and two republican premiers. In 1945 the Soviet Government attempted to unite the Azerbaijani population of Iran (Persia) with the Azerbaijan SSR, by supporting a local 'puppet' Government in Iran with military forces. Soviet troops were forced to withdraw by US-British opposition the following year, after a protest to the UN by Iran.

The most important of Azerbaijan's post-war leaders was Heydar Aliyev, installed as First Secretary of the CPA in 1969. He vastly increased the all-Union sector of the economy at the expense of local industry, while retaining popularity with his liberal attitude to local corruption. It was this corruption in the CPA that was the first target of Soviet leader Mikhail Gorbachev when he came to power. Aliyev was dismissed in October 1987, but popular dissatisfaction with the poor state of the economy and the Party élite became more vocal. Unlike most Republics, Azerbaijan had an annual trade surplus with the rest of the USSR and yet its income per head was the lowest outside Central Asia. Economic grievances were expressed at demonstrations in November 1988, which were initially concerned with the debate on the status of Nakhichevan and Nagorny Karabakh (see below), but rapidly turned to issues of economic mismanagement and privileges enjoyed by the Party leadership. Demonstrators occupied Baku's main square for 10 days before being dispersed by troops, who arrested the leaders of the demonstrations.

In mid-1989 the Popular Front of Azerbaijan (PFA) was established. Following sporadic strikes and demonstrations throughout August 1989, the PFA organized a national strike in early September and demanded discussion on the issue of sovereignty, the situation in Nagorny Karabakh, the release of political prisoners and official recognition of the PFA. After a week of the general strike the Azerbaijan Supreme Soviet agreed to concessions to the PFA, including official recognition. In addition, draft laws on economic and political sovereignty were published and, on 23 September, the Supreme Soviet adopted the 'Constitutional Law on the Sovereignty of the Azerbaijan SSR', effectively a declaration of sovereignty. An economic blockade on Armenia was also imposed at this time, although Soviet troops maintained the Baku–Yerevan rail link. Growing unrest within Azerbaijan, exacerbated by the arrival of refugees from Armenia in Baku, was directed both at the local Communist regime and at ethnic Armenians.

In January 1990 there were serious disturbances which threatened to overthrow Soviet power in Azerbaijan. Radical members of the PFA led attacks on Party and government buildings in Baku and other towns. Border posts were attacked on the Soviet–Iranian border, which separated Azerbaijanis from their co-nationals in Iran, and local nationalists rioted in the enclave of Nakhichevan. In addition, there was renewed violence against Armenians, with some 60 Armenians killed in rioting in Baku. There was a hasty evacuation of the remaining non-Azeris, including ethnic Russians, from the city.

On 19 January 1990 a state of emergency was declared in Azerbaijan and Soviet troops were ordered into Baku, where the PFA was in control and had established barricades and other makeshift defences. In the military action which ensued, lightly armed Azerbaijanis were no match for Soviet troops, who soon controlled most of the city. Officially, 124 people were killed during the Soviet intervention; unofficial sources assert that the real figure was much higher. The inability of the CPA to ensure order in the Republic led to the dismissal of Abdul Vezirov as First Secretary of the CPA; he was replaced by Ayaz Niyaz ogly Mutalibov. Order was restored in Azerbaijan by the end of January, after leading members of the PFA had been arrested, other radical nationalist organizations outlawed and decrees issued banning all strikes, rallies and demonstrations.

The continuing unrest caused the elections to the Republic's Supreme Soviet (held in most other Republics in February) to be postponed. When they did take place, on 30 September 1990, with further rounds in October, the CPA won an overall majority. In the first round alone they won 220 of the 260 seats decided. Indeed, the Democratic Alliance, which included the PFA, could only nominate 218 candidates in 350 constituencies. The CPA victory was attributed to an increasingly firm stance on the issue of Nagorny Karabakh, which attracted nationalist support, combined with a willingness to compromise with the all-Union authorities to avoid further bloodshed. Opposition figures, however, contested the validity of the elections, complaining of electoral irregularities. In addition, the continuing state of emergency, which did not permit large meetings of people, severely disrupted campaigning by the Democratic Alliance and the PFA. When the new Supreme Soviet convened in February 1991, some 80% of the deputies were members of the CPA. The small group of opposition deputies united as the Democratic Bloc of Azerbaijan.

Unlike the other Caucasian Republics, Azerbaijan declared a willingness to sign a new Union Treaty and participated in the all-Union referendum concerning the preservation of the USSR which took place in March 1991. Official results of the referendum demonstrated a qualified support for the preservation of the USSR, with 75.1% of eligible voters participating, of whom 93.3% voted for a 'renewed federation'. In Nakhichevan, however, only some 20% of eligible voters approved President Gorbachev's question. Opposition politicians also contested the results of the referendum, claiming that only 15%–20% of voters had actually participated.

In August 1991, when the State Committee for the State of Emergency (SCSE) seized power in Moscow, Mutalibov issued a statement which seemed to demonstrate support for the coup. Mutalibov denied that he had supported the SCSE, but there were large demonstrations in the last week of August, demanding his resignation, the declaration of Azerbaijan's independence, the lifting of the state of emergency, which had been imposed in January 1990, and the postponement of the presidential elections, scheduled for 8 September. The opposition was supported by Heydar Aliyev, the former First Secretary of the CPA, and the Chairman of the Supreme Majlis (parliament) of Nakhichevan, who had become increasingly critical of Mutalibov's leadership. Mutalibov responded to some of the protesters' demands by ending the state of emergency and resigning as First Secretary of the CPA, and, on 30 August, the Azerbaijani Supreme Soviet voted to 'restore the independent status of Azerbaijan'.

INDEPENDENT AZERBAIJAN

Despite continued protests from the PFA, which urged a poorly supported general strike on 3 September 1991, the elections to the presidency proceeded, although they were boycotted by the opposition, with the result that Mutalibov was the only candidate. According to official results, he won 84% of the votes cast. In the same month the PFA organized demonstrations to protest against the Government's signing a peace agreement with Armenia arranged by the leaders of Russia and Kazakhstan (see below).

Independence was formally restored on 18 October 1991, when the Supreme Soviet adopted legislation putting into effect the declaration of independence of 30 August. The Supreme Soviet also voted not to sign the Treaty on the Economic Community, which was signed by eight other Republics on the same day. In a further move towards full independence, legislation was adopted allowing for the creation of national armed forces, and Azerbaijan began to take over the military facilities of the Soviet Army in the Republic. Azerbaijan did join the Commonwealth of Independent States (CIS), however, signing the Almaty Declaration, on 21 December 1991, although it reserved its right to form a national guard rather than participate in the unified command structure agreed by most of the other Republics.

In March 1992 President Mutalibov was forced to resign as Azerbaijan had suffered military reversals. He was replaced, on an interim basis, by Yagub Mamedov, the Chairman of the Supreme Soviet, pending a presidential election in June. In early May it became apparent that Armenian units (the so-called Nagorny Karabakh Self-Defence Forces) had gained a military advantage in Nagorny Karabakh, which was blamed on Mamedov's leadership. In mid-May the Supreme Soviet voted to reinstate Mutalibov as President. His immediate declaration of a state of emergency and the cancellation of the forthcoming presidential election outraged the PFA, which organized a large-scale protest rally in Baku. The demonstrators occupied both the parliament building and the presidential palace and succeeded in deposing Mutalibov, who had held office for only one day. The Supreme Soviet was suspended, with its powers to be exercised by a National Assembly (Milli Majlis) of 50 members. The PFA's assumption of power was consolidated in the following month, when the party's leader, Abulfaz Elchibey, was elected President of Azerbaijan by direct popular vote (winning 55.1% of the votes cast against four other candidates).

The new PFA Government had to contend with a steadily deteriorating economic situation, largely as a result of the continuing conflict over Nagorny Karabakh and the collapse of the Soviet economic system. Severe shortages of food and fuel were reported throughout the country in 1992 and 1993. The urgency of the problem was compounded by the massive influx of Azerbaijani refugees, both from the embattled enclave of Nagorny Karabakh and from Armenia. The Government's failure to provide adequate support for the estimated 500,000 refugees prompted a number of protests in Baku from the middle of 1992. By April 1993 President Elchibey was forced to declare a three-month state of emergency. Furthermore, 50,000 new refugees were arriving in Baku after the latest offensive by Armenian forces. The UN began airlifts of blankets and temporary shelter for those people made homeless by the war.

Despite Elchibey's attempts to prevent any political activity likely to destabilize the Government, it appeared to be a split within the PFA itself which brought about the downfall of the increasingly unpopular regime. This dramatic fall in public esteem was attributed to the reverses in the war, economic problems compounded by the constantly increasing number of refugees and the allegedly widespread corruption in government. In early February 1993 Col Surat Husseinov, the successful commander of the Azerbaijan forces since the PFA came to power the previous June, withdrew from northern Nagorny Karabakh to Gyanja. This move allowed the Armenian militia to make significant strategic gains (see below). Elchibey accused Husseinov of attempting to destablize domestic politics and thus provide the justification for a military coup. Despite the protests of the Minister of Foreign Affairs, Rahim Gaziev (who was himself soon removed from office), Husseinov was dismissed from his posts and expelled from the PFA. However, his so-called 709th Brigade, which was effectively a private army (financed by profits from Husseinov's textile sales when director of the state wool business), remained loyal. In this situation, most of the opposition was willing to support the Government, because they hoped to gain in the parliamentary elections, but generally the PFA remained without political allies.

As the Russian troops (former Soviet army units) still based in Gyanja were rumoured to be covertly supporting Husseinov, the Government negotiated their early withdrawal from Azerbaijan. They departed before the end of May 1993, leaving considerable stocks of weaponry and ammunition, which the Government feared would be acquired by the 709th Brigade. Units of the regular Azerbaijani army were ordered to attack Husseinov's forces, which they did, on 4 June, but they were repelled after much bloodshed. Husseinov responded by holding some government negotiators hostage, assuming control of Gyanja and demanding the resignations of the Prime Minister and of Isa Gambarov, Chairman of the Supreme Soviet (and, therefore, of the Milli Majlis). He also demanded the reconvening of the Supreme Soviet (there had been an attempt in April to hold an emergency session). The premier resigned, but Elchibey's resignation was also subsequently demanded.

Elchibey was persuaded to summon to Baku the popular former Communist leader of Azerbaijan (1969–87), Heydar Aliyev, head of the Nakhichevan regional government and of the New Azerbaijan Party. He had reportedly also tried to win Aliyev's support in the previous February. Meanwhile, Husseinov began to march his forces on Baku, meeting little resistance. On 13 June 1993 Gambarov resigned and Aliyev met Husseinov, who refused to withdraw his demand for Elchibey's resignation. Two days later Aliyev was elected Chairman of the Supreme Soviet by the Milli Majlis (after constitutional amendments necessitated by Aliyev not being a member of that body). Husseinov's forces continued their approach to Baku and Elchibey was warned that the security forces would not defend him. On the night of 17–18 June President Elchibey fled to Nakhichevan.

On 18 June 1993, immediately following Elchibey's flight, Aliyev announed that he had assumed the powers of the presidency, although the Milli Majlis initially refused to transfer formal authority to him. Elchibey insisted that he remain the legally elected President. On 20 June the rebel forces of Husseinov reached Baku and he claimed 'supreme power', in the absence of any viable authority. However, Aliyev condemned the claim and, with Elchibey refusing to return to Baku, on 24 June the Milli Majlis transferred virtually all presidential powers to Aliyev (except for responsibility for foreign policy and the final legislative sanction). Husseinov, when he reached Baku a few days later, acknowledged Aliyev as the acting head of state, but was appointed premier, with control over all security services. This appointment alienated Aliyev's erstwhile ally, Etibar Mamedov, leader of the National Independence Party (Istiklal), who therefore decided to remain in opposition.

During the confusion of June 1993 a group led by Alikram Gumbatov seized control of territory around Lenkoran, in the south of the country. They proclaimed an 'Autonomous Republic of Mugan-Talysh', with Gumbatov as President. Aliyev would not countenance a referendum for the area and, on 17 August, the Milli Majlis resolved on the illegality of Gumbatov's actions. The revolt ended on 23 August, when PFA supporters attacked Gumbatov's headquarters in Lenkoran and he fled the city.

At the end of July 1993 the Milli Majlis resolved to conduct a referendum on confidence in President Elchibey. Aliyev subsequently publicly criticized Elchibey. The poll was held on 29 August and, according to official figures, some 92% of the electorate participated, with 97.5% voting against Elchibey. The PFA condemned the referendum as illegal and also claimed that there were irregularities in its conduct. The Milli Majlis, however, endorsed the results and scheduled presidential elections for the following month. Many opposition parties announced that they would boycott the contest, but Aliyev enjoyed widespread popular support (the regulation forbidding those over 65 years of age to contest the presidency was repealed) and most groups were more anxious for new parliamentary elections to be held. On 3 October Heydar Aliyev was elected President of Azerbaijan, against two other candidates, with 98.8% of the votes cast.

In foreign affairs Azerbaijan traditionally enjoyed close relations with the Russian Federation, although, under the PFA Government there had been a much closer alliance with Turkey, the ally of independent Azerbaijan in 1918–20. Azerbaijan has close linguistic and ethnic ties with Turkey and it was the first country to acknowledge Azerbaijan's declaration of independence. Under the PFA regime Azerbaijan withdrew from the CIS, although in the same month, October 1992, it signed a Treaty of Friendship, Co-operation and Mutual Security with the Russian Federation. Russian influences were alleged to have supported the overthrow of the PFA. Certainly, in September 1993, the acting head of state announced that the country would seek readmittance to the CIS (see below). It was also likely that the controversial proposed natural-gas pipeline, which had come to symbolize the conflicting foreign-policy preferences, would be through Russian territory to the Black Sea coast, rather than through Turkey. However, Turkey remained influential in the region and a strong supporter of Azerbaijan against Armenian attack.

Iran, too, was strong in condemning the incursions of the ethnic Armenian militia into Azerbaijan and, in August 1993, helped establish refugee camps near the border. In the following month it was reported that Iran had declared a 'security zone' along its border with Azerbaijan (see below). It was a mark of the closer relations that Acting President Aliyev enjoyed with Iran that his Government did not object to this situation, which included allegations that Iranian troops had entered Azerbaijani territory. Generally, however, in relations with the countries to the south of the Caucasus region, most political forces in Azerbaijan were more sympathetic to secular Turkey than the Islamic regime in Iran. Furthermore, the substantial ethnic Azerbaijani minority in northern Iran was another potential cause of tension.

By the beginning of 1993 Azerbaijan had been recognized by over 120 countries, seven of which had embassies in Baku. In March of the previous year it had been admitted to the UN and, throughout 1992, had sought to broaden its international affiliations. It became a member of the CSCE, the International Monetary Fund (IMF), the Black Sea Co-operation Accord and, with the four southern Central Asian countries, the Economic Co-operation Organization, among other bodies. Azerbaijan had voted in favour of a continued Union during the Soviet referendum on the renewal of the USSR, in March 1991, and was a founding signatory of the Almaty Declaration of December 1991, which established the CIS. However, the PFA regime (May 1992–June 1993) withdrew Azerbaijan from the CIS; the CIS treaty had never been actually ratified and, in October 1992, the Milli Majlis voted against further participation in the Commonwealth. The country remained in the 'rouble zone' (see the Economy) and, on 20 September 1993, the Milli Majlis adopted a resolution to rejoin the CIS. Azerbaijan was formally admitted to the Commonwealth on 24 September when Acting President Aliyev signed the Almaty Declaration, the Commonwealth Charter and the Treaty on Collective Security. The Milli Majlis ratified these documents on 29 September.

NAKHICHEVAN AND NAGORNY KARABAKH

The Autonomous Republic of Nakhichevan and the Nagorno-Karabakh Autonomous Oblast (Nagorny Karabakh or, self-styled, 'the Republic of Nagorny Karabakh') were two autonomous areas of Soviet Azerbaijan. The former is a territory separated from 'metropolitan' Azerbaijan by the Republic of Armenia; the latter is a predominantly ethnic Armenian enclave, surrounded by Azerbaijan proper. In October 1921 the Treaty of Kars, which agreed the borders of the Soviet Republics of Azerbaijan, Armenia and Georgia with Turkey, finally established the status of Nakhichevan and Nagorny Karabakh as territories of Azerbaijan. However, during the late 1980s and early 1990s, Armenia laid claims to both enlaves, on historical grounds, and the dispute over Nagorny Karabakh resulted in armed conflict.

Nakhichevan, despite an apparent surrender of Azerbaijan's claims to the territory in 1920, never became part of Soviet Armenia. The Soviet-Turkish Treaty of March 1921 included a clause guaranteeing Azerbaijani jurisdiction over Nakhichevan. Whereas in 1919 some 45%-50% of the region's population were ethnically Armenian, by 1989 the number was reduced to just 5%. In 1990, at the time of serious disturbances throughout Azerbaijan, local nationalists seized Party buildings in Nakhichevan and declared its secession from the USSR. This protest was soon suppressed. In September 1991 Heydar Aliyev (a native of Nakhichevan and Communist leader of Azerbaijan, in 1969-87, and again leader from June 1993—see above) was elected Chairman of the local Supreme Soviet or Supreme Majlis. Abulfaz Elchibey (President of Azerbaijan, 1992-93) was also from Nakhichevan and took refuge there, in his home town of Keleki, when he fled from Baku, in June 1993. In mid-1992 Armenian militia attacked Nakhichevan but fears that Turkey and the Russian Federation might intervene prevented the violence from escalating. (Both countries were guarantors of the territory's status; furthermore, Turkey was the traditional ally of Azerbaijan, while the Russian Federation was party to a CIS collective security treaty which included Armenia.) In May 1992 the Turkish Prime Minister, Süleyman Demirel, assured the Russian leader, Boris Yeltsin, that Turkey would not use force in Nakhichevan.

The majority of the population of Nagorny Karabakh was Armenian. Although Armenians once occupied a far larger area than that of the present-day Republic of Armenia, it has been claimed that the Armenian population of Nagorny Karabakh are descendants of ancient 'Albanians' of the Transcaucasus, augmented by Armenian settlers during the period of Tsarist Russia. The Nagorny Karabakh Armenians are more nationalist than those from the Republic of Armenia, and have closer links with the diaspora. Nagorny Karabakh was a disputed territory in 1918-20, during the period of Armenian and Azerbaijani independence. The Soviet Bureau for Caucasian Affairs (Kavburo), which was mediating in the dispute, voted, in June 1921, to unite Nagorny Karabakh with Armenia. However, some days after the Kavburo decision, following an intervention by Stalin, the decision was reversed. In 1923 it was given special status as an autonomous oblast within the Azerbaijan SSR. There were attempts to challenge Azerbaijan's jurisdiction over the region, including two petitions from the inhabitants of Nagorny Karabakh in the 1960s, but they were strongly opposed by the all-Union and Azerbaijani authorities.

Conflict over the territories began again in February 1988, when the Nagorny Karabakh regional soviet requested the Armenian and Azerbaijani Supreme Soviets to agree to the transfer of the territory to Armenia. The all-Union and Azerbaijani authorities rejected the request, which provoked huge demonstrations by Armenians, not only in Nagorny Karabakh, but also in the Armenian capital, Yerevan, where crowds of up to one million people took part in the unrest. Azerbaijanis began leaving Armenia, and rumours that refugees had been attacked led to three days of anti-Armenian violence, on 27-29 February, in the Azerbaijani town of Sumgait. According to official figures, 32 people died, 26 of whom were Armenians.

The events in Sumgait provoked widespread anger in Nagorny Karabakh, which was compounded by the decision of the Presidium of the all-Union Supreme Soviet not to transfer the region to Armenia. This official decision on the future of the enclave was a serious disappointment to many Armenians, who had expected a favourable response from the Gorbachev administration. Strikes and rallies did not abate in Armenia or Nagorny Karabakh, provoking continued unrest among Azerbaijanis in late 1988. In November thousands of people protested when an Azerbaijani was sentenced to death for his part in the Sumgait massacre; a curfew was imposed in Baku. Some 14,000 Armenians left Azerbaijan during the month as rallies and demonstrations spread to Kirovabad (now Gyanja) and other towns. Meanwhile, inter-ethnic tension in Armenia forced some 80,000 Azerbaijanis to leave Armenia during the same period.

In January 1989, in an attempt to end the violence, the Soviet Government suspended the activities of the local authorities in Nagorny Karabakh and established a Special Administration Committee (SAC), directly responsible to the USSR Council of Ministers. Although it was stressed that the region would formally retain its status as an autonomous region within Azerbaijan, the decision was widely viewed by Azerbaijanis as an infringement on Azerbaijan's territorial integrity. This imposition of 'direct rule' from Moscow and the dispatch of some 5,000 interior ministry troops did little to reduce tensions within Nagorny Karabakh, where the ethnic Armenians went on strike in May and did not resume work until September.

Following increasing popular pressure and a declaration of the Republic's sovereignty, in September 1989, Azerbaijan imposed an economic blockade of Armenia. The effect of this was only partially lessened by the use of Soviet troops to operate the Baku-Yerevan railway.

In November 1989 the Soviet Government transferred control of Nagorny Karabakh from the SAC to an Organizing Committee, which was dominated by ethnic Azerbaijanis. This decision was denounced on 1 December by the Armenian Supreme Soviet, which declared Nagorny Karabakh to be part of a 'unified Armenian republic'. This pronouncement prompted a week-long resumption of the Azerbaijani economic blockade and further outbreaks of violence in Nagorny Karabakh and along the Armenian-Azerbaijani border. In January 1990 the declaration was declared unconstitutional by the all-Union Supreme Soviet. The Armenian Supreme Soviet responded by granting itself the power to veto any all-Union legislation.

During early 1991 there was further inter-ethnic violence in the region around Nagorny Karabakh, with allegations that Soviet interior ministry troops co-operated with Azerbaijani forces to deport Armenians from villages near the Armenian-Azerbaijani border. In September 1991, however, despite the declaration of a Republic in Nagorny Karabakh, there was some progress towards peace when Boris Yeltsin of the Russian Federation and Nursultan Nazarbayev of Kazakhstan arranged negotiations between Armenia and Azerbaijan. An initial agreement was signed in Zhelenovodsk (Russian Federation), on 23 September. The agreement provided for considerable autonomy for Armenians in Nagorny Karabakh, in exchange for a renunciation by Armenia of any territorial claim to the region. However, some inter-ethnic violence was reported immediately after the agreement was signed and the PFA organized demonstrations to protest the terms. The negotiations received a serious setback when an aircraft carrying leading Azerbaijani negotiators crashed, killing all the passengers. The Azerbaijani leadership alleged that the aircraft had been shot down by Armenians, and relations between the two Republics worsened. By the end of 1991 there were increasingly violent conflicts, particularly within Nagorny Karabakh.

With the effective full independence of Armenia and Azerbaijan, following the dissolution of the USSR in December 1991, ethnic hostilities in Nagorny Karabakh intensified. In January 1992 President Mutalibov of Azerbaijan declared Nagorny Karabakh to be under direct presidential rule and ordered Armenian officials to be replaced by Azerbaijanis. International efforts to negotiate a peace settlement foundered, owing to Mutalibov's insistence that the conflict was a domestic problem. Azerbaijani forces surrounded and attacked Stepanakert, the capital of the enclave, while Armenians laid siege to Shusha, a town with a mainly Azerbaijani population.

By March 1992 the Armenian militia of Nagorny Karabakh was achieving some military success. The President of Armenia, Levon Ter-Petrosyan, stated that Armenia had no territorial claims on Azerbaijan, including Nagorny Karabakh. He supported the principle that the future of the enclave was an internal matter for Azerbaijan, although it must be agreed by both the Azerbaijan and the Nagorny Karabakh leaderships. Violence in the enclave persisted, however, despite renewed efforts by the Conference on Security and Co-operation in Europe (CSCE—both Armenia and Azerbaijan were admitted as members in February 1992) and the UN (both countries were admitted in early March) to negotiate a cease-fire.

In May 1992 the 'Nagorny Karabakh Self-defence Forces' (which the Armenian Government claimed operated outside its control) captured Shusha, thereby securing complete control of the enclave and ending the bombardment of Stepanakert. With the capture of the strategically important Lachin valley, the Armenian militia then succeeded in opening a 'corridor' through Azerbaijan territory, linking Nagorny Karabakh with Armenia.

In June 1992 there was a major counter-offensive by Azerbaijani forces, in which they retook much of the north of the enclave, prompting Armenian allegations that Turkey had provided covert military assistance to Azerbaijan. Some sources attributed Azerbaijan's success to improved army morale, following the assumption of power by the nationalist PFA and the election of Elchibey as President. Furthermore, the new commander and presidential plenipotentiary in Karabakh, Col Surat Husseinov, could bolster the regular army with forces equipped at his own expense.

In August 1992, under pressure from the Azerbaijani counter-offensive, the Nagorny Karabakh legislature declared a state of martial law in the 'republic'. The enclave's government was replaced by a State Defence Committee, which was closely linked to the Ter-Petrosyan administration of Armenia, despite that country's repeated disclaimers of ambitions on or control over Nagorny Karabakh. Armenia accused Azerbaijan of launching 'undeclared war' and appealed (without success) for assistance from the signatories of the CIS Collective Security Treaty. (The treaty was signed on 15 May 1992, by Armenia, Kazakhstan, the Russian Federation, Tajikistan, Turkmenistan and Uzbekistan, agreeing to the establishment of joint peace-making forces to intervene in CIS disputes.) By October it appeared that Azerbaijani forces had regained control of large areas of Nagorny Karabakh, although their repeated efforts to close the Lachin 'corridor' were unsuccessful. In late 1992 it was estimated that, since the beginning of the conflict in 1988, some 4,700 Azerbaijanis and 3,000 Armenians had been killed. It was also estimated that between June 1992 and June 1993 alone, some 11,000 Azerbaijanis were killed in the fighting.

In 1993 the war once more began to go against Azerbaijan. In early February Husseinov withdrew his forces from Mardakert, in northern Nagorny Karabakh, to the town of Gyanja, some 40 km from the enclave (the reasons for this were unclear and remained controversial, with allegations of coups being plotted or the PFA leadership attempting to discredit Husseinov). This move enabled the Nagorny Karabakh forces to make significant advances and, in March, they began to occupy Azerbaijani territory beyond the borders of the enclave. The offensive was concentrated on Kelbajar, to the west of Nagorny Karabakh, and Fizuli, to the south. Turkey condemned the attacks and additional troops were sent to its border with Armenia which had been closed since the fighting had begun. On 30 April the UN Security Council adopted a resolution (Resolution 822) demanding an immediate cease-fire and the withdrawal of all Armenian units from Azerbaijani territory. The UN did not, however, directly accuse Armenia itself of aggression. In June the Nagorny Karabakh leadership accepted a plan by the so-called 'Minsk Group' of nine CSCE countries (led by Italy—the plan, drawn up by Turkey, the USA and Russia, had already been signed by Armenia and Azerbaijan), having originally rejected it on the grounds that it provided insufficient guarantees for the security of the enclave. Almost immediately, however, Azerbaijan accused Armenian forces of attacking parts of the enclave and there were reports of fighting in Agdam, a town east of Nagorny Karabakh. President Elchibey of Azerbaijan appealed to the CSCE to intervene, but the political confusion in Azerbaijan during June encouraged further advances by the Armenain militia, which continued after Aliyev assumed the leadership of Azerbaijan and reappointed Husseinov as the military commander.

In early July 1993 the CSCE mediator, Mario Raffaeli, cancelled a trip to Stepanakert after it was reported that Agdam had been seized by Nagorny Karabakh forces. Attacks also resumed on Fizuli, a town linking Nagorny Karabakh to the Iranian border. (Fizuli fell on 18 August.) Azerbaijan made further appeals to the international community: since the conflict began it had lost 17% of its territory to Armenia, and one in 10 of its inhabitants was homeless. On 29 July, at an emergency session of the UN Security Council, UN Resolution 853 was adopted, based on a report submitted by the CSCE 'Minsk Group', demanding the immediate withdrawal of Nagorny Karabakh forces from Agdam and the cessation of the bombardment of civilian centres and condemning all hostilities in the region. Fighting continued into August, however, despite a series of cease-fire agreements and the first direct negotiations between the Nagorny Karabakh and Azerbaijani leaderships. In early September the Armenian President appealed to the Nagorny Karabakh regime to observe the latest cease-fire agreement. Turkey and Iran both again condemned the threat to Azerbaijan's territorial integrity, with the former threatening Armenia with war if there were any encroachments on Nakhichevan and the latter deploying 1,000 troops to set up a 'security zone' along its border with Azerbaijan. The Nagorny Karabakh leadership agreed to resume negotiations, denied any claim to territory beyond the existing borders (occupation of Azerbaijan territory was justified only on military grounds) and ordered a withdrawal from recently conquered villages in Kubatly.

On 14 October 1993 the UN Security Council adopted Resolution 874, which endorsed a schedule drawn up by the CSCE for the implementation of Resolutions 822 and 853. Under Resolution 874 the Nagorny Karabakh Armenians were recognized as a separate party in the conflict. On 27 October, following mediation by Iran, a cease-fire was signed by Armenia and Azerbaijan. The representatives of Armenia and Nagorny Karabakh accepted the CSCE schedule for the withdrawal of ethnic Armenian militia from Kelbajar, Kubatly, Fizuli, Agdam and Jebrail. The Azerbaijani delegation, however, rejected the plan on the grounds that no demand had been made for the Nagorny Karabakh forces to withdraw from the Lachin 'corridor'. In spite of the cease-fire agreement the Armenian offensive in Azerbaijan continued and, on 25 October, the Armenian militia reached the Iranian border. By the beginning of November they occupied 96 km of the Azerbaijani–Iranian border. Thousands of civilians were forced to flee their homes in south-west Azerbaijan and many died while attempting to swim across the River Araks into Iran. By this time, according to some estimates, nearly one-third of Azerbaijan was occupied by ethnic Armenian troops. The seriousness of Azerbaijan's situation prompted the re-establishment by presidential decree of Azerbaijan's Defence Council on 2 November. (The Council had first been set up by President Mutalibov but had been transformed into a Defence Committee under President Elchibey.) On 10 November nine countries from the CSCE Minsk Group issued a statement condemning the constant violation of cease-fires in Nagorny Karabakh.

The Economy

Azerbaijan is rich in natural resources, possessing fertile agricultural land and significant petroleum reserves. It has a relatively well-developed industrial base. In 1991, according to estimates by the International Monetary Fund (IMF), Azerbaijan's gross domestic product (GDP), in current prices, was 26,676m. roubles, equivalent to 3,695 roubles per head. In real terms, GDP was estimated to have declined by 0.7%, compared with the previous year, but the deterioration during 1992 was projected to be considerably greater. In 1991 net material product (NMP), measured at current prices, was estimated at 20,370m. roubles; in real terms NMP fell by 1.9%. It was estimated that NMP declined by an unprecedented 26.0%, in 1992, with the dominant sectors of industry and agriculture particularly badly affected. As well as the escalating conflict in Nagorny Karabakh, Azerbaijan was adapting to the transition to a market economy from 1992, a process slowed by political uncertainty and ineffectiveness. Reform was further impeded by the political disruptions of 1993, with war distracting resources and increasing the refugee problem and currency problems creating additional problems.

AGRICULTURE

Agriculture contributed an estimated 41.1% of NMP in 1991, compared to around 30% in the mid-1980s; but, in 1992, this share in NMP was reckoned to have declined to about one-third of NMP. These fluctuations were mainly attributable to price developments and the relative performance of the industrial sector. Most arable land requires extensive irrigation, but there are large pasture-lands, which are used by cattle, goats and sheep. The principal crops are cereals (mainly wheat, but also barley and maize—in total, 1,346,000 metric tons in 1991), grapes (1,126,000 metric tons), cotton (540,000 metric tons) and tobacco (58,000 metric tons). Other fruits and vegetables are significant. Silkworm breeding is also important. All agricultural production was estimated to fall in 1992. In 1991 32.9% of the work-force were employed in the agricultural sector, with roughly equal shares on state, co-operative (collective) and private farms. By mid-1992 some 40 of the 1,200 state and collective farms had been transferred to private control. The private sector in Azerbaijan contributed 15%–20% of agricultural production, reflecting mainly its high share in the output of vegetable, fruit and livestock production. Agricultural production was badly affected, in the late 1980s and early 1990s, by adverse weather conditions and the war over Nagorny Karabakh.

INDUSTRY

Azerbaijan has a diversified industrial sector. In 1991 industry contributed an estimated 37.1% of NMP, and employed approximately 16% of the work-force. Despite continued declines in production, price fluctuations were estimated to cause industry to increase its contribution to NMP to 48.3% in 1992. In 1991 food had the largest share in the value of industrial output (31%), followed by light processing (19%), especially wine production, the fuel industry (12%) and machine-building (11%). Light industry includes textiles, carpets and leather products, as well as toys, furniture and bicycles. The fuel industry consists of petroleum extraction and petroleum processing. In 1992 it was estimated that industrial production had declined by 27%, the fourth year in succession, with the strongest declines occurring in petrochemicals, machine-building and metallurgy. This was mainly owing to the heavy dependence of these branches on trade in the former USSR.

MINING AND ENERGY

Azerbaijan is richly endowed with mineral resources, the most important being petroleum. The country's recoverable reserves of petroleum are estimated to total about 1,000m. metric tons. Petroleum is extracted from the Apsheron Peninsula and around Siyar, Neftechala and Ali-Bayramli. Some 80% of extraction is concentrated in offshore fields, in the Caspian Sea. Petroleum, including imported crude petroleum, is refined in Baku, although refining capacity was not fully utilized from 1989, mainly because of environmental problems. In 1991 petroleum production was estimated at a total of 11,741,000 metric tons, of which 9,492,000 tons were extracted off shore and 2,249,000 tons on shore. Production fell for the fourth consecutive year, owing to a combination of inadequate investment and technological obsolescence. There are also substantial reserves of natural gas (mainly off shore), although these were largely underutilized. Total known reserves were estimated at 500,000m. cubic metres, although there are large additional offshore reserves associated with newly discovered petroleum fields and in the many undeveloped discoveries of gas. Despite the political disruptions of June 1993, the exploitation of such new fields was being negotiated with major Western companies later in the year. Other minerals extracted include iron ore, alunite (alum-stone), iron pyrites, barytes, cobalt and molybdenum.

Hydroelectricity is the principal source of electric power in Azerbaijan. It is mostly produced by plants on the River

Kura. However, many plants use natural gas and fuel oil and disruptions to this supply, as well as the general economic decline, caused a fall in electric power generation during 1992 and 1993.

TRADE

Azerbaijan is highly dependent on trade, which is still largely centralized. In 1991, according to official estimates, Azerbaijan recorded a visible trade surplus of 1,189.7m. roubles (equivalent to about 5% of annual GDP). In that year the principal trading partners were other Republics of the USSR (in total accounting for some 87% of total trade), with the Russian Federation (about 45% of total trade) and Ukraine as the two leading partners. After the collapse of the USSR Azerbaijan has sought to expand its international trading links. This was not only because of the incentives of higher international prices, but also of dislocations in the rouble area which lowered trade transactions in general (during 1992 Azerbaijan's trade with countries outside the former USSR increased from 13% of total trade, in 1991, to 47% by September 1992). In 1991 the principal foreign exports were refined petroleum products, textiles, machinery and food products. The principal imports were industrial raw materials, machinery and processed foods. In September 1993 Azerbaijan signed an agreement with the EC on the trade of textile products.

FINANCE

The current budget deficit for 1992 was estimated at 7,693m. roubles. Azerbaijan did not contract any foreign debt during 1992, and in 1993 indicated that it might adopt the 'zero option' on its share of the USSR's foreign debt, i.e. relinqish its claims on the USSR's assets, in return for being relieved of responsibility for its share of the debt. In 1991 the average annual increase in consumer prices was 87.3%

PROBLEMS AND PROSPECTS

Azerbaijan became a member of the IMF and the World Bank in 1992. It also joined the Islamic Development Bank and the European Bank for Reconstruction and Development in the same year. In 1993 Azerbaijan, Iran, Kazakhstan, the Russian Federation and Turkmenistan formed a caviar cartel which would co-ordinate the marketing of caviar around the world.

Owing to its enormous mineral wealth, Azerbaijan's prospects for eventual economic prosperity were considered to be favourable. However, major investment and foreign technological expertise were required for the full potential of Azerbaijan's unexploited reserves of petroleum and natural gas to be realized. In the early 1990s joint-venture projects emphasized the need to establish a legal and institutional framework which would encourage foreign involvement in the economy. Azerbaijan's largely obsolete extraction and refining equipment needed upgrading, likewise the methods used to produce and process petroleum, as serious environmental problems had developed, including the pollution of the Caspian Sea. Many foreign petroleum companies expressed interest in investing in Azerbaijan's petroleum industry. In October 1993 Azerbaijan signed an agreement with a Western consortium, headed by British Petroleum, for the development of the Azeri and Chirag petroleum fields. The fields are expected to be in production by 1996. Furthermore, in March 1993, Turkey and Azerbaijan signed an agreement to build a pipeline for crude-petroleum exports from Baku to the Turkish Mediterranean port of Iskenderun, via Iran and Nakhichevan (however, the new regime after June 1993 was believed to favour a northern route for the pipeline, to the Black Sea coast). Azerbaijan's capacity to develop new export markets remained contingent upon satisfying the international markets, in terms of both product and quality, as well as price. This required a major restructuring of the centrally planned economy.

A programme of reform, aimed at effecting a transition to a market economic system, was approved by the legislature in mid-1991. Further stages occurred in 1992, but the political changes of that year and of 1993, delayed implementation of necessary measure. The fighting in and around Nagorny Karabakh was also extremely disruptive of the economy. However, Azerbaijan's new currency, the manat, was introduced in August 1992. Initially it operated in parallel with the rouble. The Russian recall of all pre-1993 rouble notes prompted Azerbaijan to attempt to move away from the *de facto* 'rouble zone'. In August 1993 the Government decreed that all monetary transactions in the country should be carried out with manats, but it was forced to rescind this decision on 8 September. This demonstrated that, despite the potential of newer foreign links, Azerbaijan remained heavily dependent upon the Russian Federation. In October 1993 the Azerbaijani leadership announced its intention for the republic to leave the rouble zone within two months and declared that there was no possibility for the parallel circulation of the rouble and the manat in the future.

Statistical Survey

Principal sources: IMF, *Azerbaijan, Economic Review*; World Bank, *Statistical Handbook: States of the Former USSR*.

Area and Population

AREA, POPULATION AND DENSITY

Area (sq km)	86,600*
Population (census result)	
12 January 1989†	
Males	3,423,793
Females	3,597,385
Total	7,021,178
Population (official estimate at 1 January 1991)	7,174,000
Density (per sq km) at 1 January 1991	83.0

* 33,400 sq miles.
† Figures refer to the *de jure* population. The *de facto* total was 7,037,867.

PRINCIPAL TOWNS
(estimated population at 1 January 1990)

Baku (capital) 1,149,000; Gyanja (formerly Kirovabad) 281,000; Sumgait 235,000.

BIRTHS, MARRIAGES AND DEATHS

	Registered live births		Registered marriages		Registered deaths	
	Number	Rate (per '000)	Number	Rate (per '000)	Number	Rate (per '000)
1987	184,585	26.9	68,031	9.9	45,744	6.7
1988	184,350	26.4	68,887	9.9	47,485	6.8
1989	181,631	25.6	71,874	10.1	44,016	6.2

Source: UN, *Demographic Yearbook*.

EMPLOYMENT (annual average, '000 persons)

	1989	1990	1991
Agriculture	905	914	934
Forestry	6	5	5
Industry*	483	469	463
Construction	243	251	248
Transport and communications	133	143	143
Trade and other material services	232	230	233
Housing and municipal services	108	99	101
Science, reaserch and development	60	58	60
Education, culture and arts	329	38	341
Health care and social security	168	170	173
Government	61	62	62
Other non-material services	67	71	73
Total	2,794	2,808	2,839

* Principally mining, manufacturing, electricity, gas and water.

Agriculture

PRINCIPAL CROPS ('000 metric tons)

	1990	1991	1992
Wheat	880	889	900*
Barley	446	413	380*
Seed cotton	543	540	480†
Tobacco (leaves)	62	34	63†
Potatoes	185	180	170*
Other vegetables	1,036	955	880*
Grapes	1,196	1,126	1,100*
Watermelons*	180	150	120
Other fruit	1,515	1,622	1,580*
Tea	8	8*	7*

* FAO estimate. † Unofficial estimate.
Source: FAO, *Production Yearbook*.

LIVESTOCK ('000 head, unless otherwise indicated)

	1990	1991	1992
Cattle	1,900	1,800	1,800
Pigs	200	200	100
Sheep	5,280	5,185	5,088
Goats	220	215	212
Chickens (million)	29*	28*	27*

* Unofficial estimate.
Source: FAO, *Production Yearbook*.

LIVESTOCK PRODUCTS (metric tons)

	1990	1991	1992
Meat	176.0	156.0	145.0
Cows' milk	970.0	948.0	800.0†
Butter	3.8	3.1	2.5*
Hen eggs	54.4†	53.0†	49.5
Wool			
greasy	11.2	10.5	9.0*
scoured	6.7	6.3	5.4*

* FAO estimate. † Unofficial estimate.
Source: FAO, *Production Yearbook*.

Mining

('000 metric tons)

	1990	1991	1992
Crude petroleum	12,513	11,741	11,195*

* Provisional.

Industry

SELECTED PRODUCTS
('000 metric tons, unless otherwise indicated)

	1989	1990	1991
Steel	696	501	462
Pesticides	5.1	2.1	6.7
Sulphuric acid	768	603	552
Caustic soda	219	160	171
Radio receivers ('000)	—	6	7
Aviation fuel	113.6	88.7	58.2
Naphtha	550.4	341.0	427.0
Motor fuel	1,522.4	1,478.8	1,173.7
Jet kerosene	1,519.1	1,289.7	1,205.3
Diesel oil	4,235.5	3,898.8	3,634.9
Lubricants	933.7	817.5	762.5
Bitumen	167.0	145.6	113.1
Petroleum coke	229.8	178.5	161.3
Fuel oil	7,554.7	6,686.1	7,207.3
Electric energy (million kWh)	23,300	23,200	23,300

Finance

CURRENCY AND EXCHANGE RATES

Monetary Units

100 kopeks = 1 rubl (ruble or rouble).

Denominations

Coins: 1, 2, 3, 5, 10, 15, 25 and 50 kopeks; 1 rouble.
Notes: 1, 3, 5, 10, 25, 50 and 100 roubles.

Sterling and Dollar Equivalents (30 September 1993)

£1 sterling = 1,796.1 roubles;
US $1 = 1,201.0 roubles;
1,000 roubles = £5.568 = $8.326.

Average Exchange Rate (roubles per US $)

1989	0.6274
1990	0.5856
1991	0.5819

Note: The figures for average exchange rates refer to official rates for the Soviet rouble. However, a multiple exchange rate system was in operation, with separate non-commercial and tourist rates. A commercial exchange rate was introduced on 1 November 1990, replacing the official rate for most transactions. The commercial rate (roubles per US dollar) was: 1.692 at 31 December 1990; 1.671 at 31 December 1991. Between November 1989 and April 1991 the tourist exchange rate valued the rouble at one-tenth of the official rate. In April 1991 this rate, renamed the 'special rate', was set at $1 = 27.6 roubles. It was subsequently adjusted. The average market exchange rate in 1991 was $1 = 31.2 roubles. Following the dissolution of the USSR in December 1991, Russia and several other former Soviet republics retained the rouble as their monetary unit. In August 1992 Azerbaijan introduced a small amount of its own currency, the manat (equal to 100 gopik), to circulate alongside the rouble (at an exchange rate of 10 roubles per manat). In October 1993 it was announced that Azerbaijan intended to leave the rouble zone imminently, with the manat becoming the sole currency.

STATE BUDGET (million roubles)

Revenue	1991	1992*
Current revenue	6,690.5	50,307.0
Tax revenue	5,969.3	49,148.7
Taxes on income, profits and capital gains	2,256.3	20,430.0
of which enterprise profits tax	1,307.3	12,500.0
Property tax	15.3	250.0
Domestic taxes on goods and services	3,650.8	28,377.0
of which value added tax	2,261.0	19,000.0
Taxes on international trade and transactions	39.6	90.0
Other taxes	7.2	1.7
Non-tax revenue	721.2	1,158.3
Capital revenue	5.6	402.0
Grants	3,640.0	—
Other	—	241.0
Total	10,336.2	50,950.0

* Estimate.

Expenditure	1991	1992*
Current expenditure	8,091.4	58,000.0
General public services	177.1	2,000.0
Defence	125.5	6,070.6
Public order and safety	125.3	4,000.0
Education	1,792.6	15,800.0
Health	792.5	6,500.0
Social security and welfare	1,852.4	8,180.0
Housing and community amenities	346.2	200.0
Recreational, cultural and religious affairs and services	317.8	1,335.0
Economic affairs and services	2,170.1	10,384.4
Other expenditure	392.0	3,530.0
Net lending	1,539.1	−50.0
Total	9,630.5	57,950.0

* Estimates.

NATIONAL ACCOUNTS

Net Material Product (million roubles at current prices)

Activities of the material sphere	1990	1991	1992†
Agriculture	4,014	8,372	50,712
Industry*	3,727	7,567	73,242
Construction	1,255	1,705	14,824
Transport and communication	555	663	3,948
Other material production	1,161	2,063	8,836
Trade and catering	429	822	1,317
Total	10,712	20,370	151,562

* Including turnover taxes.
† Estimates.

External and Inter-republican Trade

PRINCIPAL COMMODITIES

Inter-republican Trade (million roubles)

Imports	1989	1990	1991*
Industrial products	3,728.6	3,984.3	8,751.8
Petroleum and gas	292.4	428.0	776.7
Ferrous metallurgy	206.0	218.5	810.6
Non-ferrous metallurgy	91.3	100.8	1,230.0
Chemicals and petrochemicals	407.1	488.0	599.3
Machines and metalworking	1,104.5	1,119.4	1,941.1
Timber, pulp and paper	99.2	117.1	293.6
Light industry (textiles)	620.0	707.9	906.1
Food	642.3	500.9	1,862.0
Agricultural products	51.8	145.8	84.6
Other commodities	13.9	117.1	—†
Total	3,794.3	4,247.2	8,836.4

Exports	1989	1990	1991*
Industrial products	6,221.8	5,845.8	11,189.0
Petroleum and gas	886.1	747.3	1,249.6
Ferrous metallurgy	88.5	71.2	268.0
Non-ferrous metallurgy	102.2	80.0	379.0
Chemicals and petrochemicals	601.0	518.0	1,131.0
Machines and metalworking	1,012.3	936.3	2,059.0
Light industry (textiles)	1,479.1	1,365.8	1,861.1
Food	1,828.5	1,748.6	3,882.2
Agricultural products	312.6	134.1	266.1
Other commodities	140.5	124.8	—†
Total	6,674.9	6,104.7	11,455.1

* Estimates.

† Distributed among the other categories shown.

PRINCIPAL COMMODITIES

External Trade (million roubles)

Imports	1989	1990	1991*
Industrial products	1,166.7	1,373.4	1,778.3
Petroleum and gas	1.5	1.9	129.1
Ferrous metallurgy	82.2	49.1	92.9
Chemicals and petrochemicals	94.4	87.5	43.6
Machines and metalworking	167.0	348.8	58.9
Light industry (textiles)	362.9	403.2	306.0
Food	409.8	431.0	1,001.4
Agricultural products	228.4	131.1	395.1
Total (incl. others)	1,395.5	1,504.9	2,173.4

Exports	1989	1990	1991*
Industrial products	434.5	319.4	730.4
Petroleum and gas	102.7	101.6	200.2
Machines and metalworking	105.9	112.4	56.1
Light industry (textiles)	172.5	61.2	408.9
Total (incl. others)	448.0	325.1	744.2

* Estimates.

PRINCIPAL TRADING PARTNERS (million roubles)

Imports	1990	1991*
Inter-republican	4,247.2	8,836.4
Belarus	264.1	248.1
Georgia	137.6	173.1
Kazakhstan	295.5	465.6
Russia	2,241.6	4,956.3
Ukraine	861.2	2,500.2
Uzbekistan	66.5	191.6
External	1,504.9	2,173.4
Total	5,752.1	11,009.8

Exports	1990	1991*
Inter-republican	6,104.7	11,455.1
Armenia	327.7	—
Belarus	190.4	569.2
Georgia	281.2	696.2
Kazakhstan	283.6	473.1
Russia	3,705.2	6,841.2
Turkmenistan	156.1	513.0
Ukraine	660.3	1,502.0
Uzbekistan	198.1	295.2
External	325.1	744.2
Total	6,429.8	12,199.3

* Estimates.

Education

(1990/91)

	Institutions	Students
Secondary schools	4,441	1,379,000
Secondary specialized institutions	80	70,000
Higher schools (incl. universities)	17	105,000

Directory

The Government

(November 1993)

HEAD OF STATE

President: HEYDAR A. ALIYEV (elected by direct popular vote, 3 October 1993).

Secretary of State: LALA S. HAJIYEVA.

COUNCIL OF MINISTERS

Prime Minister: Col SURAT D. HUSSEINOV.

Deputy Prime Ministers: ABBAS A. ABBASSOV, S. SADYKHOV, ASGHAR T. MAMMADOV, VAKHID AHMADOV, ELCHIN I. AFANDIYEV, ALI SHAHBABA TAHMAZOV.

Minister of Economy: S. SADYKHOV.

Minister of Health: ALI BINNET OGLY INSANOV.

Minister of Foreign Affairs: HASSAN A. HASSANOV.

Minister of Agriculture and Produce: R. G. ASHRAFOV.

Minister of Internal Affairs: VAGUIF NOVRUZOV.

Minister of Culture: BYUL-BYUL OGLY POLAD.

Minister of Education: LILIYA K. RASULOVA.

Minister of Land Reclamation and Water Economy: S. HAJIYEV.

Minister of Communications: S. ABBASBEILI.

Minister of Trade: RIZVAN HUSSEINOV.

Minister of Finance: SALIH M. MAMMADOV.

Minister of Grain Products: ZAKIR ABDULLAYEV.

Minister of Justice: ILYAS A. ISMAILOV.

Minister of Automobile Transport: A. A. ASLANOV.

Minister of Housing and Municipal Economy: VENIAMIN S. MAYOROV.

Minister of Labour and Social Protection: AKIF AKPER KERIMOV.

Minister of Local Industry: A. ABDULLAYEV.

Minister of National Security: NARIMAN IMRANOV.

Minister of Defence: MAMMADRAFI MAMMADOV.

Minister of External Economic Relations: KHAFIZ HUSSEIN OGLY BABAYEV.

Minister of Material Resources: FARRUKH MAMEDNABI OGLY ZEYNALOV.

Chairmen of State Committees

Chairman of the State Committee for Construction and Architectural Affairs: D. M. ASANOV.

Chairman of the State Committee for Labour and Social Questions: S. CH. KASUMOVA.

Chairman of the State Committee for Statistics: A. A. ALIYEV.

Chairman of the State Committee for Ecology and Use of Natural Resources: A. E. MANSUROV.

Chairman of the State Committee for Fuel: A. M. SHABANOV.

Chairman of the State Committee for work with people who have abandoned their place of permanent residence: SH. K. KERIMOV.

Chairman of the State Committee for Economy and Planning: Z. A. SAMED-ZADE.

Chairman of the State Committee for Supervision of Safety at Work in Industry and Mining: K. M. BAGIROV.

Chairman of the State Committee for Physical Culture and Sport: M. I. ALLAKHVERDIYEV.

Chairman of the State Committee for Geology and Mineral Resources: E. M.-E. SHEKINSKY.

Chairman of the State Committee for Press: S. K. RUSTAMKHANLY.

Chairman of the State Supply Committee: A. VELIYEV.

Chairman of the State Land Committee: D. UNAL.

Chairman of the State Committee for the Defence of State Borders: I. I. ALLAKHVERDIYEV.

Chairman of the State Committee for Foreign Investment: A. A. MASIMOV.

MINISTRIES

Ministry of Agriculture and Produce: 370016 Baku, Azadlyg Sq. 1, Government House.

Ministry of Automobile Transport: 370602 Baku, Tbilisi Ave, Block 1054; tel. (8922) 31-91-11.

Ministry of Communications: 370139 Baku, Azerbaijan Ave 35; tel. (8922) 93-00-04.

Ministry of Culture: 370016 Baku, Azadlyg Sq. 1, Government House; tel. (8922) 93-43-98, 93-72-83; fax (8922) 93-56-05.

Ministry of Defence: 370139 Baku, Azerbaijan Ave.

Ministry of Education: 370016 Baku, Azadlyg Sq. 1, Government House; tel. (8922) 93-72-66.

Ministry of External Economic Relations: 370016 Baku, Azadlyg Sq. 1, Government House.

Ministry of Finance: 370601 Baku, Samed Vurghun St 6; tel. (8922) 93-30-12.

Ministry of Foreign Affairs: 370004 Baku, Ghanjlar meydani 3; tel. (8922) 93-30-12.

Ministry of Grain Products: 370033 Baku, A. Heydarov St 13; tel. (8922) 66-74-51.

Ministry of Health: 370014 Baku, Malaya Morskaya St 4; tel. (8922) 93-29-77.

Ministry of Housing and Municipal Economy: 370016 Baku, Azadlyg Sq. 1, Government House; tel. (8922) 93-34-67.

Ministry of Internal Affairs: 370005 Baku, Gusi Hajiyev St 7; tel. (8922) 92-57-54.

Ministry of Justice: 370601 Baku, Kirov Ave 13; tel. (8922) 93-97-85.

Ministry of Labour amd Social Protection: 370016 Baku, Azadlyg Sq. 1, Government House; tel. (8922) 93-05-42; fax (8922) 93-94-72.

Ministry of Land Reclamation and Water Economy: 370016 Baku, Azadlyg Sq. 1, Government House.

Ministry of Local Industry: 370016 Baku, Azadlyg Sq. 1, Government House ; tel. (8922) 98-53-25.

Ministry of Material Resources: 370016 Baku, Azadlyg Sq. 1, Government House.

Ministry of National Security: 370016 Baku, Azadlyg Sq. 1, Government House; tel. (8922) 93-10-00.

Ministry of Trade: 370016 Baku, Azadlyg Sq. 1, Government House; tel. (8922) 98-50-74.

President and Legislature

PRESIDENT

Presidential elections were held on 3 October 1993. (President Abulfaz Elchibey, elected on 7 June 1992, was impeached on 25 June 1993. On 29 August, in a referendum of confidence in the President, 97.5% of participants voted in favour of his impeachment. The results of the referendum were endorsed by the Milli Majlis on 1 September.) According to official figures, Heydar Aliyev, Acting President of Azerbaijan, won 98.8% of votes cast. The other two candidates were Zakir Taghiyev and Kerrar Abilov. Heydar Aliyev was inaugurated as President on 10 October 1993.

MILLI MAJLIS
(National Assembly)

From May 1991, following the assumption of power by the Popular Front of Azerbaijan, the Milli Majlis was empowered to act as a standing legislative body and the Supreme Soviet (the highest representative body in the country) was suspended. The Milli Majlis was to have 50 members and was a successor body to a similar National Council or Assembly (of about 70 members) which the full Supreme Soviet voted in favour of in October 1991.

Elections to the Supreme Soviet were held on 30 September and 14 October 1990. Not all the 360 seats were filled, because, owing to security concerns, voting did not take place in 11 constituencies. Some 280 seats were won by the Communist Party of Azerbaijan (disbanded in September 1991).

The Chairman of the Milli Majlis is also Chairman of the Supreme Soviet.

Chairman of the Milli Majlis: RASUL KULIYEV.

Deputy Chairman: AFIYADDIN JALILOV.

Local Government

Azerbaijan includes one autonomous oblast and one autonomous republic.

NAKHICHEVAN AUTONOMOUS REPUBLIC:

Chairman of the Supreme Majlis: (vacant).

Chairman of the Council of Ministers: SHAMSADDIN KHANBABAYEV.

NAGORNY KARABAKH

The status of Nagorny Karabakh is disputed. In September 1991 the local authorities declared the region a republic. In a referendum on 10 December 1991 residents of Nagorny Karabakh voted overwhelmingly for independence. In response, the following month the Azerbaijani Government announced that Nagorny Karabakh was under direct presidential rule. The enclave's Government was replaced by a State Defence Committee in August 1992 when the Nagorny Karabakh legislature declared a state of martial law.

Nagorno-Karabakh Autonomous Oblast

Presidential Plenipotentiary: Col SURAT HUSSEINOV.

'Republic of Nagorny Karabakh'

Chairman of the Nagorny Karabakh Supreme Soviet: KAREN BABURYAN.

Chairman of the State Defence Committee: ROBERT KOCHARYAN.

Chairman of the Government of Nagorny Karabakh: LEVON MELIK-SHAKHNAZARYAN (acting).

Deputy Chairman of the Government: ZHIRAYR POGOSYAN.

Political Organizations

Communist Party of Azerbaijan: Baku; disbanded Sept 1991, re-established Nov. 1993; Gen. Sec. SAYAD SAYADOV.

Independent Azerbaijan Party: Baku; Leader NIZAMI SULEYMANOV.

Istiklal—National Independence: Baku; f. 1992; Chair. ETIBAR MAMEDOV.

Musavat—'Equality' Muslim Democratic Party: Baku; in existence 1911–20; re-established 1992; promotes Islamic values and the unity of Turkic peoples; Chair. ISA GAMBAROV.

Popular Front of Azerbaijan (PFA): Baku; f. 1989; Exec. Chair. IBRAHIM IBRAHIMOV.

Social Democratic Group: 370014 Baku, 28 May St 3–11; tel. (8922) 93-33-78; telex 142272; fax (8922) 98-75-55; f. 1989; 2,000 mems (1990); Chair. ARAZ ALIZADEH.

United Azerbaijan : Baku; Chair. KERRAR ABILOV.

Yeni Azerbaycan—New Azerbaijan: Baku; f. 1992; Chair. HEYDAR ALIYEV.

Other political groups include the Green Party of Azerbaijan and the Democratic Intelligentsia Alliance.

Diplomatic Representation

EMBASSIES IN AZERBAIJAN

China, People's Republic: Baku, Hotel Azerbaijan; tel. (8922) 98-00-10, 98-90-04; Ambassador SUA SUYUAN.

Egypt: Baku, Hotel Respublika; tel. (8922) 92-55-95; Ambassador FARUK AMIN AL-HAVARI.

France: Baku, Hotel Respublika; tel. (8922) 92-79-03, 92-89-77; Ambassador JEAN PERRIN.

Germany: Baku, Taghizade St 59; tel. (8922) 94-88-82; Chargé d'affaires THOMAS TERSTEGEN.

Iran: Baku, B. Sadarov St 4; tel. (8922) 92-64-53, 92-19-32; Ambassador ASGHAR NAHAVANDIAN.

Iraq: Baku, 370000 Khagani St 9; tel. (8922) 93-72-07, 93-82-83; Chargé d'affaires FARUQ SALMAN DAVUD.

Pakistan: Baku, Hotel Azerbaijan; tel. (8922) 98-90-04; Ambassador SAED ISMAT JAUDRI.

Russian Federation: Baku, Hotel Azerbaijan; tel. (8922) 98-90-04; Ambassador VALTER SHONIYA.

Sudan: Baku, Hotel Azerbaijan; tel. (8922) 92-42-81, 92-07-76; Ambassador HASSAN BASHIR ABDELVAHAB.

Turkey: 370000 Baku, Khagani St 27; (8922) 98-81-43, 98-81-35, 98-81-36; Ambassador ALTAN KARAMANOGLU.

United Kingdom: Baku; tel. (8922) 92-89-56; Ambassador THOMAS YOUNG.

USA: Baku, Prospekt Azadlyg 83; tel. (8922) 96-00-19; Ambassador RICHARD MILES.

Judicial System

Chairman of the Supreme Court: TAIR ZAIDAG OGLY KERIMLI.

Procurator-General: ALI OMEROV.

Religion

ISLAM

The majority (some 70%) of Azerbaijanis are Shi'ite Muslims; most of the remainder are Sunni (Hanafi school). The Muslim Board of Transcaucasia is based in Baku. It has spiritual jurisdiction over the Muslims of Armenia, Georgia and Azerbaijan. The Chairman of the Directorate is normally a Shi'ite, while the Deputy Chairman is usually a Sunni.

Muslim Board of Transcaucasia: Baku; Chair. Sheikh ALLASHUKUR PASHEZADE.

The Press

In 1989 there were 151 officially-registered newspaper titles being published in Azerbaijan, including 133 in Azerbaijani, and 95 periodicals, including 55 in Azerbaijani.

PRINCIPAL NEWSPAPERS

(In Azerbaijani except where otherwise stated.)

Adabiyat ve Injisenet: 370146 Baku, B. Avakyan St, Flat 529; tel. (8922) 39-50-37; organ of the Union of Writers of Azerbaijan.

Azadlyg (Liberty): Baku, Akademik Sh. Azizbeyov St 62; f. 1989; weekly; organ of the Popular Front of Azerbaijan; in Azerbaijani and Russian; Editor-in-Chief N. A. NADZAFOV; circ. 142,000.

Azerbaijan: Baku, 28 Aprel by St 4; f. 1989; weekly; publ. by the People's Committee for Relief to Karabakh; in Azerbaijani and Russian; Editor-in-Chief S. H. RUSTAMHANLI; circ. 124,000.

Azerbaijan Ganjlyari (Youth of Azerbaijan): Baku; f. 1919; 3 a week; Editor YU. A. KERIMOV; circ. 161,000.

Bakinsky Rabochy (Baku Worker): 370146 Baku, Metbuat Ave, Flat 529; tel. (8922) 32-11-10; f. 1906; 6 a week; fmrly organ of the Communist Party of Azerbaijan; in Russian; Editor GENNADI G. GLUSHKOV; circ. 68,000.

Hayat (Life): 370146 Baku, Metbuat Ave, Flat 529; f. 1991; 5 a week; publ. by the National Assembly of Azerbaijan; Editor-in-Chief A. H. ASKEROV; circ. 40,000.

Istiglal (Independence): 370014 Baku, 28 May St 3–11; tel. (8922) 93-33-78; telex 142272; fax (8922) 98-75-55; 4 a month; organ of the Social Democratic Group; Editor ZARDUSHT ALIZADEH; circ. 10,000.

Khalg Gazeti: Baku; f. 1919; fmrly *Kommunist*; 6 a week; Editor T. T. RUSTAMOV; circ. 254,000.

Molodezh Azerbaijana (Youth of Azerbaijan): Baku; tel. (8922) 39-00-51; f. 1919; weekly; in Russian; Editor V. EFENDIEV; circ. 11,000.

Respublika (Republic): 370146 Baku, Metbuat Ave, Flat 529; f. 1990; weekly; govt newspaper; Editor-in-Chief A. M. ISAYEV; circ. 57,000.

Sovet Kendi (Soviet Village): 370146 Baku, Metbuat Ave, Flat 529; f. 1923; 5 a week; fmrly publ. by the Communist Party of Azerbaijan; Editor R. M. NAGIYEV; circ. 40,000.

Veten Sesi (The Voice of the Motherland): 370146 Baku, Metbuat Ave, Flat 529; f. 1990; weekly; publ. by the Society of Refugees of Azerbaijan; in Azerbaijani and Russian; Editor-in-Chief T. A. AHMEDOV; circ. 47,000.

Vyshka (The Tower): 370146 Baku, Metbuat Ave, Flat 529; tel. (8922) 39-85-65; fax (892) 39-96-97; f. 1928; 4 a week; independent social-political newspaper; in Russian; Editor H. A. ALIYEV; circ. 50,000.

PRINCIPAL PERIODICALS

Azerbaijan: 370001 Baku, Istiglaliyat St 31; tel. (8922) 92-59-63; f. 1923; monthly; publ. by the Union of Writers of Azerbaijan; recent works by Azerbaijani authors; Editor-in-Chief YUSIF SAMEDOGLU.

Azerbaijan Gadyny (Woman of Azerbaijan): Baku; f. 1923; monthly; illustrated; Editor H. M. HASILOVA.

Dialog (Dialogue): Baku; f. 1989; fortnightly; in Azerbaijani and Russian; Editor R. A. ALEKPEROV.

Grakan Adrbejan: 370001 Baku, Istiglaliyat St 31; tel. (8922) 92-64-93; 6 a year; organ of the Union of Writers of Azerbaijan; in Armenian.

Kend Khayaty (Country Life): Baku; f. 1952; monthly; journal of the Ministry of Agriculture; advanced methods of work in agriculture; in Azerbaijani and Russian; Editor D. A. DAMIRLI.

Kirpi (Hedgehog): Baku; f. 1952; fortnightly; satirical; Editor A. M. AIVAZOV.

Literaturny Azerbaijan (Literature of Azerbaijan): 370001 Baku, Istiglaliyat St 31; tel. (8922) 92-39-31; f. 1931; monthly; journal of the Union of Writers of Azerbaijan; fiction; in Russian; Editor-in-Chief I. P. TRETYAKOV.

Ulus: 370001 Baku, Istiglaliyat St 31; tel. (8922) 92-27-43; monthly; Editor TOFIK DADASHEV.

NEWS AGENCY

Azerinform (Azerbaijan Information Agency): Baku; Dir A. A. SHARIFOV.

Publishers

Azerbaijan Ensiklopediyasy (Azerbaijan Encyclopaedia): 370004 Baku, Boyuk Gala St 41; tel. (8922) 92-87-11; f. 1965; Editor-in-Chief I. O. VELIYEV (acting).

Azerneshr (State Publishing House): Baku, Husi Hajiyev St 4; tel. (8922) 92-50-15; f. 1924; various; Dir NAZIM IBRAGIMOV.

Elm (Azerbaijani Academy of Sciences Publishing House): 370073 Baku, Narimanov Ave 37; scientific books and journals; Dir (vacant).

Gyanjlik (Youth): 370005 Baku, Husi Hajiyev St 4; books for children and young people; Dir E. T. ALIYEV.

Ishyg (Light): 370601 Baku, Gogol St 6; posters, illustrated publs; Dir G. N. ISMAILOV.

Maarif (Education): 370122 Baku, Tagizade St 4; educational books.

Madani-maarif Ishi (Education and Culture): 370146 Baku, Metbuat Ave, Block 529; tel. (8922) 32-79-17; Editor-in-Chief ALOVSAT ATAMALY OGLY BASHIROV.

Medeniyyat (Publishing House of the 'Culture' Newspaper): 370146 Baku, Metbuat Ave, Block 529; tel. (8922) 32-98-38; Dir SHAKMAR AKPER OGLY AKPERZADE.

Shur : 370001 Baku, M. Muchtarov St 6; tel. (8922) 92-93-72; Dir HASHAM ISA OGLY ISABEYLI.

Yazychy (The Writer): 370005 Baku, Natavan St 1; fiction; Dir F. M. MELIKOV.

Radio and Television

National Television and Radio Broadcasting Company: 370011 Baku, Mekhti Hussein St 1; tel. (8922) 92-90-38; telex 142214; fax (8922) 39-54-52; BABEK HUSSEIN OGLY MAMEDOV.

Radio Baku: f. 1926; broadcasts in Azerbaijani, Russian, Arabic, Persian (Farsi), English, Talish, Armenian, Kurdish, Lezgin and Turkish.

Baku Television: f. 1956; programmes in Azerbaijani and Russian.

Niyazi Symphony Orchestra of the State Radio and Television Company: tel. (8922) 39-54-80; Art Man. ISMAIL DJEVDET OGLY HADJIYEV.

Finance

BANKING

(cap. = capital; m. = million; brs = branches; amounts in roubles)

Central Bank

National Bank of Azerbaijan: Baku; f. 1992 as central bank and supervisory authority; Chair. GALIB AGAYEV.

Specialized Banks

Agroprombank—Agricultural Bank: Baku; f. 1992 from br of USSR Agroprombank; one of largest banks in Azerbaijan; 69 brs.

International Bank: 370005 Baku, H. Z. Taguiev St 3; tel. (8922) 93-18-42, 65-11-21; telex 142159, 142370; fax (8922) 93-40-91; f. 1992 to succeed br of USSR Vneshekonombank; carries out all banking services; Chair. VAGUIF K. AKHMEDOV; 2 brs.

Prominvestbank—Industrial Investment Bank: Baku; f. 1992 to succeed br of USSR Prominvestbank.

Sberbank—Savings Bank: Baku; f. 1992 to replace br of USSR Sberbank; 1,330 brs.

Commercial Banks

There are over 90 small commercial and co-operative banks (nine licensed to undertake foreign-exchange transactions during 1992), of which the largest is the following:

Azakbank: 370000 Baku, Khagani St 26; tel. (8922) 98-31-09, 93-24-91; telex 142130; fax (8922) 93-20-85; f. 1991; joint-stock bank with 100% private ownership; first Azerbaijani bank with foreign shareholders; deals with crediting and settlements carried out in local currency and trade and retail banking involving all major operations in foreign currencies; cap. 160m. plus US $400,000, total assets 4,113m. (July 1993)

Trade and Industry

CHAMBER OF COMMERCE

Chamber of Commerce and Industry: 370601 Baku, Istiglaliyat 31/33; tel. (8922) 39-85-03; Chair. KAMRAN ASAD OGLY HUSSEION.

FOREIGN TRADE ORGANIZATION

Azerbintorg: 370004 Baku, Nekrasov St 7; tel. (8922) 93-71-69; telex 212183; imports and exports a wide range of goods (80% of exports in 1991); Dir E. M. HUREYNOV.

PETROLEUM

Azerbaijan State Oil Company: Baku; f. September 1992 following a merger of the two state oil companies, Azerineft and Azneftkimiya; conducts production and exploration activities, oversees refining and capital construction activities; two separate subsidiaries of Azerineft, Azneft (for onshore areas) and Kasmorneftgaz (for offshore areas) also merged; Pres. NATIK ALIYEV.

MAJOR INDUSTRIAL ENTERPRISES

Azinmash (Azerbaijan Scientific, Research and Design Institute of Petroleum Engineering): 370029 Baku, Volodarsky St 4; tel. (8922) 67-28-88; telex 142188; f. 1930; manufactures equipment for petroleum and natural-gas industries; Dir RAUF DJABAROV.

Bakinsky Rabochy Engineering: 370034 Baku; tel. (8922) 25-93-91; telex 142445; equipment for the petroleum industry, including pumping units and pipe transporters; Dir MAMED VELIEV; 1,200 employees.

Transport

RAILWAYS

Railways connect Baku with Tbilisi (Georgia), Makhachkala (Daghestan, Russian Federation) and Yerevan (Armenia). The rail link with Armenia runs through the autonomous republic of Nakhichevan (but is currently disrupted). From Nakhichevan an international line links Azerbaijan with Tabriz (Iran). In 1991 plans were agreed with the Iranian Government for the construction of a rail line between Azerbaijan and Nakhichevan, which would pass through Iranian territory, thus bypassing Armenia.

ROADS

At 31 December 1989 the total length of roads in Azerbaijan was 30,400 km, of which 28,600 km were hard-surfaced.

SHIPPING

Shipping services on the Caspian Sea link Baku with Krasnovodsk (Turkmenistan) and the Iranian ports of Bandar Anzali and Bandar Nowshar.

Shipowning Company

Caspian Shipping Company: 370005 Baku, Rasul Zade St 5; tel. (8922) 93-20-58, 93-51-85; telex 142102; fax (8922) 93-53-39; nationalized by the Azerbaijani Govt in 1991; Pres. T. K. AKHMEDOV.

CIVIL AVIATION

Azerbaijan Airlines: Baku; f. 1992; fleet of 2 Boeing 727-200, TU-134, TU-154.

Culture

NATIONAL ORGANIZATION

Ministry of Culture: see section on The Government (Ministries); organizes International Hari Byul-Byul Folk Festival, Kara Karayev International Festival of Modern Music, Musical September in Baku International Festival.

Nakhichevan Autonomous Republic

Ministry of Culture: 373630 Nakhichevan, Revolution Ave 1; tel. (236) 42252; Minister FATTAKH SAMED OGLY HEYDAROV.

INTERNATIONAL ORGANIZATION

Bakinets: 370000 Baku, Khagani St 16; tel. (8922) 98-81-68; fax (8922) 93-53-39; Pres. FIKRET SAIB OGLY ZARBALIYEV.

CULTURAL HERITAGE

Baku State University Central Library: Baku, Patrice Lumumbu St 23; tel. (8922) 37-43-47; 1,700,000 vols; Librarian S. IBRAHIMOVA.

Central Library of the Azerbaijan Academy of Sciences: 370143 Baku, Narimanova Ave 31; tel. (8922) 38-60-17; f 1925; 2,5000,000 vols; Dir M. M. HASSANOVA.

Central State Archives of Literature and Art: 370106 Baku, S. Bahlulzade Ave 3; tel. (8922) 62-96-53; Dir MAARIF ABY OGLY TEYMUROV.

M. F. Akhundov State Public Library: 370601 Baku, Khagani St 29; tel. (8922) 93-68-01; f. 1923; 3,122,000 vols; Dir K. A. SULEYMAN-ZADE.

Manuscripts Institute of the Academy of Sciences: 370001 Baku, Istiglaliyat St 8; tel. (8922) 92-63-33; Dir Jangir Vagid ogly Kagramanov.

Museum of the History of Azerbaijan of the Azerbaijan Academy of Sciences: 370005 Baku, Malygin St 4; tel. (8922) 93-36-48; f. 1920; 120,000 exhibits on the history of the Azerbaijani people from ancient times; Dir P. A. AZIZBEKOVA.

Nizami Ganjari State Museum of Azerbaijan Literature: 370001 Baku, Istiglaliyat St 53; tel. (8922) 92-18-64; f. 1939; 75,000 exhibits on the history of Azerbaijani literature; Dir H. A. ALLAHYAROGLU.

R. Mustafaev State Art Museum: Baku, Chkalov St 9; 7,000 exhibits; Dir DrZ. M. KYAZIM.

Stepanakert Museum of History of Nagorny Karabakh: Nagorny Karabakh AO, Stepanakert, Gorky St 4; collection on the history of the Armenian people of Nagorny Karabakh (Arthakh).

PERFORMING ARTS

Drama, Opera, Dance

Azerbaijan Marionette Theatre: 370000 Baku, Khagani St 10; tel. (8922) 98-65-94; Dir TARLAN BEYBALA OGLY GORCHIYEV.

Baku Choreography School: 370014 Baku, Byul-Byul Ave 56; tel. (8922) 95-78-07; Dir RIMMA SHAKHBABA KIZI MAMEDOVA.

F. Amirov State Song and Dance Ensemble: 370001 Baku, Istiglaliyat St 2; tel. (8922) 92-51-53, 92-69-94.

Gek-Gel State Song and Dance Ensemble: 374700 Gyanja, Atayeva St 135; tel. (89522) 25321; Art Man. FIKRET SULEYMAN OGLY VERDIYEV.

Mirza Akhundov Opera and Ballet Theatre: Baku, October St 8.

State Academic Drama Theatre: 370000 Baku, Fizuli Sq.; tel. (8922) 94-49-19; Dir GASAN SATTAR OGLY TURABOV.

State Academic Opera and Ballet Theatre: 370000 Baku, Nizamy St 95; tel. (8922) 93-16-51; Dir AKIF TARAN OGLY MELIKOV.

State Dance Ensemble: 370001 Baku, Istiglaliyat St 2; tel. (8922) 92-51-53, 92-69-94; Art Man. AFAK SULEYMAN KIZI MELIKOVA.

State Drama Theatre:

Agdam State Drama Theatre: 374000 Agdam, Sahil St 34; tel. (292) 63578; Dir NAZIR MURSAL OGLY RUSTAMOV.

Fizuli State Drama Theatre: Fizuli; tel. (241) 55277; Dir VAGIF ZULFI OGLY VELIYEV.

Gyanja State Drama Theatre: 374700 Gyanja, A. Abbassade St 62; tel. (89522) 25888; Dir VAGIF ABDULLA OGLY SHARIFOV.

Lenkoran State Drama Theatre: 374311 Lenkoran, 28 May St 16; tel. (271) 54973; Dir ELSHAD ALLAHVERDI OGLY ZEYLANOV.

Mingechaur State Drama Theatre: 374311 Mingechaur, Gagarin St 5; tel. (247) 33958; Dir ZULFUGAR GULU OGLY ABBASOV.

Sheki State Drama Theatre: 374510 Sheki, Azadlyg St 174; tel. (277) 3661; Dir ALOVSAT YUSIF OGLY NASRULLAYEV.

State Musical Comedy Theatre: 3700056 Baku, Azerbaijan Ave 8; tel. (8922) 93-51-01, 93-84-68; Dir GAZANFER RAGIM OGLY TOPCHIYEV.

State Musical Drama Theatre:

Shusha State Musical Drama Theatre: Shusha, 28 May St 4; Dir YADIGAR MAMED OGLY MURADOV.

Sumgait State Musical Drama Theatre: 373200 Sumgait, Azadlyg Sq 5; tel. (264) 59121; Dir and Art Man. AGALAR IDRIS OGLY MEHTIYEV.

State Puppet Theatre: 370004 Baku, Neftyanikov Ave 36; tel. (8922) 92-64-35; Dir RAHMAN RAGIM OGLY HULIYEV.

Gyanja State Puppet Theatre: 374400 Gyanja, Djalil St 195; tel. (89522) 35728; Dir BAYREM APREL OGLY FATALIYEV.

State Russian Drama Theatre: 370000 Baku, Khagani St 7; tel. (8922) 93-40-48; Dir MARAT FARRUKH OGLY IBRAHIMOV.

State Song and Dance Ensemble of Nakhichevan Autonomous Republic: Nakhichevan; tel. (2362) 56898.

State Theatre for Young Spectators: 370000 Baku, Nizami St 72; tel. (8922) 93-88-52; Dir KAMAL GABIL OGLY AZIZOV.

State Youth Theatre: 370000 Baku, Khagani St 10; tel. (8922) 93-29-63; Dir HUSSEINAGS AGAHUSSEIN OGLY ATAKISHIYEV.

Music

Gaya State Variety Orchestra: 370004 Baku, X. Rzayeva St 5; tel. (8922) 92-48-30; Art Man. TEYMUR IBRAHIM OGLY MIRZOYEV.

Gyanja Philharmonia Society State Chamber Orchestra: 374400 Gyanja, Atayevs St 135; tel. (89522) 25321; Art Man. RASIM ISA OGLY BAGIROV.

K. Karayev State Chamber Orchestra: 370001 Baku, Istiglaliyat St 2; tel. (8922) 92-51-53, 92-69-94; Art Man. RAMIZ LYUTFALI OGLY MELIK-ASLANOV.

Model Military Brass Band of the Ministry of Defence: 370004 Baku, S. Vurgun St 12; tel. (8922) 93-64-20; Art Man. YUSIF YEVGENIEVICH AKHUNDSADE.

Mugam Folk Music Theatre: 370004 Baku, Mendjinsky St 9; tel. (8922) 92-49-98; Dir ARIF RAFI OGLY KAZIYOV.

Muslim Magomayev Philharmonia: 370001 Baku, Istiglaliyat St 2; tel. (8922) 92-51-53; Dir RAFIG HUSSEIN OGLY SEIDZEDE.

R. Beybutov State Song Theatre: 370000 Baku, R. Beybutov St 12; (8922) 93-94-15; Dir NIYAZI INGILAB OGLY ASLANOV.

State Brass Band: 370016 Baku, S. Vurgun St 79; tel. (8922) 94-90-40; Art Man. NAZIM MAGERRAM OGLY ALIYEV.

State Conservatoire: 370014 Baku, Sh. Badalbeyli St 98; tel. (8922) 932248; Rector FARHAD SHAMSI OGLY BADALBEYLI.

Tutti Youth Chamber Orchestra: 370004 Baku, Neftyanikov Ave 26; tel. (8922) 92-06-62; fax (8922) 92-48-50; Art Man. TEYMUR ENVER OGLY GEOKCHAYEV.

Uzeyir Hadjibekov State Symphony Orchestra: 370001 Baku, Istiglaliyat St 2; tel. (8922) 92-05-70; Art Man. YALCHIN VASIF OGLY ADIGEZALOV.

Nakhichevan Autonomous Republic

State Musical Drama Theatre: 373630 Nakhichevan, A. Djavad St 2; tel. (236) 2589; Dir RAMIZ OGLY BAGIROV.

State Philharmonia: 373630 Nakhichevan; tel. (236) 56898; Dir MAMED TAHIR OGLY GUMBATOV.

State Puppet Theatre: 373630 Nakhichevan; tel. (236) 43217; Dir ALEKPER HAMED OGLY KASIMOV.

State Song and Dance Ensemble: Nakhichevan; tel. (236) 56898.

ASSOCIATIONS

Azconcert (Concert Tours Union): 370010 Baku, Azerbaijan Ave 59; tel. (8922) 93-81-00; Dir-Gen. ILDRIM ALINAZIR OGLY KASIMOV.

Union of Actors of Azerbaijan: 370000 Baku, Khagani St 10; tel. (8922) 93-17-03; Pres. HASSAN SATTAR OGLY TURABOV.

Union of Composers of Azerbaijan: 370001 Baku, M. Mukhtarov St 6; tel. (8922) 92-65-75; Chair. TOFIK ALEKPER OGLY KULIYEV.

Union of Musicians of Azerbaijan: 370000 Baku, Arts St 9; tel. (8922) 92-67-04; Chair. FARHAD SHAMSI OGLY BADALBAYLI.

Union of Writers of Azerbaijan: 370000 Baku, Khagani St 25; tel. (8922) 93-66-40.

Veten: Baku; f. 1987; cultural organization for developing contacts with Azerbaijanis in other countries; Chair. V. ELCHIN.

Education

Before 1920 Azerbaijan was an important centre of learning among Muslims of the Russian Empire. Under Soviet rule, a much more extensive education system was introduced and the level of literacy was greatly increased from 8.1% in 1926 to over 99% in 1970. The main language of instruction is Azerbaijani, but there are also Russian-language schools and some teaching in Georgian and Armenian. In 1988 79.5% of pupils in general day schools were taught in Azerbaijani, 18.5% in Russian and 1.9% in Armenian. Two schools used Georgian as the language of instruction. In higher education technical subjects are often taught in Russian, but there have been demands that there should be greater use of Azerbaijani. In 1990/91 there were 105,000 students in higher education. There are a number of specialized institutes, which prepare experts for work in the major industries of the Republic. There is one university, in Baku, founded by the nationalist government of independent Azerbaijan, in 1919.

UNIVERSITY

Baku State University: 370073 Baku, Patrice Lumumbu St 23; tel. (8922) 39-01-86; f. 1919; 14 faculties; 1,093 teachers; 12,500 students; Rector M. GASYMOV.

Social Welfare

NATIONAL AGENCIES

Ministry of Health: see section on The Government (Ministries).

Ministry of Labour and Social Protection: see section on the Government (Ministries).

Employment Fund: f. 1991; extrabudgetary govt fund intended to pay unemployment benefits, but insufficient transfers; pays for vocational training.

Social Protection Fund: f. 1992 by merger of Pension Fund and Social Insurance Fund; extrabudgetary govt fund.

HEALTH AND WELFARE ORGANIZATIONS

People's Committee for Relief to Karabakh: Baku; f. 1987; Chair. B. BAIRAMOV.

Society of Refugees of Azerbaijan: Baku; humanitarian organization; aids refugees from Armenia and other regions of inter-ethnic conflict.

The Environment

Considerable environmental damage has resulted from exploitation of the petroleum and gas resources of the Caspian Sea, and from the industrial areas in the east of the Republic. Baku and Sumgait are particularly affected and are major sources of atmospheric and marine pollution. Excessive use of chemicals in agriculture has had a negative impact also. Some regulation, including a Law on the Protection of the Environment, was introduced in 1992–93.

State Committee for Ecology and Use of Natural Resources: 370016 Baku, Azadlyg Sq. 1, Government House; Chair. A. F. MANSUROV.

ACADEMIC INSTITUTES

Academy of Sciences: 370001 Baku, Istiglaliyat St 10; Pres. E. YU. SALAYEV; institutes incl.:

Commission on the Caspian Sea: Baku, Narimanova St 31; in the Dept of Earth Sciences; Chair. K. K. GYUL (acting).

Commission on Nature Conservation: 370001 Baku, Istiglaliyat St 10; in the Dept of Biological Sciences; Chair. G. A. Aliyev.

Institute for the Study of Natural Resources from Space: Baku, Novaya Ketskhoveli 9; in the Dept of Earth Sciences; researches on space and on the ground in environmental protection and information; Dir T. K. ISMAILOV.

Defence

After gaining independence in 1991, Azerbaijan began forming a national army (believed to number 30,000 in mid-1992). The Republic has a share of the Caspian Flotilla. Some mobilization of reserves was reported. The Ministry of Internal Affairs controls a militia of an estimated 20,000. Approximately 12,000 Azerbaijani volunteers (Nagorny Karabakh People's Defence) are reportedly involved in the armed conflict in the enclave. In 1992 2,847.9m. roubles, approximately 14.5% of total projected budget expenditure, was allocated to defence.

Commander: NAJAMEDDIN SADYKHOV.

Bibliography

Cox, C. *Ethnic Cleansing in Progress: War in Nagorno-Karabakh.* Zürich, Institute for Religious Minorities in the Islamic World, 1993.

Fawcett L. *Iran and the Cold War: the Azerbaijan Crisis of 1946.* Cambridge, Cambridge University Press, 1992.

Swietochowski T. *Russian Azerbaijan 1905–1920: The Shaping of National Identity in a Muslim Community.* Cambridge, Cambridge University Press, 1985.

Walker, C. (Ed.). *Armenia Karabagh: The Struggle for Unity.* London, Minority Rights Publs, 1991.

Willerton, J. *Patronage and Politics in the USSR.* Cambridge, Cambridge University Press, 1992.

BELARUS

Geography

PHYSICAL FEATURES

The Republic of Belarus (also known as Belorussia or Byelorussia and, formerly, the Byelorussian Soviet Socialist Republic—BSSR) is situated in north-eastern Europe. Historically, it was also known as White Russia or White Ruthenia. It is bounded by Latvia and Lithuania to the north-west, by Poland to the west, by Ukraine to the south and by the Russian Federation to the east. It covers an area of 207,595 sq km (80,153 sq miles).

The land is a plain with numerous lakes, swamps and marshes. There is an area of low hill country north of Minsk (Miensk), but the highest point, Mount Dzierżynski, is only 346 m (1,135 feet) above sea-level. The southern part of the country is a low, flat marshland. Forests cover some 30% of the territory. The main rivers are the Dnepr (Dnieper), which flows south to the Black Sea, and the Pripyat or Prypiać (Pripet), which flows eastwards, to the Dnepr, through a forested, swampy area, known as the Pripyat Marshes.

CLIMATE

The climate is of a continental type, with an average January temperature, in Minsk, of −5°C (23°F) and an average for July of 19°C (67°F). Average annual precipitation is between 560 mm and 660 mm.

POPULATION

Of a total population at the 1989 census of 10,199,709, 79.4% were Belarusians (also Belorussians, Belarusans or Belarus), 11.9% Russians, 4.2% Poles, 2.4% Ukrainians and 1.4% Jews. There were also small numbers of Tatars (12,436), Roma (Gypsies—10,762), Lithuanians (7,606) and other ethnic groups. From 1990 the official language of the Republic was Belarusian, an Eastern Slavonic language written in the Cyrillic script, although there is also a Belarusian version of the Latin alphabet. This, and the long domination of the area by Russia, complicates the naming and transliteration of places and people. Russified versions of names are often the most familiar, even in Belarus. Thus, at the 1989 census, only 80.2% of Belarusians considered Belarusian to be their native language. The remainder spoke Russian as their first language, although 48% of these claimed fluency in Belarusian as a second language. Some 64% of ethnic Poles claimed Belarusian as their first language, while only some 13% knew Polish.

The major religion is Christianity, the Roman Catholic Church and the Eastern Orthodox Church being the largest denominations. There are also small Muslim and Jewish communities.

At 1 January 1991 the total population was estimated to be 10,260,000. The capital is Minsk, which is situated in the centre of the country. Minsk was also declared to be the headquarters of the Commonwealth of Independent States. It had an estimated population of 1.8m. in 1992. Other important towns are Gomel (Homel or Homiel—an estimated 506,000 in January 1990), in the south-east of the country, Mogilev (Mahilou or Mahiloŭ, 363,000), near the eastern border with Russia, Vitebsk (Vitsebsk or Viciebsk, 356,000), in the north-east, and Brest (Bieraście—formerly Brest-Litovsk—269,000), on the western border with Poland.

Chronology

c. 878: Kievan Rus, the first unified state of the Eastern Slavs, was founded, with Kiev as its capital.

c. 988: Vladimir, ruler of Kievan Rus, converted to Orthodox Christianity.

10th century: The principality of Polotsk (Polatsak or Połacak) became the main centre of power on Belarusian territory, rivalling Kiev and Novgorod for predominance within Rus.

1054: Death of Yaroslav I ('the Wise') signalled the dissolution of the Kievan state into rival principalities, the main ones in Belarus being those of Polotsk and Turov (Turau).

1240–1263: Rule of Mindaugas (Mindouh), in Novogrudok (Navahradak), who formed the Grand Duchy of Lithuania (Litva) and Rus. His state covered the western territories of Rus, including Minsk, Vitebsk and Polotsk, which had not fallen to the Mongol Tatars in the previous century, and eastern Lithuania. Orthodox Slavs predominated in the state and a precursor of Belarusian was the official language. The capital was later moved to Vilnius.

1386: Marriage of Jagiełło (Jahaila, baptized Wladyslaw in 1386) of Lithuania and Jadwiga (Hedwig) of Poland established the union of the two states; subsequent treaties ensured Litva and Rus remained an autonomous Grand Duchy under Poland.

1569: The Grand Duchy of Litva, Rus and Samogitia (the latter—the 'lowlands', in western Lithuania—having been added in the 15th century) surrendered its separate status by the Union of Lublin, as part of an attempt to strengthen the Jagiellon Polish-Lithuanian state, which was threatened by Sweden, the Ottoman Turks and the Russians.

1596: The Union of Brest ('Lithuanian' Brest or Brest-Litovsk) secured the allegiance of part of the Eastern Orthodox Church for the Pope, the head of the Roman Catholic Church; the creation of this 'Greek Catholic' or Uniate Church was part of a process of attempting to catholicize the confessionally mixed Polish state, which had begun with the evangelization of the pagan ethnic Lithuanians and moved on to the repression of Protestantism.

1696: Old Belarusian was replaced by Polish as the language of official documentation in the Grand Duchy.

1772: Parts of Belarus were incorporated into the Russian Empire (the ruler of which had been proclaimed 'Tsar of all the Russias' since 1721) at the First Partition of Poland.

1793: Second Partition of Poland; acquisition by Russia of the rest of Belarus.

1839–40: The tsarist authorities intensified russification in the North-Western Territories, as Belarusian lands were known: the Uniate Church was disbanded and the terms Belarus and Belarusian were banned.

1861: Emancipation of the serfs throughout the Russian Empire.

1902: The Belarusian Revolutionary (later Socialist) Hramada was founded; it became the leading Belarusian nationalist organization.

1 August 1914: Russia entered the First World War against Germany, Turkey and Austria (the Central Powers); the tsarist military headquarters (Stavka) was based in Mogilev (Mahilou or Mahiloŭ), now in Belarus; from 1915 western Belarus was occupied by the Germans.

2 March (New Style: 15 March) 1917: Abdication of Tsar Nicholas II after demonstrations and strikes in Petrograd (St Petersburg), the imperial capital.

5 August (18 August) 1917: A Rada (Council) was proclaimed in Belarus, following the assembly of a 'national council' in the previous month; the Rada was predominantly Socialist Revolutionary in nature, aiming for an autonomous republic under the Petrograd Provisional Government.

15 November (28 November) 1917: Bolshevik troops arrived in Minsk (Miensk) from Petrograd, where Lenin (Vladimir Ilych Ulyanov) and his Bolshevik allies had assumed power; the Bolsheviks took control of the city against little resistance.

28 December 1917 (10 January 1918): An All-Belarusian Congress proclaimed Belarus a democratic republic and refused to recognize Bolshevik power on Belarusian territory; the Bolsheviks disbanded the Congress, but it elected a Rada, which continued to work in secret.

14 February (Old Style: 1 February) 1918: First day upon which the Gregorian Calender took effect in the Bolshevik territories.

21 February 1918: Bolshevik troops were forced to withdraw, as German forces occupied Minsk.

3 March 1918: By the Treaty of Brest-Litovsk, Soviet Russia ceded much territory to Germany, including Belarus, and recognized Ukrainian independence.

25 March 1918: The Belarusian Rada declared the independence of the state, as the Belarusian National Republic, but it only achieved limited autonomy under German military rule.

23 December 1918: Following the collapse of German power, the Russian Communist leadership decided a Soviet Socialist Republic (SSR) should be established in the largely reoccupied Belarus.

1 January 1919: Proclamation of an independent Belarusian SSR, despite sentiments in Russia for the absorption of the territory.

February 1919: The Bolsheviks replaced the Belarusian SSR with a short-lived Lithuanian-Belarusian SSR ('Litbel'—in recognition of their common history).

March 1919: Polish armies invaded Belarus (declared part of Poland), Lithuania and Ukraine.

11 July 1920: Soviet troops recaptured Minsk, after more than one year of civil war and war with Poland; the following day, by the Treaty of Moscow, the Soviet regime recognized Lithuanian independence and subsequently ceded some Belarusian territory; the Belarusian SSR was re-established in the following month.

16 January 1921: Soviet Russia recognized the Belarusian SSR and signed an alliance with the nominally independent state.

18 March 1921: Poland retained about one-third of Belarus, in the west, by the Treaty of Riga, which formally concluded the Soviet–Polish War.

30 December 1922: Four Soviet 'Union Republics' proclaimed the Union of Soviet Socialist Republics (USSR), of which the Belarusian SSR was a constituent and nominally independent member, despite a union with Russia being urged by Stalin (Iosif V. Dzhugashvili).

1924: The Belarusian SSR was virtually doubled in size when the territories of Vitebsk (Vitsebsk or Viciebsk) and Mogilev were formally transferred from Russian jurisdiction.

October 1926: Gomel (Homel or Homiel) was transferred from the Russian Federation to the Belarusian SSR.

1933: The Soviet Government claimed to discover a 'Belarusian National Centre', backed by Poland, which was the excuse for mass arrests of Belarusian officials and Party members; furthermore, the peasantry were enduring much hardship during the forcible collectivization of agriculture.

September 1939: The Soviet army occupied western Belarus (Polish since 1921), in accordance with the Nazi–Soviet Pact, signed in August.

3 November 1939: The Communists ensured that the new territories (which increased the Belarusian SSR by one-half in area) voted for incorporation into the USSR.

22 June 1941: The Germans violated the Nazi–Soviet Pact by invading the USSR in 'Operation Barbarossa'; under German leader Adolf Hitler's plan, Belarus was marked for ethnic German settlement (*Ostland*) and the expulsion of natives.

28 June 1941: Minsk was occupied by German forces; a 'puppet' regime under Ivan Yermachenko was subsequently established, although the Germans also encountered partisan resistance.

December 1943: At an Allied conference in Tehran (Iran), the USSR insisted that it should not only have all of Belarus and Ukraine, but its western border should be along the Oder River.

4 July 1944: Soviet troops recaptured Minsk; during the war about one-quarter of the population of Belarus died (pre-1941 population levels were not regained until 1970) and massive damage was done throughout the republic.

26 June 1945: The USSR, the USA, the United Kingdom, China and 46 other countries, including the Belarusian and Ukrainian SSRs, in their own right, signed the Charter of the United Nations.

1946–48: A mass purge of the Communist Party of Belarus (CPB) resulted in the replacement of many ethnic Belarusian officials by Russians.

October 1980: Piotr Masherau, First Secretary of the CPB since 1965, was killed in suspicious circumstances, apparently after an argument with Leonid Brezhnev, General Secretary of the all-Union Communist Party.

April 1986: An explosion occurred at a nuclear reactor in Chernobyl (Ukraine), 10 km south of the Belarusian border, which resulted in discharges of radioactive material; much of the 30-km exclusion zone around the disaster site was in Belarusian territory and over 20% of the republic was severely affected.

30 October 1988: A demonstration in Minsk to commemorate the victims of Stalinism (partly prompted by the discovery of mass graves at Kurapaty, near Minsk) was violently dispersed by security forces.

June 1989: The Belarusian Popular Front (BPF) was founded, its inaugural congress being in Vilnius (Lithuania).

28 January 1990: The Supreme Soviet (Supreme Council) enacted a law replacing Russian as the official language with Belarusian, which was also mandated as the language of education (transition periods of up to 10 years were, however, permitted).

25 February 1990: A BPF rally in Minsk was attended by some 150,000 protesters, demanding extra funds to deal with the consequences of the Chernobyl disaster, a major focus of opposition activity in Belarus.

4 March 1990: For the elections to the republican Supreme Council, the BPF was obliged to join the Belarus Democratic Bloc; although the Bloc won about one-quarter of the seats decided by popular ballot, the Communists still controlled some 84% of the total number of seats in the legislature.

27 July 1990: The Supreme Council, after increasing popular pressure, declared the state sovereignty of Belarus (claiming the right to form its own armed forces, issue its own currency and conduct its own foreign policy), but rejected the possibility of secession.

17 March 1991: In the all-Union referendum on the future of the USSR, 83% voted for a reformed Soviet federation, the highest proportion in any republic outside Central Asia.

25 August 1991: Following the collapse of the attempted coup in Moscow, the Supreme Council of Belarus adopted a declaration of independence; the Communist leadership resigned and the CPB was suspended.

19 September 1991: Formal election of Stanislau Shushkevich (Šuškevič), a physicist with a reputation as a reformist, as Chairman of the Supreme Council (head of state), replacing Nikolai Dementei (Mikalai Dzemtyantsei); the name of the state was changed to the Republic of Belarus.

18 October 1991: Representatives of Belarus joined seven other Union Republics in signing a treaty which established an Economic Community between the signatories.

8 December 1991: The leaders of Belarus, the Russian Federation and Ukraine met near Brest and agreed to form a Commonwealth of Independent States (CIS) to replace the USSR; the headquarters of the organization was to be in Minsk.

21 December 1991: At a meeting in Almaty (Kazakhstan) the leaders of 11 former Soviet Republics, including Belarus, signed a protocol on the formation of the Commonwealth.

30 December 1991: The 11 members of the CIS agreed, in Minsk, to establish a joint command for armed forces; use of nuclear weapons was to be under the control of the Russian Federation's President, after consultation with other Commonwealth leaders and the agreement of the presidents of Belarus, Kazakhstan and Ukraine.

23 June 1992: Belarus and Poland signed a Treaty of Neighbourly Relations and Friendly Co-operation, which included mutual recognition of the existing border. Later in the month a Party of Communists of Belarus (PCB) was legally recognized.

20–22 July 1992: A series of agreements between Belarus and the Russian Federation strengthened co-operation between the two countries, notably in military and economic affairs, and seemed to envisage some sort of confederation; the USA agreed to provide Belarus with US $59m. in order to assist with the removal of its nuclear weapons to Russia.

29 October 1993: The Supreme Council rejected a petition, signed by 383,000 people, in support of the BPF's demand for new parliamentary elections.

3 February 1993: The Supreme Council approved adherence to the Treaty on the Non-Proliferation of Nuclear Weapons and ratified the first Strategic Arms Reduction Treaty (START 1); the following day the Supreme Council voted to end the suspension of the CPB, which had been in force since August 1991.

9 April 1993: The Supreme Council voted to subscribe to the Tashkent Agreement (the CIS Treaty on Collective Security), but with limits on military service by Belarusian citizens outside the country; Shushkevich, however, refused to sign the Agreement, claiming it jeopardized Belarus's commitment to neutrality.

10 July 1993: The Governments of Belarus, Russia and Ukraine committed themselves to the closer economic integration of the three countries.

8 September 1993: The prime ministers of Russia and Belarus agreed to create a unified monetary system embracing the two countries; Russia also agreed to continue supplying Belarus with natural gas at subsidized prices.

26 January 1994: Shushkevich, who had yielded to pressure to sign the Tashkent Agreement the previous month, lost reformist support, enabling the conservative parliament to dismiss him from office, for 'corruption'. Vyachyslau Kuznetsou, the First Deputy Chairman of the Supreme Council, became acting head of state.

28 January 1994: Myacheslau Hryb (Gryb), a pro-Russian conservative, was elected Chairman of the Supreme Council.

15 March 1994: The Supreme Council approved the final version of a new Constitution declaring Belarus a presidential republic—elections for an executive President were subsequently scheduled for June.

History

Dr ANDREW RYDER

The area of present-day Belarus was inhabited by Slavs from at least the ninth century AD, and probably earlier. At the end of the 13th century a Grand Duchy of Lithuania and Rus was formed from Belarusian and Lithuanian lands. The Grand Duchy ('Litva'), in which Old Belarusian was the state language, united with Poland in the 16th century. Belarusian lands remained under Polish control until the partitions of Poland in 1772–95, when they became part of the Russian Empire. In the 19th century there was a growth of national consciousness among Belarusian intellectuals, but attempts to assert a Belarusian national identity were strongly opposed by the tsarist authorities, who considered the Belarusian language merely a dialect of Russian and refused to accept the concept of a Belarusian nation. Although Belarus never existed as an independent state, as such, it did have a distinct culture, mainly preserved by the peasantry, and a distinct language. However, the national movement did not initially gather significant popular support.

THE ESTABLISHMENT OF SOVIET BELARUS

With the collapse of tsarist authority, in July 1917 a Belarusian national council, or Rada, was formed in Minsk (Miensk). This move appears to have been inspired by the example of the Ukrainians to the south, who had established a similar body in April. However, the nationalists had little popular support and the declaration of a Belarusian republic, on 28 December 1917, by an All-Belarusian Congress had no lasting significance. Bolshevik forces loyal to Lenin's newly-established regime in Petrograd (St Petersburg, Russia) had seized power in Minsk, in November 1917, and they dissolved the Congress at the end of December, despite the promises of the Bolsheviks to nations of the Russian Empire that they would be permitted self-determination. Bolshevik troops only withdrew from Minsk when German troops occupied the city in February 1918. German occupation was formalized by the Treaty of Brest-Litovsk, signed by Germany and the Soviet regime in March, in the city of Brest (Bieraście). The Treaty ceded Russian control of a large swathe of western territory, running from the Baltic to the Black Sea, including Belarus. On 25 March Belarus again declared its independence, as the Belarusian National Republic (BNR), but it achieved only a limited measure of autonomy under German military rule.

The defeat of Germany in the First World War, at the end of 1918, changed the situation yet again. The Treaty of Brest-Litovsk was abrogated and German troops began to withdraw. Meanwhile, in Moscow, the Bolshevik Government of the newly created Russian Soviet Federative Socialist Republic (RSFSR) had changed its policy towards Belarus. Although earlier the Communist leadership had been unwilling to recognize the existence of a Belarusian nation, and consequently its right to self-determination, it now seemed that the Bolsheviks wanted to create a semi-independent socialist Belarusian republic, as one in a series of 'buffer' states separating Soviet Russia from Germany and central Europe. Accordingly, Bolshevik troops entered Belarus as the Germans withdrew, and a Belarusian Soviet Socialist Republic (SSR) was proclaimed on 1 January 1919.

This failed to remove the uncertainty over the future of the new Republic. In mid-January 1919 the Russian Communist Party (Bolsheviks)—RCP(B)—urged that the new Republic, as well as other newly established Soviet Republics, be absorbed by Russia. This scheme was soon replaced by a proposal for a military merger between the two. In March, however, the Belarusian SSR was merged with Lithuania, which was also then under Communist control, to form a new SSR, known as 'Litbel'. The new Republic lasted less than one month, before Polish troops invaded in April 1919, occupied most of its territory and declared Belarus part of Poland. Until 1921 control of Belarus passed back and forth between Soviet and Polish forces. Minsk was retaken by Soviet forces in July 1920 and, one month later, the Belarusian SSR was re-established. Finally, in March 1921, the Treaty of Riga was signed, which allocated the western one-third of Belarusian lands to Poland, while in the east the Belarusian SSR was firmly established.

BELARUS IN THE USSR

It was soon evident that the formal attributes of independence would not provide Belarus with control over its own affairs. The Government of the Belarusian SSR was controlled by the Communist Party of Belarus (CPB), which, in turn, was an integral part of the RCP(B). Government and state bodies of the RSFSR were increasingly taking over responsibility for Belarusian affairs. However, the Belarusian SSR was permitted to enter into diplomatic relations with other countries and to formulate and conclude its own treaties with other states. This ambiguous situation was finally resolved on 30 December 1922, when the Union of Soviet Socialist Republics (USSR) was proclaimed, with the Belarusian SSR as one of four founding members. Belarusian affairs were now largely controlled by the all-Union authorities in Moscow. Nevertheless, the Republic retained some formal vestiges of autonomy. In 1945, for example, it became one of the founding members of the United Nations (UN).

Initially, the Belarusian SSR embraced the area around Minsk and territories extending south to the border of Ukraine. Under Soviet rule, the borders of Belarus were expanded on three occasions. In 1924 Vitebsk (Vitsebsk or Viciebsk) and Mogilev (Mahilou or Mahiloŭ) provinces were transferred from Russian to Belarusian jurisdiction. In 1926 Gomel (Homel or Homiel) province was also transferred from the RSFSR. Finally, in 1939 the area of the Republic was substantially increased when western Belarus, which had been under Polish control since 1921, was annexed by the USSR and made part of the Belarusian SSR.

Under Soviet rule, the Republic suffered severely. In the early 1930s, during the programme of forced collectivization, many peasants were killed or deported. During the 1930s political repression engulfed the entire Republic, although intellectual and political leaders suffered disproportionately, with most of the Belarusian cultural and political élite executed or imprisoned. During the Second World War the Republic was occupied by German forces for three years, from 1941 to 1944. As many as 2.2m. people were estimated to have died in Belarus during the War, about 25% of the population. The Republic did not again reach its pre-1941 population until 1970. During the War as much as 80% of the Republic's housing was damaged and much of its industrial capacity and transport system was destroyed. Moreover, as a result of the War, there were significant demographic changes in Belarus. The large Jewish population was mostly destroyed by the Germans, while many Poles left the newly incorporated region of western Belarus to live in Poland. Thus post-War Belarus had a high proportion of Belarusians in the population, although large-scale immigration by ethnic Russians after 1945 undermined Belarusian dominance.

Despite the destruction during the War, and relatively late industrialization, the Belarusian SSR was one of the most prosperous regions of the USSR. By the early 1980s it also had one of the most illiberal leaderships of any Soviet Republic. Perhaps as a result of these two factors, Soviet leader Mikhail Gorbachev's policies of *glasnost* (openness) and *perestroika* (restructuring) initially had little impact in Belarus. However, towards the end of the 1980s there were growing demands for the preservation of the Belarusian language, prompted by the continuing russification of the Republic. In 1989 some 80% of ethnic Belarusians in the Republic spoke Belarusian as their native language, the remainder speaking Russian as a mother tongue. No other nationality of republican status in the USSR had such a high proportion of nationals unable to speak their own language, or such a high proportion of nationals speaking Russian. The main reason for this trend was the predominance of the Russian language in the education system. In 1980 only 35% of all pupils in the Republic were taught in Belarusian; the rest were taught in Russian. By 1989 the proportion of pupils taught in Belarusian had dropped to just 20.8% and, in the Republic's major cities, there were no Belarusian-language schools at all.

In addition to the language issue, the consequences of the Chernobyl disaster (an explosion in a Ukrainian nuclear reactor, just to the south of the border with Belarus, which was severely affected by the consequent radiation fall-out), in April 1986, led to increased activity by environmental groups. However, any overt political opposition or public criticism of the Government or of Communist Party policies was firmly stifled. This was demonstrated by the violent suppression of an anti-Stalinist demonstration in October 1988. However, despite the opposition of the republican authorities, an opposition political movement, the Belarusian Popular Front (BPF), was founded in June 1989, but its organizers were forced to hold the inaugural congress in Vilnius, Lithuania. The BPF's campaign on the use of Belarusian did have some success. The Supreme Soviet or Supreme Council (the legislature) finally voted to adopt Belarusian as the state language (in place of Russian), on 28 January 1990, and mandated the use of Belarusian in education. However, the transitional period was, in some cases, as long as 10 years.

The BPF was not officially permitted to campaign in the elections to the Belarusian Supreme Council and local councils on 4 March 1990. Instead, BPF candidates joined other opposition groups in the Belarusian Democratic Bloc. The democrats won about one-quarter of the seats decided by popular vote (310 of 360 deputies, the remainder being filled by deputies delegated from the CPB and its affiliates), a surprisingly successful outcome, considering the republican authorities' control over the mass media and the electoral procedure. However, the Supreme Council was still overwhelmingly dominated by deputies loyal to the CPB leadership (84% of deputies were members of the CPB), and the BPF faction in the parliament had only about 30 members.

Despite their limited numbers, the BPF deputies seemed to have considerable influence in the new legislature. They successfully campaigned for a declaration of state sovereignty, which the Belarusian Supreme Council adopted on 27 July 1990 (all deputies present voted for the document, but 115 did not take part in the debate at all). The declaration asserted the right of the Republic to organize its own armed forces, create a national currency, and manage its own domestic and foreign policies. However, the declaration remained little more than a symbolic document, and any attempt to put its principles into practice was firmly opposed by the Communist majority in the Supreme Council.

Little popular support for secession from the USSR was evident at the referendum on the future of the Union, in March 1991: 83% of voters supported a 'renewed union', the highest proportion in any Soviet Republic outside Central Asia. However, Belarus's reputation as one of the most stable of the Soviet Union Republics was threatened by a series of strikes in April. The strikers held large demonstrations in Minsk, demanding wage rises and the cancellation of a new sales tax, but also announced political demands, including the resignation of the Government. The strikes only ended when the Government made certain economic concessions, including high wage increases, but all the workers' political demands were rejected.

INDEPENDENT BELARUS

During the attempted coup in Moscow, in August 1991, the Belarusian Supreme Council remained ambivalent in its attitude to the putschists, but the leadership of the CPB gave the State Committee for the State of Emergency (SCSE) its full support. Following the collapse of the coup, therefore, Nikolai Dementei (Mikalai Dzemyantsei), First Secretary of the CPB and Chairman of the Supreme Council, was forced to resign. On 25 August the Supreme Council declared the formal independence of Belarus, gave the 1990 Declaration of State Sovereignty constitutional force and temporarily suspended the activities of the the CPB and the CPSU in Belarus. Dementei was replaced as Chairman of the Supreme Council (initially in an acting capacity) by Stanislau Shushkevich (Šuškevič), a centrist politician, well-known for his criticism of government negligence in the aftermath of the Chernobyl disaster. On 19 September he was formally elected to the post (equivalent to head of state) by the Supreme Council, which also voted to change the name of the country to the Republic of Belarus. Belarusian independence was confirmed on 8 December 1991, when Belarus was one of the signatories to the Minsk Agreement (together with Russia and Ukraine), which established the Commonwealth of Independent States (CIS) and effectively dissolved the USSR. The headquarters of the new organization was to be in Minsk. The foundation of the CIS was confirmed by the Almaty Declaration of 11 former Union Republics, on 21 December, and the dissolution of the USSR was finalized by the resignation of Gorbachev as the last Soviet President four days later. Belarus then gained international recognition as an independent state.

In January 1992 the BPF began a campaign for a referendum on whether elections should be held to the Supreme Council in late 1992 (more than two years earlier than required by the Constitution), and whether a new, more democratic electoral law should be introduced. By May the campaigners had collected 383,000 signatures (after the Central Electoral Commission had disqualified some 58,000 signatures) on a petition demanding a referendum, 23,000 more than were legally required to ensure that a referendum would have to take place. However, the Supreme Council session that should have met to decide a date for the referendum, was delayed for six months. When it did convene, in October, the Supreme Council rejected the petition, claiming that it suffered from massive irregularities, although no evidence was offered to support such a view. As a concession to the opposition, deputies voted to permit new elections to the legislature in March 1994, one year earlier than scheduled. Concern expressed by, among others, the US Government, concerning the banning of the referendum, was dismissed by the Supreme Council as 'interference in Belarus's internal affairs'. The dispute over the referendum demonstrated clearly that the Supreme Council remained firmly under the control of conservative deputies, largely opposed to economic and political reforms, and with some even opposed to Belarusian independence.

Belarus's still influential Communists were given considerable encouragement in June 1992, when a new Communist party, the Party of Communists of Belarus (PCB), was permitted to legally register. Operating largely in secret, it had already enroled 15,000 members and claimed to be the largest political party in the country. In February 1993, moreover, the old, Soviet-era CPB was re-legalized. Initially, there were fears that the newly legalized CPB would unite with the PCB to form a formidable political party. However, neither set of leaders was willing to be absorbed by the other party's hierarchy and the two groups continued to compete for the legacy of the pre-1991 CPB. Nevertheless, the two parties united in a loose coalition, the Popular Movement of Belarus, with 16 other extremist groups (a mixture of Communist, Russian supremacist and neo-Fascist), the avowed aim of which was to unite Belarus with Russia. Democratic and nationalist forces were also divided into several small parties and organizations, the largest of which was the BPF (not officially a political party), which claimed some 500,000 supporters. Only the BPF and the Social Democratic Assembly (Hramada) had deputies in the legislature; other parties were little more than groups of like-minded activists.

Shushkevich appeared to have been chosen as Chairman of the Supreme Council because he was not part of the Communist *apparat* (although he remained a member of the CPB until August 1991) and, indeed, had no strong links with any major political movement. Although this might have initially been considered a favourable characteristic, it left Shushkevich significantly disadvantaged in the Supreme Council. Confronted by the legislature's continued hostility towards reform, an increasingly influential Communist Party and the Government's repeated insistence that Belarus should join a Slav federation, Shushkevich became more closely associated with the opposition BPF and its allies. Relations between Shushkevich and Vyacheslau Kebich, the Chairman of the Council of Ministers (Prime Minister), became increasingly strained, reflecting a conflict between different branches of government common in much of the former USSR. Towards the end of 1992 the executive branch appeared to be increasingly strong, with Kebich and the Council of Ministers often unilaterally issuing decrees, without consulting the Supreme Council. The control of the Council of Ministers was enhanced by its ownership of most of the mass media. The Government remained in control of radio and television broadcasts and also funded about 80% of the popular press, including most national daily newspapers. In the difficult economic situation the Government remained the main source of press finance.

A draft of a new constitution was completed in late 1991, but many of its provisions were strongly opposed by the conservative factions in the Supreme Council, notably the new name of the country, the new national symbols, the provisions concerning free enterprise and private ownership and some sections on human rights. A second draft constitution was submitted to parliament in late 1992, but was also not adopted. Among other things, the new basic law, in the form discussed by the Supreme Council in October 1992, proposed replacing the 360-seat Supreme Council with a new 160-member legislature, to be called the Soim (Assembly). The final version of the Constitution, eventually adopted by the Supreme Council on 15 March 1994, provided for a directly elected executive President (elections were later scheduled for June). By this time Shushkevich had been ousted from power and replaced, on 28 January 1994, by a conservative former police chief, Myacheslau Hryb, who supported the country's moves towards closer integration with Russia. Hryb, Kebich, Shushkevich and Zianon Pazniak (Zenon Pozdnyak was the russified version of his name), the BPF leader, were likely to contest presidential elections.

FOREIGN AND DEFENCE POLICY

Although Belarus was a founding member of the UN, it had no independent foreign policy until 1991. By late 1992 it had been recognized by over 100 countries, but had done relatively little to develop contacts beyond its immediate neighbours and in the CIS. In most countries Belarus continued to be represented diplomatically under the aegis of the Russian Federation, a situation that appeared likely to persist into the mid-1990s. Belarus did develop good relations with Poland (there was a 20% increase in Polish–Belarusian trade in 1991) and, in June 1992, the two countries signed a treaty guaranteeing the inviolability of the Polish–Belarusian border. Poland also offered assistance in establishing Belarusian fishing and merchant fleets. Many more nationalist politicians encouraged a relationship with Poland as a way of reducing reliance on and dominance by the Russian Federation. In terms of trade, however, Belarus's main partner was Germany, which dominated foreign investment in the country.

The main focus of Belarus's foreign policy, however, was towards the member states of the CIS and, above all, Russia. Belarus and Russia established diplomatic relations in June 1992 and, in July, Vyacheslau Kebich and Yegor Gaydar, the premier of Russia, signed a series of documents which were intended to strengthen relations between the two countries. The accords envisaged close military and economic co-operation, to the extent that some observers argued that they almost amounted to the establishment of a Belarusian–Russian confederation within the CIS. Belarus ceded to Russia its share of Soviet assets abroad, in exchange for Russia agreeing to take responsibility for Belarus's share of the foreign debt of the former USSR.

Strengthened ties with Russia and the CIS were the subject of domestic controversy and were opposed by the BPF and its allies, who argued that they represented the renewal of Russian domination over Belarus. Shushkevich, in a more moderate form, was also wary of close ties with Russia, especially in military affairs. However, closer co-operation was strongly supported by Kebich and his supporters in the Government and by many deputies in the Supreme Council. More radical groups, ranging from neo-Communists, such as the PCB and the CPB, to right-wing, 'Great' Russian nationalist groups, such as the neo-Fascist White Rus party, were opposed to Belarusian independence in any form. They sought either the recreation of the USSR in some form or Belarusian absorption into Russia.

In July 1993 the prime ministers of the Russian Federation, Ukraine and Belarus signed a declaration on economic integration which committed them to co-ordinate more closely their economic and political policies so as to promote the re-establishment of a 'common economic space'. As was the case with the earlier agreement between Belarus and the Russian Federation, it was suggested that this would go much further than economic union and would embrace aspects of political, military and legislative affairs. The three Governments envisaged that, in the short term, the agreement would lead to the removal of trade barriers and allow citizens of each of the three countries to live, work and buy property in the others.

In military affairs, Belarus made little progress in establishing an independent defence policy. As one of the four nuclear powers created by the collapse of the USSR, in May 1992 Belarus signed the Lisbon Protocol to the Treaty on the Non-Proliferation of Nuclear Weapons, which committed it to transfer all its nuclear weapons to Russia by 1999. The Belarusian Supreme Council ratified the Treaty in February 1993. In August 1993 it was announced that all remaining nuclear missiles (about 50 SS-25 intercontinental ballistic missiles) would leave Belarus by the end of 1996. In mid-1992 Belarus took over control of former Soviet troops still on its territory, although these troops remained under joint CIS/Russian command. Officially, Belarus was to form its own armed forces, which would eventually number between 90,000 and 100,000. However, this was a long-term goal. One of the main problems was that Belarusians constituted only 20% of the staff in the Ministry of Defence and less than 30% of officers in the Belarusian armed forces, the remainder being mainly ethnic Russians.

The most controversial aspect of security policy was the dispute regarding Belarus's adherence to the Treaty on Collective Security (the so-called Tashkent Agreement), signed by six CIS states in May 1992. Belarus did not sign the Treaty initially, claiming it contradicted the Belarusian Constitution, but, in April 1993, the Supreme Council voted to authorize its Chairman, Stanislau Shushkevich, to sign the Agreement. The Supreme Council did impose conditions on Belarusian inclusion in the security pact, notably that Belarusian troops could not serve outside the country and that no foreign troops could be stationed in Belarus without the consent of the Belarusian Government. The proposal was supported by Kebich and his Government, not least because it would help to protect Belarus's large military-industrial complex, which had been severely affected by the dissolution of the USSR. It was opposed by Shushkevich and the BPF on the grounds that it would lead to continued Russian domination of the country and would commit the Republic to participate in armed conflicts in the Russian Federation and elsewhere in the CIS. Above all, they argued that accession to the Treaty would violate the 1990 declaration of state sovereignty, which committed the country to neutrality. Shushkevich ignored the vote in the Supreme Council and refused to sign the Tashkent Agreement, claiming that it would be 'a betrayal of the country's sovereignty' for the sake of Russian petroleum supplies. In December he yielded, thereby losing BPF support and thus, eventually, his post.

CONCLUSION

After two centuries of russification it was not surprising that Belarusian independence remained a controversial issue long after it was formally declared in 1991. The process of state-building which continued in the Baltic states and Ukraine was much slower in Belarus, partly because of the low level of national self-consciousness in the country. Relations with Russia dominated the political agenda in 1992–93 and most observers expected a much closer union between the two states in the near future. Economic and constitutional reform was repeatedly delayed by the Supreme Council and was hardly encouraged by the Government of Vyacheslau Kebich. Consequently, economic survival depended largely on close co-operation with Russia, with inevitable political consequences. The democratic opposition represented by the BPF was too weak to force the Government to resign or to hold new elections. Nevertheless, if elections were to take place in 1994, the BPF and the two Communist parties would probably be among the best organized political forces in the country. The political polarization which could result would represent a danger to the stability that Belarus had enjoyed so far.

The Economy

ANDREW RYDER

INTRODUCTION

Belarus had comparatively few natural resources and, at the beginning of the 1990s, an industrial base heavily dependent on the former Soviet military-industrial complex and an agricultural sector suffering from structural defects and the after-effects of the Chernobyl disaster. Nevertheless, economic performance declined slightly less drastically than in some other former Soviet states following the dissolution of the USSR. However, this was largely a result of the leadership's reluctance to embark on full-scale economic transition to a market economy. Most observers estimated that marked declines in production and the standard of living would be experienced in 1993 and 1994, possibly forcing the Government to pursue more radical economic policies, which, in turn, would have a further negative impact on the standard of living.

Within the former USSR, Belarus was generally considered a high-income Republic and its economy consistently performed at levels above the USSR average. By 1985 aggregate levels of industrialization and the industrial sector's share of employment had surpassed the all-Union average. With 3.6% of the total population of the USSR, Belarus accounted for 4.1% of industrial output and 4.0% of industrial employment. Industrial output per head was 14.5% greater than the all-Union average and, throughout the 1980s, the rate of increase in inward investment was substantially above the USSR average, showing the highest rate of increase of any Soviet Republic in 1986–88. In the 1970s and 1980s rates of return on investment also appeared to be substantially higher (18%–19%) than the all-Union average, as were rates of increase of labour productivity. The latter figure was consistently the highest in the USSR throughout the 1980s. In 1991 Belarus's gross national product (GNP) per head was put at some US $3,110, only surpassed among former Soviet states by Estonia, Latvia and the Russian Federation.

Despite these promising figures, it was extremely difficult to gauge Belarus's past economic performance. The lack of a responsive pricing mechanism, Soviet accounting practices and the Soviet method of deriving measures of national income (national income produced and net material product—NMP) tended to obscure rather than clarify economic reality. In particular, Soviet calculations did not accurately represent the Republic's balance of trade with the rest of the USSR and with foreign countries. Part of the difficulty facing Belarus's leaders was that of coming to terms with adjusted measures of economic performance which, as a rule, tend to portray Belarus as being less prosperous than had been imagined.

AGRICULTURE

Until the early 1970s Belarus's economy had a largely agricultural base and, even in the early 1990s, the agricultural sector remained a vital part of the economy. In 1990 agriculture accounted for 29.3% of NMP, although this decreased to 23.2% in 1991. Since much of the land was poor and the climate was severely continental, animal husbandry and hardier crops predominated. Major products included flax, accounting for 27% of total production in the former USSR, potatoes (15% of Soviet production), buckwheat, rye, meat and dairy products, and, increasingly since the early 1980s, sugar beet. Other important crops included barley, potatoes and animal fodder. Oats, millet, hay and tobacco were also grown in small amounts.

Agriculture in Belarus was devastated by the spread of radioactive fall-out from the accident at the Chernobyl nuclear power station, in Ukraine, in 1986. Official estimates claimed that about 20% of Belarusian territory suffered contamination, in particular the regions of Gomel (Homiel) and Mogilev (Mahiloŭ). This was the main agricultural region of Belarus and contained some 2.2m. people. By 1992 257,000 hectares (ha) of agricultural land, just over 4% of the country's total, had been removed from use, as had 1,340,000 ha of forests, about 15% of the total. Unfortunately, after 1986, the authorities in Belarus and the former USSR, and the rest of the world, were slow to recognize the extent of the disaster, hampered by a lack of information and poor access to sites. As a consequence, the local population remained largely ignorant of the problems posed by radiation, and remained uncompensated for the disaster. In the early 1990s poisoned soil continued to be dislodged by ploughing and contaminated food products were still being sold. In 1990, for example, 784,000 metric tons of contaminated meat (not much less than the total level of consumption within the Republic and over 65% of the Republic's total production) were reported to have come from contaminated zones and to have been marketed in Belarus and elsewhere in the USSR.

The problems caused by the Chernobyl disaster ensured that agricultural production had started to fall in the late 1980s. In the early 1990s agricultural NMP continued to decline, by 18% in 1990, and by a further 7% in 1991. With the collapse of the USSR, in late 1991, and the subsequent threat to inter-republican trade, Belarus was confronted by a threat to its supply of grain products, since it had always relied on imports from other Union Republics to compensate for its own production, which did not satisfy domestic demand. Between 1986 and 1990, an average of 3.5m. metric tons were imported annually to meet domestic needs. After 1990 shortages of fertilizer, fuel, spare parts and transport, as well as a gradual reorganization of agriculture, resulted in lower grain production, not only in Belarus (where it decreased by some 10% in 1990/91), but also in Kazakhstan and Ukraine, the two exporting states within the former USSR. However, in slight compensation, rising prices and falling incomes resulted in a change in consumption patterns, with less consumption of meat, and a consequent decline in the need for animal fodder. Nevertheless, Belarus was forced to arrange barter deals with other countries to acquire grain. In 1992, for example, Belarus imported 2.5m. tons of grain from Kazakhstan, in exchange for refrigerators, freezers and other manufactured goods.

Production of other crops also declined sharply in the early 1990s and, in 1993, production was badly damaged by widespread flooding in the south of the country, threatening as much as one-quarter of the grain harvest and one-half of potato production. Cattle farming also suffered, with meat production in the first six months of 1993 18% less than in the same period of 1992. Despite the continuing low level of production, which was partly attributable to the structural defects of the collective-farm system, there was little progress, in 1992–93, on plans for the privatization of agriculture. The conservative-dominated Supreme Council was largely opposed to the dissolution of collective and state farms, and the Government was concerned that a rapid move towards private farming would lead to a sharp fall in production in the short term, as had occurred in other Eastern European countries. Consequently, in early 1992 there were only 739 private farms in Belarus, which accounted for only 0.17% of all agricultural land.

MINING AND ENERGY

Peat was traditionally used locally to produce electricity and for domestic heating, particularly in rural areas, where it was still important. Its use was in decline, however, and peat extraction was also badly affected by the Chernobyl disaster: contaminated peat cannot be burned to produce electric power, since the dispersal of contaminated ash could cause further long term problems. Small deposits of petroleum and natural gas have been found and exploited, although after initial growth, output declined to relatively low levels during the 1970s and 1980s. Annual petroleum production stabilized in the late 1980s at about 2.0m. barrels per year (equivalent to almost 15% of average output in Azerbaijan) and annual production of natural gas remained at between 200m. and 300m. cubic metres. Belarus was an important producer of potassium salts, producing about one-half of the total output in the former USSR. Although there were some deposits of brown coal (lignite) and other minerals, few of them were commercially exploitable. The Republic had always been compelled to import the bulk of its raw materials and fuels.

Two important petroleum pipelines ran through the country: the Druzhba (Friendship) pipeline along the southern border; and the Soyuz (Union) pipeline along the northern border. To complement the pipelines, two refineries were built. One was at Mozyr (Mazyr), where the Druzhba pipeline split into two sections, one going towards Hungary and Slovakia, and the other towards Poland and Germany. The second refinery was at Polotsk (Polacak), where the Soyuz pipeline also split into two, one line going to Poland, and the second to Ventspils in Latvia. As a result, until 1990, the Republic was an important supplier of refined petroleum products. However, declining output in Russia, problems of supply and Russia's need to sell petroleum on the world market, to obtain convertible currency, all contributed to a decline in supplies to Belarus. Whereas in 1991 Belarus processed 35m. metric tons of petroleum in its refineries, in 1992 the amount promised by Russia was reduced to 25m. tons and Belarus was forced to search for new petroleum supplies. Throughout the year, refineries were operating at only 40%–50% of capacity and, by the end of 1992, the Mozyr refinery had stopped production. The situation worsened in 1993 as Russian production continued to fall; only limited amounts of petroleum were available to export, at low prices. Belarus began negotiations with Saudi Arabia, Kuwait and Nigeria to try and compensate for Russian supplies, but this was not expected to result in any immediate solution to the problem.

In addition to being heavily dependent on petroleum for its refineries, the country also relied on imports of petroleum, natural gas and coal for use in power stations. Despite the lack of domestic sources of coal, Belarus imported relatively little, partly because of its reliance on locally produced peat. However, imports of natural gas were vital to maintain electricity production, because in the 1980s many large power stations were converted to use natural gas, the USSR at the time being unable to consume domestic gas output. By 1993 the delivery of Russian natural gas and petroleum had become a critical problem for Belarus, because the Government could no longer afford the higher prices demanded by Russia for supplies. By August Belarus owed Russia some 100,000m. Russian roubles for gas supplies. Deliveries were sharply reduced, leading to an energy crisis in the country. In September there were renewed supplies at concessionary prices, but most observers noted that the deal was linked to Belarusian agreement to greater economic co-operation with Russia, notably a unified monetary system, based on Russia's new rouble.

Construction of a nuclear power station was continuing near Minsk (Miensk) in the early 1990s. The Government also proposed that, despite the experience of Chernobyl, two further nuclear power stations should be built, to reduce Belarus' dependence on Russian petroleum and natural gas.

INDUSTRY

Industry contributed 44% of total NMP in 1990, and 51.3% in 1991. In 1985, of total industrial output, 2.3% was accounted for by primary industry, 5.6% by fuels, 9.3% by chemical and petrochemical products, 17.7% by the food-processing industry, 20% by light industry and 32% by machine-building. Until the early 1970s Belarus specialized in light industries based on the processing of agricultural products, including tanning industries, wood and timber processing, food processing, furniture and linen manufacture, textiles and clothing production, and shoe production. During the 1970s and 1980s, however, the Republic's industrial base underwent extensive changes and, by the late 1980s, chemical and machine-building industries were well developed, although light industries continued to play an important role. Minsk also became one of the most important centres of the Soviet micro-electronics and computer industry. As a rule, major industrial enterprises were concentrated in large cities, but smaller enterprises processing agricultural and timber products were fairly evenly distributed throughout the country.

Belarus was a leading producer of consumer durables within the USSR, including radio receivers, television sets, furniture and shoes, production of which far exceeded domestic demand. It was an important manufacturer of bicycles and motor cycles, responsible for some 20% of Soviet motor-cycle production in the 1980s. Belarus was the world's third-largest producer of tractors and, in the 1980s, was increasingly successful in exporting its products. In the late 1980s one tractor firm even opened an assembly plant in Wisconsin, USA. Large lorries and trucks were also manufactured, although production in Belarus only accounted for a small fraction of total production in the former USSR. Two factories, one producing self-propelled fodder harvesters in Gomel, and another producing the important chemical dimethyl terephthalate in Mogilev, dominated production of their respective products in the former USSR, the former producing 91% of total Soviet output, and the latter 93%. However, Belarus remained dependent on other parts of the former USSR for most basic products. Those produced in the Russian Federation included cars, trolleybuses, tram rails, urban rail cars, sewing machines, automatic washing machines, hand irons, combine harvesters, potato harvesters and steam boilers. Ukraine was the country's main source of film and rolled pipe.

There was a small steel industry. Annual production of crude steel remained at an average of 1m. metric tons during the 1980s, and annual production of finished steel products remained fairly constant at some 700,000 tons. This industry was entirely dependent on imported raw materials, and was able to satisfy only a small proportion of domestic demand for steel.

A large number of enterprises in Belarus were involved in industrial production for the Soviet armed forces. With the collapse of the USSR, military orders almost halted; many such enterprises only survived during 1992 and 1993 owing to government subsidies. Attempts to convert military production to civil production were largely unsuccessful, partly because of a lack of available investment to convert machinery and production lines. In 1992 there were an estimated 120 large enterprises in Belarus dependent on military orders for survival, employing 370,000 people. Their closure would have a severe impact on unemployment, hence the enthusiasm among many of the directors of such companies for an economic union with Russia, which would allow factories to regain at least some of their pre-independence markets.

Industrial NMP did not begin to decline until 1991, and then by only 1%. However, much of this decline was concentrated in chemical and petrochemical production, and the food industry, which declined by 7.5% and 5.7%, respectively. NMP in heavy industry continued to increase, by an overall average of 1.4% in 1991, which included an increase of 3.9% for machine-building and 4.0% for petroleum refining. Industrial output declined markedly in 1992, by 11%, mainly as a result of the disruption of inter-republican trade links, vital to industries such as machine-building, which depended on the supply of components from Russia and Ukraine. Industrial output was expected to decline by 20% annually in both 1993 and 1994.

PRIVATIZATION

By 1993 there had been only limited privatization in Belarus, owing to the ideological opposition of part of the leadership, notably in the Supreme Council. In February 1993 the Supreme Council voted against a privatization scheme which would have distributed vouchers, to buy shares in state-owned enterprises, to all Belarusian citizens. The prevailing policy appeared to be to minimize economic and social disruption at any cost, and to postpone reform in favour of maintaining social stability. Nevertheless, in 1988–91 employment in the state sector (excluding collective and co-operative farms) decreased from almost 85.5% of the total labour force to 70%. However, employment in the private sector showed little growth, rising from 1.3% to only 1.8% of the labour force.

EMPLOYMENT

According to official figures, by mid-1993 unemployment had reached only some 96,000, approximately 1.0%–1.5% of the total labour force. However, several leading factories were reported to be close to bankruptcy and there was considerable potential for sharp increases in unemployment. Some Belarusian experts predicted that unemployment would reach 700,000 by early 1994. In an attempt to forestall such a possibility, the Government continued to subsidize faltering industries at the expense of more profitable ones, with a predictable affect on the budget deficit.

FOREIGN TRADE

Belarus was heavily dependent on inter-republican trade, which accounted for 44.6% of gross domestic product (GDP) in 1989, although it did appear to have a positive inter-republican trade balance in the 1980s. However, the figures tended to exaggerate the Republic's economic performance. The economic reality of trade was obscured by the Soviet pricing system, which undervalued the prices of raw materials (in comparison with world prices), in which the Republic was deficient, but tended to over-value those for machinery, in which Belarus specialized. In terms of domestic prices, Belarus had a positive inter-republican trade balance, even in 1989, of some 3,476 roubles. This fell to 2,384m. in 1990, but recovered slightly, in real terms, to 5,240m. roubles in 1991. However, when partial estimates of world market prices were used to calculate the trade balance (according to the World Bank), the Republic recorded a deficit in its trade balance with other Soviet Republics, of 812m. roubles in 1989 and 1,216m. in 1990. The main factor in this disparity was the difference between the domestic price of petroleum, produced in the Russian Federation, and the world market price of petroleum. Since Belarus was almost entirely dependent on Russia for supplies of petroleum, for which minimal charges were made, it was evident that any transfer of Belarus's trade with Russia to world prices would leave it with either a severe balance-of-payments crisis or an energy crisis. This unattractive choice was with Belarus' leaders from independence on.

In foreign (extra-Soviet) trade, Belarus appeared to have a negative balance. For example, in 1989, the foreign trade deficit was 2,522m. roubles (at domestic prices—at foreign prices, it was only 668m. roubles, there being less distortion). In that year extra-Soviet trade accounted for 23.3% of all imports and 9.8% of total exports. In 1989 the Republic was responsible for some 4% of the foreign trade of the USSR, and total foreign trade accounted for 7.4% of the Republic's GDP. The foreign-trade deficit increased to 3,155m. roubles in 1990 and to 7,040m. roubles in 1991. More recently, the World Bank estimated that, depending on the mix of exports and imports in any given year, the shift to world market prices could cause GDP to decline by 4%–7%.

Within the former USSR, in both 1989 and 1990, the main imports to Belarus from other Union Republics consisted of petroleum and petroleum products (20%), ferrous metals (7%), tools and dies (6%), tractors and agricultural equipment (5%), radio electronics (5%) and other machinery and electronics (5%). Leading exports from Belarus to other Soviet Republics were: refinery products (12%), tractors and agricultural equipment (12%), automobiles and parts (10%), tools and dies (8%), radio electronics (8%), other machinery (6%), chemical fibres (3%), meat and dairy products (3%) and textiles and hosiery (2%).

In 1991 the Republic's authorities asserted control over foreign trade, management of which was previously the preserve of the all-Union authorities in Moscow. Trade within the 'rouble zone' was conducted through bilateral government agreements and the use of quotas linked to state orders, but this system did not adequately cope with the problem of payments between fellow members of the Commonwealth of Independent States (CIS). In October 1992 the Belarusian Government noted that Russian enterprises had imported 137,000m. roubles worth of manufactured goods from Belarus, but had paid only 37,000m. roubles. However, at the same time, the Russian National Bank gave 40,000m. roubles to Belarus, to enable it to buy natural gas and petroleum, and granted a further 20,000m. roubles to the country, in the form of 'technical credits'. Nevertheless, Belarus continued to build up large debts with Russia for purchases of petroleum and gas, which led to sharp reductions in deliveries, in August 1993, since it was clear that Belarus could no longer service its debt adequately. An agreement on supplies and prices was elaborated as part of a wider agreement on economic co-operation negotiated in September 1993.

In February 1992 the Government enacted a foreign-exchange tax, which required exporters to surrender an average of 50% of their foreign-currency receipts at the extremely uncompetitive rate of 10 roubles to the US dollar, in order to enable the Government to service its external debt and pay for essential imports. This was reduced to 20% of foreign-exchange receipts in January 1993, when a single 10% tax on foreign-currency earnings was also introduced.

FINANCE

In 1991 an expected government budget deficit turned out to be a budget surplus, which amounted to 2.2% of GDP. This was partly owing to delays in passing on increases in pensions, wages and wholesale prices, but also a result of higher-than-expected tax receipts and a payment of 1,500m. roubles from the all-Union budget when the USSR collapsed. The Government responded to this relatively promising situation by increasing the level of credit offered to state enterprises through loans and grants. It was, therefore, not surprising that in 1992 the budget had a much higher-than-expected deficit. The decline in industrial production diminished tax revenues, while government expenditure increased sharply, owing to the subsidies paid to loss-making industries.

In early 1992 shortages of currency led to a requirement that substantial payments be made by cheque, rather than with cash, and the Government introduced currency coupons for use in state stores. The coupons (officially denominated as 'rubels'—roubles—but popularly known as *zaichiki*, owing to the picture of a hare on the one-rubel note) were given a value of 10 Russian roubles, and 10%–15% of salaries were paid out in coupons. In November 1992 the state halted the sale of food, tobacco and alcohol for ordinary (Russian) roubles and announced that these goods could only be purchased with coupons (Belarusian rubels). The move was apparently prompted by mass purchases of these (still subsidized) items by buyers from Lithuania and Ukraine.

During 1992 there was discussion regarding the introduction of a new Belarusian currency, the taler, a suggestion largely supported by pro-independence politicians and deplored by those keen to recreate a 'common economic space' with Russia. As late as August 1993 the introduction of a national currency was being mooted by the National Bank, and it was also reported that the rubel coupon currency would be the only legal tender from the end of August. However, an agreement with Russia, in September, to create a joint monetary system, seemed to preclude any transition to a separate currency.

In July 1993 Belarus received its first credit from the International Monetary Fund, of US $98m., granted as assistance to reduce the monthly inflation figure from 30% to 5%, improve the balance of payments, and reduce the decline in the volume of GDP from about 15% to 5%. If the targets were met, further credits would become available, but most observers doubted that the Government would be able to achieve them. Any large-scale assistance would only become available if Belarus embarked on a radical reform programme.

PROBLEMS AND PROSPECTS

Total NMP declined by 3.6% in both 1990 and 1991, and by 15% in 1992. In 1993 it was expected to decline by a further 20%. There was little expectation of growth in 1994, and the long-term prospects for the economy remained uncertain. In the first three months of 1993 NMP decreased by 14%, industrial output by 16% and agricultural output by 13.5%. Inflation remained lower than in neighbouring Ukraine and Russia, in 1992, but was expected to double during 1993, to an annual rate of some 2,000%, and the trade balance was expected to remain negative. Inflation and lack of competition made Belarusian products 25%–30%

more expensive than those sold in neighbouring Poland and Lithuania.

Continued dependence on Russia for supplies of petroleum and natural gas allowed Russia to have a significant influence on Belarus' economic policy. During 1993 Belarus gradually restored many of the economic links which had been ruptured in 1991-92, to the extent that a monetary and customs union was envisaged in September 1993. On 7 September Belarus, together with five other CIS countries, signed an agreement to remain in the rouble monetary system. Such a close economic union with Russia was strongly opposed by nationalist political forces in Belarus, who believed that it encroached on Belarusian sovereignty. However, in the absence of more radical domestic reforms, including mass privatization and a reduction in government expenditure on loss-making firms, there was little hope of assistance from international institutions. Belarus would, therefore, have little choice but to conform to Russia's economic and monetary policies.

Statistical Survey

Sources: mainly IMF, *Belarus, Economic Review* and World Bank, *Statistical Handbook: States of the former USSR.*

Area and Population

AREA, POPULATION AND DENSITY

Area (sq km)	207,595*
Population (census results)	
17 January 1979	9,560,543
12 January 1989†	
Males	4,749,324
Females	5,402,482
Total	10,151,806
Population (official estimate at 1 January 1991)	10,297,000
Density (per sq km) at 1 January 1991	49.6

* 80,153 sq miles.

† Figures refer to the *de jure* population. The *de facto* total was 10,199,709.

POPULATION BY NATIONALITY (1990)

	%
Belarusian	77.9
Russian	13.2
Ukrainian	4.1
Others	4.8
Total	100.0

PRINCIPAL TOWNS*

(estimated population at 1 January 1990)

Minsk (Miensk, capital)	1,613,000	Bobruysk (Babrujsk)	223,000
Gomel (Homiel)	506,000	Baranovichi (Baranavičy)	163,000
Mogilev (Mahiloŭ)	363,000	Borisov (Barysaŭ)	147,000
Vitebsk (Viciebsk)	356,000	Orsha (Vorša)	124,000
Grodno (Horadnia)	277,000	Pinsk	122,000
Brest (Bieraście)†	269,000	Mozyr (Mazyr)	102,000

* The Belarusian names of towns, transliterated into the Belarusian version of the Latin script, where appropriate, are given in brackets after the more widely used Russian names.

† Formerly Brest-Litovsk.

Source: UN, *Demographic Yearbook*.

BIRTHS, MARRIAGES AND DEATHS

	Registered live births		Registered marriages		Registered deaths	
	Number	Rate (per 1,000)	Number	Rate (per 1,000)	Number	Rate (per 1,000)
1987	162,937	16.1	102,053	10.1	99,921	9.9
1988	163,193	15.2	96,064	8.9	102,671	9.5
1989	153,449	15.0	97,929	9.6	103,479	10.1

1990 (registered deaths): Number 109,582; Rate (per 1,000) 10.7.

Source: UN, *Demographic Yearbook*.

EMPLOYMENT

(annual averages, '000 persons)

	1990	1991	1992
Agriculture, hunting, forestry and fishing	1,007.2	958.8	1,013.7
Industry*	1,592.9	1,565.8	1,469.8
Construction	570.4	518.5	481.3
Trade, restaurants and hotels	381.9	378.5	374.7
Transport, storage and communications	365.1	356.8	353.2
Financing, insurance, real estate and business services	28.7	29.8	31.0
Community, social and personal services	1,124.7	1,139.2	1,102.3
Activities not adequately defined	77.6	72.3	61.4
Total	5,148.5	5,019.7	4,887.4

* Principally mining, manufacturing, electricity, gas and water.

Source: ILO, *Year Book of Labour Statistics*.

Economically Active Population (persons aged 15 years and over, 1989 census, provisional): Total 5,327,000 (males 2,718,000; females 2,609,000).

Agriculture

PRINCIPAL CROPS ('000 metric tons)

	1990	1991	1992
Barley	2,908	3,032	2,400*
Rye	2,652	1,962	2,700*
Oats	806	760	800*
Other cereals	417	285	440*
Potatoes	8,591	8,958	8,000†
Sugar beet	1,479	1,147	1,350*
Raw sugar†	n.a.	85	115
Flax fibre*	52.2	76.0	n.a.

* FAO estimate.
† Unofficial estimates.
‡ IMF figures (provisional for 1991).
Source: mainly FAO, *Production Yearbook*.

LIVESTOCK ('000 head at 1 January)

	1990	1991	1992
Horses	219	217	214*
Cattle	7,166	6,975	6,660
Pigs	5,204	5,051	4,700
Sheep	500	400	400
Chickens	48,000	49,000	50,000

* FAO estimate.
Source: FAO, *Production Yearbook*.

LIVESTOCK PRODUCTS ('000 metric tons)

	1990	1991	1992
Meat (slaughter weight)	1,181	1,065	970
Milk	7,457	6,812	5,894*
Eggs	205.1	208.7	192.3

* Unofficial estimate.
Source: FAO, *Production Yearbook*.

Mining

('000 metric tons)

	1985	1989	1990
Chalk	127	122	129
Gypsum (crude)	152	154	141
Peat: for fuel	4,525	4,706	3,438
for agriculture	19,506	18,727	12,304

Source: UN, *Industrial Statistics Yearbook*.

Industry

SELECTED PRODUCTS
('000 metric tons, unless otherwise indicated)

	1989	1990	1991
Cotton yarn (pure and mixed)	49.4	50.5	50.5
Flax yarn	30.6	30.0	24.4
Wool yarn (pure and mixed)	41.6	40.2	34.1
Chemical textile fibres	450	453	443
Plywood	215	192	192
Paper	230	219	207
Paperboard	204	198	166
Quicklime	1,038	1,099	1,080
Cement	2,283	2,258	2,173
Crude steel	1,105	1,112	1,127
Refrigerators ('000)	718	728	743
Television receivers ('000)	1,102	1,302	1,103
Radio receivers ('000)	882	979	932
Bicycles ('000)	850	845	811
Motorcycles ('000)	231	225	214
Tractors ('000)	101.3	100.7	95.5
Electricity (million kWh)	38,500	39,500	38,700

Finance

CURRENCY AND EXCHANGE RATES

Monetary Units:
100 kopeks = 1 rubl (ruble or rouble).

Denominations:
Coins: 1, 2, 3, 5, 10, 15, 25 and 50 kopeks; 1 rouble.
Notes: 1, 3, 5, 10, 25, 50, 100, 200 and 500 roubles.

Sterling and Dollar Equivalents (30 September 1993)
£1 sterling = 1,796.1 roubles;
US $1 = 1,201.0 roubles;
1,000 roubles = £5.568 = $8.326.

Average Exchange Rate (US $ per rouble)
1989 0.6274
1990 0.5856
1991 0.5819

Note: The figures for average exchange rates refer to official rates for the Soviet rouble. However, a multiple exchange rate system was in operation, with separate non-commercial and tourist rates. A commercial exchange rate was introduced on 1 November 1990, replacing the official rate for most transactions. The commercial rate (roubles per US dollar) was: 1.692 at 31 December 1990; 1.671 at 31 December 1991. Between November 1989 and April 1991 the tourist exchange rate valued the rouble at one-tenth of the official rate. In April 1991 this rate, renamed the 'special rate', was set at $1 = 27.6 roubles. It was subsequently adjusted. The average market exchange rate in 1991 was $1 = 31.2 roubles. Following the dissolution of the USSR in December 1991, Russia and several other former Soviet republics retained the rouble as their monetary unit. In May 1992 the Belarusian rouble, or rubel (initially at par with the Russian rouble) was introduced as a coupon currency. The parity was subsequently ended, and the Belarusian rouble was devalued. At 30 September 1993 the exchange rate was 1 Russian rouble = 2 Belarusian roubles. The rate per Russian rouble was adjusted to 3 Belarusion roubles in October 1993, and to 4 Belarusian roubles in November.

BUDGET (million roubles)

Revenue	1990	1991	1992*
Tax revenue	12,200	21,300	87,400
Enterprise incomes	3,600	6,400	19,300
Personal incomes	900	2,400	4,700
Social security contributions	1,300	2,100	—
Turnover tax	6,200	7,700	—
Taxes on foreign transactions	—	200	100
Value-added tax	—	—	35,900
Excises	—	—	14,100
Real estate	—	—	2,000
Land	—	—	2,700
Other	200	2,600	8,600
Chernobyl tax†	—	—	7,200
Non-tax revenue	1,600	4,400	2,500
Transfers from USSR budget	1,500	5,000	—
Total	15,300	30,700	89,900

Expenditure	1990	1991	1992*
National economy	8,600	11,900	25,800
Subsidies	4,100	—	20,000
Operating expenditure	300	—	900
Capital investment	1,800	—	3,900
Other	2,300	—	1,000
Administration, law and order	200	700	4,000
Education, health and social security	4,400	8,000	36,300
Defence	—	—	8,000
Interest	—	100	1,200
Chernobyl fund†	—	5,900	10,800
Reserve fund	—	900	1,000
Other	700	1,600	8,600
Total	13,900	29,100	95,700

* Projected figures.
† Relating to measures to relive the effects of the accident at the Chernobyl nuclear power station, in northern Ukraine, in April 1986.

MONEY SUPPLY
(million roubles at 31 December)

	1989	1990	1991
Currency in circulation	3,124	3,270	5,100
Demand deposits at banks	15,601	17,992	30,885
Total	18,725	21,262	35,985

COST OF LIVING
(Consumer Price Index; base: 1980 = 100)

	1990	1991	1992
Food	125.6	236.7	2,798
Clothing (excl. footwear)	104.9	225.8	2,243
All items (incl. others)	116.1	227.3	2,579

Source: International Labour Office, *Year Book of Labour Statistics*.

NATIONAL ACCOUNTS
Net Material Product
(million roubles at current prices)

	1990	1991*
Agriculture and forestry	8,206	12,120
Industry (excluding turnover taxes)	12,333	26,847
Construction	3,293	6,409
Transport and communications	1,423	1,767
Trade and catering	1,552	2,674
Other material services	860	1,758
Sub-total	27,667	51,575
Adjustment	350	725
Total	28,017	52,300

* Estimates.

External Trade

PRINCIPAL COMMODITIES
(million roubles, at domestic prices)

Imports	1989	1990	1991*
Industry	18,251	18,457.9	38,108.0
Petroleum and natural gas	1,850	1,702.2	n.a.
Ferrous metallurgy	1,372	1,387.1	n.a.
Non-ferrous metallurgy	423	412.8	n.a.
Chemical and petrochemical industry	2,455	2,428.6	n.a.
Machine-building and metalworking	6,572	6,929.8	n.a.
Wood and paper	480	481.4	n.a.
Construction materials	283	205.1	n.a.
Consumer goods	2,606	2,714.9	n.a.
Food processing	1,699	1,523.2	n.a.
Agriculture	892	998.9	1,270
Other activities	205	308.8	686.7
Total	19,348	19,765.6	40,064.7
Inter-republican trade	14,834	14,840.7	30,363.9
Foreign trade	4,513	4,924.9	9,700.8

* Preliminary figures.

Exports	1989	1990	1991*
Industry	19,766	18,535.5	37,377.3
Petroleum and natural gas	1,498	1,444.7	n.a.
Ferrous metallurgy	190	206.9	n.a.
Chemical and petrochemical industry	2,649	2,419.0	n.a.
Machine-building and metalworking	8,871	8,742.9	n.a.
Wood and paper	508	485.8	n.a.
Construction materials	246	298.2	n.a.
Consumer goods	3,679	3,389.3	n.a.
Food processing	1,610	1,027.3	n.a.
Agriculture	283	239.2	369.1
Other activities	243	220.0	518.3
Total	20,302	18,994.7	38,264.7
Inter-republican trade	18,310	17,224.5	35,603.4
Foreign trade	1,991	1,770.2	2,661.3

* Preliminary figures.

Transport

RAILWAYS (traffic)

	1988	1989	1990
Passenger-km (million)	15,989	16,525	16,852
Freight ton-km (million)	82,231	81,734	75,430

Source: UN, *Statistical Yearbook*.

Communications Media

	1988	1989	1990
Radio receivers ('000 in use)	3,051	3,100	3,150
Television receivers ('000 in use)	2,650	2,700	2,750
Book production*:			
titles	2,962	n.a.	2,823
copies ('000)	57,524	n.a.	54,911
Daily newspapers:			
number	28	28	n.a.
average circulation ('000)	2,738	2,937	n.a.
Non-daily newspapers:			
number	n.a.	192	196
average circulation ('000)	n.a.	2,413	2,786

* Figures include pamphlets (1,135 titles and 9,465,000 copies in 1988; 978 titles and 7,796,000 copies in 1990).

Source: UNESCO, *Statistical Yearbook*.

Education

(1990/91)

	Institutions	Teachers	Students
Pre-primary	5,215	62,300	465,000
Primary	5,200	110,600	883,900
Secondary:			
general			574,600
teacher training	n.a.	n.a.	9,600
vocational	n.a.	n.a.	114,900
Higher*	n.a.	16,800	192,400

* Figures for 1989/90 (including evening and correspondence courses).

Source: UNESCO, *Statistical Yearbook*.

Directory

The Constitution

The draft of a new constitution was under discussion in 1993. Until a new one was adopted, the Constitution of 1978 remained in force, although considerably amended, notably by the inclusion of the Declaration of State Sovereignty of July 1990.

The Government

(November 1993)

HEAD OF STATE

Chairman of the Supreme Soviet: STANISLAU SHUSHKEVICH (elected 19 September 1991).

COUNCIL OF MINISTERS

Chairman: VYACHESLAU F. KEBICH.

First Deputy Chairman: MIKHAIL MYASNIKOVICH.

Deputy Chairmen: ULADZIMIER ZALAMAY, N. A. MAKAED, STANISLAU BRYL, IVAN A. KENIK, N. N. KOSTIKOU, MIKHAIL DZIAMCHUK, ALAKSEY SHAKOVICH.

Minister of Agriculture and Foodstuffs: FIODAR V. MIRACHYTSKY.

Minister of Communications and Information Technology: IVAN M. HRYTSUK.

Minister of the Construction Materials Industry: ANATOLIY F. MOISEYEVICH.

Minister of Culture: YAUHEN K. VAYTOVICH.

Minister of Defence: Lt-Gen. PAVEL KOZLOUSKY.

Minister of Education: VIKTOR A. GAYSENOK.

Minister of Energy: VALENTIN V. GERASIMOV.

Minister of Finance: STIAPAN P. YANCHUK.

Minister of Foreign Affairs: PYATRO K. KRAUCHANKA.

Minister of Forestry: GEORGI A. MARKOUSKY.

Minister of Grain Products: NIKOLAI S. YAKUSHEU.

Minister of Health: VASIL S. KAZAKOU.

Minister of Housing and Communal Services: BARYS V. BATURA.

Minister of Information: ANATOLIY I. BUTEVICH.

Minister of Internal Affairs: ULADZIMIER YAHORAU.

Minister of Justice: LEONID A. DASHUK.

Minister of Resources: VLADIMIR M. SHEPEL.

Minister of Road Construction and Utilization: STANISLAU P. YATSUTA.

Minister of Social Security: TAMARA F. KRUTOUTSOVA.

Minister of Trade: VALENTIN I. BAYDAK.

Minister of Transport: ULADZIMIER BARODZIC.

Chairmen of State Committees

Chairman of the State Committee on the Aftermath of the Chernobyl Nuclear Power Station Disaster: IVAN A. KENIK.

Chairman of the State Committee for Architecture and Construction: YURI A. PUPLIKOV.

Chairman of the State Committee on Ecology: ANATOLIY M. DOROVEYEV.

Chairman of the State Committee for the Economy and Planning: SIARHEY S. LINH.

Chairman of the State Committee for Foreign Economic Relations: ULADZIMIR V. RADKEVICH.

Chairman of the State Committee for Industry and Inter-industrial Production: ULADZIMIR I. KURENKOU.

Chairman of the State Committee for Physical Culture and Sport: ULADZIMIER RYZHANKOU.

Chairman of the State Customs Committee: GENNADY M. SHKURD.

Chairman of the State Security Committee: EDUARD SHYRKOUSKY.

MINISTRIES AND STATE COMMITTEES

Ministries

The Council of Ministers of the Republic of Belarus: 220010 Minsk, pl. Nezavisimosti, Government House; tel. (0172) 29-60-07.

Ministry of Agriculture and Foodstuffs: 220001 Minsk, Kirava 15; tel. (0172) 27-37-51; telex 252102; fax (0172) 27-53-88.

Ministry of Communications and Information Technology: 220050 Minsk, pr. F. Skariny 10; tel. (0172) 27-21-57; fax (0172) 26-08-18.

Ministry of the Construction Materials Industry: 220050 Minsk, K. Marksa 3; tel. (0172) 27-24-22.

Ministry of Culture: 220010 Minsk, Savietskaya 9; tel. (0172) 29-68-90; fax (0172) 20-91-25.

Ministry of Defence: 220029 Minsk, Kommunisticheskaya 1; tel. (0172) 39-21-15.

Ministry of Education: 220010 Minsk, Savietskaya 9; tel. (0172) 27-47-36; fax (0172) 20-80-57.

Ministry of Energy: 220077 Minsk, K. Marksa 14; tel. (0172) 29-83-59; fax (0172) 29-84-68.

Ministry of Finance: 220010 Minsk, Savietskaya 11; tel. (0172) 29-61-37.

Ministry of Foreign Affairs: 220030 Minsk, Lenina 19; tel. (0172) 27-29-22; telex 252285; fax (0172) 27-45-21.

Ministry of Forestry: 220039 Minsk, Chkalova 6; tel. (0172) 24-47-05; fax (0172) 24-41-83.

Ministry of Grain Products: 220600 Minsk, pr. Masherova 23; tel. (0172) 26-63-11; fax (0172) 26-81-72.

Ministry of Health: 220010 Minsk, Myasnikova 39; tel. (0172) 29-60-95; fax (0172) 29-62-97.

Ministry of Housing and Communal Services: 220640 Minsk, Bersana 16; tel. (0172) 20-15-45; telex 252121; fax (0172) 20-02-97.

Ministry of Information: 220617 Minsk, pr. Masherova 11; tel. (0172) 23-75-74.

Ministry of Internal Affairs: Minsk, Urytskaha 5; tel. (0172) 27-21-23.

Ministry of Justice: 220084 Minsk, Kollektornaya 10; tel. (0172) 20-96-84.

Ministry of Resources: 220099 Minsk, Kazintsa 4; tel. (0172) 78-80-17; telex 252265; fax (0172) 26-00-84.

Ministry of Road Construction and Utilization: 220097 Minsk, Myasnikova 29; tel. (0172) 20-86-94; fax (0172) 20-86-95.

Ministry of Social Security: 220010 Minsk, Savietskaya 9; tel. (0172) 29-60-35.

Ministry of Trade: 220050 Minsk, Kirava 8. kor. 1; tel. (0172) 27-61-21.

Ministry of Transport: 220612 Minsk, Valadarskaha 8; tel. (0172) 27-16-42; fax (0172) 27-19-81.

State Committees

State Committee on the Aftermath of the Chernobyl Nuclear Power Station Disaster: 220039 Minsk, Parliament House; tel. (0172) 29-63-13; fax (0172) 29-66-65.

State Committee for Architecture and Construction: 220030 Minsk, K. Marksa 32; tel. (0172) 27-80-12.

State Committee on Ecology: 220084 Minsk, Kollektornaya 10; tel. (0172) 20-66-91; fax (0172) 20-55-83.

State Committee for the Economy and Planning: 220010 Minsk, Government House; tel. (0172) 29-64-44; fax (0172) 29-63-35.

State Committee for Foreign Economic Relations: 220010 Minsk, Government House; tel. (0172) 21-17-58; telex 252292; fax (0172) 27-39-24.

State Committee for Industry and Inter-industrial Production: 220855 Minsk, Kazintsa 2; tel. (0172) 24-95-95.

State Committee for Physical Culture and Sport: 220600 Minsk, Kirava 87, kor. 2; tel. (0172) 27-72-37; telex 252175; fax (0172) 27-61-84.

State Customs Committee: 220123 Minsk, V. Khoruzhoy 29; tel. (0172) 34-43-55.

State Security Committee: Minsk, pr. F. Skariny 17; tel. (0172) 29-94-01.

Legislature

SUPREME COUNCIL

According to the Constitution, the Supreme Council (also known as the Supreme Soviet) is composed of 360 deputies. However, in 1993 several constituencies had still not elected a deputy, owing to low voter participation at successive by-elections. Its Chairman is the head of state, the *de facto* president of Belarus. Elections were held to the Supreme Soviet in March 1990. The majority of deputies elected were members of the Communist Party of Belarus, but 27 members of the Belarusian Popular Front were also elected. In mid-1993 the following parliamentary factions were operating: Belarus (120 members); Belarusian Popular Front (33); Sayuz (Union—45); Social Democratic Group (Hramada—13); Party of Communists of Belarus (10); Democratic Reforms (35); Zgoda (10–12). Other deputies were non-aligned or their affiliation was unknown. Membership of parliamentary groupings changes frequently, and some deputies may be members of more than one faction. Under the proposed new constitution, which was being drafted in 1993, the Supreme Council was to be replaced by a 160-member assembly, the Soim. Legislative elections were scheduled to take place in 1994, probably in March.

Supreme Council of the Republic of Belarus: 220016 Minsk, K. Marksa 38, Dom Urada; tel. (0172) 29-33-13.

Chairman: STANISLAU SHUSHKEVICH.

First Deputy Chairman: VYACHESLAU KUZNETSOU.

Local Government

Belarus was divided into six regions (oblasts or voblaśćs) and the capital city of Minsk (Miensk). The six regions were based around the cities of Minsk, Grodno (Horadnia), Brest (Bieraście), Vitebsk (Viciebsk), Mogilev (Mahiloŭ) and Gomel (Homiel).

Political Organizations

Belarusian Christian-Democratic Union (Belaruskaya Khrystsiyanska-Demakratychnaya Zluchnasts): 220065 Minsk-65, POB 24; tel. (0172) 23-21-18; f. 1991.

Belarusian Popular Front 'Revival'—BPF (Belaruski Narodny Front 'Adradžeńnie'): 220040 Minsk, POB 208; tel. (0172) 31-48-93; fax (0172) 39-58-69; f. 1988; anti-Communist movement campaigning for democracy, genuine independence for Belarus and national and cultural revival; Chair. ZIANON PAZNIAK; Sec. VINTSUK VIACHORKA.

Belarusian Peasant Party (Belaruskaya Syalanskaya Partiya): 220108 Minsk-108, POB 333; tel. (0172) 34-38-35; f. 1991; advocates agricultural reforms; Leader YAIGEN M. LUGIN.

Belarusian Social Democratic Assembly (Belaruskaya Satsiyal-demokratychnaya Hramada): 220026 Minsk, POB 129; tel. (0172) 46-46-91; f. 1991; Leader MIKHAS TKACHOU.

Communist Party of Belarus (CPB): Minsk; suspended in 1991, relegalized 1993.

National Democratic Party of Belarus (Natsyianal-Demokratychnaya Partiya Belarusi): Minsk; tel. (0172) 36-99-72; f. 1990; Leader MIKOLA MIKHNOUSKI.

Party of Communists of Belarus—PCB (Partiya Kommunistou Belarusi): Minsk; f. 1991; claims to be successor to the Communist Party of Belarus (suspended in Aug. 1991); 15,000 mems.

Party of People's Accord: 220041 Minsk, pr. F. Skariny 79; tel. (0172) 32-35-94; f. 1992; aims to build a civilized, law-based state.

United Democratic Party of Belarus (Abyadnanaya Demokratychnaya Partiya Belarusi): 220033 Minsk, Sudmalisa 10; tel. (0172) 29-08-34; f. 1990; Leader MIKHAIL PLISKO.

Other parties include the Belarusian United Agrarian Democratic Party, the Slavic Assembly—White Rus, the Belarusian Scientific Industrial Congress, the Polish Democratic Union and the Belarusian Green Party. In March 1993 18 organizations and parties established the Popular Movement of Belarus. The bloc included: the parliamentary factions 'Belarus' and 'Sayuz'; the PCB and the CPB; the Slavic Assembly, White Rus; the Leninist Young Communist Youth League; and other groups opposed to Belarusian independence.

Diplomatic Representation

EMBASSIES IN BELARUS

Bulgaria: 220034 Minsk, per. Bronevoi 5; tel. (0172) 27-55-02.

China, People's Republic: 220002 Minsk, Storozhevskaya 15, Hotel Belarus; tel. (0172) 69-04-01; Ambassador: WAN XINGDA.

France: 220002 Minsk, Storozhevskaya 15; tel. (0172) 69-06-02.

Germany: 220034 Minsk, Zakharova 26; tel. (0172) 33-42-16; fax (0172) 36-85-52; Ambassador: GOTTFRIED ALBRECHT.

India: 220090 Minsk, Koltsova 4, kor 5; tel. (0172) 62-93-99; Ambassador: (vacant).

Italy: 220002 Minsk, Storozhevskaya 15, Hotel Belarus; tel. (0172) 34-30-46.

Japan: 220029 Minsk, Starovilenskaya 15; tel. (0172) 39-15-87; Ambassador: SUMIO EDAMURA.

Latvia: 220004 Minsk, pr. Masherova 19; tel. (0172) 26-95-14.

Poland: 220034 Minsk, Rumyantseva 6; tel. (0172) 33-51-09; Ambassador: ELŻBIETA SMUŁEK.

Romania: 220091 Minsk, Drozdy 21, kor. 2; tel. (0172) 23-83-64.

Russia: 220002 Minsk, Starovilenskaya 48; tel. (0172) 50-36-66; Ambassador: IGOR SAPRYKIN.

Turkey: 220050 Minsk, Kirava 17; tel. (0172) 50-36-66.

Ukraine: 220088 Minsk, Traktornaya 3, Hotel '40 let pobedy'; tel. (0172) 36-70-94.

USA: 220002 Minsk, Starovilenskaya 46; tel. (0172) 34-76-42; Ambassador: DAVID H. SWARTZ.

Judicial System

Supreme Court: 220030 Minsk, Lenina 28; tel. (0172) 26-12-06; Chairman ULADZIMIER S. KARAVAY.

Procuracy: 220050 Minsk, Internatsionalnaya 22; tel. (0172) 26-41-66; Procurator-General MIKALAI IHNATOVICH.

Religion

Council of Religious Affairs of the Council of Ministers: 220050 Minsk, pl. Nezavisimosti, Government House; tel. (0172) 29-68-58; govt agency responsible for religious affairs.

CHRISTIANITY

The major denomination was the Eastern Orthodox Church, but there were an estimated 2m. adherents of the Roman Catholic Church. Of these, some 25% were ethnic Poles and there was a significant number of Uniates or 'Greek Catholics'. There was also a growing number of Baptist churches. In 1990 there were 195 Baptist churches associated with the All-Union Council and 24 independent chapels.

The Roman Catholic Church

Although five Roman Catholic dioceses, embracing 455 parishes, had officially existed since the Second World War, none of them had a bishop. In 1989 a major reorganization of the structure of the Roman Catholic Church in Belarus took place. The dioceses of Minsk (Miensk) and Mogilev (Mahiloŭ) were merged, to create an archdiocese, and two new dioceses were formed, in Grodno (Horadnia) and Pinsk. The Eastern-rite, or Uniate, Church was abolished in Belarus in 1839, but was re-established in the early 1990s.

Latin Rite

Archdiocese of Minsk and Mogilev: 231011 Grodno, Krasnopartizanskaya 1, kv. 2; tel. (01522) 23-267; Archbishop KAZIMIERZ SWIATEK.

Byzantine Rite

Belarusian Greek Catholic (Uniate) Church: 220030 Minsk, Hertsena 1.

The Eastern Orthodox Church

In 1990 Belarus was designated an exarchate of the Russian Orthodox Church, thus creating the Belarusian Orthodox Church.

Belarusian Orthodox Church: 220004 Minsk, Osvobozhdeniya 10; tel. (0172) 23-44-95.

Protestant Churches

Union of Evangelical Christian Baptists of Belarus: 220093 Minsk, 4-y Puteprovodnyi per. 2; tel. (0172) 53-92-67.

ISLAM

There were small communities of ethnic Tatars, who were adherents of Islam.

Muslim Society: 220004 Minsk, Zaslavskaya 11, kor. 1, kv. 113.

JUDAISM

Before Belarus was occupied by Nazi Germany, in 1941–44, there was a large Jewish community in Belarus, notably in Minsk. There were some 142,000 Jews at the census of 1989, but many have since emigrated.

Jewish Religious Society: 220030 Minsk, pr. F. Skariny 44A.

The Press

In September 1992 there were a total of 586 registered periodicals in Belarus, of which 140 were in Belarusian and 159 in Russian, and 241 were in both Belarusian and Russian. Other publications were in Russian in combination with one other language, or in Polish, Ukrainian or English. Most daily newspapers are government-owned, and there is only one Belarusian-language daily, *Zvyazda*. The daily newspapers with the highest circulations in 1993 were *Sovetskaya Belorossiya, Narodnaya Hazeta, Vechernii Minsk* and *Zvyazda*.

PRINCIPAL DAILIES

In Russian except where otherwise stated.

Belorusskaya Niva (Belarusian Cornfield): 220041 Minsk, pr. F. Skariny 77; tel. (0172) 32-38-95; f. 1921; 5 a week; organ of the Council of Ministers; Editor L. K. TOLKACH; circ. 150,000 (1992).

Dobry Vechar (Good Evening): 220600, pr. F. Skariny 44; tel. (0172) 33-18-58; daily; independent; in Belarusian and Russian; circ. 40,000 (1992).

Narodnaya Hazeta (The People's Newspaper): 220010 Minsk, Dom Urada; tel. (0172) 29-60-08; f. 1990; organ of the Belarusian Supreme Council; in Belarusian and Russian; Editor IOSIF P. SIAREDZICH; circ. 401,000 (1992).

Respublika (Republic): 220050 Minsk, Savietskaya 9; tel. (0172) 29-68-87; organ of the Council of Ministers; 5 a week; circ. 30,000 (1992).

Sovetskaya Belorossiya (Soviet Belorussia): 220041, pr. F. Skariny 77; tel. (0172) 32-23-52; organ of the Council of Ministers; Editor I. ASKINSKI; circ. 674,000 (1992).

Vechernii Minsk (Evening Minsk): 220005 Minsk, pr. F. Skariny 44; tel. (0172) 33-00-54; Editor S. SVERKUNOW; circ. 169,000 (1992).

Znamya Yunosti (Banner of Youth): 220041 Minsk, pr. F. Skariny 79; tel. (0172) 32-25-06; f. 1938; 5 a week; organ of the Council of Ministers; Editor A. V. KLASKOVSKY.

Zvyazda (Star): 220041 Minsk, pr. F. Skariny 77; tel. (0172) 32-51-05; f. 1917 as *Zvezda;* 6 a week; organ of the Supreme Council and Council of Ministers; in Belarusian; Editor U. B. NARKEVICH; circ. 81,000 (1992).

PRINCIPAL PERIODICALS

Belarus: 220034 Minsk, Zakharova 19, tel. (0172) 33-20-01; f. 1930; monthly; publ. by the Polymya (Flame) Publishing House; journal of the Union of Writers of Belarus; fiction and political essays; Editor-in-Chief A. A. SHABALIN.

Byarozka (Birch-tree): 220041 Minsk, F. Skariny 79; tel. (0172) 32-94-66; f. 1924; monthly; fiction; illustrated; for 10–15-year-olds; Editor-in-Chief V. V. ADAMCHIK.

Chyrvonaya Zmena (Red Rising Generation): 220041 Minsk, F. Skariny 77; tel. (0172) 32-13-54; f. 1921; weekly; Editor V. P. BELSKY.

Golas Radzimy (Voice of the Motherland): 220005 Minsk, pr. F. Skariny 44; tel. (0172) 33-03-15; f. 1955; weekly; articles of interest to Belarusians in other countries; Editor-in-Chief VATSLAV G. MATSKEVICH.

Krynitsa (Spring): 220807 Minsk, Kiseleva 11; tel. (0172) 36-61-42; f. 1988; monthly; political and literary; in Belarusian and Russian; Editor V. P. NEKLYAEV.

Litaratura i Mastatstva (Literature and Art): 220600 Minsk, Zakharova 19; tel. (0172) 33-24-61; f. 1932; weekly; publ. by the Ministry of Culture and the Union of Writers of Belarus; Editor MIKOLA S. GIL; circ. 18,000 (1992).

Maladosts (Youth): 220041 Minsk, F. Skariny 79; tel. (0172) 31-85-43; f. 1953; monthly; journal of the Union of Writers of Belarus; novels, short stories, essays, translations, etc., for young people; Editor-in-Chief A. S. GRACHANIKOU.

Mastatstva (Art): 220072 Minsk, F. Skariny 15A; tel. (0172) 39-59-37; monthly; illustrated; tel. (0172) 39-59-37; Editor-in-Chief ALYAKSEY DUDARIN.

Nabat: 220034 Minsk, Frunze 5; tel. (0172) 20-39-04; f. 1990; publ. by the Belarusian Socio-Ecological Union 'Chernobyl'; Editor VASIL YAKOVENKO.

Narodnaya Asveta (People's Education): 220023 Minsk, Makaenka 12; tel. (0172) 64-62-68; f. 1924; publ. by the Ministry of Public Education; Editor-in-Chief N. I. KALESNIK.

Neman (The River Nieman): 220005 Minsk, F. Skariny 39; tel. (0172) 33-14-61; f. 1960; monthly; publ. by the Polymya (Flame) Publishing House; journal of the Union of Writers of Belarus; fiction; in Russian; Editor-in-Chief A. P. KUDRAVETS.

Politichesky Sobesednik (Political Speaker): 220041 Minsk, F. Skariny 79; tel. (0172) 32-35-94; f. 1932; monthly; political; in Russian; Editor NIKOLAI D. ASTANEVICH; circ. 20,000.

Polymya (Flame): 220600 Minsk, Zakharova 19; tel. (0172) 33-20-12; f. 1922; monthly; publ. by the Polymya (Flame) Publishing House; journal of the Union of Writers of Belarus; fiction; Editor-in-Chief S. I. ZAKONNIKOU.

Svaboda (Freedom): 220045 Minsk, POB 17; tel. (0172) 34-22-95; fax (0172) 34-22-95; f. 1902; publ. restored 1990; organ of the Belarusian Popular Front; monthly; Editor-in-Chief IHAR HERMYANCHUK.

Vozhyk (Hedgehog): 220041 Minsk, F. Skariny 77; tel. (0172) 32-01-23; f. 1941; publ. by the Council of Ministers; fortnightly; satirical; Editor-in-Chief VALENTIN V. BOLTACH; circ. 70,000.

Vyaselka (Rainbow): 220048 Minsk, Kollektornaya 10; tel. (0172) 20-92-61; f. 1957; monthly; popular, for 5–10-year-olds; Editor-in-Chief V. S. LIPSKY; circ. 115,000.

PRESS ASSOCIATION

Union of Journalists: 220005 Minsk, Rumyantsava 3; tel. (0172) 36-51-95; 3,000 mems; Chair. LAVON YEKEL.

NEWS AGENCY

BelTA (Belarusian News Agency): Minsk, Kirava 26; tel. (0172) 27-19-92; fax (0172) 27-13-46; Dir YAKAU ALAKSEYCHYK.

Publishers

In 1989 there were 2,980 titles (books and pamphlets) published in Belarus (59m. copies), of which 439 (9.4m. copies) were in Belarusian. Most publishing houses are funded and controlled by the Ministry of Information, which also administers the main book distribution and retail organization in Belarus.

Belarus: 220600 Minsk, pr. Masherova 11; tel. (0172) 23-77-34; telex 252964; fax (0172) 20-91-25; f. 1921; political, medical and musical literature, art reproductions; Dir V. L. DUBOVSKY.

Belaruskaya Entsiklopediya (Belarusian Encyclopaedia): 220072 Minsk, pr. F. Skariny 15A; tel. (0172) 39-47-67; f. 1967; encyclopaedias, dictionaries and reference books; Editor-in-Chief I. P. SHAMYAKIN.

Mastatskaya Litaratura (Art Publishing House): 220600 Minsk, pr. Masherova 11; tel. (0172) 23-48-09; f. 1972; Dir V. GRISHANOVICH.

Narodnaya Asveta (People's Education Publishing House): 220600 Minsk, pr. Masherova 11; tel. (0172) 23-48-09; f. 1972; school textbooks and teaching aids; Dir V. N. GRISHANOVICH.

Navuka i Tekhnika (Science and Technology Publishing House): 220141 Minsk, Zhodinskaya 18; tel. (0172) 63-76-18; f. 1924; in Belarusian and Russian; Dir F. I. SAVITSKY.

Polymya (Flame Publishing House): 220600 Minsk, pr. Masherova 11; tel. (0172) 23-52-85; f. 1950; books on domestic science, sport, leisure activities, cars and radios, catalogues, calendars and magazines; Dir M. A. IVANOVICH.

Universitetskae (University Publishing House): 220048 Minsk, pr. Masherova 11; tel. (0172) 23-58-51; f. 1967; general scientific and reference; Dir V. K. KASKO.

Uradzhai (Harvest Publishing House): 220600 Minsk, pr. Masherova 11; tel. (0172) 23-64-94; f. 1961; books and booklets on agriculture; in Belarusian and Russian; Dir G. P. ZDANOVICH.

Vysheyshaya Shkola (Higher School Publishing House): 220048 Minsk, pr. Masherova 11; tel. (0172) 23-54-15; fax (0172) 23-54-15; f. 1954; textbooks and science books for higher educational institutions; Dir A. A. ZHADAN.

Yunatstva (Youth Publishing House): 220600 Minsk, pr. Masherova 11; tel. (0172) 23-24-30; fax (0172) 26-66-16; f. 1981; children's books; Dir V. A. LUKSHA.

Radio and Television

In 1990 an estimated 3.2m. radio receivers and 2.8m. television receivers were in use.

National Television and Radio Company of Belarus: 220807 Minsk, A. Makayanka 9; tel. (0172) 63-50-15; telex 25-22-67; fax (0172) 63-70-16; First Dep. Chair. PAVEL A. SHEVCHUK.

Belarusian Television: 220807 Minsk, A. Makayenka 9; tel. (0172) 33-45-01; telex 152267; fax (0172) 64-81-82; f. 1956; Chair. A. G. STOLYAROV.

Radio Minsk: 220807 Minsk, Krasnaya 4; tel. (0172) 33-88-75; fax (0172) 36-66-43.

Finance

BANKING

After Belarus gained its independence, the Soviet-style banking system was restructured and a two-tier system was introduced. In 1992 there were 26 universal commercial banks operating in Belarus (with 363 branches).

Central Bank

National Bank of Belarus: 220008 Minsk, F. Skariny 20; tel. (0172) 27-09-46; telex 252449; fax (0172) 27-64-31; f. 1991; Chair. STANISLAU BAHDANKEVICH; First Dep. Chair. NIKOLAY A. KUZMICH; 6 BRS.

Other Banks

Agro-industrial Bank (Belagroprombank): Minsk.

Bank for Foreign Economic Affairs (Belvneshekonombank—BVEB): 220004 Minsk, Zaslavskaha 10; tel. (0172) 26-96-34; telex 252426; fax (0172) 26-97-59; f. 1991; cap. R1,000m.; dep. R1,264.3m.; Pres. GENNADY ALEINIKOV; 1 br.

Joint-Stock Commerical Bank for Industry and Construction (Belpromstroibank): 220678 Minsk, bul. Lunacharskaho 6; tel. (0172) 33-21-10; telex 25-24-10; fax (0172) 31-44-76; f. 1991; provides credit to enterprises undergoing privatization and conversion to civil production; cap. R6,000m., dep. R505,500m. (Sept. 1993); Dir NIKOLAI YA. RAKOV; 46 brs.

Savings Bank (Sberbank): Minsk; 151 brs.

COMMODITY AND STOCK EXCHANGES

Gomel Regional Commodity and Raw Materials Exchange (GCME): 246000 Gomel, Sovetskaya 16; tel. (0232) 55-73-28; fax (0232) 55-70-07; f. 1991; Gen. Man. ANATOLY KUZILEVICH.

Belagroprambirzha (Belarusian Agro-Industrial Trade and Stock Exchange): Minsk, Kazintsa 86, kor. 2; tel. (0172) 77-07-26; telex 25-22-96; fax (0172) 77-01-37; f. 1991; trade in agricultural products, industrial goods, shares; 900 mems; Chair. of Bd ALEXANDER P. DECHTYAR.

Belarusian Universal Exchange (BUE): 220099 Minsk, Kazintsa 4; tel. (0172) 78-11-21; fax (0172) 78-85-16; f. 1991; Pres. ULADZIMIER SHEPEL.

Trade and Industry

CHAMBER OF COMMERCE

Chamber of Commerce and Industry of the Republic of Belarus: 220600 Minsk, pr. Masherova 14; tel. (0172) 26-99-37; telex 252190; fax (0172) 26-99-36; brs in Brest and Gomel; Chair. ULADZIMIER K. LESUN.

AGRICULTURAL AND INDUSTRIAL ORGANIZATIONS

Belarussian Peasants' Union (Syalansky Sayuz): 220199 Minsk, Brestskaya 64/327; tel. (0172) 77-99-93; Chair. KASTUS YARMOLENKA.

Confederation of Industrialists and Entrepreneurs: Minsk.

Union of Enterpreneurs and Farmers: 200079 Minsk, POB 257; tel. (0172) 20-16-16; Pres. MARK KUNIAUSKY.

Union of Small Ventures: Minsk, Bersana 1; tel. (0172) 20-92-70; Chair. VIKTAR DROZD.

FOREIGN TRADE ORGANIZATIONS

Belagrointorg: 220001 Minsk, Moskovskaya 11; tel. (0172) 25-10-42; telex 252498; fax (0172) 25-31-12; export and import of agricultural products; Gen. Dir V. V. TELUSHKIN.

Belarusintorg: 220084 Minsk, Kollektornaya 10; tel. (0172) 20-81-88; telex 252292; fax (0172) 20-94-70; import and export of consumer goods; Gen. Dir VIKTOR V. ANDRYUSHIN.

Belkoopvneshtorg: 220611 Minsk, pr. Masherova 17; tel. (0172) 26-95-89.

Belvneshpromservis: 220600 Minsk, pr. Masherova 5; tel. (0172) 26-00-84; telex 252265; fax (0172) 26-00-81.

Minskvneshservis: 220113 Minsk, Kolasa 65; tel. (0172) 66-04-60.

MAJOR INDUSTRIAL ENTERPRISES

Belarus Tyre Works (Belaruski Shynny Kambynat 'Belshyna'): 213824 Bobruisk, Minskoye shosse; tel. (02251) 3-51-11; telex 252167; fax (02251) 3-50-68; manufactures tyres for domestic and industrial use; Dir ARKADY K. POLYAKOV; 14,000 employees.

Boridovdrev: 222120 Borisov, 1840 Let Vlksm; tel. (01777) 3-16-53; telex 252299; wood products; Gen. Dir ALAKSEY G. LIVSHITS; 4,000 employees.

Brest Electric Lamp Plant (BELP): Brest, Moskovskaya 204; tel. (0162) 42-05-30; telex 229113; fax (0162) 42-60-78; f. 1966; manufactures electric incandescent lamps for automobiles, medical use, and general application; Dir ANATOLY M. SOLOGUB; 4,500 employees.

Brest Gas Apparatus Factory: 224663 Brest, Ordzhonikidze 22; tel. (01622) 64-152; telex 229114; design and manufacture of domestic gas appliances; Dir MIKHAIL F. IOFFE; 2,014 employees.

Dolomit Industrial Association: 211321 Vitebsk, Tsentralnaya 23; tel. 91-52-36; produces dolomite fertilizer; Gen. Dir M. YA. CHUMANIKHINA.

Dormash: 220736 Minsk, Ponomarenko 7; tel. (0172) 51-02-00; telex 252196; fax (0172) 51-64-55; manufactures road construction machinery, including front loaders and road rollers; Gen. Dir VASILY M. SHLYNDIKOV; 4,500 employees.

Eleventh State Bearing Plant: 220830 Minsk, Yelunovich 2; tel. (0172) 451052; telex 252176; fax (0172) 45-15-14; production of ball and roller bearings; Man. ANATOLY V. ZINKEVICH; 9,000 employees.

Gomel Machine Tool Production Group: 246640 Gomel, Internatsionalnaya 10; tel. (0232) 52-32-62; telex 252117; fax (0232) 53-04-98; production of metal-cutting machine tools; Gen. Dir G. KAZAKOV; 2,600 employees.

Industrial and Trading Amalgamation 'Polesie': Brest obl., 225710 Pinsk, Pervomaiskaya 159; tel. (01653) 3-24-41; telex 229660; fax (01653) 3-09-05; knitted products, wool and acrylic yarn; Gen. Dir V. A. NAIDENKO; 7,800 employees.

Kamerton Plant: 225710 Pinsk, Brestskaya 137; tel. (01653) 415-80; telex 229662; manufactures electronic wrist-watches and pedometers; Gen. Dir NIKOLAI S. PASS; 2,500 employees.

Minsk Chemical Plant: 220600 Minsk, Serova 8; tel. (0172) 77-19-14; produces a wide range of chemicals; Dir V. P. KORSHUNOV.

Minsk Motor Factory: 220829 Minsk-70, Vaupshasov 4; tel. (0172) 44-11-24; telex 252282; fax (0172) 44-31-88; design and manufacture of diesel engines; Gen. Dir IVAN YA. VOROBEV; 8,000 employees.

Minsk Motorcycle and Bicycle Factory: 220765 Minsk, Partizansky pr. 8; tel. (0172) 21-68-18; telex 252964; fax (0172) 21-68-06; design and manufacture of small motorcycles and a range of bicycles; Gen. Dir KONSTANTIN A. USTYMCHUK; 6,500 employees.

Mogilev Textile Factory: 212781 Mogilev, Grishina 87; tel. (0222) 23-13-12; telex 252263; produces a wide range of textiles; Gen. Dir VLADIMIR SEMYONOV; 60,000 employees.

Mogilevselmash (Mogilev Agricultural Machinery Plant): 212030 Mogilev; tel. (0222) 24-38-31; telex 252207; agricultural machinery, including front-end loaders and trailers; Dir VALERY CHERTKOV; 4,000 employees.

Pinskdrev Industrial Woodworking Association: Brest obl., 225710 Pinsk, Chuklaya vul. 1; tel. (01653) 2-50-34; telex 229110; fax (01653) 2-50-34; produces industrial and domestic furniture, matches; Gen. Dir LORAN S. ARINICH; 4,200 employees.

Vizas: 210602 Vitebsk, pr. Frunze 83; tel. (02122) 4-10-37; telex 252442; fax (02122) 4-05-17; f. 1897; manufactures tool and cutter grinders, special-purpose grinders, woodworking machinery, optical lens grinders, etc.; Dir-Gen. YEVGENY O. KISELEV; 2,000 employees.

TRADE UNIONS

Association of Independent Trade Unions of Industry of Belarus: 220126 Minsk, pr. Masherova 21; tel. (0172) 23-97-92; fax (0172) 25-97-92; f. 1991; Co-chair. ALEXANDER I. BUKHVOSTOV, GENNADY F. FEDYNICH; 600,000 mems.

Transport

RAILWAYS

At 31 December 1989 the total length of rail lines in use was 5,590 km. Minsk is a major railway junction, situated on the east-west line between Moscow and Warsaw (Poland), and north-south lines linking the Baltic countries and Ukraine. There is an underground railway in Minsk, the Minsk Metro. In 1991 plans were announced for the expansion of the Metro, beginning in 1993.

ROADS

At 31 December 1989 the total length of roads in Belarus was 265,600 km, of which 227,000 km were hard-surfaced.

Tourism

Belintourist: 220078 Minsk, pr. Masherova 19; tel. (0172) 26-98-40; telex 252270; fax (0172) 23-11-43; leading tourist org. in Belarus

Culture

NATIONAL ORGANIZATION

Ministry of Culture: see section on The Government (Ministries).

CULTURAL HERITAGE

Belarusian Humanities Centre: 220050 Minsk, Karala 16A; f. 1990; promotes the study of Belarusian culture and language.

Belarusian State Art Museum: 220030 Minsk, Lenina 20; tel. (0172) 27-56-72; f. 1939; 20,000 exhibits; Dir YURY A. KARACHUN.

Grodno State Historical Museum: Grodno, Zamkovaya 22; 90,000 exhibits.

National Library of the Republic of Belarus: 220636 Minsk, Krasnoarmeiskaya 9; tel. (0172) 22-54-63; telex 252316; f. 1922; over 7m. vols; Dir G. N. OLEINIK.

National Museum of the History and Culture of Belarus: 220050 Minsk, K. Marksa 12; tel. (0172) 27-36-65; f. 1959; over 250,000 exhibits on the history of the Belarusian people; library; Dir I. P. ZAGRISHEV.

SPORTING ORGANIZATION

State Committee for Physical Culture and Sport: see section on The Government (State Committees).

PERFORMING ARTS

Belarusian State Philharmonic Society: pr. F. Skariny; tel. (0172) 33-49-74; fax (0172) 31-90-50; f. 1936; Dir VLADIMIR P. RATOBYLSKY.

Belarusian State Theatrical and Art Institute: 220012 Minsk, pr. F. Skariny 81; tel. (0172) 32-15-42; f. 1945; training in drama, arts and applied arts; Rector YE. P. GERASIMOVICH.

State Academic Bolshoy Opera and Ballet Theatre of Belarus: 220029 Minsk, E. Pashkevich 23; tel. (0172) 34-05-84; f. 1938.

State Puppet Theatre: 220030 Minsk, Engelsa 20; tel. (0172) 27-13-65; f. 1938.

State Russian Drama Theatre of Belarus: 220050 Minsk, Volodarskaha 5; tel. (0172) 20-38-25; f. 1932.

Yanka Kupala Belarusian State Academic Drama Theatre: 220030 Minsk, Engelsa 7; tel. (0172) 27-60-81.

ASSOCIATIONS

Belarusian Cultural Fund: 220030 Minsk, Yanki Kupaly 17/30; tel. (0172) 29-34-30; Pres. IVAN CHYHRYNAY.

Belarusian Rerykhau Fund: 220050 Minsk-50, POB 177; tel. (0172) 23-07-40.

Belarusian World Association—Batskaushchyna (Fatherland): 220048 Minsk, Sukhaya 4; tel. (0172) 23-66-21; develops contacts with the Belarusian diaspora.

Francis Skarina Belarusian Language Society: 220005 Minsk, Rumyantsava 13; tel. (0172) 33-25-11.

Society for Friendship and Cultural Links with Foreign Countries: 220034 Minsk, Zakharova 28; tel. (0172) 33-18-21.

Society of Independent Cinematographers: 220005 Minsk, Frunze 3; tel. (0172) 33-51-94.

Theatrical Union of Belarus: 220029 Minsk, Kisyalova 13/6; tel. (0172) 36-69-82; Chair. MIKALAI YAROMENKA.

Union of Artists of Belarus: 220050 Minsk, K. Marksa 8; tel. (0172) 27-37-23; Chair. HIENADZ BURALKIN.

Union of Cinematographers: 220050 Minsk, K. Marksa 5; tel. (0172) 27-14-13.

Union of Composers: 220030 Minsk, plats Svabody 5; tel. (0172) 23-45-47; Chair. IHAR LUCHANOK.

Union of Designers: 220039 Minsk, Brilevskaya 14; tel. (0172) 25-83-98.

Union of Journalists: 220005 Minsk, Rumyantsava 3; tel. (0172) 36-51-95; 3,000 mems; Chair. LAVON YEKEL.

Union of Musicians of Belarus: 220030 Minsk, Yanki Kupaly 17/30; tel. (0172) 29-38-94.

Union of Writers of Belarus: 220034 Minsk, Frunze 5; tel. (0172) 36-00-12; Chair. VASIL ZUYONAK.

Education

In response to public demand, in the early 1990s the Government began to introduce greater provision for education in the Belarusian language and more emphasis on Belarusian, rather than Soviet or Russian, history and literature. Following the adoption of Belarusian as the official language, all pupils were to be taught Belarusian from primary school level onwards. In 1988 79.2% of pupils were taught in Russian, compared with 65.0% in 1980. In 1989/90 there were some 190,000 students studying at 33 higher education institutions, including three universities, four Polytechnic Institutes and several colleges specializing in technical or agricultural sciences. Two new universities were subsequently established. Research was co-ordinated by the Belarusian Academy of Sciences (see section on The Environment, below).

UNIVERSITIES

Belarusian Agricultural Technical University: 220023 Minsk, pr. F. Skariny 99; tel. (0172) 64-47-71; fmrly Belarusian Institute of Agricultural Engineering; Rector Prof. L. S. GERASIMOVICH.

Belarusian State Economic University: 220110 Minsk, pr. Partizanskii 26; tel. (0172) 49-40-32; fmrly Belarusian State Institute of National Economy; Rector F. V. BOROVIK.

Belarusian State University: 220080 Minsk, pr. F. Skariny 4; tel. (0172) 26-59-40; f. 1921; 13 faculties, 4 institutes; 1,370 teachers; 17,600 undergraduate students, 1,000 postgraduate students; Rector L. I. KISELEVSKY.

Gomel State University: 246699 Gomel, Sovetskaya 104; tel. (0232) 57-11-15; f. 1969; 8 faculties; 500 teachers; 7,000 students; Rector B. V. BOKUT.

Grodno State University: 230023 Grodno, Ozheshko 22; tel. (01522) 7-01-73; f. 1978; 7 faculties; 6,200 students.

Social Welfare

The state-funded social security system provides benefits for the unemployed, the disabled, families and the aged. There are three principal funds: the Pension Fund (covering family allowances in addition to pensions); the Social Insurance Fund (sickness and disability benefits); and the Employment Fund (administers unemployment benefit, and manages retraining and employment schemes). In 1992 projected expenditure on social security, health and education was 36,300m. roubles (some 38% of total budgeted expenditure). In 1990 there were 40.6 medical doctors and 132.3 hospital beds per 10,000 inhabitants.

GOVERNMENT AGENCIES

Belarusian Children's Fund: Minsk, Kamunistychnaya 2; tel. (0172) 36-62-67; Chair. ULADZIMIER LIPSKY.

Ministry of Health: see section on The Government (Ministries).

Ministry of Social Security: see section on The Government (Ministries).

HEALTH AND WELFARE ORGANIZATIONS

Chernobyl Children's Fund: Minsk, Staravilenskaya 14; tel. (0172) 34-21-53; fax (0172) 34-34-58; charity fund to aid the victims of the Chernobyl disaster; Chair. HYENADZ HRUSHAVY.

Society of the Deaf: 220050 Minsk, Volodarskaha 12; tel. (0172) 20-37-02.

Society of Invalids: 220012 Minsk, Kalinina 7; tel. (0172) 66-00-96.

Society of the Red Cross (Central Committee): 220030 Minsk, K. Marksa 35; tel. (0172) 27-14-17.

The Environment

In 1990 Belarus declared itself an ecological disaster area and claimed that 2.2m. people lived in areas contaminated by radioactive matter, released as a result of the Chernobyl disaster. The Chernobyl nuclear power station is situated in Ukraine, very close to the Belarusian border. When an explosion occurred, in April 1986, the radioactive discharge was carried by the prevailing winds across southern and western Belarus. The worst affected areas were Gomel and Mogilev oblasts, in the south and south-east of the country, comprising some 20% of Belarus's territory. The peaty soils and wetlands in these regions were particularly prone to contamination, since they easily absorbed radioactive particles. Later analyses suggested that the area contaminated was even greater than originally believed, including parts of Grodno and Vitebsk oblasts, and covering perhaps as much as 40% of the country.

GOVERNMENT ORGANIZATIONS

State Committee on the Aftermath of the Chernobyl Nuclear Power Station Disaster: see section on The Government (State Committees).

State Committee on Ecology: see section on The Government (State Committees).

ACADEMIC INSTITUTES

Academy of Sciences: 220072 Minsk, pr. F. Skariny 66; tel. (0172) 39-48-01; telex 252277; f. 1929; Pres. ULADZIMIER P. PLATONAU; institutes incl.:

Institute of the Problems of the Use of Natural Resources and Ecology: 220114 Minsk, Staroborisovsky trakt 10; tel. (0172) 64-26-31; f. 1932; in the Dept of Chemical and Geological Sciences; environmental research; Dir I. I. LISHTVAN.

Ecology Department, Belarusian Polytechnical Academy: 220027 Minsk, pr. F. Skariny 65; tel. (0172) 39-91-29; telex 252193; fax (0172) 32-83-16; environmental education and training; Dir Dr SERGEI DOROZHKO.

NON-GOVERNMENTAL ORGANIZATIONS

Association of Professional Ecologists: 220004 Minsk, Oboinyi per. 4; tel. (0172) 26-71-06.

'Belovezhskaya Pushcha' Museum: Brest obl., Belovezhskaya Puscha Game Preserve; works to preserve the almost extinct European bison; Dir V. S. ROMANOV.

Belarusian Ecological Union: 220030 Minsk, Lenina 15A; tel. (0172) 27-87-96; unites various groups conerned with environmental issues.

Green Party of Belarus: Minsk; active environmentalist political party.

Maladziezhny ekalagichny rukh 'Belaya Rus' (Youth Ecological Movement 'White Rus'): 220600 Minsk, K. Marksa 40; tel. (0172) 39-91-29; fax (0172) 34-53-50; distributes environmental information, organizes conferences, seminars on ecology; Co-ordinator SERGEI DOROZHKO.

Socio-Ecological Union 'Chernobyl': Minsk, 220034 Minsk, Frunze 5; tel. (0172) 20-39-04; campaigns on ecological issues; Chair. VASIL YAKORENKO.

Defence

In June 1993 the total strength of Belarus's armed forces was an estimated 102,600, comprising ground forces of 50,500, an air force of 14,100, and air defence forces of 15,600. Belarus's armed forces were to be reduced to 90,000–100,000, following the completion of the establishment of the National Armed Forces. Military service is compulsory for males and lasts for 18 months (an alternative service also exists). In 1992 there were an estimated 30,000 Russian troops stationed in Belarus (mostly engaged in work related to strategic forces), which were not due to leave until 1999.

Chief of the General Staff: Maj.-Gen. MIKALAI CHURKIN.

Bibliography

Gross, J. *Revolution from Abroad: The Soviet Conquest of Poland's western Ukraine and western Belorussia.* Princeton, New Jersey, Princeton University Press, 1988.

Kipel, V., and Kipel, Z. *Byelorussian Statehood: Reader and Bibliography.* New York, Belarusian Institute of Arts and Sciences, 1988.

Lubachko, I. S., *Belorussia under Soviet Rule, 1917–1957.* Lexington, Kentucky, University of Kentucky Press, 1972.

Marples, D. R., 'Post-Soviet Belarus and the Impact of Chernobyl' in *Post-Soviet Geography,* Vol. 33, No. 7 (September). 1992.

Martel, R. *Les Blancs-russes: Etude Historique, Geographique, Politique et Economique.* Paris, André Delpeuch, 1929.

Mienski, J., 'The Establishment of the Belorussian SSR', in *Belorussian Review,* No. 1. 1955.

Urban, M. *An Algebra of Soviet Power: Elite Circulation in the Belorussian Republic, 1966–86.* Cambridge, Cambridge University Press, 1989.

Vakar N. *Belorussia: The Making of a Nation.* Cambridge, Massachusetts, Harvard University Press, 1956.

Zaprudnik, I. *Belarus: At a Crossroads in History.* Boulder, Colorado, Westview Press, 1993.

BOSNIA AND HERZEGOVINA

Geography

PHYSICAL FEATURES

The Republic of Bosnia and Herzegovina is largely a mountainous territory with only about 20 km (12 miles) of coastline, which is of little maritime significance. Roughly triangular in shape, the Republic juts into Croatia, which forms its western border (running from north-west to south-east, along the Dinaric Alps) and its northern border. The rest of its borders are with Yugoslavia (Federal Republic): Serbia lies to the east (there is a short border with the Serbian territory of the Vojvodina in the north-east) and Montenegro to the south-east. The total area of the Republic, formerly part of the Yugoslav federation, is 51,129 sq km (19,741 sq miles).

The ancient province of Bosnia is roughly the territory bounded by the Sava, Drina and Una rivers. Along the Sava, which forms the northern border, there are fertile lowlands. The chief town, and the capital of the Republic, is Sarajevo, which is in the south, near the head-waters of the River Bosna (from which the province acquired its name). The smaller province of Herzegovina (only 18.0% of the total area) occupies the south of the Republic, with the Dalmatian coastal strip (Croatia) to the south-west and Montenegro (Yugoslavia) to the south-east. Its chief town is Mostar. Most of Herzegovina is mountainous and infertile, but there are fruitful valleys.

CLIMATE

The largely mountainous territory of Bosnia and Herzegovina had a continental climate, although this was moderated with proximity to the coast. The hinterland of the Dalmatian coast (Croatia) and the territory around Bosnia and Herzegovina's small coastal town of Neum had a Mediterranean climate.

POPULATION

The population, according to the census of 1991, totalled 4,364,574, with a density of 85.4 per sq km. No single ethnic group constituted an overall majority. The Bosnian Muslims (Bosniaks) were a Serbo-Croat-speaking people, originally Roman Catholic, who adopted Islam during the Ottoman occupation. In 1971 they were accorded separate status as a Yugoslav national unit (the term 'Muslim' not only includes the Bosnian Muslims, however, but other Slav Muslims) and they were the largest single group in the Republic. In 1991 they comprised 43.7% of the total population. The Serbs accounted for 31.4% of the population and the Croats 17.3%. Religious affiliation is roughly equated with ethnicity. Most of the Bosnian Muslims are Sunni, although a few are members of a Dervish order, introduced in 1974. The Croats are Roman Catholic, while the Serbs and Montenegrins adhere to the Eastern Orthodox Church. The principal language is Serbo-Croat; the Muslims use the Latin script, like the Croats, while the Serbs use the Cyrillic.

On 27 March 1992, shortly after the civil war began in Bosnia and Herzegovina, a 'Serbian Republic of Bosnia' was formed. In 1993 this 'Republic' covered about 72% of the total area of Bosnia and Herzegovina (most of eastern area of the country and the north-west); its administration was based in Banja Luka, the second-largest city in Bosnia and Herzegovina, but its parliament met in Pale, a suburb of Sarajevo. On 7 July 1992 a Croat state, the 'Croatian Union of Herzeg-Bosna', was declared. 'Herzeg-Bosna' originally comprised about 30% of the area of Bosnia and Herzegovina (mainly western Herzegovina), including Mostar, but by the end of 1993 had lost much of its territory to Serb and Bosnian Government forces. On 27 September 1993 the formation of the 'Autonomous Province of Western Bosnia' was announced. 'Western Bosnia' was a Muslim-dominated area, claiming the cities of Bihać, Cazin and Velika Kladusa. Its headquarters was in Velika Kladusa.

Chronology

168 BC: Illyria (which included Bosnia and Herzegovina and other former Yugoslav territories) was annexed by the Roman Empire.

395 AD: Following a division of the administration of the Roman Empire, Illyria was ruled by the Eastern Roman ('Byzantine') Emperor in Constantinople (Istanbul); this marked the beginning of the history of Bosnia and Herzegovina as a region on the borders of Western and Eastern Europe.

5th century: Southern Slav peoples began to move from the north into Illyria and the Balkans.

7th–8th centuries: Western Christian missionaries, from Aquileia (Trieste) and Salzburg, were active among the Croats and the Slovenes, respectively, introducing the Latin script and a Western cultural orientation.

863: The missionary activity of the Byzantine brothers, SS Constantine (Cyril) and Methodius, led to the conversion of the Serbs (including the ancestors of the Bosnians) and the Bulgars to Eastern Orthodox Christianity; a Slavonic liturgy was introduced with a written language, in the Cyrillic script.

11th century: Emergence of the Serb principality of Rama, the original Bosnian state, although it soon fell under the influence of the Catholic Croat kingdom.

1102: Croatia's personal union with Hungary effectively, if not finally, linked it to the Hungarian Crown.

1180–1204: The local ruler (ban) under the Hungarian Crown, Kulin, despite the disapproval of the Catholic authorities, was tolerant of the emergence of the dualist Christian heresy of the Bogomils; this was widely adopted by the local élite of a territory strongly disputed for by not only the Hungarians, but also the Serbs, Byzantines and Venetians.

1187: The Emperor in Constantinople acknowledged Serbian independence and Hungarian conquests in Croatia and Bosnia, but authority in the area remained uncertain. By the middle of the next century the local élite enjoyed sufficient independence from the Catholic and Orthodox powers that the Bogomils' Bosnian Church (*ecclesia Sclavoniae*) was virtually a state religion.

1322–53: Reign of Stjepan II Kotromanić, who established a powerful Bosnian state, nominally subject to Hungary.

1346: Coronation of Uroš IV (Stjepan Dušan of Raška, who reigned 1331–55) as Tsar of the Serbs and Greeks, at Skopje; his short-lived empire incorporated the territory subsequently known as Herzegovina.

1377: Stjepan Trvtko I (1353-91) proclaimed himself Tsar of the Bosnians and Serbs, renouncing Hungarian overlordship; his kingdom secured control of much of the Adriatic coast.

1389: The Turkish Ottoman Empire destroyed the Serbian nobility at a battle on the plain of Kosovo Polje.

1448: Herzegovina became a border duchy of Austria (*herceg* means 'duke'), as the Habsburgs attempted to improve the security of the Serbian princes and the Bosnian kingdom against the encroaching Ottomans.

1463: The Ottomans finally ended Bosnian independence.

1483: The province of Herzegovina was annexed to the Ottoman Empire.

1624: After some 150 years of Ottoman rule and the often political conversion of the Slav élite, two-thirds of the population of the provinces of Bosnia and Herzegovina were officially Muslim.

July 1878: At the Congress of Berlin, the Habsburg Empire of Austria-Hungary (already having regained Croatia) secured administration rights in Bosnia and Herzegovina; the Bosnian élite's National Muslim Organization, which sought to protect the Muslim community against competing Croat and Serb claims, was tolerated, but had less influence under the Habsburgs.

5 October 1908: Austria-Hungary formally annexed Bosnia and Herzegovina, despite international objections, following the 'Young Turk' uprising in the Ottoman Empire, which led to disturbances in the Balkans; the Habsburg ally, Germany, prevented war against Serbia.

1910: The secret 'Greater Serb' society, Union or Death (the 'Black Hand'), was founded by Col Dimitrijević-Apis.

28 June 1914: The heir to the Habsburg throne, Archduke Francis Ferdinand, and his wife were assassinated in Sarajevo, by a Bosnian student acting for the Serb Black Hand group.

28 July 1914: Austria-Hungary declared war on Serbia, which started the First World War between the Central Powers, of Austria-Hungary and Germany, and the Entente Powers, of France, Russia, Serbia and the United Kingdom.

July 1917: Serbia and the other Southern Slavs (excluding the Bulgarians) declared their intention to form a unitary state, under the Serbian monarchy.

29 October 1918: Following the defeat and dissolution of the Danubian Monarchy, the Southern Slav (Yugoslav) peoples separated from the Austro-Hungarian system of states (a Southern Slav republic was established on 15 October); Dalmatia, Croatia-Slavonia, Bosnia and Herzegovina, parts of Carinthia, Carniola and the Banat were, subsequently, ceded formally to the new state.

4 December 1918: Proclamation of the Kingdom of Serbs, Croats and Slovenes (Kingdom of Yugoslavia from 1929), which united Serbia and Montenegro with the former Habsburg lands.

1937: Josip Broz (Tito) became General Secretary of the Communist Party of Yugoslavia (CPY), which was to become the main partner in the Partisan (National Liberation Army) resistance to invasion during the Second World War.

10 April 1941: Following the German-Italian invasion and partition of Yugoslavia, an Independent State of Croatia (including Bosnia and Herzegovina) was proclaimed, with the Italian, Duke Aimone of Spoleto (Split), as King, and a Government under Ante Pavelić, leader of the Fascist Ustaša (Rebel) movement; Bosnia and Herzegovina experienced some of the worst fighting in the internecine struggles of the war period.

29 November 1943: In the Bosnian town of Jajce, following fierce resistance and civil conflict with the Serb royalist Četniks (Yugoslav Army of the Fatherland) and with the Ustaša regime, Gen. (later Marshal) Tito's Partisans proclaimed their own government for liberated areas (including much of eastern Bosnia).

29 November 1945: Following elections for a Provisional Assembly, the Federative People's Republic of Yugoslavia was proclaimed, with Tito as prime minister.

January 1946: A Soviet-style Constitution, establishing a federation of six Republics, of which one was Bosnia and Herzegovina, and two autonomous regions, was adopted. The Communist regime subsequently banned the 'Young Muslims' organization, which sought to champion the rights of Muslims, but was condemned as a terrorist group.

April 1963: A new Constitution changed the country's name to the Socialist Federal Republic of Yugoslavia (SFRY).

1971: The Slav Muslims (mainly the 'Bosnian' Muslims or Bosniaks) were granted recognition as a distinct ethnic group and the status of one of the six 'nations of Yugoslavia'. Greater autonomy was granted to the federal units and the system of collective leadership and the regular rotation of posts was adopted in the federation and in the administration of Bosnia and Herzegovina.

February 1974: A new federal Constitution was adopted.

4 May 1980: Tito died; his responsibilities were transferred to the collective federal State Presidency and to the Presidium of the LCY.

1983: The trial of the 13 'Sarajevo Muslims', of whom one of the leaders was Dr Alija Izetbegović (condemned as a 'Young Muslim' in 1946), ended in their imprisonment for allegedly favouring an Islamic state.

18 November 1990: Elections to the collective State Presidency of Bosnia and Herzegovina were held (the three nationalist parties—representing the main Bosnian Muslim, Serb and Croat ethnic groups—secured all seven seats); the first round of voting for the new, bicameral Assembly also took place (the second round was on 2 December).

9 December 1990: The final round of voting for the Assembly took place; of the 240 seats, the predominantly Muslim Party of Democratic Action (PDA) won 86, the Serbian Democratic Party (SDP) 72 and the Croatian Democratic Union of Bosnia and Herzegovina (CDU-BH) 44.

20 December 1990: The three main parties, all of them nationalist groups, announced their coalition agreement: Dr Alija Izetbegović, the leader of the PDA, was to be President of the republican State Presidency; Jure Pelivan of the CDU-BH, the Premier; and Momčilo Krajišnik of the SDP, President of the Assembly.

26 April 1991: In the first indication that the political crises in Yugoslavia could be reflected in Bosnia and Herzegovina, Serb-dominated districts in the north-west unilaterally announced the formation of the 'Municipal Community of Bosanska (Bosnian) Krajina'; the move was repudiated by the republican authorities, who feared a link with the Serb 'Krajina' territory in Croatia.

15 May 1991: The 'Serbian bloc' (the representatives of Serbia, Kosovo-Metohija, Vojvodina and Montenegro) on the federal State Presidency prevented the accession of Stipe Mesić of Croatia as the first non-Communist President of Yugoslavia, effectively depriving Yugoslavia of a head of state.

25 June 1991: The Croatian and Slovenian Assemblies declared the independence and sovereignty of their Republics, beginning the process of dissociation from the federation and the onset of armed conflicts on the territory of the old Yugoslavia.

30 June 1991: A European Community (EC) mediating team secured agreement to a cease-fire in Slovenia and Croatia, with the threat of EC sanctions, and the immediate proclamation of Stipe Mesić as President of the federal State Presidency; there was to be a three-month moratorium on further implementation of the Croatian and Slovenian declarations of dissociation.

16 August 1991: Izetbegović, President of the Presidency of Bosnia and Herzegovina, announced that a referendum on the Republic's future would be held; he repudiated a recent claim by the Serbians, Montenegrins and other Serbs to have reached an accommodation between them and the Slav Muslims.

2 September 1991: Despite the six Republics accepting the EC cease-fire plan, which provided for EC monitors and a peace conference on the future of Yugoslavia, fighting continued in Croatia. Meanwhile, in Bosnia and Herzegovina, Serb-dominated municipalities began to group together and declare 'Serbian Autonomous Regions', (SARs) in 'Eastern and Old Herzegovina', in 'Bosanska Krajina' (centred in Banja Luka), near Sarajevo in 'Romanija' and in north-eastern Bosnia (the SAR of 'Northern Bosnia').

26 September 1991: Ethnic tensions in the Republic resulted in shooting incidents along the borders with Croatia and Montenegro.

8 October 1991: The State Presidency of Bosnia and Herzegovina endorsed Izetbegović's declaration of the Republic's neutrality.

15 October 1991: The Assembly declared the Republic's sovereignty, emphasizing the inviolability of its borders and its willingness to consider a form of Yugoslav association; this declaration was rejected by the SARs, which declared themselves subject only to the federation.

24 October 1991: The Serb deputies of the republican Assembly announced the formation of an 'Assembly of the Serb Nation of Bosnia and Herzegovina' (Serb Assembly), which then proposed a referendum on a common Serb state.

9–10 November 1991: The Serb referendum was reported to have indicated overwhelming support for remaining in a common Serb state.

29 February–1 March 1992: In a referendum, boycotted by the Serb community, it was shown that 99.4% of voters (comprising 63% of the electorate) supported full independence. The Republic was declared independent by President Izetbegović and renamed the Republic of Bosnia and Herzegovina.

27 March 1992: The formation of the 'Serbian Republic of Bosnia and Herzegovina' was announced, to be headed by the leader of the SDP, Dr Radovan Karadžić.

7 April 1992: Bosnia and Herzegovina's independence was formally recognized by the EC and the USA.

2 May 1992: The siege of Sarajevo by Serb forces begins.

19 May 1992: The Jugoslavenska Narodna Armija (JNA, Yugoslav People's Army) announced the withdrawal of its troops from Bosnia and Herzegovina (ordered by the leadership of the newly established Federal Republic of Yugoslavia—FRY, which consisted of Serbia and Montenegro).

20 May 1992: The Bosnian Government declared that the JNA was now an 'occupying force' in Bosnia and Herzegovina and that a republican army would be established.

22 May 1992: Bosnia and Herzegovina was accepted as a member of the UN.

30 May 1992: The UN introduced sanctions against the FRY as a result of its continuing intervention in the civil war in Bosnia and Herzegovina.

7 July 1992: The formation of the 'Croatian Union of Herzeg-Bosna' was announced; it was to be led by Mate Boban and claimed about 30% of the territory of Bosnia and Herzegovina.

26 August 1992: The London Conference opened in the United Kingdom, co-chaired by UN and EC mediators Cyrus Vance and Lord Owen. It was decided that a permanent conference should be set up in Geneva, Switzerland.

28 October 1992: Cyrus Vance and Lord Owen announced their peace plan in Geneva; this Vance–Owen Plan envisaged the division of Bosnia and Herzegovina into 10 autonomous provinces.

22 February 1993: The UN Security Council decided to establish an international court to try those who had committed war crimes in the former Yugoslav Republics since 1991.

2 May 1993: Karadžić, under pressure from the international community, signed the Vance–Owen Plan in Geneva; on 5 May the Serb Assembly at Pale decisively rejected it.

22 May 1993: A communiqué signed by the USA, France, Russia, Spain and the United Kingdom declared that international armed forces would not intervene in the conflict on behalf of the Muslims and that the arms embargo would continue; the countries proposed the formation of six 'safe areas' for the Muslims, which came into effect on 22 July.

16 June 1993: A new peace initiative was announced in Geneva, according to which Bosnia and Herzegovina would be divided into three ethnically based states.

21 June 1993: The Bosnian State Presidency convened at Zagreb, Croatia. No consensus was reached with regard to the new peace plan; Izetbegović and his deputy, Ejup Ganić, boycotted further discussion of the plan in Geneva, while the seven remaining members of the Presidency attended the talks.

30 July 1993: Representatives of the three sides in the Bosnian conflict reached a constitutional agreement in Geneva, whereby Bosnia and Herzegovina would become the 'Union of Republics of Bosnia and Herzegovina'—a loose confederation of three states.

2 August 1993: The three Croat members of the State Presidency, Miro Lasić, Franjo Boras and Mile Akmadžić resigned from the Bosnian Government delegation at Geneva and joined the Croatian negotiating team, in protest at the treatment of Croats in central Bosnia and Herzegovina by the Bosnian army.

17 August 1993: Muslim forces were alleged to have killed and mutilated about 40 Croats in Kiseljak.

27 August 1993: During a session of the State Presidency, the Croat Prime Minister, Mile Akmadžić, was dismissed.

28 August 1993: The 'House of Representatives of the Assembly of the Croatian Republic of Herzeg-Bosna' was established in Grude; it officially proclaimed the 'Croatian Republic of Herzeg-Bosna'; the Assembly comprised members of the 'Croatian Community of Herzeg-Bosna' and deputies from the Chamber of Communes of the Bosnia and Herzegovina Assembly; the Geneva Plan was accepted by the deputies on condition that the other two sides in the conflict also accepted it. On the same day the Serb Assembly voted in favour of the plan.

31 August 1993: At a session of the Bosnia and Herzegovina Assembly the Geneva Plan was rejected in its existing form, but deputies agreed that it should be a basis for further peace negotiations.

10 September 1993: In Banja Luka members of the First Krajina Corps of the 'Serbian Republic' army seized municipal buildings and demanded improved material conditions for Serb soldiers and their families and an end to war profiteering; the operation was named 'September 93' and was led by Ostoja Zec. On the same day, in the district of Bihać in north-west Bosnia and Herzegovina, Fikret Abdić, a Muslim member of the State Presidency declared his intention to establish the 'Autonomous Province of Western Bosnia'.

17 September 1993: Following intensive negotiations with Serb leaders the blockade of Banja Luka, by members of operation 'September 93', was ended and Ostoja Zec was arrested.

27 September 1993: A 'Bosnian Convention', of Muslims, opened in Sarajevo. In Velika Kladusa the 'Autonomous Province of Western Bosnia' was officially established and Abdić was elected President by its 'Constituent Assembly'; a state of martial law was imposed by Izetbegović on the whole of 'Western Bosnia'.

28 September 1993: The Bosnian Convention declared that Bosnian Muslims would subsequently be termed 'Bosniaks'; the majority favoured the Geneva Plan, but only if the territories captured from the Muslims were returned.

3 October 1993: The Muslim Democratic Party was established in Velika Kladusa; Abdić was named Chairman. The first casualties were reported between forces loyal to Izetbegović and those supporting Abdić, when government troops stormed a radio station held by the rebels. The next day, the Constitutional Court of Bosnia and Herzegovina annulled the declaration of an 'Autonomous Province of Western Bosnia'. It was alleged that 2,500 government troops joined Abdić in the conflict, who arranged truces with the Serbs and Croats.

5 February 1994: The shelling of a Sarajevo market-place by Serb forces, causing many casualties, provoked the UN to threaten military intervention; this led to a cease-fire around Sarajevo, particularly following a Russian diplomatic initiative.

8 February 1994: Boban resigned as President of Herzeg-Bosna, to be replaced by a Presidential Council.

1 March 1994: An agreement was signed in Washington, DC (USA), between delegates of the Croats and of the Bosniak-dominated Bosnian Government, providing for a Croat-Bosniak federation in a confederal association with Croatia.

25 March 1994: The premier of the 'Serbian Republic', Vladimir Lukić, resigned. The Serb authorities continued to reject participation in the Washington Agreement.

31 March 1994: A Constituent Assembly of mainly Bosniak and Croat deputies declared the Federation of Bosnia and Herzegovina.

10 April 1994: The UN ordered the first air strike against Serb ground forces, which were attacking Goražde, such threats earlier in the year having improved the situation in Sarajevo.

History

The territory which now constitutes Bosnia and Herzegovina was settled by Southern Slavs during the Dark Ages, in the sixth century AD. The ancestors of the Bosnians spoke Serbo-Croat, but their exact ethnic identification is obscured by political controversy and their long existence on the borders of the various Eastern and Western blocs. The original Bosnian principality, Rama, which emerged in the 11th century, is often identified with the related principalities of Zeta (the original Montenegrin state) and Raška (Serbia). However, the Bosnians were also Western Catholics, which associated them with the Croats. On the borders of the surviving Roman Empire, the Eastern Empire ruled from Constantinople, Bosnia eventually fell under Hungarian domination in the 12th century. Bosnia remained a subject of dispute and rivalry between the powers, however, and was fought over by the Hungarians, the Eastern Romans or 'Byzantines', Serbs, Croats and Venetians. All these peoples did have the pursuit of one policy in common though, with their crusades against the Bogomil heresy (an ascetic, radical dualistic sect, influenced by the Manichees). The heresy, nevertheless, established itself and, in 1353, the territory gained its independence from Hungary, under Stjepan Tvrtko, who styled himself as the Tsar of the Bosnians and Serbs. Bosnia maintained a precarious independence until its final conquest by the Ottoman Turks, in 1463. Meanwhile, the territory now known as Herzegovina had become part of the Serbian Empire of Stjepan Dušan (Uroš IV). This Empire disintegrated in the latter half of the 14th century, the power of the Serbian princes finally being defeated by the Ottomans, in 1389. Herzegovina became an Austrian border duchy (hence its name, from the Serbo-Croat for 'duke', *herceg*), in 1448, but was itself incorporated into the Ottoman Empire in 1483.

From the end of the 15th century, therefore, Bosnia and Herzegovina fell under the same occupying power. During the centuries of Ottoman rule, many of the Slavs of Bosnia converted to Islam, and the Bosnian nobility enjoyed a favoured status in the region. Generally, however, the normal administration of the Ottoman Empire was based on confessional grounds. The *millet* system grouped people according to their religion, making the religious leaders responsible for the civil obedience of their followers. This was an effective means of governing the area, with its complicated ethnic and religious divisions, but it also preserved those divisions.

The Habsburg Empire, which was to the north of Bosnia, settled Serbs in the borderlands (Krajina), to defend against the Turks. With the disintegration of Ottoman power and the increasing unrest in the Balkans, the Austro-Hungarian Empire gained administration rights in Bosnia and Herzegovina by the agreements of the Congress of Berlin, in 1878. The territory was formally annexed to the Habsburg Crown, on 5 October 1908, in response to the Turkish revolution of that year. This caused the so-called Bosnian Crisis, which was among the first of the Great-Power confrontations preceding the First World War. Germany sided with Austria-Hungary, which was concerned to limit Serbian expansionism, against Russia and, to an extent, the United Kingdom. Serbian nationalist activity continued to trouble the province, despite the Trialist proposals to transform the Dual Monarchy of Austria-Hungary into a 'Triple Monarchy', with the Southern Slavs as a partner. On 28 June 1914 the heir to the Habsburg throne, Archduke

Francis Ferdinand, and his wife were assassinated in Sarajevo, while on a visit to Bosnia and Herzegovina. Their murderer, Gavril Princip, was a Bosnian student acting for a radical Serb nationalist group. The Serbian Government was not involved, but Austria-Hungary decided to use the opportunity to end the threat it perceived from Serbia. One month after the assassination the Empire declared war on Serbia and this conflict escalated into the First World War. During the War, the Serbs and Croats were among the parties to an agreement to form a common state under the Serbian monarchy. At the end of the War, therefore, Bosnia and Herzegovina became part of the Kingdom of Serbs, Croats and Slovenes, which was proclaimed on 4 December 1918 (it was renamed Yugoslavia in 1929).

With the decline of Ottoman power during the 19th century the Muslim Slavs, notably the Bosnian élite, formed the National Muslim Organization to protect their political, religious and cultural rights. It developed the policy of maximizing its influence by supporting either the Serbs or the Croats. These two ethnic groups competed for dominance in Bosnia and Herzegovina and sometimes tried to reclaim the Bosnian Muslims (Bosniaks) as their own ethnic group. Under the Habsburgs, particularly Governor Benjamin Kallay, between 1882 and 1903, the Muslims had little political influence. However, Mehmet Spaho succeeded in influencing the royal regime of the unitary Southern Slav state, after the First World War. During the Second World War some Muslims supported the Axis Powers, but many others were members of Tito's (Josip Broz) Partisans, who were dominant in most of Bosnia and Herzegovina. The province experienced the most savage strife of the civil war, which raged at the same time as the resistance to the Nazi occupation and the Ustaša Croatian regime, owing to the ethnic complexity of the area.

After the War Bosnia and Herzegovina was made a constituent Republic of the Yugoslav federation (despite Serbian pressure to make it a province, like Kosovo or the Vojvodina) and, during the 1960s, it was Tito who truly established Muslim power. This was to help counter the growing ethnic tension between the Serbs and Croats of the Republic. The federal authorities were attempting to create a Muslim power-base independent of, but equal to, the Serbs and Croats. This policy led to the Slav Muslims being granted a distinct ethnic status, as a nation of Yugoslavia, for the 1971 census. The politicians of Bosnia and Herzegovina became adept at coalition politics and, following the changes in Yugoslavia during 1990, remained committed to the institution of a collective State Presidency.

THE DEMISE OF THE YUGOSLAV FEDERATION

Rising ethnic tensions in Bosnia and Herzegovina, potentially the most dangerous in the mosaic of ethnic groups of Yugoslavia, were exemplified in September 1990. Followers of the Party of Democratic Action (PDA), the principal Muslim party of the Republic, demonstrated in the neighbouring Sandjak area of Serbia. They were supporting Muslim rights in the Novi Pazar district, but clashed with Serb nationalists. Furthermore, in the November-December republican elections for a newly reorganized Assembly of 240 seats, the three main parties to emerge were all nationalist: the Muslim PDA, with 86 seats; the Serbian Democratic Party (SDP), with 72 seats; and the Croatian Democratic Union of Bosnia and Herzegovina (CDU-BH—an affiliate of the ruling CDU party of Croatia), with 44 seats. The ruling League of Communists of Bosnia and Herzegovina gained only 19 seats, five of which were in alliance with the Socialist Alliance. The three nationalist parties also took all seven seats on the directly elected collective State Presidency and formed a coalition administration for the Republic. Dr Alija Izetbegović of the PDA was to be President of the Presidency, Jure Pelivan of the CDU-BH was to be President of the Executive Council (Premier or Prime Minister) and Momčilo Krajišnik of the SDP, President of the Assembly.

Following the declarations of independence by Slovenia and Croatia in June 1991, Izetbegović, together with the Macedonian leader, suggested a looser federation of Yugoslav Republics, but civil conflict continued. Serb-dominated territories in Bosnia and Herzegovina declared their intent to remain within the Yugoslav federation (or in a 'Greater Serbia'). In response, the republican Government rejected these moves and declared the inviolability of the internal boundaries of Yugoslavia. Armed incidents contributed to the rising tension throughout mid-1991. At this time the European Community (EC) and the USA banned arms sales to the former Yugoslav Republics; the UN followed suit in September, under Resolution 713. In October the Jugoslavenska Narodna Armija (JNA, Yugoslav People's Army) assumed effective control of Mostar, to the north-west of the Serb 'Old' Herzegovina, and began a siege of the Croatian city of Dubrovnik, which was reported to be the favoured capital of the same territory.

In October 1991 both the republican State Presidency (with the dissenting votes of the Serb members) and the PDA proposed to the Assembly that the Republic declare its independence (Macedonia had already done so in September). The proposals did favour a renewed federation, but only one in which the Republic had equal relations with both Serbia and Croatia. On 14 October, during the debate in the Assembly, the Serbs (mainly the SDP) rejected any such declaration as a move towards secession. They claimed that Serbs should live in one state. No compromise was reached and the Serb representatives withdrew from the chamber. However, on 15 October the 'rump' Assembly declared that the Republic of Bosnia and Herzegovina was a sovereign state within its existing borders.

In September 1991 several Serb-dominated areas had announced the formation of 'Serbian Autonomous Regions' (SARs): Bosanska Krajina (which in April that year had proclaimed itself the 'Municipal Community of Bosanska Krajina' and in June had declared its unification with the SAR of Krajina, in Croatia), Eastern and Old Herzegovina, Romanija and Northern Bosnia. Other ethnic groups accused the Serbs, with the backing of the JNA, of planning a Greater Serbia. The SARs rejected the republican Assembly's resolution and declared that only the federal laws and Constitution would apply on their territory; Bosanska Krajina considered that the Republic of Bosnia and Herzegovina had dissolved itself. On 24 October the Serb deputies of the Bosnia and Herzegovina Assembly constituted an 'Assembly of the Serb Nation of Bosnia and Herzegovina' at Pale, on the outskirts of Sarajevo. This body then resolved to hold a referendum on whether the Serbs of Bosnia and Herzegovina should stay in a common Yugoslav state or not and nominated Radovan Karadžić, leader of the SDP, as its representative for the federal State Presidency. At the beginning of November another SAR was proclaimed, consisting of the Serbs of Northern Bosnia, with an Assembly based in Doboj (this area did not have a Serb majority). On 9–10 November the referendum of the Republic's Serbs overwhelmingly supported staying in a Yugoslav or Serb state. However, after a referendum held on 29 February and 1 March 1992, which was boycotted by the Serbs, 99.4% of the 63% of the electorate who participated, voted in favour of full independence. President Izetbegović immediately declared independence, and omitted the word 'socialist' from the new state's official title.

The EC and the USA recognized Bosnia and Herzegovina's independence on 7 April.

CIVIL WAR

Following the declaration of independence, there were renewed hostilities between Serbs and Muslims in Sarajevo and elsewhere. On 27 March 1992 a 'Serbian Republic of Bosnia and Herzegovina', was declared, to be headed by Karadžić. The 'Republic', with its headquarters in Banja Luka, comprised about 65% of the total area of Bosnia and Herzegovina. In April the fighting intensified and several cities, including Sarajevo, were besieged by Serb troops. (A state of emergency was declared in Sarajevo in April and EC and UN peace mediators were evacuated the following month.) In early May, however, the newly established Federal Republic of Yugoslavia (FRY—composed solely of Serbia and Montenegro), in an apparent attempt to disclaim any responsibility for the civil conflict in Bosnia and Herzegovina, ordered all of its citizens in the JNA to withdraw from the Republic within 15 days. Izetbegović requested foreign intervention, but the UN decided against the deployment of a peace-keeping force in the Republic under prevailing conditions. On 22 May Bosnia and Herzegovina was accepted as a member of the UN.

At the end of May 1992 Serb forces were in control of two-thirds of the Republic's territory. On 20 May the Government of Bosnia and Herzegovina declared the JNA to be an 'occupying force' and announced the formation of a republican army. On 30 May the UN imposed economic sanctions against the FRY, for its continuing involvement in the Bosnian conflict (the EC and the USA imposed sanctions in November 1991). In June the UN Security Council decided to redeploy 1,000 troops from the United Nations Protection Force in Yugoslavia (UNPROFOR) to protect Sarajevo airport. An additional 500 troops were dispatched to Sarajevo in mid-July.

In mid-June 1992 combined Bosnian and Croat forces recaptured the city of Mostar, which had been under Serbian control since October 1991. On 7 July a major development occurred in the Bosnian conflict, when a 'Croatian Union of Herzeg-Bosna', was declared. The new state covered about 30% of the territory of Bosnia and Herzegovina and was headed by Mate Boban. Izetbegović's Government promptly declared it illegal, while the Serb leader, Karadžić, proposed that Serbs and Croats partition Bosnia and Herzegovina among themselves. Despite their political differences, Izetbegović and the President of Croatia, Franjo Tudjman (who supported the establishment of Herzeg-Bosna), signed a treaty of co-operation and friendship in late July.

Revelations about the predominantly Serb policy of 'ethnic cleansing' (involving the expulsion by one ethnic group of other ethnic groups in an attempt to create a homogeneous population) and the discovery of a number of detention camps in Bosnia and Herzegovina led to the unanimous adoption by the UN Security Council, at the beginning of August 1992, of a resolution condemning the camps and those responsible for abuses of human rights. A further resolution, adopted in mid-August, demanded unimpeded access to the detention camps for the International Committee of the Red Cross (ICRC), authorized 'all measures necessary' to ensure the delivery of humanitarian aid, and reiterated that those abusing human rights in the former Yugoslavia would be held personally responsible. The ICRC was consequently given permission to inspect the camps and, having done so, accused all three ethnic communities in Bosnia and Herzegovina of using 'systematic brutality'. Further international pressure was brought to bear at a conference in the United Kingdom. At the end of August 1992 the London Conference, co-chaired by the UN and the EC mediators, brought together representatives of all the sides involved in the Bosnian conflict, but no lasting settlement was agreed. It was decided that future negotiations should take place at a permanent conference in Geneva, Switzerland. The UN subsequently adopted measures to increase the peace-keeping forces and the amount of humanitarian aid.

In an annex to the agreement signed in July 1992, the Governments of Croatia and Bosnia and Herzegovina formed a Joint Defence Committee, in late September, and demanded that the UN remove its arms embargo on Croatia and Bosnia and Herzegovina. However, hostilities between Bosnian Croats and Muslims occurred in mid-October and Croats seized the towns of Mostar, Novi Travnik and Vitez. (Mostar was declared the capital of Herzeg-Bosna.) Furthermore, it was reported that Croat forces expelled the entire Muslim population (more than 5,000 people) from the town of Prozor. In early November 1992 the Croat Jure Pelivan resigned as Prime Minister of Bosnia and Herzegovina and was replaced by Mile Akmadžić, also a Croat. In mid-November the Government of Croatia admitted for the first time that Croatian regular army units had been deployed alongside the 'Croatian Defence Council' (HVO—Hrvatsko Vijece Obrane) forces in Bosnia and Herzegovina and agreed to withdraw them.

In December 1992 the Organization of the Islamic Conference, meeting in Jeddah, Saudi Arabia, demanded that the West intervene in Bosnia and Herzegovina and threatened to break the UN arms embargo if no action was taken by late January 1993. The US Secretary of State, Richard Cheney, subsequently threatened the Serbs with air-strikes if the UN ban on military flights (Resolution 816, October 1992) was not respected. Also in early December the UN Human Rights Commission, reiterating a statement made by the ICRC in October, declared that the Serbs were largely responsible for violations of human rights in Bosnia and Herzegovina. Following allegations of the organized rape of more than 20,000 Muslim women by Serb forces, the UN Security Council unanimously adopted, in mid-December, a resolution condemning these 'acts of unspeakable brutality' and demanding access to all Serb detention camps. On 22 February 1993 the Security Council adopted a decision to try war criminals from the former Yugoslavia in an international court.

In mid-December 1992 the Serb enclave in Bosnia and Herzegovina, now calling itself simply the 'Serbian Republic', unilaterally declared that the conflict was at an end and that the Serbs had won their own 'independent and sovereign state'. However, by late December, Muslim forces appeared to be regaining territory. Both Serb–Muslim and Croat–Muslim violence intensified in early 1993, in spite of continued efforts on the part of the UN to negotiate a peace settlement. In mid-January fighting broke out between Muslims and Croats in Gornji Vakuf (in central Bosnia and Herzegovina), which continued into February. The Serbs continued their offensive on a series of Muslim enclaves along the Drina valley in the east and finally seized the towns of Kamenica and Cerska, which for 10 months had withstood the Serb siege. In April Serb attacks on the town of Srebrenica threatened to put an end to international peace negotiations. A plan, originally proposed in October 1992 by the co-Chairmen of the Geneva Peace Conference, Lord Owen (a former British foreign minister—the EC mediator) and Cyrus Vance (a former US Secretary of State—the UN mediator), had already been approved in full by Mate Boban, leader of the Bosnian Croats, and in theory (although not in every detail) by President Izetbegović. The plan envisaged the division of Bosnia and

Herzegovina into 10 autonomous provinces (with three provinces allocated to each side in the conflict and Sarajevo as a province with special status). If they accepted the Vance–Owen Plan the Bosnian Serbs would be forced to surrender some of the territory they had won from their opponents and were therefore reluctant to do so. Under intense international pressure, Radovan Karadžić, the Bosnian Serb leader, signed the plan in Geneva on 2 May. Three days later, however, the Serb Assembly decisively rejected it.

On 22 May 1993 the USA, France, Russia, Spain and the United Kingdom signed a communiqué in Washington, DC (USA), which stated that there would be no international intervention on behalf of the Muslims, nor would the arms embargo on Bosnia and Herzegovina be lifted. Instead, the countries proposed that 'safe areas' be established for the Muslims in Sarajevo, Bihać (in the north-west), Tuzla, Goražde, Srebrenica and Zepa (in the east). In these areas Muslims would be protected from Serb attacks by UN troops. Western defence ministers, meeting in Brussels (Belgium) in the following week, failed to endorse the 'safe areas' plan, and the Muslims regarded the proposal as economically unviable as the six areas would become isolated from the rest of Muslim-held territory. However, on 22 July the plan came into effect.

Following the rejection of the Vance–Owen Plan by the Serb Assembly, on 16 June 1993 at the conference in Geneva a new set of plans was revealed. Originally conceived by President Slobodan Milošević of Serbia and President Franjo Tudjman of Croatia, the plans sought to divide Bosnia and Herzegovina into three states on ethnic grounds. On 21 June, in Zagreb (Croatia), at the second full meeting of the Bosnian State Presidency since the war in Bosnia and Herzegovina began, opinions were divided among the members of the Presidency as to whether they should agree to the plans. President of the Presidency Izetbegović had decided to boycott discussion of the plan in Geneva and he and Ejup Ganić, Vice-President of the Presidency, returned to Sarajevo while the seven remaining members attended the conference.

Despite the negotiations, in mid-1993 hostilities in Bosnia and Herzegovina continued. Muslims and Croats were no longer allies in the war and in late June, following a meeting of reconciliation between Bosnian Serbs and Croats near Konjic in the south-west of the Republic, a joint offensive began against Maglaj, a town controlled by the Muslims in the north. At the beginning of July, following the capture by Muslim forces of a Croat military base in Mostar, the two sides began to fight for control of the city. President Izetbegović continued to boycott the peace negotiations in Geneva, stating that he would only attend once Bosnian Serbs had withdrawn from Mount Igman, a Muslim-held stronghold south-west of Sarajevo which the Serbs began to attack in June. By August 1993 the Serbs controlled approximately 72% of the territory of Bosnia and Herzegovina.

On 30 July 1993 a constitutional agreement on the partition of Bosnia and Herzegovina was reached by the three warring parties in Geneva. Under this agreement, Bosnia and Herzegovina was to be reconstituted as the 'Union of Republics of Bosnia and Herzegovina', comprising a loose confederation of three ethnically based states and a weak central government. It was later agreed that nine out of the 10 municipalities (that is, all except the municipality of Pale) of Sarajevo would be placed under UN protection and administered by local police during a two-year transition period. On 2 August, in protest at the alleged brutalities committed by the predominantly Muslim Bosnian army against the population of central Bosnia, Miro Lasić, Franjo Boras and Mile Akmadžić, the Croat members of the State Presidency, left the Bosnian delegation of the Geneva talks and joined the Croatian negotiating team. Throughout August there was heavy Croat–Muslim fighting in Mostar. Thousands of Muslim civilians were expelled to the left bank of the Neretva river. Hostilities between the two sides also intensified in central Bosnia. It was alleged that on 17 August Muslim forces massacred about 40 civilians in the Croat village of Kiseljak. In mid-August the fighting spread to Bihać, in the north-west. On 27 August Akmadžić, the Croat Prime Minister of Bosnia and Herzegovina, was dismissed at a session of the State Presidency.

At the end of August 1993 the Geneva Plan was debated in Bosnia and Herzegovina by representatives of all three sides in the Bosnian conflict. The Bosnia and Herzegovina Assembly, without Croat representatives of the Sarajevo region who would attend a separate session, rejected the Plan in its existing form, but agreed that it should be used as a basis for further negotiations. Deputies at a session of the Serb Assembly at Pale voted in favour of the Plan. On 28 August members of the 'Croatian Community of Herzeg-Bosna' and deputies from the Chamber of Communes of the Bosnia and Herzegovina Assembly established the 'House of Representatives of the Assembly of the Croat Republic of Herzeg-Bosna', in Grude. A vote was passed unanimously on the formation of the 'Croatian Republic of Herzeg-Bosna'. The deputies agreed to accept the Geneva Plan, on condition that it was also accepted by the Serbs and the Muslims.

In mid-September 1993 members of the First Krajina Corps of the Serbian Republic Army, led by Ostoja Zec, imposed an eight-day blockade on strategic buildings in Banja Luka, headquarters of the 'Serbian Republic'. The operation, 'September 93', was intended as a protest against war profiteering and a call for improved material conditions for Serb soldiers, invalids and the families of soldiers killed in the conflict. After talks with the state and military delegation of the 'Serbian Republic', tanks were withdrawn from the streets of Banja Luka on 17 September and authority was restored to the municipal authorities.

On 10 September 1993 Fikret Abdić, a member of the State Presidency and an outspoken critic of Izetbegović, announced his initiative for the formation of an 'Autonomous Province of Western Bosnia'. This was to be in the Bihać region, a Muslim enclave with approximately 300,000 inhabitants, many of them refugees, and it was to exist as part of the 'Union of Republics of Bosnia and Herzegovina'. On 27 September, in Velika Kladusa, the province was declared to have been established and Abdić was elected President by the 'Constituent Assembly'. Izetbegović responded by imposing a state of martial law on the entire territory of 'Western Bosnia'. On 1 October Abdić dissolved the Velika Kladusa municipal assembly and declared that elections would be held for a new representative body. On 3 October the new Muslim Democratic Party was established, with Abdić as Chairman. The following day the Constitutional Court of Bosnia and Herzegovina annulled the act adopted by the 'Constituent Assembly' of Velika Kladusa on 27 September. Regional forces (the Fifth Corps of the Bosnia and Herzegovina Army) were deployed in the area and, on 3 October, the first bloodshed occurred when government troops stormed a radio station in Velika Kladusa. On 4 October some 2,500 soldiers from the Fifth Corps reportedly defected to the rebels. Hostilities continued in the region into 1994.

On 27 September 1993 a 'Bosnian Convention' opened in Sarajevo. The main aim of the Convention was to assess the position of the Muslims with regard to the conflict in Bosnia and Herzegovina and the Geneva Plan. Participants in the Convention included representatives from the State Presidency, the Islamic clergy, the Army, the PDA, the Bosnia and Herzegovina Assembly and Muslim associations. The majority of participants voted in favour of accepting the Geneva Plan, on the condition that the territories captured by force from the Muslims were returned. The Convention declared that Bosnian Muslims would subsequently be called by their historical name of Bosniaks, in order to strengthen their national identity.

In mid-October 1993 Serb forces resumed their bombardment of Sarajevo. By then, according to official figures, 140,878 citizens of the Republic had either been killed in the fighting in Bosnia and Herzegovina, had died of cold or starvation or were missing. Approximately 20,000 more were being held in detention camps. On 5 February 1994 a particularly high number of casualties following the shelling of a Sarajevo market-place finally provoked the threat of Western military intervention. The UN commander in Sarajevo, the British general Sir Michael Rose, succeeded in implementing a cease-fire around the city, following warnings of air strikes against the Serbs by the North Atlantic Treaty Organisation (NATO). A dramatic Russian diplomatic initiative also helped Serb compliance with the peace process.

On 1 March 1994 the US Government succeeded in securing agreement to a peace settlement between the Croats and the Bosniak Muslims. Delegations from the Bosniak-dominated Government, from Herzeg-Bosna and from Croatia, signed a proposal for a Croat-Bosniak federation, which was to be linked to Croatia. The Serbs rejected the formula, but a Federation of Bosnia and Herzegovina was proclaimed on 31 March (see Late Information). On 10 April a Serb assault on Goražde, a UN-protected 'safe' area, caused the first NATO air strike against Serb ground forces.

The Economy

The economy of Bosnia and Herzegovina was severely affected by the civil war, which began in 1992, and this made a realistic assessment of its state difficult. Before the conflicts the economy had been mainly agricultural. The Republic produced tobacco, fruit and livestock. Sheep were grazed in the mountainous terrain, where timber reserves were also exploited. There are extensive mineral resources; in peace-time the Republic was a major producer of copper, lead, zinc and gold. Iron ore was mined and there were reserves of lignite (a poor-quality brown coal). Yugoslav federal government policy favoured the development of Bosnia and Herzegovina and other poorer regions, but industrialization did not become a significant feature of the local economy. There were some light industries and, during the 1970s and 1980s, the Sava Valley (along the northern border of the Republic) became the favoured development area for some heavy industries. There were iron and steel plants at Zenica. The armaments manufacturing industry was also important. Service industries, notably tourism, were not well developed before the civil war of the early 1990s.

In general, agricultural production is estimated to have fallen in 1992. According to official figures, total fruit production fell from 255,000 metric tons in 1991 to 168,000 tons. The number of livestock (mainly pigs, sheep and cattle) also fell. Most of this was attributable to the depredations and disruptions caused by the civil war. Tobacco production in 1992, however, was estimated at 7,000 metric tons, compared to 6,000 tons in 1990. The Ministry of Agriculture estimated that the grain harvest for 1993 would be approximately 25% less than the average yield, partly owing to shortages of fuel and fertilizers.

Industrial production in Bosnia and Herzegovina was severely affected by the armed conflict both in other former Yugoslav republics, which began in June 1991, and in the Republic itself. By late May 1992 it was estimated that about four-fifths of industrial plants in Bosnia and Herzegovina had been destroyed.

Electricity output in Bosnia and Herzegovina was estimated to have fallen to 17% of normal production capacity by mid-1992. In mid-1993 hostilities between Muslim and Croat forces damaged a hydroelectric power station in Mostar and a power line used to supply Sarajevo and its surrounding area with electricity. In October supplies of power and water in the capital were reported to be minimal, as no deliveries of fuel had been made since 16 August. Some gas was supplied to the Republic by the Russian Federation, via Hungary. Petroleum was in short supply in all regions of Bosnia and Herzegovina, owing either to the effects of armed conflict, or of the sanctions imposed on Serbia and Montenegro.

In September 1993 the UN World Food Programme estimated that 2.8m. people in Bosnia and Herzegovina would require food aid during the following six months. Central Bosnia and the five Muslim enclaves in the north and east of the Republic were particularly vulnerable to food shortages, as they remained isolated from the main supply routes.

Statistical Survey

Source (unless otherwise stated): *Yugoslav Survey*, Belgrade, POB 677, Moše Pijade 8/I; tel. (11) 333610; fax (11) 332295.

Area and Population

AREA, POPULATION AND DENSITY

Area (sq km)	51,129
Population (census results)	
31 March 1981	4,124,008
31 March 1991	4,364,574
Density (per sq km) at census of 31 March 1991	85.4

PRINCIPAL TOWNS (population at 1991 census): Sarajevo (capital) 415,631; Banja Luka 142,644 (Source: *Statistički godišnjak Jugoslavije*—Statistical Yearbook of Yugoslavia).

PRINCIPAL ETHNIC GROUPS (1991 census)

	Number	% of total population
Muslims	1,905,829	43.7
Serbs	1,369,258	31.4
Croats	755,892	17.3
'Yugoslavs'	239,845	5.5
Total (incl. others)	4,364,574	100.0

Agriculture

PRINCIPAL CROPS
('000 metric tons, unless otherwise indicated)

	1990	1991	1992
Wheat	457	474*	352†
Barley	83	80*	72†
Maize	734	1,267*	873†
Rye	11	11*	10†
Oats	72	58*	40†
Potatoes	338	395*	296†
Dry beans	21	35*	19†
Soybeans (Soya beans)	12	16*	11†
Rapeseed	8	2*	2†
Cabbages	84	107*	60†
Tomatoes	18	23*	14†
Chillies and peppers (green)	11	11†	9†
Onions (dry)*	44	60	40
Garlic*	6	6	6
Beans (green)*	6	5	2
Carrots	22	25*	15*
Watermelons*	6	11	7
Grapes	31	43†	31†
Sugar beets	140	161*	96†
Apples	36	31*	27†
Pears	20	21†	17†
Peaches and Nectarines	5	4†	3†
Plums	71	119*	64*
Apricots	2	2	2
Strawberries (metric tons)*	13,056	11,039	10,809
Raspberries (metric tons)*	4,288	3,206	3,588
Almonds (metric tons)*	908	1,142	749
Chestnuts (metric tons)†	600	550	500
Walnuts (metric tons)	3,885	1,366*	1,035*
Tobacco (leaves)	6	6*	7†

* Unofficial estimate. † FAO estimate.

Source: FAO, *Production Yearbook*.

LIVESTOCK ('000 head, unless otherwise indicated)

	1990	1991	1992*
Horses	100	96	70
Cattle	874	853	826
Pigs	614	617	590
Sheep	1,319	1,317	1,287
Chickens (million)	9†	10†	8

* FAO estimate. † Unofficial estimate.

Source: FAO, *Production Yearbook*.

LIVESTOCK PRODUCTS (metric tons)

	1990	1991	1992
Beef and veal	48,000	44,000*	43,000*
Mutton and lamb	13,000	11,000*	10,000*
Pig meat†	73,000	72,000	58,000
Poultry meat	24,000	15,000	15,000*
Cows' milk	907,000	885,000*	705,000*
Sheeps' milk	13,000	13,000*	10,000*
Butter	120	45*	35*
Cheese†	19,168	21,726	17,864
Eggs*	29,300	25,500	20,000
Honey	620	590*	470*
Wool:			
greasy	1,650	1,600*	1,300*
scoured	990	960*	780*
Cattle and buffalo hides*	10,476	9,900	7,974
Sheep skins*	2,400	2,300	2,300

* FAO estimate. † Unofficial estimate.

Source: FAO, *Production Yearbook*.

Mining

('000 metric tons)

	1990
Coal	17,926

Industry

SELECTED PRODUCTS
('000 metric tons, unless otherwise indicated)

	1990
Electric energy (million kWh)	14,632
Crude Steel	1,421
Aluminium	89
Machines	16
Tractors (number)	34,000
Lorries (number)	16,000
Motor cars (number)	38,000
Cement	797
Paper and paperboard	281
Television receivers (number)	21,000

Finance

When Bosnia and Herzegovina was part of the Yugoslav federation, the currency in use was the new dinar. However, in mid-1992, after Bosnia and Herzegovina had declared its independence, the Yugoslav central bank refused to supply the country with any further currency. The Yugoslav dinar remained in use, but its value declined considerably and, under war conditions, the population increasingly relied on exchanges in kind, government rationing vouchers and the 'black market' in foreign, convertible currencies. By October 1993, owing to the effects of international sanctions and 'hyperinflation', the Yugoslav currency was of limited use even in the Federal Republic of Yugoslavia (Serbia and Montenegro). In Bosnia and Herzegovina, any monetary policy of the official Government was irrelevant—it was intended to introduce a Bosnian dinar (on 1 July 1992), but such plans were postponed indefinitely. The 'Serbian Republic of Bosnia and Herzegovina' issued its own 'national currency', but this was effectively replaced, being declared to have an official exchange rate of 1:1 with the Yugoslav new dinar. The Croatian currency circulated in areas controlled by Croat militias.

Directory

The Constitution

The Constitution of (the then Socialist Republic of) Bosnia and Herzegovina was promulgated in 1974, under the rule of the League of Communists, and extensively amended in 1989, 1990 and 1991. In 1991 the Republic's Assembly planned to draft a new constitution, on the basis of consensus, but a deterioration in relations between the three main parties, in October, delayed any implementation of this process. The existing constitutional provisions were for: a seven-member, collective State Presidency (the members elected a President from among their own number); the Government (presided over by the Prime Minister), all of whom are members of, and responsible to, the Assembly; and a legislative, bicameral Assembly, consisting of the Chamber of Citizens and the Chamber of Communes or Municipalities, with 240 deputies in total. Bosnia and Herzegovina is a multi-party, democratic state, which guarantees basic human rights and freedoms. The principles of rotating leaderships and balanced ethnic representation were preserved in the Republic, the constitutional arrangements for which were similar to those of the former Yugoslav federation itself. There is a republican Supreme Court and Constitutional Court. In March 1992, following a referendum in which the electorate voted in favour of full independence, the Republic of Bosnia and Herzegovina declared its secession from the Yugoslav federation. International recognition was confirmed upon the Republic's admittance to the UN in May 1992.

On 30 July 1993 representatives of all three sides in the civil conflict in Bosnia and Herzegovina provisionally agreed to a new constitutional settlement, according to which the state would be reconstituted as the 'Union of Republics of Bosnia and Herzegovina', comprising three ethnically based republics and a weak central government. At the end of 1993 the division of territory among the three ethnic groups had yet to be agreed upon.

The Government

(November 1993)

STATE PRESIDENCY

The republican collective State Presidency consists of seven members, except during a state of emergency when it is extended to include the Prime Minister, the President of the Assembly and the Commander of the Bosnia and Herzegovina Army. The Presidency acts as commander-in-chief of the armed forces, directs foreign policy and appoints the Prime Minister, with the approval of the Assembly. The membership of the Presidency reflects the ethnic diversity of Bosnia and Herzegovina; any vacant seat must be filled by a member of the same ethnic group. Elections to the Presidency were held on 18 November 1990. The President of the Presidency was elected on 21 December 1990 and re-elected in 1991 by the other members of the Presidency. In December 1992 the President's mandate was automatically extended, owing to the state of emergency in the Republic.

The original ruling coalition after the November elections consisted of the Party of Democratic Action (PDA), the Serbian Democratic Party and the Croatian Democratic Union (CDU). As conflict increased, however, the Serbian Democratic Party withdrew from government and relations with the CDU became disrupted. The Socialist Democratic Party (former Communists) joined the State Presidency, as did the Croatian Peasant Party (CPP).

President of the Presidency: Dr ALIJA IZETBEGOVIĆ (PDA).

Vice-President: Dr EJUP GANIĆ (PDA).

Other Members: NIJAZ DURAKOVIĆ (Socialist Democratic Party), STJEPAN KLJUIĆ (CDU), IVO KOMSIĆ (CPP), MIRKO PEJANOVIĆ (Socialist Democratic Party), Tatjana Ljuic-Mijatović (Socialist Democratic Party).

MINISTERS

Prime Minister: HARIS SILAJDŽIĆ.

Deputy Prime Minister: HADZO EFENDIĆ.

Minister of Defence: HAMDIJA HADZIHASANOVIĆ.

Minister of Foreign Affairs: IRFAN LJUBIJANKIĆ.

Minister of Internal Affairs: BAKIR ALISPAHIĆ.

Minister of Justice and State Administration: BRANKO NIKOLIĆ.

Minister of Finance: (vacant).

Minister of the Economy: RESID BEGTIĆ.

Minister of Agriculture, Water Resources and Forestry: MILIVOJE NADAZDIN.

Minister of Transport and Communications: (vacant).

Minister of Reconstruction: UGLJESA UZELAC.

Minister of Town Planning, Construction and Environmental Protection: MUSTAFA DIZDAREVIĆ.

Minister of Health, Labour and Social Security: (vacant).

Minister of Education, Science and Culture: NIHAD HASIĆ.

Minister of Information: IVO KNEZEVIĆ.

Minister of Supply: HUSEIN AHMOVIĆ.

Minister of Religion: LUKIĆ ZLATKO.

Minister for Veterans' and Disabled Veterans' Affairs: DAVID BALABAN.

Ministers without Portfolio: BOZIDAR ANTIĆ, IBRAHIM COLAKHODŽIĆ, ISMET KASUMAGIĆ, VITOMIR MIRO LASIĆ, BRANKO DERIĆ.

MINISTRIES

Office of the Prime Minister: 71000 Sarajevo, Vojvode Putnika 3; tel. (71) 213777; fax (71) 272877.

Ministry of Agriculture, Water Resources and Forestry: 71000 Sarajevo, Vojvode Putnika 3; tel. (71) 213777; fax (71) 653592.

Ministry of Defence: 71000 Sarajevo, Vojvode Putnika 3A; tel. (71) 35427; fax (71) 653592.

Ministry of the Economy: 71000 Sarajevo, Vojvode Putnika 3; tel. (71) 213777; fax (71) 653592.

Ministry of Education, Science and Culture: 71000 Sarajevo, Vojvode Putnika 3; tel. (71) 213777; fax (71) 653592.

Ministry of Finance: 71000 Sarajevo, Vojvode Putnika 3; tel. (71) 213777; fax (71) 653592.

Ministry of Foreign Affairs: 71000 Sarajevo, Vojvode Putnika 3; tel. (71) 213777; fax (71) 653592.

Ministry of Health, Labour and Social Security: 71000 Sarajevo, Vojvode Putnika 3; tel. (71) 213777; fax (71) 653592.

Ministry of Information: 71000 Sarajevo, Vojvode Putnika 3; tel. (71) 213777; fax (71) 213350.

Ministry of Internal Affairs: 71000 Sarajevo, Boriše Kovačevića 7; tel. (71) 512877; fax (71) 653592.

Ministry of Justice and State Administration: 71000 Sarajevo, Vojvode Putnika 3; tel. (71) 213777; fax (71) 653592.

Ministry of Religion: Sarajevo.

Ministry of Supply: Sarajevo.

Ministry of Town Planning, Construction and Environmental Protection: 71000 Sarajevo, Vojvode Putnika 3; tel. (71) 213777; fax (71) 653592.

Ministry of Transport and Communications: 71000 Sarajevo, Vojvode Putnika 3; tel. (71) 213777; fax (71) 653592.

Ministry of Veterans' and Disabled Veterans' Affairs: 71000 Sarajevo, Vojvode Putnika 3; tel. (71) 213777; fax (71) 653592.

Legislature

ASSEMBLY

The Assembly comprises two chambers, the Chamber of Citizens and the Chamber of Communes with 130 members and 110 members, respectively.

President: MIRO LAZOVIĆ, 71000 Sarajevo, trg Dure Pucara; tel. (71) 615355; fax (71) 217583.

Elections, 18 November, 2 and 9 December 1990

Party	Seats
Party of Democratic Action (PDA)	86
Serbian Democratic Party (SDP)	72
Croatian Democratic Union (CDU-BH)	44
League of Communists (LC-BH)*/Socialist Alliance (SA)	20†
Alliance of Reform Forces (ARF)	13
Others	5
Total	240

* The LC-BH was renamed the Socialist Democratic Party.

† The LC-BH won 14 seats alone and five in alliance with the SA; the SA won one seat alone.

Local Government

Local government was based on the commune or municipality, of which there were 109 in the Republic (Sarajevo was divided into 10 communities). Three areas declared independence from the Bosnia and Herzegovina Government but would remain within the 'Union of Republics of Bosnia and Herzegovina' (see The Constitution).

'SERBIAN REPUBLIC OF BOSNIA AND HERZEGOVINA'

On 27 March 1992 a 'Serbian Republic of Bosnia and Herzegovina' was proclaimed. It was immediately declared illegal by the President of the State Presidency. The 'Republic' comprised Serb-held areas of Bosnia and Herzegovina, including the 'Serbian Autonomous Regions' of Eastern and Old Herzegovina, Bosanska Krajina, Romanija and Northern Bosnia. Its headquarters was in Banja Luka. The 'Assembly of the Serb Nation', which was constituted on 24 October 1991 by Serb deputies of the Assembly of Bosnia and Herzegovina was based in Pale.

President: Dr RADOVAN KARADŽIĆ.

Vice-President: NIKOLA KOLJEVIĆ.

Prime Minister: VLADIMIR LUKIĆ.

Minister of Foreign Affairs: ALEKSA BUHA.

President of the Assembly of the Serb Nation: MOMČILO KRAJIŠNIK.

'CROATIAN REPUBLIC OF HERZEG-BOSNA'

The formation of the 'Croatian Union of Herzeg-Bosna' was announced on 7 July 1992 but was not recognized by the Government of Bosnia and Herzegovina. The 'Croatian Republic of Herzeg-Bosna' was officially proclaimed at the first session of the interim 'House of Representatives of the Assembly of the Croatian Republic of Herzeg-Bosna', in Grude, on 28 August 1993. It was decided that Mostar would be the capital of the republic.

President: MATE BOBAN.

Vice-President: DARIO KORDIĆ.

Prime Minister: JADRANKO PRLIĆ.

'AUTONOMOUS PROVINCE OF WESTERN BOSNIA'

The 'Autonomous Province of Western Bosnia', consisting of the predominantly Muslim Bihać region in the north-west of the Republic, was declared in the town of Velika Kladusa on 27 September 1993. Armed hostilities occurred throughout October and November, between forces loyal to the central Government and those supporting autonomy.

President: FIKRET ABDIĆ.

President of the Provincial Government (Premier): ZLATKO JUSIĆ.

First Deputy Premiers: FILIP GALIĆ, VASO BUKARIČA.

Political Organizations

Croatian Democratic Union of Bosnia and Herzegovina (CDU-BH) (Hrvatska Demokratska Zajednika—HDZ): c/o 88000 Mostar, trg Dure Pucara bb; f. 1990; affiliate of the CDU in Croatia; Croat nationalist party; Pres. MATE BOBAN, Sec.-Gen. IGNAC KOSTROMAN.

Croatian Peasants' Party (Hrvatska Seljacka Stranka): affiliated to Croatian Peasants' Party in Croatia.

Liberal Bosniak Organization: 71000 Sarajevo; f. 1992 after merger of Liberal Party of Bosnia and Muslim Bosniak Organization (f. 1990); secular Muslim party; Chair. RASIM KADIĆ, Dep. Chair. MUHAMMED FILIPOVIĆ.

Muslim Democratic Party: Velika Kladusa; f 1993; Chair. FIKRET ABDIĆ.

Party of Democratic Action (PDA) (Stranka Demokratske Akcije—SDA): c/o 71000 Sarajevo, trg Dure Pucara bb; leading Muslim nationalist party; has brs in Serbia; Leader Dr ALIJA IZETBEGOVIĆ; Sec. IRFAN AJANOVIĆ.

Serbian Democratic Party (SDP) (Srpska Demokratska Stranka—SDS): c/o Pale, 'Serb Assembly'; f. 1990; allied to SDP of Croatia; Serb nationalist party; Pres. Dr RADOVAN KARADŽIĆ.

Socialist Alliance: c/o 71000 Sarajevo, trg Dure Pucara bb; former Communist mass organization; allies of Socialist Democratic Party; left-wing.

Socialist Democratic Party (Socijalistička Demokratska Partija): 71000 Sarajevo, Dure Dakovića 41; tel. (71) 216644; fax (71) 218168; registered as political party in republican Higher Court March 1990; fmrly the ruling League of Communists of Bosnia and Herzegovina; Pres. Dr NIJAZ DURAKOVIĆ; Sec.-Gen. KRSTO STJEPANOVIĆ.

Diplomatic Representation

EMBASSIES IN BOSNIA AND HERZEGOVINA

Croatia: Medjugorje; Ambassador: ZDRAVKO SANCEVIĆ.

Iran: 71000 Sarajevo; Ambassador: MOHAMED JAVAD ASAYESH-ZARCHI.

Turkey: 71000 Sarajevo; Ambassador: SUKRU TUFAN.

USA: 71000 Sarajevo; Ambassador: VICTOR JACKOVICH.

Judicial System

The courts in Bosnia and Herzegovina were supervised by the Ministry of Justice and State Administration. The highest courts were the Supreme Court and the Constitutional Court.

Constitutional Court of the Republic of Bosnia and Herzegovina: 71000 Sarajevo, Save Kovačevića 6; tel. (71) 214555; Pres. Dr KASIM TRNKA.

Supreme Court: 71000 Sarajevo, Valtera Perića 11; tel. (71) 213577; Pres. MARTIN RAGUZ.

Office of the Public Prosecutor: 71000 Sarajevo, Valtera Perića 11; tel. (71) 214990; Public Prosecutor SLOBODAN KOVAČ.

Religion

Bosnia and Herzegovina has a diversity of religious allegiances. Just over one-half of the inhabitants were nominally Christian, but these were divided between the Serbian Orthodox Church and the Roman Catholic Church. The dominant single religion is Islam. The Reis-ul-ulema, the head of the Muslims in the territory comprising the former Yugoslavia, was resident in Sarajevo. Most of the Muslims are ethnic Muslims, or Bosnian Muslims (Slavs who converted to Islam under the Ottomans). There are, however, some ethnic Albanian and Turkish Muslims. Virtually all are adherents of the Sunni sect. There is a small Jewish community of approximately 700 members. Since 1966 there has been no rabbi in the community.

ISLAM

Islamic Community of the Sarajevo Region: 71000 Sarajevo, Save Kovačevića 2; Pres. of Massahat SALIH EFENDIJA COLAKOVIĆ; Mufti of Bosnia and Herzegovina Hadži MUSTAFA TIRIĆ.

CHRISTIANITY

The Serbian Orthodox Church

Metropolitan of Dabrobosna: VLADISLAV; (c/o Serbian Patriarchate, 11001 Belgrade, POB 182; 7 jula 5, Yugoslavia).

The Roman Catholic Church

Archbishop of Vrhbosna-Sarajevo: VINKO PULJIĆ, Nadbiskupski Ordinarijat Vrhbosanski, 71001 Sarajevo, pp 362, Radojke Lakić 7; tel. (71) 39239; fax (71) 39239.

JUDAISM

Jewish Community of the Sarajevo Region: 71000 Sarajevo; Pres. JAKOB FINCI.

The Press

PRINCIPAL DAILIES

Oslobodjenje: 71000 Sarajevo, Džemala Bijedića 185; tel. (71) 454144; telex 41136; f. 1943; morning; Editor-in-chief GORDANA KNEZEVIĆ; circ. 49,577.

Sarajevske novine: Sarajevo, Boriše Kovačevića 22; evening; Editor-in-chief IVICA BANUŠIĆ; circ. 15,671.

Večernje novine: 71000 Sarajevo, Pavla Goranina 13; tel. (71) 518497; telex 41732; fax (71) 271879; f. 1964; Editor-in-chief SERGIJE PRINCIP; circ. 61,000.

Večernje novosti: Sarajevo, Maršala Tita 13; evening; Editor Dr AZIS HADŽIHASANOVIĆ; circ. 20,000.

PERIODICALS

Socijalistička Izgradnja: Sarajevo; monthly.

Svijet: Sarajevo; illustrated; weekly; Editor-in-chief JELA JEVREMOVIĆ; circ. 115,000.

Zadrugar: Sarajevo, Omladinska 1; f. 1945; weekly; journal for farmers; Editor-in-chief FADIL ADEMOVIĆ; circ. 34,000.

The above press information was current before the worst fighting in the civil conflicts of the early 1990s. Most publications were obliged to cease in the war, although the daily newspaper *Oslobodjenje* continued throughout 1992–1993 and the siege of Sarajevo.

NEWS AGENCIES

Herzeg-Bosna News Agency: 88000 Mostar; f. 1993.

Zapadno Bosanska Informativna Agencija (ZBIA) (Western Bosnian Information Agency): Velika Kladusa; f. 1993.

The civil war disrupted services. There were a number of formally unrecognized stations operating during the conflict, such as the Croatian Radio of Herzeg-Bosna.

Publishers

Novi Glas: 78000 Banja Luka, Borisa Kidriča 1; tel. (78) 12766; fax (78) 12758; general literature; Dir MIODRAG ŽIVANOVIĆ.

Svjetlost: 71000 Sarajevo, Petra Preradovića 3; tel. (71) 212144; telex 41326; fax (71) 272352; f. 1945; textbooks and literature; Dir SAVO ZIROJEVIĆ.

Veselin Masleša: 71000 Sarajevo, Obala 4; tel. (71) 214633; telex 41154; fax (71) 272369; f. 1950; school and university textbooks, general literature; Dir RADOSLAV MIJATOVIĆ.

Radio and Television

Radio-Televizija (RTV) Bosnia and Herzegovina: 71000 Sarajevo, VI Proleterske brigade 4; tel. (71) 455107; telex 41124; fax (71) 455166 (Radio); tel. (71) 652333; telex 41122; fax (71) 461569 (TV); f. 1945 (Radio), 1969 (TV); 4 radio and 2 TV programmes; broadcasts in Serbo-Croat; Dir-Gen. MUHID MEMIU; Dir of Radio NADJA PAŠIĆ; Dir of TV BESIM CERIĆ.

Finance

The Yugoslav National Bank refused to supply Bosnia and Herzegovina with Yugoslav dinars in June 1992. A new currency, the Bosnian dinar, was to be introduced on 1 July 1992; however, its introduction was postponed indefinitely. The Croatian currency was in use in Croat-controlled areas of Bosnia and Herzegovina.

(d.d. = dioničko društvo (joint-stock company); cap. = capital; res = reserves; dep. = deposits; m. = million; amounts in Yugoslav dinars; brs = branches)

BANKS

National Bank

National Bank of Bosnia and Herzegovina: 71000 Sarajevo, Maršala Tita 25; tel. (71) 33326; Gov. JADRANKO PRLIĆ.

Selected Banks

Privredna Banka Sarajevo (Credit Bank, Shareholding Company): 71000 Sarajevo, JNA 52; tel. (71) 533688; telex 41235; fax (71) 214087; f. Dec. 1989, succeeding Privredna banka Sarajevo-Osnovna banka Sarajevo; deals with deposits, credits and other banking activities in the country and abroad; total assets 88,402,536m., dep. 31,572,486m. (Dec. 1989); Gen. Man. VOJISLAV MILIJAŠ (acting).

Privredna Banka Sarajevo d.d., Sarajevo: 71000 Sarajevo, Vojvode Stepe Obala 19, POB 160; tel. (71) 213144; telex 41280; fax (71) 219517; f. 1971; cap. 3,713.1m., res 1,131.1m., dep. 35,471.6m. (Dec. 1990); Pres. and Gen. Man. DJORDJE ZARIĆ; 13 brs.

Trade and Industry

Chamber of Economy of Bosnia and Herzegovina: 71000 Sarajevo, Mis Irbina 13; tel. (71) 211777; Pres. MENSUR SMAILOVIĆ.

MAJOR ENTERPRISES AND COMPANIES

This information was current before the civil war, which began in 1992. Updating would be difficult and unrealistic, given the disruptions caused by the fighting.

ALHOS Export-Import: 71000 Sarajevo, Tesanjska 24A; tel. (71) 39481; telex 21436; fax (71) 215999; clothing manufacturer; Dir. of Manufacture KEMAL HUJIĆ; 1,400 employees.

Aluminij: 88000 Mostar, 25 Novembra BB; tel. (88) 411333; telex 46241; fax (88) 33951; produces alumina, etc.; Gen. Man. Mijo Brajković; 4,500 employees.

Boris Kidrić Coking and Chemical Works, Lukavać (Boris Kidrić Lukavać): 75300 Lukavać, Zeljeznicka 1; tel. (75) 215151; telex 44139; production of coke, fertilizers, synthetic organic products; 5,821 employees.

Bratstvo: 72290 Pućarevo, Borisa Kidrića 1; tel. (72) 791022; telex 43139; fax (72) 791018; manufactures parts for and assembles automobiles and tractors; Gen. Dir JOZO KRIŽANOVIĆ; 11,000 employees.

Energoinvest: 71000 Sarajevo, Bratstva Jedinstva; tel. (71) 654177; telex 41221; fax (71) 656877; production, design and development of power systems; Chair. Dr BOŽIDAR MATIĆ; 47,000 employees.

Feroelektro: 71000 Sarajevo, Maršala Tita 48; tel. (71) 219611; telex 41133; fax (71) 217649; import and export of goods and services; Gen. Dir Dr MIRKO PULJIĆ; 450 employees.

Krivaja: 72220 Zavidovici; tel. (72) 871220; telex 43140; fax (72) 874341; timber industry, construction industry and metals industry; 13,000 employees.

Kula: Gradačac, Pere Bošića 23; tel. (76) 817229; telex 44726; fax (76) 818366; clothing manufacturer; Gen. Man. ŠESTAN FABIJAN; 1,570 employees.

Medic: 77226 Coraliči; tel. (77) 514222; fax (77) 511350; manufactures medical instruments and equipment; Gen. Dir ZLATKO JUŠIĆ; 530 employees.

RMK Zenica: 72000 Zenica, bul. Lenjina 1; tel. (72) 33322; telex 43129; fax (72) 419088; engineering, metal processing, casting, metallurgy and mining; Pres. MILAN MALBASIĆ.

Ro Rafinerija Ulja, Modrica: 74480 Modrica, Vjekoslava Bakulica 49; tel. (74) 880160; telex 445588; fax (74) 882541; production of base oils, paraffin waxes, special mineral oils, etc; Gen. Man. STEVO DOKIĆ; 930 employees.

Sipad Export-Import: 71000 Sarajevo, POB 56, Maršala Tita 15; tel. (71) 213188; telex 41212; fax (71) 218667; foreign trade org. dealing in forestry, industrial production, foreign trading, scientific research and internat. forwarding; Gen. Dir MORIS PAPO; 307 employees.

Sodaso: 75001 Tuzla, Bratstva i Jedinstva 17; tel. (75) 211111; telex 44141; fax (75) 212172; salt and mineral products; Gen. Man. ANTO RAOS; 6,927 employees.

Unis: 71000 Sarajevo, Trscanska 7; tel. (71) 215522; telex 41570; fax (71) 219319; a variety of businesses, incl. cars and motor accessories; 52,000 employees.

UPI Sarajevo—Associated Agriculture, Trade and Industry: 71000 Sarajevo, JNA 20; tel. (71) 518574; telex 41321; primary agriculture on socially owned land and land of co-operating farmers (246,000 ha in total); 36,000 employees.

Transport

RAILWAYS

At the beginning of the 1990s the railway system consisted of more than 1,000 km of track, of which 75% was electrified.

CIVIL AVIATION

The country has an international airport at Sarajevo, and two smaller civil airports. Civil aviation was severely disrputed by the fighting in the Republic in the early 1990s.

Air Commerce: charter flights from Sarajevo to Turkey and Egypt, and scheduled service to Switzerland; Dir MOHAMED ABADZIĆ.

Bosnaair: 71000 Sarajevo; f. 1992.

Culture

The listed institutions and societies were current before the outbreak of civil war in 1992. Since then severe damage has been done to many of the cultural monuments of Bosnia and Herzegovina. Fighting caused much damage, such as to the Stari Most (the famous 16th-century bridge at Mostar which was destroyed in early November 1993), but there was also deliberate damage by militias against the cultural heritage of other ethnic groups, notably the widespread destruction of mosques in Serb-held areas.

NATIONAL ORGANIZATIONS

Ministry of Education, Science, Culture and Physical Culture: see section on The Government (Ministries).

CULTURAL HERITAGE

Art Gallery of Bosnia and Herzegovina (Umjetnička galerija BiH): 71000 Sarajevo, JNA 38; tel. (71) 218644; f. 1946; collections of modern art; library of 3,000 vols; Dir VEFIK HADŽISMAJLOVIĆ.

'Collegium Artisticum' Gallery: 71000 Sarajevo, Skenderija; tel. (71) 35903.

Museum of Bosanska Krajina (Muzej Bosanske Krajine): 78000 Banja Luka, V. Karadžića bb; tel. (78) 35486; f. 1930; regional museum for north-west Bosnia; depts of archaeology, history, ethnography, national revolution, workers' movement; library of 9,500 vols; Dir AHMET ČEJVAN.

National Museum of Bosnia and Herzegovina (Zemaljski Muzej BiH): 71000 Sarajevo, Vojvode Putnika 7; tel. (71) 35322; f. 1888; Dir ALMAZ DAUTLEGOVIĆ.

PERFORMING ARTS

'55 Chambre' Theatre: 71000 Sarajevo, Maršala Tita 56/II; tel. (71) 39031.

National Theatre (Narodno Pozoriste): 71000 Sarajevo, Obala 9; tel. (71) 518795; Ballet and Opera Dir TEODOR ROMANIĆ.

Open Theatre 'Obala': 71000 Sarajevo, Vojvode Stepe Obala 13; tel. (71) 213692.

Music

Mostar Symphony Orchestra (Simfonijski Orkestar Mostar): 88000 Mostar, Rade Bitange 16; tel. (88) 38608; Dir/Conductor TIBOR BAUER.

Sarajevo Philharmonic Orchestra (Sarajevska Filharmonija): c/o Narodno Pozoriste, 71000 Sarajevo, Obala 9; tel. (71) 511197; Chief Conductor MIROSLAV HOMEN.

Symphony Orchestra RTV Sarajevo (Simfonijski Orkestra RTV Sarajevo): 71000 Sarajevo, VI Proleterske brigade 4; tel. (71) 461101; Chief Conductor JULIO MARIĆ.

ASSOCIATIONS

Association of Composers (Udruženje Kompozitora): 71000 Sarajevo, Radićeva 15.

Association of Musicians (Udruženje Muzičkih Umjetnika): Muzička akademija, 71000 Sarajevo, Svetozara Markovića 1; tel. (71) 25007.

Association of Writers (Udruženje Književnika): 71000 Sarajevo, Preradovićeva 3; tel. (71) 516400; f. 1945; Pres. NEDZAD IBRISOMOVIĆ.

Historical Society (Društvo Istoričara): Filozofski fakultet, 71000 Sarajevo, Račkog 1.

Society of Music Lovers and Young Musicians (Musička Omladina): Muzička akademija, 71000 Sarajevo, Sv. Markovića 1; tel. (71) 25007; f. 1958; organizes concerts, lectures, theatre events, exhibitions, film shows; 40,000 mems; library of 1,000 vols, record library of 1,000 items; Pres. KREŠIMIR BOŽIĆ; Sec. BORISLAV CURIĆ.

Education

Primary education in Bosnia and Herzegovina was free and compulsory for all children aged between seven and 15 years. Various types of secondary education were available to those who qualified; vocational and technical schools were the most popular, but children could also attend a general secondary school (gymnasium), an art school, an apprentice school or a teacher-training school. There were four universities in the Republic. Formal academic activity in Bosnia and Herzegovina was severely disrupted by the civil conflict of the early 1990s.

UNIVERSITIES

University of Banja Luka (Univerzitete u Banjaluci): 78000 Banja Luka, trg Palih Boraca 2/II; tel. (78) 35018; fax (78) 47057; f. 1975; state control; 158 teachers, 7,000 students; Rector Prof. Dr RAJKO KUZMANOVIĆ.

University of Mostar (Univerzitet 'Džemal Bijedic u Mostaru): 88000 Mostar, trg '14 Februar' bb; tel. (88) 39140; fax (88) 39141; f. 1977; 250 teachers, 5,500 students; Rector Prof. Dr BERISLAV BLAŽEVIĆ.

University of Sarajevo (Univerzitet u Sarajevu): 71000 Sarajevo, Obala vojvode Stepe 7/II, Post Fah 186; tel. (71) 211216; fax (71) 214289; f. 1949; 1,225 teachers, 24,000 full-time students, 9,000 part-time students; Rector Prof. Dr NENAD KECMANOVIĆ.

University of Tuzla (Univerzitet u Tuzli): 75000 Tuzla, M. Fizovića-Fiska 6, POB 528; tel. (75) 34650; f. 1976; Rector Prof. Dr SADIK LATIFAGIĆ.

Social Welfare

Health care in Bosnia and Herzegovina was state-administered and free. Before the civil war of the early 1990s there was one doctor to approximately every 636 inhabitants of the Republic. Since conflict began basic humanitarian welfare and food aid became increasingly dependent on international relief organizations, for example, Equilibre (a French humanitarian enterprise).

NATIONAL AGENCY

Ministry of Health, Labour and Social Security: see section on The Government (Ministries).

The Environment

GOVERNMENT ORGANIZATIONS

Ministry of Town Planning, Construction and Environmental Protection: see section on The Government (Ministries); incl.:

Institute for the Preservation of Natural and Cultural Heritage in Bosnia and Herzegovina (Zavod za Zastitu Spomenika Kulture i Prirode BiH): 71001 Sarajevo, POB 650, Obala 27 Jula 11A; f. 1947; Dir DZEMAL CELIĆ.

Most environmental activity by research bodies and the 'Green' movement took place at the federal level when the Republic was a constituent part of the Yugoslav federation. Such activity at a local level became irrelevant and ineffective with the advent of civil war, which caused immense environmental damage.

Defence

In June 1993 it was estimated that Bosnia and Herzegovina Government forces numbered around 120,000 active troops and 80,000 reservists. Serb militias totalled approximately 60,000 troops, reinforced by 20,000 soldiers from the Jugoslavenska Narodna Armija (JNA—Yugoslav People's Army). The Croatian Defence Council (HVO—Hrvatsko Vijece Obrane) consisted of between 30,000 and 35,000 troops, supplemented by 15,000 Croatian soldiers. In October 1993 more than 10,300 UNPROFOR troops were stationed in Bosnia and Herzegovina. It was reported that at least 12 units of Arabic and Islamic volunteers (mujahidin) were active in Muslim-held areas of Bosnia and Herzegovina.

Commander-in-Chief of the Bosnia and Herzegovina Army: State Presidency of the Republic of Bosnia and Herzegovina.

Chief of the General Staff of the Bosnia and Herzegovina Army: Col-Gen. RASIM DELIĆ.

'Serbian Republic'

Commander: Gen. RATKO MLADIĆ.

Chief of the General Staff: Gen. MANOJLO MILANOVIĆ.

'Herzeg-Bosna'

Chief of the General Staff of the Croatian Defence Council (HVO): Col-Gen. ANTE ROSO

Bibliography

Donia, R. *Islam under the Double Eagle: The Muslims of Bosnia and Herzegovina 1878–1914*. Boulder, Colorado, East European Monographs, 1981.

Mazower, M. *The War in Bosnia: An Analysis*. London, Action for Bosnia, 1992.

Pajic, Z. *Violation of Fundamental Rights in the Former Yugoslavia: 1. The Conflict in Bosnia-Herzegovina*. London, David Davies Memorial Institute, 1993.

Ricciuti, E. *War in Yugoslavia: The Breakup of a Nation*. London, Evans, 1993.

Schmitt. B. *The Annexation of Bosnia, 1908–1909*. Cambridge, Cambridge University Press, 1937.

Scott, N., and Jones, D. (Eds). *Bloody Bosnia: A European Tragedy*. London, *The Guardian* and Channel Four Television in association with the School of Slavonic and Eastern European Studies, University of London, 1993.

Seton-Watson, R. *The Role of Bosnia in International Politics, 1879–1951*. London, Humphrey Milford, 1931.

Tomić, I. *Whose is Bosnia-Hercegovina?* London, Zbornik, 1990.

Tvrtković, P. *Bosnia-Hercegovina: Back to the Future*. London, Paul Tvrtković, 1993.

BULGARIA

PHYSICAL FEATURES

The Republic of Bulgaria lies in south-eastern Europe, on the east of the Balkan Peninsula. The country is bordered by Romania to the north, by Yugoslavia (Serbia) to the north-west and the Former Yugoslav Republic of Macedonia to the south-west, by Greece to the south and by Turkey to the south-east. The country has an eastern coastline along the Black Sea. Its total area is 110,994 sq km (42,855 sq miles).

Central Bulgaria is traversed from west to east by the Balkan Mountains (Stara Planina), which separate the Danubian plains in the north from the Thracian plains of Eastern Rumelia in the south-east. The Rhodope Mountains (Rhodopi Planina) occupy south-west Bulgaria and separate it from Greece and Macedonia. The mountain of Musala (Riladağ, in Turkish, and also once known as Stalin Peak) is located in this range, to the south of Sofia, and is Bulgaria's highest point, rising to 2,925 m (9,596 ft). The Sofia depression, in the west of the country, is hill country which separates the Balkan Mountains from the southern mountains and is the main centre of population and communications. The general elevation slopes down from the west towards the Black Sea, and some two-thirds of Bulgaria is less than 500 m above sea level. The River Danube (Dunav) forms most of the length of Bulgaria's northern border, except between the town of Silistra (where the Danube turns north) and the Black Sea (that is, as far east as the Dobrudzha). The fertile Bulgarian plateau, between the Danubian border and the Balkan Mountains, averages some 100 km in width and is traversed by several tributaries of the Danube, the major one being the Iskur. The main rivers running south of the Balkan watershed are the Struma and the Maritza, which flow into the Aegean Sea (part of the Mediterranean Sea). The broad Maritza Valley, which leads on to the Thracian plains, is one of the principal agricultural areas of the country.

CLIMATE

The climate is continental, with hot summers and cold winters. In the south the climate is moderated by the influence of the Mediterranean Sea, which makes winters warmer and wetter. Winters on the Black Sea coast are also slightly milder, although north-easterly winds can bring very cold weather. The mean temperatures in Sofia range between 21°C (69°F) in July and −2°C (28°F) in January. Varna, on the Black Sea, has comparative mean temperatures ranging between 23°C (74°F) and 1°C (34°F). The mean annual rainfall in Sofia is 635 mm (25 in) and 485 mm (19 in) at Varna.

POPULATION

The Bulgars were a Finno-Ugrian people, whose ancestors crossed the Danube in the 7th century AD and merged with the Slavonic population. In 1981, according to official figures, 85.3% of the total population were ethnic Bulgarians, 8.5% ethnic Turks, 2.6% Roma (Gypsies), 2.5% Macedonians and there were small communities of Karakachani (Vlahs—who speak a language related to Romanian), Albanians, Sarakatsani (a Greek people), Armenians, Russians and other nationalities. Actual numbers of the minority populations were reported to be larger than official figures indicate. At the end of 1990, for instance, a revised figure of 576,926 Roma was reported by local authorities, but this was still claimed to be low. Bulgarian, the official language, is one of the Southern Slavonic tongues, closely related to Serbo-Croat and also to Russian, and is written in the Cyrillic alphabet. Minority languages include Turkish, Macedonian (a Slavonic dialect) and Romany. Most of the population are Christian and adhere to the Bulgarian Orthodox Church (some 80%), although there are small communities of Roman Catholics (including Uniates), Armenian Orthodox and Protestants. Of the 13% of the population who are estimated to profess Islam, most are ethnic Turks, but some are ethnic Bulgarians, known as Pomaks, who account for some 3% of the population. Most of the Roma are Muslim. There is also a small Jewish community.

The total population of the country was estimated to be 8,989,165 at the end of 1990, with a population density of 81.0 per sq km (209.8 per sq mile). Sofia, the capital, which is located in the central western part of Bulgaria, is the largest city, with an estimated population of 1,141,142 (1990). Other important cities include Plovdiv (379,083 in 1990), in central Bulgaria, and Varna (314,913) and Burgas (204,915) on the Black Sea coast.

Chronology

865: The Khan of the Bulgars, Boris (852–89), converted to Eastern Orthodox Christianity following the missionary activity of the Eastern Roman ('Byzantine') brothers, SS Constantine (Cyril) and Methodius ('the Apostles of the Slavs').

893–927: Reign of Simeon, first Tsar (Caesar) of the Bulgars, who failed in his ambition to take Constantinople (now Istanbul) and the Byzantine throne, but established a powerful empire and the Bulgarian Church as the first new autocephalous Orthodox church.

971: Annexation of eastern Bulgaria as a Byzantine province.

1014: The Bulgar ruler, Samuel, was defeated at the battle of Balathista by the Emperor Basil II ('the Slayer of the Bulgars'), who subsequently made western Bulgaria into a Byzantine province.

1187: A decline in Byzantine power meant that the Emperor in Constantinople recognized the establishment of the second Bulgarian Empire, under the Asen dynasty.

1330: The Bulgars were defeated by Serbian forces at the battle of Küstendil (Velbuzhde).

1396: Bulgaria became a province of the Turkish Ottoman Empire.

1870: Establishment of an autocephalous Exarchate of the Bulgarian Orthodox Church (not recognized by Constantinople until 1945).

1876: Bloody suppression of Bulgarian uprisings by the Ottomans.

1877: Russia declared war on the Turks in support of the Orthodox, Slav subjects of the Ottoman Empire.

1878: The Ottomans recognized an autonomous principality of Bulgaria, at the Congress of Berlin; Eastern Rumelia and Macedonia remained under Turkish rule.

1879: The First Grand National Assembly of Bulgaria, meeting in the town of Turnovo (now Veliko—'Grand'—Turnovo), adopted a liberal constitution (the 'Turnovo Constitution') and invited the nephew of the Russian tsarina, Alexander (Aleksandur) von Battenburg, of the House of Hesse-Darmstadt, to become the ruling prince.

1885: Eastern Rumelia was annexed by Bulgaria. Serbian forces were defeated at the battle of Slivnitsa.

1887: Election of Ferdinand of Saxe-Coburg as Prince of Bulgaria, following the abdication of Alexander.

2 August 1903: Bulgarians in Pirin Macedonia took part in the Ilinden uprising—a revolt against the Ottoman authorities organized by the Internal Macedonian Revolutionary Organization (IMRO). The revolt was suppressed.

October 1908: Upheavals in the Ottoman Empire included the proclamation of Tsar (King) Ferdinand I of an independent Bulgarian kingdom.

August 1913: The Peace of Bucharest concluded the Second Balkan War: Bulgaria lost Macedonia and Dobrudzha.

12 October 1915: Bulgaria declared war on Serbia, so entering the First World War on the side of the Central Powers of Germany, Austria-Hungary and the Ottoman Empire.

29 September 1918: Bulgaria surrendered unconditionally to the Entente Powers (consequent abdication of Ferdinand I and accession of Boris III).

29 November 1919: The Treaty of Neuilly was signed: Bulgaria was forced to cede its Thracian territories and Mediterranean coast to Greece; it ceded territory on its western frontier to Yugoslavia (then known as the Kingdom of Serbs, Croats and Slovenes); and returned the Dobrudzha (which it had regained by the Peace of Bucharest of May 1918) to Romania.

1923: A *putsch* by army officers led to the suppression of the Peasants Party and the Communist Party.

19 May 1934: A coup by two nationalist organizations, Zveno and the Association of the Officers of the Reserve, led to the establishment of the authoritarian regime of Col Georgieff.

January 1935: Resignation of Col Georgieff; authoritarian rule continued by Boris III.

30 August 1940: Second Arbitration Award of Vienna restored Southern Dobrudzha to Bulgaria (confirmed in 1947).

1 March 1941: Bulgaria signed a pact with the Axis Powers of Germany and Italy and, following the outbreak of war in the Balkans, gained western Macedonia from Yugoslavia.

August 1943: Death of Boris III; a regency established for the young Tsar Simeon II.

5 September 1944: The USSR declared war on Bulgaria.

8 September 1944: Bulgaria declared war on Germany.

9 September 1944: Following a coup by the Fatherland Front, a left-wing alliance dominated by the Bulgarian Communist Party (BCP), the Soviet army occupied Bulgaria.

28 October 1944: An armistice was signed with the Allies.

August 1945: The Agrarian and Social Democratic Parties left the Front and the Government.

15 September 1946: The formal deposition of Tsar Simeon II and the declaration of a Republic, following a referendum.

November 1946: Georgi Dimitrov, First Secretary of the BCP, became Chairman of the Council of Ministers.

22 February 1947: A peace treaty was signed with the Allies.

December 1947: A new Constitution abolished all opposition parties and established a system based on the Soviet model. Bulgaria became a People's Republic.

March 1949: Dimitrov was replaced as Chairman of the Council of Ministers by Vasil Kolarov.

July 1949: Vulko Chervenkov became leader of the BCP following Dimitrov's death.

February 1950: Chervenkov became Chairman of the Council of Ministers.

March 1954: Todor Zhivkov became leader of the BCP.

April 1956: Anton Yugov replaced Chervenkov as Chairman of the Council of Ministers.

November 1962: Zhivkov replaced Yugov as Chairman of the Council of Ministers.

1965: An army coup attempt was discovered and suppressed, enabling Zhivkov to consolidate his position.

16 May 1971: A new Constitution was adopted, following a referendum; the Constitution established the Council of State as the supreme executive and legislative body. Zhivkov relinquished his former government posts to become President of the Council of State (head of state).

June 1981: Following elections to the National Assembly, Grisha Filipov became Chairman of the Council of Ministers in succession to Stanko Todorov, who had held the post since 1971.

March 1985: Filipov was replaced as Chairman of the Council of Ministers by Georgi Atanasov.

December 1985: A national census was the occasion for accusations of a government policy ('regenerative programme') of forced assimilation of the ethnic Turkish population ('Bulgarian Muslims').

July 1987: Zhivkov promised liberalization and pluralism in his so-called 'July Concept'.

February 1988: A protocol was signed with Turkey to further economic and social relations. The dissident Independent Association for Human Rights was founded and environmental protests in northern areas led to the foundation of Ecoglasnost.

March 1988: Candidates other than those nominated by the BCP were permitted to stand in the local elections.

July 1988: Several prominent proponents of reform were dismissed from office at a plenum of the BCP, including one member of the Politburo.

November 1988: Eighty leading intellectuals founded the Club for the Support of Glasnost and Perestroika.

22 August 1989: The Turkish Government closed the border with Bulgaria, some 310,000 refugees having arrived in Turkey. In May the Government had announced its willingness to accept the entire ethnic Turkish population of Bulgaria following reports of violent suppression of protests against the programme for their assimilation.

November 1989: Zhivkov was forced to resign his post as General Secretary of the BCP, following a demonstration on environmental issues, and was replaced by the Minister of Foreign Affairs, Petur Mladenov. A week later Mladenov was elected by the National Assembly to succeed Zhivkov as President of the Council of State. The Government announced the dissolution of the secret police.

December 1989: Opposition groups, including Ecoglasnost (which became the first party to achieve legal registration), formally established the United Democratic Front (UDF). Following a strike by Podkrepa (Support), the independent trade union movement, the Government agreed to begin negotiations about 'round-table' meetings between the BCP, the Bulgarian Agrarian People's Union (BAPU) and the UDF (agreement to a multi-party system was reached in March 1990). The National Assembly began to introduce reforms, including legalizing other political parties, and the Government approved measures to end discrimination against the Muslim minority.

January 1990: A 'social council' was formed by the major political and social groups, in reaction to a week of widespread nationalist protests against the restoration of Turkish rights. The council guaranteed the rights of Turks, but outlawed any attempts to form an independent Turkish state. The National Assembly revoked the leading role of the BCP.

February 1990: Aleksandur Lilov replaced Petur Mladenov as head of the Supreme Council of the BCP. Atanasov resigned and was replaced as premier by Andrei Lukanov, who nominated a Government only comprising members of the BCP. Later, reformers from within the BCP formed the Alternative Socialist Party (ASP), and the official trade-union congress completed its renunciation of any party or state affiliations and changed its name to the Confederation of Independent Trade Unions in Bulgaria (CITUB).

3 April 1990: Petur Mladenov was elected President of the country by the National Assembly. The BCP changed its name to the Bulgarian Socialist Party (BSP).

17 June 1990: The second and final round of voting in elections to a constituent Grand National Assembly (GNA) took place amid widespread allegations of electoral irregularities. However, the BSP received 211 seats out of 400, the UDF 144 and the Muslim Movement for Rights and Freedoms (MRF) won 23.

July 1990: At a meeting of the GNA in Veliko Turnovo, seat of the first GNA 111 years previously, the premier, Lukanov, refused to head a one-party government. Nikolai Todorov (BSP) was elected President of the GNA. The ASP, a reformist group in the BSP, left the BSP and removed the majority that the BSP had held in the GNA.

August 1990: Zheliu Zhelev, leader of the UDF, was eventually elected President of the country by the GNA. Dr Petur Beron replaced him as Chairman of the Co-ordinating Council of the UDF. President Zhelev proposed that Lukanov form a new Government, although the UDF refused to join a coalition with the BSP.

November 1990: The BSP lost its overall majority in the GNA when the ASP faction joined the UDF. Despite some reforms, including renaming the country the Republic of Bulgaria, there were increasing protests at the lack of progress with a new constitution. A general strike prompted the resignation of Lukanov, after agreement on a multi-party administration under a non-party premier (Dimitur Popov).

December 1990: The major political groups signed the 'Agreement Guaranteeing the Peaceful Transition to a Democratic Society', which committed support to the Popov Government, the drafting of a new constitution, the introduction of a market economy and general elections to be held in 1991. The GNA approved Bulgaria's first coalition Government not to be controlled by the Communists since the 1940s.

14 May 1991: A group of 39 UDF deputies walked out of the GNA session, protesting at its delays (lack of progress on constitutional issues had provoked violent demonstrations in March); this action marked the beginning of a split in the UDF.

7 June 1991: Twenty-one MRF deputies joined the by-now 50 UDF deputies who were boycotting the GNA, in protest at constitutional proposals; this threatened the GNA's ability to adopt any fundamental law. A national UDF conference temporarily resolved the divisions in the alliance, by agreeing to many of the demands of the radical 'Group of 39'.

12 July 1991: The GNA finally ratified the Constitution, which was signed by 309 of the 400 deputies. The Constitution was formally promulgated and came into effect on 13 July.

August 1991: There were further splits in the UDF and its member parties, while the BSP formed an election coalition with five minor parties, most of them of a nationalist orientation. The political wing of the MRF, Rights and Freedoms, was refused registration as a party on the grounds that it was unconstitutionally based on religious and ethnic interests. (Registration was later allowed.)

13 October 1991: In the elections to the National Assembly the UDF emerged as the largest party, winning 110 seats. The BSP won 106 seats, while the balance was held by the 24 seats won by the MRF. No other party gained the 4% of the vote necessary for representation. The UDF chose the leader of the Green Party, Filip Dimitrov, as Prime Minister.

19 January 1992: Zheliu Zhelev won the presidential election after having been forced into a second round by the BSP-backed candidate, Vulko Vulkanov.

30 August 1992: President Zhelev, speaking on television, strongly criticized Dimitrov and his cabinet.

September 1992: The MRF and the BSP voted to remove Stefan Savov, the UDF-nominated Chairman of the National Assembly, from office.

December 1992: Lyuben Berov was nominated for the post of Prime Minister (Dimitrov had lost a vote of censure in October) by the MRF; he was subsequently elected by the National Assembly (his support in the Assembly consisted of the MRF, the majority of the BSP and a breakaway group from the UDF).

January 1993: The National Assembly passed a resolution not to open police files, and to withdraw the facility whereby certificates were issued to individuals, attesting that they had no links with the Communist secret police.

March 1993: A section of the UDF left the alliance and formed the New Union for Democracy (NUD). In the following month a centrist Council for Co-operation was created.

13 May 1993: The former speaker, Stefan Savov, was injured by a policeman during a demonstration outside the National Assembly building; the UDF claimed it was a deliberate attack which had been ordered by the Government, with which it had been in increasingly serious disagreement.

29 June 1993: Blaga Dimitrova, the Vice-President, resigned, alleging that she had been insufficiently consulted while in office and warned of an imminent dictatorship; this was at the end of a month of increasing demonstrations against President Zhelev, mainly organized by the UDF.

9 August 1993: Bulgaria's former leader Todor Zhivkov, former premier Georgi Atanasov (imprisoned for embezzlement in September) and seven other prominent Communists were charged over diversion of state funds abroad. On the following day began Bulgaria's first racial equality trial in Ruse (at which five police officers were charged with violation of the rights of ethnic Turks during the forced assimilation campaign of 1985).

26 August 1993: Konstantin Trenchev, leader of Podkrepa, demanded the dismissal of Deputy Prime Minister Neicho Neev following rumours of unsuitable political activities (including unauthorized discussions with Yugoslav embassy officials).

8 September 1993: A motion by Prime Minister Berov for the dismissal of Deputy Prime Minister Neicho Neev, on the grounds that he had violated the ministerial code of conduct, was approved by the National Assembly. The Ecumenical Patriarch, Bartholomeo I, arrived in the country, in an attempt to heal the rift in the Bulgarian Orthodox Church.

13 August 1993: The National Assembly resolved to establish a commission of inquiry into allegations of corruption in the executive, the legislature and the judiciary.

5 October 1993: At a session of the UN General Assembly in New York (USA), President Zhelev insisted that measures be taken to end the conflict in the former Yugoslavia; he stressed the losses suffered by Bulgaria (where there was increasing unrest at the situation) from the observance of the UN embargo against the Federal Republic of Yugoslavia (Serbia and Montenegro).

12 October 1993: The UDF National Co-ordinating Council voted to expel the Liberal Congress Party from the coalition, owing to its systematic breaches of the UDF's ethical code; at the same meeting, it was agreed that the New Social Democratic Party should be allowed to rejoin.

History

Prof. RICHARD J. CRAMPTON

BULGARIA BEFORE 10 NOVEMBER 1989

The Bulgarians established an empire in the Balkans during the ninth and 10th centuries AD, mainly at the expense of the Eastern Roman ('Byzantine') Empire, from which they received Eastern Orthodox Christianity and a powerful cultural influence. The Bulgarian state eventually succumbed to Byzantine power and, despite a revival in the 13th century, subsequently to the Turkish Ottoman Empire. Modern Bulgaria emerged from the disintegrating Ottoman realm during the 19th century. With Russian assistance, an autonomous Bulgarian principality was established and, in 1878, recognized by the Congress of Berlin. The following year an assembly adopted the constitution of a limited monarchy. In 1908, with turbulence throughout the Ottoman Empire, the Bulgarian Prince was proclaimed Tsar (King) of an independent kingdom. Balkan politics inclined Bulgaria to support Germany in both the First and the Second World Wars. Between the Wars the country was headed by an authoritarian regime, which was installed by nationalist forces but continued by Tsar Boris III. He died in 1943 and a regency was established for the young Tsar Simeon II. Despite an attempt to realign itself, Bulgaria was occupied by Soviet troops in September 1944. This resulted in the abolition of the monarchy and the rise of Communist power.

The Bulgarian Communist Party (BCP) was a member of the coalition which came to power on 9 September 1944. By the end of 1947 the BCP had neutralized all other political groups; thenceforth it was the leading force in Bulgarian society and politics. The Communists ostensibly ruled in coalition with the Bulgarian Agrarian People's Union (BAPU), a long-established Bulgarian party, which had been emasculated when its leader, Nikola Petkov, had been executed after a grotesque BCP-engineered trial in 1947.

Communist rule in Bulgaria, in the late 1940s and early 1950s, followed a pattern similar to that elsewhere in Eastern Europe. In 1954 Todor Zhivkov became First Secretary, or leader, of the BCP and, after the failure of an attempted military coup, in 1965, his power was unchallenged. Zhivkov forced Bulgaria through the familiar Communist experiences of collectivization, urbanization and industrialization. His rule was singular in the degree to which it followed the policies of the Soviet Government in Moscow, especially in foreign affairs.

In the 1980s Zhivkov's position was undermined by three main factors. The first was the appointment to the Soviet leadership of Mikhail Gorbachev, to whom the Bulgarian leader epitomized the indulgent, corrupt and inefficient ethos that existed during Leonid Brezhnev's time as First Secretary of the Central Committee of the Communist Party of the Soviet Union (1964–1982). Zhivkov's enthusiasm for all things Soviet (all Bulgarians were taught Russian and one Soviet television channel was permanently relayed to Bulgaria), however, exposed him to the new, reformist ideas from the USSR: *perestroika* ('restructuring') and *glasnost* ('openness'). The second factor was economic decline. Zhivkov had already embarked on a form of *perestroika*, economic reform, in the New Economic Mechanism of 1982. However, the initial promises were not fulfilled and the reform programme degenerated into a series of disruptive adjustments to the administration of the economy. Thirdly, there was the disastrous 'regenerative process'.

About 10% of Bulgaria's 9m. inhabitants are Turkish-speaking. In 1984 Zhivkov and some of his colleagues decided that the time had come to 'bulgarize' the Turks. Turkish broadcasts and publications were suspended and the use of the Turkish language in public was banned; most contentious of all was the order that the Turks take Bulgarian or Slavic names. The policy was a disaster. To overcome the resistance of the Turks, the Bulgarian army had to be deployed in what was probably its largest operation since the Second World War, while abroad Bulgaria was excoriated in bodies as diverse as the Islamic Conference and the Council of Europe. The 'regenerative process' also quickened internal opposition and encouraged the growth of human-rights groups. Finally, in mid-1989, some 300,000 Turks fled to Turkey, wreaking havoc with the Bulgarian economy and totally discrediting the Zhivkov regime abroad.

There was further discredit when Bulgarian police treated roughly a number of ecological protesters, amongst whom was a British journalist, on 26 October 1989. If Zhivkov's opponents in the highest levels of the Party did not actually organize this confrontation, they were certainly not slow to make use of it as yet another argument for a change of leadership. At a plenum of the BCP Central Committee, on 10 November 1989, Zhivkov was impelled to resign from office. His successor, as Party leader (First Secretary) and head of state (President of the State Council), was Petur Mladenov, who had served as Minister of Foreign Affairs for 17 years and had taken a leading part in the plot to oust Zhivkov.

THE ERA OF TRANSITION: CHANGES IN FORM BUT NOT IN STRUCTURE

Todor Zhivkov had been overthrown by his own colleagues in the upper ranks of the Party. Thus, the events of 10 November 1989 were a coup, not a revolution; 'people power' was a consequence, not a cause, of the overthrow of the old regime; revolution was the product of, not the prelude to, the change of leadership.

After this change the BCP was ready to admit that Zhivkov had brought the country close to ruin, not least in amassing a foreign-currency debt which was now revealed to be about US $11,000m. The BCP was also prepared to democratize its own procedures, but that, it seemed, was as far as it was prepared to go. However, the process of change had begun. Even before 10 November 1989 there had been indications of a revival in independent political activity, with the formation of ecological pressure groups, human-rights associations and even of an independent trade union, Podkrepa (Support). After the fall of Zhivkov political parties and civil associations proliferated. Some of them, such as the Bulgarian Social Democratic Party (BSDP), were revivals of suppressed groups; others were adaptations of previous formations, such as the Nikola Petkov Bulgarian Agrarian People's Union (BAPU-NP), established in opposition to the official, coalition BAPU; and other groups, including the Green Party, were entirely new creations. On 14 November some 15 of these bodies came together to form the Union of Democratic Forces (UDF), to which were later added other groups.

After the events of November 1989 Bulgarians were wont to refer proudly to the 'gentle revolution'. They were justified in doing so; no blood had been shed nor had significant violence occurred during the transition from totalitarianism. Yet this 'gentle revolution' did not lack tension. By the end of 1989 popular agitation, especially in the cities, was intensifying, the general demand being for an end to the domination of the Communist Party. On 14 December 1989 a massive demonstration outside the parliament building in Sofia demanded an end to the Communist grip on power and for the convocation of 'round-table' negotiations, between the official parties and the opposition, to determine the way to a new, multi-party system. The Government and the Party delayed, but, on 29 December, they did issue a decree revoking the majority of the anti-Turkish legislation passed since 1984. This produced another, but less positive, outburst of popular feeling. On 7 January 1990 a huge crowd, many of them transported to Sofia from outlying, mixed Bulgarian–Turkish areas with local BCP connivance, protested that such an important change could not be introduced without a national referendum. One week later yet another demonstration, this time organized by the UDF, insisted that there could be no going back on the decree of 29 December. The BCP and the UDF both realized that anti-Turkish chauvinism had to be resisted, not least because of Bulgaria's desperate need for financial assistance, some of which could come from the wealthy Arab states.

The common issue discovered at the beginning of January 1990, enabled the BCP and the UDF to begin effective, round-table discussions. At the same time the BCP introduced legislation to modify Article One of the Constitution, which had given it the right to political and social predominance. The appropriate legislation was eventually enacted, but only after further popular demonstrations insisting that the entire Article be removed, including the first clause, which described Bulgaria as a 'socialist state of the working people of the town and the countryside, led by the working class'. After this concession the BCP seemed to be in headlong retreat. It soon conceded the holding of multi-party elections, the rules and procedures for which were made public early in April of that year.

At the beginning of February 1990 the Party assumed sole responsibility for government. Their previous coalition partners, the official Agrarians, had responded to the taunts of the BAPU-NP (accusing them of assisting the heirs of those who had presided over the judicial murder of Nikola Petkov) and resigned from the ruling coalition. Ironically, for the first time in its history, Bulgaria had a purely Communist Government. By that time the BCP had undergone its own restructuring. During the Extraordinary 14th Congress, of 31 January–2 February, the former structures of Central Committee and Political Bureau (Politburo) were replaced by a Supreme Council and its Presidium. There were few members of the old bodies in the new organs. Mladenov relinquished his leadership of the Party to Aleksandur Lilov. On 3 April the BCP changed its name to the Bulgarian Socialist Party (BSP). Meanwhile Mladenov remained President of the country, after the dissolution of the State Council.

By then the Party had, in theory at least, abandoned, or been deprived of, much of its leading role in society. Shortly after 10 November Krustyu Petkov, a professor of sociology, successfully managed to detach the old trades union organization from domination by the Party. The newly-created Confederation of Independent Trade Unions in Bulgaria (CITUB) was to play a vital part in further political reforms. The BCP yielded to further pressure from its opponents and abolished all Party cells in the workplace. The Komsomol or Communist Youth movement, the Fatherland Front, which united various social organizations, and other pillars of the old establishment were also divorced from BCP control.

The concessions made by the BCP/BSP were important, but they could not satisfy its opponents. They would feel secure only when a new Assembly had been convened, to give legal guarantees of political freedom. From April 1990, therefore, the preoccupation of most Bulgarian political activists was with the forthcoming electoral battle.

Under the Turnovo Constitution of 1879, the first in the history of modern Bulgaria, constitutional changes could be enacted only by a Grand National Assembly, which was to be twice the size of an ordinary assembly. In 1990 the round-table parties agreed to follow this precedent. They decided that a new National Assembly should be constituted as a Grand National Assembly (GNA), which would consist of 400 deputies, one-half of whom were to be elected by proportional representation, and one-half in constituencies by a simple majority. Polling was to take place on 10 and 17 June 1990, the second date being for 'run-offs' (that is, a further election for the principal contenders in those single-member constituencies where the candidate who won the most number of votes in the first round had not reached the minimum required percentage of the total vote). There were few restrictions on the political parties, which were free to contest the election. There was, however, one regulation which caused dispute: that no political party could be based upon religious allegiance or ethnic identity.

There is little doubt that the conduct of the voting was, in general, fair. It is also widely accepted that, in the weeks before the election, the BSP exercised considerable intimidation over the electorate, particularly in the rural constituencies, where there were hints that the reformists in Sofia would be incapable of rule and would refuse to pay pensions and other benefits. The leader of the UDF, Zheliu Zhelev, summarized the electoral battle as 'free, but not fair'. The result gave an absolute majority of the seats (211) to the BSP, which had received some 47% of the votes cast. The UDF won about 38% of the votes and gained 144 seats in the GNA. The BAPU gained 16 seats, the nationalist Fatherland Party of Labour two, the Bulgarian Social Democratic Party—non-Marxist (subsequently renamed the Liberal Congress Party) one, and there were two independents. The biggest surprise was that the Movement for Rights and Freedoms (MRF), which was primarily concerned with protecting the interests of the Turkish population, gained 23 deputies in the GNA, making it the third-largest party.

THE REVOLUTION STALLED, JULY-NOVEMBER 1990

Before the second round of voting in the general election, in June 1990, considerable controversy was caused by the discovery of a video tape, in which President Mladenov was seen to advocate the use of tanks against demonstrators on 14 December of the previous year. After initial denials of the tape's authenticity, Mladenov resigned on 6 July 1990. On 1 August, after six attempts to elect a successor, Zheliu Zhelev, a former dissident and the leader of the UDF, was elected President of Bulgaria. The Vice-President was a member of the BSP, Col-Gen. Atanas Semerdzhiev.

The Mladenov affair meant that, when the GNA met on 10 July, the political atmosphere was already tense. There were also chauvinist demonstrators, claiming that the MRF was illegal because it was based on ethnic identity; the MRF responded by proving that it had ethnic Bulgarians as well as Turks amongst its members. Further tensions arose from continuing student accusations that evidence of electoral malpractice had been concealed; the students set up 'the city of truth', a tent encampment in the centre of Sofia, in which the capital's intelligentsia formulated a whole series of wide-ranging political demands.

The opening of the GNA did little to restore calm, primarily because the deputies showed a surprising reluctance to begin work. It took a threat of strike action from CITUB to initiate serious political discussions. At the same time there was growing disquiet, especially in the 'city of truth', over the real intentions of the BSP. Its promises to withdraw from its leading role, it was alleged, had been only partially implemented. Once again tension mounted and erupted on the night of 26-27 August 1990 when the BCP/BSP headquarters in Sofia was set on fire. Mystery surrounded the origins of this fire but it did bring about a greater degree of sobriety in Bulgarian politics. The tent encampments in Sofia and other cities were abandoned, in accordance with recently enacted legislation, and the GNA began serious deliberation on a number of other legislative proposals. There was still little progress, however, over another pressing question: the formation of a new Government.

Despite its electoral victory, the BSP under Lukanov was reluctant to form another one-party cabinet. Lukanov believed that the country's economic problems could be rectified only by the most extreme remedies; he argued, therefore, that, to ensure public acceptance of these remedies, all major political forces had to support them, preferably by the formation of a coalition administration. The UDF refused, arguing that the BCP/BSP was responsible for the problems and it was its responsibility to resolve them. The UDF did not want to be associated with the unpopularity which the reforms would inevitably bring. Furthermore, it argued, the BSP had a mandate and a programme and should, therefore, carry out the task for which it had been elected. In addition, the UDF insisted that it could not go into government with the BSP until the latter had purged itself of those members of the BCP who the opposition considered had exercised and abused power before 10 November 1989. Not until 20 September 1990 did Lukanov agree to form a single-party Government.

By then the chances of public support for that Government had declined sharply, with a persistent suspicion of the real intentions of the BSP. These suspicions were aggravated by the delaying tactics which the party deployed on a number of issues. A vital proposal for the reform of local government had been debated in the GNA, but had not been formally enacted by 28 August 1990, when the mandates of the existing local-government bodies, People's Councils, expired. Reform of local government was an important issue, not least because it was the locally elected officials who ran the electoral bureaux which controlled polling during general elections. After 28 August interim local councils were formed, with representation reflecting the distribution of votes in the June general elections. Another occasion for suspicion of the BSP was when a proposal to effect the depoliticization of the army, police, judiciary and diplomatic service was returned to the GNA, from the committee stage, without those clauses mentioning the diplomatic service. They were reinstated after further debate and delay. The BSP also blocked attempts to have BCP party records handed over to public archives, a fact which caused intense disquiet because of the increasingly fierce demands for the punishment of those who, it was said, had brought about 'the third national catastrophe'.

The first and second national catastrophes were the defeats in the Second Balkan War and the First World War, in 1913 and 1918, respectively. By the third such catastrophe was meant the current ruination of the Bulgarian economy. In March 1990 the Lukanov Government had suspended payment on its foreign-debt obligations, a fact which had angered the international financial community and further complicated Bulgaria's position. At home all parties were committed to de-monopolization, decentralization, the decollectivization of agriculture and the transfer to a market economy. The necessary legislation, however, was not passed. Even after forming his cabinet Lukanov refused to enact his reform programme without the support of the opposition, which they were still determined not to give. In this situation the economy became chaotic. Shortages increased, and so also prices on the unregulated and illegal 'black market' or 'parallel economy', which was frequently the only source of supply. Unemployment began to spread rapidly. In the agricultural sector, the uncertainty over land ownership was a disincentive to planting; many producers and traders were already hoarding non-perishable items for when the prices increased; thus, with the lack of foreign currency excluding the Zhivkov expedient of importing agricultural goods, food queues lengthened alarmingly. In industry, production was disrupted by the non-availability of supplies and the collapse of the Council for Mutual Economic Assistance (CMEA or Comecon) trading system with other Communist states, on which Bulgaria had depended. Furthermore, all sectors of the economy were drastically affected by the 1990–91 crisis in the Persian (Arabian) Gulf (brought about by the Iraqi invasion and attempted annexation of Kuwait). Iraq was Bulgaria's biggest foreign-currency debtor, owing some US $1,200m., which, it had been agreed in May 1990, was to be repaid to Bulgaria in the form of crude petroleum, over 600,000 metric tons of which was to be delivered that year alone. All this was lost, as was a further 200,000 tons, which was to come from Iraq via the USSR.

THE REVOLUTION RESUMED: THE POPOV GOVERNMENT

Lukanov's Government had little chance of continuing in office, given the likelihood of economic collapse and the political impasse. It was the students who struck the first blow. For much of October 1990 they had campaigned for university reforms, but they had never neglected their political objectives. On 5 November student leaders decided to occupy the buildings of the University of Sofia, and one of their demands was that the Government resign.

By the end of November 1990, with no prospect of any break in the political deadlock, workers' organizations began to support the students. On 26 November Podkrepa declared a general strike and, three days later, CITUB announced that it would ballot its members on strike action. The strike threats were accompanied by increasing signs of violence and disorder on the streets and even in the debating chamber of the GNA. On 30 November Lukanov's Government resigned, but only after talks arranged by President Zhelev had produced an agreement between the main political factions that a new, multi-party administration would be formed under a non-party premier. The new premier, confirmed by the GNA on 7 December, was Dimitur Popov, who had served as Secretary to the Electoral Commission, in June 1990. His appointment, together with the indictment of Zhivkov and one of his associates on charges of gross embezzlement, did much to calm the political atmosphere. By the middle of December the students and the trade unions had abandoned their actions.

After Popov's nomination the most important political groupings, on 14 December 1990, agreed to sign the 'Agreement Guaranteeing the Peaceful Transition to a Democratic Society'. They resolved to support the Popov Government, which was to hold office until new elections were held, originally scheduled for March 1991. During that time the Government was to devise a new constitution and enact the necessary legislation to create a market economy.

This move towards consensus was followed by general public approval of the cabinet list, which Popov presented on 20 December 1990. He skilfully balanced the existing political forces, not least by appointing an independent to the vital Ministry of Internal Affairs. On 8 January 1991 a further indication of cohesion came with the tripartite 'Social Agreement', signed by the Prime Minister, representatives from the two major trade-union organizations and the chairman of the employers' association. The agreement provided for a suspension of strike activity, sensitive management of the transition to a market system and political support for the necessary economic and social legislation. The Social Agreement was renewed in June 1991 and the tripartite commission became an important mechanism for containing and to some degree diffusing social tensions.

The conclusion of the Social Agreement allowed the Popov Government to begin real economic restructuring. The reforms to be enacted were, to a considerable degree, determined by the International Monetary Fund (IMF), to which Bulgaria had been admitted in September 1990 and which had agreed to advance a loan, on condition of real economic and fiscal reform. It was in fulfilment of these conditions that the Popov Government raised interest rates from 5% to 45% and, on 1 February 1991, abolished price controls. The latter measure brought hoarded goods into the market and, if prices were initially too high, they did respond to market forces by falling in subsequent weeks, although not to near the level they had been when regulated. The Government also abolished foreign-currency shops, with effect from 1 April. Another important enactment was a law of 1 March, by which land was to be decollectivized and returned, if it was so wished, to the families that had previously owned it.

In the constitutional sphere there was less progress. The GNA was still prone to spend time on procedural matters and, by the end of March 1991, there had been no real debate about a new basic law. There was no sign of any local elections being held, and sharp debates were developing as to when the general election should take place and whether it should be conducted simultaneously with the local elections. The BSP were considered reluctant to hold early elections and exploited the divisions in the UDF and other opposition parties. Furthermore, in April, the BSP were accused of still having access to police files, after the publication of embarrassing accusations about opposition politicians. The Minister of Internal Affairs offered his resignation, but the main consequence of the scandal was the realization by the new democratic parties that the old system had to be dismantled. Although some parties wanted to have elections before the enacting of a new constitution, some, such as the MRF, were anxious to resolve the constitutional issues before then. After several months of mounting public, and presidential, pressure the Grand National Assembly finally approved the final reading of the Constitution. It was promulgated, and took effect, on the following day, on 13 July 1991. After the promulgation of the new Constitution the Grand National Assembly became a normal legislature, or National Assembly, until new elections were held on 13 October.

PARLIAMENTARY AND PRESIDENTIAL ELECTIONS

Before the elections took place a series of splits occurred in the UDF. Disagreements over the decollectivization of agriculture, over attitudes towards the former Communists, and over the extent of welfare provision meant that by September 1991 there were three distinct UDF factions. It was the most right-wing of the three factions that carried the UDF flag in the electoral campaign. Equally serious divisions had taken place among the Agrarian parties.

Despite the splits which occurred in mid-1991 the UDF managed to emerge as the largest party in the National Assembly elected in October. It had 110 deputies, but the BSP was close behind with 106; the balance was held by the 24 deputies of the MRF which was the only other party to exceed the 4% threshold necessary for representation. The UDF faction chose the leader of the Green Party, Filip Dimitrov, as Prime Minister. In December, after its defeat, the BSP changed its leader, appointing Zhan Videnov instead. Videnov came from the neo-Marxist, rather than the liberal, wing of the party.

In January 1992 Zhelev won the first ever presidential election in Bulgaria, though many were surprised that he was forced into a second round of voting by the nationalist, BSP-backed Vulko Vulkanov. Zhelev's Vice-President, elected in the same poll, was the poetess Blaga Dimitrova.

THE POST COMMUNIST ERA: THE DIMITROV GOVERNMENT

In foreign affairs the Dimitrov Government followed much the same policies as the preceding post-1989 administrations. Relations with the USSR had long ceased to be as close as they were under Zhivkov: had not the Warsaw Pact been disbanded Bulgaria would have left it, trading links with the USSR had declined and Zhelev had been amongst the first to denounce the attempted coup of August 1991 in Moscow. Furthermore, Zhelev had deliberately made the USA the destination for his first foreign visit as President. Bulgaria also joined in discussions on the formation of the Black Sea Economic Co-operation Group, though here there were suspicions in nationalist circles that any agreement might allow the free movement into Bulgaria of Turkish capital and labour. (In June 1992 the Group, comprising Bulgaria and 10 other countries and aiming to promote regional trade and co-operation in developing transport and infrastructure, was officially founded.)

Under the Dimitrov administration closer ties were established with Western Europe. In May 1992 Bulgaria was admitted to the Council of Europe and negotiations were begun which led, in December, to the signing of an association agreement with the European Community (EC—known as the European Union from November 1993, when it had still not ratified the agreement).

Inevitably, Dimitrov's Government was greatly challenged by the problems which emerged following the disintegration of Yugoslavia. In January 1992 Bulgaria became the first country to recognize Macedonia (the Former Yugoslav Republic of Macedonia was how the UN eventually recognized it), though it specified that whilst the Government recognized a separate Macedonian state it did not acknowledge the existence of a separate Macedonian nation. The recognition of Macedonia caused the previously excellent relations between Bulgaria and Greece to decline.

At home Dimitrov's cabinet continued with economic reform and restructuring. In 1992 legislation was passed which encouraged and facilitated foreign investment, reformed the banking system, restored to its previous owners property confiscated under Communist rule and privatized industry. The driving force behind the reforms was the Minister of Finance, Ivan Kostov, who enjoyed the confidence of the important financial officials in the West.

The Dimitrov Government, however, displayed an alarming capacity to alienate its natural supporters. The trade unions had become a powerful factor, and Podkrepa remained fiercely anti-Communist. Nevertheless, the social tensions of economic reform were great and becoming greater as consumer prices increased at a much faster rate than wages, pensions and social benefits. Despite this, the Dimitrov Government dispensed with the tripartite commission which previously had helped to resolve some social tensions. It was in part his advocacy of a more co-operative attitude towards the trade unions that led to the dismissal of the Minister of Defence, Dimitur Ludiev, in May 1992. (Ludiev had been the first civilian Minister of Defence since 1947).

Even more serious was the deteriorating relationship between the UDF Government and Zhelev, its own nominee for the presidency in the January elections. Zhelev had doubts about the conduct of foreign policy, especially over Macedonia, and he was also not prepared to allow the National Assembly unlimited control over the security forces. Furthermore, there were serious disagreements over the vexed question of the alleged relationship between present politicians and the former secret police (the main issues being whether the relevant files should be published or, if not, who should have access to them). On 30 August 1992 Zhelev, speaking on television, bitterly attacked Dimitrov and his cabinet.

At the same time Dimitrov was losing the support of the MRF. The Turkish areas of Bulgaria had been extremely hard hit by economic changes; unemployment soared far above the national average and, to make matters worse, ethnic Turks in Bulgaria complained that the land privatization programme discriminated against them. The result was a second spate of emigration, a process which was ended by the reimposition of tough controls by the Turkish Government. Had it continued, it would have deprived the MRF of many of its voters. To express its concern the MRF sided with the BSP in September 1992 to remove Stefan Savov, the UDF-nominated Chairman of the National Assembly. On 28 October a similar alignment resulted in the passing of a vote of censure on Dimitrov.

THE BEROV GOVERNMENT

Dimitrov remained as Prime Minister until the National Assembly had agreed on a successor. This did not happen for almost two months, until the end of December 1992. The new head of government was Lyuben Berov, an economic historian, whose cabinet consisted mainly of non-party technocrats. Berov's name had been proposed by the MRF and his support in the National Assembly was to be based on a combination of the MRF, the majority of the BSP and a schismatic section of the UDF which, by March 1993, had come together as the New Union for Democracy (NUD). The following month a centrist Council for Co-operation was formed, aiming to promote stability and moderation in the political sphere.

The advent of the NUD considerably enhanced the chances of survival for the Berov Government. This embittered the UDF, which stepped up its criticism of the Government and of the President who had allowed it to be formed. A line of attack in UDF propaganda was that the cabinet was attempting to reintroduce socialism. Government interference in the media and the reinstatement of some dismissed ex-Communists were used justify this claim; so, too, were the January 1993 resolution of the National Assembly not to open the police files, and the withdrawal of the facility, previously agreed, which entitled individuals to certificates attesting that they had had no links with the Communist secret police. The Government countered by pointing to the facts that that property restitution was continuing and that there was no impediment in the way of the Prosecutor-General, Ivan Tatarchev, who was determined to bring former leading Communists before the courts. Indeed, Tatarchev was particularly determined to arraign Todor Zhivkov on a charge of treason, for trying, on at least two occasions, to incorporate Bulgaria into the USSR.

In mid-1993 serious confrontation occurred between the UDF on the one hand and the Government and the President on the other. On 13 May, during a demonstration outside the National Assembly building, Stefan Savov, the former parliamentary speaker, was knocked to the ground and injured by a policeman; the UDF claimed he had been deliberately attacked, on the Government's instructions. Tension increased, particularly after 7 June when Edvin Sugarev, a UDF deputy, went on 'hunger strike' until, he said, Zhelev had agreed to resign as President. On 10 June there were large UDF rallies in Sofia and other centres, all of them denouncing Zhelev for trying to restore Communism and demanding immediate elections. On 12 June demonstrators began erecting a 'tent city' outside the presidential buildings in Sofia; two days later the police estimated that 30,000 Sofiotes took part in an anti-Zhelev demonstration. The situation had become so serious that the Prime Minister cancelled a visit to a human-rights conference in Vienna (Austria). The situation, having eased slightly on 27 June when Sugarev abandoned his hunger strike, was complicated two days later when Blaga Dimitrova resigned her office of Vice-President, complaining that she had not been sufficiently consulted and that some form of dictatorship was imminent. The UDF claimed victory when Zhelev indicated that he thought elections might be held in November, although the National Assembly would still have two years of its allotted time to run. The crisis subsided with two unsuccessful UDF votes of censure on the Berov Government.

The political instability in Bulgaria did nothing to help the serious economic problems the country was facing. Berov had announced, soon after becoming premier, he would pursue the economic and financial policies of the previous cabinet; that is, large-scale privatization, support for private business and the introduction of legislation to regulate bankruptcy and the administration of state-owned companies. In its 'Plan of Action', announced in February 1993, the Government confirmed these objectives and promised also to do all it could to arrest the steep decline in overall economic output, and to concentrate its efforts on the specific problems of agriculture, light industry, tourism and parts of the machine-building and chemical industries. The Plan estimated a 4% decrease in real gross domestic product (GDP) during 1993, a 90%–100% increase in consumer prices and a budget deficit of between 8% and 10%.

The last brought a sharp reaction from the IMF, which insisted that no state borrowing from the IMF should allow a deficit of more than 5% of GDP.

The IMF, and other economic pressure groups, became increasingly concerned during the first half of 1993 at the decline in production and the increase in trade deficits. By mid-1993 it seemed that Berov's Plan was stronger on intentions than achievements. Only one major privatization had taken place, that of the Maize Products enterprise in Razgrad, and the director of the Privatization Agency had complained that the Government would not give him sufficient power to carry out his responsibilities. Only about one-quarter of the land had been returned to its previous owners and the IMF had twice expressed concern at the slow pace of economic reforms. At a press conference on 16 July 1993 the Minister of Finance, Stoyan Aleksandrov, acknowledged the need for a value added tax, a law on bankruptcy and more rapid privatization.

Despite this, some economic progress was made. Siemens, a German firm, was one of a number of important Western firms who entered into joint ventures with Bulgarian concerns (in Siemens' case, for the modernization of the telephone system). In mid-1993 Bulgaria was granted 'most-favoured-nation' status by the US Congress. This, in addition to the signing of a free-trade agreement with the European Free Trade Association (EFTA), greatly improved trading prospects, in spite of the delay of the EC in ratifying the association agreement of December 1992.

Bulgaria's most serious economic problem was not this delay on the part of the EC, nor the complaints of the IMF, but the servicing of the foreign debt. The Government had for some time argued for a decrease of 78% in its US $10,000m. debt to the 'London Club' of international bankers. In November 1993 (having rejected a reduction of 38% in March) its request of a 50% reduction was unexpectedly granted at a meeting in Frankfurt, Germany. More seriously, however, payment of interest on the debt had been suspended. This was used by the UDF as an excuse for one of its votes of censure on the Berov Government, but the administration had at least one powerful argument to justify its course of action. Bulgaria remained steadfast in its application of sanctions against the 'rump' Yugoslav state, even after the tightening of the sanctions in May caused severe disruption to Bulgaria's trade, by closing its main access route to central Europe and the West. Bulgaria's pleas for a corridor through Serbia were ignored. The total losses to the Bulgarian economy, between 1 January and 30 June 1993, according to Bulgarian estimates, amounted to $1,300m. In such circumstances, the Government argued, it was unreasonable not to make significant adjustments to Bulgaria's obligations to its debtors.

THE PROSPECTS FOR THE FUTURE

In political terms the Berov Government lasted longer than many observers had predicted. Its advent and survival forced minor realignments of political forces, which weakened the UDF and strengthened the centre. Pressure for further elections, however, were unlikely to go away and could intensify, because of the country's economic difficulties and, to a lesser degree, because of nationalist tensions. In the latter area the *de facto* parliamentary working partnership between the MRF and the BSP was weakened, though not dispelled, by the BSP's tendency to champion the 'Bulgarian' against the 'Turkish' cause. The UDF, meanwhile, also played the nationalist card, taking the lead in the campaign against the alleged 'turkification' of the Pomaks, the Bulgarian-speaking Muslims. Furthermore, both major parties supported the exercise of legal restraints on those Bulgarian citizens who wished to declare themselves of Macedonian nationality (the political establishment disapproved the foundation of a 'Union for the Prosperity of Pirin Macedonia' in September 1993. In general terms, however, ethnic tensions had been contained in Bulgaria and, in its annual report on human rights around the world, the US State Department described Bulgaria's record as generally good, though it added that more could be done to provide a legal framework for complaints of human-rights infringements.

When elections were held there would, no doubt, be some consideration of the constitutional ruling that no party could be represented in the National Assembly unless it secured 4% of the national vote. That ruling, together with the splintering of the parties, meant that almost one-quarter of the votes cast in the 1991 election went to parties which, in the event, were not represented in the National Assembly. Political rationality would also suggest that these parties should make greater efforts to come together and remain in larger units. The historical precedents, however, were not encouraging.

The constitutional court was likely to continue to play an important role in national affairs. Thus, it confirmed that the MRF did not contravene the law banning parties based on religious or ethnic affiliations and it overruled the Berov Government's dismissal of the director of the Bulgarian Telegraph Agency. Moreover, its capacity to act as an independent defender of constitutional probity was a necessary factor in a country with such limited experience of the rule of law.

In 1994 and the mid-1990s Bulgaria would, no doubt, remain at the mercy of political developments elsewhere in the Balkans. The economic hardship caused by the sanctions against the 'rump' Yugoslavia had already necessitated the serious consideration of alternative transport strategies. Thus, the European Investment Bank had agreed to grant a loan for the improvement of road connections with Greece, Romania and Turkey. The Bulgarian Government denied breaking the sanctions policy, or even intending to do so, but, in mid-1993, it was putting considerable pressure on the UN for formal recognition of its economic difficulties and for compensation. Still more money was advanced to carry out safety work at the nuclear power station at Kozlodui on the Danube. The power station provided up to 50% of the nation's electricity, but urgently needed improvements to make it safe. This is the prime example of the fact that a huge proportion of Bulgaria's resources would have to go to repairing environmental damage and preventing further degradation.

The Economy

Dr RAYMOND HUTCHINGS

INTRODUCTION

Following the overthrow of Todor Zhivkov, in November 1989, and the transition to a non-Communist Government in December 1990, the first one for 46 years, the Bulgarian economy embarked on the difficult process of transition to a market economy. The physical circumstances, much of the organizational structure and many of the attitudes inherited from the previous system remained and all the problems inherent in such a transition were encountered. These negative factors were aggravated by the previous enlargement of foreign debt, the 1990–1991 Gulf crisis in the Persian (Arabian) Gulf and the demise of the Council for Mutual Economic Assistance (CMEA), the Communist trading bloc with which Bulgaria, in particular, had traded. From 1992 there were also the problems created by the sanctions imposed by the international community on Yugoslavia (Serbia and Montenegro).

Geography and Transport

Bulgaria is a compact country, roughly rectangular and twice as long from east to west as from north to south. It is 111,000 sq km in area. Mountain chains divide it into northern and southern regions, which are of roughly equal size. Bulgaria is mainly bordered on the north by the River Danube (Dunav), which, besides being a political boundary, is useful for navigation, as cooling for industrial plant, for irrigation and, to a small extent, for fishing (but scarcely at all for recreation, owing to pollution and the strong current). Navigation is occasionally hindered by low water, while irrigation is complicated by the height of the banks along the Bulgarian side. The Danube is a considerable barrier to north–south traffic, being crossed by only one bridge between Bulgaria and Romania (just east of Ruse), which is the cause of notorious delays. Both water and sea transport primarily serve Bulgaria's external traffic. Bulgaria also lies on the main international road and rail routes between Europe and Asia Minor, although these links were disrupted by international sanctions on Yugoslavia in the early 1990s.

At the end of 1992 Bulgaria had 4,294 km of railway track, making the country slightly better endowed than Romania in terms of railway track per unit of territory. Most railways in Bulgaria were single-track; 61.4% of their total length was electrified (an unusually high proportion in Eastern Europe). Bulgaria's rail networks were not being extended. Bulgaria and Romania were about equally provided with roads per unit of territory. In 1992 the total length of roads in Bulgaria was almost 37,000 km. In mid-1993 the European Investment Bank announced that it had approved a loan of 21m. ECUs for improving Bulgaria's major roads, its links to Greece, Romania, Turkey and the Black Sea. This project was also to be financed by the European Bank for Reconstruction and Development (EBRD), which granted a US $43m. loan. Rail-freight traffic declined after 1983, while rail-passenger traffic remained constant. Car ownership per head was average for Eastern Europe, being higher than in Romania and lower than in the Czech Republic.

Bulgaria's climate is continental, especially in the north and north-east. Bulgaria is the southernmost country in Europe where the average January temperature is 0°C (32°F) or below. The soil in the Danubian plain is generally fertile, including black earths and grey forest soils; to the south it is inferior, but has proved very suitable for tobacco.

As far as water resources are concerned, Bulgaria is one of the least fortunate countries in Europe. Rivers, apart from the Danube, are mostly short and have very uneven flow, which, furthermore, is least at times when plants need it the most. Precipitation is, on the whole, adequate (650 mm annually, for the whole country) and is more suitably timed seasonally. However, it is highest in mountain areas, where it is least needed. Irrigation has, therefore, been greatly expanded: it is concentrated along the Danube, including the Vidin area. Like other Balkan countries, in the 1980s and 1990s (especially from 1985 onwards) Bulgaria suffered from repeated droughts; these affect hydro-generated electricity as well as crop yields.

Population and Labour Force

According to World Bank estimates, the population of Bulgaria reached 9m. in mid-1991, although any further increase is unlikely. Whereas national policy was generally been pro-natalist, sentiment among ethnic Bulgarians strongly favoured small families, whereas the Turkish minority and the Roma (Gypsies), favoured larger ones. There are also Bulgarians living in adjacent countries, including, it was claimed, 200,000 in Romania. Bulgaria's population density (81.0 per sq km at the end of 1990) is the lowest in Eastern Europe. The urban population was 68% of the total (in Romania, 53%). The capital city, Sofia, had a population of more than 1.1m. people; other cities of more than 150,000 included Plovdiv, Varna, Burgas, Ruse and Stara Zagora.

In 1990 some 46% of the population was within the work-force, which was a similar proportion to other countries in south-east Europe. Total employment tended to decline slightly, owing to a long-term fall in the birth-rate. In 1990 about 17% of the work-force were employed in agriculture and 38% in industry.

The transition to a market economy inevitably entails substantial unemployment. In May 1990 some 35,000–40,000 unemployed were forecast by the year's end; in actual fact the eventual total reached 70,000. Although this was a small proportion of a work-force of over 4m., it made a significant psychological impact. In mid-June 1991 unemployment reached 205,000—an increase of nearly sevenfold since July 1990. The majority of the unemployed were able-bodied and in their 30s, 40s and 50s; 44.5% were qualified specialists. In 1991 almost 10% of the registered unemployed were university graduates. By the end of August 1993 National Employment Service figures showed that a total of 603,040 were registered unemployed—a national rate of 15.96%.

Sectoral Origins of National Income

Bulgaria used to be overwhelmingly an agricultural country. It remained markedly agricultural even by the 1990s, but, according to official figures (which should be treated with caution, as the Communist regimes of Eastern Europe tended to overvalue industry and undervalue agriculture), by 1990 agriculture's contribution to the national material product (NMP) had declined to 9.1% of the total, while that of industry had risen to 56.8%. The agricultural sector, in such calculations, normally excluded forestry and the industrial sector consisted mainly of manufacturing and utilities.

Environmental Problems

As in other countries of Eastern Europe, the environment in Bulgaria suffered during the Communist period. Awareness of environmental issues was developing from the mid-1980s. A more radical ecological policy was discussed in the National Assembly in March 1990. However, the liveliest environmental issue was that of air pollution above Ruse, which the Bulgarians ascribed to a chemical plant in Giurgiu in Romania. Morbidity and mortality were claimed to be higher in Ruse than elsewhere in Bulgaria. In August 1991, partly under pressure from the European Community (EC—known as the European Union from November 1993), Romania and Bulgaria agreed to co-operate in environmental matters, to monitor atmospheric pollution in the Ruse-Giurgiu area and to accept aid in improving the area. The EC also provided funds to help rehabilitate the Bulgarian environment, during 1992 and 1993.

Statistics

In June 1991 a new National Statistical Institute was set up, which would apply uniform nomenclatures and classifications consistent with international standards. A supreme board of statistics was to be set up. Confidentiality of individual statistics would be guaranteed. The Bulgarian National Bank and the National Statistics Institute actually supplied different figures for Bulgaria's foreign trade in 1991, owing to different methods of calculation. Such difficulties were not expected to be completely resolved until the mid-1990s.

SECTORS OF THE ECONOMY

Agriculture

Over one-half (55%) of the total land area, that is, about 61,000 sq km, was farmed. In 1990 just under 5% were farmed as private plots; by mid-1993 this percentage had increased to 34%, following the programme of land privatization begun in early 1991. During the Communist regime cereals, especially wheat, were grown predominantly by 'socialized units', state and collective farms, but potatoes, meat, eggs, milk and other smaller-scale products mainly in private plots. In 1991 some 35% of the total land area of Bulgaria was arable land, compared to 42% in Romania and only 20% in Albania. Bulgaria, therefore, grew less cereals than its northern neighbour, but more tomatoes, grapes (Bulgaria was a major producer and exporter of wine) and tobacco. Bulgaria was famed for the cultivation of roses, and establishes the world standard for rose oil.

In the early 1990s the number of livestock has been steadily declining. There were some 1.3m. head of cattle, 3.0m. pigs and 6.7m. sheep in 1992. In the first seven months of 1993 the number of cattle declined by 6,845 head, and that of sows and sheep by 28,000 and 331,000 respectively. On the whole, livestock provided a smaller share of farm products in Bulgaria than in adjacent countries.

Forestry and Fishing

Like all Balkan countries, Bulgaria had a high proportion of forest and woodland (35%). Afforestation was on a very considerable scale; however, from the 1980s, the total area of woodland scarcely altered. There were both deciduous trees (including oak and beech) and conifers. Only about 15% of the forest had industrial significance. Timber is used for furniture and the manufacture of paper and cellulose. In the summer there is a significant fire risk. Forestry, with agriculture, is among the lowest paid occupations. Fishing seems to have had a low priority. Furthermore, the Iron Gates hydroelectric scheme, apparently, reduced the catch of fish in the Danube.

Industry

Industrialization took place mainly during the Communist period. According to official statistics, between 40% and 50% of gross fixed capital investments were ordinarily devoted to industry, less than 10% to agriculture. Industrial activity was not evenly distributed throughout the country. One of the main industrial areas was Sofia–Pernik (west-central Bulgaria), which was the most comprehensively developed. Efforts were made to spread industry more widely. Iron and steel industries were concentrated in the Sofia–Pernik region, in two full-cycle integrated works, at Pernik and, on a larger scale, at Kremikovtsi. A third production facility went into operation at Burgas in 1988. However, the non-Communist administrations sharply reduced investment in these projects. The food-processing industry, while constituting a smaller proportion of total industrial production in the early 1990s than before the Second World War, had greatly expanded in absolute terms and supplied both internal needs and many products for export. This industry was concentrated in the upper Thracian plains and in the Danube and Sofia basins. In engineering, the main sector was the manufacture of transport equipment, especially fork-lift trucks, electric cars, mopeds and bicycles; shipbuilding was also important. A wide range of electrical equipment (batteries, electric motors, etc.) was manufactured. Another key area was electronics (calculators, robots, etc.), which earned some export revenue in the West. The chemicals industry produced a wide range of items, from fertilizers to pharmaceuticals, including soap and petrochemicals. Ferrous metallurgy, engineering, electrical equipment and chemicals together absorbed a high proportion of total investment in the economy under the Communist regime (for example, in 1987, it was 43.5%). Garments and textiles too were manufactured, while domestic industry included the making of carpets.

One of Bulgaria's principal export industries, during the late 1970s and the 1980s, was the computer industry. Bulgaria was the CMEA country which specialized in this area. However, its advantages dissolved with the dissolution of the CMEA and exposure to the more advanced technologies of the West. By mid-1991 the industry had not yet attracted significant overseas investment or joint-venture deals. Another industry under threat from the political changes was the defence industry. In this sector changes were necessitated also by restrictions on government spending. Defence spending was included in an unspecified budgetary remainder, which rose from 12.2% of actual spending in 1985 to 15.4% in 1988. Although not itemized it was accepted that military spending ought to be reduced, with part of the industry converted for civilian manufacture. Output of this latter type was to expand almost threefold in 1989–95. In 1993 a total of 8,654m. leva was allocated to defence.

Mining and Energy

Bulgaria possessed similar mineral resources to other Balkan countries, but, on the whole, was less well endowed. Available minerals, such as iron ore, were mostly low-grade. Coal was mainly lignite (a low-grade brown coal), which is of much lower calorific value than hard coal (and causes more pollution). Hard coal was imported, both for fuel and for metallurgical purposes. Bulgaria did have some reserves of anthracite (a high-grade hard coal). There were small amounts of petroleum and natural gas, but import-dependence for each of these is over 90%. Ores of lead-zinc, iron, manganese, chrome, tin, cadmium, copper, molybdenum and silver were mined, but statistics of the amounts extracted of several of these were not published, at least under the Communists. Small quantities of fluorite and sulphur, among others, were also mined.

Like other Communist countries, Bulgaria obeyed, and exceeded, Lenin's injunctions regarding electrification. It is now admitted, for instance, that it was premature to adopt electric street-lighting. Electricity consumption was restricted after the winter of 1984/85. Other drawbacks were that the building of power stations absorbed much labour and resources, the quality of building declined and guaranteed terms of functioning were merely symbolic. Although electricity generation rose, it continued to be insufficient; a shortage of fuel for popular needs intensified the problem.

Furthermore, among the Eastern European countries, Bulgaria was unusually poorly endowed with energy sources. In 1980, for example, some three-quarters of Bulgaria's energy requirements were imported. Local resources were used increasingly, but their proportionate share tended to decrease. This dependence prompted the development of nuclear power; in 1990 Bulgaria, producing about one-third of its electricity from nuclear power, was the country which was the third-most dependent upon nuclear power in the world. The sole nuclear power station is at Kozlodui (on the Danube). It was under discussion for some time whether a second (also riverine) such station should be built at Belene. However, in May 1990, a study group of the Academy of Sciences, reversing the previous opinion of scholars, opposed this and, in mid-1991, the Government confirmed that the project had been finally abandoned. Doubts were raised about safety at Kozlodui and, in 1990, following local and international pressure, an investigatory commission of the International Atomic Energy Agency (IAEA) confirmed these doubts and recommended the plant's closure. Romania expressed particular concern at the implications and, although Bulgaria has no immediate alternatives to substantial reliance on nuclear power, in July 1991 the Bulgarian authorities agreed to close two of the six reactors at Kozlodui. This was to be done with EC aid, which Bulgaria had requested. By late November the decision had taken effect. In September 1993 the programme to improve the safety of four reactors at the power station was successfully completed, and financial aid had been guaranteed by the World Bank and Electricité de France for the next stage of the project.

Banking

In 1987 the Bulgarian State Bank, which previously monopolized domestic banking operations, was restricted to monetary issue and supervisory functions, while an Economic Bank was established to assume an important share of the financing tasks for domestic industry. The Foreign Trade Bank also continued to exist. Other banks, with sectoral and regional titles, were then established, apparently free to function on commercial lines: they could have branches anywhere, while enterprises could choose between them. Interest rates were raised in May 1990 and were entirely market-determined from 1 January 1991. At several times during 1991 the Popov Government reiterated its intention to maintain high interest rates, in order to counter inflation, and this was supported by the International Monetary Fund (IMF). An agricultural credit bank, with ambitious objectives, was founded in early 1990. Legislation in early 1991 provided for the establishment of banks with foreign capital in Bulgaria. By the end of the year the transition of the banking sector to a two-tier structure was complete. In 1993 Bulgaria was to join nine other states in setting up a Black Sea Bank of Development and Trade.

Tourism

Bulgaria's sunshine, scenery (its appreciation aided by a network of marked mountain routes) and coastline were suited to tourism, which made a significant contribution (about US $400m. annually in the late 1980s and early 1990s) to the balance of payments. In 1989 1.6% of the work-force were employed in tourism, which is a relatively low proportion (in Spain it was 5.7%). There were golden sands, with well-arranged facilities, and picturesque monasteries. However, guiding needed improvement and tourist sites more sensitive treatment. Since 1988 Bulgarians have been permitted individually to operate hotels and inns, and, in 1991, a new law on tourism was being prepared. As late as April 1993, however, the industry was stated to be in urgent need of privatization. In an effort to speed up the process a list of 300 units to be privatized had lately been approved. Foreign investment was to be directed towards new projects and infrastructure, and to the application of new technologies. Uniform standards and rules were soon to be introduced. The EC granted aid to Bulgaria for developing tourism in the period 1993–95.

Under the Communist regime, most foreign visitors were from Turkey (in transit), the former Yugoslavia or former Eastern bloc countries, particularly Poland. Therefore, they did not spend much per head or bring with them convertible currency. From Western countries, most came from the former West German state. Visits from Scandinavia have increased substantially. However, following the liberalization of travel for Eastern Europeans fewer of them holidayed within Eastern Europe; the crises in Yugoslavia had the same effect. Western participation in the industry is, nevertheless, increasing. Mitsubishi in 1990 signed a contract to manage the five-star hotel chain, Vitosha–New Otani. Traditional ties with France were also being strengthened. In 1990 the foreign exchange earned from tourism rose by about 10%, despite a 20% fall in the number of tourists.

ECONOMIC RESULTS FROM 1990

The first consequences of the overthrow of the Zhivkov regime, in the field of economics, were not favourable. During the first half of 1990 output fell by 3,400m. leva, that is, by 9.3%, relative to the same period in 1989. Almost one-half of the fall was because of the lack of raw materials, the rest to a variety of causes, including lack of sales contracts and, to a small extent, to the closure of enterprises because they polluted the environment. Industrial production fell by 10.8%, with machine-building, metalworking, chemicals, petroleum refining and food processing being responsible for more than 80% of the decline. Retail trade rose in value terms in 1990, but mainly owing to higher prices: between May and the beginning of October, the cost of living increased by a quarter. Out of 295 items supplied to the domestic market, 193 were supplied in smaller quantities. The decline in housing construction has been mentioned already. During the first 10 months of 1990 a decrease in agricultural produce, such as corn, sugar or tomatoes, was reported; also the head of cows declined by 2.8% and that of ewes by 5.6%. Overall the report depicted irregular work, a continuous and ubiquitous fall in goods production and something approaching chaos in organization and management.

By 1993, according to the National Statistical Institute, the decline in the industrial sector had begun to slow down: production had risen in the iron and steel industries, in non-ferrous metallurgy and in electronics and the petrochemical industries. In agriculture, preliminary figures for 1992 show a decline in all areas of production except sunflowers, potatoes and some fruits.

Supply and Demand

In Bulgaria, as in other centralized economies, stable prices were generally maintained by increasing budget subsidies; incomes, however, increased, producing a combination which caused suppressed inflation and shortages. Monetary emission continued. The consequence was an increasing budget deficit, an excess of money in circulation and, so, rising inflation.

There were four main reasons for the gravely aggravated supply situation in the early 1990s. One was Bulgaria's foreign-debt situation, which was aggravated over several years, revalued and increasingly became very serious. There were the travails of changing from one sort of economic system to another. Finally, there were special difficulties resulting from the Gulf crisis of 1990–91 and from the UN-imposed embargo on trade with, or through, the Federal Republic of Yugoslavia (Serbia and Montenegro) from 1992.

The outcome was severe shortages of almost every commodity. This entailed enormous queues for what goods were obtainable. Given the pervasive shortages, together with quickly changing legal and administrative arrangements, it was not surprising that a parallel or unofficial economy ('black market') was flourishing. A law against speculation was enacted in 1990, but did not cure the problem. Another result was a feverish demand for smuggled goods, even after September 1990 when rationing was eventually introduced in Sofia.

One of the items in shortest supply was petroleum. At first petroleum became more expensive, then it disappeared. Traffic came to a standstill. Following the introduction of rationing, queues at filling stations, previously kilometres long, dwindled overnight, but the black-market price reached 5 leva per litre. The most significant causes for the shortage were the Soviet decision to sell petroleum products to the Eastern European countries only in return for convertible currency, from 1 January 1991, and the Gulf crisis. The Yugoslav situation compounded the problem. Indirect causes included Bulgaria's foreign debts (see below) and poor endowment with energy resources.

Social Problems of the Transition

During 1991 inflation caused great concern. A doubling of prices proved a crushing burden for one-third of the population. The Government helped to alleviate the worst consequences of the economic transition by its Social Agreements of 1991, but some worsening in living standards seemed inevitable. Draft regulations on the restructuring of health care were published in December 1989. General policy in this sphere was substantially amended; private medical practice, it was announced in May 1990, would be permitted on equal terms to state and co-operative practice. Meanwhile medicines remained persistently short. Although the social-security system prided itself on its concern for social welfare, pension schemes were considered to be radically outdated and not to reflect the rate of inflation. Pensioners have continued to be among those who lost out.

Fiscal Trends

By the end of 1991 the rate of inflation was estimated to be four times higher than in 1990. The rate for 1992, according to the National Statistical Institute was 80%. The unreasonably large budget deficit, contraction of production, the foreign-debt burden (see below) and raised customs duties also added to inflationary pressure with (as variously estimated) either the budget deficit or the fall in production the chief factor.

Government borrowing attained large dimensions. By mid-February 1993 the central-government borrowing requirement totalled 9,420.8m. leva, more than 60% of which was needed to cover the cash deficit. The Government borrowed most of the funds in direct loans from the National Bank and by selling government securities.

Retail Trade

The retail trade amounted, annually, to some 17,000m. leva. According to official sources, the volume of trade consistently rose from year to year, but, in 1990, this was entirely because of price rises. Since both industrial and agricultural output fell, even the previous level of sales was likely to have been maintained only thanks to higher imports. (Imports of certain consumer goods, such as coffee, did in fact rise.) The larger part (63.7% in 1987) of retail trade consists of non-food items, whose share within the total rose only very slowly.

Individual items of Western provenance became available for sale in the early 1990s, or their availability expanded. An agreement was signed for Bulgaria to produce Coca Cola in quantity. Johnnie Walker whisky reached Sofia. BMW cars were selling relatively well. A significant rise in overall retail sales was registered in March 1993, owing to realization of output produced earlier, not to any improvement in the rate of production.

Foreign Trade

Foreign trade was among the sectors greatly affected by the political and economic changes of the early 1990s. Under Communist rule, Bulgaria was distinguished among other Eastern bloc countries by the unusually large proportions of its foreign trade which were conducted with other CMEA countries and with the USSR in particular. Almost 60% of Bulgaria's foreign trade was with the USSR (for Romania the corresponding percentage was only some 20%). The former German Democratic Republic (GDR) was next, but with only 6%. Bulgaria usually had a negative balance in trade with the developed West but a positive one in trade with developing countries. Industrial goods comprised the largest proportion of the items traded, especially of imports where this share exceeded 90%. The early 1990s showed a decrease in Bulgarian exports and imports. The biggest drop was in trade with developed countries, although trade with CMEA countries also declined.

In mid-1992 Bulgaria imposed sanctions on the Yugoslav Republics of Serbia and Montenegro, with stricter regulations imposed in May 1993. This move seriously affected the country's trade with central and Western Europe and, according to government estimates, would have cost the Bulgarian economy US $3,000m. by the end of 1993. One of the consequences of the trade restrictions was that transportation of goods has took much longer and, since fruit and vegetables constituted much of Bulgaria's exports, this proved particularly disastrous for the economy.

Apart from such problems, foreign trade is by no means completely liberalized. A new decree, containing export and import regulations in 1993, was to leave out certain items hitherto temporarily exempt from import duty. Part of these would be included in 'fast' liberalization schemes with the EC and EFTA. In return, the Ministry of Trade was to seek some reciprocal concessions and a reduction of tariff on others. Export taxes were to be charged at a flat rate instead of on an *ad valorem* basis.

Foreign Debts and Investments

The Communist regime having concealed the extent of Bulgaria's foreign indebtedness, the background to the pronounced fall in foreign trade was a debt situation which was revealed as much worse than was previously thought. This situation had dramatically worsened after 1984. Whereas until 1985 the country's non-socialist trade balance remained under control, the collapse of petroleum prices, in 1986, dealt a severe blow to Bulgaria's exports to the West, which consisted largely of crude or refined petroleum. The demand for Bulgarian products from petroleum-producing developing countries also fell. It was decided, nevertheless, not to reduce investments envisaged to take place during 1986–90. Furthermore, a severe drought in 1985 compelled Bulgaria to import food, which it normally exported. As a result, between 1985 and 1989, a negative balance of US $7,000m. was accumulated. Loans from abroad also went mainly towards productive and personal consumption, while even major projects that did obtain funds brought no return in earning foreign exchange. Even in December 1989 the country still had $1,000m., putting Bulgaria in fourth place among CMEA debtors (after the USSR, Hungary and Poland), but without taking into account those countries' larger populations and resources. As reported in July 1990 Bulgaria was owed money by Iran, Iraq, Ethiopia, Syria, Mozambique and Angola, but these either had no intention of paying or, in the case of Iraq, would become unable to do so. Bulgaria's losses because of the UN decision to place a full economic embargo on Iraq were estimated by the Bulgarians to reach $1,388m.; the crisis put an end to Iraqi deliveries of petroleum to Bulgaria, at a time when Iraq was repaying, in petroleum, the $1,300m. that it owed. Debt-settlement proposals were made; one presented by Bulgaria in November 1992 suggested for a 75% 'write-off, but banks found it unacceptable. In April 1993 a 38% reduction in the country's commercial foreign debt was offered.

Western and International Attitudes and Actions

The West's response to the election of the Popov Government, replacing that of Lukanov, in November 1990, was favourable and presaged increased readiness to help. France, Turkey, the Netherlands and Greece were among the countries providing aid in the early 1990s. In December 1992 draft loan agreements with Sweden, Norway and Finland were approved. The reaction from international bodies was also favourable. Bulgaria was accepted as a member of the IMF and of the World Bank in September 1990. In April 1993 the World Bank offered a 17-year $100m. loan for water development. According to official figures, direct foreign investment in Bulgaria in 1992 totalled US $41.5m. Bulgaria was expected to become a member of the General Agreement on Tariffs and Trade (GATT) in early November 1993.

Bulgaria's agreement on association with the EC, signed in Brussels on 8 March 1993, was ratified by the National Assembly on 5 April 1993. The agreement would come into force on ratification by the parliaments of the EC member states. However, by the end of 1993 this had still not been achieved. When the trade pact became effective, it would open European markets to Bulgarian goods. In April 1993 Bulgaria also reached an agreement with the EFTA. While EFTA countries did not account for any large part of Bulgaria's foreign trade, the agreement opened an opportunity to improve two-way sales. Bulgarian–British and Bulgarian–Macedonian Chambers of Commerce were set up in March 1993 and the Greek Productivity Centre was to open a subsidiary in Sofia. Bulgarian–Turkish economic structures were also formed.

Joint Ventures

Joint ventures with foreign firms (which initially were mainly German and Austrian) were launched, especially in engineering (including robotized welding and the manufacture of refrigerators) and in housing construction. Foreign concessions were granted for petroleum and natural-gas prospecting. German companies were taking an active part in furnishing and supplying department stores. Krupp was to study the Bulgarian economy, with a view to helping enterprises to become competitive. Rothmans and other leading Western manufacturers of tobacco products indicated interest in the Bulgarian tobacco market. Bulgarian tobacco lost export markets in the East; to regain its position in the world market, investment and partial retooling were required. Coca Cola bought a 49% stake in the Stara Zagora brewery. As of May 1993 there were 837 joint ventures in Bulgaria.

Restructuring

The Bulgarian economic system used to closely resemble the classic Soviet one, making allowance for Bulgaria's much smaller size; in particular, the republican division was absent. In response to Soviet *perestroika* ('restructuring'), complicated revisions of an analogous kind were announced under Zhivkov, but these, however, did not alter its essence. More fundamental changes were instituted after 1989.

Considerable measures of decentralization and the dismantling of monopolies were undertaken. In November 1990 the four biggest corporations on the home market (concerning industrial goods; car servicing and spare parts; fish and fish products; and packaging materials) ceased to exist, being divided respectively into 68, 45, 14 and 28 separate units. Bulgarplod (producing fruit and vegetables) has been divided into 67 small firms, while Vinprom (the monopoly producer of wine), Bulgartabak (tobacco) and Bulgarsko Pivo (beer) were dealt with in like manner. As long ago as June 1991, Bulgaria was the first country in Eastern Europe to draft a transport decentralization programme. The plan included dismembering up the composite companies, promoting joint ventures and attracting foreign investment. Balkanair divisions were granted independence and construction of a new airport at Sofia was put out to international tender. Only the Bulgarian Railways were expected to remain entirely state-owned, yet they too would be affected by market principles.

A draft law for privatization of land was announced in May 1990: every citizen was to have the right to own land, though priority lay with the previous owners and their heirs. By November 1990 no legislation had been enacted, the proposals only having had their first reading in parliament. Debates centred on the already-set limit of 30 ha in individual regions. The proposals stated three main principles: the right to the inviolable private ownership of land (for the state and the Church as well); non-interference in farming; and virtually no limits on land ownership, between one and 300 ha. The law was finally enacted in March 1991.

Privatization

Two co-ordinated programmes of privatization of the Bulgarian economy were proposed during the first half of 1990. One of these was prepared by US economists, headed by Dr Robert Rahn, at the invitation of the Bulgarian Government. The first programme worked out general principles, while the second dealt with various points of detail. One of the specific proposals was to establish a customs-free zone along much of the Black Sea coast. However, following the fall of the Lukanov Government these proposals and expertise were no longer available. In April 1993 a delegation of World Bank experts was to visit Bulgaria to launch private privatization projects.

However, privatization had proceeded in various sectors. As indicated above, one of the necessary steps was the dismantling of large corporations. In August 1990 there were reported to be some 30,000 private companies, although many of these were very small, local businesses. Private production was more difficult to encourage. In October 1990 the first private baker in Sofia for decades was established. A new airline, Air Via, for tourist charters and occasional freight flights, was founded by Balkanbank, Interbalkan and several private individuals. Sofia commodity exchange was reopened in June 1991, exactly 50 years after it had been closed down; there were to be weekly auctions, later on futures deals. Bulgaria's first private bank was formed.

Various obstacles to privatization were encountered. Restitution of nationalized private industrial assets ran into enormous legal and social problems: few units still existed physically as they were when originally expropriated, during the last 50 years state-owned enterprises engaged in self-financed updating, etc. Many managers, especially of profitable enterprises, considered the new policies an opportunity to convert the enterprise they were responsible for into their own property. Some managers, allegedly, sought to make their enterprises not appear profitable, so as to be able to purchase them at a lower price when they were privatized. This relationship probably helps explain the poor performance of Bulgarian industry during 1990. At December 1991 the state was still the major employer, owning some 93% of the country's capital stock. In 1992, according to official figures, the private sector accounted for 20% of GDP, while by June 1993 the sector amounted to 52.2% of retail trade.

Conclusions

The reform programmes and reorganizations both surprised and were approved of by Western governments, which, together with international institutions, responded to Bulgaria's financial needs. Stabilization measures at first proved largely successful in restraining inflation and reducing price subsidies. However, inflation grew worse and the decline in economic activity continued. Some initial indications of development appeared. Agreements were reached with the EC and EFTA. The transfer of state enterprises to private ownership was not yet fully under way (the state sector remained dominant at the end of 1993) and the problem remained of the huge foreign debt (estimated at US $13,000m. in mid-1993). By 1993 Bulgaria was being forced to choose between curbing inflation and curbing unemployment. Though comprehensive changes were being pushed ahead, the economy had not yet completed the transition to a functioning market economy, its problems compounded by the UN restrictions on its major route to the main markets of Europe.

Statistical Survey

Source (unless otherwise stated): National Statistical Institute, 1000 Sofia, 6-ti Septemvri St 10; telex 22001; fax (2) 87-78-25.

Area and Population

AREA, POPULATION AND DENSITY

Area (sq km)*	110,994†
Population (census results)	
2 December 1975	8,727,771
4 December 1985	
Males	4,433,302
Females	4,515,347
Total	8,948,649
Population (official estimates at 31 December)	
1988	8,986,636
1989	8,992,316
1990	8,989,165
Density (per sq km) at 31 December 1990	81.0

* Including territorial waters of frontier rivers (261.4 sq km).
† 42,855 sq miles.

ADMINISTRATIVE REGIONS (31 December 1990)

	Area (sq km)	Estimated population	Density (per sq km)
Sofia (capital)*	1,310.8	1,220,914	931.6
Burgas	14,656.7	875,426	59.7
Khaskovo	13,891.6	1,056,374	76.0
Lovech	15,150.0	1,048,671	69.3
Mikhailovgrad	10,606.9	655,806	61.9
Plovdiv	13,628.1	1,287,614	94.1
Razgrad (Ruse)	10,842.4	843,584	78.0
Sofia*	18,978.5	1,010,955	53.3
Varna	11,928.6	989,821	83.0
Total	110,993.6	8,989,165	81.0

* The city of Sofia, the national capital, has separate regional status. The area and population of the capital region are not included in the neighbouring Sofia region.

PRINCIPAL TOWNS
(estimated population at 31 December 1990)

Sofia (capital)	1,141,142	Stara Zagora	164,553
Plovdiv	379,083	Pleven	138,323
Varna	314,913	Dobrich*	115,786
Burgas (Bourgas)	204,915	Sliven	112,220
Ruse (Roussé)	192,365	Shumen	110,754

* Dobrich was renamed Tolbukhin in 1949, but its former name was restored in 1990.

BIRTHS, MARRIAGES AND DEATHS

	Registered live births		Registered marriages*		Registered deaths	
	Number	Rate (per 1,000)	Number	Rate (per 1,000)	Number	Rate (per 1,000)
1984	122,303	13.6	65,361	7.3	101,419	11.3
1985	118,955	13.3	66,682	7.4	107,485	12.0
1986	120,078	13.4	64,965	7.3	104,039	11.6
1987	116,672	13.0	64,429	7.2	107,213	12.0
1988	117,440	13.1	62,617	7.0	107,385	12.0
1989	112,289	12.5	63,263	7.0	106,902	11.9
1990	105,180	11.7	59,874	6.7	108,608	12.1
1991	95,910	10.7	n.a.	n.a.	110,423	12.3

* Including marriages of Bulgarian nationals outside the country but excluding those of aliens in Bulgaria.

Expectation of Life (years at birth, 1978–80): Males 68.35; Females 73.55.

ECONOMICALLY ACTIVE POPULATION
(persons aged 14 years and over, 1985 census)

	Males	Females	Total
Agriculture and hunting	392,781	379,081	771,862
Forestry and fishing; Mining and quarrying; Manufacturing; Electricity, gas and water	949,740	828,019	1,777,759
Construction	328,076	78,643	406,719
Trade, restaurants and hotels	120,624	276,807	397,431
Transport, storage and communications	234,637	79,870	314,507
Financing, insurance, real estate and business services	5,285	19,411	24,696
Community, social and personal services	419,797	572,814	992,611
Activities not adequately defined	231	324	555
Total labour force	2,451,171	2,234,969	4,686,140

Source: International Labour Office, *Year Book of Labour Statistics*.

EMPLOYMENT
(annual averages, '000 employees)

	1988	1989	1990
Agriculture*	833.9	789.1	735.2
Forestry	26.7	25.2	22.4
Mining and quarrying	115.9	114.4	113.9
Manufacturing	1,547.8	1,495.6	1,346.6
Electricity, gas and water	35.4	35.7	37.8
Construction	370.4	361.3	336.7
Commerce	386.8	395.2	372.1
Transport and storage	257.1	246.7	241.6
Communications	43.3	43.5	44.7
Finance and insurance services	25.1	25.5	24.6
Education and culture	322.0	322.5	320.0
Public health, welfare, sports and tourism	212.6	214.5	221.0
Administration	60.6	60.6	54.5
Science and scientific institutes	88.9	97.4	90.9
Housing and community services	101.4	96.6	91.7
Total (incl. others)	4,467.8	4,365.0	4,096.8

* Excluding agricultural co-operatives but including state farms and machine-tractor stations.

Source: *Bulgarian Statistical Yearbook 1991*.

Agriculture

PRINCIPAL CROPS ('000 metric tons)

	1990	1991	1992
Wheat	5,292	4,497	3,270†
Rice (paddy)	25	21	20*
Barley	1,387	1,502	1,100*
Maize	1,221	2,775	2,300†
Rye	49	46	40*
Oats	64	52	40*
Potatoes	433	498	550†
Dry beans	23	38	36*
Dry peas	53	33	30*
Soybeans	15	20	16*
Sunflower seed	389	434	470†
Seed cotton	8	18†	12*
Cabbages	115	107	100*
Tomatoes	846	646	474†
Pumpkins, squash and gourds	56	66	65†
Cucumbers and gherkins	149	152	140*
Green chillies and peppers	227	238	220*
Dry onions	76	69	65*
Green beans	14	17	15*
Green peas	14	8	7*
Water-melons	223	299	250*
Grapes	731	748	700*
Apples	411	145	130*
Pears	62	57	50*
Plums	123	103	80*
Peaches and nectarines	80	70	55*
Apricots	50	20	15*
Strawberries	19	17	15*
Sugar beets	584	856	350*
Tobacco leaves	77	72	90*

* FAO estimate(s). † Unofficial figures.

Source: FAO, *Production Yearbook*.

LIVESTOCK ('000 head at 1 January each year)

	1990	1991	1992
Horses	119	115	113
Asses	329	329	329
Cattle	1,575	1,457	1,311
Pigs	4,352	4,187	3,010
Sheep	8,130	7,938	6,703
Goats	433	498	553
Buffaloes	23	26	25
Poultry*	35,000	27,000	21,000

* Unofficial figures.

LIVESTOCK PRODUCTS (metric tons)

	1990	1991	1992
Beef and veal	120,000	108,000	103,000†
Buffalo meat	2,000	2,000	2,000*
Mutton and lamb	60,000	70,000	62,000*
Goats' meat	3,000	4,000	4,000*
Pigmeat	406,000	362,000	340,000†
Poultry meat	182,000†	100,000	100,000*
Edible offals	108,000	98,000	85,000*
Cow milk	2,101,000	1,760,000	1,550,000†
Buffalo milk	21,000	20,000	19,000*
Sheep milk	272,000	227,000	216,000*
Goat milk	64,000	59,000	55,000*
Butter	21,586	12,142	11,500
Cheese (all kinds)	192,542	126,824	120,700*
Hen eggs	135,209	102,574	88,300†
Other poultry eggs	3,192	2,380	2,400*
Honey	7,921	6,735	6,700*
Raw silk	116	95*	95*
Wool:			
greasy	27,811	23,302	21,000*
scoured	13,201	11,000†	10,000*
Cattle and buffalo hides†	18,400*	17,300*	15,500*
Sheep skins†	23,700*	26,000*	23,000*

* FAO estimate(s). † Unofficial figures.

Source: FAO, mainly *Production Yearbook*.

Forestry

ROUNDWOOD REMOVALS
('000 cubic metres, state forests only)

	1989	1990	1991
Sawlogs, veneer logs and logs for sleepers	1,033	1,041	950
Pulpwood	666	623	450
Other industrial wood	938	920	920*
Fuel wood	1,545	1,521	1,318
Total	4,182	4,105	3,638

* FAO estimate.

Source: FAO, *Yearbook of Forest Products*.

SAWNWOOD PRODUCTION ('000 cubic metres, incl. sleepers)

	1989	1990	1991
Coniferous (soft wood)	1,081	869	939
Broadleaved (hard wood)	345	257	229
Total	1,426	1,126	1,168

Source: FAO, *Yearbook of Forest Products*.

Fishing

('000 metric tons, live weight)

	1988	1989	1990
Common carp	9.5	9.2	6.2
Southern blue whiting	2.2	8.5	20.3
Patagonian grenadier	33.6	9.2	1.0
Beaked redfish	8.8	4.5	—
Cape horse mackerel	43.8	43.4	6.5
European sprat	6.2	7.4	2.7
Other fishes (incl. unspecified)	9.0	12.2	14.0
Total fish	113.1	94.4	50.6
Crustaceans and molluscs	4.0	7.6	5.6
Total catch	117.1	102.0	56.1
Inland waters	12.2	12.1	8.5
Mediterranean and Black Seas	8.2	8.6	2.9
Atlantic Ocean	96.6	81.3	43.1
Pacific Ocean	—	—	1.7

Source: FAO, *Yearbook of Fishery Statistics*.

Mining

('000 metric tons, unless otherwise indicated)

	1988	1989	1990
Anthracite	65	63	43
Other hard coal	131	130	100
Lignite	29,189	29,509	27,827
Other brown coal	4,762	4,596	3,705
Iron ore*	528	483	321
Copper ore*	50	56	24
Lead ore*	101	101	67
Zinc ore*	82	95	75
Manganese ore*	9.9	10.8	11.0
Salt (refined)	103	93	93
Crude petroleum	77	73	60
Natural gas (million cu metres)	10.2	9.3	13.6

* Figures relate to the metal content of ores.

Source: *Bulgarian Statistical Yearbook 1991*.

Industry

SELECTED PRODUCTS
('000 metric tons, unless otherwise indicated)

	1988	1989	1990
Refined sugar	361	351	185
Wine ('000 hectolitres)	3,468	n.a.	2,458
Beer ('000 hectolitres)	6,331.6	6,719.7	6,506.6
Cigarettes and cigars (metric tons)	89,219	85,750	75,812
Cotton yarn (metric tons)[1]	85,717	82,507	72,191
Woven cotton fabrics ('000 metres)[2]	361,384	357,275	290,513
Flax and hemp yarn (metric tons)	8,225	7,610	7,273
Wool yarn (metric tons)[1]	38,205	35,676	29,759
Woven woollen fabrics ('000 metres)[2]	34,417	33,902	31,398
Woven fabrics of man-made fibres ('000 metres)[3]	32,024	33,410	36,330
Leather footwear ('000 pairs)	26,437	27,468	22,154
Rubber footwear ('000 pairs)	8,606	8,072	3,243
Chemical wood pulp	168.4	166.6	109.6
Paper	395.9	378.5	271.8
Paperboard	70.9	50.1	42.3
Rubber tyres ('000)[4]	1,693.4	1,762.0	1,795.0
Sulphuric acid (100%)	839.9	846.4	521.8
Caustic soda (96%)	134.2	132.6	108.2
Soda ash (98%)	1,100.0	1,153.0	1,046.2

—continued	1988	1989	1990
Nitrogenous fertilizers (metric tons)[5]	956,270	926,046	911,147
Phosphate fertilizers (metric tons)[5]	178,550	168,753	46,557
Soap (metric tons)	26,470	28,005	11,310
Coke (gas and coke-oven)	1,457	1,561	1,376
Unworked glass—rectangles ('000 sq metres)	18,400	16,060	15,371
Clay building bricks (million)	1,049	1,089	959
Cement	5,535	5,036	4,710
Pig-iron and ferro-alloys	1,484	1,523	1,150
Crude steel	2,875	2,899	2,184
Tractors—10 h.p. and over (number)	5,309	4,956	3,120
Metal-working lathes (number)	4,953	5,438	5,014
Cranes (number)	1,456	1,688	1,467
Fork-lift trucks (number)[6]	82,485	84,473	58,075
Refrigerators—household (number)	110,570	101,001	81,558
Washing machines—household (number)	168,923	177,203	90,015
Radio receivers (number)	50,311	52,092	42,546
Television receivers (number)	181,165	185,369	218,559
Construction: dwellings completed (number)[7]	62,785	40,538	26,044
Electric energy (million kWh)	45,036	44,328	42,141

[1] Pure and mixed yarn. Figures for wool include yarn of man-made staple.
[2] Pure and mixed fabrics, after undergoing finishing processes.
[3] Finished fabrics, including fabrics of natural silk.
[4] Tyres for road motor vehicles (passenger cars and commercial vehicles).
[5] Figures for nitrogenous fertilizers are in terms of nitrogen, and for phosphate fertilizers in terms of phosphoric acid. Data for nitrogenous fertilizers include urea.
[6] Including hoisting gears.
[7] Including restorations and conversions.

Finance

CURRENCY AND EXCHANGE RATES

Monetary Units

100 stotinki (singular: stotinka) = 1 lev (plural: leva).

Denominations

Coins: 1, 2, 5, 10, 20 and 50 stotinki; 1, 2 and 5 leva.
Notes: 1, 2, 5, 10, 20 and 100 leva.

Sterling and Dollar Equivalents (30 September 1993)

£1 sterling = 39.63 leva;
US $1 = 26.50 leva;
1,000 leva = £25.23 = $37.74.

Note: For the purposes of external trade, the average value of the lev was: US $1.2703 in 1990; 6.684 US cents in 1991; 5.115 US cents in 1992.

STATE BUDGET (provisional, million leva)

Revenue	1988	1989	1990
Taxation	19,780	21,396	19,110
Taxes on income, profits, etc.	9,638	10,971	10,182
Social security contributions	3,656	3,835	4,333
Other domestic taxes on goods and services	4,571	4,537	4,082
Taxes on international trade and transactions	1,696	1,839	389
Other current revenue	8,899	8,727	12,971
Total revenue	28,679	30,123	32,081

Expenditure	1988	1989	1990
General public services	1,267	1,091	886
Defence	1,934	1,933	1,870
Public order and safety	379	379	420
Education	1,717	1,781	2,075
Health	1,125	1,200	1,612
Social security and welfare	4,431	4,887	5,703
Housing and community amenities	2,104	2,200	2,290
Recreation, culture, religious affairs	641	702	586
Economic services	14,360	13,948	15,567
Agriculture, forestry, fishing and hunting	4,025	3,537	3,855
Mining, manufacturing and construction	2,678	2,311	2,143
Other expenditures	856	1,399	2,386
Total expenditure	28,813	29,521	33,394

Source: IMF, *Government Finance Statistics Yearbook.*

COST OF LIVING

(Consumer Price Index; base: 1980 = 100)

	1988	1989	1990
Food	117.2	119.4	118.7
Others	129.8	142.6	126.9
All items	124.1	132.0	123.8

1991 (base: 1990 = 100): Food 476.6; Fuel and light 463.7; Clothing 314.1; All items (incl. others) 438.5 (Source: ILO, *Year Book of Labour Statistics*).

NATIONAL ACCOUNTS

Net Material Product* (million leva at current market prices)

Activities of the Material Sphere	1988	1989	1990
Agriculture and livestock	3,712.0	3,798.2	7,469.5
Forestry†	108.2	90.3	86.0
Industry‡	17,088.3	17,624.5	16,839.8
Construction	2,780.3	2,859.1	2,866.3
Trade, restaurants, etc.§	2,471.2	2,910.3	3,617.7
Transport and storage	2,069.1	2,224.6	2,413.0
Communications	527.3	570.5	593.7
Other activities	666.2	762.2	595.0
Total	29,422.6	30,839.7	34,481.0

* Defined as the total net value of goods and 'productive' services, including turnover taxes, produced by the economy. This excludes economic activities not contributing directly to material production, such as public administration, defence and personal and professional services.
† Including non-organized hunting and fishing.
‡ Principally manufacturing, mining, electricity, gas and water supply. The figures also include the value of hunting, fishing and logging when these activities are organized.
§ Includes material and technical supply.

External Trade

PRINCIPAL COMMODITIES (million foreign exchange leva)

Imports f.o.b.	1988	1989	1990
Machinery and equipment	5,794.7	5,459.1	4,762.8
Power and electro-technical machinery	478.4	529.4	318.9
Mining, metallurgical and oil-drilling equipment	291.4	300.4	447.6
Tractors and agricultural machinery	441.4	420.2	406.6
Fuels, mineral raw materials and metals	5,108.2	4,494.7	3,467.1
Solid fuels	374.4	336.7	323.7
Ferrous metals	854.7	673.7	467.7
Chemicals, fertilizers and rubber	755.1	639.1	464.9
Chemicals	399.3	328.5	211.6
Agricultural crop and livestock crude materials (except foods)	748.7	671.1	450.7
Timber, cellulose and paper products	225.7	214.4	162.3
Textile raw materials and semi-manufactures	248.3	217.0	146.6
Raw materials for food production	431.0	510.7	199.9
Other industrial goods for consumption	709.3	668.8	661.5
Commodities for cultural purposes	155.4	144.6	149.1
Total (incl. others)	13,928.0	12,795.8	10,314.9

Exports f.o.b.*	1988	1989	1990
Machinery and equipment	8,723.7	8,126.0	6,238.7
Power and electro-technical machinery	627.5	614.6	529.7
Hoisting and hauling equipment	1,436.6	1,427.7	1,070.2
Agricultural machinery	244.5	286.3	226.4
Fuels, mineral raw materials and metals	1,010.2	1,048.0	810.5
Ferrous metals	463.7	363.5	200.1
Chemicals, fertilizers and rubber	492.8	470.8	408.0
Chemicals	341.6	270.4	246.0
Building materials and components	273.3	273.3	204.7
Agricultural crop and livestock crude materials (except foods)	234.1	246.1	167.6
Raw materials for food production (incl. tobacco)	349.2	302.0	259.5
Foodstuffs, beverages and tobacco products	1,688.6	1,592.0	1,277.2
Meat and dairy products, animal fats and eggs	251.1	233.4	164.6
Wine, brandy and spirits	301.7	264.7	171.0
Cigarettes	672.4	654.9	602.0
Other industrial goods for consumption	1,541.7	1,517.5	1,084.9
Clothing and underwear	310.0	300.5	239.9
Total (incl. others)	14,417.4	13,672.9	10,559.5

* Figures include foreign aid and loans, and exports of ships' stores and bunkers for foreign vessels.

1991 (million leva): Imports 45,132; Exports 57,368 (Source: UN, *Monthly Bulletin of Statistics*).

PRINCIPAL TRADING PARTNERS* (million foreign exchange leva)

Imports f.o.b.	1988	1989	1990
Austria	219.5	193.4	164.9
Cuba	172.3	220.0	111.6
Czechoslovakia	751.7	630.2	478.6
France	94.8	131.0	75.3
German Democratic Republic	818.0	738.0	686.0
Germany, Federal Republic	686.1	633.1	385.8
Hungary	265.3	172.4	69.9
Italy	156.3	185.0	197.3
Japan	156.7	167.0	106.7
Libya	92.9	181.5	175.9
Poland	691.6	608.6	516.5
Romania	288.6	240.3	136.3
Switzerland	192.3	212.8	132.6
USSR	7,453.8	6,767.0	5,826.7
United Kingdom	134.8	146.7	170.5
USA	123.8	185.9	57.2
Yugoslavia	136.6	112.4	87.8
Total (incl. others)	13,928.0	12,795.8	10,314.9

Exports f.o.b.	1988	1989	1990
Cuba	258.5	184.5	106.2
Czechoslovakia	665.6	594.2	466.7
German Democratic Republic	749.9	752.4	304.6
Germany, Federal Republic	142.4	184.3	142.3
Greece	136.3	177.2	84.4
Hungary	295.2	187.8	129.6
Iraq	396.2	136.0	24.5
Italy	103.5	88.6	82.5
Libya	328.1	184.0	421.4
Poland	593.0	525.3	269.5
Romania	294.8	276.7	407.4
Switzerland	113.6	141.0	79.3
USSR	9,006.5	8,917.9	6,762.9
United Kingdom	97.4	117.2	59.3
Total (incl. others)	14,417.4	13,672.9	10,559.5

* Imports by country of purchase; exports by country of sale.

Transport

RAILWAYS (traffic)

	1988	1989	1990
Passenger-kilometres (million)	8,143	7,601	7,793
Freight ton-kilometres (million)	17,585	17,034	14,132

INLAND WATERWAYS (traffic)

	1988	1989	1990
Passenger-kilometres (million)	12	12	3
Freight ton-kilometres (million)	2,162	1,946	1,606

SEA-BORNE SHIPPING
(international and coastal traffic)

	1988	1989	1990
Passengers carried ('000)	464	392	240
Freight ('000 metric tons)	24,001	25,517	20,349

CIVIL AVIATION (traffic)

	1988	1989	1990
Passenger-kilometres (million)	3,897	3,876	3,760
Freight ton-kilometres (million)	45	39	45

Tourism

VISITORS TO BULGARIA BY COUNTRY OF ORIGIN

	1988	1989	1990
Austria	56,082	55,701	33,712
Czechoslovakia	425,934	386,593	263,275
France	34,857	32,760	29,827
German Democratic Republic	309,833	306,133	235,387
Germany, Federal Republic	276,458	236,887	
Greece	155,313	205,866	220,449
Hungary	246,561	628,329	348,172
Iran*	43,197	37,118	48,411
Italy	25,041	30,614	27,534
Poland	922,352	887,317	830,798
Romania	221,928	265,036	1,809,537
Sweden	27,549	26,364	20,581
Turkey*	3,230,528	2,970,788	3,951,758
USSR	471,560	552,561	794,742
United Kingdom	89,521	96,592	90,262
Yugoslavia	1,454,812	1,221,995	1,399,262
Total (incl. others)	8,294,985	8,220,860	10,329,537

* Mainly visitors in transit.

Communications Media

	1988	1989	1990
Telephone subscribers	2,386,462	2,515,141	2,634,892
Radio licences	1,965,117	1,941,212	1,908,898
Television licences	1,679,777	1,662,558	1,633,413
Book production:			
Titles*	4,379	4,543	3,412
Copies ('000)*	58,943	57,987	47,074
Daily newspapers:			
Titles	20	17	24
Copies ('000)†	2,396	2,389	4,065
Non-daily newspapers‡:			
Titles	361	284	516
Copies ('000)†	4,395	4,008	8,350
Other periodicals:			
Titles	994	933	907
Copies ('000)†	6,091	5,179	6,006

* Figures include pamphlets (689 titles and 7,197,000 copies in 1988; 797 titles and 7,950,000 copies in 1989).
† Average circulation.
‡ Including regional editions.

Education

(1990/91)

	Institutions	Teachers	Students
Kindergartens	4,590	28,776	303,779
Unified secondary polytechnical	3,458	72,310	1,110,733
Special	126	2,341	14,696
Vocational technical	4	54	2,631
Secondary vocational technical	236	6,602	113,139
Technical colleges and schools of arts	257	10,865	125,728
Technical colleges after secondary level	16	909	11,412
Semi-higher institutes*	30	2,038	20,531
Higher educational	38	20,716	151,510

* Including teacher-training, communications and librarians' institutes.

Directory

The Constitution

The Constitution of the Republic of Bulgaria, summarized below, took effect upon its promulgation, on 13 July 1991, following its enactment on the previous day.

FUNDAMENTAL PRINCIPLES

Chapter One declares that the Republic of Bulgaria is to have a parliamentary form of government, with all state power derived from the people. The rule of law and the life, dignity and freedom of the individual are guaranteed. The Constitution is the supreme law; the power of the State is shared between the legislature, the executive and the judiciary. The Constitution upholds principles such as political and religious freedom (no party may be formed on separatist, ethnic or religious lines, however), free economic initiative and respect for international law.

FUNDAMENTAL RIGHTS AND OBLIGATIONS OF CITIZENS

Chapter Two establishes the basic provisions for Bulgarian citizenship and fundamental human rights, such as the rights of privacy and movement, the freedoms of expression, assembly and association, and the enfranchisement of Bulgarian citizens aged over 18 years. The Constitution commits the State to the provision of basic social welfare and education and to the encouragement of culture, science and the health of the population. The study and use of the Bulgarian language is required. Other obligations of the citizenry include military service and the payment of taxes.

THE NATIONAL ASSEMBLY

The National Assembly is the legislature of Bulgaria and exercises parliamentary control over the country. It consists of 240 members, elected for a four-year term. Only Bulgarian citizens aged over 21 years (who do not hold a state post or another citizenship and are not under judicial interdiction or in prison) are eligible for election to parliament. A member of the National Assembly ceases to serve as a deputy while holding ministerial office. The National Assembly is a permanently-acting body, which is free to determine its own recesses and elects its own Chairman and Deputy Chairmen. The Chairman represents and convenes the National Assembly, organizes its proceedings, attests its enactments and promulgates its resolutions.

The National Assembly may function when more than one-half of its members are present, and may pass legislation and other acts by a majority of more than one-half of the present members, except where a qualified majority is required by the Constitution. Ministers are free to, and can be obliged to, attend parliamentary sessions. The most important functions of the legislature are: the enactment of laws; the approval of the state budget; the scheduling of presidential elections; the election and dismissal of the Chairman of the Council of Ministers (Prime Minister) and of other members of the Council of Ministers; the declaration of war or conclusion of peace; the foreign deployment of troops; and the ratification of any fundamental international instruments to which the Republic of Bulgaria has agreed. The laws and resolutions of the National Assembly are binding on all state bodies and citizens. All enactments must be promulgated in the official gazette, *Durzhaven Vestnik*, within 15 days of their passage through the legislature.

THE PRESIDENT OF THE REPUBLIC

Chapter Four concerns the Head of State, the President of the Republic of Bulgaria, who is assisted by a Vice-President. The President and Vice-President are elected jointly, directly by the voters, for a period of five years. A candidate must be eligible for election to the National Assembly, but also aged over 40 years and a resident of the country for the five years previous to the election. To be elected, a candidate must receive more than one-half of the valid votes cast, in an election in which more than one-half of the eligible electorate participated. If necessary, a second ballot must then be conducted, contested by the two candidates who received the most votes. The one who receives more votes becomes President. The President and Vice-President may hold the same office for only two terms and, during this time, may not engage in any unsuitable or potentially compromising activities. If the President resigns, is incapacitated, impeached or dies, the Vice-President carries out the presidential duties. If neither official can perform their duties, the Chairman of the National Assembly assumes the prerogatives of the Presidency, until new elections take place.

The President's main responsibilities include the scheduling of elections and referendums, the conclusion of international treaties and the promulgation of laws. The President is responsible for appointing a Prime Minister-designate (priority must be given to the leaders of the two largest parties represented in the National Assembly), who must then attempt to form a government.

The President is Supreme Commander-in-Chief of the Armed Forces of the Republic of Bulgaria and presides over the Consultative National Security Council. The President has certain emergency powers, usually subject to the later approval of the National Assembly. Many of the President's actions must be approved by the Chairman of the Council of Ministers. The President may return legislation to the National Assembly for further consideration, but can be over-ruled.

THE COUNCIL OF MINISTERS

The principal organ of executive government is the Council of Ministers, which supervises the implementation of state policy and the state budget, the administration of the country and the Armed Forces, and the maintenance of law and order. The Council of Ministers is headed and co-ordinated by the Chairman (Prime Minister), who is responsible for the overall policy of government. The Council of Ministers, which also includes Deputy Chairmen and Ministers, must resign upon the death of the Chairman or if the National Assembly votes in favour of a motion of 'no confidence' in the Council or in the Chairman.

JUDICIAL POWER

The judicial branch of government is independent. All judicial power is exercised in the name of the people. Individuals and legal entities are guaranteed basic rights, such as the right to contest administrative acts or the right to legal counsel. One of the principal organs is the Supreme Court of Cassation, which exercises supreme judicial responsibility for the precise and equal application of the law by all courts. The Supreme Administrative Court rules on all challenges to the legality of acts of any organ of government. The Chief Prosecutor supervises all other prosecutors and ensures that the law is observed, by initiating court actions and ensuring the enforcement of penalties, etc.

The Supreme Judicial Council is responsible for appointments within the ranks of the justices, prosecutors and investigating magistrates, and recommends to the President of the Republic the appointment or dismissal of the Chairmen of the two Supreme Courts and of the Chief Prosecutor (they are each appointed for a single, seven-year term). These last three officials are, *ex officio*, members of the Supreme Judicial Council, together with 22 others, who must be practising lawyers of high integrity and at least 15 years of professional experience. These members are elected for a term of five years, 11 of them by the National Assembly and 11 by bodies of the judiciary. The Supreme Judicial Council is chaired by the Minister of Justice, who is not entitled to vote.

LOCAL SELF-GOVERNMENT AND LOCAL ADMINISTRATION

Chapter Seven provides for the division of Bulgaria into regions and municipalities. Municipalities are the basic administrative territorial unit at which local self-government is practised; their principal organ is the municipal council, which is elected directly by the population for a term of four years. The council elects the mayor, who is the principal organ of executive power. Bulgaria is also divided into regions (nine in 1993, including the capital). Regional government, which is entrusted to regional governors (appointed by the Council of Ministers) and administrations, is responsible for regional policy, the implementation of state policy at a local level and the harmonization of local and national interests.

THE CONSTITUTIONAL COURT

The Constitutional Court consists of 12 justices, four of whom are elected by the National Assembly, four appointed by the President of the Republic and four elected by the justices of the two Supreme Courts. Candidates must have the same eligibility as for membership of the Supreme Judicial Council. They serve a single term of nine years, but a part of the membership changes every three years. A chairman is elected by a secret ballot of the members.

The Constitutional Court provides binding interpretations of the Constitution. It rules on the constitutionality of: laws and decrees; competence suits between organs of government; international agreements; national and presidential elections; and impeachments. A ruling of the Court requires a majority of more than one-half of the votes of all the justices.

CONSTITUTIONAL AMENDMENTS AND THE ADOPTION OF A NEW CONSTITUTION

Chapter Nine provides for constitutional changes. Except for those provisions reserved to the competence of a Grand National Assembly (see below), the National Assembly is empowered to amend the Constitution with a majority of three-quarters of all its Members, in three ballots on three different days. Amendments must be proposed by one-quarter of the parliamentary membership or by the President. In some cases, a majority of two-thirds of all the Members of the National Assembly will suffice.

Grand National Assembly

A Grand National Assembly consists of 400 members, elected by the generally-established procedure. It alone is empowered to adopt a new constitution, to sanction territorial changes to the Republic of Bulgaria, to resolve on any changes in the form of state structure or form of government, and to enact amendments to certain parts of the existing Constitution (concerning the direct application of the Constitution, the domestic application of international agreements, the irrevocable nature of fundamental civil rights and of certain basic individual rights even in times of emergency or war, and amendments to Chapter Nine itself).

Any bill requiring the convening of a Grand National Assembly must be introduced by the President of the Republic or by one-third of the members of the National Assembly. A decision to hold elections for a Grand National Assembly must be supported by two-thirds of the members of the National Assembly. Enactments of the Grand National Assembly require a majority of two-thirds of the votes of all the members, in three ballots on three different days. A Grand National Assembly may resolve only on the proposals for which it was elected, whereupon its prerogatives normally expire.

The Government

(November 1993)

HEAD OF STATE

President: ZHELIU ZHELEV (elected 1 August 1990; re-elected by direct popular vote, 19 January 1992).

Vice-President: (vacant).

COUNCIL OF MINISTERS

Prime Minister: Prof. LYUBEN BEROV.

Deputy Prime Minister and Minister of Trade: VALENTIN KARABASHEV.

Deputy Prime Minister and Minister of Labour and Social Affairs: EVGENI MATINCHEV.

Minister of Industry: RUMEN BIKOV.

Minister of Finance: STOYAN ALEKSANDROV.

Minister of Defence: VALENTIN ALEKSANDROV.

Minister of the Interior: Col VIKTOR MIKHAILOV.

Minister of Justice: PETUR KORNAZHEV.

Minister of the Environment: VALENTIN BOSSEVSKI.

Minister of Territorial Development and Construction: HRISTO TOTEV.

Minister of Transport: KIRIL ERMENKOV.

Minister of Education and Science: MARIN TODOROV.

Minister of Agriculture: GEORGI TANEV.

Minister of Health: DANCHO GOGULOV.

Minister of Culture: IVAILO ZNEPOLSKI.

Minister of Foreign Affairs: STANISLAV DASKALOV.

MINISTRIES

Office of the Presidency: Sofia.

Council of Ministers: 1000 Sofia, Blvd Dondukov 1; tel. (2) 85-01.

Ministry of Agriculture: 1040 Sofia, Blvd Botev 55; tel. (2) 85-31.

Ministry of Culture: 1540 Sofia, A Stamboliiski Blvd 18; tel. (2) 84-81; telex 22384; fax (2) 87-12-89.

Ministry of Defence: 1000 Sofia, Aksakov St 1; tel. (2) 54-60-01.

Ministry of the Environment: 1000 Sofia, ul. William Gladstone 67; tel. (2) 87-61-51; telex 22145; fax (2) 52-16-34.

Ministry of Finance: 1000 Sofia, Rakovski St 102; tel. (2) 87-06-22.

Ministry of Foreign Affairs: 1000 Sofia, Al. Zhendov St 2; tel. (2) 71-431; telex 22530.

Ministry of Health: 1000 Sofia, pl. Sveta Nedelya 5; tel. (2) 86-31.

Ministry of Industry: 1406 Sofia, Slavyanska St 8; tel. (2) 87-07-41; telex 23490; fax (2) 89-76-05.

Ministry of the Interior: 1000 Sofia, ul. Shesti Septemvri 29; tel. (2) 88-33-28, 87-86-83.

Ministry of Justice: 1000 Sofia, Blvd Dondukov 2; tel. (2) 86-01; telex 23822; fax (2) 767-32-26.

Ministry of Labour and Social Affairs: 1000 Sofia, Triaditza St 2; tel. (2) 86-01; telex 23173.

Ministry of Science and Education: 1540 Sofia, A Stamboliiski Blvd 18; tel. (2) 84-81; telex 22384; fax (2) 87-12-89.

Ministry of Territorial Development and Construction: Sofia.

Ministry of Trade: Sofia.

Ministry of Transport: 1080 Sofia, Levski St 9; tel. (2) 88-12-30; telex 23200; fax (2) 88-50-94.

President and Legislature

PRESIDENT

Presidential Election, First Ballot, 12 January 1992

Candidates	Votes	%
ZHELIU ZHELEV	2,273,468	44.66
VELKO VULKANOV	1,549,754	30.44
GEORGI GANCHEV	854,020	16.77
Others	413,867	8.13
Total	5,091,109	100.0

Second Ballot, 19 January 1992

Candidates	Votes	%
ZHELIU ZHELEV	n.a.	52.85
VELKO VULKANOV	n.a.	47.15

NARODNO SOBRANIYE
(National Assembly)

Chairman: ALEKSANDUR YORDANOV.

Deputy Chairman: YORDAN SHKOLAGEVSKI.

General election, 13 October 1991

Parties and Groups	Votes	% of votes	Seats*
Union of Democratic Forces (UDF)	1,903,567	34.36	110
Bulgarian Socialist Party (BSP)†	1,836,050	33.14	106
Movement for Rights and Freedoms (MRF)	418,168	7.55	24
Bulgarian Agrarian People's Union—United (BAPU)	214,052	3.86	—
Bulgarian Agrarian People's Union—Nikola Petkov (BAPU—NP)	190,454	3.44	—
UDF—Centre	177,295	3.20	—
UDF—Liberals	155,902	2.81	—
Others	645,349	11.65	—
Total	5,540,837	100.00	240

* Seats were allocated according to the D'Hondt system of proportional representation.

† The BSP contested the election in alliance with the Bulgarian Liberal Party, the Fatherland Party of Labour, the Christian Women's Movement, the Christian Republican Party and several other minor parties.

Local Government

At the end of 1993 Bulgaria was still divided into nine regions, administered by People's Councils. Plans to reorganize territorial administration were under consideration..

Capital People's Council: 1000 Sofia; tel. (2) 85-21.

Burgas Region People's Council: 8000 Burgas, Tsar Petar St 1; tel. (56) 4-25-65; telex 83427; fax (56) 4-54-22; Governor STEFAN KONSTANTINOV.

Haskovo Region People's Council: 6300 Haskovo; tel. (38) 21-21; Governor MIHAIL MIHAILOVICH.

Lovech Region People's Council: 5500 Lovech; tel. (68) 2-01-42; telex 37466; fax (68) 2-43-87; Governor TSANYO BOTEV.

Mikhailovgrad Region People's Council: 3400 Mikhailovgrad; tel. (96) 24-31; Governor PLAMEN MARKOV.

Plovdiv Region People's Council: 4000 Plovdiv; tel. (32) 22-22-05; Governor STEFAN STOYANOV.

Ruse Region People's Council: 7000 Ruse; tel. (82) 21-11; Governor VLADIMIR NEDYALKOV.

Sofia Region People's Council: 1000 Sofia; tel. (2) 85-171; Governor LYUBIM PRTANZHEV.

Varna Region People's Council: 9000 Varna; tel. (52) 2-12-51; Governor KIRIL YORDANOV.

Political Organizations

There are over 80 registered political parties in Bulgaria, many of them incorporated into electoral alliances. The most significant political forces are listed below:

Bulgarian Agrarian People's Union—United (BAPU) (Bulgarski Zemedelski Naroden Soyuz—BZNS): 1000 Sofia, Yanko Zabunov St 1; tel. (2) 88-19-51; telex 23302; fax (2) 80-09-91; f. 1991 by reuniting of three Agrarian parties, the official BAPU (f. 1899; in ruling coalition 1946–89), the BAPU—Nikola Petkov and the small BAPU 'Vrabcha 1'; in 1992 these three parties re-formed independently; Chair. TSENKO BAREV.

Bulgarian Communist Party (Bulgarska Komunisticheska Partiya): 1404 Sofia, Mladeshki Prokhod Blvd 5B; tel. (2) 59-16-73; f. 1990 by conservative mems of the former, ruling Bulgarian Communist Party (now the Bulgarian Socialist Party); First Sec. of the Central Cttee VLADIMIR SPASSOV.

Bulgarian Socialist Party—BSP (Bulgarska Sotsialisticheska Partiya): Sofia, 20 Positano St; POB 382; tel. (2) 85-141; telex 22268; fax (2) 87-12-92; f. 1891 as the Bulgarian Social Democratic Party (BSDP); renamed the Bulgarian Communist Party (BCP) in 1919; renamed as above in 1990; 410,850 mems (March 1993); Chair. ZHAN VIDENOV.

Christian Republican Party: 1606 Sofia, POB 113; tel. (2) 52-24-06; f. 1989; Chair. KONSTANTIN ADZHAROV.

Confederation—Kingdom Bulgaria (Tsarstvo Bulgaria): 7000 Ruse, Vassil Kolarov 45; tel. (82) 299-64; f. 1990; advocates the restoration of the former King, Simeon II; Chair. GEORGI BAKARDZHIEV.

Fatherland Party of Labour: 1000 Sofia, Slavyanska St 3, Hotel Slavyanska Beseda; tel. (2) 65-83-10; nationalist; Chair. RUMEN POPOV.

Fatherland Union: Sofia, Blvd Vitosha 18; tel. (2) 88-12-21; telex 22783; f. 1942 as the Fatherland Front (a mass organization unifying the BAPU, the BCP (now the BSP) and social organizations); named as above when restructured in 1990; a socio-political organization of independents and individuals belonging to different political parties; Chair. GINYO GANEV.

Liberal Congress Party: 1000 Sofia, Blvd Dondukov 39; tel. and fax (2) 39-00-18; f. 1989 as the Bulgarian Socialist Party, renamed Bulgarian Social Democratic Party (non-Marxist) in 1990 and as above in 1991; membership of UDF suspended 1993; c. 20,000 mems; Chair. YANKO N. YANKOV.

Movement for Rights and Freedoms—MRF (Dvizhenie za Prava i Svobodi—DPS): 1408 Sofia, Ivan Vazov, Tzarigradsko Shosse 47/1; tel. (2) 88-18-23; f. 1990; represents the Muslim minority in Bulgaria; 95,000 mems (1991); Pres. AHMED DOGAN.

New Union for Democracy: Sofia; f. 1993; fmrly section of UDF.

Party of Free Democrats (Centre): 6000 Stara Zagora; tel. (42) 2-70-42; f. 1989; Chair. Asst Prof. KHRISTO SANTULOV.

Union of Democratic Forces—UDF (Soyuz na Demokratichnite Sili—SDS): 1000 Sofia, Blvd Rakovski 134; tel. (2) 88-25-01; f. 1989; Chair. FILIP DIMITROV; alliance of the following parties, organizations and movements:

Agrarian People's Union 'Nikola Petkov'—UDF: Sofia; Chair. GEORGI PETROV.

Bulgarian Democratic Forum: 1505 Sofia, Rakovski St 82; tel. (2) 89-022-85; Chair. VASSIL ZLATAREV.

Bulgarian Social Democratic Party (United—BSDP): 1504 Sofia, Ekzarb Yossif St 37; tel. (2) 80-15-84; fax (2) 39-00-86; f. 1891; re-established 1989; Pres. IVAN KURTEV.

Christian Democratic Union: Sofia; Chair. JULIUS PAVLOV.

Christian 'Salvation' Union: Sofia; Chair. Bishop KHRISTOFOR SAHEV.

Citizens' Initiative Movement: 1000 Sofia, Blvd Dondukov 39; tel. (2) 39-01-93; Chair. TODOR GAGALOV.

Conservative Ecological Party: Sofia; Chair. KHRISTO BISSEROV.

Democratic Party: 1000 Sofia, Blvd Dondukov 34; tel. (2) 80-01-87; re-formed 1990; Chair. STEFAN SAVOV.

Ecoglasnost Movement: 1000 Sofia, Blvd Dondukov 39, 4th Floor, Rm 45; tel. (2) 80-23-23; political wing of the Ecoglasnost National Movement (f. 1989), a founding mem. of the UDF; represented in more than 50 clubs and organizations in Bulgaria; Chair. EDWIN SUGAREV; Sec. LUCHEZAR TOSHEV.

Federation of Democracy Clubs: 1000 Sofia, Blvd Dondukov 39; tel. (2) 39-01-89; f. 1988 as Club for the Support of Glasnost and Perestroika; merged with other groups, as above, 1990; Chair. YORDAN VASSILEV.

Federation of Independent Student Committees: Sofia; Leader ANDREI NENOV.

New Social Democratic Party: 1504 Sofia, POB 14; tel. (2) 44-99-47; f. 1990; membership of UDF suspended 1991, resumed 1993; Chair. Dr VASSIL MIKHAILOV.

Radical Democratic Party: 1000 Sofia, Blvd Dondukov 8, 3rd Floor, Rms 6–8; tel. (2) 80-02-99, 80-03-45; Chair. ALEXANDER YORDANOV.

Republican Party: Sofia; Chair. LENKO RUSSANOV.

United Christian Democratic Centre: 1000 Sofia, Blvd Dondukov 34; tel. (2) 80-04-09; Chair. STEFAN SOFIANSKI.

The Independent Association for Human Rights in Bulgaria (Leader STEFAN VALKOV), the Union of Victims of Repression (Leader IVAN NEVROKOPSKY) and the Union of Non-Party Members (Leader BOYAN VELKOV) all enjoy observer status in the UDF.

Diplomatic Representation

EMBASSIES IN BULGARIA

Afghanistan: Sofia, L. Karavelov St 34; tel. (2) 66-12-45; Ambassador: ABDUL ZAZAY.

Albania: Sofia, Dimitur Polyanov St 10; tel. (2) 44-33-81; Ambassador: KOCO KOTE.

Algeria: Sofia, Slavyanska St 16; tel. (2) 87-56-83; telex 22519; Ambassador: ZINE EL-ABIDINE HACHICHI.

Argentina: Sofia, Blvd Klement Gottwald 42; tel. (2) 44-38-21; Ambassador: VÍCTOR BIANCULI.

Austria: 1000 Sofia, Ruski St 13; tel. (2) 52-28-07; telex 22566; Ambassador: Dr MANFRED KIEPACH.

Belgium: Sofia, ul. Frédéric Joliot-Curie 19; tel. (2) 72-35-27; telex 22455; Ambassador: EDMOND ROOPERT.

Brazil: Sofia, Blvd Ruski 27; tel. (2) 44-36-55; telex 22099; Ambassador: GUY BRANDÃO.

Cambodia: Sofia, Mladost 1, Blvd S. Aliende, Res. 2; tel. (2) 75-51-35 Ambassador: BO RASSI.

China, People's Republic: Sofia, Blvd Ruski 18; tel. (2) 87-87-24; telex 22545; Ambassador: BAI SHOUMIAN.

Colombia: Sofia, Vasil Aprilov 17; tel. (2) 44-61-77; telex 23393; Ambassador: (vacant).

Congo: Sofia, Blvd Klement Gottwald 54; tel. (2) 44-65-18; telex 23828; Ambassador: JEAN NONO.

Cuba: 1113 Sofia, Mladezhka St 1; tel. (2) 72-09-96, 72-20-14; telex 22428; fax (2) 72-07-94; Ambassador: LUIS FELIPE VAZQUEZ.

Czech Republic: Sofia, Blvd Janko Sakazov 9; tel. (2) 44-62-81-6.

Denmark: 1000 Sofia, POB 1393, Blvd Tsar Osvoboditel 10; tel. (2) 88-04-55, 88-17-23; telex 22099; fax (2) 65-01-84; Ambassador: PREBEN STEEN SEIERSEN.

Egypt: 1000 Sofia, ul. Shesti Septemvri 5; tel. (2) 87-02-15; telex 22270; fax (2) 88-14-49; Ambassador: ALI EL NAGGARY.

Ethiopia: Sofia, Vasil Kolarov St 28; tel. (2) 88-39-24; Chargé d'affaires a.i.: AYELLE MAKONEN.

Finland: Sofia, Volokamsko St 57; tel. (2) 68-33-26; telex 23148; Ambassador: PEKKA ARTTURI OINONEN.

France: Sofia, Oborishte St 29; tel. (2) 44-11-71; telex 22336; Ambassador: JACQUES RUMMELHARDT.

Germany: 1113 Sofia, ul. Henri Barbusse 7, POB 869; tel. (2) 72-21-27; telex 22590; fax (2) 71-80-41; Ambassador: CHRISTEL STEFFLER.

Ghana: 1113 Sofia, POB 38, Pierre Degeyter St 9, Apt 37–38; tel. (2) 70-65-09; Chargé d'affaires a.i.: HENRY ANDREW ANUM AMAH.

Greece: Sofia, Blvd Klement Gottwald 68; tel. (2) 44-37-70; telex 22458; Ambassador: ANASTASIOS SIDHERIS.

Hungary: Sofia, ul. Shesti Septemvri 57; tel. (2) 66-20-21, 66-20-22; telex 22459; fax (2) 66-24-14; Ambassador: SÁNDOR SZABÓ.

India: Sofia, Blvd Patriiarkh Evtimii 31; tel. (2) 87-39-44; telex 22954; fax 87-79-84; Ambassador: BENI PRASAD AGARWAL.

Indonesia: 1504 Sofia, Veliko Turnovo St 32; tel. (2) 44-23-49; telex 22358; Ambassador: ABDEL KOBIR SASRADIPOERA.

Iran: Sofia, Blvd Tolbukhin 16; tel. (2) 44-10-13; telex 22303; Ambassador: MOHAMED ALI KOROMI NURI.

Iraq: Sofia, Anton Chekhov St 21; tel. (2) 87-00-13; telex 22307; Ambassador: FAWSI DAKIR AL-ANI.

Italy: Sofia, Shipka St 2; tel. (2) 88-17-06; telex 22173; Ambassador: AGOSTINO MATHIS.

Japan: Sofia, ul. Lyulyakova Gradina 14; tel. (2) 72-39-84; telex 22397; fax (2) 72-25-15; Ambassador: TAKASHI TAJIMA.

Korea, Democratic People's Republic: Sofia, Mladost 1, Blvd S. Aliende, Res. 4; tel. (2) 77-53-48; Ambassador: KIM PYONG IL.

Korea, Republic: 1414 Sofia, Bulgaria Sq. 1, National Palace of Culture; tel. (2) 650-162, 659-514; Ambassador: KIM HEUNG-SU.

Kuwait: Sofia, Blvd Klement Gottwald 47; tel. (2) 44-19-92; telex 23586; Ambassador: TALIB JALAL AD-DIN AL-NAQIB.

Laos: Sofia, Ovcha Kupel, Buket St 80; tel. (2) 56-55-08; Ambassador: SOMSAVAT LENGSAVAD.

Lebanon: Sofia, ul. Frédéric Joliot-Curie 19; tel. (2) 72-04-31; telex 23140; Ambassador: WALID NASSER.

Libya: Sofia, Oborishte St 10; tel. (2) 44-19-21; telex 22180; Secretary of People's Bureau: MOHAMAD GAMUDI.

Mongolia: Sofia, ul. Frédéric Joliot-Curie 52; tel. (2) 65-84-03; telex 22274; Ambassador: LHAMYN TSERENDONDOG.

Morocco: Sofia, Blvd Klement Gottwald 44; tel. (2) 44-27-94; telex 23515; Ambassador: BENASER KEYTONI.

Mozambique: Sofia; Ambassador: GONÇALVES RAFAEL SENGO.

Netherlands: Sofia, Denkoglu St 19A; tel. (2) 87-41-86, 87-65-79; telex 22686; fax (2) 87-76-46; Ambassador: F. W. J. M. BROUWERS.

Nicaragua: Sofia, Mladost 1, Blvd Aliende, Res. 1; tel. (2) 75-41-57; Ambassador: UMBERTO CARIÓN.

Peru: Sofia, Volokolamsko shose 11; tel. (2) 68-32-43; telex 23182; Chargé d'affaires: JULIO VEGA ERAUSQUÍN.

Poland: Sofia, Khan Krum St 46; tel. (2) 88-51-66; telex 22595; Ambassador: WŁADYSŁAW POZOGA.

Portugal: Sofia, Ivats Voivoda St 6; tel. (2) 44-35-48; telex 22082; fax (2) 46-40-70; Ambassador: LUIZ GONZAGA FERREIRA.

Romania: Sofia, Sitnyakovo St 4; tel. (2) 70-70-47; telex 22321; Ambassador: ALEXANDRU PETRESCU.

Russian Federation: Sofia, Blvd Dragan Tsankov 28; tel. (2) 66-88-36; fax (2) 66-88-49; Ambassador: ALEKSANDR AVDEYEV.

Slovakia: Sofia, Blvd Janko Sakazov 9; tel. (2) 44-62-81-6.

Spain: Sofia, Oborishte St 47; tel. (2) 43-00-17; telex 22308; Ambassador: JORGE FUENTES.

Sweden: Sofia, 4 Alfred Nobel Str.; tel. (2) 72-04-20; telex 22373; fax (2) 70-55-31; Ambassador: BERTIL LUNO.

Switzerland: 1000 Sofia, Shipka St 33; tel. (2) 44-31-98; telex 22792; fax (2) 44-39-47; Ambassador: HARALD BORNER.

Syria: Sofia, Hristo Georgiev 10; tel. (2) 44-15-85; telex 23464; Chargé d'affaires: SADDIK SADDIKNI.

Turkey: Sofia, Blvd Tolbukhin 23; tel. (2) 87-23-06; telex 22199; Ambassador: YALÇIN ORAL.

United Kingdom: Sofia, Blvd Vassil Levsky 38; tel. (2) 87-95-75; telex 22363; fax (2) 65-60-22; Ambassador: RICHARD THOMAS.

USA: Sofia, Blvd A. Stamboliiski 1; tel. (2) 88-48-01; telex 22690; fax (2) 88-48-06; Ambassador: WILLIAM MONTGOMERY.

Uruguay: Sofia, POB 213, Tsar Ivan Asen II St 91; tel. (2) 44-19-57; telex 23087; Ambassador: GUIDO M. YERLAS.

Venezuela: Sofia, ul. Tulovo 1; tel. (2) 44-32-82; telex 22087; fax (2) 46-52-05; Ambassador: ERIK BECKER BECKER.

Viet Nam: Sofia, Ilya Petrov St 1; tel. (2) 65-83-34; telex 22717; Ambassador: NGUYEN TIEN THONG.

Yemen: Sofia, Blvd S. Aliende, Res. 3; tel. (2) 75-61-63; Ambassador: ALI MUNASSAR MUHAMMAD.

Yugoslavia: Sofia, Veliko Turnovo St 3; tel. (2) 44-32-37; telex 23537; Ambassador: MILENKO STEFANOVIĆ.

Judicial System

The 1991 Constitution provided for justice to be administered by the Supreme Court of Cassation, the Supreme Administrative Court, courts of appeal, courts of assizes, military courts and district courts. The main legal officials are the justices, or judges, of the higher courts, the prosecutors and investigating magistrates. The Chief Prosecutor is responsible for the precise and equal application of the law. The judicial system is independent, most appointments being made or recommended by the Supreme Judicial Council. The Ministry of Justice co-ordinates the administration of the judicial system and the prisons. There is also the Constitutional Court, which is the final arbiter of constitutional issues. Under transitional arrangements attached to the Constitution, until the new system was enacted and established, the existing Supreme Court of Bulgaria was to exercise the prerogatives of the two new Supreme Courts.

Supreme Court: 1000 Sofia, Blvd Vitosha 2; tel. (2) 85-71; Chair. IVAN GRIGOROV.

Constitutional Court: 1000 Sofia; Chair. ASSEN DIMITROV MANOV.

Office of the Chief Prosecutor: 1000 Sofia, Blvd Vitosha 2; tel. (2) 85-71; fax (2) 80-13-27; Chief Prosecutor IVAN TATARCHEV; Military Prosecutor MILKO YOTSOV.

Ministry of Justice: see The Government (Ministries).

Religion

Most of the population profess Christianity, the main denomination being the Bulgarian Orthodox Church (some 88.5% of the population). The 1991 Constitution guarantees freedom of religion, although Eastern Orthodox Christianity is declared to be the 'traditional religion in Bulgaria'. In accordance with the 1949 Bulgarian Law on Religious Faith, however, all new religious denominations must be registered by a governmental board before being allowed to operate freely. There is a significant Muslim minority (some 9% of the population), most of whom are ethnic Turks, although there are some ethnic Bulgarian Muslims, known as Pomaks. There is a small Jewish community.

In 1992 a schism occurred in the Bulgarian Orthodox Church when two Metropolitans, one of whom was Bishop Pimen, established a separate synod in opposition to Bulgarian Patriarch Maksim. Bishop Pimen was subsequently demoted. In September the Ecumenical Patriarch of Constantinople, Bartholomeu I, visited Sofia and made an unsuccessful attempt to mediate between the two sides.

Directorate of Religious Affairs: 1000 Sofia, Blvd Dondukov 1; tel. and fax (2) 88-04-88; a dept of the Council of Ministers; conducts relations between govt and religious organizations; Chair. Dr CHRISTO MATANOV.

CHRISTIANITY

Bulgarian Orthodox Church: 1090 Sofia, Oborishte St 4, Synod Palace; tel. (2) 87-56-11; f. 865; autocephalous Exarchate 1870 (recognized 1945); administered by the Bulgarian Patriarchy; there are 11 dioceses in Bulgaria and two dioceses abroad (Diocese of North and South America and Australia, and Diocese of West Europe), each under a Metropolitan; Chair. of the Bulgarian Patriarchy His Holiness Patriarch MAKSIM.

Armenian Apostolic Orthodox Church: Sofia, Naicho Zanov St 31; tel. (2) 88-02-08; some 10,000 adherents (1992); administered by Bishop DIRAYR MARDIKIYAN (resident in Bucharest, Romania); Chair. of the Diocesan Council in Bulgaria GARO DERMESROBIYAN.

The Roman Catholic Church

Bulgarian Catholics may be adherents of either the Latin (Western) Rite, which is organized in two dioceses, or the Byzantine-Slav (Eastern) Rite (one diocese). All three dioceses are directly responsible to the Holy See.

Western Rite

Bishop of Nikopol: SAMUIL SERAFIMOV DZHUNDRIN, 7000 Ruse, Rostislav Blaskov St 14; tel. (82) 2-81-88; some 20,000 adherents (1993).

Diocese of Sofia and Plovdiv: GEORGI IVANOV YOVCHEV (Apostolic Administrator) 4000 Plovdiv, Lilyana Dimitrova St 3; tel. (32) 22-84-30; some 35,000 adherents (1993).

Eastern Rite

Apostolic Exarch of Sofia: METODI DIMITROV STRATIYEV (Titular Bishop of Diocletianopolis in Thrace), 1606 Sofia, ul. Bratya Pashovi 10B; tel. (2) 52-02-97; some 30,000 adherents (1993).

The Protestant Churches

Bulgarian Church of God: Sofia 1408, Petko Karavelov St 1; tel. (2) 65-75-52; fax 51-91-31; 30,000 adherents (1992); Head Pastor PAVEL IGNATOV.

Bulgarian Evangelical Church of God: Plovdiv, Velbudge St 71; tel. (32) 43-72-92; 300 adherents (1992); Head Pastor BLAGOI ISEV.

Bulgarian Evangelical Methodist Episcopal Church: 1618 Sofia, Krasno Selo Estate, Block 196/52; tel. (2) 56-13-79; 1,000 adherents (1992); Gen. Superintendent Rev. ZDRAVKO BESLOV.

Church of Jesus Christ of Latter-day Saints in Bulgaria: Sofia, Drugba estate, Bl. 82/B/6, flat 54; tel. (2) 74-08-06; f. 1991; 64 adherents (1992); Pres. VENTSESLAV LAZAROV.

Open Biblical Confraternity: 1404 Sofia, Strelbiste estate, Bl. 1A/A/1, flat 2; f. 1991; Head Pastor MARIA MINDEVA.

Union of the Churches of the Seventh-day Adventists: Sofia, Solunska St 10; tel. (2) 88-12-18; 4,659 adherents (1992); Head Pastor AGOP TACHMISSJAN.

Union of Evangelical Baptist Churches: 1303 Sofia, Ossogovo St 63; tel. and fax (2) 31-60-87; 2,500 adherents (1993); Pres. Dr TEODOR ANGELOV.

Union of Evangelical Congregational Churches: Sofia, Solunska St 49; tel. (2) 88-05-93; 4,000 adherents (1992); Head Pastor KHRISTO KULISHEV.

Union of Evangelical Pentecostal Churches: 1557 Sofia, Bacho Kiro St 21; tel. (2) 83-51-69; f. 1928; 30,000 adherents (1991); Head Pastor VIKTOR VIRCHEV.

Universal White Fraternity: 1612 Sofia, Balshik St 8/B, Flat 27; tel. (2) 54-69-43; unifies the principles of Christianity with the arts and sciences; 5,000 adherents (1992); Chair. ILIYAN STRATEV.

ISLAM

Supreme Muslim Theological Council: Sofia, Bratya Miladinovi St 27; tel. (2) 87-73-20; fax 39-00-23; adherents estimated at 9% of the actively religious population, with an estimated 708 acting regional imams; Chief Mufti of the Muslims in Bulgaria FIKRI SALI HASSAN.

JUDAISM

Central Jewish Theological Council: 1000 Sofia, Eksarkh Yosif St 16; tel. (2) 83-12-73; some 5,000 adherents (1992); Head YOSSIF LEVI.

The Press

In 1990 the press laws were liberalized, and many publications, hitherto banned, became freely available. At November 1993 over 10 new independent dailies had been established. The most important newspapers included *Demokratsiya*, published by the opposition Union of Democratic Forces, *24 Chasa* (24 Hours), a privately owned newpaper, the BSP daily, *Duma* (formerly *Rabotnichesko*

Delo) and *Trud*, the daily of the Confederation of Independent Trade Unions in Bulgaria.

PRINCIPAL DAILIES

24 Chasa (24 Hours): 1000 Sofia, Blvd Tsarigradsko shosse 47; tel. (2) 44-19-45; fax (2) 43-39-339; f. 1991; privately-owned; Editor-in-Chief VALERI NAIDENOV; circ. 320,000.

Bulgarska Armiya (Bulgarian Army): 1080 Sofia, Ivan Vasov St 12, POB 629; tel. (2) 87-47-93; telex 22651; fax (2) 87-91-26; f. 1944 as Narodna Armiya, name changed 1991; organ of the Ministry of Defence; Editor-in-Chief Col IVAN SOTIROV; circ. 60,000.

Chernomorsky Far (Black Sea Lighthouse): 8000 Burgas, Milin Kamak St 9; tel. (56) 1-22-18; telex 83464; fax (56) 1-01-78; f. 1950; independent regional since 1988; Editor-in-Chief MLADEN KARPULSKI; circ. 40,000.

Debati (Debates): 1000 Sofia, Blvd Kniyas Korsakov 2; tel. (2) 887-25-04; fax 80-05-10; f. 1990; parliamentary issues, on politics and diplomacy; independent; Editor-in-Chief DONCHO IVANOV; circ. 50,000.

Delo (Cause): 3400 Mikhailovgrad, Blvd G. Dimitrov 76; tel. (96) 2-25-01; f. 1987; fmrly *Septemvriisko Slovo*; independent regional newspaper; Editor-in-Chief BOYAN MLADENOV; circ. 20,000.

Demokratsiya (Democracy): 1000 Sofia, Rakovski St 134; tel. (2) 39-01-86; fax (2) 39-02-12; f. 1990; newspaper of the Union of Democratic Forces; Editor-in-Chief PANAYOT DENEV; circ. 160,000.

Denonoshten Novinar (Round the Clock News): 1000 Sofia, Kouzman Shapkarev St 4; tel. (2) 87-73-62; f. 1991; Editor-in-Chief CHRISTO GIULEV.

Duma (Word): 1000 Sofia, Blvd Tzarigradsko Shosse 47; tel. (2) 43-431; telex 22547; fax (2) 87-50-73; f. 1927; fmrly *Rabotnichesko Delo*; organ of the Bulgarian Socialist Party; Editor-in-Chief STEFAN PRODEV; circ. 300,000.

Faks: 1504 Sofia, Blvd Tzarigradsko Shosse 47; tel. (2) 44-81-82; fax (2) 65-94-70; f. 1991; Editor-in-Chief DIMITUR SHUMNALIEV; circ. 86,000.

Glas (Voice): 4000 Plovdiv, Lev Tolstoy St 2; tel. (32) 22-67-40; fax (32) 22-82-23; f. 1943; fmrly *Otechestven Glas*, an official organ; now independent regional newspaper for district of Plovdiv; 6 a week; Editor-in-Chief KRASIMIR OBRETENOV; circ. 90,000.

Isik/Svetlina (Light): 1000 Sofia, Blvd Tzarigradsko Shosse 47; tel. (2) 44-21-07; telex 22197; f. 1945; formerly *'Eni Isik' Nova Svetlina*; independent newspaper in Turkish and Bulgarian; Editor-in-Chief IVAN BADZHEV; circ. 30,000.

Kontinent: 1000 Sofia, Blvd Tzarigradsko Shosse 47-A; tel. (2) 46-55-07; fax (2) 44-19-04; f. 1992; independent; Editor-in-Chief BOIKO PANGELOV; circ. 60,000.

Maritza: 4000 Plovdiv, Bogomil St 59; POB 27 and 348; tel. (032) 22-59-80; fax (032) 27-47-60; f. 1991; Editor-in-Chief STEFAN VALEV.

Mladezh (Youth): 1000 Sofia, Blvd Tzarigradsko Shosse 47; f. 1990; organ of the Bulgarian Democratic Youth Org.; Editor-in-Chief VALENTIN KOLEV.

Naroden Glas (People's Voice): 5500 Lovech, G. Dimitrov St 24, 3rd Floor; tel. (68) 2-22-42; telex 37429; f. 1988; regional independent; Editor-in-Chief VENETSII GEORGIEV; circ. 50,000.

Narodno Delo (People's Cause): 9000 Varna, Blvd Khristo Botev 3; tel. (52) 23-10-71; fax (52) 23-90-67; f. 1944; regional independent; business, politics and sport; 6 days a week; Editor-in-Chief DIMITUR KRASIMIROV; circ. 56,000.

Narodno Zemedelsko Zname (People's Agrarian Banner): 1000 Sofia, Dondukov Blvd 39, POB 39; tel. (2) 39-02-16; telex 24536; fax (2) 23-90-67; f. 1945, revived 1982 (in USA); publ. in Bulgaria since 1990; organ of the 'Nikola Petkov' Bulgarian Agrarian People's Union; Editor-in-Chief ILYO DANOV; circ. 46,000.

Noshten Trud (Night Labour): 1000 Sofia, Blvd Kniyas Dondukov 52; tel. and fax (2) 87-70-63; telex 22427; f. 1992; 5 a week; Editor-in-Chief PLAMEN KAMENOV; circ. 50,000.

Otechestven Vestnik (Fatherland Newspaper): 1504 Sofia, Blvd Tzarigradsko Shosse 47; tel. (2) 43-431; telex 22555; fax (2) 46-31-08; f. 1942 as *Otechestven Front*; published by the journalists' co-operative "Okchestvo"; Editor-in-Chief LYUBEN GENOV; total circ. 70,000.

Pari (Money): 1504 Sofia, Blvd Tzarigradsko Shosse 47, POB 46; tel. (2) 44-65-73; telex 22555; fax (2) 46-35-32; f. 1991; financial and economic news; Editor-in-chief EVGENII PETROV.

Pirinsko Delo (Pirin's Cause): 2700 Blagoevgrad, Assen Khristove St 19; tel. 2-37-36; telex 26300; fax 2-31-06; f. 1945; independent regional daily since 1989; Editor-in-Chief KIRIL AKSHAROV; circ. 20,000.

Podkrepa (Support): 1000 Sofia, Ekzarkh Yosif St 37; tel. (2) 83-12-27; fax (2) 46-73-74; f. 1991; organ of the Podkrepa (Support) Trade Union Confederation; Editor-in-Chief (vacant); circ. 25,000–40,000.

Ranno Utro (Early Morning): 1000 Sofia, Blvd Kniyas Korsakov 82; tel. (2) 65-92-15; f. 1992; Editor-in-Chief IVAN STAEVSKI.

Shipka (Chilli Pepper): 6300 Khaskovo, Georgi Dimitrov St 14; tel. (38) 12-52-52; telex 43470; fax (38) 3-76-28; f. 1988; independent regional newspaper; Editor-in-Chief DIMITUR DOBREV; circ. 25,000.

Sport: 1000 Sofia, National Stadium 'Vassil Levski', Sektor V, POB 88; tel. (2) 88-03-43; telex 22594; fax (2) 81-49-70; f. 1927; Editor-in-Chief IVAN NANKOV; circ. 100,000.

Standart Daily: Sofia, Antim 1 St 53; tel. (2) 46-54-87; fax (2) 46-50-05; f. 1992; Editor-in-Chief VALERI ZHAPRIANOV.

Svoboden Narod (Free People): 1000 Sofia, Yanko Zabunov 10; tel. and fax (2) 65-74-42; f. 1944; revived 1990; organ of the Bulgarian Social Democratic Party (United); Editor-in-Chief KATIA VLADIMIROVA; estimated circ. 50,000–100,000.

Telegraf: 1113 Sofia, Blvd Tzarigradsko Shosse 72, POB 135; tel. (2) 75-11-22; fax (2) 77-04-11; f. 1990; privately-owned independent newspaper; Editor-in-Chief PLAMEN DIMITROV; circ. 30,000.

Trud (Labour): 1000 Sofia, Kniyas Korskov 82; tel. (2) 88-23-44; telex 22427; fax (2) 80-26-26; f. 1923; organ of the Confederation of Independent Trade Unions in Bulgaria; Editor-in-Chief TOSHO TOSHEV; circ. 110,000.

Vecherni Novini (Evening News): 1000 Sofia, Blvd Tzarigradsko Shosse 47; tel. (2) 44-14-69; telex 22324; fax 46-73-65; f. 1951; independent newspaper; centre-left; publ. by the Vest Publishing House; Dir GEORGI GANCHEV; Editor-in-Chief LYUBOMIR KOLAROV; circ. 35,000.

Vrabetz (Sparrow): 1000 Sofia, Blvd Tzarigradsko Shosse 47; tel. (2) 46-40-34; fax (2) 46-32-54; f. 1992; Editor-in-Chief VLADIMIR RAICHEV.

Zemedelsko Zname (Agrarian Banner): Sofia, Yanko Zabunov St 23; tel. (2) 87-38-51; telex 23303; fax (2) 87-45-35; f. 1902; organ of the Bulgarian Agrarian People's Union; Editor-in-Chief DRAGOMIR SHOPOV; circ. 178,000.

Zemya (Earth): Sofia, 11 August St 18; tel. (2) 88-50-33; telex 23174; fax (2) 83-52-27; f. 1951 as *Kooperativno Selo*; renamed 1990; fmrly an organ of the Ministry of Agriculture, now an independent; Editor-in-Chief KOSTA ANDREEV; circ. 105,000.

PRINCIPAL PERIODICALS

168 Chasa (168 Hours): 1000 Sofia, Saborna St 2A; tel. (2) 46-34-17; fax (2) 65-70-79; f. 1990; weekly; business, politics, entertainments; Editor-in-Chief PETYO BLASKOV; circ. 200,000.

166 Politzeiski Vesti (166 Police News): 1680 Sofia, J.K. Belite Brezi, Solun St bl. 25 and 26, Ground Floor; tel. (2) 82-30-30; fax 82-30-28; f. 1945; formerly *Naroden Strazh*; weekly; criminology and public security; Editor-in-Chief PETUR VITANOV; circ. 22,000.

ABV (ABC): 1000 Sofia, pl. Slaveikov 11; tel. (2) 88-08-67; fax (2) 80-37-91; f. 1972; weekly; published by Atlantida Publishing House; Editor-in-Chief PETYA MIRONOVA; circ. 10,000.

Anteni (Antennae): 1000 Sofia, Han Krum St 12; tel. (2) 87-48-95, 89-31-57; fax (2) 87-30-60; f. 1971; weekly on politics and culture; Editor-in-Chief GEORGI CHATALBASHEV; circ. 35,000–40,000.

Anti: 1000 Sofia, Blvd Kniyas Korsakov 34, 3rd Floor; tel. (2) 80-02-76; f. 1991; Editor-in-Chief VASIL STANILOV.

Avto-moto Svyat (Automobile World): 1000 Sofia, Sveta Sofia St 6, POB 1348; tel. and fax (2) 88-08-08; f. 1957; monthly; illustrated publication on cars and motor sports; Editor-in-Chief ILJA SELIKTAR; circ. 60,000.

Az Buki (Alphabet): 1113 Sofia, Blvd Tzarigradsko Shosse 125; tel. (2) 71-65-73; f. 1991; weekly; education and culture; for schools; sponsored by the Ministry of Education and Science; Editor-in-Chief MILENA STRAKOVA; circ. 24,000.

Az i Ti (Me and You): 1000 Sofia, pl. Narodno Sabranie 10; tel. (2) 87-85-66; f. 1990; independent; youth magazine on health and sexual problems; Editor-in-Chief ATANAS TEODOROV; circ. 75,000–110,000.

Bulgaria: 1184 Sofia, Blvd Tzarigradsko Shosse 113; tel. (2) 74-51-14; f. 1937; every 2 months; in English, French, German and Spanish; illustrated magazine; publ. by Sofia-Press Agency; Editor-in-Chief PETUR GERASSIMOV; circ. 17,000.

Bulgarski Biznes (Bulgarian Business): 1505 Sofia, Oborishte St 44, POB 15; tel. (2) 46-70-23; telex 22105; fax (2) 44-63-61; weekly; organ of National Union of Employers; Editor-in-Chief DETELIN SERTOV; circ. 10,000–15,000.

Bulgarski Dnevnik (Bulgarian Diary): 1080 Sofia, Vitosha Blvd 18, POB 256; tel. (2) 88-12-21; f. 1991; weekly independent magazine; Editor-in-Chief DIMITUR EZEKIEV circ. 60,000.

Bulgarski Fermer (Bulgarian Farmer): 1797 Sofia, Blvd Dr G. M. Dimitrov 89; tel. (2) 71-04-48; f. 1990; weekly; Editor-in-Chief VASSIL ASPARUHOV circ. 50,000.

Businessman: 1527 Sofia, Blvd Tzarigradsko Shosse 23; tel. and fax (2) 44-52-80; f. 1991; Editor-in-Chief EMIL ELMAZOV.

Computer World: 1421 Sofia, Blvd Hr. Smirnenski 1, Block B, Flat 11; tel. (2) 81-42-70, 68-51-76; fax (2) 80-26-52; f. 1990; weekly; US–Bulgarian joint venture; information technologies; Editor-in-Chief SNEZHINA BADZHEVA; circ. 15,000.

Delovi Sviat (Business World): 1000 Sofia, Blvd Tzarigradsko Shosse 47; tel. (2) 44-10-46; telex 22444; fax (2) 44-25-51; f. 1991; weekly; circ. 100,000.

Demokratichesko Zname (Democratic Banner): Plovdiv, Raicho Daskalov St 44; weekly; publ. by the Democratic Party; Editor-in-Chief GEORGI BOYADZHIEV.

Domashen Maistor (Household Manager): 1000 Sofia, Blvd Tolbukhin 51A; tel. (2) 87-09-14; f. 1991; monthly; magazine for household repairs; Editor-in-Chief GEORGI BALANSKI; circ. 12,000.

Durzhaven Vestnik (State Gazette): 1169 Sofia; tel. (2) 80-01-27; official organ of the National Assembly; 2 a week; bulletin of parliamentary proceedings and the publication in which all legislation is promulgated; Editor-in-Chief PLAMEN MLADENOV; circ. 60,000.

Edinstvo (Unity): 1000 Sofia, Blvd Christo Botev 48; tel. (2) 84-101 Ext. 218; f. 1991; weekly; Editor-in-Chief GENCHO BUCHVAROV.

Ekho (Echo): 1000 Sofia, Serdika St 2; tel. (2) 87-28-42; f. 1957; weekly; tourism publication; organ of the Bulgarian Tourist Union; Editor-in-Chief YASSEN ANTOV; circ. 30,000.

Ekip 10 (Team 10): 1000 Sofia, Municipality Vitosha, Tzar Boris III Blvd 223; tel. (2) 56-70-71; f. 1992; weekly; Editor-in-Chief RUMIA SAVOV.

Ekopolitika: Sofia, Blvd Dondukov 39; f. 1990; weekly; organ of the Green Party; Editor-in-Chief SARNITSA KARAMIHOVA.

Emigrant: 1000 Sofia, pl. Narodno Sobraniye 12; tel. (2) 87-23-08; fax (2) 87-46-17; f. 1991 (to replace *Kontakti*); weekly; magazine for Bulgarians living abroad; Editor-in-Chief ANDREI DZHDENEV; circ. 20,000.

Futbol (Football): 1000 Sofia, Bulgaria Blvd 1, Vassil Levski Stadium; tel. (2) 87-19-51; fax (2) 65-72-57; f. 1988; weekly; independent soccer publication; Editor-in-Chief Ivan Chomakov; circ. 130,000.

Ikonomicheski Zhivot (Economic Life): 1000 Sofia, Moskovska St 9; tel. (2) 87-65-60; f. 1970; weekly; independent; marketing and advertisement; Editor-in-Chief VASIL ALEKSIEV; circ. 31,000.

Klub M: 1000 Sofia, Blvd Vitosha 18; tel. (2) 80-23-08; f. 1990; monthly; colour magazine of Sofia-Press Agency; Editor-in-Chief KHRISTO PEEV; circ. 40,000.

Kompyutar (Computer): 1000 Sofia, Blvd Tolbukhin 51A; tel. (2) 87-50-45; f. 1985; monthly; hardware and software; Editor-in-Chief GEORGI BALANSKI; circ. 14,000.

Komunistichesko Delo (Communist Cause): 1000 Sofia, Central Post Office, POB 183; tel. (2) 598-16-73; organ of the Bulgarian Communist Party; Editor-in-Chief VLADIMIR SPASSOV; circ. 15,000–20,000.

Krile (Wings): 1184 Sofia, Blvd Tzarigradsko Shosse 111; tel. (2) 70-45-73; f. 1911; fmrly *Kam Nebeto*, renamed 1991; monthly; civil and military aviation; official organ; Editor-in-Chief TODOR ANDREEV; circ. 20,000.

Kultura (Culture): 1040 Sofia, Kniyas Alexander Battenberg St 4; tel. (2) 83-33-22; fax (2) 87-40-27; f. 1957; weekly; newspaper on arts, publicity and cultural affairs; issue of the Ministry of Culture; Editor-in-Chief KOPRINKA CHERVENKOVA; circ. 10,000.

Kurier 5 (Courier 5): 1000 Sofia, Blvd Tzarigradsko Shosse 47; tel. (2) 70-65-40; f. 1990; weekly; advertising newspaper; Editor-in-Chief EMIL KOLEV.

Liberalen Kongres (Liberal Congress): 1000 Sofia, Blvd Dondukov 39; tel. and fax (2) 39-00-18; f. 1990; weekly; organ of the Liberal Congress Party; Editor-in-Chief ROSSEN ELEZOV; circ. 20,000.

LIK: Sofia, Blvd Tzarigradsko Shosse 49; weekly publication of the Bulgarian Telegraph Agency; literature, art and culture; Editor-in-Chief SIRMA VELEVA; circ. 19,000.

Literaturen Forum (Literary Forum): 1000 Sofia, Alexandur Battenburg Ave 4; tel. (2) 88-10-69, 88-08-03, 39-02-15; fax (2) 88-10-69; f. 1990; weekly; independent; Editor-in-Chief ATANAS SVILENOV; circ. 10,000.

Makedonia (Macedonia): 1301 Sofia, Pirotska St 5; tel. (2) 87-46-64; fax 87-64-60; f. 1990; weekly; organ of the Inner Macedonian Revolutionary Organization—Union of Macedonian Societies; Editor-in-Chief LUKO ZAKHARIEV; circ. 15,000.

Missul (Thought): 1000 Sofia, Pozitano St 20, POB 382; tel. (2) 85-141; f. 1990; weekly; politics, culture; organ of the Marxist Alternative Movement; Editor-in-Chief GEORGI SVEZHIN; circ. 15,000.

Napravi Sam (Do It Yourself): 1000 Sofia, Blvd Levski 51A; tel. 87-50-45; f. 1981; monthly; Editor-in-Chief GEORGI BALKANSKI; circ. 45,000.

Nauka i Tekhnika (Science and Technology): 1040 Sofia, Blvd Tzarigradsko Shosse 49; tel. (2) 84-61; f. 1964; weekly of the Bulgarian Telegraph Agency; Editor-in-Chief VESSELIN SEIKOV; circ. 20,000.

Nie Zhenite (We the Women): 1000 Sofia, Patriarch Evtimii Blvd 84; tel. (2) 52-31-98; f. 1990; weekly; organ of the Democratic Union of Women; Editor-in-Chief EVGINIA KIRANOVA; circ. 50,000–70,000.

Nov Den (New Day): 1000 Sofia, Blvd Vallil Levski 65, 3rd Floor; tel. (2) 80-02-05; f. 1990; weekly; organ of the Union of Free Democrats; Editor-in-Chief IVAN KALCHEV; circ. 25,000.

Nova Era (New Era): 1000 Sofia, Blvd Stamboliiski 5, 4th Floor; tel. (2) 83-21-15; f. 1990; weekly; organ of the Union of Democratic Parties and Movements ERA-3; Editor-in-Chief DOBRI DOBREV; circ. 45,000–80,000.

Obshestvo i Pravo (Society and Law): 1000 Sofia, Pirotska St 7; tel. (2) 83-50-02; fax (2) 83-55-21; f. 1980; monthly of the Ministry of Justice and of the Union of Bulgarian Jurists; Editor-in-Chief Prof. BORIS SPASSOV; circ. 80,000.

Orbita: 1000 Sofia, Tsar Kaloyan St 8; tel. (2) 88-51-68; f. 1969; weekly; science and technology for youth; Editor-in-Chief NIKOLAI KATRANDZHIEV; circ. 50,000.

Paraleli: Sofia, Blvd Tzarigradsko Shosse 49; tel. (2) 87-40-35; f. 1964; weekly; illustrated publication of the Bulgarian Telegraph Agency; Editor-in-Chief KRASSIMIR DRUMEV; circ. 50,000.

Pardon: 1000 Sofia, Blvd Tzarigradsko Shosse 47; tel. (2) 43-431; f. 1991; weekly; satirical publication; Editor-in-Chief CHAVDAR SHINOV; circ. 50,000.

Pogled (Review): 1090 Sofia, pl. Slaveikov 11; tel. (2) 87-70-97; fax (2) 65-80-23; f. 1930; weekly; organ of the Union of Bulgarian Journalists; Editor-in-Chief EVGENII STANCHEV; circ. 100,000.

Prava i Svobodi (Rights and Freedoms): 1504 Sofia, Blvd Tzarigradsko Shosse 47-A, Alley 1, POB 208; tel. (2) 46-72-12; fax 46-73-35; f. 1990; weekly; politics, culture; organ of the Movement for Rights and Freedoms; Editor-in-Chief (vacant); circ. 30,000.

Progres (Progress): 1000 Sofia, Gurko St 16; tel. (2) 89-06-24; fax (2) 89-59-98; f. 1894; formerly *Tekhnichesko Delo*; weekly; organ of the Federation of Scientific and Technical Societies in Bulgaria; Editor-in-Chief PETKO TOMOV; circ. 35,000.

Reporter 7: 1124 Sofia, Evlogi Georgiev St 54; tel. (2) 44-04-05; fax (2) 46-52-76; f. 1990; weekly; private independent newspaper; Editor-in-Chief BINKA PEEVA; circ. 60,000.

Republika: 1000 Sofia, Graf Ignatiev St 2; f. 1990; weekly; publ. by the Republican Party; Editor-in-Chief DARIA TABAKOVA.

Robinson: 1592 Sofia, Iliia Beshkov St 2; tel. (2) 79-90-23; f. 1990; every 2 months; tourism, business, advertizing; Editor-in-Chief SONIA ALEKSIEVA; circ. 100,000.

Start: 1000 Sofia, Vassil Levski Stadium, POB 797; tel. (2) 88-08-48; telex 22736; fax (2) 87-83-78; f. 1971; weekly; sports, illustrated; Editor-in-Chief GRIGOR KHRISTOV; circ. 80,000.

Studentska Tribuna (Students' Tribune): 1000 Sofia, Aksakov St 13; tel. (2) 88-33-02; f. 1927; weekly; student magazine; independent; Editor-in-Chief ATANAS TODOROV; circ. 20,000.

Sturshel (Hornet): 1504 Sofia, Blvd Tzarigradsko Shosse 47; tel. (2) 44-35-50; fax 443-550; f. 1946; weekly; humour and satire; Editor-in-Chief YORDAN POPOV; circ. 200,000.

Svoboden Narod (Free People): 1000 Sofia, Ekzarch Yosis St 37, 8th Floor; f. 1990; weekly; organ of the Bulgarian Social Democratic Party; Editor-in-Chief IVAN POPOV.

Televiziya i Radio (Television and Radio): 1000 Sofia, Bulgarian National Television, San Stefano St 29; tel. (2) 44-32-94; f. 1964; weekly; broadcast listings; Editor-in-Chief LUBOMIR YANKOV; circ. 107,000.

Tempo: 1184 Sofia, Blvd Tzarigradsko Shosse 113; tel. (2) 74-54-14; f. 1990; weekly; social and political issues; also in Italian; Editor-in-Chief EKATERINA KONSTANTINOVA; circ. 15,000.

Tsarkoven Vestnik (Church Newspaper): 1000 Sofia, Oborishte St 4; tel. (2) 87-56-11; f. 1900; weekly; organ of the Bulgarian Orthodox Church; Editor-in-Chief DIMITUR KIROV; circ. 4,000.

Uchitelsko Delo (Teachers' Cause): 1113 Sofia, Blvd Tzarigradsko Shosse 125, Studentski Obshtezhitiya, Blok 5; tel. (2) 70-00-12; f. 1905; weekly; organ of the Union of Bulgarian Teachers; Editor-in-Chief YORDAN YORDANOV; circ. 24,000.

Vek 21 (21st Century): 1000 Sofia, Kaloyan St 10; tel. (2) 46-54-23; fax (2) 46-61-23; f. 1990; liberal weekly; politics and culture; organ of the Radical Democratic Party; Editor-in-Chief ALEKSANDUR YORDANOV; circ. 20,000.

Vesti (News): 1184 Sofia, Blvd Tzarigradsko Shosse 113; tel. (2) 70-20-35; f. 1991; weekly; politics, culture, society; organ of the

Bulgarian Constitutional Forum; Editor-in-Chief BOYAN OBRETENOV; circ. 25,000–40,000.

Weekend: 1592 Sofia, Iliia Beshov St 2; tel. (2) 79-90-23; f. 1990; weekly; Editor-in-Chief PLAMEN STAREV; circ. 80,000.

Zdrave (Health): 1527 Sofia, Byalo More St 8; tel. (2) 44-30-26; fax (2) 44-17-59; f. 1936; monthly; published by Bulgarian Red Cross; Editor-in-Chief YAKOV YANAKIEV; circ. 55,000.

Zhenata Dnes (Women of Today): 1000 Sofia, pl. Narodno Sabranie 12; tel. (2) 89-63-00; f. 1946; monthly organ of the Women's Democratic Union; also in Russian; Editor-in-Chief BOTIO ANGELOV; circ. 120,000.

Zname (Banner): 1184 Sofia, Blvd Kniyas Korsakov 34; tel. (2) 80-01-83; f. 1894, publ. until 1934 and 1945–49; resumed publishing 1990; weekly; organ of the Democratic Party; Editor-in-Chief BOGDAN MORFOV; circ. 20,000.

Zora (Dawn): 1000 Sofia, Blvd Tzarigradsko Shosse 77; tel. (2) 71-41-826; f. 1990; independent weekly; Editor-in-Chief MINCHO MINCHEV; circ. 20,000.

NEWS AGENCIES

Bulgarska Telegrafna Agentsia—BTA (Bulgarian Telegraph Agency): 1040 Sofia, Blvd Tzarigradsko Shosse 49; tel. (2) 84-61; telex 22821; f. 1898; the official news agency, having agreements with the leading foreign agencies and correspondents in all major capitals; publishes weekly surveys of science and technology, international affairs, literature and art; Dir-Gen. IVO INDZHEV.

Leff Information Service: 1000 Sofia, Rakovski St 127; tel. (2) 88-81-46; fax (2) 87-12-22; f. 1991; Bulgaria's only private news agency; provides international, domestic and financial and economic news and statistics; Pres. BORIS BASMADJIEV.

Sofia-Press Agency: 1040 Sofia, Slavyanska St 29; tel. (2) 88-58-31; telex 22622; fax (2) 88-34-55; f. 1967 by the Union of Bulgarian Writers, the Union of Bulgarian Journalists, the Union of Bulgarian Artists and the Union of Bulgarian Composers; publishes sociopolitical and scientific literature, fiction, children's and tourist literature, publications on the arts, a newspaper, magazines and bulletins in foreign languages; also operates **Sofia-Press Info** (tel. (2) 87-66-80; Pres. ALEKSANDUR NIKOLOV), which provides up-to-date information on Bulgaria, in print and for broadcast; Dir-Gen. VENTSEL RAICHEV.

Foreign Bureaux

Agence France-Presse (AFP): 1000 Sofia, Blvd Tolbukhin 16; tel. (2) 71-91-71; telex 22572; Correspondent VESSELA SERGEVA-PETROVA.

Agencia EFE (Spain): Sofia; tel. (2) 87-29-63; Correspondent SAMUEL FRANCES.

Allgemeiner Deutscher Nachrichtendienst (ADN) (Germany): 1000 Sofia, Moskovska 27A; tel. (2) 87-82-73; telex 22050; fax (2) 87-53-16; Correspondent HANS-PETKO TEUCHERT.

Česká tisková kancelář (ČTK) (Czech Republic): 1113 Sofia, ul. Gagarin, Bl. 154A, Apt 19; tel. (2) 70-91-36; telex 22537; Correspondent VĚRA IVANOVIČOVÁ.

Deutsche Presse Agentur (dpa) (Germany): Sofia; tel. (2) 72-02-02; Correspondent ELENA LALOVA.

Informatsionnoye Telegrafnoye Agentstvo Rossii—Telegrafnoye Agentstvo Suverennykh Stran (ITAR—TASS) (Russia): 1000 Sofia, ul. A. Gendov 1, Apt 29; tel. (2) 87-38-03; Correspondent ALEKSANDR STEPANENKO.

Magyar Távirati Iroda (MTI) (Hungary): Sofia, ul. Frédéric Joliot-Curie 15, blok 156/3, Apt 28; tel. (2) 70-18-12; telex 22549; Correspondent TIVADAR KELLER.

Novinska Agencija Tanjug (Yugoslavia): 1000 Sofia, L. Koshut St 33; tel. (2) 71-90-57; Correspondent PERO RAKOSEVIĆ.

Polska Agencja Prasowa (PAP) (Poland): Sofia; tel. (2) 44-14-39; Correspondent BOGDAN KORNEJUCK.

Prensa Latina (Cuba): 1113 Sofia, ul. Yuri Gagarin 22, Bl. 154B, Apt 22; tel. (2) 71-91-90; telex 22407; Correspondent SUSANA UGARTE SOLER.

Reuters (United Kingdom): Sofia; tel. and fax (2) 54-23-72; Correspondent NIKOLA ANTONOV.

Rossiyskoye Informatsionnoye Agentstvo—Novosti (RIA—Novosti) (Russia): Sofia, 11 Avgust St 1, Apt 3; tel. (2) 88-13-81; Bureau Man. YEVGENI VOROBYOV.

United Press International (UPI) (USA): Sofia; tel. (2) 62-24-65; Correspondent GUILLERMO ANGELOV.

Xinhua (New China) News Agency (People's Republic of China): Sofia, pl. Narodno Sobraniye 3, 2nd Floor; tel. (2) 88-49-41; telex 22539; Correspondent U. SIZIUN.

The following agencies are also represented: SANA (Syria) and Associated Press (USA).

PRESS ASSOCIATIONS

Union of Independent Bulgarian Journalists: 1000 Sofia, Graf Ignatiev St 4; tel. (2) 89-53-56; telex 22635; f. 1955; Pres. (vacant); Gen.-Sec. ALEKSANDUR ANGELOV; 4,800 mems.

Publishers

Darzhavno Izdatelstvo 'Khristo G. Danov' ('Khristo G. Danov' State Publishing House): 4005 Plovdiv, Stoyan Chalakov St 1; tel. (32) 23-12-01; fax (32) 26-05-60; f. 1855; fiction, poetry, literary criticism; Dir NACHO HRISTOSKOV.

Darzhavno Izdatelstvo 'Meditsina i Fizkultura': 1080 Sofia, pl. Slaveikov 11; tel. (2) 87-13-08; f. 1948; medicine, physical culture and tourism; Dir PETUR GOGOV.

Darzhavno Izdatelstvo 'Narodna Kultura': 1000 Sofia, ul. Gavril Genov 4; tel. (2) 87-80-63; f. 1944; foreign fiction and poetry in translation; Dir SERGEI RAIKOV.

Darzhavno Izdatelstvo 'Nauka i Izkustvo': 1080 Sofia, Blvd Ruski 6; tel. (2) 87-57-01; f. 1948; general publishers; Dir ANELIA VASSILEVA.

Darzhavno Izdatelstvo 'Prosveta': 1184 Sofia, Tsarugradsko Shosse Blvd 117; tel. (2) 75-311; f. 1948; educational publishing house; Man. Dir TSVETANA POPOVA.

Darzhavno Izdatelstvo 'Tekhnika': 1000 Sofia, pl. Slaveikov 1; tel. (2) 87-12-83; f. 1958; textbooks for technical and higher education and technical literature; Dir NINA DENEVA.

Darzhavno Izdatelstvo 'Zemizdat': 1504 Sofia, Blvd Tzarigradsko Shosse 47; tel. (2) 44-18-29; f. 1949; specializes in works on agriculture, shooting, fishing, forestry, livestock-breeding, veterinary medicine and popular scientific literature and textbooks; Dir PETUR ANGELOV.

Darzhavno Voyenno Izdatelstvo: 1000 Sofia, ul. Ivan Vazov 12; tel. (2) 88-44-31; military publishing house; Head Col TRENDAFIL VASSILEV.

Izdatelstvo na Bulgarskata Akademiya na Naukite (Publishing House of the Bulgarian Academy of Sciences): 1113 Sofia, Acad. Georgi Bonchev St, blok 6; tel. (2) 72-09-22; telex 23132; f. 1869; scientific works and periodicals of the Bulgarian Academy of Sciences; Dir TODOR RANGELOV.

Izdatelstvo 'Bulgarsky Khudozhnik': 1504 Sofia, Asen Zlatarov St 1; tel. (2) 87-66-57; fax (2) 88-47-49; f. 1952; art books, children's books; Dir STEFAN KURTEV.

Izdatelstvo 'Bulgarsky Pisatel': Sofia, ul. Shesti Septemvri 35; publishing house of the Union of Bulgarian Writers; Bulgarian fiction and poetry, criticism; Dir SIMEON SULTANOV.

Izdatelstvo 'Khristo Botev': 1504 Sofia, Blvd Tzarigradsko Shosse 47; tel. (2) 43-431; f. 1944; fmrly the Publishing House of the Bulgarian Communist Party; renamed as above 1990; Dir IVAN GRANITSKY.

Izdatelstvo Mladezh, (Youth Publishing House): 1000 Sofia, ul. Tsar Kaloyan 10; tel (2) 88-21-37; fax (2) 87-61-35; art, history, original and translated fiction and original and translated poetry for children;Gen. Dir STANIMIR ILCHEV.

Izdatelstvo 'Profizdat' (Publishing House of the Central Council of Bulgarian Trade Unions): Sofia, Blvd Dondukov 82; specialized literature and fiction; Dir STOYAN POPOV.

Knigoizdatelstvo 'Galaktika': 9000 Varna, pl. Deveti Septemvri 6; tel. (2) 22-50-77; fax (2) 22-50-77; f. 1960; popular science, science fiction, economics, Bulgarian and foreign literature; Dir PANKO ANCHEV.

Sinodalno Izdatelstvo: Sofia; religious publishing house; Dir KIRIL BOINOV.

STATE ORGANIZATION

Jusautor: 1463 Sofia, Ernst Thälmann Ave 17; tel. (2) 87-28-71; telex 23042; fax (2) 87-37-40; state organization of the Council of Ministers; Bulgarian copyright agency; represents Bulgarian authors of literary, scientific, dramatic and musical works, and deals with all formalities connected with the grant of options, authorization for translations, drawing up of contracts for the use of their works by foreign publishers and producers; negotiates for the use of foreign works in Bulgaria; controls the application of copyright legislation; Dir-Gen. YANA MARKOVA.

PUBLISHERS' ASSOCIATION

Union of Publishers in Bulgaria: 1000 Sofia, pl. Slaveikov 11; Chair. VERA GYOREVA.

WRITERS' UNION

Union of Bulgarian Writers: Sofia, Angel Kanchev 5; tel. (2) 88-00-31; f. 1913; Chair. KOLYO GEORGIEV; 400 mems.

Radio and Television

Radio and television are supervised by the Committee for Television and Radio of the Committee for Culture of the Council of Ministers.

In 1991 there were 1,983,000 licensed radio receivers and 1,692,000 licensed television receivers. Colour television was introduced in 1977.

Bulgarian Committee for Television and Radio: 1504 Sofia, ul. San Stefano 29, tel. (2) 46-81; telex 22581; Chair. (vacant).

RADIO

Four private radio stations began broadcasting in late 1992.

Bulgarsko Radio: 1040 Sofia, Blvd Dragan Tsankov 4; tel. (2) 85-41; telex 22557; fax (2) 66-22-15; f. 1929; there are two Home Service programmes and local stations at Blagoevgrad, Plovdiv, Shumen, Stara Zagora and Varna. The Foreign Service broadcasts in Bulgarian, Turkish, Greek, Serbo-Croat, French, Italian, German, English, Portuguese, Spanish, Albanian and Arabic; Dir-Gen. IVAN OBRETENOV.

Radio Alma Mater: Sofia; f. June 1993; cable radio service introduced by Sofia Univ.; culture and science programmes; almost 100,000 subscribers.

TELEVISION

Bulgarska Televiziya: 1504 Sofia, ul. San Stefano 29; tel. (2) 43-481; fax (2) 87-18-71; f. 1960; programmes are transmitted daily; there are two channels; Pres. HACHO BOYADYEV.

Finance

(cap. = capital; dep. = deposits; res = reserves; m. = million; amounts in leva)

BANKING

In 1992 the Bulgarian banking system was undergoing a process of restructuring as part of a comprehensive reform of the entire economic system to establish a market economy. By late 1991 the banking sector had already accomplished its transition to a two-tier structure. In September 1992, apart from the Bulgarian National Bank and the State Savings Bank, there were almost 80 commercial banks organized as self-managing joint-stock companies. However, only 15 of these had been licensed for cross-border foreign exchange operations, while most of the remainder were not so important in terms of size and activities. In late 1992, 22 commercial banks merged to form the United Bulgarian Bank, which opened in 1993.

Central Bank

Bulgarska Narodna Banka (Bulgarian National Bank): 1000 Sofia, 1 Aleksandur Battenberg Sq; tel. (2) 85-51; telex 24090, 24091; fax (2) 88-05-58, 88-44-01; f. 1879; bank of issue; foreign exchange reserve US $964.4m. (Sept. 1992); Gov. Prof. TODOR VULCHEV; 4 brs.

State Savings Bank

State Savings Bank: 1040 Sofia, Moskovska St 19; tel. (2) 88-10-41; telex 22719; fax (2) 54-13-55; f. 1951; provides general retail banking services throughout the country; dep. 1,700m. (1991); Pres. ASSEN DROUMEV; 481 brs.

Commercial Banks Licensed for Cross-border Foreign Exchange Operations

Agricultural and Co-operative Bank: 4018 Plovdiv, Vuzrazhdane Blvd 37; tel. (32) 56-26-68; telex 44324; fax (32) 22-39-64; f. 1993 after merging with Agro Bank, Plovdiv and with 7 other Bulgarian banks; universal commercial bank; cap. 222m. (1993); dep. 7,711m.; Chair. YULI POPOV; 41 brs.

Balkanbank: 1000 Sofia, Blvd Vitosha 18; tel. (2) 80-22-33; telex 22783; fax (2) 88-30-91; f. 1987; cap. 281m. (1991); Chair. IVAN MIRONOV.

Bank for Agricultural Credit: 1606 Sofia, Blvd Khristo Botev 55; tel. (2) 51-06-87; telex 24470; fax (2) 51-07-45; f. 1990; cap. 312m. (1992); Pres. YANKO YANEV; 15 brs.

Biochim Commercial Bank: 1040 Sofia, Ivan Vazov St 1; tel. (2) 54-13-66; telex 23862; fax (2) 54-13-78; f. 1987; cap. 80m., res 27m., dep. 1,498m. (Dec. 1989); Pres. BORIS MITEV.

Bulgarian Foreign Trade Bank: 1000 Sofia, Sveta Nedelya Sq 7; tel. (2) 8551; telex 22031; fax (2) 88-53-70; f. 1964; cap. 1,200m., res 3,659m. (Dec. 1992); Chair. and Chief Exec. CHAVDAR KANCHEV.

Bulgarian Post Bank: 1000 Sofia, Bulgaria Sq 1; tel. (2) 65-91-06; telex 22290; fax (2) 510948; Pres. VLADIMIR VLADIMIROV.

Economic Bank (Stopanska Banka): 1000 Sofia, Slavyanska St 8; tel. (2) 80-17-19; telex 23910; fax (2) 65-51-52; f. 1987; cap. 220m. (1991); Chair. TSVETAN PETKOV.

Elektronika Bank: 1000 Sofia, Blvd Vitosha 6; tel. (2) 87-85-41; telex 23789; fax (2) 88-54-67; f. 1987; cap. 121m., dep. 2,879m. (Dec. 1991); Pres. VESSELIN KARADZHOV; 4 brs.

First Private Bank: 1000 Sofia, 14 Iskar St; tel. (2) 88-54-23; telex 24540; fax (2) 80-06-19; f. 1990; cap. 534m., dep. 1,907m. (1991); Pres. VENTSISLAV YOSSIFOV; 126 brs.

Hemus Commercial Bank: 1505 Sofia, Yanko Sakuzov Blvd 25; tel. (2) 433-21; telex 22409; fax (2) 43-01-22, 44-17-61; f. 1990; cap. 121m., dep. 806m. (Dec. 1992); Pres. MARIA KOTEVA; 8 brs.

International Bank for Trade and Development: Sofia; tel. (2) 87-15-16.

Mineralbank (Bank for Economic Enterprise): 1000 Sofia, POB 589, Lege St 17; tel. (2) 83-891; telex 23390; fax (2) 51-07-45; f. 1980; cap. 292m., dep. 13,587m., res 3,936m. (Dec. 1991); Pres. RUMEN GEORGIEV; 10 brs.

Expressbank Bulgaria Commercial Bank: 9000 Varna, Shipka St 5; tel. (52) 22-30-73; telex 77293; fax (52) 23-19-64; f. 1993 from Transport Bank; cap. 611m. (1993); Chair. IVAN KONSTANTINOV; 22 brs.

United Bulgarian Bank Inc.: 1202 Sofia, Blvd Maria Luisa 70; tel. (2) 31-81-92; telex 23887; fax (2) 83-52-23; f. 1987 as Stroybank, merged with 21 other banks 1993; universal commercial bank; cap. 149m., dep. 2,721m. (Dec. 1991); Exec. Dirs DIMITUR DIMITROV, OLEG NEDYALKOV.

Vuzrazhdane Commercial Bank: 1303 Sofia, Blvd A. Stamboliiski 50; tel. (2) 87-74-31; telex 23659; fax (2) 80-20-85; f. 1990; cap. 42m., dep. 660m., res 15m. (1991); Pres. MARINA KOZOVSKA.

STOCK EXCHANGE

Bulgarian Stock Exchange: Sofia; Exec. Dir VIKTOR PAPAZOV.

INSURANCE

State Insurance Institute: 1040 Sofia, Blvd Tsar Osvoboditel 6; tel. (2) 87-93-41, 87-01-02; telex 24209; fax (2) 87-69-82; f. 1946; all insurance firms were nationalized during 1947, and were reorganized into one single state insurance company; all areas of insurance; Chair. MAKSIM SIRAKOV; 105 brs.

Bulstrad (Bulgarian Foreign Insurance and Reinsurance Co, Ltd): 1000 Sofia, Dunav St 5; POB 627; tel. (2) 8-51-91; telex 22564; f. 1961; deals with all foreign insurance and reinsurance; Chair. RUMEN YANCHEV.

Trade and Industry

INTERNATIONAL FREE ZONES

Ruse International Free Zone: 7000 Ruse, Knjazgeska St 5, POB 107; tel. (82) 27-23-06, 27-22-47; telex 62285; fax (82) 27-00-84; f. 1988; 23 employees; assets 90m. leva (mid-1993); Gen. Man. YORDAN KAZAKOV.

Free Zone Svilengrad: Khaskovo, Svilengrad, G. Dimitrov Blvd 60; tel. (359) 26-73; state firm; Gen. Dir DIMITUR MITEV.

CHAMBER OF COMMERCE

Bulgarian Chamber of Commerce and Industry: 1040 Sofia, Blvd A. Stamboliiski 11A; tel. (2) 87-26-31; telex 22374; fax (2) 87-32-09; f. 1895; promotes economic relations and business contacts between Bulgarian and foreign cos and orgs; organizes official participation in international fairs and exhibitions and manages the international fairs in Plovdiv; publishes economic publs in Bulgarian and foreign languages; patents inventions and registers trade marks and industrial designs; organizes foreign trade advertising and publicity; provides legal and economic consultations, etc.; registers all Bulgarian cos trading internationally (over 15,000 at mid-1991); Pres. BOJIDAR BOJINOV.

EMPLOYERS' ASSOCIATIONS

Bulgarian Industrial Association (BISA): 1000 Sofia, Alabin St 14; tel. (2) 88-25-01; telex 23523; fax (2) 87-26-04; f. 1980; assists Bulgarian economic enterprises with promotion and foreign contacts; analyses economic situation; assists development of small- and medium-sized firms; Chair BOJIDAR DANEV.

National Union of Employers: 1505 Sofia, Oborishte St 44, POB 15; f. 1989; federation of businessmen in Bulgaria.

Union of Private Owners in Bulgaria: 1000 Sofia, Graf Ignatiev St 2; f. 1990; Chair. DIMITUR TODOROV.

Vuzrazhdane Union of Bulgarian Private Manufacturers: 1618 Sofia, Todor Kableshkov Blvd 2; tel. (2) 55-00-16; Chair. DRAGOMIR GUSHTEROV.

FOREIGN TRADE ORGANIZATIONS AND MAJOR COMPANIES

Until 1989, foreign trade was a state monopoly in Bulgaria, and was conducted through foreign trade organizations and various state enterprises and corporations. However, in 1989, Decree 56, on economic activity, was enacted; the *firma* (firm, company) was introduced as a basic structural unit of the economy. After some delay, this law was superseded by legislation of 1991, effecting the move to a market economy, notably the Law on Commerce and the Law on Foreign Investments. The Bulgarian economy was being opened to foreign involvement; the minimum investment was stipulated to be US $50,000, with a 40% tax on any profits (if the investment was over $100,000, the tax on profit was reduced to 30%). In 1991 further reforms began the harmonization of Bulgarian regulations and practices with EC and international norms. A Law on the Protection of Competition signalled a start to the demonopolization of state enterprises (some 90% of fixed assets consisted of state and municipal enterprises) and, in August 1991, further legislative proposals aimed to hasten the transfer of companies to the private sector. In September 1993 a commission was established for registration and control of companies with a state holding abroad. Valentin Karabashev, Deputy Prime Minister and Minister of Trade, was to head the commission. The Consolid Commerce Company (see below) was also set up at this time, prompted by evidence that commercial partnerships with a state holding abroad had been misusing public funds.

Consolid Commerce Company: Sofia; f. 1993; holds share cap. of state-owned enterprises and single-person commercial partnerships to the sum of 46,000,000. Principal companies include:

Balkantourist: see section on Tourism below.

Bulgarski Morski Flot Co: see section on Transport (Shipping and Inland Waterways) below.

Bulgartabac: 1000 Sofia, Saborna 14,; tel. (2) 87-52-11; telex 23288; covers manufacture, import and export of raw and manufactured tobacco; Dir-Gen. DIMITUR YADKOV.

Chimimport: 1000 Sofia, St Karadja St 2; tel. (2) 88-38-11; import and export of pharmaceuticals, chemicals, petrochemicals, etc.; Dir-Gen. BELO BELOV.

Eltos: 5500 Lovech, Kubrat St 9; tel. (68) 2-35-50; fax (68) 2-00-69; production of electrical tools.

Hemus: 1000 Sofia, Benkovsky St 14; tel. (2) 80-03-65; telex 22267; fax (2) 80-13-41; import and export of books, periodicals, numismatic items, art products, musical instruments, gramophone records and CDs, cinematographic equipment, film and photo consumables and souvenirs; consigned paper warehouse; Exec. Dir. ANASTASIA BONEVA.

Incoms-Telecom Holding: 1309 Sofia, Kiril Ptchelinski St 1; tel. (2) 2-13-41; export and import of radioelectronic equipment and technology for the communications industry; Dir-Gen. LYUBOMIR BUTURANOV.

Interinvest Engineering Ltd: 1113 Sofia, Zhendov St 6; tel. (2) 71-00-33; fax (2) 71-00-38; engineering, trade and investment services; Dir-Gen. EMIL ALADZHEM.

Koraboimpex Co Ltd: 9000 Varna, Osmi Primorski Polk Blvd 128; tel. (52) 88-20-91; telex 77448; fax (2) 82-33-86; holding company of Koraboimpex group of companies; imports and exports ships, marine and port equipment; Exec. Dir. NIKOLAI PRASHKEVOV.

Kremikovitzi Co: 1770 Sofia, Botunetz; tel. (2) 45-70-28; telex 22478; ferrous metals.

Kvartz Co: 8800 Sliven; tel. (44) 2-32-63; fax (44) 8-06-91; glassware.

Machinoexport: 1000 Sofia, Aksakov St 5; tel. (2) 88-53-21; telex 23425; fax (2) 87-56-75; export of metal-cutting and wood-working machines, industrial robots, hydraulic and pneumatic products and other equipment, tools and spare parts; Gen. Dir HRISTO ATZEV.

Mladost: 1000 Sofia, Hristo Botev Blvd 48; tel. (2) 87-61-36; telex 22168; fax (2) 87-27-97; trade in footwear, sportswear, ready-made dresses and toys; Dir-Gen. BOJIDAR VASILEV.

Neftochim: 8104 Burgas, Industrial Zone; tel. (56) 4-59-84; petroleum products, synthetic fabrics, plastics; Dir-Gen. GANCHO NEDELCHEV.

Petur Karaminchev Ltd: 7005 Ruse, Petur Lipnik Blvd 73; tel. (82) 45-93-36; telex 62511; fax (82) 44-86-09; manufacture of floorings, synthetic leather, PVC films, etc.; Dir-Gen. GEORGUI BAIRAKOV.

Plama: 5800 Pleven, Industrial Zone; tel. (64) 2-81-11; fax (64) 3-35-76; petroleum products.

Plovdiska Conserva Co.: 4000 Plovdiv, D. Stambolov St 2; tel. (32) 55-36-34; fax (32) 55-33-71; fruit and vegetable processing.

Raznoiznos: 1040 Sofia, Tsar Assen St 1; tel. (2) 88-02-11, 87-90-84; telex 23244, 23880; fax (2) 31-70-12, 89-79-58; export and import of industrial and craftsmen's products, timber products, paper products, glassware, kitchen utensils, furniture, carpets, toys, sports equipment, musical instruments, etc.; Dir-Gen. MAKSIM SCHWARTZ.

Rudmetal: 1000 Sofia, Dobrudzha St 1; tel. (2) 88-12-71; telex 22027; fax (2) 88-45-04; f. 1952; export and import of ferrous and non-ferrous metals and products, lead zinc, copper, pure lead, coal, etc.; Dir-Gen. EMIL DELIRADEV.

Sofarma Co.: 1220 Sofia, Iliensko Shosse St 16; (2) 38-55-31; fax (2) 38-30-21; trade in chemical and pharmaceutical products, perfumery and cosmetics.

Stomana Co.: 2300 Pernik, Kv. Iztok; tel. (76) 87-20-70; telex 28501; steel products.

Technoimpex: 1000 Sofia, POB 932, Tsar Kaloyan St 8; tel. (2) 88-15-71; telex 22950; fax (2) 88-34-15; scientific and technological assistance abroad in the fields of industry, architecture, construction, transport and communications and education; representation of foreign companies, barter, import-export, re-export, specific commercial operations, leasing, etc.; Dir-Gen. SPAS PANCHEV.

Transimpex: 1606 Sofia, Skobelev Blvd 65; tel. (2) 54-91-61; telex 22123; fax (2) 52-23-25; f. 1967; import and export of railway equipment, wagons, locomotives, boats and shipping parts; Gen. Dir BORIS KHALACHEV; 520 employees.

Zarno Co.: 1000 Sofia, Vitosha Blvd 15; tel. (2) 88-23-81; telex 23441; fax (2) 83-23-38; processing and trade in grains and pulses.

Zavodi za Metalorlzheshti Machini Co.: 1220 Sofia, Iliensko Shosse St 8; tel. (2) 3-85-41; telex 22174; manufacture of machines for metal-and woodwork.

TRADE UNIONS AND CO-OPERATIVES

Confederation of Independent Trade Unions in Bulgaria (CITUB): Sofia, pl. D. Blagoev 1; tel. (2) 86-61; telex 22446; fax (2) 87-17-87; f. 1904; changed name from Bulgarian Professional Union and declared independence from all parties and state structures in 1990; still the main trade union organization; at mid-1991 there were 75 mem. federations and four associate mems (principal mems listed below); Chair. Prof. Dr KRUSTYU PETKOV; Sec. MILADIN STOYNOV; total mems 3,064,000 (mid-1991).

Edinstvo (Unity) People's Trade Union: 1000 Sofia, Moskovska St 5; tel. (2) 87-96-40; f. 1990; co-operative federation of Clubs, based on professional interests, grouped into Asscns and Regional Asscns; there are 84 asscns and 2 prof. asscns, in 14 regional groups; Chair. OGNYAN BONEV; 384,000 mems (mid-1991).

Podkrepa (Support) Trade Union Confederation: 1000 Sofia, Angel Kanchev St 2; tel. (2) 85-61; fax (2) 87-38-42; f. 1989 as an oppostion trade union (affiliated to the Union of Democratic Forces); organized into territorial (31 regions) and professional asscns (33 syndicates); Pres. Dr KONSTANTIN TRENCHEV; Gen. Sec. PETUR GANCHEV; 473,000 mems (mid-1991).

Principal CITUB Trade Unions

Federation of Independent Agricultural Trade Unions: 1606 Sofia, ul. Dimo Hadzhidimov 29; tel. (2) 52-15-40; Pres. LYUBEN KHARALAMPIEV; 640,000 mems (mid-1991).

Federation of Independent Trade Unions of Construction Workers: 1000 Sofia, pl. Sveta Nedelya 4; tel. (2) 80-16-003; Chair. NIKOLAI RASHKOV; 220,000 mems (mid-1991).

Federation of the Independent Trade Unions of Employees of the State and Social Organizations: 1000 Sofia, ul. Alabin 52; tel. (2) 87-98-52; Chair. PETUR SUCHKOV; 144,900 mems (mid-1991).

Federation of Independent Mining Trade Unions: 1000 Sofia, 6 September St 4; tel. (2) 87-72-54; fax (2) 88-45-66; f. 1909; Pres. PENCHO TOKMAKCHIEV; 42,000 mems.

Federation of Metallurgical Trade Unions: 1000 Sofia, 6 September St 4; tel. (2) 88-48-21; fax (2) 88-27-10; f. 1992; Pres. VASSIL YANACHKOV; 20,000 mems.

Federation of Light Industry Trade Unions: 1000 Sofia, ul. Shesti Septemvri 4; Chair. YORDAN VASSILEV; 217,300 mems (mid-1991).

Federation of Trade Unions of the Chemical Industry: 1040 Sofia, pl. Makedonia 1; tel. (2) 87-39-07; Pres. LYUBEN MAKOV; 60,000 mems (mid-1993).

Federation of Trade Unions of the Forestry and Timber Industries: 1606 Sofia, ul. Dimo Hadzhidimov 29; tel. (2) 52-31-21; Pres. NIKOLA ABADZHIEV; 115,000 mems (mid-1991).

Federation of Trade Unions of Health Services: 1202 Sofia, blvd Maria Louisa 45; tel. (2) 88-20-97; fax (2) 83-18-14; f 1990; Pres. Dr IVAN KOKALOV; 70,000 mems (mid-1993).

Independent Trade Union Federation of the Co-operatives: 1000 Sofia, ul. Rakovski 99; tel. (2) 87-36-74; Chair. NIKOLAI NIKOLOV; 96,000 mems (mid-1991).

Independent Trade Union Federation for Trade, Co-operatives, Services and Tourism: 1000 Sofia, ul. Shesti Septemvri 4; tel. (2) 88-02-51; Chair. PETUR TSEKOV; 212,221 mems (mid-1991).

Independent Trade Union of Food Industry Workers: 1606 Sofia, ul. Dimo Hadzhidimov 29; tel. (2) 52-30-72; fax (2) 52-16-70; Pres. SLAVCHO PETROV; 50,000 mems (mid-1992).

'Metal-electro' National Trade Union Federation: 1040 Sofia, pl. Makedonia 1, POB 543; tel. (2) 87-48-06; fax (2) 87-75-38; Pres. ASSEN ASSENOV; 90,000 mems (mid-1993).

National Federation of Energy Workers: 1040 Sofia, pl. Makedonia 1; tel. (2) 88-48-22; f. 1927; Pres. BOJIL PETROV; 15,000 mems.

Union of Bulgarian Teachers: 1000 Sofia, pl. Sveta Nedelya 4; tel. (2) 87-78-18; f. 1905; Chair. IVAN YORDANOV; 186,153 mems (mid-1991).

Union of Transport Workers: 1233 Sofia, Princess Maria Luiza Blvd 106; tel. (2) 31-51-24; fax (2) 31-71-24; f. 1911; Pres. ATANAS STANEV; 70,000 mems (mid-1991).

Other Principal Trade Unions

Bulgarian Military Legion 'G. S. Rakovski': 1000 Sofia, Ruski Blvd 9; tel. (2) 87-72-96; Chair. DOICHIN BOYADZHIEV.

Inner Macedonian Revolutionary Organization-Union of Macedonian Associations: 1000 Sofia, Treti April St 5; tel. (2) 880-56-36; Chair. DIMITUR GOTSEV.

Podkrepa Professional Trade Union for Chemistry, Geology and Metallurgy Workers: 1000 Sofia, Angel Kanchev St 2; Chair. LACHEZAR MINKOV (acting); 15,000 mems (mid-1991).

Podkrepa Professional Trade Union for the Construction Industry: 1000 Sofia, Angel Kanchev St 2; Chair. PETUR DRAGULEV; 15,000 mems (mid-1991).

Podkrepa Professional Trade Union for Doctors and Medical Personnel: 1000 Sofia, Angel Kanchev St 2; Chair. Dr K. KRASTEV; 20,000 mems (mid-1991).

Roma Democratic Union (Gypsies' Union): 1324 Sofia, Dondukov Blvd 39; tel. (2) 39-01-47; Chair. MANUSH ROMANOV.

Union of Bulgarian Architects: 1504 Sofia, Evlogi Georgiev St 1; tel. (2) 46-71-82; Chair. KHRISTO GENCHEV.

Union of Bulgarian Lawyers: 1000 Sofia, Treti April St 7; tel. (2) 87-58-59; Chair. PETUR KORNAZHEV.

Co-operatives

Central Union of Workers' Productive Co-operatives: 1000 Sofia, Dondukov Blvd 41, POB 55; tel. (2) 80-39-38; telex 23229; fax (2) 87-03-20; f. 1988; umbrella organization of 164 workers' productive co-operatives; Pres. PAVEL TSVETANSKY; 75,000 mems.

TRADE FAIR

Plovdiv International Fair: 4018 Plovdiv, Blvd Vuzrazhdane 37; tel. (32) 55-31-46; telex 44432; fax (32) 26-54-32; f. 1933; organized by Bulgarian Chamber of Commerce and Industry; Dir-Gen. KIRIL ASPARUKHOV.

Transport

Ministry of Transport: 1080 Sofia, Levski St 9–11; tel. (2) 88-12-30; telex 23200; fax (2) 88-50-94; directs the state rail, road, water and air transport organizations.

Despred: 1000 Sofia, Slavyanska St 2; tel. (2) 87-60-16; telex 23306; fax (2) 87-60-19; state firm; Man. Dir KOSTADIN KOSTADINOV.

RAILWAYS

At the end of 1992 there were 4,294 km of track in Bulgaria, of which 2,650 km were electrified. The international and domestic rail networks are centred on Sofia. Construction of an underground railway system for Sofia began in 1979, and was still in progress in 1993. The system was to have a total length of 112 km. Its first section was due to come into operation in 1993.

Bulgarian State Railways (BDZ): 1080 Sofia, Ivan Vazov St 3; tel. (2) 87-30-45; telex 22423; fax (2) 87-71-51; owns and controls all railway transport; Gen. Dir ATANAS TONEV.

ROADS

There were 36,930 km of roads in Bulgaria at the beginning of 1992: 276 km of motorways, 6,730 km of main roads and 29,924 km of secondary roads. Two important international motorways traverse the country and a major motorway runs from Sofia to the coast.

General Road Administration: 1606 Sofia, Blvd D. Blagoev 3; tel. (2) 52-17-68; telex 22679; fax (2) 87-67-98; f. 1965; Pres. DIMITAR DIMOV.

SHIPPING AND INLAND WATERWAYS

The Danube River is the main waterway, the two main ports being Ruse and Lom. In 1990 external services linked Black Sea ports (the largest being Varna and Burgas) to the former USSR, the Mediterranean and western Europe.

Bulgarian River Shipping Corporation: 7000 Ruse, pl. Otets Paisi 2; tel. (82) 700-93; telex 62403; fax (82) 701-61; f. 1935; shipment of cargo and passengers on the Danube; storage, handling and forwarding of cargo; Dir-Gen. TSONYU UZUNOV.

Bulgarski Morski Flot Co.: 9000 Varna, Panaguirishte St 17; tel. (52) 22-63-16; telex 77524; fax (52) 22-53-94; organization of sea and river transport; carriage of goods and passengers on waterways; controls all aspects of shipping and shipbuilding, also engages in research, design and personnel training; Dir-Gen. ATANAS YONKOV.

Corporation Navigation Maritime Bulgare: 9000 Varna, Primorski 1; tel. (52) 22-24-74; telex 77351; fax (52) 22-24-91; f. 1892; sole enterprise in Bulgaria employed in sea transport; owns tankers, bulk carriers and container, ferry and passenger vessels with a displacement of 1,867,857 dwt (1990); Man. Dir Capt. IVAN BORISSOV.

CIVIL AVIATION

There are three international airports in Bulgaria, at Sofia, Varna and Burgas, and seven other airports for domestic services.

Balkan Airlines: 1540 Sofia, Sofia Airport; tel. (2) 7-12-01, 7-93-21; telex 22352; fax (2) 79-12-06; f. 1947; restructured and split in 1991; designated national carrier; services to 53 international destinations; also operates domestic routes and agricultural aviation services; Dir-Gen. KONSTANTIN BOTEV.

Hemus Airlines: 1540 Sofia, Sofia Airport; tel. (2) 70-20-76; telex 22342; fax (2) 79-63-80; f. 1991; Dir-Gen. NIKOLAI BEISKI.

Jes Air: 1540 Sofia, Sofia Airport; f. 1991; Exec. Dir TATIANA STOICHKOVA.

Via Air: 1540 Sofia, Sofia Airport; f. 1990; private airline.

VSAU Helli Airlines: 1540 Sofia, Sofia Airport; tel. and fax (2) 79-11-51; telex 22498; f. 1991; Dir-Gen. GEORGUI SPASSOV.

Tourism

Bulgaria's tourist attractions include the resorts on the Black Sea coast, mountain scenery and historic centres. There were 10,329,537 foreign visitor arrivals in 1990. In 1989 tourism accounted for 10% of total income in convertible currency.

Bulgarian Tourist Chamber: Sofia, Triaditza St 5; tel. (2) 87-40-59; some 350 firms are mems, incl. state enterprises, which are in the process of privatization; Chair. TSVETAN TONCHEV.

Balkantourist: 1040 Sofia, Blvd Vitosha 1; tel. (2) 4-33-31; telex 22583; fax (2) 80-01-34; f. 1948; state tourist enterprise and leading firm; Dir ALEKSANDUR SPASSOV.

Culture

NATIONAL ORGANIZATIONS

Ministry of Culture: see section on The Government (Ministries).

National Commission for UNESCO: 1000 Sofia, Rokovski St 96B; tel. (2) 87-54-49; Vice-Chair. LYUBOMIR DRAMALIEV.

CULTURAL HERITAGE

Amateur Artists' Centre: 1000 Sofia, Ruski Blvd 8; tel. (2) 80-11-30; Man. PETUR GRIGOROV.

National Academy of Arts: 1040 Sofia, Shipka St 1; tel. (2) 88-17-01; Rector BORIS GONDOV.

National Archaeological Museum: 1000 Sofia, A. Stamboliiski 2; tel. (2) 88-24-05; f. 1892; attached to the Bulgarian Academy of Sciences; Dir I. SOTIROV.

National Art Gallery: 1000 Sofia, Moskovska St 6; tel. (2) 88-35-59; f. 1948; br. in Aleksandur Nevski Cathedral—icons and ecclesiastical art; Dir S. RUSEV.

National Museum of Applied and Decorative Arts: 1000 Sofia, Blvd Tolbukhin 49; tel. (2) 65-41-72; Dir Z. MANOLOV.

National Museum of Bulgarian Literature: 1000 Sofia, G. Rakovski St 138; tel. (2) 88-24-93; Dir G. SVEZHIN.

National Museum of Ecclesiastical History and Archaeology: 1000 Sofia, pl. V. Lenin 19; tel. (2) 88-13-43; Dir ILARION, Bishop of Trazhanopol.

National Museum of History: 1000 Sofia, Blvd Vitosha 2; tel. (2) 54-46-78; fax (2) 88-32-84; f. 1973; Dir R. KATINCHAROV.

SS Cyril and Methodius National Library: 1504 Sofia, Blvd Vassil Levski 88; tel. (2) 88-28-11; telex 22432; fax (2) 88-16-00; f. 1878; largest public scientific library in Bulgaria; publs 17 information periodicals; Dir Dr ALEXANDRA DIPCHIKOVA.

State Musical Academy: 1504 Sofia, Klement Gottwald Blvd 11; tel. (2) 47-01-81; Rector GEORGUI KOSTOV.

SPORTING ORGANIZATIONS

Olympic Committee of the Republic of Bulgaria: 1000 Sofia, Angel Kanchev St 4; tel. (2) 87-56-95; Chair. IVAN SLAVKOV.

Bulgarian Sports Union: 1040 Sofia, Blvd Vassil Levski 75; tel. (2) 86-52-22, 87-12-98; telex 22723, 22724; fax (2) 87-96-70, 80-05-20; fmrly Bulgarian Union of Physical Culture and Sports; public non-governmental sports organization; selects, educates, organizes early sport training and training and contests for children, youth, élite and professional athletes; Chair. TZVETAN TZVETANOV.

Bulgarian Workers' Sports Federation: 1040 Sofia, Makedonia Sq. 1; f. 1993; fmrly Federation of Physical Culture and Sports; trade union; Chair. KOSTADIN PARSOULOV; 10,000 mems (mid-1993).

PERFORMING ARTS

Theatre

Aleko Konstantinov State Satirical Theatre: 1000 Sofia, Stefan Karadzha St 5; tel. (2) 88-54-24; Dir PLAMEN MARKOV.

Central Puppet Theatre: 1000 Sofia, Gurko St 14; tel. (2) 87-72-88; Dir TODOR DIMITROV.

Ivan Vazov National Theatre: 1000 Sofia, Levski St 5; tel. (2) 87-78-00; Dir VASSIL STEFANOV.

N. O. Massalitinov Drama Theatre: 4000 Plovdiv; tel. (32) 22-48-67; Dir BOGOMIL STOILOV.

Salza i Smyakh (Tears and Laughter) Drama Theatre: 1000 Sofia, Slavyanska St 5; tel. (2) 87-33-89; Dir PETUR MARINKOV.

Sofia Drama Theatre: 1000 Sofia, A. Vl. Zaimov Blvd 23; tel. (2) 45-35-12; Dir VILLY TSANKOV.

Opera Houses

Sofia National Opera: 1000 Sofia, Dondukov Blvd 56; tel. (2) 88-58-69; Dir MIKHAIL ANGELOV.

National Opera in Burgas: 8000 Burgas; tel. (56) 4-30-57; Dir IVAN VULPE.

National Opera in Varna: 9000 Varna; tel. (52) 22-22-23; Dir ANTONII KAMBUROV.

ASSOCIATIONS

Asabay: Silistra; f. 1993; non-political org.; traces and preserves documents relating to the fate of the Crimean Tatars, restores Tatar folklore and publishes newspaper *Ushun*; Chair. Exec. Council ZIYA SELYAMED.

Bulgarian PEN Centre: 1040 Sofia, Angel Kanchev St 5; tel. (2) 87-47-11; affiliated to internat. writers' org.; Chair. BOGOMIL NOVEV.

Independent Federation of the Bulgarian Circus Community: 1000 Sofia, Iskar St 11; tel. (2) 83-29-22; trade union; mem. of CITUB (see section on Trade and Industry); Chair. CH. CHOHADZHIEV; 480 mems (mid-1991).

International Charity Foundation for the Development of Islamic Culture: 1000 Sofia, Ruski Blvd 8; tel. (2) 87-38-16; Chair. NEDIM HAAFUZ.

Podkrepa Trade Union Confederation: see Trade and Industry; there are Podkrepa Professional Trade Unions for: Actors (160 mems—at mid-1991); Artists (Chair. NIKOLAI RANOV; 250 mems); Culture (150 mems); Journalists (Chair. BOYAN DASKALOV; 400 mems); Musicians (1,500 mems); the Preservation of Cultural and Historical Heritage (400 mems).

Union of Bulgarian Actors: 1000 Sofia, Pop Andrei St 1; tel. (2) 88-04-40; trade union; mem. of CITUB (see section on Trade and Industry); Chair. STEFAN ILIEV; 5,000 mems (mid-1991).

Union of Bulgarian Artists: 1000 Sofia, Shipka St 6; tel. (2) 44-61-15; fax (2) 46-31-29; f. 1893; Chair. Prof. BORISLAV STOEV.

Union of Bulgarian Composers: 1000 Sofia, Ivan Vazov St 2; tel. (2) 88-15-60; f. 1947; Chair. PARASHKEV HADZHIEV.

Union of Bulgarian Film Makers: 1000 Sofia, Shesti Septemvri 7; tel. (2) 87-89-56; f. 1934; Chair. GEORGUI STOYANOV.

Union of Bulgarian Journalists: see section on The Press (Press Association).

Union of Bulgarian Musicians: 1000 Sofia, Alabin St 52; tel. (2) 87-73-32; f. 1965; Chair. Prof. G. ROBEV.

Union of Bulgarian Writers: see section on Publishers (Writers' Union).

Education

Education is free and compulsory at primary and secondary level (six to 16 years of age); higher education is also supported by the State. Children between the ages of three and six years may attend kindergartens (in 1988, of this age group, 79.1% of the total attended). Since the late 1980s plans have been under consideration to make attendance compulsory from the age of five. Education from the age of six upwards is organized into unified secondary polytechnical schools, offering an 11-year course of vocational, as well as general secondary, training. There are two types of such schools: secondary vocational-technical schools, which train the executive cadres; and technical colleges (*tekhnikums*), which offer specialized training in areas such as industry, agriculture, transport, trade and public health. Kindergarten and unified-secondary education is administered by the Ministry of Public Education, with the organs of local government. In the 1990/91 school year 303,779 children attended kindergartens and 1,110,733 pupils attended the unified secondary polytechnical schools.

Having completed secondary education, students are entitled to continue their training in semi-higher or higher education institutions. This level is the responsibility of the Ministry of Science and Higher Education. In 1989 26.2% of the relevant age-group enrolled in higher education courses. At the beginning of 1991 there were three universities, one technical university, and 16 higher institutes of university status. The system was undergoing extensive reorganization and many foundations were being renamed.

UNIVERSITIES

St Clement of Ohrid University of Sofia (Sofiiski Universitet 'Kliment Ohridski'): 1504 Sofia, Ruski Blvd 15; tel. (2) 85-81; telex 23296; f. 1909 as university; state control; 14 faculties, 1,714 teachers, 14,684 students (1990); Rector NIKOLA POPOV.

SS Cyril and Methodius University of Veliko Turnovo (Veliko Tarnovski Universitet 'Kiril i Metodi'): 5000 Veliko Turnovo, T. Tarnovski 2; tel. (62) 26-11; telex 66739; f. 1991 as university; 330 teachers, 5,463 students (1990); Rector Prof. GEORGUI DANCHEV.

University of National and World Economy: 1156 Sofia, Studentski grad. Khristo Botev; tel. (2) 6252; fax (2) 68-90-29; f. 1990 as a university (formerly Karl Marx Higher Institute of Economics, f. 1920); 21 departments, 3 faculties, 592 teachers, 13,937 students (1992); Rector Prof. KAMEN MIRKOVICH.

University of Plovdiv (Plovdivski Universitet): 4000 Plovdiv, Car Asen 24; tel. (32) 23-86-61; telex 44251; f. 1961; 6 faculties, 460 teachers, 5,761 students (1989); Rector Prof. N. BALABANOV.

Social Welfare

Since 1951 the State has provided all medical services and treatment free. In post-Communist Bulgaria, this health service has been retained and doctors' salaries increased, but private medical provision was being encouraged also (private medical and dentistry practices were banned between 1972 and November 1989). In 1984 there were 24,718 doctors. In 1988 there were 88,000 hospital beds and 22,000 beds in sanatoriums and health spas. The Ministry of Health is responsible for the health service, with the assistance of local government and the Bulgarian Red Cross. In October 1993 a bill on health insurance was passed by the Council of Ministers. The bill was founded on the principles of compulsory insurance for all citizens, competition between those providing medical care, universal access to medical services and the autonomy of the Health Insurance Fund (this fund was to be raised from a variety of sources and managed by a national insurance institute).

Other social benefits, such as unemployment and pension payments, were also being retained. In October 1993 more than 600,000 Bulgarians were without work, a situation which prompted the Government to adopt a bill on social security during unemployment. The bill provides for the establishment of an independent Occupational Training and Unemployment Fund and regulates relations between the State, the individual and his employer in cases of unemployment. Bulgarian workers enjoyed compensation during sick leave, full paid maternity leave before and after childbirth and non-contributory pensions (this last provision was, in 1991, considered likely to be adjusted). The retirement age varied between 45 and 60 years, depending on the job, and women retired five years earlier than men. State social insurance is directed by the Department of Public Insurance and the Directorate of Pensions.

NATIONAL AGENCIES

Ministry of Health: see section on The Government (Ministries).

Ministry of Labour and Social Affairs: see section on The Government (Ministries).

Department of Public Insurance: Sofia.

Directorate of Pensions: Sofia; responsible for the administration of pensions and the establishment of a pensions fund.

National Council for Employment and Occupational Training: Sofia; co-ordinates employment programmes and measures.

Agency for International Assistance (AIA): 1000 Sofia, Vrabcha St 1; tel. (2) 80-34-03; fax (2) 88-50-39; a state institution created for the purpose of receiving, storing, distributing and monitoring the use of humanitarian aid donated by foreign states, organizations and citizens; Dir STEFAN CHANEV.

HEALTH AND WELFARE ORGANIZATIONS

Bulgarian National Committee for UNICEF: 1000 Sofia, pl. Sveta Nedelya 5; tel. (2) 80-25-04; Chair. The Minister of Health.

Bulgarian Red Cross: 1527 Sofia, Biryukov Blvd 1; tel. (2) 44-14-43; Chair. of Central Cttee KIRIL IGNATOV.

Committee of Human Rights: 1000 Sofia, pl. Narodno Sabranie 12; tel. (2) 88-26-08; Chair. KONSTANTIN TELLALOV.

Foundation Against Cancer: 1000 Sofia, pl. Sveta Nedelya 5; Chair. The Minister of Health.

Union of the Blind: Sofia, Hishka St 172; tel. (2) 21-18-61; telex 23249; fax (2) 22-00-18; f. 1921; social support of the blind; production of electrical appliances, suitcases, filters, etc.; Chair. IVAN KRUMOV.

Union of the Deaf: 1000 Sofia, Denkoglu St 12–14; tel. (2) 54-50-92; Chair. VASSIL PANEV.

The Environment

Environmental concerns prompted the formation of one of the first opposition groups to the Communist regime. Ecoglasnost and the Independent Committee for the Protection of the Environment (or Ruse Committee) began the Green Movement in 1989. There are estimated to be at least 20 environmental groups in Bulgaria. The Bulgarian Government is a member of the Danube Commission (based in Hungary), the Joint Danube Fishery Commission (Slovakia) and the IUCN (Gland, Switzerland). In August 1991 Bulgaria and Romania agreed to fuller co-operation on environmental matters, in accordance with EC conditions for rendering aid to the two countries. The EC rehabilitation programme, Operation Phare, granted Bulgaria a total of 11m. ECUs in 1992 for improving environmental and nuclear safety. Much of Bulgaria's own resources are likely to be spent on repairing environmental damage, especially at Kozlodui, a nuclear-power station on the Danube which provided up to 50% of the country's electricity. Further EC (from November 1993 the European Union) aid was granted during 1993.

GOVERNMENT ORGANIZATIONS

Ministry of the Environment: see section on The Government (Ministries).

Environmental Research and Information Centre (ERIC): 1202 Sofia, Industrialna St 7; tel. (2) 39-47-25; telex 23894; fax (2) 39-21-96; co-ordinates research, analysis, environmental protection programmes, national standards; Head Assoc. Prof. TSONIO MIKHAILOV KONSTANTINOV.

The Ministry of Agriculture and Forestry is also concerned with environmental matters.

ACADEMIC INSTITUTES

Bulgarian Academy of Sciences: 1040 Sofia, 15 Noemvri 1; tel. (2) 841-41; telex 22424; fax (2) 88-04-48; f. 1869; Pres. Acad. YORDAN MALINOVSKI.

Forest Research Institute: 1756 Sofia, Kl. Ohridski Blvd 132; tel. (2) 62-20-52; studies the structure and functioning of forest ecosystems, etc.; Dir Prof. Dr ALEKSANDUR ALEKSANDROV.

Institute of Botany: 1113 Sofia, Acad. G. Bonchev St 23; tel. (2) 75-81-40; f. 1947; plant taxonomy, monitoring and conservation of rare and threatened plant species; assessment of plant resources; palaeobotany; Dir Prof. Dr EMANEL PALAMAREV.

Institute of Ecology: 1618 Sofia, Gagarin St 2; tel. (2) 71-71-95; f. 1990; Dir G. DZOLOV.

Institute of Economics: 1040 Sofia, Aksakov St 3; tel. (2) 87-30-15; fax (2) 88-21-08; f. 1949; research work, teaching, training, information services, management consultancy; main subject areas is the process of transition to a market economy; Dir Prof.K. KIRJAKOV.

Institute of Oceanology: 9000 Varna, POB 152, Asparuhovo Quarter; tel. (52) 77-20-38; telex 77237; fax (52) 77-42-56; marine ecology and research of the Bulgarian Black Sea coastline and shelf; Dir Assoc. Prof. ZDRAVKO BELBEROV.

Institute of Water Problems: 1113 Sofia, Acad. G. Bonchev St 1; tel. (2) 72-25-72; fax (2) 72-25-77; research in the field of rational planning, construction and operation of water resource systems, rehabilitation and maintenance of inland waters; Dir Prof. DrTODOR HRISTOV.

Institute of Zoology: 1000 Sofia, Tsar Osvoboditel Blvd 1; tel. (2) 88-31-63; fax 88-28-97; f. 1947; publication of two journals, *Acta Zool. Bulgarica* and *Hydrobiologia*; biological monitoring and preparation of the *Red Data* series on animal and bird life in Bulgaria; taxonomy, ecology and zoogeography of Bulgarian and Palaearctic fauna; Dir Prof. Dr VASSIL GRIGOROV GOLEMANSKI.

National Institute of Meteorology and Hydrology: 1184 Sofia, Carigradsko shosse 66; tel. and fax (2) 88-03-80; telex 22490; monitors atmospheric and ground water pollution; Dir Assoc. Prof. VASSIL ANDREEV.

Higher Institute of Forestry and Wood Technology: 1156 Sofia, Kl. Ohridski Blvd 10; tel. (2) 63-01; fax (2) 68-03-35; particular concern is acid rain; landscape restoration; Rector Prof. ANDREI RAICHEV.

National Centre of Hygiene, Medical Ecology and Nutrition: 1431 Sofia, Dimitur Nestorov Blvd 15; tel. (2) 59-10-06; fax (2) 59-81-48; fmrly Inst. of Hygiene and Occupational Health; assesses the impact of environmental damage and pollution on the health of the population; Dir Assoc. Prof. Dr EMILIA IVANOVICH.

N. Pushkarov Research Institute of Soil Science and Agroecology: 1080 Sofia, Shosse Bankya St 7; tel. (2) 24-64-41; telex 22701; fax (2) 24-77-95; monitors the pollution of soils and underground waters; Dir Assoc. Prof. Dr VULYO TENEV VULEV.

NON-GOVERNMENTAL ORGANIZATIONS

Association of Bulgarian Ecologists (ABECOL): 1040 Sofia, Blvd Vitosha 18; tel. and fax (2) 87-24-21; f. 1990; voluntary, independent, scientific and educational organization; Chair. of Board of Dirs Prof. SIMEON NEDIALKOV.

Association Ecoforum: 1113 Sofia, Gagarin St 2; tel. (2) 70-53-79; fax (2) 55-10-67; org. of scientists, businessmen and public workers committed to promoting sustainable development and conservation, particularly in the transition to a market economy; Gen. Sec. Assoc. Prof. PAVEL GEORGIEV.

Bulgarian Society for the Conservation of the Rhodope Mts: 1113 Sofia, Gagarin St 2; tel. (2) 70-51-78; fax (2) 70-54-98; f. 1991; union committed to the conservation of the natural and cultural heritage of the Rhodope Mountains; Chair. Assoc. Prof. YORDAN KIRILOV DANCHEV.

Bulgarian Society of Natural Research: 1421 Sofia, Dragan Tsankov Blvd 8, POB 1136; tel. (2) 66-65-94; f. 1896; scientific and educational society of natural scientists; promotes the study and conservation of the environment; organized into over 20 regional brs and 5 scientific sections, incl. one on ecology; over 1,500 mems; Chair. Prof. Dr VASSIL GOLEMANSKI.

Bulgarian Society for the Protection of Birds: 1421 Sofia, Dragan Tsankov Blvd 8; tel. (2) 72-06-30; fax (2) 70-54-98; f. 1988; independent ornithological assen; over 400 mems; Chair. TANIO MICHEV.

Ecoforum for Peace: 1431 Sofia, Dimitur Nestorov St 15; tel. (2) 59-61-23, 58-12-509; fax (2) 59-91-26; f. 1986 by 88 scholars from 32 countries and 12 internat. orgs; internat. movement for world peace and environmental protection; 15 brs in other countries; secretariat in Bulgaria; Gen. Sec. Vasselin Heykov.

Ecoglasnost Independent Association: 1000 Sofia, Blvd Dondukov 9, POB 548; tel. (2) 80-23-23; fax (2) 88-15-30; f. officially in 1989; mem. of the UDF, with political representation (see section on Political Organizations); 20,000 mems; Pres. EDWIN SUGAREV; Sec. LUCHEZAR TOSHEV; 147 CHAPTERS.

ECOS Foundation: 1000 Sofia, A. Stamboliiski 2A, 6th Floor; tel. (2) 71-433-71; fax (2) 87-24-00; educational foundation, intent on promoting ecological awareness; Dir Gen. OGNIAN CHAMPOEV.

Green Party: see section on Political Organizations.

Green Society Foundation: 1040 Sofia, Vitosha Blvd 18; tel. and fax (2) 87-24-21; f. 1991; co-operates in projects and campaigns with other groups; operates 7 programmes on the environment; Pres. Assoc. Prof. PETUR GULUBOV; Exec. Dir RADIANA STANOEVA.

National Ecological Club: 1000 Sofia, POB 1653; tel. (2) 70-52-25; independent public org., committed to the conservation of nature; Corresponding Mems VASSIL SGUREV, Acad. GEORGUI BLIZNAKOV.

Union for Nature Protection: 1040 Sofia, Vitosha Blvd 18; tel. (2) 83-26-72; f. 1928 as Union for Native Nature Protection; restructured 1991; independent public org.; local brs and internat. contacts; Chair. Assoc. Prof. Dr SVETOSLAV GERASIMOV.

Wilderness Fund: 1113 Sofia, Gagarin St 2; fax (2) 70-54-98; f. 1990; attached to the Instit. of Ecology; assesses the best places to establish reserves for the protection of the natural environment; Chair. JEKO SPIRODONOV.

Defence

In June 1993, according to Western estimates, the total strength of the armed forces was 98,800 (including 60,000 conscripts), comprising 52,000 in the Army, 21,800 in the Air Force and 3,000 in the Navy. Paramilitary forces included 12,000 border troops (commanded by the Ministry of the Interior) and 4,000 security police. Compulsory military service for all males was 18 months in the Army, two years in the Air Force and three years in the Air Force. Bulgaria was a member of the Warsaw Pact, which was dissolved in 1991, but had no other military alliances. The Bulgarian Government welcomed a Greek proposal, made in August 1991, to have a demilitarized zone on the Bulgarian–Greek–Turkish borders, but no further progress was made that year. In the 1993 budget 8,790m. leva were allocated to defence.

Commander-in-Chief: President of the Republic.

Chief of the General Staff: Col-Gen. LYUBEN PETROV.

Bibliography

Barnes, J. *The Porcupine.* London, Jonathan Cape, 1992.

Bell, J. D. *The Bulgarian Communist Party from Blagoev to Zhivkov.* Stanford, California, Hoover Institution Press, 1986.

Crampton, R. J. *Bulgaria 1878–1918: A History.* Boulder, Colorado, Eastern European Quarterly (Distributed by Columbia University Press), 1983.

A Short History of Modern Bulgaria. Cambridge, Cambridge University Press, 1987.

Economic Geography of the Socialist Countries of Europe. Moscow, Progress Publishers, 1985.

Feiwel, G. R., in *Osteuropa Wirtschaft,* Vol. 24, 2. June 1979.

Gehrmann, U. *Bulgariens Weg zur neuen Identität: Rückblicke und Aussichten einer unvollendeten 'Preustroystvo' auf dem Balkan.* Cologne, Bundesinstitut für ostwissenchaftliche und internationale Studien, 1993.

Grothusen, K.-D. (Ed.). *Bulgarien; Südosteuropa Handbuch, Band VI.* Göttingen, Vandenhoeck und Ruprecht, 1990.

Höpken, W., in Schönfeld, R. (Ed.). *Industrialiserung und Geselischaftlicher Wandel in Südosteuropa.* Munich, Südosteuropa-Gesellschaft, 1989.

Jackson, M. R., in *Pressures for Reform in the East European Economies,* Vol. 2. Washington, DC, USGPO (Joint Economic Committee of the US Congress), 1986.

Jelavich, B. *History of the Balkans.* Cambridge, Cambridge University Press, 1983.

Kinow D. W., in Schönfeld, R. (Ed.). *Industrialiserung und Geselischaftlicher Wandel in Südosteuropa.* Munich, Südosteuropa-Gesellschaft, 1989.

Lampe, J. R. *The Bulgarian Economy in the Twentieth Century.* London, Croom Helm, 1986.

Lang, D. M. *The Bulgarians from Pagan Times to the Ottoman Empire.* London, Thames and Hudson, 1976.

Miller, L. M. *Bulgaria during the Second World War.* Stanford, California, Stanford University Press, 1975.

Perry, D. *Stefan Stambolov and the Emergence of Modern Bulgaria, 1870–1895.* Durham, Duke University Press, 1993.

Wyzan, M. L., in *Pressures for Reform in the East European Economies,* Vol. 2. Washington, DC, USGPO (Joint Economic Committee of the US Congress), 1986.

CROATIA

Geography

PHYSICAL FEATURES

The Republic of Croatia (formerly a constituent partner in the Socialist Federal Republic of Yugoslavia) has a long western coastline on the Adriatic Sea. It is bordered by Slovenia to the north-west, Hungary to the north-east and the Vojvodina area of Serbia (Yugoslavia) to the east. Bosnia and Herzegovina abuts into Croatia, forming a southern border along the Sava River, and an eastern one inland from the Dalmatian coast which stretches southwards. At the southern tip of this narrowing stretch of Croatia, beyond a short coastal strip of Bosnia and Herzegovina, is the territory of Dubrovnik (once known as Ragusa), which has a short border with Montenegro.

Croatia, which has a total area of 56,538 sq km (21,829 sq miles), consists of two principal parts: there is a long coastal region, narrowing as it goes south, extending from the Istrian peninsula, down the Dalmatian coast to the area of the former city state of Dubrovnik; the north of this coastal region is attached, by a relatively narrow bridge of territory, to eastern Croatia, which extends inland. Beyond the 'waist' attaching it to the coast, the country widens out into Croatia proper, beyond the mountains, and stretches eastwards. Slovenia juts into this 'waist' from the north-west and Bosnia from the south-east. To the north-east of the waist of the country lies the capital, Zagreb (Agram), in the heart of old Croatia. Eastwards, is the fertile territory of Slavonia, an ancient province that lies between the Drava and the Sava rivers. Western or coastal Croatia is defined by the mountains running parallel to the littoral, which is fringed with more than 1,100 islets and islands.

CLIMATE

The climate in Croatia is Mediterranean on the coast and continental inland. The highlands have a colder climate with heavy snow in winter, but in summer it can be very hot. Temperatures inland average 10°C (50°F), while on the coast the mean temperature is 15°C (59°F). Rainfall is fairly constant throughout the year, although summer is the wettest season in the north of the country. The average annual rainfall is 890 mm (35 in) in Zagreb.

POPULATION

The total population of Croatia was 4,784,265 at the census of March 1991, and the country had a population density of 84.6 per sq km. According to the provisional results of this census ethnic Croats comprised 77.9% of the total population of the Republic (in 1981 some 78% of all Yugoslav Croats lived within the borders of the Republic). There was, in 1991, a significant Serb minority, of 12.2%; they were concentrated in certain areas, mainly along the border with Bosnia and Herzegovina. (The Habsburgs settled many Serbs along the frontier with its Muslim rival, the Ottoman Empire, in an area known as the Krajina—borderlands.) Both peoples speak versions of Serbo-Croat (or Croato-Serb), but the largely Roman Catholic Croats use the Latin script and the Eastern Orthodox Serbs use the Cyrillic script. The Roman Catholic Church is the largest religious denomination. Since 1991 the Croatians have rejected the 1954 Novi Sad Agreement, and now claim the distinctness of a Croatian language. In 1981 there was also a significant number classing themselves as ethnically neutral Yugoslavs (8.2%), but this was considerably less at the 1991 census (only 2.2%). The capital, Zagreb, was the largest city in the country (with a population of 706,770, according to the 1991 census). The most populous towns of the coast were Split (189,338), in the central coastal area, and Rijeka (Fiume—167,964), in the north. The main town of Slavonia, Osijek, in the east of the country had a population of some 104,761 in 1991.

In December 1991 a 'Republic of Serbian Krajina' (RSK) was declared. By January 1994 the borders of the RSK had still not been clearly defined (see map on p. 89) and most of the Serb territories were under the protection of UN forces, whose mandate was to demilitarize the entire area. The Serb 'Republic' controlled three regions. The Krajina region, which lay along those borders where Bosnia and Herzegovina jutted into Croatia, included the chief town of Knin. The region consisted of the districts of Eastern Dalmatia and Lika (inland from Zadar and northwards along the border with Bosnia and Herzegovina, which lay to the east); Slunj and Kordun (which straddled the apex of Bosnia and Herzegovina); and Banija (which lay between the Una and Kupa rivers, with Bosnia and Herzegovina to the south). Of Western Slavonia (a region which extended into the centre of eastern Croatia), the Serbs only securely controlled the area around the town of Okucani, near the Bosnian border. In eastern Croatia (Eastern Slavonia, Baranja and Western Srem or Syrmia), the territory held by Serb forces was contiguous with Serbia (Yugoslavia), and included the towns of Beli Manistir, Erdut and Vukovar.

Chronology

168 BC: Illyria (which included modern-day Croatia) was annexed by the Roman Empire.

AD 395: Following a division of the administration of the Roman Empire, Illyria was ruled by the Eastern Roman ('Byzantine') Emperor in Constantinople (Istanbul).

5th century: Southern Slav peoples began to move from Pannonia into Illyria and the Balkans.

7th–8th centuries: Western Christian missionaries, from Aquileia (Trieste) were active among the Croats, introducing the Latin script and a Western cultural orientation.

812: By the Treaty of Aix-la-Chapelle (Aachen), the Byzantine Emperor, Michael I, acknowledged the Frankish (German) ruler, Charles ('the Great'—Charlemagne), as Emperor in the West; Byzantine suzerainty over Istria and Dalmatia was confirmed and German influence to the north of the Croats was established.

1076: Coronation, by the Pope (the leader of the Roman Church), of Dimitar Zvonimir, who had rejected Eastern, Byzantine overlordship of the Croatian kingdom established in the 10th century.

1082: Venice was granted trading privileges in the Eastern Empire, securing their independence and their growing influence along the formerly Byzantine Dalmatian coast.

1102: Croatia's personal union with Hungary (under the *Pacta Conventa*) effectively, if not finally, linked it to the Hungarian Crown, together with parts of Dalmatia.

1187: The Emperor in Constantinople acknowledged Hungarian conquests in Croatia and Bosnia.

1490: Death of the Hungarian King, Matthias I Corvinus, who had secured modern Croatia and the Vojvodina (Slavonia and the Banat) for Hungary and, temporarily, conquered the Habsburg lands.

1526: Louis II and the Hungarian forces were destroyed by the Ottomans at the Battle of Mohács; the Hungarian Crown was claimed as a hereditary possession of the House of Habsburg, but the kingdom itself was subsequently partitioned between the Habsburgs (northern Croatia) and the Ottomans (southern Croatia and Slavonia).

1718: The Peace of Passarowitz confirmed the Habsburg liberation of Hungary, including Croatia and Slavonia; the Ottomans ceded the Banat and northern Serbia (but the latter was held only until 1739).

1815: The Congress of Vienna confirmed Austrian rule over Istria and Dalmatia, which were formerly Venetian.

1848: At a time of revolution in Habsburg and other territories, the Croatian assembly, in Agram (Zagreb), was forced to end consideration of a Southern Slav (Yugoslav) state.

1868: Croatia, united with Slavonia, was granted autonomy by Hungary, which, since the *Ausgleich* or Compromise of the previous year, was now a partner in the Habsburg 'Dual Monarchy'.

July 1878: At the Congress of Berlin, Austria-Hungary secured administration rights in Bosnia and Herzegovina.

1881: Final abolition of the 'Military Frontier' or Krajina, in which, since the 17th century, the Habsburgs had allowed some autonomy to Serb settlers defending the borders against the Ottomans in Bosnia.

1903: Accession of Petar I Karadjordjević, leader of the Radical party, to the throne of Serbia; he was anti-Habsburg and encouraged the Southern Slav movement ('Yugoslavism'), the champion of which in Croatia-Slavonia was Bishop Josip Strossmayer.

28 June 1914: The heir to the Habsburg throne, Archduke Francis Ferdinand, and his wife were assassinated in Sarajevo (Bosnia and Herzegovina).

28 July 1914: Austria-Hungary declared war on Serbia, which started the First World War between the Central Powers, of Austria-Hungary and Germany, and the Entente Powers, of France, Russia, Serbia and the United Kingdom.

July 1917: Representatives of the Croats, Serbia and the other Southern Slavs (excluding the Bulgarians) declared their intention to form a unitary state, under the Serbian monarchy.

29 October 1918: Following the defeat and dissolution of the Danubian Monarchy, the Southern Slav peoples separated from the Austro-Hungarian system of states (a Southern Slav republic was established on 15 October); Dalmatia, Croatia-Slavonia, Bosnia and Herzegovina, parts of Carinthia, Carniola and the Banat were, subsequently, ceded formally to the new state.

4 December 1918: Proclamation of the Kingdom of Serbs, Croats and Slovenes, which united the former Habsburg lands with Serbia and Montenegro.

August 1921: Prince Aleksandar, Regent of Serbia since 1914 and of the new Kingdom since its formation, became King, upon the ratification of the 'Vidovdan' Constitution.

August 1928: A separatist Croatian assembly convened in Zagreb.

3 October 1929: Following the imposition by King Aleksandar of a royal dictatorship, the country was formally named Yugoslavia.

1931: The dictatorship was suspended by the introduction of a new Constitution, although this did not prevent Croat unrest and the rise of the Fascist Ustaša (Rebel) movement.

October 1934: King Aleksandar I of Yugoslavia was assassinated in France by Croatian extremists; his brother, Prince Paul, became Regent, on behalf of the young King Petar II.

1937: Tito (Josip Broz) became General-Secretary of the Communist Party of Yugoslavia (CPY), which was to become the main partner in the Partisan (National Liberation Army) resistance to the German invasion.

March 1941: A *coup d'état* installed King Petar II, who reversed previous policies and aligned himself with the Allied Powers of the Second World War.

9 April 1941: An Independent State of Croatia was established, following the invasion of Yugoslavia by German and Italian forces; the new State included much of Bosnia and Herzegovina, while the rest of Yugoslavia was dismembered by Albania, Bulgaria, Germany, Hungary and Italy (the last annexing some of the Dalmatian coast); the Italian, Duke Aimone of Spoleto, was King of Croatia, with an Ustaša Government under Ante Pavelić.

29 November 1943: Proclamation of a government for 'liberated' areas by the Partisans, following a savage resistance struggle and civil war with the Ustaša regime and the royalist Četniks (Yugoslav Army of the Fatherland) of western Serbia; Tito's leadership was subsequently acknowledged by the Allies and the royal Government-in-Exile.

1944: King Petar II was declared deposed.

29 November 1945: Following elections for a Provisional Assembly, the Federative People's Republic of Yugoslavia was proclaimed, with Tito as prime minister.

January 1946: A Soviet-style Constitution was adopted, establishing a federation of six Republics, one of which was Croatia (including Dalmatia and western Slavonia).

1954: Istria was partitioned between Italy, which gained the city of Trieste, and Yugoslavia (mostly becoming part of Croatia, but the north going to Slovenia—denying Croatia a border with Italy). The so-called Novi Sad Agreement proclaimed Serbo-Croat to be one language with two scripts.

1966: Reformists, who had already achieved some economic liberalization, secured the fall of Vice-President Aleksandar Ranković, the head of the secret police and an advocate of strong central government.

July 1971: Following the granting of the rights of autonomy to the federal units, Tito introduced a system of collective leadership and the regular rotation of posts.

December 1971: The reformist Croatian leadership was forced to resign following criticism from Tito; the suppression of the

Croatian 'mass movement', or *Maspok,* and a purge of liberals throughout Yugoslavia followed.

1974: A new Constitution came into force, aimed at containing nationalist tendencies, particularly within Croatia.

4 May 1980: Tito died; his responsibilities were transferred to the collective State Presidency and to the Presidium of the League of Communists of Yugoslavia (LCY).

March 1989: Against a background of mounting tension in the Serbian province of Kosovo and declining economic conditions, a new Federal Government, under Ante Marković, was appointed.

September 1989: The Assembly of neighbouring Slovenia reaffirmed the sovereignty of their Republic and declared its right to secede from the Socialist Federative Republic of Yugoslavia (SFRY).

22 April 1990: The first-round elections to the three chambers of the Croatian Assembly (for a maximum of 356 seats) were held.

6–7 May 1990: A second round of voting took place; in the final results, the nationalist opposition party, the Croatian Democratic Union (CDU), gained 205 of the eventual 351 seats in the Assembly.

30 May 1990: The Assembly elected Franjo Tudjman, leader of the CDU, as President of the State Presidency of Croatia; Stjepan ('Stipe') Mesić was elected President of the Executive Council (Premier).

25 July 1990: The Croatian Assembly approved constitutional changes, including: the removal of the word 'Socialist' from the Republic's title; the redesignation of the republican Executive Council as a 'Government'; the replacement of the republican State Presidency with a President and six Vice-Presidents; and the downgrading of the use of the Cyrillic alphabet. The leaders of the Serb minority in Croatia, who had formed a 'Serb National Council', denounced the amendments and demanded a referendum on immediate cultural autonomy.

August 1990: The Assembly dismissed the Republic's member of the federal State Presidency, a Communist, and nominated the Croatian Premier, Mesić, instead (endorsed by the Federal Assembly on 19 October); Josip Manolić was elected Premier. The Assembly also outlawed 'parallel' government bodies and voluntary armed formations, as the Croatian Serbs conducted an unofficial referendum on autonomy (19 August–2 September).

1 October 1990: The Serb National Council, after announcing their referendum results, proclaimed autonomy for the Serb-dominated Krajina areas of Croatia (the 'Serb Autonomous Region—SAR—of Krajina', which was based in Knin).

November 1990: The Assembly placed the Territorial Defence Force under republican control.

21 December 1990: The Croatian Assembly promulgated a new Constitution, which proclaimed the Republic's full sovereignty and its right to secede from Yugoslavia.

20 January 1991: Croatia and Slovenia concluded a mutual defence pact, amid rising tension between the republican authorities and the Jugoslavenska Narodna Armija (JNA—Yugoslav People's Army).

25 January 1991: The JNA agreed to end its state of alert and the Croatians agreed to demobilize, if not disband, all paramilitary groups. However, 10 days later, the JNA ordered the arrest of Croatia's Minister of Defence on sedition charges.

21 February 1991: Croatia asserted the primacy of its Constitution and laws over those of the federation and declared its conditions for participation in a confederation of sovereign states.

28 February 1991: The self-proclaimed SAR of Krajina declared its separation from Croatia and its desire to unite with Serbia (on 16 March it formally resolved on its adherence to the Yugoslav federation).

March 1991: The JNA became involved, on the Serb side, in the increasing clashes with Croatian forces.

11 April 1991: Croatia established an army, the Croatian National Guard Corps (to replace the Territorial Defence Force), after increasing anxieties about the intentions of the JNA.

30 April 1991: The SAR of Krajina's self-proclaimed government or executive council announced the formation of a Krajina Assembly.

15 May 1991: The Serbian representative's term of office as President of the federal State Presidency ended; under the system of rotating leadership, Stipe Mesić was scheduled to become the first non-Communist President of Yugoslavia, but the 'Serbian bloc' of Presidency members prevented his accession.

19 May 1991: In a referendum in Croatia, some 94% of participants voted in favour of an independent Republic (possibly as part of a confederation of sovereign states).

29 May 1991: The SAR of Krajina announced that its basic statute was a constitutional law; its Assembly appointed a government led by Milan Babić.

25 June 1991: The Croatian Assembly declared the independence and sovereignty of the Republic, beginning the process of 'dissociation' from the federation at the same time as Slovenia. Two days later the union of the two Krajinas was announced: the SAR in Croatia; and Bosanska (Bosnian) Krajina in Bosnia and Herzegovina.

30 June 1991: Following fighting, mainly in Slovenia, a European Community (EC—known as the European Union from November 1993) mediating team secured agreement to a cease-fire; one condition was implemented forthwith—the proclamation of Stipe Mesić as President of the federal State Presidency; it was subsequently agreed that Croatia and Slovenia should have a three-month moratorium on further implementation of their declarations of dissociation.

18 July 1991: In Croatia, as fighting continued to escalate, Josip Manolić was appointed the head of a new war cabinet or state council, being replaced as Premier (Prime Minister) by his deputy, Franjo Gregurić.

1 August 1991: Tudjman reorganized the Croatian Government, forming an administration of 'democratic unity', with 16 of the 27 posts being filled by opposition parties.

13 August 1991: An SAR of Western Slavonia (later the SAR of Slavonia, Baranja and Western Srem) was declared.

7 September 1991: After the failure of several cease-fire arrangements, a peace conference for Yugoslavia opened in The Hague (Netherlands), chaired by a former British foreign minister, Lord Carrington.

25 September 1991: The UN Security Council unanimously ordered an arms embargo on Yugoslavia. In the SAR of Slavonia, Baranja and Western Srem, its 'Grand National Assembly' enacted a constitutional law.

8 October 1991: The Croatian Assembly declared all federal laws null and void, the EC moratorium on the Croatian and Slovenian processes of dissociation having expired the previous day. Later in the month the SAR of Krajina and Bosanska Krajina, in Bosnia and Herzegovina, announced their unification, subsequently being joined by the SAR of Slavonia, Baranja and Western Srem; Babić, leader of the Knin regime, was authorized to represent the areas at The Hague Conference.

October 1991: The siege of Dubrovnik by the JNA began (it did not end until 28 May 1992).

19 November 1991: Croatians were ordered by the Supreme Council to leave all federal offices and subsequently to serve only the Croatian state.

22 November 1991: Dobroslav Paraga, leader of the nationalist Croatian Party of Rights (CPR–Hrvatska Stranka Prava) was arrested in an attempt by the CDU to suppress political activity in the CPR's armed wing, the Croatian Defence Association.

5 December 1991: Stipe Mesić resigned as President of the Yugoslav federation; two weeks later the federal prime minister, Ante Marković, also left office.

23 December 1991: A Croatian dinar was introduced.

2 January 1992: The UN negotiated a cease-fire between the Croatian National Guard and the JNA.

15 January 1992: An independent Republic of Croatia was recognized by the EC.

February 1992: The United Nations Protection Force in Yugoslavia (UNPROFOR) was deployed in Croatia to supervise the withdrawal of the JNA and the demilitarization of Serb-held enclaves.

May 1992: Croatia was formally admitted to the UN. The Croatian People's Party left the coalition Government following the resignation of one of their members, Bosilijko Misetić, from the post of Minister of Justice; Misetić had opposed a law which gave special rights to Serbs residing in areas with a Serb majority. The JNA began to withdraw from Croatia.

June 1992: Following attacks by Croatian forces on several Serb areas, a UN Security Council resolution demanded the immediate withdrawal by Croats to the positions they had held before 21 June.

2 August 1992: Parliamentary and presidential elections were held; Tudjman, one of eight candidates, was re-elected President (winning 56% of the votes cast), and the ruling CDU obtained 85 of the 138 seats in the new Chamber of Representatives. The new Government, headed by Hrvoje Šarinić, took office on 8 September.

26 August 1992: Following the failure of the peace negotiations in The Hague in 1991, the London Conference opened in the United Kingdom; the Conference was chaired by the former US Secretary of State, Cyrus Vance, and Lord Owen, the British politician; it was decided that a permanent conference would be established in Geneva, Switzerland.

October 1992: Three members of the CPR, including Dobroslav Paraga, were charged with planning a coup. The Presidents of Croatia and Slovenia signed agreements on diplomatic and economic relations. The co-Chairman of the EC/UN peace negotiations in Geneva, Lord Owen, warned that sanctions might be imposed on Croatia if it continued to give military support to the newly proclaimed 'Croatian Union of Herzeg-Bosna' in Bosnia and Herzegovina.

November 1992: Croatia was divided, for electoral purposes, into 21 counties, 420 municipalities and 61 towns.

22 January 1993: In an effort to win control of the Maslenica bridge Croatian troops breached UNPROFOR peace-keeping lines and began an offensive in Serb-held Krajina.

7 February 1993: In elections to the Chamber of Municipalities the CDU won a majority (37 seats out of 67).

12 March 1993: A short strike by members of three trade-union confederations and several independent unions protested low wages and high inflation. There was also a strike by the staff of *Slobodna Dalmacija*, a formerly independent newspaper based in Split, which was taken over by pro-government managers; it was alleged that this was part of a continuing attempt by the Government to control the media.

29 March 1993: The Sarinić Government resigned under pressure; President Tudjman appointed Nikica Valentić as Prime Minister.

6 April 1993: The reconstruction and reopening of the Maslenica bridge, Zemunik airport and the Peruca hydroelectric plant, under UNPROFOR supervision, was envisaged in a UN-brokered agreement, signed in Geneva.

14 July 1993: Serb paramilitary forces began to reoccupy the regions of Karlovac and Zemunik, in response to the continued presence of Croatian troops in the Maslenica area.

15–16 July 1993: The so-called Erdut Agreement, negotiated by the UN, was signed by the Serbian and Croatian Presidents. On 13 August, however, the Agreement was declared null and void by the Croatian Minister of Foreign Affairs, Mate Granić.

19 July 1993: The EC again threatened sanctions against Croatia if it failed to end military involvement in the conflict in Bosnia and Herzegovina.

24 September 1993: The Croatian authorities formed a commission for relations with UNPROFOR.

4 October 1993: UN Security Council Resolution 871 required the extension of UNPROFOR's mandate; it also demanded the disarming of Serb paramilitary groups and the transferral of all 'pink zones' (areas with majority Serb populations lying outside the official UN Protected Areas—UNPAs) to Croatian control.

12 October 1993: In Beli Manastir the Krajina Serb Assembly voted to reject Resolution 871 and ordered the mobilization of all conscripts.

16 October 1993: Tudjman was re-elected President of the CDU.

History

EARLY HISTORY

From the fifth century AD the Croats (*Čorvats* or 'mountaineers') began to settle in Illyria (a Province of the Eastern Roman, or 'Byzantine', Empire since the fourth century). Despite the usually nominal overlordship of the Roman Emperor in Constantinople (now Istanbul, Turkey), the Croats were more influenced by Western Europe. Missionaries from Aquileia (Trieste) first attached them to Christianity and their allegiance remained to the Roman Church. An independent kingdom was established, in the 10th century, between the river Drava and the Adriatic Sea. The realm controlled much of Bosnia, the inhabitants of which were also Roman Catholic. To varying degrees, Byzantine influence remained along the Dalmatian coast and in Istria, thus establishing the Croatian heartland to be inland, in the mountains and around Agram (Zagreb). In 1074 Dimitar Zvonimir succeeded to the throne; he was crowned by the Pope, in 1076, having finally rejected the sovereignty of the Eastern, Byzantine Emperor. He died in 1089 and was replaced by the Hungarian king, László I. His successor, Coloman I, formalized the personal union with Hungary under the *Pacta Conventa;* he became King of Croatia, which was administered by a ban (frontier commander or marcher lord). In the late 12th century Bela III finally expelled Byzantine influence and consolidated Hungarian control of Croatia and Bosnia. Under the pressure of the Mongol invasions, particularly after the defeats of 1241, the Hungarian kingdom disintegrated. Venice consolidated its possession of the former Byzantine strongholds in Istria and along the Dalmatian coast, but, by the reign of Matthias I Corvinus (1485–90), Hungarian rule in the rest of Croatia had been re-established.

HABSBURG RULE

The Hungarians were defeated by the forces of the Ottoman Empire at the battle of Mohács, in 1526, and Croatia became a border territory between the Islamic world and the Christian West. The Habsburgs, who were the Holy Roman Emperors, had a claim to the Hungarian Crown (their hereditary possession of it was confirmed by the 1687 Imperial Diet of Pressburg). In 1529 the Habsburgs and the Ottomans divided the Hungarian territories. Northern Croatia became part of the Habsburg Kingdom of Hungary, while southern Croatia and most of Slavonia became part of the Ottoman Empire. In the 17th century the Turkish advance ended and, by 1699, the Habsburgs had secured all of modern Croatia, except for the Venetian territories of Dalmatia and Istria and the city-state of Ragusa (Dubrovnik). The Habsburg authorities settled Serbs on the borderlands with the Ottomans, in areas of Croatia hence known as the Krajina. Although part of the Habsburgs' Hungarian patrimony, Croatia, like the rest of the Empire, was more under Austrian influence during the 18th century. Between 1809 and 1813 the Croatian coast and immediate hinterland was united with Dalmatia, Istria, Ragusa and neighbouring territories to the north in French-ruled Illyria, a province created by the French Emperor, Napoleon I Bonaparte. Slavonia remained in the Austrian Empire (the Habsburg Emperor had taken the imperial title for Austria and the Holy Roman Empire had been dissolved).

The Habsburg territories were restored at the 1815 Congress of Vienna, which also bestowed Dalmatia and Istria on Austria. As a consequence of the Hungarian revolution of 1848–49 Croatia and Slavonia were made Austrian crownlands. In 1868, after the Habsburg Empire had become the 'Dual Monarchy' of Austria-Hungary under the *Ausgleich* or Compromise of the previous year, Croatia and Slavonia were restored to the Hungarian Crown. Croatia gained its autonomy and was formally joined with Slavonia in 1881. However, the central Hungarian authorities pursued policies of 'magyarization', particularly after 1875. Together with the anti-Serbian commercial practices of the Habsburgs, from 1904, this transformed traditional Croat–Serb rivalries into Southern Slav ('Yugoslav') solidarity. During the First World War representatives of the Croats met with delegates of the other Southern Slavic peoples and, in the Corfu Declaration, announced their intention to form a unitary, democratic state under the Serbian monarchy. In October 1918 the Habsburg Danubian Monarchy collapsed and the Southern Slav territories declared themselves a republic, announced their separation from the Austro-Hungarian Empire and, on 4 December, were proclaimed to be united with Serbia and Montenegro in the new Kingdom of Serbs, Croats and Slovenes.

YUGOSLAVIA

The new Kingdom, however, was dominated by the Serbs, and the Croats, the second most populous ethnic group, sought a greater share of power. They led the dissatisfaction of the non-Serb peoples against the regime. The increasing unrest within the Kingdom, symptoms of which included the meeting of a separatist assembly in Zagreb in 1928, led King Aleksandar I to impose a royal dictatorship in 1929, when the country was formally named Yugoslavia. In 1934 Aleksandar was assassinated, while in France, by Croatian extremists. At the same time the Fascist Ustaša (Rebel) movement was gaining support among the discontented Croat peasantry. They were not placated by the inclusion of Croats in the Government, in 1939. When the Germans and Italians invaded, in 1941, many Croats welcomed their support for the establishment of an Independent State of Croatia, on 9 April.

The new Croatian state invited an Italian duke, Aimone of Spoleto, to be the nominal sovereign, but government was conducted by the leader of the Ustaša, the 'Poglavnik' Ante Pavelić. His territory included most of Bosnia and Herzegovina and parts of Serbia, as well as the modern country (Istria was annexed to Italy, which also continued to hold the coastal enclave of Zara, or Zadar, until 1947). The Ustaša regime was notorious for its policies towards its minorities: a vast number of Jews, Serbs, Roma (Gypsies) and the politically 'unreliable' were murdered in extermination camps. At the same time a vicious civil war was being waged against the resistance forces, particularly the Partisans (National Liberation Army) of Tito (Josip Broz). By 1943 Tito's forces were able to proclaim a provisional government in areas under their control and the Fascist regime was beginning to lose control. The Ustaša state collapsed in 1944 and Croatia was restored to Yugoslavia as one unit of a federal Communist republic.

The legacy of the Ustaša regime was the official hostility of the Communists to any expression of Croatian nationalism. It was equated with Fascism. At the same time the development of the tourist industry along Croatia's Dalmatian coast added to the wealth of the Republic, and the Croatians resented their effective subsidy of the poorer parts of Yugoslavia, which was considered to be Serb-dominated. However, during the 1960s, there was an increase of nationalism in Croatia. This 'mass movement' (*Maspok*), which was led by organizations such as the ostensibly cultural association, Matica Hrvatska, was supported by members of the ruling League of Communists, as well as by non-Communists. The movement encouraged the local Communist leadership, which was associated with the reform wing of the Party, to defy central policy in certain areas. In December 1971 Tito committed himself to opposing the tendency: the Croatian Communist leadership was obliged to resign and they, and others prominent in the *Maspok*, were arrested. A purge of the League of Communists of Croatia followed. During 1972 many people were charged with crimes 'against the People and the State', some 427 being convicted in Croatia that year. The central authorities also moved against liberals in other Republics, notably Serbia, thus avoiding the charge of being anti-Croat. In 1974, however, Tito introduced a new Constitution, which enshrined the federal (almost confederal) and collective nature of the Yugoslav state. The Constitution was designed to placate nationalist sentiments, particularly in Croatia, and also to restrain those tendencies within a unifying framework. Any manifestations of Croatian nationalism, however, continued to be prosecuted, even after the death of Tito, in 1980.

THE ROAD TO INDEPENDENCE

An added impetus to Croatian nationalism and the perception that the Yugoslav federation was Serb-dominated, was that the League of Communists of Croatia contained a high proportion of Serbs. Any reaction against the Communists was readily associated with Croatian nationalism. When Communist power began to decline, from 1989 particularly, Croatian nationalism re-emerged as a significant force. Dissidents of the 1970s and 1980s were the main beneficiaries. Dr Franjo Tudjman, for example, an historian and former Partisan general, had been imprisoned in 1972 and 1981. In 1990 he formed the Croatian Democratic Union (CDU—Hrvatska Demokratska Zajednica). This rapidly became a mass party and the main challenger to the ruling Party, which had changed its name to the League of Communists of Croatia-Party of Democratic Reform (LCC-PDR). The Communists introduced a 'first-past-the-post' voting system (the candidate with more votes than any other single candidate won the constituency seat—to the main Socio-Political Chamber) for the multi-party elections to the republican legislature, in April 1990. Tudjman campaigned as a nationalist, causing controversy by advocating a 'Greater Croatia' (that is, including Bosnia and Herzegovina) and complaining of Serb domination, although he did promise the Croatian Serbs cultural autonomy. This rhetoric caused considerable anxiety among the Serbs, however, and there were demonstrations protesting against the CDU and accusations of reviving the Ustaša. On 18 March

1990 there was an assassination attempt made against Tudjman, which heightened ethnic tensions.

In the elections to the tricameral republican Assembly (Sabor), which took place in two rounds, on 24 April and 6–7 May 1990, the CDU gained from the voting system, taking a majority of the seats, despite only winning some 42% of the votes cast in the second round (in both the Socio-Political Chamber and the Chamber of Municipalities). In the Socio-Political Chamber the CDU gained 54 of the 80 seats; in the Chamber of Municipalities the CDU gained 68 of the 115 seats filled; in the Chamber of Associated Labour the CDU gained 83 of the 156 seats filled. Of the 351 seats of all three chambers of the Sabor (a maximum of 356 could have been filled), the CDU won 205. The next-largest party was the LCC-PDR, with a total of 73 seats. Both the leading parties won further seats in alliance with other parties. Tudjman was elected President of Croatia, but he attempted to allay Serb fears by offering the vice-presidency of the Sabor to Dr Jovan Rasković, the leader of the Serbian Democratic Party (SDP). Rasković eventually refused the post, but another Serb was appointed to it.

Serb-dominated areas were alienated by Tudjman's Croat nationalism and the Republic's adoption of a new flag (the traditional Croatian chequerboard symbol was used; although subtly altered, to the Serbs this remained balefully like the Ustaša emblem) and new police uniforms. The Serb stronghold of Knin, in the eastern hinterland of that arm of Croatia which lay along the coast, was the centre of resistance and led the moves towards claiming increased autonomy (for details, see below). By December Serb areas were issuing declarations of autonomy, the extent of which expanded as Croatia itself moved further from acceptance of the federal Yugoslav state. By October 1991 there were three 'Serbian Autonomous Regions' (SARs) in Croatia: Krajina, with its headquarters in Knin; Slavonia, Baranja and Western Srem; and Western Slavonia, most of which the Croats held. The three regions stated their determination to remain in a federal Yugoslavia or in a Greater Serbian state. In October the SARs rejected the Croatian declaration of independence and claimed representation on the federal State Presidency and at the peace conference organized by the European Community (EC—known as the European Union from November 1993).

The new Croatian Government was intent on the dismantling of the structures of Communist power. In August 1990 the Socialist Republic of Croatia became the Republic of Croatia. In the same month the Sabor voted to dismiss the sitting republican member of the federal State Presidency and replace him with Stjepan ('Stipe') Mesić, then President of the Government (Premier) of Croatia. His appointment was confirmed in October. On 21 December the Sabor enacted a new republican Constitution, which declared Croatia's sovereignty, its authority over its own armed forces and its right to secede from the federation. Tensions increased when, in January 1991, the federal State Presidency ordered the disarming of all paramilitary groups and the Croatian authorities refused to comply. The Croatian Minister of Defence was then indicted on a charge of plotting armed rebellion, but the Croatian Government refused to arrest him and boycotted negotiations on the future of the federation. On 21 February the Sabor resolved that republican legislation took precedence over federal legislation. The following month the SAR of Krajina announced its unilateral secession from the Republic; the formation of a 'Krajina Assembly' was declared on 30 April 1991. The Assembly appointed a 'Government' in May, headed by Milan Babić.

In the negotiations about the future of Yugoslavia, Croatia favoured a looser federation of sovereign states and, like Slovenia, warned that it intended to end its membership of the federation by mid-1991 if no agreement was forthcoming. In April 1991 the Croatian National Guard was formed, replacing the Territorial Defence Force, which had been under the jurisdiction of the Jugoslavenska Narodna Armija (JNA—Yugoslav People's Army). On 19 May some 94% of the votes cast in a referendum in Croatia (84% of the registered electorate voted) favoured the Republic becoming a sovereign entity, possibly within a confederal Yugoslavia (the referendum was largely boycotted by the Serb population) and 92% rejected a federal Yugoslavia. The refusal of Serbia and its allies to endorse the election of Stipe Mesić as President of the federal State Presidency had merely added to Croat anxieties. Constitutional proposals made by the Presidencies of Bosnia and Herzegovina and Macedonia did not achieve general acceptance and, on 26 June, Croatia and Slovenia declared their independence and the beginning of their process of 'dissociation' from the federation.

The JNA's first actions against the recalcitrant Republics took place in Slovenia, but the EC soon mediated a cease-fire and the JNA began its withdrawal from that Republic. The federal and Serbian authorities were, however, more anxious to maintain their influence in Croatia, where a significant Serb minority feared for itself under an independent, Croat-dominated state. During July 1991, despite the continuing EC peace efforts and the Serbian agreement to the election of Mesić as President of the Yugoslav State Presidency, civil war effectively began in Croatia. A war cabinet or state council was set up in the Republic, chaired by Josip Manolić, while his deputy, Franjo Gregurić, replaced him as Premier. On 25 September the UN placed an embargo on arms supplies to the territories of the former Yugoslavia. Three days later the International Red Cross withdrew from Croatian territory, stating that it was unable to continue its work in the existing conditions.

The initial successes of the JNA had been checked, during August and September, when the Croatians adopted the tactics of besieging army and naval bases (this strategy had proved successful in Slovenia). The JNA also encountered problems of desertion and organization, particularly because of its multi-ethnic character (although it was Serb-dominated). In October, however, it was able to mount a counter-offensive and to extend its operations beyond the neighbourhood of the military bases and the main battle-fields of Slavonia, and, by November, supported by Serb irregulars, it had secured about one-third of Croatian territory.

In October 1991, the city of Dubrovnik, which contained neither a JNA barracks nor a significant Serb minority (6.7% in 1991), came under attack. The threat to this medieval city, a UNESCO-listed World Heritage site, caused international consternation, but this did not abate the JNA siege, which did not end until May 1992. Serb and JNA attacks were also concentrated, during the last few months of 1991, on the port of Zadar, in central Dalmatia, to the west of Knin. The main theatre of war, however, remained in Slavonia, eastern Croatia (for details of the war, see Introductory Essay p. 90). There was conflict even in areas without a Serb majority, again leading to accusations that the JNA was attempting to secure the borders of a Greater Serbian state. Among the main obstacles to this ambition of linking the Krajina territories to Serbia proper were the eastern Slavonian cities of Osijek, capital of the region, Vinkovci and Vukovar. After the surrender of Vukovar, following a period of fierce resistance by the Croatians, Western nations agreed that they would be prepared to send naval detachments to ensure the safe implementation of the work of the International Red Cross and both Croatia and Serbia indicated readiness to accept a UN peace-keeping force. On 15 December, the UN Security Council resolved to send observers to Yugoslavia and a small team of civilian and military personnel to prepare for a possible peace-keeping force.

President Tudjman's administration was under domestic as well as military pressure. He was criticized for indecisiveness and for his dependence on the advice of former exiles and their unfulfilled hopes of Western military support. On 1 August 1991 Tudjman appointed a coalition Government of Democratic Unity, which was confirmed by the Sabor on 3 August. Nearly all the parties in the legislature participated, although the CDU remained the dominant partner. The SDP was not involved. The new Government continued to seek international recognition and to pursue negotiations at The Hague (Netherlands) peace conference, even after the declaration of independence, in October, following the expiry of the EC-mediated moratorium on the process of dissociation. The conference in The Hague was dissolved on 8 November, although its chairman, Lord Carrington (a former British foreign minister), continued his efforts to secure peace. In November, in accordance with the principles formulated at The Hague, the Sabor was ready to enact legislation guaranteeing minority rights, to allay the anxieties of the Serbs. However, relations between Serbs and Croats were deteriorating in the wake of reports of atrocities on both sides. The CDU was under pressure from its own right wing and more extreme groups. One of the most prominent of the nationalist parties was the Croatian Party of Rights (CPR—Hrvatska Stranka Prava). Its armed wing, the Croatian Defence Association (CDA—Hrvatska Obranje Stranka), was active in the fighting and was implicated in other anti-Serb incidents. Tudjman's ban on political activity in the armed forces was believed to be directed at the CDA, which denied accusations that it was plotting a coup. On 22 November the leader of the CPR, Dobroslav Paraga, was arrested and accused of co-operating with Croatia's enemies.

In spite of these domestic and military pressures the Croatian Government continued the process of dissociation. It proposed a new currency (kruna or crown) and, for an interim period, introduced a Croatian dinar, in December 1991. On 19 November 1991 the Supreme Council ordered all Croatians to vacate any federal offices they held and to place their services at the disposal of the Croatian state. On 5 December Mesić, Yugoslavia's nominal head of state, resigned and, on 19 December, so did Ante Marković, the federal prime minister. On 15 January 1992 the EC initiated general international recognition of Croatia.

DOMESTIC POLITICS AFTER INDEPENDENCE

In April 1992 a major government reorganization was occasioned by the resignations of two ministers, over a dispute concerning references to Yugoslavia in school textbooks. In May Bosilijko Misetić, the Minister of Justice and Administration and a member of the Croatian People's Party (CPP), resigned from his post in protest at the adoption of controversial legislation granting special status to Serbs in areas where they formed an absolute majority. A few days later the CPP withdrew its support from the coalition.

Tudjman and his party were accused of pursuing a campaign to suppress political dissent, particularly by using the tactic of threatening legal action against prominent journalists and members of the opposition. In mid-1992 the CDU attempted to take control of *Slobodna Dalmacija*, a leading newspaper based in Split, and publication of an opposition periodical, *Danas* was temporarily banned. At the beginning of October the authorities made a request to the Constitutional Court of Croatia to ban the CPR and the SDP, and later that month three CPR members (including the party leader, Paraga) were charged, following an official search of the party's headquarters in September. (Paraga was cleared of any wrongdoing in November 1993.) In December the staff of *Slobodna Dalmacija* staged a 24-hour strike in protest at state interference, following the imposition of a pro-government board of management. By mid-1993 virtually all independent newspapers and the Croatian television and radio services were effectively under government control. Even in January 1994 the editor of one of the few remaining independent publications was conscripted into military service, despite political protest.

On 2 August 1992 presidential and legislative elections were held in Croatia. These were the first elections to be held under the new Constitution (promulgated in December 1990), which provided for a bicameral legislature composed of a Chamber of Representatives and a Chamber of Municipalities. The August elections were for the Chamber of Representatives. Elections to the Chamber of Municipalities were postponed, pending the adoption of legislation on the redistribution of municipalities. The franchise was extensive because, although many ethnic Croats living in Serb areas could not vote (having been unable to claim their Croatian nationality), voting rights were afforded to Croats in Bosnia and Herzegovina and to anyone who had a Croatian parent or who intended to apply for Croatian citizenship. The elections were contested by eight presidential candidates and 37 political parties. President Tudjman was re-elected, with 56% of the votes cast, twice that of his nearest rival, Dražen Budisa of the Croatian Social-Liberal Party (CSLP—22%), while the ruling CDU obtained 85 of the 138 seats in the new Chamber of Representatives. The new Government, under the premiership of Hrvoje Šarinić (replacing Franjo Gregurić), was appointed one week after the elections and formally took office on 8 September.

In late November 1992 the Chamber of Representatives approved legislation providing for the internal reorganization of Croatia, for electoral purposes, into 21 counties, 420 municipalities and 61 towns. At the beginning of January 1993 proportional representation was introduced to replace the former plurality (first-past-the-post) electoral system. Elections to the Chamber of Municipalities were held on 7 February 1993. The CDU won 37 of the 67 seats, while the CSLP and its allies won 16, the Croatian Farmers' Party five, the Istrian Democratic Assembly three and the Social Democratic Party—Party of Democratic Reform of Croatia (SDP—PDRC) and the CPP gained one seat each. The CPR boycotted the elections, in protest at the alleged lack of impartial monitoring of the poll.

On 29 March 1993 the Croatian Government, led by Hrvoje Sarinić, resigned. The administration had come under increasing pressure to step down following a series of financial scandals and a serious deterioration in economic conditions. On 12 March 420,000 members of three trade-union confederations and several independent unions had participated in a four-hour 'warning' strike, in protest at the decline in standard of living in the country. Sarinić was replaced as Prime Minister by Nikica Valenté. However, dissatisfaction did not abate and, during 1993, Tudjman was subject to increasing criticism from the opposition, and even from members of his own party. On 5 July he stated that he was considering an exchange of territory with the Bosnian Serbs, provoking considerable controversy within Croatia. On 27 July the leaders of the 15 major political parties met to discuss the need to reverse certain government policies, in particular with regard to Bosnia and

Herzegovina. Many of them believed that continuing support of the partition of the beleaguered Republic might set a precedent for the division of Croatia on ethnic grounds. Many also feared the effects of possible international sanctions on the Croatian economy. However, in spite of growing opposition to his policies, on 16 October 1993 the CDU re-elected Tudjman as their leader.

FOREIGN RELATIONS

In January 1992 Croatia was officially recognized by the EC and was admitted to the UN in May. By September 84 states had acknowledged the country's independence. Following international recognition, Croatia enjoyed friendly relations with its neighbour, Slovenia. In October 1992 the Presidents of the two states signed agreements on diplomatic and economic relations. At this time, however, Croatia was increasingly criticized by the international community for its involvement in the conflict in Bosnia and Herzegovina. In October 1992 Lord Owen, the British co-Chairman of the EC/UN peace negotiations, threatened EC sanctions against Croatia if it did not withdraw its troops from Bosnia and Herzegovina. Croatia was being accused of supporting the 'Croatian Union of Herzeg-Bosna' (a self-styled Croat state, which proclaimed its independence on 24 October). Lord Owen also accused the Croats of 'ethnic cleansing' (the expulsion of one ethnic group by another in an attempt to create a homogeneous population) in Bosnia and Herzegovina.

During 1993 the Croatian administrations continued to attract criticism from the international community. On 19 July the EC again threatened sanctions against Croatia if it continued to make no attempt to stop Croat attacks in Bosnia and Herzegovina. President Tudjman's continued support of a plan to partition Bosnia and Herzegovina with Serbia served, in particular, to estrange Germany and Austria. In October the UN special war-crimes investigator Tadeusz Mazowiecki, the former Polish premier, accused the Croatian army of committing atrocities against Serb civilians in Krajina. He demanded that the Croatian Government investigate the alleged crimes.

ISTRIA

Istria is a peninsula in the north-west of Croatia, on the border with Slovenia. Its history is distinct from that of Croatia; the region was under Venetian rule until 1797, when it became part of Austria-Hungary. In 1919 western Istria, including the city of Trieste, came under Italian jurisdiction, while the Kingdom of Serbs, Croats and Slovenes assumed control of the eastern part. In 1954 Istria was partitioned again, Trieste being annexed to Italy and the main part of the territory to Yugoslavia. Most of Yugoslav Istria was incorporated into Croatia, although Slovenia gained a coastline in northern Istria. This arrangement was confirmed in 1975, by the Osimo Agreement between Italy and Yugoslavia. In the early 1990s it was a relatively prosperous area, earning much of its revenue from tourism and cross-border trade. Of its population of some 250,000 (in 1993), almost 30,000 were Italian and they were increasingly demanding the revision of the Osimo Agreement. The Istrian Italians claimed that the Agreement had become invalid, following the disintegration of the old Yugoslav federation.

In the local elections held on 7 February 1993, the Istrian Democratic Assembly (IDA—Istarski Demokratski Sabor), a party advocating autonomy for the region of Istria, won 72% of the votes cast. The IDA claimed that central government in Zagreb was hindering Istria's political and economic development and declared that the region should be allowed to assert its own control over the profits derived from tourism and trade. In 1993 it proposed that Istria become a trans-border region comprising the Croatian and Slovenian areas of the peninsula and the Italian town of Muggia. The Croatian Government, however, strongly opposed regional autonomy for Istria, believing it would destabilize Croatia and encourage the reconstitution of a Yugoslav federation. President Tudjman's intransigence over the issue prompted the leader of the IDA, Ivan Jakovečević, to accuse the Croatian administration of exercising totalitarian rule. A few days later, on 27 July, it was reported that the Istrian county administration had refuse to implement a series of proposed federal laws formulated by the central Government. At the beginning of 1994 it was still unclear how this direct confrontation, on the part of the IDA with the Tudjman administration, would be resolved.

THE SERBS IN CROATIA

In December 1991 a 'Republic of Serbian Krajina' (RSK) was proclaimed in Croatia, which the Croatian Government refused to recognize. In declaring their 'Republic', the Serbs in Croatia were claiming land they had inhabited since the 17th century, when the Habsburg authorities settled Serbs on the borderlands ('Krajina') with the Ottoman Empire. The Croatian Serbs' struggle for autonomy began in July 1990 with the formation of a 'Serb National Council', based in Knin (the chief town of the Krajina area). This group organized a referendum on autonomy for the Croatian Serbs, which was banned by the Croatian authorities. Amid virtual insurrection in some areas, the referendum was held between 19 August and 2 September. The results of the referendum, announced on 1 October, overwhelmingly endorsed the move for an ill-defined autonomy.

The RSK was formed by the union of three SARs: Krajina; Western Slavonia; and Slavonia, Baranja and Western Srem. The SAR of Krajina declared its autonomy on 1 October 1990 and its separation from Croatia on 16 March 1991. There was an overwhelming Serb majority in the district of Eastern Dalmatia and Lika, but in the northern areas of Krajina there were significant Croat minorities. In the SAR of Western Slavonia there was a Serb majority, but they only accounted for some 38% of the population, compared to the 36% of Croats, in 1991. This area, which declared its autonomy in August 1991, was physically isolated from other Serb-dominated areas, largely occupied by Croatian forces and declared united with Krajina in December 1991. The Serbs retained control of Okucani. In the SAR of Slavonia, Baranja and Western Srem, which declared its autonomy in August 1991 and its union with the Krajina in October, there were no districts in which the Serbs constituted an overall majority. According to the census of 1991, the largest proportion of Serbs was in Pakrac, where they accounted for 46% of the population, compared to the 36% of Croats. Baranja was in the north-east of the Republic of Croatia, bordering on Hungary and Vojvodina. Some of Baranja lay in Hungary, and the whole area had, historically, been administered as the Hungarian province of Serbian Vojvodina. In 1918 Yugoslav Baranja declared itself to be part of Serbia, and, in 1920, it was formally ceded to the new state, together with Vojvodina. Baranja became part of Croatia in 1945, partly on ethnic considerations and partly as compensation for the loss of Eastern Syrmia (Srem). In 1991 Baranja (Beli Manastir) had a Croat majority. In Western Srem there was an overall Croat majority in 1991, which was a likely explanation for the ferocity of the fighting in this area (Srem includes Vukovar and Vinkovci, and claims Osijek), during the civil war.

A UN-sponsored unconditional cease-fire was signed by the Croatian National Guard and the JNA on 2 January

1992. In late February a 14,000-strong United Nations Protection Force in Yugoslavia (UNPROFOR) was entrusted with ensuring the withdrawal of the JNA from Croatia. In February 1992 UNPROFOR forces were entrusted with the complete demilitarization of three Serb-held enclaves in the RSK (Eastern Slavonia, Western Slavonia and Krajina), which were designated UN Protected Areas (UNPAs). In the same month UNPROFOR's mandate in Croatia was extended to cover the so-called 'pink zones' (areas occupied by JNA troops and with majority Serb populations, but situated outside the official UNPAs).

In mid-May 1992 the JNA began to withdraw from Croatia, in accordance with the UN demilitarization of Serb areas, and, on 28 May, the 238-day siege of Dubrovnik ended. Sporadic shelling continued, however, and UNPROFOR proved unable to prevent the expulsion of more than 1,000 non-Serbs by Serb forces in Eastern Slavonia and had only limited success in its enforcement of the demilitarization of the UNPAs. In June Croatian forces attacked several Serb areas, including Knin, the capital of the RSK. This development provoked a UN Security Council resolution, which required the Croats to withdraw to the positions they had held prior to 21 June and to refrain from entering Serb areas. During the London Conference, arranged by the EC and the UN in the United Kingdom, agreement on economic co-operation was reached between representatives of the Croatian Government and of Krajina. At the end of September the leaders of Croatia and the Federal Republic of Yugoslavia (FRY—Serbia and Montenegro) agreed to work towards a normalization of relations between their respective countries.

In mid-January 1993 Western intelligence reports indicated that Croatian aircraft were largely to blame for breaches of the ban on military flights over Bosnia and Herzegovina, which had been imposed by the UN Security Council in October 1992. On 22 January 1993 Croatian troops crossed the UN peace-keeping lines and again attacked Serb-held Krajina, in an attempt to restore to Croatian control the Maslenica bridge (a vital communications link between northern Croatia and the Dalmatian coast), Zemunik airport and the Peruca hydroelectric plant. The Serb forces in Krajina reclaimed weapons that they had earlier surrendered to UNPROFOR in order to defend themselves. The UN responded by ordering Croatia to withdraw its troops and the Serb forces to return their weapons. Hostilities continued, however, until 6 April, when a UN-brokered agreement provided for the reconstruction and reopening of the three strategic sites under the supervision of UNPROFOR troops. The Croats, however, undertook the reconstruction of the Maslenica bridge themselves, and the bridge was reopened by President Tudjman on 18 July. The Serbs resented the continued presence of Croatian troops in the area and, on 14 July, they began to bombard the Karlovac and Zemunik areas. On 15 and 16 July the UN successfully negotiated the Erdut Agreement between the leaders of Croatia and Serbia. In return for the withdrawal of Croatian forces from Maslenica (which would then be returned to UNPROFOR) and the return of three captured villages to the Serbs, President Milošević of Serbia agreed to use his influence to dissuade Serb troops from shelling the bridge. The deadline for the Croatian withdrawal was set for 31 July. The Croatian Government claimed that Serb weaponry had not been placed under UNPROFOR control and it allowed the deadline to expire. The Serbs resumed their shelling of the bridge. In early August Croatian forces attacked the Gospić area, in retaliation for the Serb bombardment of Maslenica, and, on 13 August, in a letter to the UN Secretary-General, Dr Boutros Boutros-Ghali, the Croatian Minister of Foreign Affairs, Mate Granić declared the Erdut Agreement redundant.

Although under UNPROFOR's original mandate UN troops were entrusted with the task of ensuring the safe return of all refugees to their homes in the UNPAs and the 'pink zones', by August 1993 Croatia was still responsible for 253,000 refugees from these areas. In the same month, 278,000 Croats from Bosnia and Herzegovina were seeking refuge in Croatia. In September, according to official figures, Croatia was accommodating 524,000 refugees.

In September 1993, in response to Croatian attacks on the RSK, a full-scale mobilization was carried out among Serbs in the regions of Slavonia, Baranja and Western Srem. Serb–Croat hostilities extended to Zagreb in mid-September. By this time most of the JNA had withdrawn from Croatia and some Serb artillery had been placed under UN control, but UNPROFOR forces were not yet in effective control of Croatian borders. The Serbs still occupied approximately 30% of the territory of Croatia. On 20 September Boutros Boutros-Ghali recommended that the UNPROFOR mandate in the former Yugoslavia be extended for a further six months. (Since early 1992 12,600 foreign troops had been stationed in Croatia.) The Croatian Council of Defence and National Security, which was chaired by the President, rejected the recommendation, arguing that it failed to address certain vital issues. On 24 September a commission for relations with UNPROFOR was established in Croatia, although two days later several anti-UNPROFOR demonstrations took place across the country. On 4 October the UN Security Council voted unanimously to extend UNPROFOR's mandate. The extension was provided for by UN Resolution 871, which also required the return of all 'pink zones' to Croatian sovereignty, the restoration of all infrastructure and communications links of these regions with the rest of Croatia and the disarmament of Serb paramilitary units. It also empowered UNPROFOR forces to act in self-defence while carrying out their mandate. The Croatians accepted the Resolution. However, on 12 October the Serbs' Assembly, meeting in Beli Manastir, voted to reject it and resolved to mobilize all conscripts. At the same session a defence council was formed to investigate charges of Croat aggression against civilians in Krajina.

On 12 December 1993 parliamentary and presidential elections took place in the RSK. Some 350 candidates from 12 parties contested 84 parliamentary seats. Seven presidential candidates competed, of whom three were independent. The electorate was estimated at 250,000, of which approximately 233,000 participated in the elections. Owing to alleged electoral irregularities, the results were annulled in the counties of Benkovać and Knin and voting was repeated in these areas on 26 December. According to official results, the Serbian Democratic Party of Krajina won 31 seats (representing 36.9% of votes cast). The Serbian Radical Party won 16 seats, while the Serbian Democratic Party of All Serb Lands won 15. In the presidential elections, the Serbian Democratic Party's candidate, Milan Babić, won 49.3% of votes cast, while 25.9% of the electorate voted for Milan Martić, an independent candidate backed by the Serbian Government—a result which suggested that Serbian President Slobodan Milošević's influence among the Serbs of the RSK was weakening. However, there were allegations of voting irregularities and, in a second round (because no candidate had won an overall majority), which was contested by Babić and Martić on 23 January 1994, the latter was elected President of the RSK. Babić, as leader of the largest party, was likely to be included in a new Government.

By April 1994 there seemed more likelihood of a solution to the conflict in Croatia. This followed a series of negotiations between representatives of the RSK and Croatian administrations in Oslo (Norway) at the beginning of November 1993, new peace proposals from the European Union (formerly the EC) and from President Tudjman, and the progress of the peace process in neighbouring Bosnia and Herzegovina. On 30 March 1994, at the Russian embassy in Zagreb, Croatian Government and RSK representatives signed a cease-fire agreement, which came into effect on 4 April. The agreement provided for border territories to be under the control of UN forces and civilian police, while negotiations about a more lasting solution continued.

The Economy

Croatia was one of the richer Republics of Yugoslavia, producing some 25% of the country's gross national product (GNP) at the end of the 1980s, according to Western estimates. It was rich in mineral resources, and highly dependent on mining, quarrying and manufacturing. Tourism was also an important industry. In 1991, according to the Food and Agriculture Organization (FAO) of the UN, some 26% of the total area of Croatia was cultivated. However, it is likely that the civil conflict in Croatia, which began in 1991, destroyed much of the country's arable land.

In 1990 certain sectors of the Croatian economy were beginning to suffer. The Government claimed this was an inevitable consequence of privatization and the transition to a market-orientated economy, but the opposition accused it of lacking a coherent economic policy and providing insufficient social protection. The ethnic tensions and subsequent civil conflict in Croatia in the early 1990s resulted in a steep and rapid economic decline. Gross domestic product (GDP) was estimated to have fallen from US $13,500m. in 1990 to around $7,500m. in 1992.

The principal crops in Croatia were maize, sugar beet and wheat. Agricultural production was severely affected by the armed hostilities in Croatia: in 1992, according to the Food and Agriculture Organization (FAO) of the UN, total maize production was 1,538 metric tons, compared to 2,001 metric tons in 1991. A drought in Slavonia in the summer of 1992 reduced crop yields of maize, soya beans and sugar beet by 40% and the wheat harvest was about 47% smaller than in previous years.

The industrial sector (including mining, manufacturing and quarrying) employed just under one-third of the working population in 1992. The principal branches of the manufacturing sector were food products, light industry, fuel and construction materials. In 1991 industrial production was already falling, and, by the beginning of 1992, about 37% of Croatia's production facilities had either been destroyed or were occupied by Serb forces.

In 1991, according to official figures, total electrical energy production amounted to 8,833m. kWh—an increase of 87m. kWh since 1990. The country remained dependent on imported fuel, which accounted for some 10% of total imports in 1992.

The Croatian economy was highly dependent on tourism. However, from mid-1991 the industry was virtually eliminated by the onset of civil conflict. Tourism officials estimated, in July 1991, that losses to the Republic could total $1,200m. The civil war also caused some lasting physical damage to the environment and to the tourist infrastructure, with popular tourist destinations, such as Dubrovnik, coming under heavy bombardment and hotels suffering destruction and despoliation.

In the first nine months of 1993 foreign trade was estimated to have reached a total value of $6,500m., a decrease of 4.2% compared to the same period in 1992. Of this total, exports were estimated at approximately $3,000m.

At the beginning of 1992 the total number of unemployed persons was estimated to have reached 267,000, (excluding refugees), but by August it had risen to about 500,000. In mid-1992 approximately 15% of housing stock was destroyed and infrastructural damage caused by the war was estimated at $22,000m. The current annual inflation rate was 1,560%.

Croatia was admitted to the International Monetary Fund in January 1993 and became a member of the European Bank for Reconstruction and Development in April the same year.

In spite of a slight improvement in Croatia's economic situation in 1992, owing to the increase in foreign trade, the renewal of hostilities in January 1993, which continued throughout the year, had a drastic effect on the economy. In November 1993 the Croatian Government was forced to adopt a series of urgent measures, including the devaluation of the dinar, to protect the economy against hyperinflation.

Statistical Survey

Source (unless otherwise stated): Central Bureau of Statistics of the Republic of Croatia, 41000 Zagreb, Ilica 3; tel. (41) 454422; telex 21130; fax (41) 429413.

Area and Population

AREA, POPULATION AND DENSITY

Area (sq km)	56,538*
Population (census results)	
31 March 1981	
Males	2,226,890
Females	2,374,579
Total	4,601,469
31 March 1991	4,784,265†
Density (per sq km) at 31 March 1991	84.6

* 21,829 sq miles.

† Males 2,319,000; Females 2,465,000; Total 4,784,000.

POPULATION BY ETHNIC GROUP
(census of 31 March 1991)

	Number ('000)	%
Croat	3,736.4	78.1
Serb	581.7	12.2
Muslim	43.5	0.9
Slovene	22.4	0.5
Hungarian	22.4	0.5
Italian	21.3	0.4
Czech	13.1	0.3
Albanian	12.0	0.3
Montenegrin	9.7	0.2
Gypsy	6.7	0.1
Macedonian	6.3	0.1
Slovak	5.6	0.1
Others*	303.3	6.3
Total	4,784.3	100.0

* Including (in '000) persons who declared themselves to be Yugoslav (106.0), persons with a regional affiliation (45.5), persons of unknown nationality (62.9) and persons who refused to reply (73.4).

PRINCIPAL TOWNS
(population at 1991 census)

Zagreb (capital)	706,770	Vukovar	44,639
Split	189,388	Varaždin	41,846
Rijeka	167,964	Šibenik	41,012
Osijek	104,761	Vincovci	35,347
Zadar	76,343	Servete	35,337
Pula	62,378	Velika Gorica	31,614
Karlovac	59,999	Bjelovar	26,926
Slavonski Brod	55,683	Koprivnica	24,238
Dubrovnik	49,728	Požega	21,046
Sisak	45,792	Djakovo	20,317

BIRTHS, MARRIAGES AND DEATHS

	Registered live births		Registered marriages		Registered deaths	
	Number	Rate (per 1,000)	Number	Rate (per 1,000)	Number	Rate (per 1,000)
1984	64,909	14.0	32,161	6.9	54,169	11.7
1985	62,665	13.5	30,953	6.6	52,067	11.2
1986	60,226	12.9	30,495	6.5	51,740	11.1
1987	59,209	12.7	31,395	6.7	53,080	11.4
1988	58,525	12.5	29,719	6.3	52,686	11.3
1989	55,651	11.9	28,938	6.2	52,569	11.2
1990	55,409	11.6	27,924	5.9	52,192	10.9
1991	51,829	10.8	n.a.	n.a.	54,832	11.4

EMPLOYMENT IN THE PUBLIC SECTOR ('000)

	1990	1991	1992
Mining and industry	561	462	398
Agriculture and fisheries	54	48	43
Forestry	15	13	12
Water management	6	6	5
Construction	119	99	75
Transport and communications	125	110	96
Trade	160	142	124
Hotels, restaurants and tourism	78	61	52
Crafts and trade	34	28	24
Housing, utilities and public services	31	28	24
Financial and other services	61	56	50
Education, culture and the arts	99	94	88
Health care and social services	108	102	97
Government bodies and agencies, social and political organizations	59	54	49
Total	1,510	1,303	1,137

Agriculture

PRINCIPAL CROPS ('000 metric tons)

	1990	1991	1992
Wheat	1,602	1,496	658
Barley	197	186	107
Maize	1,950	2,001	1,538
Rye	16	14	6
Oats	62	54	45
Potatoes	609	658	480
Dry beans	18	19†	16*
Dry peas	8	10	7
Soybeans (Soya beans)	55	56	46
Sunflower seed	53	46	40
Rapeseed	33	23	24
Cabbages	104	108	63
Tomatoes	55	49	35
Cucumbers and gherkins	20	26	16
Green chillies and peppers	23	23*	18*
Onions (dry)	40	38	29
Garlic	12	11	7
Watermelons	21	18	8
Grapes	398	427	380
Sugar beet	1,206	1,244	525
Apples	70	66	62
Pears	14	16	9
Peaches and nectarines	11	10	6
Plums	31	37	62
Tobacco (leaves)	12	10	12

* FAO estimate(s). † Unofficial figure(s).

Source: FAO, *Production Yearbook*.

LIVESTOCK ('000 head)

	1990	1991	1992
Horses	39	37	27
Asses	14	14*	13
Cattle	829	757	590
Pigs	1,573	1,620	1,183
Sheep	751	753	539
Goats	174	136	114
Chickens†	15,000	15,000	13,000

* FAO estimate(s). † Unofficial figure(s).

Source: FAO, *Production Yearbook*.

LIVESTOCK PRODUCTS (metric tons)

	1990	1991	1992
Beef and veal	76,000	52,000	50,000*
Mutton and lamb	7,000	3,000	3,000*
Pigmeat†	214,000	169,000	135,000
Poultry meat	77,000	70,000	58,000*
Cows' milk	917,000	772,000	645,000*
Butter	2,256	1,969	1,672
Cheese (all kinds)	11,051†	12,760†	11,600*
Hen eggs*	51,000	44,200	38,700
Honey	917	627	500*
Wool:			
greasy	719	583	470*
scoured	430	350*	282*

* FAO estimate(s). † Unofficial figure(s).

Source: FAO, *Production Yearbook*.

Forestry

ROUNDWOOD REMOVALS ('000 cubic metres)*

	1989	1990	1991
Sawlogs and veneer logs	2,182	1,854	1,461
Pitprops (mine timber)	226	174	80
Pulpwood	466	411	298
Other industrial wood	307	252	183
Fuel wood	982	875	759
Total	4,163	3,566	2,781

* From state-owned forests only.

SAWNWOOD PRODUCTION ('000 cubic metres)

	1989	1990	1991
Coniferous (soft wood)	228	195	103
Broadleaved (hard wood)	870	744	422
Total	1,098	939	525

Fishing

('000 metric tons, live weight)

	1990	1991	1992
Freshwater fishes	11.8	6.2	6.7
Marine fishes	32.5	17.3	n.a.
Crustaceans and molluscs	2.4	1.5	n.a.
Total catch	46.7	25.0	33.2

Mining

(metric tons, unless otherwise indicated)

	1990	1991	1992
Coal	155	146	n.a.
Crude petroleum	2,497	1,903	1,743
Bauxite	309	112	n.a.
Natural gas (million cu m)	1,989	1,839	1,820

Industry

SELECTED PRODUCTS

('000 metric tons, unless otherwise indicated)

	1989	1990	1991
Canned meat (metric tons)	26,731	26,820	21,262
Canned vegetables (metric tons)†	43,533	44,429	23,043
Edible vegetable oil—crude and refined (metric tons)	48,465	49,217	46,062
Sugar	209	201	100
Wine ('000 hectolitres)‡	655	648	553
Beer ('000 hectolitres)	2,292	2,801	2,249
Cigarettes (million)	13,318	12,436	11,622
Wool yarn	13	10	6
Cotton yarn	26	20	12
Woven cotton fabrics (million sq metres)	58	40	30
Footwear ('000 pairs)	30,840	23,194	11,560
Mechanical wood pulp	33	33	34
Chemical wood pulp	14	16	1
Semi-chemical wood pulp	111	95	69
Stationery and newsprint	16	4	1
Sulphuric acid	271	242	187
Motor spirit (petrol)*	2,063	1,931	1,332
Distillate fuel oils	1,490	1,398	903
Residual fuel oil	2,237	2,624	1,760
Clay building bricks (million)	1,082	944	698
Roofing tiles (million)	109	84	55
Cement	2,891	2,653	1,706
Pig iron	240	209	69
Crude steel	486	424	214
Aluminium (unwrought)	73	74	55
Radio receivers ('000)	36	9	3
Television receivers ('000)	25	19	4
Tractors (number)	8,168	5,186	4,878
Bicycles ('000)	60	54	29
Electric energy (million kWh)	9,488	8,748	8,834

1992: Canned vegetables 25,574 metric tons†; Sugar 95,000 metric tons; Cotton yarn 12,000 metric tons; Woven cotton fabrics 12m. sq metres; Footwear 10,254,000 pairs; Cement 1,768,000 metric tons; Electric energy 8,859m. kWh.

* Not including aviation gasoline.

† Including picked vegetables, food additives, mustard and similar spices.

‡ Not including production of wine in private households.

Finance

CURRENCY AND EXCHANGE RATES

Monetary Unit

100 para = 1 Croatian dinar.

Sterling and Dollar Equivalents (30 September 1993)

£1 sterling = 9,123 dinars;
US $1 = 6,100 dinars;
10,000 Croatian dinars = £1.096 = $1.639.

Note: The Croatian dinar was introduced on 23 December 1991, replacing (and initially at par with) the Yugoslav dinar.

STATE BUDGET (million dinars)

Revenue (current)	1991	1992	1993*
Tax revenue	62,799	501,590	4,092,394
Customs duties plus import fees	5,010	99,423	847,003
Turnover and sales tax	33,215	316,332	2,886,037
Tax on incomes	24,546	83,999	336,484
Other taxes (taxes on property)	28	1,836	22,870
Non-tax revenue	972	55,489	713,302
Privatization proceeds	—	10,031	408,068
Central bank profits	—	39,780	220,000
Other non-tax revenues	972	5,678	85,234
Total	63,771	557,079	4,805,696

Expenditure	1991	1992	1993*
General public services	16,316	82,366	746,249
Defence	23,759	197,693	1,688,000
Public order and safety	4,764	21,603	210,156
Education	15,509	62,475	529,840
Health	1,199	2,310	44,474
Social security and welfare	5,802	58,360	506,705
Housing and community amenities	1,292	35,482	250,510
Recreational, cultural and religious affairs	844	2,868	24,225
Agriculture, forestry and fisheries	1,875	42,269	214,902
Mining and mineral resources	—	1,000	—
Transport and communications	8,949	35,544	445,185
Economic affairs and services	1,072	752	10,450
Other expenditure	1,748	28,470	280,000
Total	83,129	571,192	4,950,696

* Estimates.

Source: National Bank of Croatia, *Bulletin 1993*.

COST OF LIVING
(Retail price index. Base: previous year = 100)

	1990	1991	1992
All items	709.5	223.0	765.5

NATIONAL ACCOUNTS

Gross Material Product by Activities of the Material Sphere
(million Croatian dinars, at current prices)

	1988	1989	1990
Manufacturing, mining and quarrying	1,562	24,832	80,431
Agriculture and fishing	341	4,993	24,353
Forestry	42	671	3,115
Operation of irrigation systems and associated activities	12	126	912
Construction	255	3,789	20,532
Transport and communications	367	5,614	24,832
Trade	671	8,940	49,864
Catering and tourism	252	2,681	14,749
Arts and crafts (productive)	170	1,979	10,188
Public utilities (productive)	35	472	2,825
Other productive economic activities	128	2,107	10,554
Total	3,835	56,204	242,355

BALANCE OF PAYMENTS (US $ million)*

	1991	1992
Balance of trade	−536	−303
Merchandise exports (f.o.b.)	3,292	3,127
Merchandise imports (c.i.f.)	−3,828	−3,430
Exports of services	1,275	1,432
Imports of services	−1,238	−1,068
Other income received	65	49
Other income paid	−166†	−216
Private unrequited transfers (net)	−7‡	391
Unofficial unrequited transfers (net)	18	44
Current balance	−589	329
Capital (net)	−457	−220
Net errors and omissions	1,046	58
Change in foreign reserves	—	167

* Transactions without former Yugoslav Republics.
† Interest arrears included.
‡ Principal arrears included.

Source: National Bank of Croatia, *Bulletin 1993*.

External Trade

PRINCIPAL COMMODITIES
(distribution by SITC, US $ million)

Imports c.i.f.	1990	1991*	1992*
Food and live animals	719	407	468
Meat and meat preparations	130	42	n.a.
Fruit and vegetables	151	121	n.a.
Coffee, tea, cocoa and spices	98	58	n.a.
Beverages and tobacco	43	22	52
Crude materials (inedible) except fuels	306	199	263
Textiles fibres and waste	62	42	n.a.
Crude fertilizers, etc.	38	45	n.a.
Metalliferous ores and scrap	86	47	n.a.
Mineral fuels, lubricants, etc.	876	667	430
Animal and vegetable oils and fats	25	10	23
Chemicals	652	515	672
Organic chemicals	182	125	n.a.
Dyeing, tanning and colouring materials	54	45	n.a.
Medicinal and pharmaceutical products	65	55	n.a.
Plastics in primary forms	93	92	n.a.
Basic manufactures	623	347	808
Paper, paperboard, etc.	63	46	n.a.
Textile yarn, fabrics, etc.	146	89	n.a.
Non-metallic mineral manufactures	50	36	n.a.
Iron and steel	150	60	n.a.
Machinery and transport equipment	955	840	726
General industrial machinery, equipment and parts	215	156	n.a.
Road vehicles and parts (excl. tyres, engines and electrical parts)	122	296	n.a.
Miscellaneous manufactured articles	719	551	715
Other commodities and transactions	271	270	304
Total	5,188	3,828	4,461

* Preliminary figures.

Exports f.o.b.	1990	1991*	1992*
Food and live animals	286	252	459
Live animals	58	50	n.a.
Meat and meat preparations	76	55	n.a.
Fruit and vegetables	41	43	n.a.
Beverages and Tobacco	26	24	112
Crude materials (inedible) except fuels	205	171	286
Wood, lumber and cork	141	117	n.a.
Mineral fuels, lubricants, etc.	203	223	397
Animal and vegetable oils and fats	4	1	6
Chemicals	460	399	597
Medicinal and pharmaceutical products	117	68	n.a.
Fertilizers (other than crude)	41	82	n.a.
Plastics in primary forms	169	150	n.a.
Basic manufactures	670	477	820
Textile yarn, fabrics, etc.	91	74	n.a.
Non-metallic mineral manufactures	70	63	n.a.
Iron and steel	154	108	n.a.
Non-ferrous metals	121	74	n.a.
Machinery and transport equipment	961	770	849
Machinery specialized for particular industries	107	109	n.a.
Transport equipment (excl. road vehicles)	364	363	n.a.
Miscellaneous manufactured articles	1,199	971	1,044
Furniture and parts	152	128	n.a.
Clothing (excl. footwear)	641	585	n.a.
Footwear	290	152	n.a.
Other commodities and transactions	7	3	28
Total	4,020	3,292	4,597

* Preliminary figures.

PRINCIPAL TRADING PARTNERS (US $ million)

Imports c.i.f.	1990	1991	1992
Austria	283	177	190
Belgium	55	42	50
Brazil	50	37	n.a.
Czechoslovakia	147	202	215
France	99	99	72
Germany*	1,165	833	768
Hungary	162	80	103
Iran	71	175	n.a.
Italy	761	623	761
Japan	97	111	32
Libya	172	185	—
Netherlands	170	115	86
Sweden	79	46	53
Switzerland	108	87	67
USSR†	448	252	231
United Kingdom	101	111	65
USA	202	148	106
Total (incl. others)	5,188	3,828	4,461

Exports f.o.b.	1990	1991	1992
Austria	142	97	105
Belgium	38	28	32
China	3	76	n.a.
Czechoslovakia	70	51	32
France	98	66	58
Germany*	1,051	968	773
Greece	32	31	n.a.
Hungary	30	36	42
Italy	732	715	909
Kuwait	19	39	n.a.
Liberia	206	181	n.a.
Netherlands	131	126	98
Poland	31	44	32
Sweden	45	44	339
Switzerland	45	42	36
USSR†	596	247	156
United Kingdom	89	57	56
USA	194	120	69
Total (incl. others)	4,020	3,292	4,597

* Figures for the German Democratic Republic are combined with figures for the Federal Republic of Germany in 1990; figures for the united Germany are given for 1991 and 1992.

† Figures for 1992 refer to countries of the former USSR.

Transport

RAILWAYS (traffic)

	1989	1990	1991
Passengers carried ('000)	43,655	40,248	21,790
Passenger-kilometres (million)	3,664	3,429	1,503
Freight ('000 metric tons)	39,969	35,796	n.a.
Freight ton-km (million)	7,419	6,535	n.a.

1992: 17,878,000 passengers carried.

ROAD TRAFFIC (registered motor vehicles at 31 December)

	1989	1990	1991
Motor cycles (up to 50cc)	19,898	17,520	13,072
Passenger cars	796,129	795,410	735,650
Buses	6,128	5,836	4,876
Lorries	42,850	41,367	34,431
Special vehicles	15,045	15,556	14,552
Tractors	177,548	180,641	182,211

INLAND WATERWAYS (vessels and traffic)

	1989	1990	1991
Tugs	35	31	31
Motor barges	1	1	1
Barges	135	124	122
Goods unloaded (million metric tons)	3.7	2.7	1.6

INTERNATIONAL SEA-BORNE SHIPPING

	1989	1990	1991
Vessels entered (million net reg. tons)	17.1	20.6	13.1
Goods loaded ('000 metric tons)	4,720	4,124	3,261
Goods unloaded ('000 metric tons)	17,483	17,693	10,565
Goods in transit ('000) metric tons)	3,134	4,716	6,518

Tourism

FOREIGN TOURIST ARRIVALS BY COUNTRY ('000)

	1989	1990	1991
Austria	547	427	54
Czechoslovakia	193	171	12
France	200	181	37
Germany	1,874	1,486	151
Hungary	117	73	7
Italy	998	1,048	146
Netherlands	327	299	20
USSR	91	96	9
United Kingdom	457	471	66
USA	143	141	18
Total (incl. others)	5,621	5,020	629

Communications Media

	1989	1990
Telephone subscribers ('000)	761	835
Books (titles published)	2,413	2,239
Daily newspapers	8	9
Total circulation (million)	209	232
Newspapers (all frequencies)	610	572
Total circulation (million)	334	342
Periodicals	404	352
Total circulation (million)	3	6

1991: 896,000 telephone subscribers.

Education

(1991/92)

	Institutions	Students	Teachers
Elementary	1,859	415,750	22,187
Secondary	n.a.	173,727	11,705
Vocational and technical schools	3	1,839	122
Universities and art academies	54	66,881	6,303

Directory

The Constitution

The Constitution of the Republic of Croatia was promulgated in December 1990. Croatia issued a declaration of dissociation from the Socialist Federal Republic of Yugoslavia in June 1991, and formal independence was proclaimed on 8 October 1991.

The following is a summary of the main provisions of the Constitution:

GENERAL PROVISIONS

The Republic of Croatia is a democratic, constitutional state where power belongs to the people and is exercised directly and through the elected representatives of popular sovereignty.

The Republic of Croatia is an integral state, while its sovereignty is inalienable, indivisible and non-transferable. State power in the Republic of Croatia is divided into legislative, executive and judicial power.

All citizens of the Republic of Croatia over the age of 18 years have the right to vote and to be candidates for election to public office. The right to vote is realized through direct elections, by secret ballot. Citizens of the Republic living outside its borders have the right to vote in elections for the Assembly and the President of the Republic.

In a state of war or when there is a direct threat to the independence and unity of the Republic, as well as in the case of serious natural disasters, some freedoms and rights that are guaranteed by the Constitution may be restricted. This is decided by the Assembly of the Republic of Croatia by a two-thirds majority of its deputies and, if the Assembly cannot be convened, by the President of the Republic.

BASIC RIGHTS

The following rights are guaranteed and protected in the Republic: the right to life (the death sentence has been abolished), fundamental freedoms and privacy, equality before the law, the right to be presumed innocent until proven guilty and the principle of legality, the right to receive legal aid, the right to freedom of movement and residence, the right to seek asylum, inviolability of the home, freedom and secrecy of correspondence, safety and secrecy of personal data, freedom of thought and expression of opinion, freedom of conscience and religion (all religious communities are equal before the law and are separated from the State), the right of assembly and peaceful association, the right of ownership, entrepreneurship and free trade (monopolies are forbidden), the right to work and freedom of labour, the right to a nationality, the right to strike, and the right to a healthy environment.

Members of all peoples and minorities in the Republic enjoy equal rights. They are guaranteed the freedom to express their nationality, to use their language and alphabet and to enjoy cultural autonomy.

GOVERNMENT

Legislature

Legislative power resides with the Assembly (Sabor), which consists of the Chamber of Representatives (Predstavnički Dom), with no less than 100 and no more than 160 seats, and the Chamber of Municipalities (Županski Dom).

The Chamber of Representatives decides on the adoption and amendment of the Constitution, approves laws, adopts the state budgets, decides on war and peace, decides on the alteration of the borders of the Republic, calls referenda, supervises the work of the Government and other public officials responsible for their work to the Assembly, in accordance with the Constitution and the law, and deals with other matters determined by the Constitution.

The Chamber of Municipalities proposes laws and gives opinions on issues within the competence of the Chamber of Representatives; however, after the adoption of a law in the Chamber of Representatives, the Chamber of Municipalities may return the same law to the former for reconsideration. The citizens of each municipality elect, by direct and secret ballot, three deputies to the Chamber of Municipalities.

Members of the Chambers of the Assembly are elected by universal, direct and secret ballot for a term of four years, and their term is not mandatory. The Chambers of the Assembly may be dissolved, if the majority of all the deputies decides so, while the President of the Republic may, in accordance with the Constitution, dissolve the Chamber of Representatives.

President of the Republic

The President of the Republic is the Head of State of Croatia. He/she represents the country at home and abroad and is responsible for ensuring respect for the Constitution, guaranteeing the existence and unity of the Republic and the regular functioning of state power. The President is elected directly for a term of five years.

The President calls elections for the Chambers of the Assembly, calls referenda, appoints and dismisses the Prime Minister, the

Deputy Prime Ministers and members of the Government, appoints and recalls diplomatic representatives of the Republic and is the Supreme Commander of the Armed Forces of the Republic of Croatia. In the event of war or immediate danger, the President issues decrees having the force of law. The President may convene a meeting of the Government and place on its agenda items which, in his opinion, should be discussed. The President attends the Government's meetings and presides over them.

The President may dissolve the Chamber of Representatives, if it approves a vote of no confidence in the Government or if it does not approve the state budget within a specified period of time.

Ministers

Executive power in the Republic resides with the President, the Prime Minister and the Ministers. The Government of the Republic consists of the Ministers and the Prime Minister. The Government issues decrees, proposes laws and the budget, and implements laws and regulations that have been adopted by the Assembly. In its work, the Government is responsible to the President of the Republic and the Chamber of Representatives.

JUDICATURE

Judicial power is vested in the courts and is autonomous and independent. The courts issue judgments on the basis of the Constitution and the law. The Supreme Court is the highest court and is responsible for the uniform implementation of laws and equal rights of citizens. Judges and state public prosecutors are appointed and relieved of duty by the Judicial Council of the Republic, which is elected, from among distinguished lawyers, by the Chamber of Representatives for a term of eight years.

Note: Croatia received recognition as an independent state from the EC in January 1992. General international recognition followed and, in May 1992, the country was formally admitted to the UN.

The Government

(January 1994)

HEAD OF STATE

President of the Republic: Dr FRANJO TUDJMAN (elected by the Sabor on 30 May 1990, re-elected by direct vote on 2 August 1992).

Office of the President: 41000 Zagreb, Banski Dvori.

MINISTERS

Prime Minister: NIKICA VALENTIĆ.

Deputy Prime Ministers: Dr MATE GRANIĆ, Dr IVICA KOSTOVIĆ, BORISLAV ŠKEGRO, VLADIMIR ŠEKS.

Minister of Energy, Shipbuilding and Industry: FRANJO KAJFEŽ.

Minister of Finance: Dr ZORAN JAŠIĆ.

Minister of Foreign Affairs: Dr MATE GRANIĆ.

Minister of Defence: GOJKO ŠUŠAK.

Minister of Justice: IVICA CRNIĆ.

Minister of Administration: JURICA MALČIĆ.

Minister of the Economy: NADAN VIDOŠEVIĆ.

Minister of Transportation and Communications: IVICA MUDRINIĆ.

Minister of Agriculture and Forestry: Dr IVAN TARNAJ.

Minister of Education and Culture: VESNA GERARDI-JURKIĆ.

Minister of Labour and Social Welfare: IVAN PARAĆ.

Minister of Tourism: BRANKO MIKŠA.

Minister of Internal Affairs: IVAN JARNJAK.

Minister of Construction and Environmental Protection: ZLATKO TOMČIĆ.

Minister of Health: ANDRIJA HEBRANG.

Minister of Science and Technology: IVAN PARAĆ.

Ministers without Portfolio: Dr IVAN MAJDAK, Dr JURAJ NJAVRO, ČEDOMIR PAVLOVIĆ, ZLATKO MATESA.

MINISTRIES

Office of the Prime Minister: Government of the Republic of Croatia, 41000 Zagreb, Radićev trg 7; tel. (41) 444000; fax (41) 432041.

Ministry of Administration: 41000 Zagreb, Savska Cesta 41; tel. (41) 537622; fax (41) 536321.

Ministry of Agriculture and Forestry: 41000 Zagreb, Ave Vukovar 78; tel. (41) 633444; fax (41) 442070.

Ministry of Construction and Environmental Protection: 41000 Zagreb, Ave Vukovar 78; tel. (41) 536197; fax (41) 612131.

Ministry of Defence: 41000 Zagreb, Opatička 1, trg kralja Petra Krešimira IV, No. 1; tel. (41) 467111; fax (41) 451105.

Ministry of Education and Culture: 41000 Zagreb, trg Burze 6; tel. (41) 464000; fax (41) 410421.

Ministry of Energy, Shipbuilding and Industry: 41000 Zagreb, Ave Vukovar 78; tel. (41) 615111; fax (41) 613993.

Ministry of Finance: 41000 Zagreb, ul. 8 maja 42; tel. (41) 451555; fax (41) 432789.

Ministry of Foreign Affairs: 41000 Zagreb, Visoka 22; tel. (41) 451102; fax (41) 427594.

Ministry of Health: 41000 Zagreb, ul. baruna Trenka 6; tel. (41) 451555; fax (41) 431067.

Ministry of Internal Affairs: 41000 Zagreb, Savska Cesta 35, Ave Vukovar 13; tel. (41) 622111; fax (41) 443715.

Ministry of Justice: 41000 Zagreb, Savska Cesta 41; tel. (41) 537622; fax (41) 536321.

Ministry of Labour and Social Welfare: 41000 Zagreb, Prisavlje 14; tel. (41) 517000; fax (41) 613593.

Ministry of Science and Technology: 41000 Zagreb, Strossmayerov trg 4, Amruševa 4; tel. (41) 431022; fax (41) 429543.

Ministry of Tourism: 41000 Zagreb, Ave Vukovar 78; tel. (41) 613347; fax (41) 613216.

Ministry of Transportation and Communications: 41000 Zagreb, Mesnička 23; tel. (41) 444000; fax (41) 451408.

President and Legislature

PRESIDENT

Election, 2 August 1992

Candidate	Votes
Dr FRANJO TUDJMAN (CDU)	1,519,100
DRAŽEN BUDIŠA (CSLP)	585,535
SAVKA DABČEVIĆ-KUČAR (SPP)	161,242
DOBROSLAV PARAGA (CPR)	144,695
SILVIJE DEGEN	108,979
MARKO VESELICA (CDP)	45,593
IVAN CESAR (CCDP)	43,134
ANTON VUJIĆ (SDP—PDRC)	18,783

SABOR

(Assembly)

In January 1993 the plurality electoral system was replaced by proportional representation.

President: STIPE MESIĆ: 41000 Zagreb, Radićev trg 6; tel. (41) 444000.

Vice-Presidents: Dr ŽARKO DOMIJAN, KATARINA FUČEK, MILAN DJUKIĆ.

Predstavnički Dom

(Chamber of Representatives)

President: STIPE MESIĆ.

Vice-President: MILAN DJUKIĆ.

Election, 2 August 1992

Party	Seats
Croatian Democratic Union (CDU)	85
Croatian Social-Liberal Party (CSLP)	14
Croatian Party of Rights (CPR)	5
Croatian People's Party (CPP)	6
Social Democratic Party—Party of Democratic Reform of Croatia (SDP—PDRC)	11
Croatian Farmers' Party (CFP)	3
Dalmatian Action (DA)	
Istrian Democratic Assembly (IDS)	6
Rijeka Democratic Alliance (RDA)	
Serbian People's Party (SPP)	3
Independents	5
Total	138

Županski Dom

(Chamber of Municipalities)

President: JOSIP MANOLIĆ.

Vice-Presidents: IVAN ARALICA, DAMIR ZORIĆ.

Election, 7 February 1993

Party	Seats
Croatian Democratic Union (CDU)	37
Croatian Social-Liberal Party (CSLP) and allied parties	16
Croatian Farmers' Party (CFP)	5
Istrian Democratic Assembly (IDA)	3
Social Democratic Party—Party of Democratic Reform of Croatia (SDP—PDRC)	1
Croatian People's Party (CPP)	1
Total	63

Local Government

Legislation passed in November 1992 provided for the division of Croatia, for electoral purposes, into 21 counties (županije). Each county has a local assembly (županijska skupština) consisting of 40 councillors, with the exception of Zagreb City, which has 60 councillors. The head of the county administration is the župan. Local government elections were held on 7 February 1993.

Zagreb County (I): 41000 Zagreb, Skupština—Županija Zagrebačka; Župan IVICA GAŽI; Pres. of Assembly BOŽIDAR PANKRETIĆ.

Krapina and Zagorje County (II): 49000 Krapina, Skupština—Županija Krapinsko-Zagorska; tel. (49) 70557; Župan Dr FRANJO KAJFEŽ; Pres. of Assembly STJEPAN LESIČAR.

Sisak and Moslavina County (III): 47000 Sisak, Skupština—Županija Sisačko-Moslavačka; tel. (47) 23303; Župan ĐURO BRODARAC; Pres. of Assembly Prof. RUŽICA ŠIMUNOVIĆ.

Karlovac County (IV): Karlovac, Skupština—Županija Karlovačka; Župan (vacant); Pres. of Assembly IVICA CINDRIĆ.

Varaždin County (V): 42000 Varaždin, Skupština—Županija Varaždinska; tel. (42) 104100; Župan Dr ZVONIMIR SABATI; Pres. of Assembly ZORAN VIDOVIĆ.

Koprivnica and Križevci County (VI): 43000 Koprivnica, Skupština—Županija Koprivničko-Križevačka; tel. (43) 822047; Župan IVAN STANČIR; Pres. of Assembly IVAN HODALIĆ.

Bjelovar and Bilogora County (VII): Bjelovar, Skupština—Županija Bjelovarsko-Bilogorska; Župan Prof. TIHOMIR TRNSKI; Pres. of Assembly ŽELJKO LEDINSKI.

Primorje and Gorski Kotar County (VIII): 51000 Rijeka, Skupština—Županija Primorsko-Goranska; tel. (51) 36358; Župan Dr JOSIP ROJE; Pres. of Assembly Dr MILJENKO DORIĆ.

Lika and Senj County (IX): Gospić, Skupština—Županija Ličko-Senjska; Župan ANTE FRKOVIĆ; Pres. of Assembly FRANE PALČIĆ.

Virovitica and Podravina County (X): 46000 Virovitica, Skupština—Županija Virovitičko-Podravska; tel. (46) 721210; fax (46) 721683; Župan STJEPAN MIKOLČIĆ; Pres. of Assembly IVAN SANTIĆ.

Požega and Slavonia County (XI): Požega, Skupština—Županija Požeško-Slavonska; Župan ANTO BAGARIĆ; Pres. of Assembly MIROSLAV ČIČEK.

Slavonski Brod and Posavina County (XII): 55000 Slavonski Brod, Skupština—Županija Brodsko-Posavska; tel. (55) 231427; Župan Dr JOZO METER; Pres. of Assembly ŽELJKO BIGOVIĆ.

Zadar and Knin County (XIII): 57000 Zadar, Skupština—Županije Zadarsko-Kninska; tel. (57) 22890; fax (57) 312145; Župan ŠIME PRTENJAČA; Pres. of Assembly PETAR PERIĆ.

Osijek and Baranja County (XIV): 54000 Osijek, Skupština—Županije Osječko-Baranjska; Župan BRANIMIR GLAVAŠ; Pres. of Assembly ŽELJKO PONTA.

Šibenik County (XV): 59000 Šibenik, Skupština—Županija Šibenska; tel. (59) 22633; fax (59) 28966; Župan PAŠKO BUBALO; Pres. of Assembly ANTE MIKULANDRA.

Vukovar and Srem County (XVI): 56000 Vukovar, Skupština—Županija Vukovarsko-Srijemska; tel. (56) 11528; Župan MATEJ JANKOVIĆ; Pres. of Assembly (vacant).

Split and Dalmatia County (XVII): 58000 Split, Skupština—Županija Splitsko-Dalmatinska; tel. (58) 48646; Župan KRUNOSLAV PERONJA; Pres. of Assembly Dr LUKA TOMIĆ.

Istria County (XVIII): Pazin, Skupština—Županija Istarska; Župan LUCIANO DELBIANCO; Pres. of Assembly DAMIR KRAJIN.

Dubrovnik and Neretva County (XIX): 50000 Dubrovnik, Skupština—Županija Dubrovačko-Neretvanska; tel. (50) 412626; fax (50) 28398; Župan Dr JURE BURIĆ; Pres. of Assembly Prof. VINKO BRNADIĆ.

Međimurje County (XX): Čakovec, Skupština—Županija Međimurska; tel. (42) 811110; fax (42) 812112; Župan MARIJAN RAMUŠĆAK; Pres. of Assembly IVAN HRANJEC.

City of Zagreb (XXI): 41000 Zagreb, Skupština—Županija Grad Zagreb; tel. (41) 511141; fax (41) 511546; Župan BRANKO MIKŠA; Pres. of Assembly IVAN PARAĆ.

'REPUBLIC OF SERBIAN KRAJINA'

During 1991 the so-called Krajina ('borderlands') areas of Croatia, most of them with ethnic Serb majorities, constituted themselves as 'Serbian Autonomous Regions' (SAR—Srpska Autonomna Oblast), together with the Croatian parts of the historic territories of Baranja and Syrmia (Srem). These SARs subsequently announced their union and with the Bosnian or Bosanska Krajina, although the latter decision had not been effected at the beginning of 1994. These polities were not recognized by the republican authorities, but claimed representation at The Hague Conference and on the federal State Presidency. Krajina, with its capital in Knin, declared its autonomy on 1 October 1990 and its separation from Croatia on 16 March 1991. In August 1991 the formation of a second SAR, Slavonia, Baranja and Western Srem, was declared. Its headquarters were based in Vukovar, once it had been captured from the Croatians. Its union with Krajina was announced in October. The SAR of Western Slavonia also declared its autonomy in August 1991, although its three municipalities were largely in Croatian control. It announced its union with Krajina in December. In the same month a 'Republic of Serbian Krajina' (RSK) was proclaimed. The RSK headquarters was based in Knin and its local assembly met in Beli Minastir. Presidential (to succeed Goran Hadzić, 1992-94) and parliamentary elections took place in the RSK in December 1993. According to official results, in the parliamentary elections 31 seats to the Assembly were won by the Serbian Democratic Party of Krajina (SDPK), 16 by the Serbian Radical Party and 15 by the Serbian Democratic Party of All Serb Lands. None of the seven candidates in the presidential election won an overall majority and, moreover, there were allegations of electoral irregularities. The two leading candidates, therefore, Milan Babić (a former President and candidate of the SDPK with 49.3% of the votes cast) and Milan Martić (an independent candidate endorsed by President Milošević of Serbia—Yugoslavia—25.9%), contested a second round on 23 January 1994. Martić was elected the third President of the RSK with 51.7% of the valid votes (104,234) cast.

President: MILAN MARTIĆ.

Prime Minister: DJORDJE BJEGOVIĆ.

President of the Assembly: (vacant).

Political Organizations

Croatian Christian Democratic Party (CCDP) (HKDS): 41000 Zagreb, Vlahovića 2, Park V; tel. (41) 327233; fax (41) 325190; Pres. IVAN CESAR.

Croatian Democratic Party (CDP) (Hrvatska Demokratska Stranka—HDS): 41000 Zagreb, trg Kralja Tomislava 14/1; tel. (41) 431837; Pres. MARKO VESELICA.

Croatian Democratic Union (CDU) (Hrvatska Demokratska Zajednica—HDZ): 41000 Zagreb, trg hrvatskih velikana 4/III; tel. (41) 278324; fax (41) 435314; f. 1989; nationalist; Leader Dr FRANJO TUDJMAN; Pres. of Exec. Cttee SLAVKO DEGORICIJA.

Croatian Farmers' Party (CFP) (Hrvatska Seljacka Stranka—HSS): 41000 Zagreb, Trnskog 8; tel. (41) 212325; fax (41) 217411; Pres. DRAGO STIPAC.

Croatian Party of Rights (CPR) (Hrvatska Stranka Prava—HSP): 41000 Zagreb, trg Ante Starčevića 6; tel. (41) 431246; fax (41) 423929; right-wing, nationalist; armed br. is the Croatian Defence Assen or HOS; Pres. BORIS KANDARE; Chair. of Military Cttee of HOS IVAN DZAPIĆ.

Croatian Peasants' Party (Hrvatska Seljacka Stranka): 41000 Zagreb; Leader DRAGO STIPAĆ.

Croatian People's Party (CPP) (Hrvatska Narodna Stranka—HNS): 41000 Zagreb, Gajeva 12/II; tel. (41) 427749; fax (41) 425332; Pres. SAVKA DABČEVIĆ-KUČAR.

Croatian Social-Liberal Party (CSLP) (Hrvatska Socijalno-Liberalna Stranka—HSLS): 41000 Zagreb, Galovićeva 8; tel. (41) 215704; fax (41) 232887; Pres. DRAŽEN BUDIŠA.

Dalmation Action (DA) (Dalmatinska Akcija): 58000 Split, Kružićeva 2/II; tel. (41) 362060; Pres. MIRA LJUBIĆ-LORGER.

Green Action—Split (Zelena Akcija—Split): 58000 Split, Zrtava fašizma 8; tel. (58) 44421; Pres. ZORAN POKROVAC.

Green Action—Zagreb (Zelena Akcija—Zagreb): 41000 Zagreb, Radnicka c22, p.p.876.

Istrian Democratic Assembly (IDA) (Istarski Demokratski Sabor—IDS): Pula, Planajucka 29/I; tel. (41) 43702; Pres. IVAN JAKOVEČEVIĆ.

Party of Serbs: 41000 Zagreb; f. 1993 by mems of Serb cultural assn Prosveta (Enlightenment) and Serbian Democratic Forum; promotes liberal, democratic values; Leader MILORAD PUPOVAĆ.

Rijeka Democratic Alliance (RDA) (Riječki Demokratski Savez—RDS): 51000 Rijeka, Žrtava fašizma 29; tel. (51) 423713; Pres. NIKOLA IVANIŠ.

Serbian Democratic Party (SDP) (Srpska Demokratska Stranka—SDS): 59300 Knin, Jove Miodragovića 22; tel. (59) 22499; f. 1990; seeks equality with Croats for Serbs in Croatia; Pres. Dr JOVAN RAŠKOVIĆ, 41000 Zagreb, Preradovićeva 18/I; tel. (41) 423583.

Serbian People's Party (SPP) (Srpska Narodna Stranka—SNS): 41000 Zagreb, Mazuranićev trg 3; tel. (41) 451090; promotes cultural and individual rights for ethnic Serbs in Croatia; 4,500-5,000 mems; Pres. MILAN DUKIĆ.

Social Democratic Party of Croatia (Socijaldemokratska Partija Hrvatske): 41000 Zagreb, trg D. Iblera 9; tel. (41) 274463; fax (41) 423395; present name adopted 1993; formerly the ruling League of Communists of Croatia-Party of Democratic Reform, renamed Social Democratic Party-Party of Democratic Reform of Croatia 1993; 20,000 mems; Pres. IVICA RAČAN.

Socialist Party of Croatia (SPC) (Socijalistička Stranka Hrvatske—SSH): 41000 Zagreb, Prisavlje 14; tel. (41) 517835; fax (41) 510235; Pres. ŽELJKO MAŽAR.

At November 1992 there were 41 other registered political parties in Croatia.

Diplomatic Representation

EMBASSIES IN CROATIA

Austria: 41000 Zagreb, Jabukovać 39; tel. (41) 273392; fax (41) 424065; Ambassador: ANDREAS BERLAKOVICH.

Bosnia and Herzegovina: 41000 Zagreb; Ambassador: BISERA TURKOVIĆ.

Bulgaria: 41000 Zagreb, Gajeva ul. 19; Chargé d'affaires: NIKOLAI KARAKOLEV.

China, People's Republic: 41000 Zagreb, Kvaternikova 111; tel. (41) 197277; Chargé d'affaires: GUAN YUSEN.

Czech Republic: 41000 Zagreb, Prilaz Djure Deželića 10; tel. (41) 430099; fax (41) 430121.

France: 41000 Zagreb, Schlosserove stube 5; tel. (41) 272985; fax (41) 274923; Ambassador: GEORGES-MARIE CHENU.

Germany: 41000 Zagreb, Avenija Vukovar 64; tel. (41) 519200; fax (41) 518070; Ambassador: HORST WEISEL.

Holy See: 41000 Zagreb (Apostolic Delegation), Srebrenjak 116; tel. (41) 221597; fax (41) 235970; Apostolic Delegate: Most Rev. GIULIO EINAUDI, Titular Archbishop of Villamagna in Tripolitania.

Hungary: 41000 Zagreb, Il Cvijetno naselje 17b; tel. (41) 610430; fax (41) 610301; Ambassador: GÁBOR BAGI.

Iran: 41000 Zagreb, Hotel Intercontinental, Kršnjavoga 1; tel. (41) 453411; Chargé d'affaires a.i.: MOHAMED JANED ASAYESH.

Italy: 41000 Zagreb, Medulićeva 22; tel. (41) 277857; fax (41) 275106; Ambassador: SALVATORE CILENTO.

Norway: 41000 Zagreb, Andrije Hebranga 22; tel. (41) 443234; fax (41) 443234; Chargé d'affaires a.i.: LEIF H. LASSEN.

Poland: 41000 Zagreb, Krležin Gvozd 3; tel. (41) 278818; fax (41) 420305; Chargé d'affaires a.i.: Dr WIESŁAW WALKIEVICZ.

Russian Federation: 41000 Zagreb, Bosanska 44; tel. (41) 575444; fax (41) 572260; Ambassador: LEONID VLADIMIROVICH KERESTEDZHIANO.

Slovakia: 41000 Zagreb, Prilaz Djure Deželića 10; tel. (41) 430099; fax (41) 430121.

Slovenia: 41000 Zagreb, Savska cesta 41/11; tel. (41) 517401; fax (41) 517837; Ambassador: MATIJA MALEŠIĆ.

Sudan: 41000 Zagreb, Tuškanac 68; tel. (41) 276694; fax (41) 276705; Ambassador: GALLAL HASSAN ATANABI.

Sweden: 41000 Zagreb, Radićeva 14; tel. (41) 422116; fax (41) 428244; Ambassador: SUNE DANIELSSON.

Switzerland: 41000 Zagreb, Bogovićeva 3; tel. (41) 421573; fax (41) 425995; Ambassador: JACQUES RIAL.

United Kingdom: 41000 Zagreb, Ilica 12/1; tel. (41) 424888; fax (41) 420100; Ambassador: BRYAN SPARROW.

USA: 41000 Zagreb, Andrije Hebranga 2; tel. (41) 444800; fax (41) 440235; Ambassador: PETER GALBRAITH.

Judicial System

The judicial system of Croatia is administered by the Ministry of Justice. The Supreme Court is the highest judicial body in the country, comprising 15 judges who are elected for a period of eight years by the Chamber of Municipalities at the proposal of the Chamber of Representatives. The Constitutional Court consists of 11 judges, elected in the same way and for the same period.

Public Prosecutor: PETAR ŠALE.

Public Attorney: STJEPAN HERCEG.

Constitutional Court of Croatia: 41000 Zagreb, Radićev trg 4; tel. (41) 444822; Pres. Dr JADRANKO CRNIĆ.

Supreme Court: 41000 Zagreb, trg Nikole Zrinjskog 3; tel. (41) 257787; Pres. VJEKOSLAV VIDOVIĆ.

Office of the Public Prosecutor: 41000 Zagreb, Proleterskih brig. 84; tel. (41) 515422.

Religion

Most of the population are Christian, the largest denomination being the Roman Catholic Church, of which most ethnic Croats are adherents. The Archbishop of Zagreb is the most senior Roman Catholic prelate in Croatia. A Croatian Old Catholic Church does not acknowledge the authority of Rome or the papal reforms of the 19th century. There is a significant Serbian Orthodox minority (although Bishop JOVAN, Metropolitan of Zagreb and Ljubljana, was in exile in 1991–94). According to the 1991 census, 76.5% of the population of Croatia were Roman Catholics, 11.1% were Orthodox, 1.2% Muslims and there were small communities of Protestant Christians and Jews.

CHRISTIANITY

The Roman Catholic Church

Croatia comprises four archdioceses (including one, Zadar, directly responsible to the Holy See) and eight dioceses (including one for Catholics of the Byzantine rite).

Latin Rite

Archbishop of Rijeka-Senj: Dr ANTUN TAMARUT, Nadbiskupski Ordinarijat, 51000 Rijeka, Slaviše Vajnera Čiče 2; tel. (51) 37999; fax (51) 37015; 279,200 adherents (1993).

Archbishop of Split-Makarska: ANTE JURIĆ, 58001 Split, pp 142, ul. Zrinjsko-Frankopanska 14; tel. (58) 46798; fax (58) 361462; 403,187 adherents (1993).

Archbishop of Zadar: MARIJAN OBLAK, Nadbiskupski Ordinarijat, 57000 Zadar, Zeleni trg 1; tel. (57) 22395; fax (57) 25399; 145,000 adherents (1993).

Archbishop of Zagreb: Cardinal FRANJO KUHARIĆ, 41000 Zagreb, pp 553, Kaptol 22; tel. (41) 275449.

Byzantine Rite

Bishop of Križevci: SLAVOMIR MIKLOVŠ, Ordinarijat Križevačke Eparhije, 41000 Zagreb, Kaptol 20; tel. (41) 270767; 48,770 adherents (1993).

Old Catholic Church

Croatian Catholic Church: Hrvatska Katolička Crkva Ordinariat, 41000 Zagreb, ul. Kneza Branimirova 11; tel. (41) 275224; f. 894, re-established 1923; Archbishop MIHOVIL DUBRAVČIĆ.

The Press

PRINCIPAL DAILIES

Osijek

Glas Slavonije: 54000 Osijek, Prolaz Vitomira Sukića 2; tel. (54) 126722; telex 28276; fax (54) 26751; morning; independent; Editor DRAGO HEDL; circ. 21,735.

Pula

Glas Istre: 52000 Pula, Obala Maršala Tita br. 10; tel. (52) 23577; telex 25248; fax (52) 41434; morning; Dir ŽELJKO ŽMAK; circ. 25,000.

Rijeka

Novi List: 51000 Rijeka, POB 130, bul. Marksa i Englesa 20; tel. (51) 32122; telex 24236; morning; Dir ZDENKO MANCE; circ. 59,000.

La Voce del Popolo: 51000 Rijeka, bul. Marksa i Engelsa 20; f. 1944; morning; Italian; Editor MARIO BONITA; circ. 2,970.

Split

Nedjeljna Dalmacija: 58000 Split, Ivana Gundulića 23; tel. (58) 362821; fax (58) 362526; f. 1972; weekly; politics; Editor MIROSLAV IVIĆ; circ. 45,000.

Slobodna Dalmacija: 58000 Split, Splitskog odreda 4; tel. (58) 513888; telex 26124; morning; Editor JOŠKO KULUŠIĆ; circ. 103,000.

Zagreb

Novi Vjesnik: 41000 Zagreb, Slavonska Av. 4; tel. (41) 333333; telex 21121; fax (41) 341650; f. 1940; morning; Editor RADOVAN STIPETIĆ; circ. 45,000.

Sportske novosti: 41000 Zagreb, Lj. Gerovac br. 1; circ. 174,000.

Večernji list: 41000 Zagreb, Av. bratstva i jedinstva 4; tel. (41) 342780; telex 21121; fax (41) 341850; evening; Editor IVO LAJTMAN; circ. 290,850.

PERIODICALS

Arena: 41000 Zagreb, Slavonska Av. 4; tel. (41) 662796; telex 21121; fax (41) 662021; f. 1957; Croatian illustrated weekly; Editor UROŠ ŠOŠKIĆ; circ. 224,000.

Informator: 41000 Zagreb, Masarykova 1, POB 794; tel. (41) 429333; telex 21264; fax (41) 426247; f. 1952; 2 a week; economic and legal matters; Editor DUBRAVKO ABRAMOVIĆ.

Novi Danas: 41000 Zagreb, Slavonska Av. 4; tel. (41) 341971; fax (41) 341992; f. 1982; fmrly *Danas*, name changed 1992; weekly; pro-govt; news magazine; Chief and Exec. Editor ZVONIMIR LISINSKI; circ. 30,000.

Privredni vjesnik: 41000 Zagreb, Rooseveltov trg 2; tel. (41) 453422; telex 21524; fax (41) 446428; f. 1953; weekly; economic; Serbo-Croat; Man. ANTE GAVRANOVIĆ; Editor-in-Chief FRANJO ŽILIĆ.

Republika: 41000 Zagreb, Frankopanska 26; f. 1945; monthly; published by Društvo književnika Hrvatske; literary review; Editor-in-Chief VELIMIR VISKOVIĆ.

Publishers

August Cesarec: 41000 Zagreb, Prilaz Gjure Deželića 57; tel. (41) 171071; fax (41) 573695; Croatian and foreign literature.

Hrvatska Akademija Znanosti i Umjetnosti: 41000 Zagreb, Zrinski trg 11; tel. (41) 433504; fax (41) 433383; f. 1866; publishing dept of the Croatian Academy of Sciences and Arts; Pres. Dr IVAN SUPEK.

Informator IRO: Novinsko-izdavačko, štamparski i birotehnički zavod, 41000 Zagreb, Masarykova 1; tel. (41) 429333; telex 21264; newspapers, periodicals, books, forms, etc.; Dir Dr IVO BURIĆ.

Leksikografski zavod 'Miroslav Krleža': 41000 Zagreb, Frankopanska 26; tel. (41) 456244; telex 21297; fax (41) 434948; f. 1951; encyclopedias, bibliographies and dictionaries; Dir Dr DALIBOR BROZOVIĆ.

Mladost: 41000 Zagreb, Ilica 30; tel. (41) 453222; telex 21263; fax (41) 434878; f. 1947; fiction, science, art, children's books; Gen. Dir BRANKO VUKOVIĆ.

Motovun: 51424 Motovun, V. Nazora 1; tel. (53) 81722; fax (53) 81642; photomonographs and international co-productions.

Muzička naklada: 41000 Zagreb, Nicole Tesle 10/I; tel. (41) 424099; telex 22430; f. 1952; musical editions, scores; Dir RAJKO LATINOVIĆ.

Nakladni zavod Matice hrvatske: 41000 Zagreb, Ulica Matice hrvatske 2, POB 515; tel. (41) 275522; fax (41) 432430; f. 1960; fiction, popular science, politics, economics, sociology, history; Dir BORIS KREBER.

Nakladni zavod Znanje: 41000 Zagreb, Zvonimirova 17; tel. (41) 411500; f. 1946; popular science, agriculture, fiction, poetry, essays; Dir STIPAN MEDAK; Editor-in-Chief ZLATKO CRNKOVIĆ.

Naprijed: 41000 Zagreb, POB 1029, Palmotićeva 30; tel. (41) 457133; fax (41) 433424; f. 1946; philosophy, psychology, religion, sociology, medicine, dictionaries, children's books, art, politics, economics, etc.; Dir RADOVAN RADOVINOVIĆ.

Naša Djeca: 41000 Zagreb, Gajeva 7; tel. (41) 420666; fax (41) 423550; picture books, postcards, etc.; Dir Prof. DRAGO KOZINA.

Školska Knjiga: 41001 Zagreb, POB 1039; Masarykova 28; tel. (41) 420784; telex 21894; fax (41) 274360; education, textbooks, art; Dir MILJENKO ŽAGAR.

Tehnička Knjiga: 41000 Zagreb, Jurišičeva 10; tel. (41) 278172; fax (41) 423611; f. 1947; technical literature, popular science, reference books; Gen. Man. ŽVONIMIR VISTRIČKA.

PUBLISHERS' ASSOCIATION

Poslovna Zajednica Izdavača i Knjižara Hrvatske: 41000 Zagreb, Klaićeva 7; fax (41) 171624.

Radio and Television

In 1992 there were an estimated 1,002,398 television receivers in use in Croatia.

Hrvatska Radiotelevizija: 41000 Zagreb, Jurišićeva 4; govt-owned; Dir-Gen. ANTUN VRDOLJAK.

Croatian Radio: 41000 Zagreb, Jurišićeva 4; tel. (41) 426333; telex 21154; fax (41) 434369; f. 1926; 4 radio stations; broadcasts in Croat; Editor-in-Chief IVANKA LUCEV.

Croatian Television: 41000 Zagreb, Šetalište Karla Marksa bb; tel. (41) 618855; telex 21427; fax (41) 537921; f. 1956; 3 channels; broadcasts in Croat; Dir of TV BRANKO LENTIĆ; Editor-in-Chief MARIJA NEMCIĆ.

The 'Republic of Serbian Krajina' (RSK) established a separate radio and television service, based in Knin. The service was accused of being partisan during the elections in the RSK in December 1993. The Government established a rival service and banned TV Knin the following month.

RSK Radio and Television: Plitvice; f. 1994; Dir MLADEN PETROVIĆ (acting).

TV Knin: Knin; f. 1991, service suspended 1994; Dir MILAN STRBAC.

Finance

A new currency, the Croatian dinar, initially at par with the Yugoslav dinar and Slovene tolar, was introduced on 23 December 1991.

(d.d. = dioničko društvo (joint-stock company); cap. = capital; res = reserves; dep. = deposits; m. = million; amounts in convertible Yugoslav dinars unless otherwise stated; HRD = Croatian dinars; brs = branches)

BANKS

Republican National Bank

National Bank of Croatia: 41000 Zagreb, trg Burze 5; tel. (41) 464555; telex 22569; fax (41) 441684; in 1991 it assumed the responsibilities of a central bank empowered as the Republic's bank of issue; Gov. Dr PERO JURKOVIĆ.

Selected Banks

Dalmatinska Banka d.d., Zadar: 57000 Zadar, trg Sv. Stošije 3; tel. (57) 311311; telex 27224; fax (57) 433145; f. 1957; cap. US $20.3m., dep. $115.2m. (Dec. 1992); Gen. Man. NEVEN DOBROVIĆ.

Dubrovačka Banka d.d., Dubrovnik (Bank of Dubrovnik): 50000 Dubrovnik, put Republike 5; tel. (50) 32366; telex 27592; fax (50) 32939; f. 1956; Gen. Man. and Chief Exec. IVO PAVLIČEVIĆ.

Istarska Banka d.d., Pula (Bank of Istria): 52000 Pula, Premanturska 2; tel. (52) 33966; telex 24746; fax (52) 41498; Gen. Man. MARIO FLORIČIĆ.

Privredna Banka Zagreb d.d.: 41000 Zagreb, Račkoga 6; tel. (41) 450822; telex 21120; fax (41) 447234; f. 1966; commercial bank; total assets HRD 1,855m., cap. HRD 76.8m., dep. HRD 555.9m. (Dec. 1992); Man. Dir and Chief Exec. MARTIN KATIČIĆ; 21 brs.

Riječka Banka d.d.: 51000 Rijeka, POB 300, trg P. Togliatti 3a; tel. (51) 208211; telex 24143; fax (51) 30525; f. 1954 as Komunalna banka i štedionica, renamed 1967; Man. Dir NIKOLA PAVLETIC.

Samoborska Banka d.d., Samobor (Bank of Samobor): 41430 Samobor, Tomislavov trg 8; tel. (41) 782530; telex 21811; fax (41) 781523; f. 1873; total assets 2,956.4m. (Dec. 1990); Gen. Man. MARIJAN TRUSK.

Slavonska Banka d.d., Osijek (Bank of Slavonia): 54000 Osijek, POB 108, Kapucinska 29; tel. (54) 125022; telex 28090; fax (54) 124846; f. 1989; total assets 4,718.8m., dep. 3,612.4m. (Dec. 1990); Gen. Man. IVAN PATARČIĆ; 4 brs.

Splitska Banka d.d., Split: 58000 Split, R. Boskovica 16; tel. (58) 521777; telex 26162; fax (58) 526107; f. 1990; Man. Dir and Chief Exec. ANTE KRSTULOVIĆ; 32 brs.

Varaždinska Banka d.d.: 42001 Varaždin, POB 95, P. Preradovica 17; tel. (42) 55584; telex 23224; fax (42) 55114; f. 1981; Gen. Man. MATO LUKINIĆ; 15 brs.

Zagrebačka Banka Zagreb d.d. (Bank of Zagreb): 41000 Zagreb, Paromlinska 2; tel. (41) 630444; telex 21463; fax (41) 536626; f. 1978; cap. 2,458.4m., res 543.2m., dep. 26,025.3m. (Dec. 1990); Chief Exec. and Man. Dir FRANJO LUKOVIĆ; 20 brs.

STOCK EXCHANGE

Zagreb Stock Exchange: 41000 Zagreb; f. 1990.

Trade and Industry

Croatian Chamber of Commerce: 41000 Zagreb, Ruzveltov trg 1; tel. (41) 453422; telex 21524; fax (41) 448618; Pres. MLADEN VEDRIS.

Association of Independent Businessmen (Udruženje samostalnih privrednika): 41000 Zagreb.

Zagreb Trade Fair: Zagrebački Velesajam, 41020 Zagreb, POB 41020-16, Dubrovačka cesta 2; tel. (41) 623111; telex 21385; fax (41) 520643; f. 1909; International Spring Fair, annually in April; International Autumn Fair, annually in September; International Leather and Footwear Week; and numerous specialized fairs; the civil war, which began in 1991, has caused some disruption to these events.

MAJOR ENTERPRISES AND COMPANIES

ASTRA Foreign Trade Co Ltd: 41000 Zagreb, Varsavska 9; tel. (41) 457111; telex 21254; fax (41) 426296; foreign trade network incl. 29 foreign enterprises and representatve agencies for the import and export of various goods; Pres. S. R. B. VJEKOSLAV; 1,500 employees.

Auto-Hrvatska: 41000 Zagreb, Avenija Vukovar 37B; tel. (41) 533622; telex 21133; fax (41) 533810; wholesale and retail trade in vehicles, spare parts, etc; 557 employees.

Belišće d.d.: 54551 Belišće, trg Ante Starčevića 1; tel. (54) 183111; telex 28396; fax (54) 183562; f. 1884; private ownership; exports various products; Man. JOSIP LULIĆ; 3,500 employees.

Belje: 54326 Darda; tel. (54) 41026; telex 18210; primary agriculture and industrial processing of agricultual produce; 8,000 employees.

Brodogradilište Kraljevica: 51261 Kraljevica, Obala 2; tel. (51) 281222; fax (51) 281050; f. 1723; construction and repairs of sea vessels, machinery repairs; Man. VLADIMIR MAROBNIĆ; 927 employees.

Brodogradilište 'Trogir' p.o.: 58220 Trogir, put Brodograditelja 16; tel. (58) 881555; telex 26130; fax (58) 881881; f. 1944; a mem. of the Jadranbrod Shipbuilding Assen; builds and repairs ships; Man. Dir MIRKO RINČIĆ; 2,053 employees.

Brodogradilište 'Viktor Lenać': 51001 Rijeka, POB 210, Martinšćica bb; tel. (51) 442255; telex 24305; fax (51) 442433; f. 1896; private ownership; repairs and services ships; Man. DAMIR VRHOVNIK; 800 employees.

Brodokomerc d.d.: 51000 Rijeka, Jelačićev trg 4; tel. (51) 212212; telex 24245; fax (51) 213096; f. 1947; joint stock company; domestic and foreign trade; Dir MLADEN ŠEBELIĆ; 2,950 employees.

Brodomaterijal: 51000 Rijeka, Josipa Kraša 12; tel. (51) 211211; telex 24203; 1,300 employees.

Brodomerkur: 58000 Split, Poljička cesta 35; tel. (58) 301316; telex 26276; fax (58) 365673; f. 1952; import and export of goods; Man. Dir ANTE LETICA; 1,200 employees.

Brodosplit-Brodogradilište (Split Shipyards): 58000 Split, put Supavla 19; tel. (58) 521222; telex 26125; fax (58) 589269; design and manufacture and repairs of vessels; Dir SPIRO VUKMAN.

Chromos Zagreb: 41000 Zagreb, Proleterskih brig. 271; tel. (41) 334400; telex 21358; fax (41) 448814; production of paints and varnishes; Pres. VLADIMIR KONIĆ; 5,000 employees.

Dalmacija: 58315 Dugi Rat; tel. (58) 876555; telex 26146; fax (58) 876670; production of ferro-alloys; Dir NEDILJKO ERCEG.

Dalmacijacement d.d.: 58212 Kaštel-Sućurac, Cesta bb; tel. (58) 511433; telex 26155; fax (58) 211255; f. 1861; production of and trade in cement; Dir DRAGAN BOBAN; 2,080 employees.

Dina-Petrokemija: 51513 Omišalj; tel. (532) 441322; telex 2432; fax (532) 511470; f. 1991; mem. INA co; petrochemical production; Dir MARIJAN PEJČIĆ; 630 employees.

Dubrovkinja: 50000 Dubrovnik, put Republike 26; tel. (50) 27777; telex 27511; Man. DAMIR BULIĆ; 2,800 employees.

Duro Daković: 55000 Slavonski Brod, M. Budaka 1; tel. (55) 231056; telex 28616; fax (55) 232007; manufactures equipment for the engineering and construction industries, etc.; Gen. Man. ANTUN MILOVIĆ; 5,500 employees.

Duro Salaj: 54550 Valpovo, Bratstva Jedinstva 9; tel. (54) 81519; telex 28355; fax (54) 81274; manufactures food products and plastic products; Gen. Dir ANTUN SAUER; 2,800 employees.

Elektrokontakt: 41000 Zagreb, Radnicka c. bb; tel. (41) 230866; telex 21258; fax (41) 220847; manufactures signal lights, etc.; Gen. Dir ZVONKO ORINCIĆ; 1,600 employees.

Gavrilović: 44250 Petrinja, 29 Slavonske Udarne Divižije 59; tel. (44) 81126; telex 23631; fax (44) 40844; food processing; 6,000 employees.

Hidroelektra: 41000 Zagreb, Zeleni trg 6A; tel. (41) 534222; telex 21603; fax (41) 534414; civil engineering, construction; Dir STANKO KOVAĆ.

Hrvatske Ceste: 41000 Zagreb, Vončinina 3; (41) 445422; telex 21823; fax (41) 445215; f. 1991; state ownership; maintenance, protection and programming of development of road network; Man. Dir IVAN BANJAD; 3,814 employees.

Hrvatske Elektroprivreda p.o.: 41000 Zagreb, Ave Vukovar 37; tel. (41) 625111; telex 21191; fax (41) 533692; f. 1990; public ownership; production, transfer and distribution of power; import, export and exchange of electric power; Man. DAMIR BEGOVIĆ; 15,170 employees.

INA-Oki Oour Rotoform: 41000 Zagreb, Zitnjak bb; tel. (41) 231666; telex 21117; fax (41) 218124; petrochemical production; mem. co of the INA Group; Dir DAMIR LALIĆ; 1,636 employees.

Industrija Nafte—INA: 41000 Zagreb, Ave Većeslava Holjevca 10; tel. (41) 611611; telex 21188; fax (41) 539554; f. 1964; petroleum extraction and production; Dir-Gen. Dr FRANJO GREGURIĆ; 26,969 employees.

Industrijsko Poljoprivredni Kombinat, Osijek—IPK Osijek: 54000 Osijek, ul. Hrvatske Republike 45; tel. (54) 25739; fax (54) 123568; f. 1961; enterprise management, technological and business services; Dirs BRANKO NOVAK, JOSIP PAVIĆ, ZLATKO PAUKOVIĆ; 4,109 employees.

Industogradnja d.d.: 41000 Zagreb, Savska cesta 66; tel. (41) 510211; telex 21448; fax (41) 514922; construction, engineering; Dir MATO ČOP.

Jedinstvo: 41230 Krapina, Mihaljekov Jarek 33; tel. (49) 71202; telex 23134; fax (49) 71429; manufactures trapezoid aluminium and galvanized plate sections; Gen. Dir ZVONIMIR BUCONJIĆ; 740 employees.

Koka: 42000 Varaždin, Anina 2; tel. (42) 49244; telex 23240; fax (42) 51432; integrated poultry organization covering all stages of broiler-meat production; f. 1961; Gen. Man. BRANKO BOBETIĆ; 1,800 employees.

Kraš: 41000 Zagreb, Maksimirska 130; tel. (41) 232266; telex 21109; fax (41) 220522; process and manufacture confectionary products; Dir BORIS MARČAC.

Maj Brodogradilište: 51000 Rijeka, Liburnijska 3; tel. (51) 617111; telex 24137; fax (51) 617507; shipbuilding, construction of pipelines and reservoirs; Dir VLADIMIR BRUSIĆ.

Nikola Tesla Company—Telecom Systems and Equipment Co: 41000 Zagreb, Krapinska 45; tel. (41) 334433; telex 21416; fax (41) 328540; f. 1949; manufactures, installs and maintains telecommunications equipment; Gen. Man. MILIVOJ PEKOVIĆ; 4,049 employees.

Pazinka—Pazinka Kemijsko-tekstilna industrija: 51400 Pazin, Valici 1; tel. (53) 22022; telex 25137; fax (53) 22601; chemical-textile industry, manufacturing cotton bed-linen, cotton yarns, woollen and acrylic mixtures, etc; Gen. Dir BOGDAN MEDANCIĆ; 1,500 employees.

Pik 'Dakovo': 54400 Dakovo, Vladimira Nazora 2; tel. (54) 843444; telex 28064; fax (54) 845264; f. 1964; agricultural and livestock production; Dir-Gen. ZVONKO BOBETIĆ; 2,950 employees.

Pik Vrbovec-Mesna Industrija d.d.: 43216 Vrbovec, Zagrebačka 148; tel. (43) 751024; telex 23327; fax (43) 751863; f. 1962; exports meat and canned meat to Western Europe and the USA; Dir FRANJO DONCEVIĆ; 2,249 employees.

Pliva: 41000 Zagreb, Prilaz Baruna Filipovića 89; tel. (41) 181666; telex; 21246; fax (41) 576690; f. 1921; manufacture of pharmaceuticals, veterinary products, food products and cosmetics; Dir ŽELKO ČOVIĆ; 5,916 employees.

Plovidba Šibenik: 59000 Sibenik, Draga 2; tel. (59) 23755; telex 27325; fax (59) 27860; transport of goods by sea; tourism services; Dir VITOMIR JURAGA.

Podravka p.o.: 43300 Koprivnica, A. Starčevića 32; tel. (43) 827144; telex 23348; fax (43) 827064; f. 1947; agri-business, food processing, pharmaceuticals and cosmetics; Man. Dir ZVONOMIR MAJDANČIĆ; 7,525 employees.

Poduzec Pamucna Industrija 'Duga Resa': 47250 Duga Resa, Jurkas Dragutina 8; tel. (47) 8122; telex 23722; fax (47) 81904; textile production; Gen. Dir GABRIJEL PRSTEĆ; 3,806 employees.

Poslovna Zajednica Exportdrvo: 41000 Zagreb, trg Mazuranića 6; tel. (41) 446066; telex 22490; forestry, timber processing, furniture manufacture, paper production and processing and ancillary activities; 85,000 employees.

Rade Koncar: 41000 Zagreb, Fallerovo Setalliste 22; tel. (41) 336666; telex 21159; electrical industry; 23,713 employees.

Saponia p.o.: 54000 Osijek, Matije Gupca 2; tel. (54) 551622; telex 28223; fax (54) 556327; f. 1894; in the process of privatization; produces chemicals, foodstuffs, pharmaceuticals; Man. Dir MARCEL MELER; 1,873 employees.

Slavijapromet: 41000 Zagreb, Donje Svetica 127; tel. (41) 210599; telex 22683; fax (41) 22035; wholesale and retail trade in consumer goods; import and export; Dir FRANJO VOLAJ.

Tankerkomerc d.d.: 57000 Zadar, Obala Kneza Trpimira 2; (57) 311222; telex 27164; fax (57) 441826; f. 1980; foreign trade, wholesale and retail trade, catering and tourist services, public warehouses, freight forwarding, consulting services; Man. Dir Božo Jusup; 330 employees.

TLM-TVP: 59000 Šibenik, Narodnog preporoda 12; tel. (59) 35965; fax (59) 34095; f. 1955; public ownership; aluminium production; Man. Ivan Koštan; 945 employees.

Uljanik-Brodogradilište d.d.: 52000 Pula, Rade Končara 1; tel. (52) 41563; telex 25288; fax (52) 41563; shipbuilding, engineering; Dir Rudero Batelić.

Uljanik-Strojogradnja: 52000 Pula, Rade Končara 1; tel. (52) 24322, 24734; telex 24789; fax (52) 43940; manufactures engines and hydraulic motors; Dir Renato Fonović.

Varteks: 42000 Varaždin, Zagrebačka 94; tel. (42) 55555; fax (42) 44444; f. 1918; manufacture and sale of textiles and clothing; Gen. Man. Ivan Šebalj; 7,000 employees.

Zeljezara Sisak (Sisak Ironworks): 44103 Sisak, Božidara Adzije 19; tel. (44) 35844; telex 23617; fax (44) 35065; f. 1938; manufacture of coke, iron and steel; metal products; Man. Dir Marijan Balenović; 4,430 employees.

Zeljezara Sisak 'Koksar': 51222 Bakar, Nautička bb; tel. (51) 761333; telex 24427; fax (51) 761305; f. 1978; public ownership; production of coke and chemicals, collection and primary processing of industrial waste; pollution control; import and export of various products; Man. Zvonimir Vrebac; 464 employees.

'Zletovo' Battery Factory: 92210 Probistip; tel. (92) 83006; fax (92) 83656; telex 53666; production of starter batteries for motor vehicles, etc.; Gen. Dir Bona Spasovska; 1,500 employees.

Transport

RAILWAYS

In 1992 there were 2,425 km of railway lines in Croatia, of which 35% were electrified.

Hrvatske Željeznice p.o. (Croatian Railways Ltd): 41000 Zagreb, Mihanovićeva 12; tel. (41) 451111; telex 21199; fax (41) 427542; f. 1990 from Hrvatske Željeznice poduzeće, renamed 1992; state-owned; public railway transport, construction, modernization and maintenance of railway vehicles; Dir Zvonko Zdunić; 28,494 employees.

ROADS

In 1992 there 27,378 km of roads in Croatia, of which 302 km were motorways, 4,492 km were main roads and 7,984 km were secondary roads.

SHIPPING

Croatia Line: 51000 Rijeka, POB 379, Riva 8; tel. (51) 205111; telex 24218; fax (51) 211309; f. 1947; fmrly Jugolinija; cargo and passenger services from the Adriatic to North and South America, the Near and Middle East, the Indian sub-continent, People's Republic of China and the Far East; tramp service; Gen. Dir Dario Vukić.

Jadrolinija (Adriatic Shipping Line): 51000 Rijeka, Obala Jugoslovenske Mornarice 16; tel. (51) 30899; telex 24195; fax (51) 36904; f. 1947; regular passenger and car-ferry services between Italian, Greek and Croatian ports; cruises in the Mediterranean, northern Europe, etc.; Pres. J. Susanj.

Jadroplov p.o.: 58000 Split, Obala kneza Branimira 16; tel. (58) 302666; telex 26117; fax (58) 42198; f. 1947; fleet of 14 vessels and 6,000 containers engaged in linear and tramp service; Man. Nikša Giovanelli; 1,054 employees.

CIVIL AVIATION

There are eight international airports in Croatia. Zagreb airport reopened in April 1992 after being closed to civilian air traffic for seven months.

Newly-established airlines include **Bonanca Air** (based in Dubrovnik) and **Croatian Airlines** (domestic services; Dir-Gen. Matija Katičić).

Tourism

The Adriatic coast particularly made Croatia a very popular tourist destination before the 1990s. However, the civil conflict, which began in mid-1991, greatly reduced tourist activity in the country. Historic cities, notably Dubrovnik, were severely damaged in the fighting. The industry did show slight signs of recovery in 1992 (a total of 350,000 arrivals was recorded in the first nine months of the year), during a period of relative calm, but hostilities resumed in early 1993 and continued throughout the year.

Atlas: 50000 Dubrovnik, Pile 1; tel. (50) 442222; fax (50) 411100; travel agency; f. 1923; 25 branch offices; 3 overseas offices.

Dalmacijaturist: 58000 Split, Titova obala 5; tel. (58) 44666; telex 26145; fax (58) 591404; f. 1923; more than 40 branch offices; 3 offices abroad.

Generalturist: 41000 Zagreb, Praška 5; tel. (41) 450888; telex 21100; fax (41) 422633; f. 1923, renamed 1963; 40 branch offices, 3 representatives abroad.

Kvarner Express: 51410 Opatija, M. Tita 186-192; tel. (51) 271111; telex 24379; fax (51) 271741; f. 1952; arranges accommodation, tours, conventions, etc.; 40 branch offices, 1 foreign office.

Tankerska Plovidba: 57000 Zadar, B. Petranovića 4; tel. (57) 311132; telex 27127; fax (57) 437372.

Culture

The cultural organizations listed below were in existence before the outbreak of civil conflict. Armed hostilities between Serbs and Croats (which began in 1991 and continued into 1994) caused irreparable damage to Croatia's cultural heritage, most notably to the historic town of Dubrovnik, which was besieged for 238 days by the Yugoslav army and Serb paramilitaries.

NATIONAL ORGANIZATIONS

Ministry of Education and Culture: see section on The Government (Ministries).

Institute for the Preservation of Historical and Cultural Monuments: 41000 Zagreb, Ilica 44; tel. (41) 427400; fax (41) 426386; f. 1910; Dir Prof. Ferdinand Meder.

Institute for the Preservation and Scientific Study of Historical Monuments in Dalmatia (Regionalni zavod za zaštitu spomenika kulture): 58000 Split, Poljudsko šetalište 15, pp 191; tel. (58) 42327; fax (58) 48993; f. 1854; Dir Dr Josko Belamarić.

CULTURAL HERITAGE

Archaeological Museum (Arheološki muzej u Splitu): 58000 Split, Zrinjsko-Frankopanska 25; tel. (58) 44574; fax (58) 44685; f. 1820; Dir Prof. Emilio Marin.

Archaeological Museum (Arheološki muzej): 41000 Zagreb, Zrinski trg 19; tel. (41) 427600; fax (41) 427724; f. 1846; Dir Prof. Ante Rendić-Miočivić.

Archives of Croatia (Arhiv Hrvatske): 41000 Zagreb, Marulićev trg 21; tel. (41) 446325; f. 1643; Dir Josip Kolahović.

City Museum of Zagreb (Muzej grada Zagreba): 41000 Zagreb, Opatička 20-22; tel. and fax (41) 428294; f. 1907; Dir Prof. Vinko Ivić.

Gallery of Modern Art (Moderna Galerija): 41000 Zagreb, Braće Kavurića 1; tel. (41) 433802; f. 1905; Dir Prof. Igor Zidić.

Historical Museum of Croatia (Hrvatski povijesni musej): 41000 Zagreb, Matoševa 9; tel. (41) 277991; f. 1846; Dir Prof. Jasna Tomičić.

Museum of Contemporary Art (Muzej suvremene umjetnosti): 41000 Zagreb, Habdelićeva 2; tel. (41) 431343; fax (41) 431404; f. 1961; fmrly Zagreb City Galleries; controls four galleries: Contemporary Art; Benko Horvat Collection (antique and Renaissance art); Centre for Photography; Film and Television Centre; Dir Davor Matičević.

Museum and Gallery Centre: 41000 Zagreb, Jezuitski trg 4; tel. (41) 433274; fax (41) 433241; f. 1982; Dir Ante Sorić.

Museum of Modern Art (Moderna Galerija): 51000 Rijeka, Dolac 1; tel. (51) 34280; fax (51) 30982; f. 1948; Dir Prof. Berislav Valusek.

Museum of the Serbian Orthodox Church (Muzej Srpske Pravoslavne Crkve): 50000 Dubrovnik, Od Puća 2; f. 1953; collections of portraits, and over 170 icons.

Strossmayer Gallery of Old Masters (Strossmayerova gallerija starih majstora): 41000 Zagreb, trg Nikole Šubića 11; f. 1884; Dir Gjuro Vangjura.

Umjetnička Galerija Dubrovnik: 50000 Dubrovnik, Frana Supila 45; f. 1945; modern paintings and sculptures; Dir Prof. Antun Karaman.

SPORTING ORGANIZATION

Croatian Olympic Committee: 41000 Zagreb, trg Jože Vlahovića 6; f. 1991; Pres. Antun Vrdoljac.

PERFORMING ARTS

Theatre

Croatian National Theatre (Hrvatsko narodno kazalište): 41000 Zagreb, trg Maršala Tita 15; tel. (41) 449311; Dir (vacant); Opera and Ballet: tel. (41) 447644; Dir of Opera VLADIMIR BENIĆ; Dir of Ballet LEO STIPANIČIĆ.

Croatian National Theatre—Ivan Zajc (Hrvatsko narodno kazalište 'Ivan Zajc'): 51000 Rijeka, Aldo Negri 1/I; tel. (51) 424679.

Croatian National Theatre—Osijek (Hrvatsko narodno kazalište—Osijek): 54000 Osijek, A. Cesarca 9; tel. (54) 32182.

Croatian National Theatre—Split (Hrvatsko narodno kazalište—Split): 58000 Split, trg Gaje Bulata 1; tel. (58) 585999.

Jazavac Satirical Theatre: 41000 Zagreb, Ilica 31; tel. (41) 412069.

Komedija—Zagreb Municipal Theatre of Comedy: 41000 Zagreb, Kaptola 9; tel. (41) 275027.

Marin Držić Theatre: 50000 Dubrovnik, Ispred Dvora; tel. (50) 26437.

Theatre Etcetera: 41000 Zagreb, Šavska 25; tel. (41) 278068.

Visiting Theatre: 41000 Zagreb, Varšavka 16; tel. (41) 424528.

Music

Croatian Television Choir (Zbor HTV): 41000 Zagreb, Teslina 7; Chief Conductor IGOR KULJERIĆ.

Croatian Television Big Band (Plesni Orkestar HTV): 41000 Zagreb, Teslina 7; dance band; Chief Conductor MILJENKO PROHASKA.

Dubrovnik Symphony Orchestra (Dubrovački simfonijski orkestar): 50000 Dubrovnik, Kovačka 3/II; tel. (50) 26316; Chief Conductor IVO DRUŽINIĆ.

Pro-Arte String Quartet ('Pro Arte' gudački kvartet): 41000 Zagreb, Mikulićeva 22; tel. (41) 443282; fax (41) 422850.

Zagreb Concert Management (Koncertna direkcija Zagreb): 41000 Zagreb, Trnjanska bb; tel. (41) 539995; impresarios and concert promoters; Dir MIROSLAV POLJANEC.

Zagreb Philharmonic Orchestra (Zagrebačka filharmonija): 41000 Zagreb, Trnjanska bb; tel. (41) 539699; Chief Conductor KAZUSHY ONO; Permanent Conductor PAVLE DEŠPALJ.

Zagreb Soloists (Zagrebački solisti): 41000 Zagreb, trg Sv. Marka 9; tel. (41) 425551; fax (41) 423667; Sec. TONKO NINČIĆ.

Zagreb Symphony Players (Zagrebački sinfoničari): c/o HTV, 41000 Zagreb, Teslina 7; Conductor VLADIMIR KRANJČEVIĆ.

ASSOCIATIONS

Croatian Society (Matica Hrvatska): 41000 Zagreb, Matice hrvatske ul. 2; tel. (41) 278181, 275333; fax (41) 425475; f. 1842, banned 1971, re-formed 1990; soc. for cultural and educational programmes, publishing; Pres. VLADO GOTOVAC.

Federation of Museum Associations of Croatia (Savez muzejskih društava hrvatske): 41000 Zagreb, Demetrova 1; tel. (41) 428596; f. 1945; Sec. NIKOLA TVRTKOVIĆ.

Italian Union of Croatia: Pula; cultural and social org. of ethnic Italians in Istria; Pres. MAURIZIO TREMUL.

Education

Pre-school education, for children aged from one to six years, is free of charge. In 1992 approximately 110,000 children attended kindergartens. Around 7,000 teachers are employed in kindergartens. Between the ages of six and 15, all children must attend elementary school. In 1991/92 there were 1,859 such schools in the country, which were attended by an estimated 415,750 pupils and employed 22,187 teachers. Secondary school education can be free of charge (although there are private schools in Croatia) and lasts from two to five years. There are grammar schools, technical schools and mixed-curriculum schools at secondary level. In 1990/91 approximately 212,000 students attended 191 secondary schools, which employed 13,200 teachers. In 1992 there were three polytechnics and four universities in Croatia.

Ministry of Education and Culture: see section on The Government (Ministries).

UNIVERSITIES

Josip Juraj Strossmayer University of Osijek (Josip Juraj Strossmayer Sveučiliste u Osijeku): 54000 Osijek, Braće Radića 15; tel. (54) 31822; fax (54) 24750; f. 1975; language of instruction: Serbo-Croat; 588 teachers, 7,020 students; Rector Prof. IVAN MECANOVIĆ.

University of Rijeka (Sveučilište u Rijeci): 51000 Rijeka, trg Riječke rezolucije 7/1; tel. (51) 36036; fax (51) 39539; f. 1973; language of instruction: Croatian (and some courses in Italian); 10 faculties, 2 institutes; 748 teachers; 9,566 full-time students, 978 part-time students; Rector Prof. Dr KATICA IVANIŠEVIĆ.

University of Split (Sveučilište u Splitu): 58000 Split, Livanjska 5/1; tel. (58) 49966; fax (58) 49968; f. 1974; language of instruction: Croatia; 9 faculties; 907 teachers; 10,215 students; Rector (acting) Prof. Dr DRAŽEN ŠTAMBUK.

University of Zagreb (Sveučilište u Zagrebu): 41000 Zagreb, POB 815, trg Maršala Tita 14; tel. (41) 464233; fax (41) 420388; f. 1669; language of instruction: Croatian; 27 faculties; 4,050 teachers; 44,266 students.

Social Welfare

In 1993 a system of partial payment for medical care and medicines was in operation in Croatia. In 1992 health care employed 11,000 physicians, 2,500 dentists and 2,000 pharmacists. The effects of the civil conflict in the Republic, particularly the number of refugees, (estimated at 524,000 in September 1993) made foreign humanitarian assistance, from organizations such as the Open Society Fund, increasingly desirable.

NATIONAL AGENCY

Ministry of Health: see section on The Government (Ministries).

Ministry of Labour and Social Welfare: see section on The Government (Ministries).

NON-GOVERNMENTAL ORGANIZATION

Open Society Fund: 41000 Zagreb, Kravavi Most 2; tel. (41) 276819; fax (41) 275741; f. 1992; aid programmes dedicated to refugees and displaced persons; direct relief operations, psychological and trauma assistance, repatriation projects.

The Environment

Ministry of Construction and Environmental Protection: see section on The Government (Ministries); incl.:

Institute for Nature Protection: 41000 Zagreb, Ilica 44/II; tel. (41) 432022, 432023; fax (41) 431515; f. 1946; Dir Ing. MIHO MILJANIĆ.

Croatian Society for the Conservation of the Natural and Cultural Heritage Hrvatsko Udruženje za Zaštitu Prirodnog i Kulturno-Provijesnog Nasljeda: 41000 Zagreb, trg Kralja Tomislava 19; tel. (41) 274809; fax (41) 427676; Pres. Dr GORAN SUŠIĆ.

Croatian Society of Natural Sciences, Section for the Protection of Nature: Hrvatsko Prirodoslovno Društvo, 41000 Zagreb, Ilica 16/III; Pres. Prof. VLATKO SILOBRČIĆ; Sec. Prof SLOBODAN BRANT.

Hydro-Meteorological Institute of Croatia (Hidrometeoroloski Zavod Hrvatske): 41000 Zagreb, Grič 3; tel. (41) 421222; telex 21356; f. 1947; responsibilities incl. ecological studies, pollution monitoring; Dir Dipl. Eng. TOMISLAV VUČETIĆ.

Marine Research Institute (Centar za Istrazivanje Mora): 41000 Zagreb, POB 1016, Bijenicka 54; tel. (41) 425808; telex 21383; fax (41) 420437; f. 1969; concentrates on environmental concerns in the Adriatic Sea; Dir BOŽENA COSOVIĆ.

NON-GOVERNMENTAL ORGANIZATIONS

Green Action Ecological Movement (Šibenik): 59000 Šibenik, Roberta Vissiania 3; tel. (59) 29097; fax (59) 29097; Pres. PAVLE ČALA.

Green Action (Split) (Zelena Akcija—Split): see section on Political Organizations.

Green Action (Zagreb) (Zelena Akcija—Zagreb): see section on Political Organizations.

Green Alliance of Croatia (Savez Zelenih Hrvatske): 41000 Zagreb, Đorđićeva 7; tel. and fax (41) 430119; waste minimization, sustainable energy policy and environmental education.

Green Party (Rijeka): 51000 Rijeka, Ivana Rendića 8; Pres. DANKO HOLJEVIĆ.

Defence

Military service in Croatia is compulsory for men and lasts for a period of 10 months. According to Western estimates, in June 1993, Croatian armed forces totalled 103,300. This total included an army of 95,000, a navy of 4,000 and an air force of 300. Reserves numbered some 180,000. In addition, there were 40,000 armed military police and an air defence force of 4,000 at this time. Paramilitary forces consisted of 8,000 border police and 16,000 interior police. The Croatian Defence Association, the armed wing of the nationalist Croatian Party of Rights, consisting of 1,000 troops in mid-1993, was deployed in Bosnia and Herzegovina. A total of 15,400 UN troops (the United Nations Protection Force in Yugoslavia—UNPROFOR) was stationed in Croatia. The force comprised 12 UN infantry battalions and support units from 18 countries. On 4 October 1993 UNPROFOR's mandate was extended for an additional six months. In January 1993 a Council of Defence and National Security was set up; this became the Presidential Council of Defence and National Security in November. The President of the Republic is the General Secretary of the Council.

According to official sources, in December 1993 a total of 50,200 troops from the Croatian army was involved in the civil conflict in Croatia. The 'Serbian Army of Serbian Krajina' was estimated to consist of 40,000–50,000 troops in mid-1993. In October 1993 it was reported that an Italian unit, the 'Garibaldi Unit', was fighting alongside Serb paramilitary forces. Some Russian and Romanian fighters were also said to be assisting the Serbs. Serb commanders claimed that this international force totalled 6,000–7,000.

Supreme Commander of the Armed Forces of the Republic of Croatia: President of the Republic.

Chief of Staff of the Army: Gen. JANKO BOBETKO.

Bibliography

Bilandzić, D., et al. *Croatia between War and Independence.* Zagreb, University of Zagreb and OKC Zagreb, 1991.

Crnja, Z. *Cultural History of Croatia.* Zagreb, Office of Information, 1962.

Cuvalo, A. *The Croatian National Movement 1966–72.* Boulder, Colorado, East European Monographs, 1990.

Gazi, S. *A History of Croatia.* New York, Philosophical Library, 1973.

Omrcanin, I. *Diplomatic and Political History of Croatia.* Philadelphia, Pennsylvania, Dorrance, 1972.

Schödl, G. *Kroatische Nationalpolitik und 'Jugoslavenstvo': Studien zu nationaler Integration und regionaler Politik in Kroatien-Dalmatien am Beginn des 20 Jahrhunderts.* Munich, R. Oldenbourg, 1990.

Zasosek, N. *Setting up the New Institutional Framework for Croatian Politics: the Role of the Legislature.* Budapest, Hungarian Centre for Democracy Studies Foundation, 1992.

THE CZECH REPUBLIC

Geography

PHYSICAL FEATURES

The Czech Republic is a land-locked state located in central Europe, covering an area of 78,864 sq km (30,450 sq miles). It comprises the lands of Bohemia and Moravia (the latter also includes part of the historic region known as Silesia, most of which is now in Poland). The country is bordered by Poland to the north, Slovakia (which together with the Czech Republic formed Czechoslovakia between 1918 and 1992) to the east, Germany to the west and Austria to the south.

Bohemia, the westernmost of the Czech Lands, covers the region drained by the upper Labe (Elbe) and its tributary, the Vltava (Moldau), on which the capital, Prague (Praha), stands. This region is a plateau (average height 500 m), bordered to the north-west and south-west by low ranges of mountains (the Krušné Hory, or Erzgebirge, and the Český Les, or Böhmerwald, respectively), which form a natural frontier with Germany. The Krkonoše Hory (Riesengebirge) range, the highest of the Sudetic (Sudeten) mountains, marks the border with Poland, rising to 1603 m (5,259 ft) at Mt Sněžka. Several important rivers, including the Vltava and the Ohře, rise in the south-western hill country and flow north into the Labe, and hence into the North Sea. Moravia, in the east of the country, is a mainly lowland region, which has traditionally been a crossing point between Poland and south-central Europe. It is drained by the Dyje and Morava rivers; the latter forms part of the border with Slovakia and flows south to join the Danube (Dunaj) on the borders of Slovakia and Austria. Eastern Moravia is more rugged and mountainous, with the Little and White Carpathian Mountains forming the rest of the border with Slovakia.

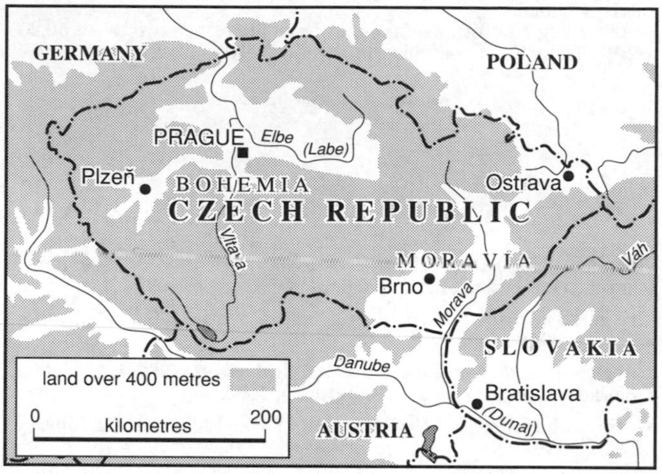

CLIMATE

The climate is typically continental, with cold, dry winters and hot, humid summers. The average July temperature in Prague is 19°C (66°F) and the average January temperature is −1°C (30°F). Prague receives an average annual rainfall of 485 mm, which often falls as snow in winter months. There is little climatic variation throughout the country.

POPULATION

At the census of March 1991 the population of the Czech Republic was 10,302,215. Of these, 81.2% were Czechs (Bohemians), 13.2% Moravian, 3.1% Slovaks, 0.6% Silesians and 2.5% of other nationalities, including small communities of Poles, Roma (Gypsies) and Germans. However, some 40% of the population live in the administrative district of Moravia. The official language was Czech, a member of the Western Slavonic group of languages. Members of ethnic minorities continued to use their own languages. The major religion was Christianity. At the census of 1991, 39.5% of the population were adherents of the Roman Catholic Church. An estimated 15% were nominally Protestant (the largest denomination, the Hussite Church, had about 400,000 members), and there were small numbers of Old Catholics and Eastern Orthodox. About 30% of the population declared themselves to have no religious beliefs.

At the census of 1991 the population density was 130.6 persons per sq km. The capital city is Prague. It is situated in central Bohemia and had a population of 1,212,000 at the 1991 census. Other important towns were Brno (population 392,614), the administrative capital of Moravia, and Ostrava (331,504), also situated in Moravia.

Chronology

5th–7th centuries: Slavic tribes migrated to central Europe from the eastern plains.

830: The establishment of the Great Moravian Empire, which comprised Bohemia, Moravia and Slovakia.

907: Following the Battle of Bratislava (Pressburg), the Great Moravian Empire was overthrown and the Kingdom of Bohemia was established.

1041: Bohemia became a fief of the Holy Roman Empire, after the subjugation of Prince Bretislav of Bohemia, by the forces of Henry III, the German Emperor.

1310: After a four-year struggle over the succession, the Bohemian nobles granted the throne to John of Luxembourg, thus ending the Přemyslid dynasty in Bohemia.

1346–78: The reign of Charles I of Bohemia (Charles IV as Holy Roman Emperor), who encouraged the cultural and commercial development of the Czech Lands.

1419: Following the martyrdom of Jan Hus (1415), the leader of a reformist religious movement centred in Prague, his followers, the Hussites, rebelled against German rule after the 'First Defenestration of Prague'.

1420–33: The Hussite Wars were fought, in which forces loyal to the Holy Roman Empire attempted to supress the Hussite rebellion.

1526: Czech nobles elected the Habsburg Archduke Ferdinand I to the throne.

1620: After a two-year rebellion, which began with the Second Defenestration of Prague, Czech troops were defeated at the Battle of the White Mountain.

1781–85: Serfdom was abolished in the Czech Lands.

1848: An unsuccessful uprising against the Habsburgs took place in Prague.

30 May 1918: The Pittsburgh Agreement, which provided for the creation of a common Czech-Slovak state, was signed between Slovak and Czech exiles.

28 October 1918: The Republic of Czechoslovakia was proclaimed; Tomáš Garrigue Masaryk was elected President.

28 June 1919: The Treaty of Versailles provided international recognition to the Czechoslovak state and confirmed its frontiers.

November 1935: Masaryk resigned as President; he was succeeded by Edvard Beneš.

29 September 1938: The Munich Conference took place between the leaders of the United Kingdom, France, Italy and Germany; an agreement was signed, which permitted the cession of the Czechoslovak territories known as Sudetenland to Germany.

5 October 1938: Beneš resigned as President.

15–16 March 1939: Hitler, the German leader, invaded the Czech Lands: Bohemia and Moravia became a German Protectorate; Slovakia was proclaimed an independent state, under the pro-Fascist leadership of Mgr Jozef Tiso.

3 April 1945: Beneš and his Government-in-exile returned to Czechoslovakia.

9 May 1945: Soviet troops entered Prague.

16 May 1946: National elections took place; the Czechoslovak Communist Party (CPCz) won 38% of the votes cast; Klement Gottwald, leader of the CPCz, was appointed Prime Minister.

25 February 1948: The Communists seized power, following the resignation of 12 non-Communist ministers.

9 May 1948: A new Constitution was approved, which declared Czechoslovakia a 'people's democracy'.

30 May 1948: Elections took place, with only Communist-approved candidates nominated.

June 1948: Beneš resigned, after refusing to sign the new Constitution.

December 1952: Rudolf Slánský, former Secretary-General of the CPCz, and other prominent Communists were executed after 'show trials'.

March 1953: Klement Gottwald died. Antonín Novotný was appointed First Secretary of the CPCz; Antonín Zápotocký became President; Viliám Široký was appointed Prime Minister.

1957: First Secretary of the CPCz, Antonín Novotný, replaced Zápotocký as President.

July 1960: A new Constitution was enacted; Czechoslovakia was renamed the Czechoslovak Socialist Republic.

1963: Prime Minister Široký was replaced by Jozef Lenárt, who launched the mildly reformist New Economic Model. Rudolf Slánský and other Communists who had been purged in the 1950s were rehabilitated.

October 1967: A student rally was violently dispersed by police.

5 January 1968: Antonín Novotný resigned as First Secretary of the CPCz; he was replaced by Alexander Dubček, leader of the Communist Party of Slovakia (CPS).

March 1968: Censorship of the press was ended.

April 1968: The Central Committee of the CPCz adopted an 'Action Programme', which proposed constitutional and economic reforms. Gen. Ludvík Svoboda was appointed President. Oldřich Černík was appointed Prime Minister.

3 August 1968: Representatives of the Communist Parties of member-countries of the Warsaw Pact (except Romania) met in Bratislava to discuss Czechoslovakia's 'Prague Spring' reforms.

20/21 August 1968: Warsaw Pact troops invaded Czechoslovakia; Dubček and other government and Party leaders were abducted to Moscow.

16 January 1969: A student, Jan Palach, immolated himself and died, in protest at the ending of reforms.

17 April 1969: Gustáv Husák replaced Dubček as First Secretary of the CPCz.

1 January 1969: A federal system of government was introduced.

January 1970: Černík was dismissed as Prime Minister.

11 December 1973: A treaty, signed between the Federal Republic of Germany and Czechoslovakia, normalized relations between the two countries and formally annulled the 1938 Munich Agreement.

May 1975: Svoboda resigned as President and was replaced by Husák.

1 January 1977: A group of dissidents, including Václav Havel, the playwright, published the 'Charter 77' manifesto, which demanded an end to the abuse of civil and political rights.

April 1987: Mikhail Gorbachev, General Secretary of the CPSU, arrived in Prague on an official visit.

December 1987: Miloš Jakeš replaced Gustáv Husák as General Secretary of the CPCz.

21 August 1988: Large anti-government demonstrations took place in Prague, on the 20th anniversary of the 1968 Soviet invasion.

10 October 1988: Lubomír Štrougal resigned as federal Prime Minister; he was replaced by Ladislav Adamec.

16 January 1989: A large demonstration took place to mark the 20th anniversary of the suicide of Jan Palach; Václav Havel and 13 other dissidents were arrested (international protests later secured Havel's release).

1 May 1989: The traditional May Day rally was disrupted when police dispersed demonstrators protesting against human rights violations.

21 August 1989: Several thousand people took part in demonstrations in Prague, on the 21st anniversary of the Soviet invasion.

28 October 1989: Anti-government demonstrations took place, on the 71st anniversary of the establishment of a Czechoslovak state.

17 November 1989: Students participating in an officially-sanctioned demonstration were attacked by riot police; 140 people were injured. Two days later some 300 opposition activists from various non-Communist organizations united to form Civic Forum, a broad anti-government coalition (in Slovakia, it's counterpart was known as Public Against Violence—PAV).

21 November 1989: Adamec began discussions with Civic Forum.

24 November 1989: With protests and strikes continuing to take place, Miloš Jakeš, General Secretary of the CPCz, and all other members of the Presidium of the Central Committee and the Secretariat of the CPCz, resigned; Karel Urbanek was elected leader of the CPCz. Alexander Dubček returned to Prague and spoke to a large crowd in Wenceslas Square.

28 November 1989: Civic Forum was officially registered as a legal organization.

29 November 1989: The Federal Assembly abolished the CPCz's constitutional monopoly of power.

7 December 1989: Adamec resigned as Prime Minister; he was replaced by Marián Čalfa.

10 December 1989: Čalfa announced a new federal Government, with a majority of non-Communist members. Gustav Husák resigned as President.

28 December 1989: Dubček was elected Chairman of the Federal Assembly. The following day it elected Václav Havel President of Czechoslovakia by the Federal Assembly.

1 February 1990: The abolition of the StB (Státni bezpečnost—the secret police) was announced.

6 February 1990: Petr Pithart was appointed Prime Minister of the Czech Republic.

7 February 1990: The National Front, the Communists' political organization, was disbanded.

27–28 March 1990: The Federal Assembly approved new laws guaranteeing freedom of association and freedom of the press, and allowing exiles to reclaim their citizenship.

29 March 1990: The name of the country was changed to the Czech and Slovak Federative Republic.

27 May 1990: Václav Klaus, federal Minister of Finance, announced a reform-orientated budget.

June 1990: Elections to the Federal Assembly took place; Civic Forum (in Bohemia and Moravia) and PAV (in Slovakia) won an overall majority. A coalition Government was formed, with participation from all major parties, except the CPCz.

5 July 1990: Havel was re-elected as President for a transitional two-year period.

12 December 1990: The Federal Assembly approved constitutional legislation delimiting the powers of the federal, Czech and Slovak governments.

23 February 1991: Civic Forum was formally disbanded; its members formed two new political parties, the conservative Civic Democratic Party (CDP) and the liberal Civic Movement.

26 February 1991: Legislation allowing privatization of state-owned enterprises was approved.

2 March 1991: Thousands of people took part in demonstrations in Moravia, demanding autonomous status for their region.

10–14 March 1991: There were large demonstrations in Slovakia, in favour of independence for the Republic; President Havel was attacked by crowds when he visited Bratislava.

27 April 1991: The Civic Movement officially constituted itself as an independent political party.

13 June 1991: The first phase of the 'large privatization' programme began, with the sale of 50 state-owned enterprises to Western companies.

21 June 1991: The withdrawal of Soviet forces, which had been stationed in Czechoslovakia since 1968, was completed.

1 July 1991: Leaders of the member countries of the Warsaw Pact met in Prague to complete the dissolution of the organization, by formally ending the work of its Political Consultative Committee.

18 July 1991: The Federal Assembly approved legislation that authorized a referendum on the future of Czech–Slovak relations.

29 August 1991: The Federal Government formally recognized the independence of Estonia, Latvia and Lithuania.

5–6 June 1992: At federal and republican legislative elections there were strong performances by the Movement for a Democratic Slovakia (MDS) and other parties favouring separation between the Czech Lands and Slovakia. However, the pro-federal CDP became the single largest party; the successors to the Communists (Left Bloc in the Czech Lands, Party of the Democratic Left in Slovakia) came third and fourth. Negotiations commenced between the CDP and MDS to form a federal government. Meanwhile Mečiar was appointed Slovak Prime Minister.

July 1992: A transitional federal Government was appointed, dominated by members of the CDP and MDS, with Jan Stráský of the CDP as Prime Minister. Czech politicians accepted that total separation of Czech Lands and Slovakia was preferable to the compromise measures proposed. Václav Klaus was appointed Prime Minister of the new Czech Government. Three rounds of voting in the Federal Assembly failed to elect a new President, with the MDS and Slovak National Party blocking re-election of Havel, who duly resigned.

26 October 1992: A Customs Union treaty and other accords were agreed between the Czech and Slovak Governments.

25 November 1992: The Federal Assembly adopted legislation enabling the constitutional disbanding of the federation, with the assets divided 2:1 in the Czech Republic's favour, in accordance with the balance of population.

December 1992: A treaty of good neighbourliness, friendly relations and co-operation was signed between the two Republics, followed by the exchange of diplomatic relations. A new Constitution of the Czech Republic was adopted; the Czech National Council became the Chamber of Deputies (lower house), retaining the existing 200 members. Czechoslovakia, Hungary and Poland signed an agreement with the European Community (EC—known as the European Union from November 1993) granting them associate member status.

1 January 1993: Separation of the Czech Republic and Slovakia took effect.

26 January 1993: Havel was elected President of the Czech Republic.

February 1993: Separate Czech and Slovak currencies (both called koruna) introduced. Final rejection of amendment to establish a Senate (upper house) with membership transferred from the former Federal Assembly; elections for the Senate were to be postponed until September 1994.

6 April 1993: Prague Stock Exchange opened.

June 1993: Parliament voted to establish a Constitutional Court and a Supreme Control Office (an independent body to audit government finances). Strict wage controls reintroduced for all companies with 25 or more employees. At the congress of the Communist Party of Bohemia and Moravia, neo-Stalinists were expelled and reformists left to form a new party, the Party of the Democratic Left.

July 1993: The former Czechoslovak Communist regime was declared illegitimate and criminal. Border controls introduced on Czech–Slovak frontier to stem flow of third-party refugees, mainly heading for Germany; Slovak citizens, however, were to be unaffected.

29 September 1993: Second round of 'voucher' privatization launched.

November 1993: The Czech Republic was elected to the 15-member UN Security Council, thus becoming the unofficial representative of post-Communist European countries, with effect from January 1994. A resolution was passed in the Chamber of Deputies requiring the Government to submit a constitutional law on new regional administrative divisions as soon as possible. The system of state prosecutors was abolished and replaced with state attorneys with effect from January 1994.

History

GORDON WIGHTMAN

INTRODUCTION

With the creation of independent Czech and Slovak Republics on 1 January 1993, the relatively short life of one of the states created following the collapse of the Austro-Hungarian Empire at the end of the First World War, the Republic of Czechoslovakia, came to an end. Founded on 28 October 1918, Czechoslovakia united the historic Czech Kingdom of Bohemia and Moravia, which had been an important power in central Europe until its incorporation into the Austrian Empire in the early 17th century, and Slovak provinces of Hungary, which had been under Magyar (Hungarian) rule for almost 1,000 years. Although created to fulfil the demands for self-determination of two of the western Slavic peoples, the Czechs and the Slovaks, the country was always more heterogeneous than the name suggests. Before the Second World War some 25% of its population were ethnic Germans, and, even though most of the German population were deported after the War, sizeable national minorities remained. The Czechoslovak census of March 1991 revealed that 9.8m. Czechs and 4.8m. Slovaks constituted 93% of a population of 15,567,550. Of other national groups, the most significant were the 600,000-strong Hungarian minority (mostly in southern Slovakia), and the Roma population, which was estimated at 500,000, although only 108,000 had registered as such in the census.

Czechoslovakia was the only country in Eastern Europe where parliamentary democracy survived intact for almost all of the period between the First and Second World Wars. Much of the credit for this success can be attributed to the influence of its first two Presidents, Tomáš Masaryk (1918–35) and Edvard Beneš (1935–38 and 1945–48). Democracy was maintained despite defects in the constitutional system. Ethnic diversity weakened a party system that was also highly fragmented by ethnic and social divisions. The system produced coalition governments of relatively short duration, which failed to provide lasting political stability. A more serious threat to the security of the country, however, was the growing disaffection felt by two of the three major ethnic groups, the Slovaks and the Germans.

Slovak disaffection with the pre-1938 Czechoslovak state (the so-called First Republic) stemmed, in part, from the predominant role played by Czechs in the country's political and economic life. It was aggravated by attempts to propagate the concept of a single Czechoslovak nation, of which Czechs and Slovaks were said to be two distinct but closely related branches. That policy tended to ignore important differences between the two nations. Although their languages are mutually comprehensible, they are as much divided by their history and divergent cultural and economic development as they are linked by linguistic and geographic proximity.

Czechs and Slovaks once shared a common state—the Great Moravian Empire, in the ninth century—but, thereafter, their histories largely diverged. While the Slovaks came under Magyar rule, the Czechs created a kingdom that was a major political and cultural force in medieval times. The first university in central Europe was established in Prague, in 1348, by Charles I of Bohemia, who was crowned Holy Roman Emperor seven years later (as Charles IV). In the early 15th century the Hussite movement (named after Jan Hus, Rector of Charles University, Prague, who was burned at the stake in 1415) established the Czech kingdom as a Protestant power. However, the Czechs were defeated by the Austrians, at the Battle of the White Mountain, in 1620. Despite this defeat and their subsequent incorporation into the Habsburg Empire and enforced conversion to Roman Catholicism, the Protestant legacy was to play an important part in the search for a Czech national identity in the 19th century. Slovakia, on the other hand, remained profoundly Roman Catholic and did not experience the same level of urbanization and industrialization as the Czech Lands. The rapid economic development in the Czech Lands, together with the nationalist emphasis on the Hussite tradition and the association of Roman Catholicism with the Austrian 'oppressors', further diluted attachment to the Roman Catholic Church among the Czechs.

It would, however, be wrong to overstate differences between the Czechs and Slovaks. Links between them were maintained, if sporadically, over the centuries. Individual Slovaks often benefited from the availability of university education and support for their studies in Prague. Indeed, the 19th-century revival of Czech nationalism owed much to the contributions of Slovak intellectuals, such as the poet Jan Kollár and the archaeologist Pavel Josef Šafařík, both of whom helped to revive the Czech literary language. Many Slovaks were as committed as Czechs to the establishment of an independent Czechoslovak state. In the diplomatic and propaganda campaign for Czechoslovak independence, which was conducted in Western Europe during the First World War, no less a role was played by the Slovak, Milan Rostislav Štefánik (Czechoslovakia's first Minister of Defence, who died in an aeroplane accident, in 1919), than by his more famous colleagues, Masaryk and Beneš. Moreover, ordinary Slovaks, exiles or prisoners of war in France, Italy and Russia, were as ready as Czechs to volunteer for the military units that were formed in those countries to fight on the side of the Allied Powers for Czechoslovak independence.

The establishment of Czechoslovakia as a unitary state was one source of increasing Slovak discontentment during the 1920s and 1930s. However, it was the dissatisfaction of the German minority which proved fatal to Czechoslovak democracy and to the survival of the state. Although many of the German inhabitants had come to terms with the Czechoslovak state and some German political parties participated in government, the rise of Nazism encouraged the emergence of an extreme German nationalism. The Sudeten German Party, led by Konrad Henlein, attracted some 67% of the votes cast by Germans in the 1935 parliamentary elections.

The problem might have been successfully contained had not the United Kingdom and France agreed, in the Munich Agreement of 29 September 1938, to Germany's annexation of Czechoslovakia's border regions (the Sudetenland—mainly inhabited by members of the German minority). Less than one week later, on 5 October, Beneš resigned as President, only three years after his election to that post. He left a country that had not only lost territory, but also its strategic defences. Six months later, on 15 March 1939, Nazi armed forces entered Prague and established a German Protectorate of Bohemia and Moravia. In Slovakia, which had been granted self-government in late 1938, a separate Slovak state was formed, ruled by the 'puppet' regime of Jozef Tiso.

CZECHOSLOVAKIA AFTER 1945

Beneš spent the Second World War campaigning for the restoration of the Czechoslovak Republic, within its pre-1938 frontiers. In 1945, after the country's liberation, he returned to Prague as President. In many other respects, however, the political situation was markedly different to that of the pre-War years. The problem of the German minority was resolved by their deportation, and an attempt was made, albeit grudgingly approved by Beneš, to satisfy Slovak demands for greater autonomy through the establishment of a legislature in Bratislava (the Slovak National Council) and an executive Board of Commissioners.

Recognition that the proliferation of political parties in the pre-War First Republic had been a major source of political instability led Beneš to favour a reduction in the number of parties that would be permitted after 1945. It was a policy, however, that contributed to the curtailment, rather than the strengthening, of parliamentary democracy. It was achieved largely through the prohibition not only of parties that had collaborated with the Nazis, but the proscription of the Agrarian Party, whose guilt was highly dubious.

As a result of that ban, the first post-War parliamentary elections, which took place in May 1946, were not wholly free, but they were, nevertheless, competitive. Their outcome indicated a marked increase in support for the Communist Party of Czechoslovakia (CPCz). With 38% of the votes cast in the country as a whole (40% in Bohemia and Moravia, but only 30% in Slovakia), it emerged as the largest party in the new Constituent National Assembly, with 114 of the 300 seats. Of the three other parties who nominated candidates in Czech constituencies, the moderate Czechoslovak Socialist Party won 55 seats, the Catholic-orientated Czechoslovak People's Party 46 and the centre-left Czechoslovak Social Democrats 37. In Slovakia, however, the Democratic Party won 62% of the popular vote, although it gained only 43 seats in the Assembly. (Two other small parties, the Labour Party and the Freedom Party, contested the elections and won two and three seats respectively.)

Before 1939 the Communists had never attracted more than 13% of the vote. However, this changed because of the Party's patriotic stance in the late 1930s, popular disillusionment with pro-Western liberal parties, after the Munich Agreement, and the benefits that accrued from association with the USSR, which had liberated most of Czechoslovakia from German occupation (US forces stopped near the western Bohemian town of Plzeň). Furthermore, Communist participation in the Provisional Government, which had governed the country until the elections, gave them a respectability they had earlier lacked. The CPCz's declared commitment, in 1946, to 'a specific Czechoslovak road to socialism' suggested that it would retain the country's democratic and parliamentary traditions, rather than introduce Stalinist practices.

For two years after the elections this apparent commitment to democracy continued. Czechoslovakia was ruled by an all-party coalition Government, in which Klement Gottwald, leader of the CPCz, the largest party in the National Assembly, was Prime Minister. However, the period of coalition government proved to be short-lived. On 20 February 1948 12 non-Communist ministers resigned, thus providing Gottwald with the opportunity to seize power by ostensibly constitutional means. On 25 February President Beneš was forced to agree to his appointment as head of a new Government, which was dominated by Communists.

During the remaining months of 1948 there was a gradual eradication of democratic practice and an emasculation of opposition to the Communists. On 9 May the National Assembly approved a new Constitution, which declared Czechoslovakia a 'people's democracy'. On 30 May elections took place to the National Assembly, with only a single list of candidates. This allowed some representation of non-Communist parties, but individuals who were unacceptable to the Communists had already been expelled from such parties. On 2 June, following his refusal to ratify the new Constitution, Beneš resigned from the presidency. The completeness of the Communists' victory was demonstrated by the election of Gottwald to that office 12 days later.

In the years that followed political repression was directed not only at the Communists' opponents, but at members of the CPCz itself, in a series of 'show trials', which were among the most severe in Eastern Europe. They reached their most extreme in November 1952, when 14 senior Party and government officials, including Rudolf Slánský, former Secretary-General of the CPCz, were found guilty on charges of conspiracy against the state. Eleven of them, including Slánský, were subsequently executed.

Gottwald's death, on 14 March 1953, only one week after the death of Stalin, the Soviet leader, was followed by a period of collective leadership in Czechoslovakia. Antonín Zápotocký, who had succeeded Gottwald as Prime Minister in 1948, became President in his place, and Antonín Novotný was appointed head of the CPCz, as First Secretary of its Central Committee. In other respects, there were few changes to the Stalinist policies conducted since 1948. The continuation of 'hardline' policies was demonstrated by the brutal suppression, in June 1953, of workers' demonstrations in Plzeň and other Czech towns. The workers were protesting against price rises and a currency reform that depleted the value of savings. Furthermore, political trials continued, notably those of alleged 'Slovak nationalists', in 1954, which led to the imprisonment of a number of leading Slovak Communists. Among them was Gustáv Husák, who had organized the Communist *coup d'état* in Slovakia, in 1947–48, and who was later to become General Secretary of the CPCz and President of Czechoslovakia.

The moderation of Stalinist policies in much of Eastern Europe in the 1950s, inspired by the new leadership in the USSR, had little effect in Czechoslovakia. Not even Khrushchev's denunciation of Stalin, at the 20th Congress of the CPSU, in February 1956, had a significant impact on the Stalinist policies still in effect in Czechoslovakia. The worst aspects of the CPCz's repressive policies were discontinued thereafter, but it was not until Khrushchev's renewed criticism of Stalin, at the 22nd Party Congress, in 1961, that genuine de-Stalinization began to be implemented in Czechoslovakia.

Recognition by Novotný (who had continued as First Secretary of the CPCz after assuming the presidency on Zápotocký's death, in 1957) that Czechoslovakia, like its neighbours, had suffered from 'a personality cult' in the 1950s, brought a partial rehabilitation for its victims. It also created the opportunity for the gradual emergence, in the 1960s, of a reform movement within the CPCz. Although Novotný encouraged the introduction of economic, and even some political, reforms, his failure to respond to growing pressure for more radical changes, combined with hostility towards him among Slovak Communists and members of the cultural intelligentsia, resulted in his dismissal as First Secretary, on 5 January 1968. He was replaced by Alexander Dubček, until then leader of the Communist Party of Slovakia (CPS), part of the CPCz. He immediately embarked on a programme of radical political and economic reforms, thus beginning a short period of political tolerance, which came to be known as the 'Prague Spring'.

THE 1968 'PRAGUE SPRING'

The reforms agreed by the new Dubček leadership were presented in an Action Programme, approved by the Central Committee of the CPCz on 6 April 1968. It envisaged the combination of a socialist economy, albeit one in which the market would have a role to play, with a democratization of the political system, which would permit the re-emergence of Czechoslovakia's democratic traditions. Recognizing that the USSR would be unlikely to accept a complete loss of power by the CPCz, Czechoslovak reformers planned to modify its traditional dictatorial role through the introduction of more genuine elections, both to parliamentary bodies and within the CPCz. In addition, greater freedom of expression was to be permitted, a greater degree of separation between Party and State was envisaged, and a federal system of government was to be introduced.

Although the Czechoslovak reforms were, in some respects, carefully controlled by the CPCz, in order to allay the fears of the Soviet leadership, the USSR and its allies were anxious to prevent Czechoslovakia's experimental 'socialism with a human face' spreading to other countries in the region, thus threatening the USSR's perceived security interests. On the night of 20/21 August 1968, troops from the other Warsaw Pact states (except Romania), led by Soviet forces, invaded Czechoslovakia. The Soviet leadership's original intention of replacing Dubček with more orthodox Communists, however, failed, owing to popular resistance and the refusal of President Ludvík Svoboda (who had replaced Novotný in that post in April) to accept pro-Soviet nominees. Nevertheless, the invasion ended the Prague Spring reforms and, eight months later, on 17 April 1969, the USSR was able to force Dubček's resignation.

SUPPRESSION OF REFORM AND THE EMERGENCE OF DISSENT

After Dubček was replaced as First Secretary of the CPCz by Gustáv Husák, all but one of the 1968 reforms were abandoned. The federal system, which had been proposed in the Action Programme and implemented on 1 January 1969, remained in place. Separate Czech and Slovak Republics were established, within a Czechoslovak federation; a Czech National Council and a Czech government were created (to parallel those established in Slovakia in 1945); and the country's legislature was transformed into a bicameral Federal Assembly. However, failure to federalize the CPCz and increasing centralization during the 1970s rendered the changes ineffective as a means of granting the Slovaks the greater autonomy which they sought (and which the 1945 changes had failed to achieve).

In other spheres Husák began reversing the 1968 reforms and attempting to ensure that Czechoslovakia conformed with a model of socialism acceptable to the USSR. In the period 1969–71 the CPCz lost some 25% of its membership, as proponents of reform left or were expelled. Reformers were dismissed from influential posts in other institutions and organizations. Newspapers, journals and organizations such as the Czechoslovak Writers' Union and the Czechoslovak Youth Union, which continued to oppose the new policies, were closed down. Opposition to the new orthodoxy was firmly suppressed. Public demonstrations on the first anniversary of the invasion, in August 1969, resulted in five deaths and the arrest of almost 1,400 people in Prague alone. Initial attempts to establish opposition movements (notably the Movement of Revolutionary Youth, in 1969, and the Socialist Movement of Czechoslovak Citizens, in 1971) failed, as their leaders were arrested and imprisoned for their activities.

It was only in the latter half of the 1970s that more durable dissident movements were established, notably Charter 77 and the Committee for the Defence of the Rights of the Unjustly Prosecuted (VONS). These differed from earlier opposition movements in that they did not propose an alternative political programme to that of the Communist leadership. Instead, they campaigned for the observance of civil and political rights, which the Communist regime ostensibly recognized. In addition, they attempted to pursue those aims in ways that were, in theory, permitted by the Constitution.

The 1975 Helsinki Final Act and Czechoslovakia's subsequent ratification of the UN's International Covenants on Civil and Political Rights and on Economic, Social and Cultural Rights gave members of the opposition greater scope to campaign on those issues. However, the direct stimulus for the creation of the Charter 77 manifesto, a document made public on 1 January 1977, was the arrest and imprisonment, in 1976, of members of The Plastic People of the Universe, a popular 'underground' rock group. One of the leaders of Charter 77 was Václav Havel, a playwright who came to prominence in the early 1960s and whose work had been banned since 1969. He later observed that the manifesto's authors (one of whom was Havel himself) had been inspired, not only by the injustice inflicted on the rock group, but also by the evident solidarity among the diverse groups of people attending the trial.

Charter 77 was initially signed by only 242 people, but, by the late 1980s, the number of signatories had risen to nearly 2,000. Its influence grew, despite a policy of repression conducted towards it by the authorities. A continual campaign was waged against it in the official media. The Charter's signatories were subject to harassment, dismissal from their jobs, arrest, imprisonment and sometimes pressure to leave the country. The sudden death, in March 1977, of one of the group's first spokesmen, Prof. Jan Patočka, may have been caused by the rough treatment he received while under interrogation.

Any assessment of the achievements of Charter 77 has to recognize that it had little success in the advancement of civil rights during the last decade of Communist rule. Nevertheless, it made a positive contribution in a number of ways. It ensured that the issue of civil and political rights was not forgotten and thus preserved the democratic values that had been revived for only a short time during the Prague Spring. Together with VONS, which dealt with wrongful arrests, it became a valued source of information about abuses of civil rights in Czechoslovakia. It sponsored a range of studies, on issues ranging from the environment to education, which remained relevant in the 1990s. As a movement which united people from diverse sections of the political spectrum, including ex-Communists, liberal democrats and members of the Christian opposition, it established a sense of community, co-operation and trust that was to bear fruit in November 1989, when the Communists' power was finally challenged.

THE END OF COMMUNIST RULE

At the time of Mikhail Gorbachev's election as General Secretary of the CPSU, in March 1985, Czechoslovakia was ruled by a Presidium of the Central Committee of the CPCz. All of its members had been in power since 1971, and, as a result, were closely identified with the suppression of the 1968 reform movement. Some undoubtedly sympathized with the aims of Gorbachev's new programme. However, the leadership as a whole was forced to choose between maintaining their traditional loyalty to the current policy in the USSR and abandoning such emulation of the Soviet example. The latter choice involved the continuation of hardline policy; the former required a new, more sympathetic attitude to reform.

In practice, the leadership adopted a compromise which involved ostensible commitment to a Czechoslovak version of *perestroika* (restructuring), while continuing to condemn the Prague Spring. Largely token gestures were made, which appeared to follow the direction of the USSR's economic and, to a lesser extent, political reforms. Husák resigned as General Secretary of the CPCz in December 1987. However, his replacement by Miloš Jakeš, a man whose hostility to reform in 1968 was well-known and who had been responsible for the purge of the CPCz after the Prague Spring, did not lead to expectations of more radical reforms. The continuing repressive character of the regime was evident in its generally harsh response to the public protests against its policies, which became a more common event from 1988 onwards. Even a peaceful candle-lit vigil, in Bratislava, in March of that year, by several thousand Roman Catholics demanding religious freedom and respect for human rights, was brutally dispersed by the police.

A greater readiness on the part of those outside traditional dissident groups to demonstrate their support for radical changes was shown on 21 August 1988, when several thousand protesters demonstrated in Wenceslas Square, in Prague. A similar protest took place on 28 October, the 70th anniversary of the foundation of Czechoslovakia. On 10 December, UN Human Rights' Day, the authorities for once agreed to an unofficial meeting that was addressed by Václav Havel.

A still more serious challenge to the authorities, however, came in early 1989, when demonstrations took place on 15–20 January, to commemorate the suicide of Jan Palach, in 1969. Palach had set himself on fire in protest at the concessions made by the Dubček leadership to the USSR's demands for the ending of the 1968 reforms. The crowds were brutally dispersed by police, leading dissidents who had been involved in the demonstrations were arrested (including Václav Havel, who was sentenced to nine-months' imprisonment) and restrictive legislation was introduced, in an attempt to prevent further protests.

None of these measures, however, seemed to have much effect. Pro-democracy demonstrations took place again, on 1 May, 21 August and 28 October 1989. Furthermore, the police brutality in January had provoked a written protest to Ladislav Adamec, the federal Prime Minister, from Cardinal František Tomášek, the Archbishop of Prague. He observed that, 'Brutal violence cannot suppress our citizens' desire to enjoy the measure of freedom which has become an accepted feature of 20th-century life.' In addition, a petition, which was signed by more than 2,000 people, condemned the police attacks on the demonstrators and demanded the release of those who had been arrested. In June 1989 another petition, entitled *A Few Sentences*, was published. Among other things, it demanded greater political freedom, the release of political prisoners and an end to censorship and to the oppression of independent initiatives.

The Velvet Revolution

Despite increasing public involvement in protest demonstrations, the collapse of Communist rule surprised most observers. It was a brutal police attack on a student demonstration, on 17 November 1989, which began what came to be known as the 'Velvet Revolution'. The march had been arranged, with the approval of the authorities, to commemorate students executed by the Nazis in 1939. After the dispersal of the crowd by security forces and police, a rumour began that one student had been killed. Although the rumour was later proved to be false, over the next few days protest demonstrations spread from Prague throughout the country.

One week after the march, on 24 November 1989, following mass demonstrations in Wenceslas Square, in Prague, the entire membership of the Presidium and Secretariat of the CPCz resigned. Adamec, the federal Prime Minister, was left with the task of negotiating a settlement with the Communists' opponents. Initially, Adamec seemed to expect the CPCz to retain a 'caretaker role' in the transition to a more democratic regime, as had happened in the German Democratic Republic and Hungary. Such expectations were quickly dispelled. On 19 November Civic Forum (Občanské fórum) was founded to represent all democratic forces in the Czech Republic; a similar movement, Public Against Violence (PAV), was established in Slovakia. These two groups, who worked in close co-operation, presented Adamec with formidable opponents. His attempt to reach agreement with Civic Forum and PAV, on the formation of a coalition government, collapsed in early December, and he resigned. On 10 December a new coalition administration, the 'Government of National Understanding', took office, with Marian Čalfa (formerly Adamec's deputy) as Prime Minister. Only 10 of the 21 members of the new Government were Communists (and two of those had been nominated by Civic Forum).

Initially Civic Forum and PAV were given only seven ministerial posts in the new Government; the remaining four went to the Czechoslovak Socialist Party and the Czechoslovak People's Party. Both these parties had been members of the CPCz-dominated National Front since 1948, but had ended their subservience to the Communists after the November 1989 revolution. In early 1990, however, Civic Forum and PAV increased their representation when Prime Minister Čalfa and three other Communist ministers resigned their membership of the CPCz and joined the new political movements. Yet, even in late 1989, it was already evident that Communist rule was ended. On 28 December Alexander Dubček, who had been expelled from the CPCz in 1970, was elected Chairman of the Federal Assembly. The next day Václav Havel, Civic Forum's leading spokesman, was elected President of Czechoslovakia. He replaced Husák, who had resigned from that post on 10 December.

Czechoslovakia thus began 1990 with an almost completely new leadership. Those associated with the suppression of the Prague Spring had been dismissed from office. In many cases they had been replaced by signatories of Charter 77, and Alexander Dubček, the symbol of 1968, had been restored to a position of political prominence. Nevertheless, it was evident that more than a revival of 'socialism with a human face' was envisaged by the new leaders. A multi-party parliamentary democracy was the aim in the political system; in the economy, a transition to a market-based structure, with at least some degree of privatization, was sought by all the non-Communist political forces.

The Return to Parliamentary Democracy

Seven months after the Velvet Revolution, on 8 and 9 June 1990, elections took place to the bicameral Federal Assembly and to the National Councils (legislatures) of the Czech and Slovak Republics. Earlier in the year legislation had been introduced, which stipulated that the elections could be contested by any party, political movement or coalition of parties with 10,000 members, or which submitted a petition containing the signatures of sufficient electors to make up for any shortfall. To win seats in each chamber of the Federal Assembly and the Czech National Council, parties were required to obtain at least 5% of the votes cast, but a lower 3% threshold applied in the case of the Slovak National Council.

The outcome of the elections was an overwhelming vote in support of parliamentary democracy. Of those eligible to vote, 96% took part. Civic Forum and PAV won a majority of the 150 seats in each chamber of the Federal Assembly (87 in the House of the People and 83 in the House of Nations). Only eight of the 22 contenders for seats in that parliament, however, passed the 5% threshold. The Communists, one of only two parties which nominated candidates in both the Czech and Slovak Republics, became the second largest party, with 23 seats in the House of the People and 24 in the House of Nations. The other party which campaigned in both republics was Coexistence (Együttélés). It sought to attract votes from all ethnic groups, including Poles and Ruthenians, as well as Czechs and Slovaks. Its main support, however, came from the Hungarian minority and it won five seats in the House of the People and seven in the House of Nations, all of them in Slovakia. In that republic, the Christian Democratic Movement (CDM), as had been expected, proved to be much more successful than its counterpart in the Czech Republic, the Christian Democratic Union (CDU). The CDM won 25 seats in the Federal Assembly, compared to 15 won by the CDU. However, PAV won more than twice as many seats as the CDM in Slovakia.

The 13% share of the votes retained by the CPCz suggested that the Communists might still regain some political influence. However, of more immediate threat to the future of federal democracy were the appeals to the electorates in both Republics which stressed regional autonomy or independence. The success of the Movement for Autonomous Democracy-The Society for Moravia and Silesia (MAD-SMS) was especially surprising. Although few observers had expected it to reach the 5% threshold, it received 8%–9% of the votes cast, which represented over 20% of the votes in the two constituencies of North and South Moravia, where it had presented a full list of candidates. This suggested that a much larger number of people than had been anticipated were attracted by its programme of greater autonomy for the regions of Moravia and Silesia. Yet that result was expected to be a relatively minor complication in the search for a lasting constitutional settlement in comparison with the question of relations between the Czechs and the Slovaks. It was the 8%–10% share of the Slovak vote received by the separatist Slovak National Party (SNP) which was the potential source of serious destabilization.

Czechoslovakia emerged from the elections, nevertheless, with a Federal Assembly which seemed capable of coping with the major tasks it expected to encounter during the two years until new elections were due to be held. By the end of June 1990, the Federal Assembly had re-elected Havel as President, confirmed Dubček as Chairman and approved Čalfa's reappointment as Prime Minister of a new coalition Government, comprising nominees from the CDM, in addition to Civic Forum and PAV.

The elections to the Czech National Council produced an overall majority for Civic Forum. Petr Pithart, Prime Minister of the Czech Republic, formed a broadly-based Government, with Civic Forum leading a coalition with the Czechoslovak People's Party (which campaigned as a part of the CDU in the elections) and the MAD-SMS. In Slovakia the election results were more fragmented. PAV was the largest party in the Slovak National Council, with 38 of the 150 seats. It formed a coalition Government with the CDM, which was the second-largest party, and the small Democratic Party, under the outgoing Interior Minister, Vladimír Mečiar.

TOWARDS THE BREAK-UP OF CZECHOSLOVAKIA

The success of Civic Forum and PAV in the June 1990 parliamentary elections reaffirmed the preference of a majority of Czechs and Slovaks for a pluralist parliamentary democracy. However, developments after the elections indicated that the re-establishment of democracy was unlikely to be smooth. The two years leading up to the second parliamentary elections, which had already been set for mid-1992, were to be marked by sharp political differentiation within each republic and a growing divergence between Czechs and Slovaks over a range of fundamental policy issues.

Divisions within Civic Forum and PAV

As broadly-based political movements, Civic Forum and PAV had proved advantageous in the first stage of the transition from Communist rule and the creation of democratic parliaments. In the longer term their effectiveness was less clear-cut. Indeed, by the end of 1990 it was already evident that Civic Forum was too disparate to survive as attempts to implement reforms exacerbated differences within its ranks over the course which should be followed.

After the election of Finance Minister Václav Klaus as Civic Forum's first Chairman, in October 1990, divisions which had remained hidden during the pre-election period were brought to the surface and led to a split within the movement in January 1991. The result was an expansion in the number of parties represented in the legislatures. Two new parties were created in the following month: a right-wing Civic Democratic Party (CDS), led by Klaus, which sought a more effectively structured organization based on individual membership and committed to a radical break with the Communist past; and a centrist Civic Movement, led by Minister of Foreign Affairs Jiří Dienstbier, which advocated the retention of a more loosely organized movement and the pursuit of a more consensual approach in the tradition of Civic Forum and Charter 77. In addition, the centre-right Civic Democratic Alliance, which had stood in the elections under Civic Forum's umbrella, emerged as an independent parliamentary group, while other Civic Forum deputies transferred to the Czechoslovak Social Democratic Party (CSDP), giving that party parliamentary seats it had failed to win at the elections.

The break-up of PAV was much less expected, since it had appeared a less disparate movement than Civic Forum. Disagreements over policy certainly played a part. The more nationalist stance adopted by Slovakia's Prime Minister Vladimír Mečiar, reflected in repeated attempts to win greater power for that Republic and his preference for a more interventionist economic policy than was thought desirable in Prague, were not universally shared within PAV. The movement's elected officials and some of its representatives in the Slovak Government, moreover, viewed Mečiar's policies, aggressive style of leadership and personal ambition as detrimental to Czech–Slovak relations and a threat to democratization. Mečiar's formation in early March 1991 of a platform within PAV called 'For a Democratic Slovakia' brought the conflict to a head. On 23 April he was dismissed as Prime Minister. In response, on 26 April, he and his allies left PAV to form a separate Movement for a Democratic Slovakia (MDS). It supported continued state intervention in the economy to protect Slovaks against the worst effects of economic liberalization and, as was made explicit at its founding congress in mid-June, the transformation of Czechoslovakia into a confederation.

Following the creation of the MDS, PAV was replaced as the largest party in the Slovak parliament by the CDM. The latter's Chairman, Ján Čarnogurský, took over as Prime Minister at the head of a coalition involving the CDM, the Democratic Party and those who had remained in PAV. The split within PAV had, in that respect, more dramatic consequences than the collapse of Civic Forum in the Czech Republic, where the Government had remained largely unaffected. In Slovakia the divisions were also more bitter and his removal from office permitted Mečiar, the most popular politician in that Republic, to portray himself as a martyr who had suffered for his defence of Slovak interests.

Czech–Slovak Disagreements

Much was achieved between 1990 and 1992 in Czechoslovakia's transformation, notably the restitution to their original owners or their descendants of small businesses and property confiscated by the Communists after 1948, and the launching of 'voucher' privatization of large-scale industry. However, the issue which appeared to dominate politics throughout that period, Czech–Slovak relations, remained unresolved, despite the efforts made to find a solution. That failure was all the more surprising as most citizens, politicians and parties (apart from the SNP) were agreed that Czechs and Slovaks should continue to live in a common state. There was also general agreement that there was a need to change the over-centralized federal system which had been inherited from the Communist regime. Beyond these two points, however, there was little common ground.

The formulation of new federal and republican constitutions had been envisaged as one of the major tasks facing the parliaments elected in 1990. However, the emergence among Czech and Slovak politicians of almost diametrically opposed views on the appropriate relationship between the central authorities and the Republics hampered agreement on a lasting constitutional settlement. In general, the Czechs favoured a degree of devolution to the two Republics that would still leave a relatively strong federal authority. They feared, moreover, that too great a transfer of power would impede economic reform and lead to the dissolution of Czechoslovakia. In Slovakia, a majority appeared to support a degree of republican autonomy that was closer to a confederacy than a federation. They suspected that too little devolution would prevent their attainment of adequate control over their own affairs. It would, they claimed, end in an effective recentralization of power in Prague, as had happened after 1945, when they had been granted their own parliament, and after 1969, when the federal system was introduced.

Despite a transfer of some powers to the Republics in December 1990, the dispute erupted once more towards the end of 1991. On this occasion an agreement reached between the Czech and Slovak parliaments, which might have formed the basis for a more lasting constitutional settlement and prevented the question becoming an issue in the 1992 elections, was thwarted by procedural obstacles when it reached the Federal Assembly. The requirement that constitutional bills obtain a qualified majority (three-fifths of all deputies in the House of the People and three-fifths of Czech and Slovak representatives in the House of the Nations, voting separately) enabled a minority to abort the agreement.

Czechoslovakia thus approached its second post-Communist parliamentary elections in June 1992 with the constitutional issue unresolved. By that time it was clear that public opinion in the two Republics diverged not only over that question, but also on a wider range of fundamental policies. The pursuit of a radical transformation of the economy—the unequivocal commitment to a market economy and a much more extensive privatization programme than had seemed likely at the time of the 1990 elections—was viewed with much less enthusiasm by Slovaks than by Czechs. That was hardly surprising given the more severe impact those policies were likely to have on an economy where unemployment had already reached 12% at the end of 1991, compared to only 4% in the Czech Lands. In that context, Slovaks believed greater control over their own affairs would afford opportunities to cushion the effects of economic change, while Czechs feared that divergent economic programmes in the two Republics would prove an obstacle to completion of that reform.

Slovaks were also less enthusiastic than Czechs on action against those too closely involved with the former Communist regime. Attempts to exclude those who were identified as collaborators of the Communist secret police from political life had been made even before the 1990 elections. New legislation, approved by the Federal Assembly in November 1991, went even further than that. It proscribed, for a five-year period, the appointment to state and public-sector posts not only of former collaborators but also of Communist Party officials elected between 1948 and 1989, of those active in the purges immediately after 1948 and after the Prague Spring, and of those who had served in the Communist Party's private army, the People's Militia. Although the new law excluded from its provisions party officials elected in 1968, it appeared a relatively draconian measure, reflecting the greater hardship experienced by the Czech population after the Prague Spring and their fear of continuing Communist influence. In Slovakia, which had benefited as a result of the Communists' industrialization policies and where repression had been less severe during the 1970s and 1980s, there was less hostility towards former Communists. Moreover, suspicions grew that the campaign waged by Czech politicians against the Communists and erstwhile collaborators was often directed against politicians who, in Slovak eyes, had defended that Republic's interests against Prague. Vladimír Mečiar, although he had been expelled from the Communist Party in 1970 for his reformist leanings, was suspected by some Czechs of involvement with the secret police. These attacks, however, together with allegations that he had destroyed some of the evidence against him during his period as Slovak Interior Minister, only served to increase his popularity with Slovaks.

The 1992 Parliamentary Elections

New elections to the Federal Assembly and the Czech and Slovak National Councils, on 5–6 June 1992, confirmed the divergence of opinion in the two Republics. In the Czech Lands the swing to the right was pronounced. The CDP, standing in coalition with the small Christian Democratic Party (Chr.DP), attracted a third of the votes for both chambers of the Federal Assembly, and 29.7% for the Czech parliament. The Christian Democratic Union–Czechoslovak People's Party (CDU–CPP), as the CDU was renamed following the departure of its coalition partner in the 1990 elections, the Chr.DP, attracted just over 6% for both legislatures. The CDA failed to reach the 5% threshold for the Federal Assembly but, with 6% of the vote for the Czech National Council, won 14 seats in that parliament.

A notable casualty of the elections was the Civic Movement, which won seats in neither Czech nor federal legislature, despite the presence on its lists of prominent members of the outgoing Governments and of well-known figures from the dissident movement. The elections in the Czech Republic nevertheless resulted in representation for a fairly broad spectrum of parties. On the far left the

Communist Party of Bohemia and Moravia (which had separated from its Slovak counterpart at the end of 1991) remained the second strongest party, with 14% of the vote. On the extreme right the Association for the Republic—Republican Party of Czechoslovakia (AFR—RSC) attracted 6%. On the more moderate left, the CSDP did less well than opinion polls had predicted but managed to secure around 7% of the vote for both parliaments. Another 6% went to the Liberal Social Union (LSU), a political movement created in 1991 by three parties which had been unsuccessful in 1990 (the moderate Czechoslovak Socialist Party, the left-wing Agrarian Party, associated with the co-operative farm movement, and the Green Party). Finally, MAD-SMS, with its autonomist programme, won enough votes in Moravia to gain representation in the Czech National Council, but failed to do so for the Federal Assembly.

In Slovakia, except for the CDM which won around 9% of the vote for both parliaments, centre-right and right-wing parties did very badly. There, support went to parties which based their appeal on their identification with the national interest or a more left-wing programme (or indeed both). The electorate swung somewhat more decisively behind the MDS than Czech voters had behind the CDP/Chr.DP coalition, giving it a similar third of the vote for the Federal Assembly and an even higher 37.3% for the Slovak National Council. The ex-Communist Party of the Democratic Left (PDL) came second, with 14%. Apart from the coalition between the Hungarian Christian Democratic Movement, the Hungarian People's Party and Coexistence, which retained the loyalty of the Hungarian minority, with a 7.4% share of the vote, which was only 1% lower than in 1990, other parties saw their vote decline. In the case of the separatist SNP, support fell by 2% for the Federal Assembly, to 9%, and by 6% for the Slovak National Council, where it attracted only 8% of the vote.

Most severely hit of all were the members of the Slovak government coalition between 1991 and 1992. The CDM vote had halved compared with 1990 while PAV, which had changed its name to Civic Democratic Union (CDU) in 1992, and the Democratic Party, which stood in the elections in coalition with Slovak representatives of Klaus's CDP, failed to reach the threshold for either parliament. The outgoing Government's record provided part of the explanation for that poor performance. More significant, however, was the identification of those parties with federalism and radical economic reform, policies lacking in appeal compared to the promises of greater autonomy and prosperity made by the MDS. That party's commitment to sovereignty for Slovakia (albeit within a common Czech and Slovak state) had clearly drawn voters not only from the CDU and CDM, but also from the SNP.

The formation of new governments in the Republics was a relatively straightforward matter. In the Czech Lands CDP leader Václav Klaus formed a coalition embracing the CDP, Chr.DP, CDU–CPP and the CDA, which held 105 of the 200 seats in the National Council. In Slovakia, the MDS, with 74 of the 150 deputies in the Slovak parliament, was only two short of an overall majority. Nevertheless, given his refusal to associate with the PDL or the Hungarian parties, Mečiar was forced to turn to the SNP, which had 15 seats, to form his administration.

The formation of republican governments with irreconcilable political programmes was ominous enough for political stability. The decisive blow to the survival of Czechoslovakia, however, was the political impasse the elections had created in the Federal Assembly, where the balance of forces provided little prospect of forming a viable government. Neither right-wing parties nor any other plausible coalition could muster even the simple majorities required in both chambers of the federal parliament, let alone the qualified majorities needed for constitutional legislation. Indeed, the CDP and the MDS each had the two fifths support among deputies in their respective sections of the House of the Nations to veto any constitutional proposals they found unacceptable.

Talks between Klaus and Mečiar, as the leaders of the largest Czech and Slovak parties, during the week following the elections established that there was no likelihood of their reaching a *modus vivendi*. In Klaus's words, Mečiar was insisting that the federation be ended and replaced, not even by a confederation, but by a common state that would be no more than 'an economic and defence community'. That was unacceptable to a party, the CDP, which believed the choice lay between federalism and separation. Instead, they agreed that the CDP and MDS would form a caretaker federal government which would oversee the dissolution of Czechoslovakia by the end of the year and its replacement on 1 January 1993 by two independent, Czech and Slovak, republics. The irrevocability of that decision seemed only to be confirmed by Klaus's decision to become head of the new Czech Government rather than, as had been expected, federal Prime Minister. That post went to his CDP colleague, Jan Stráský, with the MDS's Rudolf Filkus as his deputy.

The break-up of Czechoslovakia had not been an issue in the elections. Nor was the electorate in either Republic given the opportunity to express its view on the matter. The absence of significant protests, however, may be explained by an awareness, at least among Czechs, that the alternative was political uncertainty, a perpetuation of the disputes between the two Republics, and a probable retardation of the Czech Republic's transformation into a prosperous democracy. For Slovaks, the prospect of their own state quelled, for a time at least, any doubts they might have regarding its economic future without the protection provided by the Czechs.

The gulf between Czech and Slovak politicians was made only too clear after the elections, when a majority of Slovak representatives in the Federal Assembly refused to support Havel's re-election as the doomed federation's President. On 20 July 1992 Havel resigned from that post, more than two months before his period of office ended and on the same day as the Slovak National Council approved a declaration of sovereignty. By the end of 1992 what came to be called a 'velvet divorce' had been finalized. Czechoslovakia would cease to exist at midnight on 31 December 1992. Before then, agreement had been reached on the creation between the two successor states of what proved to be a short-lived monetary union and the maintenance of a more successful customs union. The two Republics had also gone a long way towards agreeing a property settlement (the division of federal assets between the two successor states). Although there were signs that disputes might arise over assets that remained to be shared out, hopes were high that an amicable relationship would be established between the two newly independent Czech and Slovak Republics.

THE CZECH REPUBLIC AFTER INDEPENDENCE

The Czech Republic's transition to independence on 1 January 1993 was facilitated by its emergence as a constituent unit with its own executive and parliament within the Czechoslovak federation in 1969. During the last months of 1992 legislation was approved by the Federal Assembly and Czech National Council transferring full executive authority to the Czech Government formed by Václav Klaus after the 1992 parliamentary elections. A new Constitution, adopted on 16 December 1992, provided for the transformation of the 200-member Czech National Council into a Chamber of Deputies within what was intended to be a bicameral parliament.

The transition was not entirely smooth, however. Attempts to create that parliament's second chamber through the translation of Czech members of the now defunct Federal Assembly to a Provisional Senate were unsuccessful. The idea had already been rejected in December 1992 by the Czech National Council, and the Chamber of Deputies again turned down government proposals to form the second chamber in this way early in the following year. Indeed, by spring 1993, it was clear that no second chamber would come into being until normal elections to the 81-member Senate envisaged in the Constitution could be arranged. That would not happen until autumn 1994 when they could be organized to coincide with elections that were to be held to local councils.

That was not the only controversy to arise during the new Czech Republic's first months. Another was the election of its first President. Václav Havel was the obvious candidate for the post. It was recognized that his popularity at home and reputation abroad were clear advantages for the new state. Yet it was not until 26 January 1993 that the Chamber of Deputies duly elected Havel the Czech Republic's first head of state. Behind the delay were two considerations. Firstly, Prime Minister Václav Klaus tried to secure the creation of the Provisional Senate by insisting that it should be formed before the election of the President was held. (The Constitution stipulated that the head of state should normally be elected by both houses of parliament.) Secondly, Havel no longer had the unquestioning support of parliamentary deputies. Some, from parties in the government coalition, were reluctant to see an independent figure whose politics, they believed, were not wholly consistent with those of the coalition, elected President. It was only once Klaus had abandoned his attempts to force through the second chamber and the sceptics had satisfied themselves that Havel would not be able to use a much weakened presidential office to resist parliament's wishes, that his election took place.

The Domestic Political Scene

The controversy over Havel's election reflected the degree to which the political mood had changed since the Velvet Revolution. The search for a broad consensus which had been a dominant feature during the first year of post-Communist rule had largely disappeared. Havel was one of very few former dissidents to remain in high office after the 1992 elections. Most others, like the majority of former reform Communists, adherents of the Civic Movement, had disappeared from the forefront of the political scene.

Nevertheless, the Czech parliament which had emerged from the June 1992 elections, and thus the Chamber of Deputies in the newly independent Czech Republic, appeared likely to provide a good basis for stable government. Of the 105 seats held by the right-wing parties in the government coalition, 67 had gone to the CDP and 9 to its Chr.DP partner, 15 to the CDU-CPP and 14 to the CDA. Disagreements were to surface between those parties, but none which appeared likely to undermine the cohesion of the coalition or cause the Government's collapse, at least in the short term.

The opposition benches were somewhat more disparate in political complexion. The largest group, with 35 seats, was the Left Bloc, a coalition dominated by the Communist Party of Bohemia and Moravia (CPBM). The CSDP, which was renamed the Czech Social Democratic Party at its 26th congress in February 1993, had 16 seats, as did the LSU. MAD-SMS, which was to simplify its name in January 1993 to the Movement for Autonomous Democracy of Moravia and Silesia (MADMS), retained 14 places. On the extreme right, the AFR—RSC, which like the CSDP and the parties involved in the LSU, had failed to win any parliamentary seats in 1990, had succeeded two years later by attracting what was largely a protest and anti-Roma vote. The departure before the end of 1992 of three of its deputies to form an independent group, however, left it with only 11 seats in the Chamber of Deputies.

Overall, the elections appeared to have provided some elements of a potentially durable party system. Three of the four parties within the government coalition, the CDP, the CDU-CPP and the CDA, seemed likely survivors, if for different reasons. The CDP had a strong grass-roots organization, a clearly defined programme and a popular leader in Václav Klaus. The CDU-CPP, which could trace its origins to pre-Second World War Czechoslovakia, drew its support to a large extent from among traditional Christian voters in rural areas. The CDA lacked a large membership, but had made its mark as a parliamentary party embracing a number of attractive and effective politicians. The Chr.DP, on the other hand, was in a more precarious position. Its presence in parliament was entirely due to its electoral alliance with the CDP and its political future depended on its continuing that partnership or, if that should come to an end, finding a viable alternative. (Elections to the Senate by a majority system, rather than the party-list system with its 5% threshold for allocation of parliamentary seats used for the Chamber of Deputies, might enable it to retain some representation.)

The future for the opposition parties appeared less certain. The survival of the CSDP seemed likely, despite divisions within its ranks between radicals and moderates. It had, however, done less well in the 1992 elections than had been expected and had a long way to go to regain its pre-war standing among the Czechs and to become a major force on the centre-left. The election at its 26th congress in February 1993 of a new leader, Miloš Zeman, brought some increase in its popularity according to opinion polls. There was a risk, however, that his identification with the radical wing of the party and his controversial political style might lead to a split, if internal divisions could not be healed.

Most other opposition parties had suffered from more serious internal disputes. The appeal of the AFR—RSC to the discontented and to extremist opinion may help it survive internal friction manifest in the departure of three of its deputies. The LSU, however, was already on the verge of collapse in spring 1993, as pressures increased within the Socialist Party, renamed the Liberal National Social Party (LNSP) in May, to break with its partners in that movement and move closer to the political centre. Even the CPBM failed to remain immune to internal divisions. Its refusal to abandon its traditional designation as a Communist party finally persuaded more moderate leaders, including its Chairman Jiři Svoboda, to leave its ranks at the end of June 1993 and found a new Party of the Democratic Left (PDL). However, the support which the CPBM continued to receive in the post-Communist Czech Republic after 1989 suggests that it was the 'democratic socialists' of the PDL rather than the unreformed CPBM which might suffer electorally.

The survival of MADMS was also open to question. By the next parliamentary elections, due in 1996 at the latest, the issue of regional government should have been settled and, unless voters in Moravia are particularly dissatisfied by the outcome, the basis of initial MADMS' appeal—adequate representation for that historical province—will have disappeared as an electoral issue. The victory of its more moderate, autonomist, wing at its congress in January 1993 over proponents of Moravian nationalism was one indication that MADMS was looking for a new role. Talks between MADMS and the Civic Movement, encouraged by the German Friedrich Naumann Foundation (which itself has links with the Free Democratic Party), suggested that those two parties might form a new centrist grouping, also involving the LNSP . That would afford an opportunity for politicians associated with the Civic Movement, in particular, to return to the political scene and help fill the gap in the political centre between the leftwards-leaning CSDP and the right-wing parties of the government coalition.

Foreign Relations

Two issues stood at the forefront of Czech foreign policy during the new state's first months: relations with Slovakia and the Czechs' campaign for early admission to full membership of the European Community (EC—known as the European Union since November 1993).

Despite the 'velvet divorce', the establishment of good relations with Slovakia was a primary goal of Czech Prime Minister Klaus and his Government. The agreements reached before the end of 1992 on maintenance of a common currency for the first six to nine months of independence, a customs union and a property settlement, by which the greater part of federal assets were divided between the two successor states on terms that were ostensibly generous towards Slovakia, appeared to augur well for the future in that respect.

The collapse of the monetary agreement and the creation of separate Czech and Slovak currencies in February 1993 represented an early set-back to those arrangements. The most serious risks to good relations, however, were, firstly, continuing disputes over those federal assets which had not been divided before the end of 1992, including new claims made by the Slovak Government, and, secondly, the institution by the Czechs of formal frontier posts on their border with Slovakia. Arguments over the division of property and compensation seemed likely to remain a source of friction between the two states for some time but, with a degree of good will, should be settled in the longer term. The tougher frontier regime was one which Slovakia ultimately had to accept. It was not designed, in any case, to restrict travel for Czech and Slovak citizens, but rather to inhibit entry for citizens of third countries hoping to move illegally to the West. It had been introduced, it was claimed in Prague, in response to Germany's new asylum laws.

The continuing Czech commitment to good relations with Slovakia, despite the difficulties involved, was apparent by the middle of 1993. Klaus's refusal, in July, to support Hungary's attempts to have the issue of national minorities discussed at meetings of the Central European Initiative (a forum for the discussion of common issues among Central European countries) partly reflected his belief that it was not an issue which directly concerned the Czechs. He preferred to avoid entanglement in a dispute which could, moreover, prove detrimental to the Czech Republic's relationship with Slovakia, if it was forced to participate in discussions of that country's treatment of its Hungarian citizens.

Relations between the Czech Republic and Hungary may not have been improved by Klaus's support for the Slovaks on this matter. The impediment to good relations with Hungary represented by Slovakia's attitude towards its minority was, however, no longer directly Prague's responsibility. A further area of contention between the Czechs and Hungarians which was removed by Czechoslovakia's dissolution was the transfer to Slovakia of full responsibility for the Gabčíkovo dam project on the Danube. A potential cause of poor relations with Germany was the Czech Republic's refusal to consider granting compensation to Sudeten Germans expelled after the Second World War.

Relations, not only with Hungary but also with Poland, linked with the Czech Republic and Slovakia in the Visegrad Group, retained a certain ambivalence for another reason. Klaus welcomed co-operation with his post-Communist neighbours but remained wary of any development which might divert the Czechs from their primary goal: early admission to full membership of the EC. He warned that he would not accept any institutionalization of the Visegrad grouping and suspected that Western encouragement of its activities was designed to provide grounds for delaying the admission of any post-Communist country to the Community until all were sufficiently prepared to join.

A 'return to Europe' had been a central goal of Czech policy since the Velvet Revolution and, by 1993, the EC's reluctance to accord the post-Communist states more than associate membership in the EC in the foreseeable future had created some disenchantment among the Czechs. Nevertheless, the Czech case for early accession to the Community was an issue raised on numerous foreign visits. As Klaus observed on at least one occasion, the performance of the Czech economy was better than that of some existing EC members, and the difficulties of adaptation to EC rules were, in his view, scarcely sufficient reason to exclude the country from full membership. At the time of the NATO summit held in Brussels in January 1994, the Czech Republic sought to distance itself from the other members of the Visegrad Group, and pressed for early Czech membership of NATO and, indeed, the EC.

Conclusion

The break-up of Czechoslovakia represented a failure in the process of transition from totalitarianism to democracy in east-central Europe after 1989. Nevertheless, there is every reason to anticipate that the Czech Republic will complete its journey along that path. The removal of the Czech–Slovak question from the domestic political scene left a more stable polity. Indeed the Czech Republic is a more homogeneous state than the former Czechoslovakia. Figures from the March 1991 census showed that the 9.7m. Bohemians and Moravians made up over 94% of the total population of 10.3m. Other national groups were much less numerous. Slovaks, the second largest, accounted for some 315,000, Poles around 60,000 and Germans just over 48,000. More uncertain was the size of the Roma population. Just under 33,000 had registered as such in the census, but the real figure was estimated on the basis of 1989 local government records to be closer to 170,000.

The Roma minority was the only one which seemed to present a potentially difficult political issue, fanned by the rhetoric of the extremist AFR—RSC. Suggestions by Slovak exiles in the West and by some politicians in Slovakia that their co-nationals in the Czech Republic were, or could become, the victims of discrimination seemed unlikely and found no response within a community that would probably not wish to assume the status of a conventional national minority.

Overall, the Czech Republic had, by 1993, gone a long way towards rejoining the pluralist democracies of Western Europe, to which the population believed they belonged by cultural, historical and political traditions. That path may not always be smooth but it seems reasonably assured.

The Economy

Dr PETER RUTLAND

INTRODUCTION

Of all the Eastern Europeans, the Czechs made the most successful efforts in moving towards a multi-party democracy and market economy during the early 1990s, although in their haste to 'return to Europe' they have been obliged to sacrifice their union with Slovakia.

Yet prior to 1989 Czechoslovakia was the most conservative of the central Eastern European states, both politically and economically. In the 1970s and 1980s Czechoslovakia shunned any efforts at reform, while Hungary, for example, enjoyed 30 years of steady political liberalization and economic experimentation. Poland also established extensive contacts with Western economies in the 1970s, and developed a small but thriving private sector after 1981. Despite this insulation from reform prior to the fall of Communism, the Czechs had three main advantages in comparison with neighbouring Poland and Hungary.

Firstly, the failure of the earlier partial reform experiments led to international debts of US $1,000 per head in Poland and $2,000 per head in Hungary. Czechoslovakia, in contrast, only had a $500 per head debt (which totalled $8,000m.). Secondly, by Eastern European standards, Czechoslovakia had a fairly developed and diverse economy, with a mixture of heavy and light industry and less dependence on agriculture than its neighbours (in 1992 only 8.5% of the Czech labour force was in farming). One in three families owns a car and weekend cottage, and a refrigerator and colour television are the norm. Czechoslovak families spent 35% of their income on food—double the proportion found in Western European family budgets, but half that of Poland or the former USSR.

Thirdly, after the fall of Communism there emerged a strong political leadership and the resuscitation of a consensual political culture, both of which were highly conducive to the difficult decisions needed to effect the transition to a market economy. These are deep structural characteristics of the country, which are not likely to change significantly in the short term. This means that the Czech Republic's relative economic stability and success is likely to persist in the medium to long term.

On the negative side, it must be remembered that the economy inherited from the Communist regime was in very poor shape. The gross national product (GNP) annual growth rate had steadily declined, from 6% in 1975 to less than 2% in 1988 and 1989. In 1985 Czechoslovakia had a GNP per head of $7,400 (47th highest in the world), and per head consumption of $3,390 (45th highest). Czechoslovakia's GNP per head as a proportion of that of neighbouring Austria's had fallen from 90% in 1960 to 60% in 1985. The technological level of Czech industries was also falling steadily behind that of their global competitors. Furthermore, North Bohemia, with a heavy concentration of brown coal-burning power stations and steelworks, was on the brink of an ecological catastrophe.

The Czech economy has not yet fully dealt with the inherited legacy of loss-making state-owned enterprises. Moreover, the split with Slovakia which took place in January 1993 imposed additional costs which would delay the pace of recovery.

THE POLITICAL CONTEXT

The newly reborn democracy in the Czech Republic quickly settled down into a stable pattern, which seemed likely to persist for several years. The broad coalition which emerged from the November 1989 revolution, Civic Forum, split in February 1991 into a left and right wing. The latter named itself the Civic Democratic Party (CDP), and emerged as the largest single party in the June 1992 elections under the leadership of Václav Klaus, formerly the Minister of Finance. Klaus managed to convince the voters that his policy of monetary stabilization and rapid privatization offered the best chance for a decisive break with the socialist past and a 'return to Europe'.

The CDP only won 76 of the 200 seats in the Czech parliament, and thus must rule in coalition with three other groups: the libertarian Civic Democratic Alliance, the Christian Democratic Union–Czech People's Party and the Christian Democratic Party. Prime Minister Klaus' coalition has 105 seats, which gives them a narrow majority. The Communist Party (now divided between the Communist Party of Bohemia and Moravia and the reformist Party of the Democratic Left) and their allies in the Left Bloc, together with the Social Democrats, formed the opposition (with 35 and 16 seats respectively). The political future of other parties, such as the Socialist Party (which reconstituted itself as the Liberal National Social Party) and the Movement for Autonomous Democracy of Moravia and Silesia, was uncertain, while several other smaller parties were kept out of parliament by the rule requiring parties to gain 5% of total votes cast before being eligible for seats in parliament.

Klaus' coalition was expected to stay in power at least until the next elections, scheduled for 1996. Although there is always the threat of defections from the governing coalition, no disagreement strong enough to result in this manifested itself during 1993. Even if unemployment should increase and the economy stagnate, this would probably only increase the pressure on the smaller parties to stay in the CDP-led coalition, for fear of increasing the possibility of the election of a left-wing government.

The major political challenge for the Czechs was managing the separation from Slovakia. Czechs and Slovaks have separate histories, and were only directly united in a single state in 1918. Under Communism, Slovakia was industrialized, but its large industrial plants were ill-prepared for the collapse of the USSR and the challenges of a market economy. By December 1992 unemployment had risen to 13.5% in Slovakia, while it was only 2.6% in the Czech Republic.

In the three years after 1989, Czech and Slovak politicians engaged in endless rounds of negotiations over the status of the federation. The Slovaks sought symbolic assurances from the Czechs that they were equal partners, while Czechs accused Slovaks of siphoning resources from the federal budget to prop up their ailing economy. Nevertheless, polls indicated that most Czech and Slovak citizens remained committed to the idea of a federation. Things began to change after the June 1992 elections, which saw the victory of the Movement for a Democratic Slovakia in the eastern Republic. The Slovak leader, Vladimír Mečiar, claimed that all he wanted was a new confederation, but Klaus was not prepared to meet his terms. Klaus feared that protracted negotiations with Mečiar would cause great uncertainty and could endanger the market reforms.

Klaus and Mečiar eventually agreed that a split was unavoidable, and presented their parliaments with a *fait accompli*. By November 1992 opinion polls were showing a majority of Czechs favouring separation, although only 40% of Slovaks wanted the split. The two republican parliaments approved the 'velvet divorce' arranged by Mečiar and Klaus, which came into effect at midnight on 31 December 1992. However, some crucial economic aspects of the separation were left unresolved (see below).

Despite concern over inflation and unemployment, public support among Czechs for Klaus' reform programme remained strong in 1993. A February 1993 poll showed 64% of the public expressing confidence in the Government. However, when people were invited to look back at 1992, only 18% expressed satisfaction with their standard of living, 34% with the transition to a market economy, 33% with the state of domestic politics in general and 47% with the state of democracy.

THE ECONOMIC BACKGROUND

After the surrender of power by the Communists in 1989, the new Government moved decisively to dismantle central planning controls and open the economy to foreign trade. The entire system of economic legislation was overhauled and a new commercial code introduced.

Price controls were lifted in January 1991, causing a surge in inflation to 50% during the rest of that year, but in the following two years the annual average inflation rate was limited to 12%–14%. Václav Klaus, who was finance minister between 1990 and 1992, pursued a tight monetary and fiscal policy, and made price and currency stability one of the central goals of government policy.

In 1990 the Czechoslovak crown (koruna—Kčs.) was made partially convertible, and fixed against a basket of foreign currencies (later reduced to just the German mark and US dollar). The crown (which became the Czech crown in February 1993, after the separation of the Czech and Slovak currencies) successfully held its value against other currencies over the next three years, maintaining a rate of approximately 30 koruny to the dollar.

Through the drastic reduction of industrial subsidies and investment, government spending as a share of gross domestic product (GDP) fell from 64.5% in 1989 to 52.8% in 1991 and 52.5% in 1993. Nevertheless, the government deficit crept up, from 2% to 4% of GDP (16,800m. Kčs.) in 1992. This was divided between the federal and republican governments as follows: federal 7,000m. Kčs.; Czech Republic 1,700m. Kčs.; Slovak Republic 7,900m. Kčs.

In January 1993 the old system of turnover taxes was replaced by a unified value added tax (VAT), with two rates of 23% and 5%. In 1993 the proportions of various government revenue sources were as follows: income tax 4%, corporate tax 20.5%, social security tax 32%, VAT 19% and consumption taxes 13%. The one remaining area where price controls are still in force is rent and utilities. The rent for a typical state apartment in late 1993 was 250 koruny (equivalent to US $8) per month. Rents and utilities were to be increased by 40% in 1994, but housing agencies would still require heavy subsidization.

GDP in the Czechoslovak economy (including Slovakia) fell by 16% in 1991 and 8% in 1992, with much of the decline due to a 50% fall in exports to the former USSR. Industrial output began to recover in October 1992. Viewed alone, many of the economic indicators for the Czech Republic were positive during 1992. Unemployment fell from 4.1% in 1991 to 2.6% in 1992, while wages increased by 23.4%. Inflation, meanwhile, fell from 57% in 1991 to just 10.8% in 1992. Perhaps the surest indication of underlying confidence in the economy was the increase in retail sales during 1992 of no less than 30.6%. However, the increase in retail sales was supported largely by an increase in the value of imports of 20.5%; indeed, the trade balance moved from a surplus of 25,000m. Kčs. in 1991 to a deficit of 23,000m. Kčs. in 1992.

In the first half of 1993 these trends continued. GDP fell by 0.5% (although recovery was visible during the second quarter) and industrial output 4.7%, while consumer prices rose by 12.1%, unemployment held at 2.6% and foreign trade showed a small surplus of 6,700m. koruny.

LIVING STANDARDS

Czech trade unions, politically weakened by their association with the old regime, meekly accepted a 23% drop in the real wage in 1991, in the hope that this would minimize job losses. Indeed, unemployment was maintained at a level below 3% in the Czech Republic during 1992 and 1993, although it was likely to double by the end of 1994 as privatized firms came under new management. At the end of June 1993 unemployment stood at a mere 2.8% in the Czech Republic, ranging from 0.32% in Prague to 6.16% in Znojmo, south Moravia. Due to fairly strict eligibility rules, only 50% of the 138,000 registered unemployed receive benefits.

The Government's active labour-market policy has been quite successful (promoting retraining and subsidizing the hiring of young workers), but wage restraint is the main reason for the preservation of near-full employment. Although living standards have fallen, the majority of the population are above subsistence level. In a July 1993 survey 17% of respondents reported difficulty in maintaining a basic standard of living, while 51% replied that they were just managing and 31% that they could save. (The aggregate savings rate was 2.1% in 1991, 6.3% in 1992 and 3.2% in 1993.)

The average monthly industrial wage at the end of 1992 was 5,635 Kčs., which was equivalent to a mere US $190 at the prevailing exchange rate. It is important to remember that the crown was deliberately undervalued to discourage imports, boost exports and attract foreign investors. The average Czech industrial wage is $180 per month compared to $300 in Poland, $190 in Hungary and $1,600 in Germany. The Vienna Institute for International Comparison estimates that in comparative terms GDP per head in the Czech Republic is actually $8,900, and only $6,400 in Poland. The artificially low level of real wages in the Czech Republic has been one of the key ingredients explaining their relative success, with the German newspaper *Frankfurter Allgemeine Zeitung* opining that 'Our Hong Kong lies in Prague.'

FOREIGN TRADE

Expanding foreign trade is a crucial component of the Czech economic reform strategy. Prime Minister Václav Klaus hopes that Czech firms will compensate for the collapse in the Soviet market by seeking new customers in developing countries (for example, by selling transport and power equipment to Iran and the Philippines), and by finding a niche in adjacent Western European markets as a low-cost manufacturer.

The Czech Republic has been remarkably successful at reorientating its foreign trade from East to West—all the more remarkable if one considers that it is mostly state-owned firms which are finding the new markets. The share of exports in GDP rose from 21.3% in 1990 to 35% in 1992, while the proportion going to the European Community (EC, known as the European Union from November 1993) and European Free Trade Association rose from 27% to 52% between 1989 and 1992. The Czechs felt confident enough to reduce and then abolish the 20% import tariff which they had introduced in 1990. In 1992 Germany, already by far the leading destination for Czech exports with 32.9% of the total, also overtook the former USSR countries as the largest source of imports, with 27.0%; nevertheless, the former USSR still accounted for 18.1% of Czech imports in 1992. Other leading trade partners in 1992 were Austria (which supplied 9.1% of Czech imports and took an 7.2% share of Czech exports) and Italy (4.8% of imports and 6.2% of exports). Despite these positive developments, Czech foreign trade showed a deficit of 42,638m. Kčs. in 1992, after a 24,813m. Kčs. surplus in 1991: the increased cost of petroleum and gas imports was responsible for much of the 1992 deficit.

In the first quarter of 1993 imports rose by 21% while exports fell by 2.6%, compared with the similar period in 1992 (excluding trade with Slovakia). Exports to Eastern Europe dropped by 39%, while imports from advanced market economies rose by 40%. The rise in imports may have been an indication that firms were re-equipping, but the much slower rate in the growth of exports, compared to the previous two years, was a worrying development.

The liberalization of foreign trade put the Czech Republic in the curious position of having lower barriers than most of its trading partners. In December 1992 Czechoslovakia, Poland and Hungary signed an agreement with the EC granting them associate member status. This would mean the phased elimination of tariff barriers to their exports over the next eight years. However, the small print to the agreement allowed the maintenance of quotas on steel, textiles and food, affecting about 33% of Czech exports to the EC.

On 23 June 1993 a protocol to the association agreement was drawn up, speeding up the removal of tariff barriers (for example, after three years instead of five for manufactured goods). Prime Minister Václav Klaus was confident that the Czech Republic would be able to meet the political and economic criteria for EC entry within five years. Both Klaus and President Václav Havel have urged the EC to consider Czech entry separately from the other countries of the Visegrad Group.

Trade with Poland and Hungary has fallen rapidly since 1989, accounting for only 9.4% of Czechoslovak trade in 1992 (valued at US 2,000m.), compared to 12.9% in 1989. In December 1992 the Czechs, Slovaks, Poles and Hungarians signed the Central Europe Free Trade Agreement in Kraków (Poland), pledging to remove all trade barriers over a period of five years. However, the treaty had not been ratified by late 1993, and its implementation was likely to be characterized by a large number of exemptions.

One factor contributing to the poor export performance in 1993 was the cap on steel exports to the EC, which was imposed in July 1992 and renewed for two years in April 1993. Exports of steel sheet, wire and tubes, which accounted for half of all Czech exports to the EC in 1992 (and 25% of all the steel produced in the Czech Republic), were to be held to 35% above the 1991 level until 1995. Another example of perceived unsympathetic treatment from the EC was its decision to ban all meat imports from Eastern Europe in April 1993, in response to an outbreak of foot-and-mouth disease in Croatia.

Financially, the Czech Republic is secure. Total foreign debt at the end of 1992 stood at $9,500m., with debt service payments equivalent to 11.2% of exports in 1991 and 11.7% in 1992. These figures do not include some 72,000m. koruny owed to the former Czechoslovakia by the former USSR and 16,000m. koruny by Iraq (the payment of which was considered unlikely). Total currency reserves at mid-1993 were $4,00m., up from $3,600m. at the end of 1992. The Government was confident enough to decline the provision of an additional $300m. stand-by loan. In 1992 loans from international institutions totalled $897m., sourced as follows: International Monetary Fund (IMF) $284m., World Bank $331m., EC $232m. and Group of 24 (G24) $50m. The European Bank for Reconstruction and Development (EBRD) has pledged to invest $423m. in joint ventures, including $125m. to Škoda/Volkswagen, $23m. to Čokoladovný/Nestlé, and $30m. to Czech Airlines/Air France.

FOREIGN INVESTMENT

Foreign investors, almost totally excluded from the Czechoslovak market before 1989, were initially slow to enter it. However, Czechoslovakia (and particularly the Czech Republic) became increasingly attractive to investors due to its political stability and successful stabilization programme. Between 1990 and 1 July 1993 total direct foreign investment in Czechoslovakia was US $1,898m., more than in Poland, but less than Hungary's $3,300m. Germany led the list of investors, with 32.2% of funds, followed by the USA with 29.5% and France 13.8%. Only 7% of these funds went to Slovakia. In the first half of 1993 direct foreign investment in the Czech Republic was $392m., slightly down on the first half of 1992.

By late 1993 there were 81 joint ventures with foreign partners in operation, with a total capital input of 18,000m. koruny ($600.m.). Another 54 were planned for the second phase of the privatization programme. Retailing, food processing, glass, rubber and construction materials have proved popular with foreign buyers. The largest single deal was Volkswagen's purchase of 31% of the automobile concern Škoda Mladá Boleslav, with a promise of DM5,000m. investment and a doubling of production from the 1993 current level of 200,000 units by 1995. Škoda has a 70% share of the Czech car market, and Volkswagen was promised some protection from foreign imports (which were subject to a 19% tariff) for the next several years. The largest US investor is Philip Morris, which intended to invest $420m. in the tobacco company Tabak Kutná Hora (which also held a 70% market share).

However, the overall flow of direct foreign investment has been less than the Czechs had hoped, and in 1993 several important deals fell through. Dow withdrew from its $100m. acquisition of the Sokolov chemical plant, and Mercedes pulled out of its planned deal with the Avia and Liaz truck manufacturers. More worrying still, in September 1993 Volkswagen announced that it was scaling back its planned investment programme in Škoda Mladá Boleslav.

The recession in the German economy of the early 1990s was the principal reason for these withdrawals of investment. Overall, the international business community seemed to be becoming more enthusiastic towards the Czech Republic as a target for investment. With its low-waged, and highly-skilled, labour force, a reasonable infrastructure, welcoming government and proximity to German markets, the Czech Republic remains an attractive target for foreign investors. In 1993 the country was rated 42nd in the Institutional Investor ranking of countries by degree of risk. This was ahead of all other Eastern European countries, including Slovakia (rated 59th), but lower than its previous rating as a unified country (37th). The US credit-rating agency Standard and Poors listed the Czech Republic as 'BBB' (investment grade), the same as Chile, Israel, Turkey and China, while Hungary was placed two points lower (in the speculative category). The Czech National Bank has successfully sold bonds in the European market (in March 1993) and in the Japanese public bond market (in July).

MANAGING THE SEPARATION FROM SLOVAKIA

The separation from Slovakia at midnight on 31 December 1992 added another element of uncertainty to Czech economic development. Both countries agreed to maintain a customs and currency union for an initial six months, but owing to an outflow of hard currency from Slovakia the two currencies were separated in less than six weeks, on 8 February 1993.

Confusion over tax and customs paperwork at the Czech–Slovak border caused a worrying 25% drop in trade between the two states in the first quarter of 1993. In 1992 40% of Slovak exports went to the Czech Republic and 25% of Czech exports went to Slovakia; each 10% drop in the Slovak trade translates into a 1% drop in Czech GDP. The Czechs also claimed that the Slovak Government owed 24,000m. koruny to the State Bank (which was succeeded in 1993 by the Czech National Bank and the Slovak National Bank), and on 17 March the Czech Government suspended the issue of shares to Slovak citizens under the privatization programme. Eventually, on 12 May, the two sides reached provisional agreement over several of the outstanding asset-division issues. Prime Minister Klaus reversed his earlier decision and released the privatization shares to Slovak investors.

Surprisingly, in the first quarter of 1993 the Czech Republic recorded a deficit of 1,500m. koruny with Slovakia; this was because Slovak enterprises, experiencing cash-flow problems, cut back on imports and stopped paying their debts. This allowed the Slovaks to revalue the Slovak crown by 5% on 7 May, although the underlying economic situation continued to deteriorate. Under pressure from the IMF, the Slovak crown was devalued by 10% in July 1993, and a 20% import tariff was introduced.

THE PRIVATIZATION PROGRAMME

The combined effect of privatization measures was to increase the share in GDP of the private sector from less than 1% in 1989 to 21.5% by the beginning of 1993. While the private sector still accounted for only 15% of industry in 1993, it amounted to 58% of construction and 72% of retailing. Václav Klaus' privatization programme had four main components.

Firstly, some 100,000 properties confiscated after 1948 were to be returned to their former owners, with a total value of 150,000–200,000m. koruny (equal to the assets distributed through the first phase of voucher privatization—see below). These properties include houses, shops, land and some small factories. Farmers are also eligible to regain their land from the co-operative farms, and 404,000 claims have been lodged. One-half of the nation's forests (which total 2.4m. hectares) have now been restituted.

Secondly, a 'small privatization' programme was launched in February 1991, under which five-year leases on 22,000 stores and workshops were auctioned to private bidders, raising a total of 32,000m. koruny. The small privatization programme was simple, popular and had an immediate and highly-visible impact on the general retailing environment in every Czech town. Small privatization has basically been completed, although the health-care system is now being gradually privatized. Health clinics are being sold to partnerships of their staff (with the help of subsidized loans).

Thirdly, restrictions on private enterprise were lifted, resulting in 1.1m. people (10% of the population) registering as self-employed. About one-quarter of them are working full-time, primarily in retailing and services. This rapid growth in self-employment has been a major factor in restraining the growth in unemployment.

The crucial element, however, is the programme to divest large state-owned enterprises. Early in 1992 each state-owned firm was required to prepare its own privatization project, proposing direct sale to a foreign or domestic buyer, public auction or sale through the 'voucher method'. Other citizens (for example, groups of managers within an industrial plant) could also submit rival projects. The Ministry of Privatization selected the winning projects and monitored the overall process. After privatization, state shareholding in newly-independent firms is transferred to the National Property Fund, which then disposes of them over the next several years.

The voucher method was the most innovatory aspect of Czech privatization. Recognizing that not all Czech firms would find cash buyers, Klaus issued vouchers to the general public (for a nominal sum of 1,000 koruny—US $33) which could then be used to bid for shares in state firms. By January 1992 80% of the population had bought vouchers, and 72% of the vouchers were invested with the 220 private investment funds who were allowed to pool vouchers and bid for blocks of shares. (The funds were limited to a maximum of 20% of the shares in any given firm.) The voucher method did not generate any new capital for Czech industry, but it served as a vehicle for the speedy creation of a new class of private owners (the investment funds, rather than individual citizens). Also, by giving people an individual stake in the process, it solidified public support for the privatization campaign.

The first phase of mass privatization, involving around 25% of Czech industry, began on 18 May 1992—just before the parliamentary elections in June. The timing was not coincidental: Klaus, then federal finance minister, saw the voucher method as a way of forging a political constituency for change. By the end of the first phase in January 1993, 1,320 firms valued at 343,000m. koruny ($12,000m.) had been privatized; 65% of the assets had been sold through the voucher method. The National Property Fund assumed debts of 30,000m. koruny from foreign and 12,600m. koruny from domestic buyers. The Fund still held 27% of shares in the privatized firms, which it will gradually sell.

For the second phase of voucher privatization, which started in October 1993, property valued at 500,000m. koruny was available, in 2,100 enterprises, of which 150,000m. koruny would be sold through vouchers. Slovakia did not intend to hold a second wave of voucher privatization.

Shares in the newly-privatized firms were issued in May 1993, and the new owners began to hold their first board meetings. The shares of some firms began to be traded on the Prague Stock Exchange, and through an over-the-counter system (RMS), but initial interest was slight and most share prices fell steadily. Share ownership has become concentrated in the 120 largest investment funds, which are mostly owned by banks. The leading fund-holders were the Czech Savings Bank (with about 10% of all shares issued), Investiční banka (8.2% of shares), the Harvard Fund (7.5%), the General Credit Bank of Bratislava (6.4%) and Komerční banka (about 6%).

The investment funds faced a problem in that they promised investors returns of 10,000–15,000 koruny within a year for their 1,000 koruny voucher. Observers feared that a slump in share prices would occur as the funds dumped stocks to raise cash. So far, of all the investment funds only that run by the Czech Savings Bank has honoured its 11,000 koruny profit pledge. The Harvard Fund, with 820,000 shareholders, is the largest privately-owned investment fund, under its controversial young president, Viktor Kozeny. The Harvard Fund acquired assets valued at some 45,000 koruny per 1,000-koruny voucher, but did not have the liquidity to pay the 10,000-koruny cash it had promised investors. Faced with this problem the Fund interpreted its obligation to mean that the payment was due one year after the shares in the firms were issued (in May 1993), rather than one year after the voucher had been placed with the Fund—as most investors had expected.

INDUSTRIAL RESTRUCTURING

The large privatization programme was clearly a political success, and its completion within two years is a considerable administrative achievement. However, it was still too early to predict its full economic significance in late 1993, at which time 85% of industrial output was still in the hands of state-owned firms.

While firms were awaiting privatization, there was little incentive for managers to improve performance, to invest, or to penetrate new markets. Firms did have to cover their operating costs, since they could not expect subsidies from the state budget. Thus some firms were obliged to lay off workers, in some enterprises, such as textiles and mining, amounting to 25%–40% of the work-force. For example, the Ostrava coal mines saw their total sales slump from 18m. metric tons in 1990 to 13m. tons in 1993, while the work-force fell from 100,000 to 49,500. The Poldi Kladno steel mill saw its work-force shrink from 20,000 to 9,000. However, in most cases radical decisions about closure or new investment was left to await the arrival of the new owners.

Even though most of the old debts of Czech firms were moved into a specially-created Consolidation Bank in 1991, inter-enterprise debt remained a serious problem, standing at about 220,000m. koruny in mid-1993. There is great fear of a 'domino effect'—that if some individual bankruptcies are allowed this will trigger others. Estimates of the number of Czech firms behind with their debt repayments range from 30% to 70%, although only a minority are in such bad condition as to be serious candidates for bankruptcy. A Bankruptcy Law was passed in July 1991, but was not implemented. A revised law came into effect on 22 April 1993. The Government amended the law in order to give the Ministry of Privatization a veto over court decisions affecting firms in the process of privatization. Although small firms are using the procedure, it is unlikely to trigger a wave of closures in large firms in the immediate future.

The Government remains deeply involved in the restructuring of ailing flagship enterprises. In the case of Škoda Plzeň, for example, the country's largest engineering works where 28,000 employees produce a variety of sophisticated equipment from power generators to electric locomotives, the inability of Czech, Russian and East German railways to pay their bills meant that the locomotive plant had to close temporarily in October 1992. The other divisions of Škoda Plzeň were also experiencing difficulties, for example through Eastern European nuclear plants cancelling orders. In total, Škoda Plzeň had 4,400m. koruny of outstanding bank loans. For two years Škoda had sought a foreign partner to inject capital and technology, and to help them adjust to the loss of huge Soviet orders. In 1991 the German company Siemens was selected as the partner in preference to the US firm Westinghouse. However, the signing of the Siemens deal was repeatedly postponed as the Germans tried to persuade the Government to take over Škoda's debts, and sought control over both the energy and transport divisions. After tense negotiations, the Czech Government agreed to let Lubomír Soudek, a previous director of Škoda Plzeň, buy out the firm with the aid of loans reluctantly provided by leading Czech banks. (Soudek received 20% of the shares, with 34% being sold through the voucher system.) Siemens has since taken a US $21m. stake in the Škoda Energo turbine manufacturer. Westinghouse has also signed separate deals worth $400m. to provide fuel and a control system for the Temelin nuclear plant. (Nuclear power accounts for 23% of Czech electricity, and this share will rise to 40% when Temelin starts operations.)

THE PRIVATIZATION OF BANKS

After 1991 the Czech and Slovak banking system shifted from a centralized, monobank system, to one in which commercially independent banks became the norm. The number of banks operating in the Czech Republic also increased rapidly, from nine in 1990 to 39 at the end of March 1993. While the number of banks owned by the state decreased from four to one, that of joint-stock banks (without foreign participation) increased from four to 21 and of banks partly foreign-owned from one to nine. In 1990 no entirely foreign-owned bank was operating in the Czech Republic: by the end of March 1993 there were eight such banks.

This restructuring of the banking sector looks impressive. However, in practice the changes are less radical than the increased numbers suggest. The five former state banks hold 55% of all capital, 87% of deposits and issue 83% of loans. The National Property Fund still controls 40%–50% of the shares of these banks, with the remainder mostly held by the investment funds—the largest of which are in turn owned by the banks. Thus the five leading investment funds, for example, own 35% of the largest bank, Komerční banka, with the Harvard Fund alone holding 17% of its shares. Furthermore, half of the new banks are very small; only 300m. koruny (US $10m.) of base capital is needed to start a new bank. Many enterprises took a leading role in setting up new banks, with a view to using them to generate loans for themselves. It is to be expected that there will be several bank closures and mergers among these marginal banks.

Banking has been one of the few economic sectors to experience growth in demand since 1989. Total bank credits in Czechoslovakia rose from 569,000m. koruny in 1989 to 814,000m. koruny in 1992, of which 458,000m. koruny has gone to state-owned firms, 76,000m. koruny to co-operatives, 214,000m. koruny to the private sector and 66,000m. koruny to households. The major banks seemed to be within sight of profitability, and by 1994 were to have adopted Western accounting norms (in writing off bad debts, for example).

However, the banks' performance has been widely criticized, for slowness in executing payment transfers, excessive demands for collateral, high interest rates and favouritism towards borrowers form the state sector.

AGRICULTURE

The Czech agricultural sector has been fairly successful, providing 90% of the country's food requirements. However, under the Communist economic system farms were protected by heavy state subsidies, and it is not clear how many will be viable now that subsidies have been sharply reduced. (Subsidies stood at 5,200m. koruny in 1992.) Between 1989 and 1993 the number of employees in agriculture fell dramatically, from 600,000 to 300,000. The average farm in 1992 made a loss of 10% on its capital stock, while the average farm wage is 20% below that of industrial workers. Import duties of 8%–10% have restricted imports of farm products to less than 2% of total sales.

The country's 310 state farms are being restituted to former owners or converted into joint-stock companies, while the 1,300 co-operative farms will remain more or less intact. Farms seized under the first wave of expropriations, in 1948, will not be returned to their former owners, although the Roman Catholic Church is receiving some of its former landholdings (amid considerable political controversy). It was argued that the process of identifying the current status of these assets would be too complicated, and could delay or jeopardize the entire privatization programme.

The members of co-operative farms are entitled to withdraw their land from the farm, under a procedure laid out in a law passed on 3 May 1990. To preserve the integrity of farms, smallholders might not receive their own land back, but may have to accept a plot of comparable worth on the periphery of the farm. There has been no mass exodus from co-operative farms, however. In 1993 private farmers numbered 38,269, of whom only 755 have farms with more than 100 hectares. Agricultural workers doubt the economic viability of private farming, given the elimination of farm subsidies, and new worries about the availability of credit and equipment. Surveys have shown that only 10% of farmers think that owning or renting a private farm is economically viable.

FUTURE PROSPECTS FOR THE CZECH ECONOMY

In the first quarter of 1993 GDP dropped by 4.5% and industrial output by 7.8%, owing to the drop in exports to Slovakia. The economy began to recover in the second quarter. In the first half of 1993 the rate of contraction for various economic indicators was as follows: GDP 0.5%, industrial output 4%, construction 5.2%, transport 20.1% and agriculture 1.5%. GDP and industrial output were expected to resume an upward trend by the end of 1993, although unemployment would perhaps double during 1994, from its 1993 level of 2.6%, owing to the impact of the bankruptcy law. A 10,000m. koruny balance-of-trade surplus was predicted for the whole of 1993.

The fiscal and monetary balance of the economy seemed unaffected by the separation with Slovakia. The government budget registered a surplus of 5,600m. koruny for the first half of 1993, on spending of 169,600m. koruny, and a surplus of 500m. koruny for the whole year. After an 8.5% surge in retail prices in January, caused by the introduction of VAT, monthly inflation dropped back to 0.6% per month. Annual inflation for 1993 was unlikely to exceed 16%–18%. However, there was growing concern about wage inflation, as average monthly industrial wages rose to 6,658 koruny—a 25% rise in nominal terms during the first half of 1993 (but only 5% in real terms). This led to the reimposition of wage limits for state and private firms in the fourth quarter of 1993.

In 1994 GDP growth of 2%–4% was expected, with unemployment rising to 5%–6% and inflation falling to 8%–10%. Considerable restructuring of Czech industry was due to take place during 1993–94 as the new owners of privatized firms (foreign purchasers and domestic investment funds) appointed new managers. Large-scale factory closures were unlikely, however, as the government has not put the biggest loss-makers up for privatization, and was to continue to make funding available to keep them in operation as they reduced their work-forces in an attempt to make their production more competitive.

There was also to be a further phase of privatization during 1994, probably including the telecommunications and postal monopoly, STP. STP is likely to experience dynamic growth over the next decade. The old analog phone network must be entirely replaced by a new digital system, and the number of subscribers is expected to double from its current level of 18 per 100 inhabitants. Infrastructural investment will be a significant feature of the Czech economy, with the motorway highway system set to expand from 385 km to 1,250 km. Major construction projects already agreed, or under tender, include the 75 km Ingolstadt petroleum pipeline, the 83-km Prague–Plzeň D5 motorway, and the D47 motorway from Brno to Ostrava.

CONCLUSION

It was to be expected that 1994 would be a difficult year for the Czech Republic, as it struggled to overcome the disruption caused by the split with Slovakia. The coming into effect of the new bankruptcy law would also have unwelcome repercussions for many Czech firms. However, the basic structures of a market economy were already in place: a stable currency, fiscal probity and a functioning legal framework and banking system, within a broader context of political stability.

Statistical Survey

Source: mainly Czech Statistical Office, Sokolovská 142, 186 04 Prague 8; tel. (2) 66042451; fax (2) 66310429.

Area and Population

AREA, POPULATION AND DENSITY

Area (sq km)	78,864*
Population (census results)	
3 March 1991	
Males	4,999,935
Females	5,302,280
Total	10,302,215
Population (official estimate at 31 December) 1992	10,325,697
Density (per sq km) at 31 December 1992	130.9

* 30,450 sq miles.

POPULATION BY NATIONALITY
(census of 3 March 1991)

	Number	%
Czech (Bohemian)	8,363,768	81.2
Moravian	1,362,313	13.2
Slovak	314,877	3.1
Polish	59,383	0.6
German	48,556	0.5
Silesian	44,446	0.4
Roma (Gypsy)	32,903	0.3
Hungarian	19,932	0.2
Others	34,020	0.3
Unknown	22,017	0.2
Total	10,302,215	100.0

REGIONS (census of 3 March 1991)

	Area (sq km)	Population	Density (per sq km)
Central Bohemia	10,994	1,112,882	101
Southern Bohemia	11,345	697,503	61
Western Bohemia	10,875	860,292	79
Northern Bohemia	7,819	1,174,034	150
Eastern Bohemia	11,240	1,233,187	110
Southern Moravia	15,028	2,049,386	136
Northern Moravia	11,067	1,960,757	177
Prague (city)	496	1,214,174	2,448
Total	78,864	10,302,215	131

PRINCIPAL TOWNS (census of 3 March 1991)

Praha (Prague, capital)	1,214,174	Liberec	101,162
Brno	388,296	Hradec Králové	99,917
Ostrava	327,371	České Budějovice	97,243
Plzeň (Pilsen)	173,008	Pardubice	94,636
Olomouc	103,993	Zlín*	82,869

* During the period of Communist rule this town was renamed Gottwaldov, but it has since reverted to its former name.

BIRTHS, MARRIAGES AND DEATHS

	Registered live births		Registered marriages		Registered deaths	
	Number	Rate (per 1,000)	Number	Rate (per 1,000)	Number	Rate (per 1,000)
1984	136,941	13.3	81,714	7.9	132,188	12.8
1985	135,881	13.1	80,653	7.8	131,641	12.7
1986	133,356	12.9	81,638	7.9	132,585	12.8
1987	130,921	12.7	83,773	8.1	127,244	12.3
1988	132,667	12.8	81,458	7.9	125,694	12.1
1989	128,356	12.4	81,262	7.8	127,747	12.3
1990	130,564	12.6	90,953	8.8	129,166	12.5
1991	129,354	12.5	71,978	7.0	124,290	12.1

EMPLOYMENT* (annual averages)

	1989	1990	1991
Agriculture	507,154	491,452	415,900
Forestry	63,015	78,479	56,175
Industry†	2,117,444	2,028,142	1,943,977
Construction	442,591	462,745	473,873
Wholesale and retail trade	576,908	553,089	525,097
Transport	272,392	287,391	283,386
Communications	78,006	83,542	83,110
Banking, insurance, commercial and technical services	77,256	77,650	110,581
Housing economy	75,312	74,684	59,530
Administration, justice, etc.	78,917	105,514	90,726
Municipal services	109,424	130,818	138,880
Education	307,423	299,781	285,694
Science, research and development	122,271	111,195	87,803
Health care	233,819	238,622	232,631
Culture	92,780	89,935	68,541
Total (incl. others)	5,402,533	5,351,242	5,058,633

* Excluding women on maternity leave.
† Principally mining, manufacturing, electricity and gas.

Agriculture

PRINCIPAL CROPS ('000 metric tons)

	1990	1991	1992
Wheat and spelt	4,624	4,081	3,413
Barley	3,157	2,833	2,512
Maize	98	150	104
Rye*	558	353	240
Potatoes	1,755	2,043	1,969
Rapeseed	304	348	293
Sugar beet	4,026	4,013	3,874

* Including mixed crops of wheat and rye.

LIVESTOCK ('000 head at 31 December)

	1990	1991	1992*
Horses	25	21	19
Cattle	3,360	2,950	2,512
Pigs	4,569	4,609	4,599
Sheep	430	343	254
Goats	42	43	45
Poultry	33,278	30,756	28,220

* At 1 March 1993.

LIVESTOCK PRODUCTS
('000 metric tons, unless otherwise indicated)

	1990	1991	1992
Beef and veal*	514.9	436.4	402.8
Pig meat*	739.7	680.4	704.3
Poultry meat*	210.5	218.0	193.1
Milk (million litres)	4,802	4,125	3,699
Eggs (million)	3,682	3,500	3,485

* Slaughter weight.

Forestry

LOGGING ('000 cubic metres)

	1990	1991	1992
Coniferous (soft wood)	12,175	9,510	8,700
Broadleaved (hard wood)	1,157	1,241	1,150
Total	13,332	10,751	9,850

Fishing*

(metric tons)

	1989	1990	1991
Common carp	16,740	17,624	17,280
Others	2,976	2,801	3,006
Total catch	19,716	20,425	20,286

* Figures refer only to fish caught by the Fishing Association (formerly State Fisheries) and members of the Czech and Moravian Fishing Union.

Mining

('000 metric tons)

	1991	1992
Hard coal	19,522	18,486
Brown coal and lignite	76,663	68,084
Kaolin	526	505
Crude petroleum	68.6	81.4

Industry

SELECTED PRODUCTS
('000 metric tons, unless otherwise indicated)

	1991	1992
Wheat flour and meal	559	631
Refined sugar	565	534
Wine ('000 hectolitres)	555.2	535.5
Beer ('000 hectolitres)	17,600.1	18,564.3
Cotton yarn (metric tons)	78,517	69,580
Woven cotton fabrics ('000 metres)	438,079	357,632
Woollen fabrics ('000 metres)	34,342	32,257
Linen fabrics ('000 metres)	66,122	54,088
Paper and paperboard (metric tons)	566,342	555,996
Footwear ('000 pairs)	41,400	36,572
Rubber tyres ('000)	6,733	5,891
Nitrogenous fertilizers (*a*)*	181.5	213.8
Phosphate fertilizers (*b*)*	46.3	44.6
Plastics	554	561
Motor spirit (petrol)	1,695	1,757
Diesel and fuel oil	3,553	3,437
Coke	6,467	5,701
Cement	5,610	6,111
Pig iron	5,316	5,082
Crude steel	7,972	7,334
Trucks (number)	22,227	14,127
Motor cycles and mopeds (number)	37,290	14,371
Tractors (number)	22,583	16,016
Electric energy (million kWh)	60,527	59,131
Manufactured gas (million cu metres)	1,741	1,552

* Production in terms of (a) nitrogen or (b) phospheric acid. Figures for phosphate fertilizers exclude granulated superphosphates.

Finance

CURRENCY AND EXCHANGE RATES

Monetary Units

100 haléřů (singular: haléř—heller) = 1 koruna (Czech crown or Kč.; plural: koruny).

Sterling and Dollar Equivalents (30 September 1993)

£1 sterling = 43.37 koruny;
US $1 = 29.00 koruny;
1,000 koruny = £23.06 = $34.48.

Average Exchange Rate (koruny per US $)

1990 17.95
1991 29.48
1992 28.26

Note: Figures for average exchange rates refer to the Czechoslovak koruna. In February 1993 the Czech Republic introduced its own currency, the Czech koruna, to replace (at par) the Czechoslovak koruna.

STATE BUDGET (million koruny)*

Revenue†	1990	1991	1992
Turnover tax	108,652	123,371	125,797
Transfers by economic organizations	177,693	190,980	181,253
Transfers by contribution-based organizations, banks and insurance companies	21,125	24,424	25,847
Revenues from activities of budgetary organizations	11,365	7,636	6,514
Agricultural tax	21,225	21,753	13,902
Taxes from the population and fees‡	2,279	67,292	94,945
Social insurance allowances	761	7,264	11,033
Other receipts	12,690	24,783	28,679
Total	355,790	467,503	487,970

Expenditure	1990	1991	1992
Capital construction	8,266	17,055	19,274
Material expenditure (incl. maintenance)	9,407	31,847	21,930
Non-material expenditure and services	85,987	94,037	92,640
State compensation benefit and other payments to persons	13,870	33,589	32,004
Wages and salaries	8,529	29,943	45,905
Social security benefits	95,189	121,654	133,711
Contributions to contribution-based and similar organizations and grants to co-operative organizations	28,130	30,332	75,900
Allocations to economic organizations	43,038	48,347	47,164
Total	292,416	406,804	468,528

* Figures refer to the former Czechoslovakia and represent a consolidation of the federal budget and the budgets of the Czech and Slovak Republics. For 1992 the distribution between the three units, before the allocation of grants from the federal to the republican budgets, was (in million koruny): *Revenue:* Federation 124,015, Czech Republic 248,079, Slovak Republic 115,876; *Expenditure:* Federation 126,015, Czech Republic 219,390, Slovak Republic 123,123. The data exclude the operations of units of the federal and republican governments with their own budgets. Also excluded are the budgets of local administrative organs.

† Before the allocation of grants and subsidies to local administrative organs. After adjusting for these transfers, total revenue (in million koruny) was: 296,194 in 1990; 389,348 in 1991; 451,898 in 1992.

‡ Taxes on wages accrued to local governments in 1990.

OFFICIAL RESERVES (US $ million at 31 December)*

	1990	1991	1992
Gold†	252	286	222
IMF special drawing rights	—	140	42
Foreign exchange‡	1,102	3,050	1,078
Total	1,354	3,476	1,342

* Figures refer to the former Czechoslovakia.

† Valued at market-related prices.

‡ From February 1992 figures exclude foreign exchange holdings of the Československá obchodní banka (reclassified as a deposit money bank).

Source: IMF, *International Fin ncial Statistics.*

MONEY SUPPLY ('000 million koruny at 31 December)*

	1990	1991	1992
Total money	291.15	371.44	430.50

* Figures refer to the former Czechoslovakia.

Source: IMF, *International Financial Statistics.*

COST OF LIVING
(Consumer Price Index; base: January 1989 = 100)

	1990	1991	1992
Food	110.5	159.7	174.2
Industrial goods	110.5	187.5	204.4
Public catering	110.1	174.8	189.5
Services	106.9	148.6	186.6
All items	109.9	172.2	191.3

NATIONAL ACCOUNTS

Net Material Product*
(million koruny at current market prices)

Activities of the material sphere	1989	1990	1991
Agriculture, hunting and fishing	38,609	37,767	34,764
Forestry and logging	4,046	3,860	5,188
Industry†	249,918	273,709	383,454
Construction	43,273	49,191	50,887
Trade, restaurants, etc.	72,481	87,381	107,943
Transport and storage	13,411	12,791	19,269
Communications	4,207	4,438	4,468
Others	1,996	2,359	2,789
Total	427,941	471,496	608,762

* Defined as the total net value of goods and 'productive' services, including turnover taxes, produced by the economy. This excludes economic activities not contributing directly to material production, such as public administration, defence and personal and professional services.

† Principally manufacturing, mining, electricity, gas and water supply.

Gross domestic product (million koruny at current prices): 524,565 in 1989; 567,322 in 1990; 716,593 in 1991. Source: UN, *Monthly Bulletin of Statistics.*

BALANCE OF PAYMENTS (US $ million)*

	1990	1991	1992
Merchandise exports f.o.b.	11,635	10,596	11,463
Merchandise imports f.o.b.	−13,057	−10,717	−13,297
Trade balance	−1,422	−121	−1,834
Exports of services	2,665	2,928	4,018
Imports of services	−2,424	−1,982	−2,359
Other income received	506	654	792
Other income paid	−757	−633	−790
Private unrequited transfers (net)	258	75	51
Official unrequited transfers (net)	−52	−14	90
Current balance	−1,227	908	−31
Direct investment (net)	187	586	1,073
Other capital (net)	455	−1,565	−1,319
Net errors and omissions	−543	861	−144
Overall balance	−1,127	789	−422

* Figures refer to the former Czechoslovakia.

Source: IMF, *International Financial Statistics.*

External Trade

COMMODITY GROUPS
(distribution by SITC, million koruny)

Imports f.o.b.	1991	1992
Food and live animals	14,055	17,945
Crude materials (inedible) except fuels	15,294	17,101
Mineral fuels, lubricants, etc.	50,075	45,449
Chemicals and related products	21,730	28,812
Basic manufactures	19,924	30,114
Machinery and transport equipment	67,574	119,344
Miscellaneous manufactured articles	15,717	26,879
Total (incl. others)	208,781	290,488

Exports f.o.b.	1991	1992
Food and live animals	18,429	20,008
Crude materials (inedible) except fuels	13,315	16,033
Mineral fuels, lubricants, etc.	12,747	14,050
Chemicals and related products	23,212	22,831
Basic manufactures	65,593	80,172
Machinery and transport equipment	71,005	62,926
Miscellaneous manufactured articles	26,737	29,735
Total (incl. others)	233,594	247,850

SELECTED TRADING PARTNERS (million koruny)

Imports f.o.b.	1991	1992
Austria	17,200	26,549
France	5,750	16,181
Germany	51,965	78,427
Hungary	2,927	3,333
Italy	7,747	14,086
Japan	2,947	6,527
USSR (former)	48,812	52,636
United Kingdom	5,206	7,767
USA	4,782	14,828
Total (incl. others)	208,781	290,488

Exports f.o.b.	1991	1992
Austria	13,589	17,910
France	5,594	6,314
Germany	63,947	81,460
Hungary	7,693	7,782
Italy	9,855	15,436
USSR (former)	40,841	22,126
United Kingdom	5,147	5,698
USA	2,434	4,311
Total (incl. others)	233,594	247,850

Transport

RAILWAYS (traffic)

	1990	1991	1992
Passenger-km (million)*	19,335	19,263	16,898
Freight net ton-km (million)	41,150	32,679	30,623

* Figures refer to the former Czechoslovakia.

ROAD TRAFFIC (motor vehicles in use at 31 December)

	1990	1991	1992
Passenger cars	2,366,712	2,435,645	2,522,369
Buses and coaches	26,036	26,724	26,552
Goods vehicles*	156,420	158,402	156,512
Vans	44,585	47,577	57,928
Motorcycles	453,480	453,447	455,083

* Excluding special-purpose lorries.

INLAND WATERWAYS
(freight carried, '000 metric tons)

	1990	1991	1992
Imports	645	499	364
Exports	530	472	543
Internal	5,060	4,728	3,996
Total (incl. others)	6,370	5,857	5,125

AIR TRANSPORT*

	1990	1991	1992
Kilometres flown ('000)	27,577	25,264	29,196
Passengers carried ('000)	1,290	983	1,123
Freight carried (metric tons)	24,123	23,220	26,298
Passenger-km ('000)	2,348,080	2,107,645	2,530,590
Freight ton-km ('000)	57,723	69,243	76,612

* Figures refer to the former Czechoslovakia.

Tourism

FOREIGN TOURIST ARRIVALS*

	1992
Austria	196,689
France	96,638
Germany	1,111,763
Italy	184,649
Netherlands	167,870
Poland	134,204
Spain	53,470
United Kingdom	76,211
USA	104,656
Yugoslavia (former)	50,469
Total (incl. others)	2,609,208

* Figures refer to visitors staying for at least one night at registered accommodation facilities.

Communications Media

	1990	1991	1992
Radio licences	3,095,897	2,956,017	2,882,530
Television licenses	3,348,179	3,246,205	3,184,476
Telephones in use	3,023,372	3,126,266	3,238,051
Book production*:			
Titles†	8,585	9,362	n.a.
Copies ('000)†	81,501	n.a.	n.a.
Daily newspapers*:			
Number	48	n.a.	n.a.
Average circulation ('000)	7,943	n.a.	n.a.
Non-daily newspapers*:			
Number	64	n.a.	n.a.
Average circulation ('000)	849	n.a.	n.a.
Other periodicals*:			
Number	2,513	n.a.	n.a.
Average circulation ('000)	60,061	n.a.	n.a.

* Figures refer to the former Czechoslovakia (Source: UNESCO, *Statistical Yearbook*).
† Including pamphlets (1,082 titles and 11,956,000 copies in 1990; 1,813 titles in 1991).

Education

(1992/93)

	Institutions	Teachers	Students
Pre-primary	6,979	29,942	325,735
Primary	4,142	65,186	1,115,027
Secondary:			
Grammar and vocational	997	23,111*	318,974
Apprentice-training*	702	8,276	268,154
Higher	23	12,907	114,185

* Full-time only.

Directory

The Constitution

The following is a summary of the main provisions of the Constitution of the Czech Republic, which was adopted on 16 December 1992 and entered into force on 1 January 1993:

GENERAL PROVISIONS

The Czech Republic is a sovereign, unified and democratic law-abiding state, founded on the respect for the rights and freedoms of the individual and citizen. All state power belongs to the people, who exercise this power through the intermediary of legislative, executive and judicial bodies. The fundamental rights and freedoms of the people are under the protection of the judiciary.

The political system is founded on the free and voluntary operation of political parties respecting fundamental democratic principles and rejecting force as a means to assert their interests. Political decisions derive from the will of the majority, expressed through the free ballot. Minorities are protected in decision-making by the majority.

The territory of the Czech Republic encompasses an indivisible whole, whose state border may be changed only by constitutional law. Procedures covering the acquisition and loss of Czech citizenship are determined by law. No one may be deprived of his or her citizenship against his or her will.

GOVERNMENT

Legislative Power

Legislative power in the Czech Republic is vested in two chambers,* the Chamber of Deputies and the Senate. The Chamber of Deputies has 200 members, elected for a term of four years. The Senate has 81 members, elected for a term of six years. Every two years one-third of the senators are elected. Both chambers elect their respective Chairman and Deputy Chairmen from among their members. Members of both chambers of the legislature are elected on the basis of universal, equal and direct suffrage by secret ballot. All citizens of 18 years and over are eligible to vote.

The legislature enacts the Constitution and laws; approves the state budget and the state final account; and approves the electoral law and international agreements. It elects the President of the Republic (at a joint session of both chambers), supervises the activities of the Government, and decides upon the declaration of war.

President of the Republic

The President of the Republic is Head of State. He/she is elected for a term of five years by a joint session of both chambers of the legislature. The President may not be elected for more than two consecutive terms.

The President appoints, dismisses and accepts the resignation of the Prime Minister and other members of the Government, dismisses the Government and accepts its resignation; convenes sessions of the Chamber of Deputies; may dissolve the Chamber of Deputies; names the judges of the Constitutional Court, its Chairman and Deputy Chairmen; appoints the Chairman and Deputy Chairmen of the Supreme Court; has the right to return adopted constitutional laws to the legislature; initials laws; and appoints members of the Council of the Czech National Bank. The President also represents the State in external affairs; is the Supreme Commander of the Armed Forces; receives heads of diplomatic missions; calls elections to the Chamber of Deputies and to the Senate; and has the right to grant amnesty.

Council of Ministers

The Council of Ministers is the highest organ of executive power. It is composed of the Prime Minister, the Deputy Prime Ministers and Ministers. It is answerable to the Chamber of Deputies. The President of the Republic appoints the Prime Minister, on whose recommendation he/she appoints the remaining members of the Council of Ministers and entrusts them with directing the ministries or other offices.

JUDICIAL SYSTEM

Judicial power is exercised on behalf of the Republic by independent courts. Judges are independent in the exercise of their function. The judiciary consists of the Supreme Court, the Supreme Administrative Court, high, regional and district courts.

The Constitutional Court is a judicial body protecting constitutionality. It consists of 15 judges appointed for a 10-year term by the President of the Republic with the consent of the Senate.

* The Senate was expected to be elected in autumn 1994.

The Government

(January 1994)

HEAD OF STATE

President: VÁCLAV HAVEL (elected 26 January 1993).

COUNCIL OF MINISTERS

A coalition of the Civic Democratic Party (CDP), the Christian Democratic Union-Czechoslovak People's Party (CDU-CPP), the Christian Democratic Party (Chr.DP) and the Civic Democratic Alliance (CDA).

Prime Minister: VÁCLAV KLAUS (CDP).

Deputy Prime Minister and Minister of Agriculture: JOSEF LUX (CDU—CPP).

Deputy Prime Minister: JAN KALVODA (CDA).

Deputy Prime Minister and Minister of Finance: IVAN KOČÁRNÍK (CDP).

Minister of the Interior: JAN RUML (CDP).

Minister of Foreign Relations: JOSEF ZIELENIEC (CDP).

Minister of the Economy: KAREL DYBA (CDP).

Minister of Industry and Trade: VLADIMÍR DLOUHÝ (CDA).

Minister of Privatization: JIŘÍ SKALICKÝ (CDA).

Minister of the Environment: FRANTIŠEK BENDA (Chr.DP).

Minister of Health: LUDEK RUBAS (CDP).

Minister of Culture: PAVEL TIGRID (CDU-CPP).

Minister of Justice: JIŘÍ NOVÁK (CDP).

Minister of Labour and Social Affairs: JINDŘICH VODIČKA (CDP).

Minister of Education: PETR PITHA (Chr.DP).

Minister of Economic Competition: STANISLAV BĚLEHRÁDEK (CDU-CPP).

Minister of Defence: ANTONÍN BAUDYŠ (CDU-CPP).

Minister of Transport: JAN STRÁSKÝ (CDP).

MINISTRIES

Office of the Government of the Czech Republic: Lazarská 7, 113 48 Prague 1; tel. (2) 2130111; fax (2) 2359963.

Ministry of Agriculture: Těšnov 17, 117 05 Prague 1; tel. (2) 2862111; fax (2) 2313161.

Ministry of Culture: Valdštejnské nám. 4, 118 11 Prague 1; tel. (2) 5131111; telex 122317; fax (2) 24510346.

Ministry of Defence: Dělostřelecká 11, 162 00 Prague 6; tel. (2) 341012; fax (2) 341433.

Ministry of Economic Competition: Joštova 8, 601 56 Brno; tel. (5) 2197; fax (5) 22036.

Ministry of the Economy: Staroměstké Nám. 6, 110 00 Prague 1; tel. (2) 712111; fax (2) 741957.

Ministry of Education: Karmelitská 8, 118 12 Prague 1; tel. (2) 5193111; fax (2) 5193790.

Ministry of the Environment: Vršovická 65, 100 10 Prague 10; tel. (2) 7121111; fax (2) 731357.

Ministry of Finance: Letenská 15, 118 10 Prague 1; tel. (2) 5141111; fax (2) 5142788.

Ministry of Foreign Relations: Lazarská 7, 113 48 Prague 1; tel. (2) 2350964; fax (2) 2350970.

Ministry of Health: Palackého nám. 4, 128 01 Prague 2; tel. (2) 24971111; fax (2) 24972816.

Ministry of Industry and Trade: Na Františku 32, 110 15 Prague 1; tel. (2) 2318197; fax (2) 2311970.

Ministry of the Interior: Strojnická 27/935, 170 89 Prague 7; tel. (2) 33511111; fax (2) 381769.

Ministry of Justice: Vyšehradská 16, 128 10 Prague 2; tel. (2) 294545; fax (2) 299064.

Ministry of Labour and Social Affairs: Na poříčním právu 1, 120 07 Prague 2; tel. (2) 2135111; fax (2) 2365468.

Ministry of Privatization: Senovážné nám. 32, 110 00 Prague 1; tel. (2) 2362065; fax (2) 260160.

Ministry of Transport: Nábř. L. Svobody 12, 125 11 Prague 1; tel. (2) 23031111; fax (2) 2314015.

Legislature

The Czech Constitution, which was adopted in December 1992, provided for the creation of a bicameral legislature as the highest organ of the state authority in the Czech Republic (which was established on 1 January 1993, following the dissolution of the Czech and Slovak Federative Republic). The lower house, the Chamber of Deputies, retained the structure of the Czech National Council (the former republican legislature), whose 200 deputies had been elected on 5-6 June 1992. The upper chamber, or Senate, was to be elected in autumn 1994.

CHAMBER OF DEPUTIES
(Poslanecká sněmovna)

Chairman: MILAN UHDE.

Deputy Chairmen: JAN KASAL, KAREL LEDVINKA, PAVEL TOLLNER, JIŘÍ VLACH.

Elections to the (former) Czech National Council, 5-6 June 1992

Parties and Groups	% of votes	Seats
Civic Democratic Party	29.73	76
Left Bloc*	14.05	35
Czechoslovak Social Democratic Party	6.53	16
Liberal Social Union†	6.52	16
Christian Democratic Union-Czechoslovak People's Party	6.28	15
Association for the Republic-Czechoslovak Republican Party	5.98	14
Civic Democratic Alliance	5.93	14
Movement for Autonomous Democracy-Society for Moravia and Silesia‡	5.87	14
Others	19.11	—
Total	100.00	200

* A left-wing alliance, including the Communist Party of Bohemia and Moravia.

† An alliance of the Czechoslovak Socialist Party, the Agrarian Party and the Green Party.

‡ In late 1992 renamed the Movement for Autonomous Democracy of Moravia and Silesia.

Local Government

The Constitution of the Czech Republic requires that the country should be divided into several new territorial and administrative regions. In November 1993 the Chamber of Deputies passed a resolution requiring the Government to submit a draft constitutional law on the new administrative divisions as soon as possible. Meanwhile local government continued to be the responsibility of a tier consisting of 75 districts, including the following:

Benešov (1): Masarykovo nám. 1, 256 46 Benešov; tel. (301) 55111; fax (301) 23791; Leader Ing. VÁCLAV ŠIMŮNEK.

Beroun (2): Politických vězňů 20 B.II, 266 01 Beroun; tel. (311) 53111; fax (311) 21387; Leader FRANTIŠEK MALÝ.

Kladno (3): nám. 17 listopadu 1740, 272 63 Kladno; tel. (302) 895111; fax (302) 6506; Leader Ing. VÁCLAV MIKULECKÝ.

Kolín (4): Karlovo nám. 1, 280 00 Kolín; tel. (321) 21111; fax (321) 2005; Leader Ing. JAN SOUKUP.

Kutná Hora (5): Radnická 178, 284 22 Kutná Hora; tel. (327) 51111; fax (321) 2952; Leader Ing. MIROSLAV RICHTER.

Mělník (6): nám. Míru 51, 276 01 Mělník; tel. (206) 624348; fax (206) 4549; Leader JAROSLAV HORÁK.

Mladá Boleslav (7): Staroměstské nám. 70, 293 59 Mladá Boleslav; tel. (326) 421; fax (326) 26206; Leader Ing. JOSEF TOMÁŠ.

Nymburk (8): Čs. armády 163, 288 63 Nymburk; tel. (325) 2221; fax (325) 2949; Leader Ing. VLADISLAV ŠT'ASTNÝ.

Praha–východ (9) (Prague–East): nám. Republiky 3, 110 00 Prague; tel. (2) 24225097; fax (2) 24223562; Leader Ing. VLADIMÍR HŮLKA.

Praha–západ (10) (Prague–West): Podskalská 19, 128 25 Prague; tel. (2) 297151; fax (2) 29164; Leader Dr LIBUŠE BENEŠOVÁ.

Příbram (11): nám. T. G. Masaryka 145, 261 12 Příbram; tel. (306) 511; fax (306) 21105; Leader JAROSLAV ŠTEFAN.

Rakovník (12): Na Sekyře 166/II, 269 22 Rakovník; tel. (313) 2051; fax (313) 2869; Leader Ing. JIŘÍ CHALUPECKÝ.

České Budjovice (13): Kněžská ul. 19, 370 01 České Budějovice; tel. (38) 32731; fax (38) 37436; Leader Dr MARIE MOTYČKOVÁ.

Český Krumlov (14): Plešivec 268, 381 01 Český Krumlov; tel. (337) 2011; fax (337) 2768; Leader Dr FRANTIŠEK MIKEŠ.

Jindřichův Hradec (15): Janderova 147/II, 377 36 Jindřichův Hradec; tel. (331) 2241; fax (331) 23175; Leader Dr LUKÁŠ MIKULECKÝ.

Pelhřimov (16): Pražská 127, 393 32 Pelhřimov; tel. (366) 521911; fax (366) 22979; Leader Dr ALEŠ MAREČEK.

Písek (17): Budovcova 207, 297 01 Písek; tel. (362) 2321; fax (362) 3309; Leader Ing. ZDENĚK PROKOPEC.

Prachatice (18): Velké nám. 1, 383 01 Prachatice; tel. (338) 22361; fax (338) 22291; Leader Dr KAREL ŠKÁCHA.

Strakonice (19): Smetanova 533, 386 22 Strakonice; tel. (342) 441; fax (342) 21208; Leader Ing. BŘETISLAV ŘEZNÍČEK.

Tábor (20): Na Parkánech 1623, 390 18 Tábor; tel. (361) 22011; fax (361) 62594; Leader Ing. JOSEF ČÁP.

Domažlice (21): Týnské předměstí 228, Peroutkova, 344 13 Domažlice; tel. (189) 2641; fax (189) 4802; Leader PAVEL FASCHINGBAUER.

Cheb (22): Obrněné brigády 30, 350 13 Cheb; tel. (166) 30821; fax (166) 22870; Leader OTAKAR MIKA.

Karlovy Vary (23): U spořitelny 2, 361 13 Karlovy Vary; tel. (17) 23201; fax (17) 22280; Leader Ing. JOSEF TUREK.

Klatovy (24): Plzeňská 90/III, 339 13 Klatovy; tel. (186) 22240; fax (186) 23521; Leader IVAN PETRŮ.

Plzeň–jih (25) (Pilsen–South): Radobyčická 14, 306 04 Plzeň; tel. (19) 35734; fax (19) 223392; Leader Dr VÁCLAV ČERVENÝ.

Plzeň–sever (26) (Pilsen–North): Moskevská 39, 306 06 Plzeň; tel. (19) 37381; fax (19) 37949; Leader JIŘÍ LEŠČINSKÝ.

Rokycany (27): Jiráskova 68, 337 13 Rokycany; tel. (181) 2251; fax (181) 2394; Leader Ing. JAROSLAV HELD.

Sokolov (28): ul. Jednoty 654, 356 01 Sokolov; tel. (168) 35111; fax (168) 24806; Leader Ing. JOSEF MICHALSKÝ.

Tachov (29): T. G. Masaryka 1326, 347 13 Tachov; tel. (184) 2444; fax (184) 2268; Leader Ing. JAROSLAV STEHLÍK.

Česká Lípa (30): Děčínská 389, 470 35 Česká Lípa; tel. (425) 331111; fax (425) 23233; Leader Dr HELENA BROŽOVSKÁ.

Děčín (31): ul. 28 října 2, 405 59 Děčín; tel. (412) 28221; fax (412) 28295; Leader LIBOR HOLANDA.

Chomutov (32): Masarykovo nám. 8, 430 24 Chomutov; tel. (396) 75; fax (396) 4865; Leader Dr JIŘÍ KULHÁNEK.

Jablonec nad Nisou (33): Mírové nám. 19, 467 52 Jablonec nad Nisou; tel. (428) 419111; fax (428) 23538; Leader Dr KAREL BRODSKÝ.

Liberec (34): nám. Dr E. Beneše 26, 460 01 Liberec; tel. (48) 328; fax (48) 25724; Leader JAROSLAV MRAŽ.

Litoměřice (35): Na Valech 525, 412 91 Litoměřice; tel. (416) 5721; fax (416) 3240; Leader JOSEF POL.

Louny (36): Palackého 2380, 440 27 Louny; tel. (395) 2421; fax (395) 2050; Leader JOSEF KOPIC.

Most (37): Tř budovatelů 1, 434 89 Most; tel. (35) 322201; fax (35) 42392; Leader Ing. MILAN KONEČNÝ.

Teplice (38): Husitská 2, 415 01 Teplice; tel. (417) 3131; fax (417) 29344; Leader TOMÁŠ ŘÍMAN.

Ústí nad Labem (39): Mírové nám. 36, 400 01 Ústí nad Labem; tel. (47) 214; fax (47) 23172; Leader Ing. LADISLAV CIHLÁŘ.

Havlíčkův Brod (40): Štáflova 2003, 580 31 Havlíčkův Brod; tel. (451) 327; fax (451) 22681; Leader Ing. JAROSLAVA PŘBYLOVÁ.

Hradec Králové (41): ul. ČSA, 502 06 Hradec Králové; tel. (49) 281111; fax (49) 25682; Leader Ing. JIŘÍ VLČEK.

Chrudium (42): Pardubická 62, 537 18 Chrudim; tel. (455) 2451; fax (455) 41567; Leader Ing. ONDŘEJ KUDRNÁČ.

Jičín (43): Havlíčkova 56, 506 14 Jičín; tel. (433) 412; fax (433) 23700; Leader Ing. LUDĚK PUŠ.

Náchod (44): Palachova 1303, 547 28 Náchod; tel. (441) 23251; fax (441) 21046; Leader Ing. LUBOMÍR ŠMÍDA.

Pardubice (45): nám. Republiky 12, 532 02 Pardubice; tel. (40) 584111; fax (40) 517902; Leader Dr DRAHOSLAVA BARTOŠKOVÁ.

Rychnov nad Kněžnou (46): Havlíčkova 136, 516 01 Rychnov nad Kněžnou; tel. (445) 21284; fax (445) 21687; Leader PETR NARWA.

Semily (47): Bitouchovská 1, 513 01 Semily; tel. (431) 2631; fax (431) 3278; Leader Ing. VÁCLAVA KODEJŠOVÁ.

Svitavy (48): generála Svobody 5, 568 26 Svitavy; tel. (461) 41111; fax (461) 21292; Leader Ing. JOSEF JANEČEK.

Trutnov (49): Horská 5/1, 541 18 Trutnov; tel. (439) 4251; fax (439) 5244; Leader Ing. VLASTIMIL ŠUBRT.

Ústí nad Orlicí (50): Smetanova 43/1, 562 01 Ústí nad Orlicí; tel. (465) 2011; fax (465) 4371; Leader BOHUMIL ČADA.

Blansko (51): nám. Republiky 1, 678 27 Blansko; tel. (506) 825; fax (506) 2234; Leader Ing. FRANTIŠEK SLÁMA.

Brno—venkov (52): Moravské nám. 6, 601 70 Brno; tel. (5) 42161111; fax (5) 42214576; Leader Ing. JIŘÍ BŘEZA.

Břeclav (53): T. G. Masaryka 6, 690 15 Břeclav; tel. (627) 721111; fax (627) 21501; Leader JIŘÍ PAVLOV.

Hodonín (54): Národní tř 25, 695 32 Hodonín; tel. (628) 416; fax (628) 22100; Leader Dr STANISLAV KUBRICKÝ.

Jihlava (55): Tolstého 15, 586 01 Jihlava; tel. (66) 23741; fax (23645; Leader PETR MENŠÍK.

Kroměříž (56): Husovo nám. 4, 767 37 Kroměříž; tel. (634) 514; fax (634) 20135; Leader Dr EMIL ZAVADIL.

Prostějov (57): nám. Spojenců 13, 796 01 Prostějov; tel. (508) 416; fax (508) 26589; Leader LUBOMÍR MAREŠ.

Třebíč (58): Čs. armády 6, 674 30 Třebíč; tel. (618) 775111; fax (618) 3138; Leader Ing. KAREL MULLER.

Ukerské Hradiště (59): 9 května 568, 686 01 Uherské Hradiště; tel. (632) 431; fax (632) 2181; Leader Ing. IVAN PALACKÝ.

Vyškov (60): Nádražní 7, 683 12 Vyškov; tel. (507) 411111; fax (507) 21600; Leader Ing. PAVEL VAŠÍČEK.

Zlín (61): tř Tomáše Bati, 762 69 Zlín; tel. (67) 526111; fax (67) 33359; Leader Dr ZDENĚK DOSTÁL.

Znojmo (62): nám. Armády 8, 670 39 Znojmo; tel. (624) 5201; fax (624) 5815; Leader Dr MILUŠE ŘÍČKOVÁ.

Žd'ár nad Sázavou (63): Žižkova 1, 591 12 Žd'ár nad Sázavou; tel. (616) 415; fax (616) 24717; Leader Ing. JAN TEPLÝ.

Bruntál (64): Nádražní 20, 792 11 Bruntál; tel. (646) 81; fax (646) 2193; Leader STANISLAV NAVRÁTIL.

Frýdek Místek (65): Palackého 115, 738 20 Frýdek Místek; tel. (658) 5131111; fax (658) 31576; Leader Ing. JIŘÍ ŠTÍHEL.

Karviná (66): Zakladatelská 974, 735 06 Karviná; tel. (69) 6311903; fax (69) 6311942; Leader JAN WEBER.

Nový Jičín (67): Divadelní 3, 741 11 Nový Jičín; tel. (656) 22431; fax (656) 23468; Leader Ing. JOSEF SVOBODA.

Olomouc (68): tř Kosmonautů 10, 772 55 Olomouc; tel. ((68) 510111; fax (68) 28937; Leader Dr FRANTIŠEK NEPLECH.

Opava (69): Bezručovo nám. 14, 746 84 Opava; tel. (653) 212269; fax (653) 212135; Leader ANTONÍN ŠROM.

Přerov (70): Smetanova 7, 750 83 Přerov; tel. (641) 2141; fax (641) 2808; Leader Ing. MILOSLAV PŘIKRYL.

Šumperk (71): M. R. Štefanika 20, 787 01 Šumperk; tel. (649) 5341; fax (649) 3328; Leader Ing. ADOLF JÍLEK.

Vsetín (72): nám. Míru 31, 755 11 Vsetín; tel. (657) 4001; fax (657) 4714; Leader MIROSLAV MÍRNÝ.

Political Organizations

Agrarian Party (Zemědělská strana): Prague; f. 1990; seeks compensation for farmers whose property was confiscated during collectivization; Chair. Dr FRANTIŠEK TRNKA.

Association for the Republic—Czechoslovak Republican Party (Sdružení pro republiku—Republikánská strana Československa): U zeměpisného ústavu 1, 160 00 Prague 6; tel. and fax (2) 3124392; extreme right-wing; Chair. MIROSLAV SLADEK.

Christian Democratic Party (Křesťansko-demokratická strana): Sokolská 39, 120 00 Prague 2; tel. (2) 2368429; fax (2) 2351454; f. 1989; Leader IVAN PILIP.

Christian Democratic Union-Czechoslovak People's Party (Křesťanská a demokratická unie-Československá strana lidová): Revoluční 5, 110 15 Prague 1; tel. (2) 2319329; fax (2) 2324720; f. 1992; Chair. JOSEF LUX.

Civic Democratic Alliance (CDA) (Občanská demokratická aliance): Rytirská 10, 110 00 Prague 1; tel. (2) 226898; fax (2) 227382; f. 1991 as a formal political party, following a split in Civic Forum (Občanské fórum—f. 1989); fmrly an informal group within Civic Forum; conservative; Chair. JAN KALVODA.

Civic Democratic Party (CDP) (Občanská demokratická strana): Sněmovní 3, 110 00 Prague 1; tel. (2) 3114800; fax (2) 3118273; f. 1991 following a split in Civic Forum (Občanské fórum—f. 1989); liberal-conservative; 35,000 mems; Chair. VÁCLAV KLAUS.

Communist Party of Bohemia and Moravia (Komunistická strana Čech a Moravy): Politických vězňů 9, 110 00 Prague 1; tel. (2) 2199; f. 1991 as a result of the reorganization of the Communist Party of Czechoslovakia; Leader MIROSLAV GREBENIČEK.

Czech Social Democratic Party (Česká strana sociálně demokratická): Lidový dům, Hybernská 7, 110 00 Prague 1; tel. and fax (2) 2369052; f. 1878; prohibited 1948; re-established 1989; formerly the Czechoslovak Social Democratic Party; Chair. Ing. MILOŠ ZEMAN.

Czechoslovak Socialist Party: Prague; f. 1993; formed after original party of same title renamed itself the Liberal National Social Party (see below); Chair. MILAN ADAM.

Democratic Left: Prague; f. 1993 after split from Party of the Democratic Left; Chair. LOTAR INDŘUCH.

Free Democrats (Svobodní hnutí): Prague; f. 1991, as Civic Movement, after a split in Civic Forum (Občanské fórum—f. 1989), name changed 1993; liberal; 4,000 mems; Chair. JIŘÍ DIENSTBIER.

Green Party: Křížová 60, 150 00 Prague 5; tel. and fax (2) 545243; f. 1989; Chair. JAROSLAV VLČEK .

Left Bloc: Prague; membership open to members of other political organizations with similar ideologies, incl. Communist Party of Bohemia and Moravia, and Party of the Democratic Left; Chair. MARIA STIBOROVA.

Liberal-Democratic Party: Prague; fmrly a member of the Civic Forum coalition; Chair. VOJTECH PRUŠA.

Liberal National Social Party: nám. Republiky 7, 111 49 Prague 1; tel. (2) 2367320; telex 121432; fax (2) 2369788; f. 1897 as the Czechoslovak National Socialist Party; known as Czechoslovak Socialist Party until 1993; moderate; Chair. Ing. LADISLAV DVOŘÁK.

Moravian National Party: Brno; Chair. IVAN DRIMAL.

Movement for Autonomous Democracy of Moravia and Silesia (MADMS) (Hnutí za samosprávnou demokracii Moravy a Slezska): Františkánská 1-3, 602 00 Brno; tel. (2) 15279; fax (2) 15276; fmrly the Movement for Autonomous Democracy—Society for Moravia and Silesia; renamed the Czech-Moravian Party of the Centre (Českamoravska strana stredu) in January 1994; Chair. Dr JAN KRYCER.

Party of the Democratic Left: Prague; f. 1993 following a split in the Communist Party of Bohemia and Moravia; democratic socialist; 10,000 mems; Chair. JOSEF MECL.

Radical Czech Democratic Party: Prague; f. 1993; agrarian party; Chair. MILAN GARNCARS.

Diplomatic Representation

EMBASSIES IN THE CZECH REPUBLIC

Afghanistan: V Tišině 6, 160 00 Prague 6; tel. (2) 373537; Ambassador: MOHAMMAD ARAF SAKHRA.

Albania: Pod Kaštany 22, 160 00 Prague 6; tel. (2) 379329; fax (2) 371742; Ambassador: ISMAIL ABEDIN FARKA.

Algeria: Na Marne 16, 160 00 Prague 6; tel. (2) 3120758; Ambassador: BOULAGHLEM SALAH.

Angola: Nad Štolou 18, Prague 7; tel. (2) 376260; Ambassador: MANUEL QUARTA.

Argentina: Washingtonova 25, 125 22 Prague 1; tel. (2) 223803; telex 121847; Ambassador: ABEL PARENTINI POSSE.

Austria: Viktora Huga 10, 125 43 Prague 5; tel. (2) 546550; telex 121849; fax (2) 549626; Ambassador: KARL PETERLIK.

Belgium: Valdštejnská 6, 125 24 Prague 1; tel. (2) 534051; telex 122362; fax (2) 537351; Chargé d'affaires a.i.: LUC LIEBAUT.

Bolivia: Ve Smečkách 25, 125 59 Prague 1; tel. (2) 263209; telex 122402; Ambassador: CARLOS COSTA DU RELS.

Brazil: Bolzanova 5, 125 01 Prague 1; tel. (2) 229254; telex 122292; fax (2) 228604; Ambassador: CARLOS ANTÔNIO BETTENCOURT BUENO.

Bulgaria: Krakovská 6, 125 00 Prague 1; tel. (2) 264310; telex 121381; Ambassador: BOYAN DIMITROV NICHEV.

Cambodia: Na Hubálce 1, 169 00 Prague 6; tel. (2) 352603; fax (2) 351078; Chargé d'affaires a.i.: LIM SAMKOL .

Canada: Mickiewiczova 6, 125 33 Prague 6; tel. (2) 3120251; telex 121061; fax (2) 3112791; Ambassador: PAUL D. FRAZER.

Chile: Trojská 90, 171 00 Prague 7; tel. (2) 8541495; telex 121246; fax (2) 8540668; Ambassador: ROLANDO STEIN BRYGIN.

China, People's Republic: Majakovského 22, 160 00 Prague 6; tel. (2) 3123245; Ambassador: WANG XINGDA.

Colombia: Příčná 1, 110 00 Prague 1; tel. (2) 291330; Ambassador: CAMILO REYES RODRÍGUEZ.

Costa Rica: Dlouhá 36, 110 00 Prague 1; tel. (2) 2619073; telex 121726; fax (2) 2320878; Ambassador: CARLOS E. FERNÁNDEZ GARCÍA.

Cuba: Sibiřské nám. 1, 125 35 Prague 6; tel. (2) 3122246; telex 121163; Ambassador: BENIGNO PÉREZ FERNÁNDEZ.

Denmark: U Pátě Baterie 7, 162 00 Prague 6; tel. (2) 353109; telex 122209; fax (2) 350659; Ambassador: PER POULSEN-HANSEN.

Ecuador: Opletalova 43, 125 01 Prague 1; tel. (2) 261258; telex 123286; Ambassador: OSWALDO RAMÍREZ LANDÁZURI.

Egypt: Majakovského 14, 125 46 Prague 6; tel. (2) 341051; telex 123552; fax (2) 3120861; Chargé d'affaires a. i.: Dr KHALED M. EL-KOMY.

Ethiopia: V Průhledu 9, 125 00 Prague 6; tel. (2) 352268; telex 122067; fax (2) 3123464; Ambassador: TEFERRA SHIAWL .

Finland: Dřevná 2, 125 01 Prague 2; tel. (2) 24913594; telex 121060; fax (2) 24915556; Ambassador: PAULI OPAS.

France: Velkopřevorské nám. 2, 110 00 Prague 1; tel. (2) 533042; fax (2) 539926; Ambassador: BENO&T D'ABOVILLE.

Germany: Vlašská 19, 125 60 Prague 1; tel. (2) 24510328; telex 122814; fax (2) 24510156; Ambassador: Dr ROLF HOFSTETTER.

Ghana: V Tišině 4, 160 00 Prague 6; tel. (2) 373058; telex 122263; Chargé d'affaires a.i.: KWABENA OSEI-DANQUAH.

Greece: Na Ořechovce 19, 160 00 Prague 6; tel. (2) 354279; Ambassador: CONSTANTIN POLITIS.

Holy See: Voršilská 12, 110 00 Prague 1; tel. (2) 24912192; fax (2) 24914160; Apostolic Nuncio: Most Rev. GIOVANNI COPPA, Titular Archbishop of Serta.

Hungary: Badeniho 1, 125 37 Prague 6; tel. (2) 365041; telex 123535; fax (2) 329425; Ambassador: GYÖRGY VARGA.

India: Valdštejnská 6, Mala Strana, 125 28 Prague 1; tel. (2) 532642; telex 121901; fax (2) 539495; Ambassador: D. C. MANNERS.

Indonesia: Nad Buďánkami II/7, 125 29 Prague 5; tel. (2) 526041; telex 121443; Ambassador: H. R. ENAP SURATMAN.

Iran: Na Zátorce 18, 125 30 Prague 6; tel. (2) 371480; telex 122732; Ambassador: RASUL MOVAHEDIAN ATTAR.

Iraq: Na Zátorce 10, 125 01 Prague 6; tel. (2) 375031; Ambassador: MUNTHER AHMED AL-MUTLAK.

Israel: Badeniho 2, 170 00 Prague 7; tel. (2) 322453; fax (2) 322732; Ambassador: YOEL SHER.

Italy: Nerudova 20, 125 31 Prague 1; tel. (2) 530666; telex 122704; Ambassador: FRANCESCO OLIVIERI.

Japan: Maltézské nám. 6, 125 32 Prague 1; tel. (2) 535751; telex 121199; fax (2) 539997; Ambassador: KUNIAKI ASOMURA.

Korea, Democratic People's Republic: R. Rollanda 10, 160 00 Prague 6; tel. (2) 373953; Chargé d'affaires a.i.: RI CHUN MUK.

Korea, Republic: U Mrázovky 1985/17, 125 62 Prague 5; tel. (2) 541435; fax (2) 530204; Ambassador SUN JOUN-YUNG.

Kuwait: Pod Kaštany 2, 160 00 Prague 6; tel. (2) 370180; telex 121805; fax (2) 378688; Ambassador: MOUSA SULEIMAN AL-MOUSA AL-SAIF.

Laos: Žitná 2, 125 01 Prague 2; tel. (2) 298858; Ambassador: KINDENG THAMMAVONG.

Lebanon: Masarykovo nábřeží 14, 110 00 Prague 1; tel. (2) 293633; telex 123583; Ambassador: SLEIMAN YOUNES.

Libya: Na baště sv. Jiří 5–7, 160 00 Prague 6; tel. (2) 323410; Chargé d'affaires a.i.: ABUBAKER M. SALEH.

Mexico: Nad Kazankou 8, 171 00 Prague 7; tel. (2) 8555554; telex 121947; fax (2) 8550477; Ambassador: HORACIO FLORES DE LA PEÑA.

Mongolia: Korejská 5, 160 00 Prague 6; tel. (2) 3121504; telex 121921; Ambassador: PERENLIYN NYAMAA.

Morocco: Ke starému Bubenči 4, 160 00 Prague 6; tel. (2) 329404; telex 121785; fax (2) 321758; Ambassador: OMAR BELKORA.

Myanmar: Romaina Rollanda 3, 125 23 Prague 6; tel. (2) 381140; Chargé d'affaires a.i.: U KO KO.

Netherlands: Maltézské nám. 1, 125 40 Prague 1; tel. (2) 531378; telex 122643; fax (2) 531368; Ambassador: HANS J. HEINEMANN.

Nicaragua: Vinařská 1, Prague 7; tel. (2) 373872; telex 123336; fax (2) 3121044; Ambassador: HUMBERTO CARRIÓN.

Nigeria: Před Bateriemi 18, 160 00 Prague 6; tel. (2) 354294; telex 123575; Ambassador: Prof. STEPHEN O. EMEJUAIWE.

Norway: Na Ořechovce 69, 162 00 Prague 6; tel. (2) 354526; telex 122200; fax (2) 3123797; Ambassador: JOHN EGIL GRIEG.

Peru: Hradecká 18, 125 01 Prague 3; tel. (2) 67310694; telex 123345; fax (2) 67311972; Ambassador: ADOLFO ALVARADO FOURNIER.

Poland: Valdštejnská 8, 125 42 Prague 1; tel. (2) 536951; telex 121841; fax (2) 536427; Ambassador: JACEK BALUCH.

Portugal: Bubenská 3, 170 00 Prague 7; tel. (2) 878472; telex 121354; fax (2) 802624; Ambassador: LUÍS QUARTIN.

Romania: Nerudova 5, 125 44 Prague 1; tel. (2) 533059; Ambassador: ION CIUBOTARU.

Russia: Pod Kaštany 1, 160 00 Prague 6; tel. (2) 381943; Ambassador: ALEKSANDR A. LEBEDEV.

Slovakia: Pod Hradbami 1, 160 00 Prague 6; tel. (2) 320521; fax (2) 320401; Ambassador: IVAN MJARTAN.

Spain: Pevnostní 9, 162 00 Prague 6; tel. (2) 324442; telex 121974; fax (2) 323573; Ambassador: ROBERTO BERMÚDEZ RUIZ.

Sweden: Úvoz 13, 125 52 Prague 1; tel. (2) 24510436; telex 121840; fax (2) 24510301; Ambassador: LENNART WATZ.

Switzerland: Pevnostní 7, 162 00 Prague 6; tel. (2) 320406; fax (2) 3123058; Ambassador: SYLVIA PAULI.

Syria: Pod Kaštany 16, 125 01 Prague 6; tel. (2) 3121148; telex 121532; Ambassador: SUBHI HADDAD.

Thailand: Romaini Rollanda 3, 160 00 Prague 6; tel. (2) 381140; fax (2) 370646; Ambassador: KOBSAK CHUTIKUL.

Tunisia: Nad Kostelem 8, 125 01 Prague 4; tel. (2) 460652; telex 122512; fax (2) 460825; Chargé d'affaires a.i.: ARBIA BEN AJMIA.

Turkey: Pevnostní 3, 162 00 Prague 6; tel. (2) 320597; fax (2) 3122546; Ambassador: ÜSTÜN DINCMEN.

United Kingdom: Thunovská 14, 125 50 Prague 1; tel. (2) 533347; telex 121011; fax (2) 539927; Ambassador: DAVID BRIGHTY.

USA: Tržiště 15, 125 48 Prague 1; tel. (2) 536641; telex 121196; fax (2) 532457; Ambassador ADRIAN BASORA.

Uruguay: Václavské nám. 64, 111 21 Prague 1; tel. (2) 24216590; telex 121291; fax (2) 24226684; Ambassador: ANTONIO L. CAMPS VALGOI.

Venezuela: Janáčkovo nábřeží 49, 150 00 Prague 5; tel. (2) 536051; telex 122146; Ambassador: GERMAN PÉREZ CASTILLO.

Viet Nam: Holečková 6, 125 55 Prague 5; tel. (2) 536127; telex 121824; Chargé d'affaires a.i.: DOAN DUC.

Yemen: Washingtonova 17, 125 22 Prague 1; tel. (2) 222411; telex 123300; Ambassador: ABD AL-LATIF MUHAMMAD DHAIF ALLAH.

Yugoslavia: Mostecká 15, 118 00 Prague 1; tel. (2) 24510196; telex 123284; Ambassador: STANISLAV STOJANOVIĆ.

Judicial System

According to the Constitution of the Czech Republic (adopted in December 1992), the judicial system comprises the Supreme Court (which sits in Brno), the Supreme Administrative Court, chief, regional and district courts. The judiciary was also to include military courts until 31 December 1993. There is also a 15-member Constitutional Court (to protect constitutionality).

Chairman of the Supreme Court: Dr OTAKAR MOTEJL.

Attorney-General: (vacant).

Chairman of the Constitutional Court: ZDENĚK KESSLER.

Religion

The principal religion in the Czech Republic is Christianity. The largest denomination at the 1991 (Czechoslovak) census was the Roman Catholic Church, with 4m. members representing about 40% of the total population. About 30% of the population professed no religious belief.

CHRISTIANITY

Ekumenická rada církví v České republice (Ecumenical Council of Churches in the Czech Republic): Vítkova 13, 186 00 Prague 8; tel. (2) 24231183; fax (2) 24214491; f. 1955; 9 mem. churches; Pres. Bishop VLADISLAV VOLNÝ ; Gen. Sec. NADĚJE MANDYSOVÁ.

The Roman Catholic Church

The Czech Republic comprises two archdioceses and 5 dioceses.

Bishops' Conference: Česka biskupská konference, Thákurova 3, 160 00 Prague; tel. (2) 3315201; fax (2) 24310144; f. 1990; Pres. Mgr Dr MILOSLAV VLK .

Latin Rite

Archbishop of Prague: Mgr Dr MILOSLAV VLK, Hradčanské nám. 16, 119 02 Prague 1; tel. (2) 539548.

Archbishop of Olomouc: Mgr JAN GRAUBNER, Wurmova 9, 771 01 Olomouc; tel. (68) 25726.

The Orthodox Church

Pravoslavná Církev (Orthodox Church): V Jámě 6, 111 21 Prague 1; divided into two eparchies: Prague and Olomouc; Head of the Orthodox Church, Metropolitan of Prague and of all Czechoslovakia His Holiness Patriarch DOROTEJ; Theological Faculty in Charles University, Prague.

Protestant Churches

Baptist Union in the Czech Republic: Na Topolce 14, 140 00 Prague 4; tel. (2) 430974; f. 1994; 2,221 mems; Pres. Rev. DOBROSLAV STEHLÍK ; Sec. Rev. PAVEL VYCHOPEŇ.

Brethren Church Council (Rada církve bratrské): Soukenická 15, 110 00 Prague 1; tel. (2) 2318131; 5,000 mems, 38 congregations, 140 preaching stations; Pres. PAVEL ČERNÝ; Sec. KAREL TASCHNER.

Christian Corps: Brno; 3,200 mems; 123 brs; Rep. Ing. PETR ZEMAN.

Evangelical Church of Czech Brethren (Presbyterian): Jungmannova 9, 111 21 Prague 1; tel. and fax (2) 24222217; telex 123363; f. 1781; united since 1918; activities extend over Bohemia, Moravia and Silesia; 165,196 adherents and 265 parishes (Dec. 1992); Pres. Rev. PAVEL SMETANA; Synodal Curator Dr ZDENĚK SUSA .

Silesian Evangelical Church of the Augsburg Confession in the Czech Republic (Silesian Lutheran Church): Selská 12/428, 736 01 Havířov-Bludovice; tel. (6994) 34017; founded in the 16th century during the Lutheran Reformation, reorganized in 1948; 49,583 mems (March 1991); Bishop VLADISLAV VOLNÝ.

Unitarians: Karlova 8, 110 00 Prague 1; tel. (2) 266730; f. 1923; 5,000 mems; 4 parishes; Presiding Officer Dr STREJČEK.

United Methodist Church: Ječná 19, 120 00 Prague 2; tel. (2) 290623; 3,688 mems; 21 parishes; Supt JOSEF ČERVEŇÁK.

Unity of Brethren (Jednota bratrská) (Moravian Church): Kollárova 456, 509 01 Nová Paka; tel. (434) 2343; f. 1457; 2,275 mems; 21 parishes; Pres. Rev. JAROSLAV PLEVA.

Other Christian Churches

Apostolic Church in the Czech Republic: V Zídkách 402, 280 02 Kolín; tel. (321) 20457; fax (321) 27688; f. 1989; 2,000 mems; President RUDOLF BUBIK.

Church of the Seventh-day Adventists: Zálesí 50, 142 00 Prague 4; tel. (2) 4723745; 7,336 mems; 134 churches; Pres. KAREL NOWAK.

Czechoslovak Hussite Church: Wuchterlova 5, 166 26 Prague 6; tel. (2) 24311395; fax (2) 320045; f. 1920; 170,000mems ; five dioceses divided into 322 parishes; Bishop-Patriarch Mgr VRATISLAV ŠTĚPÁNEK.

Old Catholic Church (Církev starokatolická): Hládkov 3, 169 00 Prague 6; tel. (2) 352395; f. 1871; 3,000 mems, 6 parishes; Bishop (elect) Mgr DUŠAN HEJBAL.

JUDAISM

Federation of Jewish Communities in the Czech Republic (Federace židovských obcí v České republice): Maiselova 18, 110 01 Prague 1; tel. (2) 2318559; fax (2) 2316738; 3,000 mems; Pres. JIŘÍ DANÍČEK; Chief Rabbi KAROL SIDON.

The Press

PRINCIPAL DAILIES

Brno

Brněnský Večerník (Brno Evening Paper): Jakubské nám. 7, 658 44 Brno; tel. (5) 22846; f. 1968; publ. by BV Ltd; Editor-in-Chief PETR HOSKOVEC; circ. 16,000.

Moravský demokratický deník (Moravian Democratic Daily): Moravské nám. 13, 658 22 Brno; tel. (5) 751243; fax (5) 743832; f. 1885 as *Rovnost*; morning; Editor-in-Chief JIŘÍ RUPEC; circ. 62,000.

České Budějovice

Deník Jihočeská Pravda (South Bohemia Truth Daily): Vrbenská 23, 370 45 České Budějovice; tel. (38) 22081; f. 1991; morning; publ. by Vltava Ltd; Editor-in-Chief VLADIMÍR MAJER; circ. 53,000.

Hradec Králové

Hradecké noviny—Deník Pochodeň (Hradec News—Daily Torch): Škroupova 695, 501 72 Hradec Králové; tel. (49) 613511; publ. by PN Press joint-stock co; Editor-in-Chief JAROMÍR FRIDRICH; circ. 30,000.

Karlovy Vary

Karlovarské noviny (Karlovy Vary News): Třída TGM 32, 360 21 Karlovy Vary; tel. (17) 22013; fax (17) 25115; f. 1991; Editor-in-Chief JIŘÍ LINHART ; circ. 15,000.

Ostrava

List občanů Moravy a Slezska Svoboda (Moravian and Silesian Citizens' Paper Freedom): Novinářská 3, 709 07 Ostrava; tel. (69) 262280; fax (69) 262144; f. 1991; morning; publ. by OSNA joint-stock co; Editor-in-Chief MIROSLAV MRKVICA; circ. 108,000.

Moravskoslezský den (Moravia-Silesia Daily): Havlíčkovo nábř. 32, 700 00 Ostrava 1; tel. (69) 216282; fax (69) 262144; f. 1991; Editor-in-Chief BOLESLAV NAVRÁTIL; circ. 130,000.

Moravskoslezský večerník (Moravia-Silesia Evening News): Puchmajerova 1, 701 00 Ostrava 1; tel. (69) 231046; fax (69) 232091; publ. by Rovnost joint-stock co; Editor-in-Chief ANTONÍN SIUDA; circ. 20,000.

Pardubice

Pardubické noviny—Zář (Pardubice News—Blaze): Tříd Míru 60, 530 02 Pardubice; tel. (40) 511244; fax (40) 517156; f. 1991, Editor-in-Chief ROMAN MARČÁK; circ. 15,000.

Plzeň

Plzeňský deník (Plzeň Daily): Husova 15, 304 83 Plzeň; tel. (19) 551111; fax (19) 227015; f. 1991 (fmrly *Pravda*, f. 1919); Editor-in-Chief JAN PERTL; circ. 50,000.

Prague

Československý sport (Czechoslovak Sport): Na poříčí 30, 115 23 Prague 1; tel. (2) 2322528; fax (2) 2327377; f. 1953; morning; Editor-in-Chief JIŘÍ VANÍČEK; circ. 150,000.

Český deník (Czech Daily): Na Florenci 19, 112 86 Prague 1; tel. (2) 2823249; fax (2) 2320925; morning; independent; Editor-in-Chief JAN PATOČKA; circ. 60,000.

Hospodářské noviny (Economic News): Na Florenci 19, 115 43 Prague 1; tel. (2) 2367487; fax (2) 2327236; f. 1957; morning; publ. by Economia joint-stock co; Editor-in-Chief Dr JIŘÍ SEKERA; circ. 156,000.

Lidová demokracie (People's Democracy): Na Florenci 19, 110 00 Prague 1; tel. (2) 2367487; fax (2) 2327361; f. 1945; morning; conservative; publ. by Pragoprint Publishing House; Editor-in-Chief IVAN ČERVENKA; circ. 140,000.

Lidové noviny (People's News): Národní 9, 110 00 Prague 1; tel. (2) 24811415; fax (2) 24220940; f. 1893, re-established 1990; morning; Editor-in-Chief JAROMÍR ŠTĚTINA; circ. 110,000.

Mladá fronta dnes (Youth Front Today): Na poříčí 30, 112 86 Prague 1; tel. (2) 2367487; fax (2) 2328346; f. 1990; morning; independent; Editor-in-Chief LÍBOR ŠEVČÍK; circ. 391,000.

Práce (Labour): Václavské nám. 17, 112 58 Prague 1; tel. (2) 2353732; fax (2) 2369462; f. 1945; morning; publ. by Práce Publishing House; Editor-in-Chief JAN CHÁRA; circ. 220,000.

Prostor (Area): Vyšehradská 28, 120 00 Prague 2; tel. (2) 297931; fax (2) 290423; f. 1992; morning; independent; Editor-in-Chief JAN ŠTERN; circ. 30,000.

Rudé právo (Red Right): Na Florenci 19, 111 21 Prague 1; tel. (2) 2367487; fax (2) 2321979; f. 1920; morning; publ. by Birgas joint-stock co; Editor-in-Chief ZDENĚK PORYBNÝ; circ. 370,000.

Svobodné slovo (Free Word): Václavské nám. 36, 112 12 Prague 1; tel. (2) 260341; fax (2) 266468; f. 1945; publ. by Melantrich joint-stock co; Editor-in-Chief ČESTMÍR KUBÍK; circ. 230,000.

Večerník Praha (Evening Prague): Na Florenci 19, 110 00 Prague 1; tel. (2) 2367487; fax (2) 2327361; f. 1991 (fmrly Večerní Praha, f. 1955); evening; publ. by Pragoprint Publishing House; Editor-in-Chief LADISLAV DIGRIN; circ. 130,000.

Ústí nad Labem

SD—Severočeský regionální deník (North Bohemian Regional Daily): Bělehradská 17, 400 90 Ústí nad Labem; tel. (47) 22244-6; fax (47) 23115; f. 1920; publ. by Logos joint-stock co; Editor-in-Chief JAROSLAV HAIDLER; circ. 95,000.

PRINCIPAL PERIODICALS

100+1 ZZ: Žirovnická 2389, 106 00 Prague 10; tel. (2) 7192248; fax (2) 768990; f. 1964; fortnightly foreign press digest; Editor-in-Chief VLADIMÍR PETŘÍK; circ. 60,000.

Ahoj na sobotu (Hallo till Saturday): Štefánikova 17, 150 00 Prague 5; tel. (2) 543302; fax (2) 545057; f. 1933; leisure activities weekly; Editor-in-Chief LUBOR FALTEISEK; circ. 80,000.

Ateliér (Visula Arts): Masarykovo nábř. 250, 110 00 Prague 1; tel. and fax (2) 291884.

Auto Tip: Na strži 26, 140 00 Prague 4; tel. (2) 437170; f. 1990; fortnightly for motorists; Editor-in-Chief THOMAS HYAN; circ. 40,000.

Betty: Radimova 2017, 160 00 Prague 6; tel. and fax (2) 356849; f. 1990; monthly for intellectual women; publ. by Betty Publishing House; Editor-in-Chief PETR ČERMÁK; circ. 55,000.

Český a Slovenský Profit (Czech and Slovak Profit): Karmelitská 379/18, 118 24 Prague 1; tel. (2) 534131; fax (2) 532715; weekly.

Dikobraz (Porcupine): Kubánské nám. 1391, 100 00 Prague 10; tel. (2) 742947; fax (2) 737534; f. 1945; humorous and satirical weekly; Editor-in-Chief ZDENĚK ROSENBAUM; circ. 185,000.

Divadelní noviny (Theatre News): c/o Divadelní ústav, Celetná 17, 110 00 Prague 1; tel. (2) 2328824; fax (2) 2321117; fortnightly.

Ekonom (Economist): Na poříčí 30, 112 86 Prague 1; tel. (2) 2323451; fax (2) 2321168; weekly.

Filip pro -náctileté (Filip for Teenagers): U Prašné brány 3, 116 29 Prague 1; tel. (2) 2328215; fax (2) 2328415; f. 1991; monthly cultural magazine for young people; Editors-in-Chief MARCELA TITZLOVÁ, MILAN POLÁK; circ. 125,000.

Hudební rozhledy (Musical Review): Maltézské nám. 1, 118 01 Prague 1; tel. (2) 532931; fax (2) 539062; f. 1947; monthly; publ. by the Assen of Musicians and Musicologists; Editor JAN SMOLÍK; circ. 3,000.

Katolický týdeník (Catholic Weekly): Londýnská 44, 120 00 Prague 2; tel. (2) 256473; fax (2) 533017; weekly; publ. by Czech Catholic Charity; Editor-in-Chief JOSEF GABRIEL; circ. 105,000.

Kino revue (Cinema Review): Alšovo nábř. 4, 110 00Prague 1; tel. (2) 2327000; fax (2) 2327081; f. 1991; fortnightly; Editor-in-Chief MICHAELA STORCHOVÁ; circ. 40,000.

Květy (Flowers): Na Florenci 3, 112 86 Prague 1; tel. (2) 2356775; fax (2) 2356775; f. 1834; illustrated family weekly; Editor-in-Chief JIŘÍ BLAHOTA; circ. 160,000.

Mladý svět (Young World): Na poříčí 30, 112 86 Prague 1; tel. (2) 223726; fax (2) 220039; f. 1956; illustrated weekly; Editor-in-Chief LUBOŠ BENIAK; circ. 190,000.

Obchod-Kontakt-Marketing (Trade-contact-Marketing): Efekt, Bardounova 2140, 149 00 Prague 4; tel. (2) 7940402; fax (2) 7940410; monthly.

Reflex: Alšovo nábř. 4, 110 00 Prague 1; tel. (2) 2327118; fax (2) 2327081; f. 1990; social weekly; Editor-in-Chief PETR HÁJEK; circ. 220,000.

Reportér: Pařížská 9, 110 00 Prague 1; tel. (2) 2327633; fax (2) 2326337; f. 1967 (publication suspended 1970–89); weekly news magazine; Editor-in-Chief RUDOLF MÍŠEK; circ. 25,000.

Respekt: Bolzanova 7, 110 00 Prague 1; tel. (2) 221960; fax (2) 2359983; f. 1990; political weekly; Editor-in-Chief IVAN LAMPER; circ. 80,000.

Romano Kurko (Romany Week): Černovické nábřeží 7, 618 00 Brno; tel. and fax (5) 330785; f. 1991; weekly; publ. by Civic Assen for Gypsy Press and Culture; in Czech with Romany vocabulary; Dir M. SMOLEŇ; circ. 8,000.

Signál: Jungmannova 24, 110 00 Prague 1; tel. and fax (2) 24227987; f. 1965; independent weekly; Editor-in-Chief Dr KAREL ŠIMÁNA; circ. 75,000.

SOS (Trade Union Sounds): Václavské nám. 17, 112 58 Prague 1; tel. (2) 2369197; f. 1990; fortnightly; Editor-in-Chief LADISLAV VELENSKÝ; circ. 60,000.

Stadión (Stadium): Klimentská 1, 115 88 Prague 1; tel. (2) 2314118; fax (2) 23151336; f. 1953; illustrated sports weekly; Editor-in-Chief MILAN MACHO; circ. 60,000.

Týdeník Rozhlas (Radio Weekly): Na Florenci 3, 112 86 Prague 1; tel. and fax (2) 2323261; f. 1923; Editor-in-Chief STANISLAV PSCHEIDT; circ. 170,000.

Týdeník Televize (Television Weekly): Na poříčí 30, 110 40 Prague 1; tel. (2) 2322796; fax (2) 2320127; f. 1965; weekly; cultural and television journal; Editor-in-Chief OTAKAR ŠTAJF; circ. 550,000.

Vesmír (Universe): Slezská 9, 120 00 Prague 2; tel. (2) 2153018; fax (2) 269466; f. 1871; monthly; popular science magazine; publ. by the Czech Academy of Science; Editor IVAN M. HAVEL; circ. 20,000.

Vlasta: Jindřišská 5, 116 08 Prague 1; tel. (2) 2366326; fax (2) 2362638; f. 1947; weekly; illustrated magazine for women; Editor-in-Chief MARIE FORMÁČKOVÁ; circ. 380,000.

Zahrádkář (Gardener): Kloknerova 720, 149 00 Prague 4; tel. (2) 766346; fax (2) 768042; monthly; publ. by Czech Union of Gardeners; Editor-in-Chief ANTONÍN DOLEJŠÍ; circ. 200,000.

Žena a móda (Women and Fashion): Pannská 7, 110 00 Prague 1; tel. (2) 221025; monthly; publ. by the Mona Publishing House; Editor-in-Chief HELENA ČECHOVÁ; circ. 70,000.

Zora: Krakovská 21, 115 17 Prague 1; tel. (2) 262783; f. 1917; bimonthly; for the visually handicapped; Editor-in-Chief JIŘÍ REICHEL.

FOREIGN LANGUAGES

Amaro Lav (Our Word): Černovické nábřeží 7, 618 00 Brno; tel. and fax (5) 330785; f. 1990; monthly; publ., in Romany and Czech, by Civic Assen for Gypsy Press and Culture; Dir M. SMOLEŇ; circ. 3,000.

Czech Foreign Trade: V Jirchářích 8, 110 00 Prague 1; tel. (2) 24912185; fax (2) 24912355; f. 1960; monthly; publ. in English, German and French; Editor-in-Chief Dr PAVLA PODSKALSKÁ; circ. 15,000.

Prager Wochenblatt (Prague Weekly): Pařížská 11, 116 30 Prague 1; tel. (2) 2312392; fax (2) 898571; weekly; politics, culture, economy; in German; Editor-in-Chief FELIX SEEBAUER; circ. 30,000.

Prague Post: Politických vězňů 9, 111 21 Prague 1; tel. (2) 24221076; fax (2) 265184; f. 1991; political, economic and cultural weekly; in English; Editor-in-Chief ALAN LEVY; circ. 15,000.

Prognosis: Africká 17, 160 00 Prague 6; tel. (2) 3167007; fax (2) 368139; f. 1991; political, economic and cultural fortnightly; in English; Editor-in-Chief JOHN ALLISON; circ. 10,000.

Zahraniční obchod ČR (Foreign Trade of the Czech Republic): PP Agency, V jirchářích 8, 110 00 Prague 1; tel. (2) 29329; fax (2) 203953; monthly; in English, French and German.

NEWS AGENCIES

Česká tisková kancelář (ČTK) (Czech News Agency): Opletalova 5–7, 111 44 Prague 1; tel. (2) 2147; telex 122964; fax (2) 2356980; f. Nov. 1992, assuming control of all property and activities (in the Czech Lands) of the former Czechoslovak News Agency; news and photo exchange service with all international and many national news agencies; maintains wide network of foreign correspondents; English news service; publishes daily bulletin in English and weekly bulletin in German; publishes political and economic bulletins in Czech and English, and documentation surveys in Czech; Gen. Dir Dr MILAN STIBRAL.

Foreign Bureaux

Agence France-Presse (AFP): Žitná 10, 120 00 Prague 2; tel. (2) 296927; telex 121124; fax (2) 294818; Bureau Chief BERNARD MEIXNER.

Agencia EFE (Spain): 28. října 13, 112 79 Prague 1; tel. (2) 2139246; fax (2) 2139482; Bureau Chief MIGUEL FERNÁNDEZ.

Agenzia Nazionale Stampa Associata (ANSA) (Italy): Ve Smečkách 2, 110 00 Prague 1; tel. and fax (2) 2361826; telex 122734; Bureau Chief LUCIO ATTILIO LEANTE.

Allgemeiner Deutscher Nachrichtendienst (ADN) (Germany): Milevská 835, 140 00 Prague 4; tel. (2) 6921911; fax (2) 6921627; Bureau Chief STEFFI GENSICKE.

Associated Press (AP) (USA): Růžová 7, 110 00 Prague 1; tel. (2) 2364838; telex 121987; fax (2) 260813; Correspondent ONDŘEJ HEJMA.

Deutsche Presse-Agentur (dpa) (Germany): Petrské nám. 1, 110 00 Prague 1; tel. (2) 2311810; fax (2) 2315196; Bureau Chief THOMAS WOLF.

Informatsionnoye Telegrafnoye Agentstvo Rossii—Telegrafnoye Agentstvo Suverennykh Stran (ITAR—TASS) (Russia): Pevnostní 5, 162 00 Prague 6; tel. (2) 327527; Bureau Chief A. P. SHAPOVALOV.

Magyar Távirati Iroda (MTI) (Hungary): U Smaltovny 17, 6th Floor, 170 00 Prague 7; tel. and fax (2) 801649; telex 121827; Bureau Chief JÁNOS KARPÁTI.

Novinska Agencija Tanjug (Yugoslavia): U Smaltovny 19, 170 00 Prague 7; tel. (2) 806987; Correspondent BRANKO STOŠIĆ.

Polska Agencja Prasowa (PAP) (Poland): Petrské nám. 1, 110 00 Prague 1; tel. and fax (2) 2325223; Correspondent STANISŁAW DMITREWSKI.

Rossiyskoye Informatsionnoye Agentstvo—Novosti (RIA—Novosti) (Russia): Italská 36, 130 00 Prague 3; tel. (2) 2354459; telex 122235; Bureau Chief VLADIMIR FEDOROV.

Xinhua (New China) News Agency (People's Republic of China): Majakovského 22, Prague 6; tel. and fax (2) 3123248; telex 121561; Correspondent LIU TIENPAI.

PRESS ASSOCIATION

Syndicate of Journalists of the Czech Republic: Pařížská 9, 116 30 Prague 1; tel. (2) 2325109; fax (2) 2326337; f. 1877; reorganized in 1990; 5,000 mems; Chair. RUDOLF ZEMAN.

Publishers

Academia: Vodičkova 40, POB 896, 112 29 Prague 1; tel. (2) 24223511; fax (2) 24229311; f. 1953; scientific books, periodicals; Dir ALEXANDER TOMSKÝ.

Albatros: Na Perštýně 1, 110 01 Prague 1; fax (2) 267424; f. 1949; literature for children and young people; Dir MILADA MATĚJOVIČOVÁ.

Artia: Ve Smečkách 30, 111 27 Prague 1; tel. (2) 24196206; fax (2) 24196220; f. 1953; children's books, art books and encyclopaedias; Dir MARCELA MAYEROVÁ.

Blok: Rooseveltova 4, 657 00 Brno; tel. (5) 42214516; fax (5) 42321245; f. 1957; regional literature, fiction, general; Dir JAROSLAV NOVÁK.

Horizont: Francouzská 6, 120 00 Prague 2; tel. (2) 257942; f. 1968; Dir Dr VLADIMÍR TROJÁNEK.

Kalich, evangelické nakladatelství (Evangelical Publishing House): Jungmannova 9, 111 21 Prague 1; tel. (2) 2350342; fax (2) 2357594; f. 1920; religion; Dir Ing. JAN RYBÁŘ.

Kartografie Praha, a.s.: Fr. Křížka 1, 170 30 Prague 7; tel. (2) 375541; fax (2) 375555; f. 1954; cartographic publishing and printing house; Dir Ing. JIŘÍ KUČERA.

Kruh (Circle): Dlouhá 108, 500 21 Hradec Králové; tel. (49) 22076; f. 1966; regional literature, fiction and general; Dir Dr JAN DVOŘÁK.

Lidové nakladatelství (People's Publishing House): Václavské nám. 36, 110 00 Prague 1; tel. (2) 226383; f. 1968; classical and contemporary fiction, general, magazines; Dir Dr KORNEL VAVRINČÍK.

Melantrich: Václavské nám. 36, 112 12 Prague 1; tel. (2) 260341; telex 121432; fax (2) 225012; f. 1919; general, fiction, humanities, newspapers and magazines; Dir MILAN HORSKÝ.

Merkur: Gorkého nám. 11, 115 69 Prague 1; tel. (2) 2362891; telex 121648; fax (2) 2362873; commerce, tourism, catering; Dir JIŘÍ LINHART.

Mladá fronta (Young Front): Radlická 61, 150 02 Prague 5; tel. (2) 544941; fax (2) 533492; f. 1945; literature for young people, fiction and non-fiction, magazines; Dir MARIE KOŠKOVÁ.

Nakladatelství dopravy a spojů (Transport and Communications): Hybernská 5, 115 78 Prague 1; tel. (2) 2365774; fax (2) 2356772; state publishing house for transport and communications; Dir Ing. ALOIS HOUDEK.

Nakladatelství Svoboda—Libertas (Freedom): Na Florenci 3, POB 704, 113 03 Prague 1; tel. (2) 24811874; fax (2) 24226026; f. 1945 as the publishing house of the Communist Party; restructured in 1992 as a state-owned company; politics, history, philosophy, fiction, general; Dir STEFAN SZERYŃSKI.

Odeon: Národní tř. 36, 115 87 Prague 1; tel. (2) 260179; fax (2) 2366899; f. 1953; literature, poetry, fiction (classical and modern), literary theory, art books, reproductions; Dir JIŘÍ ČERNÝ.

Olympia: Klimentská 1, 115 88 Prague 1; tel. (2) 2314861; telex 121717; f. 1954; sports, tourism, illustrated books; Dir Ing. KAREL ZELNÍČEK.

Panorama: Hálkova 1, 120 72 Prague 2; tel. (2) 2361391; Dir Ing. VLADIMÍR NEKOLA.

Panton: Radlická 99, 150 00 Prague 5; tel. and fax (2) 548627; f. 1958; publishing house of the Czech Musical Fund; books on music, sheet music, records; Dir. KAREL ČERNÝ.

Práce (Labour): Václavské nám. 17, 112 58 Prague 1; tel. (2) 266151; telex 121134; f. 1945; trade union movement, fiction, general, periodicals; Dir PAVEL LANDA.

Profil: Ciklářská 51, 702 00 Ostrava 1; regional literature, fiction and general; Dir IVAN ŠEINER.

Rapid, a.s.: 28. října 13, 112 79 Prague 1; tel. (2) 24195111; telex 121142; fax (2) 2327520; advertising; Dir-Gen. ČESTMÍR ČEJKA.

Růže (Rose): Žižkovo nám. 5, 370 96 České Budějovice; tel. (38) 38676; f. 1960; regional literature, fiction and general; Dir MIROSLAV HULE.

Severočeské nakladatelství (North Bohemian Publishing House): Prokopa Diviše 5, 400 01 Ústí nad Labem; tel. (47) 28581; regional literature, fiction and general; Dir JIŘÍ ŠVEJDA.

SNTL—Nakladatelství technické literatury (Technical Literature): Spálená 51, 113 02 Prague 1; tel. (2) 297670; fax (2) 203774; f. 1953; technology, applied sciences, dictionaries, periodicals; Dir Dr KAREL ČERNÝ (acting).

Státní pedagogické nakladatelství: Ostrovní 30, 113 01 Prague 1; tel. and fax (2) 24912206; f. 1775; state publishing house; school and university textbooks, dictionaries, literature; Dir MILAN KOVÁŘ.

Supraphon: Palackého 1, 122 99 Prague 1; tel. (2) 24230072; telex 121218; fax (2) 24228043; f. 1946; gramophone co and music publishing house; Pres. VLADISLAV KUKAČKA.

Vyšehrad: Karlovo nám. 5, POB 85, 128 00 Prague 2; tel. (2) 297726; religion, philosophy, history, fiction; Chief Editor VLASTA HESOUNOVÁ.

Západočeské nakladatelství (West Bohemian Publishing House): B. Smetany 1, 301 35 Plzeň; tel. (19) 34783; f. 1955; regional literature, fiction, general; Dir KATEŘINA RUBÍŠOVÁ.

WRITERS' UNION

Obec spisovatelů (Community of Writers): POB 669, 111 21 Prague 1; tel. (2) 2320924; f. 1989; 720 mems.

Radio and Television

Radio and television broadcasting licences are issued by the Czech Television and Radio Council.

RADIO

The national networks include Radio Prague (medium wave and VHF), Radio Vltava (VHF from Prague—programmes on Czech and world culture), Radio Regina (medium and VHF—programme of regional studios), and Interprogramme (medium and VHF—for foreign visitors to the Czech Republic, in English, German and French).

Local stations broadcast from Prague (Central Bohemian Studio), Brno, České Budějovice, Hradec Králové, Ostrava, Plzeň, Ústí nad Labem and other towns. Czechoslovakia passed a radio licensing law in 1991. By August 1993 44 private stations had been licensed, 37 of which were in operation (14 in Prague).

Český rozhlas (Czech Radio): Vinohradská 12, 120 99 Prague 2; tel. (2) 2115111; telex 121100; fax (2) 2321020; Dir VLASTIMIL JEZEK.

TELEVISION

There are television studios in Prague, Brno and Ostrava. An independent commercial station, Nova (operated by Cet-21) was to commence broadcasts in February 1994. In August 1993 about 150 cable television comapnies were operating in the country.

Česká televize (Czech Television): Česká televize, 140 70 Prague 4; tel. (2) 4134273; fax (2) 421562; f. 1992; Dir-Gen. IVO MATHÉ.

Finance

(cap. = capital; dep. = deposits; res = reserves; m. = million; Kčs. = former Czechoslovak korunas; Kč. = Czech korunas))

BANKS

With the establishment of independent Czech and Slovak Republics on 1 January 1993, the State Bank of Czechoslovakia was divided and its functions were transferred to the newly-created Czech National Bank and Slovak National Bank. Unlike its Slovak counter-part, the Czech National Bank is independent of the Government. The management and instruments of the Czech National Bank do not differ from those of the State Bank of Czechoslovakia.

Central Bank

Česká národní banka (Czech National Bank): Na Příkopě 28, 110 03 Prague 1; tel. (2) 2391-1111; telex 121555; fax (2) 2354141; f. 1993; bank of issue, the central authority of the Czech Republic in the monetary sphere, legislation and foreign exchange permission; central bank for directing and securing monetary policy, supervision of activities of other banks and savings banks; Gov. Ing. JOSEF TOŠOVSKÝ; 10 brs.

Commercial Banks

Agrobanka Praha a.s.: Rumunská 1, 120 00 Prague 2; tel. (2) 6910767; fax (2) 6911284; f. 1990; functions through a network of independent regional banks; provides a wide range of financial services, participates in privatization programmes; cap. 1,250m. Kčs. (Sept. 1992); Chair. Ing. STANISLAV LABOUNEK; 28 brs.

Banka Bohemia a.s.: Havlíčkova 3, 110 00 Prague 1; tel. (2) 222245; fax (2) 264594; f. 1991; cap. 300m. Kčs., res. 30m. Kčs., dep. 4,524m. Kčs. (June 1992); Pres. Ing. MILAN PEKAREK; Gen. Man. Ing. ARNOŠT KLESLA.

Československá obchodní banka a.s. (Commercial Bank of Czechoslovakia): Na Příkopě 14, 115 20 Prague 1; tel. (2) 2331111; telex 122201; fax (2) 2327562; f. 1965; commercial and foreign trade transactions; cap. and res. 17,173m. Kčs. (Jan. 1993); Chair. and CEO Ing. PAVEL KANÁNEK.

Investiční banka, a.s.: Senovážné nám. 32, 114 32 Prague 1; tel. (2) 24071111; telex 122459; fax (2) 24244035; f. 1990; cap. 1,000m.

Kčs., dep. 33,137m. Kčs. (Dec. 1992); Gen. Man. JIŘÍ TESAŘ; 91 brs.

Komerční banka a.s., Praha: Na Příkopě 33, POB 839, 114 07 Prague 1; tel. (2) 24021111; telex 121831; fax (2) 24243065; f. 1990; cap. 5,001m. Kčs, dep. 220,689m. Kčs. (Sept. 1992); Chair. and CEO RICHARD SALZMANN; 387 brs.

Pragobanka a.s.: Vinohradská 230, 100 00 Prague 10; tel. and fax (2) 779164; f. 1990; cap. 800m. Kč. (Sept. 1993); Gen. Man. Ing. RUDOLF KRÁL.

Živnostenská banka a.s.: Na Příkopě 20, 113 80 Prague 1; tel. (2) 21121111; telex 122313; fax (2) 21125555; f. 1868; cap. 1,360.4m. Kčs., res 114.9m. Kčs., dep. 16,514.4m. Kčs. (Sept. 1992); Pres. Ing JIŘÍ KUNERT.

Joint-Venture Banks

Bank Austria a.s.: Revoluční 15, 113 03 Prague 1; tel. (2) 2806111; fax (2) 2806180; f. 1991; shareholders: Z-Länderbank Bank Austria AG, Vienna (87%), Czech Savings Bank (13%); cap. 580m. Kčs. (Sept. 1992); Gen. Man. ANTON KNETT.

Bankovní dům SKALA a.s: Opletalova 4, 110 00 Prague 1; tel. (2) 265741-9; fax (2) 3115391; cap. 50m. Kčs. (Jan. 1991); Dir Ing. ALEXANDER SOUČEK.

EKO banka, Kroměříž a.s.: Vejvanovského 383, 767 01 Kroměříž; tel. and fax (634) 21788; cap. 51m. Kčs. (Jan. 1991); Gen. Man. Ing. RUDOLF CHURÝ.

Poštovní banka, a.s.: Voctářova 1, 180 44 Prague 8; tel. (2) 66310998; fax (2) 6842539; f. 1993; general financial services supplied through the postal network; cap. 500m. Kč. (Aug. 1993); Chair. Ing. ALFRÉD ŠEBEK; 3,520 brs.

Société Générale—Komerční banka SGKB a.s.: Pobřežní 3, POB 74, 186 00 Prague 8; tel. (2) 2323204; fax (2) 2323513; f. 1990; shareholders: Société Générale (75%), Komerční banka (25%); cap. 774m. Kč. (1993); Gen. Man. JEAN-LUIS BERGER.

Savings Bank

Česká spořitelna a.s. (Czech Savings Bank): Václavské nám. 42, 113 98 Prague 1; tel. (2) 2365325; telex 121605; fax (2) 225572; f. 1825; accepts deposits and issues loans; 15,239,363 depositors (June 1990); Gen. Man. Ing. MILOSLAV KOHOUTEK; 735 brs.

STOCK EXCHANGE

Burza cenných papírů v Praze (Stock Exchange in Prague): Na můstku 3, 110 00 Prague 1; tel. (2) 2357204; fax (2) 2356233.

INSURANCE

Česká pojišťovna a.s. (Czech Insurance and Reinsurance Corporation): Spálená 16, 114 00 Prague 1; tel. (2) 24092111; telex 121112; fax (2) 24220645; f. 1827; many home brs and some agencies abroad; issues life, accident, fire, aviation and marine policies, all classes of reinsurance; Lloyd's agency; Gen. Man. Dr VLASTIMIL UZEL.

Česká Kooperativa, družstevni pojišťovna a.s. (Czech Co-operative Insurance Company): Těšnov 5, 110 00 Prague 1; tel. (2) 2865111; fax (2) 2316235.

Pojišťovna IB, a.s.: V jámě 1, 114 09 Prague 1; tel. (2) 21422492.

Trade and Industry

STATE PROPERTY AGENCY

National Property Fund: Prague; responsible for state property and state-owned companies in the period up to their privatization; Chair. TOMÁŠ JEZEK.

CHAMBER OF COMMERCE

Česká obchodní a průmyslová komora (Czech Chamber of Commerce and Industry): Argentinská 38, 170 05 Prague 7; tel. (2) 8724111; telex 121862; fax (2) 875461; f. 1850; has more than 2,300 members (trading corporations, industrial enterprises, banks, research institutes and private enterprises); Chair. Dr Ing. VOJTĚCH BUREŠ.

INVESTMENT ORGANIZATION

Česká agentura pro zahraniční investice (Czechinvest): Politických vězňů 20, 112 49 Prague 1; tel. (2) 21261111; fax (2) 2322861; foreign investment agency; Dir Ing. arch. J. A. HAVELKA.

INDUSTRIAL AND EMPLOYERS' ASSOCIATIONS

Sdružení Podnikatelů České Republiky (Association of Entrepreneurs of the Czech Republic): Staroměstské nám. 6, 110 01 Prague 1; tel. and fax (2) 2320752; Chair. RUDOLF BARANEK.

Svaz Průmyslu České Republiky (Association of Industry of the Czech Republic): Mikulandská 7, 113 61 Prague 1; tel. (2) 299251; fax (2) 297896.

FOREIGN TRADE CORPORATIONS

Artia Ltd: Ve Smečkách 30, 111 27 Prague 1; tel. (2) 2137111; telex 121065; fax (2) 2137555; imports and exports cultural commodities; Chair. KAREL HÁJEK.

Čechofracht: Na Příkopě 8, 111 83 Prague 1; tel. (2) 2129111; telex 122221; fax (2) 2327137; f. 1949; shipping and international forwarding joint-stock co; Gen. Dir Ing. STANISLAV MACH.

Centrotex: nám. Hrdinů 3/1634, 140 61 Prague 4; tel. (2) 415; telex 121232; fax (2) 438771; imports and exports textiles; Gen. Dir Ing. MILOUŠ ČERVENCL.

Chemapol Co Ltd: Kodaňská 46, 100 10 Prague 10; tel. (2) 7151111; telex 122021; fax (2) 737007; f. 1948; imports and exports chemical and pharmaceutical products, petroleum and other raw materials; Chair. and Man. Dir VÁCLAV JUNEK.

Czechoslovak Ceramics Co: V Jámě 1, 111 91 Prague 1; tel. (2) 24161111; telex 121118; fax (2) 24229932; Gen. Dir Ing. JIŘÍ ŠUP .

Exico: Panská 9, 111 77 Prague 1; tel. (2) 24096111; telex 122211; fax (2) 2321030; f. 1966; exports and imports leather, shoes, skins; Gen. Dir Ing. LADISLAV ADAMEC.

Ferromet: Opletalova 27, 111 81 Prague 1; tel. (2) 2141; telex 121411; fax (2) 2360801; imports and exports metallurgical products; Gen. Dir Ing. JIŘÍ FRYBERT.

Filmexport Prague: Na Moráni 5, 128 00 Prague 2; tel. (2) 293275; telex 122259; fax (2) 293312; f. 1957; Man. Dir MARTIN PAPOUŠEK.

Imex: Revoluční 25, 110 15 Prague 1; tel. (2) 2311000; telex 121977; fax (2) 2317191; f. 1969; imports and exports consumer goods and sales equipment; Gen. Man. J. DANIHELKA.

Inspekta: Olbrachtova 1, 140 02 Prague 4; tel. (2) 6927628; telex 121938; fax (2) 6433520; control of goods in foreign trade; Gen. Dir Ing. JAN STRNAD.

Jablonex Co Ltd: Palackého 41, 466 37 Jablonec nad Nisou; tel. (428) 401111; telex 184462; fax (428) 29326; f. 1952; imports and exports fashion jewellery and decorations; Gen. Dir JAN BERNARD.

Koospol Ltd: Leninova 178, 160 67 Prague 6; tel. (2) 3361111; telex 121121; fax (2) 345572; imports and exports foodstuffs; Gen. Dir Ing. FRANTIŠEK HRUBÝ.

Kovo: Jankovcova 2, 170 88 Prague 7; tel. (2) 66781111; telex 121481; fax (2) 66710012; imports and exports precision engineering products; Gen. Dir OLDŘICH VACEK.

Ligna: Vodičkova 41, 112 09 Prague 1; tel. (2) 2134; telex 122066; fax (2) 263525; imports and exports timber, wood products, musical instruments and paper; Gen. Dir Ing. MIROSLAV MRNA.

Merkuria: Argentinská 38, 170 05 Prague 7; tel. (2) 6679411; telex 121022; fax (2) 66710253; exports and imports tools and consumer goods; wholesale and retail trade; Gen. Dir Ing. JOSEF CHUCHVALEC.

Metalimex: Štěpánská 34, 112 17 Prague 1; tel. (2) 2359575; telex 121405; fax (2) 2320630; imports and exports non-ferrous metals, electrical power, natural gas and solid fuels; Gen. Dir Ing. JOSEF BULVAS.

Motokov Ltd: Na Strži 63, 140 62 Prague 4; tel. (2) 4141111; telex 121882; fax (2) 434616; imports and exports vehicles, agricultural machinery and light engineering products; Gen. Dir Ing. DALIBOR MOŠOVSKÝ.

Omnipol: Nekázanka 11, 112 21 Prague 1; telex 121299; fax (2) 226792; import and export of sports and civil aircraft; Gen. Dir Ing. FRANTIŠEK HÁVA.

Pragoexport: Jungmannova 34, 112 59 Prague 1; tel. (2) 2198111; telex 121586; fax (2) 2198186; f. 1948; imports and exports consumer goods; Gen. Dir PAVEL MAJOR.

Pragoimex: Žerotínova 37, 130 00 Prague 3; tel. (2) 66035501; telex 122957; fax (2) 66035035; f. 1991; import and export of machinery, passenger cars, spare parts, school equipment and complete plant equipment; Gen. Dir DRAHOSLAV ČEČELÍN.

Skloexport: tř. 1. máje 52, 461 74 Liberec; tel. (48) 315; telex 186267; fax (48) 421027; exports glass; Gen. Dir Ing. JAROSLAV KŘIVÁNEK.

Škodaexport Co Ltd: Opletalova 41, 113 32 Prague 1; tel. (2) 265051-9; telex 122413; fax (2) 269563; exports and imports power engineering and metallurgical plants, engineering works, electrical locomotives and trolleybuses, tobacco machines; Pres. JAN RICICA.

Strojexport Co Ltd: POB 662, Václavské nám. 56, 113 26 Prague 1; tel. (2) 21311111; telex 122604; fax (2) 24811801; f. 1953; imports and exports machines and machinery equipment, civil engineering works; Gen. Dir Ing. JOSEF REGNER.

Strojimport Co Ltd: Vinohradská 184, 130 52 Prague 3; tel. (2) 67131111; telex 122241; fax (2) 777554; f. 1953; imports and exports machine tools, tools and gauges, and industrial plants; Pres. IVAN ČAPEK.

Technoexport: Václavské nám. 1, 113 34 Prague 1; tel. (2) 24226226; telex 121268; fax (2) 24224158; imports and exports chemical and foodstuff engineering plant; Pres. JOSEF CÍLEK.

Tuzex: Rytířská 13, 113 43 Prague 1; tel. (2) 220292; telex 121012; fax (2) 221808; retail goods for foreign currency; Gen. Dir JIŘÍ NEMEC.

MAJOR INDUSTRIAL COMPANIES

AERO Holdings: Beranových 130, 199 04 Prague 9; tel. (2) 66310727; telex 121893; fax (2) 886581; holding group for 10 aeronautical cos; share cap. of 7,006m. koruny; Gen. Dir ZDENĚK PERNICA; 15,000 employees.

Česká Zbrojovka a.s.: Svatopluka Čecha 1283, 688 22 Uherský Brod; tel. (633) 2303; fax (633) 2775; manufacture and sale of firearms; Dir-Gen. Ing. MIROSLAV DUDA.

ČEZ, a.s.: Jungmannova 29, 111 48 Prague 1; tel. (2) 24081111; fax (2) 24082440; electricity generation and heat production and transfer; Man. Dir Ing. HYNEK RASOCHA.

Čízkovická cementárna a.s. (Ciskovice Cement Works): 411 12 Čízkovice; tel. (419) 72511; telex 184313; fax (419) 725600; cement and hydraulic lime; Gen. Man. JOSEF ŠULC.

ČKD Blansko, a.s.: Gellhornova 1, 678 18 Blansko; tel. (506) 8213398; fax (506) 2400; heavy engineering; Man. Dir Ing. KAREL PATOHICKA.

COLORlak: Tovární 1076, 686 02 Staré Město u Uherske Hradiště; tel. (632) 47111; telex 60360; fax (632) 62601; production of coats and coatings; Man. Dir ZDENĚK TŮMA; 360 employees.

C'SVIT a.s.: Tř Tomáše Bati, 762 02 Zlín; tel. (67) 31308; fax (67) 23168; design, manufacture and retail of shoes.

DESTA Děčín a.s.: Ústecká 20, 405 28 Děčín V; tel. (412) 26911; fax (412) 8734; manufactures transport equipment, incl. fork-lift trucks; Man. Dir Ing. MIROSLAV GRÉGR.

ELECTRO-PRAGA Hlinsko a.s.: Poličská 444, 539 16 Hlinsko; tel. (454) 621111; fax (454) 22280; production of household electrical appliances; Man. Dir Ing. PAVEL SVOBODA.

Fatra: 763 61 Napajedla; tel (67) 942755; telex 67242; fax (67) 942407; manufactures plastic products, incl. PVC floorings, conveyor belts, hoses and pipes; Gen. Dir TOUFAR JAROSLAV; 1,900 employees.

Glavunion, a.s.: Sklářská 450, 416 74 Teplice; tel. (417) 342161; fax (417) 27777; glass and glass products; Man. Dir Ing. ŠTĚPÁN POPOVIČ.

Gumokov a.s.: 500 23 Hradec Králové; tel. (49) 659; telex 194246; fax (49) 616827; manufactures rubber and metal parts and products; cap. Kč. 228m.; Ing. JAROSLAVE BURDA; 900 employees.

Jihomoravské dřevařské závody Brno: Jezuitská 4, 657 49 Brno; tel. (5) 42215927; fax (5) 42211372; timber and timber products; Man. Dir Ing. KAREL HRUDA.

Kaucuk: 278 52 Kralupy nad Vltavou; tel. (205) 711111; telex 132237; fax (205) 23566; produces rubber, polystyrene and petroleum products; Gen. Dir MIROSLAV NEVOSAD; 2,649 employees.

MEX Mohelnice s.p.: Nádražní 25, 789 85 Mohelnice; tel. ((648) 451845; fax (648) 51345; production of electric motors; Man. Dir Ing. ZDENĚK ULMANN.

Nová Huť a.s.: 707 02 Ostrava 7; tel. (69) 287294; fax (69) 283877; manufacture of metallurgical products; Man. Dir Ing. SVATOPLUK VELKOBORSKÝ.

Olšanské papírny, a.s.: 789 62 Olšany; tel. (649) 98201; fax (649) 98348; paper and paper products; Man. Dir Ing. ALEXEJ KRINES.

PRECIOSA, a.s.: Opletalova 17, 466 67 Jablonec nad Nisou; tel. (428) 415111; fax (428) 28290; industrial gems, glass beads and cut crystal; Man. Dir Ing. LUDVÍK KARL.

PSP Přerovské strojírny a.s.: Kojetínská, 750 53 Přerov; tel. (641) 53111; fax (641) 4096; produces madninery and equipment for the construction industry; Man. Dir Ing. MILOŠ KRUTÁK.

Sepap, a.s.: Litoměřická 272, 411 08 Šteti; tel. (411) 92501; fax (411) 92414; paper and paper products; Chair. TOMÁŠ ŠÁBATKA.

Severočeské chemická závody (North Bohemian Chemical Works): 41017 Lovosice; tel. (419) 2541; telex 184231; fax (419) 3472; produces industrial fertilizers, viscose rayon cord, abrasive materials, concrete paving stones; Gen. Man. MILAN GALIA; 1,700 employees.

Sigma Lutín: Jana Sigmunda, 783 50 Lutín; tel. (68) 4754106; fax (68) 5221353; production and sale of pumps and pumping equipment, iron and non-ferrous metals, engineering and consulting services; Man. Dir Ing. ROSTISALV DOPITA.

ŠKODA automobilová a.s.: Václava Klementa, 293 60 Mladá Boleslav; tel. (326) 5111111; fax (326) 26757; manufacture of passenger cars; Man. Dir LUDWIK KALMA; 17,000 employees.

ŠKODA Concern, Plzeň, a.s.: Tylova 57, 316 00 Plzeň; tel. (19) 1111; fax (19) 221985; steel and steel products; Man. Dir LUBOMÍR SOUDEK; 24,000 employeees.

Spolek pro Chemickou a Hutní Výrobu, a.s. (United Chemical and Metallurgical Works, Ltd): Revolučni 86, 400 32 Ústí nad Labem; tel. (47) 22327; telex 184222; fax (47) 24597; produces chemicals and related products; Gen. Dir VÍT HROCH; 4,100 employees.

Svit Zlín, a.s.: tř. Tomáše Bati, 762 02 Zlín; tel. (67) 511; telex 67337; fax (67) 41355; footwer; Man. Dir JIŘÍ CAPEK; 10,000 employees.

Textil a oděvy Brno: Svobody nám. 4, POB 198, 657 98 Brno; tel. (5) 42210321; telex 62251; fax (5) 42213911; retail and wholesale trade; Man. Dir KOSAŘ MILOSLAV; 1,200 employees.

TOS Kuřim, a.s.: Blanenská 257, 664 35 Kuřim; tel. (5) 41321512; fax (5) 95587; manufacture of machine-tool products; Man. Dir Ing. JOSEF DRÁŽDIL.

Třinecké Železárny a.s.: 739 70 Třinec; tel. (659) 432007; fax (659) 23924; rolled metal and metal products; Man. Dir Ing. GUSTAV HOJDYSZ.

Válcovny trub Chomutov, a.s.: Libušína 4778, 430 23 Chomutov; tel. (396) 734018; fax (396) 2918; production of seamless steel tubes; Man. Dir Ing. VÁCLAV LUKÁŠ.

Vítkovice, a.s.: Ruská 101, 706 02 Ostrava 6; tel. (69) 2911111; fax (69) 52484; iron and steel, engineering; Man. Dir Ing. FRANTIŠEK HROMEK.

Východočeské chemické závody Synthesia Semtín: 532 17 Pardubice-Semtín; tel. (40) 492440; fax (40) 46465; manufacture of chemicals and explosives; Man. Dir JAROSLAV VALOUŠEK.

ŽĎAS, a.s.: Strojírenská 6, 591 71 Žďár nad Sázavou; tel. (616) 4133128; fax (616) 23380; produces plant and equipment for the iron and steel industry; Man. Dir Ing. FRANTIŠEK HAMERNÍK.

ZETOR, a.s.: Trnkova 111, 632 00 Brno; tel. (5) 5182115; fax (5) 573405; manufacture of agricultural machinery, metal foundry products; Man. Dir Ing. JAN OTOUPALÍK.

TRADE UNIONS

Českomoravská komora odborových svazů (Czech-Moravian Chamber of Trade Unions): nám. W. Churchilla 2, 113 59 Prague 3; tel. (2) 24225914; fax (2) 24215116; f. 1990; Pres. VLADIMÍR PETRUS.

Affiliated unions include the following:

Českomoravský odborový svaz pracovníků služeb (Czech-Moravian Trade Union of Workers in Services): Senovážné nám. 23, 112 82 Prague 1; tel. (2) 24242726; fax (2) 24142532; f. 1990; Pres. RICHARD FALBR; 70,000 mems.

Českomoravský odborový svaz školství (Czech-Moravian Trade Union of Workers in Education): nám. W. Churchilla 2, 113 59 Prague 3; ; tel. (2) 24226491; fax (2) 24218010; Pres. JAROSLAV RÖSSLER; 190,173 mems.

Odborové sdružení železničářů (Trade Union Association of Railwaymen): nám. W. Churchilla 2, 113 59 Prague 3; tel. (2) 2356813; fax (2) 2361928; f. 1990; Pres. ZDENĚK ŠKOP; 324,360 mems.

Odborový svaz pracovníků dřevozpracujícího odvětví, lesního a vodního hospodářství v České republice (Trade Union of Workers in Woodworking Industry, Forestry and Management of Water Supplies in the Czech Republic): nám. W. Churchilla 2, 113 59 Prague 3; tel. (2) 2350848; telex 121484; fax (2) 2365219; Pres. ROBERT ZEDNÍK; 206,391 mems.

Odborový svaz pracovníků textilního, oděvního a kožedělného průmyslu Čech a Moravy (Trade Union of Workers in Textile, Clothing and Leather Industry of Bohemia and Moravia): nám. W. Churchilla 2, 113 59 Prague 3; tel. (2) 2360782; telex 121517; fax (2) 273589; Pres. MARCEL MÖSTL; 160,514 mems.

Odborový svaz pracovníků zdravotnictví a sociální péče v ČR (Trade Union of Workers in Health Service and Social Care in the Czech Republic): nám. W. Churchilla 2, 113 59 Prague 3; tel. and fax (2) 24225819; Pres. JIŘÍ SCHLANGER; 200,000 mems.

Odborový svaz pracovníků zemědělství a výživy Čech a Moravy (Trade Union of Workers in Agriculture and Food Industry of Bohemia and Moravia): nám. W. Churchilla 2, 113 59 Prague 3; tel. (2) 2361915; fax (2) 2369661; Pres. BOHUMÍR DUFEK; 200,000 mems.

TRADE FAIRS

BVV Trade Fairs and Exhibitions: Výstaviště 1, 602 00 Brno; tel. (5) 3141111; telex 62239; fax (5) 333998; f. 1959; annual international engineering fair in September; annual international consumer goods fair in April; Gen. Dir Ing. ANTONÍN SURKA.

Prague Trade Fairs: Washingtonova 9, 111 21 Prague 1; tel. (2) 266289; fax (2) 263060.

Transport

RAILWAYS

Following the dissolution of Czechoslovakia, the administration of the railway network in the Czech Republic (formerly under the control of the Czechoslovak State Railways) was transferred to the newly-established Czech Railways. In January 1993 the total length of the Czech railway network was 9,500 km.

České dráhy (Czech Railways): nábř. L. Svobody 12, 110 15 Prague 1; tel. (2) 2891; telex 121096; Gen. Man. EMANUEL SIP.

Prague Metropolitan Railway: Dopravní podnik hlavního města Prahy, Bubenská 1, 170 26 Prague 7; tel. (2) 878278; telex 122443; fax (2) 878786; the Prague underground railway opened in 1974 and, by Nov. 1992, 38.5 km were operational; there were 41 stations; Gen. Dir Ing. MILAN HAŠEK.

ROADS

In January 1993 there were 55,517 km of roads in the Czech Republic, including 362 km of motorways.

INLAND WATERWAYS

The total length of navigable waterways in the former Czechoslovakia was 480 km. The Elbe (Labe) and its tributary, the Vltava, connect the Czech Republic with the North Sea via the port of Hamburg. The Oder provides a connection with the Baltic Sea and the port of Szczecin. The Czech Republic's river ports are Prague Holešovice, Prague Radotín, Kolín, Mělník, Ústí nad Labem and Děčín, on the Vltava and Elbe.

Česká plavba labská a.s. (Czech Elbe Navigation Ltd): K. Čapka 1, 405 91 Děčín; tel. (412) 28331; telex 184241; fax (412) 23591; f. 1922; river transport of goods to Germany, Poland, the Netherlands, Belgium, France and Switzerland; Man. Dir KAREL HORYNA.

SHIPPING

Československá námořní plavba, mezinárodní akciová společnost (Czechoslovak Ocean Shipping, International Joint-Stock Company): Počernická 168, 100 99 Prague 10; tel. (2) 778941; telex 122137; fax (2) 773962; f. 1959; shipping company operating the former Czechoslovak sea-going fleet; 18 ships totalling 443,155 dwt; Man. Dir Capt. VLADIMÍR PODLENA.

CIVIL AVIATION

There are civil airports at Prague (Ruzyně), Brno, Karlovy Vary, Mariánské Lázně, Ostrava, and Zlín, served by ČSA's internal flights. International flights serve Prague, Ostrava, Brno and Karlovy Vary.

ČSA (Československé aerolinie a.s.) (Czechoslovak Airlines): Head Office: Ruzyně Airport, 160 08 Prague 6; tel. (2) 341540; telex 120338; fax (2) 3162774; f. 1923; during 1993 ČSA was to serve as the national airline for both the Czech and Slovak Republics; external services to most European capitals, the Near, Middle and Far East, North America and North Africa; Pres. and CEO ANTONÍN JAKUBSE.

Tourism

The Czech Republic has magnificent scenery, with winter sports facilities. Prague, Karlovy Vary (Carlsbad), Olomouc, Český Krumlov and Telč are the best known of the historic towns, and there are famous castles and cathedrals, numerous resorts as well as spas with natural mineral springs.

Čedok (Travel and Hotel Corporation): Na Příkopě 18, 111 35 Prague 1; tel. (2) 24197111; telex 121064; fax (2) 2321656; f. 1920; the official travel agency; 92 domestic travel offices; 14 branches throughout Europe and in Japan and the USA; 4 hotels in Prague; 60 coaches; Pres. PETR URBAN.

ASSOCIATIONS

Culture

NATIONAL ORGANIZATIONS

Ministerstvo kultury ČR (Ministry of Culture of the Czech Republic): see section on The Government (Ministries).

Informační a poradenské středisko pro místní kulturu (Information and Consultation Centre for Local Culture): Vinohrady, Blanická 4, 120 21 Prague 2; tel. (2) 250161; fax (2) 258434; f. 1906; Dir JIŘÍ VALENTA.

Česká komise pro spolupráci s UNESCO (Czech Commission for Co-operation with UNESCO): Toskán, Hradčanské nám. 5, 125 10 Prague 1; tel. (2) 21933163.

Czech National Heritage Chamber: Prague; f. 1993; association for organizations concerned with the preservation of national monuments; Chair. KAREL LISKA.

CULTURAL HERITAGE

Národní galerie v Praze (National Gallery in Prague): Hradčanské nám. 15, 119 04 Prague 1; tel. (2) 24511167; f. 1796; Dir Dr LADISLAV DANIEL.

Národní knihovna v Praze (National Library): Klementinum 190, 110 01 Prague 1; tel. (2) 24229500; telex 121207; fax (2) 24227796; f. 1348; 6m. vols; national literature collection; national bibliography; Dir Dr VOJTĚCH BALÍK.

Národní muzeum (National Museum): Václavské nám. 68, 115 79 Prague 1; tel. (2) 24230485; fax (2) 2369489; f. 1818; Dir Dr MILAN STLOUKAL.

Historické muzeum (Historical Museum): Václavské nám. 68, 115 79 Prague 1; tel. (2) 24230484; materials relating to Czech history, ethnography; prehistoric and classical archaeology; numismatics; Dir Dr KAREL SKLENÁŘ.

Knihovna Národního muzea (National Museum Library): Václavské nám. 68, 115 79 Prague 1; tel. (2) 24230485; f. 1818; c. 3m. vols; humanities and national science; Dir Dr HELGA TURKOVÁ.

Muzeum české hudby (Museum of Czech Music): Lázeňská 2, tel. (2) 24229075; f. 1936; exhibitions on composers and collections of musical instruments; Dir Dr STANISLAV TESAŘ.

Moravská galerie v Brně (Moravian Gallery in Brno): Husova 14, 662 26 Brno; tel. (5) 26151; fax (5) 27940; Dir Dr JAROSLAV KAČER.

UMPRUM Muzeum (Museum of Applied Arts): ul. 17 listopadu 2, 110 01 Prague 1; tel. (2) 2320069; fax (2) 2322309; Dir Dr HELENA KOENIGSMARKOVÁ.

SPORTING ORGANIZATION

Československý olympijský výbor (Czechoslovak Olympic Committee): Národní 33, 110 00 Prague 1; tel. (2) 266976.

PERFORMING ARTS

Česka filharmonie (Czech Philharmonic Orchestra): Alšovo nábřeží 12, 110 00 Prague 1; tel. (2) 2489311; fax (2) 2314110; f. 1896; Chief Conductor GRED ALBRECHT; Gen. Dir LADISLAV KANTOR.

Divadelní ústav (Theatre Institute): Celetná 17, 110 01 Prague 1; tel. (2) 24812751; fax (2) 24812762; f. 1956; research and documentation on historical and contemporary Czech drama, opera and ballet; Dir HELENA ALBERTOVÁ.

Minor Theatre: Senovážné nám. 28 , 113 58 Prague 1; tel. (2) 223989; fax (2) 227223; f. 1949; puppet performances for children and adults; Dir KAREL MAKONJ.

Národní divadlo (National Theatre): Ostrovní 1, 110 00 Prague; tel. (2) 24912757; fax (2) 2321206.

Pražské jaro (Prague Spring Festival): Hellichova 18, 110 00 Prague 1; tel. (2) 533474; fax (2) 536040.

State Opera—Prague: Legerova 75, 110 00 Prague 1; tel. (2) 261450.

Stavovské divadlo (Theatre of the Estates): Ovocný tř. 1, 110 00 Prague 1; tel. (2) 24228503.

ASSOCIATIONS

Asociace českých a moravsko-slezských muzeí a galerií (Association of Bohemian, Moravian and Silesian Museums and Galleries): Východočeské muzeum, Zámek 1, 531 16 Parducbice; tel. (40) 516059; Dir Dr FRANTIŠEK ŠEBEK.

Asociace hudebních umělců a vědců (Association of Musicians and Musicologists): Maltézské nám. 1, 118 00 Prague 1; f. 1990; tel. (2) 533661; fax (2) 539062; Pres. Dr IVAN POLDEŇÁK; Exec. Sec. JAROSLAV GREGOR.

Asociace scénografu (Association of Theatre Designers): c/o Labyrint, Štefánikova 57, 150 43 Prague 5; tel. and fax (2) 544541.

Česká hudební společnost (Czech Music Society): Janačkovo nábř. 59, 150 00 Prague 5; tel. (2) 530868; f. 1934; 3,000 mems; Pres. MÍLA SMETÁČKOVÁ ; Sec.-Gen. EVA ŠTRAUSOVÁ.

Český literární fond (Czech Literature Fund): Pod nuselskými schody 3, 128 00 Prague 2; tel. (2) 6911908.

Czech Centre for International PEN: Valdštejnské nám. 4, 118 11 Prague 1; tel. (2) 5132509; f. 1924; 165 mems; Pres. JIŘÍ STRANSKÝ.

Dance Association: Štepánská 42, 120 00 Prague 2; tel. (2) 2352615; fax (2) 735409.

Divadelní obec (Theatre Association): c/o Labyrint, Štefánikova 57, 150 43 Prague 5; tel. and fax (2) 544541.

Matice moravská (Moravian Society of History and Literature): A. Nováka 1, 602 00 Brno; tel. (5) 41321258; f. 1849; 560 mems; Pres. Prof. JAN JANÁK.

Music Information Centre (HIS) of the Czech Music Fund: Besední 3, 118 00 Prague 1; tel. (2) 530546; fax (2) 539720.

Obec architektů (Community of Architects): Letenská 5, 118 45 Prague 1; tel. (2) 539741; f. 1989; 2,500 mems; Pres. ALENA ŠRÁMKOVÁ.

Obec spisovatel' (Community of Writers): POB 669, 111 21 Prague 1; tel. (2) 2358968; f. 1989; 720 mems; reorganized 1990.

Svaz českých dramatických umělců (Union of Czech Dramatic Artists): Pod Nuselskými schody 3, 120 00 Prague 2; tel. (2) 250682; f. 1978; 3,100 mems; Pres. KÁKOŠ.

Unie výtvarných umělců (Visual Artists' Association): Masarykovo nábř. 250, 110 00 Prague 1; tel. (2) 292215; fax (2) 291884.

Education

Almost all children between the ages of three and six attend kindergarten (mateřska škola). Education is compulsory between the ages of six and 16 years, when children attend basic school (základní škola). Most children continue their studies after basic school, either at a secondary grammar school or at a secondary vocational school. In both types of institution students follow four-year courses. There are also apprentice-training centres, at which courses last from two to four years, which prepare young people for workers' professions. In 1990 the establishment of private and religious schools was legalized. In the 1989/90 school year 636,622 children attended kindergarten, 1,961,742 attended basic (elementary) schools, 892,940 the different types of secondary school and there were 173,547 students in higher education (Czechoslovak figures). In the 1990/91 academic year there were 96,379 full-time students in higher education in the Czech Republic. Fees for higher education were to be introduced from September 1994.

UNIVERSITIES

České Vysoké učení Technické v Praze (Czech Technical University of Prague): Zikova 4, 166 35 Prague 6; tel. (2) 3321111; fax (2) 3117493; f. 1707; 6 faculties; 1,500 teachers; 15,000 students; Rector Prof. Ing. S. HANZL.

Univerzita Karlova (Charles University): Ovocný tř. 5, 116 36 Prague; tel. (2) 228441; f. 1348; 16 faculties; 2,785 teachers; 25,786 students; Rector Prof. Dr RADIM PALOUŠ.

Univerzita Masarykova (Masaryk University): Burešova 20, 601 77 Brno; tel. (5) 754841; f. 1919; 5 faculties; 971 teachers; 8,824 students; Rector Prof. Dr MILAN JELÍNEK.

Univerzita Palackého v Olomouci (Palacký University): Křížkovského 10, 771 47 Olomouc; tel. (68) 5508111; fax (68) 5222731; f. 1573, re-opened 1946; 7 faculties; 823 teachers; 6,154 students; Rector Prof. Dr JOSEF JAŘAB.

Univerzita Pardubice (University of Pardubice): nám. Čs. Legií 565; tel. (40) 513221; fax (40) 514530; f. 1950, renamed 1992; 3 faculties; 185 teachers; 1,600 students; Rector Prof. Ing. LADISLAV KUDLÁČEK.

Vysoká Škola Báňská v Ostravé (Technical University of Mining and Metallurgy of Ostrava): tř. 17 listopadu 15, 708 33 Ostrava 4; tel. (69) 424111; telex 52568; f. 1716; 5 faculties; 654 teachers; 7,169 students; Rector Prof. Ing. TOMÁŠ ČERMÁK.

Vysoká Škola Chemicko-Technologická v Praze (Institute of Chemical Technology, Prague): Technická 5, 166 28 Prague 6; tel. (2) 3324144; telex 122744; fax (2) 3119919; f. 1807; 4 faculties; 400 teachers; 2,500 students; Rector Prof. ČESTMÍR ČERNÝ.

Vysoká Škola Ekonomická (Prague University of Economics): nám. W. Churchilla 4, 130 67 Prague 3; tel. (2) 2353428; fax (2) 2355962; f. 1953; 5 faculties; 7,000 students; Rector Prof. ŠTĚPÁN MÜLLER.

Vysoká Škola Strojní a Textilní v Liberci (Technical University of Mechanical and Textile Engineering in Liberec): Hálkova 6, 461 17 Liberec; tel. (48) 25441; f. 1953; 4 faculties; 324 teachers; 4,661 students; Rector Prof. ZDENĚK KOVÁŘ.

Vysoká Škola Veterinární a Farmaceutická v Brně (University of Veterinary Science and Pharmacy in Brno): Palackého 1–3, 612 42 Brno; tel. (5) 7110; fax (5) 748922; f. 1918; 3 faculties; 134 teachers; 1,187 students; Rector Prof. Dr JAROSLAV KONRÁD.

Vysoká Škola Zemědělská (University of Agriculture): Zemědělská 1, 615 00 Brno; tel. (5) 45131111; telex 62489; fax (45211128; f. 1919; 4 faculties; 378 teachers; 3,337 full-time and 320 part-time students; Rector B. HRUŠKA.

Vysoká Škola Zemědělská v Praze (Prague Agricultural University): Suchdol, Kamýcká 129, 165 21 Prague 6; tel. (2) 3381111; fax (2) 341969; f. 1906; 4 faculties, 2 institutes; 429 teachers; 3,700 students; Rector Prof. Dr JIŘÍ PETR.

Vysoké učení Technické v Brné (Technical University of Brno): Opletalova 6, 601 90 Brno; tel. (5) 25831; telex 62536; f. 1899; 5 faculties; 1,026 teachers; 14,624 students; Rector Prof. Ing. FRANTIŠEK PAIL.

Západočeská Univerzita (University of West Bohemia): Americká 42, 306 14 Plzeň; tel. (19) 35551; telex 154292; fax (19) 220019; f. 1949; 5 faculties; teachers 436; students 4,114; Rector Dr JIŘÍ HOLENDA.

Social Welfare

A single and universal social security system was established in Czechoslovakia after the Second World War. Protection of health was stipulated by law, and medical care, treatment, medicines, etc. were, in most cases, available free of charge to the entire Czechoslovak population. In 1988 there were 123,000 hospital beds available. In 1989 there were 57,950 physicians, equivalent to one physician per 270 persons, and expenditure on the health service was 38,268m. koruny. There was a universal pension system, available to women at the age of 60 and to men at the age of 65.

In 1991 a new system of social security was introduced. The Government planned to guarantee a minimum level of social welfare to all citizens, in an attempt to mitigate the expected consequences of radical economic reform. In addition, benefit was made available to unemployed workers for a maximum period of 12 months, and mandatory redundancy payments, equivalent to two months wages, were introduced. In 1990 a Council of Economic and Social Consensus (the 'Tripartite Council'), composed of representatives of federal and republican governments, employers and the trade unions, was established to discuss welfare issues.

Following the dissolution of Czechoslovakia in 1993, the two successor states announced plans to introduce changes to the existing social-welfare system. In the Czech Republic the privatization programme was to extend to the health-care system, though at a slower rate than in many other parts of the economy. Health-care expenditure in 1993 was projected at 62,000m. koruny (7.7% of GDP). A new pensions insurance law was to come into effect in 1995, which would gradually increase the retirement age for men to 62 (from 60) and for women to 61 (from 55–57, depending on the number of children borne) by 2006.

GOVERNMENT AGENCIES

Board of Representatives from the Organizations of Disabled People: Na Topolce 1A, 140 00 Prague 4; tel. and fax (2) 61211588; Chair. Ing. PAVEL DUŠEK.

Česká správa sociálního zabezpečení (Czech Social Security Administration): Křížová 25, 150 00 Prague 5; tel. (2) 541141; Dir Dr LADISLAV ANTOŠIK.

Social Affairs and Health Committee: Sněmovní 4, 118 26 Prague 1; tel. (2) 530418; fax (2) 531211; parliamentary committee of the Chamber of Deputies; Chair Dr MARTYN SYKA .

Governmental Board for People with Disabilities in the Czech Republic: Na Dr Beneše 4, 118 01 Prague 1; tel. (2) 24002218; fax (2) 24002207; Exec. Dir Ing. JAROSLAV HRUBÝ.

Ministerstvo práce a sociálních věcí České republiky (Ministry of Labour and Social Affairs of the Czech Republic): see section on The Government (Ministries).

HEALTH AND WELFARE ORGANIZATION

Association of Disabled People in the Czech Republic: Karlínské nám. 12, 186 03 Prague 8; tel. (2) 2350796.

The Environment

Environmental issues caused some of the first expressions of opposition to the Communist regime. Of particular concern is the region of Northern Bohemia, where sulphur-dioxide emissions from coal-fired power stations have caused serious air pollution. According to official figures, Czechoslovakia produced more air pollutants per head of population than any other European country. There were estimated to be over 30 environmental groups in Czechoslovakia, most of which were represented in the Czech Republic from 1993.

GOVERNMENT ORGANIZATIONS

Ministry of the Environment: see section on The Government (Ministries).

Státní ústav památkové péče (State Institute for the Protection of Monuments): Valdštejnské nám. 3, 118 01 Prague; tel. (2) 5131111; fax (2) 535496.

Ustredie státnej cchrany prírody (Central Office for State Nature Conservation): Leninova 11, 031 01 Liptovský Mikulás; tel. (2) 24177; Dir ANTON LUCINKIEWICZ.

ACADEMIC INSTITUTES

Centre for Environmental Scholarship: Univerzita Karlova, Petrská 3, 110 00 Prague 1; tel. (2) 2315334; fax (2) 2315324; Dir Dr BEDŘICH MOLDAN.

Česká Akademie věd (Czech Academy of Sciences): Národní tř. 3, 111 42 Prague 1; tel. (2) and fax 24240531; telex 121040; f. 1993; Pres. Prof. R. ZAHRADNÍK.

Institute of Experimental Botany and Ecology: Na Karlovce 1A, 160 00 Prague 6; tel. (2) 24310209; fax (2) 24310113; f. 1962; plant physiology, genetics, pathology and biotechnology; Dir Dr JIŘÍ VELEMÍNSKÝ.

Institute of Industrial Landscape Ecology: Chittussiho 10, 710 00 Ostrava 2; tel. (69) 216960; promotes the application of ecology to planning industrial land use.

Institute of Landscape Ecology—Czech Academy of Sciences: Na Sádkách 7, 370 05 České Budějovice; tel. (38) 40183; fax (38) 45719; promotes the application of ecology to planning land use; Principal Officers Prof. Dr V. MESTŘIJK, J. TĚSITEL, Dr P. CUDLIN.

Institute of Physics of the Atmosphere: Bocni II-1401, 141 31 Prague 4; tel. (2) 766051; monitors atmospheric pollution.

Dřípatka Centre for Ecological Education: Rumpálova 402, 383 01 Prachatice; tel. (338) 22806; workshops and courses on nature conservation for teachers, students and children; Principal Officers HELENA KLIMEŠOVÁ, KAREL TŘÍSKA.

Ústav pro životní prostředí—pobočka Praha (Prague Institute for the Environment): U Michelského lesa 366, 140 00 Prague 4; tel. (2) 2195; fax (2) 496619.

NON-GOVERNMENTAL ORGANIZATIONS

Česky svaz ochráncu přírody—ČSOP (Czech Union for of Nature Conservation): U Michelského lesa 366, 140 00 Prague 4; tel. (2) 2195; fax (2) 496619; independent asscn of conservation groups in the Czech Republic; Pres. Assoc. Prof. Dr BEDŘICH MOLDAN.

Česky ústav ochrany přrody—ČÚOP (Czech Institute for Nature Conservation): Slezská 9, 120 00 Prague 2; tel. (2) 24172800; fax (2) 254555.

Green Party: see section on Political Organizations.

Hnuti Brontosaurus (Brontosaurus Movement): Bubenská 6, 170 00 Prague 7; tel. (2) 802910; fax (2) 802906; voluntary youth environmental movement in Bohemia and Moravia; environmental education and campaigning; conservation work; Principal Officer HELENA IZBICKÁ.

Defence

The former Czechoslovakia had one of the strongest armed forces in the Warsaw Pact (which was dissolved in 1991). In June 1991 the last of the 73,500 Soviet troops stationed in Czechoslovakia left the country. The numbers of Czechoslovak troops had already been reduced significantly, under the Conventional Forces in Europe (CFE) process, by the end of 1992, when the Czech Republic assumed responsibilty for 100,000 of the remaining 150,000 personnel. Plans were drawn up for the size of the total armed forces to be reduced to 65,000 by the end of 1995, but these were suspended in January 1994 in response to the Russian Federation's decision to abandon its own plans for force reductions. In June 1993, according to Western estimates, the total armed forces numbered 77,500 (including 40,400 conscripts); the Army numbered 41,900 (25,900 conscripts) and the Air Force 35,600 (14,500 conscripts). In addition there were an estimated 7,000 border guards, 2,000 internal security forces and 2,000 civil defence troops. About 500 Czech troops were serving with the UN in Croatia. In June 1993 a further reduction in the length of service for conscripted troops was instituted, from eighteen months to 12 months, following an earlier reduction in 1990 from two years, when an alternative of 27 months of non-military duty was also introduced. Service with the reserve lasts until 60 years of age. In 1993 a programme of screening all professional soldiers in the Czech Army commenced, intended both to reveal links with the former communist regime and to assess the performance and potential of officers. The budget allocated to the Czech armed forces in 1994 was estimated at 27,000m. koruny.

Commander-in-Chief: President of the Republic.

Chief of General Staff: Maj.-Gen. JIŘÍ NEKVASIL.

Bibliography

Korbel, J. *Twentieth Century Czechoslovakia: The Meaning of Her History.* New York, Columbia University Press, 1977.

Kusin, V. P. *From Dubček to Charter 77. A Study of 'Normalization' in Czechoslovakia, 1968–1978.* Edinburgh, Q Press, 1979.

The Intellectual Origins of the Prague Spring. Cambridge, Cambridge University Press, 1971.

Mamatey, V. S. and Luža, R. (Eds). *A History of the Czechoslovak Republic, 1918–1948.* Princeton, NJ, Princeton University Press, 1973.

Myant, M. *The Czechoslovak Economy.* Cambridge, Cambridge University Press, 1989.

Olivová, V. *The Doomed Democracy. Czechoslovakia in a Disrupted Europe, 1914–1938.* London, Sidgwick and Jackson, 1972.

Paul, D. W. *Czechoslovakia. Profile of a Socialist Republic at the Crossroads of Europe.* Boulder, Colorado, Westview Press, 1981.

Skilling, G. H. *Charter 77 and Human Rights in Czechoslovakia.* London, Allen and Unwin, 1981.

Czechoslovakia's Interrupted Revolution. Princeton, NJ, Princeton University Press, 1976.

Skilling, G. H. and Wilson, P. (Eds). *Civic Freedom in Central Europe. Voices from Czechoslovakia.* London, Macmillan, 1991.

Taborsky, E. *Communism in Czechoslovakia, 1948–1960.* Princeton, NJ, Princeton University Press, 1961.

Ulč, O. *Politics in Czechoslovakia.* San Fransisco, W. H. Freeman, 1974.

Wightman, G. 'The Collapse of Communist Rule in Czechoslovakia and the July 1990 Parliamentary Elections' in *Parliamentary Affairs*, Vol. 44, No. 1, January 1991.

ESTONIA

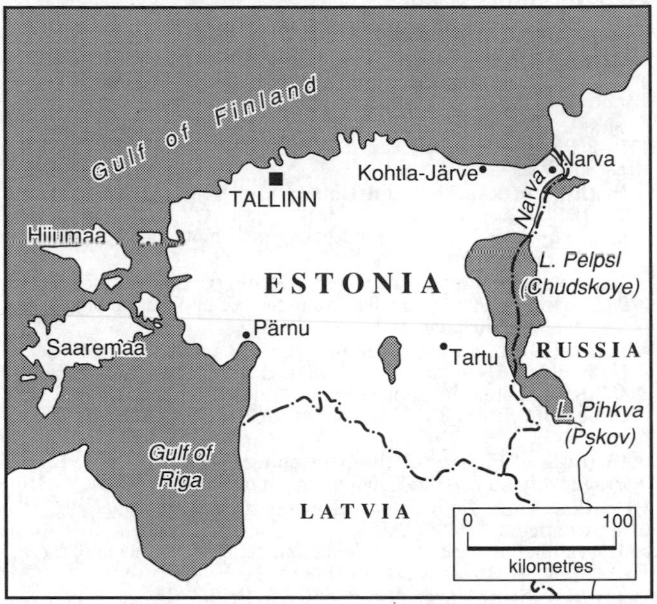

PHYSICAL FEATURES

The Republic of Estonia is situated in north-eastern Europe. It is bordered to the south by Latvia and, to the east, by the Russian Federation. Its northern coastline is on the Gulf of Finland and its territory includes over 1,520 islands, mainly off its western coastline in the Gulf of Riga and the Baltic Sea. The country covers an area of 45,226 sq km (17,462 sq miles). Before 1945, when a small amount of territory south of Lake Pihkva (Pskov) was ceded to the Russian Federation, Estonia covered an area of 47,548 sq km.

Estonia is situated on the north-western edge of the Great Russian Plain. The land is mainly flat, with some undulating terrain in the south. Forests cover some 36% of the territory. Rivers, the largest of which is the Narva, are mainly short and carry low volumes of water. There are many marshes and bogs, and more than 1,500 lakes, of which the largest are the Estonian parts of the Peipsi (Chudskoye) and Pihkva (Pskov) lakes, on the eastern border with the Russian Federation. The largest of the Republic's many islands are Saaremaa and Hiiumaa, in the Gulf of Riga.

CLIMATE

The climate is influenced by Estonia's position between the Eurasian landmass and the Baltic and North Atlantic seas. The mean January temperature in Tallinn is −5.0°C (23.0°F); in July the mean temperature is 17.1°C (62.6°F). Annual precipitation is 568 mm.

POPULATION

At the census of 1989, when the total population of permanent inhabitants was 1,565,662, 61.5% of the population were Estonians, 30.3% Russians, 3.1% Ukrainians, 1.8% Belarusians and 1.1% Finns. Other nationalities included Jews (4,613), Tatars (4,058) and Germans (3,466). In 1989 Estonian replaced Russian as the official state language. It is a member of the Baltic-Finnic group of the Finno-Ugric languages and is written in the Latin script. It is closely related to Finnish. Many Russian residents do not speak Estonian (85% in 1989) and protested at its official use. Most of the population are adherents of the Christian religion. By tradition, Estonians are Lutheran, while the Russian Orthodox Church and smaller Protestant sects were also represented in the Republic.

At 1 January 1992 the total population was estimated to be 1,562,000. The capital is Tallinn, which is situated in the north of the country, on the Gulf of Finland. It had an estimated population of 497,766 in 1991. Other important towns included the university town of Tartu (114,239), and the Russian-dominated industrial towns of Narva (86,852) and Kohtla-Järve (75,031), in the north-east of Estonia.

Chronology

***c.* 3,000 BC:** Finno-Ugric peoples, the ancestors of the Estonians, first began to migrate from Eastern Europe to the north-east coast of the Baltic Sea.

AD 1219: Valdemar II of Denmark and the German Sword Brethren, a crusading order, conquered Estonia.

1346: The Danes sold their share of Estonian territory to the Livonian Order of Teutonic Knights (an alliance of the Sword Brethren and the German Order of Teutonic Knights).

1524–39: The State of Teutonic Knights, including Estonia, renounced religious allegiance to Rome and converted to Lutheranism.

1561: In the secularization and partition of the State of Teutonic Knights, Estonia (now northern Estonia) became part of Sweden. Livonia (now Latvia and southern Estonia) was placed under Polish rule, as part of the Lithuanian–Polish Duchy of Courland (Kurland).

1595: Sweden's right to Narva and Estonia was recognized by the Peace of Teusin, signed by Sweden and the Russian Empire, although Sweden did not assume full control of Estonia until 1607.

1629: With the Armistice of Altmark, following the Swedish–Polish Wars, Sweden gained the territory of Livonia.

1721: The Treaty of Nystad, between Russia and Sweden, ended the Great Northern War and brought Estonia and Livonia under Russian rule.

1817: Serfdom was abolished in Estonia.

November 1905: Following a revolution in Russia the previous month, the increase in Estonian national feeling resulted in an all-Estonian Assembly demanding autonomy; the uprising was eventually suppressed.

1 August 1914: Russia entered the First World War against the Empires of Austria-Hungary, Germany and the Ottomans (the Central Powers).

2 March (New Style: 15 March) 1917: Abdication of the last Tsar, Nicholas II, after demonstrations and strikes in Petrograd (St Petersburg); a Provisional Government, led by Prince Lvov, took power.

30 March (12 April) 1917: The Provisional Government granted Estonia its autonomy.

24 February (Old Style: 11 February) 1918: The independent Republic of Estonia was declared; Konstantin Päts led a Provisional Government, although this was not recognized by the German occupiers.

3 March 1918: The Bolsheviks, in control of the Government of Russia, signed the Treaty of Brest-Litovsk with Germany, thereby ceding large areas of western territory to Germany, including Estonia.

November 1918: The Provisional Government assumed control in Estonia, following Germany's surrender.

2 February 1920: The Treaty of Tartu ended hostilities between Estonia and Soviet Russia; the Soviet Government recognized Estonian independence and renounced any claims on its territory.

January 1921: The West recognized Estonia as an independent state; Estonia became a member of the League of Nations.

1924: An attempt by Communists to seize power in Estonia failed.

12 March 1934: The parliamentary system in Estonia was replaced by a period of dictatorship after premier Päts seized control in a bloodless coup.

April 1938: Following the adoption of a new Constitution, which provided for a presidential system of government and a bicameral parliament, Päts was elected President of Estonia.

23 August 1939: The Treaty of Non-Aggression (the Nazi-Soviet Pact of Joachim von Ribbentrop and Vyacheslav Molotov) was signed by Germany and the USSR; the 'Secret Protocols' to this Pact provided for the annexation of Estonia and Latvia.

June 1940: The Baltic states (Estonia, Latvia and Lithuania) and Bessarabia were occupied by the USSR; the Estonian Government resigned and was replaced by a Soviet-appointed administration, led by Johannes Vares-Barbarus.

21 July 1940: The new Estonian parliament (consisting entirely of members sympathetic to the Soviet regime) proclaimed the Estonian Soviet Socialist Republic.

6 August 1940: Estonia was admitted to the USSR as a constituent Union Republic of the federation.

June 1941: In the same month that Germany invaded the USSR (Estonia was occupied by the Germans in July), more than 10,000 Estonians were deported to Siberia by the Soviet authorities; deportations continued until the death of Stalin (Iosif V. Dzhugashvili) in 1953.

September 1944: Despite expelling all German troops from Estonia, the Soviet regime had to endure a series of armed attacks by the so-called 'forest brethren' (*metsavennad*), a pro-independence guerrilla movement, which continued its campaign until 1955.

1947–March 1949: Collectivization occurred in Estonia.

October 1980: The brutal suppression of a protest by schoolchildren at the 'russification' of the Republic prompted a critical 'Letter of the Forty' from prominent intellectuals to the authorities.

23 August 1987: A crowd of 2,000 demonstrators commemorated the anniversary of the Molotov–Ribbentrop Pact; soon afterwards, an Estonian Group for the Publication of the Molotov–Ribbentrop Pact was established, becoming the Estonian National Independence Party (ENIP) in 1988.

April 1988: The Popular Front of Estonia (PFE) was formed; mass demonstrations against the Soviet regime were organized by the PFE throughout July and August.

June 1988: Vaino Vaeles replaced Karl Vaino (leader of Estonia since 1978) as First Secretary of the Communist Party of Estonia (CPE). In the following month Intermovement, a political group intended to counteract the influence of the increasingly popular opposition movements, was formed.

16 November 1988: The Estonian Supreme Soviet declared the sovereignty of the Republic.

18 January 1989: Estonian was adopted as the state language and the tricolour of independent Estonia once again became the official flag.

March 1989: In elections to the all-Union Congress of People's Deputies, the PFE won 27 of the 36 Estonian seats, while Intermovement won five. The ENIP refused to participate in the elections and proposed a rival parliament, the 'Congress of Estonia', to be elected only by citizens of pre-1940 Estonia and their descendants.

May 1989: Estonia declared its economic independence from the all-Union authorities; this decision was ratified by the Supreme Soviet of the USSR in November.

August 1989: A new electoral law stipulated that only persons who had been resident in Estonia for two years were entitled to vote in republican elections, and only those who had been resident for 10 years could stand as candidates; however, the legislation was finally suspended, following mass protests, mainly by ethnic Russians and organized by Intermovement.

November 1989: The Estonian Supreme Soviet voted to annul the 1940 decision to join the USSR.

February 1990: The legal pre-eminence of the Communists was abolished and the Estonian Supreme Soviet approved a declaration that demanded immediate negotiations with the all-Union Supreme Soviet on restoring Estonian independence.

11–12 March 1990: The Congress of Estonia, to which elections had been held in late February and early March, convened and declared itself the representative of the Estonian people.

18 March 1990: Nationalist groups won majorities in elections to the Estonian Supreme Soviet; 43 of the 105 contested seats were won by the PFE, another 35 by other pro-independence groups. Members of the Intermovement group won the remaining seats. The Communists, who were represented in several groups (both nationalist and Intermovement), subsequently split into two parties, with the majority CPE rejecting its ties with the all-Union Party, the CPSU.

30 March 1990: A transitional period towards independence was declared by the Supreme Soviet; at the same time, the validity of Soviet power in Estonia was denied.

3 April 1990: Edgar Savisaar, leader of the PFE, was elected Prime Minister by the Supreme Soviet (Supreme Council).

8 May 1990: The first five articles of the 1938 Constitution were reinstated; the formal name of independent Estonia, the Republic of Estonia, was restored, as well as the state emblems, the flag and the anthem. The following week Soviet President Mikhail Gorbachev annulled Estonia's declaration of independence and some 2,000 protesters against the declaration attempted to occupy the parliament building.

3 March 1991: In a referendum, 77.8% of the participants (comprising 82.9% of the registered electorate) voted in favour of independence.

17 March 1991: Of the 225,000 Slavs in north-eastern Estonia who participated in the all-Union referendum, approximately 95% voted in favour of keeping the USSR as a 'renewed federation'.

19 August 1991: At the same time as an attempted coup in Moscow, Soviet General Fedor Kuzmin, Commander of the Baltic Military District, declared that he was assuming control of Estonia.

20 August 1991: Military vehicles entered Tallinn; at a session of the Estonian Supreme Council full and immediate independence was declared.

21 August 1991: Soviet troops occupied the television station in Tallinn, but, in Moscow, the *coup d'état* collapsed.

22 August 1991: The Estonian Government banned the CPSU, Intermovement and the United Council of Work Collectives.

4 September 1991: The newly formed State Council of the USSR recognized the independence of Estonia, Latvia and Lithuania.

17 September 1991: Estonia (with Latvia and Lithuania) was admitted to the UN.

9 October 1991: The USSR established diplomatic relations with Estonia.

6 November 1991: A new citizenship law stated that only persons who had been citizens of Estonia prior to 1940, and their descendants, were eligible to vote.

January 1992: Edgar Savisaar resigned as Prime Minister and was replaced by Tiit Vähi.

20 June 1992: The Estonian crown or kroon replaced the rouble as sole legal tender.

June 1992: Some 91% of the electorate approved a draft Constitution proposed by the Constitutional Assembly.

20 September 1992: Some 67% of the electorate participated in legislative and presidential elections; the largest number of seats in the new legislature (now known as the Riigikogu) was won by the Isamaa (Pro Patria or Fatherland) national alliance.

5 October 1992: As no candidate for the presidency had secured an absolute majority in the direct elections, the Riigikogu had to choose between the two leading candidates: Lennart Meri, a former Minister of Foreign Affairs, and Arnold Rüütel, Chairman of the former Supreme Council. Meri was elected President and appointed a coalition Government under Mart Laar of Isamaa.

November 1992: The National Fatherland Party was formed by four out of five of the constituent parties of the Isamaa alliance; Mart Laar was elected Chairman. The CPE changed its name to the Estonian Democratic Labour Party.

February 1993: The mayor of Moscow, Yury Luzhkov, suspended commercial and economic ties with Estonia, in protest at Estonia's treatment of its Russian-speaking population.

March 1993: The withdrawal of former Soviet troops from Estonia was again halted by the Russians, this time because there had been no agreement on who was to meet the cost of relocating the servicemen.

14 May 1993: Notwithstanding opposition from the Russian Government, Estonia was admitted to the Council of Europe.

19 May 1993: The Riigikogu declared that only Estonian citizens could stand as candidates in the local elections scheduled for October that year.

21 June 1993: Despite significant protests by ethnic Russians against the citizenship laws, the Riigikogu enacted legislation requiring all non-Estonians to apply for citizenship or for a residence permit by 1 January 1996.

25–29 June 1993: The Russian Federation suspended natural-gas supplies to Estonia, in response to the law of 21 June.

16–17 July 1993: A referendum on autonomy was held in the Russian-dominated towns of Narva and Sillimae.

3 August 1993: The Minister of Defence, Hain Rebas, resigned over an incident in which a company of light infantrymen, stationed at Pullapaa, had threatened to withdraw from the command of the Ministry of Defence in late July.

17 October 1993: Local authority elections took place in Estonia; an estimated 52.6% of the electorate participated and the Government lost considerable support.

13 November 1993: Members of the PFE agreed to disband the organization.

15 November 1993: A motion of 'no confidence' in the Estonian premier, Mart Laar, was proposed by members of the opposition; however, the Prime Minister survived the vote.

20 November 1993: The Estonian National Progressive Party, led by Ants Erm, was formed.

January 1994: A cabinet reshuffle took place: Jüri Luik succeeded Trivime Velliste as Minister of Foreign Affairs and was replaced as Minister of Defence by Indrek Kannik; Toivo Jürgenson succeeded Toomas Sildmäe as Minister of the Economy; and Madis Üürike was replaced by Heiki Kranich.

History

The Estonians, a Finno-Ugric people, have inhabited the north-east coastline of the Baltic Sea for some 5,000 years. At the beginning of the 13th century AD the Estonians, who numbered some 100,000, were conquered by the German crusading order, the Sword Brethren, with the aid of the Danes, under Valdemar II. The decline of German power in the 16th century allowed Sweden to seize Northern Estonia in 1561, while Southern Estonia, or Livonia, became part of the Lithuanian-Polish Duchy of Courland (Kurland). In 1629, after the Swedish–Polish Wars, all of mainland Estonia came under Swedish rule. Russia drove the Swedes out of Estonia in 1710, and Russian annexation was formalized at the Treaty of Nystad, in 1721. During the latter half of the 19th century, as the powers of the dominant Baltic German nobility declined, Estonians experienced a national cultural revival, which culminated in political demands for autonomy during the 1905 Revolution, and for full independence after the beginning of the First World War.

INDEPENDENT ESTONIA

On 30 March 1917 the Provisional Government in Petrograd (St Petersburg), which had taken power after the abdication of Tsar Nicholas II in February, approved autonomy for Estonia. A Land Council was elected as the country's representative body. However, in October the Bolsheviks staged a *coup d'état* in Tallinn, and declared the Estonian Soviet Executive Committee as the sole Government of Estonia. As German forces advanced towards Estonia, in early 1918, the Bolshevik troops were forced to leave. The major Estonian political parties united to form the Estonian Salvation Committee, and, on 24 February 1918, an independent Republic of Estonia was proclaimed. A Provisional Government was formed, headed by Konstantin Päts, but the Germans refused to recognize Estonia's independence and the country was occupied by German troops until the end of the War. Following the capitulation of Germany, in November 1918, the Provisional Government assumed power. On 2 February 1920, after a period of armed conflict between Soviet and Estonian troops, the Republic of Estonia and Soviet Russia signed the Treaty of Tartu. By the terms of the Treaty the Soviet Government recognized Estonian independence and renounced any rights to its territory. Estonian independence was recognized by the major Western Powers, in January 1921, and Estonia was admitted to the League of Nations.

Estonia's sovereignty lasted until 1940. During most of this period the country had a liberal-democratic political system, in which the Riigikogu (parliament) was the dominant political force. Significant social, cultural and economic advances were made in the 1920s, including radical land reform and important developments in research and scholarship. However, the decline in trade with Russia and the economic depression of the 1930s, combined with the political problems of a divided parliament, caused public dissatisfaction with the regime. On 12 March 1934 Konstantin Päts, the Prime Minister, seized power in a bloodless coup and introduced a period of authoritarian rule. The Riigikogu and political parties were disbanded, but, in 1938, a new Constitution was adopted, which provided for a presidential system of government, with a bicameral parliament. In April 1938 Päts was elected President.

SOVIET ESTONIA

On 23 August 1939 the USSR and Germany signed a Treaty of Non-Aggression (the Nazi–Soviet or Molotov–Ribbentrop Pact). The Secret Supplementary Protocol to the Treaty provided for the occupation of Estonia (and Latvia) by the USSR. In September Estonia was forced to sign an agreement which permitted the USSR to base Soviet troops in Estonia. In June 1940, following the effective Soviet occupation of the country, the Government resigned, in accordance with a Soviet ultimatum. A new Government was appointed by the Soviet authorities, with Johannes Vares-Barbarus as Prime Minister. In July elections were held, in which only candidates approved by the Soviet authorities were permitted to stand. On 21 July 1940 the Estonian Soviet Socialist Republic was proclaimed by the new parliament and, on 6 August, the Republic was formally incorporated into the USSR.

Soviet rule in Estonia lasted less than a year, before German forces occupied the country. In that short period Soviet policy resulted in mass deportations of Estonians to Siberia (in one night, on 14 June 1941, more than 10,000 people were arrested and deported), the expropriation of property, severe restrictions on cultural life and the introduction of Soviet-style government in the Republic.

In July 1941 German forces entered Estonia and remained in occupation until September 1944 when, after a short-lived attempt was made to reinstate Estonian independence, Soviet troops occupied the whole of the country and the process of 'sovietization' was continued. By the end of 1949 most Estonian farmers had been forced to join collective farms. Heavy industry was expanded, with investment concentrated on electricity generation and the chemical sector. Structural change in the economy was accompanied by increased political repression, with deportations of Estonians continuing until the death of Stalin, in 1953. The most obvious form of opposition to Soviet rule was provided by the 'forest brethren' (*metsavennad*), a guerrilla movement, which continued to conduct armed operations against Soviet personnel and institutions until the mid-1950s. As in other Soviet Republics, in the late 1960s more traditional forms of dissent appeared, which concentrated on cultural issues. These were provoked by the increasing domination of the Republic by immigrant Russians and other Slavs. Before 1940 ethnic Estonians constituted nearly 90% of the population. Emigration, losses during the War and deportations, combined with in-migration by Russians to occupy political posts and to work in heavy industry, resulted in a steady decline in the proportion of ethnic Estonians in the population. By 1989 only 61.5% of the population were ethnic Estonians.

During the late 1970s and the 1980s the issues of 'russification' and environmental degradation became increasing subjects of debate in Estonia. The policy of *glasnost*, introduced by Soviet leader Mikhail Gorbachev in 1986, allowed debate to spread beyond dissident groups. The first major demonstrations of the 1980s were in protest against plans to increase greatly the scale of open-cast phosphorite mining in north-eastern Estonia. The public opposition to the plans caused the all-Union Government to reconsider its proposals. This success prompted further protests. On 23 August 1987 a demonstration attended by some 2,000 people marked the anniversary of the signing of the Nazi–Soviet Pact. Following the demonstration, an Estonian Group for the Publication of the Molotov–Ribbentrop Pact was formed. The growing opposition movement was strongly opposed by the conservative Communist Party of Estonia (CPE) leadership, but reformers within the Party began making proposals allowing more autonomy for Estonia, particularly in economic policy. The most significant document produced by the reformers was the proposal for Economic Self-Management, which advocated full republican jurisdiction over the economy, including the introduction of a convertible currency.

THE RE-EMERGENCE OF ESTONIAN NATIONALISM

During 1988 previously censored subjects, such as russification, environmental degradation and politically sensitive aspects of Estonian history, were increasingly discussed in the republican press. The opposition movement also grew in strength and, in April, a Popular Front of Estonia (PFE) was established, which organized mass demonstrations throughout July and August. The campaign led by the Estonian Group for the Publication of the Molotov–Ribbentrop Pact to publish the Nazi–Soviet Pact achieved its aim and the organization re-formed as the Estonian National Independence Party (ENIP), proclaiming the restoration of Estonian independence as its political goal. The PFE, which was formally constituted at its first Congress in October, and included many members of the CPE, was more cautious in its approach, advocating the transformation of the USSR into a confederal system. The CPE itself was forced to adapt its policies to retain a measure of public support. On 16 November the Estonian Supreme Soviet adopted a declaration of sovereignty, which included the right to annul all-Union legislation. The Presidium of the USSR Supreme Soviet declared the sovereignty legislation unconstitutional, but the Estonian Supreme Soviet affirmed its decision in December.

One of the main demands of the opposition, the adoption of Estonian as the state language, was agreed to by the Supreme Soviet in January 1989, and the tricolour of independent Estonia was also reinstated as the official flag. Despite the successes of the opposition, there were serious differences over political tactics between the radical ENIP and the PFE. ENIP refused to nominate candidates for elections to the all-Union Congress of People's Deputies in March 1989. Instead, its leadership announced plans for the registration of all citizens of the pre-1940 Estonian Republic and their descendants by 'Citizens' Committees'. An electorate registered in this way would elect a 'Congress of Estonia' as the legal successor to the pre-1940 Estonian parliament. The PFE, however, participated in the elections to the Congress of People's Deputies and won 27 of the 36 contested seats. Five seats were won by Intermovement, a political group established by the Communist authorities in July 1988 to seek to oppose the growing influence of the Estonian anti-government movements in the Republic. In August, in response to a new electoral law approved by the Supreme Soviet, which required voters in elections to have been resident in the Republic for two years and candidates to have been resident for 10 years, Intermovement organized protest rallies and strikes, in which some 30,000 people were estimated to have taken part. In response to the protests, the legislation was suspended by the Supreme Soviet.

In October 1989 delegates at the second congress of the PFE, influenced by the growing popularity of the ENIP and the Citizens' Committees, voted to adopt the restoration of Estonian independence as official policy. In November the Supreme Soviet voted to annul the decision of its predecessor in 1940 to enter the USSR, declaring that the decision had been reached under coercion from Soviet armed forces.

On 2 February 1990 a mass rally was held to mark the anniversary of the 1920 Treaty of Tartu. Deputies attending the rally later met to demand that the USSR Supreme Soviet begin negotiations on restoring Estonia's independence. The declaration was approved by the Estonian Supreme Soviet on 22 February. On 23 February the Estonian Supreme Soviet voted to abolish the constitutional guarantee of power enjoyed by the Communist Party, which was enshrined in Article Six of the Constitution. This formal decision permitted largely free elections to the Estonian Supreme Soviet to take place on 18 March 1990. The PFE won 43 of the 105 seats and 35 were won by the Association for a Free Estonia and other pro-independence groups. The remainder were won by members of Intermovement. Candidates belonging to the CPE, which were represented in all these groups, won 55 seats.

At the first session of the new Supreme Soviet, Arnold Rüütel, previously Chairman of the Presidium of the Supreme Soviet, was elected to the new post of Chairman of the Supreme Soviet, which included those state powers which had previously been the preserve of First Secretaries of the CPE. On 30 March 1990 the Supreme Soviet declared the beginning of a transitional period towards independence and denied the validity of Soviet power in the Republic.

In late February and early March 1990 elections were held to a rival parliament to the Supreme Soviet, the Congress of Estonia. The elections were organized privately by Citizens' Committees and participation was limited to those who had been citizens of the pre-1940 Estonian Republic and their descendants. Some 580,000 people took part. The Congress convened on 11–12 March and declared itself the constitutional representative of the Estonian people. Resolutions were adopted that demanded the restoration of Estonian independence and the withdrawal of Soviet troops from Estonia.

On 26 March 1990 delegates to an extraordinary congress of the CPE adopted a resolution which favoured the principle of its independence from the Communist Party of the Soviet Union (CPSU), but allowed for a transitional period of six months before a final vote on the secession of the Party would be taken. Following the Congress, some deputies, mostly non-Estonians, announced that they were planning to establish a Communist Party which would remain subordinate to the CPSU. Vaino Vaeles, who had been First Secretary of the CPE since 1988, was elected to the newly created post of Chairman of that party.

On 3 April 1990 the Supreme Soviet or Supreme Council elected Edgar Savisaar, a leader of the PFE, as Prime Minister. On 8 May the Supreme Soviet voted to restore the first five articles of the 1938 Constitution, which described Estonia's independent status. The formal name of pre-1940 Estonia, the Republic of Estonia, was also restored, as were the state emblems, flag and anthem of independent Estonia. On 16 May a transitional system of government was approved.

Although formal economic sanctions were not imposed on Estonia, as was the case with Lithuania, the Republic's declaration of independence severely strained relations with the all-Union authorities. On 14 May 1990 Soviet President Mikhail Gorbachev annulled the declaration, declaring that it violated the USSR Constitution. The Estonian leadership's request for negotiations on the status of the Republic was refused by Gorbachev, who insisted that the independence declaration be rescinded before negotiations could begin. There was also opposition within the Republic, mostly from ethnic Russians affiliated to Intermovement. On 15 May some 2,000 people protested against the declaration and attempted to occupy the Supreme Council building.

Military action by Soviet interior ministry troops in Latvia and Lithuania in January 1991 strengthened local feeling against Estonian involvement in a new Union, which was being negotiated by other Republics. Consequently, Estonia refused to participate in the all-Union referendum of 17 March on the future of the USSR, although some 225,000 people did take part in unofficial voting in the Slav-dominated north-eastern regions. Of these, some 95% approved the proposal to preserve the USSR as a 'renewed federation'. The Estonian authorities, however, had already conducted a poll on the issue of independence, on 3 March. Voters were asked the question 'Do you want the restoration of the state independence of the Estonian Republic?'. According to the official results, 82.9% of the registered electorate participated, of which 77.8% voted in favour.

When the State Committee for the State of Emergency (SCSE) announced that it had seized power in the USSR on 19 August 1991, General Fedor Kuzmin, Commander of the Baltic Military District, informed Arnold Rüütel, Chairman of the Supreme Council, that he was taking full control of Estonia. On 20 August military vehicles entered Tallinn and the following day troops occupied the television station. The military command did not prevent a session of the Estonian Supreme Council convening on 20 August. Deputies adopted a resolution declaring the full and immediate independence of the Estonian Republic, thus ending the transitional period which had begun in March 1990. Plans were also announced for the formation of a government-in-exile should the Government and the Supreme Council be disbanded by Soviet troops.

After it became evident, on 22 August 1991, that the coup had collapsed, the Government began to take measures against those who had allegedly supported the coup. The anti-government movements, Intermovement and the United Council of Work Collectives, were banned, as was the CPSU. Several directors of all-Union enterprises were dismissed and the Committee for State Security (KGB) was ordered to terminate its activities in Estonia.

As the Estonian Government moved to assert its authority over former Soviet institutions, other countries soon began to recognize Estonian independence (more than 30 countries had done so by the end of August 1991). On 4 September the Soviet State Council finally endorsed the re-establishment of the independent Estonian Republic. On 17 September Estonia, together with the other Baltic states, was admitted to the UN.

POST-SOVIET ESTONIA

In January 1992, following a series of disputes with the Supreme Council concerning economic management and the issue of citizenship, and the Government's failure to persuade the legislature to impose an economic state of emergency, Savisaar resigned as Prime Minister and was replaced by the erstwhile Minister of Transport, Tiit Vähi. A new Council of Ministers, which included seven ministers from the previous Government, was approved by the Supreme Council at the end of the month. The new Government's main aims were to solve the economic crisis, to secure the country's borders and to introduce Estonia's own currency (on 20 June 1992 the kroon replaced the rouble as the sole legal tender).

In the latter half of 1991 a Constitutional Assembly was established, composed of equal numbers of delegates from the radical Congress of Estonia and the Supreme Council, which was to draft a new Constitution. In a referendum held in late June 1992 the Constitution was approved by some 91% of the electorate. Under the citizenship law adopted in November 1991, only persons who had been citizens of pre-1940 Estonia, and their descendants, or those who had successfully applied for citizenship, were entitled to vote. The new Constitution, which entered into force in early July 1992, provided for a parliamentary system of government, with a strong presidency. A new legislature, the Riigikogu, was to replace the Supreme Council (and the Congress of Estonia), and elections to it were to be held in September. A direct presidential election was to take place simultaneously (although subsequent Presidents would be elected by the Riigikogu).

Legislative and presidential elections were held on 20 September 1992, with the participation of some 67% of the electorate. The elections to the 101-seat Riigikogu were contested by a total of 633 candidates, representing some 40 parties and movements, largely grouped into eight coalitions. The Isamaa nationalist alliance (Pro Patria or Fatherland) emerged with the largest number of seats (29). Other right-wing parties and alliances performed well. The centrist Popular Front alliance (led by the PFE) won an unexpectedly low total of 15 seats. The ENIP, which was not part of a coalition, won 10 seats. The Secure Home alliance, which comprised some former Communists, obtained 17 seats.

None of the four candidates in the presidential election, which was held simultaneously, won an overall majority of the votes. It thus fell to the Riigikogu to choose from the two most successful candidates, Arnold Rüütel, hitherto Chairman of the Supreme Council and a leading member of the Secure Home alliance, and Lennart Meri, a former Minister of Foreign Affairs, who was supported by Isamaa. In early October 1992 the Riigikogu, now dominated by members or supporters of Isamaa, elected Meri to be Estonia's President, by 59 votes to 31.

A new coalition Government, with a large representation of Isamaa members as well as members of the Moderates electoral alliance and the ENIP, was announced in mid-October 1992. Mart Laar, the leader of Isamaa, headed the new administration, the principal objectives of which, it was stated, would be to negotiate the withdrawal of all Russian troops remaining in Estonia and to accelerate the country's privatization programme. In late November four of the five constituent parties of the Isamaa alliance united to form the National Fatherland Party, with Laar as its Chairman. In the same month the CPE was renamed the Estonian Democratic Labour Party.

In the last week of July 1993 a company of light infantrymen (the Laanemaa volunteers' company), stationed at Pullapaa, signed a statement to the effect that they were withdrawing from the command of the Ministry of Defence. The rebellion was immediately suppressed and the Commander and Deputy Commander of the unit, Asso Kommer and Jaak Mosin, were arrested. On 3 August the Minister of Defence, Hain Rebas, resigned, as his proposal that the situation be dealt with by the Ministry of Justice was rejected by the Government. He was succeeded in his post by Jüri Luik, hitherto Minister without Portfolio.

Local authority elections, the first to be contested after Estonia gained independence, took place on 17 October 1993. A total of 8,738 candidates contended for 3,427 seats on 12 city councils and 241 district councils. An estimated 52.6% of the electorate participated in the elections. The ruling Isamaa party won only five seats on Tallinn city council, out of a total of 64. The Estonian Rural Centre Party also won five seats, the Consolidation Party emerged with 18, and the Russian Democratic Movement with 17. According to a law passed on 19 May, only Estonian citizens were entitled to stand as candidates (14 ethnic Russian candidates were granted citizenship immediately before the elections), but all permanent residents could vote.

In November 1993 several significant political developments occurred in Estonia. On 13 November, at its fifth congress, members of the PFE voted to disband the organization, declaring that it had largely fulfilled its aims. Two days later the Prime Minister, Mart Laar, survived a vote of 'no confidence'. The motion had been presented to the Riigikogu by 24 deputies from opposition parties on the grounds of incompetence and 'strategic errors in foreign affairs' (referring to the joint Russian–Estonian administration of Estonian border areas). On 20 November a new political party, the Estonian National Progressive Party was formed. Ants Erm, formerly Chairman of the ENIP, was to head the party.

In January 1994 Laar suffered a further crisis when the President, Lennart Meri, refused to accept two of his proposed ministerial changes. Meri believed that the government reshuffle was ill-timed, and that Laar's Government should have been more concerned with foreign affairs. The President, however, eventually agreed to sign Laar's proposals during a session of the Riigikogu on 11 January: Heiki Kranich was appointed Minister of Finance; Toivo Jurgenson became Minister of Economy; former Minister of Defence, Jüri Luik, replaced Trivimi Velliste as Minister of Foreign Affairs and was, in turn, replaced by Indrek Kannik.

WITHDRAWAL OF EX-SOVIET TROOPS

The issue of the several thousand ex-Soviet troops (for whom the Russian Government was now responsible) still stationed on Estonian territory (estimated at 7,000 in mid-1993) remained at the centre of political debate during 1992 and 1993. Although by August 1992 more than one-half of the former total had left Estonia, the Russian Government claimed that it could not comply with Estonia's demand for the rapid withdrawal of the remaining forces, as it was unable to provide housing for them. In late October the Russian President, Boris Yeltsin, announced the suspension of troop withdrawals from Estonia, as well as from Latvia and Lithuania, as a gesture of concern for the rights of the Russian-speaking population of the Baltic states. However, in apparent response to international pressure, the Russian Government abandoned its position and, in early November, it was announced that the withdrawal of ex-Soviet troops would resume.

At the end of March 1993 the operation was halted, as no agreement had been reached on how the cost of relocating the ex-Soviet servicemen was to be met. In August the joint forces of the Estonian Ministries of Defence and Internal Affairs assumed command of the military installations at Paldiski, a key naval base west of Tallinn, but the ex-Soviet navy was not due to leave until September 1994. A series of negotiations occurred in the latter half of 1993 between Russian representative Vasily Svirin and the Estonian representative Jüri Luik (who subsequently became Minister of Defence before his appointment as Minister of Foreign Affairs in January 1994), but these were inconclusive. On 15 November, however, in response to an appeal by the premiers of all three Baltic states, the UN General Assembly adopted a resolution demanding the 'early, orderly and complete withdrawal' of ex-Soviet troops from Latvia and Estonia. On 24 November the Russian delegation at the negotiations proposed that the forces withdraw from Estonia by the 31 August 1994, on the condition that Estonia provided US $23m. for the construction of housing for the retired servicemen.

THE SLAV MINORITY

A further cause of tension between Estonia and Russia was the status of ethnic minorities in the country. A citizenship law adopted on 6 November 1991, based on a law of 1938, only recognized individuals who had been citizens of Estonia prior to 1940, or their direct descendants. This ruling disqualified approximately three-quarters of the Russian-speaking population (estimated at over 500,000 in 1993) and provoked strong criticism from Russian leaders, who were concerned that the rights of the large Russian minority in Estonia were being violated. The requirements for naturalization were two years' residency, a knowledge of Estonian and an oath of loyalty. Further legislation, adopted on 6 April 1992, decreed that only citizens of Estonia could vote in national elections or stand as candidates. Since applicants for Estonian citizenship were obliged to wait one year before it was granted, this law effectively prevented ethnic Russian candidates from participating in the elections to the legislature to be held in September that year.

In late October 1992 Russian President Boris Yeltsin temporarily halted the withdrawal of ex-Soviet troops from Estonia as a gesture of support for ethnic Russians in the Baltic states. Hostility on the part of the Russian Federation towards the Estonian administration's treatment of minorities continued into 1993; in February Yury Luzhkov, the mayor of Moscow, announced that economic and commercial ties with Estonia would be suspended. On 13 May 1993, in a letter to the Secretary-General of the Council of Europe, Catherine Lalumière, the Russian Foreign Minister, Andrey Kozyrev, attempted to prevent Estonia's membership of the organization, on the grounds that its Government was depriving hundreds of thousands of people of citizenship.

On 16 June 1993 the Riigikogu passed a law which provided for the exclusive use of the Estonian language in schools (except at the elementary level) by the year 2000. However, the law was returned to the Riigikogu by President Meri and was not discussed further. On 19 June 1993, in the town of Narva in north-eastern Estonia (which, as well as the industrial towns of Kohtla-Järve and Sillimae, had a predominantly Russian population), several thousand Russian-speakers held a rally and threatened to take up arms if Russians were forced to leave the country. Two days later the Riigikogu adopted a law which stipulated that non-Estonians must apply for citizenship or for a residence permit before the end of 1995. Before the law was passed, most non-Estonian citizens were residing in Estonia with their Soviet registration (*propiska*). In response to the new legislation, President Yeltsin accused the Estonian Government of practising 'ethnic cleansing' and 'apartheid' and, on 25 June, the Russian Federation ceased to supply natural gas to Estonia, although it claimed that this was due to non-payment, rather than for political reasons. (Delivery of natural gas was resumed on 29 June.)

Following the unfavourable reaction to the law, it was suspended and submitted to the Conference on Security and Co-operation in Europe (CSCE) for approval. An amended version, in accordance with the CSCE's recommendations, was duly adopted on 12 July 1993 and was welcomed by the European Community (EC—known as the European Union from November 1993). Subsequently the Helsinki Watch human-rights organization and the UN Secretary General, Dr Boutros Boutros-Ghali, appealed for the language requirement of the law to be reduced. At home, opposition to the Government's policy on citizenship continued; on 16 and 17 July 1993 a referendum on autonomy took place in Narva and Sillimae. In Narva, out of the 54% of the population who participated, 97% voted in favour. In Sillimae 60% of inhabitants took part in the referendum, of which 95% supported autonomy. The Estonian administration refused to recognize the results, however, and the Supreme Court subsequently declared the referendum invalid, on the grounds that local governments did not have the right to conduct referendums, nor could they proclaim autonomy.

The Estonian Government did, however, make some concessions to the Russian-speaking population after the referendum on autonomy. On 6 July 1993 it registered the Representative Assembly, an organization representing the ethnic Russian community in Estonia. Moreover, following mediation by the CSCE High Commissioner on National Minorities, Max van der Stoel, the Government agreed to reconsider the language requirements for citizenship. For their part, representatives of the Russian-speaking population agreed to co-operate in negotiations on the issue. On 13 September a draft proposal was agreed which would grant special status to Narva, in the form of establishing a free economic zone in the region and allowing all residents over the age of 18 to vote. The negotiations and the relatively low level of participation in the referendum considerably reduced the threat of conflict in the region.

FOREIGN RELATIONS

Estonia's demand for the return of territories which had been ceded to Russia during the Soviet period was another factor which damaged Estonian–Russian relations. During 1992 inter-governmental talks were held on the issue, with Estonia insisting that the Russian–Estonian state border be determined by the terms of the Treaty of Tartu of 1920, as stated in its Constitution. The question remained unresolved during 1993.

Estonia actively pursued close relations with its Baltic neighbours, Latvia and Lithuania. In late 1991 the three states established a consultative interparliamentary body, the Baltic Assembly, with the aim of developing political and economic co-operation. In early 1992 it was agreed to abolish almost all trade restrictions between the three countries and to introduce a common visa policy. In November 1993, at the third session of the Baltic Assembly, it was decided that a Baltic Council would be established, comprising the Assembly and a Council of Ministers of the Baltic states.

Estonia also joined the 10-member Council of Baltic Sea States (established in March 1992). Estonia enjoyed cordial relations with Finland, with which it shared close cultural and linguistic ties. It became a member of the UN and the CSCE in September 1991 and of the Council of Europe in May 1993.

The Economy

Estonia's economy had traditionally been an agricultural one, but, owing to intensive industrialization under the Soviet administration in the 1950s and 1960s the importance of the agricultural sector significantly decreased. The country was rich in mineral resources, mainly oil shale but also phosphorite ore. By the early 1990s it had an open economy. In 1991, according to World Bank estimates, Estonia's gross national product (GNP), measured at average 1989–91 prices, was US $6,088m., equivalent to $3,830 per head. Estonia's gross domestic product (GDP) was estimated to have increased, in real terms, by an average of some 6% per year in the late 1980s. However, real GDP decreased by an estimated 12.6% in 1991, compared with the previous year, and by a further 26% in 1992. Statistics for the Estonian economy were not always reliable: those available during the Soviet period were often distorting, while the figures dating from the period of Estonia's transition to a market economy were also an unreliable indicator of the true economic condition of the country. Of the former Soviet territories, however, the Baltic states, particularly Estonia, made the most effective progress in the early 1990s. According to official figures, in the third quarter of 1993 Estonia's GDP was 6.4% higher than in the second quarter of that year: this represented the first increase in GDP since independence was restored.

AGRICULTURE

Agriculture (including forestry) contributed 15.6% of GDP in 1990, and provided 12.8% of employment in 1991. Some 30% of Estonia's land was cultivable. Animal husbandry (cattle, pigs, sheep and chickens) was the main activity in the agricultural sector. The principal crops were grain, potatoes and other vegetables. Grain production, according to official figures, amounted to 590,000 metric tons in 1992. In the same year 648,000 tons of potatoes were produced and 115,000 tons of vegetables. The large forests in Estonia provided resources for important timber-related industries, including wood-working and paper plants. By late 1991 more than 6,000 private farms had been established, while 160 collective and state farms continued to operate. Overall agricultural production declined by an estimated 21% in 1992, mainly as a result of problems in livestock rearing, owing to a decrease in imports of fodder and difficulties arising from the reorganization of state and collective farms.

INDUSTRY AND MINING

Industry was well-developed in Estonia. When it was part of the USSR the Republic was one of the largest producers of consumer goods in the Union. The industrial sector (including mining, quarrying, manufacturing, construction and power) contributed 46.8% of GDP in 1990, and provided 42.4% of employment in 1991. The manufacturing sector was dominated by machine-building, electronics and electrical engineering. Other light industries included textiles, fish- and food-processing and consumer goods. Industrial production was estimated to have declined by 32.4% in the first nine months of 1993, compared to the same period in the previous year. This was the result of the continuing problems of economic transition. The situation in the industrial sector was, however, expected to improve in 1994.

Estonia's mineral resources include an estimated 15,000m. metric tons of oil shale. An estimated 90% of oil shale produced is used in Estonia's two thermal electric power plants to generate electricity, approximately 50% of which is exported, mainly to Latvia and the Russian Federation. In 1980 extraction of oil shale reached 31m. tons but decreased to only 20m. tons in 1991. Phosphorite ore is processed to produce phosphates used in agriculture, but development of the industry has been accompanied by increasing environmental problems.

SERVICES

Estonia's services sector, accounting for 37.6% of GDP in 1990 and 44.8% of employment in 1991, was the most developed in the former USSR and was expected to adapt with relative ease to free-market conditions. In 1992 it was still principally state-owned, although the numbers of private enterprises in the tourism and retail sectors were rapidly increasing.

TRADE AND FINANCE

In 1991, according to Soviet statistics, Estonia recorded a trade surplus of 647.8m. roubles. Trade with Western countries, particularly Scandinavia and Finland, increased considerably in the early 1990s (before independence, Estonia's traditional trading partners had been other Republics of the USSR). In 1992 Estonia concluded an agreement to liberalize trade with Finland and similar agreements were expected to be concluded with the other member countries of the European Free Trade Association (EFTA). The Russian Federation, Ukraine and Germany were also important trading partners. In 1991 Estonia's principal exports were textiles, machinery, chemicals and food products. According to the International Monetary Fund (IMF), in 1991 Estonia recorded a surplus, of 972m. roubles, in its balance of payments. (A deficit had been recorded in the previous two years.) In the same year there was a surplus of 113m. roubles on the current account of the balance of payments.

In 1991 there was a budgetary surplus of 898.2m. roubles. In late 1991 Estonia had no external debt as its share of the former USSR's total external debt had not been agreed upon. The annual rate of inflation averaged 3.3% in 1980–89, rising to 17% in 1990 and to 202% in 1991. Consumer prices increased by an average rate of more than 1,000% in 1992. By May 1993, however, owing to a period of radical monetary reform, the rate of inflation had been reduced to 1.7%. Some 18,500 people (approximately 2% of Estonia's working population) were officially registered as unemployed in August 1993. Unemployment was reported to be affecting state enterprises more than private enterprises.

CONCLUSION

In the early 1990s Estonia, in common with its neighbours Latvia and Lithuania, was independent of the other former Soviet republics in its economic progress. Its traditional ties with Western, as opposed to Eastern, Europe, made it possible for Estonia to declare its economic independence from the USSR before its political independence. Furthermore, Estonia's close links with the Nordic countries, in particular Finland, increased foreign aid and investment following the country's full independence. In 1992 Estonia became a member of the IMF and the World Bank. It also joined the European Bank for Reconstruction and Development (EBRD). Estonia also hoped to expand economic contacts with the European Community (EC) and EFTA. In 1992 Estonia received financial aid from several international bodies. The EBRD granted Estonia an emergency loan of US $46.4m. to improve its energy supplies and efficiency. A further $29m. was granted by the World Bank, primarily for the energy, agricultural, transport and health sectors. The IMF approved $41m. in stand-by credits for a period of 12 months, to enable Estonia to continue its economic reforms, and the EC donated 10m. ECUs to aid privatization development, financial reforms and social-security benefits.

Even before it regained independence in mid-1991 Estonia had begun the transition to a market economic system, which included the nationalization of formerly Soviet-controlled enterprises and the establishment of a central bank as well as a private banking system. The collapse of the USSR and its internal economic system, however, resulted in serious economic difficulties. An annual decline in output was recorded in all sectors, and in 1991 Estonia's GDP decreased, in real terms, by 12.6%, with a further estimated fall of 26% in 1992. Consumer prices increased significantly (by about 200% in 1991 and 1,000% in 1992); the increased cost of petroleum and other raw materials imported from the Russian Federation was a particular problem. Nevertheless, following the introduction in June 1992 of the kroon as sole legal tender in Estonia, the granting of foreign aid and a series of comprehensive fiscal reforms, by 1993 Estonia had achieved relative economic stability. The arrival of a convertible currency in Estonia had helped to eliminate shortages of consumer goods and the process of privatization had considerably advanced (at the end of 1993 it was officially estimated that 80% of small state enterprises and 30 major concerns had been privatized). Economic conditions in Estonia were expected to improve in 1994.

Statistical Survey

Sources (unless otherwise stated): Department of Statistics, Endla 15, Tallinn 0106; tel. (2) 452-812; fax (2) 453-923; and IMF, *Estonia, Economic Review.*

Area and Population

AREA, POPULATION AND DENSITY

Area (sq km)	45,226*
Population (census result)	
12 January 1989	1,572,916
Population (official estimates at 1 January)†	
1991	1,570,390
1992	1,562,000
Density (per sq km) at 1 January 1992	34.5

* 17,462 sq miles.
† Figures refer to permanent inhabitants.

POPULATION BY NATIONALITY
(permanent inhabitants, census of 12 January 1989)

	Number	%
Estonian	963,281	61.5
Russian	474,834	30.3
Ukrainian	48,271	3.1
Belarussian	27,711	1.8
Finnish	16,622	1.1
Jewish	4,613	0.3
Tatar	4,058	0.3
German	3,466	0.2
Latvian	3,135	0.2
Polish	3,008	0.2
Others	16,663	1.1
Total	1,565,662	100.0

PRINCIPAL TOWNS
(estimated population at 1 January 1991)

Tallinn (capital)	497,766	Kohtla-Järve	75,031
Tartu	114,239	Pärnu	57,132
Narva	86,852		

BIRTHS AND DEATHS (per 1,000)

	1989	1990	1991
Birth rate	15.4	14.1	12.3
Death rate	11.7	12.3	12.6

EMPLOYMENT (state and co-operative sectors, '000 persons, excluding armed forces)

	1989	1990	1991
Agriculture, hunting, forestry and fishing	104.9	101.4	100.9
Mining and quarrying; Manufacturing; Electricity, gas and water	262.9	252.9	257.0
Construction	81.3	78.8	78.0
Trade, restaurants and hotels	73.1	69.5	69.0
Transport, storage and communications	68.2	68.3	67.5
Financing, insurance, real estate and business services	4.1	4.0	4.0
Community, social and pesonal services	200.8	199.3	198.5
Activities not adequately defined	16.2	15.0	15.1
Total	811.5	795.5	790.0

Source: ILO, *Year Book of Labour Statistics.*

Agriculture

PRINCIPAL CROPS ('000 metric tons)

	1990	1991	1992
Wheat	65	62	90
Barley	600	623	302
Rye	178	127	150
Oats	93	107	48
Potatoes	618	592	648
Tomatoes	11	9	8*
Cucumbers and gherkins	8	7	7*
Carrots	13	16	15*

* FAO estimate(s).
Source: FAO, *Production Yearbook.*

LIVESTOCK ('000 head)

	1990	1991	1992
Cattle	805	758	708
Pigs	1,080	960	799
Sheep	140	140	143
Chickens*	7,000	6,000	5,000

* Unofficial figure(s).

Source: FAO, *Production Yearbook*.

LIVESTOCK PRODUCTS
('000 metric tons, unless otherwise indicated)

	1990	1991	1992
Beaf and veal	80	64	60*
Mutton and lamb	3	2	2*
Pigmeat	115	95	90*
Poultry meat	22	22	23*
Cows milk	1,208	1,093	900†
Butter (metric tons)	29,446	28,408	26,309
Hen eggs (metric tons)†	30,640	31,340	24,100†
Honey (metric tons)	608	638	800*

* FAO estimate. † Unofficial figure(s).

Source: FAO, *Production Yearbook*.

Forestry

ROUNDWOOD REMOVALS ('000 cu m)

	1989	1990	1991
Total	2,538	1,693	1,653

SAWNWOOD PRODUCTION ('000 cu m)

	1989	1990	1991
Total	685	500	462

Fishing

('000 metric tons, live weight)

	1989	1990	1991
Total catch	401.6	370.1	317.4

Mining and Industry

SELECTED PRODUCTS

	1989	1990	1991
Peat ('000 metric tons)	216	201	195
Oil-shale (million metric tons)	23.3	22.4	19.6
Paper ('000 metric tons)	91.8	77.3	77.5
Excavators (number)	1,645	1,690	1,235
Electric energy ('000 million kWh)	17.6	17.1	14.6

Finance

CURRENCY AND EXCHANGE RATES

Monetary Units

100 cents = 1 kroon.

Sterling and Dollar Equivalents (30 September 1993)

£1 sterling = 19.604 kroons;
US $1 = 13.108 kroons;
1,000 kroons = £51.01 = $76.29.

Note: In June 1992 Estonia issued its own currency, the kroon, replacing the rouble of the former USSR, initially at a rate of one kroon per 10 roubles (for details of the rouble, see the chapter on the Russian Federation).

BUDGET (million roubles)*

Revenue	1989	1990	1991
Central government	2,308.1	2,472.5	3,064.4
Taxation	1,815.1	2,069.9	2,771.3
Taxes on income and profits	595.3	886.8	931.3
Taxes on property	—	—	16.4
Domestic taxes on goods and services	803.9	1,049.7	1,805.2
Taxes on international trade	40.6	90.1	18.4
Revenue transfers to USSR budget	375.3	43.3	—
Non-tax receipts	39.3	143.2	293.1
Transfers from USSR budget	453.7	259.4	—
Local government	232.0	375.4	1,969.8
Taxation	n.a.	n.a.	1,937.5
Taxes on income and profits	n.a.	n.a.	1,634.7
Taxes on property	n.a.	n.a.	97.0
Taxes on goods and services	n.a.	n.a.	201.8
Extrabudgetary funds	—	—	1,671.2
Taxation	—	—	1,576.5
Pollution tax	—	—	46.2
Social security tax	—	—	1,530.3
Forestry Fund receipts	—	—	66.3
Total	2,540.0	2,848.0	6,705.4

Expenditure	1989	1990	1991
Central government	1,813.7	1,927.6	1,700.5
Current expenditure	1,337.9	1,696.9	1,525.3
Goods and services	635.8	1,146.5	1,219.9
Subsidies and current transfers	702.1	550.3	305.4
Capital expenditure	261.5	230.7	175.2
Direct payments to USSR	214.3	—	—
Local government	543.3	689.2	1,952.4
Current expenditure	n.a.	n.a.	1,629.3
Capital expenditure	n.a.	n.a.	323.1
Extrabudgetary funds	—	—	2,154.3
Road Fund	—	—	173.3
Forestry Fund	—	—	85.5
Social Fund	—	—	1,722.4
Total	2,357.1	2,616.8	5,807.2

* Figures represent a consolidation of the operations of all Estonian government units, i.e. excluding transfers between different levels of government.

INTERNATIONAL RESERVES
(US $ million at 31 December, excluding gold)

	1992
IMF special drawing rights	10.62
Reserve position in IMF	—
Foreign exchange	193.69
Total	204.31

MONEY SUPPLY
(at 31 December; million roubles for 1991, million krooni for 1992)

	1991	1992
Currency outside banks	2,124	1,041
Demand deposits at banks	4,841	1,814

COST OF LIVING*
(Retail price index; base: 1980 = 100)

	1988	1989	1990
Food	128	133	168
Manufactured goods	128	136	148
All items	128	134	157

* Based on prices in state-controlled shops.

1991 (base: 1990 = 100): Food 333.0; Fuel and light 172.0; Clothing 272.8; Rent 100.0; All items (incl. others) 302.0. Source: ILO, *Year Book of Labour Statistics*.

NATIONAL ACCOUNTS (million roubles at current prices)

Expenditure on the Gross Domestic Product

	1988	1989	1990
Government final consumption expenditure	893	892	1,054
Private final consumption expenditure	3,517	3,869	5,141
Increase in stocks	204	247	516
Gross fixed capital formation	1,690	1,853	1,895
Total domestic expenditure	6,304	6,860	8,606
Exports of goods and services *Less* Imports of goods and services	−544	−437	−629
GDP in purchasers' values	5,759	6,422	7,977

Gross Domestic Product by Economic Activity

	1988	1989	1990
Agriculture and forestry	1,121.4	1,272.0	1,245.9
Industrial activity*	2,175.2	2,301.3	3,161.4
Construction	456.2	517.6	570.1
Transport and communications†	386.2	407.6	512.8
Other branches of the material sphere	434.1	516.2	644.2
Activities of the non-material sphere	1,186.2	1,407.7	1,842.5
Total	5,759.4	6,422.4	7,976.9

* Including mining, quarrying, manufacturing and the production of electricity and gas.

† Data refer only to goods transport and communications serving branches of material production.

BALANCE OF PAYMENTS (million roubles)

	1989	1990	1991
Trade with former republics of the USSR			
Exports	3,111	3,067	4,784
Merchandise trade	2,903	2,899	4,517
Retail trade	208	168	267
Imports	−3,231	−3,283	−3,617
Merchandise trade	−3,231	−3,227	−3,556
Retail trade	—	−56	−61
Trade balance	−120	−216	1,167
Services (net)	20	17	20
Trade with former CMEA countries, etc.			
Exports	64	50	17
Imports	−154	−156	−72
Trade balance	−90	−106	−54
Trade with the convertible currency area			
Exports	62	63	114
Imports	−164	−245	−276
Trade balance	−102	−182	−161
Balance on goods and services	−292	−487	972

1992 (US $ million): Merchandise exports f.o.b. 457; Merchandise imports f.o.b. −491; Trade balance −34; Net services 53; Net income −1; Net unrequited transfers 95; Current balance 113; Direct capital investment 58; Other capital (net) −51 (Source: IMF, *International Financial Statistics*).

External Trade

PRINCIPAL COMMODITIES (million roubles)

Imports	1990	1991
Vegetable products	261.4	448.5
Prepared foodstuffs, beverages, spirits, vinegar and tobacco	195.9	255.0
Mineral products	248.3	534.4
Products of the chemical or allied industries	456.3	323.8
Plastics, rubber and articles thereof	131.3	185.4
Wood pulp, paper and paperboard	68.5	81.8
Textiles and textile articles	787.7	848.2
Footwear, headgear, etc.	90.3	83.0
Pearls, precious or semi-precious stones, precious metals and articles thereof	41.1	152.2
Base metals and articles of base metal	303.0	328.9
Machinery (incl. electrical) and parts	432.9	622.9
Transport equipment	114.7	170.1
Miscellaneous manufactured articles	115.0	132.7
Total (incl. others)	3,416.1	4,454.5

Exports	1990	1991
Live animals and animal products	191.2	511.0
Animal or vegetable fats, oil and waxes	40.5	166.4
Prepared foodstuffs, beverages, spirits, vinegar and tobacco	290.8	208.9
Mineral products	83.5	265.9
Products of the chemical or allied industries	263.1	562.2
Plastics, rubber and articles thereof	114.3	242.3
Wood and cork products, etc.	26.1	113.8
Wood pulp, paper and paperboard	96.5	191.3
Textiles and textile articles	645.9	1,345.0
Footwear, headgear, etc.	79.4	95.1
Base metals and articles of base metal	64.8	108.2
Machinery (incl. electrical) and parts	265.4	590.5
Miscellaneous manufactured articles	250.9	381.6
Total (incl. others)	2,623.5	5,102.3

PRINCIPAL TRADING PARTNERS (million roubles)

Imports	1990	1991
Czechoslovakia	51.7	28.3
Finland	55.1	88.9
France	11.0	61.3
German Democratic Republic	66.2	—
India	47.8	46.0
USSR	2,802.8	3,775.4
Belarus	150.5	217.0
Georgia	31.3	63.3
Kazakhstan	52.2	108.7
Latvia	161.6	226.2
Lithuania	109.7	282.3
Moldova	89.0	105.2
Russia	1,768.3	2,045.4
Tajikistan	38.1	85.4
Turkmenistan	15.8	44.4
Ukraine	262.7	352.0
Uzbekistan	44.6	149.6
USA	30.2	157.1
Total (incl. others)	3,416.1	4,454.5

Exports	1990	1991
Finland	29.8	119.4
USSR	2,467.8	4,833.2
Armenia	37.4	62.8
Belarus	120.7	207.7
Georgia	29.8	53.9
Kazakhstan	101.2	128.2
Latvia	149.7	392.2
Lithuania	81.5	193.1
Moldova	48.6	74.7
Russia	1,443.7	2,883.5
Ukraine	345.0	655.9
Uzbekistan	47.5	90.1
Total (incl. others)	2,623.5	5,102.3

Transport

DOMESTIC PASSENGER TRAFFIC
(million passenger-kilometres)

	1989	1990	1991
Railway traffic	1,562	1,510	1,273
Road traffic (bus traffic)	4,516	4,454	3,833
Sea traffic	48	42	42
River traffic	6	6	3
Air traffic	1,261	1,244	1,046
Total public transport	7,393	7,256	6,197

DOMESTIC FREIGHT TRAFFIC (million ton-kilometres)

	1989	1990	1991
Railway traffic	7,609	6,977	6,545
Road traffic	2,319	2,097	1,662
Sea traffic	24,378	22,380	23,871
River traffic	5	2	1
Air traffic	9	8	6
Total public transport	34,320	31,464	32,085

ROAD TRAFFIC (motor vehicles in use at 31 December)

	1989	1990	1991
Passenger cars	222,094	241,664	261,086
Buses and coaches	n.a.	n.a.	8,628
Goods vehicles	n.a.	n.a.	58,877
Vans	n.a.	n.a.	18,180

Source: International Road Federation, *World Road Statistics*.

Tourism

	1991
Foreign tourist arrivals	237,944

Communications Media

	1989	1990	1991
Books published (titles)	2,070	1,628	1,654
Daily newspapers (number)	111	165	164

Education

(1991/92)

	Institutions	Students
Secondary schools	690	223,700
Vocational schools	50	18,058
Secondary specialized institutions	36	16,337
Higher schools (incl. universities)	10	25,643

Directory

The Constitution

A new Constitution, based on that of 1938, was adopted by a referendum held on 28 June 1992. The following is a summary of its main provisions:

FUNDAMENTAL RIGHTS, LIBERTIES AND DUTIES

Every child with one parent who is an Estonian citizen has the right, by birth, to Estonian citizenship. Anyone who, as a minor, lost his or her Estonian citizenship has the right to have his or her citizenship restored. The rights, liberties and duties of all persons, as listed in the Constitution, are equal for Estonian citizens as well as for citizens of foreign states and stateless persons who are present in Estonia.

All persons are equal before the law. No one may be discriminated against on the basis of nationality, race, colour, sex, language, origin, creed, political or other persuasions. Everyone has the right to the protection of the state and the law. Guaranteeing rights and liberties is the responsibility of the legislative, executive and judicial powers, as well as of local government. Everyone has the right to appeal to a court of law if his or her rights or liberties have been violated.

The state organizes vocational education and assists in finding work for persons seeking employment. Working conditions are under state supervision. Employers and employees may freely join unions and associations. Estonian citizens have the right to engage in commercial activities and to form profit-making associations. The property rights of everyone are inviolable. All persons legally present in Estonia have the right to freedom of movement and choice of abode. Everyone has the right to leave Estonia.

Everyone has the right to health care [and to] education. Education is compulsory for school-age children. Everyone has the right to instruction in Estonian.

The official language of state and local government authorities is Estonian. In localities where the language of the majorty of the population is other than Estonian, local government authorities may use the language of the majority of the permanent residents of that locality for internal communication.

THE PEOPLE

The people exercise their supreme power through citizens who have the right to vote by: i) electing the Riigikogu (legislature); ii) participating in referendums. The right to vote belongs to every Estonian citizen who has attained the age of 18 years.

THE RIIGIKOGU

Legislative power rests with the Riigikogu. It comprises 101 members, elected every four years in free elections on the principle of proportionality. Every citizen entitled to vote who has attained 21 years of age may be a candidate for the Riigikogu.

The Riigikogu adopts laws and resolutions; decides on the holding of referendums; elects the President of the Republic; ratifies or rejects foreign treaties; authorizes the candidate for Prime Minister to form the Council of Ministers; adopts the national budget and approves the report on its execution; may declare a state of emergency, or, on the proposal of the President, declare a state of war, order mobilization and demobilization.

The Riigikogu elects from among its members a Chairman (Speaker) and two Deputy Chairmen to direct the work of the Riigikogu.

THE PRESIDENT

The President of the Republic is the Head of State of Estonia. The President represents Estonia in international relations; appoints and recalls, on the proposal of the Government, diplomatic representatives of Estonia and accepts letters of credence of diplomatic representatives accredited to Estonia; declares regular (and early) elections to the Riigikogu; initiates amendments to the Constitution; nominates the candidate for the post of Prime Minister; and is the Supreme Commander of Estonia's armed forces.

The President is elected by secret ballot of the Riigikogu for a term of five years. No person may be elected to the office for more than two consecutive terms. Any Estonian citizen by birth, who is at least 40 years of age, may stand as a candidate for President.

Should the President not be elected after three rounds of voting, the Speaker of the Riigikogu convenes, within one month, an Electoral Body to elect the President.

THE GOVERNMENT

Executive power is held by the Government of the Republic (Council of Ministers). The Government implements national domestic and foreign policies; directs and co-ordinates the work of government institutions; organizes the implementation of legislation, the resolutions of the Riigikogu, and the edicts of the President; submits draft legislation to the Riigikogu, as well as foreign treaties; prepares a draft of the national budget and presents it to the Riigikogu; administers the implementation of the national budget; and organizes relations with foreign states.

The Government comprises the Prime Minister and Ministers. The President of the Republic nominates a candidate for Prime Minister, who is charged with forming a new government.

JUDICIAL SYSTEM

Justice is administered solely by the courts. They are independent in their work and administer justice in accordance with the Constitution and laws. The court system is comprised of rural and city, as well as administrative, courts (first level); district courts (second level); the National Court (the highest court in the land).

The Government

(January 1994)

HEAD OF STATE

President: LENNART MERI (elected 5 October 1992).

COUNCIL OF MINISTERS

A coalition of parties from the Pro Patria (Isamaa) and Moderates electoral alliances and the Estonian National Independence Party.

Prime Minister: MART LAAR.

Minister of the State Chancellery: ÜLO KAEVATS.

Minister of the Interior: HEIKI ARIKE.

Minister of Foreign Affairs: JÜRI LUIK.

Minister of Justice: KAIDO KAMA.

Minister of the Economy: TOIVO JÜRGENSON.

Minister of Finance: HEIKI KRANICH.

Minister of Transport and Communications: ANDI MEISTER.

Minister of the Environment: ANDRES TARAND.

Minister of Culture and Education: PAUL-EERIK RUMMO.

Minister of Agriculture: JAAN LEETSAAR.

Minister of Social Affairs: MARJU LAURISTIN.

Minister of Defence: INDREK KANNIK.

Ministers without Portfolio: PEETER OLESK, LIIA HÄNNI, ARVO NIITENBERG.

MINISTRIES

Office of the Prime Minister: Lossi 1A, Tallinn 0100; tel. (2) 316-701; fax (2) 440-372.

State Chancellery of the Republic of Estonia: Lossi 1A, Tallinn 0100; tel. (2) 316-730; fax (2) 440-372.

Ministry of Agriculture: Lai 39–41, Tallinn 0100; tel. (2) 441-166; telex 173216; fax (2) 440-601.

Ministry of Culture and Education: Tõnismägi 11, Tallinn 0106; tel. (2) 443-404; fax (2) 311-213.

Ministry of Defence: Pikk 57, Tallinn 0100; tel. (6) 444-125; fax 444-103.

Ministry of the Economy: Harju 11, Tallinn 0001; tel. (2) 440-577; fax (2) 446-860.

Ministry of the Environment: Toompuiestee 24, Tallinn 0110; tel. (2) 452-507; telex 173238; fax (2) 453-310.

Ministry of Finance: Suur-Ameerika 1, Tallinn 0100; tel. (2) 683-445; telex 173106; fax (2) 682-097.

Ministry of Foreign Affairs: Rävala 9, Tallinn 0100; tel. (6) 317-091; telex 173-269; fax (2) 771-677.

Ministry of the Interior: Pikk 61, Tallinn 0102; tel. (2) 663-611; fax (2) 602-785.

Ministry of Justice: Suur-Karja 19, Tallinn 0104; tel. (2) 445-120; fax (2) 246-235.

Ministry of Social Affairs: Gonsiori 29, Tallinn 0104; tel. (2) 423-434; fax (2) 421-862.

Ministry of Transport and Communications: Viru 9, Tallinn 0100; tel. (2) 397-613; fax (2) 397-606.

President and Legislature

PRESIDENT

Presidential Election, 20 September 1992

Candidates	Votes	%
ARNOLD RÜÜTEL	195,743	42.2
LENNART MERI	138,317	29.8
REIN TAAGEPERA	109,631	23.7
LAGLE PAREK	19,837	4.3

As none of the above candidates in the direct election of 20 September won an overall majorty of the votes, the Riigikogu was charged with electing the President from the two leading candidates. On 5 October it elected LENNART MERI to the post, by 59 votes to 31.

RIIGIKOGU

Speaker: ÜLO NUGIS.

Deputy Speakers: TUNNE KELAM, EDGAR SAVISAAR.

General Election, 20 September 1992

Parties and Coalitions	Seats
Pro Patria (Fatherland or Isamaa)	29
Secure Home	17
Popular Front	15
Moderates	12
Estonian National Independence Party (ENIP)	10
Estonian Citizen	8
Independent Royalists	8
Greens	1
Estonian Entrepreneurs' Party	1
Total	101

Local Government

For administrative purposes, Estonia is divided into 15 counties (maakonds) and six cities. Each maakond is presided over by a county government (headed by a governor) and a county council. There is also a city council and a city government, the latter headed by a mayor. Local authority elections were held on 17 October 1993.

Harju County Government: Harju Maavalitsus, Roosikrantsi 12, Tallinn 0103; tel. (2) 442-351; Gov. MATI ZERNAND.

Hiiu County Government: Hiiu Maavalitsus, Leigri 5, Kärdla 3200; tel. (46) 91-362; fax (46) 91-030; Gov. TARMO MÄND.

Ida-Viru County Government: Ida-Viru Maavalitsus, Kesk 1, Jõhvi 2045; tel. (33) 22-352; fax (33) 22-054; Gov. MÄRT MARITS.

Järva County Government: Järva Maavalitsus, Pikk 2, Paide 2820; tel. (38) 21-254; fax (38) 41-764; Gov. ARVO SARAPUU.

Jõgeva County Government: Jõgeva Maavalitsus, Suur 3, Jõgeva 2350; tel. (37) 21-956; fax (37) 21-630; Gov. PRIIT SAKSING.

Lääne County Government: Lääne Maavalitsus, Lahe 8, Haapsalu 3170; tel. and fax (47) 56-801; Gov. ANDRES LIPSTOK.

Lääne-Viru County Government: Lääne-Viru Maavalitsus, Kreutzvaldi 5, Rakvere 2100; tel. (32) 43-504; fax (32) 44-384; Gov. ANTS LEEMETS.

Pärnu County Government: Pärnu Maavalitsus, Akadeemia 2, Pärnu 3600; tel. (44) 40-193; Gov. REIN KIRS.

Põlvamaa County Government: Põlvamaa Maavalitsus, Kesk 20, Põlva 2600; tel. (30) 95-484; Gov. KALEV KREEGIPUU.

Rapla County Government: Rapla Maavalitsus, Tallinn 14, Rapla 3500; tel. (48) 55-686; fax (48) 55-672; Gov. KALLE TALVISTE.

Saare County Government: Saare Maavalitsus, Lossi 1, Kuressaare 3300; tel. (45) 54-242; fax (45) 57-448; Gov. JÜRI SAAR.

Tartu County Government: Tartu Maavalitsus, Riia 15, Tartu 2400; tel. (34) 31-384; fax (34) 31-628; Gov. KALJU KOHA.

Valga County Government: Valga Maavalitsus, Vabaduse 15, Valga 2500; tel. (42) 43-229; fax (42) 42-721; Gov. UNO HEINLA.

Viljandi County Government: Viljandi Maavalitsus, Vabaduse 2, Viljandi 2900; tel. (43) 53-202; fax (43) 53-039; Gov. REIN TRIISA.

Võru County Government: Võru Maavalitsus, Jüri 12, Võru 2710; tel. (41) 21-466; fax (41) 21-015; Gov. EINAR RANNIT.

Kohtla-Järve City Government: Kohtla-Järve Linnavalitsus, Kesk 19, Kohtla-Järve 2020; tel. (33) 47-863; fax (33) 47-218; Mayor AIN KALMARU.

Narva City Government: Narva Linnavalitsus, Peetri 5, Narva 2000; tel. (35) 22-552; fax (35) 22-555; Mayor VLADIMIR MIZHUI.

Pärnu City Government: Pärnu Linnavalitsus, Uus 4, Pärnu 3600; tel. (44) 41-656; fax (44) 43-019; Mayor REIN KASK.

Sillimae City Government: Sillimae Linnavalitsus, Kirovi 27, Sillimae 2010; tel. (49) 73-452; fax (49) 75-887; Mayor VITALY MENSHIKOV.

Tallinn City Government: Tallinn Linnavalitsus, Vabaduse 7, Tallinn 0001; tel. (2) 444-955; fax (2) 451-572; Mayor JAAK TAMM.

Tartu City Government: Tartu Linnavalitsus, Raekoda, Tartu 2400; tel. (34) 33-128; fax (34) 31-466; Mayor ANTS VEETÕUSME.

Political Organizations

Baltic Organization of Young Democrats: Tallinn; f. 1993; right-wing youth; Chair. KEN-MARTI VAHER.

Consolidation Party: Tallinn.

Estonian Democratic Labour Party (Eesti Demokraatlik Tööpartei): Kentmanni 13, Tallinn 0001; tel. (2) 445-118; fax (2) 448-554; f. 1920 as the Communist Party of Estonia; renamed as above 1992; Leader HILLAR ELLER; 2,000 mems (1992).

Estonian Entrepreneurs' Party (Eesti Ettevõtjate Erakond): Pikk 68, Tallinn 0001; tel. (2) 609-620; f. 1990; Chair. TIIT MADE.

Estonian Green Movement/Friends of the Earth Estonia (Eesti Roheline Liikumine): POB 318, Tartu 2400; tel. (34) 62-532; fax (34) 62-084; f. 1988; campaigns on environmental issues; Chair. TÕNU OJA.

Estonian National Independence Party (ENIP) (Eesti Rahvusliku Söltumatuse Partei): Piiskopi 2, Tallinn 0001; tel. (2) 445-421; fax (2) 452-864; f. 1988; Chair. TUNNE KELAM.

Estonian National Progressive Party: Tallinn; f. 1993; Chair. ANTS ERM.

Estonian Royalist Party: Tallinn; registered 1993.

Estonian Rural Centre Party (Eesti Maa-Keskerakond): Rahukohtu 1, Tallinn 0001; tel. (2) 316-651; fax (2) 449-865; f. 1990; Chair. IVAR RAIG.

Estonian Social Democratic Party (Eesti Sotsiaaldemokraatlik Partei): POB 3437, Tallinn 0090; tel. (2) 443-038; telex 173831; fax (2) 444-902; f. 1990; mem. of Socialist International; Chair. MARJU LAURISTIN.

Isamaa—National Fatherland Party: Rahukohtu 1-33, Tallinn 0100; tel. (2) 606-463; fax (2) 426-389; f. 1992 by merger of four of the five parties of the Isamaa electoral alliance; Chair. MART LAAR.

Russian Democratic Movement: Tallinn; Chair. ALEKSEY SEMENOV.

Diplomatic Representation

EMBASSIES IN ESTONIA

Denmark: Rävala 9, Tallinn 0001; tel. (2) 691-494; telex 173262; fax (2) 337-353; Ambassador: SVEN ERIK NORDBERG.

Finland: Liivalaia 12, Tallinn 0001; tel. (2) 455-903; fax (2) 455-658; Ambassador: JAAKKO KAURINKOSKI.

France: Toom-Kuninga 20, Tallinn 0001; tel. (2) 453-784; fax (2) 453-688; Ambassador: JACQUES HUNTZINGER.

Germany: Rävala 9, Floor 7, Tallinn 0100; tel. (2) 691-472; Ambassador: HENNING VON WISTINGHAUSEN.

Italy: Müürivahe 3, Tallinn 0001; tel. (2) 445-919; Ambassador: CARLO SIANO.

Latvia: Tõnismägi 10, Tallinn 0001; tel. and fax (2) 681-668; Chargé d'affaires a.i.: ALDIS BERZIŅŠ.

Lithuania: Vabaduse 10, Tallinn 0001; tel. (2) 448-917; Chargé d'affaires: DEIVIDAS MATULIONIS.

Norway: Pärnu 8, Tallinn 0100; tel. (2) 441-680; Ambassador: BRIT LØVSETH.

Russian Federation: Pikk 19, Tallinn 0100; tel. (2) 443-014; fax (2) 443-773; Ambassador: ALEKSANDR TROFIMOV.

Sweden: Endla 4A, Tallinn 0001; tel. (2) 450-350; telex 173124; fax (2) 450-676; Ambassador: LARS ARNE GRUNDBERG.

United Kingdom: Kentmanni 20, Tallinn 0001; tel. (2) 455-328; telex 173974; Ambassador: BRIAN B. LOW.

USA: Kentmanni 20, Tallinn 0001; tel. (2) 298-110; fax (2) 306-817; Ambassador: ROBERT C. FRASURE.

Judicial System

National Court: Lossi 17, Tartu 2400; tel. (72) 41-411; Chair. RAIT MARUSTE.

Public Prosecutor's Office: Wismari 7, Tallinn 0103; tel. (2) 445-226; Prosecutor-General INDREK MEELAK.

Religion

CHRISTIANITY

Protestant Churches

Association of the Estonian Evangelical Christian Baptist Communities: Pargi 9, Tallinn 0016; tel. (2) 513-005; Chair. ÜLO MERILO.

Consistory of the Evangelical Lutheran Church of Estonia: Kiriku 8, Tallinn 0106; tel. (2) 451-682; fax (2) 601-876; Archbishop KUNO PAJULA.

Estonian Conference of Seventh-day Adventists: Lille 18, Tartu 2400; tel. and fax (34) 33-924; f. 1920; Chair. TÕNU JUGAR.

Methodist Church of Estonia: Apteegi 3, Tallinn 0001; tel. (2) 499-246; f. 1907; Superintendent OLAV PÄRNAMETS.

The Eastern Orthodox Church

Council of the Estonian Orthodox Church: Pikk 64/4, Tallinn 0001; tel. (2) 601-747; Bishop KORNELIUS.

The Press

In 1991 there were 158 officially-registered newspapers being published in Estonia, including 113 in Estonian, and 327 periodicals, including 265 in Estonian.

PRINCIPAL NEWSPAPERS

In Estonian except where otherwise stated.

Äripäev (Daily Business): Raua 1A, Tallinn 0010; tel. (2) 431-201; fax (2) 426-700; f. 1989; business and finance; Editor-in-Chief PEETER RAIDLA; circ. 25,000.

The Baltic Independent: Pärnu 67A, Tallinn 0090; tel. (2) 683-074; telex 173193; fax (6) 311-232; f. 1990; weekly; political, business and cultural affairs, features; in English; Editor TARMU TAMMERK; circ. 8,500.

Eesti Ekspress (Estonian Express): Tatari 25, Tallinn 0001; tel. (2) 683-057; fax (2) 681-488; f. 1989; weekly; Editor-in-Chief HANS LUIK; circ. 42,000.

Eesti Elu (Estonian Life): Narva 5, POB 51, Tallinn 0090; tel. (2) 445-466; fax (2) 449-558; f. 1989; twice monthly; political, economic and cultural affairs; in Estonian and English; Editor-in-Chief ANN MUST; circ. 6,500–11,000.

Estonia: Pärnu 67A, Tallinn 0090; tel. (2) 681-178; fax (2) 681-167; f. 1940; six days a week; in Russian; Editor-in-Chief VYACHESLAV IVANOV; circ. 20,000.

Hommikuleht (Morning Paper): Tallinn; f. 1992; Editor-in-Chief ENNO TAMMER.

Maaleht (Land): Toompuiestee 16, Tallinn 0106; tel. (2) 453-521; fax (2) 452-902; f. 1987; weekly; problems and aspects of politics, culture, agriculture and country life; Editor-in-Chief RAUL KILGAS; circ. 70,000.

Õhtuleht (Evening Gazette): Pärnu 67A, Tallinn 0090; tel. (2) 681-154; fax (2) 441-924; f. 1944; daily; in Estonian and Russian; Editor-in-Chief TÕNIS ERILAID; circ. 50,000 (in Estonian), 20,000 (in Russian).

Päevaleht (Daily): POB 432, Pärnu 67A, Tallinn 0090; tel. (2) 681-235; fax (2) 442-762; f. 1905; daily; Editor-in-Chief PEEP KALA; circ. 30,000.

Postimees (Postman): Gildi 1, Tartu 2400; tel. (34) 33-353; fax (34) 33-348; f. 1857; daily; Editor-in-Chief VAHUR KALMRE; circ. 100,000.

Pühapaevaleht (Sunday Paper): POB 432, Pärnu 67A, Tallinn 0090; tel. (2) 681-235; fax (2) 442-762; f. 1992; weekly; Editor-in-Chief TOOMAS LIIV; circ. 33,000.

Rahva Hääl (Voice of the People): Pärnu 67A, Tallinn 0090; tel. (2) 681-202; fax (2) 448-534; f. 1940; daily; privately owned; Editor-in-Chief TOOMAS LEITO; circ. 70,000.

Sirp (Sickle): Toompuiestee 30, Tallinn 0031; tel. (2) 601-703; fax (2) 601-883; f. 1940; fmrly *Reede* (Friday); weekly; cultural affairs; Editor-in-Chief TOOMAS KALL; circ. 10,000.

PRINCIPAL PERIODICALS

Akadeemia: Küütri 1, Tartu 2400; tel. (34) 31-117; fax (34) 31-373; f. 1989; monthly; journal of the Union of Writers; Editor-in-Chief AIN KAALEP; circ. 3,400.

Eesti Loodus (Estonian Nature): Veski 4, Tartu 2400; tel. (34) 32-368; f. 1933; monthly; popular science; illustrated; Editor-in-Chief AIN RAITVIIR; circ. 8,000.

Eesti Naine (Estonian Woman): Pärnu 67A, Tallinn 0007; tel. and fax (2) 681-310; f. 1924; monthly; Editor-in-Chief AIMI PAALANDI; circ. 35,000.

Horisont (Horizon): Narva 5, Tallinn 0001; tel. (2) 437-771; fax (2) 437-722; f. 1967; 8 a year; publ. by Horisont; popular scientific; Editor-in-Chief INDREK ROHTMETS; circ. 5,200.

Keel ja Kirjandus (Language and Literature): Roosikrantsi 6, Tallinn 0100; tel. (2) 449-228; f. 1958; monthly; publ. by the Perioodika (Periodicals) Publishing House; joint edition of the Academy of Sciences and the Union of Writers; Editor-in-Chief AKSEL TAMM; circ. 1,400.

Kultuur ja Elu (Culture and Life): Narva 5, POB 51, Tallinn 0090; tel. (2) 442-900; fax (2) 449 558; f. 1958; monthly; publ. by the Perioodika (Periodicals) Publishing House; Estonian history, cultural affairs, memoirs, biographies, travel; Editor-in-Chief SIRJE ENDRE; circ. 3,300.

Linguistica Uralica: Roosikrantsi 6, Tallinn 0106; tel. (2) 440-745; f. 1965; Editor-in-Chief PAUL KOKLA; circ. 1,000.

Looming (Creation): Harju 1, Tallinn 0090; tel. (2) 441-365; f. 1923; publ. by the Perioodika (Periodicals) Publishing House; journal of the Union of Writers; fiction, poetry, literary criticism; Editor-in-Chief ANDRES LANGEMETS; circ. 5,200.

Loomingu Raamatukogu (Library of Creativity): Harju 1, Tallinn 0001; tel. (2) 449-254; f. 1957; publ. by the Perioodika (Periodicals) Publishing House; journal of the Union of Writers; poetry, fiction and non-fiction by Estonian and foreign authors; Editor-in-Chief AGU SISASK; circ. 6,000.

Noorus (Youth): Pärnu 67A, Tallinn 0007; tel. (2) 681-324; f. 1946; monthly; youth issues, contemporary life in Estonia; short stories, novels, poems, essays, etc.; Editor-in-Chief LINDA JÄRVE; circ. 27,000.

Oil Shale: Akadeemia 15, Tallinn 0026; tel. (2) 537-084; telex 173487; fax (2) 536-371; f. 1984; 4 a year; geology, mining, oil shale industry; Editor-in-Chief ILMAR ÖPIK; circ. 1,000.

Täheke (Little Star): Pärnu 67A, Tallinn 0007; tel. (2) 681-497; f. 1960; illustrated; for 6–10-year-olds; Chief Editor ELJU MARDI; circ. 22,000.

Teater, Muusika, Kino (Theatre, Music, Cinema): POB 3200, Narva 5, Tallinn 0001; tel. (2) 440-472; fax (2) 434-172; f. 1982; monthly; Editor-in-Chief MART KUBO; circ. 4,000.

Vikerkaar (Rainbow): Toompuiestee 30, Tallinn 0031; tel. (2) 601-858; fax (2) 442-484; f. 1986; monthly; publ. by the Perioodika (Periodicals) Publishing House; fiction, poetry, critical works; in Estonian and Russian; Editor-in-Chief TOIVO TASA; circ. 5,000.

NEWS AGENCY

ETA (Estonian Telegraph Agency): Pärnu 67A, Tallinn 0090; tel. (2) 681-301; telex 173193; fax (2) 441-483; f 1918; Dir PEETER TALI.

PRESS ASSOCIATION

Estonian Journalists' Union: Narva 30, Tallinn 0010; tel. (2) 443-889; (2) fax (2) 433-585; f. 1919; Chair. MÄRT MÜÜR.

Publishers

Eesti Raamat (Estonian Book): Pärnu 10, Tallinn 0090; tel. (2) 443-937; f. 1940; fiction; Dir ROMAN SIIRAK.

Estonian Encyclopaedia Publishers Ltd: Pärnu 10, Tallinn 0090; tel. (2) 449-469; fax (2) 445-720; f. 1991; Chair. of Bd TÕNU KOGER.

Huma: Pikk 2, Tallinn 0001; tel. (2) 440-955; history, tourism, maps; Dir URMAS KAUP.

Koolibri: Pärnu 10, Tallinn 0090; tel. (2) 445-223; fax (2) 446-813; f. 1991; textbooks, dictionaries, children's books; Dir ANTS LANG.

Kunst (Fine Art): Lai 34, Tallinn 0001; tel. (2) 602-035; fax (2) 443-542; f. 1957; fine arts, fiction, tourism, children's books; Dir SIRJE HELME.

Kupar: Pärnu 67A, Tallinn 0007; tel. (2) 681-257; fax (2) 442-522; f. 1987; Man. Dir IVO SANDRE.

Olion: Pikk 2, Tallinn 0090; tel. (2) 445-403; f. 1989; politics, economics, history, law; Dir HEINO KÄÄN.

Perioodika (Periodicals): Pärnu 8, Tallinn 0090; tel. (2) 441-262; fax (2) 442-484; f. 1964; newspapers, guidebooks, periodicals, politics, children's books in foreign languages; Dir UNO SILLAJÕE.

Valgus: Pärnu 10, Tallinn 0090; tel. (2) 443-702; fax (2) 445-197; f. 1965; Dir ARVO HEINING.

Radio and Television

Eesti Raadio (Estonian Broadcasting Co): Gonsiori 21, Tallinn 0100; tel. (2) 434-115; fax (2) 434-457; regular broadcasts since 1926; four programmes (three in Estonian, one in Russian and for minority groups in Ukrainian, Belarusian); external broadcasts in Finnish, Swedish, English and German; Dir-Gen. HERKKI HALDRE.

Eesti Televisioon (Estonian Television): Faehlmanni 12, Tallinn 0100; tel. (2) 434-113; telex 173271; fax (2) 434-155; regular transmissions since 1955; four channels; programmes in Estonian and Russian; Dir-Gen. HAGI SEIN.

Finance

(cap. = capital; dep. = deposits; m. = million; brs = branches; amounts in kroons, unless otherwise stated)

BANKING

Central Bank

Eesti Pank (Bank of Estonia): Estonia 13, Tallinn 0100; tel. (2) 445-331; telex 173146; fax (2) 443-395; f. 1989; central bank of Estonia; cap. 30.9m.; Pres. SIIM KALLAS.

Commercial Banks

In late 1991 there were more than 20 commercial banks operating in Estonia.

Bank of Tallinn: Vabaduse 10, Tallinn; tel. (2) 666-741; fax (2) 449-983; f. 1990; Exec. Dir JURI TRUMM.

Esttexpank Commercial Bank: Sakala 1, Tallinn 0100; tel. (2) 666-657; telex 173067; fax (2) 444-102; f. 1989; cap. 7.5m., dep. 37m.; Chair. MART SILD; 6 brs.

EVEA Bank—Commercial Bank of the Estonian Small Business Association: Narva 40, Tallinn 0100; tel. (2) 422-122; telex 173184; fax (2) 312-063; f. 1989; cap. 10m., dep. 39.3m. (July 1993); Chair. of Bd BORIS SHPUNGIN; 7 brs.

Estonian Commercial Bank of Industry and Construction: Suur-Karja 7, Tallinn 0001; tel. (2) 442-410; telex 173157; fax (2) 440-495; f. 1990; cap. 12.4m., dep. 206.4m. (Aug. 1993); Chair. of Bd ALEKSANDR GELLART; 6 brs.

Estonian Social Bank Ltd (As Eesti Sotsiaalpank): Tartu 17, Tallinn 0100; tel. (2) 433-028; telex 173139; fax (2) 397-574; f. 1990; cap. 41.1m., dep. 633.8m. (Aug. 1993); Chair. of Bd REIN MILLER; 7 brs.

Land Bank of Estonia: Estonia 11, Tallinn 0100; tel. (2) 441-797; fax (2) 454-244; f. 1990; cap. 6.53m., dep. 75.8m.; Pres. HARRY-ELMAR VOLMER; 5 brs.

South Estonian Development Bank: Kesk 42, Põlva 2600, tel. (01430) 96-239; f. 1990; Man. TOOMAS LEHISTE.

West Estonian Bank: Karja 27, Haapsalu 3170; tel. (01447) 44-091; fax (01447) 45-076; f. 1990; cap. US $500,000, dep. US $2m.; Dir AARE SOOSAAR; 30 brs.

Savings Bank

Estonian Savings Bank (Eesti Hoiupank): Kinga 1, Tallinn 0001; tel. (2) 441-758; telex 173076; fax (2) 442-840; f. 1927; Chair. OLARI TAAL; 432 brs.

STOCK EXCHANGE

Estonian Stock Exchange (Eesti Börss): Sakala 1, Tallinn 0001; tel. (2) 455-020; fax (2) 449-382.

Trade and Industry

CHAMBERS OF COMMERCE

Estonian Chamber of Commerce and Industry: Toom-Kooli 17, Tallinn 0106; f. 1925; tel. (2) 444-929; telex 173254; fax (2) 443-656; Pres. PEETER TAMMOJA.

Tartu Chamber of Commerce and Industry: Raekoja 12, Tartu 2400; tel. and fax (2) 432-991; telex 173245; Man. Dir THOMAS HANSSON.

FOREIGN TRADE ORGANIZATION

Estimpex: Uus 32–34, Tallinn 0001; tel. (2) 601-462; telex 173288; fax (2) 602-184; f. 1987; Man. Dir MÄRT KRAFT.

INDUSTRIAL ASSOCIATION

Estonian Small Business Association (EVEA): Gonsiori 29–130, Tallinn 0104; tel. (2) 423-400; fax (2) 422-279; f. 1988; Man. Dir ARNE SÕNA.

MAJOR INDUSTRIAL COMPANIES

Ahtme Building Materials Plant: Ahtme, Kohtla-Järve 2020; tel. (33) 22-405; concrete, lime and gypsum building components; Man. Dir ALEKSANDR VOROBYOV.

Aseri Ceramics Works: Tehase 1, Aseri, Ida-Virumaa 2043; tel. 51-382; bricks, roofing tiles and other building materials; Man. Dir IVO TOMERI.

Balti Manufaktuur: Kopli 35, Tallinn 0090; tel. (2) 493-511; fax (2) 444-126; cotton yarns, materials and fabrics; Man. Dir JAAGU KURG.

Desintegraator: Peterburgi 71, Tallinn 0014; tel. (2) 211-001; telex 173214; fax (2) 211-008; f. 1974; design and production of disintegrators and associated machinery; Man. Dir JURI EELMA; 100 employees.

Eesti Fosforiit: Fosforiidi 4, Maardu 0901; tel. 234-146; phosphorite mining; production of phosphorous and mixed fertilizers; Man. Dir ALEKSANDR REVKUTS.

Eksi A/S: Joe 4, Tallinn 0010; tel. (2) 435-846; fax (2) 422-049; copper and aluminium wires and cables; Man. Dir VALERY MALYSHKO.

Estonian Fuel: Tallinn; state-owned; Chair. (vacant).

Estonian Oil Shale Company: Jaama 10, Kohtla-Järve 2045; tel. (33) 94-645; fax (33) 26-654; fmrly Eesti Põlevkivi Production Assoc., renamed 1991; oil-shale mining and refining; Gen. Dir VÄINO VIILUP; 10,000 employees.

Estel: Telliskivi 6, Tallinn 0110; tel. (2) 495-410; telex 179234; fax (2) 495-489; development and manufacture of semiconductors and converters; Man. Dir VLADIMIR MIROSHNICHENKO.

Flora: Tulika 19, Tallinn 0109; tel. (2) 472-448; telex 173256; fax (2) 491-021; paints and other household chemicals; Man. Dir ELMAR KRUUSMA.

Ilmarine: Mustamäe 5, Tallinn 0108; tel. (2) 495-000; fax (2) 496-062; manufacture of equipment for industrial boilers; household goods; Man. Dir TOOMAS TALVING.

Kohtla-Järve Oil-Shale Chemicals Production Association: Narva 14, Kohtla-Järve 2020; tel. (33) 44-545; oil-shale gas and oil; Man. Dir NIKOLAY KUTASHOV.

Oru Peat Works: Oru, Ida-Virumaa 2020; tel. 27-141; production of peat, etc.; Man. Dir ANATOLY LEPETKIN.

Talleks: Mustamäe 12, Tallinn 0100; tel. (2) 449-048; telex 173201; fax (2) 498-285; produces excavators, cast-iron goods; Man. Dir PAUL TREIER.

Tallinn Engineering Plant: Kopli 68, Tallinn 0110; tel. (2) 444-621; fax (2) 444-621; Man. Dir ALEKSEY MOROZ.

Tallinn Pulp and Paper Mill: Masina 20, Tallinn 0104; tel. (2) 424-477; fax (2) 424-303; paper, pulp, etc.; Man. Dir ERNST VAHER.

Tootsi Ltd: Tootsi, Pärnumaa 3470; tel. (44) 66-221; fax (44) 43-554; f. 1971; peat, peat briquets and other peat products; Man. Dir KAI MÄELEHT; 450 employees.

Vasar: Pärnu 139C, Tallinn 0013; tel. (2) 555-143; telex 173166; fax (2) 557-596; manufactures cooling equipment and components; boilers and radiators; Man. Dir ANTS VIIGISALU.

VGT Ltd: Kreutzwaldi 59, Võru 2710; tel. (41) 21-521; fax (41) 21-651; monitoring and control equipment; Man. Dir EINAR KUUSE.

Vihur: Veerenni 56, Tallinn 0013; tel. (2) 558-900; f. 1974; electronics; Man. Dir TAIVO TANDRE; 100 employees.

Volta: Tööstuse 47, Tallinn 0110; tel. (2) 446-002; production of motors and electric radiators; Man. Dir BORIS CHURIKOV.

Võit: Kalmistu 21/23, Tartu 2400; tel. (34) 32-808; farming and forestry machinery; Man. Dir KALJU KALJUSTE.

TRADE UNIONS

Estonian Trade Union Head Office: Tartu 4, Tallinn 0100; tel. (2) 425-100; Chair RAIVO PAAVO.

Transport

RAILWAYS

In 1991 there were 1,026 km of railway track in use, of which 132 km were electrified. Main lines linked Tallinn with Narva and St Petersburg (Russia), Tartu and Pskov (Russia), and Pärnu and Riga (Latvia).

ROADS

In 1992 Estonia had 14,797 km of roads, of which 1,135 km were highways and 2,618 km secondary roads.

Roads Administration: Pärnu 24, Tallinn 0001; tel. (2) 445-829; fax (2) 440-357; Gen. Dir JURI RIIMAA.

SHIPPING

Tallinn is the main port for freight transportation. There are regular passenger services between Tallinn and Helsinki (Finland). A service between Tallinn and Stockholm (Sweden) was inaugurated in 1991.

National Maritime Board: Tartu 13, Tallinn 0105; tel. (2) 430-202; telex 173027; fax (2) 425-720; f. 1990; Gen. Dir Capt. TARMO OJAMETS.

Shipowning Company

Estonian Shipping Company Ltd: Estonia 3/5, Tallinn 0101; tel. (2) 443-802; telex 173272; fax (2) 424-958; f. 1992; Gen. Dir TOIVO NINNAS.

CIVIL AVIATION

Estonia has air links with most major cities in the former USSR and with several Western European destinations.

Estonian Civil Aviation Administration: Tartu 13, Tallinn 0105; tel. (2) 424-530; telex 173081; fax (2) 421-235; f. 1990; Dir Gen. MATI SÕRMUS.

Tourism

Estonia has a wide range of attractions for tourists, including the historic towns of Tallinn and Tartu, extensive nature reserves and coastal resorts. In 1990 the National Tourist Board was established to develop facilities for tourism in Estonia. In 1991 there were 237,944 visitors to Estonia.

Estonian Association of Travel Agents: Pikk 71, Tallinn 0101; tel. (2) 425-594; fax (2) 425-594; Pres. DAISI JÄRVA.

Estonian Marine Tourism Association: Pikk 71, Tallinn 0001; tel. (2) 601-356; fax (2) 440-533; f. 1990; Man. Dir HELLE HALLIKA.

National Tourist Board: Pikk 71, Tallinn 0001; tel. (2) 601-700; fax (2) 602-743; f. 1990; Gen. Dir SILVI BLJUMOVITS.

Culture

NATIONAL ORGANIZATIONS

Ministry of Culture and Education: see section on The Government (Ministries).

National Language Board: Roosikrantsi 6, Tallinn 0106; tel. (2) 446-906; f. 1990; fmrly Dept of Language; govt agency established to promote use of Estonian language; Gen. Dir MÄRT RANNUT.

Central Board of Antiquities: Us 18, Tallinn 0001; tel. and fax (2) 440-704; Dir Gen. JAAN TAMM.

INTERNATIONAL ORGANIZATIONS

Estonian National Commission for UNESCO: Suur-Karja 23, Tallinn 0001; tel. (2) 441-431; fax (6) 313-757; Sec.-Gen. DORIS KAREVA.

International Council of Folklore and Traditional Arts—Estonian Section (CIOFF-Estonia): Suur-Karja 23, Tallinn 0001; tel. (2) 442-927; fax (2) 313-486; Pres. INGRID RÜÜTEL.

International Council of Monuments and Sites—Estonian Committee (ICOMOS Eesti Rahvuskomitee): Pikk 46, Tallinn 0001; tel. and fax (2) 449-216.

International Council of Museums—Estonian Committee (ICOM Eesti Rahvuskomitee): Pikk 17, Tallinn 0001; tel. (2) 443-446; fax (2) 601-275.

International Music Council of UNESCO—Estonian Music Council: Vabaduse 130, Tallinn 0009; tel. (2) 446-645; (2) 313-486; Pres. Prof. LEO NORMET.

CULTURAL HERITAGE

Art Museum of Estonia: Kiriku 1, Tallinn 0103; tel. (2) 449-340; f. 1919; Dir MARIKA VALK.

Estonian Historical Archives: Liivi 4, Tartu 2484; tel. (34) 32-482; f. 1921; Dir ENN KÜNG.

Estonian History Museum: Pikk 17, Tallinn 0001; tel. (2) 443-446; Dir TOOMAS TAMLA.

Estonian National Museum: Veski 32, Tartu 2400; tel. (34) 34-279; fax (2) 32-254; f. 1909; history of the Estonian and other Finno-Ugric peoples; Dir ALEKSEY PETERSON.

Estonian State Archives: Maneeži 4, Tallinn 0100; tel. (2) 441-118; f. 1921; Dir ENDEL KUKK.

F. R. Kreutzwald Museum of Literature: Vanemuise 40, Tartu 2400; tel. (34) 30-035; f. 1940; Dir PEETER OLESK.

Library of The Estonian Academy of Sciences: Rävala 10, Tallinn 0100; tel. (2) 454-704; fax (2) 454-049; f. 1946; Dir MAIVE TRIIPAN.

National Library of Estonia: Tõnismägi 2, Tallinn 0100; tel. (2) 453-345; fax (2) 453-334; f. 1918; 4.3m. items; Dir IVI EENMAA.

SPORTING ORGANIZATIONS

Estonian Central Sports Union: Regati 1, Tallinn 0019; tel. (2) 237-959; telex 173236; fax (2) 238-387; f. 1922; Chair. TIIT NUUDI; Sec. Gen. TOOMAS TÕNISE.

Estonian Olympic Committee: Regati 1, Tallinn 0103; tel. (2) 237-277; fax (2) 238-100; f. 1923; readmitted to International Olympic Movement 1991; Pres. ARNOLD GREEN.

Estonian State Sports Department: Regati 1, Tallinn 0103; tel. (2) 238-059; fax (2) 238-355; f. 1991; govt agency; Gen. Dir MATI MARK.

PERFORMING ARTS

Estonian Drama Theatre: Parnü 5, Tallinn 0001; tel. (2) 443-378; fax (2) 440-503; f. 1920; Dir MARGUS ALLIKMAA.

Estonian National Opera: Estonia 4, Tallinn 0001; tel. (2) 443-031; fax (2) 313-806; Chief Man. JAAK VILLER.

Estonian Puppet Theatre: Lai 1, Tallinn 0001; tel. (2) 449-160; Chief Man. KALLE ARO.

Estonian Youth Theatre: Lai 23, Tallinn 0001; tel. and fax (2) 448-542; Chief Man. RAIVO PÔLDMAA.

Pärnu 'Endla' Theatre: Keskväljak 1, 3600 Pärnu; tel. (44) 42-253; Chief Man. OLAF ESNA.

Rakvere Theatre: Kreutzvaldi 2A, 2100 Rakvere; tel. (32) 45-661.

Russian Drama Theatre: Vabaduse 5, Tallinn 0001; tel. and fax (2) 443-810; Chief Man. ALEKSANDR ILJIN.

Vanalinnstuudio Theatre: Sakala 12/1, Tallinn 0001; tel. (2) 448-408; fax (2) 445-846; Gen. Man. JÜRI KARINDI.

Viljandi 'Ugala' Drama Theatre: Vaksali 7, 2900 Viljandi; tel. (43) 53-818; Chief Man. ENN KOSE.

ASSOCIATIONS

Association of Estonian Museums: Suur-Karja 23, Tallinn 0001; tel. (2) 445-164; fax (6) 313-486.

Estonian Amateur Theatre Association—SATA: Pikk 33, Tallinn 0001; tel. (2) 601-591; Chair. JAAN ULVET.

Estonian Architects' Union: Lai 29, Tallinn 0110; tel. (2) 442-337; fax (2) 441-179; f. 1921; Chair. IKE VOLKOV.

Estonian Artists' Union: Vabaduse 6, Tallinn 0105; tel. (2) 445-014; fax (2) 446-483; f. 1943; Pres. MATI KARMIN.

Estonian Authors' Society: Toompuistee 7, Tallinn 0100; tel. (2) 453-788; fax (2) 442-596; Man. Dir KALEV RATTUS.

Estonian Choral Society: Tõnismägi 8A, Tallinn 0001; tel. (2) 681-679; fax (2) 449-147; f. 1922; Chair. VENNO LAUL.

Estonian Composers' Union: Lauteri 7, Tallinn 0001; tel. (2) 454-068; Chair. LEPO SUMERA.

Estonian Cultural Foundation: Olevimägi 14, Tallinn 0100; tel. (2) 449-512; fax (2) 601-247; f. 1987; Chair. JAAK KANGILASKI.

Estonian Film-Makers' Union: Uus 3, Tallinn 0101; tel. (2) 445-337; telex 173213; fax (2) 601-423; f. 1962; Chair. REIN MARAN.

Estonian Folklore Council: Suur-Karja 23, Tallinn 0001; tel. (2) 442-927; fax (6) 313-486; Sec.-Gen. ANNE OJALO.

Estonian Heritage Society: POB 3141, Tallinn 0090; tel. and fax (2) 449-216; f. 1987; collects Estonian memoirs and documents and restores monuments; Chair. Dr JAAN TAMM.

Estonian Librarians' Association: Tônismägi 2, Tallinn 0106; tel. (2) 450-929; fax (2) 453-334; f. 1923; Pres. ANNE VALMAS.

Estonian Theatre Union: Uus 5, Tallinn 0001; tel. (2) 446-868; fax (2) 443-582; f. 1945; Chair. MIKK MIKIVER.

Estonian Writers' Union: POB 66, Harju 1, Tallinn 0001; tel. (2) 446-832; fax (2) 313-486 f. 1922; Chair. VLADIMIR BEEKMAN.

Folklore Society of Estonia: Suur-Karja 23, Tallinn 0001; tel. (2) 449-931; (6) 313-484; Chair. KRISTJAN TOROP.

International PEN—Estonian Centre (PEN Rahvusvahelise Klubi Eesti Keskus): POB 66, Tallinn 0001; tel. (2) 446-832; fax (2) 440-963.

Mother Tongue Society: Roosikrantsi 6, Tallinn 0100; tel. (2) 449-331; fax (2) 441-800; f. 1920; promotes use of Estonian; Chair. Prof TIIT-REIN VIITSO.

Society of Estonian Regional Studies: Estonia Ave 7, Tallinn 0101; tel. (2) 440-475; f. 1990; Chair. VELLO LÕUGAS.

Education

Estonian-language schools consist of 12 years of education, with nine years in elementary schools and three years in secondary schools. Russian-language schools consist of 11 years of instruction. Secondary schools were attended by a total of 223,700 students in 1991/92. There were 36 special schools, which provided education for disabled pupils and specialized instruction in music, art and sport. Higher education was provided at 10 institutes of higher education. In 1991/92 a total of 25,643 students attended higher education institutes.

UNIVERSITIES

Tallinn Technical University: Ehitajate 5, 0108 Tallinn; tel. (2) 53-72-58; telex 173276; fax (2) 53-24-46; f. 1936; 7 faculties; 650 teachers; 9,500 students; Rector Prof. B. TAMM.

Tartu University: Ülikooli 18, 2400 Tartu; tel. (34) 34-866; telex 173243; fax (34) 35-440; f. 1632; languages of instruction: Estonian and Russian; 10 faculties; 900 teachers; 7,900 students; Rector Prof. PEETER ULVISTE.

Social Welfare

In pre-1940 Estonia health care was provided by both state and private facilities. A comprehensive state-funded health system was introduced under Soviet rule. There was a relatively high number of physicians, equivalent to 39 per 10,000 inhabitants, but a shortage of auxiliary staff. In 1988 average life expectancy at birth was 71.0 years, one of the highest in the USSR. The rate of infant mortality decreased from 18.2 per 1,000 live births, in 1975, to 12.4 in 1988, but was reckoned to have increased to 14.0 in 1991.

NATIONAL AGENCIES

Ministry of Social Affairs: see section on The Government (Ministries).

HEALTH AND WELFARE ORGANIZATIONS

Estonian Children's Fund: Sakala 3, Tallinn 0105; tel. (2) 443-310; f. 1988; Chair REIN AGUR.

Estonian Committee of the Red Cross: Lai 17, Tallinn 0101; tel. (2) 444-265; f. 1919; Chair. URSEL VAGUR.

Estonian Pensioners' Union: POB 3665, Tallinn 0090; tel. (2) 666-970; f. 1990; Chair. HARRI KÄRTNER.

Union of Estonian Societies of the Disabled: Tatari 14, Tallinn 0001; tel. (2) 442-804; f. 1989; Chair. MIHKEL AITSAM.

The Environment

Environmental concerns concentrated on the high level of pollution produced in industrialized north-eastern Estonia. Of particular concern in the 1980s was the proposed expansion of open-cast phosphorite mining. After public protests, the planned expansion was suspended.

GOVERNMENT ORGANIZATION

Ministry of the Environment: see section on The Government (Ministries).

ACADEMIC INSTITUTES

Estonian Academy of Sciences: Kohtu 6, Tallinn 0001; tel. (2) 443-116; fax (2) 442-149; f. 1938; Pres. ARNO KOORNA; incl.:

Institute of Ecology: Kevade 2, Tallinn 0001; tel. (2) 451-634; fax (2) 453-748; f. 1990; Dir MATI PUNNING.

Institute of Zoology and Botany: Vanemuise 21, Tartu 2400; tel. (34) 31-331; fax (34) 33-472; f. 1946; Dir ANDRES KOPPEL.

Tallinn Botanical Gardens: Kloostrimetsa 44/52, Tallinn 0019; tel. (2) 238-913; fax (2) 238-468; f. 1961; Dir HEIKI TAMM.

Estonian Research Institute of Forestry and Nature Conservation: Rõõmu 2, Tartu 2400; tel. (34) 36-381; fax (34) 36-375; f. 1969; conducts research in forestry, forest management and nature conservation; Dir Dr KALLE KAROLES.

Estonian Institute for Information: Tõnismägi 8, Tallinn 0106; tel. (2) 440-513; telex 173178; fax (2) 682-057; f. 1972; collects data on environmental pollution; Dir GUSTAV LAIGNA (acting).

Estonian Research Institute of Agriculture and Land Reclamation: Saku Sjk., Harjumaa 3400; tel. 721-408; f. 1946; Dir VALDEK LOKO.

NON-GOVERNMENTAL ORGANIZATIONS

Commission for Nature Conservation: Vanemuise 21, Tartu 2400; fax (34) 33-472.

Estonian Fund for Nature (Eestiamaa Looduse Fond—ELF): POB 43, Struwe 2, Tartu 2400; tel. (34) 30-198; fax (34) 32-433; Pres. FRED JÜSSI.

Estonian Green Movement/Friends of the Earth Estonia (Eesti Roheline Liikumine): see section on Political Organizations.

Estonian Society for Nature Conservation: Koidu 80, Tallinn 0007; tel. (2) 681-910; fax (2) 681-010; f. 1966; organizes courses in landscape management and planning, environmental education; Chair. JAAN EILART.

Union of Protected Areas of Estonia (Eesti Kaitsealade Liit—EKAL): Lääne-Virumaa, Viitna 2128; tel. (32) 49-253; fax (32) 45-759; Chair. ARNE KAASIK.

REGIONAL ORGANIZATIONS

Association of Baltic National Parks—ABNP (Balti Rahvusparkide Assotsiatsioon): Secretariat, Lääne-Virumaa, 2128 Viitna; tel. and fax (32) 45-759; Sec. TEET KOITJÄRV.

Baltic Commission for the Study of Bird Migration: Vanemuise 21, Tartu 2400; tel. (34) 30-331; fax (34) 33-472; f. 1955; interests include effects of pollution in the Baltic Sea on migratory birds' habitats; Chair. VILJU LILLELEHT.

Defence

Prior to the dissolution of the USSR Estonia did not possess its own armed forces. In April 1992, however, a Ministry of Defence was established in Estonia and an independent military was formed. By mid-1993 total active forces were estimated to number 2,500. There was also a reserve militia of some 6,000. A navy was formed on 1 July 1993. A paramilitary border guard, consisting of 2,000 troops (including 1,200 conscripts), was under the command of the Minister of the Interior. Military service was for 12 months. At mid-1993 an estimated 7,000 ex-Soviet troops remained in Estonia. In 1992 some 3% of the budgetary government expenditure was allocated to defence.

Supreme Commander of the Armed Forces: President of the Republic.

Chief of the General Staff: ANTS LAANEOTS.

Head of the Defence Forces: Gen. ALEKSANDER EINSELN.

Bibliography

Eilart, J. *The Country and the People*. Tallinn, Eesti Raamat, 1973.

Hansson, A. *Transforming an Economy while Building a Nation: the Case of Estonia*. Stockholm, Stockholm Institute of Soviet and Eastern European Economics, 1992.

Hiden, J. and Salmon, P. *The Baltic Nations and Europe: Estonia, Latvia and Lithuania in the Twentieth Century*. London, Longman, 1991.

Laar, M. *War in the Woods: Estonia's Struggle for Survival 1944–56*. Washington, DC, Compass Press, 1992.

Lieven, A. *The Baltic Revolution: Estonia, Latvia, Lithuania and the Path to Independence*. New Haven, Yale University Press, 1993.

Misiunas, R. and Taagepera, R. *The Baltic States: Years of Dependence, 1940–1980*. Berkeley, University of California Press, 1983.

Paalberg, H. *Economy, Industry and Agriculture*. Tallinn, Eesti Raamat, 1973.

Parming, T. and Jarvesoo, E. *A Case Study of a Soviet Republic: the Estonian SSR*. Boulder, Colorado, Westview Press, 1980.

Taagapera, R. *Estonia: Return to Independence*. Boulder, Colorado, Westview Press, 1992.

von Rauch, G. *The Baltic States: the Years of Independence, 1917–1940*. London, C. Hurst and Co, 1974.

GEORGIA

Geography

PHYSICAL FEATURES

The Republic of Georgia (formerly the Georgian Soviet Socialist Republic) is situated in west and central Transcaucasia, on the southern foothills of the Greater Caucasus mountain range. There is a short frontier with Turkey to the south and a western coastline on the Black Sea. The northern border with the Russian Federation follows the axis of the Greater Caucasus, and includes borders with the Daghestan, Chechen-Ingush (Chechnya and Ingushetia), North-Ossetian and Kabardin-Balkar Autonomous Republics and the Karachay-Cherkess Autonomous Oblast. To the south lies Armenia, and to the south-east, Azerbaijan. Georgia included two Autonomous Republics (Abkhazia and Ajaria). The status of the South-Ossetian Autonomous Oblast was in dispute from 1990, when its autonomous status was abolished. Georgia has an area of 69,700 sq km (26,911 sq miles), of which Abkhazia totalled 8,600 sq km, Ajaria 3,000 sq km and South Ossetia 3,900 sq km.

Geographically, Georgia is divided by the Suram mountain range, which runs from north to south between the Lesser and Greater Caucasus mountains. To the west of the Surams lie the Rion plains and the Black Sea littoral; to the east lies the more mountainous Kura basin. The Rion, flowing westwards into the Black Sea, and the Kura, flowing eastwards through Azerbaijan into the Caspian Sea, are the country's two main rivers.

CLIMATE

The Black Sea coast and the Rion plains have a warm, humid subtropical climate, with over 2,000 mm of rain annually and average temperatures of 6°C (42°F) in January and 23°C (73° F) in July. Eastern Georgia has a more continental climate, with cold winters and hot, dry summers.

POPULATION

At the 1989 census, when the total *de facto* population was 5,443,359, 68.8% of the population were Georgians, 9.0% Armenians, 7.4% Russians, 5.1% Azerbaijanis, 3.2% Ossetians (or Ossetes), 1.9% Greeks and 1.7% Abkhazians. Other ethnic groups included Ukrainians (52,443), Kurds (33,331), Georgian Jews (14,314) and European Jews (10,312). After 1989 some non-Georgians left the Republic as a result of inter-ethnic violence, notably Ossetians seeking refuge in North Ossetia, on the other side of the Caucasus, and many Pontian Greeks. Ajarians, who are ethnic Georgians but converted to Islam under Turkish rule, were not counted separately in Soviet censuses from 1926, when Ajarians accounted for less than 4% of the population of Georgia. Until 1944 there were also some 200,000 Meskhetian Turks in Georgia, who are of mixed Turkish and Georgian descent and are predominantly Muslim. In November 1944 they were deported *en masse* to Central Asia and, although they were rehabilitated and granted the right to return to Georgia in 1968, few were actually permitted to leave Central Asia. Many were forced to flee Central Asia following inter-ethnic violence in 1989, but were refused permission by the Georgian authorities to resettle in their homelands.

Most of the population were adherents of Christianity; the principal denomination was the Georgian Orthodox Church. Islam was professed by Ajarians, Azerbaijanis, Kurds and some others. Most Ossetians in Georgia were Eastern Orthodox Christians, although their co-nationals in North Ossetia were largely Sunni Muslim. There were also other Christian groups, and a small number of adherents of the Jewish faith. The official language was Georgian, a non-Indo-European language, which was written in the Georgian script.

At 1 January 1991 the total estimated population was 5,471,000. In that year the average population density was 78.5 persons per sq km. The capital is Tbilisi, which is situated in the south-east of the country, on the River Kura. In January 1990 it had an estimated population of 1,268,000. Other important towns included the ports of Batumi (which is the capital of the Ajarian Autonomous Republic—with an estimated population of 137,000 in 1990) and Sukhumi (capital of the Abkhazian Autonomous Republic—122,000). The main town of western Georgia, however, is Kutaisi (236,000), on the Rioni plains. Rustavi (160,000) is an important industrial centre near Tbilisi.

Chronology

***c*. 299–234 BC:** Parnavaz (Farnavazi, Pharnabazus), traditionally the first king of an identifiably 'Georgian' state, reigned over eastern Georgia (anciently known as Iberia); his realm was centred on the province of Kartli; he also came to dominate the kingdom in western Georgia (Egrisi—the Colchis of the ancient Greeks).

64: The Roman general Pompey incorporated Colchis, which was part of the just-defeated kingdom of Pontus, into the Empire and secured hegemony in Kartli-Iberia and Armenia; the Persian (Parthian) Empire was soon to start disputing this control.

***c*. AD 328 :** The 'Apostle of the Georgians', St Nino (according to tradition, a Cappadocian slave woman), began the evangelization of the Georgians; the king of Kartli-Iberia, Mirian III (Meribanes, 284–361), subsequently adopted Christianity.

5th century: Invention of the Georgian alphabet, at a time when the Orthodox Georgian Church was attempting to resist Persian cultural dominance and the advance of Zoroastrianism.

523: The ruler of Lazica (established in Egrisi, Roman Colchis, in the previous century), Tsete, accepted Orthodox Christianity; the territory soon returned to dependence on the Eastern Roman ('Byzantine') Empire.

580: The Persians abolished the Kartli-Iberian monarchy, upon the death of Bakur III; the Georgian aristocracy acquiesced in the effective partition of the kingdom, between the Byzantines (based at the old capital of Mtskheta) and the Sasanian Persians (based at the new capital, to the south, Tbilisi).

645: Tbilisi fell to the Arabs and the presiding prince of Kartli-Iberia was forced to acknowledge the overlordship of the Muslim caliph.

888: The monarchy of Kartli-Iberia was restored by the Armenians, both kingdoms being ruled by branches of the Bagratuni family; there was also a kingdom in western Georgia (Egrisi), Abasgia—Abkhazia or Abkhazeti.

1008: Bagrat III, already king of Abkhazia, inherited Kartli-Iberia upon the death of his father, uniting Egrisi and Kartli into a single Georgian kingdom ('Sakartvelo', the land of the Kartvelians or Georgians); his capital was at Kutaisi.

1089–1125: Reign of King David II (the 'Restorer' or 'Builder'), who created a powerful kingdom which gained control of the remaining Georgian lands: the process began when he renounced the tribute to the Seljuq Turkish sultanate (1096); it was secured by the defeat of the Muslims at the Battle of Didgori (12 August 1121); and was symbolized by the final capture of Muslim Tbilisi, which became the royal capital (1122).

1184–1212: Reign of Queen Tamar; this marked the apogee of the independent, medieval Georgian kingdom, which witnessed the work of the 'national bard', Shota Rustaveli, repulsed the Muslims and helped establish the Byzantine 'Empire of Trebizond'.

1223–45: Reign of Queen Rusudan, under whom Georgia was devastated by Mongol and Khwarazem raiders; the power of the monarchy was destroyed, the kingdom was fractured and the Georgians became tributary to the Mongol rulers of the Persian Empire.

1554: The Russians captured the Caspian port of Astrakhan, thus first coming into contact with the territories of the Caucasus; the Georgians, divided into several kingdoms and principalities (the main ones being Imereti, in the west, and Kartli and Kakheti, in the east) struggled over by the rival Persian and Turkish Ottoman Empires, could begin to expect help from their Orthodox co-religionists, the Russians.

1783: King Irakli II, of a reunited Kartli-Kakheti (1762–98), concluded the Treaty of Giorgievski with Russia, whereby his eastern Georgian kingdom surrendered responsibility for defence and foreign affairs, but retained internal autonomy.

18 December 1800: Tsar Paul I of Russia declared Kartli-Kakheti annexed outright to the Russian Empire, although the question of the continuance of the Bagratid dynasty was left in abeyance—however, George XII, the last king of eastern Georgia, died before tsarist troops entered Tbilisi (known as Tiflis until 1936).

1801: The new Tsar, Alexander I, declared the abolition of the kingdom of Kartli-Kakheti.

December 1803: Moving westwards, the Russians placed Samgrelo (Mingrelia) under the formal protection of the Empire.

1804: King Solomon II of Imereti, the main principality of western Georgia (based at Kutaisi), was forced to accept Russian sovereignty; the last reigning Bagratid in Georgia, he, and his title, died in 1810.

1809: Safar bey Sharvashedze, preferring Russian to Ottoman overlordship, placed his principality of Abkhazia under Russian protection.

1811: Mamia Gurieli placed the principality of Guria (western Georgia, on the Black Sea coast) under the protection of the Tsar; the Russians had also seized Sukhum-Kale and other cities from the Turks.

1812: The autocephaly of the eastern Georgian Orthodox Church was ended; the western Georgian Church had a new hierarchy imposed three years later.

1828: The Treaty of Turkmenchai concluded the war between Russia and Persia, confirming the rule of Russia over the Georgians.

1864–65: Emancipation of the serfs, first in Tiflis province, then in Guria and Imereti (Kutaisi province).

1892: The first radical Marxist group, Mesami Dasi (Third Generation), was formed, being joined by Iosif Vissarionovich Dzhugashvili (Ioseb Jugashvili, when transliterated from the Georgian—later known as Stalin); the socialists were popular for opposition both to the Russian imperial system and to the Armenian bourgeoisie's dominance of the economic system.

1899: The first Tiflis committee of the All-Russian Social Democratic Labour Party (RSDLP) was formed, dominated by the Menshevik wing—the Bolsheviks of the main, Russian RSDLP were to include many prominent Georgians, notably Stalin and 'Sergo' Orjonikidze (Ordzhonikidze).

1 August 1914: Russia entered the First World War against Austria-Hungary, Germany and Ottoman Turkey.

2 March (New Style: 15 March) 1917: Abdication of Tsar Nicholas II after demonstrations and strikes in Petrograd (St Petersburg); subsequently, in Transcaucasia, the Provisional Government nominated an executive, but its power was dependent upon the soviets established in Tiflis (chaired by the Menshevik Georgian Noe Zhordania) and Baku (in Azerbaijan).

November 1917: The Georgian Mensheviks and the Armenian leaderships in Georgia and Armenia denied the legitimacy of the new, Bolshevik, central Government and established a Transcaucasian Commissariat to assume temporary authority (an assembly or Seim convened in January 1918).

14 February (Old Style: 1 February) 1918: First day upon which the Gregorian Calender took effect in Soviet Russia.

22 April 1918: The Transcaucasian Seim, following the Soviet–German Treaty of Brest-Litovsk and under pressure from a Turkish military advance into the Caucasus, declared the independence of the Democratic Federal Republic of Transcaucasia.

26 May 1918: The Georgian leadership, realizing that the new Transcaucasian state was untenable, declared an independent Georgian state, allied to Germany.

July 1920: The British withdrew the last of their forces from Batumi, having decided, like the other Western nations to have recognized the three Transcaucasian states, not to aid them militarily against Bolshevik Russia.

25 February 1921: The Menshevik Government fled Tiflis, which was occupied by the Red Army, under Orjonikidze;

Georgia, the last of the Transcaucasian states to fall to the Bolsheviks, was declared a Soviet Socialist Republic (SSR).

10 December 1922: Georgia's nominal independence ended when the Federal Union of SSRs of Transcaucasia (formed 12 March) was transformed into a single republic, the Transcaucasian Soviet Federative Socialist Republic (TSFSR), despite strong opposition from the Georgian Communists; the TSFSR, with its capital at Tiflis, became a constituent Union Republic of the Union of Soviet Socialist Republics (USSR) on 30 December.

January 1924: Death of Lenin, who was eventually succeeded by Stalin as leader of the USSR.

August 1924: A widespread revolt, led by the Mensheviks, failed; it was followed by severe repression.

5 December 1936: Under the second Constitution of the USSR, the TSFSR was dissolved and the Georgian, Armenian and Azerbaijani SSRs became full Union Republics.

1937: The leader of Georgia, Lavrenti Beria, assured Stalin of his loyalty by conducting among the most savage of the Stalinist purges, which completed the centralization of the Soviet state.

1938: A new Abkhazian alphabet, based on the Georgian script (33 characters the same and six unique ones), was introduced.

1941–45: The German–Soviet struggle during the Second World War had a severe affect on Georgia, although there was never any fighting on its territory; from a population of 3.5m., in 1939, during the War Georgia supplied some 0.5m. people to the armed forces and its total population fell to 3.2m. by 1945.

March 1956: Despite the denunciation of Stalin (died 1953) by the new Soviet leader, Nikita Khrushchev, the former's memory remained popular in Georgia and the anniversary of his death occasioned the first 'nationalist' demonstration since the 1920s.

1972: Eduard Shevardnadze became head of the Georgian Communist Party (serving until 1985 when he became Soviet Foreign Minister), as part of an anti-corruption policy by the central authorities.

April 1989: Twenty people were killed in Tbilisi when soldiers dispersed a demonstration, in support of independence and against Abkhazian secessionism, using toxic gas and sharpened shovels.

July 1989: Sixteen people were killed at Sukhumi University during fighting between students, after Georgian students had attempted to make the university a branch of Tbilisi University; a state of emergency and curfew were introduced in the Abkhazian capital.

November 1989: The Supreme Soviet of Georgia declared that republican law over-rode all-Union legislation.

December 1989: Refused demands that South Ossetia be made an autonomous republic led to violent confrontations between Ossetians and Georgians in the oblast.

February 1990: The Supreme Soviet declared Georgia an 'annexed and occupied country' and, the next month, went on to end the Communist ban on opposition parties, at whose behest the republican parliamentary elections were postponed.

25 August 1990: The Abkhazian Supreme Soviet voted to declare independence from Georgia and adopt the status of a full union republic; this declaration was pronounced invalid by the Georgian Supreme Soviet.

30 September 1990: The more radical opposition parties rejected all Soviet institutions and conducted elections to a National Congress.

28 October 1990: The Round Table-Free Georgia coalition of pro-independence parties won some 64% of the votes cast in the first round of elections to the Georgian Supreme Soviet.

14 November 1990: Zviad Gamsakhurdia, leader of the Georgian Helsinki Union and of the victorious coalition, was elected as Chairman of the Supreme Soviet; the state was renamed the Republic of Georgia.

11 December 1990: South Ossetia's autonomous status was abolished by the Georgian parliament; there was continued violence in the region between Ossetians and Georgians.

31 March 1991: Having boycotted the all-Union referendum on continued federation, the Georgian authorities conducted a republican referendum on independence, which was overwhelmingly supported.

9 April 1991: The Supreme Soviet (Supreme Council) approved a decree formally restoring Georgian independence; six days later Gamsakhurdia was appointed to the new post of executive President of the Republic.

26 May 1991: Gamsakhurdia, the incumbent, was directly elected to the presidency by 85.6% of the votes cast, although within a few months he lost support, after accusations of authoritarian rule and extreme nationalism.

21 December 1991: At a meeting in Almaty (Kazakhstan) the leaders of 11 former Union Republics of the USSR signed a protocol on the formation of the new Commonwealth of Independent States (CIS); Georgia did not sign, but sent observers to the meeting; four days later the resignation of Mikhail Gorbachev as President of the USSR confirmed the dissolution of the federation.

2 January 1992: Opposition to President Gamsakhurdia declared him deposed (he fled to Chechnya, Russia, four days later); a Military Council headed by Tengiz Kitovani and Jaba Ioseliani was formed and it subsequently appointed Tengiz Sigua premier.

January 1992: South Ossetians voted overwhelmingly in favour of becoming part of the Russian Federation; violence in the region continued; Georgian government troops arrived in South Ossetia.

10 March 1992: Eduard Shevardnadze was appointed Chairman of the newly formed State Council.

July 1992: Pro-Gamsakhurdia supporters ('Zviadists') attacked members of the paramilitary Mkhedrioni (Horsemen) group in Tskhalenjikha, who responded violently. In South Ossetia a cease-fire agreement was signed.

31 July 1992: Georgia became the last former Soviet Republic to be admitted into the UN.

11 August 1992: Zviadists kidnapped the Georgian Minister of Internal Affairs, as well as other senior officials, who had been sent to western Georgia (Mingrelia) to negotiate the release of a deputy premier, held hostage since the previous month.

14 August 1992: Three thousand National Guard members arrived in Abkhazia in order to release the hostages; Abkhazian troops responded with a series of attacks, but the Georgian forces succeeded in capturing Sukhumi.

September 1992: Abkhazian forces launched a counter-offensive and gained control of all of northern Georgia, leading Shevardnadze to claim that secessionist forces were receiving military aid from Russia.

11 October 1992: Elections to the new Supreme Soviet took place and were participated in by an estimated 75% of the electorate; Shevardnadze was overwhelmingly elected Chairman of the Supreme Soviet in direct elections (with 96% of the votes cast). The new parliament convened for the first time on 6 November.

14 May 1993: A cease-fire was agreed between Georgian and Abkhazian forces.

2 July 1993: The cease-fire in Abkhazia was broken when secessionist troops attacked Sukhumi; martial law was imposed in the region.

27 July 1993: A UN-observed cease-fire agreement was signed by the Georgian and Abkhazian leaderships; the agreement recognized both Abkhazian autonomy and the need for Georgian national integrity.

6 August 1993: Sigua and the Council of Ministers resigned after parliament rejected their proposed budget.

10 September 1993: A two-month state of emergency was declared and a new, smaller Cabinet of Ministers, under Otar Patsatsia, was appointed. Shevardnadze forced parliament to accept these measures after offering his resignation (which was refused).

15 September 1993: Forces loyal to deposed President Gamsakhurdia began an offensive to the west of Samtredia.

16 September 1993: Abkhazian forces attacked Sukhumi, breaking the cease-fire agreement; government troops were defeated after 11 days of fighting, despite the personal leadership of Shevardnadze.

30 September 1993: The last government troops were driven from Abkhazia and the region was officially declared liberated from Georgia; there were reports of ethnic Georgians being expelled and killed by victorious troops.

2 October 1993: Zviadist forces captured the port of Poti as well as gaining control of the railway line to Tbilisi, thereby blocking all rail traffic to the capital.

20 October 1993: The Supreme Soviet agreed that Georgia should join the CIS, which Shevardnadze had proposed a few days before. The next day Russian troops and supplies arrived in Georgia and government forces were able to reopen vital supply lines, while Poti and other towns were soon recaptured.

8 November 1993: Gamsakhurdia and his supporters fled to Abkhazia, after being defeated at their main base, the town of Zugdidi, by Georgian troops.

25 November 1993: The national state of emergency was extended to 20 January 1994 (and, subsequently, for a further month).

1 December 1993: Georgian officials and Abkhazian separatists signed a UN-mediated eight-point peace 'memorandum', in which the terms for the repatriation of Georgian refugees in the region were agreed.

3 December 1993: Georgia was formally admitted to the CIS.

23 December 1993: South Ossetia adopted a new Constitution, under which it was announced that parliamentary elections would be held in April 1994.

31 December 1993: Gamsakhurdia was killed, reportedly by his own hand, after being surrounded by government troops in western Georgia.

11 January 1994: The second round of UN-mediated Georgian-Abkhazian peace negotiations began in Geneva (Switzerland); a third round was scheduled for February 1994.

History

The first Georgian state was established in the fourth century BC, following the conquest of the Persian Empire by Alexander III ('the Great') of Macedon. Christianity was adopted as the state religion in the fourth century AD, but from the sixth century Georgia enjoyed only short periods of independence. Georgia regained its independence and united its territories under King David II ('the Restorer'), in the 12th century, but was conquered by the Mongols in 1236. Despite frequent attempts to preserve the country's unity and independence, Georgia became divided into principalities, which preserved only nominal independence under either Ottoman Turkish or Persian suzerainty and were frequently in conflict with each other. Kartli and Kakheti, the principalities under Persian influence, were incorporated into the Russian Empire in 1801. During the next three-quarters of a century, although mainly in the next decade, the remaining Georgian lands were annexed by Russia from Turkey.

After the collapse of the Russian Empire in 1917, an independent Georgian state was established on 26 May 1918. Independent Georgia was ruled by a Menshevik Socialist Government and received Soviet recognition by treaty in May 1920. However, against the wishes of the Bolshevik leader Lenin (Vladimir Ilych Ulyanov), Georgia was invaded by Bolshevik troops, in early 1921, and a Georgian Soviet Socialist Republic was proclaimed on 25 February of that year. In December 1922 it was absorbed into the Transcaucasian Soviet Federative Socialist Republic (TSFSR), which, on 22 December 1922, became a founder member of the USSR. The Georgian SSR became a full Union Republic, in 1936, when the TSFSR was disbanded.

Georgians were particularly subject to persecution during the period when Stalin (Iosif Dzhugashvili, when transliterated from the Russian, or Ioseb Jugashvili), an ethnic Georgian, was the Soviet leader. The first victims were opponents of Stalin during his time as a revolutionary leader in Georgia. Later, in the 1930s, the persecution became more indiscriminate. Most members of the Georgian leadership were dismissed after the death of Stalin in 1953. There was a further 'purge' in 1972, when Eduard Shevardnadze became First Secretary of the Communist Party of Georgia (CPG) and attempted to remove officials accused of corruption. Despite Soviet policy, Georgians retained a strong national identity. Opposition to a perceived policy of 'russification' was demonstrated in 1956, when anti-Russian riots were suppressed by security forces, and in 1978 when there were mass protests against the weakened status of the Georgian language in the new Constitution.

The increased freedom of expression under Soviet President Mikhail Gorbachev (1985–91) allowed the formation of unofficial groups, which campaigned on linguistic, environmental and ethnic issues. Such groups were prominent in organizing demonstrations in November 1988 against russification in the Republic. In February 1989 Abkhazians renewed a campaign, begun in the 1970s, for secession of their Autonomous Republic from the Georgian SSR. Counter-demonstrations were staged in Tbilisi by Georgians demanding that Georgia's territorial integrity be preserved. On the night of 8–9 April 1989 demonstrators in Tbilisi, who were demanding that Abkhazia remain within Georgia and advocating the restoration of independence, were brutally attacked by soldiers. Twenty people were reported killed and many more injured. Despite the resignation of Party and state officials after the incident and the announcement of an official investigation into the deaths, anti-Soviet sentiment and inter-ethnic conflict increased sharply in the Republic.

The public outrage over the April killings and the increasing influence of unofficial groups forced the CPG to adapt its policies to retain some measure of public support. In November 1989 the Georgian Supreme Soviet, at the time still dominated by CPG members, declared the supremacy of Georgian laws over all-Union laws. In February 1990 the same body declared Georgia 'an annexed and occupied country'. In March Article Six of the Georgian Constitution, which ensured that the Communist Party retained a monopoly on power, was abolished, and, in the same month, the CPG's youth wing, the Komsomol, disbanded itself. Pressure from the opposition parties also forced the elections to the Georgian Supreme Soviet, which were scheduled for 25 March, to be postponed to allow time for a more liberal election law to be drafted. Legislation permitting full multi-party elections was finally adopted in August, but only after opposition groups staged a one-week-long blockade of Georgia's main railway junction.

Despite the success of the opposition in influencing the position of the CPG, there were considerable differences between the many opposition parties. There were attempts to create a united front for the independence movement, notably the formation, in October 1989, of the Main Committee for National Salvation, which collapsed within two months. No other attempts had succeeded either. In early 1990, however, many of the principal political parties united, in the Round Table-Free Georgia coalition. This and other leading parties aimed to achieve independence by parliamentary means and were willing to participate in elections to Soviet institutions such as the Supreme Soviet. The more radical parties refused to recognize the legitimacy of Soviet institutions or elections. Many of them united in the National Forum, headed by Giorgi ('Gia') Chanturia, which announced its intention to boycott the elections to the Supreme Soviet and, instead, to elect a rival parliament, the National Congress. The announcement of elections to the Congress, to be held on 30 September 1990, thus preempting the elections to the Supreme Soviet, scheduled for 28 October, caused increased tension in relations between parties of the two tendencies. Political rivalry turned to violence in September: a leading member of the Round Table-Free Georgia coalition was kidnapped; exchanges of gunfire were reported between supporters of the two groups; and the offices of pro-Congress parties were attacked, ransacked and set on fire. The elections to the National Congress took place on 30 September, as scheduled, but only 51% of the electorate participated. Many parties did not take part, preferring to participate in elections to the Supreme Soviet.

In the elections to the Supreme Soviet, which took place on 28 October and 11 November 1990, the Round Table-Free Georgia bloc of pro-independence parties won 64% of the votes cast. This was represented by 155 seats in the 250-seat chamber. Fourteen political parties or coalitions of parties were involved in the election campaign; all of them, including the CPG, were united in seeking Georgia's independence. The CPG, despite its nationalist stance, won only 64 seats. The remainder were won by the Georgian Popular Front, smaller coalitions and independents. The elections were boycotted by many non-Georgians, since parties limited to one area of the country were prevented from participating.

THE PRESIDENCY OF ZVIAD GAMSAKHURDIA

The new Supreme Soviet convened for the first time on 14 November 1990 and elected Zviad Gamsakhurdia, a leading intellectual, the leader of the Round Table-Free Georgia group and Chairman of the Georgian Helsinki Union, as Chairman of the Supreme Soviet. Two symbolic gestures of independence were adopted: the territory was to be called the Republic of Georgia, without any reference to 'Soviet' or 'Socialist', and the white, black and plum-coloured flag of independent Georgia was adopted as the official flag. The next day Tengiz Sigua, also a member of the Round Table-Free Georgia coalition, was appointed head of government.

The new Supreme Soviet, dominated by radical nationalists, passed a number of controversial laws in its first session. On 15 November 1990 the Georgian Supreme Soviet declared illegal the conscription of Georgians into the Soviet armed forces. On 1 January 1991 only 10% of those eligible had complied with the military draft; many young men were reported to have joined nationalist paramilitary groups or were ready to join the National Guard, a *de facto* republican army, which the Supreme Soviet established on 30 January 1991.

The Georgian authorities officially boycotted the all-Union referendum on the future of the Union, held in nine other Republics, in March 1991, but polling stations were opened in South Ossetia and Abkhazia, and also in local military barracks. In South Ossetia 43,950 people took part in the referendum; of these, only nine voted against the preservation of the USSR. In Abkhazia almost the entire non-Georgian population voted to preserve the Union. The Georgian leadership refused to participate in the negotiations on a new Union Treaty. Instead, on 31 March 1991, the Government conducted a referendum asking whether 'independence should be restored on the basis of the act of independence of 26 May 1918'. Of those eligible to vote, 95% participated in the referendum, 93% of whom voted for independence.

Following the referendum, on 9 April 1991 the Georgian Supreme Soviet (Supreme Council) approved a decree formally restoring Georgia's independence. On 15 April the Supreme Soviet elected Gamsakhurdia to the newly instituted post of executive President, pending direct elections for the post on 26 May. These elections were duly won by Gamsakhurdia, who received 86.5% of the votes cast. His closest rival was Valerian Advadze, of the Georgian Union for National Accord and Rebirth, who won only 7.6%. None of the other four candidates won more than 2% of the vote. Voting did not take place in South Ossetia or Abkhazia.

Despite the high level of popular support that Gamsakhurdia received from the electorate, there was considerable opposition from other politicians to what was perceived as an authoritarian style of rule. Demands for independence by separatists in Georgia's autonomous territories (see below) increased anti-Gamsakhurdia sentiment in these regions. His actions during the failed Soviet coup attempt of August 1991 were also strongly criticized. He allegedly agreed to demands made by the members of the State Committee for the State of Emergency (SCSE) to disarm military formations in Georgia and, initially, refrained from publicly condemning the coup leaders. It was even claimed by opposition politicians that Murman Omanidze, the Minister of Foreign Affairs, had travelled to Moscow to meet members of the SCSE. After the coup had collapsed the Georgian leadership strongly denied such allegations. However, Tengiz Kitovani, the leader of the Georgian National Guard, who was officially dismissed by Gamsakhurdia on 19 August, announced that 15,000 of his men had remained loyal to him and were no longer subordinate to Gamsakhurdia. Kitovani was joined in opposition to the President by Tengiz Sigua, the former Prime Minister, who had resigned in mid-August, and Giorgi Khoshtaria, former Minister of Foreign Affairs, who was dismissed by Gamsakhurdia in the same month. In September 30 opposition parties united to demand the resignation of Gamsakhurdia and organized a series of anti-government demonstrations. Gamsakhurdia imposed a state of emergency and arrested Chanturia, the most prominent opposition politician. There were several deaths after violent clashes between the opposition and supporters of Gamsakhurdia. When opposition supporters occupied the television station in Tbilisi, several people were killed after clashes between Kitovani's troops and those forces still loyal to Gamsakhurdia.

Throughout October demonstrations by both supporters and opponents of Gamsakhurdia continued, but the strength of Gamsakhurdia's support among the rural and working-class population, his arrests of prominent opposition leaders and his effective monopoly of the national media all weakened the position of the opposition. By November Gamsakhurdia seemed to be in a more powerful position. However, continued unrest severely weakened the economy and discouraged political and economic ties with Western countries.

In December 1991 the opposition to President Gamsakhurdia resorted to force to oust him. Kitovani and Jaba Ioseliani, leader of the paramilitary Mkhedrioni (Horsemen) group, provided the main military forces, but they were joined by other opposition figures and increasing numbers of former Gamsakhurdia supporters. Chanturia and Ioseliani were released from detention early in the fighting, which was mostly confined to central Tbilisi, around the parliament buildings, where Gamsakhurdia was besieged. More than 100 people were believed to have been killed in the fighting. He escaped, on 6 January 1992, and eventually took refuge in the Chechen capital, Grozny (Russian Federation). Some days previously, on 2 January, the opposition had declared him deposed and formed a Military Council, led by Kitovani and Ioseliani, which appointed Tengiz Sigua acting Chairman of the Council of Ministers. Chanturia was reported to have refused membership of the Military Council, which declared its intention of holding power only until the Supreme Soviet could meet, later that month, and appoint an interim administration, to hold office until parliamentary elections had taken place. The office of President was to be abolished and the functions of head of state were to be exercised by the Chairman of the Supreme Soviet.

AFTER INDEPENDENCE

With the dissolution of the USSR in December 1991 (upon the creation of the Commonwealth of Independent States—CIS), Sigua was premier of a fully independent country and, soon after his appointment in January 1992, he announced plans for significant economic reform. An interim consultative council, comprising representatives of all the major political groups, was established, in an attempt to attain stability. The establishment of trade relations with members of the CIS, which consisted of 11 former Soviet republics, was considered. On 6 March Eduard Shevardnadze, the former Soviet Minister of Foreign Affairs (and previously CPG leader), returned to Georgia. A State Council, of which Shevardnadze was appointed Chairman, was created four days later to replace the Military Council as the supreme legislative and executive body, until new elections could be held. This State Council comprised 50 members, from all political parties and most ethnic minorities. Ioseliani, Kitovani and Sigua were appointed Deputy Chairmen.

Given that Gamsakhurdia refused to resign as President, claiming that the majority of the people still supported him, Shevardnadze's first priority was to restore enough political stability to allow the elections that could give legitimacy to the new regime to go ahead. He succeeded in reconciling the various factions of the State Council, as well as the leaders of the two principal military bodies, Kitovani's National Guard and the Mkhedrioni under Ioseliani. Gamsakhurdia had already returned to his home town of Zugdidi, in the Mingrelian region, in western Georgia, later in January 1992, where he attempted to incite rebellion. Although these attempts were suppressed by government troops, there were violent clashes in Tbilisi and western Georgia in February, when the National Guard acted against pro-Gamsakhurdia demonstrations. Unrest continued in March, especially in the western strongholds, where Gamsakhurdia's supporters, or 'Zviadists', systematically blew up strategic bridges and disrupted rail traffic to Tbilisi. Curfews were imposed in the capital and in other towns. However, by April government troops were reported to have re-established control in rebel areas. There were no further confrontations until 24 June, when some 300 Zviadists occupied the television building in Tbilisi, an attempt to incite insurrection which was swiftly suppressed by the National Guard. In early July members of Ioseliani's Mkhedrioni were attacked by Gamsakhurdia supporters in the western Georgian town of Tskhalenjikha and retaliated with indiscriminate violence against the local population. Shevardnadze attempted to diffuse the situation by announcing an amnesty for political prisoners. However, on 11 August, Zviadists responded by kidnapping Roman Gventsadze, the Georgian Minister of Internal Affairs, and several other senior officials, who had been sent to western Georgia to negotiate the release of deputy prime minister Sandro Kavsadze, abducted by the same group on 9 July. The State Council dispatched 3,000 National Guardsmen, led by Kitovani, to Abkhazia, where the hostages were believed to be held, prompting armed resistance by Abkhazian militia. In mid-August three of the hostages, including Gventsadze, were released.

On 31 July 1992 Georgia became the last of the former Soviet Republics to be admitted into the UN. Four days later, in an attempt to secure peaceful conditions for the planned legislative elections, Shevardnadze repealed the state of emergency, in force since late 1991, as well as the curfew in Tbilisi, and announced an amnesty for Gamsakhurdia's supporters. The elections to the new Supreme Soviet, held on 11 October, were carried out peacefully, apart from intensified fighting in Abkhazia (see below) and a boycott in South Ossetia, Mingrelia and parts of Abkhazia (by approximately 9% of the electorate). An estimated 75% of the total electorate participated. None of the more than 30 parties and alliances which contested the election succeeded in gaining a significant representation in the 235-seat legislature. At the same time there were direct elections to the post of the legislature's Chairman, effectively a presidential role. Shevardnadze was the sole candidate for the post and, although he needed only one-third of the total votes cast, he won 96% of the votes, thus obtaining the legitimate popular mandate that he had hitherto lacked.

The new Georgian Supreme Soviet convened on 6 November 1992. State power was vested in Shevardnadze as the parliament's Chairman, in conjunction with the Council of Ministers, while the Supreme Soviet remained the highest legislative body. These provisions were to remain in force until the adoption of a new constitution. Shevardnadze was also elected Commander-in-Chief of the Georgian armed forces and Tengiz Sigua was re-elected Chairman of the Council of Ministers, a body which comprised members of various parties and organizations, including former dissidents. In early 1993 a National Security and Defence Council was introduced, with the purpose of meeting one of the Government's main aims, that of creating a unified army. It comprised 11 members, including Shevardnadze as Chairman, and Sigua, Ioseliani and Kitovani as Deputy Chairmen.

As well as attempting to resolve the tensions in Georgia's autonomous territories, Shevardnadze also faced problems from his own administration. The most serious threat to his authority came from Tengiz Kitovani who, it was reported in January 1993 and again in April, was plotting a *coup d'état* against him. Shevardnadze responded by forcing Kitovani and his ally Ioseliani to resign, on 5 May, from the National Security and Defence Council. Kitovani also left his post as Defence Minister. On 6 August, however, Sigua and his Government resigned after parliament rejected their proposed budget. One month later, on 10 September, Shevardnadze announced the imposition of a two-month state of emergency in Georgia. At the same time, he appointed a new Government, with less members, renamed the Cabinet of Ministers. It was headed by Otar

Patsatsia. When accused of dictatorial methods by Ioseliani, Shevardnadze offered his resignation. Only when the Supreme Soviet refused to accept his departure, and crowds gathered in support of their beleaguered head of state, did Shevardnadze rescind his resignation, on the condition that parliament approve his proposals.

Shevardnadze's confrontation with the parliament led to Gamsakhurdia's forces, based in western Georgia, launching a new offensive against government troops, on 15 September 1993, to the west of Samtredia. At the end of July Zviadists had briefly occupied Senaki and, on 29 August, they captured the town again, as well as Abasha and Khobi. On 2 October, strengthened by the fall of Sukhumi and the defeat of government troops in Abkhazia, Gamsakhurdia's forces captured the port of Poti. Six people were reported to have been killed. They also took control of the railway junction at Samtredia, thereby blocking all rail traffic to Tbilisi, which, on 17 October, had flour supplies for only 10 more days. At the same time, Shevardnadze was facing further hostility from the Supreme Soviet because of his decision to enter Georgia into the CIS. Two days later he appealed to Russia to send aid as Zviadist troops moved eastwards and threatened to capture Kutaisi, the second city of Georgia. On 21 October, one day after the Georgian parliament agreed to membership of the CIS, Russian troops were dispatched to open vital supply lines to the Georgian capital. Georgian forces, with the assistance of newly deployed Russian troops and supplies, also recaptured Poti and, on 23 October, Samtredia and Abasha. By 8 November it was reported that Gamsakhurdia and his followers had been routed in Zugdidi, their main base, and had fled to Abkhazia. In early January 1994, however, it was reported that Gamsakhurdia had committed suicide in western Georgia, after being surrounded by Georgian troops, but the exact circumstances of his death remained controversial.

On 25 November 1993 Shevardnadze issued a decree extending the state of emergency, brought into force in September, until 20 January 1994, after which legislative elections would take place. (In January 1994 this state of emergency was extended until 20 February.) He also created his own party, the Citizen's Union of Georgia, formed from several other political parties, which seemed likely to be a leading force in Georgian politics into the mid-1990s.

Shevardnadze's gradual consolidation of power, combined with his international prestige, led to a wider recognition of Georgia. The country had not gained international recognition with the other former Soviet Republics after the formation of the CIS—the international community acknowledged that such recognition would be given, but only after the practical situation of early 1992 had been resolved. On 24 March 1993 Georgia joined the Conference on Security and Co-operation in Europe (CSCE), one day after it had been officially recognized by the European Community (EC—known as the European Union from November 1993). On 3 December Georgia finally became a member of the CIS, when all of the member states of the Commonwealth approved its admittance. However, the country was not able to develop international links after independence, owing to the urgent need to resolve the inter-ethnic tensions in Ajaria, Abkhazia and South Ossetia, which had intensified following the election of Gamsakhurdia's nationalist Government in 1990.

THE AUTONOMOUS TERRITORIES

Ajaria

The Autonomous Republic of Ajaria proved to be the least troubled of the country's self-governing regions. Despite being of ethnic Georgian origin, the Ajars, whose autonomous status was the result of a Soviet–Turkish Treaty of Friendship (1921), seem to have retained a sense of separate identity, owing to their adherence to Islam. Some Christian Georgians considered the Muslim Ajars a threat to a unified Georgian nation. Before the elections to the Supreme Soviet in October 1990, Gamsakhurdia announced that he intended to abolish the autonomous status of Ajaria. Although he did not do so, tensions between Muslims and Christians increased during 1991, particularly after the Georgian Supreme Soviet ruled as unconstitutional an election law for the Ajar Supreme Soviet. This had restricted nominations for the forthcoming elections to permanent residents of Ajaria. In April there were several days of demonstrations to protest against proposals to abolish Ajar autonomy and against perceived 'christianization' of the Muslim population. Elections took place to the Ajar Supreme Soviet in June 1991, in which Round Table-Free Georgia won the largest number of seats, but with far less support than in other regions of Georgia. Ajaria remained calm during the latter half of 1991 and during 1992. This situation continued into the beginning of 1994, apart from some reports in February 1993 of provocations against Russian troops in Ajaria by armed Ajar groups. Much of this stability was attributable to the statesmanship of Aslan Ibragimovich Abashidze, the Chairman of the Supreme Soviet of Ajaria. It was thought by many that Abashidze could become a leading force in national Georgian politics in the 1990s.

Abkhazia

Abkhazians began a campaign in 1989 for secession from Georgia, which was strongly opposed by nationalist Georgians. Abkhazians are a Turkic-speaking, predominantly Muslim, people who had enjoyed full republican status during the 1920s. However, in 1930 its status was reduced to that of an Autonomous Soviet Socialist Republic (ASSR) within Georgia, and, under Stalin, large numbers of western Georgians were resettled in the region. Consequently, by 1989, ethnic Abkhazians comprised only 17% of the area's population, while Georgians constituted 46%, the largest ethnic group. Abkhazian demands for secession were consistently rejected on these demographic grounds. In July 1989 there were violent clashes between ethnic Georgians and Abkhazians in Sukhumi, the Abkhazian capital. A state of emergency and a curfew were imposed in Sukhumi, but troops did not manage to prevent further intermittent violence throughout August.

On 25 August 1990 the Abkhazian Supreme Soviet voted to declare independence from Georgia and adopt the status of a full union republic. On the following day the declaration was pronounced invalid by the Presidium of the Georgian Supreme Soviet and Georgians living in Abkhazia staged protests and began a rail blockade of the capital, Sukhumi. On 31 August Georgian deputies in the Abkhazian Supreme Soviet reversed its previous decision and rescinded the independence declaration. During 1991 further tensions were reported as a result of Abkhazian participation in the Confederation of Mountain Peoples of the Caucasus, which united the small ethnic groups of the Northern Caucasus. The support of the Confederation for Abkhazian independence was criticized by the Georgian Government as interference in the internal affairs of Georgia. In January 1992 demonstrations in support of recently deposed President Gamsakhurdia resulted in the new Government sending troops to Abkhazia, who took control of the capital in February. Violent confrontations between the Zviadists and government troops continued for several months. A brief period of calm was disrupted in July, when the Abkhazian legislature declared Abkhazia's sovereignty as the 'Republic of Abkhazia', restoring the Constitution of

1925. This declaration was denounced by the Georgian Supreme Soviet.

In August 1992 the Georgian Government sent some 3,000 members of the National Guard to Abkhazia, supposedly in order to release the Minister of Internal Affairs and the other senior officials kidnapped by Zviadists. However, it was claimed that the covert reason for their deployment was in order to suppress the growing secessionist movement. In response to what they saw as an 'invasion', Abkhazian militias launched a series of attacks against the troops, on 14 August, but the better-equipped government forces succeeded in taking control of Sukhumi. More than 100 people were reported to have been killed in the fighting in August. The Chairman of the Abkhazian legislature and leader of the independence campaign, Vladislav Ardzinba, retreated north with his forces, to Gudauta. Russian paratroopers were dispatched to the region to protect Russian military bases. It was reported that volunteer fighters of the Confederation of Mountain Peoples of the Caucasus had joined the Abkhazian forces. The Russian President, Boris Yeltsin, appealed to Russian members of the Confederation not to participate in the conflict, and pledged support for Georgian national integrity.

Nevertheless, in September 1992, a confrontation between Georgian and Russian troops, near Sukhumi, in violation of a cease-fire agreed on 3 September, raised fears that Russia might be drawn into the conflict. In October Shevardnadze claimed that Abkhazia was receiving military support from conservative elements within the Russian armed forces and parliament. This followed a successful counter-offensive by the Abkhazians, who had regained control of all of northern Georgia and reportedly killed hundreds of ethnic Georgians. In early November, after announcing that its troops would appropriate all Russian military equipment based in the country, the Georgian Government took control of a large Russian arms depot in southern Georgia. There was a brief respite in the fighting, in mid-November, as the withdrawal of Russian and CIS troops from the conflict zone began. However, on 14 December 1992, Georgian–Russian relations deteriorated still further after Georgian forces shot down a Russian military helicopter over Abkhazia, killing all of the crew and most of the civilian passengers. The Georgians claimed that the helicopter was also carrying combat weapons, indicating 'interference' by the Russian military. In spite of this, the second round of Russian–Georgian negotiations to draft a treaty of friendship and co-operation, as well as to define the legal status of Russian regular and border troops based in Georgia (amongst other matters), still went ahead. Further negotiations were held by the Ministers of Defence of the two countries, in late December 1992 and in January 1993, and a draft treaty was concluded, whereby Russian troops were to remain in Georgia until the end of 1993.

In January 1993 Sukhumi, still held by Georgian forces, came under repeated shelling by Abkhazian troops. On 28 February President Yeltsin asserted that Russia should play a greater role in the region, although, at the same time, he claimed Russian neutrality and denied that Russian troops were fighting in the region. This neutral stance was compromised, however, when the escalation of both the fighting and of Georgian accusations of Russian involvement led to retaliatory measures being taken by Russian ground troops. When, on 14 May, a cease-fire was agreed between Georgian and Abkhazian forces, Shevardnadze maintained that the Russian authorities were not fully in control of their military.

On 2 July 1992, as peace negotiations began in Moscow (Russian Federation), Abkhazian forces attacked Sukhumi, killing at least 23 people. It was reported that the rebel troops were aided by volunteer forces from the Confederation of Mountain Peoples of the Caucasus. Four days later Shevardnadze imposed martial law in Abkhazia, in an attempt to stop mass desertion of demoralized Georgian troops to the Abkhazian forces. On 27 July, after more than three weeks of intense fighting, the Georgian and Abkhazian leaderships, following the mediation of the Russian Government, signed a UN-observed cease-fire agreement in the southern Russian town of Sochi. This so-called Sochi Agreement both recognized Abkhazian autonomy and supported Georgian national integrity. Georgian artillery and armoured vehicles withdrew from Abkhazia and prisoners of war were exchanged in accordance with the Agreement. This cease-fire lasted until 16 September, when Abkhazian forces attacked Sukhumi and the town of Ochamchire, taking advantage of their increased weaponry and of the fact that the Georgian Government's resources were diverted by a Zviadist rebellion in Mingrelia. It was reported that secessionist troops also benefited from Russian aid. After 11 days of fierce shelling Abkhazian troops finally gained control of the besieged capital and routed government troops. Shevardnadze, who had flown to Sukhumi as soon as the Abkhazian offensive was launched, was obliged to return to Tbilisi on 28 September. He blamed Russia's non-intervention for the Abkhazian capital's fall. On 30 September Abkhazian forces drove the last government forces out of the region and officially declared Abkhazia liberated from Georgia.

In the weeks that followed the capture of Sukhumi it was estimated that more than 200,000 people fled Abkhazia. There were reports of random executions and atrocities carried out by the victorious separatist troops against ethnic Georgians. On 1 December 1993 Georgian officials and Abkhazian separatists signed a UN-mediated eight-point peace 'memorandum', which agreed the terms for the repatriation of Georgian refugees in the autonomous region. However, two days later, there were reports of a renewed offensive by Abkhazian troops. On 11 January 1994 a second round of UN-mediated Georgian–Abkhazian peace negotiations began in Geneva (Switzerland), and a third round was scheduled for February.

South Ossetia

Georgian animosity towards the Ossetians stemmed partly from their pro-Soviet stance during the existence of independent Georgia in 1917–20. The Ossetians are an Eastern Iranian people who were divided under Stalin, North Ossetia falling under Russian jurisdiction and South Ossetia becoming an autonomous region of Georgia. In early 1989 leading Ossetians began to demonstrate support for the Abkhazian movement for secession. Tensions increased after the publication, in August, of legislation strengthening the status of the Georgian language in the Republic. The South-Ossetian Popular Front, Adaemon Nykhas, established earlier in the year, complained that the law discriminated against Ossetian-speakers, few of whom know Georgian. Adaemon Nykhas demanded that South Ossetia be upgraded to the status of an autonomous republic and eventually reunited with the North Ossetian Autonomous Republic, in the Russian Federation. These demands met with strong opposition from local Georgians and, in December 1989, there were violent clashes between Ossetians and Georgians. Soviet interior ministry troops were dispatched to the region in January 1990. In August the Georgian Supreme Soviet passed an electoral law which effectively banned Adaemon Nykhas from nominating candidates in elections to the Supreme Soviet. In response to what was viewed as discriminatory legislation, the South

Ossetian Supreme Soviet proclaimed the autonomous South Ossetian Soviet Democratic Republic, as a sovereign republic, on 20 September 1990. The next day this decision was declared unconstitutional by the Presidium of the Georgian Supreme Soviet.

Tension in South Ossetia increased with the election of the nationalist Gamsakhurdia to power in Tbilisi. Then the Georgian Supreme Soviet formally abolished the region's autonomous status, on 11 December 1990. In January 1991 the Soviet President, Mikhail Gorbachev, annulled both this decision and South Ossetia's September 1990 declaration of sovereignty, but violence continued between ethnic Georgians and Ossetians throughout 1991. By late 1991 an estimated 83,000 Ossetians had fled to North Ossetia and some 10,000 Georgians had left for other parts of Georgia. In December 1991 the South Ossetian legislature adopted a second declaration of the region's independence, as well as a resolution in favour of its integration into the Russian Federation. These resolutions were overwhelmingly endorsed by South Ossetians at a referendum held in January 1992. Hostilities were exacerbated by the intervention of Georgian government troops, which, by April, had surrounded and were shelling Tskhinvali, the regional capital. The Russian troops still in the region had become actively engaged in the region, albeit in a peace-keeping capacity. Their withdrawal commenced in April. A cease-fire agreed in May was almost immediately broken by Georgian militia, who attacked a convoy of South Ossetian refugees, reportedly killing 36 people.

Quadripartite negotiations, held in early July 1992 (with Russian participation), led to another cease-fire agreement, in accordance with which peace-keeping monitors were deployed in South Ossetia while all armed forces were withdrawn from the region. This cease-fire continued to be observed in 1993 and early 1994, in spite of the reiteration, in November 1992, by South Ossetia of its intention to secede from Georgia. On 23 December 1993 a new Constitution was adopted in South Ossetia, under which it was announced that parliamentary elections would take place in April 1994. The outcome of these elections would be important to the country as a whole, as any further moves by South Ossetia to secede from Georgia could jeopardize the stability of the Georgian state. This was a situation that conservative elements of the Russian establishment welcomed, but one which both the Georgian and Russian Governments had attempted to avoid by allowing Georgia the security of membership of the CIS.

The Economy

Owing to the political instability in the country following independence from the USSR, in 1991, Georgia's economy experienced a severe decline in the early 1990s. Previously, agriculture and tourism were the mainstays of the economy. As a member of the USSR, Georgia had experienced a comparatively high standard of living, owing to geography, climate and wide variety of agricultural produce. In 1992, according to International Monetary Fund (IMF) estimates, Georgia's gross domestic product (GDP), at current prices, was 134,397m. roubles. This represented an increase on 1991, when GDP was 20,766m. roubles. However, in real terms, there was a fall in GDP owing to the devaluation of the currency. In 1991 GDP per head was the equivalent of 3,796 roubles. Net material product (NMP), the measure of economic performance used under the centrally planned system, was estimated to have declined in real terms during the early 1990s: by 12.4% in 1990; by 20.6% in 1991; and by 45.6% in 1992. In the last year, measured at 1990 prices, NMP was an estimated 4,696m. roubles.

AGRICULTURE

The climate of Georgia allowed the cultivation of subtropical crops, such as tea and citrus fruits. Non-citrus fruits, flowers, wine grapes, tobacco and almonds were also produced, and some grain and sugar beet was grown. The mountain pastures were used for sheep and goat farming. In 1992 agriculture and livestock accounted for an estimated 39.2% of NMP. In the previous year the sector had accounted for an estimated 41.9% of NMP, when 27.1% of the working population were employed in the agricultural and forestry sector. The significant increase in agriculture's share of NMP (compared to some 23% in 1987–89) was not, however, an indication of the sector's vigour. The political unrest destroyed the tourist industry and disrupted trade and the import of energy and raw materials, decreasing the relative contribution of other sectors of the economy.

The principal crops, in 1992, were grapes (an estimated 550,000 metric tons), water-melons (an estimated 480,000 metric tons) and vegetables (approximately 320,000 metric tons). However, in this year, agricultural and livestock output decreased by 48.8%, accounting for 39.3% of NMP. In particular, decreases were recorded in the production of grain crops, vegetables and tea. This was caused by a reduction in cultivated land owing to civil unrest. Similarly, livestock production (per head, excluding poultry) contracted, between 1990 and 1992 by 14.8%. Poultry production decreased by an estimated 16.6%. Previously, the state-owned sector was primarily responsible for agricultural output, but, following a series of economic reforms, by 1992 some 55% of Georgia's cultivated land was privately owned (the Government intended to increase this to 75% by the end of 1993).

INDUSTRY

In 1992 industrial production, including turnover tax, was estimated at 1,899m. roubles (at 1990 prices) and accounted for 40.3% of Georgia's NMP. This was a decrease of 33.9% on industrial production one year previously, when the sector accounted for 33.3% of NMP. In the mid-1980s the sector had accounted for some 44% of NMP. In 1991 industry employed 19.4% of the working population.

The largest and most important industrial sector in the country was the production of light industrial goods, for which Georgia relied on imported raw materials and energy products. In the light industrial goods sector natural fabrics were the principal products. In 1992 output of cotton fabrics totalled an estimated 12.9m. sq m and silk 9.7m. sq m. However, this constituted a decrease of 54.4% and 64.2%, respectively, on the previous year's production. Georgia was noted for its viticulture: in 1990 wine production totalled 1,628,300 hectolitres. In 1991 this figure had dropped to 1,261,600 hectolitres and, by 1992, wine production was an estimated 713,000 hectolitres, a decrease of

43.5% on the previous year. Production of mazout, a by-product of petroleum distillation, and one of the country's main industrial products, fell by 75.2%, in 1992, to an estimated 189,000 metric tons (production had reached a peak of 1,795,000 tons in 1987). Similarly, steel production decreased by 44.4% in 1992. It was officially estimated that industrial production as a whole fell by 45% in 1992.

Unlike in agriculture, the privatization of industry had not made much progress by the end of 1993. The process was hindered by the lack of a legal framework, as well as the generally unfavourable conditions for the economy. Some small-scale privatization was achieved in 1993, particularly in the city of Tbilisi, but this was mainly of retail activities. The privatization of large industrial enterprises (about 100 of Georgia's 1,365 large enterprises had been identified by the State Property Management Agency) was intended to take the form of a mass 'voucher' privatization programme, the first stage to take place before the end of 1994.

MINING AND ENERGY

Georgia was dependent on neighbouring countries for most of its energy needs. In 1992 the country suffered severe energy shortages after civil and inter-regional conflict led to supply lines being blocked. In 1990 petroleum accounted for almost one-half of primary energy consumption, natural gas for one-third and hydroelectric power for almost one-fifth. During the 1980s domestic production of coal and crude petroleum gradually decreased. In the early 1990s, however, this fall in coal production accelerated. Between 1990 and 1992 domestic coal production decreased by 87%, to 125,000 metric tons (production had reached 1,712,000 tons in 1986). The decline in domestic coal production was largely owing to the substitution of cheap gas from other countries in the former USSR for coal in the power-generating system, the depletion of existing fields and the lack of investment in the sector. Production of crude petroleum had stabilized at about 185,000 metric tons (1989) annually between 1986 and 1990, although in 1985 production had been 552,000 tons. Output declined slightly in 1991 and was estimated to have fallen to 125,000 tons in 1992, and perhaps lower thereafter. There were also contractions in the production of natural gas (59.9m. cu m in 1990 to an estimated 12m. cu m in 1992) and electric energy (15,800m. kWh in 1989 to an estimated 11,472m. kWh in 1992).

As a result of the contraction in domestic energy production, imports of natural gas, petroleum and electricity, as a proportion of total available energy resources, increased in the early 1990s. According to estimates, almost 80% of total energy resources available, in 1990, were imported, and this percentage increased in 1991 and 1992. Imports of natural gas, the largest energy import, were an estimated 6,769m. cu m in the first nine months of 1992. This was compared to domestic production for the whole year which stood at approximately 12m. cu m. Imports of gas had been drastically reduced in 1991 (to 4,581m. cu m), as a result of the blockade of gas pipelines in South Ossetia. However, although energy imports had a larger proportion of the market, the amounts of energy imported actually decreased in 1991 and 1992. Imports of fuel oil fell from 1,652,000 metric tons, in 1991, to an estimated 261,000 tons in the first nine months of 1992. Until 1991 Russia was Georgia's main supplier of energy imports. Prompted in part by severe reductions in Russian exports to other countries of the former USSR, and also to the civil unrest in South Ossetia (which is crossed by major pipelines), Georgia began to diversify its energy sources in 1992. Azerbaijan, Iran, Turkey and Turkmenistan all became suppliers.

SERVICES, TRADE AND FINANCE

Services were an important sector in the Georgian economy and were expected to remain so in the 1990s. Before the dissolution of the USSR in December 1991 (upon the creation of the Commonwealth of Independent States—CIS), port services and the transportation of goods to other Republics formed a significant part of economic activity. It was expected that these services would increase as Georgia's neighbouring countries expanded their overseas trade. However, the services sector were particularly adversely affected by the internal conflicts in Georgia in the early 1990s.

Tourism was also an important source of revenue for the Georgian economy, owing to the favourable climate and the country's many health resorts and spas. Popular tourist destinations in Georgia included Black Sea resorts and ski resorts in the Greater Caucasian mountain range. In the late 1980s an average of 1.5m. tourists from other USSR countries visited Georgia each year. Again, however, in the early 1990s, adverse economic conditions and the worsening political situation in Georgia led to a decline in the tourism sector.

Between 1988 and 1990 Georgia suffered a slight, but increasing, trade deficit (856m. roubles in 1990). This was largely owing to the increase in the cost of energy imports. The most significant area of imports, in 1990, was in the machine-building and metal-working sector, which accounted for 23.1% of total imports. The former Soviet republics were responsible for the large majority of imports into Georgia (4,948m. roubles or 72.3% of total imports). The food industry constituted the largest area of exports, in 1990, accounting for 2,387m. roubles or 39.9% of total exports. Again, inter-republican trade constituted the largest proportion of Georgian exports, 5,724m. roubles or 95.7% of all export trade. However, following the dissolution of the USSR, in December 1991, it was estimated that the volume of external trade halved and the trade deficit expanded. This was owing to the reduction in trade links with other Soviet Republics and the worsening political and economical situation in Georgia. According to IMF estimates, despite recording a trade deficit of US $108.5m. in 1992, Georgia's current balance on its balance-of-payments, in the same year, was $23.9m.

The average annual increase in consumer prices was estimated at 3.3% in 1990 and 78.5% in 1991. In 1992 consumer prices increased by an estimated 913.1%. The steep increase in consumer prices reflected several stages of price liberalization, severe increases in imported energy prices and increasing pressure on the deteriorating economy. According to official estimates, consumer prices increased, in 1993, by an average of 20% each month. The monthly minimum wage was increased six times in 1992 but increased only slightly in real terms. In 1992 the state budget revenue amounted to an estimated 18,872m. roubles (14.0% of GDP) and expenditure to 42,672m. roubles (31.8% of GDP). The state budget deficit was 23,800m. roubles, 17.8% of GDP. In the previous year there was a budget surplus of 276m. roubles, equivalent to 1.3% of GDP.

Georgia became a member of the IMF on 5 May 1992. In the same year the country also joined the World Bank and the European Bank for Reconstruction and Development (EBRD). Membership of these institutions enabled Georgia, in April 1993, to become the sixth former Soviet Republic to abandon the rouble as its official currency. The Government introduced a temporary coupon to counter the shortage of money and as a first step towards full monetary independence. The policy was precipitated by the July 1993 decision of the Russian Central Bank to invalidate all pre-1993 roubles. The coupon was introduced on a par with the rouble, but soon lost value, and most transactions continued to make use of the old currency or (particularly in the flourishing parallel economy) of foreign convertible currencies.

PROBLEMS AND PROSPECTS

The transformation of Georgia's rigid, centrally planned economy into a market economy, following independence, proved a difficult one. Among the problems that had to be resolved were an inefficient taxation system, a one-tier banking system and a bureaucratic trade regime. The situation was exacerbated by the sustained civil and inter-regional conflicts, which further depleted the country's already low resources. The Georgian Government made some progress, in 1991, towards the resolution of these problems: the adoption of legislation approving the reconstruction of the banking system and foreign investment, price liberalization and the implementation of privatization programmes. However, in 1992, this progress slowed. In September 1993 it was reported that most factories were only operating at 15% of their full capacity and that 40% of the Tbilisi work-force was unemployed. According to official statistics, the following month, 80% of Georgians were living below the poverty line. However, further reforms were introduced later in 1992 (September and December) and in 1993. The industrial sector needed to attract foreign investors in order to gain access to technology and market-orientated management through more comprehensive privatization programmes. Financial aid and further foreign and inter-republican trade agreements were necessary if the country were to survive economically into the mid-1990s. However, the recovery of the Georgian economy was more dependent, in the early 1990s, on the political stability of the country and the cessation of its civil and inter-regional conflicts.

Statistical Survey

Principal sources: IMF, *Georgia, Economic Review*; World Bank, *Statistical Handbook: States of the Former USSR*.

Area and Population

AREA, POPULATION AND DENSITY

Area (sq km)	69,700*
Population (census result)	
12 January 1989†	
Males	2,562,040
Females	2,838,801
Total	5,400,841
Population (official estimate at 1 January 1991)	5,471,000
Density (per sq km) at 1 January 1991	78.5

* 26,911 sq miles.
† Population is *de jure*. The *de facto* total was 5,443,359.

PRINCIPAL TOWNS
(estimated population at 1 January 1990)

Tbilisi (capital)	1,268,000	Batumi	137,000
Kutaisi	236,000	Sukhumi	122,000
Rustavi	160,000		

BIRTHS, MARRIAGES AND DEATHS

	Registered live births		Registered marriages		Registered deaths	
	Number	Rate (per 1,000)	Number	Rate (per 1,000)	Number	Rate (per 1,000)
1987	94,595	17.9	39,157	7.4	46,332	8.8
1988	91,905	17.1	38,100	7.1	47,544	8.9
1989	91,138	16.7	38,288	7.0	47,077	8.6

EMPLOYMENT (annual averages, '000 persons)

	1989	1990	1991
Material sector	1,860.5	1,919.3	1,726.2
Industry	537.1	559.8	487.7
Construction	265.9	280.6	224.8
Agriculture	655.5	695.0	671.0
Forestry	12.2	11.7	11.2
Transport and communications	123.3	114.9	103.5
Trade and other services	266.5	257.3	227.0
Non-material sector	839.3	844.0	787.9
Housing and municipal services	122.6	131.4	110.1
Science, research and development	72.9	73.2	63.2
Education, culture and arts	301.4	310.0	290.1
Health, social security and sports	189.3	183.8	185.6
Banking and financial institutions	11.6	11.8	12.0
Government	55.1	51.6	48.1
Other non-material services	86.4	82.2	78.8
Total	2,699.8	2,763.3	2,514.1

Agriculture

PRINCIPAL CROPS ('000 metric tons)

	1990	1990	1992*
Wheat	258	196	180
Barley	118	75	59
Maize	270	209	210
Potatoes	294	226	200
Sunflower seed	9	16†	14
Vegetables*	443	363	320
Water-melons*	500	500	480
Grapes	691	600*	550
Sugar beet	34	18	16
Tea	126	110*	100
Tobacco (leaves)	22	22	9†

* Estimate(s). † Unofficial estimate(s).

Source: FAO, *Production Yearbook*.

LIVESTOCK ('000 head at 1 January)

	1990	1991	1992
Cattle	1,427	1,298	1,100*
Pigs	1,028	880	850*
Sheep and goats†	1,600	1,600	1,500
Poultry (million)†	24	22	20

* FAO estimate(s). † Unofficial estimate(s).

Source: FAO, *Production Yearbook*.

LIVESTOCK PRODUCTS
('000 metric tons, unless otherwise indicated)

	1990	1991	1992
Meat (slaughter weight)	170	151	133
Milk	660	602	500*
Eggs*	43,120	34,750	32,300

* Unofficial estimate(s).

Source: FAO, *Production Yearbook*.

Fishing

('000 metric tons)

	1989	1990	1991
Total catch	148	104	56

Mining

('000 metric tons, unless otherwise indicated)

	1990	1991	1992*
Coal	956	698	125
Crude petroleum	186	181	125
Natural gas (million cu m)	60	491	12
Manganese ore	1,213	491	290

* Estimates.

Industry

SELECTED PRODUCTS
('000 metric tons, unless otherwise indicated)

	1990	1991	1992*
Margarine	34.1	16.0	2.3
Vegetable oil	13.8	7.4	0.1
Wine ('000 hectolitres)	1,628.3	1,216.6	713.0
Beer ('000 hectolitres)	947.7	601.1	328.8
Cigarettes (million)	11,200	9,800	5,100
Wool yarn	8.0	4.1	n.a.
Cotton yarn	10.5	6.6	n.a.
Cotton fabrics (million sq metres)	34.1	16.7	12.9
Woollen fabrics (million sq metres)	9.8	6.1	3.4
Footwear (million pairs)	13.3	12.2	2.6
Paper	26.6	20.5	2.1
Synthetic resins and plastics	40.1	26.4	7.6
Chemical fibres and threads	32.3	20.0	4.5
Soap	12.1	6.9	n.a.
Motor spirit (petrol)	399.0	324.4	72.0
Diesel fuel	658.0	494.7	111.0
Lubricating oil	3.9	n.a.	n.a.
Mazout	898.0	736.6	189.0
Building bricks (million)	328.0	170.6	n.a.
Steel	1,316.0	961.7	535.0
Electric energy (million kWh)	14,240	13,376	11,472

* Estimate(s).

Finance

CURRENCY AND EXCHANGE RATES

Monetary Units

100 kopeks = 1 rubl (ruble or rouble).

Sterling and Dollar Equivalents (30 September 1993)

£1 sterling = 1,796.1 roubles;
US $1 = 1,201.0 roubles;
10,000 roubles = £5.568 = $8.326.

Average Exchange Rate (roubles per US dollar)

1989	0.6274
1990	0.5856
1991	0.5819

Note: The figures for average exchange rates refer to official rates for the Soviet rouble. However, a multiple exchange rate system was in operation, with separate non-commercial and tourist rates. A commercial exchange rate was introduced on 1 November 1990, replacing the official rate for most transactions. The commercial rate (roubles per US dollar) was: 1.692 at 31 December 1990; 1.671 at 31 December 1991. Between November 1989 and April 1991 the tourist exchange rate valued the rouble at one-tenth of the official rate. In April 1991 this rate, renamed the 'special rate', was set at $1 = 27.6 roubles. It was subsequently adjusted. The average market exchange rate in 1991 was $1 = 31.2 roubles. Following the dissolution of the USSR in December 1991, Russia and several other former Soviet republics retained the rouble as their monetary unit. In April 1993 the National Bank of Georgia issued coupons in various denominations to circulate alongside (and initially at par with) the Russian rouble. From August these coupons became the sole legal tender, but their value rapidly depreciated. At 29 October the exchange rate was 35 coupons per rouble.

BUDGET (million roubles)

Revenue	1991	1992*
Tax revenue	4,631	15,218
Turnover tax	2,124	697†
Sales tax	222	—
Value added tax	—	4,012
Excise taxes	—	2,623
Profit tax	1,495	5,726
State enterprises	1,236	5,254
Private sector	259	473
Individual income tax	697	1,604
Foreign trade taxes	93	554
Land tax	—	1
Non-tax revenue	1,567	3,655
Total	6,198	18,872

* Preliminary figures.
† Includes some excise tax collections during the period Jan.–April 1992.

Expenditure	1991	1992*
National economy	2,878	20,815
Social and cultural services	2,526	12,325
Education and culture	1,520	8,421
Health care and sports	812	2,996
Social needs	120	34
Science	74	874
Administration and law enforcement	242	6,559
State administration	124	1,288
Law enforcement	118	1,727
Defence†	—	3,545
Other expenditures	276	2,972
Total	5,922	42,672

* Preliminary figures.
† When not shown, separately, defence expenditure is included under law enforcement.

Capital investment for the total economy was 10,620m. roubles in 1992.

MONEY SUPPLY (million roubles at 31 December)

	1989	1990	1991
Currency in circulation	10,260	11,478	13,943
Demand deposits at banks	1,626	2,448	4,866
Total money	11,886	13,926	18,809

COST OF LIVING
(Retail Price Index; base: Dec. 1990 = 100)

	1991	1992
All items	160.5	1,626.0

NATIONAL ACCOUNTS
Net Material Product (million roubles at current prices)

	1990	1991	1992*
Agriculture and livestock	4,046	4,920	24,347
Industry†	3,800	6,148	28,201
Construction	1,194	1,318	6,453
Transport and communications	532	553	16,969
Trade and catering	613	819	1,909
Other branches of the material sphere	681	980	4,876
Total	10,866	14,737	82,755

BALANCE OF PAYMENTS (estimates, US $ million)

	1992
Merchandise exports f.o.b.	160.6
Merchandise imports f.o.b.	-269.1
Trade balance	-108.5
Services (net)	-17.8
Income	36.4
Private unrequited transfers (net)	66.2
Current balance	-23.7
Direct investment (net)	7.0
Other capital (net)	-5.0
Net errors and omissions	45.5
Overall balance	23.9

Source: IMF, *International Financial Statistics*.

External Trade

PRINCIPAL COMMODITIES (million roubles)

Imports	1988	1989	1990
Industry	6,118	6,008	6,201
Oil and gas industry	413	360	285
Ferrous metallurgy	489	443	430
Non-ferrous metallurgy	102	106	97
Chemical fuel industry	541	544	576
Machine-building and metal-working	1,533	1,522	1,580
Timber, wood, pulp and paper	248	244	279
Building materials	155	148	117
Light industry	1,221	1,287	1,372
Food industry	1,204	1,142	1,174
Agriculture	348	358	498
Other branches	27	103	140
Total	6,493	6,469	6,839
Inter-republican	5,218	4,888	4,948
Foreign	1,275	1,581	1,891

Exports	1988	1989	1990
Industry	5,610	5,789	5,486
Oil and gas industry	100	68	68
Ferrous metallurgy	375	376	318
Chemical fuel industry	316	343	339
Machine-building and metal-working	848	869	804
Light industry	1,275	1,285	1,260
Food industry	2,438	2,573	2,387
Agriculture	280	190	404
Other branches	11	105	93
Total	5,901	6,084	5,983
Inter-republican	5,508	5,719	5,724
Foreign	393	465	259

Education

(1989/90)

	Institutions	Students
Secondary schools	3,700	880,600
Secondary specialized institutions	88	44,100
Higher schools (incl. universities)	19	93,100

Directory

The Constitution

A new constitution was being drafted in 1993.

The Government

(February 1994)

HEAD OF STATE

Chairman of the Georgian Supreme Soviet: EDUARD AMVROSIS DZE SHEVARDNADZE (elected by direct popular vote 11 October 1992).

CABINET OF MINISTERS

Prime Minister: OTAR PATSATSIA.

Deputy Prime Ministers: ZURAB KERVALISHVILI, NIKOLOZ LEKISHVILI, AVTANDIL MARGIANI, AMIRAN KADAGISHVILI, IRAKLI MENAGHARISHVILI, TAMAZ NADAREISHVILI.

Minister of Agriculture and the Food Industry: GIORGI KVESITADZE.

Minister of Communications: PRIDON INJIA.

Minister for Control of State Property: AVTANDIL SILAGADZE.

Minister of Culture: DAVID MAGHRADZE.

Minister of Defence: EDUARD SHEVARDNADZE (acting).

Minister of Economic Reform: (vacant).

Minister of Education: TAMAZ KVACHANTIRADZE.

Minister of the Environment: SHOTA ADAMIA.

Minister of Finance: DAVIT IAKOBIDZE.

Minister of Foreign Affairs: ALEKSANDR CHIKVAIDZE.

Minister of Health: AVTANDIL JORBENADZE.

Minister of Industry: VLADIMER KERESELIDZE.

Minister of Internal Affairs: SHOTA KVIRAIA.

Minister of Justice: TEDO NINIDZE.

Minister of Labour and Social Security: VAZHA GUJABIDZE.

Minister of Security: IGOR GIORGADZE.

Minister of Trade and Supply: MURTAZ ZANKALIANI.

MINISTRIES

Office of the Prime Minister: 380034 Tbilisi, Ingorokva.

Ministry of Agriculture and the Food Industry: 380079 Tbilisi, Kostava 41; tel. (8832) 99-62-61.

Ministry of Communications: 380004 Tbilisi, Rustaveli 12; tel. (8832) 99-94-24.

Ministry of the Control of State Property: Tbilisi.

Ministry of Culture: 380008 Tbilisi, Rustaveli 35; tel. (8832) 93-22-55.

Ministry of Defence: Tbilisi.

Ministry of Economic Reform: 380008 Tbilisi, Rustaveli 8; tel. (8832) 99-97-58.

Ministry of Education: 380002 Tbilisi, Uznadze 52; tel. (8832) 95-88-86.

Ministry of the Environment: 380071 Tbilisi, Mindeli 9; tel. (8832) 38-58-39.

Ministry of Finance: 38008 Tbilisi, Rustaveli 8; tel. (8832) 99-97-58.

Ministry of Foreign Affairs: 380008 Tbilisi, Chitadze 4; tel. (8832) 99-72-49.

Ministry of Health: 380060 Tbilisi, K. Gamsakhurdia 30; tel. (8832) 38-70-71.

Ministry of Industry: 380060 Tbilisi, K. Gamsakhurdia 28; tel. (8832) 38-47-79.

Ministry of Internal Affairs: 380014 Tbilisi, Bolsaya 10; tel. (8832) 99-62-33.

Ministry of Justice: 380026 Tbilisi, Rustaveli 30; tel. (8832) 93-27-21.

Ministry of Labour and Social Security: 380007 Tbilisi, Leonidze 2; tel. (8832) 93-62-36.

Ministry of Security: Tbilisi.

Ministry of Trade and Supply: 380062 Tbilisi, Chavchavadze 64; tel. (8832) 29-30-61.

Legislature

GEORGIAN SUPREME SOVIET

Chairman: EDUARD SHEVARDNADZE.

Speaker: VAKHTANG GOGUADZE.

Deputy Speakers: RUSUDAN BERIDZE, VAKHTANG RCHEULISHVILI.

At the election to the 235-member Georgian Supreme Soviet, held on 11 October 1992, the largest representation was won by the following parties or groups: Peace bloc (29 seats), 11 October coalition (18), Unity bloc (14), National Democratic Party of Georgia (13), Green Party (11).

Local Government

Georgia contains two Autonomous Republics and one disputed Autonomous Oblast. In January 1991 a system of prefectures was introduced, appointed by and responsible directly to the President of the Republic. In January 1992 the ruling Military Council abolished the prefectures, along with the presidency, and appointed its own representatives in the regions.

AUTONOMOUS REPUBLICS

Abkhazia

Abkhazia is situated in the north-west of Georgia and covers an area of 8,600 sq km. In 1989 the total population was 537,000. In 1989 17.8% of the population were Abkhazians, most of the remainder being ethnic Georgians (45.7%). The capital is Sukhumi. Formerly a colony of the Eastern Roman or Byzantine Empire, Abkhazia was an important power in the ninth and 10th centuries, but it was later dominated by Georgian, Turkish and Russian rulers. The language is Abkhazian, a member of the North-Western group of Caucasian languages.

Chairman of the Supreme Soviet: VLADISLAV G. ARDZINBA.

Chairman of the Council of Ministers: ZURAB ERKVANIA.

Prime Minister: SOKRAT JINJOLIA.

Ajaria

The Autonomous Republic of Ajaria was established on 16 July 1922. It is situated in the south-west of Georgia, on the border with Turkey, and covers an area of 3,000 sq km. In 1989 the population was 393,000. The capital is Batumi. The Ajars are a Georgian people, who adopted Islam while Ajaria was under Ottoman rule. The Ajars have an unwritten language, Ajar, which is closely related to Georgian, but has been strongly influenced by Turkish.

Chairman of the Supreme Soviet: ASLAN IBRAGIMOVICH ABASHIDZE.

Chairman of the Council of Ministers: JEMAL NAKASHIDZE.

AUTONOMOUS OBLAST

South Ossetia

The South Ossetian Autonomous Oblast (Region) was established on 20 April 1922. It is situated in the north of Georgia and borders the North Ossetian Autonomous Republic (within Russia) to the north. It covers an area of 3,900 sq km. In 1989 the population was 99,000. In 1979 66.4% of the population were Ossetians and 28.8% Georgians. The capital is Tshkhinvali. The Regional Council (oblast soviet) adopted a declaration of sovereignty in September 1990 and proclaimed the territory the South Ossetian Soviet Democratic Republic. The region's autonomous status was abolished by the Georgian Supreme Soviet, in December 1990, and it was merged with adjoining areas to form an administrative region known as Shidi Kartli. The Ossetians are an Iranian (Persian) people, some of whom adopted Islam from the Kabardinians. The national language is Ossetian, a member of the North-Eastern group of Iranian languages. Jurisdiction in the region was disputed between the 'Supreme Soviet' and a Presidential Representative for Shidi Kartli. Following the ousting of President Gamsakhurdia, the Military Council released the South Ossetian leader and reformed the system of local government. Tension in the area eased, although South Ossetia persisted in its stated intent to secede.

The territory introduced a new Constitution in December 1993 and scheduled elections for April 1994.

Chairman of the Supreme Soviet of South Ossetia: LUDVIG CHIBIROV.

Chairman of the Council of Ministers: ZANAUR N. GASSIEV.

Political Organizations

The Communist Party of Georgia (CPG), which had previously held power, was disbanded in August 1991. More than 30 parties and alliances contested the legislative election of 11 October 1992. The following are among the more established parties in Georgia:

Agrarian Party of Georgia: Tbilisi; f. 1994; Chair. ROIN LIPARTELIANI.

Citizen's Union of Georgia: Tbilisi; f. 1993; 100,000 mems; Chair. EDUARD SHEVARDNADZE; Deputy Chair. REZO AMASHUKELI; Gen. Sec. ZURAB ZHVANIA.

Georgian Popular Front: Tbilisi; f. 1989; 50,000 mems; Chair. NODAR NOTADZE.

Georgian Social Democratic Party: Tbilisi; f. 1893; dissolved 1921; re-established 1990; Sec.-Gen. GURAM MUCHAIDZE.

National Democratic Party of Georgia: 380008 Tbilisi, Rustaveli 21; tel. (8832) 98-31-86; fax (8832) 98-31-88; f. 1981; Leader GIORGI CHANTURIA.

National Independence Party: Tbilisi; Chair. IRAKLI TSERETELI.

Workers' Union of Georgia: Tbilisi; f. 1993; Chair. VAKHTANG GABUNIA.

Diplomatic Representation

EMBASSIES IN GEORGIA

Germany: Tbilisi, Metechi Palace Hotel; tel. (8832) 74-45-56; fax (8832) 74-20-52; Ambassador: GÜNTHER DAHLHOFF.

Israel: Tbilisi, Metechi Palace Hotel; tel. (8832) 74-45-56; fax (8832) 74-20-52; Ambassador: BARUKH BIRENBAUM.

Kazakhstan: Tbilisi, Metechi Palace Hotel; tel. (8832) 74-45-56; fax (8832) 74-20-52.

Russia: Tbilisi; Ambassador: VLADIMIR ZEMSKIY.

Turkey: Tbilisi, Davit Aghmashenebeli 61; tel. (8832) 29-23-19; telex 212997; fax (8832) 95-18-10.

USA: Tbilisi, Atoneli 25; tel. (8832) 93-38-03; Ambassador: KENT BROWN.

Judicial System

Chairman of the Supreme Court: MINDIA UGREKHELIDZE.

Procurator-General: JAMLET BABILASHVILI.

Deputy Procurator-General: ANZOR BALUASHVILI.

Religion

CHRISTIANITY

The Georgian Orthodox Church

The Georgian Orthodox Church is divided into 15 dioceses, and includes not only Georgian parishes, but also several Russian and Greek Orthodox communities, which are under the jurisdiction of the Primate of the Georgian Orthodox Church. There are eight monasteries, a theological academy and a seminary. In 1986 the Church had an estimated 5m. members.

Patriarchate: 380005 Tbilisi, Sioni St 4; tel. (8832) 72-27-18; Catholicos-Patriarch of All Georgia ILIYA II.

ISLAM

There are Islamic communities among the Ajars, Abkhazians, Azerbaijanis, Kurds and some Ossetians. The country falls under the jurisdiction of the muftiate based in Baku (Azerbaijan).

The Press

In 1989 there were 149 officially-registered newspaper titles being published in Georgia, including 128 published in Georgian, and 75 periodicals, 61 in Georgian. Newspapers are also published in Russian, Armenian, Azerbaijani, Abkhazian and Ossetian.

Department of the Press: 380008 Tbilisi, Dzorjiashvili 12; tel. (8832) 98-70-08; govt regulatory body; Dir V. RTSKHILADZE.

PRINCIPAL NEWSPAPERS

In Georgian except where otherwise stated.

Akhalgazrda Iverieli (Young Iberian): Tbilisi; 3 a week; organ of the Supreme Soviet; Editor M. BALARJISHVILI.

Eri (Nation): Tbilisi; weekly; organ of the Supreme Soviet; Editor A. SILAGADZE.

Gurjistan: Tbilisi; in Azeri.

Iberia Spektr: Tbilisi; Editor IRAKLI GOTSIRIDZE. (In 1993 this newspaper was banned by the Georgian Government for allegedly supporting deposed President Gamsakhurdia's forces.)

Literaturuli Sakartvelo (Literary Georgia): 380004 Tbilisi, Rustaveli 7; tel. (8832) 99-84-04; weekly; organ of the Union of Writers of Georgia; Editor T. TSIVTSIVADZE.

Mamuli (Native Land): Tbilisi; fortnightly; organ of the Rustaveli Society; Editor T. CHANTURIA.

Respublika (Republic): Tbilisi; weekly; organ of the Council of Ministers; Editor J. NINUA.

Sakartvelos Respublika (Republic of Georgia): Tbilisi; 5 a week; organ of the Supreme Soviet; Editor M. PACHUASHVILI.

Svobodnaya Gruziya (Free Georgia): Tbilisi; in Russian.

Tavisupali Sakartvelo (Free Georgia): Tbilisi; 2 a week; organ of Round Table–Free Georgia.

Vestnik Gruzii (Georgian Herald): Tbilisi; 5 a week; organ of the Supreme Soviet; in Russian; Editor V. KESHELAVA.

Vrastan: Tbilisi; in Armenian.

PRINCIPAL PERIODICALS

Alashara: 394981 Sukhumi, Dom pravitelstva, kor. 1; tel. (88300) 2-35-40; organ of Abkhazian Writers' Organization of the Union of Writers of Georgia; in Abkhazian.

Dila (Morning): 380096 Tbilisi, Lenin 14; tel. (8832) 99-41-30; f. 1904; monthly; illustrated; for 5–10-year-olds; Editor-in-Chief REVAZ INANISHVILI; circ. 168,000.

Drosha (Banner): Tbilisi; f. 1923; monthly; politics and fiction; Editor O. KINKLADZE.

Fidiyag: Tskhinvali, Lenin 3; tel. 2-22-65; organ of the South Ossetian Writers' Organization of the Union of Writers of Georgia; in Ossetian.

Khelovneba (Art): Tbilisi; f. 1953, fmrly *Sabchota Khelovneba;* monthly; journal of the Ministry of Culture; Editor N. GURABANIDZE.

Kritika (Criticism): 380008 Tbilisi, Rustaveli 42; tel. (8832) 93-22-85; f. 1972; every 2 months; publ. by Merani Publishing House; journal of the Union of Writers of Georgia; literature, miscellaneous; Editor V. KHARCHILAVA.

Literaturnaya Gruziya (Literary Georgia): 380008 Tbilisi, Lenin 5; tel. (8832) 93-65-15; f. 1957; monthly; journal of the Union of Writers of Georgia; politics and fiction; in Russian; Editor R. MIMINOSHVILI.

Metsniereba da Tekhnika (Science and Technology): Tbilisi; f. 1949; monthly; publ. by the Metsniereba Publishing House; journal of the Georgian Academy of Sciences; popular; Editor Z. TSILOSANI.

Mnatobi (Luminary): 380004 Tbilisi, Rustaveli 12; tel. (8832) 93-55-11; f. 1924; monthly; journal of the Union of Writers of Georgia; fiction and politics; Editor A. SULAKAURI.

Nakaduli (Stream): Tbilisi, Kostava 14; tel. (8832) 93-31-81; f. 1926; fmrly *Pioneri*; monthly; journal of the Ministry of Education; illustrated; for 10–15-year-olds; Editor V. GINCHARADZE; circ. 35,000.

Niangi (Crocodile): Tbilisi; f. 1923; fortnightly; satirical; Editor Z. BOLKVADZE.

Politika (Politics): Tbilisi; theoretical, political, social sciences; Editor M. GOGUADZE.

Sakartvelos Kali (Georgian Woman): 380096 Tbilisi, Kostava 14; tel. (8832) 99-98-71; f. 1957; monthly; journal of the Georgian Supreme Soviet; popular, socio-political and literary; Editor-in-Chief NARGIZA MGELADZE; circ. 95,000.

Sakartvelos Metsnierebata Akedemiis Matsne (Herald of the Georgian Academy of Sciences, Biological Series): Tbilisi; f. 1975; once every two months; in Georgian and Russian; Editor-in-Chief VAZHA OKUJAVA.

Sakartvelos Metsnierebata Akedemiis Matsne (Herald of the Georgian Academy of Sciences, Chemical Series): Tbilisi; f. 1975; quarterly; in Georgian and Russian; Editor-in-Chief TEIMURAZ ANDRONIKASHVILI.

Sakartvelos Metsnierebata Akademiis Moambe (Bulletin of Georgian Academy of Sciences): 380060 Tbilisi, D. Gamrekeli 19; tel. (8832) 37-86-78; f. 1940; once every two months; in Georgian, Russian and English; Editor-in-Chief ALBERT TAVKHELIDZE.

Saunje (Treasure): 380007 Tbilisi, Dadiani 2; tel. (8832) 72-47-31; f. 1974; 6 a year; organ of the Union of Writers of Georgia; foreign literature in translation; Editor S. NISHNIANIDZE.

Tsiskari (Dawn): 380007 Tbilisi, Dadiani 2; tel. (8832) 99-85-81; f. 1957; monthly; organ of the Union of Writers of Georgia; fiction; Editor I. KEMERTELIDZE.

NEWS AGENCIES

In November 1991 the Council of Ministers disbanded Sakartvelo, the official Georgian news agency. A new government information agency was established.

Georgian News Agency: 380008 Tbilisi, Rustaveli 42; f. 1921; Dir IRAKLI KENCHOSVILI.

Iberia: Tbilisi; Chair. KAKHA GAGLOSHVILI.

Publishers

Ganatleba (Education): 380025 Tbilisi, Orjonikidze 50; f. 1957; educational, literature; Dir L. KHUNDADZE.

Georgian National Universal Encyclopaedia: Tbilisi, Tsereteli 1; Editor-in-Chief A. SAKVARELIDZE.

Khelovneba (Art): 380002 Tbilisi, Davit Aghmashenebeli 179; f. 1947; Dir N. JASHI.

Merani (Writer): 380008 Tbilisi, Rustaveli 42; f. 1921; fiction; Dir G. GVERDTSITELI.

Metsniereba (Science): 380060 Tbilisi, Kutuzov 19; f. 1941; publishing house of the Georgian Academy of Sciences; Editor S. SHENGELIA.

Nakaduli (Stream): 380060 Tbilisi, Mshvidoba 28; f. 1938; books for children and youth; Dir V. CHELIDZE.

Publishing House of Tbilisi State University: 380079 Tbilisi, I. Chavchavadze 14; f. 1933; scientific and educational literature; Editor V. GAMKRELIDZE.

Sakartvelo (Georgia): 380002 Tbilisi, Marjanishvili 16; f. 1921; fmrly *Sabchota Sakartvelo* (Soviet Georgia); political, scientific and fiction; Dir D. GVINJILIA.

Radio and Television

Department of Television and Radio Broadcasting: 380071 Tbilisi, Kostava 68; tel. (8832) 36-24-60; govt body; Dir ARCHIL GOGELIA.

Radio Tbilisi: broadcasts in Georgian, Russian, Armenian, Azerbaijani, Abkhazian and Ossetian.

Tbilisi Television: broadcasts in Georgian and Russian.

Finance

cap. = capital; res = reserves; m. = million; brs = branches; amounts in roubles)

BANKING

In August 1991 the Supreme Soviet adopted legislation which nationalized all branches of all-Union (USSR) banks in Georgia. Georgian branches of the USSR State Bank (Gosbank) were transferred to the National Bank of Georgia.

At the beginning of 1993 the Georgian banking system comprised the National Bank, five specialized government commercial banks (consisting of the domestic branches of the specialized banks of the former USSR) and 72 private commercial banks. However, of the last, only about one-half satisfied general legal provisions and only five properly complied with the paid-in capital requirement.

Central Bank

National Bank of Georgia: Tbilisi; Leonidze 3–5; tel. (8832) 99-55-89; fax (8832) 99-07-38; total assets 23,500m. (1991); Pres. NODAR JAVAKHISHVILI.

Specialized Government Commercial Banks

Agroprombank—Agroindustrial Bank: Tbilisi; f. 1991; 78 brs.

Eximbank—Export-Import Bank: Tbilisi; f. 1989; joint-stock co; res 360m.; Chair. of Bd M. L. LIKHACHEV.

Industriyabank—Industry Bank: Tbilisi; f. 1991; 28 brs.

Sberbank—Savings Bank: Tbilisi; f. 1989; 86 brs.

Zhilosotsbank—Social Development Bank: Tbilisi; f. 1991; second-largest bank in Georgia; 43 brs.

COMMODITY AND STOCK EXCHANGES

Caucasian Exchange: 380086 Tbilisi, Vazha Pshavela 72; tel. (8832) 30-25-15; telex 212945; fax (8832) 30-44-03; f. 1991; authorized cap. 80m.; Chair. of Council AMIRAN KADAGISHVILI; includes:

Caucasian Commodity and Raw Materials Exchange.

Caucasian Stock Exchange.

INSURANCE

Caucasus Insurance Co: 380086 Tbilisi, Vazha Pshavela 72; tel. (8832) 30-01-56; telex 212313; fax (8832) 30-46-64; f. 1991; authorized cap. 50m.; Chair. of Bd NUGZAR CHOKHELI.

Trade and Industry

PRIVATIZATION AGENCY

State Property Management Agency: Tbilisi; f. 1992; responsible for divestment of state-owned enterprises.

CHAMBER OF COMMERCE

Chamber of Commerce and Industry of Georgia: 380079 Tbilisi, I. Chavchavadze 11; tel. (8832) 23-00-45; telex 212183; fax (8832) 23-57-60; brs in Sukhumi and Batumi; Chair. GURAM D. AKHVLEDIANI.

FOREIGN TRADE ORGANIZATION

Georgian Import Export (Gruzimpex): 380008 Tbilisi, Georgiashvili 12; tel. (8832) 99-70-90; telex 212191; fax (8832) 99-73-13; Gen. Dir T. A. GOGOBERIDZE.

MAJOR INDUSTRIAL ENTERPRISES

Azot: 383040 Rustavi, Mira 2; tel. (8832) 12-59-90; telex 527274; f. 1956; produces mineral ferilizers, ammonia, cyanic salts; Principal Officer MURMAN ARJEVADNIDZE; 3,370 employees.

Chiaturmarganets—Chiatura Manganese Industrial Association: 393950 Chiatura, Tsereteli; tel. (8832) 5-25-35; f. 1939; Principal Officer MIKHAIL APAKIDZE; 6,523 employees.

Elektroapparat Industrial Association: 380024 Tbilisi, Tornike Eristavi 8; tel. (8832) 66-80-36; telex 212191; fax (8832) 66-72-20; f. 1971; produces a wide range of low-voltage electrical equipment and goods for general use; Gen. Dir GURAMI GZIRISHVILI; Chief Eng. VLADIMIR BIRKADZE; 3,500 employees.

Electrovozostroitel: 380092 Tbilisi, Guramushvili 24; tel. (8832) 62-81-31; f. 1948; manufactures direct-current long-haul industrial electric locomotives; Principal Officer GEORGY ZGUDADZE; 2,450 employees.

Gori Cotton and Sewing Industrial Association: 383507 Gori, Moskorskaya; tel. (8832) 2-37-70; f. 1951; Principal Officer MERAB NIZHARADZE; 3,545 employees.

Kutaisi Automobile Factory: 384007 Kutaisi, Avotstroitelya 88; tel. (8832) 6-26-95; manufactures freight containers and trailers; Principal Officer TENGIZ SHUBLADZE; 6,934 employees.

Rustavi Metallurgical Factory: 380040 Rustavi, Gagarina 12; tel. (8832) 99-50-03; f. 1950; steel manufacturer; Principal Officer GURAM KASHAKASHVILI; 8,398 employees.

Tbilisi Aircraft Manufacturers: 380036 Tbilisi, Khmelnitskogo 181; tel. (8832) 74-00-59; f. 1941; also produces agricultural equipment, bicycles and metal containers; Principal Officer AVTANDIL KHOPERIYA.

Tbilisi Instrumental Production Amalgamation: 380094 Tbilisi, Saburtalo 32; tel. (8832) 38-14-69; telex 212262; fax (8832) 38-20-07; manufactures metal-cutting and wood-processing machinery; Gen. Dir SHUKURI A. KOIAVA; 622 employees.

Tbilisi Lathe-Manufacturing Industrial Association: 380092 Tbilisi, T. Eristavil; tel. (8832) 66-22-78; f. 1934; Principal Officer ANZAR SHAUTUDZE; 1,107 employees.

TRADE UNIONS

Confederation of Independent Trade Unions of Georgia: 380122 Tbilisi, Anaga 7; tel. (8832) 38-29-95; telex 212256; fax (8832) 38-61-69; f. 1992; comprises branch unions with a total membership of *c.* 2.5m.; Chair. JRAKLI TUGUSHI.

Transport

RAILWAYS

In 1989 there were 1,570 km of railway track. The main rail links are with the Russian Federation, along the Black Sea coast, with

Azerbaijan and with Armenia. The Georgian–Armenian railway continues into eastern Turkey. The civil conflict has disrupted some of the railway network.

ROADS

At 31 December 1989 the total length of roads in use was 35,100 km, of which 31,200 km were hard-surfaced.

SHIPPING

There are international shipping services with Black Sea and Mediterranean ports. The main ports are at Batumi and Sukhumi.

Shipowning Company

Georgian Shipping Company: 384517 Batumi, Gogebashvili 60; telex 412617; fax (87314) 0-06-44; Pres. D. K. CHIGVARIYA.

CIVIL AVIATION

Orbi (Georgian Airlines): Tbilisi.

Culture

NATIONAL ORGANIZATION

Ministry of Culture: see section on The Government (Ministries).

CULTURAL HERITAGE

Georgian State Art Museum: Tbilisi, Ketskhoveli 1; Dir S. Y. AMIRANISHVILI.

Georgian State Museum of Oriental Art: Tbilisi, Azizbekova 3; large collection of Georgian art, carpets, fabrics, etc.; Dir G. M. GVISHIANI.

Georgian State Picture Gallery: Tbilisi, Rustaveli 11; Dir M. A. KIPIANI.

Kutaisi State Museum of History and Ethnography: Kutaisi, Tbilisi 1; 10,000 items; Dir M. V. NIKOLISHVILI.

State Literary Museum of Georgia: Tbilisi, Jiorjiashivili 8; f. 1929; 150,000 exhibits; library of 19,000 vols; Dir I. K. KAKABEDZE.

State Museum of the Abkhazian Autonomous Republic: Sukhumi, Lenin 22; f. 1915; 100,000 exhibits; Dir A. A. ARGUN.

State Museum of the History of Georgia: Tbilisi, Rustaveli 3; f. 1852; library of over 204,000 vols; Dir N. G. CHERKEZISHVILI.

State Public Library of the Republic of Georgia: 380007 Tbilisi, Ketskhoveli 5; tel. (8832) 99-92-86; f. 1946; 8m. vols; Dir A. K. KAVKASIDZE.

Tbilisi State Museum of Anthropology and Ethnography: Tbilisi, Komsomolsky 11; archaeological material; library of over 150,000 vols; Dir A. V. TKESHELASHVILI.

PERFORMING ARTS

Georgian Puppet Theatre: Tbilisi, Plekhanova 103.

Kote Marjanishvili Drama Theatre: Tbilisi, Marjanashvili 8.

Shota Rustaveli Drama Theatre: Tbilisi, Rustaveli 17; Dir ROBERT STURUA.

Tbilisi Musical Conservatory: Tbilisi; Dir NODAR GABURNIA.

Zakhary Paliashvili Opera and Ballet Theatre: Tbilisi, Rustaveli 25.

ASSOCIATIONS

Union of Writers of Georgia: 380000 Tbilisi, Machabeli 13; tel. (8832) 99-84-90; includes 5 regional Writers' Organizations.

Abkhazian Writers' Organization: 384000 Sukhumi, Frunze 44; tel. (88300) 2-35-34.

Ajar Writers' Organization: 384516 Batumi, Engels 21; tel. (87314) 3-29-66.

South-Ossetian Writers' Organization: 383570 Tskhinvali, Lenin 3; tel. 2-32-63.

Education

Until the late 1980s the education system was an integrated part of the Soviet system. Considerable changes were made, including the ending of teaching of ideologically orientated subjects, and more emphasis on Georgian language and history. In 1988 66.6% of all pupils were taught in Georgian-language schools, while 23.6% were taught in Russian-language schools. There was also teaching in Azerbaijani, Armenian, Abkhazian and Ossetian. In 1991 there were 19 higher education institutions.

UNIVERSITIES

Abkhazian A. M. Gorkii State University: 384900 Sukhumi, Tsereteli 9; tel. (88300) 2-25-98; f. 1985; 8 faculties; 3,800 students.

Georgian Technical University: 380075 Tbilisi, Kostava 77; tel. (8832) 36-07-62; telex 212100; fax (8832) 365590; f. 1922 (as Georgia Polytechnic Institute, renamed 1990); 15 faculties; 2,050 teachers; 28,000 students; Rector Prof. G. G. TCHOGOVADZE.

Ivan Javakhiladze University of Tbilisi: 380028 Tbilisi, Chavchavadze 1; tel. (8832) 31-47-92; f. 1918; language of instruction Georgian, with a Russian section in some faculties; 19 faculties; 1,659 teachers; 16,000 students; Rector Prof. DAVID I. CHKHIKVISHVILI.

The Environment

GOVERNMENT ORGANIZATIONS

Ministry of the Environment: see section on The Government (Ministries).

Department of Geology, Geodesy and Cartography: 380030 Tbilisi, Mosashvili 24; tel. (8832) 22-69-14; Dir VLADIMIR I. GUGUSHVILI.

ACADEMIC INSTITUTES

Georgian Academy of Sciences: 380024 Tbilisi, Jerzhinskovo 8; Pres. A. N. TAVKHELIDZE; attached institutes incl.:

Commission on Nature Conservation: Tbilisi, Z. Rukhadse 1; attached to the Presidium of the Academy; Chair. L. K. GABUNIA.

NON-GOVERNMENTAL ORGANIZATIONS

Georgia Green Movement: Tbilisi; f. 1988; activist environmental group; non-political; Pres. GIVI TUMANISHVILI; *c.*6,000 mems.

Mtsvanta Partia (Green Party of Georgia): Tbilisi; f. 1990 by mems of the Georgia Green Movement; ecological party favouring Georgian independence; Leader ZURAB ZHVANIA.

Defence

Following the dissolution of the USSR in December 1991, Georgia began to establish its own armed forces. On 1 June 1993, according to Western estimates, the Georgian Government planned to have armed forces totalling 20,000 members, including the 15,000-strong National Guard, which was being incorporated into the regular army. The paramilitary Rescue Corps, known as the Mkhedrioni (Horsemen) until February 1994, were also loyal to the Government. There were a possible 500,000 reserve troops. It was estimated that opposition troops in Abkhazia numbered 4,000 and that troops loyal to deposed President Gamsakhurdia amounted to 1,500 (many of these were reported to have made accommodations with the Government in January 1994, after the death of Gamsakhurdia). However, the continuing civil unrest in Georgia meant that these figures were uncertain. In October 1993 Russian forces and supplies arrived in the country to aid government troops. On 3 December 1993 Georgia became a member of the CIS and its collective security system. In 1992 an estimated 1.7% of budgetary expenditure (approximately 6,000m. roubles) was allocated to defence.

Commander-in-Chief of the Armed Forces: EDUARD SHEVARDNADZE.

Commander of the Internal Troops: Maj.-Gen. VLADIMER CHIKOVANI.

Bibliography

Allen, W. E. D. *A History of the Georgian People from the Beginning Down to the Roman Conquest in the Nineteenth Century.* London, Paul, 1932; New York, Barnes and Noble, 1971.

Bitov, A. *A Captive of the Caucasus: Journeys in Armenia and Georgia.* (Translated by Susan Brownsberger.) London, Harvill, 1993.

Diuk, N., and Karatnycky, A. *New Nations Rising: The Fall of the Soviets and the Challenge of Independence.* New York and Chichester, West Sussex, John Wiley and Sons, 1993.

Jones, S. 'The Establishment of Soviet Power in Transcaucasia: the Case of Georgia 1921–28' in *Soviet Studies*, Vol. 40 (4), 1982.

Kautsky, K. *Georgia, A Social-Democratic Peasant Republic, Impressions and Observations.* London, 1921.

Lang, D. M. *The Last Years of the Georgian Monarchy, 1658–1832.* New York, Columbia University Press, 1957.

A Modern History of Georgia. London, Weidenfeld and Nicolson, 1962.

The Georgians. London, Thames and Hudson, 1966.

Parsons, R. 'National Integration in Soviet Georgia' in *Soviet Studies*, Vol. 34 (4), 1982.

Suny, R. G. *The Making of the Georgian Nation.* London, I. B. Tauris and Co Ltd, 1989.

Suny, R. G. (Ed.). *Transcaucasia, Nationalism and Social Change: Essays in the History of Armenia, Azerbaijan, and Georgia.* Ann Arbor, Michigan, Michigan Slavic Publications, 1983.

HUNGARY

Geography

PHYSICAL FEATURES

The Republic of Hungary is a land-locked country in central Europe. It is bordered by Austria to the west, the Slovak Republic to the north and has a short border with Ukraine in the north-east. Romania lies to the east and Hungary's southern border is with Croatia, Slovenia, and Yugoslavia (the Vojvodina in Serbia). Hungary has a total area of 93,033 sq km (35,920 sq miles), although its territory was much reduced upon the dissolution of the Habsburg Empire.

The River Danube (Duna) forms Hungary's north-western border with Slovakia and then flows south through Budapest, bisecting the country, which is mostly low-lying and much of it prone to flooding. East of the Danube is the Pannonian or Great Hungarian Plain (*Nagyalföld*), which is also drained by the Tisza, the longest tributary of the Danube. To the west of the Danube the country is hillier, with a spur of the Alps traversing the region from the south-west to the north-east (the Bakony, Vertes and Philis ranges). South-east of these mountains lie Lake Balaton, the largest lake in central Europe, and the downlands of Transdanubia (Dunántúl). In the north-west of Hungary, between the mountains and the Danube, are the Little Hungarian Plains (*Kisalföld*). Only some 2% of the total land area of the country is over 400 m, the highest mountain being Kékestetö at 1,014 m, in the Matra range. The Matras lie east of the Danube, along Hungary's northern border, and are foothills of the Carpathian Mountains.

CLIMATE

Hungary has a continental climate, with hot summers and cold winters. In winter the Danube can freeze over for long periods and, in settled weather, fog is frequent. The mean temperatures in Budapest are a maximum of 22°C (71°F) in July and a minimum of −1°C (30°F) in January. Most rainfall is in the spring and early summer, when there are often heavy downpours; in Budapest the annual average is 610 mm. There is little regional variation in the weather.

POPULATION

The Hungarians (Magyars) are a Turkic or Finno-Ugrian people who settled on the Hungarian plains in the 7th century AD. There are still large numbers of ethnic Hungarians outside the borders of the modern state, particularly in areas which once formed part of the old kingdom, such as north-west Romania (Transylvania). In 1984, it was estimated, ethnic Hungarians accounted for 92% of the total population of Hungary. In 1990, however, official figures put the number of Romany (Gypsy) people at over 0.5m. (between 5% and 7% of the total population), Germans at over 2% of the population, Slovaks at about 1%, Southern Slavs at just under 1% and Romanians at about 0.3%. The official language is Hungarian (Magyar), but the various nationalities also speak their own languages. The predominant religion is Christianity, the largest denomination being the Roman Catholic Church (an estimated 67% of the population), followed by Calvinists (20%) and Lutherans (5%). There are also small groups of Eastern Orthodox Christians, Jews and Muslims.

The capital of Hungary is Budapest, in the north of the country. The city is located on the Danube, the ancient capital of Buda on the hillier western bank and the commercial centre of Pest on the eastern bank, with a total estimated population of 1,992,343 on 1 January 1992. Other major towns include Debrecen (214,712), Miskolc (191,623) and Szeged (177,506) east of the Danube, and Pécs (169,486) to the west. In 1991, it was estimated, some 61% of the population lived in urban areas, compared to 35% in 1945. The total population was estimated at 10,337,000 on 1 January 1992, the population density being 111.1 per sq km.

Chronology

906: The Magyars, under the leadership of Árpád (896–907), migrated to the Hungarian plains.

1001: The coronation of St Stephen I (997–1038), with a crown sent by the Pope, established Hungary as a western Christian kingdom.

1458–90: Reign of Matthias I Corvinus, who prevailed against the rival claims to the throne of the House of Habsburg, extended Hungarian hegemony and moved his capital to Vienna.

1526: The Hungarian army was destroyed by the forces of the Ottoman Empire at the battle of Mohács; with the death of Louis II, the Habsburgs inherited Hungary's Crown of St Stephen.

1533: Hungary was partitioned between the Habsburgs and the Ottomans.

1687: The Imperial Diet of Pressburg (Bratislava) declared the Hungarian Crown to be a hereditary possession of the Austrian House of Habsburg.

1699: The Ottomans ceded Hungary (including Transylvania and Slavonia) to its conqueror, the Habsburg Holy Roman Emperor.

1711: The Peace of Sathmar granted self-administration to Hungary, subject to the laws of the Imperial Diet.

6 August 1806: Francis II, under pressure from Napoleon of France, dissolved the Holy Roman Empire of the German Nation and reigned henceforth as Francis I, having assumed the imperial title for Austria in 1804.

1848: An uprising in Hungary under Louis Kossuth established a national government, but, in December, refused to recognize the new Emperor, Francis Joseph I.

1849: Imperial armies regained control of Hungary.

1867: The Compromise (*Ausgleich*) of 1867 reorganized the Habsburg empire as the Dual Monarchy of Austria (Cisleithania) and Hungary (Transleithania); Emperor Francis Joseph I was crowned as King of Hungary.

28 June 1914: The assassination of the heir to the Dual Monarchy, Archduke Francis Ferdinand, in Sarajevo (Bosnia and Herzegovina) led to the start of the First World War.

21 November 1916: Death of Francis Joseph I and accession of his grand-nephew Charles I.

4 October 1918: Austria-Hungary accepted the same armistice conditions as Germany (to take effect on 3 November).

25 October 1918: Count Mihály Károlyi established a national council following the decision of the Hungarian Diet to recall its troops and the effective dissolution of the Danubian monarchy.

31 October 1918: Károlyi became premier with the backing of Charles I, who then renounced participation in government.

16 November 1918: Hungary was declared a Republic, Károlyi becoming President.

20 December 1918: The Hungarian Communist Party was established by Béla Kun.

21 March 1919: Károlyi resigned in protest at the Allies' territorial demands; Kun formed a coalition government of Communists and Social Democrats.

August 1919: A Romanian counter-offensive, following Hungarian incursions into Slovakia and Transylvania, resulted in the flight of Kun and a brief occupation of Budapest.

March 1920: Admiral Miklós Horthy de Nagybanya restored Hungary as a monarchy, but with a vacant throne and himself as Regent.

4 June 1920: Signature of the Treaty of Trianon concluding peace at the end of the First World War: Hungary ceded Slovakia and Carpatho-Ukraine to Czechoslovakia, Transylvania to Romania, the Banat to Romania and Yugoslavia, Croatia-Slavonia to Yugoslavia and the Burgenland to Austria; the consequent desire of the Hungarians to revise the borders resulted in close relations with Germany.

February 1939: Hungary joined Germany and Italy in the Anti-Comintern Pact.

11 April 1941: Hungary entered the Second World War on the side of Germany.

March 1944: German troops occupied Hungary.

October 1944: Regent Horthy secretly concluded an armistice with the USSR, but was forced to rescind it, was arrested and replaced by the Fascist, Ferenc Szalasi.

20 January 1945: A provisional government signed an armistice with the USSR and agreed to the Hungarian borders of 1937 (as established at Trianon).

November 1945: Following a general election, the Smallholders Party (KGP), the largest party, formed a coalition Government with the Communists.

August 1947: The Communists became the largest single party in the general election, after the discrediting of the KGP.

June 1948: The Communist Party merged with the Social Democratic Party to form the Hungarian Workers' Party (HWP).

May 1949: The Hungarian People's Front for Independence (dominated by the HWP) presented a single list of candidates.

August 1949: A People's Republic was established.

1953: Imre Nagy became Prime Minister.

April 1955: Nagy was forced to resign by Mátyás Rákosi, the First Secretary of the HWP, and was expelled from the Party.

July 1956: Rákosi was forced to resign and was replaced by Ernő Gerő.

23 October 1956: Demonstrations and rioting broke out in Budapest against the Communist Government.

24 October 1956: Soviet tanks were sent in to quell the rioting.

25 October 1956: The Communist Government was replaced by a reformist regime headed by Imre Nagy; Soviet forces withdrew.

3 November 1956: Nagy established an all-party coalition Government, having already renounced membership of the Warsaw Pact.

4 November 1956: Some 200,000 Soviet troops invaded the country; Nagy was overthrown and János Kádár was installed by the USSR as the new premier in an all-Communist Government.

June 1958: Nagy and four associates were executed for their part in the 1956 uprising. Kádár became leader of the newly-formed Hungarian Socialist Workers' Party (HSWP).

1 January 1968: The New Economic Mechanism, which combined central-planning and market instruments, was introduced.

June 1985: The legislative elections permitted voters a wider choice of candidates under the terms of a new electoral law.

March 1986: Widespread disturbances occurred in Budapest, during a protest march, following violent intervention by the police.

October 1986: A group of academics, supported by Imre Pószgay and other reformers in the HSWP, drew up a paper, 'Change and Reform', which heralded the breakdown in consensus both inside and outside the Party.

June 1987: Károly Grósz was appointed Chairman of the Council of Ministers; he introduced some reforms aimed at alleviating the economic problems of the country.

15 March 1988: Some 10,000 people marched through Budapest, on the 140th anniversary of the 1848 uprising against Austrian rule, demanding the introduction of genuine reforms.

April 1988: Four reformers within the HSWP were expelled from the Party for demanding radical political and economic reform. A radical youth group formed an opposition party, the Federation of Young Democrats (FYD).

May 1988: At a special ideological conference of the HSWP János Kádár was replaced as General Secretary of the Central

Committee by Károly Grósz. Kádár also lost his membership of the Politburo. Various opposition groups formed the Network of Free Initiatives—subsequently renamed the Alliance of Free Democrats (AFD).

June 1988: Some 50,000 people demonstrated in Budapest against the Romanian Government's proposed destruction of 7,000 villages, including 1,500 ethnic Hungarian villages.

July 1988: The Central Committee of the HSWP approved an austere economic reform programme which would lead to a reduction in subsidies, a devaluation of the forint and a rapid rise in unemployment.

September 1988: The Hungarian Democratic Forum (HDF) was formally established. Some 20,000 people demonstrated in Budapest against further construction on one of the two dams in the Gabčíkovo-Nagymaros project on the Danube.

21 November 1988: Miklós Németh replaced Károly Grósz as Chairman of the Council of Ministers.

20 December 1988: The National Assembly voted to allow the right to demonstrate and the establishment of independent political organizations.

February 1989: The HSWP agreed to the establishment of a multi-party system; its Central Committee agreed to abandon the clause in the Constitution guaranteeing the HSWP's leading role in society.

15 March 1989: Some 100,000 people took part in an anti-government demonstration in Budapest.

May 1989: The Chairman of the Council of Ministers, Miklós Németh, reorganized his cabinet and declared that it would henceforth be answerable to the National Assembly before the HSWP; János Kádár was relieved of his post as Chairman of the HSWP. 'Round-table' negotiations between the HSWP and various opposition groups began.

16 June 1989: Following the rehabilitation of Imre Nagy he was reburied with four associates at a state funeral in Budapest which was attended by 300,000 people.

6 July 1989: János Kádár died.

23 July 1989: An opposition deputy was elected to the National Assembly, in a by-election, for the first time since 1947 (by September there were seven opposition deputies, who then formed a parliamentary group).

10 September 1989: The border with Austria was opened allowing the exodus of thousands of East Germans seeking to emigrate to the West.

18 September 1989: Against a background of continuing demonstrations and industrial unrest, during round-table negotiations it was decided that the Constitution and electoral law be modified and that the Presidential Council be dissolved.

7–8 October 1989: The HSWP voted to dissolve itself and reconstitute as the Hungarian Socialist Party (HSP); Rezső Nyers was elected Chairman of the new party and Imre Pozsgay was nominated as the party's candidate for the presidential elections.

18 October 1989: Mátyás Szűrös was elected to the newly created post of President of the Republic, in an acting capacity.

23 October 1989: The country was renamed the Republic of Hungary.

November 1989: The Government decided to end all participation in the Danube dam project, because of the environmental implications.

12 March 1990: Following an agreement with the USSR, the withdrawal of Soviet troops began (completed by June 1991); 10 days later the barter-trade agreement with the USSR was ended.

20 March 1990: Thousands of people demonstrated in Budapest in support of the Hungarian minority in Romania.

25 March 1990: The first round of voting in the legislative elections took place; five days later the HDF made an electoral pact with the Christian Democratic People's Party (CDPP) and the Independent Smallholders' and Peasants' Party (usually known as the Independent Smallholders' Party—ISP).

8 April 1990: The second round of voting in the legislative elections took place; the HDF won 165 of the 386 seats in the National Assembly, while the AFD gained 92, the ISP 43 and the HSP only 33. The HDF agreed a coalition government with the CDPP, the ISP and independents.

2 May 1990: When the National Assembly convened the HDF and the AFD ended their rivalry: Árpád Göncz (AFD) was elected interim President and Speaker of the National Assembly (and was supported by the HDF in the presidential election); the following day József Antall (HDF) was appointed Chairman of the Council of Ministers.

June 1990: The Ibusz travel agency became the first Hungarian company to be privatized and trading resumed on the Budapest Stock Exchange after a 42-year break. Hungary began a process of disengagement from the activities of the Warsaw Pact.

July 1990: Ministers were forced to negotiate with miners striking in protest at the widespread privatizations. The Government took over direct control of the State Property Agency in order to maintain control over its privatizations' policy.

3 August 1990: Árpád Göncz was elected President of the Republic by the National Assembly.

30 September 1990: Local elections took place; with the second round, where necessary, taking place on 14 October.

19 October 1990: The Government offered all state industries for sale; later in the month price rises had to be limited in order to end the disruptions and protests throughout the country.

22 April 1991: Negotiations with the Slovak Government (Czechoslovakia) over the Gabčikovo-Nagymarós hydroelectric scheme broke down.

17 May 1991: A new political movement, the National Democratic Federation, was formed by Imre Pozsgay, who had left the ISP the previous November.

28 June 1991: A protocol providing for the dissolution, within 90 days, of the Council for Mutual Economic Assistance (CMEA or Comecon) was signed in Budapest.

1 January 1991: An association agreement between Hungary and the European Community (EC—known as the European Union from November 1993) came into effect.

February 1992: József Torgyán, the leader of the ISP, announced his party's departure from the government coalition; however, only 13 ISP deputies followed his lead.

3 March 1992: The Constitutional Court rejected legislation that would allow the prosecution for the crimes of murder and treason committed between 1944 and 1990.

24 September 1992: Fifty thousand people demonstrated in Budapest in protest at the recent rise in right-wing sentiment in Hungary; István Csurka, the HDF Vice-Chairman, was criticized for his extreme opinions.

6 January 1993: The heads of the state radio and television corporations, Csaba Gombar and Elemer Hankiss respectively, resigned in protest at state interference in broadcasting.

5 April 1993: Hungary and Slovakia agreed to submit the dispute over Slovakia's re-routeing of the Danube, to feed the hydroelectric plant at Gabčikovo, to the International Court of Justice (based in The Hague, Netherlands), after EC mediation had failed.

May 1993: It was revealed that both the HDF and the FYD had been involved in land transactions of questionable legality.

21 June 1993: After having been expelled from the HDF at the beginning of the month, the right-winger István Csurka formed his own party, the Hungarian Justice and Life Party.

12 December 1993: Prime Minister Antall died; Péter Boross, hitherto the Interior Minister, succeeded him as premier.

History

MARTYN RADY

INTRODUCTION

The Kingdom of Hungary was established in the Middle Ages and occupied a territory some three times the size of the present-day Republic of Hungary. In 1526 the King of Hungary, Louis II, was killed by the Ottoman Turks at the Battle of Mohács, and the Kingdom was subsequently partitioned between the Ottoman Empire, the Habsburgs and the principality of Transylvania. In the later 17th century the Habsburg Emperor, Leopold I, expelled the Turks from Hungary and occupied Transylvania, reuniting it with the Hungarian Crown. Although Hungary was permitted a substantial degree of autonomy, particularly after 1867, when it became Austria's partner in the 'Dual Monarchy', the Kingdom remained part of the Habsburg empire until 1918.

Following the collapse of the Austro-Hungarian Empire, in November 1918, Hungary became a fully independent state. However, by the terms of the Treaty of Trianon (1920), Hungary lost two-thirds of its pre-1918 territories and three-fifths of its population. More than 3m. Hungarians (Magyars) were left in the neighbouring states of Austria, Czechoslovakia, Romania and Yugoslavia. The dismemberment of Hungary had a powerful impact on domestic politics in the years between the First and Second World Wars. The major parties advocated revisionist policies and the recovery of Hungary's former lands. As a consequence, Hungary inclined to the support of the Axis Powers and fought against the Allies during the Second World War.

The boundaries established by the Treaty of Trianon were confirmed in the Treaty of Paris (1947). During both the Communist and post-Communist period no Hungarian Government expressed an interest in revising the frontier. Nevertheless, during both periods there was considerable public disquiet concerning the fate of the Hungarian minorities remaining in Slovakia, Vojvodina (Yugoslavia) and Transylvania (Romania). Allegations concerning the mistreatment by the Romanian authorities of the 1.7m. ethnic Hungarians in Transylvania led to considerable tension between the Governments in Budapest and Bucharest. Likewise, in 1993 tension increased between Hungary and the newly independent Slovakia.

In 1919 a Communist Government was installed in Hungary under the leadership of Béla Kun. This proved short-lived, and the country's brief experience under it contributed to the right-wing, authoritarian character of Hungarian politics between the two World Wars. Following the defeat of the Communists the country returned to the uncodified 'royalist' Constitution of the pre-1918 period. The throne, however, was declared to be vacant, so the Head of State carried the title of Regent (*Kormányzó*). Admiral Miklós Horthy de Nagybanya was appointed to this position in 1920, and remained in office until October 1944.

Horthy proved to be an important influence in favour of stability and political conservatism in the inter-war period. The governments which he appointed consisted principally of noblemen. It was not until 1944, under pressure from the German Nazi Government, that Horthy was removed from power and a Fascist Government, headed by the leader of the Arrow Cross organization, Ferenc Szálasi, was established.

THE COMMUNIST TAKE-OVER

In 1944–45 Hungary was occupied by the Soviet army. Thereafter, Communist rule was gradually imposed on the country. Between 1945 and 1947 Hungary was governed by coalitions consisting both of Communists and of representatives from the democratic parties. At elections held in November 1945 the Communists won only 70 of the 409 seats in parliament, while the Small Landowners' Party won 245 seats. However, the Communists controlled the Ministry of the Interior and had the active support of the occupying Soviet army. With these advantages, they reduced the influence of the other parties by intimidating their leaders and by infiltrating their organizations.

In 1947 new elections were held, following the revelations of 'conspiracies' in the Small Landowners' Party. The Communists only gained 22.7% of the votes cast, but nevertheless became the largest single party, and the left-wing bloc, which they controlled, amassed 60% of the vote. The remnants of the main democratic parties were forced to join a coalition under Communist direction. Over the next year, the surviving non-Communist parties were either dissolved or absorbed into the Communist Party. In June 1948 the ruling party became known as the Hungarian Workers' Party, following the union of the Communist and Social Democratic Parties.

Under its Communist leader, Mátyás Rákosi, Hungary was transformed into a model Soviet satellite. Forced and rapid industrialization and collectivization took place and no political opposition to the regime, either real or imagined, was tolerated. The Department for the Defence of the State (ÁVO) was responsible for internal security, and under it several hundreds of thousands of people were interned in labour camps.

THE UPRISING OF 1956

The oppressive nature of Rákosi's rule led to considerable frustration and discontent, both within the Party and among the population at large. Following the death of Stalin (Iosif Vissarionovich Dzhugashvili), in 1953, a reform wing of the Hungarian Workers' Party received support from members of the Soviet Politburo. The leader of the reformers was Imre Nagy, a Communist since 1918 and a former Minister of Agriculture. The frequent changes in Soviet policy which accompanied the rise of Nikita Khrushchev led to equally rapid shuffling of the composition of the Hungarian Government. In 1953 Rákosi was forced to relinquish the premiership, although remaining First Secretary of the Party, and for the next two years Nagy headed the administration. In March 1955, at the Kremlin's insistence, Nagy was ousted and replaced with András Hegedüs, a close ally of Rákosi. However, in July 1956 Rákosi was dismissed as Party leader, even though he was succeeded by another Stalinist, Ernő Gerő.

The mood of uncertainty brought about by these changes contributed to the Uprising of 1956. Following increasing demonstrations calling for the return of Nagy, and also supporting Polish resistance to Moscow, a spontaneous rebellion against Soviet domination broke out in Budapest on 23 October and swiftly spread to other parts of the country. A reformist Government, led by Imre Nagy, was installed, and János Kádár took over as the new Party leader. On 4 November, however, Soviet troops occupied Budapest and, after bitter fighting, overthrew the revolutionary Government. Kádár, having previously lauded 'our people's glorious uprising' and given the Communist Party's 'full support for the removal of Soviet forces', now turned to support the Soviet occupiers. On 7 November Kádár was taken by Soviet armoured car to the National Assembly (parliament) building in Budapest.

KÁDÁRISM

Following the Soviet intervention, Kádár became Secretary of the renamed Hungarian Socialist Workers' Party (HSWP). Under Kádár's direction, all remaining traces of opposition to the regime were ruthlessly erased. Some 20,000 participants in the Uprising were arrested, of which 2,000 were subsequently executed, including Imre Nagy, who was hanged in June 1958. Opponents of the regime were deported to the USSR, the precise number involved being unknown. A workers' militia was established and the collectivization of agriculture was vigorously pursued.

In 1961, however, Kádár initiated a new conciliatory policy which was designed to win support for his regime. In accordance with the new principle of *ralliement* (in Hungarian, *Szövetségi politika*), Kádár was willing to enlist non-Party specialists into the bureaucracy and to allow a wider debate within the Party itself over policy. Police surveillance became less obtrusive. 'Class aliens' who, on account of their background, had been forced to take menial jobs in the countryside were also readmitted to public life.

The *ralliement* was accompanied by a reassessment of economic objectives. Under Rákosi the official policy had been that the country's economic problems had a political solution. Kádár, by contrast, endeavoured to remove political dissatisfaction by pursuing an economic solution. Under the direction of Rezső Nyers, the 'New Economic Mechanism' (NEM) was introduced, in 1968, after five years of debate. The NEM partially freed enterprises and collectives from the tutelage of central planning, and devolved initiative from the ministries to managers and farming co-operatives. At the same time, the NEM reorientated the economy away from heavy industry towards an expanding consumer sector.

THE FAILURE OF KÁDÁRISM

The introduction of the NEM led to a rapid improvement both in industrial production and in living standards. However, the economy faltered in the 1970s, giving way to inflation, declining output and a growing trade deficit. In 1974 Nyers was dismissed from the Politburo and the NEM was modified in order to satisfy conservatives in the Party. A subsequent attempt to reinvigorate the NEM failed to yield the expected dividend.

Between 1979 and 1984 Hungarians suffered a real decline in wages of 10%, and many were forced to seek second and third jobs. Popular resentment was no longer appeased by such palliatives as increasing the availability of salami (1979) or introducing scented soap to the shops (1980). The increase in alcoholism, petty corruption, crime and suicide at this time was widely considered to be a consequence of the country's economic malaise.

Within the Party itself there were growing doubts about the way the Government was managing the economy. Ever since the 1960s the HSWP had been open to reformists as well as to Party dogmatists. In the past, however, the policies of 'democratic centralism' had prevailed; conflicting opinions had been expounded and reconciled so as to yield a consensus behind which the Party might remain unified. By the mid-1980s this sort of consensus was no longer possible. Reformers within the Party advocated market solutions to the economic crisis which were entirely unacceptable to the more doctrinaire Party members. Although the Party Congress of March 1985 recognized the magnitude of the country's economic crisis, its solution was to adjust the existing structure rather than to introduce any major reform. Kádár himself delivered a special appeal for consensus within the Party and criticized the reformers for making their opposition public.

Ignoring Kádár, frustrated groups of reformers began to widen the debate by establishing informal contacts with opposition groups. During the 1970s and 1980s a number of extra-Party movements had emerged in the relatively tolerant atmosphere of Kádár's Hungary. The Party reformers eschewed, however, the 'democratic opposition' which centred upon the *samizdat* publications, *Beszélö* and *Hirmondó*. Instead they forged links with the 'populists', whose programme was more loosely concerned with national identity and traditions, and who were less dogmatically opposed to the Communist regime. In 1986 a meeting of populist writers, economists and historians at Lakitelek was attended by several reformist Party members.

By the mid-1980s, therefore, the Kádárite consensus had begun to break down in Hungary. The economy was no longer strong enough to make the regime acceptable to the majority of Hungarians; institutions were beginning to demonstrate their independence of the Party; and sections of the HSWP were no longer inclined to preserve Party unity.

THE REFORMERS TAKE CONTROL

In May 1987 János Kádár celebrated his 75th birthday. By this time it was clear that he would not survive as leader of the HSWP for much longer. Firstly, his age told against him; secondly, he plainly lacked the confidence of the new Soviet leader, the CPSU General Secretary, Mikhail Gorbachev. The collapse of the Kádárite consensus was thus combined with a prolonged leadership crisis inside the HSWP.

In June 1987 Károly Grósz was appointed Chairman of the Council of Ministers. Grósz had previously been First Secretary of the HSWP Budapest Committee, and had a reputation as a 'pragmatic realist'. He was popular among Party activists on account of his outspoken manner, and at the preceding Party Congress he had warned against the rise of social tension in the country.

Anticipating failure and a possible right-wing reaction, Grósz sought to widen responsibility for economic policy by including the National Assembly in the discussions. In September 1987 he conceded new powers of scrutiny to parliamentary committees, in return for which the deputies agreed to endorse his Consolidation Programme. The Programme imposed a purchase tax on items sold and introduced an income tax on personal salaries. The principal aim behind the Consolidation Programme, which came into effect on 1 January 1988, was to diminish the monetary overhang in the economy.

During 1987 the reform wing of the Party had become increasingly forthright in its criticism of government policy. A major focus of discontent was the Patriotic People's Front (PPF), which was an 'umbrella' organization uniting various social groups and the HSWP. Under its Secretary-General, Imre Pozsgay, the PPF sponsored a discussion paper entitled 'Turn and Reform' (1987), which advocated a thorough overhaul of the economy. Most strikingly, however, the document associated economic reform with a move towards political pluralism. In September 1987 Pozsgay attended a second meeting of the populists at Lakitelek. Under his protection, the populists established the Hungarian Democratic Forum (HDF).

As Chairman of the Council of Ministers, Grósz was caught between the Politburo, which was still headed by

Kádár and had a conservative bias, and the reformers, who were pressing for a more drastic economic solution than the Consolidation Programme and who appeared, additionally, to have the support of Mikhail Gorbachev. As Grósz wavered between the two factions, it became increasingly evident that the regime was losing control. Demonstrations and strikes became more commonplace, and the dissident and populist press flourished. In April 1988 a radical youth party, the Federation of Young Democrats (FYD), was established, while in the following month the various strands of the democratic opposition coalesced into a single confederation called the Network of Free Initiatives. The Network was subsequently renamed the Alliance of Free Democrats (AFD). These various groups joined the HDF in openly demanding the introduction of democratic reforms.

The most severe challenge, however, came from within the Party itself. In the first months of 1988 there was a periodic renewal of Party membership cards. About 45,000 members, some 6% of the total membership, did not reapply for readmission. In March and April Party organizations at all levels were canvassed on their views on economic and political reform. The responses received were so critical of the existing policies that the leadership agreed to convene a special Party Conference, to take place in May 1988.

During the early months of 1988 it had seemed that the conservatives within the Party were still in the ascendant. At a meeting of the Central Committee in March, Kádár had obtained the approval for a slowing down of the reform process and for the continued application of democratic centralism to Party discussions. Four Party members closely associated with the HDF were expelled on this occasion. Kádár probably anticipated that he could manage the Party Conference in much the same way as he had the Central Committee, and imagined that he need extend only a few concessions to the reformers.

The 986 conference delegates, however, were more amenable to the wishes of the Party members by whom they had been elected than to the organizing committee, which sought to direct proceedings. The Conference appointed a new Central Committee, rejecting one-third of its existing membership, and dismissed most of the Politburo. Kádár was ousted from the position of General Secretary and given, instead, the honorific and newly created post of Chairman of the Party; he was among those removed from the Politburo. He was removed as Chairman in May 1989, and died less than three months later. Grósz was appointed General Secretary of the Party in Kádár's place, and also retained the office of Chairman of the Council of Ministers.

During the second half of 1988 the reformers used their ascendancy in the Politburo and Central Committee to install their supporters first in the Party administration and then in the upper levels of the Government. In November members of the reform faction were appointed to the deputy premiership and the Ministries of the Interior and Foreign Affairs. In the same month, Grósz was replaced as premier by the reformist Miklós Németh.

Once established in the principal ministries, the reformers sought to introduce constitutional reform. Ten parliamentary committees, dominated by reformers, were created, with instructions to prepare legislation permitting freedom of association and assembly, the establishment of an independent judiciary and the nomination of parliamentary deputies by non-Party organizations. At the same time, a historical commission was established to investigate and report upon the Uprising of 1956. There was a relaxation of censorship laws, the HDF achieved legal recognition in September 1988 and an independent trade union (the first in Hungary for 40 years), the Democratic Union of Scientific Workers, was established. In January 1989 rights to strike, demonstrate and form associations and parties outside the HSWP were granted, and in the following month the Central Committee agreed to support the transition to a multi-party democracy.

The response of the conservatives, who had now lost influence in both the Politburo and the Government, was to draw attention to the prevailing 'counter-revolutionary atmosphere' and to hint that the Workers' Militia might be used to restore orthodoxy. Grósz, who was as anxious to conciliate the conservatives as to appease the reformers, joined in the attack in November 1988. In the now-notorious Sportcsarnok speech in Budapest, he talked of an impending 'white terror'. Grósz's intemperate address, together with his failure to obtain concessions from President Nicolae Ceauşescu of Romania over that country's mistreatment of its Hungarian minority in Transylvania, discredited him entirely. Although Grósz remained nominally in charge of the Party, hereafter he became increasingly isolated and played only a minor role in Hungarian politics. In June 1989 Grósz was effectively replaced as Party leader by a four-member Presidium. In August Grósz announced his impending resignation as General Secretary.

THE COLLAPSE OF THE HSWP

By the beginning of 1989 the conservatives within the HSWP were capable of little more than speeches, and they were depressed by the apparent disinterest of the USSR in the fate of the Hungarian regime. In the first months of the year Party organizations in the localities became dominated by reformers and opportunists, who proceeded to remove corrupt and elderly Party officials from office. Nevertheless, at this stage both the Party membership and the reforming leadership believed that the HSWP would survive as the dominant force in Hungarian politics. In particular, they anticipated negotiating a compromise with the HDF, which was closely linked, through Imre Pozsgay, to the reform wing of the Party.

In February 1989 the HSWP's historical commission published its report, which concluded that the Uprising of 1956 had indeed been a popular uprising (*népfelkelés*), rather than a counter-revolutionary movement. This was an obvious embarrassment to the Party veterans and extremists, and also compromised the HSWP's claim to act as the revolutionary instrument of the working class. Imre Nagy was rehabilitated by the HSWP Central Committee, in May; his reburial on 16 June, along with four associates, in the Rákoskeresztúr cemetery was attended by over 250,000 people.

The earliest drafts of a proposed new constitution revealed the Party leadership's limited commitment to a genuine democratic transformation. Hungary was to be 'a free, democratic and *socialist* state'; it was to remain 'a *people's* republic'; and its market economy was to be influenced 'by *socialist* socio-economic goals' (author's italics). Likewise, the law on associations, passed by the National Assembly in January 1989, postponed the regulation of new political parties (the appropriate legislation was eventually enacted in October). Clearly the Party reformers were hoping to delay the establishment of rival party organizations until as near as possible to the parliamentary elections due in 1990.

During the first months of 1989 it became increasingly evident that the HDF would not respond as the HSWP planned, and that it would be unlikely to enter into an electoral pact with the Communists. Furthermore, the advent of political pluralism, sanctioned by the law on associations, resulted in a proliferation of societies and trade unions determined to make Hungary a genuinely democratic state. New political parties were also established, despite the still-existing legal limitations on their activity. A series of serious by-election defeats, in mid-1989, also suggested that unless the Party made a genuine commitment to democracy it would not survive as a political force. Various calculations made by the leadership, however, suggested that, were the Party to pioneer a democratic transformation, then the electorate would reward it with one-third of the votes cast. Given the fragmented character of the opposition, the HSWP hoped thus to obtain the largest single share of seats in a democratically-elected Assembly. On the basis of this analysis, on 21 June the leadership of the HSWP entered into negotiations with the opposition parties on new constitutional proposals to put before the National Assembly.

The outcome of these 'round-table talks', at which the HSWP, HDF, AFD, FYD, PPF and various other Party and non-Party organizations were represented, was a series of legislative proposals which were presented to parliament, in September 1989, and rapidly enacted into law. According to this legislation, which amended the Stalinist Constitution of 1949, Hungary became a democracy, where political parties could freely operate, and where the rule of law was guaranteed by a constitutional court. A procedure for elections by a combination of party-list and member-constituencies was drawn up, and the office of President of the Republic was created. Perhaps most significantly, the separation of any party from the guidance of the state and its economic structure was formalized. Hungary formally ceased to be a People's Republic on 23 October and the red star was removed from public buildings.

In preparation for the parliamentary elections, which were to be held before June 1990, the HSWP called its party congress a year early. It was anxious to display its democratic credentials: accordingly it renamed itself the Hungarian Socialist Party (HSP), and handed over its property and control of the Workers' Militia to the state.

In the course of negotiations with the opposition, however, the Communists had obtained one important concession. It had been agreed between the then HSWP and the HDF that the President of the Republic was to be appointed by the existing Communist-dominated parliament in advance of the 1990 parliamentary elections. The aim of this measure was to ensure the selection of Imre Pozsgay, who was the only candidate acceptable both to the HSP and to the HDF.

The hasty presidential election was resisted by the AFD and the FYD, and the matter was debated in parliament. At the suggestion of the AFD, premier Miklós Németh agreed to have a national referendum on the issue. On 26 November 1989 the Hungarian electorate voted by a narrow margin to postpone the appointment of the President until after the parliamentary elections of 1990.

THE 1990 ELECTION

On 21 December 1989 the Hungarian parliament voted to dissolve itself in readiness for elections scheduled for 25 March 1990. In the intervening months the Németh Government largely confined itself to the day-to-day management of affairs. Its major achievement was to secure an agreement with the USSR on the evacuation of all Soviet troops from Hungary, a task completed in June 1991.

In the extended period of campaigning the HSP was the earliest casualty. It was alleged that the HSP was using the Ministry of the Interior to intercept the telephone conversations of opposition politicians. The HSP Interior Minister was unable to exonerate himself from the charge of political espionage and was forced to resign on 23 January 1990. The 'Danubegate' scandal deepened when opposition politicians alleged that the interior ministry was destroying records of its activities under the Communists. The HSP Minister of State, Imre Pozsgay, was also embarrassed by the accusation that he had sought to influence media coverage of the election campaign by having the head of television news removed from his post.

The opposition parties benefited from the discomfiture of the HSP. Of the 50 parties contesting the election, the principal contenders were the HDF and the AFD. The programmes of these two parties were broadly similar: both advocated political pluralism, genuine multi-party democracy, the restoration of a market economy and a 'return to Europe'. The AFD laid greater stress, however, on individual rights and endorsed a programme of rapid transition to a market economy. By contrast, the HDF espoused a more gradualist approach to the economy and emphasized 'Hungarian' national values.

During the first months of 1990 the HDF defined its policies more exactly. It ceased to be an 'umbrella' movement for disparate groups, united only by their opposition to Communism. Instead, it became a conservative (in the Western European sense of the term) and 'Christian' party. The allies of the HDF were the Christian Democratic People's Party (CDPP) and the Independent Smallholders' and Peasants' Party (usually known as the Independent Smallholders' Party—ISP), both of which broadly shared the same political outlook as the HDF leadership. The AFD, however, established close links with the anti-Communist youth organization, FYD.

Relations between the HDF and AFD were strained by personal differences. The HDF had evolved under the protection of the reformists in the HSWP; the AFD was led by former dissidents who had suffered harassment at the hands of the old Party apparatus. Moreover, the patriotism espoused by some HDF politicians occasionally gave way to nationalist and anti-Semitic statements. This was resented by the AFD, since a number of its leaders were of Jewish origin.

The election was held on 25 March 1990. A second round of voting took place on 8 April in those constituencies where no candidate had won an overall majority. Out of 386 seats in the new parliament, 176 were filled by direct elections in constituencies and 152 from 20 regional party lists. The remaining 58 seats were allocated to parties in accordance with a procedure designed to compensate for the inequities of the 'first-past-the-post' system used in the constituencies. The HDF obtained 165 seats in the new parliament, the AFD 92, the ISP 43, the HSP 33, and the FYD and CDPP 21 each. Eleven independent and joint party candidates were also elected.

THE HDF GOVERNMENT

The strength of the HDF vote allowed it to form a ruling coalition with the ISP and the CDPP. This conservative coalition controlled 229 seats in the parliament, giving it a comfortable working majority as far as normal legislation was concerned. The new coalition Government was sworn in on 23 May 1990, under the premiership of Dr József Antall, an historian who had been gaoled for his activities during the Uprising of 1956, and whose father had held high ministerial office between 1939 and 1946. The Foreign Minister was Dr Géza Jeszenszky, another historian, who had cultivated powerful connections in the USA and United Kingdom over the preceding years. Of the 16 other cabinet posts, four were given to the ISP, one to the CDPP and three to 'technocrats', specialists without party affiliation.

According to earlier legislation, a two-thirds majority in parliament was required to alter constitutional laws and to pass the budget. Since the HDF coalition controlled only 59% of the parliamentary seats, the programme of the

Government could have been impeded by the opposition. Therefore Antall began discussions with the AFD leadership. The HDF coalition agreed that the AFD spokesperson, Árpád Göncz, should be elected acting President of the Republic. In July 1990 a national referendum was held to determine the future method of electing the President (whether by direct election or by the National Assembly). However, the result was invalidated as only 14% of the electorate participated, instead of the required minimum of 50%. Consequently, on 3 August, Göncz was elected to a full five-year term; the AFD agreed to restrict the two-thirds majority rule to only the most important constitutional and legislative acts.

ECONOMIC AND SOCIAL POLICIES

The most pressing task facing the new Government was the economic situation. On 22 May 1990, Antall presented the Government's programme, the main purpose of which was the creation of a 'social market economy' based on private ownership and enterprise. Antall promised to reduce inflation, then running at an annual rate of between 25% and 30%, to reduce the US $19,500m. foreign debt and to achieve full convertibility for the forint in 1991. Although anticipating some temporary difficulties, Antall envisaged the prospect of an economic growth rate of 3%–4%. Antall's speech was criticized by opposition politicians as implausible.

In apparent confirmation of the opposition's charges, the economic situation deteriorated over 1991. By the end of the year more than 7% of the working population was unemployed. The annual inflation rate was some 34% and production also declined. The budget deficit increased to 53,100m. forint. Nevertheless, while the Hungarian economy continued to perform below the predictions of government ministers, the decline slowed by 1992, and the rate of inflation and unemployment stabilized. Largely owing to tourism, Hungary's balance of payments, in 1990–92, registered a surplus. In spite of the Government's commitment to a reform of the currency, the forint remained non-convertible and no independent central bank was established.

The pace of the Government's privatization programme was slow. In late 1990 Antall's principal economic adviser, György Matolcsy, resigned after the Government refused to implement a rapid programme of privatization. By June 1992 only 8.3% of industry had been transferred from public to private ownership, mainly through the sale of stock to foreign companies. In an attempt to hasten privatization, a State Assets Handling Company was established in late 1992, to manage nationalized industries. In January 1993 Iván Szabó replaced Mihály Kupa as Minister of Finance. Two months later the implementation of a voucher system for the sale of stock in state-run industries, similar to those adopted in the Czech Republic and Romania, was announced.

In spite of Hungary's poor economic performance, the extent of the hardship suffered in the country was less than might have been expected. Many Hungarians were able to obtain employment in the unofficial, parallel economy (the 'black market'). Furthermore, social-security payments remained relatively high. Following the social and industrial unrest which greeted the Government's austerity measures and price increases in 1990–91, the Government was reluctant to decrease subsidies and social-welfare payments again. Owing to its political and social stability, and also to its generous tax laws, Hungary continued, in the early 1990s, to be a favoured location for Western investment. The majority of this investment, led by the USA, Germany and Austria, took the form of joint ventures. In 1993, however, the small size of the Hungarian market and uncertainty over the outcome of the 1994 general elections resulted in a decline in the level of foreign investment.

FOREIGN POLICY

The HDF Government espoused a firmly European and regional foreign policy which was designed to win Hungary access to Western credit and eventual membership of the European Community (EC—known as the European Union from November 1993). On 2 October 1990 Hungary became a member of the Council of Europe and, on 1 January 1992, an associate member of the EC. The Hungarian Government signed military and economic co-operation agreements with most of its immediate neighbours, including Germany, Romania and Ukraine. Hungary, along with Poland and the Czech and Slovak Republics, was a member of the 'Visegrad Group' (originally, before the dissolution of Czechoslovakia, the 'trilateral group') which was dedicated to democratic reform and regional co-operation. It was believed that participation in the group would quicken Hungary's economic integration into the EC.

The Hungarian Government adopted a cautious stance towards the conflicts in the former Yugoslavia. The Government extended facilities to UN relief and peace-keeping forces travelling to and from the area and permitted airborne warning and control system (AWACS) aircraft to use Hungarian airspace. The country also admitted 50,000 refugees, although it was believed that the *de facto* number of refugees from the former Yugoslavia in Hungary was as many as 100,000.

Although the foreign policies pursued by the Hungarian Government in the early 1990s could largely be considered successful, political inexperience was, at times, apparent. In October 1990 the Hungarian Government was implicated in the clandestine sale of weapons to the Government of Croatia (this scandal caused the dismissal of the country's ambassador to the USA). Furthermore, Antall's statement, in August 1990, that he regarded himself 'in spirit' the Prime Minister of Hungarians living abroad was taken amiss by the Romanian Government. In July 1991 Antall further implied that the disintegration of Yugoslavia might justify Hungary making claims to some former Yugoslav territories. Relations with Slovakia were strained on account of the continued plans of the Slovak Government to re-route the Danube so as to feed the hydroelectric plant at Gabčikovo. The two countries agreed to submit this dispute to the International Court of Justice for adjudication in April 1993.

THE CONSTITUTIONAL COURT

The Hungarian Constitution was based on the Communist Constitution of 1949, although it was substantially amended. The process of amendment, together with a surfeit of new legislation (115 new laws in the first two years of the HDF Government), left a variety of constitutional uncertainties and conflicts of competence. The establishment of a Constitutional Court, in 1990, was intended to provide a mechanism for the resolution of constitutional differences. According to the Constitution, the Court's principal function was 'to contribute to the creation of a state built upon the rule of law, to protect the constitutional order and the fundamental rights of citizens, and to safeguard the separation and balance of powers'. The Court was entitled to review laws both in draft and after passage through parliament. The Court's 10 judges were appointed for nine-year terms by parliamentary committee.

On the whole, the Constitutional Court adopted a strict, constructionist view of the Constitution. While upholding the constitutional balance of powers, the Court affirmed the leading role of the parliament and of the ministers responsible to it. The Court did, however, adopt a more active stance in the defence of individual rights. In its first 18 months the Court annulled 47 laws and regulations mostly on the grounds that they interfered with the rights and liberties of the person. The Court declared both the death penalty and personal identification numbers to be unconstitutional, vetoed anti-abortion laws, and overturned legislation revoking the statute of limitations for offences committed during the period of Communist rule.

POLITICAL PARTIES

In by-elections contested after 1990 the Hungarian electorate demonstrated considerable apathy, with turn-out seldom rising above one-third of eligible voters. Disillusionment with the social and economic policies pursued by the HDF Government may partly explain this apathy as well as the general dissatisfaction with the leading political parties.

Throughout 1991 and 1992 the AFD decreased in popularity. In an attempt to improve its electoral appeal the AFD replaced its leader, the former dissident János Kis, in October 1991, with Péter Tölgessy. He, however, was replaced in November 1992, by Iván Pető. At the time, this appointment was thought to signal a leftward move in the AFD and to presage a possible coalition with the HSP.

Although its membership grew in 1991 and 1992, the HDF experienced increasing internal disputes. It was considered particularly likely to fragment into rival national-liberal and conservative-populist wings. In August 1992 the HDF's deputy leader, István Csurka, published a controversial manifesto containing racist statements. He also demanded the resignation of Antall on health grounds. Owing to the strong support for Csurka within the party, the HDF was slow to repudiate his manifesto. Csurka subsequently formed his own faction within the HDF, the 'Hungarian Road', a right-wing and nationalist pressure group. He was eventually expelled from the HDF, in June 1993, and established his own party, the Hungarian Justice and Life Party. On 12 December 1993 Antall died. Péter Boross, the Minister of the Interior, succeeded him as Prime Minister.

Although the HDF avoided dissolving into two rival parties, its coalition partner, the ISP, disintegrated. In 1990 the Constitutional Court vetoed legislation drafted by the ISP which allowed for the restitution of properties seized by the Communists after 1947. As the HDF was disinclined to seek a constitutional amendment to facilitate the passage of what was, in effect, the main aim of the ISP programme, relations between the coalition partners deteriorated. Personal rivalry between the ISP leader, József Torgyán, and Antall led, in October 1991, to Torgyán filing a suit for slander against the Prime Minister. In an attempt to bring down the Government, Torgyán announced, in February 1992, that the ISP was leaving the coalition. Only 13 ISP deputies followed Torygán's lead, the majority continuing to vote in support of the Government. The rebels were expelled from the ISP, although they retained their parliamentary seats.

Throughout 1991 and 1992 the FYD increased in popularity, although it failed to win any by-elections. In an attempt to improve its image as the unconventional junior partner of the AFD, the FYD abandoned its maximum-age qualification of 35 and began to move closer to the Government. In May 1993, however, it was revealed that the party leadership of both the HDF and the FYD had been involved in land transactions of questionable legality.

Having redefined itself as a social democratic party, the HSP, previously the vehicle of the reform Communists, moved into a commanding position as the principal electoral challenger to the HDF. Between 1990 and 1992 the HSP won five out of eight by-elections held in Budapest. In June 1992 the HSP candidate won two-thirds of the votes cast in a by-election held at Kisbér (the HDF candidate obtained only 17% of the votes cast). Although its party membership was small, the HSP's daily, *Népszabadság* (People's Freedom), was the highest-circulation newspaper in Hungary in the early 1990s. Furthermore, the Hungarian National Trade Union Organization, successor to the Communist labour organization, retained the largest membership in the Hungarian trade-union movement and was politically close to the HSP. It seemed, therefore, possible that, should the HDF coalition be defeated in the 1994 elections, the HSP would emerge as a leading parliamentary force.

The Economy

RICHARD ROSS BERRY

INTRODUCTION

The development of the Hungarian economy since the Second World War, focusing as it has on the development of heavy industry, paid little attention to the limits imposed by the country's natural assets. Although up to 70% of Hungary's total area of 93,033 sq km could be used for various agricultural purposes, the country possessed few raw materials in any sizeable quantities. Coal reserves, at 4,500m. metric tons, varied in quality and were often difficult to extract. There were deposits of crude petroleum and natural gas, but imports satisfied the vast bulk of demand for these commodities. However, Hungary did possess up to 12% of the world's total reserves of bauxite. There were also quantities of manganese ore and uranium. In general, the country had a low resource base and compensated for this by engaging actively in international trade.

At the beginning of the 1990s, in common with the other Eastern European economies, the Hungarian economy was undergoing a profound period of transition to a market economy. In the case of Hungary, however, the adoption of market mechanisms—particularly a reduction in the use of planned indicators and the implementation of a more rational price mechanism—took place over a considerable period of time, dating from the promulgation of the New Economic Mechanism (NEM) in 1968.

The erratic progress of the reform of the Hungarian economy throughout the 1970s and 1980s owed as much to political as to economic factors. The deterioration in the country's terms of trade, and continuing balance-of-payments problems, forced reform economics once again on to the agenda. The relative liberalization of the Kádár period and the emergence of Mikhail Gorbachev in the USSR further promoted the cause of reform. However, there were serious political obstacles to the marketization of the economy, chief among which was the monopoly of power held by the Communist Party. It was clear that the maintenance of this monopoly was a serious obstacle to reform and that further marketization of the economy could only be achieved along with a democratization of the political system.

At the general election held in the spring of 1990 a coalition Government, led by the Hungarian Democratic Forum (HDF), came to power. Relations between the coalition partners largely determined the pace of economic change. The main issues of the removal of subsidies, the pace and nature of privatization, the level of foreign investment and related questions of property and ownership rights ensured that the new Government's period of rule was far from uneventful. Indeed, stormy relations between the HDF and its principal partner, the Independent Smallholders' Party (ISP), had the effect of slowing down the transformation process. Once again, the development of the economy was largely dependent on politics, albeit in a democratic setting. Low turn-out in by-elections and the general apathy of the population presented considerable obstacles to the implementation of reform during the early 1990s. Moreover, there were serious divisions within the HDF which affected economic policy. In addition, it was thought likely that the 1994 general elections would result in a coalition from the opposition parties. The pace of change would depend very much on the composition of the new administration. Furthermore, regional disputes, such as those between Romania and Hungary and between Slovakia and Hungary over the issue of the Hungarian ethnic minorities, and the conflict in the former Yugoslavia, had serious repercussions for the stability of the region and its economic development.

After the 1990 general election the economy, or rather its performance, came to be a prominent feature of Hungarian life at all levels. The central issues of property rights, privatization, inflation, unemployment and debt formed the focal points of debate. In the spring of 1991 the Government introduced a four-year economic programme based on the acceleration of privatization, controlling inflation and preparing the groundwork for convertibility of the forint. The programme's aim was to integrate Hungary fully into the world economy on a competitive basis. However, the scale of the transformation envisaged was enormous; in most OECD (Organisation for Economic Co-operation and Development) countries the state controls or owns enterprises responsible for some 15% of gross domestic product (GDP), while in Hungary the state controlled or owned up to 85% of GDP.

AGRICULTURE

By 1960 Hungarian agriculture was largely collectivized. Up to 90% of farmland and 94% of agricultural workers worked in the socialized sector. In the round of economic reforms in the mid-1960s obligatory targets were removed and, after 1968, co-operative farms became largely autonomous. State farms remained under central control. Prices and subsidies were determined by the Government. In 1991 there were over 120 state farms, which cultivated about one-quarter of farmland (2,159,000 ha) and employed 17% of the 800,000-strong agricultural work-force, while 1,260 co-operatives cultivated about three-quarters of farmland and employed 75% of the agricultural work-force. Most of the co-operative and state farms are heavily indebted to the State, a condition that increased owing to the severe drought of 1990.

The changing pattern of land ownership was the result of new legislation, particularly the Compensation Act, which provided compensation to those whose property was expropriated during the Communist regime. In the early 1990s the state retained control of 20 of the larger state farms, comprising 300,000 ha out of total state farm land of 8,240,000 ha.

Up to two-thirds of the population engaged in small-scale agriculture; this included city dwellers who had weekend plots and the household plots of co-operative workers. Such plots were responsible for up to one-third of agricultural production, including over 50% of pig farming, 75% of vegetables and almost 60% of fruits. The value of gross agricultural production declined by 22.7% in 1992. Crop production decreased by an estimated 26% in the same year. Similarly, cereal production was equivalent to 63% of the 1991 figure, a decrease of approximately 6m. metric tons, worth about US $550m. Livestock production fell by 19.5% in 1992. One of the principal causes of this decline in agricultural output was the severe droughts experienced in the country in 1990 and 1992. In response to the drought of 1990 (which caused some 28,000m. forint-worth of damage) the agricultural sector received subsidies and preferential loans from the state. However, in spite of this sharp decrease in production, agricultural revenue declined by an estimated 10%–12%, in 1992, owing to the increase in prices.

Agricultural exports remained crucial to the economy and accounted for up to 25% of hard-currency exports in the early 1990s. In 1990 agriculture, hunting, forestry and fishing generated 261,236m. forint and accounted for 12.6% of GDP. In the following year the sector accounted for an estimated 10.2% of GDP.

In general, Hungarian agriculture was suffering, in the early 1990s, from a severe structural crisis, which was exacerbated by the droughts of 1990 and 1992, the collapse of the Council for Mutual Economic Assistance (CMEA) and the withdrawal of state subsidies. The establishment of trade links with the former USSR proved difficult. The old trading system in which the USSR accepted agricultural products in exchange for raw materials and machinery largely collapsed. In addition, Hungarian agricultural exporters were finding it difficult to compensate for this by establishing trade links with European Community (EC—known as the European Union from November 1993) countries. In April 1993 the EC suspended imports of livestock and dairy products from Eastern Europe owing to an outbreak of cattle disease. Although the ban was lifted in May, Hungarian sources estimated losses owing to it would be $50m. To the Hungarians this episode was an illustration of the EC's growing reluctance to increase imports from Eastern Europe. Hungary's main agricultural exports were seen as a threat by many EC countries to their own agricultural base. Hungary was active, in the early 1990s, in promoting trade liberalization within the General Agreement on Tariffs and Trade (GATT) and was also involved in the Cairns Group (an organization of major agricultural exporting countries which aimed to reform international agricultural trade). However, in order to benefit from such liberalization, Hungary's agricultural sector needed to become more self-reliant and competitive.

Livestock farming, and particularly pig farming, formed an important part of Hungarian agriculture. At the beginning of 1991 farmers had a surplus of 200,000 animals for market. Much of this surplus was accountable to the decrease in trade with the former USSR. However, the drought of 1992 and falling demand on domestic and international markets had a severe impact on this sector. In 1992 pig production decreased, according to unofficial figures, by 25.1%. In the dairy sector over-production remained a problem. Again, this was owing to the collapse of neighbouring markets and fall in domestic demand. The considerable surpluses of milk put pressure on limited storage space and on government subsidies. Milk production decreased by

4.8% in 1992, from 2,536,000 metric tons in 1991 to 2,416,000 tons in the following year.

As was the case with many other sectors in the economy, new institutions already familiar to dealers in the West began operations in the Hungarian agricultural sector following the collapse of the Communist regime. In the spring of 1991, following negotiations with commodity specialists from Chicago (USA), a meat exchange was established. Pigs and cattle formed the mainstay of trading and the exchange was to handle both spot trading and futures. This followed the establishment of a commodity exchange for wheat and maize in August 1989. The Government was keen to promote foreign investment in farming and farm-related activities, particularly food processing and canning, and sought to encourage the privatization of these activities by this method. Many of these processing plants were in need of modernization and the capital for this could only come from outside the country.

INDUSTRY

In 1992 GDP fell for the third consecutive year and was almost 20% lower than in 1989, declining by 5.0%, an improvement on the 10.0% decrease of 1991. In 1990 GDP had fallen by 4.0%. Industrial output decreased too, in 1992, by 9.8%. In the same year total industrial sales decreased by 6.4%, compared to a decline of 7.1% in 1991. However, small organizations (those with less than 50 employees) doubled their production in 1992. Consequently, their share of total industrial output increased from 6.4% at the beginning of 1992 to 14.1% at the end of the year. Industrial production in large-scale plants fell by 17.2% in 1992. The greatest decreases in production occurred in the metallurgy and engineering sectors, although there was an unexpected decline of 23% in light industry. About one-fifth of all industrial plants operated with more than 50 employees and these accounted, in 1992, for 86% of the industrial work-force. These enterprises also accounted for 93% of all industrial exports.

In the construction industry, production by enterprises employing more than 50 people decreased by 21.7%, in 1992, while small construction companies were responsible for 46% of total output. Small- and medium-sized companies have become dominant in this sector. Housing construction also declined in Hungary. Only 25,802 apartments were completed, in 1992, a decrease of 22.2%. Transport was also adversely affected by the decline in the economy: in 1992 the amount of goods transported was 27% less than in 1991.

The main problem for industry was its dependency on imported raw materials. Furthermore, given the relatively limited domestic demand, industry was adversely affected by the collapse of the CMEA and continuing restrictions on the import of industrial goods into new markets, particularly the EC. Many of the larger companies suffered financially and received government aid through the 'industrial-crisis management programme'. Although this programme prevented the bankruptcy of many plants, it was only a short-term measure. Many of these enterprises required considerable investment and lacked the necessary capital. Survival of these companies was impeded by the restrictive lending policy on the country's banks (see Finance section below). Moreover, these companies had to find new markets, a factor that was clearly not wholly within the capabilities of the enterprises themselves. In 1992 overall investment fell by 7%–8% in real terms. The construction industry was worst affected, in this respect, suffering a fall of 27%. This could be explained by the depth of the recession in the early 1990s and by the factors outlined above.

The rise in environmental problems was directly associated with the pace and nature of Hungarian economic development. The country was characterized by high sulphur-dioxide emissions and the production of high levels of hazardous waste, and consequently by polluted air and water supplies. Many towns had poor sewage facilities. The resolution of such problems has become a highly charged political question.

MINING AND ENERGY

There were major restructuring problems for the coal industry in the early 1990s. The country's eight colliery enterprises, containing 32 mining units, incurred losses in the region of 2,700m. forint in 1991 alone. Total debts amounted to more than 9,000m. forint and some collieries were closed. The Government was wary of strike action in this area and this prevented a more radical approach to the industry. Coal production declined from 17,578,000 metric tons, in 1990, to 15,836,000 metric tons in 1992. Restructuring was also taking place in the aluminium industry. The state aluminium company, MAT, was reorganized with a view to privatization. In 1990 the company produced 75,000 metric tons of aluminium ingots and 170,000 metric tons of semi-finished products. As was the case with most of the heavy industrial sector, the introduction of convertible-currency accounting and the rapid fall in trade with the former USSR gave rise to considerable fears for the future. Aluminium production decreased from 75,162 metric tons, in 1990, to 26,865 metric tons in 1992.

The energy sector accounted for about 20% of total industrial output in the early 1990s. The electricity and petroleum industries were undergoing restructuring. As with many industrial sectors, the amounts of money required for the modernization of Hungary's electricity grid were beyond the available means. As in most of the former CMEA countries, there was considerable waste; Hungary used about 2.5 times the OECD countries' average number of energy units per unit of production. Energy efficiency became a major concern for the Government. Some help was forthcoming from the UN Economic Commission for Europe, which launched an 'Energy Efficiency Project' and made available a sum of US $3.5m.–$5.5m. Most of the electricity grid remained orientated to the east, with the former USSR being a major supplier. In the early 1990s the country did not have the infrastructural capacity to accept supplementary electricity from Western European countries. Domestic electric energy production rose from 29,762m. kWh, in 1991, to 31,396m. kWh in 1992.

Similar problems were faced in the petroleum industry. Hungary needed to import some two-thirds of its petroleum requirements. In 1992 domestic crude petroleum production stood at 1.8m. metric tons. In 1989 the USSR supplied 90% of crude imports, amounting to 7.7m. tons, a figure which fell to 5m. tons in 1990. Securing petroleum supplies from the former USSR, which had previously been sold at concessionary rates, proved to be a major problem, so Hungary was forced to purchase supplies on the world market. The war in the former Yugoslavia also meant the closure of the Adria pipeline. Meanwhile the domestic industry was reorganized under the national oil and gas trust (MOL Magyar Olaj és Gáziparirt–MOL Hungarian Oil and Gas), which was responsible for all petroleum and gas production. Plans for privatization in this industry would result in a substantial reduction in the work-force from 46,000 to 18,000. There was to be considerable government control of this industry, initially up to 50%. Natural gas production fell from 5,043m. cu m, in 1991, to 4,932m. cu m in 1992.

PRIVATIZATION

The central task of restructuring and privatizing Hungary's industrial base was extremely complex, particularly in the case of the larger heavy industries. It was difficult to make comparisons with privatization in other countries, particularly the United Kingdom, where 'high-tech' profitable industries, amounting to no more than 8% of GDP, were privatized over the course of one decade. Should privatization take place at the same pace in Hungary it would take almost 100 years to arrive at a similar position. In addition, many of the Hungarian plants were in the non-profitable heavy industrial sector and existed on the basis of state subsidies. Thus, although the process of transformation resembled that in the West, the sheer scale of the task had to be taken into consideration. The process was largely controlled by the State Property Agency, which received much criticism for its bureaucratic methods. Moreover, the investigation of senior officials for corruption, in the early 1990s, damaged the Agency's image and the whole concept of privatization.

The privatization process was fundamentally affected by the removal of subsidies from uneconomic enterprises, which was a central, yet controversial, point in the Government's programme. The withdrawal or the reduction in the level of such subsidies depended on the acceptability of the social consequences of such an action. Price rises, closures and unemployment entailed by the withdrawal of subsidies were likely to result in the moderation of the programme, particularly in an election year. Total subsidies, as a percentage of GDP, amounted to 9.0% in 1990, 7.5% in 1991 and 5.3% in 1992. In 1991 subsidies totalled 172,000m. forint out of a total GDP of 2,301,500m. forint, and in 1992 149,000m. out of a total of 2,800,000m.

The role of the state in the privatization process remained controversial. The Government was to keep a majority share in certain sectors. In some cases, such as broadcasting and the state railways, this merely followed the pattern of many Western European countries. However, the Government promoted a restructuring and rationalization plan, designed to avoid making too many workers unemployed. The declared policy that 50% of the economy was to be privatized by 1994 was a considerable undertaking and was unlikely to be realized.

The privatization process was complicated by the fact that legislation forced companies to transform themselves into joint-stock units to take them out of direct state control. Thus some figures for the non-state sector appeared abnormally high. After the 1988 Associations Act there was a rapid increase in the number of organizations regarded as companies. The actual number of incorporated economic entities increased from 52,756, at the beginning of 1992, to 69,383 at the end of the year. In addition, there were 70,600 unincorporated economic associations and 600,000 individual businesses. The main problem was that the new businesses employed fewer people and could not compensate for the closure of the larger state enterprises. In 1992 many state-owned enterprises were either privatized or transformed into economic associations, and some closed. There were 4,231 bankruptcies in 1992. Hitherto the preferred means of privatization was by encouraging foreign companies to take a direct stake in a Hungarian company in a joint venture, or to allow direct foreign ownership. One of the largest privatizations of this type occurred, in March 1991, between the French company Sanofi, part of the multinational Elf Aquitaine group, and Chinoin, the leading Hungarian pharmaceutical company. After that there were notable investments by foreign companies. This involvement of foreign capital became highly controversial and the Government was sensitive to the charge of betraying national interests. Between March 1990 and the end of January 1993 679 state-owned companies were privatized.

At the end of 1992 the Government announced a new privatization scheme, under which individuals would be eligible for a loan of 100,000 forint (US $1,150) to purchase shares in privatized outlets. Such shares would not be traded until the loan was repaid. This scheme was a combination of the popular privatization programmes of Poland and of the Czech and Slovak Republics, and of the country's previous privatization programme. In addition, the Government developed legislation to provide low-interest credit for those wishing to take over an enterprise and introduced an Employee Stock Ownership Programme.

INFLATION

The problems facing the Government were compounded by the high level of inflation, which was 28.9% in 1990 and 34.2% in 1991. Prices of essential consumer goods and services were largely liberalized. In 1992 consumer prices rose by 22.9% and energy costs alone rose by 43.2%. In February 1993 an amendment to the Price Law meant that official prices barely accounted for 8.0% of overall prices. Increases in food prices continued to be a major contributory factor in fuelling the rate of inflation. These increases could be partly attributed to the monopoly some producers had on the market. Commodity purchases declined, in real terms, by 20.6% in 1992, to 723,000m. forint. This decrease was partly offset by illegal trading and non-recorded purchases, particularly by smaller businesses, but it was still indicative of the decline in real incomes and the increase in the rate of unemployment.

SERVICES

Initially retail privatization was rather slow moving. This was partly owing to the inability to establish ownership and also to the fact that the population as a whole lacked the surplus funds necessary to purchase the outlets. By the end of 1992 there were 121,000 shops and 44,000 catering units, over 9% more than at the end of 1991. The number of new shops established in 1992 was twice the number of closures. Some 61% of all shops and 64% of catering outlets were operated by private entrepreneurs. Actual retail turnover of shops and catering outlets increased by 14% and 22%, respectively, in 1992.

The liberalization of Eastern Europe greatly enhanced the prospects of the tourist industry in the region. In 1992 there were 33.5m. foreign visitors, a slight increase on the previous year. In 1992 earnings from tourism accounted for US $1,200m., making the sector one of the major earners of convertible ('hard') currency.

EMPLOYMENT AND UNEMPLOYMENT

Throughout its recent history the Hungarian economy was characterized by rapid and concentrated industrial development. In 1992 Hungary had 6,889 industrial enterprises, 770 of which had a work-force of over 300. The fall in the production of the large-scale enterprises entailed a reduction in the number of employees. Overall, some 4.2m. (41.0%) of the 10.3m. Hungarian citizens were economically active, in 1992, with many having secondary employment.

In January 1993 unemployment stood at 694,000, some 13% of the work-force. The rate of unemployment was higher amongst males. This was owing to the fact that the traditional sources of employment for this group—the steel, metallurgy and construction sectors—were the most adversely affected by the economic recession. Monthly unemployment benefit was calculated on the basis of past contributions and lasted for a limited period. Businesses paid 7% of employees' wages into the central social-security fund while workers paid 2%. Unemployment was highest in the regions: in the north-east the rate was 23%, compared to 6% in Budapest. This was partly owing to the greater opportunities for employment in the capital, but also because the Government was reluctant to create additional unemployment in the capital and tended to allow the closure of enterprises in the regions.

In 1992–93 there were a number of strikes and disputes, particularly in the coal industry. The Government was reluctant to confront the trade unions, owing to the impending general elections. Provisions made in the state budget and the Solidarity Fund—a fund set up to help manage the social effects of unemployment—were under increasing financial strain. By October 1993 the rate of unemployment had decreased slightly, to 12.6% of the work-force.

BANKING

One of the most notable changes in domestic finance has been the changing relationship between the National Bank of Hungary (Magyar Nemzeti Bank) and the Government, particularly the former's role as the central supplier of money and its role in covering the budget deficit. On the whole the National Bank sought to maintain a relatively strict control over monetary policy, largely through interest-rate policy, in order to control inflation. Many argued for an even stricter monetary regime, but there was considerable fear that the economy, already in recession, would decline further were this to be implemented.

According to law, the National Bank was limited in terms of covering the budget deficit. Therefore, commercial banks became the main purchasers of securities. Obviously this increased government debt-levels, but succeeded in reducing the growth of money. There was the additional problem of the Government competing in the money markets with the private sector. There were 31 commercial banks and 7 specialized financial institutions in Hungary in 1993. From 1990 the Government sought to introduce a series of measures designed to control the banks' operations. A Financial Institutions Act was introduced in December 1991 and new accountancy and bankruptcy laws came into effect in January 1992. The reform of the banking system, principally the introduction of a commercial sector and the ending of the monobank system (whereby the National Bank was responsible for all aspects of banking), however, actually took place in 1987. The result of this was that banks were given a particular portfolio to manage. Most of the clients allocated to the banks were not credit-worthy. As the old system did not operate an a profitability basis, the banks found themselves effectively with many clients who had low- or zero-profitability and whose financial survival was always guaranteed by the Government. The change of government which presaged an introduction of profitability criteria increased the precarious financial position of many companies and thus seriously affected the profitability of the banks.

The result was that many banks adopted a cautious lending policy. In effect, this meant the reduction of lending to the enterprise sector. The ability of companies to gain access to capital was greatly reduced by a decline in domestic demand, collapsing Eastern European markets and the introduction of high real interest rates. The more viable companies were able to raise credit abroad (more than US $700m. by the end of 1992). There was also some foreign investment.

The increasing number of unprofitable clients gave rise to a credit crisis within the banking sector. The Government responded by introducing a credit-consolidation scheme for those institutions with partial state ownership and a low capital adequacy ratio, whereby the banks were issued with negotiable government securities in return for cancelling some of the company's debts. This scheme was necessitated by the collapse of two banks in 1992.

In the increasingly uncertain economic environment of the early 1990s, actual savings ratios increased rapidly. Gross savings of households increased by 31.9% in 1992. The stock of foreign-currency deposits rose by 17.5% in the same year. Personal savings amounted to 11.6% of disposable income, in the early 1990s, compared to 4%–6% in the late 1980s. Personal savings accounted for 56% of total savings. The increasing savings ratio in a period of high inflation reflected a population which viewed the future with increasing uncertainty and were willing to hold on to wealth in cash form. However, many sectors of the population had no savings at all. Statistics showed that the vast majority of these increased savings were held by a small, wealthy section of society. In 1980 82% of Hungarians were regular savers, but by 1992 this had fallen to 38%. The worrying factor was that even these groups preferred to hold cash or government securities rather than invest in new businesses. However, there were increasing signs that domestic investment was on the increase. Some of this evidence came from the activities of the Stock Exchange, which began operations in May 1990, after an absence of more than 40 years. However, the performance of the Exchange was weak. This was mainly owing to an inflated pricing policy in 1990 and 1991.

EXCHANGE-RATE POLICY AND FOREIGN TRADE

One of the Government's declared aims was that of currency convertibility, though this was to rely largely on the state of the economy and access to hard-currency sources. A three-year stabilization plan with the International Monetary Fund (IMF) was to provide some support in this direction. In 1981 a unified exchange rate was introduced and limited convertibility became possible. In addition, the forint was adjusted on a daily basis against a basket of currencies. The forint was internally convertible, although the Government aimed to achieve full convertibility in 1994. From March 1993 the Budapest Commodity Exchange engaged in forward foreign-exchange transactions. Initially this applied to US dollar and Deutschmark transactions and it was hoped that the scheme would be extended to cover a range of currencies. This would remove the monopoly role of the central bank and should increase the volume of trade. Hungary operated an adjustable-peg exchange-rate regime: within the currency basket used to measure the value of the forint the dollar was weighted 50% with the ECU (European Currency Unit). Adjustment within a 5% range could be carried out by the National Bank, though this would be done on the basis of consultation with the Government. There were several devaluations after 1990, although in real terms the forint actually appreciated. The main reason for this was that the Government was as strict in combating inflation as it had been in implementing the exchange-rate regime.

For manufacturing companies in Hungary this meant that the prices of domestic materials were rising in line with hard-currency revenues. Thus, a company like General Electric, which took over the Tungsram light-bulb manufacturer, and which depended heavily on the export market, claimed that the exchange-rate policy was a principal reason for its losses. In general the appreciation of the forint reduced import costs and, therefore, the production costs that were based on them. The companies that supported the exchange-rate policy and benefited from it were those whose production involved the manufacture of imports using domestic labour. However, this import and re-export trade caused concern that Hungary was becoming an 'assembly' rather than a manufacturing economy.

According to official estimates (although there was some confusion in the compilation of trade statistics—it was hoped that this would be resolved by a new statistical law of April 1993), in 1992 visible exports accounted for 40% of GDP and receipts from tourism 10%. Other foreign trade and services contributed a further 1%–2% to GDP. Thus, the contribution of the external economy to GDP was over 50%. In the same year Hungarian merchandise exports grew by 4.2%, reaching a figure of US $10,097m. There was some indication that this growth of hard-currency trade was finally beginning to offset the loss of the former CMEA markets. Imports continued to remain high, reaching $10,018m. in 1992. In that year Hungary recorded a merchandise trade deficit of $11m., a decrease of $347m. on the previous year's trade surplus. However, on the current account of the balance of payments, following a deficit in 1989, Hungary consistently recorded surpluses in the early 1990s ($352m. in 1992).

The domestic difficulties of the former Soviet economy and the shortage of hard-currency trading gave rise to a severe contraction of trade between the Eastern European economies. The petrochemical, iron and steel, construction and textile industries in this region previously relied on the Soviet market. In 1992 exports by the larger enterprises in these sectors fell by 8%. However, exports by small businesses rose by 126%, although this increase in trade was largely directed to Western markets.

It was estimated that Soviet debts to Hungary amounted to 2,200m. roubles. After 1991 trade agreements between Russia (which inherited most of the Soviet debt) and Hungary were signed. However, the fulfilment of these agreements depended largely on the internal situations in the countries of the former USSR. In December 1992 an agreement was reached to enable the outstanding Russian debt to Hungary to be paid, involving the exchange of some weaponry and other imports.

After 1990 Germany replaced the USSR as the most important single trading partner. In 1990 Hungarian exports to the USSR declined to 20.1% of total exports (compared to 25.1% in 1989 and over one-third in the mid-1980s), and to 13.3% in 1991, while those to the newly united Germany rose from 19.9% in 1990, to 26.9% in 1991. In 1992 Germany accounted for some 24% of Hungarian imports and 28% of exports. The EC accounted for 50% of all merchandise exports. In 1992 approximately 72% of Hungary's trade went to developed countries. Unlike Hungary's former trading partners in the CMEA, Hungarian exports actually increased in 1992. However, exports to developing countries fell by one-third. Other important trading partners with Hungary, in the early 1990s, were Austria, Italy and the Czech and Slovak Republics.

In 1988 the Hungarian Government ended its monopoly on the conduct of foreign trade. It is important to note that more than 90% of imports were liberalized under that new Government. However, certain specific restrictions remained, either as a method of protecting certain sectors of the economy or as a means of protecting the balance of payments. In addition, there was an additional sales tax on many imported finished products and consumer goods. It should also be noted that many foreign investors, particularly in the manufacturing sector, favoured some degree of protectionism for their new industries. In the early 1990s there remained an annual quota of 120,000 passenger cars, a factor which benefited car manufacturers. In general, however, during the 1970s and 1980s there was a steady integration of Hungary into the world economy, which began, in a limited form, with membership of the GATT (1973) and the IMF (1982).

As was the case with Poland and Czechoslovakia (the Czech Republic and Slovakia from 1 January 1993), Hungary has been seeking closer co-operation with the EC. A trade and co-operation agreement was signed in June 1988 and, in mid-1991, negotiations took place on the implementation of an agreement on more free trade, known as the Association Agreement. This came into effect in March 1992. The agreement meant that some 55% of Hungary's exports to the EC, excluding steel and textiles, would no longer face quantitative restrictions, and that two-thirds of exports would be exempt from customs duties. In December 1992 a supplementary protocol was signed between Hungary and the EC, which provided for the abolition of quantitative quotas over a five-year period from 1 January 1993. There were some protectionist provisions within this agreement that were to safeguard new or restructured Hungarian industries.

In spite of attempts by the Hungarians, it was thought unlikely that Hungary would be eligible for EC membership in the short term. In September 1991 several EC member countries, including France and Germany, refused to consider allowing ready access to EC markets of Eastern European agricultural goods, and there were similar disputes in April 1993 (see Agriculture section above). Hungary benefited from participation in the Generalized System of Preferences (GSP). In the early 1990s increased access to markets was dependent on further trade liberalization. This liberalization was impeded by the slow progress of the GATT negotiations, disputes with the EC and the formation of new trading blocs in North America and, possibly, in Asia. In March 1993 the Hungarian Government signed a free-trade agreement with the European Free Trade Association (EFTA), which came into effect on 1 July. This was similar to the EC agreement, although it covered a wider range of products. In December 1992 the Central European Free Trade Agreement was signed by the countries of the Visegrad Group, which included Hungary. This came into effect in March 1993. Before this agreement was signed, trade between the countries within the Group (Czech and Slovak Republics, Hungary and Poland), amounted to no more than 7% of overall trade. It was hoped that the agreement would result in a regional trade expansion.

FINANCE

In early 1993 the Hungarian Government was granted aid from the IMF, on the condition that it adhered to its economic reform programme, which included tax increases and reductions in budgetary expenditure. Successful implementation of this programme would secure a US $400m. credit from the IMF and a $100m. structural-adjustment loan from the World Bank. In 1991 the budget deficit amounted to 53,100m. forint, compared with 700m. forint in the previous year.

Debt

Hungary had a gross debt figure of US $21,438m. in 1992, and a net debt of $13,052m. The majority of this debt was contracted under the Communist regime. Medium- and long-term debt payments, although costly, were manageable, and, unlike Poland, Hungary was not involved in any debt-reduction deals and had a reasonably good reputation in the international capital markets. Almost three-quarters of Hungarian debt was owed to Western commercial banks rather than to governments.

Foreign Investment

After being relatively isolated from many sectors of the world economy, Hungary sought to accelerate its development by encouraging foreign investment. Considerable tax incentives were available for potential investors. Despite the fact that the Government was to retain control over 'strategic industries', in particular certain defence plants, and also over some of the larger public companies (mainly for the purpose of avoiding mass unemployment), foreign investors were able to invest in the principal sectors of the economy and, in many cases, could acquire majority control. The pace of foreign investment was to depend on the political agenda, as the Government was sensitive to accusations that they were selling the country's assets to foreigners. As well as concerns about the nature of foreign investments there was also some concern about the geographical location of investment. Taking into consideration notable exceptions such as the Suzuki plant at Eger, the vast majority of capital invested went either to Budapest or to the west of the country, that is, to the areas closest to Western markets.

Liberalization of foreign-investment legislation, resulting in the abolition of special licences for joint ventures, and the introduction of limited convertibility, meant that joint ventures could use the forint to pay for imports. In 1992 some US $1,100m. was invested in joint ventures in Hungary, making a total of $4,800m. of foreign capital invested in joint ventures, by far the largest share of investment in the region. Some 60% of this investment was directed towards the manufacturing sector, providing the country not only with a major source of employment and technology, but also contributing to export growth. There were some notable international companies and banks with operations in Hungary. Germany, Austria, the USA and Italy were the principal sources of investment. In spite of these large-scale investments, much of the capital invested in the country, particularly in the form of joint ventures, remained rather small; two-thirds of all joint ventures were founded with the required minimum of equity.

CONCLUSION

In the first four months of 1993 the trade deficit increased to US $1,000m., a worrying development for such a trade-dependent nation. The budget deficit continued to rise: the Government budgeted for an annual sum of 215,000m. forint, but, by the end of May 1993, the deficit had reached 94,000m. forint. In the first half of 1993 the forint was devalued three times. However, there were signs that the decline in industrial production was slowing. The rate of unemployment decreased by 7,000 in March 1993, and by 12,000 in April. By October the rate of unemployment had fallen to 12.6%.

Hungary was at the forefront of economic change in the former Communist bloc of Eastern Europe. It was the first socialist (Communist) country to introduce Western-style personal-income and value added taxes. New Western-style accountancy and bankruptcy laws took effect in 1992. In addition, the banking system was in the process of reform.

The main problem in the Hungarian economy was the decline in the production of state-owned enterprises. However, this situation was expected to improve in 1994. The number of new businesses was continuing to rise, in spite of high interest rates and attractive alternative investments elsewhere. It was expected that the World EXPO trade fair, to be held in Budapest in 1996, would generate considerable interest for investors and raise the international profile of the country. Hungary was also taking a more active part in international negotiations, such as those held under the auspices of the GATT, the IMF and the EC, and was playing an active role in the European Bank for Reconstruction and Development (EBRD). International investors continued to have confidence in the country, which was demonstrated by the relatively high levels of investment. There was considerable opportunity for increased trade with the former members of the CMEA, although much depended on the internal situations in the countries of the former USSR. The costs of German reunification and relatively slow growth rates in that country (1.9% in 1992) also reduced export potential to Hungary's largest trading partner.

Since such a transformation of the economy had never been attempted prior to the fall of the Communist regimes in Eastern Europe and the USSR, it was difficult to measure accurately the success of the transformation process. It could be said that the early 1990s were both difficult and crucial for the Hungarian economy. Hungary's major asset was its position at the heart of Europe. When it finally joins the EC, trade will play an even more central role in the continuing modernization of the economy.

Statistical Survey

Source (unless otherwise stated): Központi Statisztikai Hivatal (Hungarian Central Statistical Office), 1525 Budapest, Keleti Károly u. 5–7; tel. (1) 202-4011; telex 22-4308; fax (1) 115-9085.

Area and Population

AREA, POPULATION AND DENSITY

Area (sq km)	93,030*
Population (census results)	
1 January 1980	10,709,463
1 January 1990	
Males	4,984,904
Females	5,389,919
Total	10,374,823
Population (official estimates at 1 January)	
1991	10,354,852
1992	10,337,000
Density (per sq km) at 1 January 1992	111.1

* 35,919 sq miles.

Languages (1990 census): Magyar (Hungarian) 98.5%; German 0.4%; Slovak 0.1%; Romany 0.5%; Croatian 0.2%; Romanian 0.1%.

ADMINISTRATIVE DIVISIONS (1 January 1992)

	Area (sq km)	Resident Population ('000)	Density (per sq km)	County Town (with population)
Counties:				
Baranya	4,487	418	93	Pécs (169,486)
Bács-Kiskun	8,362	542	65	Kecskemét (104,489)
Békés	5,631	407	72	Békéscsaba (67,731)
Borsod-Abaúj-Zemplén	7,247	755	104	Miskolc (191,623)
Csongrád	4,263	438	103	Szeged (177,506)
Fejér	4,373	423	97	Székesfehérvár (108,845)
Győr-Moson-Sopron	4,062	428	105	Győr (130,320)
Hajdú-Bihar	6,211	549	88	Debrecen (214,712)
Heves	3,637	333	92	Eger (61,917)
Jász-Nagykun-Szolnok	5,607	422	75	Szolnok (79,426)
Komárom-Esztergom	2,251	313	139	Tatabánya (72,898)
Nógrád	2,544	225	88	Salgótarján (46,877)
Pest	6,394	975	152	Budapest* (1,992,343)
Somogy	6,036	343	57	Kaposvár (70,662)
Szabolcs-Szatmár-Bereg	5,937	567	96	Nyíregyháza (114,246)
Tolna	3,704	252	68	Szekszárd (37,245)
Vas	3,336	275	82	Szombathely (85,566)
Veszprém	4,639	378	81	Veszprém (64,620)
Zala	3,784	304	80	Zalaegerszeg (62,426)
Capital City Budapest*	525	1,992	3,794	–
Total	93,030	10,337	111	–

* Budapest has separate County status. The area and population of the city are not included in the larger County (Pest) which it administers.

PRINCIPAL TOWNS (population at 1 January 1992)

Budapest (capital)	1,992,343	Nyíregyháza	114,246
Debrecen	214,712	Székesfehérvár	108,845
Miskolc	191,623	Kecskemét	104,489
Szeged	177,506	Szombathely	85,566
Pécs	169,486	Szolnok	79,426
Győr	130,320	Tatabánya	72,898

BIRTHS, MARRIAGES AND DEATHS

	Registered live births		Registered marriages		Registered deaths	
	Number	Rate (per 1,000)	Number	Rate (per 1,000)	Number	Rate (per 1,000)
1984	125,359	11.8	74,951	7.0	146,709	13.8
1985	130,200	12.3	73,238	6.9	147,614	14.0
1986	128,204	12.2	72,434	6.9	147,089	14.0
1987	125,840	12.0	66,082	6.3	142,601	13.6
1988	124,296	11.9	65,907	6.3	140,042	13.4
1989	123,304	11.9	66,949	6.4	144,695	13.9
1990	125,679	12.1	66,405	6.4	145,660	14.1
1991	127,207	12.3	61,198	5.9	144,813	14.0

ECONOMICALLY ACTIVE POPULATION*
('000 persons aged 15 years and over; at January each year)

	1990	1991	1992
Agriculture and forestry	863.3	752.2	588.9
Manufacturing, mining, electricity and water	1,510.5	1,455.2	1,286.2
Construction	332.5	328.7	272.8
Commerce	517.5	557.8	564.2
Transport and communications	410.1	417.5	372.9
Services (incl. gas and sanitary services)	1,161.3	1,157.3	1,156.8
Total	4,795.2	4,668.7	4,241.8
Males	2,594.5	2,542.9	2,276.5
Females	2,200.7	2,125.8	1,965.3

* Excluding persons seeking work for the first time.

Agriculture

PRINCIPAL CROPS ('000 metric tons)

	1990	1991	1992
Wheat	6,198	6,008	3,426*
Rice (paddy)	39	20	15†
Barley	1,369	1,555	1,721*
Maize	4,500	7,745	4,910*
Rye	232	223	134*
Oats	163	135	144*
Potatoes	1,226	1,219	1,200†
Pulses	318	284	382†
Sunflower seed	684	813	727*
Rapeseed	106	112	100*
Sugar beet	4,743	5,867	3,560*
Grapes	863	759	800†
Apples	945	859	730*
Tobacco (leaves)	14	18	15*

* Unofficial estimate(s). † FAO estimate(s).

Source: FAO, *Production Yearbook*.

LIVESTOCK
('000 head, unless otherwise indicated, at December each year)

	1989	1990	1991
Cattle	1,598	1,571	1,420
Pigs	7,660	8,000	5,993
Sheep	2,069	1,545*	1,808
Goats	16	16†	16†
Horses	75	76	75
Chickens (million)	53	43	36
Ducks (million)	2	2	2
Turkeys (million)	2	2	1

* Unofficial estimate. † FAO estimate(s).
Source: FAO, *Production Yearbook.*

LIVESTOCK PRODUCTS (metric tons)

	1990	1991	1992
Beef and veal	114,000	117,000*	105,000*
Mutton and lamb	5,000	4,000*	3,000*
Pig meat	1,018,000	965,000*	815,000*
Poultry meat	389,000	282,000	273,000†
Edible offals	50,000	43,000	38,000
Cows' milk	2,846,000	2,490,000	2,370,000*
Sheep's milk	49,000	43,000	43,000†
Goats' milk	3,000	3,000†	3,000†
Butter and ghee	38,808	28,808	25,000
Cheese	92,078	81,082	76,037
Hen eggs	259,947	246,500	228,000
Honey	16,853	10,023	10,000†
Wool:			
greasy	7,337	4,218	4,100†
clean	2,960	1,687	1,640†
Cattle hides	12,245	11,402	12,000†

*† Unofficial figure. † FAO estimate.
Source: FAO, *Production Yearbook.*

Forestry

ROUNDWOOD REMOVALS ('000 cu metres)

	1989	1990	1991
Industrial wood	3,740	3,512	3,227
Fuel wood	2,738	2,434	2,549
Total	6,478	5,946	5,776

SAWNWOOD PRODUCTION ('000 cu metres)

	1989	1990	1991
Coniferous (soft wood)	313	253	158
Broadleaved (hard wood)	350	339	313
Total	663	592	471

Fishing

(metric tons, live weight)

	1989	1990	1991
Common carp	15,029	23,057	20,131
Other cyprinids	18,341	8,899	7,839
Other fishes	2,147	1,932	1,408
Total catch	35,517	33,888	29,378

Source: FAO, *Yearbook of Fishery Statistics.*

Mining

('000 metric tons, unless otherwise indicated)

	1989	1990	1991
Hard coal	2,127	1,736	1,695
Brown coal	12,020	10,373	9,953
Lignite	5,883	5,469	5,327
Crude petroleum	1,966	1,974	1,893
Bauxite	2,644	2,559	2,037
Natural gas (million cu metres)	6,176	4,932	5,043

Industry

SELECTED PRODUCTS
('000 metric tons, unless otherwise indicated)

	1989	1990	1991
Pig iron	1,954	1,697	1,314
Crude steel	3,356	2,963	1,930
Rolled steel	2,539	2,176	1,535
Aluminium	75.2	75.2	63.3
Cement	3,857	3,935	2,529
Nitrogenous fertilizers*	580.8	534.8	281.5
Phosphatic fertilizers†	215.1	133.5	49.3
Refined sugar	508.4	512.3	605.5
Buses (number)	11,980	7,994	4,970
Cotton fabrics ('000 sq metres)	262,726	222,034	143,415
Leather footwear ('000 pairs)	29,528	24,306	18,725
Electric power (million kWh)	29,580	28,365	29,762
Woollen cloth ('000 sq metres)	32,275	20,502	12,056
Television receivers ('000)	502	492	243
Radio receivers ('000)	124	66	14

* Production in terms of nitrogen.
† Production in terms of phosphoric acid.

Finance

CURRENCY AND EXCHANGE RATES

Monetary Units
100 fillér = 1 forint.

Sterling and Dollar Equivalents (30 September 1993)
£1 sterling = 145.38 forint;
US $1 = 97.21 forint;
1,000 forint = £6.879 = $10.287.

Average Exchange Rate (forint per US dollar)
1990 63.206
1991 74.735
1992 78.988

STATE BUDGET ('000 million forint)

Revenue	1989	1990	1991
Payments made by enterprises (co-operatives) and agricultural co-operatives	443.2	537.3	492.6
Consumers' turnover tax	230.7	255.0	286.8
Payments made by the population	209.4	248.9	333.0
Payments made by organizations financed by state budget	138.8	181.0	317.9
Other receipts	41.6	56.8	158.4
Total revenue	1,063.7	1,279.0	1,588.7

Expenditure	1989	1990	1991
Investment	115.5	125.3	127.9
Industrial enterprises (co-operatives) and agricultural co-operatives	115.7	98.2	64.3
Supplement to consumers' prices	44.1	36.8	42.3
Budgetary institutions	386.5	491.9	707.2
Health and social welfare	74.7	99.0	n.a.
Culture	127.6	162.2	n.a.
Defence	62.0	72.3	n.a.
Legal and security order	6.3	8.6	n.a.
Administration	23.0	34.6	n.a.
Economic tasks	71.2	80.0	n.a.
Others	21.7	35.2	n.a.
Social security	269.5	342.5	445.5
Others	181.1	185.0	254.6
Total expenditure	1,112.4	1,297.7	1,641.8

INTERNATIONAL RESERVES (US $ million at 31 December)

	1990	1991	1992
Gold*	97	83	33
IMF special drawing rights	1	1	3
Foreign exchange	1,069	3,935	4,348
Total	1,167	4,019	4,461

* National valuation.

Source: IMF, *International Financial Statistics.*

MONEY SUPPLY (million forint at 31 December)

	1989	1990	1991
Currency outside banks	180,600	209,800	260,200
Demand deposits at commercial and savings banks	165,800	225,400	275,000

Source: IMF, *International Financial Statistics.*

COST OF LIVING (Consumer Price Index; base: 1980 = 100)

	1989	1990	1991
Food	206.0	278.5	339.5
Fuel and light	202.2	258.0	467.0
Clothing	249.0	307.0	405.6
Rent	264.5	424.0	552.5
All items (incl. others)	215.0	277.1	374.1

NATIONAL ACCOUNTS (million forint at current prices)

Expenditure on the Gross Domestic Product

	1988	1989	1990
Government final consumption expenditure	320,663	363,075	457,973
Private final consumption expenditure	716,366	844,251	1,046,338
Increase in stocks	63,929	98,200	129,605
Gross fixed capital formation	295,572	347,828	369,600
Total domestic expenditure	1,396,530	1,653,354	2,003,516
Exports of goods and services	530,395	620,857	668,979
Less Imports of goods and services	491,738	563,453	592,956
GDP in purchasers' values	1,435,187	1,710,758	2,079,539

Gross Domestic Product by Economic Activity

	1989	1990	1991‡
Agriculture, hunting, forestry and fishing*	235,893	261,236	234,803
Mining and quarrying	51,754	60,772	60,385
Manufacturing and gas	416,202	436,523	525,200
Electricity and water*	68,300	83,457	76,360
Construction	115,394	115,662	133,743
Trade, restaurants and hotels	159,513	266,560	284,910
Transport, storage and communications	124,406	143,539	192,371
Finance, insurance, real estate and business services†	116,420	145,007	179,937
Government services (incl. non-profit institutions)	190,423	251,058	343,059
Other community and social services†	19,331	22,915	
Sub-total	1,497,636	1,786,729	2,030,768
Net taxes on commodities	213,122	292,810	270,732
Total	1,710,758	2,079,539	2,301,500

* The operation of irrigation systems is included in agriculture and excluded from water. Agriculture also includes veterinary services.

† Sanitary and similar services and personal and household services are included in business services and excluded from community and social services.

‡ Preliminary figures.

BALANCE OF PAYMENTS (US $ million)

	1990	1991	1992
Merchandise exports f.o.b.	9,151	9,688	10,097
Merchandise imports f.o.b.	−8,617	−9,330	10,018
Trade balance	534	358	−11
Exports of services	2,836	2,508	3,367
Imports of services	−2,364	−1,952	−2,611
Other income received	329	340	462
Other income paid	−1,743	−1,717	−1,713
Private unrequited transfers (net)	794	834	843
Official unrequited transfers (net)	−7	34	15
Current balance	379	403	352
Capital (net)	−801	1,474	416
Net errors and omissions	10	−82	2
Overall balance	−413	1,795	770

Source: IMF, *International Financial Statistics.*

External Trade

PRINCIPAL COMMODITIES
(distribution by SITC, million forint)

Imports c.i.f.	1989	1990	1991
Food and live animals	32,259	34,537	40,741
Animal feeding-stuff (excl. cereals)	15,518	13,732	9,536
Crude materials (inedible) except fuels	33,201	28,612	36,913
Cork and wood	5,928	6,516	9,068
Mineral fuels, lubricants, etc.	61,525	77,454	130,960
Coal, coke and briquettes	8,229	5,555	14,280
Petroleum, petroleum products, etc.	28,651	48,971	66,374
Gas (natural and manufactured)	14,449	13,329	26,900
Chemicals and related products	85,075	81,383	106,570
Organic chemicals	14,472	15,383	19,446
Inorganic chemicals	10,977	10,676	11,718
Artificial resins and plastic materials, etc.	12,064	12,086	18,943

Imports c.i.f.—*continued*	1989	1990	1991
Basic manufactures	91,815	84,507	176,924
Paper, paperboard and manufactures	10,888	12,398	19,531
Textile yarn, fabrics, etc.	16,965	14,223	50,147
Iron and steel	17,113	14,453	27,340
Non-ferrous metals	15,591	13,588	22,352
Other metal manufactures	10,792	11,385	23,312
Machinery and transport equipment	175,004	188,581	263,787
Machinery specialized for particular industries	40,797	41,309	36,988
Metalworking machinery	9,797	11,085	9,148
Road vehicles and parts (excl. tyres, engines and electrical parts)	34,514	39,370	52,449
Miscellaneous manufactured articles	36,348	42,466	91,475
Total (incl. others)	523,507	544,921	855,643

Exports f.o.b.	1989	1990	1991
Food and live animals	105,976	119,707	169,276
Live animals	12,618	10,878	13,779
Meat and meat preparations	36,203	52,763	66,101
Cereals and cereal preparations	16,307	12,234	17,863
Vegetables and fruit	27,206	28,780	43,593
Beverages and tobacco	7,650	8,129	7,107
Crude materials (inedible) except fuels	23,663	28,657	45,669
Mineral fuels, lubricants, etc.	16,384	18,652	21,003
Petroleum, petroleum products, etc.	15,036	17,380	18,198
Chemicals and related products	70,615	74,998	97,694
Organic chemicals	11,580	11,459	16,545
Medicinal and pharmaceutical products	24,639	27,042	38,334
Basic manufactures	97,281	111,428	132,816
Textile yarn, fabrics, etc.	15,729	15,039	17,190
Iron and steel	26,719	30,479	28,208
Non-ferrous metals	20,955	26,655	21,033
Machinery and transport equipment	172,775	154,819	171,696
Machinery specialized for particular industries	33,854	29,981	23,193
Telecommunications and sound equipment	22,075	18,991	20,438
Other electrical machinery, apparatus, etc.	27,671	27,094	49,657
Road vehicles and parts (excl. tyres, engines and electrical parts)	44,734	41,611	41,861
Miscellaneous manufactured articles	60,148	64,598	108,461
Clothing and accessories (excl. footwear)	20,484	22,625	54,143
Footwear	7,020	6,559	11,848
Professional, scientific and controlling instruments and apparatus	13,880	13,261	8,700
Total (incl. others)	571,323	603,636	764,274

PRINCIPAL TRADING PARTNERS (million forint)*

Imports c.i.f.	1989	1990	1991
Algeria	252	10,076	9,871
Austria	44,977	54,233	114,224
Belgium and Luxembourg	8,520	9,243	11,808
Brazil	6,890	8,854	8,511
Czechoslovakia	26,966	25,383	35,503
France	11,517	11,204	22,825
German Democratic Republic	32,518	32,321	183,129
Germany, Federal Republic	83,917	94,802	
Italy	17,688	22,080	61,899
Japan	8,409	11,429	23,498
Netherlands	10,752	11,414	23,258
Poland	17,222	13,028	16,245
Romania	8,501	4,883	5,282
Sweden	6,915	8,106	13,199
Switzerland and Liechtenstein	15,328	16,767	29,049
USSR	115,513	103,889	131,262
United Kingdom	11,560	11,548	21,141
USA	13,232	14,407	22,349
Yugoslavia	18,222	12,260	11,129
Total (incl. others)	523,507	544,921	855,643

Exports f.o.b.	1989	1990	1991
Austria	37,109	45,273	82,898
Belgium and Luxembourg	4,984	6,988	11,336
Czechoslovakia	28,980	25,002	16,537
France	13,655	16,257	21,881
German Democratic Republic	30,880	18,825	205,272
Germany, Federal Republic	68,010	101,861	
Iran	5,128	7,385	16,865
Italy	26,707	35,435	57,828
Japan	6,605	6,990	13,110
Netherlands	7,584	9,143	15,844
Poland	18,091	10,044	15,746
Romania	8,317	10,730	9,943
Sweden	7,479	8,476	9,690
Switzerland and Liechtenstein	9,499	11,311	14,221
Turkey	5,479	6,600	8,521
USSR	143,587	121,854	102,276
United Kingdom	10,299	12,218	15,475
USA	19,088	21,331	24,231
Yugoslavia	23,560	28,594	27,991
Total (incl. others)	571,323	603,636	764,274

* Imports by country of production; exports by country of last consignment.

Transport

RAILWAYS (traffic)

	1989	1990	1991
Passengers carried (million)	323.2	297.0	272.0
Passenger-kilometres (million)	12,741	12,193	10,607
Net ton-kilometres (million)	19,820	16,781	11,938

ROAD TRAFFIC (motor vehicles in use at 31 December)

	1989	1990	1991
Passenger cars	1,732,385	1,944,553	2,015,455
Goods vehicles	208,306	224,061	227,818
Buses	23,793	26,121	24,181
Motor cycles	162,837	168,817	166,233

INLAND WATERWAYS (traffic)

	1989	1990	1991
Freight carried ('000 metric tons)	2,112	2,825	2,597
Freight ton-km (million)	2,109	1,883	1,599

CIVIL AVIATION (traffic)

	1989	1990	1991
Kilometres flown	23,126,780	25,776,430	21,978,970
Passengers carried	1,472,000	1,517,000	1,045,000
Passenger-km ('000)	1,576,600	1,694,800	1,286,700
Cargo carried: metric tons	8,275	9,400	7,000
Cargo ton-km	10,631,000	15,374,000	8,319,000

Tourism

('000 arrivals)

	1989	1990	1991
Foreign tourists	14,236	20,510	21,860
Foreign visitors in transit	10,683	17,122	11,405
Total	24,919	37,632	33,265

TOURISTS BY COUNTRY OF ORIGIN
('000 arrivals, including visitors in transit)

	1989	1990	1991
Austria	4,554	5,153	5,841
Bulgaria	678	924	504
Czechoslovakia	3,708	3,920	3,837
German Democratic Republic	1,573	2,633	4,004
Germany, Federal Republic	1,612		
Poland	4,481	3,791	2,549
Romania	236	9,015	6,825
USSR	2,066	1,884	1,185
Yugoslavia	4,416	8,123	5,176
Total (incl. others)	24,919	37,632	33,265

Communications Media

	1989	1990	1991
Radio receivers ('000 in use)*	6,250	n.a.	6,280
Television receivers ('000 in use)*	4,320	n.a.	4,340
Telephones in use	1,769,889	1,871,687	2,010,900
Books titles (including translations)	7,599	7,464	7,210
Daily newspapers	31	35	36
Average daily circulation	2,507,990	2,672,980	2,454,352

* Source: UNESCO, *Statistical Yearbook*.

Education

(1990/91)

	Institutions	Teachers	Students
Nursery	4,718	33,635	391,129
Primary	3,723	96,547	1,167,398
Secondary	1,192	35,808	517,358
Higher	77	17,302	102,387

Source: Ministry of Culture and Education.

Directory

The Constitution

A new Constitution was introduced on 18 August 1949, and the Hungarian People's Republic was established two days later. The Constitution was amended in April 1972 and December 1983. Further, radical amendments were made in October 1989. Shortly afterwards, the Republic of Hungary was proclaimed.

The following is a summary of the main provisions of the Constitution, as amended in October 1989.

GENERAL PROVISIONS

The Republic of Hungary is an independent, democratic constitutional state in which the values of civil democracy and democratic socialism prevail in equal measures. All power belongs to the people, which they exercise directly and through the elected representatives of popular sovereignty.

Political parties may, under observance of the Constitution, be freely formed and may freely operate in Hungary. Parties may not directly exercise public power. No party has the right to guide any state body. Trade unions and other organizations for the representation of interests safeguard and represent the interests of employees, members of co-operatives and entrepreneurs.

The State safeguards the people's freedom, the independence and territorial integrity of the country as well as the frontiers thereof, as established by international treaties. The Republic of Hungary rejects war as a means of settling disputes between nations and refrains from applying force against the independence or territorial integrity of other states, and from threats of violence.

The Hungarian legal system adopts the universally accepted rules of international law. The order of legislation is regulated by an Act of constitutional force.

The economy of Hungary is a market economy, availing itself also of the advantages of planning, with public and private ownership enjoying equal right and protection. Hungary recognizes and supports the right of undertaking and free competition, limitable only by an Act of constitutional force. State-owned enterprises and organs pursuing economic activities manage their affairs independently, in accordance with the mode and responsibility as provided by law.

The Republic of Hungary protects the institutions of marriage and the family. It provides for the indigent through extensive social measures, and recognizes and enforces the right of each citizen to a healthy environment.

GOVERNMENT

National Assembly

The highest organ of state authority in the Republic of Hungary is the National Assembly, which exercises all the rights deriving from the sovereignty of the people and determines the organization, direction and conditions of government. The National Assembly enacts the Constitution and laws, determines the state budget, decides the socio-economic plan, elects the President of the Republic and the Council of Ministers, directs the activities of ministries, decides upon declaring war and concluding peace and exercises the prerogative of amnesty.

The National Assembly is elected for a term of four years and members enjoy immunity from arrest and prosecution without parliamentary consent. It meets at least twice a year and is convened by the President of the Republic or by a written demand of the Council of Ministers or of one-fifth of the Assembly's members. It elects a President, Deputy Presidents and Recorders from among its own members, and it lays down its own rules of procedure and agenda. As a general rule, the sessions of the National Assembly are held in public.

The National Assembly has the right of legislation which can be initiated by the President of the Republic, the Council of Ministers or any committee or member of the National Assembly. Decisions are valid only if at least half of the members are present, and they require a simple majority. Constitutional changes require a two-thirds majority. Acts of the National Assembly are signed by the President of the Republic.

The National Assembly may pronounce its dissolution before the expiry of its term, and in the event of an emergency may prolong its mandate or may be reconvened after dissolution. A new National Assembly must be elected within three months of dissolution and convened within one month of polling day.

Members of the National Assembly are elected on the basis of universal, equal and direct suffrage by secret ballot, and they are accountable to their constituents, who may recall them. All citizens of 18 years and over have the right to vote, with the exception of those who are unsound of mind, and those who are deprived of their civil rights by a court of law.

President of the Republic

The President of the Republic is the Head of State of Hungary. He/she embodies the unity of the nation and supervises the democratic operation of the mechanism of State. The President is also the Commander-in-Chief of the Armed Forces. The President is elected by the National Assembly for a period of four years, and may be re-elected for a second term. Any citizen of Hungary qualified to vote, who has reached 35 years of age before the day of election, may be elected President.

The President may issue the writ for general or local elections, convene the National Assembly, initiate legislation, hold plebiscites, direct local government, conclude international treaties, appoint diplomatic representatives, ratify international treaties, appoint higher civil servants and officers of the armed forces, award orders and titles, and exercise the prerogative of mercy.

Council of Ministers

The highest organ of state administration is the Council of Ministers, responsible to the National Assembly and consisting of a Chairman, Ministers of State and other Ministers who are elected by the National Assembly on the recommendation of the President of the Republic. The Council of Ministers directs the work of the ministries (listed in a special enactment) and ensures the enforcement of laws and the fulfilment of economic plans; it may issue decrees and annul or modify measures taken by any central or local organ of government.

Local Administration

The local organs of state power are the county, town, borough and town precinct councils, whose members are elected for a term of four years by the voters in each area. Local councils direct economic, social and cultural activities in their area, prepare local economic plans and budgets and supervise their fulfilment, enforce laws, supervise subordinate organs, maintain public order, protect public property and individual rights, and direct local economic enterprises. They may issue regulations and annul or modify those of subordinate councils. Local Councils are administered by an Executive Committee elected by and responsible to them.

JUDICATURE

Justice is administered by the Supreme Court of the Republic of Hungary, county and district courts. The Supreme Court exercises the right of supervising in principle the judicial activities and practice of all other courts.

All judicial offices are filled by election; Supreme Court, county and district court judges are all elected for an indefinite period; the President of the Supreme Court is elected by the National Assembly. All court hearings are public unless otherwise prescribed by law, and those accused are guaranteed the right of defence. An accused person must be considered innocent until proved guilty.

Public Prosecutor

The function of the Chief Public Prosecutor is to watch over the observance of the law. He is elected by the National Assembly, to whom he is responsible. The organization of public prosecution is under the control of the Chief Public Prosecutor, who appoints the public prosecutors.

RIGHTS AND DUTIES OF CITIZENS

The Republic of Hungary guarantees for its citizens the right to work and to remuneration, the right of rest and recreation, the right to care in old age, sickness or disability, the right to education, and equality before the law; women enjoy equal rights with men. Discrimination on grounds of sex, religion or nationality is a punishable offence. The State also ensures freedom of conscience, religious worship, speech, the Press and assembly. The right of workers to organize themselves is stressed. The freedom of the individual, and the privacy of the home and of correspondence are inviolable. Freedom for creative work in the sciences and the arts is guaranteed.

The basic freedoms of all workers are guaranteed and foreign citizens enjoy the right of asylum.

Military service (with or without arms) and the defence of their country are the duties of all citizens.

The Government

(February 1994)

HEAD OF STATE

President of the Republic: ÁRPÁD GÖNCZ (elected 3 August 1990).

COUNCIL OF MINISTERS

A coalition of the Hungarian Democratic Forum (HDF), the Independent Smallholders' and Peasants' Party (ISP), the United Smallholders' Party (USP), the Christian Democratic People's Party (CDPP) and independents.

Prime Minister: Dr PÉTER BOROSS (Independent).

Minister of the Interior: Dr IMRE KÓNYA (HDF).

Minister of Agriculture: JÁNOS SZABÓ (USP).

Minister of Defence: LAJOS FÜR (HDF).

Minister of Justice: Dr ISTVÁN BALSAI (HDF).

Minister of Industry and Trade: JÁNOS MIKLÓS LATORCAÍ (HDF).

Minister of the Environment and Regional Planning: JÁNOS GYURKO (HDF).

Minister of Transport, Communications and Water Management: GYÖRGY SCHAMSCHULA (HDF).

Minister of Foreign Affairs: Dr GÉZA JESZENSZKY (HDF).

Minister of Labour: Dr GYULA KISS (ISP).

Minister of Culture and Education: FERENC MÁDL (Independent).

Minister of International Economic Relations: Dr BÉLA KÁDÁR (Independent).

Minister of Welfare: Dr LÁSZLÓ SURJÁN (CDPP).

Minister of Finance: Dr IVÁN SZABÓ (HDF).

Ministers without Portfolio: TIBOR FUEZESSY (CDPP), Dr BALÁZS HORVÁTH (HDF), FERENC JÓZSEF NAGY (ISP), ERNŐ PUNGOR (Independent).

MINISTRIES

Office of the Prime Minister: 1055 Budapest, Kossuth Lajos tér 1–3; tel. (1) 112-0600; telex 225547; fax (1) 153-3622.

Ministry of Agriculture: 1055 Budapest, Kossuth Lajos tér 11; tel. (1) 153-3000; telex 225445; fax (1) 153-0518.

Ministry of Culture and Education: 1055 Budapest, Szalay u. 10–14; tel. (1) 153-0600; telex 225935.

Ministry of Defence: 1055 Budapest, Balaton u. 7–11; tel. (1) 132-2500; telex 225424.

Ministry of the Environment and Regional Planning: 1011 Budapest, Fő u. 44–50, POB 351; tel. (1) 201-4572; telex 224879; fax (1) 201-2846.

Ministry of Finance: 1051 Budapest, József Nádor tér 2–4; tel. (1) 118-2066.

Ministry of Foreign Affairs: 1027 Budapest, Bem rkp. 47; tel. (1) 156-8000; telex 225571.

Ministry of Industry and Trade: 1024 Budapest, Mártírok u. 85; tel. (1) 156-5566; telex 225376; fax (1) 175-0219.

Ministry of the Interior: 1051 Budapest, József Attila u. 2–4; tel. (1) 112-1710; telex 225216.

Ministry of International Economic Relations: 1055 Budapest, Honvéd u. 13–15; tel. (1) 153-0000; telex 225578; fax (1) 153-2794.

Ministry of Justice: 1055 Budapest, Szalay u. 16; tel. (1) 131-8922.

Ministry of Labour: 1051 Budapest, Roosevelt tér 7–8; tel. (1) 132-2100; fax (1) 131-6399.

Ministry of Transport, Communications and Water Management: 1400 Budapest, Dob u. 75–81, POB 87; tel. (1) 122-6667; telex 225729; fax (1) 122-3429.

Ministry of Welfare: 1051 Budapest, Arany János u. 6–8; tel. (1) 132-3100; telex 224337; fax (1) 153-4955.

Legislature

ORSZÁGGYŰLÉS

(National Assembly)

The unicameral National Assembly consists of 386 deputies, elected for a four-year term. At elections, held in March and April 1990, 176 deputies were elected directly to represent single-member constituencies, 152 according to a system of proportional representation of parties, while the remaining 58 were elected on a national list on the basis of a nationwide summary of surplus votes. An additional eight seats were reportedly to be reserved for one deputy each from Hungary's Romany, Croat, German, Romanian, Serbian, Slovak, Slovene and Jewish minorities.

President of the National Assembly: Dr GYÖRGY SZABAD.

Deputy Presidents: Dr ALAJOS DORNBACH, MÁTYÁS SZŰRÖS, VINCE VÖRÖS.

General election, 25 March and 8 April 1990

	% of votes	Seats
Hungarian Democratic Forum (HDF)	42.74	165
Alliance of Free Democrats (AFD)	23.83	92
Independent Smallholders' Party (ISP)	11.13	43
Hungarian Socialist Party (HSP)	8.54	33
Federation of Young Democrats (FYD)	5.44	21
Christian Democratic People's Party (CDPP)	5.44	21
Others	2.88	11
Total	100.00	386

Local Government

In 1990 the National Assembly ratified a law providing for the right of citizens to participate extensively in the government of their local communities, the object being to broaden social co-operation and to prevent local politics becoming the monopoly of élite groups. Hungary is divided into 19 counties (megyei—see Statistical Survey for a complete list). There are, in addition, 168 town authorities (városi), of which 19 larger towns or cities with populations over 50,000 claim separate county status. Larger towns are subdivided into districts; for example, Budapest (with a population almost 10 times that of Debrecen, Hungary's second-biggest town) is divided into 22 districts, which send delegates to the General Assembly of the capital. In rural areas villages and large villages (with populations over 5,000) have their own representative bodies. Elections are held every four years for the county, town, district and precinct councils, or general assemblies, of which the president heads the local government. However, provisions exist for each representative body to hold a public meeting at least once a year, and for referendums to be held on significant local issues. Minimum levels of participation in elections are set, below which a result is invalidated. There is effectively no hierarchical control over local government in Hungary, each tier being regarded as equal and independent. However, the National Assembly may dissolve a local government if it is operating in contravention of the Constitution, and after consultation with the Constitutional Court. Local government decisions may be revised only by the Constitutional Court, or, in cases of illegality, by the courts. Local authorities are free to co-operate in their own representative associations.

Települési Önkormányzatok Országos Szövetsége (National Association of Local Authorities): 1056 Budapest, Váci u. 62–64; tel. (1) 118-1027; Pres. JÓZSEF OTT; Sec.-Gen. Dr FERENC KÖLLNER.

COUNTIES

Bács-Kiskun: 6000 Kecskemét, Május 1 tér 3; tel. (76) 28-788; Pres. of Council MIKLÓS KŐTÖRŐ.

Baranya: 7601 Pécs, Rákóczi út 34; tel. (72) 12-222; Pres. of Council Dr JÓZSEFS SZŰCS.

Békés: 5601 Békéscsaba, Derkovits sor; tel. (66) 21-833; Pres. of Council Dr IMRE SIMON.

Borsod-Abaúj-Zemplén: 3525 Miskolc, Tanácsház tér 1; tel. (46) 16-461; Pres. of Council GYÖRGY SZABÓ.

Csongrád: 6722 Szeged, Rákóczi tér; tel. (62) 21-622; Pres. of Council ISTVÁN LEHMANN.

Fejér: 8001 Székesfehérvár, Szent István tér 9; tel. (22) 312-360; fax (22) 314-465; Pres. of Council HUBA PAÁL.

Győr-Moson-Sopron: 9021 Győr, Árpád út 32; tel. (96) 18-122; Pres. of Council GÁBOR BOTOS.

Hajdú-Bihar: 4024 Debrecen, Piac u. 54; tel. (52) 15-255; Pres. of Council ANTAL SZEKERES.

Heves: 3300 Eger, Kossuth L. u. 9; tel. (36) 410-011; fax (36) 411-106; Pres. of Council ISTVÁN JAKAB.

Jász-Nagykun-Szolnok: 5000 Szolnok, Kossuth L. u. 2; tel. (56) 39-933; Pres. of Council LAJOS BOROS.

Komárom-Esztergom: 2001 Tatabánya, Felszabadulás tér 4; tel. and fax (34) 311-511; Pres. of Council (vacant); CEO TIBOR RUDLOF.

Nógrád: 3100 Salgótarján, Rákóczi út 192; tel. (32) 10-022; Pres. of Council FERENC KORILL.

Pest: 1052 Budapest, Városház u. 7; tel. (1) 118-0111; Pres. of Council Dr JÁNOS INCZÉDY.

Somogy: 7401 Kaposvár, Csokonai Vitéz M. u. 3; tel. (82) 15-122; Pres. of Council Dr ISTVÁN GYENESEI.

Szabolcs-Szatmár-Bereg: 4400 Nyíregyháza, Tanácsköztársaság tér 5; tel. (42) 14-111; Pres. of Council JÓZSEF MEDGYESI.

Tolna: 7100 Szekszárd, Mártírok tere 11–13; tel. (74) 11-211; Pres. of Council JÓZSEF PROGER.

Vas: 9700 Szombathely, Berzsenyi D. tér 1; tel. (94) 11-211; Pres. of Council GYULA PUSZTAI.

Veszprém: 8200 Veszprém, Megyeház tér 5; tel. (88) 324-801; fax (88) 328-893; Pres. of Council Dr GÁBOR ZONGOR.

Zala: 8900 Zalaegerszeg, Kosztolányi D. u. 10; tel. (92) 11-010; Pres. of Council Dr DÉNES PÁLFI.

Budapest

Budapest Metropolitan Area Chief Mayor's Office: 1052 Budapest, Városház u. 9–11; tel. (1) 118-6066; Chief Mayor Dr GÁBOR DEMSZKY (Alliance of Free Democrats).

Political Organizations

Alliance of Free Democrats—AFD (Szabad Demokraták Szövetsége—SzDSz): 1051 Budapest, Mérleg u. 6; tel. (1) 117-6911; fax (1) 118-7944; f. 1988; 35,000 mems (1990); Chair. IVÁN PETŐ.

Christian Democratic People's Party—CDPP (Kereszténydemokrata Néppárt—KDNP): 1126 Budapest, Nagy Jenő u. 5; tel. (1) 156-2897; fax (1) 155-5772; re-formed 1989; Chair. LÁSZLÓ SURJÁN.

Federation of Young Democrats—FYD (Fiatal Demokraták Szövetsége—FIDESz): 1062 Budapest, Lendvay u. 28 ; tel. (1) 112-1095; fax (1) 131-9673; f. 1988; 14,000 mems; Leader VIKTOR ORBAN.

Hungarian Democratic Forum—HDF (Magyar Demokrata Fórum—MDF): 1538 Budapest, POB 579; tel. (1) 115-9690; fax (1) 156-8522; f. 1988; 37,800 mems (Dec. 1991); Chair. LAJOS FÜR.

Hungarian Justice and Life Party—HJP: c/o Office of Deputies, 1357 Budapest, Széchenyi rakpart 19; tel. (1) 111-1400; fax (1) 132-8326; f. 1993; Co-Chair. ISTVAN CSURKA, LAJOS HORVATH.

Hungarian Social Democratic Party—HSDP (Magyarországi Szocialdemokrata Párt—SzDP): 1077 Budapest, Dohány u. 76; tel. (1) 142-2385; f. 1889; absorbed by Communist Party in 1948; revived 1988; 15,000 mems (Nov. 1989); Chair. ANNA PETRASOVITS.

Hungarian Socialist Party—HSP (Magyar Szocialista Párt—MSzP): 1081 Budapest, Köztársaság tér 26; tel. (1) 210-0046; fax (1) 133-0817; f. 1989 to replace the Hungarian Socialist Workers' Party; 67,000 mems (Dec. 1989); Chair. Dr GYULA HORN.

Hungarian Workers' Party—HWP (Magyar Munkáspárt—MMP): 1082 Budapest, Baross út 61; tel. (1) 134-2721; f. 1956 as Hungarian Socialist Workers' Party; dissolved and replaced by Hungarian Socialist Party in 1989; re-formed in 1989 as Hungarian Socialist Workers' Party, name changed 1992; approx. 30,000 mems (Oct. 1992); Pres. Dr GYULA THÜRMER.

Independent Smallholders' and Peasants' Party—ISP (Független Kisgazda-, Földmunkás-és Polgári Párt—FKgP): 1056 Budapest, Belgrád rkp. 24; tel. and fax (1) 1181-824; f. 1988; 60,000 mems; Chair. Dr JÓZSEF TÖRGYÁN.

Peace Party of Hungarian Gypsies (Magyar Ciganyok Bekepartja): Budapest; f. 1993; left-wing.

United Smallholders' Party—ISP: Budapest; f. 1992 as the 'Historical Section' of the ISP, renamed 1993; Chair. JÁNOS SZABÓ; Gen. Sec. ANTAL BELAFI.

Diplomatic Representation

EMBASSIES IN HUNGARY

Afghanistan: 1023 Budapest, Verhalom u. 12–16, B.ep.mfsz.1; tel. (1) 115-1094; telex 224128; fax (1) 135-4959; Ambassador: (vacant).

Albania: 1068 Budapest, Bajza u. 26; tel. (1) 122-7251; Ambassador: ISUF BASHKURTI.

Algeria: 1014 Budapest, Dísz tér 6; tel. (1) 175-9884; telex 226916; Ambassador: BACHIR ROUIS.

Argentina: 1068 Budapest, Rippl-Rónai u. 1; tel. (1) 122-8467; telex 224128; Ambassador: GUILLERMO JORGE MCGOUGH.

Australia: 1062 Budapest, Délibáb u. 30; tel. (1) 153-4233; telex 227708; fax (1) 153-4866; Ambassador: D. J. KINGSMILL.

Austria: 1068 Budapest, Benczúr u. 16; tel. (1) 269-6700; telex 224447; fax (1) 269-6702; Ambassador: Dr ERICH KUSSBACH.

Belgium: 1015 Budapest, Toldy Ferenc u. 13; tel. (1) 201-1571; telex 224664; fax (1) 175-1566; Ambassador: WILLEM VERKAMMEN.

Bolivia: 1015 Budapest, Toldy Ferenc u. 60, 1–12; tel. (1) 116-2214; Chargé d'affaires: MACARIO APARICIO BURGOA.

Brazil: 1118 Budapest, Somlói út 3; tel. (1) 166-6044; telex 225795; fax (1) 166-8156; Ambassador: IVAN VELLOSO DA SILVEIRA BATALHA.

Bulgaria: 1124 Budapest, Levendula u. 15–17; tel. (1) 156-6840; telex 223032; fax (1) 155-0998; Ambassador: VESSELIN FILEV.

Cambodia: 1121 Budapest, Budakeszi út 55D; tel. (1) 155-1128; Ambassador: UNG SEAN.

Canada: 1121 Budapest, Budakeszi út 32; tel. (1) 176-7686; telex 224588; Ambassador: R. IRWIN.

Chile: 1061 Budapest, Andrássy út 21; tel. (1) 122-4485; Ambassador: MANUEL SANHUEZA CRUZ.

China, People's Republic: 1068 Budapest, Benczúr u. 17; tel. (1) 122-4872; Ambassador: CHEN ZHILIU.

Colombia: 1024 Budapest, Vadazs u. 43–45; tel. (1) 201-3448; telex 226012; Ambassador: ALBERTO ESTEBAN ROJAS PUYO.

Costa Rica: 1118 Budapest, Iglói u. 2; Ambassador: ARNULFO HERNÁNDEZ.

Croatia: 1125 Budapest, Nogrodi út 28B; tel. (1) 155-1522; fax (1) 175-4336; Ambassador: Dr A. SOLC.

Cuba: 1021 Budapest, Budakeszi út 55D; Ambassador: FAUSTINO MANUEL BEATO MOREJÓN.

Czech Republic: 1064 Budapest, Rózsa u. 61; tel. (1) 132-5589; telex 224744; fax (1) 252-6279.

Denmark: 1122 Budapest, Határőr út 37; tel. (1) 155-7320; telex 224137; fax (1) 175-3803; Ambassador: ERIK SKOV.

Ecuador: 1021 Budapest, Budakeszi út 55D; tel. (1) 176-7593; Chargé d'affaires: ARTURO ONTANEDA.

Egypt: 1016 Budapest, Bérc u. 16; tel. (1) 166-8060; telex 225184; Ambassador: MOHAMED ALI EL-SHEREI.

Finland: 1118 Budapest, Kelenhegyi út 16A; tel. (1) 185-0700; telex 224710; fax (1) 185-0772; Ambassador: PERTTI TORSTILA.

France: 1062 Budapest, Lendvay u. 27; tel. (1) 132-4980; telex 225143; fax (1) 111-8291; Ambassador: PIERRE BROCHAND.

Germany: 1440 Budapest, Stefánia út 101–103, POB 40; tel. (1) 251-8999; telex 225954; fax (1) 160-1903; Ambassador: Dr OTTO-RABAN HEINICHEN.

Greece: 1063 Budapest, Szegfű u. 3; tel. (1) 122-8004; telex 224113; Ambassador: NICOLAS CAPELLARIS.

Holy See: 1026 Budapest, Gyimes út 1–3; tel. (1) 155-8979; fax (1) 155-6987; Apostolic Nuncio: Most Rev. ANGELO ACERBI.

India: 1025 Budapest, Búzavirág u. 14; tel. (1) 115-5211; telex 226374; Ambassador: SURINDER LAL MALIK.

Indonesia: 1068 Budapest, Gorkij fasor 26; tel. (1) 142-8508; telex 225263; Ambassador: BUSTANUL ARIFIN.

Iran: 1062 Budapest, Délibáb u. 29; tel. (1) 251-3755; telex 224129; fax (1) 251-2271; Ambassador: Dr MORTEZA SAFFARI NATANZI.

Iraq: 1145 Budapest, Szántó Béla u. 13; tel. (1) 122-6418; telex 226058; Ambassador: MOHAMMED GHANIM AL-ANAZ.

Israel: 1026 Budapest, Fullánk u. 8; tel. (1) 176-7896; telex 223274; fax (1) 176-0534; Ambassador: DAVID KRAUS.

Italy: 1143 Budapest, Stefánia út 95; tel. (1) 268-1080; telex 225294; Ambassador: VITTORIO A. FARINELLI.

Japan: 1024 Budapest, Rómer Flóris u. 56–58; tel. (1) 156-4533; telex 225048; Ambassador: KOICHI SUTSUMI.

Korea, Republic: 1125 Budapest, Mátyás király út 14C; tel. (1) 138-3388; Ambassador: HAN TAK-CHAE.

Libya: 1143 Budapest, Népstadion út 111; tel. (1) 122-6076; telex 226940; Head of People's Bureau: OMAR IBRAHIM ROKHSY.

Mexico: 1021 Budapest, Budakeszi út 55D; tel. (1) 176-7381; telex 226633; fax (1) 176-7906; Ambassador: LUCIANO JOUBLANC.

Mongolia: 1022 Budapest II, k. Bogár u. 14/C; tel. (1) 115-9625; telex 225666; fax (1) 135-9532; Ambassador: DERGELDALIJN DZAMBADZANCAN.

Morocco: 1026 Budapest, Törökvész Lejto 12A; tel. (1) 115-9251; telex 223580; Ambassador: MOHAMED CHAHID.

Netherlands: 1146 Budapest, Abonyi u. 31; tel. (1) 122-8432; telex 225562; fax (1) 268-0639; Ambassador: HENDRIK JAN VAN OORDT.

Norway: 1122 Budapest, Határőr út 35, POB 32; tel. (1) 155-1811; telex 225867; fax (1) 156-7928; Ambassador: TORMOD PETTER SVENNEVIG.

Pakistan: 1125 Budapest, Adonisz u. 3A; tel. (1) 155-8017; Ambassador: HAMIDULLAH KHAN.

Peru: 1122 Budapest, Tóth Lörinc u. 5 ; tel. (1) 155-4019; fax (1) 155-1019; Ambassador: BERTHA VEGA PÉREZ.

Philippines: 1025 Budapest II, Jozsefhegyi út 28–30; tel. (1) 115-3220; Ambassador: JUANITO P. JARASA.

Poland: 1068 Budapest, Gorkij fasor 16; tel. (1) 142-8135; Ambassador: Dr MACIEJ KOÀZMIŃSKI.

Portugal: 1118 Budapest, Kelenhegyi út 46B; tel. (1) 185-3740; telex 226509; fax (1) 166-5148; Ambassador: Dr ANTÓNIO BAPTISTA MARTINS.

Romania: 1146 Budapest, Thököly út 72; tel. (1) 142-6944; telex 225847; fax (1) 142-4938; Ambassador: IOAN DONCA.

Russia: 1062 Budapest, Bajza u. 35; tel. (1) 132-0911; Ambassador: IVAN P. ABOIMOV.

Slovakia: 1143 Budapest, Stefánia út 22-24; tel. (1) 251-1700; telex 224744; fax (1) 251-2568; Chargé d'affaires a.i.: VILIAM ROTH.

Slovenia: 1016 Budapest, Lendvay út 23; tel. and fax (1) 153-4730; Ambassador: FERENC HAJOS.

Spain: 1067 Budapest, Eötvös u. 11B; tel. (1) 153-1011; telex 224130; Ambassador: LUIS DE LA TORRE.

Sweden: 1146 Budapest, Ajtósi Dürer sor 27A; tel. (1) 122-9880; telex 225647; Ambassador: STEN STRÖMHOLM.

Switzerland: 1143 Budapest, Népstadion út 107; tel. (1) 122-9491; Ambassador: MAX DAHINDEN.

Syria: 1026 Budapest, Harangvirág u. 3; tel. (1) 176-7186; telex 226605; Ambassador: (vacant).

Thailand: 1025 Budapest, Verecke út 79; tel. (1) 250-0727; telex 202706; fax (1) 250-1580; Ambassador: TASANEE BUNNAG.

Tunisia: 1021 Budapest, Budakeszi út 55D; tel. (1) 176-7595; fax (1) 176-7336; Ambassador: MOHAMED F. CHERIF.

Turkey: 1014 Budapest, Úri u. 45; tel. (1) 155-0737; Ambassador: BEDRETTIN TUNABAS.

Ukraine: 1125 Budapest, Nogradi 8; tel. (1) 155-2443; fax (1) 202-2287; Ambassador: DMYITRO TKACH.

United Kingdom: 1051 Budapest, Harmincad u. 6; tel. (1) 266-2888; telex 224527; fax (1) 266-0907; Ambassador: Sir JOHN BIRCH.

USA: 1054 Budapest, Szabadság tér 12; tel. (1) 112-6450; telex 224222; Ambassador: CHARLES W. THOMAS.

Uruguay: 1023 Budapest 2, Vérhalom u. 12–16; tel. (1) 136-8333; fax (1) 115-0025; Ambassador: PELAYO DÍAZ MUGUERZA.

Venezuela: 1023 Budapest 2, Vérhalom u. 12–16; tel. (1) 135-3562; telex 226666; fax (1) 115-3274; Ambassador: REINALDO PABÓN.

Viet Nam: 1068 Budapest, Benczúr u. 18; tel. (1) 142-9943; Ambassador: NGUYEN VAN QUY.

Yemen: 1025 Budapest, Tömörkény u. 3A; tel. (1) 176-4048; Ambassador: MOHSEN NAGI BIN NAGOI.

Yugoslavia: 1068 Budapest, Dózsa György út 92B; tel. (1) 142-0566; Ambassador: RUDOLF-RUDI SOVA.

Judicial System

The system of court procedure in Hungary is based on an Act that came into effect in 1953 and has since been updated frequently. The system of jurisdiction is based on the local courts (district courts in Budapest, city courts in other cities), labour courts, county courts (or the Metropolitan Court) and the Supreme Court. In the legal remedy system of two instances, appeals against the decisions of city and district courts can be lodged with the competent county court and the Metropolitan Court of Budapest respectively. Against the judgment of first instance of the latter, appeal is to be lodged with the Supreme Court. The Chief Public Prosecutor and the President of the Supreme Court have the right to submit a protest on legal grounds against the final judgment of any court.

By virtue of the 1973 Act, effective 1974 and modified in 1979, the procedure in criminal cases is differentiated for criminal offences and for criminal acts. In the first instance, criminal cases are tried, depending on their character, by a professional judge; where justified by the magnitude of the criminal act, by a council composed of three members, a professional judge and two lay assessors, while in major cases the court consists of five members, two professional judges and three lay assessors. In the Supreme Court, second instance cases are tried only by professional judges. The President of the Supreme Court is elected by the National Assembly. Judges are appointed by the President of the Republic for an indefinite period. Assessors are elected by the local municipal councils.

In the interest of ensuring legality and a uniform application of the Law, the Supreme Court exercises a principled guidance over the jurisdiction of courts. In the Republic of Hungary judges are independent and subject only to the Law and other legal regulations.

The Minister of Justice supervises the general activities of courts. The Chief Public Prosecutor is elected by the National Assembly. The Chief Public Prosecutor and the Prosecutor's Office provide for the consistent prosecution of all acts violating or endangering the legal order of society, the safety and independence of the state, and for the protection of citizens.

The Prosecutors of the independent prosecuting organization exert supervision over the legality of investigations and the implementation of punishments, and assist with specific means in ensuring that legal regulations should be observed by state, economic and other organs and citizens, and they support the legality of court procedures and decisions.

President of the Supreme Court: PÁL SOLT.

Chief Public Prosecutor: KÁLMÁN GYÖRGYI.

Religion

CHRISTIANITY

Ecumenical Council of Churches in Hungary (Magyarországi Egyházak Ökuménikus Tanácsa): 1026 Budapest, Bimbó u. 127; tel. and fax (1) 115-0031; f. 1943; member churches: Baptist, Bulgarian Orthodox, Evangelical Lutheran, Hungarian Orthodox, Methodist, Reformed Church, Romanian Orthodox and Serbian Orthodox; Pres. Rev. Dr JÁNOS VICZIÁN; Gen. Sec. Rev. Dr ZOLTÁN BÓNA.

The Roman Catholic Church

In 1992 Hungary comprised three archdioceses, eight dioceses (including one for Catholics of the Byzantine rite) and one territorial abbacy (directly responsible to the Holy See). At 31 December 1991 the Church had 6,128,159 adherents in Hungary. In 1993 a fourth archdiocese, based in Veszprém, was created.

Bishops' Conference: Magyar Püspöki Kar Konferenciája, 1053 Budapest, Ferenciek tere 4–8; tel. (1) 117-4533; fax (1) 137-8016; f. 1969; Pres. Dr ISTVÁN SEREGÉLY, Archbishop of Eger.

Latin Rite

Archbishop of Eger: Dr ISTVÁN SEREGÉLY, 3301 Eger, Széchenyi u. 1, POB 80; tel. (36) 313-259; fax (36) 320-508.

Archbishop of Esztergom-Budapest: Cardinal Dr LÁSZLÓ PASKAI, Primate of Hungary, 2500 Esztergom, Mindszenty herceg-primás ter. 2; tel. (33) 313-690; fax (33) 311-085.

Archbishop of Kalocsa-Kecskemét: Dr LÁSZLÓ DANKÓ, 6301 Kalocsa, Szabadság tér 1; tel. (64) 362-166; fax (64) 362-687.

Archbishop of Veszprém: Dr JÓZSEF SZENDI, 8200 Veszprém, Vár u. 16; tel. (88) 326-088; fax (88) 326-504.

Byzantine Rite

Bishop of Hajdúdorog: SZILÁRD KERESZTES, 4401 Nyiregyháza, Bethlen u. 5, POB 60; tel. (42) 317-397; fax (42) 314-734; 252,840 adherents (Dec. 1991); the Bishop is also Apostolic Administrator of the Apostolic Exarchate of Miskolc, with an estimated 26,355 Catholics of the Byzantine rite (Dec. 1991).

Protestant Churches

Baptist Union of Hungary (Magyarországi Baptista Egyház): 1062 Budapest, Aradi u. 48; tel. (1) 132-2332; fax (1) 131-0194; f. 1846; 11,000 mems; Pres. Rev. ÁRPÁD REVESZ; Gen.-Sec. Rev. KORNÉL GYŐRI.

Hungarian Methodist Church (Magyarországi Metodista Egyház): 1068 Budapest, Felsöerdösor 5; tel. (1) 122-4723; Superintendent Dr FRIGYES HECKER.

Lutheran Church in Hungary (Magyarországi Evangélikus Egyház): 1447 Budapest, POB 500; tel. (1) 113-0886; fax (1) 138-2302; 430,000 mems (1992); Presiding Bishop Dr BÉLA HARMATI; Gen. Sec. ZOLTÁN SZEMEREI.

Reformed Church in Hungary—Presbyterian (Magyarországi Református Egyház): 1146 Budapest, Abonyi u. 21; tel. (1) 122-7870; 2m. mems (1987); 1,306 churches; Pres. of Gen. Synod Bishop Dr LORÁNT HEGEDŰS.

Unitarian Church in Hungary (Magyarországi Unitárius Egyház): 1055 Budapest V, Nagy Ignác u. 4; tel. (1) 111-2801; Bishop Rev. MARTIN BENCZE.

The Eastern Orthodox Church

Hungarian Orthodox Church (Magyar Orthodox Egyház): 1052 Budapest, Petőfi tér 2.1.2.; tel. (1) 118-4813; Administrator Archpriest Dr FERIZ BERKI.

Romanian Orthodox Church in Hungary (Magyarországi Román Ortodox Egyház): 5700 Gyula, Groza park 2; tel. (66) 61-281; Bishop PÁL ÁRDELEÁN.

Serbian Orthodox Diocese (Szerb Görögkeleti Egyházmegye): 2000 Szentendre, POB 22; Bishop Dr DANILO KRISTIC.

The Russian (6,000 mems) and Bulgarian Orthodox Churches are also represented.

BUDDHISM

Hungarian Buddhist Mission (Magyarországi Buddhista Misszió): 1221 Budapest, Alkotmány u. 83; Rep. Dr JÓZSEF HORVÁTH.

Hungarian Zen Buddhist Community (Magyarországi Csan Buddhista Közösség): Budapest; Leader FÁRAD LOTFI.

ISLAM

There are about 3,000 Muslims in Hungary. In 1987 it was announced that an Islamic centre was to be built in Budapest, with assistance from the Muslim World League.

Hungarian Islamic Community (Magyar Iszlám Közösség): 1066 Budapest, Teréz krt 65; tel. (1) 177-7602; Leader Dr BALÁZS MIHÁLFFY.

JUDAISM

The Jewish community in Hungary is estimated to number between 80,000 and 100,000 people.

Federation of Jewish Communities in Hungary (Magyarországi Zsidó Vitközségek Szövetsége): 1079 Budapest, Sip u. 12, Budapesti Zsidó Hitközség (Jewish Community of Budapest); tel. (1) 226-475; fax (1) 421-790; 80,000 mems; 40 active synagogues; Orthodox and Conservative; Man. Dir GUSZTÁV ZOLTAI; Chief Rabbi of Budapest RÓBERT DEUTSCH.

The Press

In 1988 the censorship laws were relaxed considerably, and in 1989 private ownership of publications was legalized. By late 1990 most of the former organs of political parties, trade unions, youth and social organizations had been transferred into full or partial private ownership. Most daily newspapers were partially foreign-owned.

In 1991 there were 36 dailies with an average total circulation of 2,454,352. These included more than 20 provincial dailies. Budapest dailies circulate nationally. The most popular are: *Népszabadság, Nemzeti Sport* and *Népszava. Népszabadság,* the most important daily, was formerly the central organ of the Hungarian Socialist Workers' Party, but is now independent. The paper most respected for the quality of its news coverage and commentary is *Magyar Nemzet.*

Among the most popular periodicals are the illustrated weeklies, which include the satirical *Ludas Matyi,* the women's magazine *Magyar Nők Lapja,* the illustrated news journal *Képes Újság* and the political paper *Szabad Föld.* A news magazine giving a high standard of reporting and political discussion is *Magyarország.* Specialized periodicals include cultural, medical, scientific, agricultural and religious publications (including *Új Ember, Evangélikus Élet* and *Új Élet* for Catholic, Lutheran and Jewish congregations respectively).

PRINCIPAL DAILIES

Békéscsaba

Békés Megyei Hírlap (Békés County News): 5601 Békéscsaba, Munkácsy u. 4; tel. (66) 450-450; Editor-in-Chief ZOLTÁN ÁRPÁSI; circ. 49,000.

Budapest

Daily News: 1016 Budapest, Naphegy tér 8; tel. (1) 175-6928; fax (1) 118-8384; f. 1967; published by the Hungarian News Agency; in English; Editor-in-Chief SÁNDOR KŐRÖSPATAKI KISS; circ. 10,000.

Esti Hirlap (Evening Journal): 1962 Budapest, Blaha Lujza tér 3; tel. (1) 138-2399; telex 227040; fax (1) 138-4550; 40% foreign-owned; Editor-in-Chief DÉNES MAROS; circ. 70,000.

Kurír: 1065 Budapest, Hajós u. 30–32; tel. (1) 111-2659; Editor-in-Chief GÁBOR SZÜCS.

Magyar Hirlap (Hungarian Journal): 1087 Budapest, Kerepesi út 29B; tel. (1) 210-0050; telex 224268; fax (1) 113-0249; f. 1968; 40% foreign-owned; Editor-in-Chief PÉTER NÉMETH; circ. 75,000.

Magyar Nemzet (Hungarian Nation): 1073 Budapest, Erzsébet krt 9–11; tel. (1) 141-4320; telex 224269; 45% foreign-owned; Editor-in-Chief TIBOR PETHŐ; circ. 70,000.

Mai Nap (Today): 1087 Budapest, Könyves Kálmán krt 76; tel. (1) 210-0400; telex 223634; fax (1) 133-9153; f. 1988; Editor-in-Chief FERENC GAZSÓ; circ. 90,000.

NAPI Gazdaság (World Economy): 1034 Budapest, Bécsi út 126–128; tel. (1) 168-2002; telex 227958; fax (1) 188-9504; Editor-in-Chief (vacant); circ. 15,000.

Nemzeti Sport (National Sport): 1981 Budapest, Rökk Szilárd u. 6; tel. (1) 138-4366; telex 225245; fax (1) 138-2463; Editor-in-Chief ISTVÁN SZEKERES; circ. 250,000.

Népszabadság (People's Freedom): 1960 Budapest, Bécsi út 122-124; tel. (1) 250-1680; telex 225551; fax (1) 168-2001; f. 1942; independent; Editor-in-Chief PÁL EÖTVÖS; circ. 316,000.

Népszava (Voice of the People): 1022 Budapest, Törökvész u. 30A; tel. (1) 202-7788; telex 224105; fax (1) 202-7798; f. 1873; trade unions' daily; Editor ANDRÁS DEÁK; circ. 120,000.

Pest Megyei Hirlap (Pest County Journal): 1446 Budapest, Somogyi Béla u. 6; tel. (1) 138-2399; Editor-in-Chief Dr ANDRÁS BÁRD; circ. 43,000.

Pesti Hirlap (Pest Journal): 1051 Budapest, Október 6 u. 8; tel. (1) 117-6162; fax (1) 117-6029; f. 1993; Editor-in-Chief ANDRÁS BENCSIK; circ. 50,000.

Üzlet (Business): 1055 Budapest, Bajcsy-Zsilinszky út 78; tel. (1) 111-8260; Editor-in-Chief IVÁN ÉRSEK.

Debrecen

Hajdú-Bihari Napló (Hajdú-Bihar Diary): 4024 Debrecen, Tóthfalusi tér 10; tel. (52) 12-144; Editor-in-Chief ENDRE BAKÓ; circ. 71,000.

Dunaújváros

A Hirlap (The Journal): 2400 Dunaújváros, Városháza tér 1; tel. (25) 16-010; Editor-in-Chief CSABA D. KISS.

Eger

Heves Megyei Hirlap (Heves County Journal): 3301 Eger, Barkóczy u. 7; tel. (36) 13-644; Editor-in-Chief LEVENTE KAPOSI; circ. 33,000.

Győr

Kisalföld: 9022 Győr, Szt István út 51; tel. (96) 15-544; Editor-in-Chief Dr ANDOR KLOSS; circ. 95,000.

Kaposvár

Somogyi Hirlap (Somogy Journal): 7401 Kaposvár, Latinca Sándor u. 2A; tel. (82) 11-644; Editor-in-Chief Dr IMRE KERCZA; circ. 59,000.

Kecskemét

Petőfi Népe: 6000 Kecskemét, Szabadság tér 1A; tel. (76) 27-611; Editor-in-Chief Dr SÁNDOR GÁL; circ. 59,000.

Miskolc

Déli Hirlap (Midday Journal): 3527 Miskolc, Bajcsy-Zsilinszky út 15; tel. (46) 42-694; Editor-in-Chief DEZSŐ BEKES; circ. 20,000.

Észak-Magyarország (Northern Hungary): 3527 Miskolc, Bajcsy-Zsilinszky út 15; tel. (46) 41-888; Editor-in-Chief ZOLTÁN NAGY; circ. 79,000.

Nyíregyháza

Kelet-Magyarország (Eastern Hungary): 4401 Nyíregyháza, Zrínyi u. 3–5; tel. (42) 11-277; Editor-in-Chief Dr SÁNDOR ANGYAL; circ. 80,000.

Pécs

Új Dunántúli Napló: 7601 Pécs, Hunyadi út 11; tel. (72) 15-000; Editor-in-Chief JENŐ LOMBOSI; circ. 84,000.

Salgótarján

Új Nógrád (New Nógrád): 3100 Salgótarján, Palócz Imre tér 4; tel. (32) 10-589; Editor-in-Chief LÁSZLÓ SULYOK; circ. 23,000.

Szeged

Délvilág (Southern World): 6740 Szeged, Tanácsköztársaság út 10; tel. (62) 14-911; Editor-in-Chief ISTVÁN NIKOLÉNYI; circ. 20,000.

Délmagyarország (Southern Hungary): 6740 Szeged, Tanácsköztársaság út 10; tel. (62) 24-633; Editor-in-Chief IMRE DLUSZTUS; circ. 55,000.

Székesfehérvár

Fejér Megyei Hirlap (Fejér County Journal): 8003 Székesfehérvár, Honvéd u. 8; tel. (22) 12-450; Editor-in-Chief JÁNOS Á. SZABÓ; circ. 52,000.

Szekszárd

Tolna Megyei Népújság (Tolna News): 7100 Szekszárd, Liszt Ferenc tér 3; tel. (74) 16-211; Editor-in-Chief GYÖRGYNÉ KAMARÁS; circ. 32,000.

Szolnok

Új Néplap (New People's Paper): 5001 Szolnok, Kossuth tér 1, I. Irodaház; tel. (56) 42-211; Editor-in-Chief JÓZSEF HAJNAL; circ. 46,000.

Szombathely

Vas Népe (Vas People): 9700 Szombathely, Berzsenyi tér 2; tel. (94) 12-393; Editor-in-Chief SÁNDOR LENGYEL; circ. 65,000.

Vasvármegye: 9701 Szombathely, Honvéd tér 2; tel. (94) 12-356; Editor-in-Chief LÁSZLÓ BURKON.

Tatabánya

24 Óra (24 Hours): 2801 Tatabánya, Felszabadulás tér 4; tel. (34) 10-053; Editor-in-Chief GÁBOR GOMBKÖTŐ; circ. 43,000.

Veszprém

Napló (Diary): 8201 Veszprém, Szabadság tér 15; tel. (80) 27-444; Editor-in-Chief ELEMÉR BALOGH; circ. 58,000.

Zalaegerszeg

Zalai Hirlap (Zala Journal): 8901 Zalaegerszeg, Ady Endre u. 62; tel. (92) 12-575; Editor-in-Chief JÓZSEF TARSOLY; circ. 71,000.

WEEKLIES

Élet és Irodalom (Life and Literature): 1054 Budapest, Széchenyi u. 1; tel. (1) 153-3122; fax (1) 111-1087; f. 1957; literary and political; Editor IMRE BATA; circ. 60,000.

Élet és Tudomány (Life and Science): 1088 Budapest, Bródy Sándor u 16; tel. and fax (1) 138-2472; f. 1946; popular science; Editor-in-Chief Dr WOLFNER ANDRÁS; circ. 35,000.

Evangélikus Élet (Evangelical Life): 1447 Budapest, POB 500; tel. (1) 138-2360; f. 1933; Evangelical–Lutheran Church newspaper; Editor MIHÁLY TÓTH-SZÖLLŐS; circ. 12,000.

Heti Világgazdaság (World Economics Weekly): 1126 Budapest 64, Németvölgy u. 1; tel. (1) 155-5411; telex 222556; f. 1979; Editor-in-Chief IVÁN LIPOVECZ; circ. 141,000.

Képes Újság (Illustrated News): 1085 Budapest, Gyulai Pál u. 14; tel. (1) 113-7660; f. 1960; Editor MIHALY KOVÁCS; circ. 400,000.

Ludas Matyi: 1077 Budapest, Gyulai Pál u. 14; tel. (1) 133-5718; satirical; Editor JÓZSEF ÁRKUS; circ. 352,000.

L'udové Noviny (People's News): 1065 Budapest, Nagymező u. 49; tel. (1) 131-9184; in Slovak, for Slovaks in Hungary; Editor PÁL KONDÁCS; circ. 1,700.

Magyar Mezőgazdaság (Hungarian Agriculture): 1355 Budapest, Kossuth Lajos tér 11; tel. (1) 112-2433; telex 225445; f. 1946; Editor-in-Chief Dr KÁROLY FEHÉR; circ. 24,000.

Magyar Nők Lapja (Hungarian Women's Journal): 1022 Budapest, Törökvész út 30A; tel. and fax (1) 115-4037; telex 225554; f. 1949; Editor-in-Chief LILI ZÉTÉNYI; circ. 550,000.

Magyarország (Hungary): 1085 Budapest, Gyulai Pál u. 14; tel. (1) 138-4644; telex 226351; f. 1964; news magazine; Editor DÉNES GYAPAY; circ. 200,000.

Narodne Novine (People's News): 1396 Budapest, POB 495; tel. (1) 112-4869; f. 1945; for Yugoslavs in Hungary; in Serbo-Croat and Slovene; Chief Editor MARKO MARKOVIĆ; circ. 2,800.

Neue Zeitung (New Paper): 1391 Budapest, Nagymező u. 49, POB 224; tel. (1) 132-6334; f. 1957; for Germans in Hungary; Editor JOHANN SCHUTH; circ. 4,500.

Rádió és Televízióújság (Radio and TV News): 1801 Budapest; tel. (1) 138-7210; f. 1956; Editor TAMÁS NÁDOR ; circ. 1,350,000.

Reform: 1443 Budapest, POB 222; tel. and fax (1) 122-4240; telex 223333; f. 1988; popular tabloid; 50% foreign-owned; Editor PÉTER TŐKE; circ. 300,000.

Reformátusok Lapja: 1395 Budapest, POB 424; tel. (1) 117-6809; fax (1) 117-8386; f. 1957; Reformed Church paper for the laity; Editor-in-Chief and Publr ATTILA P. KOMLÓS; circ. 30,000.

Szabad Föld (Free Earth): 1087 Budapest, Könyves Kálmán krt 76; tel. and fax (1) 133-6794; f. 1945; Editor GYULA ECK; circ. 720,000.

Szövetkezet (Co-operative): 1054 Budapest, Szabadság tér 14; tel. (1) 131-3132; National Council of Hungarian Consumer Co-operative Societies; Editor-in-Chief ATTILA KOVÁCS; circ. 85,000.

Tallózó: 1133 Budapest, Visegrádi u. 116; tel. (1) 270-3399; f. 1989; news digest; Editor-in-Chief GYÖRGY ANDAI; circ. 45,000.

Tőzsde Kurir (Hungarian Stock Market Courier): 1074 Budapest, Rákóczi út 54; tel. (1) 122-3273; fax (1) 142-8356; business; Editor-in-Chief ISTVÁN GÁBOR BENEDEK.

Új Ember (New Man): 1053 Budapest, Kossuth Lajos u. 1; tel. (1) 117-3638; fax (1) 117-3471; f. 1945; religious weekly; Editor LÁSZLÓ RÓNAY; circ. 100,000.

Vasárnapi Hirek (Sunday News): 1117 Budapest, POB 364; tel. (1) 161-2456; telex 225944; fax (1) 161-0284; f. 1984; political; Editor Dr ZOLTÁN LŐKÖS; circ. 250,000.

FORTNIGHTLIES

Foaia Noastra (Our Newspaper): 1055 Budapest, Bajcsy Zs. u. 78; for Romanians in Hungary; Editor SÁNDOR HOCOPÁN; circ. 1,500.

Magyar Hirek (Hungarian News): 1068 Budapest, Benczúr u. 15; tel. (1) 122-5616; telex 22317; fax (1) 122-2421; illustrated magazine primarily for Hungarians living abroad; Editor GYÖRGY HALÁSZ; circ. 70,000.

Pedagógusok Lapja (Teachers' Review): 1068 Budapest, Gorkij fasor 10; tel. (1) 122-8464; f. 1945; published by the Hungarian Union of Teachers; Editor-in-Chief LIEBHARDT ÁGOTA; circ. 15,000.

Szövetkezeti Hirlap (Co-operative Herald): 1052 Budapest, Pesti Barnabás u. 6; tel. (1) 117-0181; National Union of Artisans; Editor MÁRIA DOLEZSÁL; circ. 12,000.

Új Élet (New Life): 1075 Budapest, Síp u. 12; tel. (1) 122-2829; for Hungarian Jews; Editor Dr PETER KARDOS; circ. 5,000.

OTHER PERIODICALS

(Published monthly unless otherwise indicated)

Állami Gazdaság (State Farming): General Direction of State Farming, 1054 Budapest, Akadémia u. 1–3; tel. (1) 112-4617; fax (1) 111-4877; f. 1946; Editor P. GÖRGÉNYI.

Business Partner Hungary: 1051 Budapest, Dorottya u. 6; tel. (1) 117-0850; telex 225646; fax (1) 118-6483; f. 1986; quarterly; Hungarian, German, French and English; economic journal published by Institute for Economic, Market Research and Informatics (KOPINT-DATORG).

Cartactual: 1367 Budapest, POB 76; tel. (2) 694-550; telex 224964; f. 1965; every 3 months; map service periodical with supplement *Cartinform* (map bibliography); published in English, French, German and Hungarian; Editor-in-Chief ERNŐ CSÁTI.

Egyházi Krónika (Church Chronicle): 1052 Budapest, Petőfi tér 2.1.2; tel. (1) 118-4813; f. 1952; every 2 months; Eastern Orthodox Church journal; Editor Archpriest Dr FERIZ BERKI.

Elektrotechnika (Electrical Engineering): 1055 Budapest, Kossuth Lajos tér 6–8; tel. (1) 153-0117; telex 225792; fax (1) 153-4069; f. 1908; organ of Electrotechnical Association; Editor Dr TIBOR KELEMEN; circ. 3,000.

Élelmezési Ipar (Food Industry): 1361 Budapest, POB 5; tel. (1) 112-2859; fax (1) 131-022; f. 1947; Scientific Society for Food Industry; Editor Dr ISTVÁN TÓTH-ZSIGA.

Energia és Atomtechnika (Energy and Nuclear Technology): 1055 Budapest, Kossuth Lajos tér 6–8; tel. (1) 153-2751; telex 225792; fax (1) 156-1215; f. 1947; every two months; Scientific Society for Energy Economy; Editor-in-Chief Dr G. BŐKI.

Energiagazdálkodás (Energy Economy): 1055 Budapest, Kossuth Lajos tér 6; tel. (1) 153-2894; Scientific Society for Energetics; Editor Dr TAMÁS RAPP.

Ezermester (The Handyman): 1066 Budapest, Dessewffy u. 34; tel. (1) 132-0542; telex 226423; f. 1957; do-it-yourself magazine; Editor J. SZŰCS; circ. 135,000.

Forum: Budapest; f. 1989; periodical of the Hungarian Socialist Party; Editor-in-Chief ISTVÁN SZERDAHELYI.

Gép (Machinery): 1027 Budapest, Fő u. 68; tel. (1) 135-4175; telex 225792; fax (1) 153-0818; f. 1949; Scientific Society of Mechanical Engineering; Editor Dr KORNÉL LEHOFER.

Hungarian Business Herald: 1114 Budapest, Buharest u. 15; tel. (1) 186-6143; f. 1970; quarterly review published in English and German by the Ministry of International Economic Relations; Editor-in-Chief Dr GERD BIRÓ; circ. 4,000.

Hungarian Economy: 1355 Budapest, Alkotmány u. 10; tel. (1) 132-2186; telex 226613; fax (1) 132-2990; f. 1972; quarterly; economic and business review; Editor-in-Chief Dr JÁNOS FOLLINUS; circ. 10,000.

Hungarian Travel Magazine: 1088 Budapest, Múzeum u. 11; tel. (1) 138-4643; quarterly in English and German; illustrated journal of the Tourist Board for visitors to Hungary; Man. Editor JÚLIA SZ. NAGY.

Ipar-Gazdaság (Industrial Economy): 1371 Budapest, POB 433; tel. (1) 202-1083; f. 1948; Editor Dr TAMÁS MÉSZÁROS; circ. 4,000.

Jogtudományi Közlöny (Law Gazette): 1396 Budapest, POB 71; Váci út 71; tel. (1) 149-1748; f. 1866; law; Editor-in-Chief Dr IMRE VÖRÖS; circ. 2,500.

Kortárs (Contemporary): 1062 Budapest, Bajza u. 18; tel. (1) 142-1168; literary gazette; Editor-in-Chief IMRE KIS PINTÉR; circ. 5,000.

Közgazdasági Szemle (Economic Review): 1112 Budapest, Budaörsi u. 43–45; tel. (1) 185-0777; f. 1954; published by Cttee for Economic Sciences of Academy of Sciences; Editor KATALIN SZABÓ; circ. 15,000.

Made in Hungary: 1426 Budapest, POB 3; economics and business magazine published in English by Hungarian News Agency (MTI); Editor GYÖRGY BLASITS.

Magyar Jog (Hungarian Law): 1054 Budapest, Szemere u. 10; tel. (1) 131-4574; fax (1) 111-4013; f. 1953; law; Editor-in-Chief Dr JÁNOS NÉMETH; circ. 3,500.

Magyar Közlöny (Official Gazette): 1055 Budapest, Bajcsy Zs. u. 78; tel. (1) 112-1236; Editor Dr ELEMÉR KISS; circ. 90,000.

Magyar Tudomány (Hungarian Science): Hungarian Academy of Sciences, 1051 Budapest, Nádor u. 7; tel. (1) 117-9524; fax (1) 117-4017; multidisciplinary science review; Editors ÉVA CSATÓ, ZSVZSA SZENTGYÖRGYI.

Nagyvilág (The Great World): 1054 Budapest, Széchenyi u. 1; tel. (1) 132-1160; f. 1956; review of world literature; Editor LÁSZLÓ KÉRY; circ. 6,000.

New Hungarian Quarterly: 1906 Budapest, POB 223; tel. (1) 175-6722; fax (1) 118-8297; f. 1960; illustrated quarterly in English; politics, economics, philosophy, education, culture, poems, short stories, etc.; Editor MIKLÓS VAJDA; circ. 3,500.

Református Egyház (Reformed Church): 1146 Budapest, Abonyi u. 21; tel. (1) 122-7870; f. 1949; official journal of the Hungarian Reformed Church; Editor-in-Chief LAJOS TEGEZ; circ. 1,600.

Statisztikai Szemle (Statistical Review): 1525 Budapest, POB 51; tel. (1) 202-1291; f. 1923; Editor-in-Chief MARIA VISI LAKATOS; circ. 1,200.

Társadalmi Szemle (Social Science Review): 1114 Budapest, Villányi ut 11–13; tel. (1) 166-6300; fax (1) 166-7410; theoretical-political review; Editor MIHÁLY BIHARI; circ. 4,000.

Technika (Technology): 1428 Budapest, POB 12; tel. (1) 1 67-2148; telex 224244; fax (1) 118-0109; f. 1957; official journal of the Hungarian Academy of Engineering; monthly in Hungarian, annually in English, German and Russian; Editor-in-Chief EMIL SZLUKA; circ. 15,000.

Turizmus (Tourism): 1088 Budapest, Múzeum u. 11; tel. (1) 138-4638; telex 225297; Editor ZSOLT SZEBENI; circ. 8,000.

Új Technika (New Technology): 1014 Budapest, Szentháromság tér 1; tel. (1) 155-7122; telex 226490; f. 1967; popular industrial quarterly; circ. 35,000.

Vigilia: 1364 Budapest, POB 111; tel. (1) 117-7246; fax (1) 117-4895; f. 1935; Catholic; Editor LÁSZLÓ LUKÁCS; circ. 11,500.

Villamosság (Electricity): 1055 Budapest, Kossuth Lajos tér 6–8; tel. (1) 153-0117; organ of Electrotechnical Association; Gen. Editor FERENC KOVÁCS; circ. 3,000.

NEWS AGENCIES

Magyar Távirati Iroda (MTI) (Hungarian News Agency): 1016 Budapest, Naphegy tér 8; tel. (1) 175-6722; telex 224371; fax (1) 175-3973; f. 1880; 19 brs in Hungary; 18 bureaux abroad; Dir-Gen. KAROLY ALEXA.

Foreign Bureaux

Agence France-Presse (AFP): 1016 Budapest, Naphegy u. 29; tel. (1) 156-8416; telex 223831; fax (1) 201-9161; Correspondent PAOLA COLLU JUVENAL.

Agenzia Nazionale Stampa Associata (ANSA) (Italy): 1054 Budapest, Vadász u. 31; tel. (1) 135-2323; telex 224711; Bureau Chief GAETANO ALIMENTI.

Allgemeiner Deutscher Nachrichtendienst GmbH (ADN) (Germany): 1025 Budapest XIV, Szeréna út 54; tel. (1) 135-5352; telex 224675; Correspondent GERHARD KOWALSKI.

Associated Press (AP) (USA): 1122 Budapest, Maros u. 13; tel. (1) 156-9129; Correspondent GEORGE JAHN.

Česká tisková kancelář (ČTK) (Czech Republic): 1146 Budapest, Zichy Géza u. 5; tel. (1) 142-7115; telex 225367; Correspondent MICHAL STASZ.

Informatsionnoye Telegrafnoye Agentstvo Rossii—Telegrafnoye Agenstvo Suverennykh Stran (ITAR—TASS) (Russia): 1023 Budapest, Vérhalom u. 12–16; Correspondent YEVGENI POPOV.

Prensa Latina (Cuba): 1016 Budapest, Naphegy tér 8; tel. (1) 175-6722; telex 224800; Correspondent EDIT PAPP.

Reuters (United Kingdom): 1108 Budapest, Rákóczi út 1–3, East-West Business Centre; tel. (1) 266-2410; fax (1) 266-2030; Correspondent MICHAEL SHIELDS.

Rossiyskoye Informatsionnoye Agentstvo—Novosti (RIA—Novosti) (Russia): 1075 Budapest, Tanács Kőrút 9; tel. (1) 132-0594; telex 61224792; fax (1) 142-3325; Bureau Chief A. POPOV.

Xinhua (New China) News Agency (People's Republic of China): 1068 Budapest, Benczur u. 39; tel. (1) 122-8420; telex 22 5447; Chief Correspondent ZHOU DONGYAO.

PRESS ASSOCIATIONS

Magyar Újságírók Országos Szövetsége (MUOSZ) (National Association of Hungarian Journalists): 1062 Budapest, Andrássy út 101; tel. (1) 122-1699; telex 225045; fax (1) 122-1881; f. 1896; Gen. Sec. GÁBOR BENCSIK; Int. Sec. FÓZSEF HORVATH; 4,700 mems.

Association of Hungarian Newspaper Publishers: Budapest; f. 1986 by four major newspaper publishing companies, Hungarian News Agency (MTI) and local newspaper publrs; Chair. JÓZSEF BOCZ.

Publishers

PRINCIPAL PUBLISHING HOUSES

Akadémiai Kiadó: 1117 Budapest, Prielle Kornélia u. 19–35; tel. (1) 181-2134; telex 226228; fax (1) 166-6466; f. 1828; publishing house of the Hungarian Academy of Sciences; humanities, social, natural and technical sciences, dictionaries, encyclopaedias, periodicals of the Academy and other institutions, issued partly in foreign languages; Man. Dir FERENC ZÖLD.

Corvina Kiadó: 1051 Budapest, Vörösmarty tér 1; tel. (1) 117-6222; telex 224440; fax (1) 118-4410; f. 1955; Hungarian works translated into foreign languages, art and educational books, fiction and non-fiction, tourist guides, cookery books, sport, musicology, juvenile and children's literature; Man. Dir ISTVÁN BART.

Editio Musica Budapest: 1051 Budapest, Vörösmarty tér 1; tel. (1) 118-4228; telex 225500; fax (1) 138-2732; f. 1950; music publishing, engraving and printing, and books on musical subjects; Dir ISTVÁN HOMOLYA.

Európa Könyvkiadó: 1055 Budapest, Kossuth Lajos tér 13–15; tel. (1) 131-2700; telex 225645; fax (1) 131-4162; f. 1945; world literature translated into Hungarian; Man. LEVENTE OSZTOVITS.

Gondolat Könyvkiadó Vállalat: 1088 Budapest, Bródy Sándor u. 16; tel. (1) 138-3777; fax (1) 138-4540; f. 1957; popular scientific publications on natural and social sciences, art, encyclopaedic handbooks; Dir ILDIKÓ LENDVAI.

Helikon Kiadó: 1053 Budapest, Papnövelde u. 8; tel. (1) 117-4865; telex 227100; fax (1) 117-4865; bibliophile books; Dir KATALIN BERGER.

Képzőművészeti Kiadó: 1148 Budapest, Kerepesi út 26; tel. (1) 251-1527; fax (1) 251-1527; fine arts; Man. Dr ZOLTÁN KEMENCZEI.

Kossuth Könyvkiadó: 1054 Budapest, Steindl u. 6; tel. (1) 131-2111; fax (1) 111-3670; f. 1944; sociological and popular publications; Man. ANDRÁS SÁNDOR KOCSIS.

Közgazdasági és Jogi Könyvkiadó Rt: 1054 Budapest, Nagysándor József u. 6; tel. (1) 112-6430; telex 226511; fax (1) 111-3210; f. 1955; economics, law, sociology, psychology, history, politics, education, dictionaries; Man. VILMOS DALOS.

Magvető Könyvkiadó: 1806 Budapest, Vörösmarty tér 1; tel. (1) 118-5109; fax (1) 118-5364; literature; Man. MÁRIA HEGEDŐS.

Medicina Könyvkiadó Rt: 1054 Budapest, Zoltan u. 8; tel. (1) 112-2650; fax (1) 112-2450; f. 1957; books on medicine, sport, tourism; Dir BORBÁLA FARKASVÖLGYI.

Mezőgazda Kiadó: 1163 Budapest, Koronafürt u. 44; tel. (1) 183-6575; telex 202536; fax (1) 183-7571; ecology, natural sciences, environmental protection, food industry; Man. Dr LELKES LAJOS.

Móra Ferenc Gyermek és Ifjúsági Könyvkiadó: 1146 Budapest, Május 1 u. 57–59; tel. (1) 121-2390; telex 227027; fax (1) 122-4276; f. 1950; children's books, science fiction; Man. JÁNOS SZILÁDI.

Műszaki Könyvkiadó: 1014 Budapest, Szentháromság tér 6; tel. (1) 155-7122; telex 226490; fax (1) 175-5713; f. 1955; scientific and technical, fiction and non-fiction; Man. PÉTER SZŰCS.

Nemzeti Tankönyvkiadó: 1135 Budapest, Béke út 26; tel. (1) 129-1496; fax (1) 149-1709; f. 1949; school and university textbooks, pedagogical literature and language books; Man. ISTVÁN ABRAHAM.

Népszava Lap-és Könyvkiadó Vállalat: 1553 Budapest, Rákóczi u. 54; tel. (1) 122-4810; National Confederation of Hungarian Trade Unions; Man. Dr JENŐ KISS.

Statiqum Kiadó és Nyomda Kft: 1033 Budapest, Kaszásdűlő u. 2; tel. (1) 250-0311; telex 226699; fax (1) 168-8635; f. 1991; publications on statistics, system-management and computer science; Dir BENEDEK BELECZ.

Szépirodalmi Könyvkiadó: 1073 Budapest, Erzsébet krt 9–11; tel. (1) 122-1285; telex 226754; f. 1950; modern and classical Magyar literature; Man. SÁNDOR Z. SZALAI.

Zrinyi Katonai Kiadó: 1087 Budapest, Kerepesi u. 29; tel. (1) 133-4750; military literature; Man. LÁSZLÓ NÉMETH.

CARTOGRAPHERS

Cartographia (Hungarian Company for Mapping): 1443 Budapest, POB 132; tel. and fax (1) 163-4639; telex 226218; f. 1954; Dir Dr ÁRPÁD PAPP-VÁRY.

Földügyi és Térképészeti Főosztály (Department of Lands and Mapping): 1055 Budapest, Kossuth Lajos tér 11; tel. (1) 131-3736; telex 225445; fax (1) 153-0518; f. 1954; Man. SÁNDOR ZSÁMBOKI.

PUBLISHERS' ASSOCIATION

Magyar Könyvkiadók és Könyvterjesztők Egyesülése (Hungarian Publishers' and Booksellers' Association): 1051 Budapest, Vörösmarty tér 1, POB 130; tel. (1) 118-4758; fax (1) 118-4581; f. 1878; most leading Hungarian publishers are members of the Association; Pres. ISTVÁN BART; Sec.-Gen. PÉTER ZENTAI.

WRITERS' UNION

Magyar Írók Szövetsége (Association of Hungarian Writers): 1062 Budapest, Bajza u. 18; tel. (1) 122-8840; f. 1945; Pres. ANNA JÓKAI; Sec.-Gen. SÁNDOR KOCZKÁS.

Radio and Television

In 1991 there were some 6m. radio receivers and 4m. television receivers in use. Cable television systems were expanding and, before the end of the 1980s, were operating in over 12 cities. In 1988 more than 40 areas (300,000 homes) were able to receive cable and satellite services.

RADIO

Magyar Rádió: 1800 Budapest, Bródy Sándor u. 5–7; tel. (1) 138-8388; telex 225188; fax (1) 138-7004; f. 1924; stations: Radio Kossuth (Budapest), Radio Petőfi (Budapest), Radio Bartók (Budapest, mainly classical music); 6 regional studios; external broadcasts in English, German, Hungarian, Italian, Romanian, Russian, Slovak, Serbo-Croat, Spanish and Turkish; Pres. LÁSZLÓ CSUCS (acting).

Radio Danubius: f. 1986; commercial station; broadcasts news, music and information in Hungarian 21 hours a day; transmitting stations in Budapest, Lake Balaton region, Sopron, Szeged and Debrecen; Dir GYÖRGY VARGA.

TELEVISION

Magyar Televízió: 1810 Budapest, Szabadság tér 17; tel. (1) 153-3200; telex 225568; fax (1) 153-4568; f. 1957; first channel broadcasts 98 hours a week and the second channel 83 hours a week, every day, mostly colour transmissions; 100 high-capacity relay stations; Pres. Dr GÁBOR NAHLIK (acting).

Finance

In 1948 Hungary's banking system, which until then had followed the European model, was changed to the Soviet model. In this so-called single-level banking (monobank) system, the National Bank of Hungary performed not only the country's central-bank functions, but (since commercial banks had ceased to exist) it also held the current accounts of the state-owned enterprises, and provided them with credit.

The primary goal of the banking reforms, begun in 1987, was to transform the single-level banking system into a two-tier system, and thereby promote inter-bank competition, permitting the adoption of effective monetary policies and the development of healthy business relations between commercial banks and companies, free from government intervention. From January 1987 the National Bank ceased, for the most part, to act as a commercial bank, and began slowly to transform itself into a conventional central bank.

According to the method of transition to the two-tier system, and to their size and charter, Hungarian financial institutions belong to several categories: large banks, medium-sized banks, specialized financial institutions and, as a separate category, the OTP, the National Savings and Commercial Bank.

In 1987 three banks were formed to take over the commercial banking activities of the National Bank: the Hungarian Credit Bank, the Commercial and Credit Bank and the Budapest Bank. These, and one other already operating and subsequently fully chartered financial institution (the Hungarian Foreign Trade Bank), constitute the category of large banks. These operate under full commercial licences.

The medium-sized banks also operate under full commercial banking licences, and are either newly-established or have been transformed into commercial banks from specialized financial institutions.

The specialized financial institutions are licensed to perform only a limited range of financial activities, and are not authorized, for example, to hold current accounts for economic bodies.

Because of its functions and size, the National Savings and Commercial Bank forms, for the time being, a category by itself. Formerly it had the exclusive right to conduct household banking, and it remains the major bank for financial services to households. It also undertakes other, non-banking activities (real estate transactions, the management of lotteries, etc.).

The supervision and direction of the banking system in Hungary rests with several authorities. Different aspects of this work are performed, to varying degrees and in various areas of competence, by the National Bank, the State Banking Supervision (f. 1987) and the Minister without Portfolio charged with the supervision of financial institutions. The State Property Agency, in charge of the State's securities, also exercises considerable influence in decisions pertaining to the operation of the banking system.

In 1993 the Hungarian banking system consisted of the National Bank, one 'offshore' bank, 16 exclusively Hungarian-owned commercial banks, 12 jointly-owned banks and five Hungarian-owned specialized financial institutions. There were also 260 savings co-operatives and a number of state-owned specialized financial institutions.

The issue of bonds, in order to finance housing and infrastructural projects, has been of increasing significance. The bond market expanded rapidly in 1987, and by December 200 bonds, worth 24,320m. forint, were in circulation. In January 1988 the state guarantee for bonds was terminated, thus rendering the issue of bonds more difficult for less profitable organizations. The State also began to issue treasury bills in order to finance budget deficits. A national securities market opened in Budapest in January 1988. The Budapest stock exchange opened in June 1990.

BANKING

(cap. = capital; res = reserves; dep. = deposits; m. = million; Ft = forint; brs = branches)

Central Bank

Magyar Nemzeti Bank (National Bank of Hungary): 1850 Budapest, Szabadság tér 8–9; tel. (1) 153-2600; telex 22 5677; fax (1) 132-3913; f. 1924; cap. 10,000m. Ft, res 29,515m. Ft, dep. 2,298,172m. Ft (Dec. 1992); issue of banknotes; transacts international payments business; supervises banking system; 18 brs; Pres. Dr PÉTER Á. BOD.

Commercial Banks

AGROBANK Rt. (Agro Deposit and Credit Bank Ltd): 1126 Budapest, Böszörményi u. 24; tel. (1) 155-2722; telex 223111; fax (1) 155-4763; f. 1984; cap. 2,005. Ft (Dec. 1992); 50 brs; Chief Exec. Dr PÉTER KUNOS.

Általános Vállalkozási Bank Rt. (General Bank for Venture Financing Ltd): 1055 Budapest, Marko u. 9; tel. (1) 269-1473; telex 223578; fax (1) 269-1442; f. 1985; cap. 1,000m. Ft (Dec. 1991); CEO MARK PALMER.

Budapest Bank Rt.: 1052 Budapest, Deák Ferenc u. 5, POB 1852; tel. (1) 269-2333; telex 223013; fax (1) 269-2417; f. 1987; cap. 7,628m. Ft (Dec. 1992); in April 1993 it was announced that the bank was to be privatized; Pres. and Gen. Man. LAJOS BOKROS.

Duna Befektetési és Forgalmi Bank Rt. (Dunabank Co Ltd): 1054 Budapest, Báthory u. 12; tel. (1) 269-3377; telex 225595; fax (1) 269-3380; f. 1987 as Bank for Investment and Transactions; renamed 1989; cap. 1,000m. Ft; Chief Exec. TIBOR HORVÁTH; Chair. of Supervisory Bd IMRE BÓNA.

IBUSZ Bank Ltd: 1146 Budapest, Ajtósi Dürer Sor 10; tel. (1) 251-1666; fax (1) 252-1451; f. 1991; cap. 2,028m. Ft (Dec. 1990); Pres. and CEO MÁRTON NAGY-GYÖRGY.

Investbank Műszaki Fejlesztési Bank Rt. (Investbank Ltd): 1053 Budapest, Képíró u. 9; tel. (1) 117-5333; telex 223250; fax (1) 118-4400; f. 1983; cap. 1,245m. Ft (Dec. 1990); Chief Exec. Dr ANNA TEMESI.

Iparbankház Ltd (Industrial Co-operative Commercial Banking House Ltd): 1052 Budapest, Gerlóczy u. 5; tel. (1) 117-6811; telex 223042; fax (1) 117-1921; f. 1984; cap. 1,071m. Ft (Dec. 1992); 7 brs; Chair. and CEO TIBOR ROSTÁS.

Kereskedelmi Bank Rt. (Commercial and Credit Bank Ltd): 1851 Budapest, Arany János u. 24; tel. (1) 112-5200; telex 223200; fax (1) 111-4058; f. 1987; cap. 13,664m. Ft (Dec. 1991); 79 brs; in April 1993 it was announced that the bank was to be privatized; Chair. and CEO Dr GÉZA LENK.

Konzumbank Ltd: 1132 Budapest, Nyugati tér 5; tel. (1) 132-9140; telex 223305; fax (1) 131-3784; f. 1986; cap. 1,042m. Ft (Dec. 1990); Dir Dr GYÖRGY MAROSI.

Közép-Európai Hitelbank Rt. (Central-European Credit Bank Ltd): 1052 Budapest, Váci u. 16B; tel. (1) 118-8377; telex 226104; fax (1) 118-9415; f. 1988; fully-owned subsidiary of Central-European International Bank Ltd (CIB), for domestic business in the Hungarian market; cap. 1,700m. Ft (Dec. 1991); Pres. and CEO GYÖRGY ZDEBORSKY; MAN. DIR DR GYÖRGY SURÁNY.

Magyar Hitel Bank Rt. (Hungarian Credit Bank Ltd): 1054 Budapest, Szabadság tér 5–6; tel. (1) 132-7100; telex 223202; fax (1) 131-5981; f. 1987; cap. 14,000m. (Dec. 1991); activities include venture financing, securities trading, real estate investments; 100 brs; in April 1993 it was announced that the bank was to be privatized; Chief Exec. Dr ISTVÁN TÖRÖCSKEI.

Magyar Külkereskedelmi Bank Rt. (Hungarian Foreign Trade Bank Ltd): 1821 Budapest, Szent István tér 11; tel. (1) 269-0922; telex 226941; fax (1) 269-0952; f. 1950; cap. 7,155m. Ft (Dec. 1992); 7 brs; in April 1993 it was announced that the bank was to be privatized; Chair. ZSIGMOND GÁBOR ERDÉLY; CEO ÁRPÁD BARTHA.

Mezőbank Co Ltd: 1054 Budapest, Hold u. 16; tel. (1) 153-1000; telex 227615; fax (1) 112-1216; f. 1986; cap. 2,361m. Ft (Dec. 1992); 44 brs; Gen. Man. and Chair. Dr GYULA KABAI.

Országos Takarékpénztár és Kereskedelmi Bank Rt.—OTP Rt. (National Savings and Commercial Bank Ltd—NSB Ltd): 1051 Budapest, Nádor u. 16; tel. (1) 153-1444; telex 224280; fax (1) 112-6858; f. 1949; cap. 23,000m. Ft (Dec. 1991); savings deposits, credits, foreign transactions; 422 brs; Chair. and Chief Exec. SÁNDOR CSÁNYI.

Realbank Ltd: 1062 Budapest, Andrássy út 124; tel. (1) 131-7529; telex 227841; fax (1) 132-7391; f. 1989; cap. 1,000m. Ft; Gen. Dir ANDRÁS CZAKÓ.

Ybl Epítőipari Innovációs Bank Rt. (Ybl Bank Ltd): 1063 Budapest, Szív u. 53; tel. (1) 112-9010; telex 223743; fax (1) 132-0567; f. 1983; cap. 1,160m. Ft; Chair. IMRE NAGY.

Banks with Foreign Participation

Általános Értékforgalmi Bank Rt. (General Banking and Trust Co Ltd): 1055 Budapest, Markó u. 9; tel. (1) 269-1473; telex 223578; fax (1) 269-1442; f. 1922; cap. 1,000m. Ft (Dec. 1992); CEO JÁNOS ERŐS; Chair. MARK PALMER.

Banque Indosuez Hungary Ltd: 1088 Budapest, Rákóczi út 1–3; tel. (1) 266-2713; telex 222173; fax (1) 266-5231; f. 1990 as Kulturbank Ltd, changed name 1993; Chair. FERENC BARTHA; CEO CHRISTOPHER JOHNSON.

BNP-KH-Dresdner Bank Ltd.: 1056 Budapest, Molnár u. 19; 1364 Budapest, POB 263; tel. (1) 266-1447; telex 222260; fax (1) 266-1321; f. 1990; (the bank was to change address from mid-1994); cap. 1,000m. Ft (Dec. 1991); Gen. Man. LÁSZLÓ MADARÁSZ.

Citibank Budapest Ltd: 1052 Budapest, Váci u. 19–21; tel. (1) 138-2666; telex 227822; fax (1) 118-9694; f. 1985; share cap. 1,926.2m. Ft (Dec. 1991); Gen. Man. JOHN MCGLOUGHLIN.

Creditanstalt Ltd: 1054 Budapest, Akadémia u. 17; tel. (1) 269-0812; telex 223446; fax (1) 153-4959; f. 1990; commercial banking and foreign exchange services; owned by Creditanstalt (Austria) Bankverein (Austria); cap. 2,815m. Ft, dep. 16,495m. Ft (Dec. 1992); 3 brs; Man. Dir MATTHIAS KUNSCH.

Európai Kereskedelmi Bank Rt (European Commercial Bank Ltd): 1016 Budapest, Hegyalja út 7–13; tel. (1) 202-5444; telex 222190; fax (1) 202-6492; f. 1991; cap. 1,300m. Ft (Dec. 1991); Man. Dir CSABA KÓRTVÉLYESSI.

Inter-Európa Bank Ltd: 1054 Budapest, Szabadság tér 15; tel. (1) 269-1855; telex 227879; fax (1) 269-2526; f. 1980 as INTERINVEST; associated mem. of San Paolo Group; cap. 2,807.4m. Ft (Dec. 1992); Chair. GYÖRGY IVÁNYI; Man. Dir PRIER FRANCO RUBATTO.

Leumi-Hitel Bank Budapest Rt.: 1052 Budapest, Bárczy István u. 3–5; tel. (1) 117-7233; telex 222186; fax (1) 117-7328; f. 1990; cap. 1,300m. Ft (Dec. 1991); Gen. Man. DAVID EFRIMA.

MHB-Daewoo Bank Ltd (Investrade Ltd): 1088 Budapest VIII, East-West Business Center, Rákóczi út 1–3; tel. (1) 266-0200; telex 225036; fax (1) 266-5720; f. 1988; cap. 6,308m. Ft (Dec. 1992); Pres. and CEO JONG-HWAN LEE.

Nomura Magyar Befektetési Bank Rt. (Nomura Investment Bank Hungary Ltd): 1088 Budapest, East-West Business Center, Rákóczi út 1–3; tel. (1) 266-8962; fax (1) 266-8757; Pres. TAKAO SEGAWA.

Postabank Rt. (Post Bank and Savings Bank Corporation): 1051 Budapest, József Nádor tér 1; tel. (1) 118-0855; telex 223294; fax (1) 117-1369; f. 1988; cap. 6,505m. Ft (Dec. 1992); CEO GÁBOR PRINCZ.

Unicbank Ltd.: 1052 Budapest, Váci u. 19–21; tel. (1) 266-2018; telex 223172; fax (1) 266-2846; f. 1986; cap. 2,084m. Ft (Dec. 1992); Man. Dir Dr PÉTER FELCSUTI.

'Offshore' Bank

Közép-Európai Nemzetközi Bank Rt. (Central-European International Bank Ltd): 1052 Budapest, v. Váci u. 16B; tel. (1) 118-8377; telex 224759; fax (1) 118-9415; f. 1979; shareholders: National Bank of Hungary (34%), Banca Commerciale Italiana, Bayerische Vereinsbank, Long-Term Credit Bank of Japan, Société Générale, Sakura Bank (13.2% each); an offshore bank conducting international banking business of all kinds; dep. $621.8m., total resources $699.8m. (Dec. 1991); Chair. JEAN-MARIE WEYDERT; Man. Dir GYÖRGY SURÁNYI.

Specialized Financial Institutions

Corvinbank Ipari Fejlesztési Bank Rt. (Industrial Development Bank Ltd): 1054 Budapest, Hold u. 25; tel. (1) 132-0320; telex 227351; fax (1) 112-9552; f. 1984; cap. 3,200m. Ft; Gen. Man. Dr GYULA PÁZMÁNDI.

Ingatlanbank Rt. (Real Estate Bank Ltd): 1052 Budapest, Bárczy István u. 3–5; tel. (1) 117-1499; telex 225111; fax (1) 117-6302; f. 1989; cap. 840m. Ft; Chief Exec. GYÖRGY EGERSZEGI.

Innofinance Merchant Bank Plc: 1051 Budapest, Vörösmarty tér 2; tel. (1) 138-3366; telex 223182; fax (1) 117-7800; f. 1980; joint-stock company; registered cap. 500m. Ft; Chair. GÁBOR DICSŐ; Man. Dir JAN-ERIK LUNDBERG.

Merkantil Bank Ltd: 1051 Budapest, József Atilla u. 24; tel. (1) 118-2688; telex 202579; fax (1) 117-2331; f. 1988; affiliated to Commercial and Creditbank Ltd; cap. 1,100m. Ft; Pres. and Chief Exec. ÁDÁM KOLOSSVÁRY.

Portfolio Bank Ltd: 1117 Budapest, Budafoki út 79; tel. (1) 161-1050; fax (1) 162-0001; f. 1990; cap. 945m. Ft; Pres. and CEO CECÍLIA TORDAI; Chair. Dr GYÖRGY KOLLÁTH.

Other Financial Institutions

ÁFI-Állami Fejlesztési Intézet (State Development Institution): 1052 Budapest, Deák F. u. 5; tel. (1) 118-1200; telex 225672; fax (1) 118-3866; f. 1993 to succeed the State Development Institute; finance and control of governemnt investments; manages the regional development and job-creation projects subsidized by the state; manages the portfolio of assets arising from the conversion of the national debts or related to special government funds; collects and manages all liabilities of enterprises to the Government; Chair. and Dir-Gen. Dr MIKLÓS SZŐKE.

Pénzintézeti Központ (Central Corporation of Banking Companies): 1093 Budapest, Lónyai u. 38; tel. (1) 117-1255; telex 223484; f. 1916; banking, property, rights and interests, deposits, securities, and foreign exchange management; cap. 1,000m. Ft; Gen. Man. MIHÁLY BIRÓ.

STOCK EXCHANGE

Budapesti Értéktőzsde (Budapest Stock Exchange): 1052 Budapest, Deák Ferenc u. 5; tel. (1) 117-5226; fax (1) 118-1737; f. 1992; Chair. LAJOS BOKROS; Chief Exec. FARBOD LOTFI.

INSURANCE

In July 1986 the state insurance enterprise was divided into two companies, one of which retained the name of the former Állami Biztosító. Further companies have been founded since 1988.

AB-AEGON Általános Biztosító Rt. (State Insurance Co): 1813 Budapest, Üllői u. 1; tel. (1) 118-1866; telex 224875; fax (1) 117-7065; f. 1949 as Állami Biztosító, reorganized 1986, present name since 1992; handles life and property insurance, insurance of agricultural plants, co-operatives, foreign insurance, etc.; Gen. Man. Dr GÁBOR KEPECS.

Atlasz Utazási Biztosító (Atlasz Travel Insurance Co): 1052 Budapest, Deák F. u. 23; tel. (1) 118-1999; telex 226725; fax (1) 117-1529; f. 1988; cap. 1,000m. Ft; Gen. Man. GÁBOR DARVAS.

Garancia Biztosító Rt. (Garancia Insurance Co): 1052 Budapest, Semmelweis u. 17; tel. and fax (1) 117-6226; f. 1988; cap. 1,050m. Ft; Gen. Man. OTTÓ GAÁL.

Hungária Biztosító Rt. (Hungária Insurance Co): 1054 Budapest, Vadász u. 23–25; tel. (1) 269-0033; telex 222277; fax (1) 269-0679; f. 1986; handles international insurance, industrial and commercial insurance and motor-car, marine, life, household, accident and liability insurance; cap. 4,266m. Ft; Man. Dir TAMÁS UZONYI.

Trade and Industry

STATE PROPERTY AGENCY

Hungarian State Property Agency (ÁVÜ): 1133 Budapest, Pozsonyi út 56; tel. (1) 209-8600; fax (1) 120-8850; f. 1990; organizes the privatization of state-owned companies.

CHAMBERS OF COMMERCE AND AGRICULTURE

Magyar Gazdasági Kamara (Hungarian Chamber of Commerce): 1389 Budapest, POB 106; tel. (1) 153-3333; telex 224745; fax (1) 153-1285; f. 1850; federation of asscns representing Hungarian cos; develops trade with other countries; mediates between companies, etc.; mems: 66 regional and professional asscns and more than 8,000 industrial, agricultural and foreign trade orgs; Pres. LAJOS TOLNAY.

Budapesti Kereskedelmi és Iparkamara (Budapest Chamber of Industry and Commerce): 1016 Budapest, Krisztina krt 99; tel. (1) 175-6764; telex 225134; fax (1) 202-7930; Pres. IMRE TÓTH.

Magyar Agrárkamara (Hungarian Chamber of Agriculture): 1055 Budapest, Kossuth L. tér 11; tel. (1) 153-3000; Pres. KÁROLY FARKAS.

MAJOR INDUSTRIAL COMPANIES

Since 1980 Hungary's foreign trade organizations have been undergoing modernization. New regulations, introduced in 1988, permitted all business organizations to export products and to conduct business with foreign partners without the involvement of specialized traders. By the early 1990s more than 90% of all import activities had been liberalized and no special licences were required for foreign trading.

AÉV No 31: 1364 Budapest, POB 83; tel. (1) 118-0511; telex 224928; fax (1) 118-4082; f. 1951; state building factory; construction of industrial units, power plants, chemical combines, cement plants, etc.; undertakes building work abroad.

Agrária-Bábolna: 2943 Bábolna; tel. (34) 69-111; telex 226555; fax (34) 69-002; f. 1789; turn-key poultry and pig farms with breeding stock and feed premixes; hatching eggs, breeding poultry, pigs, sheep and breeding jumping and riding horses; processed chicken; rodent and insect extermination services, etc.; Gen. Dir LÁSZLÓ PAPOCSI.

Agrikon Engineering Co: 6001 Kecskemét, POB 43; tel. (76) 27-666; telex 26493; engineering and servicing for agricultural and food processing machines; Man. Dir PÁL HUGYECZ.

Agrimpex Trading Co Ltd: 1392 Budapest, POB 278; tel. (1) 111-3800; telex 225751; fax (1) 153-0658; f. 1948; agricultural products; Pres. and Gen. Man. ANDRÁS VERMES; 206 employees.

Agrober: 1518 Budapest, POB 93; tel. (1) 162-0640; fax (1) 161-2469; consulting engineers and contractors for the agriculture and food industry; Gen. Dir IMRE KONCZ.

Agrotek Mezőgazdasági Termelőeszköz Kereskedelmi V (Agrotek Agricultural Trading): 1388 Budapest, POB 66; tel. (1) 153-0555; telex 226522; fax (1) 153-4316; f. 1961; export and import of agricultural machinery and equipment, and fertilizers; Gen. Man. ÁKOS TAMÁS FEHÉR.

Alkaloida Chemical Company Ltd: 4440 Tiszavasvári, Kabay János u. 29; tel. (42) 372-511; telex 73275; fax (42) 372-512; f. 1927; production and marketing of pharmaceuticals, pesticides, etc.; cap. 4,860m. Ft; Gen. Dir LÁSZLÓ DUPCSÁK; 2,131 EMPLOYEES.

Artex International Trade Co Ltd: 1390 Budapest, POB 167; tel. (1) 153-0222; telex 224951; fax (1) 111-1295; f. 1949; furniture, carpets, household articles, sports goods, foodstuffs, hotel furnishing; Gen. Man. Dr ANDRÁS BIEBER.

BHG Telecommunication Works: 1509 Budapest, POB 2; tel. (1) 181-3300; telex 225933; fax (1) 166-7433; telecommunications; Gen. Dir LÁSZLÓ MIKICS.

Bivimpex Trading Co: 1325 Budapest, POB 55; tel. (1) 169-3522; telex 22-4279; fax (1) 169-4716; f. 1971; raw hide and leather; Dir L. VERMES.

Bőrker: 1391 Budapest, POB 215; tel. (1) 121-0760; telex 225543; fax (1) 142-9886; f. 1949; trading company for basic materials and accessories for shoes, fancy leather goods, garments and furniture; Gen. Man. LAJOS ALSÓSZENTIVÁNYI.

Buda-Flax: 1113 Budapest, Karolina ut 17; tel. (1) 166-6022; telex 225738; fax (1) 166-5486; foreign trading division of the Hungarian linen industry; Man. Dir JUDIT KOLAROVSZKI.

Budapesti Húsipari Vállalat: 1097 Budapest, Gubacsi u. 6; tel. (1) 134-3940; telex 224422; fax (1) 133-6868; meat processing factory; Man. Dir LÁSZLÓ JUHÁSZ; 597 employees.

Budavox: 1392 Budapest, POB 267; tel. (1) 181-3300; telex 225077; fax (1) 161-1288; f. 1956; exports telecommunications equipment and systems; Gen. Man. IKLODY GÁBOR.

BVM Concrete Works: 1117 Budapest, Budafoki út 209; tel. (1) 161-3810; telex 224877; fax (1) 161-2018; manufactures and exports concrete and reinforced concrete structures; Gen. Dir SÁNDOR SZIRBIK.

Chemokomplex Export-Import: 1389 Budapest, Andrássy út 60, POB 141; tel. (1) 112-2680; telex 225158; fax (1) 132-9980; machines and equipment for the chemical industry; Man. Dir FERENC NAGY.

Chemol Trading Co Ltd: 1134 Budapest, Robert Károly krt 61–65, POB 696; tel. (1) 269-8520; telex 224351; fax (1) 269-8590; export, import and domestic distribution of chemicals, agrochemicals, plastics, paints; 78% owned by Great Lakes Chemical Corpn, USA; Man. Dir ZOLTÁN GOMBOCZ; 302 employees.

Chinoin Medicine and Chemical: 1325 Budapest, POB 110; tel. (1) 169-0900; telex 224236; fax (1) 169-0293; f. 1910; pharmaceutical and chemical works; joint venture with Sanofi (France); Man. Dir M. ISTVÁN BIHARI; 3,333 employees.

CIBINTRA International Trading Company Ltd: 1051 Budapest, Bajcsy Zsilinszky u. 12; tel. (1) 118-8377; telex 226102; fax (1) 118-

5777; f. 1989; international trading house, with domestic activity also; joint venture between Közep-európai Hitelbank (50%) and Central-European International Bank (50%); Gen. Man. Dr MIKLÓS MARINOV.

Csépeli Duna: 1751 Budapest, POB 104; tel. (1) 2766-172; telex 226289; fax (1) 2768-534; steel tubes and pipes; Gen. Man. BÉLA SIMON.

Délker: 1051 Budapest, POB 70; tel. (1) 118-5888; telex 224428; fax (1) 118-1981; company for trading of tropical fruits, foodstuffs, cosmetics and household goods.

Dunaferr Acélszerkezetikft (Dunaferr Steel Works): 2400 Dunaújváros, Vasmuű tér 1–3; tel. (25) 11522; fax (25) 10929; 4,769 employees.

EMG—Electronic Measuring Gear Works: 1163 Budapest, Cziraky u. 26–32; tel. (1) 183-7751; telex 224535; fax (1) 183-7900; electronic measuring equipment; Gen. Man. ZOLTÁN K. SZABO.

Elektroimpex: 1392 Budapest, POB 296; tel. (1) 132-8300; telex 225771; fax (1) 131-0526; telecommunication and precision articles.

Elektromodul: 1390 Budapest, POB 158; tel. (1) 270-5340; telex 225154; fax (1) 140-2583; electro-technical components; Gen. Man. FERENC TIBORCZ.

ERBE Power Engineering and Consulting Ltd: 1065 Budapest, Bajosy-Zsilinszky út 57, POB 17; tel. (1) 153-0555; telex 225422; fax (1) 153-4051; power plant investment company; Man. Dir ANTAL VAVRIK.

Ferunion: 1051 Budapest, Mérleg u. 4; tel. (1) 117-2611; telex 225054; fax (1) 117-2594; tools, glassware, building materials, aluminium and steel packaging goods, stationery, various consunmer goods; Gen. Dir GYULA KOVÁCS.

FMV: 1475 Budapest, POB 215; tel. (1) 252-0666; telex 224409; fax (1) 183-5361; precision mechanics.

Folk-art: 1088 Budapest, Rákóczi u. 1-3; tel. (1) 266-6138; telex 226814; fax (1) 266-1489; f. 1948; wholesale, retail, and export sale of folk art, handicrafts and confectionery; Dir Dr JUDITH LENDVAI.

Gábor Áron Works: 1440 Budapest, POB 39; tel. (1) 133-7970; telex 224127; domestic and kitchen appliances; Dir SÁNDOR ANTAL.

Gamma Művek: 1519 Budapest, POB 330; tel. (1) 185-0800; telex 224946; fax (1) 166-5632; f. 1920; medical instruments and process control systems, elements for the instrumentation industry; Gen. Dir Dr TIVADAR MASCHEK.

Ganz Danubius Shipyard and Crane Factory: 1904 Budapest POB 280; tel. (1) 120-1625; telex 224200; fax (1) 210-1180; f. 1835.

Ganz Ansaldo Electric Ltd: 1024 Budapest, Lövőház u. 39; tel. (1) 175-3322; telex 225363; fax (1) 156-2989; f. 1878; electric power generators, transformers, switchgear, electrical vehicles.

Ganz-Hunslet Rt.: 1087 Budapest, Vajda P. u. 12; tel. (1) 133-6160; telex 202862; fax (1) 114-3481; f. 1844; railway rolling stock, underground trains, trams (light rail rolling stock); Jt CEOs S. F. KOSTYAL, G. MIXNER.

Ganz Instrument Ltd: 1191 Budapest, Üllői út 200; tel. (1) 147-0740; telex 224395; fax (1) 127-1025; all types of electrical measuring instrument; Gen. Dir ENDRE KADAS.

Generalimpex: 1518 Budapest, POB 168; tel. (1) 162-0200; telex 226758; fax (1) 165-6735; f. 1980; permitted to import or export any product; Dir LÁSZLÓ NAGY.

Geominco: 1027 Budapest, POB 92; tel. (1) 201-3122; telex 224442; geological and mining engineering; undertakes exploration and research.

Hajdú-Bihar Megyei Textilfeldolgozo Vállalat: 4220 Hajduboszormeny, Petofi u. 1–13; tel. (55) 11-833; telex 72354; fax (55) 11-034; textile and leather clothing factory; Dirs IMRE ELEK, ISTVÁN TOTH, IMRE NAGY.

Hungagent Ltd: 1374 Budapest, POB 542; tel. (1) 188-6180; telex 224526; fax (1) 188-8769; foreign representations agency; export-import.

Hungalu Kereskedelmi KFT (Hungalu Trading Ltd): 1388 Budapest, POB 63; tel. (1) 149-4750; fax (1) 140-2723; 432 employees.

Hungarocoop: 1370 Budapest, POB 334; tel. (1) 153-1711; telex 224858; fax (1) 153-3318; import and export of consumer goods.

Hungarofilm: 1054 Budapest, Báthori út 10; tel. (1) 153-3579; telex 225768; fax (1) 153-1850; f. 1956; film production and distribution; Pres. ISTVÁN VÁRADI.

Hungarofruct: 1394 Budapest, POB 386; tel. (1) 131-7120; telex 225351; fax (1) 153-1051; f. 1953; fresh, dehydrated and quick-frozen fruit and vegetables; Gen. Man. GYÖRGY TÁBORI.

Hungarotex: 1804 Budapest, POB 100; tel. (1) 117-4555; telex 224751; fax (1) 117-3410; f. 1953; textiles, garments, foodstuffs, etc; Gen. Man. LÁSZLÓ FÖLDVÁRI.

Hungexpo Publicity Co Ltd: 1441 Budapest, POB 44; tel. (1) 157-3555; telex 224188; fax (1) 183-6502; fairs, exhibitions; Dir-Gen. ISTVÁN KOVÁCS.

HUNGEXPO Advertising Agency Co Ltd: 1425 Budapest, POB 801; tel. (1) 1225-008; telex 224525; fax (1) 122-1021; advertising, printing, public relations, media buying and selling; Man. Dir MARIA VISY.

HUNICOOP Foreign Trade Company Ltd for Industrial Co-operation: 1367 Budapest 5, POB 111; tel. (1) 267-1477; fax (1) 267-1482; agency for foreign companies in Hungary, export and import.

IDEX Foreign Trading, Contracting and Engineering Co Ltd: 1011 Budapest, Fő u. 14–18; tel. (1) 201-3211; telex 22 4541; fax (1) 201-3128; f. 1953; precision engineering, electronics, construction, petroleum and gas.

Ikarus Egyedi Autobusz Gyár KFT (Ikarus Autobuses Ltd): 1630 Budapest, POB 3; tel. 252-9666; telex 224766; fax (1) 163-7066; f. 1895; construction and export of buses in complete state or in sets for assembly; Gen. Dir ANDRÁS SEMSEY; Tech. Dir JENŐ MÁDI; 8,590 employees.

Interag Holding PLC: 1136 Budapest, Pannónia u. 11, POB 184; tel. (1) 132-6770; telex 224776; fax (1) 153-0736; represents foreign firms; conducts general export-import business, domestic trade.

Intercooperation Co Ltd for Trade Promotion: 1085 Budapest, POB 136; tel. (1) 118-9966; fax (1) 118-2161; establishment and carrying out of co-operation agreements, representation of foreign companies, brands, marketing and distribution, joint ventures and import-export deals.

IPV (Publishing and Promotion Co for Tourism): 1140 Budapest, POB 164; tel. (1) 163-3652; telex 226074; fax (1) 183-7320; publishing, publicity, film-making, exhibitions, advertising; Gen. Man ISTVÁN FAZEKAS.

KGyV Metallurgical Engineering Corpn: 1138 Budapest, Révész st. 9; tel. (1) 140-3342; telex 224417; fax (1) 120-2101; f. 1951; manufacture of industrial furnaces and steel structures; Gen. Man. ANDRÁS BUDAI.

Komplex Foreign Trade Co: 1061 Budapest, Andrássy út 10, POB 125; tel. (1) 111-7010; telex 225957; fax (1) 111-7450; f. 1953; agricultural machinery, plant and equipment for food industry; Man. Dir ISTVÁN FEKETE.

Konsumex: 1446 Budapest, Hungária krt 162; tel. (1) 153-0511; telex 225151; fax (1) 141-4747; f. 1959; consumer goods, household articles, etc.; Gen. Man. MIHÁLY TEMESI.

Kopint-Datorg Economic Research Marketing and Computing Co Ltd: 1389 Budapest, POB 133; tel. (1) 266-6722; telex 266646; fax (1) 266-6483; f. 1964; economic research, information and marketing services, data processing, publishing; Gen. Dir JÁNOS DEÁK.

Kultúra Hungarian Foreign Trading Co: 1389 Budapest, POB 149; tel. (1) 201-4411; telex 224441; fax (1) 201-3207; f. 1950; books, periodicals, works of art, sheet music, teaching aids; Gen. Man. JÓZSEF MÉSZÁROS.

Labor Rt: Factory of Laboratory Instruments Co Ltd: 1450 Budapest, POB 33; tel. (1) 133-9708; telex 224162; fax (1) 134-0309; f. 1989; scientific instruments, laboratory equipment and engineering; Gen. Dir KÁROLY VARGA.

Lampart: 1475 Budapest, POB 41; tel. (1) 157-0111; telex 225365; fax (1) 157-2029; f. 1883; glass-lined processing equipment; Man. Dir ZOLTÁN RETI.

Lehel Hűtőgépgyár: 5101 Jászberény, POB 64; tel. (57) 312-014; fax (57) 311-847; export of domestic refrigerators; 3,200 employees.

Licencia: 1368 Budapest, POB 207; tel. (1) 118-1111; telex 225872; fax (1) 138-2304; f. 1950; purchase and sale of patents and inventions; Gen. Dir LAJOS VEROSZTA.

Lignitrade Co Ltd: 1393 Budapest, POB 323; tel. (1) 112-9850; telex 224251; fax (1) 132-2181; timber, paper and fuel.

Magnezitipari Movek: 1475 Budapest, POB 11; tel. (1) 157-5288; telex 225644; f. 1892; magnesium industry; Dir B. HAZAI.

Magyar Media Advertising Agency: 1392 Budapest, POB 279; tel. (1) 141-4749; telex 223040; direct mail, printing, publicity campaigns, advertising.

MAHIR Hungarian Publicity Company: 1818 Budapest, POB 367; tel. (1) 118-3444; telex 225341; fax (1) 117-9032; advertising agency; Commercial Dir MARIA JANCSO.

Margaréta GmbH: 1300 Budapest, POB 130; tel. (1) 188-8170; telex 226052; fax (1) 168-6205; textiles and textile printing; Dir Dr LÁSZLÓ MOSKOVITS.

Masped Hungarian General Forwarding Co Ltd: 1052 Budapest, Kristóf tér 2; tel. (1) 118-2922; telex 224471; fax (1) 118-8343; international forwarding and carriage; Gen. Man. ISTVÁN KAUTZ; 300 employees.

Mechaniki Művek: 1518 Budapest, POB 64; tel. (1) 227-3800; telex 225842; fax (1) 227-3827; f. 1936; electrical equipment; Man. Dir JÁNOS HEINRICH.

Medicor Trading Co Ltd: 1389 Budapest, POB 150; tel. (1) 149-5130; telex 225051; fax (1) 149-5957; medical instruments, X-ray apparatus and complete hospital installations; Dir ÁRPÁD KEVEHÁZI.

Medimpex: 1808 Budapest; tel. (1) 118-3955; telex 225477; fax (1) 117-7179; f. 1949; export, import and distribution of pharmaceutical and biological products, veterinary drugs, laboratory chemicals; Man. Dir LÁSZLÓ LOVAS; 480 employees.

Melyepterv Consulting Engineering: 1051 Budapest, Vigado tér 1; tel. (1) 117-3434; telex 224723; fax (1) 117-8623; water supply and environmental planning projects; Gen. Dir FERENC VARGA.

Mertcontrol Quality Control Co Ltd: 1245 Budapest, POB 983; tel. (1) 132-5300; telex 225777; fax (1) 111-6897; f. 1951; quality control of import and export goods.

Metalimpex Trade Co Ltd: 1393 Budapest, POB 330; tel. (1) 142-7752; telex 225251; fax (1) 122-8696; metals and metal products; Gen. Dir TIBOR TÓTH.

Metrimpex: 1391 Budapest, POB 202; tel. (1) 112-5600; telex 225451; fax (1) 131-2781; electronic, nuclear and other instruments and equipment.

MIKROMED KFT: 2500 Esztergom, Beke tér 1–11; tel. (33) 13-400; telex 027711; fax (33) 12-940; joint venture producing medical equipment; Man. Dir BÉLA BADI.

Mineralimpex: 1062 Budapest, Andrássy út 64; tel. (1) 131-6720; telex 224651; fax (1) 153-1779; oils, oil products and gas; Dir-Gen. Dr JÓZSEF TÓTH; 196 employees.

MODEXCO Trading and Servicing Ltd: 1027 Budapest 62, Csalogány u. 23, POB 475; tel. (1) 201-6333; telex 227620; fax (1) 135-9734; ready-made clothing export, fabric and machine import, leasing.

Mogürt Trading Co: 1113 Budapest, Baitás Béla út 156, POB 249; tel. (1) 118-6044; telex 225357; fax (1) 118-8895; f. 1946; motor vehicles; Gen. Man. TIBOR CSAJBI; 634 employees.

MOL Magyar Olaj és Gáziparirt (MOL Hungarian Oil and Gas): 1117 Budapest, Schönherz Zoltán u. 18; tel. (1) 166-4413; fax (1) 166-7760; responsible for all petroleum and national gas production; state shareholding company, due to be privatized in 1994; 22,091 employees.

MOM: 1525 Budapest, POB 52; tel. (1) 156-4122; telex 224151; f. 1876; laboratory and optical instruments; Man. Dir JÓZSEF SEBESFI.

Monimpex Trading House: 1392 Budapest, POB 268; tel. (1) 153-1222; telex 225371; fax (1) 112-1072; wines, spirits, spices, honey, sweets, ornamental plants, fresh and processed vegetables and fruits, coffee and cocoa.

MVMT (Hungarian Power Cos Ltd): 1011 Budapest, Vám 5–7, POB 34; tel. (1) 201-5455; telex 224382; fax (1) 202-1246; Hungarian national electricity shareholding company, due to be privatized in 1994.

Nikex Trading Co Ltd: 1016 Budapest, Mészáros u. 48–54; tel. (1) 156-0122; telex 224971; fax (1) 175-5131; industrial equipment foreign trading co; Man. Dir MIHÁLY PETRIK.

Novex: 1087 Budapest, Könyves Kálmán Krt. 76; tel. (1) 133-8933; telex 223825; fax (1) 113-8665; foreign trade; Man. Dir JÁNOS KOZMA.

Ofotért: 1135 Budapest, Reítter Ferenc 45; tel. (1) 120-3669; telex 224418; fax (1) 149-7760; f. 1949; optical and photographic articles; Gen. Dir JÁNOS SZILÁGYI.

OMKER: 1476 Budapest, POB 223; tel. (1) 112-3000; telex 224683; fax (1) 133-8718; f. 1950; medical instruments; Gen. Dir Dr RÓBERT ZENTAI; 420 employees.

ORION: 1475 Budapest, POB 84; tel. (1) 128-4830; telex 225798; fax (1) 127-2490; f. 1913; televisions, satellite receivers, digital microwave and other electrical goods; Gen. Dir CSABA NÉMETH.

Paksi Atomerőmű v Pav (Paks Nuclear Plant): 7031 Paks, POB 71; tel. (75) 11222; fax (75) 155-133; 3,698 employees.

Pannonia-Csepel International Trading Co Ltd: 1241 Budapest, POB 179; tel. (1) 132-938; telex 225128; fax (1) 132-7318; metallurgical materials, welding electrodes, cast iron fittings; steel tubes and cylinders, bicycles, industrial sewing and pressing machinery and laundry equipment, complete tube manufacturing plants, bottle palnts, etc.

Patria Nyomda: 1088 Budapest, Szentiralyi u. 47; tel. (1) 134-0186; telex 226271; fax (1) 114-0876; office stationery; Gen. Man. SÁNDOR VASS.

Pharmatrade Hungarian Trading Co: 1367 Budapest, POB 126; tel. (1) 118-5966; telex 226650; fax (1) 118-5346; medicinal plants, natural cosmetics, medicinal muds and waters, food and feed additives, seeds, honey and bee products, fruit and vegetables, radioactive products.

Philatelia Hungarica: 1373 Budapest, POB 600; tel. (1) 131-6146; telex 226508; fax (1) 111-5421; f. 1950; stamps; wholesale only; Gen. Man. ISTVÁN ZALÁVÁRI.

Phylaxia-Sanofi: 1107 Budapest, Szállás u. 5; tel. (1) 157-5454; telex 224549; fax (1) 127-4617; vaccines, veterinary products, medicines; Gen. Man. FERENC CZELLENG; 170 employees.

Precision Fittings Factory: 3301 Eger, POB 2; tel. (36) 11911; telex 63331; fax (36) 11112.

RÁBA (Hungarian Railway Carriage and Machine Works): 9002 Györ, POB 50; tel. (96) 12111; telex 024255; fax (96) 14311; f. 1896; commercial vehicles, diesel engines, agricultural tractors; Gen. Man. FERENC KÁRPÁTI; 9,545 employees.

Sasad: 1112 Budapest, Budaörsi ut 1289; tel. (1) 166-9000; telex 224789; fax (1) 186-8399; horticultural products, including bulbs, trees, shrubs and cut flowers; Pres. LÁSZLÓ MIHÁLIK.

Skála-Coop: 1300 Budapest, POB 29; tel. (1) 180-5785; telex 227637; fax (1) 168-7800; national co-operative company for purchase and disposal of goods including fine ceramics and glassware, industrial, agricultural and household metal ware, hand tools, electronic games, rubber and plastic products, cosmetics and chemicals, wood and paper industry products, leather and textile industry products, ready-to-wear clothing, vegetables and other food stuffs; Chair. and Chief Exec. ISTVÁN IMRE.

Somogyi Erdö és Fafeldolgozo Gazdaság (Somogy Forestry and Timber Company): 7400 Kaposvár, Bajcsy-Zs, u. 21; tel. (82) 315-022; telex 13348; fax (82) 310-048; wood and wood products, hunting services; Gen. Man. JÓSZEF BÓNA; 1,900 employees.

Szeged Szalamigyar és Hűsuzem: 6725 Szeged, Alsovarosi ff. 64; tel. (62) 26-033; telex 82226; fax (62) 10-643; meat-processing factory; Man. Dir VILMOS BIHARI.

Tannimpex: 1395 Budapest, POB 406; tel. (1) 112-3400; telex 224557; fax (1) 153-2170; leather, shoes, leather garments, fancy leather goods and furs.

Tatabánya Mining Co: 2803 Tatabánya, POB 323; tel. (34) 10144; telex 226206; fax (34) 11061; f. 1894; production of mining equipment and machinery, preparation of industrial and drinking water, purification of waste waters, dewatering of sludges, tunnelling; Gen. Man. LÁSZLÓ VAS; 3,040 emplyees.

Taurus Hungarian Rubber Works: 1965 Budapest, POB 48; tel. (1) 210-1010; telex 224201; fax (1) 113-5434; f. 1882; rubber; Chief Exec. Dr LÁSZLÓ PALOTÁS; 5,074 employees.

Technoimpex: 1390 Budapest, POB 183; tel. (1) 266-3611; telex 227141; fax (1) 266-6418; international trading house specializing in commodities, metals, petroleum products; organizes barter deals, co-operation, leasing and joint ventures; Chair. ISTVÁN MÁTYÁS; CEO SEBESTYÉN VÁRADI

Temaforg: 1476 Budapest, POB 114; tel. (1) 127-7880; telex 223456; fax (1) 157-4224; textile and synthetic wastes, industrial wipers, geotextiles for agriculture, road and railway construction; Dir-Gen. ANDOR SCHNEIDER.

Terta, Telefongyár: 1956 Budapest, POB 16; tel. (1) 252-6949; telex 224087; fax (1) 252-9161; f. 1876; telecommunications and data teleprocessing systems.

Tesco Co Ltd: 1367 Budapest, POB 101; tel. (1) 111-0850; telex 224642; fax (1) 153-1852; f. 1962; organization for international technical and scientific co-operation; export and import of technical services world-wide; Gen. Man. ISTVÁN BENE; 270 employees.

Tisza Chemical Works (Tiszamenti Vegyimüvek): 5007 Szolnok, Tószegi út 1; tel. (56) 35800; fax (56) 36732; 5,611 employees.

Transelektro: 1394 Budapest, POB 377; tel. (1) 132-0100; telex 224571; fax (1) 153-0308; f. 1957; generators, power stations, cables, lighting, transformers, household appliances, catering equipment, etc.; Dir-Gen. PÉTER SZÉKELY.

Tungsram Co Ltd: 1340 Budapest, Váci út 77; tel. (1) 169-2800; telex 225058; fax (1) 169-2868; f. 1896; light sources, lighting systems, lighting machinery; CEO CHARLES PIEPER .

UKM Rekard KFT: 9027 Győr, Kandó Kálmán u. 5–7; tel. (96) 313-122; telex 324360; fax (96) 313-559; farm equipment; Man. Dir IMRE SZABÓ.

Uvaterv: 1016 Budapest, Krisztina krt 99; tel. (1) 156-9000; telex 225265; fax (1) 156-7002; engineering and consultancy services, building contracting; Gen. Dir GYULA BRETZ.

Vasvill: 3520 Miskolc, Setany u. 1; tel. (46) 70-777; telex 62394; fax (46) 79-257; consumer and industrial products; Gen. Man. JENŐ MONOSTORY.

Vegyépszer Co Ltd: 1397 Budapest, POB 540; tel. (1) 135-1125; telex 226930; fax (1) 116-9470; building and assembling of chemical plant, supply of complete equipment, engineering, environment protection; Gen. Dir FERENC DERCZY.

Vetomag: 1056 Budapest, Váci u.; tel. (1) 138-2033; telex 227126; fax (1) 118-1721; horticultural seeds production; Pres. Dr JÁNOS CSISZER; GEN. DIR ENDRE TÓTH.

Videoton Rt.: 1398 Budapest, POB 557; tel. (1) 121-0520; telex 224763; fax (1) 142-1398; consumer electronics, computer technology; Gen. Dir ANDRÁS GEDE.

Volánpack Vállalat: 1108 Budapest, Kozma u. 4; tel. (1) 280-3080; telex 226935; fax (1) 127-6031; forwarding and transport, packaging, warehousing, etc.; Dir LÁSZLÓ KAPCSOS.

Zalahús: Zalaegerszeg, Balatoni út; tel. (92) 11-200; telex 33231; meat-processing factory; Man. Dir IMRE FARKAS.

TRADE FAIRS

Budapest International Fairs: Hungexpo, 1441 Budapest, POB 44; tel. (1) 157-3555; telex 224188; f. 1968; technical goods (spring), consumer goods (autumn), and other specialized exhibitions and fairs.

EXPO World Exposition Bureau: 1054 Budapest, Kossuth Lajos tér 4; tel. (1) 112-9205; fax (1) 153-0124.

CO-OPERATIVE ORGANIZATIONS

Általános Fogyasztási Szövetkezetek Országos Szövetsége (ÁFEOSz) (National Federation of Consumer Co-operatives): 1054 Budapest, Szabadság tér 14; tel. (1) 153-4222; telex 224862; fax (1) 111-3647; safeguards interests of Hungarian consumer co-operative societies, co-owner of co-operative foreign trading companies and joint ventures; Pres. Dr PÁL BARTUS; 1.2m. mems.

Ipari Szövetkezetek Országos Szövetsége (OKISz) (National Federation of Industrial Co-operatives): 1146 Budapest, Thököly u. 58–60; tel. (1) 141-5181; telex 227576; fax (1) 141-5521; safeguards interests of over 1,500 member co-operatives; Pres. CSABA SÜMEGHY.

Országos Szövetkezeti Tanács (OSzT) (National Co-operative Council): 1054 Budapest, Szabadság tér 14; tel. (1) 112-7467; telex 224862; fax (1) 111-3647; f. 1968; Pres. Dr PÁL SZILVASÁN; Sec. Dr JÓZSEF PÁL.

Termelőszövetkezetek Országos Tanácsa (TOT) (National Council of Agricultural Co-operatives): 1054 Budapest, Akadémia u. 1–3; tel. (1) 132-8167; telex 226810; f. 1967; Pres. ISTVÁN SZABÓ; Gen. Sec. Dr JÁNOS ELEKI; 1,280 co-operatives with 816,000 mems.

TRADE UNIONS

Since 1988, and particularly after the restructuring of the former Central Council of Hungarian Trade Unions (SzOT) as the National Confederation of Hungarian Trade Unions (MSzOSz) in 1990, several new union federations have been created. Several unions are affiliated to more than one federation, and others are completely independent.

Trade Union Federations

Autonóm Szakszervezetek (Autonomous Trade Unions): c/o Magyar Vegyipari Dolgozók Szakszervezeti Szövetsége, 1068 Budapest, Benczúr u. 45; tel. (1) 142-1776; Pres. LAJOS FŐCZE.

Principal affiliated unions include:

Magyar Vegyipari Dolgozók Szakszervezeti Szövetsége (Federation of Hungarian Chemical Industry Workers' Unions): 1068 Budapest, Benczúr u. 45; tel. (1) 142-1778; telex 22 3420; fax (1) 142-9975; f. 1906; Pres. LAJOS FŐCZE; 72,000 mems.

Értelmiségi Szakszervezeti Tömörülés—ÉSzT (Federation of Unions of Intellectual Workers): 1068 Budapest, Gorkij fasor 10; tel. (1) 122-8456; Pres. Dr LÁSZLÓ KIS; Gen. Sec. Dr GÁBOR BÁNK.

Független Szakszervezetek Demokratikus Ligája—FSzDL (Democratic League of Independent Trade Unions): 1146 Budapest, Thököly út 156; tel. (1) 142-6957; fax (1) 142-8143; f. 1989; Pres. CSABA ÓRY; 80,000 mems.

Principal affiliated unions include:

Tudományos Dolgozók Demokratikus Szakszervezete (TDDSz) (Democratic Trade Union of Scientific Workers): 1068 Budapest, Városligeti fasor 38; tel. (1) 142-8438; f. 1988; Chair. PÁL FORGACS.

Magyar Szakszervezetek Országos Szövetsége (MSzOSz) (National Confederation of Hungarian Trade Unions): 1415 Budapest, Dózsa György u. 84B; tel. (1) 153-2900; telex 225861; fax (1) 141-4342; f. 1898, reorganized 1990; Pres. Dr SÁNDOR NAGY; 1,700,000 mems.

Principal affiliated unions include:

Bányaipari Dolgozók Szakszervezeti Szövetsége (Federation of Mineworkers' Unions): 1068 Budapest, Városligeti fasor 46–48; tel. (1) 122-1226; telex 227499; fax (1) 142-1942; f. 1913; Pres. ANTAL SCHALKHAMMER; Vice-Pres. JÓZSEF KOCZI; 102,136 mems.

Bőripari Dolgozók Szakszervezete (Union of Leather Industry Workers): 1062 Budapest, Bajza u. 24; tel. (1) 142-9970; f. 1868; Pres. LÁSZLÓ TURZO; Gen. Sec. TIBOR TRÉBER; 48,518 mems.

Egészségügyben Dolgozók Szakszervezeteinek Szövetsége (Union of Health Service Workers): 1051 Budapest, Nádor u. 32, POB 36; tel. (1) 110645; f. 1945; Pres. Dr ZOLTÁN SZABÓ; Gen. Sec. Dr PÁLNÉ KÁLLAY; 280,536 mems.

Építő-, Fa-és Építőanyagipari Dolgozók Szakszervezeteinek Szövetsége (Federation of Building, Wood and Building Industry Workers' Unions): 1068 Budapest, Dózsa György u. 84A; tel. (1) 122-9426; f. 1906; Pres. JÁNOS NOGYMIHÓLY; Vice-Pres. ANTAL MIHALUSZ; 365,561 mems.

Helyiipari és Városgazdasági Dolgozók Szövetségének (Federation of Local Industry and Municipal Workers' Unions): 1068 Budapest, Benczúr u. 43; tel. (1) 111-6950; f. 1952; Pres. JÓZSEFNÉ SVEVER; Gen. Sec. PÁL BAKÁNYI; 281,073 mems.

Kereskedelmi Alkalmazottak Szakszervezete: (Commercial Employees' Trade Union): 1066 Budapest, Jókai u. 6; tel. (1) 131-8970; fax (1) 132-3382; f. 1900; Gen. Sec. Dr JÁNOS VÁGÓ; 149,090 mems.

Közlekedési Dolgozók Szakszervezeteinek Szövetségé (Federation of Transport Workers' Unions): 1428 Budapest, Köztársaság tér 3; tel. (1) 210-0160; f. 1898; Pres. ISTVÁN TRENKA; 5,676 mems.

Magyar Élelmezésipari Dolgozók Szakszervezeteinek Szövetsége (Federation of Food Industry Workers' Unions): 1068 Budapest, Városligeti fasor 44; tel. (1) 122-5880; fax (1) 142-8568; f. 1905; Pres. GYULA SÓKI; Gen. Sec. BÉLA VANEK; 226,243 mems.

Magyar Pedagógusok Szakszervezete (Hungarian Union of Teachers): 1068 Budapest, Városligeti fasor 10; tel. (1) 122-8456; fax (1) 142-8122; f. 1945; Gen. Sec. ISTVÁNNÉ SZÖLLŐSI; 200,000 mems.

Magyar Textilipari Dolgozók Szakszervezete (Hungarian Union of Textile Workers): 1068 Budapest, Rippl-Rónai u. 2; tel. (1) 428-196; fax (1) 122-5414; f. 1905; Pres. (vacant); Gen. Sec. TAMÁS KELETI; 70,241 mems.

Mezőgazdasági, Erdészeti és Vizgazdálkodási Dolgozók Szakszervezeteinek Szövetsége tagszervezeteiből (Federation of Agricultural, Forestry and Water Conservancy Workers' Unions): 1066 Budapest, Jókai u. 2–4; tel. (1) 131-4550; telex 227535; f. 1906; Pres. (vacant); Gen. Sec. TIBOR CZIRMAY; 389,569 mems.

Müvészeti Szakszervezetek Szövetsége (Federation of Hungarian Artworkers' Unions): 1068 Budapest, Gorkij fasor 38; tel. (1) 121-1120; fax (1) 122-5412; f. 1957; Gen. Sec. KÁLMÁN PETŐ; 32,000 mems.

Nyomdadaipari Dolgozók Szakszervezete (Printers' Union): 1085 Budapest, Kölcsey u. 2; tel. (1) 114-2413; telex 202612; fax (1) 134-2160; f. 1862; Pres. ANDRÁS BÁRSONY; Vice-Pres JÁNOS ACZÉL, ZOLTÁN GODZSA; 49,436 mems.

Postai Dolgozók Szakszervezete (Federation of Trade Unions of Postal and Communications Employees): 1146 Budapest, Cházár András u. 13; tel. (1) 142-8777; fax (1) 121-4018; f. 1945; Pres. ENIKŐ HESZKY-GRICSER; 69,900 mems.

Ruházatipari Dolgozók Szakszervezete (Union of Clothing Workers): 1077 Budapest, Almássy tér 2; tel. (1) 142-3702; f. 1892; Gen. Sec. GÁBOR VERES; 19,000 mems.

Vas-és Fémipari Dolgozók Szakszervezeti Szövetsége (Confederation of Iron and Metallurgical Industry Workers' Unions): 1086 Budapest, Magdolna u. 5–7; tel. (1) 113-5200; telex 224791; fax (1) 133-8327; f. 1877; Pres. LÁSZLÓ PASZTERNÁK; 535,000 mems.

Vasutasok Szakszervezete (Union of Railway Workers): 1068 Budapest, Benczúr u. 41; tel. (1) 122-1895; telex 226819; f. 1945; Pres. PÁL PAPP; Gen. Sec. FERENC KOSZORUS; 196,698 mems.

Szakszervezetek Együttműködési Fóruma—SzEF (Central Authority of Trade Unions): 1068 Budapest, Gorkij fasor 10; tel. (1) 122-8099; Pres. ISTVÁNNÉ SZÖLLŐSI.

Principal affiliated unions include:

Közszolgálati Szakszervezetek Szövetsége (Federation of Public Workers' Unions): 1088 Budapest, Puskin u. 4; tel. (1) 118-8900; fax (1) 118-7360; f. 1945; Pres. Dr ENDRE SZABÓ.

Transport

RAILWAYS

Magyar Államvasutak (MÁV) (Hungarian State Railways): 1940 Budapest, Andrássy ut 73–75; tel. (1) 142-8948; telex 224342; fax (1) 142-8342; state-owned since its foundation in 1868; total network 7,600 km, including 2,164 km of electrified lines; Head Int. Affairs JÓZSEF LOVAS.

Győr–Sopron–Ebenfurti-Vasut—Gysev-ROeEE (Railway of Győr–Sopron–Ebenfurt): 9400 Sopron, Matyas Kiraly u. 19;

Hungarian-Austrian-owned railway; 84 km in Hungary, 82 km in Austria, all electrified; transport of passengers and goods; Dir-Gen. Dr JÁNOS BERÉNYI.

There is an underground railway in Budapest, with a network of 23 km in 1989; in that year 296m. passengers were carried. In 1991 the total rail network in Hungary amounted to 10,607 km and carried some 272m. passengers.

ROADS

At the end of 1991 the road network totalled 105,930 km, including 351 km of motorways, 6,745 km of main or national roads and 23,151 km of secondary roads. There are extensive long-distance bus services. Road passenger and freight transport is provided by the state-owned Volán companies and by individual (own account) operators.

Hungarocamion: 1442 Budapest, POB 108; tel. (1) 157-3811; telex 225455; international road freight transport company; 17 offices in Europe and the Middle East; fleet of 1,800 lorries; Gen. Man. IMRE TORMA; 4,927 employees.

Volán Vállalatok Központja (Centre of Volán Enterprises): 1391 Budapest, Erzsébet krt 96, POB 221; tel. (1) 112-4290; telex 225177; centre of 25 Volán enterprises for inland and international road freight and passenger transport, forwarding, tourism; fleet of 17,000 lorries, incl. special tankers for fuel, refrigerators, trailers, 8,000 buses for regular passenger transport; 3 affiliates, offices and joint-ventures in Europe; Head KÁLMÁN GARAMI.

SHIPPING AND INLAND WATERWAYS

At the end of 1991 the Hungarian river merchant fleet comprised 242 vessels, with a capacity totalling 254,203 dwt, and the ocean merchant fleet comprised 11 vessels totalling 90,877 dwt.

MAHART—Magyar Hajózási Rt. (Hungarian Shipping Co): 1366 Budapest, POB 58; tel. (1) 118-1880; telex 225258; fax (1) 118-0733; carries passenger traffic on the Danube and Lake Balaton; cargo services on the Danube and its tributaries, Lake Balaton, and also Mediterranean and ocean-going services; operates port of Budapest (container terminal, loading, storage, warehousing, handling and packaging services); ship-building and ship-repair services; Dir-Gen. ANDRÁS FÁY.

MAFRACHT: 1364 Budapest 4, POB 105; tel. (1) 118-5276; telex 226128; fax (1) 118-4170; shipping agency.

CIVIL AVIATION

The Ferihegy international airport is 16 km from the centre of Budapest. Ferihegy-2 opened in 1985. Public internal air services were scheduled to resume in May 1993, after an interval of 20 years, between Budapest and Nyíregyháza, Debrecen, Szeged, Pécs, Szombathely and Győr.

Légügyi Főigazgatóság (General Directorate of Civil Aviation): 1400 Budapest, Dob u. 75–81, POB 87; tel. (1) 142-2544; telex 225729; controls civil aviation; Dir-Gen. ÖDÖN SKONDA.

Légiforgalmi és Repülőtéri Igazgatóság (LRI) (Air Traffic and Airport Administration): 1675 Budapest, POB 53; tel. (1) 157-9123; telex 224054; fax (1) 157-6982; f. 1973; controls civil air traffic and operates Ferihegy and Siófok Airports; Dir-Gen. TAMÁS ERDEI.

Magyar Légiközlekedési Részvénytársaság—MALÉV Rt. (Hungarian Airlines): 1367 Budapest, Roosevelt tér 2, POB 122; tel. (1) 266-9033; telex 224954; fax (1) 266-2417; f. 1946; regular services from Budapest to Europe, North Africa and the Middle East; Gen. Dir ANDRÁS PÁKAY.

Tourism

Tourism has developed rapidly and is an important source of foreign exchange. In 1992 convertible-currency income from tourism totalled some US $1,200m. Rouble receipts in 1990 reached 90m., considerably less than in 1989. Lake Balaton is the main holiday centre for boating, bathing and fishing. The cities have great historical and recreational attractions. The annual Budapest Spring Festival is held in March. Budapest has numerous swimming pools watered by thermal springs, which are equipped with modern physiotherapy facilities. In 1992 there were 33.5m. foreign visitors (including 11.4m. visitors in transit), a slight increase on the previous year. There were 47,317 hotel beds in 1986, and a further 8,000–10,000 were to be created by 1994.

IBUSZ—Idegenforgalmi, Beszerzési, Utazási és Szállítási Rt. (Hungarian Travel Agency): 1364 Budapest, Ferenciek tér 5; tel. (1) 118-6866; telex 224976; fax (1) 117-7723; f. 1902; has 118 brs throughout Hungary; Gen. Man. Dr ERIKA SZEMENKÁR.

Országos Idegenforgalmi Hivatal (OIH) (Hungarian Tourist Board): 1051 Budapest, Vigadó u. 6; tel. (1) 118-0750; telex 225182; fax (1) 118-5241; f. 1968; Head Dr TAMAS TEGLASSY.

Culture

NATIONAL ORGANIZATIONS

Ministry of Education and Culture: see section on The Government (Ministries).

International Cultural Institute (Nemzetközi Kulturális Intézet): 1051 Budapest, Dorottya u. 8; tel. (1) 118-3899; telex 224735; fax (1) 118-5145; co-ordinates non-governmental international cultural, educational, research and scientific relations; Dir-Gen. G. NÁDOR.

CULTURAL HERITAGE

Budapest History Museum (Budapesti Történeti Múzeum): 1014 Budapest, Szent György tér 2; tel. (1) 175-7533; fax (1) 455-9175; f. 1887; history of Budapest from Roman to modern times; fine arts; Dir-Gen. Dr GÉZA BUZINKAY.

Hungarian National Gallery (Magyar Nemzeti Galéria): 1250 Budapest, Budavári Palota; tel. (1) 175-7533; telex 223467; fax (1) 175-8898; f. 1957; collections include Hungarian art from 11th to 20th centuries; Dir Dr LÓRÁND BERECZKY.

Hungarian National Museum (Magyar Nemzeti Múzeum): 1088 Budapest, Múzeum krt 14–16, POB 364; tel. (1) 138-2122; fax (1) 117-7806; f. 1802; Dir-Gen. Dr ALÁN KRALOVÁSZKY.

Museum of Applied Arts (Iparművészati Múseum): 1091 Budapest, Üllői u. 33; tel. (1) 217-5222; fax (1) 217-5838; f. 1872; European and Hungarian decorative arts; library and publishes catalogues; Gen. Dir Dr ZSUSA LOVAG.

Museum of Fine Arts (Szépművészeti Múzeum): 1146 Budapest, Dózsa György út 41; tel. (1) 142-9759; fax (1) 122-8298; f. 1896, opened 1906; collections include Egyptian and Greco-Roman antiquities, and foreign paintings, sculptures, drawings and engravings; Dir Dr MIKLÓS MOJZER.

National Centre of Museums (Központi Múzeumi Igazgatósag): 1450 Budapest, Kinizsi u. 39; tel. (1) 117-5950; f. 1961; organizes exhibitions for museums; handles international transportation of *objets d'art* for museums; experimental, documentary and advisory centre for conservation and museological education; Dir Dr SZATMÁRI SAROLTA.

National Széchényi Library (Országos Széchényi Könyvtar): 1827 Budapest, Budavári Palota F-épulet; tel. (1) 155-6167; telex 224226; fax (1) 202-0804; f. 1802; 2.5m. books and periodicals, 4.5m. manuscripts, maps, prints, microfilms, etc.; Dir-Gen. GÉZA POPRÁDY.

SPORTING ORGANIZATIONS

National Office for Physical Education and Sport (Országos Testnevélsi és Sporthivatal—OTSH): 1054 Budapest, Hold u. 1; tel. (1) 111-9080; fax (1) 153-2950; dept of the Ministry of Culture and Education; Pres. REZSŐ GALLOV.

Olympic Committee of the Republic of Hungary: 1118 Budapest, Balogh Tihamer 4; tel. (1) 186-8000; telex 223296; fax (1) 186-9670; f. 1895; Pres. POL SCHMITT; Sec.-Gen. TAMÁS AJAN.

PERFORMING ARTS

Budapest Opera House: Budapest, Andrassy u.; f. 1884.

Erkel Theatre: Budapest, Koztársaság tér 30.

National Ballet School: Budapest, Drechsler Palace, Nepkoztarsasag út.

Film Studio

MAFILM—Magyar Filmgyarto Vállalat: Budapest, Rona u. 174; tel. (1) 251-5666; telex 226860; fax (1) 251-2896; films, videos, advertisements, management of actors; Gen. Dir LÁSZLÓ VINCZE.

ASSOCIATIONS

Federation of Hungarian Film and TV Artists (Magyar Film-és TV-Mřvészek Szövetsége): 1068 Budpaest, Gorkij fasor u. 38; tel. (1) 142-4760.

Federation of Hungarian Fine and Applied Artists (Magyar Képzőművészek és Iparművészek Szövetsége): 1051 Budapest, Vörösmarty tér 1; tel. (1) 117-6222; Pres. Dr LAJOS NÉMETH.

Hungarian Choral and Orchestra Federation (Magyar Kórusok és Zenekarok Szövetsége): 1051 Budapest, Vörösmarty tér 1; tel. (1) 117-9510; Dir JÓZSEF TÓTHPÁL.

Hungarian Theatrical Artists Federation (Magyar Színházművésti Szövetség): 1068 Budapest, Gorkij fasor 38; tel. (1) 142-0146; Mems of Man. Bd LÁSZLÓ BABARCZY, ANDRÁS BÁLINT, PÉTER HUSZTI, TAMÁS KOLTAI, GÁBOR SZÉKELY, LÁSZLÓ VÁMOS.

Education

In 1990 government spending on all levels of education amounted to approximately 143,200m. forint, 11.0% of total public expenditure. Pre-primary education in Hungary is not compulsory, but, in 1990, about 87% of children between the ages of three and six years were attending kindergartens (óvodák). Children under the age of three years attend crèches (bölcsődék). Education is compulsory for children between the ages of six and 16 years, although most continue their schooling beyond that age. Children attend a basic school (általános iskola) until they are 14, studying general subjects together with some practical training; special provision is made in basic schools for talented children, particularly those with notable ability in languages. Of children who left full-time education in 1989, 94% had completed the eight grades of primary education.

Secondary education starts at the age of 14 years. There are three principal types of secondary school: the gymnasium (gimnázium) provides a four-year course of mainly academic studies, although some vocational training is included in the curriculum; the vocational school (technikum) curriculum provides full vocational training, together with general education; and the apprentice training school (ipari tanulók gyakorló iskolai), which are attached to factories, agricultural co-operatives, etc., and provide training leading to full trade qualifications, with general education having a less prominent role. In addition, there are special schools both for children with physical and/or learning difficulties, and for the particularly gifted. Educational reform aimed at revising the curricula and the method of assessing pupils is taking place. In southern Hungary bilingual schools are being established to promote the languages of national minorities. There are 77 higher education institutes, of which 10 are universities and nine technical universities.

UNIVERSITIES

Albert Szent-György Medical University (Szent-György Albert Orvostudománti Egyetem): 6720 Szeged, Dugonics tér 13; tel. (62) 12-729; telex 82441; f. 1872, refounded 1921 as Medical Faculty of Szeged University, independent 1951; 2 faculties; 721 teachers; 2,135 students; Rector Prof. Dr L. FRATER.

Budapest University of Economic Sciences (Budapesti Közgazdaságtudományi Egyetem): 1093 Budapest IX, Fővám tér 8; tel. (1) 117-6268; telex 224186; fax (1) 117-8883; f. 1948; 574 teachers; 4,600 students; Rector R. ANDORKA.

Debrecen University Medical School (Debreceni Orvostudományi Egyetem): 4012 Debrecen, Nagyerdei krt 98; tel. (52) 317-571; telex 72411; fax (52) 319-807; f. 1918 as Faculty of Medicine of István Tirza University, independent 1951; 701 teachers; 1,400 students; Rector Dr L. GERGELY.

Janus Pannonius University of Pécs (Pécsi Janus Pannonius Tudományegyetem): 7633 Pécs, Szántó Kovács J. u. 1B; tel. (72) 310-48; telex 12301; fax (72) 310-527; f. 1367, refounded 1922; 4 faculties; 596 teachers; 4,350 students; Rector Prof. J. HÁMORI.

József Attila University (Attila József Tudományegyetem): 6720 Szeged, Dugonics tér 13; tel. (62) 324-022; telex 82401; fax (62) 310-412; f. 1872, refounded 1921; 3 faculties; 613 teachers; 4,749 students; Rector Prof. Dr JÁNOS CSIRIK.

Loránd Eötvös University (Eötvös Loránd Tudomán Yegyetem): 1364 Budapest V, Egyetem tér 1–3, POB 109; tel. (1) 267-0820; fax (1) 266-9786; f. 1635; 4 faculties; 1,426 teachers; 11,417 students; Rector MIKLÓS SZABÓ.

Louis Kossuth University (Kossuth Lajos Tudományegyetem): 4010 Debrecen, Egyetem tér 1; tel. (52) 316-666; telex 72200; fax (52) 310-007; f. 1912; 2 faculties; 488 teachers; 3,103 students; Rector Dr Z. NAGY.

Medical University of Pécs (Pécsi Orvostudományi Egyetem): 7643 Pécs, Szigeti u. 12; tel. (72) 324-122; telex 312311; fax (72) 326-244; f. 1923 as Faculty of Medicine of University of Pécs, independent 1951; 623 teachers; 1,373 students; Rector Prof. Dr G. KELÉNYI.

Postgraduate Medical University (Orvostovábbképző Egyetem): 1135 Budapest, Szabolcs u. 35, POB 112; tel. (1) 140-8900; telex 226595; fax (1) 149-8344; f. 1910 as Central Commission for Medical Post-Graduate Training, re-established 1956 as autonomous institute, university since 1987; 711 teachers; 9,903 students; Rector Prof. Dr G. BROOSER.

Semmelweis University of Medicine (Semmelweis Orvostudományi Egyetem): 1085 Budapest VIII, Üllői u. 26; tel. (1) 113-1244; telex 226720; fax (1) 113-5090; f. 1769 as Medical Faculty of University of Pest, became independent 1951; 3 faculties; 1,298 teachers; 3,983 students; Rector Prof. Dr M. RÉTHELYI.

Technical Universities

Debrecen University of Agrarian Sciences (Debreceni Agrártudományi Egyetem): 4105 Debrecen, POB 36; tel. (52) 347-888; telex 72211; fax (52) 313-385; f. 1868; 1 faculty; 2 colleges; 212 teachers; 1,055 students; Rector Dr JAKAB LOCH.

Gödöllő University of Agricultural Sciences (Gödöllői Agrártudomanyi Egyetem): 2103 Gödöllő, Páter Károly u. 1; tel. (28) 310-200; telex 224892; fax (28) 310-804; f. 1945; 3 faculties; 509 teachers; 4,242 students; Rector Dr KÁROLY KOCSIS.

Miskolc University (Miskolci Egyetem): 3515 Miskolc, Egyetemváros; tel. (46) 365-111; telex 62223; fax (46) 369-554; f. 1735 in Selmecbánya, moved to Sopron in 1919 and to Miskolc in 1949; engineering, legal and political sciences, economics; 5 faculites; 701 teachers; 3,548 students; Rector Dr F. KOVÁCS.

Pannon University of Agricultural Sciences (Pannon Agrártudományi Egyetem): 8361 Keszthely, Deák Ferenc u. 16; tel. (83) 312-652; telex 35282; fax (83) 315-105; f. 1797; 3 faculties; 250 teachers; 1,794 students; Rector Prof. GYULA SÁRINGER.

Technical University of Budapest (Budapesti Műszaki Egyetem): 1521 Budapest, Műegyetem Rkp 3; tel. (1) 166-4011; telex 225931; fax (1) 166-6808; f. 1782; 7 faculties; 1,953 teachers; 8,420 students; Rector Prof. Dr PÁL MICHELBERGER.

University of Forestry and Wood Science (Erdészeti és Faipari Egyetem): 9400 Sopron, Bajcsy-Zsilinszky u. 4; tel. (99) 311-100; telex 249126; fax (99) 311-103; f. 1808; 2 faculties; 1 college; 161 teachers; 900 students; Rector Dr ANDRÁS WINKLER.

University of Horticulture and Food Technology (Kertészeti és Élelmiszeripari Egyetem): 1118 Budapest XI, Villányi út 35–43; tel. (1) 185-0666; telex 226011; f. 1853; 4 faculties; 300 teachers; 1,828 students; Rector Prof. Dr MIHÁLY MŐCSÉNYI.

University of Veszprém (Veszprémi Egyetem): 8200 Veszprém, Egyetem u. 10; tel. (88) 322-022; telex 32397; fax (88) 326-016; f. 1949; science; 230 teachers; 2,000 students; Rector Dr J. LISZI.

University of Veterinary Sciences (Állatorvostudományi Egyetem): 1078 Budapest, István ut 2; tel. (1) 122-2660; telex 224439; fax (1) 142-6518; f. 1787; 98 teachers; 544 students; Rector Prof. Dr V. L. FRENYÓ.

Social Welfare

In 1990 state expenditure on health and social welfare amounted to 99,000m. forint, with a further 342,500m. forint allocated to social security. This represented 7.7% and 26.8% of total government expenditure, respectively. In 1991 445,500m. forint was allocated to social security, 27.1% of budgetary expenditure. Hungary's national insurance scheme is based largely on non-state contributions. Employees contribute 4% of their gross earnings as a health-care contribution and 6% to the pension fund, while employers usually pay 19% of the employees' salaries towards health insurance and 24.5% into the pension fund. The Health Insurance Act, passed in July 1992, made health insurance obligatory.

The implementation of the five-day working week was completed by 1985. There is a guaranteed minimum wage, and employment is non-discriminatory. Men are usually entitled to receive retirement pensions at the age of 60, and women at 55, drawing between 33% and 75% of their earnings, according to length of service. Unemployment benefit was introduced in January 1989. Sickness benefits are provided by social insurance: employees are usually entitled to sick pay for one year, or for two years in cases of tuberculosis, occupational disease or industrial accident. Most medical consultation and treatment is free, although there is a small charge (which rose by 80% in January 1989) for medicines, and one of between 15% and 50% of the cost of medical appliances. Social insurance also covers maternity benefits (women are entitled to 24 weeks maternity leave on full pay), invalidity pensions, widows' pensions and orphans allowances.

At the end of 1989 there were 31,537 doctors in Hungary (2.98 per 1,000 population) and 104,479 hospital beds (9.85 per 1,000). In 1990 there was one physician for every 340 people (2.94 per 1,000 population). Infant mortality was 16.0 per 1,000 live births in 1991, a slight decline on the previous year. In 1991 male life expectancy was 66, while female life expectancy was 74. The crude death rate for both sexes was 14 in the same year.

NATIONAL AGENCIES

Ministry of Social Welfare: see section on The Government (Ministries).

National Administration of Social Insurance (Országos Társadalombiztosítási Föigazgatóság): 1139 Budapest, Váci út 73; tel. (1) 129-9250; fax (1) 140-9989; finances sickness benefits, medicines and medical appliances, maternity and child-care allowances, pensions, etc.; Dir Dr ALBERT RÁCZ.

National Ambulance Service (Országos Mentöszolgálat): 1395 Budapest, Robert Károly krt 77; Dir Dr LÁSZLÓ ANDICS.

HEALTH AND WELFARE ORGANIZATIONS

'Against Cancer, for the Future of the People' Foundation ('A Rák Ellen, az Emberért, a Holnapért' Társadalmi Alapítvány): 1122 Budapest 1122, Ráth György u. 7–9.

Evangelical Health Care Service (Evangéliumi Gyógyító Szolgálat): 1118 Budapest, Torbágy u. 9; organization for the care and prevention of alcoholics and alcoholism.

'Heart Sounds' Foundation ('Szól a Szív' Alapítvány): 1146 Budapest, Ajtósi Dürer sor 39; organization for the aid of blind children.

Heart and Vasculary Diseases Foundation (Szív-és Érbetegekért Alapítvány): 1173 Budapest, Kaszáló u. 45.

Hungarian Red Cross (Magyar Vöröskereszt): 1051 Budapest, Arany János u. 31; Pres. Dr László Andics; Sec.-Gen. Dr István Szilárd.

LARES Foundation (LARES Alapítvány): Budapest, Károly krt 2; organization of family-help and self-help groups.

National Institute for Health Promotion (Nemzeti Egészségvédelmi Intézet): 1062 Budapest, Andrássy út 82; tel. (1) 132-7380; fax (1) 131-6112; f. 1990; policy planning, monitoring, evaluation and support in health promotion; Dir Dr Peter Makara.

Peter Cerny Foundation for the Treatment of Premature Babies (Peter Cerny Alapítvány a Beteg Koraszülöttek Gyógyításáért): 1126 Budapest, Királyhágó út 1–3; tel. and fax (1) 175-7616; f. 1988; Pres. Paul F. Fekete.

Semmelweis Foundation for the Development of Orthopaedics in Hungary (Semmelweis Alapítvány a Magyarországi Ortopédia Fejlesztéséért): 1113 Budapest, Karolina u. 27; tel. (1) 166-6059; fax (1) 166-8747; f. 1988; support of healing and prevention of invalidity; Pres. of the Bd Prof. T. Vizkelety.

Shelter Foundation for Mentally Retarded Children ('Hajlék' Értelmi Fogyatékosokat Segítö Alapítvány): 1051 Budapest, Október 6 u. 22.

S.O.S. Foundation (S.O.S. Alapítvány): Budapest, Attila út 71; organization for the promotion of the welfare of physically-handicapped people.

Transylvania Foundation (Transilvania Alapítvány): 1025 Budapest, Aldás u. 5; refugee organization.

The Environment

Opposition to the Danube Dam project, at Gabčíkovo-Nagymaros, produced an organized environmental movement in Hungary, as well as opposition to the Communist regime. Since the suspension of Hungarian participation in the project, however, the original Danube Circle group has not been evident. The issue continued to place a strain on relations with Slovakia during the early 1990s. In April 1993 Hungary and Slovakia agreed to refer the dispute to the International Court of Justice. There are several small Green parties in Hungary. The Hungarian Government is a member of the Danube Commission (Slovakia), the IUCN (Gland, Switzerland) and participated in the activities of the CMEA Co-ordinating Centres on environmental matters.

GOVERNMENT ORGANIZATIONS

Ministry of the Environment and Regional Planning: see section on The Government (Ministries).

Ministry of Transport, Communications and Water Management: see section on The Government (Ministries).

Environmental Protection Authority (Környezetvédelmi Főfelügyelség): 1054 Budapest, Alkotmány u. 29; tel. (1) 132-9940; Dir Dr Gyula Egerszegi.

National Committee for the Protection of Clean Air (National Planning Office): 1370 Budapest, POB 613.

ACADEMIC INSTITUTES

Hungarian Academy of Sciences (Magyar Tudományos Akadémia): 1051 Budapest, Roosevelt-tér 9; tel. (1) 138-2344; telex 224139; fax (1) 132-8943; f. 1825; Pres. Domokos Kosáry; Gen. Sec. István Láng.

Ecological and Botanical Research Institute of the Hungarian Academy of Sciences (Magyar Tudományos Akadémia Ökológiai és Botanikai Kutatóintézete): 2163 Vácrátót; tel. (27) 360-147; telex 282201; fax (27) 360-110; f. 1952; theoretical and experimental research; 130 mems; Dir Dr Edit Kovács-Láng.

Forest Research Institute (Erdeszeti Tudomanyos Intezet): 1023 Budapest, Frankel Leo ut 42–44; tel. (1) 115-0624; telex 226914; fax (1) 115-1806; f. 1949; general research in forestry and environmental matters.

NON-GOVERNMENTAL ORGANIZATIONS

Hungarian National Society of Conservationists (Magyar Természetvédok Szovetsége): 1121 Budapest, Költö u. 21; tel. and fax (1) 175-0684; organization of local conservation and environmental groups and regional and national societies; Pres. Dr Erzsébet Schmuck.

Hungarian Ornithological and Nature Conservation Society (Magyar Madartani es Termeszetvedelmi Egyesulet): 1121 Budapest, Költö u. 21; tel. (1) 156-2133; telex 226115; fax (1) 175-8327; f. 1989; Gen. Sec. Gyorgy Kallay.

ISTER (East European Environmental Research Unit): 1025 Budapest, Kapy u. 6; tel. and fax (1) 176-2288; f. 1989; aims to protect the environment through research, advisory work and publications; Pres. János Vargha; CEO György Droppa.

REGIONAL ORGANIZATIONS

Danube Commission: 1068 Budapest, Benczúr ut 25; tel. (1) 268-1976; fax (1) 268-1980; f. 1949; approves projects for river maintenance; also responsible for navigation issues; mems: Austria, Bulgaria, Hungary, Romania, Russia, Slovakia, Ukraine, Yugoslavia; Pres. I. Diaconu (Romania); Dir of Secr. Dr H. Strasser.

Environmental Partnership for Central Europe: 1023 Budapest, Frankel Leo út 102, IV 40; tel. and fax (1) 136-3370; Country Dir Zsuzsa Foltanyi.

Defence

In June 1993, according to Western estimates, Hungary's regular armed forces numbered 78,000, of which 52,000 were conscripts. The Land Forces had 60,500 forces (including 40,000 conscripts) and the Air Force 17,500 (12,000 conscripts). The armed border force of 15,900 was to be reduced to 9,000 by 1995. Hungary, formerly part of the Communist bloc of states, was prominent in advocating the dissolution of the military association dominated by the USSR. The Warsaw Pact (f. 1955) was finally dissolved in 1991, in which year the last Soviet troops left Hungary. Hungary's defence budget was estimated at 66,500m. forint in 1993.

Commander-in-Chief of the Armed Forces: Árpád Göncz.

Chief of Staff: Maj.-Gen. János Deák.

Bibliography

Ágh, A. 'The Hungarian Party System' in *Budapest Papers on Democratic Transition*, No. 51. 1993.

Batt, J. *Economic Reform and Political Change in Eastern Europe: a Comparison of the Czechoslovak and Hungarian Experiences*. Basingstoke, Macmillan, 1988.

Berend, I., and Ránki, G. (Eds). *The Hungarian Economy in the 20th Century*. London, Croom Helm, 1985.

Berend, I. *The Hungarian Economic Reforms 1953–1988*. Cambridge, Cambridge University Press, 1990.

Bozóki, A., Körösény, A., and Schöpflin, G. (Eds). *Post-Communist Transition*. London, Pinter Publishers, 1992.

Brada, J. C., and Dobozi, I. (Eds). *The Hungarian Economy in the 1980s: Reforming the System and Adjusting to External Shocks* (Industrial Development and the Social Fabric Series, Vol. 9). London, JAI Press, 1988.

Csaba, L. *Eastern Europe in the World Economy*. Budapest, 1990.

Gati, C. *Hungary and the Soviet Bloc*. Durham, North Carolina, Duke University Press, 1986.

Hahn, C. M. (Ed.). *Market Economy and Civil Society in Hungary*. London, Frank Cass, 1990.

Heinrich, H.-G. *Hungary: Politics, Economics and Society* (Marxist Regimes Series). Boulder, Colorado, Lynne Rienner, 1986.

Hoensch, J. K. *A History of Modern Hungary 1867–1986*. Harlow, Longman, 1988.

János, A. *The Politics of Backwardness in Hungary 1825–1945*. Princeton, New Jersey, Princeton University Press, 1982.

Kornai, J. *The Road to a Free Economy*. London and New York, W. W. Norton, 1990.

Koves, A. *Central and East European Economies in Transition*. Boulder, Colorado, and Oxford, 1990.

Kovrig, B. *Communism in Hungary: From Kun to Kádár*. Stanford, California, Hoover Institution Press, 1979.

Lendvai, P. *Hungary: The Art of Survival*. London, I. B. Tauris and Co Ltd, 1988.

Lomax, B. *Hungary 1956*. London, Allison and Busby, 1976.

MaCartney, C. A. *October the Fifteenth: A History of Modern Hungary, 1929–45*, 2 vols. Edinburgh, Edinburgh University Press, 1956–57.

Hungary: A Short History. Edinburgh, Edinburgh University Press, 1962.

Molnar, M. *From Béla Kun to János Kádár: Seventy Years of Communism*. Oxford, Berg Publishing Ltd, 1990.

OECD. *Economic Surveys: Hungary*. 1991 and 1992.

Révész, G. *Perestroika in Eastern Europe: Hungary's Economic Transformation, 1945–1988*. Boulder, Colorado, Westview Press, 1990.

Richet, X. *The Hungarian Model: Planning and Market in a Socialist Economy*. Cambridge, Cambridge University Press, 1989.

Schöpflin, G., and Poulton, H. *Romania's Ethnic Hungarians*. London, Minority Rights Group Report, 1990.

Shawcross, W. *Crime and Compromise: János Kádár and the Politics of Hungary Since the Revolution*. London, Weidenfeld and Nicolson, 1974.

Swain, N. *Hungary: The Rise and Fall of Feasible Socialism*. London, Verso, 1992.

Székely, I. P., and Newbery, D. M. G. (Eds). *Hungary: An Economy In Transition*. Cambridge, Cambridge University Press (Centre for Economic Policy Research), 1992.

Sugar, P. (Ed.). *A History of Hungary*. London, I. B. Tauris and Co Ltd, 1990.

Vali, F. *Rift and Reform in Hungary: Nationalism versus Communism*. Cambridge, Massachusetts, Harvard University Press, 1961.

Vass, L. 'Changes in Hungary's Governmental System and the Problems of Analysis' in *Budapest Papers on Democratic Transition*, No. 59. 1993.

KAZAKHSTAN

Geography

PHYSICAL FEATURES

The Republic of Kazakhstan (until December 1991, the Kazakh Soviet Socialist Republic) is a land-locked country in Central Asia, the western extremity of which reaches into Europe. It is the second largest country in the region, extending some 1,900 km (1,200 miles) from the Volga river in the west to the Altai mountains in the east, and about 1,300 km (800 miles) from the Siberian plain in the north to the Central Asian deserts in the south. Western geographers considered Kazakhstan to be the northernmost of five Central Asian republics, but Soviet geographers, for historical reasons, did not include it in their concept of Central Asia. After the dissolution of the USSR, however, Kazakhstan considered itself part of the Central Asian region.

To the south Kazakhstan borders Turkmenistan, Uzbekistan and Kyrgyzstan. To the east there is a frontier with the People's Republic of China. The long northern border is with the Russian Federation. In the south-west there is a 2,320-km coastline on the Caspian Sea. The total area is 2,717,300 sq km (1,049,150 sq miles), over four-fifths the size of India (but with only 2% of the population).

The relief is extremely varied. A northern belt dominated by steppes is separated by the hilly uplands of central Kazakhstan from the semi-desert and desert to the south (part of the Kzyl Kum—Red Sands—desert falls within the borders of the country). Lowlands account for more than one-third of the territory, mountainous regions cover nearly one-fifth and hilly plains and plateaux occupy the rest of the country. The western regions are dominated by the lowlands of the Caspian Depression, which is drained by the River Ural. To the east of the western lowlands is the vast Turan plain, much of which is sparsely inhabited desert. The flat north-central regions are the beginning of the West Siberian plain; to the south of the plain are the hilly uplands of central Kazakhstan. On the eastern and south-eastern borders there are high mountain ranges.

Northern Kazakhstan possesses relatively good water resources, being dominated by numerous lakes and two large river systems. In the west the Ural and the Emba drain into the Caspian Sea. In the centre of the country the Irtysh, which rises in the north-east, and its tributaries flow north, across Siberia (Russia), to empty into the Arctic Ocean. There is a shortage of water in the south, however, the only substantial river in the area being the Syr-Dar'ya, which rises in Kyrgyzstan, in the Tien Shan mountain range, and used to empty into the Aral Sea. The waters of the Syr-Dar'ya were extensively used for irrigation from the 1960s, causing serious desiccation of the Aral Sea, the northern part of which is in Kazakhstan.

The Aral Sea became one of the world's most serious areas of environmental disaster. Without the in-flow from the Syr-Dar'ya and, except in years of exceptionally high rainfall, without that from the Amu-Dar'ya either, the Sea shrank at an ever-increasing rate. By the early 1990s it had lost over one-third of its original area (to comprise less than 44,000 sq km), the surface level had fallen by 13 m and the volume reduced by 790 cu km. For many years the favoured solution for alleviating the water shortage in the southern belt and in the southern Central Asian countries, and thereby lessening the demands on the Syr-Dar'ya, was

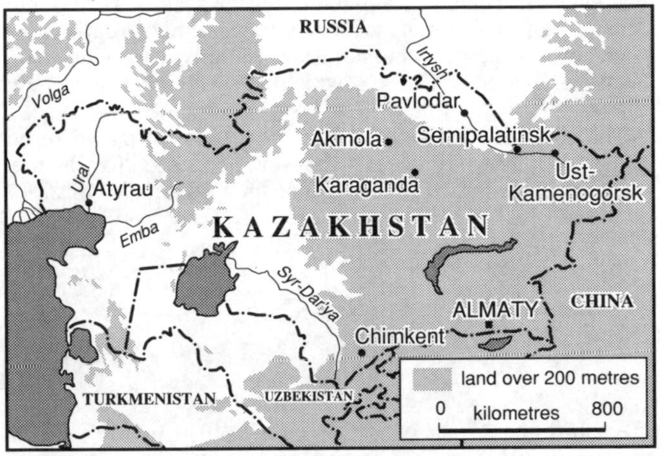

to divert the waters of the rivers that rose in central Kazakhstan (at its most extreme, the scheme aimed at the so-called reversal of the Siberian rivers; that is, to make them flow southwards rather than northwards). Even more moderate suggestions, that only some of the waters from the northern rivers should be piped to the south, provoked fierce opposition from environmentalists and Russian nationalists, who feared a detrimental effect on the ecology of Siberia. The demise of the USSR seemed to end the likelihood of this scheme being realized. Attempts were then concentrated on stabilizing the level of the Sea, to prevent any further deterioration, although the five Central Asian countries also needed the technical and financial assistance of the international community.

CLIMATE

The climate is of a strongly continental type but there are wide variations throughout the territory. Average temperatures in January range from −18°C (0°F) in the north to −3°C (27°F) in the south. Winters are long in the north, lasting from late October to mid-April. In July average temperatures are 19°C (66°F) in the north, although the north-east of the country tends to be slightly warmer, and 28°–30°C (82°–86°F) in the south. Levels of precipitation are equally varied. Average annual rainfall in mountainous regions reaches 1,600 mm, whereas in the central desert areas it is less then 100 mm. There are strong winds throughout the year, especially in the north, west and central regions; the dry sukhovej is particularly harmful to agriculture.

POPULATION

According to the census of 1989, at which the total population was 16,538,000, Kazakhs formed the largest ethnic group in the Republic, with 39.7% of the population, but they were only slightly more numerous than the Russians (37.8%), who had formed a majority of the population at the 1979 census. Other major ethnic groups were Germans (5.8%) and Ukrainians (5.4%). There were also Tatars and small numbers of Uighurs, Koreans (deported from the Soviet Far East in the late 1930s) and Dungans (Chinese

Muslims who migrated to Russian-held territory after the anti-Manzhou Muslim uprising of 1862–77).

Kazakh, a member of the Central Turkic group of languages, replaced Russian as the official language in September 1989. From 1940 it was written in a Cyrillic script of 42 characters. A Latin script was used until 1940, the traditional Arabic script having been replaced in 1928. The predominant religion was Islam; most Kazakhs were Sunni Muslims of the Hanafi school. Other ethnic groups have their own religious communities, notably the (Christian) Eastern Orthodox Church, which was attended mainly by Slavs.

The total population at 1 July 1992 was estimated to be 17,038,000. The large areas of desert accounted for the low population density of 6.3 persons per sq km in 1992. In 1991 an estimated 58% of the population lived in urban areas. The capital, Almaty (Alma-Ata), had an estimated population of 1,147,000 in January 1990. It is situated in the extreme south-east of the country, near the border with Kyrgyzstan. Other important towns included Karaganda, an industrial city in central Kazakhstan (613,000 in 1990) and Chimkent (Shymkent—401,000) in the south of the country, near the border with Uzbekistan. The main urban centres, however, were in the north-east: Semipalatinsk (339,000), Pavlodar (337,000) and Ust-Kamenogorsk (330,000). The main port on the Caspian Sea was Atyrau (formerly Guriyev—151,000). In September 1993 there were proposals to move the capital to Akmola (formerly Tselinograd—281,000), in the centre of the country, at some time in the future.

Chronology

6th century: Turkic tribes began to settle in the area of modern Kazakhstan, which was on the western borders of their empire.

1219: The Mongols conquered the area, destroying the urban culture of the south, which had emerged in the 10th century. The Golden and White Hordes (Tatars) became the dominant powers of the region.

***c.* 1511–23:** Kasym Khan established himself as leader of a loose confederation of steppe tribes, the Kazakh Orda. Some unity continued under his successor, Tahir, but did not persist.

1645: Guriyev (Atyrau), on the Caspian Sea, was acquired by the Russian Empire, which now bordered the territories of the Kazakh Hordes (the Little, the Middle and the Great).

1731: Under pressure from the Oirot Mongols, the Khan of the Little Horde was granted the protection of the Russian Tsar.

1740: The Khans of the Middle Horde gained Russian protection.

1742: Part of the Great Horde secured the protection of the Russian Empire, from the Oirot Mongols (although, in 1758, the Oirots were to be defeated by the Chinese Manzhou—Manchu—Empire, which became the ruler of the rest of the Great Horde).

1822: The absorption of the Kazakhs into the Russian Empire began with the territory of the Middle Horde, which was divided into Russian administrative units, while Russian military jurisdiction was imposed for criminal offences and Kazakhs were forbidden to acquire serfs; the Khans of the Middle Horde lost their power.

1824: The same process was implemented in the territory of the Little Horde and, despite some revolts and resistance, was followed by new taxation demands and strictures such as Kazakhs being denied the right to cultivate land.

1847: The Great Horde lost its independence when it was required to pledge its allegiance to the Russian Empire. The following year the last Khan of the Middle Horde was formally deposed.

1854: Foundation of the Russian garrison town of Vernoje (now Almaty).

1861: The emancipation of the serfs in the Russian Empire witnessed the first large influx of Slav settlers to Kazakh territory.

1895: A Russian commission set aside more land of the nomadic Kazakhs for settlement by Slav cultivators.

1906–12: The Stolypin agrarian reforms allowed another large influx of Slav (mainly Russian and Ukrainian) settlers, provoking Kazakh nationalism and resentment.

1916: An attempt to impose labour and military service on the non-Russian peoples of the Empire occasioned a widespread revolt by the Kazakhs; the rebellion was savagely crushed by the Governor-General of Turkestan, who resolved to drive the nomads from their lands.

1917: With the collapse of tsarist authority, in the Russian Revolutions, three Kazakh Conferences were held in Orenburg (now in the Russian Federation), although their narrow nationalism failed to attract widespread support. Kazakhstan became fiercely contested by the Red Army, the Whites and the Kazakh nationalists of the Alash Orda (led by Ali Bukeikhanov and Ahmed Baytursin).

26 August 1920: Following the Communist victory in the Civil War, the Russian authorities established a Kyrgyz Autonomous Soviet Socialist Republic (ASSR), in Orenburg (the Russians called the Kazakhs 'Kyrgyz' or 'Kyrgyz-Kazakhs' and knew the Kyrgyz as 'Kara-Kyrgyz').

1925: The Kyrgyz ASSR was renamed the Kazakh ASSR.

1929–30: The Arabic script was replaced by a Latin script for the written Kazakh language.

1929: The Communist authorities decided on the collectivization and the resettlement of nomads in Kazakhstan; this provoked fierce resistance.

1932: Karakalpakstan was detached from the Kazakh ASSR and made part of Uzbekistan. There was also widespread famine, because of the collectivization, and continuing Slav immigration.

5 December 1936: The Kazakh ASSR was detached from the Russian Federation and made a constituent partner of the Soviet federation, a Union Republic, the Kazakh Soviet Socialist Republic—SSR.

1940: A modified Cyrillic alphabet (with an unusually large number of characters—42) was introduced for the Kazakh language.

1944: The Soviet leader, Stalin (Iosif Dzhugashvili), ordered the deportation to Kazakhstan and Siberia of many peoples who had attracted his suspicion, including some 400,000 Chechens, 200,000 Crimean Tatars, 75,000 Ingush and 40,000 Balkars. Many of the Volga Germans had already been deported, mainly to Kazakhstan. Despite the rehabilitation of significant numbers of these peoples in 1957, many remained in Kazakhstan.

1954: A Kazakh was replaced as First Secretary of the Communist Party of Kazakhstan (CPK) by an ethnic Russian, together with a Russian Second Secretary, Leonid Brezhnev (later Soviet leader, 1964–82), who himself became leader of the CPK the following year. The official encouragement of ploughing 'Virgin Lands' began; the scheme continued to 1960 and Kazakhstan accounted for almost 60% of the extra land farmed throughout the USSR.

1956: Dinmukhamed Kunayev succeeded Brezhnev as First Secretary of the CPK, but the criticism of the Soviet leader, Nikita Khrushchev, obliged his resignation.

4 October 1957: The USSR placed the first man-made satellite (Sputnik I) in orbit around the earth; the Soviet space programme was based at the Baikonur space centre, Leninsk (Turatam).

12 April 1961: The first manned space flight was undertaken, by Maj. Yury Gagarin, on the Vostok I spacecraft.

1961–62: There was a major influx of Kazakh and Uighur refugees from the People's Republic of China.

1964: Kunayev returned as First Secretary of the CPK, later becoming the first Kazakh in the Politburo of the all-Union Party.

1984: Nursultan Nazarbayev was appointed Chairman of the Council of Ministers, the republican premier.

16 December 1986: The first nationalist riots experienced by the new Soviet leader, Mikhail Gorbachev, were in Almaty, after Kunayev was dismissed for corruption and replaced by an ethnic Russian, Gennady Kolbin.

March 1987: The Communist leadership resolved to improve the teaching of both the Kazakh and Russian languages in the Republic.

June 1989: Nazarbayev was appointed First Secretary of the CPK. The first outbreak of ethnic violence brought on by economic deprivation occurred in the western, petroleum-refining town of Novy Uzen, when Kazakh youths attacked Lezghins; the violence continued sporadically for the next few months.

September 1989: Amongst other reforms, the Supreme Soviet enacted a law making Kazakh the official language of the Republic; Russian remained the language of inter-ethnic communication (this law was upheld by the Constitution of January 1993).

February 1990: Nazarbayev was elected Chairman of the Supreme Soviet.

25 March 1990: Elections to the Supreme Soviet of Kazakhstan took place, with the Communists retaining an overwhelming majority in the legislature, despite some political reforms; in the following month the new parliament elected Nazarbayev to the new post of President.

September 1990: An explosion at a factory in Ulba, eastern Kazakhstan, contaminated a large area with toxic gases and led to several demonstrations; pollution was a major focus for opposition in the late 1980s and early 1990s, as was protest about the nuclear tests at Semipalatinsk (one of the largest opposition groups was the Nevada-Semipalatinsk movement of Olzhas Suleymenov).

25 October 1990: Kazakhstan declared itself to be a sovereign state and attempted to outlaw the storing or testing of nuclear weapons on its territory.

17 March 1991: In the referendum on the preservation of the Union, 94.1% of those who voted (89.2% of the electorate) favoured Kazakhstan remaining in the federation.

April 1991: Gorbachev and the leaders of nine Union Republics, including Nazarbayev, signed the 'Nine-Plus-One Agreement', a five-point statement on measures to stabilize the crisis situation in the country.

25 July 1991: Gorbachev announced that agreement had been reached on the substance of a new Union Treaty; Nazarbayev was prepared to sign it in August.

18–21 August 1991: An attempted coup in Moscow failed, signalling the final dismantling of institutionalized Communist authority in the USSR; the effective increase of authority for republican leaders enabled President Nazarbayev to ban nuclear testing at Semipalatinsk. In the same month Kazakhstan announced its first programme for the privatization of enterprises.

October 1991: Sergey Tereshchenko, an ethnic Ukrainian, was appointed Chairman of the Council of Ministers (Prime Minister). The representatives of Kazakhstan, the four other Central Asian Republics, Armenia, Belarus and the Russian Federation signed a treaty which established an Economic Community between the signatories.

1 December 1991: Nursultan Nazarbayev was confirmed in office as President of Kazakhstan by direct elections to that post; he was the sole candidate and won 98.8% of the votes cast.

13 December 1991: Leaders of the five Central Asian Republics met in Ashghabat (Turkmenistan) and agreed to join the Commonwealth of Independent States (CIS) which had been announced by the leaders of Belarus, Russia and Ukraine five days before.

16 December 1991: The Supreme Soviet (Supreme Kenges) declared the independence of Kazakhstan, the last Union Republic to do so.

21 December 1991: At a meeting in Almaty the leaders of 11 Union Republics signed a protocol on the formation of the new Commonwealth, thereby dissolving the USSR (Gorbachev resigned four days later).

March 1992: Kazakhstan was admitted as a member of the UN.

May 1992: Kazakhstan, anxious to maintain good relations with Russia, signed a Treaty of Friendship, Co-operation and Mutual Assistance with its northern neighbour. Nazarbayev decreed that a national army should be established.

June 1992: Some 5,000 opposition supporters demonstrated in Almaty against the continued dominance of government by former Communists.

October 1992: The three main nationalist groups, Azat (Freedom), the Republican Party and the Jeltoqsan (December) National Democratic Party, united to form the Republican Party—Azat.

28 January 1993: After public consultations lasting almost one year, the Supreme Kenges enacted a new Constitution.

March 1993: Economic reform continued with the announcement of an ambitious new privatization programme for the following two years.

June 1993: President Nazarbayev appointed a commission to examine the question of fostering a non-ethnic sense of statehood in Kazakhstan.

24 July 1993: The Russian authorities announced that pre-1993 roubles would be withdrawn from circulation, although, despite deteriorating relations between the two countries over the issue, Kazakhstan remained intent on staying within a new 'rouble zone'.

7 September 1993: Russia agreed to assume Kazakhstan's share of the Soviet debt, in return for Soviet assets in Kazakhstan. The first stage of a major privatization programme began.

9 October 1993: The People's Unity Party of Serik Abdrakhmanov held an organizational congress and announced that President Nazarbayev had agreed to be the unofficial head of the party; a Deputy Prime Minister, Kuanysh Sultanov, was elected Chairman.

15 November 1993: Amid accusations of being forced out of the rouble zone, Kazakhstan introduced its own currency, the tenge, with the support of the International Monetary Fund.

24 November 1993: Relations between Kazakhstan and Russia deteriorated, against a background of nationalist rhetoric in the Russian election campaign, when President Nazarbayev criticized Russian foreign minister Andrey Kozyrev's commitment to protect the interests of ethnic Russians even in the 'near abroad'.

8 December 1993: The Supreme Kenges announced its dissolution in preparation for elections on 7 March 1994; it then proceeded to grant the President additional powers in the interim and to ratify the Nuclear Non-proliferation Treaty; the dissolution, precipitated by 43 deputies resigning their mandates, took effect in the following week.

25 December 1993: Kazakhstan, unable to afford the maintenance of the space programme alone, agreed that Russia should lease the Baikonur facilities.

History

Dr SHIRIN AKINER

THE FORMATION OF KAZAKHSTAN

Kazakhstan, in its modern form as a unified, political entity, came into being after the establishment of Soviet rule. In 1920 the Kyrgyz Autonomous Soviet Socialist Republic (ASSR) was created, within the jurisdiction of the Russian Federation. The Kazakhs were then known to the Russians as Kyrgyz, or Kyrgyz-Kazakhs, to distinguish them from the unrelated Cossacks. As a result of the 1924–25 National Delimitation of Central Asia, some Kazakh-populated areas were transferred to the jurisdiction of the territory, which, in 1925, was formally renamed the Kazakh ASSR. In 1932 the Karakalpak region was detached from the the Republic. In 1936 Kazakhstan was elevated to the status of a full Union Republic, becoming the Kazakh Soviet Socialist Republic (SSR). Despite some redrawing of the borders, therefore, the main contours of Kazakhstan remained those that had been mapped out in the early Soviet period. With the collapse of the USSR, on 16 December 1991 the territory declared its independence as the Republic of Kazakhstan. It joined 11 other former Union Republics in the Commonwealth of Independent States (CIS), by the Almaty Declaration of 21 December, and was admitted to the UN as a member state in March 1992.

THE PEOPLES OF KAZAKHSTAN

Independent Kazakhstan was a multi-ethnic, multi-cultural country. At the beginning of the 1990s over 100 ethnic groups were represented within its borders. The two largest groups were the Kazakhs (40% of the total population according to the 1989 census) and the Russians (38%). Although accurate data were not available, it was likely that the difference in numbers increased after 1989, owing to: immigration of Kazakhs from other countries (mainly other Soviet successor states, but also including the return of a few thousand from Mongolia and Iran, descendants of those who fled the Russian Revolution and Civil War); the emigration of Russians from the country, as well as from the south of Kazakhstan into Slav-dominated areas; and, finally, the higher birth rate amongst the Kazakhs. Other groups of significant size included non-indigenous peoples such as Germans, Ukrainians and Koreans. There was some underlying friction between the immigrants and the Kazakhs, but it was mostly of low intensity and only surfaced under provocation. The main tensions were between Kazakhs and Cossacks, but there were also outbursts of violence between other groups, most notably between Kazakhs and Chechens.

Kazakhs

The Kazakhs are a Turkic people, descendants of nomadic tribes who settled on the territory of present-day Kazakhstan in the sixth century AD and possibly earlier. During the 10th century a strong urban culture developed in the south. The region lay on the transcontinental 'Silk Roads', part of the chain of trading posts that linked China, Persia (Iran) and Transoxiana (roughly the area of modern Uzbekistan). Further to the north nomadic pastoralism remained the dominant way of life. In the early 13th century (1219) Kazakhstan was conquered by the Mongols. The cities of the south, such as Otrar and Taraz, were destroyed. The trade links were eventually revived, but the urban centres never fully regained their previous levels of prosperity and sophistication.

The 14th and 15th centuries were marked by power struggles, mostly centred on the southern belt. Mongol princes from the Golden Horde and the White Horde fought amongst themselves, and also with Uzbek and Nogai contenders, for control of the region. This strife resulted in waves of migration, as whole tribes changed allegiance and moved from one area to another. There was a period of relative stability in the early 16th century, when one of the war-lords, Kasym Khan, succeeded in uniting the main tribes (Kipchaks, Naimans, Usuns, Dulats, etc.) under his rule (from about 1511 to 1523). From this time onwards it is possible to speak of a Kazakh nation, despite the fact that after Kasym's death the internecine struggles were renewed as, too, were the campaigns against Central Asian fiefdoms in the south. By the beginning of the 17th century three major groupings had emerged amongst the Kazakhs, each under the leadership of its own khan (leader): the Great Horde (Ulu Zhuz), the territory of which lay to the south-east, between the Aral Sea and Lake Balkhash; the Middle Horde (Orta Zhuz), which controlled the central zone, further north, between the Irtysh and the Tobol rivers; and the Little Horde (Kishi Zhuz), with territory to the north of the Caspian Sea, between the Emba and the Ural rivers. These Hordes were further divided into tribes and clans. There was a highly developed awareness of genealogy, since it was lineage that determined both a man's place in society as well as his rights to pasture land. These features of Kazakh society survived the later tsarist and Soviet periods.

The Kazakh aristocracy adopted Islam during the 14th and 15th centuries. Turkestan, a city in the far south, was the seat of Ahmad Yasavi (who died in the middle of the 12th century), one of the greatest Sufi mystics. His influence did much to encourage the spread of Islam in the region. By the 14th century his burial place had become a highly revered shrine (three pilgrimages to this site were supposed to equal the Pilgrimage—*hajj*—to Mecca). In 1397 the Mongol ruler, Timur (Tamerlane), built a mausoleum over Yasavi's tomb and, later, several of the Khans of the Middle and Little Hordes were buried there. The nomadic tribes in the north, however, did not have much contact with Islam. They were not fully converted until the 19th century, when, under the Russian tsarist administration, Tatar Muslim missionaries were sent to the region as part of a policy to tame these unruly subjects. A number of mosques were built during this period, but, although the Kazakhs became, by their own standards, sincere believers, they were not very devout by conventional measures. They incorporated many elements of customary law (*adat*) and animism into Islam and thus created a fusion of different traditions which was uniquely Kazakh.

The Kazakh Hordes came under Russian domination because they were divided amongst themselves and constantly under attack from their neighbours, particularly the Oirot Mongols. Thus, during the 18th century, the Kazakhs gradually had recourse to Russian protection: the Little Horde in 1731; the Middle Horde in 1740; and part of the Great Horde in 1742 (the rest of this Horde was to come under Manzhou—Manchu—rule and remained part of China). Russian influence in the steppes grew ever stronger until, eventually, the entire region was under Russian control (with the exception of the area that fell within the Chinese Empire). After a gradual policy of limiting the powers of the khans and the introduction of the Russian administrative system under Tsar Alexander I (1801–25), the last Khan of the Middle Horde was deposed in 1848. A Russian garrison named Vernoje (Faithful) was established in the far east of the territory in 1854; this town, renamed Almaty (Alma-Ata), was later to become the capital of the Kazakh SSR.

Traditionally, Kazakh culture was rooted in the nomadic way of life, expressing itself in the crafts and skills of daily life, as well as in the oral epics that encapsulated the history, wisdom and philosophy of the people. The advent of the Russians opened the door to the ideas and opportunities of a (comparatively) developed Western society. The majority of the Kazakh élite was highly responsive and came genuinely to admire Russian culture. A number of them received an excellent education in St Petersburg and other Russian cities. A member of one of the princely families, Shokan Valikhanov (1835–65), served as an officer in the imperial army and wrote numerous scholarly works in Russian. The first of several Russian-Kazakh schools was opened in 1841. Scholars such as Ibraj Altynsarin (1841–89) played an active role in the development of the Kazakh literary language (which was written in the Arabic script until 1928—previously the Kazakhs had used Tatar as a written language), as well as in the general process of educational reform. It was thanks to the pioneering efforts of this generation that, by the turn of the century, the Kazakhs were better educated and more politically aware than the other peoples of Central Asia.

Nomadism first came under threat in the second half of the 19th century, when large numbers of Russian settlers moved into northern Kazakhstan, took possession of the local population's traditional pasture lands and obstructed the routes of migration. This mass invasion of their territory was the cause of considerable resentment amongst the Kazakhs. It culminated in the fierce, though unsuccessful, uprising of 1916, which was occasioned by the introduction of a draft for labour units, even though the Kazakhs had traditionally been exempt from military service. More than 50,000 tribesmen on the steppes and in the Fergana Valley took part in the revolt, which was brutally suppressed.

Soon after, the February 1917 Revolution caused the collapse of tsarist power and, under Ali Bukeikhanov, a semi-independent Kazakh state, known as Alash Orda, was formed. However, the Kazakhs were soon brought under Bolshevik control, initially as part of the Russian Federation, although they were acknowledged as one of the nationalities of the USSR. It was under the Communists that the second and decisive onslaught on the nomadic way of life took place. This was the collectivization campaign of the 1930s, as a result of which the remaining nomads were forcibly sedentarized. It has been estimated that approximately one million Kazakhs died from starvation and other problems caused by collectivization during this period (by 1959 the Kazakh population had still not recovered from these losses, then numbering some 347,000 fewer than in 1926). Thereafter, the Kazakh population recovered and, during the 1980s, the Kazakhs once more became the largest ethnic group in their own republic (by the time of the 1989 census the Kazakhs constituted almost 40% of the total population and the Russians 38%). As well as the numerical recovery of the population, Kazakh representation in the republican government and Party institutions began to increase as, after the 1950s, a new generation of urbanized, educated Kazakhs emerged. In the 1990s, after independence, there was a revival of interest in the cultural legacy of nomadism, but it was no longer a living tradition. However, the great majority of Kazakhs still lived in rural areas, mostly in the less developed southern belt of the country. They tended to be very conservative and culturally far removed from the highly educated, Westernized, Russian-speaking Kazakhs of the urban centres.

Slavs

Slavs first began to settle in Kazakhstan in large numbers in the second half of the 19th century. The majority were farmers; there was a vast influx of land-hungry peasants after the Emancipation of the Serfs, in 1861, and the authorities continued to set aside large tracts of land for Russian and Ukrainian settlers, disrupting nomadic life and forcing many Kazakhs eastwards into Chinese territory. However, there were also industrial labourers who came to work in the nascent mining industry, as well as military personnel (including Cossack detachments) and a large civilian infrastructure. By 1926 the Russians already constituted nearly 20% (1.3m.) of the total population of Kazakhstan, while the Ukrainians, it was estimated, accounted for a further 13% (860,000). While the Kazakh population was falling, the influx of Slavs continued during the 1930s and reached a peak during the Second World War, when many industries and academic institutions were relocated to Kazakhstan. Soviet leader Nikita Krushchev's 'Virgin Lands' scheme, which aimed to raise grain production by bringing large areas of the steppe under the plough, brought new waves of Slav settlers to the region in the 1950s and early 1960s. By 1970 there were 5.5m. Russians and 933,000 Ukrainians. Both groups continued to expand, though at a slower rate than previously, with far less immigration to increase numbers. By 1989 there were some 6.3m. Russians and 896,000 Ukrainians, compared to 6.6m. Kazakhs.

As in the 19th century, the Slavs remained concentrated in the northern belt, particularly in the eastern corner of the country, where most of the industrial centres were located. They were well represented in parliament (in the early 1990s it was claimed by some Kazakhs that over one-half of the deputies were Slavs) and several of them held key positions in government. The Cossacks and other nationalist groups sometimes demanded autonomy, but, at least in the early years of independence, the majority of the Slav population seemed prepared to remain part of Kazakhstan. In the long term, however, the Slav population constituted the most serious threat to the integrity of the new state: if they should decide to press for partition, either to form their own state or to seek reunification with Russia, it was unlikely that the Kazakhs would be able to resist this pressure.

'Punished Peoples'

On the eve of the Second World War, and during the War itself, many thousands of Volga Germans, Crimean Tatars, Koreans, Greeks, Chechen, Ingush and other peoples believed to be unreliable and anti-Soviet were deported to Kazakhstan from other parts of the Union. In the post-War period they gradually succeeded in gaining acceptance in Kazakh society and some came to hold high public office. However, by the beginning of the 1990s a number of these groups were either beginning to return to their pre-deportation homes or seeking repatriation to their original homelands abroad. In 1989 the German population in Kazakhstan numbered just under one million (5.8% of the total population), but many subsequently emigrated to Germany. It seemed probable that more would follow, despite the efforts of both the German and the Kazakhstan Governments to persuade them to remain in the country. The reasons for their departure were varied, but the primary causes were undoubtedly their hope for a more secure economic future in Germany, as well as their concern over what they perceived to be an inherent instability in the existing situation in Kazakhstan. By contrast, the Koreans (numbering over 100,000) seemed determined to stay and were extremely active in business ventures involving partnerships with the Republic of Korea. The other, smaller groups of deportees had relatively limited opportunities to leave and there was little discernible reduction in their numbers during the early 1990s.

Ethnic Politics

The revival of Kazakh nationalism began during the period of *glasnost* or *aygilik* (openness), initiated by the Soviet leader Mikhail Gorbachev (1985–91). Complaints about lack of school instruction in the Kazakh language led to a decree of March 1987 which recommended improvements in the teaching of both Kazakh and Russian—an indication of the authorities' constant awareness of having to balance the demands and anxieties of both the major ethnic groups. In September 1989 the Supreme Soviet did declare Kazakh to be the official language, although Russian was to be the language of inter-ethnic communication and all officials dealing with the public were to know both languages. The issue did seem to cause some incidents of inter-ethnic tension, but, generally, it seemed to have been economic hardship that encouraged actual incidents in the Soviet period (notably the 1989 riot in Novy Uzen). The status of the two languages was confirmed in the new Constitution of January 1993.

In independent Kazakhstan the Government remained cautious of any nationalist group, discouraging extremists such as Alash or the Slav groups Yedinstvo and Lad. Kazakhs were increasingly dominant in the state, however, which fuelled ethnic Russian fears. This was a reversal of the situation in the late 1980s, when many Kazakhs feared that Russians were dominating the state and Party apparatus. Under the Kazakh Communist leader Dinmukhamed Kunayev (1956–86), Kazakhs had reached the highest positions of state in the Republic, but often as a result of nepotism and corruption. Gorbachev's dismissal of Kunayev and many of his supporters, therefore, as part of his anti-corruption campaign (part of the *perestroika* or *qayta qurilis*—restructuring—initiative), was interpreted by some as anti-Kazakh. In December 1986 there was a violent nationalist protest in Almaty, in reaction to the announcement that the new Party First Secretary was to be an ethnic Russian, Gennady Kolbin (1986–89). Kolbin remained in office and continued with his reforms, although he also recommended institutions for ensuring fair ethnic representation in the administration. The situation was only really resolved by the appointment of Nursultan Nazarbayev, an ethnic Kazakh, to the Party leadership, in June 1989.

Nazarbayev was careful to allay the fears of the Slavs and won their confidence partly because of his obvious support for the Union in the last years of the USSR. The Supreme Soviet did make a declaration of sovereignty in October 1990, and Nazarbayev was an advocate of economic sovereignty. However, in the referendum on the continuation of the Union, in March 1991, there was an overwhelming vote in favour of the federation. Although the question asked of voters in Kazakhstan was slightly different to the standard one, 94.1% of the votes cast (88.2% of those eligible voted) supported the renewal of the USSR. Kazakhstan was ready to sign the new Union Treaty in August, but the event was forestalled by the attempted *coup d'état* in Moscow. On 20 August Nazarbayev openly condemned the coup and, as it collapsed, he led the resignations from the Communist Party and ordered the depoliticization of state institutions. Nevertheless, Kazakhstan signed the Treaty of the Economic Community (October) and committed itself to a new Union in November. It had still not declared its independence (one of only two Union Republics) when the leaders of the Slav republics resolved on a CIS and the effective dissolution of the USSR. The Supreme Soviet (Supreme Kenges) declared the independence of the country before it was admitted to the CIS as a founder member, by the Almaty Declaration of 21 December.

Before independence Nazarbayev had been re-elected as President in a direct vote. He was the only candidate, but secured 98.8% of the votes cast (87.4% of the electorate participated). He had the confidence of both major ethnic groups and had gained popularity by using the greater independence of the Union Republics after the August coup attempt to ban nuclear tests at Semipalatinsk. This was an indication of his readiness to exploit issues with an appeal to both communities. Indeed, nuclear and ecological concerns had been the main focus of the emerging opposition to the Communist system during the *glasnost* years. In the early 1990s it was revealed that such issues could easily be displaced if the authorities allowed nationalism or insecurity on the part of the Slavs to polarize society. Not that tension between Kazakhs and other ethnic groups was the only problem of nationhood for the new country. There were also accusations that those ethnic Kazakhs who did hold power tended to be from Nazarbayev's Great Horde, indicating that the ancient rivalries of the Kazakh tribes had not disappeared in the years of Russian and Soviet rule. In June 1993 a commission was established to investigate ways of fostering a non-ethnic sense of nationhood.

THE POLITICAL STRUCTURES OF INDEPENDENT KAZAKHSTAN

The newly independent country had a presidential system of government, with separate executive, legislative and judicial bodies. There were three levels of administration: the national government; the provincial government of the oblasts; and the regional government in the rayons. The main organs of state were replicated at each of these levels, but, in theory, the regional administration was subordinate to the provincial, and the provincial to the centre. In practice, however, the oblasts and rayons had a considerable degree of autonomy. Local government (19 oblasts and two large metropolitan districts) had responsibility for their own budgets controlling expenditure on, for example, primary health care, education and social services. As in Russia, at the provincial level there was a lack of clarity between the functions of the legislative bodies (soviets or councils) and the executive bodies (previously known as the Ispolkom, then the Akimiyat). The latter grew increasingly powerful in the last years of the Union and the early years of independence, and came to report directly to the President, bypassing both the local soviets and the ministries of the central government.

In December 1991 Nursultan Nazarbayev became the first elected President of Kazakhstan, elected for a five-year term of office, with extensive personal powers which included the authority to appoint and dismiss officials at all levels and to issue decrees counteracting parliamentary legislation. Nazarbayev was appointed to the post of Chairman of the Council of Ministers (head of government) of Kazakhstan in 1984, then to that of First Secretary of the Communist Party of Kazakhstan (CPK) in 1989. He introduced political and administrative reforms in September 1989, including the introduction of extra executive duties (formerly the responsibility of the Party First Secretary) for the Chairman of the Supreme Soviet, the republican legislature. He was duly elected to this post in February

1990 and was, therefore, *de facto*, the republican head of state, before being elected to the new post of President by the Supreme Soviet in April (following a general election). On 1 December 1991 he was the sole candidate in elections to the presidency, in which he gained the support of 98.8% of the votes cast. He played a prominent role in all-Union politics in the last years of the Soviet regime, and then came to be regarded by many as one of the most active and internationally respected of the post-Soviet presidents. He was considered to be an astute negotiator, capable of toughness as well as flexibility. As Kazakhstan entered the mid-1990s Nazarbayev seemed to have no obvious rivals for power and was likely to remain in control for some time to come.

One of Nazarbayev's greatest assets was his ability to maintain the political balance between the Russian and Kazakh factions. This rivalry was, potentially, one of the most serious threats to the integrity of the country and if he were to be overthrown it would undoubtedly be as the result of a polarization of interest between these two groups. Thus, although his authoritarian (albeit relatively benign) style of government did not encourage the growth of multi-party democracy, it did act as a stabilizing force in the country and the region. His deputy was Vice-President Yerik Asanbayev, an economist by training and with a particular interest in the privatization process, but with little formal or political authority capable of balancing the power of the President. At the beginning of 1994 the Prime Minister remained an ethnic Ukrainian, Sergey Tereshchenko (premier since October 1991), who headed an administration which owed much in structure to its Soviet-period predecessors.

The legislative body was the Supreme Kenges (formerly the Supreme Soviet). Elections to the 360-member parliament were held on 25 March 1990—many candidates were unopposed and the system of reserving seats for CPK-affiliated candidates was retained. The result was an overwhelming Communist majority and the deputies remained docile through the period of Soviet disintegration and Kazakhstan's accession to independence, leaving the main process of decision-making to the President and his senior associates. However, in 1992 and 1993 there were some indications of the legislature showing signs of greater independence and it was critical of some government actions. Also, there was unease among some of the deputies at the way in which the power of the soviets was being undermined at provincial and regional levels, perceiving in this a threat to their own existence. However, the advantages of renewing the authority of the Supreme Kenges (and the local councils) with a mandate from the electorate, in a multi-party system and to a parliament in permanent session, clearly outweighed such anxieties. In December 1993, having enacted a new Constitution on 28 January 1993, parliament declared itself dissolved. It granted President Nazarbayev additional legislative powers for the period until after the general election, which was scheduled for 7 March 1994.

The Constitutional Court, the supreme judicial body, the function of which was to ensure that the Constitution was properly observed, was also less compliant in 1993. Despite some decisions which had been contrary to government expectations, moves to limit the powers of the Constitutional Court were not successful.

Political parties played a very minor role in the politics of Kazakhstan. It was not the President alone, but the whole of society, that preferred consensus to debate. The main parties were: the former Communist Party, disbanded in 1991, which re-emerged as the Socialist Party; the People's Congress of Kazakhstan, an umbrella organization, which had the support of a number of leading intellectuals, such as its Chairman, the poet and long-time anti-nuclear campaigner Olzhas Suleymenov; and, more recently, the People's Unity Party of Serik Abdrakhmanov, the former head of Komsomol, which, in 1993, chose Kuanysh Sultanov, a presidential adviser, as its Chairman and, reportedly, even succeeded in persuading the President to become its leader. This seemed likely to ensure victory for the new party in the parliamentary elections, scheduled for March 1994. There were a number of smaller, nationalist parties, such as the Republican Party—Azat and the more extreme Alash, but they had few members and were expected to secure little popular support.

FOREIGN RELATIONS

Given the geographic constraints of its location, the future prosperity of Kazakhstan would depend, to a very considerable degree, on the state of its relations with its immediate neighbours, namely, the Russian Federation, the People's Republic of China, the southern former Soviet Central Asian countries and, across the Caspian Sea, Iran. In the more distant past Kazakhstan was a nodal point in the Eurasian trade networks, a crossroads for the east-west, north-south routes. Later, especially after the region's incorporation into the tsarist empire, the links with Russia assumed ever greater importance until, during the Soviet period, Kazakhstan was virtually sealed off from China and Iran. Even the links with the other Central Asian republics were weaker than had formerly been the case. The relationship with Russia became the central factor in the economic life of the territory, as well as in most other spheres, including politics, defence, communications and transportation.

For independent Kazakhstan the presence of the large Russian population in Kazakhstan not only meant that these bonds had been strengthened still further, but that domestic political stability depended on good relations with Russia. The links were not something that could be destroyed immediately and, indeed, it was in the interest of both sides that they should be maintained. There was a high level of interdependency in trade between the two states (including, for Kazakhstan, the import of timber, a resource of which it had very little) and a good network of road, rail and air links and petroleum and natural-gas pipelines was already in place. In Kazakhstan the nature of the terrain was such that the routes leading westwards were always the most crucial, providing, as they did, the easiest means of access to the region. Even if (or when) other routes were developed, those that linked Kazakhstan to Russia would undoubtedly retain their importance. However, despite Kazakhstan's perception of these economic ties, it found that it was obliged to introduce its own currency (the tenge) in November 1993. This followed the country's stated intention to remain in a 'rouble zone', even after the July currency reform in Russia. However, the accompanying Russian demands were considered too great. The bitterness of this dispute was compounded by the rhetoric of many Russian politicians in the campaign for the December elections, which concerned itself with protecting ethnic Russian interests in the 'near abroad'. The Russian Minister of Foreign Affairs, Andrey Kozyrev, spoke of the need for this even in 'friendly countries' while visiting Almaty, in November, provoking a reprimand from President Nazarbayev. At the end of 1993 the relations of Kazakhstan with Russia were at an unusually low ebb.

There were also significant strategic aspects to the relationship between these two countries. For Russia, Kazakhstan had long represented part of the front line of its defence system against China. Soviet strategists may not have intended that the nuclear arsenal based on Kazakh territory should be used against China (it was, in fact, directed at the USA), but it was certainly perceived by the Chinese as a serious threat to their security. The Kazakhs, as part of the Soviet polity, shared Moscow's suspicions of Chinese expansionist intentions. They also had good historic reasons to fear their large neighbour to the east. They therefore welcomed Soviet (and, in the more distant past, tsarist) protection and, after independence, hoped that the Russians would continue to provide defence cover, at least until they had developed their own military resources. There were indications that, far from agreeing to the removal of the nuclear warheads from their territory, Kazakhstan favoured the Russians upgrading them.

However, the paradox of Kazakhstan's position lay in the fact that this same ally also constituted the most serious threat to its territorial integrity: if the Russians of Kazakhstan, either of their own volition or at the prompting of Russian nationalists in Russia, should seek autonomy, there would be very little that the Kazakhs could do to prevent them from achieving this. The only external support they would be likely to receive would be from their supposed enemies, the Chinese, who had their own reasons for not wishing to see an extension of Russian territorial claims. The Kazakhs were obliged, therefore, to perform an extremely delicate balancing act, maintaining a precise equilibrium between these two rival powers. Accordingly, after the collapse of the USSR, the Government of Kazakhstan made serious efforts to develop a good working relationship with the People's Republic of China. The interest was reciprocated by the Chinese Government and there were exchanges of high-level official delegations, as well as numerous trade, cultural and scientific missions. Both sides were eager to revive the 'Silk Roads' of old, in modern form. At the beginning of the 1990s road, rail and air links, as well as a direct telephone line, already connected Almaty and Urumchi, the capital of Xinjiang (China). There were plans to upgrade these links in the near future, so as to facilitate the eventual integration of the Chinese and Central Asian transportation and communications networks. Chinese labourers and entrepreneurs were already moving into Kazakhstan in large numbers and Chinese goods and businesses were much in evidence. The new Almaty branch of the Bank of China was also intended to give further encouragement to such activities. Such developments, however, did little to assuage popular suspicion of Chinese intentions.

Kazakhstan's relationship with Iran was far less problematic than that with either China or Russia. There was little direct contact between the two countries for many years (although there were still a few thousand Kazakhs in Iran, descendants of refugees from Soviet rule). With Kazakhstan an independent state, it was eager to develop transport and communication links to the south, through Turkmenistan, but also across the Caspian Sea. There were plans to build a petroleum pipeline through Iran. This option received considerable support from the authorities in Kazakhstan, following the political disturbances in Moscow of September–October 1993, as well as a perceptible hardening of Russian attitudes in trade and monetary policies towards its CIS partners.

Relations with the southern Central Asian republics were complicated by economic rivalry and competition for foreign aid. During the tsarist and Soviet periods Kazakhstan was always treated as a separate entity. Cultural and scientific links, as well as economic, tended to be with the centre, rather than with neighbouring Central Asia. Following independence efforts were made to develop a Central Asian political and economic grouping. However, although there were many problems that could indeed only be approached on a regional basis—for example, the question of water management—there was, as of the beginning of 1994, very little real progress in the creation of mechanisms for co-operation.

Looking beyond the adjacent countries, the Government of Kazakhstan emphasized its intention to establish good relations with the international community at large. There was an acute awareness of the need to avoid potentially provocative and divisive alliances. In joining the Economic Co-operation Organization (founded originally by Iran, Pakistan and Turkey), the Kazakhs made it clear that they were not seeking to create an Islamic bloc, but merely to facilitate mutually beneficial economic activities. Similarly, they were eager to develop relations with Turkey, but on the same basis as with other countries, and not as part of a uniquely Turkic group. President Nazarbayev also proposed an Asian equivalent of the Conference on Security and Co-operation in Europe (CSCE), although little progress was made towards developing this during 1993. The West, from which Kazakhstan hoped to receive investment, was attracted by the country's natural resources. It was also interested in the fate of the nuclear arsenal (although Kazakhstan had ratified the first Strategic Arms' Reduction Treaty—START 1—in 1992 and the Nuclear Non-proliferation Treaty in December 1993) and in the growth of the trade in illegal drugs (against which Kazakhstan sought aid from the West in 1993). This policy of encouraging international contacts, while maintaining a non-aligned stance, proved to be very effective. By the mid-1990s Kazakhstan was generally regarded as the most stable of the CIS states and it had already succeeded in attracting business partners from countries as diverse as Australia, Israel, Spain and the Republic of Korea.

The Economy

Dr SHIRIN AKINER

INTRODUCTION

Kazakhstan's extensive natural resources provided the base for a relatively diversified economy. The main sectors were agriculture and heavy industry. However, the years of central planning ensured that the economy developed into one that was highly dependent upon and vulnerable to influences from other former Soviet Republics, notably the Russian Federation. This was evident in the emphasis on trade and communications links to the west, with Russia, encouraged by geography, but in contrast to the area's historic position on the great trans-Asian trade routes of the 'Silk Road', from China to the Middle East and Europe. With the failure of the Soviet economic system and the advent of full political independence in 1991, Kazakhstan began, cautiously, but with commitment, a programme of reform. The country had significant problems to overcome in the early 1990s, and these were likely to persist into the mid-1990s, but the long-term prospects seemed secure, particularly with its natural advantages. The country encompassed approximately one-fifth of the arable land of the former USSR, although it represented only some 12% of the total territory and 6% of the population of the USSR upon the latter's dissolution in 1991. Apart from such statistics, however, many official figures should be treated with some caution, owing not only to the unreliability of many economic data, but to the added distortions of the transformation to a free-market economy.

AGRICULTURE

Kazakhstan was an important producer and exporter (mostly to other former Soviet territories) of agricultural products. It was estimated that, in 1992, this sector of the economy accounted for 37.7% of Kazakhstan's net material product (NMP) and accounted for 22.9% of those employed by the state (which still accounted for the overwhelming majority of economic activities). Animal husbandry, long a traditional occupation of the original nomads of the area, was mainly orientated towards meat production and was of major importance. There was also, however, significant output of milk and dairy products, including dried milk, butter and cheese. Wool (including the valuable Astrakhan), camel hair and hides were also produced in large quantities. Cattle were raised mainly in the north and north-east of the country, sheep and camels in the south and horses in the east. Private farms were reckoned to own some 30% of the total stock of cattle, horses and poultry at the beginning of 1993. During the 1980s brucellosis became a major health hazard; help was sought from abroad, to try to eradicate this disease.

Grain production was of crucial importance to the economy. Approximately one-half of the land under cultivation was devoted to wheat, almost entirely under state supervision. This was a legacy of Soviet leader Nikita Krushchev's 'Virgin Lands' scheme, whereby vast tracts of northern Kazakhstan were brought under the plough. Weather conditions here were excellent, although they could also be extremely disappointing. At times in the late 1980s and early 1990s it was sometimes necessary for the country to import grain in order to meet its domestic needs, but in 1992 and 1993 the grain harvest was good. Other important cereals were barley, millet and rice (cultivated in the south). Cotton, sugar beet and tobacco production were less significant, in terms of volume, than grain, but, after the dissolution of the USSR they acquired a new significance, and value. Inter-republican supplies of these commodities, especially sugar, were severely disrupted. There were plans to increase production in the mid-1990s. On the other hand, Kazakhstan remained without significant timber resources, which it imported from Russia. Foreign investors showed a particular interest in the tobacco industry; in 1993 Philip Morris, the US multinational, was about to embark on a joint venture for the production of cigarettes in Kazakhstan. However, a similar deal for a confectionary factory was not carried through, mainly owing to problems with the distribution network, which was the main interest of a company such as Philip Morris in gaining access to local markets.

In line with other sectors of the economy, agriculture performed poorly in the early 1990s. This was partly an effect of the political disruption and the uncertainties which ensued, but more because of the short-term consequences of economic reform and the general disruption being experienced by the entire, decaying Soviet economic system. Furthermore, the agricultural sector was severely affected by drought during the early 1990s and the output of most products declined. However, grain production increased to 29m. metric tons in 1992 (compared to 12m. tons in 1991), an increase of about one-quarter on the average levels for 1986–90. This helped offset the general decline in agricultural productivity. Early reports indicated that the 1993 grain harvest remained at the same level, despite the restraints imposed by the shortage of fuel in the country.

MINING AND INDUSTRY

Industry (mainly mining, manufacturing and public utilities), according to 1992 estimates, accounted for 45.4% of NMP, although this was a considerable increase on its 37% share in 1991 or the 21% of 1990. The sector typically contributed just over one-third of NMP during the late 1980s. Industry also provided an estimated 21.8% of employment (some 1.3m. jobs) in the state sector of the economy in 1992. At the end of 1992, according to official estimates, private enterprises provided some 700,000 jobs. Kazakhstan possessed large deposits of coal (it accounted for some 19% of Soviet coal production), petroleum and natural gas, and minerals such as chrome (some 90% of total Soviet reserves were located in Kazakhstan), lead, copper, zinc, wolfram and gold. Most of the industrial base of the country was connected with the extraction and processing of its resources.

The basic infrastructure of industry was good, although too orientated towards Russia. Moreover, equipment was generally old, inefficient and, environmentally, extremely harmful. There was a high degree of wastage. Karaganda (the third-largest coal basin in the former USSR) was the main centre of the Kazakhstan coal industry, although Ekibastuz, further north, was also well developed. The country produced far more coal than was needed for domestic consumption and had long been an exporter, mainly to the Volga region of the Russian Federation. Total coal production (hard coal and brown coal) of some 134m. metric tons (as in 1991) began to decline in 1992, although only slightly, to 131m. tons. However, a further fall was likely in 1993 and 1994, mainly as a result of reduced demand and excess stocks.

The proven petroleum and gas reserves were very considerable; exploration in the early 1990s, however, was far more exhaustive and it was probable that new deposits would be identified. During the Soviet period the centre of the petroleum industry was Atyrau (Guriyev), on the north-eastern shore of the Caspian Sea. Foreign petroleum and gas companies were increasingly invited to tender for exploration and development rights in this and other parts of the country. In 1993 the Kazakhstan Government finally reached agreements with the US company Chevron for the development of the Tengiz and Korolev fields and with the French Elf Aquitaine for the exploration of the Temir deposits. A consortium of Western companies agreed to exploration in the Caspian Sea, later in the year, but negotiations with other companies proceeded slowly and hesitantly.

The structural problems of the Kazakhstan hydrocarbons sector, however, were striking, despite the increasing importance of the sector, which maintained its production levels in the early 1990s. As with coal, the production of crude petroleum declined slightly during 1992, while natural gas increased in output. The dependence on Russia in the petroleum market (Kazakhstan had to import some of its petroleum needs) resulted, in the latter part of 1992, in estimates that prices for exported petroleum were about one-quarter those of imported petroleum. Thus, the three-quarters of national petroleum production from the west of the country could only be exported via Russia. On the other hand, refineries in eastern Kazakhstan could receive crude petroleum only from certain Siberian oilfields, although those producers also had alternative markets, enabling them to keep their prices high. Likewise, the main route for coal exports was by rail from Pavlodar to western Siberia and the Urals (where there were plants designed to use such supplies) and gas pipelines only went through Russia (Kazakhstan hoped to gain advantage from the proposed pipeline from Turkmenistan to Turkey via the Caucausus and Iran). Such disadvantages kept export prices for domestic production low, while the disruption to the general economic systems of the former USSR and the need for major investment in the hydrocarbons industry, after over one decade of declining investment, resulted in increased energy prices. This phenomenon was common throughout the former USSR and had adverse effects on other industrial activity.

Ferrous and non-ferrous metallurgy were highly developed. Important copper, zinc and lead works were located in the north-east of the country, while the mining and processing of iron was based in the Aktyube region in the north-west. There were also copper deposits in the centre of the country and lead and zinc in the south. Also in the north-east of the country was one of the world's largest gold deposits (estimated reserves of some 8m. troy ounces), at the extremely low-cost mines near Auezov. In 1993, following Australian and US involvement in the venture, the company operating the mines was even quoted on the London Stock Exchange, in the United Kingdom. Total gold production in Kazakhstan, in 1992, was estimated at 12 metric tons. A Metal Exchange was established in Kazakhstan in 1992.

Apart from the petrochemicals sector and the processing of agricultural products, industry was dominated by heavy engineering works, which produced a broad range of machinery and machine tools, and, a light industry, the production of textiles. These industries all suffered from the problems experienced throughout the economy of Kazakhstan (and other former Soviet Republics), such as the increase in fuel prices and the disruptions to the traditional trading partnerships. There were also problems in the supply of raw materials and with the decay of capital equipment and basic infrastructure.

OTHER SECTORS

The construction industry, which had been a strong contributor to economic activity under the Soviet system, according to official estimates, accounted for only 5.9% of NMP in 1992, and 9.9% of employment in the state sector. This was because of the decline in activity following the final collapse of the USSR and the accession to independence—in 1990 construction had contributed 14% to NMP. Transfers from the all-Union Government had been important to investment, from which construction benefited. There was an added problem in the early months of independence, when the State Committee (later the Ministry) of the Economy did not assume responsibility for investment from the all-Union authorities (defunct since December 1991) until August 1992. Moreover, apart from the economic problems of a fall in investment and, more specifically, in construction activity, was that housing and social facilities deteriorated, as did the infrastructure of the country.

This last factor was important, because transport and communications were the third most important contributor to the economy in 1992, according to estimates of the NMP. The sector accounted for 8.3% of NMP in 1992 and over 10% of state-sector employment (an estimated 8.8% for transport alone). There was a well developed transport system in Kazakhstan, which was important considering the sheer size of the country. However, it was orientated to Russia and often dependent on it and other former Soviet territories for spare parts. Thus, the railway system (the most important of the transport networks), apart from needing substantial basic investment and modernization, required spare parts, equipment and rolling stock from Russia and Ukraine. Likewise the lorry fleet (some 400,000 in 1992), upon which road transport was reliant, was affected by the rising cost and shortages of fuel, and the need for spare parts from Russia and Belarus. The disruption to trade added to the shortages created by the restraint on resources. Investment was important to maintain the transport network, particularly as Kazakhstan could benefit from this, being in a crucial position in the heart of Asia. Its existing facilities, notably its air links with Russia and Europe and with the other, southern Central Asian countries, had helped make Almaty the Central Asian city with the largest foreign population during the early 1990s.

The services sector, though less dominated by the state, remained largely dependent on government expenditure. In 1992 it was estimated that services (mainly education and health) accounted for 25.6% of employment in the state sector. Services remained a minor part of the economy, but were likely to increase in importance during the 1990s. Private retail outlets were increasing in number and it was reckoned that, by the beginning of 1993, there were some 4,000 privatized enterprises engaged in trade, catering and consumer goods.

POLICY PLANNING

Until December 1991 economic planning for Kazakhstan, as for the other Soviet Republics, was carried out at Union level, in Moscow. The role of the republican governments was, primarily, to carry out the directives which they received from the centre. Scope for formulating policies within a given Republic was extremely limited, because of the highly integrated nature of the Union economy as a whole. Detailed data were collected on a regular basis, but were transmitted to Moscow for full analysis. Several key areas of the economy, such as the military-industrial complexes, transport, communications and major industrial plants, came directly under the jurisdiction of the all-Union authorities; the republican administrations had little, if any, knowledge as to how they functioned. In Kazakhstan, strategically important facilities such as the nuclear testing site at Semipalatinsk and the Baikonur space centre were manned almost exclusively by immigrant Slavs. In effect, they represented extra-territorial enclaves. They contributed virtually nothing to the local economy and existed outside the control of the republican government. However, the activities at Semipalatinsk were suspected of causing environmental and health damage in the Republic and, with increased authority for republican government from August 1991, President Nursultan Nazarbayev gained popularity for banning future testing activities. On the other hand, at Baikonur, Kazakhstan acknowledged the inappropriateness and expense of local control at the end of 1993, when it reached an agreement, in principle, that Russia should be responsible for the space centre, under some sort of lease from the Government.

After 1991 in Kazakhstan, as elsewhere in the former USSR, the Government was trying to unravel the mysteries of its own economy. Much of the information that was available during the early 1990s was unreliable and partial. Requests for training and technical assistance were addressed to the International Monetary Fund (IMF) and other international bodies, as well as to the national governments of interested countries (India, Japan, Turkey, the United Kingdom and the USA). Some training was provided in the fields of central banking, taxation, and economic and financial management, but the technical capability in all the essential areas of economic planning was still very limited. President Nazarbayev was deeply committed to the process of economic reform, but mechanisms to implement proposed changes were often lacking. Moreover, the officials charged with the responsibility of implementing such programmes were often too conservative to sympathize with the task or too inexperienced to understand the nature of the transformation. Consequently, progress was slow. There were frequent changes in the administrative apparatus, leading to a rapid turn-over of personnel.

Nevertheless, while only 380 enterprises were privatized in 1991, some 6,000 small enterprises were sold to the private sector during the following year (out of an estimated total of some 31,000 enterprises). By the beginning of 1993 an estimated 15% of the fixed assets of Kazakhstan had been corporatized, although the state tended to be the majority shareholder in most joint stock companies. The privatization programmes, however, continued to be over-ambitious (see below).

DEVELOPMENTS AFTER INDEPENDENCE

In 1991 there were already signs of serious economic dislocation. Essential industrial supplies were disrupted as Republics, voluntarily or involuntarily, reneged on contracts with partners within the Union. This triggered a chain reaction of falling production, shortages, rising prices and, in some cases, unemployment. The Kazakhstan Government, while it had begun to advocate local control of republican economies when in the Union, was not eager to introduce economic reforms at this stage, for fear of increasing the hardships which the population was already suffering. However, because of the intimate relationship between the Russian and Kazakh economies, once the Russian Government decided on price liberalization, Kazakhstan could not but follow suit. Accordingly, on 6 January 1992, prices of all but some basic foodstuffs and essential services were deregulated. Public anger was such that some degree of control had to be reintroduced almost immediately. Salaries and social benefits were raised, and continued to be raised at regular intervals, but were unable to keep pace with inflation and the relentless, almost weekly, price increases. The most significant areas affected were fuel, staple foods (bread, milk and meat) and transportation costs (public and private).

A privatization programme was launched in 1991, but the initial results were disappointing. The original intention was that 50% of assets in industry, 40% in agriculture, all the housing stock and much of the services sector should be privatized during 1992. In the event, this proved to be an impossibly ambitious plan. No account was taken of the lack of the basic technical and professional skills which would be required (such as in law, accountancy, insurance), or of the public's fears and suspicions about private ownership. In larger enterprises, occasions of 'asset-stripping' and other corrupt practices increased dramatically; the absence of independent, but legitimate, non-state sector supply networks meant that smaller enterprises were often forced to depend on links with organized crime. The level of bankruptcy in newly privatized small enterprises within the first few months was very high (estimated by one senior official to be in the region of 90%). Consequently, the programme was largely discredited and very little real progress was made. By mid-1993 the Government (hence, by implication, the President) was being criticized for imposing privatization from above. Nazarbayev remained an advocate of the policy, however, and criticized the failure to achieve the government objective to have privatized all trading and catering establishments by the end of 1993 (only 44% were in private ownership by January 1994).

President Nazarbayev was a strong supporter of an integrated economic policy for the Commonwealth of Independent States (CIS). He suggested a number of proposals for co-ordinating economic decision-making amongst the member states and remained firmly committed to the 'rouble zone'. The announcement by the Central Bank of Russia, on 24 July 1993, that pre-1993 banknotes would no longer be legal tender was wholly unexpected. The move was clearly designed to force countries such as Kazakhstan either to introduce their own currency or to surrender their fiscal independence to Russia. The Government of Kazakhstan was reluctant to adopt the former course in haste. However, the threat to stability from the vast stocks of old roubles in existence and the Russian demands which proved too compromising for an independent state, required, on 15 November, the introduction of Kazakhstan's own currency, the tenge (which had already been printed, for such an eventuality). The Government continued to advocate closer economic integration, however, and, in January 1994, Kazakhstan and Uzbekistan announced their intention to form a common market by the year 2000—Kyrgyzstan subsequently announced its support for this ambition.

The introduction of the tenge increased international optimism that Kazakhstan would be better able to control its economy and, importantly, its fiscal deficit. Despite having to resort to *ad hoc* measures during 1992, Kazakhstan succeeded in producing a coherent budget planning government expenditure during 1993. Although unexpectedly high inflation during the year (largely caused by the monetary policies of the Russian central bank) added to the problems, the Government of Kazakhstan remained committed to improving the quality of and its control over public finances.

PROSPECTS

At the end of 1993 the short-term outlook was not encouraging. The continuing disruptions in inter-republican trade, the unpredictable monetary developments and the deteriorating political situation in some of the other former Soviet states had a disastrous effect on the economy of Kazakhstan. There was a significant decline in output in every sector. Milk and meat production were low and seemed likely to fall still further in 1994, since farmers, unable to obtain sufficient feed for their animals, had begun to slaughter their herds. In the industrial sector, too, output continued to decline. Tractor production, for example, fell by 50%, machine tools by 30% and crude petroleum production by 8% in 1992. Salaries were unable to rise in line with inflation, which was recorded as a 1,481% increase in the consumer price index in 1992, with the rate accelerating further in 1993, to an estimated 2,000%.

In the longer term, however, prospects were not so bad and, if political and social stability could be maintained, would continue to improve. By 1993 some foreign investment was already secured and more was likely to follow, particularly in the hydrocarbons sector. The country was actively trying to lessen its dependency on Russia and, thus, to protect itself against a repetition of economic shocks such as had been experienced in 1992 and 1993. Particular consideration was being given to increasing output from the Kumkol oilfield in western Kazakhstan (which, in 1993, was being exploited by German and Canadian joint ventures) in order to make the country self-sufficient with regard to its petroleum needs. There were plans, too, to make greater use of the petroleum-refining capacity in Turkmenistan and Azerbaijan and to reconstruct the domestic refineries in Chimkent (Shymkent) and Pavlodar, so as to lessen dependency on Russia. The move towards a market economy was proceeding slowly and painfully, but, in time, the reforms should begin to take effect. A private sector was emerging gradually in the early 1990s and those who grew up at the very end of the Soviet period were adapting and often showing considerable entrepreneurial ability. This, coupled with the liberal investment climate, should make Kazakhstan's mineral wealth an attractive proposition for foreign partners.

Statistical Survey

Principal sources: IMF, *Kazakhstan, Economic Review*, and *International Financial Statistics: Supplement on Countries of the Former Soviet Union;* World Bank, *Statistical Handbook: States of the Former USSR.*

Area and Population

AREA, POPULATION AND DENSITY

Area (sq km)	2,717,300*
Population (census result)	
12 January 1989†	
Males	7,974,004
Females	8,490,460
Total	16,464,464
Population (official estimates)	
1 January 1991	16,793,000
1 July 1992	17,038,000
Density (per sq km) at mid-1992	6.3

* 1,049,150 sq miles.

† Figures refer to *de jure* population. The *de facto* total was 16,536,511.

PRINCIPAL ETHNIC GROUPS
(permanent inhabitants, 1989 census)

	%
Kazakhs	39.7
Russians	37.8
Germans	5.8
Ukrainians	5.4
Others	11.3
Total	100.0

PRINCIPAL TOWNS
(estimated population at 1 January 1990)

Alma-Ata (Almaty) (capital)	1,147,000	Kustanai	228,000
Karaganda	613,000	Temirtau	213,000
Chimkent	401,000	Uralsk	207,000
Semipalatinsk	339,000	Shevchenko	165,000
Pavlodar	337,000	Kzyl-Orda	156,000
Ust-Kamenogorsk	330,000	Atyrau†	151,000
Jambul	311,000	Kokshetau	139,000
Akmola*	281,000	Ekibastuz	137,000
Aktyubinsk	260,000	Rudniy	126,000
Petropavlovsk	245,000	Taldi-Kurgan	122,000
		Jezkazgan	110,000

* Formerly Tselinograd. † Formerly Guriyev.

BIRTHS, MARRIAGES AND DEATHS

	Registered live births		Registered marriages		Registered deaths	
	Number	Rate (per 1,000)	Number	Rate (per 1,000)	Number	Rate (per 1,000)
1987	417,139	25.5	160,909	9.8	122,835	7.5
1988	407,116	24.7	162,962	9.9	126,898	7.7
1989	382,269	23.0	165,380	10.0	126,378	7.6

EMPLOYMENT* (annual averages, '000 persons)

	1990	1991	1992
Material production	4,677	4,636	4,411
Agriculture	1,202	1,194	1,355
Industry†	1,360	1,385	1,290
Construction	745	674	588
Transport	610	604	520
Other	760	779	658
Services	1,799	1,849	1,516
Public health	438	448	422
Public education	737	766	633
Banking, finance, etc.	39	42	44
Government services	258	260	159
Other	327	333	258
Total	6,476	6,485	5,927

* Figures refer to the state sector only. Total employment (in '000) was: 7,288 in 1990; 7,494 in 1991; 7,449 in 1992.

† Principally mining, manufacturing, electricity, gas and water.

Agriculture

PRINCIPAL CROPS ('000 metric tons)

	1990	1991	1992
Wheat	16,196.8	6,888.8	18,284.6
Rice (paddy)	578.7	521.0	466.9
Barley	8,500.2	3,085.1	8,510.8
Maize	442	330	500*
Rye	843	480	700*
Oats	610.6	230.9	727.3
Millet	940	235	500*
Sorghum*	15	27	27
Potatoes	2,324.3	2,143.2	2,569.7
Soybeans	32.9	16.4	11.8
Other pulses	129†	51†	84*
Sunflower seed	141	109	115*
Rapeseed	19†	20†	20*
Seed cotton	324	291	250*
Cottonseed	187†	177†	112*
Vegetables*	844	911	1,095
Water-melons*	148	120	100
Grapes	139	66	75*
Other fruit	301	98	130*
Sugarbeet	1,134	726	1,300
Tobacco (leaves)	4.6	3.9	3.7
Cotton lint	102	94	77†

* FAO estimate(s). † Unofficial estimate(s).

Source: mainly FAO, *Production Yearbook*.

LIVESTOCK ('000 head at 1 January)

	1990	1991	1992
Horses	1,618	1,666	1,688
Cattle	9,757	9,592	9,511
Pigs	8,921	9,229	9,255
Sheep and goats	35,661	34,520	34,194
Poultry	59,899	59,932	54,031

LIVESTOCK PRODUCTS
('000 metric tons, unless otherwise indicated)

	1990	1991	1992
Meat (slaughter weight)	1,559.6	1,524.4	1,257.6
Milk	5,641.6	5,555.4	5,231.0
Eggs (million)	4,185.1	4,075.3	3,541.7
Wool*:			
greasy	107.9	104.4	105.0†
scoured (clean)	67.8	62.6	63.0†

* Figures from the FAO, *Production Yearbook*.

† Estimate(s).

Mining

('000 metric tons, unless otherwise indicated)

	1990	1991	1992
Hard coal	131,443	130,382	126,543
Brown coal	3,443	3,919	4,490
Crude petroleum*	25,600	26,600	26,000
Natural gas (million cu m)	7,114	7,885	8,112
Iron ore	23,846	21,993	17,671

* Including gas condensate.

Gold: Total production, according to official estimates, was 12 metric tons in 1992.

Industry

SELECTED PRODUCTS
('000 metric tons, unless otherwise indicated)

	1990	1991
Margarine	71.4	47.6
Cotton yarn	39.9	36.9
Fabrics ('000 sq metres)	325,461	248,708
Footwear ('000 pairs)	36,464	35,410
Sulphuric acid	3,151	2,815
Synthetic rubber	32.0	25.6
Rubber tyres ('000)	2,633	3,029
Coke (6% humidity)	3,711	3,404
Building bricks (million)	2,285	2,126
Pig iron	5,226	4,952
Crude steel	6,754	6,377
Electric energy (million kWh)	87,379	86,128

1992: Cotton yarn 38,600 metric tons; Rubber tyres 2,904,000; Pig iron 4,666,000 metric tons; Electric energy 84,300 million kWh.

Finance

CURRENCY AND EXCHANGE RATES

Monetary Units

100 tein = 1 tenge.

Sterling and Dollar Equivalents (30 September 1993)

£1 sterling = 1,796.1 Russian roubles;
US $1 = 1,201.0 roubles;
10,000 roubles = £5.568 = $8.326.

Average Exchange Rate (roubles per US dollar)

1989 0.6274
1990 0.5856
1991 0.5819

Note: The figures for average exchange rates refer to official rates for the Soviet rouble. However, a multiple exchange rate system was in operation, with separate non-commercial and tourist rates. A commercial exchange rate was introduced on 1 November 1990, replacing the official rate for most transactions. The commercial rate (roubles per US dollar) was: 1.692 at 31 December 1990; 1,671 at 31 December 1991. Between November 1989 and April 1991 the tourist exchange rate valued the rouble at one-tenth of the official rate. In April 1991 this rate, renamed the 'special rate', was set at $1 = 27.6 roubles. It was subsequently adjusted. The average market exchange rate in 1991 was $1 = 31.2 roubles. Following the dissolution of the USSR in December 1991, Russia and several other former Soviet republics retained the rouble as their monetary unit. The average interbank market rate in 1992 was $1 = 222.1 Russian roubles.

On 15 November 1993 Kazakhstan introduced its own currency, the tenge (equal to 100 tein), at an exchange rate of 1 tenge = 500 roubles. Three days later a rate of 250 roubles per tenge was established.

BUDGET ('000 million roubles)*

Revenue	1991	1992	1993†
Current revenue	19.3	276.8	999.0
Taxation	17.7	261.0	944.9
Income taxes	9.9	91.6	276.0
Individual	3.1	29.9	77.2
Corporate	6.8	61.7	198.8
Taxes on property	—	2.7	2.1
Taxes on goods and services	6.6	88.1	301.6
Turnover tax/value added tax	4.4	72.5	218.4
Excises	1.5	8.7	83.2
Taxes on international trade	—	28.5	96.1
Taxes on natural resources	0.7	9.1	76.1
Tax for Investment Fund	—	39.8	190.8
Non-tax revenue	1.6	15.8	54.2
of which Foreign economic activities	—	1.4	21.6
Capital revenue	—	0.6	2.2
Grants	4.2	20.7	30.0
Net transfers from USSR budget	4.2	—	—
Total	23.5	298.2	1,031.3

Expenditure	1991	1992	1993†
Financing of the economy	12.9	78.6	207.4
Investment Fund	—	34.1	190.8
Fund for Natural Resources	—	5.6	24.1
Foreign economic activities	—	68.7	135.0
Financing of social and cultural programmes	14.2	96.9	406.2
Education	6.3	47.1	198.7
Health care	3.0	26.0	101.6
Social security	4.3	16.6	78.9
Other	0.6	7.2	27.0
Defence, public order and safety	—	23.7	140.8
State authorities and administration	1.0	9.3	44.6
Other purposes	2.9	27.4	80.7
Adjustments	—	43.1	—
Strategic defence	—	10.8	—
External interest payments due	—	32.3	—
Total	30.9	387.4	1,229.7

* Figures represent a consolidation of the operations of the central Government and local governments, excluding extrabudgetary units and social-security schemes.
† Forecasts.

INTERNATIONAL RESERVES
(US $ million at 31 December)

	1992
Foreign exchange	120.4

MONEY SUPPLY
(million roubles at 31 December)

	1991	1992
Currency outside banks	13,959	154,271

COST OF LIVING
(Consumer price index; base: 1991 = 100)

	1992
All items	1,481.3

NATIONAL ACCOUNTS
Net Material Product ('000 million roubles at current prices)

	1990	1991	1992
Agriculture and forestry	15.3	23.0	432.7
Industry*	7.7	25.1	521.1
Construction	5.9	9.1	67.7
Transport and communications	3.6	5.7	95.3
Trade and catering	1.8	2.7	16.1
Other material services	2.4	2.0	14.9
Total	36.6	67.4	1,147.8

* Principally mining, manufacturing, electricity, gas and water.

BALANCE OF PAYMENTS (US $ million)*

	1990	1991	1992
Merchandise exports	14,270	10,210	7,370
Merchandise imports	−24,550	−13,370	−9,040
Trade balance	−10,280	−3,160	−1,670
Services and transfers (net)	7,290	1,860	−410
Current balance	−2,990	−1,300	−2,080
Foreign direct investment (net)	—	—	100
Other capital (net)	−260	30	−160
Net errors and omissions	n.a.	n.a.	−50
Overall balance	n.a.	n.a.	−2,200

* Figures are rounded to the nearest $10 million.

External Trade

PRINCIPAL COMMODITIES (million roubles)

Imports	1989	1990
Petroleum and gas	1,447	1,181
Electric energy	371	420
Iron and steel	1,040	986
Non-ferrous metals	272	275
Chemicals and chemical products	1,703	1,727
Products of machine-building industry	5,359	5,510
Wood and paper products	988	832
Construction materials	313	331
Products of light industry	3,113	3,374
Products of food industry	1,871	1,880
Agricultural products (unprocessed)	457	392
Total (incl. others)	17,569	17,830
Foreign	2,998	3,516
Inter-republican (USSR)	14,571	14,314

Imports from the former USSR (million roubles): 20,049 in 1991; 494,095 in 1992.

Imports from all other countries (US $ million): 1,912 in 1991; 1,523 in 1992.

Exports	1989	1990
Petroleum and gas	875	795
Electric energy	224	233
Coal	312	306
Iron and steel	1,077	1,036
Non-ferrous metals	791	777
Chemicals and chemical products	1,121	1,082
Products of machine-building industry	836	786
Products of light industry	1,625	1,536
Products of food industry	617	612
Agricultural products (unprocessed)	1,146	1,764
Total (incl. others)	9,094	9,350
Foreign	893	906
Inter-republican (USSR)	8,201	8,443

Exports to the former USSR (million roubles): 16,512 in 1991; 324,039 in 1992.

Exports to all other countries (US $ million): 776 (mineral products 184, chemical industry products 160, base metals and products thereof 292) in 1991; 1,489 (mineral products 603, chemical industry products 243, base metals and products thereof 566) in 1992.

Education

(1989/90)

	Institutions	Students
Secondary schools	8,064	3,021,070
Secondary specialized schools	244	255,400
Higher schools (incl. universities)	55	285,600

Directory

The Constitution

The new Constitution of the Republic of Kazakhstan was adopted on 28 January 1993 and included among its principal provisions the following:

All nationalities in Kazakhstan are guaranteed equal status; Kazakh is the state language, although Russian is used as a language of inter-ethnic communication; the President of the Republic (elected by universal suffrage for a five-year term) is Head of State; he/she must have a fluent knowledge of Kazakh; the President holds supreme executive power, in conjunction with the Council of Ministers; the Prime Minister, Deputy Prime Ministers, the Ministers of Foreign Affairs, Defence, Finance and Internal Affairs (other ministers being appointed by the Prime Minister), together with the Chairman of the State Committee for National Security, and all ambassadors are appointed by the President; the supreme legislative body is the Supreme Kenges, which is directly elected by universal suffrage.

The Government

(March 1994)

PRESIDENCY

President of the Republic of Kazakhstan: NURSULTAN A. NAZARBAYEV (elected 1 December 1991).

Vice-President: YERIK M. ASANBAYEV.

CABINET OF MINISTERS

Prime Minister: SERGEY TERESHCHENKO.

First Deputy Prime Minister: KAZHEGELDIN AKEZHAN MAGZHAN ULU.

Deputy Prime Ministers: TULEGEN ZHUKEYEV, ASYGAT ZHABAGIN, SERGEY KULAGIN.

Deputy Prime Minister and Minister of External Economic Relations: SYZDYK ZH. ABISHEV.

Deputy Prime Minister and Minister of Science and New Technologies: GALYM A. ABILSIITOV.

Deputy Prime Minister and Chairman of the State Committee for State Property: ZHANIBEK KARIBZHANOV.

Minister of Defence: Col-Gen. SAGADAT NURMAGAMBETOV.

Minister of Foreign Affairs: TOLENTAI SULEYMENOV.

Minister of the Economy: MARS URKHUMBAYEV.

Minister of Justice: NAGASHIBAY AMANGALIYEVICH SHAYKENOV.

Minister of Internal Affairs: VLADIMIR SHUMOV.

Minister of Finance: YERKESHBAY DERBISOV.

Minister of Industry: ALBERT SALAMATIN.

Minister of Agriculture: BALTASH MOLDABAYEVICH TURSUMBAYEV.

Minister of Health: VASILY N. DEVYATKOV.

Minister of Communications: SABIT BAYJANOV.

Minister of Energy and Fuel Resources: K. KARABATOVICH BAYKENOV.

Minister of Material Resources: KANAT TURAKOV.

Minister of Ecology and Bioresources: SVYATOSLAV MEDVEDEV.

Minister of Highways and Transport Construction: SHAMIL KH. BEKBULATOV.

Minister of Education: SHAYSULTAN SHAYAKHMETOV.

Minister of the Press and the Media: SULTANOV.

Minister of Youth, Sport and Tourism: AYTIMOVA BYRGANYM SARIYEVA.

Minister of Social Welfare: ZAURE ZH. KADYROVA.

Minister of Trade: OKTYABR I. ZHELTIKOV.

Minister of Transport: NIGMATSHAN K. ISINGARIN.

Minister of the Forestry Industry: ALEKSANDR K. AMANBAYEV.

Chairman of the National Bank of Kazakhstan: DAULET KH. SEMBAYEV.

Chairmen of Principal State Committees

Chairman of the State Committee for Architecture and Construction: AKSAR A. KULIBAYEV.

Chairman of the State Committee for Culture: YERKEGALI RAKHMADIYEV.

Chairman of the State Committee for Geology and the Protection of Mineral Wealth: LEV M. TRUBNIKOV.

Chairman of the State Committee for Labour and Social Issues: S. D. BEYSENOV.

Chairman of the State Committee for the Limitation of Monopolization: PETR V. SVOIK.

Chairman of the State Committee for National Security: BULAT BAYEKENOV.

Chairman of the State Committee for Statistics and Analysis: T. ZH. ZHUMASULTANOV.

Chairman of the State Committee for Fuel and Power Engineering: BULAT NARYKHANOV.

MINISTRIES

Ministry of Agriculture: Almaty, Respubliki 15; tel. (3272) 63-44-44.

Ministry of Communications: Almaty, Kirova 134; tel. (3272) 62-31-94.

Ministry of Defence: Almaty; tel. (3272) 69-35-28.

Ministry of Ecology and Bioresources: 480091 Almaty, Panfilova 106; tel. (3272) 63-12-73; telex 251232; fax (3272) 63-52-44.

Ministry of the Economy: Almaty, Ablaikhana 97.

Ministry of Education: Almaty, Jambula 25; tel. (3272) 61-03-09.

Ministry of Energy and Fuel Resources: Almaty, Kirova 142; tel. (3272) 62-64-10.

Ministry of External Economic Relations: Almaty, Ablaikhana 77; tel. (3272) 62-40-57.

Ministry of Finance: Almaty, Ablaikhana 97; tel. (3272) 62-40-75; fax (3272) 62-27-70.

Ministry of Foreign Affairs: Almaty, Zheltoksan 167; tel. (3272) 63-25-38.

Ministry of Health: Almaty, Ablaikhana 63; tel. (3272) 33-46-11; fax (3272) 33-17-19.

Ministry of Highways and Transport Construction: Almaty, Panfilova 110; tel. (3272) 60-40-40.

Ministry of Industry: Almaty, Ablaikhana 93–95; tel. (3272) 62-06-03.

Ministry of Internal Affairs: Almaty, Kalinina 95; tel. (3272) 62-84-57.

Ministry of Justice: Almaty, Aiteke Bi 67; tel. (3272) 62-64-01; fax (3272) 63-84-31.

Ministry of the Press and the Media: Almaty, Mechnikova 64; tel. (3272) 67-27-56.

Ministry of Social Welfare: Almaty, Karla Marksa 122; tel. (3272) 63-67-78.

Ministry of Trade: Almaty, Ablaikhana 93–95; tel. (3272) 62-38-12.

Ministry of Youth, Sport and Tourism: Almaty, Abaya 48; tel. (3272) 67-39-86.

Principal State Committees

State Committee for Architecture and Construction: Almaty, Ablaikhana 93; tel. (3272) 62-91-00.

State Committee for Culture: Almaty.

State Committee for Fuel and Power Engineering: Almaty, Proletarskaya 80–84, ug. Jambula; tel. (3272) 61-13-91.

State Committee for Geology and the Protection of Mineral Wealth: Almaty, Lenina 85; tel. (3272) 61-60-87; fax (3272) 61-16-09.

State Committee for Labour and Social Issues: Almaty, Karla Marksa 122; tel. (3272) 62-11-68.

State Committee for the Limitation of Monopolization: Almaty; tel. (3272) 62-50-13.

State Committee for National Security: Almaty; tel. (3272) 69-35-28.

State Committee for State Property: Almaty, Ablaikhana 93–95; tel. (3272) 62-85-62.

State Committee for Statistics and Analysis: Almaty, Abaya 125; tel. (3272) 62-14-61.

Legislature

SUPREME KENGES

The Supreme Kenges was elected on 7 March 1994 and its first session was scheduled for 19 April. There were 176 deputies, of whom 42 were elected from a state list nominated by the President. The largest political party was the People's Unity Party with 30 seats, followed by the Confederation of Kazakh Trade Unions (11 seats), the People's Congress Party of Kazakhstan (9), the Socialist Party of Kazakhstan (8), the Peasants' Union (4) and Lad (Harmony—4), with one seat each for the Organization of Veterans of Kazakhstan, the Union of Kazakh Youth, the Human Rights Democratic Committee, the Association of Lawyers of Kazakhstan, the Aral-Asia-Kazakhstan International Committee and the Congress of Entrepreneurs of Kazakhstan.

Chairman: (vacant); 480091 Almaty, Dom pravitelstva; tel. (3272) 62-78-30.

Local Government

For the purposes of local government Kazakhstan was divided into 21 units: 19 oblasts and two cities. Each region had an elected assembly (soviet or council), while executive authority was represented by the akimiyat (formerly known as the ispolkom). In the early years of independence the akimiyat increasingly reported directly to the central authorities, during a period of uncertainty over the extent of jurisdiction and the powers of the various organs of government. During 1993 the President and other members of the Government urged the local soviets to resolve on their dissolution, so that new elections could be held under the 1993 Constitution. Almaty City Soviet was the first to comply with this and, with the dissolution of the national Supreme Soviet (Supreme Kenges) in December 1993, local elections were also likely in March 1994. The new representative bodies were to be known as maslikhat. The administrative regions were:

Aktyubinsk Oblast: Aktyubinsk.

Almaty City: Almaty (Alma-Ata); Mayor ZAMENBEK NURKADILOV.

Almaty Oblast: Almaty.

Eastern Kazakhstan Oblast (Vostochno-Kazakhstan Oblast): Ust-Kamenogorsk.

Guriyev Oblast: Atyrau (formerly Guriyev).

Jambul Oblast: Jambul (Dzhambul).

Jezkazgan Oblast: Jezkazgan (Dzhezhkazgan).

Karaganda Oblast: Karaganda.

Kokshetau Oblast: Kokshetau (Koktchetav).

Kustanai Oblast: Kustanai.

Kzyl-Orda Oblast: Kzyl-Orda.

Leninsk City: Leninsk (Turatam).

Mangyshlak Oblast: Shevchenko.

Northern Kazakhstan Oblast (Severo-Kazakhstan Oblast): Petropavlovsk.

Pavlodar Oblast: Pavlodar.

Semipalatinsk Oblast: Semipalatinsk.

Southern Kazakhstan Oblast (Yuzhno-Kazakhstan Oblast): Chimkent (Shymkent); Head of Admin ZAURBEK TURYSBEKOV.

Taldi-Kurgan: Taldi-Kurgan.

Tselinograd Oblast: Akmola (formerly Tselinograd).

Turgaj Oblast: Arkalyk.

Uralsk Oblast: Uralsk.

Political Organizations

People's Congress Party of Kazakhstan: Almaty; f. 1991; advocates civil peace; represents all ethnic groups in Kazakhstan; Chair. OLZHAS SULEYMENOV.

People's Unity Party: Almaty; f. 1993, originally as a socio-political movement, before becoming a political party; centrist; opposes radical nationalism, promotes social and ethnic harmony; Leader President NURSULTAN NAZARBAYEV; Chair. KUANYSH SULTANOV; Chair. of Political Bd SERIK ABDRAKHMANOV.

Republican Party—Azat: Almaty; f. 1992 by merger of three nationalist opposition parties: the Azat (Freedom) movement, the Republican Party and the Jeltoqsan (December) National-Democratic Party; Chair. KAMAL ORMANTAYEV.

Socialist Party of Kazakhstan: Almaty; f. 1991 to replace Communist Party of Kazakhstan; Chair. (vacant).

Smaller parties included the radical nationalist Kazakh movement, Alash, and the Russian nationalist groups, Yedinstvo and Lad (Harmony), and the Peasant's Union of Kazakhstan. The Ministry of Justice continued to refuse registration to the Freedom Party (which made territorial claims on parts of China), but, following the March 1994 elections, did register the Communist Party of Kazakhstan (Chair. LEONID KOROLKOV).

Diplomatic Representation

EMBASSIES IN KAZAKHSTAN

China, People's Republic: Almaty, Furmanova 137; tel. (3272) 63-93-72; fax (3272) 63-82-09; Ambassador: ZHANG DEGUANG.

France: 480110 Almaty, Furmanova 173; tel. (3272) 69-69-92; fax (3272) 62-74-12; Ambassador: BERTRAND PESSARD DE FOUCAULT.

Germany: 480110 Almaty, Furmanova 173; tel. (3272) 50-61-55; Ambassador: Dr EIKE BRACKLO.

India: Almaty, Kabanbai-Batyr 83; tel. (3272) 63-87-55; fax (3272) 53-87-64; Ambassador: KAMLESH SHARMA.

Iran: Almaty; Ambassador: RASUL ESLAMI.

Italy: Almaty; tel. (3272) 61-93-02; Ambassador: MAURIZIO TEUCCI.

Japan: 480002 Almaty, Makatayeva 47 (3rd Floor); tel. (3272) 30-42-38; fax (3272) 50-60-77.

Mongolia: Almaty; Ambassador: ERDENIYN BYAMBAJAV.

Pakistan: 480004 Almaty, Tulebaeva 25; tel. (3272) 33-35-48; Ambassador: RIAZ MOHAMMAD KHAN.

Romania: 480110 Almaty, Lenina 52, Hotel Kazakhstan, Rm 1413; tel. (3272) 61-92-30.

Turkey: 480100 Almaty, Tolebi 29; tel. (3272) 61-89-27; telex 251226.

United Kingdom: 480110 Almaty, Furmanova 173; tel. (3272) 50-61-91; fax (3272) 50-62-92; Ambassador: NOEL JONES.

USA: 480012 Almaty, Furmanova 97–99; tel. (3272) 63-17-70; fax (3272) 63-38-83; Ambassador: WILLIAM H. COURTNEY.

Judicial System

Chairman of the Supreme Court: MIKHAIL MALAKHOV.

Procurator-General: Gen. ZH. A. TUYAKBAYEV.

Chairman of the Constitutional Court: MURAT BAYMAKHANOV.

Religion

The major religion of the Kazakhs is Islam. They are almost exclusively Sunni Muslims of the Hanafi school. The Russian Orthodox Church is the dominant Christian denomination; it is attended mainly by Slavs. There are also Protestant Churches (mainly Baptists), as well as a Roman Catholic presence.

ISLAM

The Kazakhs were converted to Islam only in the early 19th century, and for many years there remained elements of animist practices among them. Over the period 1985–90 the number of mosques in Kazakhstan increased from 25 to 60, 12 of which were newly-built. By 1991 there were an estimated 230 Muslim religious communities functioning in Kazakhstan, an Islamic institute had been opened in Almaty and several translations of the Koran into Kazakh had been made. Until 1990 the Muslims of Kazakhstan were under the spiritual jurisdiction of the muftiate of Central Asia and Kazakhstan, which was based in Tashkent (Uzbekistan). In 1990 the Muslim authorities in Kazakhstan established an independent muftiate.

Mufti of Kazakhstan: RATBEK Haji RATBEK NYSANBAY-ULY, Almaty.

CHRISTIANITY

The Roman Catholic Church

Apostolic Administrator: Rt Rev. JAN PAWEŁ LENGA, Titular Bishop of Arba; 476010 Kokshetau, Krasnoarmeyskaya 56.

The Press

In 1989 there were 453 officially-registered newspaper titles being published in Kazakhstan, of which 160 were in the Kazakh language. Newspapers were also published in Russian, Uighur, German and Korean. There were 94 periodicals, including 31 in Kazakh.

GOVERNMENT AGENCY

Ministry of the Press and the Media: Almaty, Mechnikova 64; tel. (3272) 67-27-56.

PRINCIPAL DAILY NEWSPAPERS

Freundschaft (Friendship): Almaty; f. 1966; 5 a week; in German.

Kazakhstanskaya Pravda (Pravda of Kazakhstan): Almaty, Gogolya 39; tel. (3272) 63-03-98; f. 1920; 6 a week; sponsored by the Council of Ministers; independent; in Russian; Editor VYATCHESLAV M. SRYBNYH.

Kommunizm Tugi: Almaty; f. 1957; 5 a week; in Uighur.

Lenin Kichi: Almaty; f. 1938; 5 a week; in Korean.

Leninshil Zhas (Leninist Youth): 480044 Almaty, Zhibek zholy 50; tel. (3272) 33-02-19; f. 1921; 5 a week; in Kazakh; Editor U. KALIZHANOV; circ. 270,000.

Leninskaya Smena (Leninist Rising Generation): 480044 Almaty, Zhibek zholy 50; tel. (3272) 33-44-81; telex 251349; f. 1922; 5 a week; in Russian; Editor O. NIKANOV; circ. 300,000.

Sotsialistik Kazakhstan (Socialist Kazakhstan): Almaty, Gogolya 39; tel. (3272) 63-25-46; f. 1919; 6 a week; organ of the Supreme Kenges and Council of Ministers; in Kazakh; Chief Editor SH. MURTASAYEV.

OTHER PUBLICATIONS

Die Allgemeine: Almaty; f. 1966; in German; Editor-in-Chief KONSTANTIN EHRLICH; circ. 10,000.

Amanat (Voter): 480044 Almaty, Zhibek zholy 50; tel. (3272) 33-71-71; f. 1990; weekly; publ. by the Nevada-Semipalatinsk Movement; articles on disarmament and environmental protection; in Kazakh and Russian; Chief Editor E. TURSUNOV; circ. 50,000.

Ana Tili: Almaty, Pushkina 118; tel. (3272) 63-15-39; f. 1990; weekly; publ. by the Kazakh Tili society; in Kazakh; Chief Editor G. BEISENBAYULY; circ. 110,000.

Ara-Shmel (Bumble-bee): Almaty, Gogolya 39; tel. (3272) 63-59-46; f. 1956; monthly; satirical; in Kazakh and Russian; Chief Editor K. MUKAMEJANOV; circ. 53,799.

Arai-Zaria (Dawn): Almaty, Furmanova 53; tel. (3272) 32-29-45; f. 1987; monthly; socio-political; Chief Editor A. KOPISHEV.

Baldyrgan (Sprout): 480044 Almaty, Zhibek zholy 50; tel. (3272) 33-16-73; f. 1958; monthly; illustrated; for pre-school and first grades of school; in Kazakh; Editor T. MOLDAGALIYEV; circ. 150,000.

Densaulik (Health): Almaty, Ablaikhana 63; f. 1990; organ of the Ministry of Health; medicine; in Kazakh.

Ekonomika i Zhizn (Economics and Life): 480091 Almaty, Zheltoksan 118; tel. (3272) 63-96-86; f. 1926; monthly; journal of the Council of Ministers; theory and practice of economic reform and managment of the economy; in Russian; Chief Editor M. T. SARSENOV; circ. 13,000.

Kazakh Adebieti: 480091 Almaty, Ablaikhana 105; tel. (3272) 69-54-62; f. 1934; weekly; organ of the Union of Writers of Kazakhstan; weekly; in Kazakh; Chief Editor T. ABDIKOV.

Kazakhstan: Almaty; f. 1992; weekly; economic reform; in English.

Kazakhstan Aielderi (Women of Kazakhstan): 480044 Almaty, Zhibek zholy 50; f. 1929; monthly; popular women's magazine; in Kazakh; Chief Editor A. JAGANOVA; circ. 332,952.

Kazakhstan Kommunisi (Communist of Kazakhstan): Almaty, Gogolya 39; tel. (3272) 63-94-19; f. 1921; monthly; fmrly publ. by the Publishing House of the Cen. Cttee of the Communist Party of Kazakhstan; in Kazakh; Chief Editor K. SMAILOV; circ. 53,099.

Kazakhstan Mektebi (Kazakh School): 480091 Almaty, Ablaikhana 34; f. 1925; monthly; journal of the Ministry of Education; organization of public education; in Kazakh; Chief Editor S. ABISHEVA; circ. 40,033.

Kazakhstan Mugalimi: 480091 Almaty, Ablaikhana 34; f. 1952; weekly; publ. by the Ministry of Education; in Kazakh; Editor M. SERMAGAMBETOV; circ. 71,602.

Kazakstannyn Auyl Sharuashylygy (Agriculture of Kazakhstan): Almaty; f. 1936; monthly; in Kazakh and Russian.

Oasis: 484006 Jambul, Lunacharsky 42/2; tel. (32622) 5-24-83; fax (32622) 7-55-00; f. 1989; monthly; publ. by the Green Movement Centre; socio-ecological; in Kazakh and Russian; Editor A. ZAGRIBELNY.

Parasat (Intellect): 480044 Almaty, Zhibek zholy 50; tel. (3272) 33-49-29; f. 1958; monthly; publ. by the Kazakhstan Publishing House; socio-political, literary, illustrated; in Kazakh; Editor S. ELUBAYEV; circ. 135,000.

Partiinaya Zhizn Kazakhstana (Party Life of Kazakhstan): Almaty, Gogolya 39; tel. (3272) 63-32-79; f. 1920; monthly; fmrly publ. by the Communist Party of Kazakhstan; political; in Russian; Chief Editor G. M. SHESTAKOV; circ. 25,000.

Podrostok (Teenager): 480083 Almaty, Pastera 186/37; tel. (3272) 32-25-43; fortnightly; in Russian; Editor L. BALAYAN; circ. 10,000.

Pozitsia (Position): Almaty, Gogolya 49; tel. (3272) 63-28-68; f. 1990; fortnightly; Editor V. A. PARAMONOV.

Prostor (Wide Horizons): 480091 Almaty, Ablaikhana 105; tel. (3272) 69-63-19; f. 1933; monthly; journal of the Union of Writers of Kazakhstan; fiction; in Russian; Editor G. I. TOLMACHEV; circ. 127,063.

Russky Yazyk i Literatura v Kazakhskoy Shkole (Russian Language and Literature in the Kazakh School): 480091 Almaty, Ablaikhana 34; tel. (3272) 39-76-68; f. 1962; monthly; journal of the Ministry of Education; in Russian; Chief Editor B. S. MUKANOV; circ. 17,465.

Shalkar: 480044 Almaty, Zhibek zholy 50; tel. (3272) 33-86-85; f. 1976; weekly; publ. by the Kazakhstan Society; in Kazakh; Editor VAKHAP KADARKHANOV; circ. 10,500.

Sovieti Kazakhstana (Councils of Kazakhstan): Almaty; tel. (3272) 63-89-44; weekly; publ. by the Supreme Kenges of Kazakhstan; Editors S. AKTAYEV, YU. A. TARAKOV; circ. 30,000.

Sport: 480044 Almaty, Zhibek zholy 50; tel. (3272) 33-92-90; f. 1959; weekly; publ. by the Ministry of Youth, Sport and Tourism; in Kazakh and Russian; Editor-in-Chief NESIP ZHUNUSBAYEV; circ. 20,000.

Turk Birligy (Turk Unity): Almaty; f. 1993; promotes Turkic culture.

Uchitel Kazakhstana (Teacher of Kazakhstan): Almaty; f. 1952; weekly.

Ulan: 480044 Almaty, Zhibek zholy 50; tel. (3272) 33-80-03; f. 1930; 2 a week; fmrly publ. by the Leninist Young Communist League of Kazakhstan (Komsomol); Editor G. DOSKENOV; circ. 183,014.

Vestnik Selskokhozyaistvennoy Nauki Kazakhstana (Chronicle of Agricultural Science of Kazakhstan): Almaty, Janosova 51; tel. (3272) 21-48-57; f. 1958; monthly; publ. by the Kazakh Agricultural Academy; in Russian; Chief Editor K. B. IMANGALIYEV; circ. 2,235.

Zerde (Intellect): 480044 Almaty, Zhibek zholy 50; tel. (3272) 33-83-81; f. 1960; monthly; popular, scientific, technical; Editor E. RAUSHANOV; circ. 68,629.

Zhalyn: 480124 Almaty, Abaya 143; tel. (3272) 42-44-22; 6 a year.

Zhuldyz (Star): 480091 Almaty, Ablaikhana 105; tel. (3272) 62-51-37; f. 1928; monthly; journal of the Union of Writers of Kazakhstan; literary, artistic, socio-political; Editor-in-Chief MUKHTAR MAGAUIN; circ. 134,206.

Zhurnal Mod (Fashion Magazine): Almaty; f. 1958; 2 a year; publ. by the Dom Modely Odezhdy (Fashion House) Publishing House; in Kazakh and Russian.

NEWS AGENCY

KazTAG (Kazakh Telegraph Agency): Almaty, Ablaikhana 75; tel. (3272) 62-50-37; Dir AMANGELDY AKHMETALITOV.

Publishers

Gylym (Science): 480100 Almaty, Pushkina 111–113; tel. (3272) 61-18-77; f. 1946; books on the natural sciences, the humanities and scientific research journals; Dir S. G. BAIMENOV; Editor-in-Chief M. A. AIMBETOV.

Kainar (Spring): 480124 Almaty, Abaya 143; tel. (3272) 42-66-67; f. 1962; agriculture; Dir KH. A. TLEMISOV; Chief Editor I. I. ISKUZHIN.

Kazakhskaya Sovetskaya Entsiklopediya (Kazakh Soviet Encyclopaedia): Almaty, Ablaikhana 93–95; tel. (3272) 62-55-66; f. 1968; Chief Editor R. N. NURGALIEV.

Kazakhstan Publishing House: 480124 Almaty, Abaya 143; tel. (3272) 42-29-29; political and popular edns; Dir E. KH. SYZDYKOV; Chief Editor N. D. SITKO.

Oner (Art): 480124 Almaty, Abaya 143; tel. (3272) 42-08-88; f. 1980; Dir S. S. ORAZALINOV; Chief Editor A. A. ASKAROV.

Rauan (Science): 480124 Almaty, Abaya 143; tel. (3272) 42-25-37; f. 1947; fiction by young writers; Dir ZH. H. NUSKABAYEV; Editor-in-Chief K. KURMANOV.

Zhazushy (Writer): 480124 Almaty, Abaya 143; tel. (3272) 42-28-49; fiction; Dir KALDARBEK NAIMANBAYEV.

Radio and Television

Kazakhstan Broadcasting Corporation: 480013 Almaty, Zheltoksan 175; tel. (3272) 63-37-16; Chair. LEYLA BEKETOVA (acting).

Kazakh Radio: f. 1923; broadcasts in Kazakh, Russian, Uighur, German and Korean.

Kazakh Television: f. 1959; broadcasts in Kazakh, Uighur, Russian and German.

Finance

(cap. = capital; dep. = deposits; res = reserves)

BANKING

In the late 1980s major changes were introduced in the banking system of the USSR, including the establishment of a two-tier system in 1987–88. In 1990–91 the Almaty branch of the Soviet State Bank (Gosbank) was transformed into an independent Kazakh central bank (National Bank of Kazakhstan—NBK) and the establishment of private and public financial institutions was legalized. By the end of 1992 the banking system comprised the NBK, the Kazakhstan Savings Bank (renamed the People's Bank in January 1994, with 4,477 of the 5,035 bank branches in the country) and 157 other banks, 11 being co-operative banks and 48 privately owned.

Central Bank

National Bank of Kazakhstan (NBK): Almaty, Kokteli-3 21; tel. (3272) 47-37-97; Chair. DAULET KH. SEMBAYEV.

Other Banks

Agroprombank: Almaty; one of the larger banks of Kazakhstan; deals mainly with the agricultural sector; 231 brs.

Alem Bank Kazakhstan: 480100 Almaty, Lenina 39; tel. (3272) 61-83-82; telex 251206; fax (3272) 61-57-04; fmrly br. of Vneshekonombank USSR, then Kazakh Republican Foreign Trade Bank, renamed 1992; cap. 13,100m. roubles, dep. 1,600m. (July 1993); Chair. of Bd BERLIN K. IRSHIYEV; more than 20 brs.

Center Bank—Kazakh Central Joint-Stock Bank: 480096 Almaty, Bogenbay Batyr 248; tel. (3272) 53-67-64; telex 251218; fax (3272) 50-94-96; f. 1988 as Co-op Bank of the Almaty Union of Co-operatives; name changed 1991; one of the largest commercial banks of Kazakhstan; cap. 844.6m. roubles, dep. 936.4m. roubles (July 1993); Chair. of Council BAKYTBEK RYMBEKOVICH BAISEYTOV; Chair. of Bd MARAT SMAGULOVICH BISENOV; 22 brs.

Chimkent Co-op Bank—Soyuzbank: 486018 Chimkent, Lenina 2A; tel. (3252) 3-56-91; f. 1988; cap. 1m. roubles (1988); commercial bank; Chair. B. BEKTAYEV.

Kazdorbank: Almaty; tel. (3272) 32-48-61; commercial bank.

KRAMDS Bank—Innovation Commercial Bank: 480046 Almaty, Rozybakieva 101; tel. (3272) 46-29-18; telex 251309; fax (3272) 46-09-58; f. 1989; private commercial bank, financial subsidiary of KRAMDS Corpn; cap. 10,000m. roubles, dep. 5.3m. roubles (July 1993); Chair. of Bd LEONID ABLOZHEY; 33 brs.

Kredsotsbank: Almaty; one of the larger banks of Kazakhstan; commercial bank; deals mainly with housing management and municipal facilities.

People's Bank of Kazakhstan: Almaty; f. 1991 as successor to republican br. of the all-Union Sberbank (Savings Bank of Kazakhstan), renamed Jan. 1994; largest bank in Kazakhstan; 4,477 brs.

Technopolice Bank: 480013 Almaty, Respubliki 13; tel. (3272) 63-26-74; telex 251265; fax (3272) 63-23-49; f. 1991; private commercial bank; Russian ownership; cap. 175m. roubles, res 49m. roubles, dep. 5,092m. roubles (Jan. 1993); Chair. EDUARD O. AKOPIAN; Man. Dir. SERGEY F. USTINOV.

Turanbank—Kazakh Corporation Bank: 480091 Almaty, Aiteke Bi 55; tel. (3272) 62-17-74; telex 251393; fax (3272) 62-29-31; f. 1922; one of the largest commercial banks of Kazakhstan; cap. 3,576m. roubles, res 3,945m. roubles, dep. 231,050m. roubles (Jan. 1993); Chair. ORAZ M. BEYSENOV; Gen. Man. ERLAN BAIMURATOV; 78 brs.

Foreign banks with branches in Almaty included the Bank of China (China, People's Republic), Bank Stolichny (Russia), Dresdner Bank (Germany) and Neftechimbank (Russia).

Bankers' Organizations

Commercial Banks' Association of Kazakhstan: Almaty.

COMMODITY EXCHANGE

Karaganda Regional Commodity Exchange: 470074 Karaganda, Stroiteley 28; tel. (372) 74-04-82; telex 251338; fax (372) 74-43-25; f. 1991; authorized cap. 15m. roubles; Gen. Man. GEORGY REVAZOV.

Kazakhstan also has a Metal Exchange.

Trade and Industry

STATE PROPERTY AGENCY

State Committee for State Property: Almaty, Ablaikhana 93–95; tel. (3272) 62-85-62; f. 1991; responsible for the management of all and the divestment of most state-owned enterprises; Chair. ZHANIBEK KARIBZHANOV.

CHAMBER OF COMMERCE

Chamber of Commerce and Industry of Kazakhstan: 480091 Almaty, Ablaikhana 93–95; tel. (3272) 62-14-46; telex 251228; fax (3272) 62-05-94; Chair. H. RAKISHEV.

EMPLOYERS' ORGANIZATION

Union of Small Businesses: Almaty; f. 1991; Pres. CHINGIZ RYSEBEKOV.

FOREIGN TRADE ORGANIZATION

Kazakhintorg: 480091 Almaty, Gogolya 11; tel. (3272) 32-83-81; telex 251238; import and export; subsidiary of Ministry of External Economic Relations; Gen. Dir SAKEN SEYDUALIYEV.

MAJOR INDUSTRIAL ENTERPRISES

BK Gold—Bakyrchik: Auezov, Bakyrchik Mine; f. 1965, joint venture in 1992; owned by Minproc (Australia) and Chilewich (USA); operates mining at one of largest gold deposits in the world—estimated reserves of 8m. troy ounces; Chief Exec. KEVIN FOO; Operations Dir BILL HUSSEY; 1,000 employees.

Capacitor Plant: 492029 Vostochno-Kazakhstan obl., Ust-Kamenogorsk; tel. (3232) 66-02-91; produces complete capacitor installations; Dir. VLADIMIR A. NAKONETSHYJ; 2,800 employees.

Chimkent Industrial Amalgamation: 486008 Chimkent, Ordzhonikidze 28; tel. (3252) 12-29-43; telex 184112; specializes in the production of press-forging equipment; Dir-Gen. EDUARD DAVIDZHAN; 4,110 employees.

Jambul Industrial Corporation (Khimprom): 484026 Jambul; tel. (3262) 23-25-69; telex 251282; fax (3262) 23-28-73; production of phosphorus and its derivatives; Gen. Dir MUKHAN D. ATABAYEV; 6,000 employees.

Kazakhstanenergo (Kazakhstan Energy Co): Almaty, Kirova 142; state-owned electricity co.

KRAMDS Corporation: 480046 Almaty, Rozybakieva 101; tel. (3272) 46-29-18; f. 1988 as assen of state-owned enterprises and academic instits, incorporated as joint stock co in 1992; trades in a variety of industrial goods; Chair. of Bd LEONID ABLOZHEY.

Merey Furniture Company: Almaty; one of the first cos in Kazakhstan to be privatized (1991), it became a joint stock co in 1992; manufactures and exports furniture; Chair. NADJAT KADYROV; 1,500 employees.

Petroleum

Kazakhstancaspishelf (KCS): c/o Almaty, Ablaikhana 77; f. 1993 to share in and operate internat. consortium's exploration of Caspian Sea hydrocarbon resources; Chair. BALTABEK M. KUANDYKOV.

Kaznefteprodukt: c/o Almaty, Kirova 142; state petroleum and natural gas co.

Mangyshlakneft Production Association: 466200 Aktau, Atyrau Region; tel. 24-557; leading petroleum and natural gas co.

Tengizheftegas: c/o Almaty, Kirova 142; state hydrocarbons' production co for Tengiz field.

Tengiz Chevroil: c/o Almaty, Ablaikhana 77; f. 1993; joint venture with Chevron Corpn (USA).

CO-OPERATIVE ORGANIZATION

Kazakhtrebsoyuz: Almaty, Komsomolskaya 57; tel. (3272) 62-34-94; union of co-operative entrepreneurs; Chair. UMIRZAK SARSENOV.

TRADE UNIONS

Confederation of Kazakh Trade Unions: Almaty.

Transport

RAILWAYS

In 1992 the total length of rail track in use was 14,159 km, of which 3,050 km was electrified. The rail network was concentrated in the north of the country, where it joined the rail lines of the Russian Federation. From the capital, Almaty, lines run north-east, to join the Trans-Siberian Railway, and west, to Chimkent (Shymkent), and then north-west along the Syr-Dar'ya river, to Orenburg in European Russia. In June 1991 an international line was opened between Druzhba, on the eastern border of Kazakhstan, and Alataw Shankou, in the Xinjiang Uygur (Sinkiand Uighur) Autonomous Republic of the the People's Republic of China. A passenger service was inaugurated on this line in mid-1992. In January 1994 a new express passenger service from Almaty to Nukus (Karakalpakstan in Uzbekistan) opened, going via Tashkent and other cities of Uzbekistan and Turkmenistan. The country's rail services were operated by Kazakhstan Railways, which assumed responsibility for the local network from the former Soviet company in 1991. The Department of Railways at the Ministry of Transport was ultimately responsible for the state-owned Kazakhstan Railways.

Kazakhstan Railways: 480091 Almaty, Panfilova 110; tel. (3272) 60-44-70; fax (3272) 63-12-07; f. 1991; organized as three regional cos; Pres. V. T. PROTSENKO.

Almaty Railways: 480091 Almaty, Furmanova 127; tel. (3272) 60-44-70; fax (3272) 62-71-06; Dir A. J. OMAROV.

Tselinaya Railways: 473000 Akmola, Lenina 47; tel. 4-44-00; fax 2-50-95; Dir A. V. STARODUB.

Western Kazakhstan Railways: 463025 Aktyubinsk, Moldagulovoy 49; tel. (31322) 6-44-00; fax (31322) 5-39-52; Dir M. S. KHAMZIN.

ROADS

At 31 December 1989 there was a total of 164,900 km of roads, of which 99,000 km were hard-surfaced.

CIVIL AVIATION

The main international airport is at Almaty, which has scheduled links with cities in the Russian Federation and with Ashghabat (Turkmenistan), Bishkek (Kyrgyzstan), Dushanbe (Tajikistan) and Tashkent (Uzbekistan). The main operators are Aeroflot and Uzbekistan Havo Yulari. Lufthansa operates a regular service between Almaty and Frankfurt (Germany). There are some small private airline companies.

Culture

NATIONAL ORGANIZATION

State Committee for Culture: Almaty, Gogolya 35; tel. (3272) 30-63-18; Chair. E. RAKHMADIYEV.

CULTURAL HERITAGE

A. Kasteyev Kazakh State Art Museum: 480070 Almaty, Satpayeva 30A; tel. (3272) 67-99-62; f. 1976; 20,000 exhibits; library of 30,000 vols; Dir. ERMEK T. ZHANGELDIN.

State Public Library of Kazakhstan: 480021 Almaty, Abaya 14; f. 1931; over 3,458,700 vols; Dir. N. K. DAULETOVA.

Central State Museum of Kazakhstan: Almaty, Park 28 Panfilovtsev; 90,000 exhibits; Dir. R. K. KOSHAMBEKOVA.

SPORTING ORGANIZATION

Ministry of Tourism, Physical Culture and Sport: see section on The Government (Ministries).

PERFORMING ARTS

Abay Opera and Ballet Theatre: Almaty, Kalinina 112.

Auezov Drama Theatre: Almaty, Abaya 55.

Lermontov Russian Drama Theatre: Almaty, Abaya 43.

Uighur and Korean Theatre of Music and Drama: Almaty, Jerzhinskovo.

ASSOCIATION

Union of Writers of Kazakhstan: 480091 Almaty, Ablaikhana 105; tel. (3272) 62-62-95; subsid. writers' orgs in Karaganda, Semipalatinsk, Uralsk, Tselinograd and Chimkent.

Education

Education was fully funded by the state at primary and secondary level. Most pupils were taught in Russian, although, after the adoption of Kazakh as the state language, there were attempts to extend the provision of Kazakh-language education. In 1988 64.2% of all pupils at general day schools were taught in Russian, 33.0% in Kazakh, 1.9% in Uzbek, 0.4% in Uighur and 0.1% in Tajik. In 1990 there 8,308 secondary schools (including specialized establishments), with some 3.3m. students. Higher education was conducted in 55 institutions of higher education, including three universities, at which stage there were 285,600 students in total. In 1991 plans were announced for the establishment of a new university in Turkestan. Ethnic Kazakhs formed a greater proportion of students in higher education than in primary and secondary education, since many ethnic Russians chose to study at universities outside the country. In 1984/85 Kazakhs formed 46% of students in specialized secondary education, but 54% of students in higher education.

UNIVERSITIES

Al-Faraby Kazakh State National University: 480121 Almaty, Timiryazeva 46; tel. (3272) 47-25-17; fax (3272) 47-26-09; f. 1934; languages of instruction: Russian and Kazakh; 12 faculties; 1,530 teachers; 14,000 students; Rector Prof. GULZHAM JAMALIEVNA.

Karaganda State University: 470074 Karaganda, Universitetskaya 28; tel. (3212) 74-49-50; f. 1972; 10 faculties; 8,436 students.

Technical University at Karaganda Metallurgical Combine: 472300 Temirtau, Lenina 34; tel. 3-65-82; telex 251234; f. 1964; 3 faculties; Rector YU. A. MINAYEV.

Social Welfare

Even before the dissolution of the USSR reforms were aiming at making the social-security system self-financing, rather than being dependent upon transfers from the all-Union budget. The Pension and Social Insurance Funds were to be entirely financed by employer and employee contributions (26% of the total wage bill—raised to 37% in 1992—and 1% of salary, respectively). The Pension

Fund received 80.5% of all social-security contributions and the Insurance Fund was allocated 19.5%. A State Employment Fund was established in 1991, owing to the expected increase in unemployment in a free-market economy, and was financed by contributions, which in 1993 amounted to 2% of an employer's wage bill—with relatively few unemployed at this time, the Fund's responsibilities were extended to include the relief and support of Kazakh immigrants from other countries. For the same reason that there were relatively few unemployed in the early 1990s (the Government's reluctance to inflict the full consequences of a transition to a free-market economy on its population too rapidly), other social-security benefits were raised in 1992 and some were partially indexed in 1993. However, the Government intended to make the three Funds self-financing and did begin to target benefits more exactly on those with the greater needs, although an attempt to improve efficiency by uniting the Funds was rejected by parliament in 1992.

Living standards were relatively high compared to other Asian countries, with average life expectancy put at 68.7 years in 1991, when there was an infant mortality rate of 27.4 per thousand. In the same year there were an estimated 73.5 people per hospital bed in the country; there were 242 people per physician in the 1984–89 period (according to UNDP estimates).

NATIONAL AGENCIES

Ministry of Health: see section on The Government (Ministries).

Ministry of Social Welfare: see section on The Government (Ministries).

State Committee for Labour and Social Issues: see section on The Government (Ministries).

State Committee for the Supervision of Safe Working Practices in Industry and Mining: see section on The Government (Ministries).

Pension Fund: 480100 Almaty, Karla Marksa 122; tel. (3272) 63-67-37; f. 1991, after separation from Soviet system; Dir TEMIRKAN N. NURTAYEV.

Social Insurance Fund: 480003 Almaty, Zheltoksan 37–41; tel. (3272) 62-28-95; f. 1991, after separation from Soviet system; Dir MAKSUT S. NARIKBAYEV.

State Employment Fund: 480091 Almaty, Ablaikhana 93–95; tel. (3272) 62-11-68; f. 1991, in the expectation of increasing unemployment in the transfer to a free-market economy; Chair. SAYAT D. BEYSENOV.

HEALTH AND WELFARE ORGANIZATIONS

Central Committee of the Red Crescent and Red Cross of Kazakhstan: 480100 Almaty, Karla Marksa 86; tel. (3272) 61-62-91; Pres. ASYLBEK U. KONAKBAYEV.

Charity and Health Fund of Kazakhstan: 480100 Almaty, Karla Marksa 86; tel. (3272) 62-41-62.

Kazakhstan Children's Fund: 480064 Almaty, Furmanova 162; tel. (3272) 62-24-02; Chair. KOZHAKHMET B. BALAKHMETOV.

Voluntary Society of Invalids of Kazakhstan: 480100 Almaty, Karla Marksa 122; tel. (3272) 63-75-87; Chair. SEYDALIM N. TANIKEYEV.

The Environment

Kazakhstan developed severe environmental problems during the period of Soviet rule, mainly because of the considerable industrialization, but also because of ambitious agricultural projects in the region. The three main concerns of environmentalists, who led the first popular expressions of opposition to the Soviet Communist regime during the 1980s, were: atmospheric and water pollution from industrial toxins and chemical fertilizers; the desiccation of the Aral Sea, because of irrigation works; and nuclear testing. There was increasing pressure to deal with environmental pollution and some Western aid was forthcoming, although it tended to be linked to preventing further damage in new developments (such as US and World Bank aid of US $62m., in January 1994, to protect the environment during the exploration for petroleum in the Caspian Sea). The shrinking of the Aral Sea, once the world's fourth-largest fresh water lake, is one of the greatest ecological disasters in the world—in January 1994 Kazakhstan and the four other former Soviet Central Asian nations agreed, in Nukus (Uzbekistan), to establish an Aral Sea Fund, which was to receive 1% of their 1994 budgets (except from Tajikistan). Nuclear testing, which used to be carried out at Semipalatinsk, in the north of the country, was a major focus for opposition to the former Communist regime, but this was banned, with widespread popular support, in August 1991. The legacy of the nuclear industry remained of concern, as did testing in the neighbouring People's Republic of China.

GOVERNMENT ORGANIZATIONS

Ministry of Ecology and Bioresources: see section on The Government (Ministries).

Forestry Committee: Almaty, Zheltoksan 112; tel. (3272) 62-63-20; telex 251232; fax (3272) 62-20-26; f. 1946; Chair. Minister ALEKSANDR KULGANATOVICH AMANBAYEV.

International Fund for the Saving of the Aral Sea: Almaty, Respubliki 4; tel. (3272) 63-87-00; fax (3272) 63-76-33.

Kazekologiya Information Centre: Gen. Dir AMANGELDY A. SKAKOV.

State Committee for Water Resources: Almaty, Zheltoksan 118; tel. (3272) 63-76-01; Chair. NARIMAN K. KIPSHAKBAYEV.

ACADEMIC INSTITUTES

Academy of Sciences of Kazakhstan: 480021 Almaty, Shevchenko 28; tel. (3272) 69-12-12; fax (3272) 69-61-16; several attached institutes involved in environmental research; Pres. UMIRZAK M. SULTANGAZIN.

Kazekoeksp International Centre of Scientific Culture: Almaty, Shevchenko 162ZH; tel. (3272) 67-40-06; fax (3272) 63-12-07; Dir SESTAGER KHUSAINOVICH AKNAZAROV.

NON-GOVERNMENTAL ORGANIZATIONS

Aral-Asia-Kazakhstan International Public Committee: Almaty, Lenina 7; tel. (3272) 33-14-94; Pres. MUHTAR SHAHANOV.

Ecofund of Kazakhstan: Almaty; tel. (3272) 53-85-80; f. 1988; once one of largest environmental groups in Kazakhstan, but split several times; Co-Chair. LEV IVANOVICH KURLAPOV, VIKTOR ZONAV.

Eikos Organization: Almaty, Nusupbekova 32; tel. and fax (3272) 30-49-90; Gen. Dir TATYANA PILAT.

Ecology and Public Opinion—EKOM (Ekologiya i Obshchestvennoi Mneniye): 637046 Pavlodar, Suvarova 12/131; tel. 72-67-75; f. 1987; oldest registered environmental NGO in Kazakhstan; Chair. NIKOLAI STEPANOVICH SAVUKHIN; Sec. VALERI PAVLOVICH GALENKO.

Fund in Support of Ecological Education: 480005 Almaty, S. Kovalevskaya 63, kv. 13; tel. (3272) 41-29-91; telex 251232 (box 898); fax (3272) 63-66-34 (box 898); f. 1991; environmental education and ecological library; Chair. ZHARAS ABU-ULY TAKENOV.

Green Movement Centre (GMC): 484006 Jambul, Lunacharsky 42–2; tel. (32622) 5-24-83; fax (32622) 7-55-00; f. 1988; environmental education and publ. magazine *Oasis*; Chair. ALEXANDER ZAGRIBELNY; Sec. VALERIY KUKLIN.

Green Party: 480012 Almaty, Vinogradova 85, Rm. 302; f. 1991; political wing of Tabigat EcoUnion, which campaigns for environmental health and against water pollution, esp. the Sor-Bulak sewage lake near Almaty; Chair. MELS HAMSAYEVICH ELUSIZOV.

Green Salvation: 480059 Almaty, Shagabutdinova 133, kv. 66; tel. (3272) 67-89-06; f. 1990; organizes actions for groups throughout the country, collects data, raises awareness of issues; Chair. SERGEY BORISOVICH KURATOV.

International Ecology Centre (Biosphere Club): 493910 Leninogorsk, Micro-rayon 3, d. 19, kv. 10; Chair. VLADIMIR PAVLOVICH KARAMANOV.

Kazakh Community for Nature Protection (Central Council): 480044 Almaty, Zhibek zholy 15; tel. (3272) 61-65-16; Chair. KAMZA B. ZHUMABEKOV.

Nevada-Semipalatinsk Movement: 480021 Almaty, Vinogradova 85; tel. (3272) 63-49-02; fax (3272) 63-12-07; f. 1989; environmental group opposed to nuclear testing; Chair. OLZHAS SULEYMENOV; Sec. MIRZAHAN ERIMBETOV.

Lop-Nor Semipalatinsk Ecological Committee: Almaty; tel. (3272) 63-04-64; fax (3272) 63-12-07; f. 1992; semi-autonomous dept of Semipalatinsk-Nevada Movement, enjoys widespread popular support and campaigns against nuclear testing in neighbouring parts of China; Chair. AZAT MIRTAZOVICH AKIMBEK; Dep. Chair. IRKIZ ILEVA.

Tabigat EcoUnion: see entry on the Green Party above.

Defence

Kazakhstan was one of the four former Union Republics to become a nuclear power in succession to the USSR, in 1991. However, it was committed to the dismantling of its nuclear capabilities under the first Strategic Arms' Reduction Treaty (START 1—ratified by Kazakhstan in 1992) and the Nuclear Non-proliferation Treaty

(1993). In the meantime Russia effectively retained control over the nuclear weapons, with part of its small force stationed in the country. Russia and Turkmenistan also co-operated with Kazakhstan in the operation of the Caspian Sea Flotilla, another former Soviet force, which was based at Astrakhan (Russia); however, in April 1993 Kazakhstan declared its intention to create its own navy and, in February 1994, announced that it would be based near the town of Bautino, on the Caspian. In June 1993, according to Western estimates, the national army numbered some 44,000; there was also a small air force. The defence budget for 1993 was estimated 69,300m. roubles (some US $707m.).

Commander-in-Chief: President of the Republic.

Minister of Defence: Col-Gen. SAGADAT NURMAGAMBETOV.

Bibliography

Akiner, S. *Islamic People of the Soviet Union: An Historical and Statistical Handbook*, 2nd Edn. London and New York, Kegan Paul International, 1987.

Bradley, C. *The Former Soviet States: Kazakhstan.* London, Aladdin Books Ltd, 1992.

Demko, C. *The Russian Colonization of Kazakhstan, 1896–1916.* Bloomington, Mouton, 1969.

Katz, Z. *Handbook of Major Soviet Nationalities*, pp. 213–37. New York, Free Press, 1975.

International Monetary Fund. *Kazakhstan* (Economic Reviews Series). Washington, DC, IMF, 1993.

Narodnoe Khozyaistvo Kazakhstana za 70 let. Statistichekii shornik. Almaty, 1990.

Olcott, M. B. *The Kazakhs.* Stanford, California, 1987.

Qazag Sovet Enciklopedeyasi (10 Vols). Almaty, 1972–78.

KYRGYZSTAN

Geography

PHYSICAL FEATURES

The Kyrgyz Republic (formerly the Kyrgyz Soviet Socialist Republic and then, until 1993, the Republic of Kyrgyzstan) is a small, land-locked state situated in eastern Central Asia. It was also known as Kyrgyzia or Kirghizia. Kazakhstan borders it to the north, Uzbekistan to the west, Tajikistan to the south-west and south, and the People's Republic of China to the south-east. The country's western border is pincer-shaped, with the Uzbekistan part of the Fergana basin abutting into Kyrgyzstan. The country covers an area of 198,500 sq km (76,640 sq miles).

The terrain is largely mountainous, dominated by the western reaches of the Tien Shan range in the north-east and the Pamir-Alay range in the south-west. The highest mountain is Pik Pobeda (Victory Peak or Tomur Feng, 7,439 m), at the eastern tip of the country, on the border with China. Much of the mountain region is permanently covered with ice and snow, and there are many glaciers. The Fergana mountain range, running from the north-west across the country to the central-southern border region, separates the eastern and central mountain areas from the Fergana valley in the west and south-west. Other lowland areas include the Chu and Talas valleys near the northern border with Kazakhstan. The most important rivers are the Naryn, which flows through the central regions and eventually joins the Syr-Dar'ya, and the Chu, which forms part of the northern border with Kazakhstan, into the deserts of which it flows. In the north-east of the country is the world's second-largest crater lake, the Issyk-Kul.

CLIMATE

The country has an extreme, continental climate, although there are distinct variations between low-lying and high-altitude areas. In the valleys the mean July temperature is 28°C (82°F), whereas in January it falls to an average of −18°C (−0.5°F). Annual precipitation ranges from 180 mm in the eastern Tien Shan to 750–1,000 mm in the Fergana mountains. In the settled valleys the annual average varies between 100 mm and 500 mm.

POPULATION

At the census of 1989, at which the total resident population was 4,290,442, 52.4% of the population were ethnic Kyrgyz (Kirghiz), 21.5% Russians, 12.9% Uzbeks, 2.5% Ukrainians, 2.4% Germans and 1.6% Tatars. There were also small

numbers of Kazakhs (37,318), Dungans (36,928), Uighurs (36,779), Tajiks (33,518), Turks (21,294), Koreans (18,355) and others. Kyrgyz replaced Russian as the official language in September 1989. It is a member of the Southern Turkic group of languages and is written in the Cyrillic script. The Arabic script was in use until 1928 when it was replaced by a Latin script. The Latin script was replaced by Cyrillic in 1941. In 1991 it was proposed to reintroduce the use of the Latin script, although this was unlikely to occur until later in the decade. The major religion was Islam, Kyrgyz and Uzbeks traditionally being Sunni Muslims of the Hanafi school. Russians and Ukrainians were usually adherents of Eastern Orthodox Christianity.

The total population at mid-1992 was estimated to be 4,472,000. The average population density (persons per sq km) was 22.5. There was a relatively low level of urbanization, with an estimated 38% of the total population living in the major towns in 1991. Bishkek (known as Frunze, 1926–91), the capital, is situated in the Chu valley in the north of the country. It had an estimated population of 626,900 in January 1990. The only other town of significant size was Osh (218,000 in 1990), in the Fergana valley, near the border with Uzbekistan. Important regional centres include Przhevalsk, Kyzyl-Kiya, Jalal-Abad (Dzhalal-Abad) and Naryn.

Chronology

10th century: The Turkic ancestors of the Kyrgyz began to migrate from the upper reaches of the Yenisey (in the Tyva region of the Russian Federation), towards the Tien Shan.

13th century: The rise of the Mongol Empire hastened the southwards migrations, although the ancestors of the Kyrgyz remained dominated by the Eastern Turkic tribes.

1685: The Kyrgyz, reckoned to have emerged as a distinct ethnic group within the previous 200 years, came to be ruled by the Oirot Mongols, against whom the Kyrgyz rulers waged a fierce struggle.

1758: The Manzhous (Manchus) defeated the Oirots and the Kyrgyz became nominal subjects of the Chinese emperors.

1863: The northern Kyrgyz acknowledged the sovereignty of the Russian Tsar, thus providing the official date of the 'voluntary' incorporation of Kyrgyzstan into Russia.

1866: The Russians defeated the Khanate of Kokand, which had acquired suzerainty over the southern Kyrgyz earlier in the century.

1876: The Khanate of Kokand was abolished and the territory formally incorporated into the Russian Empire; however, there were several Kyrgyz uprisings in the following decades.

1916: An attempt to impose labour and military service on the non-Russian peoples of the Empire occasioned a widespread revolt in Central Asia; the savage repression of the rebellion caused many Kyrgyz to emigrate to China.

25 October (New Style: 7 November) 1917: The Bolsheviks, led by Lenin (Vladimir Ilych Ulyanov), staged a *coup d'état* and seized control of government in Petrograd (St Petersburg); the Russian Soviet Federative Socialist Republic (RSFSR or Russian Federation) was proclaimed.

14 February (Old Style: 1 February) 1918: First day upon which the Gregorian Calendar took effect in Russia.

30 April 1918: The Autonomous Soviet Socialist Republic (ASSR) of Turkestan (based in Tashkent, Uzbekistan) was proclaimed, as part of the Russian Federation; this included Kyrgyzstan, although Bolshevik control was not established here until 1919–20, because of fierce resistance to the Red Army from the 'Whites' and from local *basmachi* insurgents.

1923: The reform of the Arabic script helped the formation of a vernacular standard language.

14 October 1924: The Kara-Kyrgyz Autonomous Oblast was created, as part of the Russian Federation (until the mid-1920s the Russians knew the Kyrgyz as the 'Kara-Kyrgyz', to differentiate them from the Kazakhs who were called 'Kyrgyz').

1925: The Kara-Kyrgyz Autonomous Oblast was renamed the Kyrgyz Autonomous Oblast.

1 February 1926: Kyrgyzstan (Kyrgyzia or Kirghizia) became an ASSR, still within the Russian Federation. Also during the year, the capital of Bishkek was renamed Frunze.

1927–28: The second programme of land reform (there had been some in 1921–22) continued to aim at resettling the nomadic Kyrgyz; this policy, which had a disastrous effect on the herds and resources of the Kyrgyz, was carried out despite the protests of leading local Communists ('the Thirty'), who were subsequently purged. The agricultural reforms and, later, collectivization revived the *basmachi* struggle.

1928: A Latin script replaced the Arabic, aiding the improvement of literacy.

5 December 1936: The second Constitution of the USSR (the 'Stalin' Constitution) was adopted; Kyrgyzstan became a Soviet Socialist Republic (SSR) and, therefore, a full Union Republic in the Soviet federation.

1941: A Cyrillic script replaced the Latin.

1953: A Soviet campaign against the epic poetry of Central Asia (such as the Kyrgyz saga *Manas*) provoked strong opposition in Kyrgyzstan.

1980: The Chairman of the Council of Ministers, Sultan Ibraimov, was murdered in mysterious circumstances.

November 1985: Turdakan Usubaliyev, the First Secretary of the Kyrgyz Communist Party (KCP), was replaced by Absamat Masaliyev, who accused his predecessor of corruption and nepotism.

May 1986: Apas Jumagulov was appointed Chairman of the Council of Ministers.

September 1989: Kyrgyz replaced Russian as the official language of the Republic.

February 1990: In elections to the republican Supreme Soviet most seats were won, unopposed, by KCP candidates; those opposition candidates which were elected were united in the Kyrgyzstan Democratic Movement (KDM).

April 1990: Masaliyev was elected to the post of Chairman of the Supreme Soviet, which was effectively a republican executive head of state.

June 1990: More than 500 people were killed when ethnic Kyrgyz attacked Uzbeks in the town of Uzgen, in the Osh region, and three-quarters of the town was destroyed by fire. The state of emergency was not ended until November.

30 October 1990: The Kyrgyz SSR, or Kyrgyzia, was declared a sovereign state and renamed the Socialist Republic of Kyrgyzstan. This followed the election by the Supreme Soviet of a compromise candidate, liberal academic Askar Akayev, to the new post of executive President of the Republic—the discredited Masaliyev failed to win the post which he had designed for himself.

15 December 1990: The country was simply renamed the Republic of Kyrgyzstan (the capital, Frunze, was renamed Bishkek in the following February). In the same month Masaliyev resigned as Chairman of the Supreme Soviet.

January 1991: The Council of Ministers was replaced by a smaller Cabinet of Ministers, to head which Akayev appointed Nasirdin Isanov.

17 March 1991: In an all-Union referendum on the issue of the future state of the USSR, 87.7% of those eligible to vote approved Gorbachev's concept of a 'renewed federation'. The next month Masaliyev was replaced as leader of the KCP by Jumgalbek Amanbayev.

31 August 1991: Following the failure of the Moscow coup attempt and the banning of the KCP, the Supreme Soviet of Kyrgyzstan adopted a declaration of independence.

12 October 1991: Akayev was confirmed as President in direct elections, winning some 95% of the votes cast.

29 November 1991: Premier Nasirdin Isanov was killed in an automobile accident.

13 December 1991: Leaders of the five Central Asian Republics (Kazakhstan, Kyrgyzstan, Tajikistan, Turkmenistan and Uzbekistan) met in Ashgabat (Turkmenistan) and agreed to join the Commonwealth of Independent States (CIS).

21 December 1991: At a meeting in Almaty (Kazakhstan) the leaders of 11 former Union Republics signed a protocol on the formation of the new Commonwealth and, thereby, the effective dissolution of the USSR.

11 February 1992: Tursunbek Chyngyshev was appointed Prime Minister of Kyrgyzstan; Akayev subordinated the government to the presidency (he remained head of government until 1993) and halved the number of ministries.

June 1992: The Communists re-formed as the Party of Communists of Kyrgyzstan (PCK), led by Masaliyev and Amanbayev.

December 1992: A draft constitution was adopted for consideration by the Supreme Soviet (Uluk Kenesh), after almost one year of public debate and consultation.

March 1993: One of Akayev's closest political allies, Vice-President Feliks Kulov, had his business dealings investigated by a hostile parliament.

5 May 1993: Parliament, renamed the Jogorku Kenesh, enacted and promulgated the new Constitution of the Kyrgyz Republic.

10 May 1993: Kyrgyzstan introduced its own currency, the som; Kazakhstan and Uzbekistan immediately suspended trading relations and the latter introduced what amounted to economic sanctions for a short time.

July 1993: German Kuznetsov, the First Deputy Prime Minister, resigned and announced that he was uncertain of the future of Slavs in Kyrgyzstan and was emigrating to Russia.

10 December 1993: Kulov resigned (he was later appointed to head the administration of Chu Oblast), following further accusations of corruption against the Government by the Jogorku Kenesh.

13 December 1993: Although the parliamentary vote of confidence was inconclusive, Akayev dismissed the Chyngyshev Government in the hope of securing political stability.

21 December 1993: Apas Jumagulov returned as premier, heading a Government which included members of the PCK (one of which, Amanbayev, had to resign his parliamentary seat and party leadership in order to remain a minister).

31 January 1994: Some 96% of those who voted in a national referendum (96% participation) supported the continued presidency of Akayev; this was interpreted as a mandate for further radicalizing the economic reform programme.

16 January 1994: Kyrgyzstan signed its agreement to join an economic union proposed by Kazakhstan and Uzbekistan; the following month border restrictions between the three countries were relaxed.

History

The ancestors of the Kyrgyz were probably settled on the upper reaches of the Yenisey, around what is now the Tyva region of the Russian Federation, until about the 10th century. From there they migrated south to the Tien Shan region, a movement hastened by the rise of the Mongol Empire, in the 13th century. The Kyrgyz (believed to be of mixed Mongol, Turkic and Kypchak descent, had emerged as a distinct ethnic group by the 15th century) were ruled by various Turkic peoples until 1685, when they came under the control of the Mongol Oirots. The defeat of the Oirots by the Manzhous (Manchus), in 1758, left the Kyrgyz as nominal Chinese subjects, but the Chinese did not interfere with their independent nomadic life styles. The Kyrgyz of southern Kyrgyzstan came under the suzerainty of the Khanate of Kokand in the early 19th century and the territory was formally incorporated into the Russian Empire (which had been increasing its influence among the Kyrgyz since the mid-1800s), as part of the Khanate, in 1876. There were various revolts against tsarist authority thereafter, and many Kyrgyz moved to the Pamirs and Afghanistan. The suppression of the 1916 rebellion in Central Asia caused a major migration of the Kyrgyz to China.

Following the October Revolution of 1917 in Russia, there was a period of civil war, with anti-Bolshevik forces, including the Russian 'White' Army, and local *basmachi* armed groups of Muslim, nationalist insurgents, fighting against the Bolshevik Red Army. Soviet power was established in the region by 1919. In 1918 the Turkestan Autonomous Soviet Socialist Republic (ASSR) was established within the Russian Soviet Federative Socialist Republic (RSFSR, or Russian Federation) and included Kyrgyzstan until 1924, when the Kara-Kyrgyz Autonomous Oblast was created, also within the RSFSR (the Russians used the term Kara-Kyrgyz for the Kyrgyz until the mid-1920s, to distinguish them from the Kazakhs, who at that time were also known as Kyrgyz by the Russians). In 1925 it was renamed the Kyrgyz Autonomous Oblast and it became the Kyrgyz ASSR in February 1926. On 5 December 1936 the Kyrgyz Soviet Socialist Republic (SSR) was established as a full Union Republic of the USSR.

During the 1920s Kyrgyzstan developed considerably in cultural, educational and social life. Literacy was greatly improved and a standard literary language was introduced. Economic and social development was also notable. Land reforms were carried out in 1920–21 and 1927–28, which resulted in the settlement of many of the nomadic Kyrgyz. Land reforms were followed by the collectivization programme of the early 1930s, which was strongly opposed by many Kyrgyz, and prompted a partial revival of the *basmachi* movement, which had been largely suppressed by the mid-1920s.

Leading members of the Kyrgyz Communist Party (KCP) attempted to increase the role of ethnic Kyrgyz in the government of the Republic, but these so-called 'national Communists' were expelled from the KCP and often exiled or imprisoned, particularly during the late 1930s. Despite the suppression of nationalism during the rule of Stalin (Iosif Dzhugashvili), many aspects of Kyrgyz national culture were retained, and tensions with the all-Union authorities were evident in the post-1945 period. There were allegations that the murder of Sultan Ibraimov, the Chairman of the Kyrgyz Council of Ministers, in 1980, was a result of his support for greater republican autonomy.

The first evidence of Soviet leader Mikhail Gorbachev's new policies came with the resignation of Turdakan Usubaliyev, the First Secretary of the KCP, in November 1985. His replacement, Absamat Masaliyev, accused Usubaliyev of corruption and nepotism, and dismissed many of his closest allies from office. However, Masaliyev's commitment to *perestroika* (restructuring) did not extend beyond correcting the excesses of his predecessor. The policy of *glasnost*, which permitted greater openness in the press, was frequently criticized by Masaliyev. Nevertheless, by 1988 the Republic's press had begun to adopt a more liberal stance, notably *Literaturny Kirghizstan*, the newspaper of the Union of Writers. The conservative leadership also opposed the development of unofficial political groups, but several groups were established in 1989 with the intention of alleviating the acute housing crisis in the Republic, by seizing vacant land and building houses on it. One of these groups, Ashar, was partially tolerated by the authorities and soon developed a wider political role. Osh Aymaghi, a similar organization to Ashar, but based in Osh Oblast, where a majority of the population were ethnic Uzbeks, attempted to obtain land and homes for the ethnic Kyrgyz in the region.

Disputes over land and housing provision in the crowded Fergana valley region of Osh Oblast precipitated violent confrontation between Kyrgyz and Uzbeks in 1990. Osh had been incorporated into Kyrgyzstan in 1924, although Uzbeks formed a majority of the population, and Uzbeks had begun to demand the establishment of an Uzbek autonomous region in Osh Oblast. On 4 June 1990 at least 11 people died and more than 200 were injured as a result of conflict between Uzbeks and Kyrgyz. A state of emergency and a curfew were introduced, and the border between Uzbekistan and Kyrgyzstan was closed, but the violence escalated. Order was not restored until August. According to official reports, 230 people died in the violence, but unofficial sources claimed that over 1,000 people had been killed. The state of emergency was not lifted until November. The republican and regional leadership blamed Osh Aymaghi and other informal groups for initiating the violence, but the opposition movement criticized Masaliyev and the local KCP leadership for not responding to social and economic problems in the area. In August Renat Kulmatov, the First Secretary of the Party in Osh Oblast, was forced to resign, and the republican leadership was increasingly criticized for its role in the violence.

Despite an increase in the influence of the nascent democratic movement, the elections to the Supreme Soviet of Kyrgyzstan, in February 1990, were conducted in traditional Soviet style, with KCP candidates winning most seats unopposed. In April 1990 the Supreme Soviet elected Masaliyev to the newly instituted office of Chairman of the Supreme Soviet. He favoured the introduction of an executive presidency, as had been effected in other Union Republics. Election to the new post was to be by the Supreme Soviet, and the overwhelming KCP majority in the Supreme Soviet seemed to guarantee the election of Masaliyev. However, by October, when an extraordinary Supreme Soviet session was convened to elect the President, Masaliyev had been seriously discredited by the violence in Osh. Moreover, the democratic opposition, which had united as the Kyrgyzstan Democratic Movement (KDM), had developed into a significant political force, with support in parliament. In the first round of voting in the Supreme Soviet, Masaliyev failed to achieve the necessary percentage of votes to be elected as President. He was refused permission to be renominated. In a further round of voting, Askar Akayev, the liberal President of the Kyrgyz Academy of Sciences, was elected to the presidency. Akayev quickly allied himself with reformist politicians and economists, including leaders of the KDM, which had been influential in turning public opinion against Masaliyev following the events in Osh. Economic reformists were appointed to a State Commission on Economic Reform, and plans were announced for a programme of privatization.

In December 1990 Masaliyev resigned as Chairman of the Supreme Soviet, and was replaced by Medetkan Sherimkulov. In January 1991 Akayev introduced new government structures, replacing the unwieldy Council of Ministers with a smaller Cabinet of Ministers, and appointed a new Government, comprised mainly of younger reformist politicians. Despite opposition from the KCP, and Masaliyev in particular, in mid-December 1990 the Supreme Soviet voted to change the name of the Republic to the Republic of Kyrgyzstan. In February 1991 the capital, Frunze, named after the Red Army commander who had conquered much of Central Asia in the Civil War, reverted to its original name of Bishkek.

Although Kyrgyzstan was one of the most democratic of the Central Asian Republics, economic realities seemed to prevail against secession from the USSR. In the referendum on the preservation of the USSR, in March 1991, an overwhelming majority (87.7% of those eligible to vote) approved the proposal to retain the USSR as a 'renewed federation'.

Akayev's programme of political and economic reform had many opponents in the KCP and the security forces. In April 1991, apparently as a result of differences with President Akayev, Masaliyev resigned as First Secretary of the KCP. He was replaced by Jumgalbek Amanbayev. Although Amanbayev seemed to be more enthusiastic about Akayev's reform programme than his predecessor had been, there was much opposition in the KCP leadership to controversial plans which would lead to the 'de-partyization' (removal of Party cells from workplaces) of government and the security forces.

On 19 August 1991, when a State Committee for the State of Emergency (SCSE) announced that it had assumed power in the Soviet capital of Moscow, there was an attempt to depose Akayev in Kyrgyzstan. The KCP declared its support for the coup leaders, and the commander of the Turkestan military district threatened to dispatch troops and tanks to Kyrgyzstan. To pre-empt military action against him, Akayev dismissed Gen. Asasankulov, the Chairman of the republican KGB (State Security Committee), and ordered interior ministry troops to guard strategic buildings in Bishkek. Despite warnings from Vladimir Kryuchkov, Chairman of the all-Union KGB and a member of the SCSE, Akayev established contact with Boris Yeltsin, President of the Russian Federation, and broadcast Yeltsin's opposition to the SCSE on republican television. On 20 August 1991 Akayev publicly denounced the coup and issued a decree prohibiting activity by any political party in government or state bodies. The next day Akayev ordered all military units in Kyrgyzstan to remain in their barracks. On 26 August, after the coup had collapsed in Moscow, Akayev and Vice-President German Kuznetsov announced their resignation from the CPSU, and the entire bureau and secretariat of the KCP resigned. The KCP was dissolved, although it re-formed as the Party of Communists of Kyrgyzstan (PCK) in 1992.

Following the coup attempt, Akayev continued with his policies of seeking more independence for Kyrgyzstan and the implementation of ambitious economic reforms. On 31 August 1991 the Supreme Soviet of Kyrgyzstan voted to declare independence from the USSR. With the dissolution of the KCP and the CPSU there was little remaining organized opposition to Akayev and his policies. On 12 October 1991 Akayev was elected President by direct ballot, with 95% of the votes cast; no other candidate was nominated.

Kyrgyzstan participated in meetings of the five Central Asian Republics in 1990 and 1991, and developed relations with the European Republics of the former USSR. Together with the representatives of seven other Republics, Akayev signed the Treaty of the new Economic Community on 18 October 1991 and the republican Government also approved the draft treaty of the proposed Union of Sovereign States. When Russia, Belarus and Ukraine proposed a new Commonwealth of Independent States (CIS) to replace the USSR, Akayev was quick to announce his approval of the proposal. On 13 December all five Central Asian Republics formally agreed to join the new Commonwealth and, on 21 December, a total of 11 Republics agreed to its formation. The effective dissolution of the USSR was confirmed by the resignation of President Gorbachev on 25 December.

KYRGYZSTAN AFTER INDEPENDENCE

The early years of full independence for Kyrgyzstan were dominated by questions of economic and political reform. President Akayev, who enjoyed widespread public confidence, was committed to the reform process and was largely responsible for the introduction and implementation of what restructuring was achieved in the early 1990s. However, despite the backing of the major Western donors (including the International Monetary Fund—IMF), Kyrgyzstan had major economic difficulties during this period, mainly as a result of the disintegration of the Soviet trading bloc, and this impeded the transfer to a free-market economy. Moreover, there were problems created by the opposition from the bureaucracy and many in parliament—both the former Communists and, often, the nationalists. Thus, in the debate on a new constitution during 1992, these forces united to demand a restriction on the powers of the presidency and an enhanced role in government for the legislature (unusual in the former Soviet states). Parliament was also to insist that the Prime Minister, the chairman of the Cabinet of Ministers, be designated head of government and, less effectively, that the President should be restricted in his role as head of state. A draft document of the new basic law was adopted in December 1992, but a final version of the Constitution was not approved and promulgated until 5 May 1993. It provided for a parliamentary form of government, with legislative power vested in a 105-seat assembly or Jogorku Kenesh. However, the elected President retained considerable authority.

The Constitution of May 1993 was only adopted after a desperate appeal by President Akayev for legislative action by the Supreme Soviet (then known as the Uluk Kenesh—this body was to remain the legislature until elections to the new parliament were held, envisaged as being in 1995). Akayev cited the increasing instability and ungovernability of the country. The exact definitions of authority were often confused and disputes in local government were also frequent (thus, there was an increase in tension in Jalal-Abad, in October 1992, between the local leader and his rivals). There was also an increase in the activity of Islamic groups and many in the country, particularly the Slavs, feared that Kyrgyzstan could disintegrate, with widespread violence, in the same manner as neighbouring Tajikistan. There was also an increase in crime, much of it connected to the cultivation of and trade in illegal drugs. The leading reformers warned that this rising crime rate, and the growth of official corruption, could restrain the development of Kyrgyzstan into Akayev's vision of the 'Switzerland of Central Asia'.

President Akayev's policies were opposed by anti-reform Communists and by nationalists suspicious of his concern for the ethnic-minority groups, particularly the Slavs. This alliance caused disputes over the balance of powers in the state, over economic and political reform generally, and over language and citizenship issues (see Ethnic Politics below). However, most threatening to Akayev, in 1993 at least, were the allegations of corruption against his closest political associates. In March 1993 Vice-President Feliks Kulov was investigated for the alleged irregularity of his business dealings. Then the opposition provoked public controversy, particularly in July, over the establishment of a joint venture with a Canadian mining company to exploit the Kumtor gold deposits. The Communist forces in the Supreme Soviet wished to undermine Akayev's attempts to attract Western investment in the country, while the nationalists feared foreign exploitation. These groups united to hinder the Government, despite the accusations that they were creating unnecessary instability. However, their fears seemed justified by a scandal involving another Canadian company, Seabeco. This brokerage company was prominent in arranging business contacts between Kyrgyzstan and the West, but its association with the Government was terminated in 1993 following allegations that a significant part of the limited state gold reserves had mysteriously left the country in a Seabeco helicopter. The allegations of official misconduct reached Prime Minister Tursunbek Chyngyshev, who came under considerable pressure to resign. Chyngyshev, however, denied all charges and his supporters claimed that they were part of a right-wing conspiracy to discredit the reformers. With the report of a parliamentary commission into the 'Seabeco affair', many of the deputies again demanded a vote of confidence in the Government. The following day, 10 December, the Vice-President, Kulov, one of Akayev's strongest supporters, resigned for ethical reasons and urged that the Government do so as well. On 13 December the Supreme Soviet failed to achieve the necessary two-thirds of deputies in favour of a motion of 'no confidence' in the Chyngyshev administration, but, in the interests of the political stability which he had urged on the factions in October, Akayev dismissed the Government.

The last Communist premier, Apas Jumagulov, was asked to form a government with the help of Akayev's most implacable and best organized opponents, the PCK. However, parliament remained cautious of the new Government as well, and insisted that ministers could not retain their seats in the legislature, thereby obliging the resignation of the new deputy premier Jumgalbek Amanbayev as leader of the PCK. Furthermore, despite the preponderance of setbacks for the reformers during December 1993, Akayev received a renewed mandate to complete his term of office in a referendum on 30 January 1994. According to official results, of the 95.6% of the electorate which voted, 96.2% supported the President. Akayev therefore demanded a quickening in the pace of reform and continued his policies of fostering inter-ethnic harmony in the country. To the latter end he summoned a *kurulty* or congress of the peoples of Kyrgyzstan, in February, and again urged unity for the stability of the country.

Ethnic Politics

One of the recurring issues of politics in Kyrgyzstan was the relations between the different ethnic groups, particularly between the Kyrgyz majority and the Russians. A constant feature of the regime of President Akayev was his policy of concern for the Slav minority, even though he was the one who had led the country to independence. Initially the language issue provided the main focus of debate, with the nationalists even succeeding in omitting any reference to Russian in the draft constitution of December 1992—Kyrgyz was to be the official language and was to be spoken fluently by the President of the Republic, but there was no guarantee of the position of Russian, even as the 'language of inter-ethnic communication' as in neighbouring Kazakhstan. However, Akayev was determined to allay Slav anxieties, not only for the sake of civil order, but also in an attempt to stem the increasing rate of emigration of non-Kyrgyz from the country. The dilemma was that the departure of the skilled personnel relatively over-represented among the Russians, and other minority groups, compounded the crises in the country, further fuelling their fears of a degeneration of the situation in Kyrgyzstan.

In May 1993 Akayev succeeded in convincing parliament that it should not alter the new constitutional provisions on language. The Constitution, therefore, secured the status of the Russian language in Kyrgyzstan, but Akayev could not prevent the name of the country being changed from the Republic of Kyrgyzstan to the less ethnically neutral Kyrgyz Republic. In July the most prominent Slav in government and one of Akayev's oldest allies, the First Deputy Prime Minister and former Vice-President German Kuznetsov, announced that he was returning to Russia, because he despaired of the future for Slavs in Kyrgyzstan.

The resignation and emigration of Kuznetsov was a serious reverse to official policy of encouraging the vital minority populations to remain in the country. Government efforts continued, although Akayev thereby earned some distrust from the Kyrgyz nationalists. However, it was accepted, in mid-1993, that earlier targets to completely replace Russian with Kyrgyz in the public service by 1997 were impractical and that this should be postponed until the end of the decade. Moreover, the commitment of Kyrgyzstan to the future of the Russian language in the country was supposed to be demonstrated by the opening, later in 1993, of a Slavonic university, the Kyrgyz-Russian University, in Bishkek. In February 1994 President Akayev even agreed, in principle, to the idea of dual citizenship for ethnic Russians in Kyrgyzstan, thus, in theory, providing them with the security that might encourage them to remain in Central Asia.

FOREIGN RELATIONS

Kyrgyzstan's most important external relations were with the Russian Federation. This was partly as a result of their long association in the tsarist and Soviet empires, leading to close political and economic links, and partly because of the need for Kyrgyzstan to secure the reassurance of its ethnic Russian minority. Kyrgyzstan remained eager for close links with Russia consistently through the early 1990s. The Republic had been a strong supporter of the old Union, was committed to its membership of the CIS and was determined to remain in the rouble zone. However, as the vagaries of Russian monetary policy exacerbated the economic situation in Kyrgyzstan, it became increasingly important for the country to control and introduce its own currency (the som), which it did on 10 May 1993.

The introduction of the som, while unpopular with local Russians, was welcomed by the authorities in the Russian Federation. However, mainly because it was introduced with little notification, it occasioned a deterioration in relations with the neighbouring Central Asian states of Kazakhstan and Uzbekistan. Both countries suspended trade with Kyrgyzstan for a period and Uzbekistan even introduced restrictions which amounted to economic sanctions. They feared an influx of roubles, causing an increase in their rates of inflation. With Russia effectively forcing these and other countries from the rouble zone later in the year, however, relations did improve. Generally, Akayev was eager to maintain good relations with the other Central Asian states, particularly for economic reasons. He was eventually forced to apologize to Uzbekistan for the manner in which the new currency was introduced.

The introduction of the som also illustrated the good reputation Kyrgyzstan enjoyed among the major Western donors. Its commitment to reform seemed real and the country was viewed as a model for the other Central Asian economies. The IMF and the World Bank, with support from the USA, Japan and countries in Western Europe, were prepared to commit large amounts of support for the som, as well as other aid. Foreign investment remained cautious by the beginning of 1994, mainly because of fears for the political stability of the country and concern at the falling standards of living. Nevertheless, economic reform was progressing well and the necessary legislation was significantly more advanced than in most other former Soviet states.

Disappointment in the level of Western investment was compounded by the failure of a rapid development of Kyrgyzstan's relations with the Muslim world. However, the country did cultivate relations with the secular Turkish state, which was anxious to capitalize on its cultural and ethnic links with the region. By the beginning of 1994, though, the Turkish foreign ministry was acknowledging that the overwhelming interest of Kyrgyzstan and the other Central Asian countries was in their relations with Russia and with their former Soviet neighbours. Thus, despite initial caution, in 1992, at any involvement in the situation in Tajikistan, Kyrgyzstan did eventually contribute peacekeeping forces under Russian leadership. This followed several incursions by armed Tajik insurgents attempting to spread the idea of Islamic revolution into Kyrgyzstan.

The Kyrgyz Republic also had a long border with the People's Republic of China and the two countries had historical links. Following the dissolution of the USSR, Kyrgyzstan developed relations with China and one evident result was the dramatic increase in trade between the two.

CONCLUSION

Kyrgystan under President Akayev was determined to transform itself into a democratic, secular state with a free-market economy. In order to achieve this it needed to secure its democratic and economic reforms and its political stability, not only for the sake of internal security, but to reassure both vital Western investors and the Russian Federation. Ironically, the collapse of the economy was the most serious cause of political unrest, with the reforms being blamed rather more than the conservative forces ranged against them and the disintegration of the Soviet economic system. However, Kyrgyzstan was advanced in its reforms and even its unreformed parliament was vigorous in defence of its prerogatives. It remained attractive to the West, as the most liberal of the former Soviet Central Asian states, and as a potentially prosperous base for operations in Central Asia and with western China. Relations with Russia were also kept at an optimum level, although strained by the nationalist rhetoric of many Russian politicians in late 1993 and early 1994.

The Economy

Kyrgyzstan made considerable progress during the early 1990s in the creation of an open society which could provide the basis for a democratic system. The country was considerably in advance of the other former Soviet Central Asian states in the legislative reform of the economic system and, in May 1993, was the first to introduce its own currency, the som. However, its economic performance was very weak. As part of the USSR it was one of the poorest of the Union Republics, contributing only 0.8% of total Soviet net material product (NMP) in 1988. Of total Soviet agricultural NMP it contributed 1.2% and of industrial NMP 0.6%, although it accounted for 1.5% of the total population and 0.9% of the total area. Moreover, in 1988 50.2% of its NMP was derived from exports to other Union Republics and only 1.2% from exports to foreign countries, the lowest proportion in the USSR (in 1990 some 98% of exports were to other parts of the Union). It was, therefore, particularly badly affected by the collapse of the Soviet economic system and, in the early 1990s, its economic performance was worse than any other former Soviet state except war-torn Armenia, Azerbaijan and Tajikistan. Tajikistan even exceeded Kyrgyzstan in the production of consumer goods in 1992. The Kyrgyz Republic was, however, potentially wealthy, but it urgently needed foreign investment. A major deterrent, particularly from 1993, was the increase in political instability, which, ironically, was only likely to be calmed by an economic recovery.

AGRICULTURE

Agriculture was the principal sector of the economy, typically contributing about one-third of gross domestic product (GDP—the Western measure of economic performance, similar to the NMP of centrally planned economies) and of employment. Thus, in 1990 agriculture and forestry contributed 33.7% of total GDP (some 43% of NMP) and 32.8% of employment, although in 1991 it's share of GDP (28.4%—36.4% of NMP) declined owing to the disproportionate increase, relatively, in industrial prices.

The mountainous terrain favours livestock rearing, which remained the principal agricultural sector, as it had been throughout the largely nomadic history of the Kyrgyz. Only 7% of the agricultural land was arable, and some 70% of that depended on irrigation. The position of the country, with its often harsh climatic conditions and being in an earthquake zone, often had adverse consequences for the sector. For example, in 1992 there were earthquakes and mudslides.

The main crops were cotton, hemp, tobacco, vegetables and fruit. By the early 1990s the private sector was making an important contribution, accounting for between one-third and one-half of some harvests. The principal livestock were cattle and, particularly in the mountain areas, sheep and goats. Wool (about 38,000 metric tons per year in the late 1980s and early 1990s), leather and silk were also major products, and much of the industrial sector was devoted to agro-processing (such as the production of sugar, textiles and cigarettes). However, in common with much of the Kyrgyz economy, the sector was severely affected by the collapse of the Soviet internal market and the consequent disruption to trade: in 1991 overall agricultural production declined by 9%, although it roughly maintained its levels in 1992. Conditions deteriorated slightly in the following year and, by the beginning of 1994, the numbers of cattle had declined significantly. The sector remained one of the most important contributors to any future economic recovery, but this would be dependent upon factors common to most of the economy: an improvement in the terms of trade; a halt to the deterioration in the country's infrastructure; and foreign investment.

MINING AND ENERGY

The Kyrgyz Republic was rich in mineral resources: there were negligible petroleum and natural gas reserves, but important deposits of coal, gold, uranium, antimony and other rare metals. The main restraint on development was the inaccessibility of many of the potential resources. However, a Canadian company agreed to help exploit the Kumtor gold mines (the seventh-largest deposit in the world), in the south-east of the country, in December 1992, although conservative forces in the legislature delayed the final agreement on the joint venture by creating some political furore over the deal. The Government was also interested in establishing, with foreign co-operation, gold-processing plants in Talas and Kemin. It intended to use this resource to build up its own gold reserves by 1995, thus improving the viability of an independent economy.

The mountainous nature of the country and its plentiful water resources enabled it to be an exporter of hydro-electric energy. In 1993 there were six hydroelectric power stations, which exported electricity to neighbouring Soviet successor states and, starting in the previous year, to the People's Republic of China. The country remained a net importer of petroleum and gas, however, and as the prices of these increased to world-market levels (rather the massive subsidization of the all-Union Soviet economic system) this was likely to further undermine the country's trading position. There were plans to alleviate this situation by constructing a petroleum refinery (envisaged capacity of 100,000 metric tons per year) in the country.

INDUSTRY

Industry (including mining) contributed 37.8% of GDP in 1991 (45.3% of NMP), but this did not reflect the usual position, when the sector accounted for about one-third of total GDP (33.7% in 1990—less than the agricultural sector). Construction contributed 6.9% to GDP in 1991. Together, industry and construction employed 27.8% of those in employment. The unusual increase in the share of industry in overall economic activity was considered likely to be revealed as a temporary aberration as the consequences of the disintegration of the Soviet trading system and the increasing fuel shortages became more apparent after independence. Overall industrial output remained constant in 1991 (the main exception being food processing, where output declined by some 10%, in line with the fall in agricultural production), but deteriorated by 23% in the first three quarters of 1992. At mid-1993 official sources estimated that the volume of industrial production had fallen by 41.8% compared to the same period in the previous year, including a 63.3% decrease in the vital machine-building industry, and this also had an adverse affect on government revenue. In December 1993 there were 42 enterprises in the country which were non-active.

The industrial sector remained relatively primitive, not only in terms of technology and distribution facilities, but in terms of its basic structure. Thus, if it were to compete effectively in world markets, foreign investment was required. Some 80% of industrial output was accounted for by light industry, food processing and machine building. Light industry, based in 125 plants, consisted of textiles (26.2% of total industrial production in 1991), clothing (8.6%) and leather, shoes and fur (2.2%). Machine building was worth 17.6% of total industrial production in 1991. The metallurgy industry was important and the Government was particularly hopeful of encouraging foreign investment in it, although it also intended to emphasize paper-processing in Tokmak, the furniture factory in Bishkek and the production of household appliances. Agro-processing was the most obviously attractive proposition for foreign investors, however, as was indicated by the February 1994 agreement with the British-American Tobacco Company to invest in a cigarette factory near Bishkek (initially US $55m.).

Industry was very seriously affected by the economic crisis of the early 1990s. The general liberalization of price controls in the former USSR seriously affected supplies to Kyrgyzstan and inhibited its sales. Fuel shortages compounded the problems, as did the need to modernize production facilities. Moreover, the emigration of the productive Slav and German population (a trend which predated independence, but which the Government seemed unable to discourage even into the mid-1990s) had repercussions for the levels of skill available to industrial activity. Industrialization, like urbanization, in Kyrgyzstan, was largely a product of Slav immigration and it was seriously affected by the exodus.

SERVICES

The service sector of the economy was the least developed, most activity being accounted for by government services, which were among the first victims of post-independence austerity. Transport and communications (4.2% of GDP in

1991 and 5.4% of employment in 1990) were relatively well developed under the Soviet regime, but also suffered from being part of an integrated, all-Union system. The geography of the country meant that it had developed in conjunction with its neighbours rather than as a unit. Thus the major southern cities of Osh and Jalal-Abad were part of the Fergana valley economy, and communications between them tended to be across the territory of Uzbekistan, in which most of the Fergana basin lay. Likewise, mountain barriers encouraged the region of Talas to orientate itself on the Jambul (Dzhambul) area of Kazakhstan, rather than on the city of Bishkek. Even the remote Naryn district, in the early 1990s, was developing its links with the neighbouring regions of China. Kyrgyzstan planned to take advantage of this existing integration, however, by developing its transport links (hence its ability to export) in unison with its neighbours.

Commerce, domestically and with China, increased in the early 1990s and the private sector was influential in this activity. However, the service industry from which the country hopes to gain most in the future was tourism. The Kyrgyz Republic possessed some magnificent, snow-capped mountain scenery, including spectacular lakes, glaciers and pasturelands.

TRADE, PRICES AND FINANCE

As was indicated above, Kyrgyzstan depended on trade within the former Soviet economic system. Its principal exports (overwhelmingly to other Soviet Republics), at the beginning of the 1990s, were non-ferrous metals and minerals, woollen goods and other agricultural products, electric energy, certain engineering goods (notably agricultural machinery) and some electronic products. It relied on other former Soviet states for petroleum and natural gas, ferrous metals, chemicals, most machinery, wood and paper products, some foods and most construction materials.

The weaknesses of the country's position in free-market conditions were witnessed before the disintegration of the USSR. Even under the Soviet regime, prices began to be liberalized, most significantly in April 1991. By the end of the year, compared with the December of the previous year, consumer prices were almost three times higher and wholesale prices almost four times higher. Inflation rose, production decreased and government revenue (and its capacity for combating the deteriorating situation—particularly with the removal of the transfers from the all-Union budget) declined. A second phase of price liberalization, in January 1992, caused prices to increase by some 19 times, by the following December, compared with the previous year. The control of inflation was a major factor in the decision to introduce a national currency in Kyrgyzstan, in May 1993, and this was credited with limiting price rises (certainly compared with the average for the rouble zone), although consumer prices were still reported to have increased almost 15-fold during 1993. This had a major impact on the welfare of the population (and their enthusiasm for economic reform), but also on the national income (gross national product). This was reckoned to have declined by 26% in 1992 and 17% in 1993, according to official sources.

On 10 May 1993 Kyrgyzstan introduced its own currency, the som, and, from the close of business on 14 May, it became the sole legal tender. The currency was backed by the International Monetary Fund (IMF), the World Bank, the USA, Japan, Switzerland and the Netherlands, with a total of US $130m. Given the uncertainties of the rouble zone, most donors were anxious for the country to introduce its own currency, and its decision to do so gave it access to large amounts of foreign assistance (notably $400m. from the IMF).

The process was not without its problems, however, and created some anxieties for local businessmen and foreign suppliers. Most dramatically, and partly because of the lack of notice to the country's neighbours, Uzbekistan and Kazakhstan suspended all trading activity with the country. Furthermore, Uzbekistan even suspended petroleum and gas supplies for a few days and refused to accept any payments in soms. However, most difficulties were resolved and, by the end of the year, both these countries had left the rouble zone themselves and acknowledged that, while they favoured closer economic integration with Russia (in the Commonwealth of Independent States), greater regional co-operation was a more immediately achievable objective.

In February 1994 Kyrgyzstan, Kazakhstan and Uzbekistan began the first phase of their planned customs union, and lifted some trading restrictions on their borders. This was important to Kyrgyzstan, because of its continuing degree of integration into a regional economic system. Until it had succeeded in attracting sufficient Western investment or developing trade links with China or Turkey, for instance, it needed to maintain close relations with its neighbours in the former USSR.

CONCLUSION

The Kyrgyz Republic was the foremost of the Central Asian economies in the process of reform, although, at the beginning of 1994, it had yet to experience many benefits or the required level of foreign investment. However, President Askar Akayev claimed a mandate for accelerated reform, despite obstructionist forces in the bureaucracy and parliament, from a referendum at the end of January 1994. The Government was committed to a transfer to a free-market economic system by stabilizing the economy and implementing reforms which would encourage long-term growth. It had reduced its expenditures, ended most price subsidies (on some 90% of goods) and made such reforms as the introduction of a value added tax. The privatization programme, which began in 1991 and was accelerated in July 1992, had succeeded in putting some 26% of the economy into the private sector by the end of 1993 (compared to 11% in January). Further structural reform was likely to extend privatization, to continue the development of a suitable legal and institutional framework (including reforms in the financial sector, although the country already possessed an independent central bank) and to restructure and target more precisely social-welfare benefits. However, external factors, such as the continuing disruption to trade between the Soviet successor states and the increases in petroleum and gas prices, were likely to continue to present Kyrgyzstan with significant problems into the mid-1990s. Moreover, political instability was not conducive to the necessary foreign investment, although the natural wealth of the country, its development of political and economic reform and the backing of the major international financial institutions and donor countries were powerful incentives.

Statistical Survey

Principal source: IMF, *Kyrgyzstan, Economic Review* and *Supplement on Countries of the Former Soviet Union;* World Bank, *Statistical Handbook: States of the Former USSR.*

Area and Population

AREA, POPULATION AND DENSITY

Area (sq km)	198,500*
Population (census result)	
12 January 1989†	
Males	2,077,623
Females	2,180,132
Total	4,257,755
Population (official estimates at mid-year)	
1990	4,394,000
1991	4,453,000
1992	4,472,000
Density (per sq km) at mid-1992	22.5

* 76,600 sq miles.

† The figures refer to *de jure* population. The *de facto* total was 4,290,442.

PRINCIPAL ETHNIC GROUPS
(permanent inhabitants, 1989 census)

	%
Kyrgyz	52.4
Russian	21.5
Uzbeks	12.9
Ukrainians	2.5
Germans	2.4
Tatars	1.6
Others	6.7
Total	100.0

PRINCIPAL TOWNS (estimated population at 1 January 1990)
Bishkek (capital, formerly Frunze) 625,000; Osh 218,000.

BIRTHS, MARRIAGES AND DEATHS

	Registered live births		Registered marriages		Registered deaths	
	Number	Rate (per 1,000)	Number	Rate (per 1,000)	Number	Rate (per 1,000)
1987	136,588	32.6	40,161	9.6	30,597	7.3
1988	133,710	31.4	40,490	9.5	31,879	7.5
1989	131,508	30.4	41,790	9.7	31,156	7.2

Expectation of life (years at birth, 1991): 68.5 (males 64.3; females 72.4).

Source: UN, *Demographic Yearbook.*

EMPLOYMENT (annual averages, '000 persons)

	1988	1989	1990
Agriculture and forestry	577	577	573
Industry* Construction }	462	487	486
Transport and communications	112	96	94
Trade and other material services	117	113	115
Non-material services	450	466	479
Total	1,716	1,739	1,748

* Principally mining, manufacturing, electricity, gas and water.

1991 ('000 persons): Total 1,750.

Agriculture

PRINCIPAL CROPS ('000 metric tons)

	1990	1991	1992*
Wheat	482	434	550
Barley	592	556	550
Maize	406	365	300
Potatoes	365	303	325
Seed cotton	81	62	55
Vegetables	487	399	385
Grapes	43	29	26
Other fruit	141	85	100
Sugar beet	2	8*	10
Tobacco (leaves)	59	43	56†
Cotton lint	25	19	18†

* FAO estimate(s). † Unofficial estimate(s).

Source: FAO, *Production Yearbook.*

LIVESTOCK ('000 head, year ending September)

	1990	1991	1992*
Horses	310	313	315
Cattle	1,200	1,200	1,200
Pigs	400	400	300
Sheep	10,185	9,700	9,200
Goats	315	300	300
Chickens†	15,000	13,000	13,000

* FAO estimate(s). † Unofficial estimate(s).

Source: FAO, *Production Yearbook.*

LIVESTOCK PRODUCTS ('000 metric tons)

	1990	1991	1992*
Beef and veal	91	87	83
Mutton and lamb	70	64	60
Goatmeat	7†	7†	5
Pigmeat	41	33	30
Poultry meat	33	29	27
Cows' milk	1,185	1,132	900†
Cheese	12.5	10.0†	9.0†
Hen eggs†	39.5	36.0	31.0
Wool:			
greasy	38.6	36.6	37.0
scoured	23.2	22.0	22.2

* FAO estimate(s). † Unofficial estimate(s).

Source: FAO, *Production Yearbook.*

Mining and Industry

Production (1989, unless otherwise indicated): Coal 3,997,000 metric tons, Crude petroleum 230,000 metric tons (1975), Natural gas 1.05m. metric tons, Cement 1,165,900 metric tons, Crude steel 3,200 metric tons, Motor cars 17,700 (1975), Electric energy 14,903m. kWh.

Finance

CURRENCY AND EXCHANGE RATES

Monetary Units
100 tyiyns = 1 som.

Sterling and Dollar Equivalents (30 September 1993)
£1 sterling = 9.42 soms;
US $1 = 6.30 soms;
1,000 soms = £106.14 = $158.73.

Note: In May 1993 Kyrgyzstan introduced its own currency, the som, replacing the Russian (former Soviet) rouble. Based on the official rate of exchagne, the average value of the Soviet currency (roubles per US dollar) was: 0.6274 in 1989; 0.5865 in 1990; 0.5819 in 1991. However, a multiple exchange rate system was in operation, with separate non-commercial and tourist rates. A commercial exchange rate was introduced on 1 November 1990, replacing the official rate for most transactions. The commercial rate (roubles per US dollar) was: 1.692 at 31 December 1990; 1.671 at 31 December 1991. Between November 1989 and April 1991 the tourist exchange rate valued the rouble at one-tenth of the official rate. In April 1991 this rate, renamed the 'special rate', was set at $1 = 27.6 roubles. It was subsequently adjusted. The average market exchange rate in 1991 was $1 = 31.2 roubles. Following the dissolution of the USSR in December 1991, Russia and several other former Soviet republics retained the rouble as their monetary unit. The average interbank market rate in 1992 was $1 = 222.1 roubles.

From 15 May 1993 (having been introduced on 10 May), the som became Kyrgyzstan's sole legal currency. The initial exchange rate was $1 = 4 soms, while Russian currency was exchanged at a rate of 1 som = 200 roubles. Some of the figures in this Survey are still expressed in terms of roubles.

BUDGET (million roubles)*

Revenue	1990	1991	1992†
Taxation	2,185	2,660	11,413
Turnover tax	1,172	1,168	—
Sales tax	—	305	—
Value-added tax	—	—	5,129
Excise duties	—	—	3,256
Profits taxes	421	756	2,780
Personal income taxes‡	196	383	219
Social security contributions§	364	—	—
Other revenue	115	837	554
Grants from USSR (net)	905	1,928	—
Total	3,205	5,425	11,967

Expenditure	1990	1991	1992†
National economy	1,553	1,573	3,276
Education	604	1,096	4,231
Health	318	565	2,283
Culture and mass media	79	96	328
Social security	416	1,025	2,697
Law enforcement	n.a.	68	616
Contributions to Commonwealth of Independent States	—	—	773
Debt interest	—	—	2,196
Total (incl. others)	3,184	4,727	17,053

* Figures represent a consolidation of the operations of the central Government and local governments.

† Forecasts. Actual totals (in million roubles) were: Revenue 25,500; Expenditure 40,300, excluding lending minus repayments (12,100).

‡ Revenue was split between the USSR and the Republic in 1990. In later years all funds accrued to the Republic.

§ Collection of social security contributions was treated as extra-budgetary from 1991, when a separate pension fund was established.

MONEY SUPPLY (million roubles)

	1990	1991	1992
Currency outside banks	1,766	2,883	17,904

30 June 1993: 158 million soms.

COST OF LIVING (Retail price index; previous year = 100)

	1991	1992
All items	185.0	954.6

NATIONAL ACCOUNTS (million roubles at current prices)
Expenditure on the Gross Domestic Product

	1989	1990	1991
Government final consumption expenditure	1,250	1,370	2,510
Private final consumption expenditure	5,036	5,572	7,971
Increase in stocks	625	448	1,092
Gross fixed capital formation	2,390	2,337	4,353
Total domestic expenditure	9,301	9,727	15,926
Exports of goods and services *Less* Imports of goods and services	−1,681	−1,407	−87
GDP in purchasers' values	7,620	8,320	15,839

Gross Domestic Product by Economic Activity

	1989	1990	1991
Agriculture and forestry	2,510	2,805	4,505
Industry*	2,250	2,348	5,985
Construction	785	840	1,100
Transport and communications	357	397	672
Other material services	562	617	1,011
Non-material services	1,157	1,313	2,566
GDP in purchasers' values	7,620	8,320	15,839

* Principally mining, manufacturing, electricity, gas and water.

BALANCE OF PAYMENTS (estimates)
Inter-republican Transactions (million roubles)

	1989	1990	1991
Merchandise exports	2,549	2,446	6,331
Merchandise imports	−3,362	−2,863	−5,373
Trade balance	−813	−417	958
Services (net)	n.a.	n.a.	n.a.
Budgetary transfers from USSR (net)	540	905	1,928
Current balance*	−273	488	2,886

* Excluding services.

Foreign Transactions (US $ million)

	1989	1990	1991
Merchandise exports	81	88	23
Merchandise imports	−1,459	−1,738	−578
Trade balance	−1,378	−1,650	−555
Interest payments*	n.a.	−34	−36
Current balance	n.a.	−1,684	−590

* Kyrgyzstan's share of interest obligations on the USSR's external debt.

External and Inter-republican Trade

INTER-REPUBLICAN TRADE

PRINCIPAL COMMODITIES (million roubles)

Imports	1989	1990	1991
Industrial products	3,183	2,674	5,143
Oil and gas industry	325	269	543
Coal industry	32	3	85
Ferrous metallurgy	167	167	292
Non-ferrous metallurgy	91	96	277
Chemical and petrochemical industry	349	273	566
Machine-building and metalworking	1,020	823	1,184
Forestry, woodworking, paper and pulp	129	114	176
Construction materials industry	67	69	81
Light industry	560	522	1,238
Food industry	344	198	436
Agricultural products (unprocessed)	88	87	181
Total (incl. others)	3,361	2,863	5,373

Exports	1989	1990	1991
Industrial products	2,433	2,340	6,137
Electric power	80	67	188
Non-ferrous metallurgy	124	145	492
Chemical and petrochemical industry	24	23	121
Machine-building and metalworking	946	882	2,106
Light industry	650	640	1,898
Food industry	519	508	1,142
Agricultural products (unprocessed)	96	87	182
Total (incl. others)	2,549	2,446	6,331

EXTERNAL TRADE

PRINCIPAL COMMODITIES (US $ million)

Imports	1989	1990	1991
Industrial products	883	1,178	350
Chemical and petrochemical industry	71	62	6
Machine building and metal working	87	131	111
Light industry	133	152	23
Food industry	563	796	201
Agricultural products	94	89	93
Total (incl. others)	978	1,268	443

Exports	1989	1990	1991
Industrial products	65	85	13
Non-ferrous metallurgy	38	53	7
Total (incl. others)	67	86	20

Education

(1988/89)

	Institutions	Students
Secondary schools	1,752	928,200
Secondary specialized schools	47	49,152
Professional/Technical Schools	109	38,923
Higher schools (incl. university-level)	10	57,109

Directory

The Constitution

A new Constitution was adopted by the Supreme Soviet or Uluk Kenesh on 5 May 1993. It guaranteed basic human rights and declared the Kyrgyz Republic to be a law-governed, secular, unitary and democratic sovereign state. The Constitution provided for a parliamentary system of government, with a 105-seat legislature, the Jogorku Kenesh (as the parliament was to be known henceforth). This assembly was to be elected by universal adult suffrage for a maximum term of five years and was to be in permanent session. The existing 350-seat assembly was to continue as the legislature until a general election (due by 1995). A Prime Minister was to be head of government and responsible for choosing the Cabinet of Ministers, the members of which could not sit in the Jogorku Kenesh. The President appointed as Prime Minister someone who could command a majority in the parliament. The President of the Republic, who was to be elected by direct universal adult suffrage for a term of five years, was the head of state. The President was to be fluent in Kyrgyz, which was the official language of the state, although Russian was specifically granted equality with Kyrgyz. There was to be an independent judiciary. The provisions of and the basic rights granted by the Constitution were to be ensured by a Constitutional Court.

The Government

(March 1994)

PRESIDENCY

President of the Republic of Kyrgyzstan: ASKAR AKAYEV (elected 28 October 1990; re-elected, by direct popular vote, 12 October 1991).

Vice-President: (vacant).

CABINET OF MINISTERS

Prime Minister: APAS JUMAGULOV.

First Deputy Prime Minister (responsible for economic policy): ALMAMBET MATUBRAIMOV.

Deputy Prime Minister (responsible for privatization): ESENGUL OMURALIYEV.

Deputy Prime Minister (responsible for social policy): OSMONAKUN IBRAIMOV.

Deputy Prime Minister (responsible for agriculture): JUMGALBEK AMANBAYEV.

Deputy Prime Minister and Minister of Trade and Industry: ANDREY IORDAN.

Deputy Prime Minister: YAN FISHER.

Minister of Foreign Affairs: (vacant).

Minister of Education: ASKAR KAKEYEV.

Minister of Health: NAKEN KASIYEV.

Minister of Economics and Finance: KAMTCHYBEK SHAKIROV.

Minister of Agriculture: JALAL ASANOV.

Minister of Hydrology and Irrigation: MEYRAJDIN Z. ZULPUYEV.

Minister of Communications: EMIL BEKTENOV.

Minister of Justice: MUKAR CHOLPONBAYEV.

Minister of Labour and Social Welfare: ZAFAR KHAKIMOV.

Minister of Transport: SYDYKBEK ABLESOV.

Minister of Culture: CHOLPOBEK BAZARBAYEV.

Minister of Internal Affairs: ABDYBEK SUTALINOV.

Minister of Defence: MYRZAKAN SUBANOV.

Chairmen of State Committees

Chairman of the State Committee for the Environment: ISKENDER S. MURATALIN.

Chairman of the Commission on Foreign Investment: ASKAR SARYGULOV.

Chairman of the State Committee for National Security: ANARBEK K. BAKAYEV.

Chairman of the State Committee for Geology and the Use and Protection of the Bowels of the Earth: SHAMSHI TEKENOV.

Chairman of the State Committee for the Training of Workers and Employers: ILIYAS KASENDEYEV.

Chairman of the State Committee for Prices and Anti-monopoly Policy: BAKHTIYAR FATTAKHOV.

Chairman of the State Committee for Physical Culture, Sport and National Movement Support: KANYBEK OSMONALIYEV.

Chairman of the State Committee for Science and Technology: KUBANYTCHBEK JUMALIYEV.

Other important State Committees are for Architecture and Construction (Chair. ISHEMBAY KADYRBEKOV), the Economy (Chair. AMANGELDY MURALIYEV), Statistics (Chair. DZUMAKADYR AKINEYEV) and Tourism (Chair. ALEKSANDR MOISEYEYEV).

MINISTRIES

Office of the President: 720000 Bishkek, Government House; tel. (3312) 21-24-66; fax (3312) 21-86-27.

Office of the Prime Minister: 720000 Bishkek, Government House; tel. (3312) 22-56-56; fax (3312) 21-86-27.

Office of the Deputy Prime Ministers: 720000 Bishkek, Government House; tel. (3312) 21-89-35 (Economic Policy Dept), 21-89-35 (Privatization Dept), 21-16-52 (Social Policy Dept); fax (3312) 21-86-27.

Ministry of Agriculture: 720300 Bishkek, Kievskaya 96; tel. (3312) 22-14-35; telex 251283; fax (3312) 22-59-50.

Ministry of Communications: 720000 Bishkek, Tchu 96; tel. (3312) 22-20-34; fax (3312) 26-67-07.

Ministry of Culture: 720301 Bishkek, Abdymomunova 205; tel. (3312) 22-25-32; fax (3312) 22-50-79.

Ministry of Defence: 720001 Bishkek, Logvinenko 26; tel. (3312) 22-78-79.

Ministry of Economics and Finance: 720874 Bishkek, Erkindika 25; tel. (3312) 22-89-22; telex 227292; fax (3312) 22-74-04.

Ministry of Education: 720000 Bishkek, Tynystanova 257; tel. (3312) 26-31-52; fax (3312) 22-86-04.

Ministry of Foreign Affairs: 720301 Bishkek, Abdymomunova 205; tel. (3312) 22-05-45; telex 251384; fax (3312) 22-57-35.

Ministry of Health: 720005 Bishkek, Moskovskaya 148; tel. (3312) 22-86-97; fax (3312) 22-84-24.

Ministry of Hydrology and Irrigation: 720020 Bishkek, Sovetskaya 4; tel. (3312) 47-96-01; fax (3312) 47-97-12.

Ministry of Internal Affairs: 720011 Bishkek, Frunze 469; tel. (3312) 22-54-90; telex 288788; fax (3312) 22-38-78.

Ministry of Justice: 720321 Bishkek, Orozbekova 37; tel. (3312) 26-47-92; fax (3312) 26-53-52.

Ministry of Labour and Social Affairs: 720000 Bishkek, Jibek Jolu 356; tel. (3312) 26-42-50.

Ministry of Trade and Industry: 720000 Bishkek, Government House; tel. (3312) 21-89-35; fax (3312) 21-86-27.

Ministry of Transport: 720017 Bishkek, Isanova 42; tel. (3312) 21-66-72; fax (3312) 26-75-97.

Principal State Committees

Commission on Foreign Investments: 720002 Bishkek, Kievskaya 96; tel. (3312) 22-03-63; telex 251239; fax (3312) 22-63-91.

State Committee for the Environment: 720300 Bishkek, Isanova 131; tel. (3312) 26-42-44; telex 251329; fax (3312) 21-34-65.

State Committee for Geology and the Use and Protection of the Bowels of the Earth: 720739 Bishkek, Erkindika 2; tel. (3312) 26-46-26.

State Committee for National Security: 720000 Bishkek, Erkindika 70; tel. (3312) 22-39-29.

State Committee for Physical Culture, Sport and National Movement Support: 720033 Bishkek, Togoloko Moldo 17; tel. (3312) 22-53-95; telex 251247.

State Committee for Prices and Anti-monopoly Policy: 720001 Bishkek, Erkindika 57; tel. (3312) 22-79-24; fax (3312) 22-63-65.

State Committee for Science and Technology: 720001 Bishkek, Isanova 87; tel. (3312) 21-54-84; fax (3312) 21-54-86.

State Committee for the Training of Workers and Employers: 720000 Bishkek, Tynystanova 215; tel. (3312) 26-44-43.

Legislature

JOGORKU KENESH

Elections to the Supreme Soviet were held on 25 February 1990, the candidates of the Kyrgyz Communist Party (KCP) mostly being elected unopposed. The KCP subsequently split into factions, and, following the Soviet coup attempt of August 1991, it was formally banned. The Supreme Soviet was subsequently renamed the Uluk Kenesh and then the Jogorku Kenesh. Elections to a new, 105-seat Jogorku Kenesh, under the Constitution of May 1993, were not due until 1995.

Chairman: MEDETKAN SHERIMKULOV.

Deputy Chairman: RENAT KULMATOV.

Local Government

For the purposes of local government, Kyrgyzstan is divided into six dubans (oblasts) and the metropolitan region of Bishkek. There are regional soviets or councils, but the main executive authority is represented by the head of the local administration, who is appointed by the central government.

Bishkek City: Bishkek; Chair. of Soviet ABDYBEK ASANKULOVICH SUTALINOV.

Chu Duban: Bishkek; Chair. of Soviet (vacant); Head of Admin. FELIKS KULOV.

Issyk-Kul Duban: Przhevalsk; Chair. of Soviet TEMPI DUYSHEYEVICH OROZBAYEV.

Jalal-Abad Duban: Jalal-Abad (Dzhalal-Abad); Chair. of Soviet BEKMAMAT OSMONOVICH OSMONOV.

Naryn Duban: Naryn; Chair. of Soviet KEMEL ZHAKESHOVICH ASHIRILAYEV.

Osh Duban: Osh; Chair. of Soviet BATYRALI SYDYKOVICH SYDYKOV.

Talas Duban: Talas; Chair. of Soviet DASTAN ISLAMOVICH SARYGULOV.

Political Organizations

Agrarian Party of Kyrgyzstan: Bishkek; f. 1993; represents farmers' interests; Chair. A. ALIYEV.

Asaba: Bishkek; nationalist party.

Democratic Movement of Kyrgyzstan: Bishkek; f. 1990; co-ordinating body for democratic groups; in 1993 it intended to become a political party; campaigns for civil liberties; Pres. QAZAT AKHMATOV.

- **Aqiqat** (Truth): Bishkek; student political organization.
- **Ashar:** Bishkek; f. 1989; concerned with provision of land and homes for ethnic Kyrgyz.
- **Osh Aymaghi** (Osh Region): Osh; concerned with allocation of land in Osh region.

Erkin (Free)—Kyrgyzstan Democratic Party: Bishkek; a leading opposition party; Chair. TOPCHUBEK TURGANALIYEV.

Kyrgyz Democratic Wing: Osh; f. 1990; works for greater religious tolerance and the construction of mosques and religious schools.

National Unity: Bishkek; f. 1991; moderate democratic party, seeks to unite different ethnic groups; Leader (vacant).

Party of Communists of Kyrgyzstan: Bishkek; f. 1992 as successor to Kyrgyz Communist Party (disbanded in Aug. 1991); 10,000 mems; Leader (vacant).

Republican Popular Party of Kyrgyzstan: Bishkek; f. 1993 by prominent scientists and academics; centrist.

Slavic Association: Bishkek; represents Slavic minority in Kyrgyzstan; Vice-Pres. ANATOLY BULGAKOV.

Uzbek Adalet (Uzbek Justice): Osh; f. 1989; advocates autonomy for the Uzbeks in Osh and use of Uzbek as a state language in the region; 400,000 mems.

Diplomatic Representation

EMBASSIES IN KYRGYZSTAN

Germany: Bishkek, Petwomajskaya 28; tel. (3312) 22-48-11; fax (3312) 62-00-07; Chargé d'affaires a.i.: Dr JÜRGEN SCHELLER.

Iran: Bishkek.

Kazakhstan: Bishkek.

Russia: Bishkek; tel. (3312) 22-16-32; Ambassador: MIKHAIL ROMANOV.

Turkey: 720001 Bishkek, Moskovskaya 89; tel. (3312) 22-78-82; telex 245125; fax (3312) 26-88-35; Ambassador: METIN GÖKER.

USA: 720002 Bishkek, Erkindika 66; tel. (3312) 22-29-20; telex 245133; fax (3312) 22-35-51; Ambassador: EDWARD HURWITZ.

Judicial System

Chairman of the Supreme Court: K. D. BOOBEKOV.

Chairwoman of the Constitutional Court: CHOLPON BAYEKOVA.

Procurator-General: ASANBEK SHARSHENALIYEV.

Religion

ISLAM

The majority of Kyrgyz are Sunni Muslims (Hanafi school), as are some other groups living in the republic, such as Uzbeks and Tajiks. In 1991 there were 60 mosques operating in the republic (18 of which opened in 1991). Under Soviet rule, only small, selected groups were permitted to travel on the Muslim pilgrimage to Mecca (in Saudi Arabia), the *hajj*, but in 1991 some 500 Muslims were reported to have made the journey. Muslims in Kyrgyzstan are officially under the jurisdiction of the Spiritual Directorate of Central Asia, based in Uzbekistan. The directorate is represented in the republic by a kazi.

Kazi of Muslims of Kyrgyzstan: KIMSANBAY Haji ABDRAKHMANOV.

Islamic Centre of Kyrgyzstan: Bishkek; Pres. SADYKZHAN Haji KAMALOV.

The Press

In 1990 there were 114 newspapers published in Kyrgyzstan, including 42 published in Kyrgyz. The average circulation per issue was 1,529,000 copies (862,000 in Kyrgyz). There were 42 periodicals, including 16 in Kyrgyz, with a total circulation of 35.4m. copies (10.2m. in Kyrgyz).

PRINCIPAL NEWSPAPERS

Bishkek Shamy (Bishkek Evening Newspaper): Bishkek; f. 1989; 4 a week; official organ of the Bishkek City Soviet of People's Deputies; in Kyrgyz; Editor M. AIDARKULOV; circ. 115,000.

Kyrgyz Tuusu: Bishkek; f. 1924; 6 a week; fmrly *Sovettik Kyrgyzstan* (Soviet Kyrgyzstan); in Kyrgyz; Chief Editor T. ISHEMKULOV; circ. 180,000.

Slovo Kyrgyzstana (Word of Kyrgyzstan): Bishkek; in Russian.

Vecherny Bishkek (Bishkek Evening Newspaper): Bishkek; f. 1974; 5 a week; official organ of the Bishkek City Soviet of People's Deputies; in Russian; Editor K. Y. MUSTAFAYEV; circ. 118,500.

Zhashtyk Zharchysy (Youth Herald): Bishkek; f. 1926; 3 a week; in Kyrgyz; Chief Editor A. RYSKULOV; circ. 148,800.

PRINCIPAL PERIODICALS

Monthly, unless otherwise indicated.

Ala Too (Ala Too Mountains): 720300 Bishkek, ul. Abdymomunova 205; tel. (3312) 26-88-75; f. 1931; monthly; publ. by the Ala Too Publishing House; journal of the Union of Writers; politics, novels, short stories, plays, poems of Kyrgyz authors and translations into Kyrgyz; in Kyrgyz; Editor-in-Chief K. JUSUPOV; circ. 30,000.

Chalkan (Stinging-nettle): Bishkek; f. 1955; satirical; in Kyrgyz; Editor-in-Chief A. STAMOV; circ. 111,700.

Den Cooluk (Health): Bishkek; f. 1955; journal of the Ministry of Health; popular science; in Kyrgyz; Editor-in-Chief M. ALIYEV; circ. 125,500.

Kyrgyz Zheri (Land of Kyrgyzstan): Bishkek; f. 1955; problems of agriculture; in Kyrgyz and Russian; Editor-in-Chief T. NASIRIDINOV; circ. 14,850.

Kyrgyzstan Ayaldary (Women of Kyrgyzstan): Bishkek; f. 1951; popular; in Kyrgyz; Editor-in-Chief D. MUKAMBETOVA; circ. 79,500.

Kyrgyzstan Madaniyaty (Culture in Kyrgyzstan): 720301 Bishkek, Bokonbayeva 99; tel. (3312) 26-14-06; f. 1967; weekly; organ of the Union of Writers and the Ministry of Culture; Editor-in-Chief D. SADYKOV; circ. 87,600.

Literaturny Kirghizstan (Literary Kyrgyzstan): 720301 Bishkek, Pushkina 70; tel. (3312) 26-14-63; f. 1955; monthly; publ. by the Ala Too Publishing House; journal of the Union of Writers; fiction, literary criticism, journalism; in Russian; Editor-in-Chief A. I. IVANOV; circ. 45,000.

Zaman Jarchisi (Herald of Time): Bishkek; f. 1944 as the journal of the Kyrgyz Communist Party; socio-political; in Kyrgyz and Russian; Editor-in-Chief L. B. JOLMUKAMEDOVA; circ. 14,050.

Zdravookhraneniye Kyrgyzstana (Public Health System of Kyrgyzstan): 720000 Bishkek, Bokonbayeva 104; tel. (3312) 22-45-29; f. 1938; 6 a year; publ. by the Ala Too Publishing House; journal of the Ministry of Health; medical experimental work; in Russian; Editor-in-Chief N. K. KASIYEV; circ. 4,000.

NEWS AGENCY

Kyrgyzkabar (Kyrgyz News Agency): Bishkek; formerly KyrgyzTag—Kyrgyz Telegraph Agency.

Publishers

Adabiyat (Literature): Bishkek, ul. Sovetskaya 170; f. 1988; fiction; in Russian, Kyrgyz, Dungan and English; Dir S. D. JETIMISHEV.

Ilim (Science): Bishkek, ul. Pushkina 144; scientific and science fiction; Dir L. V. TARASOVA.

Kyrgyzskaya Sovetskaya Entsiklopediya (Kyrgyz Soviet Encyclopaedia): Bishkek, pr. Dzerzhinskova 56; dictionaries and encyclopaedias; Editor-in-Chief M. B. BORBUGULOV.

Kyrgyzstan (Kyrgyzstan Publishing House): 720737 Bishkek, ul. Sovetskaya 170; tel. (3312) 26-79-80; politics, science, economics, agriculture and fiction; Dir A. D. IMANKULOV.

Mektep (School): Bishkek, ul. Sovetskaya 170; popular for children; Dir S. N. NAMATBAYEV.

Radio

Dom Radio: 720885 Bishkek 10, pr. Molodoy gvardii 63; broadcasts in Kyrgyz, German, Dungan and Russian.

Finance

BANKING

Central Bank

National Bank of Kyrgyzstan (NBK): Bishkek, Sverdlova 101; began operations as an independent entity in Dec. 1991; Chair. of Bd S. A. BORONBAYEV; First Deputy Chair. of Bd LYUDMILA V. PISMENNAYA; Dir KEMALBEK NANAYEV.

Other Banks

Agroprombank: Bishkek; f. 1991 as a joint-stock commercial bank; formerly part of USSR Agroprombank; one of the larger banks of Kyrgyzstan; deals mainly with the agricultural sector.

Kyrgyzstan Bank (Zhilsotsbank): Bishkek; f. 1991 as a separate joint-stock commercial bank; fmrly br. of USSR Zhilsotsbank; deals with the social sector and housing; one of the main banks of Kyrgyzstan.

Promstroibank: Bishkek; f. 1991 as a separate joint-stock commercial bank; fmrly br. of USSR industrial-sector bank; one of the main banks of Kyrgyzstan.

Sberbank—Savings Bank: Bishkek; f. 1991 as a separate joint-stock commercial bank; largest bank in Kyrgyzstan.

At the beginning of 1993 there were also six other small commercial banks, four of which were established after December 1991. Three commercial banks were licensed to carry out foreign-currency transactions.

COMMODITY EXCHANGE

Kyrgyzstan Commodity and Raw Materials Exchange: 720010 Bishkek, Kievskaya 43; tel. (3312) 28-55-91; fax (3312) 28-52-31; f. 1990; auth. cap. 6m. roubles; Gen. Dir TEMIR SARIYEV.

Trade and Industry

CHAMBER OF COMMERCE

Chamber of Commerce and Industry of the Republic of Kyrgyzstan: 720300 Bishkek, ul. Abdymomunova 205; tel. (3312) 26-49-42; telex 251239; Chair. KARCHINB Y. IVANOVICH.

FOREIGN TRADE ORGANIZATION

Kyrgyzvneshtorg: 720000 Bishkek, ul. Abdymomunova 205; tel. (3312) 22-54-82; telex 251239.

MAJOR INDUSTRIAL COMPANIES

Goldstar: Tokmak; joint venture with a South Korean co; produces television sets.

Kumtor Operating Company: Issyk-Kul obl., Kumtor; f. 1992; gold-mining of seventh largest gold deposit in the world; joint venture with Canadian co, Cameco Corpn.

Kyrgyzkilem—Kara-Balty Carpet Factory: Chu Oblast, Kary-Balty; one of largest employers in Kyrgyzstan; produces carpets.

Kyrgyzneft Production Association: 715622 Kochkor-Ata, Lenina 44; tel. 91396; state-owned petroleum and natural gas co.

Torgmash: Chu Oblast, Sokuluk Rayon; machine building.

TRADE UNIONS

Kyrgyzstan Federation of Trade Unions: Bishkek.

Transport

RAILWAYS

There are no railways in Kyrgyzstan, owing to the mountainous terrain. However, from Bishkek there is relatively easy access to the railway system of Kazakhstan and, in the main centre of population, the Fergana valley region in the west, there is access to the railway network of Uzbekistan.

ROADS

In the Soviet era Kyrgyzstan acquired a good road network, with a good proportion hard-surfaced. Many of the best road links, however, are with neighbouring countries—mainly with Kazakhstan in the north and with Uzbekistan in the west.

CIVIL AVIATION

The main international airport is at Bishkek, which has links with cities in the Russian Federation and neighbouring Central Asian states. However, during 1993 most international flights had to be cancelled, owing to fuel shortages. There were also airports at Osh and other regional centres.

Kyrgyzstan Airways (Vozdushnyye Dorogi Kyrgyzstana): Bishkek; f. 1992; operated a limited service in 1993, owing to fuel shortages.

Tourism

There was little tourism in Kyrgyzstan in the Soviet period or in the first years of independence. Tourist facilities were very limited and foreign visitors tended to be mountaineers. However, the Government hoped that the country's spectacular and largely unspoilt mountain scenery might attract foreign tourists and investment. The great crater lake of Issyk-Kul and some historical and cultural sites were also likely to be of interest if the industry was able to develop.

State Committee for Tourism: 720000 Bishkek, Government House; Chair. ALEKSANDR MOISEYEYEV.

Culture

NATIONAL ORGANIZATION

Ministry of Culture: see section on The Government (Ministries).

CULTURAL HERITAGE

Bishkek Historical Museum: Bishkek; formerly the Lenin Museum.

Chernyshevsky State Public Library of Kyrgyzstan: 720873 Bishkek, Ogonbayeva 242; tel. (3312) 6-25-70; over 3,514,700 vols; Dir A. S. SAGIMBAYEVA.

State Historical Museum of Kyrgyzstan: Bishkek, Krasnooktyabrskaya 236; 20,000 items; Dir N. M. SEITKAZIYEVA.

State Museum of Fine Art of Kyrgyzstan: Bishkek, Pervomaiskaya 90; 4,000 modern exhibits; Dir K. N. UZUBALIYEVA.

PERFORMING ARTS

State Drama Theatre: Bishkek, Panfilova 273.

State Opera and Ballet Theatre: Bishkek, Sovetskaya 167.

State Philharmonia: Bishkek, Lenina.

ASSOCIATION

Union of Writers of Kyrgyzstan: 720301 Bishkek, Pushkina 70; tel. (3312) 22-26-53.

Education

Until the 1920s there was little provision for education in Kyrgyzstan, although there were some Islamic schools and colleges, and Russian-language schools were provided for the Slav population. The first Soviet schools were established in 1923; by 1988/89 there were 1,908 institutions of secondary education in the Republic. There were also 10 institutions of higher education, including one university. In 1988 52.4% of pupils in general education day-schools were taught in Kyrgyz, 34.0% were taught in Russian, 13.1% in Uzbek and 0.2% in Tajik. Following the dissolution of the USSR financial resources in Kyrgyzstan were more limited for all forms of expenditure, although the country did benefit from some foreign aid. Thus, in 1993 there were some 2,000 Kyrgyz students in Turkish universities. Also in that year a new university, for the Slavonic population, was opened.

UNIVERSITIES

State University of Kyrgyzstan: 720024 Bishkek, Frunze 537; tel. (3312) 26-26-34; f. 1951; 15 faculties; 600 teachers; 13,000 students; Rector M. Z. ZAKIROV.

Kyrgyz-Russian Slavonic University: Bishkek; f. 1993 to promote education in the Russian language.

Social Welfare

Even before the dissolution of the USSR reforms were aiming at making the social-security system self-financing, rather than being dependent upon transfers from the all-Union budget. In 1990 a Pension Fund and an Employment Fund were established in Kyrgyzstan, and began operations in 1991. The social-security (payroll) tax was paid directly into the Pension Fund (in 1991 the tax was 37% of the wage bill of enterprises and 26% for collectives and state farms, as well as a 1% tax on salaries and grants from the central government). Just over one-third of the revenue was allocated to the trade unions for social insurance, although it was planned to establish a separate scheme. In 1991 there were some 600,000 pensioners to support, mostly retired people, but also social pensioners. The Fund was also responsible for child benefits, although these grants were particularly prone to the reforms to the welfare system which aimed to target genuine need. The Employment Fund began operations in May 1991 and was intended to provide for those affected by the expected increase in unemployment. It was also responsible for retraining, public works' projects and job centres. Most of its revenue was to come from a 1% levy on enterprise wage bills.

Living standards were relatively high compared to other Asian countries, with average life expectancy at birth put at 68.5 years (males 64.3, females 72.4) in 1991, when there was an infant mortality rate of 29.9 per thousand. In the same year there were an estimated 119.8 hospital beds and 36.7 physicians per 10,000 inhabitants (according to UNDP estimates—i.e. some 83 people per bed and 273 per physician).

NATIONAL AGENCIES

Ministry of Health: see section on The Government (Ministries).

Ministry of Labour and Social Welfare: see section on The Government (Ministries).

Employment Fund: Bishkek; f. 1991; responsible for training and for the unemployed.

Pension Fund: Bishkek; f. 1990; pays retirement, veterans' and social pensions, and child and maternity benefits; funded by employer and employee contributions.

HEALTH AND WELFARE ORGANIZATIONS

Central Committee of the Red Crescent and Red Cross of Kyrgyzstan: Bishkek.

Foundation for Social Initiatives: 720075 Bishkek, 8 Micro-rayon 34, kv. 2; tel. (3312) 47-13-62; fax (3312) 22-44-14; f. 1990.

The Environment

As a result of its low level of industrialization and its distance from the ecological problems of the Aral Sea, Kyrgyzstan was less affected than some of its neighbouring countries by environmental problems. Nevertheless, the climate of the entire Central Asian region was affected by the climatic changes engendered by the desiccation of the Aral Sea. In January 1994, together with the other Central Asian states, Kyrgyzstan agreed to contribute to the Aral Sea Fund and that there should be a limit on the amount of water taken from the upper reaches of the Syr-Dar'ya (which has its sources in Kyrgyzstan) and the Amu-Dar'ya rivers. Local environmentalists were mainly concerned with the protection of the country's extensive mountain environment and the large lake of Issyk-Kul.

GOVERNMENT ORGANIZATIONS

State Committee for the Environment: see section on The Government (Ministries).

ACADEMIC INSTITUTE

Academy of Sciences: 720071 Bishkek, Tchu 265A; tel. (3312) 26-45-41; telex 251245; f. 1954; several attached institutes involved in environmental research; Pres. Acad. I. T. AITMATOV.

Centre for Independent Economic and Social Research: 720075 Bishkek, 8 Micro-rayon 34, kv. 2; tel. (3312) 47-13-62; fax (3312) 22-44-14; f. 1991; part of the Foundation for Social Initiatives; researches sustainable development and educates in ecological issues; planned an international environmental film festival for 1994; Dir VIKTOR ALEKSANDROVICH BOBROV.

NON-GOVERNMENTAL ORGANIZATIONS

Committee for the Defence of Lake Issyk-Kul: 720023 Bishkek, 10 Micro-rayon 32–31; tel. (3312) 22-19-68; f. 1990; Pres. OMOR SULTANOV.

International Physicians for the Prevention of Nuclear War: 720011 Bishkek, Pravdy 108/44; tel. (3312) 28-04-37; concerned with radiation levels in the country and with the effects of solar radiation on the mountain population; Chair. NURLAN NURGAZIEVICH BRIMKULOV.

Defence

Kyrgyzstan reorganized its armed forces in mid-1993, creating a General Staff in August. Morale was low and the rate of desertion high, despite conscription (18-month terms). In June 1993, according to Western estimates, the national army numbered some 12,000; there was also an air force, mainly because a former Soviet training base was located in Kyrgyzstan. Some units of the armed forces were serving in Tajikistan. There was also a small number of Russian troops still in the country. The defence budget for 1992 was estimated at some 800m. roubles (some US $47m.).

Commander-in-Chief: President of the Republic.

Chief of the General Staff: Lt-Gen. AKZHOL ISAYEV.

Bibliography

Akiner, S. *Islamic People of the Soviet Union: An Historical and Statistical Handbook*, 2nd Edn. London and New York, Kegan Paul International, 1987.

Dienes, L. *Soviet Central Asia: Economic Development and National Policy Choices*. Boulder, Colorado, Westview Press, 1987.

Hetmanek, A. 'Kirgizstan and the Kirgiz', in *Handbook of Major Soviet Nationalities*. New York, Free Press, 1975.

Istoriya Kirgizskoi. Frunze (Bishkek), Kyrgyzstan, 1984.

Kirgizskaya SSR. Entsiklopediya. Frunze (Bishkek), Glavnaya Redaktksiya KSE, 1982.

LATVIA

Geography

PHYSICAL FEATURES

The Republic of Latvia is situated in north-eastern Europe, on the east coast of the Baltic Sea. It is bounded by Estonia to the north and by Lithuania to the south and south-west. To thc cast there is a frontier with the Russian Federation and, to the south-east, with Belarus. Latvia covers an area of 64,589 sq km (24,938 sq miles). The present territory is essentially that of the pre-1940 Republic, except for the area around Pytalovo (formerly Jaunlatgale), which was transferred to the Russian Federation in 1945.

The country is divided into the Coastal Lowlands and three main inland regions: Western Latvia, Central Latvia and Eastern Latvia. The Coastal Lowlands comprise the low-lying littoral of the Baltic Sea and the Gulf of Rīga, along which there are several natural harbours. Western Latvia is also largely flat terrain, interrupted only by the undulating relief of the Western Kursa Upland. Central Latvia offers more varied terrain, ranging from the Zemgale plain in the south-west, part of which is below sea-level, to the Vidzeme Upland, a region of uneven relief, which includes the highest point in Latvia (Gaizinkalns, which stands at a height of 312 m or 1,030 feet). Eastern Latvia is dominated by the Latgale Upland, which extends to the south-eastern border with Belarus, and includes more than 1,000 lakes. Although there are more than 12,000 rivers in the country, the only major waterways are the Daugava (Dvina), which flows through the centre of the country and empties into the Gulf of Rīga, and the Gauja, which rises in the Vidzeme Upland.

CLIMATE

Owing to the influence of maritime factors, the climate is relatively temperate but changeable. Average temperatures in January range from −2.6°C (27.3°F) in the western, coastal town of Liepāja, to −6.6°C (20.1°F) in the inland town of Daugavpils. Mean temperatures for July range from 16.8°C (62.2°F) in Liepāja to 17.6°C (63.7°F) in Daugavpils. Average annual precipitation in Rīga is 567 mm.

POPULATION

At the census of 12 January 1989, of a total population of 2,680,000, 51.8% were Latvians, 33.8% Russians, 4.5% Belarusians, 3.4% Ukrainians and 2.3% Poles. There were also small numbers of Lithuanians (34,630), Jews (22,897), Roma (Gypsies—7,044), Tatars (4,828) and Germans (3,783).

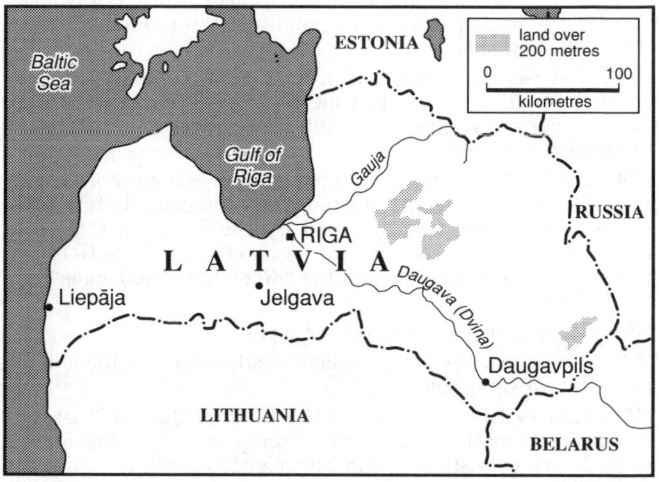

By comparison, in 1935, 75.5% of the population were ethnic Latvians. There are significant communities of Latvians in other countries, notably in the USA. The proportion of the population living in rural areas declined from 68.2% in 1935 to 28.9% in 1989. Population distribution is quite uneven, with almost 50% of the population living in the region around Rīga. The average population density (persons per sq km) was 41 in 1989, but was as low as six in parts of Western Latvia.

Latvian replaced Russian as the official language of the Republic in 1988. It is an Indo-European language, a member of the Baltic group, and is written in the Latin script. At the census of 1989 22.3% of ethnic Russians claimed fluency in Latvian. The major religion is Christianity: most ethnic Latvians are traditionally Lutheran, although smaller Protestant sects have a considerable following among the younger generation, and the Roman Catholic Church is also represented. Adherents of the Eastern Orthodox Church in Latvia are mostly ethnic Russians.

In 1993 the estimated total population of Latvia was 2,606,000. The capital is Rīga, which is an important port, situated near the mouth of the River Daugava. At 1 January 1991 it had an estimated population of 897,078. Other important cities include Daugavpils (127,279), Liepāja (113,815) and Jelgava (73,917).

Chronology

***c*. 2,000 BC:** The Balts, the ancestors of the Latvians (Letts), settled on the southern and south-eastern shores of the Baltic Sea.

AD 1201: Albert von Appeldern, the German Bishop of Livonia, founded the city of Rīga and established the crusading order of Sword Brethren.

1209: The German crusading order of the Teutonic Knights invaded Jersika, a town in southern Latvia controlled by a native ruler, Visvaldis, following his marriage to a pagan Lithuanian princess.

1290: The Teutonic Knights completed their conquest of Latvia with the capture of the kingdom of Zemgale. Latvia and Estonia were subsequently ruled by the Livonian Order of Teutonic Knights (formed in 1237 by an alliance of the German Order of Teutonic Knights and the Sword Brethren) under the name of Livonia.

1494: Serfdom was introduced in Livonia.

1524–34: Livonia renounced religious adherence to Rome and converted to Lutheranism.

1558: Ivan IV (the 'Terrible') of the Russian state of Muscovy attacked Livonia in an attempt to conquer part of the Baltic coast; his move instigated the Livonian War, which continued until 1582.

1561: The Livonian State of Teutonic Knights finally ceased to exist: northern Estonia fell under Swedish control, while the rest came under Polish–Lithuanian rule, with the kingdoms of Kurzeme and Zemgale becoming part of the autonomous Duchy of Courland (Kurland).

1629: Sweden conquered the Livonian territories of Poland.

1721: The Treaty of Nystad, concluded by Russia and Sweden, ended the Great Northern War and brought Estonia and much of Livonia under Russian rule.

1772: At the First Partition of Poland Latgale, an eastern region of Livonia, was incorporated into the Russian Empire, as part of the Russian province of Vitebsk (now in Belarus).

1795: At the Third Partition of Poland the remainder of the Duchy of Courland became part of the Russian Empire.

1817–19: Serfdom was abolished in Latvia.

1901: The Latvian Social Democratic Party was established, which advocated greater territorial autonomy for Latvia; two years later the party divided to form the Latvian Social Democratic Workers' Party and the Latvian Social Democratic Union.

October 1905: Two Latvian deputies were elected to the Duma (parliament), which was established in the tsarist capital of St Petersburg.

November 1917: The first National Council was elected in Valka, northern Latvia, at a meeting of the Rīga Democratic Bloc; the Council expressed its intention to establish Latvia as an independent sovereign state.

3 March 1918: Treaty of Brest-Litovsk: the Bolsheviks ceded large areas of western territory to Germany, including the Baltic regions.

18 November 1918: The Republic of Latvia was declared and a provisional administration, under the premiership of Kārlis Ulmanis, was formed.

3 January 1919: The Soviet Red Army captured Rīga, forcing the Provisional Government to flee to Kurzeme.

8 July 1919: Following the expulsion of the Red Army from Rīga by Latvian troops, assisted by Germany, the Provisional Government returned to the capital and the Latvian National Council reconvened.

January 1920: The last Soviet troops were finally expelled from Latvia.

1 February 1920: The Latvian and Soviet Governments signed an armistice.

April 1920: Elections were held to the Constituent Assembly.

1 May 1920: At the first session of the Constituent Assembly Jānis Čakste was elected President of the Assembly and of the Republic of Latvia.

11 August 1920: A Latvian–Soviet peace agreement, the Treaty of Rīga, was signed.

7 November 1922: Following the promulgation of the new Constitution, the first session of the new Parliament (Saeima) opened.

16 September 1922: The Saeima passed the Agrarian Reform Bill, initiating land reform in favour of the peasants.

May 1934: Ulmanis carried out a *coup d'état* and established a presidential dictatorship.

1936: Ulmanis became President of Latvia.

23 August 1939: The Treaty of Non-Aggression (the Nazi–Soviet Pact) was signed by the USSR and Germany; it included the 'Secret Protocols' which sanctioned the annexation of Latvia (as well as Eastern Poland, Estonia, Lithuania and Bessarabia).

June 1940: Red-Army troops occupied Latvia and a pro-Soviet administration, headed by Augusts Kirchenšteins, was installed.

21 July 1940: The new parliament, consisting only of members sympathetic to the Soviet regime, proclaimed the Latvian Soviet Socialist Republic (Latvian SSR) and requested to be admitted to the USSR.

5 August 1940: The Latvian SSR was incorporated into the USSR.

13–14 June 1941: The mass deportation of some 33,000 Latvians over a period of several months culminated in the expulsion from Rīga of 15,000 inhabitants overnight.

1 July 1941: German troops, which had invaded the USSR the previous week, reached Rīga.

13 October 1944: The Soviet army recaptured the Latvian capital and Courland.

24–27 March 1949: Some 70,000 Latvians, mainly inhabitants of rural areas, were deported.

1952: The process of collectivization was completed.

1959: Jānis Kalnērziņš, First Secretary of the Communist Party of Latvia (CPL) since 1940, was accused of Latvian nationalism and replaced by Arvīds Pelše.

1966: Augusts Voss succeeded Arvīds Pelše as First Secretary and continued repressive policies of russification.

1984: Boris Pugo became First Secretary of the CPL. The Environmental Protection Club was established to protest against environmental damage.

July 1986: Under the more tolerant regime of the new Soviet leader, Mikhail Gorbachev, Helsinki-86 was established in Liepāja; the group aimed to monitor observance by the authorities of the human-rights provisions of the Helsinki Final Act of 1975.

August 1986: Linards Grantinš and Raimonds Bitenieks, two leading members of Helsinki-86, were arrested and imprisoned without trial; they were conditionally released in January 1987.

14 June 1987: A mass demonstration was organized by Helsinki-86 to mark the 1941 deportation of thousands of Latvian citizens. A further demonstration was held on 23 August to commemorate the signing of the Nazi–Soviet Pact.

June 1988: A resolution was adopted by Latvia's cultural unions which demanded that Latvian become the official language, that the Secret Protocols of the Nazi–Soviet Pact of 1939 be published and that the ecological damage in the Republic be repaired.

September 1988: Jan Vigris replaced the conservative Pugo as First Secretary of the Communist Party of Latvia (CPL).

29 September 1988: Latvian was declared to be the state language and the former Latvian flag and national anthem were declared no longer illegal.

October 1988: The Latvian Popular Front (LPF) was formed by representatives of the opposition and radicals from the CPL; the new group resolved to seek sovereignty for Latvia within a renewed Soviet federation.

February 1989: The National Independence Movement of Latvia (NIML), which advocated full independence for the Republic, held its first congress.

26 March 1989: In the elections to the all-Union Congress of People's Deputies, candidates supported by the LPF won 26 of the 34 seats contested.

28 July 1989: A declaration of sovereignty and economic independence was adopted by the Latvian Supreme Soviet.

December 1989: Candidates supported by the LPF won 75% of the seats in local elections.

January 1990: The Latvian Supreme Soviet voted to end the Communist Party's monopoly of power.

15 February 1990: The decision by the Latvian Parliament in 1940 to request admission to the USSR was condemned by the Latvian Supreme Soviet; in the same month the official use of the Latvian flag, state emblems and national anthem was restored.

18 March 1990: In elections to the Latvian Supreme Soviet (subsequently renamed the Supreme Council) the LPF won 131 of the 201 seats contested; the CPL won some 59 seats (although at the party Congress of the following month a split led to the creation of a separatist independent Communist Party of Latvia) and independent candidates gained 11.

30 April–1 May 1990: A rival parliament, the Congress of Latvia, the members of which were elected only by citizens of pre-1940 Latvia, convened; the Congress announced that Latvia was an occupied country and demanded full independence and the withdrawal of Soviet troops.

3 May 1990: Anatolijs Gorbunovs was elected Chairman of the Supreme Council.

4 May 1990: The Supreme Council declared Latvia's incorporation into the USSR unlawful and announced the beginning of a transitional period towards full independence; Ivars Godmanis was elected premier of a new administration dominated by the LPF.

14 May 1990: A decree issued by President Gorbachev of the USSR annulled the declaration of independence of 4 May.

2 January 1991: Special units of the Soviet Ministry of Internal Affairs (OMON units) occupied the Rīga Press House.

20 January 1991: The 'Committee of Public Salvation', led by the First Secretary of the CPL, Alfred Rubiks, claimed authority in Latvia; four people died when OMON troops occupied the Latvian Ministry of Internal Affairs.

3 March 1991: In a referendum 73.7% of participants voted in favour of Latvian independence.

21 August 1991: Following the attempted *coup d'état* in Moscow an emergency session of the Supreme Council was convened; the Council declared full independence and pronounced that the State Committee for the State of Emergency was unconstitutional.

23 August 1991: Alfred Rubiks was arrested and the CPSU was banned in Latvia.

4 September 1991: Latvia's independence was formally recognized by the State Council of the USSR.

17 September 1991: Latvia was admitted to the UN.

15 October 1991: Legislation on citizenship was adopted by the Supreme Council; the law stipulated that all residents who were not citizens of pre-1940 Latvia or their descendants would have to apply for naturalization.

May 1992: The Latvian rouble was introduced for a transitional period until the country adopted its own currency.

October 1992: The Government survived a vote of no confidence put forward by the Satversme faction in the Supreme Council. The Minister of Foreign Affairs resigned, following a dispute with the Government on the issue of citizenship.

January 1993: Two government ministers (the Minister of Finance and the Minister of Justice) resigned.

February 1993: Members of the Satversme faction, along with other political figures, formed a new political movement, Latvian Way.

March 1993: The Minister of Foreign Trade resigned from his post.

5–6 June 1993: Elections were held to the new legislature (Saeima): Latvian Way won 37 of the 100 seats contested and formed a moderate right-wing coalition with the Latvian Farmers' Union, which won 12 seats. The remaining seats were won by the Latvian National Independence Movement, Harmony for Latvia, Equality, the Union for the Fatherland and Freedom, the Christian Democratic Union of Latvia and the Democratic Centre Party.

8 July 1993: Guntis Ulmanis of the Latvian Farmers' Union was inaugurated as President of Latvia, following three rounds of voting in the Saeima; the two other presidential candidates were Gunars Meierovics of Latvian Way and Aivars Jerumanis of the Christian Democratic Union of Latvia; Meierovics withdrew from the election after the first round of voting.

21 July 1993: The new Government, headed by Valdis Birkavs, was approved by the Saeima.

August 1993: The last former Soviet naval vessel returned to Russia from the naval base at Bolderaja.

4 August 1993: The State Minister for Culture, Raimonds Pauls, resigned in protest at the proposed disbanding of the Ministry of Culture.

September 1993: A draft law on citizenship and naturalization was submitted to the Council on Security and Co-operation in Europe (CSCE), following controversy over a similar law in neighbouring Estonia.

14 September 1993: The Government announced that from 18 October the Latvian rouble would no longer be in circulation and the lats would be the only legal tender in Latvia.

29 October 1993: The human-rights organization, Helsinki Watch, announced that many residents of Latvia had been refused registration by the Department of Citizenship and Immigration.

20 November 1993: The proposal by the Russian delegation to the Latvian–Russian negotiations to withdraw all troops from Latvia by 1 September 1994, in return for the use of the Skrunda radar base for a further six years, was rejected by premier Valdis Birkavs.

1 December 1993: The Russian Federation was strongly advised by the CSCE to remove its troops from Latvia and to draw up a schedule for the withdrawal.

10 January 1994: Latvian troops detained two Russian generals following the seizure of a Russian military base outside Rīga; the men were later released on the order of President Ulmanis. Negotiations on troop withdrawal were subsequently discontinued.

19 January 1994: Birkavs, with the Estonian and Lithuanian premiers, issued a joint declaration denouncing the statement by the Russian foreign minister, Andrey Kozyrev, that Russia had the right to station troops on the territory of the former USSR.

11 February 1994: The Russian natural-gas producer, Gasprom, threatened to halt supplies of natural gas to Latvia unless it paid a debt of 32,000m. roubles.

14 February 1994: At the North Atlantic Treaty Organisation (NATO) headquarters in Brussels (Belgium) the Latvian premier signed the Partnership for Peace association agreement, a programme which many countries of the former Soviet bloc hoped was a prelude to full membership of NATO.

History

In 1290 the German Order of Teutonic Knights completed its conquest of Latvia and established the Livonian State. In 1561, during the religious upheavals of the 16th century, Livonia was partitioned. South-western Latvia (Kurzeme and Zemgale) became part of the hereditary Duchy of Courland (Kurland), a prosperous region under the suzerainty of Poland–Lithuania. The other Livonian territories became a dependency of Poland, until they were conquered by Sweden in 1629. They remained under Swedish rule until the Great Northern War between Russia and Sweden. The conclusion of the War by the Treaty of Nystad, in 1721, brought most of Latvia under Russian rule. The eastern region of Latgale remained under Polish suzerainty until 1772, when it was annexed by Russia at the First Partition of Poland. The Duchy of Courland was absorbed into the Russian Empire at the Third Partition, in 1795. Even under Russian rule, Latvians remained divided. In west-central Latvia (the Duchy of Courland and southern Lifland) the descendants of the Teutonic Order, the Baltic Germans, or Ritterschaften, were granted considerable economic and cultural autonomy. Latgale, however, was absorbed into the Russian province of Vitebsk (now in Belarus), where the Latvian peasantry was ruled by Russian and Polish nobility.

During the latter half of the 19th century, the privileges of the Baltic nobility were gradually diminished and Latvians were permitted to become small landowners. The onset of industrialization encouraged the Latvian peasantry to move to urban areas and an indigenous middle class began to emerge. As a result of these economic and social changes, a Latvian nationalist movement developed in the 1860s, led by groups such as the Young Latvian Movement, which aimed to promote Latvian language and culture. By the early 1900s national-cultural groups had developed into a political movement which advocated territorial autonomy for Latvia within the Russian Empire, a stance which continued until after the February Revolution of 1917 in Russia, when other national groups within the Empire were demanding complete independence. However, in November 1917, representatives of most Latvian political groups, united in the Rīga Democratic Bloc, met to establish an independent Latvian state. On 18 November 1918 the independent Republic of Latvia was proclaimed.

The establishment of independence, under the nationalist Government of Kārlis Ulmanis, was only fully achieved after the expulsion of the Bolsheviks from Rīga, with the aid of German troops, and from Latgale, with Polish and Estonian assistance. Latvia's first Constitution was adopted in 1922. It introduced a democratic system of government, which, owing to an electoral system based on proportional representation, permitted a large number of small parties to be represented in the 100-member Saeima (Parliament). A series of coalition governments, dominated by the Latvian Peasants' Union, concentrated on developing the agrarian base of the economy, introducing agrarian reforms and developing the export of agricultural products to Western Europe. The economic decline of the 1930s, together with the politically fragmented Saeima, prompted a *coup d'état*, in 1934, by the Prime Minister, Kārlis Ulmanis. He introduced authoritarian rule, headed by a Cabinet of National Unity, and became President in 1936.

Under the Treaty of Non-Aggression (the Nazi–Soviet Pact), signed by Germany and the USSR on 23 August 1939, the incorporation of Latvia into the USSR was agreed by the two powers. A Treaty of Mutual Aid between the USSR and Latvia forced the Government to allow the establishment of Soviet military bases in Latvia. Under military pressure, elections were held to the Saeima, with only the nominations of candidates approved by Soviet officials permitted. The Parliament thus produced proclaimed the Latvian Soviet Socialist Republic (Latvian SSR) on 21 July 1940, and requested membership of the USSR. On 5 August 1940 the Latvian SSR was formally admitted to the USSR as a constituent Union Republic.

In 1941 Soviet rule in Latvia was ended by German occupation. Most German troops had withdrawn by 1944, although Courland was retained by Germany until the end of the War. Soviet Latvia was re-established in 1944–45 and the process of 'sovietization', begun in 1940, was continued. Independent political activities were prohibited and exclusive political power was exercised by the Communist Party of Latvia (CPL), headed by Jānis Kalnērziņš (First Secretary 1940–59), which was dominated by the so-called *latovichi*, the term used to describe russified Latvians who had spent the 1920s and 1930s in the USSR. Under Communist rule a process of industrialization was initiated, with the introduction of metal- and machine-working industries, and development of the chemical industry. This forced industrialization encouraged Russian immigration into the Republic.

Rapid development of the industrial sector left the agricultural sector neglected. By the early 1950s almost all of Latvia's privately-owned farms had been merged into collective farms, a policy which was implemented by frequent deportations and arrests of reluctant peasants. The stagnant state of agriculture was addressed when greater powers were granted the Latvian authorities as a result of the policy of economic decentralization introduced in the USSR in the mid-1950s. Increased economic independence was paralleled by a movement within the CPL for greater cultural autonomy, which focused on the need to retain the Latvian language as the predominant language in the Republic. In the late 1950s some 2,000 alleged members of this so-called 'nationalist group' were dismissed from leading government and Party positions. Among them was First Secretary of the CPL Jānis Kalnērziņš. He was replaced by Arvīds Pelše, one of the *latovichi* favoured by the Soviet authorities. Under Pelše, and under his successor Augusts Voss (First Secretary 1966–84), the limited autonomy gained in the 1950s was reversed, and repression of Latvian cultural and literary life was increased.

In the late 1970s and early 1980s there was a significant revival in traditional Latvian cultural activities, such as folk singing, and youth groups began a movement to restore historical monuments and churches. Political groups began to be established, including the Environmental Protection Club, founded in 1984 to campaign against environmental degradation, and Helsinki-86, established to monitor Soviet observance of the Helsinki human-rights accords. The latter group issued an unofficial journal, *Tevija* (Fatherland), and organized anti-Soviet demonstrations in June and August 1986, which were disrupted by the police. In November 1986 the growing influence of public opinion was demonstrated by the decision to end construction of the Daugavpils Hydroelectric Station after protests by environmentalists. In 1987 there were further demonstrations on the anniversaries of significant events in Latvian history, such as 23 August (the signing of the Nazi–Soviet Pact) and 18 November (the establishment of Latvian independence). These nascent opposition movements, engendered by the greater freedom of expression permitted by Soviet leader Mikhail Gorbachev's policy of *glasnost* (openness) were strongly opposed by the conservative republican leadership, headed since 1984 by Boris Pugo as First Secretary of the CPL.

In 1988 the opposition movements began to unite into a significant political force in the Republic. Leading intellectuals, led by Jānis Peters, the Chairman of the Writers' Union, began to criticize the CPL for its attitude to *perestroika* (restructuring) and to advocate more radical political and economic change. In June Latvia's cultural unions issued a joint resolution demanding that Latvian be made the state language, that the Secret Protocols of the Nazi-Soviet Pact be published and that measures be taken to cope with ecological degradation resulting from forced industrialization. Similar demands were made in the Republic's press. In October 1988 representatives of the leading opposition movements, together with radicals from the CPL, organized the inaugural congress of the Latvian Popular Front (LPF). The LPF quickly became the largest and most influential political force in Latvia, with an estimated 250,000 members by the end of 1988. At its inaugural congress it adopted a policy of seeking sovereignty for Latvia within a renewed Soviet federation and elected Dainis Ivans as its first President.

In September 1988 Boris Pugo, who was to be one of the leading participants in the Moscow coup attempt of August 1991, was transferred to the Soviet capital, and replaced as First Secretary of the CPL by Jan Vigris. The new Party leadership, which came increasingly under the control of members of the Popular Front (in October 1988 one-third of the Front's 120,000 members were also members of the CPL), was far more sympathetic to the Front's aims than it had been under Pugo. On 29 September 1988 Latvian was designated the state language and the symbols of national independence, such as the Latvian flag and anthem, were no longer considered illegal. During 1989 the nationalist movement began to adopt more radical policies. The National Independence Movement of Latvia (NIML), which had been formed in 1988, held its first congress in February. The NIML's policies advocated full economic and political independence for Latvia, and its influence within the opposition movement (many of its members were also members of the LPF) led to the proposal, in May, by the leadership of the LPF to conduct a referendum on full independence for Latvia.

On 26 March 1989 candidates supported by the LPF won 26 of 34 seats in the elections to the all-Union Congress of People's Deputies. On 28 July, following similar moves by Lithuania and Estonia, the Supreme Soviet adopted a declaration of sovereignty and economic independence. The growing support for full independence outside the USSR was demonstrated at the Second Congress of the LPF (7–8 October 1989), where delegates supported demands for total political and economic independence, and the introduction of a multi-party system and a market-based economy. Despite the establishment of political groups opposed to the LPF (principally Interfront, a group opposed to independence, dominated by Russian-speakers), in December 1989 candidates supported by the LPF won some 75% of seats in local elections. The high level of support for the LPF seemed to indicate a degree of indifference rather than opposition to political change among non-Latvians.

In January 1990 the Latvian Supreme Soviet voted to abolish the constitutional provisions which guaranteed the Communist Party its monopoly of political power. On 15 February the Supreme Soviet adopted a declaration condemning the decision of the 1940 Parliament to request admission to the USSR, and, in the same month, the Supreme Soviet restored the flag, state emblems and anthem of pre-1940 Latvia to official use. In the elections to the Supreme Soviet, on 18 March 1990, the LPF won a convincing victory. Candidates endorsed by the LPF, who were members of a variety of political parties which supported independence, won 131 of the 201 seats in the Supreme Soviet. Members of the CPL won about 59 seats, and there were 11 independents. In April, at an extraordinary congress, the CPL split into two parties. The majority of delegates rejected a motion to leave the Communist Party of the Soviet Union (CPSU). Instead, they voted to remain an integral part of the CPSU and elected Alfred Rubiks, a committed opponent of independence, as First Secretary. The pro-independence faction of some 260 delegates left the Congress and established the Independent Communist Party of Latvia. Ivars Kezbers was elected as Chairman of the new party and the demand for Latvian independence outside the USSR was adopted as part of a new party programme.

The new Supreme Soviet (which subsequently changed its name to the Supreme Council) convened on 3 May 1990 and elected Anatolijs Gorbunovs, a member of the CPSU-affiliated Communist Party, as its Chairman (*de facto* president of the Republic). The next day the Supreme Council adopted a resolution which declared the incorporation of Latvia into the USSR in 1940 as unlawful and announced the beginning of a transitional period which was to lead to full political and economic independence. (The resolution reinstated the Constitution of 15 February 1922 and the formal name, the Republic of Latvia. During the transitional period the 1922 Constitution was to be suspended, with the exception of four articles describing Latvia as an independent democratic state, asserting the sovereignty of the Latvian people.) Ivars Godmanis, the Deputy Chairman of the Popular Front, was elected as Prime Minister of a new Government dominated by Popular Front members.

On 30 April–1 May 1990 a rival parliament to the Supreme Council, the Congress of Latvia, convened. It had been elected in unofficial elections, in which 700,000 people were estimated to have participated. Only citizens of the pre-1940 Republic and their descendants were permitted to vote. The Congress, in which members of the radical NIML predominated, declared Latvia to be an occupied country and adopted resolutions on independence and the withdrawal of Soviet troops.

The declaration of 4 May 1990, although more cautious than independence declarations adopted in Lithuania and Estonia, severely strained relations with the Soviet authorities. On 14 May President Gorbachev issued a decree, which annulled the Latvian declaration of independence, describing it as in violation of the Soviet Constitution. The declaration was also also opposed by some non-Latvians, who organized strikes and demonstrations to protest against the decisions of the Supreme Council. Opposition to the pro-independence Government continued throughout 1990, with the all-Union authorities attempting to persuade Latvia to sign a new Union Treaty, and local anti-government movements, allied with Soviet troops stationed in Latvia, conducting a campaign of propaganda and harassment against the Government. In December a series of explosions were reported in Rīga, and the Government claimed that special units of the Soviet Ministry of Internal Affairs (OMON units) were responsible.

In January 1991 conservative forces in the Republic were involved in an apparent attempt to overthrow the Latvian Government and re-establish Soviet rule. On 2 January OMON troops seized the Rīga Press House, previously the property of the CPL. On 14 January OMON units tried to occupy a police station and attempted to remove barricades which had been erected by Latvians in anticipation of military intervention. On 20 January a 'Committee of Public Salvation', headed by Alfred Rubiks, the First Secretary of the CPL, declared itself as a rival government to that led by Godmanis. The same day four people died when OMON troops attacked the building of the Latvian Ministry of Internal Affairs.

The attempted seizure of power by the Committee for Public Salvation reinforced opposition in the Republic to inclusion in the new Union Treaty being prepared by nine other Union Republics. Latvia refused to conduct the all-Union referendum on the future of the Union, which was scheduled for 17 March (some 680,000 people did participate, on an unofficial basis, mostly Russians and Ukrainians). Instead of the official referendum, on 3 March 1991 a referendum on Latvian independence was held. Voters were asked 'Are you for a democratic and independent Latvian Republic?' Of those eligible to vote (members of the Soviet Armed Forces were excluded), 87.6% participated. According to official results, 73.7% of these voters approved an independent Latvia, a higher result than expected, given that ethnic Latvians only constituted 52% of the population.

When the State Committee for the State of Emergency announced that it had taken power in Moscow in August 1991, military intervention was immediately expected in Latvia. Preparations were made for the establishment of a government-in-exile and, despite the presence of troops in Rīga, an emergency session of the Supreme Council convened on 21 August. The Supreme Council declared the full independence of Latvia and declared the SCSE unconstitutional. When the coup collapsed the Government quickly began to assert its control over events in Latvia. On 23 August the CPSU was banned in the Republic and Alfred Rubiks, leader of the pro-CPSU Latvian Communists, was arrested. Following the recognition by several countries of Latvian independence, on 4 September 1991 the State Council of the USSR formally recognized the independent Latvian Republic. Latvia was admitted to the UN on 17 September.

INDEPENDENT LATVIA

In October 1992 the Satversme (Constitution) faction in the legislature proposed a vote of no confidence in the PFL-dominated Government which, it claimed, was responsible for the country's economic and moral decline. The Godmanis Administration survived the vote (with the exception of the Minister of Economic Reform). The following week, however, the Minister of Foreign Affairs was forced to resign (allegedly owing to disagreement with the Government over the issue of citizenship—see below). Further government resignations followed in January 1993 (the Ministers of Finance and of Justice) and in March (the Minister of Foreign Trade). Moreover, internal divisions within the PFL, which led to the formation of several factions, made the party appear increasingly unstable. A new political movement, Latvian Way, was established in February 1993: it represented a wide range of political views, and its members included Gorbunovs, as well as members of the Satversme faction.

On 5 and 6 June 1993 the first national elections to be held since independence was restored to Latvia completed the country's transition to a democratic state. A total of 874 candidates, representing some 23 electoral coalitions, political parties and organizations, contested the 100 seats to the new Parliament (Saeima). Following the citizenship law of October 1991, only 66% of Latvian residents were entitled to participate in the elections. No political organization won a majority in the elections, but the results showed that the electorate favoured moderate, right-wing parties, in particular Latvian Way, which won 36 seats in the Saeima. Latvian Way formed a parliamentary coalition with the Latvian Farmers' Union, which won 12 seats. The remaining seats were divided between the Latvian National Independence Movement (which gained 15 seats), Harmony for Latvia (13 seats), Equality (seven seats), the Union for the Fatherland and Freedom coalition (six seats), the Christian Democratic Union of Latvia (six seats) and the Democratic Centre Party (five seats). Following the election, a Law on the Cabinet of Ministers (a revised version of the 1925 legislation) had to be adopted by the Saeima before a new government could be formed. The Law was only passed after a lengthy debate in the Saeima. Among the issues to be decided upon was that of which kind of government should rule: some deputies supported the idea of a government of national unity, as opposed to the single-coalition government favoured by deputies from Latvian Way. Eventually, on 15 July, the Law was passed and six days later the Saeima endorsed the Government (comprising 13 ministers and nine state ministers) proposed by the Prime Minister, Valdis Birkavs of Latvian Way. Two further ministers of state were endorsed on 13 August. On 4 August the State Minister for Culture, Raimonds Pauls, resigned over a draft law proposing the disbanding of his Ministry. He was later replaced by Jānis Dripe.

On 6 July 1993 the first round of voting took place in the Saeima to elect the new President of the Republic. Three deputies stood as candidates: Gunars Meierovics of Latvian Way; Aivars Jerumanis of the Christian Democratic Union of Latvia; and Guntis Ulmanis of the Latvian Farmers' Union. Meierovics won 35 votes, Jerumanis 14, and Ulmanis 12. A second round of voting occurred the following day, as no candidate won the 51 votes required for election. Meierovics, however, withdrew from the elections and announced his support for Ulmanis. The results were again inconclusive, but in the third round of voting Ulmanis received 53 of the votes cast and thus became President of Latvia. He was inaugurated on 8 July.

The Issue of Citizenship

Among the most controversial political issues to emerge in Latvia was that of citizenship of the Latvian Republic. On 15 October 1991 the Supreme Council adopted legislation on citizenship, which automatically restored the citizenship status of those Latvians and their descendants who had been citizens of the pre-1940 Republic. Other residents of Latvia, according to the legislation, would have to apply for naturalization. Many Russians and other Slavs protested against the requirements for naturalization, which included 16 years' residence in Latvia and a knowledge of the Latvian language. The more radical nationalists, including members of the Congress of Latvia, protested that the Supreme Council, which they viewed as a Soviet institution, did not have the authority to make such decisions.

During 1992 the Government proceeded with a programme to register all inhabitants of Latvia and to define their citizenship status. The register was to be used in preparation for elections to the restituted Saeima, or legislature, which took place in June 1993. Final legislation governing citizenship was to be determined by the Saeima following the elections. Latvia's relations with the Russian Federation were severely affected by the issue of citizenship as the Russian community in Latvia numbered almost 1m. people—approximately one-third of the total population.

By January 1994, however, a law on citizenship and naturalization had yet to be adopted by the Saeima. In September 1993 a draft law was studied and discussed by the Council on Security and Co-operation in Europe (CSCE)

High Commissioner for Minorities, Max van der Stoel. Van der Stoel agreed that there should be a language requirement for inhabitants wishing to acquire citizenship, but stated that it should be a lenient one. The following month the human-rights organization, Helsinki Watch, announced that the Department of Citizenship and Immigration in Latvia had refused to enter many residents of Latvia in the register of inhabitants. The head of the Department was dismissed following these allegations. Towards the end of 1993 both sides in the dispute over citizenship formed groups intended to protect their interests: in November Latvia's Association of National Forces was formed to defend the draft citizenship law, while in December the Latvian Association of Noncitizens was established to preserve the rights of Latvia's minorities.

SOVIET MILITARY PRESENCE IN LATVIA

The issue of former Soviet troops still stationed in Latvia (jurisdiction over whom had been transferred to the Russian Federation) was also a significant one. Prior to Latvian independence an estimated total of 100,000 Soviet troops remained on Latvian territory. Negotiations between the two states in 1992 and early 1993 produced no definite date for the eventual withdrawal of all the troops, owing primarily to the Russian Government's difficulties in providing housing for them. Although the withdrawal of troops from Latvia did begin in early 1992, it appeared that the Russian Government was increasingly prepared to link continued withdrawals from the Baltic states with their ceasing of 'violations of the rights of the Russian-speaking populations'. However, in early November, apparently in response to international pressure, the Russian Government denied that any such order had been implemented, also claiming that Yeltsin's statement had been intended for 'internal use only'. Troop withdrawals, it was stated, would continue as before.

In August 1993 the last former Soviet vessel left the naval base at Bolderaja. However, by October of that year an estimated 17,784 officers and servicemen were still based in Latvia. At Russian–Latvian negotiations in Jūrmala the following month an agreement on the social protection of former Soviet servicemen remaining in Latvia was initialled by both delegations. Furthermore, the Russian delegation offered to withdraw all troops from Latvia by 1 September 1994 if the Russian Federation were permitted to maintain control over a radar base at Skrunda for a further six years. On 20 November Valdis Birkavs, the Latvian premier, officially rejected the Russian Federation's proposal on the grounds that it contradicted the UN Security Council Resolution of 15 November that demanded the 'early, orderly and complete withdrawal' of ex-Soviet troops from Latvia and Estonia. On 1 December the CSCE urged the Russian Federation to accelerate its withdrawal and to present a schedule for the process.

FOREIGN RELATIONS

Latvia was admitted to the UN and to the CSCE in September 1991. During 1992 Latvia initiated measures to establish relations with members of the new Commonwealth of Independent States. In March that year Latvia became a founder member of the Council of Baltic Sea States and continued to enjoy cordial relations with its Baltic neighbours, Estonia and Lithuania. In late 1991 these three former Soviet Republics formed a consultative interparliamentary body, the Baltic Assembly. At its third session, in November 1993, the Assembly agreed to establish a Baltic Council, which would consist of the Assembly and a Council of Ministers. Latvia also enjoyed good relations with the Scandinavian states and Finland. However, the most important issues in external relations involved Russia, notably the citizenship law and the military presence, but also economic matters such as energy supplies.

The Economy

Until 1990 Latvia's economy was completely integrated with the Soviet centrally planned system. Although Latvia's primary natural resource was its land, the industrial sector was greatly expanded during the Soviet period and, in 1989, its industrial output exceeded its agricultural production. Traditionally, Latvia's primary exports were foodstuffs, timber and electronic goods. Under Soviet rule, however, the machine-building, metal-working, chemical, petro-chemical and textile industries were intensively developed. In 1991, according to estimates by the World Bank, Latvia's gross national product (GNP), measured at average 1989–91 prices, amounted to US $9,193m., equivalent to $3,410 per head. In 1992, according to official figures, Latvia's gross domestic product (GDP) totalled 182,002m. Latvian roubles, equivalent to 69,840 roubles per head. This figure represented a decrease, in real terms, of some 32.9% since the previous year.

AGRICULTURE

In 1992 agriculture (including fishing) contributed 24.8% of GDP. The previous year the agricultural sector employed some 17.8% of the working population. In that year the total area of cultivated land was 2.5m. ha, of which approximately 1.7m. ha was arable land. Forested land amounted to 2.8m. ha. The principal sectors were dairy farming and pig-breeding. Flax, cereals, sugar beets, potatoes and fodder crops were the main crops grown. Livestock products accounted for approximately one-half the value of agricultural production in 1992. Agricultural output in Latvia began to decline in 1988, owing to a series of land reforms implemented by the Latvian authorities. Following Latvia's independence, however, the decrease in productivity intensified. The dramatic increase in consumer prices during 1991 and 1992, distortions in production and prices and the disruption of Latvia's trading relation with its traditional partners (namely the countries of the former USSR) all contributed to this decline. Furthermore, a drought during the growing season in 1992 compounded the problem. Overall agricultural output declined by almost 13% in 1992 and continued to decline throughout the following year. Apart from the decline in productivity of the agricultural sector, several other problems emerged in agriculture after Latvia became independent. The granting of credits to farmers ceased almost completely, the livestock sector was oversized, the many agro-industries were relying on outdated technology and equipment, and support services were insufficient. In January 1994, however, the World Bank confirmed a loan of US $25m. to assist Latvian agriculture.

Some $11.9m. of this sum was to be used on credits for farmers.

In 1992 and 1993 the Latvian Government continued the process of land privatization begun in 1990 with the Law on Land Reform in Country Districts, which provided for full private ownership for individuals. Land commissions were set up in each district to implement the reforms. By the end of 1992 some 80% of farmland was owned by approximately 700 joint stock and share companies, nearly all of which were controlled by state-appointed managements. In addition, there were some 52,000 private farms and some 80,000 private plots, which were usually farmed by employees on state or collective farms.

INDUSTRY

Industry (including mining, manufacturing and public utilities) amounted to some 44.8% of GDP in 1992. The manufacturing sector alone contributed 38.3%. In 1991 the industrial sector employed 26.6% of the working population. The principal industries within the manufacturing sectors were the engineering industries, particularly the machine-building and electronics industries. Food-processing and light industry were also important.

During Soviet rule, Latvian industry was characterized by its emphasis on defence-related production, its large enterprises with their outdated technology and the inferior quality of its products. Furthermore, industry in Latvia had depended heavily on the other Republics of the USSR for its supplies of minerals and energy, which it imported at below world market prices. In 1992 the level of industrial production began to decline: in the second six months of the year output was some 37.5% lower than in the corresponding period of 1991, with the largest declines occurring in the energy, chemical, machine-building and light industries. The fall in production continued throughout 1993, although at a slower rate, as Latvia's supplies of raw materials were exhausted and its markets amongst the former Soviet Republics disappeared.

The construction sector, previously an important activity in the economy, was seriously affected by the disintegration of the Soviet economic system. In 1992 it contributed 7.2% of GDP. It accounted for 9.3% of employment.

ENERGY

Latvia had limited natural resources (peat, dolomite, limestone, gypsum, amber, gravel and sand) and was dependent on imported fuels to provide energy. In 1991 fuel and energy imports amounted to approximately one-third of Latvia's total imports. Estonia and Lithuania were Latvia's main suppliers of electrical energy, while petroleum products were imported from Lithuania and the Russian Federation.

However, towards the end of 1993 Latvia began to develop its own petroleum industry. In September the Government signed an agreement with the US petroleum company, Amoco, to develop petroleum extraction in Latvia. (Petroleum products accounted for some 20% of total exports for the first half of 1993.) Furthermore, in January 1994 Latvian established a joint venture with the Russian Federation which would assist the petroleum-extracting complex and enable Latvia to receive cheap fuel. In February of that year Latvia and Lithuania agreed to build a terminal for the transhipment of petroleum and petroleum products at the Latvian port of Liepāja.

In February 1994 the Russian natural-gas company, Gasprom, threatened to suspend its exports to Latvia until an outstanding debt of some 32,000m. roubles had been paid. However, it was possible that Latvia would be provided with aid by the European Union (as the European Community—EC—was known from November 1993) to develop its own natural-gas deposits, which were potentially among the richest in the world.

TRADE

In 1992 some 57.5% of Latvia's trade was still conducted with former Soviet Republics, in particular with its Baltic neighbours, Estonia and Lithuania, and with the Russian Federation. In that year a trade deficit of some US $186m. was recorded, compared to a surplus of $1,171m. the previous year. In 1990 Latvia's principal exports were machinery and equipment, textiles, chemicals and food products. Its main imports were machinery and equipment, textiles, chemicals, food products, fuel and iron and steel. According to official figures, in the first half of 1993 Latvia's total foreign trade rose by 731m. lati, compared with the same period in 1992. Of this total, trade with member countries of the EC amounted to 103.8m. lati in exports and 49.2m. lati in imports. Exports to the Russian Federation were worth 100.1m. lati, and imports 49.5m. lati.

FINANCE

Latvia's state budget for 1993 envisaged a surplus of 419m. Latvian roubles, equivalent to 0.1% of GDP. Retail prices increased by 958% during 1992, compared to 262% in 1991. In January 1994, according to official figures, a total of 95,276 Latvians were unemployed, equivalent to some 8% of the working population.

Latvia joined the International Monetary Fund (IMF) and the World Bank in 1992. It also became a member of the European Bank for Reconstruction and Development (EBRD). By this time its own banking system had been reformed from the old Soviet monobank system, which existed until 1991, to a two-tier banking system with an autonomous central bank.

In May 1992 the Latvian rouble was introduced in Latvia, in response to a shortage of currency. The Latvian rouble operated in parallel to the Russian (former Soviet) rouble until it became sole legal tender on 20 July 1992. As the rate of inflation appeared to have slowed considerably, at the beginning of 1993 the Government decided gradually to introduce the lats, the name of the currency of pre-Soviet Latvia, beginning on 5 March. In June the process of introducing the lats into the economy was completed and it became the sole legal tender in October.

PROSPECTS

By the end of 1993 in Latvia there was some optimism that the end of the recession (which started in 1990) had begun. Inflation was kept largely under control, as a result of the strict monetary policies imposed by the Bank of Latvia. The reintroduction of the lats had been achieved and the supply of goods and foodstuffs was meeting consumer demand. However, unemployment was high, industrial and agricultural production were still declining, privatization was progressing slowly and Latvia was relying too heavily on imported fuel. In order to be able to complete the process of privatization and to develop its fuel industry, Latvia was likely to be dependent on loans from foreign institutions, such as the World Bank.

Statistical Survey

Source (unless otherwise stated): Latvian Encyclopaedia Publishers, Maskavas iela 68, Rīga, LV 1018; tel. (2) 220-150.

Area and Population

AREA, POPULATION AND DENSITY

Area (sq km)	64,589*
Population (census results)†	
12 January 1989	
Males	1,238,806
Females	1,427,761
Total	2,666,567
Population (official estimates at 1 January)	
1991	2,667,870
1992	2,656,958
1993	2,606,176
Density (per sq km) at 1 January 1993	40.4

* 24,938 sq miles.
† Figures refer to the *de jure* population. The *de facto* total was 2,680,029.

POPULATION BY NATIONALITY
(permanent inhabitants)

	1989 census		1992 estimates	
	'000	%	'000	%
Latvian	1,388	52.0	1,396	52.5
Russian	906	34.0	902	34.0
Belarusian	120	4.5	117	4.4
Ukrainian	92	3.5	89	3.4
Polish	60	2.3	60	2.2
Lithuanian	35	1.3	34	1.3
Total (incl. others)	2,667	100.0	2,657	100.0

PRINCIPAL TOWNS (estimated population at 1 January 1991)

Rīga (Riga, the capital)	897,078	Jelgava	73,917
Daugavpils	127,279	Jūrmala	60,901
Liepāja	113,815	Ventspils	50,435
		Rēzekne	43,073

BIRTHS, MARRIAGES AND DEATHS

	Registered live births		Registered marriages		Registered deaths	
	Number	Rate (per 1'000)	Number	Rate (per 1'000)	Number	Rate (per 1'000)
1987	42,135	16.0	25,477	9.6	32,150	12.2
1988	41,275	15.5	25,296	9.5	32,241	12.2
1989	38,922	14.5	24,496	9.1	32,584	12.1
1990	37,918	14.2	n.a.	8.8	34,812	13.0

1991 (rate per 1,000): Births 13.0; Marriages 8.4; Deaths 13.1.
1992 (provisional): Live births 31,569 (birth rate 12.0 per 1,000); Deaths 35,420 (death rate 13.5 per 1,000).

Source: mainly UN, *Demographic Yearbook* and *Population and Vital Statistics Report.*

IMMIGRATION AND EMIGRATION ('000 persons)

	1989	1990	1991
Immigrants	20.9	17.0	12.6
Emigrants	26.3	25.4	23.8

EMPLOYMENT (annual average, '000 persons)

	1990	1991
Agriculture, forestry and fishing	245	248
Mining and quarrying	4	4
Manufacturing	373	356
Electricity and water	14	11
Construction	136	130
Trade, restaurants and hotels	170	178
Transport and communications	106	107
Finance and business services	88	85
Community, social and personal services	252	254
Public administration and defence, compulsory social security	21	24
Total	1,409	1,397
Males	772	807
Females	637	590

1992 ('000): Total employment 1,350.
Total labour force ('000 persons aged 15 years and over, 1989 census): 1,470 (males 735; females 735).

Agriculture

PRINCIPAL CROPS ('000 metric tons)

	1990	1991	1992
Cereals	1,622	1,336	1,100
Potatoes	1,016	944	900
Sugar beets	439	378	350
Vegetables	169	209	230

Source: IMF, *Economic Review.*

LIVESTOCK ('000 head at 31 December)

	1990	1991	1992
Cattle	1,439	1,383	1,144
Pigs	1,401	1,246	866
Sheep	165	184	165
Poultry	10,321	10,395	5,432

Source: IMF, *Economic Review.*

LIVESTOCK PRODUCTS
('000 metric tons, unless otherwise indicated)

	1990	1991	1992
Beef and veal	125	132	128*
Mutton and lamb	4	4	4*
Pigmeat	138	126	120*
Poultry meat	40	33	30*
Cows' milk	1,892	1,739	1,530
Butter	43.6	38.3	31.8
Eggs†	46.2	42.7	40.0
Honey	3.0	2.6	2.5*
Wool (metric tons):			
greasy	347	361	370*
scoured	208	217	222

*FAO estimate(s). † Unofficial figure(s).
Source: FAO, *Production Yearbook.*

Forestry

ROUNDWOOD REMOVALS ('000 cubic metres)

	1989	1990	1991
Total	4,167	3,760	3,419

SAWNWOOD PRODUCTION ('000 cubic metres)

	1989	1990	1991
Total (incl. railway sleepers)	824.7	795.4	673.2

Fishing

('000 metric tons, live weight)

	1989	1990	1991
Freshwater fishes	n.a.	2.6	1.3
Marine fishes	n.a.	449.2	347.5
Crustaceans and molluscs	n.a.	19.5	21.1
Total catch	547.0	471.3	369.9

Mining

('000 metric tons, unless otherwise indicated)

	1990	1991
Peat	2,888	1,663
for fuel	253	298
for agriculture	2,635	1,365
Non-ore building materials ('000 cu m)	14,818	9,117

Industry

SELECTED PRODUCTS
('000 metric tons, unless otherwise indicated)

	1989	1990	1991
Refined sugar	248	230	121
Beer ('000 hectolitres)	856.3	873.8	1,295.3
Cigarettes (million)	5,522	5,209	4,765
Woven cotton fabrics (million sq metres)	55.6	48.5	45.0
Linen fabrics (million sq metres)	19.8	14.1	9.6
Leather footwear ('000 pairs)	10,175	10,648	7,773
Rubber footwear ('000 pairs)	14,516	9,717	7,571
Plywood ('000 cu metres)	95.0	64.7	43.8
Pulp	51.9	36.6	44.7
Paper	137.9	107.2	107.1
Synthetic resins and plastics	37.9	33.6	29.0
Phosphate fertilizers*	143.9	138.7	103.4
Building bricks (million)	466.1	471.8	455.7
Cement	776.0	744.3	720.0
Crude steel	555.1	550.1	373.8
Washing machines ('000)	612	570	427
Radio receivers ('000)	1,486	1,567	1,230
Buses (number)	17,034	17,100	15,849
Electric energy (million kWh)	5,801	6,647	5,644

* In terms of phosphoric acid.

Finance

CURRENCY AND EXCHANGE RATES

Monetary Units
100 santimi = 1 lats (plural: lati).

Sterling and Dollar Equivalents (30 September 1993)
£1 sterling = 92.1 santimi;
US $1 = 61.6 santimi;
100 lati = £108.55 = $162.34.

Note: Between March and June 1993 Latvia reintroduced its national currency, the lats, replacing the Latvian rouble (Latvijas rublis), at a conversion rate of 1 lats = 200 Latvian roubles. The Latvian rouble had been introduced in May 1992, replacing (and initially at par with) the Russian (formerly Soviet) rouble. Based on the official rate of exchange, the average value of the Soviet currency (roubles per US dollar) was: 0.6274 in 1989; 0.5856 in 1990; 0.5819 in 1991. However, a multiple exchange rate system was in operation, with separate non-commercial and tourist rates. A commercial exchange rate was introduced on 1 November 1990, replacing the official rate for most transactions. The commercial rate (roubles per US dollar) was: 1.692 at 31 December 1990; 1.671 at 31 December 1991. Between November 1989 and April 1991 the tourist exchange rate valued the rouble at one-tenth of the official rate. In April 1991 this rate, renamed the 'special rate', was set at $1 = 27.6 roubles. It was subsequently adjusted. The average market rate of exchange in 1991 was $1 = 31.2 roubles. Following the dissolution of the USSR in December 1991, Russia and several other former Soviet republics retained the rouble as their monetary unit. Some of the figures in this survey are still in terms of roubles.

STATE BUDGET (million roubles)*

Revenue	1992
Turnover tax	6,207.8
Excise tax	3,997.0
Profits tax	5,797.8
Property tax	15.5
Income tax of population	2,348.1
Receipts from forestry	313.2
Road tax	6.5
Natural resources tax	11.7
Customs duties	618.3
Duties and other non-tax payments	350.9
Total	26,897.8

Expenditure	1992
Financing of national economy	6,029.8
Financing of social and cultural activities	7,587.3
Education	3,235.5
Cultural activities, radio and television	822.6
Health care	2,487.2
Physical training	60.6
Social security	981.4
Financing of research and development	475.7
Maintenance of state authorities	1,041.9
Maintenance of judicial institutions	3,256.3
Grants and subsidies to local budgets	6,723.2
Total	26,859.4

* Figures refer to the budgetary accounts of the central Government only. They exclude the operations of local administrative organs and of social security funds.

INTERNATIONAL RESERVES
(US $ million, at 31 December, excluding gold)

	1991	1992
IMF special drawing rights	—	26.58
Reserve position in IMF	—	0.01
Foreign exchange	24.36	44.56
Total	24.36	71.15

Source: IMF, *International Financial Statistics: Supplement on Countries of the Former Soviet Union*.

MONEY SUPPLY (million roubles at 31 December)

	1990	1991	1992
Currency in circulation	1,863	4,000	14,661

COST OF LIVING
(Consumer price index; base: previous year = 100)

	1990	1991	1992
Food	107.5	337.0	848.0
Non-food commodities	111.5	284.2	751.7
Services	103.2	221.1	2,823.6
All items	110.5	272.2	1,051.2

NATIONAL ACCOUNTS
Gross Domestic Product by Economic Activity
(million roubles at current prices)

	1990	1991	1992
Agriculture, hunting, forestry and fishing	2,355	5,739	45,221
Mining and quarrying	25	54	313
Manufacturing	4,421	11,666	69,716
Electricity, gas and water	212	583	11,530
Construction	1,168	1,604	13,049
Services	4,307	9,019	42,173
Total	12,488	28,665	182,002

BALANCE OF PAYMENTS (US $ million)

	1991	1992
Merchandise exports f.o.b.	6,357	831
Merchandise imports f.o.b.	−5,186	−1,017
Trade Balance	1,171	−186
Services (net)	1,185	163
Unrequited transfers (net)		73
Current balance	2,536	50
Direct investment (net)	n.a.	43
Other capital (net)	n.a.	−57
Net errors and omissions	n.a.	18
Overall balance	n.a.	54

Source: IMF, *International Financial Statistics: Supplement on Countries of the Former Soviet Union.*

External Trade

PRINCIPAL COMMODITIES (million roubles)

Imports	1988	1989	1990
Electricity	134	122	111
Fuel	517	513	482
Iron and steel	411	347	355
Non-ferrous metals	136	138	140
Chemicals	718	701	733
Machinery and equipment	1,677	1,823	1,980
Forest products	160	159	155
Textiles	762	873	1,033
Food products	596	693	626
Agricultural products	263	356	288
Total (incl. others)	5,591	6,030	6,327
Inter-republican (USSR)	n.a.	4,520	4,711
Foreign	n.a.	1,510	1,616

Exports	1988	1989	1990
Iron and steel	116	117	100
Chemicals	668	693	653
Machinery and equipment	1,403	1,518	1,474
Forest products	168	148	136
Textiles	813	875	915
Food products	1,099	1,196	1,140
Agricultural products	113	143	109
Total (incl. others)	4,896	5,413	5,283
Inter-republican (USSR)	n.a.	5,039	5,028
Foreign	n.a.	374	255

Source: IMF, *Latvia, Economic Review*, and World Bank, *Statistical Handbook: States of the Former USSR.*

PRINCIPAL TRADING PARTNERS (million roubles)

Imports	1989	1990	1991
Belarus	421	370	373
Estonia	171	180	328
Germany	—	—	79
Kazakhstan	109	96	280
Lithuania	456	488	635
Russia	2,363	2,652	2,810
Ukraine	563	520	550
Total (incl. others)	6,030	6,327	6,309

Exports	1989	1990	1991
Belarus	320	368	531
Estonia	165	193	246
Germany	—	—	65
Kazakhstan	246	224	293
Lithuania	246	244	416
Russia	2,717	2,680	4,193
Ukraine	731	762	925
Total (incl. others)	5,413	5,283	7,705

Transport

RAILWAYS (traffic)

	1989	1990	1991
Passenger journeys (million)	135.1	134.4	79.4
Passenger-kilometres (million)	5,449	5,366	3,929
Freight transported (million metric tons)	20.5	18.2	16.0
Freight ton-kilometres (million)	21,132	18,538	16,739

ROAD TRAFFIC (motor vehicles in use at 31 December)

	1989	1990	1991
Passenger cars	264,084	282,688	328,436
Buses and coaches	11,197	11,722	12,647
Lorries and vans	59,857	61,000	64,343
Motorcycles and mopeds	203,720	202,860	200,859

Source: International Road Federation, *World Road Statistics.*

SHIPPING
Number of ships

	1989	1990	1991
Merchant vessels	90	87	86

Sea-borne freight traffic

	1989	1990	1991
Goods transported ('000 metric tons)	37,178	30,386	21,784
Goods turnover (million ton-kilometres)	65,156	61,328	46,991

CIVIL AVIATION (traffic)

	1990	1991	1992
Passengers carried ('000)	1,100	1,000	340
Passenger-kilometres (million)	3,357	2,999	450.5
Cargo ton-kilometres ('000).	22,052	17,975	3,069

Communications Media*

	1989	1990	1991
Radio receivers ('000 in use)	1,241	1,328	1,396
Television receivers ('000 in use)	1,122	1,136	1,126
Telephones ('000 in use)	n.a.	822	836

* At 31 December.

Education

(1992/93)

	Institutions	Students
Primary schools*	554	75,196
Latvian	414	58,621
Russian	71	16,424
Polish	2	151
Secondary schools†	374	244,985
Latvian	175	117,815
Russian	139	126,492
Polish	1	105
Ukrainian	1	72
Estonian	1	40
Jewish	1	461
Vocational schools	89	29,700
Special secondary institutions	56	31,800
Higher education institutions (incl. universities)	14	46,300
Special schools (for the physically and mentally handicapped)	52	7,482

* Including 67 schools with two languages of instruction (Latvian and Russian).

† Including 56 schools with two languages of instruction (Latvian and Russian).

Directory

The Constitution

The 1922 Constitution of the Republic of Latvia was annulled at the time of the Soviet annexation in 1940. Latvia became a Union Republic of the USSR and a new Soviet-style constitution became the legal basis for the governmental system of Latvia. The constitutional basis for Latvian membership of the USSR, the Resolution on Latvian Entry into the USSR of 21 July 1940, was declared null and void on 4 May 1990. In the same declaration the Latvian Supreme Council announced the restoration of Articles 1, 2 and 3 of the 1922 Constitution, which describe Latvia as an independent and sovereign state, and Article 6, which states that the legislature will be elected by universal, equal, direct and secret vote, on the basis of proportional representation. The 1922 Constitution was restored upon the proclamation of independence in August 1991. This provided for a parliamentary system of government, with a unicameral legislature empowered to elect a President of the Republic as head of state. The election of the new legislature (Saeima) took place on 5–6 June 1993.

The Government

(February 1994)

HEAD OF STATE

President: GUNTIS ULMANIS (inaugurated 8 July 1993).

COUNCIL OF MINISTERS

Prime Minister: VALDIS BIRKAVS.

Deputy Prime Minister and Minister of State Reform: MĀRIS GAILIS.

Deputy Prime Minister and Minister of the Economy: OJĀRS KEHRIS.

Deputy Prime Minister and Minister of Justice: EGILS LEVITS.

Minister of Agriculture: JĀNIS KINNA.

Minister of Education, Culture and Science: JĀNIS VAIVADS.

Minister of Defence: VALDIS PAVLOVSKIS.

Minister of the Environment and Regional Development: ĢIRTS LŪKINS.

Minister of Finance: ULDIS OSSIS.

Minister of Foreign Affairs: GEORGS ANDREJEVS.

Minister of the Interior: ĢIRTS KRISTOVSKIS.

Minister of Welfare: JĀNIS RITENIS.

Minister of Transport and Communications: ANDRIS GŪTMANIS.

State Minister for Energy: ANDRIS KRĒSLIŅŠ.

State Minister for Privatization: DRUVIS SKULTE.

State Minister for the Budget: JĀNIS PLATAIS.

State Minister for State Revenues: VILIS KRIŠTOPANS.

State Minister for State Property: EDMUNDS KRASTIŅŠ.

State Minister for Foreign Trade and the European Union: OLGERTS PAVLOVSKIS.

State Minister for Baltic and Northern European Affairs: GUNĀRS MEIEROVICS.

State Minister for Culture: JĀNIS DRIPE.

State Minister for Forestry: KAZIMIRS ŠĻAKOTA.

State Minister for Labour: ANDRIS BĒRKIŅŠ.

State Minister for Environmental Protection: INDULIS EMSIS.

MINISTRIES

Office of the Council of Ministers: Brīvības 36, Rīga 1170; tel. (2) 332-232; fax (2) 286-598.

Ministry of Agriculture: Republikas 2, Rīga 1841; tel. (2) 325-107; fax (2) 322-252.

Ministry of Defence: Raiņa 4, Rīga 1473; tel. (2) 210-124; fax (2) 220-274.

Ministry of the Economy: Brīvības 36, Rīga 1519; tel. (2) 288-444; fax (2) 280-882.

Ministry of Education, Culture and Science: Vaļņu 2, Rīga 1098; tel. (2) 222-415; fax (2) 213-992.

Ministry of the Environment and Regional Development: Peldu 25, Rīga 1494; tel. (2) 223-612; fax (2) 228-159.

Ministry of Finance: Smilšu 1, Rīga 1932; tel. (2) 226-672; fax (2) 227-220.

Ministry of Foreign Affairs: Brīvības 36, Rīga 1395; tel. (2) 223-307; fax (2) 227-755.

Ministry of the Interior: Raiņa 6, Rīga 1533; tel. (2) 287-260; fax (2) 212-255.

Ministry of Justice: Brīvības 34, Rīga 1536; tel. (2) 282-607; fax (2) 331-920.

Ministry of State Reform: Brīvības 36, Rīga 1050; tel. (2) 285-223.

Ministry of Transport and Communication: Brīvības 58, Rīga 1743; tel. (2) 226-922; fax (2) 217-180.

Ministry of Welfare: Skolas 28, Rīga 1331; tel. (2) 271-713; fax (2) 217-180.

Legislature

SAEIMA

(Parliament)

Chairman: ANATOLIJS GORBUNOVS.

Deputy Chairmen: AIVARS BERKIS, ANDREJS KRASTIŅŠ.

Office of the Saeima: Jēkaba 11, Rīga 1811; tel. (2) 322-938; fax (2) 211-611.

General Election, 5 and 6 June 1993

Party	Seats
Latvian Way	36
Latvian National Independence Movement	15
Harmony for Latvia, Rebirth of the National Economy	13
Latvian Farmers' Union	12
Equality	7
Christian Democratic Union of Latvia	6
Union for the Fatherland and Freedom*	6
Democratic Centre Party	5
Total	100

* An electoral coalition of the Union of 18 November and the Latvian Fatherland National Union which was formalized on 30 July 1993.

Local Government

For administrative purposes, Latvia is divided into 26 districts and seven towns. The towns are the capital, Rīga, Daugavpils, Jelgava, Jūrmala, Liepāja, Rēzekne and Ventspils.

DISTRICT ADMINISTRATION

Rīgas: Valdemāra 3, Rīga; tel. (2) 32-06-80.

Aizkraukles: Lāčplēša 1A, Aizkraukle; tel. (51) 22-766.

Alūksnes: Dārza 11, Alūksne; tel. (43) 24-292.

Balvu: Brīvības 62, Balvi; tel. (45) 22-830.

Bauskas: Uzvaras 6, Bauska; tel. (39) 22-085.

Cēsu: Raunas 4, Cēsis; tel. 22-972.

Daugavpils: K. Valdemāra 1, Daugavpils; tel. (54) 22-331.

Dobeles: Brīvības 17, Dobele; tel. (37) 22-463.

Gulbenes: Ābeļu 2, Gulbene; tel. (44) 23-194.

Jelgavas: Lielaiā 11, Jelgava; tel. (30) 47-111.

Jēkabpils: Brīvības 202, Jēkabpils; tel. (52) 32-335.

Krāslavas: Brīvības 24, Krāslava; tel. (56) 24-383.

Kuldīgas: Baznīcas 1, Kuldīga; tel. (33) 22-469.

Liepājas: Rožu 6, Liepāja; tel. (34) 22-337.

Limbažu: Rīgas 12, Limbaži; tel. (40) 21-783.

Ludzas: Raiņa 16, Ludza; tel. (57) 22-045.

Madonas: Saieta laukumā 10, Madona; tel. (48) 21-703.

Ogres: Brīvības 40, Ogre; tel. (50) 22-103.

Preiļu: Tirgus laukumā 1, Preiļi; tel. (53) 22-144.

Rēzeknes: Atbrīvošanas alejā 93, Rēzekne; tel. (46) 22-337.

Saldus: Avotu 2, Saldus; tel. (38) 22-582.

Talsu: Kareivju 7, Talsi; tel. (32) 23-320.

Tukuma: Pils 16A, Tukums; tel. (31) 22-707.

Valkas: Rīgas 13, Valka; tel. (47) 22-053.

Valmieras: Rīgas 9, Valmiera; tel. (42) 32-447.

Ventspils: Jūras 36, Ventspils; tel. (36) 24-046.

Political Organizations

In January 1990 the Latvian Supreme Soviet abolished clauses in Article 6 of the Republic's Constitution which had guaranteed a monopoly of power to the Communist Party of Latvia (CPL). In August 1991 the CPL was banned.

Christian Democratic Union of Latvia: Lāčplēša 24-4, Rīga 1050; tel. (2) 323-354; f. 1991; Chair. ANDRIS SAULĪTIS; 1,500 mems.

Democratic Initiative Centre: Rīga; f. 1991 by members of the Ravnopravic (Equality) faction in the Supreme Council; Chair. MIKHAIL GAVRILOV.

Democratic Labour Party of Latvia (Latvijas Demokratiskā Darba Partija): Kungu 8, Rīga 1581; tel. (2) 225-911; fax (2) 225-039; f. 1990, following a split in the Communist Party of Latvia; Chair. JURIS BOJĀRS; 5,000 mems.

Democratic Party: Jēkaba 16, Rīga 1811; fmrly Democratic Centre Party; Chair. AIVARS KREITUSS, ILGA GRAVA.

Equality: Jēkaba 16, Rīga 1811; coalition; Chair. FILIPS STROGANOVS.

Harmony for Latvia, Rebirth of the National Economy: Jēkaba 16, Rīga 1811; coalition; Chair. EDVINS KIDE.

Latvian Farmers' Union: Republikas 2, Rīga 1068; tel. (2) 327-163; f. 1917, re-est. 1990; nationalist; Chair. ANDREJS ROSENTALS; 2,000 mems.

Latvian Green Party (Latvijas Zaļā Partija): Kaļķu 8-1A, Rīga 1050; tel. (2) 228-892; f. 1990; Chair. OĻEGS BATAREVSKIS; 400 mems.

Latvian National Independence Movement (Latvijas Nacionālā Neatkarības Kustība): Elizabetes 23, Rīga 1050; tel. (2) 323-730; fax (2) 320-451; f. 1988; Chair. of Bd ODISEJS KOSTANDA; 12,000 mems.

Latvian Social Democratic Workers' Party (Latvijas Social Demokrātu Strādnieku Partija): Bruņinieku 29–31, Rīga 1112; tel. (2) 272-112; fax (2) 277-319; f. 1904; re-est. 1989; Chair. EGILS BALDZENS; 700 mems.

Latvian Way (Latvijas Ceļs): Rīga; tel. (2) 32-38-13; f. 1993; unites prominent political figures from Latvia and abroad; advocates a democratic state based on the principles of legality and justice, the equality and rights of all citizens, a free market economy, private ownership of land, and closer ties between Latvia, Estonia and Lithuania; Chair. ANDREJS PANTELEJEVS.

People's Harmony Party (Tautas Saskanas Partija): Rīga; f. 1993; advocates the rapid integration of noncitizens into Latvian society; Chair. JĀNIS JURKANS.

Popular Front of Latvia (Latvijas Tautas Fronte): Vecpilsētas 13-15, Rīga 1489; tel. (2) 212-286; telex 161177; fax (2) 284-771; f. 1988; Chair. ULDIS AUGSTKALNS; 150,000 mems (1992).

Union for the Fatherland and Freedom (Apvieniba Tevzemei un Brivibai): Rīga; tel. (2) 32-50-41; f. 1993; right-wing coalition of Union of 18 November and Latvian Fatherland National Union; Chair. JĀNIS STRAUME.

Youth Progress Union of Latvia: Elizabetes 45-47, Rīga 1010; tel. (2) 323-936; fax (2) 334-807; f. 1990; Chair. ANDRIS AMERIKS; 3,000 mems.

Diplomatic Representation

EMBASSIES IN LATVIA

Denmark: Pils 11, Rīga 1863; tel. (2) 226-210; telex 161213; fax (2) 229-218; Ambassador: KIRSTEN MALLING BIERING.

Estonia: Lielā Nometņu 62, Rīga 1002; tel. (2) 601-411; fax (2) 601-068; Ambassador: LEILI UTNO.

Finland: Teātra 9, Rīga 1605; tel. (2) 216-040; telex 161125; fax (2) 229-549; Ambassador: ANTTI JUHANI LÁSSILA.

France: Raiņa 9, Rīga 1050; tel. (2) 213-972; fax (8) 820-131; Ambassador: JANE DEBENEST.

Germany: Basteja 14, Rīga 1050; tel. (2) 229-096; telex 161299; Ambassador: HAGEN Graf LAMBSDORFF VON DER WENGE.

Israel: Elizabetes 2, Rīga 1010; tel. (2) 320-739.

Italy: Teātra 9, Rīga 1050; tel. (2) 216-069; telex 161235; Ambassador: UMBERTO PESTALOZZA.

Lithuania: Elizabetes 2, Rīga 1010; tel. (2) 321-519; fax (2) 321-589; Chargé d'affaires a.i.: ALGIRDAS ŽVIRENAS.

Norway: Zirgu 14, Rīga 1969; tel. (2) 216-744; fax (8) 820-195; Ambassador: TORBJØRN AALBU.

Poland: Elizabetes 2, Rīga 1010; tel. (2) 321-617; telex 161216; fax (2) 321-233; Ambassador: JAROSŁAW LINDENBERG.

Russia: L. Paegles 2, Rīga 1050; tel. (2) 332-278; Ambassador: ALEKSANDR RANNIKH.

Sweden: Lāčplēša 13, Rīga 1050; tel. (2) 286-276; telex 161114; fax (2) 288-501; Ambassador: ANDREAS ÅDAHL.

Switzerland: Elizabetes 2, Rīga 1340; tel. (2) 323-188; fax (2) 325-468; Ambassador: GAUDENZ RUF.

United Kingdom: Elizabetes, Rīga 1340; tel. (2) 320-737; fax (2) 322-973; Ambassador: RICHARD RALPH.

USA: Raiņa 7, Rīga 1050; tel. (2) 210-005; Ambassador: INTS SILINS.

Judicial System

Supreme Court: Brīvības 34, Rīga 1511; tel. (2) 289-434; following recognition of Latvian independence, the Soviet legal system ceased to be effective on Latvian territory and a complete reorganization of the judicial system was initiated. The Supreme Court is the final arbiter in criminal and civil cases.

Chairman: GVĪDO ZEMRĪBO.

Office of the Procurator-General: Kalpaka 6, Rīga 1801; tel. (2) 320-085; fax (2) 212-231.

Procurator-General: JĀNIS SKRASTIŅŠ.

Religion

From the 16th century the traditional religion of the Latvians was Lutheran Christian. Russian Orthodoxy was the religion of most of the Slav immigrants. After 1940, when Latvia was annexed by the USSR, many places of religious worship were closed and clergymen were imprisoned or exiled. In the late 1980s there was some improvement in the official attitude to religious affairs. Following the restoration of independence in 1991, religious organizations regained their legal rights, as well as property that had been confiscated during the Soviet occupation. Since 1988 some 214 new religious organizations have been officially registered in Latvia. At 1 January 1993 the statutes of 820 religious organizations were registered. The total number of congregations was 780, of which 282 were Lutheran, 190 Roman Catholic, 90 Orthodox, 54 Old Believers (Orthodox), 68 Baptists, 34 Pentecostal, 33 Adventist and five Hebrew congregations.

Department of Religious Affairs: Elizabetes 57, Rīga 1050; tel. (2) 288-879; govt agency, attached to the Ministry of Justice; Dir ARNOLDS KUBLINSKIS.

CHRISTIANITY

Protestant Churches

Consistory of the Evangelical Lutheran Church: M. Pils 4, Rīga 1050; tel. (2) 226-057; fax (8) 820-041; f. 1920; Bishop JĀNIS VANAGS.

Latvian Pentecostal Union: Laimas 14, Jelgava 3001; tel. (30) 25-011; f. 1989; Bishop JĀNIS OZOLINKEVIČS.

Union of the Latvian Baptist Congregations: Lāčplēša 37, Rīga 1050; tel. (2) 223-379; fax (2) 279-523; f. 1861; Bishop JĀNIS EISĀNS.

Union of the Seventh-day Adventists in Latvia: Vīlandes 9-1, Rīga 1010; tel. (2) 321-050; f. 1920; Chair. VIKTORS GEIDE.

United Methodist Church of Latvia: Slokas 6, Rīga 1004; tel. (2) 619-649; re-established 1991; Pastor MILDA VAINOVSKA.

The Roman Catholic Church

Latvia comprises the Archdiocese of Rīga and the Diocese of Liepāja.

Bishops' Conference (Conferentia Episcopalis Lettoniae): M. Pils 2A, Rīga 1050; tel. (2) 227-266.

Archbishop of Rīga: Most Rev. JĀNIS PUJĀTS; M. Pils 2A, Rīga 1050; tel. (2) 227-266; fax (2) 220-775.

The Orthodox Church

Although the Orthodox Church of Latvia has close ties with the Moscow Patriarchate, it has administrative independence. The spiritual head of the Orthodox Church is elected by its Saeima (or assembly).

Synod of the Orthodox Church of Latvia: M. Pils 14, Rīga 1050; tel. (2) 224-345; f. 1850; mems are mostly ethnic Slavs; Bishop ALEKSANDRS KUDRJAŠOVS.

Latvian Old Believers Pomor Church: Krasta 73, Rīga 1003; tel. (2) 222-981; f. 1760; Head of Central Council IVANS MIROĻUBOVS (Fr IOAN).

JUDAISM

Hebrew Religious Community of Rīga: Peitavas 6/8, Rīga 1050; tel. (2) 224-549; f. 1764; Head GRIGORIJS KRUPNIKOVS.

OTHER RELIGIOUS GROUPS

Dievturu sadraudze: Dārza 36A–53, Rīga 1083; tel. (2) 450-797; community celebrating the ancient Latvian animist religion; Leader JĀNIS SILIŅŠ.

The Press

Since the late 1980s, when the first independent newspapers appeared (free of the censorship of the Central Committee of the Communist Party of Latvia), both the circulation and content of newspapers and magazines have undergone considerable changes. At the end of 1992 827 publications were registered, although only 207 of these appeared regularly. A marked rise in production costs and, consequently, increased prices of newspapers and magazines, have led to a steady decline in sales. In 1991 224 magazines were published, with a total circulation of 37.5m., of which 30.4m. were in Latvian. In that year the number of newspapers published was 140, with an annual circulation of 313.8m. (of which 197.1m. were in Latvian). The joint-stock company Preses nams (Press House) is the leading publisher of newspapers and magazines in Latvia.

The publications listed below are in Latvian, unless otherwise indicated.

PRINCIPAL NEWSPAPERS

Atmoda Atpūtai (Awakening for Rest): K. Valdemāra 20, Rīga 1378; tel. (2) 289-487; fax (2) 213-978; f. 1990; 2 a week; Editor-in-Chief ELITA VEIDEMANE; circ. 20,000.

The Baltic Observer: Balasta dambis 3, Rīga 1081; tel. (2) 462-119; fax (2) 463-387; weekly; news from Estonia, Latvia and Lithuania; English; Editor-in-Chief KĀRLIS FREIBERGS; circ. 11,500.

Diena (Day): Pils 12, Rīga 1963; tel. (2) 220-019; fax (8) 820-166; f. 1990; daily; Latvian and Russian; social and political issues; Editor-in-Chief SARMITE ĒLERTE; circ. 101,600.

Dienas Bizness (Daily Business): Balasta dambis 3, Rīga 1081; tel. (2) 464-690; fax (8) 828-287; weekly; Editor-in-Chief JURIS PAIDERS; circ. 19,500.

Elpa (Breath): Smilšu 12, Rīga 1914; tel. (2) 211-776; fax (2) 212-917; f. 1990; weekly; publ. by the Club of Environmental Protection; Editor-in-Chief MAIRITA SOLIMA; circ. 8,000.

Izglītība (Education): Balasta dambis 3, Rīga 1081; tel. (2) 467-828; f. 1948; weekly; Editor ANDRA MANGALE.

Latvijas Bērnu Avīze (Latvian Children's Newspaper): Balasta dambis 3, Rīga 1081; tel. (2) 465-318; f. 1990; weekly; for 8–14-year-olds; Editor DACE KOKAREVIČA; circ. 17,200.

Latvijas Jaunatne (Latvian Youth): Balasta dambis 3, Rīga 1081; tel. (2) 467-387; fax (2) 466-221; f. 1921; daily; Editor IVARS BUŠMANIS; circ. 18,000.

Latvijas Vēstnesis (Latvian Herald): Palasta 10, Rīga 1502; f. 1993; 3 a week; official newspaper of the Republic of Latvia; Editor-in-Chief OSKARS GERTS; circ. 10,000.

Latvijas Zeme (Latvian Land): Republikas 2, Rīga 1068; tel. (2) 327-923; fax (2) 325-638; f. 1989; weekly; Latvian and Russian; Editor KSENIJA ZAGOROVSKA; circ. 50,000.

Lauku Avīze (Country Newspaper): Balasta dambis 3, Rīga 1081; tel. (2) 460-676; f. 1987; weekly; popular agriculture; Editor VOLDEMĀRS KRUSTIŅŠ; circ. 131,950.

Literatūra un Māksla (Literature and Art): Balasta dambis 3, Rīga 1081; tel. (2) 469-089; f. 1945; weekly; Editor PĒTERIS BANKOVSKIS; circ. 6,000.

Neatkarīgā Cīņa (Independent Struggle): Balasta dambis 3, Rīga 1081; tel. (2) 461-200; fax (2) 462-291; f. 1990; daily; Editor-in-Chief ANDRIS JAKUBĀNS; circ. 90,000.

Rīgas Balss (Voice of Riga): Balasta dambis 3, Rīga 1081; tel. (2) 463-842; fax (2) 465-561; f. 1957; city evening newspaper; Latvian and Russian; Editor-in-Chief VALDA KRŪMIŅA; circ. 56,525 (Mon.–Thurs.), 62,440 (Fri.).

SM-Segodņa (SM-Today): Balasta dambis 3, Rīga 1081; tel. (2) 468-383; f. 1945; daily; Russian; Editor-in-Chief ALEKSANDR BLINOV; circ. 65,000.

Solis (Step): Kijevas 14, Rīga 1003; f. 1992; weekly; promotes Christian values in society; Latvian and Russian; Editor SILVIJA FRICBERGA; circ. 12,000.

Sports: Balasta dambis 3, Rīga 1081; tel. (2) 464-117; telex 161263; fax (2) 464-458; f. 1955; 6 a week; Editor DACE MILLERE; circ. 12,000.

Svētdienas Rīts (Holy Morning): Lāčplēša 4-4, Rīga 1010; tel. (2) 334-264; f. 1920; weekly; newspaper of the Evangelical Lutheran Church of Latvia; Editor-in-Chief AIDA PRĒDELE; circ. 12,000.

PRINCIPAL PERIODICALS

Dadzis (Thistle): Balasta dambis 3, Rīga 1081; tel. (2) 460-331; f. 1957; fortnightly; satirical; Editor-in-Chief EGONS STRAUTIŅŠ; circ. 24,000.

Daugava: Balasta dambis 3, Rīga 1081; tel. (2) 465-993; f. 1977; 6 a year; literary journal; Russian; Editor-in-Chief ROALDS DOBROVENSKIS; circ. 2,000.

Draugs (Friend): Balasta dambis 3, Rīga 1081; tel. (2) 465-574; f. 1945; monthly; for 13–18-year-olds; Editor-in-Chief ANDRIS SPROĢIS; circ. 14,000.

Džentlmenis (Gentleman): Basteja 12, Rīga 1050; tel. (2) 212-223; fax (2) 213-578; f. 1992; Editor-in-Chief DAINA BEĻICKA; circ. 10,000.

Ezis (Hedgehog): Balasta dambis 3, Rīga 1081; tel. (2) 468-982; f. 1991; monthly for children; Editor MĀRIS RUNGULIS; circ. 25,000.

Karogs (Banner): Balasta dambis 3, Rīga 1081; tel. (2) 465-696; f. 1940; literary monthly; Editor-in-Chief MĀRA ZĀLĪTE; circ. 6,000.

Lauku Dzīve (Country Life): Balasta dambis 3, Rīga 1081; tel. (2) 468-095; f. 1963; monthly; popular agriculture; Editor-in-Chief ULVIS ĀBIĶIS; circ. 15,000.

Liesma (Flame): Balasta dambis 3, Rīga 1081; tel. (2) 466-470; f. 1958; monthly; for young people; Editor-in-Chief DAINIS CAUNE; circ. 35,000.

Māksla (Art): Balasta dambis 3, Rīga 1081; tel. (2) 465-543; f. 1959; illustrated monthly; Editor-in-Chief ĒVALDS STRODS; circ. 2,000.

Rīgas Modes (Riga Fashions): Kaļķu 24, Rīga 1668; tel. (2) 216-036; f. 1948; quarterly; illustrated fashion journal; Latvian and Russian; Editor RITA MUCENIECE; circ. 35,000.

Šahs Baltijā (Baltic Chess): Dzirnavu 59, Rīga 1050; tel. (2) 286-864; f. 1959; monthly; in Latvian and Russian and some articles in English, German and Esperanto; Editor-in-Chief NIKOLAJS ŽURAVLEVS; circ. 10,000.

Santa: Balasta dambis 3, Rīga 1081; tel. (2) 464-420; fax (2) 463-154; f. 1991; monthly; illustrated journal for young women; Editor-in-Chief SANTA DANSBERGA-ANČA; circ. 80,000.

Sieviete (Woman): Balasta dambis 3, Rīga 1081; tel. (2) 467-844; f. 1952; monthly; popular, for women; Editor-in-Chief MONIKA ZILE; circ. 33,000.

Skola un Ģimene (School and Family): Balasta dambis 3, Rīga 1081; tel. (2) 469-476; f. 1964; monthly; social and educational; Editor-in-Chief JĀNIS GULBIS; circ. 6,500.

Sporta Pasaule (Sports World): Balasta dambis 3, Rīga 1081; tel. (2) 465-532; f. 1992; monthly; Editor GUNTIS KEISELS; circ. 20,000.

Teātra Vēstnesis (Theatre Herald): Dzirnavu 135, Rīga 1650; tel. (2) 287-895; f. 1989; quarterly; Editor-in-Chief INGA JĒRUMA; circ. 2,000.

Tehnika (Technology): K. Valdemāra 35, Rīga 1010; tel. (2) 323-588; f. 1960; monthly; popular science and technology; Editor-in-Chief LAIMONIS ZAKSS; circ. 6,000.

Veselība (Health): Balasta dambis 3, Rīga 1081; tel. (2) 461-623; fax (2) 468-955; f. 1958; monthly; popular medical journal; Editor-in-Chief ADRIANS ĀBELTIŅŠ; circ. 20,000.

Zeltene (Maiden): Balasta dambis 3, Rīga 1081; tel. (2) 468-095; f. 1926, re-est. 1991; monthly; for girls and women; Editor-in-Chief VANDA DAVIDANOVA; circ. 25,000.

Zīlīte (Blue Titmouse): Balasta dambis 3, Rīga 1081; tel. (2) 468-867; f. 1958; monthly; illustrated; for 5–10-year-olds; Editor-in-Chief DAINA OLIŅA; circ. 23,000.

Zvaigzne (Star): Balasta dambis 3, Rīga 1081; tel. (2) 467-600; f. 1950; monthly; illustrated popular, political and fiction; Editor-in-Chief AUGUSTS LEDIŅŠ; circ. 12,000.

NEWS AGENCIES

Baltic News Service: Balasta dambis 3, Rīga 1081; tel. (2) 463-494; fax (2) 465-485; f. 1990; Dir RAITIS BIKŠE.

LETA (Latvian Telegraph Agency): Palasta 10, Rīga 1502; tel. (2) 223-462; telex 161139; fax (2) 224-502; f. 1920; govt information agency; Dir ĒRIKS KEHRIS (acting).

PRESS ASSOCIATION

Latvijas žurnālistu savienība (Latvian Journalists' Union): Basteja 4, Rīga 1862; tel. (2) 211-433; fax (8) 820-23; f. 1991; Pres. LIGITA AZOVSKA.

Publishers

In 1991 1,387 book titles were published (843 in Latvian). The total number of copies was 28.5m. (13.6m. in Latvian).

Avots (Spring Publishing House): Aspazijas 24, Rīga 1478; tel. (2) 225-824; f. 1980; fiction, children's books, agriculture, law, reference books, etc.; Dir KĀRLIS SKRUZIS.

Jana Seta: Elizabetes 83-85, Rīga 1011; tel. and fax (8) 828-039; maps, art catalogues, books.

Latvijas Enciklopēdija (Latvian Encyclopaedia Publishers): Maskavas 68, Rīga 1018; tel. (2) 220-150; f. 1963; encyclopaedias, terminological dictionaries, reference books; Dir VIKTORS TĒRAUDS.

Liesma (Flame Publishing House): Aspazijas 24, Rīga 1455; tel. (2) 223-063; f. 1965; fiction, poetry, literary criticism, fine arts; Dir VILIS JANSONS.

Preses nams (Press House): Balasta dambis 3, Rīga 1081; tel. (2) 465-732; f. 1990; Latvian fiction, translations of foreign literature, children's books; Dir MĀRA CAUNE.

Sprīdītis: Aldaru 2-4, Rīga 1836; tel. and fax (2) 224-921; f. 1990; books for children and young people; Dir JĀZEPS OSMANIS.

Vaga: Lazaretes 3, Rīga 1010; tel. (2) 336-332; fax (2) 323-825; f. 1990; fiction, children's and English textbooks; Dir MĀRIS OZOLIŅŠ.

Vieda: Elijas 17, Rīga 1018; tel. (2) 223-497; f. 1989; ecological issues; Dir-Gen. AIVARS GARDA.

Zinātne (Science Publishing House): Turgeņeva 19, Rīga 1530; tel. (2) 212-797; f. 1951; scientific and scholarly books; Dir IVARS RIEKSTIŅŠ.

Zvaigzne (Star Publishing House): K. Valdemāra 105, Rīga 1013; tel. (2) 372-396; f. 1966; textbooks, children's books, fiction, books for the blind; Dir VIJA KILBLOKA.

PUBLISHERS' ASSOCIATION

Latvijas grāmatizdevēju asociācija (Latvian Book Publishers' Association): Aspazijas 24, Rīga 1050; tel. (2) 336-332; fax (2) 228-482; f. 1993; 21 founding mems representing both state-owned and private publishing houses; Pres. MĀRIS OZOLIŅŠ.

WRITERS' UNION

Latvijas rakstnieku savienība (Latvian Writers' Union): K. Barona 12, Rīga 1427; tel. (2) 287-629.

Radio and Television

In January 1994 there were 35 television broadcasting companies in Latvia and 10 radio companies.

Latvian Radio and Television Council: Smilšu 1–3, Rīga 1939; tel. (2) 206-509; f. 1992; defends social interests and maintains free accessibility to information; Chair. ZIGMUNDS SKUJIŅŠ.

Latvijas Radio (Latvian Radio): Doma 8, Rīga 1505; tel. (2) 206-722; telex 161266; fax (8) 820-216; f. 1925; state-operated service; broadcasts in Latvian, Russian, Swedish, English and German; Dir-Gen. Dr ARNOLDS KLOTIŅŠ.

Latvijas Televīzija (Latvian Television): Zaķusalas krastmala 3, Rīga 1509; tel. (2) 200-830; telex 161188; fax (2) 200-025; f. 1954; state-operated service; two channels in Latvian (Channel II also includes Russian-language programmes); Dir-Gen. IMANTS RĀKINS.

NTV-5 (Independent Television-5): Maskavas 40–42, Rīga 1018; tel. (2) 225-758; f. 1991; entertainment programming; news reports in Latvian and English; Dir-Gen. JANIS LEJA.

Radio Rīga–Jurmala: Rīga; f. 1993; Latvian–German joint venture; news bulletins in Latvian, English, German and Russian.

Radio Sconto: Rīga; f. 1993; music and news bulletins; Dir IVO BAUMANIS.

Finance

(cap. = capital; dep. = deposits; res = reserves;
m. = million; amounts in lati, unless otherwise stated)

BANKING

Central Bank

Bank of Latvia (Latvijas banka): K. Valdemāra 2A, Rīga 1050; tel. (2) 323-863; telex 161146; fax (2) 220-543; f. 1922; cap. 366m. Latvian roubles, dep. 7,953m. Latvian roubles, res 58m. Latvian roubles; Pres. EINĀRS REPŠE; Chair of Board and Vice-Pres. ILMĀRS RIMŠEVIČS.

Commercial Banks

Atmoda–Awakening Bank (Banka Atmoda): Ganību dambis 36, Rīga 1069; tel. (2) 383-549; fax (2) 421-620; f. 1992; Pres. MARIJA VIŠŅEVSKA.

Baltic Commercial Bank (Baltija komercbanka): Brīvības 49–54, Rīga 1578; tel. (2) 228-211; fax (2) 225-024; f. 1992; Chair. of Bd TALIVALDIS FREIMANIS.

Baltic Transit Bank (Baltijas Tranzīta banka): 13. janvāra 3, Rīga 1050; tel. (2) 229-145; f. 1992; joint stock commercial bank; Pres. GALINA ALIJEVA.

Investment Bank of Latvia (Latvijas Investīciju banka): Kaļķu 15, Rīga 1050; tel. (2) 227-706; f. 1992; Pres. AIVARS JURCĀNS.

Latgale Commercial Bank (Latgales komercbanka): 18 novembra 359A, Daugavpils 5400; tel. (54) 59-646; fax (54) 31-074; f. 1991; Pres. ANATOLIJS SUŠKO.

Latvian Credit Bank (Latvijas Kredītu banka): Tirgoņu 8, Rīga 1050; tel. (2) 226-631; telex 161167; f. 1991; Pres. VILNIS BURTNIEKS.

Latvian Land Bank (Latvijas Zemes banka): Respublikas 2, Rīga 1981; tel. (2) 321-713; fax (2) 327-384; f. 1992; Chair. of Bd ANDRIS RUSELIS.

NEFTEKIMBANK—Rīga Oil and Chemicals Bank (Rīgas Naftas un ķīmijas banka): K. Valdemāra 149, Rīga 1012; tel. (2) 223-730; f. 1992; Pres. IGORS GRICEVIČS.

Olimpija Commercial Bank (Olimpija komercbanka): K. Barona 48–50, Rīga 1011; tel. (2) 217-422; telex 161658; fax (2) 217-363; f. 1991; Pres. ERVINS CEIHNERS.

PAREX banka: K. Valdemāra 8, Rīga 1010; tel. (2) 331-970; f. 1992; Pres. VALERIJS KARGINS.

Rīga Commercial Bank (Rīgas komercbanka): Smilšu 6, Rīga 1803; tel. (2) 323-647; telex 161112; fax (2) 323-449; f. 1991; cap. 1.1m., dep. 46m.; Pres. VLADIMIRS KUĻIK; 8 brs.

Savings Bank

Latvian Savings Bank (Latvijas krājbanka): Palasta 1, Rīga 1954; tel. (8) 820-167; telex 614462; fax (8) 820-083; f. 1987; cap. 48m. Latvian roubles, dep. 175m. Latvian roubles; Chair. of Bd MAIGONIS SKULTE; 37 brs.

INSURANCE

Alterna: Elizabetes 23, Rīga 1010; tel. (2) 323-441; accident, freight, building, credit insurance.

Balta Joint Stock Insurance Company: L. Paegles 7, Rīga 1010; tel. (2) 334-990; telex 161178; fax (2) 334-990; automobile, property, freight, travel insurance.

A/s Dukats: Republikas 2, Rīga 1981; tel. (2) 325-685; accident, life, credit, property insurance; brs throughout Latvia.

Balva Joint Stock Insurance Company: Eizenšteina 29, Rīga 1079 tel. (2) 538-528; f. 1991; personal transport, freight, accident, property insurance; Pres. VASILY RAGOZIN.

Estora: Ilukstes, Rīga 1082; tel. (2) 246-862; accident, life, property, credit, contract insurance.

Ezerzeme: Raiņa 28, Daugavpils 5403; tel. (54) 22-555; fax (54) 22-177; f. 1992; state, private firm, personal property, long- and short-term life, life, domestic animals, accident, freight, travel insurance.

Helga Joint Stock Insurance Company: Zvaijžņāju gatve 3–22, Rīga 1080; tel. (2) 378-549; fax (2) 574-687.

Latva: Vaļņu 1, Rīga 1912; tel. (2) 212-341; fax (2) 210-134; f. 1940; state insurance co; accident, passenger, child and adult life, transport, animals, building, property, state and co-operative property insurance; Chair. JĀNIS MEDENS.

Rīga Insurance Company: Grecinieku 22–24, Rm 314, Rīga 1050; tel. (2) 211-764; credit insurance.

Union Unlimited: Laipu 2–4, Rīga 1050; tel. (2) 213-150; fax (2) 225-397; travel, property, athletes', freight, state, co-operative, joint-stock, credit, medical, accident insurance.

COMMODITY AND STOCK EXCHANGES

Latgale Exchange (Latgales birža): Rīgas 2, Daugavpils 5400; tel. (54) 22-110.

Latvian Stock Exchange (Latvijas birža): Doma 6, Rīga 1050; tel. (2) 226-220; f. 1992; Pres. NIKOLAJS BARANOVSKIS.

Latvian Universal Exchange (Latvijas Universālā birža): K. Valdemāra 118, Rīga 1013; tel. (2) 373-173; fax (2) 370-310; f. 1991; Pres. JĀNIS VALTERS.

Rīga Exchange (Rīgas birža): Doma 6, Rīga 1050; tel. (2) 220-789; Pres. ALEKSANDRS KŅAZEVS.

Rīga Stock Exchange (Rīgas Fondu birža): Doma 6, Rīga 1927; tel. (2) 226-890; Chair. of Bd. GUNĀRS SLAVINSKIS.

Trade and Industry

STATE PROPERTY AGENCIES

Central Land Commission: Rīga; f. 1993; unites the Rural Land Commission and the Urban Land Commission of the former Supreme Council.

State Property Fund: Rīga; f. 1993; established to manage up to 80% of state enterprises and real estate.

CHAMBER OF COMMERCE

Latvian Chamber of Commerce and Industry: Brīvības 21, Rīga 1849; tel. (2) 225-595; telex 161100; fax (2) 332-276; f. 1934; re-established 1990; mem. of International Chamber of Commerce, Baltic Chambers of Commerce Association; Pres. ARNOLDS GROSBERGS.

BUSINESS AND TRADE ORGANIZATIONS

Confederation of Small and Medium Business Enterprises of Latvia: Ropazu 41, Rm 11, Rīga; tel. (2) 552-222; fax (2) 551-933; Pres. ERIKS ROZENCVEIGS.

Interlatvija: Kalpaka 1, Rīga 1010; tel. (2) 333-602; telex 161149; f. 1987; seeks to promote exports, imports and the establishment of joint ventures; Dir-Gen. MĀRIS FORSTS.

Latvia International Commerce Centre: Tirgonu 8, Rīga; tel. (2) 211-602; telex 161176; fax (2) 331-920.

Latvian Small Business Association: Elizabetes 45–47, Rīga 1010; tel. (2) 332-647; fax (2) 334-807; Chair. MĀRIS BAIDEKALNS.

PLUS (World Latvian Businessmen's Association): Jomas 83, Jūrmala; tel. (2) 764-253; telex 161196; fax (2) 764-710; Dir GVIDO VOLBRUGS.

TRADE UNIONS

Latvian Free Trade Union Association: Bruņinieku 29/31, Rīga 1103; tel. (2) 270-351; telex 161105; fax (2) 276-649; f. 1990; Chair. ANDRIS SILIŅŠ.

MAJOR INDUSTRIAL COMPANIES

Alfa: Brīvības 372, Rīga 1041; tel. (2) 553-075; telex 161160; fax (2) 520-817; production of electronic equipment, incl. measuring and testing instruments; Dir-Gen. JURIJS OSOKINS; 5,972 employees.

Broceni Cement and Slate Works: Saldus raj., Broceni 3851; tel. 65-216; fax 65-067; cement, construction lime, slate; Dir JURIS RESSONS; 1,458 employees.

Dambis Joint Stock Company: Ganību dambis 24A, Rīga 1005; tel. (2) 381-257; telex 161246; manufactures radioelectronic equipment, communication apparatus; 2,000 employees.

Dauer State Enterprise: Valkas 2, Daugavpils 5400; tel. (54) 359-43; fax (54) 302-03; construction; 1,745 employees.

Daugavpils Chain Belt Plant: Višķu 17, Daugavpils 5400; tel. (54) 231-97; manufactures roll-drive chains, double-lined plate chains, children's tricycles; Dir ALEKSANDRS KAREVS; 2,539 employees.

Era State Enterprise: Toma 4, Rīga 1018; tel. (2) 229-128; produces ship-repair equipment, lighting fixtures; 1,065 employees.

First Rīga State Construction Group: Daugavgrīvas 93, Rīga 1007; tel. (2) 469-882; construction; 731 employees.

Kompresors State Enterprise: Starta 1, Rīga 1026; tel. (2) 518-123; produces refrigeration equipment for domestic and industrial use; Dir-Gen. ALDIS ZICMANIS; 962 employees.

Laima: Miera 2, Rīga 1001; tel. (2) 379-690; produces chocolate confectionery; Dir ELMĀRS GOZĪTIS; 450 employees.

Latvija Joint Stock Company: Zilupes 7, Rīga 1019; tel. (2) 145-034; fax (2) 143-786; manufactures clothing; 3,043 employees.

Latvijas Balzams State Enterprise: A. Čaka 160, Rīga 1010; tel. (2) 272-693; produces beverages, incl. *Rīga Black Balsam* vodka; Dir-Gen. LEONS DUKULIS; 530 employees.

Latvijas Dzelzceļs State Enterprise: Gogoļa 3, Rīga 1547; tel. (2) 229-556; telex 161439; fax (2) 229-556; transports cargo; 30,000 employees.

Latvijas Stikls: Daugavgrīvas 77, Rīga 1007; tel. (2) 459-145; telex 161384; fax (2) 461-079; all types of glassware, incl. glass bottles and industrial glassware; Dir-Gen. DMITRIJS LAĻKOVS; 543 employees.

Liepājas Metalurgs State Plant: Brīvības 93, Liepāja 3400; tel. (34) 237-50; telex 161114; steel, rolled ferrous metals; 2,787 employees.

Liepāja State Machine-Building Plant: Flotes 6, Liepāja 3400; tel. (34) 245-19; produces agricultural machinery, hydrocylinders; 1,512 employees.

Lokomotīve State Enterprise: Marijas 1, Daugavpils 5400; tel. (54) 331-46; fax (54) 360-51; carries out repairs of engines; 3,200 employees.

Ogre State Enterprise: Rīgas 98, Ogre 5000; tel. (50) 226-28; fax (50) 731-00; produces wool yarn, knitted products and fabrics; 3,713 employees.

Radiotehnika: Popova 3, Rīga 226067; tel. (2) 418-088; manufacture of acoustic systems, amplifiers and other audio equipment; Dir-Gen. VLADIMIRS MARTINSONS.

REMR State Enterprise: Kr. Barona 130, Rīga 1012; tel. (2) 299-151; produces radioelectronics; 1,909 employees.

RER Rīga State Electric Engineering Plant: Ganību dambis 31, Rīga 1045; tel. (2) 382-077; fax (2) 383-417; produces electrical equipment, metal powder articles; 4,328 employees.

Rīga Asphalt-Concrete Plant: Granīta 13, Rīga 226065; tel. (2) 248-828; fax (2) 248-833; concrete and reinforced concrete; Dir JĀNIS BERTRANDS.

Rīga Carriage Building Plant: Brīvības 201, Rīga 226098; tel. (2) 365-440; telex 161124; fax (2) 555-219; produces railway rolling stock, mostly electric and diesel suburban trains; Dir-Gen. VALENTĪNS SAVINS.

Rīga Diesel Plant: Ganību dambis 40, Rīga 1005; tel. (2) 391-662; telex 161198; fax (2) 381-402; Dir ANDREJS KRASOVSKIS; 1,137 employees.

Rīga State Trawler Refrigerator Base: Atlantijas 7, Rīga 1020; tel. (2) 342-010; fish processing; 5,900 employees.

Rinar State Chemical Engineering Plant: Biķernieku 18, Rīga 1039; tel. (2) 553-290; fax (2) 563-170; produces pumps, industrial piping armature; 951 employees.

Rita State Enterprise: Valentīnas 3–5, Rīga 1046; tel. (2) 611-540; telex 161218; fax (2) 619-146; knitted products and fabrics; 1,339 employees.

RTR State Plant: Šampētera 2, Rīga 1041; (2) 613-438; manufactures metal processing equipment; 1,144 employees.

Sarkandaugava: Sliežu 6, Rīga 1005; tel. (2) 392-662; produces sheet glass, window glass; Dir PJOTRS GERAŠČENKOVS; 400 employees.

Sarma State Enterprise: Ģertūdes 46, Rīga 1011; (2) 275-285; fax (2) 282-566; production of textiles and knitted fabrics, clothing; 1,667 employees.

Second Rīga State Construction Group: Katlakalna 11, Rīga 1073; tel. (2) 242203; construction; 700 employees.

Sloka State Paper and Cellulose Factory: Fabrikas 2, Jūrmala 2000; tel. (2) 732-222; fax (2) 732-401; produces paper for specialized uses, including book covers, ice-cream holders, etc.; Dir MIHAILS PISKUNS; 1,326 employees.

Straume: E. Tēlmaņa 2, Rīga 226004; tel. (2) 627-010; fax (2) 627-997; manufactures electrical household appliances; Dir-Gen. ANATOLIJS ŠABALOVS.

VEF State Enterprise: Brīvības 214, Rīga 1039; tel. (2) 363-200; telex 16113; fax (2) 567-208; produces portable radios, telephones, cassette recorders; Dir-Gen. IVARS BRAŽIS; 13,233 employees.

Ventspils Port Plant: Dzintara 66, Ventspils 3610; tel. (36) 631-95; produces complex liquid mineral fertilizers; 1,000 employees.

Transport

RAILWAYS

In 1992 there were 2,406 km of railways on the territory of Latvia, of which 271 km were electrified. In the same year Latvian railways carried 31.8m. metric tons of freight and 83.1m. passengers.

Latvian Railways (Latvias Dzelzcelš): Gogal 3, Rīga 1951; tel. (8) 820-231; fax (2) 221-556; f. 1991; Dir-Gen. S. BAIKO.

ROADS

In 1992 there were 7,018 km of highways, main or national roads in Latvia and 13,534 km of secondary or regional roads.

SHIPPING

The major Latvian ports are at Rīga and Ventspils. The latter is particularly important for the shipping of Russian petroleum exports. In the early 1990s the conversion of the port of Liepāja from a Russian naval port into a trade port was under way. In 1991 some 21.8m. metric tons of freight were transported through Latvian ports.

Port Authorities

Liepāja Seaport: Rožu 6, Liepāja 3400; tel. (34) 21-727; Capt. EDUARDS RAITS.

Rīga Seaport: Eksporta 6, Rīga 1045; tel. (2) 322-750; Capt. KONSTANTINS GAILIŠS.

Ventspils Seaport: Jūras 36, Ventspils 3600; tel. (36) 22-586; Capt. ARVIDS BUKS.

Shipping Company

Hanza Ltd: Smilšu 14, Rīga 1050; tel. (2) 226-834; fax (2) 220-662; cargo transportation.

Janants and Co Ltd: Kr. Barona 99, Rīga 1012; tel. (2) 278-343; telex 161152; cargo transportation.

Latvian Shipping Company: Basteja 2, Rīga 1807; tel. (8) 828-105; telex 161121; fax (8) 828-106; f. 1940; sea transportation of wide variety of goods; Pres. PĒTERIS AVOTIŅŠ.

Rīgas Kugniecība State Enterprise: Smilšu 2, Rīga 1904; tel. (8) 820-095; telex 161159; fax (8) 820-096; transportation of goods by sea.

CIVIL AVIATION

In 1993 the first private airline, Rīga Airlines–Express, opened in Latvia. In 1994 there were two international airports, at Rīga and at Jelgava (south-west of Rīga). The Department of Aviation of the Ministry of Transport co-ordinates and maintains the development of air transport in Latvia.

Rīga International Airport: Lidosta Rīga, Rīga 1053; tel. (9) 348-158; fax (9) 348-654.

Department of Aviation: Brīvības 58, Rīga 1743; tel. (2) 281-247; fax (2) 217-180; Dir AUSTRIS ZOBENS.

Baltic International Airlines: Pils 4, Rīga 1050; tel. (2) 220-446; telex 161168; joint Latvian-US co; former Latvian division of Aeroflot; operates flights from Rīga to Frankfurt (Germany) and London (United Kingdom); two TU-134 B-3, two TU-154; one Douglas DC-9; Exec. Pres. PĒTERIS OZOLINS.

Inversija: Lidosta Rīga, Rīga 1053; tel. (2) 348-695; telex 614482; fax (2) 397-171; cargo service; operates routes to destinations in the CIS and in Asia, Africa and Western Europe.

Latvian Airlines (Latvijas aviolīnijas—LATAVIO): Brīvības 54, Rīga 1050; tel. (2) 225-560; fax (2) 223-659; national carrier, operating services to Russia, Western Europe and the Middle East; plans to operate flights to USA; Dir-Gen. EDUARDS MAHAREVS.

Riga Airlines Express (Rīgas gaisas linijas-Ekspress): Rīga; f. 1993; joint venture between two Latvian joint-stock cos and one Swiss co; operates services to Oslo and Amsterdam.

In addition, the airline **RAF'AVIA** operates cargo services to the CIS countries and to destinations in Asia, Africa and Western Europe.

Tourism

Since 1990 the Government of Latvia has given priority to the development of tourism, and has encouraged private and foreign investment in the sector. Many new or refurbished hotels were operating successfully in the early 1990s. Among Latvia's principal tourist attractions are the historic centre of Rīga, with its medieval and art nouveau buildings, the extensive beaches of the Baltic coastline, and Gauja National Park, which stretches east of the historic town of Sigulda for nearly 100 km along the Gauja river. Sigulda also offers winter sports facilities.

Latvian Tourist Board: Brībības 58, Rīga 1743; tel. (2) 229-945; fax (2) 217-180.

Latvian Tourism Council: Rīga; f. 1993; an administered public institution concerned with implementing state tourism policy, promoting local and international tourism and co-ordinating issues concerned with tourism.

Dēvize Ltd: Valdemāra 23, Rīga 1010; tel. (2) 334-404; telex 161176.

Lattur Ltd: Bruņinieku 29–31, Rīga 1001; tel. (2) 274-952; telex 161105; fax (2) 272-589.

Legenda-Nord Tourism Agency: Matīsa 79, Rīga 1009; tel. (2) 272-880.

Pavadonis Ltd: Elizabetes 45–47; Rīga 1010; tel. (2) 332-402; fax (2) 221-733.

Culture

NATIONAL ORGANIZATIONS

Ministry of Education, Culture and Science: see section on The Government (Ministries).

CULTURAL HERITAGE

Arsenāls Art Museum: Tornu 1, Riga 1050; tel. (2) 213-695; over 13,000 exhibits.

Central Board of Archives: Šķūņu 11, Rīga 1047; tel. (2) 212-539; Head VALDIS ŠTĀLS.

Institute of Bibliography; Anglikāņu 5, Rīga 1816; tel. (2) 225-135; f. 1989; research and compilation of a national bibliography, in co-operation with IFLA and UNESCO; Dir DZINTRA MUKĀNE.

Latvian Academy Library: Rūpniecības 10, Rīga 1235; tel. (2) 323-555; fax (2) 321-421; f. 1524; 3.1m. vols; special collection of Latvian literature; Dir E. KARNĪTIS.

Latvian Ethnographic Open-Air Museum: Brīvības 440, Rīga 1056; Dir JURIS INDĀNS.

Latvian State Museum of Foreign Fine Arts: Pils 3, Rīga 1050; tel. (2) 226-467; fax (2) 228-467; f. 1773; library of 15,000 vols; 18,668 exhibits; Dir MĀRA LAPIŅA.

Museum of Applied Arts: Skārmu 10–20, Rdiga 1050; tel. (2) 227-833; f. 1990; over 10,000 exhibits; Head ALIDA KRESLIŅA.

Museum of the History of Latvia: Pils 3, Rīga 1050; tel. (2) 223-004; f. 1869; materials on archaeology, history, ethnography; Dir INĀRA BAUMANE.

Museum of the History of Literature and Arts: Smilšu 12, Rīga 1629; tel. (2) 211-437; f. 1925; over 500,000 exhibits; materials on Latvian literature, theatre, music, folk art and cinema; Dir P. ZIRNITIS.

Museum of the History of Rīga and Navigation: Palasta 4, Rīga 1957; tel. (2) 211-358; Dir KLĀRA RADZIŅA.

National Library: Kr. Barona 14, Rīga 1423; tel. (2) 289-874; telex 161277; fax (2) 280-851; f. 1919; over 5m. vols; Dir ANDRIS VILKS.

Rundāles Castle Museum: Pilsrundāle, Bauskas raj., 3900; Dir IMANTS LANCMANIS.

State Museum of Fine Arts: Kr. Valdemāra 10A, Rīga 1342; tel. (2) 325-021; f. 1905; Dir MĀRA LĀCE.

University of Latvia Library: Kalpaka 4, Rīga 1820; tel. and fax (2) 223-984; telex 161172; f. 1862; 2.1m. vols; Dir A. LĀCIS.

SPORTING ORGANIZATIONS

Committee for Physical Culture and Sports: Tērbatas 4, Rīga 226723; tel. (2) 284-206; govt cttee; Chair. DAINA ŠVEICA.

Latvian Institute of Physical Culture: Brīvības 333, Rīga 1006; tel. (2) 520-595; telex 161172; fax (2) 225-039; educational and training establishment; 1,250 students; Rector Prof. ULDIS GRĀVĪTIS.

Latvian Olympic Committee: Elizabetes 49, Rīga 1050; tel. (2) 281-563; telex 161183; fax (2) 331-920; f. 1920; readmitted to the Olympic Movement 1991; Pres. VILNIS BALTIŅŠ.

PERFORMING ARTS

Art Theatre: Brīvības 75, Rīga 1147; tel. (2) 279-479; f. 1920; Chief Dir KĀRLIS AUŠKĀPS.

Cinematographers' House: A. Čaka 67/69, Rīga 1001; tel. (2) 297-010; fax (2) 277-300; f. 1962; Dir JĀNIS ŠULCS.

Latvian Circus: Merķeļa 4, Rīga 1050; tel. (2) 213-479; f. 1888; Chief Dir and Man. GUNĀRS KATKĒVIČS.

Latvian Puppet Theatre: Kr. Barona 16/18, Rīga 1011; tel. (2) 285-415; Artistic Dir VALDEMĀRS DZIEDĀTĀJS.

National Opera: Nometņu 62, Rīga 1002; tel. (2) 612-765; fax (2) 612-485; f. 1919; Artistic Dir VIESTURS GAILIS.

National Theatre: Kronvalda 2, Rīga 1010; tel. (2) 332-828; f. 1919; Chief Dir MĀRIS JAUNOZOLS.

Russian Drama Theatre: Kaļķu 16, Rīga 226050; tel. (2) 227-646; Dir GRIGORIJS CEHOVALS.

ASSOCIATIONS

Latvian Artists' Union: Kr. Barona 12, Rīga 1427; tel. (2) 287-432; fax (2) 287-671; f. 1941; Chair. JURIS PETRAŠKEVICS.

Latvian Cinematographers' Union: Elizabetes 49, Rīga 1050; tel. and fax (2) 288-536; f. 1962; Chair. JĀNIS STREIČS.

Latvian Composers' Union: Kr. Barona 12, Rīga 1011; tel. (2) 287-447; f. 1944; Chair. ARTURS MASKATS.

Latvian Culture Fund: Basteja 12, Rīga 1050; tel. (2) 227-230; f. 1987; promotes Latvian culture, provides scholarships for cultural studies; Chair. RAMONA UMBLIJA.

Latvian Journalists' Union: Basteja 4, Rīga 1862; tel. (2) 211-433; fax (2) 882-023; f. 1991; Gen. Sec. LEONARDS PAVILS; Chair. LIGITA AZOVSKA.

Latvian Theatrical Society: Vāgnera 5, Rīga 1050; tel. (2) 210-097; fax (2) 210-368; Chair. PAULS PUTNIŅŠ.

Latvian Writers' Union: Kr. Barona 12, Rīga 1427; tel. (2) 287-629; f. 1940; Chair. VIKTORS AVOTIŅŠ.

Education

Latvian is the main language of education, although, in 1988, 47.6% of pupils in general schools were taught in Russian. Since the adoption of Latvian as the state language, in 1988, the teaching of Latvian has become a compulsory part of the curriculum for all pupils. In 1990/91 the first schools for educating ethnic minorities were opened in Latvia. In 1992/93 a total of 75,196 students attended 554 primary schools (including 71 Russian, two Polish and 67 schools with two languages of instruction, Latvian and Russian). In the same year, 244,985 students received secondary education at 374 schools, of which 175 were Latvian and 139 Russian. There was also one Polish, one Ukrainian, one Estonian and one Jewish school. Some 56 schools used two languages of instruction, Latvian and Russian. Higher education was offered at 14 institutions, including two universities. Some 46,300 students attended institutions of higher education. In 1992 some 12% of the state budget was allocated to education.

UNIVERSITIES

Rīga Technical University: Kaļķu 1, Rīga 1658; tel. (2) 225-885; telex 161172; fax (2) 212-206; f. 1862; 12 faculties; 9,000 students; Rector Prof. EGONS LAVANDELIS.

University of Latvia: Raiņa 19, Rīga 1586; tel. (2) 229-076; fax (8) 820-113; f. 1919; language of instruction: Latvian; 12 faculties; 850 teachers; 9,500 students; Rector Prof. Dr JURIS ZAĶIS.

Social Welfare

The 1993 budget allocated a total of 45,731m. Latvian roubles to social welfare, equivalent to some 6% of GDP, of which 6,434m. roubles were to be spent on unemployment benefits. According to official figures, some 44,839 Latvians were receiving unemployment benefits in January 1994. In 1991 there were a total of 187 hospitals in Latvia with 36,100 beds available (equivalent to 135 beds per 10,000 persons). There were 393 other medical establishments and 12,203 medical doctors (equivalent to one doctor per 219 persons). In 1991 a total of 641,000 people were in receipt of pensions, of which 498,000 were on account of old age. A total of 21,639m. roubles was allocated to the payment of Ministers of pensions in that year. In December 1993 the Cabinet of Ministers approved a document on the payment of housing support to impoverished families. A total of 5.4m. lats per month was to be assigned for this purpose from the state and local government budgets.

NATIONAL AGENCIES

Ministry of Welfare: see section on The Government (Ministries).

HEALTH AND WELFARE ORGANIZATIONS

Latvian Children's Fund: Brīvības 85, Rīga 1157; tel. and fax (2) 271-662; f. 1990; independent, non-profit organization; assists deprived children; Pres. ANDRIS BERZIŅŠ.

Latvian Red Cross Society: Skolas 28, Rīga 1350; tel. and fax (2) 275-635; f. 1918; Pres. ULDIS LAUCIS.

Society of the Blind: Pāles 14, K-1, Rīga 226300; tel. (2) 532-607; f. 1926; Chair. of Cent. Bd GENRIHS LEBEDEKS.

Society of the Deaf: Jāņa sēta 5, Rīga 1350; tel. (2) 212-485; Chair. JĀNIS LIEPA.

The Environment

Degradation of the environment was one of the principal issues addressed by the political groups which emerged in the 1980s. The emission of untreated sewage and industrial waste into the Daugava, the high levels of harmful effluent from industrial plants and pollution caused by Soviet armed forces stationed in Latvia were among the major concerns of environmental groups.

GOVERNMENT ORGANIZATIONS

Ministry of the Environment and Regional Development: see section on the Government (Ministries).

ACADEMIC INSTITUTES

Latvian Academy of Sciences: Turgeņeva 19, Rīga 1524; tel. (2) 225-361; fax (2) 228-784; several instits involved in environmental research; Pres. JĀNIS LIELPETERIS.

NON-GOVERNMENTAL ORGANIZATIONS

Environmental Protection Club: Kalnciema 30, Rīga 1046; tel. (2) 612-850; f. 1984; active environmental group; Pres. ARVIDS ULME.

Latvian Green Party: see section on Political Organizations.

Defence

Until it became independent, in August 1991, Latvia had no armed forces of its own. In November 1991 a Ministry of Defence was established. Military service is compulsory from 19 years of age and lasts for 18 months. According to Western estimates, in mid-1993 Latvia possessed a total of 5,000 active troops and a Home Guard numbering 16,000. There is no air force in Latvia. In October it was estimated that 17,784 ex-Soviet troops remained on Latvian territory. In 1992 the defence budget amounted to some 1,800m. Latvian roubles.

Commander-in-Chief of the Armed Forces of Latvia: Col DAINIS TURLAIS.

Commander of Latvian Defence Forces: Gen. JONAS ANDRISKEVICIUS.

Bibliography

Van Arkadie, B. *Economic Survey of the Baltics States: the Reform Process in Estonia, Latvia and Lithuania*. London, Pinter Publishers, 1992.

Bilmanis, A. *A History of Latvia*. Princeton, Princeton University Press, 1951.

Bulletin of Latvian Economic Statistics. Rīga, The Committee, 1993.

Dreifelds, J. 'Latvian National Rebirth' in *Problems of Communism*, Vol. 38 (1989).

Grant Watson, H. *The Latvian Republic: The Struggle for Freedom*. London, G. Allen and Unwin, 1965.

Kondratev, M. (Ed.). *Latvia: A Path Chosen Twice*. Moscow, Novosti, 1987.

Latvia: An Economic Profile. Washington, DC, Document Expediting (DOCEX) Project, 1992.

Latvia: An Economic Profile for the Foreign Investor. Rīga, Ministry of Economic Reforms, 1993.

Rutkis, J. (Ed.). *Latvia: Country and People*. Stockholm, Latvian National Foundation, 1967.

Sinka, J. *Latvia and Latvians*. London, Central Board Daugavas Vanagi, 1988.

LITHUANIA

Geography

PHYSICAL FEATURES

The Republic of Lithuania is situated on the eastern coast of the Baltic Sea, in north-eastern Europe. It is bounded by Latvia to the north, Belarus to the south-east, Poland to the south-west and by the territory of the Russian Federation around Kaliningrad (formerly Königsberg) to the west. It covers an area of 65,300 sq km (25,212 sq miles).

The low-lying littoral along the Baltic coastline, known as the the Pajūrio Lowland, extends some 15–20 km from the sea. To the east of the coastal plain lies the Žemaičių Upland, which rises to a height of 234 m (772 feet) at Medvġalis. The Upland is separated from the Baltic Highlands of the south and east by a long plain across the central regions, called the Middle Lowland. The highest point in Lithuania is at Juozapinė Hill (294 m) in the east of the country. There is a dense network of waterways, the main river being the Nemunas (Neman), which flows south to north and empties into the Baltic Sea. There are also many lakes concentrated in the northern regions of the Baltic Highlands.

CLIMATE

Lithuania's maritime position moderates an otherwise continental-type climate. Temperatures range from an average in January of −4.9°C (23.2°F) to a July mean of 17.0°C (62.6°F). The level of precipitation varies considerably from region to region. In the far west average annual precipitation is 930 mm (37 in), while in the Middle Lowland it is 540 mm.

POPULATION

At the census of 1989, when the total population was 3,689,779. 79.6% of the population were Lithuanians, 9.4% Russians and 7.0% Poles. Other ethnic groups included Belarusians (63,169), Ukrainians (44,789), Jews (12,314), Tatars (5,135) and Latvians (4,229). In 1989 Lithuanian, a Baltic tongue which uses the Latin alphabet, replaced Russian as the official state language. The predominant religion in Lithuania is Christianity. Most ethnic Lithuanians are Roman Catholics by belief or tradition, but there are small communities of Lutherans and Calvinists and a growing number of modern Protestant denominations. Adherents of Russian Orthodoxy are almost exclusively ethnic Slavs. Most Tatars have retained an adherence to Islam.

At 1 January 1992 the total estimated population was 3,761,400. The capital of Lithuania is Vilnius, which is situated in the south-east of the country and was part of Poland until 1939. At 1 January 1992 it had an estimated population of 597,000. Other important towns include Kaunas (Kovno—434,000), situated on the upper reaches of the Nemunas river; Klaipėda (Memel—208,000), which is Lithuania's principal port; and Šiauliai (149,000) and Panevėžys (132,000), in the north of the country.

Chronology

1231: Mindaugas (Mindouh), a regional chieftain, united Lithuanian tribes by founding the Grand Duchy of Lithuania (Litva) and Rus (many of the ruling class were Orthodox Slavs).

1386: The personal union between Lithuania and Poland was achieved by the marriage of the Lithuanian Grand Duke Jagiełło (Jahaila, baptized Wladyslaw in 1386) and the Polish Queen Jadwiga (Hedwig). The following year Lithuania officially adopted Christianity.

1569: Lithuania (which included much of modern Belarus and, since the 15th century, the Samogitian lowlands of western Lithuania) surrendered its separate status by the Union of Lublin; the new Polish-Lithuanian Commonwealth was created to counter the threat from Sweden, the Russian state of Muscovy and the Turkish Ottoman Empire.

1795: At the Third Partition of Poland Lithuania was annexed by the Russian Empire.

1863: Following the additional rural hardships consequent to the emancipation of 1861, there was a revolt by the Lithuanian peasantry which was savagely repressed. A policy of russification was then instituted.

1915: Lithuania was occupied by German troops, following the outbreak of the First World War.

September 1917: A Lithuanian Conference was convened; the Conference adopted a resolution demanding the independence of the Lithuanian state and elected a Council of Lithuania, headed by Antanas Smetona.

16 February 1918: Lithuania's independence was formally declared by the Council of Lithuania. The declaration was contrary to the wishes of the German authorities, who had allowed the formation of the Council because they expected it to generate popular support for Germany's occupation of Lithuania.

1919: Lithuanian troops defended Lithuania's territory against invasion by Bolshevik, German and 'White' Russian forces.

April 1920: Elections were held to the Constituent Assembly.

12 July 1920: Lithuania's independence was recognized by Soviet Russia in the Treaty of Moscow.

9 October 1920: The Polish army captured Vilnius (Wilno) and its surrounding area. Poland did, however, subsequently recognize the independent state of Lithuania, with its capital at Kaunas.

1 August 1922: Lithuania's first Constitution was adopted, which declared Lithuania to be a parliamentary democracy.

1923: Lithuania occupied the territory of Klaipėda (Memel), which was under the jurisdiction of the League of Nations.

17 December 1926: Following the victory of the left wing in the May elections, Antanas Smetona seized power in a military coup and established authoritarian rule in Lithuania.

1938: Diplomatic relations with Poland were restored.

23 August 1939: In the 'Secret Protocols' to the Nazi–Soviet Pact (Treaty of Non-Agression) Lithuania was assigned to Germany.

28 September 1939: The Treaty on Friendship and Existing Borders, agreed between Germany and the USSR, permitted the USSR to occupy Lithuania.

10 October 1939: Lithuania was forced to sign a Treaty of Mutual Assistance with the USSR; the treaty provided for the return of Vilnius (previously controlled by Poland) to Lithuania. The city subsequently became its capital.

15 June 1940: The Soviet Red Army invaded Lithuania; Smetona fled the country and a 'puppet' government was formed.

3 August 1940: Lithuania was formally incorporated into the USSR.

June 1941: Some 12,000 Lithuanians were deported to Siberia (Russia), shortly before the German invasion of the USSR and occupation of Lithuania.

1944: With the defeat of Nazi Germany, Lithuania was recaptured by the Red Army. Organized partisan resistance to Soviet rule occurred throughout Lithuania until 1952.

May 1972: Anti-Communist demonstrations occurred in Kaunas.

August 1987: Dissident groups demonstrated against the signing of the Nazi–Soviet Pact.

February 1988: The security services prevented a celebration marking the 70th anniversary of Lithuanian independence.

3 June 1988: The Lithuanian Movement for Reconstruction (Sąjūdis) was formed by a group of intellectuals and writers.

11–13 August 1988: Aleksandr Yakovlev, a political ally of Mikhail Gorbachev (who had become the Soviet leader in 1985), visited Lithuania; his failure to condemn the actions of Sąjūdis served to strengthen the movement's position.

23 August 1988: At a mass rally in Vilnius the leaders of Sąjūdis denounced the Nazi–Soviet Pact and declared that the USSR had illegally occupied Lithuania.

28 September 1988: A demonstration sponsored by the radical Lithuanian Liberty League was violently dispersed by the government militia.

20 October 1988: The First Secretary of the Communist Party of Lithuania (CPL), Ringaudas Songaila, was dismissed from his post and succeeded by Algirdas Brazauskas.

March 1989: In the elections to the all-Union Congress of People's Deputies Sąjūdis won 36 out of a total of 42 contested seats in Lithuania.

20 December 1989: At a CPL Congress the Party declared its independence from the CPSU.

24 February 1990: Sąjūdis won an overall majority of seats in the elections to the Lithuanian Supreme Soviet.

11 March 1990: The Supreme Soviet (renamed the Supreme Council) declared the restoration of Lithuanian independence; on the same day it elected Vytautas Landsbergis, the leader of Sąjūdis, as its Chairman (*de facto* head of state).

17 March 1990: Kazimiere Prunskiene was appointed Prime Minister of Lithuania, the first woman premier of any of the Soviet territories.

18 April 1990: The USSR imposed an economic embargo on Lithuania, in retaliation for its declaration of independence.

30 June 1990: Lithuania agreed to a six-month moratorium on independence.

November 1990: The Supreme Council rejected the Government's plan for economic reform.

8 January 1991: Prunskiene resigned as Prime Minister; she was replaced by Gediminas Vagnorius.

13–14 January 1991: Soviet interior ministry troops (OMON) fired on civilians gathered around the Vilnius television tower; 15 people were killed and several hundred injured.

9 February 1991: A referendum on independence took place in Lithuania: some 84% of the population participated, of which 90% voted in favour of independence.

31 July 1991: Seven customs officials were killed, allegedly by OMON troops, at Medininkai, a town on the Lithuanian–Belarusian border.

4 September 1991: After Western countries had recognized Lithuania's independence the State Council of the USSR formally acknowledged it.

10 September 1991: Lithuania became a member of the Conference on Security and Co-operation in Europe (CSCE); one week later it was admitted to the UN.

January 1992: Lithuania and Poland signed a 'Declaration on Friendly Relations and Neighbourly Co-operation'.

April 1992: Ten government ministers announced that they could no longer co-operate with Vagnorius.

25 May 1992: A proposal to introduce an executive presidency was rejected in a referendum.

14 July 1992: A vote of 'no confidence' in Vagnorius won a majority in the Seimas (formerly the Supreme Council); Aleksandras Abišala replaced him as Prime Minister and subsequently announced a new council of ministers.

1 October 1992: Lithuania ceased to belong to the 'rouble zone'.

25 October 1992: A new Constitution was overwhelmingly approved in a referendum; the document stipulated that state powers were to be 'exercised by the Seimas, the President, the Government and the Judiciary'. It was adopted by the Seimas on 6 November.

15 November 1992: In the parliamentary elections the former CPL, renamed the Lithuanian Democratic Labour Party (LDLP), won 76 of the 141 seats in the Seimas; Sąjūdis won 49 seats. (The first round of voting took place on 25 October.)

14 February 1993: Algirdas Brazauskas was elected President, winning some 60% of votes cast in the Seimas (from December 1992 he had been acting head of state in his capacity as Chairman of the new Seimas); his opponent was Stasys Lozoraitis, Lithuania's ambassador to the USA.

March 1993: Adolfas Šleževičius, a member of the LDLP, was appointed Prime Minister of Lithuania.

28 June 1993: Supplies of natural gas from the Russian Federation to Lithuania were temporarily halted, owing to Lithuania's failure to pay a debt of some US $40m.; they were resumed on 9 July.

20 July 1993: The litas became the sole currency in Lithuania, replacing the interim coupon (talonas).

30 August 1993: The Presidents of Lithuania and the Russian Federation agreed that the remaining ex-Soviet troops were to be withdrawn from Lithuanian territory by the following day.

18 October 1993: The Minister of Defence, Audrius Butkevičius, resigned, following a mutiny by some 140 soldiers in Kaunas.

21 October 1993: The Seimas passed a vote of no confidence in the Chairman of the Bank of Lithuania, Romauldas Visakavičius, who had been charged with abuse of power on 8 September.

18 November 1993: Lithuania signed a number of bilateral agreements with Russia in Vilnius, including a 'most-favoured nation' treaty and social guarantees for ex-servicemen.

13 January 1994: The energy minister, Algimantas Stasiukynas, survived a vote of no confidence in the Seimas after he was accused of causing environmental damage to Lithuania by allowing imports of toxic fuel.

19 January 1994: The Lithuanian premier issued a joint declaration with the Prime Ministers of Estonia and Latvia that denounced the statement by the Russian foreign minister that Russia was entitled to station troops on the territory of the former Soviet Republics. The following day the Seimas adopted a statement which claimed that Russia was guilty of undisguised expansionism in its foreign policy.

27 January 1994: Lithuania joined the North Atlantic Treaty Organisation (NATO) programme, Partnership for Peace; earlier that month Lithuania had expressed its intent to become a full member of NATO.

11 February 1994: The Russian natural-gas producer, Gasprom, threatened to suspend its deliveries of gas to Lithuania, owing to an outstanding debt of 51,000m. roubles.

History

KESTUTIS GIRNIUS

EARLY HISTORY

The Lithuanian state emerged at the beginning of the 13th century, when the regional chieftain Mindaugas (Mindouh) imposed his rule on the majority of Lithuanian tribes. The last pagan outpost in Europe, Lithuania was under constant attack by crusaders until the 15th century. Despite being in a defensive position in the West, the Lithuanian Grand Dukes, by a skilful blend of conquest, marriage alliances and compromise with the local nobility, expanded Lithuania's southern and eastern borders to the Black Sea and beyond Smolensk (Russia). In 1386 the Lithuanian Grand Duke Jagiełło (Jahaila, baptized Wladyslaw in 1386) married the Polish Queen Jadwiga (Hedwig), instituting an alliance that would last until the latter half of the 18th century. When the Polish-Lithuanian Commonwealth was partitioned, ethnographic Lithuania was absorbed into the Russian Empire.

The alliance with Poland was a mixed blessing for Lithuania. Although its links with Poland ensured the country's integration into Western Christendom, the nobility and burghers were 'polonized', dividing the country into two distinct blocs—a literate élite which could not speak Lithuanian and the illiterate peasantry which could. During the early years of Russian rule (which lasted from 1795 to 1915) the authorities generally ignored the peasantry. Following the insurrection of 1863, however, they opted for a policy of sustained russification, even banning the publication of Lithuanian-language books in the Latin script. The tsarist government also imposed restrictions on the activity of the Roman Catholic Church. This assault on language and religion had the unforeseen effect of galvanizing the Church and a small body of intellectuals into efforts to preserve the national identity. Newspapers were published in Prussia and the USA and smuggled into Lithuania. Furthermore, political consciousness matured and there were demands for autonomy, if not independence.

INDEPENDENT LITHUANIA

The collapse of the Russian and German Empires in the aftermath of the First World War permitted the rebirth of the Lithuanian state. Germany, which occupied Lithuania in 1915, had allowed the formation of the Council of Lithuania, expecting it to supply a veneer of popular support for Lithuania's annexation. However, on 16 February 1918, the Council declared Lithuania's independence. Defeat on the western front ended German efforts to modify the declaration, and Lithuanians had begun to assume control of the country's administration by the end of the year.

Securing independence required two years of intermittent warfare and the loss of a significant amount of territory. In 1919 Lithuania's armed forces repelled an invasion by the Bolsheviks and an armed incursion into northern Lithuania by German and 'White' (anti-Bolshevik) Russian volunteers. The struggle with Poland was less successful. On 9 October 1920 Polish forces, violating a recently signed armistice, occupied Lithuania's capital, Vilnius (Wilno), and the surrounding region. Diplomatic relations between the two countries were severed and restored only in 1938, after a Polish ultimatum insisted on their resumption. Kaunas (Kovno) became the capital (until Lithuania regained Vilnius under the terms of the Treaty of Mutual Assistance in 1939). The loss of the Vilnius region was offset in part by Lithuania's seizure in 1923 of the former German territory of Klaipėda (Memel), then under the jurisdiction of the League of Nations. Most Western countries had extended diplomatic recognition to Lithuania by the end of 1922.

The Constituent Assembly, elected in April 1920, promulgated a Constitution which established a democratic republic, in which Parliament (Seimas) had extensive powers, including the right to elect the President. From 1920 to 1926 the Christian Democratic Party (CDP) and its allies dominated Parliament and adopted legislation that set the framework for communal life. Following the assumption of power by a coalition of leftists and minorities after the elections in May 1926, disgruntled army officers, Christian Democrats and members of the Nationalist Party organized a *putsch* on 16 December. Antanas Smetona, the leader of the Nationalist Party and former Chairman of the Council of Lithuania, was chosen to be President by the rightist 'rump' Parliament. Smetona maintained power until the Soviet occupation in 1940. Although opposition parties were banned, the media was censored and Smetona was portrayed as the benevolent and wise leader of the nation, the population seemed generally to tolerate this mildly authoritarian regime.

Between the First and Second World Wars the war-ravaged economy was rebuilt. The radical agrarian reform of 1922 placed agriculture on a capitalist footing and ensured a measure of social justice. Even during the economic Depression, the standard of living in Lithuania rose steadily. The country did remain underdeveloped industrially, however. Despite lack of foreign assistance Lithuania built the entire educational system, from the primary school to the university, from nothing, fostered the arts and founded an adequate health system. Its most important achievement, however, was the revival of a flagging national consciousness and the growth of civic and national pride.

THE YEARS OF OCCUPATION

The Nazi-Soviet or Molotov–Ribbentrop Pact, signed on 23 August 1939, prepared the way for Lithuania's occupation by dividing Eastern Europe into different spheres of influence. The Soviet Government wasted little time in asserting its intents under the 'Secret Protocols'. On 10 October Lithuania was coerced into signing a Treaty of Mutual Assistance that allowed the Soviet Red Army to establish bases on Lithuanian territory. On 15 June 1940, several hours after an ultimatum demanding a change of government had been issued by the USSR, large units of the Red Army marched into Lithuania. No resistance was offered, and President Smetona fled abroad. A Government compliant to the wishes of the Soviet state (the 'People's Government') was installed. In less than two months, on 3 August, Lithuania formally became a Union Republic of the USSR.

The Communist Government moved quickly to impose the Soviet model on Lithuanian society. The mass media and the educational system became instruments of government propaganda, industry was nationalized and organized religion was persecuted. All non-Communist organizations were banned. The only concession was the decision to delay the introduction of collective farms. The 'sovietization' of Lithuania was accompanied by a 'terror' that lasted for 13 years, including the period of German occupation. The deportation of more than 30,000 citizens, including women and children, only one week before Germany attacked the USSR, convinced the majority of Lithuanians that the Communists had embarked on a policy of genocide.

During the Second World War, from when the German–Soviet conflict began on 22 June 1941, many thousands of Lithuanians took up arms against the withdrawing Soviets. A Provisional Government announced the restoration of Lithuanian independence. However, the Germans replaced the Government with their own administration, the chief task of which was to ensure that Lithuania contributed to the German military campaign. Nevertheless, for many Lithuanians the Nazi German occupation was less harsh than the Soviet one. Jews were the major exception; some 90% of Lithuania's 200,000 Jews were murdered under the Nazi regime.

In 1944 most Lithuanians greeted the returning Red Army with considerable trepidation. More than 60,000 individuals, including a disproportionate number of intellectuals, fled to the West, while thousands of young men withdrew into the forest, joining partisan bands which engaged in conflict with Soviet security forces. Organized guerrilla resistance spread throughout the country and lasted until 1952. It is thought that as many as 30,000 partisans died in the struggle. The Communists retaliated with mass arrests, deportations and collectivization. Deportations occurred almost annually until 1951. Estimates of the number of victims of Communist repression vary, but 300,000, or about 15% of the total population, is a common figure.

The terror eased after the death of Stalin (Iosif V. Dzhugashvili) in 1953, as did hopes of Western intervention. The Communist Party of Lithuania (CPL), headed by its long-term First Secretary Antanas Snieckus, faithfully followed the Soviet Government's instructions and conducted the purges similar to those that devastated neighbouring Estonia and Latvia. However, owing to a higher birth-rate in the villages, a smaller influx of Russians (in part a consequence of partisan resistance) and to industrial underdevelopment, ethnic Lithuanians made up 80% of the population and, by 1970, 67% of the members of the CPL. This favourable demographic balance ensured that Lithuanians were a majority among leading government and Party officials, who, often unintentionally, hindered the process of russification.

Undeniable progress in some spheres occurred under Soviet rule. Illiteracy was eliminated and higher education was greatly improved and made accessible to a broader cross-section of the population. Medical care became universally available. After two decades of decline, agricultural output improved dramatically and surpassed that of most Soviet Republics. Industrialization gathered momentum in the 1970s, with the construction of several gigantic complexes. The standard of living rose steadily until 1985. Relative economic well-being conferred substantial legitimacy on the Soviet regime. However, there remained strong undercurrents of dissatisfaction. Although the Government's campaign against the Roman Catholic Church reduced the number of believers and banished it from public life, the Church managed to retain genuine independence and to win the sympathy of many Lithuanians, who came to consider it the prime defender of patriotic values. With renewed repression in the early 1970s, a number of militant priests began to publish the underground *Chronicle of the Catholic Church in Lithuania*, which the authorities never managed to suppress. Lay Roman Catholics and anti-Communist intellectuals followed the lead of the *Chronicle* and established a number of *samizdat* publications, most of which were rapidly suppressed and their editors imprisoned.

THE ROAD TO INDEPENDENCE

Lithuania regained its independence in an astonishingly brief period. At the end of 1987, conservative, if not reactionary, elements were firmly in control of the CPL and were planning a new campaign against clericalism and nationalism. Barely two years later, on 11 March 1991, Lithuania had declared the re-establishment of its independence. Ironically, much of the initial impetus for this change came from developments in all-Union Party and government policy. The CPL were restrained by an indecisive First Secretary, Ringaudas Songaila, and by fears that the suppression of the emergent protest movement would be interpreted by the reformist Soviet leader, Mikhail Gorbachev, as an attack on his policies of *glasnost* (openness) and *perestroika* (restructuring).

The founding meeting of the Lithuanian Movement for Reconstruction (Sąjūdis), on 3 June 1988, is generally considered to be the starting-point of Lithuania's national rebirth. Composed primarily of intellectuals from the CPL, the movement's initial goals were quite modest: co-operation with the Government in encouraging reform; the creation of separate republican citizenship; and the implementation of greater economic, cultural and political autonomy for Lithuania. Several propitious decisions ensured that Sąjūdis would become a mass movement rather than merely another group of Vilnius intellectuals. It refused the tutelage of the CPL and it began to publish an uncensored newsletter, to organize mass rallies in Vilnius and to send representatives to the countryside to speak at rock-music concerts. The visit of Gorbachev's close ally, Aleksandr Yakovlev, on 11–13 August, turned to the advantage of Sąjūdis. Yakovlev's failure to condemn Sąjūdis was broadly interpreted as an indication of the approval of the Soviet authorities and further demoralized the leadership of the CPL. On 23 August, at a mass rally in Vilnius, Sąjūdis leaders denounced the Molotov–Ribbentrop Pact and declared that Lithuania had been occupied by the USSR. Sąjūdis' agenda had changed, albeit tacitly: independence, rather than reform, had become their main objective.

Although Sąjūdis played the dominant role in mobilizing the masses, the more radical Lithuanian Liberty League took on the Socratic role of public gadfly, pointing out to Sąjūdis the inconsistencies in its policies and the problems which it failed to address. The Liberty League was the first to advocate the restoration of the flag of independent Lithuania, to insist on a meeting to condemn the Molotov–Ribbentrop Pact and to demand the release and rehabilitation of political prisoners. Finally, on 28 September 1988, the Liberty League sponsored an unofficial rally which was brutally dispersed by the militia, causing a public outcry and leading to the disgrace of the CPL First Secretary, Songaila.

On 20 October 1988, just two days before the Constituent Congress of Sąjūdis convened in Vilnius, Songaila was relieved of his duties and replaced by the reformist Algirdas Brazauskas, whose appointment was greeted with enthusiasm, even by members of Sąjūdis. Brazauskas made a number of astute political moves which increased his popularity, the decision to return the Cathedral of Vilnius to the Roman Catholic Church being the most spectacular one. The conciliatory attitude adopted by Brazauskas and the leaders of Sąjūdis seemed to usher in a new period of political harmony. However, the spirit of conciliation soon fell victim to the dictates of political reality and to rising expectations. In November Sąjūdis demanded that the Republic's Constitution be amended to state that laws passed by the central authorities were not valid until they had been ratified by the Lithuanian Supreme Soviet. In a stormy session of the Supreme Soviet on 8 November, Brazauskas ensured that the proposed amendment was defeated and he curtailed Sąjūdis' access to the mass media. The CPL and Sąjūdis, the latter now under the leadership of Vytautas Landsbergis, were once again on opposing sides. For several months both organizations vied for public support.

At the so-called 'Black Plenum' of 21 February 1989 conservative Communists led a violent tirade against reform, while even Brazauskas warned that Lithuania was close to the imposition of a special form of rule. However, Sąjūdis had won the battle for the people's support. In the March elections to the Soviet Congress of People's Deputies, Sąjūdis candidates won 37 of the 42 seats in Lithuania. The defeat in the elections was a sobering experience for the CPL, for it realized that without a radical change in policy it would be heavily defeated in the elections to the Lithuanian Supreme Soviet the following year. A series of threats and pleas from the all-Union Government gave the leadership of the CPL the opportunity to present itself as a defender of national aspirations. Brazauskas took this opportunity to recover some control over Lithuania's political agenda. In response to the mood of the public and sensing the increasing impotence of the all-Union authorities, the CPL scheduled a Party Congress for December, clearly expressing its intention to declare independence from the Communist Party of the Soviet Union (CPSU). Gorbachev's warnings of the serious consequences of such a move were ineffective as younger CPL activists, convinced that anything less than the severance of ties would be tantamount to political suicide, convinced Brazauskas to stand firm. The Congress convened as planned and, on 20 December, voted in favour of a resolution establishing an independent Communist Party of Lithuania. Despite the disapproval of the all-Union Government in Moscow and a visit by Gorbachev to Lithuania in January 1990, Lithuania's Communists did not rescind their decision.

Although its secession from the CPSU led to a surge in the popularity of the CPL, Sąjūdis easily won a majority of seats in the elections to the Lithuanian Supreme Soviet on 24 February 1990. Two weeks later, on 11 March, the newly elected parliament (which was renamed the Supreme Council) approved a declaration proclaiming the restoration of Lithuanian sovereignty. On the same day Landsbergis was elected Chairman of the Council, easily defeating Brazauskas. Kazimiere Prunskiene was appointed Prime Minister and asked to form a government.

CONSOLIDATION OF INDEPENDENCE

The Soviet central authorities reacted harshly to Lithuania's actions. A campaign of intimidation commenced almost immediately and was supplemented by an economic blockade which began on 18 April 1990. Many Western governments urged Lithuania to seek a compromise, but the Sąjūdis majority in the Supreme Council refused to accept any accord which might be interpreted as granting a mandate for the suspension of the move towards independence. Negotiations on reform were never started, partly because the all-Union Government was overwhelmed by internal problems.

Initial popular support for the Supreme Council's efforts to secure independence and mitigate the effects of the economic blockade waned as economic difficulties mounted and the inexperienced deputies struggled to agree upon legislation for the restructuring of the economy. Parliament and the Government became involved in a bitter quarrel over the division of powers and duties. In November 1990 the Supreme Council rejected the Government's economic reform plan, but Prunskiene did not resign. Landsbergis and Prunskiene strongly disagreed on the subject of Soviet policy. Prunskiene was more willing to make concessions, while Landsbergis feared that compromises on matters of principle would only encourage the Soviet authorities to increase their demands. The rancour that accompanied these disagreements diminished Sąjūdis' political influence. Despite its monolithic appearance, Sąjūdis had always been a coalition of various groups, united only in their resolve to free Lithuania from Soviet dominance. Landsbergis' considerable skills as mediator enabled him to reconcile the various factions until he lost patience with his opponents towards the end of 1991.

In January 1991 the all-Union Government resorted to force in its attempts to restore its authority in Lithuania. Airborne troops and the special units of the Soviet interior ministry, the OMON or 'Black Berets', were sent to Vilnius and began to occupy various buildings in the capital. On the night of 13–14 January a column of tanks fired on a crowd of civilians gathered around the Vilnius television tower, killing 15 and wounding hundreds. The expected assault on the Supreme Council did not take place. The violence was counterproductive. Support for independence increased, even among non-Lithuanian residents. The defence of the parliament building by many thousands of ordinary citizens convinced many in the West that Lithuania would not be subdued and that the international community would eventually have to recognize its independence. Prunskiene and her Government were forced to resign. The new Prime Minister, Gediminas Vagnorius, unequivocally supported Landsbergis' foreign policy.

Although Soviet forces did not launch any further large-scale operations, the killings created a siege mentality, which pervaded much of public life and slowed the already laggard pace of economic reform. Tension failed to ease, for OMON troops engaged in low-level harassment and even, allegedly, terrorism, culminating in the murder of seven customs officials at Medininkai on 31 July 1991. The failure of the conservative coup attempt in Moscow in August and Yeltsin's assumption of power resolved the impasse. Western countries soon began to recognize Lithuania's independence, and this was conceded by the new State Council of the USSR on 4 September.

Independence did not, however, herald an era of political consensus. Although Landsbergis and Sąjūdis now seemed invincible and their policies vindicated, political fortunes changed dramatically. Problems which had not been voiced publicly, owing to fears that they might undermine the quest for independence, emerged dramatically. From 1989 Lithuania's economy had been deteriorating uncontrollably, bringing about a drastic decline in the standard of living. Initial economic reforms had not brought the benefits many expected, while the Government's decision to disband the collective farms led to chaos and anger in rural areas. Parliamentary debate became more querulous and bitter, engendering popular disgust with politics. Internal disputes hindered the effectiveness of Vagnorius' Government, while Landsbergis pursued his efforts to establish a strong presidency, despite parliamentary opposition. Finally, in April 1992 a total of 10 ministers expressed their wish to resign, asserting that they could not work with Vagnorius. On 25 May a referendum on strengthening the role of the presidency failed to win the necessary majority. Deputies supporting Landsbergis began boycotting parliamentary sessions. On 9 July the Supreme Council decided to hold new elections and, five days later, Vagnorius was deposed by a vote of 'no confidence'. He was succeeded by a close political ally of Landsbergis, Aleksandras Abišala.

THE BRAZAUSKAS PRESIDENCY

The results of the parliamentary elections, held on 25 October and 15 November 1992, were unexpected. The former CPL, reconstituted as the Lithuanian Democratic Labour Party (LDLP), won 76 of the 141 seats in the Supreme Council (which had been renamed the Seimas), pro-Landsbergis Sąjūdis candidates won 49, with the remainder of the seats divided among several minor groupings. Few analysts had anticipated that Sąjūdis would fare so badly, and that the LDLP would come to power. Three factors played a central role in the LDLP's victory: Brazauskas' exceptional personal popularity; anger at Sąjūdis' confrontational style of politics; and dissatisfaction with the worsening economic situation. As proof that the parliamentary election results were not fortuitous, Brazauskas (who, as Chairman of the Seimas, acted as head of state from December) was elected President of the Republic by easily defeating Lithuania's ambassador to the USA, Stasys Lozoraitis, in the presidential elections, which were held on 14 February 1993.

In its election campaign the LDLP, portraying itself as the party of experienced technocrats, promised to improve the economy, especially agriculture, and to improve the economic position of the ordinary citizen. In March 1993 a new Government, headed by Adolfas Šleževičius, was appointed. It had to try and balance these popular expectations with the austerity measures that Western lending institutions considered a condition for financial aid. Success in this was limited. Industrial output and the standard of living continued to fall steadily and Lithuania's trade with its eastern neighbours failed to improve, while the spectre of mass redundancy loomed ever larger. Crime and corruption was widespread. Although disappointment with the performance of the Government increased during 1993, so too did political apathy. Nevertheless, support for the LDLP remained substantial, supported by the conviction that the opposition would do no better.

FOREIGN RELATIONS

Owing to the major issue of the withdrawal of ex-Soviet troops from Lithuania's territory, the country's foreign policy during 1993 was mainly concerned with the Russian Federation. Since national minorities in Lithuania represented only a small percentage of the country's population, all residents were eligible to apply for citizenship. Therefore, Lithuania's relations with the Russian Federation were far less strained than those of Latvia or Estonia and the problem of troop withdrawal was in no way linked to the issue of the rights of the Russian minority (which, in January 1992, represented only 9% of the population in Lithuania). On 30 August 1993 the Presidents of Lithuania and the Russian Federation agreed that the last ex-Soviet troops should leave Lithuania by the end of the month. However, the issue of compensation for weapons seized by the USSR in 1940 and for damages incurred during 50 years of Soviet rule in Lithuania remained to be resolved.

Lithuania maintained cordial relations with neighbouring Poland. In January 1992 the two countries signed a Declaration on Friendly Relations and Neighbourly Co-operation, guaranteeing the rights of the Polish minority in Lithuania (which represented only 7% of Lithuania's population in January 1992, but, nevertheless, forming a majority in two of its regions). Further agreements, on defence and visa-free travel, were signed during 1993.

Lithuania also pursued close relations with Estonia and Latvia: in 1992 almost all trade restrictions between the three countries were abolished and a common visa policy was introduced. Lithuania was admitted to the UN and the Council on Security and Co-operation in Europe in 1991. It joined the Council of Europe in May 1993.

The Economy

KESTUTIS GIRNIUS

Lithuania is a country with a total area of 65,300 sq km (25,212 sq miles), which is approximately the size of Ireland. Lithuania had few natural resources other than arable land and forests. At the beginning of 1993 it had an estimated population of 3,751,400, a decrease of approximately 10,000 from the preceding year, owing to the out-migration of Slavs and a decline in the birth-rate. In 1992 there were 14.3 births and 11.0 deaths per 1,000 inhabitants. The natural increase, amounting to some 12,200, was one of the lowest since the Second World War. During the 1980s birth-rates and the average life expectancy of inhabitants, in particular men, decreased, while the mortality rate and percentage of retired persons rose. In 1992 some 19.5% of inhabitants were of retirement age and only 23.9% were under 16 years of age. This ageing of the population was expected to continue for some time, placing added burdens on Lithuania's budget. In 1993 ethnic Lithuanians made up 80.6% of the population. Citizenship was granted to all residents, regardless of ethnic origin.

Between the First and Second World Wars Lithuania was primarily an agricultural country with a limited industrial capacity. Most of the land was owned by individual farmers and 75% of the population was employed in the agricultural sector. The restoration of Soviet control in Lithuania in 1944 was accompanied by the introduction of the Soviet centrally planned command economy. The Communist Government nationalized all branches of industry, trade and finance. It also forcibly collectivized agriculture in 1949–50 and embarked on an intensive programme of industrialization. The harsh conditions in the collective farms (*kolkhozy*) contributed to an extensive migration of the population to urban areas, which provided labour for the growing industries. Whilst in 1959 some 61% of the population lived in rural areas, in 1992 urban residents comprised 68.8% of the country's inhabitants. The Government did not allocate sufficient funds to ensure adequate housing and services for the new urban population, leading to a chronic shortage of suitable apartments.

Central planners in the USSR attempted to utilize Lithuania's advanced infrastructure and skilled work-force by establishing relatively modern, large-scale, highly specialized enterprises. Several gigantic industrial complexes were built and served as showcases of industrial progress. These included the petroleum refinery in Mazeikiai, the Azotas chemical plant in Jonava, and the nuclear reactor in Ignalina, which was originally intended to be the largest in the world. Although by 1980 Lithuanian industry compared favourably in quality, technical level and average labour productivity to the USSR as a whole, it fell far behind Western European levels and was incapable of manufacturing internationally competitive products.

Although several characteristic features of the Soviet economy were perhaps initially advantageous to Lithuania's economic development, they later served to hinder it. Owing to the availability of inexpensive energy supplies, the industrial sector became excessively energy intensive and grossly inefficient in its utilization of energy resources. The close integration of various elements in the Soviet economy radically diminished the availability of alternative responses to novel situations. In the 1980s more than 90% of Lithuanian's trade was with other parts of the USSR and much of the remainder with countries of the Council for Mutual Economic Assistance (CMEA). Trade among the three Baltic states (Lithuania, Estonia and Latvia) was minimal, accounting for approximately 3% of the total. Since Lithuania's industrial sector depended almost entirely on the Soviet Republics for the inputs of materials and as a market for outputs, the disruption of the country's trading links with the Commonwealth of Independent States (CIS) subsequently had a devastating effect on industrial production.

Lithuania's transition to a market economy was a difficult process. Plans for economic autonomy, initially formulated in 1988, failed to gain the approval of the Soviet Government. After declaring its independence in 1990, Lithuania was forced to begin restructuring its entire economy while enduring a serious economic blockade by the USSR. Disagreements soon arose over finding a suitable combination of economic incentives and social justice, the return of nationalized property and the granting of compensation to its current occupants, and attracting foreign investment and selling assets to foreigners. Lithuanians had also greatly overestimated the strength of the Lithuanian economy and the ease of the transition to market principles. The growing chaos in the Soviet Russian economy caused serious dislocations in Lithuania, further hindering efforts at reform. Even before the collapse of the USSR in August 1991, however, Lithuania enacted legislation for the privatization of state property, distributed investment vouchers to citizens in order to facilitate the sale of state property and set the foundations for the elimination of collective farms. Especially impressive was the speed with which the majority of apartments were privatized.

By liberalizing prices well ahead of the Russian Federation and the other countries of the CIS, and by utilizing its favourable terms of trade, Lithuania managed to mitigate the effects of sharp decreases in industrial production until the second quarter of 1992. At this time, however, the situation deteriorated seriously. Internal political turmoil, a severe drought, relative increases in prices for Russian natural gas and petroleum, and the cumulative effects of the industrial decline led to rapid inflation, a sharp fall in the standard of living and growing disillusionment with reform.

AGRICULTURE

In the early 1990s agriculture in Lithuania suffered its greatest crisis since collectivization. One of the principal sectors of the economy in the 1980s, it accounted for roughly 25% of Lithuania's gross national product (GNP) and employed 18% of the labour force (Lithuanian agriculture was more labour-intensive than that of the West). Lithuanian agricultural productivity was similar to that of Poland: more effective than most Eastern European and CIS countries, but less so than Western countries. In 1992, however, production fell sharply.

At the beginning of the 1990s Lithuania had 3.5m. ha of agricultural land, of which 2.3m. ha were arable. Of the arable land, roughly 50% was sown with grain, 40% with forage crops and the remainder with potatoes, flax and sugar beets. During 1982–91 the annual grain yield was slightly less than 3m. metric tons. Owing to extensive animal husbandry, 75% of grain was used as fodder for livestock, supplemented by another 1m. tons of grain and 250,000 tons of protein concentrates received from the other Soviet Republics.

On average, crops accounted for one-third of the aggregate value of agricultural production and animal husbandry for the remaining two-thirds. Cattle represented the largest component of the animal-husbandry sector (approximately 45%), while pigs accounted for 15%. In the 1980s annual meat production amounted to some 520,000 metric tons (although by 1992 this had declined to some 377,000 tons) and milk production to just over 3m. tons (2.2m. tons in 1992). The average annual yield of milk per cow was approximately 3,600 kgs. Meat and dairy products accounted for a substantial share of Lithuania's exports.

According to government statistics, agriculture's share of GNP decreased from 30% in 1989 to less than 15% in 1992. The grain harvest in 1992 was only 70% of that of 1991, while meat production was 84% and milk production 77%. The numbers of cattle and pigs also fell. The official figures probably exaggerated somewhat the scope of the decline in agricultural production. In order to avoid taxes individual farmers did not report to the Government sales in local markets or to intermediaries. A severe drought, rising prices for fuel and other imports, and a reduction in the import of fodder contributed to the crisis in agriculture. Confusion and uncertainty about land ownership, prices, the future structure of former collective farms and government policy were equally damaging. In 1993, however, owing to more favourable weather conditions, the grain harvest and the yield of potatoes and other vegetables increased.

Although the Lithuanian Government did not intend to reverse its decision to re-establish private ownership, land reform and privatization did not progress smoothly. There was not enough land to satisfy the claims of all former owners and the state lacked the funds for issuing monetary compensation in lieu of land. The pace of reform was slow. In mid-1993 there was a total of 2,900 agricultural enterprises and 105,000 individual farms. Land had been returned to approximately 20% of the 400,000 individuals who requested it. That year the Seimas (Parliament) amended the law on agrarian reform, which was passed in 1991, and slowed the process of dismantling the former collective farms.

INDUSTRY

Industry was the most important sector of the Lithuanian economy. In 1992 the industrial sector accounted for some 32% of GNP and employed approximately 30% of the working population. Industrial production grew rapidly during the years of Soviet rule, the annual rate of growth reaching almost 7% in the 1980s. In 1990 machine-building was the largest branch of the industrial sector, accounting for 27% of industrial output. Food processing and light industry each accounted for 22%. Chemicals, electronic components, computers, shipbuilding, optical equipment, building materials and forestry were also important branches of industry. Owing to the collapse of the Eastern bloc market, Lithuanian industry was forced to redirect its production capacities. The food-processing sector's share of total output rose to 33%, while the machine-building sector's fell to 18%. The greater share of industrial output (60%) was sold in Lithuania itself. Some 30% was exported to Estonia, Latvia and the CIS countries, while 10% was sold to other countries.

The characteristics of many industrial enterprises in Lithuania reflected those of their Soviet counterparts. In 1993 the 450 industrial enterprises had, on average, about 700 employees each and accounted for a large share of the market. Some factories had produced up to 80% of the USSR's share of various products. Lithuanian enterprises were closely integrated into the Soviet economy, particularly those in the machine-building, chemical and electronics sectors. Consequently, the disruption of the Soviet economy had a serious effect on Lithuania's industrial production, particularly after 1991 and the dissolution of the USSR. The decision of the Russian Federation to charge world market prices for fuel also caused great difficulties. Initially, enterprises hoarded raw materials, made barter arrangements with CIS and other Lithuanian firms, reduced working hours and resorted to other such measures. However, in 1991 not a single enterprise went bankrupt and the total number of industrial workers decreased by only 4%.

The situation worsened considerably in 1992, as the terms of trade deteriorated. In 1992 industrial output was only 55% of the 1989 total. Output continued to decline in 1993, albeit at a more moderate rate; in the first nine months of the year, overall production declined by 47.1% compared to the same period in 1992. The continuing crisis curtailed capital investment, thereby diminishing the ability of Lithuanian industry to produce quality goods that could compete in the world market. The salaries of Lithuanian industrial workers (equivalent to approximately US $50 per month) remained low, even in comparison with other Eastern European countries. Few large enterprises were privatized, and Western investment was minimal.

FISCAL POLICY AND EXTERNAL TRADE

Lithuania remained in the 'rouble zone' until 1 October 1992. The introduction of its own currency was delayed by serious disagreements between the Government and the Bank of Lithuania and by the hope that Russia would moderate the rise in energy prices if Lithuania remained in the rouble zone. However, in April 1992, owing to the shortage of roubles, the Lithuanian Government ordered that the coupon or provisional monetary unit (talonas) be accepted as substitutes for rouble notes of similar value. Initially, the Government viewed the talonas only as a temporary complement to the rouble, rather than as a transitional stage to the introduction of the litas. However, on 1 October the talonas replaced the rouble as Lithuania's official currency.

As a result of soaring inflation, in part stimulated by the Government's policy of increased wages and pensions, the value of the talonas fell against Western currencies. On 1 October 1992 one US dollar was equivalent to 260 talonas, whilst on 4 May 1993 it was worth 559. Under new leadership, the Bank of Lithuania managed to stabilize the exchange rate of the talonas and to curb inflation by ordering commercial banks to increase their reserves overall from 10% to 12% and to deposit 12% of their reserves of convertible ('hard') currency into its own hard-currency account. This reduced the number of talonas in circulation and led to a sharp decrease in the value of the dollar (from approximately 550 to 420 talonas). Furthermore, it prepared the way for the introduction of the national currency, the litas, on 25 June 1993. The talonas was exchanged for the litas at the rate of 100 to one and, one month later, it became the only legal tender in Lithuania. The official exchange rate of the litas was to depend on a 'basket' of four leading currencies: the US dollar, the Deutschmark, the pound sterling and the French franc. The Bank of Lithuania set the formal exchange rate of the litas to the US dollar at 4.5 litas to one dollar, and the rate remained stable: at the end of 1993 the rate of exchange of the litas was set at 3.9 litas to the dollar.

In the early years of independence the composition and origin of Lithuania's international trade was in flux. Before 1991 over 90% of Lithuania's total trade was with other Soviet Republics. After regaining independence in 1991, Lithuania actively sought to increase trade with the European Community (EC) and signed free-trade agreements with four member countries of the European Free Trade Association (EFTA). In 1993 the Baltic states signed a trilateral treaty instituting a free trade zone, but regional economic co-operation remained very limited. Lithuania remained dependent on the Russian Federation for petroleum, natural gas and other raw materials and as a market for its industrial and agricultural products. At the beginning of 1993 some 98% of Lithuania's petroleum was still supplied by the Russian Federation. However, in February 1994 Lithuania and Latvia agreed to build a new terminal in Latvia for the transhipment of petroleum products, which would make Lithuania's refinery at Mazekiai less reliant on Russian suppliers. For most of the period of Soviet rule Lithuania had substantial trade deficits valued at about 10% of its gross domestic product (GDP). In 1991 it had a surplus of almost 10% of GDP, owing to its favourable terms of trade.

Despite the increased cost of fuel imports, Lithuania registered a positive trade balance in 1992, as average export prices increased approximately twice as much as average import prices. Figures for that year indicated greater trade activity with Western countries. The West's share of Lithuania's trade increased from 7% in 1991 to 24% in 1992, while the former Soviet Republics' share of trade fell from 93% of the total in 1991 to 76% in 1992, (or approximately 70%, excluding Estonia and Latvia). The trade balance with both Western and CIS countries was positive, although Lithuania did register a trade deficit with the Russian Federation, its largest trading partner. In 1992 the Russian Federation accounted for 42.6% of total turnover, Ukraine for 11.7%, Belarus for 9.5% and Germany for 4.6%. Food products and chemicals were Lithuania's chief exports to the West, while the prime imports were machinery and agricultural products. A positive trade balance was also achieved in the first nine months of 1993, although there was a deficit in Lithuania's trade with Georgia, Kazakhstan, Moldova, the Russian Federation and several Western countries.

INFLATION AND THE STANDARD OF LIVING

Although Lithuania was never wealthy by Western standards, its citizens had a higher standard of living than most inhabitants of the USSR. Prior to the disintegration of the USSR, Lithuania held first place in per head consumption of meat, second place for eggs and potatoes, and fourth place for milk and dairy products. In 1988 Lithuania trailed only Estonia and Latvia in the production of consumer goods per head. Steady but unspectacular improvement in living standards occurred during the 1980s.

By liberalizing prices and reducing subsidies whilst instituting a legally binding incomes policy, the price reforms initiated by the Lithuanian Government in 1991 helped to reduce the excess demand of goods. However, in conjunction with the drastic increase in energy prices (in 1992 the cost of one unit of petroleum increased 26 times), these reforms caused a sudden rise in consumer prices and a deterioration in the terms of trade. This, in turn, resulted in a sharp decline in the standard of living, which contributed to the impoverishment of a substantial part of the population. Inflation gained momentum in 1991. During 1990–92 the purchasing power of a monetary unit fell by 65 times. The increase in consumer prices was checked somewhat in 1993, although, according to official figures, it still amounted to as much as 189%.

In 1992 tariffs and prices on consumer goods and services increased by 12.6 times, while the price of foodstuffs rose 14-fold. However, the average monthly salary increased by only four times. At the end of December 1992, an average family spent 60%–70% of their budget on food. This percentage was expected to rise still further in early 1993, had residents not changed their eating habits: in April meat prices were liberalized and soared by 100%–150%. Some estimates suggest that more than 50% of families could not afford even the most essential purchases. The price of foodstuffs continued to increase throughout 1993.

Throughout 1992 hot water was generally unavailable in Vilnius and other major cities. The temperature of apartments in the winter did not exceed 13°C (55°F). Nevertheless, more than 50% of residents did not pay their heating bills. The wages of workers in the budgetary section and social benefits for pensioners and the unemployed rose steadily; however, by December 1992 real wages had fallen by 68.5% in comparison with December 1991. The stand-by arrangement with the International Monetary Fund (IMF), signed in 1992, set an upper limit on increases in the minimum wage. Slight increases in real wages were registered in the third quarter of 1993.

PROSPECTS

Following its independence from the USSR, Lithuania embarked on the task of reorientating its economy from a centrally planned to a market system, with significant emphasis on increasing economic ties with the West. Progress was decidedly variable. By 1993 the increase in consumer prices had been checked and a stable currency had been introduced. The desire for continued Western aid made the Lithuanian authorities attentive to advice from the IMF and the World Bank, which had the means to impose fiscal and monetary discipline on the economy. In October 1993 the World Bank allocated a loan of US $60m. to the Lithuanian Government to finance enterprises and to improve the overall economic situation in the country. Lithuania's political stability, the absence of ethnic strife in the country and its geographic location between East and West were positive factors which, if properly exploited, could induce greater Western investment. By December 1993 a total of 3,172 joint ventures and foreign enterprises were active in Lithuania, of which 1,251 were owned by CIS countries and 764 by member states of the EC (known as the European Union since November).

The privatization programme in Lithuania achieved considerable success. By 1993 most Lithuanians owned their own homes and the majority of small businesses had been privatized. At the same time, however, larger enterprises remained under government control. Corruption, favouritism and the influence of criminal elements led to frequent violations of the regulations on privatization and growing public anger at what was called the 'division of Lithuania'.

The Government took energetic action to dismantle the collective-farm system, against the wishes of many rural inhabitants. Popular opposition and the return of the former Communists to power slowed the pace of reform, in particular the transfer of nationalized property to its former owners. However, the fundamental commitment to private farming remained firm. The chaos that reigned in Lithuanian agriculture in 1992 was overcome as farmers adjusted to significantly higher input prices. Nevertheless, serious problems remained, including the shortage of equipment suitable for small-scale farming and the inability of food-processing plants to pay farmers promptly for their produce.

Lithuanian industry experienced serious problems in 1993. Output decreased by more than 50%, and production seemed likely to remain depressed into the mid-1990s. Lithuanian goods were too expensive for CIS countries and of insufficient quality for the world market. Levels of investment fell sharply, as Lithuania was unable to attract Western investors, while the enterprises themselves, under government pressure, gave priority to minimizing dismissals of workers. Lack of capital limited the opportunity for the sector to make greater use of the country's skilled but inexpensive labour force and its trained scientists. The economic decline was expected to reach its lowest point in 1995, when the process of gradual improvement was expected to commence.

In 1993 Lithuania's GNP accounted for just 43% of its level in 1989. The serious economic situation in the country was exacerbated by the unwillingness of the authorities to make difficult political and economic decisions: the delayed introduction of the litas, for example, proved a negative factor. Government reluctance was strengthened, in turn, by popular dissatisfaction with the fall in the standard of living. Although the authorities realized that inefficient industrial enterprises must eventually become insolvent, they chose to continue granting subsidies in order to prevent reduced employment. Governments consistently yielded to demands for higher salaries and benefits (a further increase in pensions and wages was announced from 1 January 1994), well aware of the inflationary consequences of its actions and in spite of the IMF's insistence on a 10% rate of inflation as a condition for the granting of further aid to Lithuania. The budget for 1994 envisaged a deficit of some 164m. litai. The Seimas succumbed to the temptation to pass populist legislation, despite the deleterious effect of such legislation on the prospects for economic recovery.

Statistical Survey

Source (unless otherwise indicated): Ministry of Culture and Education of the Republic of Lithuania, Vilnius.

Area and Population

AREA, POPULATION AND DENSITY

Area (sq km)	65,300*
Population (census result)	
12 January 1989	3,689,779
Population (official estimates at 1 January)	
1991	3,739,000
1992	3,761,400
Density (per sq km) at 1 January 1992	57.6

* 25,212 sq miles.

POPULATION BY NATIONALITY
(permanent inhabitants, official estimates at 1 January 1992)

	'000	%
Lithuanian	3,000.0	80.2
Russian	334.3	8.9
Polish	262.8	7.0
Belarusian	60.8	1.6
Ukrainian	42.6	1.1
Total (incl. others)	3,760.0	100.0

PRINCIPAL TOWNS (estimated population at 1 January 1992)

Vilnius (capital)	597,000	Šiauliai	149,000
Kaunas (Kovno)	434,000	Panevėžys	132,000
Klaipėda (Memel)	208,000		

BIRTHS AND DEATHS

	1989	1990	1991
Birth rate (per 1,000)	15.0	15.1	15.0
Death rate (per 1,000)	10.3	10.6	10.9

EMPLOYMENT (annual averages, '000 employees)

	1989	1991§
Agriculture*	121.5	122.7
Industry†	507.3	566.9
Construction	194.2	182.7
Trade, restaurants and hotels‡	145.3	188.6
Transport, storage and communications	115.6	132.5
Total (incl. others)*	1,544.5	1,649.5

* Excluding employment on collective farms.
† Comprising manufacturing (except printing and publishing), mining and quarrying, electricity, gas, water, logging and fishing.
‡ Including material and technical supply.
§ Figures for 1990 are not available.

1989 census ('000 persons): Total labour force 1,926 (males 985; females 941).

Agriculture

PRINCIPAL CROPS ('000 metric tons)

	1990	1991	1992
Wheat	1,184	855	834
Barley	1,197	1,699	955
Rye	470	345	342
Oats	196	233	51
Potatoes	1,573	1,508	1,079
Pulses	229	221	27
Rapeseed	24	13	8
Fruits	87	276	118
Cabbages	100	145	112
Cucumbers and gherkins	23	34	10
Onions	16	22	13
Carrots	64	85	26
Sugar beets	912	925	622

Source: FAO, *Production Yearbook.*

LIVESTOCK ('000 head at 1 January)

	1990	1991	1992
Horses	78	80	80
Cattle	2,422	2,322	2,197
Pigs	2,730	2,436	2,180
Sheep	65	57	58
Chickens*	17,000	16,000	16,000

* Unofficial figures.
Source: FAO, *Production Yearbook.*

LIVESTOCK PRODUCTS
('000 metric tons, unless otherwise stated)

	1990	1991	1992
Beef and veal	231	209	176
Pigmeat	138	126	120*
Poultry meat	56	44	37
Cows' milk	3,157	2,916	2,245
Butter	73.9	67.2	49.2
Eggs†	71.3	69.2	53.2
Wool (metric tons):			
greasy	141	128	120*
scoured	85	77	72

* FAO estimate(s). † Unofficial figure(s).
Source: FAO, *Production Yearbook.*

Forestry

SAWNWOOD PRODUCTION ('000 cubic metres)

	1989	1990	1991
Total (incl. railway sleepers)	938	776	664

Fishing

('000 metric tons, live weight)

	1989	1990	1991
Total catch	417.9	352.5	317.0

Mining

('000 metric tons, unless otherwise indicated)

	1989	1990	1991
Dolomite ('000 cubic metres)	1,390	1,200	990
Peat	1,745	763	650
Limestone	6,800	6,850	6,370
Clay	2,601	2,911	2,353
Crude petroleum	n.a.	11.7	33.0
Sand			
quartz	120	110	110
building	5,020	3,591	3,280
Gravel	16,700	15,341	14,600

Industry

SELECTED PRODUCTS
('000 metric tons, unless otherwise indicated)

	1989	1990	1991
Refined sugar	238.6	158.6	150.5
Paper	117.2	100.7	101.2
Paperboard	138.9	116.9	113.3
Clay building bricks (million)	1,462	1,439.0	1,439.0
Television receivers ('000)	615	558.2	516.2
Domestic refrigerators ('000)	350.2	263.4	264.6
Electric energy (million kWh)	29,158	28,405	29,363

Finance

CURRENCY AND EXCHANGE RATES

Monetary Units

100 centas = 1 litas (plural: litai).

Sterling and Dollar Equivalents (30 September 1993)

£1 sterling = 6.274 litai;
US $1 = 4.195 litai;
100 litai = £15.94 = $23.84.

Note: In June 1993 Lithuania reintroduced its national currency, the litas, replacing a temporary coupon currency, the taloras, at a conversion rate of 1 litas = 100 talonai. The talonas had been introduced in May 1992, initially circulating alongside (and at par with) the Russian (formerly Soviet) rouble. Based on the official rate of exchange, the average value of the Soviet currency (roubles per US dollar) was: 0.6274 in 1989; 0.5856 in 1990; 0.5819 in 1991. However, a multiple exchange rate system was in operation, with separate non-commercial and tourist rates. A commercial exchange rate was introduced on 1 November 1990, replacing the official rate for most transactions. The commercial rate (roubles per US dollar) was: 1.692 at 31 December 1990; 1.671 at 31 December 1991. Between November 1989 and April 1991 the tourist exchange rate valued the rouble at one-tenth of the official rate. In April 1991 this rate, renamed the 'special rate', was set at $1 = 27.6 roubles. It was subsequently adjusted. The average market exchange rate in 1991 was $1 = 31.2 roubles. Following the dissolution of the USSR in December 1991, Russia and several other former Soviet republics retained the rouble as their monetary unit. From October 1992 the Russian rouble ceased to be legal tender in Lithuania. At 31 December 1992 the exchange rate was US $1 = 378.85 talonai. Some of the figures in this Survey are still expressed in terms of roubles.

BUDGET (million roubles)

	1989	1990	1991
Revenue	4,835.1	4,674.3	12,694.3
Expenditure	4,725.9	4,491.4	11,142.4

COST OF LIVING (Index of consumer prices in state and co-operative sector; base: 1985 = 100)

	1989	1990	1991
Food (excl. alcohol)	119.9	130.6	420.0
Other products	110.4	119.2	390.0
All items	114.4	124.0	402.6

NATIONAL ACCOUNTS

Gross Domestic Product by Economic Activity
(million roubles at current prices)

	1988	1989	1990
Agriculture	3,119	3,366	3,658
Industry	3,815	4,257	4,213
Construction	1,296	1,309	1,377
Transport and communications	607	653	777
Other material services	1,358	1,336	1,382
Non-material services	1,641	1,768	1,879
Total	11,836	12,689	13,287

Source: World Bank, *Statistical Handbook, States of the Former USSR*.

BALANCE OF PAYMENTS (US $ million)

	1991	1992
Merchandise exports f.o.b.	6,783	1,145
Merchandise imports f.o.b.	−4,937	−1,084
Trade balance	1,846	61
Net services	n.a.	−18
Net income	n.a.	6
Net unrequited transfers	n.a.	111
Current balance	n.a.	160
Direct capital investment (net)	n.a.	10
Portfolio investment (net)	—	—
Other capital (net)	n.a.	9
Net errors and omissions	n.a.	−128
Overall balance	n.a.	51

Source: IMF, *International Financial Statistics: Supplement on Countries of the Former Soviet Union*.

External and Inter-republican (USSR) Trade

INTER-REPUBLICAN (USSR) TRADE

PRINCIPAL COMMODITIES (million roubles)

Imports	1989	1990	1991*
Industrial products	5,603	5,502	4,554
Petroleum and gas	1,009	1,035	988
Iron and steel	311	306	232
Non-ferrous metallurgy	157	158	99
Chemicals	714	735	190
Machinery and metalworking	2,120	1,897	808
Timber, wood and paper	195	161	115
Light industry	647	664	895
Food industry	164	251	810
Other industry	83	127	262
Agricultural products	65	118	264
Other commodities	121	289	—
Total	5,789	5,909	4,819

Exports	1989	1990	1991*
Industrial products	5,550	5,622	8,174
Electricity	201	200	364
Petroleum and gas	322	389	344
Chemicals	407	370	351
Machinery and metalworking	1,849	1,832	1,875
Timber, wood and paper	238	232	126
Light industry	1,446	1,481	1,955
Food industry	927	879	2,817
Agricultural products	197	205	15
Total (incl. others)	5,850	5,975	8,194

* January–September, preliminary figures.

EXTERNAL TRADE

PRINCIPAL COMMODITIES (million roubles)

Imports	1989	1990	1991*
Industrial products	1,313	1,498	392
Chemicals	137	145	85
Machinery and metalworking	372	499	40
Light industry	406	492	176
Food industry	336	284	40
Other industry	5	36	32
Agricultural products	249	117	161
Total (incl. others)	1,563	1,616	554

Exports	1989	1990	1991*
Industrial products	468	408	295
Petroleum and gas	163	73	120
Chemicals	22	16	51
Machinery and metalworking	118	175	38
Timber, wood and paper	39	33	29
Light industry	31	32	5
Food industry	82	67	25
Total (incl. others)	475	414	301

* January–September, preliminary figures.

Source: IMF, *Lithuania, Economic Review*.

Transport

RAILWAYS (traffic)

	1989	1990	1991
Passenger journeys (million)	30.6	32.6	24.2
Passenger-kilometres (million)	3,470	3,640	3,225
Freight transported (million metric tons)	32.7	27.1	27.9
Freight ton-kilometres (million)	21,800	19,258	17,748

ROAD TRAFFIC (motor vehicles in use at 31 December)

	1989	1990	1991
Passenger cars	440,389	479,876	533,927
Buses and coaches	4,958	4,879	15,964
Motor cycles and mopeds	201,437	192,141	196,075

Lorries: 86,697 in 1991.

SHIPPING

Sea-borne freight traffic ('000 metric tons)

	1989	1990	1991
Goods loaded and unloaded	6,400	8,334	6,789

CIVIL AVIATION (traffic)

	1989	1990	1991
Passenger-kilometres (million)	2,395	2,540	2,432

Communications Media

	1991
Radio receivers (per 1,000 inhabitants)	357
Television receivers (per 1,000 inhabitants)	382
Book titles	2,482
Daily newspapers	16

Education

(1992/93)

	Institutions	Students
General-education schools*	2,189	506,563
Secondary specialized institutions	63	29,786
Higher schools (incl. universities)	17	55,516

* Including secondary schools (695 in 1992/93), elementary schools and incomplete secondary schools.

Directory

The Constitution

The Constitution was adopted in a national referendum on 25 October 1992. The following is a summary of its main provisions:

THE STATE

The Republic of Lithuania is an independent and democratic republic; its sovereignty is vested in the people, who exercise their supreme power either directly or through their democratically elected representatives. The powers of the State are exercised by the Seimas (Parliament), the President of the Republic, the Government and the Judiciary. The most significant issues concerning the State and the people are decided by referendum.

The territory of the Republic is integral. Citizenship is acquired by birth or on other grounds determined by law. With certain exceptions established by law, no person may be a citizen of Lithuania and of another state at the same time. Lithuanian is the state languge.

THE INDIVIDUAL AND THE STATE

The rights and freedoms of individuals are inviolable. Property is inviolable, and the rights of ownership are protected by law. Freedom of thought, conscience and religion are guaranteed. All persons are equal before the law. No one may be discriminated against on the basis of sex, race, nationality, language, origin, social status, religion or opinions. Citizens may choose their place of residence in Lithuania freely, and may leave the country at their own will. Citizens are guaranteed the right to form societies, political parties and associations. Citizens who belong to ethnic communities have the right to foster their language, culture and customs.

SOCIETY AND THE STATE

The family is the basis of society and the State. Education is compulsory until the age of 16. Education at state and local government institutions is free of charge at all levels. State and local government establishments of education are secular, although, at the request of parents, they may offer classes in religious instruction. The State recognizes traditional Lithuanian and other churches and religious organizations, but there is no state religion. Censorship of mass media is prohibited. Ethnic communities may independently administer the affairs of their ethnic culture, education, organizations, etc. The State supports ethnic communities.

NATIONAL ECONOMY AND LABOUR

Lithuania's economy is based on the right to private ownership and freedom of individual economic activity. Every person may freely choose an occupation, and has the right to adequate, safe and healthy working conditions, adequate compensation for work, and social security in the event of unemployment. Trade unions may be freely established and may function independently. Employees have the right to strike in order to protect their economic and social interests. The state guarantees the right of citizens to old-age and disability pensions, as well as to social assistance in the event of unemployment, sickness, widowhood, etc.

THE SEIMAS

Legislative power rests with the Seimas. It comprises 141 members, elected for a four-year term on the basis of universal, equal and direct suffrage by secret ballot. Any citizen who has attained 25 years of age may be a candidate for the Seimas. Members of the Seimas may not be found criminally responsible, may not be arrested, and may not be subjected to any other restrictions of personal freedom, without the consent of the Seimas. The Seimas convenes for two regular four-months sessions every year.

The Seimas considers and enacts amendments to the Constitution; enacts laws; adopts resolutions for the organization of referendums; announces presidential elections; approves or rejects the candidature of the Prime Minister, as proposed by the President of the Republic; establishes or abolishes government ministries, upon the recommendation of the Government; supervises the activities of the Government, with the power to express a vote of 'no confidence' in the Prime Minister or individual ministers; appoints judges to the Constitutional Court and the Supreme Court; approves the state budget and supervises the implementation thereof; establishes state taxes and other obligatory payments; ratifies or denounces international treaties whereto the Republic is a party, and considers other issues of foreign policy; establishes administrative divisions of the Republic; issues acts of amnesty; imposes direct administration and martial law, declares states of emergency, announces mobilization, and adopts decisions to use the armed forces.

THE PRESIDENT OF THE REPUBLIC

The President of the Republic is the Head of State. Any Lithuanian citizen by birth, who has lived in Lithuania for at least the three preceding years, who has reached 40 years of age and who is eligible for election to the Seimas, may be elected President of the Republic. The President is elected by the citizens of the Republic, on the basis of universal, equal and direct suffrage by secret ballot, for a term of five years. No person may be elected to the office for more than two consecutive terms.

The President resolves basic issues of foreign policy and, in conjunction with the Government, implements foreign policy; signs international treaties and submits them to the Seimas for ratification; appoints or recalls, upon the recommendation of the Government, diplomatic representatives of Lithuania in foreign states and international organizations; appoints, upon the approval of the Seimas, the Prime Minister, and charges him/her with forming the Government, and approves its composition; removes, upon the approval of the Seimas, the Prime Minister from office; appoints or dismisses individual ministers, upon the recommendation of the Prime Minister; appoints or dismisses, upon the approval of the Seimas, the Commander-in-Chief of the armed forces and the head of the Security Service.

THE GOVERNMENT

Executive power is held by the Government of the Republic (Council of Ministers), which consists of the Prime Minister and other ministers. The Prime Minister is appointed and dismissed by the President of the Republic, with the approval of the Seimas. Ministers are appointed by the President, on the nomination of the Prime Minister.

The Government administers the affairs of the country, protects the inviolability of the territory of Lithuania, and ensures state security and public order; implements laws and resolutions of the Seimas as well as presidential decrees; co-ordinates the activities of the Ministries and other governmental institutions; prepares the draft state budget and submits it to the Seimas; executes the state budget and reports to the Seimas on its fulfilment; drafts legislative proposals and submits them to the Seimas for consideration; establishes and maintains diplomatic representation with foreign countries and international organizations.

JUDICIAL SYSTEM

The judicial system is independent of the authority of the legislative and executive branches of government. It consists of a Constitutional Court, a Supreme Court, a Court of Appeal, and district and local courts (for details, see section on Judical System below).

The Government

(March 1994)

HEAD OF STATE

President: ALGIRDAS BRAZAUSKAS (elected by direct popular vote, 14 February 1993).

COUNCIL OF MINISTERS

Prime Minister: ADOLFAS ŠLEŽEVIČIUS.

Minister of the Economy: (vacant).

Minister of Energy: ALGIMANTAS VLADAS STASIUKYNAS.

Minister of Finance: EDUARDAS VILKELIS.

Minister of Defence: LINAS LINKEVIČIUS.

Minister of Culture and Education: DAINIUS TRINKŪNAS.

Minister of Forestry: (vacant).

Minister of Industry and Trade: KAZIMIERAS KLIMAŠAUSKAS.

Minister of Communications and Information: GINTAUTAS ŽINTELIS.

Minister of Social Security: LAURYNAS MINDAUGAS STANKEVIČIUS.

Minister of Housing and Urban Development: ALGIRDAS VAPŠYS.

Minister of Justice: JONAS PRAPIESTIS.

Minister of Transport: JONAS BIRŽIŠKIS.

Minister of Health: JURGIS BRĖDIKIS.

Minister of Foreign Affairs: POVILAS GYLYS.

Minister of the Interior: ROMASIS VAITIEKŪNAS.

Minister of Agriculture: RIMANTAS KARAZIJA.

Minister without Portfolio: ALGIMANTAS MATULEVIČIUS.

MINISTRIES

Office of the President: Gedimino 53, Vilnius 2026; tel. (2) 612-811; fax 226-210.

Office of the Prime Minister: Gedimino 11, Vilnius 2039; tel. (2) 629-038; telex 261105; fax (2) 619-953.

Ministry of Agriculture: Gedimino 19, Vilnius 2025; tel. (2) 625-438; fax (2) 224-440.

Ministry of Communications and Information: Vilniaus 33, Vilnius 2008; tel. (2) 624-402; telex 261166; fax (2) 225-070.

Ministry of Culture and Education: A. Volano 2/7, Vilnius 2600; tel. (2) 622-483; fax (2) 612-077.

Ministry of Defence: Totorių 25/3, Vilnius 2001; tel. (2) 624-821; fax (2) 226-082.

Ministry of the Economy: Gedimino 38/2, Vilnius 2600; tel. (2) 622-416; fax (2) 625-604.

Ministry of Energy: Gedimino 12, Vilnius 2600; tel. (2) 615-140; telex 261240; fax (2) 626-845.

Ministry of Finance: Šermūkšnių 6, Vilnius 2696; tel. (2) 625-172; telex 261252; fax (2) 226-387.

Ministry of Foreign Affairs: Tumo-Vaižganto 2, Vilnius 2600; tel. (2) 618-337; telex 261218; fax (2) 618-689.

Ministry of Forestry: Gedimino 56, Vilnius 2685; tel. (2) 626-864; fax (2) 622-178.

Ministry of Health: Gedimino 72, Vilnius 2682; tel. (2) 621-625; telex 261152; fax (2) 224-601.

Ministry of Housing and Urban Development: Jakšto 4/9, Vilnius 2694; tel. (2) 610-558; fax (2) 220-847.

Ministry of Industry and Trade: Tumo-Vaižganto 8A/2, Vilnius 2739; tel. (2) 628-830; telex 261262; fax (2) 225-967.

Ministry of the Interior: Šventaragio 2, Vilnius 2754; tel. (2) 626-752; fax (2) 698-799.

Ministry of Justice: Gedimino 30/1, Vilnius 2600; tel. (2) 624-670; fax (2) 625-940.

Ministry of Social Security: A. Vivulskio 11, Vilnius 2693; tel. (2) 651-236; fax (2) 652-463.

Ministry of Transport: Gedimino 17, Vilnius 2679; tel. (2) 621-445; fax (2) 224-335.

President and Legislature

PRESIDENT

Presidential Election, 14 February 1993

Candidates	Votes	%
ALGIRDAS BRAZAUSKAS	1,210,517	60.2
STASYS LOZORAITIS	767,345	38.1
Total*	2,011,795	100.0

* Including 33,933 spoilt voting papers (1.7% of the total).

SEIMAS

Chairman: ČESLOVAS JURŠĖNAS, Gedimino 53, Vilnius 2026; tel. (2) 621-632; telex 261138; fax (2) 620-197.

General Election, 25 October and 15 November 1992

Parties and Alliances	Seats
Lithuanian Democratic Labour Party	73
Sąjūdis/Citizens' Charter of Lithuania	30
Christian Democratic Party of Lithuania	16
Lithuanian Social Democratic Party	8
Polish Union	4
Others	10
Total	141

Local Government

In the early 1990s Lithuania was subdivided into 585 administrative territorial units, including 11 cities, 44 regions, 81 towns, 22 settlements and 427 areas. The system of local government in operation in Lithuania consisted of two levels. The lower level comprised rural districts and district towns, while the higher level comprised regions and cities. A new, one-tier system of local government, comprising approximately 10 territorial units, was to be implemented by 1995.

Vilnius City Council: Gedimino 9, Vilnius 9200; tel. (2) 62-01-60; fax (2) 22-60-57; Mayor VYTAUTAS JASULAITIS.

Alytus City Council: Rotušės 4, Alytus 4580; tel. (35) 35-804; fax (35) 35-439; Mayor VALDAS MACEDULSKAS.

Birštonas City Council: Jaunimo 2, Birštonas 4490; tel. (10) 56-233; Mayor ALGIRDAS RADAUSKAS.

Druskininkai City Council: Vilniaus 18, Druskininkai 4690; tel. (33) 51-233; fax (33) 52-253; Mayor VYTAUTAS VAIKŠNORAS.

Kaunas City Council: Laisvės 96, Kaunas 5300; tel. (7) 226-958; fax (7) 200-443; Mayor ARIMANTAS RAČKAUSKAS.

Klaipėda City Council: Liepų 11, Klaipėda 5800; tel. (61) 13-641; fax (61) 13-343; Mayor BENEDIKTAS PETRAUSKAS.

Marijampolė City Council: J. Basanavičiaus 1, Marijampolė 4520; tel. (43) 51-530; fax (43) 56-460; Mayor BRONIUS BERŽINIS.

Neringa City Council: Taikos 2, Neringa 5870; tel. (61) 52-234; fax (59) 52-856; Mayor ANDRIEJUS VAIČIULIS.

Palanga City Council: Vytauto 73, Palanga 5720; tel. (36) 53-233; fax (36) 52-284; Mayor RIMANTAS MIKALKĖNAS.

Panevėžys City Council: Laisvės 20, Panevėžys 5300; tel. (54) 63-455; fax (54) 24-721; Mayor VALDEMARAS VIZBARAS.

Šiauliai City Council: 16 Vasario 62, Šiauliai 5419; tel. (14) 33-444; fax (14) 239-88; Mayor ARVYDAS SALDA.

Akmenė Regional Council: Respublikos 2, Naujoji Akmenė 5464; tel. (95) 51-233; fax (95) 51-165; Chair. STASYS POCEVIČIUS.

Alytus Regional Council: Pulko 21, Alytus 4580; tel. (35) 51-233; fax (35) 52-760; Chair. ALOYZAS JACIUNSKAS.

Anykščiai Regional Council: J. Biliūno 23, Anykščiai 4930; tel. (51) 51-233; fax (51) 53-630; Chair. ALGIMANTAS DAČIULIS.

Biržai Regional Council: Vytauto 38, Biržai 5280; tel. (20) 51-233; fax (20) 52-485; Chair. JONAS JONUŠYS.

Ignalina Regional Council: Laisvės 76, Iganalina 4740; tel. (29) 52-442; fax (29) 53-148; Chair. BRONIUS ROPĖ.

Jonava Regional Council: Žeimiu 13, Jonava 5000; tel. (19) 51-233; fax (19) 51-309; Chair. JUOZAS JOKIMAS.

Joniškis Regional Council: Livonijos 4, Joniškis; tel. (96) 51-233; fax (96) 51-363; Chair. VOLDEMARAS BANDŽIUKAS.

Jurbarkas Regional Council: Dariaus ir Girėno 96, Jurbarkas 4430; tel. (48) 51-233; fax (48) 51-408; Chair. PRANAS VAIŠVILA.

Kaišiadoriai Regional Council: Bažnyčios 4, Kaišiadorys 4230; tel. (56) 51-233; fax (56) 51-262; Chair. VYTAUTAS STREIKAUSKAS.

Kaunas Regional Council: Savanoriu 371, Kaunas 3043; tel. (7) 714-580; fax (7) 713-797; Chair. POVILAS VENGELIAUSKAS.

Kėdainiai Regional Council: J. Basanavičiaus 36, Kėdainiai 5030; tel. (57) 53-233; fax (57) 55-809; Chair. VIKTORAS MUNTIANAS.

Kelmė Regional Council: Vytauto Didžiojo 58, Kelmė 5470; tel. (97) 51-233; fax (97) 53-393; Chair. RIMANTAS MOTUZAS.

Klaipėda Regional Council: Klaipėdos 2, Gargždai 5840; tel. (40) 52-233; fax (40) 52-182; Chair. STANISLOVAS TAMOLIS.

Kretinga Regional Council: Vilniaus 6, Kretinga 5700; tel. (58) 51-233; fax (58) 52-448; Chair. ALGIMANTAS ŠTEINYS.

Kupiškis Regional Council: Vytauto 2, Kupiškis 4880; tel. and fax (31) 51-233; Chair. LEONAS APŠEGA.

Lazdijai Regional Council: Vilniaus 1, Lazdijai 4560; tel. (68) 51-233; fax (68) 51-351; Chair. GINTAS MOCKEVIČIUS.

Marijampolė Regional Council: Vytauto 17, Marijampolė 4520; tel. (43) 51-233; fax (43) 50-248; Chair. ALBINAS MATULIS.

Mažeikiai Regional Council: Laisvės 8/1, Mažeikiai 5500; tel. (93) 34-233; fax (93) 32-244; Chair. JONAS SIMINKEVIČIUS.

Molėtai Regional Council: Vilniaus 44, Molėtai 4150; tel. (30) 51-442; Chair. VALDEMARAS KILIUS.

Pakruojis Regional Council: Kestučio 4, Pakruojis 5220; tel. (91) 51-233; Chair. BRONISLOVAS GVAZDAUSKAS.

Panevėžys Regional Council: 16 Vasario 27, Panevėžys 5300; tel. (54) 65-233; Chair. VYTAUTAS KRIAUČIŪNAS.

Pasvalys Regional Council: Vytauto Didžiojo 1, Pasvalys 5250; tel. (71) 51-233; fax (71) 52-889; Chair. ALFONSAS PULOKAS.

Plungė Regional Council: Vytauto 12, Plungė 5640; tel. (18) 52-233; fax (18) 57-804; Chair. VINCAS SENKEVIČIUS.

Prienai Regional Council: Laisvės 12, Prienai 4340; tel. (49) 51-233; fax (49) 51-680; Chair. ALVYDAS BUJAVIČIUS.

Radviliškis Regional Council: Aušros 10, Radviliškis 5120; tel. (92) 51-233; fax (92) 51-140; Chair. ALGIMANTAS RUSECKAS.

Raseiniai Regional Council: V. Kudirkos 5, Raseiniai 4400; tel. (28) 51-233; fax (28) 51-604; Chair. ERVINAS KANČAITIS.

Rokiškis Regional Council: Respublikos 94, Rokiškis 4820; tel. (78) 51-233; Chair. VITAS KAČINSKAS.

Šakiai Regional Council: Bažnyčios 4, Šakiai 4460; tel. (47) 51-332; fax (52) 560; Chair. JUOZAS URBONAS.

Šalčininkai Regional Council: Vilniaus 49, Šalčininkai 4090; tel. (50) 51-233; fax (50) 51-536; Chair. TEDAUŠAS MICKEVIČIUS.

Šiauliai Regional Council: Vilniaus 263, Šiauliai 5419; tel. (14) 30-955; fax (31) 581; Chair. VYTAUTAS KRASAUSKAS.

Šilalė Regional Council: J. Basanavičiaus 1/8, Šilalė 5920; tel. (69) 51-233; Chair. JUOZAS RAUDONIUS.

Šilutė Regional Council: Dariaus and Girėno 1, Šilutė 5730; tel. (41) 52-233; fax (41) 51-517; Chair. ALGIRDAS BALČYTIS.

Širvintos Regional Council: Vilniaus 61, Širvintos 4100; tel. (32) 51-233; fax (32) 53-770; Chair. VALENTINAS ŽIŪRA.

Skuodas Regional Council: Vilniaus 13, Skuodas 5670; tel. (16) 51-233; Chair. ALOYZAS PAULIKAS.

Švenčionys Regional Council: Vilniaus 19, Švenčionys 4730; tel. (17) 51-233; fax (17) 51-244; Chair. KESTUTIS TRAPIKAS.

Tauragė Regional Council: Respublikos 2, Tauragė 5900; tel. (46) 51-233; fax (46) 53-446; Chair. VYTAUTAS PEČIULIS.

Telšiai Regional Council: Žemaitės 14, Telšiai 5610; tel. (94) 52-233; fax (94) 51-244; Chair. PETRAS MARTINKUS.

Trakai Regional Council: Vytauto 33, Trakai 4050; tel. (38) 51-233; fax (38) 53-210; Chair. KESTUTIS VAITUKAITIS.

Ukmergė Regional Council: Kestučio 3, Ukmergės 4120; tel. (11) 52-233; Chair. PRANCIŠKUS TAMOŠEVIČIUS.

Utena Regional Council: Utenio 4, Utena 4910; tel. (39) 51-233; fax (39) 59-490; Chair. ALGIMANTAS DEMENIUS.

Varėna Regional Council: Vytauto 12, Varėna 4460; tel. (60) 51-233; fax (60) 51-200; Chair. JONAS KALANTA.

Vilkaviškis Regional Council: S. Nėries 1, Vilkaviškis 4270; tel. (42) 53-233; Chair. ALFONSAS ČELKEVIČIUS.

Vilnius Regional Council: Rinktinės 50, Vilnius 2605; tel. (2) 75-14-24; fax (2) 75-32-08; Chair. LEONIDAS BUROKAS.

Zarasai Regional Council: Sėliu 22, Zarasai 4780; tel. (70) 51-233; Chair. ALGIMANTAS CIBULSKIS.

Political Organizations

Christian Democratic Party of Lithuania: Partizanų 54-39, Kaunas 3009; tel. (3207) 770-720; f. 1905, re-est. 1989; Chair. POVILAS KATILIUS; 6,000 mems.

Lithuanian Democratic Labour Party: B. Radvilaitės 1, Vilnius 2000; tel. (2) 615-420; fax (2) 617-290; f. 1990, as successor to the Communist Party of Lithuania; Chair. Dr ADOLFAS ŠLEŽEVIČIUS; 15,000 mems.

Lithuanian Democratic Party: Gedimino 34/9, Vilnius 2001; tel. (2) 626-033; fax (2) 469-671; f. 1902, re-est. 1989; Chair. SAULIUS PEČELIŪNAS; 1,700 mems.

Lithuanian Farmers' Union: Savanorių 287, Kaunas 3009; tel. (2) 296-714; f. 1905, re-est. 1990; Chair. PETRAS BĖČIUS; 1,000 mems.

Lithuanian Green Party: Pylimo 38-1, Vilnius 2001; tel. (2) 224-215; f. 1989; seeks a demilitarized, neutral and ecologically sound Lithuania; Chair. IRENA IGNATAVIČIENĖ.

Lithuanian National Union: Gedimino 22, Vilnius 2600; tel. (2) 624-935; fax (2) 617-310; f. 1924, refounded 1989; Chair. RIMANTAS SMETONA.

Lithuanian Social Democratic Party: Basanavičiaus 16/5, Vilnius 2009; tel. (2) 652-280; fax (2) 652-157; f. 1896, re-est. 1989; Chair. ALOYZAS SAKALAS; 600 mems.

Polish Union: Didzioji 40, Vilnius 2601; tel. (2) 223-388; f. 1988; party of the Polish Union cultural assen; Chair. JAN MINCEWICZ.

Sąjūdis (Movement of Lithuania): Gedimino 1, Vilnius 2001; tel. (2) 224-881; telex 261111; fax (2) 224-890; f. 1988 as Lithuanian Movement for Reconstruction; Chair. JUOZAS TUMELIS; Sec. ANDRIUS KUBILIUS.

Diplomatic Representation

EMBASSIES IN LITHUANIA

Canada: M. K. Čiurlionio 84, Vilnius 2600; tel. (2) 661-731.

China, People's Republic: Pergalės 53, Vilnius 2048; Ambassador: CHEN DI.

Czech Republic: Gedimino 23, Vilnius 2600; tel. (2) 691-540; fax (2) 691-518.

Denmark: T. Kosciuškos 36, Vilnius 2000; tel. (2) 628-028; Ambassador: BIRGER DAN NIELSEN.

Estonia: Turniškių 14, Vilnius 2016; tel. (2) 769-848; Ambassador: VALVI STRIKAITIENĖ.

Finland: Klaipėdos 6, Vilnius 2001; tel. (2) 221-621; fax (2) 222-441; Ambassador: TAISTO VEIKKO TOLVANEN.

France: Daukanto a. 3/1, Vilnius 2600; tel. (2) 222-979; fax (2) 223-530; Ambassador: PHILIPPE DE SUREMAIN.

Germany: Z. Sierakausko 24, Vilnius 2001; tel. (2) 650-272; Ambassador: REINHART KRAUS.

Holy See: Kosciuskos 28, Vilnius 2001; tel. (2) 223-696; fax (2) 224-228; Apostolic Nuncio: Mgr JUSTO MULLOR GARCÍA, Titular Archbishop of Emerita Augusta.

Italy: Hotel Draugyste, M. K. Čiurlionio 84, Vilnius 2600; tel. (2) 661-751; telex 261005; fax (2) 290-231; Ambassador: FRANCO TEMPESTA.

Latvia: Turniškių 19, Vilnius 2016; tel. (2) 778-532, Ambassador: ALBERTS SARKANIS.

Norway: D. Poškos 59, Vilnius 2004; tel. (2) 754-202; telex 261096; fax (2) 754-149; Ambassador: PER GULLIK STAVRUM.

Poland: Aušros Vartų 7, Vilnius 2001; tel. (2) 224-444; fax (2) 223-454; Ambassador: JAN WIDACKI.

Romania: Hotel Lietuva, Rm 1718, Ukmerges 20, Vilnius 2600; tel. (2) 356-544.

Russia: Vilnius; Ambassador: NIKOLAY MIKHAILOVICH OBERTYSHEV.

Sweden: Jogailos 10, Vilnius 2000; tel. (2) 227-922; Ambassador: LARS MAGNUSON.

Turkey: Sv. Jono 3, Vilnius 2600; tel. (2) 223-380; telex 261006; fax (2) 223-277; Ambassador: ERKAN GEZER.

United Kingdom: Antakalnio 2, POB 863, Vilnius 2055; tel. (2) 222-070; Ambassador: MICHAEL PEART.

USA: Akmenų 6, Vilnius 2600; tel. (2) 223-031; fax (2) 222-779; Ambassador: DARRYL N. JOHNSON.

Judicial System

The organs of justice are the Supreme Court, the Court of Appeal, district courts and *apylinkių teismai* (local courts of administrative areas). The Seimas (legislature) appoints and dismisses from office the judges of the Supreme Court (including its Chairman) on the recommendation of the President of the Republic. Judges of the Court of Appeal are appointed by the President with the approval of the Seimas, while judges of district and local courts are appointed and dismissed by the President. All judges are appointed for a term of five years.

The Constitutional Court decides on the constitutionality of acts of the Seimas, as well as of the President and the Government. It consists of nine judges, who are appointed by the Seimas for a single term of nine years; one-third of the Court's members are replaced every three years.

The Office of the Procurator-General is an independent institution, comprising the Procurator-General and local procurators' offices which are subordinate to him. The Procurator-General and his deputies are appointed for terms of five years by the Seimas, while chief local prosecutors are appointed by the Procurator-General. The Office of the Procurator-General incorporates the Department for Crime Investigation. The State Arbitration decides cases of business litigation.

Supreme Court: Gynėjų 6, Vilnius 2755; tel. (2) 610-560; Chair. MINDAUGAS LOŠYS.

Office of the Procurator-General: Smetonos 4, Vilnius 2709; tel. (2) 611-620; fax (2) 611-826; Procurator-General ARTŪRAS PAULAUSKAS.

State Arbitration: Gedimino 39/1, Vilnius 2640; tel. (2) 622-843; Chief Arbitrator ALOYZAS MARČIULIONIS.

Religion

CHRISTIANITY

The Roman Catholic Church

The Roman Catholic Church in Lithuania comprises two archdioceses (Kaunas and Vilnius) and four dioceses (Kaišiadorys, Panevėžys, Telšiai and Vilkaviškis). At 31 December 1991 there were an estimated 2,677,400 adherents in Lithuania. There are seminaries at Kaunas and Telšiai.

Bishop's Conference (Conferentia Episcopalis Lituaniae): Vilniaus 29, Kaunas 3000; tel. (7) 222-197; Pres. Cardinal VINCENTAS SLADKEVIČIUS, Archbishop of Kaunas.

Archbishop of Kaunas: Cardinal VINCENTAS SLADKEVIČIUS, Valančiaus 6, Kaunas 3000; tel. (7) 222-197; fax (7) 226-132.

Archbishop of Vilnius: Most Rev. AUDRYS JUOZAS BAČKIS, Šv. Mikalojaus 4, Vilnius 2001; tel. (2) 627-098; fax (2) 222-807.

Orthodox Churches

Lithuanian Old Believers Pomor Church: Naujininkų 24, Vilnius 2030; tel. (2) 694-271; 54 congregations; Chair. of Supreme Pomor Old Ritualists' Council VASILJEV VASILIJ.

Vilnius and Lithuanian Eparchy of the Russian Orthodox Church: Aušros vartų 10, Vilnius 2024; tel. (2) 625-896; includes 43 congregations; Archbishop CHRIZOSTOM (Georgy Martishkin).

Protestant Churches

Consistory of the Lithuanian Evangelical Lutheran Church: Laisvės 68, Tauragė 5900; tel. (46) 52-345; Bishop JONAS KALVANAS.

Evangelical Reformed Church in Lithuania: POB 661, Vilnius 2049; tel. and fax (2) 450-656; Pres. of Collegium POVILAS A. JAŠINSKAS.

JUDAISM

Jewish Community: Pylimo 4, Vilnius 2001; tel. (2) 613-003; fax (2) 615-758; f. 1992, to replace and expand the role of the Jewish Cultural Society; Chair. SIMON ALPERAVIČIUS.

The Press

In 1991 there were 602 newspapers published in Lithuania, including 523 published in Lithuanian, and 221 periodicals, including 195 in Lithuanian.

The publications listed below are in Lithuanian, except where otherwise indicated.

PRINCIPAL NEWSPAPERS

Ekho Litvy (Echo of Lithuania): Laisvės 60, Vilnius 2056; tel. (2) 428-463; fax (2) 428-636; f. 1940; 5 a week; publ. by the Seimas and Council of Ministers; in Russian; Editor VASILY YEMELYANOV; circ. 55,000.

Kurier Wileński (Vilnius Express): Laisvės 60, Vilnius 2044; tel. (2) 427-901; fax (2) 427-265; f. 1953; 5 a week; publ. by the Seimas and Council of Ministers; in Polish; Editor ZBIGNIEW BALCEWICZ; circ. 15,000.

Lietuvos aidas (Echo of Lithuania): Maironio 1, Vilnius 2710; tel. (2) 615-208; fax (2) 224-876; f. 1917; re-est. 1990; 5 a week; Editor-in-Chief SAULIUS STOMA; circ. 75,000.

Lietuvos rytas (Lithuania's Morning): Gedimino 12A, Vilnius 2001; tel. (2) 622-680; fax (2) 227-656; f. 1990; 5 a week in Lithuanian, with a weekly Russian edition; Editor GEDVYDAS VAINAUSKAS; circ. 100,000.

Lietuvos sportas (Lithuanian Sports): Gedimino 37, Vilnius 2600; tel. (2) 616-757; f. 1922; re-est. 1992; 3 a week; Editor VYTAUTAS SAULIS; circ. 14,500.

Respublika (Republic): A. Smetonos 2, Vilnius 2600; tel. (2) 223-112; fax (2) 223-538; f. 1989; 5 a week in Lithuanian, with a weekly Russian edition; Editor-in-Chief VITAS TOMKUS; circ. 40,000–60,000.

Tiesa (Truth): Laisvės 60, Vilnius 2019; tel. (2) 429-933; fax (2) 421-790; f. 1917; 5 a week; independent newspaper supporting the Lithuanian Democratic Labour Party; Editor-in-Chief DOMIJONAS ŠNIUKAS; circ. 60,000.

Valstiečių laikraštis (Peasants' Newspaper): Laisvės 60, Vilnius 2044; tel. (2) 429-942; f. 1940; 2 a week; Editor JONAS ŠVOBA; circ. 123,641.

PRINCIPAL PERIODICALS

Aitvaras (Brownie): Smetonos 2, Vilnius 2600; tel. (2) 221-752; fax (2) 223-538; f. 1989; weekly; children's newspaper; Editor LAIMA DRAZDAUSKAITĖ; circ. 43,100.

Amžius (Century): Laisvės 60, Vilnius 2019; tel. (2) 428-554; fax (2) 429-290; f. 1992; weekly; social, cultural and political issues; Editor-in-Chief ANTANAS GAILIUS; circ. 10,000.

Atgimimas (Rebirth): T. Vrublevskio 6, Vilnius 2600; tel. (2) 614-432; f. 1988; weekly; Editor-in-Chief ROMUALDAS OZOLAS; circ. 3,000.

Caritas: Vilniaus 29, Kaunas 3000; tel. (7) 209-683; fax (7) 205-549; f. 1989; monthly; Editor ALBINA PAJARSKAITĖ; circ. 13,000.

Genys (Woodpecker): Bernardinų 8, Vilnius 2600; tel. (2) 616-334; fax (2) 227-656; f. 1940; monthly; illustrated; for 5–10-year-olds; Editor-in-Chief VYTAUTAS RAČICKAS; circ. 30,000.

Gimtasis kraštas (Native Land): Ž. Liauksmino 8/2, Vilnius 2600; tel. (2) 623-881; fax (2) 628-171; f. 1967; weekly; independent; Editor-in-Chief ALGIMANTAS BUČYS; circ. 10,000.

Hobby: Rudens 33B, Vilnius 2600; tel. (2) 696-964; f. 1991; monthly; domestic animals; Editor-in-Chief VYTAUTAS KLOVAS; circ. 10,000.

Jaunimo gretos (Ranks of Youth): Bernardinų 8, Vilnius 2600; tel. (2) 624-819; f. 1944; monthly; popular illustrated, youth issues; short stories and essays by beginners, translations; Editor-in-Chief ALGIS PETRULIS; circ. 41,000.

Kalba Vilnius (Vilnius Calling): Konarskio 49, Vilnius 2674; tel. (2) 661-022; f. 1956; weekly; Lithuanian TV and radio programmes; Editor-in-Chief ALGIRDAS KRATULIS; circ. 106,000.

Katalikų Pasaulis (Catholic World): Pranciškonų 3/6, Vilnius 2001; tel. (2) 222-141; fax (2) 222-122; f. 1989; monthly; Editor-in-Chief AUŠVYDAS BELICKAS; circ. 17,000.

Krantai (Banks): POB 511; K. Sirvydo 3/8, Vilnius 2001; tel. (2) 224-844; f. 1989; quarterly; journal of the Ministry of Culture and Education; general culture, art; Editor-in-Chief VAIDOTAS DAUNYS; circ. 2,000.

Kultūros barai (Domains of Culture): Universiteto 6, Vilnius 2600; tel. (2) 616-696; f. 1965; monthly; journal of the Ministry of Culture and Education; Editor-in-Chief BRONYS SAVUKYNAS; circ. 2,610.

Lietuvos Darbininkas (Lithuanian Worker): V. Mykolaičio-Putino 5, Vilnius 2600; tel. (2) 621-743; fax (2) 615-253; weekly; publ. by the Lithuanian Workers' Union.

Lietuvos Jeruzalė (Jerusalem of Lithuania): Vaižganto 9/1, Vilnius 2001; tel. (2) 461-208; fax (2) 224-035; f. 1989; monthly; publ. by the Jewish Community of Lithuania; in Yiddish, English, Lithuanian and Russian; Editor-in-Chief GRIGORIJUS SMOLIAKOVAS; circ. 2,000.

Lietuvos Komersantas (Lithuanian Businessman): Algirdo 9A, Vilnius 2009; tel. (2) 652-387; fax (2) 267-540; f. 1990; Editor-in-Chief ANDREJUS STEPONAVIČIUS; circ. 10,000.

Literatūra ir menas (Literature and Art): Universiteto 4, Vilnius 2600; tel. (2) 610-831; fax (2) 619-696; f. 1946; weekly; publ. by the Lithuanian Writers' Union; fiction, essays, art; Editor-in-Chief VYTAUTAS RUBAVIČIUS; circ. 5,500.

Magazyn Wileński (Vilnius Journal): a/d 1630, Vilnius 2010; tel. (2) 474-007; f. 1990; fortnightly; political, cultural; in Polish; Editor-in-Chief MICHAŁ MACKIEWICZ; circ. 8,000.

Mažoji Lietuva (Lithuania Minor): H. Manto 2, Klaipėda 5800; tel. (61) 18-074; fax (61) 13-684; f. 1932; weekly; independent; politics, social and cultural issues; Editor RYTAS STASELIS; circ. 10,000.

Metai (Year): K. Sirvydo 6, Vilnius 2600; tel. (2) 617-344; (2) 619-696; f. 1991; monthly; journal of the Lithuanian Writers' Union; fiction, criticism; Editor-in-Chief JUOZAS APUTIS; circ. 2,500.

Moteris (Woman): Laisvės 60, Vilnius 2019; tel. (2) 429-020; f. 1952; monthly; popular, for women; Editor-in-Chief ARŪNAS MARCINKEVIČIUS; circ. 100,000.

Mūsų gamta (Our Nature): Rudens 33B, Vilnius 2600; tel. (2) 696-964; f. 1964; monthly; popular science, nature preservation, tourism; Editor-in-Chief VYTAUTAS KLOVAS; circ. 6,000.

Nemunas: Gedimino 45, Kaunas 3000; tel. (7) 226-067; f. 1967; monthly; journal of the Lithuanian Writers' Union; popular, for youth; Editor-in-Chief ALGIMANTAS MIKUTA; circ. 10,000.

Politika (Politics): Laisvės 60, Vilnius 2056; tel. (2) 428-803; fax (2) 422-875; f. 1990; monthly; Editor-in-Chief ALGIMANTAS SEMAŠKA; circ. 10,000.

Šluota (Broom): Bernardinų 8/8, Vilnius 2722; tel. (2) 613-171; f. 1934; fortnightly; satirical; Editor-in-Chief ALBERTAS LUKŠA; circ. 15,000.

Švyturys (Beacon): Maironio 1, Vilnius 2600; tel. (2) 627-488; f. 1949; monthly; politics, economics, history, culture, fiction; Editor-in-Chief JUOZAS BAUŠYS; circ. 40,000.

Vasario 16 (16 February): Gedimino 34/9, Vilnius 2001; tel. (2) 626-033; fax (2) 469-671; journal of the Lithuanian Democratic Party; circ. 2,000.

NEWS AGENCY

ELTA (Lithuanian Telegraph Agency): Gedimino 21/2, Vilnius 2750; tel. (2) 613-667; telex 261196; fax (2) 619-507; f. 1920; Dir ALGIMANTAS SEMAŠKA.

Publishers

Mintis (Idea): Z. Sierakausko 15, Vilnius 2600; tel. (2) 632-943; political and popular books and booklets; Dir VIKTORAS PAPULSKIS.

Mokslo ir enciklopedijų leidykla (Science and Encyclopedia Publishers): Žvaigždžių 23, Vilnius 2050; tel. (2) 458-525; fax (2) 458-526; f. 1992; science and reference books, dictionaries, encyclopedias, textbooks for higher education establishments, books for the general reader; Dir ZIGMANTAS POCIUS.

Šviesa (Light): Vytauto 25, Kaunas 3000; tel. (7) 741-634; fax (7) 751-639; f. 1945; textbooks and pedagogical literature; Dir JONAS BARCYS.

Vaga (Furrow): Gedimino 50, Vilnius 2600; tel. (2) 626-443; fax (2) 616-902; f. 1945; fiction; Dir ALEKSANDRAS KRASNOVAS.

Vyturys (Lark): Algirdo 31, Vilnius 2600; tel. (2) 660-665; fax (2) 263-449; fiction and non-fiction for children and youth; Dir JUOZAS VAITKUS.

PUBLISHERS' ASSOCIATION

Lithuanian Publishers' Association: K. Sirvydo 6, Vilnius 2600; tel. (2) 628-945; fax (2) 619-696; f. 1989; Pres. VINCAS AKELIS.

Radio and Television

In 1991 there were 107 radio receivers per 100 families and 115 television receivers per 100 families.

Lithuanian Radio and Television: Konarskio 49, Vilnius 2674; tel. (2) 263-383; f. 1940; Dir-Gen. LAIMONAS TAPINAS.

Radio Vilnius: f. 1926; broadcasts in Lithuanian, Russian, Polish, English, Yiddish, Belarusian and Ukrainian.

TV Vilnius: f. 1957; broadcasts in Lithuanian, Russian and Polish.

Finance

(cap. = capital; dep. = deposits; m. = million; brs = branches; amounts in litas, unless otherwise stated)

BANKING

Before it regained independence, Lithuania was fully integrated into the economic and monetary systems of the USSR. In the early 1990s comprehensive reforms were made in Lithuania's banking system, beginning with the establishment of a central bank, the Bank of Lithuania. Some 20 licensed commercial banks were in operation by mid-1992.

Central Bank

Bank of Lithuania (Lietuvos Bankas): Gedimino 6, Vilnius 2600; tel. (2) 224-008; telex 261090; fax (2) 628-124; f. 1990; central bank, responsible for bank supervision; Chair. of Bd KAZYS RATKEVIČIUS.

Commercial Banks

Agricultural Bank of Lithuania: Totorių 4, Vilnius 2600; tel. (2) 628-842; fax (2) 226-047; f. 1990; cap. 2,000m. talonas, dep. 16,825m. talonas; Chair. of Bd PRANAS VILIŪNAS; 46 brs.

Balticbank: Gedimino 15, Vilnius 2001; tel. (2) 623-151; telex 261163; fax (2) 623-583; f. 1991; Chair. of Bd ROMAS JUŠKA.

Bank of Vilnius (Vilniaus Bankas): Gedimino 12, Vilnius 2600; tel. (2) 610-723; telex 261101; fax (2) 626-557; f. 1990; cap. 9.04m., dep. 109.31m.; Chair. JULIUS NIEDVARAS; 8 domestic brs, 1 overseas br.

Lithuanian Joint-Stock Innovation Bank (Lietuvos Akcinis Inovacinis Bankas): A. Jakšto 6, Vilnius 2600; tel. (2) 624-61; telex 303215; fax (2) 611-503; f. 1988; all general commercial banking services and investment banking; cap. 23.5m., dep. 30.8m. (1993); Gen. Dir ARTŪRAS BALKEVIČIUS; 14 brs.

State Commercial Bank of Lithuania: Jogailos 14, Vilnius 2631; tel. (2) 226-333; fax (2) 227-571; f. 1992; cap. 20m. talonas; Chair. of Bd ALGIMANTAS BARUSEVIČIUS; 28 brs.

Ūkio Bank (Ūkio Bankas): J. Gruodžio 9, Kaunas 3000; tel. (7) 203-651; telex 269897; fax (7) 204-296; f. 1989; cap. 5.6m., dep. 22.6m.; Chair. of Bd VALDEMARAS BŪTĖNAS; 10 brs.

Savings Bank

Lithuanian Savings Bank: Vilniaus 16, Vilnius 2736; tel. (2) 623-173; telex 261877; fax (2) 221-263; f. 1988; cap. 10m., dep. 188m. (1993); Chair. of Bd VYGINTAS BUBNYS; 53 brs.

COMMODITY EXCHANGES

Association of Lithuanian Exchanges: Savanorių 124A, Vilnius 2600; tel. (2) 261-919; fax (2) 261-397; f. 1992; 15 mems; Pres. VYTAUTAS BAJORIŪNAS.

Lithuanian Exchange Council: Pylimo 2, Vilnius 2600; tel. (2) 619-981; fax (2) 620-726; f. 1991; 16 mems; Pres. ROMUALDAS TARASEVIČIUS.

Vilnius Exchange: Gedimino 14, Vilnius 2001; tel. (2) 628-804; fax (2) 454-866; f. 1991; arranges contacts with other exchanges in the former Soviet republics; Pres. ČESLOVAS MACULEVIČIUS.

STOCK EXCHANGE

National Stock Exchange: Vilnius; f. 1993.

Trade and Industry

CHAMBERS OF COMMERCE

Association of Chambers of Commerce and Industry: Kudirkos 18, Vilnius 2600; tel. (2) 222-630; telex 261137; fax (2) 222-621; f. 1992; 6 member asscns; mem. of International Chamber of Commerce; Pres. MINDAUGAS ČERNIAUSKAS.

Vilnius Regional Chamber of Commerce and Industry: Algirdo 31, Vilnius 2900; tel. (2) 661-550; telex 261114, fax (2) 661-542; f. 1991; 178 mems; Pres. JONAS POVILAITIS.

Kaunas Regional Chamber of Commerce and Industry: Gruodžio 9, Kaunas; tel. (7) 201-294; fax (7) 208-330; Pres. VYTAUTAS ŠILEIKIS.

Klaipėda Regional Chamber of Commerce and Industry: Minijos 1A, Klaipeda; tel. and fax (61) 50-984; Pres. GINTARAS ALBRECHTAS.

Marijampolė Regional Chamber of Commerce and Industry: Kęstučio 9/20, Marijampole; tel. (43) 55-568; fax (43) 51-893; Pres. VYGANDAS MATULIS.

Panevėžys Regional Chamber of Commerce and Industry: Respublikos 54, Panevežys; tel. (54) 63-687; fax (54) 62-227; Pres. VYTAUTAS KAZAKEVIČIUS.

Šiauliai Regional Chamber of Commerce and Industry: Rūdes 17, Šiauliai 5400; tel. (14) 27-709; fax (14) 39-973; Pres. KESTUTIS VYŠNIAUSKAS.

INDUSTRIAL ASSOCIATIONS

Association of Lithuanian Businessmen: Jakšto 9, Vilnius 2600; tel. (2) 614-963; fax (2) 624-872; f. 1989; Pres. JUOZAS ŠARKUS.

Lithuanian Manufacturers' Association: Saltoniškių 19, Vilnius 2600; tel. (2) 751-278; telex 261257; fax (2) 353-320; f. 1989; Pres. ALGIMANTAS MATULEVIČIUS.

Union of Lithuanian Businessmen: Mickevičiaus 18, Kaunas 3000; tel. (7) 202-942; fax (7) 221-413; f. 1991; Pres. ARVYDAS STAŠAITIS.

MAJOR INDUSTRIAL COMPANIES AND FOREIGN TRADE CORPORATIONS

Agrolitas Imeks: J. Tumo-Vaižganto 8/27, Vilnius 2600; tel. (2) 227-908; telex 261113; fax (2) 227-489; international trading co; Man. Dir A. SMAGIN.

Akmenės Cementas: Naujoji, Akmenė 5464; tel. 58-323; telex 296419; f. 1952; produces cement, slate boards, asbestos-cement pipes, etc.; Dir LEOPOLDAS PETRAVIČIUS; 2,500 employees.

Alytus Soft Drinks and Champagne Factory: Miškininkų 17, Alytus 4580; tel. (35) 52-337; telex 269841; fax (35) 54-467; produces wines, soft drinks, concentrated juices; Dir JUOZAS DAUKŠYS.

Alytus Cotton Fabric Factory: Pramonės 1, Alytus 4580; tel. (35) 57-357; fax (35) 35-566; f. 1968; cotton yarn and fabrics; Dir GINTAUTAS ANDRIUŠKEVIČIUS; 5,634 employees.

Astra: Ulonų 33, Alytus 4580; tel. (35) 52-176; fax (35) 52-265; f. 1929; washing machines, other household goods; Dir SEMION BONDAREV.

Azotas: Taurosto 26, Jonava 5000; tel. (19) 56-621; telex 269845; fax (19) 52-074; f. 1965; produces chemical fertilizers; Dir-Gen. BRONISLAVAS LUBYS; 3,480 employees.

Banga: Draugystės 19, Kaunas 3031; tel. (7) 756-777; telex 261147; f. 1987; television broadcasting equipment; Dir-Gen. LEONAS JANKAUSKAS; 18,000 employees.

Ekranas: Elektronikos 1, Panevėžys 5300; tel. (54) 63-450; telex 287424; fax (54) 23-415; electronic components; f. 1962; Dir EIMUTIS ŽVYBAS; 6,950 employees.

Elfa: Vytenio 50, Vilnius 2654; tel. (2) 631-531; telex 261226; fax (2) 660-709; electrical household appliances; f. 1940; Dir-Gen. GINTARAS SAUNORIS; 3,500 employees.

Kėdainiai Chemical Plant: Juodkishkio 50, Kėdainiai 5030; tel. (57) 52-273; fax (57) 53-241; f. 1963; produces sulphuric acid, minieral fertilizers and other chemical products; Dir EGIDIJUS PETRAUSKAS.

Lietcom: Kauno 3A, Vilnius; tel. (2) 633-499; fax (2) 633-589; state foreign trade company; Dir J. KIRIUSHCHENKO.

Lietuvos Prekyba: Gedimino 30/31, Vilnius 2695; tel. (2) 618-001; telex 261983; fax (2) 615-296; foreign trade enterprise; Gen. Dir ALEXANDRAS GROBOVAS.

Litimpex: Verkių 37, Vilnius 2600; tel. (2) 352-544; telex 261148; fax (2) 614-194; f. 1987; foreign trade enterprise; arranges export and import of a wide range of goods; provides business services to companies engaged in foreign trade; Dir-Gen. JUSTINAS ANTANAITIS.

Neris: Pramonės 97, Vilnius 2048; tel. (2) 670-023; telex 261256; f. 1958; agricultural equipment; Dir-Gen. VYTAUTAS ŠUMAKARIS.

Nuklonas: Architektų 1, Šiauliai 5419; tel. (14) 52-235; telex 296426; fax (14) 53-504; f. 1968; electronic goods, incl. integrated circuits, household appliances; Dir VYTAUTAS SLANINA.

Panevėžys Glass-Works: Pramonės 10, Panevėžys 5319; tel. (54) 63-747; telex 287421; fax (54) 65-703; f. 1965; produces all kinds of glass; Dir STASYS STOŠKUS; 970 employees.

Šilkas: Neries kr. 16, Kaunas 3713; tel. (7) 264-235; fax (7) 261-293; f. 1956; produces textiles and fabrics; Dir-Gen. ALGIMANTAS JANKAUSKAS; 3,000 employees.

Snaigė: Pramonės 6, Alytus 4580; tel. (35) 57-580; telex 269849; fax (35) 57-612; f. 1964; produces household refrigerators and thermo-insulation panels; Pres. ANTANAS ANDRIULIONIS; 2,744 employees.

Tauras: Pramonės 15, Šiauliai 5419; tel. (14) 52-220; telex 296126; fax (14) 27-344; produces colour television sets; f. 1961; Dir RAIMUNDAS VIRBICKAS.

Vilnius Fuel Outfit Company: Kalvarijų 143, Vilnius 2650; tel. (2) 776-261; telex 261161; fax (2) 776-569; f. 1959; manufactures components for diesel engines; Dir-Gen. ALGIRDAS DIDŽIULIS; 7,110 employees.

Vilnius Fur Factory: Paupio 28, Vilnius 2600; tel. (2) 627-803; f. 1964; processes mink, rabbit, fox, musk-rat and astrakhan hides; produces fur clothes; Dir-Gen. JUOZAS MACEVIČIUS.

Vingis: Savanorių 176, Vilnius 2646; tel. (2) 653-884; f. 1959; components for television sets; Dir-Gen. ALGIRDAS LINARTAS; 3,200 employees.

Žalgiris: Vilnius 2048, Pramonės 141; tel. (14) 671-476; telex 261145; f. 1947; metal cutting machines, milling machines, other machine tools; Dir JURIJUS SIVICKIS.

TRADE UNIONS

Lithuanian Confederation of Free Trade Unions: Basanavičiaus 29A, Vilnius 2600; tel. (2) 614-888; fax (2) 226-106; f. 1990; 6 affiliated unions; Chair. ALGIRDAS KVEDARAVIČIUS; 150,000 mems.

Lithuanian Union of Trade Unions: Jasinskio 9, Vilnius 2600; tel. (2) 611-866; fax (2) 619-078; f. 1992; 7 affiliated unions; Council Chair. ALGIRDAS SYSAS; 100,000 mems.

Lithuanian Workers' Union: V. Mykolaičio-Putino 5, Vilnius 2600; tel. (2) 621-743; fax (2) 615-253; f. 1989; 37 brs; Pres. ALDONA BALSIENĖ; 110,000 mems (1993).

Transport

RAILWAYS

In 1992 there were 2,002 km of railway track in use in Lithuania, of which 122 km were electrified. Main lines link Vilnius with Rīga (Latvia), Minsk (Belarus) and Kaliningrad (Russian Federation), and Warsaw (Poland), via the Belarusian town of Grodno.

Lithuanian Railways (Lietuvos Gelezinkeliai): Mindaugo 12–14, Vilnius 2604; tel. (2) 660-041; fax (2) 618-323; f. 1991; Gen. Dir A. KLIORE.

ROADS

In 1991 the total length of the road network was 44,500 km, of which 35,800 km were asphalted.

SHIPPING

The main port is at Klaipėda.

Shipowning Company

Lithuanian Shipping Company: Juliaus Janonio 24, Klaipėda 5813; tel. (61) 19-824; telex 278111; fax (61) 18-069; f. 1969; transportation of cargo and passengers; Pres. ANTANAS ANILIONIS.

CIVIL AVIATION

Lithuania has air links with Western European destinations and with cities in the former USSR. The state airline, Leituvas Aviolinijos, is based at the international airport at Vilnius. A second airport, at Šiauliai, opened for international flights at the end of 1993.

Lithuanian Airlines (Leituvas Aviolinijos): Rodunes 8, Vilnius 2038; tel. (2) 630-116; telex 261165; fax (2) 266-828; Gen. Dir STASYS DAILYDKA.

Tourism

Tourist attractions in Lithuania include the historic cities of Vilnius, Kaunas and Klaipėda (formerly Memel), coastal resorts, such as Palanga and Kuršių Nerija, and picturesque countryside.

State Tourism Department: Gedimino 30/1, Vilnius 2695; tel. (2) 226-706; fax (2) 226-819; Dir SAULIUS ENDRIUŠKA.

Lithuania Travel Company: Ukmergės 20, Vilnius 2600; tel. (2) 356-526; fax (2) 356-270.

Culture

NATIONAL ORGANIZATION

Ministry of Culture and Education: see section on The Government (Ministries).

CULTURAL HERITAGE

Art Museum of Lithuania: Didžioji 31, Vilnius 2024; tel. (2) 628-030; f. 1941; over 297,390 items; library of 19,571 vols; Dir ROMUALDAS BUDRYS.

Institute of Culture and Arts: Gedimino 3, Vilnius; tel. (2) 613-646; f. 1990; Dir ALGIRDAS GAIZUTIS.

Institute of the Lithuanian Language: Antakalnio 6, Vilnius 2055; tel. (2) 624-726; Dir ALEKSANDRAS VANAGAS.

Kaunas State Historical Museum: Donelaitis 64, Kaunas; f. 1921; 127,459 exhibits; library of 5,510 vols; Dir A. Y. KVEDARAS.

Lithuanian Centre of Folk Culture: Barbaros Radvilaitės 8, Vilnius 2600; tel. (2) 611-190; fax (2) 224-033; Dir J. MIKUTAVIČIUS.

Lithuanian Cultural Institute: Saltoniškių 58, Vilnius 2600; tel. (2) 752-777; fax (2) 758-318; Dir K. ANTANAITIS.

Lithuanian State Jewish Museum: Pamękalnio 10, Vilnius 2001; tel. (2) 620-730; Dir E. ZINGERIS.

Martynas Mazvydas National Library of Lithuania: Gedimino 51, Vilnius 2635; tel. (2) 629-023; fax (2) 627-129; f. 1919; Dir Dr VLADAS BULAVAS.

M. K. Čiurlionis Art Museum: V. Putvinskio 55, Kaunas 3000; tel. (7) 229-738; Dir O. DAUGELIS.

Military Museum of Vytautas Magnus: K. Donelaičio 64, Kaunas 3000; tel. (7) 229-606; Dir J. JUREVIČIUS.

National Museum of Lithuania: Arsenalo 1, Vilnius 2001; tel. (2) 627-774; f. 1855; over 600,000 exhibits; special archaeological, numismatic, historical and ethnographical collections; library of over 40,000 vols; Dir BIRUTĖ KULNYTĖ.

Vilnius Contemporary Art Centre: Vokiečių 2, Vilnius 2024; tel. and fax (2) 221-936; Dir KESTUTIS KUIZINAS.

SPORTING ORGANIZATIONS

Department of Physical Training and Sports: Zemaites 6, Vilnius 2600; tel. (2) 635-363; govt agency; Dir-Gen. ALGIRDAS RASLANAS.

PERFORMING ARTS

Kaunas Academic Drama Theatre: Laisvės 71, Kaunas 3000; tel. (7) 224-198.

Klaipėda Drama Theatre: Teatro 2, Klaipėda 5800; tel. (61) 19-801.

Lithuanian Academic Drama Theatre: Gedimino 4, Vilnius; tel. (2) 621-593.

Lithuanian National Philharmonic: Aušros vartų 5, Vilnius 2001; tel. (2) 624-584; telex 261134; fax (2) 622-859; f. 1940; Dirs G. KĖVIŠAS, G. VASARIS.

Lithuanian Opera and Ballet Theatre: Vienuolio 1, Vilnius 2600; tel. (2) 620-093; fax (2) 623-503.

Lithuanian Puppet Theatre: Arklių 5, Vilnius 2600; tel. (2) 628-678.

Lithuanian Youth Theatre: Arklių 5, Vilnius 2600; tel. (2) 625-556.

Panevėžys Drama Theatre: Laisvės 5, Panevėžys; tel. (54) 92-837.

Russian Drama Theatre: Basanivičiaus 13, Vilnius; tel. (2) 620-552.

Šiauliai Drama Theatre: Tilžės 144, Šiauliai 5400; tel. (14) 32-641.

ASSOCIATIONS

Cultural Foundation of Lithuania: Jakšto 9, Vilnius 2600; tel. (2) 617-634; fax (2) 620-508; f. 1989; Chair. JURGIS DVARIONAS.

Lithuanian Artists' Union: Vokiečių 2, Vilnius 2024; tel. (2) 622-935; f. 1935; Chair. BRONIUS LEONAVICIUS; 960 mems.

Lithuanian Choirs' Union: POB 1272, Vilnius 2056; tel. (2) 711-891; telex 261140; fax (2) 622-859.

Lithuanian Choreographers' Union: Barbaros Radvilaitės 8, Vilnius 2600; tel. (2) 614-706.

Lithuanian Composers' Union: Mickevičiaus 29, Vilnius 2600; tel. (2) 752-232; telex 261140; fax (2) 351-549; f. 1941; organizes festivals, such as the Gaida Baltic Music Festival, the Lithuanian Music Spring; Chair. MINDAUGAS URBAITIS.

Lithuanian Designers' Union: Juozapavičiaus 11, Vilnius 2600; tel. (2) 351-916.

Lithuanian Film-makers' Union: Birutės 18; Vilnius 2004; tel. (2) 751-337; fax (2) 751-389; f. 1963; Chair. GYTIS LUKŠAS.

Lithuanian Folk-Art Association: Vytenio 13, Vilnius 2009; tel. (2) 662-974; f. 1966; Chair. ZILVINAS BAUTRENAS.

Lithuanian Journalists' Union: Vilniaus 35, Vilnius 2600; tel. (2) 611-790; f. 1957; Chair. RIMGAUDAS EILUNAVICIUS.

Lithuanian Photographers' Union: Universiteto 4, Vilnius 2600; tel. (2) 611-627.

Lithuanian Society for Study of Local Lore: Traku 2, Vilnius 2001; tel. (2) 622-476; f. 1926; Chair. IRENA SELIUKAITE.

Lithuanian Theatre Union: Gedimino 1, Vilnius 2001; tel. (2) 623-386; fax (2) 610-814; f. 1987; Chair. JUOZAS BUDRAITIS.

Lithuanian Writers' Union: K. Sirvydo 6, Vilnius 2600; tel. (2) 223-919; fax (2) 619-696; f. 1940; Chair. VYTAUTAS MARTINKUS.

Motherland (Teviske): Tilto 8/2, Vilnius 2600; tel. (2) 613-580; fax (2) 624-092; f. 1964; Chair. VACLOVAS SAKALAUSKAS.

PEN Centre of Lithuania: K. Sirvydo 6, Vilnius 2600; tel. (2) 619-486; fax (2) 616-902; f. 1989; 35 mems; Pres. ROMUALDAS LANKAUSKAS; Sec. GALINA BAUZYTE-CEPINSKIENE.

Polish Union: Didzioji 40, Vilnius 2601; tel. (2) 223-388; f. 1988; Chair. JAN MINCEWICZ.

Education

Under the terms of the 1992 Constitution, education in Lithuania is free of charge and is compulsory from the ages of six to 16. Lithuanian is the main language of instruction; there are, however, general-education schools in which instruction is conducted in Russian, Polish or Yiddish. There are three principal types of school: elementary, which cover the first four years of education; nine-year, which cover the first nine years; and secondary, which cover the maximum 12 years of school tuition. In the 1992/93 academic year a total of 506,563 students attended 2,189 general-education schools in Lithuania, including 43 private schools. In the same year higher education was provided in 17 institutions of higher education, including four universities, which were attended by 55,516 students.

UNIVERSITIES

Kaunas University of Technology: Donelaičio 73, Kaunas 3006; tel. (7) 227-044; telex 269880; f. 1951; Rector KESTUTIS KRIŠČIŪNAS.

Vilnius Technical University: Saulėtekio 11, Vilnius 2054; tel. (2) 769-600; fax (2) 765-210; f. 1969; Rector EDMUNDAS KAZIMIERAS ZAVADSKAS.

Vilnius University: Universiteto 3, 2734 Vilnius; tel. (2) 623-779; telex 261128; fax (2) 223-563; f. 1579; language of instruction: Lithuanian; 1,291 teachers; 15,800 students; Rector J. KUBILIUS.

Vytautas Magnus University: Daukanto 28, Kaunas 3000; tel. (7) 222-739; fax (7) 203-858; f. 1922, closed 1950, reopened 1989; 8 faculties, 3 institutes; 220 teachers; 1,880 students; Rector BRONIUS VAŠKELIS.

Social Welfare

The health-care system in Lithuania during the early 1990s was a modified version of the Soviet system. Some reforms were introduced in 1990, including the legalization of private practices. Furthermore, in October 1991 the National Health Concept was passed, which strongly criticized the Soviet health-care system and emphasized the need for more private physicians. The legislation also reformed the health-insurance system in Lithuania. At the end of 1993 the Seimas had still not adopted the necessary legislation to restructure the health-care system, although some *ad hoc* measures had been taken by the Government: for example, a commission was formed to issue licences for private practices (although by May 1993 only 1,000 out of a total of 2,200 dentists and 1,000 out of 15,000 physicians practising in Lithuania had been granted licences). The development of a private health-insurance system in Lithuania was hindered by the system of taxation, under which contributions towards health care were made automatically through deductions from the payroll. A shortage of medicines was a serious problem in Lithuania: although the country received substantial shipments of Western medicines, distribution of this foreign aid was poorly managed and little benefit was derived. In 1992 there were 46,100 hospital beds in Lithuania, equivalent to 121 beds per 10,000 inhabitants. A national social-insurance scheme covered all residents. Under the terms of the 1992 Constitution citizens were entitled to old-age and disability pensions, as well as social assistance in the event of unemployment, sickness, widowhood, etc. The 1994 budget allocated more than double the amount for public health than was allocated the previous year, although the apparent increase in expenditure was not reflected in real terms.

NATIONAL AGENCIES

Department of Labour Safety: Jaksto 1/25, Vilnius 2600; tel. (2) 661-854; Dir-Gen. JONAS SIMKUNAS.

Ministry of Social Security: see section on The Government (Ministries).

Ministry of Health: see section on The Government (Ministries).

HEALTH AND WELFARE ORGANIZATIONS

Association for the Physically Disabled of Lithuania: J. Jasinskio 9, Vilnius 2723; tel. (2) 62-98-07; fax (2) 62-74-15; Chair. JONAS MAČIUKEVIČIUS.

Children's Fund of Lithuania: Zygimantu 12, Vilnius 2600; tel. (2) 627-180; f. 1988; Chair. JUOZAS NEKROSIUS.

Lithuanian Red Cross Society: Gedimino 3A, Vilnius 2600; tel. (2) 619-923; fax (2) 614-037; f. 1919; Chair. JUOZAS SAPOKA.

Lithuanian Society of the Deaf: Šv. Kazimiero 3, Vilnius 2600; tel. (2) 628-115; Chair. ALGIRDAS JAKAITIS.

Lithuanian Union of the Blind: Labdariu 7/11, Vilnius 2001; tel. (2) 619-691; f. 1944; Chair. JUOZAS DZIDOLIKAS.

The Environment

GOVERNMENT ORGANIZATION

Department of the Environment: Juozapaviciaus 9, Vilnius 2686; tel. (2) 355-868; Dir-Gen. EVALDAS VEBRA.

ACADEMIC INSTITUTES

Lithuanian Academy of Sciences: Gedimino 3, Vilnius 2600; telex 261141; f. 1941; several attached institutes involved in environmental research; Pres. J. K. POŽELA.

Institute of Botany: Želiųjų 47, Vilnius 2021; tel. (2) 736-462; fax (2) 359-950; Dir Dr ROMAS PAKALNIS; Chair. of Bd Dr JUOZAS STANIULIS.

Institute of Ecology: Akademijos 2, Vilnius 2600; tel. (2) 359-275; f. 1958; research into degradation of water systems and affect of pollution on terrestrial ecosystems; Dir Prof. JUOZAS VIRBICKAS.

NON-GOVERNMENTAL ORGANIZATIONS

Lithuanian Green Movement: Kalvariju 130-48, Vilnius 2048; tel. (2) 765-609; fax (2) 766-737; f. 1988; directed by a Co-ordination Council.

Lithuanian Green Party: Pylimo 38/1, Vilnius 2001; tel. (2) 224-215; Chair. IRENA IGNATAVIČIENĖ.

Defence

Before regaining independence in 1991, Lithuania had no armed forces separate from those of the USSR. In October of that year the Department of State Defence (established in April 1990) was reformed as the Ministry of Defence. Military service is for a total of 12 months. According to Western estimates, in June 1993 Lithuania's total active armed forces numbered 9,800, including a border guard of 5,000. There were 11,000 reserves. A navy was being formed at Klaipėda.

Commander-in-Chief of the Lithuanian Armed Forces: President of the Republic.

Chief of the General Staff: Col STASYS KNEZYS.

Bibliography

Lukowski, J. *Liberty's Folly: The Polish-Lithuanian Commonwealth in the 18th Century, 1697–1795.* London, Routledge, 1991.

Musteikis, A. *The Reformation in Lithuania: Religious Fluctuations in the 16th Century.* Boulder, Colorado, East European Monographs, 1988.

Navickas, K. *The Struggle of the Lithuanian People for Statehood.* Vilnius, Gintaras, 1971.

Oleszczuk, J. *Political Justice in the USSR: Dissent and Repression in Lithuania.* Boulder, Colorado, East European Monographs, 1988.

Remeikis, T. *Opposition to Soviet Rule in Lithuania, 1945–1980.* Chicago, Institute of Lithuanian Studies Press, 1980.

Senn, A. *The Emergence of Modern Lithuania.* New York, Columbia University Press, 1959.

Vardys, V. *The Catholic Church, Dissent and Nationality in Soviet Lithuania.* Boulder, Colorado, and New York, East European Quarterly–Columbia University Press, 1978.

'Lithuanian National Politics', in *Problems of Communism*, Vol. 38 (1989).

MACEDONIA

Geography

PHYSICAL FEATURES

The Former Yugoslav Republic of Macedonia (or, according to its Constitution, the Republic of Macedonia) lies in south-eastern Europe, on the Balkan peninsula. Roughly rectangular in shape, Macedonia has a northern border with Yugoslavia (the Serbian province of Kosovo to the north-west and Serbia proper to the north-east). To the west lies Albania, to the south Greece and to the east Bulgaria.

The historical region of Macedonia is divided between the country which uses its name, and Greece and Bulgaria. The Republic of Macedonia, which is sometimes known as Vardar Macedonia (Pirin Macedonia is that part of the territory in Bulgaria and Aegean Macedonia in Greece), has a total area of 25,713 sq km. The country is mountainous. It is bisected by the Vardar (Axiós) river, which flows from north-west to south-east, across the centre of the country and in to Greece, where it enters the Aegean Sea.

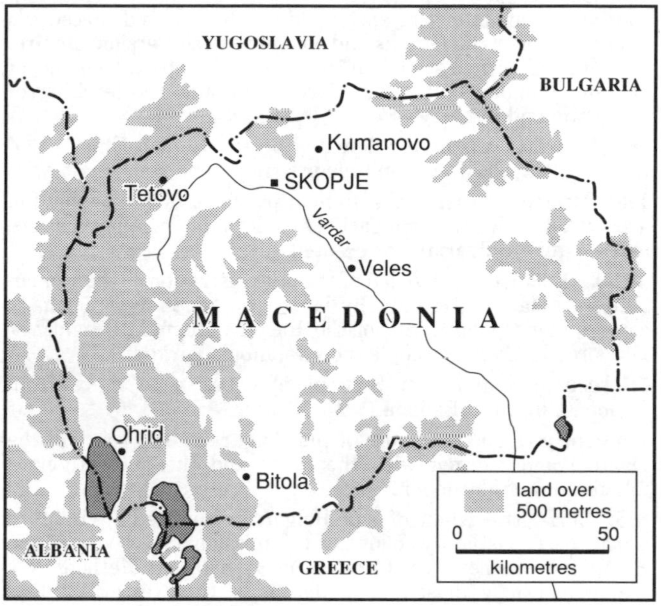

CLIMATE AND POPULATION

Macedonia has a mild climate, although winters, especially in the mountainous areas, are cold and snow cover can last for several months. According to the census of 1991 the total population of the Republic of Macedonia was 2,033,964, which gave a population density of 79.1 per sq km. The capital is Skopje (Skoplje or, in Turkish, Usküb), which is located on the Vardar, in the central north of the country. The district of Skopje, anciently a capital of the Serbs, had a population of some 563,000 in 1991. Other principal towns included Ohrid and Bitola, in south-west Macedonia, Veles, in the centre, and Tetovo, west of Skopje, the centre of Albanian settlement.

According to the census of 1991, ethnic Macedonians accounted for 64.6% of the national population (compared to some 67% in 1981) and ethnic Albanians for some 21%. The Macedonians are a Southern Slav people, closely related to Bulgarians. However, the separate existence of a Macedonian ethnic group was not acknowledged by Bulgaria, Greece (which described its own 'Macedonian' minority as Slav-speaking Greeks) or many Serbs. Most Albanians are concentrated in the west of the country, particularly the north-west, where they tend to live in distinct communities, mostly in the countryside. The official language of the country, under the Constitution of November 1991, was Macedonian, but provision was made for the use of minority languages (notably Albanian) at the local level. Most of the population was nominally Christian and of the Eastern Orthodox faith. The Macedonians were adherents of the Macedonian Orthodox Church, which was autocephalous or independent, but was not recognized by the other Orthodox. Most of the Albanians were Muslim, although there were some Roman Catholics in Skopje (immigrants from the Prizren area of Kosovo) and some Orthodox near Ohrid. Most of the remaining minority groups are also Muslim. In 1991 some 4.8% of the population were ethnic Turks, 2.7% Roma (Gypsies—for the 1991 census a separate category of Egipcani, or 'Egyptians', was allowed for those Roma renouncing their previous ethnicity and claiming to be 'descendants of the Pharaohs'), 2.1% Serbs, mostly in Skopje and Kumanovo, and 1.7% Slav Muslims (known as Torbeshes, Poturs or Pomaks). In 1981 there were also some 7,190 Vlahs (Koutsovlahs, Aromani, Cincari), Macedonia being the main former Yugoslav territory of this traditionally nomadic, Romanian-speaking people.

Chronology

6th century BC: The ancient kingdom of Macedon, with capitals at Pella and Aigai (Edessa), was established on the borders of the Hellenic territories.

336–323: Reign of Alexander III ('the Great') of Macedon, the most famous of the ancient kings; he secured Macedon's hegemony over the Greeks and conquered the Persian Empire. His empire disintegrated after his death into a number of Hellenic kingdoms, of which Macedon became the territory of the Antigonid dynasty.

168: Macedon was finally defeated by the Roman Empire and the kingdom was divided into four semi-autonomous territories.

148: After an uprising the Roman province of Macedonia (an area which included large parts of modern-day northern Greece and western Bulgaria) was created.

AD 395: Following a division of the administration of the Roman Empire, Macedonia and Illyria to the north-west formally came under the authority of the Eastern Roman ('Byzantine') Emperor in Constantinople (now Istanbul, Turkey).

5th century: Southern Slav peoples began to move from Pannonia into the Balkans.

7th century: The ancestors of the Bulgars moved south of the Danube and merged with the Slavs and the autochthonous inhabitants of Macedonia.

865: Boris, the Khan of the Bulgars, converted to Eastern Orthodox Christianity following the missionary activity of the Byzantine brothers, SS Constantine (Cyril) and Methodius; a Slavonic liturgy (based on a dialect of the western Bulgar territory of Macedonia) was introduced with a written language, in the Cyrillic script, which remains common to all the Eastern and Balkan Slavic peoples.

1014: Final defeat of the western Bulgarian, or Macedonian, realm under Samuel (Samuil) by the Byzantine Emperor, Basil II.

1187: The Emperor in Constantinople acknowledged Serbian independence and the establishment of the second Bulgarian Empire (which was to include much of Macedonia and the surrounding territories).

1330: The Serbs defeated the Bulgarians and the Greek Byzantines at the Battle of Velbuzhde (Küstendil).

1346: Establishment of a Serbian patriarchate and the coronation of Uroš IV (Stjepan Dušan of Raška, who reigned 1331–55) as Tsar of the Serbs and Greeks, at Skopje; however, he failed in his ambition to conquer Constantinople (Zarigrad).

1389: The Turkish Ottoman Empire secured its conquest of Macedonia and the region by its victory against the Serbian nobility at a battle on the plain of Kosovo Polje, 'the Field of Blackbirds'; the Ottoman Empire was administered by the confessional *millet* system, which placed the Orthodox of Macedonia (after 1453) under the jurisdiction of the Greek Ecumenical Patriarch in Constantinople.

1870: The Bulgarians declared an Exarchate for their Church—that is they proclaimed their autonomy from the Ecumenical Patriarchy and introduced the Slavonic liturgy; they contested with the Greek Church for adherents in the Macedonian region.

March 1878: The Treaty of San Stefano concluded the war between Russia, in support of the Orthodox Slavs, and the Ottomans; however, the Great Powers rejected the settlement, which created a 'Greater Bulgaria'.

July 1878: At the Congress of Berlin, Bulgaria was denied the annexation of Macedonia, while Serbia and Montenegro secured their independence; many Macedonians fled to Bulgaria after this treaty.

1893: Foundation of the Internal Macedonian Revolutionary Organization (IMRO), which opposed the partition of Macedonia, but supported the idea of a Southern Slav ('Yugoslav') federation.

1895: The foundation of the External Organization of Supremacists (based in Sofia—Bulgaria) divided Macedonian nationalism, as it favoured the incorporation of Macedonia into Bulgaria.

2 August 1903: The Ilinden uprising against the Ottomans, in what is now Bulgarian (Pirin) Macedonia, was organized by IMRO and led by Gotse Delchev; the revolt was suppressed, but remains commemorated by both Macedonian and Bulgarian nationalists.

May 1913: The Peace of London concluded the First Balkan War, in which a league of Bulgaria, Greece, Montenegro and Serbia succeeded in removing the Turks from the bulk of their European possessions.

June 1913: Hoping to secure its claim to Macedonia, Bulgaria attacked Serbia, which had occupied Skopje (Usküb) after defeating the Ottomans at nearby Kumanovo (November 1912); Serbia was supported by Greece, Montenegro, Romania and the Turks.

August 1913: The Peace of Bucharest concluded the Second Balkan War; Bulgaria lost most of Macedonia, which was divided between Serbia (Vardar Macedonia or 'South Serbia') and Greece (Aegean Macedonia); Albanian independence was recognized.

28 July 1914: Habsburg Austria-Hungary declared war on Serbia; this started the First World War between the Central Powers, of Austria-Hungary and Germany, and the Entente Powers, of France, Russia, Serbia and the United Kingdom.

1915: Serbian Macedonia was occupied by Bulgaria, which joined the Central Powers in the conquest of Serbia.

4 December 1918: Proclamation of the Kingdom of Serbs, Croats and Slovenes, which united Serbia and Montenegro with the former Habsburg lands, under the Serbian monarchy.

3 October 1929: Following the imposition of a royal dictatorship, the country was formally named Yugoslavia.

March 1941: A *coup d'état* reversed previous policies and aligned Yugoslavia with the Allied Powers of the Second World War.

April 1941: German and Italian forces invaded Yugoslavia, which was partitioned; Macedonia was again occupied by Bulgaria, which lost much local support to the Communists.

29 November 1945: Following elections for a Provisional Assembly, the Federative People's Republic of Yugoslavia was proclaimed, with Tito (Josip Broz, leader of the Communist resistance forces) as prime minister. By this time a Macedonian alphabet and orthography had been prepared and accepted by the Communist authorities, who wished to foster a distinct Macedonian identity.

January 1946: A Soviet-style Constitution established a federation of six republics and two autonomous regions; one of the Republics was Macedonia; this was not only an acknowledgement of Macedonian nationalism, but an attempt to resolve the competing claims of Serbia and Bulgaria (until 1948 Tito had ambitions of a greater federation including the latter).

1958: The archdiocese of Ohrid, an ancient see, was established, despite the protests of the Serbian Orthodox hierarchy which resented the move towards separation.

April 1963: A new Constitution changed the country's name to the Socialist Federal Republic of Yugoslavia (SFRY).

18 July 1967: The autocephaly of the Macedonian Orthodox Church was declared, but the Serbian Church refused to acknowledge it and was backed by the Ecumenical Patriarch and the other established Orthodox Churches.

November 1968: Demonstrations in Tetovo by ethnic Albanians, present in large numbers in western Macedonia, demanded the creation of a seventh federal republic, for the Albanians of Yugoslavia.

4 May 1980: Tito died; his responsibilities were transferred to the collective State Presidency and to the Presidium of the ruling League of Communists of Yugoslavia (LCY).

1981: Protests by Albanians in the neighbouring Serbian Autonomous Province of Kosovo (officially renamed Kosovo and Metohija from September 1990) provoked measures by the Macedonian authorities against Albanian nationalism.

1988: There were further demonstrations in the Republic, not only about economic conditions and in favour of reform, but also by Albanian students.

1989: The Communist regime amended the republican Constitution to allow a multi-party system; however, ethnic tension increased when further amendments declared that Macedonia was a 'nation-state' of the ethnic Macedonians, omitting mention of the Albanian minority.

February 1990: The Movement for All-Macedonian Action (MAMA) was founded; although a nationalist party, it disclaimed any territorial ambitions for the Republic.

June 1990: The Internal Macedonian Revolutionary Organization-Democratic Party for Macedonian National Unity (IMRO-DPMNU), a more extreme nationalist party, was founded and elected Ljupčo Georgievski as leader.

July 1990: Ante Marković, the federal prime minister, formed the Alliance of Reform Forces (ARF), an all-Yugoslav party which supported his Government and advocated Western-style reforms.

11 and 25 November 1990: The first and second rounds of elections to a new, unicameral 120-seat Assembly (Sobranje) were held in Macedonia.

9 December 1990: The final round of voting in Macedonia produced an inconclusive result, with the nationalist opposition, IMRO-DPMNU, winning the largest number of seats (37); the League of Communists of Macedonia-Party of Democratic Reform (LCM-PDR, the former ruling Communists) won 31 seats, the republican ARF 19 and the two predominantly Albanian parties, the Party of Democratic Prosperity (PDP) and the People's Democratic Party, together, 25.

7 January 1991: The IMRO-DPMNU, the LCM-PDR and the Macedonian ARF agreed on a coalition administration (subsequently Stojan Andov of the ARF was elected President of the Sobranje and, eventually, Kiro Gligorov of the LCM-PDR President of the Republic, with Ljupčo Georgievski of the IMRO-DPMNU as Vice-President); however, an administration under premier Milo Djukanović did not satisfy the competing demands of the parties.

25 January 1991: The Sobranje unanimously adopted a declaration of the Republic's sovereignty, including a statement of its right to secede from the SFRY.

20 March 1991: Nikola Kljusev was approved as premier of a new administration, composed of non-political 'experts'.

7 June 1991: The Sobranje changed the state's name to the Republic of Macedonia; among other constitutional amendments and against a background of increasing tension in Croatia and Slovenia, which were attempting to secede from the federation, the Sobranje declared the Republic's neutrality and also provided that it alone could authorize a state of emergency.

4 August 1991: Macedonia declared a state of emergency and, subsequently, decided to hold a referendum on independence.

23 August 1991: The Sobranje approved the draft of a proposed new constitution, amid cabinet reorganizations.

2 September 1991: Macedonia and the five other Yugoslav Republics accepted a cease-fire plan proposed by the European Community (EC—known as the European Union from November 1993); it provided for EC monitors and a peace conference (which opened later in the month) on the future of Yugoslavia.

8 September 1991: Some 95% of the two-thirds of eligible voters who participated in the referendum were in favour of an independent and sovereign Macedonia; the large ethnic Albanian minority boycotted the poll.

8 October 1991: Croatia and Slovenia declared their final independence.

23 October 1991: The IMRO-DPMNU announced that it was to leave the Government, following the resignation of Georgievski as Vice-President the previous day.

28 October 1991: The Macedonian Government announced that more than 60% of federal bases in the Republic had been evacuated, without explanation.

17 November 1991: The new Constitution was enacted, despite opposition from the majority of the ethnic Albanian deputies and three of the IMRO-DPMNU deputies; with the promulgation of the new Constitution Macedonia was declared to be an independent country.

January 1992: An unofficial referendum conducted amongst the ethnic Albanian population resulted in a 99.9% vote in favour of territorial and political autonomy for the Albanian population. The EC Commission acknowledged that Macedonia fulfilled the requirements for official recognition; however, Greek objections to the use of the name 'Macedonia' and the use of the Star of Vergina (an emblem associated with Alexander the Great) on the Macedonian national flag ensured that EC recognition for Macedonia was not forthcoming; nevertheless, on 16 January, Bulgaria became the first country officially to recognize Macedonia; Turkey followed suit early in the following month.

26 March 1992: The total withdrawal of federal troops from Macedonia was completed.

April 1992: The new Constitution of the Federal Republic of Yugoslavia referred only to Serbia and Montenegro, effectively acknowledging the secession of Macedonia. Diplomatic relations were established with Croatia.

June 1992: Negotiations between the Macedonian Minister of Foreign Relations and the Greek Prime Minister, Konstantinos Mitsotakis, ended in failure.

16 July 1992: Following a vote of 'no confidence' passed in the Sobranje nine days previously, and after demonstrations by more than 100,000 people in the capital protesting at the Government's failure to gain recognition for an independent Macedonia, the Government resigned.

4 September 1992: Branko Crvenkovski, leader of the Social Democratic Union of Macedonia (SDUM—known as the LCM-PDR until 1991), was appointed Chairman (Prime Minister) of a new coalition.

October 1992: A new citizenship law, which stipulated a 15-year residency requirement prior to granting citizenship, came into effect, angering many ethnic Albanians.

6 November 1992: Four people were killed in riots in the Bit Pazar area of Skopje over Albanian rights; the police were accused of using violence to quell the 3,000-strong crowd.

December 1992: The UN Security Council authorized the dispatch of troops, civilian police and military observers to Macedonia in order to monitor the inter-ethnic tensions.

15 December 1992: Jovan Andonov resigned as Deputy Chairman of the Cabinet of Ministers after disagreement with other members of the Government over economic policy; he was subsequently reappointed in September 1993.

8 April 1993: Macedonia was admitted to the UN despite Greek objections, but under the name of the 'Former Yugoslav Republic of Macedonia'.

May 1993: A new currency, the new Macedonian denar, was introduced.

September 1993: Negotiations between Macedonia and Greece, held in New York (USA) under UN auspices, failed to resolve the dispute over the Former Yugoslav Republic's name.

9 November 1993: A number of ethnic Albanians were arrested in Tetovo and Gosivar following the discovery of arms and ammunition; they were charged with plotting against the state.

22 November 1993: Antoni Pešev, the Minister of Urban Planning, Construction, Transport and Environmental Protection, resigned after an aeroplane crashed in Macedonia killing 115 people.

24 November 1993: Macedonia was formally admitted to the Central European Initiative (CEI) regional grouping.

16 December 1993: The United Kingdom established full diplomatic relations with Macedonia; in a co-ordinated move, Germany, France and the Netherlands agreed to recognize Macedonia before the end of the year.

10 January 1994: The Greek Government announced that it would withdraw its objection to Macedonia's accession to the Conference on Security and Co-operation in Europe (CSCE) if Macedonia would remove the Vergina Star from its national flag.

16 February 1994: Greece suspended diplomatic relations with Macedonia and prohibited the country from using the Greek port of Thessaloníki, except for humanitarian aid.

17 February 1994: At the PDP congress in Tetovo, there was a split in the party: the more moderate leadership, including members of the Government, were obliged to hold a separate assembly; the followers of Menduh Thaci, who was supported by the Albanian Government, founded the Party of Democratic Prosperity of the Albanians in the Former Yugoslav Republic of Macedonia and elected Arber Ahaferi as Chairman.

History

Macedonia is an ancient territory, covering areas in northern Greece and south-west Bulgaria, as well as the Former Yugoslav territory. The ancient kingdom of Macedon is believed to have been established in the sixth century BC; its ancient capitals, Aigai (Edessa) and Pella, are both now in Greece. Its most famous king was Alexander III ('the Great'), who succeeded to the throne in 336 BC, consolidated Macedonian rule in Greece and then campaigned against the Persian Empire, conquering Asia Minor, the Levant, Egypt, Mesopotamia, Persia and parts of India. Alexander the Great died in 323 and his empire dissolved during wars between his successors. Eventually three Hellenic monarchies were established, one of which was a Macedonian state, under the Antigonids. Macedon, however, declined in power and was finally defeated by Rome, in 168 BC, being made a province of the Roman Empire in 148.

Slavic settlers moved into the province during the sixth century AD and the Turkic ancestors of the Bulgarians moved south of the Danube in the seventh century. These peoples merged with the original population, although the predominant language was Slavonic. In the ninth century, the Eastern Roman (Byzantine) missionaries took a Macedonian dialect as the basis of a written Slavonic language (Old Church Slavonic), using the new Cyrillic script. At the time, Macedonia was dominated by the Bulgars or Bulgarians (who still claim the Macedonians to be a Bulgarian people). The Bulgar resistance to the Byzantine reconquest was led, from a base near Lake Ohrid, by Samuil (Samuel), the tsar of a western Bulgarian or Macedonian realm (the exact identification of this regime remains a matter of nationalist dispute between modern Bulgaria and Macedonia). This survived against the Emperor Basil II until 1014, after which the territory was reabsorbed into the Eastern Empire. At this time the Orthodox bishopric of Ochrida (Ohrid) was established as a metropolitan see. From the 12th century control of Macedonia was contested between the Byzantine Empire, the Bulgarians and the Serbs. These last established the first patriarchate of the autocephalous Serbian Orthodox Church at Skopje (Skoplje), in the 14th century. In 1371, however, the Serbian princes were unable to prevent the Muslim Ottomans from conquering Macedonia. The territory then remained under Ottoman rule until the 19th century.

The disintegration of the Ottoman Empire and the rise of nationalism, during the 19th century, made the fate of Macedonia and the identification of its Slavic population a matter of some political controversy. The Ottoman administration was based on the *millet* system, or confessional divisions, which effectively subordinated all the Orthodox populations to the authority of the Ecumenical Patriarch of Constantinople and the use of the Greek liturgy. In 1870 the Bulgarians declared an exarchate church (that is, independent from Constantinople and using a Slavonic liturgy), which contested the Greeks for the allegiance of the Macedonian Slavs. The Greeks continue to claim that the Macedonians are 'Slavophone Greeks'. In 1878 the Congress of Berlin thwarted the 'Greater Bulgaria' of the Treaty of San Stefano. The Bulgarian state, therefore, retained its ambitions to annex Macedonia. Meanwhile, the expansion of Austria-Hungary limited the Serbian state's ambitions to the north and west and, after defeat by the Bulgarians in 1885, the Serbs too pressed their claims to Macedonia, describing it as 'South Serbia'. Both the Serbians and the Greeks formed nationalist societies, intent on promoting their cause in Macedonia (Society of St Sava and Ethnike Hetairia, respectively). In 1895 the Greeks claimed to have retained control of 1,400 schools in Macedonia. Also in the 1890s the Bulgarians, mainly under the aegis of their Exarchate, claimed between 600 and 700 schools, while the Serbs claimed 100. By 1912 even the Romanians were subsidizing about 30 schools, based on the presence of the Vlah population in western Macedonia. The resident population, therefore, endured the competing and often violent attentions of the different claimants, as well as the depredations of their own nationalists.

In 1893 the Internal Macedonian Revolutionary Organization (IMRO) was founded, opposing the partition of Macedonia and supporting the idea of a Southern Slav federation of Macedonians, Bulgarians and Serbs. However, the unity of the nationalists was fatally distracted by a rival sentiment in favour of the incorporation of Macedonia within Bulgaria. This was advocated by the External Organization of Supremacists, founded in 1895 and based in Sofia, where there were considerable numbers of Macedonian refugees, following the failure of the San Stefano agreement. The so-called Ilinden Uprising against the Ottomans, in August 1903, led by Gotse Delchev, is commemorated as a national anniversary by both the Bulgarians and the Macedonians. The fate of the territory was to be partitioned in the Balkan Wars of 1912–13, mainly between Serbia and Greece, the ultimate victors. This was confirmed after the First World War, during which Macedonia was occupied by the Bulgarians and the Central Powers, when Vardar Macedonia became part of the new Kingdom of Serbs, Croats and Slovenes (Yugoslavia from 1929). Macedonia was placed under the authority of the Serbian Church and Serbian was made the official language, which policies helped foster pro-Bulgarian sentiments.

In the Second World War the Bulgarian occupation of 1941–44 (Nazi Germany would not sanction formal annexation) disillusioned many Yugoslav Macedonians. From 1943 the Partisan resistance of Communist leader Tito (Josip Broz) began to increase its support in the region. Since the rise of the Nazis and other Fascist parties as the leading revisionists, the Communists had rejected the idea of a united Macedonia under Bulgaria. The new Yugoslav state and its Communist rulers resolved to include a Macedonian nation as a federal partner. Furthermore, Tito regarded a Macedonian nationality as a useful link with Communist Bulgaria (the leader of which, Georgi Dimitrov, was of Macedonian parentage), with which he hoped to unite

Yugoslavia in a Balkan federation. The death of Dimitrov, in 1949, following Tito's split with the Soviet Communist bloc, began a period of tension between Bulgaria and the new Macedonian Republic.

Following the Second World War the new Communist regime began to consolidate a distinct Macedonian identity, particularly as a counter to any residual pro-Bulgarian sentiments among the population. A written language was necessary and this was, first of all, based on a northern dialect. This was not sufficiently distinct from Serbian, however, and the more southerly dialects of Bitola-Veles became the standard. These were closer to the Bulgarian literary language, but standard Bulgarian was based on its eastern dialects, which distinguished it enough from Macedonian. The alphabet and orthography were prepared and accepted in 1945 and, from then, Macedonian was encouraged and standardized by the educational and official establishment. Macedonian shares with Bulgarian most of the same distinguishing characteristics from other Slavonic languages (such as the preservation of the simple verbal forms for the perfect and imperfect tenses and the lack of cases), and whether they are separate languages can be debated. However, differences have been fostered and the obvious Serbian and Bulgarian influences among the dialects of older people were less common by the 1980s. Certainly this linguistic policy and the fostering of a historical and cultural tradition increased Macedonian self-awareness. The authorities also utilized the fundamental cultural expression of the Orthodox Slavs, the Church. In 1958 the archdiocese of Ohrid was re-established. The Serbian Orthodox Church bitterly contested this move towards separation and the loss of its jurisdiction. It refused to acknowledge the final declaration of Macedonian autocephaly, on 18 July 1967, and succeeded in persuading Constantinople and the other Orthodox patriarchs against granting recognition of this status (the Greek and Bulgarian Churches remained influenced by the political considerations of their governments). Thus surrounded by countries which denied its legitimacy, nationalism was encouraged in Macedonia, and an ambivalence developed towards the Yugoslav federation. Membership of Yugoslavia gave Macedonia a protected identity, but it feared resurgent Serbian nationalism in a federation without the balancing influence of Croatia and Slovenia. Ultimately, therefore, it seceded from Yugoslavia.

TOWARDS INDEPENDENCE

In mid-1989 the Communist regime conceded the introduction of a multi-party system in the Republic and amended the Constitution accordingly. In February 1990 the Movement for All-Macedonian Action (MAMA) was founded by a group of intellectuals. It renounced any territorial claims, but discussed co-operation with the Macedonian-nationalist Ilinden movement in Bulgaria and held several large demonstrations protesting at the oppression of fellow nationals in Albania, Bulgaria and Greece. In June a more nationalist party was founded, in the Internal Macedonian Revolutionary Organization-Democratic Party for Macedonian National Unity (IMRO-DPMNU). There were delegates from the Macedonian diaspora at the founding congress, which elected Ljupčo Georgievski, a 26-year-old unemployed university graduate, as leader. The congress declared its party's intention to seek the return of territories then within Serbia. The Communist authorities suspected the IMRO-DPMNU of favouring the Bulgarian cause (the movement was not without its factions) and of fostering inter-ethnic tension with the Serbs. However, the republican Communist leader, Petar Gošev, president of what was now named the League of Communists of Macedonia-Party for Democratic Reform (LCM-PDR), also condemned the threat of Serbian nationalism, which made explicit claims later in the year. Serbia's main opposition leader, Vuk Drasković, revived the concept of 'South Serbia' and proposed a partition of Macedonia between a 'Greater Serbia' and Bulgaria.

In November and December 1990 elections to a new, unicameral republican Assembly (Sobranje) were held in Macedonia. The MAMA and the IMRO-DPMNU formed an electoral alliance, the Front for Macedonian National Unity, to counter the strong support of the ruling LCM-PDR. The first round of the elections was held on 11 November and the nationalist Front alleged irregularities after it failed to win any seats. The Front did not boycott the subsequent rounds of voting (25 November and 9 December) and the IMRO-DPMNU emerged as the single party with the largest share of the 120 seats in the new Sobranje (37), against all expectations. The LCM-PDR gained 31 seats and the two predominantly Albanian parties a total of 25. The republican branch of the federal Alliance of Reform Forces (ARF) won 19 seats. These results were inconclusive, the uncertainty being added to by a division in the IMRO-DPMNU, when Vladimir Golubovski challenged Georgievski for the leadership (the IMRO-DPMNU factions continued to vote as a single bloc in the Sobranje). A coalition administration for Macedonia was finally agreed in January 1991: Stojan Andov of the ARF was elected President of the republican Sobranje; Kiro Gligorov of the LCM-PDR was eventually elected President of Macedonia; and Georgievski of the IMRO-DPMNU was elected Vice-President. Following some dispute over the allocation of portfolios, the three parties agreed to support a government largely consisting of independent members, without political affiliation. On 20 March the Sobranje approved a new Government, headed by an independent, Nikola Kljusev. This 'Government of experts' committed itself to concentrating on the economic problems of Macedonia, which had been exacerbated by the Sobranje's inactivity in this area over the previous months.

The Macedonians were active in attempts to mediate in the growing crisis in Yugoslavia, during 1991. The state's interests were best served by the preservation of the federation, although, on 25 January, the Sobranje had unanimously adopted a motion declaring the Republic a sovereign territory. However, after the June declarations of Croatian and Slovenian 'dissociation' and the later escalation into civil war, Macedonia became wary of Serbian domination of the 'rump' federal institutions. It declared its neutrality and emphasized its sovereign status. On 8 September a referendum vote, boycotted by the Albanian population, overwhelmingly supported the sovereignty of Macedonia, which was again declared by the Sobranje. With war in the north of Yugoslavia, there was little federal reaction to this and, in October, the evacuation of some 60% of the military bases in the Republic was reported. The Macedonian authorities had received no official explanation, but it was believed that the forces were to be used in Croatia.

In October 1991 the coalition collapsed. Georgievski resigned the Vice-Presidency on 22 October and, the following day, his party, the IMRO-DPMNU, announced that it had joined the opposition. The party complained that, although it had the largest representation in the Assembly, it was being excluded from the decision-making process. However, the IMRO-DPMNU did participate in the enactment of the new Constitution. The party proposed an introductory nationalist statement, which was strongly opposed by the predominantly Albanian parties, causing a delay in the passage of the document. The Government supported the exclusion of continual nationalist references, but did not support demands by the Party for Democratic Prosperity (PDP) to include educational and linguistic rights in the Constitution. The final version did not declare Macedonia to be the 'motherland' of the Macedonian people, but nor did it grant the Albanian language official equality with Macedonian. On 17 November the Constitution was passed by 96 of the 120 Sobranje members; the majority of Albanian deputies and three IMRO-DPMNU deputies did not support its enactment.

Having claimed independence as the Republic of Macedonia, the new country found its name a source of considerable controversy in neighbouring Greece. Negotiations with the Greek Government, which had vetoed EC recognition of Macedonia (see below), provoked a Sobranje vote against the Government and massive demonstrations in Skopje. The Government resigned on 16 July. The IMRO-DPMNU, the party with the most seats in the Sobranje, failed to form a coalition and, eventually, the Chairman of the Social Democratic Union of Macedonia (SDUM—formerly the LCM-PDR), Branko Crvenkovski, was installed as Chairman (Prime Minister) of the Cabinet of Ministers, on 4 September, at the head of a new coalition. The Cabinet of Ministers consisted of 11 SDUM members, five members of the PDP and the People's Democratic Party, four members from the Reform Forces of Macedonia—Liberal Party, and one member of the Socialist Party of Macedonia (SPM). There was a further minister representing all the coalition parties.

The new administration could not survive long without a crisis, given the extent of the country's problems. With a worsening economic situation causing widespread industrial unrest, in mid-December 1992 Deputy Prime Minister Jovan Andonov resigned after disagreement with other members of the Government over economic policy (he was subsequently reappointed in September 1993). Macedonia's economic problems were compounded by the presence of about 50,000 refugees (mainly from Bosnia and Herzegovina) and by the substantial reduction in trade caused by the UN-enforced imposition of sanctions against Serbia and Montenegro (prior to the outbreak of civil war in Yugoslavia, Serbia had been Macedonia's main trade route). The deepening economic crisis and the Government's acceptance of UN membership under the temporary name of the Former Yugoslav Republic of Macedonia provoked a motion of 'no confidence' on 13 April 1993. The Government won the Sobranje vote, however, although the economic situation could not be alleviated. Moreover, this depression contributed to the dissatisfaction of and tensions in the ethnic Albanian community.

THE ALBANIAN MINORITY IN MACEDONIA

Confidence in an independent future was not encouraged by the perceived insecurity of a large ethnic Albanian minority (some 21% of the population, according to the 1991 census) in western Macedonia. Demands for the creation of a seventh Yugoslav republic, including the Albanian areas of western Macedonia, were first expressed in 1968, following demonstrations in the neighbouring Serbian province of Kosovo. The Macedonian authorities were particularly active against Albanian nationalism from 1981, mainly in the field of education and language, which was what provoked the most reaction from the Albanian community. There had been attempts to ban personal names of an 'Albanian-nationalist' nature and to discourage the rate of births. The campaign in the education system merely exacerbated the problem of Albanians not being able to use the Macedonian language. In 1988 there were demonstrations, in which young Albanian students were prominent, and tension continued into the early 1990s, providing independent Macedonia with a potentially dangerous legacy. Most Albanian political activity in the old Yugoslav federation, however, was centred on Kosovo. Indeed, the main ethnic Albanian party in Macedonia, the PDP, was repeatedly accused of being an appendage of the Democratic Alliance of Kosovo, although the PDP reiterated its commitment to the territorial integrity and sovereignty of the country. Support for the PDP and the smaller People's Democratic Party was mainly confined to the Albanian community, although other Muslim groups also voted for them. These parties emerged as Macedonian nationalism reacted to the threat of a 'Greater Albania'. In 1989 the ruling Communists amended the republican Constitution, declaring Macedonia to be a 'nation-state' of the ethnic Macedonians, excluding mention of the 'Albanian and Turkish minorities'. Furthermore, the new Constitution of 1991 also refused to specify the Republic as a 'homeland' of the Albanians as well as the Macedonians, although it was enacted only by avoiding the specific mention of official languages.

Relations between the Macedonian authorities and the ethnic Albanian minority deteriorated further in the early years of independence. In January 1992 an unofficial referendum (declared illegal by the Government) conducted amongst the ethnic Albanian population resulted in a 99.9% vote in favour of their territorial and political autonomy. In April there were demonstrations by ethnic Albanians advocating that they be granted the status of a constituent nation of Macedonia as a precondition for international recognition of Macedonia as an independent state. In November the Vice-President of the PDP requested that the European Community (EC—known as the European Union from November 1993) postpone recognition until such a condition was met.

In October 1992 a new citizenship law was enacted, which stipulated a 15-year residency requirement before the granting of citizenship. This disqualified many ethnic Albanians then resident in Macedonia and provoked riots in the Bit Pazar region of Skopje on 6 November. These involved some 3,000 people and left four people dead (three ethnic Albanians and one Macedonian Slav) and 23 injured. The Albanian Government formally protested about the conduct of the police at these riots. Warned by the example of continuing violence elsewhere in the former Yugoslavia, in December the UN Security Council authorized the dispatch to Macedonia of a UN peace-keeping force of 700 troops, 35 military observers and 26 civilian police. However, there were further disturbances, in February 1993, when the construction of a refugee camp in Skopje led to four days of rioting by ethnic Macedonians, who feared the arrival of thousands of ethnic Albanian refugees from Kosovo.

In November 1993 a number of ethnic Albanians were arrested following the discovery of weapons and ammunition in Tetovo and Gosivar, two towns in western Macedonia with large Albanian populations. Two senior government officials were also arrested in connection with the arms discovery, and, on 29 January 1994, Mithat Emini, former Secretary-General of the PDP, was also detained. They were all charged with unlawful arms trade and plotting against the state. The Albanian Government denied any connection with the alleged conspiracy. There were reports that an Albanian republic in western Macedonia, 'Ilirida', was to have been united with Kosovo and, ultimately, Albania. Furthermore, it was claimed that this plan was not the work of an isolated group of ethnic Albanians, but was the result of continued activity by the entire Albanian separatist movement. The Ministry of Internal

Affairs justified such claims after it announced the discovery of a list of 20,000 potential supporters of the conspiracy. However, Albanian groups in the country countered that such accusations were fabricated, in an attempt to justify a suppression of the Albanian minority.

By the mid-1990s it was clear that the greatest threat to the stability of Macedonia was from the nationalism of the ethnic Albanian minority. This was compounded by the effects of the economic crisis. Government claims that the country had more to fear from Albanian separatists in Kosovo were part of official attempts to create an impression of inter-ethnic and inter-party harmony. Macedonian nationalists alleged that this policy, however, merely encouraged the separatists and allowed them to become established as ethnic-Albanian demands were met. Such demands included autonomy, equality in employment, greater representation in government and the promotion of the Albanian language in education and in the media. To the Macedonians the spectre of a 'Greater Albania' threatened not only the north-west of their country, but also compromised the communes of Prilep, Veles, Bitola and Ohrid. Yet, although ethnic Albanians held important posts in government, the Albanian parties continued to demand greater representation in such areas as the army and the police. Their reluctance to co-operate with the ruling coalition increased as the Government became less willing to satisfy their demands, mainly because of the growing pressure from Macedonian nationalists.

INTERNATIONAL RECOGNITION

The question of international recognition dominated Macedonian affairs in the first years of independence. Although the country was no longer part of Yugoslavia, it was unable to take its place as an independent nation in the international community, mainly owing to objections from Greece. The complete withdrawal of Yugoslav federal troops from Macedonia, by 26 March 1992, and the adoption, in April, of a new Constitution for a 'Federal Republic of Yugoslavia', referring only to Serbia and Montenegro, effectively signalled Yugoslav acceptance of Macedonian secession. In March Macedonia established diplomatic relations with Slovenia and, in April, with Croatia.

Bulgaria recognized Macedonia on 16 January 1992 (although it continued to deny the existence of a distinct Macedonian nationality), followed by Turkey, on 6 February. This provoked demonstrations in Thessaloníki, the capital of the Greek region of Macedonia. The Greek Government insisted that 'Macedonia' was merely a geographical term (delineating an area that included a large part of northern Greece) and maintained that the use of such a name might foster a false claim to future territorial expansion. The Greek Government was instrumental in a decision, adopted by the EC in early 1992, that Macedonia should be awarded no formal recognition of independence by EC countries until stringent constitutional requirements had been fulfilled. In May EC foreign ministers declared that the EC could, in principle, recognize Macedonia, but only 'under a name that can be accepted by all concerned'. President Gligorov condemned this statement. Negotiations in mid-June, between the Macedonian Minister of Foreign Relations and the Greek Prime Minister, Konstantinos Mitsotakis, failed to resolve the problem.

Macedonia formally began issuing passports and adopted a new flag in August 1992. Greece, however, objected to the use on the new flag of the 'Vergina Star', a symbol associated with Alexander the Great and, therefore, claimed by the Greeks as part of their ancient patrimony. In the same month Russia officially recognized Macedonia as an independent state. In July fuel rationing was introduced, following a blockade of petroleum deliveries to Macedonia by Greece. By September stocks at the Skopje petroleum refinery were exhausted. Greece was criticized by the EC for the blockade, but the domestic political benefits of such national intransigence were obvious. On 10 December more than 1m. Greeks attended a rally in Athens protesting against international recognition of the 'Republic of Macedonia' under its existing name. However, increasing EC criticism of the Greek position meant that in early February 1993 Greece accepted the idea of international arbitration over the issue of Macedonia's name, and pledged to honour any decision. On 8 April the state was admitted into the UN as, for the interim, the 'Former Yugoslav Republic of Macedonia'. One week earlier, on 1 April, Italy had angered the Greeks by unilaterally recognizing 'The Republic of Macedonia', apparently because of concern over the critical nature of the country's economic problems.

In September 1993 UN-mediated meetings began, in New York (USA), between the Macedonian and Greek Governments. This was another attempt to resolve the dispute over the territory's name, but no agreement was reached. This was not surprising given the widespread use of nationalist rhetoric in the Greek election campaign. Nevertheless, the new Government of Greece, elected in October, seemed more conciliatory and expressed concern to resolve the dispute over Macedonia. On 10 January 1994 Greece announced that it would withdraw its objection to Macedonia's accession to the Conference on Security and Co-operation in Europe (CSCE) if the latter would remove the Vergina Star from its national flag. However, on 16 February, Greece suspended diplomatic links with Macedonia and banned the country from using the Greek port of Thessaloníki, an action which was likely to exacerbate Macedonia's economic crisis.

In October 1993 the Sobranje approved the Macedonian Government's decision to apply to become a member of the North Atlantic Treaty Organisation (NATO). Although such an application was unlikely to succeed, Macedonia did have hopes of acceding to NATO's 'Partnership for Peace' scheme announced in early 1994. Macedonia became a full member of the Central European Initiative on 24 November 1993, despite the opposition of Slovenia. On 16 December the United Kingdom established full diplomatic relations with Macedonia. At the same time, in a co-ordinated move, Germany, France and the Netherlands agreed to recognize Macedonia before the end of 1993, when Greece was to assume the EC presidency for six months. On 9 February 1994 the USA recognized Macedonia, shortly before Greece increased its pressure on the Former Yugoslav Republic.

The continuing recognition of Macedonia by the international community was an essential advancement for the country. Most important was the settlement of the dispute with Greece. Given the UN-imposed sanctions on Yugoslavia, with which Macedonia had the best transport links, access to the outside world through Greece (particularly Thessaloníki) was vital. There was little assistance, in practical terms, that Albania and Bulgaria could give their neighbour. Furthermore, the Macedonian Government still faced domestic problems, not least that of ethnic Albanian separatism and the worsening economic position. At the beginning of 1994 Macedonia was finding it increasingly difficult to balance conflicting internal demands with the pursuance of a foreign policy designed to attract Western aid and recognition, both of which were necessary for Macedonia's future survival as an independent state.

The Economy

The economy of the Former Yugoslav Republic of Macedonia suffered a serious deterioration in the early 1990s. This was owing to the problems the country encountered in gaining international recognition as a nation, the consequences of the civil wars in the former Yugoslavia (the disruption of conflict and the need to adhere to the UN-imposed sanctions) and domestic instability. In 1991, according to estimates by the International Institute of Strategic Studies, Macedonia's gross domestic product (GDP) was US $5,060m. Between 1956 and 1989 the average annual real growth rate of GDP was 5.2%. However, in 1992 real GDP decreased by 14%. The situation worsened in 1993, exacerbated by the Government's decision to enforce UN-introduced sanctions against the Federal Republic of Yugoslavia (FRY) in September. Although Macedonia's main trade links were through FRY territory, it was particularly anxious to comply with US pressure. However, this emphasized the effects of the Greek policy, since 1992, of placing an embargo on food and commodity shipments to Macedonia. The country had a relatively large agricultural output, but few food reserves, and, by late 1993, there were food shortages to add to the problems of fuel supply. The Greek closure of the port of Thessaloníki to Macedonia, except for humanitarian aid, in February 1994, could only make the country's plight more extreme.

AGRICULTURE

Macedonia had an overwhelmingly agricultural economy, although the sector only contributed 14.0% of GDP in 1991. Dairy farming was the most important sector. Activity was concentrated along the Vardar and in the lowlands around other river valleys. In 1990 production of cows' milk totalled 217,000 metric tons, but, in 1991, only 123,000 tons. In 1992 output decreased by a further 19.5%, to 99,000 tons. All types of agricultural production decreased in 1992. In particular, declines were recorded in the production of grapes (by 27%, to some 191,000 metric tons), tomatoes (by 37%), and wheat (by 41%). Total cereal production in 1992 was an estimated 443,000 metric tons. Macedonia was also a major producer of apples, tobacco, cotton, rice, sunflower seed and sugar beets. The production of wine was one of the few agricultural sectors to expand: in 1990 output was 69,000 metric tons, but, by 1992, had increased to 115,000 tons. However, a decline was considered likely in 1993 and 1994.

The country's principal agricultural exports were sugar beets, cheese, lamb and tobacco. Dairy cattle made the most important contribution to the economy, but sheep farming formed the mainstay of livestock production in Macedonia. In 1990 there were some 2.5m. sheep in the country, although this total had fallen by 250,000 by 1992. In the latter year mutton and lamb production was 13,000 metric tons, although in previous years this had been exceeded by the production of pigmeat, which fell from 15,000 metric tons in 1990 and 1991 to 12,000 tons in 1992.

MINING, ENERGY AND INDUSTRY

Macedonia was famed for its gold and silver mines, and later for its petroleum resources. It also possessed moderate reserves of iron, zinc, chromium, manganese, lead and nickel ores. In 1990 coal production was 6.6m. metric tons and, in the same year, 6,000 metric tons of aluminium were produced.

Macedonia was dependent on imported energy—its only remaining hydrocarbon reserves, in significant quantities, were of coal. With the advent of independence, the Macedonian Government sought to reduce dependence on its traditional sources of energy supplies, securing agreement to the construction of a pipeline to carry natural gas from the Bulgarian border. The intermittent economic blockade imposed by Greece from 1992 onwards, however, led to severe fuel shortages. By September 1992 supplies at the Skopje petroleum refinery were exhausted and, by the end of the year, industrial production had fallen by 75%. In September 1993 production was halted at the Fenimak nickel enterprise, at Kavadarci, as a result of the UN sanctions against the FRY, as the enterprise's stocks of coal from Serbia were exhausted.

Industry contributed 52.9% of GDP in 1989. The majority of industry was focused on Skopje. The principal industrial activities were metallurgy and textile production, which accounted for approximately 20% of total industrial output. Footwear was a major industrial export. Revenue from industrial production doubled between 1953 and 1988. However, owing to fuel shortages caused by blockades by Greece, and, again, to the suspension of trade with the FRY following the imposition of UN sanctions, Macedonian industrial production declined in 1992–93. In 1990 the volume of industrial output in Macedonia declined by 10.6% (in January 1991 it was 20.9% lower than in the previous January). Industrial unrest, including strike action, in protest against deteriorating conditions of employment and the rising rate of unemployment, further exacerbated the decline in industry. In 1991 industry and the mining sector were responsible for 41.2% of the country's GDP.

TRADE

In 1990 total exports decreased by 11.8% and imports increased by 20.7%. Between January and August of 1991, Macedonia's total trade amounted to US $1,696m., which comprised $801m. in exports and $895m. in imports. In 1993 the economic embargo imposed by Greece forced Macedonia to import goods from Slovenia, where prices were higher. Furthermore, the UN-enforced imposition of sanctions against the FRY adversely affected industrial production and trade as, prior to the outbreak of civil war in Yugoslavia, Serbia was Macedonia's main trade route. Consequently, the terms of trade deteriorated.

Before independence, 50%–60% of Macedonia's trade was conducted with the internal Yugoslav market. After independence, however, the European Community (EC—known as the European Union from November 1993) was the country's main trading partner. The new regime in Albania encouraged the Macedonian Government to seek closer economic co-operation with that country from 1991. However, this did not significantly offset the loss of trade with the former Yugoslavia. With the Greek ban on Macedonian use of Thessaloníki in February 1994, Albania offered the land-locked country access to its ports. The problem remained one of infrastructure though, with few resources available to upgrade transport links between the two countries. Macedonia's proximity to the conflicts in the former Yugoslavia, the problems it experienced in attempting to gain international recognition, as well as the fact that it still had a centrally planned economy, were major discouragements to foreign investment in the country in the early 1990s.

FINANCE, PRICES AND GOVERNMENT POLICY

The average annual rate of inflation in 1990 was 120%. At the beginning of 1991 more than 20% of the labour-force were unemployed. By July 1992 the rate of unemployment in the country had reached 40%. In the latter half of 1992 strikes were organized by civil servants and railway employees, demanding large pay increases. Some 18% of those in employment (477,238 people in October 1991) worked in public administration and the decreasing government revenue meant that these demands for wage increases could not be satisfied. Macedonia's economic problems were further exacerbated by the arrival of about 50,000 refugees, mainly from Bosnia and Herzegovina, in late 1992.

The high rate of inflation prompted Macedonia to attempt to control its own monetary policy. In April 1992, at the same time as enacting economic reforms, currency coupons were introduced, as a prelude to a new currency, the Macedonian denar. Such a move succeeded in protecting Macedonia from the effects of hyperinflation in the neighbouring region of Serbia; at the end of 1993 the monthly rate of inflation in Macedonia was 15% and the monthly rate of unemployment was 35% (compared to 60% in adjacent parts of Serbia). Furthermore, in the first half of 1993, wages increased by 27% in real terms.

Owing to the earlier implementation of liberalizing market reforms, by 1993 the number of private businesses operating in Macedonia had increased to 67,000. Major industrial enterprises were still state-owned, but a privatization law passed in July opened the way for the divestment of such assets. The illegal, parallel economy, the 'black market', continued to flourish, especially in the currency exchange. Most significant, however, in the improvement of Macedonia's economic situation was the UN recognition of the country, in April 1993, which enabled Macedonia to become a member of the International Monetary Fund (IMF) and to gain access to international economic markets. In late 1993 the Macedonian Government and the IMF agreed on a stabilization programme for the country.

Although Macedonia's economy was far from healthy, following independence, it was thought by some that the situation was not as dire as the Government had claimed, when applying for aid from the IMF and the World Bank. In spite of the adverse effects caused by the UN-enforced imposition of sanctions against the FRY, and by the reduction in trade, following Greece's blockade of the country, many economists still believed that Macedonia would survive economically as an independent nation.

Statistical Survey

Sources: Statistical Office of Macedonia, Dame Gruev 4, 91000 Skopje; tel. (91) 230866; fax (91) 213311; *Yugoslav Survey*, Belgrade, POB 677, Moše Pijade 8/I; tel. (11) 333610; fax (11) 332295.

Area and Population

AREA, POPULATION AND DENSITY

Area (sq km)	25,713*
Population (census results)	
31 March 1981	1,909,136
31 March 1991	2,033,964
Density (per sq km) at census of 31 March 1991	79.1

* 9,928 sq miles.

PRINCIPAL TOWN (population at 1991 census): Skopje (capital) 563,301.

PRINCIPAL ETHNIC GROUPS (census results)

	1981	1991
Macedonians	1,279,323	1,314,283
Albanians	377,208	427,313
Turks	86,591	97,416
Romanies	43,125	55,575
Serbs	44,468	44,159
Muslims	39,513	35,256
Total (incl. others	1,909,136	2,033,964

Agriculture

PRINCIPAL CROPS
('000 metric tons, unless otherwise indicated)

	1990	1991	1992
Wheat	231	340	200*
Barley	74	164	98*
Maize	80	135	95*
Other cereals	47	62	50*
Potatoes	74	117	66*
Total pulses	18	25	17*
Sunflower seed	13	37	27†
Cabbages	55	62*	40*
Tomatoes	137	169	106*
Chillies and green peppers	89	88*	70*
Other vegetables	29	20†	14†
Water-melons	108	105*	85*
Grapes	193	264	191*
Apples	88	48	45†
Pears	17	15	22†
Plums	21	24	19*
Other fruit	34	26	17†
Walnuts	3,178	2,800	2,500*
Sugar beets	106	82	75*
Sugar (raw)	15†	13*	8†
Tobacco leaves	17	25	23†

* FAO estimate(s). † Unofficial figure(s).

Source: FAO, *Production Yearbook*.

LIVESTOCK ('000 head at 1 January)

	1990	1991	1992
Horses	66	66	48*
Cattle	288	287	282
Pigs	161	179	171
Sheep	2,496	2,297	2,250
Chickens	4,000†	5,000†	5,000*

* FAO estimate(s). † Unofficial figure(s).
Source: FAO, *Production Yearbook*.

LIVESTOCK PRODUCTS (metric tons)

	1990	1991	1992
Beef and veal	10,000	8,000*	8,000*
Mutton and lamb	14,000	13,000	13,000*
Pigmeat†	15,000	15,000	12,000
Cows' milk	127,000	123,000	99,000*
Sheeps' milk	58,000	62,000	41,000*
Cheese (all kinds)	1,149	1,240	1,100
Butter and ghee	21	15	10*
Hen eggs*	29,400	27,700	22,000
Honey	766	1,719†	1,130*
Wool:			
greasy	2,597	2,500	2,212†
scoured	1,559	1,484	1,327*
Cattle and buffalo hides*	1,926	1,800	1,465
Sheep skins*	1,284	1,264	1,144

* FAO estimate(s). † Unofficial figure(s).
Source: FAO, *Production Yearbook*.

Mining

('000 metric tons)

	1990
Coal	6,635

Industry

SELECTED PRODUCTS
('000 metric tons, unless otherwise stated)

	1990
Electric energy (million kWh)	5,755
Crude steel	504
Aluminium	6
Machines	3
Cement	639
Paper, cardboard and paperboard	43
Wine*	69

Wine (unofficial figures, '000 metric tons)*: 100 in 1991; 115 in 1992.
* Source: FAO, *Production Yearbook*.

Finance

CURRENCY AND EXCHANGE RATES

Monetary Units

100 deni = 1 new Macedonian denar.

Note: The Macedonian denar was introduced in April 1992, replacing (initially at par) the Yugoslav dinar. In May 1993 a new Macedonian denar, equivalent to 100 of the former units, was introduced. In February 1994 the exchange rate was US $1 = 47.5 new denars.

Directory

The Constitution

The Constitution of the Former Yugoslav Republic of Macedonia was promulgated on 17 November 1991. The following is a summary of the main provisions of the Constitution, which describes the country as the Republic of Macedonia:

GENERAL PROVISIONS

The Republic of Macedonia is a sovereign, independent, democratic state, where sovereignty derives from democratically elected citizens, referendums and other forms of expression. The fundamental values defined by the Constitution are: basic human rights, free expression of nationality, the rule of law, a policy of pluralism and the free market, local self-government, entrepreneurship, social justice and solidarity, and respect for international law. State power is divided into legislative, executive and judicial power.

BASIC RIGHTS

The following rights and freedoms are guaranteed and protected in the Republic: the right to life (the death penalty was abolished), the inviolability of man's physical and moral integrity, the right to freedom of speech, public appearance, public information, belief, conscience and religion, and the freedom to organize and belong to a trade union or a political party. All forms of communication and personal data are secret, and the home is inviolable.

Military and semi-military associations, which do not belong to the Armed Forces of the Republic, are prohibited.

Any citizen who has reached the age of 18 years has the right to vote and to be elected to organs of government. The right to vote is equal, general and direct, and is realized in free elections by secret ballot. Citizens enjoy equal freedoms and rights without distinction as to sex, race, colour, national and social origin, political and religious conviction, material and social position.

GOVERNMENT

Legislature

Legislative power resides with the Assembly (Sobranje), which consists of between 120 and 140 deputies elected for four years. The Sobranje adopts and amends the Constitution, enacts laws and gives interpretations thereof, adopts the budget of the Republic, decides on war and peace, chooses the Government, elects judges and releases them from duty. The Sobranje may decide, by a majority vote, to call a referendum on issues within its competence. A decision is adopted at a referendum if the majority of voters taking part in the vote has voted in favour of it and if more than one-half of the electorate has participated in the vote. The Sobranje forms a Council for Inter-Nationality Relations, consisting of the President of the Republic and two representatives from each of the ethnic Macedonian, Albanian, Turkish and Roma communities and two representatives of other nationalities living in the state.

President

The President of the Republic represents the country and is responsible for ensuring respect for the Constitution and laws. He is commander of the Armed Forces and appoints the Prime Minister, appoints and recalls ambassadors, proposes members for the Judicial Council, appoints three members of the Security Council of the Republic (of which he is president) and proposes members for the Council of Inter-Nationality Relations.

Ministers

Executive power in the Republic resides with the Prime Minister (Chairman of the Cabinet of Ministers) and Ministers, who cannot concurrently be deputies in the Sobranje. The Ministers are elected by the majority vote of all the deputies in the Sobranje. The Ministers implement laws and the state budget, and are responsible for foreign and diplomatic relations.

Judiciary

Judicial power is vested in the courts and is autonomous and independent. The Supreme Court is the highest court. The election and dismissal of judges is proposed by a Judicial Council. This body is composed of seven members, elected by the Sobranje from among the ranks of prominent lawyers.

The Government

(February 1994)

President of the Republic: KIRO GLIGOROV (elected by the Sobranje on 27 January 1991).

CABINET OF MINISTERS

A coalition of the Social Democratic Union of Macedonia (SDUM), the Party of Democratic Prosperity (PDP) and the People's Democratic Party, the Reform Forces of Macedonia—Liberal Party, and the Socialist Party of Macedonia (SPM).

Chairman (Prime Minister): BRANKO CRVENKOVSKI.

Deputy Chairmen: Dr BEĆIR ŽUTA, JOVAN ANDONOV.

Minister of Internal Affairs: Dr LJUBOMIR DANAILOV-FRČKOVSKI.

Minister of Defence: Dr VLADO POPOVSKI.

Minister of Foreign Relations: STEVO CRVENKOVSKI.

Minister of Justice: TUŠE GOŠEV.

Minister of the Economy: PETRUŠ STEFANOV.

Minister of Finance: DZEVDET HAJREDINI.

Minister of Health: Dr JOVAN TOFOVSKI.

Minister of Science: Dr ASLAN SELMANI.

Minister of Education and Physical Culture: DIMITAR BAJALDŽIEV.

Minister of Development: Dr SOFIA TODOROVA.

Minister of Urbanism, Civil Engineering, Traffic and Environment: (vacant).

Minister of Agriculture, Forestry and Water Resources Management: Dr EFTIM ANČEV.

Minister of Labour and Social Policy: ILIJAZ SABRIU.

Minister of Culture: GUNER ISMAIL.

Ministers without Portfolio: Dr JANE MILJOVSKI, Dr LJUBE TRPESKI, SERVET AVZIU, GORDANA SILJANOVSKA.

MINISTRIES

Office of the Prime Minister: 91000 Skopje, Dame Grueva 6; tel. (91) 201211; fax (91) 211393.

Ministry of Agriculture, Forestry and Water Resources Management: 91000 Skopje, Leninova 2; tel. (91) 113045; fax (91) 211997.

Ministry of Culture: 91000 Skopje, Veljko Vlahović bb; tel. (91) 220823; fax (91) 225810.

Ministry of Defence: 91000 Skopje, Dimče Mirčeva bb; tel. (91) 237373.

Ministry of Development: 91000 Skopje, Tiranska 2; tel. (91) 220678.

Ministry of the Economy: 91000 Skopje, Bihačka bb; tel. (91) 231259.

Ministry of Education and Physical Culture: 91000 Skopje, Veljko Vlahović bb; tel. (91) 223548.

Ministry of Finance: 91000 Skopje, Dame Grueva 14; tel. (91) 228411.

Ministry of Foreign Relations: 91000 Skopje, Dame Grueva bb; tel. (91) 236311.

Ministry of Health: 91000 Skopje, Dame Grueva 14; tel. (91) 228411.

Ministry of Internal Affairs: 91000 Skopje.

Ministry of Justice: 91000 Skopje, Veljko Vlahović bb; tel. (91) 223065.

Ministry of Labour and Social Policy: 91000 Skopje, Dame Grueva 14; tel. (91) 228411.

Ministry of Science: 91000 Skopje, Veljko Vlahović bb; tel. (91) 223574.

Ministry of Urbanism, Civil Engineering, Traffic and Environment: 91000 Skopje, Nikole Vapčarova bb; tel. (91) 239521.

Legislature

SOBRANJE

(Assembly)

President: STOJAN ANDOV, 91000 Skopje, 11 Oktomvri bb; tel. (91) 227111.

Elections, 11 and 25 November and 9 December 1990

Party	Seats
Internal Macedonian Revolutionary Organization-Democratic Party for Macedonian National Unity (IMRO-DPMNU)	37
League of Communists of Macedonia-Party for Democratic Reform (LCM-PDR)*	31
Party of Democratic Prosperity (PDP)	25†
Alliance of Reform Forces (ARF)	19‡
Socialist Party of Macedonia	4§
Party of Yugoslavs	1
Independents	3
Total	120

* The LCM-PDR subsequently was renamed the Social Democratic Union of Macedonia (SDUM).

† The PDP won 18 seats alone and seven in alliance with the People's Democratic Party.

‡ The ARF won 11 seats alone, six in alliance with the Young Democratic Progressive Party (YDPP) and two in alliance with the YDPP, the Socialist Party (which also won four alone) and the Roma Party. The ARF was subsequently renamed the Reform Forces of Macedonia—Liberal Party.

§ The Socialist Party of Macedonia was subsequently renamed the Socialist Alliance-Socialist Party of Macedonia, before reverting to its original name.

Political Organizations

Democratic Alliance of Serbs in the Former Yugoslav Republic of Macedonia: Skopje; f. 1994; Chair. BORA RISTIC.

Internal Macedonian Revolutionary Organization-Democratic Party for Macedonian National Unity (IMRO-DPMNU) (Vnatresna Makedonska Revolucionerna Organizacija-Demokratska Partija za Makedonsko Nacionalno Edinstvo—VMRO-DPMNE): 91000 Skopje, Petar Drapshin br. 36; tel. (91) 211586; fax (91) 111441; nationalist; Leader LJUPČO GEORGIEVSKI.

Party of Democratic Prosperity (PDP) (Partija za Demokratski Prosperitet): Tetovo, Dojce Stojcevski 14-a; tel. (94) 21380; f. 1990; predominantly ethnic Albanian and Muslim party; Chair. XHELADIN MURATI; Gen. Sec. MITHAT EMINI.

Party of Democratic Prosperity of the Albanians in the Former Yugoslav Republic of Macedonia: Tetovo; f. 1994 by Menduh Thaci in a split from the original PDP; Chair. ARBER XHAFERI.

People's Democratic Party: Tetovo, Gorna čaršija bb; tel. (94) 24604; f. 1990; predominantly ethnic Albanian and Muslim party; Gen.-Sec. ILJAZ HALILI.

Reform Forces of Macedonia—Liberal Party: Skopje, Ilinden bb; tel. (91) 213034; f. 1990 as republican br. of the all-Yugoslav Alliance of Reform Forces (ARF); name changed 1992; Pres. STOJAN ANDOV.

Social Democratic Union of Macedonia (SDUM) (Socijaldemokratski Sojuz na Makedonije—SDSM): 91000 Skopje, Bihačka 8; tel. (91) 231371; fax (91) 221071; f. 1943; name changed from League of Communists of Macedonia-Party of Democratic Reform in 1991; Sec. BLAGOJ HANDŽISKI.

Socialist Party of Macedonia (SPM): 91000 Skopje, Ilinden bb, POB 54; tel. (91) 228015; fax (91) 220025; f. 1990; left-wing.

Young Democratic Progressive Party (YDPP): 91000 Skopje, Ilinden bb; tel. (93) 89387; party of Yugoslav orientation; Pres. RISTO IVANOV.

Diplomatic Representation

EMBASSIES IN THE FORMER YUGOSLAV REPUBLIC OF MACEDONIA

Bulgaria: Skopje; Ambassador: ANGEL SIMEONOV DIMITROV.

France: Skopje.

Russia: Skopje; Ambassador: YURY PETROVICH.

Slovenia: 91000 Skopje, Partizanski odredi 3; tel. (91) 116213; fax (91) 220112; Chargé d'affaires: BORIS JELOVŠEK.

Turkey: Skopje; Ambassador: SUHA NOYAN.

United Kingdom: 91000 Skopje, Veljko Valković 26 (4th Floor); tel. (91) 116772; fax (91) 117005; Ambassador: STEPHEN NASH.

Judicial System

All courts in the former Yugoslav Republic of Macedonia are within the jurisdiction of the Ministry of Justice.

Constitutional Court of the Republic of Macedonia: 91000 Skopje, 12 Udarnas brig. bb; tel. (91) 233063; Pres. JORDAN ARSOV.

Supreme Court: 91000 Skopje, Borisa Kidriča bb; tel. (91) 234111; Pres. TIHOMIR VELKOVSKI.

Office of the Public Prosecutor: 91000 Skopje, Krste Misirkova bb; tel. (91) 229314; Public Prosecutor MARKO BUNDALEVSKI.

Religion

Most ethnic Macedonians are adherents of the Eastern Orthodox Church and, since 1967, there has been an autocephalous Macedonian Orthodox Church. However, the Serbian Church refuses to recognize it and has persuaded the Ecumenical Patriarch and other Orthodox Churches not to do so either. There are some adherents of other Orthodox rites in the country. Those Macedonian (and Bulgarian) Slavs who converted to Islam during the Ottoman era are known as Pomaks and are included as an ethnic group of Muslims. The substantial Albanian population is mostly Muslim (mainly Sunni, but some adherents of a Dervish sect); there are a few Roman Catholic Christians and some Jews.

CHRISTIANITY

Macedonian Orthodox Church: Skopje, POB 69; Metropolitan See of Ohrid revived in 1958; autocephaly declared 1967; 1m. mems; Head of Church and Archbishop of Ohrid and Macedonia: Metropolitan MIHAIL of Debar and Kičevo.

The Roman Catholic Church

The diocese of Skopje-Prizren, suffragan to the archdiocese of Vrhbosna (Bosnia and Herzegovina), includes Macedonia and southern Yugoslavia (the Kosovo region of Serbia). At 31 December 1991 there were 65,100 adherents. Most adherents followed the Latin Rite, although there were a few adherents to the Byzantine Rite.

Bishop of Skopje-Prizren: JOAKIM HERBUT, 91000 Skopje, Dimitrije Tucović 31; tel. (91) 234123.

ISLAM

Islamic Community: Skopje; formerly headquarters of the Skopje Region, one of the four administrative divisions of the Yugoslav Muslims.

The Press

PRINCIPAL NEWSPAPERS

Birlik: 91000 Skopje, Mito Hadživasilev bb; tel. (91) 116366; fax (91) 111146; f. 1944; Turkish-language newspaper; Editor-in-Chief DRITA KARAHASAN.

Flaka e Vellazerimit: 91000 Skopje, Mito Hadživasilev bb; tel. (91) 112095; fax (91) 224829; f. 1945; Albanian-language newspaper; Editor-in-Chief ABDULIADI ZULFIĆARI.

Nova Makedonija: 91000 Skopje, Mito Hadživasilev bb; tel. (91) 113586; telex 51154; fax (91) 119416; f. 1944; daily; morning; in Macedonian; Dir PANDE KOLEMOŠEVSKI; Editor-in-Chief GEORGI AJANOVSKI; circ. 25,000.

Puls: 91000 Skopje, Mito Hasživasilev bb; tel. (91) 117479; f. 1991; Editor-in-Chief VASIL MICKOVSKI.

Večer: 91000 Skopje, Mito Hadživasilev bb; tel. (91) 111537; telex 51154; fax (91) 238329; f. 1963; daily; evening; in Macedonian; Editor-in-Chief STOJAN NASEV; circ. 29,200.

PERIODICALS

21: 71000 Skopje, Ilinden bb; 2 a month; organ of the Social Democratic Union of Macedonia.

Delo: Skopje; f. 1993; weekly; nationalist.

Puls: Skopje; weekly; Editor-in-Chief SLOBOJAN PETROVIĆ.

Republika: Skopje; weekly.

Trudbenik: Skopje, Udarna brigada 12; weekly; organ of Macedonian Trade Unions; Editor SIMO IVANOVSKI.

NEWS AGENCIES

Makfaks: Skopje.

Tanjug News Agency (Yugoslavia): Skopje; Dir-Gen. IVAN MARKOVIĆ.

Publishers

Detska Radost/Nova Makedonija: 91000 Skopje, Mito Hadživasilev Jasmin bb; tel. (91) 228757; fax (91) 225830; f. 1944; children's books; Dir PETAR BAKEVSKI.

Kultura: 91000 Skopje, JNA 68A; tel. (91) 220821; fax (91) 239772; f. 1945; history, philosophy, art, poetry, children's literature and fiction; in Macedonian; Dir DIMITAR BAŠEVSKI.

Kulturen život: 91000 Skopje, Ruzveltova 6; tel. (91) 239134; f. 1911; Editor LJUBICA ARSOVSKA.

Makedonska knjiga: 91000 Skopje, 11 oktomvri bb; tel. (91) 224055; telex 51637; fax (91) 236951; f. 1947; arts, non-fiction, novels, children's books; Dir SANDE STOJČEVSKI.

Matica Makedonska: 91000 Skopje, Gradski sid 13; tel. and fax (91) 421000; f. 1991; Dir RADE SILJAN.

Metatorum: 91000 Skopje, Goce Delčev 6; tel. (91) 114890; fax (91) 115634; f. 1993; Dir RUŽICA BILKO.

Misla: 91000 Skopje, Partizanski odredi 1; tel. (91) 211619; fax (91) 118439; f. 1966; modern and classic Macedonian and translated literature; Dir VANČO SPASOVSKI.

Naša kniga: 91000 Skopje, Maksim Gorki 21, POB 132; tel. (91) 228066; fax (91) 116872; f. 1948; Dir STOJAN LEKOVSKI.

Prosvetno delo: 91000 Skopje, Veljko Vlahović 15; tel. (91) 228022; fax (91) 225434; f. 1945; works of domestic writers and textbooks in Macedonian for elementary, professional and high schools; fiction and scientific works; Dir Dr KRSTE ANGELOVSKI.

Tabernakul: 91000 Skopje, Kosturska niz 4–5; tel. and fax (91) 115329; f. 1989; Dir CVETAN VRADŽIVIRSKI.

Radio and Television

Macedonian Radio and Television (Makedonska Radio-Televizija—MRT): 91000 Skopje, Goce Delčev bb; tel. (91) 112200; telex 51157; fax (91) 111821; f. 1944 (Radio), 1964 (TV), renamed 1991; 3 radio and 3 TV programmes; broadcasts in Macedonian, Albanian and Turkish; Dir-Gen. TIHOMIR ILIEVSKI; Dir of Radio SLOBODAN ČAŠULE; Dir of TV SLOBODAN TRAJKOVSKI.

In the early 1990s there were 30 radio stations in the Former Yugoslav Republic of Macedonia.

Finance

The Former Yugoslav Republic of Macedonia declared monetary independence in April 1992, introducing its own currency (in coupon form), the Macedonian denar (initially at par with the Yugoslav dinar; in May 1993 a new Macedonian denar, equivalent to 100 of the former units, was introduced).

(a.d. = joint-stock company; cap. = capital; dep. = deposits; res = reserves; m. = million; amounts in convertible Macedonian denars; brs = branches)

BANKS

National Bank

National Bank of Macedonia: 91000 Skopje, Kompleks banki bb; tel. (91) 230111; Gov. BORKO STANOEVSKI.

Selected Banks

Komercijalna Banka a.d.–Skopje: 91000 Skopje, Kej Dimitar Vlahov 4; tel. (91) 112077; telex 51162; fax (91) 113494; f. 1955; cap. 537m., res 146m., dep. 2,316m., total assets 3,357m. (Dec. 1992); Gen. Man. Dr ALEKSANDAR MANEVSKI.

Stopanska Banka a.d.—Skopje: 91000 Skopje, 11 Oktomvri 7; tel. (91) 115322; telex 51140; fax (91) 226576; f. 1944; cap. 100.4m., res 9.8m., dep. 742.6m. (Dec. 1992); Gen. Man. and Chief Exec. LJUBOMIR POPOVSKI; 8 brs.

Trade and Industry

Chamber of Economy of Macedonia: 91000 Skopje, Ivo R. Lola 25; tel. (91) 229211; Pres. DUŠAN PETRESKI.

MAJOR INDUSTRIAL ENTERPRISES AND COMPANIES

Alumina: 91000 Skopje, Ivo R. Lola 164; tel. (91) 116422; telex 51149; fax (91) 116876; aluminium products; Gen. Dir VASIL KOSTOJČINOSKI; 1,595 employees.

Biljana: 97500 Prilep, Krusevski pat bb; tel. (98) 21140; telex 53165; fax (98) 24107; carded yarn, sanitary products, absorbent cotton, knitwear and ready-made clothing; Gen. Dir BLAGOJA PORJAZOVSKI; 1,800 employees.

Brako: 91400 Veles, Novi Veles 12; tel. (93) 26655; telex 53449; fax (93) 23210; main areas of activity incl. caravans, boat trailers, beekeepers' trailers, etc.; Dir DORDI MANČEVSKI; 650 employees.

Bucim Co—Enterprise for Mining and Metallurgy of Copper: 92420 Radovis; tel. (902) 61113; telex 53661; fax (902) 61119; mining of copper, gold and silver; manufacture of gold and silver jewellery; Gen. Man. VANCO CIFLIGANEE.

Hemteks: 91000 Skopje, Kosta Novakovik 12; tel. (91) 429112; telex 51489; fax (91) 161289; f. 1974; production of polyester fibre; Dep. Gen. Man. MIŠEV GJOKO; Commercial Man. JANČEVSKI GJORGJI; 750 employees.

Jugotutun: 91000 Skopje, Makedonska Udarna brig., 111; tel. (91) 237133; telex 51462; fax (91) 231114; responsible for a group of 31 mem. enterprises engaged in the tobacco industry.

Karpos: 91330 Kriva Palanka, Maršal Tito 7; tel. (901) 75201; telex 51245; fax (901) 74335; decorative upholstery products and taffeta fabrics; Gen. Dir RUSE DIMOVSKI.

Makpetrol Co: 91000 Skopje, POB 537, Mito Hadživasilev Jasmin bb 4; tel. (91) 230311; telex 51129; fax (91) 213377; import and export of petroleum products; Gen. Dir GAVRILO GAVRILSKI; 2,203 employees.

Metalski Zavod 'Tito': 91000 Skopje, Pero Nakov bb; tel. (91) 223111; telex 51151; fax (91) 233252; mechanical engineering industry; 9,114 employees.

Organsko Hemijska Industrija—OHIS: 91000 Skopje, Provmajska bb; tel. (91) 233111; telex 51487; fax (91) 211489; manufactures polyacrylonitrillic fibre, PVC powder, etc.; Man. Dir JORGO ČUKA; 5,774 employees.

Pelister-Bitola: 97000 Bitola, Devejani 13; tel. (97) 34544; telex 53146; fax (97) 38209; manufactures clothing; Gen. Dir DIMITAR STOJANOVSKI; 900 employees.

Rafinerija na Nafte, Skopje: 91000 Skopje, POB 66; tel. (91) 239511; telex 51366; fax (91) 236920; production of gasoline, diesel fuel, fuel oil, automobile gasoline and LPG; Gen. Dir VANGEL ARANUTOV; 1,432 employees.

Rik Sileks: Kratovo, Goce Delčev; tel. (901) 81188; telex 51345; fax (901) 81700; mining, industry, agriculture, construction, trade, tourism and hotel management; Gen. Man. LJUPČO IVANOVSKI; 3,160 employees.

Rudnici i Zelezarnica Skopje (Skopje Mines and Iron Works): 91000 Skopje, POB 54; tel. (91) 221076; telex 51136; fax (91) 221257; engaged in all stages, from iron ore mining to production of steel sheets and related products; 11,000 employees.

Ruen a.d. Industrija za Avtomobilski delovi i Traktori: Kočani, 29 Novri 32; tel. (903) 21600; telex 53644; fax (903) 21223; f. 1952; production of clutches and metal goods for all types of vehicles; Dir IVAN IVANOV; 1,500 employees.

Technometal-Vardar Export-Import: 91000 Skopje, Veljko Vlahović 11; tel. (91) 229411; telex 51453; fax (91) 113435; exports and imports metals, metal products and chemical products, machinery, vehicles and other consumer goods; Gen. Man. MILORAD ANTEVSKI; 1,000 employees.

Toranica: Palanka; tel. (901) 75478; telex 51343; fax (901) 74280; manufactures lead-zinc concentrate; Gen. Dir DUSKO ARSOVSKI.

Treska: 91000 Skopje, Ive Lole Ribara 130; tel. (91) 223222; telex 54481; timber industry and wood-working; 10,000 employees.

Zletovo—Sasa: 91000 Skopje, Partizanski odredi 18; tel. (91) 230322; telex 51199; fax (91) 211730; trading co founded by a group of zinc-mining companies; Gen. Dir TITO TRENESKI.

Transport

RAILWAYS

Owing to the economic blockade against the Federal Republic of Yugoslavia (FRY—Serbia and Montenegro), in force from September 1992, Macedonia had suspended its freight railway traffic with the rest of Europe. In September 1993 it was announced by Germany that the Munich-Athens international train link via Skopje was to be suspended. This was Macedonia's last passenger railway link with central and western Europe.

Macedonian Railways: Skopje.

ROADS

In February 1994 plans were announced for the construction of a 1,000-km highway between Istanbul (Turkey) and Durrës (Albania) via Skopje.

CIVIL AVIATION

Avioimpex: Skopje.

Palair Macedonian Airlines: Skopje; f. 1991; domestic services and flights to the USA, Canada and Australia.

Tourism

While part of the Yugoslav federation, tourism was a major source of foreign exchange in Macedonia. However, since gaining independence in 1991, the tourist industry has declined, largely owing to the country's proximity to the conflict in the former Yugoslavia, its struggle to gain international recognition, the country's domestic instability and the intermittent sanctions imposed on the region by Greece. Nevertheless, Macedonia has a mountain climate which is moderated by Mediterranean influences and possesses some spectacular mountain scenery, which contribute to a considerable potential for the tourism industry should regional problems be eased.

Culture

NATIONAL ORGANIZATIONS

Ministry of Culture: see section on The Government (Ministries).

Committee for Education, Culture and Physical Culture: 91000 Skopje, Veljko Vlahović 9; tel. (91) 223411; fax (91) 220859.

Cultural and Information Centre (Kulturno-Informativni Centar): 91000 Skopje, Moše Pijade bb; tel. (91) 236724; Dir OLGA POPOVSKA.

Republican Institute for the Protection of Cultural Monuments of Macedonia (Republički Zavod za Zaštita na Spomenicite na Kulturata): 91000 Skopje, Evlija Celebija bb; tel. (91) 116465; fax (91) 227240; f. 1949; Dir JOVAN RISTOV.

CULTURAL HERITAGE

Archaeological Museum of Macedonia (Arheološki muzej na Makedonija): 91000 Skopje, Kuršumli An; tel. (91) 116044; f. 1924; library of 5,700 vols; Dir DRAGIŠA ZDRAVKOVSKI.

Archives of Macedonia (Arhiv na Macedonia): 91000 Skopje, Grigor Prličev 3; tel. (91) 116571; fax (91) 115827; f. 1950; Dir KIRO DOJČINOVSKI.

Art Gallery (Umetnička Galerija): 91000 Skopje, Kruševska 1A; tel. (91) 233904; f. 1948; Dir DRAGAN BOŠNAKOVSKI.

Ethnological Museum (Etnološki muzej na Makedonija): 91000 Skopje, Evlija Celebija bb; f. 1949; Dir MARIJA HADŽI PECEVA.

Institute of Folklore (Institut za Folklor): 91000 Skopje, Ruzveltova 3, POB 319; tel. (91) 233876; f. 1950; Principal Officer Dr BLAGOJ STOIČOVSKI.

Institute for the Protection of Cultural Monuments in Macedonia (Zavod za Zaštita na Spomenicite na Kulturata): 91000 Skopje, Makarie Frčkovski br. 8, POB 328; tel. (91) 233812; f. 1963; Dir ŽIVKO GELEVSKI.

International Colony of Art—Prilep (Medjunaroda kolonja na sovermena umetnost vo Prilep): 98000 Prilep, Kičevsko džada bb; tel. (98) 25788; Dir BORISLAV KONESKI.

International Colony of Contemporary Art—Strumica (Medjunaroda kolonja na sovermena umetnost vo Strumica): Strumica, Dom na kulturata 'Blagoj Jankov'; tel. (92) 22788; f. 1964.

Kliment Ohridski National University Library: 91000 Skopje, Goce Delčev 6; tel. (91) 115177; fax (91) 230874; f. 1944; Dir VERA KALAJILIEVA.

Museum of Contemporary Art (Muzej na Sovremena Umetnost): 91000 Skopje, Samuilova bb, POB 482; tel. (91) 117734; f. 1964; Dir ZORAN PETROVSKI.

Museum of Skopje (Muzej na Grad Skopje): 91000 Skopje, Mito Hadživasilev bb; tel. (91) 115367; f. 1949; Dir KLIME KOROBAR.

Pane Georgievski National Library (Narodna Biblioteka Pane Georgievski): 91300 Kumanovo, Narodna revolucija 1; tel. (901) 21415; f. 1945; Dir NADA TVANOVSKA.

World Gallery of Caricatures (Svetaka galeriya na karikatura): 91000 Skopje, Mito Hadživasilev bb, POB 383; tel. and fax (91) 235051; f. 1969; Dir ANE VASILEVSKI.

Youth Cultural Centre–Skopje (Mladinski Kulturen Centar–Skopje): 91000 Skopje, Kej Dimitar Vlahov bb; tel. (91) 115225; fax (91) 115906; f. 1972; Dir GOCE DIMOVSKI.

PERFORMING ARTS

Theatre

Drama Theatre (Dramski Teatar): 91000 Skopje, Šekspirova 15; tel. (91) 250005; fax (91) 256598; f. 1965; Dir BLAGOJA ČOREVSKI.

Macedonian National Theatre (Makedonski Naroden Teater–Drama): 91000 Skopje, Dimitar Vlahov bb; tel. (91) 114511; fax (91) 114060; f. 1945; Gen. Dir SLAVKO MINOV.

Macedonian National Theatre (Opera and Ballet): 91000 Skopje, Bitpazarska bb; tel. (91) 114691; Dir LJUPČO PETRUŠEVSKI.

Pralipe Drama Group: 91000 Skopje, Kej Dimitar Vlahov bb; tel. (91) 230041.

Theatre for Children and Youth–Skopje (Teatar za Deca i Mladinci–Skopje): 91000 Skopje, POB 169, JNA bb; tel. (91) 222619; fax (91) 223118; f. 1989; Dir LJUBOMIR ČIKOVSKI.

Theatre of Minority (Teatar na Narodnostite): 91000 Skopje, Nikola Martinovski 41; tel. (91) 111017; fax (91) 222570; f. 1950; Dir Turkish Drama SALADIN BILAL; Dir Albanian Drama SEFEDIN NUREDINI.

Youth Open Theatre (Mlad otoveren teatar): c/o Youth Cultural Centre, 91000 Skopje, Kej Dimitar Vlahov bb; tel. (91) 111508; fax (91) 115906; f. 1975.

Music

International Jazz Festival of Skopje (Internacionalen Skopje džez festival): c/o Youth Cultural Centre, 91000 Skopje, Kej Dimitar Vlahov bb; tel. (91) 111508; fax (91) 115906; f. 1980.

Macedonian Philharmonic Orchestra (Makedonska Filharmonija): 91000 Skopje, JNA bb; tel. (91) 118450; fax (91) 235753; f. 1944; Chief Conductor FIMCO MURATOVSKI; Dir MELPOMENI KORNETI.

Macedonian Radio and Television Choir (Hor na Makedonskata Radio-Televizija–MRT): 91000 Skopje, Nov dom na MRT; tel. (91) 227205; Chief Conductor DRAGAN ŠUPLEVSKI.

May Opera Evenings (Majski operski večeri): 91000 Skopje, POB 153, MRT Kej Dimitar Vlahov bb; tel. (91) 114908; fax (91) 114060; f. 1973.

Skopje MRT Big Band (Plesni Orkestar MRT Skopje): 91000 Skopje, Nov dom na MRT; tel. (91) 227205; Chief Conductor ALEKSANDAR DZAMBAZOV.

Skopje MRT Chamber Orchestra (Kamerni Orkestar MRT Skopje): 91000 Skopje, Nov dom na MRT; tel. (91) 227205.

Film

Film Library of Macedonia (Kinoteka): 91000 Skopje, Goce Delčev bb; tel. (91) 228064; fax (91) 220062; organizes an annual international film festival; f. 1976.

Horizont Film: 91000 Skopje, Ruzveltova 2–8; tel. (91) 111110; f. 1993; private production company; Dir ANTONIO MITRIČEVSKI.

Macedonia Film: 91000 Skopje, POB 534, Nikola Vapoarov 7; tel. (91) 118614; fax (91) 118065; f. 1947; Dir DOBRI BOŠKOVSKI.

Pegas: 91000 Skopje, 8-mi Mart 4; tel. (91) 117038; production company; f. 1991; Dir PANTA MIŽIMAKOV.

Triangle: 91000 Skopje, Tetovska 35; tel. and fax (91) 232178; f. 1989; private production and distribution company; Dir DANČO ČEVREVSKI.

Vardar Film: 91000 Skopje, 8-mi Mart 4; tel. (91) 227674; f. 1947; production company; Dir METO PETROVSKI.

ASSOCIATIONS

Albanian Cultural Association: Tetovo; aims to preserve and foster language and culture of ethnic Albanians in Macedonia.

Association of Folklorists of Macedonia (Združenie na Folkloristite na Makedonija): Institut za folklor, 91000 Skopje, Ruzveltova 3; tel. (91) 233876; f. 1952; Pres. GORGI SMOKVARSKI; Sec. ERMIS LAFAZANOVSKY.

Association of Sciences and Arts (Društvo za nauka i umetnost): 97000 Bitola, POB 145; tel. (97) 22683; f. 1960; Pres. SOTIR PANOVSKI; Sec.-Gen. TRAJKO OGENOVSKI.

Egyptian Association of Citizens: Ohrid; f. 1990; group who reject Roma ethnicity and claim to be Egipcani or Egyptians; allowed separate registration in Macedonian census of 1991; Leader NAZIM ARIFI.

Macedonian-Turkish Friendship and Co-operation Society: Skopje; f. 1994; promotes friendly relations between Macedonia and Turkey through culture, trade, science, art, tourism and sport.

Phralipe (Brotherhood–Roma Union of Macedonia): 91000 Skopje, Suto Orizari; f. 1948; cultural asscn of the Roma (Gypsies).

Society of Literary Translators of Macedonia (Društvo na leteraturnite preveduvači na Makedonija): 91000 Skopje, POB 3; f. 1955; Pres. ILIJA KORUBIN; Sec. TAŠKO ŠIRILOV.

Society of Composers of Macedonia (Društvo na Kompozitorite na Makedonija): 91000 Skopje, Maksim Gorki 18; tel. (91) 220567; fax (91) 235854; f. 1947; Pres. VLASTIMIR NIKOLOVSKI; Sec. MARKO KOLOVSKI; 49 mems.

Society of Caricaturists of Macedonia (Združenie na karikaturistite na Makedonija): 91000 Skopje, Mito Hadživasilev bb, POB 530; tel. (91) 116366; f. 1980; Pres. ANE VASILEVSKI; 40 mems.

Society of Film Workers of Macedonia (Društvo na filmski rabotnici na Makedonija): 91000 Skopje, 8-mi mart br 4; tel. (91) 211811; f. 1950; Pres. METO PETROVSKI; 82 mems.

Society of Musical Artists of Macedonia (Združenie na muzička umetnici na Makedonija): 91000 Skopje, Maksim Gorki 18; tel. (91) 220567; fax (91) 235854; f. 1947; Pres. MILAN FIRFOV; 62 mems.

Society of Plastic Arts of Macedonia (Društvo na Likovnite Umetnike na Makedonija): 91000 Skopje, 13 Noemvri bb, POB 438; f. 1946; Pres. GLIGOR ČEMERSKI; Sec. BRANISLAV MIRČEVSKI; 333 mems.

Society of Writers of Macedonia (Društvo na Pisatelite na Makedonija): 91000 Skopje, Maksim Gorki 18; tel. (91) 117668; fax (91) 228345; f. 1947; protection of authors' rights and promotion of Macedonian literature; Pres. JOVAN PAVLOVSKI; Secs VELE SMILEVSKI, BRANKO CVETKOVSKI; 194 mems.

Union of Associations for Macedonian Language and Literature (Sojuz na Društvata za Makedonski Jakiz i Literatura): Filoški fakultet, 91000 Skopje, Krste Misirkov bb; f. 1954; Pres. KIRIL KONESKI; Sec. VANČO TUŠEVSKI; 700 mems.

Education

Elementary education is free and compulsory for all children between the ages of seven and 15. Various types of secondary school are available to those who qualify. There are Albanian-language schools. In 1993 a Serb-language school was opened in Skopska Crna Gora, an area to the north of Skopje.

UNIVERSITIES

University of Bitola (Univerzitet Bitolj): 97000 Bitola, 1 Maj bb; tel. (97) 23788; f. 1979; Rector Prof. Dr DAME NESTOROVSKI.

University of Skopje (Univerzitet 'Sv. Kiril I Metódij'): 91000 Skopje, POB 576, Krste Misirkov bb; tel. (91) 116323; fax (91) 116370; f. 1949; state-controlled; 19 faculties, 1,037 teachers, 23,746 students; Rector Prof. Dr TOMISLAV ČOKREVSKI.

Social Welfare

While Macedonia formed part of the former Yugolsav federation, the region enjoyed the same welfare provisions as the rest of the country. There was an obligatory social insurance scheme for anyone in employment and their families, which provided for health insurance, money payments and grants, in case of sickness, accident, disability and old age. All workers were entitled to annual leave, which varied between 18 and 36 days. In the 1980s the Republics assumed increasing responsibility for social welfare, for which Macedonia, following its independence in 1991, assumed total responsibility. Thereafter, resources were more severely restricted.

Ministry of Health: see section on The Government (Ministries).

Ministry of Social Security: see section on The Government (Ministries).

The Environment

GOVERNMENT ORGANIZATIONS

Ministry of Agriculture, Forestry and Water Resources Management: see section on The Government (Ministries).

Ministry of Urbanism, Civil Engineering, Traffic and Environment: see section on The Government (Ministries).

Central Institute for Safety at Work and Environmental Protection: 91000 Skopje, 13 November Quay, Bldg I/1; tel. (91) 115398; fax (91) 229706; Dir DIMCE ISJANOVSKI.

Institute for the Protection of Natural Rarities: 91000 Skopje, Rudžer Boškovič bb; tel. (91) 251133; research on natural rarities, education; Dir VASIL ANASTASOVSKI (acting).

Macedonian Public Health Institute: 91000 Skopje, 50-ta Divizija 6; tel. and fax (91) 223354; Dir Dr DANAIL SIMOVSKI.

The Ministries of Development and of Foreign Relations are also concerned with environmental matters.

ACADEMIC INSTITUTES

Macedonian Academy of Sciences and Arts (Makedonska Akademija na Naukite i Umetnostite): 91000 Skopje, Krste Misirkov bb, POB 428; tel. (91) 114200; fax (91) 115903; f. 1967; Pres. Acad. KSENTE BOGOEV.

Institute of Engineering and Scientific Societies and Unions of Macedonia: 91000 Skopje, Dame Gruev 14A, IT House, POB 139; tel. (91) 229040; conferences and seminars in the fields of engineering, technical sciences, architecture, agriculture, environmental matters and ecology; Pres. Prof. G. M. DIMIROVSKI.

Institute of Occupational Medicine: 91000 Skopje, II Makedonska Brigada Br. 43; tel. and fax (91) 264805; monitoring of the environment and assessment of the effects of the environment on human health; Principal Officers Prof. VLADIMIR CVETANOV, Prof. ELISAVETA STIKOVA, Prof. JOVANKA BISLIMOVSKA.

Macedonian Hydrometeorological Institute: 91000 Skopje, Skuppi bb; tel. (91) 363299; telex 51392; fax (91) 226839; environmental conservation (air, water, chemical pollution statistics); Principal Officers VITOMIR DIMITROVSKI, ILIJA PANOVSKI, SLAVKO KIROVSKI, ZORAN KARAMANOLEVSKI.

Water Development Institute of Macedonia (Zavod za vodostopanstvo): 91000 Skopje, Zeleznička 62, POB 310; tel. (91) 228028; fax (91) 239401; f. 1952; publication of *Water Development Problems* (Vodostopanski problemi); research in water development, ecology, applied hydraulics and erosion; Dir Ing. METODI BOEV.

NON-GOVERNMENTAL ORGANIZATIONS

Ecological Movement of Macedonia (DEM): 91000 Skopje, Ilinden bb, POB 558; tel. (91) 220518; fax (91) 117612; co-operation with Macedonian environmental non-governmental organizations; Principal Officers Dr JOSIF TANEVSKI, Prof. PANDORA NIKUŠEVA, Prof. MIHAIL TOKAREV.

Flora Environmental Association: Kriva Palanka, M. Tito bb; tel. (901) 75131; environmental conservation; Principal Officer Dr GORGI KEROVSKI.

Forum of Young Ecologists of Macedonia (FOYEC): 91000 Skopje, Ilinden bb, Block 12; tel. (91) 234373; fax (91) 116545; environmental education for young people; Pres. MARJAN MADŽOVSKI; Vice-Pres. KATERINA CVETKOVSKA.

Horticultural Society of Macedonia: 91000 Skopje, Dame Gruev 14; tel. (91) 229040; education in horticulture, urban ecosystems and environmental protection; Principal Officer BILJANA ALEKSIEVSKA.

Macedonian Ecologists' Society: 91000 Skopje, Gazi Baba bb, POB 162; tel. (91) 261330; Principal Officers Dr LJUPČO GRUPČE, LJUPČO MELOVSKI.

Macedonian Independent Association for Environmental Protection: 91000 Skopje, Ilindenska bb; tel. (91) 239470; environmental conservation; Principal Officers JELENA DIMITRIJEVIĆ, STEFANKA HADŽIPECOVA.

Macedonian Union of Clean Air Associations: 91000 Skopje, Dame Gruev 14; tel. (91) 231307; telex 51119; fax (91) 117163; monitoring of air quality, gas emissions and meteorological effects of air pollution; Principal Officers NIKOLA SRBINOVSKI, SLAVČO NOČEV.

Survival Ecological Association: 91000 Skopje, Ilinden bb; tel. (91) 220518; fax (91) 117612; monitoring of air and water pollution and industrial and urban pollution in the Skopje region; forestation; environmental education; Principal Officers SVETO STEFANOVSKI, VASILKA CVETKOVSKA, PERO STOJČEVSKI.

Defence

In June 1993, according to Western estimates, the Macedonian Armed Forces totalled 10,400 men, including 8,000 conscripts, although the recruitment of 100,000 reserves was planned. Conscription was introduced in April 1992; it lasts for nine months. The army possessed no heavy weaponry. The air force numbered 50 men, yet, although the authorities planned to purchase helicopters, there were no aircraft. There was no navy.

Chief of Staff of the Macedonian Army: Maj.-Gen. DRAGOLJUB BOCINOV.

Bibliography

Balkan Forum: An International Journal of Politics, Economics and Culture. Vol. 1, No 1. November 1992.

Barker, E. *Macedonia: Its Place in Balkan Power Politics.* Westport, Connecticut, Greenwood Press, 1980.

Bridge, F. R. (Ed.). *Austro-Hungarian Documents Relating to the Macedonian Struggle.* Thessaloníki, Institute for Balkan Studies, 1976.

Errington, R. *A History of Macedonia.* Berkeley, California, University of California Press, 1990.

Institute for Balkan Studies. *Macedonia, Past and Present: Reprints from 'Balkan Studies'.* Thessaloníki, 1992.

Pribichevich, S. *Macedonia, its People and History.* University Park, Pennsylvania, Pennsylvania State University Press, 1982.

Sowards, S. *Austria's Policy of Macedonian Reform.* Boulder, Colorado, East European Monographs, 1989.

Troebst, S. *Die bulgarisch-jugoslawische Kontroverse um Makedonien 1967–1982.* Munich, R. Oldenbourg, 1983.

Vakalopoulos, A. *History of Macedonia, 1354–1833.* Thessaloníki, Institute for Balkan Studies, 1973.

Vukmanovic-Tempo, S. *Struggle for the Balkans.* London, Merlin Press, 1990.

Wyzan, M. *First Steps to Economic Independence in Macedonia.* Stockholm, Stockholm Institute of Soviet and Eastern European Economics (Östekonomiska Institutet), 1992.

MOLDOVA

Geography

PHYSICAL FEATURES

The Republic of Moldova (formerly the Moldovan Soviet Socialist Republic, a constituent Union Republic of the USSR), is situated in south-eastern Europe. It includes only a small proportion of the historical territories of Moldova (Moldavia), most of which are in Romania, while others (southern Bessarabia and Northern Bucovina—Bukovyna) are in Ukraine. The country is bounded to the north, east and south by Ukraine. To the west there is a frontier with Romania. Moldova covers an area of 33,700 sq km (13,010 sq miles).

Moldova is a fertile plain with small areas of hill country in the centre and north of the country. The main rivers are the Dnestr (Dniestr or Dniester), which flows through the eastern regions into the Black Sea, and the Prut (Prutul), which marks the western border with Romania. The Prut joins the Dunărea (Danube) at the southern tip of Moldova.

CLIMATE

The climate is very favourable for agriculture, with long, warm summers and relatively mild winters. Average temperatures in Chişinău range from 21°C (70°F) in July to −4°C (24°F) in January.

POPULATION

At the census of 1989, at which the total population was 4,335,360, 64.5% of the population were Moldovans (ethnic Romanians), 13.8% Ukrainians, 13.0% Russians, 3.5% Gagauz, 2.0% Jews and 1.5% Bulgarians. The ethnic Moldovans speak a dialect of Romanian, a Romance language, which replaced Russian as the official language in 1989. It is now mostly written in the Latin alphabet; in 1941 the Cyrillic script had been introduced and the language referred to as 'Moldovan'. Ethnic minorities continue to use their own languages; only some 12% of them are fluent in Romanian, whereas most speak Russian. The Gagauz speak a Turkic language, written in the Cyrillic script, but 71% of them claim fluency in Russian; only 4.4% are fluent in Romanian.

Most of the inhabitants of Moldova professed Christianity, the largest denomination being the Eastern Orthodox Church. The Gagauz, despite their Turkish origins, were adherents of Orthodox Christianity. The Russian Orthodox Church (Moscow Patriarchate) had jurisdiction in Moldova, but there were Romanian and Turkish liturgies.

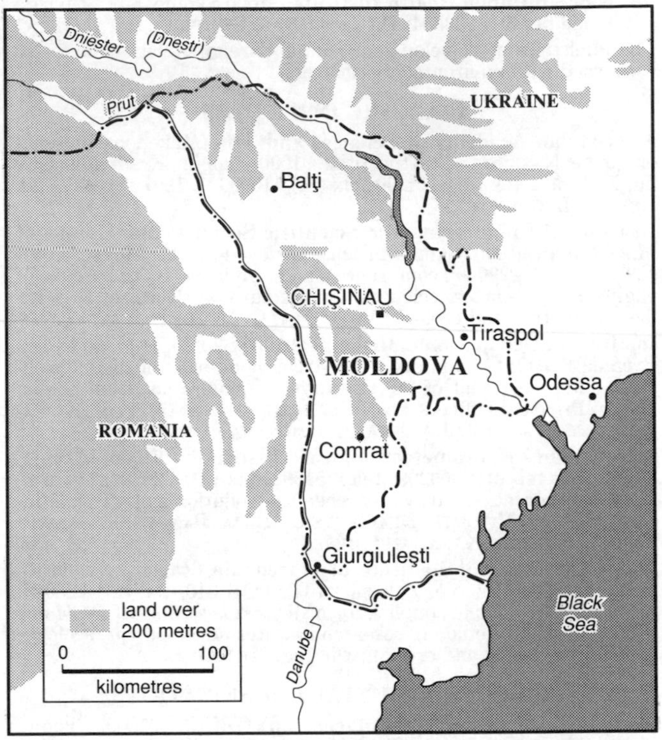

The total population at mid-1992 was an estimated 4,356,100. The population density at the same time was 129.3 per sq km. The capital is Chişinău (Kishinev), which is situated in the central region of the Republic. It had a population of 676,000 in 1990. Other important centres are the northern town of Bălţi (Beltsy—population in 1990, 162,000) and Tiraspol (184,000), which is situated on the east bank of the Dnestr, where a majority of the population were ethnic Slavs. The Gagauz mostly inhabit the southern districts, especially the region around the town of Comrat (Komrat).

Chronology

106: Emperor Trajan made Dacia a province of the Roman Empire (by 118 Rome had secured its hegemony over an area including much of modern Moldova).

270: Rome abandoned Dacia to Visigothic invaders, the first of many incursions by peoples from the north and east.

***c.* 1359:** According to tradition, a Transylvanian prince, Dragoş, became the first lord, or domn, of the region between the Carpathians and the Dnestr (a region which takes its name from the river Molda)—other independent principalities emerged at this time, on the borders of Hungarian territory (the dominant peoples of these Moldovan and Wallachian lands were Orthodox Christians speaking a Latinate tongue).

1457: Ştefan III ('the Great') came to power in Moldova, ruling until his death in 1504; under Ştefan, Moldova reached the height of its political and military power, and gained control of the lands stretching from the Carpathians to the Dnestr and the Black Sea.

1512: Moldova became a dependency of the Turkish Ottoman Empire.

1612: The Ottomans regained control of Moldova from Sigismund III of Poland.

1711: Following periodic uprisings by local nobles (boieri) in Moldova, the territory's autonomous status within the Ottoman Empire was revoked, and directly appointed Turkish administrators, Phanariots, were introduced; these Phanariots made Greek the official language and the Romanian Orthodox Church fell under Hellenic influence.

1768–74: The first Russo-Turkish war took place; the Ottomans were assisted by the Habsburg Empire in resisting a Russian attempt to occupy Moldova and Wallachia.

1806–12: In another Russo-Turkish conflict, Russian forces gained control of the lands between the Prut and the Dnestr rivers; the war was ended by the Treaty of Bucharest, under which Moldova was divided; the part west of the Prut remaining in the Ottoman Empire, while the eastern territory of Bessarabia (between the Prut and the Dnestr, extending to the Black Sea) became an autonomous region within the Russian Empire.

1815: The annexation of Bessarabia by Tsar Alexander I (1801–25) was approved by the Congress of Vienna.

1828: Bessarabia's autonomy was abolished and it became an imperial district (oblast); the use of the Romanian language in public pronouncements was suspended.

1854: Russian was made the official language of Bessarabia.

1871: Bessarabia became a province (guberniya) of the Russian Empire, by which time western Moldova (Moldavia) and Wallachia had been united into a single Romanian state (the Ottomans recognized its independence in 1878).

1905: The first Romanian-language publications appeared in Bessarabia, during a revolutionary threat to tsarist authority.

1917: With the collapse of tsarist authority in the 1917 Revolutions, revolutionary committees of soldiers and peasants quickly established a parliament (Sfatul Ţării) in the Bessarabian capital, Chişinău (Kishinev), and declared a Bessarabian Democratic Moldovan Republic.

March 1918: The Sfatul Ţării voted for union with Romania (to counter threats from Bolshevik, 'White' Russian and Ukrainian interests), which occupied the territory.

1 December 1918: The unification of Romania was declared, after Transylvania and Northern Bucovina had also voted to join the Romanian kingdom.

1924: A Moldovan Autonomous Soviet Socialist Republic (ASSR) was established in Soviet Ukraine, on the left bank of the Dnestr river; the USSR claimed that the Romanians, in occupying Bessarabia, had violated Moldova's right to self-rule.

23 August 1939: The Treaty of Non-Aggression (the Nazi-Soviet or Molotov–Ribbentrop Pact), which was signed by the USSR and Germany, included the 'Secret Protocols', sanctioning territorial gains for the USSR in Bessarabia.

27 June 1940: The Soviet Red Army entered Bessarabia.

2 August 1940: Bessarabia officially became part of the USSR; parts of annexed Moldova were united with the existing ASSR, and the resulting Moldovan Soviet Socialist Republic (SSR) was declared a Union Republic of the USSR; two Bessarabian counties on the Black Sea, one county in the north and more than one-half of the counties of the former Moldovan ASSR were apportioned to Ukraine.

1941–44: The introduction of a Cyrillic alphabet for the 'Moldovan' language was interrupted by the Romanian occupation of Bessarabia, following the German invasion of the USSR; the Romanians were expelled towards the end of the Second World War.

1950–52: Leonid Brezhnev (Soviet leader 1964–82) was First Secretary of the Communist Party of Moldova (CPM).

1961: Ivan Ivanovich Bodiul became First Secretary of the CPM.

1982: Bodiul was succeeded as Moldovan leader by Semion Kuzmich Grossu, who held the post for seven years.

May 1989: The pro-Romanian Popular Front of Moldova (PFM) was established; amongst its aims were the abolition of the use of the Cyrillic script and the return to a Latin one, and the acceptance of Romanian as the country's state language.

31 August 1989: The Moldovan Supreme Soviet adopted laws which returned 'Moldovan' to the Latin script, made it the state language of the Republic and recognized its unity with the Romanian language. After protests by the Slav population, Russian was to be retained as the language of inter-ethnic communication.

November 1989: Grossu, a conservative, was finally replaced as First Secretary of the CPM by the more reformist Petru Lucinschi (Luchinsky), an ethnic Romanian, following rioting in Chişinău.

25 February 1990: Elections to the Moldovan Supreme Soviet were held; the PFM won the largest number of seats.

April 1990: The new Moldovan Supreme Soviet convened; Mircea Snegur, a CPM member supported by the PFM, was re-elected Chairman of the Supreme Soviet.

27 April 1990: The Supreme Soviet adopted a modified version of the Romanian tricolour as Moldova's national flag.

24 May 1990: Petr Paskar's Government resigned after losing a vote of 'no confidence'; Mircea Druc was appointed Chairman of a Council of Ministers (Prime Minister) which was mainly comprised of radical reformers; the new Government immediately undertook a series of political reforms, including revoking the CPM's constitutional monopoly of power.

23 June 1990: The Moldovan Supreme Soviet adopted a declaration of sovereignty which asserted the supremacy of Moldova's Constitution and laws throughout the Republic; the 1940 annexation of Bessarabia by the USSR was declared to have been illegal, and, on the following day, thousands of Moldovans and Romanians assembled at the border in commemoration of the 50th anniversary of the occupation. The Supreme Soviet also specified the name of the Republic to be 'Moldova', rather than the russified 'Moldavia'.

19 August 1990: Five counties (raione) in southern Moldova, largely populated by ethnic Gagauz (Orthodox Christian Turks), declared a separate 'Gagauz SSR' (Gagauzia).

2 September 1990: Slavs in the territory east of the Dnestr river proclaimed their secession from Moldova and the establishment of a 'Dnestr SSR', which was based at Tiraspol.

September 1990: Snegur was elected by the Supreme Soviet to the newly instituted post of President of the Republic.

25 October 1990: Elections to a 'Republic of Gagauzia Supreme Soviet' were held, despite the opposition of some 50,000 armed Moldovan nationalists, who were prevented from violence only by Soviet troops. The Gagauz assembly subsequently convened in Comrat (Komrat) and elected Stepan Topol its president.

16 December 1990: An estimated 800,000 people, attending a 'Grand National Assembly', voted by acclamation to reject any new Union Treaty (which was being negotiated by other Soviet Republics).

19 February 1991: The Moldovan Supreme Soviet resolved not to conduct the all-Union referendum on the future of the USSR, which was scheduled for 17 March, but to endorse proposals for a confederation of states without central control.

21 May 1991: Following a vote of 'no confidence' by the legislature, Mircea Druc was replaced as Prime Minister by Valeriu Muravschi. Two days later the state was renamed the Republic of Moldova and the Supreme Soviet was renamed the Moldovan Parliament.

27 August 1991: Following the attempted coup in the Soviet capital of Moscow, Moldova declared its independence from the USSR and the CPM was banned. Romania recognized Moldova's independence and diplomatic relations between the two countries were established.

8 December 1991: The first popular presidential elections in Moldova took place; Snegur, the only candidate, received 98.2% of the votes cast.

21 December 1991: Moldova, as well as 10 other former Union Republics, signed the Almaty Declaration, by which was formed the Commonwealth of Independent States (CIS). In the same month armed conflict broke out in the Transdnestr region (Transdnestria), between the Slavic 'Dnestr Guards' and government troops.

February 1992: The PFM re-formed as the Christian Democratic Popular Front (CDPF).

March 1992: Moldova was admitted to the UN.

June 1992: The CDPF-dominated Government resigned; Andrei Sangheli was appointed Prime Minister and, over the following two months, negotiated a new coalition administration. The pro-Romanian minority in Parliament (including the CDPF) remained able to prevent the enactment of basic or constitutional legislation (which required a two-thirds majority).

21 July 1992: A peace agreement accorded Transdnestria 'special status' within Moldova; Russian, Moldovan and Dnestrian peace-keeping forces were deployed in the region to monitor the cease-fire.

12 August 1992: Moldova became a member of the International Monetary Fund.

January 1993: The Chairman of the Moldovan Parliament, Alexandru Moşanu, was replaced by Lucinschi, the former First Secretary (he was a leader of the Agrarian bloc in Parliament, which dominated the Government and enjoyed strong support in mainly rural Moldova).

4 August 1993: The Moldovan Parliament failed to secure the necessary majority for ratification of the Almaty Declaration and to formalize the country's entry into the CIS.

September 1993: The Moldovan leadership continued to favour eventual ratification of CIS entry and a sufficient majority of deputies expressed support for this; President Snegur therefore signed CIS documents on economic union and other matters.

October 1993: The parliamentary majority finally secured the enactment of a new electoral law and the dissolution of the Moldovan Parliament until after a general election (when the assembly was formally to adopt a new constitution).

19 January 1994: the President of the 'Dnestr Republic', Igor Smirnov, declared a state of emergency in Transdnestria, until 1 March, in an attempt to prevent the inhabitants of the region from participating in the legislative elections.

27 February 1994: Multi-party elections to a new 95-member unicameral Parliament took place; the Agrarian Democratic Party, which had been formed by the Agrarian bloc in the old legislature, emerged as the largest party (winning more than 40% of the votes cast), followed by the Slav-dominated former Communists, the Socialist Party, in alliance with the Yedinstvo (Unity) movement. A coalition of these leading parties, together with the loss of support for the pro-Romanian nationalists, was considered likely to secure CIS membership and a peace agreement in Transdnestria and Gagauzia.

6 March 1994: A national referendum confirmed Moldova's continuing independence.

History

CHARLES KING

INTRODUCTION

The country of Moldova (Moldavia is an anglicized version of the Russian name for the region) derives its name from a legend associated with Dragoş, a Romanian prince from Transylvania who ventured into the lands east of the Carpathian mountains in 1359. While his hunting party battled with a wild ox in a mountain stream, Dragoş's favourite hunting hound, Molda, drowned. In memory of the event, Dragoş named the river Molda and took the ox's head as his seal. Hence, the region stretching from the Carpathian Mountains to the Dnestr (Dniester) river became known as Moldova and Dragoş became the first lord (domn) of the new land. In the 15th century, the principality of Moldova emerged as a major force in south-eastern Europe. Under the powerful domn, Ştefan III ('the Great'—1457–1504), Moldova reached the zenith of its political and military power. In spite of the Tatars to the east, the Ottoman Turks to the south, and the Poles and Magyars (Hungarians) to the north and west, Ştefan was able to secure Moldovan control of the lands stretching from the Carpathians to the Dnestr and the Black Sea. A period of decline followed Ştefan's death in 1504.

By 1538 Ottoman domination of the principality had been secured. Periodic risings by local nobles (boieri) in Moldova and Wallachia (another Romanian territory south of the Carpathians) finally led to the loss of both principalities' semi-autonomous status within the Ottoman Empire, and the introduction of directly appointed Turkish administrators (in 1711 in Moldova and in 1716 in Wallachia). These administrators, known as Phanariots as they were drawn from the largely Greek Phanar, or lighthouse, district of Constantinople (now Istanbul, Turkey), brought with them the concept of a reconstituted Byzantium. Greek became the language of official communication and the Romanian Orthodox Church fell under Hellenic influence, while corruption became the hallmark of the Phanariot political system.

THE RUSSIAN ANNEXATION

After a series of wars with the Ottoman Turks, in the late 18th century, tsarist military forces finally succeeded in occupying the lands between the Prut and Dnestr rivers in 1806. Under the Treaty of Bucharest (1812), the Turks ceded the Prut-Dnestr interfluve to Russia by defining the river Prut as the border between the Russian and Ottoman Empires. The territory was mistakenly given the name Bessarabia, after the Basarab family which had ruled parts of Wallachia (not Moldova) in the 14th century. The annexation of Bessarabia divided the territory of Moldova into half: the western part, between the Carpathians and the Prut, remained under Ottoman control; and the eastern part, from the Prut to the Dnestr, was given autonomy within the Russian Empire. In spite of protestations from the Moldovan boieri at the dismemberment of the principality, the Russian annexation was approved by the Congress of Vienna in 1815. Bessarabia initially enjoyed a great deal of autonomy under Tsar Alexander I (1801–25). However, under his successor, Nicholas I (1825–55), the autonomous status of the territory was eliminated and the interfluve placed under direct imperial control, in 1828. The use of the 'Moldovan' (Romanian) language in public pronouncements ceased. In 1854 Russian was made the official language of Bessarabia. The region's autonomy was further restricted under Tsar Alexander II (1855–81), who, in 1871, changed the status of the region from an imperial district (oblast) to a province (guberniya) of Russia proper. While Bessarabia was subjected to the policy of 'russification' within the Russian Empire, the western half of historic Moldova was increasingly influenced by the awakening of pan-Romanian national consciousness. After a major rebellion, led by Tudor Vladimirescu, in 1821, Phanariot rule in Wallachia and the truncated Moldova was ended and some autonomy was restored to the local boieri. Influenced by the Greek national revival, political leaders and intellectuals in the two principalities increasingly saw themselves as Romanians, rather than as Moldovans or Wallachians. In 1859 Colonel Alexandru Ioan Cuza was elected simultaneously domn of both Wallachia and Moldova, thus effectively uniting the two principalities into a single Romanian state. Following a *coup d'état*, in 1866, Cuza was ousted and replaced by the German prince Karl von Hohenzollern-Sigmaringen. In 1877 Romania declared its independence from the Ottoman Empire. In 1881 Romania became a kingdom and Prince Karl was proclaimed King Carol I of Romania.

GREATER ROMANIA

The revolutions in Russia, in 1917, raised the possibility of Bessarabia's rejoining western Moldova inside the new Romanian kingdom. As the Russian Empire crumbled, a hastily convened citizens' assembly (Sfatul Ţării) in the Bessarabian capital of Chişinău (in Russian, Kishinev) declared a Bessarabian Democratic Moldovan Republic and, in 1918, voted for union with Romania. Following similar votes in Transylvania and Northern Bucovina (territories with sizeable ethnic Romanian populations which had been a part of the Austro-Hungarian Empire), the unification of the Romanian lands was proclaimed on 1 December 1918.

Throughout the period between the First and Second World Wars, the conflicting claims for Bessarabia caused problems in Soviet–Romanian relations. The USSR contended that the Sfatul Ţării had not been a truly representative body and that, as the USSR was the successor state to the Russian Empire, Romania had illegally occupied Bessarabia. Soviet propagandists were active in Bessarabia. Riots in Hotin and Bender, in 1919, and in Tatar Bunar, in 1924, were used by the Soviets to illustrate the Bessarabians' desire to join the USSR. In order to increase Soviet influence in Bessarabia, a Moldovan Autonomous Soviet Socialist Republic (ASSR) was established, in 1924, in Ukraine on the eastern (or left) bank of the Dnestr river. The USSR argued that the inhabitants of Bessarabia were ethnically separate from Romanians and that, by occupying Bessarabia, the Romanians had violated the right of the Moldovans to self-determination. Although relations between Romania and the USSR were finally normalized in 1934, the status of Bessarabia remained unresolved.

SOVIET MOLDOVA

Under the 'Secret Protocols' to the Treaty of Non-Aggression (the Nazi–Soviet Pact), signed on 23 August 1939, Germany recognized the USSR's interest in regaining Bessarabia. In June 1940 the USSR demanded the Romanians immediately cede Bessarabia and the northern part of Bucovina. Later the same month Soviet troops entered Bessarabia and, in August 1940, the region became a part of the USSR. Parts of Bessarabia were united with the existing Moldovan ASSR; the resulting Moldovan Soviet Socialist Republic (SSR) was declared a Union Republic of the USSR. However, a significant amount of territory was awarded to Ukraine: three Bessarabian counties (one in the north and two on the Black Sea) and more than one-half of the counties of the former Moldovan ASSR.

Given the sensitive position of the new Moldovan SSR as an object of Romanian irredentism, Soviet policy underscored the separateness of Moldovans and Romanians. The Cyrillic script was introduced in 1941, and the 'Moldovan' language was declared wholly separate from the Romanian tongue. Moldovans were portrayed as a distinct ethnic group by stressing the Slavic elements in Moldovan history and culture. Immigration of Russians and Ukrainians into the Republic was encouraged and ethnic Slavs were favoured in the Communist Party, government and enterprises. In the droughts and collectivization drive of the late 1940s, hundreds of thousands of Moldovan peasants perished or were deported to Siberia and Central Asia.

Throughout the period of Soviet rule Moldova remained an underdeveloped and politically conservative part of the USSR. Both Leonid Brezhnev (Soviet leader 1964–82) and one of his successors, Konstantin Chernenko, served in Moldova: the former as the Communist Party of Moldova's (CPM) First Secretary (1950–52) and the latter as head of the Moldovan Central Committee's propaganda department (1948–56). As Soviet–Romanian relations deteriorated, in the early 1960s, Soviet leaders feared that any instability in the Moldovan SSR might prompt the Romanians to raise the issue of the 1940 annexation. Thus, Ivan Ivanovich Bodiul, an ethnic Ukrainian who served as the CPM's First Secretary in 1961–82, was the last republican First Secretary to be replaced under Brezhnev. His successor, Semion Kuzmich Grossu, was similarly the last to be replaced under Soviet leader Mikhail Gorbachev (1985–91), in 1989. Even after the advent of *glasnost* (openness) in the USSR, leaders in Chişinău looked with nostalgia on the Brezhnev era and denounced any demands for liberalization as manifestations of 'bourgeois nationalism'.

In refusing to adopt the new thinking, the CPM leadership alienated itself not only from reformists elsewhere in the USSR, but also from local groups demanding more liberal cultural policies. Rallies were held in support of greater provision for Moldovan-language study in the Republic and the protection of national monuments. A variety of cultural and political groups were instrumental in the establishment of the Popular Front of Moldova (PFM) in May 1989. The PFM's demands focused on the language issue: the movement was in favour of a return to the Latin script and the adoption of Romanian as the state language.

While Grossu vacillated on the language issue, the Moldovan SSR Supreme Soviet moved towards meeting the PFM's demands. On 31 August 1989 the Supreme Soviet, chaired by Mircea Snegur, a CPM member supported by the PFM, adopted laws which returned 'Moldovan' to the Latin script, made it the state language of the Republic and implicitly recognized its unity with Romanian. As the notion of two distinct languages and ethnic groups—Romanian and 'Moldovan'—had been a central justification for the annexation of 1940, the language laws of 1989 thus called into question both the authority of the Communist Party in Moldova and the legitimacy of the Republic's tenure in the USSR. The PFM welcomed the laws as the first move towards spiritual and political reunion with Romania. As Chairman of the Supreme Soviet, Snegur rapidly replaced Grossu as the chief political force in Moldova. In April 1990 Snegur was re-elected as Chairman of the Supreme Soviet. (In September he was elected to the newly created post of republican President.) Under Snegur's leadership, the Moldovan SSR adopted a modified version of the Romanian tricolour as the national flag, on 27 April, declared its sovereignty within the USSR, on 23 June, and changed its name to the Republic of Moldova, on 23 May 1991.

Territorial separatism presented a major challenge to the Snegur Government. Following the adoption of Romanian as Moldova's state language, in August 1989, and the revolution in Romania, in December 1989, Moldova's ethnic minorities feared that the Republic's leaders would seek to 'romanianize' the non-Romanian population. Separate 'autonomous republics' within Moldova were declared by political leaders in southern Moldova in November, and on the eastern bank of the Dnestr in December. As Moldova moved closer to a complete separation from the USSR, the separatists likewise made plans to declare independence from Moldova. In August 1990 five counties (raioane) in southern Moldova, populated largely by ethnic Gagauzi (Orthodox Christian Turks), declared a separate 'Gagauz Soviet Socialist Republic' (Gagauzia). One month later the majority Slavic population on the left bank of the Dnestr (Transdnestria or Pridnestrove in Russian) declared a separate 'Transdnestrian Moldovan Soviet Socialist Republic'. Parliaments and administrative structures were established in the separatist regions. The Transdnestrian region, in particular, demonstrated its strength against the central Moldovan Government by suspending essential energy supplies and rail links between Chişinău and the other Soviet Republics.

INDEPENDENT MOLDOVA

Following the attempted *coup d'état* in Moscow, the Republic of Moldova declared its independence from the USSR on 27 August 1991. However, Moldova had already begun to lay the legal foundations of an independent state. The laws on language (31 August 1989), property (22 January 1991), citizenship (5 June 1991), and privatization (4 July 1991) were regarded as generally more progressive than similar laws passed in other former Soviet Republics. Moldova signed the Almaty Declaration on the creation of the Commonwealth of Independent States (CIS), on 21 December 1991. However, it declined to participate in the Treaty on Collective Security, or Tashkent Agreement, and planned to introduce its own national currency. Moldova was recognized by more than 120 countries, several of which (including four of the Permanent Members of the UN Security Council) opened embassies in Chişinău. Moldova joined the Conference on Security and Co-operation in Europe (CSCE), in January 1992, and became a member of the Black Sea Economic Co-operation Group in June of the same year. In March 1992 Moldova joined the UN as the Republic of Moldova or Moldavia, in order to avoid conflict over the region in eastern Romania which was also known as Moldova (the western part of the medieval principality).

Parliamentary elections were held in February and March 1990, while Moldova was still a part of the USSR. The Moldovan Parliament immediately after independence was thus simply the renamed Supreme Soviet. As the elections were only semi-competitive (yielding an 85% Communist-Party representation), parliamentarians had no binding party mandates, and parliamentary blocs and alliances were constantly changing. The first popular presidential elections were held on 8 December 1991. Snegur, the sole candidate, won 98.2% of the votes cast. There was a delay in preparing for new parliamentary elections, however, largely owing to the influence of the pro-Romanian nationalists, who had sufficient representation to block fundamental legislation. There were also problems with re-districting and the holding of elections in the territories which had broken away from Moldova. A new electoral law was passed in October 1993, after considerable controversy.

In mid-1993 the Moldovan Parliament began debating the draft of the new Constitution. The draft was composed by a parliamentary commission established in April 1991, but much of the progress was made only after the PFM and other pro-Romanian forces, increasingly in a minority, were ousted from control of the Government (June 1992) and the new Parliament (January 1993). The new dominant faction was the Agrarian bloc, which contested the 1994 general elections as the Agrarian Democratic Party (ADP). At least 19 of the draft Constitution's 137 articles were taken verbatim from the post-Communist Romanian Constitution (which was approved by referendum on 8 December 1991). The majority of the remaining articles bore a strong resemblance to their Romanian counterparts. The draft envisaged a semi-presidential system on the French model, with executive power divided between a popularly elected president and his appointed prime minister and government. Legislative authority would reside in a 104-member unicameral Parliament (scaled down from the previous 380). Both the President and deputies were elected for four-year terms. Before the draft was promulgated it was to be considered by the new Parliament and ratified in a national referendum. In October 1993, after enacting the new electoral law, Parliament recessed. Elections to a new Parliament were held on 27 February 1994. The ADP secured the greatest single share of the votes (43.2%) and 56 of the 104 seats in the legislature. The direct successor of the CPM, the Socialist Party, together with the Slav Yedinstvo (Unity) Movement, came second with 28 seats. The eclipse of the pro-Romanian parties was confirmed by the national referendum on 6 March, when some 90% of the voters favoured continued independence and rejected unity with Romania (see below).

TRANSDNESTRIA AND THE GAGAUZ

The most significant problem for the newly independent Moldova was the conflict over the two secessionist 'republics'. Gagauzia and Transdnestria contained about one-fifth of Moldova's population and 23% of its territory. The Transdnestr region alone accounted for over one-third of Moldova's economic revenue. With such crucial areas outside the effective control of the authorities in Chişinău, elections, large-scale privatization and administrative reform were all virtually impossible. The situation was complicated by the demographics of separatism. The separatists did not represent compact ethnic populations, and they were consequently presented with their own internal ethnic problems. Moldovans (ethnic Romanians) formed the largest ethnic group in Transdnestria (nearly 40% of the population), although Russians and Ukrainians together accounted for 54%. In Gagauzia, while ethnic Gagauz formed 47% of the total population, they represented a majority in only one of the five constituent counties. Moldovans (ethnic Romanians) represented 26% of Gagauzia's total population and were almost in the majority in two of the counties.

The Transdnestrians, in particular, presented a sizeable military threat to Moldova's nascent armed forces. Full-scale fighting broke out between the Transdnestrian army (the 'Dnestr Guards') and Moldovan police forces in December 1991, around the city of Dubăsari (Dubossary in Russian). The most serious fighting occurred in June 1992, when Transdnestrian forces attempted to take the right-bank city of Tighina (Bendery). Although the Moldovans were initially successful in repelling the Transdnestrians, the Russian Federation's 14th Army (a former Soviet force—stationed in the capital of Transdnestr, Tiraspol) intervened on the side of the separatists and drove the Moldovans from the city. The army commander justified his intervention by repeating allegations that the Moldovans were attempting 'genocide' against the city's ethnic Russian population.

From the beginning of the conflict in late 1989, the Dnestr Guards were supplied with arms by the 14th Army. Several Russian military personnel changed their allegiance to the Dnestr Guards. One of the former commanders of the 14th Army, Lt-Gen. Gennadii Iakovlev, became the head of Transdnestria's defence and security department. The Army's Commander from June 1992, Maj.-Gen. (later Lt-Gen.) Aleksandr Lebed, compared the Moldovans to Nazis, called the Moldovan-Romanian tricolour 'the flag of the Romanian fascists' and stated that the Transdnestr region should become an integral part of the Russian Federation. In April 1993 the Russian authorities attempted to restrain his outspokenness during a brief recall to Moscow.

The peace accord signed between Moldova and Russia, on 21 July 1992, brought an end to the fighting and established a security zone along the Dnestr river and in the city of Tighina. The zone was patrolled by the 10-battalion Unified Peace-Keeping Force (two battalions each from Moldova and Transdnestria, six from Russia). A tripartite Unified Control Commission supervised the Force's activities. Although numerous rounds of negotiations were held, many under CSCE auspices, no agreement was reached on the withdrawal of the 14th Army. The Moldovans demanded a full-scale withdrawal, while the Russians only agreed to hand over control of the Army to the local authorities, that is, the Transdnestrians. Furthermore, Russia demanded that any change in the status of the 14th Army be dependent on the granting of self-determination for Transdnestria. It was thought that while disputes between Russia and Ukraine over the Crimea and the Black Sea fleet remained unresolved, Russia would have a strong disincentive to remove its forces from Tiraspol, a city less than 150 km from the Ukrainian port of Odessa.

The dispute with the separatists became, from 1989, less an ethnic conflict and more a purely political struggle. In the late 1980s the success of the pan-Romanian PFM seemed to indicate a swift Moldovan unification with Romania. However, the separatists' claim that Moldova intended to unite with Romania was discredited by the progressive purge of unionists from the Moldovan Government and Parliament. The Government of Mircea Druc, in office from May 1990 and supported by the PFM, was replaced, on 21 May 1991, by a more moderate administration, led by Valeriu Muravschi. The Muravschi Government was replaced, in July 1992, by the 'national consensus' Government of Andrei Sangheli, the former head of the parliamentary conciliation commissions which negotiated with the Gagauz and Transdnestrians. Government portfolios were reserved for representatives from Transdnestria and Gagauzia, although the separatists declined to accept the posts. A further reassurance for the separatists happened in January 1993, when the pro-Romanian speaker of the Moldovan Parliament was replaced by Petru Lucinschi, the penultimate First Secretary of the CPM and Moldova's first ambassador to Russia.

This new Moldovan triumvirate—Snegur, Sangheli and Lucinschi— were all former Communist Party Politburo members. They initiated a series of direct negotiations with the Transdnestrian leadership in the hope that their political backgrounds would render them more acceptable negotiating partners than their abrasive pro-unification predecessors. However, despite the Moldovan Government's offer of local autonomy for the regions in return for loyalty to the central government, the Gagauz and Transdnestrian Supreme Soviets voted, in March 1993, to accept only a loose Moldovan-Gagauz-Transdnestrian confederation. Furthermore, they also, on occasion, demanded the transfer of Transdnestria to the Russian Federation or the re-creation of the USSR.

It seemed that the Gagauz and Transdnestrian leaders were interested less in protecting the rights of their respective ethnic groups than in maintaining the Party and state structures of the former USSR. In the Transdnestr region, in particular, the state symbols and legal code of the old Moldovan SSR were retained. The language laws of 1989 were rejected and the use of the Latin script for written 'Moldovan' was outlawed. In mid-1993 six PFM members from Tiraspol (the so-called Ilaşcu Group) went on trial in the Transdnestrian capital, accused, under the old Soviet legal code, of murder and attempting to overthrow the Transdnestrian state. In December one of the six accused, Ilie Ilaşcu, was sentenced to death. The trial was condemned as unfair by international human-rights organizations. In February 1994 the Chişinău Supreme Court annulled the sentences passed on the Group.

By late 1993 the Transdnestrian state had been recognized by only two political entities—Abkhazia (Georgia) and the 'Republic of Serbian Krajina' (Croatia). However, Russian nationalists have repeatedly proposed Russia's recognition of the secessionist republic, and, during the Moscow uprising of October 1993, pro-Communist militants from Transdnestria went to Russia to fight against President Boris Yeltsin.

On 19 January 1994 the President of the 'Dnestr Republic', Igor Smirnov, declared a state of emergency in the region until 1 March, in an attempt to discourage the area's inhabitants from participating in Moldova's legislative elections on 27 February. Furthermore, although, in January 1994, the Moldovan Government accepted the CSCE plan for peace in Transdnestria, which proposed a degree of autonomy for the area, the Transdnestrian leaders maintained their demands for full statehood for the region in a nominal confederation with Moldova. However, the results of the general election and of the referendum on continuing independence for Moldova made an agreement on a plan for peace more likely.

ROMANIA OR THE CIS?

After independence President Snegur and his supporters remained committed to the maintenance of 'two independent Romanian states', Romania and the Republic of Moldova. In contrast, the remnants of the PFM, divided mainly between the Congress of the Intelligentsia, which was formed in April 1993, and the more radical Christian Democratic Popular Front (CDPF), created in February 1992, continued to demand unification with Romania. Although the two groups differed over when unification should begin, both envisaged an independent Moldova as merely the first move towards reunion with the Romanian motherland. These parties also advocated the return of the other lands annexed by the USSR in 1940, and held by Ukraine (today the Chernovtsy and Odessa administrative districts).

Opinion polls carried out in Moldova after 1989 demonstrated that there was little support for a union with

Romania among the Moldovan population. Moreover, the Republic's majority population considered themselves Moldovan rather than Romanian. However, some, namely pan-Romanian intellectuals, saw this as merely further proof of the depth of 'denationalization' policy under the Soviet regime. The ADP, which organized the largest parliamentary faction from 1992, and other groups committed to Moldovan independence, believed that union with Romania would destroy the positions of power they enjoyed, particularly in the country's large agricultural sector. Therefore, they viewed Moldovan membership of the CIS as both an economic necessity and a safeguard against Romanian irredentism.

The pan-Romanian unionists achieved a major victory on 4 August 1993, when the Moldovan Parliament voted against the ratification of the Almaty Declaration, the founding document of the CIS. The ratification vote failed owing to a parliamentary technicality. The final vote was 162 to 22 in favour of ratification, just four votes less than the simple majority required. Some 90 unionist deputies boycotted the vote, as well as representatives from Transdnestria, who participated in the legislature only intermittently from 1990. It also seemed that several deputies from the Agrarian bloc, the largest pro-independence faction in Parliament, rebelled and voted against ratification. The Republic's failure to join the CIS raised questions about the viability of an independent Moldova and the future relationship with its former motherland, Romania. However, a majority of deputies subsequently indicated informal acceptance of the CIS, and there was sufficient confidence that a new Parliament would ratify Commonwealth membership for President Snegur to sign the Almaty Declaration in December 1993. The election victory of the ADP (parliamentary ratification was obtained in April 1994) seemed to secure an independent future for the Republic of Moldova, the second Romanian state.

The Economy

CHARLES KING

INTRODUCTION

The Republic of Moldova, the successor state to the Moldovan Soviet Socialist Republic, was a country of 33,700 sq km (13,010 sq miles) situated in south-eastern Europe, making it geographically the second-smallest of the former Soviet Republics. It was land-locked and bordered by Ukraine and Romania, although controversy surrounds Moldova's riparian frontage on the Danube (probably around 1 km). At mid-1992 Moldova had an estimated population of 4,356,000 inhabitants (the principal ethnic groups at the 1989 census were Moldovan/Romanian—64.5%, Ukrainian—13.8%, Russian—13.0%, Gagauz—3.5%, Bulgarian—2.0% and others—3.1%). The urban population accounted for 47.5% of the total, making Moldova the least urbanized of all the Soviet successor states outside Central Asia. In 1992 Moldova had the highest population density of any former Soviet Republic (129.3 per sq km), nearly 10 times the former Soviet average. In 1993 the average life expectancy at birth was 68 years (64 years for men, 71 years for women); of all the former Soviet Republics, only Turkmenistan had a lower life expectancy. The percentage of the population who were over the age of 60 totalled 12.8%, and, for every 100 people who were of productive age (16–59 years old), there were 73.8 persons of non-productive age. The infant-mortality rate, in the first five months of 1993, amounted to 20.7 per 1,000 births, one of the highest in Europe.

AGRICULTURE

As a result of Moldova's extremely fertile land and temperate climate, agriculture and related industries were the mainstays of the country's economy. Some 80% of the land was cultivated. In 1991 agriculture contributed 41.7% to net material product (NMP) and, in the following year, 40% of those employed worked in the agricultural (including hunting, forestry and fishing) sector. In relation to its size, Moldova had accounted for a significant proportion of the total agricultural-production and food-processing sectors in the USSR: in 1989 4.5% of vegetables, 19.2% of grapes, 11.2% of other fruits and berries, 30% of tobacco, 3.3% of sugar, 9.2% of cognac, 6.4% of wine and 8.3% of canned goods were produced in Moldova. By the end of the Soviet period, collective farms accounted for some 60% of agricultural production, with the remainder divided between state farms and private plots (the private ownership of land was legalized in 1991).

Principal crops in Moldova included wine grapes and other fruit, tobacco, vegatables and grain. In 1991 fruits, vegetables and tobacco accounted for 34% of total agricultural output. The wine industry traditionally occupied a central role in the economy. However, in spite of the serious disruption which the last Soviet leader Mikhail Gorbachev's anti-alcohol campaign caused the Moldovan wine industry in the mid-1980s (with some vineyards being uprooted and replaced by other crops), production revived. In 1991 wine output was 143m. litres.

Similarly, total agricultural output recovered from a brief decline in the mid-1980s; in 1989 it registered a growth of 5.2%. However, in 1990 and 1991, adverse weather conditions led to decreases of 12.9% and 10.6%, respectively, in total agricultural production. The decline continued in 1992–93. Compared with the same period in the previous year, agricultural production in the first six months of 1993 decreased by 36% (based on 1983 prices). Furthermore, there were significant declines in the production of meat (by 21%), milk (32%) and eggs (42%). In February 1991 the Moldovan Parliament approved a series of measures giving priority to agricultural reform and agricultural investment over other sectors of the country's economy. The Government pledged to make no changes in the collective-farm system without the consultation of the farm workers. They also undertook to reserve places in institutes of higher education for persons intending to work in the countryside.

INDUSTRY

Moldova's industrial capabilities were linked with its former status as a major supplier of consumer goods, particularly agricultural products, to the rest of the USSR. In 1991 the industrial sector contributed 37.6% of the country's NMP. Industry (manufacturing and public utilities) accounted for 19.9% of those in employment in 1992. A further 5.9% worked in the construction sector. In 1989 consumer goods accounted for 40% of industrial production in Moldova, compared with the Soviet average of 26%. In the consumer-goods sector, in 1991, processed agricultural goods accounted for 37% of total production and alcoholic beverages for 14%. Other consumer goods included leather and textiles, televisions, audio equipment, refrigerators and furniture.

In 1992 industrial production declined by 28%. There was a slight increase (0.9%) registered in output in the first half of 1993, compared with the same period in the previous year. However, the stability in industrial production over this period was illusory. Official government statistics were unable to calculate industrial production in the Transdnestr region, which accounted for some 30% of total state revenues. After the negotiation of the cease-fire agreement in the region, in July 1992, the Transdnestrians restored many of the energy and rail links which had been severed at the beginning of the conflict in 1989. However, the self-proclaimed Transdnestr Government began levying export duties on goods sent across the Dnestr to the rest of Moldova. Thus, the Republic experienced a massive, though incalculable, decline in industrial production owing to the effective loss of a significant part of its industrial plant.

BANKING AND MONETARY REFORM

The National Bank of Moldova was established in June 1991 and its Charter was approved in the following month. It was subordinated to the Moldovan Parliament and performed all the functions of a central state bank. As long as Moldova remained in the 'rouble zone', the instruments of monetary policy available to the National Bank were severely circumscribed. As International Monetary Fund (IMF) observers noted, in 1991, the National Bank was essentially limited to setting interest rates on lending by other banks, varying the terms of refinancing on loans to banks and, occasionally, enterprises, and changing minimum reserve requirements.

However, in January 1992, the Moldovan Parliament voted to leave the rouble zone and to introduce a national currency, the Moldovan leu (plural, lei—the same unit as in Romania). From that time transitional coupons (cupoane) issued by the National Bank of Moldova circulated alongside the Russian rouble (former Soviet rouble). By mid-1993 these coupons accounted for some 80% of banknotes in circulation. In July 1993 Moldovan President Mircea Snegur announced the creation of a commission to oversee the introduction of the leu. On 29 November the leu became Moldova's national currency. Denominations of one, 10 and 50 lei were to be introduced initially, along with the simultaneous introduction of new coupons in the value of 10,000 roubles.

The introduction of the Moldovan leu was expected to be extremely difficult, given Moldova's annual rate of increase in consumer prices (1,500% in 1992), the lack of effective central institutions to manage monetary policy and exchange-rate mechanisms, and the country's massive expenditure on energy and other industrial inputs from Russia. However, as in Kyrgyzstan, the introduction of a national currency was motivated as much by political as by economic concerns. Firstly, it was believed that the introduction of a national currency was the only way of avoiding the adverse impact on Moldova of inflationary pressures in the other former Soviet Republics, especially Ukraine. In late 1992 Moldova suffered from a surfeit of the old Soviet (Russian) roubles in the wake of monetary reform in Ukraine, where the rouble was no longer legal tender. The corresponding outflow of goods exacerbated already severe shortages in Moldova.

Secondly, the Moldovan Government hoped that a national currency would serve as a precautionary measure against the negative repercussions of monetary reform in Russia. In late July 1993 the Russian Federation's Central Bank withdrew all pre-1993 roubles, in order to facilitate the introduction of a new post-Soviet currency. The other members of the rouble zone were not consulted before the move, and President Snegur was forced to issue an emergency decree immediately withdrawing from circulation all Russian banknotes in denominations greater than 100 roubles. In August, a distinction was introduced between the Moldovan rouble and the currencies of other countries in the rouble area.

THE GENERAL REFORM PROGRAMME

The Government's draft programme on economic reform, adopted in 1991, envisaged the transition from a centralized, socialist economy to a market economy based on private ownership, although with significant government intervention. The property law, enacted in January 1991, guaranteed the right of citizens to own property privately and collectively. The right of foreign states and citizens to own property in Moldova was also guaranteed, although land may not be owned by foreign entities.

The law on privatization of July 1991 set out the general form for the privatization of state-owned enterprises and farms. Privatization in industry was to be effected through a dual voucher system. Vouchers representing each citizen's share of the national economy were to be awarded to every Moldovan citizen (including children born up to the day privatization began). An additional type of voucher was to be issued to employees of individual enterprises, representing their share of the enterprise's assets and based on the number of years they had worked in the Moldovan economy (including time spent in higher education and the armed forces). Holders were then able to sell the vouchers through an official exchange mechanism (the direct sale of vouchers between individuals was illegal) or were able to use them as credit towards the purchase of stocks in privatized companies. It was estimated that, by the end of 1994, some 40%–45% of the value of state-owned assets would have been privatized through the voucher system.

In the agricultural sector, each family unit working in state farms (sovhozuri) or collective farms (colhozuri) was to be given up to 0.75 ha of land, which could not be resold before the year 2001. However, collective farms could be initially transformed into joint-stock companies. Land and movable property would then be repartitioned in a similar way to that of privatization in industrial enterprises. By mid-1993 only 9% of Moldovan farmland (360,000 ha) had been privatized.

By the beginning of 1993 450 joint-stock companies had been registered in Moldova, 92 of which had formerly been under state control. An additional 143 enterprises had been transformed into joint-stock companies on the basis of 'mixed capital', that is, through the purchase of stocks by the enterprise's employees. State assets which were vital to national security or the social-welfare system, which formed part of the national heritage or of a state monopoly could not be privatized. On 9 October 1993 the privatization of state property began, with the auction of seven shops and two cafés. It was estimated that this sale generated 215m. Moldovan coupons (US $99,000).

Such revenues from production were likely to be useful to the Government in the 1990s. Moldova traditionally had a surplus in the government budget. In the 1980s the surplus averaged an estimated 3% of gross domestic product (GDP), in spite of the decrease in contributions from the USSR to the country's budget. In 1991 the budget surplus was 1.7m. roubles, compared with the 1990 surplus of 358.2m. roubles. This decline was partly caused by the refusal of the Transdnestr region to transfer resources to the state budget. As a response to the worsening fiscal position, the Moldovan Government introduced a series of strict budgetary measures, which included levying excise taxes on certain commodities and reducing social expenditure. However, a budget deficit of 4,800m. roubles was estimated in the first half of 1992, mainly owing to price liberalization and wage increases.

SALARIES, PRICES AND UNEMPLOYMENT

According to calculations by the Moldovan Federation of Independent Trade Unions, the minimum necessary monthly salary, in late July 1993, was 40,000 roubles. The minimum legal monthly salary in Moldova in the same period was 7,500 roubles (some US $7). The average monthly salary in the first six months of 1993 was 9,609 roubles (approximately $9). Compared with the same period in 1992, salaries were more than six times higher in the first six months of 1993, while consumer prices were almost nine times higher. Salaries, entitlements and deposit-interest rates were indexed to offset the social costs of the price liberalization initiated in 1992, although the indexation tended to exacerbate inflationary pressures. The disparity between prices and salaries led to a flourishing informal economic sector, as Moldovans attempted to supplement salaries through street sales of imported household goods, children's clothing, automobile parts and other scarce items.

By mid-1993 the massive unemployment rates, which were expected in the transitional period between a centralized economy and a market one, had not reached Moldova. This was largely owing to the reluctance of enterprises to reduce their work-force, which was made possible in part by the virtual absence of strict budgetary measures and by the willingness of the banking system to finance the companies' operating costs. In the first half of 1993 there were 22,215 people in search of work. However, only some 9,800 were registered as officially unemployed. This figure was very small in relation to the total available work-force, which was 2,463,300 in 1991. Government expenditure on unemployment entitlements in the first six months of 1993 amounted to 54,136,910 roubles, almost four times greater than in the same period of the previous year.

The official unemployment figures concealed an important aspect of the Moldovan labour market. Enterprises which sought to avoid the politically undesirable option of dismissing workers, found creative alternatives to reducing labour expenditures. The length of the average working day was reduced, employees were encouraged to take extended unpaid vacations, and, owing to energy shortages, occasionally production was halted completely for long periods. Under such conditions, employees were not eligible for unemployment benefits as they were not considered officially unemployed by the state. In September 1992 it was reported that some 24,000 people were in search of employment. Of these, however, only 66% were officially unemployed.

TRADE

While Moldova was part of the USSR, its trading relations with other Soviet Republics, as well as with foreign partners, were centrally controlled. As the other former Soviet Republics began to assert control over external economic relations, in 1990, Moldova moved to establish bilateral trade agreements with them. By February 1992 agreements had been signed with 10 former Soviet Republics. Of these, the Russian Federation remained by far the most important, receiving, in 1991, 60.5% of Moldova's inter-republican exports and providing 45.2% of its inter-republican imports. In the same year Ukraine took 18.2% of Moldova's inter-republican exports and provided 25.7% of its imports (especially refined petroleum products).

While the country's trade relations were still primarily orientated towards the former Soviet Republics (in 1991 foreign exports were worth only 6% of the value of inter-republican exports, although imports from foreign countries were worth 29% of Soviet inter-republican imports), progress was made in forging links with the West, the Black Sea zone and Asia. Romania was Moldova's largest trading partner outside the rouble zone. In 1991 16.7% of Moldovan exports went to Romania, and this country provided 21.7% of Moldovan imports from outside the Soviet Republics. Relations between the two countries were strengthened in mid-July 1993, when President Snegur and the Romanian President, Ion Iliescu, met in Bucharest (Romania). The two Presidents agreed to examine establishing a joint Romanian–Moldovan bank, organizing a joint chamber of commerce, and facilitating Moldovan access to the Cernavodă power station. Moldova signed the Declaration on Black Sea Co-operation in June 1992 and established strong trade links with other members, especially Turkey. Several joint ventures, mainly in light industry, were concluded shortly after independence, with Bulgaria, Hungary, Poland and Viet Nam. At the beginning of 1992 bilateral trade agreements had been signed with the People's Republic of China, Denmark, Sweden, the Netherlands, Italy and Spain. Moldova was also a 'most-favoured nation' trading partner of the USA.

In 1990 food and agricultural products accounted for 52% of the value of total exports, followed by light-industrial products (20%) and machines and metalworks (17%). Moldova's principal exports reflected the requirements of its agro-industrial complex: in 1990 machines and metalworks accounted for 29% of the value of all imports, while light-industrial products and energy products (including electric power) accounted for 20% and 9%, respectively.

In 1991 Moldova's total foreign-trade deficit amounted to 303.0m. Soviet roubles, just over 1% of nominal GDP. The larger trade deficit outside the rouble zone (874.7m. roubles) was offset by a trade surplus with the former Soviet Republics of 571.7m. roubles. Compared with 1990, these figures represented an overall increase in the foreign-trade deficit, primarily owing to a significant decrease in Moldova's trade surplus with the other Soviet Republics. All these figures, however, were misleading as the valuation system tended to overvalue those goods for which Moldova was a net exporter (for example, agricultural products) and to undervalue those for which Moldova was a net importer (especially energy). Calculated in terms of world prices, Moldova's trade deficit was significantly higher.

In early 1993 Moldova was accepted into the Danube Commission as a Danube riparian state and given observer status on the Commission. Moldova lost nearly all of its Danube access (around 200 km) and all of its Black Sea frontage when southern Bessarabia was apportioned to Ukraine in 1940. International recognition of Moldova's remaining Danube access was seen as a major step towards the development of stronger trade relations with countries outside the former USSR. While the amount of Danube littoral under Moldovan control (probably around 1 km) remained a source of controversy with Ukraine, the Moldovan Government proposed plans to construct port facilities on the Danube near Giurgiuleşti. Such a port would allow co-ordination of Moldovan shipping with the important Romanian port at Galaţi and would provide much-needed access to the Black Sea.

The informal economy ('black market') formed an important part of Moldova's trade with Romania. In spite of the exorbitant and arbitrary customs duties imposed by Moldova, trains between the two countries were often filled with people carrying items to sell in the markets of Iaşi and Bucharest. While the economic impact of this parallel economy on Moldovan–Romanian trade was probably relatively small, the increased contact between Moldovans and Romanians would have a significant effect on the closer integration of the two countries.

PROBLEMS AND PROSPECTS

From 1991 Moldova experienced the difficulties of the transition from a regional subdivision of an integrated national economy to a sovereign economic and political entity still dependent on the other former Soviet Republics. An example of this dependency was the refusal of natural-gas suppliers in the Russian Federation to extend credits to Moldova's main natural-gas company, MoldovaGas, which caused major shortages in the country in mid-1993. The entire capital, with its centralized heating plant, remained without hot water for several weeks. Similar shortages were envisaged in the future, many of them caused by 'chain reactions' in inter-republican trade: delays in Russian deliveries of petroleum to Ukraine caused corresponding shortages of gasoline and other refined petroleum products in Moldova in late 1993.

The failure of the Moldovan Parliament to ratify the Almaty Declaration, confirming its membership of the Commonwealth of Independent States (CIS), in August 1993, raised serious questions about the future economic orientation of the Republic. While Moldova had already established extensive bilateral links with the other former Soviet Republics, full CIS membership would have provided another forum for the resolution of common problems of energy supply, foreign investment, relations with European trading partners, and regional economic integration. Romania was swift to react to Moldova's failure to ratify membership of the CIS. In early August President Iliescu promised to use a part of the 6,000m. Romanian lei (US $7.4 million) set aside for fostering Moldovan-Romanian economic integration to ease the chronic fuel shortage in Moldova. While the offer of aid was certainly welcome to the Moldovan Government, President Snegur and his supporters were wary of the political conditions which might be attached to Romanian aid. On the other hand, the timing of the parliamentary vote which rejected ratification was prompted by a Russian decision to treat Moldova as a non-CIS country and impose punitive levies on exports. These tariffs were lifted in December, once Russia was assured of eventual ratification by Moldova of CIS membership.

The most serious problem for the Moldovan economy and the reform programme was that of territorial separatism. The effective secession of territories in southern Moldova (Gagauzia) and on the eastern bank of the Dnestr river (Transdnestria), in 1990, meant that Moldova lost effective control over some 20% of its population and 23% of its territory. Transdnestria alone accounted for more than one-third of Moldova's economic potential and provided crucial rail and energy links with the former Soviet Republics. The Moldovan Government was thus faced with a serious dilemma: to delay significant reform meant that the economic crisis in the country would deepen, yet to move ahead with reform in the parts of the Republic still under the control of the Chişinău authorities represented a *de facto* admission of the loss of the two separatist regions. Both options were economically and politically undesirable. Moldova's chief asset was its geographical position. Historically, the region has been situated at the crossroads of empires—Roman and Byzantine, Ottoman, Russian and Soviet, Austro-Hungarian—and has experienced all the traumas common to Europe's borderlands. Following independence, however, Moldova could take advantage of this position by serving as a bridge, linking eastern Europe, Turkey, the Slavic countries of the former USSR, and even Central Asia. In addition, Moldova's economic potential would be greatly increased with the construction of a port on the Danube, thus diminishing the perennial problem of transport costs, and allowing Moldova to take advantage of access to Europe's most important waterway.

Statistical Survey

Principal sources (unless otherwise indicated): IMF, *Moldova, Economic Review* and *International Financial Statistics: Supplement on Countries of the Former Soviet Union;* World Bank, *Statistical Handbook: States of the Former USSR.*

Area and Population

AREA, POPULATION AND DENSITY

Area (sq km)	33,700*
Population (census result)	
12 January 1989†	
Males	2,063,192
Females	2,272,168
Total	4,335,360
Population (official estimates at mid-year)	
1990	4,364,000
1991	4,363,000
1992	4,356,000
Density (per sq km) at mid-1992	129.3

* 13,010 sq miles.

† Figures refer to the *de jure* population. The *de facto* total was 4,337,592.

PRINCIPAL ETHNIC GROUPS

(permanent inhabitants, 1989 census)

	Number ('000)	%
Moldovan (Romanian)	2,795	64.5
Ukrainian	600	13.8
Russian	562	13.0
Gagauzi	153	3.5
Bulgarian	88	2.0
Jewish	66	1.5
Other	71	1.6
Total	4,335	100.0

PRINCIPAL TOWNS

(estimated population at 1 January 1990)

Chişinău (Kishinev) (capital)	676,000	Bălţi (Beltsy)	162,000
Tiraspol	184,000	Bender (Benderi)	132,000

Source: UN, *Demographic Yearbook.*

BIRTHS, MARRIAGES AND DEATHS (per 1,000)

	Registered live births		Registered marriages		Registered deaths	
	Number	Rate (per 1,000)	Number	Rate (per 1,000)	Number	Rate (per 1,000)
1987	91,762	21.4	39,084	9.1	40,185	9.4
1988	88,568	20.5	39,745	9.2	40,912	9.5
1989	82,221	18.9	39,928	9.2	40,113	9.2

Source: UN, *Demographic Yearbook.*

1992: Live births 70,102 (birth rate 16.1 per 1,000); Deaths 44,637 (death rate 10.2 per 1,000). Source: UN, *Population and Vital Statistics Report.*

EMPLOYMENT (annual averages, '000 persons)

	1990	1991	1992
Agriculture, hunting, forestry and fishing	700	865	820
Manufacturing	443	363	394
Electricity, gas and water	13	13	14
Construction	144	121	120
Trade, restaurants and hotels	138	111	111
Transport, storage and communications	111	105	102
Financing, insurance, real estate and business services	9	10	9
Community, social and personal services	444	422	422
Services not adequately defined	69	60	58
Total	2,071	2,070	2,050

1989 census (persons aged 15 years and over): Total labour force 2,117,592 (males 1,084,504; females 1,033,088).

Source: ILO, *Year Book of Labour Statistics.*

Agriculture

PRINCIPAL CROPS ('000 metric tons)

	1990	1991	1992
Wheat	1,129	1,057	1,000*
Barley	419	427	400*
Maize	885	1,501	700*
Other cereals*	6	6	6
Potatoes	295	291	300*
Total pulses	97	106	80*
Sunflower seed	252	169	175*
Vegetables	1,657	1,443	1,300*
Water-melons*	480	454	450*
Grapes	940	774	720
Other fruit	901	698	650*
Sugar beets	2,374	2,262	2,200*
Tobacco (leaves)	73	69	51

* FAO estimate(s).

Source: FAO, *Production Yearbook.*

LIVESTOCK ('000 head at 1 January)

	1990	1991	1992*
Horses	46	47	48*
Cattle	1,100	1,100	1,021
Pigs	2,000	1,800	1,404
Sheep†	1,168	1,189	1,189
Goats†	10	10	10
Poultry†	25,000	25,000	24,000

* FAO estimate(s). † Unofficial figure(s).

Source: FAO, *Production Yearbook.*

LIVESTOCK PRODUCTS
('000 metric tons, unless otherwise indicated)

	1990	1991	1992
Beef and veal	114	96	68*
Pigmeat	177	145	99*
Poultry meat	66	56	37*
Cows' milk	1,512	1,300	1,200*
Butter and ghee	27.0	21.8	20.0*
Eggs (metric tons)*	63,300	72,400	45,360
Wool:			
greasy	3,100	2,900	3,200†
scoured	1,850	1,750	1,900†

* Unofficial figure(s). † FAO estimate(s).

Source: FAO, *Production Yearbook.*

Industry

SELECTED PRODUCTS
('000 metric tons, unless otherwise indicated)

	1989	1990	1991
Vegetable oil	117.6	125.6	117.9
Flour	640.2	633.9	576.7
Sugar	446.1	435.8	236.9
Wine from grapes (million litres)	124	163	143
Soft drinks (million litres)	123.3	130.6	86.4
Cigarettes (million)	9,500	9,100	9,200
Cloth (million sq m)	224.2	244.2	228.1
Footwear (million pairs)	23.2	23.2	20.8
Refrigerators and freezers ('000)	204	133	118
Washing machines ('000)	280	298	194
Television receivers ('000)	121	138	173
Tractors ('000)	12.1	9.8	6.6
Electric energy (million kWh)	17,022	15,690	n.a.

Finance

CURRENCY AND EXCHANGE RATES

Monetary Units

A temporary coupon currency, the Moldovan rouble, was in use prior to the introduction of the leu on 29 November 1993 (see below).

Sterling and Dollar Equivalents (30 September 1993)
£1 sterling = 3,053.4 Moldovan roubles;
US $1 = 2,041.6 roubles;
10,000 Moldovan roubles = £3.275 = $4.898.

Note: Until July 1993 the Russian (formerly Soviet) rouble was legal tender in Moldova. Based on the official rate of exchange, the average value of the Soviet currency (roubles per US dollar) was: 0.6274 in 1989; 0.5856 in 1990; 0.5819 in 1991. However, a multiple exchange rate system was in operation, with separate non-commercial and tourist rates. A commercial exchange rate was introduced on 1 November 1990, replacing the official rate for most transactions. The commercial rate (roubles per US dollar) was: 1.692 at 31 December 1990; 1.671 at 31 December 1991. Between November 1989 and April 1991 the tourist exchange rate valued the rouble at one-tenth of the official rate. In April 1991 this rate, renamed the 'special rate', was set at $1 = 27.6 roubles. It was subsequently adjusted. Following the dissolution of the USSR in December 1991, Russia and several other former Soviet republics retained the rouble as their monetary unit. The Moldovan rouble, initially at par with the Russian rouble, was introduced in June 1992 as a coupon currency. The average interbank market rate in 1992 was $1 = 222.1 Russian roubles. In July 1993 all pre-1993 Russian roubles were withdrawn from circulation in Moldova, and from August a distinction was introduced between Moldovan roubles and the currencies of other countries in the rouble area. On 29 November 1993 the Moldovan leu (plural: lei) was introduced as the national currency. The leu comprises 100 bani (singular: ban). The former currency was exchanged at a rate of 1 leu = 1,000 Moldovan roubles. Some of the figures in this Survey are still expressed in terms of roubles.

STATE BUDGET (million Soviet roubles)

Revenue	1990	1991
Tax revenue	2,910.8	5,525.2
Taxes on income and profits	1,299.9	2,216.3
Individual income tax	305.9	501.0
State enterprises	821.7	1,391.9
Co-operatives and social organizations	172.3	323.5
Turnover tax	1,556.1	2,830.3
Sales tax	n.a.	453.4
Other revenue	1,376.8	877.9
Fees and charges	54.4	93.6
Transfers from Social Security Fund	426.5	n.a.
Re-evaluation of inventories	n.a.	91.0
Receipts from USSR budget	423.1	4.3
Surplus from previous budget	319.0	177.8
Unallocated receipts	181.0	n.a.
Total	4,468.6	6,403.1

Expenditure	1990	1991
National economy	2,179.5	2,445.4
Subsidies	n.a.	1,280.0
Social and cultural activities	1,702.0	3,261.2
Education	793.4	1,370.2
Health care	409.0	781.4
Transfers to Social Security Fund	485.4	981.9
Culture and art	n.a.	127.6
Science	n.a.	63.1
Internal affairs	5.0	161.2
Administration and state control	63.0	110.2
Expenditure on all-Union programmes	n.a.	217.5
Total (incl. others)	4,110.4	6,401.4

INTERNATIONAL RESERVES (US $ million at 31 December)

	1992
Reserve position in IMF	0.01
Foreign exchange	2.43
Total (excl. gold)	2.44

MONEY SUPPLY (million roubles at 31 December)

	1991	1992
Currency outside banks	1,827	9,444
Demand deposits at banks	7,260	5,808

COST OF LIVING
(Consumer Price Index; base: 1991 = 100)

	1992
All items	1,208.7

NATIONAL ACCOUNTS (million Soviet roubles at current prices)
Net Material Product by Use

	1989	1990	1991
Personal consumption	6,102	6,907	13,862
Material consumption in the units of the non-material sphere serving individuals	629	680	1,109
Consumption of the population	6,731	7,587	14,970
Material consumption in the units of the non-material sphere serving the community as a whole	129	190	170
Net fixed capital formation	1,295	1,065	1,280
Increase in material circulating assets and in stocks	1,057	824	3,662
Losses	52	141	226
Net exports of goods and material services / Net errors and omissions	−992	−364	−1,555
Total	8,272	9,443	18,753

1992: Net material product 192,533 million roubles.

Net Material Product by Economic Activity

	1989	1990	1991
Agriculture	3,312	3,934	7,823
Industry	2,913	3,245	7,048
Construction	826	852	1,296
Transport and communications	316	452	711
Trade and catering	817	871	1,757
Other activities of the material sphere	88	89	118
Total	8,272	9,443	18,753

External and Inter-republican (USSR) Trade

INTER-REPUBLICAN (USSR) TRADE
PRINCIPAL COMMODITIES (million Soviet roubles)

Imports	1988	1989	1990
Industrial products	4,863.7	4,883.2	4,618.9
Petroleum and gas	513.9	519.6	424.6
Coal	135.8	128.6	119.1
Iron and steel	310.6	310.8	285.8
Non-ferrous metallurgy	157.3	154.7	150.4
Chemical products	582.1	588.9	581.3
Machine-building and metalworking	1,603.7	1,610.4	1,504.4
Wood and paper products	223.0	223.6	205.0
Building materials	105.1	119.2	117.3
Light industry	718.8	704.3	769.0
Food industry	367.4	364.6	256.6
Agricultural goods	98.9	90.3	149.6
Other commodities	23.9	218.0	223.1
Total	4,986.5	5,191.5	4,991.6

Exports	1988	1989	1990
Industrial products	4,475.9	4,822.7	5,388.3
Chemical products	190.2	195.5	206.2
Machine-building and metalworking	924.4	983.1	978.0
Wood and paper products	104.9	109.3	80.8
Light industry	1,066.1	1,148.7	1,148.7
Food industry	1,924.2	2,101.5	2,621.1
Agricultural goods	318.2	319.4	426.5
Total (incl. others)	4,800.3	5,186.4	5,853.3

1991 (million roubles): *Imports c.i.f.:* Energy products 1,354.9; Other industrial goods 4,833.8; Consumer goods 1,048.6; Total 7,237.3. *Exports c.i.f.:* Agricultural products and processed food 3,200.7; Industrial goods 2,663.6; Consumer goods 1,944.7; Total 7,809.0.
1992 (estimates, million roubles): Imports 79,900; Exports 47,800.

PRINCIPAL TRADING PARTNERS
(million Soviet roubles)

	1991	
	Imports	Exports
Armenia	68.2	71.4
Azerbaijan	81.7	106.2
Belarus	598.2	508.7
Estonia	73.8	103.4
Georgia	122.6	60.9
Kazakhstan	260.6	180.2
Latvia	100.5	150.1
Lithuania	160.5	170.1
Russia	3,269.8	4,724.7
Ukraine	1,863.0	1,418.8
Uzbekistan	258.9	166.4
Total (incl. others)	7,237.3	7,809.0

EXTERNAL NON-USSR TRADE
PRINCIPAL COMMODITIES (million Soviet roubles)

Imports	1988	1989	1990
Industrial products	976.5	1,292.6	1,347.6
Iron and steel	8.2	11.3	21.8
Non-ferrous metallurgy	22.2	26.6	1.1
Chemical products	98.5	122.3	150.1
Machine-building and metalworking	192.5	250.6	356.7
Wood and paper products	38.9	37.9	19.1
Building materials	14.9	31.5	26.3
Light industry	427.7	570.1	538.4
Food industry	170.1	239.4	204.5
Agricultural goods	117.0	126.3	121.2
Total (incl. others)	1,093.9	1,420.0	1,469.8

Exports	1988	1989	1990
Industrial products	253.0	266.8	300.4
Electric power	94.3	87.9	58.8
Iron and steel	9.1	7.2	10.9
Machine-building and metalworking	38.8	50.3	67.1
Light industry	21.6	34.0	41.8
Food industry	84.2	81.2	111.7
Agricultural goods	2.6	2.6	22.6
Total (incl. others)	257.2	270.0	323.4

1991 (million roubles): Imports 1,206.5; Exports 331.8.
1992 (estimates, million roubles): Imports 162.7; Exports 118.2.

PRINCIPAL TRADING PARTNERS
(million Soviet roubles)

	1991	
	Imports	Exports
Austria	78.6	49.5
Bulgaria	48.1	37.3
Canada	53.5	8.1
Cuba	30.9	4.9
Czechoslovakia	52.6	9.5
France	53.5	6.4
Germany	64.6	58.3
Hungary	14.4	18.3
Italy	19.4	11.2
Japan	27.9	10.0
Poland	22.8	8.7
Romania	261.8	55.3
United Kingdom	6.8	14.0
USA	239.0	4.7
Total (incl. others)	1,206.5	331.8

Transport

ROAD TRAFFIC (motor vehicles registered at 31 December)

	1990	1991	1992
Passenger cars	209,013	218,059	221,883
Goods vehicles	11,060	10,528	9,297
Buses and coaches	11,308	11,226	11,112
Motor cycles and scooters	196,354	198,809	n.a.

Source: International Road Federation, *World Road Statistics*.

Education

(1987/88)

	Institutions	Students
Secondary schools	1,617	731,000
Secondary specialized institutions	52	52,084
Higher schools (incl. universities)	9	58,970

Directory

The Constitution

A new constitution was drafted in 1992 and 1993. It was to be ratified only after the new Moldovan Parliament (elected in February 1994) had approved it.

The Government

(April 1994)

HEAD OF STATE

President: MIRCEA ION SNEGUR (directly elected 8 December 1991).

COUNCIL OF MINISTERS

Prime Minister: ANDREI SANGHELI.

Deputy Prime Ministers: VALENTIN PETRU CUNEV, ION GUTU, VALERIU BULGARI*.

Minister of State: GHEORGHE DAVID GUSAC.

Minister of the Economy: VALERIU BOBUTAC.

Minister of Finance: VALERIU CHITAN.

Minister of Privatization and Administration of State Property: CESLAV CIOBANU.

Minister of Industry: GRIGORE TRIBOI.

Minister of Agriculture and Food: VITALIE VASILE GORINCIOI.

Minister of Informatics, Information and Telecommunications: ION LEON CASIAN.

Minister of Labour and Social Security: DUMITRU ION NIDELCU.

Minister of Health: TIMOFEI MOSNEAGA.

Minister of Education: PETRU GAUGAS.

Minister of Culture: VALERIU PAVEL CIBOTARU.

Minister of Justice: VASILE STURZA.

Minister of Defence: PAVEL SIMION CREANGĂ.

Minister of the Interior: CONSTANTIN GRIGORE ANTOCI.

Minister of National Security: VASILE PAVEL CALMOI.

Minister of Foreign Affairs: MIHAI POPOV.

Minister of Transport: VASILE IOVV.

Minister of Public Services: MIHAI STEFAN SEVEROVAN.

Minister of Relations with Parliament: VICTOR PUSCAS.

* Another Deputy Prime Minister was to be appointed.

CHAIRMEN OF STATE DEPARTMENTS

Chairman of the State Department for Customs: GHEORGHE HIOARĂ.

Chairman of the State Department for Energy Resources: VALERIU IUREVICI ICONNICOV.

Chairman of the State Department for Environmental Protection and Natural Resources: ION I. DEDIU.

Chairman of the State Department for the Gas Industry: BORIS GHEORGHE CARANDIUC.

Chairman of the State Department for Languages: ION CIOCANU.

Chairman of the State Department for Privatization: VISARION CEŞUEV.

Chairman of the State Department for Publishing: AUREL ANDREI SCOBIOALĂ.

Chairman of the State Department for Technology: DUMITRU CIMPOIEŞ.

MINISTRIES

(March 1994)

Ministry of Agriculture and Food: Chişinău, Ştefan cel Mare; tel. (2) 23-35-36.

Ministry of Architecture and Construction: 277012 Chişinău, Cosmonautilor 9; tel. (2) 23-35-17.

Ministry of Culture and Religion: 277033 Chişinău, Piaţa Marii Adunări Naţionale 1; tel. (2) 22-76-20; telex 163137; fax (2) 23-23-88.

Ministry of Defence: Chişinău, str. Hînceşti 1; tel. (2) 23-26-31.

Ministry of the Economy: 277033 Chişinău, Piaţa Marii Adunări Naţionale 1; tel. (2) 23-31-35; fax (2) 23-40-64.

Ministry of Finance: 277033 Chişinău, Cosmonautilor 7; tel. (2) 23-35-75.

Ministry of Foreign Affairs: 277033 Chişinău, Piaţa Marii Adunări Naţionale 1; tel. (2) 23-39-40; telex 163130; fax (2) 23-23-02.

Ministry of Foreign Economic Relations: 277033 Chişinău, Piaţa Marii Adunări Naţionale 1; tel. (2) 23-39-40; telex 163130; fax (2) 23-23-02.

Ministry of Health: Chişinău, str. Hînceşti 1; tel. (2) 72-10-10.

Ministry of Informatics, Information and Telecommunications: Chişinău, Ştefan cel Mare; tel. (2) 24-27-47.

Ministry of the Interior: Chişinău, Ştefan cel Mare 67; tel. (2) 23-35-69.

Ministry of Justice: 277001 Chişinău, Ştefan cel Mare 73; tel. (2) 24-50-87; fax (2) 26-51-67.

Ministry of Labour and Social Security: Chişinău, str. Hînceşti 1; tel. (2) 73-75-72; fax (2) 73-51-81.

Ministry of National Security: Chişinău, Ştefan cel Mare 166; tel. (2) 23-93-09.

Ministry of Public Housing: Chişinău, str. Secenov 3; tel. (2) 72-95-47.

Ministry of Science and Education: 277033 Chişinău, Piaţa Marii Adunări Naţionale 1; tel. (2) 23-35-15; fax (2) 23-34-74.

Ministry of Trade and Material Resources: Chişinău, Ştefan cel Mare 77; tel. (2) 23-35-82; telex 163115; fax (2) 22-44-47.

Ministry of Transport: 277004 Chişinău, Bucuriey 12A; tel. (2) 62-05-70; fax (2) 62-48-75.

Ministry of Youth, Sport and Tourism: 277001 Chişinău, Ştefan cel Mare 73; tel. (2) 22-60-61.

State Departments

State Department for Customs: Chişinău.

State Department for Energy Resources—MOLDENERGO: 277612 Chişinău, Khynchesht 1; tel. (2) 72-96-89; telex 163196; fax (2) 25-31-41.

State Department for Environmental Protection and Natural Resources: 277001 Chişinău, Ştefan cel Mare 73; tel. (2) 22-18-61; fax (2) 23-38-06.

State Department for the Gas Industry: Chişinău, str. Albisoara 38; tel. (2) 24-05-29.

State Department for Languages: Chişinău.

State Department for Privatization: Chişinău.

State Department for Publishing: Chişinău, str. Albisoara 38; tel. (2) 24-65-25.

State Department for Technology: Chişinău.

Legislature

MOLDOVAN PARLIAMENT

The draft of a new constitution proposed that legislative authority should reside in a 104-member unicameral Parliament (compared to the previous 380). Both the President of the Republic and the deputies were to be elected for four-year terms. Before this draft constitution was promulgated it was to be considered by the new Parliament (elected 27 February 1994) and ratified in a national referendum.

According to the final election results, the Agrarian Democratic Party won 43% of the votes cast (56 seats), the Socialist Party-Yedinstvo (Unity) Movement bloc 22% (28), the Peasants' Party of Moldova-Congress of the Intelligentsia electoral alliance 9% (11) and the CDPF 8% (9). The Social Democratic Party of Moldova won 3.5%, the Democratic Labour Party of Moldova 2.6%, and the Reform Party 2.5% of the votes cast, but did not gain representation.

Chairman: PETRU LUCINSCHI.

Deputy Chairmen: DUMITRU MOTPAN, NICOLAE ANDRONIC.

Secretary: GHEORGHE GHIMPU.

Local Government

For administrative purposes, Moldova is divided into 10 cities and 40 districts or counties (raioane). Each unit of local government is named for the town in which it is based, where the head of the administration, a governor, sits. However, not all territories acknowledged the authority of the central government. In 1991 the region east of the Dnestr river (Transdnestria), which was dominated by ethnic Russians, declared the independence of a 'Dnestr Soviet Socialist Republic', based in Tiraspol. In the south of Moldova, five districts dominated by the Gagauz (Turkish Christians) declared a 'Gagauz Soviet Socialist Republic', based in Comrat (Komrat).

CITIES

Bălti: Bălti; tel. (31) 2-31-81; Gov. VLADIMIR TONCIUC.

Bender: Bender; tel. (32) 2-30-50; Gov. VECESLAV COGUT.

Cahul: Cahul; tel. (39) 2-24-00; Gov. SIMION PLATON.

Chişinău: Chişinău; tel. (2) 23-72-55; Gov. NICOLAE COSTIN.

Dubăsari: Dubăsari; tel. (45) 2-23-32; Gov. VLADISLAV FINAGIN.

Orhei: Orhei; tel. (35) 2-42-66; Gov. VLADIMIR POPUŞOI.

Rîbnita: Rîbnita; tel. (55) 3-09-77; Gov. ALEXANDRU IULIN.

Soroca: Soroca; tel. (30) 2-26-60; Gov. ANATOL CHUŞNER.

Tiraspol: Tiraspol; tel. (33) 3-14-55; Gov. VLADIMIR RÎLEACOV.

Ungheni: Ungheni; tel. (36) 2-23-36; Gov. VASILE PARA.

DISTRICTS

Anenii Noi: Anenii Noi; tel. (65) 2-26-50; Gov. ANATOL BARBĂROŞIE.

Basarabeasca: Basarabeasca; tel. (67) 2-26-50; Gov. GRIGORE OJOG.

Briceni: Briceni; tel. (47) 2-26-50; Gov. VALERIU BULGARI.

Cahul: Cahul; tel. (39) 2-23-04; Gov. VASILE VLADARCIUC.

Camenca: Camenca; tel. (66) 2-35-40; Gov. LEONID MATEICIUC.

Cantemir: Cantemir; tel. (73) 2-26-50; Gov. PINTILIE PÎRVAN.

Căinari: Căinari; tel. (77) 2-26-50; Gov. ALEXANDRU SÎRBU.

Clăraşi: Clăraşi; tel. (44) 2-26-50; Gov. ION MALCOCI.

Căuşeni: Căuşeni; tel. (43) 2-26-50; Gov. EUGEN PÎSLARU.

Ciadîr-Lunga: Ciadîr-Lunga; tel. (61) 2-26-50; Gov. DUMITRU CROITOR.

Cimişlia: Cimişlia; tel. (41) 2-26-50; Gov. ANDREI COADĂ.

Comrat: Comrat; tel. (38) 2-26-50; Gov. VICTOR VOLCOV.

Criuleni: Criuleni; tel. (48) 2-26-50; Gov. VLADIMIR CEBAN.

Donduşeni: Donduşeni; tel. (51) 2-26-50; Gov. ANATOL VASCĂUTAN.

Drochia: Drochia; tel. (52) 2-26-50; Gov. PETRU AVASILOAE.

Dubăsari: Dubăsari, Cocieri; tel. (78) 22-51-38; Gov. ŞTEFAN BEŞLEAGA.

Edinet: Edinet; tel. (46) 2-26-50; Gov. DUMITRU PUNTEA.

Făleşti: Făleşti; tel. (59) 2-26-50; Gov. CONSTANTIN COMAN.

Floreşti: Floreşti; tel. (50) 2-26-50; Gov. NICOLAE BARBĂSCUMPĂ.

Glodeni: Glodeni; tel. (49) 2-26-50; Gov. LEONID ISTRATI.

Grigoriopol: Grigoriopol; tel. (40) 2-39-93; Gov. SERGIU LEONTIEV.

Hînceşti: Hînceşti; tel. (34) 2-26-50; Gov. ION DONICĂ.

Ialoveni: Ialoveni; tel. (68) 22-83-76; Gov. GRIGORE GOLOGAN.

Leova: Leova; tel. (63) 2-26-50; Gov. VICTOR ANDONI.

Nisporeni: Nisporeni; tel. (64) 2-26-50; Gov. MIHAI CIORICI.

Ocnita: Ocnita; tel. (71) 2-26-50; Gov. ION GUTU.

Orhei: Orhei; tel. (35) 2-26-50; Gov. VLADIMIR BOBEICĂ.

Rezina: Rezina; tel. (54) 2-26-50; Gov. NICOLAE PROCA.

Rîbnita: Rîbnita; tel. (55) 3-26-50; Gov. NICOLAE MACUŞINSCHI.

Rîşcani: Rîşcani; tel. (56) 2-26-50; Gov. ALEXANDRU SCORPAN.

Sîngerei: Sîngerei; tel. (62) 2-26-50; Gov. MIHAI CUCOŞ.

Slobozia: Slobozia; tel. (57) 2-46-50; Gov. VASILE VACARCIUC.

Soroca: Soroca; tel. (30) 2-26-50; Gov. VASILE LUPUŞOR.

Străşeni: Străşeni; tel. (37) 2-26-50; Gov. NICOLAE ALEXEI.

Şoldăneşti: Şoldăneşti; tel. (72) 2-26-50; Gov. VASILE MACOVEI.

Ştefan Vodă: Ştefan Vodă; tel. (42) 2-26-50; Gov. VASILE VARTIC.

Taraclia: Taraclia; tel. (74) 2-36-50; Gov. DUMITRU CEREŞ.

Teleneşti: Teleneşti; tel. (58) 2-26-50; Gov. TUDOR LEFTER.

Ungheni: Ungheni; tel. (36) 2-26-50; Gov. TUDOR GONCIARUC.

Vulcňeşti: Vulcňeşti; tel. (53) 2-20-50; Gov. CONSTANTIN CARAGHIAUR.

SEPARATIST REGIONS

Transdnestria ('Dnestr SSR')

President of the Dnestr SSR: IGOR N. SMIRNOV.

Vice-President of the Dnestr SSR: ALEKSANDR KARAMAN.

Gagauzia ('Gagauz SSR')

President of the Gagauz SSR: STEPAN TOPOL.

Vice-President of the Gagauz SSR: MIKHAIL KENDIGELYAN.

Political Organizations

In August 1991 the Moldovan Parliament voted to ban the Communist Party of Moldova. In 1993 there were more than 20 political parties and movements registered in Moldova, among the most prominent of which were the following:

Agrarian Democratic Party (ADP): Chişinău; f. by moderates from both the Popular Front of Moldova and the Communist Party; supports Moldovan independence, CIS membership and economic and agricultural reform; Leader PETRU LUCINSCHI; Chair. K. ANDREYEV.

Christian Democratic Popular Front—CDPF: 277014 Chişinău, str. Nicolae Iorga 5; tel. (2) 22-50-64; fax (2) 23-44-80; f. 1989 as the Popular Front of Moldova, renamed 1992; advocates Moldova's reintegration into Romania; Pres. MIRCEA DRUC.

Congress of the Intelligentsia: Chişinău; f. 1993 by former Popular Front of Moldova members; favours union with Romania.

Democratic Labour Party of Moldova: Chişinău; f. 1993; Pres. ALEXANDRU ARSENI.

Gagauz Halky (Gagauz People): Comrat; represents the ethnic Gagauz population.

Peasants' Party of Moldova: Chişinău; nationalist, moderate party; formed electoral alliance with the Congress of the Intelligentsia in 1994.

Reform Party: Chişinău; f. 1993; centre-right party which seeks to represent middle-class interests; Leader ANATOL SALARU; Chair. STEFAN GORDA.

Social Democratic Party of Moldova: Chişinău; f. 1990; based on support from urban professional groups and ethnic minorities; supports independence and economic reform.

Socialist Party: Chişinău; successor to the former Communist Party; favours socialist economic and social policies, defends the rights of Russian and other minorities and advocates CIS membership; Leader VALERIU SENIC.

Yedinstvo (Unity) Movement: Chişinău; Leader PETR SHORNIKOV.

Diplomatic Representation

EMBASSIES IN MOLDOVA

China, People's Republic: Chişinău; Chargé d'affaires a.i.: TIANG BENLIANG.

Germany: 277012 Chişinău, M. Cebotari, Hotel Seabeco, Suite 622; tel. (2) 23-73-63; fax (2) 23-28-70; Chargé d'affaires a.i.: JOHANNES GIFFELS.

Kazakhstan: Chişinău.

Romania: Chişinău, Vlaicu Pîrcălab 39; tel. (2) 22-75-83; Ambassador: MARIAN ENACHE .

Russia: Chişinău; tel. (2) 22-85-73; fax (2) 23-26-00; Ambassador: VLADIMIR PLECHKO.

Ukraine: Chişinău; Ambassador: VITALII BOIKO.

USA: Chişinău, Alexi Mateevich 103; tel. (2) 23-37-72; fax (2) 23-24-94; Ambassador: MARY C. PENDLETON.

Judicial System

President of the Supreme Court: PAVEL BARBALAT.

Procurator: DIMITRIE POSTOVAN.

Religion

The majority of the inhabitants of Moldova profess Christianity, the largest denomination being the Eastern Orthodox Church. The Gagauz, although of Turkic descent, are also adherents of Orthodox Christianity.

Roman Catholic Church

The diocese of Tiraspol was founded in 1848, but has been inoperative for many years.

Russian Orthodox Church

In December 1992 the Patriarch of Moscow and All Russia issued a decree altering the status of the Eparchy of Chişinău and

Moldova to that of a Metropolitan See. The Government accepted this decree, thus tacitly rejecting the claims of the Metropolitan of Bessarabia.

Archbishop of Chişinău and Moldova: VLADIMIR.

The Press

In 1989 there were 200 officially-registered newspapers being published in Moldova (including 85 published in Romanian), and 65 periodicals (including 30 in Romanian). In 1990 the number of Romanian-language newspapers and periodicals increased, and most publications began using the Latin script.

The publications listed below are in Romanian, except where otherwise indicated.

PRINCIPAL NEWSPAPERS

Glasul (The Voice): Chişinău.

Moldova Suverană (Sovereign Moldova): 277012 Chişinău, str. Puşkin 22; tel. (2) 23-35-38; fax (2) 23-35-01; f. 1924; 5 a week; organ of the Govt of Moldova; Editor TUDOR TSOPA; circ. 100,000.

Nezavisimaya Moldova (Independent Moldova): 277612 Chişinău, str. Puşkin 22; tel. (2) 23-35-59; fax (2) 23-36-08; f. 1925; 5 a week; independent; in Russian; Editor BORIS MARIAN; circ. 46,660.

Rabochy Tiraspol (Working Tiraspol): Tiraspol; main newspaper of the east-bank Slavs; anti-Govt; in Russian; Editor VALENTIN LESNICHENKO.

Sovetskaya Moldova (Soviet Moldova): 277612 Chişinău, str. Puşkin 22; tel. (2) 23-36-05; f. 1925; morning.

Ţara (Homeland): Chişinău; organ of the Christian Democratic Popular Front; circ. 8,000.

Tinerimya Moldovei/Molodezh Moldovy (Youth of Moldova): Chişinău; f. 1928; 3 a week; editions in Romanian (circ. 12,212) and Russian (circ. 4,274); Editor V. BOTNARU.

Viaţă Satului (Life of the Village): 277612 Chişinău, str. Puşkin 22, Casa presei, et. 4; tel. (2) 23-03-68; f. 1945; 3 a week; govt publ.; Editor V. S. SPINEY; circ. 50,000.

PRINCIPAL PERIODICALS

Basarabia (Bessarabia): Chişinău; f. 1931; fmrly *Nistru*; monthly; journal of the Union of Writers of Moldova; fiction; Editor-in-Chief D. MATKOVSKY; circ. 4,500.

Chipăruş (Peppercorn): 277612 Chişinău, str. Puşkin 22; tel. (2) 23-38-16; f. 1958; fortnightly; satirical; Editor-in-Chief ION VIKOL; circ. 6,000.

Femeile Moldova (Moldovan Woman): 233470 Chişinău, 28-vo Iyunya 45; f. 1951; monthly; popular, for women; circ. 25,468.

Lanterna Magică (Magic Lantern): Chişinău, str. Bucureşti 39; tel. (2) 26-51-77; telex 163137; fax (2) 23-23-88; f. 1990; publ. by the Ministry of Culture and Religion; 6 a year; art, culture; circ. 2,500.

Literatură şi Artă: 277009 Chişinău, str. Sfatul Tării; tel. (2) 24-92-96; f. 1954; weekly; organ of the Union of Writers of Moldova; literary; Editor NICOLAE DABIJA; circ. 100,000.

Moldova: Chişinău; f. 1966; monthly; illustrated popular and fiction; circ. 4,855.

Noi (Us): Chişinău; tel. (2) 23-31-10; f. 1930; fmrly *Scînteia Leninista*; monthly; fiction; for 10–15-year-olds; Man. VALERIU VOLONTIR; circ. 8,900.

Sud-Est (South East): Chişinău, str. Maria Cebotari 16; tel. (2) 23-26-05; fax (2) 23-22-42; f. 1990; publ. by the Ministry of Culture and Religion; quarterly; art, culture; Editor-in-Chief VALENTINA TASLAUANA; circ. 5,000.

NEWS AGENCY

Moldovan Information Agency—Moldovapres: 277012 Chişinău, str. Puşkin 22; tel. (2) 23-34-95; telex 163140; fax (2) 23-43-71; f. 1990.

Publishers

In 1989 there were 1,479 titles (books and pamphlets) published in Moldova (21.3m. copies), of which 522 titles were in Romanian (9.5m. copies).

Editura Enciclopedică: 277612 Chişinău, Ştefan cel Mare 180; tel. (2) 24-68-92; Editor-in-Chief ION GROSU.

Humanitas: Chişinău, Ştefan cel Mare; political and fiction; in Romanian, Russian, Ukrainian, Gagauz and Bulgarian; Dir N. N. MUMZHI.

Hyperion: 277004 Chişinău, Ştefan cel Mare; tel. (2) 24-64-14; f. 1977; fiction, non-fiction, poetry, art books; in Romanian, Russian, English, French, Spanish, Gagauz and Bulgarian; Dir VALERIU MATEI.

Lumina (Light): Chişinău, Ştefan cel Mare 180; tel. (2) 24-63-95; f. 1966; educational textbooks; Man. VLADIMIR I. KISTRUGA; Editor-in-Chief CHIRIL T. VAKULOVSKY.

Ştiinţa: Chişinău, str. Academic 3; tel. (2) 73-96-16; f. 1959; scientific literature; in Romanian and Russian; Dir G. N. PRINI.

Universitas: Chişinău; Editor-in-Chief IURIE KOLESNIK.

GOVERNMENT AGENCY

State Department for Publishing: 277004 Chişinău, Ştefan cel Mare 180; tel. (2) 24-65-25; fax (2) 24-64-12; Chair. AUREL A. SCOBIOALĂ.

Radio and Television

Radio Chişinău: 277028 Chişinău, str. Prerezhnikov 1; broadcasts in Romanian and Russian; Gen. Dir Radio and Television ADRIAN USATII.

Chişinău Television: 277028 Chişinău, str. Prerezhnikov 1.

Finance

(cap. = capital; res = reserves; dep. = deposits)

BANKING

Restructuring of Moldova's banking system was begun in 1991 with the establishment of a central bank, the National Bank of Moldova (NBM), which was formerly a branch of the USSR Gosbank (state bank). The NBM is independent of the Government (but subordinate to Parliament) and has the power to regulate monetary policy and the financial system. In 1993, apart from the NBM, the banking system comprised the State-Commercial Savings Bank (which had more than 1,000 branches nation-wide, with a total of 4.5m. accounts) and 17 other commercial banks.

Central Bank

National Bank of Moldova: 277006 Chişinău, Renasterii 7; tel. (2) 22-16-79; fax (2) 22-95-91; res. 1,375.9m. roubles, dep. 42.2m. roubles (1993); Dir LEONID TALMACH.

Commercial Banks

Banca socială: 277006 Chişinău, str. Banulescu Bodony 61; tel. (2) 22-63-68; telex 163265; fax (2) 22-24-45; f. 1991; joint-stock commercial bank; cap. 1,074.4m. roubles, dep. 384.4m. roubles; Pres. VLADIMIR SUETNOV; Vice-Pres. AGLAYA KRIVCHANSKAYA; 2 brs.

Bancosind: 277036 Chişinău, str. Puşkin 26; tel. (2) 22-36-31; fax (2) 22-55-86; trade-union bank; Chair. BORIS COJUHARI.

Commercial Besarabiabank: 277006 Chişinău, str. Puşkin 42; tel. (2) 24-07-57; fax (2) 24-47-54; Chair. GHEORGHE ANDRIES.

Intreprinzbank: 277036 Chişinău, str. Sfatul Ţării 16; tel. (2) 47-11-89; fax (2) 22-51-70; Chair. PAVEL VIZER.

Moldmebelbank: 277001 Chişinău, str. Tighina 65; tel. (2) 22-89-50; telex 163169; fax (2) 22-50-11; Chair. NICOLAI DORIN.

Moldindconbanc SA: 277006 Chişinău, Renasterii 7; tel. (2) 22-76-80; telex 163228; fax (2) 22-93-82; joint-stock commercial bank; Chair. ANATOL I. TURCANU.

Moldova-Agroindbanc SA: 277006 Chişinău, str. Renasterii 7; tel. (2) 22-83-17; telex 163263; fax (2) 23-27-06; f. 1991; joint-stock commercial bank; cap. 2,725m. roubles, dep. 1,030m. roubles (August 1993); Chair. GRIGORE FURTUNĂ; 43 brs.

Promstroibank: 129700 Ribnita, Promislennii 2; tel. (55) 5-00-39; fax (55) 3-23-95; Chair. NINA IUSUPOVA.

Victoriabank: 277004 Chişinău, str. Augusta 31 141; tel. (2) 23-30-65; telex 163188; fax (2) 23-39-33; Chair. VICTOR TURCANU.

Savings Bank

State-Commercial Savings Bank of Moldova: 277006 Chişinău, Cosmonautilor 9; tel. (2) 22-52-27; fax (2) 24-47-31; Chair. CONSTANTIN BULGAC.

Foreign Bank

Finist Bank (Russia): 278000 Tiraspol, str. K. Libknehta; tel. (33) 3-64-75.

Trade and Industry

CHAMBER OF COMMERCE

Chamber of Commerce and Industry of the Republic of Moldova: 277012 Chişinău, M. Eminescu 28; tel. (2) 22-15-52; telex 163118; fax (2) 23-38-10; f. 1969; Chair. VASILY D. GANDRABURA.

FOREIGN TRADE ORGANIZATIONS

Moldimpex: 277018 Chişinău, Botanicheskaya 15; tel. (2) 55-70-36; Gen. Dir V. D. VOLODIN.

MAJOR INDUSTRIAL COMPANIES

Agromashina Production Association: 277034 Chişinău, Uzinelor 21; tel. (2) 47-12-16; telex 163147; fax (2) 47-22-00; f. 1949; machines for cultivation, sowing and processing, for use in horticulture, viniculture, arboriculture and fruit-growing.

Alfa Production Association: 277051 Chişinău, Alba Yuliya 75; tel. (2) 62-75-58; telex 163129; fax (2) 62-78-04; televisions, radios, medical appliances.

Bender Mechanical Engineering Factory: 278100 Bender, Benderskogo vosstaniya 5; tel. (32) 2-68-43; telex 163177; fax (32) 22-24-73; f. 1972; specialized electronic aviation equipment.

Chişinău Refrigerator Factory: 277036 Chişinău, Meshterul Manolye 9; tel. (2) 47-42-71; telex 163175; fax (2) 47-16-17; f. 1964; manufactures Giochel freezers.

Compecs Factory: 277075 Chişinău, Mikhay Cadovyany 20/2; tel. (2) 33-36-34; telex 163171; fax (2) 33-36-76; f. 1986; computers, radio-electronic equipment, electronic components, washing machines.

Elektromash: 278000 Tiraspol, Sekriery; tel. (33) 3-32-59; telex 163177; fax (33) 5-19-70; f. 1959; synchronized diesel generators, transformers, synchronized electric motors.

MoldovaGas: Chişinău; natural-gas company.

Rif Scientific Research Institute: 279200 Bălti, Bykoviney 13; tel. (31) 2-11-47; telex 163177; fax (31) 2-10-17; f. 1957; navigation equipment for river- and sea-vessels, sonar equipment.

Sigma Production Association: 277032 Chişinău, Dechebal 99; tel. (2) 56-57-82; telex 163177; fax (2) 56-57-82; f. 1963; computers, stereo headphones.

Topaz Factory: 277004 Chişinău, pl. Frunze 1; tel. (2) 62-47-50; telex 163177; fax (2) 62-17-20; f. 1977; computerized navigation systems for ships; machines for the textile, petroleum-processing and natural-gas industries.

Tractor Factory Production Association: 277004 Chişinău, Kontemira 170; tel. (2) 63-29-33; telex 136224; fax (2) 22-24-73; f. 1961; caterpillar tractors, stone-cutting machines, heating equipment.

CONSUMER ORGANIZATION

Union of Consumers' Societies of Moldova: 277001 Chişinău, Ştefan cel Mare 67; tel. (2) 23-35-95; telex 163155; fax (2) 26-24-84; Chair. PAVEL G. DUBALAR.

Transport

RAILWAYS

Moldovan Railways: 277012 Chişinău, str. Vlaiku Pirkelab 48; tel. (2) 23-35-83; f. 1992 following the dissolution of the former Soviet Railways (SZD) organization; total network 1,338 km; Pres. I. MIKENBERG.

Tourism

Ministry of Youth, Sport and Tourism: see section on The Government (Ministries).

Moldova-Tur: Chişinău; tel. (2) 26-66-79; Dir-Gen. NICOLAE CHERNOMAZ.

Culture

NATIONAL ORGANIZATIONS

Ministry of Culture and Religion: see section on The Government (Ministries).

State Department for Architecture and Town Planning: Chişinău; tel. (2) 23-39-20; Chair. ALEXEI G. PALADI.

CULTURAL HERITAGE

Institute of Ethnography and Folklore: 277612 Chişinău, Ştefan cel Mare 1; tel. (2) 26-14-45; attached to the Moldovan Academy of Sciences; Dir N. A. DEMCENCO.

Moldovan State Art Museum: Chişinău, Lenina 115; 22,000 exhibits; Dir T. V. STAVILA.

National Library of the Republic of Moldova: 277612 Chişinău, str. Augusta 31 78A; tel. (2) 22-14-75; f. 1832; 3,500,000 vols; Dir A. RĂU.

PERFORMING ARTS

Chekhov Russian Drama Theatre: Chişinău, 28-vo Iyunya 75.

Opera and Ballet Theatre: Chişinău, Ştefan cel Mare 180.

Likurich Puppet Theatre: Chişinău, Kievskaya 121.

Moldova National Philharmonic: 277012 Chişinău, Metropolit Varlaam 78; tel. (2) 22-40-16; fax (2) 23-23-88; Dep. Dir VALENTIN GOGA; Dir IGOR BOLBOCHANU.

ASSOCIATION

Union of Writers of Moldova: 277612 Chişinău, Kievskaya 98; tel. (2) 22-73-73.

Education

Until the late 1980s the system of education was an integral part of the Soviet system, with most education in the Russian language. In 1990 and 1991 there were extensive changes to the education system, with Romanian literature and history added to the curriculum. In the period 1980–88 the percentage of pupils in general day-schools taught in Russian increased from 36.9% to 40.9%, although this trend was reversed in the early 1990s. In 1991 the state budget allocated 1,370.2m. roubles (or 21.4% of total budgetary spending) to education.

UNIVERSITY

Moldovan State University: 277014 Chişinău, Livezilor 60; tel. (2) 24-00-41; telex 163645; languages of instruction: Russian and Romanian; f. 1945; 13 faculties; 950 teachers; 11,800 students; Rector B. E. MELNIK.

Social Welfare

The social-security and health systems provided a comprehensive service. In 1991 a Social Security Fund was established in order to dispense a system of social benefits, including family benefits and allowances, pensions and social insurance. Social security provided allowances for families, especially those with low incomes, pensioners and invalids. Women aged 55 who have worked for at least 20 years, and men who are 60 and who have worked for at least 25 years, were eligible for a pension. In early 1992 some 900,000 people were in receipt of pensions. In February 1994 President Snegur announced a 50% increase in pensions. In 1990 there were 129.2 hospital beds per 10,000 inhabitants and one doctor for every 250 people. In the following year the state budget allocated 781.4m. roubles to health care (some 12.2% of budgetary expenditure), while a further 981.9m. roubles (15.3%) was transferred to supplement the Social Security Fund.

NATIONAL AGENCIES

Ministry of Health: see section on The Government (Ministries).

Department of Pensions and Social Welfare: Chişinău, str. Hînceşti 1; tel. (2) 72-99-85; Dir ALEXEI A. SÎCI.

Social Security Fund: Chişinău, str. Hînceşti 1; tel. (2) 72-99-55; Dir GHEORGHE A. CIUMAK.

HEALTH AND WELFARE ORGANIZATIONS

Invalids' Society of Moldova: Chişinău; tel. (2) 72-80-63; Pres. MARICICA P. LEVITSKAYA.

Moldovan Charity and Health Fund: 277028 Chişinău, Khynchesht 1; tel. (2) 72-96-89; fax (2) 73-53-22; f. 1988; provides social, moral, medical and material assistance for pensioners, invalids, families with many children and other needy people; Pres. ION P. CUZUIOC.

Organization of the Red Cross in Moldova: Chişinău; tel. (2) 72-97-00; Pres. ION P. DUMITRAŞ.

The Environment

GOVERNMENT ORGANIZATIONS

State Department for Energy Resources—MOLDENERGO: see section on The Government (Ministries).

State Department for Environmental Protection and Natural Resources: see section on The Government (Ministries).

ACADEMIC INSTITUTES

Academy of Sciences of Moldova: 277612 Chişinău, Ştefan cel Mare 1; tel. (2) 26-14-78; fax (2) 26-20-91; f. 1961; Pres. A. ANDRIESH ; attached institutes incl.:

Commission on Nature Conservation: 277612 Chişinău, Ştefan cel Mare 1; attached to the Presidium of the Academy; Chair. S. I. TOMA.

Institute of Biological Protection of Plants: 277072 Chişinău, Păcii 58; tel. (2) 57-04-66; Dir N. A. FILIPPOV.

Republic of Moldova Committee on the UNESCO 'Man and Biosphere' Programme: Chişinău; attached to the Presidium of the Academy; Chair. M. F. LUPAŞCU.

NON-GOVERNMENTAL ORGANIZATIONS

Ecological Movement of Moldova: Chişinău; f. 1990; local Green movement and political party.

Moldovan Society of Animal Protection: Chişinău, str. Serghei Lazo 17, apt 6; tel. (2) 24-75-99; environmental education, co-operates with government agencies and non-governmental organizations with interests in animal welfare and the environment; Pres. Prof. P. I. NESTEROV.

Defence

Following independence from the USSR (declared in August 1991), the Moldovan Government initiated the creation of national armed forces. In June 1993, according to Western estimates, these numbered 9,400, including 3,500 Ministry of Defence and rear services staff. There were some 300,000 reserves. There was a national guard, attached to the Ministry of the Interior, numbering 2,500 men. The air force totalled 2,100 men, including air defence staff. Opposition forces, from the Transdnestr region ('Dnestr Guard'), were estimated to number 10,000, in mid-1993. This amount included some 1,000 Cossacks. In early 1994 the former Soviet 14th Army was still stationed in Moldova (under Russian jurisdiction): negotiations with a view to its eventual withdrawal were still being conducted by the Moldovan and Russian Governments. A Unified Peace-Keeping Force, consisting of six batallions from Russia and two battalions each from Moldova and the Transdnestr, was also present in the country.

Bibliography

Dailey, E. *Human Rights in Moldova: The Turbulent Dniester.* New York, Helsinki Watch, 1993.

Dima, N. *From Moldavia to Moldova: The Soviet-Romanian Territorial Dispute.* Boulder, Colorado, East European Monographs, 1991.

Hill, R. *Soviet Political Élites: The Case of Tiraspol.* London, Martin Robertson, 1977.

Manoliu-Manea, M. (Ed.). *The Tragic Plight of a Border Area: Bessarabia and Bucovina.* Humboldt, California, Humboldt State University Press, 1983.

Stoilik, G. *Moldavia.* Moscow, Novosti Press Agency Publishing House, 1987.

POLAND

Geography

PHYSICAL FEATURES

The Republic of Poland is located to the north of central Europe, with a 520-km coastline along the Baltic Sea. To the west lies Germany, to the south-west the Czech Republic and to the south Slovakia. The eastern frontiers are with former Soviet states; to the north is the Russian Federation enclave around Kaliningrad on the Baltic coast; there is a short border with Lithuania to the north-east; while Belarus lies beyond the northern part of the eastern border, and Ukraine the southern. After the Second World War Poland lost a considerable amount of territory to the USSR, while gaining the former German provinces of Pomerania and Silesia in the west, and part of East Prussia in the east. Poland's borders are now marked by the Oder (Odra) and Neisse (Nysa) rivers in the west, the River Bug in the east, the Sudetic Mountains in the south-west and the Carpathian range of mountains in the south-east. The country has an area of 312,685 sq km (120,728 sq miles), some 20% less than in 1939.

Poland is a predominantly low-lying country, the average altitude being only 173 m. The highest point in the country is 2,499 m, at Rysy on the border with Slovakia. The most developed and most highly-populated region is the central plain, which covers more than one-third of the country. The plain is crossed by Poland's two major rivers, the Oder and the Vistula (Wisła), which rise in the Sudetic and Carpathian mountains, respectively, along the southern borders, and flow into the Baltic Sea. South of the plain there is a plateau (average height 700 m) which is drained by the Bug, San and Wisła rivers. On the southern border of Poland, between the Sudetic range in the west and the western reaches of the Carpathians in the east, lies the broad depression of the Moravian Gate, which is the traditional route into central Europe. North of the central plains there are belts of shallow lakes, surrounded by undulating and wooded countryside. North of this lake district are the coastal lowlands, which are most extensive near the estuaries of the Oder and Vistula. Most of the coastline is covered by sand dunes. There are many beaches and lagoons and few natural harbours.

CLIMATE

Poland's climate is largely continental, with hot summers and cold winters, although it is more temperate in the west than in the east. The average July temperature in Warsaw is 18°C (65°F), while the average for January is −4°C (25°F). Warsaw has an average annual rainfall of 560 mm, whereas Kraków, in the south, has an annual average of 745 mm.

POPULATION

Ethnic Poles now constitute some 98% of the total population. Most of the substantial pre-1939 Ukrainian and Jewish populations either fled the country or were killed during the Nazi occupation. There are still minor communities of Belarusians, Ukrainians and Jews, and small numbers of Greeks, Macedonians, Russians, Lithuanians, Slovaks, Czechs and Roma (Gypsies). Some ethnic Germans remain in the former German territories of Silesia and Pomerania, but most of the Germans living in Poland or in the lands granted to Poland in 1945 were deported after the War. The official language is Polish, a member of the Western Slavonic group. Most of the inhabitants profess Christianity, an estimated 95% of the population being adherents of the Roman Catholic Church.

The total population in December 1992 was estimated at 38,417,000; the population density was 122.9 persons per sq km. In December 1991 it was estimated that 1,653,300 people lived in the capital, Warsaw (Warszawa). Other important towns included Łódź (population 844,900), a major industrial centre, and Kraków (population 751,300), an important centre of culture and learning. Since the Second World War there has been a significant movement of the population from rural to urban areas: in 1988 only 38.8% of the population lived in the countryside, compared with 68% in 1946.

Chronology

966: The first historical ruler of Poland, Prince Mieszko I, converted to Latin Christianity.

1320: Lidisław I was crowned King of a reunited Poland.

1386: Vladisław II, Grand Duke of Lithuania, became King of Poland by marriage, founded the Jagiellonian dynasty (1386–1572) and established a personal union with Lithuania.

1493: A two-chamber Sejm (Parliament) was established.

1569: Under Sigismund II a permanent union with Lithuania was established, by the Union of Lublin, which was to last until the final dismemberment of the Commonwealth in 1795.

1764: Election of Stanisław II, who ruled until 1795.

1772: The First Partition of Poland, between Russia, Prussia and Austria, took place.

1791: Stanisław II created Europe's first modern constitution.

1793: The Second Partition of Poland.

1795: The Third Partition extinguished the Polish state.

1807: The Grand Duchy of Warsaw was established by Napoleon.

1815: The 'Congress Kingdom of Poland' was formed under Russian patronage.

1905–07: Revolution in Russian Poland.

1915: The Russian occupation was ended by German victory on the Eastern Front in the First World War.

1916: Restoration of an 'independent' Kingdom of Poland by Germany.

3 June 1918: Allied Governments recognized the principle of Polish independence.

11 November 1918: Józef Piłsudski assumed power in Warsaw. Poland was declared an independent Republic.

28 June 1919: The Treaty of Versailles recognized Polish independence.

13–19 August 1920: Soviet forces were defeated at the Battle of Warsaw.

18 March 1921: The Treaty of Riga was signed by Poland, Ukraine and Soviet Russia, formally concluding the Soviet-Polish war and defining the frontiers in the region.

1922: Stanisław Wojsiechowski was elected Head of State.

12 May 1926: Piłsudski seized power in a *coup d'état*.

25 January 1932: A non-aggression pact was signed with the USSR.

26 January 1934: A non-aggression pact was signed with Germany.

23 March 1935: A new Constitution was enacted.

12 May 1935: Death of Piłsudski.

31 March 1939: France and the United Kingdom announced guarantees of Poland's independence, in response to German territorial demands.

23 August 1939: The Nazi–Soviet Pact was signed, including a secret agreement between the USSR and Germany to partition Poland.

1 September 1939: Germany invaded Poland, which caused the start of the Second World War.

17 September 1939: The USSR invaded Poland.

30 September 1939: A Government-in-Exile was formed in Paris (France) under Gen. Sikorski, moving to London (United Kingdom) in 1940.

22 June 1941: Germany invaded the USSR; all of Poland was occupied by Nazi forces.

30 July 1941: The Polish Government-in-Exile established diplomatic relations with the USSR.

5 January 1942: The Polish Workers' Party (PWP) was founded.

April 1943: The Warsaw Ghetto uprising was suppressed by German troops.

25 April 1943: German investigators discovered, at Katyn in the USSR, the bodies of 4,000 Polish officers, who had been murdered by Soviet secret police in 1940.

26 April 1943: The USSR severed diplomatic relations with the Polish Government-in-Exile.

4 July 1943: Gen. Sikorski, Prime Minister of the Government-in-Exile, died in an air crash.

23 July 1944: The Polish Committee of National Liberation (Lublin Committee—PKWN) was established under Soviet auspices.

1 August–2 October 1944: The Warsaw Rising was eventually suppressed by German troops.

February 1945: German forces withdrew from Warsaw. The British, Soviet and US leaders, Winston Churchill, Stalin (Iosif Dzhugashvili) and Franklin D. Roosevelt, met in the Crimean town of Yalta (now in Ukraine): the 'Curzon line' was agreed as Poland's eastern border; Stalin promised 'free and unfettered elections' in Poland after the War.

21 April 1945: A Soviet–Polish Treaty of Friendship was signed.

28 June 1945: The USA and the United Kingdom recognized the 'Provisional Government of National Unity', which was dominated by members of the Soviet-backed PKWN, but included Stanisław Mikołajczyk and a few others from the Government-in-Exile.

17 July–2 August 1945: The Potsdam Conference: the Allies agreed to give former German territories east of the Oder–Neisse line to Poland.

19 January 1947: Elections to the Sejm were won by the Democratic Bloc, a grouping dominated by the PWP and led by Władysław Gomułka; the United Kingdom and the USA complained that the elections did not meet the requirements agreed at Yalta.

6 February 1947: The People's Republic of Poland was declared; Bolesław Bierut took office as President.

October 1947: Mikołajczyk fled to London after threats to his life.

September 1948: Gomułka was forced to admit 'political errors' and was dismissed as Party leader.

December 1948: The founding congress of the Polish United Workers' Party (PUWP) took place after the PWP merged with the Polish Socialist Party; Bierut was appointed Party First Secretary.

1949: Gomułka was arrested, accused of 'rightist and nationalist deviations'.

22 July 1952: A new Soviet-style Constitution was adopted.

1954: Bierut was succeeded by Józef Cyrankiewicz as Chairman of the Council of Ministers.

14 May 1955: The Treaty of Warsaw founded the Soviet bloc military organization known as the Warsaw Pact.

March 1956: The First Secretary of the PUWP, Bolesław Bierut, died in the Soviet capital, Moscow.

28–29 June 1956: Seventy-four people died in riots in Poznań protesting against food price rises.

October 1956: Władysław Gomułka was appointed First Secretary by the Eighth Party Plenum and began to introduce some political liberalization.

March 1968: Nation-wide anti-government student protests took place, followed by a Party-inspired campaign against Jews and intellectuals.

April 1968: Marshal Marian Spychalski was appointed Head of State.

November 1968: Soviet leader Leonid Brezhnev announced the 'Brezhnev Doctrine' (declaring the right of the USSR to intervene in the affairs of its Warsaw Pact allies) in Warsaw.

December 1970: Gomułka and Spychalski resigned after workers were killed when police suppressed strikes and protests in the Baltic ports; Piotr Jaroszewicz replaced Józef Cyrankiewicz (who became Head of State) as Chairman of the Council of Ministers; Edward Gierek was appointed First Secretary.

7 December 1970: A treaty was signed by Poland and the Federal Republic of Germany ('West Germany'), confirming the post-1945 Polish western border.

1972: Gierek launched a 'modernization programme' of large-scale investment funded chiefly by Western banks.

June 1976: Strikes and demonstrations prevented planned food price rises from being implemented.

September 1976: The Workers' Defence Committee (KOR) was formed after striking miners were arrested at Radom.

16 October 1978: Cardinal Karol Wojtyła, Archbishop of Kraków, was elected head of the Roman Catholic Church as Pope John Paul II.

February 1980: Piotr Jaroszewicz was replaced as Chairman of the Council of Ministers by Edward Babiuch at the Party Congress.

July 1980: Food price rises led to strikes and workers' protests; unofficial strike committees were formed to press for pay increases and, subsequently, for political demands to be met.

24 August 1980: Babiuch resigned and was replaced by Józef Pińkowski as Chairman of the Council of Ministers.

14 August 1980: Some 17,000 workers at the Lenin Shipyards in Gdańsk went on strike and issued a list of economic and political demands; the strike spread to Szczecin one week later and involved over 150,000 workers.

31 August 1980: Following negotiations between Mieczysław Jagielski, a member of the Politburo, and Lech Wałęsa and other union delegates, the Gdańsk and Szczecin agreements were signed: the Government agreed to the unions' demands, including the right to form free trade unions and the right to strike.

5 September 1980: Gierek was replaced as First Secretary by Stanisław Kania.

17 September 1980: Representatives from some 35 independent trade union committees met to form the independent trade union, Solidarity (Solidarność).

10 November 1980: Solidarity was officially recognized.

1 January 1981: The Central Council of Trade Unions was dissolved.

10–11 February 1981: Pińkowski was replaced as Chairman of the Council of Ministers by Gen. Wojciech Jaruzelski.

12 May 1981: Rural Solidarity was officially recognized.

14–18 July 1981: The Ninth (Extraordinary) Party Congress of PUWP was held: multi-candidate secret ballots were introduced for elections; only four former Politburo members were re-elected.

5–10 September 1981: Solidarity's first National Congress took place.

October 1981: Jaruzelski replaced Kania as Party First Secretary.

13 December 1981: Jaruzelski declared martial law; a Military Council of National Salvation was established; Lech Wałęsa and other Solidarity activists were arrested and imprisoned.

1 May 1982: Anti-government demonstrations were dispersed by the police.

31 August 1982: Demonstrations took place to mark the second anniversary of the Gdańsk Accords.

8 October 1982: The Trade Union Bill was introduced, outlawing independent union activity.

12 November 1982: Wałęsa was released from prison.

13 December 1982: Martial law was suspended.

22 July 1983: Martial law was formally lifted; the Military Council of National Salvation was dissolved.

5 October 1983: Lech Wałęsa was awarded the Nobel Peace Prize.

22 November 1983: Jaruzelski resigned as Minister of Defence to become Chairman of the newly formed National Defence Committee.

October 1984: Jerzy Popiełuszko, a pro-Solidarity priest, was murdered by security forces.

October 1985: Some multi-candidate ballots were allowed in legislative elections; Solidarity urged a boycott.

6 November 1985: Jaruzelski resigned as the Chairman of the Council of Ministers, becoming President of the Council of State (Head of State); he was succeeded by Prof. Zbigniew Messner.

February 1986: Wałęsa was put on trial for disputing the voting figures for the elections held in October 1985; the charges were subsequently dropped.

May 1986: Zbigniew Bujak, a leading Solidarity activist, was detained after spending nearly five years in hiding; large demonstrations took place in protest at his arrest.

July 1986: Legislation was passed to allow the release of political prisoners.

May 1987: Anti-government protests resulted in 158 arrests.

October 1987: The Government announced plans for radical economic and political reforms, which were to be submitted to popular approval in a referendum.

November 1987: The Government failed to achieve the necessary majority in the referendum, partly owing to a Solidarity-backed boycott.

March 1988: Security forces dispersed student demonstrations commemorating the 1968 protests.

April–May 1988: Widespread strikes and demonstrations took place.

June 1988: Only 55% of the electorate participated in local elections after Solidarity urged a boycott.

August 1988: The Government offered 'round-table' negotiations with labour groups after coal-miners went on strike.

19 September 1988: Zbigniew Messner's Government resigned; Dr Mieczysław Rakowski became Chairman of a more reformist Council of Ministers.

31 October 1988: Large-scale protests took place after the Government announced the closure of the Lenin Shipyards in Gdańsk.

18 January 1989: The Central Committee of the PUWP agreed to negotiate towards the re-legalization of Solidarity.

6 February 1989: Round-table negotiations between the Government and opposition leaders, headed by Lech Wałęsa, opened in Warsaw.

7 March 1989: The Polish Government for the first time accused the USSR of committing the 1940 Katyn massacre (the USSR admitted liability in April 1990).

5 April 1989: A negotiated agreement was reached at the round-table negotiations: Solidarity was to be re-legalized; partly-free elections were to be held; economic reforms were promised.

7 April 1989: Constitutional amendments resulting from the round-table talks were adopted, including the creation of a new, bicameral National Assembly.

17 May 1989: Laws were adopted granting full legal status to the Roman Catholic Church (diplomatic relations with the Holy See were restored in July) and guaranteeing freedom of conscience.

4 June 1989: Elections to the National Assembly took place: Solidarity won 99% of the freely-elected seats.

18 June 1989: The second round of elections were held.

4 July 1989: The new National Assembly convened in Warsaw.

19 July 1989: The National Assembly re-elected Jaruzelski as President by a narrow margin.

25 July 1989: Lech Wałęsa rejected an offer for Solidarity to join a coalition government.

28–29 July 1989: Jaruzelski resigned as First Secretary of the PUWP and from the Politburo and Central Committee; he was replaced as First Secretary by Mieczysław Rakowski.

2 August 1989: Lt-Gen. Czesław Kiszczak was elected Chairman of the Council of Ministers; he resigned, however, on 17 August, after failing to form a government.

7 August 1989: Solidarity proposed that it should form the administration in alliance with the United Peasants' Party (UPP) and the Democratic Party (DP).

20 August 1989: Jaruzelski accepted Solidarity's proposal and asked Tadeusz Mazowiecki to lead a new administration.

12 September 1989: The Sejm approved Mazowiecki's 23-member cabinet, which included ministers from all four major parties.

29–30 December 1989: The National Assembly approved amendments to the Constitution, including an end to the PUWP's monopoly of power, and the restoration of the official name and flag of pre-war Poland. Finance Minister Leszek Balcerowicz's economic reform plan (already approved by the International Monetary Fund—IMF) was approved by the Sejm.

2 January 1990: Sharp price rises and currency devaluation were introduced as part of an austerity programme.

28 January 1990: The PUWP changed its name to Social Democracy of the Polish Republic at its 11th Congress.

13 July 1990: A Bill was passed by the National Assembly allowing for the sale of state-owned companies to the private sector.

November 1990: Poland's western border was confirmed by the signature of a treaty with the reunified Germany.

25 November 1990: The presidential election took place: Wałęsa received some 43% of the votes cast, but premier Mazowiecki was forced into third place by a maverick candidate, Stanisław Tymiński.

26 November 1990: The Mazowiecki Government resigned.

9 December 1990: Wałęsa won the second round of the presidential election with 74% of the vote.

4–5 January 1991: Jan Bielecki was approved as Chairman of the Council of Ministers by the Sejm, and his proposed Government was also accepted. The Citizens' Parliamentary Club (OKP—the group of Solidarity deputies in the National Assembly) was split by the formation of the Democratic Union.

23 February 1991: Marian Krzaklewski was elected Chairman of Solidarity in succession to Lech Wałęsa.

9 March 1991: The Sejm rejected President Wałęsa's suggestion of immediate parliamentary elections, voting to postpone elections until October.

15 March 1991: The 'Paris Club' of 17 Western countries cancelled 50% of Poland's US $33,000m. foreign debt.

4 April 1991: The first of the 50,000 Soviet troops remaining in Poland were withdrawn; some Soviet troops were to remain until the end of 1993 to support the transit of 380,000 Soviet troops leaving the former German Democratic Republic.

12 May 1991: The Democratic Union party was strengthened by the merger of three groupings of former Solidarity politicians.

1 July 1991: President Wałęsa approved an electoral law authorizing Poland's first fully free parliamentary elections; he had earlier twice vetoed the Sejm's proposals, fearing that it would lead to a fragmented legislature.

11 July 1991: The Sejm rejected Wałęsa's new draft electoral law, intended to replace the law approved on 1 July, which would have entailed voting for party lists rather than for individual candidates.

30 August 1991: The Bielecki Government offered its resignation after repeated obstruction by the Sejm of its policies for economic reform; parliament rejected the resignation the following day.

2 September 1991: Premier Bielecki and President Wałęsa discussed special economic powers for the Government, and later formally requested such powers in the Sejm (where they were denied).

27 October 1991: Only 43.2% of the electorate participated in elections to the Senat (the upper house of the National Assembly) and the Sejm; a total of 29 parties won representation in the Sejm, the largest, with 62 of the 460 seats (12.3% of the vote), being the Democratic Union; the electoral alliance of Social Democracy of the Republic of Poland (SDRP) and the All Poland Trade Unions Alliance, the Democratic Left Alliance (Sojusz Lewicy Demokratycznej—SLD), won 60 seats (11.9% of the votes cast). The Democratic Union also gained the greatest representation in the Senate (21 of the 100 seats), while Solidarity took 11 seats.

6 December 1991: Following weeks of negotiations, Jan Olszewski of the Centre Alliance was appointed Chairman of the Council of Ministers (Prime Minister).

17 February 1992: Minister of Finance Karol Lutkowski unexpectedly resigned shortly before the new Government was due to present formally its economic programme.

6 April 1992: The Minister of National Defence, Jan Parys, was temporarily removed from office after he accused President Wałęsa of attempting to conspire with the armed forces against the Government.

6 May 1992: The Olszewski Government's second Minister of Finance, Andrzej Olechowski, resigned.

4–5 June 1992: A motion of 'no confidence' in the Government was passed by the Sejm; on the following day the leader of the Polish Peasant Party (Polskie Stronnictwo Ludowe—PSL), Waldemar Pawlak, was appointed premier.

2 July 1992: Pawlak resigned his post after failing to form a government; a coalition of eight parties nominated Hanna Suchocka of the Democratic Union to form a government.

11 July 1992: Suchocka's appointment as Prime Minister was approved by the Sejm; she proceeded to form a seven-party coalition.

8 December 1992: An interim Constitution, the 'Small Constitution', entered into force while a comprehensive revision of the 1952 Constitution was in progress.

13 January 1993: Legislation which ended the state monopoly over radio and television and introduced a system of licensing for commercial broadcasters took effect. Amid some controversy the Sejm approved legislation that imposed strict limitations on the availability of abortion.

28 May 1993: As a result of continuing dissatisfaction over government economic and social policies, a vote of 'no confidence' in the Suchocka Government was passed in the Sejm; however, President Wałęsa refused to accept the Prime Minister's resignation and dissolved parliament.

19 September 1993: General elections took place; the SLD and the PSL gained the most number of votes cast (20.4% and 15.4%, respectively) and took 303 seats between them; the Democratic Union gained 74 seats in the new Sejm (11.0% of the votes cast); President Wałęsa's newly formed Non-Party Bloc for Reform (Bezpartyjny Bloc Wapierania Reform—BBWR) won 5.4% of the vote and 16 seats. Furthermore, the SLD and the PSL gained almost three-quarters of the 100 seats in the Senate.

18 October 1993: The PSL leader Waldemar Pawlak was nominated as Prime Minister by President Wałęsa; his nomination was subsequently approved by the Sejm.

10 November 1993: Premier Pawlak's Cabinet, comprised of members from the SLD and the PSL, was installed in government.

History

KEITH SWORD

EARLY HISTORY

Present day Poland traces its origins to the unification, in the second half of the 10th century, of a group of Slavic tribes which lived in the basin of the Warta River. In 966 their King, Mieszko, introduced Christianity, ensuring that henceforth Poland's cultural development would be linked to that of Western Europe. The centre of the state moved gradually southwards to settlements on the upper Vistula (Kraków, Sandomierz). Casimir the Great (1333–70), the last of the Piast kings, strengthened state organization through measures such as monetary reform and codifying the law, and founded the country's first university at Kraków. In 1386 the Polish Queen, Jadwiga, married Jagiełło (baptized as Vladisłav), the Grand Duke of Lithuania. This alliance was eventually to pave the way for full political union (the Union of Lublin, 1569) which was to last until the late 18th century. At its height the combined kingdom stretched from the Baltic to the Black Sea.

In 1572 the last of the Jagiellons died, leaving no heir. For the next 200 years Poland experienced a period of elective monarchy. It was an era marked by numerous wars and military campaigns (against Muscovites, Turks, Tatars, Cossacks, Swedes) but little economic progress. Shaken increasingly by factional conflict and the decline of royal authority, the Polish-Lithuanian Commonwealth began to fragment into a federation of minor states ruled by magnates. The Polish Sejm (parliament) was powerless to prevent a partition of Polish territory in 1772 by Russia, Prussia and Austria.

The last king, Stanisław Poniatowski, attempted to introduce reforms and galvanize the political structure. He created the world's first ministry of education and introduced a liberal Constitution in May 1791. This was not enough to prevent further partitions of the country in 1793 and 1795. The former provoked an unsuccessful insurrection led by Tadeusz Kościuszko, while the latter signalled the disappearance of Poland from the map of Europe.

During the long years of partition (1795–1918) Polish hopes for national rebirth focused initially on the French leader Napoleon. His creation of the Duchy of Warsaw (1807–15) encompassed only a small part of Polish territory, however, and this ceased to exist after the Emperor's downfall. The Kingdom of Poland was formed from an area of the Duchy allocated to Russia at the Congress of Vienna (1815). The harsh policies of tsarist Russia led to two unsuccessful insurrections, in 1830–31 and in 1863. The incorporation of Polish territories into the three neighbouring empires meant suppression of political and cultural life (less so under Austrian Hapsburg rule) and economic stagnation. One result was the early emigration of many intellectuals and writers (such as Mickiewicz, Słowacki and Norwid) and potential soldiers (to Napoleon's legions). Towards the end of the 19th century emigration from the Polish lands took on a mass character as peasants looked for land and work in the New World.

REBIRTH OF THE POLISH STATE

After the First World War Poland was restored to statehood at the Treaty of Versailles (1919), following the collapse of the three empires which had partitioned it. However, the borders were not finally fixed until a number of plebiscites and further military activity had taken place. The eastern frontier, for example, was only fixed when the Treaty of Riga (1921) marked an end to the Polish–Soviet War of 1919–20. The problems of unifying the three separate partition regions, devastated by the passage of armies, were considerable.

Poland was between the World Wars a parliamentary republic, but the dominant figure was Marshal Józef Piłsudski. The country was afflicted with economic problems, experienced difficulty in dealing with its large minority populations, and suffered from political instability. Impatient with the lack of political stability Piłsudski led a *coup d'état* in 1926 and became virtually a dictator. His followers continued to rule in his name after Piłsudski's death in 1935.

THE SECOND WORLD WAR

In 1939, with the outbreak of the Second World War, Poland was partitioned once again—this time between Nazi Germany and the USSR. France and the United Kingdom declared war in defence of Poland, but could do little to aid it. During a horrendous six-year period of occupation Poland lost one-sixth of its population, including virtually all its Jewish community, and 38% of its national wealth. Resistance activity continued throughout the War, and was crowned by the ill-fated Warsaw Rising in 1944, during which 250,000 civilian casualties occurred. Political leadership, in the form of a Government-in-Exile, was organized in Paris (France) and, from 1940, in London (United Kingdom), under General Władysław Sikorski. Following Sikorski's death in an air crash at Gibraltar, in 1943, he was replaced as premier by the Peasant Party leader, Stanisław Mikołajczyk.

Poland was liberated by the Red Army. In July 1944, when Red Army units crossed the River Bug, a Committee of National Liberation (PKWN) was established at Lublin. The 'Lublin Committee' consisted of Polish Communists subservient to the Soviet leader Stalin. They immediately took over the administration of the territory liberated by the Soviet advance and became a *de facto* Government.

The new Poland had a different shape to that of the pre-War Republic. At the conferences of Teheran and Yalta, the Great Power leaders had agreed that Poland should lose almost one-half of its territory to the USSR, but should receive compensation in the north and west at the expense of Germany. These border changes were followed by the expulsion of some 3.5m. Germans from the western territories. At the same time 'repatriation' agreements with the neighbouring Soviet Republics provided for the transfer of ethnic Poles from land seized by the USSR in the east. Poland's population was much reduced from its wartime level. It was also more homogeneous, because of losses (particularly the wholesale destruction of the Jewish community by the Nazis), border changes and population transfers.

THE IMPOSITION OF COMMUNIST RULE

In January 1945 the PKWN was transformed into a Provisional Government. Stalin had demonstrated that he did not trust the Polish authorities in London and that he was determined to have the dominant voice in how Poland was ruled after the War. As a concession to Western leaders he allowed the Provisional Government to be reconstituted, with the participation of a small group of 'London' politicians headed by Mikołajczyk. Importantly though, the

Communists retained hold of key ministries such as defence and internal security. This Government—the Provisional Government of National Unity—was recognized by the United Kingdom and the USA on 6 July 1945.

The Communists had pledged to hold 'free and unfettered' elections as soon as was possible after the liberation of the country, but they were aware that their support was weak. They therefore delayed the elections and set about using the Soviet-trained secret police to confuse and terrorize their opponents. The elections, which were eventually held in February 1947, resulted in a victory for the Polish Workers' Party (that is, the Communists). The Peasant Party leader, and main focus of opposition to the Communists, Mikołajczyk, fled to the West in October 1947, his attempts to prevent the Communist domination of his homeland having failed.

The first post-War Communist leader was Władysław Gomułka, a patriotic Pole and not as subject to the USSR's influence as some of his colleagues. He was against slavishly imitating the Soviet pattern of social and economic organization in all countries which came under Soviet influence. In particular, he opposed the wholesale collectivization of agriculture, which he feared would alienate the large number of peasant farmers. Gomułka's advocacy of a 'Polish road to socialism' eventually brought his downfall. In 1948 he was dismissed and placed under house arrest.

His successor was Bolesław Bierut, a long-term Comintern agent. Bierut took power as the Cold War was beginning in earnest, and his period of office marked Poland's darkest period of repressive Stalinism. Bierut's succession was accompanied by a massive expansion of the internal security forces (UB), the beginning of a programme to collectivize agriculture, the development of heavy industry, and the expansion of the military-defence sector in line with the wishes of the Soviet bloc's Warsaw Pact military alliance.

On the political front, the Polish Workers' Party was merged with the Socialist Party to form the Polish United Workers' Party (PUWP). The continuing existence of minor parties—a United Peasant Party (UPP) and a Democratic Party (DP)—were meant to provide the semblance of a continued multi-party democracy. In fact these parties were completely subservient to the Communists; Poland had become a one-party state on the Soviet model.

One centre of recalcitrance which the Communists found difficult to suppress was the Roman Catholic Church. The Concordat with the Vatican had been renounced in 1945 and a major campaign waged against the Church's influence. In September 1953 the Polish Primate himself, Cardinal Wyszyński, was barred from exercising his functions and compelled to retreat to a monastery. The Church nevertheless grew in stature and became, as it was to remain throughout the period of Communist rule, a source of enduring national and family values, a haven from the ideological slogans and exhortations of the Communists.

In 1953 Stalin died. Khrushchev's denunciation of Stalin's excesses (in 1956) was quickly followed by the death of the Polish Party leader, Bierut. A major crisis in Polish politics developed in the summer of 1956, when workers in a rolling-stock factory in Poznań demonstrated in the city centre. The demonstration developed into a violent display of dissatisfaction with conditions under Communist rule and included an attack on the Party headquarters. It was only finally suppressed when the army was called in. Fifty-three people died in the violence that resulted.

THE GOMUŁKA PERIOD

An immediate result of the crisis was the political rehabilitation of Władysław Gomułka, and the onset of a period during which, for the first and last time, a Communist leader in Poland enjoyed a measure of popularity. For the next decade there was to be relative stability in Poland. In the eyes of the people, Communist rule, temporarily at least, ceased to be synonymous with Soviet control; for the first time Poles were able to feel that their leaders were acting in *their* interests. There was also increasing freedom from the attentions of the secret police, with greater tolerance extended towards elements previously characterized as 'reactionary' or 'anti-socialist'. The Church, too, was allowed greater freedom of activity and a cautious *modus vivendi* was reached between Church and State. Poles also found it easier to travel abroad—an important consideration for those many Poles who had relatives in the West. There was also greater freedom of expression, with the relaxation of censorship over cultural life.

In the economic sphere Gomułka embarked on his promised 'Polish road' to socialism by abandoning the collectivization of agriculture. His reforms included a partial dismantling of the central-planning structure and devolving a large measure of decision-making to local enterprises and workers' councils. By the mid-1960s, however, it had become clear that gains had been at best modest. In spite of Gomułka's reforms the economy remained over-centralized, bureaucratic and unresponsive both to demands of the market-place and to those of the work-force. Real wages rose by only 20% in Poland during the 1960s—the slowest rate of increase in Eastern Europe.

In December 1970 violent unrest broke out again in Poland, this time on the Baltic coast at Gdańsk. Workers, whose wages had been held down, demonstrated in protest at rises in the price of meat. Army units were used to quell the protests and once more considerable bloodshed resulted. This unrest highlighted the failure of Gomułka's policies and proved the signal for his removal as Party leader. His successor was Edward Gierek, a former coal-miner from Silesia, who had spent many years working in Western Europe.

THE GIEREK YEARS

Gierek attempted to revitalize the economy—essential for political stability and for the survival of Party leaders. In the atmosphere of détente which characterized the early 1970s, he authorized massive borrowings from Western banks in order to fund investment and the purchase of numerous licences from Western firms. He had a vision of a 'Polish economic miracle' to rival those of the Far East, founded on Poland's availability of, by Western standards, cheap labour. In the short term the economy certainly improved. Industrial production rose and living standards increased. A growth in real earnings was accompanied by the appearance of cheap and plentiful food in the shops, and reasonably priced consumer durables. For the first time, Poles could feel that they were part of the 'consumer society' as the numbers of televisions, washing machines and cars increased rapidly.

However, Gierek's plan misfired. The Polish economy was incapable of making efficient use of the loans and credits, and of producing the increase in exports that the plan required. By the mid-1970s a debt crisis had appeared which was to burden the Polish economy for more than a decade. Ironically, the former emigrant who had seen the salvation of his country in attempting to emulate the West, was now forced to go to the USSR to ask for loans. When his economic 'miracle' began to pale, support for Gierek evaporated. A series of strikes, again in protest against food price rises, occurred in 1976, significantly on the 20th anniversary of the Poznań troubles. The authorities' harsh suppression of protest in Ursus and Radom led to the creation of the Committee for Workers' Defence (KOR).

By the end of the decade the Party leadership was demoralized. It had no coherent strategies for finding a way out of the intractable morass of political and economic problems that it had helped to generate. The vacuum in moral and spiritual leadership from the Government and Party was highlighted, in October 1978, when Cardinal Karol Wojtyła of Kraków was elected to the papacy, as Pope John Paul II—the first Pole to fill that office. His triumphant return to his homeland, in the following year, brought people out on to the streets in their tens of thousands. It was not difficult to see this as a turning-point in post-War Polish history. It was the moment at which the Polish people became confident of their own strength and shared values, in the face of the now enfeebled Communist giant.

A desperate set of economic manoeuvres, in late 1979 and early 1980, culminated in yet another attempt to raise meat prices in June. The inevitable strikes followed and Gierek resigned, retiring because of 'ill health'. Stanisław Kania became leader of a Party which by now had lost all semblance of authority and credibility.

FROM GDAŃSK TO THE 'ROUND TABLE'

The summer of discontent in 1980 led to confrontation between Gdańsk shipyard workers and government officials and to the birth of Solidarity (Solidarność), the first independent trade union in the Soviet bloc. Its leader was Lech Wałęsa, a shipyard electrician. Solidarity was soon claiming 10m. members, including many in the PUWP. In the countryside, Rural Solidarity also came into being to represent the interests of farmers. In the ensuing months, however, Solidarity's demands became more diffuse and its discipline slackened. Strikes broke out randomly as isolated groups of workers sought to take advantage of the Government's weakness to air their grievances.

The first tentative move towards political pluralism ended suddenly, in December 1981, when martial law was declared. Gen. Wojciech Jaruzelski attempted to restore the 'leading role' of the Communist Party in political life, seizing power as leader of a Military Council of National Salvation (WRON). In the course of the 1980s the Jaruzelski regime struggled to establish normality on the domestic front and to secure recognition internationally. These efforts received a set-back, in October 1984, when the murder of a pro-Solidarity priest, Father Jerzy Popiełuszko, brought to the world's attention the methods being used by the interior ministry to re-establish the Party's authority. In the latter half of the decade there was a softening of official policies. This was partly owing to Poland's deteriorating economic situation and to the recognition by the authorities that while the population could be controlled by force, it could not be forced to co-operate. A further important factor was the accession of Mikhail Gorbachev to power in the USSR. Gradually, his more liberal policies permeated the political structures of the Warsaw Pact states.

In 1989 'round table' negotiations between Communists and opposition leaders, headed by Lech Wałęsa, resulted in the legalization of Solidarity and in agreement on reform of the political system along more democratic lines. Changes agreed included the restoration of a second parliamentary chamber (the upper house had been abolished in 1946) and of the presidency, and a gradual return to multi-party, competitive elections. Importantly, restrictions on the freedom of the press were also removed.

SOLIDARITY TAKES POWER

The first election under the new rules was held in June 1989. All 100 seats to the upper chamber (Senat) were to be freely contested, but 65% of seats in the lower chamber (Sejm) were reserved for the Communists and their associates. Solidarity representatives won all but one of the seats in the Senat and all 35% of seats which they were free to contest in the Sejm. Although in a minority in the lower chamber, they had achieved such an overwhelming mandate from the electorate that their moral right to participate in government could not be denied.

Immediately following the elections, parliamentary delegates were asked to vote for a President. The surprising election of Gen. Jaruzelski, the architect of martial law and, less than a decade earlier, the most unpopular man in Poland, could be attributed to two factors: Solidarity deputies were in a minority, and there were worries about the reaction of the USSR to the dramatic political changes taking place. Jaruzelski's election, it was thought, would be a reassuring sign of continuity and stability.

When the Communists' former allies in the Sejm turned against them, the way was cleared for Tadeusz Mazowiecki, formerly a Roman-Catholic journalist, to become, on 24 August 1989, the first non-Communist prime minister in the Soviet bloc. The Council of Ministers which was formed over the following weeks included 11 posts for Solidarity, four for the PUWP (Communists), four to the UPP, and three to the DP. Among the ministers was Jacek Kuroń (Minister of Labour) who had been a dissident since the 1960s.

Two main tasks faced the new Government. One was a reform of the political structure in order to rid it of the trappings of Communist rule which had become so irksome to the Polish people during the previous four decades. The other was a resolution of the urgent economic problems. Work began immediately on drafting a completely new Constitution to serve Poland during its coming period of parliamentary democracy. Further changes included the reversion of the country to being, as it was in pre-War days, a Republic (Rzeczpospolita Polska) rather than a People's Republic. Symbols of Communist rule were erased or torn down, and the country's symbol, the white eagle, had its royal crown restored. In February 1990 the PUWP was dissolved and replaced by a new party, Social Democracy of the Republic of Poland—SDRP.

The economic problems faced by the incoming Polish Government towards the end of 1989 were daunting. A foreign debt of over US $40,000m., with inflation running in excess of 50% per month, were the immediate problems which had to be addressed. A radical series of budgetary measures was introduced, in January 1990, with International Monetary Fund (IMF) approval. The measures, named the 'Balcerowicz Plan' after the young Finance Minister, Leszek Balcerowicz, aimed at a rapid move from a centrally planned economy to one run along market lines. A key aim was to free prices from government influence by removing subsidies. At the same time wages would be restrained, in an attempt to ease the rate of inflation. It was hoped that by devaluing the złoty and introducing limited convertibility, Polish exporters would be helped. To this end also the Government undertook to adopt responsible monetary policies and to encourage the private sector.

During its 15-month period of office the Mazowiecki Government was subjected to increasing pressures from sectors of the working population, owing to the punishing effects of its economic policies. The mood of optimism which had greeted the formation of the 'Solidarity' Government disappeared by mid-1990 as productivity and real wages decreased. Unemployment too rose rapidly and, by the autumn, the official figure was over one million. The farmers were particularly restive, finding that the free markets in produce for which they had long campaigned were not what they had anticipated, and complaining that the Government's agricultural policies did little to help them.

The pressures soon began to show within the Solidarity movement, and criticism of the Government's performance came from none other than the leader of the trade union, Lech Wałęsa. When President Jaruzelski offered his resignation, in the latter half of 1990, the stage was set for a confrontation between Wałęsa and his former adviser, premier Mazowiecki, for the vacant presidency. The campaign aroused much emotion and confirmed the division in the Solidarity movement. In the first round, Mazowiecki was eclipsed by a hitherto unknown Polish-Canadian businessman, Stanisław Tymiński. Wałęsa triumphed in the second round, but his success was overshadowed by the Tymiński factor. Tymiński had gained 23.1% of the votes cast in the first round, proving how volatile the electorate was and how unpopular the policies of the Solidarity Government (with which, of course, Wałęsa was also associated) had become.

Mazowiecki resigned as premier, unable to continue under Wałęsa's presidency. His successor was Jan Krzysztof Bielecki, a 39-year old economist and journalist. Of the former administration only two ministers were retained; the Finance Minister Leszek Balcerowicz (despite being responsible for the unpopular economic reforms) and the Foreign Minister, Krzysztof Skubiszewski. Their retention was a clear indication of the desire to retain confidence abroad, and, in particular, in the West, from whence much-needed investment and loans were being sought.

The development of independent political parties in Poland began in late 1989, but was given greater impetus during the summer of 1990 by the dissolution of the Solidarity movement. (Previously the Solidarity imprimatur had been essential for any candidate who wished to attain office.) Leading parties which emerged by the spring of 1991 included the Centre Alliance (Porozumienie Centrum), based upon those Solidarity members who had supported Wałęsa's candidacy for president. This had begun to develop into a right-of-centre Christian democratic party. The Citizen's Movement-Democratic Action (CMDA), which was created by former Solidarity activists, Adam Michnik and Jacek Kuroń, to support Mazowiecki for the presidency, looked an influential rival, but had perhaps an over-heavy dependence upon the support of the intelligentsia. However, in May, the CDMA merged with two other organizations to form the Democratic Union. This party was led by Mazowiecki, in an attempt to regain representation in parliament. Other parties included the Polish Peasant Party (Polskie Stronnictwo Ludowe—PSL), the former Communist SDRP, the right-wing National Christian Union and Party X. The last was the creation of defeated presidential candidate Stanisław Tymiński. In September, however, Party X was barred from standing for election in 32 districts, following the discovery of falsified candidature documentation.

On 30 August 1991 the Bielecki Government offered its resignation, exasperated by the constant obstructiveness of a politically unsympathetic Sejm. Although the legislature rejected the resignation, Poland's first free parliamentary elections were arranged for 27 October. They were contested by a great number of political parties. However, only 43.2% of the electorate participated. Owing to the extreme form of proportional representation adopted, no clear winner emerged. Twenty-nine parties eventually earned representation in the Sejm. The most successful parties were the Democratic Union, with 12.3% of the votes cast (62 seats), and the electoral coalition of the SDRP and the All Poland Trade Unions Alliance (OPZZ), the Democratic Left Alliance (Sojusz Lewicy Demokratycznej—SLD), with 11.9% of the electoral vote (60 seats).

Following several weeks of negotiations, in December 1991, a centre-right coalition was formed by Jan Olszewski, a lawyer and former Solidarity activist. The Finance Minister, Balcerowicz, was replaced, although the control of economic policy passed, in any case, to Jerzy Eysymont, the Minister-Head of the Central Planning Office. Although Poland (together with Hungary and Czechoslovakia) obtained the long sought after association agreement with the European Community (EC—known as the European Union from November 1993), on 16 December, which would facilitate access to Western markets, and in spite of the fact that the country continued to attract foreign investment, Poland's economic problems continued. There were strikes in protest against increases in energy prices in February 1992. In the same month the złoty was devalued by 12%. In March the Sejm failed to agree on budget proposals, effectively sabotaging the agreements which the Finance Minister had reached with the IMF. It was a weak, unstable and ineffective administration, consisting of members first from five, and later from seven, political parties, who failed to function as a coherent unit, and gave the impression of lacking authority. Moreover, the Olszewski Government became involved in bitter disputes with President Wałęsa. The defence minister even accused Wałęsa of attempting to gain control of the armed forces in order to organize a *coup d'état*, an accusation which resulted in the minister's temporary removal from office.

Political instability was the result of the fragmented parliament following the 1991 legislative elections. However, it was accentuated by the uncertain delineation of presidential powers. There was frustration as political infighting prevented effective decision-making, particularly with regard to the economy, where the privatization process was effectively halted. The number of unemployed had reached 2,155,000 (11.8% of the work-force), at the end of 1991, and there was a common perception that the Government was doing nothing to remedy the situation. On the night of 4–5 June 1992, after only seven months in office, the Olszewski Government was obliged to resign. Following the failure of Waldemar Pawlak, of the PSL, to form a government, and his subsequent resignation on 2 July, a coalition of eight parties nominated Hanna Suchocka of the Democratic Union as Prime Minister. Her appointment to the post was approved by the Sejm on 11 July. She proceeded to form a seven-party coalition.

Suchocka's premiership began with a month-long strike by 40,000 workers at a copper combine in Legnica and a budgetary crisis. In the late summer of 1992 strikes broke out in the motor industry, while, in December, miners withdrew their labour; production in the Silesian coalfields was almost completely halted for three weeks. However, the Government's concessions in the face of industrial unrest were minimal. In February 1993, following a threat to dissolve parliament, the Sejm finally accepted, by a narrow majority, the Government's budgetary proposals.

Prime Minister Suchocka quickly gained the respect and support not only of her coalition partners, but also, importantly, of the President. Although political infighting continued in the first twelve months of her Government's term of office, Suchocka herself remained largely insulated from it. In contrast, Wałęsa's conflicts with his former colleagues and confidants increased. Accusations were levelled against Wałęsa of past co-operation with the Communist security services. Politicians continued to be wary of Wałęsa's alleged authoritarian tendencies, and were irritated by the creation of presidential councils which became involved in policy-making decisions. In late December 1992 Wałęsa created a 47-member Committee on Economic Development, led by Andrzej Olechowski, the former finance minister in the Olszewski Government. The creation of this committee met with much criticism from ministers.

On 28 May 1993 a vote of 'no confidence' in the Suchocka Government was passed by a margin of one vote in the Sejm. The vote was a response by the Solidarity caucus to the Government's economic and social policies, and, more specifically, to its unflinching stance towards industrial unrest. However, President Wałęsa refused to accept Prime Minister Suchocka's resignation and instead dissolved the Sejm, scheduling new general elections for 19 September 1993.

The elections' rules excluded from parliamentary representation any parties receiving less than 5% of the votes cast. The aim was to reduce the number of parties in the Sejm and, hopefully, to create a more stable system of government. Of the 52% of voters who participated (an increase of 9% on voter turn-out in the 1991 general elections), approximately one-third cast votes for parties which, ultimately, did not receive more than 5% of the electorate's support. Only six parties earned representation in the parliament, apart from the German minority for whom four seats were reserved. The SLD, the electoral alliance dominated by the former Communists, and the PSL, the former associates of the Communists, emerged as the two strongest parties, together claiming 35.8% of the votes cast. However, under the new rules, they won over 65% of the seats in the lower chamber. In an attempt to exert greater influence on the parliamentary process, President Wałęsa created a Non-Party Bloc for Reform (Bezpartyjny Bloc Wapierania Reform—BBWR), which succeeded in attracting 5.4% of the votes cast.

In the Senat the victory of the left was even more complete. Seventy-three of the 100 seats were won by the SLD or the PSL. Owing to the fact that the abolition of the Senate was included in both the SLD's and the PSL's manifestos, there were doubts as to whether Poland would retain a bicameral parliamentary system.

The success of the left had been widely predicted. However, the extent of the political right's electoral defeat was unexpected. They were almost completely excluded from parliamentary representation. The Centre Alliance and the Christian National Union (CNU) were among the parties which failed to gain any seats. Following the elections, right-wing forces began to regroup. The success of the left wing could not be seen as a desire by the Polish people to return to Communism, although there was a certain degree of nostalgia for the certainties of the Communist period, but rather as a wish for changes which would ease the pain of economic reform. The SLD gained support not only among former Communists, but also among those who had been most adversely affected by the economic policies of the early 1990s: industrial workers, the unemployed, pensioners and others on fixed incomes. The PSL gained most of its support in the countryside, where the economic reform programme also had a severe effect. It was also thought that the right-wing, Christian parties had suffered electorally from increasing anti-clericalism.

Ironically, the former Communists were returned to parliament as the largest single party at the precise moment that another legacy of the past, the presence of former Soviet troops on Polish soil, was ending. The last elements of the Red Army garrison withdrew from the country on the day before the elections were held. In spite of the comprehensiveness of the left's victory, negotiations on the formation of a coalition Government proved difficult at first. Aleksander Kwasniewski, leader of the SLD, was thought to be an obvious choice as the next Prime Minister, but, on 18 October 1993, Waldemar Pawlak, the PSL leader, was nominated as premier by President Wałęsa. One week later, following tense negotiations between the PSL and the SLD, Pawlak presented his new Council of Ministers, comprised of politicians from the two parties, which was approved by the Sejm on 10 November.

It was still uncertain, in early 1994, how a Government containing former Communists would affect Poland's domestic politics and the country's international relations, an area of government policy where, hitherto, there was continuity. Full membership of the EC looked unlikely in any case much before the end of the 1990s. However, the previous Government had declared its intention to gain membership of North Atlantic Treaty Organisation (NATO). Nevertheless, despite earlier misgivings about the consequences of the former Communists regaining power, Pawlak pledged his Government to continuing to seek EC and NATO membership. Certainly NATO seemed wary of a Polish candidature for membership, but, in January 1994, it resolved to reorganize its structure and redefine its aims, in order to accommodate, at least in part, the aspirations for security guarantees by most of the former Communist states. In early February Poland acceded to NATO's 'Partnership for Peace' association.

The Economy

KEITH SWORD

INTRODUCTION

Poland is a country of some 312,685 sq km (120,728 sq miles) situated in north-central Europe on the Baltic coast. At the end of 1992 it had an estimated 38,417,000 inhabitants. This was an increase of 378,600 (1.0%) over the 1989 figure. While the birth-rate decreased slightly to approximately 513,600 (from 562,530 in 1989), the mortality rate increased from 381,173 to 393,400. The natural increase was therefore 120,200—the lowest recorded in the post-Second World War period. The percentage of the population of productive age (18–59 for women, 18–64 for men) was 57% of the total. For every 100 men in the population there were 105 women.

In the decades following the Second World War Poland became transformed into an industrialized country. Although lagging behind the economies of the West in terms of efficiency and standards of living, gross domestic product (GDP) per head (as estimated by the World Bank) had risen to US $1,860 by 1988. Any economic portrait of the country, however, must take account of two recent historical factors; the calamitous effects of the Second World War and the policies pursued during the resulting four-and-a-half decades of Communist rule.

During the War, Poland's losses were severe: the level of destruction of buildings in many Polish towns varied between 40% and 80%. Some 353,876 farms (up to 42% of the total in some areas) had been destroyed, with large-scale losses of livestock. Its industries had been destroyed by military activity, or else looted by the invaders (from both west and east). Poland's population was reduced by some 11m. people (from 35m. to 24m.) as a result of military losses, population movement and border changes. This included disproportionate losses among the cultural and technical intelligentsia. The population of Poland did not return to its pre-War levels until 1975.

In 1945 Poland was moved physically to the west, losing almost one-half of its pre-War territory to the USSR and gaining former German territory in the north and south. Although the changes meant an overall reduction in the area of the country, the territories acquired included superior arable farming land, a longer stretch of coastline (an additional 400 kms, including the ports of Gdańsk—Danzig and Szczecin—Stettin), and the Silesian coalfields. These advantages more than outweighed the loss of the Drohobycz oilfield and the large expanses of forest in the eastern regions.

The new Communist rulers of Poland set about implementing their economic programme. This involved nationalizing all branches of industry, trade and finance without compensation. Land reform was attempted. Larger estates, including those belonging to the Church and to the aristocracy, were divided up and distributed to landless peasants. A start was made to collectivization along the lines of the Soviet model, but this was abandoned in the 1950s. Strong emphasis was placed upon education and training. Illiteracy rates had been high before the War; the new authorities sought to eliminate illiteracy and to train rapidly a new generation of teachers, scientists, engineers, administrators and technicians to carry through the complete economic transformation which they planned.

The Communists aimed to transform Poland into a major industrial economy, and, following the Stalinist model, great emphasis was placed on engineering and heavy industry. With the help of Soviet investment and technology several prestige developments were embarked upon. One of the best-known was the giant iron and steel mills complex at Nowa Huta (New Foundry), near Kraków. The programme of rapid industrialization had the desirable effect from the Communists' point of view of drawing in workers from the countryside and creating an industrial proletariat.

The extent of this migration was astonishing. Whereas, in 1946, 68% of the population lived in the countryside, by 1988 this figure had been reduced to 39%. If the fact that Poland had one of the fastest rates of population growth in Europe after the Second World War (between 1947 and 1975 alone its population increased by some 45%) is taken into account, then the true rate of urban growth can be appreciated. Unfortunately, the infrastructure of housing and services was not enough to cope with this speed of rural depopulation; the house-building programme, in particular, could not keep up and housing remained one of the key areas of inadequacy in the economy. A 1990 World Bank estimate put the shortage of accommodation at about 1.3m. apartments.

The high rate of economic development over the first three post-War decades owing to 'socialist industrialization' was accompanied by other changes. In 1949 Poland joined the Council for Mutual Economic Assistance (CMEA or Comecon), the Soviet bloc's trading organization. Poland's economic development and, in particular, its foreign trade therefore became intertwined with that of its Communist partners and particularly with the dominant partner, the USSR. The overall costs and benefits of this association on Poland's trade were difficult to estimate, since foreign trade was not measured in convertible currency. However, the losses which Poland suffered by selling ships and vehicles at below market prices were, to some extent, compensated by receiving manufactured goods and raw materials, particularly energy (petroleum), at prices well below the world level.

National income and per head incomes were estimated to have increased sixfold in the three decades to 1975 although, with priority given to heavy industry and defence spending, there was little availability of consumer goods. In any case, this date marked the high point of the Gierek period, when economic indicators were falsely buoyed by the large-scale borrowing which the Gierek administration had made in the early 1970s.

Following the fall of Gierek in 1979, economic activity suffered from the series of strikes and protests which accompanied the birth of the Solidarity (Solidarność) trade union. The declaration of martial law in December 1981 did little to improve matters, since, with the opposition harried and political dialogue suppressed, the economy became the arena for political struggle. The deteriorating economic situation, while caused by the colossal mistakes of the Gierek era, was exacerbated by industrial stoppages, rising wages, a short working week and the rejection of necessary price increases. Attempts to modify or reform economic policy during the mid- to late 1980s had little effect, and, by 1989, not only was output falling but the rate of inflation had exceeded 100% and was continuing to rise.

At the beginning of the 1990s, following the collapse of Communist rule, Poland was one of several states in east-central Europe which were attempting to shake off the legacy of central planning of the economy. However, Poland was not only the largest of these states, but also had the most severe economic problems. Its new leaders felt unable to wait for gradual reforms to take effect and so, with International Monetary Fund (IMF) approval, embarked upon a series of radical market-orientated reforms. The first moves in this 'shock therapy' were taken in January 1990. They involved the liberalization of trade policy, encouragement of the private sector, and reduction of subsidies and defence spending. Further moves included maintaining a balanced budget and a strict monetary policy. The partial liberalization of the złoty and its 'pegging' against the US dollar were seen as further necessary stabilizing elements. (Seventeen countries contributed to a stabilization fund for the złoty which, by the end of 1990, amounted to more than US $1,000m.) Although finance minister Leszek Balcerowicz left office at the end of 1991, the market reforms which he initiated were continued by his successors, albeit with minor adjustments.

AGRICULTURE

In the four decades from 1946 to 1988, the proportion of the population living in rural areas declined from over 68% to 38.8%. Nevertheless, despite large-scale migration of the rural population to the cities and an ageing of the remaining rural population, by 1968 annual agricultural production was double that of the 1930s. This was the result of the partial reform of the agricultural sector carried out during the early 1950s, notably the creation of state farms, and a major investment of material resources and finance. In spite of the moves made towards collectivization, the state sector farmed only some 18%–20% of cultivated land in the post-War era. In 1989 some 4,068,000 people were employed in private-sector agriculture (a significant decline from 4,871,000 in 1960), whereas some 745,000 were employed in the state sector. The market reforms introduced from 1990 had an adverse effect on the farming sector. Although prices were no longer controlled in the market place, the removal of subsidies, the rapid decrease in purchasing power of incomes and limited access to the affluent markets of Western Europe have affected Polish farmers. In addition, the cost of farming equipment, fertilizer and other inputs rose severely, while credit became more expensive.

The situation was aggravated by a drought in 1992 which caused crop yields to fall by 20% and livestock production by 3.9%—a total decrease in agricultural output of 11.9%. Funds which were designated for the restructuring of the agricultural sector were redirected towards drought relief. The drought, and the shortages which resulted, brought some significant price increases, but these were enjoyed by only a few farmers. Farm incomes dropped by one-half in the period from 1988 to the early 1990s, and in 1992 there was a further 4% decrease overall. Unsurprisingly, therefore, Polish farmers reacted militantly. There were demands for state intervention and frequent protests. The dissatisfaction felt among farmers accounted for the electoral gains made by the Polish Peasant Party (Polskie Stronnictwo Ludowe—PSL) in 1993.

Although there were some grounds for optimism over the future of the agricultural sector, for example in 1992 there was a modest, but significant, US $193m. surplus in food trade with the European Community (EC—known as the European Union from November 1993), it seemed that long-term structural changes were inevitable. Although agricultural production increased by 2.2% in 1993, it was unlikely that Polish agriculture would be able to support over 30% of the population for much longer, especially if the EC continued to impede Polish imports. In the most developed countries of Western Europe, less than 5% of the population make their living on the land. In the absence of subsidies from central government, rationalization of private smallholdings must take place and modern farming methods be introduced. There was also the possibility that, eventually, land would have to be taken out of production.

In 1992 an Agricultural Ownership Agency was established to sell off the 1,495 state farms. By the end of March 1993 the state had taken over 873 of these farms and had succeeded in leasing or selling 8% of them to the public. Although these larger holdings were more suited to modern farming methods and were more efficient than the holdings of the private sector, there were doubts about the privatization. Most large state farms were in the western territories, 'recovered' from Germany in 1945. In the Szczecin, Koszalin, Gorzów, Zielona Góra and Elbląg districts, state farms accounted for more than 50% of arable land. Prospective foreign, and especially German, buyers of land in this area were regarded with suspicion. There was no wish for it to be recolonized by German capital. However, it was uncertain if domestic buyers could be found.

Crops

In 1988 the total area sown with crops was 14,359,000 ha, or 46% of the area of the country. Crop production generally holds a dominant position in agricultural production, but the major source of increase in crop production over the first 25 post-War years was a systematic increase in yields owing to the use of fertilizers, pesticides and machinery, rather than from any growth in its share of the land. Cereals accounted for about two-fifths of this total and production totals, in 1992, included 7.4m. metric tons of wheat, 4.0m. tons of rye, 2.8m. tons of barley and 1.2m. tons of oats. Total cereal output was 20.0m. tons, a decrease of 28.2% on 1991. Production of potatoes and sugar beet experienced a gradual decline in the 1980s and early 1990s, both in terms of the area sown and also in total production. By 1992 output had decreased to 23.4m. tons (a decrease of 35.6% from 1990 alone), and 11.1m. tons (a decline of 33.9% from 1990), respectively.

Livestock

Cattle were kept in Poland both for beef and dairy production. Their numbers doubled in the period between 1950–75 to just over 13m. head, although this number fell back in the 1980s; in 1992 cattle numbered 8.2m. Large numbers of pigs were kept since the Polish diet traditionally included a lot of meat. Pigs numbered 18.9m. in June 1993, a significant decrease on the previous year (22.1m.). A high slaughter rate had resulted from the shortage of animal feedstuff following the 1992 drought. Sheep were kept mainly for their wool or hides. Their milk or meat was largely seen as a by-product, neither lamb nor mutton being very popular with the Poles. In 1992 their number declined to 1.9m., a decrease of 42.2% on the 1991 figure. The greatest concentration of flocks was in the Carpathian-Sudeten highlands to the south.

MINERALS AND ENERGY

In 1991 Polish hard-coal exports accounted for 6.8% of foreign earnings and there were possibilities for further exports, as industrial unrest adversely affected Soviet coal production. However, the increase in exports did not occur. Instead, production decreased; 1993 hard-coal output was estimated to be less than 120m. metric tons (in 1991 production stood at 140.4m. tons), some 60% of production in the 1980s. The Government was forced to restrict exports to ensure that domestic users (power stations in particular) facing shortages were not forced to import coal. Until the summer of 1993 the coal-mining industry suffered from the Government's reluctance to sanction an increase in the price of coal. As a consequence, losses increased and miners' earnings were adversely affected. The industrial action which the miners took, in late 1992 and early 1993, brought little benefit. In mid-1993 a formula for gradual increases in the price of coal supplied to power stations seemed close to agreement.

Rich natural-gas deposits exist in the Lubaczów region (near the Ukrainian frontier) and there were also reserves in the Sudety region. The Polish Government also intended to invite foreign companies to extract methane gas from coal seams. However, it was unlikely that the production of natural gas in this way would occur quickly or have any impact on the pattern of energy use for future decades.

Poland's known reserves of petroleum were insignificant. Some reserves have been exploited in the Sub-Carpathian Depression, east of Kraków, and deposits were also found during the 1970s on the Baltic coast. By mid-1993 petroleum-exploration licences had been issued to Western companies such as Shell, Amoco, Exxon and British Gas for blocks in the Carpathian and Lublin areas, and further 'auctions' were planned. It was unlikely though, given the inevitable rise in consumption, that Poland would significantly reduce its petroleum imports. Most of Poland's petroleum was imported. However, the erratic nature of deliveries from its traditional supplier, Russia, forced Polish leaders to look elsewhere for petroleum supplies. In 1990 Poland imported just under 2.2m. tons of refined products, of which 1.7m. tons (77%) came from the West. In 1990 imports of crude petroleum amounted to 11,354,885m. złotys, 12.5% of Poland's total imports. Much of this petroleum was brought to German ports, owing to limited capacity on the Polish coast, and thus incurred high transportation costs.

The Poles intended to increase their refining capacity by building a new plant near the Baltic coast ports. Furthermore, a number of Western companies were reported to be interested in developing refining capacity at Gdańsk and Płockie. The overall aim was to increase petroleum consumption by 43% by the year 2000. Government plans involved reducing the country's dependence upon coal which, in 1990, accounted for 74% of energy consumed. A restructuring of the industry, agreed in early 1993, could reduce this figure to 50% within the next two decades. There were enough coal supplies to last for many decades, but the environmental costs of burning so much coal were considered to be unacceptable. Poland's use of energy was, in any case, inefficient. Since its decision, in September 1990, not to proceed with the exploitation of nuclear energy, even more determined efforts would have to be made to enhance efficient energy use.

Plans to privatize the petroleum industry, which covered exploration, production, refining, marketing and distribution, were being discussed in 1993. However, it seemed that the state companies themselves were reluctant to hand over control to private enterprises, especially in refining and marketing. There was particular concern that such important state enterprises would be transferred to foreign control.

Poland is a significant producer of a number of metal ores, the most important being copper and zinc. In the late 1950s large deposits of copper were found in the Legnica-Głogów region in the west of the country. In 1990 copper was one of Poland's most successful exports, accounting for US $470m. of foreign earnings. Zinc and lead ores are found in the Bytom-Chrzanów-Olkusz region. In 1990 output of these two ores was 200,200 metric tons. Iron ore is found in the Częstochowa area and near Łęczyca, but the iron content is low, barely reaching 30%. More valuable deposits of iron ore in the Suwałki region lie at a considerable depth and are difficult to exploit. Poland's iron ore output is therefore negligible, and, by the end of the 1980s, the Polish iron and steel industry came to rely almost entirely on Soviet imports of raw materials.

Poland also has large reserves of sulphur and rock salt. The sulphur, discovered in the 1950s, is mined in the Tarnobrzeg and Staszów regions. In 1991 3.9m. metric tons of sulphur were produced. Exports amounted to some $236m. in 1990. Large deposits of silver and smaller deposits of aluminium are also exploited, and some of the output exported. In 1991 products of basic metal industries (including raw materials) generated 25,128,700m. złotys in foreign-exchange earnings.

MANUFACTURING

After the introduction of the 'Balcerowicz Plan' for reform, in January 1990, production in state-owned industry decreased, by an estimated 23% by the end of that year. The consumer-goods sector was the most adversely affected: in 1990 production of washing-machines declined by over 40%, radios by 42% and footwear by more than 34%.

The removal of subsidies and central planning meant that managers in state enterprises had to learn quickly about concepts such as profitability and motivation, and to come to terms with skills such as balancing accounts and marketing, before the inevitable privatization of their business took place. Several closures of factories and enterprises occurred which rapidly increased the level of unemployment. Much attention was paid to the fate of the textile industry in Łódź. However, in general, the level of bankruptcies was less than anticipated. Four years after the 'shock therapy' programme was initiated, there were encouraging signs that some state enterprises were being run efficiently. Significantly, output of steel and heavy engineering, key sectors of the centrally planned economy, had decreased over the same period; in the case of the steel sector, by one-half since 1989. In contrast, the private sector's share in industrial output increased in the early 1990s. The dynamism of the private sector was the main reason why industrial production increased by 6.2% in 1993. Strong growth in the chemical, electrical machinery and construction industries was one factor which would help Poland recover from the recession of the early 1990s.

FOREIGN TRADE

In 1989–90, owing to political and economic changes in the region, and particularly to the collapse of the CMEA, Poland, along with other former Communist states, began once more to look to the West for trading partners. The shift in the orientation of Poland's trade became immediately clear in 1990. While the principal destination for Poland's exports in 1989 was the USSR (20.8%), followed by West Germany (14.2%), in 1990 the newly reunified Germany took 25.1% of exports and the USSR only 15.3%. In 1991, Germany took 29.4% of Polish exports and the USSR only 10.9%, followed by the United Kingdom (7.1%), the Netherlands (5.2%), Czechoslovakia (4.6%) and Austria (4.5%). Following the dissolution of the USSR, in December 1991, Poland's trade with the market economies of the West (72.1% of the country's total trade in 1992) far exceeded trade with the rest of Eastern Europe (15.9%).

The fate of economic reforms in Eastern Europe, following the fall of Communism, depended upon how successful the reforming countries were in penetrating Western markets. There was a strong realization of this fact in Poland, combined with frustration that the EC, and France in particular, were proving so reluctant to admit Polish goods into their markets. Although, from March 1992, Polish trade with the EC was regulated by an Association Agreement intended to establish, within a decade, a free-trade area which would include central Europe, this commitment did not apply to all economic sectors. Some restrictions on agricultural produce looked set to remain and concessions on exports of textiles and clothing were still undecided.

In 1992 Poland's trade deficit was US $86m., compared to $786m. in 1991. However, Poland's creditable export performance deteriorated at the beginning of 1993. A decline in foreign trade was accompanied by a marked growth in imports. In the first quarter of 1993 Poland registered a $370m. trade deficit. Import tariffs of 6% were introduced, in an attempt to reduce imports. The decline in exports in 1993 was worrying, given Poland's lack of reserves and its need to service its huge overseas debt.

The level of foreign investment in Poland, following the introduction of market reforms, was disappointing in some respects. By the end of 1991 there had been total investment of $700m. in Poland, compared with a total of $2,000m. in the much smaller Hungarian economy. However, the rate of investment subsequently improved, and foreign companies involved in take-overs or joint ventures in 1992–93 included major European and US firms such as Unilever, Philips, Pilkington, Volvo, General Motors and Coca Cola. However, it was clear that many Western firms were still cautious about investing in the country. It was possible that Poland's political instability contributed to this caution, and it was thought that the return to power of former Communist parties, in September 1993, would not encourage further foreign investment. In its favour, however, Poland's capacity to absorb foreign investment grew steadily from 1990. In 1993 it had the most privatized (most foreign trade came from the private sector) and, potentially, the most dynamic economy in the region. In July 1993 the British Export Credits Guarantee Department (ECGD) resumed cover for Poland, originally withdrawn in 1982. The ECGD was influenced by Polish attempts to resolve its debt problem and by positive reports from the IMF on Polish economic performance.

FINANCE, TAXATION AND NATIONAL DEBT

A common feature of post-Communist Governments in Poland was their strict control over the national budget. All administrations promised balanced budgets, control of the money supply and a reduction in the proportion of government spending directed towards subsidies and defence. The Solidarity Government's stabilization plan of January 1990 allowed for a 31.5% devaluation (from 6,500 złotys to 9,500 złotys per US dollar) and, at the same time, provided for the złoty to become internally convertible. The złoty-dollar rate held throughout 1990. However, in May 1991, the rate was increased to 11,000 złotys to the dollar—a devaluation of some 15%. A further 12% devaluation took place in February 1992. From then the National Bank managed a 'creeping devaluation' of 1.85% per month in order to maintain the price advantage of Polish exports. This meant a 25% devaluation over the 12 months to July 1993. Given the decrease in exports, at the beginning of 1993, even this was considered insufficient and, in August 1993, a further 8% devaluation took place. By this point the exchange rate had reached almost 20,000 złotys to the dollar, although officially the złoty was measured against a 'basket' of currencies (the US dollar, the Deutschmark, the pound sterling and the French and Swiss francs).

A number of changes occurred in the relative weighting of revenue sources as the Polish tax system was reformed. A personal taxation scheme was introduced in January 1992, and, on 5 July 1993, the long-awaited introduction of a value added tax (VAT) took place. It was applied in three bands; a standard band of 22%; a preferential band of 7%; and a zero rating for certain items. At the same time, excise duties were announced on alcohol, tobacco and a range of luxury goods. The Government's aim was to shift the burden of taxation to consumers and, in the process, to simplify the tax system. In 1992 the Government attempted to reduce tax evasion, which was believed to be widespread.

In March 1990 the 'Paris Club' of debtor nations agreed to a suspension of interest payments for 12 months. (Poland was fortunate in having a greater proportion of its debt owed to foreign governments than to commercial banks.) In the spring of 1991 the USA agreed to cancel 70% of the debt owed it and encouraged its allies to follow their lead. The Paris Club agreed on a 50% reduction of the current value of the US $33,000m. official debt. However, the 'London Club' of 360 commercial creditors (mostly Western banks) proved reluctant to match these terms. Negotiations were suspended again, in July 1993, with the London Club prepared to concede only a 30% reduction in the $12,000m. debt. An agreement was important to Poland in order to attract foreign-equity investment and remove the last obstacle to normalizing relations with the commercial banking system. Servicing the debt burden was set to rise from $3,200m. a year to $5,400m. in 1994.

The IMF agreed a stand-by loan of $660m. in March 1993. In May the World Bank made two further loans of $750m. to help finance farm reforms, bank restructuring and debt repayment. The Suchocka Government had agreed to maintain the budget deficit at 5% of GDP. Budget plans for 1993 provided for spending to grow more slowly than revenue, involving a deficit of 81,000m. złotys, in line with the 5% threshold. A crucial element in maintaining this budgetary discipline was the Government's insistence that pensions and public sector wages be restrained. However, it was the Suchocka Government's determined resistance to demands for higher pay and pensions which eventually brought it down.

Banking

The National Bank of Poland (Narodowy Bank Polski) was formed in January 1945 as a central bank with the exclusive right to print currency. For most of the Communist period it was the basic organ of the entire banking system, financing state credit requirements, the needs of other banks, and supplying credit to industry, trade, the construction sector, transport and communications. In 1988 this began to change. Many of the functions and responsibilities of the National Bank were divided up to new commercial banks, and by early 1993 licences had been granted for more than 84 commercial banks. More than a dozen banks were given foreign-exchange licences and a new Export Development Bank (Bank Rozwoju Eksportu) was set up. In April 1993 the Credit Bank in Poznań (Wielkopolski Bank Kredytowy w Poznaniu) became the first of Poland's commercial banks to be privatized. The offer attracted interest from home and overseas and was considerably over-subscribed. A further eight regional banks were expected to be sold off before the end of 1996.

ECONOMIC GROWTH

In the period following the introduction of the Balcerowicz Plan, the Polish economy improved. GDP decreased sharply in the initial stages, by 12% in 1990 and 8% in 1991. However, in 1992 GDP grew by 1.5%, and would have increased further had not agricultural production been affected by drought. In the private sector, significantly, growth for the same year was 11.3%. In 1993 GDP increased by some 3% and there were expectations that GDP would continue to grow by 5% or more per year for the rest of the decade.

There was also a steady reduction of the level of inflation, in the early 1990s, which had reached a rate of 3,900% in the last quarter of 1989. In 1990 it fell to a monthly average of 4%–5%. In 1992 the annual rate of consumer prices was 43%. The Government intended to reduce inflation to 32% in 1993 and this was likely to be achieved. Although the introduction of VAT in July had been expected to increase inflation, the effect seemed to have been less than was anticipated. Consumer prices rose by only 1.1% in the same month. Inflation prospects for 1994 were reasonably good, since government-induced price rises in fuel and energy would not be included. There remained concerns, however, that the policy of gradual devaluation, or the spending policies of the new Government, might cause price increases.

WAGES AND THE LABOUR MARKET

Real earnings struggled to keep up with inflation and, in the first half of 1993, the real value of earnings fell by 1.2%. In part, this was owing to the effects of a high rate of unemployment. However, it was also partly owing to continuing government controls over wages in the state sector, where increases have been limited to 60% of the increase in consumer prices. If increases were exceeded, the employer risked invoking a punitive tax (known as the *popiwek*). The *popiwek* led to a decline in the earnings of employees in state enterprises, and hence industrial unrest. However, it also acted as an incentive to workers to speed the privatization of their own companies (since private firms are free from the *popiwek* wage restrictions). A reduction of 5.3% in the number of public enterprises in the first six months of 1993 seemed to demonstrate the efficiency of the *popiwek* in this area.

Against these achievements, however, was an increase in labour unrest. The number of recorded strikes was higher during the first half of 1993 than the corresponding period twelve months earlier (7,341 compared with 5,916), more people were involved in industrial action and more working days were lost. Public-sector workers also became more involved in strike activity—protests from teachers closed many schools temporarily in May 1993.

Unemployment continued to rise as the restructuring of industry reduced work-forces. It was estimated that the level of unemployment would reach 3.0m. by the end of 1993. It had already reached 2.8m. by the end of July, or 15.2% of the available labour-force. Major centres of the new prosperity such as Warsaw (7.3%), Kraków (8.1%), Katowice (8.5%) and Poznań (8.6%) still had relatively low unemployment. However, the smaller, peripheral towns such as Suwałki, Olsztyn, Koszalin and Słupsk, had levels of between 20%–25%, which led to demands for a regional aid programme. The number of young people without jobs was also cause for concern, as was the increasing number of long-term unemployed.

PRIVATIZATION

In 1990 the Mazowiecki Government had planned to sell state-owned enterprises in a major privatization campaign. It had undertaken to sell one-half of the state enterprises within five years, a considerable undertaking given that Poland had some 8,000 state enterprises of any size. The privatization legislation was passed by the Sejm in July 1990 and a Ministry of Ownership Transformation established to handle the operation. The operation was slow to begin, however. The delay was partly owing to legislative and administrative problems and partly to indecision over which enterprises to privatize. The first group of five large firms was eventually offered to the public in November 1990. These included Exbud (building and construction), Krosno (glassware) and Prochnik (clothing manufacturer).

The process of privatization by individual enterprise proved both slow and costly, and an alternative was sought. The mass privatization scheme was approved by parliament in April 1993. The scheme would ultimately involve some 600 large- and medium-sized state enterprises from a broad range of industrial sectors. Under an Enterprise Pact signed between the Government, trade unions and enterprise representatives, in February 1993, each enterprise was to be given six months to decide whether it wanted to take the route of privatization. In addition to tax advantages, workers were promised representation on the supervisory boards of the companies privatized.

By the autumn of 1993 the first 195 candidates had been selected, a condition being that they must be running at a profit. The enterprises were to be grouped and managed within some 20 investment trusts (called National Investment Funds or NIFs). Although some foreign experts were recruited to manage these trusts, two-thirds of the governing boards were Polish. Shares in the trusts were to be distributed to those who wished, for a small fee (expected to be US $15–20, or about 5% of an average monthly salary), to take part. Workers would be entitled to a free allocation of 15% of the shares in their own firm. Later, the shares in individual companies were to be floated on the stock exchange.

PROBLEMS AND PROSPECTS

Most outside observers agreed that, in the early 1990s, Poland experienced strong export growth to Western markets, sharp productivity gains and budgetary discipline. There were realistic hopes that GDP would double over the ensuing decade. When this situation is contrasted with the economic disarray in the successor states of the USSR, it must seem that the countries of the former Communist bloc were developing at two speeds (Hungary and the Czech Republic having also made considerable progress with their economic reforms). The 'prosperity frontier' between East and West, which once ran along the German-Polish border was perceptibly shifting to Poland's eastern frontier.

The success of the former Communist Democratic Left Alliance (Sojusz Lewicy Demokratycznej—SLD) in the 1993 elections came as something of a set-back to investors. There were fears that the moves that were made towards transforming the economy from a centrally planned one to a market-orientated one over the previous four years would be reversed. However, it was unlikely that the election results would make any difference to the progress of the economic reforms. The SLD expressed their support for the market reforms and in fact voted for the mass privatization. They intended, however, to alleviate the effects of the changes on lower-income groups, just as the Polish Peasant Party (Polskie Stronnictwo Ludowe—PSL), their coalition partner, intended to aid the agricultural sector. There were concerns, however, as to how these electoral commitments could be kept without exceeding the 5% budget deficit agreed by all parties as a prerequisite for obtaining IMF economic aid.

Statistical Survey

Principal sources: *Rocznik Statystyczny, Biuletyn Statystyczny* and *Concise Statistical Yearbook of Poland*, all published by Główny Urząd Statystyczny (Central Statistical Office), 00-925 Warsaw, Al. Niepodległości 208; tel. (22) 252431; telex 814581.

Area and Population

AREA, POPULATION AND DENSITY

Area (sq km)	
Land	304,465
Inland water	8,220
Total	312,685*
Population (census results)†	
7 December 1978	35,061,450
6 December 1988	
Males	18,464,373
Females	19,414,268
Total	37,878,641
Population (official estimates at 31 December)†	
1990	38,183,200
1991	38,309,200
1992	38,417,000
Density (per sq km) at 31 December 1992	122.9

* 120,728 sq miles.

† Figures exclude civilian aliens within the country and include civilian nationals temporarily outside the country.

VOIVODSHIPS (estimated population at 31 December 1991)

	Area (sq km)	Total ('000)	Density (per sq km)	Capital* ('000)
Warszawskie	3,788	2,419.6	639	1,653.3
Bialskopodlaskie	5,348	306.2	57	54.1
Białostockie	10,055	695.2	69	273.3
Bielskie	3,704	906.7	245	184.4
Bydgoskie	10,349	1,116.0	108	383.6
Chełmskie	3,866	248.1	64	67.7
Ciechanowskie	6,362	429.8	68	44.7
Częstochowskie	6,182	777.0	126	258.7
Elbląskie	6,103	481.0	79	126.9
Gdańskie	7,394	1,438.9	195	466.5
Gorzowskie	8,484	502.8	59	125.2
Jeleniogórskie	4,379	518.6	119	93.5
Kaliskie	6,512	713.5	110	106.5
Katowickie	6,650	4,006.6	603	366.9
Kieleckie	9,211	1,127.3	122	215.0
Konińskie	5,139	470.7	92	81.1
Koszalińskie	8,470	511.1	60	109.8
Krakowskie	3,254	1,234.5	379	751.3
Krośnieńskie	5,702	497.9	87	50.1
Legnickie	4,037	518.5	128	106.1
Leszczyńskie	4,154	389.4	94	59.5
Lubelskie	6,792	1,019.6	150	352.5
Łomżyńskie	6,684	348.2	52	60.7
Łódzkie	1,523	1,136.6	746	844.9
Nowosądeckie	5,576	703.3	126	79.0
Olsztyńskie	12,327	757.2	61	164.8
Opolskie	8,535	1,021.2	120	128.9
Ostrołęckie	6,498	398.8	61	51.8
Pilskie	8,205	483.5	59	73.3
Piotrkowskie	6,266	643.0	103	81.0
Płockie	5,117	517.8	101	125.3
Poznańskie	8,151	1,339.4	164	589.7
Przemyskie	4,437	408.3	92	69.2
Radomskie	7,294	753.2	103	229.7
Rzeszowskie	4,397	728.8	166	154.8
Siedleckie	8,499	653.6	77	72.9
Sieradzkie	4,869	408.6	84	43.6
Skierniewickie	3,960	420.7	106	46.7
Słupskie	7,453	416.8	56	102.4
Suwalskie	10,490	474.1	45	62.8
Szczecińskie	9,982	975.9	98	414.2
Tarnobrzeskie	6,283	601.7	96	49.5
Tarnowskie	4,151	674.6	163	121.9
Toruńskie	5,348	660.6	124	202.0
Wałbrzyskie	4,168	740.5	178	141.2
Włocławskie	4,402	430.1	98	122.8
Wrocławskie	6,287	1,130.7	180	643.6
Zamojskie	6,980	490.5	70	63.1
Zielonogórskie	8,868	662.5	75	114.9
Total	312,685	38,309.2	123	—

* Each Voivodship is named after the town from which it is administered.

PRINCIPAL TOWNS
(estimated population at 31 December 1991)

Warszawa (Warsaw)	1,653,300	Ruda Śląska	171,600
Łódź	844,900	Olsztyn	164,800
Kraków (Cracow)	751,300	Rzeszów	154,800
Wrocław	643,600	Rybnik	144,800
Poznań	589,700	Wałbrzych	141,200
Gdańsk	466,500	Dąbrowa Górnicza	139,200
Szczecin	414,200	Chorzów	131,500
Bydgoszcz	383,600	Opole	128,900
Katowice	366,900	Elbląg	126,900
Lublin	352,500	Gorzów Wielkopolski	125,200
Białystok	273,300	Płock	125,300
Sosnowiec	259,000	Włocławek	122,800
Częstochowa	258,700	Tarnów	121,900
Gdynia	251,800	Zielona Góra	114,900
Bytom	232,200	Wodzisław Śląski	112,200
Radom	229,700	Koszalin	109,800
Gliwice	215,700	Kalisz	106,500
Kielce	215,000	Legnica	106,100
Zabrze	205,800	Jastrzębie Zdrój	104,600
Toruń	202,000	Grudziądz	102,900
Tychy	138,800	Słupsk	102,400
Bielsko-Biała	184,400		

BIRTHS, MARRIAGES AND DEATHS

	Registered live births		Registered marriages		Registered deaths	
	Number	Rate (per 1,000)	Number	Rate (per 1,000)	Number	Rate (per 1,000)
1984	699,041	18.9	285,258	7.7	364,862	9.9
1985	677,576	18.2	266,816	7.2	381,457	10.3
1986	634,748	17.0	257,887	6.9	376,316	10.1
1987	605,492	16.1	252,819	6.7	378,365	10.1
1988	587,741	15.5	246,791	6.5	370,821	9.8
1989	562,530	14.8	255,643	6.7	381,173	10.0
1990	545,800*	14.3	255,369	6.7	388,440	10.2
1991	546,000*	14.3	233,206	6.1	404,000*	10.6
1992*	513,600	13.4	217,900	5.7	393,400	10.3

Average life expectation at birth (1989): Males 66.8 years; Females 75.5 years.

* Provisional.

IMMIGRATION AND EMIGRATION*

	1989	1990	1991
Immigrants	2,230	2,626	5,040
Emigrants	26,645	18,440	20,977

* Figures refer to immigrants arriving for permanent residence in Poland and emigrants leaving for permanent residence abroad.

EMPLOYMENT (persons aged 15 years and over, 1988 census)

	Males	Females	Total
Agriculture, hunting and forestry*	2,772,496	2,361,330	5,133,826
Coal mining	450,893	62,490	513,383
Industry†	2,729,081	1,815,043	4,544,124
Electricity, gas and water	146,159	40,860	187,019
Construction	1,236,934	228,137	1,465,071
Trade (wholesale and retail) and restaurants	414,039	1,079,006	1,493,045
Transport, storage and communications	913,535	321,855	1,235,390
Financing, insurance, real estate and business services	111,119	211,302	322,421
Community, social and personal services (incl. hotels); Activities not adequately defined	1,295,749	2,262,202	3,557,951
Total	10,070,005	8,382,225	18,452,230

* Including fishing from inland waters.
† Including sea fishing, manufacturing, gas production and mining and quarrying other than coal mining.

CIVILIAN LABOUR FORCE EMPLOYED ('000 persons)

	1989	1990	1991
Agriculture, hunting, forestry and fishing	4,729.5	4,597.0	4,415.2
Mining and quarrying	614.7	607.9	480.8
Manufacturing	4,680.6	4,335.9	4,026.9
Electricity, gas and water	195.1	148.7	147.2
Construction	1,432.3	1,320.9	1,203.8
Trade, restaurants and hotels	1,787.0	1,652.9	1,750.5
Transport, storage and communications	1,303.2	1,127.2	999.7
Financing, insurance, real estate and business services	395.4	337.8	341.7
Community, social and personal services	3,066.6	3,084.3	3,099.3
Activities not adequately defined	233.6	339.5	95.2
Total	18,438.0	17,552.1	16,560.3

Source: ILO, *Year Book of Labour Statistics*.

Agriculture

PRINCIPAL CROPS ('000 metric tons)

	1990	1991	1992
Wheat	9,026	9,270	7,368
Barley	4,217	4,257	2,819
Maize	290	340	206
Rye	6,044	5,899	3,981
Oats	2,119	1,873	1,236
Other cereals	6,318	6,173	4,359
Potatoes	36,313	29,038	23,388
Dry beans	116	132	99
Other pulses	493	548	499
Rapeseed	1,206	1,043	758
Cabbages	1,749	1,848	1,286
Tomatoes	414	450	404
Cauliflower	224	254	198
Cucumbers and gherkins	388	463	395
Onions (dry)	568	669	539
Carrots	822	842	672
Sugar beets	16,721	11,412	11,052
Sugar (raw)	2,219	1,677	1,520*
Apples	812	1,146	1,570
Pears	35	53	67
Plums	43	67	97
Strawberries	241.3	262.6	204.5
Raspberries	28.5	31.7	28.1
Currants	130.4	169.2	213.4
Tobacco leaves	59	57	45
Flax fibre and tow	16	5	2

* Unofficial figure.
Source: FAO, *Production Yearbook*.

LIVESTOCK ('000 head, year ending September)

	1990	1991	1992
Horses	941	939	900
Cattle	10,049	8,844	8,221
Pigs	19,464	21,868	22,086
Sheep	4,158	3,234	1,870
Goats*	12	14	10
Chickens	63,000	52,000	50,000
Ducks	6,000	7,000	7,000
Turkeys	1,000	1,000	1,000

* FAO estimate(s).
Source: FAO, *Production Yearbook*.

LIVESTOCK PRODUCTS (metric tons)

	1990	1991	1992
Beef and veal	725,000	663,000	617,000*
Mutton and lamb	29,000	33,000	18,000†
Pig meat	1,855,000	2,013,000*	1,998,000*
Horse meat	4,000	4,000	3,000†
Poultry meat	332,000	333,000	330,000
Cows' milk	15,832,000	14,442,000	12,800,000
Sheep's milk	7,000	6,000	4,000†
Cheese	332,699	294,637	288,260
Butter and ghee	300,000*	220,000*	180,000
Dried milk	216,121	212,139	175,144
Hen eggs	422,375	361,833	389,000*
Honey	13,794	14,100	13,800†
Wool:			
greasy	14,783	10,738	5,000*
scoured	8,870	6,443	3,000*
Cattle hides†	74,000	70,000	59,000
Sheepskins†	5,000	5,600	3,000

* Unofficial figure(s). † FAO estimate(s).
Source: FAO, *Production Yearbook*.

Forestry

('000 cu metres)

	1989	1990	1991
Roundwood removals	21,254	17,617	17,026
Sawnwood production*	5,159	3,995	3,378

* Excluding railway sleepers. Industrial production only.

Fishing

('000 metric tons, live weight)

	1989	1990	1991
Common carp	21.8	22.0	25.0
Atlantic cod	31.9	28.8	25.8
Alaska (Walleye) pollack	268.6	223.5	230.6
Southern blue whiting	33.7	50.6	24.8
North Pacific hake	18.2	3.7	5.8
Patagonian grenadier	10.3	4.0	1.2
Atlantic herring	58.6	60.9	45.9
European sprat	20.6	14.3	23.2
Other fishes (incl. unspecified)	32.6	32.4	37.6
Total fish	496.3	440.1	419.9
Crustaceans	7.8	1.3	9.6
Squids	60.7	31.6	33.2
Total catch	564.8	473.0	457.4
Inland waters	34.2	45.0	48.0
Atlantic Ocean	242.8	200.8	220.7
Pacific Ocean	287.8	227.2	236.5

Source: FAO, *Yearbook of Fishery Statistics*.

1992 ('000 metric tons): Sea fishing 445.

Mining

('000 metric tons, unless otherwise indicated)

	1989	1990	1991
Hard coal	177,633	147,736	140,376
Lignite	71,816	67,584	69,406
Iron ore[1]:			
gross weight	7.4	2.4	0.1
metal content[2]	2	n.a.	n.a.
Crude petroleum	159	163	158
Salt (unrefined)	4,670	4,055	3,840
Native sulphur (per 100%)	4,864	4,660	3,935
Copper ore (metric tons)[2,3]	405,400	396,600	n.a.
Lead ore (metric tons)[2,3,4]	51,100	45,400	n.a.
Magnesite—crude (metric tons)[2,3]	24,100	23,300	n.a.
Silver (metric tons)[3]	1,003	832	899
Zinc ore (metric tons)[2,3,4]	170,000	154,800	n.a.
Natural gas (million cu metres)	5,368	3,867	4,132

[1] Including the iron content of iron pyrites.
[2] Source: UN, *Industrial Statistics Yearbook*.
[3] Figures refer to the metal content of ores.
[4] Estimated by Metallgesellschaft Aktiengesellschaft, Frankfurt am Main.

Industry

SELECTED PRODUCTS
(metric tons, unless otherwise indicated)

	1989	1990	1991
Sausages and smoked meat	767,000	714,000	676,000
Refined sugar ('000 metric tons)	1,710	1,971	1,636
Margarine	222,000	179,000	194,000
Wine and mead ('000 hectolitres)	2,556	2,114	2,970
Beer ('000 hectolitres)	12,082	11,294	13,600
Cigarettes (million)	81,342	91,497	90,400
Cotton yarn[1]	195,500	126,700	73,200
Woven cotton fabrics ('000 metres)[2]	760,200	427,500	286,000
Flax and hemp yarn[1]	27,400	14,900	9,500
Linen and hemp fabrics ('000 metres)[2]	75,000	35,500	26,600
Wool yarn[1]	77,200	55,000	37,400
Woven woollen fabrics ('000 metres)[2]	96,800	64,700	44,323
Cellulosic continuous filaments	18,600	13,900	n.a.
Cellulosic staple and tow	66,700	35,600	25,500
Leather footwear ('000 pairs)	55,092	43,273	28,500
Mechanical wood pulp	105,000	81,300	84,200
Chemical wood pulp	582,000	523,000	509,000
Newsprint	8,400	25,000	64,200
Other paper	1,156,000	899,000	885,000
Paperboard	241,000	141,000	111,000
Synthetic rubber	125,000	103,000	79,500
Rubber tyres ('000)[3]	6,025	4,704	4,516
Ethyl alcohol ('000 hectolitres)	2,687	2,304	n.a.
Sulphuric acid—100% ('000 metric tons)	3,114	1,721	1,088
Nitric acid—100% ('000 metric tons)	2,175	1,577	1,438
Caustic soda—96%	452,000	404,000	324,000
Soda ash—98%	1,005,000	968,000	962,000
Nitrogenous fertilizers (*a*) ('000 metric tons)[4]	1,642.6	1,303	1,148
Phosphate fertilizers (*b*) ('000 metric tons)[4]	945	467	253
Plastics and synthetic resins	721,000	627,000	596,000
Motor spirit—Petrol ('000 metric tons)[5]	4,407	3,586	3,307
Distillate fuel oils ('000 metric tons)	4,861	3,905	3,694
Residual fuel oils ('000 metric tons)	2,956	2,883	2,655
Coke-oven coke ('000 metric tons)	16,323	13,490	11,317
Gas coke ('000 metric tons)	223	155	55
Cement ('000 metric tons)	17,125	12,518	12,012
Pig-iron ('000 metric tons)[6]	9,488	8,658	6,515
Crude steel ('000 metric tons)	15,094	13,625	10,432
Rolled steel products ('000 metric tons)	11,272	9,836	8,036
Aluminium—unwrought[7]	47,809	45,974	45,793
Refined copper—unwrought	390,268	346,083	378,479
Refined lead—unwrought	78,200	64,800	50,800
Zinc—unwrought[7]	163,727	132,131	126,067
Radio receivers ('000)	2,523	1,433	581
Television receivers ('000)	772	748	438

—continued	1989	1990	1991
Merchant ships launched (gross reg. tons)	94,000	136,000	219,000
Passenger motor cars (number)	285,497	266,421	168,791
Lorries (number)	43,853	38,956	21,625
Domestic washing machines (number)	811,000	482,000	336,000
Domestic refrigerators (number)	516,000	604,000	553,000
Construction: dwellings completed (number)	150,159	134,215	136,790
Electric energy (million kWh)	145,467	136,311	134,697
Manufactured gas:			
from gasworks (million cu metres)	109	75.8	27.3
from cokeries (million cu metres)	6,456	5,475	4,702

1 Pure and mixed yarns. Cotton includes tyre cord yarn.
2 Pure and mixed fabrics, after undergoing finishing processes. Cotton and wool include substitutes.
3 Tyres for passenger motor cars and commercial vehicles, including inner tubes and tyres for animal-drawn road vehicles, and tyres for non-agricultural machines and equipment.
4 Fertilizer production is measured in terms of (*a*) nitrogen or (*b*) phosphoric acid. Phosphate fertilizers include ground rock phosphate.
5 Including synthetic products.
6 Including blast-furnace ferro-alloys.
7 Figures refer to both primary and secondary metal. Zinc production includes zinc dust and remelted zinc.

Finance

CURRENCY AND EXCHANGE RATES

Monetary Units

100 groszy (singular: grosz) = 1 złoty.

Sterling and Dollar Equivalents (30 September 1993)

£1 sterling = 29,514 złotys;
US $1 = 19,735 złotys;
100,000 złotys = £3.388 = $5.067.

Average Exchange Rate (złotys per US dollar)

1990 9,500
1991 10,576
1992 13,626

BUDGET ('000 million złotys)

Revenue	1988	1989	1990
Turnover tax	3,214.6	8,818.3	39,600.8
Share in profits and income tax of state enterprises*	3,960.6	12,048.3	n.a.
Taxes from the private sector	470.8	1,490.4	n.a.
Taxes from population	230.1	970.4	n.a.
Surplus of financial sector	363.0	2,953.1	n.a.
Total (incl. others)	10,088.7	30,108.5	196,240.5
of which:			
Central government	6,702.1	19,394.0	137,795.1
Local authorities	3,386.6	10,759.5	58,445.4

* Including income tax from financial institutions and co-operative organizations.

Expenditure	1988	1989	1990
National economy	4,196.8	11,941.4	50,104.5
Science	68.6	109.1	421.9
Education	1,010.7	4,342.5	28,249.9
Culture	164.2	638.8	3,115.7
Public health } Social welfare }	1,093.3	4,015.8	32,671.3
Physical culture and tourism	51.7	199.5	1,029.5
Social insurance	432.7	2,344.4	16,543.4
National defence	742.2	2,118.0	13,598.8
Public administration and jurisdiction	541.0	1,997.9	13,615.0
Current expenditure (incl. others)	8,430.6	29,617.5	172,165.3
Investment expenditure	1,579.6	4,069.6	21,636.0
Total	10,010.2	33,687.1	193,801.3
of which:			
Central government	6,315.3	20,933.5	121,330.8
Local authorities	3,694.9	12,753.6	72,470.5

INTERNATIONAL RESERVES (US $ million at 31 December)

	1990	1991	1992
Gold*	189.0	189.1	189.0
IMF special drawing rights	0.8	7.7	1.1
Reserve positition in IMF	—	—	106.1
Foreign exchange	4,491.3	3,624.9	3,992.0
Total	4,681.1	3,821.7	4,288.1

* National valuation (US $400 per troy ounce).

Source: IMF, *International Financial Statistics.*

MONEY SUPPLY ('000 million złotys at 31 December)

	1990	1991	1992
Currency outside banks	39,336	56,177	77,984
Demand deposits at commercial banks	54,114	51,128	70,957

From December 1991 figures were based on a new system of accounts and an improved reporting system.

Source: IMF, *International Financial Statistics.*

COST OF LIVING (Consumer Price Index; base: 1980 = 100)

	1990	1991	1992
Food	24,985	37,727	51,611
Fuel and light	29,935	85,135	165,332
Clothing	13,790	26,132	36,533
Rent	33,873	75,909	121,151
All items (incl. others)	22,362	38,082	54,458

Source: ILO, *Year Book of Labour Statistics.*

NATIONAL ACCOUNTS

Gross Domestic Product by Economic Activity
('000 million złotys at current market prices)

	1990	1991
Industry*	265,717.7	331,358.5
Construction	54,590.2	84,349.4
Agriculture	42,832.0	51,091.8
Forestry	6,952.6	5,403.4
Transport	23,794.6	32,103.0
Communications	4,922.9	14,064.3
Trade	75,293.7	107,713.7
Other activities of the material sphere	9,222.5	16,757.2
Community services	9,374.3	18,928.9
Other non-material services	128,368.6	194,563.1
Sub-total	621,069.1	856,333.3
Less Imputed bank service charge	29,551.5	32,003.4
GDP in purchasers' values	591,517.6	824,329.9

* Principally manufacturing, mining, sea fishing, electricity, gas and water.

BALANCE OF PAYMENTS (US $ million)

	1990	1991	1992
Merchandise exports f.o.b.	11,329	13,846	13,887
Merchandise imports f.o.b.	-9,919	-14,632	-13,972
Trade balance	1,410	-786	-85
Exports of services	2,138	2,232	2,327
Imports of services	-1,886	-1,704	-1,614
Other income received	581	541	527
Other income paid	-3,910	-3,404	-4,723
Private unrequited transfers (net)	2,196	724	213
Official unrequited transfers (net)	305	45	253
Current balance	834	-2,352	-3,102
Direct investment (net)	88	256	577
Other capital (net)	5,457	-3,337	-1,670
Net errors and omissions	-62	-1,084	-102
Overall balance	6,317	-6,517	-4,297

Source: IMF, *International Financial Statistics.*

External Trade

PRINCIPAL COMMODITIES (million złotys)

Imports f.o.b.	1989	1990	1991
Fuels and power	1,882,732	18,942,000	30,922,000
Natural gas	369,166	1,351,213	n.a.
Crude petroleum	1,011,410	11,354,885	n.a.
Petroleum products and synthetic liquid fuels	411,079	4,022,702	n.a.
Products of basic metal industries*	1,298,006	6,075,000	6,587,000
Iron ore (crude and enriched)	113,605	918,997	n.a.
Rolled iron and steel products	165,779	637,030	n.a.
Steel tubes and pipes	116,695	462,032	n.a.
Products of electro-engineering industries	5,505,261	36,355,000	61,802,000
Products of chemical industry*	2,237,022	10,390,000	20,626,000
Products of wood and paper industry	285,286	1,430,000	4,048,000
Products of light industry (textiles, clothing and leather)*	1,126,930	5,520,000	10,085,000
Textiles	505,858	n.a.	n.a.
Products of food industry	1,349,710	6,879,000	17,016,000
Agricultural products	678,228	1,711,000	5,019,000
Total (incl. others)	14,864,175	90,512,747	164,259,298

Exports f.o.b.	1989	1990	1991
Fuels and power	1,873,686	13,789,000	16,803,800
Hard coal	1,294,193	9,191,611	9,797,300
Products of basic metal industries*	2,035,384	19,822,000	25,128,700
Rolled iron and steel products	606,988	5,363,476	8,648,000
Products of electro-engineering industries	7,475,108	39,909,000	35,338,500
Products of chemical industry*	2,050,184	16,340,000	18,273,000
Products of wood and paper industry	570,865	5,516,000	10,316,600
Products of light industry (textiles, clothing and leather)*	1,072,873	8,711,000	9,639,200
Textile clothing and underwear	268,477	2,432,600	3,170,100
Products of food industry	1,868,635	13,630,000	15,762,300
Agricultural products	806,082	7,338,000	10,362,600
Total (incl. others)	19,476,174	136,055,235	157,715,913

* Including raw materials.

PRINCIPAL TRADING PARTNERS* (million złotys)

Imports f.o.b.	1989	1990§	1991
Austria	886,892	4,403,499	10,335,869
Belgium	224,203	1,096,453	4,376,671
China, People's Republic	458,045	1,382,606	454,635
Czechoslovakia	846,166	2,761,817	5,487,430
Denmark	145,237	881,464	3,486,496
Finland	101,189	984,523	1,738,681
France	464,981	2,343,890	5,951,717
German Democratic Republic	662,884	15,586,565‡	43,596,839‡
Germany, Federal Republic†	2,337,781		
Hong Kong	24,212	129,214	1,307,646
Hungary	236,580	720,237	1,447,962
Iran	36,408	1,641,596	4,461,057
Italy	615,761	5,796,152	7,323,313
Japan	202,397	1,789,640	2,650,846
Korea, Republic	19,129	45,553	1,736,691
Netherlands	444,980	2,037,532	8,115,391
Norway	111,263	1,029,897	2,642,931
Singapore	21,619	96,563	1,605,498
Spain	62,122	404,013	1,537,132
Sweden	257,336	1,513,612	2,901,426
Switzerland	782,392	4,988,089	5,649,703
USSR	2,688,802	15,369,501	23,193,059
United Kingdom	663,918	4,382,049	6,531,089
USA	201,193	1,259,663	3,716,660
Yugoslavia	611,778	1,585,990	2,082,039
Total (incl. others)	14,864,175	77,519,855	164,259,298

Exports f.o.b.	1989	1990§	1991
Austria	690,865	4,988,514	7,162,379
Belgium	220,603	2,075,609	3,163,910
Brazil	133,506	1,341,706	1,275,104
China, People's Republic	444,935	1,826,340	426,686
Czechoslovakia	1,075,301	5,282,084	7,284,159
Denmark	266,797	2,270,812	3,657,472
Finland	354,476	2,030,871	2,312,277
France	474,767	4,171,145	5,969,690
German Democratic Republic	815,520	32,502,840‡	46,427,896‡
Germany, Federal Republic†	2,757,736		
Hungary	312,965	1,271,207	1,161,612
Italy	448,584	3,810,638	6,466,460
Netherlands	505,851	4,057,300	8,172,363
Romania	214,593	1,208,448	433,986
Sweden	421,338	3,392,827	4,146,936
Switzerland	504,375	6,078,434	7,031,753
Turkey	165,014	1,580,739	1,161,278
USSR	4,048,255	19,767,703	17,311,671
United Kingdom	1,262,563	9,227,183	11,210,833
USA	540,116	3,527,296	3,923,877
Yugoslavia	582,241	2,021,429	2,153,598
Total (incl. others)	19,476,174	129,454,947	157,715,913

* Imports by country of purchase; exports by country of sale.
† Excluding West Berlin.
‡ Figures for 1990 and 1991 are for the united Germany.
§ Excluding trade by privately-owned Polish enterprises.

Transport

POLISH STATE RAILWAYS (traffic)

	1989	1990	1991
Paying passengers ('000 journeys)	951,544	789,922	651,991
Freight ('000 metric tons)	388,920	281,658	227,797
Passenger-kilometres (million)	55,888	50,373	40,115
Freight ton-kilometres (million)	111,140	83,530	65,146

ROAD TRAFFIC (motor vehicles registered at 31 December)

	1989	1990	1991
Passenger cars	4,846,411	5,260,646	6,112,171
Goods vehicles*	976,986	1,044,641	1,004,780
Buses and coaches	91,092	92,080	86,951
Motor cycles and scooters	1,410,859	1,356,553	1,235,640

* Including non-agricultural tractors.

INLAND WATERWAYS (traffic)

	1989	1990	1991
Passengers carried ('000)	5,770	3,816	975
Freight ('000 metric tons)	14,040	9,795	7,828
Passenger-kilometres (million)	68	28	21
Freight ton-kilometres (million)	1,193	1,034	737

MERCHANT SHIPPING FLEET (at 30 June)

	1989	1990	1991
Number of vessels	710	698	673
Displacement ('000 gross registered tons)	3,416	3,369	3,348

Source: *Lloyd's Register of Shipping*.

SEA TRANSPORT (Polish merchant ships only)

	1989	1990	1991
Passengers carried ('000)	667	569	573
Freight ('000 metric tons)	28,299	28,477	27,563
Passenger-kilometres (million)	251	193	195
Freight ton-kilometres (million)	212,259	207,430	202,281

INTERNATIONAL SEA-BORNE SHIPPING AT POLISH PORTS

	1989	1990	1991
Vessels entered ('000 net reg. tons)	27,066	28,024	26,795
Passengers (number):			
Arrivals	274,585	247,963	270,185
Departures	274,918	236,727	255,505
Cargo* ('000 metric tons):			
Loaded†	28,700	29,362	n.a.
Unloaded†	16,660	17,915	n.a.

* Including ships' bunkers. † Including transhipments.

CIVIL AVIATION

Polish Airlines—'LOT' (scheduled and non-scheduled flights)

	1989	1990	1991
Passengers carried	2,305,000	1,715,000	1,208,000
Passenger-kilometres ('000)	4,887,000	4,430,000	3,589,000
Cargo (metric tons)	12,000	14,000	11,000
Cargo ton-kilometres ('000)	40,000	57,000	45,000

Tourism

FOREIGN TOURIST ARRIVALS (including visitors in transit)

Country of Residence	1988	1989	1991
Austria	53,000	75,000	133,000
Bulgaria	52,000	55,000	83,000
Czechoslovakia	1,417,000	1,503,000	6,102,000
Finland	24,000	33,000	30,000
France	56,000	75,000	197,000
German Democratic Republic	1,081,000	1,195,000	20,885,000
Germany, Federal Republic	416,000*	596,000*	
Hungary	567,000	698,000	180,000
Italy	40,000	60,000	123,000
Netherlands	46,000	56,000	159,000
Romania	22,000	19,000	276,000
Sweden	69,000	115,000	144,000
USSR	1,739,000	2,899,000	7,546,000
United Kingdom	34,000	47,000	85,000
USA	58,000	96,000	124,000
Yugoslavia	193,000	248,000	67,000
Total (incl. others)	6,196,000	8,233,000	36,846,000

* Excluding visitors from West Berlin: 36,000 in 1988; 53,000 in 1989.

Communications Media

	1989	1990	1991
Radio licences*	11,120,000	10,944,000	10,783,000
Television licences*	10,055,000	9,919,000	9,809,000
Telephones in use*	5,039,000	5,232,000	5,480,000
Book titles produced†	10,286	10,242	10,688
Daily newspapers	48	67	68
Non-daily newspapers	63	63	54
Newspaper circulation:			
Dailies (average)	6,715,000	4,889,000	5,258,000
Non-dailies (average)	3,193,000	2,058,000	1,604,000

* At 31 December.
† Including pamphlets (1,820 in 1989; 1,651 in 1990; 1,776 in 1991).

Education*

(1991/92)

	Institutions	Teachers ('000)	Students ('000)
Primary	18,578	321.5	5,302.7
Secondary (General)	1,565	26.6	548.8
Technical, art and vocational	9,729	89.5	1,787.5
Higher	117	63.2	428.2

* Including part-time courses for workers.

Directory

The Constitution

The Constitution that had been adopted on 22 July 1952 was amended in 1989, to incorporate reforms such as the establishment of an upper legislative chamber, and again in 1990, to permit the holding of direct presidential elections. In April 1992 the procedural law for the drafting of a new constitution was approved by the Sejm. In December 1992 an interim 'Small Constitution' came into force, designed principally to regulate relations between the legislative and executive authorities, pending a full revision of the Constitution, which was initiated in November 1992. The following is a summary of the provisions of the amended 1952 Constitution:

STATE AUTHORITIES

The Sejm consists of 460 deputies, elected for a four-year term, subject to dissolution. Its prerogatives include the adoption of laws; the adoption of the national socio-economic plans and state financial plans; the appointment and recall of the Chairman of the Council of Ministers (at the motion of the President); the appointment and recall of the members of the Council of Ministers (at the motion of the Chairman presented in conjunction with the President or on the Chairman's own initiative); the appointment of the Civil Rights Ombudsman (with consent of the Senate); the adoption of a resolution concerning a state of war; the expression of consent for prolongation (at most for three months) of a state of emergency imposed by the President (consent for such a decision must also be given by the Senate). The Speaker (Marshal) of the Sejm acts in the capacity of President if this office is vacant.

The Senate is made up of 100 members. Its term coincides with that of the Sejm, subject to dissolution. The Senate reviews the laws adopted by the Sejm; it may proffer its comments and proposals on these laws or even propose their rejection in full. The Senate can be overridden by the Sejm by a qualified majority of two-thirds. Its also reviews drafts of national socio-economic plans and financial plans of the State. It has the right of legislative initiative.

The National Assembly is the combined Sejm and Senate. It should be convened by the Sejm Speaker (Marshal) within two months of elections to the Sejm and the Senate. The National Assembly may be convened in order to declare the permanent incapacity of the President to serve his office and to consider impeaching the President in the Tribunal of State.

The President of the Republic of Poland is the highest representative of the Polish State in domestic and international relations. He is to monitor observance of the Constitution, safeguard the sovereignty and security of the State, inviolability of its territory and observance of political and military alliances entered into by the State. Any Pole aged over 35 years with full electoral rights may stand as a presidential candidate, a minimum of 100,000 signatures being required to secure nomination. The President is directly elected for a five-year term and may be re-elected only once. The President's duties include the calling of elections to the Sejm, Senate and local councils; heading the armed forces; proposing a motion in the Sejm for the appointment or recall of the Chairman of the Council of Ministers; (when necessary) imposing martial law on a segment or the entire territory of the country if such is dictated by defence considerations or an outside threat to state security (the President may announce a partial or general mobilization for the same reasons); (when necessary) introducing a state of emergency on a segment or the entire territory of the country when there is a threat to the domestic security of the State or in case of a natural disaster; the President may introduce it for a period not longer than three months and prolong it (with the consent of the Sejm and the Senate) for another three months.

The Council of Ministers is the supreme executive and managing agency of state authority, serving functions typical of the executive branch and carrying out the decisions adopted by the Sejm. It is appointed by the Sejm which may recall the entire Council of Ministers or its individual members. The Council is responsible to the Sejm and reports to it on its activities. In periods between Sejm terms, this function towards the Council is served by the President. The Council of Ministers co-ordinates actions of the entire state administration.

CONSTITUTIONAL TRIBUNAL AND TRIBUNAL OF STATE

The Constitutional Tribunal pronounces judgment on the consistence with the Constitution of laws and other normative acts issued by the supreme and central state organs. Its decisions are binding. Members of the Tribunal are independent and are subject only to the Constitution.

The Tribunal of State pronounces judgment on the responsibility of persons holding high state positions for violation of the Constitution and laws; it can also pass judgment on penal responsibility of those persons for offences committed in connection with the positions which they have held. Its head is the first president of the Supreme Court. Judges of the Tribunal are independent and subject only to the law.

LOCAL ORGANS OF STATE ADMINISTRATION

Poland comprises 49 voivodships, a government-appointed official supervising state administration in each area. The members of each provincial assembly are elected by local councils. Local councils are directly elected and are completely autonomous, territorial self-government being the basic form of the organization of public life in the rural community.

COURTS AND PUBLIC PROSECUTOR'S OFFICE

The administration of justice is carried out by the Supreme Court, the Supreme Administrative Court, General Courts and Courts Martial. The Supreme Court is the highest judicial organ, and is to be appointed by the Sejm for an unlimited term.

FUNDAMENTAL RIGHTS AND DUTIES OF CITIZENS

The Republic of Poland strengthens and extends the rights and liberties of citizens. Citizens have equal rights, irrespective of sex, origin, education, occupation, nationality, race, religion, descent or social status. Citizens have the right to work and the right to rest; the right to health protection, and the right to education. Women are guaranteed equal rights with men. Freedom of conscience is guaranteed. The Church is separated from the State. Citizens are guaranteed freedom of speech, of the press, of meetings etc.; the right to unite in public organizations; and the inviolability of the person and of the home.

PRINCIPLES OF ELECTORAL LAW

Election to the Sejm and Senate, and to People's Councils, is universal, equal, direct and carried out by secret ballot. At the age of 18 every citizen has the right to vote, and is eligible for election to People's Councils; at the age of 21 every citizen is eligible for election to the Sejm and Senate. Candidates to the Sejm and Senate are nominated by political and social organizations uniting citizens of town and country.

COAT-OF-ARMS, COLOURS AND CAPITAL OF THE REPUBLIC OF POLAND

The coat-of-arms of the Republic of Poland is a white eagle with a golden crown on the head, and with golden beak and claws, on a red field. The National Anthem is the *Mazurka Dabrowskiego.* The capital of the Republic of Poland is Warsaw.

The Government

HEAD OF STATE

President: LECH WAŁĘSA (sworn in 22 December 1990).

THE CABINET
(March 1994)

The Government is a coalition of the Democratic Left Alliance (Sojusz Lewicy Demokratycznej—SLD), the Polish Peasant Party (Polskie Stronnictwo Ludowe—PSL), the Union of Labour (Unia Pracy—UP) and independents.

Prime Minister: WALDEMAR PAWLAK (PSL).

Deputy Prime Minister (responsible for state administration) and Minister of National Education: ALEKSANDER LUCZAK (PSL).

Deputy Prime Minister (responsible for social policy), Minister of Justice and Attorney-General: WLODZIMIERZ CIMOSZEWICZ (SLD).

Minister-Head of the Office of the Cabinet: MICHAŁ STRAK (PSL).

Minister of Foreign Affairs: ANDRZEJ OLECHOWSKI.

Minister of Internal Affairs: ANDRZEJ MILCZANOWSKI.

Minister of National Defence: Adm. (retd) PIOTR KOLODZIEJCZYK.

Minister-Head of the Central Planning Office: MIROSŁAW PIETREWICZ (PSL).

Minister of Finance: HENRYK CHMIELAK (acting).

Minister of Foreign Economic Relations: LESŁAW PODKAŃSKI (PSL).

Minister of Agriculture: ANDRZEJ SMIETANKO (PSL).

Minister of Transport and Maritime Economy: BOGUSŁAW LIBERADZKI.

Minister of Environmental Protection, Natural Resources and Forestry: STANISŁAW ZELICHOWSKI (PSL).

Minister of Labour and Social Policy: LESZAK MILLER (SLD).

Minister of Culture: KAZIMIERZ DEJMAK (PSL).

Minister of Health: RYSZARD JACEK ZOCHOWSKI (SLD).

Minister of Industry and Trade: MAREK POL (UP).

Minister of Regional Planning and Construction: BARBARA BLIDA (SLD).

Minister of Communication: ANDRZEJ ZIELIŃSKI (PSL).

Minister of Ownership Transformation (Privatization): WIESŁAW KACZMAREK (SLD).

Head of Scientific Research Committee: Prof. WITOLD KARCZEWSKI.

MINISTRIES

Office of the Prime Minister: 00-567 Warsaw, Al. Ujazdowskie 1/3.

Ministry of Agriculture: 00-930 Warsaw, ul. Wspólna 30; tel. (22) 296127; telex 814597; fax (22) 212326.

Ministry of Communication: 90-940 Warsaw, pl. Małachowskiego 2; tel. (22) 275089; telex 813601; fax (22) 273256.

Ministry of Culture: 00-071 Warsaw, ul. Krakowskie Przedmieście 15/17; tel. (22) 267331; fax (22) 267533.

Ministry of Environmental Protection, Natural Resources and Forestry: 00-067 Warsaw, ul. Wawelska 52/54; tel. (22) 253355; telex 812816; fax (22) 253355.

Ministry of Finance: 00-916 Warsaw, ul. Świętokrzyska 12; tel. (22) 200311; telex 815592.

Ministry of Foreign Affairs: 00-580 Warsaw, Al. Szucha 23; tel. (2) 6239000; fax (2) 6257652.

Ministry of Foreign Economic Relations: 00-950 Warsaw, Pl. Trzech Krzyży 5; tel. (2) 6935000; telex 814501; fax (22) 286808.

Ministry of Health: 00-923 Warsaw, ul. Miodowa 15; tel. (22) 312144; telex 817441; fax (2) 6359245.

Ministry of Industry and Trade: 00-926 Warsaw, ul. Wspólna 4; tel. (22) 210351; telex 814261; fax (22) 295043.

Ministry of Internal Affairs: 00-904 Warsaw, ul. Rakowiecka 2B; tel. (22) 210251; telex 813681.

Ministry of Justice: 00-950 Warsaw, Al. Ujazdowskie 11; tel. (2) 6284431; telex 813891; fax (22) 281692.

Ministry of Labour and Social Policy: 00-513 Warsaw, ul. Nowogrodzka 1/3/5; tel. (2) 6289041; telex 814710; fax (22) 296750.

Ministry of National Defence: 00-909 Warsaw, Któlewska 1; tel. and fax (22) 260586.

Ministry of National Education: 00-918 Warsaw, Al. Szucha 25; tel. (22) 297241; telex 813523; fax (2) 6288561.

Ministry of Ownership Transformation (Privatization): 00-522 Warsaw, ul. Krucza 36; tel. (2) 6280281; fax (22) 213361.

Ministry of Regional Planning and Construction: 00-926 Warsaw, ul. Wspólna 2; tel. (22) 212725; telex 814411; fax (2) 6284030.

Ministry of Transport and Maritime Economy: 00-928 Warsaw, ul. Chałubińskiego 4/6; tel. (22) 215676; telex 813614; fax (22) 219968.

Central Planning Office: 00-507 Warsaw, Pl. Trzech Krzyży 5; tel. (2) 6935000; telex 814698.

President and Legislature

PRESIDENT

Presidential elections, 25 November and 9 December 1990

	Votes	
	First ballot	Second ballot
LECH WAŁĘSA	6,569,889	10,622,696 (74.25%)
STANISŁAW TYMIŃSKI	3,797,605	3,683,098 (25.75%)
TADEUSZ MAZOWIECKI	2,973,264	—
WŁODZIMIERZ CIMOSZEWICZ	1,514,025	—
ROMAN BARTOSZCZE	1,176,175	—
LESZEK MOCZULSKI	411,516	—

ZGROMADZENIE NARODOWE
(National Assembly)

The National Assembly consists of an upper chamber (Senat, created in 1989) and a lower chamber (Sejm, the former unicameral legislature).

Senat

Marshal: ADAM STRUZIK.

Election, 19 September 1993

Party	Seats
Democratic Left Alliance*	37
Polish Peasant Party	36
Solidarity	9
Democratic Union	4
Union of Labour	2
Non-Party Bloc for Reform	2
Others	10
Total	100

* See footnotes under Sejm.

Sejm

Marshal: JOZEF OLEKSY.

Deputy Marshal: OLGA KRZYZANOWSKA.

Election, 19 September 1993

Party	% of votes cast	Seats
Democratic Left Alliance*	20.41	171
Polish Peasant Party	15.40	132
Democratic Union	10.59	74
Union of Labour	7.28	41
Confederation for an Independent Poland	5.77	22
Non-Party Bloc for Reform	5.41	16
German Minority of Lower Silesia	0.44	3
Social and Cultural Association of Germans from Upper Silesia	0.10	1
Others†	34.60	—
Total	100.00	460

* Electoral coalition of Social Democracy of the Republic of Poland and the All Poland Trade Unions Alliance (OPZZ).

† The other parties which also participated in the elections were not represented in parliament as they failed to secure the percentage of votes necessary.

Local Government

A new system of local government was established by a law adopted by the Sejm in March 1990. The lowest tier of local government is the commune, of which there were 2,394 in January 1991. Poland is also divided into 49 voivodships, each named after the town from which they are administered. Each voivodship is administered by a local governor (voivode). District agencies act as an intermediate tier between local government and the central state administration, through which additional responsibilities may be delegated to communes where requested.

In May 1990 the Competence Act defined the respective functions and areas of competence of local government and the central state administration in 540 specific tasks. Of these tasks, 45% were considered to be the exclusive function of local governments, 17% to be the delegated function of local governments, 35% to be the function of district agencies and only 3% to be the function of the voivodships. Local government operations are financed partly by local taxes and administrative fees, and partly by taxes collected by central government.

VOIVODSHIPS

Warszawskie: 00-950 Warszawa, pl. Bankowy 3–5; tel. (22) 200271; Gov. BOHDAN JASTRZEBSKI.

Bialskopodlaskie: 21-500 Biała-Podlaska, ul. Brzeska 41; tel. (80) 437030; Gov. TADEUSZ KORSZEN.

Białostockie: 15-213 Białystok, ul. Mickiewicza 3; tel. (85) 439; Gov. STANISŁAW PRUTIS.

Bielskie: 43-300 Bielsko-Biała, ul. Piastowska 40; tel. (30) 36200; Gov. MIROSŁAW STYCZEN.

Bydgoskie: 85-950 Bydgoszcz, ul. Jagiellońska 3; tel. (52) 221831; Gov. (vacant).

Chełmskie: 22-100 Chełm, pl. Niepodległości 1; tel. (82) 55211; Gov. LESZEK BURAKOWSKI.

Ciechanowskie: 06-400 Ciechanów, ul. 17 Stycznia 7; tel. (23) 2051; Gov. (vacant).

Częstochowskie: 42-201 Częstochowa, ul. Sobieskiego 7; tel. (33) 245031; Gov. JERZY GULA.

Elbląskie: 82-300 Elbląg; ul. Wojska Polskiego 1/3; tel. (50) 337001; Gov. ZDZISŁAW OLSZEWSKI.

Gdańskie: 80-958 Gdańsk; ul. Okopowa 21/27; tel. (58) 377294; Gov. MACIEJ PLAZYŃSKI.

Gorzowskie: 66-400 Gorzów Wielkopolski, ul. Jagiellończyka 8; tel. (60) 75600; Gov. ZBIGNIEW PUSZ.

Jeleniogórskie: 58-500 Jelenia Góra, pl. Ratuszowy 58; tel. (75) 26001; Gov. JERZY NALICHOWSKI.

Kaliskie: 62-800 Kalisz, pl. Sw. Józefa 5; tel. (62) 57292; Gov. EUGENIUSZ MALECKI.

Katowickie: 40-032 Katowice, ul. Jagiellońska 25; tel. (32) 1554161; Gov. (vacant).

Kieleckie: 25-955 Kielce, al. IX Wieków Kielc 3; tel. (41) 21222; Gov. ZYGMUNT SZOPA.

Konińskie: 62-510 Konin, al. 1 Maja 7; tel. (63) 423890; Gov. MAREK NAGLEWSKI.

Koszalinskie: 75-950 Koszalin, ul. A. Lampego 34; tel. (94) 428281; Gov. JERZY MOKRZYCKI.

Krakowskie: 31-004 Kraków, ul. Basztowa 22; tel. (12) 160200; Gov. TADEUSZ PIEKARZ.

Krośnieńskie: 38-400 Krosno, ul. Bieszczadzka 1; tel. (98) 24211; Gov. PIOTR KOMORNKKI.

Legnickie: 59-208 Legnica, pl. Slowiański 1; tel. (76) 66444; Gov. (vacant).

Leszczyńskie: 64-100 Leszno, pl. Kościuszki 4; tel. (65) 209400; Gov. (vacant).

Lubelskie: 20-914 Lublin, ul. Spokojna 4; tel. (81) 20041; Gov. (vącant).

Łomzyńskie: 18-400 Łomza, ul. Nowa 2; tel. (86) 4271; Gov. (vacant).

Łódzkie: 90-925 Łódź, ul. Piotrkowska 104; tel. (42) 329040; Gov. WALDEMAR BOHDANOWICZ.

Nowosądeckie: 33-300 Nowy Sacz, ul. Jagiellońska 52; tel. (18) 23371; Gov. JÓZEF JUNGIEWICZ.

Olsztyńskie: 10-959 Olsztyn, al. J. Piłsudskiego 7/9; tel. (89) 232200; Gov. ROMAN PRZEDWOJSKI.

Opolskie: 45-082 Opole, ul. Piastowska 14; tel. (77) 24100; Gov. RYSZARD ZEMBACZYNSKI.

Ostrołęckie: 07-400 Ostrołęka, pl. Gen. J. Berna 3; tel. (88) 3281; Gov. (vacant).

Pilskie: 64-920 Piła, al. Niepodległości 33/35; tel. (67) 125101; Gov. WALDEMAR JORDAN.

Piotrkowskie: 97-300 Piotrków Tribunalski, ul. Sienkiewicza 16A; tel. (41) 473635; Gov. (vacant)

Płockie: 09-402 Płock, ul. Kolegialna 15; tel. (24) 623031; Gov. KRZYSZTOF KOLACH.

Poznańskie: 60-967 Poznań, al. Niepodległości 16–18; tel. (61) 521071; Gov. WLODZIMIERZ LECKI.

Przemyskie: 37-700 Przemyśl, pl. Dominikański 43; tel. (10) 5051; Gov. (vacant).

Radomskie: 26-600 Radom, ul. Zeromskiego 53; tel. (48) 20000; Gov. (vacant).

Rzeszowskie: 35-959 Rzeszów, ul. Grunwaldzka 15; tel. (17) 37511; Gov. (vacant).

Siedleckie: 08-100 Siedlce, ul. Piłsudskiego 40; tel. (25) 22080; Gov. (vacant).

Sieradzkie: 98-200 Sieradz, pl. Wojewódzki 3; tel. (49) 5501; Gov. JAN RYS.

Skierniewickie: 96-100 Skierniewice, ul. Jagiellońska 29; tel. (26) 2010; Gov. ANDRZEJ CHARZEWSKI.

Słupskie: 76-200 Słupsk, ul. Wałowa 1; tel. (59) 36008; Gov. KAZIMIERZ KLEINA.

Suwalskie: 16-400 Suwalki, ul. Noniewicza 10; tel. (87) 62220; Gov. CEZARY CIESLUKOWSKI.

Szczecińskie: 70-502 Szczecin, ul. Wały Chrobrego 4; tel. (91) 303200; Gov. MAREK TALASIEWICZ.

Tarnobrzeskie: 39-400 Tarnobrzeg, ul. Kościuszki 32; tel. (15) 221595; Gov. JANINA SAGATOWSKA.

Tarnowskie: 33-100 Tarnów, ul. Narutowicza 38; tel. (14) 217641; Gov. (vacant).

Toruńskie: 87-100 Toruń, pl. Teatralny 2; tel. (56) 18200; Gov. BERNARD KWIATKOWSKI.

Wałbrzyskie: 58-300 Wałbrzych, ul. Zamkowa 4; tel. (74) 26201; Gov. HENRYK GOLEBIEWSKI.

Włocławskie: 87-800 Włoclawek, ul. Cyganka 28; tel. (54) 326201; Gov. KAZIMIERZ TULODZIECKI.

Wrocławskie: 50-951 Wrocław, pl. Powstańców Warszawy 1; tel. (71) 446000; Gov. JANUSZ ZALESKI.

Zamojskie: 22-400 Zamość, ul. Partyzantów 3; tel. (84) 71661; Gov. STANISŁAW ROCZKOWSKI.

Zielonogórskie: 65-954 Zielona Góra, ul. Podgórna 7; tel. (68) 79898; Gov. JAROSŁAW BARANCZAK.

Political Organizations

Under the 1990 law, political parties are not obliged to file for registration, but by 1 May 1992 a total of 135 parties had been registered.

Centre Alliance (Porozumienie Centrum): 02-927 Warsaw, ul. Zawojska 47; tel. (22) 6428289; fax (22) 6426987; f. 1990 by supporters of Lech Wałęsa; Christian democratic party; main component of **Centre Citizens' Alliance,** coalition formed to contest 1991 elections; supports market economy based on private ownership; 10,000 mems; Chair. JAROSŁAW KACZYŃSKI.

Christian Democratic Party: (Pracy Chrześcijanska Demokracja—PChD): Warsaw; f. 1991; right-wing; Chair. PAWEL LACZKOWSKI.

Christian Democratic Labour Party—CDLP (Chrześcijanska Demokracja Stronnictwo Pracy—ChDSP): 00-585 Warsaw, ul.

Bagatela 10, m. 7; tel. (22) 291611; fax (2) 6252095; f. 1937, reactivated 1989, merged with Christian Democracy group in 1994; 1,800 mems; Chair. TOMASZ JACKOWSKI; Deputy Chair. LESZEK STYPULA.

Christian National Union—CNU (Zjednoczenie Chrześcijańsko-Narodowe—ZChN): 00-853 Warsaw, ul. Twarda 28; f. 1989; about 6,000 mems; Leader STEFAN NIESIOLOWSKI; Gen. Sec. MIROSŁAW JAKUBOWSKI.

Confederation for an Independent Poland (Konfederacja Polski Niepodległej—KPN): 00-920 Warsaw, ul. Nowy Świat 18/20; tel. (22) 261043; fax (22) 261400; f. 1979; centre-right; Chair. LESZEK MOCZULSKI.

Democratic Left Alliance (Sojusz Lewicy Demokratycznej—SLD): Warsaw; f. 1991; Leader ALEKSANDER KWASNIEWSKI; electoral coalition of Social Democracy of the Republic of Poland and the All Poland Trade Unions Alliance:

Social Democracy of the Republic of Poland—SDRP (Socjaldemokracja Rzeczypospolitej Polskiej—SRP): 00-419 Warsaw, ul. Rozbrat 44A; tel. (22) 210341; telex 825581; fax (22) 216657; f. 1990 to replace Polish United Workers' Party—PUWP (Polska Zjednoczona Partia Robotnicza—PZPR; f. 1948), which held power until 1989; over 60,000 mems (May 1991); Chair. ALEKSANDER KWAŚNIEWSKI; Gen. Sec. LESZEK MILLER.

All Poland Trade Unions Alliance (Ogólnopolskie Porozumienie Związków Zawodowych—OPZZ): see section on Trade and Industry (Trade Unions).

Democratic Party—DP (Stronnictwo Demokratyczne—SD): 00-021 Warsaw, ul. Chmielna 9; tel. (22) 261001; telex 812502; f. 1939; recruits its members mainly from among progressive intellectuals and craftsmen, inhabitants of towns and cities; 80,000 mems (1991); Chair. ZBIGNIEW ADAMCZYK.

Democratic Union (Unia Demokratyczna): 00-024 Warsaw, Al. Jerozolimskie 30; tel. (22) 275047; fax (22) 277851; f. 1991 by merger of Citizens' Movement-Democratic Action (Ruch Obywatelski-Akcja Demokratyczna—ROAD), Democratic Right Forum and the former Democratic Union; 15,000 mems; Leader TADEUSZ MAZOWIECKI; Gen. Sec. PIOTR NOWINA-KONOPKA. (In March 1994 it was announced that the Democratic Union was to merge with the Liberal Democratic Congress.)

German Minority of Lower Silesia (Mniejszisc Niemiecka Slaska Opolskiego): Leader HENRYK KROL.

Liberal Democratic Congress—LDC (Kongres Liberalno-Demokratyczny—KLD): 00-031 Warsaw, ul. Szpitalna 8; tel. and fax (22) 274813; f. 1988; 3,000 mems; Chair. DONALD TUSK; Sec.-Gen. GRZEGORZ SCHETYNA. (In March 1994 it was annnounced that the LDC was to merge with the Democratic Union.)

Non-Party Bloc for Reform (Bezpartyjny Bloc Wapierania Reform—BBWR): Warsaw; f. 1993 by Lech Wałęsa; Leader ANDRZEJ OLECHOWSKI; Chair. Prof. ZBIGNIEW RELIGA.

Party X: 00-137 Warsaw, ul. Elektoralna 21 m. 19; tel. and fax (22) 242777; f. 1991; advocates free-market economy, expansion of industry and agriculture, gradual elimination of unemployment and universal access to education, culture and health; 9,000 mems; Leader STANISŁAW TYMIŃSKI.

Peasant Christian Party (Polskie Stronnictwo Ludowe—Chrześcijańskie): 00-020 Warsaw, ul. Chmielna 24, m. 1; tel. (22) 262614; f. 1989; fmrly Polish Peasant Party—Solidarity; 20,000 mems; Leader JÓZEF ŚLISZ.

Polish Beer Lovers' Party: c/o The Sejm, Warsaw; f. 1991 by LESZEK BUBEL; contested legislative elections with support of business executives; subsequently split into 'Large Beer' (now Polish Economic Programme, see below) and 'Small Beer'.

Polish Economic Programme (Polski Program Gospodarczy—PPG): c/o The Sejm, Warsaw; f. following split in Polish Beer Lovers' Party; Leader TOMASZ BANKOWSKI.

Polish Peasant Party—PPP (Polskie Stronnictwo Ludowe—PSL): 00-131 Warsaw, ul. Grzybowska 4; tel. (22) 200251; telex 814367; f. 1990 to replace United Peasant Party (Zjednoczone Stronnictwo Ludowe; f. 1949) and Polish Peasant Party—Rebirth (Polskie Stronnictwo Ludowe—Odrodzenie; f. 1989); stresses development of agriculture and food-processing; 200,000 mems; Pres. WALDEMAR PAWLAK; Leader GABRIEL JANOWSKI.

Polish Socialist Party (Polska Partia Socjalistyczna—PPS): 00-325 Warsaw, ul. Krakowskie Przedmieście 6; tel. (22) 266908; fax (22) 266908; f. 1892, re-established 1987; 3,000 mems; Chair. PIOTR IKONOWICZ; Chair. Cen. Exec. Cttee JAN MULAK.

Social and Cultural Association of Germans from Upper Silesia (Towarzyctwo Spoleczno-Kulturalne Niemcow wojew katowickiego): Silesia; independent party.

Solidarity (Solidarność): c/o The Sejm, Warsaw; the electoral wing of the trade-union movement (see section on trade unions); Chair. MARIAN KRZAKLEWSKI.

Union of Labour (Unia Pracy—UP): Warsaw; f. 1993; Leader RYSZARD BUGAJ.

Diplomatic Representation

EMBASSIES IN POLAND

Afghanistan: 03-933 Warsaw, Obroncow st. 33; tel. (22) 172471; Ambassador: AZIZULLAH KARZI.

Albania: 00-789 Warsaw, Słoneczna 15; tel. (22) 498516; Ambassador: SUZANA FAJA.

Algeria: 03-932 Warsaw, ul. Dąbrowiecka 21; tel. (22) 175855; telex 817019.

Argentina: 03-928 Warsaw, Styki 17/19; tel. (22) 176028; telex 812412; Ambassador: NICOLÁS A. E. GARCÍA PINTO.

Australia: 03-903 Warsaw, Estońska 3/5; tel. (22) 176081; telex 813032; fax (22) 176756; Ambassador: ANTHONY C. KEVIN.

Austria: 00-748 Warsaw, ul. Gagarina 34; tel. (22) 410081; telex 813629; fax (22) 410085; Ambassador: GERHARD WAGNER.

Bangladesh: 02-516 Warsaw, Rejtana 15, m. 20/21; tel. (22) 497610; telex 816409; Ambassador: KHAIRUL ANAM.

Belarus: 03-978 Warsaw, ul. Ateńska 76; tel. (22) 173954; Ambassador: VLADIMIR SENKO.

Belgium: 00-095 Warsaw, Senatorska 34; tel. (22) 270233; telex 813340; fax (22) 355711; Ambassador: FRANÇOIS RONSE.

Brazil: 03-931 Warsaw, Poselska 11; tel. (22) 174800; telex 813748; Ambassador: JOÃO AUGUSTO DE MEDICIS.

Bulgaria: 00-540 Warsaw, Al. Ujazdowskie 33/35; tel. (22) 294071; Ambassador: YANI MILCHAKOV.

Canada: 00-481 Warsaw, Matejki 1/5; tel. (22) 298051; telex 813424; fax (22) 296457; Ambassador: ANNE LEAHY.

Chile: 02-932 Warsaw, ul. Morszyńska 71B; tel. (2) 6428155; telex 814542; fax (22) 409041; Ambassador: MAXIMO LIRA ALCAYAGA.

China, People's Republic: 00-203 Warsaw, Bonifraterska 1; tel. (22) 313836; telex 813589; fax (22) 409041; Ambassador: LIU YANSHUN.

Colombia: 03-936 Warsaw, Zwycięzców 29; tel. (22) 177157; telex 816496; fax (22) 176684; Ambassador: CARLOS BULA CAMACHO.

Costa Rica: 02-516 Warsaw, ul. Starościńska 1, m. 17; tel. (22) 481478; Ambassador: CARLOS ALBERTO VARGAS SOLÍS.

Cuba: 03-932 Warsaw, ul. Katowicka 22; tel. (22) 178428; telex 813588; Ambassador: ANA MARÍA ROVIRA INGIDUA.

Czech Republic: 00-555 Warsaw, Koszykowa 18; tel. (2) 6287221; fax (22) 298045; Ambassador: MARKÉTA FIALKOVÁ.

Denmark: 02-517 Warsaw, ul. Rakowiecka 19; tel. (22) 490056; telex 813387; fax (22) 494485; Ambassador: NIELS PETER GEORG HELSKOV.

Egypt: 03-972 Warsaw, ul. Alzacka 18; tel. (22) 176973; telex 813605; Ambassador: MOHAMED MAHMOUD SOLIMAN.

Finland: 00-559 Warsaw, Chopina 4/8; tel. (22) 294091; telex 814286; fax (22) 216010; Ambassador: JYRKI AIMONEN.

France: 00-477 Warsaw, Piękna 1; tel. (2) 6288401; telex 825580; fax (22) 291239; Ambassador: ALAIN BRY.

Germany: 03-932 Warsaw, Dąbrowiecka 30; tel. (22) 173011; telex 813455; Ambassador: Dr FRANZ BERTELE.

Greece: 01-640 Warsaw, Jana Paska 21; tel. (2) 3334889; telex 813692; fax (22) 331735; Ambassador: GEORGE ALEXANDROPOULOS.

Holy See: 00-580 Warsaw, Al. Szucha 12 (Apostolic Nunciature); tel. (22) 212337; telex 816493; fax (2) 6284556; Apostolic Nuncio: Most Rev. JÓZEF KOWALCZYK, Titular Archbishop of Heraclea.

Hungary: 00-559 Warsaw, Chopina 2; tel. (2) 6284451; telex 814672; fax (22) 218561; Ambassador: ÁKOS ENGELMAYER.

India: 02-516 Warsaw, Rejtana 15; tel. (22) 495800; telex 814891; fax (22) 496705; Ambassador: JAGANNATH DODDAMANI.

Indonesia: 00-950 Warsaw, Wąchocka 9, POB 33; tel. (22) 172935; telex 813680; Ambassador: ABDUL SALAM GANI.

Iran: 03-928 Warsaw, Królowej Aldony 22; tel. (22) 174293; telex 813823; fax (22) 178452; Ambassador: MOHAMMAD REZA ASTANEH.

Iraq: 03-932 Warsaw, Dąbrowiecka 9A; tel. (22) 175773; telex 813918; fax (22) 177065; Ambassador: MOHAMMED FADL HUSSAIN AL-HABOUBI.

Ireland: 02-614 Warsaw, ul. Lenartowicza 18; tel. (22) 446440; telex 812305; fax (22) 480211; Ambassador: RICHARD ANTHONY O'BRIEN.

Israel: 02-078 Warsaw, Krzywickiego 24; tel. (22) 250028; telex 817660; fax (22) 251607; Ambassador: GERSHON ZOHAR.

Italy: 00-055 Warsaw, Plac Dąbrowskiego 6; tel. (22) 263471; telex 813742; fax (22) 278507; Ambassador: VINCENZO MANNO.

Japan: 02-548 Warsaw, ul. Grażny 11; tel. (22) 498781; fax (22) 498494; Ambassador: NAGAO HYODO.

Korea, Democratic People's Republic: 00-728 Warsaw, ul. Bobrowiecka 1A; tel. (22) 405813; telex 812707; Ambassador: PAK YONG DOK.

Korea, Republic: 02-611 Warsaw, ul. Ignacego Krasickiego 25; tel. (2) 4833337; telex 817069; Ambassador: WOONG CHOI.

Laos: 02-516 Warsaw, Rejtana 15, m. 26; tel. (22) 484786; telex 8135932; Ambassador: SITHONG CHITNHOTHINH.

Libya: 03-934 Warsaw, Kryniczna 2; tel. (22) 174822; telex 825508; fax (22) 175091; Chargé d'affaires: MOHAMED M. MATMATI.

Lithuania: 00-580 Warsaw, ul. J. Ch. Szucha 5; tel. (2) 6253410; fax (2) 6253440; Ambassador: DAINIUS JUNEVIČIUS.

Malaysia: 03-902 Warsaw, ul. Gruzińska 3; tel. (22) 174413; telex 825368; fax (22) 177920; Ambassador: ABDUL RAHMAN BIN ABDUL RAHIM.

Mexico: 02-516 Warsaw, Starościńska 1B, m. 4/5; tel. (22) 495250; telex 814629; fax (22) 487617; Ambassador: JOSÉ LUIS VALLARTA MARRON.

Mongolia: 00-478 Warsaw, Al. Ujazdowskie 12; tel. (2) 6281651; telex 814399; fax (2) 6284864; Ambassador: BAJARCHUGIJN NANZAD.

Morocco: 02-516 Warsaw, Starościńska 1, m. 11/12; tel. (22) 496341; telex 813740; Ambassador: ABDELMAJID ALEM.

Netherlands: 00-791 Warsaw, ul. Chocimska 6; tel. (22) 492351; telex 813666; fax (22) 488345; Ambassador: JOHAN WILLEM SEMEIJNS DE VRIES VAN DOESBURGH.

Nigeria: 00-791 Warsaw, Chocimska 18; tel. (22) 486944; telex 814675; fax (22) 485379; Chargé d'affaires a.i.: ONUORAH OBODOZIE.

Norway: 00-559 Warsaw, Chopina 2A; tel. (22) 214231; telex 813738; fax (2) 6280938; Ambassador: ARNT RINDAL.

Pakistan: 02-516 Warsaw, Starościńska 1, m. 1/2; tel. (22) 494808; telex 816063; Ambassador: S. M. INAAMULLAH.

Peru: 01-555 Warsaw, Felińskiego 25; tel. and fax (22) 399766; telex 814320; Ambassador: (vacant).

Philippines: 00-484 Warsaw, ul. Górnośląska 22, m. 5; tel. (22) 219523; Chargé d'affaires: CHARLIE PACAÑA MANANGAN.

Portugal: 03-910 Warsaw, Dąbrowiecka 19; tel. and fax (22) 176021; telex 815509; Ambassador: RUI FERNANDO MEIRA FERREIRA.

Romania: 00-559 Warsaw, Chopina 10; tel. (2) 6283156; telex 813420; Ambassador: JOAN GRIGORESCU.

Russia: 00-761 Warsaw, Belwederska 49; tel. (22) 213453; fax (2) 6253016; Ambassador: YURI KACHLEV.

Slovakia: 00-581 Warsaw, ul. Litewska 6; tel. (2) 6284051; telex 813585; fax (2) 6284055; Ambassador: (vacant).

Spain: 02-516 Warsaw, Starościńska 1B; tel. (22) 499926; telex 814515; fax (22) 491297; Ambassador: JOSÉ ANTONIO LÓPEZ ZATÓN.

Sweden: 00-585 Warsaw, ul. Bagatela 3; tel. (22) 493351; telex 813457; fax (22) 495243; Ambassador: KARL VILHELM WÖHLER.

Switzerland: 00-540 Warsaw, Ujazdowskie 27; tel. (2) 6280481; telex 813528; fax (22) 210548; Ambassador: J. RICHARD GAECHTER.

Syria: 02-536 Warsaw, Narbutta 19A; tel. (22) 491454; telex 825465; Ambassador: AHMAD SAKER.

Thailand: 02-516 Warsaw, Starościńska 1B, m. 2/3; tel. (22) 494730; telex 825392; fax (22) 492630; Ambassador: Dr SOMKIATI ARIYAPRUCHYA.

Tunisia: 00-459 Warsaw, Myśliwiecka 14; tel. (2) 6286330; telex 812827; fax (22) 216298; Ambassador: HOUCINE LONGO.

Turkey: 02-622 Warsaw, Malczewskiego 32; tel. (22) 443201; fax (22) 443737; Ambassador: HATAY SAVAŞÇI.

Ukraine: Warsaw, Ave Szucha 7; tel. and fax (22) 296449; Ambassador: GENNADY YOSIPOVICH UDOVENKO.

United Kingdom: 00-556 Warsaw, Al. Róż 1; tel. (2) 6281001; telex 813694; fax (22) 217161; Ambassador: MICHAEL LLEWELLYN SMITH.

USA: 00-540 Warsaw, Al. Ujazdowskie 29/31; tel. (2) 6283041; telex 813304; fax (2) 6257290; Ambassador: NICHOLAS A. REY.

Uruguay: 02-516 Warsaw, Rejtana 15, m. 12; tel. (22) 495040; telex 814647; Chargé d'affaires a.i.: MARINÉS BENAVIDES.

Venezuela: 02-011 Warsaw, Al. Jerozolimskie 101, m. 7; tel. (2) 6289651; telex 812788; fax (2) 6286740; Ambassador: GUILLERMO HERRERA HURTADO.

Viet Nam: 02-589 Warsaw, ul. Kazimierzowska 14; tel. (22) 446723; Ambassador: DAO THITAM.

Yemen: 02-686 Warsaw, ul. Olimpijska 11; tel. (22) 440234; fax (22) 446129; Ambassador: MANSOOR ABDUL GALIL ABDUL RAB.

Yugoslavia: 00-540 Warsaw, Al. Ujazdowskie 23/25; tel. (2) 6285161; fax (22) 297173; Chargé d'affaires a.i.: VLADIMIR STANIMIROVIĆ.

Zaire: 02-954 Warsaw, Kubickiego 11; tel. (2) 6422369; telex 816015; Ambassador: (vacant).

Judicial System

SUPREME COURT

The Supreme Court: 00-9518 Warsaw, ul. Ogrodowa 6; tel. (22) 203975; telex 817989; fax (2) 2031714; the highest judicial organ; exercises supervision over the decision-making of all other courts; its functions include: the examination of extraordinary appeals brought against final decisions of other courts and bodies; the adoption of resolutions aimed at providing interpretation of legal provisions that give rise to doubts. Justices of the Supreme Court are appointed by the President of the Republic on motions of the National Council of Judiciary and serve until the age of retirement (life tenure). The First President of the Supreme Court is appointed (and dismissed) from among the Supreme Court Justices by the National Assembly of Poland on the motion of the President of the Republic. The other presidents of the Supreme Court are appointed by the President of the Republic.

First President: Prof. Dr hab. ADAM STRZEMBOSZ.

OTHER COURTS

The Supreme Administrative Court examines, in one procedure, complaints concerning the legality of administrative decisions; it is vested exclusively with the powers of court of cassation.

The General Courts review civil, criminal, family cases and cases of minors, questions of labour and insurance law. They also have the right to try all economic cases.

The office of Prosecutor-General was subordinated to the Ministry of Justice (rather than to the President of Poland) in 1990.

Religion

CHRISTIANITY

The Roman Catholic Church

The Roman Catholic Church was granted full legal status in May 1989, when three laws regulating aspects of relations between the Church and the State were approved by the Sejm. The legislation guaranteed freedom of worship, and permitted the Church to administer its own affairs. The Church was also granted access to the media, and allowed to operate its own schools, hospitals and other charitable organizations.

For ecclesiastical purposes, Poland comprises 14 archdioceses and 25 dioceses (including one for the Catholics of the Byzantine-Ukrainian Rite and one Military Ordinariate). In 1985 an estimated 95% of Poland's inhabitants were adherents of the Roman Catholic Church.

Bishops' Conference: Konferencja Episkopatu Polski, 01-015 Warsaw, Skwer Kardynała Stefana Wyszyńskiego 6; tel. (22) 389251; telex 816550; fax (22) 389250; f. 1969 (statutes approved 1987); Pres. Cardinal JÓZEF GLEMP, Archbishop of Warsaw; Sec.-Gen. Bishop TADEUSZ PIERONEK.

Latin Rite

Archbishop of Warsaw and Primate of Poland: Cardinal JÓZEF GLEMP, Sekretariat Prymasa Polski, 00-246 Warsaw, ul. Miodowa 17/19; tel. (22) 312157; telex 817000; fax (2) 6358745.

Archbishop of Białystok: Most Rev. STANISŁAW SZYMECKI, 15-087 Białystok, ul. Kościelna 1; tel. (85) 416473.

Archbishop of Częstochowa: Most Rev. STANISŁAW NOWAK, 42-200 Częstochowa, Al. Najśw. Maryi Panny 54; tel. (34) 43375.

Archbishop of Gdańsk: Most Rev. TADEUSZ GOCŁOWSKI, 80-330 Gdańsk, ul. Cystersów 15; tel. (58) 522808.

Archbishop of Gniezno: Most Rev. HENRYK MUSZYŃSKI, 62-200 Gniezno, ul. Kanclerza Jana Łaskiego 7; tel. (661) 2102; fax (661) 1285.

Archbishop of Katowice: Most Rev. DAMIAN ZIMOŃ, 40-027 Katowice, ul. Francuska 47; tel. (3) 1554673.

Archbishop of Kraków: Cardinal FRANCISZEK MACHARSKI, 31-004 Kraków, ul. Franciszkańska 3; tel. (12) 211533; telex 0322700; fax (12) 215012.

Archbishop of Łódź: Most Rev. WŁADYSŁAW ZIÓŁEK, 93-423 Łódź, ul. Rudzka 55/57; tel. (42) 844343.

Archbishop of Lublin: Most Rev. BOLESŁAW PYLAK, 20-105 Lublin, ul. Kard. S. Wyszyńskiego 2; tel. (81) 23468.

Archbishop of Olsztyn (Warmia): Most Rev. EDMUND PISZCZ, 10-025 Olsztyn, ul. Staszica 5A; tel. (89) 272291.

Archbishop of Poznań: Most Rev. JERZY STROBA, 61-109 Poznań, ul. Mieszka I 1; tel. (61) 528556; fax (61) 526797.

Archbishop of Przemyśl: Most Rev. IGNACY TOKARCZUK, 37-700 Przemyśl, Pl. Katedralny 4; tel. (10) 2674.

Archbishop of Szczecin-Kamień: Most Rev. MARIAN PRZYKUCKI, 71-423 Szczecin, ul. Piotra Skargi 30; tel. (91) 225157.

Archbishop of Wrocław: Cardinal HENRYK ROMAN GULBINOWICZ, 50-328 Wrocław, ul. Katedralna 11; tel. (71) 224214.

In addition, BRONISŁAW DĄBROWSKI, the General Secretary of the Bishops' Conference, and KAZIMIERZ MAJDAŃSKI hold the personal title of Archbishop.

Byzantine-Ukrainian Rite

Bishop of Przemyśl: Rt Rev. JAN MARTYNIAK, 37-700 Przemyśl, ul. Fryderyka Chopina 8; tel. (10) 3523.

Old Catholic Churches

Mariavite Catholic Church (Kościół Katolicki Mariawitów): Felicjanów, 09-470 Bodzanów, k. Płocka; tel. Bodzanów 10; f. 1893; 3,012 mems (1992); Archbishop JÓZEF M. RAFAEL WOJCIECHOWSKI.

Old Catholic Mariavite Church (Starokatolicki Kościół Mariawitów): 09-400 Płock, ul. Wieczorka 27; f. 1907; 25,250 mems (1992); Chief Bishop STANISŁAW KOWALSKI.

Polish Catholic Church (Kościół Polskokatolicki): 00-464 Warsaw, ul. Szwoleżerów 4; tel. (22) 413743; f. 1920; 52,400 mems (1991); Prime Bishop Most Rev. TADEUSZ R. MAJEWSKI.

The Orthodox Church

Polish Autocephalous Orthodox Church (Polski Autokefaliczny Kościół Prawosławny): 03-402 Warsaw, Al. Solidarności 52; tel. (22) 190886; 870,600 mems (1989); Archbishop of Warsaw and Metropolitan of All Poland BAZYLI (WŁODZIMIERZ DOROSZKIEWICZ); Archbishop of Białystok and Gdańsk SAWA (MICHAŁ HRYCUNIAK); Archbishop of Łódź and Poznań SZYMON (SZYMON ROMAŃCZUK); Bishop of Przemyśl and Nowy Sącz ADAM (ALEKSANDER DUBEC); Bishop of Wrocław and Szczecin JEREMIASZ (JAN ANCHIMIUK); Bishop of Lublin and Chełm ABEL (ANDRZEJ POPŁAWSKI).

Protestant Churches

There are approximately 100,000 Protestants in Poland.

Baptist Union of Poland (Polski Kościół Chrześcijan Baptystów): 00-865 Warsaw, ul. Waliców 25; tel. and fax (22) 242783; f. 1858; 3,335 baptized mems; Pres. Rev. KONSTANTY WIAZOWSKI; Gen. Sec. RYSZARD GUTKOWSKI.

Evangelical Augsburg Church in Poland (Kościół Ewangelicko-Augsburski): 00-246 Warsaw, ul. Miodowa 21; tel. (22) 315187; fax (22) 312348; 90,000 mems (1992); Bishop and Pres. of Consistory JAN SZAREK.

Evangelical-Reformed Church (Kościół Ewangelicko-Reformowany): 00-145 Warsaw, Al. Solidarności 76A; tel. (22) 314522; fax (22) 310827; f. 16th century; 4,500 mems (1992); Bishop ZDZISŁAW TRANDA; Pres. of the Consistory Prof. JAROSŁAW ŚWIDERSKI.

Pentecostal Church (Kościół Zielonoświątkowy): 00-825 Warsaw, Sienna 68/70; tel. (22) 248575; fax (22) 204073; f. 1910; 14,500 mems (1992); Pres. MICHAŁ HYDZIK.

Seventh-day Adventist Church in Poland (Kościół Adwentystów Dnia Siódmego): 00-366 Warsaw, ul. Foksal 8; tel. (22) 277611; telex 812359; fax (22) 278619; f. 1921; 9,673 mems, 74 preachers (1991); Pres. WŁADYSŁAW POLOK; Sec. ROMAN R. CHALUPKA.

United Methodist Church (Kościół Ewangelicko-Metodystyczny): 00-561 Warsaw, ul. Mokotowska 12; tel. and fax (2) 6285328; f. 1921; 5,000 mems; Gen. Supt Rev. EDWARD PUŚLECKI.

There are also several other small Protestant churches, including the Church of Christ, the Church of Evangelical Christians, the Evangelical Christian Church and the Jehovah's Witnesses.

ISLAM

In 1989 there were about 4,000 Muslims of Tartar origin in Białystok Province (eastern Poland), and smaller communities in Warsaw, Gdańsk and elsewhere.

Religious Union of Muslims in Poland (Muzułmański Związek Religijny): 15-426 Białystok, Rynek Kosciuszki 26, m. 2; tel. (85) 414970; Chair. STEFAN MUCHARSKI.

JUDAISM

Union of Jewish Communities in Poland (Związek Gmin Żydowskich w Rzeczypospolitej Polskiej): 00-950 Warsaw, ul. Twarda 6; tel. (22) 204324; 21 synagogues and about 3,220 registered Jews; Pres. PAWEŁ WILDSTEIN.

The Press

Legislation to permit the formal abolition of censorship and to guarantee freedom of expression was approved in April 1990. Many newspapers, however, were in serious financial difficulties, largely owing to the steep increase in the cost of newsprint.

Following the political changes of 1989, hundreds of new newspapers were established. In 1991 there were 68 daily newspapers in Poland with a total circulation of 5,258,000. In 1989 there were 3,189 periodicals with a combined circulation of 46.5m. copies.

PRINCIPAL DAILIES

Białystok

Gazeta Współczesna: 15-950 Białystok, POB 193, ul. Suraska 1; tel. (85) 23241; f. 1951; Editor ADAM JERZY SOCHA; circ. 35,000.

Bydgoszcz

Gazeta Pomorska: 85-011 Bydgoszcz, ul. Śniadeckich 1; tel. (52) 221928; telex 056-2386; fax (52) 221542; f. 1948; local independent newspaper for the provinces of Bydgoszcz, Toruń and Włocławek; Editor MACIEJ KAMIŃSKI; circ. 100,000 (weekdays), 300,000 (weekends).

Ilustrowany Kurier Polski: 85-950 Bydgoszcz, ul. Marshala Focha 20; tel. (52) 225501; telex 056-2387; f. 1945; regional; Editor-in-Chief MAREK FAŚCISZEWSKI; circ. 40,000.

Gdańsk

Dziennik Bałtycki: 80-886 Gdańsk, Targ Drzewny 3/7; tel. and fax (58) 313560; f. 1945; non-party; Editor JAN JAKUBOWSKI; circ. 80,000.

Głos Wybrzeża: 80-886 Gdańsk, ul. Targ Drzewny 3/7; tel. (58) 311572; f. 1991; Editor-in-Chief ZBIGNIEW ZUKOWSKI; circ. 50,000.

Katowice

Dziennik Zachodni: 40-925 Katowice, ul. Młyńska 1; tel. (32) 539984; telex 0315455; f. 1945; non-party; Chief Editor WŁODZIMIERZ PAŹNIEWSKI; circ. 100,000.

Trybuna Śląska: 40-098 Katowice, ul. Młyńska 1; tel. (32) 537703; telex 0312432; fax (32) 537997; f. 1945; fmrly Trybuna Robotnicza; independent; Editor TADEUSZ BIEDZKI; circ. 180,000 (weekdays), 800,000 (weekends).

Kielce

Słowo Ludu (Word of the People): 25-953 Kielce 12, Targowa 18; tel. (41) 42480; fax (41) 46979; f. 1949; independent; Editor KRZYSZTOF FALKIEWICZ; circ. 50,000 (weekdays), 130,000 (weekends).

Koszalin

Głos Pomorza (Voice of Pomerania): 75-604 Koszalin, ul. Zwycięstwa 137/139; tel. (94) 22693; f. 1952; Editor-in-Chief WIESŁAW WISNIEWSKI; circ. 60,000 (weekdays), 130,000 (weekends).

Kraków

Czas Krakowski: 31-015 Kraków, ul. Pijarska 9; tel. (12) 225355; telex 0322717; fax (12) 217502; f. 1848, reactivated 1990; independent; Editor JAN POLKOWSKI; circ. 150,000 (weekdays), 260,000 (weekends).

Echo Krakowa: 31-072 Kraków, ul. Wielopole 1; tel. (12) 224678; f. 1946; independent; evening; Editor WITOLD GRZYBOWSKI; circ. 60,000 (weekdays), 90,000 (weekends).

Gazeta Krakowska: 31-072 Kraków, ul. Wielopole 1; tel. (12) 220985; telex 0325785; fax (12) 221563; f. 1949; Editor-in-Chief JERZY SADECKI; circ. 60,000 (weekdays), 150,000 (weekends).

Łódź

Dziennik Łódzki: 90-113 Łódź, ul. Sienkiewicza 315; tel. (42) 364585; telex 886138; fax (42) 322832; f. 1945; non-party; Editor MACIEJ ROSALAK; circ. 65,000 (weekdays), 130,000 (weekends).

Głos Poranny: 90-113 Łódź, ul. Sienkiewicza 3/5; tel. (42) 366785; f. 1945; fmrly Głos Robotniczy; Editor GUSTAW ROMANOWSKI; circ. 52,000 (weekdays), 118,000 (weekends).

Lublin

Dziennik Lubelski: 20-601 Lublin, ul. Zana 38C; tel. (81) 558000; f. 1990; fmrly Sztandar Ludu; Editor ALOJZY LESZEK GZELLA; circ. 45,000 (weekdays), 210,000 (weekends).

Kurier Lubelski: 20-950 Lublin, ul. Armii Wojska Polskiego 5; tel. (81) 26634; fax (81) 26835; f. 1830; independent; evening; Editor WŁODZIMIERZ WÓJCIKOWSKI; circ. 40,000 (weekdays), 100,000 (weekends).

Olsztyn

Gazeta Olsztyńska (Olsztyn Gazette): 10-417 Olsztyn, ul. Towarowa 2; tel. (889) 330277; telex 0526371; fax (889) 332691; f. 1886, renamed 1970; independent; Editor-in-Chief TOMASZ ŚRUTKOWSKI; circ. 53,000 (weekdays), 101,000 (weekends).

Opole

Trybuna Opolska: 45-086 Opole, ul. Powstańców Śląskich 9; tel. (77) 33870; telex 732131; fax (77) 38822; f. 1952; local organ of SDRP; Editor MARIAN SZCZUREK; circ. 80,000.

Poznań

Gazeta Poznańska: 60-782 Poznań, ul. Grunwaldzka 19; tel. (61) 665568; f. 1991; independent; Editor PRZEMYSŁAW NOWICKI; circ. 80,000 (weekdays), 320,000 (weekends).

Głos Wielkopolski: 60-959 Poznań, ul. Grunwaldzka 19; tel. (61) 45409; telex 0413410; f. 1945; independent; Editor MAREK PRZYBYLSKI; circ. 110,000 (weekdays), 160,000 (weekends).

Rzeszów

Gazeta Codzienna 'Nowiny': 35-959 Rzeszów, ul. Unii Lubelskiej 3; tel. (17) 628471; telex 0632220; fax (17) 626754; f. 1949; evening; Editor JAN MUSIAŁ; circ. 100,000.

Szczecin

Głos Szczeciński (Voice of Szczecin): 70-550 Szczecin 2, Pl. Hołdu Pruskiego 8; tel. (91) 334864; telex 0422242; fax (91) 334864; f. 1947; Editor-in-Chief ZBIGNIEW JASINA; circ. 60,000 (weekdays), 180,000 (weekends).

Warsaw

Express Wieczorny: 02-017 Warsaw, Al. Jerozolimskie 125/127; tel. (2) 6285231; telex 825466; fax (2) 6284929; f. 1946; non-party; evening; Editor ANDRZEJ URBAŃSKI; circ. 140,000 (weekdays), 400,000 (weekends).

Gazeta Wyborcza: 00-732 Warsaw, ul. Czerska 8/10; tel. (22) 415513; telex 825703; fax (22) 416920; f. 1989; non-party; weekend edn: Gazeta Świateczna; Editor ADAM MICHNIK; circ. 540,000 (daily), 780,000 (weekends).

Kurier Polski: 00-018 Warsaw, ul. Zgoda 11; tel. (22) 278081; telex 814725; fax (22) 270552; f. 1729; Editor ANDRZEJ NIERYCHEO; circ. 200,000 (weekdays), 300,000 (weekends).

Polska Zbrojna: 00-950 Warsaw, ul. Grzybowska 77; tel. (22) 204293; fax (22) 202127; f. 1943; fmrly Żołnierz Wolności, name changed 1990; Editor ANTONI BARTKIEWICZ; circ. 50,000.

Przegląd Sportowy: 02-017 Warsaw, Al. Jerozolimskie 125/127, POB 181; tel. (2) 6289116; telex 814731; fax (22) 218697; f. 1921; Editor MACIEJ POLKOWSKI; circ. 110,000.

Rzeczpospolita (The Republic): 02-015 Warsaw, Pl. Starynkiewicza 7; tel. (2) 6280493; telex 817131; fax (2) 6280588; f. 1982; Editor-in-Chief DARIUSZ FIKUS; circ. 250,000.

Słowo-dziennik Katolicki: 00-551 Warsaw, ul. Mokotowska 43; tel. (22) 297767; telex 814434; f. 1993; fmrly Słowo Powszechne, organ of the 'Pax' Catholic Association; Editor JERZY MARCHLEWSKI; circ. 150,000.

Sztandar Młodych: 00-687 Warsaw, ul. Wspólna 61; tel. (2) 6287661; telex 814767; fax (2) 6282049; f. 1950; Editor GRAZYNA MINKOWSKA; circ. 110,000 (weekdays), 500,000 (weekends).

Trybuna: 04-029 Warsaw, Al. Stanów Zjednoczonych 53; tel. (22) 132040; telex 816302; fax (22) 100592; f. 1991; fmrly Trybuna Ludu; organ of the SDRP; Editor DARIUSZ SZYMCZYCHA; circ. 120,000 (weekdays), 250,000 (weekends).

Życie Warszawy (Warsaw Life): 00-575 Warsaw, Al. Armii Ludowej 3/5; tel. (2) 6256990; telex 814507; fax (22) 252829; f. 1944; independent; Editor KAZIMIERZ WÓYCICKI; circ. 250,000 (weekdays), 460,000 (weekends).

Wrocław

Gazeta Robotnicza: 50-010 Wrocław, ul. Podwale 62; tel. (71) 357356; telex 712665; fax (71) 357356; f. 1948; Editor ANDRZEJ BUŁAT; circ. 150,000 (weekdays), 520,000 (weekends).

Zielona Góra

Gazeta Lubuska: 65-042 Zielona Góra, POB 120, Al. Niepodległości 25; tel. (68) 70955; telex 0432262; fax (68) 3707; f. 1952; independent; Editor MIROSŁAW RATAJ; circ. 100,000 (weekdays), 200,000 (weekends).

PERIODICALS

Fantastyka: 00-640 Warsaw, ul. Mokotowska 5/6; tel. (22) 253475; f. 1982; monthly; science fiction and fantasy; Editor MACIEJ PAROWSKI; circ. 100,000.

Filipinka: 00-236 Warsaw, Świętojerska 5/7; tel. (22) 312221; f. 1957; fortnightly; illustrated for teenage girls; Editor HANNA JAWOROWSKA-BŁOŃSKA; circ. 125,600.

Film: 02-595 Warsaw, Puławska 61; tel. (22) 455325; fax (22) 454651; f. 1946; weekly; illustrated magazine; Editor MACIEJ PAWLICKI; circ. 105,000.

Forum: 00-678 Warsaw, ul. Śniadeckich 10; tel. (22) 256150; f. 1965; weekly; survey of foreign press; political, social, cultural and economics; Editor-in-Chief BOHDAN HERBICH; circ. 33,000.

Gazeta Bankowa: 00-696 Warsaw, Pankiewicza 3; tel. (2) 6287272; fax (22) 212653; f. 1988; weekly; business and finance; Editor ANDRZEJ WRÓBLEWSKI; circ. 40,000.

Głos Nauczycielski (Teachers' Voice): 00-389 Warsaw, ul. Spasowskiego 6/8; tel. (22) 276630; telex 816896; fax (22) 263420; f. 1916; weekly; organ of the Polish Teachers' Union; Editor WOJCIECH SIERAKOWSKI; circ. 40,000.

Gromada-Rolnik Polski: 00-375 Warsaw, ul. Smolna 12; tel. (22) 278815; telex 814741; fax 278815; f. 1951; 3 a week; agricultural; Editor ZBIGNIEW LUBAK; circ. 281,800.

IMT Światowid: 00-695 Warsaw, ul. Nowogrodzka 49; tel. (22) 215762; fax (22) 212376; f. 1955; monthly; illustrated tourist magazine; Editor BEATA TALLAR; circ. 50,000.

Karuzela (The Merry-Go-Round): 90-113 Łódź, ul. Sienkiewicza 3/5; tel. (42) 339083; f. 1956; satirical; Editor HALINA SIBIŃSKA; circ. 60,000.

Kobieta i Życie (Women and Life): 00-564 Warsaw, ul. Koszykowa 6A; tel. and fax (2) 6287811; f. 1946; weekly; women's; Editor ZOFIA KAMIŃSKA; circ. 400,000.

Literatura: 00-562 Warsaw, Koszykowa 6A; tel. (22) 214856; f. 1972; monthly; literary; Editor JACEK SYSKI; circ. 40,000.

Morze: 00-023 Warsaw, ul. Widok 10; tel. and fax (22) 273551; f. 1924; illustrated monthly; maritime affairs; Editor-in-Chief JANUSZ WOLNIEWICZ; circ. 50,000.

Nie: 00-789 Warsaw, ul. Słoneczna 25; tel. (22) 484420; fax (22) 497258; f. 1990; satirical weekly; Editor JERZY URBAN; circ. 500,000.

Nie z tej Ziemi (Not from that World): 00-840 Warsaw, Wronia 23; tel. (22) 241485; fax (22) 241481; f. 1990; monthly; para-science, ghost stories, etc.; Editor TADEUSZ LACHOWICZ; circ. 150,000.

Nowa Wieś: 00-480 Warsaw, ul. Wiejska 17; tel. and fax (2) 6284583; f. 1948; weekly; peasant illustrated magazine; Editor KAZIMIERZ DŁUGOSZ; circ. 60,000.

Panorama: 40-003 Katowice, Rynek 13; tel. (32) 538595; telex 031-5212; fax (32) 538374; f. 1960; weekly; socio-cultural magazine; Editor ANDRZEJ WRAZIDŁO; circ. 200,000.

Państwo i Prawo (State and Law): 00-490 Warsaw, ul. Wiejska 12; tel. (2) 6288296; f. 1946; monthly organ of the Polish Academy of Sciences; Editor Dr LESZEK KUBICKI; circ. 3,000.

Polityka (Politics): 00-182 Warsaw, ul. Dubois 9; tel. (2) 6353091; telex 812546; fax (2) 6351797; f. 1956; weekly; political, economic, cultural; Editor JAN BIJAK; circ. 350,000.

Polska Dziś (Poland Today): 04-028 Warsaw, Al. Stanów Zjednoczonych 53; tel. (22) 106568; telex 814775; fax (2) 6284651; f. 1991; Editor CEZARY LEŻEŃSKI; circ. 10,000.

Poradnik Gospodarski: 60-837 Poznań, ul. A. Mickiewicza 33; tel. (61) 476001; fax (61) 411881; f. 1889; monthly; agriculture; Editor-in-Chief WAWRZYNIEC TRAWIŃSKI; circ. 10,000.

Prawo i Życie (Law and Life): 00-028 Warsaw, ul. Bracka 20A; tel. (22) 272466; fax (22) 267585; f. 1965; weekly; legal and social; Editor ANDRZEJ DOBRZYŃSKI; circ. 120,000.

Przegląd Tygodniowy: 00-950 Warsaw, POB 992, ul. Bracka 22; tel. (22) 271899; telex 816400; fax (22) 279128; f. 1981; weekly; political, economic, social, historical, cultural, scientific and artistic; Editor-in-Chief ANDRZEJ NIERYCHŁO; circ. 130,000.

Przekrój: 31-012 Kraków, ul. Reformacka 3; tel. (12) 221833; telex 0322733; fax (12) 214929; f. 1945; weekly; illustrated; Editor-in-Chief MIECZYSŁAW CZUMA; circ. 190,000.

Przyjaciółka (The Friend): 00-490 Warsaw, ul. Wiejska 16; tel. (2) 6280583; fax (2) 6285866; f. 1948; weekly; women's magazine; Editor EWA ŁUSZCZUK; circ. 1,300,000.

Res Publica Nowa: 00-950 Warsaw 1, POB 856, ul. Smolna 12; tel. (22) 263047; fax (22) 262329; f. 1987; monthly; political and cultural; Editor MARCIŃ KRÓL; circ. 5,000.

Sport: 40-053 Katowice, ul. Młyńska 1; tel. (32) 53995; telex 0312436; fax (32) 537138; f. 1945; 5 a week; Editor ADAM BARTECZKO; circ. 135,000.

Sportowiec (Sportsman): 00-543 Warsaw, ul. Mokotowska 40; tel. (22) 216208; f. 1949; weekly; Chief Editor LECH UFEL; circ. 70,000.

Spotkania: 01-756 Warsaw, ul. Przasnyska 6; tel. (22) 399022; telex 817403; fax (22) 241423; f. 1990; weekly; illustrated; political, social, economic, cultural and scientific magazine; Editor MACIEJ IŁOWIECKI; circ. 80,000.

Sprawy Międzynarodowe (International Affairs): 00-950 Warsaw, ul. Warecka 1A; tel. (22) 278888; fax (22) 274738; f. 1948; every 3 months; published by the Polski Instytut Spraw Międzynarodowych; Editor HENRYK SZLAJFER; circ. 1,200.

Szpilki: 00-490 Warsaw, Pl. Trzech Krzyży 16A; tel. (2) 6280429; f. 1935; weekly; illustrated satirical; Editor JACEK JANCZARSKI; circ. 100,000.

Teatr: 03-902 Warsaw, ul. Jakubowska 14; tel. (22) 175594; f. 1945; monthly; illustrated; theatrical life; Editor ANDRZEJ WANET; circ. 4,500.

Twoje Dziecko: 02-548 Warsaw, ul. Grażyny 13; tel. (22) 452742; fax (22) 454216; f. 1951; monthly; women's magazine concerning children's affairs; Editor-in-Chief EWA SZPERLICH; circ. 150,000.

Tygodnik Solidarność: 00-950 Warsaw, POB P-6, ul. Czackiego 15/17; tel. (22) 273303; telex 816992; fax (22) 264451; f. 1981, reactivated 1989; weekly; Editor ANDRZEJ GELBREG; circ. 60,000.

The Warsaw Voice: 00-950 Warsaw, POB 28; tel. (22) 375138; fax (22) 371995; f. 1988; weekly; economic, political, social, cultural and economic; in English for foreigners; Editor ANDRZEJ JONAS; circ. 15,000.

Zielony Sztandar (Green Banner): 00-950 Warsaw, ul. Grzybowska 4; tel. (22) 207554; fax (22) 207557; f. 1931; weekly; main organ of the Polish Peasant Party (PPP); Editor PAWEŁ POPIAK; circ. 100,000.

Żołnierz Polski: 00-800 Warsaw, ul. Grzybowska 77; tel. (22) 204286; fax (22) 202127; f. 1945; monthly; illustrated magazine primarily about the armed forces; Editor IRENEUSZ CZYŻEWSKI; circ. 40,000.

Życie Gospodarcze: 00-490 Warsaw, ul. Wiejska 12; tel. (2) 6280628; fax (2) 6288392; f. 1945; weekly; economic; Editor KAROL SZWARC; circ. 35,700.

NEWS AGENCIES

Polska Agencja Prasowa—PAP (Polish Press Agency): 00-950 Warsaw, Al. Jerozolimskie 7; tel. (2) 6280001; telex 812509; fax (22) 218518; f. 1944; brs in 28 Polish towns and 22 foreign capitals; 274 journalist and photojournalist mems; information is transmitted abroad in English only; Pres. IGNACY RUTKIEWICZ; Dir-Gen. JERZY WYSOKIŃSKI.

Polska Agencja Informacyjna (Polish Information Agency): 00-585 Warsaw, ul. Bagatela 12; tel. (2) 6250822; telex 816170; fax (2) 6284651; f. 1967; multi-lingual books, magazines, bulletins and news, television films, feature and photo services on Polish culture, foreign policy and economics; press centre for foreign journalists and publishers; advertising and promotional services; Editor-in-Chief ZBIGNIEW DOMARAŃCZYK.

Redakcja Fotograficzna PAP/CAF (Photographic Department of the Polish Press Agency): 00-372 Warsaw, ul. Foksal 16; tel. (22) 262229; telex 814801; fax (22) 266118; f. 1951; fmrly Centralna Agencja Fotograficzna; supplies photographs to Polish press and to foreign press photo agencies; serves photographic publishing houses, and advertising agencies; Editor-in-Chief IZABELA WOJCIECHOWSKA.

Krajowa Agencja Wydawnicza—KAW (National Publishing Agency—KAW): 00-950 Warsaw, ul. Wilcza 46; tel. (2) 6286481; telex 813487; fax (22) 296007; f. 1974; publishes children's and youths' fiction, history, art, popular reference books, postcards, posters and calendars, and audio records, cassettes and compact discs; Dir and Editor-in-Chief JAN WYSOKIŃSKI.

Foreign Bureaux

Allgemeiner Deutscher Nachrichtendienst (ADN) (Germany): 00-116 Warsaw, ul. Świętokrzyska 36, m. 61; tel. (22) 201152; fax (22) 201015; Chief Correspondent JÖRG SCHREIBER.

Agence France-Presse (AFP): 00-672 Warsaw, ul. Piękna 68, p. 305; tel. (22) 216747; telex 813620; Correspondent MICHEL VIATTEAU.

Agencia EFE (Spain): 00-656 Warsaw, Śniadeckich 18, Lokal 16; tel. (2) 6282567; telex 7849; fax (22) 215989; Bureau Chief JORGE RUIZ LARDIZABAL.

Agenzia Nazionale Stampa Associata (ANSA) (Italy): 00-672 Warsaw, ul. Piękna 68, p. 301; tel. (22) 298413; telex 813724; fax (22) 299843; Bureau Chief MAURIZIO SALVI.

Associated Press (AP) (USA): 00-433 Warsaw, ul. Profesorska 4; tel. (2) 6287231; telex 813440; fax (22) 295240; Correspondent PAUL ALEXANDER.

Bulgarska Telegrafna Agentsia (BTA) (Bulgaria): 00-019 Warsaw, Kniewskiego 9, m. 14; tel. (22) 278059; telex 813720; Correspondent WESELIN JANKOW.

Česká tisková kancelář (ČTK) (The Czech Republic): 00-116 Warsaw, ul. Świętokrzyska 36, m. 46; tel. (22) 204504; telex 813746; Correspondent MILAN SYRUČEK.

Deutsche-Presse Agentur (dpa) (Germany): 03-908 Warsaw, ul. Saska 7A; tel. (22) 171058; telex 813374; Correspondent RENATA MARSCH-POTOCKA.

Informatsionnoye Telegrafnoye Agentstvo Rossii—Telegrafnoye Agentstvo Suverennykh Stran (ITAR—TASS) (Russia): 00-581 Warsaw, ul. Litewska 10, m. 18; tel. (22) 293161; telex 814425; Correspondent ALEKSANDR POTOMKIN.

Inter Press Service (IPS) (Netherlands): 00-116 Warsaw, ul. Jana Pawła II 23, m. 133; tel. (22) 243982; fax (22) 205508; Correspondent IWONA DMOCHOWSKA-KNOTHE.

Kyodo Tsushin (Japan): 00-679 Warsaw, ul. Waryńskiego 9 m. 56; tel. (22) 298416; telex 816997; fax (2) 6282045; Chief SUSUMU SOKATA.

Magyar Távirati Iroda (MTI) (Hungary): 02-954 Warsaw, ul. Jakuba Kubickiego 19/22, m. 21; tel. (22) 420089; telex 8144460; Correspondent JÁNOS BARABÁS.

Reuters (United Kingdom): 00-695 Warsaw, ul. Nowogrodzka 47A, IV Floor; tel. (2) 6256303; telex 813821; fax (2) 6257501; Correspondent TIMOTHY HERITAGE.

Rossiyskoye Informatsionnoye Agentstvo—Novosti (RIA—Novosti) (Russia): 00-582 Warsaw, Al. Szucha 5; tel. (2) 6283092; telex 813355; 6 Correspondents.

United Press International (UPI) (USA): 00-672 Warsaw, ul. Piękna 68, p. 306; tel. (2) 6280704; telex 813417; Chief Correspondent PATRICIA KOZA.

Xinhua (New China) News Agency (People's Republic of China): 00-203 Warsaw, ul. Bonifraterska 1; tel. (22) 313876; telex 813357; Correspondents TANG DEQIAO, DONG FUSHENG, SCHAO JIN.

PRESS ASSOCIATION

Stowarzyszenie Dziennikarzy Polskich—SDP (Polish Journalists' Association): 00-366 Warsaw, ul. Foksal 3/5; tel. (22) 278720; f. 1951, dissolved 1982, legal status restored 1989; over 3,000 mems; Pres. IGNACY RUTKIEWICZ (acting).

Publishers

A total of 10,242 titles (books and pamphlets) were published in 1990.

AGPOL (Foreign Trade Publicity and Publishing Enterprise): 00-957 Warsaw, ul. Kierbedzia 4, POB 7; tel. (22) 416061; telex 813364; fax (22) 405607; f. 1956; foreign trade publicity services for Polish firms, export-import of goods and services; Man. Dir TADEUSZ POLANOWSKI.

Instytut Prasy i Wydawnictw 'Novum' Unii Chrześcijansko-Społecznej: 00-580 Warsaw, ul. I. Armii Wojska Polskiego 3; tel. (22) 213413; telex 816721; religious books; Dir KRZYSZTOF BIELECKI.

Instytut Wydawniczy Pax (Pax Publishing Institute): 00-743 Warsaw, ul. Nabielaka 16; tel. (22) 415231; telex 813434; fax (22) 418702; f. 1949; theology, philosophy, religion, history, literature; Editor-in-Chief AMELIA SZAFRAŃSKA.

Instytut Wydawniczy Związków Zawodowych (Trade Unions' Publishing Institute): 00-950 Warsaw, ul. Spasowskiego 1/3; tel. (22) 279011; f. 1950; social, economic, scientific, cultural, labour safety and trade union literature and fiction; Dir and Editor-in-Chief STANISŁAW GRZEŚNIAK.

Księgarnia św. Wojciecha (St Adalbert Printing and Publishing Co): 60-967 Poznań, Pl. Wolności 1; tel. (61) 529186; telex 0414220; f. 1895; textbooks and Catholic publications; Dir Rev. BOLESŁAW JURGA; Editor-in-Chief BOZYSŁAW WALCZAK.

Ludowa Spółdzielnia Wydawnicza (People's Publishing Co-operative): 00-131 Warsaw, ul. Grzybowska 4/8; tel. (22) 205718; fax (22) 207277; f. 1949; fiction and popular science; Chair. and Editor-in-Chief KRZYSZTOF RAJEWSKI.

Niezależna Oficyna Wydawnicza NOWA (Independent Publishing House NOWA): 00-929 Warsaw, ul. Truskawiecka 1; tel. (22) 423073; belles-lettres, poetry, memoirs, essays, recent history, politics; Pres. GRZEGORZ BOGUTA; Editor-in-Chief MIROSŁAW KOWALSKI.

Oficyna Literacka: 30-112 Kraków, ul. Smoleńsk 38, m. 12; tel. (12) 218472; f. 1982 clandestinely, 1990 officially; belles-lettres, poetry, including débuts, essays; Editor-in-Chief HENRYK KARKOSZA.

Oficyna Wydawnicza Volumen: 02-759 Warsaw, ul. Złotych Piasków 3, m. 10; tel. (22) 425013; f. 1984 (working clandestinely as WERS), 1989 officially; science, popular history, anthropology and socio-political sciences; Dir ADAM BOROWSKI.

Pallottinum—Wydawnictwo Stowarzyszenia Apostolstwa Katolickiego: 60-959 Poznań, Al. Przybyszewskiego 30; tel. (61) 417212; fax (61) 417217; f. 1947; religious books; Dir Mgr STEFAN DUSZA.

Państwowe Wydawnictwo Ekonomiczne (State Publishing House for Economic Literature): 00-098 Warsaw, ul. Niecała 4A; tel. and fax (22) 275567; f. 1949; economics books and magazines; Dir and Editor-in-Chief ALICJA RUTKOWSKA.

Państwowe Wydawnictwo Rolnicze i Leśne (State Agricultural and Forestry Publishers): 00-950 Warsaw, Al. Jerozolimskie 28; tel. and fax (22) 276338; f. 1947; for professional publications on agriculture and forestry; Dir and Editor-in-Chief JOLANTA KUCZYŃSKA.

Państwowy Instytut Wydawniczy (State Publishing Institute): 00-950 Warsaw, POB 377, ul. Foksal 17; tel. (22) 260201; telex 814306; fax (22) 261536; f. 1946; Polish and foreign classical and contemporary literature, fiction, literary criticism, biographies, performing arts, culture, history, popular science and fine arts; Dir ANDRZEJ GRUSZECKI; Editor-in-Chief ALOJZY KOŁODZIEJ.

Państwowy Zakład Wydawnictw Lekarskich (State Medical Publisher): 00-950 Warsaw, POB 379, ul. Długa 38/40; tel. (22) 312161; fax 310054; f. 1945; school textbooks for children with learning difficulties and literature on special pedagogy for parents and children; Dir and Editor-in-Chief (vacant).

Polska Oficyna Wydawnicza BGW (Polish Publishing House BGW): 02-001 Warsaw, Al. Jerozolimskie 91; tel. (22) 217546; fax (2) 6284652; telex 817-965; f. 1990; encyclopaedias, compendia of knowledge, books for children; Pres. ROMAN GÓRSKI.

Polskie Przedsiębiorstwo Wydawnictw Kartograficznych im. Eugeniusza Romera (Romer Polish Cartographical Publishing House Co): 00-410 Warsaw, ul. Solec 18/20; tel. (22) 283251; f. 1951; maps, atlases, books on geodesy and cartography, and a quarterly review; Dir ALINA MELJON.

Polskie Wydawnictwo Muzyczne (PWM—Edition): 31-111 Kraków, Al. Krasińskiego 11A; tel. (12) 227328; telex 813370; fax (12) 220174; f. 1945; music and books on music; Dir JAN BĘTKOWSKI; (see also under Foreign Trade Organizations).

Spółdzielnia Wydawnicza Czytelnik (Reader Co-operative Publishing House): 00-490 Warsaw, ul. Wiejska 12A; tel. (2) 6281441; fax (2) 6283178; f. 1944; general, especially fiction and contemporary Polish literature; Chair. MAREK BOGUCKI; Editor-in-Chief HENRYK CHŁYSTOWSKI.

Wydawnictwa Artystyczne i Filmowe (Art and Film Publications): 02-595 Warsaw, ul. Puławska 61; tel. (22) 455301; fax (22) 455584; f. 1959; theatre, cinema, photography and art publications and reprints; Man. Dir JANUSZ FOGLER.

Wydawnictwa Komunikacji i Łączności (Transport and Communications Publishing House): 02-546 Warsaw, ul. Kazimierzowska 52; tel. and fax (22) 492322; telex 812736; f. 1949; technical books on motorization, electronics, radio engineering, television and telecommunications, road, rail and air transport; Dir JERZY KOZŁOWSKI; Editor-in-Chief BOGUMIŁ ZIELIŃSKI.

Wydawnictwa Naukowo-Techniczne (Scientific-Technical Publishers): 00-950 Warsaw, ul. Mazowiecka 2/4, POB 359; tel. (22) 267271; fax (22) 268293; f. 1949; scientific and technical books on mathematics, physics, chemistry, foodstuffs industry, electrical and electronic engineering, computer science, automation, mechanical engineering, light industry; technological encyclopaedias and dictionaries, children's dictionaries; Gen. Man. Dr ANIELA TOPULOS.

Wydawnictwa Normalizacyjne Alfa (Standardization Publishing House): 00-950 Warsaw, ul. Nowogrodzka 22; tel. (22) 216751; telex 812374; f. 1956; standards, catalogues and reference books on standardization, periodicals; popular science for children, science fiction, household directories; Dir and Editor-in-Chief JERZY WYSOKIŃSKI.

Wydawnictwa Polskiej Agencji Ekologicznej (Polish Ecological Publishing House): 00-975 Warsaw, ul. Rakowiecka 4; tel. (22) 494927; fax (22) 495081; f. 1953; geology; Dir JERZY CHODKOWSKI.

Wydawnictwa Szkolne i Pedagogiczne—WSiP (Polish Educational Publishers): 00-950 Warsaw, POB 480, Pl. Dąbrowskiego 8; tel. (22) 268382; telex 816132; fax (22) 279280; f. 1945; school textbooks and popular science books, scientific literature for teachers, visual teaching aids, periodicals for teachers and youth; Man. Dir ANDRZEJ CHRZANOWSKI.

Wydawnictwo Adamski i Bieliński: 00-420 Warsaw, ul. Szara 10A, rms 302/303; tel. and fax (22) 294930.

Wydawnictwo Arkady: 00-959 Warsaw, ul. Dobra 28, POB 169; tel. (22) 269316; fax (22) 274194; f. 1957; publications on building, town planning, architecture and art; Dir and Pres. JANINA KRYSIAK.

Wydawnictwo Bellona: 00-873 Warsaw, ul. Grzybowska 77; tel. (22) 204291; f. 1947; fiction, history and military; Dir Col JÓZEF SKRZYPIEC.

Wydawnictwo Czasopism i Książek Technicznych Sigma NOT, Spółka z o.o. (Sigma Publishers of Technical Periodicals and Books, Ltd): 00-950 Warsaw, ul. Biała 4, POB 1004; tel. (22) 203118; telex 814550; fax (22) 203116; f. 1949; popular and specialized periodicals and books on general technical subjects; Dir and Editor-in-Chief Dr ANDRZEJ KUSYK.

Wydawnictwo Interpress (Interpress Publishers): 04-028 Warsaw, Al. Stanów Zjednoczonych 53; tel. (22) 134669; telex 816170; fax (22) 134924; Poland past and present, handbooks, monographs, guide-books, albums; publishing co-operation and printing services; Editor-in-Chief BOHDAN GAWROŃSKI.

Wydawnictwo 'iskry' Spółka z o. o. (Iskry Publishing House Ltd): 00-375 Warsaw, ul. Smolna 11/13; tel. (22) 279415; fax (22) 279415; f. 1952; travel, Polish and foreign fiction, science fiction, essays, popular science, history, memoirs; Dir and Editor-in-Chief Dr WIESŁAW UCHAŃSKI.

Wydawnictwo Literackie (Literary Publishing House): 31-147 Kraków, ul. Długa 1; tel. (12) 224644; fax (12) 225423; f. 1953; works of literature and belles-lettres; Dir Dr JERZY KOWALCZYK.

Wydawnictwo Łódzkie: 90-447 Łódź, ul. Piotrkowska 171/173; tel. (42) 360331; fax (42) 368524; f. 1957; contemporary and classical Polish literature, juvenile literature, memoirs, essays, translations, popular science; Dir and Editor-in-Chief BRONISŁAWA STOLARSKA.

Wydawnictwo Lubelskie (Lublin Publishing House): 20-022 Lublin, ul. Okopowa 7; tel. (81) 27344; f. 1957; social and political literature, memoires, essays, fiction, poetry, translations from Ukrainian literature; Dir and Editor-in-Chief IRENEUSZ CABAN.

Wydawnictwo Morskie (Maritime Publishing House): 80-835 Gdańsk, ul. Szeroka 38/40; tel. (58) 311031; f. 1951; popular science, humanities, maritime economy, belles-lettres, encyclopaedias, dictionaries, children's books; Dir and Editor-in-Chief JOANNA KONOPACKA (acting).

Wydawnictwoy Nasza Księgarnia Spólka z o. o. (Publishing House Nasza Księgarnia Ltd): 00-389 Warsaw, ul. Smulikowskiego 4; tel. (22) 263648; fax (22) 263646; f. 1921; books and periodicals for children and educational publications; Pres. MIROSŁAW TOKARCZYK.

Wydawnictwo Naukowe PWN, Sp. z o. o. (Scientific Publishers Ltd): 00-251 Warsaw, ul. Miodowa 10; tel. (22) 312738; fax (22) 267163; f. 1951; publications and journals on all sciences, encyclopaedias, university textbooks, dictionaries; Dir GRZEGORZ BOGUTA; Editor-in-Chief JAN KOFMAN.

Wydawnictwo Ossolineum (Ossolineum Publishing House): 50-106 Wrocław, Rynek 9; tel. (71) 38625; telex 712771; fax (71) 448103; f. 1817; humanities and sciences; Dir BARBARA KOCOWSKA; Editor-in-Chief JAN STANISŁAW MIŚ.

Wydawnictwo Prawnicze (Legal Publishing House): 02-520 Warsaw, ul. Wiśniowa 50; tel. (22) 494705; f. 1952; Dir PIOTR SZCZEŚNIEWSKI.

Wydawnictwo Śląsk Sp. z o.o. (Silesia Publishing House Ltd): 40-161 Katowice, Al. W. Korfantego 51; tel. (32) 580756; fax (32) 583229; f. 1954; belles-lettres, social, popular science, juvenile books and regional literature; Pres. TADEUSZ SIERNY.

Wydawnictwo Spółdzielcze: 00-013 Warsaw, ul. Jasna 1; tel. (22) 271524; telex 813622; books, periodicals, information bulletins, catalogues, albums; Dir SYLWESTER KOMARNICKI.

Wydawnictwo Sport i Turystyka (State Sport and Tourism Publishers): 00-021 Warsaw, ul. Chmielna 7/9; tel. (22) 271303; telex 816578; fax (22) 274250; f. 1953; publications in the field of tourism, sports, popular topography, and artistic albums; Dir and Editor-in-Chief KATARYNA BALICKA.

Wydawnictwo Spotkania: 00-867 Warsaw, ul. Chłodna 29; tel. (22) 241615; fax (22) 207092; f. 1976 (outside Poland), f. 1990 (officially in Poland); memoirs, books on history, including military history, albums, postcards, cassettes, weekly *Spotkania*; Propr PIOTR JEGLIŃSKI.

Wydawnictwo Wiedza Powszechna (Popular Knowledge): 00-054 Warsaw, ul. Jasna 26; tel. (22) 269592; fax (22) 268594; f. 1952; popular scientific books, Polish and foreign language dictionaries, teach-yourself handbooks, foreign language textbooks, encyclopaedias and lexicons; Dir JÓZEF CHLABICZ.

Zakład Wydawnictw Statystycznych (Statistical Publishing Establishment): 00-925 Warsaw, Al. Niepodległości 208; tel. (22) 252724; telex 814581; fax (22) 259545; f. 1971; statistics and theory of statistics, periodicals; Dir ANDRZEJ STASIUN.

Zakłady Wydawniczè, Produkcyjne i Handlowe Epoka: 00-950 Warsaw, ul. Zgoda 11, POB 393; tel. (22) 272495; fax (22) 277042; f. 1957; newspapers, periodicals, political and social publs of Democratic Party (DP); Pres. ADAM KARAS.

Znak Społeczny Instytut Wydawniczy (Znak Social Publishing Institute): 30-105 Kraków, ul. Kościuszki 37; tel. (12) 219776; telex 0325707; fax (12) 219814; f. 1959; religion, philosophy, belles-lettres, essays, history; CEO HENRYK WOŹNIAKOWSKI; Editor-in-Chief JERZY ILLG.

PUBLISHERS' ASSOCIATION

Polskie Towarzystwo Wydawców Książek (Polish Association of Book Publishers): 00-048 Warsaw, ul. Mazowiecka 2/4; tel. (22) 260735; f. 1926; Chair. ANDRZEJ KARPOWICZ; 1,000 mems.

WRITERS' ORGANIZATION

Agencja Autorska (Authors' Agency): 00-950 Warsaw, ul. Hipoteczna 2; tel. (22) 278396; telex 812470; f. 1964; represents Polish writers, composers, graphic artists and photographers; publishes monographs on contemporary Polish writers, and periodicals; places foreign books with Polish publishing houses; Dir EWA MICHAŁSKA; Pres. ANTONI MARIANOWICZ.

Radio and Television

At the end of 1992 there were 10.9m. radio and 9.0m. television subscribers. By late 1988 3,500 licences for the reception of satellite television had been issued. Legislation passed by the National Assembly in December 1992 brought to an end the state monopoly over broadcasting. In January 1994 Poland's first national commercial television licence was controversially awarded to PolSat, a Polish satellite television company.

National Council for Radio and Television: Warsaw; f. 1993; regulatory body; Chair. (vacant).

RADIO

Polskie Radio (Polish Radio): 00-950 Warsaw, Al. Niepodległości 77/85, POB 46; tel. (22) 445280; telex 814825; Chair. KRZYSZTOF MICHALSKI; Dir of International Relations HANNA DĄBROWSKA.

Home Service: there are four national channels broadcasting 80 hours per day; one long-wave transmitter (600 kW) broadcasting on 225 kHz; 14 medium-wave transmitters and 18 relay stations; 98 VHF transmitters covering all four programmes and 17 local programmes; Head of Radio JAN MAREK OWSIŃSKI.

Foreign Service: Seven transmitters broadcast on ten frequencies on short-wave, one transmitter broadcasting on medium-wave. Beamed programmes in Polish, English, Esperanto, German, Russian, Belarusian, Ukrainian, Lithuanian and Czech.

TELEVISION

There are two national public channels, one broadcasting for 22 hours, the other for 16 hours per day via 84 transmitters and 134 relay stations, and one national private channel, broadcasting for 18 hours per day. Moreover, there is one satellite channel of Polish Television, TV Polonia, broadcasting for 16 hours per day. In addition to the various local programmes for Gdańsk, Katowice, Szczecin, Wrocław (seven hours per day) and Lublin (four hours per day), there are regional programmes for Bydgoszcz, Kraków, Łódź, Poznań, Rzeszów and Warsaw (three hours per day). Poland's first private (commercial) TV station began operating in Wrocław in early 1990. Broadcasting is regulated by the Broadcasting Bill, enacted in 1993.

Telewizja Polska (Polish Television): 00-950 Warsaw, ul. Woronicza 17, POB 211; tel. (22) 478501; telex 825331; fax (22) 435779; f. 1952; Chair. WIESŁAW WALENDZIAK; Man. Dir BARBARA BORYS-DAMIECKA.

PolSat: Warsaw; f. 1992; Polish satellite company, awarded Poland's first national, private television licence in 1994; Owner ZYGMUNT SOLORZ.

Finance

(cap. = capital; res = reserves; dep. = deposits; m. = million; amounts in złotys unless otherwise stated; brs = branches)

BANKING

A major restructuring of the Polish banking system began in 1987, numerous new banks subsequently being established. The Banking Law of January 1989 allowed the involvement of foreigners in Polish banking.

National Bank

Narodowy Bank Polski (National Bank of Poland): Head Office: 00-950 Warsaw, ul. Świętokrzyska 11/21, POB 1011; tel. (22) 200321; telex 814681; fax (22) 263932; f. 1945; state central bank; 53 brs throughout Poland; by early 1993 nine independent regional banks (since 1991 joint-stock companies), two state banks, three foreign banks and 84 commercial banks (joint-stock companies, including eight with foreign capital) had been granted licences by the National Bank; Pres. HANNA GRONKIEWICZ-WALTZ; First Deputy Pres. WITOŁD KOZIŃSKI.

Other Banks

Bank-Agrobank SA: 04-398 Warsaw 44, ul. Minska 25, POB 2; tel. (22) 102930; telex 816883; fax (22) 103355; f. 1989; Pres. ALEKSY MISIEJUK; 15 brs.

Bank Depozytowo-Kredytowy w Lublinie SA (Deposit and Credit Bank in Lublin): 20-954 Lublin, ul. Lubomelska 1/3, POB 184; tel. (81) 21712; telex 642015; fax (81) 713171; f. 1989; cap. 291,000m., res 1,250,797m., dep. 8,625,436m. (Dec. 1992); Pres. WŁODZIMIERZ KOSACKI.

Bank of Economic Initiatives BIG SA: 00-950 Warsaw, Al. Jerozolimskie 44, POB 97; tel. (22) 272391; telex 814869; fax (22) 271330; f. 1989; 63.4% private cap.; cap. and res US $32.2m., dep. $335.2m. (June 1993); Chair. BOGUSŁAW KOTT; 7 brs.

Bank Gdański: 80-958 Gdańsk, ul. Targ Drzewny 1, POB 436; tel. (58) 379222; telex 513220; fax (58) 311570; f. 1989; cap. 490,300m., dep. 14,070,863m. (Dec. 1990); Pres. EDMUND TOLWIŃSKI; 48 brs.

Bank Gospodarki Żywnościowej (Bank of Food Economy): 00-131 Warsaw, ul. Grzybowska 4; tel. (22) 257206; telex 825775; fax (22) 206112; f. 1975; finances agriculture, forestry and food processing; res 2,484,200m., dep. 32,350,200m. (Dec. 1991); Chair. KAZIMIERZ OLESIAK; 102 brs.

Bank Gospodarstwa Krajowego: 00-958 Warsaw, ul. Grzybowska 80/82, POB 57; tel. (2) 6615106; telex 813232; fax (2) 6615133; f. 1924; cap. 58,747m., res 32,000m., dep. 162,785m. (Dec. 1992); Pres. MARIUSZ STOLARZ.

Bank Handlowo-Kredytowy SA: 40-163 Katowice, Plac Gwarków 1, POB 189; tel. (32) 592542; telex 315792; fax (32) 582410; f. 1990; Pres. FRANCISZEK SOBCZAK; brs in Szczecin, Warsaw, Wrocław and Zielona Góra.

Bank Handlowy w Warszawie SA: 00-950 Warsaw, ul. Chałubińskiego 8, POB 129; tel. (22) 303000; telex 814811; fax (22) 300113; f. 1870; authorized foreign exchange bank; cap. 2,583,000m., res 2,111,932m., dep. 73,378,943m. (Dec. 1992); Pres. CEZARY STYPULKOWSKI; 20 brs.

Bank Polska Kasa Opieki SA (Pekao): 00-844 Warsaw, ul. Grzybowska 53/57, POB 1008; tel. (22) 269211; telex 817755; fax (22) 273465; f. 1929; state savings bank; domestic and foreign business; cap. 400,000m., res 2,820,764m., dep. 80,586,223m. (Dec. 1992); Chair. STEFAN KAWALEC; 31 brs.

Bank Przemysłowo-Handlowy w Krakowie SA (Industrial and Commercial Bank in Kraków): 31-027 Kraków, ul. św. Tomasza 43, POB 57; tel. (12) 223333; telex 0326426; fax (12) 216914; f. 1989; was to be privatized in 1994; cap. and res 2,456,840m., dep. 18,566,503m. (Dec. 1992); Pres. JANUSZ QUANDT; 59 brs.

Bank Rozwoju Eksportu SA (Export Development Bank SA): 00-950 Warsaw, POB 728, Plac Bankowy 2; tel. (2) 6355926; telex 817118; fax (2) 6358071; f. 1986; joint-stock co, with Ministry of Foreign Trade as main shareholder; privatization in progress in 1993; provides credit for ventures that promote export growth; cap. 400,000m., res 444,345m., dep. 4,031,499m. (Dec. 1992); Pres. KRZYSZTOF SZWARC; 10 brs.

Bank Rozwoju Rolnictwa SA: 61-773 Poznań, ul. Stary Rynek 85/86; telex 413218; fax (61) 525194; f. 1990; commercial bank; cap. 111,300m., res 27,100m., dep. 1,121,200m.; Pres. JERZY MAŁECKI; 19 brs.

Bank Rozwoju Rzemiosła, Handlu i Przemysłu Market SA: 61-773 Poznań, Stary Rynek 73/74, POB 72; tel. (61) 528231; telex 0413375; fax (61) 528237; Pres. ERYK WOJCIECHOWSKI.

Bank Śląski SA w Katowicach: 40-950 Katowice, ul. Warszawska 14, POB 137; tel. (32) 537281; telex 312809; fax (32) 537364; f. 1989; commercial bank; was privatized in 1993; cap. 926,000m., dep. 18,086,412m. (Dec. 1992); Pres. BRUNO BARTKIEWCZ (acting); 52 brs.

Bank Staropoloski SA w Pozaniu: 60-967 Poznań, ul. Nowowiejskiego 5; tel. (61) 522568; telex 424782; fax (61) 522568; f. 1990; commercial bank; cap. 102,149m., dep. 823,280m. (Dec. 1992); Pres. JULIUSZ BARSZCZEWSKI.

Bank Turystyki SA: 00-030 Warsaw, ul. Mysia 3; tel. (2) 6265565; telex 815059; fax (2) 6256505; commercial bank for tourism industry; cap. and res 69,927m., dep. 246,908m. (Dec. 1992); Pres. STEFAN JERZAK.

Bank Zachódni Spólka Akcyjna (Western Bank): 50-950 Wrocław, ul. Ofiar Oświęcimskich 41/43, POB 1109; tel. (71) 446621; telex 712369; fax (71) 34917; f. 1989; res 1,259,180m., dep. 11,663,447m. (Dec. 1992); Pres. TADEUSZ GŁUSZCZUK.

Bank Ziemi Radomskiej SA: 26-600 Radom, ul. Zeromskiego 75; tel. (48) 455271; telex 0672469; fax (48) 455120; f. 1990; Pres. LOUIS MONTMORY.

Bydgoski Bank Budownictwa SA: 85-065 Bydgosz, ul. Chodkiewicza 15; tel. (52) 212661; telex 563178; fax (52) 212009; f. 1990; savings bank; cap. 51,741m., res 8,853m., dep. 370,650m. (Dec. 1992); Pres. BOGUSŁAW SALAMOPŃSKI; 7 brs.

Bydgoski Bank Komunalny SA: 85-097 Bydgoszcz, ul. Jagiellońska 34; tel. (52) 229061; telex 562404; fax (52) 211902; f. 1989; commercial bank; cap. 24,000m., res 108,936m., dep. 133,768m. (Dec. 1991); Pres. MAREK JAROCIŃSKI; 9 brs.

Polski Bank Rozwoju SA (Polish Development Bank SA): 00-680 Warsaw, ul. Zurawia 47/49; tel. (2) 6300402; telex 812698; fax (2) 6300403; f. 1990; cap. and res 1,252,000m., dep. 3,543,328m. (Dec. 1992); Pres. WOJCIECH KOSTRZEWA.

Pomorski Bank Kredytowy SA (Pomeranian Credit Bank): 70-952 Szczecin, Pl. Zołnierza 16, Polskiego, POB 613; tel. (91) 34769; telex 422239; fax (91) 533114; f. 1989; cap. 354,000m., res 740,297m., dep. 6,473,272m. (Dec. 1991); Pres. TADEUSZ ZYWCZAK; 55 brs.

Powszechna Kasa Oszczędności—Bank Państwowy (State Savings Bank): 00-950 Warsaw, POB 639; tel. (22) 261310; telex 816829; fax (22) 261489; f. 1919; cap. 540,000m., dep. 77,798,980m. (Dec. 1992); Chair. STANISŁAW PIETRASIEWICZ; 800 brs and sub-brs.

Powszechny Bank Gospodarczy w Łodzi (Universal Economic Bank in Łódàz): 90-950 Łódź, Al. Piłsudskiego 12, POB 12; tel. (42) 366244; telex 885411; fax (42) 341470; f. 1989; cap. 331,500m., res 439,783m., dep. 16,386,740m. (Dec. 1992); Pres. ANDRZEJ SZUKALSKI; 33 brs.

Powszechny Bank Kredytowy SA w Warszawie (Warsaw Credit Bank): 00-400 Warsaw, 6/12 Nowy Świat; tel. (22) 210321; telex 815027; fax (2) 6257664; f. 1989; cap. and res 2,625,411m., dep. 20,876,342m. (Dec. 1992); Pres. EWA KAWECKA-WLODARCZAK; 47 brs.

Prosper-Bank SA w Krakowie: 30-960 Kraków, ul. Solskiego 43; tel. (12) 225872; telex 0325403; f. 1990; Pres. ADAM KAWALEC.

Warszawski Bank Zachodni SA: 00-973 Warsaw 37, Al. Jerozolimskie 91, POB 57; tel. and fax (2) 6255248; Pres. WOJCIECH MIERNIK.

Wielkopolski Bank Kredytowy w Poznaniu SA (Credit Bank in Poznań): 60-967 Poznań 9, Pl. Wolności 15, POB 516; tel. (61) 542900; telex 0414501; fax (61) 521113; f. 1989; privatized in 1993; cap. 457,400m., res 211,330m., dep. 10,856,594m. (Dec. 1992); Pres. FRANCISZEK POŚPIECH; 48 brs.

Foreign Banks

By the early 1990s many foreign banks, including Banque Nationale de Paris, Société Générale (France), Deutsche Bank AG, Dresdner Bank AG (Germany), Banca Commerciale Italiana (Italy) and Citibank NA (USA) had opened representative offices in Poland. The Bank Amerykański w Polsce SA (American Bank in Poland) was established in late 1989 with US and Polish capital.

STOCK EXCHANGES

The stock-exchange service was re-established in April 1991. The Warsaw securities exchange reopened in July of that year.

Warsaw Stock Exchange: 00-920 Warsaw, Nowy Świat 6; opened for trading in 1991; Pres. WIESŁAW ROZLUCKI.

INSURANCE

Until 1991 the Polish insurance market was dominated by Polish National Insurance (Państwowy Zakład Ubezpieceń—PZU), which had 60% of business, and Warta Insurance and Reinsurance, which had 30%; the remaining 10% was held by about 20 recently-created private insurance companies. PZU was due to be privatized and replaced by smaller, more specialized, companies during 1992–93.

Państwowy Zakład Ubezpieczeń—PZU (Polish National Insurance): 00-916 Warsaw, ul. Traugutta 5; tel. (22) 269115; telex 814487; fax (22) 269743; f. 1803; state insurance company dealing in all types of insurance; Chair. KRZYSZTOF JARMUSZCZAK; 400 brs.

Towarzystwo Ubezpieczeń i Reasekuracji Warta SA (Warta Insurance and Reinsurance Co Ltd): 00-697 Warsaw, Al. Jerozolimskie 65/79; tel. (22) 272625; telex 817026; fax (22) 300336; f. 1920; marine, air, motor, fire, illness, luggage and credit; deals with all foreign business; Pres. ANDRZEJ WOJTYŃSKI; 13 brs; representatives in London and New York.

Trade and Industry

STATE PROPERTY AGENCY

General Privatization Programme: c/o Department of National Investment Funds, Ministry of Ownership Transformation (Privatization), 00-522 Warsaw, ul. Krucza 36; tel. (2) 292587; fax (2) 297129; responsible for the divestment of various state-owned enterprises.

CHAMBERS OF COMMERCE

Krajowa Izba Gospodarcza (Polish Chamber of Commerce): Head Office: 00-074 Warsaw, Trębacka 4, POB 361; tel. (22) 260221; telex 814361; fax (22) 274673; 28 regional offices; f. 1990; Pres. ANDRZEJ ARENDARSKI.

The Chamber of Industry and Trade of Foreign Investors and the Economic Chamber of Private Industry were founded in 1989. The National Federation of Employers (Pres. ANDRZEJ MACHALSKI) was established in 1991.

FOREIGN TRADE ORGANIZATIONS AND MAJOR COMPANIES

Under new measures introduced in 1982, foreign trade organizations, hitherto operating as state enterprises, began a conversion into joint-stock companies with limited liability, the former Ministry of Foreign Trade holding 51% of the stock and producers and commercial enterprises holding 49%.

Agromet-Motoimport Spółka z o.o.: 00-950 Warsaw, Plac Bankowy 2, POB 990; tel. (22) 285071; telex 813665; fax (22) 284180; import and export of agricultural machinery and equipment; Gen. Dir STANISŁAW RUBAJ.

Agros Spółka z o.o.: 00-950 Warsaw, Chałubińskiego 8; tel. (22) 302742; telex 814391; fax (22) 300791; import of tea, coffee, cocoa beans, tobacco products, citrus fruit, alcoholic drinks, wines, dried fruit and spices; export of vodkas, beer, wines, tobacco, confectionery, fruits, vegetables, etc.

Agros Holding SA: 00-613 Warsaw, Chałubińskiego; tel. (22) 302742; telex 814391; fax (22) 300615; Gen. Dir ZOFIA GABER-SOBIERALSKA.

Animex Export-Import, Spółka z o.o.: 00-613 Warsaw, Chałubińskiego 8; tel. (22) 300810; telex 814491; fax (22) 300537; imports and exports slaughtering and breeding animals, meat and meat products, poultry, game; Dir WITOLD PERETA.

Ars Polona: 00-068 Warsaw, Krakowskie Przedmieście 7, POB 1001; tel. (22) 261201; telex 813498; fax (22) 266240; f. 1953; import and export of books, newspapers, stamps, coins, musical instruments, records, contemporary works of art and silver jewellery; Gen. Dir MONIKA BIAŁECKA.

AUTOSAN—Sanocka Fabryka Autobusow: 38-500 Sanok, ul. Lipinskiego 109; tel. (137) 50126; telex 065577; fax (137) 50430; manufacture and export of motor buses, and agricultural and goods trailers; Chair. ANDRZEJ KRZANOWSKI.

Azoty Puławy—Zakłady Azotowe Puławy w Puławach: 24-110 Puławy, Al. 1000-lecia, Państwa Polskiego 13; tel. (831) 75555; telex 642316; fax (831) 75444; f. 1961; chemicals, incl. fertilizers, melamine, nitrates and polyethelene; Gen. Dir MIROSŁAW MALINOWSKI.

Baltona SA: 81-963 Gdynia, Pułaskiego 6, POB 365; tel. (58) 202357; telex 054361; fax (58) 203825; f. 1946; import and export of food and industrial goods; supplier to retail shops, ships, airlines, duty-free shops, diplomatic offices; Pres. and Gen. Dir JERZY MROZOWICKI.

Befama: 43-300 Bielsko Biała, Powstańców Śląskich 6; tel. (30) 23061; telex 35333; fax (30) 21293; f. 1851; textile machinery; Man. Dir ANDRZEJ JEREMIENKO.

Bomis Spółka z o.o.: 00-926 Warsaw, ul. Zurawia 6/12; tel. (22) 288181; telex 812773; fax (22) 295354; exports and imports machines, raw and reclaimed materials; co-operation in trade turnover, custom storehouses; Dir ZYGMUNT MAJZEL.

Budex: 42-200 Częstochowa, Sobieskiego 9; tel. (34) 44627; telex 037443; fax (34) 44761; civil and industrial construction; Gen. Dir LECH REGULSKI.

Budimex Spółka z o.o.: 00-926 Warsaw, Marszałkowska 82; tel. (22) 292397; telex 813473; fax (22) 213853; industrial building, civil engineering, housing, assembly works, land reclamation; Dir GRZEGORZ TUDEREK.

Bumar: 00-828 Warsaw, Al. Jana Pawla II 11; tel. (22) 295270; telex 814805; fax (22) 243807; f. 1971; construction equipment; Dir BOGUSŁAW JARZYŃSKI.

Bumar-Labedy: 44-109 Gilwice, ul. Mechaników 9; tel. (32) 345111; telex 036553; fax (32) 342514; f. 1951; steel machinery and parts for agriculture and construction; Pres. and Gen. Dir JÓZEF JĘDRUCH.

H. Cegielski: 60-965 Poznań, ul. 28 Czerwca 1956 r. 223/229; tel. (61) 333954; telex 0413451; fax (61) 321541; f. 1846; exports power equipment, marine engines, railway locomotives and carriages, etc.; Man. Dir ZBIGNIEW ROSOLSKI; 8,200 employees.

Centromor SA: 80-819 Gdańsk, ul. Okopowa 7; tel. (58) 380000; telex 512161; fax (58) 319428; f. 1950; import and export of ships and marine equipment; Man. Dir RYSZARD FERWORN.

Centrozap Co Ltd: 40-085 Katowice, ul. Mickiewicza 29; tel. (32) 513401; telex 0315771; fax (32) 598658; imports and exports complete plants, machines and equipment for the metallurgical, foundry and mining industries, air conditioning, etc.; Dir-Gen. STANISŁAW LABIŚ.

Cepelia Spółka z o.o.: 00-950 Warsaw, ul. Łucka 11; tel. (22) 205001; telex 813671; fax (22) 204002; export of artistic and folk handicraft articles; Man. Dir TADEUSZ KUBICKI.

Chemobudowa: 30-104 Kraków, ul. Stachowicza 18, POB 7; tel. (12) 228066; telex 0322371; fax (12) 210333; civil engineering; Dir-Gen. JERZY MALOST.

Ciech Spółka z o.o.: 00-950 Warsaw, Powazkowska 46–50; tel. (2) 6391000; telex 814561; fax (2) 6391451; imports and exports organic and inorganic chemicals, dyestuffs, fertilizers, paints, varnishes, enamels, cosmetics, petroleum products, rubber and synthetic rubber products, plastics, sulphur and pharmaceutical products; Dir MARIAN MAŁECKI.

Confexim Spółka z o.o.: 90-950 Łódź, ul. Kościuszki 123; tel. (42) 363522; telex 886877; fax (42) 363045; import and export of garments, fabrics and other textile products; Gen. Dir ANDRZEJ KEMP.

Coopexim Ltd: 00-975 Warsaw, Puławska 14, POB 215; tel. (22) 494851; telex 814211; fax (22) 492851; import and export of household goods, toys, folk art; Dir PRZEMYSŁAW DELATKIEWICZ.

M. Czarnecki SA: 00-950 Warsaw, ul. Marszałkowska 87, POB 215; tel. (2) 6280296; telex 813278; fax (22) 295943; representation of foreign firms in Poland; Dir TADEUSZ WYZGAL.

Dal SA: 00-683 Warsaw, Al. Jerozolimskie 65/79; tel. (22) 300460; telex 817226; fax (22) 300461; international trading company, barter and compensation transactions, mediation through its affiliated companies all over the world; Dir MAREK PIETKIEWICZ.

Diora: 58-200 Dzierzoniow, ul. Swidnicka 38; tel. (74) 322200; telex 0745231; fax (74) 318561; audio and visual electronic equipment; Chair. and Gen. Dir EUGENIUSZ NOWAK.

Dromex: 02-105 Warsaw, Trojańska 7; tel. (22) 463901; telex 815473; fax (22) 461319; f. 1967; export of road, bridge, railway and airfield construction work; Gen. Man. JERZY TREPIŃSKI.

Dynamo: 00-950 Warsaw, ul. Stawki 2; tel. (2) 6356864; telex 813428; fax (2) 6356838; import-export and barter business, representation of foreign firms in Poland; Dir HENRYK KOZIARA.

Elana: 87-100 Toruń, Curie-Skłodowskiej 73; tel. (56) 484345; telex 0555161; fax (56) 398406; synthetic fibres; Gen. Dir STANISŁAW CZUSZEL.

Elektrim SA: 00-950 Warsaw, Chałubińskiego 8, POB 638; tel. (22) 301000; telex 814351; fax (22) 300841; f. 1945; imports and exports power engineering technology, transmission, electrical and telecommunication equipment; Man. Dir ANDRZEJ SKOWROŃSKI.

Elwro: 53-238 Wrocław, Ostrowskiego 30; tel. (71) 610621; telex 0712423; fax (71) 617233; manufacture and export of computer systems, microcomputers, industrial automation and control systems, teleprocessing systems, other computer equipment (hardware and software), calculators, etc.; Man. Dir WŁADYSŁAW KIERZKOWSKI.

Energomontaz-Polnac: 00-950 Warsaw, ul. Nowy Swiat 9; tel. (22) 282392; telex 813429; fax (22) 296324; manufacture and service of power and industrial engineering installations; Man. Dir KAZIMIERZ ZUKOWSKI.

Energopol: 00-950 Warsaw, ul. Nowogrodzka 21, POB 367; tel. (22) 298081; telex 813663; fax (22) 290412; f. 1974; contractors and designers, civil engineering projects, pipelines; Dir JANUSZ GÓRZNY.

Exbud SA: 25-363 Kielce, Wesola 51; tel. (41) 43445; telex 613396; fax (41) 48894; construction company; privatized; Pres. WITOLD ZARASKA.

Eximpol SA: 00-950 Warsaw, Stawki 2, POB 810; tel. (2) 6357641; telex 814640; fax (2) 6353544; representation of foreign firms in Poland; Gen. Dir MAREK DZIUGIEŁŁ.

Expolco Holding SA and Expolco Trading Spółka z o.o.: 01-698 Warsaw, ul. Smoleńska 1/10; tel. (22) 332086; telex 816029; fax (22) 332084; international trade, financial transactions, export of wood, metal and plastic goods, ready-made clothing, knitwear, foodstuffs, technical service; import of consumer goods, materials and instruments; Gen. Dir KRZYSZTOF SRTRZAŁKOWSKI.

Fabryka Samochodow Ciezarowych—FSC: 27-200 Starachowice, ul. Maja 1; tel. 8831; telex 612571; fax 7038; goods vehicles, parts and assemblies; Gen. Dir JANUSZ KROLIKOWSKI.

Fabryka Samochodow Malolitra Zowych—FSM: 43-301 Bielsko-Biała, ul. Komorowicke 79; tel. (30) 20264; telex 0355753; fax (30) 35330; passenger car manufacture (incl. Fiat 126 and Cinquecento).

Fabryka Samochodow Osobowych—FSO: 03-215 Warsaw, ul. Stalingradzka 50; tel. (22) 110211; telex 814571; passenger car manufacture (incl. Fiat 125); Gen. Dir Dr HENRYK OLENIAK.

Film Polski Film Agency: 00-048 Warsaw, Mazowiecka 6/8; tel. (22) 268455; telex 813640; fax (22) 275784; f. 1964; promotion of Polish film, imports and exports films for television and the cinema, production services, distribution; Gen. Man. ADAM LASKOWSKI.

Furnel International Ltd Spółka z o.o.: 00-950 Warsaw, Al. Jerozolimskie 65/69, POB 670; tel. (22) 300467; telex 817543; fax (22) 306525; 8 regional offices; production and export of furniture, wooden goods, electronic and telecommunication equipment; Pres. JAN BANDURSKI.

Gdanska Stocznia Remontowa: Gdańsk 80-958, ul. Ostrowiu 1; tel. (58) 371300; telex 311281; ship repairs and conversions; Gen. Dir PIOTR SOYKA.

Geokart: 00-950 Warsaw, ul. Jasna 2/4; tel. (22) 273278; telex 812770; fax (22) 277629; geodesic and cartographic work and service; Dir JERZY WYSOCKI.

C. Hartwig: 00-950 Warsaw, Poznańska 15, POB 375; tel. (22) 296031; telex 814601; fax (22) 291581; f. 1858; also Katowice, Gdynia, Gdańsk, Szczecin; sole forwarding agent for rail, air, sea, river and road transport; Dir ZYGMUNT KORDECKI.

Hortex: 00-034 Warsaw, ul. Warecka 11A; tel. (22) 277174; telex 816611; fax (22) 270251; exports fresh, frozen and processed fruits and vegetables, forest fruits, mushrooms, honey and flowers, potatoes and potato products, seeds, herbs and snails; imports fresh and processed fruit and vegetables, foodstuffs, manufactured consumer articles, machinery, equipment, etc.; Dir LUDWIK OLEJARZ.

Hortex-Trading Spółka z o.o.: 31-027 Kraków, ul. Legnicka 5; tel. (12) 229801; telex 0322602; fax (12) 270522; export-import and sale of items of food, sporting and leisure equipment; Dir ZOFIA BURDA.

Huta Katowice SA: 41-308 Dabrowa Gornicza; tel. (32) 622256; telex 0315562; fax (32) 255200; steel mill; Pres. EMIL WASACZ.

Huta Sendzimira: 30-969 Kraków, ul. Ujastek; tel. (12) 448866; telex 0322441; fax (12) 447496; f. 1954; rolled steel, galvanized steel and steel products; Gen. Dir JERZY KNAPIK.

Huta Stalowa Wola: 37-450 Stalowa Wola, ul. Kwiatkowskiego 1; tel. (16) 435261; telex 062233; fax (16) 425566; heavy construction equipment, steel foundry products; Gen. Dir RYSZARD KAPUSTA.

Impexmetal: 00-842 Warsaw, Łucka 7/9, POB 62; tel. (2) 6586000; telex 814371; fax (22) 200544; f. 1953; imports and exports non-ferrous metals, ball and roller bearings; Dir EDWARD WOJTULEWICZ.

Interpegro SA: 03-839 Warsaw, ul. Grochowska 320; tel. (22) 106375; fax (22) 135585; export-import foodstuffs, agricultural products, flowers, fresh and processed fruit and vegetables, electronic, telecommunication equipment and service, etc.; Pres. JAN ZBIGNIEW HRYNIEWICZ.

Intraco: 00-950 Warsaw, POB 912, ul. Stawki 2; tel. (2) 6356002; telex 812341; fax (2) 6355418; exports building services, interior architecture; imports equipment and spare parts; Dir JERZY PIETRULA.

KGHM Polska Miedz SA: 59-301 Lublin, ul. M. Skłodowskiej-Curie 48; tel. (70) 461110; telex 782277; fax (70) 461100; f. 1961; mining of copper ore and processing of refined copper; Exec. Chair. KRZYSZTOF SĘDZIKOWSKI; 28,000 employees.

Kolmex: 00-844 Warsaw, Grzybowska 80/82, POB 236; tel. (2) 6615000; telex 813270; fax (22) 209381; imports and exports railway rolling-stock and containers; Dir ANDZREJ NAŁĘCZ.

Kopex: 40-952 Katowice, Grabowa 1, POB 245; tel. (32) 581631; telex 315681; fax (32) 580040; exports and imports machinery, equipment and appliances for mining, drilling and other engineering industries; consultancy services; Gen. Dir EUGENIUSZ KUCZKA.

Krakowskie Przedsibiorstwo Instalacji Sanitarnych: 31-503 Kraków, ul. Lubicz 27; tel. (12) 211099; telex 0325428; fax (12) 212193; construction of domestic and industrial sanitary installations; Gen. Dir STANISŁAW ZIMNY.

Labimex Spółka z o.o.: 00-950 Warsaw, Krakowskie Przedmieście 79, POB 261; tel. (22) 266431; telex 814230; fax (22) 261941; f. 1973; exports and imports medical, scientific and research apparatus, teaching aids, laboratory equipment, optical and geodetic instruments; Dir-Gen. JERZY RYCHTER.

Metalexport Ltd: 00-950 Warsaw, Mokotowska 49, POB 642; tel. (2) 6282291; telex 814241; fax (2) 6286561; f. 1949; exports and imports technological equipment, complete engineering plants, tools and machine tools; Dir Dr JERZY ZIELIŃSKI.

Metronex Spółka z o.o.: 00-950 Warsaw, Mysia 2, POB 198; tel. (22) 291699; fax (2) 6288274; exports and imports measurement instruments, process control devices, nuclear engineering equipment, computers, software, office equipment, etc.; Dir ANDRZEJ ZIAJA.

Minex Spółka z o.o.: 00-950 Warsaw, Chałubińskiego 8, POB 1002; tel. (22) 300500; telex 814401; fax (22) 300448; f. 1949; exports and imports minerals, cement, glass and ceramics; Dir JÓZEF KOSTERA.

Mundial Spółka z o.o.: 00-717 Warsaw, Czerniakowska 58; tel. (22) 414015; telex 813689; fax (22) 402006; representation of foreign firms in Poland, import-export; Dir WALDEMAR PIOTROWSKI.

Navimor Import-Export Co. Ltd: 80-890 Gdańsk, ul. Heweliusza 11, POB 423; tel. (58) 316821; telex 0512453; fax (58) 314497; ship repairs, import and export of shipyard installations, floating docks and pontoons, yachts, river vessels and coasters, fishing vessels, marine equipment, motors for small craft; Dir KRZYSZTOF BANASZAK.

Pagart: 00-078 Warsaw, Pl. Marszałka Józefa Piłsudskiego 9; tel. (22) 260145; telex 813639; fax (22) 275397; f. 1957; represents Polish artists abroad and organizes guest performances of foreign artists in Poland; Gen. Dir WŁODZIMIERZ SANDECKI.

Paged: 00-950 Warsaw, Pl. Trzech Krzyży 18, POB 991; tel. (2) 6238100; telex 814221; fax (2) 6281396; f. 1932; imports machinery and equipment for wood and paper industries, exports furniture, pulp and paper, boards and wooden products; Dir-Gen. MIRON TRZECIAK.

Petrochemia Plock SA: 09-403 Plock, ul. Chemikow 7; tel. (24) 653150; telex 83341; fax (24) 653180; crude petroleum processing and manufacture of petrochemical products; state-owned joint-stock co; Gen. Dir KONRAD JASKOLA.

Pewex: 00-697 Warsaw, Al. Jerozolimskie 65/79, POB 240; tel. (22) 300170; telex 815404; fax (22) 300172; import of consumer goods, raw materials, etc.; Dir MARIAN W. ZACHARSKI.

Pezetel Spółka z o.o.: 00-991 Warsaw 44, Al. Stanów Zjednoczonych 61; tel. (22) 108001; telex 812815; fax (22) 132356; import and export of aircraft, helicopters, sailplanes, turboshaft, jet, and radial-piston aircraft engines, diesel engines, generators, air equipment, electric carts, pneumatics, hydraulics, motor cycles, aviation and agricultural services; Dir JERZY KRĘŻLEWICZ.

Polcargo Inspection: 81-963 Gdynia, ul. Żeromskiego 32, POB 223; tel. (58) 205371; telex 054247; fax (58) 216819; f. 1949; international superintendence and testing services; Dir SŁAWOMIR WŁADYKO.

Polcomex SA: 00-061 Warsaw, Marszałkowska 140, POB 478; tel. (22) 266810; telex 813452; fax (22) 278441; representation of foreign firms in Poland; Dir ANDRZEJ ONACIK.

Polcoop SA: 00-950 Warsaw, Kopernika 30, POB 199; tel. (22) 262363; telex 814451; fax (22) 271053; f. 1957; exports foodstuffs, agricultural products, incl. fruit, vegetables and meat; imports fertilizers, fresh and processed fruit and vegetables, machinery, equipment, spare parts, etc.; Pres. JAN WAGA.

Polexpo: 02-232 Warsaw, Łopuszańska 38, POB 125; tel. (22) 460401; telex 813633; fax (22) 464591; f. 1950; design, construction and display of international fairs, exhibitions; Dir JERZY KARAIM.

Poliglob SA: 00-950 Warsaw, ul. Stawki 2, POB 40; tel. and fax (2) 6353689; telex 813557; f. 1950; representation of foreign firms in Poland; brs in Gdańsk, Katowice and Łódź; Dir RYSZARD JAROSZYŃSKI.

Polimar SA: 00-950 Warsaw, ul. Stawki 2, POB 151; tel. (2) 6350187; telex 814895; fax (2) 6355154; international trading company; Dir WALERIAN CHRYSZCZANOWICZ.

Polimex-Cekop Ltd: 00-950 Warsaw, Czackiego 7/9, POB 815; tel. (2) 6237101; telex 814231; fax (22) 260493; f. 1945; exports and imports machines and complete plants; Dir MAZIEJ MĘCLEWSKI.

Polmos: 00-006 Warsaw, ul. Szkolna 2/4, POB 160; tel. (22) 265031; telex 813445; alcoholic beverages.

POL-MOT Co Ltd: 03-370 Warsaw, Stalingradzka 23; tel. (22) 111093; telex 813901; fax (22) 111826; f. 1968; import and export of cars, lorries, buses, service stations, repair equipment, etc.; Gen. Dir ANDRZEJ ZARAJCZYK.

Polservice: 00-613 Warsaw, Chałubinskiego 8; tel. (22) 300522; telex 813539; fax (22) 300076; export and import of consulting and technical services, transfer of technology; Dir JERZY FIJAŁKOWSKI.

Polskie Wydawnictwo Muzyczne: 31-111 Kraków, Al. Krasińskiego 11A; tel. and fax (12) 220174; f. 1945; import and export of musical material; Dir ADAM NEUER; see also under Publishers.

PZL-Mielec Transport Equipment Corporation: 39-300 Mielec, ul. Wojska Polskiego 3; tel. (196) 7000; telex 0632293; fax (196) 7451; manufactures aircraft and vehicles; Gen. Dir JAN M. SZYMAŃSKI; 10,400 employees.

Remex Spółka z o.o.: 00-950 Warsaw, Bracka 25; tel. (22) 276021; telex 815387; fax (22) 274472; f. 1977; export of Polish handicraft articles and services; Gen. Dir JÓZEF GŁOWANIA.

Rolimpex: 00-613 Warsaw, ul. Chałubińskiego 8, POB 364; tel. (22) 300636; telex 814341; fax (22) 301867; f. 1951; exports and imports agricultural products of vegetable origin; Dir ROMAN MŁYNIEC.

RYBEX Co Ltd: 70-656 Szczecin, ul. Energetyków 3/4; tel. (91) 624490; telex 0422326; fax (91) 34247; sole exporter and importer of fish and fish products; exports technical service for fishing and fish processing; Gen. Man. WOJCIECH POLACZEK.

SGS-PTK Supervise Ltd: 81-369 Gdynia, Derdowskiego 7, POB 167; tel. (58) 206001; telex 054446; fax (58) 207975; f. 1947; quality and quantity control, supervisions, appraisals and evaluations for privatizations and joint ventures, environmental services; Dir MAREK SZWAJ.

Shipcontrol: 81-334 Gdynia, Polska 21; tel. (58) 207096; telex 054271; fax (58) 210212; f. 1963; tallying, weighing and gauging of cargo, stowage plans and supervision, inspection of containers, etc.; Dir BOGDAN OBSZARSKI.

Skórimpex Spółka z o.o.: 90-950 Łódź, Traktorowa 128, POB 133; tel. (42) 524000; telex 885251; fax (42) 521306; imports skins, hides, leathers, footwear, fur and leather goods, etc.; exports shoes, leather, fur and sheepskin garments, skins, hides, etc.; Dir IRENEUSZ MINTUS.

Spedrapid Spółka z o.o.: 81-361 Gdynia, Zgoda 8, POB 201; tel. (58) 216085; telex 054321; fax (58) 216614; f. 1949; freight-forwarding company; Chair. PAVEL MÜLLER; Dir WITOLD GÓRSKI.

Stalexport: 40-085 Katowice, Mickiewicza 29, POB 401; tel. (32) 512211; telex 0315751; fax (32) 511941; exports and imports rolled steel products, high quality steel, tubes, ores, pig iron, ferro alloys, power-generating units, ceramic tiles; Gen. Dir RYSZARD HARHALA.

Textilimpex Spółka z o.o.: 90-950 Łódź, ul. Traugutta 25, POB 320; tel. (42) 361638; telex 886471; fax (42) 788375; import and export of textile goods and raw materials for the textile industry; Dir DONAT ŁAWNICZAK.

Timex Spółka z o.o.: 00-238 Warsaw, ul. Długa 23/25; tel. (2) 6354824; telex 812396; fax (2) 3115148; f. 1947; import, export and representation of foreign firms; Dir Dr STANISŁAW LESZKOWICZ.

Torimex Spółka z o.o.: 00-691 Warsaw, ul. Nowogrodzka 35/41, POB 394; tel. (22) 216652; telex 813611; fax (22) 211796; import and export within exchange market, suppliers of stores in Poland and abroad with imported consumer goods, compensatory transactions, rustic restaurant interiors; Dir RYSZARD BACHURA.

Transactor SA: 00-950 Warsaw, Stawki 2, POB 276; tel. (2) 6355221; telex 813288; fax (2) 6357017; representation of foreign firms in Poland; Gen. Dir STANISŁAW JAKUBCZYK.

Tricot Spółka z o.o.: 90-361 Łódź, ul. Piotrkowska 270, POB 278; tel. (42) 810211; telex 884545; fax (42) 817936; became limited liability company in Jan. 1983, continuing activities of former state-owned Textilimpex-Tricot; import and export of textile goods, especially knitwear; Man. Dir ANDRZEJ MORYC.

Unitech: 02-237 Warsaw, ul. Instalatorów 7; tel. (22) 464078; telex 825524; marine service bureau; servicing of equipment on ships in foreign and Polish ports; brs in Gdynia and Szczecin; Man. Dir JERZY JACNIACKI.

Unitex SA: 00-950 Warsaw, Stawki 2, POB 404; tel. (2) 6353619; telex 817478; fax (2) 6356545; Dir CZESŁAW GRAD.

UNITRA Trading and Industrial Corporation: 00-950 Warsaw, ul. Nowogrodzka 50, POB 66; tel. (22) 213382; telex 814878; fax (22) 214761; hi-tech equipment, industrial systems, electronic and other goods; consultancy and promotional services; Dir JAN BRUKSZO.

Universal SA: 00-950 Warsaw, Al. Jerozolimskie 44, POB 370; tel. (2) 6936091; telex 814431; fax (22) 278312; export and import of electrical household appliances, metal, plastic and glass household goods, sports and camping equipment, metal goods, food and agricultural products, chemical goods; Gen. Dir DARIUSZ PRZYWIECZERSKI.

Universal-Kraktrade SA: 30-960 Kraków, ul. Floriańska 3, POB 181; tel. (12) 222398; telex 0326335; fax (12) 222398; export and import of commercial articles, building design and consultancy services, etc.; Dir MAREK STRUTYŃSKI.

Ursus: 02-945 Warsaw, Traktorzystów 10; tel. (2) 6626713; telex 813939; fax (2) 6670545; tractor manufacturers; Gen. Dir (vacant).

Varimex: 00-950 Warsaw, Wilcza 50/52, POB 263; tel. (22) 288041; telex 814311; fax (22) 218519; f. 1945; import and export of medical and photographic equipment, valves and fittings, fire-fighting equipment, building hardware, catering and typographic equipment; import of textile machines; Dir ANDRZEJ SOBCZYK.

Węglokoks: 40-185 Katowice, ul. A. Mickiewicza 29; tel. (32) 582431; telex 0315641; fax (32) 515453; imports and exports coal, coke, gas; Dir JAN BARAŃSKI.

Zakłady Wlokien Chemicznych Wistom: 97-200 Tomaszów Mazowiecki, ul. Spalska 103/105; tel. (45) 2301; telex 886214; fax (45) 5248; synthetic fibres; Gen. Man. ZDZISŁAW RACZYŃSKI ; 3,800 employees.

ZELMER—Zakłady Zmechanizowanego Sprzetu Domwego: 35-016 Rzeszów, ul. Hoffmanowej 19; tel. (17) 37431; telex 0632389; fax (17) 36178; domestic and kitchen appliances; Gen. Dir BOGUSŁAW MADERA; 3,900 employees.

TRADE UNIONS

In April 1989, after two months of 'round-table' talks, Solidarity and the Government reached agreement on extensive political and economic reforms, as a result of which legal status (removed upon the declaration of martial law in December 1981) was restored to Solidarity and to Rural Solidarity, the independent farmers' union.

All Poland Trade Unions Alliance (Ogólnopolskie Porozumienie Związków Zawodowych—OPZZ): 00-924 Warsaw, Kopernika 36/40; tel. (22) 267102; telex 813834; fax (22) 265102; f. 1984; 4.5m. mems (1991); Chair. EWA SPYCHALSKA.

Independent Self-governing Trade Union Solidarity National Commission (NSZZ Solidarność Komisja Krajowa): 80-855 Gdańsk, Wały Piastowskie 24; tel. (58) 316722; telex 513170; fax (58) 316722; f. 1980; outlawed 1981–89; 2.5m. mems; Chair. MARIAN KRZAKLEWSKI.

Rural (Private Farmers') Solidarity: Leader PIOTR BAUMGART.

TRADE FAIRS

Poznań International Fair Ltd: 60-734 Poznań, ul. Głogowska 14; tel. (61) 692592; telex 413251; fax (61) 665827; f. 1921; international fair of investment goods in June and 24 other fairs (one in Katowice); 14,000 exhibitors, 1m. visitors annually; Pres. STANISŁAW LASKOWSKI.

Transport

RAILWAYS

At the end of 1992 there were 25,254 km of railway lines making up the state network, of which 11,496 km were electrified and 1,855 km were narrow gauge. Substantial modernization, with assistance from the World Bank and other sources, was planned for the 1990s.

Polish State Railways (Polskie Koleje Państwowe—PKP): 00-928 Warsaw, ul. Chałubińskiego 4; tel. (22) 244400; telex 816651; fax (22) 212705; f. 1842; Dir-Gen. ALEKSANDER JANISZEWSKI.

ROADS

In December 1991 there were 365,365 km of roads, of which 257 km were motorways, 45,342 km were national roads and 128,705 km were provincial roads.

PKS/Państwowa Komunikacja Samochodowa (Polish Motor Communications): 00-973 Warsaw, ul. Grójecka 17; tel. (22) 220011; telex 816598; f. 1945; state enterprise organizing inland road transport for passengers and goods. Bus routes cover a total of 121,000 km; passengers carried 2,553,968 (1989); freight 7,650m. ton-kilometres (1989).

Pekaes Auto-Transport SA: 01-204 Warsaw, ul. Siedmiogrodzka 1/3; tel. (2) 3222519; telex 817419; fax (22) 321092; f. 1958; road transport of goods to all European and Middle East countries.

INLAND WATERWAYS

Poland has 6,850 km of waterways, of which 3,997 km were navigable in 1989. The main rivers are the Vistula (1,047 km), Oder (742 km in Poland), Bug (587 km in Poland), Warta (808 km), San, Narew, Noteć, Pilica, Wieprz and the Dunajec. There are some 5,000 lakes, the largest being the Śniardwy, Mamry, Łebsko, Dąbie and Miedwie. In addition, there is a network of canals (approximately 1,215 km).

About 3,816,000 passengers and 9,795,000 tons of freight were carried on inland water transport in 1990.

Zjednoczenie Żeglugi Śródlądowej (United Inland Navigation and River Shipyards): 50-149 Wrocław 2, Wita Stwosza 28; includes five inland navigation enterprises and eight inland shipyards.

SHIPPING

Poland has three large harbours on the Baltic Sea: Gdynia, Gdańsk and Szczecin. The Polish merchant fleet had 673 ships in June 1991, with a total displacement of 3,348,443 grt.

Principal shipping companies:

Polskie Linie Oceaniczne—PLO (Polish Ocean Lines): 81-364 Gdynia, ul. 10 Lutego 24, POB 265; tel. (58) 201901; telex 054231; fax (58) 278480; f. 1951; 16 ships totalling 163,474 dwt and serving all five continents; Dir-Gen. HENRYK DĄBROWSKI; Exec. Dir ANDRZEJ WALENCIAK.

Polska Żegluga Morska—PZM (Polish Steamship Co): 70-419 Szczecin, Plac Rodła 8; tel. (91) 533958; telex 422136; fax (91) 344346; f. 1951; world-wide tramping; fleet of 118 vessels totalling 3,008,775 dwt (Dec. 1991); Chair. and Dir-Gen. FRANCISZEK MAKAREWICZ.

Przedsiębiorstwo Połowów Dalekomorskich i Usług Rybackich Gryf: 70-952 Szczecin, Port Rybacki, ul. Władysława IV 1; tel. (91) 533772; telex 0425491; fax (91) 47989; f. 1957; deep-sea fishing and fish-processing; Man. Dir PIOTR JASNOWSKI.

CIVIL AVIATION

Okęcie international airport is situated near Warsaw. A city terminal was completed in October 1989 under a joint-venture scheme with Austrian and US interests. A new airport terminal was scheduled for completion in 1992. There are also international airports at Kraków and Gdańsk. Domestic flights serve Gdańsk, Goleniow, Katowice, Kraków, Poznań, Rzeszów, Szczecin, Warsaw and Wrocław.

Polskie Linie Lotnicze—LOT (Polish Airlines—LOT): 00-697 Warsaw, Al. Jerozolimskie 65/79; tel. (2) 6283443; telex 813552; fax (22) 305860; f. 1929; domestic services and international services to the Middle East, Africa, Asia, Canada, USA, and throughout Europe; privatization announced, Feb. 1991; Pres. JAN LITWIŃSKI.

Tourism

The Polish Tourist and Country Lovers' Society is responsible for tourism and maintains about 420 branches across the country. The Society runs about 250 hotels, hostels and campsites. Poland is rich in historic cities, such as Gdańsk, Wrocław, Kraków and Warsaw. There are 30 health and climatic resorts, while the mountains, forests and rivers provide splendid scenery and excellent facilities for touring and sporting holidays. In 1991 Poland was visited by 36.8m. foreign tourists. In 1993 some 4.5m. foreign tourists visited Warsaw; about 50% of these were from the former USSR.

Polish Tourist and Country-Lovers' Society (Polskie Towarzystwo Turystyczno-Krajoznawcze): 00-075 Warsaw, ul. Senatorska 11; tel. (22) 265735; telex 812441; fax (22) 262505; f. 1950; Chair. ADAM CHYŻEWSKI; the Society has about 250 tourist accommodation establishments; 145,000 mems (1993).

Orbis SA: 00-028 Warsaw, str. Bracka 16; tel. (22) 260271; telex 814757; fax (22) 273301; f. 1923; national tourist enterprise; Gen. Man. JACEK WRÓBEL; 162 branch offices and 54 tourist hotels.

Culture

NATIONAL ORGANIZATIONS

Ministry of Culture: see section on The Government (Ministries); includes:

Institute of Culture (Instytut Kultury): 00-075 Warsaw, ul. Senatorska 13/15; tel. (22) 262477; fax (22) 261069; f. 1974; research centre for Polish culture; Dir Prof. TERESA KOSTYRKO.

Polish Cultural Foundation (Fundacja Kultury Polskiej): 00-252 Warsaw, ul. Podwale 1/3; tel. (2) 6357628; telex 812732; f. 1988; promotes Polish culture of all kinds both in Poland and world-wide; Chair. Prof. STANISŁAW WISŁOCKI; Pres. Dr TADEUSZ POLAK.

CULTURAL HERITAGE

History Museum of the City of Kraków (Muzeum Historyczne m. Krakowa): 31-011 Kraków, Krzysztofory, Rynek Główny 35; tel. (12) 223264; f. 1899; Dir ANDRZEJ SZCZYGIEŁ.

History Museum of the City of Warsaw (Muzeum Historyczne m. st. Warszawy): 00-272 Warsaw, Rynek Starego Miasta 28; tel. (2) 6351625; f. 1947; collections covering the history of Warsaw from the 10th century onwards; Dir Prof. Dr JANUSZ DURKO.

Jagiellonian Library (Biblioteka Jagiellońska): 30-059 Kraków, ul. Mickiewicza 22; tel. (12) 336377; telex 325682; f. 1364; national library for books up to 1800; Dir Dr KRZYSZTOF ZAMORSKI.

National Library (Biblioteka Narodowa): 00-973 Warsaw, Al. Niepodległości 213; tel. (22) 259270); telex 817183; f. 1928; Dir Dr STANISŁAW CZAJKA.

National Museum (Muzeum Narodowe): 00-495 Warsaw, Al. Jerozolimskie 3; tel. (22) 211031; f. 1862; historical and art collections; Dir Dr MARIAN SOŁTYSIAK.

National Museum in Kraków (Muzeum Narodowe w Krakowie): 31-109 Kraków, ul. Piłsudskiego 12, POB 875; tel. (12) 221528; f. 1879; historical and art collections; Dir TADEUSZ CHRUŚCICKI.

State Archaeological Museum (Państwowe Muzeum Archeologiczne): 00-950 Warsaw, ul. Długa 52, POB 69; tel. (22) 313221; telex 816700; fax (22) 315195; f. 1923; Dir Dr JAN JASKANIS.

State Ethnographic Museum in Warsaw (Państwowe Muzeum Etnograficzne w Warszawie): 00-056 Warsaw, ul. Kredytowa 1; tel. (22) 277641; f. 1888; Polish and non-European collections; Dir Dr JAN WITOLD SULIGA.

SPORTING ORGANIZATION

Olympic Committee of the Republic of Poland: 00-483 Warsaw, ul. Frascati 4; tel. (2) 6285038; telex 813522; fax (22) 813522;

f. 1918; Pres. ALEKSANDER KWASNIEWSKI; Sec.-Gen. TADEUSZ WROBLEWSKI.

PERFORMING ARTS

Theatre

National Folk Theatre of Kraków (Państwowy Teatr Ludowy w Krakowie): 31-943 Kraków, ul. ós Teatralne 34.

Warsaw Contemporary Theatre (Teatr Współczesny w Warszawie): 00-640 Warsaw, ul. Mokotowska 13.

National Theatre of Poland in Warsaw (Państwowy Teatr Polski w Warszawie): 00-327 Warsaw, ul. Karasia 2.

National Modern Theatre in Warsaw (Państwowy Teatr Nowy w Warszawie): 02-503 Warsaw, ul. Puławska 37/39.

Opera Houses

Kraków Opera and Operetta (Opera i Operetka w Krakowie): 31-002 Kraków, ul Skarbowa 2.

Warsaw National Operetta (Państwowa Operetka w Warszawie): Warsaw, ul. Nowogrodzka 49.

Warsaw Chamber Opera (Warszawska Opera Kameralna): Warsaw, ul. Nowogrodzka 49.

Orchestras

Kraków National Philharmonic (Karol Szymanowski) Orchestra (Państwowa Filharmonia im. Karola Szymanowskiego w Krakowie): 31-103 Kraków, ul. Zwierzyniecka 1.

Warsaw National Philharmonic Orchestra (Filharmonia Narodowa w Warszawie): Warsaw, ul. Jasna 5.

ASSOCIATIONS

Art Historians Association: (Stowarzyszenie Historyków Sztuki): 00-272 Warsaw, Rynek Starego Miasta 27; tel. (22) 313773; Pres. Prof. Dr hab. MARIA POPRZECKA; 1,602 mems.

Association of Polish Film Artists (Stowarzyszenie Filmowców Polskich): 00-071 Warsaw, ul. Krakowskie Przedmieście 21/23; tel. (22) 263096; fax (2) 6351927; f. 1966; Pres. JAN KIDAWA-BŁOŃSKI.

Association of Polish Musicians (Stowarzyszenie Polskich Artystów Muzyków): 00-526 Warsaw, ul. Krucza 24/26; tel. (22) 218647; Pres. EUGENIUSZ SĄSIADEK.

Plastic Arts Association of Poland (Związek Polskich Artystów Plastyków): 00-554 Warsaw, ul. Marszałkowska 34/50; tel. (22) 211365; Pres. ZBIGNIEW MAKAREWICZ.

Polish Federation of Photographic Societies (Polska Federacja Stowarzyszeń Fotograficznych): 00-566 Warsaw, ul. Sniadeckich 10; tel. (22) 282862; Pres. ANDRZEJ PROTASIUK.

Polish PEN Club (Polski PEN Club): 00-079 Warsaw, ul. Krakowskie Przedmieście 87/89; tel. (22) 26-57-84; Pres. ARTUR MIĘDZYRZECKI.

Polish Society of Graphic Arts and Design (Stowarzyszenie Polskich Artystów Grafików, Projektantów): 00-496 Warsaw, ul. Nowy Świat 7, m. 6; tel. (22) 217819; Pres. STANISŁAW WIECZOREK.

Education

Children up to the age of seven years may attend crèches (złobki) and kindergartens (przedszkola). In 1990 46% of children between the ages of three and six years attended kindergarten, with 98% of all six-year olds attending a pre-school establishment. Education is free and compulsory for all children between the ages of seven and 14 years. Basic schooling begins at the age of seven years with the eight-year school (szkoła podstawowa), for which there is a common curriculum throughout the country.

Four years of free education leading to college or university entrance is available at general secondary schools (liceum ogólnokształcące) to pupils who are successful in the entrance examination. Other pupils, about 75% of those continuing their education beyond the age of 14, attend vocational and technical schools (technika zawodowe) or basic vocational schools (zasadnicze szkoły). Vocational and technical schools provide five-year courses combining vocational and general secondary education, and can lead to qualifications for entry into higher education. Basic vocational schools provide three-year courses consisting of three days' theoretical and three days' practical training per week; in addition, some general secondary education is provided.

There is a small number of private schools, administered under state supervision, and, in 1989, the Roman Catholic Church was granted the right to operate its own schools. In 1993 there were 117 higher education establishments in Poland, including 11 universities and 17 technical and agricultural universities. In 1990 government expenditure on education amounted to 28,249,900m. złotys, which was 14.6% of total budgetary expenditure.

UNIVERSITIES

Adam Mickiewicz University in Poznań (Uniwersytet im. Adama Mickiewicza w Poznaniu): 61-712 Poznań, ul. Henryka Wieniawskiego 1; tel. (61) 699251; telex 0413260; fax (61) 535535; f. 1919; 11 faculties; 1,917 teachers; 12,770 students; Rector Prof. Dr hab. JERZY FEDOROWSKI.

Catholic University of Lublin (Katolicki Uniwersytet Lubelski): 20-950 Lublin, al. Racławickie 14; tel. (81) 30426; telex 643235; fax (81) 30433; f. 1918; 5 faculties; 736 teachers; 8,000 students; Rector Rt Rev. Prof STANISŁAW WIELGUS.

Jagiellonian University (Uniwersytet Jagielloński): 31-007 Kraków, Gołębia 24; tel. (12) 221033; telex 322297; fax (12) 226306; f. 1364; 10 faculties; 2,800 teachers; 17,500 students; Rector Prof. Dr hab. ALEKSANDER KOJ.

Marie Curie-Skłodowska University (Uniwersytet Marii Curie-Skłodowskiej): 20-031 Lublin, Plac Marii Curie-Skłodowskiej 5; tel. (81) 375107; f. 1944; 9 faculties, 1 institute; 1,583 teachers; 19,500 students, incl. 6,650 extra-mural students; Rector Prof. Dr hab. EUGENIUSZ GASIOR.

Nicholas Copernicus University of Toruń (Uniwersytet Mikołaja Kopernika w Toruniu): 87-100 Toruń, ul. Gagarina 11; tel. (56) 22694; telex 0552412; fax (56) 24602; f. 1945; 9 faculties; 1,100 teachers; 12,000 students; Rector Prof. Dr hab. ANDRZEJ JAMIOŁKOWSKI.

Szczecin University (Uniwersytet Szczeciński): 70-540 Szczecin, ul. Korsarzy 1; tel. (91) 42992; telex 0422719; fax (91) 342992; f. 1985; 6 faculties, 1 institute; 900 teachers; 14,000 students; Rector Prof. Dr hab. HUBERT BRONK.

University of Gdańsk (Uniwersytet Gdański): 80-952 Gdańsk, ul. Bażyńskiego 1A; tel. (58) 525071; f. 1970; 7 faculties; 1,473 teachers; 12,394 students; Rector Prof. Dr hab. ZBIGNIEW GWIZDALA.

University of Łódź (Uniwersytet Łódzki): 90-131 Łódàz, Narutowicza 65; tel. (42) 354001; telex 886291; fax (42) 783958; f. 1945; 7 faculties; 1,901 teachers; 15,640 students; Rector Prof. Dr hab. MICHAŁ SEWERYŃSKI.

University of Silesia (Uniwersytet Śląski): 40-007 Katowice, Bankowa 12; tel. (32) 587231; telex 0315584; f. 1968; 10 faculties; 1,665 teachers; 27,876 students; Rector Prof. Dr MAKSYMILIAN PAZDAN.

University of Warsaw (Uniwersytet Warszawski): 00-325 Warsaw, Krakowskie Przedmieście 26/28; tel. (22) 200381; telex 815439; fax (22) 267520; f. 1818; 23 faculties, 1 institute, 1 affiliated college in Białystok; 839 teachers; 25,476 students; Rector Prof. ANDRZEJ WRÓBLEWSKI.

University of Wrocław (Uniwersytet Wrocławski): 50-137 Wrocław, Plac Uniwersytecki 1; tel. (71) 402212; telex 0712791; fax (71) 402800; f. 1702; 6 faculties; 1,710 teachers; 14,553 students; Rector Prof. Dr WOJCIECH WRZESIŃSKI.

Technical Universities

Agricultural University of Poznań (Akademia Rolnicza w Poznaniu): 60-637 Poznań, ul. Wojska Polskiego 28; tel. (61) 470334; telex 0413322; fax (61) 411022; f. 1951; 7 faculties; 724 teachers; 3,714 students; Rector Prof. Dr RYSZARD GANOWICZ.

Białystok Technical University (Politechnika Białostocka): 15-351 Białystok, ul. Wiejska 45A; tel. (85) 22393; telex 852424; f. 1949; 4 faculties, 1 institute; 440 teachers; 2,600 students; Rector Prof. Dr KAZIMIERZ PIEŃKOWSKI.

Częstochowa Technical University (Politechnika Częstochowska): 42-201 Częstochowa, ul. Dąbrowskiego 69; tel. (34) 252580; telex 037341; fax (34) 252385; f. 1949; 4 faculties; 427 teachers; 2,981 students; Rector Prof. Dr hab. Inż. JANUSZ BRASZCZYŃSKI.

Kielce University of Technology (Politechnika Świętokrzyska): 25-314 Kielce, al. Tysiąclecia Państwa Polskiego 7; tel. (41) 24100; f. 1965; 3 faculties; 340 teachers; 3,200 students; Rector Prof Dr hab. ANDRZEJ NEIMITZ.

Kraków University of Technology (Politechnika Krakowska im. Tadeusza Kościuszki): 31-155 Kraków, Warszawska 24; tel. (12) 330300; telex 0322468; fax (12) 348451; f. 1945; 6 faculties; 1,027 teachers; 5,224 students; Rector Prof. Dr hab. J. NIZIOŁ.

Łódź Technical University (Politechnika Łódzka): 90-924 Łódź, Żwirki 36; tel. (42) 312000; telex 886136; fax (42) 368522; f. 1945; 7 faculties, 2 institutes; 1,300 teachers; 8,200 students; Rector Prof. Dr hab. JAN KRYSIŃSKI.

Poznań Technical University (Politechnika Poznańska): 60-965 Poznań, pl. Skłodowskiej-Curie 5; tel. (61) 332581; telex 413250; fax (61) 330217; f. 1919; 5 faculties; 985 teachers; 4,253 students; Rector Prof. Dr hab. Inż. JAROSŁAW STEFANIAK.

Rzeszów Technical University (Politechnika Rzeszowska): 35-959 Rzeszow, ul. W. Pola 2; tel. (17) 43281; telex 0632224; fax (17) 41260; f. 1974 as a university; 4 faculties; 460 teachers; 5,500 students; Rector Prof. KAZIMIERZ OCZOŚ.

Silesian Technical University (Politechnika Śląska im. W. Pstrowskiego): 44-100 Gliwice, ul. Pstrowskiego 7; tel. (32) 312349; telex 036304; fax (32) 318085; f. 1945; 12 faculties; 1,600 teachers; 14,000 students; Rector Prof. Dr hab. Inż. WILIBALD WINKLER.

Szczecin Technical University (Politechnika Szczecińska): 70-310 Szczecin, al. Piastów 17; tel. (91) 347326; f. 1946; 5 faculties; 600 teachers; 4,150 students; Rector Prof Dr hab. Inż. STEFAN BERCZYŃSKI.

Technical University of Gdańsk (Politechnika Gdańska): 80-952 Gdańsk, ul. G. Narutowicza 11/12; tel. (58) 415791; fax (58) 415821; f. 1904; 10 faculties; 1,115 teachers; 8,400 students; Rector Prof. EDMUND WITTBRODT .

Technical University of Lublin (Politechnika Lubelska): 20-109 Lublin, ul. Bernardyńska 13; tel. (81) 22201; telex 642745; fax (81) 27364; f. 1953; 4 faculties; 485 teachers; 4,520 students; Rector Prof. Dr hab. Inż. WŁODZIMIERZ KROLOPP.

University of Agriculture in Lublin (Akademia Rolnicza w Lublinie): 20-934 Lublin, ul. Akademicka 13; tel. and fax (81) 33549; telex 0643176; f. 1955; 5 faculties; 599 staff; 5,100 students; Rector Prof. Dr hab. JÓZEF NURZYŃSKI.

University of Agriculture and Technology in Olsztyn (Akademia Rolniczo-Techniczna w Olsztynie im. Michała Oczapowskiego): 10-957 Olsztyn, Kortowo; tel. (89) 273310; telex 0526419; fax (89) 273908; f. 1950; 8 faculties; 5,000 students; Rector Prof. Dr hab. ANDRZEJ HOPFER.

University of Mining and Metallurgy (Akademia Górniczo-Hutnicza im. Stanisława Staszica w Krakowie): 30-059 Kraków, Al. Mickiewicza 30; tel. (12) 337600; telex 0322203; fax (12) 331014; f. 1919; 13 faculties; 1,519 teachers; 9,300 students; Rector Prof. Dr hab. Inż. MIROSŁAW HANDKE.

Warsaw University of Technology (Politechnika Warszawska): 00-661 Warsaw, Pl. Politechniki 1; tel. (22) 210070; telex 813307; fax (22) 292962; f. 1826; 16 faculties; 2,600 teachers; 18,500 students; Rector Prof. Dr Inż. MAREK DIETRICH.

Wrocław Technical University (Politechnika Wrocławska): 50-370 Wrocław, Wybrzeże Wyspiańskiego 27; tel. (71) 227336; telex 0712559; fax (71) 223664; f. 1945; 11 faculties; 1,750 teachers; 10,600 students; Rector Prof. ANDRZEJ WISZNIEWSKI.

Social Welfare

The Polish social-welfare system is controlled by the Ministries of Health and of Labour and Social Policy. Locally, the system is administered by the Health and Social Welfare Departments of the Presidiums of the National Councils. Medical care is provided free for all workers and rural population. Radical reforms to the health insurance scheme have been under consideration since 1989. The 1990 central government budget allocated a total of 32,671,300m. złotys, which was 16.9% of total budget expenditure, to public health and social welfare, and a further 16,543,400m. złotys (8.5% of budget expenditure) to social insurance.

At the end of 1990 there were 81,641 physicians and 18,205 dental surgeons in practice. There were 218,560 general hospital beds and a total of 3,328 health centres in operation. The Polish Red Cross organizes and undertakes the care of the sick at home and general home assistance to those who are incapacitated through ill health, etc. Alimony is assured by law to single mothers. Welfare benefits are available to the unemployed. Pensions are organized and managed by the Union of Pensioners, Invalids and Retired Persons.

NATIONAL AGENCIES

Ministry of Health: see section on The Government (Ministries).

Ministry of Labour and Social Policy: see section on The Government (Ministries).

HEALTH AND WELFARE ORGANIZATIONS

Institute of Labour and Social Affairs (Instytut Pracy i Spraw Socjalnych): 00-496 Warsaw, ul. Mysia 2; tel. (22) 219334; fax (2) 6284535; f. 1963; research on labour, wages, income distribution, living standards, social security and social insurance, and labour laws; Dir STANISŁAWA GOLINOWSKA.

Marie Skłodowska-Curie Memorial Cancer Centre and Institute of Oncology (Centrum Onkologii, Instytut im. Marii Skłodowskiej-Curie): 00-973 Warsaw, ul. Wawleska 15; tel. (22) 221276; telex 812704; fax (22) 222429; f. 1932; Dir Prof. A. KUŁAKOWSKI.

National Institute of Cardiology (Instytut Kardiologii): 04-628 Warsaw, ul. Alpejska 42; tel. (22) 153011; telex 816052; Dir Prof. ZYGMUNT SADOWSKI.

Tuberculosis and Pulmonary Diseases Institute (Instytut Gruàzlicy i Chorób Płuc): 01-138 Warsaw, ul. Płocka 26; tel. (22) 324451; f. 1948; Dir Prof. Dr hab. med. LILIA PAWLICKA.

The Environment

The environmental movement in Poland became of significance in the early 1980s, with several groups emerging from within the Solidarity trade union movement. There are more than 40 major ecological groups and several Green parties. The Polish Government maintains membership of the World Conservation Union—IUCN (based in Gland, Switzerland) and the Environmental Partnership for Central Europe.

GOVERNMENT ORGANIZATIONS

Ministry of Environmental Protection, Natural Resources and Forestry (Ministerstwo Ochrony Srodowiska, Zasobów Naturalnych i Leśnictwa): see section on The Government (Ministries); incl.:

Forestry Research Institute (Instytut Badawczy Leśnictwa): 00-973 Warsaw, ul. Bitwy Warszawskiej 1920, r. 3; tel. (22) 223201; telex 812476; fax (22) 224935; f. 1930; comprises 23 scientific sections covering all aspects of forestry, incl. environment; Dir Prof. Dr Eng. ANDRZEJ KLOCEK.

National Council for the Protection of Nature in Poland (Państwowa Rada Ochrony Przyrody): 00-922 Warsaw, ul. Wawelska 52–54; tel. (22) 251114; telex 812816; advises the Government on environmental matters; Sec. JAN LAPACZEWSKI.

The Ministry of Agriculture is also concerned with environmental matters (see section on The Government—Ministries).

Regional Organizations

Environmental Partnership for Central Europe: 50-020 Wrocław, Dom Technika NOT, ul. Piłsudskiego 74; tel. and fax (71) 31611; Principal Officer KRYSTYNA WOLNIAKOWSKI.

European Association of Environment and Resource Economists, Polish Division: 31-510 Kraków, ul. Rakowicka 27, Rm 155; tel. (12) 210099; fax (12) 212182; Head Dr KAZIMIERZ GURKO.

International Baltic Sea Fishery Commission: 00-528 Warsaw, ul. Hoza 20; tel. (2) 6288647; telex 817421; fax (2) 6253372; eight mems.

ACADEMIC INSTITUTES

Polish Academy of Sciences—PAN (Polska Akademia Nauk—PAN): 00-901 Warsaw, POB 24, Palac Kultury i Nauki; tel. (22) 200211; telex 813929; fax (22) 207651; f. 1952; Pres. Prof. ALEKSANDER GIEYSZTOR; attached research insts incl.:

Institute of Ecology (Instytut Ekologii PAN): 05-092 Łomianki, Dziekanów Lesny; tel. (22) 513047; telex 817378; f. 1952; Dir Prof. Dr KAZIMIERZ DOBROWOLSKI.

Institute of Environmental Engineering (Instytut Podstaw Inżynierii Środowiska PAN): 41-800 Zabrze, ul. M. Skłodowskiej-Curie 34; tel. (32) 716481; telex 036401; fax (32) 717470; f. 1961; air and water pollution control; Dir Assoc. Prof. JAN KAPALA.

Institute of Environmental Protection (Instytut Ochrony Środowiska—IOS): 00-548 Warsaw, ul. Krucza 5/11; tel. (22) 299254; telex 813493; research centre into major environmental issues.

Institute of Nature Conservation: 31-512 Kraków, ul. Lubicz 46; tel. (12) 210348; telex 322630; fax (12) 210348; research into natural biological processes, preservation of biodiversity and rare and threatened plant and animal species; research into the degradation of natural resources, changing ecosystems, water resources and landscape; Dir Prof. Dr ZYGMUNT DENISUK.

Institute of Physical Planning and Municipal Economy (Instytut Gospodarki Przestrzennej i Komunalnej): 02-078 Warsaw, Krzywickiego 9; tel. and fax (22) 250937; telex 813493; f. 1949; research on physical planning, municipal economy and architecture; Dir Prof. Dr ZYGMUNT NIEWIADOMSKI.

Institute of State and Law, Research Group on Environmental Law (Instytut Państwowa i Prawą PAN, Zespół Prawnych Problemow Ochrony i Kształtowania Środowiska): 00-330 Warsaw, Nowy Świat 72 (Palac Staszica); tel. (22) 267853; Dir Prof. JANUSZ ŁETOWSKI.

Research Centre for Agricultural and Forest Environmental Studies PAN (Zakład Badan Środowiska Rolniczego i Leśnego PAN): 60-479 Poznań, ul. Bukowska 19; tel. (61) 45601; fax (61) 43668; f. 1979; Dir Prof. Dr hab. LECH RYSZKOWSKI.

Silesian Technical University, Faculty of Environmental Protection: 44-100 Gliwice, ul. Pstrowskiego 7, Politechnika Śląska im. W. Pstrowskiego; tel. (32) 312349; telex 036304; fax (32) 318085; Faculty Dean Prof. Dr hab. Inż. MARIA ZDYBIEWSKA.

NON-GOVERNMENTAL ORGANIZATIONS

Biuro Obsługi Ruchu Ekologicznego (BORE—Service Office for the Environmental Movement—SOEM): 00-420 Warsaw, ul. Szara

14, m. 34; tel. and fax (22) 296433; Principal Officer JOLANTA PAWLAK.

Ecological Library Foundation: 61-715 Poznań, ul. Kościuszki 79; tel. (61) 521325; fax (61) 528276; ecological library, protects endangered species in Poland; Pres. JACEK PURAT; DIR JAREK FISZER.

Ecology and Health Foundation: 00-215 Warsaw, Al. Ujazdowskie 13; tel. and fax (2) 6942153; provides information on environmental threats to health; Principal Officers Drs MAREK SIEMIŃSKI, STEFAN BOGUSŁAWSKI.

League for the Conservation of Nature in Poland (Liga Ochrony Przyrody): 00-922 Warsaw, ul. Reja 3-5; tel. and fax (22) 253593; nature conservation; Pres. Dr JANUSZ JANECKI; Gen. Sec. ZYGMUNT TRZEBIATOWSKI.

Nature Conservation League (Liga Ochrony Przyrody—LOP): 02-067 Warsaw, ul. Wawelska 52/54, Zarzad Glowny; f. 1928; official nature conservation asscn.

Polish Ecological Club (Polski Klub Ekologiczny—PKE): 31-010 Kraków, Rynek Glowny 27; f. early 1980s as part of Solidarity; major independent asscn, affiliated to Friends of the Earth Int.; promotes sustainable development, human ecology, environmental education, waste recycling, conservation strategies; federation of regional groups; Mem. Bd Prof. STANISŁAW JUCHNOWICZ.

Polish Green Party: 30-960 Kraków, POB 783; f. 1988; environmental issues.

Defence

In June 1993 Poland's armed forces numbered 287,500 people, of which 162,400 were conscripts. Of the total, 188,500 were in the army, 19,200 in the navy and 79,800 in the air force. In addition, the border troops numbered 16,000 and the prevention units of the police 7,400. Military service lasted for 18 months in all services. Since 1988 conscientious objectors have been permitted to perform an alternative community service. The defence budget for 1993 totalled 37,487,300m. złotys, an increase of 31.6% on the budget of the previous year.

Poland was a member of the Warsaw Pact until its final dissolution in July 1991. Withdrawals of all former Soviet troops from Poland were completed by November 1992. Some 5,000 Russian troops from the Military Mission remained in Poland, in mid-1993, in order to supervise the transit arrangements for troops withdrawing from Germany. In January 1994 the restructuring of the armed forces was announced in order to allow for the implementation of NATO's 'Partnership for Peace' scheme, of which Poland was a member.

Commander-in-Chief of the Armed Forces: President of the Republic.

Chief of Staff of the Defence Forces: Gen. TADEUSZ WILECKI.

Bibliography

Ascherson, N. *The Polish August: the self-limiting revolution*. Harmondsworth, Penguin, 1981.

The Struggles for Poland. London, Michael Joseph, 1987.

Brock, P. de Beauvoir. *Nationalism and Populism in Partitioned Poland*. London, Orbis, 1973.

Bromke, A. *Poland's Politics: idealism vs. realism* (Russian Research Center Studies). Cambridge, MA, Harvard University Press, 1967.

Davies, N. *God's Playground: a history of Poland*, 2 vols. Oxford, Oxford University Press, 1982.

Dziewanowski, M. K. *The Communist Party of Poland: an outline history* (Russian Research Center Studies). Cambridge, MA, Harvard University Press, 1967.

Garlinski, J. *Poland in the Second World War*. Basingstoke, Macmillan, 1985.

Garton Ash, T. *The Polish Revolution: Solidarity 1980–82* (revised edn). London, Granta (in assen with Penguin), 1991.

Gomułka, S. and Polansky, A. (Eds). *Polish Paradoxes*. London, Routledge, 1990.

Kolankiewicz, G. and Lewis, P. *Poland. Politics, Economics, Society* (Marxist regimes series). London, Pinter, 1988.

Landau, Z. and Tomaszewski, J. *The Polish Economy in the Twentieth Century*. London, Croom Helm, 1985.

Lane, D. and Kolankiewicz, G. (Eds). *Social Groups in Polish Society*. London, Macmillan, 1973.

Majkowski, W. *People's Poland: patterns of social inequality and conflict*. Westport, CN, Greenwood, 1985.

Miłosz, C. *The Captive Mind* (translated by Jane Zielomko, new edn). Harmondsworth, Penguin, 1980.

Polonsky, A. *Politics in Independent Poland: the crisis of constitutional government, 1921–39*. Oxford, Clarendon Press, 1972.

The Great Powers and the Polish Question, 1941–45: a documentary study in Cold War origins. London, London School of Economics, 1976.

Roos, H. *A History of Modern Poland: from the foundation of the State in the First World War to the present day* (translated by J. R. Foster). London, Eyre and Spottiswoode, 1966.

Sachs, J. *Poland's Jump to the Market Economy*. Cambridge, Massachusetts, The MIT Press, 1993.

Sanford, G. *Military Rule in Poland: the rebuilding of Communist power, 1981–83*. London, Croom Helm, 1986.

Staniszkis, J. *Poland's Self-Limiting Revolution* (edited by Jan. T. Gross). Princeton, NJ, Princeton University Press, 1984.

Swidlicki, A. *Political Trials in Poland, 1981–86*. London, Croom Helm, 1987.

Szajkowski, B. *Next to God . . . Poland: politics and religion in contemporary Poland*. London, Frances Pinter, 1983.

Wandycz, P. *The Lands of Partitioned Poland, 1795–1918* (A History of East Central Europe, vol. 7). Seattle, WA, University of Washington Press, 1975.

Weydenthal, J. B. de. *The Communists of Poland: an historical outline*. Stanford, CA, Hoover Institution Press, 1986.

Woodall, Jean (Ed.). *Policy and Politics in Contemporary Poland*. London, Frances Pinter, 1982.

ROMANIA

Geography

PHYSICAL FEATURES

Romania (formerly the the Socialist Republic of Romania) is a republic in south-eastern Europe; much of the country forms part of the Balkan Peninsula. In the south-east of the country there is a coastline of about 250 km (150 miles) along the Black Sea. The southern border is with Bulgaria and the south-western border with Yugoslavia (Serbia). Hungary lies to the north-west, Ukraine to the north and Moldova to the north-east. Romania has a total area of 237,500 sq km (91,699 sq miles).

The Carpathian Mountains form a horseshoe through central Romania, running south-east from the northern border and then, as the Transylvanian Alps or Southern Carpathians, traversing central Romania from east to west. The Transylvanian Alps rise to over 2,000 m in places, the mountain of Negoiul being the highest point in Romania, at 2,548 m (8,360 ft). South and east of the mountains lies the fertile Romanian Plain, the lowlands of Wallachia (along the Danube) and Moldavia (along the Siret and Prut Rivers, tributaries of the Danube). Most of the southern confines of Romania are marked by the River Danube (Dunărea). However, in the west of the country, the Banat region has a land border with Yugoslavia (Vojvodina, a part of Serbia). The Iron Gates hydroelectric power and navigation system is on the border with Serbia. In the east, before it reaches the Black Sea, the Danube turns north and flows parallel to the coast before entering the sea at the Delta Dunării (Mouths of the Danube), which forms a border with Ukraine. This area between the Danube and the Black Sea, which forms Romania's only land border with Bulgaria, is the Dobrogea (Dobrudzha). The River Prut defines the north-eastern border and divides Romanian Moldavia from the republic of that name. The plateau-land of north-west Romania, across the Carpathians from the plains, is known as Transylvania and was formerly a province of Hungary.

CLIMATE

The climate is continental, with cold, snowy winters and hot summers. Summers are milder and wetter in the mountains, and the Black Sea moderates the winters on the coast. The north and east suffer from drought if the summer is dry. The average annual rainfall for the whole of Romania is 637 mm (25 in), ranging from 1,000 mm in the mountains to 400 mm in the Danube delta.

POPULATION

Romanian is a Romance language, which evolved from the Latin spoken in central Europe at the time of the Roman Empire, but with many archaic forms and influences from the Slavonic languages, Hungarian, French and Turkish. It is the official language, although Hungarian (Magyar), German and other minority languages are also spoken. In 1987, according to official figures, 89% of the total population were ethnic Romanians, 7.9% were ethnic Hungarians

and 1.6% ethnic Germans (however, it was estimated that about one-half of Romania's German population migrated to Germany during 1990). There are also communities of Roma (Gypsy) people, Ukrainians (Ruthenians), Serbs, Croats, other Slavic peoples, Jews, Turks, Tatars and small groups of Greeks and Armenians. Most of the population profess Christianity and are adherents of the Eastern Orthodox Church; about 80% of the population are members of the Romanian Orthodox Church. About 6% of the population are members of the Roman Catholic Church, using not only the Latin rite, but also Romanian (Uniate) and Armenian rites. Protestant churches are particularly strong among the Hungarian and German populations. There are also communities of the Old-Rite Christian Church (an Orthodox sect) and the Armenian-Gregorian Church. The Turks and Tatars are predominantly Muslim and, despite the decline in numbers caused by emigration, there is still a significant Jewish community.

The principal and capital city is Bucharest (Bucureşti), which is located in the south of the country, in the east of the historic territory of Wallachia. At the census of January 1992 it had an estimated population of 2,064,474. Other major cities are: Constanţa (350,476), a port on the Black Sea; Iaşi (342,994), in the north-east, near the border with Moldova; Timişoara (334,278) in the west, in what was known as the Banat; Cluj-Napoca (328,008) in central Transylvania; Galaţi (325,788), on the Danube near the borders with Moldova and Ukraine; Braşov (323,835), in the centre of the country; and Craiova (303,520), in the Jiu valley in the south. The total population of the country at the 1992 census was 22,760,449, and the population density was 95.8 per sq km. The Bucharest Municipality was the most densely populated region (1,291.7 per sq km).

Chronology

106: Emperor Trajan made Dacia a province of the Roman Empire.

270: Rome abandoned Dacia to Visigothic invaders, the first of many incursions by peoples from the north and east.

1365: Emergence of independent principalities in Moldavia (now north-east Romania and parts of the Republic of Moldova and Ukraine) and Wallachia (now south-west Romania), having formerly been Hungarian banates or border lordships.

1394: Wallachia became a dependency of the Ottoman Empire.

1457–1504: Reign of Stephen III ('the Great') of Moldavia.

1512: Moldavia recognized Ottoman overlordship.

April 1856: Under the terms of the Treaty of Paris the principalities of Wallachia and Moldavia were unified, but remained under Turkish suzerainty; the Moldavian Bojar, Cuza, became the ruler.

1866: A prince of the House of Hohenzollern-Sigmaringen replaced the ousted Cuza as Carol I of Romania.

13 July 1878: By the Treaty of Berlin Romania was recognized as an independent state and was ceded part of the Dobrogea.

27 March 1881: Romania was recognized as a kingdom.

1916: Romania entered the First World War after generous promises of territory by the Entente Powers; however, much of the country was occupied by the Axis Powers.

1919–20: Following the post-First World War peace treaties, Romania received Bessarabia, Bucovina, Transylvania, the Banat and Crisana-Maramureş.

27 June 1940: Romania ceded Bessarabia and Northern Bucovina to the USSR.

1938: King Carol II established a royal dictatorship, suspending the Constitution and banning political parties.

August 1940: Romania ceded southern Dobrogea to Bulgaria and northern Transylvania to Hungary.

September 1940: Carol II abdicated in favour of his son, Michael, after having appointed Gen. Ion Antonescu as Prime Minister.

22 June 1941: Romania joined the German invasion of the USSR.

23 August 1944: Antonescu was arrested and Romania became a supporter of the Allied cause.

31 August 1944: Soviet troops entered Bucharest.

6 March 1945: The Soviets installed a 'puppet' government under Petru Groza.

November 1946: Elections were held and won by the Communist-led National Democratic Front.

30 December 1947: The Romanian People's Republic was proclaimed following the abdication of King Michael under pressure from the ruling Romanian Workers' Party (RWP).

24 September 1952: A new Constitution, based on the Soviet model, was approved by the Grand National Assembly.

30 November 1952: Elections were held for the Grand National Assembly. Gheorghe Gheorghiu-Dej, First Secretary of the RWP, became absolute leader.

March 1965: Following Gheorghiu-Dej's death, Nicolae Ceauşescu was elected First Secretary of the RWP.

June 1965: The RWP changed its name to the Romanian Communist Party (RCP).

August 1965: A new Constitution was adopted. The country's name was changed to the Socialist Republic of Romania.

December 1967: Ceauşescu became President of the State Council.

1968: Romania refused to join in the Warsaw Pact's suppression of the 'Prague Spring' revolt in Czechoslovakia.

1971: Romania was admitted to the General Agreement on Tariffs and Trade (GATT).

1972: Romania was admitted to the International Monetary Fund (IMF) and the World Bank.

March 1974: Ceauşescu became President of the Republic.

July 1987: An Amnesty International report condemned the lack of human rights in Romania, particularly for the Hungarian community.

15 November 1987: Thousands of workers in Braşov demonstrated against the Government's economic policy. The local RCP headquarters was sacked.

December 1987: Protests took place in Timişoara and other cities. Following a three-day conference of the RCP, Ceauşescu announced improvements in food supplies and wage increases.

March 1988: Ceauşescu announced plans for the complete 'systematization' of the country by the year 2000.

June 1988: Following a demonstration by 50,000 Hungarians outside the Romanian embassy in Budapest, the Romanian Government ordered the closure of the Hungarian consulate in Cluj-Napoca.

March 1989: In an open letter to the President, six retired RCP officials questioned Ceauşescu's uncompromising policies, accusing him of disregard for the Constitution.

15–17 December 1989: Mounting protests in Timişoara over attempts to arrest László Tőkes, an ethnic Hungarian pastor, culminated in the army opening fire on demonstrators.

21 December 1989: Ceauşescu was interrupted by hostile chanting during a speech in the centre of Bucharest. During a subsequent demonstration the police and army shot dead many of the protesters.

22–25 December 1989: Nicolae and Elena Ceauşescu were forced to escape by helicopter from the roof of the Central Committee Building. They were later captured near Tîrgovişte, summarily tried by a military tribunal, and executed. Meanwhile, anti-Ceauşescu forces seized control of the radio and television stations, and a Council of the National Salvation Front (NSF) was formed.

26 December 1989: Ion Iliescu was declared President, and Petre Roman was made Prime Minister of the NSF-appointed Government. The ban on abortion was overturned.

27 December 1989: A final Securitate assault on the television station was driven back by the army. The death penalty was abolished.

28 December 1989: The name of the country was changed by decree to Romania.

29 December 1989: The ideologue of the NSF, Silviu Brucan, announced that the NSF would not become a political party.

1 January 1990: The NSF Council abolished the Securitate. Ion Iliescu announced that food exports had been halted.

7 January 1990: Students demonstrated in Bucharest against the policies of the NSF and its alleged links with the RCP.

23 January 1990: Silviu Brucan confirmed that the NSF would stand in the elections, which were to be held in May.

24 January 1990: Demonstrators in Bucharest protested against the NSF's decision to stand in the elections.

28–29 December 1990: Anti-NSF demonstrations were dispersed by NSF loyalists, who later attacked the offices of parties opposed to the NSF.

February 1990: The NSF and opposition parties agreed on the formation of a 253-seat Provisional National Unity Council (PNUC), which elected a 21-member Executive Bureau with Iliescu as its President. A demonstration against Iliescu and the NSF was followed by one in support of the NSF by miners from the Jiu valley.

March 1990: Opposition groups led by George Serban drew up the Timişoara Declaration, which called for the banning of former Communists from office and for democratic reforms. There were disturbances between ethnic Hungarians and nationalist Romanians.

22 April 1990: Opposition supporters began an occupation of University Square in Bucharest.

5 May 1990: Opposition leader Radu Câmpeanu was attacked in Braila while attempting to address an election rally.

11 May 1990: Opposition leader Ion Raţiu was prevented from addressing an election rally in Oradea.

20 May 1990: The NSF won decisively in the first free elections since 1937. Ion Iliescu was elected President with over 85% of the vote.

13–15 June 1990: Police forcibly removed the opposition supporters who had been occupying University Square, prompting unrest in which the police headquarters was set on fire and there was an attempt to take over the television station. Miners from the Jiu valley were transported to the capital by the Government, and later attacked anyone in Bucharest suspected of being an anti-government sympathizer; at least six people were killed. The miners were later congratulated on their efforts by President Iliescu.

20 June 1990: Ion Iliescu was sworn in as President and called on Petre Roman to head a new Government.

6 July 1990: President Iliescu resigned as head of the NSF in accordance with the terms of the electoral law.

25 and 31 July 1990: The Grand National Assembly first approved a bill reorganizing state economic enterprises into autonomous units and commercial companies, and then a privatization law.

August 1990: Anti-government demonstrations resumed in University Square, but the mayor of Bucharest subsequently declared an indefinite ban on meetings and demonstrations in Bucharest's squares.

September 1990: Former Securitate chief Col-Gen. Iulian Vlad went on trial charged with being an accomplice to mass murder; Nicu Ceauşescu, son of the former President, was sentenced to 20-years' imprisonment for instigating 'extremely grave murder'; however, in November 1992 he was released 'on health grounds'.

18 October 1990: Petre Roman announced emergency measures to deal with the disastrous state of the economy. These included devaluation and convertibility of the currency, privatizations and the removal of price controls.

19 October 1990: The mass murder charges against former Securitate chief Col-Gen. Iulian Vlad were dropped.

November 1990: Prime Minister Roman was granted special powers by the Grand National Assembly to rule by decree and speed up the reforms for the free-market economy. There were various demonstrations, in Bucharest and elsewhere, against the Government's economic policies, against the re-emergence of the RCP as the Socialist Party of Labour, and demanding the reunification of Soviet Moldova with Romania.

11 December 1990: President Iliescu met union leaders in an attempt to avoid a general strike being called over worsening living conditions. The Government agreed to demands that the second stage of its price liberalization programme be postponed until 1 June 1991 (but it was later brought forward to 1 April 1991).

26 December 1990: The former sovereign, King Michael, was expelled from the country during a 24-hour visit.

30 January 1991: The Group of 24 countries admitted Romania to its Eastern Europe aid programme, having initially excluded the country after the violent suppression of the demonstrations in Bucharest in June 1990.

February 1991: The Government announced the temporary closure of nearly 200 industrial units and factories during February and March in order to conserve energy; the 247,000 workers temporarily made redundant were to receive 60% of their wages. Trading in foreign currencies commenced at six authorized Romanian banks. Land reform law came into effect returning between 0.5 and 10 hectares of arable land to agricultural workers, according to the size of the family plot nationalized by the Communists.

16–17 March 1991: A national convention of the NSF approved a programme by its leader, Prime Minister Petre Roman, which would reshape the NSF as a social democratic party.

18 March 1991: Former Securitate chief Col-Gen. Iulian Vlad was sentenced to three-and-a-half years in prison, after being found guilty of illegal arrest and detention of demonstrators. Later in the month 13 former politburo members were sentenced to between two and five-and-a-half years imprisonment, two to lesser sentences, and six acquitted on mass murder charges.

1 April 1991: The second stage of the Government's price liberalization programme was introduced; prices of essential foodstuffs rose by up to 125%; individual income tax was introduced, with rates between 6% and 45%; the leu was devalued against the US dollar by 72%. The National Assembly subsequently passed legislation allowing direct foreign investment in Romanian enterprises and the IMF approved a 12-month loan package valued at US $748m.

29–30 April 1991: Nine ministers were dismissed in a reshuffle of the Council of Ministers; three non-NSF members were appointed ministers; however, the National Assembly vetoed the appointment of two radical ministers, including one non-NSF member.

10 June 1991: Talks between the NSF and the opposition parties to form a coalition government broke down.

18 June 1991: Miners demonstrated against the Government in Bucharest.

5 July 1991: The Civic Alliance movement of extra-parliamentary opposition groupings voted to form a political party parallel to the existing organization.

9 July 1991: Romania's draft constitution was presented to the Constituent Assembly (the combined chambers of parliament).

22 July 1991: Col-Gen. Iulian Vlad was sentenced to nine years' imprisonment for supporting mass murder.

14 August 1991: The Privatization Law was approved, providing for the distribution of 30% of the capital of state commercial companies by voucher to the general public, and for the sale of the remaining 70%; overall some 47% of state capital was to remain under government control.

27 August 1991: The Government announced its recognition of Moldova immediately after the Republic's parliament had declared its independence from the USSR.

28 August 1991: President Iliescu referred to the inevitability of Moldova and Romania being reunited. The Party of the Civic Alliance declared its intention to join the National Convention for Establishing Democracy, ruling out the possibility of making an alliance with the NSF.

1–3 September 1991: The price of motor fuel was doubled, bringing it into line with international prices, but price ceilings were introduced for some foodstuffs; meat prices fell by up to 50%.

23–26 September 1991: Coal-miners in the Jiu valley went on strike over pay and conditions. They subsequently hijacked trains and travelled to Bucharest, attacked government buildings and fought with police, and demanded the resignations of the Government and President Iliescu. Prime Minister Roman and his Government resigned to enable the creation of a government of 'national opening', but vowed to continue in office in the current climate of unrest.

October 1991: Theodor Stolojan (former Finance Minister and President of the National Privatization Agency), at the invitation of President Iliescu, formed a new Government, which included members of the NSF, the National Liberal Party, the Agrarian Democratic Party and the Romanian Ecological Movement.

November 1991: The National Assembly approved the new Constitution, which was endorsed by the electorate in a referendum held in the following month (8 December).

February–April 1992: Local elections were conducted, which confirmed the decline in the popularity of the NSF, with many seats won by candidates of the Democratic Convention, an alliance of opposition parties.

27–29 March 1992: The Third National Convention of the NSF was held, at which the party split into pro-Iliescu (Democratic National Salvation Front—DNSF) and pro-Roman (NSF) wings; Roman was confirmed as NSF President.

27 September 1992: Legislative and presidential elections were held. The DNSF won the greatest number of seats, with 117 of the 328 elective seats in the Assembly of Deputies and 49 of the 143 seats in the Senate. The Democratic Convention of Romania (DCR) won 82 seats in the Assembly of Deputies and 34 seats in the Senate. Ion Iliescu, with 47% of the votes cast, failed to win the required majority for election as President.

11 October 1992: In a second round of voting, Iliescu, with 61% of the votes cast, defeated Emil Constantinescu, of the DCR, to be elected President.

November 1992: After extended negotiations, Nicolae Vacaroiu, a nominally-independent bureaucrat, formed a Government consisting equal numbers of DNSF members and independents.

March 1993: A motion of 'no confidence' in the Government's economic programme was defeated at a joint session of both houses of parliament.

May 1993: Price subsidies for many basic commodities and services were abolished, precipitating renewed industrial unrest. Minimum wages in the public sector were increased by about 75%.

11 May 1993: Romania's application for membership of the Council of Europe was rejected owing to its poor record concerning civil liberties.

29 May 1993: The NSF changed its name to the Democratic Party—NSF.

1 July 1993: Value added tax was introduced at the rate of 18%.

3 July 1993: The Party of the Civic Alliance split when the majority of its parliamentary members resigned and joined the Liberal Party 1993.

9–10 July 1993: At its second national conference, the DNSF changed its name to the Party of Social Democracy of Romania (PSDR); the merger of the party with the Democratic Cooperationist Party, the Republican Party and the Romanian Socialist Democratic Party was confirmed.

23 July 1993: Romania was refused further IMF loans owing to its failure to reform the largest state-owned enterprises and to control inflation.

August 1993: There were strikes over wages levels by coal-miners and railway workers.

28 August 1993: Misu Negritoiu, the leading economic reformer in the Government, was replaced, along with three other ministers.

7 October 1993: Romania was admitted to the Council of Europe (Hungary abstained from voting).

9 December 1993: An 18-month stand-by loan of US $700m. was agreed with the IMF.

17 December 1993: The Vacaroiu Government survived a motion of 'no-confidence', over the lack of progress in the economic reform programme, by 13 votes.

26 January 1994: Romania became the first former Communist country to sign a 'Partnership for Peace' agreement with the North Atlantic Treaty Organisation (NATO).

January–February 1994: The PSDR entered into negotiations with various other parties in an attempt to form, by 1 March, a new coalition Government.

9 February 1994: The Senate approved the economic reform programme, including the liberalization of the exchange rate (by April 1994), measures to reduce inflation and the restructuring and privatization of the state sector.

6 March 1994: Four new ministers were appointed, marking a failure of the PSDR's attempts to broaden the Government coalition.

History

Dr TOM GALLAGHER

INTRODUCTION

Nationalism has been a primary force in Romanian political life this century, despite a succession of political ruptures as right-wing dictatorship replaced constitutional monarchy in 1938, followed by the triumph of Russian-imposed Communism in 1947, and the emergence of a qualified democracy in 1990 out of the ruins of Ceauşescu's National Communist state. The basic elements of Romanian national identity, the Latinity of the people and their language, their Orthodox faith, the long struggle for independence and suspicion of neighbouring peoples, have proved cohesive and long-lasting. However, in practice, nationalism has often been defined and shaped by those in charge of the state in order to obtain consent for projects that result in the enrichment of a restricted class, circle or even family (in the case of the Ceauşescus), or the imposition of a particular ideology. The refusal of a succession of different rulers either to broaden participation or to allow citizens greater access to decision-making, while constantly invoking the people and the nation as guarantors of their policy, has created deep-seated tensions, with the result that regimes lacking legitimacy have often succumbed to internal collapse or foreign invasion. The recent history of Romania explains the resilience of nationalism, despite its failure to integrate citizens into a balanced political community or to offer the means for the sustained economic development of the country.

The nucleus of an independent state only emerged in 1856 when two principalities, Wallachia and Moldavia, under Turkish suzerainty since the 16th century, became self-governing. In 1878 the new state finally won its independence from the Ottoman Empire, and in 1881 it became a kingdom under a branch of the German Hohenzollern dynasty. A sense of vulnerability, stemming from centuries of foreign overlordship or occupation and a realization that independence had been acquired in part as a result of the shifting balance of power, meant that national self-assertion was the dominant note in political life. The legacy of tyranny and systematic exploitation associated with the rule of the Ottoman Turks and the Phanariot Turks would be difficult to eradicate. However, under King Carol I (1866–1914), Romania enjoyed a lengthy, uninterrupted period of stability which made it unique in Eastern Europe. In 1916 nearly all of the country was occupied by the Axis Powers after Romania had been induced to enter the First World War on the Allied side by lavish promises of territory. At the post-1918 peace conferences Romania more than doubled its area and population as it acquired Transylvania, with its Romanian majority, from Hungary, and Bessarabia and Bucovina from Russia.

The wealth and importance of Romania were thus increased, as the gains of the Versailles peace settlement turned it into a medium-sized European power. However, with 30% of the population consisting of Hungarians, Saxons (Germans), Jews, Ukrainians and other minorities, it was also one of Europe's most ethnically-mixed states. Such diversity was regarded as a potential threat rather than an enriching factor, and the minorities were treated as subordinates to be assimilated into a single national culture based on the Romanian language. Deep-seated social and economic divisions also resulted in the elevation of nationalism almost to the status of a secular religion in order to superimpose a sense of unity on a country that soon revealed itself to be internally fragmented. The peasantry, despite being hailed as the well-spring of the nation, was excluded from political life. Land reform had been carried out to avert unrest of the kind which, in 1907, had given rise to modern Europe's most violent peasant rebellion. However, rural over-population, high illiteracy, and state neglect of agriculture rekindled peasant alienation and made parts of the countryside a recruiting ground for the Iron Guard, Romania's indigenous fascist movement.

The National Liberal Party dominated politics until 1928. Its emphasis on industrial self-sufficiency (based partly on Romania's oil wealth) and on foreign alliances that lessened dependence on powerful neighbours evoke parallels with the Ceauşescu era. The 1930s were a decade of mounting tension as the traditional parties were marginalized by an unscrupulous monarch, Carol II, who imposed a royal dictatorship in 1938 and suppressed the Iron Guard. Romania's native fascists had drawn increasing support from intellectuals and other groups which had gravitated to extremism as their chances of remunerative state employment were dashed by the 1930s' economic depression.

The Second World War swept away the fragile and disunited Greater Romania which had emerged in 1918. Carol II was forced to abdicate, in favour of his son, Michael, in September 1940, after Stalin had seized Bessarabia and Hungary was granted a large swathe of Transylvania as the dictators carved out spheres of influence in Eastern Europe. Marshal Ion Antonescu then established a dictatorship which lasted until his overthrow on 23 August 1944. In June 1941 Antonescu joined the German invasion of the USSR, fighting as far as Stalingrad and recovering Bessarabia in the process. Antonescu's contribution to the Axis war effort was more substantial than that of any other German partner, and the Romanian army sustained about 500,000 deaths during the Second World War. A portion of these occurred after Romania changed sides following the palace coup by King Michael which brought Romania on to the Allied side on 23 August 1944.

COMMUNIST ROMANIA

The USSR became a decisive force in Romanian affairs after 23 August 1944. The February 1945 Yalta conference, whereby Romania was assigned to the Soviet sphere of influence with the agreement of the Western allies, confirmed Romania's role of Soviet satellite. However, it was not immediately clear to the Soviets what political arrangements would bolster their power in Romania. The Romanian Communist Party (RCP) possessed no more than 1,000 members in 1944 and had never organized any serious guerrilla or resistance movements. Between 1926 and 1944 each of its general secretaries had been non-Romanians. After the idea was proposed of installing Antonescu as the head of a 'puppet' regime (the wartime dictator refused and was executed in 1946), a popular front government was set up on 6 March 1945 under Petru Groza, whose wealth and social standing briefly obscured Soviet intentions for Romania. Land reform, followed by the return of northern Transylvania to Romanian jurisdiction, were designed to create popular support for the pro-Communist government as the RCP expanded its size and role under Soviet tutelage, prior to taking complete control of the country.

Once the RCP's domination over traditional parties was felt to be assured, elections were held on 19 November 1946. They were won by the Communist-led National Democratic Front, the old Romanian tradition of vote-rigging, combined with Communist methods of intimidation, crushing the opposition. The anti-Communist parties were unrealistically reliant on the USA (and were not discouraged from being so by the West) until the arrest of Iuliu Maniu, the symbol of democratic Romania, who was sentenced to life imprisonment in 1947. On 30 December 1947 King Michael was forced to abdicate and on 13 April 1948 Romania formally became 'a people's democracy'.

The weak implantation of the RCP in national life helps to explain the ruthlessness with which the old social order was demolished after 1947. Sweeping attacks were made on personal liberty, property rights and national cultural values. Businessmen, army officers, churchmen, intellectuals and any political activists who were felt to pose a challenge to the new Marxist-Leninist rulers were imprisoned, and it is reckoned that many tens of thousands of people perished in captivity during the 1948–56 period. The Communists were in complete charge by the 1950s, and an internecine power struggle followed, won by the leading national Stalinist, Gheorghe Gheorghiu-Dej, who purged the Party of his opponents to establish his mastery after 1952. He then showed great skills in responding to the upheavals in the Soviet camp that followed the death of Stalin in 1953, and culminated in the open denunciation of Stalin by Nikita Khrushchev in 1956 and the Hungarian revolution. The stern orthodoxy of the Romanian regime, and the assistance it gave to the USSR over Hungary, persuaded the Kremlin in 1958 that it was safe to withdraw its troops from Romania. However, thereafter Romania began to drop its subservience to the USSR. It is clear that Gheorghiu-Dej saw Khrushchev's anti-Stalinist campaign as a serious threat to his regime, and saw little future in controlled liberalization given the drastic steps that had been needed to begin the transformation of a traditional rural society into a Marxist collectivist state. In 1959 he opted for a policy of intensive industrialization in defiance of Moscow's policy for turning Romania into the 'bread-basket' of the Soviet bloc. Following the eruption of the Sino–Soviet dispute in 1961, he took advantage of the disarray in the Soviet camp, and the erosion of Khrushchev's authority, to pursue an autonomous foreign policy while remaining inside the Warsaw Pact. Gheorghiu-Dej consolidated his authority by pursuing a Stalinist model of economic development with the emphasis being on heavy industry. The proportion of people employed in agriculture fell from 75% in 1950 to under 30% in the late 1980s, while the percentage of those working in industry rose from 11% in 1950 to 37% in 1988. To bolster support for what was a strategy of National Communism, the official ideology was revamped to include populist and nationalist themes. Historic figures associated with past struggles for Romania's independence were rehabilitated. In 1964 Russian ceased to be a mandatory foreign language taught in all Romanian schools. Trade with the West increased and was assisted by the release of surviving political prisoners in 1964. Many Romanians saw the new policy departure, at a time of less economic stringency, as an improvement on what had gone before and their approval broadened the base of the regime.

THE CEAUŞESCU ERA

Upon the death of Gheorghiu-Dej, his successor, Nicolae Ceauşescu, who was elected First Secretary of the Party in 1965, chose to build upon the nationalist strategy. Adherence to the Chinese view that there can be no one centre of international Communism and hence no heretics, blossomed into outright rejection of Moscow's overlordship during the 1968 Czechoslovak crisis. Ceauşescu refused to participate in the Warsaw Pact invasion of Czechoslovakia, and the public adulation he received when he openly condemned the Soviet invasion on 21 August 1968 suggested that he enjoyed genuine popularity. Ceauşescu had emphasized socialist legality and individual rights, and had rehabilitated figures purged by his predecessor. Political control over cultural matters was also relaxed. But this was soon revealed merely to be clever power-broking, as he consolidated his rule over potential rivals, rather than a shift towards the limited pluralism allowed in Tito's Yugoslavia. A turning point occurred in June 1971 when Ceauşescu returned from a visit to the Democratic People's Republic of Korea and the People's Republic of China. He had been impressed by the social engineering, regimentation and cult of personality that personified the regimes of Kim Il Sung and Mao Zedong. Encouraged by his wife Elena, whose political influence was steadily to increase in years to come, he launched a mini-cultural revolution designed to eradicate signs of undisciplined liberalism and individualism which were felt to pose a danger to the Party's monopoly of power. Ceauşescu revealed himself to be a dogmatic Communist who was prepared to create a highly centralized and ethnically homogeneous state. He used the autonomy acquired from the Soviet Union to establish a personal dictatorship.

In 1974 the office of President was created and Ceauşescu became President of the Socialist Republic of Romania and Commander-in-Chief of the Romanian Army. Despite a worsening human-rights record, under which the people were increasingly shielded from Western contacts, Romania continued to receive 'rewards' from the West for its defiance of the USSR, including: state visits to and from the USA and the United Kingdom; membership of GATT (General Agreement on Tariffs and Trade) in 1971 and the International Monetary Fund (IMF) and the World Bank in 1972; the accordance of preferential trading status with the European Community (EC—known as the European Union from November 1993) in 1973; and 'most-favoured nation' status with the USA in 1975.

The commitment to rapid industrialization, with the emphasis on heavy and extractive industries, was taken to even more extreme lengths in the 1970s. The aim was to create 'the new socialist man and woman', which also lay behind efforts in the 1980s to move inhabitants from traditional dwellings into apartment blocks and 'agro-industrial complexes'. However, the financing of forced industrialization schemes through loans from the West led to massive indebtedness; by the end of 1981 Romania's foreign debt had risen to US $10,200m., which Ceauşescu then set out to repay by 1990. Food rationing and restrictions on the use of energy steadily mounted in the 1980s, as Ceauşescu slashed imports and increased exports of food and fuel in an attempt to meet his target, all of which led to considerable financial and personal suffering among the general population.

During the 1980s all remaining power drained from the RCP and became concentrated in a clique which included many family members of the presidential couple; Elena Ceauşescu, now First Deputy Premier, managed her husband's schedule. Backed by an all-pervasive secret police (the Securitate), the dynastic socialism of the Ceauşescus appeared entrenched even after the emergence of Mikhail Gorbachev, a reform Communist, as leader of the USSR in 1985. However, eventually President Ceauşescu's control was fatally undermined by Moscow's refusal to prop up threatened Communist regimes. Ironically, a regime which had enjoyed misplaced admiration in the West because of the autonomy it had acquired from Moscow in the 1960s fell under threat once Moscow allowed the same degree of autonomy to other Soviet bloc countries in the late 1980s. The 14th Party Congress went ahead on 20–25 November 1989 following the collapse of Communist rule in other Warsaw Pact states. Ceauşescu, shielded by his self-serving entourage from understanding the precariousness of his position, received 67 standing ovations and pledged to continue with the same unyielding policies.

THE DOWNFALL OF THE CEAUŞESCU REGIME

When serious disturbances broke out in the city of Timişoara on 16 December 1989, which soon spread into a generalized revolt, Ceauşescu still felt secure enough to make a brief visit to Iran. Upon his return, he addressed a public rally of support on 21 December, which had to be abandoned amid heckling from the crowd, all of which was broadcast live on television and radio. An improvised group of Party officials, along with some army and Securitate officers, then attempted to oust Ceauşescu against a background of huge demonstrations which were fired upon indiscriminately by members of the security forces still loyal to the regime. (The Minister of National Defence, Col-Gen. Vasile Milea, was shot by a member of the Securitate after refusing to order his troops to open fire on the demonstrators.) On 22 December 1989, the day that Nicolae Ceauşescu acknowledged the effective collapse of his rule by fleeing with his wife by helicopter from the Central Committee Building in Bucharest, the National Salvation Front (NSF) was formed. In the hours and days ahead, Ceauşescu's self-appointed successors, drawn from out-of-favour members of the Communist establishment, struggled to assert their authority. Relatively few Romanians had heard of 59-year-old Ion Iliescu, the Chairman of the NSF, who had been a rising political figure until, in 1971, he had disagreed with the rigid course being adopted by Ceauşescu, or of his associate, Petre Roman, the son of a veteran Communist who had played a leading role in reshaping the armed forces after 1946. Important assistance in the task of legitimizing their authority was provided by Hungary, which became the first country to recognize the new authorities on 23 December.

On 25 December 1989 Nicolae and Elena Ceauşescu were executed after being captured and summarily tried by a military tribunal. An NSF spokesman had promised on 22 December that they would be put on public trial, but Iliescu later insisted that the drastic action taken against them had been vital in order to save many lives, by making Securitate 'terrorists' loyal to Ceauşescu see that they were fighting for a lost cause. Fierce fighting, which had continued in central Bucharest, did indeed stop; but as no such 'terrorists' were ever subsequently made to stand trial, there was speculation that the revolutionary upheaval had been superseded by an anti-Ceauşescu coup organized by disenchanted members of the Party, army and Securitate bureaucracies. Certainly, no Communists would be tried for the atrocious crimes committed in Romania before 1989. It had been charges of 'genocide' during the December fighting which had led to the Ceauşescus facing a firing squad, and leading accomplices, such as Col-Gen. Iulian Vlad, the former chief of the Securitate, and the Ceauşescus' son, Nicu, were eventually convicted of lesser charges and treated relatively leniently.

THE NATIONAL SALVATION FRONT

The fragile consensus between Communist insiders, dissidents and newly politicized elements held for some weeks amid the general euphoria which greeted the demise of the Ceauşescus. The Council of the National Salvation Front filled the political vacuum and assumed control of the machinery of government. On 26 December Ion Iliescu was appointed interim President and Petre Roman Prime Minister. Over the next few weeks visits by leading officials from the USA, the USSR and Western European countries that had been quick to recognize the new regime strengthened Iliescu's authority. He also won popular backing following a series of television broadcasts in which he promised to end the policies which had led to severe material privations, to reconstruct the national economy 'in accordance with the criteria of profitability and efficiency', to safeguard human rights and freedoms, and to observe the rights and freedoms of national minorities. For almost a month the NSF conveyed the impression that it would be content to play a caretaker role, winding up one-party rule and creating the conditions which would enable Romania to become a pluralist democratic state. But on 24 January 1990 protesters were back on the streets of Bucharest following an announcement by Silviu Brucan, the NSF's chief spokesman, that it would be a challenger in elections due to be held in the spring. Those who remembered his earlier statement, on 29 December, that there was no need for the NSF to become a political party, were appalled by this volte-face. Dissidents resigned from the political offices to which they had been co-opted. A serious of street confrontations took place between 25 and 29 January 1990 which gave the NSF the upper hand against its opponents, but only after it had used methods that rested uncomfortably with its self-proclaimed mission of bringing democracy to Romania: calls were made on television for workers to rush to the centre of the capital to protect the Government; unarmed opponents were beaten up on 28 January and the offices of newly constituted parties, now in opposition to the Front, were stormed on 29 January. On 6 February the NSF registered as a political party and soon after announced that Ion Iliescu would be its candidate for Romania's presidency.

Against a background of international concern about what had just occurred, the provisional Government made some concessions to its opponents. The NSF Council, from which well-known anti-Communists had resigned, was replaced on 1 February by a Provisional National Unity Council. Critics were represented, but it soon emerged that two-thirds of the 253-member body were NSF members or supporters. The events of late January showed that the agencies of manipulation and control which had enabled Romania to be dominated by unaccountable leaders had not perished with Ceaușescu. Ion Iliescu's reluctance to yield power, or to allow that power to be shared out among interests he could not control, also revealed certain continuities with the past. As the NSF had spread out from Bucharest, it had absorbed the local RCP organization in nearly all parts of the country.

The collapse of the short-lived revolutionary front of December 1989 meant that Iliescu was reliant on former Ceaușescu loyalists to secure a majority for the NSF in hastily-arranged elections. In parts of Transylvania this meant that he depended on individuals who had risen to prominence as a result of steps taken by Ceaușescu to marginalize the Hungarian population, actions which the NSF had condemned in its earliest statements. The NSF briefly found itself in a contradictory position. If it was to honour commitments made to the national minorities on 5 January 1990 for a ministry that would provide them with group rights, this would offend officials who had achieved career fulfilment during a period when Hungarian schools and cultural institutions had been diluted of their Hungarian character. In February a radical nationalist pressure group, Vatra Românească (Romanian Hearth), emerged, designed to block Hungarian demands, which it depicted as threatening to the territorial survival of Romania. The pernicious effects of decades of nationalist mobilization under Ceaușescu, the precipitate action of certain Hungarians in seeking to reclaim their schools and Vatra's access to the resources of the local state enabled a nationalist backlash to get under way. It culminated, on 19–20 March, in severe rioting in Tirgu Mureș, the Transylvanian city where Romanians and Hungarians were most evenly balanced in terms of numbers. Peaceful rallies by Hungarians met with a violent response from Romanians (many being villagers bused in from distant neighbourhoods who had been alerted by rumours about Hungarian attacks on their children who were educated in the city). Local Hungarians retaliated and community relations were left in ruins. Inter-state relations between Romania and Hungary also deteriorated rapidly: Bucharest blamed the troubles on foreign interference, while Budapest alleged that inter-ethnic peace had been sacrificed to internal power struggles.

While claiming to play a balancing role, the NSF distanced itself from the Hungarians, who had earlier been much more willing to co-operate with the Government than with Romanian dissidents, and it began to play the nationalist card in its own right as elections drew nearer. The Tirgu Mureș violence had shown that the state-licensed chauvinism, promoted under Ceaușescu and feeding on conflicts from the recent and more distant past, had not abated with the collapse of his regime. Indeed, the potential for an ethnic collision had increased owing to the replacement of a totalitarian state which monopolized expressions of chauvinism by a relatively liberal state prepared to exploit nationalism in order to boost its authority, but unable or unwilling to prevent others going much further to fulfil their nationalist objectives.

THE MAY 1990 ELECTIONS

However, inter-ethnic disputes were soon eclipsed by bitter recriminations among Romanians as campaigning got under way for elections due on 20 May 1990. Opponents of the NSF accused it of seeking to impose a neo-Communist solution by holding a poll less than 20 weeks after Ceaușescu's overthrow, and before its competitors had had a chance to organize themselves. From the outset the NSF enjoyed crucial advantages over a weak and fragmented opposition. Its position as the dominant force in government gave it control over state assets, ranging from access to printing presses and transportation, to control over radio and television. The last advantage was a crucial one in a society where television had shaped the outlook of millions of people, particularly the poorly educated living in small towns and villages in those remoter areas which received few other sources of information about the outside world. The totalitarian state had always found it easier to manipulate rural dwellers than other sections of the population. Thousands had demonstrated outside the headquarters of 'Free Romanian Television' on 4 February because of what they viewed as the state media's capacity for bias, distortion and character assassination.

State television's handling of the election campaign triggered off an occupation of Bucharest's University Square on 22 April 1990 by students, intellectuals and others making up the informal opposition, who claimed that former Communists were trying to create a democratic Romania in their own distorted image. Their demand that RCP leaders, members of the Securitate and leading nomenklatura officials should be barred from competing in the first three elections for any public office, including the presidency, was Article 8 of the Timișoara Proclamation released on 11 March by opponents of the NSF. The conviction of anti-government protesters that cosmetic changes were leaving old power structures intact was strengthened when, on 24 April, it was announced that a new 'information service' was being formed to replace the Securitate. The Romanian Information Service (RIS) was to employ 6,000 of the 15,000 personnel who had belonged to the Securitate up to 1989. The need to protect Romania from external threats to its security was cited as the reason for creating this successor service. But to vocal critics, statements that the Securitate of old no longer existed were as bogus as the claim that the NSF had no connection with the party that had been the dominant force in Romanian society until the previous December. Many, far beyond their ranks, wondered what had happened to the RCP and why Romania was exceptional among post-Communist states in that none of the 82 parties competing in its election admitted to having had any connection with the previous ruling Party.

Those Romanians whose reference-point in measuring change in their country was how elections were conducted in Western Europe, or in recently liberated neighbours, proved only to be a minority. Most citizens, owing to the isolation they had endured for 45 years, had much narrower horizons. They compared Iliescu's performance not with a Havel or even a Gorbachev, but with the rule of the person who made life so exacting in the 1980s. Ceaușescu, 'the bad father', had been replaced by Iliescu, 'the good father'. Perhaps it was too much to expect that a people with traditionally low expectations, for whom a benevolent ruler was a rarity, would cast out a ruler who, in his first months in office, had undoubtedly lightened the burdens of daily life: supplies of heat and light had been restored; peasants were being promised access to private land; rationing was being scaled down despite continuing food shortages; and a full television service was being provided, which offered entertainment as well as coverage of the exploits of those in power.

The close identification between one party and the state, distasteful to many urbanized Romanians who wished to see a complete break with the past, was not necessarily viewed in this way by the more traditional citizens from in the villages and provincial towns, among whom Ion Iliescu received his most tumultuous welcomes on the campaign trail. Many Romanians had had no alternative but to get used to being ruled by an authority figure in charge of a powerful set of centralized institutions, given the nature of their history. Perhaps not without reason, they feared that anarchy might ensue should a dissident with no administrative experience or first-hand knowledge of the country (Iliescu's two presidential challengers, Ion Rațiu and Radu Câmpeanu, had both spent long periods abroad) came to power. Iliescu emphasized his readiness to defend national security and the material interests of ordinary people by shielding them from a rapid transition to a market economy, with the result that he was the overwhelming choice of the great majority of voters.

Ion Iliescu won 85% of the valid vote in the ballot cast for President. In the parliamentary voting, the NSF won 65% of the vote giving it 263 of the 387 seats in the Chamber of Deputies, and 91 of the 119 seats in the Senate. Foreign observers found irregularities in the electoral process, particularly in rural areas, but it was clear that the NSF was the preferred choice of an overwhelming majority of the electorate. Iliescu's message of social and economic paternalism was appealing to millions of people, who regarded it as a genuine advance over anything they had been offered by Romanian rulers for a long time.

In second place to the NSF was the Hungarian Democratic Union of Romania (HDUR), with 7.2% of the vote, which campaigns for cultural and educational rights that will protect the identity of the 1.7m. Hungarians, while firmly disavowing irredentism. The ability of the Transylvanian Hungarians to maintain a united front was in contrast to the main Romanian anti-Communist parties, which might have seemed more credible had they compromised over their differences and formed an opposition alliance. In the campaign they often failed to make a distinction between crying 'Down with Communism' and 'Down with the Communists'. The first slogan had to do with the destruction of a system, while the second implied a clear threat to the welfare of millions of Romanians who had joined the RCP out of necessity or convenience, rather than conviction. The scattered forces of intellectual dissent also failed to produce a party capable of making any electoral impact.

THE VIOLENT SUPPRESSION OF DISSENT

However, attention remained focused on the informal opposition which remained encamped in Bucharest's University Square, until their removal in a police operation on 13 June 1990 in which participants were beaten and arrested. Groups protesting this action attacked the police headquarters, the offices of Romanian Television and the Foreign Ministry, where Iliescu and the Government were based. When the police failed to disperse them, Iliescu went on television to appeal for loyal citizens to come to the aid of the Government. Seven thousand miners from the Jiu valley arrived in the capital on 14 June, on board special trains and armed with staves and clubs. They were joined by vigilantes, some of whom were later identified in the press as having been former members of the Securitate. For the next two days they went on the rampage, attacking, under the direction of unknown persons, the headquarters of the main opposition parties, the offices of opposition newspapers and the University, where they beat up students. On 15 June President Iliescu, in an address ridden with clichés from the pre-1989 era, thanked the miners for having shown 'workers' solidarity' in the face of a plot which had 'been hatched' by those who were of the view that 'right-wing forces should come to power in all East European countries'. Before departing from Bucharest, some miners went on the rampage through the city's Roma (Gypsy) quarter, the authorities standing aside as a group that had few defenders in Romanian society once more found itself the scapegoat for the country's ills.

The international condemnation resulting from the Government's role in the 13–15 June violence was virtually unanimous. Members of the Romanian leadership increased their discomfiture by giving explanations for the events that differed sharply from initial statements. Economic assistance from the EC was frozen immediately after the June violence. In October 1990 Iliescu was the only Eastern European leader not received by US President Bush when he attended the UN General Assembly meeting in New York. Later, Prime Minister Roman's request that Romania be included in the Visegrad Group of former Warsaw Pact countries which were closing ranks in order to speed up the process of integrating with Western European institutions met with a rebuff. President Havel of Czechoslovakia felt that the Visegrad partners' agenda would be hampered if they were associated with a country whose level of democracy was regarded with disfavour in the West.

THE ROMAN GOVERNMENT

The Bucharest authorities quickly took steps to repair their international image which suggested that a return to isolationism was not an option felt by them to be open. The scale of the economic damage inflicted during Ceaușescu's relentless bid to impose economic self-sufficiency did not make autarky an attractive alternative, even for those public figures clearly ill at ease with having to operate in a democratic environment. The appointment by Iliescu of a Government headed by Petre Roman demonstrated a desire to develop economic and political links with the West that would enable the country to emerge from isolation, albeit on its own terms. Only two members of Roman's 23-member Government could be described as being members of the former nomenklatura, or neo-Communist in outlook. The important economic portfolios were filled by ministers who gradually convinced a stream of Western visitors of their seriousness in wishing to discard past economic models and to press ahead with a rapid liberalization of the economy. Indeed, the Roman Government borrowed much of its economic rhetoric from the opposition, whose pro-capitalist proposals it had denounced as an economic sell-out of the country during electioneering. Privatization measures, just as radical as the ones the opposition had earlier promised, were announced in August 1990. These made an impression in Western European capitals and financial centres among experts unfamiliar with the fact that, in Romania, government programmes and rhetoric often bore even less relation to intentions than in other Eastern European countries.

Petre Roman's cosmopolitan outlook and economic radicalism concealed the fact that there was no equivalent policy of political openness at home. Perhaps the clearest example of the Government's definition of democracy was provided by the decisions it took on the subject of local government. In July 1990 Roman began replacing mayors appointed on an interim basis after December 1989 because they reflected local opinion, with pro-NSF appointees, even in cities where the party had got well under half the votes cast in the national elections of May 1990. The office of prefect was also re-established, the unelected holder being the highest authority in each Romanian county and answerable directly to the Prime Minister. In the city of Cluj-Napoca, where the NSF had only obtained 28% of the vote, the appointment of a city mayor and a county prefect who had been members of the RCP establishment led opposition parties to combine in forming an Anti-Totalitarian Front, which then spread to other cities.

Although the opposition's more mature political strategy, emphasizing programmes which related to people's needs, increased its standing, popular involvement in politics failed to increase. Many citizens were too absorbed with the increasingly arduous battle for material existence to engage in an activity which offered few psychological rewards. The turbulence of 1989–90 suggested to many that overt political activity contained too many risks. The Government's own stance suggested that it had no wish to alter Romanian political culture, which had traditionally placed a low value on political participation and access to decision-making by the mass of the population.

Nationalism was promoted as a unifying factor to overcome a set of cleavages (urban–rural, generational, inter-ethnic and intellectuals–workers) which had emerged with differing degrees of intensity in 1990. Choosing as the new national day 1 December, the day in 1918 when Transylvania was united with Romania, rather than 16 December, the day in 1989 when Timişoara's citizens first went on to the streets to defy oppression, showed a concern to shift attention away from the disputed circumstances in which the NSF came to power. In several Transylvanian cities, former party officials, by stressing an internal enemy or an external threat, were able to manage change on their own terms. Hungarians fared badly when the county prefect in Cluj-Napoca declared that he was only prepared to allow property to be sold to people who could be trusted not to harm 'the national interest'. Transylvania's principal city was the clearest example of selective privatization being pursued according to nationalist criteria, enabling former members of the nomenklatura to relaunch themselves as entrepreneurs. Unwilling to challenge the nationalist lobby in Transylvania, where its own support was weak, the NSF endured criticism from the lively opposition press that its economic programme amounted to 'Communism with a capitalist face' or else to 'market Communism'.

The NSF's failure to acquire a secure political identity based on a consistent programme or set of philosophical ideas meant that going down the nationalist route was difficult to resist. But in relations with the USSR, this temptation was resisted. In April 1991 Iliescu evoked surprise when he signed a treaty in Moscow which endorsed existing borders and was interpreted as giving the USSR a veto over the alliances that Romania could enter into. He also held back from endorsing the independence of Moldova, the Soviet republic including Russian and Gagauz minorities but largely carved from the Romanian province of Bessarabia annexed by Stalin.

The media outcry against the treaty was so strong that the Romanian parliament postponed the treaty's ratification indefinitely. Following the failure of the August 1991 coup, in Moscow, the treaty rapidly became obsolete when large parts of the USSR declared independence from Moscow. One of them was the Republic of Moldova, which was proclaimed on 27 August 1991. Disappointment unconfined to either pro-government or opposition circles greeted the realization that there was little enthusiasm among the Romanian-speaking majority in Moldova for rejoining Romania. However, Bucharest came to accept the Moldovan Government's desire to establish its own sovereignty, and advanced the formula of one Romanian people currently residing in two states.

THE FALL OF ROMAN

The instability which, along with poor living standards, made Moldova wary of integration with Romania was underlined in September 1991 with the violent ejection from office of Petre Roman. The agents of his fall were the miners of the Jiu Valley, whose previous onslaughts on the capital had been at the invitation of the NSF but who, by the autumn of 1991, had turned against the Government owing to its failure to shield them from the mounting social costs of the transition to a market economy. Unemployment was becoming an unaccustomed menace for Romanians, and wages had failed to keep step with prices, which increased by 219% in the year up to November 1991. Industrial output had fallen by 30% in the twelve months following September 1990 and food and fuel were to be rationed in order to get the country through the winter of 1991–92. Like Ceauşescu, Roman was destined to fall in little over 24 hours, being unable to mobilize popular support against his extra-parliamentary foes in the way that Boris Yeltsin had managed to do in Moscow in August against pro-Communist conspirators. If Roman had used his period in office to create an accessible democracy based on the rule of law, he might not have found himself so alone in his hour of need. Even the security forces melted away before several thousand miners, who were able to occupy parliament on 26 September after having seized trains to take them to Bucharest.

Roman handed in his mandate to facilitate a political solution to the crisis, saying afterwards that he had no intention of resigning. Police and soldiers were then able to restore order and the miners went home. But President Iliescu refused to annul the resignation and reinstate Roman, which fuelled speculation about an internal power struggle. 'Under circumstances of violence', Roman affirmed, 'there can be no resignation' and he criticized Iliescu's willingness to negotiate under the threat of force as 'an act of cowardice' bound to prove disastrous for democracy. In previous months, Iliescu's backing for his premier's economic strategy had become increasingly lukewarm. The Western-orientated technocrats with whom Roman had surrounded himself remained a minority in the NSF. Conservative, party-educated deputies, with a background in the state bureaucracy, had already established their strength in the autumn of 1990 by blocking proposals that civil servants should be appointed on the basis of proven competence. By the end of 1991, Eugen Dijmarescu, economy minister in the former Roman Government, was complaining about 'an unseen but operational establishment' formed after the revolution by 'a conservative strata of the former nomenklatura' intent on retaining control of Romanian society. Roman spoke on 29 October 1991 of the dangers facing Romania as a result of the survival of 'the mentality and methods of the Securitate'. However, the appointment of another reformer, Theodor Stolojan, as his successor, signified that things were not quite so simple. Stolojan's new Government of 'national openness' was confirmed in office by parliament on 16 October; it was a four-party coalition, dominated by the NSF, which included members of the opposition National Liberal Party (NLP). However, Stolojan was to show surprising freedom of action in his 11-month premiership and, despite further austerity measures, he gained a measure of popularity for his openness which had eluded his predecessor.

POLITICAL DEVELOPMENTS IN 1991–92

A coalition of mainstream democratic parties, called the Democratic Convention, had been formed in the autumn of 1991 to enable the opposition to provide a united challenge to the NSF and its satellites in local elections due in 1992. The stature of the opposition increased as the NSF plunged into the worst disarray it had faced since coming into existence. However, when one of the opposition parties, the NLP, decided to enter the Stolojan Government for modest terms, which did not include strengthening the regime's democratic character by opening up the state media or making the security services more accountable, the initiative slowly passed back to Iliescu and the main governing party.

A new Constitution for Romania was successfully steered through parliament in the last months of 1991. It made Romania a unitary state with a parliamentary form of government. Romanian was the sole official language and the president enjoyed important discretionary powers. The HDUR voted *en bloc* against the document, given the absence of specific measures guaranteeing minority rights. Most other opposition members voted against it because it continued with the republican form of government which had been imposed arbitrarily under the Communists in 1947. A referendum was held on 8 December 1991, but the electorate was given the choice only of accepting or rejecting the Constitution as a whole, rather than being able to express a preference for a republican or monarchical form of government. However, royalist sentiments lacked widespread backing and it was government over-reaction which prevented the exiled former king, Michael I, returning to Romania except for a brief visit made at Easter 1991.

Of the 69.1% of the electorate who voted on 8 December, 77.3% approved the new Constitution. The NSF had thus received a convincing endorsement for the Constitution, despite its own widening splits and the collapse of governmental authority in September. Largely single-handedly, it had drawn up the new political structures for a post-Communist Romania, making concessions to Western viewpoints but effectively ignoring the domestic opposition.

A test of its standing with the voters was provided by local elections to elect mayors, local councils and county councils, due to be held on 9 February 1992. For the first time in over 50 years, Romanians were to elect from among themselves citizens entrusted with the task of providing effective and accessible local government. The outbreak of internal strife within the NSF placed that party at a disadvantage, except in its rural and small town strongholds where the opposition was too weak to exploit the governing party's difficulties. Local NSF activists who had, in many cases, enrolled in the party not for ideological reasons but in order to obtain the benefits associated with belonging to a ruling party, were unsure which of the former partners, Iliescu and Roman, to support. Petre Roman had been deprived of his powers of patronage, but Iliescu's re-election prospects were far from assured. The President felt it necessary to intervene openly in the NSF's factional struggles to rally his own supporters, despite the Constitution forbidding the head of state from membership of any party.

The Democratic Convention captured the large cities, with the exception of Cluj-Napoca, which was won by an extreme nationalist with NSF support. In March 1992 the NSF finally split into two rival and separate parties. Roman's group was strong enough to retain the name, but a majority of the parliamentary party went over to the Democratic National Salvation Front (DNSF), which was less of a political party and more of a personal platform for Iliescu. Almost a dozen deputies were also to defect to the most extreme of the nationalist parties, the Greater Romania (România Máre) party, in the period of realignment that preceded the general election which was due to be held one year after the ratification of the Constitution. This was a period when ultra-nationalists emerged as a distinctive force in their own right, rather than as a group which operated in the shadows of the ruling party. Corneliu Vadim Tudor, the leader of România Máre and an agile and uninhibited self-publicist who had produced skilful propaganda for Ceauşescu, proved able to exploit the disgruntlement of those Romanians unhappy with the post-1989 changes and who could be persuaded, by selective evocation of the past, that the Ceauşescu era had been one of stability and achievement. In Transylvania, Gheorghe Funar, Cluj-Napoca's newly elected mayor, quickly emerged as a figure of national prominence, owing to a series of controversial decisions aimed at the Hungarian minority (some of doubtful constitutional legality), designed, in his own words, to allow the Romanians to be 'masters in their own house'.

Mounting economic hardship and the collapse of the country's Yugoslav and Soviet neighbours provided rich opportunities for populists to stress an internal enemy or an external threat to Romania. The democratic opposition was hampered by the withdrawal of the NLP from its electoral alliance. However, this party broke up and mainstream democrats rallied around a strong challenger for the presidency, Prof. Emil Constantinescu, rector of Bucharest University. He had spent all his life in Romania and was more in touch with national realities than the *émigrés* who had been opposition standard-bearers in 1990. He fought a spirited and professional campaign, but it was hampered by lack of resources and by the fact that Constantinescu was little known, having only been chosen as the Democratic Convention of Romania's (DCR) candidate in the summer.

The one-month campaign for the elections on 27 September 1992 was not marred by the types of incidents which had made that of May 1990 so controversial, and television coverage of the opposition was much fairer. In the presidential contest, Iliescu obtained 47.34% of the vote; Constantinescu received 31.24%; and the nationalist Gheorghe Funar, leader of the Romanian National Unity Party (RNUP) came third with 10.87%. A run-off for the presidency took place on 11 October between the two front-runners, nobody having reached 50%. The failure of any party to gain a parliamentary majority enabled Iliescu, once again, to present himself as a rock of stability in a fluid political situation. This message appealed to many middle-aged and elderly Romanians, influenced by a lifetime of state paternalism and who feared any uncertainty or interruption of established routines; on a high turn-out of 73.20%, Ion Iliescu was re-elected, with 61.43% of the vote to Constantinescu's 38.57%, for a four-year term.

In the parliamentary contest, the DNSF emerged as the largest party on 27.71%, the pro-reform forces of the DCR came second on 20.16%, Petre Roman's NSF was a distant third on 10.18%, the Hungarian HDUR got 7.45% and ultra-nationalists and neo-Communists shared most of the rest of the vote between them. The parties making up the DCR had done much better than in 1990, but expectations that they would emerge as the main political force had not been fulfilled. The DNSF proved to be the largest party in the south and in Moldavia, to the north-east, but in Transylvania it could only manage 12% of the vote, given the high level of urbanization and the nationalist factor. The President's first task was to break the impasse resulting from an inconclusive parliamentary result and appoint a new government. The DNSF was reluctant to govern alone and to take responsibility for difficult economic portfolios which the parliamentary party had few suitable people able to fill. The DCR conditions for being in government were too onerous for Iliescu to accept, so, finally, in November 1992, a non-party government was sworn in under Nicolae Vacaroiu, a senior bureaucrat close to Iliescu. It was sustained in parliament by the DNSF, as well as by ultra-nationalists who expected concessions in return for their support.

THE PROBLEMS FACING THE VACAROIU GOVERNMENT

Romania's isolation was underscored on 30 September 1992 when the US House of Representatives rejected a bilateral trade agreement which included the restoration of 'most-favoured nation' trading status. Although the country had enjoyed a year of stability under Stolojan, its mixed human-rights record and the Vacaroiu Government's reliance on the votes of extremist deputies, some of whom made no secret of their anti-Semitism, kept alive Western suspicions about Romania's direction. Romania's difficulty in gaining access to the Council of Europe as a full member (it retained guest status long after most other Soviet bloc countries had joined) reflected external concern about the degree of continuity with the Communist era in some aspects of internal affairs. Aid, investment and training from Western European institutions and individual states had been channelled increasingly to the country since 1991, but had made little impact on the economic crisis which had intensified as a deeply entrenched socialist economy was led in a haphazard fashion towards the market. Gross domestic product (GDP) fell by 16.5% in 1992, and the decline in industrial production was even steeper (23.5%). The crisis in industry meant that 9% of the labour force was unemployed by the end of 1992, with a further sharp rise projected for 1993. The de-indexation of prices for a range of basic goods and services led to an inevitable sharp fall in living standards, which affected those citizens without the mobility, language, skills, technical expertise and access to hard currency that enabled them to benefit from the movement towards economic liberalization.

Some 362,000 private businesses had been set up by the end of September 1992, but they were generally small-scale in terms of investment and the size of their work-force. Younger, better-educated Romanians, and those with a background of decision-making before 1989, have been able to do well in the shift away from the command economy, but millions of Romanians—particularly the elderly, the barely-educated and those working in factories whose products lack markets—are in danger of falling victim to what has been a badly co-ordinated and rushed drive towards a market economy. By 1993 the disenchantment with the rigours of a capitalist democracy were being reflected in poll findings. When asked what sort of government they would like, 27% of respondents expressed a preference for 'an authoritarian iron-fisted leadership'. In 1992 polls were finding that as many as two in five respondents believed that they had fared better before the overthrow of Ceaușescu. Increasingly, the numbers of those who felt Romania was going in the right or wrong directions were converging.

In past moments of political uncertainty and economic hardship, with the low repute of the political class and serious disagreement about future options generating tension, nationalism has been summoned up as a panacea to overcome current difficulties and place Romania on the road to national redemption. The nationalist bloc in parliament, with around 15% of the seats, held the fate of the Vacaroiu Government in its hands. Its support enabled it to survive an opposition confidence motion in March 1993. But, in return, the Government came under pressure to appoint nationalists, many of whom were influential before 1989, to diplomatic posts, to administrative jobs in ethnically-mixed areas, and to head the state television service.

The nationalist bloc does not hide its support for Slobodan Milošević's attempt to carve a Greater Serbia out of the former Yugoslavia in defiance of Western opinion. However, the Government's Yugoslav policy has been cautious. Like the West, it opposed the breakup of Yugoslavia, the Romanian foreign ministry issuing a statement in June 1991 expressing the hope that 'a country which is a neighbour and friend' would maintain 'its territorial integrity and stability'. Later, Romania joined in the United Nations' economic embargo on Serbia, but without severing political and diplomatic ties. Romania offered to mediate in contacts there and, in June 1992, Prime Minister Stolojan declared that Romania would never participate in any international military intervention against Belgrade.

Policy has been influenced by the way that the disintegration of Yugoslavia might affect Romanian unity. Official caution towards the prospect of reunification with Moldova also stems partly from the fear that a change of borders might encourage Hungarian irredentism in Transylvania. Hungary long ago dropped any territorial claim over neighbouring territories where Hungarian-speakers are found, and the HDUR rejects irredentism. However, a Romanian-Hungarian friendship treaty may be blocked as long as Hungary seeks to include provisions on the protection of the Hungarian minority, while Romania insists on a clause concerning the inviolability of borders. Even when Romania was eventually admitted to the Council of Europe, Hungary abstained from voting.

The ruling party, the DNSF, changed its name to the Party of Social Democracy of Romania (PSDR) in July 1993, shortly before the publication of a report for the Organisation of Economic Co-operation and Devlopment (OECD) which found that the shift away from state control of the economy had been 'diluted and distorted' by bureaucratic interventionism. The report found that state-owned enterprises still accounted for 90% of industrial production, many in the loss-making metallurgy, machine-building and chemicals industries. The OECD report concluded that the economic situation 'remains critical, with the foundations for a sustained recovery and transformation not yet laid'. The DNSF's name change had been preceded by a similar change by Petre Roman's National Salvation Front, to the Democratic Party—NSF. These moves symbolized the desire of both wings of the former NSF to distance themselves from the events of 1989–90.

In July 1993 the PSDR absorbed three other left-wing parties, confirming its position as Romania's principal party of the left. However, the parliamentary position of the Vacaroiu Government remained precarious, not least because its membership, drawn as it was from the PSDR and assorted independent technocrats, had the direct support of barely one-third of the seats in the Assembly of Deputies. For survival it depended on parliamentary support from the Socialist Labour Party and the extreme nationalist parties, the RNUP and România Máre. Towards the end of 1993 there were clear signs of a deepening political crisis. In December the Government survived another motion of 'no confidence', this time by only 13 votes. In the following months the PSDR undertook a vigorous round of talks with other parties, both those on which it could traditionally rely for support, and opposition parties such as the DCR alliance and the Democratic Party—NSF, in an attempt to forge a new government coalition. However, these talks proved to be inconclusive, and in March 1994 the exercise appeared to have been concluded when a relatively minor government reshuffle occurred, which continued the pattern of single-party rule supplemented by 'independent' technocrats. The only discernible change was that the nationalist parties appeared to be wielding more influence over who was appointed to government posts.

Compared to the 1989 revolution and the months following it Romania has enjoyed a period of relative calm. However, Government and opposition remain polarized, and some kind of unconstitutional seizure of power would seem just as likely as a peaceful handover to the opposition should the disastrous situation bequeathed by the Ceauşescu regime prove too much for President Iliescu.

The Economy

ALAN H. SMITH

DOMESTIC DEVELOPMENT POLICIES UNDER COMMUNISM

Romanian economic policy from the end of the Second World War until the overthrow of the Ceauşescu regime in December 1989 can be seen as an extreme version of the pursuit of the traditional Stalinist model of economic development. This involved the rapid construction of a heavy industrial base in a predominantly agrarian economy, by means of a highly-centralized system of economic management. This pattern of development also reflected the economic priorities of the Romanian Communist Party, which were influenced by the theories of protectionist and nationalist-minded Romanian economists from the inter-War period, who rejected the idea that Romania should remain a predominantly agrarian country.

The strategy of Romanian industrialization in the Communist era was similarly motivated by the desire to create a form of economic independence by reducing the demand for imported manufactured goods and generating exports of manufactures in place of food and raw materials. This policy was extended by Ceauşescu to include a policy of import substitution which involved the domestic production of a wide range of industrial products to minimize dependence on imports. Ironically, this pattern of industrialization, which both neglected the country's traditional comparative advantage in agriculture and drastically increased domestic consumption of energy and raw materials, increased Romania's dependence on imported raw materials and foodstuffs.

The growth of the industrial capital stock was achieved by allocating a large (and growing) proportion of national income to investment, concentrated in heavy industry. A relatively low priority was attached to investment in infrastructure and social and cultural facilities, including housing, health and scientific research. About 50% of investment during the Communist period was concentrated in industry, four-fifths of which was devoted to industrial producers' goods. A further 10% of total investment was allocated to transport. In the 1950s and 1960s, industrial investment was largely concentrated on the development of the energy sector (including petroleum) and of the iron and steel, machine-tool and chemical industries. When Ceauşescu came to power in 1965, a growing share of industrial investment was concentrated on the development of the machine-tool and chemical industries (including petrochemicals), while the energy sector received a smaller proportion of total investment.

According to official statistics, the industrial labour force increased from 800,000 in 1950 to 4.2m. in 1989. From 1956 onwards (when labour shortages started to appear in urban areas) the growth of the industrial labour force was largely achieved by the movement of labour from rural areas to the towns. This policy was facilitated by collectivization, and also coincided with a shift in industrial location policy away from traditional industrial regions towards the construction of large greenfield sites, to provide employment and accommodation for workers migrating from rural areas (Ronnas, 1991—see Bibliography). A major consequence of this policy is that Romania currently has a high proportion of workers of first (or second) generation peasant origin in its industrial labour force.

Romanian economic policy under Ceauşescu (1965–89) was increasingly dominated by the tendency to set over-ambitious central plan targets, which reflected the personal preferences of Ceauşescu himself, and which ignored the strains imposed on other sectors of the economy. The major features which differentiate Romanian economic policy from that of the other Eastern European economies during this period were the high degree of concentration of economic power and authority in the hands of the leadership, and the virtual absence of any attempts to reform the economy that would have involved a genuine decentralization of economic decision-making to either enterprises or non-party organizations.

Until the late 1970s the major objective was to maximize the rate of industrial growth, which was achieved by devoting a growing proportion of national income to investment in order to compensate for declining investment efficiency. These plans were badly affected by a major earthquake on 4 March 1977, with its epicentre in the oilfields of Ploieşti, which contributed to a longer-term decline in crude petroleum output from a peak of 14.7m. metric tons in 1976 to 11.5m. tons in 1980, and to below 10m. tons by the late 1980s (*Anuarul Statistic*, various years). The fall in crude petroleum production, combined with the expansion of the oil refining and petrochemicals sectors in the mid-1970s, was sufficient to turn Romania into a net petroleum importer (in value terms) from 1977 onwards.

The already over-ambitious plan targets for the 1976–80 five-year plan were revised upwards in October 1977, despite the damage the earthquake had inflicted on both the industrial capital stock and domestic energy production, not to mention popular morale, which was reflected in strikes and riots in the principal coal-mining regions in the Jiu valley in the summer of 1977. The planned expansion of industrial output (of just under 12% a year) placed further strain on domestic energy production, and on electric power generation in particular, and further aggravated shortages. The planners' response to energy shortages was to increase targets for coal production (including low-quality and highly-polluting brown coal and lignite), despite the disturbances in the mining regions, and to launch a series of unattainable proposals for the expansion of hydroelectric power and the construction of nuclear power. In practice, targets for coal-fired power generation could not be realized, and petroleum and natural gas had to be diverted from exports to power generation (Smith, 1982 and 1987).

The causes of the crisis which overtook the Romanian economy in the 1980s can be largely dated to the response to the problems of the late 1970s. From 1977–80, the domestic imbalances created by unattainable plan targets were partly relieved by increasing imports of not only machinery and equipment, to meet investment targets, but also by increased imports of energy, raw materials (including iron ore) and even food, the majority of which had to be paid for in hard currency as a result of Romania's isolation within the Council for Mutual Economic Assistance (CMEA).

ROMANIAN FOREIGN ECONOMIC RELATIONS UNDER COMMUNISM

The Rift with the CMEA

Romanian foreign economic relations in the Communist period were influenced by the policy of national independence, which was interpreted in the West (to Romania's undoubted advantage) as a desire for independence from the USSR. In practice, Romania's 'independent line' in economic policy was largely the result of a dispute with the more-industrialized Eastern European nations over the economic role that Romania should play within the CMEA, rather than a reflection of a conscious desire to improve economic relations with the West.

Romania, in common with the other CMEA economies, was initially forced to accelerate its plans for the development of heavy industry following the outbreak of the Korean War in 1950. Following the death of Stalin in 1953, the Soviet Government scaled down the priority attached to heavy industrial production in the CMEA in favour of increased production of consumer goods (the 'New Course'). Romania responded to the lower level of Eastern bloc demand for iron and steel and engineering products by reducing its imports of capital goods from CMEA partners and increasing the proportion of investment that was met from domestic production, thereby reducing its trade levels with the other CMEA economies. This resulted in a major conflict with the more-industrialized members of the CMEA, who felt that the less-industrialized Balkan economies should concentrate on the production of food and agrarian products, and meet a greater proportion of their demand for machinery and engineering goods by importing from the central East European countries, which were now faced with excess capacity for industrial products (Montias, 1967).

Similar concerns were expressed by the Soviet authorities, who were concerned with the increasing cost to the Soviet economy of meeting Eastern European demand for energy and raw materials. Soviet concerns were reflected in a series of proposals for specialization agreements in the late 1950s and early 1960s, which were intended to limit Eastern European production of steel and engineering goods to countries which either had a clear comparative advantage in these industries, or had adequate sources of iron ore and coking coal. The Soviet proposals were welcomed by the German Democratic Republic and Czechoslovakia, but were greeted with far less enthusiasm by the Balkan economies, who interpreted the policies as a deliberate attempt to restrict their plans to industrialize, and which would commit them to a permanent agrarian status. Romania, in particular, was reluctant to abandon proposals to build a major metallurgical complex at Galaţi, with Soviet assistance, close to the mouth of the Danube, which would have relied on iron ore imported from the USSR.

The dispute came to a crisis in November 1962 when the USSR indicated its unwillingness to assist in the production of the Galaţi steel mill. A special Central Committee plenum was convened on 21–23 November, following which it was announced that the construction of the Galaţi metallurgical combine would now go ahead on the basis of assistance provided by an Anglo-French consortium (Fischer-Galati, 1967 and Smith, 1983).

The Romanian rift with the CMEA was accentuated following Ceauşescu's accession to power in 1965. In the late 1960s Romania did not fully participate in a number of CMEA investment projects which were designed to provide Eastern European assistance in the development of Soviet natural resources for bloc consumption. This economic 'independence' was achieved at a substantial cost to the Romanian economy, as Romania did not benefit from preferential terms of trade with which the USSR supplied crude oil to the other East European economies, but was forced to import crude oil from hard currency sources.

The Diversion of Trade to the West: the Import-Led Growth Strategy

Romania's trade with the West was insignificant in the early 1960s and grew only modestly until 1967, despite Galaţi affair. In 1967 Romania became the first East European country to embark on the strategy of 'import-led growth', which involved making relatively costless political concessions to the West (including the recognition of the Federal Republic of Germany) in exchange for improved economic relations. The economic goal of the strategy was the modernization of the industrial capital stock, which involved a combination of direct imports of Western machinery and equipment (largely supplied on credit) and the encouragement of a number of different types of 'co-operation ventures' with Western multinational corporations. It was hoped that the latter would provide Romania with technology embodied in machinery and equipment, together with technical documentation and know-how, in exchange for repayment in products which would (at least theoretically) be produced by the newly-installed plant and equipment, and by the new industrial processes. In 1971 Romania became the first CMEA country to enact joint-venture legislation, which enabled Western multinationals to take a minority (up to 49%) equity holding in ventures on Romanian territory. At the same time Romania joined GATT (the General Agreement on Tariffs and Trade) in 1971, and the IMF (International Monetary Fund) and the World Bank in 1972.

The strategy of the acquisition of foreign technology, within the framework of a highly centralized system of economic administration, suffered from a number of basic flaws. Firstly, the strategy placed excessive emphasis on building up a technological base in engineering industries, in which Romania had little or no experience or expertise (for example, aerospace and car production), rather than building on Romania's traditional strengths in agriculture, textiles, furniture and footwear. More critically, Romania offered Western multinationals a far less attractive economic environment than the newly-industrializing economies of South-East Asia. Central government controls were maintained over a myriad of enterprise decisions, including manning levels, wage and price policy, and quality control. As a result, co-operation ventures and joint ventures proved to be far less attractive to Western multinationals than the Romanian authorities had anticipated (only five joint ventures were established), and Romania was forced to rely on straightforward purchases of industrial licences and machinery and equipment to a far greater degree than intended.

Romania was unable to generate the volume of hard-currency exports required to finance a continued flow of imports of machinery and equipment, and the increased demand for energy, raw materials and components and spare parts, required to keep imported plants in operation and to service fully its debt. As a net petroleum exporter Romania benefited from the increase in world petroleum prices in 1973–74 and managed to stabilize its net debt at about US $2,500m. from 1974 to 1976. The fall in crude petroleum output in 1977, following the earthquake, turned Romania into a net petroleum importer and created additional balance-of-payments problems, which were aggravated by the second increase in world petroleum prices in 1979. Crude petroleum imports cost Romania $3,800m. in hard currency in 1980, which, together with rising interest rates on existing debt, pushed the current account deficit in its balance of payments in convertible currencies to $2,400m. Despite cuts in imports of $1,000m. in 1981, interest charges pushed the current account into deficit by $800,000, and gross debt rose to $10,500m. at the end of 1981. With payments arrears of $1,100m. Romania was forced to make a formal request for the rescheduling of its debt and the suspension of interest payments in 1982 (Jackson, 1986 and Smith, 1983 and 1987).

THE DEBT REPAYMENT PROGRAMME

The need to reschedule debt resulted in an abrupt change in Romanian economic policy in the 1980s. The goal of the maximization of industrial output was suddenly replaced by the goal of the elimination of hard-currency debt. The low level of competitiveness of Romanian exports in Western markets, meant that surpluses in the balances of trade and payments could only be achieved by a drastic reduction in imports, followed by the export of items with a low level of processing, such as food and energy, which were in high domestic demand. Hard-currency imports were cut from US $8,000m. in 1980 to $4,700m. in 1982, and to only $3,400m. (in current prices) in 1989. Imports from the industrialized West were reduced from a peak of $3,900m. in 1980 to $1,300m. in 1983, reaching their lowest in 1989, at $1,200m.

The major burden of the reduction in imports from the industrialized West was borne by cuts in imports of machinery and equipment. The net effect of import cuts was that a hard-currency trade deficit of $2,400m. in 1980 had been turned into trade surpluses in the region of $2,000m. a year in the mid-1980s, climbing to $2,500m. in 1988. Ceauşescu announced, in April 1989, that Romanian debt had been eliminated.

The repayment of debt had been accomplished at an enormous human and economic cost. In 1982 Romania became a major net exporter of food, while severe food shortages and food queues appeared in major cities. Bread, sugar and cooking oil were rationed (if available at all), and meat, apart from occasional items of poultry, was virtually unobtainable (Jackson, 1986).

The position with energy supplies was even more acute, and became critical in the severe winter of 1984/85, when temperatures in some parts of the country were reported to have fallen below −25°C. Communal heating systems were switched off for most of each day, while gas pressures were too low for heating or cooking; electric power supplies were frequently interrupted and the use of electric heaters, refrigerators and vacuum cleaners was banned and household electricity consumption was virtually reduced to the equivalent of a single 40-watt light bulb per household. The use of private cars was banned for three months, while the public transportation networks collapsed, forcing workers to trudge many miles to work in deep snow. In addition, a virtual ban on public lighting and lighting in stairways of apartments was imposed; offices and shops were required to operate during daylight hours only and, even in tourist areas, bars and cafés had to close at 9 p.m. Hospitals were frequently without heating, adequate lighting or power for operations, and deaths from hypothermia were reported. Similar restrictions were imposed in the following winters although, fortunately, weather conditions were not so severe (Smith, 1987).

Although Western attention has largely concentrated on the human costs of the debt repayment policy, the efficiency and competitiveness of Romanian industry was also seriously affected. Cuts in imports of machinery and equipment have resulted in the failure to modernize industry, inadequate investment in infrastructure, including transport and telecommunications, while valuable resources allocated to investment were squandered on grandiose 'prestige' investment projects such as the Presidential Palace in Bucharest and the Danube–Black Sea Canal. Similarly, industrial investment that did take place appears to have been directed towards obsolete industries. As a result, after the revolution the new Prime Minister, Petre Roman, claimed that the majority of industrial plants were using technology that was, in some cases, 30 to 40 years old, and that the technological level of Romanian industry was 15 to 20 years behind that of the West (Smith, 1991).

THE ECONOMY AFTER THE REVOLUTION

Economic Performance 1990–92

The process of transition to a market economy has proved to be far more difficult in Romania than elsewhere in central and eastern Europe, and has been associated with a greater loss of output and economic welfare. Romanian economic performance in 1992 was the worst of the Eastern European economies which had been members of the CMEA (i.e. excluding Albania and former Yugoslavia) on the majority of indicators. According to official statistics gross domestic product (GDP) fell by 15.4% in 1992, the largest recorded fall in the region. This followed falls of 7.4% and 13.7% in 1990 and 1991, respectively, resulting in a cumulative reduction in GDP of 33% since the fall of Communism. Industrial output fell by 22.5% in 1992, and by 1993 stood at less than half its 1989 level. However, a limited recovery did start in 1993, with GDP increasing by 1%; agriculture was the sector which performed best, with a growth rate of 12.4%, while industry grew by 1.3% and construction by 0.7%. The rate of consumer price inflation in 1992, at 210%, was the highest in the former CMEA zone, and increased further in 1993, to 296%.

Romania was the only country to record a fall in its exports to the industrialized West, as exports fell from US $3,900m. in 1989 to $2,400m. in 1992. In other former

CMEA countries the growth of exports to the industrialized West has been a major factor offsetting the fall in demand from their former Eastern partners (and the former USSR in particular), and in limiting the fall in output in the other Eastern European countries, and is expected to play a major role in ending the recession. In Romania the fall in exports to the West has exacerbated the fall in exports to the CMEA, leading to an overall reduction of exports of more than 50% since the end of 1989. Although some of this can be explained by the reduction in exports of refined oil products from imported crude petroleum, which was of limited profitability, it will still damage Romania's prospects of economic recovery.

At the same time, imports from the industrialized West grew from $1,200m. in 1989 to $3,000m. in 1992. This has contributed to balance-of-payments deficits of $1,700m. in 1990 and $1,400m. in both 1991 and 1992, resulting in a net foreign debt of around $3,000m. at the end of 1992 compared to a net creditor position of $1,200m. at the end of 1989. Although the stock of foreign debt remains low in comparison with the other Eastern European countries, a significant improvement in export performance will be required if Romania is not to face continued long-term financing problems. The inflow of finance from private commercial banks and multinational investment into Romania between 1989 and 1992 were negligible. This has forced Romania to depend on financial support from multilateral financial institutions (the IMF, World Bank, European Bank for Reconstruction and Development and the European Investment Bank), which requires them to comply with IMF targets for economic stabilization and structural adjustment. In July 1993 Romania failed to secure further financing from the IMF, which was dissatisfied with the progress made in reforming large state enterprises and in controlling inflation. This, in turn, would block loans from the European Community and G24. Between 1990 and late 1993 total foreign investment in Romania registered at only $729m., with Italy, France, the United Kingdom and Germany among leading investors.

The pace of structural adjustment in Romania has also been slow, particularly in comparison with other central and eastern European countries. The major successes have been recorded in the privatization of agriculture, where 70% of farmland had been nominally returned to private ownership by the end of 1992, although many issues relating to titles of ownership remained unresolved. The development of a small-scale private sector has also proceeded fairly well, although not as rapidly as countries such as the Czech Republic, Hungary and Poland. By the end of 1992 the small-scale private sector employed around 600,000 people and contributed 10% of GDP. The majority of these businesses were involved in services and trade (with 45% of retail turnover in private hands), but some were also involved in manufacturing. The biggest weakness has been in the privatization of state industry. A complicated scheme initially involved the redesignation of state enterprises as joint stock companies. A State Ownership Fund, which holds 70% of shares in a state industry prior to privatization, and five private ownership funds, which hold the remaining 30% for free distribution to the public, were established in 1992. Adult citizens were issued with 'Certificates of Ownership' providing them with a title to the private ownership funds during 1992. Each certificate contained one coupon for each of the funds. Certificates can also be sold (but not to foreigners) or used to buy shares directly in small- and medium-scale enterprises. In practice, the private ownership funds do not appear to be capable of exercising much control over enterprises, particularly as it was not planned to hold shareholders' meetings for five years. By September 1993 only 1% of the equity of the 6,280 companies scheduled for privatization had been sold, even though the privatization law introduced in 1991 had stipulated that 10% of the equity should be sold each year.

Economic Policy since the Revolution

The first priority of the National Salvation Front (NSF), which took power following the December 1989 revolution, was to win popular support by improving consumption, which had been suppressed during the debt-repayment policy. This was effectively the opposite of the austere macroeconomic policies pursued in Poland. Similarly, structural adjustment programmes were postponed until after the elections scheduled for the spring of 1990. Macroeconomic policy involved easing the constraints on domestic consumption and the continuation of central controls over prices, accompanied by substantial subsidies for basic staple goods funded by the state budget. Exports of food and energy were restricted, while imports of the most urgent deficit items were increased. Many of the harshest measures of factory discipline that had been imposed in the 1980s were relaxed. The working week was reduced and many older workers took early retirement on favourable terms.

The relaxation of factory discipline and a fall in working hours of 16.6% contributed to a fall in industrial output of 16.6%, and to the reduction in GDP of 7.4%, in 1990 while wages continued to rise, by 11%. This led to a widening gap between domestic demand and supply, which was partly alleviated by doubling imports from the West, thus compounding the problems of shortages of hard-currency, but was also reflected in growing shortages in domestic markets.

The NSF indicated in its election programme that the transition to a market economy would be gradual. Following the election on 20 May 1990, the Prime Minister, Petre Roman, nominated a young, essentially meritocratic, Government and awarded the principal economic portfolios to economists who supported a rapid transition to a market economy, and whose views appeared to conflict with those of President Ion Iliescu. In the autumn of 1990 Roman argued that the economic problems had become so serious that it was necessary to accelerate the economic reforms and proposed a programme of structural reforms, and a macroeconomic stabilization programme that was largely modelled on the plan drawn up by Jeffrey Sachs for Poland with IMF advice.

Roman introduced a detailed package of reforms which was to involve the transition to a Western European style of market economy within a two-year period. This would involve measures to make the currency fully convertible in the long term, and to expose domestic enterprises to international competition; the introduction of a two-tier banking system, incorporating a central national bank and independent commercial banks; liberalization of both wholesale and retail prices; the restructuring of industry away from 'smoke-stack' industries to modern light industry; the removal of existing restrictions on small-scale private enterprises and the privatization of state industry; land reform; tax reform; and the creation of a state welfare system (Roman, 1990).

The level of excess demand in the economy meant that these reforms had to be accompanied by a severe 'deflationary' macrostabilization package, which was intended to equilibriate supply and demand on domestic markets and to draw out repressed inflation. This was to be achieved by gradually allowing prices to rise to market clearing levels in a series of steps, and by reducing and eliminating the budget deficit through the removal of subsidies to industrial enterprises and to food, rents, etc. The macroeconomic stabilization programme came into effect in November 1990 and initially involved the removal of state subsidies to consumer goods, except for basic foodstuffs, housing and heating. This resulted in price rises for the affected goods which ranged between 100% and 300%, and resulted in a general increase in consumer prices of 40% in the last two months of 1990.

Consumer price inflation had slowed to a monthly rate of 6%–7% by March 1991 before a second round of price increases, which affected many food products, was introduced in April 1991, leading to a second sharp increase of 26.5% in the consumer price index. At the same time, a new stabilization programme, involving tight fiscal and monetary policies, was drawn up with the approval of the IMF, who, together with the World Bank, provided financial support for the programme. Wages and salaries were only partially to be indexed to price rises, to prevent an inflationary wage-price spiral. The initial plan proposed that real wages would fall by an average of 25% in 1991, and real wages had indeed been reduced by 10% in August 1991. These measures provoked public hostility, which threatened not only the implementation of the reform programme, but also popular support for the Front itself and the social cohesion of the country. This was vividly reflected in the further violent demonstrations by miners in Bucharest in September 1991, which led directly to the fall of Roman.

Roman's replacement as Prime Minister, Theodor Stolojan, was also seen as committed to economic reforms. The Stolojan Government attempted to accelerate the liberalization of foreign trade and announced the introduction of internal convertibility of the leu, which permitted enterprises to obtain foreign currency for trade purposes, in November 1991. A single fixed exchange rate of 180 lei to the US dollar was introduced (compared with the official rate of 60 lei to $1 and the market auction rate of 260 lei to $1), which increased both import prices and the profitability of exports. However, a complicated system of price controls limited the ability of enterprises to pass on the increased cost of imported materials in product prices, and contributed to the suspension of the convertibility of the leu in May 1992.

Critically, the Stolojan Government was unable to bring inflation under control. Consumer price inflation averaged over 10% per month in the period from October 1991 to March 1992, and real wages were cut by a further 20%. The average growth in consumer prices rose from 161% in 1991 to 210% in 1992, with the inflation rate over the preceding 12 months reaching 264% in March 1992. Further reductions in subsidies for food and housing in May and September 1992 drove the monthly rate of inflation over 10% for those two months. In May 1993 subsidies were removed from most commodities, and in July value added tax was introduced at the rate of 18%; in the 12 months to October 1993 inflation measured 314%.

The inability to control inflation can be attributed to two major factors. Firstly, the phasing in of price liberalization in a series of pre-announced stages led to the general expectation that prices and costs would continue to rise. This has made it exceedingly difficult to control wages and social expenditures, which were also increased in stages to accommodate the announced price increases. At the same time, staged increases in domestic prices and wages meant that it was virtually impossible to introduce a fixed external rate of exchange, as exports became progressively less competitive and imports more attractive. Since the suspension of fixed exchange rates in May 1992, the leu subsequently floated down to 615 lei per US dollar by the end of April 1993, less than one-third of its value of a year earlier, contributing to a 300% increase in the domestic price of imported goods.

The second factor contributing to the failure to contain inflation was that an apparently tight monetary policy in 1991 was undermined by the practice of industrial suppliers effectively granting their customers credit by not demanding payment from illiquid state enterprises. Similarly, enterprises 'financed' this credit by not paying their own suppliers, thereby establishing a chain of inter-enterprise debt. The absence of a bankruptcy law meant that enterprises had few powers to force business customers to pay their debts. Creditors' willingness to continue supplying state enterprises, despite the non-payment of bills, reflected their perception that the Government would eventually be forced to underwrite the debts of illiquid state enterprises, rather than close them down and create large-scale unemployment.

The build-up of enterprise arrears had become critical by late 1991 (reaching 80% of GDP), and by now affected viable enterprises who could not obtain the cash to pay workers. In December 1991 parliament required the National Bank of Romania to advance credit to enterprises to clear the chain of inter-enterprise debt. This contributed to a doubling of the money supply at the end of 1991 and reinforced enterprise managers' expectations that similar write-offs could be expected in the future. As a result, attempts to impose a strict monetary policy in 1992 were again undermined by the expansion of inter-enterprise arrears after the initial clearance of inter-enterprise debts. Monetary policy was again relaxed towards the end of 1992, and a scheme to help reduce these arrears, under stricter conditions than in 1991, was introduced at the beginning of 1993. Nevertheless, inter-enterprise debts had reached US $2,400m. by mid-1993. The monthly rate of inflation rose to 10% in the first quarter of 1993. In May 1993 the final round of subsidies on food and heating were removed, which resulted in price increases for bread (350%), butter and milk (400%), and electricity (350%), which led to an increase in the consumer price index of 30%.

Parliamentary and presidential elections in September and October 1992 returned President Iliescu, with a reduced majority, while Iliescu's party, the Democratic National Salvation Front (broadly committed to gradualist reforms, the DNSF changed its name to the Party of Social Democracy of Romania), became the largest party in parliament, although with only 27% of the popular vote. A minority Government was formed, composed of independent technocrats, chosen by the DNSF, and of DNSF members, with Nicolae Vacariou (a former taxation official at the Ministry of Finance) as Prime Minister. Both Vacariou and Florin Georgescu, the new Minister of Finance, were advocates of gradualist reforms. The need for continued external finance to fund basic imports will require them to comply with IMF targets for fiscal and monetary policy. The IMF and other external agencies were also attempting to tie further financial assistance to the acceleration of structural reforms, including the introduction of bankruptcy laws, the elimination of industrial subsidies and the privatization of large-scale state industry. Although progress in implementing these policies was partially slow, and led to a delay in reaching an agreement for new financing with the IMF which only came to an end in December 1993, the effects on the economy and people of Romania meant that the policies encountered major opposition inside parliament and from trade unions. Between the revolution of 1989 and the end of 1993 it was estimated that real wages levels had lost about 45% of their value.

Statistical Survey

Source (unless otherwise stated): *Romanian Statistical Yearbook*, published by the Comisia Natională de Statistică (National Statistics Commission), Bucharest, Str. Stavropoleos 6; tel. (1) 158200; telex 111153.

Area and Population

AREA, POPULATION AND DENSITY

Area (sq km)	
Land	229,077
Inland water	8,423
Total	237,500*
Population (census results)	
5 January 1977	
Total	21,559,910
7 January 1992	
Males	11,182,290
Females	11,578,159
Total	22,760,449
Density (per sq km) at January 1992	95.8

*91,699 sq miles.

ADMINISTRATIVE DIVISIONS (at 1992 census)

	Area (sq km)	Population ('000)	Density (per sq km)	Administrative capital (with population)
Alba	6,231	414	66.5	Alba Iulia (71,254)
Arad	7,652	487	63.7	Arad (190,088)
Argeş	6,801	681	100.1	Piteşti (179,479)
Bacău	6,606	736	111.4	Bacău (204,495)
Bihor	7,535	634	84.2	Oradea (220,848)
Bistriţa-Năsăud	5,305	327	61.7	Bistriţa (87,793)
Botoşani	4,965	459	92.4	Botoşani (126,204)
Braşov	5,351	643	120.1	Braşov (323,835)
Brăila	4,724	392	83.0	Brăila (234,706)
Buzău	6,072	516	85.0	Buzău (148,247)
Caraş-Severin	8,503	376	44.2	Reşiţa (96,798)
Călăraşi	5,074	339	66.8	Călăraşi (76,886)
Cluj	6,650	735	110.5	Cluj-Napoca (328,008)
Constanţa	7,055	748	106.0	Constanţa (350,476)
Covasna	3,705	233	62.8	Sfîntu Gheorghe (68,070)
Dîmboviţa	4,036	560	138.7	Tîrgovişte (97,876)
Dolj	7,413	761	102.7	Craiova (303,520)
Galaţi	4,425	640	144.6	Galaţi (325,788)
Giurgiu	3,511	313	89.2	Giurgiu (74,236)
Gorj	5,641	400	70.9	Tîrgu Jiu (98,267)
Harghita	6,610	348	52.6	Miercurea-Ciuc (46,029)
Hunedoara	7,016	548	78.1	Deva (78,366)
Ialomiţa	4,449	304	68.3	Slobozia (55,614)
Iaşi	5,469	807	147.5	Iaşi (342,994)
Maramureş	6,215	539	86.7	Baia Mare (148,815)
Mehedinţi	4,900	332	67.8	Drobeta-Turnu Severin (115,526)
Mureş	6,696	607	90.7	Tîrgu Mureş (163,625)
Neamţ	5,890	578	98.1	Piatra-Neamţ (123,175)
Olt	5,507	521	94.6	Slatina (85,336)
Prahova	4,694	873	186.0	Ploieşti (252,073)
Satu Mare	4,405	400	90.8	Satu Mare (131,859)
Sălaj	3,850	266	69.2	Zalău (68,322)
Sibiu	5,422	453	83.5	Sibiu (169,696)
Suceava	8,555	701	81.9	Suceava (114,355)
Teleorman	5,760	482	83.7	Alexandria (58,582)
Timiş	8,692	700	80.6	Timişoara (334,278)
Tulcea	8,430	270	32.1	Tulcea (97,500)
Vaslui	5,297	458	86.4	Vaslui (80,151)
Vîlcea	5,705	436	76.5	Rîmnicu Vîlcea (113,356)
Vrancea	4,863	393	80.7	Focşani (101,296)
Bucharest Municipality	1,820	2,351	1,291.7	Bucharest (2,064,474)
Total	237,500	22,760	95.8	

PRINCIPAL TOWNS

(estimated population at 7 January 1992)

Bucureşti (Bucharest, the capital)	2,064,474	Sibiu	169,696
Constanţa	350,476	Tirgu Mureş	163,625
Iaşi	342,994	Baia Mare	148,815
Timişoara	334,278	Buzău	148,247
Cluj-Napoca	328,008	Satu Mare	131,859
Galaţi	325,788	Botoşani	126,204
Braşov	323,835	Piatra-Neamţ	123,175
Craiova	303,520	Drobeta-Turnu-Severin	115,526
Ploieşti	252,073	Suceava	114,355
Brăila	234,706	Rîmnicu-Vîlcea	113,356
Oradea	220,848	Focşani	101,296
Bacău	204,495	Tirgu Jiu	98,267
Arad	190,088	Tîrgovişte	97,876
Piteşti	179,479	Tulcea	97,500
		Reşiţa	96,798

BIRTHS, MARRIAGES AND DEATHS

	Registered live births		Registered marriages		Registered deaths	
	Number	Rate (per 1,000)	Number	Rate (per 1,000)	Number	Rate (per 1,000)
1984	350,741	15.5	164,110	7.3	233,699	10.3
1985	358,797	15.8	161,094	7.1	246,670	10.9
1986	376,896	16.5	167,254	7.3	242,330	10.6
1987	383,199	16.7	168,079	7.3	254.286	11.1
1988	380,043	16.5	172,527	7.5	253,370	11.0
1989	369,544	16.0	177,943	7.7	247,306	10.7
1990	314,746	13.6	192,652	8.3	247,086	10.6
1991	275,275	11.9	183,388	7.9	251,760	10.9

CIVILIAN LABOUR FORCE EMPLOYED (official estimates)

	1989	1990	1991
Industry*	4,169,000	4,015,000	3,817,400
Agriculture and forestry	3,056,300	3,096,900	3,133,100
Construction	766,700	653,100	462,700
Transport and communications	757,100	752,300	680,900
Trade	648,900	678,500	871,900
Housing, communal and other services	533,600	527,700	705,800
Public education, culture and arts	372,800	452,200	467,900
Science and science services	141,200	133,300	109,000
Public health, social welfare and physical culture	292,300	303,900	297,800
State and local administration	53,800	67,900	83,200
Total (incl. others)	10,945,700	10,839,500	10,785,800

* Manufacturing, mining, quarrying, electricity, gas, water and sanitary services.

Agriculture

PRINCIPAL CROPS ('000 metric tons)

	1990	1991	1992*
Wheat and rye	7,379	5,559	3,228†
Rice (paddy)	67	31	39
Barley	2,680	2,951	1,678
Maize	6,810	10,497	6,829
Oats	234	258	508
Potatoes	3,186	1,873	2,600†
Sunflower seed	556	612	774
Cabbages	552	617	850†
Tomatoes	814	693	850†
Onions (dry)	225	219	200†
Grapes	954	849	906
Sugar beet	3,278	4,703	2,875
Apples	683	505	545
Pears	74	58	70†
Peaches	53	44	42†
Plums	450	419	350†
Apricots	48	26	42†
Strawberries	18	14	22†
Walnuts	26	18	30‡

* Source: FAO, *Production Yearbook*.
† Unofficial figure(s).
‡ FAO estimate(s).

LIVESTOCK ('000 head at 1 January)

	1990	1991	1992
Horses	663	670	749
Cattle	6,291	5,381	4,355
Pigs	11,671	12,003	10,954
Sheep	15,435	14,062	13,879
Chickens	113,968	121,379	106,032

LIVESTOCK PRODUCTS ('000 metric tons)

	1990	1991	1992
Meat	1,555	1,453	1,397
Cows' milk	3,242	3,150*	2,838*
Cheese	106	83	72
Butter	33	23	20*
Hen eggs	385	341	340*
Honey	11	10*	10*
Wool:			
greasy	38	33	32*
clean	27	23*	21*

* FAO estimate(s).

Source: FAO, *Production Yearbook*.

Forestry

ROUNDWOOD REMOVALS
('000 cubic metres, excluding bark)

	1989	1990	1991
Sawlogs, veneer logs and logs for sleepers	5,075	5,164	4,386
Pulpwood	3,900	4,090	3,887
Other industrial wood*	4,500	4,500*	4,500*
Fuel wood	2,790	2,579	1,996
Total	12,625	16,333	14,769

* FAO estimate(s).

Source: FAO, *Yearbook of Forest Products*.

SAWNWOOD PRODUCTION
('000 cubic metres, incl. railway sleepers)

	1989	1990	1991
Coniferous (soft wood)	1,673	1,357	1,127
Broadleaved (hard wood)	1,178	1,554	1,329
Total	2,851	2,911	2,456

Source: FAO, *Yearbook of Forest Products*.

Fishing

('000 metric tons, live weight)

	1989	1990	1991
Common carp	16.7	13.4	9.4
Goldfish	12.8	4.2	5.7
Silver carp	14.3	13.9	11.9
Bighead carp	11.9	7.3	6.9
Other freshwater fishes	8.9	8.6	6.1
Cape horse mackerel	51.0	7.2	—
Other jack and horse mackerels	25.0	8.6	16.9
False scad	3.4	5.5	10.0
Round sardinella	14.8	14.4	18.6
Madeira sardinella	4.2	5.7	7.2
European pilchard (sardine)	29.4	16.8	19.9
Chub mackerel	7.2	6.0	5.8
Other fishes	25.1	18.2	6.4
Total catch	224.8	127.7	124.9
Inland waters	66.8	48.2	40.5
Mediterranean and Black Sea	13.8	6.3	1.2
Atlantic Ocean	144.1	73.2	83.2

Source: FAO, *Yearbook of Fishery Statistics*.

Mining

	1989	1990	1991
Hard coal ('000 metric tons)	8,300	4,446	3,836
Brown coal ('000 metric tons)	61,343	38,183	32,414
Crude petroleum ('000 metric tons)	9,173	7,928	6,791
Iron ore ('000 metric tons)*	2,482	2,002	1,461
Salt ('000 metric tons)	5,038	4,262	3,255
Methane gas (million cu metres)	22,222	19,154	17,252

* Figures refer to gross weight. The estimated metal content is 26%.

Industry

SELECTED PRODUCTS

('000 metric tons, unless otherwise indicated)

	1989	1990	1991
Canned fish	8	18	16
Canned vegetables	257	190	140
Canned fruits	117	124	77
Refined sugar	716	538	344
Margarine	48	29	26
Wine ('000 hectolitres)	4,632	4,705	4,805
Beer ('000 hectolitres)	11,513	10,527	9,757
Tobacco products	33	27	26
Cotton yarn—pure and mixed	158	130	92
Cotton fabrics—pure and mixed (million sq metres)	709	536	444
Woollen yarn—pure and mixed	67	59	49
Woollen fabrics—pure and mixed (million sq metres)	141	107	93
Silk fabrics—pure and mixed (million sq metres)*	142	107	98
Flax and hemp yarn—pure and mixed	34	24	22
Linen and hemp fabrics—pure and mixed (million sq metres)	123	95	76
Chemical filaments and fibres	276	209	142
Footwear (million pairs)	118	88	68
Chemical wood pulp	592	388	259
Paper and paperboard	709	540	380
Synthetic rubber	149	102	55
Rubber tyres ('000)	6,687	5,143	4,363
Sulphuric acid	1,687	1,111	745
Caustic soda	763	552	461
Soda ash	889	632	471
Chemical fertilizers	2,805	1,744	1,080
Insecticides, fungicides, etc.	33	24	17
Plastics and resins	640	474	350
Motor spirit (Petrol)	6,074	4,667	3,122
Distillate fuel oils	8,435	6,426	3,951
Residual fuel oils	10,172	8,126	4,969
Lubricating oils	516	401	273
Coke	5,870	3,942	2,550
Cement	13,265	10,383	7,405
Unworked glass ('000 sq metres)	76,199	56,649	45,711
Pig-iron	9,052	6,355	4,525
Crude steel	14,411	9,761	7,110
Rolled steel products	10,263	6,727	5,161
Steel tubes	1,360	1,041	627
Aluminium—unwrought	269	168	158
Electric motors ('000 kilowatts)	6,945	5,115	4,030
Electric generators ('000 kilovoltamperes)	664	589	382
Radio receivers ('000)	590	438	435
Television receivers ('000)	511	401	389
Merchant ships launched ('000 deadweight tons)	502	238	264
Passenger motor cars ('000)	123	85	74
Motor tractors, lorries and dump trucks (number)	13,515	8,457	7,592
Tractors (number)	17,124	25,640	22,453
Sewing machines ('000)	39	39	30
Combine harvester-threshers (number)	5,649	4,111	1,274
Freight wagons (number)	11,274	7,495	3,675
Domestic refrigerators ('000)	470	393	389
Domestic washing machines ('000)	204	205	188
Gas cookers ('000)	518	435	413
Construction: new dwellings completed ('000)	60	49	n.a.
Electric energy (million kWh)	75,851	64,309	56,912

* Including fabrics of artificial silk.

Finance

CURRENCY AND EXCHANGE RATES

Monetary Units

100 bani (singular: ban) = 1 leu (plural: lei).

Sterling and Dollar Equivalents (30 September 1993)

£1 sterling = 1,360.9 lei;
US $1 = 910.0 lei;
10,000 lei = £7.348 = $10.989.

Average Exchange Rate (lei per US $, commercial rate)

1990 22.43
1991 76.39
1992 307.95

Note: In February 1990 the two exchange rates which had hitherto operated in relation to convertible currencies (a commercial and a non-commercial rate) were unified. In February 1991 an interbank rate was introduced. Since November 1991 all foreign exchange transactions have been effected through the free market.

STATE BUDGET ('000 million lei)

Revenue	1989	1990	1991
Tax revenue	94.88	265.37	724.19
Taxes on income and profits	—	55.85	277.04
Social security contributions	53.94	67.57	227.83
Taxes on payroll and work force	40.94	43.95	—
Domestic taxes on goods and services	—	96.40	182.48
Import duties	—	1.60	24.63
Other taxes	—	—	12.21
Entrepreneurial and property income	255.37	29.57	55.75
Administrative fees, charges and non-industrial sales	1.02	—	—
Other current revenue	35.06	0.42	8.00
Total current revenue	386.33	295.36	787.94
Capital revenue	—	2.55	34.87
Total	386.33	297.91	822.81

Expenditure	1989	1990	1991
General public services, incl. public order	1.90	8.46	33.65
Defence	29.33	29.81	80.42
Education	16.08	7.86	78.16
Health	16.20	25.20	71.75
Social security and welfare	75.40	91.23	206.81
Housing and community amenities	25.10	—	0.61
Recreational, cultural and religious affairs and services	0.28	1.84	3.69
Economic affairs and services	153.29	110.94	257.45
Fuel and energy	26.51	18.28	12.14
Agriculture, forestry, fishing and hunting	18.60	30.46	43.22
Mining, manufacturing and construction	35.94	31.99	96.93
Transportation and communication	19.51	10.88	36.85
Other economic affairs and services	52.73	19.33	68.31
Other purposes	2.97	14.53	47.43
Total	320.55	289.87	779.98

Source: IMF, *Government Finance Statistics Yearbook*.

INTERNATIONAL RESERVES (US $ million at 31 December)

	1990	1991	1992
IMF special drawing rights	—	58	11
Foreign exchange	373	637	815
Total (excl. gold)	373	695	826

Source: IMF, *International Financial Statistics*.

MONEY SUPPLY (million lei at 31 December)

	1990	1991	1992
Currency outside banks	92.37	176.49	411.68
Demand deposits at deposit money banks	140.61	554.83	599.83
Total money	232.98	731.32	1,011.51

Source: IMF, *International Financial Statistics.*

BALANCE OF PAYMENTS (US $ million)

	1990	1991	1992
Merchandise exports f.o.b.	5,770	4,266	4,364
Merchandise imports f.o.b.	−9,114	−5,372	−5,558
Trade balance	−3,344	−1,106	−1,194
Exports of services	610	680	659
Imports of services	−787	−819	−946
Other income received	175	104	54
Other income paid	−14	−89	−144
Private unrequited transfers	—	20	19
Official unrequited transfers (net)	106	198	46
Current balance	−3,254	−1,012	−1,506
Direct investment (net)	−18	37	73
Other capital (net)	1,631	283	1,307
Net errors and omissions	147	15	−12
Overall balance	−1,494	−677	−138

Source: IMF, *International Financial Statistics.*

External Trade

PRINCIPAL COMMODITIES (million lei)

Imports f.o.b.	1988	1989	1990
Fuel, mineral raw materials and metals	65,244	75,633	99,923
Industrial equipment and means of transportation	32,284	34,361	49,843
Chemicals, fertilizers and rubber	7,611	7,471	13,308
Raw materials (other than foodstuffs	5,964	7,329	13,769
Manufactured consumer goods	5,514	4,613	9,848
Foodstuffs	1,268	1,981	10,834
Total (incl. others)	122,263	134,982	209,912

Exports f.o.b.	1988	1989	1990
Industrial equipment and means of transportation	57,508	49,067	41,665
Fuels, mineral raw materials and metals	51,164	53,922	45,545
Manufactured consumer goods	33,819	30,401	28,670
Chemicals, fertilizers and rubber	19,233	15,933	8,758
Foodstuffs	8,299	7,163	1,024
Raw materials (other than foodstuffs)	7,464	6,929	5,627
Total (incl. others)	182,258	167,780	135,191

PRINCIPAL TRADING PARTNERS (million lei)

Imports f.o.b.	1989	1990	1991*
Austria	879.2	3,469.6	16,610.5
Brazil	406.6	881.6	2,537.0
Bulgaria	3,451.9	3,451.9	4,778.3
China, People's Republic	5,148.0	5,369.8	10,360.5
Cuba	1,875.3	1,265.8	128.0
Czechoslovakia	6,172.9	6,588.5	5,122.4
Egypt	2,447.2	7,636.7	17,156.1
France	786.3	4,013.8	15,234.7
Germany†	12,869.0	24,017.1	45,135.9
Hungary	4,379.5	5,119.0	10,134.3
India	614.4	1,072.3	2,630.0
Iran	16,216.6	12,319.5	34,143.0
Iraq	908.4	3,525.7	—
Italy	834.0	2,500.9	19,780.1
Japan	714.3	1,778.7	4,046.7
Libya	184.3	5,082.3	6,037.6
Netherlands	707.7	3,053.9	8,092.2
Poland	5,395.6	8,962.9	7,137.3
Saudi Arabia	8,463.2	17,350.0	17,664.1
Switzerland	668.4	4,230.8	9,190.2
Syria	2,246.1	368.9	1,594.7
Turkey	774.4	1,760.4	7,182.3
USSR	42,493.3	49,487.0	74,265.5
United Kingdom	1,146.4	3,868.6	13,710.4
USA	2,735.8	9,607.3	10,587.2
Yugoslavia	2,452.7	4,835.8	15,850.5
Total (incl. others)	134,982.3	209,911.8	432,405.8

* 1991 imports are c.i.f.
† Including the former German Democratic Republic.

Exports f.o.b.	1989	1990	1991
Austria	2,689.2	1,648.9	9,530.9
Brazil	198.2	150.7	935.1
Bulgaria	2,791.8	2,510.5	5,180.5
Canada	1,043.1	636.2	767.5
China, People's Republic	5,657.7	3,541.6	11,670.1
Cuba	2,224.7	1,480.0	48.3
Czechoslovakia	5,234.4	4,348.2	3,169.6
Egypt	3,092.8	1,860.9	3,832.4
France	3,997.9	4,643.7	13,730.0
Germany*	19,965.1	14,883.3	38,062.0
Greece	2,616.9	1,979.8	3,638.4
Hungary	4,516.6	3,550.3	5,887.4
India	1,141.5	595.4	1,329.6
Iran	5,009.3	1,798.9	4,099.2
Iraq	2,168.2	970.0	—
Italy	15,980.6	11,963.4	17,741.8
Japan	2,754.8	2,148.9	5,783.2
Lebanon	955.9	2,022.9	4,427.5
Libya	187.2	816.7	273.7
Netherlands	2,385.9	3,596.8	18,233.5
Poland	5,079.2	1,913.3	3,926.2
Switzerland	1,393.6	2,044.4	6,232.5
Syria	744.2	506.2	3,338.8
Turkey	4,968.3	3,735.6	8,590.1
USSR	37,981.8	34,102.9	73,153.1
United Kingdom	4,050.1	2,929.8	11,301.2
USA	9,127.7	7,875.1	6,166.3
Yugoslavia	2,814.8	3,163.4	15,117.1
Total (incl. others)	167,779.5	135,191.4	323,693.1

* Including the former German Democratic Republic.

Transport

RAILWAYS (traffic)

	1989	1990	1991
Passenger-km (million)	35,456	30,582	25,429
Freight ton-km (million)	81,131	57,253	37,853

INLAND WATERWAYS (traffic)

	1989	1990	1991
Passenger-km (million)	72	58	33
Freight ton-km (million)	3,666	2,090	2,030

INTERNATIONAL SEA-BORNE SHIPPING
(freight traffic, '000 metric tons)

	1988	1989	1990
Goods loaded	13,800	14,060	6,578
Goods unloaded	33,300	33,690	33,480

Source: UN, *Monthly Bulletin of Statistics.*

CIVIL AVIATION (traffic)

	1989	1990	1991
Passenger-km (million)	3,842	3,418	2,694
Freight ton-km (million)	78	57	26

Tourism

FOREIGN TOURIST ARRIVALS BY COUNTRY OF ORIGIN
('000)

Country of origin	1990	1991
Bulgaria	1,057.8	797.5
Czechoslovakia	210.4	151.7
France	59.7	55.6
Germany	293.5	214.1
Hungary	998.3	760.1
Italy	44.9	51.5
Poland	813.8	377.8
USSR	2,216.0	2,171.9
Yugoslavia	264.3	179.7
Total (incl. others)	6,531.9	n.a.

Communications Media

	1988	1989	1990
Radio licences	3,112,000	3,073,000	2,982,852
Television receivers	3,740,000	3,696,000	3,675,140
Telephone subscribers	2,207,000	2,287,868	2,358,041
Book production:			
Titles	2,478	2,159	1,475
Copies ('000)	60,095	62,399	55,751
Daily newspapers	36	36	65
Annual circulation ('000)	1,145,603	1,138,684	1,245,000
Weeklies	24	24	n.a.
Annual circulation ('000)	39,863	42,218	n.a.

Education

(1991/92)

	Institutions	Pupils	Teachers
Kindergartens	12,600	742,232	36,326
Primary and gymnasium schools	13,985	2,639,279	159,199
Secondary schools	1,209	778,420	55,013
Vocational schools	717	375,303	5,319
Tertiary-level technical education	384	54,907	1,300
Other tertiary education	257*	215,226	17,615

* Number of faculties.

Directory

The Constitution

Following its assumption of power in December 1989, the National Salvation Front decreed radical changes to the Constitution of 1965. The name of the country was changed from the 'Socialist Republic of Romania' to 'Romania'. The leading role of a single political party was abolished, a democratic and pluralist system of government being established.

Under the electoral law of March 1990 political power in Romania belongs to the people and is exercised according to the principles of democracy, freedom and human dignity, of inviolability and inalienability of basic human rights. Romania is governed on the basis of a multi-party democratic system and of the separation of the legal, executive and judicial powers. Romania's legislature, consisting of the Chamber of Deputies (with 387 seats—subsequently reduced to 341 seats, of which 13 are reserved for various ethnic minorities) and the Senate (with 119 seats—subsequently increased to 143 seats), and Romania's President are elected by universal, free, direct and secret vote, the President serving a maximum of two terms. Citizens have the right to vote at the age of 18, and may be elected at the age of 21 to the Assembly of Deputies and at the age of 30 to the Senate, with no upper age limit. Those ineligible for election include former members of the Securitate (the secret police of President Ceaușescu) and other former officials guilty of repression and abuses. Independent candidates are eligible for election to the Assembly of Deputies and to the Senate if supported by at least 251 electors and to the Presidency if supported by 100,000 electors. Once elected, the President may not remain a member of any political party.

The combined chambers of the legislature elected in May 1990, working as a constituent assembly, drafted a new constitution (based on the Constitution of France's Fifth Republic), which was approved in a national referendum on 8 December 1991.

The Government

HEAD OF STATE

President: ION ILIESCU (assumed power as President of the National Salvation Front 26 December 1989, confirmed as President of Provisional National Unity Council 13 February 1990; elected by direct popular vote 20 May 1990, re-elected 11 October 1992).

COUNCIL OF MINISTERS
(March 1994)

Composed of independents (Ind.) and members of the Party of Social Democracy of Romania (PSDR).

Prime Minister: NICOLAE VACAROIU (Ind.).

Deputy Prime Minister and Chairman of the Council for Economic Strategy and Reform: MIRCEA COSEA (Ind.).

Deputy Prime Minister and Minister of Employment and Social Protection: DAN MIRCEA POPESCU (PSDR).

Deputy Prime Minister and Minister of Finance: FLORIN GEORGESCU (Ind.).

Deputy Prime Minister and Minister of Foreign Affairs: TEODOR VIOREL MELESCANU (Ind.).

Minister of Justice: IOSIF GAVRIL CHIUZBAIAN (Ind.).

Minister of National Defence: Lt-Gen. GHEORGHE TINCA (Ind.).

Minister of the Interior: IOAN DORU TARACILA (PSDR).

Minister of Industry: DUMITRU POPESCU (PSDR).

Minister of Agriculture and Food: IOAN OANCEA (PSDR).

Minister of Transport: AUREL NOVAC (Ind.).

Minister of Communications: ANDREI CHIRICA (Ind.).

Minister of Commerce: CRISTIAN IONESCU (PSDR).

Minister of Tourism: MATEI AGATEN DAN (PSDR).

Minister of Public Works and Physical Planning: MARIN CRISTEA (PSDR).

Minister of Waters, Forestry and Environmental Protection: AUREL CONSTANTIN ILIE (Ind.).

Minister of Education: LIVIU MAIOR (PSDR).

Minister of Research and Technology: DORU DUMITRU PALADE (Ind.).

Minister of Health: Prof. IULIAN MICU (PSDR).

Minister of Culture: PETRE SALCUDEANU (PSDR).

Minister of Youth and Sports: ALEXANDRU MIRONOV (PSDR).

Minister for Relations with Parliament: VALERIU DORNEANU (Ind.).

MINISTRIES

Office of the Prime Minister: 71201 Bucharest, Piaţa Victoriei 1; tel. (1) 143400; telex 11057; fax (1) 592018.

Ministry of Agriculture and Food: 70433 Bucharest, Bd. Carol I 24; tel. (1) 154412; telex 11217; fax (1) 130322.

Ministry of Commerce: 70663 Bucharest, Str. Apolodor 17; tel. (1) 141141; telex 10564; fax (1) 3122342.

Ministry of Communications: 70005 Bucharest, Bd. Libertăţii 14; tel. (1) 401100; telex 11372; fax (1) 401742.

Ministry of Culture: 71341 Bucharest, Piaţa Presei Libere 1; tel. (1) 170906; fax (1) 594781.

Ministry of Education and Science: 70749 Bucharest, Str. Berthelot 30; tel. (1) 144588; telex 11637; fax (1) 157736.

Ministry of Employment and Social Protection: 70119 Bucharest 1, Str. Demetru I. Dobrescu 2–4; tel. (1) 6156563; fax (1) 6156563.

Ministry of Finance: 70663 Bucharest, Str. Apolodor 17; tel. (1) 311784; telex 11239; fax (1) 121630.

Ministry of Foreign Affairs: 71274 Bucharest, Al. Modrogan 14; tel. (1) 334060; telex 11220; fax (1) 127589.

Ministry of Health: 70109 Bucharest, Str. Ministerului 1–3; tel. (1) 141526; telex 11982; fax (1) 156192.

Ministry of Industry: 71101 Bucharest, Calea Victoriei 152; tel. (1) 503168; telex 11109; fax (1) 503029.

Ministry of the Interior: 70622 Bucharest, Str. Mihai Voda 6; tel. (1) 6151108; fax (1) 3113555.

Ministry of Justice: 70602 Bucharest, Bd. M. Kogălniceanu 33; tel. (1) 148623; telex 11964; fax (1) 131219.

Ministry of National Defence: 77303 Bucharest, Intrarea Drumul Taberei 9; tel. (1) 6315553; fax (1) 7450238.

Ministry of Public Works and Physical Planning: 70663 Bucharest, Str. Apolodor 17; tel. (1) 141690; telex 11727; fax (1) 121130.

Ministry of Tourism: 70663 Bucharest, Str. Apolodor 17; tel. (1) 6310455; fax (1) 3122342.

Ministry of Transport: 77113 Bucharest, Bd. Dinicu Golescu 38; tel. (1) 6387886; telex 11372; fax (1) 3120984.

Ministry of Waters, Forestry and Environmental Protection: 70005 Bucharest, Bd. Libertăţii 12; tel. (1) 7816394; telex 11457; fax (1) 3124227.

Ministry of Youth and Sports: 70139 Bucharest, Str. Vasile Conta 16; tel. (1) 3120160; telex 11180; fax (1) 3120161.

Council for Economic Co-ordination, Strategy and Reform: Bucharest.

President

Presidential Election, 27 September and 11 October 1992

Candidates	First ballot votes cast: Number	First ballot votes cast: %	Second ballot votes cast %
ION ILIESCU (DNSF)	5,633,456	47.34	61.43
EMIL CONSTANTINESCU (DCR)	3,717,006	31.24	38.57
GHEORGHE FUNAR (RNUP)	1,294,388	10.88	—
CAIUS DRAGOMIR (NSF)	564,655	4.75	—
ION MANZATU (RP)	362,485	3.05	—
MIRCEA DRUC (Independent)	326,866	2.75	—
Total	11,898,856	100.00	100.00

In addition, a total of 554,948 invalid votes were cast in the first ballot.

Legislature

President of the Assembly of Deputies: ADRIAN NASTASE (PSDR).

Speaker of the Senate: OLIVIU GHERMAN (PSDR).

General Election, 27 September 1992

	Seats: Assembly of Deputies	Seats: Senate
Democratic National Salvation Front (DNSF)*	117	49
Democratic Convention of Romania (DCR) Alliance	82	34
Christian Democratic National Peasants' Party	42	21
Party of the Civic Alliance†	13	7
National Liberal Party—Democratic Convention†	2	4
National Liberal Party—Youth Wing†	11	1
Romanian Social Democratic Party	10	1
Romanian Ecology Party	4	—
National Salvation Front (NSF)‡	43	18
Romanian National Unity Party (RNUP)	30	14
Hungarian Democratic Union of Romania (HDUR)	27	12
Greater Romania Party (România Máre)	16	6
Socialist Labour Party (SLP)	13	5
Agrarian Democratic Party of Romania	—	5
Total	328§	143

* Name changed to Party of Social Democracy of Romania (PSDR) in 1993.
† United in 1993 to form the Liberal Party 1993.
‡ Name changed to Democratic Party—NSF in 1993.
§ In addition, a total of 13 seats were reserved in the Assembly of Deputies for ethnic minorities, giving an overall total of 341 seats.

Local Government

The system of local government in Romania was to be reformed under the terms of the new Constitution, which was approved by referendum on 8 December 1991. According to the Constitution, the basic principle of local government was to be local autonomy and the decentralization of public services. The lowest tier of local government was to be the local council of a city or commune; these were to have mayors and council members elected by constituents in each relevant area. The activities of local councils were to be co-ordinated by county councils, which were also to be elected by their constituents. A prefect for each county was to be appointed by the central Government as its representative at the local level, and would have the power to challenge acts of all tiers of local government. Romania has 40 administrative divisions (counties), and the municipality of Bucharest, the capital city, which is itself divided into administrative sectors.

Political Organizations

Following the downfall of President Ceauşescu in December 1989, numerous political parties were formed or re-established in preparation for the holding of free elections. By April 1990 more than 80 parties had been registered by the Bucharest Municipal Court, and by the time of the September 1992 general election there were 91 registered political parties. The financing of political parties from abroad is not permitted.

Agrarian Democratic Party of Romania/Partidul Democrat Agrar din România: Bucharest, Al. Alexandru 45; tel. (1) 336672; f. 1990; supported by agricultural workers; advocates defence of the Romanian villagers' way of life; Pres. VICTOR SURDU.

Christian Democratic National Peasants' Party/Partidul Naţional Ţărănesc-Creştin şi Democrat: 70433 Bucharest, Bd. Carol 34; tel. (1) 147819; fax (1) 154533; f. 1990 by merger of centre-right Christian Democratic Party and traditional National Peasant Party (f. 1869, banned 1947, revived Dec. 1989; original party re-established in Aug. 1990 by separate group); supports pluralist democracy; advocates a return to a market economy and the restoration of peasant property, the reorganization of education, the separation of powers in the State, the free election of management bodies and the equality of all nationalities and religious beliefs; supports Christian morals; 615,000 mems; Pres. CORNELIU COPOSU.

Civic Alliance/Alianţa Civică: Bucharest; f. 1990 as alliance of opposition groupings outside legislature; voted, in July 1991, to create a parallel political party, the Party of the Civic Alliance (see below); Chair. ANA BLANDIANA.

Democratic Convention of Romania (DCR) Alliance: 70001 Bucharest, Splaiul Unirii 5, ap. 1, sect. 3; tel. (1) 3124014; fax 3124041; f. 1992; alliance of 18 parties and other organizations, including the Christian Democratic National Peasants' Party, the Party of the Civic Alliance, the Civic Alliance, the Liberal Party 1993, the Romanian Social Democratic Party, the Romanian Ecological Party; Pres. EMIL CONSTANTINESCU.

Democratic Party—NSF: 70024 Bucharest, Al. Modrogan 1; tel. (1) 6337232; fax (1) 6335332; f. Dec. 1989, as National Salvation Front, changed name in May 1993; centre-left; advocates a free-market economy, privatization of state property, encouragement of foreign investment, reorganization of education, freedom of the press and of religion, respect for the rights and freedoms of the national minorities, curbing of pollution and Romania's observance of international agreements; Pres. PETRE ROMAN.

Greater Romania/România Máre: Bucharest; nationalist; Leader CORNELIU VADIM TUDOR.

Hungarian Democratic Union of Romania (HDUR)/Uniunea Democrată Maghiară din România: Bucharest, str. Herăstrău 13; tel. (1) 6333569; fax (1) 6796675; f. 1990; supports the rights of Hungarians in Romania; Hon. Pres. LÁSZLÓ TÖKES; Pres. BÉLA MARKÓ.

Liberal Monarchist Party of Romania/Partidul Liberal Monarhist din România: Bucharest, Bd. George Coşbuc 1; tel. (1) 6134940; f. 1990; advocates the restoration of the monarchy; Pres. DAN CERNOVODEANU.

Liberal Party 1993: Bucharest; f. 1993 by merger of the National Liberal Party—Democratic Convention and the Liberal Party—Youth Wing; later joined by faction of the Party of the Civic Alliance; Pres. DINU PATRICIU.

Liberal Union 'Bratianu'/Uniunea Liberală 'Bratianu': Bucharest, Calea Victoriei 95–97, Sector 1; tel. (1) 6594487; fax (1) 3120808; f. 1990 following split in National Liberal Party; Pres. ION I. BRATIANU.

National Liberal Party/Partidul Naţional Liberal: Bucharest, Bd. Bălcescu 21; tel. (1) 6143235; fax (1) 6157638; f. 1869, banned 1947; merged with Socialist Liberal Party in 1990; advocates separation of powers in the State, restoration of democracy, freedom of expression and religion, observance of the equal rights of all minorities, the abolition of collectivization and nationalization in agriculture, the gradual privatization of enterprises, trade union freedom and the right to strike; Chair. MIRCEA IONESCU-QUINTUS.

Party of the Civic Alliance (PCA)/Partidul Alianţei Civice: 73311 Bucharest, Bd. Matiunilor Unite 5, block 110; tel. (1) 615310; f. 1991; set up by Civic Alliance to contest elections; Pres. NICOLAE MANOLESCU.

Party of Social Democracy of Romania (PSDR): Bucharest, Str. Filioara 3, Sector 2; tel. (1) 611777; f. 1992 (as National Salvation Front—22 December, later known as the Democratic National Salvation Front) by supporters of Ion Iliescu, following split in the National Salvation Front (f. 1989); social-democratic party; Chair. OLIVIU GHERMAN; Exec. Pres. ADRIAN NASTASE.

Romanian Ecological Movement/Mişcarea Ecologistă din România: Bucharest, Al. Alexandru Phillippide 11; tel. (1) 6142943; f. 1990; advocates protection of the environment and the pursuit of democratic pacifist and humanist values; Chair. TOMA GEORGE MAIORESCU.

Romanian Ecological Party/Partidul Ecologist Român: Bucharest, Bd. George Coşbuc 1, block P58; tel. (1) 6312350; supports protection of the environment; Chair. OTTO WEBER.

Romanian National Unity Party/Partidul Unităţii Naţionale Române: 4300 Tîrgu Mureş, Str. Bolyai F30; tel. (95) 433619; f. 1990; political wing of the Nationalist Romanian movement, Vatra Românească; Leader GHEORGHE FUNAR.

Romanian Social Democratic Party/Partidul Social-Democrat Român: 70119 Bucharest, Str. Dem Dobrescu 9; tel. (1) 6146110; fax (1) 6146089; f. 1893; centre-left; Exec. Pres. SERGIU CUNESCU.

Romanian Unity Alliance—AUR: advocates national unity.

Socialist Labour Party/Partidul Socialist al Muncii: Bucharest, Str. Olari 12; tel. (1) 6351375; f. 1990 by Romanian Communist Party members and left-wing Democratic Labour Party; Exec. Pres. ILIE VERDEŢ.

Traditional Social Democratic Party of Romania/Partidul Social Democrat Traditional din România: Bucharest 2, Str. Aron Florian 1; tel. (1) 6110479; f. 1991 by merger of Traditional Social Democratic Party and National Democratic Party; a member of the Social-Democratic Alliance, supports the Democratic Party—NSF; centre-left; Sec.-Gen. PASCU BOGDAN.

Diplomatic Representation

EMBASSIES IN ROMANIA

Albania: Bucharest, Str. Ştefan Gheorghiu 4; Ambassador: FRAN ZEF CUKAJ.

Algeria: Bucharest, Bd. Ana Ipătescu 29; Ambassador: LIAMINE ZEROUAL.

Argentina: Bucharest, Str. Drobeta 11; telex 11412; Ambassador: OSCAR EDUARDO TORRES AVALOS.

Austria: 70254 Bucharest, Str. Dumbrava Roşie 7; tel. (1) 6119377; telex 11333; fax (1) 3128508; Ambassador: CHRISTOPH PARISINI.

Bangladesh: Bucharest, Bd. Kiseleff 55; tel. (1) 171544; telex 10197; Chargé d'affaires a.i.: MOHAMMED HASIB AZIZ.

Belgium: 79359 Bucharest, Bd. Dacia 58; tel. (1) 3122968; telex 11482; fax (1) 3122903; Ambassador: IGNACE VAN STEENBERGE.

Brazil: 71248 Bucharest, Str. Praga 11; tel. (1) 129823; telex 11307; fax (1) 127549; Ambassador: MARCEL DEZON COSTA HASLOCHER.

Bulgaria: Bucharest, Str. Rabat 5; tel. (1) 332150; fax (1) 127654; Ambassador: STEFAN NAUMOV.

Canada: 71118 Bucharest, Str. N. Iorga 36; tel. (1) 3128345; telex 10690; fax (1) 3120366; Ambassador: MURRAY FAIRWEATHER.

Chile: Bucharest, Bd. Ana Ipătescu 8; tel. (1) 115691; telex 11197; Ambassador: SERGIO MIMICA BEZMALINOVIC.

China, People's Republic: Bucharest, Şos. Nordului 2; tel. (1) 6331925; telex 11316; fax (1) 3127523; Ambassador: LI FENGLIN.

Colombia: Bucharest, Str. Polonă 35, ap. 3; tel. (1) 6115108; telex 10498; fax (1) 3120155; Ambassador: CÉSAR PARDO VILLALBA.

Congo: Bucharest, Str. Armeneasca 35; tel. (1) 3128296; Ambassador: (vacant).

Costa Rica: Bucharest, Str. Lt. Dumitru Lemnea 3–5, et. 1, ap. 4; tel. (1) 592008; telex 11939; Chargé d'affaires: ELIZABETH SEGURA HERNÁNDEZ.

Cuba: Bucharest, Al. Alexandru 33; tel. (1) 796895; telex 11305; Ambassador: NIEL RUÍZ GUERRA.

Czech Republic: Bucharest 3, Str. Ion Ghica 11; tel. (1) 6159142; fax (1) 3122539; Chargé d'affaires: JAROMÍR KVAPIL.

Denmark: 73102 Bucharest, Str. Dr Burhelea 3; tel. (1) 3120352; telex 11325; fax (1) 3120358; Ambassador: ULRIK HELWEG-LARSEN.

Ecuador: Bucharest, Str. Polonă 35, ap. 1; tel. (1) 110503; telex 10836; Chargé d'affaires: RAFAEL VEINTIMILLA C.

Egypt: Bucharest, Bd. Dacia 21; tel. (1) 110138; telex 11549; Ambassador: SAAD ABOU EL-KHEIR.

Finland: Bucharest, Str. Atena 2 bis; tel. (1) 335440; telex 11293; Ambassador: BO ADAHL.

France: Bucharest, Str. Biserica Amzei 13–15; tel. (1) 110540; telex 11320; fax (1) 506576; Ambassador: RENAUD VIGNAL.

Germany: 79449 Bucharest, Str. Rabat 21; tel. (1) 792580; telex 11292; fax (1) 796854; Ambassador: Dr KLAUS TERFLOTH.

Greece: Bucharest, Str. Orlando 6; tel. (1) 503988; telex 11321; Ambassador: GIORGIOS LINARDOS.

Guinea: Bucharest, Str. Bocşa 4; tel. (1) 111893; telex 10255; Ambassador: ABEL NIOUMA SANDOUNO.

Holy See: 70749 Bucharest, Str. Pictor C. Stahi 5–7 (Apostolic Nunciature); tel. (1) 139490; fax (1) 120316; Apostolic Nuncio: Most Rev. JOHN BUKOVSKY, Titular Archbishop of Tabalta.

Hungary: Bucharest, Str. J. L. Calderon 63; tel. (1) 146621; telex 11323; fax (1) 142846; Ambassador: ERNŐ RUDAS.

India: 71274 Bucharest, Str. Brîncuţei 11; tel. (1) 797630; telex 11619; Ambassador: JULIO FRANCIS RIBEIRO.

Indonesia: Bucharest, Orlando 10; tel. (1) 507720; telex 11258; Ambassador: LAMTIUR ANDALIAH PANGGABEAN.

Iran: Bucharest, Bd. Ana Ipătescu 39; tel. (1) 334471; telex 11507; Ambassador: ABDOUL RASOUL MOHAGER HEGEAZI.

Iraq: Bucharest, Str. Polonă 8; tel. (1) 110835; Ambassador: SULTAN IBRAHIM SHUJA.

Israel: 73102 Bucharest, Str. Dr Burghelea 5; tel. (1) 132634; telex 11685; fax (1) 120431; Ambassador: AVSHALOM MEGIDDON.

Italy: Bucharest, Str. I. C. Frimu 7–9; tel. (1) 6505110; telex 11602; fax (1) 3120422; Ambassador: BERNARDO UGUCCIONI.

Japan: Bucharest, Str. Polonă 4, Sector 1; tel. (1) 3120790; telex 11322; fax (1) 3120272; Ambassador: YOSHIKI SUGIURA.

Jordan: Bucharest, Str. Dumbrava Roşie 1; tel. (1) 104705; telex 11477; Ambassador: YASIN ISTANBULI.

Korea, Democratic People's Republic: Bucharest, Şos. Nordului 6; tel. (1) 331926; Chargé d'affaires: MUN BIONG ROK.

Korea, Republic: 70412 Bucharest, Calea Victoriei 2; tel. (1) 137941; Ambassador: YI HYUN-HONG.

Lebanon: Bucharest, Str. Atena 28; tel. (1) 118343; telex 11645; fax (1) 127534; Ambassador: EMILE BEDRAN.

Liberia: Bucharest, Str. Mihai Eminescu 82–88; tel. (1) 6193029; Chargé d'affaires: G. MARCUS KELLEY.

Libya: Bucharest, Bd. Ana Ipătescu 15; tel. (1) 505511; telex 10290; Secretary of People's Bureau: MUHAMMAD AL-BARUNI.

Malaysia: Bucharest, Bd. Dacia 30; tel. (1) 113801; Ambassador: ZAINUDDIN BIN ABDUL RAHMAN.

Mauritania: Bucharest, Str. Duiliu Zamfirescu 7; tel. (1) 592305; telex 10595; Ambassador: KANE CHEIKH MOHAMED FADHEL.

Moldova: Bucharest, Al. Alexandru 40, sector 1; tel. and fax (1) 3129790; telex 10910; Ambassador: M. AURELIAN DANILA.

Mongolia: Bucharest, Str. Făgăraş 6; tel. (1) 507237; telex 11504; Ambassador: DOSORYN GHENDEN.

Morocco: Bucharest, Bd. Dacia 25; tel. (1) 192945; telex 11687; Ambassador: MOHAMED HALIM.

Netherlands: 71271 Bucharest, Str. Atena 18; tel. (1) 6332292; telex 11474; fax (1) 3127620; Ambassador: COENRAAD FREDERIK STORK.

Nigeria: Bucharest, Str. Orlando 9; tel. (1) 6504050; telex 10478; Ambassador: Dr L. E. OKOGWU.

Pakistan: Bucharest, Str. Barbu Delavrancea 22; tel. (1) 177402; Ambassador: RASHEED AHMAD.

Peru: Bucharest, Str. Paris 45A; tel. (1) 331124; telex 11566; Ambassador: GUILLERMO GERDAU O'CONNOR.

Philippines: Bucharest, Stirbei Voda 87; tel. (1) 137643; telex 10237; Ambassador: ALICIA C. RAMOS.

Poland: Bucharest, Al. Alexandru 23; tel. (1) 6794530; telex 11302; fax (1) 3129832; Ambassador: ZYGMUNT KOMOROWSKI.

Russia: Bucharest, Şos. Kiseleff 6; tel. (1) 170120; Ambassador: EVGENII OSTROVENKO.

Slovakia: Bucharest 2, Str. Otetari 3; tel. (1) 3123352; telex 11548; fax (1) 3122435; Ambassador: M. RESUTÍK.

Spain: Bucharest, Str. Tirana 1; tel. (1) 335730; telex 11508; Ambassador: ANTONIO NÚÑEZ GARCÍA-SAUCO.

Sudan: Bucharest, Bd. Dacia 35; tel. (1) 118352; telex 10855; Ambassador: LAWRENCE MODE TOMBE.

Sweden: Bucharest, Str. Sofia 5; tel. (1) 173184; telex 11313; Ambassador: NILS G. ROSENBERG.

Switzerland: 70152 Bucharest 1, Str. Pitar Moş 12; tel. (1) 3120298; telex 11579; fax (1) 3120324; Ambassador: SVEN BEAT MEILI.

Syria: Bucharest, Bd. Ana Ipătescu 50; tel. (1) 503195; telex 10061; Ambassador: HICHAM KAHALEH.

Thailand: Bucharest, Str. Mihai Eminescu 44–48; tel. (1) 114686; telex 10247; Ambassador: PRAPHOT NARITHRANGURA.

Tunisia: Bucharest, Str. Mihai Eminescu 50–54; tel. (1) 111895; telex 11829; Ambassador: RAUF SAID.

Turkey: Bucharest, Calea Dorobanţilor 72; tel. (1) 193625; Ambassador: TUGAY ULUCEVIK.

Ukraine: Bucharest, Rabat Str. 1; tel. (1) 124547; fax (1) 124514; Ambassador: LEONTII IVANOVICH SANDULYAK.

United Kingdom: 70154 Bucharest, Str. Jules Michelet 24; tel. (1) 3120303; telex 11295; fax (1) 3120229; Ambassador: ANDREW P. F. BACHE.

USA: Bucharest, Str. Tudor Arghezi 7–9; tel. (1) 3124042; telex 11416; fax (1) 3120395; Ambassador: JOHN R. DAVIS, Jr.

Uruguay: Bucharest, Str. Polonă 35; tel. (1) 6118212; telex 10475; fax (1) 3120342; Ambassador: GASTON SCIARRA.

Venezuela: Bucharest, Str. Pictor Mirea 18, sector 1; tel. (1) 3120311; telex 10470; fax (1) 3120311; Ambassador: GUSTAVO GARAICOECHEA.

Viet Nam: Bucharest, Str. Gr. Alexandrescu 86; tel. (1) 116120; telex 11604; Ambassador: NGUYEN TRONG LIEU.

Yugoslavia: Bucharest, Calea Dorobanţilor 34; tel. (1) 119871; telex 92535; fax (1) 191752; Ambassador: Dr DESIMIR JEVTIĆ.

Zaire: Bucharest, Al. Alexandru 41; tel. (1) 795717; telex 11503; Ambassador: MUSUNGAYI NKUEMBE MAMPUYA.

Judicial System

The judicial system was to be reorganized and reformed under the terms of the new Constitution, which was approved by referendum in December 1991.

SUPREME COURT

The Supreme Court of Justice, which was reorganized under Law 56 of 9 July 1993, exercises control over the judicial activity of all courts. It ensures the correct and uniform application of the law. The members of the Supreme Court are appointed by the President of Romania at the proposal of the Superior Council of Magistrates.

President: VALERIU BOGDĂNESCU; 70503 Bucharest, Calea Rahovei 4; tel. (1) 133736; telex 11165.

COUNTY COURTS AND LOCAL COURTS

The judicial organization of courts at the county and local levels was established by Law 92 of 4 August 1992. In each of the 40 counties of Romania there is a county court and between three and six local courts. The county courts also form 15 circuits of appeal courts, where appeals against sentences passed by local courts are heard, which are generally considered courts of first instance. There is also a right of appeal from the appeal courts to the Supreme Court. In both county courts and local courts the judges are professional magistrates.

MILITARY COURTS

Military courts were reorganized through Law 54 of 9 July 1993. Generally they judge contraventions of the law by service personnel at one of the two military courts in the country. These are the Territorial Military Court, with a right of appeal to the Appeal Military Court. There is also a military department within the Supreme Court which judges appeals in some special cases. The judges are professional lawyers and career officers.

GENERAL PROSECUTING MAGISTRACY

The General Prosecuting Magistracy functions under Law 92 of 4 August 1992. There are prosecuting magistracies operating through each court, under the authority of the Minister of Justice.

Prosecutor-General: VASILE MANEA-DRĂGULIN; tel. (1) 812727.

Religion

In Romania there are 15 religious denominations and more than 120 religious associations recognized by the State. About 87% of believers belong to the Romanian Orthodox Church.

The State Secretariat for Religious Affairs: 70136 Bucharest, Str. Snagov 40; tel. (1) 6112125; f. 1990; Minister Sec. of State: Prof. GHEORGHE VLĂDUŢESCU.

CHRISTIANITY

The Romanian Orthodox Church

The Romanian Orthodox Church is the major religious organization in Romania (with more than 18m. believers) and is organized as an autocephalous patriarchate, being led by the Holy Synod, headed by a patriarch. The Patriarchate consists of five metropolitanates, nine archbishoprics and nine bishoprics.

Holy Synod: 70666 Bucharest, Str. Antim 29; tel. (1) 313413; Sec. NIFON PLOIEŞTEANUL.

Patriarhia Română: 70526 Bucharest 4, Al. Patriarhiei 2; tel. (1) 6156772; fax (1) 3128056.

Patriarch, Metropolitan of Muntnia and Dobrogea and Archbishop of Bucharest: TEOCTIST ARĂPAŞU.

Metropolitan of Moldavia and Bukovina and Archbishop of Iaşi: Dr DANIEL CIOBOTEA (resident in Iaşi).

Metropolitan of Transylvania and Archbishop of Sibiu: Dr ANTONIE PLĂMĂDEALĂ (resident in Sibiu).

Metropolitan of Oltenia and Archbishop of Craiova: Dr NESTOR VORNICESCU (resident in Craiova).

Metropolitan of Banat and Archbishop of Timişoara and Caransebeş: Dr NICOLAE CORNEANU (resident in Timişoara).

Archbishop of the Lower Danube: ANTIM NICA (resident in Galaţi).

Archbishop of Tomis: LUCIAN FLOREA (resident in Constanţa).

Archbishop of Vad, Feleac and Cluj: BARTOLOMEU ANANIA (resident in Cluj-Napoca).

Archbishop of Tîrgovişte: Dr VASILE COSTIN (resident in Tîrgovişte).

Archbishop of Suceava and Rădăuti: PIMEN ZAINEA (resident in Suceava).

The Roman Catholic Church

Catholics in Romania number 1.35m., and include adherents of the Armenian, Latin and Romanian (Byzantine) Rites.

Latin Rite

There are two archdioceses and four dioceses. At 31 December 1991 there were 1,481,434 adherents of the Latin Rite (about 6.5% of the total population).

Archbishop of Alba Iulia: Most Rev. LAJOS BÁLINT, 2500 Alba Iulia, Str. Mihai Viteazul 21; tel. (968) 11689; fax (968) 11454 .

Archbishop of Bucharest: Most Rev. IOAN ROBU, 70749 Bucharest, Str. Gral Berthelot 19; tel. (1) 133936.

Romanian Rite

There is one metropolitan and four dioceses.

Metropolitan of the Romanian Uniate Church and Archbishop of Făgăraş and Alba Iulia: Cardinal ALEXANDRU TODEA, 3175 Blaj, Str. P. P. Poni 2; tel. (96) 712057.

Protestant Churches

Baptist Union of Romania: 78152 Bucharest 1, Bd. N. Titulescu 56/A; tel. (1) 6173705; 1,300 churches; Pres. Rev. VASILE AL. TALOŞ.

The Evangelical Church of the Augsburg Confession: 2400 Sibiu, Str. General Magheru 4; tel. (92) 433789; Gen. Sec. HANS-GERALD BINDER; tel. (92) 433680; telex 69200; fax (92) 433680; founded in the 16th century, comprises some 25,500 mems, mainly of German nationality; Bishop of Sibiu Dr CHRISTOPH KLEIN.

The Reformed (Calvinist) Church: 700,000 mems; two bishoprics:

Bishop of Cluj-Napoca: Dr KÁLMÁN CSIHA, 3400 Cluj-Napoca, Str. I. C. Brătianu 51; tel. (95) 112453.

Bishop of Oradea: LÁSZLÓ TŐKES, 3700 Oradea, Str. Craiovei 1; tel. (991) 31710.

The Synodo-Presbyterian Evangelical Church: 3400 Cluj-Napoca, Bd. 22 Decembrie 1; tel. (51) 16614; comprises about 25,000 mems of Hungarian, 4,000 mems of Slovak and 200 mems of Romanian nationality; Superintendent PAUL SZEDRESSY.

The Unitarian Church: 3400 Cluj-Napoca, Bd. 22 Decembrie 9; tel. (51) 15927; fax (51) 15927; f. 1568; comprises about 75,000 mems of Hungarian nationality; Bishop LAJOS KOVÁCS.

Other Christian Churches

The Armenian-Gregorian Church: 70334 Bucharest, Str. Armenească 9; tel. (1) 140208; 5,000 mems.; Archbishop TIRAIR MARTICHIAN.

The Old-Rite Christian Church: 6100 Brăila, Str. Zidari 1; 50,000 mems. of Russian nationality; Metropolitan TIMON GAVRILA.

The Pentecostal Church: Bucharest, Str. Carol Davila 81; tel. (1) 6384425; 250,000 mems; Pres. Rev. EMIL BULGĂR.

The Seventh-day Adventist Church: Bucharest, Str. Plantelor 12; tel. (1) 3129253; fax (1) 3129255; 64,000 mems; Pres. of the Union: Rev. NELU DUMITRESCU.

Christians according to the Gospel: Bucharest, Str. 7 Noiembrie 60A; tel. (1) 557865; Head: Dr SILVIU CIOATĂ.

Open Brethren Church: Head: MELITON LAZAROVICI.

ISLAM

The Muslim Community comprises some 55,000 members of Turkish-Tatar nationality.

Grand Mufti: OSMAN NEGEAT, 8700 Constanţa, Bd. Tomis 41.

JUDAISM

In 1990 there were about 18,000 Jews, organized in 68 communities, in Romania.

Federation of Jewish Communities: 70478 Bucharest, Str. Sf. Vinieri 9–11; tel. (1) 132538; telex 10798; fax (1) 130911; Chief Rabbi Dr MOSES ROSEN.

The Press

The Romanian press is highly regionalized, with newspapers and periodicals appearing in all of the administrative districts. Many newspapers and periodicals are published in the languages of co-inhabiting nationalities in Romania, including Hungarian, German, Serbian, Ukrainian, Armenian and Yiddish. The Ministry of Culture relinquished control of the press in June 1990.

The publications listed below are in Romanian, unless otherwise indicated.

PRINCIPAL NEWSPAPERS

Academia Catavencu (Dubious Academy): Bucharest; f. 1990; weekly; satirical; Editor SORIN VULPE; circ. 100,000.

Adevărul (Truth): 71341 Bucharest, Piaţa Presei Libere 1; tel. (1) 6181982; telex 11342; fax (1) 6175540; f. 1989; daily except Sun.; independent; Editor-in-Chief D. TINU; circ. 239,000.

Alianţa Civică (Civic Alliance): 71102 Bucharest, Calea Victoriei 133-135, Sc. A, et. 3; tel. and fax (1) 595909; f. 1991; daily; organ of the Civic Alliance.

Allgemeine Deutsche Zeitung für Rumänien: 79777 Bucharest, Piaţa Presei Libere 1; tel. (1) 6181723; fax (1) 6183758; f. 1949; fmrly *Neuer Weg*; daily except Sun. and Mon.; political, economic, social and cultural news; in German; Editor-in-Chief EMMERICH REICHRATH; circ. 10,000.

Azi (Today): 70101 Bucharest, Calea Victoriei 39A; tel. (1) 133147; telex 11054; f. 1990; daily; organ of National Salvation Front; Editor-in-Chief OCTAVIAN ŞTIREANU.

Cotidianul (The Daily): 77103 Bucharest, Calea Plevnei 114; tel. (1) 6377795; fax (1) 6377840; f. 1991; daily except Sat. and Sun.; Founder ION RAŢIU; Editor DOINA BÂSCĂ.

Cronica Română: Bucharest; daily.

Curierul Naţional (National Messenger): 70109 Bucharest, Ministerului 2–4; tel. (1) 6159512; telex 10250; fax (1) 3121300; f. 1990; daily; Dir-Gen. VALENTIN PAUNESCU; Editor OPREA GEORGESCU.

Dreptatea (Justice): 71102 Bucharest, Calea Victoriei 133–135, et. 2; tel. (1) 504125; f. 1990; daily evening newspaper published by Christian Democratic National Peasants' Party; Dir PAUL LĂZĂRESCU.

Evenimentul Zilei (Event of the Day): Bucharest, Piaţa Presei Libere 1; tel. (1) 3127080; fax (1) 3128381; f. 1992; tabloid daily; Editor-in-Chief ION CRISTOIU; circ. 600,000.

Gazeta Sporturilor (Sports Gazette): 79778 Bucharest 2, Str. Vasile Conta 16; tel. (1) 113288; fax (1) 113459; f. 1924; daily except Sun.; independent; Editor-in-Chief CONSTANTIN MACOVEI; circ. 250,000.

Informatia Zilei: 70711 Bucharest, Str. Brezoianu 23-25, Sector 1; tel. (1) 3120383; telex 10169; fax (1) 3120393; f. 1953; Editor-in-Chief OCTAVIAN ANDRONIC.

Libertatea (Freedom): 70711 Bucharest, Str. Brezoianu 23–25; tel. (1) 3120383; telex 10169; fax (1) 3120393; f. 1989; daily except Sun.; evening paper; Editor-in-Chief OCTAVIAN ANDRONIC; circ. 105,000.

Ora (Hour): 71102 Bucharest, Calea Victoriei 133-135; tel. (1) 6596239; fax (1) 6117938; f. 1992; independent; Dir NICOLAE CRISTACHE.

România Liberă (Free Romania): 71341 Bucharest, Piaţa Presei Libere 1; tel. (1) 6177849; telex 11179; fax (1) 3128271; f. 1943; daily except Sun.; independent; Editor-in-Chief PETRE MIHAI BACANU; circ. 200,000.

Romániai Magyar Szó (Hungarian Word from Romania): 79776 Bucharest, Piaţa Presei Libere 1; tel. (1) 6180302; fax (1) 6181562; f. 1947; daily except Sun. and Mon.; in Hungarian; Editor-in-Chief GYARMATH JÁNOS.

Tineretul Liber (Free Youth): 71341 Bucharest, Piaţa Presei Libere 1; tel. (1) 176736; fax (1) 177876; f. 1989; daily except Sun. and Mon.; Editor-in-Chief AUREL PERVA.

Viitorul Românesc (Future of Romania): 71102 Bucharest, Calea Victoriei 133–135, et. 5; tel. (1) 596239; fax (1) 117938; f. 1991; daily; organ of the New Liberal Party; Dir VLADIMIR SIMON.

DISTRICT NEWSPAPERS

Alba

Ardealul: 2500 Alba Iulia, Piaţa Iuliu Maniu 29; tel. (968) 13026; f. 1990; daily; organ of the National Salvation Front; Editor-in-Chief IOAN MAIER.

Unirea (The Union): 2500 Alba Iulia, Str. Decebal 27; tel. (968) 11420; f. 1990; independent daily; Editor-in-Chief HORIA SANDU.

Arad

Adevărul (The Truth): 2900 Arad, Bd. Revoluţiei 81; tel. (966) 13302; fax (966) 16854; f. 1990; independent; daily; Dir TRISTAN MIHUŢA.

Jelen Tükör (Present Mirror): 2900 Arad, Bd. Revoluţiei 81; tel. (966) 12414; telex 76373; f. 1989; fmrly Vörös Lobogó; daily except Sun. and Mon.; independent; in Hungarian; Editor-in-Chief KÁROLY KISS; circ. 8,000.

Argeş

Argeşul Liber (Free Argeş): 0300 Piteşti, Bd. Republicii 988; tel. (976) 30490; f. 1990; independent; daily; Editor-in-Chief MARIN MANOLACHE.

Bacău

Deşteptărea (The Awakening): 5500 Bacău, Str. Vasile Alecsandri 63; tel. (93) 111272; telex 21205; fax (93) 125466; f. 1989; Man. CORNEL GALBEN; Editor-in-Chief IOAN ENACHE; circ. 50,000.

Glasul Moldovei (Voice of Moldova): 5500 Bacău, Str. Nicolae Bălcescu 1; tel. (93) 126789; f. 1990; socio-political and cultural; weekly; Dir VASILE MIHĂILESCU.

Moldova: 5500 Bacău, Str. Eliberării 7; tel. (93) 134752; f. 1990; opinion weekly; Editor-in-Chief VIOREL SAVIN.

Moldova Sport: 5500 Bacău, Str. Vasile Alecsandri 63; tel. (93) 111272; telex 21205; fax (93) 125466; f. 1990; weekly; Man. CORNEL GALBEN; Editor-in-Chief IOAN ENAĆHE; circ. 20,000.

Bihor

Bihari Napló: 3700 Oradea, Str. Stadionului 25; tel. (99) 112727; fax (99) 115450; f. 1990; daily except Mon.; in Hungarian; Editor-in-Chief ANDRÁS BOKOR; circ. 25,000.

Crişana: 3700 Oradea, Str. Română 3; tel. (99) 117421; f. 1946; daily except Mon.; Editor-in-Chief ION CREŢU.

Erdélyi Napló (Chronicle of Ardeal): 3700 Oradea, Stadionului 25; tel. (99) 117158; fax (99) 117126; f. 1990; in Hungarian; weekly; Editor-in-Chief ISTVÁN STANIK.

Bistriţa-Năsăud

Răsunetul (The Sound): 4400 Bistriţa, Str. Bistricioarei 6; tel. (990) 11684; f. 1990; journal of the National Salvation Front, Bistriţa-Năsăud County; Editor-in-Chief VASILE TABĂRĂ.

Botoşani

Gazeta de Botoşani: 6800 Botoşani, Bd. Mihai Eminescu 91; tel. (98) 511106; f. 1990; fmrly *Clopotul*; 33; weekly; Editor-in-Chief GHEORGHE ZANEA.

Brăila

Libertatea (Freedom): 6100 Brăila, Piaţa Independenţei 1; tel. (94) 635946; f. 1989; independent daily; Editor-in-Chief RODICA CANĂ.

Braşov

Brassói Lapok (Braşov Gazette): 2200 Braşov, Str. M. Sadoveanu 3; tel. (92) 144047; telex 61224; f. 1849; weekly; in Hungarian; Editor-in-Chief GELLERT LAJOS.

Gazeta de Transilvania: 2200 Braşov, Str. M. Sadoveanu 3; tel. (92) 142029; telex 61224; fax (92) 152927; f. 1838, ceased publication 1946, re-established 1989; daily except Mon.; independent; Editor-in-Chief EDUARD HUIDAN.

Karpatenrundschau (Carpathian Panorama): 2200 Braşov, Str. M. Sadoveanu 3; tel. and fax (92) 143624; f. 1968; weekly; in German; Editor-in-Chief DIETER DROTLEFF; circ. 2,000.

Buzău

Opinia (The Opinion): 5100 Buzău, Str. Chiristigii 3; tel. (974) 12764; f. 1969; independent; daily; Editor-in-Chief CORNELIU ŞTEFAN.

Călăraşi

Pămîntu l Liber (Free Earth): 8500 Călăraşi, Str. Bucureşti 187; tel. (911) 15840; f. 1990; socio-political; weekly; Editor-in-Chief GHEORGHE FRANGULEA.

Caraş-Severin

Timpul (The Times): 1700 Reşiţa, Piaţa Republicii 7; tel. (96) 412739; telex 74235; fax (96) 416709; f. 1990; independent daily; Editor-in-Chief GHEORGHE ZINCESCU.

Cluj

Adevărul de Cluj (The Truth of Cluj): 3400 Cluj-Napoca, Str. Napoca 16; tel. (95) 111032; f. 1990; daily; independent; Editor-in-Chief ILIE CĂLIAN; circ. 8,000.

Atlas-Clusium (Atlas Free Cluj): 3400 Cluj-Napoca, Piaţa Unirii 1; tel. (95) 116940; f. 1990; weekly; independent; Gen. Man. VALENTIN TAŞCU.

Mesagerul transilvan (Transylvanian Messenger): 3400 Cluj-Napoca; daily; independent; circ. 250,000.

Nu (No): 3400 Cluj-Napoca, Calea Motilor 18; tel. and fax (95) 195269; f. 1990; weekly; opinion and culture for youth; Editor-in-Chief LIVIU MAN.

Szabadság (Freedom): 3400 Cluj-Napoca, Str. Napoca 16, POB 340; tel. (95) 118985; telex 31447; fax (95) 117206; f. 1989; daily except Sun. and Mon.; in Hungarian; Editor-in-Chief TIBORI SZABÓ ZOLTÁN; circ. 30,000.

Constanţa

Cuget Liber (Free Thinking): 8700 Constanţa, Bd. I. C. Brătianu 5; tel. (91) 665605; telex 14385; fax (91) 665606; f. 1990; independent; daily; Dir ARCADI STRAHILEVICI.

Covasna

Cuvîntul nou (The New World): 4000 Sfîntu Gheorghe, Str. Pieţei 8; tel. (92) 311388; f. 1968; new series 1990; daily except Mon.; Editor-in-Chief DUMÎTRU MÂNOLĂCHESCU.

Háromszék (Three Chairs): 4000 Sfîntu Gheorghe, Str. Pieţei 8A; tel. (92) 311504; fax (92) 311135; f. 1989; socio-political; daily; in Hungarian; Editor-in-Chief ÁRPÁD FARKAS.

Dîmboviţa

Dîmboviţa: 0200 Tîrgovişte, Str. Unirii 32; f. 1990; independent; daily; Editor-in-Chief ALEXANDRU ILIE.

Dolj

Cuvîntul Libertăţii (The Word of Liberty): 1100 Craiova, Str. Lyon 8; tel. (41) 12457; fax (41) 13833; f. 1989; daily except Mon.; Editor-in-Chief DAN LUPESCU; circ. 60,000.

Galaţi

Viaţa Libera (Free Life): 6200 Galaţi, Str. Domnească 48; tel. (93) 414620; f. 1990; independent; daily; Dir RADU MACOVEI.

Giurgiu

Cuvintul Liber (Free World): 8375 Giurgiu, Str. 1 Dec. 1918 60A; tel. (912) 21227; f. 1990; weekly; Editor-in-Chief ION GAGHII; circ. 10,000.

Gorj

Gorjanul: 1400 Tîrgu Jiu, Str. Constantin Brâncuşi 15; tel. (929) 17464; telex 45203; f. 1990; socio-political; daily; Editor-in-Chief NICOLAE BRÎNZAN.

Harghita

Adevărul Harghitei (Truth of Harghita): 4100 Miercurea-Ciuc, Str. Leticeni 45; tel. (958) 13019; f. 1990; independent; daily; Editor-in-Chief MIHAI GROZA.

Új Sport (New Sport): 4100 Miercurea-Ciuc; tel. (958) 15940; telex 67228; fax (92) 152514; independent sports; daily; in Hungarian; Editor-in-Chief LÁSZLÓ DOBOS.

Hunedoara

Cuvîntul Liber (The Free Word): 2700 Deva, Str. 1 Decembrie 35; tel. (956) 11275; fax (956) 18061; f. 1949; daily except Mon.; Editor-in-Chief NICOLAE TÎRCOB; circ. 25,000.

Ialomiţa

Tribuna Ialomiţei (The Ialomiţa Tribune): 8400 Slobozia, Str. Dobrogeanu-Gherea 2; f. 1969; weekly; Editor-in-Chief TITUS NIŢU.

Iaşi

Monitorul: 6600 Iaşi, Str. Smirdan 5; tel. (98) 172557; fax (98) 144577; daily; Editor-in-Chief DAN RADU; circ. 25,000 (30,000 Sunday).

Opinia (Opinion): 6600 Iaşi, Str. Vasile Alecsandri 8; tel. (98) 145105; f. 1990; social, political and cultural; daily; Editor-in-Chief VÂSILE FILIP.

Opinia Studenţească (Students' Opinion): 6600 Iaşi, Bd. Copou 18; tel. (98) 145610; f. 1990; independent; weekly; Editor-in-Chief DANIEL CONDURACHE; circ. 15,000.

Maramureş

Graiul Maramureşului (Voice of Maramureş): 4800 Baia Mare, Bd. Bucureşti 25; tel. (99) 431035; telex 33221; fax (99) 430870; f. 1989; independent; daily; Editor-in-Chief AUGUSTIN COZMUŢA.

Bányavidéki Új Szó (Miner's New Word): 4800 Baia Mare, Bd. Bucureşti 25; tel. (99) 432585; f. 1989; weekly; in Hungarian; Editor-in-Chief CSOMA GYÖRGY.

Mehedinţi

Datina (Tradition): 1500 Drobeta-Turnu Severin, Str. Traian 89; tel. (978) 11995; f. 1990; independent; daily; Editor-in-Chief GHEORGHE BUREŢEA.

Mureş

Cuvîntul Liber (Free Word): 4300 Tîrgu Mureş, Str. Gh. Doja 9; tel. (954) 36636; f. 1990; independent; daily; Editor-in-Chief LAZĂR LADARIU.

Népújság (People's Journal): 4300 Tîrgu Mureş, Str. Gh. Doja 9; tel. (954) 36881; f. 1990; daily; in Hungarian; Editor-in-Chief JÁNOS MAKKAI.

Neamţ

Ceahlăul: 5600 Piatra Neamţ, Al. Tiparului 14; tel. (936) 25282; f. 1990; weekly; Editor-in-Chief VIOREL TUDOSE.

Olt

Glasul Adevărului (Voice of the Truth): 0500 Slatina, Str. Filimon Sîrbu 5; tel. (944) 22131; f. 1990.

Prahova

Curierul de Prahova (Courier of Prahova): 2000 Ploieşti, Bd. Republicii 2; tel. (97) 143192; organ of the National Salvation Front—Prahova County; weekly; Editor-in-Chief IÓAN POPESCU.

Prâhova: 2000 Ploieşti, Bd. Republicii 2; tel. (97) 145691; f. 1990; independent; daily; Editor-in-Chief OCTAVIAN GÎLĂ.

Sălaj

Graiul Sălajului (Voice of Sălaj): 4700 Zalău, Piaţa Unirii 7; tel. (99) 614120; f. 1990; daily; Editor-in-Chief IOAN LUPA.

Szilágyaság (Word from Sălaj): 4700 Zalău, Piaţa Libertăţii 9, POB 68; tel. (99) 633736; f. 1990; organ of Hungarian Democratic Union of Romania; weekly; Editor-in-Chief JÁNOS KUI.

Satu Mare

Ardealul: 3900 Satu Mare, Bd. Republicii 24; tel. (99) 730661; f. 1990; organ of Christian and Democratic National Peasants' Party; weekly; Dir NAE ANTONESCU.

Szatmári Hirlap (Satu Mare Journal): 3900 Satu Mare, Calea Traian 1; f. 1968; daily except Mon.; in Hungarian; Editor-in-Chief STEFAN IOSIF STHAL.

Sibiu

Dimineaţa (Morning): 2400 Sibiu, Str. Samuel Brukenthal 2; tel. (92) 418103; f. 1990; independent socio-cultural; daily; Editor-in-Chief TRAIAN SUCIUI.

Tribuna: Sibiu, Str. George Coşbuc 38; tel. (92) 412810; telex 69247; fax (92) 412026; Bd. Victoriei 8; f. 1884; daily; independent; Editor-in-Chief OCTAVIAN RUSU; circ. 40,000.

Suceava

Crai nou: 5800 Suceava, Str. Stefan cel Mare 36; tel. (987) 14723; f. 1990; daily; Editor-in-Chief ION PARANICI.

Teleorman

Teleormanul Liber (Free Teleorman): 0700 Alexandria, Str. Dunării 178; tel. (913) 11950; f. 1990; daily; Editor-in-Chief GHEORGHE FILIP.

Timiş

Gazeta de Timişoara (Timişoara Gazette): 1900 Timişoara, C P 1127; f. 1990; independent opinion and news; weekly; Dir PREDA MARIA IRINA.

Neue Banater Zeitung: 1900 Timişoara, Bd. Revoluţiei din Decembrie 1989 8; tel. (96) 115586; fax (96) 115586; f. 1957; daily except Sun. and Mon.; in German; Editor-in-Chief GERHARD BINDER; circ. 5,000.

Timişoara: 1900 Timişoara, Str. Proclamatia de la Timişoara 5; tel. and fax (96) 190120; f. 1990; daily; Dir GEORGE SERBAN; Editor-in-Chief IOSIF COSTINAS.

Tulcea

Delta (The Delta): 8800 Tulcea, Str. Spitalului 4; tel. (915) 12406; telex 52235; f. 1885; new series 1990; daily except Mon.; Editor-in-Chief NECULAI AMIHULESEI.

Vaslui

Adevărul (Truth): 6500 Vaslui, Str. Stefan cel Mare 79; tel. (983) 12203; social-cultural publication; twice weekly; f. 1990; Editor-in-Chief TEODOR PRAXIU.

Vîlcea

Curierul de Vîlcea (Courier of Vîlcea): 1000 Rîmnicu Vîlcea, Calea lui Traian 127; tel. (94) 712326; fax (94) 718265; f. 1990; independent; daily; Editors IOAN BARBU, SILVIU POPESCU, GHEORGHE SMEOREANU, PETRE TĂNĂSOAICA, PETRINEL STEFĂNESCU.

Vrancea

Milcovul Liber (Free Milcov): 5300 Focşani, Bd. Unirii 18; tel. (939) 14579; f. 1989; weekly; Editor-in-Chief IONEL NISTOR.

PRINCIPAL PERIODICALS

Bucharest

22: 70179 Bucharest, Calea Victoriei 120; tel. (1) 141776; fax (1) 141525; f. 1990; weekly; published by the Group for Social Dialogue; Editor-in-Chief GABRIELA ADAMEŞTEANU; circ. 12,000.

Agricultura României (Agriculture of Romania): 71341 Bucharest, Piaţa Presei Libere 1; tel. (1) 176020; f. 1974; weekly; published by the Ministry of Agriculture and Food; Editor-in-Chief LUCIAN ROŞCA.

A Hét (The Week): 79776 Bucharest, Piaţa Presei Libere 1; tel. (1) 6184939; f. 1970; weekly; in Hungarian; social, cultural, scientific and ecological review; Editor-in-Chief GÁLFALVI ZSOLT.

Albina (The Bee): 71341 Bucharest, Piaţa Presei Libere 1; tel. (1) 6173487; f. 1897; monthly; social and cultural review; Editor-in-Chief VLADIMIR PANĂ.

Anticipaţia: 79781 Bucharest, Piaţa Presei Libere 1; f. 1990; monthly; science-fiction literature; Editor-in-Chief PAVELESCU MIHAI-DAN.

Arhitectura (Architecture): 70109 Bucharest, Str. Academiei 18–20; f. 1906; published twice a year in 6 issues; review of the Union of Romanian Architects; Editor AUGUSTIN IOAN.

Armata României (The Armed Forces of Romania): Bucharest, Str. General Cristescu 5; tel. (1) 6133393; telex 11243; fax (1) 6159456; f. 1859; weekly; published by Ministry of National Defence; Editor-in-Chief GHEORGE VĂDUVA.

Arta (Art): Bucharest 13, POB 13-80; tel. (1) 6131380; fax (1) 3121008; f. 1953; 6 a year; visual arts and media magazine; Editor-in-Chief CĂLIN DAN.

Biserica Ortodoxă Română (The Romanian Orthodox Church): 70526 Bucharest, Intrarea Patriarhiei 9; tel. (1) 234449; f. 1822; monthly; official bulletin of the Romanian Patriarchate; Editor Rev. DUMITRU SOARE.

Bucuria Copiilor—Luminiţa (Children's Happiness—The Little Light): 71341 Bucharest, Piaţa Presei Libere 1; tel. (1) 176010; telex 11272; f. 1949; monthly; Editor-in-Chief DUMITRU DOBRICĂ; circ. 50,000.

Business Club: 70711 Bucharest, Str. Brezoianu 23-25, Sector 1; tel. (1) 3120383; telex 10169; fax (1) 3120393; f. 1990; quarterly; Editor-in-Chief OCTAVIAN ANDRONIC; circ. 5,000.

Cimboro (Friend): 71341 Bucharest, Piaţa Presei Libere 1; tel. (1) 176010; f. 1922; monthly; in Hungarian; for children; Editor-in-Chief GABRIELLA CSIRE.

Contemporanul—Ideea Europeană: 71341 Bucharest, Piaţa Presei Libere 1; tel. (1) 177316; f. 1881; weekly; cultural, political and scientific review, published by the Ministry of Culture; Dir NICOLAE BREBAN.

Curierul Comercial (Commercial Messenger): 71341 Bucharest, Piaţa Presei Libere 1; tel. (1) 181387; f. 1898, re-established Dec. 1989; weekly trade journal; Editor-in-Chief SILVIU SORIN TRUSCĂ.

Curierul Românesc: 71273 Bucharest, Al. Alexandru 38; tel. (1) 6797510; fax (1) 3127559; f. Dec. 1989 to replace Tribuna României; monthly; cultural and social; published by the Romanian Cultural Foundation; circulated internationally; Pres. AUGUSTIN BUZURA; circ. 10,000.

Cuvîntul (The Word): 70112 Bucharest, Bd. N. Balcescu 23A; tel. (1) 6157813; fax (1) 3110516; opinion; weekly; f. 1990; Editor-in-Chief MIRCEA ŢICUDEAN; circ. 50,000.

Democratia (Democracy): 70101 Bucharest, Calea Victoriei 39A; tel. (1) 130190; f. 1990; independent periodical; supports National Salvation Front; Editor-in-Chief EUGEN FLORESCU.

Expres: 71102 Bucharest, Calea Victoriei 135; tel. (1) 503041; fax (1) 507994; f. 1990; independent; weekly; Editor-in-Chief ILIE ŞERBĂNESCU.

Expres Magazin: 71341 Bucharest 1, Piaţa Libere 1; tel. (1) 6173523; fax (1) 3128381; independent; weekly; Editor-in-Chief ION CRISTOIU.

Falvak Népe (Peasants): 71341 Bucharest, Piaţa Presei Libere 1; tel. (1) 185292; f. 1945, new series 1990; weekly; in Hungarian; Editor-in-Chief FERENCZ L. IMRE.

Fapta (The Deed): 70317 Bucharest, Str. Olari 12; tel. (1) 331577; f. 1990; weekly; published by Democratic Labour Party; Editor-in-Chief PETRU ŞTEŢ.

Femeia (Woman): 71341 Bucharest, Piaţa Presei Libere 1; f. 1948; monthly; published by National Women's Council; Editor-in-Chief CONSTANŢA NICULESCU.

Filatelia: 70100 Bucharest, POB 1-870; tel. (1) 6131007; f. 1950; monthly; published by Philatelists' Federation; Editor-in-Chief AURELIAN DÂRNU.

Flacăra (The Flame): 71341 Bucharest 1, Piaţa Presei Libere 1; tel. (1) 6175969; fax (1) 3128289; f. 1911; weekly; Editor-in-Chief LIVIU TIMBUS; circ. 50,000.

Gazeta cooperaţiei: 71341 Bucharest, Piaţa Presei Libere 1; tel. (1) 176020; weekly; published by Centrocoop; Editor-in-Chief GHEORGHE ANGELESCU.

Ifi Fórum (Youth Forum): POB 95, 4100 Miercurea-Cluc; tel. (1) 968-16940; fax (1) 92-162614; f. 1990; organ of Hungarian youth in Romania; weekly; in Hungarian; Editor-in-Chief ISTVÁN FERENCZES.

Közoktatás (Public Education): 71341 Bucharest 33, Piaţa Presei Libere 1, Corpul Central, Etajul 9, camera 902; tel. (1) 6171796; f. 1957, known as *Tanügyi Ujság* until 1989; monthly; published by Ministry of Education and Science; in Hungarian; Editor LÁSZLÓ GERGELY.

Luceafărul (The Morning Star): 71102 Bucharest, Calea Victoriei 133; tel. (1) 596760; f. 1958; weekly; published by the Writers' Union; Dir LAURENTIU ULICI.

Lumea Azi (The World Today): 71341 Bucharest, Piaţa Presei Libere 1; tel. (1) 185081; telex 11272; f. 1963; weekly; independent review of international affairs; Dir MAGDALENA BOIANGIU; circ. 20,000.

Lupta CFR (Romanian Railway Workers' Struggle): 77113 Bucharest, Bd. Dinicu Golescu 38; telex 10876; f. 1932; weekly; Editor-in-Chief IONEL CHIRU.

Magazin istoric (Historical Magazine): 70100 Bucharest, Str. Ministerului 2; tel. (1) 150200; f. 1967; monthly; review of historical culture; Chief Editor CRISTIAN POPIŞTEANU.

Manuscriptum: Bucharest, Str. Fundaţiei 4; tel. (1) 6502096; telex 10376; f. 1970; quarterly; published by the Ministry of Culture; Editor-in-Chief PETRU CRETIA; circ. 2,000.

Modelism—International: 71341 Bucharest, Piaţa Presei Libere 1, POB 33-126; quarterly; hobbies; Editor-in-Chief Dr CRISTIAN CRĂCIUNOIU; circ. 60,000.

Neamul Românesc (Serie Nouă) (The Romanian Nation—New Series): 6600 Iaşi, Str. Anastasi Panu 60; f. 1990; independent periodical of opinion, information, science and culture; Editor-in-Chief DUMITRU POPA.

Noul Cinema: 71341 Bucharest, Piaţa Presei Libere 1; fax (1) 3127668; f. 1963; monthly; Editor-in-Chief ADINA DARIAN; circ. 130,000.

Novîi vik (New Age): 71341 Bucharest, Piaţa Presei Libere 1; f. 1949; fortnightly; social, political and cultural journal for the Ukrainian population; Editor-in-Chief ION COLESNIC.

Panoramic Radio-TV: 70747 Bucharest, Str. Gral Berthelot 60–62; tel. (1) 1593050; fax (1) 156992; weekly.

PC World Romania: 72231 Bucharest, Calea Floreasca 167, Rm 412; tel. (1) 6797140; fax (1) 3127612; monthly; computing magazine; Editor-in-Chief ION DIAMANDID.

Pentru patrie (For the Motherland): 70622 Bucharest, Sector 5, Str. Mihai Vodă 17; tel. (1) 143795; telex 88810; f. 1949; monthly; illustrated; published by Ministry of the Interior; Editor-in-Chief OLIMPIAN UNGHEREA.

Psihologia: 79781 Bucharest, Piaţa Presei Libere 1; f. 1991; 6 a year; psychology; Editor-in-Chief ADINA CHELCEA.

Rebus: 71341 Bucharest 1, Piaţa Presei Libere 1; tel. (1) 6175969; fax (1) 3128289; f. 1931; monthly; Editor-in-Chief ALEXANDRU PĂSĂRIN; circ. 300,000.

Revista Cultului Mozaic (Review of the Mosaic Creed): 70478 Bucharest, Popa Rusu 24; tel. (1) 118080; telex 10798; fax (1) 130911; f. 1956; fortnightly; English, Romanian, Hebrew and Yiddish; published by Federation of Jewish Communities; Pres. Dr MOSES ROSEN.

Revista Română de Statistică (Romanian Review of Statistics): Bucharest, Str. Stavropoleos 6; tel. (1) 6138876; f. 1952; monthly; organ of the National Statistics Commission; Editor-in-Chief NICOLAE GÂRCEAG.

România apicolă (Apicultural Romania): 70231 Bucharest, Str. I. Fuçik 17; tel. (1) 137877; telex 11205; f. 1926; monthly; review of apiculture published by the Beekeepers' Association; Editor ELISEI TARŢA.

România Literară (Literary Romania): 71102 Bucharest, Calea Victoriei 133; tel. (1) 506286; fax (1) 128253; f. 1968 as successor to *Gazeta Literară*; weekly; literary, artistic and political magazine; published by the Writers' Union; Editor-in-Chief GABRIEL DIMISIANU.

România Máre: 70702 Bucharest, Calea Victoriei 39A; tel. 156093; f. 1990; weekly; independent nationalist; Editor-in-Chief CORNELIU VADIM TUDOR.

România pitorească (Picturesque Romania): 70148 Bucharest, Str. Gabriel Péri 8; tel. (1) 597474; telex 11724; f. 1972; monthly; published by the Ministry of Commerce; Editor-in-Chief ANDA RAICU.

Romanian Foreign Trade: 79502 Bucharest, Chamber of Commerce and Industry, Bd. Nicolae Bălcescu 22; f. 1952; quarterly; in English, French, German, Russian and Spanish.

Romanian Insight: 79502 Bucharest, Chamber of Commerce and Industry, Bd. Nicolae Bălcescu 22; tel. (1) 6132379; telex 11374; fax (1) 3122091; f. 1952; in English; Editor CONSTANTIN GOLIAT; circ. 5,000.

Romanian Panorama: 71341 Bucharest, Piaţa Presei Libere 1, Corp B, POB 33–38; tel. (1) 6173836; fax (1) 3110526; f. 1955; monthly; in Chinese, English, French, German, Russian and Spanish; economy, politics, social questions, science, history, culture, sport, etc.; published by the Foreign Languages Press Group; Dir NICOLAE ŞARAMBEI; circ. 166,000.

Romanian Review: 71341 Bucharest, Piaţa Presei Libere 1; tel. (1) 6173836; fax (1) 3110526; f. 1946; monthly; in English, French, German and Russian; literature, the arts, history, philosophy, sociology, etc.; published by Foreign Languages Press Group; Editor-in-Chief MIHAESCU F. VALENTIN; circ. 51,000.

Satul Românesc (Romanian Village): 71341 Bucharest, Piaţa Presei Libere 1; tel. (1) 170304; weekly; publ. by Federation of Agricultural Cos of Romania; Editor-in-Chief TITU CONSTANTIN.

Sănătatea (Health): 70172 Bucharest, Str. Biserica Amzei 29; tel. (1) 506233; f. 1952; monthly; published by the National Council of the Red Cross; Editor-in-Chief GHEORGHE M. GEORGE.

Secolul 20 (20th Century): 71102 Bucharest, Calea Victoriei 115; f. 1961; monthly; published by the Writers' Union; Editor-in-Chief DAN HĂULICĂ.

Sportul Ilustrat: 79778 Bucharest 2, Str. Vasile Conta 16; tel. (1) 113288; telex 10350; fax (1) 120153; f. 1947; monthly; illustrated magazine; Editor-in-Chief CONSTANTIN MACOVEI; circ. 50,000.

Start 2001: 71341 Bucharest, Piaţa Presei Libere 1; tel. (1) 181361; f. 1990; monthly review; Editor-in-Chief IOAN VOICU.

Ştiinţă şi Tehnică (Science and Technology): 71341 Bucharest, Piaţa Presei Libere 1; tel. (1) 176010; f. 1949; monthly; Editor-in-Chief VOICHITA DOMANEANTU.

Studentimea Democrata: 77119 Bucharest, Str. Ştefan Furtună 140; tel. (1) 157086; f. 1990; independent students' weekly.

Tehnium: 79784 Bucharest, Piaţa Presei Libere 1; tel. (1) 6183566; f. 1970; monthly; hobbies; Editor-in-Chief Ing. ILIE MIHĂESCU; circ. 100,000.

Totusi iubirea: 70184 Bucharest, Str. Dionisie Lupu 84; tel. (1) 115533; f. 1990; culture and civilization; weekly; Dir ADRIAN PĂUNESCU.

Tribuna economică (Economic Tribune): 70159 Bucharest, Bd. Magheru 28–30; tel. (1) 595158; f. 1886; weekly; Editor-in-Chief BOGDAN PADURE.

Tribuna învăţământului (Education's Tribune): 71341 Bucharest, Piaţa Presei Libere 1; tel. (1) 6181508; f. 1990; weekly; guide to schools and colleges; Editor-in-Chief RECEAN DUMITRU MIRCEA.

Universul cărtii: 71341 Bucharest, Piaţa Presei libere 1; tel. (1) 176010; 173306; f. 1991; monthly; published by Ministry of Culture; Editor-in-Chief PAUL DUGNEANU.

Urzica (Stinging Nettle): 79751 Bucharest, Str. Brezoianu 23–25, Sector 1; f. 1949; monthly; humour and satire; Editor-in-Chief TUDOR POPESCU.

Viaţa (The Life): Bucharest, CP 22-105; tel. and fax (1) 135617; f. 1990 to replace *Săptămina culturală a capitalei*; weekly sociocultural review; Editor-in-Chief FLORIN BOLOLOI.

Viaţa Armatei (Army Life): 70764 Bucharest, Str. Gen. Cristescu 5, Sector 1; tel. (1) 6142012; telex 11243; fax (1) 6159456; f. 1947; fmrly *Viaţa Militară*; monthly illustrated review of the Ministry of National Defence; Editor-in-Chief ION JIANU.

Viaţa Românească (Romanian Life): 77112 Bucharest, Str. N. Golescu 15, tel. (1) 142512; monthly; published by Writers' Union; Editor-in-Chief CEZAR BALTAG.

Vânătorul şi Pescarul Român (The Romanian Hunter and Angler): 70344 Bucharest, Calea Moşilor 128; tel. (1) 6136698; fax (1) 6136804; f. 1948; monthly review; published by the General Association of Hunters and Anglers; Editor-in-Chief GABRIEL CHEROIU.

Volk und Kultur: 71341 Bucharest, Piaţa Presei libere 1; tel. (1) 176010; monthly; published by Ministry of Culture; Editor-in-Chief ANNA BRETZ.

Zig-Zag Magazin: 70602 Bucharest, Bd. M. Kogălniceanu 25; tel. (1) 141250; f. 1990; independent; weekly; Editor-in-Chief ION MATEI.

Bacău

Ateneu (Atheneum): 5500 Bacău, Str. V. Alecsandri 7; tel. (93) 112497; f. 1964; monthly; cultural review; Editor-in-Chief SERGIU ADAM.

Braşov

Astra: 2200 Braşov, Str. M. Sadoveanu 3; tel. (92) 143179; f. 1966; monthly; literature, art, culture, philosophy; Editor-in-Chief VASILE GOGEA.

Cluj-Napoca

Családi Tükör (Family Mirror): Cluj-Napoca, Str. Napoca 16; tel. (95) 111734; f. 1945; fmrly *Dolgozó Nő*; monthly; in Hungarian; Editor-in-Chief Dr MAGDA KOVÁCS; circ. 40,000.

Helikon: 3400 Cluj-Napoca, Str. Eroilor 2; tel. (95) 112420; weekly; organ of the Writers' Union; in Hungarian; Editor-in-Chief ISTVÁN SZILÁGYI.

Korunk (Our Time): 3400 Cluj-Napoca, Str. Iasilor 14; tel. (95) 194836; f. 1926; monthly; social review; in Hungarian; Editor-in-Chief LAJOS KÁNTOR.

Napsugár (Sun Ray): 3400 Cluj-Napoca, Piaţa Păcii 1–3, POB 137; tel. (95) 111184; fax (95) 157295; f. 1957; monthly illustrated literary magazine for children aged 7–10 years; in Hungarian; Editor-in-Chief EMESE ZSIGMOND; circ. 22,000.

Steaua (Star): 3400 Cluj-Napoca, Piaţa Libertăţii 1; tel. (95) 115852; f. 1949; monthly review of the Writers' Union; Editor-in-Chief AUREL RĂU; circ. 2,000.

Szivárvány (Rainbow): 3400 Cluj-Napoca, Piaţa Păcii 1–3, POB 137; tel. (95) 111184; fax (95) 157295; f. 1979; monthly illustrated literary magazine for children aged 3–6 years; in Hungarian; Editor-in-Chief EMESE ZSIGMOND; circ. 23,000.

Tribuna: 3400 Cluj-Napoca, Str. Universităţii 1; tel. (95) 117548; f. 1884; weekly; cultural review; Editor-in-Chief AUGUSTIN BUZURA.

Constanţa

Tomis: 8700 Constanţa, Str. J. Lahovari 87; tel. (91) 611172; f. 1966; monthly review; Chief Editor CONSTANTIN NOVAC.

Craiova

Ramuri (Branches): 1100 Craiova, bis Str. Săvineşti 3; tel. (94) 114414; f. 1964; monthly; review of culture; Editor-in-Chief R. DIACONESCU.

Iaşi

Convorbiri literare (Literary Conversations): 6600 Iaşi, Str. Dimitrov 1; tel. (98) 116242; f. 1867, new series 1972; weekly; review of literature; published by the Writers' Union, Iaşi branch; Editor-in-Chief AL DOBRESCU.

Cronica: 6600 Iaşi, Str. Vasile Alecsandri 8; tel. (98) 146433; f. 1966; weekly; political, social and cultural review; Editor-in-Chief IOAN HOLBAN; circ. 8,000.

Oradea

Familia (Family): 3700 Oradea, Str. Romană 3; tel. (99) 114129; f. 1865, new series 1965); monthly; social and cultural review; Editor-in-Chief IOAN MOLDOVAN; circ. 4,000.

Piteşti

Calende: 0300 Piteşti, Bd. Republicii Bl. G 1, et. 2; tel. (97) 633592; f. 1966, known as *Argeş* until 1991; monthly; literary review; Editor-in-Chief NICOLAE OPREA.

Sibiu

Transilvania: 2400 Sibiu, Str. Dr I Raţiu 2; tel. (92) 413377; f. 1868; 2 issues quarterly; political, social and cultural; Editor-in-Chief ION MIRCEA.

Tribuna Sporturilor: 2400 Sibiu, Str. George Coşbuc 38; tel. (92) 412810; telex 69247; fax (92) 412026; f. 1990; weekly; sports magazine; Editor-in-Chief MIRCEA BIŢU.

Timişoara

Orizont (Horizon): 1900 Timişoara, Piaţa Sf. Gheorghe 3; tel. (61) f. 1949; weekly; review of the Writers' Union (Timişoara branch); Editor-in-Chief MIRCEA MIHAIES.

Tîrgu Mureş

Erdélyi Figyelő (Transylvanian Observer): 4300 Tîrgu-Mures, Str. Primăriei 1; tel. (954) 26780; f. 1958; fmrly *Új Élet*; fortnightly; illustrated magazine; Editor-in-Chief WELEMAN JÓZSEF.

Látó (Visionary): 4300 Tîrgu Mureş, Str. Primăriei 1; tel. (954) 26610; f. 1953; fmrly *Igaz Szó*; monthly; in Hungarian; literature; Editor-in-Chief BÉLA MARKÓ; circ. 2,500.

Vatra (Home): 4300 Tîrgu Mureş, Str. Primăriei 1; tel. (954) 35005; f. 1894, 1971; monthly; review of literature, arts, sociology; published by the Writers' Union, Mureş branch; Editor-in-Chief CORNEL MORARU.

NEWS AGENCIES

Rompres (Romanian News Agency): 71341 Bucharest, Piaţa Presei Libere 1; tel. (1) 6182878; telex 11272; fax (1) 6170487; f. 1949; fmrly Agerpres; co-operates with, and provides news and photo services to, 64 overseas news agencies; daily news released in English, French, Russian and Spanish; publs news and feature bulletins in English, French, Russian and Spanish; Dir-Gen. NEAGU UDROIU.

Nord-Est Press: 6600 Iaşi, Str. Smirdan 5; tel. and fax (98) 144776; independent regional news agency for north-east Romania; Editor MONA DIRTU.

Foreign Bureaux

Agence France-Presse (AFP): Bucharest; tel. (1) 135226; telex 10848; Correspondent MARIE-FRANCE OSENDA.

Agenzia Nazionale Stampa Associata (ANSA) (Italy): 70185 Bucharest, Bd. Dacia 9A, ap. 2; tel. (1) 335325; telex 11642; Correspondent GIAN MARCO VENIER.

Allgemeiner Deutscher Nachrichtendienst (ADN) (Germany): 70256 Bucharest, Bd. Dacia 37B, ap. 3; tel. (1) 111214; telex 11327; Correspondent MICHAEL HUBE.

Bulgarska Telegrafna Agentsia (BTA) (Bulgaria): Bucharest, Str. Mihai Eminescu 124, Inter B et 5 ap. 12; tel. (1) 191880; telex 11484; Correspondent PETYO PETKOV.

Česká tisková kancelář (ČTK) (Czech Republic): Bucharest, Str. Drobeta 4–10, ap. 12, Sector 2; tel. (1) 114473; telex 11301; Correspondent JAN KOKES.

Deutsche Presse-Agentur (dpa) (Germany): Bucharest, Bul. Jancu Hunedoara 66 (fost Ilie Pintelie), ap. 45 et 4; tel. (1) 121481; fax (1) 123079; Correspondent JOACHIM SONNENBERG.

Informatsionnoye Telegrafnoye Agentstvo Rossii—Telegrafnoye Agentstvo Suverennykh Stran (ITAR—TASS) (Russia): Bucharest, Str. General Praporgescu 33; tel. (1) 134802; telex 11317; Chief Correspondent DMITRII DIAKOV.

Magyar Távirati Iroda (MTI) (Hungary): 72238 Bucharest, Al. Alexandru 10, ap. 1; tel. (1) 3127745; telex 11211; Correspondent DÉNES BARACS.

Novinska Agencija Tanjug (Yugoslavia): Bucharest, Str. Drobeta 4–10; tel. (1) 116208; telex 11304; Correspondent PETAR TOMICI.

Polska Agencja Prasowa (PAP) (Poland): Bucharest; tel. (1) 206870; telex 11298; Correspondent STANISŁAW WOJNAROWICH.

Rossiyskoye Informatsionnoye Agentstvo—Novosti (RIA—Novosti) (Russia): Bucharest; tel. (1) 795648; telex 11300; Correspondent VYACHESLAV SAMOSHIN.

Xinhua (New China) News Agency (People's Republic of China): Bucharest, Şos. Nordului 2; tel. (1) 331927; telex 11308; Correspondent ZHANG HANWEN.

PRESS ASSOCIATIONS

Societatea Ziariştilor din România-Federaţia Sindicatelor din Întreaga Presă (Society of Romanian Journalists-Federation of All Press Unions): Bucharest, Piaţa Presei Libere 1; tel. (1) 6171591; fax (1) 3128266; f. 1990; affiliated to International Organization of Journalists and to International Federation of Journalists; Pres. MIOARA VERGU IORDACHE; 1,600 mems.

The **Union of Professional Journalists** (Pres. STEFAN MITROI) was established in 1990, as was the **Democratic Journalists' Union** (Pres. P. M. BACANU).

Publishers

In 1990 some 1,475 book titles (55.8m. copies) were published.

Editura Academiei Române (Publishing House of the Romanian Academy): 79717 Bucharest, Calea Victoriei 125; tel. (1) 6502130; f. 1948; important books and periodicals on original scientific work, 95 periodicals in Romanian and foreign languages; Dir CONSTANTIN BUSUIOCEANU.

Editura Albatros: 71341 Bucharest, Piaţa Presei Libere 1, Of. 33; tel. (1) 6180448; f. 1971; Editor-in-Chief GEORGETA DIMISIANO.

Editura Artemis (Artemis Publishing House): 71341 Bucharest, Piaţa Presei Libere 1; tel. (1) 6181699; fine arts, fiction, children's literature, history; Dir VASILE FLOREA.

Editura Cartea Românească (Publishing House of The Romanian Book): 79721 Bucharest, Str. Gral Berthelot 41; tel. (1) 149352; f. 1969; Romanian contemporary literature; Dir MARGARETA BEDROSIAN.

Editura Ceres: 79722 Bucharest, Piaţa Presei Libere 1; tel. (1) 180174; f. 1953; books on agriculture and forestry; Dir Eng. ECATERINA MOŞU.

Editura Ion Creangă (Ion Creangă Publishing House): 71341 Bucharest, Piaţa Presei Libere 1; tel. (1) 182525; f. 1969; children's books; Dir DANIELA CRĂSNARU.

Editura Dacia (Dacia Publishing House): 3400 Cluj-Napoca, Str. Emil Isac 23; tel. and fax (95) 194912; telex 31347; f. 1969; classical and contemporary literature, art books, literary, philosophical and scientific books in Romanian, Hungarian and German; Dir VASILE IGNA.

Editura Didactică şi Pedagogică (Educational Publishing House): 79724 Bucharest, Str. Spiru Haret 12; tel. (1) 152455; telex 011352; f. 1951; school, university, technical and vocational textbooks; pedagogic literature and methodology; teaching materials; Dir CONSTANTIN FLORICEL.

Editura Mihai Eminescu (Mihai Eminescu Publishing House): 71341 Bucharest, Piaţa Presei Libere 1; tel. (1) 177380; f. 1969; contemporary original literary works and translations of world literature; Dir EUGEN NEGRICI.

Editura Enciclopedică (Encyclopaedic Publishing House): 71341 Bucharest, Piaţa Presei Libere 1; tel. (1) 6175168; f. 1968, merged with Scientific Publishing House, as Editura Ştiinţifică şi Enciclopedică, 1974–90; encyclopaedias, dictionaries, bibliographies, chronologies and reference books; popular and informational literature; provides photographs and encyclopaedic and statistical data about Romania for publishing houses abroad; Dir MARCEL POPA.

Editura Humanitas (Humanitas Publishing House): 79734 Bucharest, Piaţa Presei Libere 1; tel. (1) 6172987; fax (1) 3128250; philosophy, religion, political and social sciences, economics, history, fiction; Dir GABRIEL LIICEANU.

Editura Junimea (Junimea Publishing House): 6600 Iaşi, O. P. 1, POB 28; tel. (81) 17290; f. 1970; Romanian literature, art books, translations, scientific and technical books; Dir NICOLAE CREŢU.

Editura Kriterion (Kriterion Publishing House): 71341 Bucharest, Piaţa Presei Libere 1; tel. (1) 6174060; fax (1) 6182430; f. 1969; classical and contemporary literature, reference books in science and art in Hungarian, German, Romanian, Russian, Serbian, Slovak, Tatar, Turkish, Ukrainian and Yiddish; translations in Romanian, Hungarian and German; Dir GYULA H. SZABÓ.

Editura Litera (The Letter Publishing House): 71341 Bucharest, Piaţa Presei Libere 1; tel. (1) 182471; 1969; original literature; Dir VIORICA OANCEA.

Editura Medicală (Medical Publishing House): 79728 Bucharest, Str. Smîrdan 5; tel. (1) 6143252; fax (1) 3124879; f. 1954; medical literature; Dir Prof. AL. C. OPROIU.

Editura Meridiane (Meridiane Publishing House): 71341 Bucharest, Piaţa Presei Libere 1; tel. (1) 181087; f. 1952; fine arts, theatre, cinema, architecture; art history, theory and criticism; picture art books, monographs, postcards; Dir CORINA POPA.

Editura Militară (Military Publishing House): 70764 Bucharest, Str. General Cristescu 3–5; tel. (1) 6133601; f. 1950; military history, theory, science, technics and medicine, and fiction; Dir CORNEL BARBULESCU.

Editura Minerva (Minerva Publishing House): 71341 Bucharest, Piaţa Presei Libere 1; tel. (1) 6184464; f. 1969; Romanian classical literature, world literature, original literary works, literary criticism and history; Dir ZIGU ORNEA.

Editura Muzicală (Musical Publishing House): 70718 Bucharest, Str. Poiana Narciselor 6; tel. (1) 138743; f. 1957; books on music, musicology and musical scores; Dir VLAD ULPIU.

Editura pentru Turism (Tourism Publishing House): 70161 Bucharest, Bd. Gh. Magheru 7; tel. (1) 145160; telex 11270; f. 1990; tourism; Dir VICTOR CRĂCIUN.

Editura Porto-Franco (Porto-France Publishing House): 6200 Galati, Bd. George Coşbuc 223A; tel. (934) 27602; f. 1990; literary and scientific books, translations; Dir RADU DORIN MIHĂESCU.

Editura Presa Libera (Free Press Publishing House): 71341 Bucharest, Piaţa Presei Libere 1; f. 1954; newspapers, magazines; Dir (vacant).

Editura Scrisul Românesc (Romanian Writing Publishing House): 1100 Craiova, Str. Mihai Viteazul 4; tel. (41) 13763; f. 1972; socio-political, technical, scientific and literary works; Dir MARIN SORESCU.

Editura Sport-Turism (Sport-Tourism Publishing House): 79736 Bucharest, Str. Vasile Conta 16; tel. (1) 107480; f. 1968; sport, tourism, monographs, translations, postcards, children's books; Dir MIHAI CAZIMIR.

Editura Ştiinţifică (Scientific Publishing House): 71341 Bucharest, Piaţa Presei Libere 1; tel. (1) 6176689; f. 1990; fmrly Editura Ştiinţifică şi Enciclopedică; language dictionaries, bibliographies, monographs, chronologies, reference books, popular and informational literature; Dir DINU GRAMA.

Editura Tehnică (Technical Publishing House): 71341 Bucharest, Piaţa Presei Libere 1; tel. (1) 180630; f. 1950; technical and scientific books, technical dictionaries; Dir Dr Eng. IOAN GANEA.

Editura Univers: 71341 Bucharest, Piaţa Presei Libere 1; tel. (1) 6181762; fax (1) 3129470; f. 1961; translations from world literature; Dir MIRCEA MARTIN.

Editura de Vest (West Publishing House): 1900 Timişoara, Piaţa Sfîntul Gheorghe 2; tel. (61) 18218; fax (1) 14212; f. 1972 as Editura Facla; socio-political, technical, scientific and literary works in Romanian, Hungarian, German and Serbian; Dir VASILE POPOVICI.

Întreprinderea de Stat pentru Imprimate şi Administrarea Publicaţiilor (State Enterprise for Printed Matter and Periodicals): 71341 Bucharest, Piaţa Presei Libere 1; f. 1951; general publications; Dir NICOLAE BAZAC.

Tribuna Press and Publishing House: 2400 Sibiu, Str. George Coşbuc 38; tel. (24) 12810; telex 69247; fax (24) 12026; f. 1991; Dir EMIL DAVID.

PUBLISHERS' ASSOCIATIONS

Romlibri: 79715 Bucharest, Piaţa Presei Libere 1; tel. (1) 181255; f. 1962 as Centrala Editorală; a state organization which co-ordinates book production and distribution throughout Romania as well as the economic and financial activities of the publishing houses; organizes the import and export of books and other cultural goods; Man. Dir DUMITRU CONSTANTINESCU.

Societatii Patronilor de Edituri din România: Braşov, Bd dul 15 Noeimbrei 3; tel. (92) 114876; fax (92) 150394; f. 1993; 50 mems; Pres. DANIEL DRAGAN.

WRITERS' UNION

Uniunea Scriitorilor din România (Romanian Writers' Union): Bucharest, Calea Victoriei 133; tel. (1) 6507245; telex 11796; fax (1) 3129634; f. 1949; Pres. MIRCEA DINESCU.

Radio and Television

In March 1991 there were 2,355,800 radio subscribers and 3,640,791 television subscribers. Romania's first regional TV station (at Timişoara) was registered in December 1989. Plans exist for the reception of satellite TV in Romania.

Radioteleviziunea Română (Romanian Radio and Television): Bucharest, Calea Dorobanţilor 191, POB 63–1200; tel. (1) 334710; telex 11251; fax (1) 337544; Pres. Prof. Dr RĂZVAN THEODORESCU.

RADIO

Radiodifuziunea Română: Bucharest, Str. Gral Berthelot 61–62, POB 63-1200; tel. (1) 6334710; telex 11252; fax (1) 3123640; f. 1928; 39 transmitters on medium-wave, 69 transmitters on VHF; First, Second, Third and Fourth Programme; foreign broadcasts on one medium-wave and eight short-wave transmitters in Arabic, English, French, German, Greek, Hungarian, Italian, Persian, Portuguese, Romanian, Russian, Serbian, Spanish and Turkish; Dir-Gen. EUGEN PREDA.

Radio 'Nord-Est': 6600 Iaşi, Str. Smirdan 5; tel. (98) 145530; fax (98) 146363; f. 1991; independent; Dir ALEXANDRU LAZESCU.

TELEVISION

Televiziunea Română—Telecentrul Bucureşti (Romanian Television—Bucharest TV Centre): Bucharest, Calea Dorobanţilor 191, POB 63-1200; tel. (1) 6334710; telex 11251; fax (1) 6337544; 39 transmitters; daily transmissions; Dir-Gen. DUMITRU POPA.

Channel 2 TV Română: Bucharest; f. 1992 as a jt venture; 80% owned by Atlantic Television Ltd (UK-Canada), 20% by Radioteleviziunea Română; independent commercial channel; to broadcast six hours of programmes daily; Man. Dir ROBIN EDWARDS.

Soti: independent co; began broadcasting on state TV's second channel in Dec. 1991; Exec. Man. RADU BUDEANU.

Finance

(cap. = capital; res = reserves; dep. = deposits; m. = million; amounts in lei; brs = brs)

BANKING

Central Bank

Banca Naţională (National Bank of Romania): 70421 Bucharest, Str. Lipscani 25; tel. (1) 6140262; telex 11136; fax (1) 6415055; f. 1880; until 1948 was the Banca Natională a României; from 1948–65 was the Banca Republicii Populare Române; central bank and bank of issue; manages monetary policy; supervises commercial banks and credit business; Gov. MUGUR ISĂRESCU; 141 brs.

Other Banks

Banca Agricolă SC (Agriculture Bank): 70006 Bucharest, Str. Smîrdan 3; tel. (1) 144260; telex 11622; fax (1) 120340; f. 1968; fmrly Banca pentru Agricultură şi Industrie Alimentară, present name since 1990; cap. 29,000m. (May 1993), res 1,145m., dep. 365,029m. (Dec. 1991); state-owned; Pres. GHEORGHE BĂRBULESCU; 41 brs.

Banca Comerciala Română SA (Romanian Commercial Bank): 70348 Bucharest, Bd. Republicii 14; tel. and fax (1) 612166; telex 10893; f. 1990; commercial banking services for domestic and foreign customers; subscribed cap. 30,000m., res 1,682m., dep. 686,109m. (Dec. 1992); Pres. ION GHICA; 184 brs and agencies.

Banca Română de Comerţ Exterior SA (Romanian Bank for Foreign Trade): 70012 Bucharest, Calea Victoriei 22–24; tel. (1) 6149190; telex 11703; fax (1) 6141598; f. 1968, reorganized 1991; cap. 14,000m., res 40,813m., dep. 361,196m. (Dec. 1992); state-owned; Pres. and CEO DAN PASCARIU; 12 brs.

Banca Română Pentru Dezvoltare (Romanian Bank for Development): 70016 Bucharest 3, Str. Doamnei 4; tel. (1) 6133200; telex 10138; fax (1) 6157603; f. 1990 to replace Investment Bank (f. 1948); financial and banking services and operations to all economic units, public enterprises and individuals for investment, production and commercial activities, etc.; cap. 21,000m.; state-owned; Chair. and CEO MARIAN CRIŞAN; 160 brs.

Bankcoop SA (The Cooperative Credit Bank): 70418 Bucharest, Str. Ion Ghica 13; tel. (1) 3120035; telex 11202; fax (1) 3120037; f. 1990; cap. 2,500m., dep. 37,747m. (Nov. 1992); Pres. Mr DINULESCU; 41 brs.

Bank for Small Industry and Free Enterprise—Mindbank: Bucharest, 46–48 Calea Plevnei; tel. (1) 6130788; telex 10228; fax (1) 3120031; f. 1990; cap. 1,500m., res 1,607m., dep. 12,230m. (Dec. 1992); privately-owned; Chair. IOAN PRUNDUS; 3 brs.

Casa de Economii şi Consemnaţiuni—CEC (Savings and Consignation Bank): Bucharest, Calea Victoriei 13; tel. (1) 6154810; telex 11466; fax (1) 3123159; f. 1864; handles private savings and loans for the inter-banking market; cap. 17,400m., dep. 389,800m. (Dec. 1992); state-owned; Pres. EMIL ACHIM BADIU; 42 brs.

Other private banks founded since 1990 include the Banca Comerciala Ion Tiriac SA, Bankost, Creditbank, the Romanian Bank and the Export Import Bank (initial cap. 20,000m. lei).

A supervisory authority, the Romanian Banking Institute, was scheduled to commence operations in early 1992.

BANKING ASSOCIATION

Romanian Banking Association: Bucharest; Chair. DAN PASCARIU.

INSURANCE

Asigurarea Românească SA (Asirom): 70406 Bucharest 3, Str. Smîrdan 5; tel. (1) 3125020; telex 11269; fax (1) 3124819; f. 1991; all types of insurance, including life insurance; Gen. Man. GHEORGHE PARASCHIV; 41 brs.

Insurance and Reinsurance Company SA (Aatra): 79118 Bucharest, Str. Smîrdan 5; tel. (1) 150986; telex 11209; fax (1) 139306; all types of insurance, including commercial insurance; Gen. Man. EMIL BOLDUŞ.

Trade and Industry

STATE PROPERTY AGENCIES

National Agency for Privatization: Bucharest; Pres. (vacant).

State Ownership Fund: Bucharest; responsible for the sale of shareholdings totalling 70% in about 6,000 state-owned enterprises; Chair. EMIL DIMA.

INVESTMENT ORGANIZATION

Romanian Development Agency: Bucharest; promotes foreign investment in Romanian industry; Pres. (vacant).

CHAMBER OF COMMERCE AND INDUSTRY

There are chambers of commerce throughout Romania.

Chamber of Commerce and Industry of Romania: 79502 Bucharest, Bd. Nicolae Bălcescu 22; tel. (1) 3121312; telex 11374; fax (1) 3122091; f. 1868; Pres. AUREL GHIBUTIU.

FOREIGN TRADE ORGANIZATIONS AND MAJOR COMPANIES

Arcif SA: 70448 Bucharest, Str. Scaune 1–3; tel. (1) 6155996; telex 12688; fax (1) 3121115; f. 1982; export of land reclamation work, water course regulation works, water supply and treatment plants, sewerage works, agricultural and civil construction works, studies, surveys, etc.; Dir VIOREL GIHAC.

Arcom International SA: Bucharest, Str. Scaune 1–3; tel. (1) 153632; telex 11490; f. 1969; civil and industrial constructions, mechanical and electrical installations, engineering and technical assistance services; Pres. and Dir-Gen. MARCEL FLORESCU.

Arpimex Trading SA: Bucharest, Str. Lipscani 19, Sector 3, POB 1-130; tel. (1) 144140; telex 11472; fax (1) 145464; f. 1970; export of footwear, leather goods, leather and fur garments, gloves; import of raw hides, organic dyes, chemical auxiliaries; Gen. Dir MIRCEA STADOLEANU.

Auto-Dacia SA: Piteşti, Str. Mircea Vodă 42; tel. (97) 634978; telex 18296; fax (97) 636762; manufacture, export and import of road vehicles, vehicle parts and special purpose vehicles; Dir CONSTANTIN STROE.

Confex: Bucharest, Bd. Armata Poporului 5–7; tel. (1) 814450; telex 011195; fax (1) 316170; exports ready-made clothes and knitwear.

Contransimex: 77115 Bucharest, Bd. Dinicu Golescu 38, POB 2006; tel. (1) 180042; telex 11606; fax (1) 180042; civil engineering and construction projects; import and export of transport and telecommunication equipment and installations; Gen. Man. ALFONS IRINESCU.

Electra Trading SA: Bucharest, Calea Victoriei 216, POB 22; tel. (1) 3124778; telex 11388; fax (1) 3129706; f. 1950; export and import of electric motors, electrical cables and conductors, power transformers and other industrial and household electronic goods, and medical equipment and instruments; Gen. Dir P. TUDOR; 150 employees.

Electronum: Bucharest, Bd. Magheru 28–30; tel. (1) 137081; telex 11547; fax (1) 506940; exports and imports computer parts and accessories, telecommunication equipment, radio receivers, TV sets, components, etc.; Dir M. TUDOR.

Fructexport-Agroexport: 70714 Bucharest, Str. Brezoianu 43, POB 790; tel. (1) 136563; telex 10963; fax (1) 149747; f. 1950; exports fruit and vegetable produce, wine, spirits, medicinal herbs, aromatic seeds, technical assistance; imports agricultural products, veterinary supplies, etc.; Gen. Dir VICTOR STOICULESCU.

Ilexim: Bucharest, Str. 13 Decembrie 3, POB 1-136; tel. (1) 148530; telex 11226; exports carpets, toys, furniture, handicrafts, ready-made clothes, metal and rubber goods, wooden articles, foodstuffs, agricultural products, cultural goods; Dir BUJOR URSULESCU.

Industrialexport SA: 70185 Bucharest 1, Bd. Dacia 13; tel. (1) 6118905; telex 10052; fax (1) 3120312; exports and imports oilfield and mining equipment, complete chemical, petro-chemical, oil refining and food industry plants and equipment, gears, pumps and industrial valves and fittings; barter operations and general trading; Pres. and Gen. Man. Eng. GEORGES CONSTANTIN.

Maşinexportimport Industries SA: 70033 Bucharest, Bd. Carol I 32, Sector 3, POB 37-152; tel. (1) 3124314; fax (1) 3120150; exporter and importer of machine tools for metal-working and manufactured and consumer goods; also exports woodworking and textiles machinery; Gen. Dir TRAIAN CRUCERU.

Mecanoexportimport SA: 79522 Bucharest, Bd. Dacia 30, POB 22-107; tel. (1) 119855; telex 10269; fax (1) 116650; imports and exports road construction equipment, metal railway sleepers, diesel and electric railway engines, rolling stock, air compressors, lifting and conveying equipment; Gen. Dir CORNEL ANGHEL.

Mercur Trading SA: Bucharest, Calea Victoriei, Sector 1; tel. (1) 503784; telex 11368; fax (1) 506375; importer and exporter of food and consumer goods; barter trade; Gen. Man. SERBAN ALTANGIU.

Metalexportimport: Bucharest, Str. Mendeleev 21–25; tel. (1) 593850; telex 11515; fax (1) 507922; exports and imports rolled steel products, welded and seamless tubes, ferro-alloys, non-ferrous metals; Gen. Man. CONSTANTIN GHITA.

Mineralimportexport SA: Bucharest, Bd. Republicii 16; tel. (1) 139167; telex 11873; fax (1) 126927; f. 1962; exports coal-tar, graphite electrodes, abrasives, etc.; imports iron ore, manganese ore, pyrite, bauxite, coal, coke, anthracite, potassium fertilizers, refractory materials, abrasive materials, etc.; Dir DAN GEORMANEANU.

Mondexim SA: 70701 Bucharest, Str. Constantin Mille 17; tel. (1) 149548; telex 11496; fax (1) 149404; exports metallurgical products, chemicals, wood products; imports raw materials for metallurgical industry, electronics, spare parts, etc.

Navlomar SA: Bucharest, Bd. Republicii 16, POB 851; tel. (1) 132279; telex 11783; fax (1) 144071; f. 1969; shipbrokers, Danube River chartering agents, cargo transit and transhipment, ship agents, ship-chandlers, consultancy and legal assistance; Gen. Dir VIOREL COVRIG.

Petrolexportimport: Bucharest, Bd. Magheru 1–3; tel. (1) 133045; telex 11519; fax (1) 156550; export of petroleum products; import of raw materials for petrochemical industry; Dir GHEORGHE ALBU.

Prodexport: Bucharest, Str. Valter Mărăcineanu; tel. (1) 3122695; telex 11527; fax (1) 6152107; f. 1948; exports and imports livestock, meat, sugar, vegetable oils, tobacco, spices, food additives, etc.; Dir MIHAI STURZ.

Romănoexport: 70014 Bucharest, Str. Doamnei 17–19, POB 594; tel. (1) 133699; telex 11186; fax (1) 131841; f. 1948; exports: fabrics, knitwear, carpets, and blankets; imports: wool, cotton, jute, dyestuffs, felts, etc.; Man. Dir PETRU CRIŞAN.

Romelectro SA: Bucharest, Calea Dorobanţilor 60; tel. (1) 3120364; telex 10449; fax (1) 3124440; export and import of power equipment, electrical appliances, spare parts, etc.; Dir-Gen. CORNELIU LAZĂR.

Romenergo SA: 71101 Bucharest, Calea Victoriei 91-93, POB 22–153; tel. (1) 506682; telex 11525; fax (1) 506682; import and export of power generation equipment for hydro, thermal and nuclear power projects, boilers, turbines, generators; studies, training, service, etc.; Gen. Man. ALEXANDRU PÂRVESCU.

Romferchim SA: Bucharest, Splaiul Independenţei 202A, POB 12-226; tel. (1) 6385305; telex 11489; fax (1) 3121141; exports fertilizers, pharmaceuticals, cosmetics, cellulose, fibres, chemical products, etc.; imports phosphorites, apatite, acids, complete plants and equipment for chemical and petro-chemical industry; Man. Dir MIHAI IONESCU.

Rompetrol: 70176 Bucharest, Calea Victoriei 109; tel. (1) 594325; telex 10155; fax (1) 595405; provides geological survey and geophysical prospecting, drilling works, construction of pipelines and storage tanks for crude oil, LPG and petroleum products, technical assistance; Gen. Man. NELU IONESCU.

Romproiect SA: 70704 Bucharest 1, Str. Matei Millo 13; tel. (1) 154237; telex 11785; fax (1) 158523; f. 1969; exports design and drafting services, technical assistance for building and irrigation works, mass housing programmes, construction management; Dir DOREL RĂDULESCU.

Romsit: 70418 Bucharest, Str. Doamnei 15–17, Sector 3; tel. (1) 156821; telex 11836; f. 1972; export of glassware, lead crystal, tableware and ornamental porcelain, hotel porcelainware, ornamental earthenware, clear sheet glass; Man. Dir I. SPIRIDON.

Romtrans SA: 75260 Bucharest, Calea Rahovei 196; tel. (1) 236040; telex 11346; fax (1) 413516; f. 1952; international forwarding agency; Dir EUGEN BÂR.

Tehnoforestexport SA: Bucharest, Piaţa Rosetti 4; tel. (1) 6136717; telex 10330; fax (1) 6154020; f. 1948; exports furniture and other finished wooden products; imports raw materials for wood-working industry; timber processing; marketing; Man. Dir CONSTANTIN POPA.

Tehnoimportexport: Bucharest, Str. Doamnei 2, POB 110; tel. (1) 152653; telex 10254; fax (1) 132526; imports and exports bearings and technical goods, aircraft, helicopters, spare parts, etc.; Gen. Dir MIRCEA BORTEŞ.

Terra SA: Bucharest, Bd. Republicii 16, POB 86; tel. (1) 6155938; telex 11571; fax (1) 3120954; imports and exports various commodities; co-operation ventures, etc.; technical assistance; Gen. Man. FLORIN CASPRUF.

Universal-Trading SA: 2200 Braşov, Str. Turnului 5; tel. (92) 162661; telex 61335; exports tractors and farming machinery, lorries, buses; Dir SAVA RADU BASARAB.

Uzinexportimport SA: 70033 Bucharest, Bd. Republicii 32; tel. (1) 132959; telex 11214; fax (1) 139389; f. 1966; export and import of complex installations and basic equipment for the machine-building industry and ships and shipbuilding industry and cement industries, metallurgical and iron and steel plants; Man. Dir MATACHE NICOLAIDE.

Vitrocim SA: Bucharest, Str. Blănari 18; tel. (1) 131638; telex 11330; fax (1) 142412; f. 1970; import and export of building materials and machinery for the building industry; Gen. Dir CONSTANTIN MĂRGINEANU.

CO-OPERATIVE ORGANIZATIONS

Federaţia agricultorilor privatizaţi din România (Romanian Private Farmers' Federation): 70111 Bucharest, Bd. Nicolae Bălcescu 17–19, Sector 1; tel. (1) 131869; f. 1989; represents 4,000 farming co-operatives and 41 district unions; Pres. AUREL STIRBU.

Uniunea centrală a cooperativelor de consum şi de credit—Centrocoop (Central Union of Consumer and Credit Co-operatives): Bucharest, Str. Brezoianu 31; tel. (1) 6144800; telex 11591; fax (1) 6142991; f. 1950; 2,500 producer and 850 credit co-operatives were affiliated to the Central Union in 1992; represents 10m. members.

Uniunea centrală a cooperativelor meşteşugăresti—UCECOM (Central Union of Handicrafts Co-operatives): Bucharest, Calea Plevnei 46; tel. (1) 151810; Chair. Ing. DUMITRU DĂNGĂ.

TRADE UNIONS

The regulations governing trade unions were liberalized in early 1990. The Uniunea Generală a Sindicatelor din România (UGSR) was dissolved. Several new trade union organizations have since been established.

Alianţa Confederativă Intersindicală 15 Noiembrie: Braşov; f. 1991; 120,000 mems; Leader MIRCEA SAVACIUC.

Blocul Naţional Sindical: Bucharest; f. 1991; 500,000 mems; Chair. MATEI BRĂTIANU.

Cartelul Alfa: f. 1990; 1.1m. mems; Leader BOGDAN HOSSU.

Confederaţia COSIN: f. 1990; 10,000 mems.

Confederaţia Fides: 180,000 mems; Leader CĂTĂLIN CROITORU.

Confederaţia Hercules: Bucharest; f. 1990; transport workers.

Confederaţia Naţională a Sindicatelor Libere din România—FRATIA (CNSLR-FRATIA—National Free Trade Union Confederation of Romania): 70109 Bucharest, Str. Ministerului 1–3; tel. (1) 3125292; telex 10844; fax (1) 6133883; f. 1990, merged with Confederaţia Naţională a Sindicatelor Libere Frăţia in 1993; 3.5m. mems (1993); 52 professional or branch federations, in all sectors of the economy, and 41 territorial leagues; Pres VICTOR CIORBEA; Exec. Pres. MIRON MITREA.

Other organizations include Infratirea, the Justice and Brotherhood Union and the Convention of Non-Affiliated Trade Unions of Romania.

TRADE FAIRS

Romexpo SA (Fairs and Exhibitions Co): 71331 Bucharest, Bd. Mărăşti 65–67, POB 32-3; tel. (1) 6181160; telex 11108; fax (1) 6183724; f. 1970; Gen. Dir GEORGE COJOCARU.

Transport

RAILWAYS

In 1991 there were 11,127 km of track, of which 2,367 km were electrified lines.

Societatea Natională a Căilor Ferate Române—CFR (Romanian Railways): 79684 Bucharest 1, Bd. Dinicu Golescu 38; tel. (1) 6386550; telex 10633; fax (1) 3123205; f. 1880; Pres. AUREL DUMITRESCU.

Metropolitan Transport

The Bucharest underground railway network, sections of which were opened between 1979 and 1989, totals 60 km in length.

Regia de Éxploatare a Metroului Bucureşti: 79917 Bucharest 1, Bd. Dinicu Golescu 38; tel. (1) 6387515; telex 11665; fax (1) 3125149; f. 1977; Gen. Man. VIRGIL DASCHIEVICI.

ROADS

At the end of 1992 there were 72,816 km of roads, of which 113 km were motorways, 14,570 km national roads and 58,133 km secondary roads. In addition, there were 308,867 km of other (non-public) roads. Under the 1991–2005 road development programme, more than 3,000 km of motorways were to be built and 4,000 km of existing roads were to be modernized.

Administraţia Naţională a Drumurilor (National Administration of Roads): Ministerul Transporturilor, Bucharest 1, Bd. Dinicu Golescu 38; tel. (1) 6387886; telex 10835; fax (1) 3120984; Dir-Gen. Dr Ing. MIHAI BOICU.

INLAND AND OCEAN SHIPPING

Navigation on the River Danube is open to shipping of all nations. The Danube–Black Sea Canal was officially opened to traffic in May 1984, and has an annual handling capacity of 80m. metric tons. Work on the 85-km Danube–Bucharest Canal was abandoned in early 1990. A new port was planned at Bucharest. The first joint Romanian-Yugoslav Iron Gates (Porţile de Fier) power and navigation system on the Danube was completed in 1972, and Iron Gates-2 opened to navigation in December 1984. Romania's principal seaports are Constanţa (on the Black Sea), Tulcea, Galaţi, Brăila and Giurgiu (on the Danube). In June 1991 Romania's merchant fleet had 469 vessels, with a total displacement of 3,838,034 grt.

NAVROM (Romanian Shipping Co): 8700 Constanţa; tel. (91) 615821; telex 14217; fax (91) 618413; organizes sea transport; operates routes to most parts of the world; Gen. Man. MANEA GHIOCEL.

Petromin SA: Constanţa; operates merchant fleet of 92 ships and tankers totalling 4.6m. gross registered tons.

Romline: Constanţa; merchant shipping company.

CIVIL AVIATION

There are international airports at Bucharest-Otopeni, M. Kogălniceanu-Constanţa, Timişoara and Arad.

Transporturile Aeriene Române—TAROM (Romanian Air Transport): Bucharest, Otopeni Airport; tel. (1) 333137; telex 11181; fax (1) 330356; f. 1954; services to 40 destinations throughout Europe, the Middle East, Africa, Asia and the USA and extensive internal flights; Dir-Gen. NICOLAE BRUTARU.

Liniile Aeriene Române—LAR: Bucharest, Baneasa Airport; tel. (1) 336551; telex 113779; fax (1) 120148; f. 1975 by TAROM to operate passenger charter services; re-established as independent airline in 1990; Man. Dir DORIN IVAŞCU.

Tourism

The Carpathian mountains, the Danube delta and the Black Sea resorts (Mamaia, Eforie, Mangalia and others) are the principal attractions. The Danube delta development programme, instigated in 1983, is to affect only half the total area of the delta, the remainder being designated a nature reserve. In 1990 there were 6.5m. tourist arrivals. In 1988 receipts from tourism totalled US $170m.

National Tourist Office, Carpaţi: Bucharest 1, Bd. Magheru 7; tel. (1) 6145160; telex 11270; fax (1) 3122594; f. 1936; Gen. Man. MIHAI VOICU.

Litoral SA: 8741 Mamaia-Constanţa, Hotel Bucureşti B; tel. (18) 31152; telex 14267; fax (18) 31276; f. 1970; Gen. Dir CORNELIU CULEŢU.

S. C. Postavural—Tourism Co: 2200 Braşov, Str. Mureşenilor 12; tel. (92) 144622; fax (92) 150496; f. 1990; fmrly National Tourist Office; promotes tourism in Braşov; Gen. Man. NICOLAE ALBU.

Culture

NATIONAL ORGANIZATIONS

Ministry of Culture: see section on The Government (Ministries).

Romanian Cultural Foundation (Fundaţia Culturală Română): Bucharest, Al. Alexandru 38; tel. (1) 6333372; fax (1) 3127559; f. 1990; aims to promote Romanian culture world-wide; Pres. AUGUSTIN BUZURA; Sec. CARMEN FIRAN.

Romanian National Commission for UNESCO (Comisia Naţională a României pentru UNESCO): 71291 Bucharest 1, Str. Anton Cehov 8; tel. (1) 6333223; telex 11657; fax (1) 3127636; f. 1956; Pres. Prof. MIHAI GOLU; Sec. GEORGE VAIDEANU.

CULTURAL HERITAGE

Historical Museum of Bucharest (Muzeul de Istorie şi Artă al Municipiului Bucureşti): Bucharest, Bd. Brtianu 2; tel. (1) 6132154; f. 1984; 11 affiliated museums; Dir Dr VASILE BORONEANŢ.

Library of the Romanian Academy (Biblioteca Academiei Române): 71102 Bucharest, Calea Victoriei 125; f. 1867; 9.4m. items; Dir Prof. VICTOR SAHINI.

Museum of Romanian Literature (Muzeul Literaturii Române): Bucharest, Str. Fundaţiei 4; tel. (1) 6503395; fax (1) 503922; f. 1957; 5 affiliated museums; Dir ALEXANDRU DAN CONDEESCU.

National Museum of Art (Muzeul Naţional de Artă): Bucharest, Calea Victoriei 49–53; tel. (1) 6155193; fax (1) 3124327; f. 1950; 1 affiliated museum; Dir THEODOR ENESCU.

National History Museum of Romania (Muzeul Naţional de Istorie a României): Bucharest, Calea Victoriei 12; tel. (1) 157055; f. 1972; historical artefacts from all periods; archaeological and numismatic research; Dir Prof. Dr RADU FLORESCU.

National Library (Biblioteca Naţională): Bucharest, Str. Ion Ghica 4; tel. (1) 6157063; fax (1) 3123381; f. 1955; 8.5m. items; Dir GHEORGHE-IOSIF BERCAN.

State Archives (Arhivele Statului): Bucharest, Bd. M. Kogălniceanu 29; tel. (1) 152446; f. 1831; Gen. Dir ION ALEX MUNTEANU.

Village Museum (Muzeul Satului): 71321 Bucharest, Şos. Kiseleff 28–30; tel. (1) 6171732; fax (1) 6180861; f. 1936; ethnographic open-air museum, folk art, rural architecture, agricultural machinery, etc.; Dir Dr IOAN GODEA.

SPORTING ORGANIZATION

Olympic Committee of Romania: Bucharest 1, Str. Vasile Conta 16; tel. (1) 6107600; telex 11180; fax (1) 3120450; f. 1914; Pres. LIA MANOLIU; Sec.-Gen. ALEXANDRU MOGOS.

PERFORMING ARTS

Theatre

Caragiale National Theatre: Bucharest, Bd. Nicolae Bălcescu 2.

Comedy Theatre: Bucharest, Str. Mandineşti.

Romanian Athenaeum: Bucharest, Str. Franklin 1.

Tandarica Puppet Theatre: Bucharest, Calea Victoriei 50.

Opera Houses

Opera House: Bucharest, Bd. Gheorghiu-Dej 70.

Operetta House: Bucharest, Piaţa Natiunile Unite 1.

ASSOCIATIONS

Architects' Union of Romania (Uniunea Arhitecţilor din România): 79182 Bucharest, Str. Academiei 18–20; tel. (1) 6140743; f. 1952; Pres. Arch. ALEXANDRU BELDIMAN.

Association of Photographic Artists (Asociaţia Artistilor Fotografi—AAF): 70700 Bucharest, POB 1-223; tel. (1) 6149558; f. 1956.

Bessarabia and Bucovina Cultural Association (Asociaţia culturală 'Pro Basarabia şi Bucovina'): 70601 Bucharest, Bd. Mihail Kogîniceanu 19; tel. (1) 6193126; f. 1983; Exec. Pres. VASILE LUPU.

Cinema Workers' Union of Romania (Uniunea Cineaştilor din România): 70169 Bucharest, Str. Mendeleev 28–30; tel. (1) 6507245; f. 1963, reorganized 1990; Pres. MIHNEA GHEORGHIU; Dir CONSTANTIN PIVNICIERU.

Ethnology Society of Romania (Societatea de Etnologie din România): 70714 Bucharest, Str. Zalomit 12; tel. (1) 6535846; f. 1990; Pres. Dr ROMULUS VULCĂNESCU; Sec. ION MOANŢA.

European Centre of Culture (Centrul European de Cultură): 71268 Bucharest, Bd. Primŷerii 50; tel. (1) 6185004; fax (1) 3128327; Pres. RĂZVAN THEODORESCU.

PEN Club: Bucharest, Casa Scriitorilor Mihail Sadoveanu, Calea Victoriei 113; Pres. ANA BLANDINA.

Romanian Composers' and Musicologists' Union (Uniunea Compozitorilor şi Musicologilor din România): 71102 Bucharest, Calea Victoriei 141; tel. (1) 6502838; fax (1) 145608; f. 1920, reorganized 1949; Pres. ADRIAN IORGULESCU.

Romanian Union of Fine Arts (Uniunea Artiştilor Plastici din România): 71118 Bucharest, Str. Nicolae Iorga 21; tel. (1) 6507380; f. 1950; Pres. MIHAI MĂNESCU.

Romanian Writers' Union: see section on Publishers (Writers' Union).

Education

Education is free and compulsory between the ages of six and 16 years. Before reaching the age of six years, children may attend crèches (creşe) and kindergartens (grădinițe de copii); in 1991 75% of pre-school age children were attending kindergarten. Between the ages of six and 16 years children attend the general education school (şcoală de cultură generală de zece ani).

There are five types of secondary school. The general secondary school (şcoala medie de cultură generală), for which there is an entrance examination, provides a specialized education suitable for preparation of students for admission to university or college. Vocational secondary schools (şcoli profesionale de ucenici), where training is given for careers in, for example, industry or agriculture, along with some general education. (Courses in these schools are also available to adults requiring retraining.) Secondary art schools (şcoală medie de artă) provide a general secondary education, but with an emphasis on music, art and the theatre. Secondary physical education schools (şcoala medie de educaţie fizică) also provide a general secondary education, but with an emphasis on physical fitness and training. Finally, teacher training secondary schools (şcoala pedagogică de învăţători and şcoală pedagogică de educatoare) provide courses to prepare students for work as kindergarten and general education teachers.

Tuition in minority languages, particularly Hungarian and German, is available. There are 48 higher educational institutes in Romania, with 186 faculties, including eight universities and eight technological universities. In 1991 spending of 78,160m. lei, or 10.0% of the state budget, was allocated to education. Following the revolution of 1989, education was to be reorganized, including the elimination of ideological training.

UNIVERSITIES

Bucharest University (Universitatea Bucureşti): Bucharest, Bd. M. Kogălniceanu 64; tel. (1) 3120419; fax (1) 6131760; f. 1694 (refounded 1864); 16 faculties; 2,065 teachers; 24,785 students; Rector Dr EMIL CONSTANTINESCU.

Cluj-Napoca University 'Babeş-Bolyai' (Universitatea 'Babeş-Bolyai' Cluj-Napoca): 3400 Cluj-Napoca, Str. M. Kogălniceanu 1; tel. (95) 116101; fax (95) 111905; f. 1919; 11 faculties; 1,425 teachers; 12,597 students; Rector Prof. Dr IONEL HAIDUC.

University 'Al. I. Cuza' of Iaşi (Universitatea 'Al. I. Cuza' Iaşi): Iaşi, Bd. Copou 11; tel. (98) 140559; telex 22371; fax (98) 146330; f. 1860; 12 faculties; 776 teachers; 12,009 students; Rector Prof. Dr GHEOFGHE POPA .

University of Braşov 'Transylvanian' (Universitatea 'Transilvania' din Braşov): 2200 Braşov, Bd. Eroilor 29; tel. (92) 141580; f. 1971; 10 faculties; 617 teachers; 8,500 students; Rector Prof. Dr Eng. SERGIU CHIRIACESCU.

University of Craiova (Universitatea din Craiova): 1100 Craiova, Str. 'Al. I. Cuza' 13; tel. (94) 114398; fax (94) 111688; f. 1966; 13 faculties; 950 teachers; 14,000 students; Rector Prof. Dr MIRCEA IVANESCU .

University of Galaţi 'Dunarea de Jos' (Universitatea 'Dunarea de Jos' din Galaţi): 6200 Galaţi, Str. Domnească 47; tel. (93) 461904; fax (93) 461353; f. 1974 as university; 7 faculties; 506 teachers; 7,916 students; Rector Prof. MIHAI JĂŞCANU.

University of Ploieşti (Universitatea din Ploieşti): 2000 Ploieşti, Bd. Bucareşti 39; tel. (97) 173171; fax (97) 171974; f. 1948 as Institute of Oil and Gas, 1992 as a university; 4 faculties; 410 teachers; 3,340 students; Pres. Prof. Dr CONSTANTION IONESCU.

University of Timişoara (Universitatea din Timişoara): 1900 Timişoara, V. Pârvan 4; tel. (96) 112805; fax (96) 116722; f. 1962; 6 faculties; 500 teachers; 6,500 students; Rector E. TODORAN.

Technological Universities

Cluj-Napoca University of Medicine and Pharmacy (Universitatea de Medicină şi Farmacie Cluj-Napoca): 3400 Cluj-Napoca, Str. Constantin Daicoviciu 13; tel. and fax (95) 197257; f. 1919; 3 faculties; 537 teachers; 3,578 students; Rector Prof. Dr OLIVIU PASCU.

Cluj-Napoca Technical University (Universitatea Tehnica din Cluj-Napoca): 3400 Cluj-Napoca, Str. Constantin Daicoviciu 15; tel. (95) 134565; fax (95) 112055; f. 1948; 7 faculties; 596 teachers; 7,559 students; Rector Dr Eng. HANDRA-LUCA VIOREL .

'Gheorghe Asachi' Technical University (Universitatea Technică 'Gheorghe Asachi'): Iaşi, Bd. Copou 22; tel. (98) 146577; telex 22368; fax (98) 147923; f. 1912; 10 faculties; 1,140 teachers; 13,600 students; Rector Prof Dr Ing. VITALIE BELOUSOV.

Iaşi University of Medicine and Pharmacy 'Gr. T. Popa' (Universitatea de Medicină şi Farmacie 'Gr. T. Popa' Iaşi): 6600 Iaşi, Str. Universităţii 16; tel. (98) 116104; fax (98) 117845; f. 1879; 3 faculties; 522 teachers; 3,898 students; Pres. Prof. Dr CAROL STANCIU.

Technical University of Timişoara (Universitatea Tehnică din Timişoara): Timişoara, Piaţa Victoriei 2; tel. (96) 134717; fax (96) 190321; f. 1920; 9 faculties; 1,358 teachers; 12,238 students; Rector Prof Dr Ing. NICHICI ALEXANDRU .

University of Agricultural Science of the Banat in Timişoara (Universitatea de Ştiinţe Agricole a Banatului Timişoara): 1900 Timişoara, Calea Aradului 119; tel. (96) 143016; telex 71386; fax (96) 141563; f. 1945; 3 faculties; 263 teachers; 1,200 students; Rector Prof. Dr IOAN PĂUN OTIMAN.

University of Medicine and Pharmacy (Universitatea de Medicină şi Farmacie): 4300 Tîrgu-Mureş, Str. Gheorghe Marinescu 38; tel. (95) 413127; fax (95) 430804; f. 1945; 3 faculties; 281 teachers; 1,780 students; Rector Prof. Dr ION PASCU.

University 'Politehnica' of Bucharest (Universitatea 'Politehnica' din Bucureşti): 77206 Bucharest, Splaiul Independenţei 313; tel. (1) 3127044; telex 10252; fax (1) 3120188; f. 1819; 11 faculties; 1,800 teachers; 27,800 students; Rector Prof. Dr GHEORGHE ZGURA.

Social Welfare

Romania has a comprehensive state insurance scheme, premiums being paid by enterprises and institutions on behalf of their employees. A new law on unemployment allowance was adopted in January 1991. In addition, funds are allotted to sickness benefits, children's allowances, pensions and the provision of health resorts. There were 215,796 hospital beds in service, and 41,813 doctors and 6,717 dentists in practice, in 1990. Spending of 213,000m. lei (8.2% of the state budget) was allocated to health in 1993.

Following the revolution of December 1989, international attention was focused on the orphanages in Romania housing large numbers of unwanted and neglected children (contraception and abortion having been illegal during the Ceauşescu years), many of whom were found to be suffering from AIDS, hepatitis and other serious illnesses, due to poor medical treatment. Owing to persistent shortages of foodstuffs and high levels of pollution, many Romanians were believed to be suffering from malnutrition and other serious conditions. The incidence of tuberculosis increased during the early 1990s (from 64 sufferers per 100,000 in 1990 to 92.7 per 100,000 in the first quarter of 1993), and up to 10% of the population were reported to be carrying the hepatitis B virus. In 1992 Romania had the highest infant mortality rate in Europe, at 23.4 per thousand births, which was more than twice the European average.

NATIONAL AGENCIES

Ministry of Health: see section on The Government (Ministries).

Ministry of Labour and Social Protection: see section on The Government (Ministries).

Department of Labour: Bucharest, Str. Oneşti 2, Sector 1; Secretary of State OCTAVIAN PARTENIE.

Department of Social Protection: Bucharest, Str. Oneşti 2, Sector 1; Secretary of State MIHU BIJI.

HEALTH AND WELFARE ORGANIZATIONS

Institute of Hygiene and Public Health (Institutul de Igienă şi Sănătate Publică Bucureşti): 76256 Bucharest, Str. Dr Leonte 1–3; tel. (1) 6383970; fax (1) 3123426; f. 1927; Dir Prof. MANOLE CUCU.

Institute of Research for the Quality of Life (Institutul de Cercetare a Calităţii Vieţii): Bucharest 6, Splaiul Independenţei 202A; f. 1990; formulates economic and social policy for improvement of standards of living in Romania; Dir Dr CĂTĂLIN ZAMFIR.

National Committee for Child Protection: Bucharest; Dir ALEXANDRU ZUGRAVESCU.

Research Institute for Labour Safety (Institutul de Cercetări pentru Protecţia Muncii): 70744 Bucharest 1, Str. Gral. Budişteanu 15; tel. (1) 6150531; f. 1951; Dir Dr Ing. ALEXANDRU DARABONT.

Union of Societies of Medical Sciences of Romania (Uniunea Societăţilor de Ştiinţe Medicale din România): 70754 Bucharest, Str. Progresului 10; tel. (1) 141817; f. 1877; Pres. Prof. Dr ZOREL FILIPESCU; Sec.-Gen. Prof. Dr EMANOIL POPESCU.

The Environment

Environmental problems caused some concern under the Communist regime, but the most controversial issue was the threatened destruction of traditional villages (see History). The extent of heavy pollution and environmental damage in Romania became apparent after the revolution of December 1989. The many examples included the town of Copsa Mica, where lead and cadmium pollution was 10 times the internationally accepted level, and surfaces and inhabitants were covered in black soot. Estimates have claimed as many as 112 local environmental groups in existence, with some 100,000 members, in Romania. The Romanian Government is a member of the Danube Commission (based in Hungary), the Joint Danube Fishery Commission (Slovakia) and the IUCN (Gland, Switzerland). Romania's Danube Delta Project is considered to be the most important bird preservation scheme in Europe. In August 1991 Romania and Bulgaria agreed to fuller co-operation on environmental matters, in accordance with EC conditions for rendering aid to the two countries.

GOVERNMENT ORGANIZATIONS

Ministry of the Environment: see section on The Government (Ministries).

National Council for Environmental Protection: Bucharest, Piaţa Victoriei 1; tel. (1) 143400; incl. Commissions for Air Protection and Noise Abatement, Water Protection, Soil and Subsoil Protection, the Protection of Flora, Fauna and the Monuments of Nature and the Protection of Human Settlements.

ACADEMIC INSTITUTES

Academy of Agricultural and Forest Sciences 'Gheorghe Ionescu-Şişeşti' (Academia de Ştiinţe Agricole şi Silvice 'Gheorghe Ionescu-Şişeşti'): Bucharest, Bd. Mărăşti 61; tel. (1) 6180699; telex 11394; f. 1969; Pres. TIBERIU MUREŞAN; particularly involved in environmental matters through the activities of:

Central Research Station for Soil Erosion Control (Staţiunea Centrală de Cercetări pentru Combatarea Eroziunii Solului): Perieni jud. Vaslui; Dir Eng. D. NISTOR.

Danube Delta Institute (Institutul Delta Dunării) 8800 Tulcea, Str. Babadag 165; tel. (91) 524546; fax (91) 524547; f. 1970; conservation of the diverse ecology of the Danube delta, monitoring of the wetlands, fish ecology, tourism research; Dir Eng. ROMULUS STIUCA.

Forest Research and Management Plans Institute (Institutul de Cercetări şi Amenajări Silvice—ICAS): Bucharest 2, Şos. Stefăneşti 128; tel. and fax (1) 6556845; f. 1933; silviculture, genetics, ecology, game managements, trout farming, protection against soil erosion; Gen. Man. Dr M. IANCULESCU.

Romanian Marine Research Institute (Institutul Român de Cercetări Marine): 8700 Constanţa 3, Bd. Mamaia 300; tel. (91) 643288; telex 14418; fax (91) 831274; f. 1970; studies Black Sea hydrology, ecosystems and pollution; biochemistry, extraction and utilization of aquatic living resources; aquaculture; fishery resources; marine technology; Dir Dr Eng. S. NICOLAEV.

Energy Information and Documentation Office (Oficiul de Informare Documentară pentru Energetică): 79619 Bucharest, Bd. Energeticienilor 8, Sector 3; tel. (1) 206730; telex 10783; f. 1966; Dir V. PLEŞCA.

National Institute of Metrology (Institutul Naţional de Metrologie): 75669 Bucharest, Şos. Vitan-Bîrzeşti 11; tel. (1) 6343520; telex 11871; fax (1) 3121533; f. 1951; Dir A. MILLEA.

Romanian Academy (Academia Română): 71102 Bucharest, Calea Victoriei 125; tel. (1) 507680; telex 11907; f. 1866 as Societatea Literară Română, present name 1948; concerned with protection of both natural and human environments; Pres. MIHAI DRĂGĂNESCU.

NON-GOVERNMENTAL ORGANIZATIONS

The **Romanian Ecological Movement** (Mişcarea Ecologistă din România) and the **Romanian Ecological Party** (Partidul Ecologist Român) (see section on Political Organizations) are members of the Democratic Convention of Romania. There are several other small Green parties.

Defence

Prior to its dissolution in 1991, Romania was a member of the Warsaw Pact, although it allowed no Pact troops on to its soil and did not participate in military exercises. Military service is compulsory and lasts for 12 months in the army and air force, and for 18 months in the navy. In June 1993, according to Western estimates, regular forces totalled 203,100 (including 125,000 conscripts); of these, 161,000 were in the army, 23,100 in the air force and 19,000 in the navy. In addition, there were 43,000 paramilitary forces, including 12,000 border guards and 10,000 security troops (both under Ministry of Interior control), and 21,000 construction troops. Spending of 298,000m. lei was allocated to defence in the 1993 state budget.

Commander-in-Chief of the Armed Forces: President of Romania.

Chief of Staff of the Army: Lt-Gen. DUMITRU IOAN CIOFLINA.

Bibliography

Almond, M. *The Rise and Fall of Nicolae and Elena Ceausescu*. London, Chapman, 1992.

Behr, Edward. *Kiss the Hand You Cannot Bite: the Rise and Fall of the Ceauşescus*. London, Hamish Hamilton, 1991.

Fischer, M. *Nicolae Ceausescu. A Study in Political Leadership*. Boulder, Colorado, and London, Lynn Rienner Publishers, 1989.

Fischer-Galati, S. *The New Rumania*. Cambridge, Massachusetts, MIT Press, 1967.

Twentieth Century Romania. New York and London, Columbia University Press, 1991.

Georgescu, V. *The Romanians: A History*. London, I. B. Tauris, 1991.

Gilberg, T. *Nationalism and Communism in Romania*. Boulder, Colorado, and Oxford, Westview Press, 1990.

Ionescu, G. *Communism in Rumania, 1944-62*. London, Oxford University Press, 1962.

Jackson, M. *Romania's Debt Crisis: Its Causes and Consequences*, Vol. 3 of East European Economies: Slow Growth in the 1980s. Washington, DC, USGPO (Joint Economic Committee of the US Congress), 1986.

Kideckel, D. *The Solitude of Collectivism, Romanian Villagers to the Revolution and Beyond*. Ithaca, New York and London, Cornell University Press, 1993.

Montias, J. M. *Economic Development in Communist Romania*. Cambridge, Massachusetts, MIT Press, 1967.

Nelson, D.N. (Ed.). *Romania After Tyranny*. Boulder, Colorado, and London, Westview Press, 1992.

Otetea, A. (Ed.). *A Concise History of Romania*. London, Hale, 1985.

Rady, M. *Romania in Turmoil*. London and New York, I. B. Tauris, 1992.

Roberts, H. *Rumania, Political Problems of an Agrarian State*. New Haven, Connecticut, Yale University Press, 1951.

Roman, P. 'Report on the Stage of Implementation of Economic Reform and the Demand to Step up its Pace'. Copy of speech of 18 October 1990.

Ronnas, P. *Urbanization in Romania*. Stockholm, Economic Research Institute, Stockholm School of Economics, 1984.

'The Economic Legacy of Ceauşescu' in *Economic Change in the Balkan States*, Orjan Sjoberg and Michael L. Wyzan (Eds). London, Frances Pinter, 1991.

Shafir, M. *Romania: Politics, Economics and Society*. London, Frances Pinter, 1985.

Smith, A. H. 'Is There a Romanian Crisis? The Problems of Energy and Indebtedness' in *Crisis in the East European Economy*, J. Drewnowski (Ed.). Beckenham, Croom Helm, 1982.

The Planned Economies of Eastern Europe. Beckenham, Croom Helm, 1983.

'Romania: international economic developments and foreign economic relations' in *The Economies of Eastern Europe and their Foreign Economic Relations*, P. Joseph (Ed.). Brussels, NATO, 1987.

'The Romanian Economy: policy and prospects for the 1990s' in *The Central and East European Economies in the 1990s: Prospects and Constraints*, R. Weichardt (Ed.). Brussels, NATO, 1991.

THE RUSSIAN FEDERATION

Geography

PHYSICAL FEATURES

The Russian Federation (formerly the Russian Soviet Federative Socialist Republic of the USSR) is bounded to the west by Norway (in the far north-west), Finland, Estonia and Latvia. Belarus and Ukraine lie to the south-west of European Russia, the southern borders of which are with the Transcaucasian states of Georgia and Azerbaijan, and with Kazakhstan. There is a short coastline in the north-west, near St Petersburg, where the country has access to the Baltic Sea via the Gulf of Finland. In the south, towards the Caucasus, European Russia has a coastline on the Black Sea in the south-west, with the Caspian Sea to the east. Beyond the Ural Mountains, the Siberian and Far Eastern regions have southern frontiers with the People's Republic of China, Mongolia and, in the south-east, the People's Democratic Republic of Korea. The eastern coastline is on the Sea of Japan, the Sea of Okhotsk, the Pacific Ocean and the Barents Sea. The northern coastline is on the Arctic Ocean. The region around Kaliningrad (formerly Königsberg in East Prussia), on the Baltic Sea, became part of the Russian Federation in 1945. It is separated from the rest of the Russian Federation by Lithuania and Belarus. It borders Poland to the south, Lithuania to the north and east and has a coastline on the Baltic Sea. The Russian Federation covers an area of 17,075,400 sq km (6,592,812 sq miles), making it by far the largest country in the world. Its territory consists of 89 federal units, including the cities of Moscow, the capital, and St Petersburg (Leningrad 1924–91, the old tsarist capital).

The territory includes a wide variety of physical features. European Russia (traditionally meaning that part of Russia to the west of the Urals) and western Siberia form a vast plain, interrupted only by occasional outbreaks of hill-country and wide river-valleys. In the south, between the Black and Caspian Seas, the territory is more undulating, until it reaches the foothills of the Caucasus mountain range in the far south. The Ural Mountains provide only a symbolic barrier between Siberia and European Russia, their mean altitude being only 500 m. Beyond them the Great Russian Plain extends for some 2,000 km, before reaching the Mid-Siberian Plateau and high mountain ranges on the southern border with Mongolia. The territory of Eastern Siberia and the Far East is dominated by several mountain ranges (notably the Verkhoyansk, Chersky and Anadyr mountains) which extend off shore in a series of islands and peninsulas. The Kamchatka peninsula, which extends 1,200 km south to the northernmost of the Kurile Islands, has 100 active volcanoes, the highest being Klyuchevskaya Sopka at an altitude of 4,800 m. Only the basins of the Amur and Ussuri rivers in the south of the Far Eastern Region can support any significant population. The northern regions of both Asian and European Russia are inhospitable areas, much of the territory being covered by permafrost.

CLIMATE

The climate of Russia is extremely varied. The central regions experience the climatic conditions characteristic of central and eastern Europe, although in a more extreme form. There are wide temperature differences between summer and winter, and there is considerable snow in winter. The average temperature in Moscow in July is 19°C (66°F); the average for January is −9°C (15°F). Average annual precipitation in the capital is 575 mm. Further south the climate is more temperate, especially along the Black Sea coastline. Average temperatures in Rostov-on-Don (Rostov-na-Donu) range from −5.3°C (22.5°F) in January to 23.5°C (74.3°F) in July. In the northern areas of Russia and in much of Siberia the climate is severe, with Arctic winters and short, hot summers. Only the northern fringe is under the polar ice-cap; the zone of permafrost is, however, extensive. Average temperatures in the southern Siberian town of Irkutsk range from −20.8°C (−5.4°F) in January to 17.9°C (64.2°F) in July. Average annual rainfall is 458 mm, most of which falls in the summer months. In Verkhoyansk, in the far north of Siberia, the average January temperature is −46.8°C (−52.2°F). The Far Eastern region combines the extreme temperatures of Siberia with monsoon-type conditions common elsewhere in Asia, although they are not so pronounced, owing to the protection of mountain ranges on the Pacific coast. The mean temperature in January in the eastern port of Vladivostok is −14°C (7°F); in August the average is 21°C (70°F).

POPULATION

At the 1989 census, Russians formed the largest ethnic group in the Republic, accounting for 82.6% of the population. Other important ethnic groups included Tatars (3.6%), Ukrainians (2.7%) and Chuvash (1.2%). There were also Belarusians, Bashkirs, Jews, Mordovians, Mari, Chechens, Kazakhs and Uzbeks. Religious adherence was equally varied, with many religions closely connected with particular ethnic groups. Christianity was the major religion, mostly adhered to by ethnic Russians and other Slavs. The Russian Orthodox Church was the largest denomination. The main concentrations of Muslims were among Volga Tatars, Chuvash and Bashkirs, and the peoples of the Northern Caucasus, including the Chechen, Ingush, Ossetians, Kabardinians and the peoples of Daghestan. Buddhism was the main religion of the Buryats, the Tyvans and the Kalmyks. The large pre-1917 Jewish population was depleted by war and emigration, but there remained some 2m. Jews in the Russian Federation in the early 1990s.

The official language in the Russian Federation was Russian, but a large number of other languages were in daily use. The majority of the population lived in European Russia, the population of Siberia and the Far East being only some 32m. in 1989, approximately 22% of the total. In 1991 it was estimated that some 74% of the population lived in urban areas, although there were substantial regional differences, with 83% of the inhabitants of central Russia living in towns, compared with only 57% in the North Caucasus region.

The capital of the Russian Federation is Moscow (Moskva), which had an estimated population of 8,801,000 in 1990. The second city is St Petersburg (Sankt Peterburg), with a population of 4,468,000. Other important regional centres are Nizhny Novgorod (formerly Gorky—1,443,000), the Siberian cities of Novosibirsk (1,443,000) and Omsk (1,159,000), the industrialized Ural towns of Yekaterinburg (formerly Sverdlovsk—1,367,000) and Chelyabinsk (1,148,000), the regional centre of Siberia, Irkutsk (635,000),

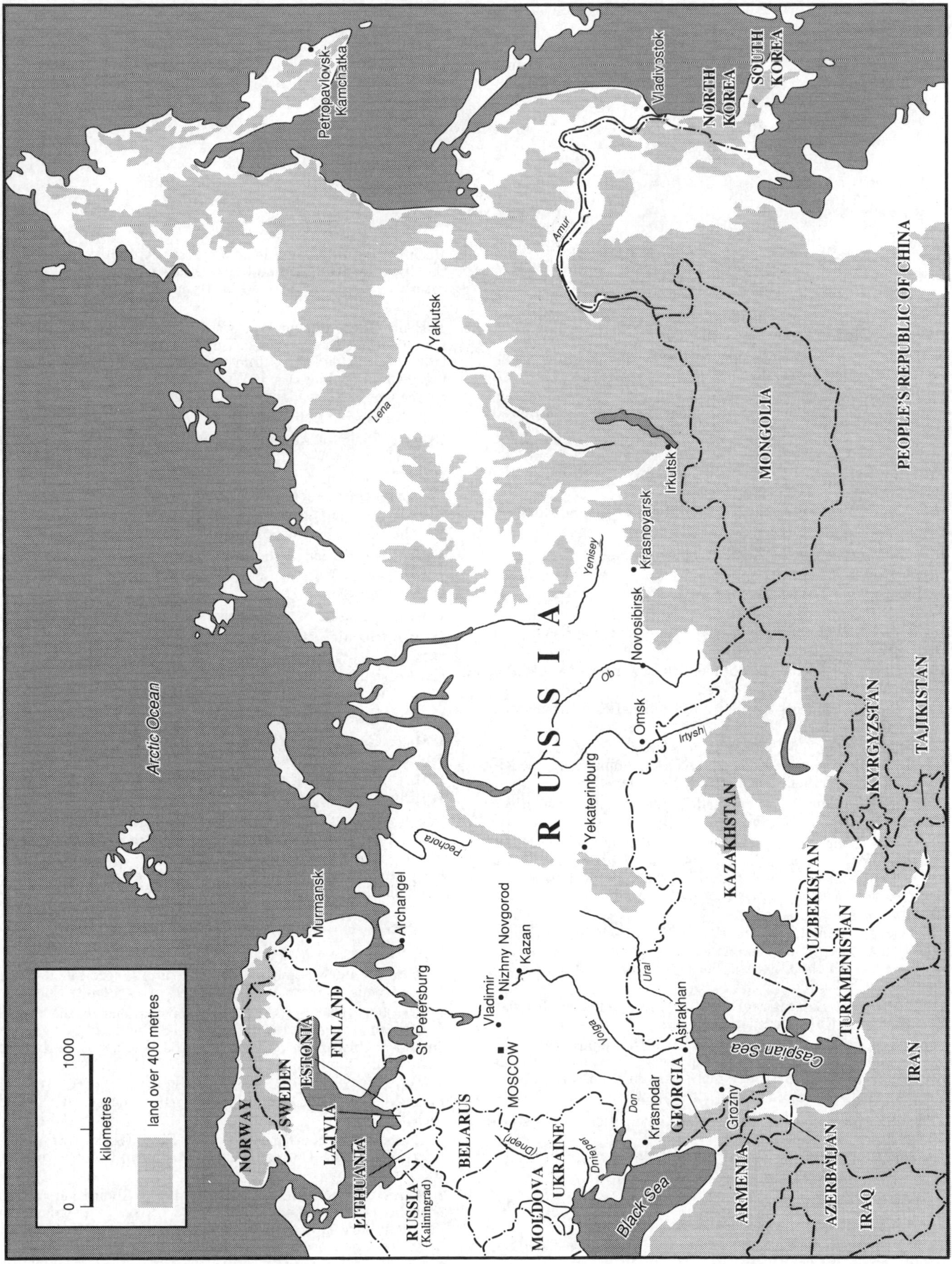
0
1000
kilometres
land over 400 metres
Arctic Ocean
RUSSIA
Murmansk
Archangel
Pechora
St Petersburg
Vladimir
Nizhny Novgorod
Kazan
MOSCOW
Yekaterinburg
Omsk
Irtysh
Ob
Novosibirsk
Yenisey
Krasnoyarsk
Irkutsk
Lena
Yakutsk
Amur
Vladivostok
Petropavlovsk-Kamchatka
NORTH KOREA
SOUTH KOREA
MONGOLIA
PEOPLE'S REPUBLIC OF CHINA
KAZAKHSTAN
UZBEKISTAN
TURKMENISTAN
KYRGYZSTAN
TAJIKISTAN
IRAN
IRAQ
AZERBAIJAN
ARMENIA
GEORGIA
Grozny
Krasnodar
Don
Volga
Ural
Astrakhan
Caspian Sea
Black Sea
Dniepr
Dnieper
UKRAINE
MOLDOVA
BELARUS
RUSSIA
(Kaliningrad)
LITHUANIA
LATVIA
ESTONIA
FINLAND
SWEDEN
NORWAY

and the Far Eastern towns of Khabarovsk (608,000) and Vladivostok (643,000).

Many ethnic Russians lived beyond the borders of the Russian Federation, in the other countries of the former USSR. They formed significant minorities in the neighbouring countries of Estonia, Latvia, Belarus, Ukraine and Kazakhstan. Large Russian communities were also present in Moldova and the Central Asian countries. The Russian Federation also inherited various border disputes from the USSR, notably with Japan over the northern Kurile Islands (annexed by the USSR in 1945).

Chronology

RUSSIA AND THE RUSSIAN EMPIRE

***c.* 878:** Kievan Rus, the first unified state of the Eastern Slavs, was founded, with Kiev (Kiyv) as its capital.

***c.* 988:** Volodymyr I (Vladimir 'the Great'), ruler of Kievan Rus, converted to Orthodox Christianity.

1237–40: The Russian principalities were invaded and conquered by the Mongol Tatars.

1462–1505: Reign of Ivan III of Muscovy (Moscow), who consolidated the independent Russian domains into a centralized state.

1480: Renunciation of Tatar suzerainty.

1533–84: Reign of Ivan IV ('the Terrible'), who began the eastern expansion of Russian territory.

1547: Ivan IV was crowned 'Tsar of Muscovy and all Russia'.

1552: Subjugation of the Khanate of Kazan.

1556: Subjugation of the Khanate of Astrakhan.

1581: The Russian adventurer, Yermak, led an expedition to Siberia, pioneering Russian expansion beyond the Ural Mountains.

1645: A Russian settlement was established on the Sea of Okhotsk, on the coast of eastern Asia.

1654: Eastern Ukraine came under Russian rule as a result of the Treaty of Pereyaslavl.

1679: Russian pioneers reached the Kamchatka peninsula and the Pacific Ocean.

1682–1725: Reign of Peter I ('the Great'), who established Russia as a European Power, expanded its empire, and modernized the civil and military institutions of the state.

1703: St Petersburg was founded at the mouth of the River Neva, in north-west Russia.

1721: The Treaty of Nystad with Sweden ended the Great Northern War and brought Estonia and Livonia (now Latvia and parts of Estonia) under Russian rule. Peter I, who was declared the 'Tsar of all the Russias', proclaimed the Russian Empire.

1762–96: Reign of Catherine II ('the Great'—Princess Sophia of Anhaldt-Zerbst), who expanded the Empire in the south, after wars with the Ottoman Turks, and in the west, by the partition of Poland.

1772: Parts of Belarus were incorporated into the Russian Empire at the First Partition of Poland.

1774: As a result of the Treaty of Kuchuk Kainardji with the Turks, the Black Sea port of Azov was annexed and Russia became protector of Orthodox Christians in the Balkans.

1783: Annexation of the Khanate of Crimea.

1793: Second Partition of Poland; acquisition of western Ukraine and Belarus.

1795: Third Partition of Poland.

1801–25: Reign of Alexander I.

1801: Annexation of Georgia.

1809: Finland became a possession of the Russian Crown.

1812: Bessarabia was acquired from the Turks. Napoleon I of France invaded Russia.

1815: The Congress of Vienna established 'Congress Poland' as a Russian dependency (annexed 1831).

1825: On the death of Alexander I, a group of young officers, the 'Decembrists', attempted to seize power; the attempted *coup d'état* was suppressed by troops loyal to the new Tsar, Nicholas I.

1853–56: The Crimean War was fought, in which the United Kingdom and France aided Turkey against Russia, after the latter had invaded the Ottoman tributaries of Moldavia (including modern Moldova) and Wallachia; the War was concluded by the Congress of Paris.

1825–55: Reign of Nicholas I.

1855–81: Reign of Alexander II, who introduced economic and legal reforms.

1859: The conquest of the Caucasus was completed, following the surrender of rebel forces.

1860: Acquisition of provinces on the Sea of Japan from China and the establishment of Vladivostok.

1861: Emancipation of the serfs.

1867: The North American territory of Alaska was sold to the USA for US $7m.

1868: Subjugation of the Khanates of Samarkand and Bukhara.

1873: Annexation of the Khanate of Khiva.

1875: Acquisition of Sakhalin from Japan in exchange for the Kurile Islands.

1876: Subjugation of the Khanate of Kokand.

1881: Assassination of Alexander II.

1881–94: Reign of Alexander III, who re-established autocratic principles of government.

1891: Construction of the Trans-Siberian railway was begun.

1894–1917: Reign of Nicholas II, the last Tsar.

1898: The All-Russian Social Democratic Labour Party (RSDLP), a Marxist party, held a founding congress in Minsk (Belarus). In 1903, at the Second Congress in London (United Kingdom), the party split into 'Bolsheviks' (led by Lenin—Vladimir Ilych Ulyanov) and 'Mensheviks'.

WAR AND REVOLUTION

1904–05: Russia was defeated in the Russo-Japanese War.

22 January 1905: Some 150 demonstrators were killed by the Tsar's troops, in what came to be known as 'Bloody Sunday'.

17 October 1905: Strikes and demonstrations in the capital, St Petersburg, and other cities forced the Tsar to introduce limited political reforms, including the holding of elections to a Duma (parliament).

January 1912: At the Sixth Congress of the RSDLP the Bolsheviks formally established a separate party, the RSDLP (Bolsheviks).

1 August 1914: Russia entered the First World War against Austria-Hungary, Germany and the Ottoman Empire (the Central Powers).

2 March (New Style: 15 March) 1917: Abdication of Tsar Nicholas II after demonstrations and strikes in Petrograd (as St Petersburg was renamed in 1914); a Provisional Government, led by Prince Lvov, took power.

9 July (22 July) 1917: In response to widespread public disorder, Prince Lvov resigned; he was replaced as Prime Minister by Aleksandr Kerensky, a moderate socialist.

1918–21: The Civil War was fought between the Bolshevik Red Army and various anti-Communist leaders ('the Whites'), who received support from German and Allied forces.

25 October (7 November) 1917: The Bolsheviks, led by Lenin, staged a *coup d'état* and overthrew Kerensky's Provisional Government; the Russian Soviet Federative Socialist Republic (RSFSR or Russian Federation) was proclaimed.

6 January (19 January) 1918: The Constituent Assembly, which had been elected in November 1917, was dissolved on Lenin's orders.

14 February (Old Style: 1 February) 1918: First day upon which the Gregorian Calender took effect in Russia.

3 March 1918: Treaty of Brest-Litovsk: the Bolsheviks ceded large areas of western territory to Germany, including the Baltic regions, and recognized the independence of Finland and Ukraine. Belarus, Georgia, Armenia and Azerbaijan subsequently proclaimed their independence.

6–8 March 1918: The RSDLP (Bolsheviks) was renamed the Russian Communist Party (Bolsheviks)—RCP (B).

9 March 1918: The capital of Russia was moved from Petrograd (renamed Leningrad in 1924) to Moscow.

10 July 1918: The first Constitution of the RSFSR was adopted by the Fifth All-Russian Congress of Soviets.

18 July 1918: Tsar Nicholas II and his family were murdered in Yekaterinburg (Sverdlovsk 1924–91) by Bolshevik troops.

11 November 1918: The Allied Armistice with Germany (which was denied its gains at Brest-Litovsk) ended the First World War.

4 March 1919: Establishment of the Third Communist International (Comintern).

8–16 March 1921: At the 10th Party Congress of the RCP (B), the harsh policy of 'War Communism' was replaced by the New Economic Policy (NEP), which allowed peasants and traders some economic freedom.

18 March 1921: A rebellion by Russian sailors in the island garrison of Kronstadt was suppressed by the Red Army. Signing of the Treaty of Riga between Russia, Ukraine and Poland, which formally concluded the Soviet–Polish War of 1919–20, with territorial gains for Poland.

3 April 1922: Stalin (Iosif V. Dzhugashvili) was elected General Secretary of the RCP (B).

18 April 1922: The Soviet–German Treaty of Rapallo was signed, which established diplomatic relations between the two powers.

THE UNION OF SOVIET SOCIALIST REPUBLICS

30 December 1922: The Union of Soviet Socialist Republics (USSR) was formed at the 10th All-Russian (first All-Union) Congress of Soviets by the RSFSR, the Transcaucasian Soviet Federative Socialist Republic (TSFSR), the Ukrainian SSR (Soviet Socialist Republic) and the Belarusian SSR.

6 July 1923: Promulgation of the first Constitution of the USSR.

21 January 1924: Death of Lenin.

31 January 1924: The first Constitution of the USSR was ratified by the Second All-Union Congress of Soviets.

October 1927: Expulsion of Trotsky (Lev Bronstein) and other opponents of Stalin from the Communist Party.

1928: The NEP was abandoned; beginning of the First Five-Year Plan and forced collectivization of agriculture, which resulted in widespread famine, particularly in Ukraine.

November 1933: Recognition of the USSR by the USA.

18 September 1934: The USSR was admitted to the League of Nations.

1 December 1934: Sergey Kirov, a leading member of the Political Bureau (Politburo) of the Communist Party, was shot in Leningrad, allegedly on the orders of Stalin; following the shooting, Stalin initiated a new campaign of repression.

25 November 1936: The anti-Comintern Pact was signed between Japan and Germany.

26 September 1936: Nikolay Yezhov replaced Genrikh Yagoda as head of the security police, the People's Commissariat for Internal Affairs; a series of mass arrests and executions, which came to be known as the 'Great Purge' or the 'Yezhovshchina', began.

5 December 1936: The second Constitution of the USSR (the 'Stalin' Constitution) was adopted; two new Union Republics (the Kyrgyz and Kazakh SSRs) were created, and the TSFSR was dissolved into the Georgian, Armenian and Azerbaijani SSRs.

March 1938: Nikolay Bukharin, Aleksey Rykov and other prominent Bolsheviks were sentenced to death at the Moscow 'Show' Trials.

23 August 1939: Signing of the Treaty of Non-Aggression with Germany (the Nazi–Soviet Pact), including the 'Secret Protocols' which sanctioned territorial gains for the USSR in eastern Poland, the Baltic states (Estonia, Latvia and Lithuania) and Bessarabia (Romania).

17 September 1939: Soviet forces invaded eastern Poland.

28 September 1939: The Treaty on Friendship and Existing Borders was signed by Germany and the USSR, by which the two powers agreed that the USSR should annex Lithuania.

30 November 1939: The USSR invaded Finland.

14 December 1939: The USSR was expelled from the League of Nations.

June 1940: The Baltic states and Bessarabia were annexed by the USSR.

21 August 1940: Trotsky was murdered in Mexico by a Soviet agent.

22 June 1941: Germany invaded the USSR.

2 February 1943: German forces surrendered at Stalingrad (now Volgograd), marking the first reverse for the German Army. Soviet forces began to regain territory.

15 May 1943: The Comintern was dissolved.

8 May 1945: German forces surrendered to the USSR in Berlin and Germany subsequently capitulated; most of eastern and central Europe had come under Soviet control.

26 June 1945: The USSR, the USA, the United Kingdom, China and 46 other countries, including the Belarusian and Ukrainian SSRs, signed the Charter of the United Nations.

8 August 1945: The USSR declared war on Japan and occupied Sakhalin and the Kurile Islands.

September 1947: The Communist Information Bureau (Cominform) was established, to control and co-ordinate Communist Parties that were allied to the USSR.

25 January 1949: The Council for Mutual Economic Assistance (CMEA or Comecon) was established, as an economic alliance between the USSR and its Eastern European allies.

14 July 1949: The USSR exploded its first atomic bomb.

5 March 1953: Death of Stalin; he was replaced by a collective leadership, which included Georgy Malenkov and Nikita Khrushchev.

17 June 1953: Soviet troops suppressed demonstrations in Berlin.

September 1953: Khrushchev was elected First Secretary of the Central Committee of the Communist Party of the Soviet Union (CPSU).

14 May 1955: The Warsaw Treaty of Friendship, Co-operation and Mutual Assistance was signed by Albania, Bulgaria, Czechoslovakia, the German Democratic Republic (GDR), Hungary, Romania, Poland and the USSR. The Treaty established a military alliance between these countries, known as the Warsaw Treaty Organization (or the Warsaw Pact).

14–25 February 1956: At the 20th Party Congress Khrushchev denounced Stalin in the 'secret speech'.

17 April 1956: The Cominform was abolished.

26 August 1956: The first Soviet inter-continental ballistic missile (ICBM) was launched.

4 November 1956: Soviet forces invaded Hungary to overthrow Imre Nagy's reformist Government.

June 1957: Malenkov, Molotov and Kaganovich (the so-called 'Anti-Party' group) were expelled from the CPSU leadership after attempting to depose Khrushchev.

4 October 1957: The USSR placed the first man-made satellite (Sputnik I) in orbit around the earth.

March 1958: Khrushchev consolidated his position in the leadership by being elected Chairman of the Council of Ministers (premier), while retaining the office of CPSU First Secretary.

August 1960: Soviet technicians were recalled from the People's Republic of China, as part of the growing dispute between the two countries.

12 April 1961: The first manned space flight was undertaken by Maj. Yury Gagarin on the Vostok I spacecraft.

3–4 June 1961: US President John F. Kennedy met Khrushchev for official talks in Vienna (Austria).

30 October 1961: Stalin's body was removed from its place of honour in the mausoleum in Red Square, in Moscow.

18–28 October 1962: The discovery of Soviet nuclear missiles in Cuba by the USA led to the 'Cuban Missile Crisis'; tension eased when Khrushchev announced the withdrawal of the missiles, following a US blockade of the island.

5 August 1963: The USSR signed the Partial Nuclear Test Ban Treaty.

13–14 October 1964: Khrushchev was deposed from the leadership of the CPSU and the USSR and replaced as First Secretary by Leonid Brezhnev and as premier by Aleksey Kosygin.

20–21 August 1968: Soviet and other Warsaw Pact forces invaded Czechoslovakia to overthrow the reformist Government of Alexander Dubček.

12 August 1970: A non-aggression treaty was signed with the Federal Republic of Germany ('West Germany').

May 1972: US President Richard Nixon visited Moscow, thus marking a relaxation in US–Soviet relations, a process which came to be known as *détente*.

1 August 1975: Signing of the Helsinki Final Act by 32 European countries, plus the USA and Canada, committing all signatories to approve the post-1945 frontiers in Europe and to respect basic human rights.

16 June 1977: Brezhnev became Chairman of the Presidium of the Supreme Soviet (titular head of state).

7 October 1977: The third Constitution of the USSR was adopted.

24 December 1979: Soviet forces invaded Afghanistan (the last troops were not to be withdrawn until February 1989).

October 1980: Kosygin was replaced as premier by Nikolay Tikhonov.

10 November 1982: Death of Leonid Brezhnev; Yury Andropov, former head of the Committee for State Security (KGB), succeeded him as General Secretary of the CPSU.

9 February 1984: Death of Andropov; Konstantin Chernenko succeeded him as General Secretary.

THE GORBACHEV ERA AND THE END OF THE USSR

10 March 1985: Death of Chernenko; he was succeeded as General Secretary by Mikhail Gorbachev.

2 July 1985: Andrey Gromyko was replaced as Minister of Foreign Affairs by Eduard Shevardnadze; Gromyko became Chairman of the Presidium of the Supreme Soviet.

27 September 1985: Nikolay Ryzhkov replaced Tikhonov as Chairman of the Council of Ministers.

24 February–6 March 1986: At the 27th Congress of the CPSU Gorbachev proposed radical economic and political reforms and 'new thinking' in foreign policy; emergence of the policy of *glasnost* (meaning a greater degree of freedom of expression).

26 April 1986: An explosion occurred at a nuclear reactor in Chernobyl (Ukraine), which resulted in discharges of radioactive material.

December 1986: Andrey Sakharov, the prominent human-rights campaigner, returned from internal exile in Gorky (now Nizhny Novgorod); rioting occurred in Almaty (Kazakhstan).

January 1987: At a meeting of the CPSU Central Committee Gorbachev proposed plans for the restructuring (*perestroika*) of the economy and some democratization of local government and the CPSU.

21 June 1987: At local elections the CPSU nominated more than one candidate in some constituencies.

21 October 1987: Boris Yeltsin, who had been appointed First Secretary of the Moscow City Party Committee in 1985, resigned from the Politburo.

7 November 1987: Gorbachev rehabilitated many of the victims of Stalin's purges.

8 December 1987: In Washington, DC (USA), Gorbachev and US President Ronald Reagan signed a treaty to eliminate all intermediate-range nuclear forces (INF) in Europe.

27–29 February 1988: In the first serious inter-ethnic conflict under Gorbachev, 32 people died in attacks on Armenians in Sumgait (Azerbaijan).

5–17 June 1988: A millennium of Christianity in Russia was celebrated with official approval.

1 July 1988: The 19th Party Conference of the CPSU ended, after approving extensive political and legal reforms, including partly free elections to a new legislature, the Congress of People's Deputies.

October 1988: As the pace of reform quickened, Andrey Gromyko resigned as Chairman of the Presidium of the Supreme Soviet; he was succeeded by Gorbachev.

1 December 1988: The all-Union Supreme Soviet approved constitutional amendments creating a new legislative system, consisting of the Congress of People's Deputies and a full-time Supreme Soviet.

6 December 1988: In a speech at the UN, Gorbachev outlined his 'new thinking' on foreign policy and announced troop withdrawals from Eastern Europe.

25 March 1989: Multi-party elections to the newly established Congress of People's Deputies took place; several prominent 'hardliners' were defeated by radical candidates.

9 April 1989: Twenty people were killed in Tbilisi (Georgia) when soldiers dispersed a demonstration.

18 May 1989: The Lithuanian Supreme Soviet issued declarations of political and economic sovereignty.

25 May 1989: The Congress of People's Deputies convened for the first time; Gorbachev was elected Chairman of the Presidium of the Supreme Soviet.

27 May 1989: Congress elected an all-Union Supreme Soviet, which would act as a full-time legislature, but there were protests when only a few radicals managed to gain seats.

6 December 1989: The Supreme Soviet of Lithuania abolished the Communist Party's constitutional right to power, thus establishing the first multi-party system in the USSR.

January 1990: A state of emergency was declared in Baku (Azerbaijan), following widespread disturbances. Later in the month Democratic Platform, a reformist faction within the CPSU, held its founding conference.

4 February 1990: Some 150,000 people joined a pro-reform march in the centre of Moscow. Three days later the CPSU Central Committee approved draft proposals to abolish Article 6 of the Constitution, which had guaranteed the CPSU's monopoly of power.

4 March 1990: Elections took place to the local and republican soviets of the Russian Federation; reformists made substantial gains in the larger cities, notably Moscow and Leningrad (elections to the Supreme Soviets of Belarus, Estonia, Kazakhstan, Kyrgyzstan, Latvia, Lithuania, Moldova, Tajikistan, Ukraine and Uzbekistan also took place in February–March, producing overtly nationalist majorities in the Baltic Republics and Moldova).

11 March 1990: The new Supreme Soviet of Lithuania declared the re-establishment of Lithuanian independence.

15 March 1990: Congress approved the establishment of the post of President of the USSR and elected Mikhail Gorbachev to that office.

29 May 1990: Boris Yeltsin was elected as Chairman of the Supreme Soviet of the Russian Federation.

5 June 1990: More than 500 people were killed in inter-ethnic violence in Kyrgyzstan, as protests increased throughout the USSR.

16 July 1990: The Supreme Soviet of Ukraine declared Ukraine to be a sovereign state, with the right to maintain its own armed forces.

2 August 1990: The USSR condemned the invasion of Kuwait by Iraq, a Soviet ally.

22 August 1990: Turkmenistan declared itself to be a sovereign state.

24 August 1990: Tajikistan declared itself to be a sovereign state.

3 September 1990: Boris Yeltsin announced a 500-day programme of economic reform to the Supreme Soviet of the Russian Federation.

1 October 1990: In New York (USA) France, the United Kingdom, the USA and the USSR, the four Occupying Powers of the GDR ('East Germany'), formally recognized the full sovereignty of a unified Germany.

October 1990: Legislation allowing freedom of conscience and the existence of other political parties, apart from the CPSU, was adopted by the all-Union Supreme Soviet. It also approved a reform programme designed to establish a market economy. In Georgia pro-independence parties won an overall majority in the Supreme Soviet.

25 October 1990: Kazakhstan declared itself to be a sovereign state and outlawed the storing or testing of nuclear weapons on its territory.

30 October 1990: Kyrgyzstan declared itself to be a sovereign state.

November 1990: Gorbachev announced constitutional changes and a draft of the proposed new Union Treaty was published.

December 1990: Eduard Shevardnadze resigned as Minister of Foreign Affairs (on 21 December), claiming that the country was moving towards dictatorship. Later in the month Congress granted Gorbachev extended presidential powers. Ryzhkov was succeeded as Soviet premier by Valentin Pavlov, while Gennady Yanayev was eventually endorsed as Vice-President.

13 January 1991: Thirteen people died and some 500 were injured when Soviet troops occupied radio and television buildings in Vilnius (Lithuania). One week later four people died in Rīga (Latvia) when Soviet troops occupied government buildings.

22 February 1991: Some 400,000 people demonstrated in Moscow, in support of Boris Yeltsin, who had demanded Gorbachev's resignation, and reform.

17 March 1991: In an all-Union referendum on the issue of the future state of the USSR, some 75% of participants approved Gorbachev's concept of a 'renewed federation' (several Republics did not participate, including Lithuania where a referendum had already produced a result in favour of independence).

23 April 1991: Gorbachev and the leaders of nine Union Republics, including Yeltsin, signed the 'Nine-Plus-One Agreement'.

12 June 1991: Yeltsin was elected President of the Russian Federation in direct elections, with Aleksandr Rutskoy as Vice-President; residents of Leningrad voted to change the city's name back to St Petersburg.

1 July 1991: The USSR, together with the other member countries of the Warsaw Pact, signed a protocol which formalized the dissolution of the alliance. Eduard Shevardnadze and Aleksandr Yakovlev, together with other reformists, announced the formation of a new reformist movement, later known as the Movement for Democratic Reforms.

16 August 1991: Yakovlev resigned from the CPSU (which a few weeks previously had abandoned Marxism-Leninism), warning of the possibility of a coup against Gorbachev.

18 August 1991: Gorbachev was placed under house arrest in his Crimean *dacha* (summer residence), following his refusal to declare a state of emergency and transfer power to Vice-President Gennady Yanayev, as demanded by a delegation from the self-proclaimed State Committee for the State of Emergency in the USSR (SCSE).

19 August 1991: It was announced that Yanayev had assumed power as Acting President, owing to the inability of Gorbachev to continue in office as a result of 'ill health'; an eight-member SCSE was announced; the Soviet Cabinet of Ministers met and approved the new conservative leadership; military vehicles moved into the centre of Moscow. Yeltsin, however, declared the SCSE illegal and its members guilty of treason; thousands of people demonstrated against the coup in St Petersburg; in Moscow, despite a state of emergency, some 5,000 people gathered to support Yeltsin at the 'White House', where the administration of the Russian Federation was based.

20 August 1991: Yeltsin demanded the restoration of Gorbachev to power; some 200,000 people demonstrated in Moscow and three were killed by armoured vehicles. Estonia declared independence.

21 August 1991: The *coup d'état* collapsed: an emergency session of the Russian Supreme Soviet was convened; the Presidium of the all-Union Supreme Soviet declared the seizure of power by Yanayev illegal and formally reinstated Gorbachev as President, who was released. Latvia declared independence.

23 August 1991: Gorbachev, replacing supporters of the coup attempt, appointed Vadim Bakatin Chairman of the KGB, Gen. Yevgeny Shaposhnikov Minister of Defence and Viktor Barannikov Minister of Internal Affairs. Aleksandr Bessmertnykh was dismissed as Minister of Foreign Affairs. Yeltsin suspended the activities of the Russian Communist Party (RCP) and the publication of six CPSU newspapers, including *Pravda* (the RCP was formally banned in November).

24 August 1991: Gorbachev resigned as General Secretary of the CPSU, nationalized the Party's property, demanded the dissolution of the Central Committee and banned party cells in the Armed Forces, the KGB and the police. The Supreme Soviet of Ukraine adopted a declaration of independence, pending approval by referendum on 1 December (90% of the participating voters were to approve the decision).

25 August 1991: Gorbachev established an interim government, the Committee for the Operational Management of the National Economy, headed by Ivan Silayev. The Supreme Soviet of Belarus adopted a declaration of independence.

27 August 1991: The Supreme Soviet of Moldova proclaimed the Republic's independence.

30 August 1991: The Supreme Soviet of Azerbaijan voted to 're-establish' the independent status it had enjoyed until 1920.

31 August 1991: The Supreme Soviets of Uzbekistan and Kyrgyzstan adopted declarations of independence.

6 September 1991: The newly formed State Council, which comprised the supreme officials of the Union Republics, recognized the independence of Estonia, Latvia and Lithuania.

9 September 1991: The Supreme Soviet of Tajikistan adopted a declaration of independence.

23 September 1991: Armenia declared its independence, following a referendum two days previously.

27 September 1991: Ivan Silayev officially resigned as Prime Minister of the Russian Federation, following his appointment as Soviet Prime Minister; he was one of a number of reformers promoted by Gorbachev.

28 September 1991: The Leninist Young Communist League of the Soviet Union (Komsomol) voted to disband itself.

5 October 1991: The USSR was officially admitted as an associate member of the International Monetary Fund.

18 October 1991: A treaty, which established an Economic Community between its signatories, was signed by representatives of the Russian Federation and Armenia, Belarus, Kazakhstan, Kyrgyzstan, Tajikistan, Turkmenistan and Uzbekistan; four other Republics had earlier agreed to some form of economic co-operation.

21 October 1991: The first session of the newly established all-Union Supreme Soviet was attended by delegates of the Russian Federation, Belarus, Kazakhstan, Kyrgyzstan, Tajikistan, Turkmenistan and Uzbekistan. Representatives of Azerbaijan and Ukraine attended as observers.

27 October 1991: Following a referendum, Turkmenistan declared its independence.

November 1991: President Yeltsin announced the formation of a new Russian Government, with himself as Chairman (Prime Minister) and Gennady Burbulis as First Deputy Chairman. Later in the month the RSFSR Supreme Soviet refused to endorse Yeltsin's decree of a state of emergency in the Chechen Autonomous Republic, following unrest there.

8 December 1991: The leaders of the Russian Federation, Belarus and Ukraine met in Brest (Belarus) and agreed to form a Commonwealth of Independent States to replace the USSR.

16 December 1991: Kazakhstan declared its independence, following a decision by it and the four other Central Asian Republics to join a Commonwealth.

21 December 1991: At a meeting in Almaty the leaders of 11 former Union Republics of the USSR signed a protocol on the formation of the new Commonwealth of Independent States (CIS). Georgia did not sign, but sent observers to the meeting.

25 December 1991: Mikhail Gorbachev formally resigned as President of the USSR, thereby confirming the effective dissolution of the Union.

30 December 1991: The 11 members of the CIS agreed, in Minsk (Belarus), to establish a joint command for armed forces, although several member states were also to establish independent armies; use of nuclear weapons was to be under the control of the Russian Federation's President, after consultation with other Commonwealth leaders and the agreement of the presidents of Belarus, Kazakhstan and Ukraine.

POST-SOVIET RUSSIA

1992

January

2: A radical economic reform programme was introduced, under which most consumer prices were liberalized.

February

14: At a meeting of the CIS member states in Minsk it was agreed that the commander of strategic forces was subordinate to the Council of Heads of State; Marshal Yevgeny Shaposhnikov was formally appointed Commander-in-Chief of the Joint Armed Forces; agreements were also reached on retaining the rouble as the common currency for inter-state trade and on the free movement of goods between member countries.

March

31: Eighteen of the 21 autonomous republics of the Russian Federation, the leaders of the Russian administrative regions and the mayors of Moscow and St Petersburg signed the Russian Federation Treaty; representatives from the Chechen Republic and Tatarstan did not participate.

April

13–14: The member states of the CIS were admitted to the European Bank for Reconstruction and Development (EBRD).

May

15: At a meeting of the CIS Heads of State in Tashkent (Uzbekistan) a Five-Year Collective Security Agreement was signed by Armenia, Kazakhstan, Russia, Tajikistan, Turkmenistan and Uzbekistan.

June

15: Yeltsin appointed Yegor Gaidar, an economist and supporter of radical market reform, as Acting Prime Minister (he had been joint First Deputy Prime Minister since May).

September

16: The first CIS Inter-Parliamentary Assembly took place in Bishkek (Kyrgyzstan); the session was attended by delegates from Armenia, Belarus, Kazakhstan, Kyrgyzstan, Russia and Tajikistan.

October

1: The Government's privatization programme was initiated with the issue of a 10,000-rouble privatization voucher to every Russian citizen.

7: Azerbaijan effectively withdrew from the CIS, following the failure of its legislature to ratify the founding treaty.

28: A presidential decree was issued, ordering the disbandment of the National Salvation Front (a recently formed political organization dominated by pro-Communists and nationalists) and of a 5,000-strong parliamentary security force under the command of the Chairman of the Russian Supreme Soviet, Ruslan Khasbulatov.

November

2: Yeltsin declared a one-month state of emergency in North Ossetia and Ingushetia, following an outbreak of hostilities between Ingush and Ossetian forces.

25: Yeltsin accepted the resignation of one of his Deputy Prime Ministers, Mikhail Poltoranin, as a concession to the conservative opposition in the Congress of People's Deputies.

30: The Constitutional Court announced its verdict concerning Yeltsin's ban on the CPSU and the RCP of November 1991: the Court upheld the abolition of the national structures of the two parties and the decision to confiscate Communist properties, but declared the ban on local party branches illegal.

December

1: The seventh Congress of People's Deputies convened.

9: The Congress rejected Yeltsin's nomination of Gaidar as Prime Minister; Yeltsin subsequently appointed Viktor Chernomyrdin to the post.

17: The dismissal of Gennady Burbulis, a reformer, as a senior presidential adviser, was confirmed.

1993

March

11: Congress reduced the powers of President Yeltsin by once more granting itself the right to suspend any presidential decrees that contravened the Constitution, pending a ruling by the Constitutional Court.

20: Following the rejection by Congress of his proposal to hold a referendum on the issue of the respective powers of the presidency and the legislature, Yeltsin announced his intention to rule Russia by decree until such a referendum could take place.

28: A proposal to impeach President Yeltsin was narrowly defeated; however, a majority of deputies also voted against the dismissal of the parliamentary Chairman, Ruslan Khasbulatov.

April

25: Some 65.7% of the registered electorate participated in the referendum, of which 57.4% endorsed President Yeltsin and 70.6% voted in favour of early elections to the Congress of People's Deputies.

May

11: Yeltsin dismissed Yury Skokov, the Secretary of the State Security Council, and Georgy Khizha, the Deputy Prime Minister for the Military-Industrial Complex; both men were opponents of reform.

June

5: President Yeltsin formally opened the Constitutional Convention in Moscow; the Convention comprised 760 delegates and was assigned the task of drafting a new Russian constitution.

16: The Constitutional Convention ended, having failed to finalize a draft constitution; its work was to be continued by a conciliation commission of 60 members.

July

9: A joint session of parliament voted in favour of reclaiming the Crimean port of Sevastopol (Ukraine), where the Black Sea fleet was based, and to nullify an agreement to divide the fleet between Russia and Ukraine.

10: Russia, Belarus and Ukraine agreed to work towards a market union.

12: At the Constitutional Convention a compromise draft constitution, based on the presidential and parliamentary drafts, was approved by 433 of a total 585 delegates.

21: Anatoly Chubays was dismissed by parliament from his post of Chairman of the State Committee for the Management of State Property.

23: The parliamentary session ended but Khasbulatov ordered the Presidium of the Supreme Soviet to remain in session during the recess.

24: In an attempt to control inflation in Russia, all rouble notes printed between 1961 and 1992 were withdrawn from circulation and replaced with new ones; no new notes were issued to any other country until January 1994, when Tajikistan agreed effectively to surrender control of its monetary policy to Russia; Belarus agreed to similar conditions in April 1994.

27: Viktor Barannikov, the Minister of Security, was dismissed for the 'violation of ethical norms and serious failures in the leadership of his ministry'; Nikolay Golushko was appointed acting security minister; the Presidium of the Supreme Soviet condemned Barannikov's dismissal.

August

5: Yury Kalmykov was confirmed as Minister of Justice by presidential decree.

12: President Yeltsin vetoed legislation on the mass media approved by the Supreme Soviet.

20: Mikhail Fedotov, the Minister of the Press and Information, resigned in protest at the amendments made by parliament to the Law on Mass Media, which envisaged the establishment of supervisory councils for the media. The following day, Sergey Glazyev, the Minister of External Economic Relations, resigned, following allegations of corruption.

31: Following a series of meetings in Moscow, the heads of administration from 58 constituent parts of the Russian Federation and 45 heads of regional legislative bodies approved President Yeltsin's proposal for the establishment of a Federation Council.

September

1: Yeltsin ordered the temporary dismissal of Vice-President Rutskoy and First Deputy Prime Minister Vladimir Shumeyko, because of the problems inflicted on the Government by mutual accusations of corruption.

3: The Supreme Soviet suspended the presidential decree ordering Rutskoy's removal from office and voted to refer the issue to the Constitutional Court.

7: Russia and five other member states of the CIS (Armenia, Belarus, Kazakhstan, Tajikistan and Uzbekistan) signed a protocol agreement on the establishment of a new 'rouble zone'.

14: Ukraine agreed to join the rouble zone.

16: It was announced that Yegor Gaidar would return to the Government as First Deputy Prime Minister.

18: The first session of the Federation Council convened. Sergey Golushko was appointed Minister for Security.

20: Azerbaijan was formally readmitted to the CIS.

21: Yeltsin issued a decree On Gradual Constitutional Reform (Decree 1,400), which suspended the powers of the legislature with immediate effect and set the date for elections to a new bicameral legislature, the Federal Assembly. The President assumed control of the Prosecutor-General's office and the Russian Central Bank. An emergency session of the Supreme Soviet appointed Rutskoy Acting President. The Constitutional Court ruled that the decree failed to comply with the Constitution.

22: The Council of Ministers issued a statement in support of Yeltsin's decree; the defence minister, Pavel Grachev, and the Chief of the General Staff of the Russian Armed Forces, Col.-Gen. Mikhail Kolesnikov, affirmed their loyalty to the President.

23: The Government assumed control of those media organs previously controlled by the Supreme Soviet; Rutskoy demanded simultaneous presidential and parliamentary elections; the Chairman of the Constitutional Court, Valery Zorkin, proposed early parliamentary and presidential elections and that both parties should annul their recent resolutions; the President announced that presidential elections would be held in June 1994. An emergency session of the Congress of People's Deputies was convened.

24: At a meeting of the CIS Council of Heads of State in Moscow, an agreement was reached on a framework for economic union, including the gradual removal of tariffs and a currency union; nine states signed the agreement, while Turkmenistan and Ukraine agreed to be associate members of such a union. President Yeltsin ordered the parliamentary guard to be temporarily subordinated to the Ministry of Internal Affairs. Nikolay Ryabov, a former deputy chairman of the Supreme Soviet, was appointed Chairman of the Central Electoral Commission, which was formed to organize the forthcoming parliamentary elections.

25: Khasbulatov announced the need for military units to defend the White House (which had housed the Russian Parliament since the Government had moved to the Kremlin, following the disintegration of the USSR); Vladislav Achalov, the 'defence minister' appointed by parliament, declared that a motorized infantry regiment was being formed.

26: Some 10,000 demonstrators attended a rally outside the White House in support of the legislators.

27: Regional leaders meeting in St Petersburg demanded simultaneous presidential and parliamentary elections before the end of the year.

28: President Yeltsin attended meetings with a group of legal experts and members of the Presidential Council; an unarmed militia-man was killed in disturbances in the centre of Moscow as a crowd of several thousand attempted to break through the police cordon around the White House.

29: The Council of Ministers warned Khasbulatov and Rutskoy to surrender, while the Patriarch of All-Russia, Aleksey II, offered to mediate in the dispute; further hostilities occurred between supporters of the parliament and the militia and special interior ministry troops (OMON); forces inside the White House threatened to open fire if the police blockade moved any closer.

30: A conference of regional representatives opened in Moscow, attended by representatives of 62 of the Russian Federation's 89 regions; the delegates demanded the lifting of the blockade on the White House.

October

1–3: Representatives of the Government and the parliament attended a series of negotiations, mediated by the Russian Orthodox Church, but no compromise was reached.

2: The Congress of People's Deputies instructed Rutskoy as 'Acting President' to form a new cabinet.

3: A crowd of more than 3,500 attended a rally organized by Working Moscow, a pro-Communist group; the demonstrators broke through a militia cordon and reached the parliament building. Rutskoy urged this crowd to storm the Mayor of Moscow's office and the Ostankino television station; this they did, taking the Deputy Mayor, Aleksandr Braginsky, hostage, while some 1,000, headed by Viktor Anpilov, attacked the Ostankino television building; government forces subsequently regained control. President Yeltsin announced a state of emergency in Moscow. Rutskoy was formally dismissed from office. Khasbulatov and Rutskoy issued an 'appeal to the people' to defend the parliament.

4: During the night some 20,000 pro-Yeltsin demonstrators assembled near the Kremlin. At dawn government armoured personnel carriers surrounded the White House; exchanges of fire occurred between the Russian army and forces inside and outside the parliament building. The White House was shelled and severely damaged by fire. Over 100 people were reported to have been killed during the violence. The Prosecutor-General ordered the arrest of the organizers of the anti-government insurrection; the Minister of Justice suspended seven political organizations, including the National Salvation Front, the Russian Communist Workers' Party and Working Russia; several opposition newspapers were suspended. Later that day Khasbulatov and Rutskoy surrendered; Rutskoy was condemned by his party, the People's Party of Free Russia; the perpetrators of the violence were arrested.

5: Vladimir Shumeyko was appointed acting press and information minister. The newspapers *Nezavisimaya Gazeta* and *Izvestiya* were reportedly under censorship. Valentin Stepankov was replaced as Prosecutor-General by Aleksey Kazannik. Yury Luzhkov, the Mayor of Moscow, announced the disbandment of Moscow's city and district soviets. A curfew was introduced in the capital.

6: Yeltsin declared an end to all censorship measures.

7: The Constitutional Court was suspended pending the adoption of a new constitution and the election of new judges.

9: Two more political parties, the Free Russia People's Party and the Communist Party of the Russian Federation, were suspended.

12: Yeltsin established a state chamber and a public chamber of the Constitutional Convention; the Convention reopened on 15 October.

13: Several opposition newspapers, including *Den*, were banned by the Ministry for the Press and Information, while the editors-in-chief of *Pravda* and *Sovetskaya Rossiya* were dismissed from their posts.

15: The leaders of the anti-government insurrection, including Khasbulatov, Rutskoy, Barannikov and Achalov, were charged with incitement to riot. Yeltsin decreed that a nation-wide plebiscite would be held on the draft constitution.

18: The state of emergency was suspended in Moscow.

November

3: The President presented a new draft constitutional document at a meeting of the leaders of the constituent territories of the Russian Federation.

6: Yeltsin repealed his decree of 12 June on early presidential elections.

10: The Constitutional Convention finally agreed on a draft of a new basic law.

30: The double-headed eagle was restored as Russia's state emblem by presidential decree.

December

3: Some 1,500 delegates arrived in Moscow to debate the constitutional proposals; some aspects of the draft were criticized, such as the difficulties in impeaching the President or amending the Constitution, and the simplified procedure for dissolving parliament. Georgia joined the CIS.

5: Yeltsin issued a decree freeing the media from future legislative regulation.

12: The Constitution was approved by 58.4% of participating voters in a plebiscite; on the same day elections to the new Federal Assembly (consisting of the Federation Council and the State Duma) were held, producing an unexpected number of votes for Vladimir Zhirinovsky's radical nationalist Liberal Democratic Party (approximately 22.8% of votes cast) and for the Communists (some 12.35%).

21: The Ministry of Security was abolished and the Federal Counter-Intelligence Service established in its place.

22: It was announced that the Ministry of the Press and Information and the Federal Information Centre would be disbanded by 15 February 1994. The news agency, ITAR-TASS, was returned to government control by presidential decree.

24: At a meeting of heads of state in Ashgabat (Turkmenistan) Yeltsin was elected Chairman of the CIS for the following year.

1994

January

5: A presidential decree was issued which guaranteed freedom of information.

11: The first sessions of the Federation Council and the State Duma were held.

13: Vladimir Shumeyko, the First Deputy Prime Minister, was elected Chairman of the Federation Council. Representatives of the Communist Party in the State Duma established a conservative parliamentary bloc with the Democratic Party and the Agrarian Party; this bloc controlled 115 seats out of a total of 450 in the State Duma, while the liberal bloc occupied some 196 seats and the Liberal Democratic Party 64 seats.

14: Ivan Rybkin of the Agrarian Party was elected Chairman of the State Duma.

16: Ella Pamfilova, the social welfare minister, submitted her resignation; Viktor Chernomyrdin refused to accept it, although he did make concessions to the nationalist and conservative forces in parliament. Pamfilova was finally relieved of her duties by President Yeltsin on 25 February.

18: Boris Fedorov, a prominent reformer, offered to resign as finance minister; his resignation was finally accepted by Yeltsin on 26 January.

February

8: At a meeting of the council of the CIS Interparliamentary Assembly in St Petersburg, Shumeyko was elected its Chairman.

15: Yeltsin signed a treaty with Mintimer Shamiyev, President of the federal Republic of Tatarstan, which devolved considerable powers to the Republic.

23: The State Duma granted an amnesty to the members of the SCSE of the 1991 coup attempt in Moscow and to the organizers of the parliamentary resistance of September–October 1993. Rutskoy and Khasbulatov were amongst those released three days later.

26: The Prosecutor-General, Aleksey Kazannik, resigned after he refused an appeal by Yeltsin for him to suspend the State Duma's powers to grant amnesty.

28: Following the exposure of Aldrich Ames, a former leading figure in the US Central Intelligence Agency (CIA), as a Soviet spy and the USA's subsequent expulsion of a Russian diplomat, the Russian Government retaliated by demanding the immediate departure of an employee of the US embassy in Moscow.

History

ANGUS ROXBURGH

THE EMERGENCE OF RUSSIA

The Russians are Eastern Slavs, inhabitants of the huge Eurasian land mass, which is a territory with no great natural frontiers. This fact has made the Russians throughout history both vulnerable to invaders and themselves inclined to migration and expansion. Their first state was established towards the end of the ninth century, around Kiev (now in Ukraine). Kievan Rus (forerunner not only of the 'Great' Russians, but also of the Belarusians or 'White Russians' and the Ukrainians or 'Little Russians') was a slave-holding society, which was officially Christianized in the year 988. The state did not exist for long, however. Much of its population, tired of constant enemy attacks from the south and west, gradually migrated to the north and east. By the late 12th century the early Russians were scattered over a large area in what is now western Russia, Belarus and Ukraine. Their territory was fragmented among a large number of (usually warring) principalities, the most powerful centred on the town of Vladimir.

The disintegration of the Russian nation was halted, ironically, by outsiders. In 1237 ferocious invaders from the east, the Mongol Tatars, led by Batu (a descendant of Chinghiz or Genghis Khan), crossed the River Volga and imposed almost 250 years of subjugation on the Russian people. Mongol rule established in Russia a social, political, administrative and military system quite unlike that of Western Europe. It was based on the unquestioning submission of all individuals to the group and to the absolute power of the ultimate ruler, the Khan. Russia's feuding princes all became vassals of the Golden Horde, as the Khan and his entourage were known. One of the smallest principalities, Muscovy (based in the town of Moscow), rose to prominence, largely as a reward for its devotion to the Khan and its position as chief tax-collector for the Golden Horde.

From the late 14th century the Mongol empire began to disintegrate into smaller khanates. In 1480 a new Russian state finally emerged, when the Muscovite prince, Ivan III, proclaimed complete independence from the Tatar yoke. Moreover, with the fall of Constantinople (Istanbul) to the Turks in 1453, Moscow could lay claim to being the 'Third Rome', the capital of the most pre-eminent Orthodox state. However, the new state retained many features of the Mongol system, including the supremacy of the state over the individual and the principle of universal compulsory service to the state. The Russian historian, Nikolay Berdyayev, described Muscovite Russia as a 'Christianized Tatar kingdom'. Ivan IV ('the Terrible') was the first of many a Russian Tsar (Caesar or Emperor) to use his unquestioned rights as supreme ruler to establish a despotic regime in which terror was, effectively, an instrument of state policy. His *oprichniki*, a dreaded secret police force, were used to suppress dissent, whether real or imagined, in the most barbaric fashion. Ivan IV annexed the Mongol khanates of Kazan and Astrakhan to Moscow and began to colonize the middle and upper reaches of the Volga. This led to a mass migration of peasants to these more fertile areas. It was under Ivan's rule that the Cossack leader, Yermak, began Russia's expansion eastwards beyond the Ural Mountains into Siberia, where villages, forts and trading posts were soon established. For the first time the Russian Empire extended into two continents. In 1645, under the first Tsar of the Romanov dynasty, Muscovite rule reached the Sea of Okhotsk and the port town of Okhotsk was founded.

Over subsequent centuries, Russia's development was marked both by almost continuous expansionism and by arguments over whether to follow a 'Western', European model of civilization, or to create a peculiarly Russian one, informed more by the country's geographical position on the frontier between Europe and Asia. Peter I ('the Great') combined despotic methods with a determination to modernize Russia and establish it as a great European Power. To symbolize this, in 1712 he moved the capital from Moscow to a newly built city on the Baltic coast, St Petersburg, which he called his 'window on the West'. Under Catherine II ('the Great') the Russian Empire was expanded south to the Black Sea and west into Poland. The Tsars Alexander I (1801–25) and Nicholas I (1825–55) extended the Russian frontiers into the Caucasus and some of Central Asia. The cities of Bukhara and Samarkand fell to Russia under Alexander II in 1868. In 1885 the Turkmens became the last of the Muslim peoples of Central Asia to be incorporated into the Empire. During this period, new territories were also claimed in the Far East, reaching Vladivostok in 1860. Politically, 19th-century Russia alternated between reactionary Tsars, such as Nicholas I, and enlightened ones, such as Alexander II (whose most famous act was the Emancipation of the Serfs in 1861). European liberal and revolutionary ideas constantly threatened the political stability and the last Tsar, Nicholas II, was obliged to introduce elements of parliamentary democracy, with the establishment of a legislative assembly, the Duma, in 1906.

In 1917 the pressures of defeats in the First World War and growing economic and social chaos in the country at large brought two revolutions. The first, which occurred in March, overthrew the Tsar and established a Provisional Government which, however, soon found itself sharing power with new workers' councils known as soviets. The second, the Bolshevik Revolution, on 7 November (25 October, Old Style), brought the Communists to power in the capital (renamed Petrograd in 1914) and, after three years of civil war, throughout the territory of the Russian Empire.

RUSSIA IN THE USSR

In the new Union of Soviet Socialist Republics (USSR—established in 1922), Russia (the Russian Soviet Federative Socialist Republic or RSFSR) became just one of 15 national republics, itself containing 31 ethnically defined autonomous republics or regions. In the 1920s genuine attempts were made to encourage other nationalities to develop their own identities and cultures under local leaderships. Under Stalin (Iosif Vissarionovich Dzhugashvili), however, especially after a surge of Russian nationalism during the Second World War, the accepted dogma was that the Soviet nations would not merely 'come together' (*sblizheniye*) but eventually 'merge' (*sliyaniye*—which most understood to mean the subjugation of the other nations by the Russian people). Even after Stalin, despite concessions to the other nations in terms of limited cultural, linguistic and administrative rights, Russians remained the colonial masters, their Empire simply renamed the USSR. Many of the characteristics of pre-Soviet Russia came to dominate the political culture of the USSR. The Communist regime was highly centralized. It encouraged and relied upon traditions of collectivism in the population. The Soviet secret police, censorship and the policy of russification all had equivalents before the Revolution. The three basic principles of tsarism; orthodoxy, autocracy and nationality (*pravoslaviye, samoderzhaviye* and *narodnost*) were transmuted into the Communist doctrines of Marxism-Leninism, Communist Party dictatorship and the idealization of the People (*narod*). In both cases the vision was of a nation ruled by a tyrannical leader, who allegedly embodied the people's faith or ideology. Russia ensured the loyalty of non-Russian parts of the Soviet empire by a system of 'viceroys' (second secretaries in the republican Communist Party organizations were always Russian), by establishing Russian as the language of the Soviet state, and by making the Republics' economies dependent on each other and on the all-Union Government in Moscow. Russian migration to the other Republics was encouraged. So strongly was the USSR identified with Russia that, until 1990, the Communist Party itself had no separate organization in the Russian Federation: unlike all other Republics, Russia's Communists were members simply of the Communist Party of the Soviet Union (CPSU). Owing to total ideological control, this policy was not unsuccessful: in the Soviet period there was little ethnic violence in the non-Russian Republics. Russian domination may have been resented, but, until Mikhail Gorbachev's policy of *glasnost* (openness) in the late 1980s, the colonized Soviet nations rarely protested in public. When the Georgian Party leader, Eduard Shevardnadze, told his people that 'for us the sun rises in the north', it was more a statement of political reality than of Georgian submissiveness. However, the suppression of non-Russian nationalities caused bitter resentment throughout the Soviet period. When the Communist monopoly on power ended in the late 1980s, the very first demand of the national independence movements in the Baltic Republics (Estonia, Latvia and Lithuania), Armenia and elsewhere was to have the indigenous tongues re-established as state languages within the Republics.

THE REBIRTH OF RUSSIA AS A SEPARATE POLITY

Post-Soviet Russia emerged from the USSR almost by default. Under Gorbachev, other Republics (especially the Baltic states, Armenia and Georgia) led the way in fighting for greater autonomy from the all-Union Government. For the Republics, this movement was perceived as a struggle against Russian rule, as well as against Soviet power. Russia was a latecomer to the 'national movement': from mid-1990 its newly elected parliament (a 1,068-member Congress of People's Deputies, which elected a standing parliament or Supreme Soviet of 274 members, both then chaired by Boris Yeltsin) began to oppose 'Soviet' centralism and demand the right to raise its own taxes and pay selectively into the central budget. These rights were inscribed in a Declaration of Sovereignty passed by the RSFSR Congress of People's Deputies (then a minor body compared to the USSR Congress elected one year earlier) on 12 June 1990, a date now commemorated as Independence Day. One year later Yeltsin became Russia's first directly elected executive President, with 57.3% of the votes cast, and, from that moment, Russia's political power matched, or even outweighed, that of the Soviet central authorities. Unlike the Soviet President, Mikhail Gorbachev (the leader of the USSR between 1985 and 1991), who had never faced a popular election, Yeltsin had a real mandate for reform. Confronted by 15 Republics all demanding autonomy, Gorbachev tried to negotiate a Union Treaty which would preserve the USSR, at least as some kind of confederation. However, the signing of the Treaty, scheduled for 20 August 1991, was pre-empted by a conservative coup, led by Communists determined to keep the old Union together at all costs. Their plan had unforeseen consequences, for when Gorbachev returned to Moscow from his brief detention in the Crimea (Ukraine), Yeltsin led an invigorated crusade against both central Soviet power and Communist rule. In the months that followed, the Russian Supreme Soviet adopted numerous decrees which removed the all-Union Government's control over key economic and financial levers. At the end of November even the Soviet foreign ministry was subordinated to the Russian foreign ministry. Gorbachev continued to try to revive and revise the Union Treaty, but he became more and more of a peripheral figure as Yeltsin began to deal directly with the leaders of the other Republics. On 7–8 December 1991, the presidents of Russia, Ukraine and Belarus met in a hunting lodge at Belovezhskaya Pushcha (Belarus), near Brest on the border with Poland, and signed a treaty, according to which the USSR had ceased to exist and was replaced by a new Commonwealth of Independent States (CIS). The CIS was soon joined by most of the other Republics (by the founding Almaty Declaration, signed in Kazakhstan on 21 December), and, on 25 December, President Gorbachev accepted that he should resign. His resignation signified the end of the USSR. Above the Kremlin, the red Soviet flag was replaced by the white, blue and red tricolour of independent Russia (which was formally renamed the Russian Federation on 25 December). When Yeltsin moved into the former General Secretary's office in the Kremlin, he was the first Russian leader for centuries to rule over such a truncated territory, stripped of all its colonies other than those peoples physically within Russian frontiers. The population of Russia was less than 150m., compared to the 290m. of the USSR. It remained, however, the largest country in the world.

POST-SOVIET ECONOMIC REFORM

President Yeltsin had two principal aims as Russia emerged as a new state from the ruins of the USSR. First, to turn the country into a genuine democracy, something it had never been either before or after the Bolshevik Revolution. Secondly, to abandon the Communist centrally planned economy and recreate capitalism, based on a free market and private ownership. A far-reaching economic reform, termed 'shock therapy', was introduced from 2 January 1992. In the first stage of the reform, almost all prices were freed and allowed to reach levels dictated by the market, though state subsidies remained on some foodstuffs, rents and energy costs. Wages paid by state enterprises were slow to follow suit and, consequently, the first and most obvious effect of this policy was a marked increase in poverty throughout the country. This change was evident both in the growing numbers of poor people and beggars in the streets and in official figures, which soon placed between 40% and 80% of the population below the poverty line. (The disparities in the figures suggested they were unreliable, however, and possibly manipulated by opponents of the reforms.) The West responded by providing substantial humanitarian and food aid, which undoubtedly helped Russia to avoid starvation and civil unrest during the first winter of the reforms.

In 1992 prices in the Russian Federation rose by 2,500%. Worst affected were pensioners and those who had saved large amounts of money under the safe, low-inflation conditions of the USSR. Even relatively large savings were quickly eliminated. Many Russians had to resort to selling their belongings at the pavement markets that appeared in most towns. Although these markets were dictated by necessity, they also soon proved inadvertently to be the first links in the new market economy. Some of the vendors graduated from selling their own possessions to trading in scarce commodities, which they bought in the shops specifically for resale on the streets at a profit. This chaotic 'pavement capitalism' proliferated after the rouble was made internally convertible in July 1992. This meant that, while the Russian currency remained unconvertible on world markets, Russians and foreigners could trade roubles and dollars freely inside the country. Thousands of currency-exchange offices were set up, at which Russian traders could freely buy US dollars with which to travel abroad (mainly to neighbouring Poland, Turkey and the People's Republic of China) to buy cheap clothes, foodstuffs and other goods for resale in Russia. From the pavement markets emerged small kiosks, and from the kiosks small shops, or even chains of retail outlets as the system expanded. One year after the start of the reform, the term 'capitalism' embraced everything from individuals selling a few Western chocolate bars from a box at their feet on the pavement to prosperous new concerns trading in Japanese computers. For the Russian consumer, the economic developments brought more choice in the shops than at any time since the Revolution, but at prices that many people could not afford. Prices, rather than the notorious queues of the Soviet period, became the main principle in the distribution and allocation of goods. The laws of supply and demand began to function. The Russian Government, led by a radical young economist, Yegor Gaidar, tried hard to satisfy conditions stipulated by the International Monetary Fund (IMF) before the West would agree to provide large-scale economic aid. The conditions were low inflation and reductions in public spending, including the abolition of massive state subsidies, in order to achieve a budget deficit not exceeding 5% of gross national product (GNP). Neither condition was met, and much of a US $24,000m. allocation of economic aid for the former Soviet Republics, promised by the 'Group of Seven' (G7) major industrial nations in 1992, was never dispatched.

In April 1993 the G7 offered an even larger amount of aid, totalling $43,400m., mostly in the form of tied credits and relief on Russia's $80,000m. foreign debt. Industrial production fell by about 20% in the first year of the reforms, and the value of the rouble, initially pegged at 90 roubles to the US dollar, dropped to about 1,000 by mid-1993. Inflation was fuelled by the feverish printing of money by the Central Bank of the Russian Federation, largely in order to issue credits to inefficient parts of the state sector. As a result, the money supply increased over 1992 by 10.4 times. President Yeltsin frequently criticized the Central Bank for this policy but was unable to prevent it because, under the Constitution, the Bank was controlled not by the Government but by parliament. A majority in parliament favoured the policy of supporting former Soviet industries, rather than allowing them to fend for themselves in the market economy. Parliament also impeded the implementation of other reforms, in a struggle sometimes known as the 'war of laws'.

Despite such political problems, the Gaidar administration continued with the second stage of the reform from mid-1992: privatization of state industries. The process was overseen by the State Committee for the Management of State Property, known as Goskomimushchestvo (GKI). At first, small-scale enterprises employing fewer than 200 workers (mainly shops and services) were sold, usually to their employees. Cities such as Nizhny Novgorod (formerly Gorky) led the way, holding the first public auctions of municipally owned enterprises. By July 1993, after a year of privatization, almost 72,000 firms were in private hands, including 57% of the country's small enterprises. Meanwhile, a start was also made on the more complex task of privatizing medium- and large-scale enterprises, including huge industrial concerns employing tens of thousands of workers. In preparation for privatization, thousands of state-owned enterprises were turned into joint-stock companies.

A vital instrument in the privatization process was the issue, from October 1992, of privatization cheques or vouchers to all Russian citizens. In practice, many preferred to sell their vouchers for cash (invariably at considerably less than their nominal value), so that the cheques tended to accumulate in the hands of a growing class of investors. Investment funds were also set up, giving individuals the chance to use their privatization cheques profitably without having to become expert in the financial markets. In early 1993, the first major industries, such as the huge Zil car and truck manufacturer in Moscow, were privatized, either at auctions or through privatization offices at which individuals could use their vouchers. It was noteworthy, however, that no major enterprises, however overmanned or inefficient, were closed down, or even dismissed significant numbers of workers, despite a law permitting bankruptcies. After almost two years of economic reform, predictions of mass unemployment remained unfulfilled. In July 1993 there were only one million registered unemployed, out of a work-force of 70m. This was fortunate for workers, and for the Government, which feared social unrest if there were large-scale redundancies. It was, however, a sign that the transition to a market economy was still progressing slowly, and that the Government was afraid of allowing market mechanisms to function freely.

Two matters somewhat overshadowed the overall success of the privatization programme. One was the incontrovertible fact that many private companies were set up using former Communist Party funds, turning the country's former political rulers into its new economic bosses. In the months before the collapse of Communism, as members of the Party predicted its fate they tried to save its considerable fortune either by secretly transferring it to foreign bank accounts or by setting up commercial companies in Russia. Many of these members became leaders in the new market economy. Most major state industries also remained in the hands of managers appointed under the Soviet system, where Communist loyalty was judged more important than business acumen. This was inevitable, though, and it was likely to be a long time before a new generation of managers, trained in Western economics, would emerge.

The second problem was the growth of organized crime, known, not without justification, as the 'mafia'. Almost every company, whether privatized or simply private, whether purely Russian or partly foreign-owned, was controlled or 'protected' by one of 3,000 mafia gangs which operated throughout the country, grouped in about 150 criminal fraternities. Moscow, for example, was divided territorially among several groups, which extorted up to 40% of the profits of all businesses, ostensibly in return for protection from other criminal groups. Armed hostilities became common in Moscow as members of the mafia sought to punish businessmen who failed to pay their protection money, or rival gangs attempting to operate on their territory.

Organized crime was but one of many deterrents to large-scale Western investment in the Russian economy. Western businesses complained of the continuing instability of the economic and political situation and of the uncertainty surrounding the reform programme. Laws were continually revised, as the Government and its opponents in parliament argued over the course of the reforms, especially the privatization programme. Western companies were subject to a bewildering array of taxes, import-export duties and other regulations, which also changed from month to month, making forward planning difficult.

POLITICS AND DEMOCRACY

President Yeltsin found greatest support for his reforms among the Democratic Russia movement, which had helped his rise to power by organizing large demonstrations during Mikhail Gorbachev's period in office, and from the Russian Movement for Democratic Reforms, which included prominent radical intellectuals such as Gavriil Popov, the former Mayor of Moscow, and Anatoly Sobchak, Mayor of St Petersburg. The economic reforms also found a natural constituency among Russia's nascent business class. The Economic Freedom Party, led by one of the most successful entrepreneurs, Konstantin Borovoy, urged an even faster move towards capitalism, and a complete end to subsidies for bankrupt Soviet industries.

Opposition to Yeltsin's reforms came from two main groups. The fiercest criticism emanated from a loose coalition of neo-Communists and Russian nationalists, termed the 'red-brown plague' by their opponents. This group claimed that Yeltsin was capitulating to the West or to the 'Zionists', allowing economic policy to be dictated by the IMF and the World Bank. They accused the Government of humiliating Russia in every way: in losing its empire; in abandoning 25m. Russians to live in foreign countries which were once part of the USSR; and in 'betraying' ordinary citizens by promising them prosperity and turning them, instead, into paupers. These critics demanded that Russia rely on its own resources and return to the social guarantees and state planning of the Soviet period. (It should be noted that few, however, advocated a return to old-style Communist Party rule.) Such views were held by a variety of groups, many of whom were part of a co-ordinating body, the National Salvation Front, set up in October 1992. A more moderate, centrist group supported the general move towards a market economy but demanded a shift in tactics and a significant slowing down of the reforms. A leading role here was played by Civic Union, a co-ordinating body which included centrist political parties and the influential Union of Industrialists (called the 'Red Directors' since most of them were in charge of huge Soviet enterprises), led by a former Party central committee functionary, Arkady Volsky.

Civic Union described itself as a 'constructive opposition' to Yeltsin's Government. It called for government intervention to halt the disastrous decline in industrial production, as well as broad social guarantees. It developed an 'alternative plan' for a more moderately paced transition to capitalism than that devised by Gaidar. With Civic Union and the outright opposition controlling a majority in parliament (both the Congress of People's Deputies and the Supreme Soviet), Yeltsin was obliged to moderate his policies, abandoning some of the financial austerity measures, and to reorganize his Governments throughout 1992 and 1993. In December 1992 the seventh Congress refused to endorse Yegor Gaidar as Prime Minister and forced Yeltsin to nominate a centrist figure, Viktor Chernomyrdin, instead. Yeltsin was also obliged to dismiss his closest liberal adviser, Gennady Burbulis. By appointing another liberal, Boris Fedorov, as finance minister, Yeltsin was, nevertheless, able generally to adhere to his programme for reform. Congress failed by a few votes to deprive him of the emergency presidential powers granted him the previous April to introduce reforms by decree.

By March 1993, however, serious problems began to occur for President Yeltsin. The eighth Congress of People's Deputies created a series of obstacles to his programme. It cancelled his emergency powers, and rejected almost all of his proposals, including one designed to overcome the paralysis of power by holding a referendum on whether parliament or President should rule Russia. On 20 March President Yeltsin inflicted a crisis on the country by introducing emergency rule, effectively by-passing parliament, in an attempt to end the political stalemate. One week later, an emergency session of the Congress of People's Deputies attempted to impeach Yeltsin for violating the Constitution. His opponents narrowly failed to achieve the required two-thirds majority, but a national vote of confidence in Yeltsin was arranged. The referendum, held on 25 April, included four questions: on confidence in Yeltsin as President; on support for his economic reforms; and on whether to hold early presidential and early parliamentary elections. The result confounded the President's enemies. Not only did he win 57.4% in the personal vote of confidence, but a majority even endorsed his economic policies. There was less support, however, for new elections, which meant Yeltsin would have to continue working with a hostile legislature.

A major part in the political struggle was played by Yeltsin's two most implacable political opponents: Ruslan Khasbulatov, who became Chairman of the Supreme Soviet after Yeltsin's election as President in June 1991; and the Russian Vice-President, Aleksandr Rutskoy. Both men had stood close by Yeltsin in his fight against Soviet power, notably during the coup attempt of August 1991. However, when it came to reforming independent Russia, they had very different agendas. Khasbulatov, though unpopular in the country (largely because of his Chechen nationality), used his influence in parliament to obstruct many reforms and undermine Yeltsin. Rutskoy, who was elected as Yeltsin's colleague in the presidential election, soon revealed that his opposition to the then-ruling Communist Party did not imply his support of Western-style capitalism. He derided Yeltsin's privatization programme as a 'swindle', which was only intended to impoverish the country. Rutskoy demanded harsh measures against the mafia and intervention in other former Soviet Republics to defend their Russian inhabitants against discrimination. As his opposition became more outspoken, Yeltsin deprived Rutskoy of all his assignments, leaving him Vice-President in name only. Rutskoy ceased to attack Yeltsin's policies and began, instead, to make allegations of corruption against the President's most senior ministers. A corruption commission, which Rutskoy had previously headed, made serious allegations in turn about Rutskoy's own financial machinations and the alleged existence of a Swiss bank account in his name. Opinion polls consistently placed Rutskoy second in popularity after Yeltsin, and occasionally even above him, making him the strongest rival candidate in the event of a presidential election.

With the opposition's case against Yeltsin's economic reforms weakened by his victory in the referendum, the key political issue became the question of what kind of democratic system Russia should have: essentially, whether it should be a presidential or a parliamentary republic. The existing Constitution was based on the old Soviet one but incorporated hundreds of amendments to annul the Communist Party's leading role and introduce the quasi-democratic parliamentary structures invented by Gorbachev: namely, the Congress of People's Deputies, which met for short sessions about twice a year; and the smaller, permanent body, the Supreme Soviet, elected by the Congress. It was the failure of this Constitution to define properly the powers of the legislature and the executive that resulted in the constant political impasse between

President Yeltsin and the Congress. A totally new constitution was needed to redefine Russia's basic law for the future. Yeltsin's own team and a parliamentary committee headed by Oleg Rumyantsev each drew up rival drafts of a new organic law. However, little progress was made towards actually adopting one until Yeltsin forced the issue by calling a Constitutional Convention, with some 760 representatives from the main political and social organizations and from 88 autonomous regions and republics of the Russian Federation. (The 89th territory, Chechnya, part of the former Chechen-Ingush Autonomous Soviet Socialist Republic, had declared independence in November 1991 and boycotted the conference, as it had all other dealings with the central Government in Moscow.)

Although Yeltsin had insisted that only his draft for a new constitution be taken as a basis for discussion, the delegates in fact discussed the parliamentary version too, and formulated a compromise draft which was approved on 12 July 1993. The draft provided for a presidential republic in some ways similar to the French model. According to its terms, the legislature (to be known as the Federal Assembly) would consist of a directly elected 400-member lower house, the State Duma, and an upper house (to be known as the Federation Council), which consisted of two members from each republic and region (178 members in all). The directly elected President would have the right to dissolve the State Duma in certain circumstances and to set new elections. The Federation Council would have the right to impeach the President in the event of treason or other grave crimes. The Government would report to both President and Parliament.

Huge problems remained, however. First, the existing People's Deputies insisted that only they had the right, under the old Constitution, to adopt a new one; and a majority of them, including Khasbulatov, were opposed to the Conference's draft, which would, inevitably, abolish the Congress of People's Deputies. Secondly, the draft did not find a satisfactory balance between the federal Government and Russia's regions and ethnically based republics. Some of the 21 ethnic minorities, which had been granted a certain degree of autonomy under the Soviet system and who now had their own republics in the Russian Federation, wanted greater economic and political independence from the federal Government. Many of the 68 non-national regions wanted similar rights, particularly as many of them wielded considerably greater economic might than some of the republics.

While no agreement could be reached with the Supreme Soviet on either the new constitution or on holding parliamentary elections, Yeltsin continued with political changes. In August 1993 he persuaded the leaders of 88 republics and regions to create a consultative body, also known as the Federation Council, which he hoped to turn into a prototype of the future upper house of parliament. Whatever the outcome of the political struggle between the executive and legislature, the regions seemed destined to play a key role in the future, with greater power than ever before devolved from the centre.

Despite the political conflicts, by August 1993 it appeared that Russia had made steady progress from Communism to democracy. Apart from some trouble in the Caucasus region, it had generally avoided the bloody ethnic conflicts which affected many other former Soviet Republics. Apart from one death in a May Day demonstration in 1993, there had been no major social conflicts either; indeed, anti-reform demonstrations had even grown smaller as time went by. Politics tended to be dominated by 10 or so personalities rather than by political parties, which remained too numerous and too small to be a major influence on the country's democratic development. However, a return to the past seemed unlikely, even if institutions such as television and the press still saw their role as propagandists rather than informants. Television, in particular, was frequently accused of pro-government bias. President Yeltsin himself was trusted by most Western governments as the guarantor of both political and economic reform in Russia. Despite his sometimes erratic decision-making (his sudden declaration of emergency rule in March 1993 and frequent reversals of policy), he did not seem to evince the dictatorial ambitions attributed to him by his enemies. Indeed, he stated on several occasions that he would not stand again for President when his present term expired, although he seemed likely to ignore his pledge if forced to call elections before the end of his term. In general, Yeltsin gave the impression that he would be happy to see his place in history as the man who helped destroy Soviet Communism and put a democratic system in place in Russia.

In mid-1993 a new generation of politicians, many of whom played no part at all in the old Communist structures, were waiting to take their turn when the time came. The search for a post-Communist future involved a resurrection of past traditions, the Cossack movement and the Orthodox Church to name but two, as well as the adoption of Western democratic values. It seemed that a balance was likely to be struck, in time-worn fashion, between Slavophiles and Westernizers, with Russia remaining something unique, with its own model of statehood and political culture. What was underestimated by both liberals and centrists, however, was the increasing disenchantment with the politicians and the appeal of simplistic but extremist solutions, notably those espoused by the nationalists.

In September 1993 the tension between the legislative and the executive branches of power turned into serious confrontation. Frustrated with attempts by the legislature to hinder his reforms, on 21 September Yeltsin dissolved parliament and announced that elections would be held to two houses of a new body, the Federal Assembly. The Supreme Soviet responded by summoning an emergency session of the Congress of People's Deputies. In spite of the suspension of power supplies to the parliament building (the White House, formerly the seat of the Russian administration) some 180 parliamentary deputies remained inside the parliament building, including Rutskoy and Khasbulatov. Attempts by the Constitutional Court and the Orthodox Church to mediate in the conflict proved useless. On 3–4 October armed hostilities occurred between supporters of the defiant deputies and the army and interior ministry troops. On 3 October the Ostankino television station was attacked by anti-Yeltsin demonstrators. The following day government troops bombarded the White House and overcame the resistance. Over 100 people were reported to have died in the conflict.

Having suppressed the rebellion by opponents to his reforms, Yeltsin sought to finalize a draft constitution. On 10 November 1993 the Constitutional Convention agreed upon a version which was put to a nation-wide vote in a plebiscite on 12 December. According to the final results issued by the Central Electoral Commission, a total of 58,187,755 citizens (comprising 54.8% of registered voters in Russia) participated in the plebiscite. The Constitution was endorsed by 58.4% of participants (some 32,937,630 voters) and rejected by 41.6% (23,431,333). The Constitution provided for a strong presidency with few legislative checks on its power and differed in some respects from the draft worked out by the Constitutional Convention in May; most significantly, the status of the constituent territorial units of the Russian Federation was reduced. According to the final version of the Constitution, the country would be a presidential republic with a bicameral legislature and an independent judiciary.

On 12 December 1993 (the same day as the plebiscite was held) elections were held to the new legislature, the Federal Assembly. This was to consist of a lower chamber, the State Duma (comprising 450 deputies), and an upper chamber, the Federation Council (consisting of a total of 179 members elected in two-member constituencies as independent candidates). In the State Duma, 225 deputies were elected in single-member constituencies (a 'first-past-the-post' system), while the remaining 225 seats were contested by proportional representation on the basis of party lists. A total of 13 parties and blocs qualified to stand for election to the State Duma. Of these movements, the Liberal Democratic Party, a right-wing nationalist party led by Vladimir Zhirinovsky, won a surprisingly large percentage of the votes cast (some 22.8%) but few individual candidates from the party were elected. The Liberal Democrats won a total of 63 seats in the State Duma. Far fewer votes than expected were cast in favour of Russia's Choice (15.4% and 40 seats), a coalition of democrats led by Yegor Gaidar. However, the pro-reform coalition did win the majority of seats contested by individual candidates, thereby making them the largest faction in the lower chamber, with a total of 76 seats. The centrist Agrarian Party won 7.9% of the votes cast on party lists (21 seats) and the Communist Party of the Russian Federation 12.35% (32 seats). The second largest faction in the State Duma, however, was New Regional Policy, a centrist grouping comprising 65 members who had been elected as independent candidates.

Few members of the Federation Council acknowledged party affiliations. However, it was estimated that supporters of President Yeltsin far outnumbered the radical Communist and nationalist opposition. The majority of members of the Council (a total of 81 deputies) were senior officials in the executive and legislative branches of the Russian Federation's republics and regions.

The prospects for Yeltsin's reforms remained unclear at the beginning of 1994. The lower chamber of the new legislature promised to be more conservative than its predecessor, the Congress of People's Deputies. Less than two months after the opening of its first session, the State Duma voted to end criminal proceedings against the State Committee for the State of Emergency in the USSR (SCSE—the leaders of the 1991 coup attempt), against the organizers of the violent demonstration which took place on 1 May 1993 and against the perpetrators of the anti-government uprising of October that year. Only the Russia's Choice faction opposed the resolution. However, the distribution of seats in the Duma among democrats, centrists and radical conservative opposition promised to make any form of consensus unlikely. The Federation Council, although more pro-Yeltsin in its composition, would probably choose to promote their own regional interests, rather than help strengthen Yeltsin's position.

FOREIGN RELATIONS

Foreign policy in the Russian Federation underwent a significant change in 1993–94. The Government's stance with regard to the former Soviet Republics (the 'near-abroad') became more aggressive, culminating, in January 1994, in the controversial claim by the foreign minister, Andrey Kozyrev, that Russian (former Soviet) troops had the right to remain on the territory of the countries of the former USSR to protect the interests of their Russian minorities. At this time Russia also expressed increasing concern over the possible incorporation of the countries of Eastern Europe (its former 'sphere of influence') into the North Atlantic Treaty Organisation (NATO), which it perceived as increasingly adopting the role of the UN's military arm. In February the Russian Government intervened in the civil war in Bosnia and Herzegovina by persuading Serb forces to withdraw from their positions in Sarajevo and offering to send reinforcements to join the UN peacekeeping forces there. This involvement in the conflict in the former Yugoslavia and Russia's increasing domination of the CIS confirmed that the country was again asserting its significance in international politics.

The Economy

Prof. PHILIP HANSON

INTRODUCTION

To judge by the official statistics, the decline in economic activity in Russia between 1989 and mid-1993 was one of the most dramatic economic collapses experienced by any large country this century. The reality was indeed dramatic but the collapse was less than the official data reported. Nevertheless, the attempt to change the Russian economic system from centrally administered socialism to market capitalism was implemented in a confused and confusing fashion. Political resistance to change was even stronger than in Poland or Hungary, and the course of reform followed an irregular and devious pattern.

According to received wisdom with regard to the 'transformation' of former Communist economies, there are four main elements in the process of change: liberalization, stabilization, privatization, and internationalization. In other words, state administrative controls over prices and outputs, and imports and exports, must be largely removed; the initial upsurge in prices which this is likely to produce must be prevented from causing an inflationary spiral and the purchasing power of the currency must be stabilized; most state enterprises should be transferred to private ownership; and the economy should be substantially opened to the outside world, particularly to imports and foreign investment.

No detailed prescription for the sequence and timing of these changes is possible. Political circumstances affect what can be done and how quickly. These circumstances varied among the former Communist economies. The inherited levels of economic development, economic structures and cultural traditions were also different from one country to another. Russia began its attempt at transformation later than some central and eastern European countries. The Russian Government, led by President Boris Yeltsin (who was also initially Chairman or Prime Minister of the cabinet), initiated a general price liberalization on 2 January 1992. This occurred two years after the launch of Poland's so-called 'shock therapy' and one year after similar steps were taken in Czechoslovakia. It was also 24 years after Hungary had begun a far more limited and tentative process of institutional reform while still under Communist rule. Even within the former USSR, in 1991 Estonia and

Latvia had begun to dismantle price controls. Most other ex-Communist countries, however, made slower, more confused changes to their economies. All registered sharp declines in officially recorded output. The case of Russia was no exception. Official statistics show a decline of about 30% in Russian real gross domestic product (GDP) between 1989 and 1992, and a fall of 17% between the first quarter of 1992 and the corresponding period in 1993. For several reasons, these figures exaggerated the true decline in the population's economic welfare. First, state enterprise managers had previously overstated their output in order to qualify for plan-fulfilment bonuses. This incentive to exaggerate output figures disappeared with the abandonment of planning. So, therefore, did the exaggerated part of reported output. Secondly, some of the output actually produced before the changes was an unwanted, wasteful side-effect of the planning system, the loss of which caused no reduction in welfare. Thirdly, some of the loss of output was a loss of military production that made no contribution to consumption or the growth of capital stock. Fourthly, there was a far greater fall in investment than in consumption; though potentially damaging for future prosperity, this entailed no immediate loss to the population. Fifthly, the movement of prices towards market equilibrium levels meant a reduction in shortages and, therefore, in time spent queueing—a welfare gain not reflected in output figures. Finally, the private sector's output was not adequately reported in the official statistics and was more dynamic than that of the state sector. The new private firms were increasing output rapidly, though from very low levels. Other important, long-established private-sector activities, such as household production of food (which was extensive amongst the urban as well as the rural population), had always been important and under-represented; such production declined only slightly, or even increased.

For these reasons, the decline in officially measured output suggested a more desperate situation than actually prevailed. Substantial numbers of people who started their own businesses, were employed in the private sector, or who had other new opportunities created by the changes actually benefited. At the same time, however, economic conditions became more uncertain for everyone and some sections of the population, particularly large families with low incomes, experienced a significant deterioration in their standard of living. Moreover, many of Russia's 'entrepreneurs' were members of criminal gangs, which operated an illegal ('black') market with a level of violence hitherto unknown in Russian cities.

Liberalization was far from complete, despite the large rise in prices. Housing rent and most fuel prices remained under state control. Territorial authorities within Russia retained a range of price controls on basic food items, which they supported with subsidies. Local capacities to subsidize and local policies varied; consequently, the cost of a basket of basic food items varied substantially across the country. By the same token, some elements of the shortage economy remained. Open inflation was, nevertheless, extremely rapid. The official consumer price index showed a rise of 2,500% between December 1991 and December 1992, which included the price leap of January 1992, when prices were freed. By mid-1993 inflation had slowed somewhat but was still at an annual rate of 500%–600%.

Stabilization policy in Russia, in other words, was largely unsuccessful in 1992 and the first half of 1993. Budgetary expenditure outran revenue by a wider margin than the Russian Government had intended. Foreign funding alleviated some of the budget deficit, which reduced its domestic inflationary impact. Meeting the remaining deficit by the domestic issue of government bonds was, however, impossible for as long as capital markets scarcely existed. (Some progress in this direction was made in May 1993—see below.) A substantial expansion of cash emission and credit was therefore unavoidable, given the size of the budget deficit. Actual credit expansion was probably greater than that generated by the deficit. For this the Central Bank, at any rate from mid-1992, was partly responsible. Money supply, therefore, grew rapidly, sustaining an inflationary spiral. In the course of 1992, money wages at first lagged behind, then caught up with, price rises.

External finances were no healthier. Imports were curbed in 1992 and early 1993, so that official sources recorded a merchandise trade surplus. However, large amounts of foreign currency were deposited off shore, foreign debt-service payments could not be met, current payment arrears on trade shipments increased and the low level of foreign direct investment meant that Russia had, overall, a large external financing gap. This situation, together with the continuing domestic inflation, ensured that the rouble's exchange rate with Western currencies began to fall precipitately in early 1992 and continued to decline in 1993.

In general, the outcome of economic reform in Russia by mid-1993 was less promising than had been the case after 18 months in Poland and the Czech Republic (which separated from Slovakia on 1 January 1993). This appeared to reflect the stronger entrenched opposition to real reform in Russia. Despite all the failures of Russian reform, however, developments in the Russian economy were not all unfavourable. The new private sector grew fast, and people's attitudes changed in ways that were often helpful to transformation. Opinion polls showed that tolerance of price rises increased as experience of them grew, and the case for privatization was widely accepted. The privatization process moved ahead reasonably fast in late 1992 and early 1993. The support shown for Boris Yeltsin in the referendum of 25 April 1993 no doubt indicated a widespread distrust of his main opponents as much as anything else, but it did confirm what many opinion polls had been suggesting: the Russian people's acceptance of the need for radical change and their capacity to endure the upheavals involved, were greater than the centrist and nationalist politicians in Moscow claimed. However, in December these same politicians secured an unexpectedly high level of support in the general election. While this restrained the liberal element in government, the powers of the presidency had been enhanced by the new Constitution, introduced in the same month, and Yeltsin committed himself to continue the reforms.

GROSS DOMESTIC PRODUCT

For the reasons given above, data on the Russian economy, always problematic, in many ways became even less reliable in 1992. In addition to the statistical problems already noted, there still existed a statistical reporting system that was generally rather weak. An extremely rapid increase in consumer prices, as well as substantial changes in the composition of output, presented that statistical system with challenges which would have proved difficult to meet for more advanced statistical offices. The figures that are quoted here must, therefore, be treated with extreme caution.

Gross domestic product at current prices was 14,956,000m. roubles in 1992, and approximately the same (15,000,000m. roubles) in the first quarter of 1993 alone. The equality of the two figures entirely reflected inflation, for real output continued to decline in 1993. In 1992 Russian GDP by sector of origin, according to official data, was 37.5% industrial (including mining and public utilities) and 10.9% agricultural, while 3.5% came from transport and communications, 11.0% from construction, 18.6% from other material-production sectors (mostly retail and wholesale distribution), and 13.0% came from services other than distribution. The remainder, some 5.5%, was attributed by Russian government statisticians to amortization, which apparently was not identified by sector.

The sectoral composition of total output appeared to have shifted somewhat from 1990, with industry apparently increasing in relative importance, within a declining total, and the agricultural sector declining. This was almost certainly the result of relative price changes, rather than changes in the relative levels of real output in the various sectors. In constant prices, the agricultural sector fared better than the average for the whole economy; but monopoly power was stronger in industry, and price rises there were relatively large. By Western standards, in 1990 and in 1992 the shares of the industrial and agricultural sectors were large and that of services small. Whatever the reality in 1990, the share of services was likely to be understated in 1992, because the growth of the private sector that was not sufficiently recorded was concentrated in services (in business services as well as in retailing and other consumer-related activities).

The distribution of GDP by end-use also changed and in a more straightforward way. In 1990 household consumption was approximately 50% of the total, gross fixed and inventory investment about 30% and public-sector consumption about 20%. Equivalent data for 1992 have not been found, but the reported fall in investment between 1990 and 1992 was approximately 54%. Therefore, in rough terms, the share of gross fixed and inventory investment in 1992 GDP at 1990 prices was some 20%—a 10% decrease since 1990. One can only estimate how that 10% shift was shared between household and public consumption. According to official figures, taxes accounted for 33.6% of GDP and public expenditure for 39.9%.

INDUSTRY

Like the economy as a whole, industrial-sector output underwent some restructuring in 1990–92, despite the virtual absence of net investment. The composition of the installed capacity of machinery and equipment must have altered little, apart from any effects of differential rates of retirements of capital assets in different lines of production. However, the rates of utilization of capacity, though generally declining, must have declined in very different proportions in different lines of production. In the extractive industries the situation was slightly different. Generally, in the fuel and energy sector, insufficient development of new capacity (for example, through petroleum exploration) combined with a reduction in the supply of current material input and capital equipment, and general disarray, to reduce production substantially.

Supply problems (even when production was maintained) troubled all sectors, and were especially acute in the case of equipment for the petroleum industry, since much of the Soviet production of such equipment was in Azerbaijan, where production and delivery were disrupted by war. Crude petroleum output in 1992, at 393m. metric tons, was 31% below its highest level in 1987. Petroleum production in the first quarter of 1993 was at a rate of 7m. barrels per day, against 11.4m. in 1987. Output, therefore, was still falling. Natural-gas output, which had hitherto risen continuously, though at an increasingly slow rate, actually fell fractionally in 1992, to 625,000m. cu m. Coal production in 1992, at 337m. tons, was 21% below its highest level, which had been reached in 1988.

The agricultural sector experienced particular difficulties, owing to the fact that it possessed less monopoly power than industry. This was reflected in steep falls in the ability of farms to pay for agricultural machinery. The agricultural-machinery industry, therefore, encountered falling demand and was forced to reduce output. Broadly speaking, the demand for all investment goods was reduced.

Russian state enterprises did not adapt output to demand as a matter of course, however. A tendency to continue producing for stock was widely observed. So, too, was a practice of delivering output even to customers likely to be insolvent and billing them through the banking system in the old way. The implicit assumption in many cases was that either customer or payee would receive assistance from the state. Moreover, Russian state enterprise managers often gave as a reason for continuing to deliver to insolvent customers the need to have money owing them recorded in their accounts. Cash was still used to pay wages, and cash and bank money were still not, for many enterprises, freely interchangeable. The enterprise could often acquire cash from the bank to pay wages, however, if it could show that it had accounts receivable which would, under the old system, have come in reliably and covered the wages involved. The fact that payment would probably never materialize seemed not to be a matter of concern. In this way, arrears among enterprises increased sharply in early 1992.

In 1992 industrial production of consumer goods, including food processing, declined slightly less than production in the sector as a whole in 1992—by 15% compared to 19%. The same pattern could be observed in the period January–March 1992 and the same period in 1993, when the decline amounted to 12% and 19% respectively. This reflects, though to a much smaller degree, the steep relative decline of investment as against consumption in the economy as a whole. This, admittedly somewhat attenuated, similarity between industrial supply-side developments and final demand suggests that part of the industrial decline was determined by demand and that the decline in industrial activity might not all be attributable to supply 'bottlenecks' or other supply-side factors.

Many, if not most, industrial enterprises in Russia, were subject to declines in real demand and a need to make major changes to the quality and range of their products if they were to survive in the long-term. Despite their doubtful prospects, however, the process of privatization began to develop fairly rapidly in the industrial sector. In Russia, as in other former Communist countries, industrial privatization entailed substantially greater difficulties than the privatization of small-scale non-agricultural concerns, such as shops, cafés, road haulage businesses and local housing construction. Small-scale, or so-called 'petty', privatization may be carried out by auction sales of the assets to individuals or small partnerships. Many people could raise the money required. The value of the assets (that is, the present value of the expected future income to be generated from them) is not subject to very great uncertainties, at any rate by comparison with the industrial sector.

Privatizing state industrial enterprises or other large concerns is much more difficult. To begin with, the average industrial enterprise in Russia and in other Communist countries was very much larger than the average Western industrial plant; small-scale industrial production scarcely existed, and it was seldom easy to divide large state enterprises into small units for separate sale. The valuation of such assets was far more vulnerable to uncertainties about prices and government policies than was generally the case with a shop or a café. As a result of all these considerations the sale of large state industrial enterprises was not easily achieved anywhere in the former Communist bloc.

Privatization policy in Russia was developed mainly by the deputy premier responsible for privatization, Anatoly Chubays. His aim was to achieve rapid large-scale privatization on the basis of the free issue of privatization vouchers to the entire population. He argued that this would finally detach the enterprises concerned from state control and protection, and help to create a new property-owning class that would resist any moves in the direction of the old order. Chubays was well aware of the risks of worker ownership, but saw no politically feasible alternative for securing a rapid change in property rights for a large section of the economy. He contended that disposal mainly to workers at the outset could be followed by a rapid restructuring of ownership through subsequent share-trading, and that any attempt by the Government to dispose of shares to outsiders would be resisted by both management and workers alike.

The vouchers had a nominal value of 10,000 roubles but could be freely bought and sold at whatever price they would fetch. Medium and large state companies (defined as enterprises employing more than 200 people or with capital assets with a July 1991 book value of 1m. roubles or more) could be privatized, under Russian legislation, in one of several prescribed ways. All the variants provided the opportunity for at least a 50% equity stake being acquired by the enterprise's own managers and workers on favourable terms. The most popular variant, giving at least a 51% insider stake, was chosen by the great majority of the enterprises embarking on the process in 1992–93. A further share of 30% of the equity could be sold for vouchers at auctions, but not on favourable terms.

By the end of April 1993, more than 1,500 medium and large enterprises had been formally privatized, and perhaps 10% of the stock of vouchers issued had been used to acquire shares. This was a relatively rapid start to the process. The total of available medium and large enterprises was said to amount to 26,000 although the process had only started in mid-1992. Moreover, some 3,000 out of 450,000 state retail and catering outlets had been sold by June 1993. Some 28% of retail sales in the first five months of 1993 were reported to be from private outlets, presumably from new private retail outlets plus the 7% of state outlets that had been privatized by that time.

In general, therefore, formal privatization in Russia had developed quite rapidly in a short time. There were, however, considerable doubts about the nature of the privatization process in the industrial sector. In particular, it did not appear to be changing enterprise behaviour patterns or leading to a purposeful reorganization of the internal structure of the enterprises concerned. One reason for this was that state enterprises had not undergone a phase of commercialization beforehand, in which they would have had to adjust to 'hard' budget constraints. Instead, they had been operating in what was still a 'soft' financial environment, in which subsidies could still be obtained, and pressures to adapt to competition and customers' choice were weak. In most cases, the management wanted to preserve this situation. The second reason was that the preferential arrangements for workers and managers to gain control of their own enterprises gave them the chance to avoid real change. Studies of enterprises undergoing privatization found that the main force in insider privatization was the desire to defend 'the collective' against other owners, who might cut jobs and impose tougher terms on both labour and management.

These studies also found that there was some readiness on the part of the new worker-owners and manager-owners to dismiss some of the existing work-force. This readiness, however, seemed to come from the widespread perception that there were easily identifiable drunkards and shirkers in the work-force, whose departure would not be regretted by the majority of their colleagues. The notion of restructuring and large-scale reductions in the work-force was much less acceptable.

Newly privatized enterprises rarely established the marketing and finance departments they would need in a market economy. The management team generally remained unchanged. In mid-1993, however, some instances could be found of outside investors trying to gain control of a number of privatized firms. In the medium term, improved performance by these firms could be expected only if certain conditions were met: stricter monetary control, producing a stable currency and rigid budgetary constraints for most firms; the development of a capital market on which shares could by exchanged freely; and an active and successful anti-monopoly policy.

AGRICULTURE

State and collective farms had played their part in the downfall of the Soviet regime. The stagnation of Soviet agricultural output after 1978 was a significant factor in the general deterioration of morale in the USSR towards the end of Leonid Brezhnev's rule. Until that time, farm output had grown substantially since the death of Stalin (Iosif V. Dzhugashvili) in 1953. This, together with a new readiness to import grain when domestic supplies were low, had allowed a general improvement in the diet of Soviet citizens. The 25-year growth in Soviet agriculture had, admittedly, been secured by massive inputs of capital and additional land; labour productivity at the end of this period was still pitifully low by Western European standards. Nevertheless, the Soviet consumer had experienced a sustained improvement in food supplies. The end of that improvement, during the early 1980s, resulted in an absolute decline in food consumption per head. Retail food prices were kept artificially low while costs rose and availability in many cities fell. Local food rationing was widespread in 1981–84.

Despite the seriousness of the problem, the approach to agricultural reform in the USSR was notoriously more cautious and less effective than in the People's Republic of China. In China, from the late 1970s, agricultural land was effectively reprivatized and peasant farming was allowed, even encouraged, to flourish. In the USSR, on the other hand, reform, when it came, was focused on industry. In the countryside very little changed. This was all the more remarkable since Mikhail Gorbachev (who became General Secretary of the Communist Party of the Soviet Union in 1985) had spent his entire Party career in a rural area before he joined the national leadership and had entered the Politburo (the Communist Party's inner leadership group) as a specialist in agricultural policy.

The reasons for the lack of reform in agriculture seem to have been political. The Party apparatus in the countryside was, perhaps, especially resistant to change. So too, and less predictably, was the rural population in general. Opinion surveys around 1989–90 tended to find that the privatization of farmland was supported by a majority of city-dwellers, but not by a majority of rural residents. That in turn may have been connected with the characteristics of the Soviet farm labour force. For many years the agricultural sector had been given low priority. The social infrastructure in rural areas was even worse than in the cities. Pay and working conditions in most regions were less favourable and young and enterprising people had left the land in large numbers over several generations. Military service provided a special opportunity for young men to leave their home villages and not return. As a result, the farm labour force was comprised largely of older people and women. Their expectations were, typically, low and their scepticism about any government reforms was profound.

Under Gorbachev, there was a relaxation of the restrictions on the subsidiary household plots which most rural and many urban households possessed. However, the prime constituent of the agricultural sector, the giant state and collective farms, was barely affected. Some effort was made to encourage the establishment of small working groups, in some cases family-based, within these farms and to give them more independence and control over a particular piece of land or activity. However, these tentative changes were implemented *pro forma*, not seriously. They had no discernible effect.

Russia inherited about 26,000 Soviet state and collective farms. Some 11m. people were employed on them, an average of over 400 per farm. Some experiments during Gorbachev's leadership had shown that a few peasant families, working on their own and appropriately motivated, could easily outperform these giant farms in the livestock sector. So far as crop production was concerned, the advantage of a much smaller size was less obvious, but there was little doubt that efficient large farms would employ far fewer people than were currently working on Russian state and collective farms.

The Russian Government's policy, announced in December 1991, was to require all state and collective farms to hold meetings of their employees in early 1992, at which decisions would be taken on the future form of organization of the farm. In this way, the most radical and politically provocative option, namely, enforcing the disbandment of these 'socialized' farms, was avoided. By the end of the year over three-quarters of the farms had taken their decision and been re-registered. About one-third of those re-registered, some 7,000 farms, had opted to keep their previous status as a collective or a state farm. Another 9,000 had elected to be registered as companies and 1,700 as farm co-operatives. Exactly what most of the changes of status really signified was unclear. In many cases they signified very little.

It was officially reported that only one in five peasants in the re-registered farms had proceeded to transform their 'share' in the original collective into an independent peasant farm. The reallocation of land to facilitate the creation of private farms was the responsibility either of the former state- or collective-farm management or of the local council. Both were usually traditionalist in orientation, and did little to help the new independent farmers. For similar reasons, supplies of machinery, fertilizer, seed, etc., for the new private sector were problematic.

One fundamental problem was that property rights to land were not radically reformed. Under certain circumstances households could acquire legal title to plots of land but the Russian parliament resisted legislation which would have allowed the free buying and selling of plots of land, whether farm land or urban sites. Therefore, where private farms were established, the right of the owners to sell the land was limited, as was the ability to purchase additional land. In October 1993, however, following his dissolution of parliament, Yeltsin issued a decree suspending restrictions on the transfer of private land. Moreover, on 10 March 1994 Viktor Chernomyrdin, the Russian premier, announced that all collective farms would be disbanded and ordered the nation-wide implementation of a process of land reform, by which all land and machinery owned by collective farms was to be sold, but the farms' employees were to combine their plots in order to form sizeable private farms.

In early 1993 there were 184,000 peasant farms, occupying some 3%–4% of Russian farmland. At the same time, the long-established household subsidiary plots were being increased in size and various pre-existing 'orchard-and-garden' associations in urban areas were also being encouraged. This combination of private farming and horticulture was devoted mainly to subsistence production for the households which worked the plots of land in question. It was important because its contribution to the nation's food consumption was substantial. However, as a source of supplies to Russian shops and markets, it was still relatively small.

In the short term, the administrative problems encountered by the new private farms were less important than the deteriorating terms of trade which confronted the entire farm sector. It was estimated that in the course of 1992 the prices of farm inputs of machinery, fertilizer, fuel, etc., increased by 20 times, while purchase prices for farm produce rose only 10.6 times. This decline in the ratio of output prices to input prices was owing partly to governmental decisions (the state remained a major purchaser of agricultural output) and partly to the fact that industrial suppliers of the agricultural sector had greater monopoly power than the farms had. One result of this was the further rapid growth of state subsidies to agriculture. In 1992 these totalled 542,000m. roubles, or 3.6% of GDP. Another result was the steep decline in farm purchases of machinery and other inputs (see above). A less obvious but, nonetheless, important development was that the linking of state subsidies to deliveries to state procurement retarded the growth of private food distribution channels.

Despite all these complications, officially recorded agricultural output fell by only 8% between 1991 and 1992, which was less than the decline in either GDP or industrial production. The reduction in agricultural output was concentrated in the livestock sector, where partially controlled prices were less favourable than for cereals and vegetables. It was also the case that the decline in many households' purchasing power produced a shift in the composition of retail food buying away from meat and milk and towards bread and potatoes.

The privatization of the farm and agricultural distribution sectors continued in 1992–93. The 'old' agricultural private sector, the household subsidiary plots, was less affected by the various difficulties than the large farms. Russian government estimates put the share of household plots in total agricultural output in 1992 at about one-third. At the same time, despite the linking of subsidies to state deliveries, direct sales by producers through private distribution channels continued to increase. Some two-fifths of the potatoes produced in 1992 were sold outside the state procurement system, and 25% of green vegetables, compared with 24% and 11%, respectively, in 1991.

Other institutional changes in food trading included the introduction of sugar-futures contracts on the Moscow Commodity Exchange in January 1993. The first such contract was for deliveries from the Kursk region. It was planned to develop futures contracts further in 1993.

In general, in 1992–93 food production in Russia seemed to be relatively resilient in the midst of pervasive economic turmoil. However, longer-term reform was impeded, above all, by the impasse between the Government and parliament over private property rights in land. President Boris Yeltsin and the economic reformers tried in 1993 to end this impasse, along with the whole political stalemate, by incorporating full private property rights to land in the presidential draft Constitution. The issue of land ownership had assumed a prominent position in the conflict between the old order and the new in Russia.

FOREIGN TRADE AND PAYMENTS

For Russia, the meaning of the words 'foreign trade' became ambiguous when the USSR disintegrated at the end of 1991. After that, by convention, Russia's trade outside the former USSR was treated as 'foreign', and transactions with other ex-Soviet Republics were treated as a special category. This is reasonable. Inter-republican transactions continued throughout 1992 to possess some of the characteristics of domestic trade. The former USSR was a single currency area for part of the year and most former Republics continued to use the same cash roubles as Russia throughout the year. The 'rouble zone' contracted, however, and there ceased to be a single currency area in the full sense. In July 1993 Russia effectively ended the rouble zone by the withdrawal of pre-1993 currency. By the beginning of 1994 only the regime in Tajikistan had entered a new rouble zone; in April Belarus also agreed to do so, although Russian conditions were still being condemned as too onerous in March. Nevertheless, the paucity of border controls and the prevalence of barter and cash transactions in roubles across the borders of former Soviet Republics made the remnants of the old inter-republican trade a rather different business from trade outside the former USSR.

Russia's foreign trade cannot, however, be considered in complete isolation from Russia's trade with other former Soviet Republics. There are three reasons for this. First, the Russian balance of payments is affected by the treatment of the inherited Soviet debt. If Russia is assumed to be responsible for all the ex-Soviet debt, interest and principal repayments due on 100% of that debt have to be included; if not, only 61% of the debt has to be allowed for in this way. In the first case, Russia would be aiming to obtain resource transfers from the other ex-Soviet Republics which would offset 'their' element in the debt-service burden. Secondly, some transactions between the successor states were being settled in convertible ('hard') currency, which had an impact on Russian international reserves. Thirdly, the distinctions between Russian exports which were delivered across the territories of other Republics and items which were apparently sold to buyers in the other Republics and then re-exported, or simply sold to other Republics, were far from clear. Deliveries of petroleum and natural gas through pipelines across Ukraine and Belarus should fall in the first category. Metals bought by firms in the Baltic states and then re-sold with little or no processing would not present a great difference in substance, but were often reported merely as sales to, for example, Latvia.

As officially recorded, at all events, Russia's foreign trade fell steeply in 1990–93. Merchandise exports to all non-Soviet partners amounted to US $81,000m. in 1990, $53,000m. in 1991, $40,000m. in 1992 ($38,000m. according to some Russian official sources) and approximately $7,000m. in the first quarter of 1993. Imports fell even more steeply, so the merchandise balance changed from a deficit of $2,000m. in 1990 to a surplus of $3,100m. in 1992 and of slightly more than this in January–March 1993. International Monetary Fund (IMF) figures for merchandise imports differ slightly, however, recording a trade surplus of $8,700m. in 1991 and $4,200m. in 1992.

The change in trade balances suggests a strengthening of Russia's external finances, albeit at a high cost in domestic supplies of goods foregone. In fact, the external financial position was as weak in 1993 as it was in 1991, if not weaker. In 1992 Russia's balance on service transactions was marginally negative, net interest payments due were approximately $5,000m., capital repayments due were about $12,000m., and net foreign direct investment was reckoned by the Russian authorities to be only $100m. The Russian authorities also estimated that $5,000m. were deposited in foreign bank accounts (most of it illegally) and that there was a further 'outflow' in the form of a negative errors and omissions item of approximately the same amount. The flow of capital from Russia, which other sources estimated at between $8,000m. and $13,000m. in 1992, may be very roughly represented by this total of $10,000m.

The net result of these flows would have been a fall of about $32,000m. in Russia's reserves if there had been no assistance from the West and if Russia had had $32,000m. of reserves to lose. What happened, according to the Russian official version of events, was that Russia accepted Western bilateral credits (mostly official export credits) worth $10,800m. and $1,000m. of an IMF stand-by loan. It also benefited from agreements with Western Governments and banks to defer $19,000m. of debt-service due.

There were many problems with these or any other data concerning Russia's external finances. It was obvious, however, that Russia was unable to meet its international payments. Even with substantial flows of Western assistance, arrears of trade payments continued in 1992–93 to worry Western firms trading with Russia. The inconvertible rouble, rapid domestic inflation and the unreliability of many Russian trade partners all acted as deterrents to Western direct investment in Russia and, to some extent, even to regular trading. The steep fall in imports and the shift to a 'favourable' trade balance in 1992–93 had to be seen against this background.

Russian trade was changing substantially both in the composition of commodities and the composition of its trading partners. As in so much else, the information available was too poor to allow precise conclusions to be drawn, but the broad changes in trade patterns were clear. Russian trade with Eastern Europe fell to only 18% of total Russian foreign trade turnover in 1992, according to the Russian State Statistics Committee. (Data from the Ministry of Foreign Economic Relations were slightly different.) Trade with the developed countries of the West had risen to 62% of the greatly reduced total and the remainder was with China and the developing world. The decline in trade with Eastern Europe was partly the result of the disintegration of the old Council of Mutual Economic Assistance (CMEA) in 1990–91. Russian trade with Eastern Europe was beginning to operate in terms of world prices and hard-currency settlements. Therefore, the relative attractiveness of the old Eastern bloc trade was greatly reduced.

Russia continued to be dependent on fuel and raw materials as staple export earners. Petroleum, petroleum products, natural gas and coal provided approximately one-half of 1992 hard-currency earnings. Fuel and raw materials in total accounted for just over 80%. Arms exports fell sharply, in spite of the efforts of Russian arms producers. New strategic export-control machinery was introduced. The fall in arms sales, however, probably owed more to unplanned production declines and Russia's new image as an unreliable source of spare parts and follow-on supplies.

In general, the rates of delivery of particular export items were highly unpredictable. The fluctuations were caused both by production cuts enforced by supply problems and by the Russian Government's constant adjustment of trade regulations and incentives. Export licensing, quotas and taxes were widely but inconsistently used. The fact that the Government sought to limit exports was a reflection of the continued shortages and instability arising from domestic price controls. In particular, owing to the control of domestic energy prices throughout 1992, it was vastly more profitable for producers to export than to supply the domestic market. This distortion was compounded by the

Government's ceaseless variation of the rules of trade. The rates and coverage of export duties, for example, were substantially changed five times in the first five months of 1992. Compulsory conversion of one-half of an exporter's convertible-currency earnings into roubles stimulated the illegal depositing of hard currency abroad. Conversion into roubles, after all, meant an enforced exchange into a rapidly depreciating currency. This measure was modified in July 1993 so as to be less damaging to exporters, but the impediments to normal export activity remained considerable.

Imports were severely restricted by Russia's limited ability to pay. Much depended on the availability of Western credits (usually tied to particular Western nations' suppliers and to particular product groups). Grain imports, at a total of 29.5m. metric tons, were almost two-fifths higher than in 1991. Hard-currency imports of medicines remained high, at over US $1,000m., partly because of the curtailment of past Eastern European sources of supply on soft terms. Machinery imports decreased slightly, although at $13,500m. they remained remarkably high in view of the collapse of domestic investment.

The atmosphere of chaos and decline was unhealthy for Western commercial investment in Russia. Admittedly, the numbers of foreign firms and joint ventures registered in Russia continued to rise, reaching 3,106 at the end of 1992. However, the rate of increase was slowing and the average size of the initial capital was falling. The sales of foreign firms and joint ventures on the Russian market fell in real terms, with the volume of their sales for roubles falling twice as fast as national income. Their exports, on the other hand, grew rapidly as they expanded their activities in petroleum trading and other fuel and raw material exports.

Had it been possible to stabilize the rouble and make it freely convertible the outcome of foreign trade in Russia would have been very different. As it was, the rouble was endowed with a limited internal convertibility by the merging of the Central Bank and black-market exchange rates in July 1992. The rate of exchange was left to float, with the Moscow Inter-Bank Currency Exchange providing the main market. This was a very narrow market, on which the exchange rate bore no relationship whatever to the domestic purchasing power of the rouble, except that both decreased rapidly. Beginning at around 100 roubles to the dollar in mid-1992, the rouble sank to 450 at the end of the year and to 1,100 in June 1993. In June–July 1993 it recovered slightly, reaching about 1,000 in late July. At this point, the volume of currency-market transactions had risen to an annual rate of approximately US $8,000m., so the market was no longer a marginal one. This was helped by the withdrawal of all rouble notes printed between 1961 and 1992, announced by the Central Bank on 24 July 1993. Making only 1993 notes legal tender (in most cases) caused considerable controversy, but was part of an attempt to control monetary policy more strictly.

BUDGET AND FINANCES

Austere fiscal and monetary policies are the banal but unavoidable prescription for dealing with a rise in consumer prices. In 1991–93 Russian policy-makers failed to follow the prescription. This failure in stabilization, though neither complete nor irredeemable, was of the greatest significance. The control of inflation is desirable in all circumstances. When government and people are trying to move from a centrally administered to a market economy, however, it is vital. The currency has to be reasonably stable if the institutions of a market economy are to be established and to function properly. The initial freeing of previously controlled prices usually means a sudden increase in the price level. This increase can easily turn into a continuing upward trend if strong action is not taken to prevent an escalating, or 'spiralling', increase in prices and wages. If inflation remains out of control investment is deterred, hard currency flows abroad and there is a risk of hyperinflation, causing a complete breakdown of monetary transactions.

Russia avoided hyperinflation in 1991–93 but the rate of growth of consumer prices remained high. The immediate causes, themselves closely related, were a large budget deficit and an excessive expansion of credit. According to the Russian Ministry of Finance, the consolidated (federal plus local) budget revenue in 1992 was 5,330,000m. roubles and expenditure was 5,970,000m. This apparently signified a budget deficit of only 4% in a GDP of 15,000,000m. roubles. The data, however, were again extremely doubtful. There existed various extra-budgetary funds that were not included (though several of these should have been in surplus). More important was the measurement of expenditure by actual disbursement rather than by expenditure commitments, so that failures to service debt, for instance, were not included as they would be in standard international practice. IMF economists and other knowledgeable observers calculated that the 'true' deficit, on an internationally comparable basis, was a great deal larger. Some of the true budget deficit had no immediate inflationary impact on the domestic economy because it was financed by foreign credits. However, these would have to be repaid.

Another part of the deficit might have been funded by the issue of government securities without increasing the money supply; but the absence of capital markets meant that such instruments of policy were not available. In May 1993, however, a small start was made in this direction when a trial issue of three-month government bills was made. The issue was successfully taken up but the scale of the operation was small and the inflationary environment precluded the issue of longer-term securities for the time being.

The net result was that a substantial amount of the budget deficit could only be covered by expanding the money supply. The Russian Central Bank in fact expanded credit in 1992 by 6,100,000m. roubles. Only 1,260,000m. roubles of this was lent to the Government to finance budgetary expenditure. It was widely argued, therefore, that the credits to state enterprises (3,300,000m. roubles) and to other ex-Soviet Republics (1,500,000m. roubles) were the result of irresponsible inflationary activity on the part of the Central Bank, and were not to be blamed on the Government. This was plausible, as the Central Bank was answerable to the traditionalist parliament rather than to the Government, and because its Chairman from mid-1992, Viktor Gerashchenko, was a member of the old, Soviet-era establishment. The reality, however, was not so simple. The Central Bank of the Russian Federation under Gerashchenko certainly did not pursue a tough anti-inflationary policy. However, a large part of the credits going from the Bank through the commercial banks to enterprises (at interest rates of one-tenth of the rate of inflation) was apparently initiated by the Government. Central Bank economists argued that these credits were really a disguised budget subsidy: if they had been presented as such, the counterpart would have been a much larger volume of bank lending to the Government to cover a larger deficit. The precise merits of the case are not clear. What is clear is that the Government itself in 1992–93 was divided over the permissible extent of subsidization, and that subsidies of one sort or another remained extremely high. At the same time, budgetary spending was in excess of revenue on any reckoning, in part because of weaknesses in tax collection.

More than two-thirds of 1992 budget revenue came from a value added tax at the high rate of 28%, plus a profits tax. Those who had to pay complained of the high rates involved, but many enterprises, especially in the new private sector, were able to evade taxes. The development of an efficient tax and customs service was bound to take time. Meanwhile, corruption and tax evasion were endemic. The soft-money inclinations of the Russian Central Bank leadership did not help. They were compounded by a weak commercial banking sector: there were about 2,000 commercial banks at mid-1993, most of them lacking basic banking skills and laden with bad debt to practically bankrupt state enterprises. Only a handful of these banks were reckoned to be operating in an internationally acceptable fashion. Indeed, the books of the Central Bank itself were found by Western auditors in 1993 to be highly unsatisfactory, with substantial sums unaccounted for.

In 1993 a major effort to renew the fight against inflation was made by Boris Fedorov. He had been appointed finance minister in December 1992 and became, in effect, the leader of the reformers in the Government after the enforced resignation of Yegor Gaidar. In May he secured an agreement with the Central Bank on a gradual reduction of the growth of the money supply. The extension of automatic credits to other ex-Soviet Republics was meanwhile being curbed and Fedorov also appeared to have some success in reducing credits to Russian enterprises. The monthly inflation rate, having risen almost to 30% at the end of 1992, was down to 17% in June 1993. The stabilization of the rouble exchange rate in June–July reflected the resulting improvement in inflationary expectations. The withdrawal of pre-rouble notes also enabled the authorities henceforth to maintain stricter control over monetary emissions. This was reinforced by the signs of success in the privatization programme, which encouraged holders of foreign currency to convert some of their holdings into roubles in order to buy shares in privatized enterprises. The parliament and the Central Bank, however, employed a variety of spoiling tactics in July, which cast doubt upon the durability of the recent stabilization. The disbanding of the old legislature and the reinforcement of presidential powers in the 1993 Constitution did, however, reduce the obstacles to reform. However, the election of another conservative parliament, notably the State Duma (the lower house of the Federal Assembly), seemed to encourage the restraint of reform. The most serious casualty of the government reorganization of early 1994 was Fedorov, who was dismissed.

PROBLEMS AND PROSPECTS

Economic change in Russia was partly change from below. By mid-1993 this was proceeding fairly rapidly with the creation of new firms, banks and other commercial organizations. It would be halted only by a clear shift in political power to an authoritarian and anti-Western regime. But it was not enough by itself to turn Russia into a properly functioning market economy with low inflation and growing output. Part of the process of change necessarily comes from above, with legislation on property rights, control of the money supply, the removal of the remaining administrative impediments to free commerce, the provision of effective state machinery (such as tax collection) to support the functioning of the market economy and some degree of state management of the process of privatization. This element of change from above was impeded in Russia by political incoherence. In mid-1993, as throughout Russia's short life as a post-Communist state, the political strength of the reformers was limited. This situation was only marginally improved by a new Constitution and general elections in December 1993. As a result, reform measures were constantly moderated or undermined. The transforming of ex-Communist economies encountered resistance throughout Eastern Europe and the former USSR. However, a clear reform consensus amongst most of the politically active part of the population and a reform-minded Government with the impetus of a clear mandate for change, and no fundamental challenge to its right to govern, made a difference. This was evident in the early 1990s in the Czech Republic, Estonia, Hungary, Latvia, Poland and Slovenia. It was not the case in Russia and seemed unlikely to become the case in 1993–94.

Until its dissolution in September–October 1993, the old Soviet-era Congress of People's Deputies and its standing Supreme Soviet were not proponents of reform and there was a sufficient conservative majority to act as a major hindrance to liberalization of the economy. Its opposition to Yeltsin derived strength from the unclear delineation of powers between legislative and executive authorities causing the so-called 'war of laws', a conflict of jurisdiction. Two other elements in the political situation were especially debilitating, so far as the development of a functioning market economy was concerned. One was the fact that the Government itself was divided, with centrists holding key positions within it (they were strengthened by the strong support for centrists and the right-wing in the December 1993 elections). The other was that the 89 administrative councils in the federal territories were, in almost all cases, more traditionalist than modernizing. In 1992–93 the issue of the Federation became a dominant one. Yeltsin had tried to counter the territories' traditionalism by appointing local governors of a more reformist cast, but his ability to impose his preferences even on them was limited. Moreover, Russia had its own nationality problem, which was far less acute than that of the old USSR but still troublesome. Twenty-one of the administrative territories were formally republics, the identity of which was based on a territorial connection with a non-Russian nationality. Some had pursued greater autonomy on quasi-nationalist grounds. Still other territories had rich endowments of natural resources which they considered were being exploited by the central authorities to their disadvantage. Moreover, all of the territories had real grievances over the division of budget revenues and expenditure responsibilities between themselves and the centre.

In his efforts to outmanoeuvre the old parliament and establish a new Constitution, Boris Yeltsin tried in 1993 to use the federal territories against the parliament. This promoted a competitive advancing of demands against the centre on the part of the various territories. Even with the introduction of a new Constitution and Federation Treaty, and in spite of a strengthened presidency, at the beginning of 1994 the forces opposed to reform seemed likely to be able to hinder the implementation of a thorough restructuring of the economy for some time into the future. The political legitimacy needed to impose financial stabilization seemed to be lacking. However, a credible stabilization of the rouble was required to encourage a return flow of hard currency from abroad, a stimulation of investment and the reduction of the pervasive corruption and law-breaking which impeded most business. In the short term high inflation and stagnant or declining output were therefore likely. In the longer term, however, the impetus towards an effective market economy would be hard to resist.

Statistical Survey

Sources (unless otherwise indicated): State Committee of Statistics of the USSR; State Committee of Statistics of the Russian Federation, 103616 Moscow, Maly Cherkassky per. 2/6; tel. (095) 921-47-68; fax (095) 921-39-65.

Area and Population

AREA, POPULATION AND DENSITY

Area (sq km)	17,075,400*
Population (census result) 12 January 1989	147,400,537†
Population (official estimate at 1 January) 1991	148,485,000
Density (per sq km) at 1 January 1991	8.7

* 6,592,812 sq miles.
† The *de jure* population was 147,021,869 (males 68,713,869; females 78,308,000).

REPUBLICS WITHIN THE FEDERATION
(census of 12 January 1989)

Republic	Area (sq km)	Population ('000)	Capital (with population, '000)
Adygheya*	7,600	432	Maikop (149)
Altay*	92,600	192	Gorno-Altaysk (40‡)
Bashkortostan	143,600	3,952	Ufa (1,083)
Buryatia	351,300	1,042	Ulan-Ude (353)
Chechen Republic-Ichkeria†	n.a.	n.a.	Grozny (401)
Chuvashia	18,300	1,336	Cheboksary (420)
Daghestan	50,300	1,792	Makhachkala (315)
Ingushetia†	n.a.	n.a.	Nazran (n.a.)
Kabardin-Balkaria	12,500	760	Nalchik (235)
Kalmykia	75,900	322	Elista (120)
Karachay-Cherkessia*	14,100	418	Cherkessk (113)
Karelia	172,400	792	Petrozavodsk (270)
Khakassia	61,900	569	Abakan (153)
Komi	415,900	1,263	Syktyvkar (233)
Mari-El	23,300	750	Yoshkar-Ola (242)
Mordovia	26,200	964	Saransk (312)
North Ossetia	8,000	634	Vladikavkaz (300)
Sakha (Yakutia)	3,103,200	1,081	Yakutsk (187)
Tatarstan	68,000	3,640	Kazan (1,094)
Tyva	170,500	309	Kyzyl (n.a.)
Udmurt Republic	42,100	1,609	Izhevsk (635)

* Under the terms of the 1992 Federation Treaty, these former autonomous oblasts (regions) were granted the status of republic.
† Until 1992 the territories of the Republic of Chechnya and the Ingush Republic were combined in the Chechen-Ingush autonomous republic.
‡ At 1 January 1976.

PRINCIPAL TOWNS
(estimated population, in '000, at 1 January 1990)

Moskva (Moscow, the capital)	8,801	Astrakhan	510
Sankt Peterburg (St Petersburg)*	4,468	Naberezhnye Chelny*	507
Nizhny Novgorod*	1,443	Tomsk	506
Novosibirsk	1,443	Tyumen	487
Yekaterinburg*	1,367	Viyatka*	487
Samara*	1,258	Ivanovo	482
Omsk	1,159	Murmansk	472
Chelyabinsk	1,148	Bryansk	456
Kazan	1,103	Lipetsk	455
Perm	1,094	Tver*	454
Ufa	1,094	Magnitogorsk	443
Rostov-na-Donu	1,025	Nizhny Tagil	440
Volgograd	1,005	Kursk	430
Krasnoyarsk	922	Cheboksary	429
Saratov	909	Arkhangelsk	419
Voronezh	895	Kaliningrad	406
Vladivostok	643	Grozny	401
Izhevsk*	642	Chita	372
Tolyatti	642	Kurgan	360
Simbirsk*	638	Ulan-Ude	359
Yaroslavl	636	Vladimir	353
Irkutsk	635	Smolensk	346
Krasnodar	627	Orel	342
Khabarovsk	608	Sochi	339
Barnaul	603	Makhachkala	327
Novokuznetsk	601	Stavropol	324
Orenburg	552	Komsomolsk-na-Amure	318
Penza	548	Saransk	316
Tula	543	Kaluga	314
Ryazan	522	Cherepovets	313
Kemerovo	521	Tambov	307
		Belgorod	306
		Vladikavkaz*	303

* Some towns that were renamed during the Soviet period have reverted to their former names: St Petersburg (Leningrad); Nizhny Novgorod (Gorky); Yekaterinburg (Sverdlovsk); Samara (Kuybyshev); Izhevsk (Ustinov); Simbirsk (Ulyanovsk); Naberezhnye Chelny (Brezhnev); Viyatka (Kirov); Tver (Kalinin); Vladikavkaz (Ordzhonikidze).

BIRTHS AND DEATHS (per '000)

	1982	1983	1984
Birth rate	18.9	20.1	16.9
Death rate	10.1	10.3	11.6

1989: Registered live births 2,160,559 (birth rate 14.6 per 1,000); Registered deaths 1,583,743 (death rate 10.7 per 1,000).

EMPLOYMENT (annual averages, '000 employees)

	1988	1989	1990
Agriculture and forestry	10,122	10,073	9,967
Industry and construction	31,940	32,322	31,836
Transport and communications	6,298	5,938	5,876
Trade and other material services	6,073	5,938	5,876
Science, education, culture and arts, health care and social security	14,245	14,507	14,505
Government and finance	1,799	1,729	1,711
Other non-material services	4,499	4,660	4,612
Total	74,976	75,168	74,382

1989 census ('000 persons aged 15 years and over): Total labour force 77,283 (males 39,767; females 37,516).

Agriculture

PRINCIPAL CROPS ('000 metric tons)

	1990	1991	1992
Wheat	49,596	38,899	46,000*
Rice	896	773	800†
Barley	27,235	22,174	25,500†
Maize	2,451	1,969	2,100†
Rye	16,431	10,639	13,900†
Oats	12,326	10,372	11,500†
Millet	1,946	1,041	1,500†
Potatoes	30,848	34,329	37,800
Peas, dry	4,321	2,039	3,800†
Soybeans	717	622	500
Sunflower seed	3,427	2,896	3,070
Rapeseed*	246	327	189
Vegetables	2,997	2,747	2,723
Grapes	612	543	520†
Sugar beets	32,327	24,280	25,500

* Unofficial figure(s). † FAO estimate(s).
Source: FAO, *Production Yearbook*.

LIVESTOCK
('000 head at 1 January, unless otherwise indicated)

	1990	1991	1992
Horses	2,620	2,618	2,610*
Cattle	58,800	57,043	54,677
Pigs	40,000	38,314	35,384
Sheep	58,400	55,200	52,535
Goats	2,900	3,000	2,765
Chickens (million)†	628	634	628
Turkeys (million)†	26	26	24

* FAO estimate(s). † Unofficial figure(s).
Source: FAO, *Production Yearbook*.

LIVESTOCK PRODUCTS ('000 metric tons)

	1990	1991	1992
Beef and veal	4,329	3,989	3,500
Mutton and lamb	390	342	280*
Pigmeat	3,480	3,190	2,700
Poultry meat	1,801	1,751	1,577†
Cows' milk	55,615	51,890	46,930
Butter	832.5	729	746
Hen eggs†	2,641	2,623	2,370
Wool:			
greasy	226.7	204.5	179
scoured	136.1	122.7	107.4

* FAO estimate(s). † Unofficial figure(s).
Source: FAO, *Production Yearbook*.

Mining

('000 metric tons, unless otherwise indicated)

	1989	1990	1991
Crude petroleum*	552,200	516,200	461,100
Coal	409,900	395,400	353,300
Natural gas (million cu m)	615,800	640,600	642,900

* Including gas condensates.

Industry

SELECTED PRODUCTS
('000 metric tons, unless otherwise indicated)

	1988	1989	1990
Granulated sugar	3,945	4,216	3,758
Margarine	809	820	833
Vegetable oil	1,080	1,127	1,159
Cigarettes (million)	170,000	162,000	151,000
Paper	5,334	5,344	5,240
Leather footwear ('000 pairs)	368,700	377,700	385,300
Crude steel	94,085	92,752	89,622
Radio receivers ('000)	4,984	5,562	5,760
Television receivers ('000)	4,370	4,465	4,717
Cameras: photographic ('000)	1,701	1,761	1,856
Watches and clocks ('000)	57,600	58,500	60,100
Domestic refrigerators and freezers ('000)	3,492	3,594	3,774
Motor cycles, scooters, etc. ('000)	828	736	765
Bicycles ('000)	3,443	3,444	3,671
Domestic washing machines ('000)	4,110	4,501	5,419
Electric energy (million kWh)	1,065,504	1,076,592	1,082,152

Finance

CURRENCY AND EXCHANGE RATES

Monetary Units

100 kopeks = 1 rubl (ruble or rouble).

Sterling and Dollar Equivalents (30 September 1993)

£1 sterling = 1,796.1 roubles;
US $1 = 1,201.0 roubles;
10,000 roubles = £5.568 = $8.326.

Average Exchange Rate (roubles per US dollar)

1989 0.6274
1990 0.5856
1991 0.5819

Note: The figures for average exchange rates refer to official rates for the Soviet rouble. However, a multiple exchange rate system was in operation, with separate non-commercial and tourist rates. A commercial exchange rate was introduced on 1 November 1990, replacing the official rate for most transactions. The commercial rate (roubles per US dollar) was: 1.692 at 31 December 1990; 1,671 at 31 December 1991. Between November 1989 and April 1991 the tourist exchange rate valued the rouble at one-tenth of the official rate. In April 1991 this rate, renamed the 'special rate', was set at $1 = 27.6 roubles. It was subsequently adjusted. Following the dissolution of the USSR in December 1991, Russia and several other former Soviet Republics retained the rouble as their monetary unit. On 24 July 1993 the Central Bank of the Russian Federation (CBRF) announced that all rouble notes issued between 1961 and 1992 were to be withdrawn from circulation. No other country was issued with the 1993 notes until January 1994, when Tajikistan joined the new 'rouble zone' and surrendered control of its monetary policy to the CBRF. In April Belarus agreed likewise.

COST OF LIVING
(Consumer price index; base 1985 = 100)

	1989	1990	1991
All items*	110	116	222

* Weighted average of prices in the state and co-operative sector and prices on *kolkhoz* (collective farm) markets.

NATIONAL ACCOUNTS (million roubles at current prices)
Net Material Product by Economic Activity

	1988	1989	1990
Agriculture and forestry	72,000	77,500	88,475
Industry	171,600	183,600	187,621
Construction	50,400	53,500	56,464
Transport and communications	25,400	24,100	30,677
Other material services	66,000	74,000	81,362
Total	385,400	412,700	444,600

BALANCE OF PAYMENTS
External Transactions (US $ million)

	1991	1992
Merchandise exports f.o.b.	53,200	41,100
Merchandise imports f.o.b.	−44,500	−36,900
Trade balance	8,700	4,200
Services (net)	−2,400	−4,000
Income (net)	−2,200	−4,500
Unrequited transfers (net)	1,600	3,000
Current balance	5,700	−1,300
Direct investment (net)	−100	700
Other capital (net)	2,100	−3,700
Net errors and omissions	−1,800	−8,402
Overall balance	5,900	−12,702

Inter-republican Transactions ('000 million roubles): *1991:* Merchandise exports f.o.b. 135, Merchandise imports f.o.b. −103, Trade balance 32. *1992:* Merchandise exports f.o.b. 2,147, Merchandise imports f.o.b. −1,849, Trade balance 298; Current balance 298; Other capital (net) 264; Net errors and omissions 465; Overall balance 1,027.

Source: IMF, *International Financial Statistics: Supplement on Countries of the Former Soviet Union.*

External Trade

PRINCIPAL COMMODITIES
(million roubles, including trade with other former Republics of the USSR)

Imports f.o.b.	1989	1990
Petroleum and natural gas	2,216	2,546
Iron and steel	8,271	7,137
Non-ferrous metals	3,243	2,936
Chemicals and products	12,082	10,621
Machine-building industry	48,094	51,577
Wood and paper products	2,059	2,122
Light industry	28,367	29,149
Food industry	23,718	23,823
Agricultural products (unprocessed)	9,208	6,188
Total (incl. others)	144,267	142,563
Inter-republican	70,668	67,284
Foreign	73,599	75,280

Exports f.o.b.	1989	1990
Petroleum and natural gas	18,046	15,652
Iron and steel	7,450	7,364
Non-ferrous metals	5,103	5,134
Chemicals and products	11,515	11,316
Machine-building industry	37,997	37,361
Wood and paper products	7,635	6,837
Light industry	8,180	8,654
Food industry	4,072	4,093
Total (incl. others)	109,607	106,795
Inter-republican	75,067	74,710
Foreign	34,540	32,084

Communications Media

	1988	1989	1990
Books published (number of titles)*	49,603	46,023	41,234
Newspapers: titles	4,696	4,772	4,808
Annual circulation (million copies)	37,108	38,250	37,849
Periodicals: titles†	4,060	3,781	3,681
Annual circulation (million copies)	3,462.1	4,264.9	5,010.2

* Including books and pamphlets.
† Including weekly newspapers.

Education

(1990/91)

	Institutions	Students
Secondary schools	69,600	20,900,000
Secondary specialized institutions	2,603	2,270,000
Higher schools (incl. universities)	514	2,824,500

Directory

The Constitution

The current Constitution of the Russian Federation came into force on 12 December 1993, following its approval by a majority of participants in a nation-wide plebiscite. It replaced the Constitution (Fundamental Law) originally passed on 12 April 1978 but amended many times after 1990.

THE PRINCIPLES OF THE CONSTITUTIONAL SYSTEM

Chapter One of Section One declares that the Russian Federation (Russia) is a democratic, federative, law-based state with a republican form of Government. Its multi-ethnic people bear its sovereignty and are the sole source of authority. State power in the Russian Federation is divided between the legislative, executive and judicial branches, which are independent from one another. Ideological pluralism and a multi-party political system are recognized. The Russian Federation is a secular state and all religious associations are equal before the law. All laws are made public and in accordance with universally acknowledged principles and with international law.

HUMAN AND CIVIL RIGHTS AND FREEDOMS

Chapter Two states that the basic human rights and freedoms of the Russian citizen are guaranteed regardless of sex, race, nationality or religion. It declares the right to life and to freedom and personal inviolability. The principles of freedom of movement, freedom of expression and freedom of conscience are upheld. Censorship is prohibited. Citizens are guaranteed the right to vote and stand in state and local elections and to participate in referendums. Individuals are to have equal access to state employment and the establishment of trade unions and public associations is permitted. The Constitution commits the State to protection of motherhood and childhood and to granting social security, state pensions and social benefits. Each person has the right to housing. Health care and education are free of charge. Basic general education is compulsory. Citizens are guaranteed the right to receive qualified legal assistance. Payment of statutory taxes and levies is obligatory, as is military service.

THE ORGANIZATION OF THE FEDERATION

Chapter Three names the 89 members (federal territorial units) of the Russian Federation. Russian is declared the state language, but all peoples of the Russian Federation are guaranteed the right to preserve their native tongue. The state flag, emblem and anthem of the Russian Federation are to be established by a federal constitutional law. The Constitution defines the separate roles of the authority of the Russian Federation, as distinct from that of the joint authority of the Russian Federation and the members of the Russian Federation. It also establishes the relationship between federal laws, federal constitutional laws and the laws and other normative legal acts of the subjects of the Russian Federation. The powers of the federal executive bodies and the executive bodies of the members of the Russian Federation are defined.

THE PRESIDENT OF THE RUSSIAN FEDERATION

Chapter Four describes the powers and responsibilities of the head of state, the President of the Russian Federation. The President is elected to office for a term of four years by universal, direct suffrage. The same individual may be elected to the office of President for no more than two consecutive terms. The President may appoint the Chairman of the Government of the Russian Federation, with the approval of the State Duma, and may dismiss the Deputy Chairmen and the federal ministers from office. The President is entitled to chair sessions of the Government. The President's responsibilities include scheduling referendums and elections to the State Duma, dissolving the State Duma, submitting legislative proposals to the State Duma and promulgating federal laws. The President is responsible for the foreign policy of the Russian Federation. The President is Commander-in-Chief of the Armed Forces and may introduce martial law or a state of emergency under certain conditions.

If the President is unable to carry out the presidential duties, these will be assumed by the Chairman of the Government. The Acting President, however, will not possess the full powers of the President, such as the right to dissolve the State Duma or order a referendum. The President may only be removed from office by the Federation Council on the grounds of a serious accusation by the State Duma.

THE FEDERAL ASSEMBLY

Chapter Five concerns the Federal Assembly, which is the highest representative and legislative body in the Russian Federation. It consists of two chambers: the Federation Council and the State Duma. The Federation Council comprises two representatives from each member of the Russian Federation, one from its representative and one from its executive body (178 deputies in total). The State Duma is composed of 450 deputies. The State Duma is elected for a term of four years. The procedures for forming the Federation Council and for electing the State Duma are to be determined by federal legislation. The deputies of the Russian Federation must be over 21 years of age and may not hold government office or any other paid job. (Section Two of the Constitution states that the State Duma and the Federation Council of the first convocation are to be elected for a term of two years and that a deputy of the State Duma of first convocation may concurrently be a member of the Government.) The Federal Assembly is a permanently working body.

Both chambers of the Federal Assembly may elect their Chairman and Deputy Chairmen, who preside over parliamentary sessions and supervise the observance of their regulations. Each chamber adopts its code of procedure. The powers of the Federation Council include the approval of the President's decrees on martial law and a state of emergency, the scheduling of presidential elections and the impeachment of the President. The State Duma has the power to approve the President's nominee to the office of Chairman of the Government of the Russian Federation. Both chambers of the Federal Assembly adopt resolutions by a majority vote of the total number of members. All federal and federal constitutional laws are adopted by the State Duma and submitted for approval first to the Federation Council and then to the President. If the Federation Council or the President reject proposed legislation it is submitted for repeat consideration to one or both chambers of the Federal Assembly.

The State Duma may be dissolved by the President if it rejects all three candidates to the office of Chairman of the Government or adopts a second vote of 'no confidence' in the Government. However, it may not be dissolved during a period of martial law or a state of emergency or in the case of charges being lodged against the President. A newly elected State Duma should be convened no later than four months after dissolution of the previous parliament.

THE GOVERNMENT OF THE RUSSIAN FEDERATION

The executive authority of the Russian Federation is vested in the Government, which is comprised of the Chairman, the Deputy Chairmen and federal ministers. The Chairman is appointed by the President and his nomination approved by the State Duma. If the State Duma rejects three candidates to the office of Chairman, the President will appoint the Chairman, dissolve the State Duma and order new elections. The Government's responsibilities are to submit the federal budget to the State Duma and to supervise its execution, to guarantee the implementation of a uniform state policy, to carry out foreign policy and to ensure the country's defence and state security. Its duties also include the maintenance of law and order.

Regulations for the activity of the Government are to be determined by a federal constitutional law. The Government can adopt resolutions and directives, which may be vetoed by the President. The Government must submit its resignation to a newly elected President of the Russian Federation, which the President may accept or reject. A vote of no confidence in the Government may be adopted by the State Duma. The President can reject this decision or demand the Government's resignation. If the State Duma adopts a second vote of no confidence within three months, the President will announce the Government's resignation or dissolve the State Duma.

JUDICIAL POWER

Justice is administered by means of constitutional, civil, administrative and criminal judicial proceedings. Judges in the Russian Federation must be aged 25 or over, have a higher legal education and have a record of work in the legal profession of no less than five years. Judges are independent, irremovable and inviolable. Proceedings in judicial courts are open. No criminal case shall be considered in the absence of a defendant. Judicial proceedings may be conducted with the participation of a jury.

The Constitutional Court comprises 19 judges. The Court decides cases regarding the compliance of federal laws and enactments, the constitutions, statutes, laws and other enactments of the members of the Russian Federation, state treaties and international treaties which have not yet come into force. The Constitutional Court settles disputes about competence among state bodies. Enactments or their individual provisions which have been judged unconstitutional by the Court are invalid. At the request of the Federation Council, the Court will pronounce its judgment on bringing an accusation against the President of the Russian Federation.

The Supreme Court is the highest judicial authority on civil, criminal, administrative and other cases within the jurisdiction of the common plea courts. The Supreme Arbitration Court is the highest authority in settling economic and other disputes within the jurisdiction of the courts of arbitration.

The judges of the three higher courts are appointed by the Federation Council upon presentation by the President. Judges of other federal courts are appointed by the President.

The Prosecutor's Office is a single centralized system. The Prosecutor-General is appointed and dismissed by the Federation Council upon presentation by the President. All other prosecutors are appointed by the Prosecutor-General.

LOCAL SELF-GOVERNMENT

Chapter Eight provides for the exercise of local self-government through referendums, elections and through elected and other bodies. The responsibilities of local self-government bodies include: independently managing municipal property; forming, approving and executing the local budget; establishing local taxes and levies; and maintaining law and order.

CONSTITUTIONAL AMENDMENTS AND REVISION OF THE CONSTITUTION

Chapter Nine states that no provision contained in Chapters One, Two and Nine of the Constitution is to be reviewed by the Federal Assembly, while amendments to the remaining Chapters may be passed in accordance with the procedure for a federal constitutional law. If a proposal for a review of the provisions of Chapters One, Two and Nine wins a three-fifths majority in both chambers, a Constitutional Assembly will be convened.

CONCLUDING AND TRANSITIONAL PROVISIONS

Section Two states that the Constitution came into force on the day of the nation-wide vote, 12 December 1993. Should the provisions of a federal treaty contravene those of the Constitution, the constitutional provisions will apply. All laws and other legal acts enforced before the Constitution came into effect will remain valid unless they fail to comply with the Constitution. The President of the Russian Federation will carry out the presidential duties established by the Constitution until the expiry of his term of office. The Council of Ministers will acquire the rights, duties and responsibility of the Government of the Russian Federation established by the Constitution and henceforth be named the Government of the Russian Federation. The courts will administer justice in accordance with their powers established by the Constitution and retain their powers until the expiry of their term.

The Federation Council and the State Duma of first convocation will both be elected for a term of two years. A deputy of the State Duma of first convocation may also be a member of the Government. Deputies to the Federation Council of first convocation will carry out their duties on a part-time basis.

The Government

HEAD OF STATE

President of the Russian Federation: BORIS N. YELTSIN (elected President 12 June 1991).

THE GOVERNMENT
(March 1994)

Chairman: VIKTOR S. CHERNOMYRDIN.

First Deputy Chairman (responsible for investment policy and the defence industry): OLEG N. SOSKOVETS.

Deputy Chairman (responsible for agriculture and hydrometeorology): ALEKSANDR K. ZAVERYUKHA.

Deputy Chairman and Chairman of the State Committee for State Property Management): ANATOLY B. CHUBAYS.

Deputy Chairman (responsible for social policy and co-operation between the Government and representative bodies, political parties and public organizations): YURY F. YAROV.

Minister of Agriculture and Food: VIKTOR N. KHLYSTUN.

Minister of Civil Defence, Emergencies and Natural Disasters: SERGEY K. SHOYGU.

Minister of Communications: VLADIMIR B. BULGAK.

Minister of Culture: YEVGENY YU. SIDOROV.

Minister of Defence: Gen. PAVEL S. GRACHEV.

Minister of the Economy: ALEKSANDR N. SHOKHIN.

Minister of Education: YEVGENY V. TKACHENKO.

Minister of Environmental Protection and Natural Resources: VIKTOR I. DANILOV-DANILYAN.

Minister of Finance: SERGEY DUBININ (acting).

Minister of Foreign Affairs: ANDREY V. KOZYREV.

Minister of Foreign Economic Relations: OLEG D. DAVYDOV.

Minister of Fuel and Power Engineering: YURY K. SHAFRANIK.

Minister of Health and the Medical Industry: EDUARD A. NECHAYEV.

Minister of Internal Affairs: Lt-Gen. VIKTOR F. YERIN.

Minister of Justice: YURY KH. KALMYKOV.

Minister of Labour: GENNADY G. MELIKYAN.

Minister of Nationalities and Regional Policy: SERGEY M. SHAKHRAY.

Minister of Nuclear Energy: VIKTOR N. MIKHAILOV.

Minister of Railways: GENNADY M. FADEYEV.

Minister of Science and Technical Policy: BORIS G. SALTYKOV.

Minister of Social Welfare of the Population: (vacant).

Minister of Transport: VITALY B. YEFIMOV.

Chairmen of Principal State Committees

Chairman of the State Committee for Anti-Monopoly Policy and Support for New Economic Structures: LEONID A. BOCHIN.

Chairman of the State Committee for Architecture and Construction: YEFIM V. BASIN.

Chairman of the State Committee for Statistics: YURI A. URKOV.

Chairman of the State Customs Committee: ANATOLY S. KRUGLOV.

The Chairman of the Central Bank of the Russian Federation (VIKTOR GERASHCHENKO), the Chairman of the Russian Federal Property Fund (FIRYAT TABEYEV) and the Chairman of the Board of the Pension Fund of the Russian Federation (V. BARCHUK) are *ex officio* members of the Russian Federation Government.

MINISTRIES

Office of the Government: Moscow, Staraya pl. 4; tel. (095) 206-25-11.

Ministry of Agriculture and Food: 107139 Moscow, Orlikov per. 1/11; tel. (095) 207-42-43.

Ministry of Civil Defence, Emergencies and Natural Disasters: 103012 Moscow, Teatralny pr. 4.

Ministry of Communications: 103375 Moscow, ul. Tverskaya 7; tel. (095) 292-10-75.

Ministry of Culture: 103693 Moscow, Kitaysky proezd 7; tel. (095) 220-45-00; fax (095) 975-24-20.

Ministry of Defence: 103160 Moscow, ul. Myasnitskaya 37; tel. (095) 293-56-83.

Ministry of the Economy: 103009 Moscow, Okhotny ryad 6; tel. (095) 292-91-39.

Ministry of Education: 101856 Moscow, Chistoprudny bul. 6; tel. (095) 924-84-68.

Ministry of Environmental Protection and Natural Resources: 123812 Moscow, Bolshaya Gruzinskaya ul. 4/6; tel. (095) 252-23-05.

Ministry of Finance: 103097 Moscow, ul. Iliynka 9; tel. (095) 206-21-71.

Ministry of Foreign Affairs: 121200 Moscow, Smolenskaya-Sennaya pl. 32/34; tel. (095) 244-40-21.

Ministry of Foreign Economic Relations: 121200 Moscow, Smolenskaya-Sennaya pl. 32/34; tel. (095) 244-10-46.

Ministry of Fuel and Power Engineering: 103693Moscow, Kitnysky pr. 7; tel. (095) 220-52-00.

Ministry of Health and the Medical Industry: 101474 Moscow, Vadkovsky per. 18/20; tel. (095) 923-84-06.

Ministry of Internal Affairs: 117049 Moscow, Zhitnaya ul. 16; tel. (095) 239-65-32.

Ministry of Justice: 101434 Moscow, ul. Yermolovoy 10A; tel. (095) 209-60-55.

Ministry of Labour: 103706 Moscow, pl. Kuybysheva 1; tel. (095) 928-06-83.

Ministry of Nationalities and Regional Policy: 117292 Moscow, ul. Ivana Babushkina 16; tel. (095) 125-21-50.

Ministry of Nuclear Energy: 109180 Moscow, Starometny per. 7; tel. (095) 239-49-08; fax (095) 230-24-20.

Ministry of Railways: Moscow, Novobasmannaya ul. 2; tel. (095) 262-10-02; telex 411832.

Ministry of Science and Technical Policy: 103905 Moscow, ul. Tverskaya 11; tel. (095) 229-25-01.

Ministry of Social Welfare of the Population: 103715 Moscow, Slavianskaya pl. 4, korpus 1; tel. (095) 220-92-01; fax (095) 924-36-90.

Ministry of Transport: 101433 Moscow, Sadovo-Samotechnaya ul. 10; tel. (095) 200-08-03.

State Committees

State Committee for Administration of State Property: 103685 Moscow, pr. Vladimirova 9; tel. (095) 924-67-04.

State Committee for Anti-Monopoly Policy and Support for New Economic Structures: 117947 Moscow, pr. Vernadskogo 41; tel. (095) 434-27-47.

State Committee for Architecture and Construction: 101819 Moscow, Furkassovsky per. 12/5; tel. (095) 209-60-55.

State Committee for State Property Management: Moscow, Staraya pl. 4; tel. (095) 206-25-11.

State Committee for Statistics: 103616 Moscow, Maly Cherkassky per. 2/6; tel. (095) 921-47-68; fax (095) 921-39-65.

State Customs Committee: 107842 Moscow, Komsomolskaya pl. 1A; tel. (095) 975-32-89.

President and Legislature

PRESIDENT

Election, 12 June 1991

Candidate	Votes	% of total
BORIS N. YELTSIN	45,552,041	57.30
NIKOLAI RYZHKOV	13,395,335	16.85
VLADIMIR ZHIRINOVSKY	6,211,007	7.81
AMAN-GELDY TULEYEV	5,417,464	6.81
VADIM BAKATIN	2,719,757	3.42
ALBERT MAKASHOV	11,136	0.7

FEDERAL ASSEMBLY

The Federal Assembly is a bicameral legislative body, comprising the Federation Council and the State Duma. Elections to the Federal Assembly were held on 12 December 1993. There were no elections in some constituencies or, in others, an insufficient number of electors participated to validate the ballot. Further rounds of voting took place at subsequent dates.

Federation Council

The Federation Council is the upper chamber of the Federal Assembly. It comprises 178 deputies, two from each of the constituent members (federal territorial units) of the Russian Federation.

Federation Council: Moscow, 26 Bolshaya Dmitrovka ul.

Chairman: VLADIMIR SHUMEYKO.

Deputy Chairmen: RAMAZAN ABDULATIPOV, VALERYAN VIKTOROV.

State Duma

The State Duma is the 450-seat lower chamber of the Federal Assembly. Members of the State Duma are elected for a term of four years.

State Duma: Moscow, Novy Arbat 36.

Chairman: IVAN RYBKIN.

First Deputy Chairman: MIKHAIL MITYUKOV.

Deputy Chairmen: VALENTIN KOVALEV, ALEVTINA FEDULOVA, ALEKSANDR VENGEROVSKY.

General election, 12 December 1993

	Party lists			
Party	% of vote	Seats	Single-member constituency seats	Total seats*
Liberal Democratic Party	22.79	59	5	64
Russia's Choice	15.38	40	18	58
Communist Party of the Russian Federation	12.35	32	16	48
Women of Russia	8.10	21	2	23
Agrarian Party	7.90	21	12	33
Yavlinsky-Boldyrev-Lukin	7.83	20	2	22
Party of Russian Unity and Concord	6.76	18	1	19
Democratic Party of Russia	5.50	14	1	15
Democratic Russia Movement			5	5
Russian Movement for Democratic Reforms	13.39	—	4	4
Others			153†	153
Total	100.00	225	219‡	444‡

* In mid-January 1994, according to Western estimates, the parliamentary factions in the State Duma were as follows: Russia's Choice (76 seats); New Regional Policy (centrist faction comprising independents—65); Liberal Democratic Party (63); Agrarian Party (55); Communist Party of the Russian Federation (45); Party of Russian Unity and Concord (30); Yavlinsky-Boldyrev-Lukin (Yabloko—25); Women of Russia (23); Democratic Party of Russia (15). Two further factions were expected to be formed by independents.

† Including 130 members without parliamentary affiliations.

‡ Totals exclude six Tatarstan deputies for which results were not yet available.

Local Government

The Russian Federation comprises 89 federal territorial units (for details, see below on p. 587). The basic divisions of local government are autonomous republics, oblasts (regions), krays (provinces), okrugs (districts), cities, rayons, and municipal and village authorities.

The Federation Treaty, which was signed on 31 March 1992, provided for a Russian Federation composed of 20 republics (16 of which were autonomous republics under the previous system of local goverment, and four of which were autonomous oblasts), one autonomous oblast and six krays (provinces). There are also 10 autonomous okrugs (districts), which are under the jurisdiction of the oblast or kray within which they are situated. A further republic, the Ingush Republic, was created in June 1992. Two cities, Moscow and St Petersburg, subsequently assumed the status of federal cities.

On 21 September 1993 President Yeltsin issued a decree (No. 1,400) entitled On Gradual Constitutional Reform, which dissolved the bicameral Russian legislature but did not affect the powers of local government bodies. On 6 October, however, the President 'invited' those local soviets (at kray, oblast and lower levels) that had rejected Decree No. 1,400 to disband themselves. The following day Yeltsin announced that heads of local administration were to be appointed and dismissed by presidential decree. On 9 October Yeltsin ordered the dissolution of all soviets at the lowest levels of the administrative structure and the assumption of their powers by the local administrators. In addition, all provincial (kray) or regional (oblast) soviets unable to achieve a quorum were to be disbanded and their powers transferred to the local administrator. Later that month a presidential decree ordered elections to be held in krays, oblasts and lower territorial subdivisions betweeen December 1993 and March 1994. Republics were advised to do the same.

Political Organizations

Following the anti-government uprising in October 1993 several opposition movements, including the National Salvation Front, the Free Russian People's Party, the Communist Party of the Russian Federation and the Russian Communist Workers' Party, were suspended by the Ministry of Justice. Some of these organizations were permitted to register for the parliamentary elections in December of that year.

Agrarian Party: Moscow; Leader MIKHAIL LAPSHIN.

Civic Union: Moscow, ul. Shabolovka 8; f. 1992; Chair. ARKADY VOLSKY; centrist coalition including:

All-Russian Union for Renewal: Moscow; advocates gradual economic reform, combined with a strong industrial policy; Co-Chair. ALEKSANDR VLADISLAVLEV, IGOR SMIRNOV.

Democratic Party of Russia: Moscow, ul. Shabolovka 8; tel. (095) 237-09-22; f. 1990 by the radical wing of the Democratic Platform in the CPSU and the Moscow Society of Electors; liberal-conservative; advocates centralized Russian state and stronger CIS structures; Leader NIKOLAY TRAVKIN; 28,600 mems.

People's Party of Free Russia: Moscow; f. 1991 as Democratic Party of Communists of Russia within the CPSU; Pres. ALEKSANDR RUTSKOY; Chair. of Bd. VASILY LIPITSKY; 100,000 mems.

Communist Party of the Russian Federation: Moscow: f. 1993; claims succession to the Russian Communist Party which was banned in 1991; Chair. of Central Cttee GENNADY ZYUGANOV; c. 500,000 mems.

Liberal Democratic Party: Moscow; right-wing nationalist; Leader VLADIMIR ZHIRINOVSKY.

Majority Party (Partiya Bolshinstva): Moscow; f. 1994; conservative; Chair. VYACHESLAV GRECHNEV; 150,000 mems.

Movement for Russia's National Revival: Moscow; f. 1994; nationalist organization; est. by the Pamyat nationalist front and several centrist and conservative parties; Chair. DMITRY VASILYEV.

Party of Economic Freedom: Moscow; f. 1992; advocates economic liberalism, but supports Civic Union on some policies; Co-Chair. KONSTANTIN BOROVOY, SERGEY FEDEROV; 100,000 mems.

Party of Russian Unity and Concord: Moscow; f. 1993; democratic bloc; Leader SERGEY SHAKRAY.

Russian Christian-Democratic Movement: Moscow; f. 1990; alliance of groups advocating application of Christian principles to society; conservative-nationalist; Chair. of Political Cttee VIKTOR AKSYUCHITS; c. 6,000 mems.

Russia's Choice: Moscow; f. 1993; democratic bloc; Leader YEGOR GAIDAR; the following are mems or affiliates of Russia's Choice:

Democratic Russia Movement: 109180 Moscow, 36 Starometny per.; tel. (095) 233-00-23; f. 1990; alliance of democratic parties; Co-Chair. GLEB YAKUNIN, ELLA PAMFILOVA; c. 150,000 mems.

Free Democratic Party of Russia: 198255 St Petersburg, pr. Veteranov 55, kv. 94; tel. (812) 356-84-27; f. 1990 as a result of a split in the DPR; radical democratic party; Co-Chair. MARINA SALYE, LEV PONOMAREV, IGOR SOSHNIKOV; c. 1,000 mems.

Free Labour Party: 109193 Moscow, ul. Petra Romanova 18/2/8; tel. (095) 277-67-02; f. 1990; party of business people and professionals; advocates economic liberalism; Chair. of Political Cttee IGOR KOROVIKOV; c. 1,500 mems.

Party of Constitutional Democrats: Moscow;tel. (095) 244-70-21; mem. of Liberal Union; Chair. VLADIMIR ZOLOTAREV.

Peasants' Party of Russia: 119619 Moscow, ul. Narfominskaya 2-192; tel. (095) 189-89-51; f. 1990; advocates agricultural reform, and the return of collectivized land to individual farmers; Chair. YURI CHERNENKO; c. 1,500 mems.

Republican Party of the Russian Federation: 109044 Moscow, 11/31-6 Siminovsky val; tel. (095) 298-13-49; f. 1990 by former members of the Democratic Platform in the CPSU; advocates a mixed economy, defence of sovereignty of Russia; mem. of Liberal Union; Co-Chair. VLADIMIR LYSENKO, VLADISLAV SHOSTAKOVSKY, IGOR YAKOVENKO, PETR FILIPPOV; c. 7,000 mems.

Russia's Future—New Names: Moscow; f. 1993; formed as electoral bloc by the Free Russia youth movement; advocates ideas of nonconfrontational policy and national statehood; Chair. OLEG SOKOLOV.

Russian All-People's Union: Moscow; f. as party 1994; Leader SERGEY BABURIN.

Russian Movement for Democratic Reforms (RMDR): 103050 Moscow, ul. Tverskaya 22; tel. (095) 299-15-01; f. 1991 by reformist members of the CPSU; unites several democratic groups; Chair. GAVRIIL POPOV; 10,000–12,000 mems.

Socialist Workers' Party (SWP): Moscow; f. 1991; moderate socialist party; rejects Stalinism, advocates mixed economy; Co-Chair. IVAN RYBKIN, ROY MEDVEDEV.

Social Democratic Party of the Russian Federation (SDPRF): 109044 Moscow, POB 35; tel. (095) 202-14-87; fax (095) 202-15-65; f. 1990; advocates democratic society, social forms of 'privatization', a social partnership between government, employers and trade unions; Chair. IGOR AVERKYEV (acting); 5,600 mems.

Women of Russia: Moscow; Leader ALEVTINA FEDULOVA.

Yavlinsky–Boldyrev–Lukin (Yabloko): Moscow; f. 1993; democratic-centrist; Leaders: GRIGORY YAVLINSKY, YURY BOLDYREV, VLADIMIR LUKIN.

The KEDR (Cedar) Constructive Ecological Movement (Leader ANATOLY PANFILOV) and the Dignity and Charity electoral bloc (comprising the All-Russian Organization of Veterans of War, the All-Russian Society of the Disabled and the Chernobyl Union; Co-Chair. MIKHAIL TRUNOV) also participated in the elections.

Diplomatic Representation

EMBASSIES IN RUSSIA

Afghanistan: Moscow, Sverchkov per. 3/2; tel. (095) 928-50-44; telex 413270; fax (095) 924-04-78; Ambassador: MUHAMMAD DAOUD RAZMYAR.

Albania: Moscow, ul. Mytnaya 3, kv. 25; tel. (095) 230-78-75; telex 414506; fax (095) 230-76-35; Ambassador: CICI ARBEN.

Algeria: Moscow, Krapivinsky per. 1A; tel. (095) 200-66-42; telex 413273; fax (095) 200-22-25; Ambassador: HADJ MUHAMMAD YALA.

Angola: ul. Olof Palme 6; tel. (095) 143-63-24; telex 413402; Ambassador: MANUEL BERNARDO DE SOUZA.

Argentina: Moscow, ul. Sadovo-Triumfalnaya 4/10; tel. (095) 299-03-67; telex 413259; Ambassador: JUAN CARLOS OLIMA.

Australia: Moscow, Kropotkinsky per. 13; tel. (095) 246-50-12; telex 413474; fax 230-26-06; Ambassador: CAVAN O. HOGUE.

Austria: Moscow, Starokonyushenny per. 1; tel. (095) 201-73-79; telex 413398; fax (095) 230-23-65; Ambassador: FRIEDRICH BAUER.

Bahrain: Moscow, Berezhkovskaya nab. 2, Hotel Slavyanskaya; tel. (095) 941-80-20; Ambassador: Dr SALMAN AL-SOFFAR.

Bangladesh: Moscow, Zemledelchesky per. 6; tel. (095) 246-79-00; telex 413196; fax (095) 248-31-85; Ambassador: MUSTAFIZUR RAHMAN.

Belgium: Moscow, ul. Malaya Molchanovka 7; tel. (095) 291-60-27; telex 413471; fax (095) 291-60-05; Ambassador: Baron THIERRY DE GRUBEN.

Benin: Moscow, Uspensky per. 4A; tel. (095) 299-23-60; telex 413645; fax (095) 200-02-26; Ambassador: BABATOUNDÉ CONSTANT KOUKOUI.

Bolivia: Moscow, Lopukhinsky per. 5; tel. (095) 201-25-08; telex 413356; Ambassador: Dr JAVIER MURILLO DE LA ROCHA.

Brazil: Moscow, ul. Gertsena 54; tel. (095) 290-40-22; telex 413476; fax (095) 200-12-85; Ambassador: SEBASTIÃO DO REGO BARROS NETTO.

Bulgaria: Moscow, ul. Mosfilmovskaya 66; tel. (095) 143-90-27; Ambassador: VLADIMIR VELCHEV.

Burkina Faso: 129090 Moscow, Meshchanskaya ul. 17; tel. (095) 971-37-49; telex 413284; Ambassador HANITAN JONAS YÉ.

Burundi: Moscow, Uspensky per. 7; tel. (095) 299-72-00; telex 413316; Ambassador: ILDEPHONSE NKERAMIHIGO.

Cambodia: Moscow, Starokonyushenny per. 16; tel. (095) 201-47-36; telex 413261; fax (095) 201-76-68; Ambassador: BO RASY.

Cameroon: Moscow, ul. Vorovskovo 40; tel. (095) 290-65-49; telex 413445; Ambassador: Alhadji YÉRIMA SOUAIBOU HAYATOU.

Canada: Moscow, Starokonyushenny per. 23; tel. (095) 241-11-11; telex 413401; fax (095) 241-44-00; Ambassador: JEREMY KINSMAN.

Cape Verde: Moscow, Bolshaya Spasskaya ul. 9; tel. (095) 208-08-56; telex 413929; fax (095) 208-72-83; Ambassador: LUIS DE MATOS MONTEIRO DA FONSECA.

Central African Republic: 117571 Moscow, ul. 26-Bakinskikh-Kommissarov 9, kv. 124–125; tel. (095) 434-45-20; telex 413737; Ambassador: CLAUDE BERNARD BELOUM.

Chad: Moscow, Rublevskoye Chaussée 26, kor. 1, kv. 20–21; tel. (095) 415-41-39; telex 413623; Chargé d'affaires a.i.: BRAHIM MAHAMAT BRAHIM.

Chile: Moscow, ul. Yunosti 11; tel. (095) 373-9176; telex 413751; fax (095) 373-77-25; Ambassador: JAMES HOLGER.

China, People's Republic: Moscow, Leninskiye Gory, ul. Druzhby 6; tel. (095) 143-15-40; telex 413981; Ambassador: WANG JINQING.

Colombia: Moscow, ul. Burdenko 20; tel. (095) 248-30-42; telex 413206; fax (095) 248-30-25; Ambassador: RICARDO EASTMAN DE LA CUESTA.

Congo: Moscow, Kropotkinsky per. 12; tel. (095) 246-02-34; telex 413487; Ambassador: GABRIEL EMOUENGUÉ.

Costa Rica: Moscow, Rublevskoye shosse 26, kv. 23–25; tel. and fax (095) 415-40-42; telex 413963; Ambassador: ARTURO ROBLES ARIAS.

Côte d'Ivoire: Moscow, Molochny per. 9/14; tel. (095) 201-24-00; telex 413091; Ambassador: Moïse Aka.

Croatia: Moscow, Krasnopresnenskaya nab. 12; tel. (095) 253-12-53; fax (095) 253-12-70; f. 1992; Ambassador: Niko Bezmalinovic.

Cuba: Moscow, ul. Mosfilmovskaya 40; tel. (095) 147-43-12; Ambassador: (vacant).

Cyprus: 121069 Moscow, ul. Gertsena 51; tel. (095) 290-21-54; telex 413477; fax (095) 200-12-54; Ambassador: Charalambos Christoforou.

Czech Republic: Moscow, ul. Yuliusa Fuchika 12/14; tel. (095) 251-05-40; Ambassador: (vacant).

Denmark: Moscow, per. Ostrovskogo 9; tel. (095) 201-78-60; telex 413378; fax (095) 201-53-57; Ambassador: Henrik Ree Iverson.

Ecuador: Moscow, Gorokhovsky per. 12; tel. (095) 261-55-44; telex 413174; Ambassador: Pedro Antonio Saad Herrería.

Egypt: Moscow, Skatertny per. 25; tel. (095) 291-32-09; telex 413276; fax (095) 291-46-09; Ambassador: Ahmed Mahir al-Sayyid.

Equatorial Guinea: Moscow, Kutuzovsky pr. 7/4, kor. 5, kv. 37; tel. (095) 243-96-11; Ambassador: Policarpo Mensuy Mba.

Estonia: Moscow, Sobinovsky per. 5; tel. (095) 290-50-13; fax (095) 202-38-30; Ambassador: Jüri Kahn.

Ethiopia: Moscow, Orlovo-Davydovsky per. 6; tel. (095) 230-20-36; telex 413980; Chargé d'affaires a.i.: Belayneh Mengesha.

Finland: Moscow, Kropotkinsky per. 15/17; tel. (095) 246-40-27; telex 413405; fax (095) 230-27-21; Ambassador: Heikki Talvitie.

France: Moscow, ul. Bolshaya Yakimanka 45/47; tel. (095) 236-00-03; telex 413290; fax (095) 230-21-69; Ambassador: Pierre Morel.

Gabon: Moscow, ul. Vesnina 16; tel. (095) 241-00-80; telex 413245; fax (095) 244-06-94; Ambassador: Marcel Ondongui-Bonnard.

Germany: 119285 Moscow, Mosfilmovskaya ul. 56; tel. (095) 956-10-80; telex 413411; fax (095) 938-23-54; Ambassador: Dr Klaus Blech.

Ghana: Moscow, Skatertny per. 14; tel. (095) 202-18-70; telex 413475; Ambassador: Chris Hesse.

Greece: Moscow, ul. Stanislavskogo 4; tel. (095) 290-22-74; telex 413472; fax (095) 200-12-52; Ambassador: Elias Gounaris.

Guinea: Moscow, Pomerantsev per. 6; tel. (095) 201-36-01; telex 413404; Ambassador: Cherif Diallo.

Guinea-Bissau: Moscow, ul. Bolshaya Ordynka 35; tel: (095) 231-79-28; telex 413055; Ambassador: Chérif Turé.

Holy See: 117049 Moscow, ul. Mytnaya, kv. 19/30; tel. and fax (095) 230-29-94; Apostolic Pro-Nuncio: Mgr Francesco Colasuonno.

Hungary: Moscow, ul. Mosfilmovskaya 62; tel. (095) 143-86-11; telex 414428; fax (095) 143-46-25; Ambassador: Sándor Györke.

Iceland: Moscow, Khlebny per. 28; tel. (095) 290-47-42; telex 413181; fax (095) 200-12-64; Ambassador: Ólafur Egilsson.

India: Moscow, ul. Obukha 6–8; tel. (095) 297-08-20; telex 413409; fax (095) 274-00-42; Ambassador: Ronen Sen.

Indonesia: Moscow, ul. Novokuznetskaya 12; tel. (095) 231-95-49; telex 413444; fax (095) 230-22-13; Ambassador: Janwar Marah Djani.

Iran: 109028 Moscow, Pokrovsky bul. 7; tel. (095) 227-57-88; telex 413493; Ambassador: Nematollah Izadi.

Iraq: Moscow, Pogodinskaya ul. 12; tel. (095) 246-55-06; telex 413184; fax (095) 230-29-22; Ambassador: Ghafil Jassim Hussain.

Ireland: Moscow, Grokholsky per. 5; tel. (095) 288-41-01; telex 413204; Ambassador: Patrick McCabe.

Israel: Moscow, ul. Bolshaya Ordynka 56; tel. (095) 238-27-32; fax (095) 238-13-46; Ambassador: Chaim Bar Lev.

Italy: Moscow, ul. Vesnina 5; tel. (095) 241-15-33; telex 413453; fax (095) 253-92-89; Ambassador: Federico di Roberto.

Jamaica: Moscow, Korovy val 7, kv. 70–71; tel. (095) 237-23-20; telex 413358; fax (095) 230-21-02; Chargé d'affaires a.i.: Paul A. Bobotham.

Japan: Moscow, Kalashny per. 12; tel. (095) 291-85-00; telex 413141; fax (095) 200-12-40; Ambassador: Koji Watanabe.

Jordan: Moscow, per. Sadovskikh 3; tel. (095) 299-95-64; telex 413447; fax (095) 299-43-54; Ambassador: Dr Mohammed Adwan.

Kenya: Moscow, ul. Bolshaya Ordynka 70; tel. (095) 237-47-02; telex 413495; fax (095) 230-23-40; Ambassador: D. I. Kathambana.

Korea, Democratic People's Republic: Moscow, ul. Mosfilmovskaya 72; tel. (095) 143-62-49; telex 413272; Ambassador: Son Song-Pil.

Korea, Republic: 119121 Moscow, ul. Gubkina 14; tel. (095) 938-28-02; Ambassador: Ro-Myung Gong.

Kuwait: Moscow, 3-Neopalimovsky per. 13/5; tel. (095) 248-50-01; telex 413353; fax (095) 230-24-23; Ambassador: Abdulmohsin Y. al-Duaij.

Laos: Moscow, ul. Bolshaya Ordynka 18/1; tel. (095) 233-20-35; telex 413101; Ambassador: Khamphong Phanhvongsa.

Latvia: Moscow, ul. Chaplygina 3; tel. (095) 925-27-07; fax (095) 925-92-95; Ambassador: Janis Peters.

Lebanon: Moscow, Sadovo-Samotechnaya ul. 14; tel. (095) 200-00-22; telex 413120; fax (095) 200-32-22; Ambassador: Selim Tadmoury.

Libya: Moscow, ul. Mosfilmovskaya 38; tel. (095) 143-03-54; telex 413443; fax (095) 143-76-44; Secretary (Ambassador): Ahmed Mohamed Rhaim.

Lithuania: Moscow, Borisoglebsky per. 10; tel. (095) 291-16-98; fax (095) 202-35-16; Ambassador: Romualdas Kozyrovičius.

Luxembourg: Moscow, Khrushchevsky per. 3; tel. (095) 202-53-81; telex 413131; fax (095) 200-52-43; Ambassador: Jean Hostert.

Madagascar: Moscow, Kursovoy per. 5; tel. (095) 290-02-14; telex 413370; Ambassador: Simon Raboara Rabe.

Malaysia: Moscow, ul. Mosfilmovskaya 50; tel. (095) 147-15-14; telex 413478; fax (095) 147-15-26; Ambassador: Mohamed Haron.

Mali: Moscow, Novokuznetskaya ul. 11; tel. (095) 231-06-55; telex 413396; Ambassador: Cheick A. T. Cissé.

Malta: Moscow, Korovy val 7, kv. 219; tel. (095) 237-19-39; telex 413919; fax (095) 237-21-58; Ambassador: George Saliba.

Mauritania: Moscow, ul. Bolshaya Ordynka 66; tel. (095) 237-37-92; telex 413439; Ambassador: Aly Gueladio Kamara.

Mexico: Moscow, ul. Shchukina 4; tel. (095) 201-25-53; telex 413125; fax (095) 230-20-42; Ambassador: Carlos Tello.

Mongolia: Moscow, ul. Pisemskovo 11; tel. (095) 290-30-61; Ambassador: Nyamyn Mishigdorj.

Morocco: Moscow, per. Ostrovskovo 8; tel. (095) 201-73-51; telex 413446; fax (095) 230-20-67; Ambassador: Abdeslam Znined.

Mozambique: Moscow, ul. Gilyarovskovo 20; tel. (095) 284-40-07; telex 413369; Ambassador: José Rui Mota do Amaral.

Myanmar: Moscow, ul. Gertsena 41; tel. (095) 291-05-34; telex 413403; fax (095) 956-31-86; Ambassador: U Khin Maung Soe.

Namibia: Moscow, Kazachny per. 7; tel. (095) 230-01-13; telex 413827; fax (095) 230-22-74; Ambassador: N. P. Nashandi.

Nepal: Moscow, 2-Neopalimovsky per. 14/7; tel. (095) 244-02-15; telex 413292; Ambassador: Kumar P. Gyawali.

Netherlands: Moscow, Kalashny per. 6; tel. (095) 291-29-99; telex 413442; fax (095) 200-52-64; Ambassador: Godert W. de Vos van Steenwijk.

New Zealand: 121069 Moscow, ul. Vorovskovo 44; tel. (095) 290-34-85; telex 413187; fax (095) 290-46-66; Ambassador: Gerald McGhie.

Nicaragua: Moscow, Mosfilmovskaya ul. 50, kor. 1; tel. (095) 938-27-01; telex 413264; Ambassador: Adolfo Evertz Vélez.

Niger: Moscow, Kursovoy per. 7/31; tel. (095) 290-01-01; telex 413180; fax (095) 200-42-51; Ambassador: Moutari Ousmane.

Nigeria: Moscow, ul. Kachalova 13; tel. (095) 290-37-83; telex 413489; Ambassador: Jibrin D. Chinade.

Norway: Moscow, ul. Vorovskovo 7; tel. (095) 290-38-72; telex 413488; fax (095) 200-12-21; Ambassador: Dagfinn Stenseth.

Oman: Moscow, per. Obukha 6; tel. (095) 928-56-30; telex 411432; fax (095) 975-21-74; Chargé d'affaires a.i.: Ahmed Mohammad al-Riyami.

Pakistan: Moscow, Sadovo-Kudrinskaya ul. 17; tel. (095) 254-97-91; telex 413194; Ambassador: Ashraf Jahangir Qazi.

Peru: Moscow, Smolensky bul. 22/14, kv. 15; tel. (095) 248-77-38; telex 413400; fax (095) 230-20-00; Ambassador: Dr Armando Lecaros de Cossío.

Philippines: Moscow, Karmanitsky per. 6; tel. (095) 241-38-70; telex 413156; fax (095) 956-60-87; Ambassador: Romualdo A. Ong.

Poland: Moscow, ul. Klimashkina 4; tel. (095) 255-00-17; telex 414362; fax (095) 254-22-86; Ambassador: Stanisław Ciosek.

Portugal: Moscow, Botanichesky per. 1; tel. (095) 230-24-35; telex 413221; fax (095) 230-26-51; Ambassador: António Costa Lobo.

Qatar: Moscow, Korovy val 7, kv. 197–198; tel. (095) 230-15-77; telex 413728; fax (095) 230-22-40; Ambassador: Fahd al-Khater.

Romania: Moscow, ul. Mosfilmovskaya 64; tel. (095) 143-04-24; telex 414355; fax (095) 143-04-49; Ambassador: Vasile Sandru.

Rwanda: Moscow, ul. Bolshaya Ordynka 72; tel. (095) 237-32-22; telex 413213; Ambassador: Anastase Ntezilyayo.

Saudi Arabia: Moscow, Balaklavsky pr. 2, kor. 2; tel. (095) 316-81-63; Ambassador: Abdul-Aziz Mohiddin Khojah.

Senegal: Moscow, ul. Donskaya 12; tel. (095) 236-20-40; telex 413438; Ambassador: PASCAL-ANTOINE SANÉ.

Sierra Leone: Moscow, ul. Paliashvili 4; tel. (095) 203-62-00; telex 413461; Ambassador: OLU WILLIAM HARDING.

Singapore: Moscow, per. Voyevodina 5; tel. (095) 241-37-02; telex 413128; fax (095) 230-29-37; Ambassador: JOSEPH FRANCIS CONCEICAO.

Slovakia: Moscow, ul. Yuliusa Fuchika 17–19; tel. (095) 250-56-09; telex 414480; fax (095) 973-20-81; Ambassador: ROMAN PALDAN.

Somalia: Moscow, Spasopeskovskaya pl. 8; tel. (095) 241-96-24; telex 413164; Ambassador: ABDULLAHI EGAL NUR.

South Africa: 113054 Moscow, B. Strochenovsky per. 22/25; tel. (095) 230-68-69; fax (095) 230-68-65; Ambassador: Dr GERRARD C. OLIVIER.

Spain: Moscow, ul. Gertsena 50/8; tel. (095) 202-21-61; telex 413220; fax (095) 200-12-30; Ambassador: EUGENIO BREGOLAT OBIOLS.

Sri Lanka: Moscow, ul. Shchepkina 24; tel. (095) 288-16-51; telex 413140; Ambassador: NISSANKA PARAKRAMA WIJEYERATNE.

Sudan: Moscow, ul. Vorovskovo 9; tel. (095) 290-39-93; telex 413448; Ambassador: IBRAHIM MOHAMMED ALI.

Sweden: Moscow, ul. Mosfilmovskaya 60; tel. (095) 147-90-09; telex 413410; fax (095) 147-87-88; Ambassador: ÖRJAN BERNER.

Switzerland: Moscow, per. Stopani 2/5; tel. (095) 925-53-22; telex 413418; fax (095) 200-17-28; Ambassador: JEAN-PIERRE RITTER.

Syria: Moscow, Mansurovsky per. 4; tel. (095) 203-15-21; telex 413145; Ambassador: MUHAMMAD ISSAM NAEB.

Tanzania: Moscow, ul. Pyatnitskaya 33; tel. (095) 231-81-46; telex 413352; fax (095) 230-29-68; Ambassador: WILSON TIBAIJUKA.

Thailand: Moscow, Eropkinsky per. 3; tel. (095) 201-48-93; telex 413309; Ambassador: KASIT PIROMYA.

Togo: 103001 Moscow, ul. Shchuseva 1; tel. (095) 290-65-99; telex 413967; fax (095) 200-12-50; Ambassador: CHARLES DJABABOU NANA.

Tunisia: Moscow, ul. Kachalova 28/1; tel. (095) 291-28-58; telex 413449; Ambassador: SLAHEDDINE ABDELLAH.

Turkey: Moscow, Vadkovsky per. 7/37; tel. (095) 972-69-00; telex 413731; fax (095) 200-22-23; Ambassador: VOLKAN VURAL.

Uganda: Moscow, per. Sadovskikh 5; tel. (095) 251-00-60; telex 413473; fax (095) 200-42-00; Ambassador: FELIX OKOBOI.

United Arab Emirates: Moscow, Olof Palme ul. 4; tel. (095) 147-62-86; telex 413547; fax (095) 938-21-37; Ambassador: NASSER SALMAN AL-ABOODI.

United Kingdom: Moscow, nab. Morisa Toreza 14; tel. (095) 230-63-33; telex 413341; fax (095) 233-35-63; Ambassador: Sir BRIAN FALL.

USA: Moscow, Bolshoy Devyatinsky per. 8; tel. (095) 252-24-51; telex 413160; Ambassador: THOMAS PICKERING.

Uruguay: 117330 Moscow, Lomonosovsky pr. 38; tel. (095) 143-04-01; telex 413238; fax (095) 938-20-45; Ambassador: ALEJANDRO LORENZO Y LOSADA.

Venezuela: Moscow, ul. Ermolovoi 13–15; tel. (095) 299-96-21; telex 413119; fax (095) 200-02-48; Ambassador: RAFAEL LEÓN MORALES.

Viet Nam: Moscow, Bolshaya Pirogovskaya ul. 13; tel. (095) 247-02-12; Ambassador: NGUYÊN MANH CÂM.

Yemen: Moscow, 2-Neopalimovsky per. 6; tel. (095) 246-15-31; telex 413214; Ambassador: ALI ABDULLA AL-BUGERY.

Yugoslavia: Moscow, ul. Mosfilmovskaya 46; tel. (095) 147-41-06; Ambassador: ANJELKO RUNIĆ.

Zaire: Moscow, per. N. Ostrovskovo 10; tel. (095) 201-76-64; telex 413479; fax (095) 201-79-48; Ambassador: MITIMA K. MURAIRI.

Zambia: Moscow, pr. Mira 52A; tel. (095) 288-50-01; telex 413462; Ambassador: OBINO RICHARD HAAMBOTE.

Zimbabwe: Moscow, Serpov per. 6; tel. (095) 248-43-67; telex 413029; fax (095) 230-24-97; Ambassador: Dr MISHECK J. M. SIBANDA.

PERMANENT REPRESENTATIVES OF COMMONWEALTH OF INDEPENDENT STATES MEMBERS

Armenia: Moscow, Armyansky per. 2; tel. (095) 924-12-69; fax (095) 923-09-85; Permanent Representative: FELIKS MAMINOKYAN.

Azerbaijan: Moscow, ul. Stanislavskogo 16; tel. (095) 229-16-49; Permanent Representative: V. R. VERDIYEV.

Belarus: Moscow, ul. Maroseyka 17/6; tel. (095) 924-30-31; Permanent Representative: VIKTOR DANILENKO.

Georgia: Moscow, ul. Paliashvili 6; tel. (095) 291-21-36; Permanent Representative: P. P. CHKHEIDZE.

Kazakhstan: Moscow, Chistoprudny bul. 3A; tel. (095) 208-98-52; Permanent Representative: VALERI TIMERBAYEV.

Kyrgyzstan: Moscow, ul. Bolshaya Ordynka 64; tel. (095) 237-48-82; Permanent Representative: AKMATBEK NANAYEV.

Moldova: Moscow, Kuznetsky most 18; tel. (095) 928-54-05; Permanent Representative: ION CHEBUK.

Tajikistan: Moscow, Skatertny per. 19; tel. (095) 290-61-02; Permanent Representative: ABDUMALIK ABDULLOJONOV (designate).

Turkmenistan: Moscow, per. Aksakova 22; tel. (095) 291-66-36; Permanent Representative: NIYAZ NURKLICHEV.

Ukraine: Moscow, ul. Stanislavskogo 18; tel. (095) 229-34-22; fax (095) 229-35-42; Permanent Representative: VOLODYMYR KRYZHANIVSKIY.

Uzbekistan: Moscow, Pogorelsky per. 12; tel. (095) 230-00-76; fax (095) 238-89-18; Permanent Representative: AKMAL SAIDOV.

Judicial System

Constitutional Court of the Russian Federation: 103132 Moscow, ul. Ilyinka 21; tel. (095) 206-78-74; fax (095) 206-92-15; f. 1991; Chair. NIKOLAY VITRUK.

Supreme Arbitration Court of the Russian Federation: Moscow; f. 1993.

Supreme Court of the Russian Federation: 103289 Moscow, ul. Ilyinka 7/3; tel. (095) 924-23-47; Chairman of the Supreme Court VYACHESLAV M. LEBEDEV.

Office of the Prosecutor-General: 103760 Moscow, Kuznetsky most 13; tel. (095) 928-90-43; Prosecutor-General (vacant).

Religion

The majority of the population of the Russian Federation are adherents of Christianity, but there are significant Islamic, Buddhist and Jewish minorities.

CHRISTIANITY

The Russian Orthodox Church

The Russian Orthodox Church is the dominant religious organization in the Russian Federation, with an estimated 35m. adherents. In May 1991 the Russian Orthodox Church announced plans to begin building 542 churches throughout Russia. In 1988–92 more than 2,000 churches were returned to religious use. The Church's jurisdiction is challenged by the Russian Orthodox Church Abroad, which was established in the Soviet period and rejects the hierarchy of the Moscow Patriarchy.

Moscow Patriarchate: 113191 Moscow, Danilov Monastery, Danilovsky val 22; tel. (095) 954-04-54; fax (095) 230-26-19; Patriarch ALEKSEY II.

The Roman Catholic Church

In May 1991 Tadeusz Kondrusiewicz became the first Roman Catholic Archbishop of Moscow for more than 50 years. In February 1991 the Russian 'Greek Catholic' (Uniate) Church, users of the Byzantine Rite, was re-established.

Protestant Churches

Euro-Asiatic Federation of the Unions of Evangelical Christians-Baptists: Moscow, Vuzovsky per. 3; tel. (095) 297-89-47; telex 412426; fax (095) 227-39-90; Pres. GRIGORY KOMENDANT; Gen. Sec. ALEKSANDR HRISLUK.

Other Christian Churches

Armenian Apostolic Church: Moscow, ul. Sergeya Makeyeva 10; tel. (095) 255-50-19.

Old Believers (The Old Faith): Moscow, Rogozhovsky pos. 29; tel. (095) 361-51-92; divided into three branches: the Belokrinitsky Concord, under the Metropolitan of Moscow and All-Russia, the Bezpopovtsy Concord and the Beglopopovtsy Concord; Metropolitan of Moscow and All-Russia: Bishop ALIMPI.

ISLAM

Most Muslims in the Russian Federation are adherents of the Sunni sect. Muslims in the Russian Federation come under the spiritual jurisdiction of the Muslim Board of European Russia and Siberia and the Muslim Board of the North Caucasus.

JUDAISM

Although many Jews emigrated from the USSR in the 1970s and 1980s, there are still significant Jewish communities in the Russian Federation, particularly in the larger cities. There are a small number of Jews in the Jewish Autonomous Oblast, in the Far East of the Russian Federation. There is an Orthodox Jewish Seminary (yeshiva) in Moscow. In the Jewish Autonomous Oblast the teaching of Yiddish has begun in schools and institutes.

Chief Rabbi of Moscow: ADOLF SHAYEVICH.

BUDDHISM

Buddhism is most widespread in the Republic of Buryatia, where the Central Spiritual Department of Buddhists of Russia has its seat, the Republics of Kalmykia and Tyva and in some districts of the Irkutsk and Chita Oblasts. There are also newly established communities in Moscow and St Petersburg. Before 1917 there were more than 40 datsans (monasteries) in Buryatia, but by 1990 only two of these remained in use. Estimates of the number of Buddhists range from Soviet estimates of some 200,000 to Western estimates of more than 600,000. In July 1991 the Dalai Lama, the spiritual leader of many Buddhists, visited Buryatia to attend the celebrations marking the 250th anniversary of the recognition of Buddhism as an official religion in Russia.

Chairman of the Central Spiritual Department of Buddhists: (vacant).

The Press

In 1990 there were 4,808 officially-registered newspaper titles published in the Russian Federation, of which 4,488 were in Russian. There were also 3,681 periodicals, including 3,389 in Russian. Owing to the economic situation, almost all newspapers and periodicals suffered a sharp decrease in circulation in 1992 and 1993. Despite losing some 20m. subscribers, *Argumenty i Fakty* remained the best-selling Russian weekly newspaper, while *Izvestiya*, *Moskovsky Komsomolets* and *Trud* were the most popular dailies. Many of the large number of new newspapers which emerged in the early 1990s were strongly partisan in their political stance. Following the disturbances in Moscow in October 1993 the Ministry of Press and Information suspended the publication of several opposition publications, most notably *Den*, *Pravda* and *Sovetskaya Rossiya*. Some 16 newspapers, including *Den*, were subsequently banned, and the editors of *Pravda* and *Sovetskaya Rossiya* were dismissed.

Russian Federation Press Committee: 101409 Moscow, Strastnoy bul. 5; tel. (095) 209-60-26; f. 1993 to replace the Ministry of Press and Information and the Federal Information Centre of Russia; central organ of federal executive power; Chair. BORIS S. MIRONOV.

PRINCIPAL NEWSPAPERS

Moscow

Argumenty i Fakty (Arguments and Facts): 101000 Moscow, ul. Myasnitskaya 42; tel. (095) 923-23-82; telex 114769; fax (095) 200-22-52; f. 1978; weekly; Editor VLADISLAV A. STARKOV; circ. 12,500,000.

Glasnost (Openness): 103132 Moscow, Novaya pl. 14; tel. (095) 206-40-37; weekly; publ. by Pressa Publishing House; left-wing; Editor-in-Chief YU. P. IZYUMOV; circ. 155,000 (1993).

Izvestiya (News): 103791 Moscow, Pushkinskaya pl. 5; tel. (095) 209-91-00; telex 411121; fax (095) 230-23-03; f. 1917; fmrly organ of the Presidium of the Supreme Soviet of the USSR; independent; Editor I. GOLEMBIOVSKY; circ. 2,000,000.

Komsomolskaya Pravda (Komsomol Pravda): 125865 Moscow, ul. Pravdy 24; tel. (095) 257-21-39; telex 111551; fax (095) 200-22-93; f. 1925; fmrly organ of the Leninist Young Communist League (Komsomol); independent; Editor VLADISLAV A. FRONIN; circ. 600,000.

Krasnaya Zvezda (Red Star): 123826 Moscow, Khoroshevskoye shosse 38; tel. (095) 941-21-58; fax (095) 941-40-57; f. 1924; organ of the Ministry of Defence; Editor V. L. CHUPAKHIN; circ. 223,000.

Krestiyanskaya Rossiya (Peasant Russia): 123022 Moscow, ul. 1905 goda 7; tel. (095) 259-47-98; fax (095) 259-93-37; weekly; f. 1906; Editor-in-Chief KONSTANTIN LYSENKO; circ. 90,000 (1993).

Kuranty (Chimes): 103009 Moscow, ul. Stankevicha 12; tel. (095) 203-06-10; fax (095) 292-55-15; f. 1991; 5 a week; Editor-in-Chief ANATOLY PANKOV; circ. 150,000 (1993).

Moskovskaya Pravda (Moscow Pravda): 123846 Moscow, ul. 1905 goda 7; tel. (095) 259-82-33; fax (095) 259-63-60; f. 1918; fmrly organ of the Moscow city committee of the CPSU and the Moscow City Soviet; 5 a week; independent; Editor SH. S. MULADZHANOV; circ. 362,000 (1993).

Moskovsky Komsomolets (Member of the Leninist Young Communist League of Moscow): 123848 Moscow, ul. 1905 goda 7; tel. (095) 259-50-36; fax (095) 259-43-58; f. 1919; 5 a week; independent; Editor-in-Chief PAVEL GUSEV; circ. 1,400,000.

Nezavisimaya Gazeta (The Independent Newspaper): Moscow, ul. Myasnitskaya 13; tel. (095) 925-94-63; f. 1990; independent; Editor-in-Chief VITALY TRETYAKOV; circ. 100,000.

Pravda (Truth): 125867 Moscow, ul. Pravdy 24; tel. (095) 257-37-86; telex 411209; fax (095) 200-22-91; f. 1912; fmrly organ of the Cen. Cttee of the CPSU; independent; left-wing; Editor-in-Chief ALEKSANDR ILYIN; circ.610,000 (1993).

Rabochaya Tribuna (Workers' Tribune): 125880 Moscow, ul. Pravdy 24; tel. (095) 257-27-51; telex 114040; f. 1969; fmrly organ of the Cen. Cttee of the CPSU; organ of the Federation of Independent Trade Unions of the Russian Federation and the Russian Union of Industrialists and Businessmen; Editor-in-Chief ANATOLY YURKOV; circ. 210,000 (1993).

Rossiskaya Gazeta: 125881 Moscow, ul. Pravdy 24; tel. (095) 257-22-52; fax (095) 973-22-56; f. 1990; organ of the Russian Government; publication suspended in Nov. 1993 owing to shortage of funds; 5 a week; Editor-in-Chief VALENTIN LOGUNOV; circ. 768,000 (1993).

Rossiiskiye Vesti (Russian News): 103379 Moscow, ul. Bolshaya Sadovaya 8, podyezd 4; tel. (095) 209-98-22; fax (095) 209-98-22; organ of the Russian Govt; Editor-in-Chief VALERY KUCHER; circ. 150,000 (1993).

Rossiya (Russia): 125865 Moscow, ul. Pravdy 24; tel. (095) 257-24-91; independent; weekly; Editor-in-Chief ALEKSANDR DROZDOV.

Selskaya Zhizn (Country Life): 125869 Moscow, ul. Pravdy 24; tel. (095) 257-29-36; fax (095) 257-28-39; f. 1918; 3 a week; fmrly organ of the Cen. Cttee of the CPSU; independent; Editor-in-Chief ALEKSANDR P. KHARLAMOV; circ. 1,350,000 (1993).

Sovetskaya Rossiya (Soviet Russia): 125868 Moscow, ul. Pravdy 24; tel. (095) 257-28-84; fax (095) 200-22-90; f. 1956; fmrly organ of the Cen. Cttee of the CPSU and the Russian Federation Supreme Soviet and Council of Ministers; 5 a week; independent; Editor (vacant); circ. 580,000 (1993).

Trud (Labour): 103792 Moscow, Nastasyinsky per. 4; tel. (095) 292-49-47; f. 1921; 6 a week; independent trade union newspaper; Editor ALEKSANDR S. POTAPOV; circ. 3,059,000 (1993).

Vechernyaya Moskva (Moscow Evening): 123846 Moscow, ul. 1905 goda 7; tel. (095) 259-33-33; f. 1923; Editor S. INDURSKY; circ. 630,000.

St Petersburg

Chas Pik (Rush Hour): 191040 St Petersburg, Nevsky pr. 81; tel. (812) 279-25-65; weekly; publ. by St Petersburg Union of Journalists; Editor-in-Chief NATALIYA CHAPLINA; circ. 80,000 (1993).

Sankt-Peterburgskiye Vedomosti (St Petersburg News): 191023 St Petersburg, Fontanka 59; tel. (812) 314-71-76; f. 1918; fmrly *Leningradskaya Pravda* (Leningrad Truth); organ of the St Petersburg Mayoralty; Editor O. KUZIN; circ. 350,000.

Vecherny Sankt Petersburg (St Petersburg Evening): St Petersburg, Fontanka 59; f. 1946; organ of the St Petersburg City Council; Editor G. F. KONDRASHEV.

PRINCIPAL PERIODICALS

Agriculture, Forestry, etc.

Agrokhimiya (Agricultural Chemistry): Moscow, Podsosensky per. 21; f. 1964; monthly; publ. by the Nauka (Science) Publishing House; journal of the Russian Academy of Sciences; results of theoretical and experimental research work; Editor N. N. MELNIKOV; circ. 5,900.

Doklady Rossiiskoy Akademii Selskokhozaistvennykh Nauk (Reports of the Russian Academy of Agricultural Sciences): 117218 Moscow, ul. Krzhizhanovsky 15; tel. (095) 207-76-60; f. 1936; 6 a year; the latest issues in agriculture; Editor-in-Chief N. S. MARKOVA; circ. 1,040.

Ekonomika Selskokhozyaistvennykh i Pererabatyvayushchikh Predpriyatiyakh (Economics of Agricultural and Processing Enterprises): 107807 Moscow, Sadovaya-Spasskaya ul. 18; tel. (095) 207-15-80; f. 1926; monthly; publ. by Kolos Publishing House and Ministry of Agriculture and Food; Editor V. A. ORLOV; circ. 25,970.

Lesnaya Promyshlennost (Forest Industry): 125047 Moscow, Bokzal pl. 3; tel. (095) 250-46-23; f. 1926; 3 a week; fmrly organ of the USSR State Committee for Forestry and the Cen. Cttee of the Timber, Paper and Wood Workers' Union of the USSR; Editor V. A. ALEKSEYEV; circ. 250,000.

Mekhanizatsiya i Elektrifikatsiya Selskovo Khozyaistva (Mechanization and Electrification of Agriculture): 107807 Moscow, Sadovaya-Spasskaya ul. 18; f. 1930; monthly; Editor I. E. CHESNOKOV; circ. 27,890.

Mezhdunarodny Selsko-Khozhiaistveny Zhurnal (International Agricultural Journal): 107807 Moscow, Sadovaya-Spasskaya ul. 18; tel. (095) 207-16-56; monthly.

Molochnoye i Myasnoye Skotovodstvo (Dairy and Meat Cattle Breeding): Moscow, Sadovaya-Spasskaya ul. 18; tel. (095) 207-21-20; f. 1956; 6 a year; Editor V. V. KORGENEVSKY; circ. 39,800.

Selskokhozyaistvennaya Biologiya (Agricultural Biology): Moscow, Sadovaya-Spasskaya ul. 18; f. 1966; 6 a year; publ. by the

Russian Academy of Agricultural Sciences; Editor V. M. ANANINA; circ. 1,980.

Svinovodstvo (Pig Breeding): Moscow, Sadovaya-Spasskaya ul. 18; f. 1930; 6 a year; Editor K. D. BAYEV; circ. 37,830.

Tekhnika v Selskom Khozyaistve (Agricultural Technology): 107807 Moscow, Sadovaya-Spasskaya ul. 18; tel. (095) 207-37-62; fax (095) 207-28-70; f. 1941; 6 a year; journal of the Ministry of Agriculture and Food Production and the Russian Academy of Agricultural Sciences; Editor-in-Chief PETR S. POPOV; circ. 4,000.

Vestnik Selskokhozyaistvennoy Nauki (Agricultural Scientific Bulletin): Moscow, Sadovaya-Spasskaya ul. 18; f. 1956; monthly; journal of the Russian Academy of Agricultural Sciences; Editor-in-Chief A. A. NIKONOV; circ. 6,460.

Veterinariya (Veterinary Science): Moscow, Sadovaya-Spasskaya ul. 18; tel. (095) 207-10-60; fax (095) 207-20-70; f. 1924; monthly; Editor V. A. GARKAVTSEV; circ. 19,000.

Zashchita Rastenii (Plant Protection): 107807 Moscow, Sadovaya-Spasskaya ul. 18; tel. (095) 207-21-30; f. 1932; monthly; Editor V. E. SAVZDARG; circ. 22,000.

Zemledeliye (Farming): Moscow, Sadovaya-Spasskaya ul. 18; f. 1939; monthly; Editor V. IVANOV; circ. 53,000.

Zhivotnovodstvo (Cattle Breeding): Moscow, Sadovaya-Spasskaya ul. 18; f. 1928; monthly; Editor A. T. MYSIK; circ. 106,870.

For Children

Koster (Campfire): 193024 St Petersburg, Mytninskaya ul. 1/20; tel. (812) 274-15-72; telex 321584; f. 1936; monthly; fmrly journal of the Union of Pioneer Organizations (Federation of Children's Organizations) of the USSR; fiction, poetry, sport, reports and popular science; for 10–14 years; Editor-in-Chief O. A. TSAKUNOV; circ. 800,000 (1991).

Murzilka: 125015 Moscow, Novodmitrovskaya ul. 5A; tel. (095) 285-18-81; f. 1924; monthly; publ. by the Molodaya Gvardiya (Young Guard) Publishing House; fmrly journal of the Union of Pioneer Organizations (Federation of Children's Organizations) of the USSR; illustrated; for first grades of school; Editor T. ANDROSENKO; circ. 2,960,000.

Pioner (Pioneer): 101459 Moscow, Bumazhny proyezd 14; tel. (095) 212-14-17; f. 1924; monthly; fmrly journal of the Cen. Cttee of the Leninist Young Communist League; fiction; illustrated: for children of fourth–eighth grades; Editor A. S. MOROZ; circ. 1,770,000.

Pionerskaya Pravda (Pioneer Pravda): 101502 Moscow, Sushchevskaya ul. 21; tel. (095) 972-22-38; f. 1925; 3 a week; fmrly organ of the Union of Pioneer Organizations (Federation of Children's Organizations) of the USSR; Editor O. I. GREKOVA; circ. 3,600,000.

Veselye Kartinki (Merry Pictures): 125015 Moscow, Novodmitrovskaya ul. 5A; tel. (095) 285-80-90; f. 1956; monthly; publ. by the Molodaya Gvardiya (Young Guard) Publishing House; humorous; for pre-school and first grades; Editor R. A. VARSHAMOV; circ. 9,350,000.

Yuny Naturalist (Young Naturalist): Moscow, Novodmitrovskaya ul. 5A; f. 1928; monthly; publ. by the Molodaya Gvardiya (Young Guard) Publishing House; fmrly journal of the Union of Pioneer Organizations (Federation of Children's Organizations) of the USSR; popular science for children of fourth–10th grades who are interested in biology; Editor A. G. ROGOZHKIN; circ. 1,500,000.

Yuny Tekhnik (Young Technologist): 125015 Moscow, Novodmitrovskaya ul. 5A; tel. (095) 285-80-81; f. 1956; monthly; publ. by the Molodaya Gvardiya (Young Guard) Publishing House; popular science for schoolchildren; Editor BORIS CHEREMISINOV; circ. 1,095,000.

Culture and Arts

Avrora (Aurora): 191065 St Petersburg, ul. Millionaya 4; tel. (095) 312-13-23; fax (095) 312-59-76; f. 1969; monthly; journal of the Russian Union of Writers; fiction; Editor-in-Chief E. SHEVELYOV; circ. 1,090,000.

Biblioteka 'V Pomoshch Khudozhestvennoy Samodeyatelnosti' (Amateur Art): Moscow; f. 1945; 2 a month; publ. by the Sovetskaya Rossiya (Soviet Russia) Publishing House; songs, plays and articles by leading actors; Editor N. M. SERGOVANTSEV; circ. 72,000.

Dekorativnoye Iskusstvo (Decorative Art): 103009 Moscow, ul. Tverskaya 9; tel. (095) 229-19-10; fax (095) 200-42-44; f. 1957; monthly; all aspects of contemporary visual art; illustrated; Editor S. B. BAZAZIANTS; circ. 7,000.

Ekran (Screen): Moscow, ul. Chasovaya 5B; tel. (095) 152-79-37; fax (095) 152-97-91; f. 1925; fortnightly; publ. by the Pressa Publishing House; journal of the Confederation of Film-makers' Unions; Russian and foreign cinema; Editor V. P. DEMIN; circ. 50,000.

Film (Film): 103009 Moscow, B. Gnezdnikovsky per. 9; tel. (095) 229-06-43; telex 411143; fax (095) 200-12-56; f. 1957; monthly; Russian, English, French, German and Spanish; illustrated; Russian and foreign films; Editor VALERY S. KICHIN; circ. 130,000.

Foto (Photography): Moscow, ul. Malaya Lubyanka 16; tel. (095) 925-10-07; fax (095) 200-42-37; f. 1926; 6 a year; journal of the Confederation of Journalists' Unions; Editor G. M. CHUDAKOV; circ. 35,000.

Govorit i Pokazyvayet Moskva: Programmy Tsentralnovo Televideniya i Radioveshchaniya (Moscow Speaks and Shows: Central Television and Radio Programmes): Moscow, Vtoroy Troitsky per. 4; f. 1967; Editor N. F. IVANKOVICH; circ. 1,650,000.

Iskusstvo (Art): Moscow, Vorotnikovsky per. 11; f. 1933; monthly; publ. by the Iskusstvo (Art) Publishing House; journal of the Union of Artists of Russia and the Russian Academy of Arts; fine arts; Editor V. ZIMENKO; circ. 18,500.

Iskusstvo Kino (Cinema Art): 125319 Moscow, Usievicha 9; tel. (095) 151-02-72; telex 411939; fax (095) 151-02-72; f. 1931; monthly; journal of the Confederation of Film-makers' Unions; Editor DANIIL DONDUREY; circ. 18,000.

Knizhnoye Obozreniye (Book Review): 129272 Moscow, Sushchevsky val 64; tel. (095) 281-62-66; fax (095) 281-62-66; f. 1966; weekly; summaries of newly published books; Editor E. S. AVERIN; circ. 105,000.

Kultura (Culture): 101484 Moscow, ul. Novoslobodskaya 73; tel. (095) 214-60-31; f. 1929; fmrly *Sovetskaya Kultura* (Soviet Culture); weekly; Editor A. A. BELYAYEV; circ. 75,000.

Kultura i Zhizn (Culture and Life): 103674 Moscow, proyezd Sapunova 13–15; tel. (095) 921-35-60; f. 1957; monthly; Russian, English, French, Spanish and German; publ. by the Society for Cultural and Friendly Relations with Foreign Countries; Editor ADO KUKANOV; circ. 130,000.

Literaturnaya Gazeta (Literary Newspaper): 103654 Moscow, Kostyansky per. 13; tel. (095) 200-24-17; telex 411294; fax (095) 200-02-38; f. 1830; publ. restored 1929; weekly; independent; fmrly organ of the USSR Writers' Union; Editor-in-Chief ARKADY UDALTSOV; circ. 210,000.

Literaturnaya Rossiya (Literary Russia): 103662 Moscow, Tsvetnoy bul. 30; tel. (095) 200-41-58; fax (095) 200-27-55; f. 1958; weekly; essays, verse, literary criticism, political reviews; Editor ERNST I. SAFONOV.

Moskva (Moscow): 121918 Moscow, Arbat 20; tel. (095) 291-71-10; f. 1957; monthly; journal of the Russian Federation Union of Writers and its Moscow branch; fiction; Editor-in-Chief MIKHAIL N. ALEKSEYEV; circ. 800,000.

Muzykalnaya Akademiya (Musical Academy): 103009 Moscow, ul. Ogareva 13; tel. (095) 229-81-66; f. 1933; fmrly *Sovetskaya Muzyka* (Soviet Music); quarterly; publ. by the Kompozitor (Composer) Publishing House; journal of the Union of Composers of the Russian Federation and the Ministry of Culture; Editor YU. S. KOREV; circ. 3,158.

Muzykalnaya Zhizn (Musical Life): 103006 Moscow, Sadovaya-Triumfalnaya ul. 14-12; tel. (095) 209-75-24; f. 1957; fortnightly; publ. by the Kompozitor (Composer) Publishing House; journal of the Union of Composers of the Russian Federation and the Ministry of Culture; development of music; Editor INNOKENTI YE. POPOV; circ. 131,000.

Neva (The River Neva): 191065 St Petersburg, Nevsky pr. 3; tel. (812) 312-65-37; fax (812) 311-08-17; f. 1955; monthly; journal of the St Petersburg Writers' Organization; fiction, literary criticism; Editor B. NIKOLSKY; circ. 46,000 (1993).

Oktyabr (October): Moscow, ul. Pravdy 11; tel. (095) 214-62-05; f. 1924; monthly; published by the Pressa Publishing House; independent literary journal; new fiction and essays by Russian and foreign writers; Editor A. A. ANANIYEV.

Teatr (Theatre): 121069 Moscow, ul. Gertsena 49; tel. (095) 291-57-88; monthly; publ. by the Izvestiya (News) Publishing House; journal of the Theatrical Workers' Union and the Russian Federation Union of Writers; new plays by Russian and foreign playwrights; Editor A. SALYNSKY; circ. 50,000.

Televideniye i Radioveshchaniye (Television and Radio Broadcasting): 113326 Moscow, Pyatnitskaya ul. 25; tel. (095) 292-82-68; f. 1952; monthly; Editor-in-Chief N. S. BIRYUKOV; circ. 50,000.

Economics, Finance

Dengi i Kredit (Money and Credit): 103016 Moscow, Neglinnaya ul. 12; tel. (095) 925-45-03; f. 1927; monthly; publ. by the Finansy i statistika (Finances and Statistics) Publishing House; all aspects of banking and money circulation; Editor Y. G. DMITRIEV; circ. 29,190.

Ekonomika i Matematicheskiye Metody (Economics and Mathematical Methods): 117418 Moscow, ul. Krasikova 32; tel. (095) 332-46-39; fax (095) 310-70-15; f. 1965; 4 a year; publ. by the Nauka (Science) Publishing House; journal of the Institute of Economics and Mathematics and the Institute of Market Problems; theoretical and methodological problems of economics, econometrics; Editor V. L. MAKAROV; circ. 1,675.

Ekonomika i Zhizn (Economics and Life): 101462 Moscow, Bumazhny proyezd 14; tel. (095) 250-57-93; fax (095) 212-30-93; f. 1918; weekly; fmrly *Ekonomicheskaya gazeta*; news and information about the economy and business; Editor YURI YAKUTIN; circ. 600,000.

Finansy (Finances): 103050 Moscow, ul. Tverskaya 22B; tel. (095) 299-43-33; fax (095) 299-93-06; f. 1991; monthly; publ. by the Finansy (Finances) Publishing House; fmrly journal of the Ministry of Finance; theory and information on finances; compiling and execution of the state budget, insurance, lending, taxation etc.; Editor YU. M. ARTEMOV; circ. 80,000.

Kommersant: Moscow, Khoroshovskoye Shosse 41; tel. (095) 941-09-00; f. 1989; independent; economics, business and politics; Editor MIKHAIL ROGOZHNIKOV.

Mir Daidzhest Pressi (Business World Press Digest): 191180 St Petersburg, POB 55; f. 1989; 8 a year; publ. by St Petersburg branch of Union of Journalists; all aspects of finance; Editors YAN STRUGACH, SERGEI GRACHEV.

Mirovaya Ekonomika i Mezhdunarodniye Otnosheniya (World Economy and International Relations): Moscow, Profsoyuznaya ul. 23; tel. (095) 128-08-83; telex 411687; fax (095) 31-07-27; f. 1957; monthly; publ. by the Nauka (Science) Publishing House; journal of the Institute of the World Economy and International Relations of the Russian Academy of Sciences; problems of theory and practice of world socio-economic development, international policies, international economic co-operation, economic and political situation in different countries of the world, etc.; Editor Prof. G. G. DILIGENSKY; circ. 26,000.

Rossiisky Ekonomishesky Zhurnal (Russian Economic Journal): 109542 Moscow, Ryazansky pr. 99; tel. (095) 377-25-56; f. 1958; monthly; fmrly Ekonomicheskiye Nauki (Economic Sciences); theory and practice of economics and economic reform; Editor A. YU. MELENTEV; circ. 23,600.

Voprosy Ekonomiki (Problems of Economics): 117218 Moscow, ul. Krasikova 27; tel. (095) 129-04-44; fax (095) 310-70-01; f. 1929; monthly; journal of the Institute of Economics of the Russian Academy of Sciences; theoretical probelems of economic development, market relations, social aspects of transition to a market economy, international economics, etc.; Editor A. ABALKIN; circ. 24,000.

Education

Pedagogika (Pedagogics): 119034 Moscow, Smolensky bul. 4; tel. (095) 248-51-49; f. 1937; monthly; publ. by Academy of Pedagogical Sciences; Chief Editor G. N. FILONOV; circ. 46,500.

Professionalno-tekhnicheskoye Obrazovaniye (Vocational and Technical Education): 125319 Moscow, ul. Chernyakhovskovo 9; tel. (095) 152-75-41; f. 1941; monthly; Editor-in-Chief VLADIMIR G. CHERNYKH; circ. 35,000 (1991).

Rodnoy Yazyk (The Mother Tongue): 121819 Moscow, Trubnikovsky per. 19; f. 1993; 6 a year; Editor M. I. ISAYEV; circ. 2,000.

Semya (Family): Moscow; f. 1988; weekly; fmrly publ. by Soviet Children's Fund; Editor-in-Chief SERGEY A. ABRAMOV; circ. 4,600,000.

Semya i Shkola (Family and School): 129278 Moscow, ul. Pavla Korchagina 7; tel. (095) 283-80-09; f. 1871; monthly; Editor V. F. SMIRNOV; circ. 125,000.

Shkola i Proizvodstvo (School and Production): 107847 Moscow, Lefortovsky per. 8; tel. (095) 246-65-91; f. 1957; monthly; publ. by the Pedagogika (Pedagogics) Publishing House; Editor YU. YE. RIVES-KOROBKOV; circ. 205,000.

Uchitelskaya Gazeta (Teachers' Gazette): 103012 Moscow, Vetoshny per. 13/15; tel. (095) 928-82-53; f. 1924; weekly; independent pedagogical newspaper; distributed throughout the CIS; Editor P. POLOZHEVETZ; circ. 250,000.

Vestnik Vysshey Shkoly (Higher Schools' Review): 103031 Moscow, ul. Rozhdestvenka 11; tel. (095) 924-73-43; f. 1940; monthly; Editor O. V. DOLZHENKO; circ. 17,000.

Vospitaniye Shkolnikov (The Upbringing of Schoolchildren): Moscow, Lefortovsky per. 8; f. 1966; 6 a year; publ. by Pedagogika (Pedagogics) Publishing House; Editor L. V. KUZNETSOVA; circ. 733,230.

International Affairs

Ekho Planety (Echo of the Planet): 103009 Moscow, Tverskoy bul. 10–12; tel. (095) 202-69-96; fax (095) 290-66-45; f. 1988; weekly; Russian; publ. by ITAR—TASS; international affairs, economic, social and cultural; Editor-in-Chief YURY PEVNEV; circ. 150,000.

Mezhdunarodnaya Zhizn (International Life): 103064 Moscow, Gorokhovsky per. 14; tel. (095) 265-37-81; f. 1954; monthly; Russian, English and French; publ. by the Pressa Publishing House; problems of foreign policy and diplomacy of Russia and other countries; Editor B. D. PYADYSHEV; circ. 71,620.

Novoye Vremya (New Times): 103782 Moscow, pl. Pushkina 5; tel. (095) 229-88-72; telex 411164; fax (095) 200-41-92; f. 1943; weekly; Russian, English, French, German, Spanish, Portuguese, Italian, Polish, Greek and Czech; publ. by the Moskovskaya Pravda Publishing House; foreign and Russian affairs; Editor V. IGNATENKO; circ. 500,000.

Za Rubezhom (Abroad): 125865 Moscow, ul. Pravdy 24; tel. (095) 257-23-87; telex 411421; fax (095) 200-22-96; f. 1960; weekly; publ. by the Pressa Publishing House; review of foreign press; Editor-in-Chief S. MOROZOV; circ. 650,000.

Language, Literature

Filologicheskiye Nauki (Philological Sciences): Moscow, prospekt Marksa 18; f. 1958; 6 a year; publ. by the Vysshaya Shkola (Higher School) Publishing House; reports of institutions of higher learning on the most important problems of literary studies and linguistics; Editor P. A. NIKOLAYEV; circ. 2,960.

Lepta (Mite): 121248 Moscow, Kutuzovsky pr. 1/7; tel. (095) 243-38-78; fax (095) 243-03-66; f. 1931; fmrly *Sovetskaya Literatuta* (Soviet Literature); monthly; English and Russian; novels, short stories, verses, poems, literary criticism, non-fiction and topical articles; Editor ALEKSEY BARKHATOV; circ. 50,000.

Russkaya Literatura (Russian Literature): 199164 St Petersburg, nab. Makarova 4; f. 1958; quarterly; journal of the Institute of Russian Literature of the Russian Academy of Sciences; development of Russian literature from its appearance up to the present day; Editor V. V. SKATOV; circ. 13,149.

Russkaya Rech (Russian Speech): Moscow, ul. Volkhonka 18/2; f. 1967; 6 a year; publ. by the Nauka (Science) Publishing House; journal of the Institute of Russian Language of the Academy of Sciences; popular; history of the development of the literary Russian language; Editor V. P. VOMPENSKY; circ. 30,000.

Russky Yazyk za Rubezhom (The Russian Language Abroad): 117485 Moscow, ul. Volgina 6; tel. (095) 336-66-47; f. 1967; 6 a year; publ. by the Russky Yazyk (Russian Language) Publishing House; journal of the Pushkin Institute of the Russian Language; current problems of methodology of teaching the Russian language to foreigners; Editor A. V. ABRAMOVICH; circ. 44,300.

Voprosy Literatury (Questions of Literature): 103009 Moscow, Bolshoy Gnezdnikovsky per. 10; tel. (095) 229-49-77; f. 1957; monthly; publ. by the Izvestiya (News) Publishing House; joint edition of the Institute of World Literature of the Academy of Sciences and the Literary Thought Foundation; theory and history of modern literature and aesthetics; Editor L. I. LAZAREV; circ. 18,500.

Voprosy Yazykoznaniya (Questions of Linguistics): 121019 Moscow, Volkhonka 18/2; tel. (095) 201-74-42; f. 1952; 6 a year; publ. by the Nauka (Science) Publishing House; journal of the Department of Literature and Language of the Russian Academy of Sciences; actual problems of general linguistics on the basis of different languages; Editor T. V. GAMKRELIDZE; circ. 2,800.

Leisure, Physical Culture and Sport

Filateliya (Philately): 121069 Moscow, Khlebny per. 8; f. 1966; monthly; journal of the Russian Philatelic Society; Editor-in-Chief ZH. G. BEKHTEREV; circ. 70,000.

Fizkultura i Sport (Physical Culture and Sport): Moscow, Kalyayevskaya ul. 27; f. 1922; monthly; publ. by the Beta-print Publishing House; fmrly journal of the USSR State Committee for Physical Culture and Sport; activities and development of Russian sport; Editor A. CHAIKOVSKY; circ. 717,000.

Mir Puteshestvy (World of Travels): 107078 Moscow, Bolshoi Kharitonyevsky per. 14; tel. (095) 921-13-90; telex 111777; f. 1929, fmrly *Turist*; journal of the Sputnik tourist company; monthly; publ. by the Profizdat (Trade Union Literature) Publishing House; articles, photo-essays, information, recommendations about routes and hotels for tourists, natural, cultural and historical places of interest; Editor BORIS V. MOSKVIN; circ. 20,000.

Shakhmatny Vestnik (Chess Herald): 121019 Moscow, POB 10, Gogolevsky bul. 14; tel. (095) 291-87-70; f. 1921; fmrly *Shakhmaty v SSSR* (Chess in the USSR); monthly; publ. by the Beta-print Publishing House; journal of the Russian Chess Federation and International Chess Players' Union; Editor Y. AVERBAKH; circ. 15,000.

Sportivnye Igry (Sports): 101421 Moscow, Kalyayevskaya ul. 27; tel. (095) 258-06-56; fax (095) 200-12-17; f. 1955; monthly; publ. by the Fizkultura i Sport (Physical Culture and Sport) Publishing House; fmrly journal of the USSR State Committee for Physical Culture and Sport; Editor D. L. RYZHKOV; circ. 160,000.

Sport: 103772 Moscow, ul. Moskvina 8; tel. (095) 229-46-59; f. 1963; monthly; Russian, English, Spanish, and Hindi; publ. by Voskresenye Publishing Corporation; illustrated; Editor O. D. SPASSKY.

Teoriya i Praktika Fizicheskoy Kultury (Theory and Practice of Physical Culture): Moscow, Kalyayevskaya ul. 27; f. 1925; monthly; publ. by the Fizkultura i Sport (Physical Culture and Sport) Publishing House; fmrly journal of the USSR State Committee for Physical Culture and Sport; Editor A. V. SEDOV; circ. 16,200.

Politics and Military Affairs

Ekspress-Khronika (Express-Chronicle): 111399 Moscow, POB 5; tel. (095) 264-97-91; fax (095) 264-57-42; f. 1987; weekly; independent chronicle of events throughout the former USSR; also an edition in English; Editor ALEKSANDR PODRABINEK.

Moskovskiye Novosti (Moscow News): 103829 Moscow, ul. Tverskaya 16/2; tel. (095) 209-19-84; fax (095) 209-17-28; f. 1930; weekly; Russian, English; independent; Editor-in-Chief LEN KARPINSKY; circ. 500,000.

Politicheskoye Obrazovaniye (Political Education): Moscow, ul. Pravdy 24; f. 1957; monthly; publ. by the Pressa Publishing House; fmrly journal of the Cen. Cttee of the CPSU; Editor N. Y. KLEPACH; circ. 1,862,000.

Rossiyskaya Federatsiya: Moscow, Staraya pl. 4; f. 1994; journal of the Russian Govt.

Sovetsky Voin (Soviet Soldier): 123831 Moscow, 32A/3 Khoroshevskoye Shosse; tel. (095) 198-55-63; f. 1919; fortnightly in Russian, monthly in English and German; publ. by Voyenizdat (Military Publishing House); Editor-in-Chief LEONID GOLOVNYOV; circ. 1,000,000.

Svobodnaya Mysl (Free Thought): 119875 Moscow, ul. Marksa i Engelsa 5; tel. (095) 291-60-67; f. 1924; fmrly *Kommunist* (Communist), the theoretical journal of the Cen. Cttee of the CPSU; 18 a year; problems of political theory, philosophy, economy, etc.; Editor-in-Chief N. B. BIKKENIN; circ. 995,000.

Popular, Fiction and General

Druzhba Narodov (Friendship of Peoples): 121827 Moscow, ul. Vorovskovo 52; tel. (095) 291-62-27; f. 1939; monthly; publ. by the Izvestiya (News) Publishing House; independent; prose, poetry and literary criticism; Editor A. RUDENKO-DESNYAK; circ. 250,000.

Inostrannaya Literatura (Foreign Literature): Moscow, Pyatnitskaya ul. 41; tel. (095) 233-51-47; fax (095) 230-23-03; f. 1955; monthly; publ. by the Izvestiya (News) Publishing House; independent; Russian translations of modern foreign authors; Editor-in-Chief VLADIMIR LAKSHIN; circ. 200,000.

Moskva (Moscow): Moscow, ul. Arbat 20; f. 1957; monthly; publ. by the Khudozhestvennaya Literatura (Fiction) Publishing House; Editor M. N. ALEKSEYEV; circ. 760,000.

Nash Sovremennik (Our Contemporary): Moscow, Tsvetnoy bul. 30; f. 1933; monthly; publ. by the Literaturnaya Gazeta (Literary Gazette) Publishing House; Editor STANISLAV KUNAYEV; circ. 270,000.

Novy Mir (New World): 103806 Moscow, Maly Putinkovsky per. 1/2; tel. (095) 200-08-29; f. 1925; monthly; publ. by the Izvestiya (News) Publishing House; new fiction and essays; Editor SERGEY P. ZALYGIN; circ. 1,560,000.

Ogonek (Beacon): 101456 Moscow, Bumazhny per. 14; tel. (095) 212-23-27; fax (095) 943-00-70; f. 1923; weekly; independent; popular illustrated; Editor LEV GUSHCHIN; circ. 1,500,000.

Rodina (Motherland): Moscow; f. 1989; monthly; publ. by the Pressa Publishing House; social, political and scientific; illustrated.

Roman-Gazeta (Novels): Moscow, Novo-Basmannaya ul. 19; tel. 261-49-29; f. 1927; fortnightly; publ. by the Khudozhestvennaya Literatura (Fiction) Publishing House; contemporary fiction including translations into Russian; Editor V. GANICHEV; circ. 3,500,000.

Stolitsa (Capital): 101425 Moscow, ul. Petrovka 22; tel. (095) 928-23-49; telex 413739; fax (095) 921-29-85; f. 1990; weekly; general; Editor ANDREY MALGIN; circ. 100,000.

Vokrug Sveta (Around the World): 125015 Moscow, Novodmitrovskaya ul. 5A; tel. (095) 285-88-83; fax (095) 972-05-72; f. 1861; monthly, including the supplement *Iskatel* (Seeker) in alternate issues and the book supplement *Library of Vokrug Sveta*; publ. by Vokrug Sveta joint stock co; geographical, travel, adventure and science fiction, detective stories; illustrated; Editor A. A. POLESHCHUK; circ. 210,000.

Voskreseniye (Resurrection): 103772 Moscow, ul. Moskvina 8; tel. (095) 229-14-19; fax (095) 229-74-14; f. 1930; monthly; Russian, English, French, German, Spanish; publ. by the New Russia Publishing Corporation; illustrated; Editor A. N. MISHARIN.

Zakon (Law): 103798 Moscow, Pushkinskaya pl. 5; tel. (095) 299-74-55; f. 1991; publ. by the Izvestiya printing house; publishes legislation relating to business and commerce; legal issues for businessmen; Editor YURY FEOFANOV.

Znamya (Banner): Moscow, ul. Nikolskaya 8/1; f. 1931; monthly; independent; novels, poetry, essays; Editor-in-Chief GRIGORY YA. BAKLANOV; circ. 80,900.

Zvezda (Star): St Petersburg, Mokhovaya 20; f. 1924; monthly; publ. by the Khudozhestvennaya Literatura (Fiction) Publishing House; journal of the Russian Federation Union of Writers; novels, short stories, poetry, art and literary criticism; Editor G. KHOLOPOV; circ. 215,000.

Popular Scientific

HF Magazine: 103045 Moscow, Selivertsov per. 10; tel. (095) 292-65-11; f. 1992; 6 a year; supplement to *Radio*; Chief Editor B. G. STEPANOV; circ. 5,000.

Meditsinskaya Gazeta (Medical Gazette): 129010 Moscow, Sukharevskaya pl. 1/2; tel. (095) 208-86-95; f. 1938; 2 a week; organ of the Union of Medical Workers of Russia; Editor K. V. SHEGLOV; circ. 1,430,000.

Modelist-Konstruktor (Modelling-Designing): 125015 Moscow, Novodmitrovskaya ul. 5A; tel. (095) 285-17-04; f. 1962; monthly; publ. by the Molodaya Gvardiya (Young Guard) Publishing House; designs and descriptions of technical models; Editor Y. STOLYAROV; circ. 1,200,000.

Nauka i Religiya (Science and Religion): 109004 Moscow, Ulyanovskaya 43; f. 1959; monthly; Editor V. F. PRAVOTVOROV; circ. 480,000.

Nauka i Zhizn (Science and Life): 101877 Moscow, ul. Myasnitskaya 24; tel. (095) 923-21-22; fax (095) 200-22-59; f. 1934; monthly; publ. by the Pressa Publishing House; popular; recent developments in all branches of science and technology; Chief Editor I. K. LAGOVSKY; circ. 141,800.

Priroda (Nature): 117069 Moscow, Maronovsky per. 26; tel. (095) 238-26-33; f. 1912; monthly; publ. by the Nauka (Science) Publishing House; journal of the Presidium of the Academy of Sciences; popular; natural sciences; Editor A. F. ANDREYEV; circ. 25,000.

Radio: 103045 Moscow, Seliverstov per. 10; tel. (095) 207-68-89; fax (095) 208-13-11; f. 1924; monthly; audio, video, communications, practical electronics, computers; Editor A. V. GOROKHOVSKY; circ. 270,000.

Tekhnika-Molodezhi (Engineering—For Youth): 125015 Moscow, Novodmitrovskaya ul. 5A; tel. (095) 285-89-81; f. 1933; monthly; publ. by the Molodaya Gvardiya (Young Guard) Publishing House; fmrly journal of the Cen. Cttee of the Leninist Young Communist League; popular; engineering and science; Editor S. V. CHUMAKOV; circ. 1,819,000.

Vrach (Physician): 119435 Moscow, ul. Pogodinskaya 7; tel. (095) 248-20-55; fax (095) 248-02-14; f. 1990; monthly; publ. by Meditsina Publs; medical, scientific and socio-political; illustrated; Editor-in-Chief MIKHAIL A. PALTSEV; circ. 100,000.

Zdorovye (Health): Moscow, Bumazhny per. 24; f. 1955; monthly; publ. by the Pressa Publishing House; publ. by the Ministry of Health; popular scientific; medicine and hygiene; Editor M. D. PIRADOVA; circ. 16,800,000.

Zemlya i Vselennaya (Earth and Universe): Moscow, Maronovsky per. 26; tel. (095) 238-42-32; f. 1965; 6 a year; publ. by the Nauka (Science) Publishing House; joint edition of the Academy of Sciences and the Society of Astronomy and Geodesy; popular; current hypotheses of the origin and development of the earth and universe; astronomy, geophysics and space research; Editor V. K. ABALAKIN; circ. 49,000.

Znaniye-Sila (Knowledge is Strength): 113114 Moscow, Kozhevnicheskaya ul. 19; tel. (095) 235-89-35; f. 1926; monthly; publ. by the Znaniye (Knowledge) Publishing House; general scientific; Editor G. A. ZELENKO; circ. 350,000.

The Press, Printing and Bibliography

Bibliografiya (Bibliography): 129272 Moscow, Sushchevsky val 64; tel. (095) 284-57-65; f. 1929; 6 a year; publ. by the Knizhnaya Palata (Book Chamber) Publishing House; theoretical, practical and historical aspects of bibliography; Editor G. A. ALEKSEEVA; circ. 6,000.

Knizhnaya Letopis (Book Chronicle): 127018 Moscow, Oktyabrskaya ul. 4; tel. (095) 288-92-01; f. 1907; weekly; publ. by the Knizhnaya palata (Book Chamber) Publishing House; registration of all books published in the CIS, with description of books; Editors V. N. TYURICHEVA, G. N. DMITRIYENKO; circ. 1,600.

Notnaya Letopis (Chronicle of Music): 127018 Moscow, Oktyabrskaya ul. 4; tel. (095) 288-92-38; f. 1931; monthly; publ. by the Knizhnaya palata (Book Chamber) Publishing House; registration of issues of music in the CIS; Editors N. A. ROSTOVSKAYA, G. N. DMITRIYENKO; circ. 776.

Poligrafiya (Printing): 129272 Moscow, Sushchevsky val 64; tel. (095) 281-74-81; fax (095) 288-97-66; f. 1924; 6 a year; equipment and technology of the printing industry; Dir A. I. OVSYANNIKOV; circ. 8,000.

V Mire Knig (In the World of Books): 129272 Moscow, Sushchevsky val 64; tel. (095) 281-50-98; f. 1936; monthly; publ. by the Knizhnaya

Palata (Book Chamber) Publishing House; reviews of new books, theoretical problems of literature, historical and religious; Editor A. V. LARIONOV; circ. 147,000.

Zhurnalist (Journalist): 101453 Moscow, Bumazhny proyezd 14; tel. (095) 257-30-58; fax (095) 257-35-89; f. 1920; monthly; journal of the Confederation of Journalists' Unions; problems of professionalism, journalistic ethics and the life of journalists; Editor D. S. AVRAAMOV; circ. 10,000.

Religion

Bratsky Vestnik (Herald of the Brethren): 101000 Moscow, POB 520, Maly Vuzovsky per. 3; tel. (095) 297-96-26; f. 1945; 6 a year; organ of the Euro-Asiatic Federation of the Unions of Evangelical Christian-Baptists; Chief Editor A. M. BICHKOV.

Pravoslavnaya Beseda (Orthodox Discussion): Moscow; f. 1991; publ. by the Orthodox Brotherhood.

Zhurnal Moskovskoy Patriarkhii (Journal of the Moscow Patriarchate): 119435 Moscow, Pogodinskaya 20; tel. (095) 246-98-48 (Russian), (095) 245-14-41 (English); fax (095) 230-27-35; f. 1931; monthly; publ. by the Patriarchate in Russian and English; Editor Metropolitan PITIRIM (K. V. NECHAEV); circ. 40,000.

Satirical

Krokodil (Crocodile): 101455 Moscow, Bumazhny proyezd 14; tel. (095) 250-10-86; f. 1922; 3 a month; publ. by the Pressa Publishing House; Editor A. S. PYANOV; circ. 2,200,000.

Trade, Trade Unions, Labour and Social Security

Chelovek i Trud (Man and Labour): 103062 Moscow, Lyalin per. 14; tel. (095) 297-29-67; monthly; employment issues and problems of unemployment; Editor-in-Chief G. L. PODVOYSKY; circ. 40,000.

Profsoyuzy (Trade Unions): 101000 Moscow, ul. Myasnitskaya 13; tel. (095) 921-36-73; f. 1917; monthly; fmrly publ. by the General Confederation of Trade Unions of the USSR; Editor M. P. MUDROV; circ. 50,000.

Sotsialnoye Obespecheniye (Social Security): Moscow, ul. Shabolovka 14; f. 1926; monthly; journal of the Ministry of Social Welfare of the Population; Editor L. S. MALANCHEV.

Torgovlya (Trade): Moscow, Berezhkovskaya nab. 6; tel. (095) 240-48-37; f. 1927; monthly; fmrly *Sovetskaya Torgovlya*; Editor M. M. LYSOV; circ. 50,000.

Vneshnyaya Torgovlya (Foreign Trade): 121108 Moscow, ul. Minskaya 11; tel. (095) 145-68-94; fax (095) 145-51-92; f. 1921; monthly; Russian and English; fmrly organ of the Ministry of Foreign Economic Relations; Editor-in-Chief V. N. DUSHENKIN; circ. 25,000.

Transport and Communication

Avtomatika, Telemekhanika i Svyaz (Automation, Telemechanics and Communication): Moscow, Krasnovorotsky proyezd 3B; f. 1923; monthly; publ. by the Transport Publishing House; fmrly journal of the USSR Ministry of Railway Transport; utilization of new equipment in rail transport; Editor L. P. SLOBODYANYUK; circ. 27,780.

Grazhdanskaya Aviyatsiya (Civil Aviation): Moscow; f. 1931; monthly; journal of the Union of Civil Aviation Workers; development of air transport; utilization of aviation in construction, agriculture and forestry; Editor A. M. TROSHIN.

Radiotekhnika (Radio Engineering): Moscow, Kuznetsky most 20; f. 1937; monthly; publ. by the Svyaz (Communication) Publishing House; journal of the A. S. Popov Scientific and Technical Society of Radio Engineering, Electronics and Electrical Communication; theoretical and technical problems of radio engineering; Editor A. L. MIKAELYAN.

Radiotekhnika i Elektronika (Radio Engineering and Electronics): Moscow, Mokhovaya ul. 11; tel. (095) 203-47-89; f. 1956; monthly; journal of the Russian Academy of Sciences; theory of radio engineering; Editor N. D. DEVYATKOV; circ. 8,098.

Vestnik Svyazi (Herald of Communication): Moscow, ul. Kazakova 8A; tel. (095) 261-05-55; f. 1917; monthly; publ. by the Svyaz (Communication) Publishing House; mechanization and automation of production; Editor E. B. KONSTANTINOV; circ. 63,000.

For Women

Krestyanka (Peasant Woman): 101460 Moscow, Bumazhny per. 14; tel. (095) 212-20-63; f. 1922; monthly; publ. by the Pressa Publishing House; popular; Editor G. V. SEMENOVA; circ. 20,500,000.

Moda i Mir (Fashion and the World): 103031 Moscow, Kuznetsky Most 7/9; tel. (095) 921-73-93; annually; Editor (vacant); circ. 250,000.

Modeli Sezona (Models of the Season): Moscow, Kuznetsky Most 7/9; tel. (095) 921-73-93; f. 1945; 4 a year; Editor (vacant); circ. 600,000.

Rabotnitsa (Working Woman): 101460 Moscow, Bumazhny per. 14; f. 1914; monthly; publ. by the Pressa Publishing House; popular; Editor Z. P. KRYLOVA; circ. 20,500,000.

Zhenshchina (Woman): 103764 Moscow, Kuznetsky Most 22; tel. (095) 221-04-81; f. 1945; monthly; Russian, Chinese, English, French, German, Hindi, Hungarian, Japanese, Korean, Bengali, Arabic, Spanish, Portuguese, Finnish and Vietnamese; fmrly publ. by the Soviet Women's Committee and the General Confederation of Trade Unions; popular; illustrated; Editor-in-Chief V. I. FEDOTOVA.

Zhurnal Mod (Fashion Journal): 103031 Moscow, Kuznetsky Most 7/9; tel. (095) 921-73-93; f. 1945; 4 a year; Editor (vacant); circ. 1,000,000.

Youth

Molodaya Gvardiya (Young Guard): 125015 Moscow, Novodmitrovskaya ul. 5A; tel. (095) 285-88-58; f. 1922; monthly; publ. by the Molodaya Gvardiya (Young Guard) Publishing House; fiction, criticism, popular science; Editor A. IVANOV; circ. 640,000.

Perspektivy (Perspectives): 125015 Moscow, Novodmitrovskaya ul. 5A; tel. (095) 285-88-05; telex 411261; fax (095) 972-05-82; f. 1918; monthly; publ. by the Molodaya Gvardiya (Young Guard) Publishing House; fmrly *Molodoy Kommunist* (Young Communist), the journal of the Cen. Cttee of the Leninist Young Communist League; Editor Z. G. APRESYAN; circ. 630,000.

Rovesnik (Contemporary): 125015 Moscow, Novodmitrovskaya ul. 5A; tel. (095) 285-89-20; f. 1962; publ. by the Molodaya Gvardiya (Young Guard) Publishing House; fmrly journal of the Cen. Cttee of the Leninist Young Communist League and the Publishing-Printing Unit of Molodaya Gvardiya; popular illustrated monthly of politics, fiction, verses, songs, etc.; Editor A. A. NODIYA; circ. 2,050,000.

Selskaya Molodezh (Rural Youth): Moscow, Novodmitrovskaya ul. 5A; f. 1925; monthly; publ. by the Molodaya Gvardiya (Young Guard) Publishing House; fmrly journal of the Cen. Cttee of the Leninist Young Communist League; popular illustrated, fiction, verses, problems of rural youth; Editor O. POPTSOV; circ. 1,450,000.

Smena (Rising Generation): 101457 Moscow, Bumazhny proyezd 14; tel. (095) 212-15-07; fax (095) 250-59-28; f. 1924; monthly; publ. by the Pressa Publishing House; popular illustrated, short stories, essays and problems of youth; Editor-in-Chief M. G. KIZILOV; circ. 400,000.

Yunost (Youth): Moscow, ul. Tverskaya 32/1; f. 1955; monthly; publ. by the Pressa Publishing House; journal of the Russian Federation Union of Writers; novels, short stories, essays and poems by beginners; Editor A. DEMENTEV; circ. 3,300,000.

NEWS AGENCIES

Informatsionnoye Telegrafnoye Agentstvo Rossii—Telegrafnoye Agentstvo Suverennykh Stran (ITAR—TASS) (Information Telegraphic Agency of Russia—Telegraphic Agency of the Sovereign Countries): Moscow, Tverskoy bul. 10; tel. (095) 229-79-25; telex 411186; f. 1925; state information agency; Dir-Gen. VITALY IGNATENKO.

Interfax: 103006 Moscow, 1-aya Tverskaya-Yamskaya ul. 2; tel. (095) 250-98-40; telex 612176; fax (095) 250-97-27; f. 1989; independent news agency; Pres. M. KOMISSAR.

Postfactum: Moscow; f. 1990; independent news agency; Pres. MIKHAIL V. KOMISSAR.

Rossiyskoye Informatsionnoye Agentstvo—Novosti (RIA—Novosti) (Russian Information Agency—Novosti Press Agency): Moscow, Zubovsky bul. 4; tel. (095) 201-24-24; telex 411321; fax (095) 201-21-19; f. 1961; collaborates by arrangement with foreign press and publishing organizations in 110 countries of the world; Chair. VLADIMIR MARKOV.

Foreign Bureaux

Agence France-Presse (AFP): Moscow, Sadovo-Samotechnaya ul. 12/24, kv. 67–68; tel. (095) 200-12-44; telex 413321; fax (095) 200-19-46; Dir BERNARD ESTRADE.

Agencia EFE (Spain): 103051 Moscow, Sadovo-Samotechnaya ul. 12/24, kv. 23; tel. (095) 200-15-32; telex 413114; fax (095) 200-02-19; Bureau Chief SILVIA ODORIZ GONZÁLEZ.

Agenzia Nazionale Stampa Associata (ANSA) (Italy): 121248 Moscow, Kutuzovsky pr. 9, kv. 12–14; tel. (095) 230-27-54; telex 413451; fax (095) 243-06-37; Bureau Chief ALESSANDRO SERPIERI.

Anatolian News Agency (Turkey): Moscow, Rublevskoe Chausée 26, kor. 1, kv. 279; tel. (095) 415-29-34; telex 413641; Correspondent MUSTAFA KEMAL ERICH.

Associated Press (AP) (USA): Moscow, Kutuzovsky pr. 7/4, kor. 5, kv. 33; tel. (095) 243-51-53; telex 413422; fax (095) 230-2845; Bureau Chief BARRY RENFREW.

Bulgarska Telegrafna Agentsia (BTA) (Bulgaria): Moscow, Kutuzovsky pr. 9, kor. 2, kv. 64–65; tel. (095) 243-65-80; telex 414494; Correspondent NACHO HALACHEV.

Česká tisková kancelář (ČTK) (Czech Republic): 121069 Moscow, Novinsky bul. 28, kv. 4; tel. (095) 203-04-24; telex 414463; Correspondent VACLAV FRANK.

Dan News Agency (Argentina): Moscow, pl. Vosstaniya 1, kv. 371; tel. (095) 255-47-21; telex 413361; Correspondent ILDA RANDI.

Deutsche Presse-Agentur (DPA) (Germany): Moscow, Kutuzovsky pr. 7/4, kv. 210; tel. (095) 243-97-90; telex 413122; Correspondent Dr FRANZ SMETS.

Excelsior (Mexico): 123056 Moscow, Bolshoy Gruzinsky per. 3, kv. 266; tel. (095) 250-41-65; telex 413013; Correspondent MIGUEL ANGEL BARBERENA.

Interpress (Poland): 121248 Moscow, Kutuzovsky pr. 7/4, kor. 6, kv. 63; tel. (095) 243-75-23; telex 414376; Bureau Chief TOMAS PIVOVARUN.

Iraqi News Agency: Moscow, Simferopolsky bul. 7, kv. 119–120; tel. (095) 316-94-92, telex 413484; Correspondent AHMED SAKRAN KDEP.

Jiji Tsushin-sha (Jiji Press) (Japan): Moscow, Sadovaya-Samotechnaya ul. 12/24, kv. 21; tel. (095) 200-10-17; telex 413137; fax (095) 200-02-31; Bureau Chief KENRO NAGOSHI.

Korea Central News Agency (Democratic People's Republic of Korea): Moscow, ul. Mosfilmovskaya 72; tel. (095) 143-90-71; Bureau Chief CHAN KON SOB.

Kuwait News Agency (KUNA): Moscow, Korovy val 7, kv. 52; tel. (095) 237-49-32; telex 413463; fax (095) 230-25-10; Correspondent ADIB AL-SAYYED.

Kyodo News Service (Japan): 121059 Moscow, B. Dorogomilovskaya 12; tel. (095) 956-60-24; fax (095) 956-60-27; Bureau Chief KAZUHIRO EZAWA.

Magyar Távirati Iroda (MTI) (Hungary): Moscow, Bolshaya Spasskaya ul. 12, kv. 46; tel. (095) 280-04-21; telex 414419; fax (095) 280-04-21; Bureau Chief SÁNDOR DOROGI.

Middle East News Agency (MENA) (Egypt): Moscow, Sokolnichesky val 24, kor. 2, kv. 176; tel. (095) 264-82-76; fax (095) 288-95-27; Correspondent Dr MAMDOUH MUSTAFA.

Mongol Tsahilgaan Medeeniy Agentlag (Montsame) (Mongolia): Moscow, ul. Gilyarovskovo 8, kv. 81–82; tel. (095) 284-48-14; Bureau Chief CH. TUMENDELGER.

News Agency of Nigeria (NAN) (Nigeria): Moscow, Leninsky pr. 148, kv. 231; tel (095) 434-73-07; telex 413914; Correspondent VICTOR A. UDOM.

News Agencies of Sweden, Norway, Denmark and Finland: Moscow, Kutuzovsky pr. 7/4, 196; tel. (095) 243-06-74; telex 413469; Correspondents THOMAS HAMBURG, BERIT HAMBURG.

Novinska Agencija Tanjug (Yugoslavia): Moscow, pr. Mira 74, kv. 125; tel. (095) 971-19-21; Bureau Chief MIHAILO SARANOVIĆ.

Polska Agencja Prasowa (PAP) (Poland): Moscow, Leninsky pr. 45, kv. 411; tel. (095) 135-78-75; telex 414367; Bureau Chief JERZY MALCZYK.

Prensa Latina (Cuba): 103031 Moscow, ul. Petrovka 15, kv. 22; tel. (095) 208-10-51; telex 414476; fax (095) 921-76-98; Chief Correspondent LAZARO MÁLVAREZ.

Press Trust of India: 129041 Moscow, Bolshaya Pereyaslavskaya ul. 7, kv. 133–134; tel. (095) 280-27-49; telex 413319; Correspondent V. S. KARNIC.

Reuters (United Kingdom): Moscow, Berezhkovskaya nab. 2; tel. (095) 941-85-00; telex 413342; fax (095) 941-85-19; Chief Representative MIKHAIL SCHUBAKOV.

Rompres (Romania): Moscow, Kutuzovsky pr. 14, kv. 21; tel. (095) 243-67-96; Bureau Chief NICOLAE CRETU.

Syrian Arab News Agency (SANA): Moscow, Kutuzovsky pr. 7/4, kv. 184–185; tel. (095) 243-13-00; Dir SULEIMAN ABU DIAB.

United Press International (UPI) (USA): Moscow, Kutuzovsky pr. 7/4, kv. 67; tel. (095) 243-68-29; telex 413424; Bureau Chief GERALD NADLER.

Viet Nam News Agency (VNA): Moscow, Leninsky pr. 45, kv. 326–327; tel. (095) 137-38-67; telex 414490; Correspondent PHAM QUE LAM.

Xinhua (New China) News Agency (People's Republic of China): Moscow, ul. Druzhby 6, kor. 4, kv. 118; tel. (095) 143-15-64; telex 413983; fax (095) 938-20-07; Chief Correspondent TANG XIUZHE.

PRESS ASSOCIATIONS

All-Russian Association of Publishers and Newspapers: Moscow; f. 1993; Dir-Gen. IVAN LAPTEV.

Confederation of Journalists' Unions: 119021 Moscow, Zubovsky bul. 4; tel. (095) 201-77-70; telex 411421; fax (095) 200-42-37; f. 1991; fmrly Union of Journalists of the USSR; Chair. EDUARD SAGALAYEV.

Publishers

Following the failure of the coup attempt in the USSR in 1991, all publishing houses affiliated to the Communist Party of the Soviet Union (CPSU) were transferred to the jurisdiction of the Russian Federation Government. Many were subsequently privatized.

Agropromizdat (Agricultural Industry Publishing House): 107807 Moscow, Sadovaya-Spasskaya ul. 18; tel. (095) 207-29-92; f. 1985; all aspects of agricultural production; Dir (vacant).

Avrora (Aurora): 191065 St Petersburg, Nevsky pr. 7/9; tel. (095) 312-37-53; telex 121562; fax (095) 312-54-70; f. 1969; fine arts; published in foreign languages; Pres. BORIS PIDEMSKY; Dir ZENOBIUS SPETCHINSKY.

Bolshaya Rossiyskaya Entsiklopediya (The Great Encyclopedia of Russia): 109817 Moscow, Pokrovsky bul. 8; tel. (095) 297-74-83; fax (095) 227-56-24; f. 1925; universal and special encyclopedias; Dir V. G. PANOV.

Detskaya Entsiklopediya: 107042 Moscow, Bakuninskaya ul. 55; tel. (095) 269-52-76; f. 1933; science fiction, literature, poetry, biographical and historical novels.

Detskaya Literatura (Children's Literature): Moscow, Maly Cherkassky per. 1; tel. (095) 928-08-03; f. 1933; State Publishing House of Children's Literature (other than school books); Dir T. M. SHATUNOVA.

Ekologiya (Ecology): 101000 Moscow, ul. Myasnitskaya 40A; tel. (095) 928-78-60; fmrly *Lesnaya Promyshlennost* (Forest Industry); publications about environmental protection, forestry, wood and paper products, nature conservation; Dir P. P. TIZENGAUZEN.

Ekonomika (Economy): 121864 Moscow, Berezhkovskaya nab. 6; tel. (095) 240-48-77; fax (095) 240-58-18; f. 1963; various aspects of economics, management and marketing; Dir G. I. MAZIN.

Energoatomizdat: 113114 Moscow, Shluzovaya nab. 10; tel. (095) 925-99-93; f. 1981; different kinds of energy, nuclear science and technology; Dir A. P. ALESHKIN.

Finansy i Statistika (Finances and Statistics): 101000 Moscow, ul. Chernishevskovo 7; tel. (095) 925-47-08; f. 1924; banking, taxation, accountancy, etc.; Dir A. N. ZVONOVA.

Fizkultura i Sport (Physical Culture and Sport): 101421 Moscow, Kalyayevskaya ul. 27; tel. (095) 258-26-90; fax (095) 200-12-17; f. 1923; books and periodicals relating to all forms of sport, chess and draughts, etc.; Dir V. A. ZHILTSOV; Editor-in-Chief V. I. VINOKUROV.

Iskusstvo (Art): 103009 Moscow, Sobinovsky per. 3; tel. (095) 203-58-72; f. 1938; fine arts, architecture, cinema, photography, television and radio, theatre; Dir O. A. MAKAROV.

Izdatelstvo Novosti (Novosti Publishers): 107082 Moscow, Bolshaya Pochtovaya ul. 7; tel. (095) 265-63-35; telex 412474; fax (095) 975-20-65; f. 1964; fmrly *Izdatelstvo Agenstva Pechati Novosti* (Novosti Press Agency Publishing House); politics, economics, fiction, translated literature; Dir ALEKSANDR YEIDINOV.

Izobrazitelnoye Iskusstvo (Fine Art): Moscow, Sushchevsky val 64; tel. (095) 281-65-48; reproductions of pictures, pictorial art, books on art, albums, calendars, postcards; Dir V. S. KUZYAKOV.

Izvestiya (News): 103798 Moscow, Pushkinskaya pl. 5; tel. (095) 209-91-00; publishes the newspaper *Izvestiya* (News) with weekly supplement *Nedelya* (Week), and other publications and journals; Dir Y. I. BALANENKO.

Khimiya (Chemistry): Moscow B-76, ul. Strominka 21, kor. 2; tel. (095) 268-29-76; f. 1963; chemistry and the chemical industry; Dir BORIS S. KRASNOPEVTSEV.

Khudozhestvennaya Literatura (Fiction): Moscow, Novo-Basmannaya ul. 19; tel. (095) 261-88-65; telex 412162; fax (095) 261-83-00; fiction and works of literary criticism, history of literature, etc.; Dir G. A. ANDJAPARIDZE.

Khudozhnik (Artist): 125319 Moscow, ul. Chernyakhovskovo 4; tel. (095) 151-25-02; f. 1969; art reproduction, art history and criticism; Dir V. V. GORYAINOV.

Kniga and Business Ltd: 125047 Moscow, ul. 1-Tverskaya-Yamskaya 22; tel. (095) 251-60-03; telex 411871; fax (095) 250-04-89; books on publishing, printing and bookselling; facsimiles and reprints of literary classics; fiction and biographies and criticism of popular writers and their works; historical works, guidebooks; Dir VIKTOR N. ADAMOV.

Kompozitor (Composer): 103006 Moscow, Sadovaya-Triumfalnaya ul. 12-14; tel. (095) 209-23-84; f. 1957; established by the Union of Composers of the USSR; music and music criticism; Dir Y. Y. BELAYEV.

Legprombytizdat (Light Industry and Consumer Services Literature): 113035 Moscow, 1 Kadashevsky per. 12; tel. (095) 233-09-47; f. 1932; scientific and technical publishing house on light industry (clothing, footwear, sewing, etc., welfare services, domestic science); Dir T. G. GROMOVA.

Malysh (Little One): 121352 Moscow, Davydkovskaya ul. 5; tel. (095) 443-06-54; fax (095) 443-06-55; f. 1958; books, booklets and posters for children aged between 3–10 years; Dir V. A. RYBIN.

Mashinostroyeniye (Machine Building): 107076 Moscow, Stromynsky per. 4; tel. (095) 268-38-58; fax (095) 269-48-97; f. 1931; books and journals on mechanical engineering, aerospace technology, computers; Dir MAKSIM A. KOVALEVSKY.

Meditsina (Medicine): 101000 Moscow, Petroverigsky per. 6/8; tel. (095) 924-87-85; telex 412282; fax (095) 928-60-03; f. 1918; books and journals on medicine and health; Dir A. M. STOCHIK.

Metallurgiya (Metallurgy): 119034 Moscow, 2 Obydensky per. 14; tel. (095) 202-55-32; f. 1939; metallurgical literature; Dir A. G. BELIKOV.

Mezhdunarodnye Otnosheniya (International Relations): 107078 Moscow, Sadovaya-Spasskaya ul. 20; tel. (095) 207-67-93; fax (095) 200-22-04; f. 1958; international questions, economics and politics of foreign countries, foreign trade, international law, foreign language textbooks and dictionaries, translations and publications for UN and other international organizations; Dir B. P. LIKHACHEV.

Mir (Peace): 129820 Moscow, Pervy Rizhsky per. 2; tel. (095) 286-17-83; telex 411466; fax (095) 288-95-22; f. 1946; Russian translations of foreign scientific, technical and science fiction books; translations of Russian books on science and technology into foreign languages; Dir G. B. KURGANOV.

Molodaya Gvardiya (Young Guard): 103030 Moscow, Sushchevskaya ul. 21; tel. (095) 972-05-46; telex 411261; fax (095) 972-05-82; f. 1922; fmrly publishing and printing combine of the Leninist Young Communist League; joint-stock co; books and magazines, newspaper for children and for adolescents; Gen. Dir V. F. YURKIN.

Moscow University Press: 103009 Moscow, ul. Gertsena 5/7; tel. (095) 229-50-91; telex 411483; f. 1756; more than 200 titles of scientific, educational and reference literature annually, 19 scientific journals; Dir N. S. TIMOFEYEV.

Moskovsky Rabochy (Moscow Worker): 101854 Moscow, Chistoprudny bul. 8; tel. (095) 921-07-35; f. 1922; publishing house of the Moscow city and regional soviets; all types of work, including fiction; Dir D. V. YEVDOKIMOV.

Muzyka (Music): 103031 Moscow, Neglinnaya ul. 14; tel. (095) 923-04-97; fax (095) 200-52-48; f. 1861; sheet music, music scores and related literature; Dir LEONID S. SIDELNIKOV.

Mysl (Idea): Moscow, Leninsky pr. 15; tel. (095) 234-07-22; f. 1964; science, popular science, economics, philosophy, demography, history, geography; Dir V. M. VODOLAGIN.

Nauka (Science): 117864 Moscow, Profsoyuznaya ul. 90; tel. (095) 336-02-66; telex 411612; fax (095) 420-22-20; f. 1964; publishing house of the Academy of Sciences; general and social science, mathematics, physics, chemistry, biology, earth sciences, oriental studies, books in foreign languages, university textbooks, scientific journals, translation, typesetting and printing services; Dir-Gen. V. VASILIYEV.

Nedra (Natural Resources): 125047 Moscow, Tverskaya zastava 3; tel. (095) 250-52-55; fax (095) 250-27-72; f. 1963; geology, natural resources, mining and coal industry, petroleum and gas industry; Dir YU. B. KUPRIYANOV.

Pedagogika Press (Pedagogics Press): 100034 Moscow, Smolensky 4; tel. (095) 246-59-69; fax (095) 246-59-69; f. 1969; scientific and popular books on pedagogics, didactics, psychology, developmental physiology; young people's encyclopaedia, dictionaries; Dir I. KOLESNIKOVA.

Planeta (Planet): Moscow, ul. Petrovka 8/11; tel. (095) 923-04-70; telex 411733; fax (095) 200-52-46; f. 1969; postcards, calendars, guidebooks, brochures, illustrated books; co-editions with foreign partners; Dir V. G. SEREDIN.

Pressa: 125865 Moscow, ul. Pravdy 24; tel. (095) 257-31-11; fax (095) 200-22-95; f. 1934 as Pravda (Truth) Publishing House; publishes booklets, books and many newspapers and periodicals; Dir V. P. LEONTEV.

Profizdat (Trade Union Literature): 101000 Moscow, ul. Myasnitskaya 13; tel. (095) 924-57-40; fax (095) 975-23-29; f. 1930; publishing house of the CIS Labour Union Federation; economic, legal and other matters; Dir ALEKSANDR GAVRILOV.

Progress (Progress): 119847 Moscow, Zubovsky bul. 17; tel. (095) 246-90-32; telex 411800; fax (095) 246-07-56; f. 1931; translations of Russian language books into foreign languages and of foreign language books into Russian; political and scientific, fiction, literature for children and youth, training and reference books; Dir A. K. AVELICHEV.

Prosveshcheniye (Education): 127521 Moscow, POB 24; tel. (095) 289-14-05; fax (095) 200-42-66; f. 1969; textbooks; Dir D. D. ZUEV.

Radio i Svyaz (Radio and Communication): 101000 Moscow, ul. Myasnitskaya 40; tel. 258-53-51; telex 411665; f. 1981; radio engineering, electronics, communications, computer science; Dir YE. N. SALNIKOV; Editor-in-Chief I. K. KALUGIN.

Raduga (Rainbow): 121839 Moscow, Sivtsev Vrazhek 43; tel. (095) 241-68-15; telex 411826; fax (095) 241-63-53; f. 1982; translations of Russian fiction into foreign languages and of foreign authors into Russian; Dir NINA S. LITVINETS.

Respublika (Republic): Moscow, Miusskaya pl. 7, A-47; tel. (095) 251-45-94; fax (095) 200-22-54; f. 1918; fmrly *Politizdat* (Political Publishing House); books on politics, human rights, philosophy, history, economics, religion, fiction, children's literature; Dir A. P. POLYAKOV.

Russkaya Kniga (Russian Book): 123557 Moscow, per. B. Tishinsky 38; tel. (095) 205-34-59; fax (095) 205-37-08; f. 1957 as Sovetskaya Rossiya; fiction, politics, history, social sciences, health, do-it-yourself, children's; Dir B. S. MIRONOV.

Russky Yazyk (Russian Language): 103012 Moscow, Staropansky per. 1/5; tel. (095) 928-37-55; telex 411603; fax (095) 928-89-06; f. 1974; textbooks, reference, dictionaries; Dir V. I. NAZAROV.

Sovremenny Pisatel (Contemporary Writer): 121069 Moscow, ul. Povarskaya 11; tel. (095) 202-50-51; f. 1934; fiction and literary criticism, history, biography; publ. house of the International Confederation of Writers' Unions and the Union of Russian Writers; Dir A. N. ZHUKOV.

Stroyizdat (Construction Literature): 101442 Moscow, Kalyayevskaya ul. 23A; tel. (095) 251-69-67; f. 1932; building, architecture, environmental protection, fire protection and building materials; Dir V. A. KASATKIN.

Sudostroyeniye (Shipbuilding): 191065 St Petersburg, ul. Gogolya 8; tel. (821) 312-44-79; fax (821) 312-07-12; f. 1940; shipbuilding, ship design, navigation, marine research, underwater exploration; Dir and Editor-in-Chief A. A. ANDREYEV.

Transport (Transport): 107174 Moscow, Basmanny tupik 6A; tel. (095) 262-67-73; f. 1923; publishes works on all forms of transport; Dir V. P. TITOV.

Vneshtorgizdat (The Foreign Trade Economic Printing and Publishing Association): 125047 Moscow, ul. Fadeyev 1; tel. (095) 250-51-62; telex 411238; fax (095) 253-97-94; f. 1925; publishes foreign technical material translated into Russian, and information on export goods, import and export firms, joint ventures; in several foreign languages; Dir-Gen. V. I. PROKOPOV.

Voyenizdat (Military Publishing House): Moscow K-160, Voyennoye Izdatelstvo; tel. (095) 195-45-95; military theory and history, general fiction; Dir YURY I. STADNIUK.

Vysshaya Shkola (Higher School): Moscow, Neglinnaya ul. 29/14; tel. (095) 200-04-56; fax (095) 973-21-80; f. 1939; textbooks for higher-education institutions; Dir M. I. KISELEV.

Yuridicheskaya Literatura (Law Literature): 121069 Moscow, ul. Kachalova 14; tel. (095) 202-83-84; fax (095) 973-21-80; f. 1917; law subjects; official publishers of enactments of the Russian President and Govt; Dir I. A. BUNIN.

Znaniye (Knowledge): 101835 Moscow, proyezd Serova 4; tel. (095) 928-15-31; f. 1951; popular books and brochures on politics and science; Dir V. K. BELYAKOV.

Radio and Television

In December 1993 the Russian Federal Television and Radio Broadcasting Service was established to replace the Ministry of Press and Information and the Federal Information Service of Russia. Its function was to co-ordinate the activity of national and regional state television and broadcasting organizations. At the beginning of 1994 it was reported that the two major broadcasting companies in Russia owed the Ministry of Communications some 60,000m. roubles. This debt consisted of non-payment for television programmes, power, equipment and premises. The television channel Russian TV announced that its broadcasts would be reduced by almost one-half, owing to a significant decrease in grants from the Government.

Federal Television and Radio Broadcasting Service of Russia: 101409 Moscow, Strastnoy bul. 5; tel. (095) 209-60-26; Chair. ALEKSANDR N. YAKOVLEV.

All-Russian State Television and Radio Broadcasting Company (Vserossiyskaya Gosudarstvennaya Teleradiokompaniya—VGTRK): 125124 Moscow, ul. Yamskogo Polya 5-ya 19/21; tel. (095) 251-40-50; telex 411252; fax (095) 214-47-67; f. 1991; the main television channel is Russian TV, a nation-wide channel for the

Russian Federation; Chair. OLEG POPTSOV; Dir-Gen. ANATOLY LYSENKO

Voice of Russia (Golos Rossii): 113326 Moscow; tel. (095) 233-68-68; telex 411136; fax (095) 233-64-49; f. 1993; Man. Dir T. ADROSOV.

Ostankino Russian State Television and Radio Broadcasting Company (Rossiyskaya Gosudarstvennaya Teleradiokompaniya 'Ostankino'): 127000 Moscow, ul. Akademika Koroleva 12; tel. (095) 217-99-62; the main television channel is Ostankino; Gen. Dir ALEKSANDR YAKOVLEV.

Radio Moscow International: 113326 Moscow; tel. (095) 233-78-01; telex 411137; fax (095) 233-76-48; Man. Dir ARMEN OGANESYAN.

Finance

(cap. = capital; dep. = deposits; res = reserves; m. = million; brs = branches; amounts in roubles, unless otherwise stated)

BANKING

The structure of the banking system in the Russian Federation was legally defined by the Law on Co-operatives, which was passed in 1988 and allowed the establishment of commercial banks, and the 1990 Laws on Central Banking and Banking Activity. At mid-1993 there were some 2,000 commercial banks in Russia. The five Soviet sectoral banks (Sberbank, Vneshtorgbank, Promstroibank, Agroprombank and Zhilsotsbank) were reorganized according to the 1990 Laws. Zhilsotsbank was closed in mid-1991.

Central Bank of the Russian Federation: 103016 Moscow, ul. Neglinnaya 12; tel. (095) 237-30-65; telex 411283; fax (095) 921-64-65; Chair. VIKTOR GERASHCHENKO.

Rosvneshtorgbank (Bank for Foreign Trade of the Russian Federation): 103031 Moscow, Kuznetsky most 16; tel. (095) 925-52-31; telex 414726; fax (095) 973-20-96; Chair. VALERY M. TELEGUIN.

Major Commercial and Co-operative Banks

Agroprombank—Agricultural Bank: 103780 Moscow, ul. Neglinnaya 12; tel. (095) 921-38-38.

Alfa Bank Commercial Innovation Bank: 107078 Moscow, ul. Mashy Poryvayevoy 11; tel. (095) 204-96-39; telex 412089; fax (095) 207-61-36; f. 1991; cap. 429m., dep. 3,659.5m. (Dec. 1992); Pres. M. M. FREEDMANN.

Bank Vozrozhdeniye: 103696 Moscow, Khrustalny per. 1; tel. (095) 298-30-47; telex 412735; fax (095) 925-73-04; f. 1991; public joint stock co; cap. 1,247.3m., dep. 63,774m., res 2,155.1m. (Dec. 1992); Chair. DMITRY L. ORLOV.

Conversbank Ltd: 109017 Moscow, ul. Bolshaya Ordynka 24/26; tel. (095) 239-21-29; telex 911591; fax (095) 233-25-40; f. 1989; specializes in financing conversion programmes for the mining and defence industry; cap. 200m., dep. 77,694m., res 4,272.8m. (Jan. 1993); Chair. NIKOLAS G. PISSEMSKY; 7 brs.

Credo Bank: 103009 Moscow, ul. Stanislavkogo 10; tel. (095) 229-77-88; telex 412308; fax (095) 925-80-74; f. 1989; cap. 16,756.4m.; Pres. YURI AGAPOV; 24 brs.

Ekonombank: 410753 Saratov, ul. Radishcheva 28; tel. (095) 24-06-13; telex 241124; fax (095) 26-61-98; f. 1990; cap. 630.7m., dep. 1,339.2m., res 501.7m. (Dec. 1992); Chair. ALEKSNANDR V. SUSLOV.

Elektrobank: 103074 Moscow, Kitaysky proezd 7; tel. (095) 220-52-15; telex 207063; fax (095) 220-54-71; f. 1990; Chair. VIKTOR V. MUZHITSKIKH; 15 brs.

Imperial Bank: 113162 Moscow, ul. Mytnaya 23/14; tel. (095) 958-03-10; telex 412093; fax (095) 958-02-92; f. 1990; reorganized as joint stock bank 1992; cap. 411,000m., dep. 163,000m., res 1,378.1m. (Jan. 1993); Pres. VLADIMIR G. CHIRSKOV.

Inkombank: 117420 Moscow, ul. Nametkina 14, korp. 1; tel. (095) 322-06-99; telex 412345; fax (095) 331-88-33; f. 1991; total assets US $456.6m. (Dec. 1992); Pres. VLADIMIR P. GROSHEV; 20 brs.

International Moscow Bank: 103009 Moscow, ul. Pushkinskaya 5/6; tel. (095) 292-96-32; telex 412284; fax (095) 975-22-14; f. 1989 and opened for operations 1990; joint venture between Banca Commerciale Italiana (12%), Bayerische Vereinsbank (12%), Creditanstalt-Bankverein (12%), Credit Lyonnais (12%), Kansallis-Osake-Pankii (12%) and three former credit banks of the USSR banking system, Vneshekonombank (20%), Promstroibank (10%) and Sberbank (10%); specializing in the financing of joint ventures, investments and projects of domestic and foreign customers and international trade deals; cap. 110m., dep. 1,360.862m. (Dec. 1992); Chair. OTTO K. FINSTERWALDER.

Kuzbassprombank: Kemerovo, Ostrovskogo 12; tel. (384) 226-62-43; telex 215122; fax (384) 226-84-84; f. 1922; commercial and joint stock bank; cap. 1,200m., dep. 33,989m., res 27,105m. (Jan 1993); Pres. NIKOLAY N. ZHURAVLEV; 22 brs.

Mezhkombank—InterBranch Commercial Bank: 125319 Moscow, Dmitrovsky per. 3/4; tel. (095) 152-70-83; telex 612642; fax (095) 155-72-33; f. 1990; cap. 762.3m., dep. 2,813.9m., res 2,813.9m. (Dec. 1992); Pres. A. KOZLOV.

Moskovsky Industrialny Bank (Moscow Industrial Bank): 117419 Moscow, Ordzhonikidze 5; tel. (095) 952-74-08; telex 613055; fax (095) 952-77-94; f. 1990; cap. 1,337.1m., dep. 2,189.1m., res 91,389.9m. (Jan. 1993); Pres. F. A. PLESKANOVSKY; 27 brs.

Novobank: 173000 Novgorod, ul. Slavnaya 50; tel. (81600) 361-67; telex 237111; fax (81600) 323-19; cap. 150m., dep. 4,301m., res 271.1m. (Jan. 1993); Pres. VIKTOR KRESTYANINOV.

Permkombank: 614000 Perm, ul. Sovetskaya 6; tel. (3422) 65-57-29; telex 614215; fax (3422) 48-18-33; f. 1989; cap. 1,680m., dep. 35,362m., res 632m. (Jan. 1993); Chair. ANATOLY V. FEDYANIN; 15 brs.

Petroagroprombank—Joint Stock Commercial Agro-industrial Bank of St Petersburg: 191186 St Petersburg, nab. kan. Griboyedova 13; tel. (812) 315-44-92; telex 121205; fax (812) 314-83-42; cap. 240m., dep. 30,480m., res 601m. (April 1993); Pres. YURY V. TRUSOV; 22 brs.

Promstroibank: 103867 Moscow, Tverskoy bul. 13; tel. (095) 229-22-92; telex 111506; fax (095) 200-71-51; f. 1922; Chair. YAKOV N. DUBENETSKY.

Rodina Bank: 123812 Moscow, ul. B. Gruzinskaya 4/6; tel. (095) 252-52-62; telex 411772; fax (095) 254-09-47; f. 1990; Pres. KONSTANTIN A. FOKIN.

Ruskobank: 191065 St Petersburg, ul. Bolshaya Morskaya 15; tel. (812) 315-73-89; telex 121669; fax (812) 311-21-35; f. 1989; cap. 119.8m., dep. 2,428.8m., res 179.6m. (Dec. 1992); Chair. MIKHAIL A. BABICH.

Sberbank—Savings Bank of the Russian Federation: 103473 Moscow, ul. Seleznevskaya 40; tel. (095) 281-84-67; telex 412487; fax (095) 224-10-41; f. 1842 as a deposit taking institution, reorganized as a joint-stock commercial bank in 1991; cap. 5,045.6m., dep. 789,053.6m., res 53,245.1m.; Pres. of Council VIKTOR V. GERASHCHENKO; Chair. OLEG V. YASHIN.

Stolichny Joint-Stock Commercial Bank: 113095 Moscow, ul. Pyatnitskaya 70; tel. (095) 233-35-85; telex 412086; fax (095) 237-29-93; f. 1989; provides finance for small manufacturing companies; cap. 25,000m.; Pres. ALEKSANDR P. SMOLENSKY.

Stroynovatsiya Commercial Bank: 103655 Moscow, ul. Petrovka 14; tel. (095) 200-43-97; telex 411191; full range of commercial banking services including credits, factoring and leasing; Chair. of Bd ALEKSANDR V. KOVYZHENKO.

Stroysevzapbank Commercial Innovation Bank: 117916 Moscow, ul. Stroiteley 8, kv. 2; tel. (095) 930-61-21; telex 111849; fax (095) 930-12-77; f. 1990; cap. 315m.; Chair. G. V. KULAKOV; 7 brs.

TverUniversal Bank:170000 Tver, Voldarsky 34; tel. (08222) 312-43; telex 171215; fax (08222) 261-20; f. 1990; cap. 990m., dep. 85,696m., res 2,646.7m. (July 1993); Pres. ALEKSANDRA KOZYREVA; 17 brs.

Unikombank: 103699 Moscow, Khrustalny per. 1; tel. (095) 284-10-66; telex 612443; fax (095) 286-73-14; f. 1990; cap. 474.6m., dep. 8,545.6m., res 155.8m. (Jan. 1992); Pres. IGOR V. ANTONOV.

Uralkombank—Ural Commercial Bank: 620219 Yekaterinburg, M. Sibiryaka 58; tel. (73432) 55-83-70; telex 721028; fax (73432) 22-81-46; f. 1989; cap. 283.2m., dep. 3,223.4m., res 200.9m.; Chair. OLEG A. ILYINIKH.

INSURANCE

Ingosstrakh Insurance Co. Ltd: 113805 Moscow, Pyatnitskaya ul. 12; tel. (095) 231-16-77; telex 411144; fax (095) 230-25-18; f. 1947; undertakes all kinds of insurance and reinsurance; Chair. VLADIMIR P. KRUGLIAK.

COMMODITY EXCHANGES

Baikal Commodity Exchange (BCE): 670000 Ulan-Ude, 23 ul. Sovetskaya, kom. 37; tel. (30122) 2-26-81; fax (30122) 2-26-81; f. 1991; Chair. ANDREY FIRSOV.

Commodity and Raw Materials Exchange 'Konversia': 140056 Moscow, 6 ul. Sovetskaya; tel. (095) 551-01-88; fax (095) 175-24-94; f. 1991; Gen. Dir VADIM IVANOV.

Khabarovsk Commodity Exchange (KHCE): 680037 Khabarovsk, ul. Karla Marksa 66; tel. (81422) 33-65-60; fax (81422) 33-65-60; f. 1991; Pres. GEORGY GAPONENKO.

Komi Commodity Exchange (KOCE): 167610 Syktyvkar, Komi Republic, pr. 16 October; tel. (82122) 2-32-86; fax (82122) 3-84-43; f. 1991; Pres. MIKHAIL GLUZMAN.

Kuzbass Commodity and Raw Materials Exchange (KECME): 650043 Kemerovo, 7 ul. Yermaka; tel. (3842) 26-85-02; f. 1991; Gen. Man. FEDOR MYASIPOV.

Kuznetsk Commodity and Raw Materials Exchange (KCME): 650079 Novokuznetsk, 2 ul. Nevskogo; tel. (83843) 42-15-29; fax (83843) 42-22-75; f. 1991; Gen. Man. YURY POLYAKOV.

Moscow Commodity Exchange (MCE): 129223 Moscow, pr. Mira, Russian Exhibition Centre, Pavilion 4; tel. (095) 187-83-07; fax (095) 187-99-82; f. 1990; organization of exchange trading (cash and futures market); Pres. and Chair. of Bd YURY MILIUKOV.

Moscow Exchange of Building Materials (ALISA): 117334 Moscow, 45 Leninsky pr.; tel. (095) 137-00-06; fax (095) 137-67-23; f. 1990; Chair. of Exchange Cttee GERMAN STERLIGOV.

Petrozavodsk Commodity Exchange (PCE): 185028 Petrozavodsk, 31 Krasnaya ul.; tel. 7-80-57; fax 7-80-57; f. 1991; Gen. Man. VALERY SAKHAROV.

Russian Commodity and Raw Materials Exchange (RCME): 103070 Moscow, ul. Myasnitskaya 26; tel. (095) 262-80-80; fax (095) 262-57-57; f. 1990; Chief. Man. ALEKSEY VLASOV.

Russian Commodity Exchange of the Agro-Industrial Complex (ROSAGROBIRZHA): Moscow, 11 Volokolamskoye shosse; tel. (095) 209-52-25; f. 1990; Chairman of Exchange Committee: ALEKSANDR KHOLOSTOV.

St Petersburg Commodity and Stock Exchange (CSE St Petersburg): 199026 St Petersburg, 26-aya liniya v.o. 15; tel. (812) 355-68-67; fax (812) 355-68-63; f. 1990; Pres. and CEO VIKTOR NIKOLAYEV.

Siberia Commodity Exchange (SCE): 630106 Novosibirsk, 25 Krasny pr.; tel. (3832) 22-30-95; fax (3832) 22-03-90; f. 1991; Chair. OLEG FILCHENKO.

Surgut Commodity and Raw Materials Exchange (SCME): 626400 Surgut, ul. Lyet Pobedy 30; tel. (34561) 2-05-69; tel. (Moscow) (095) 315-09-56; telex 412 547; f. 1991.

Tyumen Commodity and Stock Exchange (TCE): 625026 Tyumen, ul. Geologorazvedchikov 8A; tel. (3452) 25-24-12; fax (3452) 25-24-31; f. 1991; cap. 119m.; Pres. SERGEY DENISOV; 5 brs.

Udmurt Commodity Universal Exchange (UCUE): 426000 Izhevsk, tel. (3412) 69-64-87; f. 1991; Pres. YURY UTEKHIN.

Ural Commodity Exchange (UCE): 620012 Yekterinburg, 23 pr. Kosmonavtov; tel. (3432) 55-69-61; fax (3432) 51-53-64; f. 1991; Chair. of Exchange Cttee KONSTANTIN ZHUZHLOV.

Trade and Industry

STATE PROPERTY AGENCY

Russian Federal Property Fund: Moscow; Chair. FIRYAT TABEYEV.

CHAMBER OF COMMERCE

Chamber of Commerce and Industry of the Russian Federation: 103684 Moscow, ul. Ilyinka 6; tel. (095) 923-43-23; telex 411126; fax (095) 230-24-55; f. 1991.

FOREIGN TRADE ENTERPRISES

The status and structure of many former Soviet foreign trade enterprises were undergoing reorganization in the early 1990s.

Agrochimexport: 119900 Moscow, ul. Gritsevetskaya 2; tel. (095) 202-51-58; telex 411678; fax (095) 200-12-16; f. 1987; joint-stock co; exports and imports nitrogen and potassium fertilizers, phosphate fertilizers, raw materials; Dir-Gen. YURY A. ORLOV.

AKP Sovkomflot: 103759 Moscow, ul. Rozhdestvenka 1/4; tel. (095) 926-14-34; telex 411170; fax (095) 975-26-37; leasing, purchase and sales of vessels, containers and equipment; Chair. VADIM D. KORNILOV.

Almazyuvelireksport: 119021 Moscow, Zubovsky bul. 25, kor. 1; tel. (095) 245-34-10; telex 411115; fax (095) 200-52-67; exports jewellery, gems, precious metals and stones; imports equipment for diamond cutting and polishing; Chair. I. V. GORBUNOV.

Atomenergoexport: 113324 Moscow, Ovchinnikovskaya nab. 18/1; tel. (095) 220-14-36; telex 411397; fax (095) 230-21-81; export and import of equipment for nuclear power generation and research; undertakes projects and services in the field of nuclear science and technology; Chair. V. V. KOZLOV.

Aviyaeksport: 121817 Moscow, Trubnikovsky per. 19; tel. (095) 203-10-79; telex 411555; fax (095) 290-01-71; f. 1961; export and import of aircraft, air navigational aids and other civil aviation equipment, consumer goods; Gen. Dir FELIKS N. MYASNIKOV.

Avtotraktoroeksport (ATEX Ltd): 119902 Moscow, ul. Marks-Engels 8; tel. (095) 202-92-71; telex 411135; fax (095) 202-60-75; f. 1990; joint stock holding company; engaged in economic, financial and investment activities in the Russian Federation and abroad; has five main subsidiary joint-stock companies, Avtoeksport, Avtoimport, ASTO, East-West Investment Bank and Traktoroeksport; Pres. E. N. LYUBINSKY.

Avtoeksport: renders services on publicity and promotion of sales, engineering, marketing and after-sale servicing of motor vehicles and equipment; Dir-Gen. I. A. AKSENOV.

Avtoimport: imports motor vehicles and equipment and sets up and develops commodity circulation networks, and organizes after-sale service; Dir-Gen. N. V. CHUMAKOV.

Traktoroeksport: offers same services as Avtoeksport with regard to tractors and agricultural machinery and equipment; Dir-Gen. V. A. TSUKANOV.

Dalintorg: 692904 Nakhodka (Primorsky Kray), Nakhodkinsky pr. 16A; tel. 4-48-77; telex 213814; f. 1964; Eastern Siberian and Far Eastern trade with Japan, Australia, China and North and South Korea; Dir G. N. MURZAYEV.

Eksportkhleb: 121200 Moscow, Smolenskaya-Sennaya pl. 32/34; tel. (095) 244-47-01; telex 411145; fax (095) 253-90-69; f. 1923; involved in the export and import of wheat, rye, barley, oats, maize, rice, pulses, flour, oil seeds and other grain and fodder products; also engaged in barter, futures operations, consulting and joint ventures involving these products; Chair. O. A. KLIMOV.

Eksportles: 121803 Moscow, Trubnikovsky per. 19; tel. (095) 291-61-16; telex 411229; fax (095) 200-12-19; f. 1926; joint stock co; exports and imports sawn and round timber, wooden articles, woodpulp, paper and cardboard; imports machines and equipment for timber enterprises, consumer goods and foodstuffs; sets up joint-ventures, carries out import and export operations under compensation agreements, conducts market research and consulting services; Chair. of Bd V. A. RADZISHEVSKY.

ELORG Corporation: 121099 Moscow, Novinsky bul. 11A; tel. (095) 205-38-72; telex 612044; fax (095) 205-34-92; imports computer hardware, software and associated equipment; exports computer software, advertising services; Gen. Dir ZH. V. TRIFONOV.

Energomasheksport: 129010 Moscow, Protopopovsky per. 25A; tel. (095) 288-84-56; telex 411965; fax (095) 288-79-90; f. 1966; exports metallurgical and mining equipment, equipment for thermal and hydroelectric power stations and industrial utilities, diesel engines, generators, railway equipment; Pres. and Gen. Dir MIKHAIL V. NOSANOV.

Gammachim: 121200 Moscow, Smolenskaya-Sennaya pl. 32/34; tel. (095) 244-18-14; telex 411297; fax (095) 244-21-81; f. 1990 as a foreign trade stock corporation to replace Soyuzkhimeksport; exports and imports chemical and other products; imports machinery and equipment for industry; Gen. Dir IGOR S. VOROBIEV.

Koopvneshtorg: 103626 Moscow, Bolshoy Cherkassky per. 15; tel. (095) 924-81-71; telex 411127; fax (095) 230-28-19; exports raw materials, medicinal drugs, minerals, etc.; imports consumer goods, household appliances, etc.; Chair. A. N. STARYKH.

Lenfintorg: 196084 St Petersburg, Moskovsky pr. 98; tel. (812) 296-11-65; telex 121518; fax (812) 292-56-33; f. 1960; export and import trade in consumer goods, timber goods and semi-finished timber goods of the timber industry (including paper and packing materials), building and finished materials, feeds and foodstuffs, chemicals, industrial equipment, medicines; Gen. Dir A. G. ANIKIN.

Litsenzintorg: 121108 Moscow, Minskaya ul. 11; tel. (095) 145-11-11; telex 411415; fax (095) 142-59-02; export and import of patents; Chair. V. V. IGNATOV.

Mashinoeksport: 117330 Moscow, ul. Mosfilmovskaya 35; tel. (095) 147-15-42; telex 411207; fax (095) 938-21-16; f. 1952; imports and exports machinery, goods and services; deals with investment and innovation programmes; participates in regional development programmes, etc.; Chair. V. N. SIOMIN.

Mashinoimport: 121200 Moscow, Smolenskaya-Sennaya pl. 32/34; tel. (095) 244-33-09; telex 411231; fax (095) 244-38-07; exports services associated with the construction of pipe-lines, coal mines, etc.; imports power engineering and pumps, compressors, hoisting and conveying equipment, extracting equipment for the petroleum and natural gas industries, industrial fittings; Chair. O. F. KLIMENKO.

Mashpriborintorg: 117909 Moscow, 2 Spasonalivkovsky per. 6; tel. (095) 238-81-31; telex 411235; fax (095) 230-21-26; f. 1959; exports and imports wire and wireless communication equipment, electronic measuring instruments, electronic components; exports timber and steel products, aluminium, nickel; Chair. V. G. LOZHNIKOV.

Medeksport: 113461 Moscow, ul. Kakhovka 31, kor. 2; tel. (095) 331-82-00; telex 411247; fax (095) 331-89-88; exports and imports medicines, pharmaceutical raw materials, medical equipment and instruments, serums, vaccines and medicines; Chair. I. N. FILIMONOV.

Metallurgimport: 117393 Moscow, ul. Arkhitektora Vlasova 33; tel. (095) 128-09-32; telex 411388; imports mining and ore-dressing equipment, metallurgical and foundry equipment, iron and steel works machinery and equipment, rotor excavators; Gen. Dir N. P. MAKSIMOV.

Mezhdunarodnaya Kniga: 113095 Moscow, ul. Dimitrova 39; tel. (095) 238-46-00; telex 411160; fax (095) 230-21-17; exports and imports books, periodicals, newspapers, pictures, maps, gramophone records, postage stamps, slides and film-strips; Chair. Y. B. LEONOV.

Morsvyazsputnik: 103030 Moscow, ul. Novoslobodskaya 14/19; tel. (095) 258-70-45; telex 411197; fax (095) 253-99-10; communications and navigational aids; Pres. V. A. BOGDANOV.

Novoeksport: 117393 Moscow, ul. Arkhitektora Vlasova 33; tel. (095) 218-07-86; telex 411204; fax (095) 128-16-12; exports textile fibres, petroleum products, raw materials, ferrous and non-ferrous metals and products, porcelainware, furs; Chair. ANATOLY N. GROMOV.

Obschemashexport: 101444 Moscow, Krasnoproletarskaya ul. 9; tel. (095) 258-66-56; telex 411836; fax (095) 200-22-68; exports tractors, industrial processing equipment, medical and domestic appliances; imports accessories, equipment for developing new technologies; Gen. Dir YU. S. TIKHONOV.

Prodintorg: 121200 Moscow, Smolenskaya-Sennaya pl. 32/34; tel. (095) 244-20-60; telex 411206; fax (095) 244-26-29; f. 1952; exports and imports meat, sugar, milk powder, butter, tobacco and tobacco products, vegetable oil, other oils; export of raw materials; import of consumer goods, equipment for food industry; Chair. V. GOLANOV.

Prommashimport: 121200 Moscow, Smolenskaya-Sennaya pl. 32/34; tel. (095) 244-43-57; telex 411261; imports equipment for the pulp and paper, woodworking and timber and electrical industries; Chair. G. F. RAKHIMBAYEV.

Promsyrioimport: 121834 Moscow, Novinsky bul. 13; tel. (095) 203-06-46; telex 411152; fax (095) 203-61-77; f. 1936; exports and imports pig iron and ferro alloys, steel wire and metal products; Chair. O. M. SMIRNOV.

Radioeksport: 101959 Moscow, ul. Myasnitskaya 35; tel. (095) 923-79-49; telex 411376; export and import of computers and technical maintenance.

Raznoeksport: 107896 Moscow, ul. Verkhnaya Krasnoselskaya 15; tel. (095) 264-56-56; telex 411408; fax (095) 288-95-39; exports and imports light industrial and consumer goods; Chair. YURY KOSTROV.

Raznoimport: 113324 Moscow, Ovchinnikovskaya nab. 18/1; tel. (095) 233-22-79; telex 411118; fax (095) 200-32-18; f. 1936; imports and exports non-ferrous metal and alloys, rolled iron and rare-earth metals; Chair. R. A. PETROSYAN.

Russian Independent Oil Co: 121200 Moscow, Smolenskaya-Sennaya pl. 32/34; tel. (095) 253-94-88; telex 411148; fax (095) 244-22-91; fmrly Soyuznefteksport; exports and imports petroleum, petroleum products; declared itself a private co 1991; Chair. VLADIMIR A. ARUTUNYAN.

Selkhozpromeksport: 113324 Moscow, Ovchinnikovskaya nab. 18/1; tel. (095) 220-16-92; telex 411933; fax (095) 921-93-64; assists in construction of hydrotechnical and irrigation facilities, storage plants and the other agricultural projects; also involved in the fishing industry, petroleum extraction and the timber, microbiological and confectionary industries; Chair. A. A. YELISEYEV.

Skotoimport: Moscow, Skatertny per. 8; tel. (095) 290-24-07; telex 411645; imports slaughtered livestock, exports racehorses and breeding stock of cattle, horses, sheep and goats.

Soveksportfilm: 103009 Moscow, Kalashny per. 14; tel. (095) 290-50-09; telex 411143; fax (095) 200-12-56; imports and exports films; joint film production; Chair. V. Y. MAYATSKY.

Sovbunker: 103030 Moscow, ul. Novoslobodskaya 14/19, kor. 7; tel. (095) 258-91-22; telex 411134; fax (095) 288-95-69; export, import and bunkering operations; Pres. Y. P. DROBININ.

Sovfrakht: 103030 Moscow, ul. Novoslobodskaya 14/19; tel. (095) 926-11-18; telex 411168; fax (095) 230-26-40; chartering and broking of tanker, cargo and other ships; forwarding agents; ship management; legal and consultative services; Gen. Dir A. I. KOLTYPIN.

Soyuzgazeksport: 117071 Moscow, Leninsky pr. 20; tel. (095) 244-22-84; telex 411987; exports and imports natural gas, liquefied petroleum gas, inert and other gases; Chair. Y. V. BARANOVSKY.

Soyuzkinoservice: 121069 Moscow, Skatertny per. 20; tel. (095) 290-10-00; telex 411114; fax (095) 200-12-86; establishes and co-ordinates commercial ties between film studios and foreign firms; Chair. A. K. SURIKOV.

Soyuzplodoimport: 121200 Moscow, Smolenskaya-Sennaya pl. 32/34; tel. (095) 244-22-58; telex 411262; fax (095) 244-36-36; f. 1966; exports and imports fruit, vegetables, foodstuffs and beverages, incl. Pepsi-Cola; exports Stolichnaya and Moskovskaya vodka; Chair. E. F. SOROCHKIN.

Soyuzpromeksport: 121200 Moscow, Smolenskaya-Sennaya pl. 32/34; tel. (095) 244-19-79; telex 411268; fax (095) 244-37-93; exports coal and coal by-products, manganese, chrome and iron ore, asbestos and other mineral and semi-finished products; Chair. B. K. KOSOLAPOV.

Soyuzpushnina: 103012 Moscow, ul. Ilyinka 6; tel. (095) 923-09-23; telex 411150; exports and imports furs, bristles, animal hair, hides, skins and casings, casein products, oils, etc.; organizes fur auctions in St. Petersburg, concludes long-term agreements for deliveries of fur goods to foreign firms; Chair. V. M. IVANOV.

Soyuzregion: 103055 Moscow, ul. 2-Lesnoy per. 10; tel. (095) 251-18-19; telex 412306; fax (095) 258-04-16; exports raw materials; imports equipment and consumer goods.

Soyuztransit: 121200 Moscow, Smolenskaya-Sennaya pl. 32/34; tel. (095) 244-39-51; telex 411266; fax (095) 230-28-50; f. 1963; reorganized as an independent organization 1980; handles transit of goods through the territory of Russia and the neighbouring states, incl. the Trans-Siberian Container Service and combined transport of cargoes to and from Iran; effects transport-forwarding operations and storage of transit and bilateral trade cargoes, etc.; Pres. S. G. MELNIK.

Soyuzvneshtrans: 121019 Moscow, Gogolevsky bul. 17/16; tel. (095) 203-11-79; telex 411441; fax (095) 200-02-90; handles transport and forwarding of imports, exports and transit goods; Pres. OLEG A. NIKITIN.

Stankoimport: 117342 Moscow, ul. Obrucheva 34/63; tel. (095) 333-51-01; telex 411991; fax (095) 310-70-19; f. 1930; exports and imports machine tools and precision instruments; Dir-Gen. E. A. KHUDYAKOV.

Stroydormashexport: 121019 Moscow, Suvorovsky bul. 7; tel. (095) 291-49-31; telex 411063; fax (095) 202-90-56; f. 1988; exports and imports construction and road-building machinery; Gen. Dir YU. A. MALYSHEV.

Stroymaterialintorg: 121059 Moscow, ul. Kievskaya 19; tel. (095) 243-71-86; telex 411887; fax (095) 243-90-86; export and import of cement, glass, asbestos and other building materials; Chair. V. V. DEVYATOV.

Sudoeksport: 123231 Moscow, ul. Sadovaya-Kudrinskaya 11; tel. (095) 255-44-91; telex 411116; fax (095) 200-22-50; exports ships, ships' equipment and equipment for ship-building; Gen. Dir VLADIMIR A. CHMYR.

Sudoimport: 103006 Moscow, Uspensky per. 10; tel. (095) 299-02-14; telex 114393; fax (095) 209-13-31; exports and imports all kinds of ships and marine equipment, licences and allied consultancy services; provides maintenance and repairs of ships and marine equipment; Chair. B. A. YAKIMOV.

Tekhmasheksport: 101850 Moscow, Mosfilmovskaya ul. 35; tel. (095) 202-48-00; telex 411068; fax (095) 291-58-08; exports machinery and equipment for the textile industries; Dir-Gen. V. F. FADEYEV.

Tekhmashimport: 121819 Moscow, Trubnikovsky per. 19; tel. (095) 290-48-53; telex 411194; fax (095) 291-58-09; f. 1959; imports and exports refrigeration equipment and machinery for chemical and textile plants; completes projects for the petroleum, petrochemical, pulp-and-paper and microbiological industries; Chair. V. I. GRIB.

Tekhnoeksport: 121200 Moscow, Ovchinnikovskaya nab. 18/1; tel. (095) 220-10-09; telex 411338; fax (095) 230-20-80; assists in petroleum production; construction of industrial plants, pharmaceutical plants, hospitals, schools; Chair. V. I. VELICHKO.

Tekhnointorg: 113836 Moscow, ul. Pyatnitskaya 64; tel. (095) 231-26-22; telex 411200; fax (095) 230-26-42; commercial, consultancy, information and trade intermediary activities in Russia and abroad; Chair. V. N. BOSSENKO.

Tekhnopromeksport: 113324 Moscow, Ovchinnikovskaya nab. 18/1; tel. (095) 220-15-23; telex 411158; fax (095) 233-33-73; assists construction of thermal and diesel power stations; exports electric power, coal, ferrous and non-ferrous metals, sawn timber; imports technology and consumer goods; Pres. S. M. BOKOV.

Tekhnopromimport: 113324 Moscow, Ovchinnikovskaya nab. 18/1; tel. (095) 220-12-18; telex 411233; fax (095) 230-21-11; f. 1930; import of equipment for the light, food, polygraphic and electronics industries; export of raw materials and industrial and household goods; Chair. V. I. BOYKO.

Tekhnostroyeksport: 113324 Moscow, Ovchinnikovskaya nab. 18/1; tel. (095) 220-14-48; telex 411474; assists construction of plants producing building materials; Chair. D. M. SHPILEV.

Tekhsnabeksport: 109180 Moscow, Staromonetny per. 26; tel. (095) 233-48-60; telex 411328; fax (095) 230-26-38; f. 1963; export and import of isotopes, ionizing radiation sources; export of heat-producing elements for various types of atomic reactors, components and parts for nuclear-power stations, rare and rare-earth metals, nuclear physics equipment, consumer goods; imports vehicles, computers, televisions and video recorders; Dir-Gen. A. A. SHISHKIN.

Tsvetmetpromeksport: 113324 Moscow, Ovchinnikovskaya nab. 18/1; tel. (095) 220-18-61; telex 411983; assists construction of non-ferrous metallurgy projects, mines, quarries, metallurgical works; Chair. R. I. KUPREVICH.

Tyazhpromeksport: 113324 Moscow, Ovchinnikovskaya nab. 18/1; tel. (095) 220-16-10; telex 411931; fax (095) 230-22-03; f. 1957; assists construction and extension of integrated iron and steel mining complexes and hardware plants; Chair. V. A. YEGOROV.

Vneshintorg: 109147 Moscow, Marksistskaya ul. 5; tel. (095) 271-90-12; telex 411250; fax (095) 274-01-02; f. 1992 by merger of Vneshposyltorg and Vostokintorg; exports and imports foodstuffs, consumer goods and raw materials; participates in joint-venture operations and wholesale and retail trade; Dir-Gen. NAZAR I. BELIAYEV.

Vneshstroyimport: 103009 Moscow, Tverskoy bul. 6; tel. (095) 290-06-84; telex 411434; fax (095) 973-21-48; f. 1974; arranges joint construction projects with foreign firms; exports raw materials; Chair. G. I. VOROBEV.

Vneshtorgreklama: 113461 Moscow, ul. Kakhovka 31, kor. 2; tel. (095) 331-83-11; telex 411265; fax (095) 310-70-05; export and import of advertising services; Dir-Gen. E. P. ZUYEV.

MAJOR INDUSTRIAL ENTERPRISES

10th State Ball-Bearing Factory: 344717 Rostov-na-Donu, ul. Peskova 1; tel. (8632) 22-56-72; telex 123122; fax (8632) 22-56-71; production of bearings; Gen. Dir IGOR O. SHCHERBINA; 8,500 employees.

23rd State Bearing Factory: 160028 Vologda, Okruzhnoe shosse 13; tel. (81722) 2-23-91; fax (81722) 3-43-93; manufactures ball-bearings; Gen. Dir ALEKSANDR I. YELPERIN.

Agrovod: 125040 Moscow, Leningradsky pr. 22/2; tel. (095) 213-40-36; telex 411614; fax (095) 213-02-56; design and construction of irrigational systems, roads, dams and agricultural equipment; Pres. GEORGY G. GULYUK; 150,240 employees.

Almetyevsk Electrical Submersible Pumps Plant (Alnas): Tatarstan, 423400 Azpen, Almetyevsk 11; tel. 8-43-12; telex 224843; fax 2-73-64; produces electrical pumps; Dir-Gen. PAUL R. SHOTTER; 2,600 employees.

Altay Tractor Factory: 658212 Altay kray, Rubtsovsk, ul. Traktornaya 17; tel. 2-86-45; telex 233515; fax 3-74-72; design and production of 'Crawler' tractors; Gen. Dir ARTHUR A. DERFLER; 23,000 employees.

Altay Motorworks: 656023 Altay kray, Barnaul, pr. Kosmonavtov 8; tel. 77-01-17; telex 133145; manufactures diesel engines, fuel pumps, etc.; Gen. Dir VLADIMIR ZAKHAROV; 18,000 employees.

Altayselmash Production Association: 658202 Altay kray, Rubtsovsk, ul. Krasnaya 100; tel. 2-26-65; telex 233129; fax 2-76-72; design and manufacture of all types of agricultural machinery and hand tools; Gen. Dir VICTOR K. TOLSTOV; 5,139 employees.

Apatit Industrial Association: 184230 Murmansk obl., Kirovsk, ul. Lenengradskaya; production of apatite concentrate; 21,500 employees.

Applied Chemistry: 197198 St Petersburg, Dobrolyubov pr. 14; tel. (812) 238-95-36; telex 121986; fax (812) 233-89-89; research and development of chemical products, etc.; Gen. Dir GENNADY TERESCHENKO; 7,500 employees.

Automobile and Tractor Electrical Equipment Plant: 309530 Belgorod obl., Stary Oskol, ul. Vatutina 54; tel. (075) 22-09-65; fax (075) 241015; produces spare and assembly parts for automobiles, etc.; Plant Man. ANATOLY M. MAMONOV; 4,500 employees.

Automobile and Tractor Electrical Equipment Plant: 625000 Tyumen, ul. Tsoilkovskogo 1; tel. 26-15-90; telex 235151; produces coil distributors, plugs, electric stoves, electric immersion heaters; Plant Dir. VLADISLAV P. ZAGVAZDIN; 2,500 employees.

Avtogreid Road-Machine Factory: 241000 Bryansk, ul. Kalinina 98; road-building machines, road graders, concrete- and asphalt-laying machines, bitumen pumps; 5,500 employees.

Azot Industrial Association: 650099 Kemerovo, Predzavodskoy; produces ammonia fertilizers and caprolactam; 10,000 employees.

Carburettor and Fittings Factory: 192102 St Petersburg, Samoilovoy 5; tel. (812) 166-48-05; telex 321245; design, development and manufacture of carburettors for automobiles; Dir GENNADY B. ORLOV.

Cheboksary Tractor Works: 428033 Cheboksary, pr. Tractorostroiteley; tel. (095-8350) 23-37-48; telex 412627; fax (095-8350) 23-76-36; production of heavy-duty tractors and their maintenance and repair; Gen. Dir HANIF H. MINGAZOV; 25,000 employees.

Chelyabinsk Tractor Plant: 454007 Chelyabinsk, pr. Lenina 3; tel. 77-14-51; fax 73-07-65; telex 124886; design and manufacture of caterpillar tractors; Chief Dir NIKOLAY R. LOSHENENKO.

Cherepovets Steel Plant: 162600 Vologda obl., Cherepovets, ul. Mira 30; coke, cast iron, steel, rolled steel, consumer goods; 43,000 employees.

Cherepovets Steel-Rolling Mill: 162600 Vologda obl., ul. 50-letiya Oktyabrya 1/33; hardware, cold-extended steel, ropes; 10,000 employees.

Dzerzhinsky Tractor Plant: 400061 Volgograd; tel. (844) 77-26-22; produces agricultural machinery and equipment; Dir N. M. BUDKO; 35,000 employees.

Electropribor Production Association: 428000 Cheboksary, Yakovlevsky pr. 3; tel. 22-25-73; fax 20-50-02; produces electronic measuring instruments, microprocessor controllers and analog-digital converters; Gen. Dir LEONID V. YAKOVLEV; 5,300 employees.

Esta Joint-Stock Company: 430001 Republic of Mordovia, Saransk, ul. Proletarskaya 126; manufactures conversion equipment and semi-conductor instruments; 8,600 employees.

Fifth State Bearing Plant Productive Amalgamation: 634006 Tomsk-6, Severny Gorodok GPZ-5; tel. 75-15-01; produces all types of bearings; Gen. Dir YURY GALVAS; 6,500 employees.

First State Bearing Plant: 109088 Moscow, Sharikopodshipnikovskaya ul. 13; tel. (095) 275-08-29; design and manufacture of over 2,000 types of bearings; Gen. Dir VALERY B. NOSOV; 20,000 employees.

GAZ Joint-Stock Company: 603046 Nizhny Novogorod, pr Lenina; tel. (8312) 56-42-06; telex 151127; fax (8312) 53-05-57; holding co. preparing works for privatization; Dir-Gen. BORIS P. VIDYAYEV.

GAZ—Gorky Automobile Plant: f. 1932; manufactures trucks and cars, bicycles, Elita washing-machines, etc.; 106,400 employees.

Gidromash: 129626 Moscow, 2-aya Mytischinskaya ul. 2; tel. (095) 287-78-20; fax (095) 287-11-81; development and manufacture of pumps and other products; Pres. VLADIMIR KARAKHANYAN; 21,000 employees.

Kabardino-Balkarian Diamond Tool Factory: 361200 Terek, Yubileinaya ul. 1; tel. 9-11-76; produces diamond-boring tools, diamond drills, etc; Factory Dir VLADIMIR SH. KHAZHUYEV; 2,880 employees.

Kaliningrad Elektrosvarka Experimental Factory: 236012 Kaliningrad, ul. Dzerzhinskogo 136; manufactures electric welding equipment and ballast rheostats; 731 employees.

Kaluzhsky Turbinny Zavod Industrial Association: 248632 Kaluga, ul. Moskovskaya 255; produces steam turbines; 11,703 employees.

Kamaz: 423808 Naberzhnyye Chelny, pr. Musy Dzhalilya 29; tel. (855) 42-20-16; manufactures and distributes heavy trucks; Gen. Dir NIKOLAY H. BEKH; 150,000 employees.

Kaprolaktam Industrial Association: 606000 Nizhny Novgorod obl., Dzerzhinsk; produces caustic soda, mineral fertilizers, synthetic resins and plastics; 11,960 employees.

Kaskad: 125047 Moscow, 1-aya Brestskaya ul. 35; tel. (095) 250-38-87; fax (095) 973-20-48; telex 412310; research, development and manufacture of electronic and cybernetic systems; Dir-Gen. ANATOLY V. MYSCHLEZOV; 40,000 employees.

Kazanresinotekhnika: 420026 Tatarstan, Kazan, Tekhnicheskaya 2; tel. (8432) 37-28-84; manufactures rubber products; Dir VENIAMIN GRIGORIEV; 5,000 employees.

Kostroma Motordetal Factory: 156604 Kostroma, ul. Moskovskaya 92A; manufactures automobile spare parts; 4,104 employees.

Krasnoyarsk Grain-Harvester Industrial Association: 660049 Krasnoyarsk, ul. Profsoyuzov 3; production of grain-harvesters; 14,231 employees.

Krasny Oktyabr Steel Plant: 40060 Volgograd, 60, ZKO; manufacture of grade steels, round rolled products, rolled wire, hexahedron, drilling hollow rolled sheets, ingots, cableware; 15,339 employees.

Krasny Proletary Machine-Tool Building Factory: 117071 Moscow, Malaya Kaluzhskaya ul. 15; tel. (095) 232-27-66; fax (095) 310-70-03; telex 411017; manufactures lathes, and loading and production-processing robots; Gen. Man. YURY I. KIRILLOV; 6,000 employees.

Kristall Industrial Association: 300600 Tula, pr. Lenina 85; alcohol, liquor and vodka products; 1,955 employees.

Kvant Industrial Association: Novgorod, ul. Sankt-Peterburgskaya 73/1; manufacture of televisions, radio communication complexes, satellite television systems; 5,000 employees.

Kzame Production Association: 248631 Kaluga, Azarovskaya 18; tel. (0842) 2-53-09; fax (0842) 2-75-16; telex 412691; design and manufacture of a wide range of electronic motors and control units for the automobile industry; 8,500 employees.

Lenin Autoworks: 432008 Ulyanovsk, ul. Moskovskoye sh.; part of Avtotouaz Industrial Assen; manufacture of UAZ-enhanced cross-country capability vehicles; 23,858 employees.

Leningradsky Metallichesky Zavod: 195108 St Petersburg, Sverdlovskaya nab. 18; produces steam, gas and hydraulic turbines; 11,286 employees.

Lipetsk Tractor Factory: 398030 Lipetsk, ul. Krasnozavodskaya 1; manufactures 0.9 wheel tractors; 19,131 employees.

Middle Volga Chemical Plant: 446100 Samara obl., Chapayevsk, ul. Ordzhonikidze 1; tel. (84639) 2-39-09; fax (84639) 2-39-55; f. 1912; manufactures chemical products; Dir E. MORKOVKIN; 4,000 employees.

Moscow Rubin Television Factory: 121087 Moscow, Bagrationovsky pr. 7; manufactures televisions; 4,400 employees.

Moskvich Production Association: 109316 Moscow, Volgogradsky pr. 42; tel. (095) 276-32-96; telex 411333; fax (095) 274-00-49; design and manufacture of automobiles, consumer goods, hand tools and machine tools; Gen. Dir VALENTIN P. KOLOMNIKOV; 25,000 employees.

Murmanrybprom: 183011 Murmansk, ul. Tralovaya 38; manufacture of fish food products; 10,500 employees.

Ninth State Bearings Factory: 443008 Samara, GPZ-9; tel. (846) 56-36-04; design and manufacture of roller bearings; Gen. Dir IGOR SHVIDAK.

Novolipetsk Yu. V. Andropov Steel Plant: 398040 Lipetsk, pl. Metallurgov 2; production of cast-iron, rolled stock, dynamo steel, transformer steel, etc.; 40,010 employees.

Orsko-Khalilovsky Metallurgical Integrated Works: 462353 Orenburg obl., Novotroisk, ul. Zavodskaya 1; manufacture of rolled ferrous metals, cast iron, coke, benzine and resin; 26,260 employees.

Pervouralsky Novotrubny Zavod (First Ural Tube Manufacturing Plant): Yekaterinburg obl., 623112 Pervouralsk, Torgovaya ul. 1; tel. (343) 7-56-56; telex 348715; fax (343) 2-44-78; production of steel piping and steel cylinders; Dir V. N. DUYEV; 25,000 employees.

Petrovsky Molot Electro-Mechanical Factory: 412520 Petrovsk, ul. Gogolya 40; auto-steering devices, washing-machines; 6,000 employees.

Plodoovshchkhoz Association: Tambov, ul. Kommunalnaya 10; produces fruit, vegetables and canned fruit and vegetables; 8,755 employees.

Pressmash Taganrog Production Association: 347927 Taganrog, Polyakovskaya ul.; tel. (863) 4-91-23; telex 123249; manufacture of sheet stamping presses and smelting machinery; Gen. Dir ANATOLY FILIPPOV; 10,075 employees.

Progress Factory: 414056 Astrakhan, Savushkina ul. 61; household appliances, computers, lighting equipment; 4,800 employees.

Pskovelektromash Scientific-Industrial Association: 180000 Pskov, Oktyabrsky pr. 27; manufactures DC generators, low-capacity electric motors, low-voltage units; 4,553 employees.

Rossvyazinform GPSI: 344007 Rostov, pr. Budyennovsky 50; provides communications services, telephone exchanges, etc.; 21,439 employees.

Schetmash Industrial Association: 305901 Kursk, ul. Republikanskaya 6; production of personal computers; 11,372 employees.

Second Watch Factory: 125040 Moscow, Leningradsky pr. 8; tel (095) 251-29-37; fax (095) 257-15-02; produces mechanical and electronic watches and clocks; Gen. Dir VLADIMIR M. KOROLEV; 10,000 employees.

Severonikel Integrated Works: 184280 Murmansk obl., Monchegorsk; production of electrical nickel, copper, metallic cobalt and sulphuric acid; 12,700 employees.

Severostokzoloto Association: Magadan, ul. Proletarskaya 12; production of gold, silver, tin and mining equipment; 80,000 employees.

Sibenergomash Industrial Association: 656037 Altay kray, Barnaul, pr. Kalinia 57; forging and pressing machines, automatic machines and semi-automatic machine-tools; 1,930 employees.

Sixth State Bearings Plant: 620075 Yekaterinburg, Shartashskaya ul. 13; tel. (343) 55-21-48; telex 221153: manufactures roller bearings; Plant Dir VLADIMIR B. TERESCHENKO.

Stalkonstruktsiya: 103001 Moscow, Sadovaya Kudrinskaya 8/12; tel. (095) 209-95-60; fax (095) 975-22-17; f. 1989; manufacture and erection of steel structures and erection of concrete structures; Pres. VIKTOR K. VOROBIOV; 50,000 employees.

Stroytechsteklo: 117036 Moscow, ul. Kedrova 15; tel. (095) 129-09-09; telex 411737; produces glassware, crystalware and patterned tiles; Gen. Dir NIKOLAY V. FEDULOV; 30,000 employees.

Tulamashzavod State Enterprise: 300002 Tula, ul. Mosina 2; manufactures scooters and spare parts; 15,733 employees.

Tulaugol Industrial Association: 300600 Tula, ul. 9 Maya 1; production of fuel; 37,605 employees.

Ufa Electric Lamp Factory: Bashkiria, 450029 Ufa, Yubileynaya ul. 1; tel. 42-52-11; fax 42-52-30; produces electric light bulbs and lamps; Plant Man. TIMERBAY A. GASHIMOV.

Ust-Ilim Lesopromyshlenny Kompleks State Enterprise: 665770 Irkutsk obl., Ust-Ilimsk, POB 353; produces cellulose, forest chemistry products, sawn timber, splint slabs, round timber; 21,914 employees.

Vostsibugol Industrial Association: 664674 Irkutsk, ul. Sukhe-Batora 6; produces coal; 15,166 employees.

Vladimir Tractor Factory: 600005 Vladimir, Traktornaya ul. 43; tel. 3-84-86; telex 412528; design and manufacture of tractors; Gen. Man. ANATOLY V. GRISHIN; 15,253 employees.

Volgokhemmash United Enterprises: Samara obl., 445621 Tolyatti, ul. M. Gorkogo 96; tel. (848) 22-33-53; telex 214137; manufactures equipment for cement production, crushing equipment for construction-materials and ore-mining industries, autoclaves; Dir-Gen. VIKTOR A. KOPIN; 10,000 employees.

Vologdalesprom Timber Industrial Association: 160600 Vologda, ul. Lermontova 15; produces birch and coniferous sawn timber, plywood, etc.; 30,093 employees.

Yamalneftegazgeologia Geological State Enterprise: 626608 Yamal-Nenets okrug, Salekhard, ul. Matrosova 26; produces natural-gas condensate, natural gas and petroleum; provides geological information; 5,070 employees.

Yantar Baltic Ship-Building Factory: 236002 Kaliningrad, ul. Transportny tupik 1; ship-building, ship repair; 7,822 employees.

Yuzhnouralsky Machine-Building Factory: 462425 Orenburg obl., Orsk, pr. Mira 12; manufactures blast-furnace and steel-casting equipment, power shovel ladles; 10,000 employees.

ZIL: 109280 Moscow, Avtozavodskaya ul. 23; tel. (095) 275-33-28; telex 411006; fax (095) 274-00-78; manufactures trucks, engines, industrial ovens and washing machines; also automobiles, particularly luxury limousines; Dir-Gen. YEVGENY A. BRAKOV.

TRADE UNIONS

Until 1990 trade unions were united in the All-Union Central Council of Trade Unions (ACCTU), which operated strictly under the control of the CPSU. During the late 1980s, however, several informal, independent labour movements were established by workers dissatisfied with the official organizations. Prominent among the new movements was the Independent Trade Union of Miners (ITUM), formed by striking miners in 1989. In 1990, in response to the growing independent labour movement, several branch unions of the ACCTU established the Federation of Independent Trade Unions of Russia (FITUR), which took control of part of the property and other assets of the ACCTU. The ACCTU was itself reformed as the General Confederation of Trade Unions of the USSR, which was in turn renamed the CIS Labour Federation in 1992. In November of that year, in an attempt to challenge the influence of the FITUR, the ITUM and several other independent trade unions established a consultative council to co-ordinate their activities.

CIS Labour Union Federation: 117119 Moscow, Leninsky pr. 42; tel. (095) 938-70-00; telex 411010; fax (095) 938-21-55; f. 1990; fmrly the General Confederation of Trade Unions of the USSR; co-ordinating body for trade unions in CIS member states; Pres. VLADIMIR I. SHCHERBAKOV.

Federation of Independent Trade Unions of the Russian Federation (FITUR): 117119 Moscow, Leninsky pr. 42; tel. (095) 938-83-13; fax (095) 137-06-94; f. 1990; Chair. MIKHAIL SHMAKOV; unites 38 branch unions, including:

Aircraft Engineering Workers' Union: Moscow, Leninsky pr. 42; tel. (095) 930-81-06; fax (095) 930-97-84; f. 1934; Pres. A. F. BREUSON.

Automobile, Tractor and Farm Machinery Industries Workers' Union: Moscow, Leninsky pr. 42; Pres. A. P. KASHIRIN.

Automobile Transport and Highway Workers' Union: Moscow V-218, ul. Krzhizhanovskovo 20/30, kv. 5; Pres. LEV A. YAKOVLEV.

Civil Aviation Workers' Union: Moscow V-218, ul. Krzhizhanovskovo 20/30, kor. 5; Pres. A. G. GRIDIN.

Coal Mining Industry Workers' Union: Moscow, Zemlyanoy val 64, kor. 1; Pres. M. A. SREBNY.

Construction and Building Materials Industry Workers' Union: 117119 Moscow, Leninsky pr. 42; f. 1957; tel. (095) 938-76-62; Pres. G. D. ARJANOV.

Educational and Scientific Workers' Union: Moscow, Leninsky pr. 42; f. 1919; Pres. R. M. PAPILOV.

Engineering and Instrument-Making Industries Workers' Union: 117119 Moscow, Leninsky pr. 42; tel. (095) 930-85-25; fax (095) 930-80-25; Pres. ANATOLI Y. RYBAKOV.

Federation of the Agroindustrial Unions of the CIS: 117119 Moscow, Leninsky pr. 42; tel. (095) 938-75-95; f. 1919, merged with Food Workers' Union in 1986; Pres. M. B. RYZHIKOV; 37m. mems.

Federation of Chemical Industries Workers' Unions of the CIS: 117119 Moscow, Leninsky pr. 42; tel. (095) 938-83-70; Pres. V. K. BORODIN.

Federation of Communication Workers' Unions of the CIS: 117119 Moscow, Leninsky pr. 42; tel. (095) 930-84-58; fax (095) 938-21-63; f. 1905; Pres. ANATOLY NAZEYKIN.

Federation of Cultural Workers' Unions: 109004 Moscow, Zemlyanoy val 64, kor. 1; tel. (095) 297-86-12; fax (095) 925-85-17; Pres. I. A. NAUMENKO.

Federation of Timber and Related Industries Workers' Unions of the CIS: 117119 Moscow, Leninsky pr. 42; tel. 938-82-02; fax (095) 938-82-04; Pres. VIKTOR P. KARNIUSHIN.

Federation of Trade Unions 'Electrounion': 117119 Moscow, Leninsky pr. 42; tel. (095) 938-86-80; telex 411010; fax (095) 938-83-14; f. 1905; electrical workers; Pres. NIKOLAI A. PUGACHEV.

Geological Survey Workers' Union: Moscow V-218, Leninsky pr. 42; Pres. M. GOUBKIN.

Heavy Engineering Workers' Union: Moscow, Leninsky pr. 42; Pres. N. I. ZINOVIYEV.

Independent Trade Union of Railwaymen and Transport Construction Workers: 107217 Moscow, Sadovo-Spasskaya ul. 21; tel. (095) 262-58-73; Pres. I. A. SHINKEVICH.

International Trade Union Alliance of Municipal, Local Industry and Communal Services Workers and Allied Trades: 117119 Moscow, Leninsky pr. 42; tel. (095) 938-85-12; f. 1991 to replace the Local Industries and Public Services Workers' Union Federation; Pres. Y. Y. ABRAMOV.

International Trade Union Federation of State and Public Employees: 117119 Moscow, Leninsky pr. 42; tel. (095) 938-80-53; telex 411010; fax (095) 938-21-55; f. 1918; Pres. I. L. GREBENSHIKOV.

Medical Workers' Union: Moscow, Leninsky pr. 42; Pres. L. I. NOVAK.

Moscow Federation of Trade Unions: Moscow; largest regional branch of FITUR; Chair. MIKHAIL V. SHMAKOV; 6m. mems.

Oil and Gas Workers' Union: Moscow, Leninsky pr. 42; Pres. V. T. SEDENKO.

Radio and Electronics Industry Workers' Union: Moscow, Pervy Golutvinsky per. 3; Pres. V. N. TUZOV.

Russian Fishing Industry Workers' Union: 117119 Moscow, Leninsky pr. 42; tel. (095) 938-77-82; fax (095) 930-77-31; f. 1986; Pres. V. A. ZYRIANOV.

Sea and River Workers' Union: 109004 Moscow, Zemlyanoy val 64, kor. 1; tel. (095) 227-29-96; Pres. K. YU. MATSKYAVICHYUS.

Shipbuilding Workers' Union: Moscow, Leninsky pr. 42; Pres. A. G. BURIMOVICH.

State Trade and Consumer Co-operative Workers' Union: Moscow, Leninsky pr. 42; Pres. G. N. ZAMYTSKAYA.

Textile and Light Industry Workers' Union: Moscow, Leninsky pr. 42; tel. (095) 938-74-70; Pres. M. V. IKHARLOVA.

Independent Trade Unions

Federation Union of Air Traffic Controllers: Moscow; Chair. ALFRED MALINOVKSY.

Independent Trade Union of Miners: Moscow; f. 1989 in opposition to the official coal-miners' union; Chair. ALEKSANDR SERGEYEV; 50,000 mems.

Metallurgical Industry Workers' Union: Moscow; Puchkinskaya ul. 5/6; left the FITUR in 1992 to form independent organization; Pres. BORIS MISNIK.

Russian Union of Sailors: Moscow; Pres. V. NEKRASOV.

Russian Union of Locomotive Workers: Moscow; Chair. V. KUROCHIN.

Russian Union of Dock Workers: Moscow; Chair. V. VASILYEV.

Transport

RAILWAYS

In 1993 the total length of railway track in use was 87,079 km, of which 37,365 km were electrified. The railway network is of great importance in the Russian Federation, owing to the poor road system and relatively few private vehicles. The Trans-Siberian Railway provides the main route connecting European Russia with Siberia and the Far East.

Russian Railways: 107174 Moscow, ul. Novobasmannaya 2; tel. (095) 262-16-28; fax (095) 262-65-61; comprises 17 of the 32 regional divisions of the former Soviet Railways (SZD); in 1992 these were reorganized into 19 operating divisions; Gen. Mans A. SEDENKO, V. N. SHATAYEV.

ROADS

At 31 December 1990 the total length of roads was 879,100 km, of which 652,500 km were hard-surfaced. The road network is of most importance in European Russia; in Siberia and the Far East there are few roads, and they are often impassable in winter. At the beginning of 1994 the World Bank granted Russia a loan of US $300m. to finance the construction of 10,000 km of roads to the west of the Urals.

SHIPPING

The seaports of the Russian Federation provide access to the Pacific Ocean, in the east, the Baltic Sea and the Atlantic Ocean, in the west, and the Black Sea, in the south. Major eastern ports are at Vladivostok, Nakhodka, Magadan and Petropavlovsk. In the west St Petersburg and Kaliningrad provide access to the Baltic Sea, and the northern port of Murmansk has access to the Atlantic Ocean, via the Barents Sea. Novorossiysk and Sochi are the principal Russian ports on the Black Sea.

Principal Shipowning Companies

Baltic Shipping Company: 198035 St Petersburg, Mezhevoy kanal 5; tel. (812) 216-93-26; telex 121501; fax (812) 186-85-44; freight and passenger services; Pres. VIKTOR I. KHAVCHENKO; 30,000 employees.

Far Eastern Shipping Company: 690019 Vladivostok, ul. Aleutskaya 15; tel. (4232) 2-24-32; telex 213115; Pres. MIKHAIL A. ROMANSKY.

Kamchatka Shipping Company: 683600 Petropavlovsk-Kamchatsky, ul. Radiosvyazi 65; tel. 2-22-63; telex 244112; fax 2-19-60; f. 1949; freight services; Pres. V. G. KULAGIN.

Murmansk Shipping Company: 183636 Murmansk, ul. Kominterna 15; tel. (4785) 1-04-91; telex 126113; fax (4785) 1-04-95; f. 1939; shipping and icebreaking services; Gen. Dir Capt. N. I. MATYUSHENKO.

Northern Shipping Company: 163061 Arkhangelsk, nab. Sev. Dviny 36; tel. (818) 44-74-00; telex 242111; fax (818) 3-83-10; f. 1870; Pres. A. N. GAGARIN.

Novorossiysk Shipping Company: 353900 Novorossiysk, ul. Svobody 1; tel. 6-42-71; telex 279113; fax 140-12-56; Pres. LEONID I. LOZA.

Primorsk Shipping Company: 692900 Nakhodka, ul. Pogranichnaya 6; tel. (42366) 5-53-09; telex 213812; fax (42366) 5-60-78; f. 1972, reorganized as joint-stock co 1992; Pres. A. D. KIRILICHEV.

Sakhalin Shipping Company: 694620 Sakhalin, Kholmsk, ul. Pobedy 16; tel. 2-28-03; telex 412613; fax 2-55-84; Pres. M. A. ROMANOVSKY.

White Sea and Onega Shipping Company: Petrozavodsk, ul. Rigachin 7; tel. 6-13-33; telex 121591; fax 5-77-17.

CIVIL AVIATION

In 1991 the establishment of a Russian transcontinental airline, Air Rossiya, was announced. The airline was to be a joint venture between British Airways and the Russian Government, and was expected to commence services, based at Domodedovo airport in Moscow, by 1994. In 1992 some 30 independent state-owned airlines were founded in Russia on the basis of Aeroflot's former regional directorates and several small commercial airlines were established during the early 1990s. In the first nine months of 1993 Aeroflot's services to remote regions of Russia declined by an estimated 46%, owing to a sharp increase in fuel prices. In general, air travel in Russia declined by one-third in 1993.

Aeroflot—Russian International Airlines: 125167 Moscow, Leningradsky pr. 37; tel. (095) 155-66-48; telex 411967; fax (095) 155-66-47; f. 1923 as Dobrolet, restyled Aeroflot in 1932; the world's largest airline and the operator of all kinds of air services in the former USSR, which, apart from scheduled flights, include agricultural, survey and ambulance services and the maintenance of airfields and navigation aids. Its extensive domestic network, which covers more than 1m. km, serves the capitals of all the former Republics of the USSR and over 3,600 other towns, while international flights, covering about 250,000 km, serve 120 destinations in 102 countries in Europe, Africa, Asia and the Americas. In 1990 Aeroflot transported 137m. passengers and 2,548,000 metric tons of freight; Chair. of Bd VLADIMIR V. POTAPOV.

Nebo: Khabarovsk; f. 1993; private airline; operates route from Moscow to Petropavlovsk-Kamchatsky via Khabarovsk.

Orel Avia: Orel; f. 1993; 15 passenger and cargo aircraft operating domestic flights.

Rossiya State Transport Company: Moscow; f. 1993; Dir ALEKSANDR LARIN.

Tourism

Intourist: 103009 Moscow, ul. Mokhovaya 13; tel. (095) 292-22-60; telex 411211; fax (095) 203-52-67; f. 1929; branches throughout Russia and in other countries; Pres. VLADIMIR MALININ.

Intourist Holdings: 103009 Moscow, ul. Pushkinskaya 26; tel. (095) 292-30-13; telex 411211; fax (095) 292-43-34; f. 1991 as a result of reorganization within Intourist; manages tourist facilities, incl. hotels and catering facilities; Chair. IGOR KONOVALOV.

Culture

NATIONAL ORGANIZATIONS

Ministry of Culture: see section on The Government (Ministries).

Cultural Foundation: 121019 Moscow, 6 Gogolevsky bul.; tel. (095) 291-27-48; telex 411071; fax (095) 200-12-38; f. 1986 as Cultural Foundation of the USSR; encourages interest in and study of cultural heritage, especially architecture, literature, music and education; Chair. DMITRY LIKHACHEV; Deputy Chair. GEORGY MYASNIKOV.

Russian Association for International Co-operation: 103885 Moscow, ul. Vozdvizhenka 14; tel. (095) 290-69-32; telex 411286; fax (095) 200-12-20; f. 1992; unites 56 societies of friendship and cultural relations with foreign countries; Chair. V. V. TERESHKOVA; 65,000 mems.

INTERNATIONAL ORGANIZATION

National Commission of the United Nations Educational, Scientific and Cultural Organization (UNESCO): Moscow, ul. Vozdvizhenka 9; tel. (095) 290-08-53; telex 411587; fax (095) 202-10-83.

CULTURAL HERITAGE

Moscow

A. V. Shchusev State Research Architectural Museum: 121019 Moscow, pr. Vozdvizhenka 5; tel. (095) 291-21-09; fax (095) 291-21-09; f. 1934; over 70,000 sheets of architectural drawings; over 300,000 negatives and 400,000 photographs of architectural monuments; library of 50,000 vols; Dir I. A. KASUS.

Andrey Rublev Museum of Ancient Russian Art: 107120 Moscow, pl. Pryamikova 10; tel. (095) 278-14-29; fax (095) 291-19-78; f. 1947; important collection of Russian icons; library of 22,000 vols; Dir S. V. VASHLAYEVA.

Central A. A. Bakhrushkina State Theatrical Museum: 113054 Moscow, ul. Bakhrushina 31/12; tel. (095) 233-44-48; telex 412101; f. 1894; over 1m. exhibits; library of 100,000 vols; Dir V. V. YUBIN.

Folk-Art Museum: 103009 Moscow, ul. Stanislavskogo 7; tel. (095) 290-52-22; f. 1885; about 50,000 exhibits; Dir G. A. YAKOVLEVA.

Kremlin Museums: 103073 Moscow, Kremlin; tel. (095) 928-44-56; Dir I. A. RODIMTSEVA.

M. I. Glinka State Central Museum of Musical Culture: 125047 Moscow, ul. Fadeyeva 4; tel. (095) 251-31-43; fax (095) 972-32-55; f. 1943; some 700,000 items; Dir A. D. PANYUSHKIN.

Novodevichy Monastery Museum: 119435 Moscow, Novodevichy pr. 1; tel. (095) 246-85-26; Russian fine and decorative art; Dir V. G. VERZHBITSKY.

Obraztsov's Central State Puppet Theatre Museum: Moscow, Sadovo-Samotechnaya ul. 3; f. 1937; over 2,600 dolls from 50 countries; library of over 5,300 books; Dir N. KOSTROVA.

Russian State Art Library: 103031 Moscow, Pushkinskaya ul. 8/1; tel. (095) 292-09-84; f. 1922; over 1.75m. items; Dir T. I. SILINA.

Russian State Library: 10100 Moscow, pl. Vozdvizhenka 3; tel. (095) 202-57-90; telex 411167; f. 1862 as the Rumyantsev Library, reorganized 1925; fmrly State V. I. Lenin Library; over 30m. books, periodicals and serials; Dir Dr IGOR FILIPPOV.

State Archives of the Russian Federation: 119817 Moscow, Bolshay Pirogovskaya ul. 17; tel. (095) 244-81-41; fax (095) 245-12-87; f. 1920 as Central State Archives of the October Revolution and Higher State Bodies, reorganized 1992; 4,947,871 items; Dir SERGEY V. MIRONENKO.

State Historical Museum: 103012 Moscow, Krasnaya pl. 1/2; tel. (095) 921-43-11; fax (095) 292-47-35; f. 1872; 4,500,000 exhibits on Russian history; Dir A. I. SHKURKO.

State Literature Museum: 103051 Moscow, ul. Petrovka 28; tel. (095) 925-12-26; f. 1934; library of 250,000 vols; 6 brs; Keeper-in Chief VERONIKA V. AKOPDZHANOVA.

State Museum of Ceramics and the Kuskovo Estate: 111402 Moscow, Yunosti ul. 2; tel. (095) 370-01-50; fax (095) 370-79-61; large collection of Russian and foreign art, ceramics and glass; Dir E. S. ERITSYAN.

State Museum of Oriental Art: 107120 Moscow, Suvorovsky bul. 12A; tel. (095) 291-96-14; f. 1918; large collection of Middle and Far Eastern art; Dir V. A. NABACHIKOV.

State Pushkin Museum of Fine Arts: 121019 Moscow, Volkhonka 12; tel. (095) 203-69-74; fax (095) 203-46-74; f. 1912; some 550,000 items of ancient Eastern, Graeco-Roman, Byzantine, European and American art; library of 200,000 vols; Dir I. A. ANTONOVA.

State Tretyakov Gallery: 117049 Moscow, Krymsky val 10–14; tel. (095) 230-77-88; f. 1856; collection of 40,000 Russian icons and works of Russian and Soviet painters, sculptors and graphic artists, Dir P. I. LEBEDEV.

Tolstoy State Museum: 119034 Moscow, ul. Prechistenka 11; tel. (095) 201-58-11; f. 1911; library of 71,000 works by or about Tolstoy; over 42,000 exhibits; Dir L. M. LUBIMOVA.

St Petersburg

Central Music Library, attached to the State Academic Theatre of Opera and Ballet: St Petersburg, ul. Zodchego Rossi 2; contains one of the largest collections in the world of Russian music; Dir S. O. BROG.

Literary Museum of the Institute of Russian Literature: 199034 St Petersburg, Pushkinsky dom, nab. Makarova 4; tel. (812) 218-05-02; 95,000 exhibits and over 120,000 items of reference material; Dir T. A. KOMAROVA.

Museum of the Academic Maly Theatre of Opera and Ballet: St Petersburg, pl. Iskusstv 1; f. 1935; collection of materials depicting the history of the theatre and its work; Dir V. LIPHART.

Peter the Great Museum of Anthropology and Ethnography: St Petersburg B-034, Universitetskaya nab. 3; tel. (812) 218-14-12; f. 1714; 900,000 items; Dir Prof. R. F. ITS.

Pushkin Museum: 191186 St Petersburg, nab. Moyki 12; tel. (812) 311-38-01; f. 1938; 50,000 exhibits illustrating the life and work of Pushkin and his epoch; Dir S. M. NEKRASOV.

State Circus Museum: 191011 St Petersburg, ul. Fontanka 3; tel. (812) 210-44-13; telex 187500; f. 1928; some 80,000 exhibits; library of 4,000 items; Dir NATALYA KUZNETSOVA.

State Hermitage Museum: St Petersburg, Dvortsovaya nab. 34; f. 1764 as a court museum; richest collection in Russia of the art of prehistoric, ancient Eastern, Graeco-Roman and medieval times; Dir M. B. PIOTROVSKY.

State Museum of Theatrical and Musical Arts: 191011 St Petersburg, pl. Ostrovskogo 6; tel. (812) 315-52-43; fax (812) 314-77-46; f. 1918; over 380,000 exhibits; library of 5,000 vols; 3 brs; Dir I. V. EVSTIGNEYEVA.

State National Ethnographical Museum: St Petersburg, Inzhenernaya ul. 4/1; 300,000 exhibits; 150,000 photographs; library of 105,000 vols; Dir Prof. I. V. DUBOV.

State Russian Museum: St Petersburg, Inzhenernaya ul. 4; f. 1898; 400,000 exhibits of Russian art; Dir V. A. YUSEV.

Other Regions

Archangel State Museum: 163061 Arkhangelsk, pl. Lenina 2; tel. (818) 3-66-79; telex 02242518; f. 1737; 150,000 items; library of 30,000 vols; Dir YU. P. PROKOPEV.

Mordovian Museum of Fine Arts: Saransk, Kommunisticheskaya ul. 61; tel. (83422) 17-56-38; f. 1960; 8,977 exhibits; painting, sculpture, prints, decorative arts; library of 10,000 vols; Dir M. N. BARANOVA.

North-Ossetian K. L. Khetagurov Memorial Museum: Republic of North Ossetia, Vladikavkaz, pr. Mira 12; collection of materials on Caucasian poetry and literature.

Sergiev Posad State History and Art Museum: Moscow obl., Sergiev Posad, Lavra; tel. 4-13-58; f. 1920; 100,000 items dealing with the development of Russian art; library of 17,000 vols; Dir K. V. BOBKOV.

Stalsky Memorial Museum: Republic of Daghestan, Kasumkentsky rayon, Ashaga-stal; exhibits on the history of Daghestani literature; library of 20,000 vols.

State Museum of Tatarstan: Republic of Tatarstan, Kazan, ul. Lenina 2; f. 1894; over 500,000 exhibits; library of 5,000 vols; Dir V. M. DYAKONOV.

Tolstoy Museum Estate: Tula obl., Shchekinsky rayon, Yasnaya Polyana; f. 1921; 27,695 exhibits; Dir S. Yu. Bunin.

Yaroslavl State Historical Museum: 150000 Yaroslavl, pl. Bogoyavlenskaya 25; tel. (0852) 22-02-72; f. 1864; over 370,000 exhibits; library of 35,000 vols; Dir V. I. Lebedev.

SPORTING ASSOCATIONS

National Olympic Committee of the Russian Federation: 119871 Moscow, Luzhnetskaya 8; tel. (095) 248-00-44; telex 411287; fax (095) 248-08-14; f. 1989; Pres. Vitaly Smirnov; Sec. Gen. Yury Yuryev.

Russian Central Council of the Sports Society of Trade Unions: 109017 Moscow, Maly Tolmachevsky per. 4; tel. (095) 238-61-44; fax (095) 230-76-26; Pres. Gennady S. Shibayev.

PERFORMING ARTS

Bolshoy Theatre: Moscow, Teatralnaya pl. (095) 928-40-91; f. 1824; opera and ballet company; Dir Yury N. Grigoriyevich.

Leninsky Komsomol Theatre: Moscow, ul. Chekova 6; tel. (095) 299-96-68.

Maly Drama Theatre: Moscow, Teatralnaya 1/6; tel. (095) 925-98-68.

Mayakovsky Theatre: Moscow, ul. Gertsena 19; tel. (095) 290-62-41; f. 1922; Dir Mikhail P. Zaitsev.

Sovremenik Theatre: Moscow, Chistoprudny bul. 19a; tel. (095) 921-17-90.

State Conservatoire: Moscow, ul. Gertsena 13; tel. (095) 229-81-83.

State Kirov Academic Ballet: St Petersburg, Teatralnaya pl. 2; Dir O. Vinogradov.

Taganka Comedy and Drama Theatre: Zemlyanoy val 76; tel. (095) 271-28-26; Dir Yury Lyubimov.

Teatr-Studio na Yugo-Zapade (Theatre-Studio of the South-West): Moscow, pr. Vernadskogo 125; tel. (095) 434-74-83.

ASSOCIATIONS

All-Russian Culture Fund: 103051 Moscow, ul. Petrovka 28/2; tel. (095) 924-63-73.

All-Russian Musical Society: 103009 Moscow, Sobinovsky per. 9; tel. (095) 290-56-47.

Russian Branch of the All-Union Znaniye Society: 101814 Moscow, Novaya pl. 3/4; tel. (095) 921-90-58.

Russian PEN Centre: 103031 Moscow, Neglinnaya ul. 18/1, kor. 2; tel. (095) 209-45-89; fax (095) 200-02-93; f. 1989; Pres. Andrey Bitov; Dir-Gen. Vladimir Stabnikov; 143 mems.

Theatre Union of the Russian Federation: 103009 Moscow, ul. Tverskaya 16/2; tel. (095) 229-91-52; telex 411030; f. 1986; fmrly All-Russia Theatrical Society; 30,124 mems; library of 300,000 vols; Chair. M. A. Ulyanov.

Theatrical Fund of the Russian Federation: 103031 Moscow, Pushkinskaya 34/10; tel. (095) 200-13-56.

Union of Architects of the Russian Federation: 103001 Moscow, ul. Shchuseva 22; tel. (095) 291-55-79.

Union of Artists of the Russian Federation: 103062 Moscow, ul. Chernyshevskogo 37; tel. (095) 297-56-52.

Artistic Fund: 103726 Moscow, Tverskoy bul. 26/5; tel. (095) 229-90-50.

Union of Composers of the Russian Federation: 103009 Moscow, ul. Nezhdanovoy 8/10, kor. 2; tel. (095) 229-52-18.

Musical Fund of the Russian Federation: 103006 Moscow, Sadovaya-Tirumfalnaya 14/12; tel. (095) 200-19-14.

Union of Russian Writers (Soyuz Rossiyskikh Pisateley): Moscow; f. 1991 as an alternative to the Union of Writers of the Russian Federation; 1,300 mems.

Union of Writers of the Russian Federation: 119087 Moscow, Komsomolsky pr. 13; tel. (095) 246-75-65; Chair. Yury Bondarev.

Education

Education in the Russian Federation is compulsory for all children between the ages of seven and 17 years. State primary and secondary education is provided free of charge although, in the early 1990s, some higher education establishments were charging tuition fees. In 1991 there were 27 graduates per 10,000 of the population of the Russian Federation.

Following the disintegration of the USSR, there were extensive changes to the curriculum, with particular emphasis on changes in the approach to Soviet history, and the introduction of the study of literary works which had previously been banned. At this time a number of private schools and colleges were introduced. In 1992 there were some 300 non-state schools, attended by more than 20,000 pupils, and 40 non-state higher education institutions. In the academic year 1990/91 there were a total of 72,203 institutions of secondary education (including secondary specialized institutions) attended by some 23,170,000 students. Higher education establishments totalled 514 and were attended by a total of 2,824,500 students.

UNIVERSITIES

Altay State University: 656099 Barnaul, ul. Dimitrova 66; tel. 22-18-07; f. 1973; 10 faculties; 516 teachers; 5,470 students; Chancellor Valery Mironov.

Bashkir State University: 450074 Bashkortostan, Ufa, ul. Frunze 32; tel. 22-63-70; telex 162125; f. 1957; 10 faculties; 525 teachers; 8,300 students; Rector Raghib N. Guimayev.

Chechen-Ingush State University: 364907 Chechen Republic-Ichkeria, Grozny, ul. Sheripova 32; tel. 3-40-89; f. 1972; 10 faculties; 5,600 students; Rector M. P. Pavlov.

Chelyabinsk State Technical University: 454080 Chelyabinsk, pr. Lenina 76; tel. (3512) 33-58-82; fax (3512) 65-36-77; f. 1943; 11 faculties, 1,500 teachers, 15,000 students; Rector German P. Vyatkin.

Chelyabinsk State University: 454136 Chelyabinsk, ul. Br. Kashirinykh 129; tel. (3512) 42-12-02; fax (3512) 42-08-59; f. 1976; 8 faculties; 2,100 students; Rector Valentin D. Batukhin.

Chuvash I. N. Ulyanov State University: 428015 Chuvash Republic, Cheboksary, Moskovsky pr. 15; tel. 24-03-79; telex 658127; fax 42-80-90; f. 1967; 12 faculties; 940 teachers; 10,600 students; Rector Prof. Dr L. P. Kurakov.

Daghestan V. I. Lenin State University: 36700 Daghestan Republic, Makhachkala, Sovetskaya ul. 8; tel. (872) 7-29-50; telex 175126; fax (872) 4-75-36; f. 1957; 14 faculties; 590 teachers; 8,800 students; Rector Prof O. A. Omarov.

Far Eastern State University: 690600 Vladivostok, ul. Sukhanova 8; tel. (4232) 22-47-00; telex 213218; f. 1920; 16 faculties; 635 teachers; 10,000 students; Rector Prof Vladimir I. Kurilov.

Irkutsk State University: 664003 Irkutsk, ul. K. Marksa 1; tel. (3952) 33-33-43; telex 231511; f. 1918; 10 faculties; 700 teachers; 7,000 students; Rector Prof. Fedor K. Shmidt.

Ivanovo State University: 153377 Ivanovo, ul. Yermaka 39; tel. 4-02-16; f. 1974; 10 faculties; 5,000 students.

Kabardino-Balkar State University: 360004 Kabardino-Balkarian Republic, Nalchik, ul. Chernyshevskovo 173; tel. (8600) 2-52-58; fax (8600) 337-99-55; f. 1957; 13 faculties; 780 teachers; 9,000 students; Rector Prof. V. Tlostanov.

Kaliningrad State University: 236041 Kaliningrad, ul. A. Nevskovo 14; tel. (0112) 46-59-17; telex 262116; fax (0112) 46-58-13; f. 1967; 11 faculties; 240 teachers; 6,000 students; Rector Prof. N. A. Medvedev.

Kalmyk State University: 358000 Republic of Kalmykia , Elista, ul. Pushkina 11; tel. 2-50-60; f. 1970; 9 faculties; 5,000 students; Rector N. P. Krasavchenko.

Kazan State University: 320008 Republic of Tatarstan, Kazan, ul. Lenina 18; tel. (8432) 38-70-69; telex 224641; fax (8432) 38-09-94; f. 1804; 14 faculties; 750 teachers; 9,000 students; Rector Prof. Yu. G. Konoplev.

Kemerovo State University: 650043 Kemerovo, Krasnaya ul. 6; tel. (3842) 23-12-26; fax (3842) 23-38-85; f. 1974; 9 faculties; 544 teachers; 6,000 students; Rector U. A. Zakharov.

Krasnoyarsk State University: 660062 Krasnoyarsk, pr. Svobodny 79; tel. 25-64-00; telex 288020; f. 1969; 416 teachers; 3,561 students; Rector N. D. Podufalov.

Kuban State University: 350751 Krasnodar, ul. Karla Libknekhta 149; tel (861) 33-75-37; f. 1970; 14 faculties; 9,800 students; Rector K. A. Novikov.

Mari University: 424001 Mari-El, Yoshkar-Ola, pl. Lenina 1; tel. 6-20-90; f. 1972; 5 faculties; 3,400 students; Rector V. P. Ivshin.

Mordovian N. P. Ogarev State University: 430000 Republic of Mordovia, Saransk, Bolshevistskaya ul. 68; tel. 4-45-63; f. 1957; 18 faculties; 16,000 students; Rector A. I. Sukharev.

Moscow M. V. Lomonosov State University: 117234 Moscow, Leninskiye gory; tel. (095) 939-53-40; f. 1755; 19 faculties; 8,000 teachers; 28,000 students; Rector Viktor Sadovnichy.

Nizhny Novgorod N. I. Lobachevsky State University: 603600 Nizhny Novgorod, pr. Gagarina 23; tel. (8312) 65-84-90; telex 224846; f. 1918; 9 faculties; 800 teachers; 9,500 students; Rector Prof. A. F. Khoklov.

North-Ossetian K. L. Khetagurov State University: 362000 Republic of North Ossetia, Vladikavkaz, ul. Vatutina 46; tel. 3-98-24; f. 1969; 11 faculties; 7,000 students; Rector A. K. Gudev.

Novosibirsk State University: 630090 Novosibirsk, ul. Pirogova 2; tel. (3832) 35-35-60; f. 1959; 6 faculties; 600 teachers; 3,700 students; Rector Prof. YU. L. ERSHOV.

Omsk State University: 644077 Omsk, pr. Mira 55A; tel. (38112) 64-25-87; fax (38112) 64-60-60; f. 1974; 8 faculties; 354 teachers; 3,634 students.

Patrice Lumumba People's Friendship University: 117198 Moscow, ul. Miklukho-Maklaya 6; tel. (095) 234-00-11; telex 411768; f. 1960; 7 faculties; 1,500 teachers; 6,700 students from Africa, Asia and Latin America; Rector V. F. STANIS.

Perm A. M. Gorky State University: 614600 Perm, ul. Bukireva 15; tel. (3422) 33-61-83; telex 134249; fax (3422) 33-80-14; f. 1916; 12 faculties; 683 teachers; 9,167 students; Rector V. V. MALANIN.

Petrozavodsk State University: 185640 Republic of Karelia, Petrozavodsk, pr. Lenina 33; tel. 7-17-91; telex 121399; fax 7-10-21; f. 1940; 10 faculties; 637 teachers; 6,101 students; Rector VIKTOR VASILYEV.

Rostov State University: 344066 Rostov-on-Don, ul. Bolshaya Sadovaya 105; tel. (8632) 22-68-36; telex 123228; fax (8632) 24-43-11; f. 1915; 11 faculties; 940 teachers; 9,600 students; Rector Prof. A. V. BELOKON.

St Petersburg State University: 199034 St Petersburg, Universitetskaya nab. 7/9; tel. (812) 218-97-88; telex 121481; fax (812) 218-51-52; f. 1724; 17 faculties; 2,086 teachers; 21,035 students; Rector Prof. (vacant).

St Petersburg Technical University: 195251 St Petersburg, Politekhnicheskaya ul. 29; tel. (821) 247-20-28; telex 121187; fax (821) 552-60-86; f. 1899; 10 faculties, 1,400 teachers, 16,000 students; Rector Prof. Dr YU. S. VASILYEV.

Samara State University: 443086 Samara, ul. Akademika Pavlova 1; tel. (8462) 34-54-02; f. 1969; 8 faculties; 4,500 students; Rector A. I. MEDVEDEV.

Saratov N. G. Chernyshevsky State University: 410600 Saratov, Astrakhanskaya ul. 83; tel. 24-16-96; telex 241125; fax 24-04-46; f. 1909; 8 faculties; 808 teachers; 9,800 students; Rector Prof. ANATOLY BOGOMOLOV.

Syktyvkar State University: 167001 Republic of Komi, Syktyvkar, Oktyabrsky pr. 55; tel. (82122) 3-68-20; fax (82122) 3-18-88; f. 1972; 7 faculties; 3,000 students; Pres. SERGEY I. KHUDYAYEV.

Tomsk State University: 634010 Tomsk, pr. Lenina 36; tel. 23-44-65; telex 128258; fax 22-24-66; f. 1880; 11 faculties; 700 teachers; 10,000 students; Rector Prof M. SVIRIDOV.

Tver State University: 170000 Tver, ul. Zhelyabova 33; tel. 3-15-50; telex 412556; f. 1971; 10 faculties; 600 teachers; 8,000 students; Rector A. N. KUDINOV.

Tyumen State University: 625610 Tyumen 3, ul. Semakova 10; tel. (3452) 6-19-30; 9 faculties; 6,000 students.

Udmurt State University: 426037 Udmurt Republic, Izhevsk, Krasnogeroyskaya ul. 71; tel. 75-16-10; telex 255154; fax 75-15-38; f. 1972; 10 faculties; 631 teachers; 7,235 students; Rector VITALY A. ZHURAVLEV.

Urals A. M. Gorky State University: 620083 Yekaterinburg, pr. Lenina 51; tel. (3432) 255-74-20; fax (3432) 255-59-64; f. 1920; 9 faculties; 1,000 teachers; 7,000 students; Rector Prof. VLADIMIR E. TRETYAKOV.

Volgograd State University: 400062 Volgograd, 2-ya Prodolnaya ul. 30; tel. (8442) 43-81-24; f. 1978; 5 faculties; 1,000 students.

Voronezh State University: 394693 Voronezh, Universitetskaya pl. 1; tel. (0732) 55-29-83; telex 153153; fax (0732) 56-65-51; f. 1918; 15 faculties; 1,000 teachers; 12,500 students; Rector Prof. V. V. YUSEV.

Yakutsk State University: 677000 Sakha Republic (Yakutia), Yakutsk, ul. Belinskogo 58; tel. (41122) 6-33-44; f. 1956; 12 faculties; 671 teachers; 7,000 students; Rector Prof. V. V. FILIPPOV.

Yaroslavl State University: 150000 Yaroslavl, Sovetskaya ul. 14; tel. (0852) 22-24-56; telex 217271; fax (0852) 22-52-32; f. 1970; 9 faculties; 520 teachers; 2,906 students; Rector G. S. MIRONOV.

Social Welfare

A basic social-security and health system exists in the Russian Federation. The Social Insurance Fund provides maternity benefit (which is payable for up to 18 weeks) and payments for the loss of earnings owing to ill-health. Old-age pensions are provided from a Pension Fund. Women over the age of 55 years and men over the age of 60 are entitled to receive old-age pensions if they have worked for at least 20 years. A social pension, equivalent to two-thirds of the minimum pension, may be paid to citizens who have worked a maximum of five years less than the qualifying period. Disability benefits are also payable from the Pension Fund. Child-care allowances exist for all children under six years of age, and further allowances were introduced in 1991 for children aged between six and 16 years. According to official estimates, in December 1993 some 49m. people (approximately one-third of the total population) had incomes below the subsistence level. The minimum living standard at this time was about 39,000 roubles per month, while the minimum wage stood at 15,000 roubles per month.

Unemployment benefit in the Russian Federation is paid to those who have been without employment for a period of more than three months. It is usually payable for a maximum period of 12 months. On 1 November 1993 the number of Russian citizens claiming unemployment benefit was 728,000. However, experts believed that large-scale 'hidden' unemployment existed in the form of part-time employment, compulsory unpaid leave, etc. The actual number of unemployed at this time was estimated at between 7m. and 9m. people, or 8%–11% of the able-bodied population.

All health care in the Russian Federation was previously financed by the State. In 1991, however, a law on health insurance was adopted, whereby employers would pay. By 1993 little progress had been made in establishing the new system, owing to the economic situation, technical difficulties and concerns regarding the ability of non-state organizations to support such a system. Very few private medical facilities were in existence at this time. In 1991 there were 47 doctors, 123 auxiliary staff and 137 hospital beds per 10,000 of the population. From 1 January 1994 all medical establishments in the Russian Federation were to be licensed.

In 1992 some 6.2% of the total state budget (representing 2.3% of GDP) was allocated to health care. In real terms, this represented less than the 1991 budgetary allocation. During the early 1990s wages in the health sector fell, in real terms, and there was a severe shortage of medical supplies. As in most other former Soviet Republics, medical production in Russia effectively collapsed as most newly privatized pharmacies became unprofitable. The difficulties experienced by the health-care system were reflected by a serious deterioration in the health of the population. Throughout 1993 the number of cases of typhoid, diphtheria and dysentery rose significantly. The reasons cited for this increase were unsatisfactory environmental conditions, a decline in immunity, a shortage of vitamins and medicine, and insufficient innoculations. In November that year, according to official figures, some 35% of children in Russia were suffering from chronic illnesses and only 14% of children were healthy. Foreign aid programmes existed at this time but they were insufficient to compensate for the severe problems in the health-care system.

GOVERNMENT AGENCIES

Ministry of Social Welfare of the Population: see section on The Government (Ministries).

State Committee for Sanitary and Epidemiological Inspection: Moscow; Chair. YEVGENY BELYAYEV.

Federal Employment Fund: Moscow; f. 1991; financed by employer contributions and govt funds.

Pension Fund of the Russian Federation: 117934 Moscow, ul. Shabolovka 4; tel. (095) 237-09-58; telex 207050; fax (095) 230-09-58; f. 1991; financed by contributions from employers and employees; Chair. of Bd VASILY BARCHUK.

Social Insurance Fund of the Russian Federation: Moscow; f. 1991; financed by employers on behalf of their workers; administered by the Federation of Independent Trade Unions of Russia.

HEALTH AND WELFARE ORGANIZATIONS

All-Russian Association of the Blind: 103672 Moscow, Novaya pl. 14; tel. (095) 923-91-49; fax (095) 925-46-92; Chair. A. YA. NEUMYVAKIN.

All-Russian Society of the Deaf: 123022 Moscow, ul. 1905 goda 10A; tel. (095) 255-67-04; fax (095) 255-04-17; f. 1926; Chair. V. A. KORABLINOV.

All-Russian Society of the Disabled: 121165 Moscow, Kutuzovsky pr. 30/32; tel. (095) 241-22-86; fax (095) 241-81-80; f. 1988; private voluntary organization; concerned with the protection of the rights and interests of disabled people and the integration of disabled people into Russian society; Chair. ALEKSANDR V. LOMAKHIN.

All-Russian Society of Invalids: 121099 Moscow, 2-Smolensky per. 3/4; tel. (095) 241-22-86; Chair. A. V. Deryugin.

Central Committee of the Russian Federation Red Cross: 103031 Moscow, Kuznetsky most 18/7; tel. (095) 925-58-48; fax (095) 928-20-74; Chair. of Central Committee O. M. SUDOROV.

Russian Charity and Health Fund: 100062 Moscow, ul. Chernyshevskogo 22; tel. (095) 227-18-88; fax (095) 975-22-45; Chair. A. K. KISILEV.

The Environment

Serious environmental problems developed in the Russian Federation during the Soviet period. Prolonged nuclear testing at the testing-range in Semipalatinsk (Kazakhstan) caused substantial damage in the neighbouring Altay Kray. The accident at the Chernobyl nuclear power station in Ukraine in 1986 resulted in widespread contamination, in particular of the Bryansk, Orel and Tula Oblasts. Accidents connected with outdated, Soviet-designed nuclear reactors continued to occur in the early 1990s: in early 1992 a fire occurred at a nuclear installation in Sosnovy Bor, near St Petersburg; and, in April 1993, an explosion at the closed city of Tomsk-7 in Siberia contaminated an area of 40 sq km. The issue of disposing of radioactive waste at sea, which the USSR had done for over 30 years, was also an important environmental issue at this time. In 1991 Russia temporarily ceased depositing toxic waste at sea only to resume in October 1993 in the Sea of Japan, some 150 km south of the Russian port of Nakhodka. In response to protests from environmental activists and from the international community, the Russian Government announced that Russia would be able to stop disposing of nuclear waste in this manner in 1994 or 1995, depending on the financial support it received for the construction of storage facilities on land. In December 1993, according to an official environmental report, some 15% of Russian territory was an 'ecological disaster zone' and only one-half of the country's arable land was suitable for agriculture. No improvement in the situation was expected before the late 1990s.

GOVERNMENT ORGANIZATIONS

Ministry of Environmental Protection and Natural Resources: see section on The Government (Ministries).

Arctic and Antarctic Research Unit: 199226 St Petersburg, ul. Bering 38; tel. (812) 352-03-19; telex 121423; fax (812) 352-26-88; f. 1920; research into ecology of the Artic and Antarctic; responsible for Russian Antarctic Expedition; Dir Dr B. A. KRUTSKIKH.

Interdepartmental Commission for Ecological Security: Moscow; f. 1993; commission of the Security Council; Chair. ALEKSEY YABLOKOV.

Russian Federal Hydrometeorology and Environmental Monitoring Service: Moscow.

State Committee for Hydrometeorology and Environmental Control: Moscow, ul. Kuybysheva 4.

State Committee for Social Protection of Citizens and the Rehabilitation of Territories Affected by Chernobyl and Other Radiation Accidents: 103132 Moscow, Staraya pl. 8/2, pod. 3; tel. (095) 206-48-81; Chair. VASILY Y. VOZNYAK.

RUSSIAN ACADEMY OF SCIENCES

Russian Academy of Sciences: 117901 Moscow, Leninsky pr. 14; tel. (095) 954-21-53; telex 411964; fax (095) 938-21-44; f. 1725; renamed Academy of Sciences of the USSR 1925; original name reinstated 1991; Pres. YURY S. OSIPOV; a Commission on Problems of Ecology is attached to the Presidium of the Academy; the principal sections and institutes involved in environmental matters incl.:

All-Union Scientific Research Institute for Nature Conservation and Reserves (Vsesoyuzny Nauchno-issledovatelsky Institut Okhrany Prirody i Zapovednovo Dela): Moskovskaya obl. M-628, Leninsky rayon, 142790 P/O VILR, Znamenskoye-Sadki; applied research inst.; major repository of research material.

Section of Chemical, Technological and Biological Sciences

A. N. Severtsov Institute of Evolutionary Morphology and Animal Ecology (Institut evolyutsionnoy morfologii i ekologii zhivotnykh imeni A. N. Severtsova): 117071 Moscow, Leninsky pr. 33; tel. (095) 954-47-56; fax (095) 954-55-34; in the Dept of General Biology; research of general ecology, morphology, ecology and ethology of animals, animal evolution, problems of biodiversity and nature preservation; Dir Acad. V. E. SOKOLOV.

Institute of the Biology of Inland Waters: 152742 Yaroslavl obl., Nekuzsky rayon, P/O Borok; tel. 349; telex 412583; in the Dept of General Biology; incl. Commission on the Conservation of Natural Waters; Dir N. P. SMIRNOV.

Institute of the Ecology of the Volga River Basin: Samara obl., 445003 Toglyatti, ul. Komzina 10; tel. 23-56-85; f. 1983; in the Dept of General Biology; monitors the environment of the lower Volga; Dirs G. P. KRASNOSHCHEKOV, G. S. ROZENBURG.

Institute of Soil Science and Photosynthesis: 142292 Moscow obl., Serpukhovsky rayon, Pushchino; tel. (095) 923-95-58; telex 205128; in the Dept of Biochemistry, Biophysics and Physiological Chemistry; research incl. soil conservation and land reclamation; Dir V. I. KEFELYA.

Section of Earth Sciences

Institute of Water Problems: 107078 Moscow, POB 524, ul. Novobasmannaya 10; tel. (095) 208-46-11; fax (095) 265-18-87; f. 1968; in the Dept of Oceanology, Atmospheric Physics and Geography; Dir M. G. KHUBLARYAN.

Laboratory for the Monitoring of the Environment and Climate: c/o Dept of Oceanology, Atmospheric Physics and Geography, 117901 Moscow, Leninsky pr. 14; tel. (095) 234-14-24; Dir (vacant).

Research Co-ordination Centre 'Aral': c/o Dept of Oceanology, Atmospheric Physics and Geography, 117901 Moscow, Leninsky pr. 14; tel. (095) 234-14-24; responsible for researching the environmental spoilation of the Aral Sea region; Dir V. M. KOTLYAKOV.

The Section of Earth Sciences also includes the Instiitute of Lake Conservation and the Scientific Council on Study of the Caspian Sea.

Section of Social Sciences

Institute of State and Law, Sector on Environmental Law: 119841 Moscow, ul. Znamenka 10; tel. (095) 291-33-81; f. 1925; research into Soviet and Russian environmental law; in the Dept of Philosophy and Law; Dir BORIS N. TOPORNIN.

Siberian Division

630090 Novosibirsk, pr. Akademika Lavrenteva 17; tel. (3832) 35-05-67; Chair. Acad. V. A. KOTYUG; institutes involved in environmental matters incl:

Chita Institute of Natural Resources: 672014 Chita 14, ul. Nedorezova 16; tel. 1-24-81; f. 1981; scientific research into the region's ecosystems; Dir V. V. MAZALOV; Scientific Sec. T. A. STRIZHOVA.

Institute of Limnology: 666063 Irkutsk, ul. Lermontova 281; tel. (3952) 46-05-04; telex 133163; fax (3952) 46-69-33; studies the ecology of lakes; particularly concerned with the conservation programme in Lake Baikal; Dir M. A. GRACHEV.

Institute of Water and Ecological Problems: 656009 Barnaul, ul. Papanintseva 105; tel. (3852) 25-21-40; fax (3852) 24-03-96; f. 1987; research into water-resource use, land reclamation and environmental protection in Siberia; experimental and mathematical methods for analysis of hydrophysical, hydrochemical and other natural processes in the water environment; environmental assessment of large-scale engineering projects; Dir Prof. OLEG F. VASILIYEV.

Far Eastern Division

690600 Vladivostok, ul. Leninskaya 50; tel. (4232) 22-25-28; Chair. G. B. YELYAKOV; environmental research by:

Institute of Biological Problems of the North: 685000 Magadan, ul. K. Marksa 24; tel. 2-65-00; telex 145123; Dir A. A. AIDARALIYEV.

Institute of Water and Ecological Problems: 680063 Khabarovsk, ul. Kim Yu Chena 65; tel. 33-39-48; telex 141359; fax 33-33-42; f. 1968; research into use and management of water resources; Dir I. P. DRUZHININ; Vice-Dir V. A. VORONOV.

Urals Division

620219 Yekaterinburg, ul. Pervomaiskaya 91; tel. (343) 44-02-23; Chair. G. A. MESYATS; attached institutes incl.:

Institute of Industrial Ecology: 620219 Yekaterinburg, ul. Pervomayskaya 91; tel. and fax (3432) 44-07-71; f. 1992; environmental research; Dir Prof. V. N. CHUKANOV.

Institute of Plant and Animal Ecology: 620008 Yekaterinburg, ul. 8-vo Marta 202; tel. (3432) 22-05-70; environmental research; Dir V. N. BOLSHAKOV.

NON-GOVERNMENTAL ORGANIZATIONS

All-Russian Society for Nature Conservation (Vserossiiskoe Obshchestvo Okhrany Prirody): 103012 Moscow L-12, Kuybyshevsky pr. 3; tel. (095) 924-77-65; f. 1924; civilian assen focusing on environmental education; Chair. I. F. BAZISHPOL.

Association of Ecological Centres: 107078 Moscow, ul. Novobasmannaya 10.

Association for the Support of Ecological Issues: Moscow, Lomonosovsky pr. 111–119; co-ordinating group.

Environmental Education Association: 249020 Kaluga obl., Obninsk, POB 152; tel. (8439) 3-86-48; telex 64412633; fax (095) 255-22-25; concerned with environmental education in the former USSR; Co-ordinator VADIM KALININ.

Green World Environmental Association (Zelyony Mir): 603047 Nizhny Novgorod, ul. Krasniye Zory 15, kv. 409; tel. (831) 224-39-41; fax (831) 244-02-85; Gen. Co-ordinator VALENTINA MALAKHOVA.

Greenpeace Russia: 103006 Moscow, ul. Dolgorukovskaya 21; tel. (095) 251-90-73; fax (095) 251-90-88; Exec. Dir ALEKSANDR KNORRE.

International Foundation for the Survival and Development of Humanity (IF): c/o Yevgeny Velikhov, Vice-President of the Academy of Sciences: 117901 Moscow, Leninsky pr. 14; tel. (095) 232-29-10; f. 1988; international environmental asscn; Dir YE. P. VELIKHOV.

Krasnoyarsk Green World (Krasnoyarsky Zeleny Svet): Krasnoyarsk; local environmental group opposed to nuclear power and weapons.

Moscow Ecological Federation: 121019 Moscow, POB 211; tel. (095) 206-88-94; concerned with Moscow's ecological problems; provides environmental information; assists with urban development plans; Co-Chairs. LYUBOV RUBINCHIKA, VADIM DAMIE.

Moscow Society of Naturalists: 103009 Moscow, ul. Gertsena 6; tel. (095) 203-67-04; f. 1805; 2,700 mems; library of 500,000 vols; Chair. A. L. YANSHIN.

Movement for a Nuclear-Free North: Murmansk; advocates demilitarization of the Kola peninsula and an end to nuclear testing on Novaya Zemlya.

Prikamya Green Party (Partiya Zelyenykh Prikamya): 614006 Perm, ul. Kuybysheva 14, kom. 318; Chair. MARCEL AKHMETOV.

Rostov Regional Ecological Centre: Rostovsky Oblastnoy Ekologichesky Tsentr: 344007 Rostov, ul. Stanislavskogo 114, kv. 1; tel. (863) 62-14-47; Pres. VALERY PRIVALENKO.

Russian Green Party: Moscow; Chair. DMITRY LIKHACHEV.

Socio-Ecological Union: 125319 Moscow, ul. Krasnoarmeyskaya 25, kv. 85; tel. (095) 928-76-08; fax (095) 206-82-73; co-ordinates 180 environmental committees, clubs and societies in 11 of the former Soviet Republics; campaigns on environmental issues; Chair. SVYATOSLAV ZABELIN.

Perm Department: 614081 Perm, POB 5786; tel. (3422) 33-48-58; Chair. YURY SCHIPAKIN.

Tambov Green Party: 392032 Tambov, bul. Entuziastov 32, kv. 47; tel. (752) 35-01-33; Chair. LUDMILA SPIRIDONOVA.

Defence

In May 1992 the Russian Federation established its own armed forces, on the basis of former Soviet forces on the territory of the Russian Federation and those former Soviet forces outside Russian territory that were not subordinate to other former republics of the USSR. In June 1993 the total active armed forces in Russia numbered some 2,030,000. (This figure includes some 165,000 staff of the Ministry of Defence but excludes approximately 130,000 railway and construction personnel.) Military service is compulsory for men over 18 years of age. It lasts for a term of 18 months for conscripts to the army and two years for conscripts to the navy. In addition, there were some 20m. reserves. Ground forces in the Russian army consisted of some 1m. troops, including 450,000 conscripts. There was a navy of 300,000, including 180,000 conscripts, and an airforce of 170,000, some 85,000 of which were conscripts. There were a further 220,000 paramilitary troops, including 100,000 border guards. According to Western estimates, the defence budget for 1993 amounted to 3,115,510m. roubles.

At the end of 1993 Russian forces remained on the territory of most of the former Soviet Republics. The issue of control of the Black Sea Fleet had yet to be resolved by the Governments of Russia and Ukraine.

Commander-in-Chief of the Armed Forces of the Russian Federation: President of the Federation.

Chief of the General Staff: Col-Gen. MIKHAIL KOLESNIKOV.

Members of the Russian Federation

There are 89 members (federal territorial units) of the Russian Federation. According to the Constitution of December 1993, the recognized members consisted of 21 autonomous republics, six krays (provinces), 49 oblasts (regions), two cities of federal status, one autonomous oblast and 10 autonomous okrugs (districts). Their status had begun to be regularized by the Federation Treaty of 31 March 1992, which had provided for a union of 20 republics (16 of which had been Autonomous Soviet Socialist Republics—ASSRs under the old regime, and four of which were autonomous oblasts), six krays and one autonomous oblast. There were also 10 autonomous okrugs, which were also under the jurisdiction of the kray or oblast within which they were located. A further republic, Ingushetia, was acknowledged in June 1992. Moscow and St Petersburg subsequently assumed the status of federal cities. The 89 members of the Russian Federation were each administered by a local administration, the head of which (governor) was the highest official in the territory, and a representative assembly (usually known as a soviet or duma).

On 21 September 1993 President Yeltsin issued a decree (No. 1,400) entitled On Gradual Constitutional Reform, which dissolved the bicameral Russian legislature. On 6 October the President 'invited' those local soviets (at kray, oblast and lower levels) that had rejected Decree No. 1,400 to disband themselves. The following day Yeltsin announced that heads of local administration were to be appointed and dismissed by presidential decree. On 9 October Yeltsin ordered the dissolution of all soviets at the lowest levels of the administrative structure and the assumption of their powers by the local administrators. In addition, all provincial (kray) or regional (oblast) soviets unable to achieve a quorum were to be disbanded and their powers transferred to the local administrator. Later that month a presidential decree ordered elections to be held in krays, oblasts and lower territorial subdivisions betweeen December 1993 and March 1994. Republics were advised to do the same, although some exceptions were made. The following is a list of the 89 regions (for maps, see pp. 46 and 96), listing the main officials at March 1994. Not all election results were available at the time of going to press.

AUTONOMOUS REPUBLICS

Republic of Adygheya

The Republic of Adygheya (an Autonomous Oblast until the signing of the Federation Treaty in March 1992, when it was reorganized as a Republic) is situated in the foothills of the Greater Caucasus, in the basin of the Kuban river. It forms part of Krasnodar Kray. The Republic's agricultural production consists mainly of grain, sunflower, sugar beets, tobacco and vegetable production, cucurbit (gourds and melons) cultivation and viniculture. Animal husbandry and bee-keeping are also important. Its industry is based on processing of agricultural and timber products, machine-building and production of natural gas. Its major industrial centres are at the two cities of Maikop and Kamennomostsky. The Republic occupies an area of 7,600 sq km and had a population of 432,000 in 1990. Its administrative centre is at Maikop.

President: ASLAN A. DJARIMOV; tel. 2-19-00.

Chairman of the Supreme Soviet: ADAM K. TLEUJ.

Chairman of the Council of Ministers: MUGDIN S. TLEKHAS.

Permanent Representative in Moscow: PSHIMAF A. SHEVOTSUKOV; tel. (095) 202-77-90.

Head of Maikop City Administration: MIKHAIL N. CHERNICHENKO; tel. 2-17-08.

Republic of Altay

The Republic of Altay was the Gorno-Altay Autonomous Oblast until the signing of the Russian Federation Treaty in March 1992, when it became an autonomous republic. On 14 October 1993, at an extraordinary session of the Supreme Soviet, a resolution was adopted which provided for the establishment of a State Assembly (El Kurultay). The Assembly would comprise 27 deputies and be the highest body of power in the Republic. Elections to the Assembly were held on 12 December.

The Republic of Altay is situated in the Altay mountains in the basin of the river Ob. It has one lake—Teletskoye—and one-quarter of its territory was forested. The Republic forms the eastern part of the Altay Kray and has international borders with Kazakhstan in the south-west, a short border with the People's Republic of China to the south, and Mongolia to the south-east. Its agriculture consists mainly of livestock breeding, bee-keeping, grain production and hunting. Its main industries are timber and food processing, light industry and the electrotechnical industry. The major industrial centre is at Gorno-Altaysk. The Republic occupies an area of 92,600 sq km and had a population of 192,000 in 1990. Its administrative centre is at Gorno-Altaysk.

Chairman of the Government: VLADIMIR I. PETROV; tel. 2-60-71.

Chairman of the State Assembly: (vacant).

Permanent Representative in Moscow: ALEKSANDR P. MANZYROV; tel. (095) 202-12-23.

Head of Administration: ALEKSANDR P. OBLOGIN; tel. 2-07-31.

Republic of Bashkortostan

Bashkiria was annexed by Russia in 1557. The Bashkirs are a Turkic Muslim people. The Bashkir ASSR was established on 23 March 1919. The Republic declared sovereignty on 11 October 1990. On 23 September 1993 the Supreme Soviet adopted a resolution suspending President Yeltsin's decree No. 1,400 on the territory of the Republic. However, on 12 October it reversed this decision. Legislative and presidential elections were held in the Republic on 12 December to a new post of President of the Republic. The election was won by Murtaza Rakhimov, former Chairman of the Supreme Soviet. The same day, a majority in the Republic voted against acceptance of the Russian Constitution, which was approved in the Federation as a whole. On 24 December the republican Supreme Soviet adopted a new Constitution which stated that its own laws had supremacy over federal laws.

The Republic of Bashkortostan is situated on the slopes of the southern Urals. Its major rivers are the Belaya and the Ufa. It formed part of the Urals Economic Area. Its principal agricultural products are grain, sugar beets, sunflowers and vegetables. Animal husbandry and bee-keeping are also important. The Republic's industries include processing of agricultural and forestry products, petroleum refining, machine-building, metal-working, and the production of petroleum, coal, iron and copper-zinc ores. Its major industrial centres are at Ufa, Sterlitamak, Salavat and Ishimbay. Bashkortostan occupies an area of 143,600 sq km and comprises 54 administrative districts and 17 cities. In 1990 it had a population of 3,952,000. In 1989 21.9% of the population were Bashkirs and 39.3% Russians; there was also a large Tatar community. The capital is at Ufa.

President of the Republic: MURTAZA G. RAKHIMOV.

Chairman of the Supreme Soviet: (vacant).

Chairman of the Council of Ministers: MARAT P. MIRGAZYAMOV; tel. 23-37-01.

Permanent Representative in Moscow: ABRAR B. YARLYKAPOV; tel. (095) 291-45-14.

Head of Ufa City Administration: MIKHAIL A. ZAITSEV; tel. 22-83-60.

Republic of Buryatia

Russian influence reached Buryatia in the 17th century but possession was contested with China until 1727. The Buryats are native Siberian people of Mongolian descent, who were converted to Buddhism in the 18th and 19th centuries by Mongolian and Tibetan missionaries. An ASSR was established on 1 March 1920, although its territory was considerably reduced in 1937. In 1958 the Buryat-Mongol ASSR was renamed the Buryat ASSR. On 14 October 1993 the Supreme Soviet in the Republic rescinded its earlier decision to condemn President Yeltsin's Decree No. 1,400. On 30 December a draft constitution of the Republic of Buryatia was published. It was adopted by the Supreme Soviet on 4 March 1994. The Constitution provides for Buryatia as a sovereign, democratic law-governed state within the Russian Federation.

The Republic of Buryatia is situated in the Transbaikal region and within the eastern Sayan mountains. It forms part of the Eastern Siberian Economic District and has an international boundary with Mongolia in the south. At its extreme south-western end it has a border with the Russian federal territory of Tyva. Buryatia's largest rivers are the Selenga, the Barguzin, the Upper Angara and the Vitim. Its one lake, Baikal, is the deepest in the world, possessing over 80% of Russia's freshwater resources, and 20% of the world total. Four-fifths of Buryatia's territory is taiga (forested marshland). Its agriculture consists mainly of animal husbandry, grain production and hunting. Its main industries are mining, machine-building, metal-working, timber, wood-working and mineral production. Its major industrial centre is at Ulan-Ude. The Republic's territory covers 351,300 sq km and comprises a total of 20 administrative districts and 6 cities. It had a population of 1,042,000 in 1990. In 1989 some 24.0% of the total number of inhabitants were Buryats and 70.0% were Russians. The capital is at Ulan-Ude.

Chairman of the Supreme Soviet: LEONID V. POTAPOV.

Chairman of the Council of Ministers: VLADIMIR B. SAGANOV; tel. 2-45-63; fax 2-47-03.

Permanent Representative in Moscow: NIKOLAY I. KRYUCHKOV; tel. (095) 291-45-14.

Head of Ulan-Ude City Administration: VIKTOR K. KUKSHINOV; tel. 2-32-52.

Chechen Republic-Ichkeria

The Chechens and Ingush were conquered by Russia in the late 1850s. The Chechens are closely related to the Ingushetians (both of whom are known collectively as Vainakhs). Their language is a Nakh dialect and they are Sunni Muslims. A Chechen Autonomous Oblast was established on 30 November 1922. An Ingush Autonomous Oblast was established on 7 July 1924. In 1924 the two regions were combined, and, in 1936, consituted as the Chechen-Ingush ASSR. Many of the Chechen and Ingush were deported to Central Asia in 1944 and their autonomous republic was dissolved. On 9 January 1957 the ASSR was reconstituted but certain Ingush territories, which had been absorbed by North Ossetia, were not included. In 1991 an All-National Congress of the Chechen People gradually seized effective power in the territory and, on 27 October, held elections to the presidency of a 'Chechen Republic' (Chechnya). The Republic, although unrecognized internationally, continued to insist on its independence and did not take part in the elections to the Russian State Duma, which were held on 12 December 1993. On 16 December the Republic rejected the new Russian Constitution. On 19 January 1994 Ichkeria was added to the Republic's name by presidential decree.

The territory of the former Chechen-Ingush ASSR is located in the North Caucasus, on the Russian border with Georgia. North Ossetia lies to the west and Daghestan to the east. The exact delineation of Chechnya and Ingushetia had not been decided at the beginning of 1994, although, in the previous year, the peaceful resolution of border questions had been resolved upon. The Chechens dominate the east of the territory and the old ASSR capital, Grozny, is the chief town of the Chechen Republic-Ichkeria.

President: Gen. JOKHAR M. DUDAYEV.

Vice-President: ZELIMKHAN IYANDERBIYEV (acting).

Chairman of Parliament: HUSSEIN S. AKHMADOV.

Head of Grozny City Administration: MAIRBEK E. BAIMURAZOV; tel. 22-01-42.

Chuvash Republic (Chuvashia)

Russia annexed Chuvash lands in the 16th century. A Chuvash Autonomous Oblast was established on 24 June 1920 and was subsequently upgraded to the status of an ASSR. In March 1992 its name was changed to the Chuvash Republic. On 19 October 1993 the Supreme Soviet in the Republic refused to dissolve itself or to rescind its earlier condemnation of Yeltsin's Decree No. 1,400. On 12 December, in the nation-wide plebiscite, a majority in the Republic voted against the new Russian Constitution. On 26 December a second round of voting took place for the post of President of the Republic (as none of the seven candidates won the required 35% of the vote in the first round). Nikolay Fedorov, one of two candidates standing in the second round, won the majority of the votes cast.

The Chuvash Republic is situated in the north-west of European Russia, on the East European Plain on the middle reaches of the Volga. The Republics of Mari-El (north-east), Tatarstan (east) and Mordovia (south-west) neighbour Chuvashia. Its major rivers are the Volga and the Sura, and one-third of its territory is covered by forest. It forms part of the Volga-Vyatka Economic Area. Its agriculture consists mainly of grain, hops, hemp and tobacco production, horticulture and animal husbandry. Its main industries are machine-building, chemicals, light, wood-working and food. Its major industrial centres are at Cherboksary, Novocheboksarsk, Kanash, Alatyr and Shumerlya. It occupies 18,300 sq km and consists of 21 administrative districts and nine cities. In 1989 the total population of the Republic was 1,336,000, of which 67.8% were Chuvash and 26.7% Russians. Its capital is at Cheboksary (Shupashkar).

President of the Republic: NIKOLAY FEDOROV.

Chairman of the Supreme Soviet: EDUARD A. KUBAREV.

Chairman of the Council of Ministers: VALERYAN N. VIKTOROV; tel. 22-01-71.

Permanent Representative in Moscow: ANDRIAN G. NIKOLAYEV; tel. (095) 291-45-32.

Head of Cheboksary City Administration: VITALY V. ALEKSEYEV (acting); tel. 22-35-76.

Republic of Daghestan

Daghestan (Dagestan) came under Russian rule in 1723, when the various Muslim khanates on its territory were annexed from Persia (now Iran). A Daghestan ASSR was established on 20 January 1920. The Republic of Daghestan acceded to the Federation Treaty in March 1992. On 22 October 1993 the Supreme Soviet in the Republic rescinded its previous decision to condemn President Yeltsin's Decree No. 1,400 and agreed to hold early local elcetions. In December 1993 the Republic voted against the new Russian Constitution.

The Republic of Daghestan is situated in the North Caucasus on the Caspian Sea. Azerbaijan lies to the south and Chechnya to the west. Its largest rivers are the Terek, the Sulak and the Samur. It forms part of the Northern Caucasus Economic Area. Its agriculture consists mainly of grain production, viniculture and horticulture. Its main industries are petroleum and natural-gas production, machine-building, metal-working, food processing, light industry and handicrafts. Its major industrial centres are at the main port of Makhachkala, Derbent, Kaspiisk, Izberbash, Khasavyurt, Kizlyar, Kizilyurt and Buinaksk. It occupies an area of 50,300 sq km. The Republic is made up of 39 administrative districts and eight cities and had a population of 1,823,000 in 1990. In 1989 some 27.5% of the population were Avars, 15.6% Darghins, 12.9% Kumyks, 11.3% Lezghis, 5.1% Laks, 1.6% Nogays, 0.8% Rutuls, 0.8% Aguls, 4.3% Tabasarans and 0.3% Tsakhurs, while ethnic Russians formed the fifth-largest nationality, with 9.2%. Its capital is at Makhachkala.

Chairman of the Supreme Soviet: MAGOMEDALI M. MAGOMEDOV.

Chairman of the Council of Ministers: ABDURAZAK M. MIRZABEKOV; tel. 7-22-34.

Permanent Representative in Moscow: GADZHI-KURBAN G. SHAIDAYEV; tel. (095) 227-15-36.

Head of Makhachkala City Administration: ALIMIRZA A. BAIBOLOTOV; tel. 7-26-70.

Ingush Republic (Ingushetia)

Prior to 1990, the Ingush Republic was part of the Chechen-Ingush ASSR (see Chechen Republic-Ichkeria above). In June 1992 the Supreme Soviet of the Russian Federation formalized Ingushetia's separate existence and adopted the law On the Formation of the Ingush Republic within the Russian Federation. The exact borders internal to the old ASSR were not defined, but the Ingush dominated the western territories. In addition the new Republic claimed the eastern regions of the Republic of North Ossetia and part of the North Ossetian capital, Vladikavkaz (formerly Ordzhonikidze). The rayon of Prigorodny was at the centre of the dispute. Armed hostilities between the two Republics began in October 1992 and continued into 1994. A state of emergency was introduced almost immediately and continued, like the dispute, into 1994. On 1 August 1993 the head of the state-of-emergency area was assassinated. On 27 February 1994 simultaneous parliamentary and presidential elections were held in the Republic, as was a referendum on a draft constitution. A total of 97% of the inhabitants of Ingushetia voted in favour of the draft. The administrative centre is at Nazran.

President: RUSLAN S. AUSHEV.

Vice-President: BORIS AGAPOV.

Speaker of the Ingush Parliament: MURAT KELIGOV.

Head of the Provisional Administration on the Territory of the North Ossetia and Ingushetia: VLADIMIR LAZOVOY.

Representative of the President of the Russian Federation: ISA KOSTOYEV.

Chairman of the Council of Ministers: TAMERLAN DIDIKOV; tel. 22-11-26.

Head of Nazran City Administration: MAGOMED A. SULTYGOV (acting).

Kabardino-Balkar Republic (Kabardin-Balkaria)

The Turkic Kabardins, a Muslim people of the North Caucasus, came under Russian rule in the 16th century. The Kabardino-Balkar ASSR was established on 5 December 1936. On 18 November 1991 the first congress of the National Council of the Balkar People declared the sovereignty of Balkaria and the formation of a Republic of Balkaria within the Russian Federation. This formation, and many of the Russian and Cossack population, opposed the presidential elections for the whole region, the second round of which was held on 5 January 1992. These were won by the former Chairman of the Supreme Soviet. The Supreme Soviet initially rejected President Yeltsin's Decree No. 1,400 of 21 September 1993. However, on 16 October, the Supreme Soviet rescinded its previous decision and declared that elections to the Republic's legislature would take place simultaneously with the elections to the Federal Assembly. On 22 October the Supreme Soviet transferred its powers to the President of the Republic. On 10 March 1994 the President of Kabardin-Balkaria decreed that a Chamber of Nationalities, in which Kabardins, Russians and Balkars would be equally represented, would be formed within the Supreme Soviet.

The Kabardino-Balkar Republic (Kabardino-Balkar ASSR prior to March 1992) is situated on the northern slopes of the Greater Caucasus and the Kabardin Flatlands between North Ossetia to the east and Karachay-Cherkessia to the west. There is an international border with Georgia to the south. Its major rivers are the Terek, the Malka and the Baskan. It forms part of the Northern Caucasus Economic Area. Its main agricultural products are grain and sunflowers. Animal husbandry, horticulture and viniculture are also important. The Republic's main industries are machine-building, metal-working, non-ferrous metallurgy, food processing and light industry. Its major industrial centres are at Nalchik, Tyrnauz and Prokhladny. The territory of the Republic occupies an area of 12,500 sq km. It consists of eight administrative districts and seven cities. In 1990 the population of the Republic totalled 768,000. In 1989 some 48.2% of inhabitants were Kabardins, 9.4% were Balkars and 32.0% were Russian. The capital of the Republic is at Nalchik.

President: VALERY M. KOKOV; tel. 2-20-64.

Vice-President: GENNADY S. GUBIN; tel. 2-21-18.

Chairman of the Supreme Soviet: KHACHIM M. KARMOKOV.

Prime Minister: GEORGY M. CHERKESOV; tel. 2-21-26.

Representative of the President of the Russian Federation: AZIRATALI N. AKHMETOV; tel. 2-20-04.

Permanent Representative in Moscow: VLADIMIR K. MASTAFOV; tel. (095) 205-50-63.

Head of Nalchik City Administration: SULTAN B. ABROKOV; tel. 2-20-04.

Republic of Kalmykia (Khalmg Tangch)

A Kalmyk Autonomous Oblast was established on 4 November 1920. Its status was upgraded to that of an ASSR in 1935, which was dissolved in 1943, when the Kalmyks were deported to Central Asia. A Kalmyk Autonomous Oblast was reconstituted in 1957 and an ASSR in 1958. A declaration of sovereignty was adopted on 18 October 1990. In April 1993 the President of Kalmykia, Kirsan Ilumjinov, dissolved all soviets on the Republic's territory. On 28 December the Kalmyks were formally rehabilitated by the Russian President. On 11 March 1994 Ilumjinov abrogated the republican Constitution and decreed that from 25 March only the Russian basic law would be valid in the Republic.

The Republic of Kalmykia is situated in the western part of the Caspian Sea lowlands. The south-eastern part of the Republic lies on the Caspian Sea. It has a southern border with the Republic of Daghestan. Kalmykia forms part of the Volga Economic Area. Its agriculture consists mainly of grain production and animal husbandry. Its industry consists mainly of machine-building, metal-working, production of building materials, food processing and the production of petroleum and natural gas. Its major industrial centres are at Elista and Kaspiysk. The Republic occupies an area of 75,900 sq km and comprises 13 administrative districts and three cities. In 1990 it had a population of 325,000. In 1989 some 45.4% of the total population were Kalmyks (a Buddhist people) and 37.7% Russians. The capital is at Elista.

President: KIRSAN N. ILUMJINOV.

Chairman of the Council of Ministers: BATYR C. MIKHAILOV; tel. 6-27-41; fax 6-28-80.

Permanent Representative in Moscow: HEINRICH A. DJIMBINOV; tel. (095) 291-48-32.

Head of Elista City Administration: IOSIF B. SHARAPOV; tel. 5-23-11.

Republic of Karachay-Cherkessia

On 14 February 1994 the Republic's Supreme Soviet appointed the Chairman of the Council of Ministers acting head of state in Karachay-Cherkessia. The Republic's constitutional system was to be formed in accordance with the results of a subsequent referendum on a republican presidency.

The Republic of Karachay-Cherkessia (formerly an Autonomous Oblast) is situated on the northern slopes of the Greater Caucasus. Another Russian federal territory, Kabardin-Balkaria, lies to the east, but there is an international boundary with Georgia (mainly with Abkhazia) to the south. The Karachay and the Cherkessk were among the peoples Stalin (Iosif V. Dzhugashvili) deported during the Second World War (they were moved to Central Asia in late 1943). They were permitted to return in the late 1950s and an Autonomous Oblast was created. Its major river is the Kuban. The Republic forms part of Stavropol Kray. Its agriculture consists mainly of animal husbandry and production of grain, sunflower seeds, sugar beets and vegetables. Its main industries are petrochemicals, chemicals, machine-building and metal-working. Light industry, timber processing and coal production are also important. Its major industrial centres are at Cherkessk, Karachayevsk and Zelenchukskaya. The total area of the Republic occupies some 14,100 sq km. Karachay-Cherkessia consists of 15 administrative districts and four cities and has a population of 422,000 (in 1990). Its capital is at Cherkessk.

Chairman of the Supreme Soviet: (vacant).

Chairman of the Council of Ministers (Acting Head of State): VLADIMIR I. KHUBIYEV; tel. 2-40-40.

Chairman of the Regional Soviet: VIKTOR N. SAVELYEV.

Permanent Representative in Moscow: (vacant).

Head of Cherkessk City Administration: GENNADY M. KLYUSHNIKOV; tel. 2-42-24.

Republic of Karelia

Karelia was an independent, Finnish-dominated state in medieval times. In the 16th century the area came under Swedish hegemony, before being annexed by Russia in 1721. A Karelian Labour Commune was formed in June 1920 and became an autonomous republic in July 1923. A Karelo-Finnish SSR, including territory annexed from Finland, was created in 1940 as a Union Republic of the USSR. However, part of its territory was ceded to the Russian Federation in 1946 and Karelia subsequently resumed its status of an ASSR within the Russian Federation. The Republic declared sovereignty on 10 August 1990. It was renamed on 13 November 1991 as the Republic of Karelia. In October 1993, having refused to disband, the Supreme Soviet in the Republic announced that elections to a new bicameral legislature, the Legislative Assembly, were to take place on 17 April 1994. The upper chamber of the Assembly would comprise 25 deputies and would work on a professional basis.

The Republic of Karelia is situated in the north-west of the country, on the edge of the East European Plain. It is bordered by Finland to the west. The White Sea lies to the north-east. Its major rivers are the Kem and the Vyg. It has two lakes, the Ladoga and the Onega, and one-half of its territory is forested. It forms part of the Northern Economic Area. Its agriculture consists mainly of animal husbandry, fur farming and fishing. Its main industries are the processing of forestry products, machine-building, metallurgy and mining. Its major industrial centres are at Petrozavodsk, Sortavala, Kem, Kondopoga, Medvezhiegorsk, Belomorsk and Segezha. Karelia occupies an area of 172,400 sq km and consists of 15 administrative districts and 12 cities. In 1990 it had a population of 796,000. In 1989 some 10.0% of the population were Karelians (Finnish) and 73.6% Russians. The capital is at Petrozavodsk.

Chairman of the Council of Ministers: SERGEY P. BLINNIKOV; tel. 7-24-44.

Chairman of the Supreme Soviet: VIKTOR N. STEPANOV.

Permanent Representative in Moscow: ALEKSANDR S. ZAUDALSKY; tel. (095) 241-19-87.

Head of Petrozavodsk City Administration: SERGEY L. KATANANDOV; tel. 7-49-89.

Republic of Khakassia

The Republic of Khakassia was formerly an Autonomous Oblast. It was upgraded to the status of an Autonomous Republic under the terms of the Federation Treaty of March 1992. The nationwide plebiscite on the Russian Constitution, held on 12 December 1993, was declared invalid in the Republic, owing to a shortage of participants. On 25 December, the Supreme Soviet of the Republic adopted a decree on its own reform by which its powers were extended for the period required to formulate and adopt a constitution and to hold early elections.

The Republic of Khakassia is situated in the western area of the Minusinsk hollow, on the left bank of the river Yenisey, on the eastern slopes of the Kuznetsk Alatau and the northern slopes of the western Sayan mountains. It forms part of Krasnoyarsk Kray. Tyva lies to the south-east and Altay to the south-west. Its major rivers are the Yenisey and the Abakan. Its agriculture consists mainly of grain production and animal husbandry. Its main industries are ore mining, light manufacturing, machine-building, non-ferrous metallurgy and processing of forestry and agricultural products. Its major industrial centres are at Abakan, Sorsk, Sayanogorsk, Chernogorsk and Balyksa. It occupies 61,900 sq km and has five cities. In 1990 it had a population of 573,000. Its capital is at Abakan.

Chairman of the Supreme Soviet: VLADIMIR N. SHTYGASHEV.

Chairman of the Council of Ministers: YEVGENY A. SMIRNOV; tel. 6-33-22.

Permanent Representative in Moscow: ANDREY S. ASOCHAKOV; tel. (095) 202-75-89.

Head of Abakan City Administration: SERGEY M. KREMENTSKY; tel. 6-37-91.

Republic of Komi

The territory of the Komi Autonomous Republic was conquered by Russia in the 14th century. A Komi Autonomous Oblast was established in 1921 and an ASSR in 1936. The Republic declared its sovereignty on 30 August 1990. On 23 September the Komi Supreme Soviet denounced Decree No. 1,400. On 28 October the Supreme Soviet voted to hold early elections to the republican bodies of regional representation no later than June 1994. The nation-wide plebiscite on the Russian Constitution, which was held on 12 December 1993, failed to be validated in the Republic, owing to the low number of participants. A republican referendum was held on the same day: participants were asked whether they agreed with the creation of an executive presidency within the Republic. A new draft constitution was published on 23 January 1994 and was adopted by the Supreme Soviet on 17 February. Under the terms of the new Constitution, the nationally elected Head of the Republic of Komi would have functions and powers equal to those of a President and would appoint the cabinet of ministers. The Republic's legislative body, the State Soviet, would be a permanent body. Elections were scheduled to be held before mid-1994.

The Republic of Komi is situated in the north-east of European Russia. Its eastern part is taken up by mountains of the Northern, Circumpolar and Polar Urals. Its major rivers are the Pechora and the Vychegda. It forms part of the Northern Economic Area. Its agriculture consists mainly of animal husbandry. Its industry is based on the processing of forestry products, the production of coal and the production and processing of petroleum and natural gas. Its major industrial centres are at Syktyvkar, Ykhta and Sosnogorsk. The Republic of Komi occupies an area of 415,900 sq km. It comprises 16 administrative districts and 10 cities and had a population of 1,265,000 in 1990. In 1989 some 23.3% of the Republic's inhabitants were Komis and 57.7% were Russians. The capital is at Syktyvkar.

Chairman of the State Soviet: YURY A. SPIRIDONOV.

Chairman of the Council of Ministers: VYACHESLAV I. KHUDAYEV; tel. 7-24-44.

Permanent Representative in Moscow: NIKOLAY N. KOCHURIN; tel. (095) 291-48-23.

Head of Syktyvkar City Administration: ANATOLY A. KARAKCHIYEV; tel. 2-41-20.

Republic of Mari-El

The Mari were under the suzerainty of the Khanate of Kazan until it was annexed by Russia in 1552. A Mari Autonomous Oblast was established in 1920. On 5 December 1936 the territory became the Mari ASSR. The Republic declared sovereignty on 22 October 1990. Presidential elections were held on 14 December 1991. In December 1993 elections were held to a new 300-seat parliament, the State Assembly.

The Republic of Mari-El is situated in the east of the East European Plain in the middle reaches of the Volga river and forms part of the Volga-Vyatka Economic Area. The Republics of Chuvashia and Tatarstan neighbour it to the south-west and to the south-east, respectively. Its major rivers are the Volga and the Vetluga and about one-half of its territory is forested. Its agriculture consists mainly of animal husbandry and flax and grain production. Its main industries are machine-building, metal-working, light industry and the processing of forestry products. Its major industrial centres are at Yoshkar Ola and Volzhsk. Mari-El occupies an area of 23,300 sq km and consists of 14 administrative districts and four cities. In 1989 the total population was 750,000, of which 43.3% were Maris (also known as Cheremiss) and 47.5% Russians. The capital is at Yoshkar-Ola.

President: VLADISLAV M. ZOTIN; tel. 5-66-64.

Vice-President: VIKTOR A. GALAVTEYEV; tel. 5-68-33.

Chairman of the State Assembly: ANATOLY SMIRNOV.

Permanent Representative in Moscow: (vacant); tel. (095) 291-48-38.

Head of Yoshkar-Ola City Administration: VENIAMIN V. KOZLOV; tel. 5-64-01.

Republic of Mordovia

The Mordovian territories came under Russian rule in the 13th century. A Mordovian Autonomous Oblast was established in 1930 and the territory became the Mordovian ASSR in 1934. In September 1993 the Mordovian legislature declared President Yeltsin's decree dissolving the Russian parliament unconstitutional. However, a mass rally was held on 13 October, at which a resolution was passed demanding the dissolution of the Republic's parliament. On 22 October the Supreme Soviet decided not to disband itself and proposed that elections be held in the Republic in June 1994. The territory was renamed the Republic of Mordovia in January 1994 (dispensing with the words Soviet and Socialist from the title).

The Republic of Mordovia occupies a section of the Oka-Don plain and the Volga area uplands. It forms part of the Volga-Vyatka Economic Area, like its eastern neighbour, Chuvashia. Its major rivers are the Moksha and the Insa (upon which the capital lies), and one-quarter of its territory is forested. Its principal crops are grain, sugar beets and hemp. Animal husbandry and bee-keeping are also important. Its main industries are machine-building, metal-working, light industry, production of chemicals and construction materials, and food processing. Its major industrial centres are at Saransk and Ruzayevka. The territory of Mordovia occupies an area of 26,200 sq km. The Republic consists of 21 administrative districts and seven cities and in 1990 had a population of 964,000. In 1989 some 32.5% of the total population were Mordovians and 60.8% Russians. The capital is at Saransk.

President: VASILY D. GUSLYANNIKOV; tel. 4-78-42.

Vice-President: VLADIMIR P. NAREZHNY; tel. 4-29-22.

Chairman of the Supreme Soviet: NIKOLAY M. BIRYUKOV.

Permanent Representative in Moscow: VALENTIN V. KONAKOV; tel. (095) 202-12-23.

Head of Saransk City Administration: VASILY T. TARATOV; tel. 17-64-16.

Republic of North Ossetia

Ossetia was ceded to Russia by the Ottoman Turks at the Treaty of Kuchuk Kainardji in 1792. Transcaucasian Ossetia, or South Ossetia, became part of Georgia. In North Ossetia an Autonomous Oblast was established in 1924, which became an ASSR on 5 December 1936. In 1944 its territory was expanded to the east by the inclusion of former Ingush territories. From 1991 there was considerable debate about some form of unification with South Ossetia. The Republic's administration refused to recognize claims by Ingushetia to territory in the east of North Ossetia, which led to the onset of violence in October 1992 and the imposition of a state of emergency in the affected areas (see Ingush Republic above). In October 1993 the Supreme Soviet in the Republic announced that new elections would be held on 27 March 1994. Presidential elections were held on 16 January.

The Republic of North Ossetia is situated on the northern slopes of the Greater Caucasus. The other Russian federal units of Kabardin-Balkaria to the west and Ingushetia and Chechnya to the east, border it. Georgia lies to the south. North Ossetia forms part of the Northern Caucasus Economic Area. Its major river is the Terek. Its agriculture consists mainly of vegetable and grain production, horticulture, viniculture and animal husbandry. Its main industries are non-ferrous metallurgy, machine-building, wood-working, light industry, chemicals and glass-making. Its major industrial centres are at Vladikavkaz (formerly Ordzhonikidze), Mozdok and Beslan. The territory of North Ossetia covers a total of 8,000 sq km. The Republic comprises eight administrative districts and six cities and had a population of 638,000 in 1990. In 1989 some 53.0% of the population were Ossetians and 29.9% Russians. The capital is at Vladikavkaz, in the east of the Republic.

President of the Republic: AKHSARBEK K. GALAZOV.

Chairman of the Supreme Soviet: YURY BIRAGOV.

Chairman of the Council of Ministers: SERGEY V. KHETAGUROV; tel. 3-36-44; fax 3-39-8.

Head of the Provisional Administration on the Territory of North Ossetia and Ingushetia: VLADIMIR LAZOVOY.

Plenipotentionary Representative in Moscow: KAZBEK M. DULAYEV; tel. (095) 239-38-57.

Republic of Sakha (Yakutia)

The Yakuts came under Russian rule in the late 17th century. Apart from the Buryats, they are the only native Siberian peoples still surviving in significant numbers. Their language is Turkic, but with considerable Mongolian influence. Having briefly been united by the toion (chief) Tygyn before falling under Tsarist rule, the economic resources of the territory enabled the Yakut to secure a measure of autonomy, as an ASSR established in 1922 (its first leader was the Yakut poet, Platon Oyunsky). Cultural, ecological and economic concerns led to the proclamation of a Yakut-Sakha SSR on 27 April 1990. On 22 December 1991 elections for an executive presidency were held, and were won by the former Chairman of the Supreme Soviet. It became the Republic of Sakha in March 1992. On 12 October 1993 the Supreme Soviet dissolved itself and set elections to a new 60-seat bicameral legislature for 12 December. Following the failure of 12 of the 254 candidates in the elections to win the required percentage of votes, a second round of voting was scheduled for 24 December. On 26 January 1994 the new parliament named itself the State Assembly (previously the Legislative State Assembly).

The Republic of Sakha (Yakutia) is situated in Eastern Siberia. Its major rivers are the Lena, the Olenek, the Yana, the Indigirka and the Kolyma, and four-fifths of its territory is taiga (forested marshland). It forms part of the Far Eastern Economic Area. Its agriculture consists mainly of animal husbandry, hunting and fishing. Its main industries are ore mining, wood-working and food processing. Its major industrial centres are at Yakutsk, Mirny, Neryungry, Aldan and Lensk. Its main port is Tiksi on the Arctic Sea. The Republic occupies an area of 3,103,200 sq km and consists of 34 administrative districts and 11 cities. In 1992 it had a population of 1,077,000. In 1989 some 33.4% of the total population were Yakuts and 50.3% Russians. The capital is at Yakutsk.

President: MIKHAIL E. NIKOLAYEV; tel. 2-36-27; fax 4-35-14.

Vice-President: VYACHESLAV A. SHTYROV; tel. 4-16-20.

Chairman of the State Assembly: (vacant).

Permanent Representative in Moscow: ZOYA A. KORNILOVA; tel. (095) 926-82-98.

Head of Yakutsk City Administration: PAVEL P. BORODIN; tel. 2-30-26; fax 4-35-14.

Republic of Tatarstan

After the dissolution of the Mongol empire the region became the Khanate of Kazan, the territory of the Golden Horde. It was conquered by Russia in 1552. Some of the Muslim Tatars succumbed to Russian pressures to convert to Orthodox Christianity (the Staro-Kryashens still exist, using Tatar as their spoken and liturgical tongue), but most did not. A modernist school of thought in Islam, Jadidism, originated among the Volga Tatars, who attained an exceptionally high cultural level in the 19th-century Russian Empire, despite being a subject people. A Tatar Autonomous Republic was established on 27 May 1920. The Republic declared sovereignty on 31 August 1990. On 18 October 1993 the Supreme Soviet in the Republic refused to disband itself. Tatarstan did not participate in the elections to the Russian Federal Assembly held on 12 December 1993, owing to a shortage of candidates. The nation-wide plebiscite on the Russian Constitution, which was held on the same day, was invalidated in Tatarstan as only 13.9% of registered electors participated. On 15 February 1994 the President of Tatarstan signed a treaty with Russian President Boris Yeltsin, which ceded extensive powers to the Republic and allowed it to retain its own Constitution. Following this resolution of the political crisis between the Republic and the federal Government, further elections to the Federal Assembly were held on 13 March.

The Republic of Tatarstan is situated in the east of European Russia. It forms part of the Volga Economic Area and neighbours several other Republics: Bashkortostan to the east (Urals Economic Area); Udmurtia in the north-east (Urals); Mari-El in the north-west; and Chuvashia to the west (both Volga-Vyatka). Its major rivers are the Volga and the Kama and one-fifth of its total area is forested. Its agriculture consists mainly of grain production, animal husbandry, horticulture and bee-keeping. Its main industries are natural-gas production, manufacture of chemicals and petrochemicals, machine-building, light industry and food processing. Its major industrial centres are at Kazan, Naberezhnye Chelny, Zelenodolsk, Nizhnekamsk, Almetyevsk, Chistopol and Bugulma. Tatarstan occupies 68,000 sq km and is divided into 39 administrative districts and 18 cities. In 1990 it had a population of 3,658,000. In 1989 some 48.5% of the total population were Tatars and 32.0% Russians. The capital is at Kazan.

President: MINTIMER S. SHAMIYEV; tel. 32-70-01.

Vice-President: VASILY N. LIKHACHEV; tel. 32-05-90.

Chairman of the Supreme Soviet: FARID K. MUKHAMETSHIN.

Prime Minister: MUKHAMMAT G. SABIROV; tel. 32-66-98.

Permanent Representative in Moscow: ISKANDER U. YUSUPOV; tel. (095) 975-17-36.

Head of Kazan City Administration: KAMIL S. ISKHAKOV; tel. 35-56-94.

Republic of Tyva

Tyva, as the Republic of Tannu-Tuva, was a nominally independent state until 1944, when it was incorporated into the USSR. It became an ASSR on 10 October 1961, within the Russian Federation, prior to which it had been an Autonomous Oblast. On 22 October 1993 the Tyvan (Tuvin) Supreme Soviet resolved that the Republic's name was Tyva (as opposed to the russified Tuva) and adopted a new Constitution which came into effect immediately. The Constitution provided for a 32-member working parliament, the Supreme Hural, and a supreme constitutional body, the Grand Hural. The new parliament was elected on 12 December. On the same day, the new Constitution was approved by 62.2% of registered voters in Tyva. Only 32.7%, however, voted in favour of the Russian Constitution.

The Republic of Tyva is situated in the south of Eastern Siberia. Tyva has an international border with Mongolia (the two peoples are closedly related, by tradition being Buddhist nomads) to the south. The Republic of Buryatia lies to the east, Khakassia to the north-west and Altay to the south-west. It forms part of the Eastern Siberian Economic Area. Almost all the rivers in the Republic belong to the Yenisey basin. Its agriculture consists mainly of animal husbandry and hunting. Its main industries are ore mining, the processing of agricultural and forestry products, light manufacturing and metal-working. Its major industrial centres are at Kyzyl and Ak-Dovurak. Tyva occupies 170,500 sq km and consists of 14 administrative districts and five cities. In 1990 it had a population of 314,000. In 1989 some 64.3% of inhabitants were Tyvans and 32.0% Russians. The capital is at Kyzyl.

President: SHERIG-OOL D. OORZHAK; tel. 3-73-00.

Vice-President: ALEKSEY A. MELNIKOV.

Chairman of the Supreme Hural: KAADYR-OOL BICHELDEY.

Permanent Representative in Moscow: IVAN M. SUVANDIN; tel. (095) 291-45-25.

Head of Kyzyl City Administration: ZOYA N. SAT; tel. 3-50-55.

Udmurt Republic (Udmurtia)

The territories inhabited by Votyaks (the former name for Udmurts) came under Russian rule in the 15th century. A Votyak Autonomous Oblast was established on 4 November 1920. In 1934 it became the Udmurt ASSR. The Republic declared sovereignty on 19 September 1990. In early November 1993 the Supreme Soviet in the Republic announced that elections would be held on 6 March 1994 to a new post of president of the Republic. On 12 December 1993 the nation-wide plebiscite on the Russian Constitution was declared invalid in the Republic, owing to the low level of participation. In the same month the Udmurt Supreme Soviet announced that a new bicameral parliament would be established, comprising a 50-seat Council of Representatives and a 35-seat lower, legislative chamber.

The Udmurt Republic occupies part of the Upper Kama highlands. Tatarstan lies to the south-west and Bashkortostan to the south-east. Udmurtia forms part of the Urals Economic Area. Its major rivers are the Kama and the Vyatka and about one-half of its territory is forested. Its agriculture consists mainly of livestock breeding, grain production and flax growing. Its main industries are machine-building, metal-working, metallurgy, processing of forestry and agricultural products, petroleum production, glass-making, light manufacturing and the production of peat. Its major industrial centres are at Izhevsk, Sarapul and Glazov. Its total area covers some 42,100 sq km. The Republic consists of 25 administrative districts and six cities and had a population of 1,619,000 in 1990. In 1989 some 30.9% of the total population were Udmurts and 58.9% Russians. The capital is at Izhevsk.

Chairman of the Supreme Soviet: VALENTIN K. TUBYLOV.

Chairman of the Council of Ministers: ALEKSANDR VOLKOV; tel. 25-45-67.

Permanent Representative in Moscow: ANATOLY N. KOVIN; tel. (095) 202-60-89.

Head of Izhevsk City Administration: ANATOLY I. SALTYKOV; tel. 22-45-90.

KRAYS (PROVINCES)

Altay Kray

In December 1993 the Provincial Soviet of the Altay Kray scheduled elections to a new legislature for 13 March 1994. The legislature was to be bicameral, comprising a lower chamber of 25 deputies and an upper chamber of 73 deputies (one from each district in the Kray).

Most of Altay Kray lies within the West Siberian Plain. Part of the Western Siberian Economic Area, it has international boundaries with Kazakhstan, the People's Republic of China and Mongolia. The eastern part of the Kray is constituted as the Republic of Altay (formerly the Gorno-Altay Autonomous Oblast—see above). Its major river is the Ob with its tributaries. It has one lake, the Teletskoye, and about one third of its total area is forested. The Kray's principal crops are grain, flax and sugar beets. Horticulture, animal husbandry, bee-keeping and hunting are also important. Its main industries are machine-building, chemicals and petrochemicals, ore mining, food processing and light manufacturing. Its main industrial centres are at Barnaul, Biysk, Rubtsovsk, Novoaltaysk and Slavgorod. The Kray occupies a total area of 261,700 sq km and is divided into 65 administrative districts and 12 cities, and includes one autonomous republic. It has a population of approximately 3m. (1990). Its administrative centre is at Barnaul.

Head of the Provincial Administration: LEV KORSHUNOV; tel. 22-68-14.

Chairman of the Provincial Soviet: ALEKSANDR A. SURIKOV.

Representative of the President of the Russian Federation: NIKOLAY M. SHUBA; tel. 22-28-36.

Head of the Provincial Representation in Moscow: VIKTOR A. PISARENKO; tel. (095) 202-44-43.

Head of Barnaul City Administration: VLADIMIR N. BAVARIN; tel. 23-32-95.

Khabarovsk Kray

On 5 October 1993 the Provincial Soviet in Khabarovsk Kray rescinded its earlier decision to condemn Decree No. 1,400. On 1 November the decision was taken to hold local elections in the Kray on 6 March 1994.

Khabarovsk Kray is situated in the Far East on the Sea of Okhotsk and the Tatar straits. There is a short international border with the People's Republic of China in the south-west. Its main river is the Amur. More than one-half of its territory is forested. Its agriculture consists mainly of grain production, animal husbandry, bee-keeping, fishing and hunting. Its main industries are machine-building, metal-working, ferrous metallurgy, the processing of forestry products, ore mining and petroluem refining. Its main industrial centres are at Khabarovsk, Komsomolsk-on-Amur (Komsomolsk-na-Amurye), Sovetskaya Gavan, Nikolayevsk-on-Amur (Nikolayevsk-na-Amurye) and Amursk. The Kray's main ports are Vanino, Okhotsk (both seaports) and Nikolayevsk-on-Amur. It occupies a total area of 824,600 sq km and is divided into 21 administrative districts and nine cities. The population is approximately 2m. Its administrative centre is at Khabarovsk.

Head of the Provincial Administration: ISHAYEV; tel. 33-55-40; fax 33-87-56.

Chairman of the Provincial Soviet: (vacant).

Representative of the President of the Russian Federation: KONDRAT YEVTUSHENKO; tel. 33-70-88.

Head of Khabarovsk City Adminstration: VIKTOR M. TEVELEVICH; tel. 33-53-46.

Krasnodar Kray

On 22 September 1993 the Krasnodar Provincial Soviet condemned Russian President Boris Yeltsin's Decree No 1,400. The following month the Soviet refused to dissolve itself but announced that elections would be held to a new 32-member legislative assembly on 6 March 1994. The elections were subsequently postponed until 12 June.

Krasnodar Kray is situated in the south of European Russia, in the western region of the Greater Caucasus and Kuban-Azov lowlands. Part of the Northern Caucasus Economic Area, its territory includes and encloses the Republic of Adygheya. The Kray lies on the Black Sea in the south-west and the Sea of Azov and the Kerch gulf in the north-west. Its major river is the Kuban. The Kray's principal crops are grain, sugar beets, tobacco, essential oil plants, tea and hemp. Horticulture, viniculture and animal husbandry are also important. Its main industries are food processing, light manufacturing, machine-building, metal-working and the production and processing of petroleum and natural gas. Its main industrial centres are at Krasnodar, Armavir, Novorossiysk, Kropotkin, Tikhoretsk and Eisk. Its main ports are Novorossiysk and Tuapse. The Kray covers an area of 83,600 sq km and is divided into 44 administrative districts and 28 cities, as well as the autonomous republic, Adygheya. The population is over 5m. The administrative centre is at Krasnodar.

Head of the Provincial Administration: NIKOLAY D. YEGOROV; tel. 52-57-16; fax 52-85-40.

Chairman of the Provincial Assembly: (vacant).

Representative of the President of the Russian Federation: VASILY N. TETERIN; tel. 52-45-63.

Head of Krasnodar City Administration: VALERY A. SAMOILENKO; tel. 55-43-48.

Krasnoyarsk Kray

In November 1993 the Provincial Soviet in Krasnoyarsk Kray agreed to hold elections to a new legislature on 6 March 1994 and to cease its own activities immediately.

Krasnoyarsk Kray extends from the Arctic Ocean coast to the southern Siberian mountains. Its major river is the Yenisey. Most of its area is covered by taiga (forested marshland). The Kray forms part of the Eastern Siberia Economic Area and its territory includes one autonomous republic (Khakassia—formerly an autonomous oblast) and two autonomous okrugs (Evenk and Taymyr). Its principal crops are grain, flax, and hemp. Animal husbandry, fur farming and hunting are also important. Its main industries are non-ferrous metallurgy, machine-building, metal-working, ore mining, chemicals, forestry, light manufacturing and food processing. The major industrial centres in the Kray are at Krasnoyarsk, Abakan, Chernogorsk and Minusinsk. It occupies an area of 2,401,600 sq km and is divided into 55 administrative districts and 27 cities. The Kray had a total population of around 4m. in the early 1990s. Its administrative centre is at Krasnoyarsk.

Head of the Provincial Administration: VALERY M. ZUBOV (acting); tel. 22-22-63; fax 22-11-75.

Chairman of the Provincial Assembly: (vacant).

Representative of the President of the Russian Federation: YURY N. MOSKVICH; tel. 22-46-12.

Head of Krasnoyarsk City Administration: VALERY A. POZDNYAKOV; tel. 22-22-31.

Maritime Kray (Primorye)

The territories of the Maritime Kray became part of the Russian Empire in 1860, being ceded by China, and the port of Vladivostok was founded. Maritime Kray declared itself of a republic in mid-1993 but was not recognized as such by the federal authorities. On 28 October 1993 the governor disbanded the Provincial Soviet as it had failed to muster a quorum.

Maritime Kray (Primorye) is situated in the extreme south-east of the country on the Sea of Japan. Part of the Far Eastern Economic Area, the Kray has international borders with the People's Republic of China to the west and the People's Democratic Republic of Korea to the south. Its major river is the Ussuri. It has one lake, the Khanka. Its agriculture consists mainly of grain and soya production, animal husbandry, fur farming, bee-keeping and fishing. Its main industries are non-ferrous metallurgy, ore mining, the processing of forestry products, machine-building, metal-working and chemicals. Its major industrial centres are at Vladivostok, the terminus of the Trans-Siberian Railway, Ussuriysk, Nakhodka, Dalnegorsk, Lesozavodsk, Dalnorechensk and Partizansk. The Kray's most important ports are Vladivostok, Nakhodka and Vostochny. It occupies 165,900 sq km, is divided into 24 administrative districts and nine cities, and has a population of over 2m. The administrative centre is at Vladivostok.

Head of the Provincial Administration: YEVGENY I. NAZDRATENKO; tel. 2-38-00.

Chairman of the Provincial Soviet: DMITRY N. GRIGOROVICH.

Representative of the President of the Russian Federation: VLADIMIR IGNATENKO; tel. 2-39-13.

Head of the Provincial Representation in Moscow: Mikhail M. Sitnikov; tel. (095) 203-53-36.

Head of the Vladivostok City Administration: K. TOLSTOSHEIN (acting).

Stavropol Kray

Stavropol city was founded in 1777 as part of the consolidation of Russian rule in the Caucasus. The city was named Voroshilovsk in 1935–43. On 19 October 1993 the Stavropol Provincial Soviet reversed its earlier decision to condemn Russian President Boris Yeltsin's Decree No. 1,400 and agreed to suspend its activities and transfer its powers to the Provincial Administration. On 20 January 1994 elections to a new representative body, the Kray State Duma, were set for 27 March.

Stavropol Kray is situated in the central Caucasus region on the northern slopes of the Greater Caucasus. It is part of the Northern Caucasus Economic Area and, in the south-west, it includes the Republic of Karachay-Cherkessia (formerly an autonomous oblast—see above). The Kray's major rivers are the Kuban, the Kuma and the Yegorlyk. Its agricultural production consists mainly of grain, sunflower seeds, sugar beets and vegetables. Horticulture, viniculture and animal husbandry are also important. The Kray's main industries are food processing, light manufacturing, machine-building, chemicals and the production of natural gas, petroleum, non-ferrous metal ores and coal. Its main industrial centres are at Stavropol, Nevinomyssk, Cherkessk, Georgyevsk and Budennovsk. It occupies a total area of 80,600 sq km and is divided into 34 administrative districts and 22 cities. The population of Stavropol Kray numbered approximately 3m. in the early 1990s. Its administrative centre is at Stavropol.

Head of the Provincial Administration: YEVGENY S. KUZNETSOV; tel. 5-22-52.

Representative of the President of the Russian Federation: ALEKSEY V. KULAKOVSKY; tel. 4-82-85.

Head of Stavropol City Administration: MIKHAIL V. KUZMIN; tel. 3-03-10.

OBLASTS (REGIONS)

Amur Oblast

On 21 July 1993 Amur Oblast declared itself a republic, a move which was condemned by the federal authorities. On 4 October the head of the Regional Administration, Aleksandr Surat, was dismissed by President Russian President Boris Yeltsin for denouncing Decree No. 1,400. Following the failure of the Regional Soviet to reverse its condemnation of Russian President Boris

Yeltsin's Decree, on 20 October the acting head of the Regional Administration disbanded the Soviet and assumed its executive and administrative functions.

Amur Oblast is situated in the extreme south-east of the Russian Federation, to the east of Khabarovsk Kray and on the Chinese border. Its main river is the Amur. More than one-half of its territory is forested. It forms part of the Far Eastern Economic Area. Its agriculture consists mainly of grain production, animal husbandry and bee-keeping. Industry in the Oblast is based on ore mining, machine-building, electrotechnical industry and the processing of agricultural and forestry products. Its main industrial centres are at Blagoveschensk, Belogorsk, Raichikhinsk, Zea, Shimanovsk, Svobodny and Tynda. Its territory occupies 363,700 sq km and is divided into 20 administrative districts and nine cities. In 1989 the population of the Amur Oblast was 1,058,000. Its administrative centre is at Blagoveschensk.

Head of the Regional Administration: VLADIMIR P. POLEVANOV; tel. 4-03-22.

Chairman of the Regional Soviet: ANATOLY N. BELONOGOV.

Representative of the President of the Russian Federation: GRIGORY A. NIKANDROV; tel. 4-68-32.

Head of Blagoveschensk City Administration: YURY G. LIASHKO; tel. 2-49-85.

Archangel Oblast

Founded in the 16th century, to further Muscovite trade, it was the first Russian seaport and its main one until the building of St Petersburg. On 13 October 1993 the Archangel (Arkhangelsk) Regional Soviet transferred its responsiblities to the Regional Administration. The following month, the head of the Regional Administration decreed that elections to a new representative body would be held on 12 December, simultaneously with the elections to the Russian Federal Assembly. The new parliament, the Deputies' Assembly, consisted of an upper chamber of 27 members and a lower chamber of 11 members.

Archangel Oblast is situated in the north of the East European Plain. It lies on the White, Barents and Kara Seas. Its main rivers are the Severnaya Dvina, the Onega, the Mezen and the Pechora. It forms part of the Northern Economic Area and its territory includes the Nenets Autonomous Okrug. Its agriculture consists mainly of animal husbandry and hunting. Its industry is based on the processing of agricultural and forestry products, and machine-building. Its main industrial centres are at Archangel, Kotlas, Severodvinsk and Novodvinsk. Its main ports are Archangel, Onega, Mezen and Naryan Mar (sea- and river-ports). The Oblast occupies an area of 587,400 sq km and is divided into 19 administrative districts and 13 cities. The population in 1989 was 1,570,000. Its administrative centre is at Archangel (Arkhangelsk).

Head of the Regional Administration: PAVEL N. BALAKSHIN; tel. (818) 3-79-12; fax (818) 3-40-29.

Representative of the President of the Russian Federation: VALERY S. KRIMNUS; TEL. (818) 3-74-82.

Head of the Archangel City Administration: ANATOLY A. BRONNIKOV; tel. (818) 3-86-84.

Astrakhan Oblast

The Khanate of Astrakhan was conquered by the Russians in 1556. The Astrakhan Oblast is situated in the Caspian lowlands. The Caspian Sea lies to the south of the Oblast and Kazakhstan to the east. It has one lake, the Baskunchak. It forms part of the the Volga Economic Area. Its principal crops are grain, vegetables and cucurbits (gourds and melons). Animal husbandry is also important. Its main industries are light manufacturing, food processing, machine-building, metal-working, wood-working, pulp and paper manufacturing, chemicals and the production of petroleum and natural gas. Its main industrial centres are at Astrakhan and Akhtyubinsk. The Oblast occupies some 44,100 sq km and is divided into 11 administrative districts and five cities. In 1989 its total population was 998,000. Its administrative centre is at Astrakhan.

Head of the Regional Administration: ANATOLY P. GUZHVIN; tel. 2-17-67.

Chairman of the Regional Soviet: VALERY I. VINOKUROV.

Representative of the President of the Russian Federation: VALERY M. ADROV; tel. 2-56-44.

Head of Astrakhan City Administration: VLADIMIR R. SCHERBAKOV; tel. 22-55-88.

Belgorod Oblast

On 11 October 1993 Russian President Boris Yeltsin dismissed the head of the Regional Administration in Belgorod Oblast, Viktor Berestovoy. He had failed to support the President during his confrontation with the Russian parliament.

Belgorod Oblast is situated in the south-west of the Central Russian highlands. Its main rivers are the Severny Donets and the Oskol. It forms part of the Central Chernozem Economic Area and is on the border with Ukraine. Its principal crops are grain, sugar beets, sunflower seeds and essential-oil plants. Horticulture and animal husbandry are also important. The Oblast's main industries are ore mining, machine-building, metal-working, chemicals, the manufacture of building materials and food processing. Its main industrial centres are at Belgorod, Shebekino, Alexeyevka and Valuiki. It occupies 27,100 sq km and is divided into 18 administrative districts and nine cities. The population in 1989 was 1,381,000. Its administrative centre is at Belgorod.

Head of the Regional Administration: YEVGENY S. SAVCHENKO; tel. 2-42-47.

Chairman of the Regional Soviet: MIKHAIL I. BESKHMELNITSYN.

Representative of the President of the Russian Federation: NIKOLAY I. MELENTYEV; tel. 2-46-89.

Head of Belgorod City Administration: YURY I. SELIVERSTOV; tel. 7-72-06.

Bryansk Oblast

On 23 September 1993 both the head of the Regional Administration, Yury Lodkin, and the Regional Soviet declared Decree No. 1,400 to be unconstitutional. Two days later President Russian President Boris Yeltsin dismissed Lodkin from his post and appointed his deputy in his place. On 19 October the head of the Regional Administration ordered the closure of the Regional Soviet.

Bryansk Oblast is situated in the central part of the Central Russian highlands. Its main river is the Desna. It forms part of the Central Economic Area. Its agriculture consists mainly of grain and vegetable production and animal husbandry. Its main industries are machine-building, metal-working, the manufacture of building materials, light manufacturing, food processing and timber working. Its main industrial centres are at Bryansk and Klintsy. The Oblast occupies 34,900 sq km of territory, is divided into 24 administrative districts and 15 cities and had a population of 1,475,000 in 1989. Its administrative centre is at Bryansk.

Head of the Regional Administration: VLADIMIR A. KARPOV; tel. 4-21-40.

Chairman of the Regional Soviet: VLADIMIR P. SIDORENKO.

Representative of the President of the Russian Federation: VLADIMIR A. BARABANOV; tel. 6-14-98.

Head of Bryansk City Administration: (vacant); tel. 4-30-13.

Chelyabinsk Oblast

On 8 October 1993 the Chelyabinsk Regional Soviet agreed to rescind its earlier decision to condemn Russian President Boris Yeltsin's Decree No. 1,400 and to hold early local elections, but refused to dissolve itself.

Chelyabinsk Oblast is situated in the southern Urals and in the Transural (Asian Russia). Its major rivers are the Ural and the Miass. It has two lakes—Uvildy and Turgoyak. It forms part of the Urals Economic Area. The Oblast's agriculture consists mainly of animal husbandry, horticulture and the production of grain and vegetables. Its main industries are ferrous and non-ferrous metallurgy, ore mining and the manufacture of building materials. The major industrial centres are at Chelyabinsk, Magnitogorsk, Miass, Zlatoust, Kopeysk, Korkino and Troytsk. The territory of the Oblast covers an area of 87,900 sq km and is divided into 24 districts and 27 cities. The population in 1989 was 3,626,000. The Oblast's administrative centre is at Chelyabinsk.

Head of the Regional Administration: VADIM P. SOLOVYOV; tel. (3512) 33-92-41; fax (3512) 33-12-83.

Chairman of the Regional Soviet: PETR I. SUMIN.

Representative of the President of the Russian Federation: VLADIMIR V. SELEZNEV; tel. (3512) 33-30-67.

Head of Chelyabinsk City Administration: VYACHESLAV M. TARASOV; tel. (3512) 33-38-05.

Chita Oblast

The town of Chita was established by the Cossacks in 1653, at the confluence of the Chita and Ingoda rivers. It was named Ingodinskoye Zirnovye for a time. On 27 September 1993 the Regional Soviet in Chita Oblast reversed its previous decision to condemn Decree No. 1,400. The following month a joint commission was set up to examine ways in which to reform the local-government system in the Oblast.

Chita Oblast is situated in Transbaikal. Its territory surrounds and includes the Autonomous Okrug of Aga-Buryat. Its major rivers are those in the Baikal, the Lena and the Amur basins. More than one-half of the Oblast's territory is forested. It forms part of the Eastern Siberian Economic Area. Its agriculture consists mainly of animal husbandry and hunting. The Oblast's major industries are ore mining, ferrous metallurgy, machine-building and the processing of forestry products. Its main industrial centres are at Chita, Nerchinsk, Darasun, Olovyannaya and Tarbagatay. Its territory covers an area of 431,500 sq km and is divided into 31 districts and 10 cities. The total population of the Oblast was 1,378,000 in 1989. Its administrative centre is at Chita.

Head of the Regional Administration: BORIS P. IVANOV; tel. 3-34-93; fax 3-02-22.

Chairman of the Regional Soviet: ALEKSANDR F. YEPOV.

Representative of the President of the Russian Federation: VLADIMIR I. MELNIKOV; tel. 3-34-92.

Head of Chita City Administration: RAVIL F. GENIATULIN; tel. 3-21-01.

Ivanovo Oblast

The Ivanovo Regional Soviet ceased to function in October 1993.

Ivanovo Oblast is situated in the central part of the East European Plain. Its main river is the Volga. It forms part of the Central Economic Area. Its agriculture consists mainly of grain, flax and vegetable production and animal husbandry. Its main industries are light manufacturing, machine-building, chemicals, food processing, wood-working and handicrafts. Its main industrial centres are at Ivanovo, Kineshma, Shuya, Vichuga, Furmanov, Teikovo and Rodniki. The Oblast's territory occupies 23,900 sq km. It has 17 cities and the total population in 1989 was 1,317,000. Its administrative centre is at Ivanovo.

Head of the Regional Administration: ADOLF F. LAPTEV; tel. 32-81-25.

Chairman of the Regional Soviet: VLADISLAV N. TIKHOMIROV.

Representative of the President of the Russian Federation: VLADIMIR I. TOLMACHEV; tel. 32-70-05.

Head of Ivanovo City Administration: SERGEY V. KRUGLOV; tel. 32-70-20.

Irkutsk Oblast

The city of Irkutsk was founded in 1661, at the confluence of the Irkut and Angara rivers (the latter is the only river to drain Lake Baikal, which lies 66 km to the east of the city). It became one of the largest economic centres of Eastern Siberia. On 13 October 1993 the Regional Soviet in Irkutsk Oblast transferred its responsibilities to the Regional Administration. On 28 December the head of the Regional Administration suspended completely the work of the Soviet.

Irkutsk Oblast is situated in Eastern Siberia in the south-east of the Central Siberian Plateau. Its main rivers are the Angara, the Nizhnyaya Tunguska, the Vitim and the Kirenga. Its one lake, Baikal, is the deepest in the world, possessing over 80% of Russia's, and 20% of the world's, freshwater resources. Four-fifths of its territory are forested. It forms part of the Eastern Siberian Economic Area and its jurisdiction includes the Autonomous Okrug of Ust-Orda Buryat. Its agriculture consists mainly of grain production, animal husbandry, hunting and fishing. The Oblast's main industries are ore mining, machine-building, chemicals and petrochemicals, and the processing of forestry products. Its main industrial centres are at Irkutsk, Bratsk, Ust-Ilimsk, Angarsk and Usoliye Sibirskoye. It occupies 767,900 sq km and is divided into 27 administrative districts and 22 cities. The population in 1989 was 2,831,000. Its administrative centre is at Irkutsk.

Head of the Regional Administration: YURY A. NOZHIKOV; tel. 27-64-15; fax 24-44-74.

Chairman of the Regional Soviet: VIKTOR V. IGNATENKO.

Representative of the President of the Russian Federation: IGOR I. SHIROBOKOV; tel. 24-77-75.

Head of the Regional Representation in Moscow: VLADIMIR B. MAZUR; tel. (095) 215-50-96.

Head of Irkutsk City Administration: BORIS A. GOVORIN; tel. 24-44-10.

Kaliningrad Oblast

The city of Kaliningrad was founded in 1255, as Königsberg, during German expansion eastwards. The chief city of East Prussia, it was the original royal capital of the Hohenzollerns (later the German Emperors). After the Second World War it was annexed by the USSR and received its current name (1945). Most of the German population were deported. In mid-1993 Kaliningrad Oblast requested the status of a republic, which was refused by the federal authorities. On 15 October the Regional Soviet was disbanded by the head of the Regional Administration for failing to rescind its decision to reject President Russian President Boris Yeltsin's decree of 21 September.

Kaliningrad Oblast is the westernmost part of the Russian Federation, being an enclave separated from the rest of the country by Lithuania (which borders it to the north and east) and Belarus. Poland lies to the south. The Oblast is part of the Baltic Economic Area, which it had constituted with the former Soviet Baltic states. The city of Kaliningrad is sited at the mouth of the river Pregolya (Pregel), where it flows into the Vistula Lagoon, an inlet of the Baltic Sea. The other main river is the Neman (Memel). Its agricultural sector consists mainly of animal husbandry, vegetable growing and fishing. Its main industries are machine-building, electrotechnical industry, the processing of agricultural and forestry products, natural-gas production, light manufacturing and the production and processing of amber. Its main industrial centres are at Kaliningrad, Gusev, Sovetsk (formerly Tilsit) and Chernyakhovsk (formerly Insterburg). Its main ports are Kaliningrad and Baltiysk (formerly Pillau). The Oblast occupies 15,100 sq km, is divided into 13 administrative districts and 22 cities, and had a population of 871,000 in 1989. Its administrative centre is at Kaliningrad.

Head of the Regional Administration: YURY S. MATOCHKIN; tel. (0112) 46-42-31; fax (0112) 46-35-54.

Chairman of the Regional Soviet: YURY N. SEMENOV.

Representative of the President of the Russian Federation: TAMARA A. POLUYEKTOVA; tel. (0112) 46-46-22.

Head of Kaliningrad City Administration: VITALY V. SHIPOV; tel. (0112) 21-48-98.

Kaluga Oblast

The Regional Soviet in Kaluga Oblast, having refused to disband itself, was closed by the head of the Administration at the end of 1993. In January 1994 elections to a new representative body, the Guberniya Legislative Assembly, were set for 27 March. The new Assembly would consist of 27 deputies.

Kaluga Oblast is situated in the central part of the East European Plain, the city being 188 km south-west of Moscow. Its main river is the Oka. It forms part of the Central Economic Area. Its agriculture consists mainly of animal husbandry and production of vegetables, grain and flax. Its main industries are machine-building, wood-working and light manufacturing. Its main industrial centres are at Kaluga, Lyudinovo, Kirov, Maloyaroslavets, Sukhinichi and Borovsk. It occupies 29,900 sq km, is divided into 23 administrative districts and 17 cities, and had a population of 1,067,000 in 1989. Its administrative centre is at Kaluga, a river-port.

Head of the Regional Administration: ALEKSANDR V. DERYAGIN; tel. and fax 7-23-57.

Chairman of the Guberniya Legislative Assembly: (vacant).

Representative of the President of the Russian Federation: OLEG V. SAVCHENKO; tel. 7-46-37.

Head of Kaluga City Administration: VITALY A. CHERNIKOV; tel. 7-26-46.

Kamchatka Oblast

Both the Regional Soviet and the Regional Administration in Kamchatka Oblast supported President Russian President Boris Yeltsin following his dissolution of the Russian parliament on 21 September 1993.

Kamchatka Oblast is situated in the Far East. Its main rivers are the Kamchatka and the Avacha. Its agriculture consists mainly of fishing, animal husbandry and hunting. The Oblast's industry is based on the processing of agricultural and forestry products and coal production. Its main industrial centres are at Petropavlovsk-Kamchatka and Ust-Kamchatka, which are also its main ports. Its territory covers an area of 472,300 sq km and is divided into 11 administrative districts and three cities. In 1989 the population was 466,000. Its administrative centre is at Petropavlovsk-Kamchatka.

Head of the Regional Administration: VLADIMIR A. BIRYUKOV; tel. (415) 2-20-91.

Chairman of the Regional Soviet: PETR G. PREMYAK.

Representative of the President of the Russian Federation: IGOR A. SIDORCHUK; tel. (415) 2-29-88.

Head of the Regional Representation in Moscow: ALEXANDRA G. BALENKO; tel. (095) 415-68-84.

Head of Petropavlovsk-Kamchatka City Administration: ALEKSANDR K. DUDNIKOV; tel. (415) 2-49-13.

Kemerovo Oblast

On 14 October the Kemerovo Regional Soviet was disbanded and its functions taken over by the Regional Administration. Elections to a bicameral Regional Assembly were scheduled to take place in March 1994.

Kemerovo Oblast is situated in the Kuznetsk hollow, to the west and north-west of the Republic of Khakassia. Its main river is the Tom. It forms part of the Western Siberian Economic Area. Its agriculture consists mainly of vegetable production, animal husbandry, bee-keeping and hunting. Its main industries are the production of coal, iron and complex ores, ferrous and non-ferrous metallurgy, chemicals, machine-building, metal-working, food processing, light manufacturing and wood-working. Its main industrial centres are at Kemerovo, Novokuznetsk, Prokopyevsk, Kiselevsk, Leninsk-Kuznetsky, Anzhero-Sudzhensk and Belovo. The territory of the Oblast occupies 95,500 sq km and is divided into 16 administrative districts and 19 cities. In 1989 the total population was 3,175,000. Its administrative centre is at Kemerovo.

Head of the Regional Administration: Mikhail B. Kislyuk; tel. (3842) 26-43-33; fax (3842) 26-34-09.

Chairman of the Regional Assembly: (vacant).

Representative of the President of the Russian Federation: Anatoly V. Malykhin; tel. (3842) 26-41-54.

Head of the Regional Representation in Moscow: Igor S. Kozhuhovsky; tel. (095) 202-00-63.

Head of Kemerovo City Administration: Vladimir V. Mikhailov; tel. (3842) 23-39-92.

Kirov Oblast (Vyatka)

Until 1934 the city and its region were called Vyatka. In September 1993 a draft constitution for Kirov Oblast was prepared which referred to the Oblast as Vyatka Kray and provided for a universally elected Governor and a new legislature, the Kray Duma. On 18 October the Kirov Regional Soviet voted to disband itself. By the beginning of 1994 the federal authorities had not acknowledged the area's redesignation as a kray (province).

Kirov Oblast is situated in the east of the East European Plain. Its main rivers are the Kama and the Vyatka. It forms part of the Volga-Vyatka Economic Area. Its agriculture consists mainly of animal husbandry and production of grain, flax and vegetables. Its main industries are machine-building, metal-working, ferrous and non-ferrous metallurgy, chemicals, the processing of agricultural and forestry products, light manufacturing and phosphorite production. The Oblast's main industrial centres are at Kirov, Slobodsky, Kotelnich, Omutninsk, Kirovo-Chepetsk and Vyatskiye Poliany. It occupies a total area of 120,800 sq km and is divided into 39 administrative districts and 19 cities. The total population in 1989 was 1,694,000. Its administrative centre is at Kirov.

Head of the Regional Administration: Vasily A. Desyatnikov; tel. 62-95-64.

Chairman of the Regional Soviet: Aleksandr Y. Kostin.

Representative of the President of the Russian Federation: Veniamin M. Sumarokov; tel. 62-24-94.

Head of Kirov City Administration: Anzheli M. Mikheyev.

Kostroma Oblast

The Kostroma Regional Soviet declared Decree No. 1,400 to be unconstitutional, but was subsequently obliged to recognize the authority of the federal Government.

Kostroma Oblast is situated in the central part of the East European Plain. Its main rivers are the Volga, the Kostroma and the Vetluga. It forms part of the Central Economic Area. Its agriculture consists mainly of production of grain, flax and vegetables and animal husbandry. The main industries in the Oblast are light manufacturing, wood-working, machine-building, food processing and handicrafts. Its main industrial centres are at Kostroma, Sharya, Nerekhta, Galich, Bui, Manturovo and Krasnoye-on-Volga (Krasnoye-na-Volgye). The total area of Kostroma Oblast is 60,100 sq km. It is divided into 24 administrative districts and 11 cities and had a population of 809,000 in 1989. Its administrative centre is at Kostroma.

Head of the Regional Administration: Valery P. Arbuzov; tel. 7-34-72; fax 7-70-90.

Chairman of the Regional Soviet: Rudolf A. Kartashov.

Representative of the President of the Russian Federation: Yury A. Litvinov; tel. 7-24-82.

Head of the Regional Representation in Moscow: Boris G. Vasilyev; tel. (095) 203-41-56.

Head of Kostroma City Administration: Yury A. Korobov; tel. 7-87-71.

Kurgan Oblast

At a session on 19 October 1993 the Kurgan Regional Soviet refused to disband itself, resolving to continue its work until the elections on 12 December.

Kurgan Oblast is situated in the south of the West Siberian Plain. Its main rivers are the Tobol and the Iset. It forms part of the Urals Economic Area. Its agriculture consists mainly of grain production and animal husbandry. Its main industries are machine-building, light manufacturing and food processing. Its main industrial centres are at Kurgan and Shadrinsk. The Oblast occupies 71,000 sq km and is divided into 23 administrative districts and nine cities. It has a population of 1,105,000 in 1989. Its administrative centre is at Kurgan.

Head of the Regional Administration: Valentin P. Gerasimov; tel. 2-25-34; fax 2-74-64.

Chairman of the Regional Soviet: Oleg A. Bogomolov.

Representative of the President of the Russian Federation: Nikolay Davidov; tel. 2-22-33.

Head of Kurgan City Administration: Anatoly F. Yelchaninov; tel. 2-24-52.

Kursk Oblast

In October 1993 the Regional Soviet in Kursk Oblast refused to disband itself but agreed to hold early elections.

Kursk Oblast is situated within the Central Russian highlands. Its main river is the Seym. It forms part of the Central Chernozem Economic Area. Its main industries are production and enrichment of iron ores, machine-building, electrotechnical products and chemicals, food processing, light manufacturing and production of building materials. Its main industrial centres are at Kursk and Zeleznogorsk. Its agriculture consists mainly of sugar beets and grain production, horticulture and animal husbandry. The Oblast occupies 29,800 sq km, is divided into 28 administrative districts and 10 cities, and had a population of 1,329,500 in 1989. Its administrative centre is at Kursk.

Head of the Regional Administration: Vasily I. Shuteyev; tel. (071) 2-62-62; fax (071) 2-65-62.

Chairman of the Regional Soviet: Vladimir N. Likhachev.

Representative of the President of the Russian Federation: Aleksandr A. Kureninov; tel. (071) 2-30-02.

Head of Kursk City Administration: Yury B. Ivanov; tel. (071) 2-62-62.

Leningrad Oblast

The Leningrad region did not change its name when the city reverted to the name of St Petersburg. In October 1993 the head of the Regional Administration in Leningrad Oblast decided not to disband the Regional Soviet. Elections to the legislative assembly in the Oblast were set for 20 March 1994.

The Leningrad Oblast is situated in the north-west of the East European Plain. It lies on the Gulf of Finland, an inlet of the Baltic Sea. Its main rivers are the Neva, the Volkhov, the Svir and the Vuokha. It has two lakes—the Ladoga and the Onega. It forms part of the North-Western Economic Area. Its agriculture consists mainly of animal husbandry and vegetable production. Its major industries are machine-building, ferrous and non-ferrous metallurgy, chemicals, petroleum refining, the processing of forestry and agricultural products, light manufacturing and the production of building materials, bauxites, slate and peat. Its main industrial centres are at St Petersburg, Sestroretsk, Vyborg and Kingisepp. Its main ports are St Petersburg and Vyborg. The Oblast occupies 85,900 sq km and is divided into 17 administrative districts and 26 cities. The total population in 1989, excluding the St Petersburg City region, was 2,147,000. Its administrative centre is in St Petersburg.

Head of the Regional Administration: Aleksandr S. Belyakov; tel. (812) 274-35-63; fax (812) 274-59-86.

Chairman of the Regional Soviet: Vadim A. Gustov.

Representative of the President of the Russian Federation: (vacant); tel. (812) 310-45-36.

Head of the Regional Representation in Moscow: Boris I. Aristov; tel. (095) 203-48-41.

Lipetsk Oblast

In September 1993 both the Regional Soviet and the head of the Regional Administration in Lipetsk Oblast denounced President Russian President Boris Yeltsin's dissolution of the Russian parliament. Subsequently the territory was obliged to comply with the directives of the federal Government. Legislative elections were held in the region on 6 March 1994 but were invalidated, owing to a low level of attendance. Further elections were to be arranged.

Lipetsk Oblast is situated within the Central Russian highlands. Its main river is the Don. It forms part of the Central Chernozem Economic Area. Its agriculture consists mainly of animal husbandry, horticulture and the production of grain, sugar beets, tobacco and vegetables. Its main industries are ferrous metallurgy, machine-building, metal-working, electrotechnical industry, food processing and the production of building materials. Its main industrial centres are at Lipetsk, Yeletsk, Dankov and Gryazi. The Oblast occupies 24,100 sq km, is divided into 18 administrative districts and eight cities and had a population of 1,231,000 in 1989. Its administrative centre is at Lipetsk.

Head of the Regional Administration: Mikhail Narolin; tel. 24-25-65.

Chairman of the Regional Soviet: Oleg P. Koroloyev.

Representative of the President of the Russian Federation: RAVIL A. KASYMOV; tel. 24-03-65.

Head of Lipetsk City Administration: ANATOLY I. SAVENKOV; tel. 77-66-17.

Magadan Oblast

On 19 October 1993 the Regional Soviet in Magadan Oblast refused to disband itself but agreed to suspend its activities indefinitely.

Magadan Oblast is situated in the north-east of Russia, east of Yakutia in the Far Eastern Economic Area. It has a coastline on the Sea of Okhotsk and, in the north-east where it constitutes the Chukchi Autonomous Okrug, on the Arctic Ocean and the Bering Sea. Its main rivers are the Kolyma and the Anadyr. Its agriculture consists mainly of fishing, animal husbandry and hunting. Its main industries are ore mining, food processing, machine-building and metal-working. Its main industrial centres are at Magadan, Susuman, Pevek and Anadyr. Its main ports are Nagayevo, Pevek, Providenia and Anadyr. The territory of the Oblast occupies 1,199,100 sq km. It is divided into 16 administrative districts and four cities and had a population of 543,000 in 1989. Its administrative centre is at Magadan.

Head of the Regional Administration: VIKTOR G. MIKHAILOV; tel. 2-31-34; fax 2-04-25.

Chairman of the Regional Soviet: VYACHESLAV I. KOBETS.

Representative of the President of the Russian Federation: SERGEY S. PETRISCHEV; tel. 2-55-32.

Head of Magadan City Administration: GENNADY E. DOROFEYEV; tel. 2-50-47.

Moscow Oblast

On 9 October 1993 the Moscow Regional Soviet voted to rescind its earlier decision condemning President Russian President Boris Yeltsin's decree of 21 September. Elections to a new 50-seat Duma were held on 12 December.

Moscow Oblast is situated in the central part of the East European Plain at the Volga-Oka confluence. It forms part of the Central Economic Area. The Oblast's agriculture consists mainly of animal husbandry and the production of vegetables and grain. Its major industries are machine-building, radio electronics, chemicals, light manufacturing, ferrous metallurgy, metal-working, manufacture of building materials, wood-working and handicrafts. The main industrial centres are at Khimki, Podolsk, Volokolamsk, Noginsk, Serpukhov, Orekhovo-Zuevo and Yegoriyevsk. The territory of the Oblast covers an area of 47,000 sq km and has 71 cities. Its total population in 1989 was 6,686,000 (excluding Moscow City region). The Oblast's administrative centre is at Moscow.

Head of the Regional Administration: ANATOLY S. TYAZHLOV; tel. (095) 206-60-93.

Chairman of the Regional Duma: (vacant).

Representative of the President of the Russian Federation: (vacant).

Murmansk Oblast

Murmansk city was founded in 1916, as a fishing port on the Barents Sea. Until 1917 it was called Romanov-na-Murmane. On 23 September 1993 the Regional Soviet denounced Russian President Boris Yeltsin's Decree No. 1,400. On 10 October the Soviet was disbanded by the head of the Regional Administration.

Murmansk Oblast occupies the Kola peninsula, with Norway and Finland to the west. It lies on the Barents and White Seas. Its major rivers are the Ponoy, the Varguza, the Umba, the Niva and the Tulona. It has three lakes—Imandra, Umbozero and Lovozero. It forms part of the Northern Economic Area. Its agriculture consists mainly of fishing and animal husbandry. The Oblast's major industries, which have been accused of causing major environmental damage by the neighbouring Nordic nations, are the production and enrichment of ores and ferrous metals, ore-mining, ferrous metallurgy and food processing. Its principal industrial centres are at Murmansk, Monchegorsk, Kirovsk, Zapolyarny, Apatity and Kandalaksha. It has one port, Murmansk. The territory of the Oblast covers an area of 144,900 sq km. Its total population was 1,146,000 in 1989. It is divided into five districts and 11 cities. Its administrative centre is at Murmansk.

Head of the Regional Administration: YEVGENY B. KOMAROV; tel. 5-65-40; fax 5-46-25.

Chairman of the Regional Soviet: YURY A. YEVDOKIMOV.

Representative of the President of the Russian Federation: IVAN I. MENSHIKOV; tel. 5-51-31.

Permanent Representative in Moscow: PETR I. ZELENOV; tel. (095) 299-37-59.

Head of Murmansk City Administration: OLEG P. NAYDENOV; tel. 5-51-60.

Nizhny Novgorod Oblast

Nizhny Novgorod city was founded in 1221. For much of the Soviet period the city and oblast were known as Gorky, but they reverted to the original name in 1990. At the end of September 1993 the Regional Soviet in Nizhny Novgorod rescinded its original condemnation of Russian President Boris Yeltsin's Decree No. 1,400.

Nizhny Novgorod Oblast is situated in the middle reaches of the Volga river. Its major rivers are the Volga, the Oka, the Sura and the Vetluga. It forms part of the Volga-Vyatka Economic Area. Its agriculture consists mainly of the production of grain, sugar beets, flax, onions and vegetables. Animal husbandry is also important. The Oblast's principal industries are machine-building, ferrous metallurgy, chemicals, the processing of agricultural and forestry products, and light manufacturing. Its major industrial centres are at Nizhny Novgorod, Dzerzhinsk and Arzamas. The Oblast occupies a total area of 74,800 sq km and is divided into 47 administrative districts and 25 cities. In 1989 it had a total population of 3,713,000. Its administrative centre is at Nizhny Novgorod.

Head of the Regional Administration (Governor of the Oblast): BORIS Y. NEMTSOV; tel. (8312) 39-10-12; fax (8312) 39-06-29.

Chairman of the Regional Soviet: YEVGENY V. KRESTYANINOV.

Representative of the President of the Russian Federation: (vacant); tel. (8312) 39-12-88.

Head of Nizhny Novgorod City Administration: DMITRY I. BEDNYAKOV; tel. (8312) 39-15-06.

Novgorod Oblast

One of the oldest Russian cities, it remained a powerful principality after the dissolution of Kievan Rus and even after the Mongol incursions. In 1478 Ivan III ('the Great'), prince of Muscovy and the first Tsar of All Russia, destroyed the Republic of Novgorod. On 20 October 1993 the Novgorod Regional Soviet dissolved itself and transferred its powers to the Regional Administration.

Novgorod Oblast is situated in the north-west of the East European Plain. Its major rivers are the Msta and the Lovat. It has one lake—Ilmen—and one-half of its territory is forested. It forms part of the North-Western Economic Area. Its agriculture consists mainly of flax production and animal husbandry. It major industries include machine-building, chemicals, wood-working, light manufacturing and food processing. The Oblast's principal industrial centres are at Novgorod and Staraya Russa. Its territory covers an area of 55,300 sq km and is divided into 21 administrative districts and 10 cities. In 1989 the population of the Oblast was 753,000.

Head of the Regional Administration: MIKHAIL M. PRUSAK; tel. 7-47-79; fax 7-71-81.

Chairman of the Regional Soviet: NIKOLAY I. GRAZHDANKIN.

Representative of the President of the Russian Federation: (vacant); tel. 7-40-46.

Head of the Regional Representation in Moscow: YELENA A. KUCHEROVA; tel. (095) 203-95-46.

Head of Novgorod City Administration: VIKTOR N. IVANOV; tel. 7-25-40.

Novosibirsk Oblast

On 5 October 1993 Russian President Boris Yeltsin dismissed the head of the Regional Administration in Novosibirsk, Vitaly Mukha, because of the latter's outspoken criticism of the President. In the same month the Regional Soviet refused to disband itself until new elections were held. In December 1993 it was announced that elections to a new representative body, consisting of 48 members, would take place on 27 March 1994.

Novosibirsk Oblast is situated in the south-east of the West Siberian Plain, at the Ob-Irtysh confluence. The city of Novosibirsk (formerly Novonikolayevsk) was founded in 1893, during the construction of the Trans-Siberian Railway. The region's major rivers are the Ob and the Om. The Oblast has four lakes—Chany, Sartlan, Ubinskoye and Uryum. About one-third of its territory is swampland. It forms part of the Western Siberian Economic Area. The Oblast's agriculture consists mainly of animal husbandry and the production of grain, vegetables, flax and sunflower seeds. Its main industries are the production of coal, petroleum, natural gas, peat, marble, limestone and clay, machine-building, ferrous and non-ferrous metallurgy, chemicals, food processing and the production of building materials. The principal industrial centre is at Novosibirsk. The Oblast occupies an area of 178,000 sq km and is divided into 30 administrative districts and 14 cities. In 1989 it had a population of 2,782,000. Its administrative centre is at Novosibirsk.

Head of the Regional Administration: IVAN I. INDINOK (acting); tel. (3832) 23-08-62; fax (3832) 23-57-00.

Chairman of the Regional Soviet: ANATOLY P. SYCHEV.

Representative of the President of the Russian Federation: ANATOLY N. MANOKHIN; tel. (3832) 23-08-13.

Head of the Regional Representation in Moscow: NINA M. MIKHAILOVNA; tel. (095) 203-27-20.

Head of Novosibirsk City Administration: IVAN I. INDINOK; tel. (3832) 22-07-43.

Omsk Oblast

In September 1993 the Regional Soviet in Omsk denounced President Russian President Boris Yeltsin's Decree No. 1,400 and subsequently refused to disband itself.

Omsk Oblast is situated in the south of the West Siberian Plain in the middle reaches of the Irtysh river. Its major rivers are the Irtysh, the Ishim, the Om and the Tara. About one-quarter of its territory is forested. It forms part of the Western Siberian Economic Area. The Oblast's agriculture consists mainly of the production of grain, flax, sunflower seeds and vegetables, and animal husbandry and hunting. Its main industries are machine-building, petroleum refining, chemicals, light manufacturing and food processing. The territory of Omsk Oblast covers some 139,700 sq km. It is divided into 31 districts and six cities. In 1989 the population of the Oblast was 2,140,000. The administrative centre is at Omsk.

Chief of the Regional Administration: LEONID K. POLEZHAYEV; tel. (38112) 24-14-15; fax (38112) 24-23-72.

Chairman of the Regional Soviet: ANATOLY P. LEONTYEV.

Representative of the President of the Russian Federation: BORIS TYULKOV; tel. (38112) 23-18-20.

Head of Omsk City Administration: (vacant); tel. (38112) 24-30-33.

Orel Oblast

On 12 January 1994 the Orel Regional Soviet was abolished by presidential decree and elections to a new legislature, a Duma, were scheduled for 20 March.

Orel Oblast is situated in the central part of the East European Plain within the Central Russian highlands. Its major river is the Oka. The Oblast forms part of the Central Economic Area. Its agriculture consists mainly of grain, sugar beets, sunflower seeds, hemp and animal husbandry. Its main industries are machine-building, metallurgy, chemicals, light manufacturing and food processing. The principal industrial centres are at Orel, Livny and Mtsensk. The territory of Orel Oblast covers an area of 24,700 sq km and is divided, for administrative purposes, into 19 districts and seven cities. In 1989 the population of the Oblast was 891,000. Its administrative centre is at Orel.

Head of the Regional Administration: (vacant).

Chairman of the Regional Duma: (vacant).

Representative of the President of the Russian Federation: NIKOLAY P. UDIN; tel. 4-26-24.

Head of Orel City Administration: ALEKSANDR G. KISLYAKOV; tel. 6-33-12.

Orenburg Oblast

On 11 October 1993 the Orenburg Regional Soviet agreed to repeal its condemnation of Decree No. 1,400 issued by President Russian President Boris Yeltsin on 21 September. It refused to disband itself, however.

Orenburg Oblast is situated in the foothills of the southern Urals and it borders Kazakhstan. Its major river is the Ural. Its agriculture consists mainly of grain production and animal husbandry. Its major industries are ferrous and non-ferrous metallurgy, machine-building, metal-working, natural-gas production, chemicals, light manufacturing, food processing and the production of petroleum, ores, asbestos and salt. The Oblast's principal industrial centres are at Orenburg, Orsk, Novotroysk, Mednogorsk, Buzuluk, Buguruslan and Gay. It occupies a total area of 124,000 sq km and is divided into 35 districts and 12 cities. In 1989 the total population of the Oblast was 2,174,000. Its administrative centre is at Orenburg.

Head of the Regional Administration: VLADIMIR V. YELAGIN; tel. 47-69-31.

Chairman of the Regional Soviet: VALERY N. GRIGORYEV.

Representative of the President of the Russian Federation: VLADISLAV A. SHAPOVALENKO; tel. 47-34-46.

Head of the Regional Representation in Moscow: NIKOLAY D. TUTOV; tel. (095) 415-53-46.

Head of Orenburg City Administration: GEORGY P. SOLDATOV (acting); tel. 47-50-55.

Penza Oblast

Penza Oblast is situated in the Volga area highlands. Its major river is the Sura. It forms part of the Volga Economic Area. Agriculture in the Oblast consists mainly of the production of grain, sugar beets, sunflower seeds and hemp. Animal husbandry is also important. The main industries are machine-building, light manufacturing, the processing of timber and agricultural products and the production of building materials. The Oblast's principal industrial centres are at Penza and Kuznetsk. Its territory covers an area of 43,200 sq km and is divided into 28 districts and 10 cities. In 1989 the population of the Oblast was 1,502,000. Its administrative centre is at Penza.

Head of the Regional Administration: (vacant).

Chairman of the Regional Soviet: ALEKSANDR R. LYCHAGIN.

Representative of the President of the Russian Federation: IGOR KUDINOV; tel. 63-47-35.

Head of the Regional Representation in Moscow: GENNADY A. FRANK; tel. (095) 202-82-89.

Head of Penza City Administration: FEODOSY F. DUBINCHUK; tel. 63-14-67.

Perm Oblast

Perm city was founded in 1723, when a copper foundry was built there. Industrial development was such that by the latter part of the 20th century the city extended for some 80 km along the banks of the Kama river. In the Soviet period it was, for a time, called Molotov, and the city was forbidden to foreigners until 1989. Until 1991 it was the site of the last Soviet camp for political prisoners (Perm-35). In December 1993 there were elections in Perm Oblast for a new legislative body, the Duma.

Perm Oblast is situated on the western slopes of the central and northern Urals and the adjacent eastern edge of the East European Plain. Apart from the Kama, its major rivers are the Chusovaya, the Kosva and the Vishera. It forms part of the Urals Economic Area. Agriculture in the Oblast consists mainly of grain and vegetable production and animal husbandry. The main industries are coal, petroleum, natural-gas, potash and salt production, machine-building, electrotechnical industries, chemicals and petrochemicals, petroleum refining, the processing of forestry products, ferrous and non-ferrous metallurgy, and printing. The major industrial centres are Perm, Berezniki, Solikamsk, Chusovoy, Krasnokamsk and Chaykovsky. The territory of the Oblast covers an area of 160,600 sq km and is divided into 37 districts and 25 cities. Its population in 1989 was 3,100,000. The administrative centre is at Perm.

Head of the Administration of Perm Oblast and the Western Urals: BORIS Y. KUZNETSOV; tel. (3422) 34-07-90; fax (3422) 39-46-00.

Chairman of the Regional Duma: (vacant).

Representative of the President of the Russian Federation: SERGEY B. KALYGIN; tel. (3422) 34-33-44.

Head of Perm City Administration: VLADIMIR Y. FIL; tel. (3422) 32-40-84.

Pskov Oblast

Pskov Oblast is situated on the East European Plain. Its major river is the Velikaya. On its border with Estonia lie the Pskov (Pihkva) and Chudskoye (Peipsi) lakes. The Oblast forms part of the North-Western Economic Area. Its agriculture consists mainly of animal husbandry and the production of grain, vegetables and flax. Its major industries are machine-building, light manufacturing, food processing and wood-working. The principal industrial centres are at Pskov and Velikiye Luki. The territory of the Pskov Oblast covers an area of 55,300 sq km and is divided into 24 districts and 14 cities. The population in 1989 was 847,000. The administrative centre is at Pskov.

Head of the Regional Administration: VLADISLAV N. TUMANOV; tel. 2-22-03.

Chairman of the Regional Soviet: VITALY N. PUSHKAREV.

Representative of the President of the Russian Federation: DMITRY K. KHRITONENKOV; tel. 2-26-46.

Head of Pskov City Administration: ALEKSANDR V. PROKOFIEV; tel. 2-26-67.

Rostov Oblast

On 24 October 1993 the Rostov Regional Soviet adopted a decision to suspend its activities pending local elections.

Rostov Oblast is situated in the south of the East European Plain, in the North Caucasus area. It lies on the Taganrog gulf of the Sea of Azov. Its major rivers are the Don and the Severny Donets. The Volga–Don Canal runs through its territory. The Oblast's agriculture consists mainly of the production of grain, sunflower seeds, coriander, mustard, vegetables and cucurbits (gourds and melons). Viniculture and horticulture are also important. Its principal industries are machine-building, food processing, light manufacturing, chemicals, ferrous and non-ferrous metallurgy, and coal production. Its industrial centres are at Rostov-on-Don (Rostov-na-Donu), Taganrog, Novocherkassk, Shakhty, Kamensk-Shakhtinsky, Novoshakhtinsk and Volgo-Donsk. Its ports are Rostov-on-Don and Ust-Donetsky (both river-ports). The territory of the Rostov Oblast covers an area of 100,800 sq km and consists of 41 districts and 22 cities. The population in 1989 was 4,304,000. Its administrative centre is at Rostov-on-Don.

Head of the Regional Administration: VLADIMIR F. CHUB; tel. (8632) 66-78-10; fax (8632) 65-36-26.

Chairman of the Regional Soviet: ALEKSANDR V. POPOV.

Chairman of the Regional Government: VIKTOR N. ANPILOGOV.

Representative of the President of the Russian Federation: VLADIMIR N. ZUBKOV; tel. (8632) 24-34-38.

Head of Rostov-on-Don City Administration: YURY B. POGREBSCHIKOV; tel. (8632) 62-48-48.

Ryazan Oblast

At the end of October 1993, following its failure to muster a quorum, the Supreme Soviet was disbanded.

Ryazan Oblast is situated in the central part of the East European Plain. Its major rivers are the Oka and its tributaries. It forms part of the Central Economic Area. The Oblast's agriculture consists mainly of grain and vegetable production, horticulture and animal husbandry. Its main industries are machine-building, petroleum processing, chemicals, the production of building materials, light manufacturing, food processing and peat and coal production. The major industrial centres are at Ryazan, Skopin, Kasimov and Sasovo. The territory of the Oblast covers 39,600 sq km and is divided into 25 districts and 12 cities. In 1989 its population was 1,346,000. Its administrative centre is at Ryazan.

Head of the Regional Administration: (vacant); tel. 77-40-32.

Chairman of the Regional Soviet: VIKTOR V. PRIKHODKO.

Representative of the President of the Russian Federation: NIKOLAY V. MOLOTKOV; tel. 77-21-47.

Head of Ryazan City Administration: VALERY V. RYUMIN; tel. 77-27-85.

Sakhalin Oblast

On 16 October 1993 the Regional Soviet in Sakhalin Oblast was disbanded by the head of the Regional Administration. The Soviet had previously denounced Decree No. 1,400.

Sakhalin Oblast comprises the island of Sakhalin and the Kurile Islands in the Pacific Ocean. The latter are claimed by Japan, from which they were seized in 1945. It forms part of the Far Eastern Economic Area. Its agriculture consists mainly of vegetable production, animal husbandry, fishing and fur farming. Its major industries are fish processing, the production of petroleum, natural gas and coal, and the processing of forestry products. The Oblast's principal industrial centres are at Yuzhno-Sakhalinsk, Kholmsk, Okha, Nevelsk, Dolinsk, Korsakov, Uglegorsk and Poronaisk. Its ports are Kholmsk, Korsankov and Aleksandrov-Sakhalinsky. The Oblast covers an area of 87,100 sq km and is divided into 17 districts and 19 cities. The population in 1989 was 709,000. Its administrative centre is at Yuzhno-Sakhalinsk.

Head of the Regional Administration (Governor of the Oblast): YEVGENY A. KRASNOAROV; tel. (424) 3-14-02.

Chairman of the Regional Soviet: ANATOLY P. AKSENOV.

Representative of the President of the Russian Federation: VITALY V. GULY; tel. (424) 3-50-70.

Head of Yuzhno-Sakhalinsk City Administration: IGOR P. FARKHUTDINOV; tel. (424) 2-25-11.

Samara Oblast

The Samara Regional Soviet was disbanded on 20 October 1993, following its refusal to repeal its condemnation of Russian President Boris Yeltsin's Decree No. 1,400.

Samara Oblast (Kuybyshev prior to 1991) is situated in the south-east of the East European Plain. Its major river is the Volga. It forms part of the Volga Economic Area. Agriculture in the Oblast consists mainly of animal husbandry and the production of grain, sugar beets and sunflower seeds. The main industries are machine-building, metal-working, petroleum production and petrochemicals. The major industrial centres are at Samara, Togliatti, Syzran and Novokuybyshevsk. The Samara Oblast covers 53,600 sq km. It is divided into 25 districts and 10 cities. The population in 1989 was 3,266,000. The administrative centre is at Samara (formerly Kuybyshev).

Head of the Regional Administration: KONSTANTIN A. TITOV; tel. (8462) 32-22-68.

Chairman of the Regional Soviet: OLEG N. ANISCHIK.

Representative of the President of the Russian Federation: YURY BORODULIN.

Head of Samara City Administration: OLEG N. SYSUYEV; tel. (8462) 32-20-68.

Saratov Oblast

On 12 October 1993 the Regional Soviet in Saratov Oblast was closed by the head of the Regional Administration after it had become inquorate.

Saratov Oblast is situated in the south-east of the East European Plain. Its main river is the Volga. It forms part of the Volga Economic Area. The Oblast's agriculture consists primarily of animal husbandry and the production of grain, sunflower seeds and sugar beets. Its main industries are machine-building, petroleum refining, chemicals, the manufacture of building materials, woodworking, light manufacturing, food processing and the production of petroleum and natural gas. The main industrial centres are at Saratov, Engels and Balakovo. The territory of the Saratov Oblast covers an area of 100,200 sq km. It comprises 38 districts and 17 cities. In 1989 the population was 2,690,000. Its administrative centre is at Saratov.

Head of the Regional Administration: YURY V. BELYKH; tel. 24-14-16; fax 24-20-89.

Chairman of the Regional Soviet: NIKOLAY S. MAKAREVICH.

Representative of the President of the Russian Federation: VLADIMIR G. GOLOVACHEV; tel. 24-10-25.

Head of Saratov City Administration: YURY B. KITOV; tel. 24-24-57.

Smolensk Oblast

At an emergency session on 22 September 1993, the Regional Soviet in Smolensk Oblast declared Decree No. 1,400 unconstitutional. On 14 October 1993 the powers of the Smolensk Regional Soviet were suspended by the head of the Regional Administration, pending the election of a new legislature.

Smolensk Oblast is situated in the central part of the East European Plain. Its major river is the Dnepr (Dnieper). The Oblast forms part of the Central Economic Area. Its agriculture mainly consists of animal husbandry and the production of grain, sugar beets and sunflower seeds. Its main industries are machine-building, chemicals, light manufacturing, food processing and the production of coal and peat. The major industrial centres are at Smolensk, Roslavl, Safonovo, Vyazma, Yartsevo, Gagarin and Verkhnedneprovsky. The territory of the Oblast covers an area of 49,800 sq km and is divided into 25 districts and 14 cities. The population was 1,158,000 in 1989. Its administrative centre is at Smolensk.

Head of the Regional Administration: (vacant).

Chairman of the Regional Soviet: MIKHAIL I. SEMENOV.

Representative of the President of the Russian Federation: (vacant); tel. 3-65-23.

Head of Smolensk City Administration: MIKHAIL G. ZYAMANOV; tel. 3-11-81.

Sverdlovsk Oblast

Sverdlovsk Oblast did not change its name when, in 1990, its chief city (which bore the same name) reverted to the name of Yekaterinburg (famed as where the last Tsar—Nicholas II—and his family were killed in 1918). On 29 September 1993 the Sverdlovsk Regional Soviet adopted a draft constitution for a 'Ural Republic'. The 'Republic' was officially proclaimed on 27 October by the Regional Soviet and the head of the Regional Administration. It was also announced on that day that the Regional Soviet would continue its work until parliamentary elections were held on 12 December. The Ural Republic was dissolved by presidential decree and Eduard Rossel, the head of the Regional Administration, was dismissed on 9 November.

Sverdlovsk Oblast is situated on the eastern, and partly on the western, slopes of the middle and northern Urals. Its major rivers are those of the Ob and Kama basins. It forms part of the Urals Economic Area. The Oblast's agriculture consists of grain production and animal husbandry. The main industries are ferrous and non-ferrous metallurgy, machine-building, chemicals, the processing of forestry and agricultural products, light manufacturing and the production of copper and other ores, bauxite, asbestos and coal. The most important industrial centres are at Yekaterinburg, Nizhny Tagil, Pervouralsk, Krasnouralsk, Serov, Alapayevsk and Kamensk-Uralsky. The territory of the Oblast covers an area of 194,800 sq km and is divided into 30 districts and 44 cities. In 1989 the population totalled 4,721,000. The administrative centre is at Yekaterinburg.

Head of the Regional Administration: ALEKSEY STRAKHOV; tel. (3432) 51-13-65; fax (3432) 58-91-03.

Chairman of the Regional Soviet: ANATOLY V. GREBENKIN.

Representative of the President of the Russian Federation: VITALY V. MASHKOV; tel. (3432) 51-21-61.

Head of Yekaterinburg City Administration: ARKADY M. CHERNETSKY; tel. (3432) 58-92-18.

Tambov Oblast

On 22 October the head of the Regional Administration of Tambov adopted a decree dissolving the Regional Soviet.

Tambov Oblast is situated in the central part of the Oka-Don plain. It forms part of the Central Chernozem Economic Area. Its agriculture consists mainly of the production of grain, sugar beets, sunflower seeds and vegetables. Animal husbandry and horticulture are also important. The principal industries in the Oblast are machine-building, chemicals, light manufacturing and food processing. The major industrial centres are at Tambov, Michurinsk, Morshansk, Kotovsk and Rasskazovo. Its territory occupies 34,300 sq km. The Oblast is divided into 23 districts and eight cities. In 1989 its population totalled 1,320,000. The administrative centre is at Tambov.

Head of the Regional Administration: VLADIMIR D. BABENKO (acting); tel. 22-25-28.

Chairman of the Regional Soviet: ALEKSANDR I. RYABOV.

Representative of the President of the Russian Federation: (vacant); tel. 22-33-01.

Head of Tambov City Administration: VALERY N. KOVAL (acting); tel. 2-84-40.

Tomsk Oblast

At a session of the Tomsk Regional Soviet on 16 October 1993 the resolution which had declared President Russian President Boris Yeltsin's decree of 21 September null and void was rescinded. The Soviet was subsequently disbanded and elections to a new parliament were held on 12 December, simultaneously with the elections to the State Duma.

Tomsk Oblast is situated in the south-east of the West Siberian Plain. Its major rivers are the Ob, the Tom, the Chylym and the Vasyugan. More than one-half of its territory is forested. It forms part of the Western Siberian Economic Area. Its agriculture consists mainly of animal husbandry, the production of grain, vegetables and flax, fishing, hunting and fur farming. Its main industries are petroleum production, machine-building, metal-working, electrotechnical industry, the processing of forestry and agricultural products and chemicals. The major industrial centres in the Oblast are at Tomsk, Kopashevo, Asino and Strezhevoy. Its territory occupies 316,900 sq km and is divided into 16 districts and five cities. In 1989 its total population was 1,001,000. The administrative centre of the Oblast is at Tomsk.

Head of the Regional Administration: VIKTOR M. KRESS; tel. 22-25-05; fax 22-48-84.

Chairman of the Regional Assembly: (vacant).

Representative of the President of the Russian Federation: ANATOLY KOBZEV; tel. 22-20-30.

Head of Tomsk City Administration: VLADIMIR V. GONCHAR; tel. 23-32-32.

Tula Oblast

On 7 October 1993 the Tula Regional Soviet refused to disband itself but over 100 deputies resigned, thereby making the Soviet inquorate. The Soviet was subsequently dissolved and its functions transferred to the Regional Administration.

Tula Oblast is situated in the central part of the East European Plain in the northern section of the Central Russian highlands. Its major rivers are the Oka, the Upa and the Osetr. It forms part of the Central Economic Area. The Oblast's agriculture consists primarily of animal husbandry and production of grain and sugar beets. Its main industries are machine-building, chemicals, ferrous metallurgy, manufacture of building materials, light manufacturing, food processing and the production of brown coal. The major industrial centres are at Tula, Novomoskovsk, Schekino, Aleksin, Uzlovaya and Yefremov. The territory of the Oblast covers an area of 25,700 sq km and is divided into 23 districts and 21 cities. Its total population in 1989 was 1,868,000. The Oblast's administrative centre is at Tula.

Head of the Regional Administration: NIKOLAY V. SEVRYUGIN; tel. (0872) 27-84-36.

Chairman of the Regional Soviet: YURY I. LITVINTSEV.

Representative of the President of the Russian Federation: VIKTOR G. KUZNETSOV; tel. (0872) 31-41-62.

Head of Tula City Administration: NIKOLAY Y. TYAGLIVY; tel. (0872) 27-80-88.

Tver Oblast

In October 1993 the Tver Regional Soviet refused to disband itself. It was subsequently obliged to comply with the directives of the federal authorities.

Tver Oblast (Kalinin prior to 1990) is situated in the central part of the East European Plain. Its major rivers are the Volga, the Mologa and the Tvertsa. It has more than 500 lakes, the largest of which is Seliger. About one-third of the territory of the Oblast is forested. Its agriculture consists mainly of animal husbandry and production of vegetables and flax. Its major industries are machine-building, light manufacturing, chemicals, wood-working, printing and glass- and china-making. The principal industrial centres are Tver, Vyshny Volochek, Rzhev, Torzhok and Kimry. It occupies 84,100 sq km and is divided into 36 districts and 23 cities. The population in 1989 was 1,670,000. The administrative centre is at Tver (formerly Kalinin).

Head of the Regional Administration: VLADIMIR A. SUSLOV; tel. 3-10-50.

Chairman of the Regional Soviet: MIKHAIL A. SHESTOV (acting).

Representative of the President of the Russian Federation: VIKTOR I. BELOV; tel. 3-50-25.

Head of Tver City Administration: ALEKSANDR P. BELUSOV; tel. 3-01-31.

Tyumen Oblast

On 21 October the Regional Soviet in Tyumen Oblast repealed its earlier condemnation of President Russian President Boris Yeltsin's Decree No. 1,400 but refused to disband itself. Legislative elections were held in the Oblast on 6 March 1994, but the results in several constituencies were declared invalid, owing to a low level of participation.

Tyumen Oblast is situated in the West Siberian Plain. Its major rivers are the Ob, the Taz, the Pur and the Nadym. It forms part of the Western Siberian Economic Area. The Oblast's agriculture consists mainly of animal husbandry, the production of grain, flax and vegetables, fur farming and hunting. The major industries are the production and processing of petroleum and natural gas, machine-building, metal-working, chemicals and the processing of agricultural and forestry products. The main industrial centres are at Tyumen, Tobolsk, Surgut, Nizhnevartovsk and Nadym. The territory of the Oblast occupies an area of 1,435,200 sq km and is divided into 37 districts and 20 cities. The total population in 1989 was 3,083,000. The administrative centre is at Tyumen.

Head of the Regional Administration: LEONID U. ROKETSYE; tel. (3452) 26-51-80.

Chairman of the Regional Soviet: VLADIMIR I. ULYANOV.

Representative of the President of the Russian Federation: GENNADY A. SHERBAKOV; tel. (3452) 26-29-84.

Head of Tyumen City Administration: GENNADY I. RAYKOV; tel. (3452) 24-67-34.

Ulyanovsk Oblast

Ulyanovsk city (formerly Simbirsk) was founded in 1648. Lenin (Vladimir Ilych Ulyanov) was born here in 1870, living in the city until 1887. The city and region were named after his family name following his death in 1924. The Regional Soviet in Ulyanovsk Oblast decided to cease its activities on 1 November 1993.

Ulyanovsk Oblast is situated in the Volga Area. It forms part of the Volga Economic Area. Its agriculture consists primarily of animal husbandry and the production of grain, sunflower seeds and sugar beets. It main industries are machine-building, light manufacturing, manufacture of building materials and wood-working. The Oblast's major industrial centres are at Ulyanovsk and Melekess. Its territory covers an area of 37,300 sq km and is divided into 20 districts and six cities. The total population of the Oblast was 1,400,000 in 1989. The administrative centre is at Ulyanovsk.

Head of the Regional Administration: YURY F. GORYACHEV; tel. 31-25-06.

Chairman of the Regional Soviet: VLADIMIR L. RAZUMOV.

Representative of the President of the Russian Federation: GEORGY I. STUPNIKOV; tel. 31-91-30.

Head of Ulyanovsk City Administration: SERGEY N. YERMAKOV; tel. 31-30-80.

Vladimir Oblast

Founded in 1108 as a frontier fortress, the city is one of the oldest in Russia. In October 1993 the Vladimir Regional Soviet was dissolved by the head of the Regional Administration and the soviet apparatus was abolished.

Vladimir Oblast is situated in the central part of the East European Plain. Its main rivers are the Oka and the Klyazma. It forms part of the Central Economic Area. Its agriculture consists mainly of animal husbandry, vegetable growing and horticulture. Its main industries are machine-building, metal-working, light manufacturing, chemicals, glass-making and handicrafts. Its main industrial centres are at Vladimir, Kovrov, Murom, Alexandrov, Kolchugino, Vyazniki and Gus-Khrustalny. It occupies a total of 29,000 sq km. The Oblast is divided into 16 administrative districts and 21 cities and had a population of 1,654,000 in 1989. Its administrative centre is at Vladimir.

Head of the Regional Administration: YURY V. VLASOV; tel. 2-52-52.

Chairman of the Regional Soviet: VLADIMIR A. KALYAGIN.

Representative of the President of the Russian Federation: NIKOLAY S. YEGOROV; tel. 2-53-62.

Head of Vladimir City Administration: IGOR V. SHAMOV; tel. 3-28-17.

Volgograd Oblast

In October 1993 the Regional Soviet in Volgograd Oblast eventually agreed to a reform of the system of local goverment in the Oblast. It decided to hold elections to a new 30-seat Duma.

Volgograd Oblast is situated in the south-east of the East European Plain. Its main rivers are the Volga and the Don. It forms part of the Volga Economic Area. Its principal agricultural products are grain, sunflower seeds, mustard and cucurbits (gourds and melons). Horticulture and animal husbandry are also important. The main industries in the Oblast are petroleum refining, chemicals and petrochemicals, machine-building, metal-working, ferrous and non-ferrous metallurgy, the manufacture of building materials, wood-working, light manufacturing, food processing and the production of petroleum and natural gas. The Oblast's main industrial centres are at Volgograd, Bolzhsky and Kamyshyn. It occupies 113,900 sq km and is divided into 33 administrative districts and 18 cities. In 1989 it had a population of 2,593,000. Its administrative centre is at Volgograd.

Head of the Regional Administration: IVAN P. SHABUNIN; tel. 33-66-88; fax 33-47-57.

Chairman of the Regional Soviet: ALEKSANDR G. MOROZOV.

Representative of the President of the Russian Federation: YEVGENY S. KUZNETSOV; tel. 33-28-20.

Head of Volgograd City Administration: YURY V. CHEKHOV; tel. 33-50-10.

Vologda Oblast

In mid-1993 the Vologda Oblast declared itself a republic but failed to be acknowledged as such by the federal authorities. On 13 October the Regional Soviet transferred its responsibilities to the Regional Administration.

Vologda Oblast is situated in the south-west of the East European Plain. Its main rivers are the Sukhona, the Yug, the Sheksna and the Mologa. It forms part of the Northern Economic Area. Its agriculture consists mainly of animal husbandry and production of flax and vegetables. Its main industries are ferrous metallurgy, the processing of forestry products, machine-building, glass-making, light manufacturing, food processing and handicrafts, such as lace-making. Its main industrial centres are at Vologda, Cherepovets, Veliky Ustyug and Sokol. It occupies 145,700 sq km and is divided into 26 administrative districts and 15 cities. The population in 1989 was 1,354,000. Its administrative centre is at Vologda.

Head of the Regional Administration: NIKOLAY M. PODGORNOV; tel. 2-07-64.

Chairman of the Regional Soviet: GENNADY T. KHRIPEL.

Representative of the President of the Russian Federation: GURI V. SUDAKOV; tel. 2-93-95.

Head of the Regional Representation in Moscow: LEONID A. GORSHKOV; tel. (095) 202-20-34.

Head of Vologda City Administration: BORIS V. UPADYSHEV; tel. 2-00-42.

Voronezh Oblast

In October 1993 the Regional Soviet in Voronezh rescinded its earlier condemnation of Russian President Boris Yeltsin's Decree No. 1,400, but refused to disband itself. It was finally dissolved on 21 October by the head of the Regional Administration.

Voronezh Oblast is situated within the Central Russian highlands. Its main rivers are the Khoper and the Bityug. It forms part of the Central Chernozem Economic Area. Its agriculture consists mainly of the production of grain, sugar beets, sunflower seeds and vegetables. Animal husbandry is also important. Its main industries are machine-building, metal-working, chemicals, manufacture of building materials and food processing. The region's main industrial centres are at Voronezh, Borisoglebsk, Georgy u-Dezh, Rossosh and Kalach. It occupies an area of 54,400 sq km and is divided into 32 administrative districts and 14 cities. Its population in 1989 was 2,470,000. Its administrative centre is at Voronezh.

Head of the Regional Administration (Governor of the Oblast): ALEKSANDR Y. KOVALEV; tel. (0732) 55-27-37.

Chairman of the Regional Soviet: IVAN M. SHABANOV.

Representative of the President of the Russian Federation: VIKTOR A DAVYDKIN; tel. (0732) 55-34-24.

Head of the Regional Representation in Moscow: VIKTOR I. IVANENKO; tel. (095) 239-37-01.

Head of Voronezh City Administration: ANATOLY S. GOLTS (acting); tel. (0732) 55-04-27.

Yaroslavl Oblast

On 27 October 1993 the Yaroslavl Regional Soviet ceased its functions. Elections were held to a new legislature, a 23-seat Duma, on 27 February 1994.

Yaroslavl Oblast is situated in the central part of the East European Plain. Its major river is the Volga, and Yaroslavl city is reputed to be the oldest town on the river (founded *c.* 1024). It has two lakes—Nero and Plescheyevo. It forms part of the Central Economic Area. Agriculture in the Oblast consists primarily of animal husbandry and the production of vegetables, flax and grain. The main industries are machine-building, chemicals, petroleum processing, light manufacturing, peat production and the processing of agricultural and forestry products. The major industrial centres are at Yaroslavl, Rybinsk, Tutayev, Uglich, Pereslavl-Zalessky, Rostov and Gavrilov-Yam. The territory of the Oblast covers a total area of 36,400 sq km and is divided into 17 districts and 10 cities. The total population in 1989 was 1,471,000. The administrative centre is at Yaroslavl.

Head of the Regional Administration: ANATOLY I. LISTISYN; tel. 22-23-28; fax 22-34-25.

Chairman of the Regional Duma: (vacant).

Representative of the President of the Russian Federation: VLADIMIR G. VARUKHIN; tel. 22-09-05.

Head of Yaroslavl City Administration: VIKTOR V. VOLONCHUNAS; tel. 22-08-41.

FEDERAL CITIES

Moscow

Moscow (Moskva) was founded in about 1147. In 1325 Moscow became the seat of the Eastern Orthodox Metropolitan of Russia (subsequently the Patriarchate of the Russian Orthodox Church) and the steadily expanding Muscovite state became the foundation for the Russian Empire. The capital of the tsarist state was moved to St Petersburg in 1712, but Moscow was restored as the Russian capital, and became the Soviet capital, in March 1918. In the 1980s and 1990s, while reformists enjoyed considerable support in the city there were also powerful forces of conservatism. On 4 October 1993 President Russian President Boris Yeltsin ordered the offices of the Moscow City Soviet to be closed. On 7 October the powers of the City Soviet were suspended by presidential decree. Elections to a new 35-member Municipal Duma were held on 12 December 1993. The Duma held its first session on 10 January 1994.

Moscow is located in the west of European Russia, on the river Moskva. It is connected to the Volga river system by canal. Moscow is the largest city in the Russian Federation. The total population of the Moscow city region in 1989 was 8,769,000.

Mayor: YURY M. LUZHKOV; tel. (095) 200-54-45.

Speaker of the Municipal Duma: VIKTOR MAKSIMOV.

Representative of the President of the Russian Federation: VLADIMIR F. KOMCHATKOV; tel. (095) 202-92-32.

St Petersburg

St Petersburg (Sankt-Peterburg) was founded by the Tsar Peter I ('the Great') in 1703 and became the Russian capital in 1712. At the beginning of the First World War, in 1914, the city was renamed Petrograd. Following the fall of the Tsar and the Bolshevik Revolution in 1917, the Russian capital was moved back to Moscow. In 1924 the city was renamed Leningrad. In June 1991 the citizens of Leningrad voted to restore the old name of St Petersburg and their decision was effected in October. On 8 October 1993 the St Petersburg City Soviet voted to cancel its resolution of 23 September, which condemned President Russian President Boris Yeltsin's decree dissolving the Russian parliament. The Soviet also agreed to hold early elections. On 22 October elections to the new body of local representative power were set for 12 June 1994. On 16 November the City Soviet voted to defy President Russian President Boris Yeltsin's order that it should disband. The City Soviet was finally dissolved by presidential decree on 22 December.

St Petersburg is a seaport at the mouth of the Riva Neva, which debouches into the Gulf of Finland (part of the Baltic Sea). The population of the city was some 4,456,000 in 1989, making it Russia's second-largest city.

Mayor: ANATOLY A. SOBCHAK (elected 12 June 1991); tel. (812) 319-98-65.

Chairman of the City Soviet: ALEKSANDR N. BELYAYEV.

Representative of the President of the Russian Federation: SERGEY A. TSYPLYAYEV; tel. (812) 319-93-54.

AUTONOMOUS OBLAST

Jewish Autonomous Oblast

The Soviet regime established an autonomous Jewish province at Birobidzhan in 1928, but it never became the centre of Soviet (or Russian) Jewry. Despite the advice of President Russian President Boris Yeltsin, at a session on 14 October 1993 the Regional Soviet in the Jewish Autonomous Oblast announced that it would not disband itself.

The Jewish Autonomous Oblast is in the Far Eastern Economic Area (Khabarovsk Kray), on the border with the People's Republic of China to the south, and is part of the Amur river basin. More than one-third of its territory is covered by forest. Its agriculture consists mainly of grain production, animal husbandry, bee-keeping, hunting and fishing. Its main industries are machine-building, wood-working, light manufacturing and food processing. Its major industrial centre is at Birobidzhan. It occupies 36,000 sq km and has two cities. Its population in 1990 was 218,000. The regional capital is at Birobidzhan.

Chairman of the Regional Soviet: ALEKSANDR A. SKACHKOV.

Head of the Regional Administration: NIKOLAY M. VOLKOV; tel. 6-32-04.

Representative of the President of the Russian Federation: IOSIF D. NEKHIN; tel. 6-98-92.

Head of Birobidzhan City Administration: VIKTOR V. BOLOTNOV; tel. 6-22-02.

AUTONOMOUS OKRUGS (DISTRICTS)

Aga-Buryat Autonomous Okrug

Aga-Buryat Autonomous Okrug is situated in the south-east of Transbaikal. Its major river is the Onon, and about one-third of its territory is forested. It forms part of the Chita Oblast. Its agriculture consists mainly of animal husbandry and grain production. Its main industries are ore mining, and processing of forestry and agricultural products. The territory of Aga-Buryat occupies a total of 19,000 sq km. It has four urban-type settlements (towns) and its population in 1990 was 77,000. Its administrative centre is at the Aga town.

Head of the District Administration: GURODARMA TSEDASHIEV; tel. 3-41-52.

Chairman of the District Representation in Moscow: BAIR B. JAMSUYEV; tel. (095) 202-37-89.

Chukchi Autonomous Okrug

Chukchi Autonomous Okrug is situated on the Chokotka peninsula and the adjacent mainland portion. It is the easternmost part of mainland Russia and is washed by the Arctic Ocean and the Bering Sea. Its major river is the Anadyr. It forms part of the Magadan Oblast in the Far East, and was formerly known as the Chukot Autonomous Okrug. Its agriculture consists mainly of fishing, animal husbandry and hunting. Its main industries are ore mining and food processing. The Okrug's major ports are at Pevek, Providenia, Anadyr, Egvekinot and Beringovsky. It occupies an area of 737,700 sq km and has two towns. The population in 1990 was 156,000. The Okrug's administrative centre is at Anadyr.

Head of the District Administration: ALEKSANDR V. NAZAROV; tel. 4-61-75.

Chairman of the District Soviet: VLADIMIR M. ETYLEN.

Representative of the President of the Russian Federation: YURY A. YEREGIN; tel. 4-21-02.

Evenk Autonomous Okrug

Evenk Autonomous Okrug is a land-locked territory situated on the Middle Siberian Plateau. Its major rivers are the Nizhnaya Tunguska and the Podkammenaya Tunguska. The Okrug forms part of Krasnoyarsk Kray. Its agriculture consists mainly of fishing, hunting, reindeer breeding and fur farming. Its main industries are the production of graphite and Iceland spar, and food processing. It occupies a total area of 767,600 sq km. In 1990 the population of Evenk Autonomous Okrug was 25,000. Its administrative centre is at Tura town.

Head of the District Administration: ANATOLY M. YAKIMOV; tel. 2-24-02.

Chairman of the District Soviet: VALERY I. NOVOSELTSOV.

Khanty-Mansi Autonomous Okrug

Khanty-Mansi Autonomous Okrug is situated in the West Siberian plain and the Ob-Irtysh basin. It forms part of Tyumen Oblast. Its agriculture consists mainly of fishing, reindeer breeding, fur farming, hunting and vegetable production. Its industry is based on the processing of agricultural and forestry products, and the production of petroleum and natural gas. The Okrug occupies a total of 523,100 sq km. It has 11 towns and its population in 1990 numbered 1,301,000 in 1990. Its administrative centre is at Khanty-Mansiysk.

Head of the District Administration: ALEKSANDR V. FILIPENKO; tel. 2-20-27.

Chairman of the District Soviet: VALERY A. CHURILOV.

Representative of the President of the Russian Federation: (vacant); tel. 2-33-06.

Head of the District Representation in Moscow: VLADIMIR A. KHARITON; tel. (095) 347-25-26.

Komi-Permyak Autonomous Okrug

Komi-Permyak Autonomous Okrug is situated in the Urals area on the upper reaches of the Kama river. It forms part of Perm Oblast and has a border with the Komi Republic to the north. A largely forested territory, its agriculture consists mainly of grain production, animal husbandry and hunting. Its industry is based on the processing of forestry and agricultural products, and light manufacturing. It occupies an area of 32,900 sq km and its population was 160,000 in 1990. The capital is at Kudymkar.

Head of the District Administration: NIKOLAY A. POLUYANOV; tel. 2-09-03.

Chairman of the District Soviet: IVAN V. CHETIN.

Representative of the President of the Russian Federation: VYACHESLAV N. DELIDOV; tel. 2-17-17.

Head of the District Representation in Moscow: VASILY D. LUNEGOV; tel. (095) 202-37-82.

Koryak Autonomous Okrug

Koryak Autonomous Okrug comprises the northern part of the Kamchatka peninsula and the adjacent area of mainland. Chukchi district lies to the north. Its coastline lies on the Bering Sea and the Sea of Okhotsk. It forms part of Kamchatka Oblast. Its agriculture consists mainly of fishing, reindeer breeding, fur farming and hunting. Its main industries are food processing and the production of brown coal. It occupies 301,500 sq km and has five urban-type settlements. In 1990 its population was 39,000. Its capital is at Palana town.

Head of the District Administration: (vacant).

Chairman of the District: ANATOLY I. DELYANSKY.

Representative of the President of the Russian Federation: GRIGORY M. OINVID; tel. 3-20-87.

Head of the District Representation in Moscow: STANISLAV S. NIKITIN; tel. (095) 932-25-49.

Nenets Autonomous Okrug ('Nenets Republic')

On 11 March 1994 Russian President Boris Yeltsin suspended a resolution, by the District Administration, ordering a referendum to be held on the territory of the Okrug. Participants in the referendum were to vote on the status of the Okrug within the Russian Federation.

Nenets Autonomous Okrug (the self-proclaimed Nenets Republic) is situated in the north-east of European Russia. It lies on the White, Barents and Kara Seas. Its major river is the Pechora. The Okrug forms part of Archangel (Arkhangelsk) Oblast. Its agriculture consists mainly of reindeer breeding, fishing, hunting and fur farming. Its industry is based on the processing of forestry and agricultural products. Its major ports are at Naryan-Mar and Amderma. It occupies an area of 176,700 sq km. In 1990 the total population of Nenets Autonomous Okrug was 55,000. Its capital is at Naryan-Mar.

Head of the District Administration: (vacant).

Chairman of the District Soviet: BORIS F. SLEZKIN.

Representative of the President of the Russian Federation: ALEKSANDR I. VYUCHEYSKY; tel. 28-64.

Head of the District Representation in Moscow: ANATOLY A. SANDYGO; tel. (095) 202-63-74.

Taymyr (Dolgan-Nenets) Autonomous Okrug

Following President Russian President Boris Yeltsin's forcible dissolution of the Russian parliament and his advice to the federal units, on 18 October 1993 the Taimyr District Soviet voted to disband itself.

Taymyr (Dolgan-Nemets) Autonomous Okrug is situated on the Taymyr peninsula. Its major rivers are the Yenisey, the Pyasina and the Khatanga. It forms part of Krasnoyarsk Kray, like its southern neighbour, Evenk Autonomous Okrug. Its agriculture consists mainly of fishing, animal husbandry and hunting. Its main industries are ore mining and food processing. Its major ports are Dudinka, Dixon and Khatanga. It occupies a total area of 862,100 sq km and the population was 55,000 (in 1990). Its administrative centre is at Dudinka.

Head of the District Administration: GENNADY P. NEDELIN; tel. 2-11-60.

Chairman of the District Soviet: GENNADY N. MAIMAGO.

Ust-Orda Buryat Autonomous Okrug

Ust-Orda Buryat Autonomous Okrug is situated in the southern part of the Lena-Angara plateau. Its major river is the Angara. It forms part of Irkutsk Oblast and lies to the north of Irkutsk city, west of Lake Baikal. The Okrug's agriculture consists mainly of grain production and animal husbandry. Its main industries are the production of coal and gypsum and the processing of agricultural and forestry products. It occupies an area of 22,400 sq km and has four urban-type settlements. In 1990 the population was 137,000. The capital is at Ust-Ordynsky town.

Head of the District Administration: ALEKSEY N. BATAGAYEV; tel. 2-11-60.

Chairman of the District Soviet: LEONID A. KHUTANOV.

Representative of the President of the Russian Federation: PAVEL M. IMEDOYEV; tel. 2-10-41.

Head of the District Representation in Moscow: OLEG B. BATOROV; tel. (095) 202-89-39.

Yamal-Nenets Autonomous Okrug

Yamal-Nenets Autonomous Okrug is situated on the West Siberian Plain on the lower reaches of the Ob river. It lies on the Asian side of the Ural Mountains and has a deeply indented northern coastline. The Yamal-Nenets district borders three other Autonomous Okrugs (Taymyr to the east, Khanty-Mansi to the south, and Nenets in the north-west) and the Komi Republic to the west. Apart from the Ob, its other major rivers are the Nadym, the Taz and the Pur. It forms part of the Tyumen Oblast. Its agriculture consists mainly of fishing, reindeer breeding, fur farming and hunting. Its main industries are the production of natural gas and petroleum, and the processing of agricultural and forestry products. The territory of the Yamal-Nenets Autonomous Okrug occupies an area of 750,300 sq km. It has five towns and a total population (in 1990) of 495,000 inhabitants. Its administrative centre is at Salekhard.

Head of the District Administration: (vacant); tel. 26-02.

Chairman of the District Soviet: ALEKSANDR I. KUZIN.

Representative of the President of the Russian Federation: SERGEY P. YAR; tel. 35-63.

Bibliography

Aganbegyan, A. *The Challenge: Economics of Perestroika.* London, Hutchinson, 1988.

Andrew, C., and Gordievsky, O. *KGB, the Inside Story.* London, Hodder and Stoughton, 1990.

Brown, A. (Ed.). *The Soviet–East European Relationship in the Gorbachev Era.* Boulder, Colorado, Westview, 1990.

Campbell, K. M., and MacFarlane, S. N. (Eds). *Gorbachev's Third World Dilemmas.* London, Routledge, 1989.

Clarke, R. A., and Matko, D. J. I. *Soviet Economic Facts, 1917–81.* London, Macmillan, 1983.

Dawisha, K. *Eastern Europe, Gorbachev and Reform: The Great Challenge,* 2nd Edn. Cambridge, Cambridge University Press, 1988.

Dawisha, K., and Valdes, J. 'Socialist Internationalism in Eastern Europe', in *Problems of Communism,* Vol. 36, No. 2 (March/April). 1987.

Desai, P. *The Soviet Economy.* Oxford, Basil Blackwell, 1987.

Doder, D., and Branson, L. *Heretic in the Kremlin.* London, Futura, 1990.

Galbraith, J. K., and Menshikov, S. *Capitalism, Communism and Co-existence: From the Bitter Past to a Better Prospect.* Boston, Massachusetts, Houghton Mifflin Co, 1989.

Gorbachev, M. *Perestroika,* 2nd Edn. London, Fontana Collins, 1988.

Grancelli, B. *Soviet Management and Labor Relations.* Boston, Massachusetts, Unwin Hyman, 1988.

Gray, K. R. (Ed.). *Soviet Agriculture: Comparative Perspectives.* Ames, Iowa, Iowa State University Press, 1990.

Hanson, P. *Trade and Technology in Soviet–Western Relations.* London, Macmillan, 1981.

Hedlund, S. *Crisis in Soviet Agriculture.* London, Croom Helm, 1984.

Private Agriculture in the Soviet Union. London, Routledge, 1990.

Hewett, E. A. *Reforming the Soviet Economy: Equality versus Efficiency.* Washington, DC, Brookings Institution, 1989.

Holden, G. *The Warsaw Pact: Soviet Security and Bloc Politics.* Oxford, Basil Blackwell, 1989.

Hudson, G. E. (Ed.). *Soviet National Security Policy under Perestroika,* Mershon Center Series on International Security and Foreign Policy (Vol. IV). Boston, Massachusetts, Unwin Hyman, 1990.

Kittrie, N., and Volgyes, I. (Eds). *The Uncertain Future: Gorbachev's Eastern Bloc.* New York, Paragon House, 1988.

Kochan, L., and Abraham, R. *The Making of Modern Russia,* 2nd Edn. London, Penguin, 1983.

Kozlov, V. I. *The People's of the Soviet Union.* London, Hutchinson, 1988.

Laird, R. F., and Hoffman, E. P. (Eds). *Soviet Foreign Policy in a Changing World.* New York, Aldine de Gruyter, 1986.

Light, M. *The Soviet Theory of International Relations.* Brighton, Wheatsheaf, 1988.

Linden, R. H. (Ed.). *Studies in East European Foreign Policy.* New York, Praeger, 1980.

Litvin, V. *The Soviet Agro-Industrial Complex.* Boulder, Colorado, Westview, 1987.

Lynch, A. *The Soviet Study of International Relations.* Cambridge, Cambridge University Press, 1988.

McGwire, M. *Perestroika and Soviet National Security.* Washington, DC, Brookings Institution, 1991.

Malcolm, N. *Soviet Policy Perspectives on Western Europe,* Chatham House Paper. London, Routledge (for the Royal Institute of International Affairs), 1989.

Medvedev, Z. A. *Soviet Agriculture.* New York and London, Norton, 1977.

Mellor, R. E. H. *The Soviet Union and its Geographical Problems.* London, Macmillan, 1982.

Menon, R., and Nelson, D. (Eds). *Limits to Soviet Power.* Lexington, Massachusetts, Lexington Books, 1989.

Miller, J. *Mikhail Gorbachev and the End of Soviet Power.* New York, St Martin's Press, 1993.

Moskoff, W. (Ed.). *Perestroika in the Countryside: Agricultural Reform in the Gorbachev Era.* Armonk, New York, M. E. Sharpe, 1990.

Motyl, A. J. (Ed.). *The Post-Soviet Nations: Perspectives on the Demise of the USSR.* New York, Columbia University Press, 1992.

Nahaylo, B., and Swoboda, B. *Soviet Disunion: A History of the Nationalities Problem in the USSR.* London, Hamish Hamilton, 1990.

Nelson, D. N. 'Europe's Unstable East', in *Foreign Policy,* No. 82 (Spring). 1991.

de Nevers, R. 'The Soviet Union and Eastern Europe: the End of an Era', in *Adelphi Papers,* No. 249. London, Brasseys and International Institute for Strategic Studies, 1990.

Nogee, J. L., and Donaldson, R. H. (Eds). *Soviet Foreign Policy since World War II,* 3rd Edn. Oxford, Pergamon, 1988.

Nove, A. *An Economic History of the USSR,* Revised Edn. Harmondsworth, Penguin, 1982.

Pipes, R. *The Formation of the Soviet Union: Communism and Nationalism, 1917–23.* Cambridge, Massachusetts, Harvard University Press, 1964.

Remnick, D. *Lenin's Tomb: The Last Days of the Soviet Empire.* London, Viking, 1993.

Roxburgh, A. *The Second Russian Revolution.* London, BBC Books, 1991.

Ryan, M. (Ed.). *Contemporary Soviet Society: A Statistical Handbook.* Aldershot, Edward Elgar, 1990.

Saikal, A., and Maley, W. (Eds). *The Soviet Withdrawal from Afghanistan.* Cambridge, Cambridge University Press, 1989.

Sakwa, R. *Russian Politics and Society.* London, Routledge, 1993.

Smith, A. *Russia and the World Economy: Problems of Integration.* London, Routledge, 1993.

Smith, G. *The Nationalities Question in the Soviet Union.* London, Longman, 1990.

Smith, H. *The New Russians.* London, Hutchinson, 1990.

Steele, J. *Eternal Russia.* London, Faber and Faber, 1994.

Symons, L., and White, C. (Eds). *Russian Transport: An Historical and Geographical Survey.* London, G. Bell and Sons, 1975.

Terry, S. M. *Soviet Policy in Eastern Europe.* New Haven, Connecticut, Yale University Press, 1984.

Turnbull, M. *Soviet Environmental Policies and Practices: The Most Critical Investment.* Aldershot, Dartmouth, 1991.

Urban, G. R. *End of Empire: The Demise of the Soviet Union.* Washington, DC, American University Press, 1993.

Wädekin, K.-E. (Ed.). *Communist Agriculture.* London, Routledge, 1990.

White, S. *Gorbachev in Power.* Cambridge, Cambridge University Press, 1990.

White, S., Pravda, A., and Gitelman Z. (Eds). *Developments in Soviet Politics.* London, Macmillan, 1990.

White, S., di Leo, R., and Cappelli, O. (Eds). *The Soviet Transition: From Gorbachev to Yeltsin.* London, Frank Cass, 1993.

Whiting, A. S. *Siberian Development and East Asia.* Stanford, California, Stanford University Press, 1981.

SLOVAKIA

Geography

PHYSICAL FEATURES

The Slovak Republic, or Slovakia, which, together with the Czech Republic, formed Czechoslovakia between 1918 and 1922, is bordered to the west by the Czech Republic, to the north by Poland, to the east by Ukraine, to the south by Hungary and to the south-west by Austria. The country covers an area of 49,035 sq km (18,934 sq miles).

The terrain is largely mountainous, rising, in the north, to Slovakia's highest point, Gerlach (Gerlachovsky) Peak (2,655 m—8,711 ft), in the High Tatras. The High Tatras (Vysoké Tatry), on the northern border with Poland, and the Low Tatras (Nízké Tatry), in the centre and east, are the principal mountain ranges. They form the westernmost branch of the Carpathian mountain chain. The mountains are drained by numerous rivers, flowing south to the lowland areas, including the Váh, the Nitra, the Hron and the Hornád. Part of the southern border is marked by the River Danube (Dunaj). There are lowland areas in the south-west and south-east of the country, which are extensions of the Pannonian Plain and are the main areas for settlement and agriculture. More than two-fifths of Slovakia is forested, and only one-third is cultivated land.

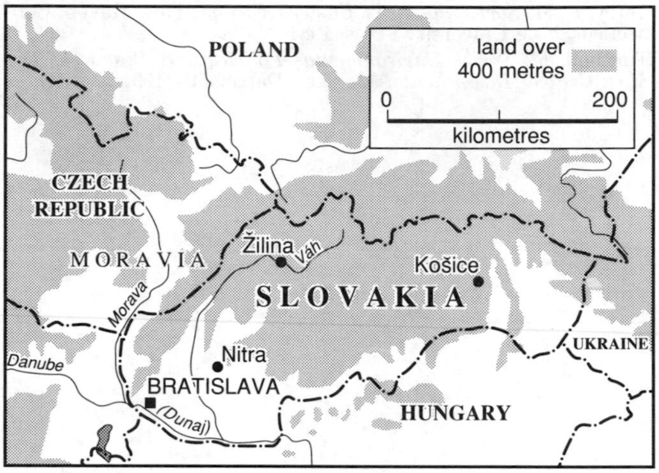

CLIMATE

The climate is of a typical continental type, with average temperatures in Bratislava varying from −0.7°C (30.7°F) in January to 21.1°C (70.0°F) in July. However, average temperatures in the mountainous centre of the country are as much as 10°C lower. Temperature inversions during the winter frequently cause pollution problems in the more populous and industrialized areas. Average annual rainfall in Bratislava is 649 mm.

POPULATION

At the census of March 1991, the total population of Slovakia was 5,274,335. Of these, 4,519,328 (85.7%) were ethnic Slovaks, 567,296 (10.8%) Hungarians, who are concentrated along the southern border with Hungary, 75,802 Roma (Gypsies) and 59,326 Czechs (including Moravians and Silesians). There were also small communities of Ruthenians and Ukrainians (30,478), Germans (5,414) and Poles (2,657). (It was believed that there was considerable underenumeration of the Roma community, many of whom claimed other nationalities, particularly Hungarian.) Slovak, a member of the Western Slavonic group of languages (and closely related to Czech), is the official language. The Hungarian (Magyar) community use their own language; there are Hungarian-language newspapers and periodicals and Hungarian-language broadcasting. The language law of 1990, which established Slovak as the official language in the Slovak Republic, over two years before formal separation, restricted official use of minority languages to areas where at least 20% of the population were members of an ethnic minority. Christianity is the major religion, the Roman Catholic Church being the largest denomination.

The capital of Slovakia is Bratislava (formerly known as Pressburg), situated in the extreme south-west of the country, on the River Danube, and only 50 km from Vienna (the capital of Austria). At the March 1991 census it had a population of 442,197. Other important towns include Košice (235,160), in the east, Nitra (89,969), in the south, Prešov (87,765), in the east, Banská Bystrica (85,030), in the centre, and Žilina (83,911), on the River Váh in the north. About 71% of the population is urbanized, living in towns of more than 5,000 inhabitants.

Chronology

5th 7th centuries: Slavic tribes migrated to central Europe from the eastern plains.

830: The Great Moravian Empire was established, eventually including Slovakia and Bohemia.

907: The Hungarians destroyed the Moravian forces at the Battle of Bratislava (Pressburg).

11th century: Slovakia was incorporated into the Kingdom of Hungary, although parts were subsequently claimed by the Kingdom of Bohemia.

1491: The Peace of Pressburg acknowledged Habsburg claims to the throne of Hungary.

1526: The Austrian Habsburgs inherited their claim to Hungary upon the death of Louis II, at the battle of Mohács. The Kingdom was partitioned between the victorious Ottomans, the principality of Transylvania and the Habsburgs, who retained control of the Slovak territories; Pressburg became the capital of Hungary, and Hungarian monarchs were crowned there for the next three centuries.

1781–85: Serfdom was abolished in both the Czech and Slovak lands.

1844: The first grammar of the Slovak language was published.

1848: There was an unsuccessful Slovak rebellion against Hungarian rule.

1861: A National Congress of Slovaks issued the Memorandum of the Slovak Nation, which demanded autonomy for Slovakia.

1867: The *Ausgleich* (Compromise) creating the Habsburg Dual Monarchy of Austria-Hungary restored full Hungarian control over Slovakia; a policy of 'magyarization' soon commenced, contributing to a high rate of emigration.

30 May 1918: The Pittsburgh Agreement, which provided for the creation of a common Czech-Slovak state, was signed between Slovak and Czech exiles.

28 October 1918: The Republic of Czechoslovakia was proclaimed (for details on Czechoslovakia, see chapter on the Czech Republic).

29 September 1938: The Munich Agreement between the United Kingdom, France, Italy and Germany permitted the cession of the Czechoslovak territories known as Sudetenland to Germany. This also caused the collapse of the Czechoslovak First Republic.

October 1938: Slovakia and Carpatho-Ruthenia (after 1945 part of the USSR—Ukraine) gained autonomy; the Hlinka Slovak National People's Party (HSNNP), under the pro-Fascist leadership of Mgr Jozef Tiso, was declared the only authorized party in Slovakia.

2 November 1938: Hungary annexed parts of southern Slovakia.

14 March 1939: The day before Nazi Germany began the occupation of the Czech Lands Adolf Hitler, the German leader, agreed to a separate Slovak state.

1941: The Tiso regime adopted a Jewish Code that enabled it to begin a policy of extermination of Jews.

29 August 1944: An uprising against HSNNP rule began in Slovakia. By the end of October it had been suppressed by German troops.

April 1945: The Government-in-Exile returned to Czechoslovakia; it agreed to some limited Slovak autonomy.

16 May 1946: In national elections the Czechoslovak Communist Party (CPCz) won 38% of the votes cast; in Slovakia, however, it won only some 30%, with the Democratic Party winning 62%.

1947: Gustáv Husák organized a Communist 'coup' in Slovakia, by accusing many members of the Democratic Party of being sympathetic to the HSNNP; Tiso was hanged.

February–June 1948: The Communists effectively seized power in the whole country and introduced a new Constitution.

1954: Husák and other prominent Slovak Communists, accused of 'Slovak nationalism', were the latest victims of the purges in the CPCz.

1960: A new Constitution formally limited Slovak autonomy, dissolving the local executive and removing legislative authority from the Slovak National Council.

January 1968: Alexander Dubček, leader of the Communist Party of Slovakia (CPS), became First Secretary of the CPCz and initiated the so-called 'Prague Spring' reforms.

August 1968: After a meeting in Bratislava the countries of the Warsaw Pact (except Romania) sent troops to invade Czechoslovakia; Dubček and other government and Party leaders were abducted.

1 January 1969: A federal system of government was introduced, despite the ending of other reforms, with the country comprising the Slovak and Czech Socialist Republics.

April 1969: Husák, rehabilitated in the early 1960s, replaced Dubček as First Secretary of the CPCz.

1975: Svoboda resigned as President and was replaced by Husák.

1 January 1977: A group of Czechoslovak dissidents published the 'Charter 77' manifesto, which demanded an end to the abuse of civil and political rights.

1987: Miloš Jakeš replaced Husák as leader of the CPCz.

1988: Towards the end of the year large anti-government demonstrations began to occur and this continued to escalate in 1989.

November 1989: Opposition activists formed an anti-government coalition known as Public Against Violence—PAV (the Czech equivalent was Civic Forum). The leadership of Civic Forum and PAV began discussions with the Communist leadership, as protests continued to increase throughout the country. At the end of the month the Federal Assembly had abolished the CPCz constitutional monopoly on power.

December 1989: Demonstrators in Prague and other cities continued. A new federal Government was announced, with a majority of non-Communist members. Dubček was elected Chairman of the Federal Assembly. Husák resigned as President and was replaced by the dissident Czech playwright Václav Havel.

April 1990: As part of a continuing process of reform and liberalization the name of the country changed to the Czech and Slovak Federative Republic.

June 1990: Elections to the Federal Assembly took place; PAV (in Slovakia) and Civic Forum (in Bohemia and Moravia) won an overall majority. In elections to the Slovak National Council, the republican legislature, PAV emerged as the largest party, with some 35% of the votes cast and 48 of the 150 seats; Vladimir Mečiar of PAV was elected premier of Slovakia.

December 1990: Constitutional changes delimited the powers of the federal, Czech and Slovak governments.

March 1991: Mečiar, the premier of the Slovak Republic, left PAV over the issue of Czech–Slovak relations and his advocacy of more autonomy. There were also large demonstrations in favour of independence; President Havel was attacked by crowds when he visited Bratislava.

April 1991: Mečiar and seven members of his cabinet were dismissed by the Presidium of the Slovak National Council, because of their defection from PAV; Jan Čarnogurský, leader of the Christain Democratic Movement (CDM), was appointed as premier instead.

June 1991: Jozef Kučerák, the Chairman of PAV, announced that PAV would become a formal political party, but it was already in the process of dissolution. Mečiar was elected Chairman of the newly-formed Movement for a Democratic Slovakia (MDS).

July 1991: The Federal Assembly approved legislation which authorized a referendum on the future of Czech–Slovak relations.

August 1991: Some 700 people were evacuated from the area between the controversial Gabčíkovo hydroelectric dam and the River Danube because of fears that the dam might break.

September 1991: A group of Slovak politicians, mostly members of the MDS and the Slovak National Party (SNP), formed the Initiative for a Sovereign Slovakia (mainly as an attempt to forestall a referendum).

5–6 June 1992: Elections to the federal and republican legislatures took place; the MDS emerged as the dominant Slovak party, winning some 37% of the votes cast and 74 seats in the Slovak National Council. The former Communists, the Party of the Democratic Left (PDL) won 29 seats, the CDM 18 and the SNP 15. The remaining 14 seats were won by a coalition of Hungarian parties; Mečiar was elected to lead an MDS-dominated Slovak Government.

17 July 1992: The Slovak National Council overwhelmingly approved a declaration of sovereignty and the dissolution of the federation came to appear inevitable.

1 September 1992: The Slovak National Council adopted a new Constitution for the Republic, which was to come into effect upon the dissolution of Czechoslovakia.

24 October 1992: Slovakia unilaterally (i.e. without the agreement of Hungary) started to divert the River Danube into a newly-constructed canal, part of the Gabčíkovo dam scheme.

November 1992: At the third attempt, and by only three votes, the Federal Assembly approved the legislation which would end the federation, despite opposition even by Slovak deputies.

1 January 1993: With the dissolution of all federal structures, the Slovak Republic became a sovereign nation, as did the Czech Republic.

February 1993: Separate Slovak and Czech currencies (both called koruna) were introduced. The parliament, the National Council of the Slovak Republic, finally elected a President for the country, Michal Kováč, deputy leader of the MDS and a former Chairman of the Czechoslovak Federal Assembly.

March 1993: Growing divisions within the Government culminated in the dismissal of Mečiar's main critic within the MDS, Milan Kňažko (who announced the formation of an opposition liberal party, the Alliance of Independent Democrats) and, later, the resignation of L'udovít Černák, leader of the SNP.

April 1993: The dispute between Slovakia and Hungary over the Gabčíkovo-Nagymaros dam scheme was referred to the International Court of Justice.

June 1993: Slovakia became a member of the Council of Europe, finalized its association agreement with the European Communities (EC—known as the European Union from November 1993) and signed a loan agreement with the International Monetary Fund.

July 1993: Border controls were introduced on the Czech–Slovak border to stem the flow of third-country immigrants.

October 1993: The MDS and SNP agreed to form a new coalition Government.

8 November 1993: President Kováč approved six of the seven new ministers proposed by Mečiar for the coalition Government, but rejected Ivan Lexa as minister responsible for privatization.

17 November 1993: Viliam Sobona, Minister of Health and a close ally of Mečiar, was forced to resign after losing a vote of confidence in the National Council.

7 December 1993: Lexa was charged with defaming President Kováč, an offence carrying a possible two-year prison sentence.

22 December 1993: The National Council passed the 1994 budget.

8 January 1994: Representatives of the ethnic-Hungarian community, at a meeting in Komarno, made proposals for the local government of the southern areas with majority Hungarian population.

28 January 1994: The National Council rejected legislation which would have allowed bilingual city names in areas with significant ethnic minorities.

February 1994: Six SNP members of the National Council, led by L'udovít Černák, left the party to form the National Democratic Party; 10 MDS members formed a new Alternative of Political Realism faction; Roman Kováč, First Deputy Prime Minister, and Jozef Moravčík, Minister of Foreign Affairs, resigned after being expelled from the MDS.

March 1994: The Mečiar Government left office after being defeated in a motion of 'no confidence' in the National Council; a new Government was formed, with Jozef Moravčík as Prime Minister, which included representatives of six former opposition parties and groupings; the holding of early elections on 30 September and 1 October 1994 was approved.

History

ANDREW RYDER

INTRODUCTION

The territory now known as Slovakia was initially settled by Illyrian, Celtic and then German tribes. Slavic tribes arrived from the east in the sixth or seventh centuries AD. In the ninth century it was part of the Great Moravian Empire, which also included Bohemia and neighbouring territories. Following the dissolution of the Great Moravian Empire, however, in the 10th century, the Czechs and Slovaks were divided, as the latter came under Hungarian rule.

Slovakia remained under Hungarian rule, in different forms, for some 1,000 years. Even when it was part of the Austrian Empire, the transport infrastructure and economy of Slovakia remained orientated towards Budapest, the leading city of the Hungarian dominated area, rather than towards Vienna, the capital of the Austrian Empire. The Czech Lands (Bohemia and Moravia), however, were orientated towards Vienna. Slovaks were heavily influenced by the Protestant ideas disseminated in Bohemia by the Hussites, but Roman Catholicism was largely restored by the Habsburg rulers, who succeeded to the Hungarian throne in 1526. There was little evidence of significant cultural development in Slovakia until the late 18th century, when a movement of national renaissance began. Slovak was not recognized as an independent language until the mid-19th century, and the first grammar was not written until 1844. However, it continued often to be treated as a dialect of Czech rather than as a language in its own right (indeed, the first Czechoslovak constitution referred to a single Czechoslovak language). In the 19th century Slovak nationalists were supported by the Austrian Habsburgs, who were attempting to limit the growing influence of the Hungarians. A Slovak legion came to the assistance of Emperor Francis Joseph I in suppressing the Hungarian revolt of 1848–49; in return the Slovaks were granted a limited amount of autonomy. In 1861 a National Congress, organized by leading Slovak intellectuals, issued a Memorandum, demanding autonomy for Slovakia. However, after the Austro-Hungarian *Ausgleich* (Compromise) of 1867, the Hungarians regained full control over Slovakia and instituted a policy of 'magyarization', which resulted in considerable emigration, in particular to the USA. While Slovakia was a mainly agricultural country with few large cities and little industry, the Czech Lands were relatively urbanized and became the leading industrial region of the former Austro-Hungarian Empire, supplying a market which stretched across central Europe. During the First World War Slovaks joined with Czechs in campaigning for an independent state, composed of the Czech Lands and Slovakia. In 1918, in the USA, the leading campaigners signed the Czech-Slovak Pittsburgh Agreement, in which the Czech and Slovak exile groups agreed to coexistence in a common, democratic state.

The Pittsburgh Agreement envisaged considerable autonomy for Slovakia, but, when Czechoslovakia's first Constitution was promulgated, in 1920, there was no provision for a proper federal system. During the existence of the First Republic (1918–38) the authorities in Prague rejected proposals to grant Slovakia genuine self-government, although, from 1928, the country was divided into four territorial-administrative areas: Bohemia, Moravia-Silesia, Slovakia and Carpatho-Ruthenia. The early years of the Czechoslovak state found both the Czech Lands and Slovakia disadvantaged. The collapse of the Austro-Hungarian Empire meant that many traditional markets for both Czech manufactured goods and Slovak agricultural products disappeared. Moreover, although the Czech Lands experienced considerable economic development between the First and Second World Wars, Slovakia remained largely undeveloped. Therefore the new Czechoslovak republic was characterized by great disparities in living standards, infrastructure and economic development between different regions, and by poor east–west transport links between the Czech and Slovak parts of the country and within Slovakia itself. Slovaks constituted 23% of the population of the new state, but produced only 12% of the national income and 8% of the total national industrial product. Moreover, the productivity of Slovak agriculture was only 60% of that in the Czech Lands, and Czech output was far greater than Slovak: Slovakia produced only 22% of the country's agricultural output. Per-head incomes in Slovakia were only 42% of the Czech average. These differences persisted throughout the first two decades of Czechoslovakia's existence.

The centrist policies of the Czechoslovak Government, dominated by Czech rather than Slovak interests, paid most attention to maintaining and safeguarding the nation's industrial base, and tended to ignore problems which were specific to Slovakia. This led, therefore, to a more radical approach on the part of the Slovaks. The main Slovak national party, the Hlinka Slovak National People's Party (HSNPP), combined elements of Fascism with a fusion of Roman Catholicism and nationalism. In October 1938, following the Munich Agreement (which permitted the cession of the Czechoslovak Sudetenland territories to Germany) and the end of the First Republic, the HSNPP declared autonomy for Slovakia and became the only authorized party there, after banning all other political groups. However, in November Hungary annexed some southern parts of Slovakia where the population was predominantly Hungarian. On 14 March 1939, the day before the German occupation of the Czech Lands, Hitler agreed to the establishment of a separate Slovak state, under the leadership of Jozef Tiso, a Slovak nationalist and Roman Catholic priest, and Slovakia became independent for the first time in its history.

The wartime Slovak state (March 1939–April 1945) was based on a combination of German and Italian Fascist principles. Any opposition to the Tiso regime was ruthlessly suppressed and the treatment of Jews, especially after the adoption of the Jewish Code in 1941, was particularly severe. Between March and October 1942 an estimated 58,000 Jews were deported to Nazi extermination camps. In August 1944, however, an armed uprising against the Fascist regime began. It lasted two months before being suppressed by German troops, which were invited into Slovakia by Tiso.

Despite the failure of the Slovak National Rising, it did provide legitimacy for Slovak exiles abroad who were opposed to Tiso. The Czechoslovak Government-in-Exile, however, was unwilling to grant genuine autonomy to the Slovaks in a post-Second World War state, and Slovakia and the Czech Lands were reunited; the Slovak territory seized by Hungary was returned to Czechoslovak control. Although economic and other disparities between Slovakia and the Czech Lands persisted, the relative differences between the two parts of the country had changed for several reasons. Ethnic Germans were expelled from the re-created Czechoslovak state and, as a result, the relative share of the Slovak population in it increased. Likewise, the loss of Carpatho-Ruthenia to the USSR (Ukraine) in 1945 had a similar effect on the balance of population. Moreover, Czech industry, controlled by Germany for six years, had not only been reorientated towards military needs, but had suffered from over-intensive use and insufficient new investment. Finally, Slovakia's distance from Germany had prompted the creation of defence industries in the country as early as the 1930s, a pattern which was reinforced by the country's ostensibly neutral status during the War. Consequently, by 1948, Slovakia had almost 28% of the country's population, and produced over 19% of the national income, over 13% of the national industrial output and almost 31% of agricultural output.

There were certain political concessions, including the devolution of some powers to the Slovak National Council and the establishment of a weak governmental structure in Slovakia, the Board of Commissioners. Even this small degree of federalization was largely negated by the seizure of power by the Communists, in Slovakia, in late 1947, and in the whole of the country, in 1948. The Communist *coup d'état* in Slovakia was led by Gustav Husák, later to be General Secretary of the Communist Party of Czechoslovakia (CPCz), on the pretext of preventing the re-emergence of supporters of the Tiso regime (Tiso himself was hanged in 1947).

In the aftermath of the Communist take-over of the country the new leadership attempted to reduce any sense of Slovak nationhood. Husák did not long remain in power in Slovakia. In 1954 he was sentenced to life imprisonment, along with four other Slovak Communists, on charges of Slovak separatism. Under the Communist regime expressions of Slovak nationalism were severely suppressed, and any formal power that Slovak national institutions maintained was nullified by the highly centralized structure of the CPCz.

It was not until the 1960s, with the appointment of Alexander Dubček (an ethnic Slovak) as leader of the Communist Party of Slovakia (CPS) and the beginning of the reform movement, that the issue of Slovak autonomy re-emerged in public debate. In 1968 the Government approved plans for the creation of a federal system of two equal republics. Despite the Soviet invasion, in August, the new federal system was introduced on 1 January 1969. Slovakia became the Slovak Socialist Republic, with a Slovak government and a National Council with wide constitutional powers. However, the reimposition of centralized Communist rule, under the leadership of Husák, left these new institutions largely powerless.

The Communist Government pursued a policy of industrializing the entire country, and paid special attention to Slovakia. As had been the case during the 1930s, the drive to industrialize Slovakia was also prompted by strategic considerations. Slovakia's eastern border was, at that time, with the USSR; furthermore, the fraternal socialist (Communist) states of Poland and Hungary virtually surrounded the territory, which was a comfortable distance away from the border with the Federal Republic of Germany, the main focus of interest for the North Atlantic Treaty Organisation (NATO). Investment and production in the defence industry increased sharply, as did investment in those industries which relied on imports from the USSR, such as the steel industry, which used iron ore from Ukraine. Moreover, the state made a concerted effort to distribute employment and production in such a way as to reflect the relative proportions of population between the Czech and Slovak parts of Czechoslovakia, and also concentrated on eliminating differences in wages and living standards. Although disparities persisted, they were relatively slight: by 1989, the Slovak Republic contained 34% of the Federation's population, produced 30.4% of its national income, 33% of its gross agricultural output and almost 30% of gross industrial output. Labour productivity increased from 62% percent of the Czech average to 96%, and the average wage increased to 99.1% of the Czech average. Within Slovakia, the share of industry in total production rose from 43% in 1948 to over 68% in 1989, and the share of agriculture dropped from 37% to 13%.

POST-COMMUNIST CZECHOSLOVAKIA

With the Velvet Revolution of 1989, Slovaks began to demand real changes in their status within the federation. It was at this time that political and economic differences between the two Republics again became evident. Policies at the federal level were adopted on economic and moral grounds, regardless of their regional impacts, and before a consensus had been reached on how to mitigate their effects. These effects were felt more strongly, and more rapidly, in Slovakia than in the Czech Republic, and the free-market policies espoused by the new Federation were seen as being particularly harmful to the Slovak economy. In November 1989 a coalition of independent groups, called Public Against Violence (PAV), was formed in opposition to the Communist regime. (PAV was the Slovak counterpart to, and ally of, the Czech Civic Forum.) It retained a wide degree of support at the first free elections to be held since 1946, both to the Federal Assembly and to the Czech and Slovak National Councils, which took place on 8 and 9 June 1990. PAV won 34.5% of the vote and took 48 of the 150 seats in the Slovak National Council. Vladimír Mečiar, the leader of PAV, was elected Prime Minister of the Slovak Republic. At the federal level PAV, in alliance with its Czech partner, Civic Forum, was also the dominant party.

However, as its name implies, PAV was less a political party than a loose coalition of reformers and, by 1991, the coalition had split apart under the strain of the difficult relations between the Czech and Slovak Republics. Mečiar himself was forced to resign over this issue, and founded his own party, the Movement for a Democratic Slovakia (MDS). Meanwhile, Ján Čarnogurský of the Christian Democratic Movement, the second largest party in the Slovak National Council, became Prime Minister. Mečiar and the MDS became a rallying point for those in Slovakia who favoured outright independence. Further general elections at federal and republican levels were held in June 1992. Not only did the MDS establish itself as the dominant party in the Slovak National Council, where it won 74 of the 150 seats (but only 37% of votes cast), but it also won a sizeable block of seats, 57, in the 300-member Federal Assembly, where it was second only to the Civic Democratic Party, the principal party to emerge from the Czech Civic Forum, with 85 seats. In the Slovak National Council the principal advocate of a continued federation, the Christian Democratic Movement, gained only 18 seats. Mečiar once again became Prime Minister in Slovakia, and relentlessly moved the Republic towards independence. On 17 July the Slovak National Council approved a declaration of Slovak sovereignty by an overwhelming majority. Although the Civic Democratic Party and the MDS did agree to form a new federal government in late July, its objective was merely to supervise the dissolution of Czechoslovakia by the end of the year, after Czech politicians realized that Slovak opposition would curtail or even block their economic reform programme. Mečiar favoured a continuation of government intervention in the economy, and Slovaks stood to suffer economically far more than their Czech neighbours, with unemployment already three times higher, at 12%, in Slovakia than in the Czech Republic.

INDEPENDENT SLOVAKIA

During the following months the method of enabling the separation of the two Republics was discussed and debated, both in the Federal Assembly and in the National Councils. The new Slovak Constitution was adopted, with overwhelming support in the Slovak National Council, on 1 September 1992. However, there was surprising resistance in the Federal Assembly to adoption of legislation allowing the dissolution of Czechoslovakia. The suggestion is that many Slovak politicians, including some leading MDS members, had been seeking a more decentralized federation, but were eventually left with no alternative but a complete division of the Republics, largely because Czech politicians did not wish Slovakia to be able to interfere with their economic reform programme. It was only in late November, at the third attempt and by the very narrow margin of three votes, that the Federal Assembly finally approved the necessary legislation. During all of this period, opinion polls never indicated that there was majority public support for the dissolution of the federation.

One technical requirement was the division of federal assets and liabilities, and the armed forces, between the Czech and Slovak Republics. Initially it was agreed that some federal property would continue to be shared by the two Republics, and also that the Czechoslovak currency, the koruna (crown), would remain, at least for the first six months of independence. However, in practice there was some urgency in the setting up of separate national institutions in Slovakia, and, in February 1993, separate currencies were established, prompted by an outflow of convertible ('hard') currency from Slovakia. Slovakia experienced problems in finding sufficient numbers of appropriately-skilled personnel to fill its enlarged governmental offices, and to staff its own diplomatic corps.

The existing MDS-dominated Government remained in place, and the Slovak National Council became the unicameral legislature, with the new official title of the National Council of the Slovak Republic. The President was to be elected by the National Council to serve a five-year term of office. It had been anticipated that the veteran politician and 1960s' Communist reformer, Alexander Dubček, would be elected as Slovakia's first President. However, he died in November 1992 as the result of injuries received in an automobile accident. In two rounds of voting in January 1993 none of the four presidential candidates, one from each of the leading parties, obtained the necessary 60% of votes cast. In mid-February Michal Kováč, Deputy Chairman of the MDS, was presented to the National Council as the sole candidate and was duly appointed President.

Mečiar had attempted to broaden his support in parliament and within the country at large by bringing the leader of the Slovak National Party, L'udovít Černák, into his Government. However, the early months of independence were marked by political in-fighting, not only between parties (Černák resigned as Minister of the Economy over the appointment of a former Communist as minister responsible for defence), but also within the MDS. In March 1993 the MDS member Milan Kňažko was obliged to resign his position as Deputy Prime Minister and Minister for Foreign Affairs, after unsuccessfully standing for the leadership of the party against Mečiar; he, and seven other members of the National Council, left the MDS and announced their intention to form a rival party, the Alliance of Independent Democrats. His previous outspoken criticism of Mečiar had included urging MDS members not to vote for the party's own candidate in the earlier rounds of presidential voting. Kňažko was also a leading advocate of Westernization, whereas Mečiar at this stage favoured preserving an eastwards orientation towards Ukraine and Russia. Slovaks were generally less inclined to exclude former Communists from official positions than their counterparts in the Czech Republic.

The resignation of Kňažko and his allies weakened the Government's position in parliament. From the middle of the year onwards Mečiar embarked on a series of protracted attempts to construct a new coalition government with the Slovak National Party to consolidate his position, but did not finally achieve this objective until November. The new coalition was founded more on the two parties' common fear of defeat at the hand of the former Communists, the PDL, should the calling of early elections be forced, rather than any close harmony between their policies. Even then Mečiar's attempts to nominate a close ally, Ivan Lexa, as Minister of Privatization, led to him becoming embroiled in a constitutional struggle with the President, Michal Kováč, who refused to ratify Lexa's nomination. Lexa subsequently came under investigation by the state prosecutor for allegedly addressing the President in an irreverent manner.

By February 1994 Mečiar's Government had again lost majority support in the National Council, with only part of the SNP giving him support. The party split later in the month, with L'udovít Černák forming a new party, the National Democratic Party (whose members included six of the SNP's 14 National Council members); Ján Slota became leader of the SNP. There was also a further round of defections from the MDS when several members formed a grouping known as the Alternative of Political Realism. Two of the most prominent ministers, Jozef Moravčík (Minister of Foreign Affairs) and Roman Kováč (First Deputy Prime Minister) submitted their resignations. These new factions, along with the Alliance of Democrats of Slovakia formed by Milan Kňažko, entered into negotations to form a moderate party capable of replacing the MDS-SNP coalition, which they accused of becoming increasingly authoritarian and ultra-nationalist. Meanwhile Mečiar launched a petition to enable a referendum to be held, with the object of authorizing the holding of early elections, on the grounds that the members of the National Council who had subsequently left the parties which they were elected for no longer had a mandate.

Amid increasingly bitter relations between Mečiar and President Kováč, a motion of 'no confidence' was tabled against the Government. The motion was voted upon on 12 March 1994, and resulted in defeat for Mečiar's Government, which was duly dismissed two days later. President Kováč invited Jozef Moravčik to form a new Government, and a six-party coalition was hastily agreed. It was made clear that the coalition, which included former Communists from the PDL and right-wing Christian Democrats as well as members from the parties formed by exiled MDS politicians, was intended as no more than an interim arrangement to govern the country until early elections could be held. The new Government's first act was to approve the holding of early elections on 30 September and 1 October 1994.

SLOVAK-HUNGARIAN RELATIONS

There are two subjects of serious dispute between Slovakia and Hungary: the construction of the Gabčíkovo dam on the River Danube border between the two countries, and the treatment of Slovakia's Hungarian minority. Although Hungary had been a joint partner in the Danube dam project, since its inception in the late 1950s, and was a signatory to contract with Czechoslovakia in 1977, it withdrew from the scheme in 1989. The Hungarian objections to the project were largely environmental, but an additional factor was the destruction of ethnic Hungarian villages in southern Slovakia by the canalization of the Danube. In 1989 the Communist Czechoslovak Government vowed to continue with the project alone, insisting that too much money had already been spent. Although after the fall of Communism the Federal Government had begun to reassess the project, with independence imminent, Slovakia proceeded unilaterally to divert the Danube's water into the newly-constructed canal in October 1992. Slovakia claimed that the advantages of a new source of electricity, which could replace the heavy dependence on polluting thermal power stations and dangerous nuclear reactors, and more reliable river-freight access to the Rhine-Main-Danube network, were essential for its economic future. The issue was referred to the International Court of Justice (based in The Hague, Netherlands) in April 1993 but, as no judgment would be made for several years, the issue continued to be a subject of dispute. Meanwhile, Hungary started to dismantle its Nagymaros dam, completed in 1988 as part of the project.

In January 1994 representatives of the Hungarian community in southern Slovakia, meeting in Komarno, made proposals for the future of the local government of areas which had ethnic-Hungarian majorities. Their preferred options were for the creation of either one or three new administrative units, covering an area running from just south of Bratislava along the Hungarian border to eastern Slovakia, in which the ethnic Hungarian population would average about 60%. These proposals were counter to the Slovakian Government's intentions to divide the entire country into four administrative regions with their borders running from north to south, thus effectively splitting the ethnic Hungarian population, and leaving them as a minority in each region. The meeting also demanded the right to use the Hungarian language in official matters: a particularly virulent dispute had arisen over the removal of bilingual signs for town names in the summer of 1993, and over the state's insistence that female Hungarian names should carry the Slavic suffix '-ova'. The issue of the Hungarian minority threatened to prevent Slovakia's admittance to the Council of Europe. Hungary only removed its objection to Slovakia's membership when the Council of Europe recommended to Slovakia, in June 1993, that it should introduce legislation improving conditions for the ethnic minorities. However, by early 1994 this legislation had still not been introduced. The Slovaks' antipathy towards the Hungarian minority dates to their 1,000-year domination by Hungary, which only ended in 1918, and, more recently, to the seizure of southern Slovakia by Hungary in 1938. There were fears, heightened by some statements from Hungarian politicians, that Hungary had not given up hopes of expanding its boundaries. Although Hungary had signed a treaty recognizing the inviolability of its boundaries with Ukraine, it had notably failed to do so with Slovakia.

FOREIGN POLICY

Early post-independence relations with the Czech Republic were dictated by the aftermath of the division of the previous Czechoslovak state's assets. As the Czechs retained control of certain pivotal assets, such as the state airline and travel agency, the Slovaks claimed that they were entitled to some form of compensation. Furthermore, Slovaks were initially prevented from taking up the shares which they had bought in Czech companies privatized during 1992. In July 1993 border controls were introduced on the Czech–Slovak border, in a development triggered by the increased movement of immigrants around central and eastern Europe, particularly of those hoping to reach and settle in Germany. However, an agreement ensured that restrictions on movement between the two countries would not apply to nationals of the Czech Republic and Slovakia.

Slovakia is a member of the Visegrad Group, along with the Czech Republic, Hungary and Poland. In the early months of independence it appeared that Mečiar still saw Slovakia's foreign policy orientation in terms of Russia and the east. However, by the middle of 1993 leading government officials were unanimous in stressing, repeatedly, that Slovakia saw its future as a member of the EC and NATO. Nevertheless, Slovakia wished the Visegrad Group to become a more permanent structure, whereas the other members, particularly the Czech Republic, were more intent on pursuing their integration with Western European organizations as soon as possible. In June 1993 Slovakia finalized its association agreement with the EC and joined the Council of Europe, as well as signing an agreement on a loan with the International Monetary Fund (IMF).

The Economy

ANDREW RYDER

INTRODUCTION

Before independence, not only was Slovakia characterized by a standard of living lower than that in the Czech Republic, but also by higher unemployment and inflation. Furthermore, the affects of the economic reform programme were sharper on the Slovak economy than on that of the Czech Republic. In 1990 prices and the rate of inflation in the Czech and Slovak Republics were virtually the same, but in 1991 Slovak inflation accelerated, and the general price index was four points ahead of the Czech index. Higher inflation was initially expected to persist throughout 1992, but in fact, inflation turned out to be lower than that in the Czech Lands, reaching 10.1%, one point lower than the Czech rate. Inflation rose only modestly in the first few months of 1993, reaching an annual rate of 13.8% in May. However, the devaluation of the Slovak koruna by 10% was expected to contribute at least an additional 5% to the inflation rate by the end of the year. National income also contracted, falling by an estimated 36% by the end of 1992.

At the time of separation, Slovakia agreed to assume responsibility for US $2,600m. dollars of Czechoslovakia's $9,500m. debt, and agreed to adhere to a Free Trade Zone with its partners in the Visegrad Group, the Czech Republic, Hungary and Poland, which came into effect at the beginning of March 1993. However, separation failed to clarify the long-term economic relations between the two Republics. Moreover, it imposed new costs on the country, such as those involved in setting up diplomatic representation abroad, new ministries and state bureaux, customs bureaux and armed forces, and other parts of the state administration.

At the time of its occurrence, the separation of the two Republics was hailed as a 'velvet divorce', and public statements suggested that they would continue to maintain close economic and political relations. However, the plan that the two new countries should continue to use a common currency for at least six months proved short lived. Fears that a devaluation in Slovakia would cause the destabilization of the Czechoslovak crown (koruna) led to the Czech Government withdrawing from the currency agreement within six weeks of the separation. Each country then issued new banknotes, and stamped old banknotes with a national symbol which made it possible to distinguish Czech from Slovak crowns. By the middle of the year the process of minting new coins had also started although, for the time being, coins from the former Federation remained legal tender in both countries. Almost immediately, there was pressure to devalue the Slovak crown, but central bankers insisted on maintaining parity with the Czech crown until July 1993. Even so, Czech currency traders continued heavily to discount the Slovak crown in commercial transactions. Inflation accelerated, owing in part to the imposition of value added tax (VAT), but also owing to the need to eliminate subsidies. Rail fares, the costs of transporting goods by train, bus fares and telephone costs all increased.

Although the economies of the two Republics were highly interdependent, the system of payments between enterprises in different Republics was thrown into confusion by the creation of separate currencies. This, in turn, affected the eagerly anticipated privatization programme, which had started before the dissolution of the Federation. At the beginning of 1993 Slovak commercial banks owed 24,700m. koruny to the successor to the Central Bank of the federal republic, an amount equal to the former subsidy paid by the Czechs to the Slovaks. By early March Slovak firms owed 16,800m. koruny to the Czech Republic. Moreover, there was still debate over the proper division of federal assets. Although the Slovaks maintained their level of repayments, the Czech Government decided to apply pressure to the Slovak Government. During the first round of privatization carried by the Federal Government in 1992, Slovak investment in Czech firms had considerably exceeded that of Czechs in Slovak firms, and the Czech Government refused to distribute vouchers for Czech firms to Slovak citizens.

Talk of a customs union also proved to have no foundation: shortly before the separation of the two countries took place, customs posts appeared at 18 crossings along the new border. Telephone calls between the Czech and Slovak Republics, formerly charged at a domestic rate, were now charged at an international one, and quintupled in price. Inter-republican traders were forced to go through complicated VAT payment procedures, money clearing procedures between the two countries were found to take up to two months, and banking relations were strained.

Even before the dissolution of Czechoslovakia trade between the two Republics had dropped sharply. The Czech Government estimated that in 1992 Czech exports to Slovakia had contracted by 20%, and exports from Slovakia to the Czech Republic had dropped by 17%. During the first few months of 1993 inter-republic trade contracted still more sharply—some estimated by up to 60% compared with 1992. This worsened an already difficult economic situation. The shift to world market prices for fuel and raw materials, and the collapse of traditional markets in Eastern Europe and the former USSR affected the balance of trade, and hampered the performance of the manufacturing sector and exporters in general. Gross domestic product (GDP) within the Republic dropped steadily after 1990, and although the rate of decline was expected to become slower, continued contraction of GDP seemed likely until the end of 1994. Rates of decline were 2.5% in 1990, 15.8% in 1991, 8.3% in 1992, and were expected to be at least 5% in 1993 and 2% in 1994. Industrial output also dropped sharply, by over 25% during 1990–91, and by an estimated 12.9% in 1992. Continued decline was expected, by up to 8% in 1993, and 3% in 1994.

AGRICULTURE

Agriculture, like climate, is shaped by relief. The country's farming regions can be divided into four east–west zones which follow the relief from north to south. These are the warm southern plains, which are suitable for the cultivation of maize and grapes for wine; a cooler zone, which, with some interruptions, extends across the entire country and in which wheat, barley and sugar beets are grown; a slightly larger belt suitable for growing rye, oats and potatoes; and a mountain region, which dominates the central part of the country, covering about one-quarter of the total area. This last region is of limited agricultural value, and is used mainly for grazing. In total, 51% of the area of the country is used for farming, and just over 40% of the territory is covered by forests.

Leading cereal crops include wheat, barley, maize and fodder, although smaller amounts of rye, oats and barley are grown. Other major crops include sunflowers, rape, sugar beets, strawberries, grapes for wine and poppy seeds. Fruits and vegetables are also important, and include celery, tomatoes, peppers, cucumbers, melons, parsley and garlic.

Agricultural output has also declined in the early 1990s, by 11.9% in 1992, reflecting a decline of 11.7% in crop production and 12.1% in animal farming. Cereal production fell by 13% in 1992 and, with a reduction in the area sown in 1993, output was likely to fall again. The entire sector is plagued by shortages of investment and of essential equipment; in addition, agricultural subsidies have been reduced by over 40%. When inflation is taken into account, subsidies have been reduced by over one-half, and agricultural incomes have dropped sharply in real terms. To some extent this represented a much needed reform in the sector. The Communist Government had pursued a policy of self-sufficiency which often encouraged the production of food in economically unsuitable districts. Not only were massive subsidies required to make this possible, but investment was also frequently diverted away from other activities which might have been more productive. Long-term plans call for the privatization of agriculture, which at independence was almost entirely collectivized or organized in co-operatives. In 1990 14.65% of the labour force was engaged in agriculture. Employment in the sector was expected to contract sharply, adding further to Slovakia's unemployment problem.

INDUSTRY

Slovakia had a narrower industrial base than the Czech Lands, and much of its industrial capacity was concentrated in large and unwieldy enterprises which employed many thousands of employees. Companies employing 500 or more people accounted for 62% of the industrial labour force. Moreover, within Czechoslovakia and the Council for Mutual Economic Assistance (CMEA or Comecon) region, the Republic had specialized in armaments, electrical goods, and quality steel. Within the former federation, Slovakia was the only producer of refrigerators, freezers, colour televisions, and motorcycles with engines under 100 cc. Not only did these industries require considerable hidden subsidies for energy, raw materials and transport, but they often relied on obsolete technology. Heavy industry consumed 60% of Slovakia's electricity, and 60% of this consumption was accounted for by just 20 large industrial enterprises. Two, a steel works at Košice, and an aluminium works at Žiar nad Hronom, each consumed almost 10% of total electricity output.

There are also some positive aspects to the post-independence Slovak economy. Despite the country's financial difficulties, a growing number of companies have opened up branch or representative offices in Bratislava, rather than serving Slovakia from Prague, as had been the case in the past. Some major investments also took place after independence, including one by Nestlé (of Switzerland) in the food industry, one by Reemtsma Cigarettenfabrik in the tobacco industry, and an investment by Siemens (of Germany) to build motors for small machines. A cable telecommunications system was to be built in Bratislava, and the French firm Matra also announced plans to build an underground railway system in the capital. In addition to the privatization of large firms through the voucher scheme, the Slovak Republic sponsored the privatization of small-scale firms, which were often sold to employees who worked in them as well as to outside buyers. By mid-1992 almost 10,000 small shops and enterprises had been privatized, and the number was expected eventually to reach 40,000. In addition, 10,000 individuals were listed on the Republic's private enterprise register, and the country had over 200,000 more unregistered small-scale entrepreneurs. Moreover, companies with less than 75 employees showed considerable growth during 1992, and small firms in the construction sector, with more than 25 employees, increased production by almost 16%. Although the state still owned 91% of industry at the end of 1992, the private sector was growing rapidly and, by the start of 1993, was responsible for almost 21% of the national income, compared to less than 0.5% in 1989. However, progress towards further privatization was very slow during 1993, partly owing to the lack of foreign investment, although a succession of political arguments over the appointment of a minister responsible for privatization contributed to the problems.

Slovakia had about one-half of the petroleum-refining capacity of the former Czechoslovakia, and is crossed by petroleum and gas pipelines which were supplied by the former USSR. A transit agreement was made to supply the Czech Republic with 8,000m. cu m of natural gas, and plans have been announced to link the pipeline system directly with Western European networks. Recently a new natural-gas field has been discovered in the eastern part of the country, which is expected to produce between 200m. and 250m. cu m of gas annually, doubling the country's previous output. Production was expected to start in 1994.

EXTERNAL TRADE

Trade with other countries has also been adversely affected. Shortages of hard currency led to changes in foreign-exchange laws. Companies importing goods with a value of over US $30,000 were unable to receive hard currency until the goods had cleared customs, VAT had been paid and the goods had been in the country for over three months. For imports valued at less than $30,000, importers received advances of only 15% of the hard-currency value. As a result, Slovak companies have been forced to operate on credit, which has both compromised the security of the Slovak crown, and affected the perception of their credit-worthiness.

Within the Czechoslovak federation, the Slovak economy was much more reliant on exports to the Czech Republic than vice versa, and the Slovak economy was also more reliant on exports to other countries within the socialist bloc. Before the dissolution of the Federation, sales to the Czech Lands accounted for almost 27% of all Slovak goods sold. For the Czech Republic the corresponding figure was only 11.5%. Overall, the Slovak economy was also more dependent on imports than was the Czech economy, and a substantially higher proportion of its imports came from the USSR and other socialist countries than did those to the Czech Republic. Imports of fuel were the largest single item, accounting for 43% of all imports for production use. This is because the Republic has virtually no domestic sources of fuel, and relies on imports from the Czech Lands or from the former USSR. The collapse of the socialist system has left Slovakia disadvantaged. Fuel prices have increased sharply, and this has had repercussions throughout the economy, increasing the cost of transport and manufacturing. It was evident that the future existence of some of the Republic's main employers (and main consumers of energy) were directly threatened by federal free-market policies.

Although the Czech Republic remains Slovakia's principal trade partner, accounting for 48.5% of Slovak exports in 1992, there were fears that trade between the two Republics would decline following independence. By 1992 Slovakia's other trading patterns had already become orientated towards Western Europe rather than the former Communist bloc; 21.4% of Slovak exports went to EC countries and a further 6.5% to other developed Western countries, compared to 8.5% to the former USSR and 8.6% to other Eastern European nations (excluding the Czech Republic).

ECONOMIC POLICY AND UNEMPLOYMENT

In 1993 and 1994 the Government was aiming to restrict its budget deficit to 5% of GDP (equivalent to about 16,000m. koruny), which was the limit set by the International Monetary Fund (IMF). On 1 January 1993 a new tax system was introduced in Slovakia, as it also was in the Czech Republic. A value added tax (VAT) was introduced, at 23% for most goods and 5% for certain services (these levels were increased to 25% and 6% respectively in July). There are also personal and corporate income taxes, and a social-security tax.

Meanwhile, although unemployment had declined from an earlier high of over 12.7% in early 1992, to just over 10% by the end of the year, it increased again in 1993, reaching 14% by the end of the year. In some areas, particularly in southern regions where there was a large ethnic-Hungarian population, levels of unemployment surpassed 20%. To some extent there appears to be a seasonal trend of variation in unemployment, which has not yet been incorporated into statistical reports. Nevertheless, Slovakia's unemployment rate was not high compared to that of several of its post-Communist neighbours (although the contrast with the Czech Republic was admittedly stark), and even to some Western European economies. However, there were fears that the general level of unemployment could rise as high as 20%, and, in October 1994, the Government accepted in its budget that unemployment would rise to 17% during 1994. The problems of unemployment are not only caused by lay-offs, but also by the large number of newcomers entering the labour force who are unable to find jobs in traditional sectors. Moreover, government representatives have argued that figures may have been artificially inflated owing to the promise of unemployment benefits, enticing many who were not formerly part of the labour force to register as unemployed. Between 1990 and 1991 the labour force increased from 2,382,800 individuals to 2,465,500, an unusually high increase. The normal rate of increase is between 5,000 and 10,000 annually.

In the immediate period after independence economic policy appeared to be orientated towards limiting the growth of unemployment by protecting those large firms which were leading employers in their districts. These include the steel works at Košice, and an aluminium works at Žiar nad Hronom, as well as several large chemical works and other large enterprises. However, it would only be possible for this policy to be maintained in the short term. Protection requires subsidies, and attempts to find new export markets have been hindered by protectionism among potential trading partners. This is particularly true of the European Community (EC—known as the European Union from November 1993) and the steel industry. Therefore, additional efforts have been made to attract joint ventures to regions which are heavily dependent on a single industry, and to attract new capital to help modernize and streamline production.

INVESTMENT

Between 1990 and 1992 Slovakia received only 12.8% of the total of US $1,801m. foreign investment in Czechoslovakia. As the country moved towards independence, foreign investment dropped sharply. It was hoped that independence would change this situation, but the banking and foreign-exchange problems faced by the new country initially had an inhibiting effect on investment.

It rapidly became evident that foreign exchange requirements were having an adverse effect on trade and investment. Plans were therefore announced to grant tax 'holidays' for new foreign firms until the end of the first year in which they showed a profit. Joint ventures which had over 30% foreign ownership were to receive an extra two years' tax holiday, and those firms which established operations in the 17 most depressed districts, and with a pay-roll of at least 75 employees, were also to obtain an extra two years' tax holiday.

PROSPECTS

The immediate outlook for the Slovak economy was not encouraging. In the eyes of Western investors, the country has been overshadowed by the higher profile and relative successes of the privatization programme of the Czech Republic. The traditional industrial strengths of Slovakia were in the heavy-industry and defence sectors. Some estimates indicated that production capacity in the latter had fallen by as much as 90% since 1989, and was unlikely to recover significantly. The transition to a modern market and service economy was, therefore, likely to be a lengthy and painful procedure.

Statistical Survey

Source: Statistical Office of the Slovak Republic, Miletičova 3, 824 67 Bratislava; tel. (7) 201-8111; fax (7) 214-601.

Area and Population

AREA, POPULATION AND DENSITY

Area (sq km)	49,035*
Population (census results)	
3 March 1991	
Males	2,574,061
Females	2,700,274
Total	5,274,335
Population (official estimates at 31 December)	
1989	5,287,663
1990	5,310,711
1991	5,289,608
Density (per sq km) at 31 December 1991	107.9

* 18,932.4 sq miles.

POPULATION BY NATIONALITY
(census result, 3 March 1991)

	'000	%
Slovak	4,519,328	85.69
Hungarian	567,296	10.75
Gypsy	75,802	1.44
Czech, Moravian, Silesian	59,326	1.12
Ruthenian and Ukrainian	30,478	0.58
German	5,414	0.10
Polish	2,657	0.05
Russian	1,391	0.03
Others (incl. undeclared)	12,643	0.24
Total	5,274,335	100.00

DISTRICTS

	Area (sq km)	Population (31 Dec. 1990)	Density (per sq km)
Western Slovakia	14,492	1,730,786	119
Central Slovakia	17,982	1,622,380	90
Eastern Slovakia	16,193	1,512,506	93
Bratislava (city)	368	444,482	1,208
Total	49,035	5,310,154*	108

* Revised official estimate 5,310,711.

PRINCIPAL TOWNS
(census result, 3 March 1991)

Bratislava (capital)	442,197	Trnava	71,783
Košice	235,160	Martin	58,393
Nitra	89,969	Trenčín	56,828
Prešov	87,765	Prievidza	53,424
Banská Bystrica	85,030	Poprad	52,914
Žilina	83,911		

BIRTHS, MARRIAGES AND DEATHS

	Registered live births		Registered marriages		Registered deaths	
	Number	Rate (per 1,000)	Number	Rate (per 1,000)	Number	Rate (per 1,000)
1989	80,116	15.2	36,525	6.9	53,902	10.2
1990	79,989	15.1	40,435	7.6	54,619	10.3
1991	78,570	14.9	32,714	6.2	54,621	10.4

EMPLOYMENT (at 31 December)*

	1989†	1990	1991
Activities of the material sphere	1,845,510	1,793,565	1,527,306
Agriculture	304,081	294,390	235,942
Forestry	40,806	32,125	35,847
Industry‡	836,169	812,634	691,609
Water works and supply	16,361	16,047	15,269
Construction	258,604	251,461	217,771
Trade	229,857	233,044	184,181
Material and technical supplies	16,125	14,828	11,853
Freight transport	80,755	79,478	77,697
Communications	15,497	16,274	15,948
Activities of the non-material sphere	652,873	665,050	624,278
Trade and technical services	20,555	20,089	46,118
Passenger transport	49,641	48,966	47,883
Communications	15,497	16,273	15,949
Finance and insurance	9,484	11,179	15,100
Education	172,347	172,737	159,366
Culture	35,732	34,551	20,069
Science, research and development	60,079	48,640	36,351
Public health and social care	133,553	135,400	128,734
Administration and justice	35,836	49,053	56,531
Accommodation, travel and communal services	68,373	82,470	54,660
Total	2,498,383	2,458,615	2,151,584

* Figures exclude women on maternity leave (annual averages): 124,886 in 1989; 137,881 in 1990; 152,568 in 1991.
† Annual averages.
‡ Principally mining, manufacturing, electricity and gas.

Agriculture

PRINCIPAL CROPS ('000 metric tons)

	1989	1990	1991
Wheat	2,266	2,083	2,124
Barley	936	914	960
Maize	825	370	711
Rye	151	178	131
Oats	50	47	44
Potatoes	745	779	669
Dry peas	75	73	96
Sunflower seed	64	56	101
Rapeseed	73	76	97
Cabbages	142	124	133
Tomatoes	69	69	96
Peppers	48	37	41
Onions	61	54	53
Carrots	75	66	62
Grapes	115	140	119
Sugar beet	1,876	1,581	1,501
Apples	125	82	96
Tobacco (leaves)	5	5	5
Flax fibre	16	12	2

LIVESTOCK ('000 head at end of year)

	1989	1990	1991
Cattle	1,623	1,563	1,397
Pigs	2,708	2,521	2,428
Sheep	621	600	531
Goats	9	10	16
Horses	15	14	13

LIVESTOCK PRODUCTS
('000 metric tons, unless otherwise indicated)

	1989	1990	1991
Beef and veal*	211.2	212.6	207.9
Mutton, lamb and goats' meat*	12.8	10.1	8.9
Pig meat*	382.0	375.6	328.4
Poultry meat*	111.3	116.4	98.7
Cows' milk (million litres)	1,995	1,920	1,566
Butter†	n.a.	38.9	29.0
Cheese†	n.a.	55.5	33.5
Eggs (million)	1,985	1,983	1,931
Wool	3.0	3.0	1.3

* Slaughter weight. † Factory production only.

Forestry

ROUNDWOOD REMOVALS ('000 cubic metres)

	1989	1990	1991
Production	5,579	5,277	4,399
Deliveries	5,575	5,361	4,339
Industrial	5,163	4,880	3,834
Fuel wood	412	481	505

SAWNWOOD PRODUCTION ('000 cubic metres)

	1989	1990	1991
Coniferous (soft wood)	866	876	641
Broadleaved (hard wood)	519	395	343

Mining

('000 metric tons, unless otherwise indicated)

	1989	1990	1991
Brown coal	3,893	3,456	2,810
Lignite	1,376	1,310	1,338
Iron ore (gross weight)	1,674	1,728	1,627
Crude petroleum	n.a.	73	72
Salt (refined)	n.a.	50	54
Magnesite (crude)	n.a.	2,704	1,553
Antimony concentrate (metric tons)*	n.a.	2,256	—
Copper concentrates (metric tons)*	15,363	13,477	11,313
Lead concentrates (metric tons)*	3,124	3,853	4,634
Mercury (metric tons)	129	124	75
Zinc concentrates (metric tons)*	4,369	5,164	6,851

* Figures refer to the metal content of ores and concentrates.

Industry

SELECTED PRODUCTS
('000 metric tons, unless otherwise indicated)

	1990	1991
Wheat flour	374	333
Refined sugar	165.5	189.0
Beer ('000 hectolitres)	3,988	3,387
Cigarettes (million)	8,589	8,721
Cotton yarn (metric tons)	27,929	18,931
Cotton fabrics ('000 metres)	93,338	62,335
Woollen fabrics ('000 metres)	12,709	8,379
Linen fabrics ('000 metres)	31,867	19,929
Footwear ('000 pairs)	40,038	24,633
Paper and paperboard	333.6	331.6
Sulphuric acid (100%)	178.2	93.7
Nitrogenous fertilizers (a)*	268.8	175.2
Phosphate fertilizers (b)*	110.8	122.0
Potassic fertilizers (c)*	54.5	11.5
Chemical fibres	124.5	85.6
Plastic materials	482.0	403.9
Coke	2,340	2,137
Cement	3,781	2,680
Pig iron	3,561	3,163
Crude steel	4,779	4,106
Copper (metric tons)	24,606	25,273
Aluminium (metric tons)	30,076	49,387
Household refrigerators and freezers (number)	448,992	514,745
Washing machines (number)	202,478	144,112
Radio receivers (number)	157,344	65,110
Television receivers (number)	498,552	201,851
Passenger cars and delivery vans (number)	3,453	3,806
Lorries (number)	12,648	6,877
Motor cycles (number)	48,207	33,222
Electric energy (million kWh)	24,082	22,731

* Production in terms of (a) nitrogen; (b) phosphoric acid; or (c) potassium oxide.

Finance

CURRENCY AND EXCHANGE RATES

Monetary Units

100 halierov (singular: halier) = 1 Slovenská koruna (Slovak crown or Sk; plural: koruny).

Sterling and Dollar Equivalents (30 September 1993)

£1 sterling = 48.3 koruny;
US $1 = 32.3 koruny;
1,000 koruny = £20.70 = $30.96.

Average Exchange Rate (Czechoslovak koruny per US $)

1990	17.95
1991	29.48
1992	28.26

Note: The foregoing information on average exchange rates refers to the Czechoslovak koruna, but the sterling and dollar equivalents apply to the Slovak koruna. In February 1993 Slovakia had introduced its own currency, to replace (at par) the Czechoslovak koruna.

BUDGET (million koruny)

Revenue	1990	1991
Receipts from production	70,163	99,332
Taxes and payments from population	460	16,395
Other receipts from own activity	1,442	1,155
Subsidies from Czechoslovak federal budget	23,275	—
Total	95,340	116,881

Expenditure	1990	1991
Production	28,108	23,388
Science and technology	2,192	2,327
Monetary and technical services	1,903	3,755
Social services and activities	40,832	83,001
Defence and security	2,215	3,521
Administration	1,596	3,156
Subsidies to local budgets	18,962	7,961
Total	95,808	127,109

COST OF LIVING (Consumer Price Index for employee households; base: January 1989 = 100)

	1990	1991
Food	114.2	172.7
Beverages	102.2	135.7
Other goods	112.2	191.1
Services	105.3	147.7
All items	110.6	172.4

NATIONAL ACCOUNTS

Gross Domestic Product by Economic Activity
(million koruny at current prices)

	1988	1989	1990
Activities of the material sphere	188,853	195,306	202,629
Agriculture	13,554	19,758	16,041
Forestry	1,531	2,103	1,917
Industry*	112,866	114,476	120,142
Water works and supply	1,267	1,035	1,454
Construction	21,125	21,418	22,414
Trade and catering	24,171	22,043	25,326
Material and technical supplies	2,447	2,656	3,265
Freight transport	9,036	8,434	8,470
Communications	1,787	1,845	2,045
Activities of the non-material sphere	31,724	34,147	35,958
Trade and technical services	n.a.	1,822	2,449
Personal transport	895	1,514	846
Communications	1,831	1,911	2,185
Finance and insurance	n.a.	1,803	782
Education	6,741	6,892	7,288
Culture	−405	−488	−356
Science, research and development	n.a.	3,862	3,518
Health services and social care	4,833	5,239	5,991
Administration and justice	n.a.	5,458	5,695
Accommodation, travel and communal services	2,263	2,617	4,395
Non-material services of inhabitants	2,221	2,847	3,103
Total	222,798	232,300	241,690

* Principally mining, manufacturing, electricity and gas.

External Trade

Note: Figures exclude trade with the Czech Republic.

COMMODITY GROUPS
(distribution by SITC, million koruny)

Imports f.o.b.	1991
Food and live animals	5,023
Crude materials (inedible) except fuels	14,069
Mineral fuels, lubricants, etc.	39,080
Chemicals and related products	9,722
Basic manufactures	8,848
Machinery and transport equipment	26,449
Miscellaneous manufactured articles	6,668
Total (incl. others)	110,864

Exports f.o.b.	1991
Food and live animals	6,671
Crude materials (inedible) except fuels	4,352
Chemicals and related products	11,790
Basic manufactures	35,065
Machinery and transport equipment	21,783
Miscellaneous manufactured articles	15,181
Total (incl. others)	96,800

PRINCIPAL TRADING PARTNERS (million koruny)

Imports f.o.b.	1989	1990	1991
Austria	3,426	8,277	9,215
Belgium	499	495	1,061
Brazil	808	1,063	1,465
Bulgaria	1,362	707	538
China, People's Republic	1,898	2,696	839
France	563	1,007	2,104
German Democratic Republic	3,315	3,470	15,553
Germany, Federal Republic	5,391	8,835	
Hungary	3,230	2,742	3,284
Iran	13	36	1,625
Italy	1,292	1,631	3,113
Netherlands	797	855	1,463
Poland	5,210	5,458	3,990
Romania	1,035	606	415
USSR	10,764	9,674	47,489
United Kingdom	1,156	1,674	1,043
USA	281	243	1,250
Yugoslavia	1,784	2,201	2,518
Total (incl. others)	n.a.	n.a.	110,864

Exports f.o.b.	1989	1990	1991
Austria	3,357	3,769	5,702
France	1,240	2,106	2,364
German Democratic Republic	3,541	1,514	19,154
Germany, Federal Republic	4,785	7,180	
Hungary	2,977	2,801	6,582
Italy	1,165	1,895	4,947
Netherlands	880	1,313	2,614
Poland	5,607	3,401	7,729
Romania	690	481	1,188
Syria	48	67	2,511
USSR	16,560	13,065	24,139
United Kingdom	760	1,232	1,064
Yugoslavia	2,470	3,038	3,910
Total (incl. others)	n.a.	n.a.	96,800

Transport

	1989	1990	1991
Railway transport			
Freight ('000 tons)	127,974	117,237	83,873
Passengers (million)	122	119	112
Public road transport			
Freight ('000 tons)	105,472	83,571	34,921
Passengers (million)	944	937	939
Waterway transport			
Freight ('000 tons)	5,618	3,715	1,946

ROAD TRAFFIC (motor vehicles in use)

	1989	1990	1991
Passenger cars	837,221	875,550	906,129
Buses and coaches	13,736	14,301	13,770
Goods vehicles	139,543	145,531	150,156
Motorcycles and scooters	106,505	107,139	103,908

Tourism

FOREIGN TOURIST ARRIVALS*
(visitors at accommodation facilities)

Country of origin	1991
Austria	30,959
France	15,681
Germany	128,872
Hungary	72,674
Italy	36,627
Netherlands	16,908
Poland	92,311
USSR	13,116
USA	16,430
Yugoslavia	64,602
Total (incl. others)	576,299

* Excluding visitors from the Czech Republic.

Communications Media

	1989	1990	1991
Telephones in use	1,193,000	1,248,000	1,300,000
Radio receivers (licensed)	1,103,000	1,094,000	1,094,000
Television receivers (licensed)	1,310,000	1,309,000	1,309,000
Book production: titles*	3,096	2,734	3,305
Periodicals	772	1,870	1,553

* Including printed music, teaching materials, maps and atlases.

Education

(1991/92)

	Institutions	Teachers*	Students
Kindergarten	3,759	17,342	188,821
Primary (basic)	2,415	37,244	716,416
Secondary			
Grammar	147	3,875	59,347
Specialized	204	6,343	99,751
Vocational	317	6,076	143,282
Higher	13	7,873	61,272

* Teachers in full-time employment.

Directory

The Constitution

On 1 September 1992 the Slovak National Council adopted the Constitution of the Slovak Republic (which entered into force on 1 January 1993), the main provisions of which are summarized below:

FUNDAMENTAL PROVISIONS

The Slovak Republic is a democratic and sovereign state, ruled by law. It is bound neither to an ideology, nor to a religion. State power belongs to the people, who exercise it either through their representatives or directly. The state authorities shall act only on the basis of the Constitution and to the extent and in the manner stipulated by law.

The territory of the Slovak Republic is integral and indivisible. The conditions for naturalization or deprival of state citizenship of the Slovak Republic are regulated by law. No person may be deprived of citizenship against his will. The Slovak language is the state language in the Republic. The use of languages other than the state language in administrative relations is regulated by law. The capital of the Republic is Bratislava.

BASIC RIGHTS AND FREEDOMS

The people are free and equal, and the rights and freedoms of every citizen are guaranteed, irrespective of sex, race, colour, language, faith, political or other conviction, national or social origin, nationality or ethnic origin. No person may be tortured, nor be subjected to cruel, inhuman or humiliating treatment or punishment. Capital punishment is not practised.

Every person has the right to own property. The place of abode is inviolable. The freedom of migration and the freedom of domicile are guaranteed.

The freedom of expression and the right to information are guaranteed. Censorship is prohibited. The right to assemble peacefully is guaranteed. Every person has the right to be a member of a union, community, society or any other association. Citizens have the right to found political parties and movements. Such parties and movements, as well as other associations, are separate from the state.

The citizens have the right to participate in the administration of public affairs, either directly or through the free election of their representatives. The right to vote is universal, direct and equal and is exercised by secret ballot.

The universal advancement of citizens who are members of national minorities and ethnic groups is guaranteed, above all the right to develop their own culture, to broadcast and receive information in their mother tongue, to join national associations and to found and maintain educational and cultural institutions. The languages of national minorities may also be used in administrative relations.

Every person has the right to the free choice of profession and vocational training as well as to do business and to perform other commercial activities. Employees are entitled to fair and satisfactory working conditions. Citizens may form free associations to protect their economic and social interests. Trade unions are independent of the state. The right to strike is guaranteed.

Every citizen is entitled to adequate old-age and disability benefits; widow's allowances; free health care; family suppport; and education.

NATIONAL COUNCIL OF THE SLOVAK REPUBLIC

Supreme legislative power is vested in the National Council of the Slovak Republic, which has 150 deputies, elected for a four-year term. The deputies represent the citizens and are elected by them in general, equal and direct elections, by secret ballot.

The National Council has the power to: adopt the Constitution, constitutional and other laws and supervise their execution; elect and recall the President of the Slovak Republic by secret ballot; decide on proposals to call a referendum; prior to their ratification, give consent to international political, economic or other agreements; establish ministries and other bodies of state administration; supervise the activities of the Government and pass a vote of confidence or censure on the Government or its members; approve the state budget and supervise its execution; elect judges, including the Chairman and Vice-Chairmen of the Supreme Court and of the Constitutional Court; adopt a resolution to declare war if the Slovak Republic is attacked, or if such a declaration ensues from the obligations of international treaties.

THE PRESIDENT OF THE REPUBLIC

The President is the Head of State of the Slovak Republic. He/she is elected by the National Council by secret ballot for a five-year term. The President is responsible to the National Council. He/she may not be elected for more than two consecutive terms.

The President represents the Slovak Republic internationally, negotiates and ratifies international agreements; receives and gives credentials to envoys; convenes constituent sessions of the National Council; may dissolve the National Council; signs laws; appoints and recalls the Prime Minister and other members of the Government and receives their resignation; grants amnesty, pardons and commutes sentences imposed by courts; is the Commander-in-Chief of the Armed Forces; may declare a state of emergency on the basis of constitutional law; may declare a referendum.

THE GOVERNMENT

The Government of the Slovak Republic is the highest organ of executive power. It is composed of the Prime Minister and Ministers. The Prime Minister is appointed by the President of the Republic. On the Prime Minister's recommendation, the President appoints and recalls the members of the Government and puts them in charge of their ministries. For the execution of office, the Government is responsible to the National Council.

The Government has the power to prepare bills; issue decrees; adopt fundamental provisions for economic and social policy; authorize drafts for the state budget and closing account of the year; decide international agreements; decide principal questions of internal and international policy; submit bills to the National Council; request the legislature for a vote of confidence.

The Government

HEAD OF STATE

President of the Republic: MICHAL KOVÁČ (elected 15 February 1993).

GOVERNMENT
(March 1994)

The Government is composed of members of the Party of the Democratic Left (PDL), the Democratic Union of Slovakia (DUS), the Alliance of Democrats of Slovakia (ADS), the National Democratic Party (NDP) and the Christian Democratic Movement (CDM).

Prime Minister: JOZEF MORAVČÍK (DUS).

Deputy Prime Minister: ROMAN KOVÁČ (DUS).

Deputy Prime Minister and Minister for Economic Reform: BIRGITA SCHMOEGNEROVA (PDL).

Deputy Prime Minister and Minister for Legislative Affairs: IVAN SIMKO (CDM).

Minister of the Economy: PETER MAGVASI (PDL).

Minister of Finance: REDOLF FILKUS (ADSR).

Minister of Foreign Affairs: EDWARD KUKAN (ADS).

Minister of Defence: PAVOL KANIS (PDL).

Minister of Culture: LUBO ROMAN (CDM).

Minister of Agriculture: PAVEL KONCOS (PDL).

Minister of Labour, Social Affairs and the Family: JULIUS BROCKA (CDM).

Minister of the Interior: LADISLAV PITTNER (CDM).

Minister of Transport, Communications and Public Works: MIKULAS DZURINDA (CDM).

Minister of Health: TIBOR SAGAT (DUS).

Minister of Education and Science: LUBOMÍR HARACH (PDL).

Minister of Justice: MILAN HANZEL (PDL).

Minister for the Environment: JURAJ HRASKO (PDL).

Minister for the Administration and Privatization of National Property: MILAN JANICINA (NDP).

MINISTRIES

Office of the Government of the Slovak Republic: nám. Slobody 1, 813 70 Bratislava; tel (7) 415-111; fax (7) 497-595.

Ministry for the Administration and Privatization of National Property: Drieňová 24, 820 09 Bratislava; tel. (7) 234-332; fax (7) 233-335.

Ministry of Agriculture: Dobrovičova 12, 812 66 Bratislava; tel. (7) 490-581.

Ministry of Culture: Dobrovičova 12, 813 31 Bratislava; tel. (7) 368-7813; fax (7) 323-528.

Ministry of Defence: Kutuzovova 7, 831 03 Bratislava; tel. (7) 2799; fax (7) 258-871.

Ministry of the Economy: Mierová 19, 827 15 Bratislava; tel. (7) 299-8111; fax (7) 237-827.

Ministry of Education and Science: Hlboká 2, 813 30 Bratislava; tel. (7) 492-002.

Ministry for the Environment: Hlboká 2, 812 35 Bratislava; tel. (7) 492-002; fax (7) 311-368.

Ministry of Finance: Štefanovičova 5, 813 08 Bratislava; tel. (7) 490-426; fax (7) 498-042.

Ministry of Foreign Affairs: Stromová 1, 833 36 Bratislava; tel. (7) 370-4111; fax (7) 376-364.

Ministry of Health: Špitálska 6, 813 05 Bratislava; tel. (7) 300.

Ministry of the Interior: Pribinova 2, 812 72 Bratislava; tel. (7) 206-1111.

Ministry of Justice: Župné nám. 13, 813 11 Bratislava; tel. (7) 353-111; fax (7) 315-952.

Ministry of Labour, Social Affairs and the Family: Špitálska 4, 816 43 Bratislava; tel. (7) 300.

Ministry of Transport, Communications and Public Works: Miletičova 19, 820 06 Bratislava; tel. (7) 254-753; fax (7) 254-800.

Legislature

NATIONAL COUNCIL OF THE SLOVAK REPUBLIC

Following the division of Czechoslovakia on 1 January 1993, the former Slovak regional legislature, the Slovak National Council, was retained as the new Slovak Republic's supreme legislative body (although it was officially renamed the National Council of the Slovak Republic). Its 150 members were last elected in June 1992. The next election was not scheduled to be held until June 1996, but, in March 1994, it was agreed to have a general election on 30 September–1 October.

Chairman: IVAN GAŠPAROVIČ.

First Deputy Chairman: PETER WEISS.

Deputy Chairmen: L'UDOVÍT ČERNÁK, AUGUSTÍN MARIÁN HÚSKA.

Elections to the (former) Slovak National Council, 5–6 June 1992

Parties and Groups	% of votes	Seats
Movement for a Democratic Slovakia	37.3	74*
Party of the Democratic Left	14.7	29†
Christian Democratic Movement	8.9	18
Slovak National Party	7.9	15‡
Coexistence§	7.4	14
Others	23.8	—
Total	100.0	150

* By March 1994, following a series of defections, the number of seats held by the Movement for a Democratic Slovakia had fallen to 52.

† By March 1994 the number of seats held by the Party of the Democratic Left had fallen to 28.

‡ By March 1994 the number of seats held by the Slovak National Party had fallen to 9.

§ A coalition of the Hungarian Christian Democratic Movement, Együttélés (Coexistence) and the Hungarian People's Party.

Local Government

The country is divided into 38 administrative districts, called okres. Before 1990 it was also divided into 3 larger regions, called kraj, but, after the collapse of Communist rule, the kraj disappeared. However, there are plans to reintroduce a regional tier of government.

Political Organizations

Alliance of Democrats of the Slovak Republic: Bratislava; f. 1993; Leader MILAN KŇAŽKO.

Christian Democratic Movement (Kresťanskodemokratické hnutie): Žabotova 2, 814 02 Bratislava; tel. (7) 492-541; fax (7) 496-313; f. 1990; Chair. JÁN ČARNOGURSKÝ.

Coexistence (Coexistencia/Együttélés): Pražská 7, Bratislava; Leader MIKLÓS DURAY.

Democratic Party (Demokratická strana): Malinovského 70, 812 78 Bratislava; tel. (7) 498-020; fax (7) 492-273; f. 1944; merged with Civic Democratic Union, Civic Democratic Party of Slovakia, Democrats '92, Czech-Slovak Understanding and the Green League in 1994; right-wing; Chair. PAVOL HAGYARI; 5,000 mems.

Democratic Union of Slovakia: Bratislava; f. 1994; formed by former members of the Movement for a Democratic Slovakia; Leaders JOZEF MORAVČÍK, ROMAN KOVÁČ.

Hungarian Christian Democratic Movement: Žabotova 2, Bratislava; Leader BÉLA BUGÁR.

Hungarian People's Party: Bratislava; Leader GYULA POPÉLY.

Movement for a Democratic Slovakia (Hnutie za demokratické Slovensko): Tomašíkova 32, 823 69 Bratislava; tel. (7) 231-769; f. 1991; Chair. ARPAD MATEJKA.

National Democratic Party: Bratislava; f. 1994; centre party; Chair. of Preparatory Cttee L'UDOVÍT ČERNÁK.

Party of the Democratic Left (Strana demokratickej l'avice): Gundulovičova 12, 816 10 Bratislava; tel. (7) 335-475; telex 92722; fax (7) 235-323; f. 1991 to replace the Communist Party of Slovakia; Chair. PETER WEISS.

Slovak National Party (Slovenská národná strana): Štefánikova 47, 814 99 Bratislava; tel. (7) 496-977; Chair. JÁN SLOTA.

Social Democratic Party in Slovakia (Sociálnodemokratická strana na Slovensku): Žabotova 2, 812 02 Bratislava; tel. (7) 494-700; fax (7) 494-681; re-established 1990; Chair. JAROSLAV VOLF.

Diplomatic Representation

EMBASSIES IN SLOVAKIA

Austria: Holubyho 11, 811 03 Bratislava; tel. (7) 311-103; fax (7) 313-145.

Bulgaria: Kuzmányho 1, 811 06 Bratislava; tel. (7) 333-677.

China, People's Republic: Jančova 8, 811 06 Bratislava; tel. (7) 314-577; Ambassador: TANG ZHANQIN.

Cuba: Jančova 9, 811 06 Bratislava; tel. (7) 311-529.

Czech Republic: Bratislava; Ambassador: FILIP ŠEDIVÝ.

France: POB 152 810 00 Bratislava; tel. (7) 340-311; fax (7) 340-302; Ambassador: MICHEL PERRIN.

Germany: Palisády 47, 813 03 Bratislava; tel. (7) 315-300; fax (7) 315-363; Ambassador: HEIKE ZENKER.

Hungary: Sedlarska St., Bratislava; tel. (7) 335-601; fax (7) 509-00; Ambassador: JENOE BOROS.

Italy: Červeňova 19, 811 03 Bratislava; tel. (7) 313-195; fax (7) 313-202.

Poland: Hummelova 4, 814 91 Bratislava; tel. and fax (7) 315-143.

Romania: Fraňa Kráľa 11, 811 05 Bratislava; tel. (7) 491-665.

Russia: Godrova 4, 811 06 Bratislava; tel. (7) 313-468; fax (7) 334-910; Chargé d'affaires a.i.: VLADIMIR M. POLYAKOV.

South Africa: Jančova 8, 811 02 Bratislava; tel. (7) 311-582; fax (7) 312-581; Ambassador: R. V. FRANKEN.

USA: Hviezdoslavovo nám. 4, 811 02 Bratislava; tel. (7) 330-861; fax (7) 335-439; Chargé d'Affairs a.i.: PAUL HACKER.

Judicial System

Justice in Slovakia is performed by the district courts (first level), county courts (second level) and the Supreme Court of the Slovak Republic. The Constitutional Court, restored in 1993, protects constitutionality.

Chairman of the Supreme Court: Prof. KAROL PLANK.

Procurator-General: VOJTECH BACHO.

Chairman of the Constitutional Court: MILAN ČÍČ.

Religion

The principal religion in Slovakia is Christianity. The largest denomination, in 1991, was the Roman Catholic Church, with 3.2m. members, representing some 60% of the total population. About 10% of the population professed no religious belief.

CHRISTIANITY

The Roman Catholic Church

Slovakia consists of one archdiocese and 5 dioceses, including one (directly responsible to the Holy See) for Catholics of the Slovak (Byzantine) rite, also known as 'Greek' Catholics or Uniates.

Latin Rite

Archbishop of Trnava: Mgr JÁN SOKOL, Svätoplukovo 3, 917 66 Trnava; tel. (805) 262-35.

Slovak Rite

Bishop of Prešov: Mgr JÁN HIRKA, Greckokatolický biskupský úrad, Hlavná ulica 8, Prešov; tel. (91) 346-22; 188,397 adherents (March 1991); 201 parishes.

The Orthodox Church

The Orthodox Church of the Czech Lands and Slovakia: V Jámě 6, POB 655, 111 21 Prague 1, Czech Republic; tel. (2) 260-017; divided into four eparchies in the former Czechoslovakia: Prague and Olomouc (Czech Republic), Prešov and Michalovce (Slovak Republic); Archbishop of Prague and Metropolitan of the Czech Lands and Slovakia DOROTHEOS; 53,613 mems (March 1991); 127 parishes; Theological Faculty in Charles University, Prague, Czech Republic.

Archbishop of Prešov: Rev. NIKOLAJ, Budovatelská 1, 080 01 Prešov.

Bishop of Michalovce: Rev. JOHN, Štefánikova, 071 44 Michalovce.

Protestant Churches

Baptist Union in Slovakia: Súlovská 2, 821 05 Bratislava; tel. (7) 221-145; f. 1994; 1,843 mems; Pres. Rev. JURAJ KOHÚT; Sec. JURAJ PRIBULA.

Brethren Church Council (Rada církve bratrské): Soukenická 15, 110 00 Prague 1, Czech Republic; tel. (2) 231-8131; 10,000 mems, 45 congregations, 190 preaching stations; Pres. PAVEL ČERNÝ; Sec. KAREL TASCHNER.

Evangelical Church of the Augsburg Confession in Slovakia (Lutheran Church in the Slovak Republic): Palisády 46, 811 06 Bratislava; tel. (7) 332-842; fax (7) 330-500; presided over by the Bishop-General, assisted by bishops of the Western and Eastern districts; 327 parishes in 14 seniorates; 329,390 mems (March 1991); Bishop-Gen. PAVEL UHORSKAI.

Reformed Christian Church of Slovakia: Jókaiho 34, 945 01 Komárno; tel. (819) 2788; fax (819) 3716; 89,295 mems and 310 parishes (March 1991); Bishop Dr EUGEN MIKÓ; Gen. Sec. Mgr BARTOLOMEJ GÖÖZ.

Other Christian Churches

Apostolic Church: Sreznevského 2, 831 03 Bratislava; tel. and fax (95) 644-1422; f. 1956; 2,000 mems; Pres. JOZEF BRENKUS .

Church of the Seventh-day Adventists: Zálesí 50, 142 00 Prague 4, Czech Republic; tel. (2) 472-3745; 1,924 mems; 40 churches; Pres. KAREL NOWAK.

Old Catholic Church (Církev starokatolická): Hládkov 3, 169 00 Prague 6, Czech Republic; tel. (2) 352-395; f. 1871; 3,000 mems, 6 parishes; Bishop (elect) Mgr DUŠAN HEJBAL.

JUDAISM

Union of the Jewish Religious Communities in the Slovak Republic (Ústredný zväz židovských náboženských obcí ve Slovenskej republike): Kozia ul. 21/II, 814 47 Bratislava; tel. (7) 312-167; fax (7) 311-106; 3,300 mems; Chair. FERO ALEXANDER; Chief Rabbis BARUCH MYERS (Bratislava), LAZAR KLEINMAN (KOŠICE).

The Press

In 1992 there were approximately 700 newspapers and periodicals (130 of which were new titles) being published in Slovakia. These included 26 publications in Hungarian, three in Ukrainian and two in Romany.

PRINCIPAL DAILIES

(In Slovak, unless otherwise indicated.)

Banská Bystrica

Smer Dnes (Course Today): Čs. armády 10, 975 43 Banská Bystrica; tel. (88) 254-78; telex 70261; fax (88) 255-06; f. 1948; independent; Editor-in-Chief IVAN BAČA; circ. 45,000.

Bratislava

Hlas l'udu (Voice of the People): Sliačska 1, 830 08 Bratislava; tel. (7) 251-383; fax (7) 251-268; f. 1949; morning; West Slovakia region; Editor-in-Chief PAVOL DINKA; circ. 28,800.

Národná obroda (National Renewal): Trnavská cesta 112, POB 63, 830 00 Bratislava; tel. (7) 220-433; telex 92738; fax (7) 296-281; f. 1990; independent; Editor-in-Chief JURAJ VEREŠ; circ. 80,000.

Nový čas (New Time): Gorkého 5, 812 78 Bratislava; tel. (7) 36-30-70; fax (7) 36-31-04; f. 1991; morning; Editor-in-Chief JOZEF BIELIK; circ. 250,000.

Nový Slovák (New Slovak): Teslova 26, POB 254, 814 99 Bratislava; tel. (7) 672-39; fax (7) 670-42; Editor-in-Chief PETER ŠKULTÉTY; circ. 18,000.

Práca (Labour): Odborárské nám. 3, 812 71 Bratislava; tel. (7) 650-60; telex 93283; fax (7) 212-985; f. 1946; publ. by the Confederation of Trade Unions of the Slovak Republic; Editor-in-Chief MILOŠ NEMEČEK; circ. 135,000.

Pravda (Truth): Pribinova 25, 819 08 Bratislava; tel. (7) 552-33; telex 92702; fax (7) 583-05; f. 1920; independent; left-wing; Editor-in-Chief PETER SITÁNY; circ. 250,000.

Rol'nícke noviny (Agricultural News): Dobrovičova 12, 813 78 Bratislava; tel. (7) 555-15; telex 93211; fax (7) 512-82; f. 1946; Editor-in-Chief JURAJ ŠESTÁK; circ. 27,000.

Slovenský denník (Slovak Daily): Žabotova 2, 811 04 Bratislava; tel. (7) 491-137; f. 1990; Editor-in-Chief RÓBERT RÓM; circ. 27,000.

Smena (Shift): Dostojevského rad 1, 819 24 Bratislava; tel. (7) 368-255; fax (7) 362-655; f. 1947; youth daily; Editor-in-Chief GABA BARANOVIČOVÁ; circ. 80,000.

Sme na každý deň: Pribinova 25, 819 13 Bratislava; tel. (7) 210-4566; fax (7) 550-58; Editor-in-Chief KAROL JEŽÍK; circ. 70,000.

Šport (Sport): Svätoplukova 2, 819 23 Bratislava; tel. (7) 600-53; telex 93334; fax (7) 211-380; Editor-in-Chief ZDENO SIMONIDES; circ. 65,000.

Szabad Újság (Free Journal): Michalská 9, 811 01 Bratislava; tel. (7) 333-012; fax (7) 334-215; f. 1991; Hungarian-language economic daily; Editor-in-Chief GÉZA SZABÓ; circ. 20,000.

Új Szó (New World): Pribinova 25, 819 15 Bratislava; tel. (7) 532-20; telex 92308; fax (7) 505-29; f. 1948; midday; Hungarian-language paper; Editor-in-Chief JOZEF SZILVÁSSY; circ. 56,000.

Večerník (Evening Paper): Pribinova 25, 819 16 Bratislava; tel. (7) 210-4517; telex 92296; fax (7) 210-4521; f. 1956; evening; Editor-in-Chief Dr RUDOLF MACHALA; circ. 42,000.

Košice

Lúč: B. Němcovej 32, 042 62 Košice; tel. (95) 345-38; fax (95) 359-090; East Slovakia region; Editor-in-Chief IMRICH ŠTELIAR; circ. 15,000.

Košický večer (Košice Evening): tr. SNP 24, 042 97 Košice; tel. (95) 420-021; fax (95) 421-214; f. 1990; Editor-in-Chief MIKULÁŠ JESENSKÝ; circ. 22,400.

Slovenský východ (Slovak East): Letná 45, 042 66 Košice; tel. (95) 539-79; fax (95) 539-50; East Slovakia region; Editor-in-Chief DUŠAN KLINGER; circ. 56,000.

Prešov

Prešovský večerník (Prešov Evening Paper): Jarkova 4, 080 01 Prešov; tel. (91) 245-63; fax (91) 233-98; f. 1990; Editor-in-Chief PETER LIČÁK; circ. 13,000.

PRINCIPAL PERIODICALS

(In Slovak, unless otherwise indicated.)

Avízo: Teslova 26, 821 02 Bratislava; tel. (7) 627-10; fax (7) 331-373; weekly; advertising and information; Editor-in-Chief VIKTOR KUBAL; circ. 45,000.

Dievča (Girl): Mudroňova 12, 811 01 Bratislava; tel. (7) 311-920; every 2 months; publ. by the Slovak Union of Women; Editor-in-Chief Dr ELENA GIRETHOVÁ; circ. 28,000.

Domino: Košice; weekly; Editor-in-Chief ANDREJ HRICO.

Elektrón + Zenit: Pražská 11, 812 84 Bratislava; tel. (7) 491-606; fax (7) 493-385; monthly; science and technology for young people; Editor-in-Chief LADISLAV GYORFFY; circ. 25,000.

Eurotelevízia (Eurotelevision): Pribinova 25, 819 14 Bratislava; tel. (7) 210-4194; telex 92661; fax (7) 509-95; weekly; Editor-in-Chief TAŇA LUCKÁ; circ. 400,000.

Eva: Pribinova 25, 815 85 Bratislava; tel. (7) 522-71; every 2 months; magazine for women; Editor-in-Chief Dr GITA PECHOVÁ; circ. 150,000.

Express: Pribinova 25, 819 05 Bratislava; tel. (7) 210-4031; fax (7) 551-85; f. 1969; weekly digest of the foreign press; Editor-in-Chief JÁN MACHAJ; circ. 85,000.

Expres International: Brečtanova 1, 833 49 Bratislava; tel. (7) 321-308; fax (7) 372-486; weekly; current affairs; Editor-in-Chief GENAD PEŇKOVSKÝ; circ. 68,000.

Extra S: Tomášikova 32A, 821 01 Bratislava; tel. (7) 293-807; fax (7) 293-925; social, economic and political weekly; Editor-in-Chief IMRICH DEMOVIČ; circ. 40,000.

Kamarát (Friend): POB 73, 820 14 Bratislava; f. 1950; magazine for teenagers; Editor-in-Chief VLADIMÍR TOPERCER; circ. 25,000.

Katolícke noviny (Catholic News): Kapitulská 20, 815 21 Bratislava; tel. (7) 335-216; fax (7) 333-178; f. 1849; weekly; Editor-in-Chief JOZEF ZAVARSKÝ; circ. 140,000.

Krásy Slovenska (Beauty of Slovakia): Vajnorská 100A, 832 58 Bratislava; illustrated monthly; Editor-in-Chief ELENA PUKOVÁ; circ. 19,000.

Línia: Kapitulská 3, 816 26 Bratislava; tel. (7) 332-743; quarterly; life-style; Editor-in-Chief MARTA MASARYKOVÁ; circ. 40,000.

Móda (Fashion): Mudroňova 12, 811 01 Bratislava; tel. (7) 311-920; monthly; publ. by the Slovak Union of Women; Editor-in-Chief EMILIA ŠANDOROVÁ; circ. 35,000.

Nové slovo bez rešpektu (New Word Without Respect): Pribinova 25, 819 07 Bratislava; tel. (7) 503-34; telex 92702; fax (7) 583-05; f. 1944; weekly; politics, culture, economy; Editor-in-Chief EMIL POLÁK; circ. 15,000.

Ohník (Little Flame): Pražská 11, 812 84 Bratislava; tel. (7) 561-68; fortnightly; youth; Editor-in-Chief STANISLAV BEBJAK; 60,000.

Plus 7 dní: Ružová dolina 27, 824 65 Bratislava; tel. (7) 201-6369; fax (7) 640-56; weekly social magazine; Editor-in-Chief MILOŠ LUKNÁR; circ. 50,000.

Populár: Špitálska 35, 815 85 Bratislava; tel. (7) 586-79; fax (7) 400-395; monthly music magazine for young people; Editor-in-Chief BARBARA MOKRÁ; circ. 70,000.

Poradca Podnikatel'a (Entrepreneurs' Advice): Predmestská 1395, 010 01 Žilina; tel. (89) 465-87; fax (89) 222-56; monthly; circ. 35,000.

Romano L'il: Prešov; f. 1991; in Romany; publ. by the Cultural Union of the Roma in Slovakia.

Slobodný piatok (Free Friday): Križkova 9, 815 32 Bratislava; tel. (7) 496-517; fax (7) 496-334; f. 1990; weekly; independent; Editor-in-Chief JOZEF SITKO; circ. 90,000.

Slovenka (Slovak Woman): Jaskový rad 5, 833 80 Bratislava; tel. (7) 373-169; fax (7) 376-118; f. 1949; weekly; illustrated magazine; Editor-in-Chief ALŽBETA REMIÁŠOVÁ; circ. 195,000.

Slovenské národné noviny (Slovak National News): Matica slovenská, Mudroňova 26, 036 52 Martin; tel. and fax (842) 345-35; f. 1845; weekly; organ of Matica slovenská cultural organization; Editor-in-Chief MILOŠ MAJER.

Slovenský národ (Slovak Nation): Vajanského 15, 811 02 Bratislava; tel. and fax (7) 556-10; f. 1990; weekly; Editor-in-Chief BIBIÁNA HROMADOVÁ; circ. 20,000.

Stop Auto-Moto Revue: Brečtanova 1, 833 49 Bratislava; tel. (7) 373-403; fax (7) 372-486; fortnightly; motoring; Editor-in-Chief JÁN KORECKÝ; circ. 45,000.

Technické noviny (Technica Newspaper): Štefánikova 19, 812 71 Bratislava; tel. (7) 330-051; fax (7) 330-838; f. 1953; weekly; Editor-in-Chief PAVOL MARUŠINEC; circ. 16,000.

Trend: Jakubovo nám. 14, 814 61 Bratislava; tel. (7) 325-287; fax (7) 367-873; f. 1991; weekly; for entrepreneurs; publ. by Trendy Ltd; Editor-in-Chief TATIANA REPKOVÁ; circ. 24,000.

Vasárnap (Sunday): Martanovičova 25, 819 15 Bratislava; tel. (7) 532-20; telex 92308; fax (7) 505-29; f. 1948; weekly; independent Hungarian-language magazine; Editor-in-Chief JOZEF SZILVÁSSY; circ. 130,000.

Výber (Digest): Pribinova 25, 819 45 Bratislava; tel. (7) 210-3936; fax (7) 334-534; f. 1968; weekly; digest of home and foreign press; Editor-in-Chief RICHARD SZABÓ; circ. 20,000.

Život (Life): Pribinova 25, 819 17 Bratislava; tel. (7) 490-121; fax (7) 593-91; f. 1951; illustrated family weekly; Editor-in-Chief MILAN VÁROŠ; circ. 230,000.

Zmena (Change): Záhradnícka 93, POB 7, 818 07 Bratislava; tel. and fax (7) 211-754; f. 1989; weekly; independent; Editor-in-Chief VLADO MOHORITA; circ. 80,000.

NEWS AGENCIES

Tlačová agentúra Slovenskej republiky (TASR) (News Agency of the Slovak Republic): Pribinova 23, 819 28 Bratislava; tel. (7) 362-578; fax (7) 332-333; f. 1992; has overseas bureaux in Washington (USA) and Budapest (Hungary); bureaux in Russia, Belgium and Germany to be opened in 1993; Gen. Man. DUŠAN KLEIMAN.

Foreign Bureaux

The following news agencies are represented in Slovakia: Reuters (UK), Deutsche Presse-Agentur (Germany), Česká tisková kancelář (Czech Republic) and Austria Presse-Agentur (Austria).

PRESS ASSOCIATION

Slovenský syndikát novinárov (Slovak Syndicate of Journalists): Župné nám. 7, 815 68 Bratislava; tel. (7) 335-071; fax (7) 334-534; f. 1968; reorganized 1990; 2,400 mems; Chair. JÚLIUS GEMBICKÝ.

Publishers

Alfa: Hurbanovo nám. 3, 815 89 Bratislava; tel. (7) 331-441; fax (7) 594-43; technical and economic literature, dictionaries; Dir MARTIN PARAJKA.

Církevné vydavatel'stvo: Palisády 64, 801 00 Bratislava; religious literature; ŠTEFÁNIA HREBÍKOVÁ.

Matica slovenská: Novomeského 32, 036 52 Martin; tel. (842) 313-71; telex 75331; (842) 331-88; f. 1863; literary science, bibliography, biography and librarianship; literary archives and museums; Man. Š. HANAKOVIČ.

Mladé letá (Young Years): nám. SNP 12, 815 19 Bratislava; tel. (7) 364-475; telex 92721; fax (7) 364-563; f. 1950; literature for children and young people; Dir Ing. OLDRICH POLÁK.

Obzor (Horizon): Špitálska 35, 815 85 Bratislava; tel. (7) 361-015; fax (7) 490-395; f. 1953; educational encyclopaedias, popular scientific, fiction, textbooks, law; Editor-in-Chief MARGITA SVITKOVÁ.

Osveta (Education): Osloboditel'ov 21, 036 54 Martin; tel. (842) 341-21; fax (7) 350-36; f. 1953; medical, health, photographic, fiction; Gen. Dir Ing. MARTIN FARKAŠ.

Práca (Labour): Štefánikova 19, 812 71 Bratislava; tel. (7) 333-779; fax (7) 330-046; f. 1946; law, guides, cookery, fiction, etc.; Dir MIROSLAV BERNÁTH.

Príroda a.s. (Nature): Križkova 9, 815 34 Bratislava; tel. (7) 497-241; fax (7) 496-360; agriculture, ecology, forestry, natural history, medicine, veterinary medicine, gardening; books and journals; Chair. Ing. JÁN ODZGAN.

Slovenské pedagogické nakladetel'stvo: Sasinková 5, 891 12 Bratislava; pedagogical literature, educational, school texts, dictionaries; Dir Dr SERGEJ TROŠČÁK.

Slovenský spisovatel a.s. (Slovak Writer): Laurinská 2, 813 67 Bratislava; tel. (7) 333-903; fax (7) 335-411; publishing house; fiction, poetry; Dir MARTIN CHOVANEC.

Smena (Change): Pražská 11, 812 84 Bratislava; tel. (7) 498-018; fax (7) 493-305; f. 1949; fiction, literature for young people, newspapers and magazines; Dir Ing. JAROSLAV ŠIŠOLÁK.

Šport: Vajnorská 100/A, 832 58 Bratislava; tel. (7) 691-95; telex 93330; sport, physical culture, guide books, periodicals; Dir Dr BOHUMIL GOLIAN.

Tatran: Michalská 9, 815 82 Bratislava; tel. (7) 335-849; fax (7) 335-777; f. 1949; fiction, art books, children's books, literary theory; Dir Ing. PETER TVRDOŇ.

Veda (Science): Klemensova 19, 814 30 Bratislava; tel. (7) 583-15; f. 1953; publishing house of the Slovak Academy of Sciences; scientific and popular scientific books and periodicals; Man. EVA MAJESKÁ.

Východoslovenské vydaveatel'stvo (East Slovakia Publishing House): Alejová 3, 040 11 Košice; tel. (95) 765-206; fax (95) 765-204; f. 1960; regional literature, children's literature, fiction, general; Dir Dr IMRICH GOFUS.

PUBLISHERS' ASSOCIATIONS

Združenie vydavatel'ov a kníhkupcov (Publishers' and Booksellers' Association): Michalská 9, 815 82 Bratislava; tel. (7) 330-141; Sec. MARTIN UŠIAK.

WRITERS' UNION

Asociácia organizácií spisovatel'ov Slovenska (Asscn of Writers' Organizations in Slovakia): Laurinská 2, 815 08 Bratislava; tel. (7) 335-368; f. 1949; reorganized 1990; 330 mems; Pres. JÁN BUZÁSSY; Sec. PETER ANDRUŠKA.

Radio and Television

There were 1.1m. licences for radio receivers and 1.3m. licences for television receivers in 1991. Radio and television stations are licensed through the Slovak Council for Radio and Television.

RADIO

Slovenský rozhlas Bratislava (Slovak Radio Bratislava): Mýtna 1, 812 90 Bratislava; tel. (7) 494-464; telex 93352; fax (7) 498-923; f. 1926; Dir-Gen. Dr VLADIMÍR ŠTEFKO.

TELEVISION

Slovenská televízia (Slovak Television): Staré grunty 28, 845 45 Bratislava; telex 92277; fax (7) 729-440; f. 1956; public broadcasting co; Dir-Gen. PETER MALEC.

Finance

cap. = capital; res = reserves; dep. = deposits; m. = million; brs = branches; amounts in Slovak koruny)

BANKING

Central Bank

Národná banka Slovenska (National Bank of Slovakia): Štúrova 2, 818 54 Bratislava; tel. (7) 323-511; fax (7) 364-721; f. 1993; determines monetary policy, issues banknotes and coins, manages circulation of money, co-ordinates payment connections and accounting of banks, supervises activities of banks; Gov. VLADIMÍR MASAR; Vice-Gov. Ing. MARIÁN TKÁČ.

Commercial Banks

Devín banka, a.s.: Františkánske nám. 8, 811 10 Bratislava; tel. (7) 333-479; fax (7) 334-652; f. 1992; cap. 499m.; Gen. Dir Ing. VLADISLAV BACHÁR.

Investičná a rozvojová banka, a.s. Bratislava (Investment and Development Bank, Inc.): Štúrova 5, 818 55 Bratislava; tel. (7) 361-051; telex 92309; fax (7) 363-252; f. 1992; cap. 500m., res 169.7m., dep. 39,146.7m. (Dec. 1992); Gen. Dir Ing. JOZEF TKÁČ; 24 brs.

Istrobanka, a.s.: Laurinská 1, POB 109, 810 00 Bratislava; tel. (7) 332-604; fax (7) 331-744; f. 1992; cap. 597m., dep. 1,289m.; Man. Dir Ing. IVAN ŠRAMKO; 2 brs.

L'udová banka Bratislava, a.s. (People's Bank, Inc.): nám. SNP 15, 810 09 Bratislava; tel. (7) 367-049; fax (7) 363-794; f. 1992; cap. 300m.; Commercial Man. Ing. JOZEF KOLLÁR.

Poštová banka, a.s. Bratislava (Postal Bank, Inc.): Gorkého 3, 814 99 Bratislava; tel. (7) 335-771; fax (7) 331-413; f. 1991; cap. 350m.; Pres. Ing. VLADIMÍR ULMAN.

Priemyselná banka, a.s. Košice (Industrial Bank, Inc.): Boženy Němcovej 30, 042 18 Košice; tel. (95) 353-26; fax (95) 303-11; f. 1992; cap. 330m.; Gen. Dir Doc. Ing. JAROSLAV MARIČÁK; 3 brs.

Prvá komunálna banka, a.s. (First Communal Bank, Inc.): ul. Horný Val 24, 010 10 Žilina; tel. (89) 450-35; fax (89) 488-37; f. 1993; cap. 300m.; Gen. Dir Ing. JOZEF MIHALIK.

Slovenská kreditná banka, a.s. (Slovak Credit Bank, Inc.): nám. SNP 13, 814 99 Bratislava; tel. and fax (7) 321-021; f. 1993; cap. 411.5m.; Gen. Dir ŠTEFAN VESELOVSKÝ.

Slovenská pol'nohospodárska banka, a.s. (Slovak Agricultural Bank, Inc.): Vajnorská 21, 832 65 Bratislava; tel. (7) 202-1211; telex 927315; fax (7) 215-121; f. 1990; cap. 800m.; Gen. Dir Ing. L'UDOVÍT PÓSA; 15 brs.

Slovenská záručná banka š.p.ú. (Slovak Guarantee Bank): Kutlíkova 17, POB 223, 852 99 Bratislava; tel. (7) 836-732; fax (7) 836-909; f. 1991; cap. 376.2m.; Gen. Dir Ing. JOZEF DRŠKA; 2 brs.

Tatra banka, a.s.: Vajanského nábr. 5, 810 06 Bratislava; tel. (7) 331-351; telex 92644; fax (7) 334-656; f. 1991; cap. 401.7m., res. 153.8m., dep. 2,290.0m. (Dec. 1992); Gen. Dir Ing. MILAN VRŠKOVÝ.

Všeobecná úverová banka, a.s. (General Credit Bank, Inc.): nám. SNP 19, 818 56 Bratislava; tel. (7) 367-428; telex 93346; fax (7) 326-867; f. 1990; cap. 2,039m., res 6,830m., dep. 110,831m.; Chair. and Pres. Ing. JOZEF MUDRÍK; 39 brs.

Savings Bank

Slovenská štátna sporitel'ňa (Slovak State Savings Bank): nám. SNP 18, 816 07 Bratislava; tel. (7) 367-300; fax (7) 367-087; f. 1967; cap. 2,129.9m., res 4,057.1m., dep. 117,206.0m. (Dec. 1992); Dir ALOJZ ONDRA; 680 brs and agencies.

COMMODITY AND STOCK EXCHANGES

Bratislavská medzinárodná komoditná burza (Bratislava Commodity Exchange): Záhradnicka 153, 821 08 Bratislava; tel. (7) 211-454; fax (7) 213-585.

Burza cenných papierov v Bratislave a.s. (Bratislava Stock Exchange): Hlavné nám. 8, POB 151, 814 99 Bratislava; tel. (7) 335-844; fax (7) 335-725; Man. MARIÁN SASIK.

INSURANCE

Slovenská poist'ovňa (Slovak Insurance Co): Strakova 1, 815 74 Bratislava; telex 93375; fax (7) 330-879; Gen. Dir VLADIMÍR HORVÁTH.

Trade and Industry

CHAMBER OF COMMERCE

Slovenská obchodná a priemyselná komora (Slovak Chamber of Commerce and Industry): Gorkého 9, 816 03 Bratislava; tel. (7) 316-402; fax (7) 330-754; Pres. Ing. PETER MIHÓK.

INVESTMENT AGENCY

Slovak National Agency for Foreign Investment and Development (SNAFID): Manesovo nám. 2, 851 01 Bratislava; tel. (7) 847-219; fax (7) 849-806; Dir RADOVAN PEKNIK.

FOREIGN TRADE CORPORATIONS AND MAJOR INDUSTRIAL COMPANIES

Chirana-Prema a.s.: 916 01 Stará Turá; tel. (834) 963-721; telex 93675; fax (834) 963-911; production and distribution of medical equipment and measuring devices; Gen. Dir JURAJ BOROVSKÝ.

Drevounia: Jašíkova 6, 826 10 Bratislava; tel. (7) 237-723; telex 93292; fax (7) 236-164; f. 1974; exports wood and furniture; Gen. Dir Ing. JIŘÍ JIRAVA; 120 employees.

Intercoop: Dr V. Clementisa 10, 826 08 Bratislava; tel. (7) 229162; telex 93365; fax (7) 224393; imports and exports toys, fruits, vegetables, honey and wine.

Martimex Ltd: Červenej armády 1, 036 65 Martin; tel. (842) 33311; telex 75488; fax (842) 39118; f. 1970; imports and exports construction and roadbuilding machinery, fork-lift trucks; Pres. MILAN LAUKO.

Petrimex, a.s.: Dr V. Clementisa 10, 826 02 Bratislava; tel. (7) 290-2111; telex 92525; fax (7) 238-148; imports and exports chemicals, raw materials and pharmaceutical products; Man. Dir ANTON RAKICKÝ.

TRADE UNIONS

Confederation of Trade Unions of the Slovak Republic (Konfederácia odborových zväzov Slovenskej republiky): Odborárské nám. 3, 815 70 Bratislava; tel. (7) 622-65; fax (7) 213-303; Pres. ALOJZ ENGLIŠ.

Affiliated unions include the following:

Trade Union of Metal Workers: Vajnorská 1, 815 70 Bratislava; tel. (7) 214-225; fax (7) 213-326; Pres. JOZEF KRUMPOLEC.

Trade Union of Workers in Agriculture: Vajnorská 1, 815 70 Bratislava; tel. (7) 213-942; fax (7) 211-673; Pres. EMIL KUČERA.

Trade Union of Workers in the Chemical Industry: Vajnorská 1, 815 70 Bratislava; tel. (7) 213-408; fax (7) 214-308; Pres. JURAJ BLAHÁK.

Trade Union of Workers in Construction: Vajnorská 1, 815 70 Bratislava; tel. (7) 214-180; fax (7) 212-764; Pres. RUDOLF HORVÁTH.

Trade Union of Workers in Cultural and Social Organizations: Vajnorská 1, 815 70 Bratislava; tel. and fax (7) 213-760; Pres. JARMILA JÁNOŠOVÁ.

Trade Union of Workers in Energy: Vajnorská 1, 815 70 Bratislava; tel. (7) 211-622; fax (7) 211-692; Pres. JOZEF KOLLÁR.

Trade Union of Workers in the Food-processing Industry: Vajnorská 1, 815 70 Bratislava; tel. (7) 678-24; Pres. MILAN PIEŠŤANSKÝ.

Trade Union of Workers in the Glass Industry: Studentská, 911 01 Trenčín; tel. (831) 372-00; Pres. MILAN MLYNČÁR.

Trade Union of Workers in the Health and Social Services: Vajnorská 1, 815 70 Bratislava; tel. (7) 213-965; fax (7) 215-330; Pres. DANIEL REPÁŠ.

Trade Union of Workers in Radio, Television and Newspapers: Vajnorská 1, 815 70 Bratislava; tel. (7) 211-844; Pres. PETER JÁCHIN.

Trade Union of Workers in the Textile, Clothing and Leather Industry: Vajnorská 1, 815 70 Bratislava; tel. (7) 213-389; fax (7) 651-82; Pres. Ing. PAVOL JAKUBÍK.

Trade Union of Workers in the Wood-working, Furniture and Paper Industries: Vajnorská 1, 815 70 Bratislava; tel. (7) 213-660; fax (7) 213-163; Pres. BORISLAV MAJTÁN.

Transport

RAILWAYS

In 1993 the total length of railways in Slovakia was 3,661 km, of which 1,373 km were electrified. A 43-km underground railway system in Bratislava was scheduled for completion in 1997.

Železnice Slovenskej republiky (Slovak State Railways): Klemensova 8, 813 61 Bratislava; tel. (7) 325-242; fax (7) 362-341; f. 1993; Dir ALBERT VEREŠ.

ROADS

In 1993 there were 17,737 km of roads in Slovakia, including 210 km of motorways.

Cestná a mestská doprava, Ministerstvo dopravy, spojov a verejných prác (Road and Urban Transport Department, Ministry of Transport, Communications and Public Works): Miletičova 19, 820 06 Bratislava; tel. (7) 255-741; fax (7) 211-221; Dir Ing. PAVOL REICH.

INLAND WATERWAYS

The total length of navigable waterways in Slovakia (on the River Danube) is 172 km. The Danube provides a link with Germany, Austria, Hungary, Yugoslavia, Bulgaria, Romania and the Black Sea. The main river ports are Bratislava and Komárno.

Štátna plavebná správa (State Administration of Shipping): Prístavná 10, 816 14 Bratislava; tel. (7) 363-022; fax (7) 323-286; Dir Ing. ANDA KAROL.

Slovenská plavba Dunajská (Slovak Danube Shipping): Pribinova 24, 815 24 Bratislava; tel. (7) 367-504, fax (7) 363 002; Ing. JURAJ PAVELEK.

CIVIL AVIATION

There are civil airports at Bratislava (M. R. Štefanik Airport), Košice, Piešt'any, Poprad and Sliač (Banská Bystrica).

Slovenská správa letísk (Slovak Airports Administration): Letisko Ivánka, 823 11 Bratislava; tel. (7) 224-633; fax (7) 222-146; Man. Dir IVAN SCHLOSSER.

Tatra Air Group, a.s.: Letisko M. R. Štefanika, 823 12 Bratislava; tel. (7) 291-408; fax (7) 223-175; f. 1990; joint-stock airline co; Dir DUŠAN PODHORSKÝ.

Tourism

Slovakia's tourist attractions include ski resorts in the High and Low Tatras and other mountain ranges, more than 20 spa resorts (with thermal and mineral springs), numerous castles and mansions and historic towns, including Bratislava, Košice, Nitra, Bardejov, Kežmarok and Levoča. In 1991 576,299 foreign tourists visited Slovakia.

Slovakotour: Michálska 2, Bratislava; tel. (7) 332-962.

Slovakoturist: Volgogradská 1, Bratislava; tel. (7) 552-47.

Tatratour: Františkánské nám. 7, Bratislava; tel. (7) 335-536.

Culture

NATIONAL ORGANIZATION

Ministry of Culture: see section on The Government (Ministries).

CULTURAL HERITAGE

Galéria mesta Bratislavy (Gallery of Bratislava): Mirbachove palač, Františkánske nám. 11, 815 35 Bratislava; tel. and fax (7) 332-611; Dir FEDOR KRIŠKA.

Matica Slovenská: L. Novomeského 32, Martin; tel. (842) 324-54; telex 75331; f. 1863; Slovak cultural org.; Chair. Ing. IMRICH SEDLÁCH.

Slovenská národná galéria (Slovak National Gallery): Riečna 1, 815 13 Bratislava; tel. (7) 330-437; fax (7) 333-971; f. 1948; paintings, sculpture, prints, drawings, applied art and facsimilies; scientific library; Dir Dr JURAJ ŽÁRY.

Slovenské národné múzeum (Slovak National Museum): Vajanského nábr. 2, 814 36 Bratislava; tel. (7) 330-479; fax (7) 335-471; f. 1924; archaeology, ethnography, musicology, numismatics, history of Slovakia, natural history; Dir Dr BRANISLAV MATOUŠEK.

Stredoslovenská galéria: nám. SNP 7, 974 00 Banská Bystrica; tel. (88) 248-64; art gallery; Dir Dr VILIAM DÚBRAVSKÝ.

Východoslovenská galéria: Leninova 72, 040 01 Košice; tel. (95) 211-87; art gallery; Dir Dr LADISLAV ZOZUL'ÁK.

PERFORMING ARTS

Bratislavské hudobné slávnosti (Bratislava Music Festival): Michalská 10, 815 36 Bratislava; tel. (7) 334-528; telex 92785; fax (7) 332-652; Dir Dr LADISLAV MOKRÝ.

Divadlo korzo '90: Suché mýto 17, Dunajská 1, Bratislava; tel. (7) 330-739; theatre; Dir L'UBOMÍR GREGOR.

Nová scéna: Živnostenská 1, 812 92 Bratislava; tel. (7) 532-30; theatre; Dir L'UBO ROMAN.

Slovenská filharmónia (Slovak Philharmonic Orchestra): Medená 3, 816 01 Bratislava; tel. (7) 333-351; fax (7) 335-956; Dir ALŽBETA RAJTEROVÁ; Principal Conductor ALDO CECCATO.

Slovenské národné divadlo (Slovak National Theatre): Gorkého 4, 815 86 Bratislava; tel. (2) 323-861; f. 1920; comprises separate opera, ballet and drama ensembles; Gen. Dir DUŠAN JAMRICH.

Štátna filharmónia Košice (Košice State Philharmonic Orchestra): Dom umenia, Moyzesova 66, 041 23 Košice; tel. (95) 245-14; Dir Dr IRENA MEDŇANSKÁ; Principal Conductor Dr JOHANNES WILDNER.

Štátne divadlo: Šrobárova 14, 042 77 Košice; state theatre, opera and ballet house; Dir ANTON GREGA.

Symfonický orchester slovenského rozhlasu (Slovak Radio Symphony Orchestra): Mýtna 1, 812 90 Bratislava; tel. (7) 444-62; Principal Conductor ADRIAN LEAPER.

ASSOCIATIONS

Asociácia organizácií spisovatel'ov Slovenska (Association of Writers' Organizations in Slovakia): Laurinská 2, 815 08 Bratislava; tel. (7) 335-368; f. 1949, reorganized in 1990; 330 mems; Pres. JÁN BUZÁSSY; Sec. PETER ANDRUŠKA.

Association of Hungarian Writers: Bratislava; f. 1989.

Fond výtvarných umení (Fine Art Foundation): Trnavská 112, 826 33 Bratislava; tel. (7) 235-340; fax (7) 236-282.

Hudobné informačné stredisko (Music Information Centre): Medená 29, 811 02 Bratislava; tel. (7) 335-569; telex 92575; Dir Dr VIERA POLAKOVIČOVÁ.

Slovenská hudobná asociácia (Slovak Music Association): Jakubovo nám. 12, 811 06 Bratislava; tel. (7) 333-794.

Slovenská hudobná únia (Slovak Music Union): Michalská 10, 815 36 Bratislava; tel. (7) 335-291; fax (7) 330-188; Chair. PETER DVORSKÝ.

Slovenská výtvarná únia (Slovak Fine Art Union): Partizánska 21, 811 01 Bratislava; tel. (7) 331-078; fax (7) 335-744.

Slovenské Design centrum: Baštová 4, 811 01 Bratislava; tel. (7) 331-371.

Slovenský filmový zväz (Slovak Film Union): Mostová 6, 811 02 Bratislava; tel. (7) 331-071; Chair. ILJA RUPPELDT; Sec. PETER ŇUKOVIČ.

Slovenský hudobný fond (Slovak Music Foundation): Fučíková 29, 811 02 Bratislava; tel. (7) 333-412; telex 92575; Dir Ing. MILOŠ KOCIÁN.

Spolok architektov Slovenska (Slovak Architects' Society): Panská 15, 811 01 Bratislava; tel. (7) 335-711; fax (7) 335-744; 1,300 mems; Pres. Ing. arch STEFAN SLACHTA; Sec. PATRIK GULDAN.

Ústredie l'udovel umeleckej výroby (Craft Art Centre): Obchodná 64, 816 11 Bratislava; tel. (7) 335-296.

Združenie divadelníkov na Slovensku: Gorkého 4, 812 92 Bratislava; tel. (7) 334-434; theatrical association; Contact Dr JANA MELICHÁRKOVÁ.

Zväz slovenských dramatických umelcov (Union of Slovak Dramatists): Gorkého 4, 812 92 Bratislava; Pres. OSVALD ZAHRADNIK.

Zväz slovenských skladatelov a koncertných umelcov) (Union of Slovak Composers and Concert Performers): Sládcovičova 11, Bratislava; tel. (7) 330-188; f. 1955; 290 mems; Pres. Prof. Dr OTO FERENCZY; Sec. ALOJZ LUKNÁR.

Education

Education is fully funded by the state at all levels. Most children between the ages of three and six attend kindergarten (materška škola). Education is compulsory between the ages of six and 16 years, when children attend basic school (základní škola). Most children continue their studies after basic school, either at a secondary grammar school, of which there were 165 in the 1992/93 academic year, a secondary specialized school (stredná odborná škola), of which there were 315, or a secondary vocational school (stredné odborné učilište), of which there were 348. In each type of institution students follow four-year courses. In 1990 the establishment of private and religious schools was legalized. In the 1991/92 school year 188,821 children attended kindergarten, 716,416 attended basic (elementary) schools, 302,380 the different types of secondary school and there were 61,272 students in higher education.

UNIVERSITIES

Ekonomická Univerzita v Bratislave (University of Economics in Bratislava): Odbojárov 10, 832 20 Bratislava; tel. (7) 605-61; fax (7) 630-45; f. 1940; 5 faculties, 1 attached institute; 519 teachers; 7,270 teachers; Rector Prof. Ing. MIKULÁŠ SEDLÁK.

Slovenská Technická Univerzita v Bratislave (Slovak Technical University in Bratislava): nám. Slobody 17, 812 43 Bratislava; tel. (7) 323-740; fax (7) 361-652; f. 1938; 6 faculties; 1,869 teachers; 12,576 students; Chancellor Ing. HELENA ŽIDEKOVÁ.

Technická Univerzita v Košiciach (Košice Technical University): Letná, 041 87 Košice; tel. (95) 399-062; telex 77410; fax (95) 327-48; f. 1952; 7 faculties; 809 teachers; 5,683 students; Rector Prof. Dr IVAN HRIVŇÁK.

Technická Univerzita vo Zvolene (Technical University in Zvolen): T. G. Masaryka 24, 960 53 Zvolen; tel. (855) 601; telex 72267; fax (855) 200-27; f. 1807, reorganized as College of Forestry and Wood Technology 1952, acquired university status 1991; 3 faculties; 193 teachers; 1,470 students; Rector Assoc. Prof. VILÉM ŠTEFKA.

Univerzita Komenského Bratislava (Comenius University of Bratislava): Šafárikovo nám. 6, 818 06 Bratislava; tel. (7) 321-594; f. 1919; 12 faculties; 1,931 teachers; 20,000 students; Chancellor Prof. Dr JURAJ ŠVEC.

Univerzita Pavla Jozefa Šafárika (Šafárik University): Šrobárova 2, 041 80 Košice; tel. (95) 622-2608; telex 77562; fax (95) 766-959; f. 1959; 7 faculties; 727 teachers; 6,118 students; Rector Prof. Dr LEV BUKOVSKÝ.

Univerzita Veterinárskeho Lekárstva (University of Veterinary Medicine): Komenského 73, 041 81 Košice; tel. (95) 321-11; telex 77322; fax (95) 767-675; f. 1949; 155 teachers; 755 students; Rector Assoc. Prof. RUDOLF CABADAJ.

Vysoká Škola Dopravy a Spojov (University of Transport and Telecommunications): Moyzesova 20, 010 26 Žilina; tel. (89) 217-81; telex 75630; fax (89) 543-84; f. 1953; 5 faculties; 567 teachers; 4,973 students; Rector Ing. MIROSLAV KOPECKÝ.

Social Welfare

A single and universal social-security system was established in Czechoslovakia after the Second World War. Protection of health was stipulated by law, and medical care, treatment, medicines, etc. were, in most cases, available free of charge to the entire Czechoslovak population. In 1992 there were 6.5 physicians and 76.7 hospital beds per 1,000 inhabitants of Slovakia. There was a universal pension system, available to women at the age of 60 and to men at the age of 65.

In 1991 a new system of social security was introduced. The Government planned to guarantee a minimum level of social welfare to all citizens, in an attempt to mitigate the expected consequences of radical economic reform. In addition, benefit was made available to unemployed workers for a maximum period of 12 months, and mandatory redundancy payments, equivalent to two months' wages, were introduced. In 1990 a Council of Economic and Social Consensus (the 'Tripartite Council'), composed of representatives of federal and republican governments, employers and the trade unions, was established to discuss welfare issues.

Following the dissolution of Czechoslovakia in 1993, the two successor states announced plans to introduce changes to the existing social-welfare system. The health service was to remain largely under state control in Slovakia, although there were plans to privatize certain elements, particularly spas and pharmacies. A National Insurance Company came into being on 1 January 1993 and consisted of separate funds for general health insurance, sickness insurance and pensions insurance. Payments into the funds were to be made by employees, employers, the self-employed and the state. Further reforms to the social-welfare system were hampered by policitical uncertainties, which included the forced resignation of the Minister of Health.

GOVERNMENT AGENCIES

Ministry of Labour, Social Affairs and the Family: see section on The Government (Ministries).

Národná poisťovňa (National Insurance Company): ul. 29 augusta 8-10, 813 63 Bratislava; tel. (7) 323-592; fax (7) 323-168; f. 1993; administers health, sickness and pension insurance schemes; Dir Ing. PETER MAGVAŠI.

The Environment

GOVERNMENT ORGANIZATIONS

Ministry for the Environment: see section on The Government (Ministries).

Národny Park Nízke Tatry—NAPANT (Low Tatras National Park): Horná 67, 974 00 Banská Bystrica; tel. (88) 543-72; fax (88) 247-28; Dir Dr LUBOŠ ČILLAG.

Ústredie štátnej ochrany prírody—UŠOP (State Centre for Nature Conservation): Leninova 11, 031 01 Liptovský Mikuláš; Dir ANTON LUCINKIEWICZ.

Ústredie Statnej Pamatkove Pece a Ochrany Prirody—USPPOP (State Institute for the Protection of Monuments and Nature Conservancy): Mostova 6, 811 02 Bratislava.

ACADEMIC INSTITUTES

Slovenská Akadémia Vied (Slovak Academy of Sciences): Štefánikova 49, 814 38 Bratislava; tel. (7) 492-751; telex 93261; fax (7) 496-849; f. 1953; Pres. Acad. LADISLAV MACHO.

Arboretum Mlyňany—Ústav dendrobiológie (Institute of Dendrobiology): 951 52 Slepčany; tel. (814) 948-33; fax (814) 948-36; f. 1892, re-established 1954; research into horticulture and landscape architecture; Dir Assoc. Prof. IVAN TOMAŠKO.

Botanický ústav (Institute of Botany): Dúbravská cesta 14, 842 23 Bratislava; tel. (7) 373-507; fax (7) 371-948; f. 1964; research into the flora and vegetation of Slovakia, plant physiology, embryology and pathology; Dir Dr OTÍLIA GAŠPARÍKOVÁ.

Geografický ústav (Institute of Geography): Štefánikova 49, 814 73 Bratislava; tel. (7) 492-751; f. 1943; research in geography, regional matters and the environment; Dir Assoc. Prof. ANTON BEZÁK.

Ústav ekológie lesa (Institute of Forest Ecology): Štúrova 2, 960 53 Zvolen; tel. (855) 22-312; fax (855) 274-85; Dirs Dr OL'GA KONTRIŠOVÁ, Ing. VINCENT ŠTRBA.

Ústav hydrológie a hydrauliky (Institute of Hydrology and Hydraulics): Trnavská 32, 826 51 Bratislava; tel. (7) 63561.

Ústav krajinnej ekológie (Institute of Landscape Ecology): Štefánikova 3, POB 254, 814 99 Bratislava; tel. (7) 334-311; fax (7) 332-560; br. in Nitra.

Ústav zoológie a ekosozológie (Institute of Zoology and Ecosociology): Mánesovo nám. 2, 851 01 Bratislava; tel. (7) 846184.

Centre for Environmental Impact Assessment: Faculty of Natural Sciences, Comenius University, Mlynská Dolina B-2, 842 15 Bratislava; tel. (7) 720-642; fax (7) 729-064; Dirs Dr MARÍA KOZOVÁ, Dr KATARÍNA PAVLIČKOVÁ.

ENVIRO—Information Branch: c/o Ministry for the Environment, Hlbolá 2, 812 35 Bratislava; tel. (7) 725-968; fax (7) 728-441.

Lesnícky výskumný ústav (Forest Research Institute): T. G. Masaryka 22, 960 92 Zvolen; tel. (855) 273-11; fax (855) 233-97; f. 1898; forestry management and ecological research; Dir JOZEF REMIŠ.

Výskumný ústav vodného hospodárstva (Water Research Institute): nábr. L. Svobodu 5, 812 49 Bratislava; tel. (7) 343-111; fax (7) 315-743; f. 1951; Dir Ing. VLADIMÍR HOLČÍK.

NON-GOVERNMENTAL ORGANIZATIONS

Environmental Partnership for Central Europe: Skvteckého 30, 974 00 Banská Bystrica; tel. (88) 294-259; fax (88) 294-220; Country Dir JURAJ MESIK.

Greenpeace Slovakia: POB 58, 815 99 Bratislava.

Nadácia Zelená Alternatíva (Green Alternative Foundation): Vajanského 3, 921 01 Piešt'any; tel. (838) 239-27; presents ecologically sound alternatives to present ways of living; environmental education; Pres. Dr PETER SABO.

Nadácia Zelená Nádej (Green Perspective Foundation): Levočská 5, 080 01 Prešov; tel. (91) 345-00; fax (91) 314-45; campaigns for environmental conservation and responsible use of biosystems; campaigns to save the Čergov forest in north-east Slovakia; Dirs JURAJ LUKÁČ, RADOSLAV POTOČNÝ, DAGMAR BALÁŽOVÁ.

Slovensky zväz ochrancov prírody a krajiny—SZOPK (Slovak Union of Nature and Landscape Conservationists): Gorkého 6, 811 01 Bratislava; tel. (7) 364-665; fax (7) 335-422; environmental education; protection of natural resources and biodiversity; protection of historical monuments and the landscape; Dirs Dr MIROSLAV FULÍN, Dr JOZEF GREGOR; 353 local groups; 14,000 mems.

Strana Zelených na Slovensku (Green Party in Slovakia): Laurinská 1, 811 01 Bratislava; tel. (7) 332-604; f. 1990; 4,000 mems.

Strom života (Tree of Life): Pražská 11, 813 36 Bratislava; tel. (7) 498-473; fax (7) 498-703; organizes environmental education projects for young people; tel. (7) 498-473; fax (7) 498-703; Dirs OTO MAKÝŠ, PETER HRABINA.

Defence

The former Czechoslovakia had one of the strongest armed forces in the Warsaw Pact (which was dissolved in 1991). In June 1991 the last of the 73,500 Soviet troops stationed in Czechoslovakia left the country. The numbers of Czechoslovak troops had already been reduced significantly, under the Conventional Forces in Europe (CFE) process, by the end of 1992, when Slovakia assumed responsibilty for 50,000 of the remaining 150,000 personnel. Military service is compulsory and lasts for 12 months. In June 1993, according to Western estimates, the total armed forces numbered 47,000; the Army numbered 33,000 and the Air Force 14,000. In addition there were an estimated 600 border guards, 250 internal security forces and 3,100 civil defence troops. About 400 Slovak troops were serving with UNPROFOR in Croatia. The budget allocation for defence spending in 1993 was estimated at 8,200m. koruny.

Commander-in-Chief: President of the Republic.

Commander of the Slovak Army: Lt-Gen. JÚLIUS HUMAJ.

Bibliography

For publications on Czechoslovakia see the Bibliography of the Czech Republic, p. 285.

Brock, P. *The Slovak National Awakening: An Essay in the Intellectual History of East-Central Europe*. Toronto, University of Toronto Press, 1976.

Jablonický, J., and Pivovarči, J. *The Slovak National Uprising*. Bratislava, Obzor, 1969.

Kirschbaum, S. J., and Roman, C. R. (Eds). *Reflections on Slovak History*. Toronto, Slovak World Congress, 1987.

Lettrich, J. *History of Modern Slovakia*. Toronto, Slovak Research and Studies Centre, 1987.

Steiner, E. *The Slovak Dilemma*. Cambridge, Cambridge University Press, 1973.

SLOVENIA

Geography

PHYSICAL FEATURES

The Republic of Slovenia, formerly a constituent partner in the Socialist Federal Republic of Yugoslavia (SFRY), lies in south-central Europe. Slovenia has frontiers with Italy in the west, Austria to the north, Hungary along a short border in the east, and its southern border is with Croatia. In the south-west of the country there is a short coastal strip (40 km—24.9 miles) on the Adriatic Sea, around the Istrian port of Koper.

Slovenia is an Alpine area, being dominated by the Julian and Karawanken Alps (Julijske Alpe and Karavanke). Slovenia's highest peak, Triglav (2,863 m—9,394 ft), is in the Julian Alps, close to the northern part of the border with Italy. Most of the territory is mountainous, the main areas of lower land being in the south-west near the coast, in the central southern areas, along the Sava river, and in the north-east around the Mura river, where Slovenia becomes a narrowing strip of territory abutting onto the Pannonian plains. The river valleys and karst lands of the Adriatic contribute to the agricultural territory and there is considerable woodland.

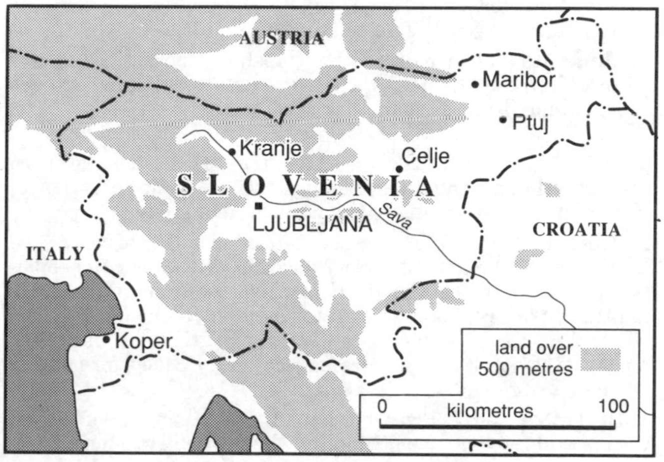

CLIMATE

The climate in Slovenia is Mediterranean on the coast and continental inland. Mountainous areas have a colder climate with heavy snowfall in winter. Average daily temperatures range from between 0°C (32°F) and 22°C (71.6°F) inland, and between 2°C (35.6°F) and 24°C (75.2°F) on the coast. Average annual rainfall ranges from 800 mm in the east to 3,000 mm in the north-west.

POPULATION

At the census of March 1991, the total population of Slovenia was 1,965,986, which gave it a population density of 97.1 per sq km. Most of the population were ethnic Slovenes (87.8% in 1991). There were also Slovene communities in other former Republics of the SFRY, and in Austria and Italy. The largest minority ethnic groups in Slovenia were Croats (2.8% of the total population in 1991), Serbs (2.4%) and Slav Muslims (1.4%). The official language is Slovene, a Southern Slavonic tongue, related to but distinct from Serbo-Croat. The traditional religion of the Slovenes is Christianity, as practised by the Roman Catholic Church, to which most of the population adhere. There are small communities of other Christian denominations, including Eastern Orthodox Christians, of Muslims (mainly guest workers) and Jews. The capital of Slovenia is Ljubljana, the largest city in the country, with a population of 276,133 at the 1991 census. It is located in the centre-west of Slovenia. Other important towns include Maribor (108,122 in 1991), Celje (41,279) and Kranj (37,318).

Chronology

168 BC: Illyria (in the north of which lay the territory which is now Slovenia) was annexed by the Roman Empire.

AD 395: Following a division of the administration of the Roman Empire, Illyria was ruled by the Eastern Roman ('Byzantine') Emperor in Constantinople (now Istanbul, Turkey).

5th century: Southern Slav peoples began to move from Pannonia into Illyria and the Balkans.

7th century: Western Slavic tribes associated themselves with the Slavic Duchy of Carinthia (based in modern Austria), while Western Christian missionaries from Salzburg were active among these ancestors of the Slovenes, introducing the Latin script and a Western cultural orientation.

745: Carinthia fell under the influence of the Frankish (German) empire, becoming a mark or marcher lordship in 788; the Slav conversion to Christianity was, therefore, secured.

812: By the Treaty of Aix-la-Chapelle (Aachen), the Byzantine Emperor, Michael I, acknowledged the Frankish ruler, Charles ('the Great'—Charlemagne), as Emperor in the West; German influence over the Slovene-inhabited areas of Carinthia and Carniola was thus established, although Byzantine (and Venetian) influence remained on the Istrian coast.

869–74: Kocelj briefly established a Slovene principality in Lower Pannonia (southern Hungary).

1335: Carniola and Carinthia became hereditary possessions of the Austrian House of Habsburg, within the Holy Roman Empire.

1490: Death of the Hungarian King, Matthias I Corvinus, who had, temporarily, conquered the Habsburg lands.

1551: A minister of the Protestant (Calvinist) Church of Carniola, Primož Trubar, published a catechism which was the first book in the Slovene language.

1584: Jurij Dalmatin translated the Bible into Slovene and Adam Bohorič wrote a Slovene grammar.

1599: The Counter-Reformation secured the Slovenes for Roman Catholicism by the final extinction of the Church of Carniola, the writings of which, however, had already provided the basis of Slovene literature.

1815: The Congress of Vienna confirmed Austrian rule over Istria and Dalmatia, which were formerly Venetian.

1848: A group of Slovene intellectuals formulated the first political manifesto advocating a united Slovenia.

1867: The *Ausgleich* or Compromise created, in the Habsburg territories, the 'Dual Monarchy' of Austria-Hungary; the Slovenes were found in four of the 15 Austrian crownlands: Carniola (where they formed a majority); Carinthia; Styria; and the Coastal Lands around Trieste (ancient Aquileia).

28 June 1914: The heir to the Habsburg throne, Archduke Francis Ferdinand, and his wife were assassinated in Sarajevo (Bosnia and Herzegovina), which led to the start of the First World War.

July 1917: Prominent Slovenes, together with other Southern Slavs (excluding the Bulgarians), declared their intention to form a unitary state, under the Serbian monarchy.

29 October 1918: Following the defeat and dissolution of the Danubian Monarchy, the Southern Slav (Yugoslav) peoples separated from the Austro-Hungarian system of states (a Southern Slav republic was established on 15 October); Carniola and parts of the Coastal Lands, Styria and Carinthia, among other territories, were subsequently ceded formally to the new state.

4 December 1918: Proclamation of the Kingdom of Serbs, Croats and Slovenes, which united the former Habsburg lands with Serbia and Montenegro.

3 October 1929: Following the imposition of a royal dictatorship, the country was formally named Yugoslavia.

1937: Josip Broz (Tito) became General-Secretary of the Communist Party of Yugoslavia (CPY), which was to become the main partner in the Partisan (National Liberation Army) resistance to the German invasion.

April 1941: German and Italian forces invaded Yugoslavia, which was dismembered, with Germany annexing Lower Styria and parts of Carinthia, and Italy annexing Ljubljana (Laibach) and Istria; the Liberation Front, which was to become the Slovene wing of the Partisan movement, was founded.

29 November 1945: A Provisional Assembly proclaimed the Federative People's Republic of Yugoslavia, elections having taken place after fighting ended in Carinthia and Styria in May.

January 1946: A Soviet-style Constitution, establishing a federation of six republics (including a Socialist Republic of Slovenia) and two autonomous regions, was adopted.

November 1952: The Communist Party was renamed the League of Communists of Yugoslavia (LCY) and several liberal reforms were adopted.

1954: Istria was partitioned between Italy (which gained the city of Trieste) and Yugoslavia (most of the territory was awarded to Slovenia, which thereby gained a coastline, but the southern Istrian peninsula became part of Croatia).

April 1963: A new Constitution changed the country's name to the Socialist Federal Republic of Yugoslavia (SFRY).

1971: Following the granting of the rights of autonomy to the federal units, Tito introduced a system of collective leadership and the regular rotation of posts; a collective State Presidency for Yugoslavia was established, with Tito as its head. However, later in the year, there was a purge of 'nationalist' liberals throughout Yugoslavia.

1975: The Treaty of Osimo formally established the Yugoslav–Italian borders.

4 May 1980: Tito died; his responsibilities were transferred to the collective State Presidency and to the Presidium of the LCY.

1988: Against a background of increasing dissatisfaction with the state of the economy, the military trial of journalists on *Mladina* magazine and of an army officer provoked the first demands for Slovenian independence.

September 1989: With rising dissatisfaction throughout Yugoslavia and tension increasing in Kosovo (Serbia), the Slovenian Assembly reaffirmed the sovereignty of their Republic and declared its right to secede from the SFRY.

December 1989: Serbian enterprises were instructed to sever all links with Slovenia, which retaliated by closing its borders to Serbian goods and implementing reciprocal economic sanctions. Six of the main opposition parties united in the Democratic Opposition of Slovenia (DEMOS), which advocated economic independence.

20–23 January 1990: At its 14th (Extraordinary) Congress, the LCY voted to abolish its leading role in society, but rejected Slovenian proposals to restructure the federal Party; the Slovenian delegation withdrew from the Congress and the League of Communists of Slovenia suspended its links with the LCY; the Congress adjourned following its decision not to continue without the Slovenian delegation.

4 February 1990: A conference of the League of Communists of Slovenia renounced its links with the LCY and decided to change its name to the Party of Democratic Reform. Slovenia withdrew its police contingent from Kosovo.

8 March 1990: The Slovenian Assembly renamed the territory the Republic of Slovenia.

8 April 1990: The opposition DEMOS coalition won the direct elections to the Assembly's main Socio-Political Chamber (gaining 47 of the 80 seats); there were also the first-round elections to the Chamber of Municipalities, to the Chamber of Associated Labour (on a non-party basis) and for the President of the republican State Presidency.

22 April 1990: The second round of voting for the parliamentary and presidential elections was held: Milan Kučan, the leader of the former Communists, was elected as President of the republican Presidency; DEMOS emerged as the winner in the Chamber of Municipalities. The following month Lojze Peterle, leader of the Slovenian Christian Democratic Party (a member of DEMOS), was elected President of the Executive Council (Premier).

2 July 1990: The Assembly proclaimed the full sovereignty of Slovenia.

28 September 1990: The Assembly asserted its jurisdiction over the Slovenian Territorial Defence Force; the move was denounced by the federal authorities, which soon ordered the Jugoslavenska Narodna Armija (JNA—Yugoslav People's Army) to occupy the force headquarters.

23 December 1990: A referendum, in which an overwhelming majority voted in favour of secession, was held in Slovenia, despite federal warnings of unconstitutionality and economic sanctions.

January 1991: The federal State Presidency ordered that all 'unauthorized' armed units should surrender their weapons, causing tension between the JNA and forces controlled by Slovenia and Croatia. Later the two Republics concluded a mutual defence pact.

20 February 1991: The Slovenian Assembly adopted a resolution initiating its process of 'dissociation' from Yugoslavia, although it declared its willingness to negotiate on the federation's future as well as the details of secession.

8 May 1991: With the failure of various attempts to negotiate a new federation, Slovenia announced that it would secede from Yugoslavia by 26 June; increasing tension between the Territorial Defence Force and the JNA followed. One week later a crisis involving the federal State Presidency began—the Croatian member was prevented from becoming President of the body.

25 June 1991: The Slovenian and Croatian Assemblies declared the independence and sovereignty of their Republics, formally beginning dissociation from the federation. Slovenia had enacted enabling legislation, formed a new Slovenian Territorial Army and attempted to take receipt of customs duties.

27 June 1991: The JNA began military operations in Slovenia, mobilizing to secure the international borders of the SFRY and bombing Ljubljana airport. Fighting continued intermittently over the next few weeks, despite European Community (EC) efforts to negotiate a cease-fire.

7–8 July 1991: Representatives of the EC, Slovenia, Croatia and the Yugoslav State Presidency met on the Adriatic island of Brioni (Croatia); their final agreement resolved that all fighting should cease immediately and that Slovenia and Croatia should have a three-month moratorium on further implementation of their declarations of dissociation.

2 October 1991: The Slovenian Assembly resolved to end all involvement in Yugoslavia after 7 October, the last day of the EC-negotiated moratorium. When this independence declaration took effect, the country introduced its own currency and recalled all its citizens in federal institutions (the last JNA troops left Slovenia, by sea, on 26 October). Later in the month the ruling DEMOS became a coalition of seven, rather than six, parties, following a split in the Slovenian Democratic Union.

23 December 1991: The Slovenian Constitution was enacted, providing for a bicameral legislature, with elections scheduled for 1992. In the same month the DEMOS coalition was dissolved.

15 January 1992: Slovenia was officially recognized by the EC, having been recognized by Germany the previous month. The USA recognized the country in April.

22 May 1992: Slovenia was admitted to the UN.

May 1992: As a result of a vote of 'no confidence' by the National Assembly, Lojze Peterle resigned as Prime Minister. His successor was Dr Janez Drnovšek, leader of the Liberal Democratic Party (LDP) and a former President of the SFRY State Presidency.

August 1992: The USA ended for Slovenia the sanctions which it had imposed on the entire SFRY.

7 November 1992: The National Assembly adopted a law on the privatization of socially owned companies, with the aim of abolishing them.

November 1992: Drnovšek postponed a visit to Italy after a large demonstration was held in Trieste to demand revision of the Italian–Slovenian border.

6 December 1992: The first presidential and parliamentary elections since Slovenian independence were held; Kučan, the incumbent head of state, was elected President of the Republic and Drnovšek was confirmed as Prime Minister, leading a coalition government composed mainly of members of the Liberal Democratic Party, the Slovenian Christian Democrats and the Associated List (subsequently known as the Associated List of Social Democrats).

February 1993: Slovenia began negotiations with Italy to revise the Treaty of Osimo of 1975.

23 July 1993: Arms illegally destined for Bosnia and Herzegovina were discovered at Maribor airport. Several leading Slovenian politicians were implicated in the scandal, including the Minister of Defence, Janez Janša.

August 1993: Italy placed army units on the Slovenian border, officially in response to the illegal arms affair.

January 1994: The Krsko nuclear power station occasioned a deterioration in relations with Croatia. Moreover, Slovenian companies near the border with Croatia were reported to have dismissed around 3,000 Croatian employees. At the end of the month, however, Drnovšek announced that relations with Croatia were improving.

History

Dr CATHIE CARMICHAEL

The Republic of Slovenia came into independent political existence in 1991 with the disintegration of the Socialist Federal Republic of Yugoslavia (SFRY). The idea of a 'Slovenian' state inhabited chiefly by Slovene speakers was not novel, whereas its political existence was. Any history of 'Slovenia' must therefore be considered as a narrative of cultural as much as political events.

EARLY HISTORY

Slavic tribes, including proto-Slovenes, arrived in south-east Europe in the fifth century. The extent of Slovene autochthonous territory was initially much wider, covering large areas of present-day Austria, Italy and Hungary, but the Alpine Slavs experienced a gradual contraction of their ethnic territory in subsequent centuries. By the end of the 20th century the Slovene language was only spoken in Slovenia itself and by minorities in the Italian province of Friuli-Venezia Giulia, in several villages in Hungary and in the Austrian province of Carinthia. The Slovenes did not form a completely autonomous nation-state before the late 20th century, although Slovene political customs, including the ritual of investiture (*ustoličenje*) by peasant voting, were apparent in the duchy of Carinthia (Karantanija) during the seventh century. After 745, the Slovenes lived under the domination of the Franks and were incorporated into the Holy Roman Empire and the Western Catholic Church.

THE SLOVENES UNDER HABSBURG DOMINATION

During the 13th and 14th centuries, Slovene-speaking territories were acquired by the Habsburg family; Styria in 1278, followed by Carniola and Carinthia in 1335 and Trieste in 1385. Most Slovenes, excluding a small minority in northern Italy, continued to live as subjects of the Habsburg monarch until 1918. Within these territories, the Slovenes formed a class of peasant farmers ruled by German-speaking feudal lords. Sections of the lower nobility spoke Slovene, and Italian and German were spoken in the towns. Although they were never conquered by the Ottoman Turks they were subject to frequent incursions during the 16th century. In the early 16th century there was a serious peasant uprising led by Matija Gubec, but the cultural and economic position of the Slovene peasants was altered only after Emperor Joseph II abolished serfdom in 1782. Slovene culture was preserved from complete German domination by the development of the literary language during the Protestant Reformation, which included the publication of a Slovene catechism by Primož Trubar in 1551 and a translation of the Bible by Jurij Dalmatin in 1584. There was a reduction in Slovene-language publication in the 17th and 18th centuries and Protestantism was outlawed in Inner Austria in 1628. Baron Valvasor's *Glory of the Duchy of Carniola*, an encyclopedic study of Slovene culture, was published in German in 1689. The use of the Slovene language was revived by the activities of intellectuals, often under the patronage of Baron Žiga Zois, in the late 18th century. Marko Pohlin published a Slovene Grammar (*Kraynska Gramatika*) in 1768 and in 1791 Anton Linhart, one of the first writers to define the Slovenes as a distinct national ethnic community, completed a history of Carniola. The poet Valentin Vodnik produced the first Slovene-language newspaper in 1797.

In 1809–13 the Slovene lands were incorporated into the French Napoleonic Empire as the Illyrian Provinces. Although they were then regained by the Habsburgs in 1815, the French occupation had a lasting impact on Slovene national consciousness. In the period up to 1848 Slovene intellectuals continued to create a new national and cultural identity along Herderian lines (the German philosopher Johann Gottfried Herder, 1744–1803, believed that nations were natural units, and that people were defined by their belonging to a specific culture and nation). The linguist Jernej Kopitar produced a standardized Slovene grammar in 1808 and the poet France Prešeren (1800–49) produced some of the greatest work in the language, including the National Anthem, *Zdravljica*. In 1848 the Habsburg dominions were shaken by revolutions in the provincial capitals and some Slovene intellectuals openly proclaimed a policy of *Zedinjena Slovenija* (United Slovenia). They continued their nationalist activities after the revolutions, with the foundation of two cultural societies to disseminate Slovene literature: the Society of St Hermagoras in 1851, and the Slovene Society (Slovenska Matica—literally, the Slovene Queen-Bee) in 1864.

The 19th century also saw the beginnings of Slovene political organization within the Habsburg empire. In 1843 Janez Bleiweis created the agricultural society which evolved to become the Slovene People's Party in 1905. From 1867 the realm was reorganized as the 'Dual Monarchy' of Austria and Hungary, with the Slovenes living in the western or Austrian part, known as Cisleithania. Some Slovenes sought a 'Trialist' solution to the Monarchy's national problems, with Slavs recognized as the third element in the Habsburg lands, and the Southern Slav or Yugoslav movement became increasingly significant in Slovene political life. During the years 1911–12 a student group, Preporod, demanded the formation of a Yugoslav state, but liberals still firmly believed that there was an 'Austroslav' solution to the national question inside the Habsburg Monarchy. Yugoslavism grew in importance during the First World War, particularly with the activities of the Yugoslav Committee in London (United Kingdom). Between August and September 1918, national councils (Narodni sveti) were formed all over Slovene ethnic territory, which became the basis for a 'home rule' administration.

THE SLOVENES AND THE TWO YUGOSLAVIAS

Yugoslavia was an immediate product of the First World War, formed as the Kingdom of Serbs, Croats and Slovenes (formally renamed Yugoslavia in 1929) in December 1918, after the collapse of Austria-Hungary on 29 October. The Slovenes of the new Yugoslav state were organized into the banovina (banate) of Dravska, but their national position was weakened by the division of territories between neighbouring states. The border with Austria was resolved after a plebiscite in the Klagenfurt basin in October 1920, but a Slovene minority was left inside Austrian Carinthia. Some of the heaviest fighting of the War was along the front on the Soča river and, in return for their military support for the Allied side, the Italians had been promised areas of South Slav territory in the Treaty of London, drawn up secretly in 1915. Italy formally gained parts of the Adriatic littoral, Gorizia and a large section of the Julian Alps by the Treaty of Rapallo in November 1920.

The first Yugoslavia was poor, politically unstable and ruled from the former Serbian capital of Belgrade. The Slovene leader, the priest Anton Korošec, became Prime Minister, but growing inter-ethnic tension led King Aleksander to suspend the Vidovdan Constitution and rule by dictatorship from 6 January 1929 until his assassination in 1934. By 1939 the first Yugoslavia was disintegrating, with Croatia gaining its autonomy and some Slovenes pressing for a similar national settlement. Yugoslav resistance was crushed within a few days when the German army invaded in April 1941 and King Petar and his ministers fled to London where they established a government-in-exile. Slovene Styria and a part of Carniola were directly annexed to the German Third Reich, while the Italians controlled the south, including Ljubljana (Laibach). A Liberation Front was formed on 27 April 1941 to oppose the occupation and was composed of Christian Socialists, including the writer Edvard Kocbek, Liberals and Communists, led by Boris Kidrič and Edvard Kardelj. Their liberation struggle occurred simultaneously with internal fighting between the Domobranci (White Guards) and other opposition forces. The civil war was won decisively by the all-Yugoslav Partisans (National Liberation Army), led by the Communist leader Josip Broz (Tito). The alleged dispatch of 10,000 Domobranci to their enemies by British occupying forces in Carinthia remained a cause of controversy for decades after. The Partisans proceeded to form a second, multinational Yugoslavia based on their policy of brotherhood and unity. As a proposed solution to the pre-War nationalities problem, they created a new federal structure of 'national' republics, modelled on the USSR.

The second Yugoslavia obtained the Adriatic littoral, previously under Italian occupation, and at this time the territorial basis for a future Slovenian state was created. Through the insistence of Edvard Kardelj, the newly created Socialist Republic of Slovenia was given the Istrian towns of Koper, Izola and Piran, creating a distinctively Slovenian coastline. Although the Yugoslav Partisans had liberated Trieste on 1 May 1945, the Allies insisted that the status of the city be resolved by the establishment of the Free Territory of Trieste in 1946, under the control of the UN. The UN then divided Trieste into zones A and B, the latter being under the control of Yugoslavia. The formal military occupation of the territory ended in 1954, when a settlement granted Slovenia *de jure* possession of an Istrian coastline. The existence of a sizeable Slovene minority in Italy proved not only to be a focus for disputes between the two states but also to be a continual problem for the Yugoslav regime. In 1967 the writer Marjan Rožman was jailed for six months after publishing an article in the Triestine journal *Most* which criticized Yugoslavism. During the 1970s and 1980s, the cultural activities of the Triestine Slovene community further undermined Yugoslav cohesion. In contrast, the Slovenes of Carinthia tended to integrate much more with Austrian-German culture after 1918, rather than identifying primarily with other Slovenes.

In the 1960s there was a radical restructuring of the Yugoslav economy directed by Edvard Kardelj. Some market mechanisms and worker self-management were introduced and more autonomy was given to the Republics. This in turn created structural tensions between republican and federal authorities which were only partially resolved by the abilities of Tito and his ministers. Inter-republican tensions erupted in mid-1969 when the Slovenians protested to Belgrade over the redirection of funds lent by the World Bank, originally obtained in order to build a motorway linking Slovenia to Austria and Italy. Following nationalist tension in Croatia in the early 1970s several Slovenians, including the former Communist chief Stane Kavčič, were removed from power in 1972. The introduction of a new constitution in 1974, which gave the Republics more autonomy, was intended to diffuse national problems.

THE DISINTEGRATION OF YUGOSLAVIA 1980–91

After the death of President Tito in May 1980, there was effectively a power vacuum and the federal balance that he had created was gradually eroded, leaving Slovenia and Serbia increasingly pitted against each other in various disputes over civil liberties, the position of the Albanians of Kosovo (Kosovars) and the economy. There was a great deal of sympathy among the Slovenians, particularly younger intellectuals, for the situation of the Kosovars following the uprising in 1981 and the implementation of martial law. In February 1989 the Serbian Association of Writers ended relations with its Slovenian counterpart because its members had spoken out against the stationing of 15,000 federal troops in Kosovo and the striking miners of Trebća. In November of that year the Slovenian Youth Federation spoke out in defence of Azem Vllasi, the imprisoned leader of the Kosovars. In retaliation, the Kosovo Polje Committee of Kosovo Serbs and other Serb nationalists planned to travel to Ljubljana for a rally on 1 December 1989, to intimidate the Slovenian public into withdrawing their support for the Kosovars. On 21 November the Slovenian authorities prevented the possibility of violence on the streets of Ljubljana by prohibiting open-air meetings of more than 30 people. They also closed the Slovenian borders to any vehicles carrying Serb demonstrators. The Serbian leader Slobodan Milošević responded by urging an economic boycott of Slovenia, to which the Slovenians retaliated by withholding part of their contribution to the federal budget. There followed a series of economic disputes between the two Republics and, by 23 October 1990, Yugoslavia's internal market was effectively ended when the Serbian parliament passed a number of economic measures placing import duties on goods from Slovenia.

In the late 1980s Slovenians also showed particular concern about the role of the Jugoslavenska Narodna Armija (JNA—Yugoslav People's Army), one of the most powerful armies in Europe and a vestige of Tito's regime. In early 1988, three journalists and a junior army officer were tried for criticizing the JNA in the pages of the youth newspaper *Mladina*. The Slovenian public was particularly horrified that the defendants were tried and sentenced in Serbo-Croat, the language of the army command. This was criticized both by a nascent opposition, which formed the Committee to Defend Janez Janša (an imprisoned journalist), and by the republican Communist chief Milan Kučan.

Issue antagonism towards Serbia and the remnants of the Titoist regime coincided with a 'cultural revolution' in Ljubljana during the 1980s, led by intellectuals such as Slavoj Žižek, Tomaž Mastnak and many others, including those attached to the Neue Slovenische Kunst (New Slovenian Art) movement. In 1987 the journal *Nova Revija* published a collection of articles devoted to the 'Slovenian National Programme', which was particularly concerned with the perceived negative position of the Slovene language within Yugoslavia. Young people circulated their ideas and criticisms of the regime in the pages of the journals *Mladina* and *Katedra*, and on the independent Radio Študent. Slovenia also experienced a cultural reorientation away from the Balkans towards Western Europe during the 1980s, fostered in part by membership of the Alpe-Adria Organization and articulated in 1990 by the renamed Communist publication *Europe Now*.

These developments were paralleled by political developments within the League of Communists of Slovenia (LCS) and from organized political opposition. On 27 September 1989 a majority in the Slovenian Assembly adopted a constitutional amendment which asserted republican sovereignty. On 13 December the newly formed coalition of DEMOS (Democratic Opposition of Slovenia) announced its alternative political programme, which included economic sovereignty for Slovenia, the suspension of federal legislation, the introduction of a temporary Slovenian monetary unit and a commitment to a plebiscite on independence. In January 1990 the entire Slovenian delegation withdrew from an emergency congress of the League of Communists of Yugoslavia (LCY). In February the LCS, which had extended its name to include the Party of Democratic Renewal (LCS-PDR), officially left the Yugoslav Communist Party and arranged for democratic elections to be held. Although DEMOS won an overall majority of seats in the Republic's elections of April with 126 of the 240 contested seats, the LCS-PDR candidate Milan Kučan defeated the DEMOS leader Joze Pučnik to be President of the republican state Presidency. The Christian Democrat Lojze Peterle became Prime Minister. On 2 July, by an overwhelming majority, the Slovenian National Assembly declared Slovenia to be a sovereign state, without explicitly confronting the issue of secession. From that time on Slovenian laws were to take precedence over federal laws. In September the Slovenians refused to accept the authority of the federal Constitution, on the grounds that the Kosovars had effectively been excluded from the Federal Assembly.

The question of Slovenian involvement in the JNA also resurfaced in 1990. After withdrawing its police units from Kosovo, the Slovenian Government then announced its right to control its frontier posts and the JNA units stationed within the Republic. In July the JNA seized territorial defence weapons, including most of the Republic's heavy artillery, from warehouses in Slovenia and ignored requests to return them by 10 August. When the JNA also refused to allow Slovenian recruits to perform their military service solely in Slovenia, the Slovenian Government suspended territorial defence payments in retaliation, on 6 September. Following the army crisis in 1988, the Slovenians had started to build their own republican army upon the existing structures of their territorial forces. This move was overseen by Janez Janša, who had become Minister of Defence in March 1990. Work on these plans was accelerated after 4 October when the JNA forcibly took control of the Republic's defence headquarters in Ljubljana.

On 5 October Croatia and Slovenia proposed a plan to restructure Yugoslavia into an alliance of sovereign states. These states would have control of their own military forces and diplomats, but a federal court and a consultative parliament, including a council of ministers and an executive commission, would remain in Belgrade. The Slovenian Government then organized a plebiscite to determine whether Slovenia should be an independent and autonomous state. Of the 93.5% of the electorate who voted on 26 December, 88.5% were in favour and Slovenia then declared itself to be an independent state. The plebiscite was followed by security and legislative measures. In January 1991 Croatian-Slovenian defence and security agreements were signed. During the next six months the Slovenian Government made further constitutional amendments which finalized the transfer of power from federal to republican bodies and, in March, it suspended the sending of conscripts to the JNA.

THE REPUBLIC OF SLOVENIA FROM 1991

On 25 June the parliaments of Slovenia and Croatia declared their independence and the Slovenians ordered their own police force and army to take control of borders. JNA troop movement was initially restricted to the seizure of international border posts on 27 and 28 June, but the Slovenian authorities refused a cease-fire until the JNA had returned to barracks. Over the following 10 days, aerial bombing of Ljubljana's airport, ambushes, blockades of military bases and mass desertions from the JNA occurred on Slovenian territory, resulting in the loss of 79 lives, according to official figures. A 'diplomatic' war also ensued, which effectively secured Slovenian independence and a non-military defeat of Yugoslav forces.

On 28 June 1991 a 'troika' of EC foreign ministers from Italy, Luxembourg and the Netherlands initiated negotiations for a cease-fire between the federal authorities, the

JNA and the Slovenian Government, the terms of which included the return of federal troops to barracks and a three-month suspension of implementation of the Slovene declaration of independence. These terms were broken within hours. Two days later Milan Kučan and Lojze Peterle met Ante Marković, the federal prime minister, and they agreed that the JNA should return to barracks on 1 July. On 2 July Stipe Mesić, the newly elected President of the federal State Presidency, and Kučan sent a joint statement to Marković and General Veljko Kadijević, the Federal Secretary for National Defence, reiterating these demands. Although disputes continued around the control of frontier posts and barracks, by 5 July Slovenia had demobilized 10,000 men and the EC had imposed an arms embargo on Yugoslavia. A second cease-fire plan, which called for an unarmed European observer mission to monitor the cease-fire during the three-month moratorium on independence, was drawn up by the EC ministers on 7 July. It also stipulated that the JNA was to withdraw to barracks, the blockades of barracks by Slovenian forces were to be lifted, and the Slovenian police were to control the international borders. This was then ratified by the Slovenian parliament on 11 July and, one week later, the federal authorities guaranteed that all troops would be withdrawn from Slovenia by 25 October. On 7 October 1991 the moratorium on independence lapsed and Slovenia issued its own currency. A new Slovenian Constitution was adopted on 23 December 1991, based upon the principle of the division of power between the judiciary, executive and legislature. The 90-member National Assembly was to be elected for a four-year term and the directly elected President was to serve a five-year term.

After independence, the political life of Slovenia was dominated by the struggle to achieve international recognition, the issue of Slovenia's borders and the disintegration of the pre-war consensus amongst politicians. In December 1991 the DEMOS coalition effectively split up and was dissolved the following February. In May 1992 Peterle resigned as Prime Minister in favour of Janez Drnovšek, leader of the Liberal Democratic Party (LDP) and a former Yugoslav President. The subsequent organization of Slovenian political parties was largely based on individual personalities.

The first elections since independence were held on 6 December 1992 and confirmed Milan Kučan as President. On 25 January 1993 Janez Drnovšek was confirmed as Prime Minister of a coalition administration in which the main partners were the Liberal Democrats, the Christian Democrats and the Associated List (an alliance including some reformed Communists, later renamed the Associated List of Social Democrats). The continued involvement of former Communist personnel within the government and in commerce and public institutions was criticized in some quarters during 1993. The most notable of these critics was Janez Janša, leader of the Social Democratic Party of Slovenia, although, during that year, he was discredited by his alleged involvement in an arms-trade scandal (see below).

FOREIGN RELATIONS

On 15 January 1992 the countries of the EC officially recognized the independence of Slovenia and Croatia. This was followed on 7 April 1992 by recognition by the USA. By May 1992, 76 countries had extended recognition and Slovenia was admitted to the UN. In mid-1992 a Slovenian national team participated in the Olympic Games in Barcelona (Spain).

Slovenia's efforts to achieve international recognition continued in 1993. On 2 November Hungary ratified a treaty of friendship and co-operation with Slovenia which guaranteed minority rights in both countries. The Prime Ministers of Slovenia and the Czech Republic signed a free-trade agreement on 4 December, abolishing customs tariffs on 83% of trade, with effect from 1 January 1994. Later in December Slovenia made a similar accord with Slovakia and signed a co-operative treaty with Poland on 14 February 1994. In September 1993 a visiting EC commissioner had spoken of an imminent EC association agreement with Slovenia and in February 1994 the Minister of Foreign Affairs (the former premier, Lojze Peterle) stated that Slovenia's membership of the Consultative Council of the Western military alliance, the North Atlantic Treaty Organisation (NATO), was dependent on such an agreement. Slovenia had not yet received an official response from the Council regarding its request to join the 'Partnership for Peace' programme.

Slovenia was in dispute with a number of its neighbours. There were eight areas of disputed border territory with Croatia in 1993, of which the Bay of Piran in Istria was the most controversial. The question of the status of Istria's ethnic Italians was raised in February 1993, when negotiations began with Italy to revise the Treaty of Osimo (Osim), which had settled the Italian–Yugoslav borders in 1975. However, Italy's main concern was the restitution of property formerly belonging to Italians who had left Yugoslavia before 1945. In August 1993 the Italian Army moved units to the Slovenian border, ostensibly because of an illegal arms scandal. In October there were signs of a growing movement for autonomy in Slovenian Istria, supported by the Italian minority in Slovenian and Croatian areas of Istria. Concern over this issue provided a useful point of agreement between the Slovenian and Croatian Governments in 1993 and 1994. In January 1994 Slovenia began a dispute with Croatia over the supply of electricity generated at the Krsko nuclear power station, situated in Slovenia but constructed with Croatian support before the disintegration of the old Yugoslav federation. In the same month Slovenian companies near the border with Croatia were reported to have dismissed around 3,000 Croatian employees, apparently for political reasons. At the end of January, however, Drnovšek announced that relations with Croatia were improving in spite of continuing border disputes. A trade agreement between the two countries was expected in February.

National minorities within Slovenia were officially protected by the Constitution and Yugoslavs resident within Slovenia were permitted to apply for citizenship before 25 December 1991. Many thousands of refugees from the fighting in Bosnia and Herzegovina and Croatia arrived in Slovenia after 1991, but in April 1993 the Slovenian Government took sanctions against Serbia and Montenegro by restricting the entry of Yugoslav citizens. Moreover, many high-ranking Slovenian politicians, including Janez Janša, were implicated in an international scandal when, on 23 July 1993, 150 metric tons of military hardware was discovered at Maribor airport, destined for use against the Serbs by Muslim forces in Bosnia and Herzegovina. This incident indicated that Slovenia was still divided between its ties with the former Yugoslavia and its desired orientation towards Western Europe.

The Economy

Dr JOHN B. ALLCOCK

THE LEGACY OF THE PAST

Located on major communications routes linking the industrial and commercial centres of the Habsburg Empire to the Adriatic Sea, the Slovene lands became integrated into the modern economy during the 19th century more rapidly than the rest of the Balkans. By the outbreak of the First World War Ljubljana (Laibach) had a modern credit bank and a growing industrial base, principally owned by Austrian and German interests. The Slovenes were predominantly an agricultural people, whose small farms coexisted with centres of industrial activity. Nevertheless, their participation in the modernization process is suggested by an extensive network of agrarian co-operatives and by the fact that around 85% of the population were literate.

This relative economic advantage was maintained after the formation of the 'First Yugoslavia'. In 1938 the Dravska banovina (roughly equivalent to modern Slovenia) boasted one-fifth of the invested capital, industrial utilization of energy, employed labour and factories of the entire kingdom. Of particular importance were the steel works at Jesenice, founded by Austrian capital in 1891, and timber and wood-processing capacities.

Although committed to the development of underdeveloped areas of the federation, using redistributed levies imposed upon the wealthier areas, socialist (Communist) Yugoslavia never succeeded in diminishing Slovenia's economic primacy. Indeed, the gap between economically advanced Slovenia and less developed areas grew steadily throughout the post-Second World War years.

SLOVENIA IN THE YUGOSLAV ECONOMY

With 8% of the total population of Yugoslavia in 1991 (10% of its economically active population), Slovenia delivered around one-fifth of its social product. Social product per head was approximately twice the average for the federation. Net personal incomes were 144% of the Yugoslav average. Slovenes produced 60% of Yugoslavia's glass, 36% of its industrial machinery, 32% of its paper products, 28% of its cotton yarn, 26% of its agricultural machinery, 23% of its steel and 22% of its household furniture and woollen yarn. Nor was this success confined to manufacturing industry. With only 7% of Yugoslavia's agricultural area, Slovenian farms delivered 30% of its fruit products, 20% of its pasta and flour products, 15% of its forest products, 14% of its meat and 12% of its milk. Overall, the Republic accounted for 22% of Yugoslav imports before independence, and 26% of its export trade.

Slovenia specialized in high-quality products demanding relatively high levels of capitalization and skill. Slovenian producers of electrical and electronic goods (such as Iskra) or of heating equipment (such as Gorenje) dominated the Yugoslav market in their sectors, as well as contributing significantly to exports. Slovenian pharmaceutical producers Lek and Krkaalways regarded themselves as more sophisticated than Pliva (Croatia) or Alkaloid, and manufacturers of the Renault car in Novo Mesto claimed superiority in terms of quality to the Yugo made in Kragujevac (Serbia).

THE ECONOMIC BACKGROUND TO SECESSION

With this secure position within the Yugoslav market, why should the Slovenians have pursued independence? Although the disintegration of the Yugoslav federation was often simply attributed to 'nationalism', it is important to attend to the economic causes of its collapse. In the case of Slovenia three principal economic reasons may be cited.

As the wealthiest of Yugoslavia's six Republics Slovenia suffered most from the federal policy of inter-republican redistribution: in 1990 net transfers to the rest of Yugoslavia were estimated at 6.5% of gross domestic product (GDP). This process was regulated through federal agencies in which Slovenia's voice was only one among eight (six Republics and two Autonomous Provinces). A high proportion of this redistribution, nominally directed to the task of promoting economic development, was devoted to prestigious but non-productive cultural or administrative projects, reflecting political patronage rather than genuine economic opportunity.

When the federal government began to deal with the need for economic restructuring, different strategies were proposed. Slovene interests placed them broadly in sympathy with the programme promoted in 1989 by Ante Marković, President of the Federal Executive Council. This envisaged rapid structural and institutional reform leading to the strengthening of a federation-wide market economy, and the reduction of the traditional practice of political economic intervention by republican élites. This economic orientation was accompanied by support for multi-party democracy in place of the monopolistic position of the League of Communists. The Slovenes found themselves engaged in increasingly severe conflict with other republics, especially Serbia, the natural interests of which favoured a continuing role for a paternalistic and interventionist state.

These different regional attitudes to economic reform were conditioned in part by their different orientations to the external world, especially in areas such as currency reform and the restructuring of the banking system. The Slovenian share of foreign trade was heavily orientated towards Western Europe: that of the more easterly Republics towards members of the Council for Mutual Economic Assistance (CMEA). A key element in Slovenian 'nationalism' and 'separatism', therefore, was the emerging sense of an urgent need to establish proper control over their own economic destiny, rather than to allow their advantages to be dissipated in the pursuit of policies and the defence of structures which undermined rather than served Slovenian interests.

THE CONTINUING INFLUENCE OF YUGOSLAVIA

In spite of the fact that Slovenia was described as 'the Republic that escaped to freedom and prosperity', it continued to experience the adverse effects of Yugoslavia's proximity after secession.

The military struggle within Slovenia lasted a mere 10 days and resulted in very little damage and few casualties; but the war elsewhere in the former Yugoslavia continued to overshadow Slovenia's development. The border of the Serb Krajina, within Croatia, was less than 20 km from the Slovenian border near Karlovac (in late 1993 missiles fired by the Serbs against the Croatian army landed within 5 km of the border). This was the most sensitive and exposed part of the contested area of Croatia, control of which was of vital significance for both Serb secessionist and Croatian government forces. It seemed highly likely that it would become a focus for renewed military activity in 1994. War so close to its borders would do nothing to enhance either the sense of normality which Slovenia was trying to foster abroad, as the basis for attracting foreign economic involvement, or the security and confidence of its own population.

That Slovenia could not simply ignore events in the Balkans and enjoy the benefits of independence was underlined by the problem of international indebtedness. This was one of the most severe economic difficulties under which the former federal authorities laboured. The national debt of the old Socialist Federal Republic of Yugoslavia (SFRY) was around US $15,000m. in 1991. Slovenia remained responsible after secession for a part of that debt, only some $1,700m. of which could be unambiguously allocated to it. The share of the unallocated debt which would fall to Slovenia could only be determined by international agreement, which would not be possible until the conclusion of the various conflicts. Whereas it is not in doubt that the sums involved would leave Slovenia with a manageable debt service ratio, their indeterminacy did have a bearing upon the Government's ability to negotiate additional credits.

Calculations regarding the economic viability of an independent Slovenia took great account of its relative integration into foreign (especially European) markets. Even so, roughly 60% of Slovenian external trade (25% of all sales) before secession was with other Yugoslav Republics. In spite of the tendencies towards republican economic autarky in the former SFRY, Slovenia could count in effect upon a 'domestic' market of 23m. people, which following independence shrank to fewer than 2m. The Slovenian business community was vigorous in the pursuit of alternative markets, entailing the evasion of international trade sanctions against 'Yugoslavia' to an extent rarely recognized. These attempts coincided with two developments which were not foreseen. The European recession made penetration of new markets much more difficult than was anticipated. The collapse of the CMEA placed member states in competition for exactly the same markets and sources of foreign direct investment. It was by no means easy for Slovenia to distinguish itself in such a competitive and hostile market. From its position as supplier of relatively high-quality goods to a Balkan market, Slovenia risked becoming perceived as one among many providers of relatively low-quality goods in a European market.

A closely related issue is the extent to which secession from Yugoslavia undermined the real integration of production in many Slovenian firms. The Slovenian-based company Gorenje, for example, had subsidiary plants in Bihać and Tuzla, both of which were isolated from their parent by the war in Bosnia and Herzegovina. Taking a second example, the Yugoslav defence production industry, in which Slovenian firms were deeply implicated, spread a network across the entire federation. Similarly, the relatively high-technology products and research-and-development activities, for which several Slovenian firms were noted, were sometimes heavily dependent upon the activities of consortia covering the whole of the SFRY.

THE ECONOMIC STRUCTURE OF INDEPENDENT SLOVENIA

The dominant sector of the Slovenian economy was manufacturing industry, which accounted for one-third of GDP and 38% of the employed labour force in 1993 (in 1991 manufacturing accounted for 33% of GDP and, with mining and public utilities, employed 36% of the working population). Although relatively urbanized, the population was mainly located in small towns. Ljubljana had fewer than 300,000 inhabitants, or 15% of the total population of Slovenia; nine other towns with populations of more than 20,000 accounted for a further 30% of the total. Although no single industry determined the fate of the national economy, the fortunes of a locality could be decided by the success or failure of one industrial branch, or even of one plant, as in the case of the steel plant in Jesenice and the TAM (Tovarna Automobilov In Motorjev) plant in Maribor. Consequently the impact of economic restructuring was extremely varied.

Machine-building and metal-working remained the largest sectors of manufacturing industry and, although these greatly reduced their labour force after independence, they still accounted for around one-quarter of manufacturing value added in 1993. Also important were chemicals and pharmaceuticals, textiles and garment making, footwear, paper making and furniture. The electrical and electronic industries were successful, and notably active in export markets, to which construction also made a significant contribution.

Farming was dominated by small family holdings which provided ancillary sources of income and, although there were some notable areas in which food-processing industries had developed, its greatest importance probably lay in the support which home-grown fruit and vegetables gave to family budgets.

Before independence the Yugoslav tourist industry was dominated by Croatia. With only around 40 km of Adriatic coastline Slovenia was unable to compete in the market for seaside holidays. Nevertheless, efforts were made to develop Slovenia's assets, including the Julian Alps, particularly in the provision of specialist holidays. After the collapse of the tourism industry in 1991 as a result of war, there was a small but useful recovery of foreign interest.

Slovenia was relatively deficient in energy resources. Coal and lignite (a brown coal of low calorific value) of poor quality were mined, but the economic viability of these workings was in doubt. A nuclear reactor was shared with Croatia, at Krško. This met about one-quarter of Slovenia's electricity requirements, but it was politically unpopular and there was strong pressure for its closure. Hydroelectricity provided most of local needs. Having limited potential for expansion and lacking important reserves of petroleum and natural gas, unless more acceptable means of utilizing its small uranium deposits could be devised, Slovenia seemed likely to remain a net energy importer.

Slovenia reported a positive balance of trade in goods in 1992, although in significant measure this could be explained by the decline in imports as a result of economic dislocation. Moreover, during the first half of 1993 the trading surplus became a deficit. Overall, however, there were surpluses on the current account of the balance of payments in the early 1990s. Machinery and transport equipment were the most significant items of export (around 38%), followed by manufactured goods, chemicals and related products. During the decade from 1983 to 1993 the orientation of Slovenian trade changed dramatically. In the mid-1980s around 40% of exports and 44% of imports were exchanged with the countries of the European Community (EC). These proportions had grown to 58% in each case by 1993. Although trade with the European Free Trade Association (EFTA) and other economically developed countries decreased slightly over the same period, those who lost the greatest amount of business were the CMEA states and, particularly, developing countries.

THE RESTRUCTURING PROCESS

The most immediate priority of Slovenia's ruling coalitions was to dissociate the Slovenian economy as much as possible from that of the former Yugoslavia. The second was to increase involvement in the international division of labour.

Financial restructuring was seen as a precondition for the achievement of both of these aims.

Slovenia introduced its own currency, the tolar (SlT), in October 1991, without any external support. This was almost fully convertible by 1993. When the tolar was first introduced foreign-exchange reserves of less than US $200m. provided import cover for around 14 days. Careful economic management increased reserves to $1,231m. by May 1993, providing around 2.3 months of import cover.

By the end of February 1993 Slovenia had been admitted to the International Monetary Fund (IMF), the World Bank group and the European Bank for Reconstruction and Development (EBRD). Negotiation with the IMF was complicated by the political question of 'succession to membership' and the unclear status of the new Federal Republic of Yugoslavia (Serbia and Montenegro). Slovenia accepted 16.4% of the 'Yugoslav' quota of special drawing rights (SDRs)—or $99m.—later in the same year. The link with the World Bank was viewed as important largely because of its potential impact upon Slovenia's competitive bidding for contracts financed by the Bank in its member countries, although in July 1993 a structural adjustment loan of $80m. from the World Bank was also taken up. The EBRD committed 225m. European Currency Units (ECUs) to various projects in Slovenia in 1993.

A precondition for external financial recognition was the rehabilitation of the Slovenian banking system. In the SFRY the banks had been governed by consortia composed of a mixture of republican and municipal political functionaries and the representatives of their principal creditors. Not surprisingly, they functioned as ill-regulated sources of cheap credit, often serving to support unviable enterprises and permitting government at all levels to operate within extremely flexible budgetary constraints. The system was highly centralized within each Republic, with the Ljubljanska Banka dominating the structure in Slovenia. The rehabilitation process began before independence, under the federal Banking Law of February 1989, although a fundamental role was played by the establishment of a Bank Rehabilitation Agency (BRA), which began operation in 1992. The process of rehabilitation comprised two essential tasks: reorganization and recapitalization.

Reorganization consisted in part of the division of the Ljubljanska Banka into viable and competitive units. At the same time, the new legal framework permitted the rapid creation of around 25 new banking institutions, encouraged largely by very low capitalization requirements. It was doubtful whether 32 separate banks could survive, serving a population of under 2m., and the BRA expected to promote an orderly consolidation during 1994, partly through raising capitalization requirements.

The processes of reorganization and recapitalization were linked and Slovenian banks sought to improve both their financial position and their managerial functioning through links with foreign banks. Austrian interests acquired controlling shares in at least five of the larger Slovenian banks. This significant investment in the Slovenian banking system by Austrian banks was not achieved without attracting strongly adverse political comment and remained a sensitive political issue. Also, the blockage of Slovenian foreign-exchange deposits within the Belgrade banking system continued to pose problems for Slovenian banks and their creditors.

As in all of the former Communist states, the focus of the economic restructuring process in Slovenia was the privatization of the public sector. Here, as elsewhere, that process was politically controversial and the Ownership Transformation Law of November 1992 embodied several compromises.

The Law established two bodies through which the disposal of socially owned assets was to be managed: a Privatization Agency (PA) and a Development Fund (DF). The disposal of equity was to be divided between a mandatory proportion of 40% of the total, and 60% available for voluntary disposal. Under the mandatory provision, 10% of the total equity was to be transferred to a restitution fund through which former private owners would be compensated. (This avoided some of the obvious practical difficulties experienced elsewhere with attempts at direct restitution.) A similar proportion was allocated to the state pension fund and the remaining half (20% of the total) to special investment funds controlled by the DF, which would distribute vouchers to Slovene citizens. One-third of the voluntary proportion of the equity was to be distributed in the first instance to the employees of the enterprises, the remainder offered through a discounted option scheme to retired employees, and the residue sold on the open market. Only the last of these categories was to be open in the first instance to foreign purchasers; the transfer of other categories was limited to Slovene citizens during an initial period of two years.

The new law clarified the acute ambiguity and consequent uncertainty about property rights which attached to what was previously 'social property', but a number of larger enterprises interested in engaging foreign direct investment were unhappy about the scheme and approaches were made to the PA requesting exemption from the restrictions on the sale of equity. These arrangements did not apply to public utilities, nor to the restitution of socially owned land. Here the great size of the former land holdings of the Roman Catholic Church proved particularly contentious.

The privatization process was relatively straightforward in the case of smaller enterprises, but more difficult to accomplish in larger units, especially where an enterprise was composed of both profitable and unprofitable sectors, complicating the transfer of ownership with questions of organizational restructuring.

An important aspect of the restructuring of the Slovene economy was its geographical location. The continuation of the Yugoslav wars compelled the Slovenians to rethink the post-1945 tendency to see themselves as located on a major transcontinental route, on a north-west to south-east axis, from Jesenice to Zagreb. There was a reversion to the 19th century view of Slovenia as central Europe's means of access to the Adriatic. This was reflected very directly both in substantial road-building projects linking Maribor with Graz (Austria) to the north and with Hungary to the east, and in the development of Koper as a port.

ASSESSING THE BALANCE

Economists are prone to concentrate their attention upon problems and these were not difficult to find in Slovenia. Output declined by 13% in 1992 and by a similar proportion in 1993, while real GDP also decreased slightly (by approximately 2%–3%) during 1993. Unemployment continued to rise, standing in mid-1993 at around 14%. Enterprise losses persisted and prospects for reversing this trend quickly were poor. The tolar continued to depreciate against internationally traded currencies. Average net personal incomes declined by around 3% in real terms in 1992. Whereas net wages per worker were projected to grow by 6% in 1993, retail prices increased by approximately 20%. Although important measures were taken, aimed at the restructuring of the economy, in many ways these did not immediately prove their worth. A number of vital issues relevant to the reform of the legal and fiscal systems were not seriously addressed. Forecasts made at the time of secession, that five years would be needed to return to 'normality', quickly proved excessively optimistic.

The attraction of foreign direct investment was taken by the Slovenians themselves as an indication of the success or otherwise of the restructuring process. Substantial growth in this area was reported following independence, including some very large projects. At the end of 1988 there had been only 44 joint ventures with DM 146.1m. of invested capital. By May 1993 the number of such projects had increased to 3,224 and the value of capital invested had increased to DM 1,600m. German, Austrian and Italian firms were particularly active in this process, investing more than 70% of the total. Nevertheless, it is important to recognize the small scale of the majority of such deals, nearly one-half of which involved less than DM 1,000. Significant international financial integration was dependent upon the clearer outcome of the process of institutional restructuring.

With an estimated GDP per head in 1992 of US $6,052, Slovenia compared favourably with the countries of the Visegrad Group (the then Czechoslovakia, Hungary and Poland) and this figure was substantially above the average for Eastern Europe in general. If the Slovenians could moderate the sentimental presentation of their location 'on the sunny side of the Alps' and give more sustained attention to the identification of their real comparative advantages, then it seemed possible that the eventual conclusion of the 'Third Balkan War' would see them in a position to realize the economic advances which they had hoped independence would bring.

Statistical Survey

Source: *Statistični letopis* (Statistical Yearbook), published by Statistical Office of the Republic of Slovenia, 61000 Ljubljana, Vožarski pot 12; tel. (61) 1255322; fax (61) 216932.

Area and Population

AREA, POPULATION AND DENSITY

Area (sq km)	20,254*
Population (census results)	
31 March 1981	1,891,864
31 March 1991	
Males	952,611
Females	1,013,375
Total	1,965,986
Density (per sq km) at 31 March 1991	97.1

* 7,820 sq miles.

POPULATION BY ETHNIC GROUP (1991 census)

Ethnic group	Number	%
Slovenes	1,727,018	87.8
Croats	54,212	2.8
Serbs	47,911	2.4
Slav Muslims	26,842	1.4
Yugoslavs	12,307	0.6
Hungarians	8,503	0.4
Macedonians	4,432	0.2
Montenegrins	4,396	0.2
Albanians	3,629	0.2
Italians	3,064	0.2
Total (incl. others)	1,965,986	100.00

PRINCIPAL TOWNS (population at 1991 census)

Ljubljana (capital)	276,133	Velenje	27,665
Maribor	108,122	Koper	25,272
Celje	41,279	Novo Mesto	22,760
Kranj	37,318		

BIRTHS, MARRIAGES AND DEATHS

	Registered live births		Registered marriages		Registered deaths	
	Number	Rate (per 1,000)	Number	Rate (per 1,000)	Number	Rate (per 1,000)
1984	26,274	13.5	11,386	5.9	20,214	10.4
1985	25,933	13.1	10,579	5.4	19,854	10.0
1986	25,570	12.9	10,621	5.4	19,499	9.8
1987	25,592	12.9	10,307	5.2	19,837	10.0
1988	25,209	12.6	9,217	4.6	19,126	9.6
1989	23,447	11.7	9,776	4.9	18,669	9.3
1990	22,368	11.2	8,517	4.3	18,555	9.3
1991	21,583	10.8	8,173	4.1	19,324	9.7

ECONOMICALLY ACTIVE POPULATION
(persons aged 10 years and over, 1991 census)

	Males	Females	Total
Agriculture, hunting, forestry and fishing	61,947	58,548	120,495
Mining and quarrying, manufacturing, electricity, gas and water	178,557	135,476	314,033
Construction	33,819	6,824	40,643
Trade, restaurants and hotels	38,722	65,669	104,391
Transport, storage and communications	37,631	8,947	46,578
Financing, insurance, real estate and business services	25,206	23,544	48,750
Community, social and personal services	85,261	114,469	199,730
Activities not adequately defined	2,543	1,626	4,169
Total employed	463,686	415,103	878,789
Unemployed	40,696	26,281	66,977
Total labour force	504,382	441,384	945,766

Agriculture

PRINCIPAL CROPS ('000 metric tons)

	1990	1991	1992
Wheat	200	181	186
Barley	25	27	27
Maize	338	336	207
Rye	7	7	7
Oats	7	5	6
Potatoes	413	425	368
Cabbages	69	50	48
Tomatoes	7	7	7
Onions (dry)	9	9	9
Carrots	6	6	5
Grapes	214	294*	213*
Sugar beet	167	166	97
Apples	94	73	85
Pears	20	14	17
Peaches and nectarines	5	7	9
Plums	5	5	9

* FAO estimate(s).

Source: FAO, *Production Yearbook*.

LIVESTOCK ('000 head, year ending September)

	1990	1991	1992
Cattle	546	533	484
Pigs	554	588	529
Sheep	23	20	28
Horses	11	10	11
Poultry*	13,000	12,000	12,000

* Unofficial estimate(s).

Source: FAO, *Production Yearbook*.

LIVESTOCK PRODUCTS
('000 metric tons)

	1990	1991	1992
Beef and veal	57	51	50*
Pigmeat†	81	80	75
Poultry meat	79†	73	53*
Milk	597	643	352*
Cheese	11.2	12.3	12.4
Eggs	23.8	26.5	15.8*

* FAO estimate(s). † Unofficial estimate(s).

Source: FAO, *Production Yearbook*.

Forestry

ROUNDWOOD REMOVALS ('000 cubic metres)

	1991
Sawlogs and veneer logs	812
Pitprops (mine timber)	26
Pulpwood	173
Other industrial wood	239
Fuel wood	164
Total	1,414

SAWNWOOD PRODUCTION ('000 cubic metres)

	1991
Coniferous (soft wood)	432
Non-coniferous (hard wood)	187
Total	619

Fishing

(metric tons, live weight)

	1991
Freshwater fishes	805
Marine fishes	4,865
Crustaceans and molluscs	147
Total catch	5,817

Mining

('000 metric tons, unless otherwise indicated)

	1991
Coal	5,159
Crude petroleum	2
Lead and zinc ore	162
Natural gas ('000 cubic metres)	19

Industry

SELECTED PRODUCTS
('000 metric tons, unless otherwise indicated)

	1991
Sugar	50
Wine ('000 hectolitres)	173
Beer ('000 hectolitres)	2,287
Cigarettes (million)	4,798
Wool yarn	4
Cotton yarn	13
Footwear (excl. rubber) ('000 pairs)	9,124
Mechanical woodpulp	61
Chemical woodpulp	85
Stationery and newsprint	291
Sulphuric acid	86
Motor spirit (petroleum)	104
Distillate fuel oils	241
Residual fuel oils	8
Clay building bricks (million)	240
Roofing tiles (million)	26
Cement	974
Steel	287
Aluminium	90
Refined lead	10
Television receivers ('000)	101
Motor cars (number)	82,536
Lorries (number)	1,378
Bicycles ('000)	218
Electric energy (million kWh)	12,669

Finance

CURRENCY AND EXCHANGE RATES

Monetary Units
100 stotins = 1 tolar (SlT).

Sterling and Dollar Equivalents (30 September 1993)
£1 sterling = 173.9 tolars;
US $1 = 116.3 tolars;
1,000 tolars = £5.75 = $8.60.

Average Exchange Rate (tolars per US $)
1992 81.299

Note: The tolar was introduced in October 1991, replacing (initially at par) the Yugoslav dinar.

BUDGET (million tolars)

Revenue	1991	1992
Taxation	132,967	437,072
Personal income tax	23,451	69,057
Corporate income tax }	2,961	8,733
Payroll tax }		—
Social insurance taxes	67,493	224,977
Sales tax	27,883	101,491
Customs and import duties	10,878	32,412
Other receipts	13,256	16,600
Total	146,222	453,671

Source: Bank of Slovenia, *Monthly Bulletion.*

BANK OF SLOVENIA RESERVES
(US $ million at 31 December)

	1991	1992
Foreign exchange	112.1	715.6

Source: Bank of Slovenia, *Monthly Bulletin.*

COST OF LIVING
(Index of retail prices; base: previous year = 100)

	1990	1991	1992
All items	649.7	217.7	301.3

Source: Bank of Slovenia, *Monthly Bulletin.*

NATIONAL ACCOUNTS (million tolars at current prices)
Gross Domestic Product by Economic Activity

	1989	1990	1991
Agriculture, hunting, forestry and fishing	1,520.9	9,232.7	19,333.5
Mining and quarrying	283.8	2,022.5	4,015.8
Manufacturing	12,823.4	58,363.3	115,085.9
Electricity, gas and water supply	756.7	5,083.6	16,047.7
Construction	1,584.2	8,388.6	12,881.5
Wholesale and retail trade	2,391.8	21,388.4	29,695.8
Hotels and restaurants	755.4	4,484.5	6,600.4
Transport, storage and communications	2,203.2	12,824.1	21,250.3
Finance and insurance services	1,208.5	8,845.6	38,891.6
Real estate and business services	3,130.4	20,202.1	33,371.9
Public administration and defence	1,527.7	7,427.7	14,627.5
Education	1,290.9	6,959.0	11,660.4
Health and social work	1,985.0	9,490.3	15,934.5
Other community, social and personal services	835.2	4,727.7	6,688.3
Sub-total	32,297.1	179,440.1	346,035.1
Import duties	1,213.7	9,733.4	12,555.3
Other indirect taxes	2,045.3	12,310.4	24,682.3
Less Imputed bank service charge	751.1	5,640.7	32,623.4
GDP in purchasers' values	34,805.0	195,843.2	350,649.3

BALANCE OF PAYMENTS (US $ million)

	1989	1990	1991
Merchandise exports f.o.b.	3,382.5	4,118.0	3,869.1
Merchandise imports c.i.f.	−3,201.3	−4,727.0	−4,131.3
Trade balance	181.2	−609.0	−262.2
Exports of services	1,352.4	1,695.2	1,013.0
Imports of services	−403.7	−492.1	−413.8
Other income received	25.3	59.7	42.0
Other income paid	−146.5	−229.2	−217.7
Private unrequited transfers (net)	71.6	87.2	15.1
Official unrequited transfers (net)	25.8	46.9	34.5
Current balance	1,106.1	558.7	210.9
Direct investment (net)	−14.4	−2.1	41.3
Portfolio investment (net)	0.1	2.5	n.a.
Other capital (net)	−17.3	−73.2	−255.0
Net errors and omissions	−1,102.2*	−481.2*	85.6
Overall balance	−27.7	4.6	82.8

* Including sales of claims from bilateral agreements to the National Bank of Yugoslavia (NBY) and purchases of foreign currency by the NBY through Slovenian exchange offices.

Source: Bank of Slovenia, *Monthly Bulletin.*

Balance of Payments (current balance, US $ million): 526 in 1990; 190 in 1991; 764 in 1992. Source: World Bank, *Trends in Developing Economies Extracts.*

External Trade

PRINCIPAL COMMODITIES
(distribution by SITC, million tolars)

Imports c.i.f.	1991
Food and live animals	5,418
Beverages and tobacco	450
Crude materials (inedible) except fuels	8,645
Pulp and waste paper	2,040
Mineral fuels, lubricants, etc.	9,095
Chemicals	16,457
Chemical elements and compounds	5,441
Basic manufactures	19,804
Textile yarn, fabrics, etc.	3,781
Iron and steel	5,241
Machinery and transport equipment	36,119
Miscellaneous manufactured articles	7,946
Total (incl. others)	104,498

Exports f.o.b.	1991
Food and live animals	4,768
Crude materials (inedible) except fuels	2,975
Wood, lumber and cork	2,012
Chemicals	8,496
Basic manufactures	28,726
Wood and cork manufactures (excl. furniture)	2,860
Textile yarn, fabrics, etc.	3,597
Non-metallic mineral manufactures	3,252
Iron and steel	2,399
Non-ferrous metals	3,629
Other metal manufactures	4,401
Machinery and transport equipment	38,892
Miscellaneous manufactured articles	16,929
Furniture	5,897
Total (incl. others)	102,158

Principal Commodities (US $ million): *1990:* Imports c.i.f. 4,727 (Food 889, Capital goods 841); Exports f.o.b. 4,118 (Manufactures 1,833). *1991:* Imports c.i.f. 4,131 (Food 657, Capital goods 765); Exports f.o.b. 3,869 (Manufactures 1,723). *1992:* Imports c.i.f. 4,133 (Food 631, Capital goods 734); Exports f.o.b. 4,185 (Manufactures 1,973). Source: World Bank, *Trends in Developing Economies Extracts.*

PRINCIPAL TRADING PARTNERS (million tolars)

Imports c.i.f.	1991
Austria	10,091
Czechoslovakia	2,649
France	12,690
Germany	25,749
Hungary	1,969
Italy	16,764
Japan	2,275
Netherlands	2,598
Sweden	1,574
Switzerland	2,472
USSR	6,877
United Kingdom	1,922
USA	3,659
Total (incl. others)	104,498

Exports f.o.b.	1991
Austria	5,931
Czechoslovakia	1,618
France	11,769
Germany	27,091
Hungary	1,006
Iran	1,284
Italy	19,364
Netherlands	1,372
Poland	2,701
Switzerland	1,024
USSR	8,078
United Kingdom	2,825
USA	4,364
Total (incl. others)	102,158

Transport

RAILWAYS (traffic)

	1992
Passenger journeys ('000)	12,286
Passenger-kilometres (million)	547
Freight carried ('000 metric tons)	13,045
Freight ton-kilometres (million)	2,574

Source: Slovenske Železnice (SZ—Slovenian Railways).

ROAD TRAFFIC
(registered motor vehicles in use at 31 December)

	1991
Motor cycles (up to 30 cc)	14,344
Passenger cars	594,289
Buses	2,855
Lorries	30,772
Special vehicles	8,592
Tractors	96,280

CIVIL AVIATION (traffic)

	1991
Kilometres flown ('000)	8,035
Passengers carried ('000)	697
Passenger-kilometres (million)	577
Cargo carried (tons)	1,670
Ton-kilometres ('000)	1,216

Tourism

FOREIGN TOURIST ARRIVALS
(by country of origin)

	1991
Austria	38,601
Czechoslovakia	4,662
France	10,716
Germany	47,893
Hungary	3,852
Italy	7,060
Netherlands	6,295
USSR	5,453
United Kingdom	21,620
USA	4,583
Total (incl. others)	969,591

Communications Media

	1991
Telephone subscribers ('000)	459
Radio licences ('000)	591
Television licences ('000)	444
Books (titles published)	2,459
Daily newspapers	5
Non-daily newspapers	199
Other periodicals	484

Education

(1991/92)

	Institutions	Students	Teachers
Primary education; Secondary education (first stage)	824	225,640	14,655
Secondary education (second stage)	149	92,060	6,701
General secondary	n.a.	61,973	n.a.
Teacher training	n.a.	3,907	n.a.
Technical and vocational	n.a.	26,094	n.a.
Religion and theology	2	86	50
Higher education	28	36,504	2,575

1992/93 (institutions): Primary education and secondary education (first stage) 821; Secondary education (second stage) 145; Higher education 28. Source: Statistical Office of the Republic of Slovenia.

Directory

The Constitution

The Constitution of the Republic of Slovenia was enacted on 23 December 1991. Under its terms, the President of the Republic, who is head of state, is elected by direct, secret and universal adult suffrage for a term of five years, renewable only once. The President is Commander-in-Chief of the Armed Forces, calls elections to the National Assembly (Drzavni Zbor), convenes parliament, promulgates laws adopted by the National Assembly, proposes a candidate for Prime Minister and accredits ambassadors.

There is a unicameral legislature, the National Assembly, with 90 members (38 directly elected by universal suffrage, 50 selected by an electoral commission, on the basis of proportional representation, and two who are non-elected representatives of the country's Hungarian and Italian minorities). Elected for four years, it holds effective legislative power, while the National Council (Drzavni Svet), which is elected for five years, has mainly advisory functions; it may, however, veto decisions of the National Assembly. The National Council has 40 members (22 directly elected, 18 appointed by an electoral college to represent various social, economic, trading, political and local interest groups). The Prime Minister must be able to command a majority in parliament, and the composition of any Government must be approved by the National Council. The Government is the highest executive body, but is responsible to the National Assembly.

The Government

HEAD OF STATE

President: MILAN KUČAN (directly elected on 6 December 1992).

Office of the President: 61000 Ljubljana, Erjavčeva 17; tel. (61) 1259280; fax (61) 1251275.

COUNCIL OF MINISTERS
(March 1994)

The Government consists of a coalition of the Liberal Democratic Party (LDP), the Associated List of Social Democrats (ALSD), the Social Democratic Party of Slovenia (SDPS), the Slovenian Christian Democrats (SCD), the Greens of Slovenia (GS) and two independents (Ind.).

Prime Minister: Dr JANEZ DRNOVŠEK (LDP).

Minister of Economic Affairs: Dr MAKS TAJNIKAR (ALSD).

Minister of Economic Relations and Development: Dr DAVORIN KRAČUN (LDP).

Minister of Finance: MITJA GASPARI (Ind.).

Minister of Defence: JANEZ JANŠA (SDPS).

Minister of Internal Affairs: IVAN BIZJAK (SCD).

Minister of Justice: MIHA KOZINC (LDP).

Minister of Labour, Family and Social Affairs: JOŽICA PUHAR (ALSD).

Minister of the Environment and Regional Planning: MIHA JAZBINŠEK (LDP).

Minister of Foreign Affairs: LOJZE PETERLE (SCD).

Minister of Agriculture and Forestry: Dr JOŽE OSTERC (SCD).

Minister of Transport and Communications: IGOR UMEK (SCD).

Minister of Health: Dr BOŽIDAR VOLJČ (GS).

Minister of Education and Sport: Dr SLAVKO GABER (LDP).

Minister of Culture: SERGIJ PELHAN (ALSD).

Minister of Science and Technology: Dr RADO BOHINC (ALSD).

Minister without Portfolio (responsible for legislation): LOJZE JANKO (Ind.).

MINISTRIES

Office of the Prime Minister: 61000 Ljubljana, Gregorčičeva st. 20; tel. (61) 224200; telex 06231284; fax (61) 224240.

Ministry of Agriculture and Forestry: 61000 Ljubljana, Parmova st. 33; tel. (61) 323643; fax (61) 313631.

Ministry of Culture: 61000 Ljubljana, Cankarjeva st. 5; tel. (61) 1259071; fax (61) 210814.

Ministry of Defence: 61000 Ljubljana, Kardeljeva ploščad 24–26; tel. (61) 1331111; fax (61) 1319145.

Ministry of Economic Affairs: 61000 Ljubljana, Kotnikova 5; tel. (61) 1323177; fax (61) 1331031.

Ministry of Economic Relations and Development: 61000 Ljubljana, Kotnikova 5; tel. (61) 1323177; fax (61) 1713599.

Ministry of Education and Sport: 61000 Ljubljana, Župančičeva ul. 6; tel. (61) 1254208; fax (61) 214820.

Ministry of the Environment and Regional Planning: 61000 Ljubljana, Župančičeva ul. 6; tel. (61) 1254208; fax (61) 224548.

Ministry of Finance: 61000 Ljubljana, Župančičeva st. 3; tel. (61) 1765211; fax (61) 214640.

Ministry of Foreign Affairs: 61000 Ljubljana, Gregorčičeva st. 25; tel. (61) 1250300; fax (61)1256275.

Ministry of Health: 61000 Ljubljana, Štefanova 5; tel. (61) 1251028; fax (62) 217752.

Ministry of Internal Affairs: 61000 Ljubljana, Štefanova 2; tel. (61) 1325125; fax (61) 214330.

Ministry of Justice: 61000 Ljubljana, Župančičeva st. 3; tel. (61) 1765279; fax (61) 210200.

Ministry of Labour, Family and Social Affairs: 61000 Ljubljana, Kotnikova 5; tel. (61) 1713311; fax (61) 1713456.

Ministry of Science and Technology: 61000 Ljubljana, Slovenska 50; tel. (61) 1311107; fax (61) 1324140.

Ministry of Transport and Communications: 61000 Ljubljana, Prešernova st. 23; tel. (61) 1256256; fax (61) 218707.

President and Legislature

PRESIDENT

Presidential Elections, 6 December 1992

Candidate	% of votes
MILAN KUČAN	63.8
IVAN BIZJAK	21.2
JELKO KACIN	7.2
STANKO BUSER	1.9
DARJA LAVTIŽAR-BEBLER	1.8
ALENKA ŽAGAR-SLANA	1.7
LJUBO SIRC	1.4
FRANCE TOMŠIČ	0.6
Total	100.0

DRZAVNI ZBOR
(National Assembly)

President: HERMAN RIGELNIK; 61000 Ljubljana, Šubičeva st. 4; tel. (61) 1258022; fax (61) 1258160.

General Election, 6 December 1992

	Seats		
Party	Directly elected	Indirectly elected	% of votes
Liberal Democratic Party	17	5	23.7
Slovenian Christian Democrats	8	7	14.5
Associated List*	8	6	13.6
Slovenian National Party†	3	9	9.9
Slovenian People's Party	2	8	8.8
Democratic Party of Slovenia‡	—	6	5.0
Greens of Slovenia§	—	5	3.7
Social Democratic Party of Slovenia	—	4	3.3
Others	—	—	17.9
Total¶	38	50	100.0

* Later renamed the Associated List of Social Democrats.

† Five deputies from the Slovenian National Party (SNP) subsequently formed the Independent SNP Deputy Group and a sixth member left the party to become an independent deputy.

‡ One deputy left the Democratic Party of Slovenia to become an independent deputy.

§ All five deputies elected as candidates of the Greens of Slovenia later joined the Greens of Slovenia—Eco-Social Party.

¶ Two of the 90 seats in the Assembly are reserved for representatives of the Italian and Hungarian minorities.

DRZAVNI SVET
(National Council)

President: Dr IVAN KRISTAN; 61000 Ljubljana, Šubičeva st. 4; tel. (61) 1257311; fax (61) 1258160.

Local Government

The system of local government in Slovenia was restructured during 1994 and the number of municipal units was expected to increase to around 200 by the end of the year.

Political Organizations

Associated List of Social Democrats (ALSD): 61000 Ljubljana, Levstikova 15; tel. (61) 215897; fax (61) 1261170; f. 1992 as the Associated List, an electoral alliance of the Democratic Party of Pensioners, Social Democratic Reform of Slovenia, the Social Democratic Union and the Workers' Party of Slovenia; in 1993 it became a single party and adopted its current name; Pres. JANEZ KOCIJANČIČ.

Democratic Party of Slovenia (Demokratska stranka—DSS): 61000 Ljubljana, Breg 12; tel. (61) 1252203; fax (61) 1253316; f. 1991 after split in Slovenian Democratic Union (SDU—f. 1989, first opposition party to Communists); minority faction, but retained SDU leadership and liberal orientation; centrist party; Pres. IGOR BAVČAR.

Greens of Slovenia—Eco-Social Party: 61000 Ljubljana, Komenskega 11; tel. (61) 311629; fax (61) 313065; f. 1989 as Greens of Slovenia (Zelena Slovenije—ZS), one of first opposition groups to Communists; party split into two factions in 1993; advocates protection of the environment and demilitarization of an independent Slovenia; Pres. Dr PETER TANCIG.

Greens of Slovenia (Zelena Slovenije—ZS): 61000 Ljubljana; f. 1989 as one of first opposition groups to Communists; following a split in 1993 all five deputies in the National Assembly formed the Greens of Slovenia—Eco-Social Party; Leader VANE GOŠNIK.

Independent SNP Deputy Group: 61000 Ljubljana; tel. (61) 150256; f. 1993 by five deputies from the Slovenian National Party (SNP); Leader SAŠO LAP.

Liberal Democratic Party (LDP) (Liberalno demokratska stranka—LDS): 61000 Ljubljana, Dalmatinova 4; tel. (61) 312659; fax (61) 312381; former Union of Socialist Youth, a Communist youth org., it changed its name and renounced its previous character in 1990; centre-left party; Pres. Dr JANEZ DRNOVŠEK; Sec.-Gen. GREGOR GOLOBIĆ.

Liberal Party: f. 1989 as the Slovenian Artisans' Party; changed name 1990; supports a free-market economy; right-wing; Pres. and Parl. Leader FRANC GOLIJA.

National Democratic Party (Narodni Demokrati—ND): 61000 Ljubljana, Beethovnova 4; tel. (61) 1262179; fax (61) 211788; f. 1992 following split in Slovenian Democratic Union; Chair. Dr RAJKO PIRNAT; Sec.-Gen. MATJAŽ KONCILJA.

Party of Democratic Reform (PDR) (Stranka Democratskih Reformi—SDP): 61000 Ljubljana, Šubičeva st. 4; former League of Communists of Slovenia, disaffiliated from the League of Communists of Yugoslavia (LCY) and changed name in 1990; left-wing; Pres. CIRIL RIBIČIČ; Parl. Group Leader MIRAN POTIČ.

Slovenian Christian Democrats: 61000 Ljubljana, Beethovnova 4; tel. (61) 1262179; fax (61) 211738; f. 1989; centrist, conservative party; mem. of European Union of Christian Democrats and of European Democratic Union (EDU); Pres. LOJZE PETERLE; Sec.-Gen. EDVARD STANIČ; Parl. Group Leader IGNAC POLAJNAR.

Slovenian National Party (SNP) (Slovenska nacionalna stranka—SNS): 61000 Ljubljana, Tivolska 13; tel. (61) 224241; fax (61) 213294; f. 1991; right-wing nationalist party; Pres. ZMAGO JELINČIČ; Sec.-Gen. JURE JESENKO.

Slovenian People's Party (SPP) (Slovenska ljudska stranka—SLS): 61000 Ljubljana, Zarnikova 3; tel. (61) 301891; fax (61) 301878; f. 1989 as the Slovenian Farmers' Association; Pres. MARJAN PODOBNIK.

Social Democratic Party of Slovenia (SDPS) (Socialdemokratska stranka Slovenije—SDSS): 61000 Ljubljana, Komenskega 11; tel. (61) 314086; fax (61) 301143; f. 1989; workers' party of nationalist orientation; centre-left; Pres. JANEZ JANŠA; Sec.-Gen. BRANKO GRIMS; Parl. Group Leader Dr JOŽE PUČNIK.

Socialist Party of Slovenia (SPS) (SSS): 61000 Ljubljana, Šubičeva st. 4; former Communist org., the Socialist Alliance of Slovenia, changed name and became independent party in 1990; left-wing; Pres. VIKTOR ŽAKELJ; Parl. Group Leader DUŠAN SEMOLIČ.

Diplomatic Representation

EMBASSIES IN SLOVENIA

Albania: 61000 Ljubljana, Ob Ljubljanici 12; tel. (61) 1322324; fax (61) 1323129; Ambassador: NAPOLEON DHIMITER ROSHI.

Austria: 61000 Ljubljana, Štrekljeva 5; tel. (61) 213436; fax (61) 221717; Ambassador: Dr JUTTA STEFAN-BASTL.

Bosnia and Herzegovina: 61000 Ljubljana, Likozarjeva 6; tel. (61) 1322214; fax (61) 1322230; Ambassador: UGLJEŠA UZELAC.

Bulgaria: 61000 Ljubljana, Hotel Turist, Dalmatinova 15; tel. (61) 1322343; fax (61) 319291; Chargé d'affaires: GANČO GANEV.

China, People's Republic: 61000 Ljubljana, Cesta na Brdo 115; tel. (61) 272283; fax (61) 272283; Ambassador: LU PEIXIN.

Croatia: 61000 Ljubljana, Grubarjevo nabrežje 6; tel (61) 211635; fax (61) 1258106; Ambassador: MILJENKO ŽAGAR.

Czech Republic: 61000 Ljubljana, Kolarjeva 30; tel. and fax (61) 318423; Ambassador: PETR KYPR.

France: 61109 Ljubljana, Robbova 18/VI; tel. (61) 1734441; fax (61) 1734442; Ambassador: BERNARD PONCET.

Germany: 61000 Ljubljana, Prešernova 27, p.p. 85; tel. (61) 216166; fax (61) 1254210; Ambassador: Dr GÜNTHER SEIBERT.

Holy See: 61000 Ljubljana, Tabor 3; tel. (61) 1314133; fax (61) 1315130; Apostolic Nuncio: Dr PIER LUIGI CELATA, Titular Archbishop of Doclea (resident in Malta).

Hungary: 61000 Ljubljana, Dunajska 22, VI; tel. (61) 1315168; fax (61) 1317143; Ambassador: Dr ISTVÁN BALOGH.

Italy: 61000 Ljubljana, Snežniška 8; tel. (61) 1262194; fax (61) 1253302; Ambassador: LUIGI SOLARI.

Macedonia: 61000 Ljubljana, Dunajska 104; tel. (61) 1684454; fax (61) 1685181; Ambassador: DIMITAR MIRČEV.

Romania: 61000 Ljubljana, Nanoška 8; tel. (61) 268702; Chargé d'affaires: MARIAN PAVELESCU.

Russian Federation: 61000 Ljubljana, Rožna dolina, Cesta II, št 7; tel. (61) 261189; fax (61) 1254141; Chargé d'affaires: JURIJ STEPANOVIČ GIRENKO.

Turkey: 61000 Ljubljana, Livarska 4; tel. (61) 1332012; fax (61) 1323158; Ambassador: ILHAN YIGITBASIOGLU.

United Kingdom: 61000 Ljubljana, trg republike 3; tel. (61) 1257191; fax (61) 1250174; Ambassador: GORDON MACKENZIE JOHNSTON.

USA: 61000 Ljubljana, Pražakova 4; tel. (61) 301427; fax (61) 301401.

Judicial System

In Slovenia the judiciary is independent of the Government. Ordinary courts are divided into three instances: basic courts, higher courts and the Supreme Court. The eight basic courts make rulings on almost all civil and criminal cases, and the four higher courts make rulings on appeals against decisions made by the basic courts. The Supreme Court is the highest authority for civil and criminal law. There is also a constitutional court, composed of nine judges, each elected for nine years, which determines the conformity of national legislation with the Constitution.

Constitutional Court of Slovenia: 61000 Ljubljana, Beethovnova 10; tel. (61) 210448; Pres. Dr PETER JAMBREK.

Supreme Court: 61000 Ljubljana, Tavčarjeva 9; tel. (61) 1323133; Pres. FRANCKA STRNOLE-HLASTEC.

Office of the Public Prosecutor: 61000 Ljubljana, Tavčarjeva 9; Public Prosecutor ANTON DROBNIČ.

Office of the Public Attorney: 61000 Ljubljana, Cankarjeva 5; Public Attorney JOŽE GREGORIČ.

Religion

Most of the population are Christian, predominantly adherents of the creeds of the Roman Catholic Church. The Archbishop of Ljubljana is the most senior Roman Catholic prelate in Slovenia. The Roman Catholic Church in Slovenia comprises one archdiocese (Ljubljana) and two dioceses (Koper and Maribor). There is also a Slovene Old Catholic Church, but there are few Protestant Christians, despite the importance of a Calvinist sect (Church of Carniola) to the development of Slovene literature in the 16th century. There are some members of the Eastern Orthodox Church, some who profess Islam and a small Jewish community.

CHRISTIANITY

The Roman Catholic Church

Archbishop of Ljubljana: Dr ALOJZIJ ŠUŠTAR, 61001 Ljubljana, p.p. 121/III, Ciril-Metodov trg 4; tel. (61) 310673; fax (61) 314169.

Old Catholic Church

Slovene Old Catholic Church: Ljubljana, trg Francoske revolucije 1/I; Maribor, Vita Kraigherja 2; f. 1948; Bishop Rev. JOSIP KVOČIĆ.

The Protestant Church

Evangelical Lutheran Church of Slovenia: Headquarters: 69000 Murska Sobota, Slovenska 15; tel. and fax (69) 22304; f. 1561; 18,900 mems; Chair. LUDVIK NOVAK.

The Press

PRINCIPAL DAILIES

Delo: 61000 Ljubljana, Dunajska 5; tel. (61) 1318255; telex 31255; fax (61) 1334032; f. 1959; morning; in Slovene; Editor TIT DOBERŠEK; circ. 90,000.

Dnevnik: 61000 Ljubljana, Kopitarjeva 2; tel. (61) 1325261; telex 31177; fax (61) 1321020; f. 1951; evening; independent; Chief Editor ZLATKO ŠETINC; Exec. Editor ROBERT MECILOŠEK; circ. 74,000.

Primorski Dnevnik: CP 559, Trieste, Italy; tel. (40) 7796600; fax (40) 772418; Man. Editor VOJIMIR TAVCAR.

Republika: 61000 Ljubljana, Slovenska 54; tel. (61) 1313121; fax (61) 1320126; f. 1992; Editor-in-Chief MARJAN SEDMAK; circ. 30,000.

Slovenec: 61000 Ljubljana, Dunajska 9; tel. (61) 320841; fax (61) 320179; f. 1991; Editor-in-Chief JANI VIRK; circ. 32,000.

Slovenske novice: 61000 Ljubljana, Dunajska 5; tel. (61) 1318255; fax (61) 318193; f. 1991; Editor-in-Chief and Man. Editor MARJAN BAUER; circ. 46,000.

ČZP Večer: 62000 Maribor, Svetozarevska 14; tel. (62) 224221; telex 33183; fax (62) 227736; f. 1945; in Slovene; Man. Dir BOŽO ZORKO; Editor-in-Chief MILAN PREDAN; circ. 65,000.

PERIODICALS

Antena: 61000 Ljubljana, Slovenska 15; tel. (61) 221991; fax (61) 221967; f 1964; weekly; youth magazine concerned with popular culture; Editor-in-Chief JASMIN PETAN MALAHOVSKY; circ. 25,000.

Auto magazin: 61000 Ljubljana, Dunajska 5; tel. (61) 319180; telex 31255; fax (61) 319873; f. 1967; car, motorcycle and sports magazine; Editor MARTIN ČESENJ; circ. 26,000.

Delavska enotnost: 61000 Ljubljana, Dalmatinova 4; tel. (61) 311956; fax (61) 317298; Dir and Editor-in-Chief MARJAN HORVAT.

Delo Plus: 61000 Ljubljana, Dunajska 5; tel. (61) 118255; fax (61) 302339; Editor-in-Chief MARJAN RAZTRESEN.

Dolenjski List: 68000 Novo Mesto; tel. (68) 23606; fax (68) 24898; Editor-in-Chief DRAGO RUSTJA.

Druzina: 61000 Ljubljana, p.p. 95, Trubarjeva 82; tel. (61) 329793; fax (61) 116152; Editor-in-Chief JANEZ GRIL.

Ekipa: 61260 Ljubljana, Vevska 52; tel. (61) 482469; fax (61) 483710; Editor-in-Chief SLAVKO SAKELSEK.

Finance: 61000 Ljubljana, Dunajska 5; tel. (61) 302287; fax (61) 121012; Editor-in-Chief DUSAN SNOJ.

Gorenjski glas: 64000 Kranj, Zoisova 1; tel. (64) 223111; fax (64) 222917; f. 1947; twice weekly; Editor-in-Chief MARKO VALJAVEC; circ. 25,000.

Gospodarski vestnik: 61000 Ljubljana, Dunajska 5; tel. (61) 318389; fax (61) 122115; f. 1920; Slovenian; business weekly; Editor-in-Chief DUŠAN SNOJ.

Jana: 61000 Ljubljana, Dunajska 5; tel. (61) 118255; fax (61) 319873; Editor-in-Chief BERNARDA JEKLIN; circ. 62,000.

Kaj: 62000 Maribor, Svetozarevska 14; tel. (62) 26951; fax (62) 27736; Man. Editor ZARE ROJC; circ. 16,500.

Kmecki glas: 61000 Ljubljana, p.p. 47, Celovska 43; tel. (61) 318855; fax (61) 321651; Editor-in-Chief BORIS DOLNICAR; circ. 38,000.

Mladina: 61000 Ljubljana, Resljeva 16; tel. (61) 321954; fax (61) 329589; f. 1942; weekly; news magazine; Editor-in-Chief ROBERT BOTTERI; circ. 25,000.

Nas Cas: 63320 Velenje, Frantiska Foita 10; tel. (63) 853451; fax (63) 851990; Editor-in-Chief BORIS ZAKOSEK; circ. 6,250.

Nedeljski Dnevnik: 61000 Ljubljana, Kopitarjeva 2; tel. (61) 125261; telex 31177; fax (61) 312775; f. 1961; weekly; popular; Exec. Editor ZLATKO ŠETINC; circ. 185,000.

Nova doba: 63000 Celje, Askerceva 15; tel. (63) 441215; fax (63) 25849; Editor-in-Chief JANEZ SEVER.

Nova Proizvodnja: Ljubljana, Erjavceva 15; tel. (61) 212139; f. 1949; bi-monthly; technics and economics; organ of the Association of Engineers and Technicians of the Republic of Slovenia; Editor MARJAN LAČIĆ.

Novi tednik: 63000 Celje, p.p. 161, V. Kongresa trg 3A; Editor-in-Chief JOZE CEROVSEK; circ. 16,980.

PIL: 61000 Ljubljana, Nazorjeva 1; tel. (61) 210261; fax (61) 210313; Editor-in-Chief SUZANA SOSTER.

Radio tednik: 62250 Ptuj, Raiceva 6; tel. (62) 771261; fax (62) 771223; Editor-in-Chief FRANC LACEN.

Razgledi: 61001 Ljubljana, Dunajska 5, POB 188; tel. (61) 318445; telex 31255; fax (61) 311871; f. 1952; political and cultural fortnightly; Editor MARKO CRNKOVIČ; circ. 8,000.

Salomonov oglasnik: 61000 Ljubljana, Nazorjeva 6; tel. (61) 223328; Editor-in-Chief LENART ŠKOK.

Slovenian Business Report: 61000 Ljubljana, Dunajska 5; tel. (61) 318389; fax (61) 122115; monthly; business magazine; publ. in English; Dir SLOBODAN SIBINČIČ; Editor-in-Chief DUŠAN SNOJ; Editor TOMAŽ GERDINA.

Slovenske brazde: 61000 Ljubljana, Zarnikova 3; tel. (61) 301891; fax (61) 301871; Editor-in-Chief BOŽA GREŠOVNIK (acting).

Stop: 61001 Ljubljana, Dunajska 5; tel. and fax (61) 319190; f. 1967; weekly magazine covering leisure, film, theatre, pop music, radio and television programmes; Editor IGOR SAVIČ; circ. 50,000.

Tretji dan: 61000 Ljubljana, Jurcicev trg 2; tel. (61) 211136; fax (61) 223836; Editor-in-Chief JOZE KURILCIC.

Tribuna: 61000 Ljubljana, Kersnikova 4; tel. (61) 319496; fax (61) 319448; Editor-in-Chief BOJAN KORENINI.

Vestnik: 69000 Murska Sobota, Titova 29/1; tel. (69) 21383; fax (69) 22419; Editor-in-Chief IRMA BENKO.

Yugoslav Echo: 61000 Ljubljana, Titova 35; tel. (61) 318389; telex 31255; fax (61) 311871; quarterly; in English; economy, finance, trade.

PRESS AGENCIES

Slovenska Tiskovna Agencija (STA): 61101 Ljubljana, Cankarjeva 5, p.p. 145; tel. (61) 211706; fax (61) 301321; f. 1991; Dir DUŠICA JURMAN; Editor-in-Chief TADEJ LABERNIK.

Publishers

Cankarjeva založba: 61000 Ljubljana, Kopitarjeva 2; tel. (61) 323841; telex 31821; fax (61) 318782; f. 1945; philosophy, science and popular science; dictionaries and reference books; Yugoslav and translated literature; import and export; international co-productions; Dir-Gen. JANEZ STANIČ.

Državna založba Slovenije (DZS): 61000 Ljubljana, Mestni trg 26; tel. (61) 211711; fax (61) 215675; f. 1945; Slovenian textbooks, manuals, Slovenian authors, world classics, natural sciences, art books, dictionaries; import and export; Mans ANDREJ POGLAJEN, IRENA JUNKAR.

Mladinska knjiga: 61000 Ljubljana, Slovenska 29; tel. (61) 161300; telex 31345; fax (61) 215320; f. 1945; books for youth and children, including general, fiction, science, travel and school books; international co-operation; Dir MILAN MATOS.

Slovenska Matica: 61000 Ljubljana, Kongresni trg 8; tel. (61) 214200; f. 1864; poetry, science, philosophy; Pres. Prof. Dr PRIMOŽ SIMONITI.

Založba Obzorja: 62000 Maribor, Partizanska 3–5; tel. (62) 28971; telex 33255; fax (62) 26696; f. 1950; popular science, general literature, periodicals, etc.; Man. Dir FRANC FILIPIĆ.

Zdo Založba Lipa Koper: 66000 Koper, Muzejski trg 7; tel. (66) 23291; fax (66) 23293; fiction; Dir Prof. JOŽE A. HOČEVAR.

Radio and Television

RADIO

Radio Slovenija: 61000 Ljubljana, Tavčarjeva 17; tel. (61) 1311333; fax (61) 1334007; f. 1928; 3 programmes nationally; main MW stations at Ljubljana, Koper and Maribor; broadcasts in Slovene, Hungarian and Italian languages; foreign broadcasts in English and German; Editor-in-Chief FRANCE VURNIK (acting).

TELEVISION

Televizija Slovenija: 61000 Ljubljana, Kolodvorska 2-4; tel. (61) 1311333; telex 32283; fax (61) 1335079; f. 1958; 2 programmes nationally; studios at Ljubljana, Maribor and Koper; Editor-in-Chief JANEZ LOMBERGER (acting).

A-Kanal (Channel A): 61000 Ljubljana, Tivolska 50; tel. (61) 1334133; fax (61) 1334222; private company; Editor-in-Chief BRANKO ČAKARMIŠ.

Finance

BANKS

(d.d. = dioničko društvo (joint-stock company); cap. = capital; dep. = deposits; m. = million; amounts in Slovene tolars (SlT) unless otherwise stated; brs = branches)

National Bank

Banka Slovenije (Bank of Slovenia): 61001 Ljubljana, Slovenska 35, p.p. 440; tel. (61) 1257333; telex 31214; fax (61) 215516; formerly National Bank of Slovenia, as part of the Yugoslav banking system; assumed central bank functions in 1991; bank of issue since Oct. 1991; Gov. Dr FRANC ARHAR; Dep. Gov. BOGOMIR KOS.

Selected Banks

Abanka d.d. Ljubljana (Abanka Joint-Stock Company): 61001 Ljubljana, Slovenska 58, POB 368; tel. (61) 112112; telex 31228; fax (61) 314535; f. 1955 as Ljubljana Branch of Yugoslav Bank for Foreign Trade, adopted current name 1989; total assets US $277.5m. (Sept. 1992); Gen. Dir MIROSLAV KERT; 31 brs.

Bank Austria d.d.: 61000 Ljubljana, Wolfova 1; tel. (61) 214009; fax (61) 212977; Dir PETER SETZER.

Creditanstalt Nova Banka d.d. Ljubljana: 61000 Ljubljana, Šubičeva 3; tel. (61) 215877; fax (61) 125206; Dir IGOR KADUNC.

Hipotekarna Banka Brezice d.o.o. Brezice: 68250 Brezice, Cesta prvih borcev 11; tel. (608) 62232; fax (608) 62231; Dir BOJAN PETAN.

Kreditna banka Maribor d.d. (Credit Bank, Maribor): 62000 Maribor, Vita Kraigherja 4; tel. (62) 223311; telex 33167; fax (62) 224333; f. 1955; cap. 805.3m., dep. 28,473.6m. (mid-1993); Pres. and Chief Exec. A. HAZABENT; Exec. Man. DARKO TOLAR; 32 brs.

Ljubljanska Banka d.d. Ljubljana: 61001 Ljubljana, POB 534, trg republike 2; tel. (61) 150155; telex 31256; fax (61) 222422; f. 1955; commercial, investment and savings bank; total assets 2,899.3m., dep. 1,206.1m. (Jan. 1993); Pres. and Chief Exec. MARKO VOLJČ; 57 brs.

Probanka d.d. Maribor: 62000 Maribor, Razlagova ul. 22; tel. (62) 26370; telex 33245; fax (62) 24978; Gen. Man. ROMANA PAJENK.

SKB Banka d.d.: 61000 Ljubljana, Ajdovščina 4; tel. (61) 132132; telex 39144; fax (61) 302808; f. 1965; cap. US $103.2m., dep. $317.3m. (Dec. 1992); Man. Dir IVAN NERAD; 37 brs.

Slovenska Investicijska Banka d.d. Ljubljana: 61000 Ljubljana, Copova 38; tel. (61) 161181; fax (61) 217095; Dir VLADO KLEMENČIČ.

Slovenska Zadruzna Kmetijska Banka d.d.: 61000 Ljubljana, Miklošičeva 4; tel. (61) 153251; telex 39154; fax (61) 217057; f. 1990; cap. US $12.354m., dep. $19.583m. (mid-1993); Man. Dir MILAN KNEŽEVIČ: Dep. Man. Dir LADISLAV SAMEC; 2 brs.

UBK Banka d.d. Ljubljana: 61111 Ljubljana, Tržaška 116, p.p. 87; tel. (61) 272073; fax (61) 273082; Dir MATJAŽ KAŠTRUN.

STOCK EXCHANGE

Ljubljana Stock Exchange d.d.: 61000 Ljubljana, Slovenska c. 56; tel. (61) 1710211; fax (61) 1710213; f. 1989, operative 1990; Gen. Man. DRAŠKO VESELINOVIČ.

Trade and Industry

STATE PROPERTY AGENCIES

Agency for Restructuring and Privatization: 61000 Ljubljana, Kotnikova 28; tel. (61) 1312122; fax (61) 1316011; Dir MIRA PUC.

Development Fund of the Republic of Slovenia: 61000 Ljubljana, Kotnikova 28; tel. (61) 1312122; fax (61) 1316011; Dir UROŠ KORŽE.

CHAMBERS OF COMMERCE

Chamber of Economy of Slovenia: 61000 Ljubljana, Slovenska 41; tel. (61) 1250122; fax (61) 315944; Pres. DAGMAR ŠUSTER.

Chamber of Small Businesses of Slovenia: 61000 Ljubljana, Celovška 71; tel. (61) 1593241; fax (61) 559270; Pres. MIHA GRAH; 50,000 mems.

MAJOR ENTERPRISES AND COMPANIES

ABC Pomurka—Zunanja Trgovina: 69000 Murska Sobota, POB 127, Lendavska 11; tel. (69) 31580; telex 35219; fax (69) 32670; federation of 39 work orgs and 4,000 co-operating agricultural producers; largest food producer in Slovenia; Dir DARKO PEJNOVIČ; 12,000 employees.

Adria Caravan: 68000 Novo Mesto, Zagrebska 20; tel. (68) 23311; fax (68) 23224; Dir DANILO PLESNICAR.

Avtoimpex: 61000 Ljubljana, Celovška del 150; tel. (61) 551686; fax (61) 551477; Dir ANDREJ KOŽELJ.

Avtotehna: 61000 Ljubljana, Slovenska 54; tel. (61) 117144; fax (61) 320589; Dir STEFAN KRAJNC.

Cimos International: 66000 Koper, Marežganskega Upora 2; tel. (66) 31131; fax (66) 34490; Dir BORIS BERNETIČ.

Cinkarna: 63000 Celje, Kidričeva 26; tel. (63) 33112; fax (63) 34640; Dir MARJAN PRELEC.

Exim: 62000 Maribor, Ljubljanska 9; tel. (62) 33411; Dir MAGDA ŠPARAŠ.

Gorenje G.A.: 63320 Velenje, Partizanska 12; tel. (63) 853321; fax (63) 854475; manufacturers of heating equipment; Dir JOŽE STANIČ.

Gostol: 65001 Nova Gorica, Prvomajska 37; tel. (65) 23411; telex 38106; fax (65) 23495; production and sale of machines and equipment for bakeries, foundries, and associated technology; Gen. Dir DRAGAN MOZETIČ; 500 employees.

Hidria Trading: 65281 Spodnja Idrija, Staneta Rozmana 19A; trading company; Dir ANDREJKA REJC KRAPŠ.

IBN—JT: 61000 Ljubljana, Slovenska 27; tel. (61) 159160; fax (61) 157181; Dir ANTON HRASTELJ.

Impol: 62310 Slovenska Bistrica, Partizanska 38; tel. (62) 811521; fax (62) 811219; Dir JERNEJ ČOKL.

Industrija Usnja: 61360 Vrhnika, Tržaška 31; tel. (61) 752211; fax (61) 751330; Dir ANTON DEBEVC.

Iskra Stevci: 64000 Kranj, Savska Loka 4; tel. (64) 221321; fax (64) 223644; Dir NIKOLAJ BEVK.

Kamnik Co: 61241 Kamnik, Fužine 9; tel. (61) 831011; telex 31264; fax (61) 832735; produces aluminium pastes and powders, explosives, other plastics, etc.; Gen. Dir PETER ŠKUFCA; 700 employees.

Kemofarmacija Ljubljana: 61000 Ljubljana, Na Brdo 100; tel. (61) 268145; fax (61) 271362; pharmaceutical products; Dir MIRKO KORINŠEK.

Krka Tovarna Zdravil: 68000 Novo Mesto, Herojev 45; tel. (68) 22441; fax (68) 21537; pharmaceutical products; Dir MILOŠ KOVAČIČ.

Lek d.d., Ljubljana: 61107 Ljubljana, Verovškova 57, POB 81; tel. (61) 182161; telex 39403; fax (61) 183517; pharmaceuticals, chemicals, cosmetics and medical products; Dir METOD DRAGONJA; 2,164 employees.

Mehano: 66310 Izola, Polje 9; tel. (66) 62121; telex 34134; fax (66) 62983; manufacturer of battery-operated toys; Gen. Dir MARJAN STARČ; Gen. Man. MARINO ANTOLOVIČ; 500 employees.

Merkur: 64000 Kranj, Koroška 1; tel. (64) 26461; fax (64) 21088; Dir JAKOB PISKERNIK.

Mura—European Fashion Design: 69000 Murska Sobota, Plese 2; tel. (69) 21535; telex 35215; fax (69) 25510; production of ready-made garments and fashion design; Gen. Man. BOŽO KUHARIČ; 6,500 employees.

Nafta: 69220 Lendava, Rudarska 1; tel. (69) 75301; fax (69) 75621; Dir MILOŠ OŠLAJ.

OMV—Istra: 66000 Koper, Ferrarska 7; Dir PETER POŽRL.

Paloma—Sladkogorska Tovarna Papirja: 62214 Sladki VRH, Sladki VRH 1; tel. (62) 644460; fax (62) 644458; Dir IGOR POGLEJ.

Papirnica Vevče: 61000 Ljubljana, Vevška 52; tel. (61) 485535; fax (61) 485450; Dir MILAN ŠETINC.

Peko: 64290 Tržič, Ste Marie aux Mines 5; tel. (64) 50260; fax (64) 50887; Dir FRANC GRAŠIČ.

Petrol Trgovina: 61000 Ljubljana, Dunajska del 50; tel. (61) 312755; fax (61) 318770; Dir FRANC PREMK.

Planika: 64000 Kranj, Savska Loka 21; tel. (64) 222721; fax (64) 222431; Dir ANTON GROS.

Revoz: 68000 Novo Mesto, Zagrebska 20; tel. (68) 23311; fax (68) 21300; Dir BERNARD COURSAT.

Sava: 64000 Kranj, Skofjeloška 6; tel. (64) 222241; fax (64) 221114; Dir VILJEM ŽENER.

Skupina Emona R.O.: 61000 Ljubljana, Šmartinska 130; tel. (61) 442544; telex 31205; fax (61) 101321; production, trading, tourism, catering and engineering; 6,000 employees.

Slovenske Železarne: 61000 Ljubljana, Mala 5; tel. (61) 311633; fax (61) 318556; Dir ANDREJ OCVIRK.

Talum: 62325 Kidričevo, Tovarniška 10; tel. (62) 796110; fax (62) 796269; Dir DANILO TOPLEK.

Tehno-Impex International: 61000 Ljubljana, Kersnikova 2; Dir ARNE MISLEJ.

Unior: 63214 Zreće, Kovaska 10; tel. (63) 761122; telex 33527; fax (63) 761643; producer of hand tools, etc.; other activities incl.

machine manufacture and tourism; Dir JANEZ ŠPES; 2,300 employees.

Unitex: 61000 Ljubljana, Dunajska del 51; tel. (61) 116166; fax (61) 316546; Dir FRANC LUCKMANN.

TRADE UNIONS

The Association of Independent Trade Unions of Slovenia: 61000 Ljubljana, Dalmatinova 4; tel. (61) 317983; fax (61) 316895; Pres. DUŠAN SEMOLIČ.

Independence—Confederation of New Trade Unions of Slovenia: 61000 Ljubljana, Linhartova 13; tel. (61) 1329141; fax (61) 302868; Pres. FRANCE TOMŠIČ.

Transport

RAILWAYS

The rail link between the countries of the European Union (formerly the European Community) and Greece, Turkey and the Near and Middle East runs through Slovenia. In 1992 there were 1,201 km of railway lines in Slovenia, of which 499 km were electrified.

Slovenske Zeleznice (SŽ—Slovenian Railways): 61000 Ljubljana, Kolodvorska 11; tel. (61) 318878; fax (61) 317262.

ROADS

There are two motorways in Slovenia, with a total combined length of 81 km. In 1992 the country had 14,794 km of roads.

SHIPPING

The principal ports of Slovenia are Koper-Capodistria, Portorož and Izola. The port of Koper-Capodistria alone handles an annual traffic of 5m. tons.

Principal Shipping Company

Splošna Plovba Piran: 66320 Portorož, Obala 55; tel. (66) 73881; telex 34122; fax (66) 75867; transport of all types of cargo; regular liner service.

CIVIL AVIATION

There are three international airports in Slovenia, at Brnik (Ljubljana), Maribor and Portorož.

Adria Airways: 61001 Ljubljana, Kuzmičeva 7; tel. (61) 313366; telex 31268; fax (61) 323356; f. 1961; operates international scheduled services to destinations in Europe and the Near and Middle East; Pres. JANEZ KOCIJANČIČ.

Solinair commenced a daily service to Vienna (Austria) in April 1992.

Tourism

Slovenia offers a variety of attractions for the tourist, including Mediterranean beaches to the west, the Alps to the north and the 'karst' limestone regions, with more than 6,000 caves. In 1991 and 1992 Slovenia recorded 1.4m. tourist arrivals per year, compared with 2.5m. in 1990. According to the Bank of Slovenia income from tourism was over US $728m. in 1993.

Centre of Tourist and Economic Promotion (Chamber of Economy of Slovenia): 61000 Ljubljana, Igriška 5; tel. (61) 156172; fax (61) 157323; Dir RUDI TAVČAR.

Emona Globtour: 61000 Ljubljana, Šmartinska 130/X; tel. (61) 444177; telex 39606; fax (61) 441325; f. 1968; 13 branch offices, 9 foreign offices; Gen. Man. BOGO UMEK.

Tourist Association of Slovenia: 61000 Ljubljana, Milošičeva 38; tel. (61) 120141; fax (61) 301570; Pres. Dr MARJAN ROŽIČ.

Culture

NATIONAL ORGANIZATIONS

Ministry of Culture: see section on The Government (Ministries).

Festival Ljubljana: 61000 Ljubljana, trg francoske revolucije 1–2; tel. (61) 221948; annual cultural event; Dir VLADIMIR VAJDA.

Cankarjev dom: 61000 Ljubljana, Prešernova 10; tel. (61) 1258121; impresarios and sponsors of cultural events; Dir MITJA ROTOVNIK.

CULTURAL HERITAGE

Archives of the Republic of Slovenia (Arhiv Republike Slovenije): 61000 Ljubljana, Zvezdarska 1, p.p. 70; tel. (61) 151222; fax (61) 216551; f. 1945; collection of material from the 12th century onwards dealing with the territory of Slovenia; Chief VLADIMIR ŽUMER.

International Graphic Arts Centre (Mednarodni Grafični Likovni Center): 61000 Ljubljana, Grad Tivoli, Pod turnom 3; tel. (61) 219744; f. 1986; Dir Prof. ZORAN KRŽIŠNIK.

Museum of Modern Art (Moderna galerija): 61000 Ljubljana, Tomšičeva 14; tel. (61) 214101; fax (61) 214120; f. 1948; 20th-century Slovenian art collection; temporary exhibitions of national and international contemporary art; maintains an information centre, a photographic archive, a library and a restoration studio; Dirs Dr JURE MIKUŽ, ZDENKA BADOVINAC.

National Art Gallery (Narodna galerija): 61000 Ljubljana, Prežihova 1; tel. (61) 219740; f. 1918; Dir Dr ANDREJ SMREKAR.

National Museum (Narodni muzej): 61000 Ljubljana, Prešernova 20; f. 1821; Dir Dr BORIS GOMBAČ.

PERFORMING ARTS

City Theatre of Ljubljana: 61000 Ljubljana, Čopova 14; tel. (61) 214188; Dir JANEZ PRETNAR.

Slovenian National Theatre (Slovensko narodno gledališče): 61000 Ljubljana, Erjavčeva 1; tel. (61) 221492; Dir POLDE BIBIČ.

Slovenian National Theatre—Maribor: 62000 Maribor, Slovenska 27; tel. (62) 224421; fax (62) 221207; Dir TEO PAJNIK.

Slovenian National Theatre—Opera and Ballet: 61000 Ljubljana, Zupančičeva 1; tel. (61) 214148; Dir IGOR ŠVARA.

Mladinsko Theatre (Slovensko mladinsko gledališče): 61000 Ljubljana, Vilharjeva 11; tel. (61) 310610: Dir PETAR JOVIČ.

Music

Slovenian Philharmonic Orchestra (Slovenska filharmonija): 61000 Ljubljana, Kongresni trg 10; tel. (61) 213554; Chief Conductor MARKO LETONJA.

Slovenian RTV Big Band (Plesni orkester RTV Slovenija): 61000 Ljubljana, Tavčarjeva 17; tel. (61) 1211333; Chief Conductor JOŽE PRIVŠEK.

Slovenian RTV Chamber Orchestra (Komorni orkester RTV Slovenija): 61000 Ljubljana, Tavčarjeva 17; tel. (61) 1211333.

Slovenian RTV Symphony Orchestra (Simfonijski orkester RTV Slovenija): 61000 Ljubljana, Tavčarjeva 17; tel. (61) 1211333; Chief Conductor ANTON NANUT.

ASSOCIATIONS

Historical Association of Slovenia (Zveza zgodovinskih društev Slovenije): 61000 Ljubljana, Aškerčeva 12; tel. (61) 1250001; fax (61) 332659; f. 1839; Pres. Dr DARJA MIHELIČ.

Slovene Society (Slovenska matica): 61000 Ljubljana, Kongresni trg 8; tel. (61) 214200; f. 1864; Pres. Prof. Dr PRIMOŽ SIMONITI; Sec. DRAGO JANČAR.

Society for Slavic Studies of Slovenia (Slavistično društvo Slovenije): 61000 Ljubljana, Aškerčeva 2/II; tel. (61) 1250001; f. 1935; Chair. Dr FRANCE NOVAK.

Society for Slovene Composers (Društvo slovenskih skladateljev): 61000 Ljubljana, trg francoske revolucije 6/I; f. 1945; Sec. MAKS STRMČNIK.

Education

Education in Slovenia is compulsory between the ages of seven and 15 years. In 1992/93 there were 28 institutions of higher education, 1.9% of the total population were students in higher education and there was one teacher for every 19.8 students. In the same year there were 145 second stage secondary schools, 4.9% of the population were pupils in secondary education and there was one teacher for every 14 secondary pupils. There were a total of 821 primary and first stage secondary schools. In 1993 49% of children of pre-school age attended kindergarten.

Ministry of Education and Sport: see section on The Government (Ministries).

UNIVERSITIES

University of Ljubljana (Univerza v Ljubljani): 61000 Ljubljana, Kongresni trg 12; tel. (61) 1254055; fax (61) 1254053; f. 1595, reconstituted 1809, reopened 1919; state control; 25 faculties; 1,768 teachers, 26,190 students; Rector Prof. Dr MIHA TIŠLER.

University of Maribor (Univerza v Mariboru): 62000 Maribor, Krekova 2; tel. (62) 212281; telex 33334; fax (62) 23541; f. 1975; state control; 419 teachers, 12,498 students; Rector Prof. Dr LUDVIG TOPLAK.

Social Welfare

There is an extensive system of social welfare in Slovenia, including a state pension fund. In 1992 for every 100,000 inhabitants there were 46 general practitioners, 149 medical specialists, 640 hospital beds and 57 dentists.

NATIONAL AGENCIES

Ministry of Health: see section on The Government (Ministries).

Ministry of Labour, Family and Social Affairs: see section on The Government (Ministries).

Secretariat for War Veterans and the War-Disabled: 61000 Ljubljana, Tržaška st. 42; tel (61) 261124; fax (61) 261958; f. 1993; formerly Ministry of War Veterans and War-Disabled; Sec. of State JANKO SEBASTIJAN STUŠEK.

Government Office for Women's Affairs: 61000 Ljubljana, Tomšičeva 4; tel. (61) 1251112; fax (61) 1256057; Dir VERA KOZMIK.

The Environment

Environmental concerns are not as prevalent in Slovenia as in other Eastern European countries, although in 1989 the Citizens' Green Party of Slovenia (later the Greens of Slovenia) was the first formal party of opposition to the League of Communists in the old Yugoslav federation. In July 1991, shortly before Slovenia's secession, the federal government signed a declaration on the ecological protection of the Adriatic, implementing the Adriatic Initiative agreed with Albania, Greece and Italy in 1989. Slovenia accepted its obligations under this accord.

GOVERNMENT ORGANIZATION

Ministry of the Environment and Regional Planning: see section on The Government (Ministries).

ACADEMIC INSTITUTES

Slovenian Institute for the Preservation of Natural and Cultural Heritage (Zavod Republike Slovenije za varstvo naravne in kulturne dediščine): 61000 Ljubljana, Plečnikov trg 2; tel. (61) 213012; fax (61) 213120; f. 1913; Dir JELKA PIRKOVIČ.

University of Ljubljana—Faculty of Biotechnical Engineering: 61000 Ljubljana, Kongresni trg 12; departments include forestry and agronomy; Dean Prof. Dr ANDREJ SALEHAR.

NON-GOVERNMENTAL ORGANIZATIONS

Greens of Slovenia—Eco-Social Party: see section on Political Organizations.

Greens of Slovenia (Zelena Slovenije—ZS): see section on Political Organizations.

Society for Natural Sciences of Slovenia: 61000 Ljubljana, Novi trg 4/IV; f. 1934; 3,000 mems; Pres. R. KAVČIČ; Sec. T. WRABER.

Defence

Military service in Slovenia is compulsory and lasts for a period of seven months. In June 1993, according to Western estimates, Slovenia had active armed forces of 15,000, with an estimated 85,000 reserves. The total included an army of 13,000, which was planned to increase to 20,000, with territorial defence units of army reserves. A small coastal defence unit was formed in 1993. Slovenian paramilitary forces comprise 4,500 armed police and 5,000 reserves. The defence budget for 1992 was an estimated 15,000m. tolars (US $340.9m.).

Commander-in-Chief of the Armed Forces: President of the Republic.

Chief of Staff of the Slovenian Territorial Army: Maj.-Gen. JANEZ SLAPAR.

Headquarters of the Territorial Defence: 61000 Ljubljana, Prežihova 4; tel. (61) 219748; fax (61) 219764.

Bibliography

Belic, D. and Bilbija, D. *Srbija i Slovenija: od Cankarevog doma do 'Jugoalata' i Gazimestana: dokumenti*. Belgrade, Tera, 1989.

Chetkovich, S. and Chetkovich, S. *Monetary reform: the case of Slovenia*. Stockholm Institute of Soviet and East European Economics, 1992.

Country Report: Slovenia. London, Economist Intelligence Unit, 1993.

Englefield, G. *Yugoslavia, Croatia, Slovenia: Re-emerging Boundaries*. Durham, International Boundaries Research Unit (IBRU) Press, 1992.

Fink Hafner, D. *The Transition of the Space of Political Intermediation and New Patterns of Policy-Making in Slovenia*, Papers on Democratic Transition, No. 26. Budapest, Hungarian Center for Democracy Studies Foundation, 1992.

Gow, J. 'Slovenia: Stabilization or Stagnation?', in *RFE/RL Research Report*, Vol. 3, No. 1. Munich, Radio Free Europe/Radio Liberty Research Institute, 1994.

Presern, N., et al. (Eds). *Slovenia: Economic Facts and Figures*. Ljubljana, Republic of Slovenia Institute of Social Planning, 1991.

Slovenian Economic Monitor. Washington, DC, PlanEcon Report, 1993.

Tollefson, J. W. *The Language Situation and Language Policy in Slovenia*. Washington, DC, University Press of America, 1981.

TAJIKISTAN

Geography

PHYSICAL FEATURES

The Republic of Tajikistan (formerly the Tajik or Tadzhik Soviet Socialist Republic) is situated in the south-east of Central Asia. To the north and west it is bounded by Uzbekistan, and to the north-east by Kyrgyzstan. Its eastern boundary is with the People's Republic of China, while to the south lies Afghanistan. Its territory includes the autonomous region of Gorno-Badakhshon (of which the capital is Khorog), in the east of the country. Tajikistan covers an area of 143,100 sq km (55,250 sq miles).

The terrain is almost entirely mountainous, with more than one-half of the country above 3,000 m. The main agricultural areas are in the lower-lying regions of the south-west (Hatlon Oblast) and the north-west—the latter region, north of the mountains separating Leninabad Oblast from the rest of the country, around the city of Khojand (Khodzhent—formerly Leninabad), is part of the prosperous Fergana basin. The major mountain ranges are the western Tien Shan in the north, the southern Tien Shan in the central region and the Pamirs in the south-east. The highest mountains of Tajikistan, and of the former USSR, Lenin Peak (7,134 m) and Communism Peak (7,495 m), are situated in the northern Pamirs. There is a dense river network, which is extensively used to provide hydroelectric power. The major rivers are the upper reaches of the Syr-Dar'ya and of the Amu-Dar'ya, which forms the southern border with Afghanistan, as the Pyanj. The Zeravshen river flows through the centre of the country. Most settlement is in the valleys of the south-west and the northern areas around Khojand.

CLIMATE

The climate varies considerably according to altitude. The average temperature in January in Khojand (lowland) is −0.9°C (30.4°F); in July the average is 27.4°C (81.3°F). In the southern lowlands the temperature variation is somewhat more extreme. Precipitation is low in the valleys, ranging from 150–250 mm per year. In mountain areas winter temperatures can fall below −45°C (−51°F); the average January temperature in Murgab, in the mountains of south-east Gorno-Badakhshon, for example, is −19.6°C (−3.3°F). Levels of rainfall are very low in mountain regions and seldom exceed 60–80 mm per year. Snow and ice, however, can make many parts of the country inaccessible for many months of the year.

POPULATION

At 1 January 1991 the total population was estimated to be 5,357,000. In 1992–93, however, owing to the civil war, many were killed (estimates range from 20,000 to 50,000 or more) and some 600,000 were reckoned to have become refugees. The largest ethnic group is the Tajiks (62.3% of the population in 1989), followed by Uzbeks (23.5%), Russians (7.6%) and Tatars (1.4%). In the 1989 census the Pamiri Peoples (also known as Mountain Tajiks or Galchaks), who inhabit Gorno-Badakhshon, were counted as Tajiks, although they have distinct languages (Eastern Iranian or Persian group) and cultural traditions. Other ethnic minorities included Kyrgyz (63,832), Ukrainians (41,375), Germans (32,671), Turkmen (20,487) and Koreans (13,431). In 1989 Tajik replaced Russian as the official language of the Republic. Tajik belongs to the South-Western Iranian group of languages and is closely related to Farsi (Persian). From 1940 the Cyrillic script was used.

The major religion was Islam. Most Tajiks and Uzbeks followed the Sunni tradition, but the Pamiris were mostly Isma'ilis, members of a Shi'ite sect. There were also representatives of the Russian Orthodox Church and a small minority of Protestant groups. There was a small Jewish community, which, in 1989, included 9,701 European Jews and 4,879 Central Asian Jews.

The capital was Dushanbe (Stalinabad 1929–61), which is situated in the west of the country, and had an estimated population of 602,000 in 1990. Khojand, to the north, was Tajikistan's second largest city (163,000). Important regional centres were the towns of Kurgan-Tyube and Kulyab, in Hatlon Oblast to the south of Dushanbe, and Khorog, on Gorno-Badakhshon's western border with Afghanistan. The level of urbanization, put at 31% by the UN Development Programme in 1991, was the lowest in the former USSR.

Chronology

7th century: The Arabs, the latest non-Iranian (Persian) invaders of the area, conquered and converted to Islam the peoples of the great 'Silk Road' cities (notably Samarkand and Bukhara), anciently the provinces of Sogdiana and Bactria.

8th century: The Persic, islamicized urban dwellers began to be identifiable as a distinct Tajik people, distinguished from their Turkic neighbours.

16th century: The Turkic Uzbek people were established as the rulers of the previously Tajik cities and were overlords of the Tajik clans of modern Tajikistan; a variety of khanates, notably those based in the cities of Bukhara, Samarkand and Kokand, struggled for control in the following centuries.

1868: The Emirate of Bukhara became a Russian protectorate and ceded some of what is northern Tajikistan to the Russian Empire, but retained the central and southern regions.

1876: The Khanate of Kokand, conquered in 1866, was abolished and parts of northern Tajikistan and the Eastern Pamir were incorporated into the Russian Empire.

1895: Russia acquired the Western Pamir, after it and the United Kingdom defined their spheres of influence in Afghanistan.

November 1917: Khojand (Khodzhent—later renamed Leninabad until 1991) fell to the Bolsheviks, mainly helped by soviets of Slavs, but there were also Tajik groups such as the Union of Muslim Workers; most of the rest of north and east Tajikistan was in Bolshevik control by the end of the next year.

September 1920: The Emir of Bukhara was driven from his city by the Bolsheviks, but his supporters retained control of much of the south and centre of modern Tajikistan for another two years, with the help of fierce *basmachi* resistance, some of which lasted until the 1930s.

15 March 1925: A Tajik Autonomous Soviet Socialist Republic (ASSR) was formed, with its capital at Dushanbe (called Stalinabad 1929–61), by uniting parts of the old Turkestan ASSR and eastern territories of the Bukharan People's Soviet Republic.

1927: It was decided to replace the Arabic script with a Latin alphabet for the Tajik language.

16 October 1929: The Tajik ASSR, now including the territory of Khojand, became a full Union Republic and no longer part of the Uzbek Soviet Socialist Republic (SSR).

1940: A Cyrillic script replaced the Latin one.

1978: Against a background of increasing Islamic influence, there were reports of anti-Russian riots in Tajikistan.

1982: Previously the republican premier, Rakhmon Nabiyev became First Secretary of the Communist Party of Tajikistan (CPT).

1985: Nabiyev was replaced as leader of the CPT by Kakhar Makkhamov, who criticized his predecessor and acknowledged the economic problems of the Republic (not least brought on by a high birth rate—the population increased by 34% between 1979 and 1989).

1989: Increasing nationalism was evidenced by a law making Tajik the state language and by ethnic clashes.

March 1990: Elections to the Supreme Soviet produced an overwhelmingly Communist legislature; they took place under a state of emergency prompted by riots the previous month, after which the leadership became less tolerant of dissent.

25 August 1990: The Supreme Soviet declared the sovereignty of the Republic.

November 1990: Makkhamov was elected to the new post of President of the Republic, by the Supreme Soviet, opposed only by Nabiyev.

17 March 1991: In an all-Union referendum on the future of the USSR, 90% of the participating electorate favoured a 'renewed federation'.

31 August 1991: Mass demonstrations forced the resignation of President Makkhamov, who had failed to condemn the abortive coup attempt in Moscow. Demonstrations continued into the following month, organized by the opposition: the nationalist Rastokhez (Rebirth) movement; the secular, Westernized Democratic Party of Tajikistan (DPT); and the unregistered Islamic Renaissance Party (IRP).

9 September 1991: The Supreme Soviet declared the independence of the renamed Republic of Tajikistan.

22 September 1991: Conceding the demands of the continuing demonstrations, the Chairman of the Supreme Soviet and acting head of state, Kadriddin Aslonov, banned the Communist Party and nationalized its assets. The next day the Supreme Soviet rescinded his decree, declared a state of emergency and replaced Aslonov with Nabiyev.

2 October 1991: The Supreme Soviet reimposed the ban on the Communist Party (known as the Socialist Party, September 1991–February 1992), after Nabiyev had conceded to key opposition demands some days previously. The IRP was legalized and the state of emergency ended.

24 November 1991: Nabiyev (who had resigned the presidency on 6 October to contest the presidential elections) won 57% of the votes cast, compared to 30% for his main rival, the opposition-backed liberal, Davlat Khudonazarov.

21 December 1991: Tajikistan and 10 other former Soviet Republics declared the foundation of the Commonwealth of Independent States (CIS), thereby finally dissolving the USSR.

January 1992: The premier since the previous September, Izatullo Khayeyev, resigned and was replaced by Akbar Mirzoyev.

March–April 1992: Opposition demonstrations were provoked by President Nabiyev's dismissal of prominent sympathizers of the opposition, the Islamic and democratic elements of which were co-ordinated into a united front largely through the efforts of the Chief Kazi, Hajji Akbar Turajonzoda.

3 May 1992: Pro-Communist counter-demonstrators engaged in the first armed conflicts with the opposition supporters; this marks the start of the civil war.

6 May 1992: Shocked at the violence, Nabiyev and the opposition agreed a new 'Government of National Reconciliation' including eight opposition ministers. Peace was secured in Dushanbe, but there was fighting in the south as pro-Communists based in Kulyab formed militias to harass the opposition.

7 September 1992: Dispossessed, captured and threatened by demonstrators supporting the Islamic-democratic parties, President Nabiyev resigned and his powers were assumed by the Chairman of the Supreme Soviet, Akbarsho Iskandarov. The latter supported the continuing coalition Government, the authority of which was steadily being rejected by the establishment outside the capital, but Mirzoyev resigned and the new premier was a Khojand Communist, Abdumalik Abdullojonov.

25 October 1992: Safarli Kenjayev, leader of a southern militia, was expelled from Dushanbe, having entered and attempted to proclaim himself head of state. He then placed the city under siege.

10 November 1992: With civil war still raging and having agreed to a session of the Supreme Soviet, Iskandarov and the Government resigned.

19 November 1992: The Supreme Soviet having convened in Khojand, it instituted a Communist reaction by abolishing the presidency and appointing a Kulyabi, Imamali Rahmonov, its Chairman (head of state), and dismissing all opposition figures from the Government.

10 December 1992: The pro-Communist Kulyabi militias seized control of the capital; there were allegations of widespread atrocities against supporters of the Islamic-democratic opposition, most of the leaders of which fled into exile or to the eastern mountains.

22 January 1993: A collective security treaty signed by Tajikistan, Kazakhstan, Kyrgyzstan, Russia and Uzbekistan marked the end of formal CIS neutrality in the civil war (the new regime received particular support from the latter two).

23 May 1993: A bilateral treaty between Tajikistan and Russia re-emphasized the latter's concern for the southern borders, now that the armed Tajik opposition had fled to Afghanistan. By this time most internal resistance had been crushed and even Gorno-Badakhshon, sympathetic to the Islamic-democratic coalition, was indicating that it would acknowledge central authority in return for urgent food and medical aid.

29 June 1993: The European Community (known as the European Union from November 1993) condemned the human-rights abuses of the regime in Tajikistan.

13 July 1993: An attack which killed 25 Russian soldiers at a border post increased Russian concerns at Tajik opposition incursions and there were warnings of Islamic fundamentalism and illegal-drugs smugglers.

17 July 1993: Both the Tajik Government and Afghanistan complained to the UN about border violations, which continued throughout the summer.

24 July 1993: In Russia, the pre-1993 rouble notes were withdrawn from circulation; Tajikistan was not issued with the new notes until it had negotiated terms for entry into a new 'rouble zone'.

31 August 1993: Although the Gorno-Badakhshon authorities complained that government troops had attacked the oblast's forces in the operation to clear the Dushanbe–Khorog road, a convoy reached the Pamiri chief town for the first time in 10 months.

27 November 1993: With mounting inflation and a generally worsening economic situation, the Tajik Government agreed to Russian demands for joining a new 'rouble zone'.

27 December 1993: Abdujalil Samadov was approved by the Supreme Soviet as the new Chairman of the Council of Ministers, following the resignation of Abdullojonov nine days previously.

5–8 January 1994: Tajikistan effected the introduction of the new Russian rouble, formalizing its economic subjection to Russia, which had insisted that the Communist regime introduce political and economic reforms in the same year.

April 1994: The Government and the Islamic-democratic opposition began negotiations in Moscow (Russia).

History

The ancient territories of Sogdiana and Bactria were part of the Persian Empire when they were conquered by Alexander III ('the Great') of Macedon in the fourth century BC. An independent kingdom, Kushan, based on the city of Bactra (Bacharia or Bukhara), was established by nomads from the north some 200 years later. The Arabs conquered the area in the seventh century AD and the great cities of the 'Silk Road' adopted Islam. Under the caliphate the Western Iranian language of Persian displaced the previous, Eastern Iranian tongues in the area, including the Sogdian lingua franca of the trade routes (these languages survived in the inaccessible Pamir mountain valleys). The Persian-speaking, largely urban Tajiks (Tadzhiks) were probably a distinct ethnic group by about the eighth century. Their name originated from an Arab tribal name, Taiy (Sogdian, Tazik), which was used by the peoples of Central Asia to describe the Arab invaders and, by extension, the islamicized city-dwellers who administered the Persian-speaking empire established by the Arabs. The Tajiks were distinguished from their Turkic neighbours by their sedentary life style and Farsi (Persian) language. The great Tajik cities of Bukhara and Samarkand (Marakanda) were important Muslim cultural centres, which survived the successive invasions of Turkic and Mongol peoples. By the 16th century the Uzbeks were the dominant group. The Tajiks in the territory of modern Tajikistan formed several semi-independent territories under Uzbek suzerainty, but, as the Russian Empire expanded southwards in the 19th century, the northern Tajik principalities came under Russian rule. The southern regions were annexed by the expanding Emirate of Bukhara.

SOVIET TAJIKISTAN

In 1918 the Bolsheviks re-established control over northern Tajikistan, which was incorporated into the Turkestan Autonomous Soviet Socialist Republic (ASSR) of Russia, but did not conquer Dushanbe and the other territories subject to Bukhara until 1921. Opposition to Soviet rule was led by the *basmachis* (local guerrilla fighters) and foreign interventionists. Full Soviet control was not established in the remote south-east of Tajikistan until 1925. In 1924 the Tajik ASSR was established, as a part of the Uzbek Soviet Socialist Republic (SSR). On 2 January 1925 the south-east of Tajikistan was designated a Special Pamir Region (later renamed the Gorno-Badakhshon Autonomous Oblast) within the Tajik ASSR. On 16 October 1929 the Tajik ASSR became a full Union Republic of the USSR, as the Tajik SSR, and was enlarged by the addition of the Khojand (Khodzhent) Okrug, a district previously in Uzbekistan. This wealthy area, organized as an oblast (renamed Leninabad—the city reverted to the name of Khojand in February 1991) came to dominate the Republic. However, the historic cities of the largest Tajik communities, and much of their population, remained outside the borders of Tajikistan.

Soviet power brought economic and social benefits to Tajikistan, but living standards remained low even by Soviet standards. Cattle breeding, the main occupation in the uplands, was severely disrupted by collectivization. During the repressions of the 1930s almost all Tajiks in the republican government were removed and replaced by Russians, sent from the Soviet capital Moscow. After the Second World War, mainly in the 1950s when an increase in the production of cotton was being encouraged, important internal demographic changes were instituted by the republican leadership. Many Tajiks from the east of the Republic, particularly from the Garm valley and Gorno-Badakhshon, were resettled in the south-west of the country, in the oblasts of Kurgan-Tyube and Kulyab (merged as Hatlon Oblast in late 1992). There was considerable friction between these large communities of new arrivals and the existing natives, many of whom were ethnic Uzbeks. During the 1970s there were reports of increased Islamic influence and violence towards non-indigenous nationalities. In 1978 there were reports of an anti-Russian riot, involving some 13,000 people, and, after 1979, there were arrests of some activists opposed to Soviet intervention in Afghanistan.

As in other Central Asian Republics, the first manifestation of the new policies of Soviet leader Mikhail Gorbachev was a campaign against corruption. Rakhmon Nabiyev, who had been First Secretary of the Communist

Party of Tajikistan (CPT) since 1982, was replaced, in 1985, by Kakhar Makkhamov, who accused his predecessor of tolerating nepotism and corruption. Makkhamov was also openly critical of the economic situation in the Republic, admitting that there were high levels of unemployment and that many people lived in poverty, particularly in the south and east. Censorship was also relaxed and there was increased discussion of perceived injustices, such as alleged discrimination against Tajiks in Uzbekistan. In June 1989 there were violent confrontations between villagers on the Kyrgyz-Tajik border and there was debate in the media about the fairness of the Uzbek-Tajik boundary.

Increased freedom of expression allowed discussion of Tajik culture and language, and greater interest in Iranian cultures in other countries. Links with Iran had been limited since the 1979 Iranian Revolution, but the pro-Soviet regime in Afghanistan developed cultural contacts with Tajikistan and many Tajiks served in Afghanistan as interpreters. Tajik was declared the state language in 1989, and the teaching of the Arabic script (used by Tajiks prior to sovietization) was begun in schools.

In February 1990 rioting occurred in Dushanbe, after rumours that Armenian refugees were to be settled there. The scarcity of housing and work seemed to be the cause of the protests, which were directed against the Communist authorities in the Republic. Demonstrators demanded democratic reforms and more radical economic reform. Violence broke out at a protest rally of about 3,000 people, when demonstrators clashed with police, overturned cars and looted shops. A state of emergency was declared and a night-time curfew was imposed in Dushanbe. Makkhamov requested aid from the all-Union authorities and some 5,000 Soviet interior ministry troops were dispatched to the city. In conjunction with 'civilian militia' units, they suppressed the demonstrations; 22 people were reported dead and 565 injured.

The events of February 1990 prompted a more inflexible attitude towards political pluralism from the Republic's leadership. The state of emergency was not lifted during 1990 and two nascent opposition parties, Rastokhez (Rebirth), which was involved in the February demonstrations, and the Democratic Party of Tajikistan (DPT), were refused official registration. In addition, the Islamic Renaissance Party (IRP) was refused permission to hold a founding congress in Dushanbe. However, all three groups continued to attract popular support. In the elections to the Supreme Soviet, held in March 1990, opposition politicians were refused permission to participate and 94% of the deputies elected were members of the CPT.

In an apparent concession to growing Tajik nationalism, the Tajik Supreme Soviet adopted a declaration of sovereignty, on 25 August 1990. Although the declaration emphasized the equality of all nationalities living in Tajikistan, the growth in Islamic influence, the rediscovery of the Tajiks' Iranian heritage and language and the uncertain political situation all contributed to an increase in emigration from the Republic, mainly by ethnic Slavs and educated Tajiks. In November 1990 Makkhamov was elected to the new post of President of the Republic by the Supreme Soviet. His only opponent was former Party leader Rakhmon Nabiyev.

The Tajik Government, possibly anxious about increased Turkic dominance in Central Asia, displayed great enthusiasm for a new Union Treaty and Tajikistan was the first Republic to declare its willingness to sign such a document. Tajiks voted overwhelmingly for preservation of the USSR in the all-Union referendum of March 1991. According to official figures, 90% of the electorate voted to preserve the Union.

In August 1991, before the new Union Treaty could be signed, conservative leaders of the CPSU and the security forces attempted a *coup d'état* in Moscow. Makkhamov did not oppose the coup, which failed, and, on 31 August, he resigned as President. His resignation had been forced by mass demonstrations, which continued throughout much of September. They were organized by the three main opposition parties (the DPT, the IRP and Rastokhez). On 9 September, following Uzbekistan's declaration of independence, the Tajik Supreme Soviet voted to proclaim Tajikistan an independent state, based on democratic principles and the rule of law. The Tajik SSR became the Republic of Tajikistan. This did not, however, satisfy the demonstrators, who demanded the dissolution of the CPT and new, multi-party elections.

Finally, on 22 September 1991 Kadriddin Aslonov, the Chairman of the Supreme Soviet and Acting President, issued a decree which banned the Communist Party and nationalized its assets (earlier in September the CPT had reorganized as the Socialist Party of Tajikistan, but the original name was reinstated in January 1992). In response, at an emergency session of the Supreme Soviet the following day, the Communist majority demanded Aslonov's resignation, declared a state of emergency in the Republic and rescinded the prohibition of the Party. Aslonov resigned and was replaced by former CPT leader, Rakhmon Nabiyev. Within one week, however, Nabiyev was obliged to concede many of the opposition's demands and required the Supreme Soviet to ratify the attempts to allay growing popular protest. On 2 October 1991 the Supreme Soviet rescinded the state of emergency, suspended the CPT and legalized the IRP, which had previously been banned under legislation prohibiting the formation of religious parties.

On 6 October 1991 Nabiyev resigned as Acting President, in advance of the presidential elections. There were seven candidates in the elections, which took place on 24 November 1991. The main contenders were Nabiyev and Davlat Khudonazarov, the liberal Chairman of the USSR Cinematographers' Union, who was supported by the main opposition parties. Mostly as a result of strong support in rural areas, Nabiyev won 57% of the votes cast, compared with 30% for Khudonazarov. The latter claimed that there were electoral malpractices, but his complaints were not upheld and Nabiyev took office in early December. In early January 1992 a new premier, Akbar Mirzoyev, was appointed to head the Government, replacing Izatullo Khayeyev, who resigned for reasons of health.

Tajikistan, as was expected, signed the Treaty on the Economic Community, on 19 October 1991, and demonstrated its willingness to join the proposed Union of Sovereign States. When a Commonwealth of Independent States (CIS) was suggested in December, initially by the three Slav Republics, Tajikistan expressed its desire to become a co-founder, along with the other Central Asian Republics. The Republic was a signatory of the Almaty Declaration, on 21 December.

INDEPENDENT TAJIKISTAN

The Republic of Tajikistan was one of the few of the newly independent Soviet successor states in which ethnic tensions were not the major political problem. Instead it was beset by a complexity of other divisions and rivalries. These were basically regional and political.

The main regional groupings among the Tajiks were based on the towns of Khojand (formerly Leninabad), Kulyab and Kurgan-Tyube. The mainly Isma'ili Pamirs of Gorno-Badakhshon were an additional regional interest group. The northern city of Khojand provided the traditional élite of Communist Tajikistan. It was the wealthiest part of the country and every Communist First Secretary from 1943 until the end of Soviet rule was from the so-called 'Khojand mafia'. This group also dominated the economy throughout the country and it was probably the Leninabad area that benefited most from the years of Soviet rule. It was not surprising that this region supported the Communist system and the status quo, although there was some support for economic reform and privatization. Khojand's power was aided by its physical isolation from the rest of the country (it was linked by a single pass across the dividing mountains, which was not traversable during the winter) and its ability, therefore, to implement a threat of secession from the impoverished south, if necessary. The area was free from fighting during the civil war and Russian and Uzbek emigration was not so great from here—the Khojand regional group best represented the interests of the vital, skilled ethnic minorities.

The south of the country did not benefit so greatly from the period of Soviet rule and this ensured that much opposition support came from the poorer suburbs of Dushanbe and the eastern territories of Garm and Gorno-Badakhshon. However, there was little solidarity in the south and southern divisions were exploited by the Khojand élite. Most importantly, the provinces of Kulyab and Kurgan-Tyube were traditional rivals. In the 1980s Kulyab's attempt to merge with Kurgan-Tyube was supported by Khojand. Kurgan-Tyube was, therefore, inclined to support the opposition.

Tensions created by the post-1945 settlement of eastern Tajiks (notably Garmis) in the south-west further complicated the situation. The presence of such settlers was resented by the established clans, who tended to support the regime. There was a higher proportion of these newcomers in Kurgan-Tyube and, most affected by the increasing unemployment of the 1980s, they were ready to support advocates of a new system, whether democratic or Islamic. Likewise, those whose interests were vested in the Communist system identified with the so-called Kulyab group, although many were actually from Kurgan-Tyube and, notably, the Hissar valley (just south of Dushanbe), but were enemies of the Garmis.

The usual late- and post-Soviet tensions between reformers and old-guard Communists, therefore, was complicated by a regional and intra-ethnic rivalry. Moreover, the resurgence of Islam raised the fears not only of the Communist ruling class, but amongst the secular, pro-Western reformers. However, the Islamic opposition was relatively moderate and was able to evolve a working alliance with the democratic, nationalist groups. Much of this co-ordination was achieved by the Muslim spiritual leader Hajji Akbar Turajonzoda (kazi of Tajikistan from 1990), who constantly rejected accusations that the opposition intended to create an Islamic state. Although the Islamic-democratic parties were opposed by a particularly entrenched and, thus, conservative establishment, by 1991 Tajikistan had a seemingly healthy multi-party system. Apart from the CPT, there was the moderate Islamic party, the IRP, the Tajik-nationalist Rastokhez party, the pro-Western and democratic DPT, and the Pamiri-nationalist Lale Badakhshon.

Civil War

Despite Nabiyev gaining the presidency, the opposition had demonstrated a considerable degree of popular support in the elections. Nabiyev's attempts in early 1992 to consolidate the conservative hold on government merely served to unite the democratic and Islamic opposition. By March the first anti-government demonstrations in Dushanbe had been provoked by the dismissal of Mamadayez Navzhuvanov, a Pamiri, as Minister of Internal Affairs. Lale Badakhshon (a party advocating greater autonomy, and even independence, for Gorno-Badakhshon), which had organized the protests, was soon joined by the three other opposition groups. They also objected to the April arrest of the mayor of Dushanbe, Maksud Ikramov, who was a reformist.

Throughout April and May 1992 opposition demonstrators, mainly from the poorer parts of Dushanbe and Kurgan-Tyube, were encamped in the city centre and it was to counter this that the Government organized its own demonstrations of popular support. These rallies at the end of April, for which many had been brought in from Kulyab and even Khojand, increased tensions. Furthermore, troops fired on the opposition demonstrators and, in the first week of May, the National Security Committee (NSC—formerly the republican KGB) allegedly distributed weapons to pro-Communist supporters. The violent clashes then escalated into civil war.

The first fighting prompted President Nabiyev to negotiate a new 'Government of National Reconciliation'. The opposition parties provided eight of the 24 ministers, including Navzhuvanov, the prominent IRP leader Davlat Usmon, and Mirbobo Mirrakhimov of Rastokhez, who was appointed to direct the national broadcast media. Nabiyev remained dissatisfied that he had been forced to this compromise. The regions of Khojand and Kulyab rejected the authority of the administration, claiming it was unconstitutional (technically they were correct, because without the deputies from these areas attending, the Supreme Soviet was inquorate and could not approve the Government). Thus, while the announcement of the new Government secured peace in the capital, there was widespread violence in the south, particularly in Kulyab. The arming of the dispute, usually from ex-Soviet (Russian) garrisons, meant that the war escalated despite the various attempts to negotiate cease-fires. Moreover, the opposition also armed, and their main obvious source of weaponry was from the Afghan *mujahidin*, which seemed to justify many of the establishment fears of the rise of Islamic fundamentalism.

The pro-Communist militias of Kulyab, who rejected the compromise with the opposition, spread the fighting into Kurgan-Tyube, a stronghold of the Islamic-democratic movement, in late May 1992. The main militia force was the Tajik Popular Front (TPF), led by Sangak Safarov, recently released from 23 years in prison, but a leader of the Kulyab faction. With the increasing ferocity of the fighting in the south, by August 1992 demonstrations resumed in Dushanbe. This enabled the 'opposition', the Islamic-democratic coalition, to secure dominance of the administration: at the end of the month anti-government youths occupied the presidential palace; then, on 7 September, demonstrators captured Nabiyev and forced him to resign the presidency. Although Mirzoyev also resigned, the coalition Government continued in office with the support of the acting head of state, the Chairman of the Supreme Soviet, Akbarsho Iskandarov, who attempted to mediate a settlement. However, the authority of this administration was largely confined to the capital: the south was controlled by the TPF; and Leninabad Oblast, fearing an Islamic state and the loss of power for the Khojand nomenklatura, even threatened secession. This was despite an attempt to placate the powerful Khojand Communists by appointing one of their number, Abdumalik Abdullojonov, to the premiership.

In late October 1992 the Islamic-democratic alliance's control of Dushanbe was challenged. A former Supreme Soviet Chairman, Safarali Kenjayev, a Hissarite of the

Kulyab group and a supporter of Nabiyev, led his forces into the capital. He attempted to proclaim himself head of state, but was driven out by forces loyal to the regime. Kenjayev thereupon enforced a blockade of the city throughout November and into December. Under pressure from this siege and with mounting international concern, the Islamic-democratic-supported Government agreed that a session of the Supreme Soviet should be convened. Having failed to secure an end to the civil war, and in advance of the legislature's meeting, Iskandarov and the Government resigned on 10 November. Five days later the Supreme Soviet met in Khojand.

On 27 November 1992 the Communist reaction, co-ordinated by an alliance of the traditional élite of Khojand and the new power of the Kulyabi militias, began to move against the Islamic-democratic movement. Abdullojonov, from Khojand, assured the Supreme Soviet that Leninabad Oblast would not insist on Nabiyev being retained as President. Abdullojonov was then formally confirmed as Chairman of a Council of Ministers purged of opposition representatives and dominated by Kulyabis and the traditional Khojand figures. On 19 November the presidency had been abolished and the new head of state, the Chairman of the Supreme Soviet, was elected: Imamali Rahmonov, formerly a collective-farm manager from Kulyab, was supported by Safarov of the TPF. The Kulyabi group also secured, with the support of the Leninabad deputies, the merging of the provinces of Kulyab and Kurgan-Tyube into the single Hatlon Oblast on 2 December. Moreover, with the flight and condemnation of Turajonzoda, who remained the pre-eminent opposition figure in exile, the former mullah of Kulyab, Fatkhullo Sharifov, was elevated to the new post of Chief Mufti of Tajikistan.

On 10 December 1992, despite the continued resistance of the Islamic-democratic forces (organized as the Popular Democratic Army—PDA), the TPF and the Kulyabi/Hissarite militias retook Dushanbe. Opposition figures, most of whom fled abroad, accused the militias of atrocities both in the capital and in the south, particularly against people from Garm and Gorno-Badakhshon. It was to these areas, indeed, the mountains east of Dushanbe, that the opposition 'rebels' fled. In February 1993 some of the insurgents in Garm attempted to declare an 'autonomous Islamic republic' and there were rumours that a 'Pamir republic' was to be announced, but the Government had secured control of most of the country by March. The end of the civil war was then marked by the deaths of Safarov, who was shot in a dispute with one of his lieutenants, and, in April, of Nabiyev, from a heart attack. The casualties of the civil war, according to probably conservative government estimates, included some 20,000 people who had been killed and 600,000 who were refugees (many fled to Gorno-Badakhshon and to Afghanistan). Other estimates put the number of dead in the civil war and its immediate aftermath as high as 50,000 or even 100,000.

The Rahmonov Administration

Although the civil war as such ended at the beginning of 1993, the continued insurgency of Islamic-democratic forces, notably from across the Afghan border, continued to destabilize the country. This situation was perpetuated by the regime's repression and its refusal to negotiate with the opposition. Such intransigence was made possible by the continuing threat to the regime's security—Russia and the CIS, with tacit Western approval, were anxious to preserve Tajikistan from becoming an Islamic state. The flight of the Islamic-democratic party leaders and their increased dependence on the *mujahidin* of Afghanistan, where there were large numbers of Tajik refugees, increased fears of a Muslim revolution. However, the regime also suffered from internal weaknesses, as the interests of the Khojand and Kulyab groups began to diverge. Increasingly, under Rahmonov, the country had to be underwritten by the Russian Federation, both in terms of security and economically, suborning its sovereignty to the interests of the regime and of Russian concerns for its 'sphere of influence'.

In March 1993 government forces ended rebel resistance near Garm. Gorno-Badakhshon remained sympathetic to the opposition cause, and isolated from the rest of the country, because of winter conditions and the rebels' control of the crucial Dushanbe–Khorog road. However, this deprived the impoverished mountain territory, its population swollen by refugees, of vital supplies (although some were transported via the road from Osh in Kyrgyzstan). By June, when the roads became passable, the threat of famine and malnutrition in Gorno-Badakhshon was serious. The Pamiri administration therefore agreed to abandon claims for independence and greater autonomy, after assurances that government troops would not enter the Autonomous Oblast and the local self-defence forces would be responsible for sealing the borders. However, fighting blocked the Dushanbe–Khorog road for much of the summer (it was alleged that government troops not only attacked rebel troops, but also the Gorno-Badakhshon forces) and it was only at the end of August that a convoy of vital supplies could cross the Khaburabot Pass and reach Khorog. Government efforts were, of course, helped by the Russians and Central Asians (mainly Uzbeks), although this official aid was primarily intended to prevent border incursions from Afghanistan.

The Communist Government effectively suspended press freedom in January and February 1993, and the arrest of Mirrakhimov ended opposition control of the broadcasting media in early February. In June the Supreme Court formally outlawed the IRP, Lale Badakhshon, Rastokhez and the DPT, leaving the CPT the only legal party in the country. Even the new parties established later in the year were associated with the ruling CPT: the Party of Economic Freedom was associated with premier Abdullojonov; the People's Democratic Party was founded in December by another of the Khojand élite, Abdujalil Homidov, until shortly after the head of Leninabad Oblast; and the People's Party was founded in August by the First Deputy Chairman of the Supreme Soviet, Abdulmajid Dostiyev. The re-establishment of an uncompromising Communist system, which even gave control of compulsory political education in schools to the CPT, was not without critics. While the West was reluctant to encourage Islamic fundamentalism, it did disapprove of the suppression of the free press, the widespread reports of human-rights abuses (particularly by Kulyabi militiamen) and the outlawing of opposition parties. In June the European Community (known as the European Union from November) condemned the Tajik regime and even Russia, anxious not to become immersed in a prolonged struggle, brought pressure on the Government to negotiate with the opposition and begin reforms.

The main threat to the Government came from the potential for a factional dispute between the Khojand élite and the newly dominant Kulyab faction. The former, as the traditional economic as well as political leaders, were anxious to begin some reforms or, at least, the revitalization of the economy. Moreover, the Khojand group, having gained the most benefit from the Communist state hitherto, found that it was their own affiliation which was most disadvantaged by the Kulyabi consolidation of their new position. Furthermore, the Kulyabi claim to power, based as it was on their militias and a continuing threat from insurgents, ran directly counter to the Khojand desire for greater stability. Rahmonov did achieve some success in beginning to incorporate the Kulyabi militias into the national security services and the new army (although this thereby began the institutionalization of Kulyab influence), but this was only after the death of Safarov. On the other hand, that event meant that, thereafter, no one was certain to what extent the Kulyabi leaders could actually control their armed supporters.

In December 1993 Abdullojonov resigned as premier. This was perceived as a reverse for the Khojand faction, although the new Chairman of the Council of Ministers, Abdujalil Samadov, was also from Leninabad Oblast. Ultimately, it seemed that the wealth of the north ensured that the Kulyab faction would seek a compromise with their colleagues in power, although, at the beginning of 1994, a split in the regime remained a possibility, rooted in their different motives for restoring the old order. The Khojand élite wished to preserve their traditional leadership, but were prepared to acknowledge that this could be in a new context. The Kulyab faction wished to achieve power at the centre of the old, centralized structure, and realized that they had gained access to that position through the civil war.

At the end of 1993 and in early 1994 Rahmonov, who had secured to his own office responsibility for the powerful ministries of defence and the interior and for the National Security Committee (and, in February 1994, operational supervision of the broadcast media), began to show signs of compromise. When the new Government was appointed Rahmonov announced that a priority would be the enactment of a new constitution and elections towards the end of 1994: he favoured a presidential system of government, with a smaller, permanent legislature. Also in December the Supreme Court only imposed a nominal sentence on the opposition poet, Bozor Sobir, after appeals from the international community and, indeed, from Rahmonov. Then, in March 1994, Rahmonov announced that he was willing to negotiate with the Islamic-democratic opposition.

Foreign Involvement

Tajikistan differs from many of the former Soviet states in that its national minority of ethnic Russians was relatively small. Thus, at least the regional and political rivalries were not compounded by ethnic tensions. The authorities were prepared to allow the ethnic Russians to vote in the December 1993 Russian Federation elections, and the main ethnic group, the Uzbeks, identified with the Communist order. The Communist regime was, therefore, able to secure the backing of Uzbekistan and of Russia. However, aware of the parallels with the Soviet débâcle in Afghanistan in the early 1980s, Russia ensured that the problems arising from the Tajikistan civil war were dealt with through the CIS and with the involvement of the other Central Asian states.

A vestige of the USSR was the presence of the Russian 201st Motorized Rifle Division in Tajikistan. Throughout the civil war of 1992 it remained strictly neutral and was important in the defence of government buildings and vital installations such as the Nurek Dam. Although Russia was accused of supplying the pro-Communist forces with arms, this seemed not to be official policy. Indeed, Russian troops, helped repel Kenjayev from Dushanbe in October, not by taking the offensive, but because of their defence of certain roads and ministries. However, following the Communist victory, Russia and Uzbekistan abandoned their neutrality—the Uzbek air force was active in crushing the rebels in Garm in March 1993 (there were reports of Uzbek forces supporting the pro-Communists as early as September the previous year) and Russian border troops became embroiled in preventing insurgents crossing from Afghanistan. Certainly, Russia was concerned to protect the CIS borders as if they were its own, and the West did not object to this, no doubt prompted by the association of the Islamic-democratic forces with the *mujahidin* and the trade in illegal drugs. In January 1993 a collective security treaty committed Kazakhstan, Kyrgyzstan (parliament prevented participation until later in the year), Russia and Uzbekistan to the defence of Tajikistan's southern frontiers. In May a bilateral Tajik–Russian treaty prompted an unusual display of co-operation by the Russian President and parliament, when a Tajik rebel attack on a border post in July inspired immediate ratification of the treaty by the parliament. A peace-keeping force was established in August, following a summit meeting of the leaders of Russia and the Central Asian states (except Turkmenistan, which refused any involvement in the Tajik situation) in Moscow. Nevertheless, border skirmishes continued throughout the summer and autumn of 1993, a situation largely determined by the weather, which permitted military activity only outside the winter.

Afghanistan was also interested in Tajikistan, but to what extent it was involved was complicated by its own internal divisions. It had traditional links with its Persic neighbour and, certainly, many of the Islamic opposition were welcomed to the country, which was the refuge of some 80,000 Tajiks by the beginning of 1993. Rahmonov was eager to begin the repatriation of refugees, particularly because many were likely to be recruits to a newly radicalized insurgency, trained by the Afghan *mujahidin* (the main opposition force was known as the Defence of the Fatherland, led by a warlord whose *nom de guerre* was Rizvon). The location of most of the border violations indicated that the principal supporter of the Tajik resistance was Gulbuddin Hekhmatyar, who was also Prime Minister of Afghanistan. This prompted considerable diplomatic tension between that country, Tajikistan and Russia. The situation deteriorated when the Russians responded to attacks on their border troops with the bombardment of Afghan villages, although generally the international participants were eager to avoid an escalation of such confrontations. Certainly Uzbekistan's links with the Afghan warlord Gen. Abdul Rashid Dostam, an ethnic Uzbek, secured the western frontiers from being an area of friction. The position of a further Afghan warlord, Ahmed Shah Masud, an ethnic Tajik, was more ambivalent—he was considered likely to become involved if Russia became permanently committed to the conflict. There was, of course, some uncertainty as to the extent of control over the various armed groups, which made the prospect of a successful peace settlement on the border more unlikely.

CONCLUSION

At the beginning of 1994 an unreconstructed Communist regime was securely in control of Tajikistan. However, it was composed of two factions with conflicting interests. Reform and stability remained necessary, but unlikely without some compromise with the Islamic-democratic opposition. The Afghans, who could influence a radicalization of the exiled groups, were training them in the successful tactics for small, lightly armed groups which would avoid open confrontation. The Russians, seemingly resolved to assert their traditional interests in the area, remained reluctant to become embroiled in a long struggle against guerrilla fighters. While Russia was prepared to support the Communist regime, to the extent of subsidizing it through a monetary union (effected in January 1994), it consistently urged the necessity of negotiations. It was apparent that the mid-1990s would provide another opportunity for the Tajik establishment to attempt to retain its hegemony in a reformed state, although the chances for peace remained tenuous.

The Economy

Tajikistan had a limited role in the economy of the USSR. It was the poorest of the Union Republics and constituted 0.6% of the total territory and 1.8% of the population of the federation at the beginning of 1991. In 1988 Tajikistan provided only 0.8% of total Soviet net material product (NMP), including only 0.4% of industrial NMP and 1.2% of agricultural NMP. However, in comparison with some other regions of the Union, it was relatively self-sufficient, with 41.8% of its NMP derived from exports to other Republics. Exports to other countries constituted 6.9% of NMP. The Republic was very dependent upon transfers from the all-Union budget and was severely affected when these ceased after 1991. With its economic situation exacerbated by civil war and insurgency in 1992–94, the system unreformed and instability discouraging economic activity of any kind, let alone development, Tajikistan was once more a dependency of the Russians.

Russian military assistance to the Communist regime in Dushanbe was followed by an effective subsidy, when Tajikistan joined a new 'rouble zone' in January 1994, subordinating its monetary policy to the control of the Central Bank of the Russian Federation. This did, however, increase pressure on the Tajik Government to negotiate with the opposition. The need to reconstruct the economy and deal with post-conflict problems such as refugees were bedevilled by the factional nature of Tajik politics. The newly ascendant Kulyab group were eager to maintain the Russian and Uzbek military support for the regime. They therefore emphasized the need to fight the threat of Islamic fundamentalists and halt their financing by ending the smuggling of illegal drugs. This certainly secured political support, or at least tolerance, for the Government from the CIS and from the West, but perpetuated the armed instability which discouraged investment. This was a source of frustration to the traditional Khojand élite, who tended to be neo-Communists not unopposed to reform, particularly if it reinforced their command of the economy.

AGRICULTURE

Agriculture was the principal economic sector of Tajikistan, although it was obviously severely affected by the fighting in 1992, which discouraged farmers and disrupted harvesting. In 1990 agriculture (including forestry) contributed 38.3% of NMP and provided 42.9% of employment. The major crop was cotton, over one-half of which was produced in the south-west of the country, in Hatlon Oblast. Production declined from 1980s' totals of over 900,000 metric tons of seed cotton, and barely reached 420,000 tons in the war year of 1992, but recovered in 1993 to over 500,100 tons. This last figure, however, was only some two-thirds of the target, adverse weather conditions (cold temperatures and heavy rains) hindering production towards the end of the year. Cotton remained fundamental to the economy, although yields were low in international terms. It was hoped that Western investment might overcome this—in 1993 a consortium of Turkish interests announced that it was to help build cotton mills in the south-west.

Other arable activities included wheat-farming and horticulture. The sector was dependent on irrigation, which covered about three-quarters of Tajikistan's arable land and was provided by a complex network of canals and reservoirs. The generally mountainous terrain limited potential arable land, although there were more areas available for pasture and livestock-rearing (mainly sheep, goats and dairy cattle). The sector remained the most important in the economy, although, in November 1993, the Chairman of the Supreme Soviet, Imamali Rahmonov, reported that it had been devastated by the civil war. Reforms were to be proposed during 1994, but little progress had been made since 1991, when the share of private farming in the total labour force of Tajikistan was amongst the highest of all the Soviet Republics (some 22% were employed by co-operatives or worked on private farms).

MINING, ENERGY AND INDUSTRY

There were considerable mineral deposits in Tajikistan, including gold, iron, lead, mercury and tin. There were important coal deposits and small reserves of petroleum and natural gas. Extraction was often difficult, given the extreme terrain and the lack of infrastructure in many areas. The precipitous mountain ranges of the country did, however, provide a river system widely used for hydroelectric power generation. At the beginning of the 1990s, following years of Soviet investment in capital development, the hydroelectric system provided some three-quarters of Tajikistan's electricity requirements. This relative abundance of power enabled the Republic to have some energy-intensive industries (such as the production of aluminium). On the other hand, most of Tajikistan's hydrocarbon-fuel requirements had to be imported, certainly of refined petroleum products. With the collapse of the Soviet trading system and integrated economy, and the further disruptions of civil war, the country experienced widespread fuel shortages during 1992 and 1993. This affected industrial production, transport and, even, harvesting (particularly cotton).

Industry accounted for 28.6% of NMP and 13.4% of employment in 1990. Some 98% of fixed assets in the industrial sector were held by 373 state enterprises, with a relatively small number dominating the sector. There was little heavy industry, apart from mineral exploitation, hydroelectric power generation and the aluminium plant at Regar, near Dushanbe. The last, in 1991, had a capacity of 500,000 metric tons per year and accounted for some 15% of total aluminium capacity in the then USSR, although the process is energy intensive and required imported alumina. A few other heavy and intermediate industrial activities included engineering plants and metal works, the main products being agricultural equipment and machinery for power stations. Light industry tended to process domestic raw materials, although a significant number of industries relied on imports, from the days of the integrated Soviet economic system. Food processing concentrated on local produce, such as fruit, natural oils and tobacco. Textile industries included cotton mills, silk factories, clothing and footwear; there was also tanning and carpet-making.

The civil war and the deterioration of socio-economic conditions in Tajikistan compounded the problems of an industrial sector beset by problems such as the collapse of the Soviet internal market and the need to compete with ageing machinery on the international market. Apart from fuel shortages and disruptions caused by the fighting, there was capital damage (which continued into 1993 and 1994—such as the explosion on the Kurgan-Tyube railway to Termez in Uzbekistan, in November 1993)—and an unwillingness by potential investors to commit themselves in an unstable environment. It was estimated by the Government that the civil war caused losses to Tajik industry worth 500,000 roubles, and, in Dushanbe alone, by mid-1993 the war was estimated to have caused a fall of some 50% in industrial production.

However, there was rather less damage to the basic infrastructure of the country than might have been expected. During the civil war itself, before Russia and Uzbekistan became supporters of the new Communist Government in 1993, the neutral Russian (ex-Soviet) garrison was important in the defence of vital installations, such as the Nurek Dam (one of the highest in the world), and the transport network. However, the lawlessness enabled the pilfering of what valuable resources there were. This did not only include supplies of food or weaponry, but, in the cold winters in fuel-starved Dushanbe, it was estimated that as of December 1993 some 15%–20% of the electricity supply was being taken from the national grid illegally.

SERVICES AND GOVERNMENT FINANCE

As the poorest Republic of the USSR Tajikistan had a limited services sector, most of the activity being accounted for by government services (hence, largely financed by transfers from the all-Union budget). Consequently, basic service-sector activities (trade, supply and other services) only contributed 14.3% of NMP in 1990. Transport and communications accounted for 4.2% of NMP and construction 14.7% in the same year.

With independence, Soviet subsidies ended and Tajikistan found that it was obliged to operate with a large government deficit, forecast to be 1,103m. roubles in 1992, even before the outbreak of hostilities in the country. By 1993 it was estimated that some 40% of the government budget was expended on defence and security, and the budget deficit for that year was expected to exceed the equivalent of 50% of gross domestic product (GDP). Although the international community was willing to send humanitarian aid to Tajikistan thereafter, the political instability and allegations of human-rights abuses prevented any long-term assistance from the West. Thus, the European Community (known as the European Union from November 1993) condemned the regime in June 1993 and in September the US Government refused development aid on the grounds of the country's poor democratic credentials. The Communist regime, therefore, was almost exclusively supported by Russia and Uzbekistan. In return Tajikistan had to surrender its economic independence almost completely. It already had to have Russian approval for every part of its budget and, in November, the Russian Government granted the country a credit of US $100m. to facilitate its transfer to the new rouble and support its money supply—$40m. had been received by the beginning of January 1994. The country already owed some 700,000m. roubles to CIS countries and $220m. to the West by October 1993.

REFORM

Thus, the rigorous Communist reaction against the emerging democratic system, in 1992, came to be backed by Russia and most of Central Asia and tacitly accepted by the West, which responded to fears of Islamic fundamentalism and reports of extensive drugs smuggling. The introduction of reform before 1992 had been tardy as it was, and the restoration of a Brezhnevite political system, combined with the instability created by an armed opposition, impeded renewed attempts. The Government and many of the Khojand élite had been willing to implement reforms of the economy, such as privatization, but many measures were reversed or neutralized by the conservative, Communist parliament. However, although the Communists were restored with the help of the Russians, they then came under considerable pressure to introduce economic reforms, as well as negotiating a political settlement with the Islamic-democratic opposition. Russia was unwilling to subsidize the inefficient and bankrupt Tajik state indefinitely.

The Government responded remarkably quickly after the late-1993 agreement to introduce the new rouble and the accompanying Russian demands that the Tajiks should open the economy to foreign investment (only to be achieved from the USA and the EC with democratic reforms) and stabilize the country by negotiating with the opposition. Before the end of the year Rahmonov announced that a new, democratic constitution would be introduced towards the end of the following year, when there would also be parliamentary and presidential elections. He also promised an increased rate of privatization for the larger state enterprises. Later the Government, which had been changed, expressed willingness to negotiate with the opposition.

The Russian subsidy of the economy was effected through monetary union between Tajikistan and the Russian Federation. The 1993 Russian rouble was introduced as the currency of Tajikistan on 5–8 January 1994, after the Tajik Government had accepted conditions which had driven every other country from the 'rouble zone' (monetary policy, as well government expenditure and foreign reserves, was effectively to be controlled by the Central Bank of the Russian Federation). Since July 1993 and the withdrawal from circulation in Russia of the old Soviet (Russian) roubles issued between 1961 and 1992, the old rouble had continued as the currency of Tajikistan and other countries in the rouble zone. The inflationary effects of being in the old rouble zone were exacerbated as the old currency continued a half-life outside Russia. As the year progressed and the remaining countries of Central Asia were forced to introduce their own currencies, the rate of increase in prices escalated. By November Tajikistan was judged to have hyperinflation, as the old notes increasingly appeared in the country which alone accepted them. Under this final pressure the Government had little option but to accept the Russian conditions. The move received some initial justification upon being effected in January 1994: that month retail food prices declined considerably.

One consequence of the Russian assistance was the Tajik Government's assurance that it would introduce privatization. At the end of 1993 there was still no private ownership of land, and there were widespread allegations of corruption by those in power. Even the Khojand élite, which reportedly wished to secure its dominant economic position in a new system, was reluctant to lose existing privileges. Thus, the privatization of small retail businesses and minor services, which normally took place early in the transfer to a market economy, had not occurred in Tajikistan because it was a source of profit to officials controlling the state's assets. Likewise, the large state farms continued to exist because they were alleged to be a valuable source of bribes. In December 1993 the Government committed itself to privatization and promised to introduce the necessary legislative framework for a market economy during the ensuing year.

CONCLUSION

Tajikistan possessed significant reserves of natural resources, but there seemed little likelihood of these being properly exploited in the mid-1990s. The general problems of a loss of Soviet investment, and the destruction of the old trading system upon which the country had depended, were compounded by a serious loss of wealth during the civil war and the continuing troubles thereafter. It was estimated, by the European Bank for Reconstruction and Development, that Tajikistan's GDP declined, by 31% in 1992 alone, and again in 1993, although not by as great a proportion. New trading links would be important (inter-republican trade had accounted for between 80% and 90% of Tajik trade in the 1980s), but could only be established by a reformed and more efficient economic system. The old Communist nomenklatura were reluctant to sacrifice their position, but were under pressure from their Russian backers and their own reformists. The latter were eager to secure the economic dominance of Khojand (Leninabad Oblast was estimated to account for some 65% of gross national product in 1991), which was not likely to be difficult, given the skilled human resources in the province and the infrastructure links of the prosperous Fergana basin (most of it in Uzbekistan). The essential factor in restoring the existing economic enterprises and promoting new investment was the establishment of stability. By the beginning of 1994 the Government seemed decided on reform and reconciliation, but the commitment of its factions was uncertain and the opposition uncowed by the vicious civil war.

Statistical Survey

Principal sources: IMF, *Tajikistan, Economic Review*; World Bank, *Statistical Handbook, States of the Former USSR.*

Area and Population

AREA, POPULATION AND DENSITY

Area (sq km)	143,100*
Population (census result) 12 January 1989	5,108,576
Population (official estimate at 1 January 1991)	5,357,000
Density (per sq km) at 1 January 1991	37.4

* 55,251 sq miles.

POPULATION BY NATIONALITY
(1989 census result)

	%
Tajik	62.3
Uzbek	23.5
Russian	7.6
Tatar	1.4
Others	5.2
Total	100.0

PRINCIPAL TOWNS (estimated population at 1 January 1990)
Dushanbe (capital) 602,000; Khojand (Leninabad) 163,000.

BIRTHS, MARRIAGES AND DEATHS

	Registered live births		Registered marriages		Registered deaths	
	Number	Rate (per 1,000)	Number	Rate (per 1,000)	Number	Rate (per 1,000)
1987	126,787	37.2	31,484	9.2	26,802	7.9
1988	125,887	36.0	33,008	9.4	27,317	7.8
1989	124,992	34.9	34,890	9.8	27,609	7.7

Source: UN, *Demographic Yearbook*.

EMPLOYMENT (annual averages, '000 persons)

	1988	1989	1990
Activities of the material sphere	1,364.4	1,411.1	1,463.0
Agriculture and forestry	726.5	790.1	831.0
Industry	251.4	254.4	260.7
Construction	131.7	160.0	160.8
Transport and communications	83.6	68.3	64.7
Trade, supply and other material services	135.2	138.3	145.8
Activities of the non-material sphere	455.9	467.5	475.3
Government and finance	41.0	39.2	39.7
Education, culture and arts	199.3	210.5	217.3
Medical care, physical training and social security	95.2	101.7	103.7
Science, research and development	29.8	30.2	28.5
Housing and municipal services	50.4	50.8	50.8
Other non-material services	40.2	35.1	35.3
Total	1,820.3	1,878.6	1,938.3

Agriculture

PRINCIPAL CROPS ('000 metric tons)

	1990	1991	1992
Grain	300	283	318*
Wheat	134	141	200*
Rice (paddy)	26	24	20*
Barley	46	47	40*
Maize	85	60	50*
Potatoes	207	181	165*
Seed cotton	842	828	420
Cotton (lint)	256	247	109†
Vegetables	528	628	620*
Water-melons*	200	200	150
Grapes	189	121	100*
Other fruits	217	177	150*
Tobacco (leaves)	12	11	8*

* FAO estimate(s). † Unofficial estimate(s).

Source: FAO, *Production Yearbook*.

LIVESTOCK ('000 head year ending September)

	1990	1991	1992
Horses	51	52	53*
Cattle	1,363	1,349	1,400
Pigs	217	210	100
Sheep	2,620	2,540	2,620
Goats	780	760	780
Chickens†	9,000	8,000	6,000

* FAO estimate(s). † Unofficial estimate(s).

Source: mainly FAO, *Production Yearbook*.

LIVESTOCK PRODUCTS ('000 metric tons)

	1990	1991	1992
Beef and veal	55	48	43*
Mutton and lamb	25	21	20*
Pigmeat	12	6	5*
Poultry meat	15	10	8*
Cows' milk	540	557	475†
Butter and ghee	6	5	4†
Hen eggs†	32.8	25.2	18.0
Wool:			
greasy	4.6	4.4	4.0*
scoured	2.8	2.7	2.4*

* FAO estimate(s). † Unofficial estimate(s).

Source: FAO, *Production Yearbook*.

Mining and Industry

Production (1989, unless otherwise stated): Coal 515,000 metric tons, Crude petroleum 190,000 tons, Natural gas 303 million cu m, Mineral fertilizers 88,100 tons, Domestic refrigerators 170,500, Copper cable (by copper weight) 16,200 tons, Technical lighting equipment 8.9 million roubles, Cotton yarn 129,000 tons, Woven cotton fabrics 125 million m, Knitted garments 13,200,000 (1986), Hosiery 36.1 million pairs (1986), Leather footwear 10.8 million pairs, Carpets and rugs 10.8 million sq m, Vegetable oil 93,200 tons, Tinned goods 374 million cans, Cement 1,111,0000 tons, Reinforced concrete 1,169,000 cu m, Bricks 320.0 million, Electric energy 15,277 million kWh.

Finance

CURRENCY AND EXCHANGE RATES

Monetary Units

100 kopeks = 1 rubl (ruble or rouble).

Sterling and Dollar Equivalents (30 September 1993)

£1 sterling = 1,796.1 roubles;
US $1 = 1,201.0 roubles;
10,000 roubles = £5.568 = $8.326.

Average Exchange Rate (roubles per US dollar)

1989 0.6274
1990 0.5856
1991 0.5819

Note: The figures for average exchange rates refer to official rates for the Soviet rouble. However, a multiple exchange rate system was in operation, with separate non-commercial and tourist rates. A commercial exchange rate was introduced on 1 November 1990, replacing the official rate for most transactions. The commercial rate (roubles per US dollar) was: 1.692 at 31 December 1990; 1.671 at 31 December 1991. Between November 1989 and April 1991 the tourist exchange rate valued the rouble at one-tenth of the official rate. In April 1991 this rate, renamed the 'special rate', was set at $1 = 27.6 roubles. It was subsequently adjusted. Following the dissolution of the USSR in December 1991, Russia and several other former Soviet Republics retained the rouble as their monetary unit. Tajikistan continued to use the old rouble when Russia withdrew all pre-1993 rouble notes in July 1993. By November the Tajik Government had agreed to the conditions of the Central Bank of the Russian Federation for readmission to a new 'rouble zone'. The new roubles were brought into circulation on 5–8 January 1994.

STATE BUDGET (million roubles)

Revenue	1991	1992*
Turnover tax	955	—
Tax on sales	219	—
Value-added tax	—	5,140
Excises	—	5,070
Enterprise profits tax	604	1,821
Revaluation enterprise stocks	393	2,263
Income from privatizations	—	1,363
Personal income taxes	333	522
Duties and local taxes	169	130
Import and export taxes	2	233
Land tax	7	310
Transfers from USSR budget	2,543	—
Balance from previous year	209	—
Total (incl. others)	5,457	16,875

Expenditure	1991	1992*
Economy	1,315	1,326
Social and cultural services	3,138	9,737
Science	18	98
Law enforcement	49	4,159
Authorities, agencies, courts	82	201
Cabinet reserve fund	—	170
Other expenditure	418	1,178
Capital export union enterprises	—	600
Commonwealth of Independent States	—	500
Total	5,020	17,978

* Forecast.

NATIONAL ACCOUNTS

Net Material Product (million roubles at current prices)

	1988	1989	1990
Agriculture	1,794.3	1,793.2	2,014.6
Industry	1,508.6	1,284.5	1,503.0
Construction	710.7	737.1	771.7
Transport and communications	184.0	185.1	221.0
Trade, supply and others	680.0	817.5	750.7
Total	4,877.6	4,817.4	5,261.0

1991 (estimates, million roubles): Total net material product 9,616.8.

External Trade

PRINCIPAL COMMODITIES
(million roubles at current prices)

Imports	1989	1990
Petroleum and gas	300	271
Electric energy	83	71
Iron and steel	116	117
Non-ferrous metallurgy	243	232
Chemicals and chemical products	367	379
Machine-building	932	909
Wood and paper products	126	137
Light industry	769	856
Food industry	568	576
Agricultural products (unprocessed)	190	263
Total (incl. others)	3,930	4,127
Foreign	681	767
Inter-republican	3,249	3,359

Exports	1989	1990
Electric energy	46	63
Non-ferrous metallurgy	443	466
Chemicals and chemical products	115	121
Machine-building	249	232
Light industry	1,234	1,187
Food industry	235	410
Agricultural products (unprocessed)	81	96
Total (incl. others)	2,527	2,686
Foreign	351	308
Inter-republican	2,176	2,377

Education

(1989/90)

	Institutions	Students
Secondary schools	3,101	1,258,800
Secondary specialized schools	42	41,694
Higher schools (incl. universities)	10	65,586

Directory

The Government

HEAD OF STATE

Chairman of the Supreme Soviet of the Republic of Tajikistan: IMAMALI SHARIPOVICH RAHMONOV (elected by the Supreme Soviet on 19 November 1992).

COUNCIL OF MINISTERS
(March 1994)

Chairman (Prime Minister): ABDUJALIL AHADOVICH SAMADOV.

First Deputy Chairman: RAHIMJON GHAFOROV.

Deputy Chairman and Administrator of the Affairs of the Council of Ministers: RAMAZON MIRZOYEV.

Deputy Chairman and Minister of the Economy and Forecasting: RUSTAM MIRZOYEV.

Deputy Chairmen: JURA SHOKIROV, MAYONSHO NAZARSHOYEV.

Minister of Finance: MAHMAD YUNUSOV.

Minister of Foreign Economic Relations: IZZATULLO HAYOYEV.

Minister of Industry: SHAVKAT UMAROV.

Minister of Construction: ODIL OCHILOV.

Minister of Grain Products: MAKHMUJON N. SABIROV.

Minister of Transport: FARIDDUN MUHIDDINOV.

Minister of Education: BOZGUL DODKHUDOYEVA.

Minister of Culture: ATO KHOJAYEV.

Minister of Health: ALAMKHON AHMEDOV.

Minister of Environmental Protection and Water Resources: SAYDULLO KHAYRULLOYEV.

Minister of Security: Maj.-Gen. SAYDAMIR ZUHUROV.

Minister of the Press and Information: BOBOKHON MAHMADOV.

Minister of Labour and Employment: SHUKURJON ZUHUROV.

Minister of Communications: IBRAHIM USMONOV.

Minister of Defence: Maj.-Gen. ALEKSANDR SHISHLYANNIKOV.

Minister of Internal Affairs: YAKUB SALIMOV.

Minister of Justice: SHAVKAT ISMOILOV.

Minister of Social Security: ABDUSSATOR JABBOROV.

Minister of Foreign Affairs: RASHID ALIMOV.

Minister of Agriculture: HABIBULLO TABAROV.

Minister of Trade and Material Resources: HAKIM SOLIYEV.

Chairmen of State Committees

Chairman of State Committee for Construction and Architecture: BAHAVADDIN ZUHURUDDINOV.

Chairman of State Committee for State Property: MATLUBKHON S. DAVLYATOV.

MINISTRIES

Office of the Chairman of the Supreme Soviet: Dushanbe.

Secretariat of the Council of Ministers: Dushanbe; tel. (3772) 23-27-93.

Ministry of Agriculture: 734025 Dushanbe, Lenina 46; tel. (3772) 22-82-68.

Ministry of Communications: Dushanbe.

Ministry of Construction: Dushanbe.

Ministry of Culture: Dushanbe.

Ministry of Defence: Dushanbe.

Ministry of the Economy and Forecasting: Dushanbe.

Ministry of Education: Dushanbe.

Ministry of Environmental Protection and Water Resources: Dushanbe.

Ministry of Finance: Dushanbe.

Ministry of Foreign Affairs: 734051 Dushanbe, Rudaki 42; tel. (3772) 23-29-71; telex 116277; fax (3772) 23-29-64.

Ministry of Foreign Economic Relations: Dushanbe.

Ministry of Grain Products: Dushanbe.

Ministry of Health: 734026 Dushanbe, I. Somoni 59; tel. (3772) 36-16-37.

Ministry of Industry: Dushanbe.

Ministry of Internal Affairs: Dushanbe.

Ministry of Justice: Dushanbe.

Ministry of Labour and Employment: Dushanbe.

Ministry of the Press and Information: Dushanbe.

Ministry of Security: Dushanbe.

Ministry of Social Security: Dushanbe.

Ministry of Trade and Material Resources: Dushanbe.

Ministry of Transport: Dushanbe.

Principal State Committees

State Committee for Construction and Architecture: Dushanbe.

State Committee for State Property: Dushanbe.

Other important State Committees are those for Customs (Chair. KH. HAMROKULOV) and Statistics (Chair. KHOLMAMED AZIMOV).

Legislature

SUPREME SOVIET

Elections to the Supreme Soviet were held in March 1990. Of those deputies elected, 94% were members of the Communist Party of Tajikistan. In May 1992 it was decided to replace the Supreme Soviet with a new transitional legislature, to be known as the Majlis, but this was not instituted. The 230-member Supreme Soviet remained the country's highest legislative body, with its Chairman as head of state (the presidency was abolished in November 1992). A proposed new constitution, reportedly to be approved by referendum at the same time as new parliamentary elections (scheduled for September or October 1994), provided for a smaller, permanent legislature and a presidential system of government.

Chairman: IMAMALI SHARIPOVICH RAHMONOV.

Local Government

From February 1991 Tajikistan had a three-tier system of local government, when the highest level of local government consisted of one autonomous oblast, three oblasts and the capital city of Dushanbe. In December 1992 the two oblasts to the south of Dushanbe, Kurgan-Tyube and Kulyab, were merged into a single oblast, Hatlon, which occupies the south-west of Tajikistan. Leninabad Oblast lies in the north-west, while the Autonomous Oblast of Gorno-Badakhshon consists of the eastern part of the country. The rayons (districts) of the central belt of territory were not united in an oblast. In all of Tajikistan there were 52 rayons, which were part of the second tier of local government, which also included 21 municipalities and four municipal regions (in Dushanbe). Finally, at the lowest level, there were 340 kishlak or village soviets and 47 other settlements. Each unit of local government had a soviet (council) and an executive committee (administration).

Dushanbe City: 734000 Dushanbe, Rudaki 48; tel. (3772) 23-22-14; Chair. of Exec. Cttee JAMOLIDIN M. MANSUROV.

Hatlon Oblast: 735140 Kurgan-Tyube, Gogolya 2; tel. (37744) 2-54-35; f. 1992 by union of Kurgan-Tyube and Kulyab Oblasts; Chair. of Exec. Cttee ABDUJALIL SALIMOV.

Leninabad Oblast: 735700 Khojand (Khodzhent), Dzerzhinskaya 45; tel. 4-02-44; fax 6-77-55; Chair. of Exec. Cttee SOLEKHUJA MAHMUDZODA.

AUTONOMOUS OBLAST

Gorno-Badakhshon

The Autonomous Oblast of Gorno-Badakhshon is situated in the south-east, consisting of the entire eastern part of Tajikistan. The territory is dominated by the Pamir mountain range. Its chief town is Khorog, in the west of the territory, near the border with Afghanistan (there are also international borders with the People's Republic of China in the east and Kyrgyzstan in the north). The population, at the beginning of the 1990s, was some 175,000, of which some 35,000 lived in Khorog. In 1993 an estimated 80,000 refugees from other parts of Tajikistan arrived in the region. The local administration consists of seven rayons (regions).

Gorno-Badakhshon was dominated by the Pamiri people, distinct from the Tajiks in both language and religion (many were Isma'ilis and spoke one of six Eastern Iranian languages). The territory was only acquired by the Russian Empire at the very end of the 19th century and was long an area of disputed sovereignty. Under the Soviets it gained a special administrative status, but remained one of the poorest regions in the USSR. During the late 1980s a separatist movement, Lale Badakhshon, emerged, which allied itself with the Islamic and democratic opposition to the Communist establishment of Tajikistan. In 1993, however, severely affected by the civil war and with the main road from Dushanbe to Khorog closed until August, the local administration pledged its loyalty to the Tajik state and appealed for urgent food and medical aid. Supplies were difficult to obtain from the end of 1992 and there were also the many refugees.

Chairman of the Oblast Soviet: GARIBSHO SHABOZOV.

Chairman of the Oblast Executive Committee: BALKHIER ZAMIROV.

Administration Headquarters: 736000 Khorog, Lenina 26; tel. 25-22.

Political Organizations

Communist Party of Tajikistan: Dushanbe; f. 1924; only registered party until 1991 and during 1993; First Sec. of Cen. Cttee SHODI SHABDOLLOV.

Party of Economic Freedom: Dushanbe; f. 1993; represents interests of northern Tajikistan; Leader ABDUMALIK ABDULLOJONOV.

People's Party of Tajikistan: Dushanbe; f. 1993; pro-Communist; Leader ABDULMAJID DOSTIYEV.

People's Democratic Party (Hizb-i Khalq-i Demokrati): 735700 Khojand, Dzerzhinskaya 45; f. 1993; seeks to represent northern economic interests; Leader ABDUJALIL HOMIDOV.

The following parties were formally banned by the Supreme Court in June 1993:

Democratic Party of Tajikistan (DPT): f. 1990; secular nationalist and pro-Western; First Sec. of Cen. Cttee SHODMAN YUSUPOV; *c.* 15,000 mems (1991).

Islamic Renaissance Party (IRP): believed to be based in Jalalabad, Afghanistan; formally registered in 1991; br. of what was the Soviet IRP; formerly a moderate Islamic party; Leader SAYED ABDULLO NURI; Dep. Leader DAVLAT USMON; *c.* 10,000 mems (1990).

Lale Badakhshon: f. 1991; sought greater autonomy for Gorno-Badakhshon and the resident Pamiri peoples.

Rastokhez (Rebirth): f. 1990; nationalist-religious party favoured by intellectuals; Chair. TAKHIR ABDUJABOROV.

Many of the supporters of these parties maintained guerrilla warfare against the Communist regime, often with the support of the Afghan *mujahidin.* The main opposition paramilitary grouping was known as **Defence of the Fatherland** (Najot-i Vatan; f. 1992 by MUHAMMED SHARIF HIMMATZODA, a leader of the IRP). The leader of the opposition delegation to the April 1994 negotiations with the Government was Hajji Akbar Turajonzoda.

Diplomatic Representation

EMBASSIES IN TAJIKISTAN

China, People's Republic: Dushanbe; Ambassador: XI ZHAOMING.

Iran: Dushanbe; Ambassador: ALI ASHRAF MOJTAHED-SHABESTARI.

Pakistan: 734001 Dushanbe, Hotel Tajikistan; tel. (3772) 27-53-74; telex 201114; fax (3772) 27-51-55; Chargé d'affaires a.i.: MUDASSAR NOOR.

Russia: Dushanbe; Ambassador: MECHISLAV SENKEVICH.

Turkey: 734001 Dushanbe, Hotel Tajikistan; tel. (3772) 27-53-05; telex 201220.

USA: Dushanbe, Ainii 39; tel. (3772) 24-82-33; Ambassador: STANLEY T. ESCUDERO.

Judicial System

Chairman of the Supreme Court: S. MAKHMUDOV.

Procurator-General: MUHMADNAZAR SOLIHOV.

Religion

The majority of Tajiks are adherents of Islam and are mainly Sunnis (Hanafi school). Some of the Pamiri peoples, however, are Isma'ilis (followers of the Aga Khan), a Shi'ite sect. Under the Soviet regime the Muslims of Tajikistan were subject to the Muslim Board of Central Asia and a muftiate, both of which were based in Tashkent (Uzbekistan). The senior Muslim cleric in Tajikistan was the Chief Kazi. In late 1992 the incumbent, Hajji Akbar Turajonzoda, fled to Afghanistan after the civil war. The new regime subsequently replaced him as the spiritual leader of Tajikistan's Muslims and established an independent muftiate. Most of the minority Christian population is Slav, the main denomination being the Russian Orthodox Church. There are some Protestant and other groups, notably a Baptist Church in Dushanbe.

Chief Mufti: FATKHULLO SHARIFOV, Dushanbe.

The Press

In 1990, according to official statistics, there were 74 newspaper titles being published in Tajikistan, including 66 published in Tajik. The daily circulation was 1,598,000 copies (1,239,000 in Tajik). There were 48 periodicals being published, including 13 in Tajik, with a total annual circulation of 16.2m. copies (9.2m. in Tajik).

PRINCIPAL NEWSPAPERS

Adabiyet va sanat (Literature and Art): Dushanbe, Ismail Somoni 8; tel. (3772) 24-57-39; f. 1959; weekly; organ of the Union of Writers and Ministry of Culture; in Tajik; Editor A. KHAKIMOV.

Djavononi Tochikiston (Tajikistan Youth): Dushanbe; f. 1930; 5 a week; fmrly organ of the Cen. Cttee of the Leninist Young Communist League of Tajikistan; in Tajik; Editor O. FAKHRIEV.

Komsomolets Tajikistana (Member of the Leninist Young Communist League of Tajikistan): Dushanbe; f. 1938; 5 a week; fmrly organ of the Cen. Cttee of the Leninist Young Communist League of Tajikistan; in Russian; Editor V. V. KRASOCHIN.

Narodnaya Gazeta: Dushanbe; f. 1929; fmrly *Kommunist Tajikistana* (Tajik Communist), the organ of the Communist Party of Tajikistan; 5 a week; in Russian; Editor N. N. KUZMIN.

Omuzgor (Teacher): Dushanbe; f. 1932; weekly; organ of the Ministry of Education; in Tajik; Editor B. NASRIDDINOV.

Sadoi mardum (The Voice of the People): Dushanbe; f. 1991; 5 a week; organ of the Supreme Soviet; in Tajik; Editor MIRZOMAHMUD MIRBOBOYEV.

Sovet Tochikistoni (Soviet Tajikistan): Dushanbe; f. 1929; 5 a week; organ of the Supreme Soviet; in Uzbek; Editor T. A. JURABOYEV.

Tochikistoni (Tajikistan): Dushanbe; f. 1925; 5 a week; fmrly organ of the Communist Party of Tajikistan; in Tajik; Editor M. MUHABBATSHOYEV.

PRINCIPAL PERIODICALS

Monthly unless otherwise indicated.

Hajoti dehot (Village Life): 734025 Dushanbe, Lenina 46; tel. (3772) 22-82-68; f. 1947; journal of the Ministry of Agriculture; in Tajik; Editor-in-Chief K. YA. AFZALI.

Khorpushtak (Hedgehog): Dushanbe; f. 1953; fortnightly; satirical; in Tajik.

Mashal (Torch): Dushanbe, Rudaki 33; tel. (3772) 24-83-17; f. 1952; fmrly journal of the Cen. Cttee of the Leninist Young Communist League and Republican Council of the Pioneer Organization of Tajikistan; juvenile fiction; in Tajik; Editor-in-Chief T. NIGOROVA; circ. 120,000.

Pamir: 734001 Dushanbe, Ismail Somoni 8; tel. (3772) 24-56-56; f. 1949; journal of the Union of Writers of Tajikistan; fiction; in Russian; Editor-in-Chief BORIS PSHENICHNY.

Sadoi shark (Voice of the East): 734001 Dushanbe, Ismail Somoni 8; tel. (3772) 24-56-79; f. 1924; journal of the Union of Writers; fiction; in Tajik; Editor-in-Chief (vacant).

Selskaya zhizn (Agriculture): Dushanbe; in Russian.

Tochikiston (Tajikistan): Dushanbe; f. 1938; social and political; in Tajik and Russian; Editor-in-Chief (vacant).

Zanoni Tochikiston (Women of Tajikistan): Dushanbe; f. 1954; popular; in Tajik; Editor-in-Chief M. KHAKIMOVA.

Zdravookhraneniye Tajikistana (Tajikistan Public Health System): 734026 Dushanbe, I. Somoni 59; tel. (3772) 36-16-37; f. 1933; 6 a year; journal of the Ministry of Health; medical research; in Russian; Editor-in-Chief AZAM T. PULATOV; circ. 5,000.

NEWS AGENCY

Khovar (East): Dushanbe, Lenina 37; f. 1991 to replace TajikTA (Tajik Telegraph Agency); govt information agency; Dir Z. NASRIDDINOV.

Publishers

Adib (Literary Publishing House): Dushanbe, kuchai Ayni 126; f. 1987; juvenile and adult fiction; Dir K. MIRZOYEV.

Irfon (Light of Knowledge Publishing House): Dushanbe, kuchai Ayni 126; politics, science, economics and agriculture; Dir A. SANGINOV.

Maorif (Education Publishing House): Dushanbe, kuchai Ayni 126; educational; Dir A. GHAFUROV.

Sarredaksiyai Ilmii Entsiklopediyai Tajik (Tajik Scientific Encyclopaedia Publishing House): Dushanbe, kuchai Ayni 126; tel. (3772) 25-18-41; f. 1969; Editor-in-Chief J. AZIZQULOV.

Radio and Television

The broadcast media were state-owned and under government control. The extent of this control was reinforced by a decree of February 1994, which placed the State Committee for Television and Radio under the direct operational supervision of the head of state, the Chairman of the Supreme Soviet. The Government was also responsible for 'jamming' (blocking the signals) of the US broadcaster, Radio Liberty (based in Germany), during 1993. In the same year there were transmissions of a rebel opposition group, calling itself Voice of Free Tajikistan.

State Committee for Television and Radio: 734013 Dushanbe, Bekhzod 7A; Chair. BOBOKHON IKRAOMOV.

Tajik Radio: 734025 Dushanbe, kuchai Chapayev 25; broadcasts in Russian, Tajik, Farsi (Persian) and Uzbek.

Tajik Television: 734013 Dushanbe, Bekhzod 7A; broadcasts on four channels in Tajik, Russian and Uzbek.

Finance

BANKING

In mid-1992 Tajikistan's banking system comprised the National Bank of Tajikistan, the Savings Bank (Sberbank), the Bank for Foreign Economic Activity (Vneshekonombank), three large banks (Promstroibank, Agroprombank and Tajikbankbusiness) which originated from former state banks, and three smaller commercial banks (all branches of Russian commercial banks). The National Bank of Tajikistan is the central bank of the country, but its role is circumscribed by Tajikistan's membership of the 'rouble zone', wherein the Central Bank of the Russian Federation largely determines monetary policy and controls foreign reserves.

Central Bank

National Bank of Tajikistan: 734004 Dushanbe, Lenina 24; f. 1991; Chair. of Board KAYLIM KAVMIDDINOV.

Other Banks

Agroprombank—Agricultural Bank: Dushanbe; f. as independent bank in 1991; formerly specialized in agriculture sector; largest commercial bank (41% of total bank lending in 1991).

Bank for Foreign Economic Activity: Dushanbe; fmrly br. of USSR Vneshekonombank; Chair. I. L. LALBEKOV.

Orienbank—Tajik Joint Stock Commercial, Industrial and Construction Bank: 734001 Dushanbe, Rudaki 95/1; tel. (3772) 24-59-20; telex 201226; fax (3772) 24-52-24; f. 1991; fmrly Promstroibank; cap. 92.7m. roubles, res 423.9m. roubles, dep. 23,649.1m. roubles (Jan. 1993); commercial bank (almost 18% of total lending in 1991); Pres. ABDULMUTALIB ABDUSATTAROV; Chair. BAHROM SIROGEV; 5 brs.

Sberbank—Savings Bank: Dushanbe; f. 1991; fmrly br. of all-Union Sberbank; licensed by presidential decree and not subject to the same controls as the commercial and trading banks.

Tajikbankbusiness: Dushanbe; f. 1987 to assume commercial banking activities of the former Soviet Gosbank; second-largest bank in the country (some 37% of total lending in 1991).

In January 1994 the Council of Ministers resolved to form a development bank for Tajikistan, the State Bank for Development and Reconstruction, based in Dushanbe.

COMMODITY EXCHANGES

Tajik Republican Commodity Exchange—NAVRUZ: 374001 Dushanbe, Orjonikidze 37; tel. (3772) 23-48-74; telex 116249; fax (3772) 27-03-91; f. 1991; Chair. SULEYMAN CHULEBAYEV.

Vostok-Mercury Torgovy Dom: 734026 Dushanbe, Lomonosova 162; tel. and fax (3772) 24-60-61; f. 1991; trades in a wide range of goods.

Trade and Industry

CHAMBER OF COMMERCE

Chamber of Commerce and Industry: 734012 Dushanbe, Mazayeva 21; tel. (3772) 27-95-19; Chair. KAMOL SUFIYEV.

COMMERCIAL AND INDUSTRIAL ORGANIZATIONS

National Association of Small- and Medium-Sized Businesses of Tajikistan: Dushanbe; f. 1993, with govt support; independent org.

Tajikvneshtorg: 734051 Dushanbe, Lenina 42; tel. (3772) 23-29-03; co-ordinates foreign trade in a wide range of goods; Gen. Dir YU. G. GAYTSGORI.

Tajikvneshtorg Industrial Association: 734025 Dushanbe, POB 48; tel. (3772) 23-29-03; telex 116119; fax (3772) 22-81-20; est. by Council of Ministers to encourage trade and economic relations with foreign countries; Gen. Dir ABDURAKHMON MUKHTASHOV.

TRADE UNIONS

Council of Trade Unions of Tajikistan: Dushanbe; confederation of the trade unions of the country.

SELECTED INDUSTRIAL COMPANIES

Aluminium Works of Tajikistan: Regar; capacity of 500,000 metric tons per year; one of largest aluminium producers in former USSR.

Bokhtar: 735140 Kurgan-Tyube, Karl Marx 9; tel. (37744) 2-31-57; clothing, footwear, furniture; Gen. Dir SAYIFOV MUHIDDIN; 2,000 employees (1992).

Vakhsh Fertilizer Factory: Hatlon Oblast; producer of nitrogenous fertilizers.

Vostokredmet Industrial Association: 735730 Chkalovsk; formerly processed uranium for Soviet nuclear industry, but converted to gold refining in 1993; 35,000 employees (1993).

Transport

RAILWAYS

There were few railways in Tajikistan, and those were lines linking the major centres of the country with the railway network of Uzbekistan. Thus, Khojand was connected to the Fergana valley lines and the cotton-growing centre of Kurgan-Tyube was linked to Termez. The predominantly mountainous terrain made a more extensive network unlikely.

ROADS

The principal highway of Tajikistan was the road that linked the northern city of Khojand, across the Anzob Pass (3,372 m), with the capital, Dushanbe, went on to the border town of Khorog (Gorno-Badakhshon), before wending through the Pamir Mountains, north, to the Kyrgyz city of Osh, across the Akbaytal Pass (4,655 m). This arterial route exhibited problems common to much of the country's land transport: winter weather was likely to cause the road to be closed by snow for up to eight months of the year. There were also roads of a reasonable standard in the Leninabad region of Khojand, and linking Dushanbe to the south-western cities of Kurgan-Tyube and Kulyab.

CIVIL AVIATION

The main international airport is at Dushanbe, although there is also a major airport at Khojand. The country is linked to cities in the Russian Federation and neighbouring Central Asian states. During the early 1990s, however, many flights, both domestic and international, were cancelled owing to the civil war or fuel shortages. In late 1993 a joint venture with a British company established commercial flights from Dushanbe to London (United Kingdom), and also planned links with the USA, Iran and Pakistan.

TAL—Tajikistan Air Lines: Dushanbe; f. 1993; joint venture between state airline co and British Airways; operated a limited service in 1993; scheduled flights to Iran, Pakistan, the United Kingdom and the USA.

Tourism

There was little tourism in Tajikistan even before the civil war of 1992. There was some spectacular mountain scenery, hitherto mainly visited by climbers, and, particularly in the Fergana valley, in the north of the country, there were sites of historical interest, notably the city of Khojand (Khodzhent).

State Committee for Youth, Sport and Tourism: Dushanbe; Chair. ZEBINISO RUSTAMOVA.

Culture

NATIONAL ORGANIZATION

Ministry of Culture: see section on The Government (Ministries).

CULTURAL HERITAGE

Firdousi State Public Library of the Republic of Tajikistan: 734610 Dushanbe, Lenina 34; tel. (3772) 22-33-16; 2,839,329 vols; Dir S. GOIBNAZAROV.

Tajik United Historical and Regional Fine Arts Museum: 730418 Dushanbe, Ayni 31; tel. (3772) 23-15-44; f. 1934; museum and art gallery; 55,000 items; library of over 17,000 vols; Dir MAZBUT M. MAKHMADOV.

ASSOCIATION

Union of Writers of Tajikistan: 734001 Dushanbe, Putovskogo 8; tel. (3772) 24-57-37.

Education

Education is controlled by the Ministry of Education and was, under the Soviet system, fully funded by the state at all levels. The majority of pupils received their education in Tajik (66.0% of pupils in general day schools in 1988); other languages used included Uzbek (22.9%), Russian (9.7%), Kyrgyz (1.1%) and Turkmen (0.3%). Following the adoption of Tajik as the state language, pupils in Russian-language schools were to learn Tajik from the first to 11th grades. Greater emphasis was made in the curriculum on Tajik language and literature, including classical Persian literature.

UNIVERSITIES

Khojand State University: Khojand; f. 1991; fmrly Khojand Pedagological Institute; 12 faculties.

Tajik State University: 734025 Dushanbe, Rudaki 17; tel. (3772) 22-77-11; f. 1948; languages of instruction: Tajik and Russian; 14 faculties; 1,005 teachers; 6,026 full-time, 1,772 evening and 4,453 extra-mural students; Rector Prof. F. T. TAKHIROV.

Social Welfare

Under the Soviet system there was a fully state-funded health and social-welfare system, largely dependent upon transfers from the all-Union budget. There were reforms aimed at making the social-security system self-financing to a greater degree, notably with the help of employee and employer contributions. At the beginning of 1992 an Employment Fund was established and the Pension Fund and Fund for Social Expenditure (social insurance) were reformed. Even before the problems of the civil war their operations were expected to produce a deficit.

Tajikistan, although one of the poorest regions in the USSR, had a population which had the highest life expectancy at birth in the region (69.6 in 1990). There was a relatively low rate of maternal mortality and yet some 362 members of the population per physician. This situation deteriorated considerably on account of the civil war of 1992–93, which produced some 600,000 refugees, both internally and in neighbouring countries. The situation was particularly bad in Gorno-Badakhshon, which was largely isolated from supplies from November 1992 until August 1993, although the Aga Khan Foundation managed to get some aid to the largely Isma'ili population on the road from Osh (Kyrgyzstan).

The Environment

Tajikistan was less affected than other former Soviet Central Asian countries by the consequences of over-irrigation, which caused major environmental problems in other regions. The country was important as a water source for Turkmenistan in particular. There was anxiety about the effect on the extensive glaciers of the Pamir mountains of wind-borne pesticides and other chemicals from the Aral region.

GOVERNMENT ORGANIZATION

Ministry of Environmental Protection and Water Resources: see section on The Government (Ministries).

ACADEMIC INSTITUTES

Academy of Sciences of the Republic of Tajikistan: 734025 Dushanbe, Lenina 33; tel. (3772) 22-50-83; f. 1951; Pres. S. K. NEGMATULLAYEV; institutes incl.:

Department of Conservation and the Rational Use of Natural Resources: 734025 Dushanbe, Kommunisticheskaya 42; in the Dept of Biological Sciences; Dir K. A. NASREDDINOV.

NON-GOVERNMENTAL ORGANIZATION

Tajikistan Socio-Ecological Union: 734043 Dushanbe, Mayakovskogo 46/2, kv. 34; tel. (3772) 36-86-29; Chair. MUAZAMA ALIKULOVNA BURKHANOVA; Sec. HAMID ABDULLAYEVICH ATAKHANOV.

Defence

Tajikistan began to form its own national armed forces and border guard during 1993. Many of the personnel were from the pro-Communist militias of the civil war, but were to be trained by

Russian army officers. At mid-1993 Western estimates put the total of armed formations at only a maximum of 3,000. An air force was also planned, with four fighter aircraft due in the country by the end of the year. There was also a CIS peace-keeping force in the country—in October this numbered some 25,000, including the Russian (ex-Soviet) 201st Motorized Rifle Division, which was permanently stationed in Tajikistan. A considerable proportion of government expenditure was on defence and security.

Bibliography

Akiner, S. *Islamic People of the Soviet Union: An Historical and Statistical Handbook*, 2nd Edn. London and New York, Kegan Paul International, 1987.

Rumer, B. Z. *Soviet Central Asia: A Tragic Experiment*. Boston, Unwin Hyman, 1989.

Martin, K. 'Tajikistan: Civil War without End?' in *RFE/RL Research Report*, Vol. 2, No. 33. RFE/RL, 1993.

McCagg, W. O., and Silver, B. (Eds). *Soviet Asian Ethnic Frontiers*. New York and Oxford, Pergamon, 1979.

Rakowska-Harmstone, T. *Russia and Nationalism in Central Asia: The Case of Tadzhikistan*. Baltimore, Maryland, Johns Hopkins University Press, 1970.

TURKMENISTAN

Geography

PHYSICAL FEATURES

The Republic of Turkmenistan, or Turkmenia (formerly the Turkmen Soviet Socialist Republic), is situated in the south-west of Central Asia. It is bordered on the north by Uzbekistan, on the north-west by Kazakhstan and on the west by the Caspian Sea. To the south lies Iran and, to the south-east, Afghanistan. The country has an area of 488,100 sq km (188,456 sq miles).

The Kara-Kum (Black Sand) desert, one of the largest sand deserts in the world, covers more than four-fifths of Turkmenistan, occupying the entire central region. There are mountainous areas along the southern and north-western borders, including the Kopet-Dag range, along the frontier with Afghanistan, which is prone to earthquakes. The main river is the Amu-Dar'ya (Oxus), which flows through the eastern regions of the country and used to empty into the Aral Sea. The Kara-Kum Canal, which was begun in 1954, carries water from the Amu-Dar'ya to the arid central and western regions of Turkmenistan where there are no significant natural waterways. However, the existence of this Canal is one of the main factors contributing to the desiccation of the Aral Sea, as the Amu-Dar'ya dries up before reaching it. The other major rivers are the Murgab, which flows south into Afghanistan, and the Tejen, which also flows south and forms part of the border with Iran.

CLIMATE

The climate is severely continental, with extremely hot summers and cold winters. The average temperature in January is −4°C (25°F), but winter temperatures can fall as low as −33°C (−27°F). In summer temperatures often reach 50°C (122°F) in the south-east Kara-Kum; the average temperature in July is 28°C (82°F). Precipitation is slight throughout much of the region. Average annual rainfall ranges from only 80 mm in the north-west to about 300 mm per year in mountainous regions.

POPULATION

The largest ethnic group is the Turkmen (72.0% of the total population in 1989). Minority groups included Russians (9.5%), Uzbeks (9.0%) and Kazakhs (2.5%). There were small communities of other ethnic groups, such as Tatars (39,245), Ukrainians (35,578), Azerbaijanis (33,365), Armenians (31,829) and Baluchis (an Iranian people, most of whom live in Pakistan and Iran—28,280). Among the Turkmen there remains a strong sense of tribal loyalty, reinforced by dialect. The largest tribes are the Tekke in central Turkmenistan, the Ersary in the south-east, and the Yomud in the west of the country. Other Turkmen tribes live in Iran. In 1990 Turkmen was declared the official language of the Republic. Russian is also used, but, in 1989, only some 25% of Turkmen claimed fluency in Russian. Turkmen is a member of the Southern Turkic group of languages; in 1929 the traditional Arabic script was replaced by a Latin script, which was, in turn, replaced by a Cyrillic script in 1940. In the 1990s there were investigations into the possibility of restoring a Latin script. Most of the population are Sunni Muslims. Islam in Turkmenistan traditionally featured elements of Sufi mysticism and shamanism, and pilgrimages to local religious sites were reported to be common.

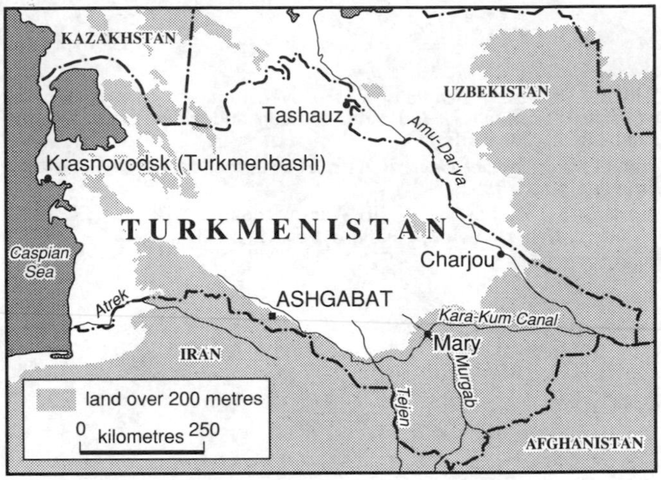

The total estimated population at 1 January 1993 was 4,254,000. Most non-Turkmen live in urban areas: 41% of the population of Ashgabat (Ashkhabad) were Russian in 1990. The capital, Ashgabat, is in the south of the country, near the border with Iran. In 1990 it had an estimated population of 407,200. Charjou (Chardzhou—161,000), situated on the Amu-Dar'ya, is the second largest city. Other important centres include Tashauz, Mary (formerly Merv) and the Caspian port of Krasnovodsk (also known as Turkmenbashi).

Chronology

552–659: Turkic tribes moved west and settled in the area of modern Turkmenistan.

644–661: Southern areas of modern Turkmenistan, including Mary (Merv), were conquered for Islam under the Caliphs 'Uthman and 'Ali.

661–750: Central and eastern areas of Turkmenistan were taken by Muslims during the Umaiyad dynasty.

10th century: Turkic Oghuz tribes, ancestors of the Turkmen, migrated to Turkmenistan.

1038–1194: Southern and eastern areas of Turkmenistan formed part of the territory of the Seljuq Turkic dynasty.

1219–25: Mongolian forces under Temujin (Chinghiz or Genghis Khan) attacked Khwarezm, formerly a territory owing allegiance to the Abbasid caliphate, establishing the Empire of the Khwarezm Shah.

1251–65: Hulagu, a grandson of Chinghiz Khan, established the Empire of the Il-Khans, which included all but the extreme north-west of modern Turkmenistan.

1353: The Il-Khans were replaced by a local Turkmen dynasty who established beyliks, administrative areas ruled by beys (princes).

1370–80: A Turkmen from Transoxania, in modern Uzbekistan, Timur (Tamerlane), founded the second Mongol Empire, which included the territories of the Turkmen. Timur's empire disintegrated rapidly after his death in 1405 and control of Transoxania passed to the Uzbek tribes.

16th–17th centuries: Southern areas of Turkmenistan, including Mary, were dominated by the Safavid dynasty of Persia (Iran).

1868–73: The Uzbek-ruled khanates of Bukhara and Khiva, which had disputed Persia for control of Turkmen territories for more than a century, were made protectorates of the Russian Empire. The Russians also gained control of western areas of Turkmenistan adjacent to the Caspian Sea.

1881: After a four-year campaign by the Russians against the tribes of central Turkmenistan, an estimated 150,000 Turkmen were killed at the battle of Gök Tepe (near Ashgabat—Ashkhabad).

1884: Persia ceded control of the territories near Mary, which became the southernmost part of the Russian Empire.

1895: The United Kingdom and Russia established the southern boundary of modern Turkmenistan, when they demarcated the British and Russian 'spheres of influence'.

1917: Following an unsuccessful Bolshevik attempt to gain power, an anti-Bolshevik Russian Provisional Government of Transcaspia and a Turkmen Congress were established.

30 April 1918: The Turkestan Autonomous Soviet Socialist Republic, including Transcaspia, was proclaimed after Bolshevik forces had occupied Ashgabat.

July 1918: Turkmen nationalists, with limited support from the British, overthrew the Bolshevik regime and created an independent state based in Ashgabat; this fell after the British withdrawal from the area, and Ashgabat was captured by the Red Army in 1920.

27 October 1924: The Turkmen Soviet Socialist Republic (SSR) was established, becoming a Union Republic of the Soviet federation the following May.

1928: The Soviet authorities began to outlaw religious practices in Turkmenistan and the majority of mosques and other Islamic institutions were closed down.

1929: An agricultural collectivization programme was begun, under which nomadic tribespeople were forced to settle in collective farms. In the same year the traditional Turkmen Arabic script was replaced by a Latin script.

***c.* 1937:** The execution of Nederbai Aitakov, 'nationalist' Chairman of the Turkmen Supreme Soviet, was the most notable example of the persecution of Turkmen intellectuals, politicians and even Communist officials which was prevalent during the 1930s.

1940: The Latin alphabet introduced in 1929 was replaced by a Cyrillic script.

1954: Construction work began on the Kara-Kum Canal, which conveys water from the Amu-Dar'ya river (the Oxus of ancient times) on the eastern border of Turkmenistan, to irrigate dry central and western areas of the country; the Canal is a principal cause of the desiccation of the Aral Sea.

1958: Babayev, First Secretary of the Communist Party of Turkmenistan (CPT), proposed an increase in the number of ethnic Turkmen in positions of importance, many of which were held by Russians; subsequently Babayev and a large number of his political colleagues were dismissed from office.

1985: Saparmurat Niyazov became First Secretary of the CPT.

September 1989: Turkmen intellectuals formed Agzybirlik, a 'popular-front' organization concerned with cultural, economic and environmental issues; the movement was officially registered in the following month.

7 January 1990: Only the CPT and other approved organizations were allowed to participate in elections to the Supreme Soviet and local councils; consequently the CPT gained the majority of seats; Niyazov was later elected Chairman of the new Supreme Soviet.

February 1990: Agzybirlik held its founding congress, despite having been banned in the previous month.

May 1990: Turkmenistan followed the example of other Soviet Republics by replacing Russian with the local tongue (Turkmen) as the official language.

22 August 1990: The Turkmen Supreme Soviet adopted a declaration of sovereignty, which asserted Turkmenistan's right to secede from the USSR.

27 October 1990: Niyazov was unopposed in direct elections for the first executive President of the Republic, receiving 98.3% of the votes cast.

17 March 1991: After several months of negotiations for a new Union Treaty, an all-Union referendum was held and 95.7% of the participating electorate in Turkmenistan approved the 'renewal' of the USSR.

June 1991: The Turkmen Supreme Soviet adopted a Law on Freedom of Conscience and Religious Organizations.

18–21 August 1991: There was little official reaction to the attempted conservative coup in Moscow; however, opposition groups such as Agzybirlik publicly denounced it and attempted to form a coalition, resulting in the arrest of several of their leaders.

27 October 1991: The Supreme Soviet declared the country independent the day after 94.1% of voters opted for independence in a national referendum on the issue; the name of the Turkmen SSR was changed to the Republic of Turkmenistan.

November 1991: The Turkmen Government agreed to draft proposals to establish a 'Union of Sovereign States', a political grouping of Soviet Republics.

December 1991: The CPT became known as the Democratic Party of Turkmenistan (DPT) under the chairmanship of Niyazov.

21 December 1991: Turkmenistan and 10 other former Soviet Republics signed the Almaty Declaration establishing the Commonwealth of Independent States (CIS) and effectively dissolving the USSR.

18 May 1992: A new Constitution was adopted which increased the powers of the President of the Republic, who became, conjointly, Prime Minister and Supreme Commander of the Armed Forces; the Supreme Soviet was to continue to act as the legislature, the Majlis, until elections were held, after which the body would have 50 members; the Constitution also established the Khalk Maslakhaty (People's Council) as a supervisory national assembly.

21 June 1992: Niyazov was re-elected unopposed as President, receiving 99.5% of the votes cast.

August 1992: Abdy Kuliyev resigned as Minister of Foreign Affairs, allegedly over Niyazov's growing authoritarianism.

November–December 1992: Elections for the 50 regional representatives to the People's Council were held (the first session of the Council took place in mid-December).

2 January 1993: Electricity, gas and water supplies were made free to all citizens of Turkmenistan.

22 January 1993: At a CIS summit meeting held in Minsk (Belarus), Turkmenistan was one of three countries which refused to sign a treaty on closer economic and political integration; Turkmenistan favoured closer relations with the other four Central Asian CIS member states.

2 February 1993: President Niyazov announced economic reforms which intended to achieve the privatization of land ownership within a period of 10 years.

3 April 1993: The Minister of Internal Affairs, S. Charyyarov, was dismissed, for the poor performance of his ministry.

14 May 1993: Turkmenistan alone declined to sign a declaration of intent to form a CIS economic union; Turkmenistan's position had not changed substantially by the time a subsequent meeting was held in late September.

1 November 1993: Turkmenistan introduced its own currency, the manat, and a number of economic reforms. Later in the same month the Minister of Foreign Affairs, Khalykberdy Atayev, reportedly resigned in protest at proposals to extend Niyazov's presidency; however, Atayev's resignation was not effected.

23 December 1993: Niyazov and Russian President Boris Yeltsin signed an agreement, unique in the former Soviet countries, granting ethnic Russians in Turkmenistan dual nationality with the Russian Federation. At the same CIS summit meeting in Ashgabat Turkmenistan and six other countries signed defence agreements with the Russian Federation which abolished centralized military command for former Soviet forces.

27 December 1993: President Niyazov announced that he would allow the eventual registration of a second political party, the Peasants' Party, in order to promote Turkmenistan's development into a multi-party democracy.

15 January 1994: In a referendum proposed by the DPT, 99.9% of the electorate voted to exempt President Niyazov from having to seek re-election in 1997 in order to allow him time to complete his programme of economic reforms.

History

The Turkmen are descendants of the Oghuz tribes who migrated to Central Asia in about the 10th century AD. By the 15th century, they had emerged as a distinct ethnic group, but were divided by tribal loyalties and territorial division between neighbouring powers. From the 15th to the 17th centuries the southern tribes were under Persian rule, while the north was under the suzerainty of the (Uzbek) khanates of Khiva and Bukhara. In the early 18th century the Persians annexed Khivan and Bukharan territories, but Bukhara regained its power in the latter half of the century and retook Merv (now Mary) and deported its entire population to Bukhara. Meanwhile, the Russians had begun their expansion into Central Asia and, during the 19th century, they gradually reduced the Khanates to the status of protectorates. In 1877 the Russians began a campaign against the Turkmen, which culminated in the battle of Gök Tepe, in 1881, at which some 150,000 Turkmen are estimated to have been killed. In 1895 the Russian conquest was confirmed by agreement with the British; the international boundary thus established divided some Turkmen under Russian rule from others in the British sphere of influence.

In 1917 the Bolsheviks attempted to take power in the region, but there was little support for them among the local population. An anti-Bolshevik Russian Provisional Government of Transcaspia was formed and a Turkmen Congress was also established. Soviet forces were sent to Ashgabat, and a Turkestan Autonomous Soviet Socialist Republic (ASSR), which included Transcaspia, was declared on 30 April 1918. In July, however, nationalists, aided by British forces, overthrew the Bolshevik Government and established an independent administration in Ashgabat, protected by a British garrison. After the British withdrew, however, the regime was soon overthrown and, by 1920, the Red Army, under the control of Frunze, was in control of Ashgabat. As part of the National Delimitation of Central Asia, the Turkmen SSR was established on 27 October 1924.

After the establishment of a Soviet Republic in Turkestan, resistance to Soviet forces continued for some years. The collectivization programme, which was begun in 1929 and entailed the forced settlement of traditionally nomadic people in collective farms, provoked further military resistance; guerrilla warfare against Soviet power continued until 1936. In 1928 a campaign against the practice of religion in Turkmenistan was launched: almost all Muslim institutions were closed, including schools, courts and mosques. In 1917 an estimated 500 mosques were functioning in the region (by 1979 only four were still operating). In the early 1930s there was a campaign among the Turkmen intelligentsia for greater political autonomy for Turkmenistan. As a result many Turkmen intellectuals were imprisoned or executed. The scope of the 'purges' widened, in the late 1930s, to include government and Party officials.

Despite the repressions, advances were made in the provision of social and health facilities among the Turkmen. Campaigns against illiteracy had a high rate of success, despite two changes in the written script of the Turkmen language. According to official figures, the level of literacy rose from 2.3% of the population, in 1926, to 99%, in 1970.

There was some small-scale industrialization of the Republic in the 1920s, but after the early 1930s there was little development in the industrial sector. Agriculture was encouraged and irrigation extended, although with little regard for the possible ecological effects. Irrigation projects such as the Kara-Kum Canal, the largest irrigation project in the USSR, enabled rapid development of cotton-growing, especially after 1945. However, the ecological consequences for the Aral Sea, to the north of the Republic, were so catastrophic that, by January 1994, it had become necessary for the five former Soviet Central Asian countries to establish a joint fund and a permanent committee to save it. (Turkmenistan, Kazakhstan, Kyrgyzstan and Uzbekistan were sufficiently concerned to allocate 1% of their budgets for 1994 to the fund.)

The immigration of Russians into the urban areas of Turkmenistan, during and after the 1920s, gradually diminished the proportion of Turkmen in leading posts in the Republic. In 1958 the First Secretary of the Communist Party of Turkmenistan (CPT), Babayev, proposed that Turkmen should occupy more leading positions. He was dismissed, together with many of his colleagues in government.

The major issues in Turkmenistan in the late 1980s were economic, environmental and cultural. Turkmenistan's position as a provider of raw materials (mainly natural gas and cotton) to more developed Republics, in the European parts of the USSR, provoked strong criticism of the relationship between Turkmenistan and the all-Union authorities. The environmental and health hazards connected with over-intensive agriculture, notably the cultivation of cotton, were also widely discussed in the republican media. These issues, combined with those of language and history, all provoked dissatisfaction with the relationship with the Union. However, the geographical remoteness of the Republic and its poor level of communications with other parts of the USSR inhibited its involvement in the political changes occurring in other Soviet Republics. Moreover, the lack of any history of a unified nation, together with the continuing tribal divisions, did not engender any mass movement for national autonomy, as occurred elsewhere.

In the absence of any significant democratic movement, the CPT dominated elections to the all-Union Congress of People's Deputies, in early 1989. However, in September 1989, Turkmen intellectuals met to form Agzybirlik, a popular-front style organization concerned with the status of the Turkmen language, indigenous arts in the Republic, environmental matters and economic issues. In October 1989 it was officially registered with some reluctance, but, after support for the movement had increased, it was banned in January 1990. Nevertheless, Agzybirlik's founding congress took place in February 1990. As a result of the official animosity towards the nascent democratic movement, the CPT was the only party permitted to participate in elections to the republican Supreme Soviet and local soviets, which took place on 7 January 1990. Communist Party members won most of the seats. When the new Supreme Soviet convened Saparmurat Niyazov (First Secretary of the CPT) was elected Chairman of the Supreme Soviet, the highest government office in the Republic.

Despite the continuing dominance of the CPT, some concessions were made to popular pressure. In May 1990 the Turkmen language was introduced as the state language; Turkmenistan was the last Republic to introduce such legislation. On 22 August 1990 the Turkmen Supreme Soviet adopted a declaration of sovereignty, which declared the Republic a zone free of nuclear and chemical weapons, and asserted the right of the Republic to determine its own political and social system and to secede from the USSR. On 27 October 1990 Niyazov was elected, by direct ballot, as President of Turkmenistan. He was unopposed in the election and received 98.3% of the votes cast.

In late 1990 and early 1991 Turkmenistan participated in negotiations about a new Union Treaty. The backward state of the economy and the Republic's dependence on the all-Union Government for subsidies ensured that the republican leadership was one of the most enthusiastic proponents for retaining the Union. When the all-Union referendum on the status of the USSR was conducted in Turkmenistan, 95.7% of all eligible voters approved the preservation of the USSR as a 'renewed federation', the highest proportion of any Soviet Republic.

There was little response in Turkmenistan to the attempted conservative coup of August 1991. President Niyazov made no public announcements either opposing or supporting the self-proclaimed 'Emergency Committee' in Moscow. The two small opposition groups, the Democratic Party (which ceased to exist after 1991) and Agzybirlik, publicly opposed the coup, but when democratic groups attempted to form a coalition opposed to the coup, some opposition leaders were arrested.

Following the coup attempt, Niyazov remained in power and announced that the Communist Party would be retained as the ruling party, unlike in other Republics, where it had been suspended or dissolved. In December 1991 it changed its name to the Democratic Party of Turkmenistan (DPT). On 26 October 1991 a national referendum took place, on the issue of independence. According to the official results, 94.1% of the electorate voted for independence. On 27 October the Turkmen Supreme Soviet adopted a law on independence and declared 27 October to be Independence Day. The name of the Republic was changed from the Turkmen SSR to the Republic of Turkmenistan, and a new state emblem, flag and national anthem were adopted. On 19 October 1991 the Republic's representatives signed the Treaty on the Economic Community and the Turkmen leadership agreed to the draft proposals for a new political union, the 'Union of Sovereign States', in November. However, when this plan was superseded by the Commonwealth of Independent States (CIS), initially proposed by the Slav Republics, Turkmenistan indicated its wish to become a founder member. On 21 December it became a signatory of the Almaty Declaration, which decision was subsequently ratified by the Supreme Soviet.

INDEPENDENT TURKMENISTAN

In May 1992 a new Constitution was adopted in Turkmenistan. According to its terms, the 50-member Majlis replaced the Supreme Soviet as Turkmenistan's legislature and the People's Council (Khalk Maslakhaty) was established as the 'supreme representative body of popular power'. This was a purely supervisory body with authority to suggest changes to the Constitution and to declare 'no confidence' in the President of the Republic should his actions be considered unconstitutional. Headed by the President, it was to be composed of the 50 members of the Majlis, 60 additional representatives from the electoral districts of Turkmenistan and a number of important officials, including members of the Council of Ministers and the Chairman of the Supreme Court. The Constitution also conferred on the President the additional positions of Prime Minister (Chairman of the Council of Ministers) and Supreme Commander of the Armed Forces. The President was also authorized to legislate by decree in certain circumstances.

Internal affairs after independence were characterized by the increasingly authoritarian leadership of President Niyazov. Niyazov was apparently widely popular, and this was helped by concessions such as free electricity, gas and water supplies for all citizens from January 1993 (and the possibility of free bread in 1996), as well as additional promises of future economic prosperity based on the exploitation of Turkmenistan's natural gas and petroleum reserves. Moreover, the lack of a free press and the Government's restriction of opposition activity (such as confining opposition leaders to their homes when important foreign visitors were in the country) limited the possibility of widespread criticism.

In June 1992 Niyazov was unopposed in direct presidential elections and re-elected, receiving an estimated 99.5% of the votes cast. However, the resignation in August of the Minister of Foreign Affairs, Abdy Kuliyev, was apparently in reaction to the growing 'personality cult' associated with Niyazov. Similarly, in November 1993, when the DPT proposed to cancel the presidential elections scheduled for 1997 and to grant Niyazov life presidency, Kuliyev's successor, Khalykberdy Atayev, was reported to have resigned in protest. However, Atayev continued to act as foreign minister and any disagreements within the Government appeared to have been resolved. One month later the Majlis voted to extend Niyazov's presidency until 2002 without re-election, in order to allow the President time to implement his 10-year programme of economic reforms. This decision was confirmed by 99.9% of the electorate in a referendum held on 15 January 1994.

Niyazov claimed to envisage Turkmenistan's future as a multi-party democracy, but maintained that premature political pluralism would threaten the nation's undeniable stability. In fact, Niyazov announced in December 1993 that a second party, the Peasants' Party, would eventually be granted official registration, as the first step in Turkmenistan's progress towards a multi-party system. However, at that time the organization lacked the minimum number of members required for registration.

FOREIGN RELATIONS

Subsequent to the final dissolution of the USSR and the achievement of full independence, Turkmenistan began to distance itself from other CIS countries, particularly the Russian Federation. In May 1992, at a meeting of CIS heads of state in Tashkent (Uzbekistan), Turkmenistan was not a signatory of the Collective Security Agreement and in January 1993, at another such meeting held in Minsk (Belarus), Turkmenistan, Moldova and Ukraine did not sign a charter on closer economic and political co-operation. Similarly in May, during a meeting in Moscow, Turkmenistan was the only country not to declare its support for closer economic integration. At the end of September, when the other CIS countries agreed on a framework for economic union, Turkmenistan and Ukraine would only agree to be associate members of the group. President Niyazov often sent a representative to meetings of CIS heads of state, suggesting that he regarded the CIS as primarily a consultative body.

Turkmenistan did develop closer relations with the other Central Asian CIS countries, namely Kazakhstan, Kyrgyzstan, Tajikistan and Uzbekistan. In early 1993 the five countries agreed, in principal, to the eventual creation of a Central Asian economic community, although President Niyazov's enthusiasm for the project subsequently appeared to diminish. By mid-January 1994, Kazakhstan, Uzbekistan and Kyrgyzstan had signed agreements to form a separate economic area, without Turkmenistan. With other CIS members, the Turkmen Government proved even less positive, causing many of them considerable economic difficulty by introducing world market prices for natural gas supplies during the early 1990s. Likewise, the involvement of Russia appeared to deter Turkmen involvement in the civil war in Tajikistan, and it remained neutral. Unlike Kazakhstan, Kyrgyzstan, Uzbekistan and Russia, in January 1993 Turkmenistan did not sign the treaty to protect Tajikistan's southern borders and in August, at a summit meeting held in Moscow, Niyazov refused to contribute troops to the proposed joint CIS peace-keeping force. In September Turkmenistan was not party to the protocol agreement on the formation of a new 'rouble zone'. On 1 November, the country issued its own currency, the manat. The purpose of its introduction, other than to combat high inflation, was to maximize Turkmenistan's control of its economy.

Although it might have seemed that Turkmenistan risked provoking a deterioration in relations with Russia in its attempts to evade what remained of Russia's influence over the former Soviet states, Turkmenistan in fact maintained a relatively cordial rapport with Moscow. On 23 December 1993 Niyazov and President Yeltsin signed an accord granting dual Russian and Turkmen citizenship to ethnic Russians in Turkmenistan. Ethnic Russians constituted an estimated 9.8% of the total population in 1993. This was the first such agreement to be made between former states of the USSR and was intended to ease ethnic conflict, which was, nevertheless, negligible by comparison with neighbouring countries.

After independence Turkmenistan began to develop political and economic relations with several foreign countries. It concentrated on developing contacts with its neighbour, Iran, and during 1992 several agreements were made relating to closer economic and political links, in addition to the construction of a railway line between the two countries. Turkmenistan also joined the Economic Co-operation Organization (ECO), a union of Asian countries originally founded by Iran, Pakistan and Turkey. In common with the other Turkic Republics, Turkmenistan was also anxious to develop economic, cultural and political relations with Turkey (the Turkmen have common ancestry with the Turks). In late 1992 the two countries reached an agreement to co-operate on the eventual construction of a pipeline to convey natural gas from Turkmenistan to Europe via Turkey. However, the exact route of the link remained a controversial issue more than a year later, although by early 1994 Iran had agreed that the pipeline could cross its territory. The Turkmen administration appeared to have decided that the nation's future prosperity lay with more economically developed countries in Europe, rather than with other former Soviet republics.

CONCLUSION

Although, in many ways, little changed in Turkmenistan in the years immediately following independence, the country enjoyed a greater degree of stability than many of its neighbours. As President Ter-Petrosyan of Armenia was reported to have said in late 1993, apart from the Baltic states, Turkmenistan was the only former Soviet Republic to be truly independent of the Russian Federation.

The Economy

The desert republic of Turkmenistan still had an economy dominated by agriculture at the beginning of the 1990s. However, its future lay in the development of its huge reserves of natural gas and petroleum. Following independence at the end of 1991 the country increased its revenues from sales of gas, and was developing the exploitation of petroleum. Foreign investment was available for such projects because of the potential of Turkmenistan's hydrocarbons reserves and because of the political stability of the country. Existing wealth encouraged such stability, with the Government able to support gestures such as providing the population with free supplies of gas, water and electricity during 1993. Moreover, Turkmenistan was able to afford to introduce its own currency without the financial backing (but with the advice) of the International Monetary Fund (IMF).

The introduction of the manat towards the end of 1993, in replacement of the rouble, also marked a further effort by the authorities to reduce the dependence of the Turkmen economy on the Russian Federation and other former Soviet countries. The disintegration of the internal market of the former USSR had a severe effect on Turkmenistan, as it did on other states. Despite its efforts, it inevitably remained linked to the economic system of the former Soviet Republics and would do so for some years. Another consequence of the years of Soviet rule was the ecological legacy, notably the catastrophic drying out of the lower reaches of the Amu-Dar'ya and the Aral Sea. This was largely the result of the ambitious Soviet project to make the deserts of Turkmenistan (the Kara-Kum Desert covered almost 90% of the country) cultivable. The deteriorating ecology was believed to be responsible for the failure to raise the standards of many of the social development indicators, as compared with other Soviet Republics. Thus, in the early 1990s Turkmenistan had the highest infant mortality rate and the lowest life expectancy at birth of any former Soviet state (in 1990 average life expectancy at birth was 66.4 years, the next lowest being 68.7 in Moldova). The maintenance of a stable polity into the late 1990s obviously depended on the Government being able to improve such conditions and raise the population's standard of living with the expected increase in national wealth.

AGRICULTURE

Only some 2% of Turkmenistan's land area was arable, but, in 1991, the agricultural sector contributed 46.4% of net material product (NMP) and employed 42.4% (including workers on private plots) of the working population. The sector is heavily dependent on irrigation (one-half of the arable land was irrigated in 1990), crucial to which is the massive Kara-Kum Canal, noted as one of the few man-made features discernible from space. When it was begun in the 1950s the Canal was intended to link the Amu-Dar'ya river with the Caspian Sea and, by the early 1990s, it extended over 1,200 km. However, apart from the diverting of the Aral Sea's water supply and the immense environmental consequences there, the unsuitable land irrigation, the inefficient use of water, the increasing salination of the soil and the excessive development of cotton cultivation combined to keep agricultural yields low.

The major crop was cotton—in 1991 the crop was planted on some 50% of arable land and accounted for 60% of agricultural production. The Turkmen cotton crop alone accounted for 1.2% of Soviet agricultural NMP. Other crops included cereals, vegetables and grapes, melons and other fruits. The country was also a major producer of such high-value crops as liquorice root, of which it exported (including extracts) some 1,300 metric tons in 1992. However, the extent of specialization meant that Turkmenistan did not satisfy a considerable proportion of its own food needs. Thus, in 1991, it imported: 65% of its grain consumption; 70% of its potatoes; all of its sugar; and 45% of its dairy products.

Livestock was also important, contributing one-quarter of agricultural production in 1991. There was more pasture than arable land in the country. Sheep, notably the Karakul sheep with its distinctive soft, curled pelt, horses (Turkoman horses) and camels are bred. The major products are astrakhan and karakul wools. Silkworms are also bred. Overall agricultural NMP fell slightly in 1991 (by 1.6%) and continued to decline in the next two years.

MINING, ENERGY AND INDUSTRY

Turkmenistan is rich in natural resources. The importance of energy reserves and other mineral resources, as well as the dominance of cotton in the agricultural sector, could be seen in the structure of the industrial sector. In 1991 about one-third of total industrial production was accounted for by 61 textile enterprises, and a further one-third was contributed by 38 large enterprises in the chemicals, gas, petroleum and electricity-generating industries. Most of the hydrocarbons reserves were located in the west of the country and off shore, under the Caspian Sea. In 1993 it was estimated that Turkmenistan had reserves of between 10,000,000m. and 15,000,000m. cu m of natural gas and 6,300m. metric tons of petroleum (proven reserves of the latter were 213m. tons). Despite these natural endowments, however, the weakness of the industrial sector left Turkmenistan in the position of being the least productive Republic in the former USSR (in 1988 it accounted for only 0.6% of total Soviet NMP and provided the lowest proportion of total Soviet industrial NMP, 0.4%—compared to 2.2% of the land area and 1.2% of the population of the USSR in that year).

The extraction of natural gas was overwhelmingly important to the economy. By 1993 the country was producing some 85,000m. cu m of gas per year and, with no facilities for chemical processing of it, most of this production was exported. The main domestic use of gas was for thermal power stations, some two-thirds of the electricity produced also being exported. Such exports were vital sources of convertible ('hard') currency, particularly as Turkmenistan introduced increased prices for its main, CIS customers (under the Soviet system energy and raw materials were greatly underpriced relative to world markets). By March 1994 the CIS gas debt was put at some US $1,500m. The economic straits of the former Soviet territories, however, encouraged Turkmenistan to seek greater access to Western and world markets for its gas and it proposed a pipeline to the Turkish coast. In January 1994 Iran agreed that such a pipeline could cross its territory, although interested US companies were anxious to minimize the extent to which Turkmen exports would be dependent upon Iran. This was emphasized by an agreement from the same time which proposed that increased petroleum exports should be piped across Iran to the Persian (Arabian) Gulf.

Turkmenistan intended to increase petroleum production during the mid-1990s and attracted several Western companies to invest in development and exploration (such as Elf Aquitaine of France). This followed the stagnation of the industry in the last years of the Soviet regime, as the all-Union authorities displayed reluctance to invest in the region. Where major investment in the sector occured, with the Charjou petroleum refinery built in the late 1980s (capacity of 6m. metric tons per year), supplies of crude petroleum were to be from Western Siberia, in Russia. In 1993, however, there were proposals from an Italian firm (Tecnologie Progetti Lavori—TPL) to invest some US $1,000m. in a refinery in the east of the country, to augment the Krasnovodsk (Turkmenbashi) refinery, which had a capacity of 5.5m. tons per year.

There were also significant deposits of iodine-bromine, sodium sulphate and various mineral salts. The processing of such minerals, particularly the mineral salts from the Kara Bogaz gulf, supported a fairly large chemicals industry, mainly based in Charjou. It was believed that there might, in addition, be reserves of gold and platinum in the country. Other industries included, predominantly, textiles, cotton-ginning and hand-woven carpets. Western investment was also evidenced in these activities, with Turkish firms showing a particular interest and TPL investing some $250m. in a textile plant near Ashgabat (when agreed in July 1992, one of the largest foreign investment deals for the country hitherto). There was also considerable construction activity (22.7% of NMP in 1991), owing to extensive industrial and infrastructure projects, although these were severely affected by the collapse of the USSR. However, the need to develop transport and communications links in the 1990s, as well as the availability of Western assistance to such a potentially wealthy country as Turkmenistan, indicated that such projects were likely to continue. In 1991 industry and construction contributed 42% of NMP and employed 20% of the working population.

FINANCE AND REFORM

On 1 November 1993 Turkmenistan introduced its own currency, the manat, initially at a rate of one manat for 500 Russian roubles (or for US $0.5). Backed by its hydrocarbons wealth and reserves of some $300m., the country could dispense with IMF financial assistance, but the international financial institutions and Russia supported the move. By the beginning of 1994, despite an intitial increase in prices and some popular suspicion of the new currency, it had proved to be one of the more successful currency introductions of the region (the official rate had only fallen to one manat for 600 roubles at the end of 1993). From 15 March, in an effort to stabilize circulation of the currency, the manat was floated, a measure largely supported by the gas debts of CIS member states. Turkmenistan had, of course, benefited from the preparation time, as the manat had been planned before the Russian currency reforms of July had increased pressures on other former Soviet states to withdraw from the high-inflation 'rouble zone'. Nevertheless, the exchange rate of the new currency still suffered a serious deterioration, even if not as dramatic as the currencies of other former Soviet states: from a rate of two manats per US $1 when it was introduced, following the floating of the currency in March the rate reached 10 manats per $1 (although there were reports of 'black-market' rates of 55–70 manats per $1). This was part of a process of Turkmenistan exercising increased control over its own economic policy.

The Turkmen Government ended the use of the rouble as part of its withdrawal from the old Soviet economic space into world markets. However, it was also reluctant to become over-reliant on the West and the IMF; this enabled it to dictate the manner and rate at which the country made the transition to an economy operated on market principles. Even in the early years of independence President Saparmurat Niyazov stated his intent to create a free-market economy which maintained a role for the state in the development of industry, social policy, health and a national culture. With unemployment already high in the Republic before the dissolution of the USSR (reported to be between 18% and 40% in 1990, although official figures stated only some 2.5% of the labour force in mid-1992), the Government was anxious to avoid further widespread social consequences, typical for extensive restructuring of a formerly centrally planned economic system. Even the start of privatization, with unprofitable enterprises, in 1993, was controlled so as alternative employment was available in the event of business failure. Other forms of privatization were slow to be introduced. Thus, the housing privatization proposed in 1991 was, by the end of 1993, being severely limited, at least until the end of the decade.

Turkmenistan was one of the poorest of the former Soviet Republics, with NMP per head estimated at 61% of the all-Union average in 1988. It was also highly integrated into the Soviet economic system, with 84% of its trade being with other Union Republics in 1991 (despite a decline in the proportion since the late 1980s). However, that trade was in surplus (1,095m. roubles), while there was a deficit in trade with other countries (197m. roubles). Imported fininshed and intermediate goods were vital for Turkmen industrial activity, but it also imported consumer goods and foods. Many of these products were obtained by barter agreements, even in 1993, indicating the limits to the economic reforms and the attempt to integrate into the world economy rather than remain a part of the decaying former Soviet system.

However, even in the first year of independence the gross domestic product of Turkmenistan declined by only 5%, in real terms, compared with figures for the fall in other Central Asian countries in 1992: Kazakhstan 13%; Kyrgyzstan 25%; and Tajikistan 31%. The profitability of the natural-gas sector helped finance the policies of the Turkmen Government, which was able to attract foreign investment mainly on the strength of its political security and the country's natural resources, rather than the force of its reformist credentials.

Statistical Survey

Principal sources (unless otherwise stated): IMF, *Turkmenistan, Economic Review*; World Bank, *Statistical Handbook, States of the Former USSR.*

Area and Population

AREA, POPULATION AND DENSITY

Area (sq km)	488,100*
Population (census result)	
12 January 1989	3,533,925
Population (official estimate at 1 January)	
1991	3,714,000
1993†	4,254,000
Density (per sq km) at 1 January 1993	8.7

* 188,456 sq miles.
† Figure for 1992 not available.

POPULATION BY NATIONALITY
(official estimates at 1 January 1993)

	Number	%
Turkmen	3,118,000	73.3
Russian	419,000	9.8
Uzbek	382,000	9.0
Kazakh	87,000	2.0
Tatar	39,000	0.9
Ukrainian	34,000	0.8
Azeri	34,000	0.8
Armenian	32,000	0.8
Belarusian	9,000	0.2
Others	100,000	2.4
Total	4,254,000	100.00

PRINCIPAL TOWNS (estimated population at 1 January 1990)
Ashgabat (capital) 517,200*; Charjou 164,000; Tashauz 114,000.
* At 1 January 1993.

BIRTHS, MARRIAGES AND DEATHS

	Registered live births		Registered marriages		Registered deaths	
	Number	Rate (per 1,000)	Number	Rate (per 1,000)	Number	Rate (per 1,000)
1987	126,787	37.2	31,484	9.2	26,802	7.9
1988	125,887	36.0	33,008	9.4	27,317	7.8
1989	124,992	34.9	34,890	9.8	27,609	7.7

Source: UN, *Demographic Yearbook.*

EMPLOYMENT ('000 persons)

	1989	1990	1991
Material sphere	1,111.5	1,148.9	1,175.0
Agriculture	622.7	648.5	673.0
Forestry	1.8	1.7	1.8
Industry	159.5	166.4	168.0
Construction	149.1	154.4	151.3
Trade and catering	89.7	87.5	90.0
Transport and communications	64.7	62.5	63.5
Other activities	24.0	27.9	27.4
Non-material sphere	382.9	396.8	410.4
Education, culture and arts	167.8	175.5	184.4
Health care and social security	81.4	86.4	91.0
Science, research and development	27.5	28.3	28.5
Housing services and transport	68.9	67.8	65.0
Other services	37.3	38.8	41.5
Total	1,494.4	1,545.7	1,585.4

Agriculture

PRINCIPAL CROPS ('000 metric tons)

	1990	1991	1992
Grain	447	485	780*
Wheat	130	206	400*
Rice (paddy)	42	54	60
Barley	140	129	160*
Maize	135	96	160*
Potatoes	35	30	32*
Seed cotton	1,457	1,433	1,290
Cottonseed	803†	710†	709*
Vegetables	411	388	360*
Grapes	169	167	170*
Other fruit	47	56	58*
Tobacco (leaves)	3	3	2*
Cotton (lint)	437	430	395†

* FAO estimate(s). † Unofficial estimate(s).
Source: FAO, *Production Yearbook.*

LIVESTOCK ('000 head at 1 January)

	1990	1991	1992
Horses	18	19	20*
Cattle	800	800	900
Pigs	300	300	300
Sheep	5,185	5,280	5,380
Goats	215	220	220
Chickens†	8,000	7,000	8,000

* FAO estimate(s). † Unofficial estimate(s).
Source: FAO, *Production Yearbook.*

LIVESTOCK PRODUCTS ('000 metric tons)

	1990	1991	1992
Beef and veal	47	44	45*
Mutton and lamb	27	30	30*
Goatmeat	8†	6†	4*
Pigmeat	10	9	10*
Poultry meat	9	7	8†
Cows' milk	436	458	400†
Butter ghee	4.5	4.3	4.0†
Hen eggs	18.0	16.6	15.0
Wool:			
greasy	16.0	16.3	17.0*
scoured	9.6	9.8	10.2*

* FAO estimate(s). † Unofficial estimate(s).

Source: FAO, *Production Yearbook*.

Mining

	1989	1990	1991
Natural gas (million cu metres)	89,900	87,800	84,300

Crude petroleum ('000 metric tons): 5,812 in 1987.

Industry

SELECTED PRODUCTS
('000 metric tons, unless otherwise indicated)

	1989	1990	1991
Motor spirit (petrol)	758.5	773.3	813.9
Kerosene	69.1	110.4	98.1
Diesel oil	1,618.3	1,572.5	2,236.1
Mazout (heavy fuel oil)	1,302.9	1,218.0	1,991.0
Electric energy (million kWh)	16,624.3	16,637.2	17,171.4

Finance

CURRENCY AND EXCHANGE RATES

Monetary Units

100 tenge = 1 manat.

Sterling and Dollar Equivalents (30 September 1993)
£1 sterling = 1,796.1 Russian (ex-Soviet) roubles;
US $1 = 1,201.0 roubles;
10,000 roubles = £5.568= $8.326.

Average Exchange Rate (roubles per US dollar)
1989 0.6274
1990 0.5856
1991 0.5819

Note: The figures for average exchange rates refer to official rates for the Soviet rouble. However, a multiple exchange rate system was in operation, with separate non-commercial and tourist rates. A commercial exchange rate was introduced on 1 November 1990, replacing the official rate for most transactions. The commercial rate (roubles per US dollar) was: 1.692 at 31 December 1990; 1.671 at 31 December 1991. Between November 1989 and April 1991 the tourist exchange rate valued the rouble at one-tenth of the official rate. In April 1991 this rate, renamed the 'special rate', was set at $1 = 27.6 roubles. It was subsequently adjusted. Following the dissolution of the USSR in December 1991, Russia and several other former Soviet Republics retained the rouble as their monetary unit.

On 1 November 1993 Turkmenistan introduced its own currency, the manat, initially at a rate of 500 roubles per manat (or $0.5 per manat). By the end of 1993 this rate had deteriorated to 600 roubles per manat. From 15 March 1994 the manat was floated.

BUDGET (million roubles)

Revenue	1990	1991	1992*
Taxation	1,038	1,972	22,352
Turnover tax	780	669	—
Value-added tax	—	—	14,058
Tax on company profits	—	518	5,696
Excises	—	—	1,502
Sales tax	—	314	—
Tax on co-operatives and public companies	92	122	76
Personal income tax	166	349	1,020
Income from sale of goods imported with convertible currencies	—	11	7,100
State duties	15	34	274
Funds from social security	187	—	—
Transfers from state-owned enterprises (formerly of the USSR)	312	—	—
Transfers from state-owned gas and cotton corporations	—	1,551	17,354
Other revenue	920	1,506	884
Transfers from the USSR	764	1,419	—
Total	3,236	6,489	47,964
Central government	1,648	4,413	38,039
Local government	1,589	2,075	9,924

Expenditure	1990	1991	1992*
Financing of national economy	1,848	2,302	25,952
Social and cultural services	1,162	3,356	15,479
Education and science	655	1,159	7,833
Health care	283	556	3,458
Social security	207	1,572	4,101
Administration	49	161	1,445
Other purposes	55	78	9,275†
Total	3,114	5,897	52,151
Central government	1,597	3,822	41,735
Local government	1,517	2,074	10,415

* Projections.

† Including appropriations for acquiring foreign exchange from exporters.

COST OF LIVING (Index of retail prices; base: previous year = 100)

	1989	1990	1991
Food	100.2	102.7	171.3
Other commodities	103.4	105.9	205.1
All items	102.1	104.6	190.4

NATIONAL ACCOUNTS

Net Material Product by Economic Activity
(million roubles at current prices)

	1989	1990	1991
Agriculture and forestry	2,095	2,549	6,390
Industry	1,101	835	2,699
Construction	874	952	3,126
Transport and communications	309	452	578
Other material services	454	537	978
Total	4,828	5,321	13,771

BALANCE OF PAYMENTS (million roubles)

	1990	1991
Exports f.o.b.:		
Inter-republican	2,469	6,731
Foreign	172	1,105
Imports f.o.b.:		
Inter-republican	2.927	5,636
Foreign	685	1,302
Trade balance:		
Inter-republican	-458	1,095
Foreign	-513	-197
Services (net):		
Inter-republican	-172	-422
Foreign	-77	-422
Public unrequited transfers (net):		
Inter-republican	600	2,222
Current balance:		
Inter-republican	-30	2,894
Foreign	-590	-341
Capital (net):		
Inter-republican	-1,062	-447
Foreign	18	60
Net errors and omissions:		
Inter-republican	542	113
Foreign	86	22
Overall balance:		
Inter-republican	-549	2,561
Foreign	-487	-259

External Trade

INTER-REPUBLICAN (USSR) TRADE
PRINCIPAL COMMODITIES (million roubles)

Imports	1988	1989	1990
Petroleum and gas	100.2	100.0	79.3
Iron and steel	107.0	83.9	105.8
Chemicals and petrochemicals	200.1	209.4	202.6
Machine-building	925.6	949.4	958.8
Timber, woodwork and paper	103.1	124.9	96.7
Light industry	395.1	453.3	550.7
Agricultural products	28.2	33.6	132.1
Food	433.9	477.9	444.7
Total (incl. others)	2,486.0	2,746.1	2,927.4

1991: Total imports (estimated) 5,636.4m. roubles.

Exports	1988	1989	1990
Electric power	58.9	69.6	67.0
Petroleum and gas	800.6	745.1	705.1
Chemicals and petrochemicals	150.4	151.5	146.7
Light industry	1,066.1	1,073.8	1,073.2
Agricultural products	137.2	127.6	123.6
Food	95.3	85.1	205.9
Total (incl. others)	2,389.2	2,418.2	2,469.0

1991: Total exports (estimated) 6,731.1m. roubles.

FOREIGN TRADE
PRINCIPAL COMMODITIES (million roubles)

Imports	1988	1989	1990
Iron and steel	8.3	18.5	7.3
Chemicals and petrochemicals	8.7	21.0	26.6
Machine-building	21.3	92.6	119.5
Timber, woodwork and paper	25.7	12.1	9.2
Light industry	195.6	243.3	254.5
Agricultural products	42.4	50.7	60.1
Food	122.8	143.5	185.1
Total (incl. others)	432.2	589.1	685.3

1991: Total imports (estimated) 1,302.1m. roubles.

Exports	1988	1989	1990
Petroleum and gas	—	2.1	9.3
Chemicals and petrochemicals	1.5	0.8	6.7
Light industry	206.6	223.1	138.9
Agricultural products	22.0	4.9	3.5
Food	3.6	1.5	7.1
Total (incl. others)	245.0	241.2	171.9

1991: Total exports (estimated) 1,104.6m. roubles.

Education

(1984/85)

	Institutions	Students
Secondary schools	1,900	800,000
Secondary specialized schools	35	36,900
Higher schools (incl. universities)	9	38,900

Directory

The Constitution

A new Constitution was adopted on 18 May 1992, and included the following among its main provisions:

The President of the Republic is directly elected by universal adult suffrage for a five-year term. A President may only hold office for a maximum of two terms. The President is not only head of state, but also head of government (Prime Minister in the Council of Ministers) and Supreme Commander of the Armed Forces. The President must ratify all parliamentary legislation and in certain circumstances may legislate by decree. The President appoints the Government and chairs sessions of the Khalk Maslakhaty (People's Council).

Supreme legislative power resides with the 50-member Majlis, a unicameral parliament which is directly elected for a five-year term (the first Majlis was to be the 175-seat former Supreme Soviet, elected in 1990 for five years). Sovereignty, however, is vested in the people of Turkmenistan and the supreme representative body of popular power is the Khalk Maslakhaty. This is described as a supervisory organ with no legislative or executive functions, but it is authorized to perform certain duties normally reserved to a legislature or constituent assembly. Not only does it debate and approve measures pertaining to the political and economic situation in the country, but it examines possible changes to the Constitution and may vote to express 'no confidence' in the President of the Republic, on grounds of unconstitutionality. The Khalk Maslakhaty is comprised of all the deputies of the Majlis, a further 50 elected and 10 appointed representatives from all districts of the country, the members of the Council of Ministers, the Chairmen of the Supreme Court and the Supreme Economic Court, the Procurator-General and the heads of local councils.

The Constitution, which defines Turkmenistan as a democratic state, also guarantees the independence of the judiciary and the basic human rights of the individual. The age of majority is 18 years (parliamentary deputies must be aged at least 21). Ethnic minorities are granted equality under the law, although Turkmen is the only official language.

Note: On 16 January 1994 a referendum confirmed President Saparmurat Niyazov's exemption from the need to be re-elected in 1997.

The Government

HEAD OF STATE

President of the Republic: Gen. SAPARMURAT ATAYEVICH NIYAZOV (directly elected 27 October 1990; re-elected 21 June 1992—a referendum on 16 January 1994 extended his term of office until 2002).

COUNCIL OF MINISTERS
(March 1994)

Prime Minister (Chairman): Gen. SAPARMURAT A. NIYAZOV.

Deputy Prime Minister and Minister of the Economy and Finance: VALERY OTCHERSOV.

Deputy Prime Ministers: ORAZGEDI AYDOGDYEV, JORAKULY BABAKULYEN, YAGMUR OVEZOV, REJEP SAPAROV, NAZAR SUYUNOV, REJEPMAMMET PUKHANOV, BORIS SHIKHMURATOV, MATKARIM RAZHAPOV, SPARGELDY MOTAYEV, KURBAN ORAZOV, PIRKULY ODEYEV, JUMAGELDY AMANSAKHATOV, GURBANMUKHAMMET KASYMOV, ABAD SEHEDOVNA IRZAYEVA.

Minister of Agriculture, Food and the Processing Industries: PAYZGELDY MEREDOV.

Minister of Agricultural Construction: R. ABDYEV.

Minister of the Building Materials Industry: KHALMUKHAMMET ORAZSAKHATOV.

Minister of Communications: AMANMURAT JUMMYEV.

Minister of Construction: N. O. ORAZMUKHAMMETOV.

Minister of Consumer Goods: ASHIR ATAYEV.

Minister of Culture and Tourism: GELDYMURAT NURMUKHAMMETOV.

Minister of Defence: Lt-Gen. DANATAR KOPEKOV.

Minister of Education: N. BAYRAMSAKHATOV.

Minister of Foreign Affairs: KHALYKBERDY ATAYEV.

Minister of Forestry: T. CHOREKLIYEV.

Minister of Grain Products: A. CHARYYAROV.

Minister of Health: (vacant).

Minister of Internal Affairs: AMMANGELDY GELDYKURBANOV (acting).

Minister of Justice: TAGANDURDY KHALLYEV.

Minister of Local Industry: (vacant).

Minister of Motor Transport: KAKJAN ACHYROVICH ACHYROV.

Minister of Natural Resources and Environmental Protection: NURMAKHAMMET ASHIROV.

Minister of Petroleum and Natural Gas: BERDYEV (acting).

Minister of Social Security: AKSOLTAN TOREYEVNA ATAYEVA.

Minister of State Property and Enterprise Support: MATKARIM RAZHAPOV.

Minister of Trade: KH. A. AGAKHANOV.

Minister of Water Management: (vacant).

Chairmen of State Committees

Chairman of the State Committee for Fish Management: GELDYKURBAN IBRAGIMOV.

Chairman of the State Committee for Land Use, Land Organization and Land Reform: A. NOBADOV.

Chairman of the State Committee for Material-Technical Supply: NURMUKHAMMET KHANAMOV.

Chairman of the State Committee for National Security: SAPARMURAT SEYIDOV.

Chairman of the State Committee for Preservation of State Secrets in the Press and Other Media: KAKABAY ATAYEV.

Chairman of the State Committee for Publishing, Printing and the Book Trade: KH. DIVANKULIYEV.

Chairman of the State Committee for Statistics: B. ANNAYEV.

Chairman of the State Committee for the Supervision of Industrial Safety and Mining Inspection: N. D. KLYCHEV.

Chairman of the State Committee for the Supply of Petroleum Products: A. S. KANAYEV.

MINISTRIES

Office of the President and the Council of Ministers: Ashgabat.

Ministry of Agriculture, Food and the Processing Industries: Ashgabat.

Ministry of Agricultural Construction: Ashgabat.

Ministry of the Building Materials Industry: Ashgabat.

Ministry of Communications: Ashgabat.

Ministry of Construction: Ashgabat.

Ministry of Consumer Goods: Ashgabat.

Ministry of Culture and Tourism: Ashgabat; tel. (3632) 25-35-60.

Ministry of Defence: Ashgabat.

Ministry of the Economy and Finance: Ashgabat.

Ministry of Education: Ashgabat.

Ministry of Foreign Affairs: Ashgabat; tel. (3632) 26-62-11; fax (3632) 25-35-83.

Ministry of Forestry: Ashgabat.

Ministry of Grain Products: Ashgabat.

Ministry of Health: Ashgabat.

Ministry of Internal Affairs: Ashgabat.

Ministry of Justice: Ashgabat.

Ministry of Local Industry: Ashgabat.

Ministry of Motor Transport: Ashgabat.

Ministry of Natural Resources and Environmental Protection: Ashgabat.

Ministry of Petroleum and Natural Gas: Ashgabat.

Ministry of Social Security: Ashgabat.

Ministry of State Property and Enterprise Support: Ashgabat.

Ministry of Trade: Ashgabat.

Ministry of Water Management: Ashgabat.

All the principal state committees are also based in Ashgabat.

KHALK MASLAKHATY (PEOPLE'S COUNCIL)

Under the Constitution of May 1992, the People's Council was established as the supreme representative body in the country. The People's Council is composed of all the Majlis deputies, 50 directly elected representatives from all districts of Turkmenistan, 10 appointed representatives, the members of the Council of Ministers, the Chairman of the Supreme Court, the Chairman of the Supreme Economic Court, the Procurator-General and the heads of the local councils. It is headed by the President of the Republic. Elections for the 50 members were held in November and December 1992; the Council convened for the first time later in December.

Legislature

MAJLIS

The Supreme Soviet of Turkmenistan, with 175 seats, was elected on 7 January 1990, for a term of five years, in elections contested only by the Communist Party of Turkmenistan (CPT) and its approved organizations. The main parliamentary factions were: Democratic (members of the Democratic Party, the successor organization of the CPT); the Agrarian or Peasant; the War Veterans; and the Intelligentsia. Under the Constitution of 1992, which was promulgated on 18 May, the highest legislative body was to be a 50-member Majlis, directly elected for a term of five years. Until the expiry of its term or until elections to the new body were held, the former Supreme Soviet was to act as the Majlis. The deputies of the Majlis also form part of the Khalk Maslakhaty (see above).

Chairman: SAKHAT N. MURADOV.

Deputy Chairman: ALEKSANDR D. DODONOV.

Local Government

Turkmenistan was divided into five oblasts (regions) for administrative purposes. Each area had an elected council (soviet) and a local administration, based in the town for which the oblast had been named (however, where a town had changed its name, the region often retained the old designation).

Ashgabat Oblast: Ashgabat.

Charjou Oblast: Charjou.

Krasnovodsk Oblast: Turkmenbashi (Krasnovodsk).

Merv Oblast: Mary (Merv).

Tashauz Oblast: Tashauz.

Political Organizations

Agzybirlik: Ashgabat; f. 1989; popular front organization, denied official registration except from Oct. 1991 to Jan. 1992.

Democratic Party of Turkmenistan: 744014 Ashgabat 14, Gogolya 28; tel. (3632) 25-12-12; name changed from Communist Party of Turkmenistan in 1991; Chair. Gen. SAPARMURAT A. NIYAZOV; 116,000 mems (1991).

Peasants' Party: Ashgabat; f. 1993 by deputies of the agrarian faction in parliament; was considered likely to be registered in 1994.

There were several unregistered opposition groups, such as the Islamic Renaissance Party, which had been an all-Union Muslim party in the former USSR, and the remnants of another Democratic party. The main opposition organization was Agzybirlik, although in early 1994 President Niyazov indicated that the Peasants' Party would be permitted registration in the near future.

Diplomatic Representation

EMBASSIES IN TURKMENISTAN

Iran: Ashgabat; Ambassador: GHOLAMREZA BAQERI.

Kazakhstan: Ashgabat.

Turkey: Ashgabat, Shevchenko 9; tel. (3632) 29-42-50; telex 228117.

USA: Ashgabat, Yubilenaya Hotel; tel. (3632) 24-49-08; Ambassador: JOSEPH S. HULINGS, III.

Judicial System

Chairman of the Supreme Court: N. M. YUSUPOV.

Procurator-General: V. M. VASILIUK.

Religion

The majority of the population were adherents of Islam. In June 1991 the Turkmen Supreme Soviet adopted a Law on Freedom of Conscience and Religious Organizations.

ISLAM

Turkmen are traditionally Sunni Muslims, but with elements of Sufism. Islam, the religion of the Turkmen for many centuries, was severely persecuted by the Soviet regime from the late 1920s. Until July 1989 Ashgabat was the only Central Asian capital without a functioning mosque. The Muslims of Turkmenistan were officially under the jurisdiction of the Muslim Board of Central Asia, based in Tashkent (Uzbekistan). The Board was represented in Turkmenistan by a kazi.

Kazi of Turkmenistan: NASRULLO IBADULLAYEV.

The Press

In 1989, according to official statistics, 66 newspaper titles were being published in Turkmenistan, including 49 published in Turkmen. There were 34 periodicals, including 16 in Turkmen. All publications are in Turkmen except where otherwise stated.

PRINCIPAL NEWSPAPERS

Edebiyat ve sungat (Literature and Art): 744604 Ashgabat, Atabayeva 20; tel. (3632) 5-30-34; f. 1958; 2 a week; publ. by the Ministry of Culture and the Union of Writers of Turkmenistan; Editor TIRKISH JUMAGELDIYEV.

Novcha: Ashgabat, Atabayeva 20; tel. (3632) 25-68-02; f. 1930; weekly; for children and teenagers; in Russian; Editor-in-Chief BABANIYAZ KAYUMOV.

Turkmenskaya iskra (Turkmen Spark): Ashgabat; f. 1924; 6 a week; organ of the Majlis and Council of Ministers; in Russian; Editor V. V. SLUSHNIK.

Syyasy sokhbetdesh (Political Symposium): 744014 Ashgabat 14, Gogolya 28; tel. (3632) 25-12-12; weekly; organ of the Democratic Party of Turkmenistan; circ. 14,500.

PRINCIPAL PERIODICALS

Monthly unless otherwise indicated.

Ashgabat: 744000 Ashgabat, Makhtumkuli 5; tel. (3632) 09-65-44; journal of the Union of Writers of Turkmenistan; popular; in Russian; Editor V. N. POU; circ. 6,000.

Ovadan: Ashgabat; f. 1952; for women; Editor A. B. SEITKULIYEVA.

Pioner (Pioneer): Ashgabat; f. 1926; fmrly journal of the Republican Council of the Pioneer Organization of Turkmenistan; juvenile fiction; Editor A. RAKHMANOV.

Politichesky sobesednik (Political Symposium): 744014 Ashgabat 14, Gogolya 28; tel. (3632) 25-12-12; 6 a year; in Russian; publ. by the Democratic Party of Turkmenistan; circ. 2,300.

Sovet edebiyaty: 744000 Ashgabat, Makhtumkuli 5; tel. (3632) 5-14-33; journal of the Union of Writers of Turkmenistan; fiction and literary criticism.

Tokmak (Beetle): 744000 Ashgabat, Atabayeva 20; tel. (3632) 25-10-39; f. 1925; satirical; Editor TACHMAMED JURDEKOV.

Turkmenistanyn oba khozhalygy (Agriculture of Turkmenistan): Ashgabat; f. 1957; journal of the Ministry of Agriculture; Editor B. POLLIKOV.

NEWS AGENCY

Turkmen Press: Ashgabat; Dir MURAD KARANOV.

Publishers

Magaryf Publishing House: Ashgabat; Dir N. ATAYEV.

Turkmenistan Publishing House: Ashgabat, Gogolya 17A; politics and fiction; Dir A. M. JANMURADOV.

Ylym Publishing House: 744000 Ashgabat, Engelsa 6; tel. (3632) 9-04-84; f. 1952; science; Dir B. M. AKMAMEDOV.

Radio and Television

State Committee for Television and Radio: 744024 Ashgabat, Kurortnaya III; Chair. ANNAGELDY ORAZDURDYEV.

Turkmen Radio: broadcasts local programmes and relays from Russia in Turkmen and Russian.

Turkmen Television: Ashgabat; broadcasts local programmes and relays from Russia in Turkmen and Russian.

Finance

BANKING

Reforms in the financial system of the USSR were initiated in 1988 with the introduction of a two-tier banking system. Further restructuring of the banking sector took place even before the attainment of full independence during 1991, after which time the republican State Bank was forced to become a full central bank. In November 1993 a Turkmen currency, the manat, was introduced, supported by the country's international reserves.

Central Bank

State Bank of Turkmenistan: Ashgabat; central monetary authority, issuing bank and supervisory authority; Chair. of Bd A. B. BORJAKOV; 3 brs.

Other Banks

Agroprombank: Ashgabat; f. 1989 as independent bank; specializes in agricultural sector; commercial bank.

Foreign Trade Bank of Turkmenistan: Ashgabat; f. 1991 as independent from Soviet Vneshekonombank.

Industry and Construction Bank: Ashgabat; f. 1989 as independent bank; specializes in industrial and construction sector; commercial bank.

Republican Commercial Bank: Ashgabat; f. 1989 as independent bank; fmrly the main commercial bank.

Sberbank—Savings Bank: Ashgabat; f. 1989 as independent bank; 50 brs (1992).

Trade and Industry

CHAMBER OF COMMERCE

Chamber of Commerce and Industry: 744000 Ashgabat, Lakhuti 17; tel. (3632) 25-57-56; Chair. LIDIA N. OSIPOVA.

SELECTED INDUSTRIAL ENTERPRISES

Balkanneftekhimprom: Ashgabat; f. 1992; state petroleum and natural-gas company; operates joint ventures with foreign cos.

Turkmenprod Aktsiyoner (Turkmen Food Joint-Stock Co): Ashgabat; f. 1994; state owned; Dir NEDIRMAMMET ALOVOV.

TRADE UNIONS

Federation of Trade Unions of Turkmenistan: Ashgabat.

Transport

RAILWAYS

The main rail line in the country runs from Krasnovodsk (Turkmenbashi), on the Caspian Sea, in the west, via Ashgabat, to Charjou in the east. From Charjou one line runs to the east, to the other Central Asian countries of the former USSR, while another runs north-west, via Uzbekistan and Kazakhstan, to join the rail network of the Russian Federation. In 1989 the total length of rail track in use was 2,120 km. In 1992 plans were approved for a rail link with Iran on the route Tejen–Sarakhs–Mashhad. From the Iranian town of Mashhad, the railway would be able to join the Iranian rail network and thus provide the possibility of rail travel between Turkmenistan and Istanbul (Turkey).

ROADS

At 31 December 1989 there was a total of 22,600 km of roads, of which 17,800 km were hard-surfaced. In November 1991 a 600-km road was opened between Ashgabat and Tashauz.

SHIPPING

Shipping services link Krasnovodsk (Turkmenbashi) with Baku (Azerbaijan) and the major Iranian ports on the Caspian Sea. The Amu-Dar'ya river is an important inland waterway.

Shipowning Company

Middle-Asia Shipping Company: 746100 Charjou, Flotilskaya 8; Pres. N. B. BAZAROV.

CIVIL AVIATION

Turkmenistan National State Aviacompany: Ashgabat.

Culture

NATIONAL ORGANIZATION

Ministry of Culture and Tourism: see section on The Government (Ministries).

Committee for Physical Culture and Sport (attached to the Cabinet of Ministers): Ashgabat; Chair. A. M. SHANIYAZOV.

CULTURAL HERITAGE

National Library of Turkmenistan: 744000 Ashgabat, K. Marksa; tel. (3632) 25-32-54; f. 1895; 5.5m. vols; Dir S. A. KURBANOV.

National UNESCO Committee: Ashgabat; Chair. GELDYMURAT NURMUKHAMMEDOV.

Turkmen State Museum of Fine Art: 744000 Ashgabat, Pushkina 9; tel. (3632) 25-63-71; f. 1938; 60 mems; library of 6,100 vols; Dir N. SHABUNTS.

Turkmen State United Museum of History and Ethnography: Ashgabat, Shevchenko 1; tel. (3632) 5-58-16; f. 1899; 200,000 exhibits; library of 3,000 vols; Dir A. TADYEV.

PERFORMING ARTS

Makhtumkuli Opera and Ballet Theatre: Ashgabat, Engelsa 9.

Turkmen Drama Theatre: Ashgabat, Kemineh 42.

Pushkin Russian Drama Theatre: Ashgabat, 1-ovo Maya 15.

State Philharmonia of Turkmenistan: Ashgabat, Oktyabrskaya 13.

ASSOCIATION

Union of Writers of Turkmenistan: 744000 Ashgabat, Makhtumkuli 5; tel. (3632) 5-51-78; brs in Mary, Tashauz and Charjou.

Education

There were few educational establishments in pre-revolutionary Turkmenistan, but a state-funded education system was introduced under Soviet rule. Most school education is conducted in Turkmen (76.9% of all pupils at general day-schools in 1988), but there are also schools using Russian (16.0%), Uzbek (6.1%) and Kazakh (1.0%). Until the early 1990s most institutions of higher education used Russian, but there have been attempts to increase the provision of Turkmen-language courses. In 1989 8.3% of the population over 15 years of age had completed courses of higher education. In 1992 it was reported that some 30% of schoolchildren in Turkmenistan studied in shifts, owing to the inadequate provision of staffing and facilities. That year's budget projected that 30% of total expenditure would be allocated to education and science.

UNIVERSITY

Makhtumkuli State University: 744014 Ashgabat, Lenina 31; tel. (3632) 5-11-59; f. 1950 as A. M. Gorky State University; 10 faculties; 11,000 students; Rector Prof. S. N. MURADOV.

Social Welfare

In 1990 the average life expectancy at birth was 66.4 years, the lowest of all the Soviet Republics. In 1989 the rate of infant mortality reached 54.2 per 1,000 live births, the highest rate of any Union Republic. However, under-reporting of mortality rates is widespread and it was estimated that true figures might be 50%–100% higher than offically reported. A basic, state-funded health system was introduced under Soviet rule, but the system was of low quality and underfunded. In 1984–89 there were 274 people per physician and, by the early 1990s, there were 111 hospital beds per 10,000 inhabitants. The high levels of disease in Turkmenistan (among adults as well as children) were attributed to poor overall medical and sanitary conditions, and the critical state of the environment.

In 1991 and the early years of independence, the Turkmen Government introduced extensive social protection measures (mostly the responsibility of a Pension Fund), relatively more generous than in other former Soviet states. Its unemployment compensation scheme was less successful and was abandoned by the end of 1991. Improvements were likely later in the decade, as the benefits of the potential gas and petroleum wealth in the country were realized. In 1993 electricity, gas and water was free for all citizens of the country.

Ministry of Health: see section on The Government (Ministries).

Ministry of Social Security: see section on The Government (Ministries).

The Environment

Turkmenistan experienced severe ecological problems as a result of the desiccation of the lower reaches of the Amu-Dar'ya and the Aral Sea. From the dehydrated sea-bed of the Aral Sea large amounts of salted dust and sand are blown on to fertile areas in northern Turkmenistan, particularly in Tashauz Oblast. Excessive use of chemical pesticides and herbicides in cotton-growing areas also caused severe problems. The chemicals enter the soil and the water supply, and, since only 13% of the population was provided with piped water at the end of the 1980s, most water for domestic use was drawn directly from polluted water channels. In January 1994 Turkmenistan and the four other Central Asian countries agreed to take co-ordinated action against a further deterioration of the Aral Sea ecology and to attempt to restore some of the damage. A joint fund was established for this purpose.

GOVERNMENT ORGANIZATIONS

Ministry of Natural Resources and Environmental Protection: see section on The Government (Ministries).

Ministry of Water Management: see section on The Government (Ministries).

ACADEMIC INSTITUTES

Academy of Sciences of the Republic of Turkmenistan: 744000 Ashgabat, Gogolya 15; tel. (3632) 25-49-49; telex 228164; Pres. A. G. BABAYEV; institutes incl.:

Commission on Nature Conservation: 744000 Ashgabat, Gogolya 15; attached to the Presidium; Chair. A. O. TASHILIYEV.

Desert Research Institute: 744000 Ashgabat, Gogolya 15; tel. (3632) 29-54-27; fax (3632) 25-37-16; f. 1962; programmes incl. research into desert resources and arid environment problems; incl. International Centre for Research and Training in the Problems of Desertification; Dir A. G. BABAYEV; Dep. Dir A. P. ZHUMASHOV.

Scientific Consultative Ecological Centre (EKOTSENTR): Ashgabat, Gogolya 15; Chair. A. G. BABAYEV.

NON-GOVERNMENTAL ORGANIZATIONS

Turkmenistan Society for the Conservation of Nature: Ashgabat, 1-ovo Maya 62; Dir A. K. RUSTAMOV.

Dashkhovuz Ecology Club: 746301 Dashkhovuz, Micro-rayon Ts-1, d. 8, kv. 23; tel. (36022) 2-62-23; only registered grass-roots environmental org.; enforces anti-poaching regulations; Co-Chair. VALERI DAVIDOV, ANDREY LVOVICH ZATOKA.

Defence

The national armed forces of Turkmenistan began to be formed in mid-1992, based on former Soviet forces which had been based in the territory of the Republic. By agreement with Russia, these forces were under the joint control of Turkmenistan and the Russian Federation, although this was a transition agreement, with the intention of introducing autonomous Turkmen control by the mid-1990s. In June 1993, according to Western estimates, the national army, which was under the joint control of Turkmenistan and the Russian Federation, numbered some 28,000; there was also an air force. Russia and Kazakhstan co-operated with Turkmenistan in the operation of the Caspian Sea Flotilla, another former Soviet force, which was based at Astrakhan (Russia). However, Turkmenistan did intend to form its own navy. In September 1993 the country's first military institute opened (formerly a department of Makhtumkuli University). In December Turkmenistan agreed that Russian troops should be stationed on its southern borders.

Supreme Commander of the Armed Forces: President of the Republic.

Chief of the General Staff: Maj.-Gen. ANNAMYRAT SOLTANOV.

Bibliography

Akiner, S. *Islamic People of the Soviet Union: An Historical and Statistical Handbook*, 2nd Edn. London and New York, Kegan Paul International, 1987.

Akiner, S. (Ed.). *Cultural Change and Continuity*. London, KPI, 1991.

McCagg, W. O., and Silver, B. (Eds). *Soviet Asian Ethnic Frontiers*. New York and Oxford, Pergamon, 1979.

Rumer, B. Z. *Soviet Central Asia: A Tragic Experiment*. Boston, Unwin Hyman, 1989.

Saray, M. *The Turkmen in the Age of Imperialism: A Study of the Turkmen People and their Incorporation into the Russian Empire*. Ankara, Turkish Historical Society Printing House, 1989.

Wheeler, G. *The Modern History of Soviet Central Asia*. London and New York, Weidenfeld and Nicholson, 1964.

UKRAINE

Geography

PHYSICAL FEATURES

The Republic of Ukraine (formerly the Ukrainian Soviet Socialist Republic, a constituent part of the USSR) is situated in eastern Europe. It is bordered by Poland and Slovakia to the west and by Hungary, Romania and Moldova to the south-west. In the western part of the country the northern border is with Belarus, while in eastern Ukraine the northern and eastern borders are with the Russian Federation. To the south lie the Black Sea and the Sea of Azov. Ukraine covers an area of 603,700 sq km (233,089 sq miles) and is the largest country entirely within Europe. Its territory includes the Autonomous Republic of Crimea, which lies on a peninsula in the south of the country, with the Sea of Azov, to the east, and the Black Sea to the south, west and north-west almost completely surrounding it.

The relief consists of a steppe lowland, bordered by uplands to the west and south-west, and by the Crimean mountains in the south, on the Crimean Peninsula. The main rivers are the Dnieper (Dnipro), which drains the central regions of the country and flows into the Black Sea, and the Dniester (Dniestr), which flows through Western Ukraine and Moldova before also entering the Black Sea, near Odessa. In the south, to the south-west of Odessa, Ukraine has a short border on the Danube (Dunay) delta.

CLIMATE

The climate is temperate, especially in the south. The north and north-west share many of the continental climate features of Poland or Belarus, but the Black Sea coast is noted for its mild winters. Droughts are not infrequent in southern areas. Average temperatures in Kiev range from −6.1°C (21°F) in January to 20.4°C (69°F) in July. Average annual rainfall in Kiev is 615 mm.

POPULATION

According to official estimates, the total population at 1 January 1992 was 52,057,000. At the 1989 census Ukrainians formed the largest ethnic group, comprising 72.7% of the total population, while 22.1% were Russians. There were also significant minorities of Belarusians, Moldovans (Romanians) and Poles. The official state language is Ukrainian, an Eastern Slavonic language written in the Cyrillic script. Most of the population are adherents of Christianity, the major denominations being the Ukrainian Orthodox Church (an Exarchate of the Russian Orthodox Church), the Ukrainian Autocephalous Orthodox Church and the Roman Catholic Church (mostly 'Greek' Catholics or Uniates, users of the Byzantine Rite). There are also a number of Protestant churches and small communities of Jews and Muslims. During the 1990s numerous pseudo-Christian and apocalyptic sects appeared.

The capital is Kiev (Kyiv), which had a population of 2,616,000 in 1990. It is situated in the north of the country, on the Dnieper river. Other large towns include Kharkov (Kharkiv, population 1,618,000 in 1990), Dnepropetrovsk (Dnipropetrovsk, 1,187,000—formerly Yekaterinoslav), the port of Odessa (Odesa, 1,106,000), Donetsk (Donetsk, 1,117,000) and Lvov (Lviv, 798,000—formerly Lemberg). The capital of the Crimea is Simferopol (349,000 in 1990), although its largest town is Sevastopol (Sebastopol—361,000).

Chronology

***c.* 878:** The Eastern Slavs founded the state of Kievan Rus, with Kiev (Kyiv) as its capital.

***c.* 988:** Kievan Rus officially converted to Orthodox Christianity, following the baptism of its ruler, Volodymyr I (Vladimir 'the Great').

1237–40: As a result of internecine feuds over the succession, the defenceless Kievan state was captured by invading Mongol Tatars.

1596: By the Union of Brest a number of Orthodox bishops, mainly in what is modern Western Ukraine and Belarus, acknowledged the primacy of the Roman Catholic spiritual leader, the Pope.

1648: Bohdan Khmelnitsky led a rebellion by Ukrainian Cossacks against their Polish overlords, which resulted in the formation of a Cossack state in eastern Ukraine.

1654: Eastern Ukraine came under Russian rule under the terms of the Treaty of Pereyaslavl.

1667: Ukraine was divided between the Polish-Lithuanian Commonwealth (which gained the western region) and the Russian Empire (which gained Ukrainian territory east of the Dnieper).

1709: Ivan Mazeppa, Hetman (ruler) of the Ukrainian Cossack state, supported Charles XII of Sweden in his invasion of Ukraine; the Russian army defeated the Swedes and the Cossack state was incorporated into the Russian Empire.

1793: At the Second Partition of Poland the regions of Galicia, Transcarpathia (Carpatho-Ruthenia) and Bukovyna (Bucovina) were acquired by the Habsburgs, while the rest of Western Ukraine came under Russian rule.

1861: Emancipation of the Serfs throughout the Russian Empire.

1917: Following the collapse of the Russian Empire, Ukrainian nationalists formed a Central Rada (council or soviet) in Kiev.

9 January 1918: The Rada proclaimed a Ukrainian People's Republic.

9 February 1918: The Central Powers (Germany and Austria-Hungary) recognized the independence of the new country in a peace treaty.

April 1918: Following the signing of the Treaty of Brest-Litovsk, under which the Bolshevik Russian authorities ceded Ukraine to Germany, the Government of the Ukrainian People's Republic was replaced by a pro-German administration, headed by Hetman Pavlo Skoropadsky.

December 1918: With the defeat of Germany, Skoropadsky was deposed and a liberal Directorate Government was established in Ukraine.

1919: The Ukrainian People's Republic was united with the Western Ukrainian People's Republic (formed after the collapse of the Habsburg Monarchy the previous year).

December 1920: A Ukrainian Soviet Socialist Republic (SSR) was proclaimed in eastern Ukraine, following the occupation of the area by the Soviet Red Army; later that month (20 December) the Republic signed a Treaty of Alliance with the Bolshevik administration in Russia.

18 March 1921: The Soviet–Polish War was formally ended by the signing of the Treaty of Riga; the Treaty provided for the division of Western Ukraine between Poland (Galicia), Czechoslovakia (Transcarpathia) and Romania (Bucovina—Romania had also acquired the previously Russian territory of Bessarabia).

30 December 1922: At the 10th All-Russian (first All-Union) Congress of Soviets the Union of Soviet Socialist Republics (USSR) was proclaimed; the Ukrainian SSR was a founding member.

1928: The New Economic Policy (NEP), in effect since 1921 and under which Ukraine had thrived, was abandoned by the all-Union Government; it was replaced by a system of forced collectivization of agriculture.

1929: The right-wing Organization of Ukrainian Nationalists (OUN) was founded in Galicia.

1932–33: The Great Famine, the direct result of Stalin's (Iosif V. Dzhugashvili) policy of collectivization, claimed the lives of some 6m.–7m. Ukrainian peasants.

1933: Mykola Skrypnyk, the moderate leader of the Communist Party of Ukraine (CPU), committed suicide; Stalin appointed a close political ally, Lazar Kaganovich, to replace him.

1936–38: Large numbers of the Ukrainian cultural and political élite suffered in what came to be known as the 'Great Purge', a series of mass arrests and executions by the Soviet security police, the NKVD (People's Commissariat for Internal Affairs), under the leadership of Nikolay Yezhov.

June 1941: The German army invaded Ukraine, as part of 'Operation Barbarossa'. Later in the year, in Lvov (Lviv), Ukrainian nationalists declared independence from the Soviet Government.

1943: The Ukrainian Insurgent Army (UPA) was established by the OUN; the partisans continued to carry out attacks against the Communist Government into the early 1950s.

9 May 1945: Following Germany's unconditional surrender the Second World War ended in Europe; Ukraine had suffered considerable damage during the conflict and some 6m. inhabitants were estimated to have died. The hitherto Czechoslovak region of Transcarpathia subsequently became part of the Ukrainian SSR; Northern Bucovina and southern Bessarabia (Romanian territories between the World Wars) became part of Ukraine, and it regained some of the territories on the Dniester taken to form a Moldovan (Moldavian) autonomous region in 1924.

26 June 1945: The Ukrainian SSR was one of 50 countries to sign the Charter of the United Nations.

1954: During Nikita Khrushchev's period as Soviet leader Ukraine gained the territory of the Crimea, a peninsula on the Black Sea previously controlled by Russia. The Crimea's Tatar population had been deported to Central Asia by Stalin in 1944.

1963: Petro Shelest became First Secretary of the CPU; during his time in office a nationalist intellectual movement developed in Ukraine and many independent (*samizdat*) publications were produced.

1972: Shelest was replaced as Communist leader by Volodymyr Shcherbytsky, a politician loyal to the all-Union Government.

1976: The Helsinki Group was founded in Ukraine to monitor the effects in the Republic of the Helsinki Final Act (the human-rights final agreement signed by 32 European countries, Canada and the USA in Finland the previous year). The Group was subsequently suppressed, but re-emerged as the Ukrainian Helsinki Union in 1988.

26 April 1986: A serious explosion took place at the Chernobyl nuclear power station in northern Ukraine; large discharges of radioactive material occurred but information concerning the accident was suppressed for a time.

1987: Mikhail Gorbachev, the Soviet leader, granted amnesty to a large number of Ukrainian political prisoners.

November 1988: The Ukrainian People's Movement for Restructuring (Rukh) was founded in Kiev.

10–19 July 1989: Miners in the Donbass region of Ukraine went on strike in protest at their living conditions.

September 1989: Rukh, headed by Ivan Drach, held its founding conference. On 28 September Vladimir Shcherbitsky resigned, following his failure to control the opposition movement and the miners' unrest; Volodymyr Ivashko replaced Shcherbitsky as First Secretary.

December 1989: The Soviet leader granted official recognition to the Ukrainian Uniate Church (users of the Roman Catholic Byzantine Rite), following a meeting with Pope John Paul II.

4 March 1990: Elections were held to the Ukrainian Supreme Soviet; Rukh, participating as a member of the Democratic Bloc electoral coalition, won 108 of a total of 450 seats.

June 1990: Ivashko was elected Chairman of the republican Supreme Soviet and subsequently resigned as First Secretary of the CPU, following protests by opposition deputies at his holding the two posts simultaneously. He was succeeded by Stanislav Hurenko.

16 July 1990: The Ukrainian Supreme Soviet adopted a declaration of sovereignty, which asserted the right of Ukraine to possess its own military and proclaimed the supremacy of republican law on its territory. In the same month, Ivashko was appointed Deputy General Secretary of the Communist Party of the Soviet Union (CPSU).

23 July 1990: Leonid Kravchuk, formerly Second Secretary of the CPU, was elected Chairman of the Ukrainian Supreme Soviet in succession to Ivashko.

17 October 1990: Vitaly Masol, Chairman of the Council of Ministers (Prime Minister), was forced to resign, following two weeks of protests by students in Kiev. Vitold Fokin was elected to replace him the following month.

20 January 1991: In a referendum the inhabitants of the Crimea voted to restore to the region the status of an autonomous republic.

17 March 1991: In an all-Union referendum on the issue of the future status of the USSR, 70.5% of Ukrainian participants approved Gorbachev's concept of a 'renewed federation'; an additional question on Ukrainian sovereignty gained 80.2% of the vote, while a third question on outright independence (which was held only in parts of Western Ukraine) won 88.4% support.

24 August 1991: Following the attempted *coup d'état* in Moscow, the Ukrainian Supreme Soviet adopted a declaration of independence, by 346 votes to one, pending approval by referendum on 1 December.

30 August 1991: The CPU was declared illegal.

1 December 1991: Presidential elections were held simultaneously with a referendum on Ukraine's declaration of independence, in which 90.3% of participants voted in favour; Leonid Kravchuk was elected to the new post of executive President of the Republic, with 61.3% of the votes cast.

8 December 1991: At a meeting in Belarus the leaders of Ukraine, Belarus and the Russian Federation agreed to form a Commonwealth of Independent States (CIS) to replace the USSR.

21 December 1991: At a meeting in Almaty (Kazakhstan) a protocol on the formation of the Commonwealth was signed by the leaders of 11 former Republics of the USSR; the resignation of Gorbachev as Soviet President (25 December) confirmed the dissolution of the Union.

30 December 1991: In Minsk (Belarus) members of the CIS agreed to establish a joint command for armed forces; use of nuclear weapons was to be under the control of the President of the Russian Federation, in consultation with the leaders of the other nuclear states: Ukraine, Belarus and Kazakhstan.

January 1992: New Ukraine, a grouping of parliamentary deputies whose aim was to promote radical economic reform, was formed in the Supreme Soviet (subsequently known as the Supreme Council—Verkhovna Rada).

5 May 1992: The Crimean parliament voted to declare independence from Ukraine. The resolution was annulled the following week by the Ukrainian legislature.

June 1992: Fokin's administration narrowly avoided defeat in a 'no-confidence' vote proposed by New Ukraine. The Crimean peninsula was granted full autonomy by the Ukrainian Government.

July 1992: The Ukrainian Government ended all price controls, a move which provoked strong criticism from the opposition and resulted in the dismissal by President Kravchuk of Volodymyr Lanovy, the Minister of the Economy; he was replaced by Volodymyr Symonenko, a less radical figure.

30 September 1992: Fokin's Government resigned, having been heavily defeated in a vote of 'no confidence'; the premier was held responsible for the rapid price increases in Ukraine and the country's budget deficit.

13 October 1992: Leonid Kuchma was approved as Prime Minister by the Verkhovna Rada; several members of Rukh and New Ukraine were appointed to the new Government.

13 November 1992: The rouble ceased to be legal tender in Ukraine; it was was replaced by the karbovanets, a currency coupon, which was intended as a transitionary stage to the introduction of a new Ukrainian currency.

21 November 1992: The Verkhovna Rada granted Kuchma emergency powers to rule by decree for a period of six months.

February 1993: In response to a campaign to reinstate the CPU a group of some 30 political organizations established the Anti-Communist and Anti-Imperialist Front.

March 1993: In the wake of sharp criticism by President Kravchuk of the Government's budget proposals a leading reformist, Ihor Yukhnovsky, resigned as deputy premier (Yuhym Zvyahilsky succeeded him in June). The following month Viktor Pynzenyk, who had headed the Government's reform programme, was relieved of his duties as economy minister. Pynzenyk was replaced by a conservative, Yury Bannikov.

20 May 1993: Following the Verkhovna Rada's refusal to extend his emergency powers, and a bid by President Kravchuk to head the Government (now known as the Cabinet of Ministers) himself, Kuchma tendered his resignation. The following day both Kuchma's resignation and Kravchuk's request were refused by parliament.

May 1993: The Presidium of the Verkhovna Rada decided to allow the re-establishment of the CPU.

16 June 1993: An emergency committee, headed by Leonid Kuchma, was established by presidential decree to deal with the critical political and economic situation in Ukraine, following widespread industrial action in the east. The following day the Verkhovna Rada submitted to the demand of the strikers to hold a nation-wide vote of confidence in the President and the parliament. (The referendum was cancelled in mid-August.)

17 June 1993: The Presidents of Ukraine and Russia agreed to divide the 350-vessel Black Sea Fleet, based at Sevastopol, equally between the two states, but agreed to delay the division of the Fleet until 1995. At the end of June this decision was rejected by the officers of the Fleet, who demanded that it be placed solely under Russian jurisdiction.

2 July 1993: The Verkhovna Rada declared the right to own all Soviet nuclear weapons (a total of 176 ballistic missiles) on its territory, but announced that it intended to become a non-nuclear state in the future. This stance was officially supported by Kravchuk the following week.

14 July 1993: The Verkhovna Rada adopted a resolution condemning the claim by the Russian Supreme Soviet to Sevastopol. Two days later several thousand inhabitants of the Crimea (now recognized as an Autonomous Republic) supported the claim.

27 August 1993: Pynzenyk resigned from his post as deputy premier.

30 August 1993: Yury Bannikov was relieved of his duties as Minister of the Economy at his own request, and was replaced by his deputy, Roman Shpek. Kuchma presented an emergency programme of anti-inflationary measures to the Verkhovna Rada, which was rejected two days later.

3 September 1993: Following a meeting at Massandra, Kravchuk and Russian President Boris Yeltsin announced that former Soviet nuclear warheads (estimated to number between 1,600 and 1,800) on the territory of Ukraine would be transferred to Russia for dismantling; an agreement was also reached whereby Ukraine would sell its share of the Black Sea Fleet to Russia in return for the supply of nuclear fuel; the accord was reached under pressure from Ukraine's outstanding debt to Russia for petroleum and natural gas (estimated at some US $2,500m).

9 September 1993: Kuchma resigned for the third time in four months, in protest at parliamentary opposition to his economic programme. The premier's resignation was accepted by the Verkhovna Rada two weeks later, which simultaneously passed a vote of 'no confidence' in the entire Cabinet.

22 September 1993: Kravchuk appointed Yuhym Zvyahilsky, a proponent of increased state involvement in the economy, acting premier. Three days later, plans for a general strike to be held on 28 September were cancelled, owing to the decision by the Verkhovna Rada to hold early parliamentary and presidential elections (on 27 March 1994 and 26 June respectively).

27 September 1993: Kravchuk assumed direct leadership of the Cabinet of Ministers.

4 October 1993: Kostyantyn Morozov, the Minister of Defence (a member of the old nomenklatura, whose reappointment by Kravchuk had elicited some criticism), resigned and was succeeded by Col-Gen. V. Radetsky.

21 October 1993: The Verkhovna Rada voted to abandon plans to close the three surviving nuclear reactors at the Chernobyl nuclear power station. Four days later Ukraine agreed with the USA that it would dismantle its ex-Soviet nuclear warheads; in return the country was to receive some US $175m. in US economic aid. (On 20 December Ukraine announced that 17 of its 46 SS-24 strategic nuclear missiles had been deactivated.)

30 October 1993: The Ukrainian draft constitution was published.

18 November 1993: A draft resolution ratifying the first Strategic Arms' Reduction Treaty (START 1) was approved by parliament, but with major conditions which seemed likely to delay implementation of the accord for some time.

8 December 1993: The Cabinet of Ministers declared a state of emergency in Ukraine, owing to the critical economic situation in the country.

14 January 1994: President Kravchuk signed an agreement on nuclear disarmament in Moscow (Russia) with the US and Russian Presidents; Ukraine was to give up its warheads in return for security guarantees and financial aid amounting to US $1,000m.

20 January 1994: Iskender Memetov, the Crimean Tatar leader, was shot in the Crimean capital, Simferopol. He died two days later.

30 January 1994: The final round of voting took place for the Crimean presidential elections; Yury Meshkov, a Russian nationalist, won 72.9% of the votes cast, while his rival, Nikolay Bahrov, won 23.5%.

3 February 1994: The Verkhovna Rada agreed to remove the conditions it had previously placed on ratification of the START 1 agreement but refused to join the Nuclear Non-Proliferation Treaty.

8 February 1944: Ukraine became a signatory to 'Partnership for Peace', the security arrangement for Eastern Europe and the former Soviet states proposed by the North Atlantic Treaty Organisation (NATO).

2 March 1994: Meshkov demanded the withdrawal of all Ukrainian troops stationed in the Crimea.

3 March 1994: The Russian Federation drastically reduced natural-gas deliveries to Ukraine, claiming that Ukraine owed US $700m. for fuel received. The previous month Turkmenistan had ceased to supply Ukraine with natural gas for the same reason.

27 March 1994: Elections were held to the all-Ukrainian and Crimean parliaments. After a second round of voting to the Verkhovna Rada, on 12 April, the CPU had gained a total of 75 seats—the largest representation of any party. Rukh came second with 26.

History

Dr ANDREW WILSON

EARLY HISTORY

Kievan Rus, the first state of the Eastern Slavs (Ukrainians, Belarusians and Russians) existed on the territory of what is now Ukraine from the ninth to the 11th centuries. Its great princes, Volodymyr I (Vladimir 'the Great', who ruled from 980 to 1015) and Yaroslav 'the Wise' (1034–1054), led their subjects in conversion to Orthodox Christians (Volodymyr himself was baptized in 988) and made Rus the dominant power in Eastern Europe and an integral part of the European system of states. From the 12th century onwards, however, Rus declined, as rival princes quarrelled over the succession, leaving the state defenceless against the invading Mongol Tatars, who captured Kiev (Kyiv), the capital of Rus, in 1240. The tradition and culture of Rus was subsequently dispersed among several states. The Russians would later claim that the states of Novgorod and Muscovy were the main direct descendants of Rus, the Belarusians would point to the Polish-Lithuanian Commonwealth (the Grand Duchy of Lithuania was largely founded by Orthodox Eastern Slavs), while the Ukrainians claim that the traditions of Rus continued to thrive in the kingdom of Galicia-Volyn and elsewhere. Certainly, modern Ukrainians are fond of reminding Russians that Kievan civilization is much older than that of Moscow. However, there can be no doubt that what are now Ukrainian lands fell under the domination of foreign overlords (Poles, Lithuanians and Belarusians, Mongols and Ottoman Turks) for several centuries until a Ukrainian revival began in Kiev in the 16th and 17th centuries. This was based in the restoration of the local Orthodox Church and in the foundation of free Cossack settlements throughout southern Ukraine. The national revival culminated in the large-scale Ukrainian Cossack rebellion led by Bohdan Khmelnytsky in 1648. Khmelnytsky established a short-lived Cossack state after a series of overwhelming military victories against the Poles, but his search for allies led him to sign the Treaty of Pereyaslavl with Russia in 1654, under which Khmelnytsky recognized the suzerainty of the Russian Tsar in return for Russia's protection against the Poles. During the rule of Khmelnytsky's weaker successors, the Russian tsars used the Treaty as a means of incorporating Ukrainian territory (sometimes known as 'Little Russia') into their Empire. Ukrainian dreams of independence finally ended, after the rebellion of Ivan Mazeppa was defeated at the Battle of Poltava in 1709. The Russian tsars gained further Ukrainian territory with the Partitions of Poland in 1793–95, while other lands in the west (Galicia, Transcarpathia and Bukovyna) came under Habsburg rule. Even at the end of the 20th century marked differences in culture, religion (most Western Ukrainians are adherents of the Uniate, or 'Greek' Catholic Church—originally created by Eastern Orthodox bishops being persuaded to acknowledge the jurisdiction of the Roman Catholic Church of their rulers—see p. 19) and levels of national consciousness existed between Western and eastern and central Ukraine as a consequence of their separate historical development.

NATIONAL REVIVAL

In the 19th century, when it seemed that Ukrainian traditions and culture were on the verge of disappearing, a strong Ukrainian national revival occurred. A standardized Ukrainian language emerged out of the several Ukrainian dialects and became a codified literary language (although its use was banned by the Russian rulers in 1863 and 1876). Its most gifted exponent was the greatest of all Ukrainian national heroes, the poet Taras Shevchenko (1814–61). The small Ukrainian intelligentsia of this period formed a series of 'underground' patriotic organizations, which developed into political parties when political conditions in Ukraine became less repressive after the 1905 revolution. Even after the fall of the tsarist regime in February 1917, however, such parties still commanded little support. Most Ukrainian political activists continued to support the ideas of Mykhaylo Drahomanov (1841–95), who had proposed a federal union between Ukraine and Russia.

Nevertheless, the Ukrainian political parties and the population as a whole were quickly radicalized by the events of 1917. A Central Rada (council or soviet) was established in Kiev in mid-1917, headed by the historian Mykhaylo Hrushevsky (1866–1934). On 9 January 1918, in the aftermath of the Bolshevik Revolution, the Rada proclaimed a Ukrainian People's Republic. From this time until 1921 a series of weak governments ruled Ukraine, while Ukrainians, Bolsheviks, 'Whites' (anti-Bolshevik forces) and Poles fought for possession of the Republic. Even the union in January 1919 of the Ukrainian People's Republic with the Western Ukrainian People's Republic (formed out of those Ukrainian lands under Habsburg rule when the Austro-Hungarian Empire disintegrated in late 1918) failed to protect Ukraine against foreign invasion.

In April 1918 the liberal Government of the Ukrainian People's Republic was overthrown by 'Hetman' Pavlo Skoropadsky, a powerful conservative backed by the German army. (The Bolsheviks had been forced to cede Ukraine to Germany under the terms of the Treaty of Brest-Litovsk, signed on 3 March 1918.) Skoropadsky's rule ended in December 1918, with the Germans' defeat, and the politicians of the Ukrainian People's Republic returned to form a more left-wing Directorate Government under Volodymyr Vynnychenko and Symon Petlyura. However, this administration was unable to defend Ukraine against repeated invasions by the Bolshevik Red Army and in 1920 a Ukrainian Soviet Socialist Republic (SSR) was established. By 1921 Soviet rule over most of Ukraine was secure. Western Ukraine, however, continued its separate path of development, despite the attempted union of 1919, because the Polish army had occupied most of it. At the end of the Soviet–Polish War, under the terms of the Treaty of Riga (concluded on 18 March 1921), Galicia fell under Polish rule, Transcarpathia became part of the new Czechoslovak state (and was known as Carpatho-Ruthenia—Ruthenians are usually considered to be a Ukrainian people), and Bukovyna (Bucovina) was assigned to the Romanians. Ukraine was one of the founding members of the Union of Soviet Socialist Republics (USSR), which was established on 30 December 1922.

SOVIET UKRAINE

Ironically, the Ukrainians prospered under Soviet rule in the 1920s. The New Economic Policy (NEP), introduced in 1921, benefited Ukraine's peasant agriculture, and Ukrainian language and culture was recognized, and even promoted, in a manner unthinkable under the tsars. A cultural 'Golden Age' produced writers such as Mykola Khvylovy and Borys Antonenko-Davydovych. Moreover, the leadership of the Ukrainian SSR was entrusted to local Ukrainian leaders such as Mykola Skrypnyk, who began to promote Ukrainian interests aggressively. However, this caused a defensive reaction amongst Ukraine's ethnic Russian population, which was still predominant in the cities and in working class organizations, especially in eastern Ukraine. Soviet leader Stalin (Iosif V. Dzhugashvili), moreover, began to suspect that he was encouraging the development of a new generation of nationalists. The Ukrainian leaders were all purged in the early 1930s and Stalin appointed Lazar Kaganovich, the notorious executor of his repressive policies, to run Ukraine. Skrypnyk committed suicide in 1933.

The collectivization of agriculture (begun in 1928, after the abandonment of the NEP) affected Ukraine worst of all the Soviet Republics. Between 6m. and 7m. Ukrainian peasants perished in the Great Famine of 1932–33, which some claimed was deliberately engineered to weaken Ukrainian resistance to Stalin's rule. The Ukrainian political élite again suffered heavily in the Great Purge of 1936–38. The outbreak of the Second World War in 1939 gave Stalin the opportunity to seize the Western Ukrainian territories, briefly reunited with central and eastern Ukraine in 1919. Galicia was annexed with the partition of Poland in 1939 and Bukovyna (Northern Bucovina) was taken from Romania in 1940. The territories were lost to Germany, following that country's invasion of the USSR in 1941, but were regained in 1944. The USSR also gained the Romanian territory of Bessarabia, most of which became part of the Moldovan (Moldavian) SSR, which had originally been formed as the Autonomous Soviet Socialist Republic in 1924 from Ukrainian territory on the east bank of the Dniester river. Some of this territory was formally restored to Ukraine in 1940, which also gained southern Bessarabia (the coastal regions south-east of Odessa). Transcarpathia was added to the Ukrainian SSR in 1945.

The incorporation of Western Ukraine into the USSR proved a mixed blessing for Stalin, however. A more extreme style of Ukrainian nationalism had developed in Galicia, in particular under the relatively liberal conditions of Habsburg and then Polish rule. The extreme right-wing Organization of Ukrainian Nationalists (OUN), established in Galicia in 1929, first fought against Polish rule and then took the opportunity provided by the German invasion in 1941 to initiate an armed uprising against Soviet rule in Ukraine. A symbolic declaration of Ukrainian independence in the Western Ukrainian centre of Lvov (Lviv) in 1941 was soon suppressed, but the OUN founded the Ukrainian Insurgent Army (UPA) in 1943. Inevitably, the UPA attracted many disaffected Ukrainians (some 50,000–100,000) to its ranks and continued to fight in apparently hopeless conditions until the early 1950s.

Stalin's victory in the Second World War resulted in the unification of most ethnically Ukrainian territory into the Ukrainian SSR (Ukraine gained more territory than any other European nation in the post-War settlement). Further expansion of its territory occurred in 1954, when the Crimea (formerly part of Russia) was granted to Ukraine. The Republic remained a multi-ethnic state. (In 1989, of its population of 51.5m., 72% were Ukrainians, 22% Russians and 6% other minorities.) Substantial minority problems existed amongst the Russian population in eastern Ukraine and the Crimea, amongst the Hungarians and Ruthenians of Transcarpathia, and the Romanians of Bukovyna. Nationalist sentiment was again suppressed in Stalin's later years, but after the dictator's death in 1953 ethnic Ukrainians once again began to head the Communist Party of Ukraine (CPU) and the Republic slowly and carefully began to reassert its distinct national interests. In particular, Petro Shelest, the leader of the CPU in 1963–72, attempted to maximize Ukrainian independence from the all-Union Government and to protect the dissident movement which revived in the 1960s. Shelest's policies resulted in his replacement in 1972 by the arch-conservative Volodymyr Shcherbytsky, who maintained strict control over Ukraine on behalf of the all-Union Government until his final departure in September 1989, several years after the reformist, Mikhail Gorbachev, became First Secretary of the CPSU.

Shcherbytsky oversaw a widespread purge of all dissident elements in Ukrainian society in 1972–73, which halted the nationalist movement for several years. Although attempts were made to revive nationalist dissent, as with the establishment of the Ukrainian Helsinki Group in 1976, they were suppressed. On the eve of the Gorbachev era, therefore, Ukraine appeared to be a bastion of Communist orthodoxy.

THE ERA OF REFORM IN UKRAINE: 1985–91

Although Gorbachev came to power in 1985, little changed in Ukraine until Shcherbytsky's departure in 1989. The accident at the Chernobyl nuclear power station on 26 April 1986 was to have serious long-term consequences in discrediting the Ukrainian regime, but it was initially kept secret. Dissident groups began slowly to revive in Ukraine in 1987–88, with the mass release of Ukrainian political prisoners, but the Ukrainian Helsinki Union, refounded in 1988, was harassed at every turn. Attempts to form a Ukrainian popular front, after the fashion of the Baltic Republics, were constantly frustrated by the Ukrainian Government. In September 1989, however, the opposition Ukrainian Movement for Restructuring (Rukh), which had been formed in November 1988, was finally permitted to hold its inaugural congress. In the same month Shcherbytsky resigned, following his dismissal from the CPSU Politburo.

Rukh was able to participate indirectly, as part of the Democratic Bloc, in the republican elections held in Ukraine on 4 March 1990. It won almost one-quarter of the seats in the Ukrainian Supreme Soviet (108 parliamentary seats out of a total of 450). The Democratic Bloc was mainly successful in Western Ukraine and Kiev (the opposition also took over the three Galician local councils and some towns in Central Ukraine). Nevertheless, Shcherbytsky's successor, Volodymyr Ivashko, continued to maintain a pro-Union line. In July, however, Ivashko abandoned his political posts in Ukraine to become Deputy General Secretary of the CPSU under Gorbachev. This resulted in a sudden radicalization of the political mood in Ukraine. Moreover, Ivashko's functions were subsequently divided between two officials. Stanislav Hurenko became First Secretary of the CPU, and continued to pursue the conservative policies of Shcherbytsky and Ivashko, but the chairmanship of the increasingly powerful Ukrainian Supreme Soviet was granted to CPU Second Secretary Leonid Kravchuk, who was soon pursuing a more nationalist course and forging links with Rukh. The Ukrainian Supreme Soviet passed the radical Declaration of Ukrainian Sovereignty by 355 votes to four in July 1990. This stressed the supremacy of Ukrainian legislation over all-Union law and asserted Ukraine's right to issue its own currency, to chart an independent foreign policy and even to possess its own armed forces. Many Communists had voted for the Declaration simply as a means of increasing their popularity and several months of bitter political struggle now ensued. Most of the CPU majority in the Supreme Soviet (the so-called 'Group of 239') blocked attempts by the nationalist opposition to adopt measures which would give the Declaration real political content. The first trial of strength between the two rival groups were the 'hunger strikes' by radical students which occurred in Kiev between 2 and 16 October. The participants in the strike won the public's sympathy and a series of mass demonstrations took place. The Chairman of the Council of Ministers, Vitaly Masol, was forced to resign and the authorities were obliged to make a series of important concessions to the students, including the promise of new elections and the nationalization of the property of the CPU. (Masol was succeeded in November by Vitold Fokin.) Moreover, it was agreed that Ukraine would not sign Gorbachev's proposed new Union Treaty until a new constitution had been agreed.

Most of these concessions were soon forgotten, however, as Hurenko and the conservative members of the all-Union Government engineered a dramatic change in the political climate in Ukraine at the end of 1990 and the beginning of 1991. The right to public demonstration was curtailed in the Republic and parliamentary rules were changed so that the opposition could no longer disrupt proceedings simply by leaving the chamber. In November 1990 the radical deputy Stepan Khmara was deprived of his parliamentary immunity and arrested on fraudulent charges of assault. In January 1991 Hurenko supported the all-Union Government's use of force in the Baltic Republics and it was suspected that the radical local councils (rada) of Western Ukraine would be the next target of repression. At this point, however, Kravchuk broke away from the rest of the CPU and signed a resolution of the Presidium of the Ukrainian Supreme Soviet condemning the killings in Latvia and Lithuania. Fearful that they too would soon be the victims of force, the Supreme Soviet began to adopt measures to defend their sovereignty. They were further encouraged to do so after Gorbachev retreated from his aggressive position with regard to the Baltic Republics, as it now appeared that the all-Union Government was unwilling or unable to use force to prevent the Republics seceding. Kravchuk skilfully avoided confrontation over the issue of the preservation of the USSR in Gorbachev's referendum of 17 March 1991 by adding a second question on to the Ukrainian ballot, concerning the need to defend Ukrainian sovereignty. Gorbachev's question received 70.5% support in Ukraine, but Kravchuk's question received an 80.2% vote in favour. (Some 88.4% of participants supported a third question on outright independence, asked only in Western Ukraine, in the Lvov, Ternopol and Ivano-Frankovsk Oblasts.)

Kravchuk was able to play for time during Gorbachev's negotiations on the future of the Union, while simultaneously taking practical measures to boost Ukrainian sovereignty. Work on the drafting of a new Ukrainian constitution continued and, in June 1991, Ukraine established its own National Bank, claimed jurisdiction over all enterprises operating in Ukraine and declared that the Ukrainian authorities had the sole right to levy taxes on their territory. On 27 June the Ukrainian parliament voted to have no part in the negotiations on the Union Treaty until it reconvened in September. (Kravchuk's supporters could now command a majority in parliament when they voted with the former opposition. Ironically, conservative Communist supporters of Hurenko were now in the minority.) It was this event more than any other which provoked the attempted *coup d'état* in Moscow on 19 August, the day before Gorbachev's new Union Treaty was to be signed.

THE ATTEMPTED COUP AND UKRAINIAN INDEPENDENCE

During the three days of the attempted coup (19–21 August 1991) Ukraine remained peaceful and there was no direct attempt to impose the new regime on Ukraine, although General Varrenikov was sent to Kiev by the self-proclaimed State Committee for the State of Emergency (SCSE) to try to persuade the Ukrainians to conform. Kravchuk in fact prevaricated, preferring to wait and see who emerged victorious from the power struggle in Moscow. Russian President Boris Yeltsin's victory revealed powerful anti-Communist feeling throughout Ukraine. Most CPU conservatives therefore decided that the only way to protect their careers was by supporting the nationalists' demand for a declaration of independence. Kravchuk, moreover, had to restore his reputation as a nationalist. Therefore, it came as no surprise when an extraordinary session of the Ukrainian Supreme Soviet voted to declare independence on 24 August, by 346 votes to one. It was decided that the declaration of independence would be subject to ratification by a popular referendum on 1 December, when Ukraine's first free presidential elections (which had been set before the coup) would also be held.

Although the CPU was banned in Ukraine on 30 August 1991, there was no purge of those Communists who had supported the attempted coup. On the whole, the same people remained in charge, both at national and local levels. Ukraine immediately began a series of measures to reinforce its declaration of independence. In particular, plans to form Ukrainian armed forces were announced in October. With all significant political forces now campaigning for independence, an overwhelming majority of 90.3% voted in favour of independence on 1 December, while Kravchuk won an impressive victory in the presidential elections with 61.6% of the votes cast. His nearest rival, the nationalist and former dissident Vyacheslav Chornovil, won 23.3%.

Ukraine's new leaders faced increasing problems with three main separatist movements among the ethnic minorities in the country: the Russian population of the Crimea; the Ruthenians in Transcarpathia; and the Romanians of Bukovyna. The Crimean threat was the most serious. The Ukrainian Government was obliged to grant the peninsula full autonomy in June 1992. Kravchuk, Yeltsin and the Belarusian leader Stanislau Shushevich then met in Belarus on 8 December and announced the dissolution of the USSR and its replacement by the Commonwealth of Independent States (CIS). This declaration was reiterated by 11 of the 12 remaining Republics in Almaty on 21 December (the independence of the three Baltic Republics had been acknowledged in September). Gorbachev resigned as Soviet President on 25 December.

UKRAINE AS AN INDEPENDENT STATE

Although Ukraine was now independent, Ukraine's ex-Communist élite soon acquired a conservative reputation, especially in comparison to the radical economic reforms initiated by Yegor Gaidar's Government in Russia. Kravchuk was much criticized by Ukrainian reformists for allowing the administration of Vitold Fokin, appointed in October 1990, to continue in office. In July 1992 the only radical member of the Government, the economy minister and deputy premier Volodymyr Lanovy, who had advocated accelerated economic reforms, was unceremoniously dismissed and replaced by a more conservative figure, Volodymyr Symonenko. Fokin and his Government were eventually heavily defeated in a vote of 'no confidence' in September. Kravchuk himself had accumulated many extra powers: an advisory council or Duma, which the Supreme Council (Verkhovna Rada—as the Supreme Soviet was now known) considered was usurping its functions; a system of presidential prefects in the provinces; and a Presidential Commission for Economic Reform. However, the President proved unwilling to use these powers in order to implement radical reform. In October, however, a new Government was formed under Leonid Kuchma. The administration included many members of the former opposition (several from Rukh and from New Ukraine, a parliamentary faction formed in January that year to promote radical economic reforms).

When, in November 1992, Kuchma forced Kravchuk to dissolve the Duma and the Commission for Economic Reforms and persuaded the Verkhovna Rada to grant him the power to rule by emergency decree for six months, it seemed that Ukraine might be on the point of implementing a radical programme of economic reform. However, the new Government still contained many old-style conservatives and the premier was unable to acquire as many powers from parliament as he desired—in particular, control over the National Bank of Ukraine and the State Property Fund (the privatization agency). Moreover, by early 1993 the Government also had to cope with increasing pressure from revivalist neo-socialist groups and from the Russian-speaking population in eastern Ukraine. The latter may have voted for independence on 1 December 1991 in the hope of a better standard of living in an independent Ukraine, but the reverse had proved to be the case. Russophone organizations, campaigning for more autonomy for eastern Ukraine, began to gather strength in late 1992.

In January 1993, some 150 deputies from eastern Ukraine provoked a political crisis by demanding that a special session of the Verkhovna Rada consider their demands for a federal Ukraine, equal status for the Russian language at the local level, joint citizenship of Ukraine and Russia, and closer integration of Ukraine into the CIS. The opposition prevented debate taking place by leaving the chamber, but confrontation in the parliament continued. In December 1992 the Socialist Party of Ukraine (SPU) and the Communists had begun a campaign to revoke the ban on the CPU, which had been in effect since August 1991. In retaliation, an Anti-Communist and Anti-Imperialist Front was formed in February 1993 by some 30 political movements, headed by Rukh and the Congress of National Democratic Forces (CNDF). The following month the conservative majority attempted to staff the new Ukrainian Supreme Court with conservative former Communists and in May the Presidium of the Verkhovna Rada agreed to allow former members of the CPU to re-establish a Communist Party.

By this time, Rukh was hopelessly split. As the Ukrainian economy plunged even deeper into recession, the growing confidence of the neo-Communists was given further impetus when they were able to drive leading reformist ministers, such as the first deputy premier, Ihor Yukhnovsky (who left his post in March 1993), out of office. In the same month, President Kravchuk sharply criticized the Government's budget proposals. The minister in charge of Ukraine's economic reform programme, Viktor Pynzenyk, lost his portfolio in April, but remained a deputy premier. He was replaced by a conservative industrialist from eastern Ukraine, Yury Bannikov. The Verkhovna Rada, which also disapproved of the Government's economic programme, refused to grant Kuchma his request for an extension of his emergency powers and he resigned on 20 May. Since President Kravchuk was also urging the Verkhovna Rada to increase his authority, Ukraine seemed set for a prolonged period of political and constitutional uncertainty. Despite the Verkhovna Rada's failure to accept Kuchma's resignation, the premier was given little opportunity to implement his reforms. On 27 August Pynzenyk, who represented the last reformist element in the Cabinet of Ministers, resigned, and Kuchma was left without support amongst his Government. When, at the beginning of September, the Verkhovna Rada rejected a series of emergency measures on the economy, the premier once again resigned. This time his resignation was accepted and, on 27 September, Kravchuk appointed himself head of government.

DEFENCE AND FOREIGN POLICY

The first priority of Ukraine's leaders after gaining independence was to build strong armed forces. This surprised many observers and quickly led to a deterioration in

Ukraine's relations with Russia. However, it is axiomatic amongst Ukrainian politicians that Ukraine's bid for independence in 1917–21 had basically failed because of a lack of military preparedness. Instead of the Baltic option of expelling former Soviet forces within their borders, or the Georgian option of building a parallel military, Ukraine sought from December 1991 to nationalize all armed forces on its territory. By promising servicemen improved salaries and social rights, Ukraine had, by the end of 1992, established armed forces of some 700,000 men (only 12,000 refused to take the oath of loyalty to Ukraine and were subsequently transferred elsewhere in the former USSR). It was envisaged that gradual professionalization and a natural decrease would reduce this number to 250,000 by the year 2000.

Ukraine was not, however, able to secure control over the Black Sea Fleet, which was based in the Crimean port of Sevastopol. Most of its 350 vessels and 75,000–100,000 servicemen preferred to serve Russia, and leading Russian politicians were determined to retain control of such a potent historical and military symbol. Although an agreement was concluded at Yalta in July 1992 to establish joint Ukrainian and Russian control over the Fleet for an interim period of three years, renewed controversy over the fleet occurred in 1993 when several of the fleet's warships were used to bomb Abkhazia (Georgia) without Ukrainian permission, and when Russian sailors raised Russian flags on 115 of the Fleet's ships in May. In June Presidents Yeltsin and Kravchuk agreed to divide the Fleet equally, but three months later, at a summit held at the Crimean town of Massandra on 3 September, the extent of Ukraine's indebtedness to the Russian Federation for supplies of petroleum and natural gas forced Kravchuk to make several concessions on defence issues, including an offer to sell his country's half of the Black Sea Fleet.

Ukrainian policy on nuclear weapons caused much controversy in the early 1990s. Following the dissolution of the USSR, Ukraine inherited 176 intercontinental ballistic missiles (ICBMs), some 2,600 tactical nuclear weapons (all of these were withdrawn to Russia by May 1992) and around 40 nuclear bombers. Ukraine had promised in its July 1990 Declaration of Sovereignty 'not to produce, receive or acquire' nuclear weapons. This promise was repeated in its Declaration of Non-Nuclear Status of October 1991. Moreover, Ukraine signed the Lisbon Protocols to the first Strategic Arms' Reduction Treaty (START 1) in May 1992, which committed Ukraine to ratifying and implementing the Treaty and to achieving non-nuclear status in the future. The West therefore expected Ukraine to disarm and to sign the Nuclear Non-Proliferation Treaty. However, growing tension with Russia and the repeated threats against Ukraine's territorial integrity by leading Russian politicians led many Ukrainians to reconsider this policy. So too did the sense that Ukraine had a valuable asset that it would be foolish to give away for nothing and the country's growing irritation with the West for its obsession with the nuclear question. In April 1993 162 Ukrainian deputies (out of a total of around 400) signed a motion demanding that Ukraine should remain a nuclear state. Western threats to suspend aid to Ukraine had little effect as such assistance had not yet been provided on a significant scale. Ukraine prolonged the process of parliamentary ratification of START 1 (without which the second Treaty, START 2, could not proceed) for as long as possible, in the hope of receiving Western security guarantees or economic assistance in return for disarmament. Ukraine's promise to ratify the treaty by December 1992 was broken, and the Verkhovna Rada again refused to debate the treaty in June 1993. In that month, the CIS joint military command was dissolved and operational control of all nuclear weapons was devolved to the Russian Ministry of Defence. The transfer of these weapons was provided for by the Massandra agreement of 3 September 1993, which stated that all nuclear weapons would be returned to Russia for dismantling and that Ukraine would receive reprocessed reactor fuel as compensation. The agreement failed to be implemented. The intention of the President and the Verkhovna Rada to affirm Ukraine's claim to ownership of nuclear weapons and to demand extensive compensation for the process of denuclearization was further demonstrated in November, when the parliament adopted a controversial resolution on ratification of START 1. The most significant aspect of the resolution was the contention that the terms of the Treaty only applied to Ukraine's older ICBMs (SS-19s, rather than SS-24s) which represented a mere 36% of the total.

In 1994, however, important progress was made towards the denuclearization of Ukraine. A trilateral agreement between Ukraine, Russia and the USA was signed on 14 January. The terms of this were similar to those agreed at Massandra, but also included important provisions concerning compensation and security guarantees to be granted to Ukraine. The country was to receive some US $1,000m. in compensation for weapons removed from its territory, mainly in the form of reactor fuel, and a further $175m. to assist with dismantling nuclear weapons. These terms evidently satisfied the Verkhovna Rada, who voted to ratify START 1 unconditionally on 3 February 1994.

As regards foreign policy, Ukraine has traditionally stood at the the crossroads of three great civilizations: Russia, Europe and Islam. Having been under Russian domination since 1654, Ukraine was keen to 'rejoin Europe' once it had independent status. However, in the early 1990s most Ukrainian government and business officials remained committed to the CIS as a means of preserving the economic links established in the Soviet period and on which it seemed the Ukrainian economy would have to depend for the foreseeable future. Nationalists, on the other hand, were strongly opposed to the Commonwealth and instead favoured the creation of a Baltic-Black Sea alliance of anti-Russian states. However, the defection of Belarus into a close military alliance with Russia in early 1993 and a closer economic union in early 1994 reduced the likelihood of such an alliance. Ukraine was forced to content itself with a series of small measures designed to create links with central and eastern European states and to establish Ukraine's claim to eventual participation in the process of European union. The Carpathian Euro-Region, established in February 1993 between Poland, Hungary and Ukraine, was a typical example of such steps. Ukrainian relations with Poland were good, owing to common security fears concerning Russia. Hungary and Ukraine had excellent relations, partly because of a mutual antipathy towards Romania, which claimed the territories of Bukovyna (Bucovina) and southern Bessarabia from Ukraine. Relations with Slovakia remained poor because of claims on each other's territory by extreme nationalists and strong links between Slovakia and Russia.

In general, however, Ukraine was severely disappointed by the pace of its 'return to Europe'. It would have little to offer Europe until its economy began to improve from its catastrophic condition. Hence, in the early 1990s Ukraine tried increasingly to rebuild traditional ties in the Middle East, if only to secure petroleum supplies and to sell arms. Relations with Turkey were particularly cordial, as both sides had an interest in working against Russian domination of the Black Sea. Ukraine was a founder member of the Black Sea Economic Co-operation Group established in

June 1992, and joined the Black Sea Inter-Parliamentary Assembly in February 1993.

THE CRIMEAN REPUBLIC

One of the most serious issues to confront President Kravchuk's administration was the status of the Crimea within Ukraine. The Crimea had been granted to the Ukrainian SSR in 1954 and its population was predominantly Russian (some 67% in 1989). During the early 1990s the inhabitants of the peninsula increasingly asserted their claim to independence from the mainland. In January 1991 they voted in favour of the region becoming autonomous. In May 1992 the Crimean assembly declared the territory independent of Ukraine, although this decision was rejected by the Verkhovna Rada. However, in June the Crimea was granted the status of an Autonomous Republic. As well as the increasing discontent on the part of the Crimea's Russian population, that they should have to suffer the consequences of Ukraine's disastrous economic policies, the controversy over the future of the Black Sea Fleet, which was based in Sevastopol, a Crimean port, also caused considerable tension. Furthermore, there was the problem of resettling some 280,000 Crimean Tatars, who had returned from Central Asia where they had been exiled by Stalin in 1944.

The Ukrainian Government granted some concessions to the Crimean Republic in late 1993 and early 1994. In mid-October 1993 President Kravchuk, the Chairman of the Crimean Verkhovna Rada and the Chairman of the Crimean Council of Ministers signed a protocol on implementing an open-economy regime in Crimea, including setting up a central bank and a currency exchange in the Republic. Moreover, in January 1994, it was agreed that taxes levied from the inhabitants of the peninsula would go directly to the Republic's budget, while 5% of Ukraine's state budget would be paid by the Crimea. However, in the same month, Ukraine's apprehension was increased by the election victory of a Russian nationalist, Yury Meshkov, as President of the Autonomous Republic. During his campaign Meshkov had advocated the reintegration of the Crimea into the Russian Federation. On 24 February the Verkhovna Rada adopted a resolution on the status of the Crimea, which obliged the Crimean parliament to ensure that the republican Constitution and other legislative acts conformed with all-Ukrainian law. In a referendum held on 27 March, 70% of those voting demonstrated their support for Meshkov (who by this time had somewhat moderated his anti-Ukrainian stance).

CONCLUSION

In the six months that followed Leonid Kuchma's resignation as head of the Ukrainian Government, until elections were held to the Verkhovna Rada (the first elections to be held in an independent Ukraine), President Kravchuk's reputation continued to decline, both in Ukraine and in the international community. The lack of a coherent programme of economic reform had serious effects, including hyperinflation and a severe energy crisis. Kravchuk's indecision on the crucial issue of disarmament and Ukraine's nuclear status alarmed Western governments. Furthermore, it antagonized Ukrainian nationalists, who perceived the denuclearization of Ukraine as the end to any hope of the country playing an important strategic role in Europe, or as a rival to its powerful neighbour, the Russian Federation. The fragmentation of Ukraine, on political and ethnic grounds, was demonstrated by the large number—some 6,000—of candidates competing in the parliamentary elections on 27 March and 12 April. It was likely that conflicting ethnic interests would continue to threaten economic collapse and political disintegration in Ukraine. Furthermore, despite a major electoral victory for the CPU over its rival, Rukh (after early election results it had gained 75 seats, as opposed to Rukh's 26), it was unclear whether the new legislature would be as fragmented as the last.

The Economy

Dr ANDREW WILSON

INTRODUCTION

Ukraine has a surface area of 603,700 sq km. In January 1992 it had a population of 52.1m. (72% of whom were ethnic Ukrainians). Some 68% of the population were urban dwellers, and 32% rural. The most heavily populated parts of Ukraine were the five oblasts of eastern Ukraine, which accounted for 23.8% of Ukrainian territory, 33.5% of its population and 44.9% of its industrial output. Those employed in Ukraine, in 1991, totalled 25.0m., of which 7.8m. worked in the industrial sector and 4.8m. in agriculture. A total of 7m. workers in Ukraine had some form of higher or specialized education.

AGRICULTURE

Agriculture traditionally provided the basis of the Ukrainian economy. In the 19th century Ukraine gained a reputation as the 'bread-basket of Europe', as large grain surpluses were exported from the 'black earth' of its fertile central plains (often at the expense of the local population). However, collectivization in the early 1930s (and, in Western Ukraine, in the late 1940s), the Great Famine of 1932–33 and the post-Second World War population drift to the cities combined to leave Ukrainian agriculture in a relatively poor state. Although 32% of the population still lived on the land in the early 1990s, it was usually aged and female, as the younger and more dynamic elements of the rural population traditionally migrated to the cities. Rural alcoholism was a serious problem amongst those who remained.

Moreover, rural areas were still under the domination of collective-farm chairmen and heads of agro-industry (except in Western Ukraine, where the memory of private farming was more recent, and easier to revive), who also formed a powerful lobby of nearly 100 members of the 450-seat Ukrainian legislature, the Verkhona Rada (Supreme Council), which was able to prevent radical land reform. The average size of a Ukrainian collective farm was an enormous 2,650 ha (compared to 10.5 ha for the average farm in France). Land and produce waste was endemic. It was estimated that up to one-half of Ukraine's total agricultural output disappeared before it reached retail outlets, through decay, wastage and corruption. Moreover, its final quality was generally poor.

Most collective farms were still poorly mechanized (68% of their work-force consisted of manual workers in 1991), and many lacked basic social amenities (although Ukrainian villages, particularly in Western Ukraine, were usually better kept and organized than most Russian villages). The machinery which did exist often could not be used because of spare-part shortages and repair problems. As elsewhere in the former USSR, however, private plots added disproportionately to overall production, producing over 33% of total output on less than 10% of the land. In the early 1990s Ukraine had 42m. ha of agricultural land, of which 34m. ha was arable land. Some 15% of this, however, was unusable, owing to the consequences of the explosion at the nuclear power station in Chernobyl, in northern Ukraine, in April 1986.

The central, 'black earth' region remained as fertile as ever, but, in the 1980s and early 1990s, irrigation of the dry, southern coastlands became an increasingly acute problem. Nevertheless, in 1990, Ukrainian land was able to produce 25% of the total agricultural output of the USSR. In 1992 potato production amounted to 20.4m. metric tons, an increase of 40.4% on the 1991 output. Wheat production in 1992 was 19.5m. metric tons and output of sugar beets totalled 28.5m. tons. This was a decrease in production from the previous year of 8% and 21%, respectively. In 1992 there were 23.7m. head of cattle and 17.8m. head of pigs. Ukraine also produced, in 1992, some 19m. metric tons of cows' milk and an estimated 1.7m. tons of beef and veal.

ENERGY

Ukraine had a serious energy problem in the early 1990s. When the country was a part of the USSR, more than 90% of its petroleum and natural gas was supplied from the Russian Federation, which, following the dissolution of the USSR, in 1991, rapidly moved towards charging world market prices for both commodities. Traditionally, Ukraine needed some 40m.–50m. metric tons of Russian petroleum annually, and some 60,000m. cu m of gas, not just for domestic consumption, but also to meet the large energy demands of the highly inefficient metallurgical and petrochemicals industries. In 1993 Ukraine was promised only 15m. tons of petroleum, and barely one-half of its traditional gas deliveries, resulting in drastic shortages of fuel for everyday transport. In March 1993 the Government was compelled to prohibit the use of private cars.

Nevertheless, some 90% of Russian gas exports to Europe passed through Ukrainian territory, giving it some economic bargaining power. In negotiations between Ukraine and Russia, held in Kiev (Kyiv), in May 1993, Russia openly insisted on linking energy prices and deliveries to the broader questions of Ukraine's political and economic co-operation with Russia. Ukraine was offered gas at 43,000 roubles per 1,000 cu m, still only one-third of the world price, whilst the more compliant Belarus enjoyed a price of 28,600 roubles. Ukraine's search for alternative energy supplies in the Middle East and elsewhere was not very successful, given Ukraine's lack of convertible ('hard') currency. In February 1993 Turkmenistan agreed to deliver 29,000m. cu m of gas to Ukraine in that year, but, one year later, deliveries were suspended because of Ukraine's outstanding debt.

Ukraine has some hydroelectric power stations, mainly those built on the central Dnieper (Dnipro) river in the 1930s, but its other main source of power was its nuclear power stations. Following the expansion programme of the early 1980s Ukraine possessed some 35% of Soviet nuclear-energy capacity. It had large nuclear power stations at Chernobyl, Rovno (Rivne), South Ukraine and Zaporozhye (Zaporizhzhia—the largest nuclear complex in Europe), with expansion planned at Khmelnitsky (Khmelnytskyi), Odessa (Odesa), Kharkov (Kharkiv) and Cherkassy (Cherkasy). Plans for power stations near Kiev, and near an earthquake zone in the Crimea, were abandoned in the wake of the 1986 Chernobyl disaster. The energy crisis meant that the Chernobyl reactors, scheduled to close in 1992, continued to operate throughout 1993 (with little popular opposition). Again, however, Ukraine was dependent on Russia for the supply of nuclear fuel to its reactors. To secure this, Ukraine was eager to include guaranteed supplies in return for disarmament (which it did by agreements in both September 1993 and January 1994).

MILITARY PRODUCTION

Many large military-industrial complexes were sited on Ukrainian territory. As in other parts of the former USSR, these were often the most advanced sectors of the Ukrainian economy. The most famous site was the Pivmash missile-building factory in Dnepropetrovsk (Dnipropetrovsk), the largest in the world, responsible for building Scud, SS-4, SS-5 and SS-18 missiles, and employing some 50,000 people. The director of this company, Leonid Kuchma, became Ukrainian Prime Minister in October 1992. Missiles were also produced at Pivmash's sister factory in Pavlograd (Pavlohvad).

Ukraine had some small uranium mines near the town of Dnepropetrovsk. Much of the research and production facilities for the Soviet space shuttle were located in Ukraine. The town of Kharkov in eastern Ukraine was the site of one of the world's largest tank factories. Weapons production was concentrated in Kharkov and in central Ukrainian towns such as Dnepropetrovsk, although Ukraine did not have much of a small-arms industry. Kharkov was also the centre of the Ukrainian electronics industry and the scientific-research establishment. Lasers and radio-electronic equipment were produced in Lvov (Lviv), Kiev was host to the design headquarters for the giant Antonov aircraft manufacturers, and Zaporozhye in eastern Ukraine produced aero-engines.

The Ukrainian aero-industry concentrated on heavy transport aeroplanes, such as the giant Ruslan. Military warship production was concentrated on the Black Sea coast. According to the Ministry of Engineering Military-Complex Industries and Conversion, some 1,840 defence industries in Ukraine employed some 2.7m. people in 1993, and were responsible for 30% of Ukraine's total industrial output. However, less than 1,000 of these were in fact exclusively concerned with military production. Even Pivmash always produced tractors, and was moving into trolley-bus production. Crucially, however, nearly all of Ukraine's defence industry was highly integrated with the rest of the Soviet military economy. There was no self-sufficient Ukrainian defence industry as such. Although Ukraine was trying to save an industry bereft of orders by recapturing former Soviet arms markets, especially in developing countries (Ukraine reportedly sold sea-launched cruise missiles to Iran and was frequently accused of supplying the combatants in the former Yugoslavia), it did not have closed production cycles for most products, and was only able to sell the hardware already located on its territory. A case in point was the giant aircraft carrier, Variag, which languished in Nikolayev (Mikolaiv) docks from 1992. A proposed sale to the People's Republic of China failed because Ukraine did not have the capacity to equip the carrier with all the technology and weapons systems originally planned. Such factors influenced many to favour a restoration of the old Union, or at least increased economic co-operation in the Commonwealth of Independent States (CIS).

THE DONBASS REGION

The Donbass, or Don Basin territory, 15% of which was in Russia, was the economic heartland of Ukraine. It consisted of the two modern oblasts of Donetsk and Lugansk (Luhansk). The area was first developed under the tsars in the late 19th century, and then expanded further during the great Soviet industrialization programme begun by Stalin (Iosif V. Dzhugashvili) in the 1930s. Unfortunately, much of the area's mines, plants and machinery still dated from this period. The main industry of the Donbass region was traditionally coal-mining. The region still possessed an estimated 103,000m. metric tons of reserves, or some 300 years' of mining (there were also some smaller coalfields near Lvov in Western Ukraine). However, the coal was increasingly only to be found in older, deeper and less accessible seams. Furthermore, working conditions underground were notoriously difficult.

The area was the centre of the first serious labour unrest of the modern Soviet period, in 1989, and the independent miners' unions created after the 1989 strikes remained a formidable political force. The Donbass also had significant reserves of rock salt, chalk (for the production of soda), sand (for glass), marl and gypsum, and was a centre of metallurgy, machine-building and petroleum refining. A high concentration of petrochemicals industries and thermal power plants meant that the region was one of the most heavily polluted in Ukraine.

SOUTHERN UKRAINE

Southern Ukraine, which consisted of the coastal oblasts of Odessa, Kherson and Nikolayev, and the Crimean peninsula, is the traditional centre of Ukraine's shipbuilding, petroleum refining and trading industry. In the early 1990s, following independence, the huge shipyards at Nikolayev and Kherson were attempting to convert to civilian production under the guidance of the European Bank for Reconstruction and Development (EBRD). The Crimea, the most southerly region in Ukraine, was famous for its fruit and wine, and as a holiday destination. It had the most well-developed tourist infrastructure in Ukraine (mainly in the southern coastal region), but communications to the region remained poor. Ukraine's large trading combines operated out of southern ports such as Odessa. Sanctions imposed by the UN from May 1992, against Serbia and Montenegro (Federal Republic of Yugoslavia), adversely affected the Danube Shipping Company and others, with Ukraine claiming that it had lost up to US $10,000m. of traditional business by mid-1993.

TRADE

Ukraine's foreign-trade balance was difficult to estimate, as, in the early 1990s, the majority of its trade was in the form of barter. Some 80% of Ukrainian trade was with Russia, with which Ukraine had a substantial structural deficit, providing Russia with considerable political influence over Ukraine after independence. In the first 10 months of 1992, Ukraine's trade deficit with the rest of the former USSR totalled 48,400m. roubles, and in the first quarter of 1993 the country accumulated a deficit with Russia alone of 734,000m. coupons (see Monetary Policy—below). Outstanding payments from Ukrainian enterprises to Russian ones in 1992 amounted to 570,000m. roubles. However, official customs returns in 1992 did indicate that Ukraine had a trade surplus of some US $4,300m. with countries not belonging to the CIS. Nearly all such Ukrainian export trade, however, was in raw materials or agricultural produce. One-third of trade even outside the CIS remained in the form of barter agreements. Moreover, Ukraine had a substantial problem in controlling foreign-currency earnings, because of corruption and punitive withholding taxes of 60% or more. Most foreign-currency earnings therefore remained in the illegal, parallel economy ('black market') or in foreign bank accounts. Consequently, Ukraine's total official foreign-exchange reserves were less than $100m. in 1993.

MONETARY POLICY

Until 1990 Ukraine was an integral part of the 'rouble zone', with no independent monetary policy as such. In late 1990, however, Ukraine began to issue non-reusable coupons with all salaries, which were to be used in parallel with roubles to purchase consumer goods (for example, a 20-rouble bottle of vodka could only be bought with 20 roubles and 20 coupons). The aim was to protect the domestic consumer market from rouble-rich Russians. In June 1991 Ukraine began to assert its economic independence more aggressively, by creating a National Bank of Ukraine (NBU).

Following the dissolution of the USSR, a highly inflationary situation was created, whereby 15 central banks (in each of the former Republics) could all create money within a single currency zone, exporting inflation between them. In Ukraine, moreover, the situation was exacerbated by the decision, in January 1992, to introduce a second type of coupon. The new coupons (karbovantsi) were again designed to protect the Ukrainian consumer market, as Russian wages and prices were liberalized by a reformist premier, but were now reusable. They gradually became the only legal tender for cash transactions in Ukraine. Their rate of emission was even more uncontrolled than that of the rouble, however, as the NBU maintained a policy of credit on favourable terms to state enterprises. In March 1993 alone, the NBU issued new agricultural credits of 1,300,000m. coupons. As a result, the rate of inflation in Ukraine was even higher than that in Russia, reaching 50% per month in the first quarter of 1993, compared to 20% in Russia.

By June 1993 the coupon was worth only one-quarter of a rouble, and exchanged at 3,100 roubles per US dollar. As a result of the NBU's relaxed monetary control, Ukraine had been forced to leave the rouble zone in November 1992, and the karbovanets became the only legal tender in the country. Plans to introduce a permanent, convertible Ukrainian currency, the hryvnya, were repeatedly delayed, although the banknotes were already printed. Ukraine had few foreign-exchange reserves and, by mid-1993, still had not received any significant financial support from the International Monetary Fund (IMF), the EBRD or the World Bank. Only Canada, owing to its large ethnic Ukrainian community, provided the country with a loan, of US $50m., in 1992. Hence, it was generally recognized that the introduction of the hryvnya would have to be delayed until monetary stability was achieved. Early in 1994 the Government announced that any such move seemed unlikely in the near future. Prices in Ukraine were never liberalized in the same manner as most Russian prices in January 1992. Instead, Ukraine was compelled to make a series of administered price increases after January 1992. In December of the same year many price controls, particularly on monopoly enterprises, were in fact restored, so that 42% of all prices remained state-controlled.

FISCAL POLICY

In 1991–93 it proved impossible for the new state to establish financial discipline. Only one-third of tax revenues were collected, as Kiev's practical control over state enterprises, particularly in periphery areas, decreased. Moreover, state expenditure was profligate and populist. Ukraine had yet to organize a truly consolidated budget, and control over state spending was shared between the Government and the Verkhona Rada. The latter repeatedly intervened in the budgetary process to increase social expenditure (32% of the total state budget), and to defer large restrictions in expenditure, even after the Kuchma Government was installed in October 1992. State subsidies to energy, agriculture and manufacturing amounted to 9.5% of total expenditure, and the state was also burdened with continued costs in the wake of the accident at the nuclear power-station at Chernobyl. Reductions in expenditure seemed even less likely under Kravchuk's premiership (from September 1993) and the March 1994 elections were unlikely to resolve the situation.

In April 1993 the parliament adopted a new budget, which set expenditure at 5,600,000m. coupons, and receipts at 4,600,000m. The resulting planned deficit of 1,000,000m. would represent some 15% of gross national product (GNP). However, as in the past, little credence could be placed in such figures, which were likely to be overtaken quickly by events. Prime Minister Kuchma had indicated, in November 1992, that the budget deficit was estimated at an incredible 44% of GNP. Ukrainian tax rates remained at Soviet levels. Export-import trade regulations were actually increased in December 1992 (although this had little impact on black-market trade) and, in February 1993, a decree was passed to force all Ukrainian enterprises to sell 50% of their foreign-currency earnings through official inter-bank currency auctions. It was estimated that more than 60% of enterprises in Ukraine withheld taxes. In January 1993, however, the Government began to liberalize the tax regime by reducing value added tax (VAT) from 28% to 20%, and Enterprise Tax from 45% to 30%. Moreover, the latter began to be charged on net profit, rather than on gross income, as previously.

PRIVATIZATION

In theory, Ukraine had one of the most impressive privatization programmes in Eastern Europe, following the passage of the key laws in March 1992. However, the practical implementation of these laws was constantly delayed. The first full privatizations only began in Lvov in early 1993, when Deputy Prime Minister Pynzenyk announced that the state would organize the auction of most small enterprises (defined as those with a book value of less than 50m. coupons on 1 January 1993) in Ukraine, at the rate of 20% of the total, every three months. Privatization in the second quarter of 1993 was still proceeding slowly, however. Because most small enterprises were considered to be the property of local authorities, the implementation of small-scale privatization depended on the attitudes of the local leadership.

The first privatization of a medium-sized company in Ukraine began in Odessa in early 1993. Large enterprises, meanwhile, were to be converted into joint-stock companies by 1 July 1993, while the prospects of their long-term privatization seemed even more distant. However, the semi-privatization of companies, the forerunner of complete ownership transformation, was more advanced; by October 1992 some 9,700 retail shops and 5,900 catering establishments, accounting for 21% of retail sales, had been leased to private management.

CONCLUSION

Not surprisingly, therefore, Ukrainian economic performance was even worse than that of Russia. When part of the USSR, Ukraine had been heavily industrialized, with the large part of industry related, directly and indirectly, towards military production. With the dissolution of the USSR, in December 1991, the demand for production from this sector severely decreased. Thus, the need to restructure the economy was even more urgent than in other former Soviet Republics. Furthermore, Ukraine found it difficult to expand its foreign trade and was still heavily dependent on Russia for its export-import earnings. At the same time, Russia began to reduce its subsidies on energy supplies to the other countries of the former USSR, and as Ukraine relied greatly on imports to meet its energy needs, the country suffered a deterioration in its terms of trade.

In 1992, according to the Ministry of Statistics, GNP decreased by 14% (the EBRD estimated a fall in net material product of 16%), the average national income declined by 16%, industrial output decreased by 9%, labour productivity fell by 13% and the output of foodstuffs by 15.6%. The fact that the level of unemployment in Ukraine was still only officially 161,000 in late 1993 (less than 1% of the work-force) indicated that the real problems of economic adjustment were still to come. Throughout 1992 the Ukrainian Government was more concerned with mitigating the adverse effects of economic shocks rather than actually undertaking a specific economic course. This was reflected in the introduction, in early 1992, of coupons as a parallel currency, following anxiety about protecting the domestic market against foreign interest, and the liberalization of prices after similar price reforms in Russia.

The rate of decline moderated slightly in the first quarter of 1993, but it was predicted there would be a similar economic performance overall in 1993 to that in 1992, when the rate of inflation increased from an average of 18% in the first quarter of 1992 to almost 30% in the last three months of the year. The Government's Plan of Action, presented to parliament in January 1993, aimed to reassert control over consumer prices, foreign trade and state-owned enterprises as a necessary prerequisite to an organized programme of liberalization and economic reform. By early 1993 serious signs of labour unrest were beginning to appear in Ukraine, especially in the Donbass region, where 450,000 miners took industrial action in February. It was likely, therefore, that such unrest would increase as the adverse consequences of the transformation from a centrally planned economy to a market one began to take effect.

Statistical Survey

Principal sources (unless otherwise stated): IMF, *Ukraine, Economic Review* and *International Financial Statistics: Supplement on Countries of the Former Soviet Union*; World Bank, *Statistical Handbook: States of the Former USSR.*

Area and Population

AREA, POPULATION AND DENSITY

Area (sq km)	603,700*
Population (census results)	
17 January 1979	49,754,642
12 January 1989†	
Males	23,959,000
Females	27,745,000
Total	51,704,000
Population (official estimate at 1 January)	
1991	51,944,000
1992	52,057,000
Density (per sq km) at 1 January 1992	86.2

* 233,090 sq miles.

† Figures are provisional. The revised total is 51,706,742.

POPULATION BY NATIONALITY
(permanent inhabitants, census of 12 January 1989)

	'000	%
Ukrainian	37,419.1	72.7
Russian	11,355.6	22.1
Jewish	486.3	0.9
Belarussian	440.0	0.9
Moldovan	324.5	0.6
Bulgarian	233.8	0.5
Polish	219.2	0.4
Hungarian	163.1	0.3
Romanian	134.8	0.3
Greek	98.6	0.2
Tatar	86.9	0.2
Roma (Gypsy)	47.9	0.1
Crimean Tatar	46.8	0.1
Armenian	38.6	0.1
Others	356.8	0.7
Total	51,452.0	100.0

ADMINISTRATIVE DIVISIONS

	Area ('000 sq km)	Population ('000, 1 Jan. 1991)	Density (per sq km)
Regions*			
Cherkasy (Cherkassy)	20.9	1,530.9	73.2
Chernihiv (Chernigov)	31.9	938.6	44.1
Chernivtsi (Chernovtsy)	8.1	1,405.8	115.6
Dnipropetrovsk (Dnepropetrovsk)	31.9	3,908.7	122.5
Donetsk	26.5	5,346.7	201.8
Ivano-Frankivsk (Ivano-Frankovsk)	13.9	1,442.9	103.8
Kharkiv (Kharkov)	31.4	3,194.8	101.7
Kherson	28.5	1,258.7	44.2
Khmelnytskyi (Khmelnitsky)	20.6	1,520.6	73.8
Kyiv (Kiev)†	28.9	4,589.8	158.8
Kirovohrad (Kirovograd)	24.6	1,245.3	50.6
Luhansk (Lugansk)	26.7	2,871.1	107.5
Lviv (Lvov)	21.8	2,764.4	126.8
Mikolaiv (Nikolayev)	24.6	1,342.4	54.6
Odesa (Odessa)	33.3	2,635.3	79.1
Poltava	28.8	1,756.9	61.0
Rivne (Rovno)	20.1	1,176.8	58.5
Sumy	23.8	1,430.2	60.1
Ternopil (Ternopol)	13.8	1,175.1	85.2
Transcarpathia	12.8	1,265.9	98.9
Vinnytsia (Vinnitsa)	26.5	1,914.4	72.2
Volyn (Volin)	20.2	1,069.0	52.9
Zaporizhzhia (Zaporozhye)	27.2	2,099.6	77.2
Zhytomyr (Zhitomir)	29.9	1,510.7	50.5
Republic			
Crimea	27.0	2,549.8	94.4
Total	603.7	51,944.4	86.0

* With the exception of Crimea and Transcarpathia, the names of regions are given in Ukrainian, with the Russian version in brackets where it differs.

† Combines Kyiv metropolitan area and Kyiv region, although they are administered separately.

PRINCIPAL TOWNS*
(estimated population at 1 January 1990)

Kyiv (Kiev, capital)	2,616,000	Poltava	317,000
Kharkiv (Kharkov)	1,618,000	Chernihiv (Chernigov)	301,000
Dnipropetrovsk (Dnepropetrovsk)	1,187,000	Cherkasy (Cherkassy)	297,000
Donetsk	1,117,000	Sumy	296,000
Odesa (Odessa)	1,106,000	Zhytomyr (Zhitomir)	296,000
Zaporizhzhia (Zaporozhye)	891,000	Dniprodzerzhynsk (Dneprodzerzhinsk)	284,000
Lviv (Lvov)	798,000	Kirovohrad (Kirovograd)	274,000
Kryvyi Rih (Krivoi Rog)	717,000	Chernivtsi (Chernovtsy)	257,000
Mariupol†	520,000	Khemelnytskyi (Khmelnitsky)	241,000
Mikolaiv (Nikolayev)	508,000	Kremenchug	238,000
Luhansk (Lugansk)‡	501,000	Rivne (Rovno)	233,000
Makayevka	427,000	Ivano-Frankivsk (Ivano-Frankovsk)	220,000
Vinnytsia (Vinnitsa)	379,000	Ternopil (Ternopol)	212,000
Kherson	361,000	Lutsk	204,000
Sevastopol	361,000		
Simferopol	349,000		
Gorlovka	338,000		

* As far as possible, the names of towns are given in transliterated Ukrainian, with the Russian version in brackets where it differs.

† Known as Zhdanov from 1948 to 1989.

‡ Known as Voroshilovgrad from 1935 to 1958 and from 1970 to 1989.

Source: UN, *Demographic Yearbook*.

BIRTHS, MARRIAGES AND DEATHS (per 1,000)

	Registered live births		Registered marriages		Registered deaths	
	Number	Rate (per 1,000)	Number	Rate (per 1,000)	Number	Rate (per 1,000)
1988	744,056	14.4	455,700	8.8	600,725	11.7
1989	690,981	13.4	489,330	9.5	600,590	11.6
1990	657,200	12.7	482,800	9.3	629,602	12.1

Source: UN, *Demographic Yearbook*.

EMPLOYMENT (annual averages, '000 employees)

	1989	1990	1991
Agriculture	4,801	4,960	4,762
Industry	7,981	7,830	7,769
Construction	2,396	2,422	2,267
Transport and communications	1,793	1,788	1,774
Trade and material services	1,896	1,892	1,863
Health and social services	1,480	1,502	1,521
Education and culture	2,361	2,360	2,367
Other activities	2,712	2,647	2,655
Total	25,420	25,401	24,977

Agriculture

PRINCIPAL CROPS ('000 metric tons)

	1990	1991	1992
Wheat	30,374	21,155	19,473
Barley	9,169	8,047	10,106
Maize	4,737	4,747	2,851
Rye	1,260	982	1,156
Oats	1,303	945	1,246
Millet	338	338	226
Potatoes	16,732	14,550	20,427
Dry peas	3,029	1,782	2,776
Sunflower seed	2,725	2,448	2,100
Cabbages	1,891	1,299	1,140*
Tomatoes	1,633	1,682	1,480*
Cucumbers and gherkins	300	382	336*
Dry onions	850	801	715*
Carrots	401	322	290*
Water-melons	792	766	800†
Grapes	836	673	655
Sugar beets	44,265	36,168	28,546
Raw sugar*	5,360	3,600	3,850
Apples	1,968	798	900†
Pears	212	118	150†
Plums	315	256	266†

* Unofficial figure(s). † FAO estimate(s).

Source: FAO, *Production Yearbook*.

LIVESTOCK ('000 head, year ending September)

	1990	1991	1992
Horses	754	738	730*
Cattle	25,195	24,623	23,700
Pigs	20,000	19,400	17,800
Sheep	8,545	7,332	7,332*
Goats	458	523	468
Poultry†	255,000	247,000	243,000

* FAO estimate(s). † Unofficial figure(s).

Source: FAO, *Production Yearbook*.

LIVESTOCK PRODUCTS ('000 metric tons)

	1990	1991	1992
Beef and veal	1,985	1,878	1,676*
Mutton and lamb	44	38	35†
Goatmeat	2	2	2†
Pigmeat	1,576	1,421	1,209*
Poultry meat	708	654	605*
Cows' milk	24,360	22,312	19,000*
Sheep's milk	22	15	8†
Goats' milk	126	82	70†
Butter and ghee	44.4	37.6	34.5*
Eggs	973.6	913.8	854.1
of which: hen eggs	944.3	886.3	830.0
Wool:			
greasy	29.8	26.6	22.4†
scoured	18.0	16.0	13.4†

* Unofficial figure(s). † FAO estimate(s).

Source: FAO, *Production Yearbook*.

Mining

('000 metric tons, unless otherwise indicated)

	1988	1989	1990
Hard coal	181,800	180,200	155,532
Brown coal (incl. lignite)	9,900		9,280
Crude petroleum*	5,400	5,400	5,252
Natural gas (million cu metres)	32,400	30,800	28,082
Iron ore:			
gross weight	116,000	n.a.	104,982
metal content	64,371	61,665	58,988
Manganese ore†	n.a.	2,279.5	2,208.3
Magnesite	855	851	828
Chalk	665	652	1,082
Potash salts (crude)	1,077	851	585
Native sulphur	2,556	2,407	2,118
Salt (unrefined)	8,186	8,338	8,309
Gypsum (crude)	1,030	1,034	1,014
Peat:			
for fuel	2,007	2,366	1,619
for agricultural use	21,957	18,225	14,680

* Including gas condensates.

† Figures refer to the metal content of ore extracted.

Source: mainly UN, *Industrial Statistics Yearbook*.

1991: Coal 135.6m. metric tons; Crude petroleum 4.9m. metric tons; Natural gas 24,400m. cu m.

1992: Coal 133.6m. metric tons; Crude petroleum 4.5m. metric tons; Natural gas 20,900m. cu m.

Industry

SELECTED PRODUCTS
('000 metric tons, unless otherwise indicated)

	1988	1989	1990
Margarine	308.1	318.4	288.5
Flour	7,534	7,614	7,671
Raw sugar*	4,646	5,177	5,388
Ethyl alcohol ('000 hectolitres)	2,776	4,911	5,394
Wine ('000 hectolitres)	3,165	3,258	2,723
Beer ('000 hectolitres)	12,951	13,749	13,778
Cigarettes (million)	81,659	78,446	69,397
Wool yarn: pure and mixed	47.7	48.9	47.5
Cotton yarn: pure and mixed	160.5	161.8	157.1
Flax yarn	27.8	27.2	24.7
Woven cotton fabrics (million sq metres)	613	620	614
Woven woollen fabrics (million sq metres)	86.9	89.8	86.0
Linen fabrics (million sq metres)	107.3	109.0	102.4

—continued	1988	1989	1990
Footwear, excl. rubber ('000 pairs)	190,583	193,673	196,466
Paper	343	353	369
Hydrochloric acid	270.5	279.3	273.7
Sulphuric acid	4,339	4,268	4,194
Nitric acid	214	244	229
Phosphoric acid	695	694	692
Caustic soda (Sodium hydroxide)	494	472	444
Soda ash (Sodium carbonate)	1,340	1,263	1,120
Nitrogenous fertilizers (a)†	3,635	3,275	3,022
Phosphatic fertilizers (b)†	1,725	1,695	1,648
Potassic fertilizers (c)†	203	170	143
Rubber tyres ('000)‡	8,783	8,730	8,539
Rubber footwear ('000 pairs)	30,618	31,626	32,290
Clay building bricks (million)	6,792	7,118	7,241
Quicklime	8,929	8,931	8,677
Cement	23,533	23,416	22,729
Pig-iron	43,930	43,061	41,906
Crude steel:			
for castings	2,156	2,014	1,920
ingots	54,282	52,772	50,702
Tractors (number)§	130,705	115,913	106,221
Household refrigerators ('000)	843	882	903
Household washing machines ('000)	533	651	788
Radio receivers ('000)	432	574	n.a.
Television receivers ('000)	3,434	3,572	3,773
Passenger motor cars ('000)	155	155	156
Buses and motor coaches (number)	14,834	14,561	12,713
Lorries (number)	29,789	28,111	27,680
Motorcycles, scooters, etc. ('000)	112	109	103
Bicycles ('000)	891	838	800
Electric energy (million kWh)	297,229	295,300	298,500

*Production from home-grown sugar beet.
† Production of fertilizers is in terms of (a) nitrogen; (b) phosphoric acid; or (c) potassium oxide.
‡ Tyres for road motor vehicles.
§ Tractors of 10 horse-power and over, excluding industrial tractors and road tractors for tractor-trailer combinations.

Source: mainly UN, *Industrial Statistics Yearbook*.

Electric energy: 278,700m. kWh in 1991; 252,600m. kWh in 1992.

Finance

CURRENCY AND EXCHANGE RATES

Monetary Units (temporary)

A currency coupon, the karbovanets (plural: karbovantsi), is in use.

Sterling and Dollar Equivalents (30 September 1993)

£1 sterling = 27,632 karbovantsi;
US $1 = 18,477 karbovantsi;
100,000 karbovantsi = £3.619 = $5.412.

Note: Based on the official rate of exchange, the average value of the Soviet currency (roubles per US dollar) was: 0.6274 in 1989; 0.5856 in 1990; 0.5819 in 1991. However, a multiple exchange rate system was in operation, with separate non-commercial and tourist rates. A commercial exchange rate was introduced on 1 November 1990, replacing the official rate for most transactions. The commercial rate (roubles per US dollar) was: 1.692 at 31 December 1990; 1.671 at 31 December 1991. Between November 1989 and April 1991 the tourist exchange rate valued the rouble at one-tenth of the official rate. In April 1991 this rate, renamed the 'special rate', was set at $1 = 27.6 roubles. It was subsequently adjusted. Following the dissolution of the USSR in December 1991, Russia and several other former Soviet republics retained the rouble as their monetary unit. In November 1992 the rouble ceased to be legal tender in Ukraine, and was replaced by the karbovanets (see above) for a transitional period. The exchange rate deteriorated rapidly ($1 was equivalent to approximately 700 karbovantsi by the beginning of 1993), but improved in the final quarter of 1993 (at the beginning of 1994 $1 bought some 12,000 karbovantsi). Ukraine has announced an intention to introduce its own permanent currency, the hryvnya, but, in early 1994, the Government announced that it envisaged no immediate prospect for such a move.

BUDGET (million roubles)

Revenue	1991	1992	1993*
Taxation	70,200	1,121,100	7,112,800
Turnover tax	27,800	485,000	1,995,200
Excises	—	59,400	808,100
Profits tax on enterprises	28,400	277,000	1,346,100
Individual income tax	9,300	148,400	554,800
Chernobyl contribution†	2,700	122,800	611,300
Foreign-trade taxes	900	7,200	1,005,600
Other tax revenue	1,100	21,200	791,700
Non-tax revenue	6,700	102,300	1,008,500
Total	76,900	1,223,400	8,121,300

Expenditure	1991	1992	1993*
Current expenditure by state budget	99,800	1,831,200	8,405,200
Social safety net	50,200	361,700	1,849,700
Subsidies	38,400	234,900	1,145,700
National economy	13,100	597,200	1,326,400
Education and health	} 29,300	431,500	2,276,900
Other social and cultural services		39,200	357,100
Science	—	39,900	178,600
Administration and justice	—	75,400	575,500
Defence	—	112,300	547,100
Chernobyl disbursement†	4,500	115,000	415,300
Other current expenditure	2,700	59,000	878,600
Capital expenditure by state budget	9,000	89,200	689,400
Total	108,800	1,920,400	9,094,600

* Projections.
† Relating to measures to relieve the effects of the accident at the Chernobyl nuclear power-station in April 1986.

MONEY SUPPLY (million roubles at 31 December)

	1989	1990	1991
Currency in circulation	17,200	17,400	29,800
Demand deposits at banks	61,800	76,200	143,600
Total money	79,000	93,600	173,400

COST OF LIVING
(Index of retail prices; base: previous year = 100)

	1989	1990	1991
Food	100.6	101.5	179.2
Other commodities	103.5	106.2	188.3
All items	102.2	104.2	184.2

NATIONAL ACCOUNTS (million roubles at current prices)
Net Material Product by Economic Activity

	1990	1991	1992*
Agriculture and fisheries	35,800	67,800	852,100
Industry and mining	48,700	95,000	1,921,500
Construction	11,500	24,400	558,700
Trade and catering	6,500	13,000	160,700
Transport and communications	7,100	11,000	177,800
Other activities of the material sphere	8,400	13,100	119,900
Total	118,000	224,300	3,790,700

* Preliminary figures.

External Trade

PRINCIPAL COMMODITIES (million roubles)

Imports	1989	1990
Petroleum and gas	4,381	3,875
Iron and steel	2,893	2,679
Non-ferrous metals	2,188	2,136
Chemicals and chemical products	5,883	5,711
Machine-building	18,046	18,745
Wood and paper products	1,933	1,856
Light industry	9,694	9,738
Food industry	5,058	4,046
Agricultural products (unprocessed)	1,409	1,402
Total (incl. others)	54,540	54,059
Foreign	14,569	15,071
Inter-republican (USSR)	39,971	38,989

Exports	1989	1990
Iron and steel	8,088	7,619
Non-ferrous metals	965	914
Chemicals and chemical products	3,944	3,923
Machine-building	18,164	17,881
Light industry	2,674	2,326
Food industry	7,790	6,659
Agricultural products (unprocessed)	1,495	1,651
Total (incl. others)	48,062	45,606
Foreign	7,595	7,287
Inter-republican (USSR)	40,467	38,319

Communications Media

	1988	1989	1990
Radio receivers ('000 in use)	38,655	40,414	41,200
Television receivers ('000 in use)	16,000	16,752	16,950
Book production*:			
Titles	8,311	n.a.	7,046
Copies ('000)	184,588	n.a.	170,476
Daily newspapers:			
Titles	n.a. †	n.a.	127
Circulation ('000)	n.a. †	n.a.	13,026
Non-daily newspapers:			
Titles	n.a. †	n.a.	1,660
Circulation ('000)	n.a. †	n.a.	11,893
Other periodicals:			
Titles	n.a.	n.a.	185
Circulation ('000)	n.a.	n.a.	9,957

* Including pamphlets (2,771 titles and 53,600,000 copies in 1988; 1,878 titles and 53,874,000 copies in 1990).
† Daily and non-daily newspapers totalled 1,794, with a combined circulation of 24,000,000.
Source: UNESCO, *Statistical Yearbook.*

Education

(1990)

	Institutions	Teachers	Students
Pre-primary	23,600	212,600	1,939,600
Primary } General secondary }	20,900	473,100	3,990,500 / 2,863,900
Specialized Secondary			
Teacher training	n.a.	n.a.	20,700
Vocational	n.a.	n.a.	522,900
Higher*	n.a.	72,300	889,574

* Including evening and correspondence courses.
Source: UNESCO, *Statistical Yearbook.*

Directory

Constitution

Ukraine's Constitution was adopted in 1978, and was modelled on the 1977 Constitution of the USSR. In the early 1990s significant amendments were made to the Constitution to reflect Ukraine's status as an independent, non-socialist state. In 1991 the institution of an executive presidency was introduced into the Constitution. A draft of a new constitution was prepared in 1992, but adoption of a new document was delayed by disagreements concerning the division of power, and notably the role of the President in any constitutional order. A further draft was published in October 1993. Formal ratification of any new fundamental law awaited a new parliament (elected in March 1994).

The Government

HEAD OF STATE

President: Leonid M. Kravchuk (elected 1 December 1991).

CABINET OF MINISTERS
(March 1994)

Prime Minister: Yuhym Zvyahilsky (acting).
Deputy Prime Minister: Volodymyr V. Demyanov.
Deputy Prime Minister: Vasyl Yevtukhov.
Deputy Prime Minister: Valentyn Landyk.
Deputy Prime Minister: Valery Shmarov.
Deputy Prime Minister: Mykola H. Zhulynsky.
Minister of the Cabinet: Ivan Dotsenko.
Minister of Agriculture: Yury Karasyk.
Minister of Communications: Oleh P. Prozhyvalsky.
Minister of Construction: Yury Serbin.
Minister of Culture: Ivan Dzhyuba.
Minister of Defence: Col-Gen. Vitaly Radetsky.
Minister of the Economy: Roman Shpek.
Minister of Education: Petro M. Talanchuk.
Minister of Energy: Vilen Symenyuk.
Minister of Engineering, Military-Complex Industries and Conversion: Dmytro Chernenko.
Minister of Environmental Protection: Yury I. Kostenko.
Minister of Finance: Hrihory O. Pyatachenko.
Minister of Foreign Affairs: Anatoly M. Zlenko.
Minister of Foreign Economic Relations and Trade: Ivan I. Herts.
Minister of Forestry: Valery I. Samoplavsky.
Minister of Health Care: Yury P. Spizhenko.
Minister of Industry: Anatoly K. Holubchenko.
Minister of Internal Affairs: Andrey V. Vasylyshyn.
Minister of Justice: Vasyl V. Oponenko.
Minister of Labour: Mykhailo H. Kaskevych.
Minister of National Minorities and Migration: Oleksandr Yemets.
Minister for Protection of the Population against the Consequences of Chernobyl: Heorhy O. Hotovchits.
Minister of Social Welfare: Arkady V. Yershov.
Minister of Statistics: Mykola Borysenko.
Minister of Transport: Orest D. Klympush.
Minister of Youth and Sport: Valery P. Borzov.

The following are ex-officio members of the Cabinet of Ministers:
Chairman of the State Security Service: Evhen K. Marchuk.
Chairman of the State Committee for Customs: (vacant).
Chairman of the State Committee for Defence of State Borders: Valery O. Hubenko.
Chairman of the State Resources Fund: Volodymyr V. Predkov.
Chairman of the State Committee for Demonopolization: Oleksandr L. Zavada.
Chairman of the Board of the National Bank: Viktor Yushchenko.

MINISTRIES

Cabinet of Ministers: 252008 Kiev, vul. M. Hrushevskoho 12/2; tel. (044) 293-52-27.
Ministry of Agriculture: 252001 Kiev, vul. Kreshchatik 24; tel. (044) 226-25-04; fax (044) 229-87-56.
Ministry of Communications: 252001 Kiev, vul. Kreshchatik 22; tel. (044) 226-21-40.
Ministry of Construction: Kiev.
Ministry of Culture: 252030 Kiev, vul. Ivan Franka 19; tel. (044) 224-49-11.
Ministry of Defence: 252005 Kiev, vul. Bankova 6; tel. (044) 226-26-56.
Ministry of the Economy: 252008 Kiev, vul. M. Hrushevskoho 12/2; tel. (044) 293-44-65.
Ministry of Education: 252001 Kiev, vul. Kreshchatik 34; tel. (044) 226-32-31; fax (044) 226-33-23.
Ministry of Energy: 252001 Kiev, vul. Kreshchatik 30; tel. (044) 224-93-88.
Ministry of Engineering, Military-Complex Industries and Conversion: Kiev, vul. Pushkinska 8; tel. (044) 291-50-53.
Ministry of Environmental Protection: 252001 Kiev, vul. Kreshchatik 5; tel. (044) 228-06-44; fax (044) 229-83-83.
Ministry of Finance: 252008 Kiev, vul. M. Hrushevskoho 12/2; tel. (044) 293-53-63; fax (044) 293-21-78.
Ministry of Foreign Affairs: 252018 Kiev, Mykhaylivska pl. 1; tel. (044) 226-33-79; fax (044) 226-31-69.
Ministry of Foreign Economic Relations and Trade: 252053 Kiev, Lvivska pl. 8; tel. (044) 226-27-33.
Ministry of Forestry: 252001 Kiev, vul. Kreshchatik 5; tel. (044) 226-32-53; fax (044) 228-77-94.
Ministry of Health Care: 252021 Kiev, vul. M. Hrushevskoho 7; tel. (044) 226-22-05; fax (044) 293-69-75.
Ministry of Industry: 253167 Kiev, vul. M. Paskovoy 15; tel. (044) 226-26-23.
Ministry of Internal Affairs: 252024 Kiev, vul. Bohomoltsa 10; tel. (044) 291-18-30; fax (044) 291-31-82.
Ministry of Justice: 252030 Kiev, vul. M. Kotsyubynskoho 12; tel. (044) 226-24-16.
Ministry of Labour: 252004 Kiev, vul. Pushkinska 28; tel. (044) 224-63-47; fax (044) 224-59-05.
Ministry for Protection of the Population against the Consequences of Chernobyl: 254655 Kiev, 8 Lvivska pl.; tel. (044) 212-50-19; fax (044) 212-50-69.
Ministry of Social Welfare: 252053 Kiev, vul. Kudriavska 26/28; tel. (044) 212-25-55.
Ministry of Statistics: 252023 Kiev, vul. Shota Rustaveli 3; tel. (044) 226-20-21; telex 132368; fax (044) 227-42-66.
Ministry of Transport: 252113 Kiev, Peremohy pr. 57; tel. (044) 446-30-30.
Ministry of Youth and Sport: 252023 Kiev, vul. Esplanadna 42; tel. (044) 220-02-00; fax (044) 220-12-94.
Security Service of Ukraine: 252003 Kiev, vul. Volodymyrska 33; tel. (044) 226-24-16.

President and Legislature

PRESIDENT

Election, 1 December 1991

Candidate	Votes	% of total
Leonid M. Kravchuk	19,643,481	61.59
Vyacheslav M. Chornovil	7,420,727	23.27
Levko G. Lukyanenko	1,432,556	4.49
Vladimir B. Grinov	1,329,758	4.17
Ihor P. Yukhnovsky	554,719	1.74
Leopold I. Taburyansky	182,713	0.57

VERKHOVNA RADA
(Supreme Council)

The Supreme Council is the highest legislative body in Ukraine. It comprises 450 deputies, who were elected in March 1990 (when the body was known as the Supreme Soviet). Elections to the Supreme Council took place on 27 March and 12 April 1994. After initial election results, the largest parties were expected to be the Communist Party of Ukraine, followed by the People's Movement of Ukraine (Rukh).

Supreme Council: 252019 Kiev, vul. M. Hrushevskoho 5; tel. (044) 291-51-00.

Chairman: IVAN PLYUSHCH.

First Deputy Chairman: V. V. DURDYNETS.

Local Government

Ukraine is divided for administrative purposes into 24 regions (oblasts), one metropolitan area (Kiev) and one Autonomous Republic (Crimea). The oblasts are governed by councils (rada), although there was also a system of provincial prefects appointed by the President of the Republic. Their administrative centres are situated in the following towns: Cherkassy (Cherkasy), Chernigov (Chernihiv), Chernovtsy (Chernivtsi), Dnepropetrovsk (Dnipropetrovsk), Donetsk, Ivano-Frankovsk (Ivano-Frankivsk), Kharkov (Kharkiv), Khmelnitsky (Khmelnitskyi), Kherson, Kiev (Kyiv, excluding the city of Kiev), Kirovograd (Kirovohrad), Lugansk (Luhansk—formerly Voroshilovgrad), Lutsk (Volyn), Lvov (Lviv), Nikolayev (Mykolaiv), Odessa (Odesa), Poltava, Rovno (Rivne), Sumy, Ternopol (Ternopil), Uzhgorod (Uzhorod—centre of Transcarpathian Oblast), Vinnitsa (Vynnytsa), Zaporozhye (Zaporizhzhya) and Zhitomir (Zhytomyr). Elections to local councils were scheduled for January 1994.

CRIMEAN REPUBLIC

The Crimean peninsula was originally colonized by the ancient Greeks in the seventh century BC and subsequently invaded by the Goths (AD 250), the Huns (373), the Khazars (eighth century), the Eastern Roman or Byzantine Greeks (1016), the Kipchaks (1050), the Mongol Tatars (13th century) and the Ottoman Turks (end of the 15th century). An independent Crimean Khanate was founded by the Tatars in northern and central Crimea (Krym) in 1475, and survived until the late 18th century, when the Russian Empire made repeated incursions into the peninsula. The Khanate was finally annexed in 1783. The Russians were defeated in the Crimean War (1854–55) by the Western Powers (United Kingdom, France and the Kingdom of Sardinia) and the Ottoman Turks. The Crimea formed part of the short-lived republic of Taurida (established in 1918), until 18 October 1921, when the Crimean Autonomous Soviet Socialist Republic (ASSR) was created.

The Crimean ASSR was abolished on 30 June 1945 and the peninsula became merely an oblast (region) in the Russian Soviet Federative Socialist Republic (RSFSR or Russian Federation). However, on 19 February 1954, the Crimea was transferred to the control of the Ukrainian Soviet Socialist Republic (SSR). Following a referendum held on 20 January 1991 the status of an autonomous republic was claimed by the Crimea. On 5 May 1992 the Crimean Supreme Soviet declared independence from Ukraine, but the decision was annulled by the republican parliament the following week. However, in June the Ukrainian authorities recognized Crimea as an Autonomous Republic. On 16 January 1994 elections were held to the new presidency of the Crimea. Following a second round of voting, in which 1,427,419 inhabitants (or 75.1% of the electorate) participated, the contest was won by Yury Meshkov, a Russian nationalist. Meshkov was supported in his candidacy by 1,040,888 voters (72.92% of participants), while his rival, Chairman of the Crimean Supreme Council Mykola Bahrov, gained 333,243 votes (23.35%). Meshkov was inaugurated as President on 4 February. On 10 March the Cabinet of Ministers was dismissed by presidential decree and its Chairman, Yevgeny Saburov, was invited to head a new Government. Elections to the Supreme Council of the Crimea were held on 27 March, as was a referendum on various issues, which included the right of the population of the Crimea to dual citizenship, the authority of the President and relations between the Crimea and mainland Ukraine.

The Crimea is bounded to the south and west by the Black Sea and is separated from mainland Ukraine (to the north) by the Perekop Isthmus and from the Taman Peninsula (situated in the Russian Federation, to the east) by the Kerch Strait. The Republic covers a total area of 25,900 sq km, some 80% of which is dry steppeland. It is rich in minerals. The region's main cities are Simferopol, Sevastopol and Kerch. The towns of the south coast, particularly Yalta, are popular tourist resorts. In 1989 an estimated 26% of the population of the Crimea were Ukrainian and 67% Russian. By 1984 there were some 280,000 Crimean Tatars in the region, who had returned from Central Asia where they were deported by Stalin in 1944. The capital of the Crimean Republic is at Simferopol.

President of the Republic: YURY MESHKOV.

Chairman of the Presidium of the Supreme Council: MYKOLA BAHROV.

Prime Minister: YEVGENY SABUROV (designate).

Political Organizations

Until 1990 the only legal political party in Ukraine was the Communist Party of Ukraine (CPU), an integral part of the Communist Party of the Soviet Union. In 1988, however, a Ukrainian People's Movement for Restructuring (known as Rukh) was established to support greater democratization and freedom of speech, and several other political organizations were also founded. In 1990, after the CPU's constitutional monopoly was abolished, many new political parties were established. In 1992 several coalitions were formed, notably the Congress of National Democratic Forces, which unites conservative, nationalist parties, and New Ukraine, which has the support of centrist parties and many business executives. Rukh, which had been the main coalition of forces opposed to the CPU in 1988–91, became a political party (as the People's Movement of Ukraine) in 1993. At the beginning of 1994 both extreme left-wing and extreme right-wing parties had been formed in Ukraine, including the Ukrainian National Assembly and the National Fascist Party, and the extreme left-wing Socialist Party of Ukraine. The CPU, which was banned after the coup attempt in Moscow in August 1991, was officially reinstated by the Presidium of the Supreme Council in May 1993 and registered by the Ministry of Justice in October. Some 32 Ukrainian political parties were registered for the elections held to the Supreme Council on 27 March 1994.

All-Ukrainian Centrist Party of Civil Accord: Kiev; f. 1993; 20,000 mems.

Anti-Communist and Anti-Imperial Front of Ukraine (AAFU): Kiev; f. 1993; loose alliance of more than 30 parties, inc. Rukh, the CNDS, the URP, the UDP; advocates new local and parliamentary elections, adoption of a new constitution; opposes end to ban on the Communist Party of Ukraine.

Christian Democratic Party of Ukraine (KhDPU): Kiev; democratic nationalist party; Leader V. ZHURAVSKY; 12,000 mems.

Civic Congress of Ukraine (HKU): Kiev; centrist; Leader O. BAZYLYUK; 1,500 mems.

Communist Party of Ukraine (KPU): Kiev; banned in August 1991, re-established in May 1993; registered as a political party in October; Leader P. SYMONENKO; 120,000 mems.

Congress of National Democratic Forces (CNDS): Kiev; f. 1992; alliance of 20 nationalist-conservative groups and parties; advocates strong presidency, a unitary state, secession from the CIS, 'socially-just' market economy; Chair. MYKHAILO HORYN; includes:

Democratic Party of Ukraine (DPU): Kiev; f. 1990; democratic nationalist party; opposes CIS membership, advocates national cultural and linguistic policies to support Ukrainian heritage; Chair. VOLODYMYR YAVORISKY; c. 3,000 mems.

Ukrainian National Conservative Party (UNKP): Kiev; f. 1992 by merger of Ukrainian National Party and Ukrainian People's Democratic party; radical nationalist party; Leader V. RADIONOV; 500 mems.

Ukrainian Peasant Democratic Party (USDP): Lviv, vul. 700-richya Lviva 63, kv. 712; tel. (0322) 59-97-37; f. 1990; democratic nationalist party, advocates private farming, dissolution of collective farms; Chair. SERHIY PLACHYNDA; 5,000 mems.

Ukrainian Republican Party (URP): Kiev; f. 1990 as successor to Ukrainian Helsinki Union (f. 1988); democratic nationalist party; advocates immediate departure from the CIS, consolidation of independence; Chair. MYKHAILO HORYN; 12,000 mems.

Congress of Ukrainian Nationalists (KUN): Kiev; radical nationalist party; Leader S. STESTKO.

Constitutional Democratic Party (KDPU): Kiev; centrist party; Leader V. ZOLOTAREV.

Green Party of Ukraine (Partiya Zelenykh Ukrayiny—PZU): 252024 Kiev, vul. Luteranska 24; tel. (044) 293-69-09; fax (044) 293-52-36; f. 1990 as political wing of environmental organization, Zeleny Svit (Green World—f. 1987); democratic nationalist party; Pres. VITALY KONONOV; Chair. SERHIY KURYKIN; 1,500 mems.

Labour Congress of Ukraine (TKU): Kiev; centrist party; Leader A. MATVIYENKO; 2,000 mems.

Liberal Democratic Party of Ukraine (LDPU): Kiev; democratic nationalist party; Leader V. KLYMCHUK; 1,000 mems.

Liberal Party of Ukraine (LPU): Kiev; centrist party; Leader IHOR MARKULOV; 10,000 mems.

Organization of Ukrainian Nationalists (Orhanizatisya Ukrayinskykh Natsionalistiv—OUNvU): Kiev; registered as a political party in 1993; radical nationalist; Leader M. SLYVKA.

National Fascist Party: Lviv; f. 1993; advocates supremacy of the Ukrainian nation and the extension of Ukrainian borders to the scale of Kievan Rus.

New Ukraine: Kiev; f. 1992; alliance of centrist parties and moderate left-wing groups; advocates radical economic reform and improvement of links with Russia and the CIS; Chair. VOLODYMYR FILENKO; c. 30,000 mems; includes:

Party for Democratic Renewal of Ukraine (PDVU): 252034 Kiev, Proreznaya vul. 13, Flat 64; tel. (044) 229-29-68; (044) 224-23-12; f. 1990 as the Democratic Platform within the CPU; centrist party; advocates close economic links with Russia and the CIS, a market economy and privatization; Leaders VOLODYMYR FILENKO; 2,500 mems.

Party of Free Peasants of Ukraine (PVSU): Kiev; democratic nationalist party; Leader V. HORDIYENKO; 4,500 mems.

Party of Labour (PP): Kiev; centrist party; Leader N. AZAROV; 10,000 mems.

Party for the National Salvation of Ukraine (Partiya Natsionalnoho Vryatuvannya Ukrayiny—PNPU): Kiev; registered as a political party in 1993; centrist; Leader LEONID YERSHOV; 1,500 mems.

Party for the Protection of Disabled and Socially Disadvantaged Citizens of Ukraine: Kiev; f. 1993.

Party of Slavic Unity (PSYeU): Kiev; centrist party; Leader I. KARPENKO.

Peasants' Party of Ukraine (SelPU): Kiev; f. 1992; centrist party; advocates retention of collective farm system, opposed to radical economic reform and land privatization; Leader SERHIY DOVHAN; 7,000 mems.

People's Movement of Ukraine (Rukh): Kiev; f. 1989 as popular front (Ukrainian People's Movement for Restructuring); registered as political party in 1993; democratic nationalist party; Leader VYACHESLAV CHORNOVIL; 62,000 full mems, 500,000 assoc. mems (1993).

People's Party of Ukraine (NPU): Kiev; centrist party; Leader L. TABURYANSKY; 3,671 mems.

Social Democratic Party of Ukraine (SDPU): f. 1990; advocates federal Ukraine, economic and political reform; centrist party; Leader YURY SBITNEV; 2,000 mems.

Socialist Party of Ukraine (SPU): Kiev; f. 1991; formed as partial successor to CPU; advocates retention of large state role in the economy, stronger links with CIS, priority for workers in privatization; strongly anti-nationalist; Leader OLEKSANDR MOROZ; c. 90,000 mems.

State Independence of Ukraine (DSU): Kiev; f. 1990; radical nationalist party; Co-Leaders V. SHLEMKO, HEORHY HREBENYUK.

Ukrainian Beer Lovers' Party (UPShP): Kiev; centrist party; Leader V. YERMAKOV; 2,500 mems.

Ukrainian Christian Democratic Party (UKhDP): Kiev; democratic nationalist party; Leader V. SICHKO; 350 mems.

Ukrainian Conservative Republican Party (UKRP): Kiev; radical nationalist party; Leader S. KHMARA; 3,000 mems.

Ukrainian National Assembly: Kiev; neo-fascist; Leader DMYTRO KORCHYNSKY.

Ukrainian Party of Justice (UPS): Kiev; centrist party; Leader M. HRECHKO; 20,000 mems.

United Social Democratic Party of Ukraine (USDPU): Kiev; f. 1990; left-wing democratic party; advocates comprehensive social-welfare system, gradual approach to economic reform, and continued Ukrainian membership of the CIS; Leader OLEKSANDR ALIN; c. 1,000 mems.

CRIMEAN POLITICAL ORGANIZATIONS

Like its Ukrainian counterpart, the Communist Party of Crimea was banned in August 1991. The following month, however, several local Communist Unions were established, which united in June 1992 to form the Union of Communists of Crimea. On 18 June 1993 the Union was renamed the Communist Party of Crimea and was officially registered on 15 September. Despite the anti-government violence in Moscow (Russia) in September–October 1993, at the beginning of 1994 the party enjoyed considerable support among the inhabitants of Crimea. However, several other powerful political interest groups were emerging at this time: various pro-Russian parties, including the Republican Party of Crimea, whose former leader, Yury Meshkov, won the Crimean presidential elections in January 1994; several parties promoting business interests, the most powerful of which was the Party for the Economic Renewal of Crimea; and Crimean Tatar movements. There was also one centrist organization, the Democratic Party of Crimea. In July 1993 a law was passed by the Crimean Supreme Soviet, which stated that all-Ukrainian political parties would not be entitled to participate in the elections to the Crimean legislature (scheduled for 27 March 1994) unless they registered locally. The Ukrainian Civic Forum of Crimea was formed as a result of this legislation. The Ukrainian Republican Party and the Democratic Party of Ukraine did, nevertheless, have some support amongst the population of the Crimea.

Agrarian Party of Crimea: Simferopol; f. 1994; Leader IVAN DEZHEMERYV.

Communist Party of Crimea: Simferopol; registered as political party in 1993; constituent part of CPU; Leader LEONID HRACH; 28,000 mems.

Crimean Party of Social Guarantees (Partiya Sotsialnykh Harantiy): Simferopol; f. 1993; envisages the development of a socially oriented economy by way of the independent development of both state and private sectors; Leader YUKHYM FIKS.

Crimean Tatar National Movement: Simferopol; registered as public organization in 1993; Leader: VASHTIY ABDURAYIMOV.

Democratic Party of Crimea: Simferopol; f. 1993; social-democratic party, supports Crimean autonomy within Ukraine and the establishment of confederative relations between the former Soviet Republics; Leader ANATOLY FILATOV.

Milli Firka: Simferopol; f. 1918; re-established in 1993; radical nationalist Tatar organization; Leader ILMY UMEROV.

National Movement of the Crimean Tatars: Simferopol; f. 1967; moderate nationalist organization; Leader (vacant).

National Movement of Tatars: Simferopol; Leader MUSTAFA CEMILOGLU.

Organization of the Crimean Tatar National Movement: Simferopol; f. 1989; promotes the aims of the Crimean Tatar parliament (Majlis), which include exclusive sovereignty over the territory of the Crimea and compensation for the victims of deportation; Leader REJEP KHAIREDINOV; 600–800 mems.

Party for Economic Revival of Crimea (PEVK): Simferopol; f. 1992; registered as political party in 1993; Crimean and all-Ukrainian organization; centrist; supports the establishment of an open economy; Co-Leaders VLADIMIR SHEVIOV, VLADIMIR YEGUDIN, VITALY FERMANCHUK; 30,000 mems.

Republican Party of Crimea: Simferopol; formed from the Republican Movement of Crimea (f. 1991) which opposed Ukrainian independence; registered as a political party in 1993; Chair. SERHIY TSEKOV.

Russian-Language Movement of Crimea: Simferopol; faction of the Republican Movement of Crimea; advocates the union of the Crimea with Russia.

Russian Party of Crimea: Simferopol; f. 1993; faction of the Republican Movement of Crimea; supports the return of the Crimea to Russia; Chair. (vacant); 1,000 mems.

Ukrainian Civic Congress of Crimea (Ukrayinsky Hromadyanskyy Konhres Krymu—UHKK): Simferopol; f. 1993.

Union for the Support of the Republic of Crimea: Kerch; f. 1993; Co-Leaders YAKOB APTER, SERGEY KUNITSYN.

Diplomatic Representation

EMBASSIES IN UKRAINE

Austria: 252021 Kiev, vul. Lipska 5, Hotel Natsionalny; tel. (044) 291-88-40; fax (044) 291-89-66; Ambassador: Dr GEORG WEISS.

Belgium: 252024 Kiev, vul. Chovkovichna 26/4; tel (044) 293-21-10; telex 131177; fax (044) 226-36-47; Ambassador: INGEBORG KRISTOFFERSEN.

Bulgaria: Kiev, vul. Hospitalna 1; tel. (044) 224-53-60; Ambassador: DIMITAR TSEROV.

Canada: 252034 Kiev, POB 200, 31 Yaroslaviv val; tel. (044) 212-35-50; fax (044) 291-54-68; Ambassador: FRANÇOIS MATHYS.

China, People's Republic: Kiev, vul. Hospitalna 4, Hotel Rus; tel. (044) 227-84-02; Ambassador: CHIANG CHEN.

Croatia: Kiev, vul. Volodymyrska 45; tel. (044) 224-05-00; fax (044) 225-20-14; Ambassador: IVICA TRNKOP.

Cuba: Kiev, Bekhterevsky prov. 5; tel. (044) 216-29-30; Ambassador: DIOGENES HERNÁNDEZ ASTORGA.

Czech Republic: 252034 Kiev, Yaroslaviv val 34; tel. (044) 229-79-22; Ambassador: ROBERT HARENCAR.

Denmark: Kiev, vul. Volodymyrska 4; tel. (044) 229-45-37; fax (044) 229-18-31; Ambassador: CHRISTIAN FABER-ROD.

Finland: Kiev, vul. Striletska 14; tel. (044) 227-84-34; fax (044) 227-84-56; Ambassador: ERIK ULFSTEDT.

France: Kiev, vul. Reytarska 39; tel. (044) 228-87-28; Ambassador: HUGUES PERNET.

Germany: 252054 Kiev, vul. Chkalova 84; tel. (044) 216-67-94; fax (044) 216-92-33; Ambassador: HENNECKE Graf VON BASSEWITZ.

Holy See: 250005 Kiev, vul. Chervonoarmiyska 96; tel. (044) 268-95-05; fax (044) 269-24-17; Apostolic Nuncio: Most Rev. ANTONIO FRANCO, Titular Bishop of Gallese.

Hungary: Kiev; Ambassador: ISTVÁN VARGA.

India: Kiev, Hotel Kiev; tel. (044) 227-88-60; Ambassador: S. T. DEVARE.

Iran: 252021 Kiev, vul. Lipska 5, Hotel Natsionalny; tel. (044) 291-88-69; fax (044) 291-54-68; Ambassador: BEHZAD MAZAHEVI.

Italy: 252021 Kiev, vul. Lipska 5, Hotel Natsionalny; tel. (044) 291-88-98; telex 131462; fax (044) 291-88-97; Ambassador: VITTORIO SURDO.

Japan: 252021 Kiev, vul. Lipska 5, Hotel Natsionalny; tel. and fax (044) 291-88-72.

Kazakhstan: Kiev.

Mongolia: Kiev, vul. Kotsyubynskoho 3; tel. (044) 216-88-91; Ambassador: DASHNYAM YADMAAGIIN.

Poland: Kiev, Yaroslaviv val 12; tel. (044) 255-51-14; Ambassador: JERZY KOZAKIEWICZ.

Romania: 252030 Kiev, vul. Kotsyubynskoho 8; tel. (044) 224-52-61; fax (044) 293-69-50; Ambassador: LEONTIN PASTOR.

Russia: 252021 Kiev, vul. Lipska 5, Hotel Natsionalny; tel. (044) 291-83-13; fax (044) 291-54-68; Ambassador: LEONID SMOLYAKOV.

Slovakia: 252034 Kiev, Yaroslaviv val 34; tel.(044) 229-79-22; fax (044) 212-32-71; Ambassador: (vacant).

Spain: Kiev, vul. Hospitalna 4, Hotel Rus; tel. (044) 229-77-09; Ambassador: EDUARDO JUNCO BONET.

Sweden: 252021 Kiev, vul. Lipska 5, Hotel Natsionalny, Suite 1109; tel. (044) 291-89-19; fax (044) 291-62-33; Ambassador: MARTIN HALLQVIST.

Turkey: 252021 Kiev, vul. Lipska 5, Hotel Natsionalny; tel. (044) 291-88-72; fax (044) 291-54-68; Ambassador: ACAR GERMEN.

United Kingdom: Kiev, vul. Desiatynna 9; tel. (044) 228-05-04; fax (044) 228-39-72; Ambassador: SIMON HEMANS.

USA: Kiev, vul. Kotsyubynskoho 10; tel. (044) 244-73-44; fax (044) 244-73-51; Ambassador: WILLIAM G. MILLER.

Judicial System

Constitutional Court: Kiev; Chair. Prof. LEONID YUZKOV.

Supreme Court: 252601 Kiev, vul. Chekistiv 4; tel. (044) 226-23-04; Chair. HEORHY BUTENKO.

Supreme Arbitration Court: 252001 Kiev, vul. Kreshchatik 5; tel. (044) 226-32-39; fax (044) 228-70-42; f. 1991; Chief Justice DMYTRO M. PRYTYKA.

Procurator-General: 252601 Kiev, vul. Riznitska 123/15; tel. (044) 226-20-27; Procurator-General VLADISLAV DOTSYUK.

Religion

CHRISTIANITY

The Eastern Orthodox Church

Eastern Orthodoxy is the principal religious affiliation in Ukraine. Until 1990 all Orthodox churches were part of the Ukrainian exarchate of the Russian Orthodox Church. In that year the Russian Orthodox Church in Ukraine was renamed the Ukrainian Orthodox Church (UOC), partly to counter the growing influence of the Ukrainian Autocephalous Orthodox Church (UAOC). In the early 1990s there was considerable tension between the UOC and the UAOC over the issue of church property seized in 1930. A third Orthodox church was formed in June 1992, when Filaret, the disgraced former Metropolitan of Kiev, united with part of the UAOC to form the Kievan Patriarchate of the UOC, with himself as Patriarch. Patriarch Filaret had failed to secure canonical recognition for the Kievan Patriarchate of the UOC by January 1994.

Ukrainian Autocephalous Orthodox Church: Kiev; established in 1921 as part of the wider movement for Ukrainian autonomy, but forcibly incorporated into the Russian Orthodox Church in 1930; continued to operate clandestinely and among Ukrainian exiles; formally revived in Ukraine in 1990; Patriarch of Kiev and All Ukraine His Holiness DMYTRO.

Ukrainian Orthodox Church: Kiev, Pechersk Monastery, Sichnevoho povstannia 21; tel. (044) 290-08-66; exarchate of the Russian Orthodox Church; owes allegiance to the Moscow Patriarchate; Metropolitan of Kiev VLADIMIR.

Ukrainian Orthodox Church (Kievan Patriarchate): Kiev; f. 1992; Patriarch of All Ukraine VOLODYMYR ROMANYUK.

Roman Catholicism

Most Roman Catholics in Ukraine are adherents of the Byzantine Rite, the so-called Uniate ('Greek' Catholic) Church, which is based principally in Western Ukraine and Transcarpathia. In June 1992 there were 2,700 Uniate churches in Ukraine and 452 Roman Catholic churches of the Latin Rite. Adherents of Latin-Rite Catholicism in Ukraine are predominantly ethnic Poles.

Metropolitan See of Lvov (Latin Rite): Lubaczów, Poland; Archbishop MARIAN JAWORSKI.

Ukrainian Catholic (Uniate) Church: Lviv, St George's Cathedral; established in 1596 by the Union of Brest, which permitted Orthodox clergymen to retain the Eastern rite, but transferred their allegiance to the Pope; in 1946 at the Synod of Lvov (Lviv Sobor) the Uniates were forcibly integrated into the Russian Orthodox Church, but continued to function in an 'underground' capacity; an estimated 4m.–5m. adherents; Archbishop-Major of Lvov Cardinal MYROSLAV I. LUBACHIVSKY.

The Press

In 1990 there were 1,787 officially-registered newspaper titles being published in Ukraine, of which 1,253 were in Ukrainian. There were also 185 periodicals, 97 in Ukrainian.

The publications listed below are in Ukrainian, except where otherwise stated.

PRINCIPAL NEWSPAPERS

Demokratychna Ukraina (Democratic Ukraine): 252047 Kiev, pr. Peremohi 50; tel. (044) 441-85-46; f. 1918; fmrly *Radyanska Ukraina* (Soviet Ukraine); fmrly organ of the Communist Party of Ukraine, the Supreme Soviet and Council of Ministers; 6 a week; independent; Editor V. Y. STADNICHENKO; circ. 311,300.

Holos Ukrainy (Voice of Ukraine): 252047 Kiev, vul. Nesterova 4; tel. (044) 441-89-46; fax (044) 224-72-54; organ of the Supreme Council; in Ukrainian and Russian; supplements in other languages used in Ukraine; circ. 448,000 (1992).

Literaturna Ukraina: 252601 Kiev, bul. Lesi Ukrainki 20; tel. (044) 296-36-39; f. 1927; weekly; organ of the Union of Writers of Ukraine; Editor-in-Chief VASIL PLYUSHCH; circ. 45,000 (1992).

News from Ukraine: 252107 Kiev, vul. O. Shmidta 35/37; f. 1964; weekly; publ. by the joint-stock co. News from Ukraine; in English; readership in 70 countries; Editor V. P. KANASH; circ. 20,000.

Nezavizimost (Independence): 252047 Kiev, Peremohy pr. 50; tel. (044) 441-83-33; fmrly *Komsomolskoe Znamya* (Komsomol Banner); independent; Editor-in-Chief VOLODYMR KULEBA.

Pravda Ukrainy (Ukrainian Pravda): 252047 Kiev, Peremohy pr. 50; tel. (044) 225-51-42; f. 1938; 6 a week; organ of the Supreme Council; Editor A. T. ZONENKO; circ. 358,300.

Rabochaya Gazeta/Robitnycha Hazeta (Workers' Gazette): Kiev, pr. Pobedy 50; tel. (044) 441-86-57; fax (044) 446-02-98; f. 1957; 5 a week; publ. by the Cabinet of Ministers and Inter-regional Association of Manufacturers; editions in Russian and Ukrainian; Editor-in-Chief EVELINA V. BABENKO-PIVTORADNI; circ. 176,000 (1993).

Silski Visti (Rural News): Kiev, Peremohy pr. 50; tel. (044) 441-83-33; f. 1920; 6 a week; fmrly publ. by the Cen. Cttee of the Ukrainian Communist Party; Editor I. V. SPODARENKO; circ. 550,000 (1992).

Uryadoviy Kuryer (Official Courier): 252008 Kiev, vul. Sadova 1; tel. (044) 293-55-09; 3 a week (organ of the Supreme Council; Editor-in-Chief MIKHAILO SOROKA.

Vecherniy Kyiv (Evening Kiev): 252136 Kiev, vul. Marshala Hrechka 13; tel. (044) 434-61-09; fax (044) 443-96-09; Editor-in-Chief VITALII KARPENKO.

Za Vilnu Ukrainu: 290000 Lviv, vul. Voronoho 3; tel. (0322) 72-89-04; fax (0322) 72-95-27; f. 1990; 3 a week; independent; Editor-in-Chief BOGDAN VOVK; circ. 135,000 (1993).

Zemlia i Volia (Land and Freedom): Lviv, vul. 700-richya Lviva 63, kv. 213; tel. (0322) 59-96-71; f. 1991; organ of the Ukrainian Democratic Peasant Party.

PRINCIPAL PERIODICALS

Barvinok (Periwinkle): 254119 Kiev, vul. Degtyarivska 38–44; tel. (044) 211-04-98; f. 1928; 2 a month; illustrated popular fiction for school-age children; in Ukrainian and Russian; circ. 500,000.

Berezil (March): 310078 Kharkiv, vul. Chernyshevskoho 59; tel. (0572) 43-41-84; f. 1956; fmrly *Prapor;* monthly; publ. by the Berezil (March) Publishing House; journal of Union of Writers of Ukraine; fiction; Editor-in-Chief YURIY STADNYCHENKO; circ. 10,000.

Dnipro (The Dnieper River): 252119 Kiev, vul. Degtyarivska 38–44; tel. (044) 213-98-79; f. 1927; monthly; publ. by the Molod (Youth)

Publishing House; fmrly journal of the Cen. Cttee of the Leninist Young Communist League of Ukraine; novels, short stories, essays, poetry; social and political topics; circ. 71,900.

Donbass (The Donets Coal Basin): 340055 Donetsk, vul. Artema 80A; tel. (0622) 93-82-26; f. 1923; monthly; journal of Union of Writers of Ukraine; fiction; in Ukrainian and Russian; circ. 20,000 (1991).

Dzvin (Bell): 290005 Lviv, vul. Vatutina 6; tel. (0322) 72-36-20; f. 1940; monthly; publ. by the Kamenyar Publishing House; journal of Union of Writers of Ukraine; fiction; Editor ROMAN FEDORIV; circ. 152,500.

Khronika 2,000—Nash Kray (Chronicle 2,000—Our Land): 252001 Kiev, vul. M. Hrushevskoho 1D; tel. (044) 296-33-77; fax (044) 228-88-62; f. 1992; Ukrainian cultural almanac; Editor-in-Chief YURY BURYAK; circ. 15,000.

Kiev: 252025 Kiev, vul. Desyatinna 11; tel. (044) 229-02-80; f. 1983; monthly, publ. by the Ukrainsky Pysmennyk (Ukrainian Writer) Publishing House; journal of the Union of Writers of Ukraine and the Kiev Writers' Organization; fiction; Editor-in-Chief PETR M. PEREBEINOS; circ. 39,000.

Kommunist Ukrainy (Communist of Ukraine): 252009 Kiev, vul. Bankova 8; tel. (044) 291-57-72; f. 1925; monthly; publ. by the Presa Ukrainy (Press of Ukraine) Publishing House; political; in Ukrainian and Russian; circ. 21,700 in Ukrainian, 11,200 in Russian.

Lel: 254119 Kiev, vul. Degtyarivska 38–44; tel. (044) 211-02-89; fax (044) 228-88-62; f. 1992; monthly; erotic fiction and arts; Editor-in-Chief SERHIY CHIRKOV; circ. 120,000.

Lyudina i Svit (Man and World): 254025 Kiev, Rylsky pr. 10; tel. (044) 228-23-87; f. 1960; monthly; publ. by the Presa Ukrainy (Press of Ukraine) Publishing House; journal of the Ukrainian Society Znanye (Knowledge); popular scientific; religious; Editor-in-Chief MIKOLA RUBANETS; circ. 46,000.

Malyatko (Child): 254119 Kiev, vul. Degtyarivska 38–44; tel. (044) 213-98-91; f. 1960; monthly; illustrated; for pre-school children; Editor-in-Chief SVITLANA YEFIMENKO; circ. 240,000 (1993).

Muzyka (Music): 252601 Kiev, vul. Yanvarskoho Vosstaniya 21, kor. 20; tel. (044) 290-49-70; f. 1923; 6 a year; organ of the Ministry of Culture, of the Union of Ukrainian Composers and the Musicians' Society of Ukraine; musical culture and aesthetics; circ. 8,200.

Nauka i Suspilstvo (Science and Society): 252047 Kiev, Peremohy pr. 50; tel. (044) 441-88-10; f. 1923; monthly; publ. by the Presa Ukrainy (Press of Ukraine) Publishing House; journal of the Ukrainian Society Znanye (Knowledge); popular scientific; illustrated; Editor-in-Chief YURY ROMANYUK; circ. 48,800.

Novini Kinoekranu (Screen News): 252033 Kiev, vul. Saksahanskoho 6; tel. (044) 227-47-07; f. 1961; monthly; journal of the Ukrainian Union of Cinematographers; cinema criticism and information; circ. 410,000.

Obrazotvorche Mistetstvo (Fine Arts): 254655 Kiev, vul. Artema 1–5; tel. (044) 212-02-86; f. 1935; 4 a year; publ. by the Artists' Union of Ukraine; journal of the Artists' Union of Ukraine; fine arts; Editor-in-Chief MYKOLA MARYCHEVSKY; circ. 5,200.

Odnoklasnnik (Classmate): 254119 Kiev, vul. Degtyarivska 38–44; tel. (044) 211-02-78; f. 1923; monthly; fiction; for teenagers; in Ukrainian and Russian; Editor-in-Chief SERGIY CHIRKOV; circ. 100,000 in Ukrainian, 55,200 in Russian.

Perets (Pepper): 252047 Kiev, vul. P. Nesterova 4; tel. (044) 441-82-14; f. 1927; fortnightly; publ. by the Presa Ukrainy (Press of Ukraine) Publishing House; satirical; circ. 1,946,900.

Politika i Chas (Politics and Time): 252025 Kiev, vul. Desyatinna 4–6; tel. (044) 229-75-73; f. 1992; monthly; publ. by the Presa Ukrainy (Press of Ukraine) Publishing House; international affairs and foreign relations of Ukraine; Editor-in-Chief L. S. BAYDAK; circ. 10,000.

Raduga (Rainbow): 252047 Kiev, Peremohy pr. 50; tel. (044) 224-91-98; f. 1950; monthly; publ. by the Ukrainsky Pysmennyk (Ukrainian Writer) Publishing House; journal of the Union of Writers of Ukraine; fiction and politics; in Russian; circ. 51,140.

Ranok (Morning): 252119 Kiev, vul. Degtyarivska 38–42; tel. (044) 213-15-96; f. 1953; monthly; publ. by the Molod (Youth) Publishing House; for young people; social, political and fiction; circ. 105,000.

Start (Start): 252033 Kiev, vul. Tarasovska 6; tel. (044) 224-71-20; f. 1922; monthly; publ. by the Molod (Youth) Publishing House; organ of the State Cttee for Sports and Physical Culture; sports news; circ. 115,000.

Ukraina (Ukraine): 252047 Kiev, Peremohy pr. 50; tel. (044) 441-88-31; f. 1941; weekly; publ. by the Presa Ukrainy (Press of Ukraine) Publishing House; social and political life in Ukraine; illustrated; Editor-in-Chief ANATOLY MIKHAILENKO; circ. 70,000.

Ukrainsky Teatr (Ukrainian Theatre): Kiev, vul. Yanvarskoho Vosstaniya 21, kor. 20; tel. (044) 290-79-49; f. 1936; 6 a year; publ. by the Mistetstvo (Fine Art) Publishing House; journal of the Ministry of Culture and the Union of Theatrical Workers of Ukraine; Editor-in-Chief TAMARA ANUFRIENKO; circ. 4,100.

Vavylon-XXI (Babylon-XXI): 252195 Kiev, Lesi Ukrainki bul. 26; publ. by the Dovira Publishing House; tel. (044) 296-52-51; fax (044) 228-88-62; f. 1990; cinema; Editor-in-Chief MYKHAYLO SLABOSHPITSKY; circ. 4,000.

Visti z Ukrainy (News from Ukraine): Kiev, Zoloti Vorota 6; tel. (044) 229-65-71; fax (044) 228-04-28; f. 1960; monthly; aimed at Ukrainian diaspora; Editor VALERY STETSENKO; circ. 50,000.

Vitchizna (Fatherland): 252021 Kiev, vul. M. Hrushevskoho 34; tel. (044) 293-28-51; f. 1933; monthly; publ. by the Ukrainsky Pysmennyk (Ukrainian Writer) Publishing House; journal of the Union of Writers of Ukraine; Ukrainian prose and poetry; circ. 50,100.

Vsesvit (All the World): 252021 Kiev, vul. M. Hrushevskoho 34; tel. (044) 293-13-18; f. 1925; monthly; publ. by the Ukrainsky Pysmennyk (Ukrainian Writer) Publishing House; joint edition of the Union of Writers of Ukraine and the Ukrainian Peace Council; foreign fiction, critical works and reviews of foreign literature and art; Editor-in-Chief OLEG MIKITENKO; circ. 30,000.

Zhinka (Woman): 252047 Kiev, Peremohi pr. 50; tel. (044) 446-90-34; f. 1920; monthly; publ. by Presa Ukrainy (Press of Ukraine) Publishing House; social and political subjects; fiction; for women; circ. 750,000.

Znannya ta Pratsya (Knowledge and Labour): 252047 Kiev, vul. Degtyarivska 38–42; tel. (044) 211-02-51; f. 1929; monthly; publ. by the Molod (Youth) Publishing House; fmrly journal of the Leninist Young Communist League of Ukraine; popular science and technology; circ. 28,000.

NEWS AGENCIES

Respublika: Kiev-140, POB 136, vul. Nyzhny Val 23D; tel. (044) 417-13-32; independent press agency; Dir S. NABOKA.

Rukh Press: 252032 Kiev, Shevchenka bul. 37/122; tel. and fax (044) 244-64-00; affiliated to the Rukh political movement; f. 1989 as Rukh Inform, renamed 1990; issues information in Ukrainian and English; Dir DMYTRO PONAMARCHUK.

Ukrainian National Information Agency (UKRINFORM): 252601 Kiev, vul. Bohdana Khmelnytskoho 8/16; tel. (044) 226-32-30; telex 131210; fax (044) 229-24-39; official news agency, covering political, economic, diplomatic, cultural and sporting information; Dir VITALY F. VOZIANOV.

Ukrainian Press Agency: Kiev, vul. Baumana 53/16; tel. (044) 221-55-07; fax (044) 221-55-07; independent news agency; Dir T. KUZIO.

Foreign Bureau

Reuters Ltd (United Kingdom): Kiev, vul. Bohdana Khmelnytskoho 8/16, office 112; tel. (044) 229-22-64; Chief Correspondent R. POPESKI.

Publishers

In 1990 there were 7,046 book titles (including pamphlets and brochures) published in Ukraine (total circulation, 170m., including 95m. in Ukrainian).

Berezil (March): 310002 Kharkiv, vul. Chubarya 11; tel. (044) 47-72-52; fiction and criticism; in Ukrainian and Russian; Dir A. M. KUMAKA.

Budivelnik (Building): 254053 Kiev, Observatorna vul. 25; tel. (044) 212-10-90; f. 1947; books on building and architecture; in Ukrainian and Russian; Dir S. N. BALATSKY.

Carpaty (Carpathian Mountains): 294000 Ushhorod, Radyanska pl. 3; tel. (03100) 3-25-13; fiction and criticism; in Ukrainian and Russian; Dir V. I. DANKANICH.

Dnipro (The Dnieper River): 252601 Kiev, Volodymyrska vul. 42; tel. (044) 224-31-82; f. 1919; fiction, poetry and critical works; in Ukrainian and Russian; Dir TARAS I. SERGIYCHUK.

Donbass (The Donets Coal Basin): 340002 Donetsk, vul. Bohdana Khmelnytskoho 102; tel. (0622) 93-25-84; fiction and criticism; in Ukrainian and Russian; Dir B. F. KRAVCHENKO.

Kamenyar (Stonecrusher): 290006 Lviv, vul. Pidvalna 3; tel. (0322) 72-19-49; fiction and criticism; in Ukrainian; Dir M. V. NECHAY.

Mayak (Lighthouse): 270001 Odesa, vul. Zhukovskoho 14; tel. (048) 22-35-95; fiction and criticism; in Ukrainian and Russian; Dir D. A. BUKHANENKO.

Mistetstvo (Fine Art): 252034 Kiev, vul. Zolotovoritska 11; tel. (044) 225-53-92; fax (044) 229-05-64; f. 1932; fine art criticism, theatre and screen art; in Ukrainian, Russian, English, French and German; Dir VALENTIN M. KUZMENKO.

Molod (Youth): 252119 Kiev, vul. Degtyarivska 38–44; tel. (044) 213-11-60; fax (044) 213-98-29; in Ukrainian; Dir A. I. Davidov.

Muzichna Ukraina (Music of Ukraine): 252004 Kiev, Pushkinska vul. 32; tel. (044) 225-63-56; f. 1966; books on music; in Ukrainian; Dir N. P. Linnik; Chief Editor B. R. Vereshchagin.

Naukova Dumka (Scientific Thought Publishing House): 252601 Kiev, vul. Tereshchenkivska 3; tel. (044) 224-40-68; fax (044) 224-70-60; f. 1922; scientific books and periodicals in all branches of science; research monographs; in Ukrainian, Russian and English; Dir S. S. Radchenko.

Osvita (Education): 252053 Kiev, vul. Y. Kotsyubynskoho 5; tel. (044) 216-58-02; textbooks for secondary schools; Dir A. F. Denisov.

Politvidav Ukrainy (Ukraine Political Publishing House): 254025 Kiev, vul. Desyatinna 4/6; tel. (044) 229-16-92; academic, reference and popular works; law, social and economic issues, religion; calendars, posters, etc.; in Ukrainian, Russian and other European languages; Dir G. F. Nemazany.

Sich: 320070 Dnipropetrovsk, K. Marks pr. 60; tel. (0562) 45-22-01; f. 1964; fiction, juvenile, socio-political, criticism; in Ukrainian, English, German, French and Russian; Dir V. A. Sirota; Editor-in-Chief V. V. Levchenko.

Tavria: 330000 Simferopol, vul. Gorkoho 5; tel. (0652) 7-45-66; fiction and criticism; in Ukrainian and in Russian; Dir I. N. Klosovsky.

Tekhnika (Technical Publishing House): 252601 Kiev, vul. Khreshchatik 5; tel. (044) 228-22-43; f. 1930; industry and transport books, popular science, posters and booklets; in Russian and Ukrainian; Dir M. G. Pisarenko.

Ukrainska Encyclopedia (Ukrainian Encyclopedia): 252030 Kiev, vul. Bohdana Khmelnytskoho 51; tel. (044) 224-80-85; encyclopaedias, dictionaries and reference books; Dir A. V. Kudritsky.

Ukrainsky Pysmennyk (Ukrainian Writer Publishing House): 252054 Kiev, vul. Chkalova 52; tel. (044) 216-25-92; f. 1933; publishing house of the Ukrainian Union of Writers; fiction; in Ukrainian; Dir V. P. Skomarovski.

Urozhai (Crop Publishing House): 252035 Kiev, Yaroslaviv val 10; tel. (044) 245-11-96; f. 1925; books and journals about agriculture; Dir V. G. Prikhodko.

Veselka (Rainbow Publishing House): 252050 Kiev, vul. Melnikova 63; tel. (044) 213-96-01; f. 1934; books for pre-school and school age children; in Ukrainian and foreign languages; Dir Yarema Hoyan.

Vyscha Shkola (Higher School): 252054 Kiev, vul. Hoholivska 7; tel. (044) 216-33-05; f. 1968; educational, scientific, reference, etc.; Dir V. P. Taranik.

Zdorovya (Health Publishing House): 252601 Kiev, vul. Chkalova 65; tel. (044) 216-89-08; books on medicine, physical fitness and sport; in Ukrainian; Dir A. P. Rodziyevsky.

Radio and Television

In 1990 there were a total of 794 radio receivers and 327 televisions in Ukraine per 1,000 of the population.

National Council for Television and Radio Broadcasting Issues (Natsionalna Rada z Pytan Telebachennya i Radiomovlennya): Kiev; f. 1994; a state, extradepartmental body functioning in accordance with regulations approved by the Supreme Council.

State Television and Radio Broadcasting Company of Ukraine: 252001 Kiev, vul. Khreshchatik 26; tel. (044) 226-31-44; telex 131359; fax (044) 229-11-70; f. 1924; television and radio broadcasts in Russian and Ukrainian; also broadcasts to Europe, Australia, the CIS and North America in Ukrainian, English, German and Romanian.

Crimea (Krym) Television and Radio Company: Simferopol; Pres. Valery Astakhov.

Finance

(cap. = capital; res = reserves; dep. = deposits; K = karbovantsi; brs = branches; m. = million; amounts in karbovantsi, unless otherwise stated)

BANKING

Central Bank

National Bank of Ukraine: 252007 Kiev, vul. Zhovtnevoi Revolutsii 9; tel. (044) 293-42-64; fax (044) 293-16-98; Chair of Board Viktor Yushchenko; Vice-Chairman Dr Oleksandr Savchenko.

Other State Banks

State Bank of Crimea: Simferopol.

Ukrainian Export-Import Bank: 252001 Kiev-1, vul. Khreshchatik 8; tel. (044) 226-27-45; fax (044) 229-80-82; fmrly br. of USSR Vneshekonombank; deals with foreign firms, joint ventures and import-export associations; Chair. S. O. Yarmenko.

Commercial Banks

Commercial Bank for Development of Construction Materials Industry: Kiev, vul. Artema 73; tel. (044) 211-39-13; telex 631266; fax (044) 216-75-95; cap. K1,000m., dep. K1,500m. (1993); Chair. of Bd. V. I. Gorbovsky; 2 brs.

Inko Joint-Stock Bank: 252021 Kiev, vul. Mechnikova 10; tel. (044) 432-45-66; fax (044) 294-87-90.

Kiev Narodny Bank: Kiev, vul. Sofiyevska 1; tel. (044) 228-74-51; telex 631334; fax (044) 229-35-55; f. 1989; cap. K496.8m. (Jan. 1993); Chair. of Bd Valery I. Ohiyenko; 4 brs.

Kievcoopbank: Kiev-5, vul. Anry Barbyusa 9; tel. (044) 268-32-04.

Perkombank—Joint-Stock Commercial 'Personal Computer' Bank: 254070 Kiev, vul. Sagaydachny 17; tel. (044) 291-86-20; telex 131420; fax (044) 291-86-60; f. 1989; cap. K2,700m., dep. K4,500m.; Chair. of Bd Sergey P. Bely.

Slaviansky Bank: 330600 Zaporizhzhia, vul. Elektrozavodska; tel. (0612) 52-13-25; fax (0612) 52-13-80.

Ukrinbank—Ukrainian Innovation Bank: 252601 Kiev, vul. Institutska 12a; tel. (044) 229-38-04; telex 131320; fax (044) 229-02-75; f. 1989; long-term investment credits; commercial and foreign exchange transactions; cap. K2,859m.; Chair. Viktor M. Kravets.

Ukrlegbank—Commercial Bank for Development of Light Industry in Ukraine: 252023 Kiev, vul. Kuybysheva 8/10; tel. (044) 220-81-36.

West-Ukrainian Commercial Bank: 290017 Lviv, vul. Levitskoho 67; tel. (0322) 75-03-96; telex 234199; fax (0322) 75-05-41; f. 1990; cap. 16.8m. roubles, res 867,000 roubles, dep. 87.0m. roubles (Dec. 1991); Pres. Oleksandr Ya. Dzhubenko; Chair. Volodymyr E. Shestopalov.

Zakhidkoopbank: Ivano-Frankivsk; tel. 2-50-02; fax 2-38-82; f. 1990; cap. K500m., dep. K6,000m.; Dep. Chair. Nela Politiko; 6 brs.

Banking Association

Association of Ukrainian Banks: Kiev; fmrly Commercial Bank Assn; Pres. Oleksandr Suhonyako.

COMMODITY EXCHANGES

Dnepropetrovsk Commodity Exchange (DCE): 320006 Dnipropetrovsk, 3 Turbinny spusk; tel. (0562) 42-03-14; f. 1991; Gen. Man. Vadim Komeko.

Kharkov Commodity and Raw Materials Exchange (KHCME): 310022 Kharkiv, Office 307, Gosprom; tel. (057) 47-82-78; fax (057) 22-82-01; f. 1991; Chair. of Exchange Cttee Zakhar Bruk.

Kiev Universal Commodity Exchange (KUCE): 252015 Kiev, vul. Leyptsihska 1a; tel. (044) 290-27-14; fax (044) 290-15-57; f. 1990; Pres. Nikolay Detochka.

Odessa Commodity Exchange (OCE): 270114 Odesa, 43 Leninskoy Iskri proyezd; tel. (048) 44-81-56; f. 1991; Gen. Man. Anatoly Glushkov.

South Universal Commodity Exchange (SUCE): 327015 Mikolaiv, vul. Rabochaya 2a; tel. (0510) 37-55-74; telex 272125; fax (0510) 36-08-52; f. 1990; Gen. Dir Nikolay Kozhemyakin.

INSURANCE

State Insurance Company

Ukrainian Commercial Insurance Organization: 252021 Kiev, vul. M. Hrushevskoho 34/1; tel. (044) 293-62-31; state insurance grouping; inc. State Insurance Company of Ukraine; Head of Directorate S. P. Hrusha.

Commercial Insurance Companies

Inderzhstrakh: Kiev-034; vul. Chekistiv 14/26; tel. (044) 212-29-19.

Inkomrezerv: Kiev-035, vul. Uritskoho 45; tel. (044) 244-09-80.

OMETA Inster: Kiev-053, vul. Artema 18; tel. (044) 212-09-26.

Revival Insurance Company: Kiev-024, vul. Kruhlouniversytetska 3; tel. (044) 224-71-50.

ROSTOK Insurance Company: Kiev-139, vul. Akademika Hlushkova 1, Pavilion 1; tel. (044) 261-75-55.

SKAID Insurance Corporation: Kiev-001, vul. Sofiyivska 9; tel. (044) 228-05-22; fax (044) 228-05-22.

Trade and Industry

STATE PROPERTY AGENCY

State Property Fund: 252008 Kiev, vul. M. Hrushevskoho 12/2.

TRADE DIRECTORATE

Chief Trade Directorate: 252053 Kiev, Lvivska pl. 8; tel. (044) 226-27-33; f. 1993; a section of Ministry of Foreign Economic Relations and Trade.

CHAMBERS OF COMMERCE

Ukrainian Chamber of Commerce and Industry: 254601 Kiev, vul. B. Zhytomyrska 33; tel. (044) 212-29-11; telex 131379; fax (044) 212-33-53; f. 1973; nine brs; Chair. OLEKSY P. MIKHAILICHENKO.

Congress of Business Circles of Ukraine: 252601 Kiev, vul. Proresnaya 15; tel. (044) 228-64-81; fax (044) 229-63-76; Pres. VALERY G. BABICH.

FOREIGN TRADE ORGANIZATION

Ukrimpex: 252054 Kiev, vul. Vorovskoho 22; tel. (044) 216-21-74; telex 131384; fax (044) 216-29-96; f. 1987; imports and exports a wide range of goods; organizes joint ventures, exhibitions; provides marketing expertise and business services; Dir-Gen. STANISLAV I. SOKOLENKO.

MAJOR INDUSTRIAL ENTERPRISES

Aviaagregat State Enterprise: 320600 Dnipropetrovsk, vul. Shchepkina 53; tel. (0562) 42-22-10; fax (0562) 59-02-37; manufacture and sale of hydraulics, centrifugal pumps and vacuum cleaners; Dir VLADIMIR MAZHARA; 6,000 employees.

Avtozaz Production Association: 330063 Zaporizhzhia, Leninsky pr. 8; tel. 64-36-89; telex 127437; fax 64-54-53; produces small passenger cars; Gen. Dir STEPAN I. KRAVCHUN; 20,000 employees.

Azovmash: 341035 Mariupol, pr. Ilyicha 145/147; tel. 47261; telex 115172; Gen. Dir ANATOLY E. ANTIFEYEV; 37,000 employees.

Belotserkovshina Production Association: 256400 Kiev, Belaya Tserkov, vul. Levanevskoho 91; tel. (044) 5-54-39; telex 131486; manufactures tyres for cars, trucks, etc.; Gen. Dir YURY V. KRASOTKIN; 10,000 employees.

Chemical Reagent Plant: 257036 Cherkasy; tel. 43-21-63; development and manufacture of chemical reagents; Dir VALENTIN V. BYHOV; 3,000 employees.

Chimprom Production Association: Donetsk obl., 343204 Slavyansk, vul. Chubarska 91; tel. (06262) 3-51-38; telex 115767; fax (06262) 2-48-69; production of various chemical products, including detergents, fire extinguishing powders, soda products, etc.; Dir EDVARD E. KRECH; 4,000 employees.

Donetsk Excavator Plant: 346338 Donetsk; tel. (0622) 5-22-32; telex 123235; produces excavators for use in industry, agriculture, etc; Plant Dir ALBERT V. KRUGLOV; 4,000 employees.

Donetskgormash Industrial Association: 340005 Donetsk, 1 vul. Tkachenko 189; tel. (0622) 61-45-08; fax (0622) 63-14-76; telex 115114; research, design and production of mining equipment; Gen. Man. VLADIMIR F. OSMERIK.

Electric Machine Building Plant: 325000 Kherson, vul. Ushakov 57; tel. 2-62-68; telex 273134; produces starter motors and alternators for car, tractor and motorcycle engines, car engine fans, etc; Dir Z. I. GORLOVSKY; 3,000 employees.

Kamenka Engineering Plant: Cherkasskoy obl., 258450 Kamenka, vul. Lenina 40; tel. 2-14-55; telex 147685; manufactures industrial pumps; Plant Dir ALEKSANDR V. ZHEVCHENKO; 2,500 employees.

Karpatpressmash Production Association: 284023 Ivano-Frankovsk, Yunosti vul. 16; tel. 2-34-83; design and manufacture of metal-plate pressing machinery, washing machines and a wide range of other consumer goods; Gen. Dir NIKOLAY SHINKARENKO; 3,600 employees.

Kharkov Tractor Plant: 310007 Kharkiv, Moskovsky pr. 275; tel. (057) 93-00-69; telex 115163; fax (057) 94-17-60; production of all types of tractors; Dir NIKOLAY A. PUGHIN.

Mayak Kiev Plant: 252073 Kiev, pr. Krasnikh Kozakov 8; tel. (044) 435-12-44; fax (044) 410-26-67; telex 131068; manufacture of audio equipment; Dir NIKOLAY I. PIVEN; 7,100 employees.

Pivmash: Dnipropetrovsk; largest missile-building factory in the world; Dir LEONID KUCHMA; 50,000 employees.

Preobrazovatel: 330069 Zaporizhzhia, Dnipropetrovskoye Shosse; tel. (0612) 52-71-31; fax (0612) 52-03-71; telex 127446; manufacture of power-conversion equipment and electrical household appliances; Gen. Dir MIKHAIL D. KOBLITSKY; 7,000 employees.

Stankiev Machine-Tool Production: 252062 Kiev, pr. Pobedy 67; tel. (044) 449-97-46; fax (044) 443-79-86; telex 131426; production of automatic lathes and other machinery; Chair. YURY E. ZABRODSKY; 7,000 employees.

Ukrelektromash Scientific and Industrial Association: 310005 Kharkiv, Iskrinskaya vul. 37; tel. (057) 21-45-50; fax (057) 21-84-92; telex 115170; produces electric motors; Gen-Dir NIKOLAY P. BELOUS.

Vinnitsa Plant of Tractor Units: 287100 Vynnytsa, Kotsubinsky 4; tel. 7-05-15; telex 119173; specializes in the production of hydraulic gear pumps and cylinders, and high-pressure hoses; Gen. Dir VLADIMIR A. BEDENKO.

Yuzhelektromash: Kakhovka obl., 326840 Novaya Kakhovka, Pervomaiskaya vul. 35; tel. 4-23-80; design and manufacture of electric motors; Gen. Dir DMITRY I. MOTSYO; 11,000 employees.

TRADE UNIONS

Federation of Trade Unions of Ukraine: 252012 Kiev, Maydan Nezalezhnosti 2; tel. (044) 228-87-88; fax (044) 229-00-87; f. 1990; fmrly Ukrainian branch of General Confederation of Trade Unions of the USSR; affiliation of 41 br. trade unions and 26 regional trade union federations; Chair. OLEKSANDR M. STOYAN.

Transport

RAILWAYS

In 1990 there were 22,780 km of railway track in use, with lines linking most towns and cities in the Republic. Kiev is linked by rail to all the other Republics of the former USSR, and there are direct lines to Warsaw (Poland), Budapest (Hungary) and Bucharest (Romania).

State Railway Transport Administration: 252034 Kiev, vul. Lysenka 6; tel. (044) 223-42-13; Pres. B. S. OLIYNYK.

ROADS

In 1990 there was a total of 273,700 km of roads, of which 236,400 were hard-surfaced.

INLAND WATERWAYS

In 1990 there were 4,400 km of navigable waterways. The Dnieper (Dnipro) river, which links Kiev, Cherkassy, Dnepropetrovsk and Zaporozhye with the Black Sea, is the most important route for river freight.

SHIPPING

The main ports are Yalta and Yevpatoriya in the Crimea, and Odessa. In addition to international shipping lines, there are services to the Russian ports of Novorossiysk and Sochi, and Batumi and Sukhumi in Georgia.

Shipping Companies

Azov Shipping Company: 341010 Mariupol, pr. Admirala Lunina 89; tel. 5-80-33; telex 115156; Pres. A. I. BANDURA.

Black Sea Shipping Company (BLASCO): 270026 Odesa, vul. Lastochkina 1; tel. (048) 25-21-60; telex 232248; Pres. PAVEL KUDYUKIN.

Danube Shipping Company: 272630 Izmail, pr. Suvorova 2; telex 232817; Pres. A. F. TEKHOV.

CIVIL AVIATION

Ukraine has air links with cities throughout the former USSR and with several major European and North American cities. The principal international airport is at Boryspil (Kiev).

National Airline

Ukrainian Airlines: 252135 Kiev, Peremohy pr. 1; tel. (044) 216-62-27; fax (044) 216-72-06; Gen. Dir V. S. RASHCHUK.

Tourism

The Black Sea coast of Ukraine has several popular resorts, including Odessa and Yalta. The Crimean peninsula is a popular tourist centre in both summer and winter, owing to its temperate climate. Kiev and Odessa have important historical attractions. The tourist industry is little developed outside Kiev and the Black Sea resorts, and the number of hotels and other facilities is low.

Association of Foreign Tourism: Kiev, Yaroslaviv val 36; tel. (044) 212-55-70; VLADIMIR I. SKRINNIK.

Culture

NATIONAL ORGANIZATION

Ministry of Culture: see section on The Government (Ministries).

CULTURAL HERITAGE

Kamenets-Podolsk State Historical Museum-Preserve: Khmelnitskaya obl., Kamenets-Podolsk, vul. K. Marksa 20; Dir K. G. MIKOLAIOVICH.

Kiev Lesya Ukrainka State Literature Museum: 252032 Kiev, vul. Saksaganskoho 97; tel. (044) 220-57-52; f. 1962; exhibits on the life of the Ukrainian poets and artists of the 19th and early 20th centuries; library of 5,000 vols: Dir IRINA L. VEREMEYEVA.

Kiev Museum of Russian Art: 252004 Kiev, vul. Tereschenkovska 9; tel. (044) 224-82-88; f. 1922; 10,000 exhibits; library of 17,000 vols; Dir G. N. SOLDATOVA.

Kiev Museum of Ukrainian Art: 252004 Kiev, vul. Kirova 6; 11,000 items; Dir V. F. YATSENKO.

Kiev-Pechersky State Historical Museum: Kiev, vul. Yanvarskoho Vosstaniya 21; tel. (044) 290-66-46; ancient monastery; large collection of icons.

Kiev State Historical Museum: Kiev, vul. Vladimirska 2; tel. (044) 228-65-45; 53,000 exhibits; Dir I. E. DUDNIK.

Kiev State Museum of Western and Oriental Art: Kiev, vul. Tereschenkovska 15–17; tel. (044) 225-02-06; 16,000 items; Dir V. F. OVCHINNIKOV.

Kiev T. G. Shevchenko State Museum: Kiev, bul. Shevchenko 12; tel. (044) 224-25-23; f. 1940; 21,000 exhibits on the life and work of Taras Shevchenko; Dir O. I. POLYANICHKO.

Kiev T. G. Shevchenko State University Library: 252601 Kiev, vul. Vladimirska 58; tel. (044) 266-54-77; some 2.7m. vols; Dir V. G. CHUBUK.

Lvov Historical Museum: Lviv, pl. Rynok 4/6; tel. (0322) 74-33-04; f. 1893; 300,000 exhibits; Dir B. N. CHAIKOVSKY.

National Archive: 252601 Kiev, Solomyanska 24; tel. (044) 277-12-33.

Odessa Archaeological Museum: Odesa, vul. Lastochkina 4; tel. (0482) 22-01-71; f. 1825; about 200,000 items; library of some 26,000 vols; Dir V. P. VANTCHUGOV.

Sofiysky Historical and Architectural State Museum: 252601 Kiev, vul. Vladimirska 24; tel. (044) 228-67-06; f. 1934; comprises 11th-century Sofiysky cathedral, frescoes, paintings, applied decorative arts, architectural monuments; Curator VALENTINA N. ACHKASOVA.

State History Library: 252601 Kiev, vul. Yanvarskoho Vasstaniya 21, kor. 24; tel. (044) 290-46-17.

State Public Library of Ukraine: 252001 Kiev, vul. M. Hrushevskoho 1; tel. (044) 228-85-12; f. 1866; 3.5m. vols; Dir A. P. KORNIENKO.

Ukrainian Museum of Folk and Decorative Art: Kiev, vul. Yanvarskoho Vosstaniya 21; f. 1954; 54,834 exhibits from 16th century onward; library of 3,180 vols; Dir V. G. NAGAY.

Ukrainian State Museum of Theatrical, Musical and Cinematographic Art: Kiev, Sichnevoho Povstanya 21/24; tel. (044) 290-51-31; 223,000 exhibits; Dir L. N. MATAT.

PERFORMING ARTS

Ivan Franko Ukrainian Drama Theatre: Kiev, 3 pl. Franko.

Kiev State Philharmonic Society: Kiev, 2 Vladimirsky Spusk; tel. (044) 229-62-51; fax (044) 228-03-30; f. 1863; Artists' Man. DMITRY I. OSTAPENKO.

Lesya Ukrainka Russian Drama Theatre: Kiev, vul. Lenina 5.

Taras Shevchenko Opera and Ballet Theatre: Kiev, vul. Vladimirska 50.

Ukrainian Puppet Theatre: Kiev, 13 vul. Rustaveli.

ASSOCIATION

Union of Writers of Ukraine: 252024 Kiev, vul. Bankova 2; tel. (044) 93-45-86; fax (044) 293-61-63; f. 1934; incl. 25 regional Writers' Organizations; Chair. YURY M. MUSHKETIK.

Education

The reversal of perceived 'russification' of the education system was one of the prinicipal demands of the opposition movements which emerged in the late 1980s. In the period 1980–88 the proportion of pupils who were taught in Russian increased from 44.5% to 51.8%, while the proportion taught in Ukrainian decreased from 54.6% to 47.5%. After Ukrainian was adopted as the state language, in 1990, policies were adopted to ensure that all pupils were granted the opportunity of tuition in Ukrainian. In 1988 there was also tuition in Romanian (0.6% of all school pupils), Hungarian (0.3%) and a small number of pupils were taught in Polish. In the early 1990s there were significant changes to the curriculum, with more emphasis on Ukrainian history and literature. Some religious and private educational institutions were established in 1990–91, including a private university, the Kiev Mihyla Academy, which had been one of Europe's leading educational establishments before 1917. In 1990 there were 23,600 pre-primary educational establishments in Ukraine, which employed 212,600 teachers and provided for some 1,939,600 students. In the same year a total of 6,854,400 students attended 20,900 primary and general-secondary institutions. There were approximately 473,100 teachers of primary and general secondary education in that year. Some 889,574 students attended institutions of higher education, which employed 72,300 teachers.

UNIVERSITIES

Chernovtsy State University: 274012 Chernivtsi, vul. Kotsyubinskoho 2; tel. (03722) 2-62-35; telex 149193; f. 1875; languages of instruction: Russian and Ukrainian; 12 faculties; 652 teachers; 9,733 students; Rector S. S. KOSTYSHIN.

Dnepropetrovsk State University: 320625 Dnipropetrovsk, pr. Gagarina 72; tel. (0562) 39-46-71; fax (0562) 46-55-23; f. 1918; 15 faculties; 1,042 teachers; 13,042 students; Rector Prof. V. F. PRISNYAKOV.

Donetsk State University: 340055 Donetsk, vul. Universitetska 24; tel. (0622) 93-30-28; telex 115102; f. 1965; languages of instruction: Russian and Ukrainian; 11 faculties; 900 teachers; 12,000 students; Rector V. P. SHEVCHENKO.

Kharkov State University: 310077 Kharkiv, pl. Svobody 4; tel. (0572) 45-61-96; fax (0572) 47-12-72; f. 1805; languages of instruction: Russian, Ukrainian; 13 faculties, 2 research institutes; 1,200 teachers; 12,000 students; Rector V. A. SVICH.

Kiev T. G. Shevchenko State University: 252601 Kiev, Vladimirska vul. 64; tel. (044) 220-86-91; fax (044) 224-61-66; f. 1834; 16 faculties, 12 institutes; 2,000 teachers; 20,000 students; Rector Acad. V. V. SKOPENKO.

Lvov State University: 290602 Lviv, Universitetska vul. 1; tel (0322) 72-20-68; language of instruction: Ukrainian; f. 1661; 13 faculties; 700 teachers; 13,000 students; Rector Prof. N. G. MAKSIMOVICH.

Odessa I. I. Mechnikov State University: 270100 Odesa, vul. Petra Velokoho 2; tel. (0482) 23-52-54; telex 232229; (0482) 23-35-15; f. 1865; languages of instruction: Russian and Ukrainian; 10 faculties; 800 teachers; 12,000 students; Rector Acad. I. P. ZELINSKY.

Simferopol State University: 333036 Simferopol, Yaltinska vul. 4; tel. (0652) 23-22-80; telex 861; fax (0652) 23-39-30; f. 1918; 9 faculties; 559 teachers; 6,600 students; Rector VYACHESLAV G. SIDYAKIN.

Uzhgorod State University: 294000 Uzhorod, vul. M. Gorkoho 46; tel. (03122) 3-42-02; f. 1945; 11 faculties; 8,000 students; Rector VLADIMIR SLIVKA.

Zaporozhye State University: 330600 Zaporizhzhia, vul. Zhukovskoho 66; tel. (0612) 64-45-46; telex 127447; fax (0612) 62-71-61; f. 1985; languages of instruction: Russian and Ukrainian; 11 faculties; 530 teachers; 6,300 students; Rector Prof. V. A. TOLOK.

Social Welfare

Until Ukrainian independence, the Soviet state-funded system of social welfare was in existence. In 1991, however, certain changes were made in the system, including the creation of three extra-budgetary funds, the Pension Fund, the Social Insurance Fund and the Employment Fund. These funds were intended to administer most of Ukraine's social-security benefits. All three remained financially viable throughout 1992, with the surplus of the Pension Fund increasing by four times. An extensive programme of family allowances and compensation for price increases, to be directly financed by the state budget, was also formulated at this time.

In 1989 the average life expectancy for Ukrainians at birth was 70.9 years, while the rate of infant mortality was 13.0 per 1,000 live births (considerably lower than the Soviet average of 22.7). In the same year there were, respectively 44 physicians and 135 hospital beds per 10,000 inhabitants. The compulsory retirement age in Ukraine at the beginning of the 1990s was 55 years for women and 60 years for men. At this time, approximately 25% of the population was in receipt of a pension. In September 1993 the minimum wage in Ukraine was raised to 20,000 karbovantsi per month, and the minimum old-age pension to 40,000 karbovantsi per month. On 5 October the World Bank agreed to provide Ukraine with US $2.5m. worth of aid to finance three projects, including one on health care and one on social protection. However, the allocation of funds was conditional on the Ukrainian Government presenting the bank with a coherent programme for implementing the projects.

Ministry of Social Welfare: see section on The Government (Ministries).

The Environment

An explosion at the Chernobyl nuclear power station in April 1986 resulted in serious contamination of many areas in the Ukraine, as well as in many other European countries. In addition, as well as 31 killed in the initial explosion, at least 200 people suffered from acute radiation sickness and many more, possibly numbering several thousand, died from related diseases. The incident, particularly the secrecy surrounding it and the subsequent decontamination operation, led to the formation of several environmental campaigning and political organizations.

GOVERNMENT ORGANIZATIONS

Ministry of Environmental Protection: see section on The Government (Ministries).

Standing Governmental Commission for Questions of Technological and Ecological Safety and Emergency Situations: Kiev; f. 1993; Chair. YU. ZVYAHILSKY.

Ministry for Protection of the Population against the Consequences of Chernobyl: see section on The Government (Ministries).

ACADEMIC INSTITUTES

Ukrainian Academy of Sciences: 252601 Kiev, vul. Vladimirska 54; tel. (044) 225-63-66; telex 131376; fax (044) 224-32-43; f. 1919; Pres. B. E. PATON; attached instits incl.:

Ukrainian State Steppe Reservation: Donetsk obl., Khomutoho, Novoazov rayon; in the Dept of General Biology; has some environmental responsibilities; Dir A. P. GENOV.

NON-GOVERNMENTAL ORGANIZATIONS

Zeleny Svit (Green World): 254070 Kiev, Kontraktovna pl. 4; tel. (044) 417-02-83; fax (044) 417-43-83; f. 1988; ecological assn of various Ukrainian groups; affiliated to Rukh and to the Ukrainian Peace Council's campaign against nuclear power; Exec. Dir YURY SCHERBAK.

Green Party of Ukraine: see section on Political Organizations.

Defence

In December 1991 an independent Ukrainian military was established. In June 1993 there were an estimated 450,000 active troops in the Ukrainian armed forces, including 217,000 ground forces, an air force of 171,000 and a navy of an estimated 3,000. Reserves numbered approximately 1m. In addition, at the beginning of 1994 Ukraine still owned a share of the former Soviet Black Sea Fleet. However, according to an agreement signed by Russia and Ukraine on 3 September 1993, Ukraine was to allow the sale of its share of the Fleet to Russia. Military service in Ukraine was compulsory for males over 18 years of age, for a period of 18 months, although there were plans for a transition to a two-year period of service.

In June 1993 Ukraine still possessed 176 intercontinental ballistic missiles on its territory, in addition to 42 nuclear-armed bombers. In February 1994 the Ukrainian Supreme Council agreed to ratify unconditionally the first Strategic Arms Reduction Treaty (START 1), which provided for the transfer of all nuclear weapons on its territory to the Russian Federation.

Supreme Commander of the Armed Forces of Ukraine: President of the Republic.

Chief of the General Staff: (vacant).

Bibliography

Gow, J. 'Independent Ukraine: The Politics of Security', in *International Affairs*, Vol. 11, No. 3 (December). 1992.

Krartnychy, A. 'The Ukrainian Factor', in *Foreign Affairs*, Vol. 71, No. 3 (Summer). 1992.

Krawchenko, B. *Social Change and National Consciousness in Twentieth Century Ukraine.* London, Macmillan, 1985.

Kuzio, T. 'Nuclear Weapons and Military Policy in Independent Ukraine', in *Harriman Institute Forum*, Vol. 6, No. 9 (May). 1993.

Ukraine: The Unfinished Revolution. London, Institute for European Defence and Strategic Studies, 1992.

Kuzio, T., and Wilson, A. *Ukraine: Perestroika to Independence.* London, Macmillan, 1993.

Marples, D. *Ukraine Under Perestroika: Ecology, Economics and the Workers' Revolt.* London, Macmillan, 1991.

Nahaylo, B. *The New Ukraine.* London, Royal Institute of International Affairs, 1992.

Rudnytsky, I. L. *Essays in Modern Ukrainian History.* Edmonton, CIUS, 1987.

Smith, M. *The Eastern Giants: Russia, Ukraine and European Security.* London, Royal United Services Institute for Defence Studies, 1992.

Solchanyk, R. *Ukraine: From Chernobyl to Sovereignty.* London, Macmillan, 1992.

'Ukraine: The Former Centre, Russia and Russia', in *Studies in Comparative Communism*, Vol. 24, No. 1 (March). 1992.

Subtelny, O. *Ukraine: A History.* Toronto, University of Toronto Press, 1988.

Wilson, A. *Ukraine.* Longman Series on Russia and the Post-Soviet Successor States, No. 1 (March). 1993.

Wilson, A., and Bilous, A. 'Political Parties in Ukraine', in *Europe-Asia Studies*, Vol. 45, No. 4. 1993.

UZBEKISTAN

Geography

PHYSICAL FEATURES

The Republic of Uzbekistan (formerly the Uzbek Soviet Socialist Republic, a constituent part of the USSR) is located in the heart of Central Asia. The country lies along a north-west to south-east axis and its eastern extremity, the Fergana valley region, abuts into Kyrgyzstan to the east, with Tajikistan to the south, forming the south-eastern border of the country. Uzbekistan has a short border with Afghanistan in the south, near the town of Termez, and Turkmenistan lies to the south-west. The north-western end of the country consists of the Kara-Kalpak Autonomous Republic (Karakalpakstan), to the west of which is Kazakhstan, which also lies to the north, beyond the Aral Sea, and forms the entire north-eastern border of Uzbekistan. The country covers an area of 447,400 sq km (172,740 sq miles), of which 165,600 sq km constitutes Karakalpakstan.

Much of the land is desert, including the south-western part of the Kyzyl Kum or Red Sands desert, but the western reaches of the Tien Shan range extend into the south-east of the country. The two main rivers are the Amu-Dar'ya (anciently the Oxus) and the Syr-Dar'ya (Jaxartes), both of which rise in the mountainous regions of the Tien Shan and flow north-westwards, to drain into the Aral Sea. However, severe over use of these water resources for irrigation (notably the Kara-Kum Canal in Turkmenistan) from the 1950s, caused a dramatic depletion of the waters reaching the Aral Sea. The consequent fall in its water level and the increase in the area of toxic (because of the use of chemical fertilizers) desert had severe environmental implications for the whole region. The Amu-Dar'ya is the worst affected of the two rivers and usually dries up far short of the Aral Sea, in the region of Nukus. It is the more southerly river and flows through Turkmenistan, parallel to the Uzbek border, before forming that border until it reaches the oasis towns of Khorezm where it enters Uzbek territory and heads towards the Aral Sea. The Syr-Dar'ya waters the prosperous Fergana valley region, crosses the Kojand region of Tajikistan, and then cuts north across Uzbekistan before entering Kazakhstan.

CLIMATE

The climate is marked by extreme temperatures and low levels of precipitation. Summers are long and hot with average temperatures in July of 32°C (90°F); daytime temperatures often exceed 40°C (104°F). During the short winter there are frequent severe frosts and temperatures can fall as low as −38°C (−36°F).

POPULATION

Uzbeks form the largest ethnic group in the Republic (71.4% of the total population in 1989); the remainder includes Russians (8.3%), Tajiks (4.7%), Kazakhs (4.1%) and Tatars (2.4%). Other ethnic groups include Karakalpaks (411,878), most of whom are resident in Karakalpakstan, Crimean Tatars (188,772), who were deported from their homeland in 1944, Koreans (183,140), Kyrgyz (174,907), Ukrainians (153,197), Turkmen (121,578) and Turks (106,302). The population of Karakalpakstan was 6.1% of the total population in 1989, although its area is 37% of the total of the country. According to unofficial figures, there were some 200,000 Arabs in Kaskadarin Oblast in 1990.

Islam was the predominant religion. Most Uzbeks were Sunni Muslims (Hanafi school), but there were small communities of Wahhabis, whose influence was reported to be growing. Some unusual Muslim sects were reported to be represented in the ancient cities of Samarkand and Bukhara (see p. 20). There were also Orthodox Christians among the Slavic communities, and some 65,000 European Jews and 28,000 Central Asian Jews. The official language was Uzbek, a member of the Eastern Turkic language group. From the 1940s it was written in Cyrillic (replacing a Latin alphabet introduced in the late 1920s), but in 1993 it was decreed that the country would proceed with the transition to the official use of a Latin script. The language is closely related to modern Uighur. Minority communities continued to use their own languages and Russian was still widely used in business and official circles, although, in 1989, only 49% of Uzbeks claimed fluency in Russian.

According to official estimates, the total population at 1 January 1991 was 20,739,000, and the population density was 46.4 persons per sq km. In 1991 it was estimated that 40% of the population lived in urban areas. The capital is Tashkent, with an estimated population of 2,093,900 in 1990, making it the USSR's fourth largest city. Other important urban centres were the historic towns of Samarkand (370,000 in 1990), Bukhara (228,000) and Kokand (176,000), the industrial, Fergana valley towns of Namangan (312,000), Andijan (297,000) and Fergana itself (198,000), and Nukus (169,000), the capital of Karakalpakstan.

Chronology

7th century: The Arabs conquered and brought Islam to the ancient provinces of Sogdiana and Bactria, notably the 'Silk Road' trading cities of Samarkand (Marakanda) and Bukhara (Bactra or Bacharia, previously the Kushan capital).

13th century: Nomadic Mongols settled among the predominantly Turkic population of Central Asia.

1313–41: Reign of Uzbeg, a khan of the Golden Horde, after whom the Uzbeks were named.

1370–1405: Reign of Timur (Tamerlane), originally from Transoxania (in modern Uzbekistan), who established a second Mongol Empire, which disintegrated rapidly after his death; his capital was in Samarkand.

16th century: Competing Uzbek khanates had established their dominance in the territory of modern Uzbekistan, especially Bukhara, Khiva, Kokand and Samarkand.

1866: The Khanate of Kokand was conquered by Russia, which was expanding southwards. In the following year much of the area which is now Karakalpakstan was annexed by Russia from the Khanate of Khiva.

1868: With the fall of Samarkand to the Russians, the Emirate of Bukhara surrendered and became a protectorate of the Russian Empire, following over a century of struggle by the Uzbek khanates with Persia; Samarkand and Tashkent were ceded to Russia.

1873: The Khanate of Khiva, which controlled much of what is western Uzbekistan, became a protectorate of the Russian Empire.

1876: The Khanate of Kokand was abolished and its territory absorbed into the Russian Empire.

November 1917: The Bolsheviks gained control of areas of Uzbekistan.

30 April 1918: The Turkestan Autonomous Soviet Socialist Republic (ASSR) was formed, covering an area that included Uzbekistan; Soviet forces withdrew temporarily when confronted by the nationalist *basmachi* movement, supported by British and 'White' (anti-Bolshevik) forces.

September 1919: Soviet forces re-established control over much of Uzbek territory.

February 1920: Khiva fell to the Red Army and the Khorezm People's Socialist Republic was proclaimed.

September 1920: The Emir of Bukhara fled as the city and most of his territory was conquered by the Red Army, although *basmachi* resistance continued in the east for some years. A Soviet Republic of Bukhara, also nominally independent, was declared.

December 1922: Bukhara and Khorezm were founding states of the USSR.

27 October 1924: The Uzbek Soviet Socialist Republic (SSR) was established.

May 1925: The Uzbek SSR formally became a constituent Union Republic of the Union of Soviet Socialist Republics (USSR).

1929: The Tajik ASSR, formerly part of the Uzbek SSR, became a full Union Republic of the USSR; the Khojand (Leninabad) area of the Uzbek SSR was also incorporated within the Tajik SSR.

1932: Karakalpakstan (which included much of the territory of Khiva, to the north and east of the city), to the south-east of the Aral Sea, passed from Kazakhstan (then part of the Russian Federation) to the Uzbek SSR.

1940: The Uzbek Latin script imposed in the late 1920s was replaced with a Cyrillic script.

1943: The Muslim Board of Central Asia was founded in Tashkent as part of the Soviet Government's more liberal attitude towards religion; in the same decade two religious colleges and a small number of mosques were allowed to open in Uzbekistan.

1954–60: The 'Virgin Lands' scheme brought more land into agricultural use, particularly for cotton, but the accompanying irrigation works eventually caused the environmental catastrophe of the Aral Sea and its environs.

1983: A major fraud was revealed in the cotton industry, involving some 3,000m. roubles—it led eventually to the removal from office of Uzbek Party leader Inamzhon Usmankhojayev (January 1988), the Chairman of the Uzbek Supreme Soviet, Akil Salimov, and the Party leaders in Bukhara and Samarkand; the son-in-law of the late Soviet leader Leonid Brezhnev, Yuri Churbanov (deputy interior minister of Uzbekistan 1980–83), was also accused and convicted of involvement.

November 1988: A group of Uzbek intellectuals founded Birlik (Unity), the first significant movement of opposition to the Communist Party of Uzbekistan (CPU).

25 March 1989: Birlik failed in its attempt to put forward a candidate in elections to the Congress of People's Deputies of the USSR, having previously been refused official registration.

June 1989: More than 100 people died in riots resulting from conflict between ethnic Uzbeks and members of the minority Meskhetian Turk community; First Secretary of the CPU Rafik Nishanov was replaced by Islam Karimov, for his failure to deal with the problem effectively.

October 1989: Legislation was adopted which made Uzbek (rather than Russian) the official state language.

18 February 1990: Members of Birlik were prevented from standing as candidates in elections to the Uzbek Supreme Soviet; in many constituencies CPU candidates were elected unopposed.

February–March 1990: There were further outbreaks of inter-ethnic conflict in Uzbekistan, culminating in three deaths during confrontations between the police and demonstrators in Parkent, near Tashkent.

24 March 1990: Islam Karimov was elected to the new position of executive President of the Republic at the first session of the Supreme Soviet; Shakurulla Mirsaidov was elected Chairman of the Council of Ministers (Prime Minister).

20 June 1990: Uzbekistan made a declaration of sovereignty.

November 1990: The Council of Ministers was abolished and replaced by the Cabinet of Ministers under the leadership of the President of the Republic; the position of Prime Minister ceased to exist and Mirsaidov was appointed to the new position of Vice-President.

April 1991: In the month following an all-Union referendum on the issue of the future state of the USSR (an overwhelming majority in Uzbekistan had favoured a 'renewed federation'), Uzbekistan and eight other Union Republics agreed to sign a new Union Treaty.

19–21 August 1991: President Karimov did not condemn the attempted conservative coup in Moscow until it became apparent that it had failed.

31 August 1991: The Supreme Soviet voted to declare the Uzbek SSR independent and, on the following day, its name was changed to the Republic of Uzbekistan.

November 1991: Having previously voted to sever links with the Communist Party of the Soviet Union, the CPU reorganized itself as the People's Democratic Party of Uzbekistan (PDPU) under the continued leadership of Karimov.

21 December 1991: Although it had remained a supporter of a new federation, Uzbekistan agreed to join 10 other former Soviet Republics in signing the Almaty Declaration, which established the Commonwealth of Independent States (CIS) and signalled the final dissolution of the USSR.

29 December 1991: Karimov was re-elected as President, receiving an estimated 86% of votes cast in direct popular elections; on the same day 98.2% of voters supported independence when a referendum was held on the issue.

8 January 1992: The post of Vice-President was abolished and that of Prime Minister (Chairman of the Cabinet of Ministers) was restored; Abdulkhashim Mutalov was appointed to the latter position. Mirsaidov was appointed State Secretary, but soon resigned, later to be accused of financial improprieties.

15 May 1992: Uzbekistan signed a collective security agreement with five other CIS countries, in Tashkent.

August 1992: A defence law was adopted which provided for the establishment of national armed forces.

September 1992: Uzbekistan, which supported the pro-Communist forces in the Tajik civil war, first indicated that it would be prepared to send troops into neighbouring Tajikistan.

8 December 1992: The Supreme Soviet adopted a new Constitution, which declared Uzbekistan to be a secular, democratic republic and made provision for a Supreme Assembly (Oly Majlis) to replace the Supreme Soviet as highest legislative body following elections scheduled for 1994. Three Uzbeks attending a human-rights conference in Kyrgyzstan were arrested for sedition by Uzbek security police and, on the following day, the opposition movement Birlik, which had never been permitted to register as a political party, was banned for supposedly subversive activities; the ban was later extended until mid-April 1993.

January 1993: Uzbekistan, the main regional supporter of the new regime in Tajikistan, signed a security agreement with that country, Russia, Kazakhstan and Kyrgyzstan to provide troops for the defence of Tajikistan's southern borders. Uzbek forces were also reported to have acted directly against Tajik rebels.

2 February 1993: President Karimov appointed Sadyk Safayev as Minister of Foreign Affairs, replacing Ubaidulla Abdurazzakov.

May 1993: Shukhrat Ismatullayev, a leader of the Birlik movement, was attacked, possibly by government agents; several other opposition members were put on trial or intimidated during 1993.

June 1993: Mirsaidov, former premier and Vice-President, was found guilty of the misuse of state funds, but was pardoned by President Karimov; he was also subjected to physical intimidation and eventually declared his decision to unite with the opposition to Karimov.

6 August 1993: Uzbekistan agreed to contribute troops to the CIS peace-keeping force to be sent to Tajikistan.

September 1993: It was decreed that the Latin script should be used for the Uzbek language, rather than the Cyrillic script; however, the new alphabet was different from the common script agreed upon earlier in the year by representatives from the other Central Asian states.

1 October 1993: The Government used technical pretexts to prevent both Birlik and Erk (Freedom), the opposition party established in 1990, from registering with the Ministry of Justice; consequently both organizations were permanently banned. Two days later Erk's newly elected First Secretary, Samad Muratov, was assaulted by anonymous attackers.

15 November 1993: Despite earlier intentions to continue participation in the 'rouble zone', Uzbekistan condemned Russia's conditions and introduced a new currency, the sum coupon, announcing that roubles would no longer be legal tender after December; food prices increased when Uzbek citizens attempted to spend their old currency.

December 1993: A compulsory re-registration of the mass media excluded all independent publications.

10–16 January 1994: Uzbekistan signed agreements to form an economic union with Kazakhstan and Kyrgyzstan; in February border controls between the three countries were relaxed.

19 January 1994: President Karimov appointed Bakhtiyar Khamidov as a deputy premier and as Erkin Bakibayev's replacement at the Ministry of Finance; a week later Karimov appointed Viktor Chzhen as a deputy premier and as Chairman of the State Committee for Property and Privatization.

22 January 1994: Karimov issued a decree permitting the sale by auction of state-owned shops, the abolition of restrictions on the import and export of foreign currency and the removal of all customs tariffs on imported goods until 1 July 1995.

4 February 1994: Afghanistan protested to Uzbekistan over its alleged interference in Afghan internal affairs; it was claimed that Uzbekistan had given aid to Gen. Rashid Dostam, an Afghan warlord and an ethnic Uzbek, although this was subsequently denied by the authorities of Uzbekistan.

2–3 March 1994: Karimov and Russian President Boris Yeltsin signed treaties on military and economic co-operation between Uzbekistan and the Russian Federation.

History

SOVIET UZBEKISTAN

The Uzbeks are descendants of nomadic Mongol tribes who mixed with the sedentary inhabitants (mainly of Turkic stock) of Central Asia, in the 13th century AD. In the 18th and 19th centuries the most prominent political formations in the territory were the khanates of Bukhara, Khiva, Kokand and Samarkand. Russian conquest of the region between the Syr-Dar'ya and the Amu-Dar'ya was completed when the Khanate of Kokand was formally annexed in 1876.

Soviet power was first established in Tashkent in November 1917. The Turkestan Autonomous Soviet Socialist Republic (ASSR) was proclaimed in April 1918, but Soviet forces then withdrew before opposition from the nationalist *basmachi* movement, the 'White' army and a British expeditionary force. Soviet power was re-established in September 1919, although armed opposition continued until the early 1920s. Bukhara and Khiva became nominally independent people's republics in 1920, but, together with the rest of Turkestan, were reorganized under the National Delimitation of Central Asia (1924–25, the process of creating nation-states, under the appropriate ethnonyms, from the ethnic mosaic of the region). On 27 October 1924 the Uzbek Soviet Socialist Republic (SSR) was established, including, until 1929, the Tajik ASSR. In 1932 Karakalpakstan was transferred from the RSFSR (Russian Federation) to the Uzbek SSR, retaining, however, its autonomous status.

The National Delimitation of Central Asia created an Uzbek nation-state for the first time. Its formation was accompanied by the creation of corresponding national symbols, including the development of a new literary language (the ancient Uzbek literary language, Chatagai, was accessible only to a small minority of the population). Campaigns promoting literacy were an integral part of the establishment of the Soviet ideology in the region, and the level of literacy rose from 3.8%, at the 1926 census, to 52.5% in 1932. There was an increase in the provision of educational facilities, which formed an important part in the policy of secularization in the region. The campaign against religion, initially promoted by educational means, became a repressive policy against all who admitted their adherence to Islam. Muslim schools, courts and mosques were closed and Muslim clergy were subject to persecution. However, there was a considerable improvement in the status of women, particularly in urban areas, under the Soviet regime.

There had been little industrial development in Central Asia under tsarist rule, although the extraction of raw materials was developed. Under the first two Five-Year Plans (1928–33 and 1933–38), however, there was considerable economic growth, aided by the immigration of skilled workers from the Slavic Republics. Although economic growth continued at quite high rates after the Second World War (when Uzbekistan's industrial base was enlarged by the transfer of industries from the war-zone), most Uzbeks continued to lead a traditional rural life style, affected only by the huge increase in the amount of cotton grown in the Republic.

The policies of *glasnost* and *perestroika* introduced by Soviet leader Mikhail Gorbachev (1985–91) did not result in significant political changes in the short term. The traditional respect for authority and the relatively small intelligentsia in the Republic allowed the leadership to hinder, or actively oppose, attempts at political or economic reform. Nevertheless, there was some greater freedom of the press in the late 1980s, allowing discussion of previously unexamined aspects of Uzbek history and contemporary ecological and economic problems. Moreover, a major financial scandal, first discovered in 1983, was thoroughly investigated under Gorbachev and led to the downfall of the corrupt Brezhnevite Party leadership in Uzbekistan in 1988.

The poor condition of the environment was one major source of popular dissatisfaction. The over-irrigation of land to water the vast cotton-fields caused both salination of the soil and, most importantly, the desiccation of the Aral Sea, the southern part of which is in the Kara-Kalpak Autonomous Republic (Karakalpakstan), and is a vital element in the ecology of the entire region. By the early 1980s it was evident that excessive drainage of the Amu-Dar'ya and Syr-Dar'ya rivers was resulting in dangerously low levels of water reaching the Aral Sea. Decisive measures to remedy the problem were not taken until January 1994, when the five former Soviet Central Asian countries established a joint fund and a permanent committee to save the Aral Sea and improve the health of those living in its basin. Uzbekistan, Kazakhstan, Kyrgyzstan and Turkmenistan each committed 1% of their total budgets for 1994 to the fund (Tajikistan was exempted from this commitment). Foreign funding was also available, but the scale of the problem was immense.

Environmental problems and the status of the Uzbek language were among the issues on which Uzbekistan's first major non-Communist political movement, Birlik (Unity), campaigned. It was formed in late 1989, by a group of intellectuals in Tashkent, but quickly grew to be the main challenger to the ruling Communist Party of Uzbekistan (CPU). However, the movement was not granted official registration, and its attempts to nominate a candidate in the 1989 elections to the all-Union Congress of People's Deputies were unsuccessful. Nevertheless, its campaign for recognition of Uzbek as the official language of the Republic led to the adoption of legislation in October 1989, which declared Uzbek to be the state language.

On 18 February 1990 elections were held to the Uzbek Supreme Soviet. Members of Birlik were not permitted to stand as candidates and many leading members of the CPU stood unopposed, as had been the tradition in old-style Soviet elections. In such constituencies there were isolated protests by opposition groups. During 1990 a branch of Birlik, Erk (Freedom), was founded as an opposition party.

The new Supreme Soviet convened in March 1990 and elected Islam Karimov to the newly created post of executive President. Shakurulla Mirsaidov was elected Chairman of the Council of Ministers (Prime Minister). In November 1990 there was a reorganization of government. The Council of Ministers was abolished and replaced by a Cabinet of Ministers, headed by the President of the Republic. Shakurulla Mirsaidov was appointed to the newly established post of Vice-President.

In June 1989 inter-ethnic conflict had been reported between Uzbeks and the Meskhetian Turk minority. The origins of the conflict were unclear, but seemed to stem from high levels of unemployment and the shortage of housing in the Fergana Oblast. During a two-week period in early June at least 100 people died during rioting, most of them Meskhetians. In February and March 1990 there was a resurgence of inter-ethnic conflict. On 3 March, in Parkent, near Tashkent, three people died after clashes between demonstrators and the police. There was further inter-ethnic tension in connection with clashes in Osh, a city in Kyrgyzstan with an Uzbek majority, in June 1990. Border crossings were sealed to prevent up to 15,000 armed Uzbek citizens crossing the Kyrgyz–Uzbek border to join their co-nationals in Kyrgyzstan. President Karimov declared a state of emergency in Andijan Oblast (which borders Kyrgyzstan's Osh Oblast). Particularly after independence, there was also some increase of tension with the largely urban Persic Tajiks of Bukhara and Samarkand.

In April 1991 Uzbekistan agreed, together with eight other Republics, to sign a new Union Treaty. However, on 19 August, the day before the signing was to take place, a State Committee for the State of Emergency (SCSE) attempted to stage a *coup d'état* in Moscow. President Karimov did not initially oppose the coup, and some opposition leaders in Uzbekistan were temporarily detained. However, once it was clear that the coup had failed, Karimov declared that the orders of the SCSE were invalid. On 31 August, after the coup had collapsed, an extraordinary session of the Supreme Soviet voted to declare the Uzbek SSR independent and changed its name to the Republic of Uzbekistan.

INDEPENDENT UZBEKISTAN

In November 1991 the ruling CPU renamed itself the People's Democratic Party of Uzbekistan (PDPU), having previously voted to dissociate itself from the all-Union Party. The PDPU remained under the leadership of Karimov, who was re-elected as President of the Republic on 29 December, receiving a reported 86% of the votes cast in direct popular elections. The only other candidate, who received 12% of the votes, was Muhammad Solikh, Chairman of the Erk party. The Birlik movement was not permitted to put forward a candidate as it had still not been granted official registration as a political party. On the same day as the presidential elections, 98.2% of voters endorsed Uzbek independence in a referendum. However, Uzbekistan's sovereignty had already been effected by the Almaty Declaration (see below) and Gorbachev's resignation earlier in the month, which had finally dissolved the USSR.

In early January 1992 the post of Vice-President was abolished. Mirsaidov was appointed State Secretary under the President and Abdulkhashim Mutalov was appointed to the newly re-established prime ministerial post (Chairman of the Cabinet of Ministers). Throughout the year the PDPU dominated Uzbek affairs and President Karimov's leadership became increasingly authoritarian. The Uzbek Government used the civil war in neighbouring Tajikistan as justification for the repression of opposition movements and Muslim groups such as the Islamic Renaissance Party, having passed a law the previous year which banned religious political parties.

On 8 December 1992 the Supreme Soviet adopted a new Constitution. This confirmed the authority of the President of the Republic as head of state and established that the Supreme Soviet would be replaced by a new, smaller legislature, the 150-member Oly Majlis (Supreme Assembly), after elections had been held in 1994. Until then the Supreme Soviet was to continue as the legislature. The Constitution also declared Uzbekistan to be a secular, democratic republic and guaranteed freedom of expression and of religion for its citizens.

On the day that the Constitution was adopted, three opposition leaders, including Abdumannob Pulatov, the head of the Human Rights Association in Uzbekistan, were arrested by Uzbek security police while attending a conference in Bishkek (Kyrgyzstan) and charged with sedition. Pulatov was sentenced to three years in prison on 28 January 1993, but released one day later under a general amnesty which had been introduced by Karimov in September 1992. On 9 December 1992 Birlik was banned because of its allegedly subversive intentions and the ban was later extended until mid-April 1993.

Throughout late 1992 and 1993 a number of opposition leaders disappeared, were kidnapped or assaulted in mysterious circumstances. Others were tried for offences such as defamation of the President. Many of those put on trial were, like Pulatov, released immediately after sentencing; some commentators suggested that the Government's intention was merely to issue a warning to opposition leaders without estranging them further. The most important trial was that of six opposition activists, including leading members of Erk and Birlik, in July–August 1993. The six defendants were accused of numerous acts of subversion, notably of attempting to convene an alternative parliament, or Melli Majlis. They were found guilty and sentenced to several years' imprisonment, but immediately released in accordance with the amnesty.

In March 1993 the Government had announced that any political movements or parties which had not obtained or renewed official registration with the Ministry of Justice by 1 October would be permanently banned. When the deadline arrived, neither Birlik nor Erk was able to comply with the decree, as they no longer had headquarters at which to be registered (following separate government action). Similarly, in December the State Committee for the Press conducted an obligatory re-registration of the media, during which only government publications were eligible for registration.

In January 1993 both the US State Department and the human-rights committee of the Russian parliament expressed alarm at alleged abuses of human rights in Uzbekistan. International concern at Karimov's style of leadership continued throughout the year. Karimov, however, like President Niyazov of Turkmenistan, maintained that unity was essential for preserving the country's stability, which would in turn attract foreign investors to Uzbekistan. Tajikistan, on the other hand, had been the first former Soviet Central Asian country to have a truly multi-party political system, but it also became the scene of one of the worst civil wars in any former territory of the USSR.

FOREIGN RELATIONS

One of Karimov's primary concerns was to prevent the growth of Islamic fundamentalism in Uzbekistan and this influenced foreign affairs inasmuch as it was in his interests to forestall its spread from neighbouring countries. Karimov was therefore anxious that the democratic and Islamic opposition in Tajikistan should not regain the power which it had shared in May–November 1992. Accordingly, in December 1992 and January 1993 Uzbek aircraft were reported to have bombed opposition groups resisting the restored Communist regime in Tajikistan. Uzbekistan signed a collective security agreement in January 1993, which formally ended CIS neutrality in the Tajik civil war and led to the immediate deployment of Uzbek, Russian and Kazakh troops on the Tajik–Afghan border.

In 1993 Tajik opposition refugees in Afghanistan made a number of incursions across the border with Tajikistan. General Rashid Dostam, an ethnic Uzbek and head of a northern Afghan faction, was reported to have reached an agreement with the Uzbek and Tajik Governments, to the effect that refugees in areas under his control would not be involved in any such incidents. Furthermore, in May there were unsubstantiated claims that Dostam and Karimov had negotiated the establishment of a 'buffer' state in northern Afghanistan, immediately south of the border with Uzbekistan and Tajikistan. In early February 1994 Afghanistan protested at Uzbekistan's alleged involvement in Afghan internal affairs, claiming that it had supplied assistance, in the form of money and military hardware, to General Dostam. This allegation was strongly denied by the Uzbek authorities.

After its declaration of independence in 1991, Uzbekistan attempted to develop relations with other former Soviet Republics and with other countries. Diplomatic efforts were directed towards developing relations with Turkey, while relations with other former Soviet Republics were largely limited to ties with the other Central Asian countries. Uzbekistan, which had previously favoured some form of renewal for the Soviet federation, nevertheless agreed to the dissolution of the USSR and participation in a Commonwealth of Independent States (CIS) as first proposed by the Slavic Republics in early December 1991. The Commonwealth was founded by the Almaty Declaration of 11 former Soviet Republics, including Uzbekistan, on 21 December.

In August 1993 Uzbekistan agreed to form a new economic union with Kazakhstan and the Russian Federation. One month later Uzbekistan and three other countries signed an agreement with the Russian Federation to remain within the 'rouble zone', but in doing so were obliged to comply with a series of Russian conditions. The terms attached to continued use of the rouble rapidly became so rigorous that they could be perceived as an infringement of sovereignty and, on 15 November, in spite of previous agreements, Uzbekistan introduced its own currency, the sum coupon, and declared that roubles would not be legal tender from December. Earlier, more ambitious agreements to form CIS or Central Asian economic communities having resulted in little progress, in mid-January 1994 Uzbekistan signed agreements establishing an economic union with Kazakhstan and Kyrgyzstan and, the following month, border restrictions between the member states were relaxed.

CONCLUSION

Uzbekistan made relatively little progress towards the Western conception of democracy after gaining independence, but avoided any overt expressions of political, social or ethnic tension. However, at the heart of Central Asia and with only one, short southern border with a non-CIS country, Uzbekistan remained deeply integrated within the Commonwealth and maintained close relations with all the other former Soviet Central Asian countries. Nevertheless, Karimov was anxious to encourage Western investment, which required a certain measure of reform, and the Government's commitment to some reorientation of the country was evidenced by its moves to adopt the Latin alphabet (decreed in 1993).

The Economy

Uzbekistan was rich in natural resources, but one of the poorest countries of the former USSR. In 1991 its gross national product (GNP) per head was an estimated US $1,350. However, according to the World Bank, by the next year, this was put at some $860 per head—only Kyrgyzstan and war-torn Armenia, Georgia and Tajikistan were poorer. Over 60% of the territory was arid steppe or desert, but the country was the most populous in Central Asia (41% of the total population of the five countries). Most of this population was rural (60% in 1991) and about one-half were under the age of 19 years (1992 estimate). Much of the population resided in the Fergana basin, in the east of the country, where a mix of ethnic groups and a social environment in decay since the 1980s created a dangerous background for a further deterioration in economic conditions. Thus, the cautious approach of President Islam Karimov's regime to the transition to a market economy was explained by the need to maintain social and political stability.

The country accounted for an estimated 3.3% of gross domestic product (GDP) of the USSR in 1990. In 1988 it had also contributed 3.3% of all-Union net material product (NMP—a similar economic measure to GDP used in centrally planned economies); Uzbekistan contributed only 2.3% of total Soviet industrial NMP, but 5.2% of agricultural NMP. According to estimates for 1991, the last year of the Soviet federation, Uzbekistan accounted for 7.1% of the total population (it was the third most populous Union Republic) and for only 2.0% of the area. However, in terms of its major exports, cotton and gold, the country was an important producer in terms of the world market, as well as within the former USSR.

AGRICULTURE

In 1991 agriculture, including forestry, accounted for an estimated 43.2% of NMP and 40.6% of employment. According to World Bank figures, agricultural NMP provided 39% of the total NMP in the following year (35.9% of GNP). Some 40% of agricultural production was accounted for by a single crop, cotton. By far the largest producer in the Commonwealth of Independent States (CIS—as it had been in the former USSR), Uzbekistan was the world's fourth largest producer and third largest exporter of cotton. With most fertile land confined to the valleys of the great rivers Amu-Dar'ya and Syr-Dar'ya, ambitious irrigation works from the 1950s onwards considerably increased the available arable land, although this was to have long-term environmental effects. Most of the land so gained was used for cotton. Production declined in the early 1990s, not least because of the disruption caused by the collapse of the Soviet trading system, but reforms in agriculture were likely to bear results during the mid-1990s.

Although agriculture was dominated by cotton, Uzbekistan was also the largest producer of fruit (especially grapes) and vegetables in the CIS. The country was the main CIS producer of kanaf (jute), a plant used to make sacking. Other crops included grain and water-melons. Animal husbandry was also important; at the beginning of the 1990s two-thirds of the agricultural land was actually used for livestock rearing. There were numerous cattle, but most significant were sheep, which were bred for wool and, notably, astrakhan pelts.

Agriculture, although important, was inefficient and wasteful of both land and water resources. The severe depletion in the flow of the major rivers, as a result of extensive irrigation, had severe regional consequences for the Aral Sea. In 1960 it was the fourth largest inland lake in the world, with a surface area of some 68,000 sq km. By 1989 the water level had fallen by 14.3 m, reducing the surface area by some 46% to 37,000 sq km and increasing its salinity by 280%. Inefficient irrigation systems, mainly in Uzbekistan and Turkmenistan, suffered from considerable loss of water through leakage and evaporation, and also led to waterlogging and increased salinity of the soil. Together with the excessive use of chemical fertilizers and pesticides, the emphasis on the cultivation of cotton and rice, and other unsuitable development policies, the Aral Sea has been reduced, its aquatic ecosystem destroyed and its immediate environment fundamentally jeopardized. The deterioration in soil quality, the pollution and limitation of water supplies, and the economic effects also had serious repercussions for the health of the population.

Moreover, the entire Aral Sea basin (including most of Central Asia, but with some headwaters in Afghanistan, the People's Republic of China and Iran) was affected by the massive changes in the lacustrine environment. It was estimated, in 1992, that unless urgent action was taken, the Aral Sea's surface area would continue to shrink, to perhaps 9,000 sq km by 2015, and it would be reduced to a few residual brine lakes. International environmental scientists consider the Aral Sea to be one of the most serious ecological disasters of the 20th-century world, but no specific plans were evolved. At the beginning of 1994 the Central Asian countries agreed to co-operate, financially as well, to at least mitigate the effects of the desiccation of the Aral Sea and prevent any further dramatic deterioration. The scale of the problem was such that the political and financial costs of beginning to restore the Sea were uncertain but considerable, while restoring it to pre-1960 conditions seemed impossible. Probably the most effective measure likely to be taken in the 1990s, which would also be of economic benefit, would be to improve the management of water resources, especially reducing waste and diversifying crops.

MINING, ENERGY AND INDUSTRY

Industry (including the mining sector) accounted for an estimated 33% of total NMP in 1992 (28.5% of GNP), according to the World Bank, and in 1991 the sector provided 23.0% of employment. The predominant industrial sector was the extraction and processing of Uzbekistan's considerable mineral wealth. This included huge reserves of natural gas and significant deposits of coal, petroleum and several other minerals, including gold, uranium, copper, tungsten, silver and aluminium ore. Apart from the established industry of the extraction and refining of gold, and the developing hydrocarbons sector, the most promising resource was copper.

In 1993 Uzbekistan was the world's sixth largest producer of gold, its 65 metric tons or so annually accounting for about one-third of production in the former USSR. Most of the gold mining was done in the deserts of central Uzbekistan, to the north of Bukhara, including activity at Murantau, which was claimed to be the largest single gold mine in the world: it accounted for about 70% of total Uzbek production. Further reserves were also being brought into production; in 1993 the British company Lonhro agreed to set up joint-ventures with two Uzbek companies to begin exploiting new fields. Earlier that year the first major investment in the sector by the West was promised by a US company, Newmont Mining Co, which committed US $75m. to a joint venture.

Hydrocarbon reserves are another significant resource of Uzbekistan, and with considerable potential for improving the country's export earnings as well as for satisfying its energy requirements. Uzbekistan was the third largest natural gas producer of the former USSR and the 10th largest exporter in the world. In 1992 some 42,800 cu m of natural gas was produced, mostly for domestic consumption. However, Western experts believed that the export potential for the resource was underestimated by the Government, which was not fully accounting for the savings that could be made in the domestic market by greater efficiency of energy use. In addition, known petroleum reserves were greatly increased by two major discoveries in 1993, which was likely to lead to increased petroleum production, above the 3.3m. metric tons of 1992. In this sector French companies were foremost in investment: Elf Aquitaine was the first major Western company to agree an exploration deal with the Uzbek Government (February 1993), and in the same year a French bank agreed to finance the construction of a refinery at Bukhara. In February 1994 the European Union (until November 1993 known as the European Community) agreed to aid the country in developing self-sufficiency in petroleum and natural gas by the end of the decade. The prospects for the mining and energy sectors were, in general, very good.

Industrial production consisted mainly of light industries (45% of total industrial production in 1991—mainly textiles, clothing, etc.) and food processing (14%). The major subsectors of heavy industry (36%) were machine-building (itself 10% of total industrial production), the fuel-energy sector (7%), metallurgy (5%) and construction materials (4%). The importance of the agricultural sector was reflected in industrial activity, a major product being agricultural machinery and, from the chemicals industry, fertilizers. By the end of 1993, for the first time in two years, industrial production had increased (by 3.4% in the first 11 months of the year), especially in the fuel, machine-building and light industry sectors.

FINANCE AND REFORM

Uzbekistan, based as it was on the ancient cities of the 'Silk Road' trading routes, was very dependent on commerce. After more than one century of being integrated into the Russian/Soviet economy, the country was severely affected by the collapse of the USSR and the wider Soviet trading bloc: many of its industries had been organized on a Union-wide basis and its agriculture did not produce a diversity of produce. The orientation of transport perpetuated Uzbek reliance on Russia, but the need for different CIS countries to control their varied paces of economic transformation encouraged the final demise of the 'rouble zone' in 1993. The Karimov regime introduced a national currency, the sum coupon, in tandem with Kazakhstan's introduction of the tenge, but otherwise remained tardy in adopting economic restructuring. The Government was reluctant to exacerbate economic hardship for its population and stated, as a matter of policy, that it believed that the state should play the major role in the reform of the economy and the transformation to a free-market system.

Traditionally, Uzbekistan sustained considerable visible trade deficits. However, much of this was because of the under-pricing of raw materials in the Soviet trading system and, following a 10% deterioration in the terms of trade in 1992, it was thought that any further problems with import costs would be offset by the increase of natural-gas and petroleum prices to world market levels (virtually achieved by 1993). The economic crises in the former USSR, however, created continuing problems for Uzbekistan, because this was its traditional market (in 1990 83% of trade had been with other Union Republics). By 1992, according to World Bank estimates, external trade accounted for 55% of total trade, and the deficit was some US $60m., compared to the inter-republican deficit of $199m. Prior to 1992, Uzbekistan had relied on transfers from the all-Union budget, although in that year foreign direct investment began, which helped offset the deficit of $369m. on the current account of the balance of payments.

Towards the end of 1992 Uzbekistan resolved another obstacle to foreign investment, when it improved its creditworthiness by settling the Soviet debt issue. As a successor state of the USSR it agreed, in November, on the so-called 'zero option' with the Russian Federation, whereby Uzbekistan renounced all claims to Soviet assets in return for responsibility for Soviet debt being assumed by Russia. Western assistance was forthcoming for a variety of projects thereafter, and was important in supporting the introduction of the national currency.

In July 1993 the Central Bank of the Russian Federation declared that all pre-1993 rouble notes in circulation (1961–92 notes) were to be withdrawn. It refused to issue new, 1993 notes to other CIS countries still in the rouble zone. The old rouble therefore continued as the currency of Uzbekistan. This arrangement was obviously unsatisfactory and potentially destabilizing, but the Government hoped to resolve it by negotiating its participation in a new rouble zone. However, the stringency of Russian conditions meant that Uzbekistan introduced a currency coupon, the sum, on 15 November, phasing it in as the only legal tender by the beginning of 1994 (later in the year the permanent sum currency was to be introduced). The new currency was not the most successful of those introduced by the Central Asian states, and it caused price increases in the country, but Uzbekistan's potential wealth was considered likely to support it in the long-term.

Uzbekistan had been most reluctant to introduce its own currency and, even after its departure from the rouble zone, the Government remained committed to economic co-operation with the CIS, especially with Russia and the other Central Asian states. However, despite several sonorous declarations on increased integration and agreements to a variety of customs and economic unions, few practical measures were taken. In January 1994, therefore, Uzbekistan and Kazakhstan and, later, Kyrgyzstan, agreed on the creation of a more limited free-trade area between their own territories. In February certain border restrictions were lifted. This was in addition to the continuation of a policy by Uzbekistan of not levying a variety of foreign-trade tariffs, in an effort to encourage commerce. The Government had also introduced a measure of general tax reform and implemented some of the legislative framework necessary to the proper functioning of a free-market economy, but was far from adopting the 'shock therapy' of some Eastern European and former Soviet countries.

By 1993 the private sector was reckoned, according to government sources, to contribute some 23.1% of GDP, compared to 15.7% in the same period one year earlier. The number of private enterprises had increased from 1,600 to 5,800. The intermediate stage of privatizing state concerns was also proceeding, with the number of leased or floated enterprises increasing fivefold over the year. Most progress was made with retail outlets, which international financial institutions recommended the development of in the private sector in order to provide employment for at least some of the population likely to be affected by the widespread loss of work, which usually accompanied structural reform of a former Communist economy. Land reform was another priority recommendation, because of the relatively short time it took to achieve improved results in agriculture, particularly in Uzbekistan where the sector was so important. However, although private farming had been legalized in 1992 and the number of peasant holdings had doubled over the course of 1993, reform of the state sector had made more apparent than real progress. By November 1993 it was reported that all 712 state farms had been converted to collective or co-operative farms, or to leasehold ventures. However, this was often a nominal redesignation that, in some cases at least, merely protected the interests of the powerful nomenklatura managers of the concerns.

Certainly the Government, with its gradualist approach to economic reform, had succeeded in maintaining employment levels (although some unemployment had existed before 1991, notably in the major cities and the Fergana valley region). However, this was at the cost of a decline in real wages and a high rate of inflation (wholesale prices increased by some 2,700% in 1992). Real GDP had not declined by as much as in some former Soviet countries (some 10% in 1992), although the future of the economy demanded that investment and consumption levels regained something approaching their former levels. Transport and communications infrastructure, although adequate, also needed investment and improvement. Uzbekistan was in a good position, a traditional one on the great Eurasian trade routes, to take advantage of this sector. Thus, schemes for improving rail links with Kazakhstan, Kyrgyzstan and Tajikistan were announced during 1993 and foreign investment was forthcoming for a major new international air terminal in Tashkent. Turkey was prominent in improving telecommunications for the region as a whole, an appropriate role in view of its encouragement of pan-Turkic cultural links and support for the adoption of a Latin alphabet.

CONCLUSION

Uzbekistan was implementing structural reform of the economy with caution during the early 1990s. Although it was committed to the introduction of a free-market system, it was equally determined to preserve a prominent role for the state in managing the transition and to protect the population from excessive hardship during the process. Given the variety of social problems which had already emerged during the 1980s, this was understandable, but also made the case for the benefits of reform more urgent. Moreover, given the poor health conditions of the population, improvements in the agricultural and infrastructure sectors, in particular, were of importance. Apart from the Aral Sea environmental problems (see above), industrial pollution in the Fergana valley and general problems with water supplies were also serious. The need for returns on investment also risked a lack of attendance to the environmental consequences of mining. Educational standards were also important to maintain, with additional demands on government expenditure likely from new social problems such as large-scale unemployment (which the Government wished to avoid) and the use of and trade in illegal drugs (in the first 10 months of 1993 some 300 ha of opium plantings were destroyed and there was an increase of 150% in the amount of illicit produce confiscated since 1992).

Uzbekistan suffered many problems common to most of the former Soviet countries: inefficient and outdated production methods; the demise of central planning and the sudden responsibility for their own economies foisted on to the republican authorities in 1991; the collapse of the inter-republican trade and payments system; monopolistic market structures; the decline in output; repressed inflation; and the loss of all-Union budget transfers. In addition, in the early 1990s, world market prices for both cotton and gold, Uzbekistan's main exports, were falling. The developing hydrocarbons industries needed easier access to Western markets, which required investment, and the Government's reluctance to hasten economic reform (being unwilling to exacerbate social tensions) discouraged foreign investment. However, the country's potential wealth and its political stability were likely more than to compensate for this, particularly as the gradualist approach began to show results.

Statistical Survey

Principal sources (unless otherwise indicated): IMF, *Uzbekistan, Economic Review*; World Bank, *Statistical Handbook, States of the Former USSR.*

Area and Population

AREA, POPULATION AND DENSITY

Area (sq km)	447,400*
Population (census result) 12 January 1989	19,905,158
Population (official estimate at 1 January 1991)	20,739,000
Density (per sq km) at 1 January 1991	46.4

* 172,740 sq miles.

POPULATION BY NATIONALITY
(census of 12 January 1989)

	%
Uzbek	71.4
Russian	8.3
Tajik	4.7
Kazakh	4.1
Tatar	2.4
Others*	9.1
Total	100.0

* Including Karakalpaks, Crimean Tatars, Koreans, Kyrgyz, Ukrainians, Turkmen and Turks.

PRINCIPAL TOWNS
(estimated population, at 1 January 1990)

Tashkent (capital)	2,094,000	Karshi	163,000
Samarkand	370,000	Chirchik	159,000
Namangan	312,000	Angren	133,000
Andizhan	297,000	Urgench	129,000
Bukhara	228,000	Margilan	125,000
Fergana	198,000	Almalyk	116,000
Kokand	176,000	Navoi	110,000
Nukus	175,000	Jizak	108,000

Source: UN, *Demographic Yearbook*.

BIRTHS AND DEATHS (per 1,000)

	1985	1988	1989
Birth rate	37.2	35.1	33.3
Death rate	7.2	6.8	6.3

Birth rate (per 1,000): 37.8 in 1986; 36.9 in 1987.

EMPLOYMENT (annual averages, '000 persons)

	1989	1990	1991
Agriculture and forestry	2,938	3,120	3,291
Industry Construction	1,873	1,911	1,867
Transport and communications	242	250	250
Trade and catering Other activities of the material sphere	594	602	592
Government	114	119	122
Other non-material services	1,863	1,938	1,989
Total	7,624	7,941	8,111

Agriculture

PRINCIPAL CROPS ('000 metric tons)

	1990	1991	1992
Wheat	553	610	900*
Rice	503	515	530*
Barley	385	324	300*
Maize	431	431	445*
Potatoes	336	351	335
Sunflower seed	5†	5†	5*
Seed cotton	5,058	4,646	4,000
Cottonseed	2,926†	2,644†	2,100*
Vegetables‡	3,343	3,858	3,750*
Grapes	745	481	460*
Other fruit	656	517	500*
Tobacco (leaves)	31	21	19†
Cotton (lint)	1,593	1,443	1,735†

* FAO estimate(s). † Unofficial figure(s).
‡ Including water-melons, melons, pumpkins and squash.
Source: FAO, *Production Yearbook*.

LIVESTOCK ('000 head at 1 January)

	1990	1991	1992
Horses	97	105	108*
Cattle	4,200	4,600	5,100
Pigs	700	700	700
Sheep	8,000	8,370	9,200
Goats	800	830	900
Chickens†	36,000	35,000	34,000

* FAO estimate(s). † Unofficial figure(s).
Source: FAO, *Production Yearbook*.

LIVESTOCK PRODUCTS ('000 metric tons)

	1990	1991	1992
Beef and veal	295	323	340*
Mutton and lamb	67	62	58*
Pigmeat	50	44	50*
Poultry meat	67	60	60†
Cows' milk	2,922	3,207	2,860†
Butter and ghee	15.9	14.6	14.0†
Hen eggs†	135.8	130.0	90.0
Wool:			
greasy	25.8	25.3	26.0*
scoured	15.5	15.2	15.6*

* FAO estimate(s). † Unofficial figure(s).
Source: FAO, *Production Yearbook*.

Mining and Industry

Production (1989): Paper 25,700 metric tons, Cardboard 56,100 metric tons, Plastics 158,100 metric tons, Sulphuric acid 2,641,900 metric tons, Mineral fertilizers 1,899,900 metric tons, Coal 2,673,000 metric tons, Gas 41,092m. cu m, Electric energy 55,900m. kWh.

Finance

CURRENCY AND EXCHANGE RATES

Prior to the introduction of the sum-coupon in November 1993 (see below), Russian currency was in use.

Monetary Units
100 kopeks = 1 rubl (ruble or rouble).

Sterling and Dollar Equivalents (30 September 1993)
£1 sterling = 1,796.1 Russian roubles;
US $1 = 1,201.0 Russian roubles;
10,000 Russian roubles = £5.568 = $8.326.

Average Exchange Rate (roubles per US dollar)
1989 0.6274
1990 0.5856
1991 0.5819

Note: The figures for average exchange rates refer to official rates for the Soviet rouble. However, a multiple exchange rate system was in operation, with separate non-commercial and tourist rates. A commercial exchange rate was introduced on 1 November 1990, replacing the official rate for most transactions. The commercial rate (roubles per US dollar) was: 1.692 at 31 December 1990; 1.671 at 31 December 1991. Between November 1989 and April 1991 the tourist exchange rate valued the rouble at one-tenth of the official rate. In April 1991 this rate, renamed the 'special rate', was set at $1 = 27.6 roubles. It was subsequently adjusted. Following the dissolution of the USSR in December 1991, Russia and several other former Soviet republics retained the rouble as their monetary unit. The average interbank market rate in 1992 was $1 = 222.1 Russian roubles. On 16 November 1993 Uzbekistan introduced a transitional currency, the sum-coupon, to circulate alongside (and initially at par with) the Russian rouble. At 31 December 1993 the official exchange rate was $1 = 1,150 sum-coupons. The transitional currency was to become the sole legal tender on 1 January 1994, and there were plans to establish a permanent currency, the sum, later in 1994.

BUDGET (million roubles)*

Revenue	1990	1991	1992†
Corporate income tax	1,900	3,500	9,500
Individual income tax	900	1,600	4,100
Turnover tax	4,000	5,800	—
Value added tax	—	—	19,600
Excise tax	—	—	9,500
Social security tax	1,100	—	—
Price differential tax	—	—	27,000
Revenue from privatization	—	—	3,300
Other receipts	400	5,100	1,700
Grants from USSR budget (net)	6,300	12,000	—
Total	14,600	28,000	74,700

Expenditure	1990	1991	1992†
National economy	8,100	11,100	—
Social and cultural services	6,200	11,000	23,500
Subsidies	—	5,300	21,300
Other current expenditure	600	3,700	12,200
Capital expenditure	—	—	7,900
Total	14,900	31,100	86,200

* Excluding the operations of the Pension Fund, the State Insurance Fund and the Employment Fund.

† Projections.

COST OF LIVING

(Index of retail prices; base: previous year = 100)

	1989	1990	1991
All items	100.7	103.1	182.2

Index of retail prices (base: previous year = 100): *1991* 161.0; *1992* 787.0 (Source: IMF, *Supplement on Countries of the Former Soviet Union*).

NATIONAL ACCOUNTS (million roubles at current prices)

Gross National Product by Economic Activity

	1991	1992
Agriculture (incl. forestry)	22,900	149,500
Industry (incl. mining)	15,600	119,000
Construction	6,400	54,400
Trade	2,400	10,300
Transport and communications	2,600	20,200
Other services	11,600	63,500
Total	61,500	416,900

Source: *World Bank Country Study: Uzbekistan.*

BALANCE OF PAYMENTS (US $ million)

	1992
Merchandise exports	869
Merchandise imports	−929
Inter-republican trade balance	−199
Trade balance	−259
Services (net)	−110
Current balance	−369
Capital investment (net)	165
Net errors and omissions	97
Overall balance	−107

Source: *World Bank Country Study: Uzbekistan.*

External Trade

PRINCIPAL COMMODITIES (million roubles)

Imports	1989	1990
Petroleum and gas	1,032	888
Iron and steel	676	661
Non-ferrous metals	424	409
Chemicals and products	1,111	1,147
Machine-building	3,553	3,625
Wood and paper products	725	560
Construction materials	228	205
Light industry	2,761	2,963
Food industry	2,156	1,983
Agricultural products (unprocessed)	661	1,309
Total (incl. others)	14,158	14,662
Foreign	2,112	2,798
Inter-republican (USSR)	12,046	11,864

Exports	1989	1990
Petroleum and gas	646	598
Electric energy	214	207
Non-ferrous metals	468	447
Chemicals and products	894	853
Machine-building	1,190	1,231
Light industry	4,659	4,242
Food industry	795	824
Agricultural products (unprocessed)	757	447
Total (incl. others)	10,169	9,351
Foreign	1,628	1,182
Inter-republican (USSR)	8,542	8,169

1992 (US $ million): Imports 929.3; Exports 869.3 (Source: *World Bank Country Study: Uzbekistan*).

Education

(1989/90)

	Institutions	Students
Secondary schools	8,329	4,649,000
Secondary specialized schools	244	277,300
Higher schools (incl. universities)	44	331,600

Directory

The Constitution

A new Constitution was adopted by the Supreme Soviet on 8 December 1992. It declares Uzbekistan to be a secular, democratic and presidential republic. Basic human rights are guaranteed.

The highest legislative body is the Oly Majlis (Supreme Assembly), comprising 150 deputies. It is elected for a term of five years, and the first such elections were to take place in 1994, until when the 500-member Supreme Soviet was to continue to exercise legislative power. Parliament may be dissolved by the President (by agreement with the Constitutional Court). The Oly Majlis enacts normal legislation and constitutional legislation, elects its own officials, the judges of the higher courts and the Chairman of the State Committee for Environmental Protection. It confirms the President's appointments to ministerial office, the procuracy-general and the governorship of the Central Bank. It must ratify international treaties, changes to borders and presidential decrees on emergency situations. Legislation may be initiated by the deputies, by the President, by the higher courts, by the Procurator-General and by the Autonomous Republic of Karakalpakstan.

The President of the Republic, who is directly elected by the sovereign people for a five-year term, is head of state and holds supreme executive power. However, an individual may only be elected President for a maximum of two consecutive terms. The President is required to form and supervise the Government, appointing the Prime Minister and Ministers, subject to confirmation by parliament, the Oly Majlis. The President also nominates the candidates for appointment to the higher courts and certain offices of state, subject to confirmation by the Oly Majlis. The President appoints the judges of the lower courts and the khokims (governors) of the regions. Legislation may be initiated, reviewed and returned to the Oly Majlis by the President, who must promulgate all laws. The President may dissolve the Oly Majlis. The President is also Commander-in-Chief of the Armed Forces and may declare a state of emergency or a state of war (subject to confirmation by the Oly Majlis within three days).

The Cabinet of Ministers is the Government of the country; it is subordinate to the President, who appoints its Chairman (Prime Minister), Deputy Chairmen and Ministers, subject to the approval of the legislature. Local government is carried out by elected soviets (councils) and appointed khokims, the latter having significant personal authority and responsibility.

The exercise of judicial power is independent of government. The higher courts, of which the judges are nominated by the President and confirmed by the Oly Majlis, consist of the Constitutional Court, the Supreme Court and the High Economic Court. There is also a Supreme Court of the Autonomous Republic of Karakalpakstan. Lower courts, including economic courts, are based in the regions, districts and towns. The Procurator-General's office is responsible for supervising the observance of the law.

The Government

HEAD OF STATE

President of the Republic: ISLAM A. KARIMOV (elected 24 March 1990; re-elected, by direct popular vote, 29 December 1991).

CABINET OF MINISTERS
(March 1994)

Chairman (Prime Minister): ABDULKHASHIM M. MUTALOV.

First Deputy Chairman: ISMAIL KH. JURABEKOV.

Deputy Chairmen: ERKIN K. KHALILOV (Acting Chairman of the Supreme Soviet), ANATOLY N. VOZNENKO, KAYIM KHAKKULOV, KAZIM N. TULYAGANOV, MUKHMAJON K. KARABAYEV.

Deputy Chairman and Minister of Foreign Economic Relations: UKTUR S. SULTANOV.

Deputy Chairman and Minister of Finance: BAKHTIYAR KHAMIDOV.

Deputy Chairman and Chairman of the State Committee for the Management of State Property and for Privatization: VIKTOR A. CHZHEN.

Minister of Foreign Affairs: SAIDMUKHTAR S. SAIDKAZYMOV.

Minister of Defence: Maj.-Gen. RUSTAM U. AKHMEDOV.

Chairman of the National Security Service: GULYAM A. ALIYEV.

Minister of Higher and Specialized Secondary Education: AZIL U. SALIMOV.

Minister of the Interior: ZOKIRJON A. ALMATOV.

Minister of Health: SHAVKAT I. KARIMOV.

Minister of Culture: ERKIN K. KHAITBAYEV.

Minister of Land Improvement and Water Resources: RIM A. GINIYATULLIN.

Minister of Education: JURA G. YULDASHEV.

Minister of Agriculture: NORBEK K. KAYUMOV.

Minister of Communications: KAMILZHAN R. RAKHIMOV.

Minister of Social Security: BAKHODYR K. UMURZAKOV.

Minister of Labour: AKILJON ABIDOV (acting).

Minister of Energy and Electrification: VALERY Y. ATAYEV.

Minister of Justice: ALISHER MARDIYEV.

MINISTRIES

Office of the President: 700163 Tashkent, ul. Uzbekistanskaya 43; tel. (3712) 39-57-46; fax (3712) 39-55-25.

Office of the Cabinet of Ministers: 700008 Tashkent, Government House; tel. (3712) 39-82-95; fax (3712) 39-86-01.

Ministry of Agriculture: Tashkent; tel. (3712) 41-00-20.

Ministry of Communications: Tashkent, ul. A. Tolstovo 1; tel. (3712) 33-65-03.

Ministry of Culture: Tashkent; tel. (3712) 44-18-30.

Ministry of Defence: Tashkent; tel. (3712) 39-46-69.

Ministry of Education: Tashkent, alleya Paradov 5; tel. (3712) 39-47-38.

Ministry of Finance: 700078 Tashkent, alleya Paradov 6; tel. (3712) 39-15-69; fax (3712) 44-56-43.

Ministry of Foreign Affairs: 700047 Tashkent, ul. Gogolya 87; tel. (3712) 33-64-75; telex 116116; fax (3712) 32-37-57.

Ministry of Foreign Economic Relations: 700077 Tashkent, ul. Bujuk Ipak Yuli 75; tel. (3712) 68-92-56; telex 116294; fax (3712) 68-72-31.

Ministry of Health: Tashkent, ul. Navoi 12; tel. (3712) 44-12-02.

Ministry of Higher and Specialized Secondary Education: Tashkent, alleya Paradov 5; tel. (3712) 33-64-41.

Ministry of the Interior: Tashkent, ul. Germana Lopatina 1; tel. (3712) 33-95-32.

Ministry of Justice: Tashkent, ul. A. Kadiry 1; tel. (3712) 41-42-33.

Ministry of Land Improvement and Water Resources: Tashkent, ul. A. Kadiry 5A; tel. (3712) 41-18-04; telex 116198; fax (3712) 41-49-24.

Ministry of Social Security: Tashkent, ul. Babura 20A; tel. (3712) 53-53-71.

Principal State Committees

National Information Agency: 700000 Tashkent, ul. Hamza 28; tel. (3712) 33-16-22; fax (3712) 33-24-45; Dir MAMATCKUL KHAZRATCKULOV.

National Security Service: Tashkent; tel. (3712) 33-56-48; Chair. GULYAM ALIYEV.

State Committee for Environmental Protection: Tashkent, ul. A. Kadiry 5A; tel. (3712) 41-08-81; fax (3712) 41-39-90; Chair. ASKHAT SH. KHABIBULLAYEV.

State Committee for Forecasting and Statistics: 700000 Tashkent, ul. Uzbekistanskaya 45A; tel. (3712) 39-46-80; telex 116108; fax (3712) 39-86-39; Chair. (vacant).

State Committee for the Management of State Property and for Privatization: 700008 Tashkent, pl. Mustakilik 6; tel. (3712) 39-82-03; fax (3712) 39-46-66; Chair. V. CHZHEN.

State Committee for Precious Metals: 700019 Tashkent, proezd Turakorgan 26; tel. (3712) 48-07-20; fax (3712) 44-26-03; Chair. SH. NAZHIMOV.

State Committee for Science and Technology: 700017 Tashkent, Hadicha Suleymonova 29; tel. (3712) 39-18-43; fax (3712) 39-12-43; Chair. NODIRBEK YUSULBEKOV.

State Tax Directorate: 700195 Tashkent, ul. Abai 4; tel. (3712) 41-78-70; telex 116054; Chair. SHAMIL GATAULIN.

Legislature

SUPREME SOVIET

The Supreme Soviet, which was comprised of 500 members, was the supreme legislative organ in Uzbekistan. Under the 1992

Constitution it was to continue as such until the election of a new parliament, the Oly Majlis (Supreme Assembly), which was scheduled for 1994. The majority of deputies elected in 1990 were members of the Communist Party of Uzbekistan (CPU). In late 1992 320 seats in the Supreme Soviet were held by the People's Democratic Party of Uzbekistan, which succeeded the CPU in November 1991. In 1993 it was reported that there were only 15 deputies who could be readily identified as from the opposition.

Chairman: ERKIN KHALILOV (acting); 700008 Tashkent, Government House; tel. (3712) 39-87-40; fax (3712) 39-87-49.

Local Government

Uzbekistan contained one Autonomous Republic (Karakalpakstan) and 12 oblasts (regions). There were further local subdivisions. From January 1992 the main figure in local government was the khokim (governor), who was appointed as the chief executive figure in the region by the President of the Republic. There was also a regional soviet (council) of people's deputies.

OBLASTS

Andijan Oblast: Andijan.

Bukhara Oblast: Bukhara.

Fergana Oblast: Fergana.

Jisak Oblast: Jisak.

Khorezm Oblast: Urgench.

Kashkadarin Oblast: Karshi.

Namangan Oblast: Namangan.

Novoi Oblast: Novoi.

Samarkand Oblast: Samarkand; Khokim PULAT ABDURAKHMANOV.

Surhandarin Oblast: Termez.

Syr-Dar'ya Oblast: Gulistan.

Tashkent Oblast: Tashkent.

AUTONOMOUS REPUBLIC

The Kara-Kalpak Autonomous Republic (Karakalpakstan) became part of Uzbekistan in 1932. Prior to that it had been an autonomous territory attached to Kazakhstan, within the Russian Federation. Russia had annexed the region from the Khanate of Khiva. It is an integral part of Uzbekistan. Karakalpakstan is the main habitation of the Kara-Kalpak ethnic minority. The capital is Nukus, on the Amu-Dar'ya river. The territory is amongst the worst affected by the Aral Sea environmental problems. There is a directly elected President and a legislative Supreme Soviet.

President of the Kara-Kalpak Autonomous Republic: D. N. SHAMSHETOV; Karakalpakstan, Nukus.

Permanent Representation in Tashkent: 700078 Tashkent, pl. Mustakilik 5; tel. (3712) 39-40-72; fax (3712) 39-48-48.

Political Organizations

Following Uzbekistan's independence (achieved in August 1991), the ruling People's Democratic Party took increasingly repressive measures against opposition and Islamic parties; all religious political parties were banned in 1991, and in the following year the leading opposition group, Birlik, was likewise outlawed.

Birlik (Unity): c/o Union of Writers of Uzbekistan, 700000 Tashkent, ul. Pushkina 1; tel. (3712) 33-79-21; f. 1989; leading opposition group, banned in 1992; registered as a social movement; Chair. Prof. ABDURAKHIM PULATOV.

Erk (Freedom): Tashkent; f. 1990; only registered opposition party; Chair. MUHAMMAD SOLIKH; Sec. DIKH EGITALIYEV; 5,000 mems (1991).

Islamic Renaissance Party: Tashkent; banned in 1991; advocates introduction of a political system based on the tenets of Islam; Leader ABDULLAH UTAYEV.

People's Democratic Party of Uzbekistan: 700163 Tashkent, ul. Uzbekistanskaya 43; f. 1991 to replace Communist Party of Uzbekistan; Leader ISLAM A. KARIMOV; 340,000 mems (1993).

Other political organizations include the Progress of the Fatherland Party (registered), Human Rights Committee of Uzbekistan (Chair. ABDUMANOB PULATOV), the Free Peasants' Party (affiliated to Birlik) and Islamic groups, mainly based in the Fergana valley, such as the conservative Adolat (Justice—f. and banned in 1992).

Diplomatic Representation

EMBASSIES IN UZBEKISTAN

China, People's Republic: Tashkent; Ambassador: GUAN HENGGUANG.

France: Tashkent.

Germany: 700067 Tashkent, pr. Sharaf-Rashidov 15; tel. (3712) 34-66-96; Ambassador: Dr KARL-HEINZ KUHNA.

India: Tashkent, ul. A. Tolstovo 5; tel. (3712) 33-82-67; fax (3712) 33-56-65; Ambassador: DALIP MEHTA.

Italy: Tashkent; tel. (3712) 77-69-21; Ambassador: CARLO UNGARO.

Japan: 700031 Tashkent, ul. G. Lopatina 64, Hotel Turkiston, Rm 4; tel. and fax (3712) 56-46-43.

Kazakhstan: Tashkent.

Pakistan: 700115 Tashkent, ul. Chilanzarskaya 25; tel. (3712) 77-10-03; telex 116431; fax (3712) 77-14-42; Ambassador: SHAFQAT ALI SHEIKH.

Russia: Tashkent.

Turkey: Tashkent, Gogol kucesi 87; tel. (3712) 33-21-07; telex 116167; fax (3712) 33-13-58.

United Kingdom: Tashkent, Hotel Uzbekistan, Rm 1001–02; tel. (3712) 33-82-31; fax (873) 1447203; Chargé d'affaires a.i.: PAUL BERGNE.

USA: 700115 Tashkent, ul. Chelanzarskaya 55; tel. (3712) 77-14-07; fax (3712) 77-10-81; Ambassador: HENRY LEE CLARK.

Judicial System

Chairman of the Supreme Court: M. IBRAGIMOV.

Procurator-General: BURITOSH MUSTAFAYEV.

Religion

The Constitution of 8 December 1992 stipulates that, while there is freedom of worship and expression, there may be no state religion or ideology. The most widespread religion in the country is Islam; the majority of ethnic Uzbeks are Sunni Muslims (Hanafi school), but the number of Wahhabi communities is increasing. Most ethnic Slavs in Uzbekistan are adherents of Orthodox Christianity. In the early 1990s there were reported to be some 65,000 European Jews and 28,000 Central Asian Jews.

State Committee for Religious Affairs: 700000 Tashkent, ul. Ulyanova, 1-ogo proezd 14; tel. (3712) 33-41-50; Chair. ABDUGANY ABDULLAYEV.

ISLAM

Muslim Board of Central Asia: Tashkent 2, Zarkainar 103; tel. (3712) 40-39-33; fax (3712) 40-08-31; f. 1943; has spiritual jurisdiction over the Muslims in the Central Asian republics of the former USSR; Chair. MUHAMMAD SODIK MUHAMMAD YUSUF, Chief Mufti of Mowarounnahr (Central Asia).

The Press

In 1990, according to official statistics, there were 279 newspapers being published in Uzbekistan, including 185 published in Uzbek. The average daily circulation was 5,158,400 copies (4,120,500 in Uzbek). There were 93 periodicals being published, including 33 in Uzbek. Newspapers were also published in Russian, Greek, Tajik, Crimean Tatar and Karakalpak. In December 1993 the Government ordered all publications to be re-registered with the State Committee for the Press, but did not license any of the independent publications.

The publications listed below are in Uzbek, unless otherwise stated.

State Committee for the Press: Tashkent, ul. Navoi 30; tel. (3712) 44-32-87; telex 116108; fax (3712) 44-26-03; Chair. RUSTAM SH. SHAGULYAMOV.

PRINCIPAL NEWSPAPERS

Khaik suzi (The People's World): Tashkent; f. 1991; 5 a week; organ of the Supreme Soviet; Editor N. MUKHTAROV.

Molodets Uzbekistana (Young Person of Uzbekistan): 700083 Tashkent, ul. Leningradskaya 32; tel. (3712) 32-56-51; f. 1926; 5 a week; in Russian; Editor A. PUKEMOV; circ. 30,000.

Narodnoye Slovo: 700163 Tashkent, ul. Uzbekistanskaya 43; official gazette.

Pravda Vostoka (Eastern Truth): 700008 Tashkent, Government House; f. 1917; 6 a week; organ of the Supreme Soviet and Cabinet of Ministers; in Russian; Editor R. SAFAROV.

Tashkentskaya Pravda (Tashkent Truth): 700008 Tashkent, Government House; major local paper.

Turkiston (Turkestan): 700083 Tashkent, ul. Leningradskaya 32; tel. (3712) 33-89-61; f. 1925 as *Yash Leninchy* (Young Leninist), renamed as above 1992; 3 a week; Editor ZHABBAR RAZZAKOV; circ. 70,000.

Uzbekiston adabieti va sanyati (Literature and Art of Uzbekistan): 700000 Tashkent, ul. Leningradskaya 32; (3712) 32-54-66; f. 1956; weekly; organ of the Union of Writers of Uzbekistan; Editor N. MELIBAYEV.

PRINCIPAL PERIODICALS

Monthly, unless otherwise indicated.

Chelovek i politika (Man and Politics): Tashkent; f. 1920; political; in Uzbek and Russian.

Fan va turmush (Science and Life): 700000 Tashkent, ul. Gogolya 70; tel. (3712) 33-69-61; f. 1933; publ. by the Fan (Science) Publishing House; journal of the Academy of Sciences of Uzbekistan; popular scientific.

Gulistan (Flourishing Area): Tashkent; f. 1925; fiction.

Gulkhan (Bonfire): 700083 Tashkent; tel. (3712) 32-78-85; f. 1929; illustrated juvenile fiction.

Guncha (Small Bud): Tashkent, Buyuk Turon 41; tel. (3712) 32-78-80; f. 1958; illustrated; literary, for pre-school-age children; Editor-in-Chief Y. U. SAGDULLAYEVA; circ. 111,000.

Mushtum (Fist): Tashkent; f. 1923; fortnightly; satirical.

Obshchestvennye nauki v Uzbekistane (Social Sciences in Uzbekistan): 700000 Tashkent, ul. Gogolya 70; tel. (3712) 33-69-61; f. 1957; publ. by the Fan (Science) Publishing House of the Academy of Sciences of Uzbekistan; history, oriental studies, archaeology, economics, ethnology, etc.; in Russian.

Saodat (Happiness): Tashkent; f. 1925; women's popular.

Shark yulduzi (Star of the East): 700000 Tashkent, pr. Lenina 41; tel. (3712) 33-21-81; f. 1932; journal of the Union of Writers of Uzbekistan; fiction.

Uzbekistan-Contact: 700083 Tashkent, ul. Leningradskaya 32; tel. (3712) 33-02-15; f. 1984; publ. by National Assen for Cultural-Educational Relations; history, politics, culture, general interest; in Uzbek, English, Russian, Arabic, Turkish, Farsi (Persian), Hindi and Urdu; Editor-in-Chief KAKHAR F. RASHIDOV; circ. 25,000.

Uzbek tili va adabyati (Uzbek Language and Literature): 700000 Tashkent, ul. Gogolya 70; f. 1958; fortnightly; publ. by the Fan (Science) Publishing House; journal of the Academy of Sciences of Uzbekistan; history and modern development of the Uzbek language, folklore, etc.

Uzbekiston kishlok khuzhaligi (Agriculture of Uzbekistan): Tashkent; f. 1925; journal of the Ministry of Agriculture; cotton-growing, cattle-breeding, forestry.

Zvezda vostoka (Star of the East): 700000 Tashkent, ul. gazety Pravda 41; tel. (3712) 33-42-68; f. 1932; publ. by Gafur Gulyam Publishers; journal of the Union of Writers of Uzbekistan; fiction; translations into Russian from Arabic, English, Hindi, Turkish, Japanese, etc.; Editor-in-Chief SABIT MADALIYEV; circ. 82,678.

NEWS AGENCY

UzTAG (Uzbek Telegraph Agency): Tashkent, ul. Khamza 2; tel. (3712) 39-49-82; Dir ERKIN K. KHAITBAYEV.

Publishers

In 1989 there were 2,336 book titles (including pamphlets and brochures) published in Uzbekistan, in a total of 48m. copies, including 929 (28.6m. copies) in Uzbek.

Chulpon (Little Star): Tashkent, ul. gazety Pravda; Dir N. NORBUTAYEV.

Esh Gvardiya (Young Guard Publishing House): Tashkent, ul. Navoi 30; juvenile books and journals; Dir KH. E. PIRMUKHAMEDOV.

Fan (Science Publishing House): Tashkent, ul. Gogolya 70, k. 105; tel. (3712) 33-69-61; scientific books and journals; Dir N. T. KHATAMOV.

Gafur Gulyam Publishers: 700129 Tashkent, ul. Navoi 30; tel. (3712) 44-22-53; fax (3712) 44-11-68; f. 1957; fiction, the arts; books in Uzbek, Russian and English; Dir B. S. SHARIPOV.

Meditsina (Medicine Publishing House): Tashkent, ul. Navoi 30; tel. (3712) 44-51-72; f. 1958; medical sciences; Editor-in-Chief R. RESKIN.

Sharq Publishing House: 700000 Tashkent, ul. Buyuk Turon 41; tel. (3712) 33-47-86; fax (3712) 33-18-58; largest publishing house; govt-owned.

Ukituvchi (Teacher): Tashkent, ul. Navoi 30; tel. (3712) 44-23-86; fax (3712) 44-32-04; f. 1936; literary textbooks, education manuals, scientific literature, juvenile; Dir M. MIRZAYEV.

Uzbekistan Publishing House: Tashkent, ul. Navoi 30; tel. (3712) 44-38-10; fax (3712) 44-11-35; f. 1924; socio-political, economic, illustrated; Dir R. SAFAYEV.

Uzbekskoy Sovetskoy Entsiklopedii (Uzbekistan Soviet Encyclopaedia): Tashkent, ul. Zhukovskovo 52; tel. (3712) 33-50-17; f. 1968; encyclopaedias, dictionaries and reference books; Editor-in-Chief N. TUCHLIYEV.

WRITERS' UNION

Union of Writers of Uzbekistan: 700000 Tashkent, ul. Pushkina 1; tel. (3712) 33-79-21; Pres. JAMAL KEMAL.

Radio and Television

State Television and Radio Broadcasting Company: 700047 Tashkent, ul. Khorezmskaya 49; tel. (3712) 41-05-51; Dir-Gen. SHAVQAT G. YAKHYAYEV.

Radio Tashkent: 700047 Tashkent, ul. Khorezmskaya 49; tel. (3712) 33-02-49; telex 116139; f. 1947; broadcasts in Uzbek, English, Urdu, Hindi, Farsi (Persian), Arabic, Chinese and Uighur.

Tashkent Television Studio: Tashkent, ul. Navoi 69.

Finance

(cap. = capital; res = reserves; dep. = deposits; m. = million; amounts in roubles, unless otherwise stated; brs = branches)

BANKING

State Banks

Central Bank of the Republic of Uzbekistan: 700001 Tashkent, ul. Uzbekistanskaya 6; tel. (3712) 33-68-29; telex 116396; fax (3712) 33-35-09; Chair. of Bd FAIZULLA M. MULLAJANOV; Vice-Chair. of Bd ALIKUL H. ERDONAYEV.

Uzbek National Bank for Foreign Economic Activities: 700015 Tashkent, ul. Tarasa Shevchenko 29; tel. (3712) 54-59-01; telex 116194; fax (3712) 55-13-51; f. 1991; Chair. RUSTAM AZIMOV.

Other Banks

Sberbank—Savings Bank of Uzbekistan: Tashkent; f. 1991; fmrly a br. of the USSR Savings Bank; holds almost all household deposits; state-controlled.

Rustambank: 700000 Tashkent, Frunze 27; tel. (3712) 33-21-18; telex 116547; fax (3712) 33-77-49; f. 1992; private, commercial bank; cap. 181.6m., res 1.1m., dep. 378.4m. (Dec. 1992); Pres. RUSTAM T. USMANOV; Gen. Man. RAHIM S. RAJABOV.

Uzbek Commercial Bank: 700015 Tashkent, ul. Poltoratskovo 73B; tel. (3712) 54-79-51.

Uzbek Joint-Stock Innovation Bank: 700015 Tashkent, ul Pavla Rzhevskovo 3; tel. (3712) 55-82-59; telex 116152; fax (3712) 55-76-16; f. 1988; cap. 37.5m., dep. 117.9m.; Man. Dir YU P. GORDEYEV.

Uzagroprombank—Agroindustrial Bank of Uzbekistan: 700096 Tashkent, Mukimi 43; tel. (3712) 78-21-77; telex 116412; fax (3712) 78-12-96; f. 1991 (fmrly part of USSR Agroprombank); joint-stock commercial bank; total assets US $911m. (Jan 1993); 185 brs.

Uzpromstroibank—Uzbek Joint-Stock Commercial Industrial Construction Bank: 700000 Tashkent, ul. 1-vo Maya 3; tel. (3712) 33-34-26; telex 116342; fax (3712) 33-63-54; f. 1922; cap. 3,054m., res 760m., dep. 471,097m. (Jan. 1993); Chair. AKHMED I. IBOTOV; Gen. Man. MARIA V. BONDAREVSKY.

In 1992 there were 16 other joint-stock commercial banks. Four of the commercial banks were licensed to carry out foreign-exchange transactions. However, Uzagroprombank and Uzpromstroibank were the largest banks, providing 96% of total credit to enterprises at the end of 1991. The Savings Bank was the institution most widely used by private individuals.

COMMODITY EXCHANGE

Tashkent Commodity Exchange (TACE): 700003 Tashkent, ul Uzbekistanskaya 45; tel. (3712) 45-71-41; fax (3712) 45-62-79; Chair. Exchange Cttee KABUL USMANOV.

Trade and Industry

STATE PRIVATIZATION AGENCY

State Committee for the Management of State Property and for Privatization: 700008 Tashkent, pl. Mustakilik 6; tel. (3712) 39-82-03; fax (3712) 39-46-66; Chair. V. CHZHEN.

CHAMBER OF COMMERCE

Chamber of Commerce and Industry: 700017 Tashkent, pr. Timura 16A; tel. (3712) 33-62-82; Chair. DELBART YU. MIRSIAADOVA.

EMPLOYERS' ORGANIZATIONS

Employers' Association of Uzbekistan: 700017 Tashkent, ul. Abdullah Kadyri 2; tel. (3712) 34-06-71; fax (3712) 34-13-39.

Union of Entrepreneurs of Uzbekistan: Uzbek Expo Information Centre, 700000 Tashkent, alleya Paradov 6; tel. (3712) 33-67-00; fax (3712) 33-32-00.

SELECTED INDUSTRIAL COMPANIES AND ENTERPRISES

Amantaytau Goldfields: c/o 700077 Tashkent, ul. Bujuk Ipak Yuli 75; f. 1993; joint venture between two state-owned Uzbek cos and British co Lonhro; gold mining near Zerafshan; scheduled to start production in 1995.

Sredazelektroapparat: 700005 Tashkent, Manjara 1; tel. (3712) 291-29-04; engaged in the production of low-voltage equipment, incl. packet-type switches, cam switches, etc.; Gen. Dir ALIM ABDURAIMOVICH; 9,000 employees.

Tashkent Industrial Amalgamation: 700090 Tashkent, Barbur 73; tel. (3712) 55-17-23; fax (3712) 44-30-43; produces diamond and elbor grinding wheels, instruments of galvanic binder, etc.; Gen. Man. ANATOLY HEGAY; 1,100 employees.

Usselchosmash: Tashkent; state-owned; produces variety of motor vehicles; largest industrial concern in the country; operates joint venture to produce heavy trucks with Mercedes-Benz of Germany; 36,000 employees (1993).

Uzbekneftgaz (State Petroleum and Natural Gas Co): Tashkent; f. 1991; responsible for the operation of the hydrocarbons industry; participates in joint ventures with foreign investors; Chair. KAYIM ZH. KHAKKULOV.

Uzbektelekom (Telecommunications of Uzbekistan): Tashkent, ul. A. Tolstova 1; f. 1992; consists of 14 regional enterprises; controls local telecommunications, with subsidiary controlling international and regional links; dept of Ministry of Communications; Chair. K. R. RAKHIMOV.

Zerafshan Gold Refinery: Bukhara obl., Zerafshan; f. 1967; main gold refinery in country; Dir VALERY NIKOLAYEVICH; 3,000 employees (1993).

TRADE UNIONS

Federation of Trade Unions of Uzbekistan: Tashkent; Chair. of Council ALLA MURODOV.

Transport

INLAND WATERWAYS

The extensive use of the waters of the Amu-Dar'ya and Syr-Dar'ya for irrigation lessened the flow of these rivers and caused the desiccation of the Aral Sea. This reduced a valuable transport asset. However, the Amu-Dar'ya Steamship Co still operated important river traffic and was able to add two vessels to its fleet in mid-1993.

RAILWAYS

Uzbekistan's railway network is connected to those of the neighbouring republics of Kazakhstan, Kyrgyzstan, Tajikistan and Turkmenistan, and it dominates the operation of the system in the latter three countries. All track is standard gauge. The Tashkent Metro was inaugurated in 1977; in 1991 two new stations were opened, giving a total of 23, with 31 km of track.

Middle Asian Railway: 700061 Tashkent, Gogolya 94; f. 1991; tel. (3712) 32-44-00; Dir V. M. ZHELTOUKHOV.

CIVIL AVIATION

Uzbekistan Airlines (Uzbekistan Havo Yulari): 700060 Tashkent, Proletarskaya 41; tel. (3712) 33-73-57; telex 116169; fax (3712) 33-18-85; f. 1992; operates flights to Central Asian and other destinations; Dir-Gen. GANI RAFIKOV.

Tourism

Uzbekistan, at the time of independence, was not a major tourist destination. However, it has a large number of historical sites, notably the ancient cities of Samarkand and Bukhara.

Uzbektourism: 700027 Tashkent, ul. Khorezmskaya 47; tel. (3712) 33-54-14; fax (3712) 32-79-48; Chair. BAKHODYA P. KAYUMOV.

Culture

Uzbekistan has a rich cultural heritage, particularly in the ancient cities of the 'Silk Road'. Islam, together with Persic (Tajik) and Turkic and Mongol (Uzbek) traditions, provided a varied legacy. Samarkand, the capital and site of the mausoleum of the medieval khan Tamerlane (Timur 'the Lame'), was also reviving as a pilgrimage site in the early 1990s. The city is the site of the Shah-e-Zinda shrine (formerly a museum), dedicated to Muhammad's nephew, Kussam Ibn Abbas, who, according to tradition, evangelized the area for Islam. Tashkent, long a centre of Russian influence in the territory, is the base for many cultural activities.

NATIONAL ORGANIZATIONS

Ministry of Culture: see section on The Government (Ministries).

CULTURAL HERITAGE

Alisher Navoi State Public Library of Uzbekistan: 700000 Tashkent, alleya Narodov 5; tel. (3712) 33-05-47; f. 1870; 4,157,500 vols; Dir D. TAJIYEVA.

Karakalpak Historical Museum: Nukus, ul. Rakhmatova 3; contains material on the history of Karakalpakstan and the Uzbek people.

Museum of Uzbek History, Culture and Arts: Samarkand, ul. Sovetskaya 51; f. 1874; over 100,000 items; Dir N. S. SADYKOVA.

Tashkent Historical Museum of the People of Uzbekistan: 700047 Tashkent, ul. Kuibysheva 15; tel. (3712) 33-57-32; f. 1876; over 200,000 exhibits; Dir G. R. RASHIDOV.

Uzbek State Museum of Art: 700060 Tashkent, Proletarskaya 16; tel. (3712) 32-34-44; f. 1918; library of 22,700 vols; Dir D. S. RUSIBAYEV.

SPORTING ORGANIZATION

State Committee for Physical Education and Sport: 700027 Tashkent, ul. Furkat 1; tel. (3712) 45-16-18; fax (3712) 45-08-52; Chair. SABYR S. ROUZIYEV.

PERFORMING ARTS

Alisher Navoi Opera and Ballet Theatre: Tashkent, ul. Pravdy Vostoka 31.

Central Puppet Theatre of Uzbekistan: Tashkent, pr. Kosmonavtov 1.

Khamza Uzbek Drama Theatre: Tashkent, pr. Navoi 34.

Maxim Gorky Russian Drama Theatre: Tashkent, ul. K. Marksa 28.

ASSOCIATION

National Association for International Cultural and Humanitarian Relations: 700003 Tashkent, T. Tula 1; tel. (3712) 45-55-54; telex 116570; fax (3712) 45-55-53; f. 1992 by merger of Society for Friendship and Cultural Relations with Foreign Countries and Vatan (Motherland) Society for Cultural Relations with Uzbeks Abroad; promotes cultural and educational relations with other countries; Chair. NAIM JA. GAYBOV.

Union of Writers of Uzbekistan: 700000 Tashkent, ul. Pushkina 1; tel. (3712) 33-79-21; Sec. MUKHAMMAD SOLIKH.

Education

Until the early 1990s education was based on the Soviet model, but some changes were introduced, including a greater emphasis on Uzbek history and literature, and study of the Arabic script. From 1993 a Latin script was to be introduced. In 1988/89 76.8% of pupils at day schools were educated in Uzbek. Other languages used include Russian (15.0%), Kazakh (2.9%), Karakalpak (2.4%), Tadzhik (2.3%), Turkmen (0.4%) and Kirghiz (0.2%). Higher education is provided in several specialized institutes and four universities. In 1993 private education was banned.

UNIVERSITIES

Bukhara State University: 705017 Bukhara, pr. Leninskogo Komsomola 15; tel. (36522) 3-04-02; 5 faculties.

Nukus State University: 742012 Nukus, ul. Universitetskaya 1; tel. (36122) 3-23-72; f. 1979; 11 faculties; 7,000 students; Rector Prof. K. ATANIYAZOV.

Samarkand State University: 703004 Samarkand, ul. Universitetskaya 15; tel. (36622) 35-26-26; fax (36622) 35-03-40; f. 1933; 16 faculties; 1,235 teachers; 18,650 students; Rector Prof. Acad. T. M. MUMINOV.

Tashkent State University: 700095 Tashkent, Vozgorodok, Universitetskaya ul. 95; tel. (3712) 46-02-24; f. 1920; 17 faculties; 1,480 teachers; 19,300 students; Rector Dr S. K. SIRAJINOV.

Social Welfare

In the early 1990s the Government was anxious to minimize the social and economic consequences on the population of a transfer to a free-market economy. Provision was made for a deterioration in employment levels and for welfare and pension benefits, however, with the establishment of three extrabudgetary funds: the Employment Fund, the Pensions Fund and the Social Insurance Fund. Government social protection policy, while not efficient and properly co-ordinated nor fully adapted to a society with a free-market economy, consisted of three essential components. These were: an anti-poverty policy, designed to improve real incomes; an income-maintenance policy for those unable to continue in employment; and an employment policy for those who had lost their jobs. Subsidies of essential items had also formed part of social protection, but the phasing out of such price-support mechanisms was essential to the process of economic reform, although some still continued after the January 1994 deadline for their elimination. Other reforms still outstanding were the more precise targeting of the needy and the reorganization of health services.

Health standards were relatively poor in the country, which was severely affected by environmental problems. Average life expectancy at birth, according to the World Bank, was 69.5 years in 1992. In 1990 there were 297 people per physician.

NATIONAL AGENCIES

Ministry of Health: see section on The Government (Ministries).

Ministry of Social Security: see section on The Government (Ministries).

HEALTH AND WELFARE ORGANIZATION

Uzbek Institute of Sanitation and Hygiene: Tashkent, ul. K. Marksa 85.

The Environment

The principal environmental concerns in Uzbekistan revolve around the desiccation of the Aral Sea, to which the extensive use of the Syr-Dar'ya and Amu-Dar'ya rivers for irrigation purposes is a major contributing factor (see The Economy above). Water resources generally are the main environmental concern in the country, although industrial pollution in Tashkent and the Fergana valley also caused disquiet to local groups. Environmental activists were not encouraged by the authorities.

GOVERNMENT ORGANIZATION

State Committee for Environmental Protection: Tashkent, ul. A. Kadiry 5A; tel. (3712) 41-08-81; fax (3712) 41-39-90; Chair. ASKHAT SH. KHABIBULLAYEV; First Deputy Chair. VLADIMIR G. KONJUKHOV.

ACADEMIC INSTITUTE

Uzbek Academy of Sciences: 700000 Tashkent, ul. Gogolya 70; tel. (3712) 33-38-02; telex 116320; fax (3712) 33-49-01; f. 1943; several attached institutes involved in environmental research; Pres. M. S. SALAKHIDDINOV.

Academy of Sciences of Karakalpakstan: Karakalpakstan, 742000 Nukus; Pres. SABIR KAMALOV.

NON-GOVERNMENTAL ORGANIZATIONS

Bukhara State University Ecology Club: 705017 Bukhara, Bukhara State University, pr. Leninskogo Komsomola 15; f. 1993; Chair. MAJDU ARYNOVICH ABDYLGAYEV.

Committee to Save the Aral Sea: 700132 Tashkent, Perviya Proen, ul. Sadokat 14; tel. (3712) 47-11-95; Chair. PRIMAT SHERMUKHAMEDOV.

Ekolog Children's Club: 704114 Samarkand obl., Ziadin, ul. Lenina 20; tel. (36627) 3-10-67; f. 1978; youth group; Chair. BAKHODIR JUMAYEVICH KHUDAYBERDIYEV.

Ekolog Club: 700105 Tashkent, Gaydara 11A/10; tel. (3712) 91-39-35; once a large group, but reduced by adverse circumstances and official pressure; Chair. OLEG IVANOVICH TSARUK.

Ekosan: Tashkent, ul. Uzbekistanskaya 43; tel. (3712) 39-84-01; f. 1992; environmental health; Chair. YUSUFJAN SHADIMETOVICH SHADIMETOV.

Ekosan Karakalpakstan: Karakalpakstan, Nukus; tel. (36122) 2-42-20; f. 1993; Chair. MARINA ALEKSANDROVNA KOGAY.

Eremurus: 700171 Tashkent, Lisunova 1/1; tel. (3712) 33-41-46; city youth group; Chair. ELENA VLADIMIROVNA MELNIKOVA.

Lop-Nor Semipalatinsk Ecological Committee (Tashkent): Tashkent; tel. (3712) 46-35-27; f. 1993 as br. of anti-nuclear group based in Kazakhstan; registered as Uighur social org.; Chair. ABDULJAN BARAYEV.

Union in Defence of the Amu-Dar'ya and the Aral Sea: Karakalpakstan, 742000 Nukus, ul. Gogolya tup. Lenina 1; tel. (36122) 2-37-30; most active environmental org. in Uzbekistan; Chair. ORAZBAY ABDIRAKHMANOV; Deputy Chair. YUSUP SABIROVICH KAMALOV.

Defence

Uzbekistan, according to Western estimates, at June 1993, possessed total armed forces of 40,000 personnel. This included an army of some 38,000 and an air force of 2,000. There was a small Russian (ex-Soviet) force based in the country. Uzbekistan participated in a defence pact with the Russian Federation and several other Central Asian states, committing it to the defence of Tajikistan's southern borders. During 1993 the Uzbek air force in particular was involved in supporting the Government of Tajikistan against insurgents, action which allegedly included raids into Afghanistan.

Commander-in-Chief: President of the Republic.

Minister of Defence: Maj.-Gen. RUSTAM AKHMEDOV.

Bibliography

Akiner, S. (Ed.). *Cultural Change and Continuity*. London, Kegan Paul International, 1991.

Aminova, R. Kh. *The October Revolution and Women's Liberation in Uzbekistan*. Moscow, Nauka, 1972.

Allworth, E. (Ed.). *Central Asia: A Century of Russian Rule*. London and New York, Columbia University Press, 1967.

Bennigsen, A., and Lemercier-Quelquejay, C. *Islam in the Soviet Union*. London, Pall Mall, 1967.

Bromlei, Ju. *Present-day Ethnic Processes in the USSR*. Moscow, Progress, 1977.

Carrere d'Encausse, H. *Decline of an Empire*. New York, Newsweek Books, 1980.

Dienes, L. *Soviet Asia: Economic Development and National Policy Choices*. Boulder, Colorado, Westview Press, 1987.

McCagg, W. O., and Silver, B. (Eds). *Soviet Asian Ethnic Frontiers*. Oxford and New York, Pergamon Policy Studies, 1979.

Medlin, W. K., Carpenter, F., and Cave, W. M. *Education and Development in Central Asia: A Case Study on Social Change in Uzbekistan*. Leiden, Brill, 1971.

Rumer, B. Z. *Soviet Central Asia: A Tragic Experiment*. Boston, Unwin Hyman, 1989.

YUGOSLAVIA

Geography

PHYSICAL FEATURES

The Federal Republic of Yugoslavia (FRY), formerly part of the Socialist Federal Republic of Yugoslavia, is situated in the central Balkan Peninsula, in south-eastern Europe. It has a western coastline along the Adriatic Sea (part of the Mediterranean). The country is a federation of two Republics: Montenegro (with an area of 13,182 sq km), in the south-west, on the Adriatic coast, and the land-locked territories of Serbia (with an area of 88,361 sq km), occupying the rest of the country; Yugoslavia has a total area of 102,173 sq km (39,449 sq miles). Serbian territory includes the Autonomous Province of Kosovo and Metohija (formerly known as Kosovo) and the Autonomous Province of Vojvodina. Kosovo-Metohija (with an area of 10,887 sq km) occupies the plateau-lands in the south-west of Serbia and Vojvodina (21,506 sq km) is in the north of the Republic. The FRY is bordered by Hungary to the north, Romania and Bulgaria to the east, Macedonia to the south-east and Albania to the south. In the extreme south-western corner there is a short border with Croatia on the Adriatic coast, but the main border with that country is in the north-west, and the central western border is with Bosnia and Herzegovina.

The River Danube (Dunav) forms part of the FRY's western border with Croatia and runs across the northern half of the country to form part of the eastern frontier with Romania. The fertile plains of Vojvodina and northern Serbia are also watered by the Tisa (Tisza), Drava and Sava rivers, the last of which flows eastwards from Bosnia and Herzegovina to join the Danube at Belgrade (Beograd). Another river to join the Danube on these plains is the Morava, which passes through a deep valley from the mountainous south. The FRY has a rugged mountainous terrain, except in the north where the Pannonian plains begin. The highlands of the south-west are known as the Black Mountains (Crna Gora), from which Montenegro takes its name. The Republic is also traversed by some fertile river valleys which cut southwards towards the lowlands around Lake Scutari (Skadarsko Jezero). There are some coastal lowlands around the harbour of Kotor (formerly Cattaro—on the Boka Kotorska bay) and to the south of the Adriatic city of Bar and Lake Scutari.

CLIMATE

The climate is continental in the hilly interior and Mediterranean on the coast, with steady rainfall throughout the year. The average summer temperature in Belgrade is 22°C (71°F) and in winter the average temperature is 0°C (32°F). The average annual rainfall is 635 mm (25 in) in Belgrade.

POPULATION

The FRY is dominated by Southern Slavic (Yugoslav) peoples, predominantly the Serbs. The Serbs made up 62% of the country's total population, according to the census of 1991. The principal language in the country is Serbo-Croat in its Serbian form (written in the Cyrillic script). The Montenegrins (5% of the total population at the 1991 census, but 62% of the population of Montenegro) also speak a Serbo-Croat dialect, use the Cyrillic script and are a Serbian people. The non-Slavic ethnic Albanians were actu-

ally the second-largest group in the country (17% of the total population in 1991). They were predominantly present in the Autonomous Province of Kosovo-Metohija. The other main non-Slavic group in the country was that of the Hungarians (Magyars—3%). The Autonomous Province of Vojvodina, in the north of the country, was formerly part of the Banat, a border territory of the Habsburg realm. Although it is an area of very mixed ethnic composition, originally it had a large Hungarian population. However, by the latter part of the 20th century it was dominated by Serbs. Those, usually of mixed parentage, who chose to define themselves as ethnic 'Yugoslavs' also make up some 3% of the country's total population. The Slav Muslims (3%) lived mainly in the Sandžak region, on the Serbian–Montenegrin border and to the north of Kosovo-Metohija (the chief city of the region is Novi Pazar—anciently Raška). Other minority communities in the FRY include Roma (Gypsies), Vlahs, Bulgarians, Czechs, Slovaks and Ruthenians (Ukrainians).

A reflection of the Serb and Montenegrin majority in the FRY is the predominance of Orthodox Christianity. Some 41% of the population adhered to the Eastern Orthodox Church (which introduced the Cyrillic alphabet), as represented by the Serbian Orthodox Church. There are followers of other Orthodox rites, some Roman Catholics (in Vojvodina and among the Albanian minority) and a few Protestants. Islam is the religion of a significant minority, but it is concentrated in the south of the country amongst Slav Muslims and most of the Albanian population. There are also some Jews.

According to the March 1991 census, the FRY had a total population of 10,406,742. The population density was 102 per sq km. The capital and largest city is Belgrade (in

Serbia—also the capital of that Republic) which had a population of 1,087,915 in 1991. The Montenegrin capital is Podgorica (formerly Titograd) which had a population of 96,074 in 1991. The Autonomous Province of Kosovo-Metohija had a population of 1,954,747 in 1991 (an increase of some 23% on 1981, the highest rate of population growth of any region in the former Yugoslavia). The provincial capital is Priština (108,020). The other Autonomous Province of Vojvodina had a population of 2,102,517; its capital is Novi Sad, which had 170,029 inhabitants in 1991. Other important towns in the FRY include Niš (161,376 in 1991), Kragujevać (108,020), Subotica (100,219) and Zrenjanin (81,328).

Chronology

168 BC: Illyria (which included modern-day Yugoslavia) was annexed by the Roman Empire and Macedonia was finally defeated.

AD 395: Following a division of the administration of the Roman Empire, Illyria was ruled by the Eastern Roman ('Byzantine') Emperor in Constantinople (now Istanbul, Turkey).

5th century: Southern Slav peoples began to move from Pannonia into Illyria and the Balkans.

812: By the Treaty of Aix-la-Chapelle (Aachen), the Byzantine Emperor, Michael I, acknowledged the Frankish (German) ruler, Charles ('the Great'—Charlemagne), as Emperor in the West; German influence over the Slovene-inhabited areas of Carinthia and Carniola was established.

863: The missionary activity of the Byzantine brothers, SS Constantine (Cyril) and Methodius, led to the conversion of the Serbs (including the ancestors of the Bosnians and Montenegrins) and the Bulgars (and Macedonians) to Eastern Orthodox Christianity; a Slavonic liturgy (based on a Macedonian dialect) was introduced with a written language, in the Cyrillic script, which remains common to all the Eastern and Balkan Slavic peoples.

1014: Final defeat of the western Bulgarian, or Macedonian, realm under Samuel by the Byzantine Emperor, Basil II. Later in the century Byzantine influence began to decline.

1102: Croatia's personal union with Hungary effectively, if not finally, linked it to the Hungarian Crown.

1151: Accession of Stjepan (Stephen) I Nemanja as Grand Žhupan; he united the Serb tribes and established the Serbian Empire.

1187: The Emperor in Constantinople acknowledged Serbian independence, Hungarian conquests in Croatia and Bosnia and the establishment of the second Bulgarian Empire.

1219: St Sava, brother of the Serbian king, Stjepan II, was consecrated the first autocephalous archbishop of the Serbian Orthodox Church, at Nicasa.

1330: The Serbs defeated the Bulgarians and the Greek Byzantines at the Battle of Velbuzhde (Küstendil).

1346: Establishment of a Serbian patriarchate and the coronation of Uroš IV (Stjepan Dušan of Raška, who reigned 1331–55) as Tsar of the Serbs and Greeks, at Skopje; however, he failed in his ambition to conquer Constantinople (Zarigrad).

1377: Stjepan Trvtko (1353–91) proclaimed himself Tsar of the Bosnians and Serbs, ruling a Bosnia which was now dominated by the dualist Christian heresy of the Bogomils.

28 June 1389: The Turkish Ottoman Empire, which had already conquered Macedonia, destroyed the Serbian nobility at a battle on the plain of Kosovo Polje, 'the Field of Blackbirds'.

1459–83: The Ottomans finally incorporated the rest of Serbia into the Empire, following the fall of the Serbian stronghold of Smederovo, and completed the subjugation of Bosnia and Herzegovina; the Montenegrins (Serbs of the principality of Zeta) maintained a semi-independence.

1490: Death of the Hungarian King, Matthias I Corvinus, who had secured modern Croatia and Vojvodina (Slavonia and the Banat) for Hungary and, temporarily, conquered the Habsburg lands.

1526: Louis II and the Hungarian forces were destroyed by the Ottomans at the Battle of Mohács; the Hungarian Crown was claimed as a hereditary possession of the House of Habsburg, but the kingdom itself was subsequently partitioned between the Habsburgs (Croatia) and the Ottomans (Slavonia).

1690: Serbs ('the 30,000 Families', led by Patriarch Arsenije III Crnojević), retreating with Habsburg armies, first settled in Vojvodina.

1718: The Peace of Passarowitz confirmed the Habsburg liberation of Hungary, including Croatia and Slavonia; the Ottomans ceded the Banat and northern Serbia (but the latter was held only until 1739).

1796: Montenegro, never completely subdued by the Ottomans, was acknowledged as an independent principality.

1804–12: A revolt of the Serbian peasantry against the local Turkish garrison, became a popular revolt for autonomy (the First Serbian Uprising), led by Kara Djordje ('Black George') Petrović.

1815: The Congress of Vienna confirmed Austrian rule over Istria and Dalmatia, which were formerly Venetian.

1817: Serbia became an autonomous principality, after the Second Serbian Uprising under Miloš Obrenović, whose house was, from then on, in constant rivalry with the Karadjordjević dynasty.

1848: At a time of revolution in Habsburg and other territories, the Croatian assembly, in Agram (Zagreb), was forced to end consideration of a Southern Slav state.

1868: Croatia, united with Slavonia, was granted autonomy by Hungary, which, since the *Ausgleich* or Compromise of the previous year, was now a partner in the Habsburg 'Dual Monarchy'.

March 1878: The Treaty of San Stefano concluded the war between Russia, in support of the Orthodox Slavs, and the Ottomans, but the Great Powers rejected the settlement.

July 1878: At the Congress of Berlin, Bulgaria was denied the annexation of Macedonia, Montenegro's independence was confirmed, Serbia's tributary status was ended and it was awarded territory around Niš, and Austria-Hungary secured administration rights in Bosnia and Herzegovina and ensured that the Ottomans remained in the Sandžak of Novi Pazar and Kosovo, as a restraint on Serbian expansion.

1881: Final abolition of the 'Military Frontier' or Krajina (now Croatia), in which, since the 17th century, the Habsburgs had allowed some autonomy to Serb settlers defending the borders against the Ottomans.

1882: Serbia was proclaimed a kingdom under Milan Obrenović, whose regime was conservative and pro-Habsburg.

1903: Assassination of King Aleksandar I of Serbia; accession of Petar I Karadjordjević, leader of the Radical Party, who was anti-Habsburg and saw the rise of the Southern Slav movement ('Yugoslavism').

1908: The 'Young Turk' uprising in the Ottoman Empire led to disturbances in the Balkans; Austria-Hungary annexed Bosnia and Herzegovina, despite international objections, but its ally, Germany, prevented war against Serbia.

1910: Nikita I of Montenegro proclaimed himself king. The secret, Greater Serb society, Union or Death (the 'Black Hand'), was founded by Col Dimitrijević-Apis.

May 1913: The Peace of London concluded the First Balkan War, in which a league of Bulgaria, Greece, Montenegro and Serbia succeeded in removing the Turks from the bulk of their European possessions.

June 1913: Bulgaria attacked Serbia, which was supported by Greece, Montenegro, Romania and the Turks.

August 1913: The Peace of Bucharest concluded the Second Balkan War; Bulgaria lost Macedonia, which was divided between Serbia and Greece; the Sandžak was divided between Serbia and Montenegro; but Austria-Hungary and Italy succeeded in preventing Serbia gaining access to the Adriatic, notably by the recognition of Albanian independence.

28 June 1914: The heir to the Habsburg throne, Archduke Francis Ferdinand, and his wife were assassinated in Sarajevo, by a Bosnian student, Gavrilo Princip, acting for the Serb Black Hand group.

28 July 1914: Austria-Hungary declared war on Serbia, which started the First World War between the Central Powers, of Austria-Hungary and Germany, and the Entente Powers, of France, Russia, Serbia and the United Kingdom.

1915: Serbia, including Macedonia, was conquered by the Central Powers and Bulgaria.

1916: Habsburg troops invaded Montenegro.

July 1917: Serbia and the other Southern Slavs (excluding the Bulgarians) declared their intention to form a unitary state, under the Serbian monarchy.

YUGOSLAVIA 1918–91

29 October 1918: Following the defeat and dissolution of the Danubian Monarchy, the Southern Slav (Yugoslav) peoples separated from the Austro-Hungarian system of states (a Southern Slav republic was established on 15 October); Dalmatia, Croatia-Slavonia, Bosnia and Herzegovina, parts of Carinthia, Carniola and the Banat were, subsequently, ceded formally to the new state.

4 December 1918: Proclamation of the Kingdom of Serbs, Croats and Slovenes, which united Serbia and Montenegro with the former Habsburg lands.

August 1921: Prince Aleksandar, Regent of Serbia since 1914 and of the new Kingdom since its formation, became King, upon the ratification of the 'Vidovdan' Constitution.

August 1928: A separatist Croatian assembly convened in Zagreb.

3 October 1929: Following the imposition of a royal dictatorship, the country was formally named Yugoslavia.

1931: The dictatorship was suspended by the introduction of a new Constitution, although this did not prevent Croat unrest and the rise of the Fascist Ustaša (Rebel) movement.

October 1934: King Aleksandar I of Yugoslavia was assassinated in France by Croatian extremists; his brother, Prince Paul, became Regent, on behalf of the young King Petar II.

1937: Josip Broz (Tito) became General-Secretary of the Communist Party of Yugoslavia (CPY), which was to become the main partner in the Partisan (National Liberation Army) resistance to the German invasion.

March 1941: A *coup d'état*, by air-force officers, ousted the Regent and installed King Petar II, who reversed previous policies and aligned himself with the Allied Powers of the Second World War.

10 April 1941: An Independent State of Croatia was established (including much of Bosnia and Herzegovina), with an Ustaša Government under Ante Pavelić.

17 April 1941: German and Italian forces invaded Yugoslavia: Germany annexed Lower Styria and parts of Carinthia; Italy annexed Ljubljana (Laibach) and Dalmatia, and the nominally independent Montenegro became its client; Albania (in personal union with the Italian Crown) annexed Kosovo; part of Vojvodina (eastern Slavonia) was annexed by Hungary; Macedonia was occupied by Bulgaria; the remainder of Serbia was placed under German military administration.

29 November 1943: In the Bosnian town of Jejce, following fierce resistance and civil conflict with the royalist Četniks (Yugoslav Army of the Fatherland) of western Serbia and with the Ustaša regime, Gen. (later Marshal) Tito's Partisans proclaimed their own government for liberated areas (mainly in Bosnia, Croatia and Montenegro); Tito's leadership was subsequently acknowledged by the Allies and the royal Government-in-Exile, although the following year King Petar II was declared deposed.

20 October 1944: Aided by the Soviet Red Army, Belgrade was liberated from German occupying forces.

29 November 1945: Following elections for a Provisional Assembly, the Federative People's Republic of Yugoslavia was proclaimed, with Tito as prime minister.

January 1946: A Soviet-style Constitution, establishing a federation of six republics and two autonomous regions, was adopted.

28 June 1948: Yugoslavia was expelled from the Soviet-dominated Cominform; the break with the USSR ended Yugoslav ambitions for a Balkan federation with Albania and Bulgaria.

November 1952: The Communist Party was renamed the League of Communists of Yugoslavia (LCY) and several liberal reforms were adopted.

January 1953: A new Constitution was adopted, with Tito becoming President of the Republic.

1954: Istria was partitioned between Italy, which gained the city of Trieste, and Yugoslavia. The so-called Novi Sad Agreement proclaimed Serbo-Croat to be one language with two scripts.

1955: Relations with the USSR were normalized.

April 1963: A new Constitution changed the country's name to the Socialist Federal Republic of Yugoslavia (SFRY).

1966: Monetary reform and economic liberalization were introduced; later in the year the reformists secured the fall of Vice-President Aleksandar Ranković, the head of the secret police and an advocate of strong central government.

July 1971: Following the granting of the rights of autonomy to the federal units, Tito introduced a system of collective leadership and the regular rotation of posts; a collective State Presidency for Yugoslavia was established, with Tito as its head.

November 1971: Tito criticized the reformist Croatian leadership, causing them to resign; the suppression of the Croatian 'mass movement', or *Maspok*, and a purge of liberals throughout Yugoslavia followed.

February 1974: A new Constitution was adopted.

May 1979: The principle of rotating leadership was extended to the secretaryship of the LCY.

4 May 1980: Tito died; his responsibilities were transferred to the collective State Presidency and to the Presidium of the LCY.

March 1981: Protests by students in Priština led to demonstrations by Albanian nationalists throughout Kosovo; a state of emergency was declared after rioting broke out in the Province.

March 1982: Further demonstrations took place in Kosovo.

December 1985: Demonstrations again took place in Kosovo.

1986: Slobodan Milošević, leader of the Belgrade Communists, became leader of the League of Communists of Serbia.

March 1987: There was widespread strike action throughout Yugoslavia, following the implementation of a government policy refusing to grant any wage increases.

24–25 April 1987: Thousands of Serbs and Montenegrins, who had gathered at Kosovo Polje to protest at harassment by the Albanian population, clashed with police.

October 1987: Emergency security measures were introduced in Kosovo, following further ethnic unrest.

June 1988: Widespread strike action was initiated by workers protesting against the decline in living standards; in the following month protesting workers forced their way into the Federal Assembly building in Belgrade.

October 1988: The Presidium of the League of Communists of Vojvodina resigned, following protests in Novi Sad.

November 1988: Some 100,000 ethnic Albanians demonstrated in Priština, demanding the reinstatement of two Kosovo Party leaders who had been pressured into resigning. An estimated 1m. people demonstrated in Belgrade, against alleged discrimination by the Albanian population of Kosovo. Public demonstrations were banned in Kosovo.

December 1988: Branko Mikulić, the President of the Federal Executive Council (Yugoslav prime minister), and his Government were forced to resign following the Federal Assembly's rejection of the proposed state budget for 1989.

January 1989: In Montenegro, the State Presidency and the Presidium of the local League of Communists resigned as a result of public pressure.

February 1989: Azem Vlasi, a prominent Albanian from Kosovo, was dismissed from the LCY Central Committee, provoking protests in Kosovo, during which federal troops intervened.

March 1989: A new Federal Government, under Ante Marković, was appointed. Azem Vlasi and other Albanian leaders were arrested on suspicion of inciting unrest; a curfew was imposed in Kosovo.

May 1989: Slobodan Milošević was elected President of the Serbian State Presidency (and re-elected, in direct elections, in November).

September 1989: The Slovenian Assembly reaffirmed the sovereignty of their Republic and declared its right to secede from the SFRY; thousands demonstrated in Serbia and Montenegro against the perceived threat to the unity of the SFRY.

November 1989: The first direct, secret ballot in Serbia since before the Second World War was held for local, parliamentary and presidential elections, although the Communists continued to dominate the electoral and candidate lists.

December 1989: Serbian enterprises were instructed to sever all links with Slovenia, which retaliated by closing its border with Serbia and implementing reciprocal economic sanctions.

2 January 1990: The new, fully convertible dinar, worth 10,000 old dinars, was introduced.

20–23 January 1990: The LCY voted to abolish its leading role in society, but rejected Slovenian proposals to restructure the federal Party; the League of Communists of Slovenia suspended its links with the LCY.

27 January 1990: At least nine Albanians were killed by the police in Kosovo, following several days of rioting; there were demands that the Jugoslavenska Narodna Armija (JNA—Yugoslav People's Army) be used to quell the disturbances.

February 1990: Federal troops were deployed in Kosovo for the first time and the federal State Presidency subsequently approved any action by the JNA needed to maintain the *status quo* in Kosovo; a curfew was imposed in Priština. The Slovenian Communists changed the name of their party and renounced its links with the LCY.

3 April 1990: Yusuf Zehjnulahu, the Chairman of the Executive Council (Premier) of Kosovo, resigned his post in protest at the excessive force used against the ethnic Albanians in the Province; however, in the following month, the provincial Assembly refused to accept his resignation.

17 April 1990: Milošević announced that the Serbian internal affairs ministry had assumed the federal ministry's responsibility for security in Kosovo; the following day, the federal State Presidency ended the special measures imposed in Kosovo.

22 April 1990: In Slovenia, the second round of voting for the parliamentary and presidential elections was held: Milan Kučan, the leader of the former Communists, was elected as President of the republican Presidency; the opposition DEMOS coalition, which had already won the direct elections to the main Socio-Political Chamber, emerged as the winner in the Chamber of Municipalities.

24 April 1990: Azem Vlasi, the former Party leader of Kosovo, was released from custody.

6–7 May 1990: A second round of voting took place in elections to the Croatian Assembly; the nationalist opposition party, the Croatian Democratic Union (CDU), gained 205 of the eventual 351 seats in the Assembly.

15 May 1990: Dr Borisav Jović (Serbia) took over as President of the federal State Presidency.

26 June 1990: The Kosovo Assembly was suspended and its responsibilities assumed by the Serbian Assembly.

2 July 1990: The Slovenian Assembly proclaimed the full sovereignty of the Republic. In a referendum, a majority of Serbians approved the proposed new republican Constitution, which, among other matters, effectively removed the distinct status of the Autonomous Provinces of Kosovo and Vojvodina; 114 deputies of the 180-member Kosovo Assembly declared that Kosovo was, thenceforth, independent of Serbia and a constituent republic of the SFRY.

5 July 1990: The Serbian Assembly voted to dissolve the Kosovo Assembly permanently.

17 July 1990: The League of Communists of Serbia merged with the republican Socialist Alliance of the Working People (a Communist mass organization), to form the Socialist Party of Serbia (SPS); Slobodan Milošević was elected leader.

25 July 1990: The Croatian Assembly approved constitutional changes which reasserted Croatian sovereignty. The leaders of the Serb minority in Croatia, who had formed a 'Serb National Council', proclaimed the right to sovereignty and autonomy for all Croatian Serbs.

29 July 1990: The federal prime minister, Ante Marković, formed the Alliance of Reform Forces (ARF), an all-Yugoslav party which supported his Government and advocated Western-style reforms.

8 August 1990: The Federal Assembly finalized their approval of constitutional amendments establishing a multi-party system.

13 September 1990: The 111 members of the Kosovo Assembly, who, at a secret session in Kačanik on 7 September, had declared the Assembly to have been re-formed, proclaimed a 'Constitution of the Republic of Kosovo'.

28 September 1990: Serbia's new Constitution formally took effect: the word 'Socialist' was removed from the Republic's title; a multi-party system was established; the independence of the institutions of the Autonomous Provinces was effectively removed; and Kosovo was renamed Kosovo and Metohija.

19 October 1990: Stipe Mesić was endorsed, by the Federal Assembly, as the new Croatian member of the State Presidency and Vice-President of the collective body.

23 November 1990: The Serbian opposition parties refused to participate in the republican elections, following the Serbian Assembly's rejection of five demands designed to prevent electoral fraud.

9 December 1990: Three nationalist parties won most of the seats after the final round of elections to the Assembly of Bosnia and Herzegovina. In similar elections in Macedonia, the nationalist opposition, the Internal Macedonian Revolutionary Organization-Democratic Party for Macedonian National Unity (IMRO-DPMNU) won the largest number of seats in the Assembly. In Serbia, a presidential election was won by Milošević, with 65% of the votes cast; the first round of the elections to the Assembly was held. The first-round elections to the presidency and to a new, unicameral Assembly were also held in Montenegro.

16 December 1990: The final round of voting in the Montenegrin Assembly elections took place; the ruling League of Communists of Montenegro won 83 of the 125 seats.

21 December 1990: The Croatian Assembly promulgated a new Constitution, which proclaimed the Republic's full sovereignty and its right to secede from Yugoslavia.

23 December 1990: A referendum, in which an overwhelming majority voted in favour of secession, was held in Slovenia, despite federal warnings of unconstitutionality and economic sanctions. No candidate having won an overall majority in the Montenegrin presidential election, a second round was held and won by Momir Bulatović, of the League of Communists.

The second round of elections to the Serbian Assembly was held; the final results gave 194 of the 250 seats to the ruling SPS.

8 January 1991: Yugoslavia's international financial reputation was damaged by revelations that the Serbian National Bank had issued an unauthorized 18,300m. dinars to the Serbian Government.

15 January 1991: The Serbian Assembly elected Dragutin Zelenović, until then the Vojvodina member of the federal State Presidency, as the republican Premier.

20 January 1991: Croatia and Slovenia concluded a mutual defence pact, amid rising tension between the republican authorities and the JNA.

25 January 1991: The Macedonian Assembly unanimously adopted a declaration of the Republic's sovereignty, including a statement of its right to secede from the federation.

14 February 1991: The Presidency of Vojvodina nominated its President, Jugoslav Kostić, to act as its member on the federal State Presidency.

20–21 February 1991: Slovenia initiated its process of 'dissociation' from Yugoslavia, and Croatia asserted the primacy of its Constitution and laws over those of the federation; both Republics declared their willingness to negotiate a future for Yugoslavia.

9 March 1991: Massive demonstrations, demanding less confrontational policies by the SPS and resignations from the Serbian Government began in Belgrade; many opposition leaders were among those arrested, notably Vuk Drasković of the nationalist Serbian Renewal Movement; President Milošević demanded the deployment of federal troops to suppress the disturbances.

15–21 March 1991: Jović, the President of the federal State Presidency, resigned and supported by the members for Kosovo-Metohija, Montenegro and Vojvodina, demonstrated the power of the 'Serbian bloc' to render the State Presidency inquorate; however, the JNA rejected political involvement (which was what the Serbian Government was demanding) and the crisis passed when Jović withdrew his resignation.

16 April 1991: The Serbian Government agreed to many of the demands of textile, leather and metallurgical workers, who staged Yugoslavia's biggest strike since the Second World War.

6 May 1991: The USA suspended all economic aid to Yugoslavia, because of alleged human-rights abuses in Kosovo-Metohija and for the 'destabilization' of the State Presidency.

THE DEMISE OF THE SFRY

15 May 1991: Against a background of increasing tension in Croatia and Slovenia, Jović's term of office as President of the federal State Presidency ended; under the system of rotating leadership, Stipe Mesić of Croatia was scheduled to become the first non-Communist President of Yugoslavia, but the Serbian bloc on the Presidency refused to endorse this.

6 June 1991: A summit of the republican presidents considered a proposal to make Yugoslavia an alliance of states; by this time an overwhelming majority had voted for independence in Croatia (although the Serb region of Krajina rejected such moves) and Slovenia had enacted legislation enabling its eventual assumption of independent power.

25 June 1991: The Croatian and Slovenian Assemblies declared the independence and sovereignty of their Republics, beginning the process of dissociation from the federation.

27 June 1991: The JNA began military operations, mainly in Slovenia, mobilizing (with the support of the Federal Government, in the absence of the State Presidency) to secure the international borders of the SFRY. The union of the two Krajinas was announced by the local Serbs: the 'Autonomous Republic' in Croatia and Bosanska (Bosnian) Krajina in Bosnia and Herzegovina.

30 June 1991: Mediation efforts by the European Community (EC—known as the European Union from November 1993) secured agreement to a cease-fire, under the threat of EC sanctions; one condition was implemented forthwith—the proclamation of Stipe Mesić as President of the federal State Presidency.

1–5 July 1991: The emergency committee of senior officials of the Conference on Security and Co-operation in Europe (CSCE) and the CSCE Conflict Prevention Centre met for the first time, to discuss the situation in Yugoslavia; the CSCE meetings supported the EC's peace efforts, which continued with agreement on an arms embargo (endorsed by the USA on 8 July), a decision to send in cease-fire observers and the suspension of financial aid to Yugoslavia.

7–8 July 1991: The EC mediating team and representatives of the State Presidency, Croatia and Slovenia met on the Adriatic island of Brioni; their final agreement included: all fighting should cease immediately; Slovenia and Croatia should have a three-month moratorium on further implementation of their declarations of dissociation. However, fighting continued to escalate in Croatia, although JNA troops had withdrawn from Slovenia by October.

21 August 1991: The federal State Presidency and the republican authorities reached an agreement that provided for the basic economic and political operation of the federation for three months, but only after controversy was caused by a Serbian claim to the Serb territories of Croatia.

26 August 1991: The presidential cease-fire commission collapsed with the resignation of its secretary, who stated that the Brioni agreement of August had been breached some 200 times and that more than 70 people had been killed. The next day condemnation of Serbia, as the aggressor in the Yugoslav conflict, was general at an EC meeting (a view echoed by the USA on 29 August); the EC proposed new peace measures, but Milošević refused to endorse them.

7 September 1991: An EC-sponsored peace conference on the future of Yugoslavia opened in The Hague (Netherlands), chaired by the former British foreign minister and NATO Secretary-General, Lord Carrington; the federal State Presidency met with all eight members for the last time.

25 September 1991: The UN Security Council unanimously ordered an arms embargo on Yugoslavia. Despite various attempts to arrange cease-fires, fighting continued in Croatia, and tensions were increasing in Bosnia and Herzegovina.

26 September 1991: A referendum on independence for Kosovo, announced by the provincial Assembly-in-Exile (based in Zagreb), began, despite Serbian determination to prevent it; the result was an overwhelming endorsement of independence.

3 October 1991: The Serbian bloc on the federal State Presidency announced that, because of the imminent threat of war, Serbia was to assume certain powers of the Federal Assembly; the other four Presidency members were not present and repudiated the decision of this 'rump' Presidency and refused to participate in further activities of the body.

8 October 1991: The Croatian Assembly declared all federal laws null and void. Slovenia's independence declaration took effect and recalled all its citizens in federal institutions.

15 October 1991: The Assembly of Bosnia and Herzegovina declared the Republic's sovereignty, emphasizing the inviolability of its borders and its willingness to consider a form of Yugoslav association. As in Croatia, however, the Serb areas rejected such declarations.

19 October 1991: The Kosovo Assembly-in-Exile, citing their referendum results, declared Kosovo to be an independent and sovereign Republic; the Assembly appointed a provisional coalition government.

24 October 1991: In Bosnia and Herzegovina, the Serb deputies announced the formation of an 'Assembly of the Serb Nation of Bosnia and Herzegovina', which then proposed a referendum on a common Serb state, to be held on 9–10 November (there was overwhelming support for remaining in a common Serb state).

26 October 1991: In the Sandžak region (mainly in Serbia, but partly in Montenegro), the Slav Muslims voted for autonomy in a referendum banned by the Serbian authorities.

17 November 1991: A new Constitution was enacted in Macedonia, which declared it to be an independent country.

5 December 1991: Stipe Mesić resigned from his post as President of the federal State Presidency, declaring that Yugoslavia had ceased to exist.

12 December 1991: The Government of Serbia was reorganized.

20 December 1991: Ante Marković, the federal prime minister, resigned following a vote of 'no confidence'; further resignations followed.

10 January 1992: Sanctions, imposed on Montenegro and Serbia by the EC in the previous year, were lifted from Montenegro.

15 January 1992: The EC recognized the independence of Croatia and Slovenia; numerous countries followed suit. The Montenegrin Constitution, adopted in November 1991, was amended in order to comply with EC criteria for recognition.

9 March 1992: The first UN peace-keeping forces arrived in the former Yugoslavia, following the endorsement of their deployment by the 'rump' federal State Presidency the previous December.

9–12 March 1992: Mass protests were organized in Belgrade by opponents of the Serbian Government; Drašković proposed a campaign of civil disobedience in order to force the resignation of President Milošević.

27 April 1992: By adopting a new Constitution, Montenegro and Serbia effectively acknowledged the secession of the other four Republics, although they claimed to be a continuation of the SFRY, rather than one of a number of successor states and claimed all international functions of the Federation. Under the new Constitution a Federal Republic of Yugoslavia (FRY) was created, with a bicameral legislature and a single head of state replacing the collective State Presidency; the 1990 Serbian abolition of the autonomous status of Kosovo and Vojvodina was confirmed.

11 May 1992: Alleging Serbian involvement in the continued fighting in Croatia and in Bosnia and Herzegovina, the Governments of the EC countries announced their decision to withdraw their ambassadors from the FRY.

24 May 1992: Elections, declared illegal by the Serbian authorities, were held in Kosovo-Metohija; the Democratic Alliance of Kosovo (DSK) won a majority of seats in this Assembly and its leader, Ibrahim Rugova, was elected President of the self-proclaimed 'Republic of Kosovo'. The 'Kosovo Assembly' was prevented from holding its inaugural session by several hundred Serbian police.

30 May 1992: Economic sanctions were imposed on Serbia and Montenegro by the UN, because of their involvement in the wars in Croatia and Bosnia and Herzegovina.

31 May 1992: The opposition boycotted elections to the new Federal Assembly and the SPS won an overwhelming number of seats in the parliament. There were anti-government protests in Belgrade and the Serbian Democratic Movement (DEPOS) was formed by a broad alliance of opposition parties; Vuk Drašković was elected leader.

15 June 1992: Dobrica Ćosić was elected President of the FRY.

14 July 1992: Milan Panić, a US businessman of Serbian origin, was elected Prime Minister of the FRY.

26–27 August 1992: At the conference on the former Yugoslavia, held in London (United Kingdom), Panić declared that there was no federal involvement in the conflict in Bosnia and Herzegovina. The state of emergency in Kosovo-Metohija (in force from 1989) was revoked, following a visit to the area by Panić.

10 September 1992: The Federal Minister of Foreign Affairs resigned in protest at the policies of Prime Minister Panić; there were further departures from the Federal Executive Council in November.

12 October 1992: A new Montenegrin Constitution was adopted, defining the Republic as part of the FRY.

12–13 October 1992: There was rioting in Kosovo following the arrest of two ethnic Albanian deputies from the 'Kosovo Assembly' and the banning of the Albanian-language newspaper, *Bujiku*; Panić attended negotiations in Priština with Cyrus Vance and Lord Owen (Co-Chairmen of the joint UN-EC negotiating initiative on former Yugoslavia) to discuss the reopening of Albanian schools in Kosovo. There were terrorist attacks on Muslims in Pljevlja, in the Sandžak. Supporters of President Milošević surrounded the Federal Ministry of Internal Affairs with 48,000 Serbian police and blockaded the building for several weeks.

20 December 1992: Ćosić was re-elected President of Yugoslavia, in direct elections, with some 85% of the votes cast. The SPS won 47 of the 138 seats in the Federal Assembly. The SPS was also successful in the republican elections, winning 101 of the 250 seats in the Serbian Assembly; the nationalist Serbian Radical Party (SRS) gained 73 seats. The SPS leader, Milošević, was re-elected President of Serbia, with 56% of the votes cast, compared to Panić who gained 34%. The opposition accused the SPS of electoral malpractice.

29 December 1992: Following a vote of 'no confidence' in the Federal Assembly, Panić was replaced as federal Prime Minister by a Montenegrin, Rade Kontić.

10 January 1993: Momir Bulatović, of the ruling Democratic Party of Socialists, was re-elected President of Montenegro in a second round of voting, defeating his nationalist rival, Branko Kostić, by a substantial margin.

3 February 1993: A new federal Government, comprising the SPS and the Montenegrin Democratic Party of Socialists, was formed. DEPOS, which had won 49 seats at the December elections, began a boycott of the Serbian Assembly.

10 February 1993: A new Serbian Government, comprised of SPS members and led by Nikola Sainović, officially took office.

5 March 1993: Milo Djukanović formed a new coalition Government in Montenegro.

April 1993: More UN sanctions were imposed against the FRY, in an attempt to ensure that the Bosnian Serbs would be persuaded to accept the UN-EC proposed peace plan. However, the Bosnian Serbs' assembly later rejected the plan.

1 June 1993: Ćosić was removed from office by the Federal Assembly, following accusations that he had conspired with army generals to oust Milošević; there were mass demonstrations in Belgrade in protest at his dismissal, during which the opposition leader, Vuk Drašković, was arrested and severely beaten by Serbian police. Miloš Radulović was appointed Acting President by the Federal Assembly.

25 June 1993: Zoran Lilić was elected President of the FRY.

26 August 1993: Col-Gen. Momcilo Perisić became Commander-in-Chief of the Yugoslav Army (formerly the JNA); at the same time, many army officers were replaced with ones thought to be more loyal to Serbian President Milošević.

October 1993: A vote of 'no confidence' in the Serbian Government was debated in the Serbian Assembly, but, owing to a parliamentary technicality, no vote was taken. Later in the month Milošević dissolved the Serbian parliament.

19 December 1993: In the Serbian parliamentary elections the SPS received some 37% of votes cast and 123 seats in the Assembly; the opposition DEPOS gained 18% of the ballot and 45 seats; the SRS came third with 15.6% of the votes cast and 39 seats. The Democratic Party of Serbia (DSS) won seven seats.

20 December 1993: The Deputy Prime Minister of Montenegro, Mihailo Ljesar, was assassinated in Podgorica (formerly Titograd).

24 January 1994: The newly elected Serbian Assembly convened for the first time. On the same day the Federal Government began an economic recovery programme, and, at the same time, issued another new dinar, the latest in a series of attempts to control hyperinflation by manipulation of the currency.

17 March 1994: The Serbian Assembly approved the election of a new republican Government, with Mirko Marjanović as premier.

History

DAVID NORRIS

EARLY HISTORY

The Federal Republic of Yugoslavia (FRY) declared on 27 April 1992 consisted of the Republics of Serbia and Montenegro from the former Socialist Federal Republic of Yugoslavia (SFRY), which had, in addition, included the Republics of Bosnia and Herzegovina, Croatia, Macedonia and Slovenia. The Serbs of Serbia, Bosnia and Herzegovina, and Croatia, and most Montenegrins regarded themselves as part of the Serb nation. They dated the beginning of their statehood from 1151 when Stjepan (Stephen) I of the Nemanjid dynasty declared himself the Grand Župan of Raška (Rascia—now Novi Pazar). His oldest son, Stjepan, was recognized as king and his youngest son, Sava, became archbishop of the first Serbian autocephalous church, based at Nicasa, in 1219. The kingdom gradually grew in wealth and political prestige under the influence of Eastern Roman (Byzantine) culture. During the reign of Stjepan ('the Great') Dušan of Raška (1331–55) Serbia reached its furthest territorial extent, from the Danube (Dunav) in the north to the Peloponnese in the south.

The medieval Serbian Empire began to disintegrate following the death of Stjepan Dušan and could not resist the attempts of the Turkish Ottoman Empire to gain a foothold in Europe. The two sides met at the Battle of Kosovo Polje ('the Field of Blackbirds'), on 28 June 1389, but the Ottoman victory was not complete until the capture of the last Serbian stronghold of Smederovo in 1459. Montenegro, then known as Zeta, was an integral part of the Serb state with the same cultural traditions stemming from Orthodox Christianity. Its mountainous terrain saved it from Ottoman conquest.

Cultural and economic life in Serbia stagnated under the centuries of Ottoman domination. Deprived of a political role, many Serbs emigrated at the end of the 17th century into the Habsburg Empire. They were given land in the border regions (Krajina) with the Ottoman Empire where they served as frontier guards. Settled in large areas of modern Croatia and Vojvodina in northern Serbia, they were granted semi-autonomous legal and economic institutions. The Serbs of Vojvodina experienced the beginning of a national cultural revival during the 18th century.

INDEPENDENCE IN THE 19TH CENTURY

Political independence was first gained to the south of the Danube. The First Serbian Uprising, 1804–12, arose as a result of local conditions rather than against the Sultan's authority. It became a national liberation movement under the leadership of Kara Djordje ('Black George') Petrović. The rebels captured Belgrade in 1806 and secured their rule over the region of Sumadija, to the south of the city, but were defeated in 1812. The Sultan granted a degree of local autonomy to Miloš Obrenović, leader of the Second Serbian Uprising, in 1815–17. The houses of Obrenović and Karadjordjević became rivals for power in Serbia. Prince Mihail Obrenović secured the removal of the last Ottoman garrisons from Serbia in 1867. His successor, Milan, was recognized as king of a sovereign state in 1882. The successor to Milan, King Aleksandar I Obrenović of Serbia, a conservative and pro-Habsburg monarch, was deposed by a *coup d'état* in 1903 and Petar Karadjordjević, leader of the Radical Party, acceded to the throne.

Petar I Karadjordjević restored constitutional government and his pro-Russian policies prompted the Habsburg Empire, now organized as the Dual Monarchy of Austria-Hungary, to begin a trade war against the kingdom in 1906–11. The Ottoman Empire lost most of its European possessions during the Balkan Wars of 1912–13 when Serbia also expanded into Macedonia. Serbia and Montenegro now shared a common border. King Nikita I of Montenegro, crowned in 1910, entered negotiations for a formal union between the two states which were interrupted by the outbreak of the First World War.

Habsburg annexation of Bosnia and Herzegovina in 1908 was designed to intimidate Serbia. A majority of Bosnia and Herzegovina's population was Orthodox Serb, some 43.5%, according to the 1910 census, with 32.4% Muslim and 22.8% Roman Catholic, and Austro-Hungarian land now obstructed Serbia's easy outlet to the sea. Bosnian resentment at Habsburg imperialist policy motivated Gavrilo Princip, a student acting for the secret Serb 'Black Hand' Group, to assassinate the heir to the Habsburg throne, Archduke Francis Ferdinand, on 28 June 1914. On 28 July Austria-Hungary declared war on Serbia, which started the First World War between the Central Powers of Austria-Hungary, Germany and their allies, and the Entente Powers of France, Russia, Serbia and the United Kingdom.

KINGDOM OF SERBS, CROATS AND SLOVENES

Serbia, after some initial military success against the Habsburg Empire, was conquered in 1915. The Serbian Government-in-Exile met Croat and Slovene representatives on Corfu (then a British territory, now Greek) in 1917. They agreed to form a unitary Southern Slav state under the Karadjordjević dynasty after the War. Such a state had been the aim of the Southern Slav—'Yugoslavist' movement which had developed during the 19th century. The Kingdom of Serbs, Croats and Slovenes was proclaimed on 4 December 1918, uniting Serbia and Montenegro with the former Habsburg lands. The Serbs were the largest single national group and maintained a monopoly of political power. Croatian opposition led a Serb nationalist deputy to assassinate the leader of the Croatian Peasant Party in June 1928. In August a separatist assembly convened in Zagreb (formerly Agram), the Croatian capital. Confronted with the breakdown of parliamentary government, King Aleksandar I installed himself as dictator. The country was formally named Yugoslavia on 3 October 1929.

In 1931 the dictatorship was suspended with the introduction of a new Constitution. However, this was not enough to prevent Croat unrest and the rise of the Fascist Ustaša (Rebel) movement. King Aleksandar I of Yugoslavia was assassinated by Ustaša extremists in 1934, in France. His brother, Prince Paul, became Regent on behalf of Aleksandar's son, Petar II, but he too failed to solve the problem of Serb-Croat relations, although he granted limited local autonomy to Croatia in 1939.

Prince Paul signed a treaty with the Axis Powers of Germany and Italy in March 1941, in the hope of preventing an Axis invasion of his divided country. A *coup d'état* followed, on 26–27 March, in which Petar was installed as monarch and the treaty revoked. King Petar II aligned himself with the Allied Powers in the Second World War. German and Italian forces invaded Yugoslavia in early April, and, on 17 April, the Yugoslav high command surrendered. Yugoslavia was dismembered: Germany annexed

Lower Styria and parts of Carinthia; Italy annexed Ljubljana (Laibach) and Dalmatia, and the nominally independent Montenegro became its client; Albania (in personal union with the Italian Crown) annexed Kosovo; part of Vojvodina was annexed by Hungary; Macedonia was occupied by Bulgaria; the remainder of Serbia was placed under German military administration (nominally under the leadership of Nedić). On 10 April an Independent State of Croatia (including much of Bosnia and Herzegovina) had been formed, with an Italian, Duke Aimone of Spoleto (Split), as King and an Ustaša Government headed by Ante Pavelić. Atrocities committed by the Ustaša against the Serbs forced many to resist this new order.

There were two resistance groups against the Ustaša regime, organized by the royalist Četniks (Yugoslav Army of the Fatherland), and the Partisans (National Liberation Army) led by Gen. (later Marshal) Josip Broz (Tito) and his Communist Party of Yugoslavia (CPY). A civil war was fought between the various internal forces. The United Kingdom shifted its support from the Četniks to the Partisans in mid-1943 and began supplying them with arms. Belgrade was liberated from German occupying forces, on 20 October 1944, with the help of the Soviet Red Army. The Partisans alone pressed the occupying forces until the liberation of Ljubljana (Slovenia), on 7 May 1945, and Zagreb, on 9 May.

On 29 November 1943, in the Bosnian town of Jejce, Tito's Partisans had proclaimed their own government for liberated areas (mainly in Bosnia, Croatia and Montenegro), the Anti-Fascist Council (AVNOJ). The AVNOJ formed the basis for the Provisional Assembly of August 1945. By manipulating the electoral process the CPY won an overwhelming majority in the Constituent Assembly, on 11 November, which voted to abolish the monarchy and establish the Federal People's Republic of Yugoslavia (FPRY), with Tito as prime minister, on 29 November. In January 1946 a new, Soviet-style Constitution was adopted which established a federation of six republics and two autonomous regions.

THE TITO YEARS

The six republics of the Federal People's Republic of Yugoslavia (FPRY) were based on the country's five principal nationalities (Croat, Macedonian, Montenegrin, Serb, Slovene) and Bosnia and Herzegovina. Serbia was subdivided into three parts: 'Narrow' or 'Inner' Serbia (comprising Belgrade, Šumadija and southern Serbia), and the Autonomous Provinces of Kosovo and Vojvodina. Kosovo contained a large Albanian minority and Vojvodina a substantial Hungarian minority. The borders of the Republics held some historical justifications although the practical result was to isolate the two largest nationalities, the Serbs and the Croats, from their compatriots in Bosnia and Herzegovina and to reduce their effective influence in the federation. The Federal Assembly had two chambers: the Federal Council, and the Council of Nationalities in which Republics and Provinces had equal representation. Routine business was dealt with by a small group in the Presidium of the Federal Assembly, although the real power was held by the CPY's Central Committee. The centralization of functions was symbolized by Tito simultaneously holding the posts of prime minister, leader of the CPY and Commander-in-Chief of the Jugoslavenska Narodna Armija (JNA—Yugoslav People's Army).

Between 1945 and 1948 nationalization of all major industries, transport and banks was completed, while land belonging to the Serbian Orthodox Church, collaborators and foreign nationals was redistributed to landless peasants. In 1947 the Yugoslav Government presented its first Five-Year Plan. However, ambitious hopes for economic recovery were delayed after Yugoslavia's independent policies led to its expulsion from the Soviet-dominated Cominform on 28 June 1948.

Isolated from its former partners in the Communist bloc of Eastern Europe, the FPRY was guided by two aims: firstly, to obtain trade treaties and credits from Western countries without having to establish Western parliamentary pluralism; secondly, to distance itself from the highly centralized Soviet system. To these ends, Yugoslav self-management developed, combining the principles of workers' co-operatives with a mass participatory political system of interlocking delegations. Rudimentary and limited economic decentralization was adopted in the 1950 Basic Law on the Management of State Economic Enterprises by Working Collectives. Workers' councils operated factories alongside managers appointed by the CPY. In 1952 further political decentralization was attempted when local authorities were given more powers and were linked to the workers' councils under their administration. The January 1953 Constitution extended this system to the republican and federal levels. In the same Constitution, Tito became President of the Republic. The Party was renamed the League of Communists of Yugoslavia (LCY) at its Sixth Congress in November 1952, when it was decided that Party members should play a more educative role in their drive to further socialism. This apparent liberalism did not extend to internal discipline and when one of Tito's close associates, Milovan Djilaš, demanded further reform he was imprisoned.

The system contained obvious contradictions. During the 1960s Western countries continued to support Yugoslavia, a Communist country which had resisted the Soviet leader Stalin and survived. Decentralization continued with individual enterprises and local councils taking more responsibility for fixing prices, wage levels and investment priorities. Standards of living rose rapidly. The country was renamed the Socialist Federal Republic of Yugoslavia (SFRY) in April 1963. In July 1965 a series of economic measures was approved which further relaxed state controls on foreign investment and the banking system. The principle of 'market socialism' was introduced in an attempt to reduce the gap between economic decision-making and economic realities.

However, increased standards of living were bought at the expense of Western credits and loans. Many commercial decisions were still taken for political reasons. In the mid-1960s the Federal Government began an expensive undertaking of transferring resources from the wealthy north of the country (Slovenia and parts of Croatia) to the poorer southern areas (Kosovo, Bosnia and Herzegovina, Macedonia, Montenegro). The rate of unemployment was rising, in spite of the fact that some 1m. Yugoslavians were working abroad. In the liberal atmosphere of the 1960s the LCY strictly maintained its political monopoly.

The tension between decentralization and the LCY's political power led to demands for political change. These demands were, in part, stimulated by the fall of Vice-President Aleksandar Ranković, the head of the secret police and an advocate of strong central government in 1966. This was mistakenly taken as evidence of the LCY's more liberal policies. The armed forces succeeded in quelling the November 1968 demonstrations in Kosovo in support of the Province becoming a Republic.

Following the granting of the rights of autonomy to the federal units, Tito introduced a system of collective leadership and the regular rotation of posts, in July 1971. A collective State Presidency for Yugoslavia was established, with Tito as its head. Croatian opposition to such decisions combined the desire for economic reform with Croatian nationalist opinion. In November the Croatian leadership resigned and student activists in the region were imprisoned. The Croatian 'mass movement', or *Maspok*, was suppressed. Tito then began a purge of reformers and liberals in other Republics, such as the head of the Serbian League of Communists, Marko Nikezić, who was removed from his post in October 1972. In the previous month Tito reaffirmed the principle of democratic centralism in a letter to all branches of the LCY. Adherence to this principle was repeated at the 10th Party Congress, in May 1974, and at the 11th, in June 1978.

Initial repressive measures were followed by concessions. Belgrade's University College in Priština, capital of the Autonomous Province of Kosovo, became an independent university in 1970. The 1974 Constitution strengthened the status of the Republics and granted similar internal powers to Serbia's Autonomous Provinces. The collective federal State Presidency, introduced in 1971, was reformed to include one representative from each of the eight constituent parts of the SFRY. The concept of consensus government was introduced, by which federal policy had to be approved by all members of the collective State Presidency, effectively giving rights of veto. This principle was extended to all levels within the self-management system. Delegated authority at the federal level became more dependent on power bases in the Republics. Consequently, local interests tended to foreshadow collective issues.

In foreign affairs, the SFRY resisted all overtures from Soviet leader Nikita Khrushchev (1953–64) to return to the Soviet bloc, although relations did improve (Yugoslav–Soviet relations were normalized in 1955). Eastern Europe became Yugoslavia's most important trading partner as it had proved impossible to break into Western markets. Foreign policy focused on fostering relations with developing and newly independent countries to form a bloc able to act internationally. The first conference of this Non-aligned Movement, which Tito co-founded, was held in Belgrade in 1961. The Movement never united as a third force in international politics, nor did it help to increase Yugoslavia's export trade. It did, however, give the SFRY a visible international role and made both East and West wary of forcing the country to align itself with either side of the 'Iron Curtain'. The policy was also a useful adjunct to the general aim of balancing relations between East and West during the Cold War.

The many contradictions of Tito's regime deepened in the last years before his death in May 1980. The competition between jealously guarded local autonomy and the need for overall central controls was countered by appeals to the principles of self-management on which the state had been founded, by the propagation of Wartime myths of great Partisan heroism, and by comparisons between Yugoslavia's prosperous and relatively open society with other states in Eastern Europe. In reality, unity was bought through spreading fear of hostile neighbours and because of mutual animosity between different national groups. The nationality issue was partially resolved through compromise. Positions of power and influence rotated amongst representatives of different national groups in sensitive areas. However, this system tended to reinforce nationality as an administrative category. Federal cohesion was promoted by Tito's personal influence, which he used to persuade dissenters to conform, and by the combined power of the LCY and the JNA, which were virtually the only two institutions to recognize their base within a pan-Yugoslav framework.

AFTER TITO: 1980–87

Following Tito's death on 4 May 1980, his responsibilities were passed smoothly to the collective State Presidency and to the Presidium of the LCY. The President of the State Presidency acted as titular head of state, a post which rotated annually amongst the delegates. Major problems arose owing to nationalist tensions and the worsening economic situation. Self-management as it had developed after the 1974 Constitution had serious structural deficiencies. The delegate system was cumbersome and expensive and there had been a shift of real power from the federal to the republican governments. In May 1982 a new Federal Executive Council or cabinet was appointed, chaired by Milka Planinć, former leader of the Croatian Party.

Protests by students over living conditions, in Priština, beginning in March 1981, led to demonstrations by Albanian nationalists throughout Kosovo. The Government declared a state of emergency in the Autonomous Province, and the ensuing riots resulted in several deaths and many injuries. Numerous changes in the leadership of Kosovo followed, and Yugoslav–Albanian relations deteriorated. Demonstrations recurred intermittently in Kosovo in the mid-1980s and hundreds of Albanian nationalists were convicted and imprisoned on charges of conspiracy against the state. From 1986 the Presidency of Serbia, and the Serbian delegate to the federal State Presidency, Ivan Stambolić, demanded constitutional reform which would give the Serbian parliament more control over its Provinces. The demands were refused, however, as other delegates sensed an attempt to increase Serbian influence in the federation.

The 1974 Constitution had shifted the balance of power in Kosovo to the Albanian community. It was claimed that 100,000 Serbs were coerced into leaving the region during the 1970s, and a further 30,000 in 1981–87. On 24–25 April 1987 thousands of Serbs and Montenegrins attended a rally, addressed by the leader of the Serbian Communists, Slobodan Milošević, at Kosovo Polje, in order to protest at harassment by the Albanian population. Violent clashes between protesters and police occurred. There was further unrest throughout the year, and, in October, emergency security measures were once again introduced in the Autonomous Province.

The SFRY was fractured under a leadership which was cast in the mould of the old, Titoist one-party system and was unable to deal with new circumstances and pressures. Proposals to increase the role of market forces were unacceptable, for both ideological and political reasons. However, there was growing dissent, in the 1980s, from both nationalist and liberal forces, against the LCY's monopoly of political power.

THE DISSOLUTION OF THE SFRY: 1987–92

The late 1980s and early 1990s in Serbian and Montenegrin politics were dominated by Slobodan Milošević's rise to power and the dissolution of the SFRY. Milošević was supported by Stambolić in his early Party career. Given responsibility for economic issues, in 1982, Milošević became leader of the Belgrade League of Communists in 1984, and of the Serbian League of Communists in 1986. He succeeded in bringing about the fall of Stambolić by the end of 1987. As leader of the Serbian Party, Milošević already had control over many committees; he proceeded to strengthen his position through purges of all those associated with Stambolić. He was elected President of the State Presidency of Serbia in May 1989, giving rise to increased fears of Serbian domination of the SFRY, and, in November, he was re-elected to the post by a direct popular vote. He continued to lead the Serbian Communists, from 17 July 1990 under a new name, the Socialist Party of Serbia (SPS).

Milošević widened his popular appeal by manipulating discontent in Serbia and Montenegro. It was felt that Serbia's division into three virtually independent constituent parts of the SFRY was unfair, as Inner Serbia could be vetoed by its Provinces. He organized mass demonstrations throughout Serbia in support of Serbs in Kosovo, and began a campaign, known as the 'Anti-Bureaucratic Revolution'. Demonstrations in Novi Sad caused the resignation of the Presidium of the Vojvodina League of Communists in October 1988. In the following month tension between the respective Party leaderships of Serbia and of Kosovo increased, following several resignations (under pressure from Serbia) from the leadership of the Kosovo Party. As many as 100,000 ethnic Albanians took part in a protest march against the resignations. In the same month, in Belgrade, a rally by Serbs protesting against alleged discrimination by the Albanian population of Kosovo, attracted almost 1m. people. Mass demonstrations had also taken place in the Montenegrin capital of Titograd (Podgorica) and in Nikšić, in October, in support of the Serbs in Kosovo and in protest at the Montenegrin Government, which subsequently resigned. Momir Bulatović, a Milošević supporter, became President of the Presidium of Montenegro's League of Communists in January 1989.

In February 1989 the dismissal from the LCY Central Committee of Azem Vlasi, a prominent Albanian from Kosovo, and the changes to the Serbian Constitution, led to renewed disturbances in Kosovo and the intervention of federal troops. In early March Vlasi and two other Albanian leaders were arrested on charges of inciting unrest and a curfew was imposed in the region. In an attempt to redress the demographic balance, a campaign to attract Serbs to settle in Kosovo was announced (a total of 50,000 Serbs and Montenegrins had left the Province since 1981). The President of the Presidency of Kosovo resigned in early April.

On 1 February 1990 federal troops arrived in Kosovo, following an escalation of the violence in the region. The release from custody of Vlasi, in April 1990, led to hopes that Serbia's control of Kosovo might be weakened. However, in a referendum held on 2 July, a majority of Serbians approved the proposed new republican Constitution, which effectively removed the autonomous status of the Provinces of Kosovo and Vojvodina. The Kosovo provincial Assembly and Government were dissolved by the Serbian authorities three days later. Leaders of the other Republics did not object to Milošević's claim that amendments to the Serbian Constitution were an internal republican matter.

However, differences between the Serbian and the Slovenian leadership did worsen in 1989. Both sides wished to maintain the unity of the SFRY but by incompatible means. The Slovenians argued in favour of a confederation with looser links between central government and the Republics, while Milošević insisted on the collective responsibility imposed by democratic centralism. An Emergency Congress of the LCY was held on 20–22 January 1990, when the Congress approved the abolition of the LCY's leading role in society and the introduction of a multi-party system. However, Slovenian proposals to restructure the federal Party were rejected. The Slovenian delegation withdrew from the Congress and the Republic's League of Communists suspended its links with the LCY. The LCY as a federal organization no longer existed.

In February 1990 the Slovenian Party confirmed its formal secession from the federal LCY and changed its name to the Party of Democratic Reform. The Communists of Croatia and Macedonia subsesquently made similar changes. Slovenia and Croatia elected nationalist governments in April and May 1990. Fear for Serbs outside Serbia increased and demands for a confederal structure met with the demand for border changes to include the Serbs in one state. On 15 May, under the continuing system of rotating leadership, Dr Borisav Jović of Serbia replaced Janez Drnovšek of Slovenia as President of the SFRY State Presidency.

In December 1990 multi-party elections were held in several Republics. In Montenegro the Communists succeeded in retaining the Presidency and in securing a majority of seats in the Assembly. In Serbia, amid allegations of electoral irregularities, Milošević was elected sole President, under the new Serbian Constitution. However, opposition to his Government grew in 1991. Workers' demonstrations in January were followed by a large rally in Belgrade, demanding his resignation on 9 March. Some 100,000 people took part in the demonstrations. Milošević urged the federal State Presidency to deploy troops in order to quell the rioting. However, after the body failed to meet Milošević's demand, President Jović submitted his resignation. The Montenegrin Presidency member resigned on the following day, and the Kosovo member was dismissed by the Serbian authorities and its provincial Presidency temporarily suspended. However, the JNA refused to get involved in politics and, after an appeal by the Serbian Assembly, Jović rescinded his resignation.

The six Republican Presidents met in late March 1991, in a renewed attempt to resolve their country's crisis. Both Croatia and Slovenia declared their intention to secede from the SFRY if a solution was not found. Tension between Serbs and Croats increased when, on 15 May, the normally automatic transfer of the federal State Presidency to the Croatian delegate, Stjepan ('Stipe') Mesić, was not endorsed by the Serbian, Kosovan and Vojvodinian members (the Montenegrin member abstained). Croatia and Slovenia declared their independence from the SFRY on 25 June 1991. Federal premier Ante Marković ordered the JNA to re-take the Slovenian borders as the legitimate territory of the SFRY. The Serbian-dominated army advanced into Slovenia but had retreated by the end of June. At the same time, a cease-fire agreement, brokered by the European Community (EC—known as the European Union from November 1993), resulted in Serbian acceptance of Mesić as President of the federal State Presidency. In Croatia, meanwhile, hostilities broke out in Eastern Slavonia and in the newly established self-styled 'Serbian Autonomous Region of Krajina', where the JNA worked with local Serb paramilitary units. The withdrawal of federal troops from Slovenia began in July and, in the same month, discussions on the future of Yugoslavia between the State Presidency members and the six republican Presidents began.

On 6 August 1991 the first of many ineffective cease-fires was declared in eastern Croatia. The Croatian leader, President Franjo Tudjman, demanded a withdrawal of all federal troops from his Republic, however, fighting intensified and spread to other parts of Croatia in the latter half of 1991. On 8 October the Croatian and Slovenian declarations of independence took effect, while later in the month the Republic of Bosnia and Herzegovina proclaimed its sovereignty. Serbia rejected an EC proposal to establish a loose association of sovereign states. By November the conflict had spread to Serbian territory, with reported incursions by Croatian forces. Marković and the federal Secretary for Foreign Affairs resigned from their posts after a vote of 'no confidence' in the Federal Assembly in November and, in the following month, Mesić resigned, claiming that Yugoslavia had ceased to exist.

On 15 January 1992 the EC, at Germany's insistence, initiated general recognition of Slovenian and Croatian independence. A UN peace-keeping force (UN Protection Force in Yugoslavia—UNPROFOR) was deployed in Croatia, in March, a move supported by the remaining members of the federal State Presidency, which was dominated by Serbia. The West's readiness to assist Yugoslavia in its economic and other problems had disappeared in the changed geo-political conditions following the end of the Cold War. International recognition of Bosnia and Herzegovina as an independent state, on 7 April 1992, led to an escalation of the civil war there also.

THE FEDERAL REPUBLIC OF YUGOSLAVIA

As the other Republics had formally seceded from the SFRY, in April 1992 Serbia and Montenegro claimed all international functions of the SFRY. On 27 April the 83 deputies of Serbia and Montenegro to the Federal Assembly of the SFRY voted to adopt a Constitution which created the Federal Republic of Yugoslavia (FRY), comprising Serbia and Montenegro. The new Constitution reflected the Serbian Constitution of 1990 which defined Serbia as including the 'formerly autonomous provinces of Kosovo and Vojvodina'. Both Republics kept their own governments and established a bicameral Federal Assembly. The lower federal chamber was elected by constituencies while the upper house had equal numbers of Serbian and Montenegrin deputies. The Constitution contained few details on the exact nature of the FRY and was lacking specific regulations on citizenship. By early 1994 the state had not been recognized by the international community and this seemed unlikely until a general resolution of the conflicts in the former Yugoslavia.

Elections, held on 31 May 1992, in Serbia and Montenegro, for representatives to the Federal Assembly, resulted in widespread success for the SPS, owing to a boycott by opposition parties. However, Milošević faced strong opposition in mid-1992, with attacks from the Serbian Orthodox Church, the appearance in Belgrade of the pretender to the Serbian (Yugoslavian) throne, Aleksandar Karadjordjević, and the formation, in late May, of a broad opposition alliance, the Serbian Democratic Movement (DEPOS). Dobrica Ćosić was appointed federal President and, on 14 July, a US businessman of Serbian origin, Milan Panić, became federal Prime Minister. In the remainder of 1992 a political battle developed between Milošević and Panić. At the London Conference on the former Yugoslavia held in the United Kingdom, in August, Panić dismissed Milošević's political ally, Mihalj Kertes, from his ministerial post and condemned the policy of 'ethnic cleansing' (involving the expulsion by one ethnic group of other ethnic groups in an attempt to create a homogeneous population) by Serbs in Bosnia and Herzegovina. Milošević's attempt in the Federal Assembly, on 4 September, to engineer a vote of 'no confidence' in Panić's Government failed, as Montenegrin deputies supported the Prime Minister. Instead, presidential and parliamentary federal and republican elections were scheduled for 20 December 1992, while Panić and Ćosić demanded Milošević's resignation. Milošević's supporters retaliated in October by surrounding the Federal Ministry of Internal Affairs with 48,000 Serbian police and taking control of the federal police headquarters within it. The building was blockaded for several weeks. Panić, standing against Milošević for the Serbian presidency, publicly attacked the Serb leaders in Croatia and Bosnia and Herzegovina, Goran Hadzić and Radovan Karadžić, respectively. Recognizing the territorial integrity of the former Yugoslav Republics, furthermore, he offered appeasement to ethnic Albanians in Kosovo and, at the end of November, he requested the UN to suspend sanctions for 60 days over the election period, a request which was denied.

In the elections the federal President, Ćosić, was re-elected with some 85% of the votes cast. Milošević was re-elected President of Serbia and the SPS won 47 of the 138 seats in the Federal Assembly. Monitors from the Conference on Security and Co-operation in Europe (CSCE) contested that the elections were seriously flawed. The Albanians in Kosovo and Muslims in the Sandžak did not take part in the elections. Panić was removed from office on 29 December 1992, following a vote of 'no confidence' in the new Federal Assembly. He was replaced as federal Prime Minister by the Montenegrin Rade Kontić. On 3 February 1993 a new Federal Government, comprising the SPS and the Montenegrin Democratic Party of Socialists, was formed.

The FRY's first years were largely shaped by the civil wars in the territories of the former Yugoslavia, and by international sanctions imposed against Serbia and Montenegro. The FRY was left with a substantial part of the JNA under its control. Its forces in Bosnia and Herzegovina constituted an occupying force there, and conscripts from Serbia and Montenegro were withdrawn. Milošević strengthened his control of the JNA by dismissing 39 high-ranking officers in May 1992. The international community pressured Milošević to influence the Bosnian Serbs to halt their offensive against the Muslim and Croat forces in Bosnia and Herzegovina. Governments of EC countries announced their decision to withdraw their ambassadors from Yugoslavia on 11 May 1992, and, on 30 May, UN sanctions were imposed against Serbia and Montenegro.

The FRY was severely affected by the UN-imposed economic sanctions. By late 1992 there were shortages of many basic items, there was hyperinflation, productivity was decreasing rapidly and the rate of unemployment was rising, as all international trade and banking relations were suspended. In the first three months of 1993 the FRY's economy survived through private banks, which offered interest rates of 12%–14% per month on foreign-currency accounts. The two biggest were Jugoskandić and Dafiment Banks, which also held substantial business interests in the illegal import of petroleum and other commodities. It was suspected that they operated with the knowledge and support of the Serbian Government, which prevented further social unrest in the Republic by printing money and encouraging citizens to live off foreign-currency savings. The private banks began to close in mid-March, as the supply of foreign-currency deposits which were used to pay the high interest rates ended. In mid-July 1993 the inflation rate was calculated to be 20,000%. The Governor of the National Bank of Yugoslavia announced a new approach to the monetary crisis, in which the state would print money to finance public works. In September rationing of basic foodstuffs to pensioners was introduced and medicines, not formally covered by sanctions rules, were scarce in all areas of the FRY.

Greater sanctions were imposed against the FRY in April 1993, in an attempt to persuade the Bosnian Serbs to accept the plan for the 'cantonization' of Bosnia and Herzegovina, proposed by Cyrus Vance and Lord Owen, the Co-Chairmen of the UN-EC negotiating initiative on the former Yugoslavia. Milošević and Ćosić persuaded the President of the 'Serbian Republic of Bosnia and Herzegovina', Radovan Karadžić, to accept the Vance–Owen Plan on 2 May. His acceptance, however, was rejected by the Bosnian Serb Assembly three days later. Milošević called a meeting of Serb representatives from all the territories of the former SFRY on 14 May. Many boycotted it, on the grounds that the Serbian President was betraying the Bosnian Serbs by signing the Plan. By mid-June it was clear that the Vance–Owen Plan could not be implemented without force.

However, Western Governments were not willing to begin a military campaign in Bosnia and Herzegovina. President Milošević, his Croatian and Bosnian counterparts, Franjo Tudjman and Alija Izetbegović, as well as the Bosnian Serb Karadžić and the Bosnian Croat leader, Mate Boban, attended a summit meeting, in Geneva (Switzerland), on 16 June, where the Serbian and Croatian sides agreed a peace initiative under which Bosnia and Herzegovina would be divided into three ethnically based states. The Bosnian leader Izetbegović refused to ratify any plans until the Serbs had lifted their siege of the Bosnian capital, Sarajevo.

Milošević consolidated his position as Serbian President in 1993. It was estimated that he had increased the internal security forces to 70,000 personnel. Federal President Ćosić was dismissed on 1 June, and replaced, on 25 June, by the less-influential Zoran Lilić, when it was alleged that he had held secret negotiations with military commanders to depose Milošević. His dismissal was followed by a large demonstration in Belgrade on 2 June, during which Vuk Drašković was arrested and badly beaten by police. On 26 August a new Commander-in-Chief of the Yugoslav Army was appointed, Col-Gen. Momcilo Perisić, and 42 members of the General Staff were retired and replaced. The new military cadres were thought to be more loyal to the Serbian President.

In July 1993 a dispute between the Serbian and Montenegrin elements of the FRY emerged over constitutional arrangements. Montenegro opposed a plan to abolish the republican ministries of defence, foreign affairs and foreign economic relations, and transfer all responsibility to the corresponding federal ministries. The Montenegrin foreign minister, Miodrag Lekić, announced that international observers would be allowed to monitor the Montenegrin–Bosnian border despite protests from Serbia that federal policy opposed such action. Serbia expelled international monitors working in Kosovo, where Serb–Albanian relations were still tense. The Montenegrin Government wanted firm, local autonomy and was beginning increasingly to resent Serbian attempts to dominate the government of the FRY. Milošević's administration favoured strong, central government. Therefore, in 1993 and early 1994, the divisions between the two Republics of the FRY increased, as Montenegro began to distance itself from its dominant partner, and the economy of the FRY further deteriorated under the weight of UN sanctions. Serbia could not afford to alienate Montenegro, as a united, stable FRY was one of the prerequisites to the relaxation of UN sanctions. It was also essential that the FRY establish a stable *modus vivendi* between itself and its former Yugoslav neighbours, a relationship which the newly created country had hitherto lacked.

The Economy

Dr DAVID A. DYKER

INTRODUCTION

By 1993 the crisis in the Yugoslav lands had reached a level of political and social dissolution unimaginable only one year or so earlier. Perhaps more significant than the dissolution of the country itself was the fact that none of its successor states—with the exception of Slovenia—had succeeded in creating a stable, policy-making social and political environment. This political failure had an extremely adverse effect on the economy. Furthermore, its origins must be sought partly in earlier economic failures of the Tito (Yugoslavian leader until 1980) and post-Tito periods. The most significant of those economic failures was the 'debt-shock' period (see below), which began in 1982, and its aftermath, which was characterized by industrial stagnation and a decline in the standard of living. However, the origins of that shock must, in turn, be sought in earlier periods and, to a degree, in the whole pattern of economic development of the country following the formation of a Communist Federal People's Republic of Yugoslavia in 1945.

The Communist Party of Yugoslavia (CPY) was independent of the Communist Party of the Soviet Union (CPSU) and enjoyed considerable popular support among the Yugoslav population, owing to its leadership of the Second World War Partisan (National Liberation Army) resistance to the German invasion. However, in the initial post-War period of 1945–48, it was distinguished by a passion for imitating all things Soviet, including grossly over-centralized five-year planning exercises. When Stalin (Iosif Dzhugashvili) denounced Tito, in 1948, and declared an economic blockade of Yugoslavia, following a period of worsening relations, he cited Tito's revisionism as a root cause of the rift. It was difficult to take this charge seriously, certainly on the economic side, and, indeed, the Yugoslav leadership initially reacted by even closer adherence to the Soviet model. The disastrous collectivization campaign of 1949, which brought the Yugoslav peasantry to the brink of insurrection, was the result. It was towards the end of that year that a process of reappraisal began, which eventually produced a complete rejection of the Soviet economic-planning style. By 1953 directive planning had been abandoned. Astonishingly, for a Communist regime in the early 1950s, the Yugoslav Communists publicly proclaimed the need to abandon target planning completely, and to reinstate the market as the focal point of economic activity. To reinforce the socialist credentials of all this, workers' councils were created in each enterprise, with the prerogative, theoretically at least, of making all major decisions of business strategy.

While the break with the Soviet economic system was complete, however, that with Soviet development strategy was not. The Soviet-Marxist tendency to overemphasize industrial development, in particular, heavy industrial development, was almost as marked in Yugoslavia, in the 1950s and early 1960s, as it had been in the USSR in the 1930s. However, this was more dangerous in the Yugoslav case, in that the weight of comparative advantage for Yugoslavia clearly lay with agriculture and services. Nevertheless, market-socialist Yugoslavia performed very impressively, in growth terms, in 1953–65. A certain element of political enthusiasm apart, however, that growth performance was based largely on the massive transfer of unskilled labour, from the over-populated countryside into the towns, and the virtually unlimited support which US aid afforded the Yugoslav balance of payments up to 1961. This latter factor, in turn, made it possible for Yugoslavia to import food, petroleum and equipment at a very low real cost. By the early 1960s the process of indiscriminate transfer of labour from the countryside was clearly approaching its natural limits, while US aid stopped altogether in 1962. The growth strategy based on cheap labour, cheap food and cheap energy was over. Further growth would have to be based on high productivity performance and efficient assimilation of technology.

Yugoslavia was already a market economy, of sorts, by the early 1960s. Theoretically, the reforms of 1965 heralded a transition to a much more 'full-blooded' form of market socialism. The capital-investment sector and, implicitly, growth strategy were now also to be subordinated to the market mechanism, through the development of an autonomous banking system. In this context it was striking that Yugoslavia's failure to make the transition from 'extensive' to 'intensive' growth was almost as complete as that of the Soviet bloc countries, the majority of which continued to struggle with some variant of the central-planning model. The explanation for this was to be found in a complex of inter-related factors, with the political dimension playing a key role. The attempt to extend the market principle into the area of capital formation exacerbated nationality tensions, which, previously, had been, to a degree, repressed or subdued. By the early 1970s nationalist ferment, especially in Croatia, had provoked a reaction on the part of the central authorities, in Belgrade, which sought increasingly to subordinate the market principle to the principle of the 'planning agreement'. This latter tended to produce a peculiarly Yugoslav pattern of cartelization. At the same time the central Communist leadership placed its faith in regional League of Communists activists, which they hoped would bind multi-national Yugoslavia together. In the event, it was precisely these regional élites who were primarily to blame for the progressive disintegration of central economic policy-making in Yugoslavia, in the 1970s, as they sought to consolidate their own prerogatives. The planning-agreement system proved to be particularly vulnerable to the petty corruption which became increasingly the stock-in-trade of League of Communists élites.

The 1970s were years of faltering growth, this reflecting stagnating labour productivity, a loss of technological dynamism and increasing wastefulness in the utilization of material inputs. Behind these unsatisfactory trends lay: failures of industrial policy, as import-substitution programmes, often promoted by regional leaderships, simply created new import needs; failures of foreign trade policy, as plans to transfer resources to 'assured' exports achieved nothing; and failures of regional policy, as development funds were wasted on prestige projects. It was against this background that Yugoslavia had to face the challenges of the 'oil crises', as international petroleum prices increased significantly in the 1970s.

The huge escalation in the price of petroleum posed challenges to the efficiency of the Yugoslav economy which it was ill-equipped to meet. More insidiously, the excess supply of 'petro-dollars' in the international banking system, which the oil crises produced, made it too easy for medium-developed countries, like Yugoslavia, to ignore underlying structural problems and simply to borrow in order to remain viable. One of the crucial areas that the central authorities lost control of, in the mid-1970s, was the balance of payments. The National Bank of Yugoslavia was unable to prevent enterprises and regional governments continuously borrowing from international bankers, who paid little heed to the likely efficiency with which the funds lent would be used. In 1979 the current-account deficit reached a new record level of US $3,700m.

It was the sharp increase in international interest rates, in 1980, which finally condemned Yugoslavia to international insolvency. Though the current-account deficit was reduced, in the early 1980s, the rapidly growing burden of interest and amortization payments forced the Yugoslav Government to seek rescheduling of the debt at the end of 1982. The rescheduling was not, in itself, difficult to negotiate and, indeed, Yugoslavia managed to achieve a surplus on the current account of its balance of payments as early as 1983, which was maintained until 1989. In this respect, the Yugoslav case differed sharply from the typical Eastern European scenario of the 1980s, in which initial debt-service crisis was followed by pronounced failure to remove current-account deficits, so that total debt continued to grow. In Yugoslavia, by contrast, net debt was reduced by a total of some $3,000m., between 1983 and 1989. This re-establishment of a degree of international financial equilibrium was not, however, without its negative consequences. The improvement in the current account was largely based on reduction of imports, including imports of raw materials and equipment, and this produced an almost complete cessation of economic growth in Yugoslavia. The failure of the economy to generate any significant new exporting dynamic, following the 'debt-shock' period, indicated a continuing failure to address underlying structural problems, which, in turn, reflected a deepening tendency for the old, Titoist one-party system to fragment and lose impetus. Those political trends were also partly responsible for a rapid escalation in the problem of inflation, as regional leaderships used their 'decentralized' prerogative to create primary money as a way of shoring up existing structures. By the end of 1989 the annual rate of inflation had reached 2,500%.

THE MARKOVIĆ PLAN: YUGOSLAVIA'S LAST CHANCE

Ante Marković succeeded Branko Mikulić as the Yugoslav prime minister, the President of the Federal Executive Council, at the beginning of 1989. He came to the premiership with a reputation as a highly efficient technocrat, and quickly made it clear that he intended to remain largely aloof from the political and ethnic tensions which were becoming critical in that year. Then, at the end of 1989, he announced a programme of radical economic reforms, to be implemented from 1 January 1990. The key measures, which were influenced by the Polish experience and the ideas of the economist Geoffrey Sachs are summarized below (including a number of details, which were subsequent to, but augmented the original proposals):

A new dinar was introduced, to exchange for the old one at the rate of 10,000 old to 1 new;

the new dinar was linked or 'pegged' to the Deutschmark at a rate of 7:1;

the new dinar was to be internally convertible, that is, Yugoslav citizens were to be allowed to convert unlimited amounts of dinars into convertible or 'hard' currency, for current-transaction purposes;

imports would be liberalized, although foreign-exchange quotas for broad bands of imports (such as consumer goods) were retained;

a process of deregulation and privatization was initiated, which was to increase the share of the private sector in the Yugoslav economy to some 35%, by 1995, leaving the socialized sector with a reduced, but still substantial, share of the economy. Agencies for restructuring and development, modelled on the German Treuhandanstalt (the government agency responsible for privatization in the former German Democratic Republic—GDR), were to be established at the republican level, to implement privatization plans and restructuring programmes within the socialized sector;

joint-venture regulations were liberalized and it became possible, for the first time, for foreigners to own 100% of Yugoslav companies. These changes represented the main policy of a strategy designed to open the Yugoslav economy to foreign private capital.

Behind these six key points lay a seventh, which was less explicitly iterated, but was, ultimately, the most important of them. For Marković, the significance of 'shadowing the Deutschmark' lay in the fact that it provided an automatic and accurate guideline on which to base domestic macroeconomic policy. The parity of seven new dinars to the Deutschmark would only remain tenable if the value of the dinar remained at least as stable as that of the German currency. If not, against a background of liberalization of import controls, the balance of trade would start to fall into critical disequilibrium. Thus, the enemy that Marković was really countering, with his internal convertibility proposals, was domestic inflation. This could only be controlled, however, if the National Bank was able to reclaim the authority over vital, 'high-powered', monetary emissions, which it had lost during the 1970s, and finally to stop the process of politically-inspired accommodation of inflationary pressures.

THE MARKOVIĆ PLAN: OUTCOMES AND PROBLEMS

Domestic Macroeconomic Balance

The internal convertibility strategy was initially remarkably successful in its attack on inflation. Within six months the annual rate of inflation had been reduced from 2,500% to under zero. It was equally successful in restoring confidence in the dinar, which, in turn, induced a massive conversion of private hard-currency holdings into dinars, and a substantial resultant increase in national hard-currency reserves. Net inflows of foreign exchange into the Yugoslav banking system, in the first six months of 1990, totalled more than US $1,900m. The impact of this on the current account of the balance of payments was amplified by a strong tendency, in the first six months of 1990, for Yugoslavia to export for cash and import on credit. As a result, by August 1990, foreign-exchange reserves grew by about 80%, to reach some $10,000m., or approximately two-thirds of the annual value of hard-currency imports. All of this enabled Yugoslavia to improve relations with the International Monetary Fund (IMF). A stand-by arrangement was concluded, in early 1990, and this facilitated the extension of substantial new World Bank credits.

However, in imposing this new macroeconomic discipline, Marković, the technocrat, had made a direct attack on the most cherished prerogative of the regional political élites, the 'licence to print money'. This action brought him into conflict with the most powerful member of those élites—the Communist-populist President of Serbia, Slobodan Milošević.

The sharp decrease in output, particularly industrial output, in 1990, was in itself no particular cause for anxiety. The new monetary rigour was designed to force firms to restructure in order to eliminate loss-making activities. Most enterprises reacted to the January 1990 programme by reducing output in all areas, including exports, while largely maintaining employment levels. Between August 1989 and August 1990 employment in the socialized sector fell by just 4.1%. Firms were able to do this without going bankrupt because they received substantial, and, essentially, unlimited support from commercial banks. In particular, the banks showed a willingness, throughout the first part of 1990, to capitalize unpaid interest on loans. In effect, then, they simply assumed the role that the National Bank had previously fulfilled. This was to give general support to all enterprises of the socialized sector which wanted to continue in their traditional manner, rather than addressing the priorities of the future. This did not solve the problem of insolvency. Rather, it shifted it from the level of the enterprise to that of the commercial banking system. By the end of 1990 the banking system faced collapse. Irrecoverable or 'bad' debts were estimated at three times the value of capital, and 57.8% of total deposits. This put tremendous pressure on the National Bank to relax its strict monetary policy.

The matter came to a head at the end of November 1990, with a bizarre development, the so-called 'Great Bank Robbery'. The republican Government of the Socialist Party of Serbia (SPS—formerly the League of Communists) prevailed upon the National Bank of Serbia to re-discount bank loans to the value of 18,000m. dinars ($1,700m.). This, effectively, created new, 'high-powered' money, equivalent to some 10% of the total Yugoslav stock of money at that time. This enabled Milošević to pay salaries and pensions to millions of state employees, retirees, invalids, etc., for the first time in months, just a few days before Serbia's first democratic election since the Second World War. A few months later the Government of Montenegro gained finance in exactly the same way, to compensate for federal funds which it should have received (for the payment of such things as pensions, hard-currency obligations and export support), but had not.

It was inevitable that these developments should compromise Yugoslavia's new-found macroeconomic equilibrium. From July 1990 the National Bank again started to increase the supply of primary money. After the extraordinary 0.6% inflation rate recorded for June 1990, the monthly rate of increase in the retail price index once more began to escalate. It was already 8.2% in October and, although it then fell again (as low as 2.7% in December), it had increased to 9.2% by February 1991. Considering the pressures they were under, the Federal Government and the National Bank had done well to keep the inflation rate still well below the hyperinflationary threshold. Even before the onset of civil war, in mid-1991, however, all the signs were that the situation would get worse rather than better in the immediate future. A massive labour strike in Serbia, in April 1991, in protest at another period of unpaid wages and salaries, was only ended when President Milošević promised that all claims would be settled. It was clear that the inflationary emission of currency was the only way Milošević could keep his promise.

Balance of Payments

The loss of macroeconomic control had an immediate and dramatic effect on the balance of payments and reserves situation. By December 1990 all the balance-of-payments gains made via hard-currency deposits over the first seven months of the year had been lost. At 31 December hard-currency reserves were US $6,700m., which was only a little more than at December 1989. With the hard-currency balance of trade for 1990 recording a deficit of nearly $5,000m., and the balance of cash and credits on imports and exports now level, there was a current-account deficit for the first time since 1982. International developments beyond the control of the Yugoslav Government sharply reinforced negative trends in the trade balance in 1990–91, as traditional markets in Eastern Europe contracted, following the collapse of the Council for Mutual Economic Assistance (CMEA), and the conflict in the Persian (Arabian) Gulf destroyed one of Yugoslavia's biggest export markets for construction services. Furthermore, Serbia suffered proportionately more than the other Republics. The civil war in Yugoslavia also virtually destroyed the tourist industry, a perennial source of foreign exchange (although mainly for Croatia).

By October 1991, with Slovenia and Croatia reinforcing their June 1991 declarations of independence (Slovenia introduced its own currency, the tolar, in that month), and with civil war heightening political pressures and adversely affecting economic activity and infrastructure, Marković's administration became increasingly powerless and federal economic objectives became increasingly irrelevant. On 19 December 1991 Marković finally resigned as President of the Federal Executive Council, signalling the end of the Socialist Federal Republic of Yugoslavia (SFRY).

THE ECONOMIC IMPACT OF FRAGMENTATION

The fragmentation of the Yugoslav market started well before the final collapse of the SFRY. Indeed, there was a degree of continuity between the politically inspired regional autarkism of the late Communist period and the more explicit isolationism pursued by President Milošević. From 1989 Serbia became involved in a series of bizarre 'trade wars' with, first, Slovenia, and then Croatia, extending to the imposition of a kind of import tariff on 'foreign' goods, and culminating in the sequestration of many Slovenian and Croatian businesses located in Serbia. However, while the Serbian Government continued to proclaim national self-sufficiency as a goal, it was clear that the dissolution of Yugoslavia, in conditions of civil war, adversely affected the economies of the two Republics remaining in the new Federal Republic of Yugoslavia (FRY).

In 1991 gross domestic product (GDP), at constant prices, decreased by 11.1% and industrial output fell by 17.6% in Yugoslavia. This decline accelerated in 1992, with GDP decreasing by an estimated 27% and industrial production falling by about 23%, compared to 1991. In terms of international purchasing power, it was estimated that real GDP per head in Serbia increased by 3.4% per year in 1985–89, but declined by 4.4% in 1990 and by 6.7% in 1991. On the same basis, Montenegro's GDP per head rose by 1.8% per year in 1985–89, but fell by 6.6% in 1990 and by 8.0% in 1991. The population of the FRY, which accounted for 44.2% of the SFRY's total in 1991, increased at an average rate of 0.5% per year in 1981–91. The SFRY recorded a visible trade surplus of US $512m. in 1991. However, in the same year, the Serbian trade deficit was $700m., and it reached the same figure in the first five months of 1992 alone. The FRY's exports declined, in volume terms, by 17% in 1991, while imports fell by 24%.

It would be incorrect to impute completely the deterioration of the FRY's economy to the fragmentation of the Yugoslav market. The effects of the demise of the CMEA and the conflict in the Persian (Arabian) Gulf apart, the poor production and trading figures of 1991 and 1992 simply represented, to a degree, a continuation of the negative structural tendencies of the 1980s. There was, however, a sharp acceleration in the rate of decline from 1991, and the fragmentation of Yugoslavia was clearly one of the main reasons for this.

The impact of the disintegration on industries dependent on a national grid, for example electricity, was enormous. However, the impact on the manufacturing industry was also severe. The Zastava motor manufacturer, based in Belgrade, for example, found that with the loss of component suppliers in Croatia and Slovenia it was extremely difficult to maintain production of passenger cars—although it did, at the same time, discover that circumstances were conducive to the expansion of its (previously subsidiary) weapons output. The Serbian chemicals industry was also adversely affected by the dissolution of the federation, and this had consequences for the agricultural sector. Agricultural production in Serbia and Montenegro declined by 6.9% in 1990, by 9.7% in 1991 and by an estimated 22% in 1992. Production of most major crops was sharply reduced in 1992; wheat by 48.9%, maize by 44.9% and sugar beets by 42.1%. By 1993 supplies of fertilizer and pesticides were at a critically low level and many farmers were sowing with unselected seeds.

THE IMPACT OF SANCTIONS

In May 1992 the UN Security Council imposed a range of sanctions on Serbia and Montenegro as a way of applying pressure on the authorities to stop Serb military action in Bosnia and Herzegovina. The sanctions included a trade embargo (subsequently made more specific in terms of a list of key commodities—crude petroleum, petroleum products, coal, power-plant machinery, iron, steel, other metals, chemicals, rubber, plastics, motor vehicles, aircraft and all types of engines—humanitarian supplies were explicitly excepted), a partial freeze on assets abroad, a suspension of transport links, and the termination of all agreements on scientific co-operation. In April 1993 these sanctions were extended; the transport blockade on the Adriatic coast and the River Danube (Dunav) was enforced more strictly, there was an effective ban on transit across Serbia, and a much more comprehensive blocking of Yugoslav financial assets abroad.

However, the UN imposition of sanctions could not be held completely responsible for the deterioration of the FRY's economy from May 1992, although it was evident that it was the major contributor to the worsening situation. In 1992 the FRY's exports declined, in volume terms, by 46%, while imports declined by 30%. That imports decreased less than exports was testimony to the effectiveness of the FRY's breaking of sanctions in the first months after their imposition. However, 'sanctions-busting' proved expensive: the trade deficit in 1992 totalled US $1,500m., more than double that of 1991. By the end of 1992 the FRY's hard-currency reserves had decreased to less than $1,000m. Between March 1992 and March 1993 exports fell by 69%. Strikingly, though, imports in March 1993 were 8.1% more than 12 months previously. It was this minor increase in imports which formed the immediate background to the extension of sanctions in April 1993. In that month the FRY Government ceased publishing statistics on foreign trade.

The decline in industrial production accelerated in 1993. In June output was 35.8% lower than in the same month of the previous year. The most adversely affected sectors included engineering and machine-building, for which total output in 1992 had declined to the 1966 level. Output declined by a further 49.7% between June 1992 and June 1993. The Zastava motor manufacturer saw the rate of capacity utilization on its car-production lines fall to 10%–20% in late 1992. Zastava attempted initially to compensate for the loss of its Yugoslav partners by attracting business from Western companies. However, this business ceased on the imposition of UN sanctions. It seemed likely that these sanctions would prove to have administered the *coup de grâce* to the Yugoslav car industry.

The impact of sanctions on the chemicals and pharmaceuticals industry was even more devastating. Because the industry was so dependent on crude petroleum, the trade embargo simply halted production in a number of base chemicals plants, which, in turn, affected other parts of the sector. By early 1993 there was not a single fertilizer factory in operation in the country. It was estimated, in June 1993, that production in this sector had declined by 50% compared to the same month in the previous year.

Steel production was also virtually suspended, owing to the loss of raw material supplies and export markets.

In spite of the petroleum embargo 4m. metric tons of petroleum products were consumed in Serbia and Montenegro in 1992, estimated to be only 2m. tons less than what would have been consumed in the absence of those restrictions. As well as petroleum shortages and the disruption of the old Yugoslav grid, the FRY's energy sector faced shortages of (normally imported) spare parts and the loss of its export markets as an outlet for surplus output during the summer (July–September). This last problem was particularly damaging as Serbia had already lost its 'export' markets in other parts of the former Yugoslavia. As a result, the FRY was left with a number of very large power-stations which could not be run at even their minimum production levels in the summer, and therefore had to be shut down. The volume of output in this sector decreased by an estimated 33.5% between June 1992 and June 1993.

The increase in the official rate of unemployment in the FRY from May 1992, however, was relatively small. This was owing to the Government's politically motivated decision not to reduce the work-force because of the sanctions. Instead, employees were kept on in enterprises, but with little or no work to do, or were forced to take indefinite leave.

THE GROWING IMPORTANCE OF THE INFORMAL ECONOMY

The figures for 'official' production were, in a sense, misleading. The parallel or informal economy, known as the 'black economy', covering everything from the merely unreported (and therefore untaxed) to the criminal, grew vigorously in the 1980s, as official gross national product (GNP) stagnated. It was estimated that by 1991 the informal sector accounted for 23.7% of real GNP. Inevitably, the imposition of sanctions further increased the black economy, as illegal imports and exports increasingly came to represent the most important activity in the FRY economy. In 1992 it was estimated that the contribution of the informal economy to real GNP was as high as 29.4%. As official GNP continued to fall in 1993, it must be assumed that the share of the black economy in real GNP increased further.

Obviously, taking the informal sector into consideration improves any assessment of the Yugoslav economy as a whole. However, the benefits from this sector were only felt by a minority, and the structural shift in the FRY economy towards the informal sector produced a greater inequality in the distribution of income. This change was exacerbated by the decrease in the average monthly net personal income in hard-currency terms in 1992 and 1993. Furthermore, there were numerous scandals relating to government involvement in black marketeering, most notoriously in early 1993, when ministers were implicated in the smuggling of petroleum and food.

One of the reasons why the informal sector did comparatively little for the living standards of the Yugoslav population was that it was concentrated in the trading sectors, rather than the production sectors. In particular, the illegal foreign-currency market grew to such an extent that it effectively took over as the official foreign-currency market. This market was used by individuals, but was dominated by banks, including the new private banks, many of which operated on the borderline of legality, and by the state itself. By early 1993 40% of the domestic money supply was being diverted to the currency black market.

INFLATION AS ECONOMIC POLICY

The successive transitions from the hyperinflation of the Communist period to Marković's dramatic macroeconomic stabilization, followed by a return to hyperinflation, this time post-Communist, occurred with breathtaking speed. By June 1992 the monthly rate of inflation had increased to 102.3%. Crude price-control measures then reduced the rate to 33.3% in November 1992, but, by March 1993, it had risen again to 228.3%, and, by June, to 366.7%.

Government measures to combat inflation were ineffectual. However, there was some reason to doubt the seriousness of those measures. Insistence on the prerogative of using the printing press to finance preferred schemes, and, more generally, to cover any budget deficits which might arise, was one of strongest elements of continuity between the Communist and post-Communist periods. However, the nature of the preferred schemes changed. Under Communist rule, heavy industrial projects were favoured, but in the Milošević period it was ethnic wars. As much as 60%–70% of the FRY's GNP was used on public expenditure, the most part of it spent on the military (it was estimated that as much as 20% of the country's national income was being transferred to the Serb-controlled areas of Croatia and Bosnia), and on social support. As the legal economy contracted dramatically, attempts to increase budget revenue through increased taxation succeeded only in further damaging morale in that sector, while increasing the advantages of conducting transactions in the informal sector. The impact on the budget deficit was negligible, and it was left to the printing press to cover the greater part of that deficit. As noted earlier, this in turn supplied the foreign-currency black market. Thus, the link between the progressive criminalization of the FRY economy and the hyperinflationary financial policies of its Government was a close one.

IS THERE A FUTURE FOR THE YUGOSLAV ECONOMY?

By early 1994 UN sanctions against Serbia had not succeeded in stopping the conflict in Bosnia. They had, however, already greatly damaged the Serbian and Montenegrin (FRY) economy. By the end of 1993 the annual rate of inflation was in excess of 3,000,000,000%. It was impossible to gauge precisely the extent of that damage, because other factors—the dissolution of the SFRY, the weakness of government economic policy, among others—exacerbated the economic situation. Nevertheless, it was clear that the imposition of sanctions substantially accelerated a decline which was probably inevitable. Perhaps more insidiously, sanctions might increasingly be pre-empting Yugoslavia's chances of economic recovery in a (putative) post-civil-war setting. The full extent of the damage that was being done to the technological- and human-capital base of the country, as technology and equipment imports ceased and the FRY experienced the emigration of much of its intelligentsia (around 120,000 from 1989), would only become evident towards the end of the century. It was difficult, in 1994, to perceive any clear prospect of a recovery of sustained economic development in Yugoslavia in the immediate future.

Statistical Survey

Source: *Statistički godišnjak Jugoslavije* (Statistical Yearbook of Yugoslavia), published by Savezni zavod za statistiku (Federal Statistical Office), 11000 Belgrade, Kneza Miloša 20; tel. (11) 681999; telex 11317; fax (11) 642368.

Note: Unless otherwise indicated, figures in this Survey refer to the territory of the Federal Republic of Yugoslavia (FRY), comprising the two republics of Serbia and Montenegro. Where data for the FRY are not available, the Survey has retained tables relating to the former Socialist Federal Republic of Yugoslavia (SFRY), which comprised six republics. Such tables are indicated by the phrase 'former SFRY' after the heading.

Area and Population

AREA, POPULATION AND DENSITY

Area (sq km)	102,173*
Population (census results)	
31 March 1981	
Males	4,919,066
Females	4,978,920
Total	9,897,986
31 March 1991	10,406,742
Density (per sq km) at census of 31 March 1991	101.9

* 39,449 sq miles.

Estimated population: 10,630,000 (104.0 per sq km) at mid-1992 (Source: UN, *Monthly Bulletin of Statistics*).

REPUBLICS (Census of 31 March 1991)

Republic	Area (sq km)	Population	Density (per sq km)	Capital (with population)
Serbia	88,361	9,791,475	111	Belgrade (1,087,915)
Vojvodina*	21,506	2,012,517	94	Novi Sad (170,029)
Kosovo and Metohija*	10,887	1,954,747	179	Priština (108,020)
Montenegro	13,812	615,267	45	Podgorica† (96,074)
Total	102,173	10,406,742	102	–

* Provinces within Serbia. † Formerly Titograd.

PRINCIPAL TOWNS (population at 1991 census)

Beograd (Belgrade, the capital)	1,087,915	Subotica	100,219
Novi Sad	170,029	Podgorica*	96,074
Niš	161,376	Zrenjanin	81,328
Kragujevać	146,607	Pančevo	72,717
Priština	108,020	Čačak	72,092

* Formerly Titograd.

POPULATION BY ETHNIC GROUP
(1991 census, preliminary results)

Ethnic Group	Population ('000)	%
Serbs	6,486	62.3
Albanians	1,728	16.6
Montenegrins	521	5.0
Hungarians	345	3.3
Yugoslavs	344	3.3
Muslims	327	3.1
Total (incl. others)	10,407	100.0

BIRTHS, MARRIAGES AND DEATHS

	Registered live births		Registered marriages		Registered deaths	
	Number	Rate (per 1,000)	Number	Rate (per 1,000)	Number	Rate (per 1,000)
1984	172,800	17.0	72,421	7.1	97,230	9.6
1985	166,587	16.3	70,140	6.9	97,588	9.6
1986	164,393	16.0	68,497	6.7	98,345	9.6
1987	165,067	16.0	70,502	6.8	97,723	9.4
1988	163,944	15.7	70,403	6.8	97,534	9.4
1989	154,560	14.8	69,438	6.6	99,270	9.5
1990	155,022	14.7	64,856	6.2	97,665	9.3
1991*	149,221	14.1	55,326	5.6	97,645	9.2

* Provisional.

ECONOMICALLY ACTIVE POPULATION
(persons aged 10 years and over, 1981 census)

	Males	Females	Total
Agriculture, hunting, forestry and fishing	807,196	681,594	1,488,790
Mining and quarrying, Manufacturing, Electricity, gas and water	598,354	267,919	866,273
Construction	250,883	23,799	274,682
Trade, restaurants and hotels	175,723	153,501	329,224
Transport, storage and communications	151,273	23,819	175,092
Financing, insurance, real estate and business services	40,489	38,963	79,452
Community, social and personal services	389,002	284,945	673,947
Activities not adequately defined	46,054	16,203	62,257
Total employed	2,458,974	1,490,743	3,949,717
Unemployed	288,447	190,064	478,511
Total labour force	2,717,421	1,680,807	4,428,228

EMPLOYMENT IN THE 'SOCIALIZED' SECTOR
('000 employees, average of March and September each year)

	1989	1990	1991
Agriculture, forestry and fishing	143	144	137
Mining and quarrying	64	64	55
Manufacturing	1,060	1,026	951
Electricity, gas and water	57	59	56
Construction	221	209	188
Trade, restaurants and hotels	369	349	310
Transport, storage and communications	205	197	178
Financing, insurance, real estate and business services	82	76	73
Community, social and personal services	532	517	490
Total	2,733	2,641	2,438
Males	1,700	1,622	1,479
Females	1,033	1,019	959

Agriculture

PRINCIPAL CROPS ('000 metric tons)

	1990	1991	1992
Wheat	3,869	4,109	2,101
Barley	313	299	250
Maize	3,623	7,818	4,311
Oats	135	128	130
Other cereals	27	27	23
Potatoes	737	867	711
Dry beans	49	85*	61
Soybeans	89	115	91
Sunflower seed	351	380	362
Hempseed	164†	85†	60*
Cabbages	287	344	226
Tomatoes	181	230	202†
Green chillies and peppers	135	161	103*
Dry onions	144	168	140*
Carrots	58	74	47*
Other vegetables	117	62	109
Water-melons and melons	201	198†	160†
Grapes	273	497†	384
Sugar beets	4,363	4,713	2,730
Pears	371	365	379
Oranges	3	3	3*
Apricots	32	17	16*
Strawberries	35	31	27
Raspberries	56	42	44
Chestnuts†	1.9	1.7	1.5
Walnuts	17.5	20.9	15.6

* FAO estimate(s). † Unofficial figure(s).

Source: FAO, *Production Yearbook*.

LIVESTOCK ('000 head, year ending 30 September)

	1990	1991	1992
Horses	97	94	89
Cattle	2,168	2,102	2,189*
Pigs	4,329	4,374	3,844
Sheep	3,006	3,043	2,715
Poultry	30,000	30,000	26,000

* Unofficial figures.

Source: FAO, *Production Yearbook*.

LIVESTOCK PRODUCTS (metric tons)

	1990	1991	1992*
Beef and veal	162,000	163,000*	159,000
Mutton and lamb	33,000	29,000	27,000
Pigmeat	434,000	378,000	340,000
Poultry meat	113,000†	73,000	71,000
Cows' milk	1,957,000	1,829,000	1,700,000
Sheep's milk	62,000	54,000	50,000
Cheese	78,000	87,000	77,000
Butter and ghee	11,329	4,112	2,500
Hen eggs	98,000	84,600	80,000
Honey	2,848	1,934	1,800
Wool:			
greasy	4,729	3,990	3,600
scoured	2,837	2,394	2,160
Cattle hides*	22,011	21,483	17,294
Sheep skins*	1,700	1,900	1,700

* FAO estimate(s). † Unofficial figure(s).

Source: FAO, *Production Yearbook*.

Forestry

ROUNDWOOD REMOVALS ('000 cubic metres)*

	1989	1990	1991
Sawlogs and veneer logs	1,304	1,177	1,113
Pitprops (mine timber)	56	59	59
Pulpwood	472	344	277
Other industrial wood	128	102	104
Fuel wood	730	687	703
Total (incl. others)	2,704	2,385	2,267

* From socially-owned forests only.

SAWNWOOD PRODUCTION ('000 cubic metres)

	1989	1990	1991
Coniferous (soft wood)	758	643	555
Non-coniferous (hard wood)	4,225	3,708	3,599
Total	4,983	4,351	4,154

Fishing

(metric tons, live weight)

	1989	1990	1991*
Freshwater fishes	9,263	7,658	1,983
Marine fishes	482	460	170
Crustaceans and molluscs	26	29	15
Total catch	9,771	8,147	2,168

* Preliminary figures.

Mining

('000 metric tons, unless otherwise indicated)

	1989	1990	1991
Coal	44,503	45,491	40,410
Crude petroleum	1,090	1,063	1,100
Copper ore*	26,252	26,463	25,758
Lead and zinc ore*	1,920	1,573	1,237
Bauxite	979	940	900
Natural gas ('000 cu m)	660	646	745

* Figures refer to gross weight of ores extracted. In the former Socialist Federal Republic of Yugoslavia the copper content of copper ore was about 0.5% in 1989 and 1990, while lead and zinc ore contained 2.7% lead and 2.3% zinc in the same years.

Industry

SELECTED PRODUCTS
('000 metric tons, unless otherwise indicated)

	1989	1990	1991
Electric energy (million kWh)	42,546	40,949	39,453
Motor spirit (petrol)	1,259	1,335	983
Distillate fuel oils	985	985	578
Residual fuel oil	2,238	1,804	1,104
Pig iron	881	767	526
Crude steel	1,170	1,012	725
Electrolytic copper	151	151	134
Refined lead	70	48	44
Electrolytic zinc	69	61	39
Aluminium ingots	74	81	76
Tractors (number)	47,102	31,224	23,865
Lorries (number)	8,319	8,421	8,508

—continued	1989	1990	1991
Motor cars ('000)*	223	179	97
Bicycles ('000)	156	191	200
Sulphuric acid	1,022	886	582
Soda ash	91	88	51
Clay building bricks (million)	1,886	1,623	1,512
Roofing tiles (million)	288	300	223
Cement	2,931	2,723	2,411
Chemical woodpulp and cellulose	222	190	138
Stationery and newsprint	93	86	73
Cotton yarn (metric tons)†	40,139	32,163	20,275
Woollen yarn (metric tons)†	22,710	17,815	11,795
Woven cotton fabrics ('000 sq metres)†	81,507	65,398	45,698
Footwear (excl. rubber) ('000 pairs)	30,005	26,191	17,965
Radio receivers ('000)	47	24	55
Television receivers ('000)	215	144	80
Refined sugar	630	619	470
Edible vegetable oils	119	100	112
Wine ('000 hectolitres)	1,088	1,029	1,194
Beer ('000 hectolitres)	4,991	6,105	5,622
Cigarettes (million)	15,701	16,389	17,501

* Including cars assembled from imported parts.
† Including yarn and fabrics produced from cellulosic fibres.

Finance

CURRENCY AND EXCHANGE RATES

Monetary Unit
100 para = 1 new Yugoslav dinar.

Sterling and Dollar Equivalents (31 December 1992)
£1 sterling = 1,135.5 new dinars;
US $1 = 750.0 new dinars;
10,000 new Yugoslav dinars = £8.807 = $13.333.

Average Exchange Rate (new dinars per US $)
1989 2.876
1990 11.318
1991 19.638

Note: On 1 January 1990 the new dinar, equivalent to 10,000 old dinars, was introduced in the Socialist Federal Republic of Yugoslavia (SFRY). After the disintegration of the SFRY, the Federal Republic of Yugoslavia (FRY) continued to use the Yugoslav dinar as its currency. Meanwhile, the other republics of the former SFRY introduced their own currencies to replace (initially at par) the Yugoslav dinar. As a result of rapid inflation in the FRY, the value of the Yugoslav dinar depreciated sharply. By the end of May 1993 the exchange rate was about 89,000 dinars per US dollar. After further devaluations, the currency was redenominated from 1 October, with the introduction of another new dinar, worth 1,000,000 of the former units. However, the depreciation of the currency continued, and on 30 December the new dinar was replaced by a further dinar, worth 1,000 million of its predecessors. In January 1994 there was another currency reform, with the establishment of a dinar officially valued at 1 Deutsche Mark.

BUDGETS (million new dinars)*

	Federal budget		Other budgets†	
Revenue	1989	1990	1989	1990
Total receipts	11,376.5	92,082.5	8,782.3	109,826.3

	Federal budget		Other budgets†	
Expenditure	1989	1990	1989	1990
Schools	—	—	155.2	9,682.0
Science and culture	—	—	39.3	4,457.2
Public health and social welfare	1,105.7	8,269.0	308.9	1,758.0
National defence	6,112.4	4,693.1	37.2	487.0
Non-economic investment	44.1	195.0	154.8	1,480.6
Government	1,163.4	7,838.9	5,140.4	41,107.3
Investment and interventions in the economy	1,579.1	24,713.3	351.9	16,606.8
Other	822.1	8,522.6	2,487.9	33,622.5
Total	10,826.9	96,451.9	8,675.6	109,201.4

* Figures refer to the former Socialist Federal Republic of Yugoslavia.
† Republican, Provincial (Vojvodina and Kosovo) and Communal Budgets.

INTERNATIONAL RESERVES (former SFRY, US $ million at 31 December)

	1989	1990	1991
Gold*	80	81	81
IMF special drawing rights	—	13	—
Foreign exchange	4,136	5,461	2,682
Total	4,216	5,555	2,763

* Valued at US $42.22 per troy ounce.
Source: IMF, *International Financial Statistics.*

MONEY SUPPLY (former SFRY, million new dinars at 31 December)

	1988	1989	1990
Notes in circulation	585	12,375	52,517
Private-sector deposits at national banks	24	896	175
Deposit money at basic and associated banks	1,798	37,759	73,591
Total money	2,407	51,030	126,283

Source: IMF, *International Financial Statistics.*

NATIONAL ACCOUNTS (former SFRY, million new dinars at current prices)

Gross Material Product by Activities of the Material Sphere*

	1988	1989	1990
Manufacturing, mining and quarrying	7,099	109,928	368,402
Agriculture and fishing	1,520	23,570	107,364
Forestry	127	1,937	8,701
Operation of irrigation systems and kindred activities	32	423	2,636
Construction	867	13,713	72,047
Transport and communications	1,045	15,099	76,438
Trade	2,448	33,085	181,054
Catering and tourism	508	6,278	37,003
Arts and crafts (productive)	565	7,746	35,669
Public utilities (productive)	151	2,094	11,967
Other productive economic activities	470	7,556	40,464
Sub-total	14,832	221,430	941,744
Statistical discrepancy	24	432	2,548
Total	14,856	221,862	944,292

* By establishment principle.

BALANCE OF PAYMENTS (former SFRY, US $ million)

	1989	1990	1991
Merchandise exports f.o.b.	13,560	14,308	13,799
Merchandise imports f.o.b.	−13,502	−16,984	−13,287
Trade balance	58	−2,676	512
Exports of services	5,441	6,374	2,465
Imports of services	−8,245	−15,012	−5,586
Other income received	403	789	470
Other income paid	−1,872	−1,667	−1,154
Private unrequited transfers (net)	6,645	9,830	2,134
Official unrequited transfers (net)	−3	−2	−2
Current balance	2,427	−2,364	−1,161
Capital (net)	−697	3,504	−2,133
Net errors and omissions	201	228	497
Overall balance	1,931	1,368	−2,797

Source: IMF, *International Financial Statistics*.

External Trade

Note: Figures exclude trade with other former republics of the Socialist Federal Republic of Yugoslavia.

PRINCIPAL COMMODITIES
(distribution by SITC, million new dinars)

Imports c.i.f.	1989	1990	1991
Food and live animals	129	800	796
Fruit and vegetables	n.a.	135	143
Coffee, tea, cocoa and spices	n.a.	131	202
Beverages and tobacco	3	40	84
Crude materials (inedible) except fuels	154	547	525
Textile fibres and waste	n.a.	146	125
Mineral fuels, lubricants, etc.	263	1,331	1,985
Animal and vegetable oils and fats	9	25	23
Chemicals	233	955	1,429
Chemical elements and compounds	n.a.	119	160
Medicinal and pharmaceutical products	n.a.	140	222
Basic manufactures	317	1,256	1,502
Textile yarn, fabrics, etc.	n.a.	281	339
Non-metallic mineral manufactures	n.a.	110	143
Iron and steel	n.a.	326	297
Non-ferrous metals	n.a.	151	167
Other metal manufactures	n.a.	118	192
Machinery and transport equipment	464	2,066	2,374
Miscellaneous manufactured articles	89	846	1,087
Other commodities and transactions	1	492	652
Total	1,661	8,363	10,459

Exports f.o.b.	1989	1990	1991
Food and live animals	119	473	1,056
Meat and meat preparations	n.a.	126	126
Cereals and cereal preparations	n.a.	90	270
Fruit and vegetables	n.a.	120	330
Beverages and tobacco	56	44	120
Crude materials (inedible) except fuels	79	302	293
Mineral fuels, lubricants, etc.	21	220	397
Animal and vegetable oils and fats	2	6	11
Chemicals	197	640	819
Basic manufactures	381	1,794	2,435
Textile yarn, fabrics, etc.	n.a.	215	382
Non-metallic mineral manufactures	n.a.	106	162
Iron and steel	n.a.	342	483
Non-ferrous metals	n.a.	706	810
Machinery and transport equipment	413	1,615	1,760
Miscellaneous manufactured articles	215	1,409	2,046
Furniture	n.a.	112	149
Clothing (excl. footwear)	n.a.	808	1,278
Footwear	n.a.	270	349
Other commodities and transactions	5	36	34
Total	1,450	6,539	8,971

PRINCIPAL TRADING PARTNERS (million new dinars)

Imports c.i.f.	1989	1990	1991
Austria	59	339	409
Czechoslovakia	48	220	292
France	55	329	397
Germany	338	1,680	2,109
Hungary	62	277	347
Iran	8	160	180
Iraq	78	72	n.a.
Italy	159	932	1,109
Japan	22	125	240
Libya	7	21	516
Netherlands	30	135	186
Poland	72	231	183
Romania	32	87	214
Sweden	17	82	100
Switzerland	32	190	207
USSR	264	1,223	1,319
United Kingdom	n.a.	198	306
USA	74	381	423
Total (incl. others)	1,661	8,363	10,459

Exports f.o.b.	1989	1990	1991
Austria	43	240	253
Bulgaria	19	80	191
Czechoslovakia	65	250	113
Egypt	20	110	144
France	33	228	259
Germany	160	1,254	2,704
Greece	30	131	276
Hungary	43	121	141
Iran	10	64	85
Iraq	35	45	310
Italy	121	875	1,253
Netherlands	19	70	110
Poland	69	114	156
Romania	24	141	383
Switzerland	17	94	682
USSR	382	1,334	1,598
United Kingdom	46	221	212
USA	60	259	398
Total (incl. others)	1,450	6,539	8,971

Transport

RAILWAYS (traffic)

	1989	1990	1991
Passenger journeys (million)	n.a.	n.a.	31
Passenger-kilometres (million)	4,654	4,794	2,926
Freight carried (million metric tons)	n.a.	n.a.	25
Freight ton-kilometres (million)	8,707	7,744	5,348

ROAD TRAFFIC (registered motor vehicles at 31 December)

	1988	1989	1990
Motor cycles (up to 50 cc)	40,821	42,261	43,414
Passenger cars	1,225,043	1,309,681	1,405,455
Buses	12,390	12,693	13,133
Lorries	34,558	88,700	92,874
Special vehicles	24,486	25,789	26,475
Tractors	289,834	306,610	318,312

INLAND WATERWAYS

Fleet (number of vessels)

	1991
Tugs	188
Motor barges	73
Barges	424
Tankers	93
Passenger vessels	8

Traffic ('000 metric tons)

	1989	1990	1991
Goods unloaded	14,111	12,946	11,638

SEA-BORNE SHIPPING (international freight traffic)

	1989	1990	1991
Vessels entered ('000 net reg. tons)	6,939	5,469	2,394
Goods loaded ('000 metric tons)	636	727	705
Goods unloaded ('000 metric tons)	1,744	1,321	847
Goods in transit ('000 metric tons)	27	4.2	6.8

CIVIL AVIATION (traffic)

	1989	1990	1991
Passengers carried ('000)	5,189	5,304	5,146
Passenger-kilometres (million)	6,693	7,102	3,443
Cargo carried (tons)	47,840	37,141	16,122
Ton-kilometres ('000)	153,337	134,745	61,885
Kilometres flown ('000)	60,076	59,232	34,257

Tourism

FOREIGN TOURIST ARRIVALS (by country of origin)

	1989	1990	1991
Austria	64,700	50,500	9,100
Czechoslovakia	34,300	35,100	12,200
France	44,300	43,000	15,200
Germany, Federal Republic	260,000	236,000	81,400*
Hungary	57,900	28,600	9,000
Italy	91,500	91,800	22,800
Netherlands	39,600	37,300	6,500
USSR	217,000	188,000	30,400
United Kingdom	81,900	86,400	21,700
USA	34,300	33,500	9,700
Total (incl. others)†	5,350,000	5,062,000	3,508,000

* Including arrivals from the former German Democratic Republic.
† Including internal tourism.

Communications Media

	1988	1989	1990
Telephones ('000 in use)	1,824	1,948	1,839
Radio licences ('000)	1,926	1,907	1,877
Television licences ('000)	1,714	1,704	1,690
Books (titles published)	5,538	5,190	4,180
Daily newspapers	12	12	15
Average circulation ('000)	1,091	956	1,084
Newspapers (all frequencies)	1,152	1,046	962
Average circulation ('000)	10,784	12,554	11,275
Periodicals	988	645	569
Average circulation ('000)	1,930	1,388	1,659

Education

(1991/92)

	Institutions	Teachers	Students
First level	4,424	21,399	470,669
Second level (first stage)	1,746	29,994	465,800
Second level (second stage)	538	14,977	347,916
General secondary (public general)	n.a.	n.a.	74,626
Teacher training	n.a.	n.a.	3,568
Technical and vocational	n.a.	n.a.	269,722
Religion and theology (private)	2	194	2,427
Institutions for higher education	145	9,599	132,814

Directory

The Constitution

The Constitution of the Federal Republic of Yugoslavia, comprising Serbia and Montenegro, was adopted on 27 April 1992, and is summarized below.

The Federal Republic of Yugoslavia (FRY) is a sovereign federal state, based on the principle of equality of its citizens and its member republics. The FRY comprises the Republic of Serbia and the Republic of Montenegro, and there are constitutional provisions for it to be joined by other republics. The FRY covers a unified territory consisting of the territories of the member republics. The FRY borders are inviolable.

Each member republic will have sovereignty over issues which, under the Federal Constitution, do not come within the competence of the FRY. In the FRY, power is in the hands of citizens, who exercise it either directly or through their freely-elected representatives. The FRY is based on the rule of law. The FRY recognizes and guarantees human liberties and citizens' rights as recognized by international law. The FRY recognizes and guarantees the rights of national minorities to preserve, develop and express their ethnic, cultural, linguistic and other characteristics, and their right to use their own national symbols in accordance with international law.

Authority in the FRY is shared between legislative, executive and judicial organs of state. Under the Constitution, the FRY is a single economic space with a single market. Political pluralism is a condition for, and a guarantee of, a democratic political system in the FRY.

In the FRY all citizens are equal before the law, regardless of their national affiliation, race, sex, language, religion, political or other convictions, education, social origin, property status and any other personal characteristic. Each citizen has a duty to respect the freedoms and rights of others and will be accountable for it.

The freedom of work and enterprise is guaranteed in the FRY. The right to private ownership is guaranteed. Nobody can be deprived of property, nor can it be limited (except when general interests require, as envisaged by the law and provided that compensation not lower than the market value of the property is paid to the owner). A foreigner assumes the right to private ownership and the right to enterprise under the conditions of reciprocity.

The FRY establishes policies, adopts and implements federal laws, other regulations and general documents, and secures constitutional and judicial protection in the following areas: human liberties, citizens' rights and duties as laid down in the Federal Constitution, the single market, the development of the FRY, communications and technical and technological systems, safety in all types of transport, the health service, international relations, and the defence and security of the FRY.

Bodies of the FRY are: the Federal Assembly, the President of the Republic, the Federal Government, the Federal Court, the Federal State Prosecutor and the National Bank of Yugoslavia. Provision is made for the power and composition of the Federal Constitutional Court.

The FRY has an army which protects its sovereignty, territory, independence and constitutional system. The Yugoslav Army has both active and reserve staff. The active staff comprises professional soldiers and conscripts engaged in national service. The President of the Republic commands the Army both in time of peace and in time of war, in accordance with decisions of the Supreme Defence Council. The Supreme Defence Council consists of the President of the Republic and presidents of member republics. The FRY President is the president of the Supreme Defence Council. National service in the FRY is compulsory. A citizen who does not wish to perform regular military service on account of religious or other conscientious objections can participate in national service in the Yugoslav Army without weapons or in civilian service.

The Government

HEAD OF STATE

President: ZORAN LILIĆ (elected 25 June 1993).

FEDERAL GOVERNMENT

(March 1994)

Prime Minister: RADOJE KONTIĆ.

Deputy Prime Ministers: JOVAN ZEBIĆ, ZELJIKO SIMIĆ, NIKOLA ŠAINOVIĆ, UROS KLIKOVAĆ.

Federal Minister of Foreign Affairs: VLADISLAV JOVANOVIĆ.

Federal Minister of National Defence: PAVLE BULATOVIĆ.

Federal Minister of Internal Affairs: DJORDJE BLAGOJEVIĆ.

Federal Minister of the Economy: TOMISLAV SIMOVIĆ.

Federal Minister of Finance: VUK OGNJANOVIĆ.

Federal Minister of Foreign Trade: MILORAD UNKOVIĆ.

Federal Minister of Transport and Communications: BLAGOJE LUCIĆ.

Federal Minister of Justice: ZORAN STOJANOVIĆ.

Federal Minister of Employment, Health and Social Affairs: VELIBOR POPOVIĆ.

Federal Minister of Agriculture: LOVRO KOVILJKO.

Federal Minister of Science: MILAN DMITRIJEVIĆ.

Federal Minister of Education and Culture: SLAVO GORDIĆ.

Federal Minister of Human Rights and National Minority Affairs: MARGIT SAVOVIĆ.

Federal Minister of Information: SLOBODAN IGNJATOVIĆ.

Federal Minister of Commerce: MIROSLAV IVANISEVIĆ.

Federal Minister of Sports: ZORAN BINGULAĆ.

Federal Minister of the Environment: SLOBODANKA DJORDAN.

Federal Minister without Portfolio: RADONJA MINIĆ.

MINISTRIES

Office of the Federal Government: 11070 Belgrade, Lenjina 2; tel. (11) 334281.

Federal Ministry of Agriculture: 11070 Belgrade, AVNOJ-a 104; tel. (11) 602555; telex 11062; fax (11) 195244.

Federal Ministry of Development: 11070 Belgrade, Omladinskih brigada 1; tel. (11) 2223550; telex 11062; fax (11) 195244.

Federal Ministry of the Economy: 11070 Belgrade, Omladinskih brigada 1; tel. (11) 2223550; telex 11062; fax (11) 195244.

Federal Ministry of Education and Culture: 11070 Belgrade, Lenjina 2; tel. (11) 2222900; fax (11) 602391.

Federal Ministry of Employment, Health and Social Affairs: 11070 Belgrade, AVNOJ-a 104, SIV-II; tel. (11) 602555; telex 11062; fax (11) 195244.

Federal Ministry of Energy and Industry: 11070 Belgrade, AVNOJ-a 104; tel. (11) 602555; telex 11062; fax (11) 195244.

Federal Ministry of Finance: Belgrade.

Federal Ministry of Foreign Affairs: 11000 Belgrade, Kneza Miloša 24; tel. (11) 682555; telex 11173; fax (11) 682668.

Federal Ministry of Foreign Trade: 11070 Belgrade, Omladinskih brigada 1; tel. (11) 2223550; telex 11062; fax (11) 195244.

Federal Ministry of Internal Affairs: 11000 Belgrade, Kneza Miloša 92; tel. (11) 685555; telex 11185; fax (11) 2351005.

Federal Ministry of Justice: 11070 Belgrade, AVNOJ-a 104; tel. (11) 602555; telex 11062; fax (11) 195244.

Federal Ministry of National Defence: 11000 Belgrade, Kneza Miloša 29; tel. (11) 656122; telex 12216.

Federal Ministry of Commerce: 11070 Belgrade, AVNOJ-a 104; tel. (11) 602555; telex 11062; fax (11) 195244.

Federal Ministry of Transport and Communications: 11070 Belgrade, AVNOJ-a 104; tel. (11) 602555; telex 12062; fax (11) 2223946.

Federal Legislature

SAVEZNA SKUPŠTINA

(Federal Assembly)

The Federal Assembly is composed of two chambers: the Chamber of Republics and the Chamber of Citizens, both comprising representatives of Serbia and Montenegro.

Chamber of Citizens

Elections, 20 December 1992

Party	Seats
Socialist Party of Serbia	47
Serbian Radical Party	34
Democratic Movement of Serbia	20
Democratic Party of Socialists	17
Democratic Party	5
Socialist Party of Montenegro	5
People's Party	4
Democratic Community of Vojvodina Hungarians	3
Others	3
Total	138

Chamber of Republics

The Chamber of Republics comprises 40 members (20 each for Montenegro and Serbia), selected on a proportional basis to reflect the composition of the republican legislatures.

Local Government

Local government is based on the municipality or commune. For administrative purposes, Montenegro is divided into municipalities (for details, see below on p. 749), of which there are 21. Serbia is divided into administrative regions (for details, see below on p. 753), of which there are 29, including the territories of the formerly autonomous provinces of Kosovo-Metohija and Vojvodina. Following the enactment of the 1990 Serbian Constitution, and, subsequently, of the FRY Constitution of 27 April 1992, Vojvodina retained its provincial Assembly. However, the provincial Assembly of Kosovo-Metohija was dissolved. In October 1991 the Slav Muslims of the Sandžak area voted for autonomy in a banned referendum. Their leader was SULEJMAN UGLJANIN.

Political Organizations

Alliance of Peasants of Serbia Party: 11000 Belgrade, Srpskih Vladara 81; tel. (11) 789235; Pres. MILOMIR BABIĆ.

Alliance of Reform Forces for Montenegro: Podgorica; republican branch of federal, pro-Yugoslav party; favours free-market economic reform.

Citizens' Group (Željko Ražnjatović): Belgrade.

Democratic Action Party: Podgorica; mem. of Democratic Coalition of Muslims and Albanians in Montenegro.

Democratic Alliance: Podgorica; mem. of Democratic Coalition of Muslims and Albanians in Montenegro.

Democratic Alliance of Kosovo (Demokratski Savez Kosovo—DSK): 38000 Priština; f. 1990 by dissidents and take-over of provincial brs of the Socialist Alliance of Working People; ethnic Albanian grouping; Chair. Dr IBRAHIM RUGOVA.

Democratic Community of Vojvodina Hungarians (Demokratska zajednica vojvodjanskih Madjara—DZVM): Ada, trg Oslobodjenja 11; tel. (24) 852248; f. 1990; supports interests of ethnic Hungarian minority in the Vojvodina; c. 20,000 mems; Pres. ANDRAŠ AGOŠTON.

Democratic Movement of Serbia (Demokratski Pokret Srbije—DEPOS): Belgrade, Masarikova 5/VIII; tel. (11) 685490; f. 1992 as a coalition of four parties and a party faction; Pres. VUK DRAŠKOVIĆ; Sec. MILENKO PALIĆ.

Democratic Party (Demokratska stranka): 11000 Belgrade, Terazije 3/IV; tel. (11) 338078; fax (11) 623686; nationalist; Leader ZORAN DJINDJIĆ.

Democratic Party of Albanians: Preševo.

Democratic Party of Serbia (Demokratska stranka Srbije—DSS): Belgrade; f. 1992 following split from Democratic Party; Leader VOJISLAV KOSTUNICA.

Democratic Party of Socialists (DPS) (Demokratska Partija Socijalista): Podgorica; name changed from League of Communists of Montenegro in 1991; supports continued federation; Chair. MOMIR BULATOVIĆ; Gen. Sec. SVETOZAR MAROVIĆ.

Democratic Party of Vojvodina: Novi Sad.

Democratic Reform Party of Muslims: 38400 Prizren, Koritnik 3; tel. (29) 22322; party of ethnic Muslims; left-wing; Pres. AZAR ZULJI.

Equality Party: Podgorica; mem. of Democratic Coalition of Muslims and Albanians in Montenegro.

League of Social Democrats of Vojvodina: Novi Sad; Leader NENAD ČANAK.

Liberal Alliance of Montenegro: Podgorica; pro-independence; Leader SLAVKO PEROVIĆ.

Liberal Party (Liberalna Stranka): Valjevo, POB 148; tel. (14) 22627; favours a free-market economy; Leader NIKOLA MILOŠEVIĆ.

Muslim Democratic Party.

National Peasant's Party: Novi Sad; Pres. DRAGAN VESELINOV.

New Democracy: Belgrade; Leader DUSAN MIHAILOVIĆ.

New Socialist Party of Montenegro: Podgorica; f. 1992 by merger of the People's Party (Leader NOVAK KILIBARDA) and the Socialist Party of Montenegro.

Party of Democratic Action: Preševo; party of ethnic Albanians; Leader RIZA HALILI.

Party of Democratic Action of Kosovo-Metohija (PDA-KM): Vitomirića; party of ethnic Muslims; affiliated to the PDA of Bosnia and Herzegovina; Chair. NUMAN BALIĆ.

Party of Democratic Action—Montenegro: Rozaj; Slav Muslim party, affiliated to PDA of Bosnia and Herzegovina; support mainly in Sandžak region; Leader HARUN HADŽIĆ.

Party of Democratic Action of the Sandžak (PDA-S): 36300 Novi Pazar, E. Redzepagića 54; tel. (20) 25626; party of ethnic Muslims; affiliated to the PDA of Bosnia and Herzegovina; advocates autonomy for the Sandžak region; Chair. SULEJMAN UGLJANIN.

Peasant Party: Belgrade; Leader MILOMAR BABIĆ.

People's Party (Narodna Stranka): 11000 Belgrade, Srpskih Vladara 14; Leaders MILAN PAROSKI, DRAGOSLAV PETROVIČ.

Reform Democratic Party of Vojvodina (Reformska Demokratska Stranka Vojvodine): Novi Sad, Ilije Ognjanović 7/I; Pres. Dr DRAGOSLAV PETROVIĆ.

Republican Party of Kosovo: Leader RESHAT NURBOJA.

Serbian National Restoration: Belgrade; pro-monarchist party, favours restoration of a 'Greater Serbia'.

Serbian Radical Party (Srpska Radikalna Stranka—SRS): 11000 Belgrade, Ohridska 1; tel. (11) 457745; right-wing; nationalist; armed br. supported war in Croatia in 1991; Leader Dr VOJISLAV SESELJ.

Serbian Renewal Movement (SRM) (Srpski Pokret Obnove—SPO): 11000 Belgrade, Andre Nikolića 1–3; tel. (11) 684223; f. 1990; right-wing; nationalist; Pres. VUK DRAŠKOVIĆ.

Serbian Unity Party: Belgrade; f. 1993; nationalist; Leader ZELJKO RAZNJATIVIĆ (alias ARKAN).

Social Democratic Party: Belgrade; Leader NENAD CANAK.

Socialist Party of Serbia (SPS) (Socijalistička Partija Srbije): 11000 Belgrade, bul. Lenjina 6; tel. (11) 627804; f. 1990 by merger of League of Communists of Serbia and Socialist Alliance of the Working People (SAWP) of Serbia; Pres. SLOBODAN MILOŠEVIĆ; Gen. Sec. MILOMAR MINIĆ.

Yugoslav Green Party: Belgrade, Mutapova 12; tel. (11) 4447030; f. 1990; open to all citizens regardless of national, religious or racial affiliation; Pres. DRAGAN JOVANOVIĆ.

Diplomatic Representation

EMBASSIES IN YUGOSLAVIA

Many countries have withdrawn their ambassadors from Belgrade; where known, the date of withdrawal is indicated below.

Afghanistan: 11000 Belgrade, Njegoševa 56/1; tel. (11) 4448716; Ambassador: SARWAR MANGAL (withdrawn 1992).

Albania: 11000 Belgrade, Kneza Miloša 56; tel. (11) 646864; telex 12294; Chargé d'affaires: JONUZ BEGAJ.

Algeria: 11000 Belgrade, Maglajska 26B; tel. (11) 668211; telex 12343; Ambassador: AHMED ATTAF (withdrawn May 1992).

Angola: 11000 Belgrade, Tolstojeva 51; tel. (11) 663199; telex 11841; fax (11) 662916; Ambassador: EVARISTO DOMINGOS.

Argentina: 11000 Belgrade, Knez Mihajlova 24/I; tel. (11) 621550; telex 12182; Ambassador: FEDERICO CARLOS BARTTFELD.

Australia: 11000 Belgrade, Čika Ljubina 13; tel. (11) 624655; telex 11206; fax (11) 624029; Ambassador: (vacant).

Austria: 11000 Belgrade, Kneza Sime Markovića 2; tel. (11) 635955; telex 11456; fax (11) 638215; Ambassador: Dr WALTER SIEGL (withdrawn May 1992).

Belgium: 11000 Belgrade, Proleterskih brigada 18; tel. (11) 330016; telex 11747; fax (11) 330016; Ambassador: Baron ALAIN GUILLAUME (withdrawn May 1992).

Brazil: 11000 Belgrade, Proleterskih brigada 14; tel. (11) 339781; telex 11100; Ambassador: ANTÔNIO AMARAL DE SAMPAIO.

Bulgaria: 11000 Belgrade, Birčaninova 26; tel. (11) 646222; telex 11665; Ambassador: MARKO MARKOV.

Cambodia: 11000 Belgrade, Gospodar Jovanova 67; tel. (11) 631151; Ambassador: RENE VANHON.

Canada: 11000 Belgrade, Kneza Miloša 75; tel. (11) 644666; telex 11137; fax (11) 641480; Ambassador: JAMES B. BISSETT.

Chile: 11000 Belgrade, Vasilija Gaćeše 9A; tel. (11) 648340; Ambassador: LUIS JEREZ RAMÍREZ.

China, People's Republic: 11000 Belgrade, Kralja Milutina 6; tel. (11) 331484; telex 11146; Ambassador: ZHU ANKANG.

Colombia: 11000 Belgrade, Njegoševa 54/II–5; tel. (11) 457246; telex 12530; fax (11) 457120; Ambassador: (vacant).

Cuba: 11000 Belgrade, Kneza Miloša 14; tel. (11) 657694; Ambassador: ZOILA ROSALES BRITO.

Cyprus: 11040 Belgrade, Diplomatska Kolonija 9; tel. (11) 663725; telex 12729; fax (11) 665348; Ambassador: ANDRESTINOS N. PAPADOPOULOS.

Czech Republic: 11000 Belgrade, bul. Revolucije 22; tel. (11) 330134; fax (11) 336448.

Denmark: 11040 Belgrade, Neznanog Junaka 9A; tel. (11) 667826; telex 11219; fax (11) 660759; Ambassador: HANS JESPERSEN (withdrawn May 1992).

Ecuador: 11000 Belgrade, Kneza Miloša 16; tel. (11) 684876; telex 12751; fax (11) 684876; Ambassador: FRANCISCO PROAÑO ARANDI.

Egypt: 11000 Belgrade, Andre Nikolića 12; tel. (11) 651225; telex 12074; Ambassador: Dr HUSSEIN HASSOUNA.

Ethiopia: 11000 Belgrade, Knez Mihajlova 6/IV; tel. (11) 628666; telex 11818; Ambassador: (vacant).

Finland: 11000 Belgrade, Birčaninova 29; tel. (11) 646322; telex 11707; fax (11) 683365; Ambassador: MAUNO CASTRÉN.

France: 11000 Belgrade, Pariska 11; tel. (11) 636555; telex 11496; Ambassador: MICHEL CHATELAIS (withdrawn May 1992).

Gabon: 11000 Belgrade, Dragorska 3; tel. (11) 669683; telex 12019; Ambassador: EMMANUEL MENDOUME-NZE.

Germany: 11000 Belgrade, Kneza Miloša 74–76; tel. (11) 645755; telex 11107; fax (11) 656989; Ambassador: Dr HANSJÖRG EIFF (withdrawn May 1992).

Ghana: 11000 Belgrade, Ognjena Price 50; tel. (11) 4442445; telex 11720; fax (11) 436314; Ambassador: THOMAS BENJAMIN SAM.

Greece: 11000 Belgrade, Francuska 33; tel. (11) 621443; telex 11361; Ambassador: ELEFTHERIOS KARAYANNIS (withdrawn May 1992).

Guinea: 11000 Belgrade, Ohridska 4; tel. (11) 431830; telex 11963; Ambassador: MOROU BALDE.

Holy See: 11000 Belgrade, Svetog Save 24; tel. (11) 432822; fax (11) 434631; Apostolic Pro-Nuncio: Most Rev. GABRIEL MONTALVO, Titular Archbishop of Celene.

Hungary: 11000 Belgrade, Proleterskih brigada 72; tel. (11) 4440472; Ambassador: ISTVÁN ÖSZI.

India: 11070 Belgrade, B-06/07 Genex International Centre, Vladimira Popovića 6; tel. (11) 2223325; telex 71127; fax (11) 2223357; Ambassador: (vacant).

Indonesia: 11000 Belgrade, bul. Oktobarske Revolucije br. 18; tel. (11) 662122; telex 11129; Ambassador: (vacant).

Iran: 11000 Belgrade, Proleterskih brigada 9; tel. (11) 338782; telex 11726; fax (11) 338784; Ambassador: NASROLLAH KAZEMI KAMYAB.

Iraq: 11000 Belgrade, Proleterskih brigada 69; tel. (11) 434688; telex 12325; Ambassador: Dr WAHBI AL-QARAGULI.

Italy: 11000 Belgrade, Birčaninova 11; tel. (11) 659722; telex 12082; Ambassador: SERGIO VENTO (withdrawn May 1992).

Japan: 11000 Belgrade, Ilirska 5; tel. (11) 768255; telex 11263; fax (11) 762934; Ambassador: TAIZO NAKAMURA (withdrawn June 1992).

Jordan: 11000 Belgrade, Kablarska 28; tel. (11) 651642; telex 12904; Ambassador: HANI B. TABBARA (withdrawn May 1992).

Korea, Democratic People's Republic: 11000 Belgrade, Dr Milutina Ivkovića 9; tel. (11) 668739; telex 11577; Ambassador: CHI JAE RYONG.

Korea, Republic: 11070 Belgrade, Genex International Centre, Vladimira Popovića 6; tel. (11) 2223531; Ambassador: DOO BYONG SHIN.

Kuwait: 11000 Belgrade, Čakorska 2; tel. (11) 664961; telex 12774; Ambassador: ISSA AHMAD AL-HAMMAD.

Lebanon: 11000 Belgrade, Vase Pelagića 38; tel. (11) 651290; telex 11049; Ambassador: (vacant).

Libya: 11000 Belgrade, Generala Ždanova 42; tel. (11) 644782; telex 11787; Secretary of People's Committee: ASSUR MUHAMED KARKUM.

Mali: 11000 Belgrade, Generala Hanrisa 1; tel. (11) 493774; telex 11052; Ambassador: N'TJI LAICO TRAORÉ.

Mexico: 11102 Belgrade, trg Republike 5/IV; tel. (11) 638111; telex 12141; fax (11) 629566; Ambassador: AGUSTÍN GARCÍA-LÓPEZ SANTAOLALLA.

Mongolia: 11000 Belgrade, Generala Vasića 5; tel. (11) 668536; telex 12253; Ambassador: LUDEVDORJYN KHASHBAT.

Morocco: 11000 Belgrade, Sanje Živanović 4; tel. (11) 651775; Ambassador: HASSAN FASSI FIHRI.

Myanmar: 11000 Belgrade, Kneza Miloša 72; tel. (11) 645420; telex 72769; Ambassador: U HLA MAUNG.

Netherlands: 11000 Belgrade, Simina 29; tel. (11) 626699; telex 11556; fax (11) 628986; Ambassador: J. H. W. FIETELAARS (withdrawn May 1992).

Nigeria: 11000 Belgrade, Geršićeva 14A; tel. (11) 413411; telex 12875; fax (11) 418562; Ambassador: EZEKIEL GOTOM DIMKA.

Norway: 11000 Belgrade, Kablarska 30; tel. (11) 651626; telex 11668; fax (11) 651754; Ambassador: GEORG KRANE.

Pakistan: 11000 Belgrade, bul. Oktobarske Revolucije 62; tel. (11) 661676; fax (11) 660219; Ambassador: Adm. TARIQ K. KHAN.

Panama: 11000 Belgrade, Strahinjića Baua 51/II-5; tel. (11) 620374; telex 11451; Ambassador: RICARDO T. PEZET H.

Peru: 11000 Belgrade, Baba Višnjina 26/II-10; tel. (11) 454943; telex 12272; Ambassador: EDUARDO LLOSA.

Poland: 11000 Belgrade, Kneza Miloša 38; tel. (11) 644866; telex 72006; fax (11) 646275; Ambassador: JERZY CHMIELEWSKI.

Portugal: 11110 Belgrade, Stojana Novakovića 19; tel. (11) 750358; telex 11648; fax (11) 754421; Ambassador: JOÃO MORAIS DA CUNHA MATOS (withdrawn May 1992).

Romania: 11000 Belgrade, Kneza Miloša 70; tel. (11) 646071; telex 11318; fax (11) 646071; Chargé d'affaires a.i.: CONSTANTIN GHIRDĂ.

Russia: 11000 Belgrade, Deligradska 32; tel. (11) 657533; Ambassador: GENNADY SHIKIN.

Slovakia: 11070 Novi Belgrade, Ho Ši Minova 18; tel. (11) 2222432; telex 6272790; fax (11) 134520; Ambassador: J. LIPKA.

Spain: 11000 Belgrade, Moravska 5; tel. (11) 454777; telex 12864; fax (11) 4440614; Ambassador: JOSÉ MANUEL ALLENDESALAZAR (withdrawn May 1992).

Sri Lanka: 11000 Belgrade, Lepenička 10; tel. (11) 460661; telex 12475; Ambassador: RAZIK ZAROOK.

Sudan: 11000 Belgrade, Maglajska 5; tel. (11) 667762; telex 12479; Ambassador: IBRAHIM A. HAMRA (withdrawn May 1992).

Sweden: 11000 Belgrade, Pariska 7; tel. (11) 626422; telex 11595; fax (11) 626492; Ambassador: JAN AF SILLEN.

Switzerland: 11000 Belgrade, Birčaninova 27; tel. (11) 646899; telex 11383; fax (11) 657253; Ambassador: (vacant).

Syria: 11000 Belgrade, Mlade Bosne 31; tel. (11) 4449985; telex 11889; fax (11) 453367; Ambassador: ISMAIL AL-KADI.

Thailand: 11000 Belgrade, Molerova 11/V; tel. (11) 454053; telex 12657; Ambassador: (vacant—withdrawn September 1992).

Tunisia: 11000 Belgrade, Vase Pelagića 19; tel. (11) 652966; telex 11461; fax (11) 647656; Ambassador: RAOUF SAID.

Turkey: 11000 Belgrade, Proleterskih brigada 1; tel. (11) 335431; telex 12081; Ambassador: BERHAN EKINCI.

United Kingdom: 11000 Belgrade, Generala Ždanova 46; tel. (11) 645055; telex 11468; fax (11) 659651; Ambassador: (vacant).

USA: 11000 Belgrade, Kneza Miloša 50; tel. (11) 645655; telex 11529; fax (11) 645221; Ambassador: WARREN ZIMMERMANN (withdrawn May 1992).

Uruguay: 11000 Belgrade, Vasina 14; tel. (11) 620994; telex 12650; Ambassador: Dr FERNANDO GÓMEZ FYNS.

Venezuela: 11000 Terazije 45/II; tel. (11) 331604; telex 12856; Ambassador: FREDDY CHRISTIANS.

Viet Nam: 11000 Belgrade, Lackovićeva 6; tel. (11) 663527; telex 11292; Ambassador: VO ANH TUAN.

Yemen: 11000 Belgrade, Vasilija Gaćeše 9C; tel. (11) 653932; Ambassador: MOHAMED MAHMOOD HASSAN AL-BAIHI.

Zaire: 11000 Belgrade, Oktobarske revolucije 47; tel. (11) 668931; telex 11491; Ambassador: LUNDUNGE KADAHI CHIRI-MWAMI.

Zimbabwe: 11000 Belgrade, Perside Milenković 9; tel. (11) 647047; Ambassador: CHIMBIDZAYI E. C. SANYANGARE.

Judicial System

Judicial functions are to be discharged within a uniform system, and the jurisdiction of the courts shall be established and altered only by law. In general, court proceedings are conducted in public (exceptionally the public may be excluded to preserve professional secrets, public order or morals) in the national language of the region in which the court is situated. Citizens who do not know the language in which the proceedings are being conducted may use their own language.

The judicial system comprises courts of general jurisdiction, i.e. communal courts, county courts, republican supreme courts and the Federal Court. The courts of general jurisdiction are organized in accordance with individual republican legislation. In general, the courts are entitled to proceed in criminal, civil and administrative matters. Military courts, headed by the Supreme Military Court, proceed in criminal and administrative matters connected with military service or national defence. Economic or trade matters are under the jurisdiction of economic courts. They proceed also in penal-economic matters.

Judges are elected or relieved by the republican assemblies or the Federal Assembly.

THE FEDERAL JUDICIARY

Constitutional Court

This court decides on the conformity of the Constitutions of the member republics with the federal Constitution, whether or not a republican regulation is contrary to federal statute and on the conformity of enactments of federal agencies with the Constitution and federal statute. The court has seven judges, who elect the president of the Court from among themselves.

President of the Constitutional Court: MILOVAN BUZADZIĆ.

Federal Court

This is the highest organ of justice. In the final instance, it decides on appeals in cases when the death sentence has been passed for criminal offences defined by federal statutes. It decides on extraordinary legal remedies against decisions of republican courts and military courts in cases involving federal statutes. The Court also decides disputes between the republics and between the Federation and its member republics, as well as disputes related to the protection of property rights of Yugoslavia, in the case of non-implementation or violation of federal statute. The Federal Court assesses the legality of irrevocable administrative decisions of federal authorities adopted in the implementation of federal laws. The Federal Court consists of 11 judges who are elected and relieved by the Federal Assembly. The judges of the Federal Court elect the president of the Court from among themselves.

President of the Federal Court of Yugoslavia: Dr RAFAEL CIJAN, 11000 Belgrade, Svetozara Markovića 21; tel. (11) 333911.

Office of the Public Prosecutor

The Federal Public Prosecutor is elected or dismissed by the Federal Assembly.

Federal Public Prosecutor: LJUBO PRLJETA.

Office of the Public Attorney

Represents proprietary rights and interests of the federation, republics, autonomous provinces, towns and communes. The Federal Attorney-General is appointed by the Federal Assembly.

Federal Attorney-General: SAŠO IVANOVSKI.

Federal Social Attorney of Self-Management: carries out his or her function within the framework of federal rights and duties.

Social Attorney of Self-Management: IVICA ČAČIĆ.

THE REPUBLICAN JUDICIARIES

Montenegro

The courts in Montenegro are supervised by the republican Ministry of Justice. The highest courts in the republican judicial system are the Supreme Court and the Constitutional Court. Final appeal lies to the Yugoslav Federal Court and, in constitutional matters, to the federal Constitutional Court.

Constitutional Court of the Republic of Montenegro: 81000 Podgorica, Lenjina 3; tel. (81) 41846; Pres. LJUBOMIR SPASOJEVIĆ.

Supreme Court: 81000 Podgorica, Njegoševa 6; tel. (81) 43070; Pres. MARKO MARKOVIĆ.

Office of the Public Prosecutor: 81000 Podgorica, Njegoševa 6; tel. (81) 43053; Public Prosecutor VLADIMIR ŠUŠOVIĆ.

Serbia

All courts in Serbia are within the jurisdiction of the republican Ministry of Justice. The Federal Court and the federal Constitution Court are the final courts of appeal. Serbia also provides for economic courts, in certain cases.

Constitutional Court of the Republic of Serbia: 11000 Belgrade, Nemanjina 22–26; tel. (11) 658755; Pres. Dr BALŠA SPADIJER.

Supreme Court of Serbia: 11000 Belgrade, Nemanjina 22–26; tel. (11) 658755; Pres. CASLAV IGNJATOVIĆ.

Office of the Public Prosecutor of the Republic of Serbia: 11000 Belgrade, Nemanjina 22–26; tel. (11) 658755; Public Prosecutor MILOMIR JAKOVLJEVIĆ.

Provincial Secretariat of Justice for the AP of Kosovo-Metohija: 38000 Priština, Zejnel Salihu br. 4; fax (38) 31929.

Provincial Secretariat of Justice for the AP of Vojvodina: 21000 Novi Sad, Srpskih Vladara; fax (21) 56672.

Religion

Most of the inhabitants of Yugoslavia and its successor states are, at least nominally, Christian, but there is a significant Muslim minority. The main Christian denomination is Eastern Orthodox, but there is a strong Roman Catholic presence. There are also small minorities of Old Catholics, Protestants and Jews.

CHRISTIANITY

The Eastern Orthodox Church

Serbian Orthodox Church: Headquarters: 11001 Belgrade, 7 jula 5, POB 182; tel. (11) 638161; fax (11) 182780; 11m. adherents (mainly in Yugoslavia); Patriarch of Serbia: His Holiness PAVLE, Archbishop of Peć and Metropolitan of Belgrade-Karlovci; Sec. Archdeacon MOMIR LEČIĆ.

Montenegrin Orthodox Church: Cetinje; established 1993; its jurisdiction is denied by the Serbian Church and not acknowledged by the Ecumenical Patriarch; Patriarch of Montenegro: His Holiness ANTONIJE ABRAMOVIĆ.

The Roman Catholic Church

The Federal Republic of Yugoslavia and the former Yugoslav Republic of Macedonia together comprise two archdioceses (including one, Bar, directly responsible to the Holy See) and four dioceses. At 31 December 1991 the territories contained an estimated 550,000 adherents (about 4% of the population), of whom the majority were in the Serbian province of Vojvodina.

Archbishop of Bar: PETAR PERKOLIĆ, Nadbiskupski Ordinarijat, 85000 Bar, Popovići 98; tel. (85) 21705.

Archbishop of Belgrade: Dr FRANC PERKO, Nadbiskupski Ordinarijat, 11000 Belgrade, Svetozara Markovića 20; tel. and fax (11) 334846.

Old Catholic Church

Old Catholic Church in Serbia and Vojvodina: 11000 Belgrade; Dir of Bishop's Diocese JOVAN AJHINGER.

Protestant Churches

Baptist Union of Yugoslavia: 21000 Novi Sad, Koruška 24; tel. (21) 623273; f. 1922; Sec. ŽELIMIR SRNEC.

Christian Assemblies—Church of Christ's Brethren: 21470 Bački Petrovac, Janka Kralja 4; tel. (21) 780153; Pres. of Elders SAMUEL RYBAR.

Christian Church Jehovah's Witnesses: 11000 Belgrade, Milorada Mitrovića 4; tel. (11) 450383.

Christian Nazarene Community: Hrišćanska nazarenska zajednica, 21000 Novi Sad, Vodnikova br. 12; tel. (21) 390577; Pres. KAROL HRUBIK VLADIMIR.

Christian Reformed Church: 24323 Feketic, Bratsva 26; tel. (11) 738070; f. 1919; 22,000 mems; Bishop IMRE HODOSY.

Evangelical Church of Republic of Croatia, Republic of Bosnia and Herzegovina and Vojvodina: 41000 Zagreb, Gundulićeva 28; tel. (41) 420685; 4,950 mems; Pres. Dr VLADO L. DEUTSCH.

Evangelical Hungarian Church: Subotica, Brace Radiča 17; Pastor DANNY NOVÁK.

Seventh-Day Adventist Church: Hrišćanska adventistička crkva, 11000 Belgrade, Božidara Adzije 4; tel. (11) 453842; telex 72645; fax (11) 458604; Pres. JOVAN LORENCIN; Sec. NEDELJKO KAČAVENDA.

Slovak Evangelical Church of the Augsburg Confession: 21000 Novi Sad, Karadžićeva 2; tel. (21) 611882; Lutheran; 51,500 mems (1990); Bishop Dr ANDREJ BEREDI.

United Methodist Church: 21000 Novi Sad, L. Mušičkoga 7; tel. (21) 610377; f. 1898; 3,000 mems; Superintendent MARTIN HOVAN.

ISLAM

Almost 20% of the Montenegrin population profess Islam as their faith, many being ethnic Muslims of the Sandžak area (which was partitioned between Montenegro and Serbia in 1913). Most Muslims of Serbia and its two Provinces are in Kosovo-Metohija and are ethnic Albanians. Most of the ethnic Slav Muslims are those of the Sandžak, in south-west Serbia. Serbian Islam is predominantly Sunni, although a Dervish sect, introduced in 1974, is popular among the Albanians (some 50,000 adherents, mainly in Kosovo-Metohija).

Islamic Community in the Republic of Serbia: 38000 Priština; Pres. of the Mesihat Dr REDZEP BOJE.

JUDAISM

Federation of Jewish Communities in Yugoslavia: Belgrade, 7 jula 71A/III, POB 841; tel. (11) 624359; fax (11) 626674; f. 1919, revived 1944; Pres. of Federation of Jewish Communities in Yugoslavia DAVID ALBAHARI.

The Press

In 1990, prior to the country's disintegration, 34 dailies were published in Yugoslavia, printed in Serbian (Cyrillic alphabet), Croatian (Roman), Slovene, Macedonian, Hungarian, Italian, English and Albanian. Important newspapers include *Borba* and *Politika* (Belgrade), and *Pobjeda* (Podgorica). Evening papers are also popular, notably *Večernje novosti* (Belgrade).

PRINCIPAL DAILIES

(In Serbo-Croat except where otherwise stated)

Belgrade

Borba: Belgrade, trg Nikole Pašića 7; tel. (11) 334531; telex 11104; fax (11) 344913; f. 1922; morning; Dir IVAN MRDJEN; Editor-in-Chief GORDANA LOGAR; circ. 46,000.

Newsday: 11001 Belgrade, Obiličev Venac 2, POB 439; f. 1983; Mon.–Fri; published in English by Tanjug and *Privredni Pregled.*

Politika: 11000 Belgrade, Makedonska 29; tel. (11) 321836; telex 11416; fax (11) 633083; f. 1904; morning; non-party; Dir-Gen. ZIVORAD MINOVIĆ; Editor-in-Chief MOMČILO PANTELIĆ; circ. 110,000.

Politika Ekspres: 11000 Belgrade, Makedonska 29; tel. (11) 325630; telex 11852; evening; Editor-in-Chief JEVREM DAMNJAVIĆ; circ. 76,000.

Privredni Pregled: 11000 Belgrade, M. Birjuzova 3; tel. (11) 182888; telex 11509; fax (11) 627591; f. 1950; economics; Dir and Chief Editor DUŠAN DJORDJEVIĆ; circ. 14,000.

Sport: 11000 Belgrade, trg Nikole Pašića 7; tel. (11) 333429; telex 12022; fax (11) 455862; f. 1945; Editor SLAVOLJUB VUKOVIĆ; circ. 100,000.

Večernje novosti: 11000 Belgrade, trg Nikole Pašića 7; tel. (11) 334531; telex 12200; fax (11) 344913; f. 1953; evening; Chief and Executive Editor RADISAV BRAJOVIĆ; circ. 169,000.

Niš

Narodne Novine: 18000 Niš, Vojvode Gojka 14; morning; Chief Editor LJUBIŠA SOKOLOVIĆ (acting); circ. 7,210.

Novi Sad

Dnevnik: 21000 Novi Sad, 23; f. 1942 as *Slobodna Vojvodina*; morning; Editor-in-Chief DRAGAN RADEVIĆ; circ. 61,000. (In December 1993 publication of this newspaper was suspended owing to lack of production materials.)

Magyar Szó: 21000 Novi Sad, V. Mišića 1; f. 1944; morning; in Hungarian; Editor-in-Chief (vacant); circ. 25,590.

Podgorica

Pobjeda: Podgorica, Marka Milanova 7; daily; morning; Editor-in-Chief VIDOJE KONTAR (acting); circ. 17,959.

Priština

Bukju: Priština; Albanian language newspaper; banned by Serbian authorities October 1992; Editor-in-Chief HIDAJET HISENI (acting).

Jedinstvo: 38000 Priština, Srpskih Vladara 41; morning; Editor-in-Chief DRAGAN MALOVIĆ; circ. 2,465.

Rilindja: 38000 Priština, Druga Zejnel Salihi 1; morning; in Albanian; Editor MEHMET EMERLLAHU; circ. 80,000; banned by Serbian authorities, 1990; resumed publication in Switzerland, May 1992.

PERIODICALS

Belgrade

4. Jul.: Belgrade, trg Bratstva i Jedinstva 9/III–IV; weekly; organ of Federation of Veterans of the People's Liberation War of Yugoslavia; Dir and Editor-in-Chief RAJKO PAVIČEVIĆ; circ. 10,000.

Duga: Belgrade; news magazine; Editor-in-Chief ILIJA REPAIĆ.

Ekonomist: Belgrade, Nušićeva 6/III; f. 1948; quarterly; journal of the Yugoslav Association of Economists; Editor Dr HASAN HADŽIOMEROVIĆ.

Ekonomska Politika: 11000 Belgrade, trg Nikole Pašića 7; tel. (11) 335355; telex 11410; f. 1952; weekly; Editor-in-Chief MILOŠ MARKOVIĆ.

Finansije: Belgrade, Jovana Ristića 1; f. 1945; 6 a year; organ of the Federal Ministry of Finance; Editor BOGOLJUB LAZAREVIĆ.

Front: Belgrade, Proleterskih brigada 13; f. 1945; fortnightly; illustrated review; Editor-in-Chief STEVAN KORDA; circ. 263,000.

Ilustrovana Politika: Belgrade, Makedonska 29; tel. (11) 326938; telex 11099; f. 1958; weekly illustrated review; Editor-in-Chief RADE ŠOŠKIĆ; circ. 100,000.

Intervju: Belgrade; news magazine; Editor-in-Chief DRAGAN VLAHOVIĆ; circ. 20,000.

Jež: Belgrade, Nušićeva 6/IV; f. 1935; humorous weekly; Editor RADIVOJE IVANOVIĆ; circ. 50,000.

Književne Novine: Belgrade, Francuska 7; f. 1948; fortnightly; review of literature, arts and social studies; Editor-in-Chief (vacant); circ. 7,500.

Književnost: Belgrade, Čika Ljubina 1; tel. (11) 620130; fax (11) 182581; f. 1946; monthly; literary review; Editor VUK KRNJEVIĆ; circ. 1,800.

Medjunarodna Politika (Review of International Affairs): Belgrade, Nemanjina 34, POB 413; f. 1950 by the Federation of Yugoslav Journalists; fortnightly; published in English, French, Russian, German, Spanish and Serbo-Croat; Dir and Editor-in-Chief Dr RANKO PETKOVIĆ.

Medjunarodni Problemi: Belgrade, Makedonska 25; tel. (11) 321433; fax (11) 324013; f. 1949; quarterly; review of the Institute of International Politics and Economics; Editor B. MARKOVIĆ; circ. 1,000.

NIN (Nedeljne informativne novine): Belgrade, Cetinjska 1, POB 208; tel. (11) 324410; telex 12000; fax (11) 633368; f. 1935; weekly; Editor-in-Chief MILO GLIGORIJEVIĆ; circ. 35,000.

Official Gazette of the Federal Republic of Yugoslavia: 11000 Belgrade, Jovana Ristića 1; f. 1945; editions in Serbo-Croat, Slovene, Albanian, Hungarian and Macedonian; Dir VELJKO TADIĆ; circ. 73,000.

Politikin Zabavnik: Belgrade, Makedonska 29; f. 1939; weekly; comic; Editor RADOMIR ŠOŠKIĆ; circ. 41,000.

Pravoslavlje: 11000 Belgrade, 7 Jula 5; tel. (11) 635699; fax (11) 630865; fortnightly; religious; published by the Serbian Orthodox Church; Editor Dr SLOBODAN MILEUSNIĆ; circ. 22,500.

Rad: Belgrade, trg Nikole Pašića 5; tel. (11) 330927; telex 11121; weekly; organ of the Confederation of Trade Unions; Dir RADOSLAV ROSO; Editor-in-Chief STANISLAV MARINKOVIĆ; circ. 70,000.

Tehničke novine: 11000 Belgrade, Vojvode Stepe 89; tel. (11) 468596; fax (11) 473442; monthly; technical; Chief Editor SAŠA IMPERL; circ. 70,000.

Vojska: Belgrade, Proleterskih brig. 13; f. 1945; weekly; Yugoslav Army organ; Dir MILAN KAVGIĆ; Editor-in-Chief GAJA PETROVIĆ.

Yugoslav Law (1975–): Belgrade, Terazije 41; tel. (11) 333213; fax (11) 329; 3 a year in English and French; publ. by the Institute of Comparative Law and the Union of Jurists' Assen; Editor Dr VLADIMIR JOVANOVIĆ.

Yugoslav Survey: Belgrade, Moše Pijade 8/1, POB 677; tel. (11) 333610; fax (11) 332295; f. 1960; quarterly; general reference publication of basic documentary information about Yugoslavia in English; Editor-in-Chief IKA BOROVNJAK (acting); circ. 3,000.

Niš

Bratstvo: Niš; Bulgarian-language magazine; Dir VENKO DIMITROV.

Novi Sad

Letopis Matice Srpske: Novi Sad, Matice srpske 1; f. 1825; monthly; literary review; Editor BOŠKO IVKOV.

Podgorica

Koha (Time): Podgorica; f. 1978; Albanian-language magazine; circ. 2,000 (estimated).

Stvaranje: Podgorica, Revolucije 11; f. 1946; monthly; literary review; publ. by the Literary Assen of Montenegro; Man. SRETEN ASANOVIĆ.

Priština

Koha (Time): Priština; f. 1994; Albanian-language magazine; Editor-in-Chief VETON SUROI.

Zeri: Priština; political weekly; Albanian; Editor-in-Chief BLERIM SHALA.

NEWS AGENCY

Novinska Agencija Tanjug: 11001 Belgrade, Obilićev Venac 2, POB 439; tel. (11) 332230; telex 11220; f. 1943; 90 correspondents in Yugoslavia and 50 offices abroad; press and information agency governed by self-management; news service for Yugoslavia press, radio and television; news and features service for abroad in English, French, Spanish, Russian and German; also features service in Arabic; photo and telephoto service; economic and financial services for home and abroad; publishes EITI, service for trade, industry and banking in Serbo-Croat, English, French, German and Spanish; computerized commodity service for Yugoslav businesses and banks; Dir DUŠAN RADOVANOVIĆ; Editor-in-Chief DUŠAN ZUPAN.

Foreign Bureaux

Agence France-Presse (AFP) (France): 11000 Belgrade, trg Marksa i Engelsa 2; tel. (11) 332622; telex 11262; fax (11) 620638; Correspondent NICOLAS MILETITCH.

Agenzia Nazionale Stampa Associata (ANSA) (Italy): 11000 Belgrade, Braće Jugovića 5; tel. (11) 620221; telex 11680; Bureau Chief ALBERTO PIAZZA.

Allgemeiner Deutscher Nachrichtendienst (ADN) (Germany): 11000 Belgrade, Šiva Stena 1A; tel. (11) 461752; telex 11338; Correspondent Dr WILLFRIED MUCH.

Associated Press (AP) (USA): 11000 Belgrade, Dositejeva 12; tel. (11) 631553; telex 11264; Correspondent IVAN STEFANOVIĆ.

Bulgarska Telegrafna Agentsia (BTA) (Bulgaria): Belgrade, Gospodar Jevremova 41; tel. (11) 636361; telex 11114; fax (11) 636361; Correspondent NIKOLA KITSEVSKI.

Česká tisková kancelář (ČTK) (Czech Republic): 11070 Belgrade, 190/Stan. 6/III, Blok 37; tel. (11) 134892; telex 11657; Correspondent MIROSLAV JILEK.

Informatsionnoye Telegrafnoye Agentstvo Rossii—Telegrafnoye Agentstvo Suverennykh Stran (ITAR—TASS) (Russia): 11000 Belgrade, Ognjena Price 17; tel. (11) 4446928; Correspondent MIKHAIL ABELEV.

Korean Central News Agency (KCNA) (Democratic People's Republic of Korea): Belgrade, Dr Milutina Ivkovića 9; tel. (11) 668426; telex 11577; Bureau Chief KIM ZONG SE.

Magyar Távirati Iroda (MTI) (Hungary): 11030 Belgrade, Vladimira Rolovica 176; tel. (11) 506508; telex 11783; Correspondent GYÖRGY WALKO.

Rossiyskoye Informatsionnoye Agentstvo—Novosti (RIA—Novosti) (Russia): Belgrade, Strahinjića Bana 50; tel. (11) 629419; Bureau Chief SERGEY GRIZUNOV.

United Press International (UPI) (USA): 11000 Belgrade, Generala Zdanova 19; tel. (11) 342490; telex 11250; Correspondent NESHO DJURIĆ.

Xinhua (New China) News Agency (People's Republic of China): Belgrade, Bože Jankovica 23; tel. (11) 493789; telex 11375; Correspondent YANG DAZHOU.

PRESS ASSOCIATIONS

Independent Association of Journalists of Serbia: Belgrade; f. 1994; Pres. DRAGAN NIKITOVIĆ.

Savez Novinara Jugoslavije (Federation of Yugoslav Journalists): Belgrade, trg Republike 5/III; tel. (11) 624993; f. 1945; 11,500 mems; Pres. MILISAV MILIĆ.

Yugoslav Newspaper Publishers' Association: Belgrade; Dir RASTKO GUZINA.

There is also an **Association of Professional Journalists of Montenegro.**

Publishers

BIGZ—Beogradski izdavačko-grafički zavod: 11000 Belgrade, vojvode Mišića 17; tel. (11) 651666; telex 11855; fax (11) 651841; f. 1831; literature and criticism, children's books, pocket books, popular science, philosophy, politics; Gen. Dir ILIJA RAPAIĆ.

Dečje novine: 32300 Gornji Milanovac, T. Matijevića 4; tel. (32) 711195; telex 13731; fax (32) 711248; general literature, children's books, science, science fiction, textbooks; Gen. Dir MIROSLAV PETROVIĆ.

Forum: Novinsko-izdavačka i štamparska radna organizacija, 21000 Novi Sad, Vojvode Mišića 1, POB 200; tel. (21) 611300; telex 14199; f. 1957; newspapers, periodicals and books in Hungarian; Dir MIKLOS MAROTI.

Gradjevinska Knjiga: 11000 Belgrade, trg Nikole Pašića 8/II; tel. (11) 333565; fax (11) 333565; f. 1948; technical, scientific and educational textbooks; Dir MILAN VIŠNJIĆ.

IP Matice srpske: 21000 Novi Sad, trg Heroja Toze Markovića 2; tel. (21) 615599; Yugoslav and foreign fiction and humanities; Dir DRAGOLJUB GAVARIĆ.

Jedinstvo: 38000 Priština, Dom štampe bb, POB 81; tel. (38) 27549; telex 18285; fax (38) 29809; poetry, novels, general literature, science, children's books; Dir JORDAN RISTIĆ.

Jugoslovenska knjiga: 11000 Belgrade, trg Republike 5/VIII, POB 36; tel. (11) 621992; telex 12466; fax (11) 625970; art and culture; Dir ŽIVORAD JAKOVLJEVIĆ.

Medicinska knjiga: 11001 Belgrade, Mata Vidakovića 24–26; tel. (11) 458165; f. 1947; medicine, pharmacology, stomatology, veterinary; Dir MILE MEDIĆ.

Minerva: Izdavačko-štamparsko preduzeće, 24000 Subotica, trg 29 novembra 3; tel. (24) 25712; fax (24) 23208; novels and general; Dir LADISLAV ŠEBEK.

Narodna knjiga: 11000 Belgrade, Šafarikova 11; tel. (11) 328610; f. 1950; economics, scientific and popular literature, reference books, dictionaries; Dir NEDELIKO DRČELIĆ.

Naučna knjiga: 11000 Belgrade, Uzun Mirkova 5; tel. (11) 637220; f. 1947; school, college and university textbooks, publications of scientific bodies; Dir Dr BLAŽO PEROVIĆ.

Nolit: 11000 Belgrade, Terazije 27/II; tel. (11) 345017; fax (11) 627285; f. 1929; Yugoslav and other belles-lettres, philosophy and fine art; scientific and popular literature; Dir-Gen. RADIVOJE NESIĆ; Editor-in-Chief MILOŠ STAMBOLIĆ.

Obod: 81250 Cetinje, Njegoševa 3; tel. (86) 21331; fax (86) 21953; general literature; Dir VLADIMIR MIRKOVIĆ.

Pobjeda: 81000 Podgorica, Južni bul. bb; tel. (81) 44433; f. 1974; poetry, fiction, lexicography and scientific works.

Proex: 11000 Belgrade, Terazije 16; tel. (11) 688563; fax (11) 641052; editorial and typographic co-productions; export and import of books and periodicals.

Prosveta: 11000 Belgrade, Čika Ljubina 1/I; tel. (11) 629843; fax (11) 182581; f. 1944; general literature, art books, dictionaries, encyclopaedias, science, music; Dir BUDIMIR RUDOVIĆ.

Rad: 11000 Belgrade, M. Pijade 12; tel. (11) 339998; f. 1949; labour and labour relations, politics and economics, sociology, psychology, literature, biographies, science fiction; Man. Dir VESNA ALEKSIĆ; Editor-in-Chief DRAGAN LAKIĆEVIĆ.

Rilindja: 38000 Priština, Dom štampe; tel. (38) 23868; telex 18163; popular science, literature, children's fiction and travel books, textbooks in Albanian; Dir NAZMI RRAHMANI.

Savremena administracija: 11000 Belgrade, Crnotravska 7–9; tel. (11) 663824; telex 11233; fax (11) 667277; f. 1954; economy, law, science university textbooks; Dir MILUTIN SRDIĆ.

Sportska knjiga: 11000 Belgrade, Makedonska 19; tel. (11) 320226; f. 1949; sport, chess, hobbies; Dir BORISLAV PETROVIĆ.

Srpska književna zadruga: 11000 Belgrade, Srpskih Vladara 19/I; tel. (11) 330305; fax (11) 626224; f. 1892; works of classical and modern Yugoslav writers, and translations of works of foreign writers; Pres. RADOVAN SAMARDŽIĆ; Editor RADOVAN RADOVANAC.

Svetovi: 21000 Novi Sad, Arse Teodorovića 11; tel. (21) 28036; general; Dir JOVAN ZIVLAK.

Tehnička Knjiga: 11000 Belgrade, Vojvode Stepe 89; tel. (11) 468596; fax (11) 473442; f. 1948; technical works, popular science, reference books, 'how to' books, hobbies; Dir RADIVOJE GRBOVIĆ.

Vuk Karadžič: 11000 Belgrade, Kraljevića Marka 9, POB 762; tel. (11) 628066; fax (11) 623150; scientific literature, popular science, children's books, general; Gen. Man. VOJIN ANČIĆ.

Zavod za udžbenike i nastavna sredstva: 11000 Belgrade, Obilićev Venac 5; tel. (11) 638463; fax (11) 630014; f. 1958; textbooks and teaching aids; Dir TOMISLAV BOGAVAC.

PUBLISHERS' ASSOCIATION

Udruženje izdavača i knjižara Jugoslavije (Association of Yugoslav Publishers and Booksellers): 11000 Belgrade, Kneza Miloša 25, POB 883; tel. (11) 642533; fax (11) 646339; f. 1954; organizes Belgrade International Book Fair; Dir OGNJEN LAKIĆEVIĆ; 101 mem. organizations.

Radio and Television

Jugoslovenska Radiotelevizija (JRT) (Association of Yugoslav Radio and Television Organizations): 11000 Belgrade, Generala Ždanova 28; tel. (11) 330194; telex 12158; fax (11) 434023; f. 1952; Exec. Dir ALEKSANDAR TODOROVIĆ.

Radio Jugoslavija: 11000 Belgrade, Hilandarska 2/IV, POB 200; tel. (11) 346884; telex 12432; fax (11) 332014; f. 1951; foreign service; broadcasts in Serbo-Croat, Arabic, English, French, German, Russian and Spanish; Dir Dr DRAGAN MARKOVIĆ.

Radiotelevizija Crne Gore: 81000 Podgorica, Cetinjski put bb; tel. (81) 41800; telex 61133; fax (81) 43640; f. 1944 (Radio), 1971

(Television); 2 radio and 2 television programmes; broadcasts in Serbo-Croat; Dir-Gen. (vacant); Dir of Radio ZORAN JOCOVIĆ; Dir of Television MILUTIN RADULOVIĆ (acting).

Radiotelevizija Srbije (RTS): 11000 Belgrade, Takovska 10; tel. (11) 342001; telex 11884; fax (11) 543178; f. 1992; Dir-Gen. MILORAD VUČELIĆ; comprises:

Radiotelevizija Beograd: 11000 Belgrade, Hilandarska 2; tel. (11) 346801; telex 11727; fax (11) 326768 (Radio); 11000 Belgrade, Takovska 10; tel. (11) 342001; telex 11884; fax (11) 543178 (Television); f. 1929 (Radio), 1958 (Television); 5 radio programmes, plus 1 experimental, and 3 television programmes in Serbo-Croat; Dir-Gen. DOBROSAV BJELETIĆ; Dir of Radio DRAGOSLAV NIKITOVIĆ (acting); Dir of Television SLOBODAN IGNJATOVIĆ.

Radiotelevizija Novi Sad: 21000 Novi Sad, Žarka Zrenjanina 3; tel. (21) 611588; telex 14127; fax (21) 26624 (Radio); 21000 Novi Sad, Kamenički put 45; tel. (21) 56855; telex 14303; fax (21) 52079 (Television); f. 1949 (Radio), 1975 (Television); 7 radio and 2 television programmes; broadcasts in Serbo-Croat, Slovak, Romanian, Hungarian and Ruthenian; Dir-Gen. MILAN TODOROV; Dir of Radio MIROSLAV BONDZIĆ; Dir of Television PETAR LJUBOJEV.

Radiotelevizija Priština: 38000 Priština, Srpskih Vladara bb; tel. (38) 26255; telex 18134; fax (38) 25355 (Radio); 38000 Priština, Zejnel Ajdini 12; tel. (38) 31211; telex 18186; fax (38) 32073 (Television); f. 1944 (Radio), 1975 (Television); 3 radio and 1 television programme; broadcasts in Albanian, Serbo-Croat, Romany and Turkish; Dir-Gen. PETAR JAKŠIĆ; Dir of Radio MILORAD VUJOVIĆ; Dir of Television NIKOLA SARIĆ.

B92: Belgrade; f. 1989; independent radio station; aims to oppose war 'with humour and creativity'; Editor-in-Chief SASHA VUČINIĆ.

Finance

(cap. = capital; res = reserves; dep. = deposits; m. = million; amounts in convertible Yugoslav dinars unless otherwise stated; br. = branch)

BANKING

Central Banking System

The National Bank of Yugoslavia is the country's central bank, its powers and obligations being determined by law. Its functions include the issue of money, provision of credit to banks and government authorities, control of credits and bank activities, recommendation of legislation relating to the activities, recommendation of legislation relating to the foreign exchange system and its implementation, management of gold and foreign exchange reserves, control of foreign exchange operations and other special activities.

Narodna banka Jugoslavije (National Bank of Yugoslavia): 11000 Belgrade, revolucije 15, POB 1010; tel. (11) 332001; telex 72000; f. 1883 as Banque Nationale Privilégiée du Royaume du Serbie; in 1920, name changed to Banque Nationale du Royaume des Serbes, Croates et Slovenes and in 1929 to Banque Nationale du Royaume de Yougoslavie; in 1946 name changed to Banque Nationale de la République Fédérative Populaire de Yougoslavie; received its present name 1963; Gov. DRAGOSLAV AVRAMOVIĆ.

National Bank of Montenegro: 81000 Podgorica, Blaža Jovanovića 7; tel. (81) 43381; Gov. KRUNISLAV VUKČEVIĆ.

National Bank of Serbia: 11000 Belgrade, 7 jula 12; tel. (11) 625555; Gov. BORISLAV ATANACKOVIĆ.

Bank for International Economic Co-operation

Jugoslovenska Banka Za Medjunarodnu Ekonomsku Saradnju—JUBMES (Yugoslav Bank for International Economic Co-operation): Head Office: 11070 Belgrade, AVNOJ-a 121, POB 219; tel. (11) 143004; telex 11710; fax (11) 131457; f. 1979; replaced the Export Credit and Insurance Fund and assumed the assets and liabilities of the Fund; established by a special Law; grants export credits; underwrites insurance of exports against non-commercial risks, etc.; total assets 2,556,604m. old dinars (1988); Pres. IVAN STAMBOLIĆ; Deputy Pres. MOMČILO PEJIĆ.

Other Banks

Beogradska Banka d.d., Beograd: 11001 Belgrade, POB 955, Knez Mihajlova 2–4; tel. (11) 624455; telex 11712; fax (11) 633128; f. 1978; cap. 28,077m., res 5,249m., dep. 206,168m. (Dec. 1991); Pres. LJUBISA IGIĆ.

Glavna filijala Beobanka, Beograd: 11000 Belgrade, Zeleni Venac 16; tel. (11) 629455; telex 11802; f. 1978; main br. within Beogradska Banka d.d., Belgrade; total assets 60,597.1m. (Sept. 1989); Man. Dir and Chief Exec. PETAR VASILJEVIĆ (acting).

Glavna filijala Investbanka, Beograd: 11000 Belgrade, Terazije 7–9; tel. (11) 335201; telex 11147; f. 1862; main br. within Beogradska Banka d.d., Belgrade; total assets 83,499,532 (Sept. 1989); Man. Dir and Chief Exec. Dr STOJAN DABIĆ (acting).

Investicion a Banka Podgorica: 81000 Podgorica, Revolucije 1; tel. (81) 42922; telex 61118; f. 1966; total assets 1,606,826m. old dinars (Dec. 1987); in process of reorganization.

Jugobanka d.d., Beograd: 11000 Belgrade, POB 400, 7 Jula 19–21; tel. (11) 630022; telex 71004; fax (11) 635085; f. 1955 as Yugoslav Bank for Foreign Trade; name changed 1971; cap. 10,912m., res 1,781m., dep. 68,256m. (Dec. 1991); Chair. MILOŠ MILOSAVLJEVIĆ.

Jugobanka d.d., Beograd, Jugobanka Beograd: 11000 Belgrade, Srpskih Vladara 11; tel. (11) 334931; telex 11280; f. 1956; total assets 4,019,740m. old dinars (Dec. 1988); Gen. Man. LJUBOMIR POTKONJAK.

Jugobanka d.d., Beograd, Jugobanka k.b. Beograd: 11000 Belgrade, Radivoja Koraća 6; tel. (11) 455666; telex 12133; fax (11) 458396; f. 1970 as br. of Sremska banka, joined Jugobanka 1977; total assets 3,500m. (March 1991); Gen. Man. LJUBOMIR POTKONJAK.

Jugoslovenska izvozna i kreditna banka d.d. (Yugoslav Export & Credit Bank Inc.): 11000 Belgrade, Knez Mihailova 42, POB 234; tel. (11) 632822; telex 12906; fax (11) 183198; f. 1946; cap. and res 16,151m., dep. 182,580m. (Dec. 1992); Pres. MIODRAG PRICA.

Montex Bank: 11000 Belgrade, Kneza Miloša 61; tel. (11) 646797; telex 72080; fax (11) 659995; f. 1991; cap. 176,414.1m., res 1,213.8m., dep. 807,591.7m. (Dec. 1991); Pres. ILIJA ČULJKOVIĆ.

Kosovo

Udružena Kosovska Banka (Kosovo Associated Bank): 38000 Priština, Srpskih Vladara 4; tel. (38) 34111; telex 18149; cap. 316,474.8m., res 112,184.5m., dep. 6,300,309.9m. old dinars (Dec. 1988); Pres. MUHAREM ISMAILJI.

Vojvodina

Privredna Banka d.d., Novi Sad: 21001 Novi Sad, POB 302, Grčkoškolska 2; tel. (21) 412277; telex 15457; fax (21) 623025; f. 1956; cap. 440.1m., res 2.6m., dep. 3,557m. (Dec. 1990); Gen. Man. GOJKO BJELICA.

Vojvodjanska Banka, d.d.: 21001 Novi Sad, POB 391, Srpskih Vladara 14; tel. (21) 57222; telex 14129; fax (21) 624940; f. 1978; res 8,995.6m., dep. 51,807m. (Dec. 1991); Gen. Dir ŽIVOTA MIHAJLOVIĆ.

Banking Association

Udruženje banaka Jugoslavije (Association of Yugoslav Banks): 11001 Belgrade, Masarikova 5/IX; tel. (11) 684797; telex 11767; fax (11) 684947; f. 1955; association of Yugoslav business banks; works on improving inter-bank co-operation, organizes agreements of mutual interest for banks, gives expert assistance, establishes co-operation with foreign banks, other financial institutions and their associations, represents banks in relations with the Yugoslav Government and the National Bank of Yugoslavia; Pres. DJORDJE ZARIĆ; Sec.-Gen. MILOVAN MILUTINOVIĆ.

STOCK EXCHANGE

Belgrade Stock Exchange: Belgrade; f. 1886, ceased operation 1941, reopened 1990.

INSURANCE

'DUNAV' Deoničko Društvo za Osiguranje (Dunav Insurance Company): 11001 Belgrade, Makedonska 4, POB 624; tel. (11) 324001; telex 11359; fax (11) 624652; f. 1974; all types of insurance.

Trade and Industry

CHAMBERS OF ECONOMY

Privredna Komora Jugoslavije (Yugoslav Chamber of Economy): 11000 Belgrade, Terazije 23, POB 1003; tel. (11) 339461; telex 11638; fax (11) 631928; independent organization affiliating all Yugoslav economic organizations; promotes economic and commercial relations with foreign countries.

Chamber of Economy of Montenegro: 81000 Podgorica, Novaka Miloševa 29/II; tel. (81) 31071; fax (81) 34926.

Chamber of Economy of Serbia: 11000 Belgrade, Gen. Zdanova 13–15; tel. (11) 340611; fax (11) 330949; Pres. Dr VLAJKO STOJILJOVIĆ.

The **Yugoslav Chamber of Commerce** was established in December 1990.

FOREIGN TRADE INSTITUTE

Institut za Spoljnu Trgovinu: 11000 Belgrade, Moše Pijade 8; tel. (11) 339041; telex 12214; Dir Dr SLOBODAN MRKŠA.

MAJOR ENTERPRISES AND COMPANIES

Agrooprema: 11000 Belgrade, Balkanska 44; tel. (11) 658655; telex 11124; fax (11) 684842; manufacture of agricultural machinery, vehicles and chemicals, etc.; 1,100 employees.

Agrovojvodina: 21000 Novi Sad, M. 17 Tita 6 VI; tel. (21) 21661; telex 14150; fax (21) 52068; wholesale and retail trade of agricultural machinery, construction equipment, chemicals, tools, etc.; Dir of Trade PETKO SEKULIĆ; 5,500 employees.

Beko: 11000 Belgrade, Donjogradski 6–8; tel. (11) 620122; telex 11403; fax (11) 620847; produces and exports clothing; Gen. Man. TOMAS ZUGIĆ; 5,058 employees.

Beocinaska Fabrika Cementa: 21300 Beocin, trg Ive Lole Ribara 1; tel. (21) 870030; telex 14161; f. 1839; cement manufacturer.

BIP—Unified Beer, Malt and Soft Drinks Industry: 11000 Belgrade, Bulevar Vojvode Putnika 5; tel. (11) 652322; telex 11880; brewing and soft drinks manufacture; 2,600 employees.

Centroprom: 11000 Belgrade, Knez Mihailova 20; tel. (11) 622730; telex 11971; fax (11) 624630; wholesale and retail trading; 7,322 employees.

Centrotextil: 11000 Belgrade, Knez Mihailova 1–3; tel. (11) 185333; telex 11150; fax (11) 630565; design, manufacture and sale of textiles, clothing, leather goods and footwear; 2,600 employees.

DMB—Dvadesetprvi Maj: 11090 Rakovica, Oslobodenja 1; tel. (11) 592111; telex 72718; fax (11) 593967; production of engines, transmissions and equipment; Dir-Gen. ALEKSANDAR LAKOVIĆ; 5,500 employees.

Fabrika Vagona-Kraljevo (FVK): 36000 Kraljevo, Industriska 27; tel. (36) 333455; telex 17625; fax (36) 339919; manufactures all types of freight wagons, tanks for transport of acids, etc; Gen. Dir TOMISLAV SIMOVIĆ; 3,100 employees.

F-KA Pumpi Jastrebac, Niš: 18000 Niš, 12 februara br. 82; tel. (18) 42047; telex 16237; fax (18) 42362; manufacture of pumps for all types of liquids and operations; Gen. Dir DRAGOSLAV MILUTINOVIĆ; 1,700 employees.

Galenika-Oour—Galenika Farmaceutsko-Hemijska Industrija: 11080 Zemun, Batajnicki Drum bb; tel. (11) 190810; telex 11289; fax (11) 199424; pharmaceutical and chemical production; 6,000 employees.

Genex—Generalexport: 11070 Belgrade, Narodnih Heroja br. 43; tel. (11) 696992; telex 11228; fax (11) 609228; general trading internationally and in the execution of export-import business on a large scale; Gen. Dir MILORAD SAVICEVIĆ; 5,228 employees.

Goša Holding Corporation: 11420 Smederevska Palanka, Industrijska 70; tel. (26) 31253; telex 11684; fax (26) 31472; f. 1923; state-owned company; design, production and assembly of vehicles, engineering, power-generating and agricultural equipment; 13,000 employees.

Goša-Commerce: 11000 Belgrade, Kolarceva 8; tel. (11) 628337; telex 11568; fax (11) 650773; Pres. MOMIR PAVLICEVIĆ; 8,500 employees.

Hemijska Industrija, Pancevo (Pancevo Chemical Industry): 26000 Pancevo, Spoljnostarcevacka 80; tel. (13) 44122; telex 13124; engaged in the production of petrochemicals, inorganic chemicals, fine and special chemicals, etc.; 11,700 employees.

IHP Prahovo: 19330 Prahovo; tel. (19) 512551; telex 19138; fax (19) 513885; production of mineral fertilizers; Gen. Dir RADOMIR SLADOJEVIĆ; 3,400 employees.

Industriaimpex: 81000 Podgorica, Marka Miljanova 17; tel. (81) 32811; telex 61132; fax (81) 22152; foreign trading co; 350 employees.

Industriaimport: 81000 Podgorica, Vuka Karadžića 41; tel. (81) 31322; telex 61138; import-export trading; 3,500 employees.

Industrija Masina i Traktora—IMT: 11000 Belgrade, Novi Beograd, Tosin Bunar 268; tel. (11) 150747; telex 11518; manufacture of agricultural machinery; 13,500 employees.

Industrija Stakla, Pancevo: 26000 Pancevo, Prvomajska 10; tel. (13) 47255; telex 13266; fax (13) 47993; production of flat glass; Gen. Man. Dr VIDOMIR J. PAREŽANIN; 2,400 employees.

Industrija Kablova Svetozarevo Yugoslavia (Cables Manufacturing Industry of Svetozarevo): 35000 Svetozarevo; tel. (35) 221102; telex 17845; fax (35) 231446; Yugoslavia's largest cables manufacturer; 9,038 employees.

Industrija Kotrljajucih Lezaja—IKL: 11000 Belgrade, Kneza Danila 23–25; tel. (11) 331472; telex 12105; fax (11) 339417; manufacture of ball bearings; 2,400 employees.

Inex: 11000 Belgrade, Marta 69 27: tel. (11) 621149; telex 72963; import and export, manufacturing, tourism and transportation.

Istra—Fabrika Armatura Istra Deonicarsko Drustvo: 25230 Kula, Ise Sekičkog 30; tel. (25) 722122; telex 15346; fax (25) 722173; manufactures sanitary fittings; Gen. Dir ROMODA DJORDJE; 1,500 employees.

Ites Lola Ribar: 25250 Odžaci, POB 5, Lola Ribar 40; tel. (25) 742113; telex 15336; fax (25) 742419; manufactures hemp yarn, twines, cordage and polypropylene products; Gen. Man. METODIJE KOSTIĆ; 1,500 employees.

Ivo Lola Ribar: 11000 Belgrade, Revolucije 84; tel. (11) 4440884; telex 72788; fax (11) 431494; designs and manufactures drilling and milling machinery, industrial cranes and computers, etc; Gen. Dir STANOJE KONSTANTINOVIĆ; 9,500 employees.

Jadran: 85336 Boka Kotorska, Obala Marka, Martinovića bb Perast; tel. (82) 25003; telex 61392; fax (82) 14799; manufactures heavy garments; Gen. Dir VLADIMIR POCANIĆ; 700 employees.

Jugodent: 21000 Novi Sad, Futoski put 10; tel. (21) 394566; telex 14423; fax (21) 396365; produces dental equipment; Gen. Dir BRANKO ZMUKIĆ; 930 employees.

Jugopetrol: 11070 Belgrade, Milentija Popovića 66; tel. (11) 2223311; telex 12311; sale and distribution of petroleum derivatives.

Kolor Konfekcija Drustveno Preduzeće Konfekcija Kolor: 31230 Arile, Svetolika Lazarevića 22; tel. (31) 892461; telex 13665; fax (31) 891970; manufactures and exports clothing; Gen. Man. SLAVKO PAVLOVIĆ; 1,100 employees.

Kombinat Aluminijuma, Podgorica: 81000 Podgorica, POB 22; tel. (81) 53011; telex 61114; metal processing; 4,948 employees.

Komgrap—DP Komgrap Gradevinski Kombinat: 11000 Belgrade, Terazije 4; tel. (11) 688155; telex 118185; 7,858 employees.

Krusik Metalopreradjivacka Industrija: 14000 Valjevo, Beogradski put bb; tel. (14) 23121; telex 10232; manufactures textile machinery; 16,000 employees.

Lece: 16240 Medvedja, B. Stojanovića br. 1; tel. (16) 84020; telex 19745; fax (16) 84047; Gen. Dir RADOVAN MILLIOEVIĆ.

Leskoteks: 16000 Leskovac, AVNOJ-a 95; tel. (16) 43042; telex 19648; fax (16) 53364; manufacture of woollen fabrics and garments; Gen. Dir JELICA KOCIĆ; 9,550 employees.

Metallurgical and Metalworking Corporation (MMK): Nikšić; tel. (83) 41422; telex 61120; fax (83) 44750; manufacture of crude steel, steel castings, etc.; Pres. ZARKO MIJUSKOVIĆ; 6,500 employees.

Metalservis: 11000 Belgrade, POB 337, Karadjordjeva 65; tel. (11) 186333; telex 11546; fax (11) 626325; supplies tools, machines and equipment, building materials, electrical meterials, chemical products; Gen. Dir MILOVAN MILOŠEVIĆ; 1,140 employees.

Metalurski Kombinat Smederevo: 11300 Smederevo, Goranska 12; tel. (26) 23413; telex 11621; production of iron and steel; 10,300 employees.

Metalursko Metalski Kombinat, Nikšić: 81400 Nikšić; tel. (83) 31422; telex 61120; metallurgy and foreign work, processing and provision of related services.

Milan Blagojević: 32240 Lucani, Radnicka bb; tel. (32) 817100; telex 13715; fax (32) 818916; f. 1948 as manufacturer of defence products, has developed a chemical industry with a wide product assortment; Gen. Dir MILIJA JANKOVIĆ; 3,700 employees.

Miloje Zakić: 37000 Krusevac, Srpskih Vladara bb; tel. (37) 22328; telex 17454; fax (37) 23517; rubber processing, manufacture of industrial explosives and production of environmental protection equipment; 7,000 employees.

Minel: 11000 Belgrade, Cara Lazara br. 3; tel. (11) 181181; telex 11643; fax (11) 623566; produces thermal power equipment, electrical power equipment and food-processing facilities; Pres. MILOSAV FILIPOVIĆ; 13,000 employees.

Naftagas-Hip-Jugopetrol: 21000 Novi Sad, Sutjeska 1; tel. (21) 615144; telex 14196; f. 1990 by merger of 42 social enterprises, previously affiliated to 3 composite orgs of associated labour; petroleum and natural gas exploration and production in Yugoslavia and abroad; refines crude petroleum and natural gas, producing a variety of petroleum derivatives and associated products, incl. mineral fertilizers and synthetic rubber; also operates petrochemical and chemical plants; 36,000 employees.

Naftagas Promet: Novi Sad, 23 Oktobra 27; tel. (21) 29682; telex 14130; fax (21) 614692; wholesale and retail distribution of petroleum products; Gen. Man. MLADEN MARKOVIĆ; 2,956 employees.

Pik-Bicej: 21220 Becej, Mose Pijade 2; tel. (21) 811180; fax (21) 812049; telex 14101; agricultural production, being one of Yugoslavia's largest producers of milk and meat; 4,500 employees.

PKB-Belgrade Agricultural Combine: Belgrade, 11213 Padinska Skela; tel. (11) 769181; telex 11457; fax (11) 754426; agricultural production, industrial production, catering and tourism; 36,000 employees.

Proleter: 23000 Zrenjanin, Temisvarski drum bb; tel. (23) 44210; telex 15518; fax (23) 49138; produces machine-woven carpets, machine-tufted carpets and yarn; Gen. Dir JOKO IVANCEVIĆ; 1,500 employees.

Prvi Maj: 18300 Pirot; tel. (10) 32255; telex 16810; fax (10) 35116; produces clothing and knitwear; Gen. Man. HRISTIVOJE KOSTIĆ; 6,000 employees.

Ratko Mitrović: 11000 Belgrade, Koste Glavinića 8; tel. (11) 650522; telex 11649; fax (11) 650356; design, construction, civil engineering and manufacture of building materials; 7,000 employees.

Reik Kolubara: 14220 Lazarevac, Slobonana Kozareva bb; tel. (11) 810226; telex 12840; mining of lignite coal (estimated production of 33m. metric tons in 1992); 15,500 employees.

Rudarsko Topionicarski Basen, Bor: 19210 Bor, Srpskih Vladara 29; tel. (30) 230252; telex 19204; fax (30) 34462; extraction and processing of copper, precious metals and minerals; manufacture of chemicals and provision of engineering services; 24,000 employees.

Rudnici Boksita Nikšić Oour Prerada (Nikšić Bauxite Mines): 81000 Nikšić, var 13 Jula 30; tel. (83) 24122; telex 61216; non-ferrous metallurgy; 1,600 employees.

Rudnik Olova i Činka, Mojkovac: 84205 Mojkovac, Vojvode Scepanovića bb; tel. (84) 72137; telex 61351; manufacture of lead, zinc and pyrites concentrates; Gen. Dir MILIJA ZEJAK.

Servo Mihalj IPK: 23000 Zrenjanin, Petra Drapšina 1; tel. (23) 44410; telex 15511; primary agricultural production, food processing, chemicals and services; 21,893 employees.

Simpo: 17500 Vranje, Radnicka 6; tel. (17) 22280; telex 16766; fax (17) 24136; manufacturer and exporter of furniture, mattresses and decorative upholstery fabrics; Gen. Man. DRAGAN TOMIĆ; 5,000 employees.

Sintelon: 21400 Backa Palanka, Salas 1; tel. (21) 742012; telex 14122; fax (21) 742677; manufacture of PVC floor coverings and machine-woven carpets; 2,330 employees.

Sirmium: 22000 Sremska Mitrovića, trg Brace Radica 4; tel. (22) 221122; telex 15721; primary agriculture, food processing, trade, catering and tourism services; 21,000 employees.

Sloboda: 25230 Kula, Josipa Kramera 27; tel. (25) 722444; telex 15360; fax (25) 723620; produces textiles; Gen. Dir BORISA CALASAN; 1,100 employees.

Sport—Jugoslovenski Kombinat 'Sport': 11060 Belgrade, Visnijicka 84; tel. (11) 771333; telex 11850; fax (11) 782882; produces and sells sporting goods; Gen. Man. DRAGAN VOSTINIĆ; 1,950 employees.

Srbocoop: 11000 Belgrade, Sredacka 2A; tel. (11) 431657; telex 11702; meat processing; 1,200 employees.

Tamis: 26000 Pancevo, POB 116, trg Borisa Kidrića 6; tel. (13) 44999; telex 13113; primary agriculture and food processing; 13,000 employees.

Valjaonića Bakra i Aluminijuma 'Slobodan Penezić' (Krcun—Copper and Aluminium Rolling Mill): 31205 Sevojno; tel. (31) 21015; telex 13611; processing metal into products; 7,870 employees.

Veljko Vlahović: 85343 Bijela; tel. (82) 81122; telex 61179; fax (82) 82303; shipyard, providing building and repair services for vessels of various sizes; Gen. Dir ILIC VASILIJE; 1,100 employees.

Viskoza Loznića: 15300 Loznića, Gradiliste bb; tel. (15) 82411; telex 101718; fax (15) 82047; production and processing of viscose fibres and foils; Pres. PAVLE DJOKIĆ; 10,386 employees.

Vojvodina: 22000 Sremska Mitrovića, Parobrodska 2/I; tel. (22) 222284; telex 15701; forestry, processing of timber; manufacture of furniture, cellulose, paper; foreign trade; 14,000 employees.

Vrbas: 21460 Titov Vrbas, Srpskih Vladara 89; tel. (21) 701045; telex 14181; primary agricultural production, food processing, chemicals and trade; 14,780 employees.

Zastava SDP: 34000 Kragujevac, Spanskih boraca br. 4; tel. (34) 224011; telex 17128; fax (34) 215542; manufacture, sales and maintenance of passenger vehicles, lorries and firearms for hunting and sports use; Gen. Dir RADOLJUB MICIĆ; 52,161 employees.

Zavarivac: 11000 Belgrade, Brankova 23; tel. (11) 633125; telex 12247; fax (11) 620560; manufactures load-bearing steel structures, steel locks and specialist processing equipment for the petrochemical, chemical and food industries; Gen. Dir NOVIĆA JANKOVIĆ; 2,400 employees.

Zmaj Co: 11080 Zemun-Belgrade, Autoput 18; tel. (11) 600452; telex 11579; fax (11) 676867; production and development of agricultural machinery and equipment; Gen. Man. RADOSLAV MITROVIĆ; 4,200 employees.

TRADE UNIONS

Council of Confederation of Trade Unions of Yugoslavia (Veće Saveza sindikata Jugoslavije): 11000 Belgrade, trg Marksa i Engelsa 5 (Dom sindikata); tel. (11) 330481; telex 11121; 6,348,858 mems.

Trade unions forming the Confederation of Trade Unions of Yugoslavia (address, telephone and telex number as above unless otherwise stated):

Agricultural, Food and Tobacco Industry Workers' Union (Sindikat radnika poljprivrede, prehrambene i duvanske industrije): Pres. Federal Cttee ERNE KIČI.

Building Workers' Union (Sindikat radnika gradjevinarstva): Pres. Federal Cttee MILOŠ ŽORIĆ.

Catering and Tourism Workers' Union (Sindikat radnika u ugostiteljstvu i turizmu): Pres. Federal Cttee MILAN FRKOVIĆ.

Chemistry and Non-Metallic Industry Workers' Union (Sindikat radnika hemije i nemetala): Pres. Federal Cttee STOJMIR DOMAZETOVSKI.

Commerce Workers' Union (Sindikat radnika u trgovini): Pres. Federal Cttee LJUBICA BRAČKO.

Education, Science and Culture Workers' Union (Sindikat radnika delatnosti vaspitanja, obrazovanja, nauke i kulture): Pres. Federal Cttee BORIS LIPUŽIĆ.

Energy Workers' Union (Sindikat radnika energetike): Pres. Federal Cttee VASKRSIJE SAVIČIĆ.

Forestry and Wood Industry Workers' Union (Sindikat radnika šumarstva i prerade drveta): Pres. Federal Cttee DRAGOLJUB OBRADOVIĆ.

Health and Social Care Workers' Union (Sindikat radnika delatnosti zdravstva i socijalne zaštite): Pres. Federal Cttee LJILJANA MILOŠEVIĆ.

Metal Production and Manufacturing Workers' Union (Sindikat radnika proizvodnje i prerade metala): Pres. Federal Cttee SLAVKO URŠIĆ.

Public Utilities and Handicrafts Workers' Union (Sindikat radnika u komunalnoj privredi i zanatstvu): Pres. Federal Cttee JOSIP KOLAR.

Printing, Newspaper, Publishing and Information Workers' Union (Sindikat radnika grafičke, novinsko-izdavačke i informativne delatnosti): Pres. Federal Cttee BORIS BIŠĆAN.

State Administration and Finance Workers' Union (Sindikat radnika državne uprave i finansijskih organa): Pres. Federal Cttee RAM BUĆAJ.

Textile, Leather, and Footwear Workers' Union (Sindikat radnika industrije tekstila, kože i obuće): Pres. Federal Cttee JOZEFINA MUSA.

Transport and Communications Workers' Union (Sindikat radnika saobraćaja i veza): 11000 Belgrade, Miloša Pocerca 10; tel. (11) 646321; Pres. Federal Cttee HASAN HRNJIĆ.

Federation of Independent Trade Unions of Yugoslavia: Pres. MOMO COLAKOVIĆ.

TRADE FAIRS

Belgrade Fair: Belgrade, Vojvode Mišića 14, POB 408; tel. (11) 655555; telex 11306; fax (11) 688173; Internat. Technical Fair, annually in May; Internat. Motor Show, annually in April; Internat. Chemical Fair, annually in May; Internat. Clothing Fair 'Fashions in the World', annually in October; Internat. Book Fair, annually in October; Internat. Furniture Fair, annually in November; and other fairs; Pres. SINIŠA ZARIĆ.

Novi Sad: Novosadski Sajam, Novi Sad, Hajduk Veljkova 11; tel. (21) 25155; telex 14180; fax (21) 616121; Novi Sad Internat. Agricultural Fair, annually in May; Internat. Fair of Hunting, Fishing, Sports and Tourism, annually in October; Internat. Autumn Fair, annually in October; and other fairs; Dir-Gen. JOVAN NEŠIN.

Transport

Much international transport activity to or from Yugoslavia has been halted as a result of UN sanctions.

RAILWAYS

Zajednica Jugoslovenskih Železnica (Community of Yugoslav Railways): 11000 Belgrade, Nemanjina 6, POB 553; tel. (11) 685822; telex 12495; Gen. Man. N. ZURKOVIĆ.

ROADS

The road network is the responsibility of the Federal Ministry of Transport and Communications.

INLAND WATERWAYS

Inland waterways are supervised by the Federal Ministry of Transport and Communications.

SHIPPING

With the dissolution of the SFRY, Yugoslavia lost much of its access to the sea; the principal coastal outlet is the Montenegrin port of Bar.

Jugoslovenska Oceanska Plovidba (Yugoslav Ocean Lines): 85330 Kotor; tel. 25011; telex 61116; Pres. ANTON MOŠKOV.

Jugoslovenska Pomorska Agencija (Yugoslav Shipping Agency): Belgrade, bul. Lenjina 165A, POB 210; tel. (11) 130004; telex 11140; f. 1947; charter services, liner and container transport, port agency, passenger service, air cargo service; Gen. Man. STEVAN OBRADOVIĆ.

CIVIL AVIATION

There are international airports at Belgrade and Podgorica, as well as several domestic airports.

Jugoslovenski Aerotransport (JAT) (Yugoslav Airlines): 11070 Belgrade, Ho Ši Minova 16; tel. (11) 2224222; telex 12035; fax (11) 2221082; f. 1947; 51% owned by Govt of Serbia; international operations curtailed by imposition of sanctions in mid-1992; operates two domestic routes; Pres. and Dir-Gen. ZIKA PETROVIĆ.

Smaller operators, the international operations of which have also been suspended, included:

Air Jugoslavia: 11000 Belgrade, Moše Pijade 1/III; tel. (11) 338812; telex 12125; fax (11) 327832; f. 1969; wholly-owned subsidiary of JAT; Gen. Man. A. SKEPANOVIĆ.

Air Montenegro: Podgorica; tel. (81) 43020; telex 61425; fax (81) 41939.

Aviogenex: 11070 Belgrade, Milentija Popovića 9; tel. (11) 149729; telex 11711; fax (11) 2222439; f. 1968; passenger and cargo flights within Europe, the Mediterranean and the Middle East; Gen. Man. MIROSLAV SPASIĆ.

Tourism

Prior to the disintegration of the SFRY, tourism was a major source of foreign exchange (receipts were estimated at US $2,700m. in 1990); most foreign tourists were, however, attracted to Croatia and Slovenia. The great lake of Scutari, in Montenegro, is a notable tourist attraction, as is Montenegro's Adriatic coastline. The Yugoslav tourist industry was adversely affected by the imposition of UN sanctions against it, in May 1992; as well as the suspension of foreign visits, most domestic tourists were unable to travel, owing to their reduced incomes.

Turistički savez Jugoslavije (Tourist Association of Yugoslavia): 11001 Belgrade, Moše Pijade 8/IV, Poštanski fah 595; tel. (11) 339041; telex 11863; fax (11) 634677; f. 1953; produces tourist information in foreign languages; Pres. (vacant); Sec.-Gen. GEORGI GOŠEV.

Yugotours: 11000 Belgrade, Djure Djakovića 31; tel. (11) 764622; telex 11000; fax (11) 766447; f. 1957; organizes travel and accommodation arrangements for foreign and domestic tourists; 9 branch offices, 26 European and overseas offices; Man. Dir DANILO TODOROVIĆ.

Culture

GOVERNMENT ORGANIZATIONS

Federal Ministry of Education and Culture: see section on The Federal Government (Ministries—above).

Ministry of Culture of the Republic of Montenegro: see section on The Federal Republics—Government of Montenegro (Ministries—below).

Ministry of Culture of the Republic of Serbia: see section on The Federal Republics—Government of Serbia (Ministries—below).

Cultural Centre of Novi Sad (Kulturni Centar grada Novog Sada): 21000 Novi Sad, Katolička porta 5; tel. (21) 25539; Dir DJORDJE KAĆANSKI.

Historical Institute of Montenegro (Istoriski Institut Crne Gore): 81000 Podgorica, Naselje Kruševac; f. 1948.

Montenegrin Centre for Cultural and Artistic Activities (Republički Centar za Kulturno-umjetničke Delatnosti): 81000 Podgorica, Vasa Raičkovića 27; tel. (81) 44270; Dir MILAN POPOVIĆ; Programme Organizer VESELIN RADUNOVIĆ.

Montenegrin Institute for the Protection of Cultural Monuments (Republički Zavod za Zaštitu Spomenika Kulture): 81205 Cetinje, Bajova 150; tel. (86) 21182; f. 1948; Dir CEDOMIR MARKOVIĆ.

CULTURAL HERITAGE

Archiv Jugoslavije: 11000 Belgrade, Vase Pelagića 33, POB 65; tel. (11) 650755; f. 1950; Dir Prof. ZEČEVIĆ MIODRAG.

Art Gallery: 38000 Priština, POB 267; tel. (38) 27833.

Cvijeta Zuzorić Gallery: 11000 Belgrade, Mali Kalemegdan 1; tel. (11) 621585.

Ethnographical Museum (Etnografski muzej): 11000 Belgrade, trg Studentski 13, p.p 357; tel. (11) 181888; fax (11) 621284; f. 1901; Dir BRANKO RADIVOJEVIĆ.

Maritime Museum of Montenegro (Pomorski muzej Crne Gore): 81330 Kotor; f. 1900; Dir JOVAN MARTINOVIĆ.

Museum of Applied Arts (Muzej primenjene umetnosti): 11000 Belgrade, Vuka Karadžića 18; tel. (11) 626494; f. 1951; Dir SVETLANA ISAKOVIPĆ.

Museum of Contemporary Art: 11071 Belgrade, Novi Beograd, Ušće Save; tel. (11) 145900; fax (11) 222955; f. 1958, opened 1965; Dir ZORAN GAVRIĆ.

Museum of Vojvodina (Muzej vojvodine): 21000 Novi Sad, Dunavska 35; tel. (21) 26766; f. 1947; Dir LUBIVOJE CEROVIĆ.

National Museum (Narodni muzej): 11000 Belgrade, trg Republike 1A; tel. (11) 624322; fax (11) 627721; f. 1844; archeological collections and art gallery; Dir JEVTA JEVTOVIĆ.

Serbian Society Gallery ('Matica Srpska' Galerija): 21000 Novi Sad, trg Galerija 1; tel. (21) 24155; f. 1847; Dir LEPOSAVA ŠELMIĆ.

State Museum of Montenegro (Državni muzej Crne Gore): 81250 Cetinje, trg Titov; Dir STANISLAV-RAKO VUJOŠEVIĆ.

PERFORMING ARTS

'Atelier 212' Theatre: 11000 Belgrade, Lole Ribara 21; tel. (11) 346731.

Belgrade Drama Theatre: 11000 Belgrade, Save Kovačevića 64A; tel. (11) 423183.

Bitef Theatre: 11000 Belgrade, Terazije 29/I; tel. (11) 343109.

National Theatre of Montenegro (Crnogorsko Narodno Pozoriste): 81000 Podgorica, Stanka Dragojevića 12; tel. (81) 43293; drama, ballet, opera; Dir BLAGOTA ERAKOVIĆ.

National Theatre of Serbia (Narodno Pozorište Srbije): 11000 Belgrade, Francuska 3; tel. (11) 622469; Dir of Opera KONSTANTIN VINAVER; Dir of Ballet BORE MARKOVIĆ.

National Theatre—Subotica: 24000 Subotica, Ive Vojnovića 2; tel. (24) 25507; Dir LJUBISA RISTIĆ.

Provincial National Theatre—Kosovo-Metohija (Pokrajinsko Narodno Pozorište): 38000 Priština, Srpskih Vladara 21; tel. (38) 22396.

Serbian National Theatre (Srpsko Narodno Pozorište): 21000 Novi Sad, trg Pozorišni 1; Drama: tel. (21) 621411 (Drama), (21) 52399 (Opera and Ballet); Opera and Ballet Dir MLADEN SABLJIĆ.

Terazije Theatre: 11000 Belgrade, trg Marksa i Engelsa 3; tel. (11) 334037.

Ujvideki Szinhaz Theatre of Novi Sad: 21000 Novi Sad, Jovana Subotica 3–5; tel. (21) 622306.

Yugoslav Drama Theatre: 11000 Belgrade, Srpskih Vladara 50; tel. (11) 657766.

Yugoslav National Theatre: Belgrade; Dir ALEXANDER BERCEK.

Zvezdara Theatre: 11000 Belgrade, Revolucije 77A; tel. (11) 422170.

Music

Belgrade Opera Orchestra (Orkestar Beogradske opere): 11000 Belgrade, trg Republike 1; tel. (11) 615085; Conductors ANTON KOLAR, NIKOLAJ ŽLIČAR.

Belgrade Philharmonic Orchestra (Beogradska Filharmonija): 11000 Belgrade, trg Studentski 11; tel. (11) 635518; Chief Conductor VASILIJ SINAIJSKI.

Collegium Musicum Choir ('Collegium Musicum' hor): c/o Fakultet muzičke umetnosti, 11000 Belgrade, Srpskih Vladara 50; tel. (11) 642414; Chief Conductor DARINKA MATIĆ MAROVIĆ.

Dušan Skovran Chamber Orchestra (Kamerni orkestar 'Dušan Skovran'): c/o Jugokoncert, 11000 Belgrade, Terazije 4/I; tel. (11) 339916; Chief Conductor ALEKSANDAR PAVLOVIĆ.

Jugokoncert: 11000 Belgrade, Terazije 41/I; tel. (11) 339916; Dir EDUARD ILLE.

Marković Jazz Sextet (Jazz sekstet Marković/Gut): c/o RTV Beograd, 11000 Belgrade, Hilandarska 2; tel. (11) 346801.

Niš Symphony Orchestra (Niški Sinfonijski Orkestar): 18000 Niš, Stanka Paunovića 16a; tel. (18) 23047; Chief Conductor DEJAN SAVIĆ.

Pro Musica Chamber Orchestra (Kamerni Orkestar 'Pro Musica'): c/o Djura Jakšić, 11000 Belgrade, Požeška 92; tel. (11) 552580; Conductor DJURA JAKŠIĆ.

Radio-television Belgrade (RTV Belgrade) Jazz Band (Jazz orkestar RTV Beograd): 11000 Belgrade, Hilandarska 2; tel. (11) 346801; Conductors VOJISLAV SIMIĆ, ZVONIMIR SKERL.

RTV Belgrade Mixed Choir (Mešoviti hor RTV Beograd): 11000 Belgrade: Hilandarska 2, tel. (11) 346801; Chief Conductor VLADIMIR KRANJČEVIĆ.

RTV Belgrade Symphony Orchestra (Simfonijski orkestar RTV Beograd): 11000 Belgrade, Hilandarska 2; tel. (11) 346801; Conductor VANCO CAVDARSKI.

RTV Novi Sad Big Band (Plesni orkestar RTV Novi Sad): 21000 Novi Sad, Žarka Zrenjanina 3; tel. (21) 611588; Chief Conductor RUDOLF TOMŠIĆ.

Renaissance Ensemble of Ancient Music (Ansambl stare muzike 'Renesans'): c/o Zorž Grujić, 11000 Belgrade, Kneza od Semberije 16; tel. (11) 440476.

Symphony Orchestra of Montenegro RTV (Simfonijski orkestar Crnogorske RTV): 81000 Podgorica, Cetinjski put bb; Chief Conductor RADOVAN PAPOVIĆ.

Yugoslav Army Choir: 11000 Belgrade, Braće Jugovića 19; tel. (11) 339551; Conductor DJORDJE MINOV.

Yugoslav Army Symphony Orchestra (Sinfonijski orkestar umetničkog ansambla JNA): Dom JNA, 11000 Belgrade, Braće Jugovića 19; tel. (11) 339551; Chief Conductor MAJOR ILIJA ILIJEVSKI

ASSOCIATIONS

Historical Society of Serbia: 11000 Belgrade, Faculty of Philosophy, Čika Ljubina 18–20; f. 1948; Pres. Prof. Dr LJUBOMIR MAKSIMOVIĆ.

Library Association of Serbia (Bibliotekarsko društvo Srbije): 11000 Belgrade, Skerlićeva 1; tel. (11) 451242; telex 12208; fax (11) 452952; f. 1947; Pres. DOBRIVOJE MLADENOVIĆ; Sec. VERA CRLJIĆ.

Montenegrin PEN Centre: 81250 Cetinje, Njegoševa 7, POB 117; tel. (86) 21303; f. 1990; Pres. PAVLE MIJOVIC; Sec. MLADEN LOMPAR.

Roma Union of Serbia (Društva Rom Srpska): 11000 Belgrade; f. 1930; federation of some 60 local asscns; Pres. SAIT BALIĆ.

Serbian Literary Association (Srpska književna zadruga): 11000 Belgrade, Srpskih vladara 19/I; tel. (11) 330305; f. 1892; Pres. RADOVAN SAMARDŽIĆ; Sec.-Gen. RADIVOJE KONSTANTINOVIĆ.

Serbian PEN Centre: 11000 Belgrade, Francuska 7; f. 1926, reformed 1962; Pres. Dr MILEVA SLADIĆ-TRIFUNOVIĆ; Sec. KOSTA ČAVOŠKI.

Serbian Society (Matica srpska): 21000 Novi Sad, Matice srpske 1; f. 1826; Sec. Dr DUŠAN POPOV.

Society of Serbian Language and Literature (Društvo za srpski jezik i književnost): University of Belgrade, 11000 Belgrade, trg Studentski 1; f. 1910; Pres. P. STEVANOVIĆ.

Education

The educational system of Yugoslavia is organized at republican level. Elementary education is free and compulsory for all children between the ages of seven and 15, when children attend the 'eight-year school'. Various types of secondary education are available to all who qualify, but the vocational and technical schools are the most popular. Alternatively, children may attend a general secondary school (gymnasium) where they follow a four-year course which will take them up to university entrance.

At the secondary level there are also a number of art schools, apprentice schools and teacher-training schools. In 1990/91 the total enrolment at elementary and secondary schools was equivalent to 96.13% and 86.99% respectively of school-age population. Those who have attended the technical schools may pursue their education further at one of the two-year post-secondary schools, created in response to the needs of industry and the social services. Higher education is offered at six universities and the post-secondary schools. Courses are of four to six years' duration. There are facilities for adult education at evening schools and in part-time studies.

From 1990 ethnic Albanian schools in the province of Kosovo have been closed. In 1992 about 250,000 ethnic Albanian children did not attend school.

UNIVERSITIES

Kragujevac University (Univerzitet u Kragujevcu): 34000 Kragujevac, trg Slobode 1; tel. (34) 65424; f. 1976; 8 faculties; 773 teachers; 6,501 students; Rector Prof. Dr ILIJA ROSIĆ.

University of Arts in Belgrade (Univerzitet Umetnosti u Beogradu): 11000 Belgrade, Kosančićev venac 29; tel. (11) 629785; fax (11) 629785; f. 1957 as Academy of Arts, became University in 1973; 4 faculties; 387 teachers; 1,602 students; Rector Prof. DARINKA MATIĆ-MAROVIĆ.

University of Belgrade (Universizitet u Beogradu): 11001 Belgrade 6, trg Studentski 1; tel. (11) 635153; f. 1863, reorganized 1905 and 1954; 24 faculties; 3,702 teachers; 57,200 students; Rector Prof. Dr SLOBODAN UNKOVIĆ.

University of Montenegro, Podgorica (Univerzitet Crne Gore, Podgorica): 81000 Podgorica, Cetinjski put bb; tel. (81) 14484; telex 61439; fax (81) 11301; f. 1974; 10 faculties, one Academy of Music; 833 teachers; 8,000 students; Rector Prof. Dr BOŽIDAR NIKOLIĆ.

University of Niš (Univerzitet u Nišu): 18000 Niš, trg Bratstva i Jedinstva 2; tel. (18) 25544; telex 16362; fax (18) 24488; f. 1965; 9 faculties; 982 teachers; 16,121 students; Rector Prof. Dr BRANIMIR DJORDJEVIĆ.

University of Novi Sad (Univerzitet u Novi Sadu): 21000 Novi Sad, POB 7, trg Dositeja Obradovića 5; tel. (21) 350622; fax (21) 611725; f. 1960; 11 faculties; 1,967 teachers; 22,000 students; Rector Prof. Dr DRAGOSLAV HERCEG.

University of Priština (Universiteti i Prishintës/Univerzitet u Prištini): 38000 Priština, Vidovdanska bb; tel. (38) 24970; fax (38) 27628; f. 1970; 13 faculties; 756 teachers; 10,230 students; Rector Prof. Dr RADIVOJE PAPOVIĆ.

Social Welfare

All employed persons and their families are covered by obligatory social insurance schemes, providing for health insurance, money and grants in kind in case of sickness, accidents, disablement, old age and death. Insured persons are entitled to medical care, including compensation for an unlimited period during sick leave, rehabilitation and preventive care. The retirement pension is usually equivalent to 85%–87% of average monthly income during the last five years of employment. Women and young children enjoy special protection under the health insurance scheme. Employed women are entitled to at least 270 days' paid leave before and after childbirth. Confinements in hospital and maternity care are free of charge. Women are entitled to shorter working hours when their child is ill. All workers are entitled to annual leave which varies from 18 to 36 days.

GOVERNMENT AGENCIES

Federal Ministry of Employment, Health and Social Affairs: see section on The Federal Government (Ministries—above).

Ministry of Labour, Social Welfare and Protection of Veterans and Disabled Persons of the Republic of Montenegro: see section on The Federal Republics—Government of Montenegro (Ministries—below).

Ministry of Labour, Veterans' and Social Affairs of the Republic of Serbia: see section on The Federal Republics—Government of Serbia (Ministries—below).

Red Cross of Yugoslavia: 11000 Belgrade; national federation of republican societies.

HEALTH AND WELFARE ORGANIZATION

Serbian Society for the Fight against Cancer: 11000 Belgrade, Pasterova 14; tel. (11) 656386; telex 11077; fax (11) 685300; Pres. Dr PREDRAG BRZAKOVIĆ.

The Environment

GOVERNMENT ORGANIZATIONS

Federal Ministry of the Environment: see section on The Federal Government.

Ministry of Agriculture, Forestry and Water Resources Management of the Republic of Montenegro: see section on The Federal Republics—Government of Montenegro (Ministries—below).

Ministry of Health and the Environment of the Republic of Montenegro: see section on The Federal Republics—Government of Montenegro (Ministries—below).

Ministry of Agriculture, Forestry and Water Resources Management of the Republic of Serbia: see section on The Federal Republics—Government of Serbia (Ministries—below).

Ministry of Environmental Protection of the Republic of Serbia: see section on The Federal Republics—Government of Serbia (Ministries—below).

Co-ordinating Committee for the Environment: 11070 Belgrade, SIV, Lenjina 2; tel. (11) 330349; telex 11448.

Hydrometeorological Service of the Republic of Serbia: 11000 Belgrade, POB 100, Kneza Višeslava 66; tel. (11) 545240; telex 11748; fax (11) 545378; network of stations involved in meteorological and hydrological forecasting, agricultural meteorology, environmental control and radar monitoring; Dir NIKOLA DUTINA; Deputy Dir VLADIMIR DIMITRIJEVIĆ.

ACADEMIC INSTITUTES

Academy of Sciences and Arts of Kosovo (Akademia e Shkencave dhe e Arteve e Kosovës/Akademija Nauka i Umetnosti Kosova): 38000 Priština, Milladin Popoviqi 10; f. 1976, reorganized 1978; Pres. Dr VUKASIN FILIPOVIĆ; Sec.-Gen. OSMAN IMAMI.

Montenegrin Academy of Sciences and Arts (Crnogorska Akademija Nauka i Umjetnosti): 81000 Podgorica, Rista Stijovića 5; tel. (81) 31095; Pres. DRAGUTIN VUKOTIĆ; Sec.-Gen. BOŽIDAR GLUŠČEVIĆ.

Serbian Academy of Sciences and Arts (Srpska Akademija Nauka i Umetnosti): 11000 Belgrade, Knez Mihailova 35, POB 366; tel. (11) 187144; fax (11) 182825; f. 1886; Pres. DUŠAN KANZIR; Gen. Sec. DEJAN MEDAKOVIĆ.

Institute for Plant Protection: 11000 Belgrade, T. Drajzera 9, POB 936; tel. (11) 660049; f. 1945; Dir Dr MIRKO DRAGANIĆ.

NON-GOVERNMENTAL ORGANIZATION

Yugoslav Green Party: Belgrade, Mutapova 12; tel. (11) 4447030; f. 1990; environmental party open to all citizens regardless of national, religious or racial affiliation; Pres. DRAGAN JOVANOVIĆ.

Defence

Before the outbreak of civil war in the former SFRY, in 1991, the Jugoslavenska Narodna Armija (JNA—Yugoslav People's Army) was responsible for the country's defence. The JNA was a multi-ethnic, conscript-based force of 180,000. Serbs made up 36% of its conscripts and 42% of the total forces. Of the officer corps, 60% were of Serbian or Montenegrin stock, although these nationalities formed only some 40% of the Yugoslav population. By March 1992, however, it was estimated that there were only 11,000 non-Serbs or non-Montenegrins in the JNA, less than 3% of the total armed forces. In May 1992 the JNA was formally disestablished and divided into two halves, the Army of the Serbian Republic (of Bosnia and Herzegovina) and the Yugoslav Army.

The Yugoslav Army comprises land, air and sea services. The ground forces are divided into three armies, with headquarters at Belgrade, Podgorica and Niš. In June 1993, according to Western estimates, the FRY armed forces totalled 136,500 (including 60,000 conscripts), comprising an army of 100,000, a navy of 7,500 and an air force of 29,000. Military service was compulsory for men and lasted for 12 months. Voluntary military service for women was introduced in 1983. In 1992 the defence budget amounted to an estimated 245,000m. dinars (an estimated US $3,760m., or 27.8% of gross domestic product).

Chief of Staff of the Yugoslav Army: Col-Gen. MOMCILO PERIŠIĆ.

The Federal Republics

Under the Constitution adopted on 27 April 1992, the Federal Republic of Yugoslavia (FRY) comprised the Republics of Montenegro and Serbia. The abolition of the autonomy of the Serbian provinces of Kosovo and Metohija and Vojvodina was confirmed.

Montenegro

The Republic of Montenegro lies in the south-west of the FRY, on the Adriatic Sea. Montenegro has an area of 13,812 sq km, and its population was 615,267 in March 1991. The old royal capital, in the highlands above the Adriatic, is Cetinje. The federal capital of Montenegro is Podgorica (formerly Titograd), with a population of 96,074 at the 1991 census.

Montenegro is a Serb territory, first settled by the Slavs in the sixth century AD. The Serbs converted to Eastern Orthodox Christianity in the ninth century. Mihajlo (Michael) of Zeta first united the Serbs in one kingdom, in the 11th century. The principality of Zeta was the original Montenegrin state, consisting of the Southern Slav tribes in the inaccessible mountains of the modern Montenegro ('Black Mountains'). Zeta shared the fate of the Serbs generally for the rest of the Middle Ages, eventually falling under Serbian (Raška) rule. Despite the Ottoman advance into Europe, the Montenegrins maintained a precarious independence, emerging as an identifiable political entity by the 15th century. The Montenegrins resisted complete domination by the Venetians or, from the 16th century, by the Ottoman Turks. They remained faithful to the Serbian Orthodox Church, but did not establish a unitary state, being ruled by a succession of different dynasties. The modern principality emerged during the 19th century, its independence being acknowledged in 1796 and confirmed in 1878.

With the revival of a Serbian principality, Montenegrin policy was guided by its ethnic-Serb roots and an alignment with its co-religionists. In 1910 Montenegro was proclaimed a kingdom, under Nikita I. Montenegro supported Serbia in the Balkan Wars of 1912–13 and gained part of the Sandžak, on its north-eastern borders. Montenegro also supported Serbia in the First World War, but was occupied by Habsburg troops in 1916. During the War the Montenegrins joined in negotiations to form a common Southern Slav state. The Montenegrin royal family acquiesced in the loss of its power and the Serbian dynasty occupied the new throne of the Kingdom of Serbs, Croats and Slovenes (from 1929, Yugoslavia). In the Second World War Montenegro regained a nominal independence, as a client of Fascist Italy, but support for Tito's Partisan resistance was strong and after the War Montenegro, with the additional territory of the city-state of Cattaro (now Kotor), became a Republic of federal Yugoslavia.

The Montenegrins were well represented in the ruling Communist party and in the Jugoslavenska Narodna Armija (JNA—Yugoslav People's Army). During the 1980s, following the death of Tito, Montenegro's traditional alliance with Serbia once more became evident. In 1988 this was ensured by allegedly Serbian-organized demonstrations, which brought about the replacement of the Montenegrin Communist leadership with conservatives in sympathy with the Serbian leader, Slobodan Milošević. Similarity to the Serbian situation was further demonstrated by the elections of 1990. The ruling Communists amended the republican Constitution, which then provided for a unicameral Assembly, with 125 seats, and a directly-elected State President, replacing the previous collective Presidency. In the elections of 9 December the ruling League of Communists of Montenegro (subsequently named the Democratic Party of Socialists—DPS) won a majority of seats (83), while the republican branch of the Alliance of Reform Forces (ARF) won 17. The Communist presidential candidate, Momir Bulatović, defeated the ARF candidate in a second round of voting, on 23 December.

During the early 1990s Montenegro loyally supported Serbia in the political crises of Yugoslavia. Bulatović, the President of Montenegro, did cause some surprise when he accepted EC peace proposals, in October 1991. Serbia, alone of the Yugoslav republics, had rejected the plan. There was some tension in relations between Montenegro and Serbia, following this action and a declaration of sovereignty by the Montenegrin Assembly, on 18 October. The assertion of republican over federal law was prompted by uneasiness with the civil war and, it was believed, as a pragmatic response to the disintegration of Yugoslavia. It was a formality, intended to ensure proper representation at any future negotiations on the federation, more than a symptom of a distinct Montenegrin nationalism. On 10 January 1992 EC sanctions, imposed on Montenegro in the previous year, were lifted, and, five days later, the Montenegrin Constitution, adopted in November 1991, was amended in order to comply with EC criteria for recognition.

In April 1992 Montenegro joined with Serbia in claiming all the international functions of the SFRY, following the secession from it of the other four Republics. The Federal Republic of Yugoslavia (FRY), comprising Serbia and Montenegro, was created on 27 April. From 30 May UN sanctions were imposed on the new country. On 12 October Montenegro adopted a new Constitution, in which the Republic was defined as part of the FRY. On 10 January 1993 Bulatović was re-elected President of the Republic, after defeating his nationalist rival, Branko Kostić, by a substantial margin. On 5 March Milo Djukanović, the republican premier, formed a coalition Government.

Montenegro's relations with Serbia deteriorated in mid-1993. Following the imposition of an import-export licensing system by Serbia, Montenegro retaliated by introducing similar trade controls. Furthermore, Serbia's endeavours to disestablish both Republics' defence and foreign ministries were seen as further attempts to erode Montenegrin sovereignty and to undermine Bulatović's power. Increasingly, in 1993, Montenegro pursued foreign relations independently of Serbia. The Montenegrin foreign minister tried to station UN monitors on the Republic's borders with Bosnia and Herzegovina to ensure no sanctions were being broken. Although the various elements of the Montenegrin coalition Government held differing views on the future form that their state should take, all agreed on the preservation of the Republic's sovereignty when confronted with Serbia's attempts to erode it.

THE GOVERNMENT

State President

President of the Republic: MOMIR BULATOVIĆ (elected by popular vote on 23 December 1990; re-elected 10 January 1993).

Ministers
(March 1994)

Prime Minister: MILO DJUKANOVIĆ.

Deputy Prime Ministers: KRUNISLAV VUKCEVIĆ, RADE PEROVIĆ, ZORAN ŽIŽIĆ.

Minister of Internal Affairs: NIKOLA PEJAKOVIĆ.

Minister of Finance: BOŽIDAR GAZIVODA.

Minister of Foreign Affairs: MIODRAG LEKIĆ.

Minister of National Defence: Col BOŽIDAR BABIĆ.

Minister of Justice: FILIP VUJANOVIĆ.

Minister of Labour, Social Welfare and the Protection of Veterans and Disabled Persons: MILIVOJE JAUKOVIĆ.

Minister of Agriculture, Forestry and Water Resources Management: BRANKO ABRAMOVIĆ.

Minister of Culture: GOJKO CELEBIĆ.

Minister of Health and the Environment: MIOMIR MUGOŠA.

Minister of Education and Science: Dr PREDRAG OBRADOVIĆ.

Minister of Maritime Affairs and Transport: JUSUF KALAMPEROVIĆ.

Minister of Energy, Mining and Industry: MIODRAG GOMILANOVIĆ.

Minister of Tourism: DRAGAN MILIĆ.

Minister of Trade: DUSKO LAUĆEVIĆ.

Ministers without Portfolio: MILADIN VUKOTIĆ, MEVLUDIN NUHODŽIĆ.

Ministries

Office of the President: Podgorica; fax (81) 42329.

Office of the Prime Minister: Podgorica, Jovana Tomaševića bb; tel. (81) 52833; fax (81) 52246.

Ministry of Agriculture, Forestry and Water Resources Management: Podgorica, Omladinskih brig. 2; tel. (81) 31287; fax (81) 52935.

Ministry of Culture: Podgorica, Vuka Karadžića 3; tel. (81) 51355; fax (81) 42028.

Ministry of the Economy: Podgorica, Stanka Dragojevića 2; tel. (81) 42104; fax (81) 42028.

Ministry of Education and Science: Podgorica, Ulica slobode bb; fax (81) 612780.

Ministry of Energy, Mining and Industry: Podgorica.

Ministry of Finance: Podgorica, Blaža Jovanovića 2; tel. (81) 42835; fax (81) 42028.

Ministry of Foreign Affairs: Podgorica, Stanka Dragojevića 2; tel. (81) 52821; fax (81) 45752.

Ministry of Health and the Environment: Podgorica, Stanka Dragojevića 2; fax (81) 42028.

Ministry of Internal Affairs: Podgorica, Lenjina 6; tel. (81) 5223; fax (81) 52919.

Ministry of Justice: Podgorica, Vuka Karadžića 3; tel. (81) 51355; fax (81) 612780.

Ministry of Labour, Social Welfare and Protection of Veterans and Disabled Persons: Podgorica, Vuka Karadžića 3; tel. (81) 51255; fax (81) 612912.

Ministry of Maritime Affairs and Transport: Podgorica, Pete proleterske brig. 36; tel. (81) 2142; fax (81) 52246.

Ministry of National Defence: Podgorica, Blaža Jovanovića 4; tel. (81) 42396; fax (81) 45431.

Ministry of Tourism and Trade: Podgorica; fax (81) 42028.

LEGISLATURE

Republican Assembly

Chairman: RISTO VUKČEVIĆ.

Elections to the Montenegrin Assembly took place on 20 December 1992. The party enjoying the greatest success was the Democratic Pary of Socialists, which took 42.5% of the votes cast.

LOCAL GOVERNMENT

For administrative puposes, Montenegro is divided into 21 municipalities.

Andrijevica (1): Andrijevica; tel. (871) 53505; fax (871) 53171; Pres. of the Assembly SCEPAN DRAGOVIĆ.

Bar (2): Bar; tel. (81) 12065; fax (81) 12833; Pres. of the Assembly ZARIJE LEKIĆ.

Bijelo Polje (3): Bijelo Polje; tel. (84) 22630; fax (84) 22825; Pres. of the Assembly VELIMIR RADOJEVIĆ.

Berane (4): Berane; tel. (871) 31954; fax (871) 61820; Pres. of the Assembly MOMČILO MICOVIĆ.

Budva (5): Budva; tel. (86) 51211; fax (86) 52649; Pres. of the Assembly ZARKO MIKOVIĆ.

Danilovgrad (6): Danilovgrad; tel. (81) 812022; fax (81) 812682; Pres. of the Assembly MILORAD KADIĆ.

Zabljak (7): Zabljak; tel. (83) 88216; fax (83) 88222; Pres. of the Assembly RADOJICA POPOVIĆ.

Kolašin (8): Kolašin; tel. (81) 87177; fax (81) 87004; Pres. of the Assembly DRAGOLJUB MEDENICA.

Kotor (9): Kotor; tel. (82) 13150; fax (82) 13404; Pres. of the Assembly VIDOSAVA KASCELAN.

Mojkovać (10): Mojkovać; tel. (84) 72117; fax (84) 72715; Pres. of the Assembly RADENKO BOSKOVIĆ.

Nikšić (11): Nikšić; tel. (83) 24670; fax (83) 24780; Pres. of the Assembly Dr BLAGOJE CEROVIĆ.

Plav (12): Plav; tel. (871) 51475; fax (871) 51420; Pres. of the Assembly SADRIJA BALIĆ.

Pluzine (13): Pluzine; tel. (83) 71103; fax (83) 71139; Pres. of the Assembly DJORDJIJE BOSNJAK.

Pljevlja (14): Pljevlja; tel. (872) 81013; fax (872) 81601; Pres. of the Assembly MOMČILO BOJOVIĆ.

Rozaje (15): Rozaje; tel. and fax (871) 54383; Pres. of the Assembly NUSRET KALAĆ.

Tivat (16): Tivat; tel. (82) 61225; fax (82) 61301; Pres. of the Assembly LJUBO SAMARDZIĆ.

Podgorica (17): Podgorica; tel. (81) 43351; fax (81) 45035; Pres. of the Assembly ZORAN KNEZEVIĆ.

Ulcinj (18): Ulcinj; tel. (85) 81413; fax (85) 51909; Pres. of the Assembly MAHMUR BARDHLI.

Herzeg-Novi (19): Herceg-Novi; tel. (82) 51564; fax (82) 53976; Pres. of the Assembly STEVAN MITROVIĆ.

Cetinje (20): Cetinje; tel. (86) 21755; fax (86) 21891; Pres. of the Assembly DJORDJIJE VUSUROVIĆ.

Šavnik (21): Šavnik; tel. (83) 73127; Pres. of the Assembly RADOMIR KANDIĆ.

POLITICAL ORGANIZATIONS

Alliance of Reform Forces for Montenegro: Podgorica; founded as republican branch of federal, pro-Yugoslav party; favours free-market economic reform.

Democratic Action Party: Podgorica; mem. of Democratic Coalition of Muslims and Albanians in Montenegro.

Democratic Alliance: Podgorica; mem. of Democratic Coalition of Muslims and Albanians in Montenegro.

Democratic Party of Socialists (DPS) (Demokratska Partija Socijalista): Podgorica; name changed from League of Communists of Montenegro in 1991; supports continued federation; Chair. MOMIR BULATOVIĆ; Gen. Sec. SVETOZAR MAROVIĆ.

Equality Party: Podgorica; mem. of Democratic Coalition of Muslims and Albanians in Montenegro.

Liberal Alliance of Montenegro: Podgorica; pro-independence; Leader SLAVKO PEROVIĆ.

New Socialist Party of Montenegro: Podgorica; f. 1992 by merger of the People's Party (Leader NOVAK KILIBARDA) and the Socialist Party of Montenegro.

Party of Democratic Action—Montenegro: Rozaj; Slav Muslim party, affiliated to PDA of Bosnia and Herzegovina; support mainly in Sandžak region; Leader HARUN HADŽIĆ.

Serbian Radical Party: see Political Organizations in Serbia—below.

There were 31 registered political parties in Montenegro in October 1992. Other parties active in the republic included the Montenegro Social Democratic Party, the Montenegrin Liberal Alliance, the Yugoslav National Party, the Party of Socialists of Montenegro and the Independent Organization of Communists.

Serbia

The Republic of Serbia is a land-locked territory forming the most part of the FRY. The Republic also includes the Province of Kosovo and Metohija (formerly known as Kosovo) and the Province of Vojvodina, both of which were formerly federal units of the old Yugoslav federation (as Autonomous Republics within Serbia). Kosovo-Metohija occupies the south-west corner of the Republic and Vojvodina comprises the northern part. The capital of the Republic of Serbia is the federal capital, Belgrade (Beograd), which lies in the very north of 'Inner' Serbia. At the census of March 1991, the total population of the Republic was 9,791,475.

Serbs settled in the Roman province of Illyria in the sixth century AD. Their conversion to Eastern Orthodox Christianity strengthened the claims of the Eastern Roman (Byzantine) Empire to suzerainty, although, in the ninth and 10th centuries, the main Southern Slav power was the Bulgarian Empire. Despite Bulgarian, Byzantine and Hungarian pressures, a Serbian kingdom was established in the 12th century. It did not include the northern parts of modern Serbia; the territories of the Serbs were in southern and central Serbia, based on the principality of Raška (Rascia—Novi Pazar), but including the principalities of Zeta (Montenegro) and Rama or Bosnia. Stjepan (Stephen) I of the Nemanjid dynasty was able to end Byzantine rule and, in 1187, Serbian independence was acknowledged by the Emperor. In 1219 St Sava was consecrated the autocephalous archbishop of the Serbs. The Serbian Orthodox Church was to become the repository of national culture and identity, particularly following the destruction of the medieval empires.

The Serbian state of the Nemanjids declined, but a period of Balkan pre-eminence was secured by the destruction of the Bulgarian and Byzantine armies at Velbuzhde (Küstendil), in 1330. The following year Stjepan Dušan succeeded to the principality of Raška and he led the Serbs in campaigns against the other Orthodox powers for dominance in the Balkans. In 1346, as Uroš IV, he was crowned Tsar of the Serbs and Greeks and established a Serbian patriarchate. His capital was at Skopje (Macedonia), although he hoped to conquer Constantinople (now Istanbul, Turkey) and inherit the legitimate claims of the Roman Empire. Uroš IV was succeeded by Uroš V (1355–67), under whom the kingdom disintegrated into feudal 'despotates'. One of the more powerful of the ruling noblemen, Lazar of Raška, attempted to unite the despotates against the advance of the Ottoman Turks, but the power of the Serbs was crushed on the plains of Kosovo Polje ('the Field of Blackbirds'), in 1389. In 1459 Serbia was finally absorbed by the Ottoman Empire. During the following centuries, the Serbs preserved their Orthodox Christian culture and proved to be valuable recruits against the Turks, even for the Roman Catholic Habsburgs (Vojvodina became a Habsburg territory, as was, in the early 18th century, northern Serbia).

The modern Serbian state was established during the 19th century. For the details of this, see the Chronology (p. 716) and History (p. 721) above. Serbian expansion was opposed by Austria-Hungary, and this consequent involvement of Great-Power politics in the Balkans led to the First World War. Thus, from 1915, Serbia was occupied by forces of the Central Powers, and the exiled Serbian Government agreed to the formation of a Southern Slav (Yugoslav) state to include Montenegro and various Habsburg territories. With the defeat of the Central Powers and the dissolution of the Habsburg Monarchy, this decision was effected. On 4 December 1918 a Kingdom of Serbs, Croats and Slovenes was proclaimed, uniting Serbia, including Macedonia and Kosovo, with Montenegro and the Habsburg lands (modern Croatia, Slovenia and Vojvodina). In August 1921, upon the agreement and ratification of the Constitution, the Serbian Regent from 1914, Prince Aleksandar Karadjordjević, became King Aleksandar I of a Serb-dominated state.

The other nationalities resented Serbian domination of the Kingdom (known as Yugoslavia from 1929) and this added to the violence of the civil war, which erupted after the German invasion of 1941, during the Second World War. The royal family and the Government fled into exile and Serbia was partitioned between the Fascist Croatian state, Hungary and Bulgaria; the 'rump' Serbia was placed under German military administration, the nominal leader being the quisling Nedić. The occupation was fiercely resisted, however, and the Allied Powers gave their support to the Communist-dominated Partisans of Josip Broz (Tito). They declared King Petar II deposed, in 1944, and, after the War, Serbia became part of a federal Yugoslav state. Serbia was one of the constituent Republics of Communist Yugoslavia, but it included two autonomous regions, Kosovo and Vojvodina, which were also distinct units of the federation (see below).

Serbia remained dissatisfied with the federal arrangement, as the two Autonomous Provinces were *de facto* republics, particularly after the adoption of a new Constitution in 1974. Tito had supported the gradual decentralization of Yugoslavia, but Serb aspirations were placated by their domination of the JNA and of the Communist Party. After Tito's death, in 1980, the Serbian authorities began to seek a rearrangement of the balance of power within the Republic and in the federation.

In May 1989 Slobodan Milošević became President of the republican State Presidency. A conservative Communist, he appealed to Serbian nationalism and granted some constitutional reforms. Thus, in November 1989, he secured his position by being re-elected President of the Presidency, in the first direct, secret ballot in Serbia since before the Second World War. On 9 December 1990 he was elected, with over 65% of the votes cast, as the sole President of Serbia, under the new Serbian Constitution. This Constitution made Serbia a Republic, rather than a Socialist Republic, and effectively removed the autonomy of Kosovo (which was renamed Kosovo-Metohija) and Vojvodina. It was approved by referendum in July 1990. The Constitution (which effectively gave Serbia control of three votes, instead of one, in the federal institutions) was not entirely in accordance with the federal Constitution, but Milošević was not challenged. Serbia continued to veto proposals for federal reform and, instead, advocated more centralization.

Opposition to Milošević's Government increased in 1991. The main opposition to Milošević's Socialist Party of Serbia (SPS—as the Serbian League of Communists was renamed in July 1990) was the nationalist Serbian Renewal Movement (SRM). In early 1991 the SRM leader, Vuk Drašković, emerged as the main figure in an anti-Communist alliance of opposition parties, which found increasing support in the Republic. In March there were mass anti-Communist demonstrations in Belgrade against Milošević's policies.

With the onset of civil war, in June 1991, however, the immediate pressure of the opposition abated and the SPS was again able to exploit the nationalism engendered by the conflict, although opposition criticism did not cease completely. With the support of the State Presidency members for Kosovo-Metohija, Vojvodina and Montenegro, Serbia took effective control of the 'rump' federal Presidency. Internationally, Serbia was widely held to be primarily responsible for the civil war and, in May 1992, UN sanctions were imposed on Serbia.

Following the secession of the other Republics from the SFRY, in April 1992, Serbia, along with Montenegro, claimed to be the legitimate successor of the old federation, renaming the country the Federal Republic of Yugoslavia (FRY). In late May a broad opposition alliance, the Serbian Democratic Movement (DEPOS) was formed, partly as a response to the electoral success that the SPS had enjoyed in the recent federal elections. Republican elections were scheduled for 20 December and Milan Panić, the Federal Prime Minister, stood against Milošević for the post of Serbian President.

Although Panić's electoral campaign was initially popular it began to lose momentum in late 1992. The opposition to Milošević was fragmented and the UN did not respond to

Panić's request to suspend sanctions during the election period. Milošević, on the other hand, had inherited the property and organization of the Communists, controlled most of the mass media and exploited his opponent's failure to secure UN concessions. Consequently, he succeeded in being re-elected President, winning 56.3% of the votes cast. His party, the SPS, won the largest share of the seats (101) in the 250-seat Serbian Assembly. The ultra-nationalist Serbian Radical Party (SRS), led by Vojislav Seselj, took 73 seats and DEPOS 49. However, the leader of DEPOS and the Serbian Renewal Movement (SRM), Vuk Drašković, claimed that the election was fraudulent and, from 3 February 1993, the DEPOS deputies began a boycott of the Serbian Assembly. On 2 June, during anti-government demonstrations in Belgrade, Drašković and his wife were detained by police and badly beaten.

Throughout 1993 tension within the government coalition of the SPS and Seselj's SRS, increased. On 7 October Seselj levelled numerous accusations against the SPS, including attempting to betray the FRY's national interests by negotiating with the international community with the aim of ending the war in Bosnia and Herzegovina. A motion of 'no confidence' in the Government was debated, and supported by the opposition SRM. Threatened by the imminent fall of his Government, President Milošević, on 20 October, dissolved the Serbian parliament and scheduled elections for 19 December.

The political issues of the election campaign were overshadowed by personal rivalry between Milošević and Seselj. On 5–6 November 1993 numerous SRS members were arrested for various capital crimes. The parts of the media under the Serbian Government's control made much of the events, linking Seselj to various war crimes in Bosnia and Herzegovina. Seselj retaliated with counter-accusations of atrocities. An estimated 62% of those able to vote participated in the elections. The SPS received 49.2% of the votes cast and 123 seats in the Assembly. DEPOS gained 18% of the votes cast (45 seats) and the SRS 15.6% of the ballot (39). The Democratic Party, led by Zoran Djindjić, made the largest gains in the elections, winning 11.6% of the votes cast and 29 seats (compared to the seven it had previously held). The nationalist Democratic Party of Serbia won seven seats (2.8% of the votes cast). The remaining seven seats went to ethnically based political groups, the Democratic Community of Vojvodina Hungarians and the Albanian Party of Democratic Action coalition.

Thus, Milošević succeeded in reaffirming his control of the Serbian Government, and in increasing the representation in the Serbian Assembly of the SPS. However, his party still lacked a parliamentary majority and it appeared unlikely that an alliance would be formed with any opposition party in 1994. This political instability, combined with the worsening economic situation in the Republic, owing to the continuing UN sanctions, and the tensions in the Autonomous Provinces, made Serbia's situation a bleak one.

KOSOVO

The former autonomous province of Kosovo and Metohija lies in south-west Serbia. Its capital is Priština. Kosovo is populated by a large Albanian majority. The region was important historically to the Serbs as well as to the Albanians (the Albanian national revival began here, in 1878, with the foundation of the League of Prizren). The Serbs remained suspicious of ambitions for a 'Greater Albania' and seldom tolerated nationalist aspirations. Under President Milošević, the Serbian Government implemented policies designed to encourage resettlement of Kosovo-Metohija by ethnic Serbs, a total of 50,000 Serbs and Montenegrins having left the province from 1981.

The Albanians did achieve some national rights under the federal state, notably the achievement of the status of an Autonomous Province and participation in the state as a federal unit. Serbs and Montenegrins dominated the provincial administration and the Communist apparatus until the fall of the Serb head of the security services, Aleksandar Ranković, in 1966. There were then demands for a Kosovo republic, and some concessions were granted to both the Autonomous Provinces (the other being Vojvodina—see below) by the federal authorities in 1968. These rights were confirmed in the new Yugoslav Constitution of 1974. However, the federal and Serbian authorities remained repressive of nationalist groups, accusing them of separatist sympathies. Certainly the Albanians of Kosovo were not culturally threatened and the leadership of the local League of Communists and provincial administration was predominantly ethnic Albanian. The main demand of the nationalists was for republican status.

In March and April 1981 there were nationalist riots in Kosovo, mainly in Priština, which were vigorously repressed after a state of emergency had been declared. The Communist authorities instituted a policy of 'differentiation', which involved the purging of any Party member or official who did not actively denounce the campaign for a seventh republic. Between 1981 and 1990, according to the human-rights group, Amnesty International, over 7,000 Albanians were arrested and imprisoned in Kosovo, for nationalist activities.

The rise of Serb nationalism, from the mid-1980s, exacerbated tensions in the Province. From 1985 the issue of Serb and Montenegrin emigration became of note in the Serbian media, with allegations of harassment by the Albanians. By 1987 Serbian nationalists were regularly citing incidents of what was increasingly described as 'genocide'. The rise of Slobodan Milošević to the Presidency of Serbia was indicative of the increasingly nationalist mood of the Serbs. The 1974 Constitution was now perceived to be against Serbian interests and the new leadership sought to reduce the autonomy of the two Provinces.

In November 1988, under pressure from Serbia, the prominent Albanian politician, Azem Vlasi, resigned from the Kosovo politburo, causing widespread protests in the Province. In February 1989 he was dismissed from the Central Committee of the League of Communists of Yugoslavia, causing further protests in Kosovo. In March he was arrested, together with other Albanian leaders, and charged with 'counter-revolutionary' activities; their trial became a source of continuing tension, until their release, in April 1990. The situation deteriorated in this year and, in March, Serbia assumed direct control of the Kosovo police force, causing the resignation of the Premier of Kosovo and, by May, of every ethnic Albanian member of the provincial Government.

The new Serbian Constitution of 1990 removed the remaining vestiges of autonomy from the two Provinces. A Republic-wide referendum on the new Serbian Constitution, largely boycotted by the Albanians, was conducted on 2 July (it was formally promulgated on 28 September, from when Kosovo was known as the Autonomous Province of Kosovo and Metohija) resulted in a majority of Serbs approving the new Constitution. On 5 July the Serbian authorities dissolved the provincial Assembly and Government. The Kosovo Presidency resigned in protest and Serbia introduced a special administration. By September some 15,000 ethnic Albanian officials had been dismissed and measures limiting the number of Albanians in the education system had been implemented.

The dependence of the provincial administration on central Serbian authority, however, was demonstrated in the federal constitutional crisis of March 1991. The Albanian member for Kosovo-Metohija on the federal State Presidency was dismissed by the Serbian Assembly on 16 March, and, on 18 March, the functions of the Kosovo-Metohija Presidency were temporarily suspended. This action by Serbia, and alleged rights abuses in Kosovo-Metohija, however, was what the USA used to justify its termination of economic aid to Yugoslavia. Meanwhile the Kosovo Assembly-in-Exile, based in Zagreb, organized a referendum on independence, on 26–30 September (although it was banned by Serbia) which overwhelmingly was in favour of Kosovo becoming a sovereign republic. Elections, also declared illegal by Serbian authorities, were held in the Province on 24 May 1992. The Democratic Alliance of Kosovo (DSK) secured the most seats in the 130-seat Assembly, and the DSK leader, Ibrahim Rugova, was elected President of the self-proclaimed 'Republic of Kosovo'.

The new Yugoslav Constitution of April 1992 confirmed Kosovo's loss of status as according to the 1990 Serbian Constitution: the Federal Republic of Yugoslavia (FRY) comprised only the Republics of Montenegro and Serbia, with reference made to Kosovo-Metohija and to Vojvodina as 'former autonomous provinces'. The ethnic Albanians in Kosovo did not participate in the 1992 Serbian presidential and parliamentary elections and there were allegations of malpractice by Serbian authorities. In March 1993, following reports of increased harassment of Albanians in Kosovo, the USA threatened to send troops to the area. In July Serbia expelled international monitors working in the region. Controversy continued in 1993–94 over issues such as the closure of Albanian-language schools, the dissolution of the Kosovo Academy of Sciences and renewed Serbian attempts to settle Slavs in the province. In December 1993 republican elections were boycotted in Kosovo, and, in early 1994, the situation remained tense, with reports of a growing armed resistance by ethnic Albanians, and a large Serbian police and military presence.

VOJVODINA

The other former autonomous province, Vojvodina, was also affected by the changes in Serbia, although the ethnic Serb majority there made them less controversial. Vojvodina had originally been a Hungarian marcher territory or banate, in which the Habsburgs had settled other ethnic groups to defend Christendom against the Ottomans. A large Serb population had first settled there in 1690, when the so-called '30,000 Families', led by Patriarch Arsenije III Crnojević, migrated from the Ottoman-dominated south. In the 19th century the Habsburgs had created a province of Serbian Vojvodina, hoping to satisfy the aspirations of the Serb nationalists. At the end of the Second World War more Serbs had settled there and they became the dominant ethnic group.

Until the late 1980s Vojvodina retained some provincial independence. In October 1988 demonstrations allegedly organized by the Milošević faction secured a Communist leadership sympathetic to the new Serbian leadership. The Hungarian Government expressed concern for the rights of the ethnic Hungarian minority, during 1990 and 1991, particularly following the effective removal of Vojvodina's autonomous status in the 1990 Serbian Constitution. This was confirmed by the April 1992 Constitution of the new Federal Republic, which recognized these changes introduced in Serbia's organic law. However, Vojvodina did retain a provincial Assembly to represent the region as a whole. There were a great number of ethnic minorities in Vojvodina, all of which had political or social organizations to represent them. The largest was the Democratic Community of Vojvodina Hungarians (DCVH), which, unlike the Albanian parties of Kosovo, did not boycott the Serbian elections of December 1993 and secured representation in the new parliament. With a Serb majority in the province, the republican authorities were more tolerant of manifestations of cultural autonomy for minorities in Vojvodina than in Kosovo.

THE GOVERNMENT

State President

President of the Republic: SLOBODAN MILOŠEVIĆ (took office as President of the collective Presidency in May 1989 and re-elected, by direct ballot, in November 1989; elected as sole President on 9 December 1990, re-elected 20 December 1992 and 19 December 1993).

Ministers
(March 1994)

Prime Minister: MIRKO MARJANOVIĆ.

Deputy Prime Ministers: SLOBODAN RADULOVIĆ, RATKO MARKOVIĆ, SLOBODAN UNKOVIĆ, SVETOZAR KRSTIĆ.

Minister of Internal Affairs: ZORAN SOKOLOVIĆ.

Minister of Finance: DUSAN VLATKOVIĆ.

Minister of Justice: ARANDJEL MARKICEVIĆ.

Minister of Agriculture, Forestry and Water Resources Management: IVKO DJONOVIĆ.

Minister of Industry: OSKAR FODOR.

Minister of Mining and Energy: DRAGAN KOSIĆ.

Minister of Transport and Communications: ALEKSA JOKIĆ.

Minister of Urban Planning and Construction: BRANISLAV IVKOVIĆ.

Minister of Trade and Tourism: SRDJAN NIKOLIĆ.

Minister of Labour, Veterans' and Social Affairs: JOVAN RADIĆ.

Minister of Education: DRAGOSLAV MLADENOVIĆ.

Minister of Culture: NADA POPOVIĆ-PERIŠIĆ.

Minister of Health: LEPOSAVA MILICEVIĆ.

Minister of Environmental Protection: JORDAN ALEKSIĆ.

Minister of Youth Affairs and Sport: VLADIMIR CVETKOVIĆ.

Minister of Religious Affairs: DRAGAN DRAGOJLOVIĆ.

Minister responsible for Liaison with Serbs outside Serbia: RADOVAN PANKOV.

Minister of Information: RATOMIR VITO.

Minister of Private Enterprise: RADOJE DJUKIĆ.

Government Co-ordinator for Local Self-Management: ANDO MILOŠAVLJEVIĆ.

Government Co-ordinator for Economic Affairs in Kosovo-Metohija: VEKOSLAV SEŠEVIĆ.

Government Co-ordinator responsible for the Technological Development of the Serbian Economy: MILAN BABIĆ.

Ministries

Office of the President: 11000 Belgrade, Andrićev venac 1.

Office of the Prime Minister: 11000 Belgrade, Nemanjina 11; tel. (11) 685872; fax (11) 659682.

Ministry of Agriculture, Forestry and Water Resources Management: 11000 Belgrade, Nemanjina 26; tel. (11) 642276; fax (11) 659146.

Ministry of Culture: 11000 Belgrade, Nemanjina 11; tel. (11) 657347; fax (11) 683854.

Ministry of Education: 11000 Belgrade, Nemanjina 22–26; tel. (11) 659595; fax (11) 683724.

Ministry of Environmental Protection: 11000 Belgrade, Nemanjina 22–26; (11) 657143; fax (11) 642242.

Ministry of Finance: 11000 Belgrade, Nemanjina 22–26; tel. (11) 658883; fax (11) 646436.

Ministry of Health: 11000 Belgrade, Nemanjina 22–26; tel. (11) 642291; fax (11) 642684.

Ministry of Industry: 11000 Belgrade, Nemanjina 22–26; (11) 659247; fax (11) 642681.

Ministry of Information: 11000 Belgrade, Nemanjina 11; tel. (11) 657056; fax (11) 685937.

Ministry of Internal Affairs: 11000 Belgrade, Kneza Miloša 103; tel. (11) 685157; fax (11) 641867.

Ministry of Justice: 11000 Belgrade, Nemanjina 26; tel. (11) 657866; fax (11) 659147.

Ministry of Labour, Veterans' and Social Affairs: 11000 Belgrade, Nemanjina 22-26; tel. (11) 659547; fax (11) 682758.

Ministry of Mining and Energy: 11000 Belgrade, Nemanjina 22-26; tel. (11) 658755.

Ministry of Private Enterprise: Belgrade.

Ministry of Religious Affairs: 11000 Belgrade, Nemanjina 11; tel. (11) 682185; fax (11) 688841.

Ministry of Trade and Tourism: 11000 Belgrade, Nemanjina 22-26; tel. (11) 658855; fax (11) 642148.

Ministry of Transport and Communications: 11000 Belgrade, Nemanjina 22-26; tel. (11) 661666; fax (11) 659379.

Ministry of Urban Planning and Construction: 11000 Belgrade, Nemanjina 22-26; tel. (11) 659078; fax (11) 659055.

Ministry of Youth Affairs and Sport: 11000 Belgrade, Nemanjina 11; tel. (11) 685353; fax (11) 682167.

Ministry responsible for Liaison with Serbs outside Serbia: 11000 Belgrade, Nemanjina 11; tel. (11) 684148; fax (11) 659798.

LEGISLATURE

National Assembly

Chairman: DRAGAN TOMIĆ.

Elections, 19 December 1993

Party	Seats
Socialist Party of Serbia	123
Democratic Movement of Serbia	45
Serbian Radical Party	39
Democratic Party	29
Democratic Party of Serbia	7
Democratic Community of Vojvodina Hungarians	5
Coalition of the Party of Democratic Action and the Democratic Party of Albanians	2
Total	250

LOCAL GOVERNMENT

For administrative purposes, Serbia is divided into regions, of which there are 29, including territories of the formerly autonomous provinces of Kosovo and Metohija and Vojvodina. Following the enactment of the 1990 Serbian Constitution and, subsequently, of the federal Constitution of 1992, Vojvodina retained its provincial Assembly. However, the provincial Assembly of Kosovo-Metohija was dissolved, although a 'Kosovo Assembly-in-Exile' was formed, based in Zagreb, which proclaimed a 'Republic of Kosovo'. In October 1991 the Slav Muslims of the Sandžak area voted for autonomy in a banned referendum. Their leader was SULEJMAN UGLJANIN.

North Bačka (1): Subotica, trg Slobode 1; tel. (24) 26112; CEO DRAGAN BOZINIVIĆ.

Central Banat (2): Zrenjanin, trg Slobode 10; tel. (23) 64586; CEO JOVAN SUBOTIĆ.

North Banat (3): Kikinda, trg Titov 12; tel. (230) 21008; fax (230) 22921; CEO ZDRAVKO GALIĆ.

South Banat (4): Pancevo, trg Borisa Kidrica 2; tel. (13) 46940; CEO VLADIMIR SARIĆ.

Western Bačka (5): Sombor, trg Cara Urisa 1; tel. (25) 56311; CEO MILE CAPIĆ.

Southern Bačka (6): Novi Sad, Maršala Tita 16; tel. (21) 56311; CEO JOVO UBIPARIP.

Srem (7): Sremska Mitrovica, trg Brace Radica 13; tel. (22) 221053; CEO ZIKICA DRONJAK.

Macva (8): Sabac, Maršala Tita 6/III; tel. (15) 25500; fax (15) 24203; CEO RADENKO STEPIĆ.

Kolubara (9): Valjevo, Vuka Karadzica 16/II; tel. (14) 21655; fax (14) 26112; CEO ALEKSA JOKIĆ.

Podunavlje (10): Smederevo, trg Republike 5; tel. (26) 223636; fax (26) 223646; CEO STEVAN ZEZELJ.

Branicevo (11): Pozarevać, Drinska 2; tel. (12) 223999; fax (26) 223646; CEO MIROSLAV SRETENOVIĆ.

Sumadija (12): Kragujeva, Save Kovacevica 7; tel. (34) 69206; CEO VLADETA MILETIĆ.

Pomoravlje (13): Svetozarevo (Jagodina), Maršala Tita 82; tel. (35) 221516; fax (35) 224515; CEO VLADIMIR JOVANOVIĆ.

Bor (14): Por, Moše Pijade 5; tel. (30) 23970; fax (30) 21749; CEO NEDELJKO MAGDALENOVIĆ.

Zaječar (15): Zaječar, Generala Gambete 44; tel. (19) 21587; fax (19) 21626; CEO SRETEN TROJANECEVIĆ.

Zlatibor (16): Uzice, Maršala Tita 52; tel. (31) 22262; CEO SLOBODAN VERMEZOVIĆ.

Morava (17): Cacak, Maršala Tita 2; tel. (32) 23310; CEO MILOS NEŠOVIĆ.

Raška (18): Kraljevo, trg Bratstva i Jedinstva 3; tel. (36) 332133; fax (36) 22235; CEO MILOS NEŠOVIĆ.

Resava (19): Krusevać, Pana Djukica 1; tel. (37) 24538; CEO VLADIMIR TASIĆ.

Nišava (20): Niš, Vozdova 11; tel. (18) 40626; fax (18) 23742; CEO JOVAN ZLATIĆ.

Toplica (21): Prokuplje, Tatkova 2; tel. (27) 21070; fax (27) 24316; CEO RATKO ZECEVIĆ.

Pirot (22): Pirot, Maršala Tita 125; tel. (18) 22471; CEO NESKO MADIĆ.

Jablanica (23): Leskovać, Predsednika Tita 124; tel. (16) 44312; CEO ZIVOJIN STEFANOVIĆ.

Pčinja (24): Vranje, Matije Gupca 2; tel. (17) 23133; fax (17) 31330; CEO SVETISLAV LJUBIĆ.

Kosovo (25): Priština, Vidovdanska 2; tel. (38) 27790; fax (38) 27791; CEO MILOS SIMOVIĆ.

Peć (26): Peć; tel. (39) 21514; fax (39) 22257; CEO MILADIN IVANOVIĆ.

Prizren (27): Prizren, Zgrada Opstinskog fonda zdravstene zastite, Mose Pijade bb; tel. (29) 44322; CEO BLAZO DAMJANOVIĆ.

Kosovska Mitrovica (28): Kosovska Mitrovica, Zgrada Kulturnog Centra; tel. (28) 82024; CEO DRAGAN PELEVIĆ.

Kosovsko Pomoravlje (29): Gnjilane, Borisa Kidrica 11; tel. and fax (280) 20249; CEO PREDRAG KOVACEVIĆ.

Kosovo-Metohija

Government Co-ordinator for Economic Affairs in Kosovo-Metohija: VEKOSLAV SEŠEVIĆ.

'Republic of Kosovo'

In 1990 between 110 and 120 deputies of the Kosovo (now Kosovo-Metohija) provincial Assembly rejected the Serbian constitutional reforms and the dissolution of that Assembly. They formed a 'Kosovo Assembly-in-Exile', which proclaimed Kosovo a Republic, and formed an interim Government, based in Zagreb (Croatia). This body organized a referendum in the province, at the end of September 1991, the result of which was overwhelmingly in favour of Kosovo becoming a sovereign republic. The Assembly-in-Exile also arranged elections to a new 130-seat provincial assembly on 24 May 1992 (the Democratic Alliance of Kosovo won the most seats and its leader became the 'President of Kosovo'). Both referendum and elections were declared illegal by the Serbian and federal authorities.

President of the Republic: Dr IBRAHIM RUGOVA.

Chairman of the Provisional Government: Dr BUJAR BUKOSHI.

Vojvodina

Provincial Assembly: Novi Sad; Pres. of the Provincial Assembly Dr MILUTIN STOJKOVIĆ; Pres. of the Provincial Govt BOŠKO PEROŠEVIĆ; Prime Minister KOVILJKO LOVRE.

POLITICAL ORGANIZATIONS

Alliance of Peasants of Serbia Party: 11000 Belgrade, Srpskih Vladara 81; tel. (11) 789235; Pres. MILOMIR BABIĆ.

Citizens' Group (Željko Ražnjatović): Belgrade.

Democratic Alliance of Kosovo (Demokratski Savez Kosovo—DSK): 38000 Priština; f. 1990 by dissidents and take-over of provincial brs of the Socialist Alliance of Working People; ethnic Albanian grouping; Chair. Dr IBRAHIM RUGOVA.

Democratic Community of Vojvodina Hungarians (Demokratska zajednica vojvodjanskih Madjara—DZVM): Ada, trg Oslobodjenja 11; tel. (24) 852248; f. 1990; supports interests of ethnic Hungarian minority in the Vojvodina; c. 20,000 mems; Pres. ANDRAŠ AGOŠTON.

Democratic Movement of Serbia (Demokratski Pokret Srbije—DEPOS): Belgrade, Masarikova 5/VIII; tel. (11) 685490; f. 1992 as a coalition of four parties and a party faction; Pres. VUK DRAŠKOVIĆ; Sec. MILENKO PALIĆ.

Democratic Party (Demokratska stranka): 11000 Belgrade, Terazije 3/IV; tel. (11) 338078; fax (11) 623686; nationalist; Leader ZORAN DJINDJIĆ.

Democratic Party of Albanians: Preševo.

Democratic Party of Serbia (Demokratska stranka Srbije—DSS): Belgrade; f. 1992 following split from Democratic Party; Leader VOJISLAV KOSTUNICA.

Democratic Party of Vojvodina: Novi Sad.

Democratic Reform Party of Muslims: 38400 Prizren, Koritnik 3; tel. (29) 22322; party of ethnic Muslims; left-wing; Pres. AZAR ZULJI.

League of Social Democrats of Vojvodina: Novi Sad; Leader NENAD ČANAK.

Liberal Party (Liberalna Stranka): Valjevo, POB 148; tel. (14) 22627; favours a free-market economy; Leader NIKOLA MILOŠEVIĆ.

Muslim Democratic Party.

National Peasant's Party: Novi Sad; Pres. DRAGAN VESELINOV.

New Democracy: Belgrade; Leader DUSAN MIHAILOVIĆ.

Party of Democratic Action: Preševo; party of ethnic Albanians; Leader RIZA HALILI.

Party of Democratic Action of Kosovo-Metohija (PDA-KM): Vitomirića; party of ethnic Muslims; affiliated to the PDA of Bosnia and Herzegovina; Chair. NUMAN BALIĆ.

Party of Democratic Action of the Sandžak (PDA-S): 36300 Novi Pazar, E. Redzepagića 54; tel. (20) 25626; party of ethnic Muslims; affiliated to the PDA of Bosnia and Herzegovina; advocates autonomy for the Sandžak region; Chair. SULEJMAN UGLJANIN.

Peasant Party: Belgrade; Leader MILOMAR BABIĆ.

People's Party (Narodna Stranka): 11000 Belgrade, Srpskih Vladara 14; Leaders MILAN PAROSKI, DRAGOSLAV PETROVIČ.

Reform Democratic Party of Vojvodina (Reformska Demokratska Stranka Vojvodine): Novi Sad, Ilije Ognjanović 7/I; Pres. Dr DRAGOSLAV PETROVIĆ.

Republican Party of Kosovo: Leader RESHAT NURBOJA.

Serbian National Restoration: Belgrade; pro-monarchist party, favours restoration of a 'Greater Serbia'.

Serbian Radical Party (Srpska Radikalna Stranka—SRS): 11000 Belgrade, Ohridska 1; tel. (11) 457745; right-wing; nationalist; armed br. supported war in Croatia in 1991; Leader Dr VOJISLAV SESELJ.

Serbian Renewal Movement (SRM) (Srpski Pokret Obnove—SPO): 11000 Belgrade, Andre Nikolića 1-3; tel. (11) 684223; f. 1990; right-wing; nationalist; Pres. VUK DRAŠKOVIĆ.

Serbian Unity Party: Belgrade; f. 1993; nationalist; Leader ZELJKO RAZNJATIVIĆ (alias ARKAN).

Social Democratic Party: Belgrade; Leader NENAD CANAK.

Socialist Party of Serbia (SPS) (Socijalistička Partija Srbije): 11000 Belgrade, bul. Lenjina 6; tel. (11) 627804; f. 1990 by merger of League of Communists of Serbia and Socialist Alliance of the Working People (SAWP) of Serbia; Pres. SLOBODAN MILOŠEVIĆ; Gen. Sec. MILOMAR MINIĆ.

Bibliography

Allcock, J. B. 'Tourism and Social Change in Dalmatia' in *Journal of Development Studies*, Vol. 20, No. 1. 1983.

Auty, P. *Tito: A Biography*. Harmondsworth, Penguin, 1974.

Berg, S. *Conflict and Cohesion in Socialist Yugoslavia: Political Decision Making Since 1966*. Princeton, New Jersey, Princeton University Press, 1983.

Biberaj, E. 'Kosovo: The Struggle for Recognition' in *Conflict Studies*, No. 137/138. 1982.

Banać, I. *The National Question in Yugoslavia: Origins, History, Politics*. Ithaca, New York, Cornell University Press, 1984.

Bićanić, R. *Economic Policy in Socialist Yugoslavia*. Cambridge, Cambridge University Press, 1973.

Bojičić, V. and Dyker, D. 'Sanctions on Serbia: Sledgehammer or Scalpel?' in *Working Papers in Contemporary European Studies*, No. 1. Sussex European Institute, University of Sussex, 1993.

Cohen, L. J. *The Socialist Pyramid: Elites and Power in Yugoslavia*. London, Tri-Service Press, 1989.

Broken Bonds: The Disintegration of Yugoslavia. Boulder, Colorado, Westview Press, 1993.

Djilas, M. *Tito: The Story from Inside*. London, Weidenfeld and Nicolson, 1981.

Dragnich. A. N. *Serbs and Croats: The Struggle in Yugoslavia*. London, Harcourt Brace Jovanovich, 1992.

Dyker, D. *Yugoslavia: Socialism, Development and Debt*. London, Routledge, 1990.

Glenny, M. *The Fall of Yugoslavia: The Third Balkan War*. London, Penguin, 1992.

Gruenwald, O. *The Yugoslav Search for Man: Marxist Humanism in Contemporary Yugoslavia*. South Hadley, Massachusetts, J. F. Bergin, 1983.

Kardelj, E. *Reminiscences: the Struggle for Recognition and Independence: The New Yugoslavia 1944–57*. London, Blond and Briggs, 1984.

Lydall, H. *Yugoslav Socialism: Theory and Practice*. Oxford, Clarendon Press, 1984.

Yugoslavia in Crisis. Oxford, Clarendon Press, 1989.

Magaš, B. *The Destruction of Yugoslavia: Tracking the Break-Up 1980–92*. London and New York, Verso, 1993.

Minić, J. 'The Black Economy in Serbia: Transition from Socialism?' in *RFE/RL Research Report*, Vol. 2, No. 34. Munich, 1993.

Pavlowitch, S. K. *Yugoslavia*. London, Ernest Benn, 1971.

'Kosovo: An Analysis of Yugoslavia's Albanian Problem', in *Conflict Studies*, No. 137/138. 1982.

The Improbable Survivor: Yugoslavia and its Problems 1918–1988. London, C. Hurst, 1988.

Tito—Yugoslavia's Great Dictator: A Reassessment. London, C. Hurst, 1993.

Ramet, S. *Nationalism and Federalism in Yugoslavia, 1963-1990*. Bloomington, Indiana, Indiana University Press, 1992.

Shoup, P., Palmer, S., and King, R. *Yugoslav Communism and the Macedonian Question*. Hamden, Connecticut, Archon Books, 1971.

Singleton, F. *A Short History of the Yugoslav Peoples*. Cambridge, Cambridge University Press, 1985.

Singleton, F., and Carter, B. *The Economy of Yugoslavia*. London and Canberra, Croom Helm, 1982.

Tudjman, F. *Nationalism in Contemporary Europe*. Boulder, Colorado, East European Monographs, 1981.

Wilson, D. *Tito's Yugoslavia*. Cambridge, Cambridge University Press, 1979.

World Directory of Minorities. London, Longman (for Minority Rights Group), 1989.

PART THREE
Political Profiles of the Region

POLITICAL PROFILES

ABASHIDZE, Aslan Ibragimovich: Georgian (Ajarian) politician; b. 20 June 1938, Batumi. *Career:* a descendant of the dynasty which ruled Ajaria from 1463 until the late nineteenth century, he was an economist and philologist who worked for Komsomol for three years before becoming a teacher in Batumi. He was Ajar Minister of Communal Services before being appointed Georgian First Deputy Minister of Communal Services in 1986. He became Minister in 1990. He was appointed Chairman of the Supreme Soviet of the Autonomous Republic of Ajaria in April 1991. *Address:* Supreme Soviet, Batumi, Ajaria, Georgia.

ABDIĆ, Fikret: Bosnian politician and President of the 'Autonomous Province of Western Bosnia'; b. 1940; ethnic Bosnian Muslim (Bosniak). *Career:* in 1967 he became manager of Agrokomerc, a state agroindustrial company, which he built into a large, successful enterprise, thereby bringing prosperity to the surrounding region of Cazinska Krajina (north-west Bosnia) and earning popularity among its inhabitants (who named him 'Babo', an affectionate term for father). He was a member of the Presidium of the Central Committee of the League of Communists of Bosnia and Herzegovina and was a representative in the Federal Chamber of the Yugoslav Federal Assembly in the 1980s. In August 1987 he was accused of corruption and imprisoned for almost two years during his investigation and trial. He was eventually acquitted, owing to insufficient evidence against him. In mid-1990 he joined the predominantly Bosniak Party for Democratic Action (PDA), declaring that he was acting according to the will of the people of Cazinska Krajina, and was elected to the Bosnian State Presidency in November, winning more votes than any other candidate. He increasingly opposed the President of the State Presidency, Alija Izetbegović (q.v.), after the outbreak of civil war in Bosnia and Herzegovina, arguing for the partition of the Republic and an end to the 'suicidal war'. On 27 September 1993 a 400-member constituent assembly, meeting in Velika Kladusa (Cazinska Krajina), proclaimed the 'Autonomous Republic of Western Bosnia' and elected him President. He was subsequently expelled from the PDA and dismissed from the State Presidency, and his control of territory in the Bihać region was contested by Bosnian government troops. He founded the Muslim Democratic Party in October. Having continued to remain on friendly terms with both Serbs and the Croats during the Bosnian crisis (maintaining that business was more important than politics), he has been consistently accused of opportunism by his opponents. *Address:* Muslim Democratic Party of Western Bosnia, Bosnia and Herzegovina, Velika Kladusa.

ABDRAKMANOV, Serik: Kazakh politician and writer. *Career:* a noted writer and poet, he was a member of the Communist Party, although he embarked on a political career only during the 1980s. In February 1993 he formed the People's Unity movement, but it remained inhibited as a genuine political force because of the perception that it was a vehicle for Abdrakmanov's personal ambitions. The movement was broadly supportive of the President, Nursultan Nazarbayev (q.v.), and enjoyed support from figures in a variety of the ethnic communities of Kazakhstan. It became more credible as a political force when Abdrakmanov persuaded the President to become the leader of People's Unity and a congress in October elected a close colleague of Nazarbayev, Kuanysh Sultanov (q.v.), Chairman. Abdrakmanov became Chairman of the Political Board. The movement was subsequently reorganized as the People's Unity Party of Kazakhstan (SNEK) and participated in the general election of March 1994. It emerged as the single largest group in the new parliament, with 30 of the 176 seats, one of which was won by Abdrakmanov. *Address:* Office of the Supreme Kenges, Kazakhstan, 480091 Almaty, Dom pravitelstva.

ABDULLOJONOV, Abdumalik: Tajik politician and former premier; b. Leninabad (now Khojand). *Education:* Technical Institute of Odessa, Ukraine. *Career:* a member of the Khojand élite, he returned to Tajikistan to work in the Party-state apparatus (Komsomol and and the Ministry of Grain Production). He was appointed Minister of Grain Production in 1987. In 1990 he became head of the powerful Non (Bread) state corporation. He was a prominent supporter of fellow Khojandi, Rakhmon Nabiyev (1930–93), in the 1991 presidential elections. However, the independent media soon focused on his business dealings, and there were allegations that his business success was less due to his acumen than to his complicity in 'mafia' (organized criminal syndicates) hierarchies. In early 1992 the Procurator-General instituted criminal proceedings against him, alleging financial improprieties, but the case was dismissed. In September 1992 Abdullojonov was nominated as Chairman of the Council of Ministers (Prime Minister) by the Islamic-democratic parties in the coalition Government. They hoped thereby to placate the opposition of the traditional ruling élite of Tajikistan, the powerful Khojand Communist clans. However, Abdullojonov denied reformist involvement in his elevation and succeeded in persuading the reconvened Supreme Soviet (legislature) of this fact in November 1992. He was therefore confirmed as Prime Minister of a Government purged of Islamic-democratic elements. There were reports that the price was Khojand agreement to abandonment of Nabiyev as President and the election of a new head of state (Chairman of the Supreme Soviet), Imamali Rahmanov, a member of the newly dominant Kulyabi clans. However, the economy continued to deteriorate, despite the end to the civil war, allegations of corruption re-emerged, and there were other signs of tensions between the traditional ruling class of Khojand (Leninabad Oblast) and the *arriviste* victors of the civil war from Kulyab. In December 1993 he was dismissed, without explanation save for the technical reason that he was being appointed temporary ambassador in Moscow (Russia). *Address:* Embassy of Tajikistan, Russian Federation, Moscow, Skatertni per. 19.

ABILOV, Kerrar: Azerbaijani politician. *Career:* as Chairman of the United Azerbaijan party, he was one of only two rival candidates to Heydar Aliyev (q.v.), in the presidential elections held on 3 October 1993. *Address:* United Azerbaijan, Azerbaijan, Baku.

AGOŠTAN, Andraš: Yugoslav (Vojvodina/Serbian) politician; b. in Vojvodina, Republic of Serbia; ethnic Hungarian (Magyar). *Career:* the deputy director of the Forum publishing house, he was elected to the Serbian Assembly as leader of the main ethnic Hungarian party of Yugoslavia, the Democratic Community of Vojvodina Hungarians. This party was founded in August 1990 and is one of the better-organized political opposition groups of Serbia. It had five seats in the Serbian parliament. He was a prominent opponent of the fighting in Croatia and Bosnia and Herzegovina in the early 1990s. *Address:* Democratic Community of Vojvodina Hungarians, Federal Republic of Yugoslavia, Vojvodina, Ada, trg Oslobodjenja 11.

AKAYEV, Askar: President of Kyrgyzstan; b. 1944, in Kyzyl-Bayzak Keminsky rayon; m., four c. *Career:* he was a mathematics professor who joined the CPSU in 1981 (resigning from it in 1991). He was a member of the Central Committee of the Kyrgyz Communist Party, President of the Kyrgyz Academy of Sciences in Frunze (now Bishkek) and a member of various all-Union committees. A known liberal, he was elected by the republican Supreme Soviet as executive President in October 1990, after the Communist leader (for whom the post had been designed) failed to win a majority. He was a compromise candidate, who favoured reform and was unconnected with the dominant factions, having been in Leningrad (now St Petersburg) for many years of his academic career. He favoured the introduction of economic reform before political changes, although he also achieved some consensus with the opposition. He ensured that Kyrgyzstan was one of the most ostensibly liberal of the Central Asian Republics. He condemned the coup attempt against President Mikhail Gorbachev (q.v.) of the USSR, in August 1991, and was himself threatened by Communist putschists. He took precautionary measures, however, and, when the Moscow coup attempt failed, he resigned from the Communist Party, which was subsequently dissolved. In October Akayev was unopposed in direct presidential elections. He resolved to make independent Kyrgyzstan the 'Switzerland of Central Asia', and urged economic reform on an untypically (for Central Asia) critical parliament. During 1993 parliament obliged him to cease being head of government (he had subordinated the premier and cabinet to his authority in February 1992) and he suffered the hostile investigations of many of his closest political colleagues for corruption. Both the Vice-President (Feliks Kulov—q.v.) and the premier (Tursunbek Chyngyshev—q.v.) were obliged to resign in December. The new premier appointed some of Akayev's most implacable Communist critics to his Government, but, in January 1994, the President secured what was interpreted as an overwhelming endorsement of his reform programme in a referendum on his completing his term of office. *Address:* Office of the President of the Republic, Kyrgyzstan, 720003 Bishkek, Government House.

AKMADŽIĆ, Mile: Bosnian politician and Minister of Inter-republican and International Relations of the 'Croatian Republic of Herzeg-Bosna'; ethnic Croat. *Career:* a Croat who supported a multi-ethnic Bosnian state, he was appointed Prime Minister of Bosnia and Herzegovina (and consequently a member of the extended State Presidency) in November 1992, following the resignation of a fellow Croat, Jure Pelivan. On 2 August the following year, during peace negotiations in Geneva (Switzerland), he and two other Croat members of the State Presidency left the Bosnian negotiating team and joined the Croatian delegation, in protest at the actions of the Bosnian army against the Croat population of central Bosnia. He was dismissed as Prime Minister at the end of the month, and was subsequently appointed a member of the Government of 'Herzeg-Bosna' a self-proclaimed Croat republic based in Mostar, central Bosnia. Owing to his increasingly significant role as Bosnian Croat representative at peace negotiations (he attended the talks in Washington, USA, in February 1994, at which an agreement was signed on the creation of a Croat-Muslim federation within Bosnia and Herzegovina) there was increasing speculation that he might succeed Mate Boban (q.v.) as President of Herzeg-Bosna.

ALEXSEY II, His Holiness Patriarch: Head of the Russian Orthodox Church, Chairman of the Moscow Patriarchy; b. 23 Feb. 1929, in Tallinn, Estonia; of Baltic German and ethnic Russian descent. *Education:* a graduate of the Leningrad (now St Petersburg) Theological College. *Career:* originally Aleksey M. Ridiger, his early career in the Russian Orthodox Church was in his native Estonia, and he became Bishop of Tallinn and Estonia in 1961. He moved to the Moscow Patriarchate in 1962, where he was Vice-Chairman of the Dept of External Affairs. In 1964 he became an Archbishop, the Administrative Manager of the Patriarchate and a permanent member of the Holy Synod. In 1968 he became Metropolitan of Tallinn and Estonia and, in 1986, Metropolitan of Leningrad (now St Petersburg) and Novgorod. In 1990 he succeeded Patriarch Pimen as Patriarch of Moscow and All Russia. He is considered theologically conservative, but relatively liberal in politics (he condemned the attempted *putsch* of August 1991 and mediated between Boris Yeltsin (q.v.) and the Russian parliament in the crisis of September–October 1993). *Address:* Russian Federation, 113191 Moscow, Danilovsky val 22.

ALIA, Ramiz: Albanian politician and former President; b. 1925, in Shkodër. *Career:* he joined the Communist Party (later renamed the Party of Labour of Albania, and then, in 1990, the Socialist Party of Albania—SPA) in 1943 and achieved responsibility in the National Liberation Army and the youth movement before moving into the Party hierarchy. He became a full member of the Politburo in 1961 and, in 1982, head of state. He was responsible for introducing moderate reforms after the death of Enver Hoxha, in 1985, particularly with the increase in popular opposition from 1990. He formally left the SPA in April 1991, upon being elected to the post of President of the Republic, a post he held until April 1992, when following the electoral defeat of the SPA, he resigned. On 12 September 1992 Alia was placed under house arrest and charged with corruption, although it was claimed that the real reason for his arrest was his strong criticism of the new Government. He was imprisoned in August 1993. *Address:* Office of the President, Albania, Tirana.

ALIYEV, Heydar Ali Rza ogly: President of Azerbaijan; b. 1923. *Education:* graduate of Azerbaijan State University (1957). *Career:* already active in the administration of his home territory of Nakhichevan, he joined the CPSU in 1945 and was prominent in the republican apparatus by the 1960s. He became First Secretary of the Azerbaijan Communist Party, and thus leader of the Republic, in 1969. In 1982 he was appointed First Deputy Chairman of the USSR Council of Ministers in Moscow. He was dismissed in 1987, a victim of Mikhail Gorbachev's (q.v.) drive against corruption. He left the Communists in July 1991, alleging their suppression of the democratic movement, and, in September, was elected Chairman of the Supreme Majlis (parliament) of the Autonomous Republic of Nakhichevan. Aliyev was prevented from contesting the presidential elections of June 1992 because he exceeded the maximum age limit of 65 years. In the same year he founded the New Azerbaijan Party (Yeni Azerbaijan), support for which demonstrated his continuing popularity in the country. In early June 1993, threatened by revolt, President Abulfaz Elchibey (q.v.) summoned Aliyev to Baku and offered him the premiership, which Aliyev refused. On 13 June Aliyev attempted to negotiate with Col Surat Husseinov (q.v.), a rebel army commander. Two days later, Aliyev was elected Chairman of the Supreme Soviet. On 18 June Aliyev declared that he had appropriated the presidential powers of Elchibey, who had fled to Nakhichevan the previous night. One week later the Milli Majlis granted Aliyev the majority of these powers, despite the claims of both Elchibey and Husseinov to be in control of the country. However, when Husseinov arrived in Baku on 28 June he recognized Aliyev as Acting President. Aliyev was elected President by direct popular vote on 3 October, receiving 98.8% of the votes cast, and was inaugurated one week later. *Address:* Office of the President, Azerbaijan, Baku.

AMANBAYEV, Jumgalbek: Deputy Prime Minister of Kyrgyzstan. *Career:* he became leader of the republican Communist Party in April 1991, to replace the discredited Absamat Masaliyev. By this time the Party had already lost its crucial advantage of leadership by failing to secure the new post of executive President, which, instead, went to the liberal, Askar Akayev (q.v.). Following the failed Moscow coup attempt of August 1991, the Kyrgyz Communist Party was banned, but, in June 1992 Masaliyev and Amanbayev re-formed the party as the Party of Communists of Kyrgyzstan (PCK). Those deputies who were members of the PCK, Amanbayev among them, were prominent in opposition to the Government and secured a strong parliamentary system for the country, by limiting the powers of the President. However, Akayev complained that this unremitting opposition was impeding governance and he appealed for an end to factionalism. Having made this appeal he decided to dismiss his Government (which had technically survived a motion of 'no confidence' in the Jogorku Kenesh—legislature), in December. The new Prime Minister, Apas Jumagulov (q.v.), had been the last Communist premier of Kyrgyzstan and he appointed Amanbayev and other Communists to the Government. However, the Jogorku Kenesh remained suspicious of government in general and insisted that if Amanbayev wished to retain his position as Deputy Prime Minister responsible for agriculture, he must resign both his parliamentary seat and the leadership of the PCK, which he did at the end of 1993. *Address:* Office of the Deputy Prime Ministers, Kyrgyzstan, 720000 Bishkek, Government House.

ANDOV, Stojan: President of the Macedonian Assembly (parliamentary speaker). *Career:* he was in public service, serving as ambassador to Iraq during the late 1980s. He was a supporter of the federal prime minister, Ante Marković's, economic reforms and favoured gradual political reform, but the maintenance of a Yugoslav federation. He became leader of the Macedonian branch of the federal party of Ante Marković, the Alliance of Reform Forces, which was one of the major parties in Macedonia following the parliamentary elections of November–December 1990. Helped by his reputation as a skilled negotiator, and with the need for political compromise in the Assembly apparent, Andov was elected President (speaker) of the Sobranje (Assembly) on 8 January 1991. His party was subsequently renamed the Reform Forces of Macedonia—Liberal Party. *Address:* Sobranje, Macedonia, 91000 Skopje, 11 Octomvri bb.

ARARKTSYAN, Babken: Chairman of the Armenian Supreme Council (parliamentary speaker). *Career:* he succeeded Levon Ter-Petrosyan (q.v.) as Chairman of the Supreme Soviet following the latter's election as President of the Republic in October 1991. He remained Chairman when the legislature changed its name to the Supreme Council (Geraguin Khorhurt) during 1992. *Address:* Geraguin Khorhurt, Armenia, Yerevan.

ARDZINBA, Vladislav Grigoriyvich: Georgian (Abkhazian) politician and historian; b. 1945, in Eshera, Abkhazia. *Education:* he studied at Sukhumi Pedagogical Institute. *Career:* having been a researcher at the Institute of Oriental Sciences in Moscow since 1969, he became Director of the D. Gulia Abkhaz Institute of Language, Literature and History (Georgian Academy of Sciences) in 1987 and remained in that post until 1990. He was a member of the CPSU in 1967–91 and was a People's Deputy of the USSR in 1989–91. He became Chairman of the Abkhazian Supreme Soviet in 1990 and was leader of the independence movement. He returned to Sukhumi following the defeat of the Georgian Government's forces in September 1993, but later agreed to negotiations on the future status of Abkhazia. Previously enjoying covert Russian support, Abkhazia seemed less likely to retain this after Georgia joined the Commonwealth of Independent States in October 1993. *Address:* Supreme Soviet, Sukhumi, Abkhazia, Georgia.

ARUTYUNYAN, Gagik Garushevich: Vice-President of Armenia; b. 1948. *Education:* a graduate in economic sciences. *Career:* an economist by profession (a lecturer and writer), he was a head of the Armenian Communist Party's Central Committee. He joined the nationalist opposition and, from August 1990, was a Deputy Chairman of the Armenian Supreme Soviet. In October 1991, with the support of President Levon Ter-Petrosyan (q.v.), he was elected Vice-President of the Republic. On 22 November he was appointed Chairman of the Council of Ministers (Prime Minister). He was succeeded as Prime Minister by Khosrov Arutyunyan (q.v.) in the second half of 1992, but he remained Vice-President. *Address:* Office of the Vice-President, Armenia, Yerevan.

ARUTYUNYAN, Khosrov: Armenian politician and former premier; b. 1948. *Education:* he studied at Yerevan Polytechnic Institute. *Career:* a former mechanical engineer, he was director of a state knitted-goods factory. He was a member of the Supreme Soviet from 1990 and in 1990–92 he was Chairman of a commission on problems of local self-government. He was appointed as Prime Minister in the latter half of 1992, but was dismissed in early February of the following year because of disagreements over social and economic policy, particularly the budget for 1993.

ASANBAYEV, Yerik Magzumovich: Vice-President of Kazakhstan; b. 10 March 1936. *Career:* he joined the CPSU in 1967 and was Chairman of the republican Supreme Soviet from April 1990 until December 1991. A reformist Communist, he was a supporter and deputy of President Nursultan Nazarbayev (q.v.). He was popularly elected as Vice-President of the Republic, in December 1991. An economist by training, he had a particular interest in the privatization process, but his contribution to government was based on the President's indulgence, rather than any formal authority or the support of an important political interest group. *Address:* Office of the Vice-President of the Republic, Kazakhstan, 480091 Almaty, Respubliki 4.

BABIĆ, Milan: Croatian ('Serbian Krajina') politician; ethnic Serb. *Career:* a former dentist, he was leader of the Croatian Serbs who began the formation of an autonomous area in Croatia, when that Republic began moves towards secession from the old Yugoslav federation. A member of the Serbian Democratic Party (SDP), he gained influence and popularity among the Serbs in the Krajina region for his belief that they should not be separated from the Yugoslav (Serbian) state against their will. Consequently, in mid-1990, allegedly with the support of the federal armed forces, the ethnic Serbs of Croatia established a large measure of effective self-rule in a large part of Croatia. As head of government in Krajina, based in Knin, he immediately sought to establish a military force which would be capable of defending the region's independence. He also seized control of the media in Krajina, to ensure public support for his actions. At the end of 1991, was declared to be President of the 'Republic of Serbian Krajina' (RSK), which claimed membership of the Yugoslav federation and its separation from Croatia. Previously supported by the Serbian authorities, he would not concur in their agreement to the UN-brokered peace plan, objecting to the presence of peace-keeping forces in Krajina. The split became public in January 1992. He resigned the presidency and subsequently became mayor of Knin, but stood as the SDP candidate in the presidential elections held in December 1993–January 1994. He won 49.3% of the votes cast in the first round, but owing to allegations of irregularities and to the fact that none of the seven candidates had won an overall majority, on 23 January 1994 he contested a second round with Milan Martić, an independent candidate (endorsed by the Serbian President, Slobodan Milošević—q.v.) who had gained 25.9% of the votes. Although it was predicted that Babić would gain the most support from the electorate, Martić was elected President. Babić's party, however, was the largest in the RSK parliament and it was considered likely that he would be a member of any coalition government agreed (he was reportedly offered a deputy premiership and the portfolio of foreign affairs in March 1994). *Address:* Serbian Democratic Party, Croatia, 59300 Knin, Jove Miodragovića 22.

BAGRATYAN, Hrand: Prime Minister of Armenia; b. 1958. *Career:* an economist with a reputation as an economic reformist. Having previously been Chairman of the State Committee for the Economy and one of three joint First Deputy Chairmen of the Council of Ministers, in early 1992 he became Deputy Prime Minister, retaining his post at the State Committee for the Economy. Later in the year he also became Minister of the Economy. He was appointed as Prime Minister in February 1993. *Address:* Office of the Prime Minister, Armenia, 375010 Yerevan, Parliament Sq. 1, Government House.

BALCEROWICZ, Dr Leszek: Polish politician and economist; b. 19 January 1947, in Lipno; m., with three c. *Education:* graduated from the Main School of Planning and Statistics in Warsaw (1970); studied business administration at St John's University, New York (USA), until 1974. *Career:* staff member at the Institute of International Economy Relations, 1970–80, then worked at the Economic Development Institute. He was a member of the Polish Union of Workers' Party, 1969–81. In 1989–91 he was Minister of Finance and introduced reforms (the so-called Balcerowicz Plan) which provided for a 'shock therapy' move to a free-market economy. *Address:* 00-916 Warsaw, ul. Świętokrzyska 12, Poland.

BERISHA, Dr Sali: President of Albania; b. 1 Aug. 1944, in Tropoje. *Education:* he studied at Tirana University. *Career:* a cardiologist, he co-founded the main anti-Communist opposition group, the Democratic Party of Albania (DPA), with Gramoz Pashko (q.v.), in December 1990. In December 1991 he withdrew DPA support from the Bufi Government, in protest at the failure to satisfy opposition demands. The move was also believed to bolster his own authority as head of the radical, more militant wing of the party. On 9 April 1992, after the electoral defeat of the Communists, he was elected to the presidency by a large parliamentary majority. In the following month, as the new President, he toured Europe and addressed the Council of Europe's Parliamentary Assembly in Strasbourg (France) in an attempt to increase foreign investment. He pursued close relations with Muslim countries and, on Berisha's initiative, Albania became a member of the Organization of the Islamic Conference in December 1992, a decision which met with some controversy. There were accusations that he was undemocratic in conducting Albania's foreign policy. However, the limits to his tolerance of the right-wing were demonstrated in August 1993, when he dismissed a popular minister for allegedly pro-Fascist remarks. *Address:* c/o Office of the Council of Ministers, Këshilli i Ministrave, Tirana, Albania.

BEROV, Lyuben: Prime Minister of Bulgaria. *Career:* an historian and former economic advisor to President Zheliu Zhelev (q.v.), he was nominated to the post of Prime Minister by the Movement for Rights and Freedoms in December 1992, replacing Filip Dimitrov (q.v.). Against a background of political instability, he pursued a policy of large-scale privatization and support for private enterprise. Although criticized by his opponents for achieving little to improve the economic situation in Bulgaria, he maintained sufficient support in the National Assembly to survive two votes of censure proposed by the Union of Democratic Forces during 1993. In early 1994 he was temporarily incapacitated by a heart attack. *Address:* Council of Ministers, Bulgaria, 1000 Sofia, Blvd Dondukov 1.

BIRKAVS, Valdis: Prime Minister of Latvia; b. 28 July 1942, in Rīga. *Education:* he obtained an honours degree in law from the University of Latvia where he also studied philosophy. *Career:* having graduated, he worked for the Ministry of Justice and simultaneously taught law and criminology at the University of Latvia, where he became a full-time lecturer in 1986. A member of the Latvian Communist Party, in 1990 he was elected to the Supreme Council. In June 1993 he won a seat in the newly formed legislature, renamed the Saeima, as a member of Latvian Way, a democratic coalition which won a total of 36 seats. He formed a coalition Government comprising members of Latvian Way and the Latvian Farmers' Union, which was endorsed by the Saeima on 20 July. The aims of his premiership included an acceleration of the process of privatization, the implementation of a large number of legal reforms, the adoption of fair legislation on the status of the non-Latvian population, and the development of cordial relations with the other Baltic states. However, since the parliamentary coalition of Latvian Way and the Latvian Farmers' Union did not command an absolute majority in the Saeima, he was likely to experience some difficulty in implementing his policies. *Address:* Office of the Council of Ministers, Brīvības 36, Rīga 1170, Latvia.

BOBAN, Mate: Bosnian politician and former President of the 'Croat Republic of Herzeg-Bosna'; ethnic Croat. *Career:* the 'Croatian Union of Herzeg-Bosna', a Croat state comprising some 30% of the territory of Bosnia and Herzegovina, was declared on 7 July 1992, with Boban as its President. Although an extreme nationalist, he claimed to be committed to securing peace in the country and approved international peace proposals in January 1993. He also attempted (unsuccessfully) to end the Croat-Muslim violence in central Bosnia during 1993. On 22 October he made a joint statement with the Bosniak Fikret Abdić (q.v.), to the effect that both sides intended to establish peace in the newly proclaimed 'Republic of Western Bosnia'. In February 1994, in an attempt to aid the peace process, he was reported to have resigned as President of Herzeg-Bosna. According to the Presidential Council which formed to carry out the functions of the presidency, however, he remained President, although the formation of the Federation of Bosnia and Herzegovina, in March, was likely to render his post redundant.

BOROSS, Dr Péter: Hungarian Prime Minister; b. 28 Aug. 1928, in Nagybajom. *Education:* he studied law at Budapest University, graduating in 1951. *Career:* he worked for Budapest city council until January 1957, when he was dismissed for his membership of the revolutionary committee in the previous year. He was subsequently arrested and imprisoned and remained under surveillance by the security services until late 1959. For several years he was engaged in menial employment until he became a restaurant manager. He became deputy director of a catering company in 1965 and was appointed director in 1971. He retired from that position in February 1989, but was nominated as Minister of the Interior in December 1990. In August 1992 he joined the Hungarian Democratic Forum and in December 1993, following the death of József Antall (b. 1932), he was appointed Prime Minister. *Address:* Office of the Prime Minister, Hungary, 1055 Budapest, Kossuth Lajos tér 1–3.

BRAZAUSKAS, Algirdas-Mikolas Kazevich: President of Lithuania; b. 22 September 1932, in Rokishkis; m. with two d. *Education:* Polytechnic of Kaunas. *Career:* a member of the Communist Party of Lithuania (CPL), his first political appointment was in 1965, when he became Lithuanian Minister for the Construction Materials Industry. He was First Secretary of the CPL from 1988–1990 (during which time it seceded from the Communist Party of the Soviet Union) and Deputy Chairman of the all-Union Supreme Soviet in 1990. In 1990–91 he served as Deputy Prime Minister of Lithuania, under the premiership of Kazimiere Prunskiene. Following elections to the parliament (Seimas) in October–November 1992, in which the former Communists (renamed the Lithuanian Democratic Labour Party) won 76 seats out of a total of 141, he was elected Chairman of the Seimas. In this capacity, he was also acting head of state, until presidential elections were held. He was elected President by the Seimas. gaining some 60% of the votes cast, on 14 February 1993. He immediately distanced himself from the CPL and advocated pragmatism in relations with the Russian Federation, as well as gradual economic reform. *Address:* Office of the President, Gedimino 53, Vilnius 2026, Lithuania.

BULATOVIĆ, Momir: Yugoslav politician, President of Montenegro; b. 1928, in Montenegro. *Career:* a Communist, he became prominent in the leadership of the League of Communists of Montenegro, following the protests of early 1989, which caused the resignation of the old leadership. Bulatović became leader of the republican Communists (who were renamed the Democratic Party of Socialists in 1991) and secured the Party's nomination for the presidential elections, in December 1990. On 23 December he was elected President of the seven-member State Presidency of Montenegro. He was re-elected, by popular vote, to be President of the Republic on 10 January 1993. Under him, Montenegro was a loyal supporter of Serbia, in Yugoslavia's crises in the early 1990s. However, he was anxious to maintain a distinct Montenegrin identity and did, at times, distance himself from the more aggressive Serbian policies, particularly in neighbouring Bosnia and Herzegovina. In 1993 he refused to endorse a plan whereby the republican foreign ministries, among others, would be abolished. *Address:* Office of the President of the Republic of Montenegro, Federal Republic of Yugoslavia, Podgorica.

BURBULIS, Gennady: Russian politician; b. 1945, in Pervouralsk, Sverdlovsk (now Yekaterinburg) region; of mixed Lithuanian and ethnic Russian parentage. *Education:* graduate of Ural State University, in Philosophical Sciences; speaks German. *Career:* a philosopher, he first worked in factories and the Soviet Rocket Forces, before going to the Ural State University. He then lectured on Marxism-Leninism at the Institute of the All-Union Ministry of Non-Ferrous Metallurgy, in Sverdlovsk, until he was elected to the Soviet Congress of People's Deputies. He joined the CPSU in 1970, but, in 1988, he formed a political club in favour of democratization, the Discussion Tribune, in Sverdlovsk. He was elected to Congress in 1989 and was a prominent member of the radical Inter-Regional Group. He became a supporter of Boris Yeltsin (q.v.) and, after Yeltsin's election as Chairman of the Supreme Soviet of the Russian Federation, his chief of staff. A Russian nationalist, Burbulis is the leader of the 'Young Turks' (*Mladoturki*), a radical group of young politicians, who opposed the Union. In 1991 he was appointed State Secretary, the head of the Russian Federation State Council, an advisory body to President Yeltsin. On 6 November 1991 Yeltsin formally formed a new Government of the Russian Federation, with himself as Chairman. Burbulis was appointed First Deputy Chairman and granted additional powers to act for the Chairman. He was dismissed, however, as a concession by Yeltsin to the conservative Russian parliament, on 17 December 1992.

In December 1993 he was elected to the State Duma, the lower chamber of the new Federal Assembly, as a member of the democratic Russia's Choice electoral coalition (headed by Yegor Gaidar—q.v.). However, he had yet not decided on whether or not to join the Russia's Choice party, when its formation was announced by Gaidar on 29 March 1994. *Address:* State Duma, Russian Federation, Moscow, Novy Arbat 36.

ČARNOGURSKÝ, Ján: Slovak politician and former premier; b. 1 Jan. 1944, in Bratislava. *Education:* graduated in law from Charles University, Prague (Czech Republic). *Career:* he practised law until he was banned in 1981, after defending a teacher accused of sedition. In 1981–87 he worked as a company lawyer, while, at the same time, dealing with human-rights cases. He was unemployed for two years and was then detained in prison, from August to November 1989, charged with incitement. In December 1989 he was made Deputy Federal Prime Minister and remained in the Federal Government until June 1990. He was a founder of the Christian Democratic Movement (CDM), a predominantly Slovak party favouring a looser federation, in early 1990. In June 1990 he was invited to join the new coalition Federal Government, but he declined the offer, preferring to take office in the Slovak Republic as First Deputy Premier. He became the republican Premier in April 1991, but was replaced in June 1992, following legislative elections in which his party won only 18 seats in the Slovak National Council. He subsequently remained a deputy in the Slovak parliament and Chairman of the CDM, a party which was strongly represented in the coalition Government formed in March 1994. *Address:* Christian Democratic Movement, Žabotova 2, 814 02 Bratislava, Slovakia.

CHANTURIA, Georgi ('Gia'): Georgian politician; b. 1960. *Career:* a member of the nationalist opposition to Communist rule, he was leader of the National Forum (subsequently the National Democratic Party of Georgia) and one of the most serious political opponents of Zviad Gamsakhurdia (1939–93). He urged the boycott of the 1990 Supreme Soviet elections and the election of a National Congress instead. This was to act as a parliament until Georgia gained its independence. He was arrested by the Gamsakhurdia regime, but released by rebel forces during the civil war, in December 1991. In this conflict he and other radicals were allied with more moderate opposition figures. He became a member of the Georgian Supreme Soviet in 1992. *Address:* National Democratic Party of Georgia, Georgia, 380008 Tbilisi, Rustaveli 21.

CHERNOMYRDIN, Viktor Stepanovich: Chairman of the Government (Prime Minister) of the Russian Federation; b. 9 April 1938, in Cherny-Otrog, Orenburg obl. *Education:* Kuybyshev Polytechnic. *Career:* he served in the Soviet army in 1957–60 before becoming involved in industry. In 1973–78 he was deputy chief engineer of the Orenburg natural-gas plant. A member of the CPSU since 1961, he held various posts in the state and Party bureaucracy until he was appointed Soviet Minister of Gas in 1985. In 1989 he oversaw the transition of the Ministries of Oil and Gas into the highly successful state energy company, Gasprom, of which he was Chairman. He was Minister of Fuel and Energy in June–December 1992. On 9 December President Boris Yeltsin (q.v.) nominated him as Chairman of the Council of Ministers, following the conservative Russian parliament's rejection of Yeltsin's original proposal of Yegor Gaidar (q.v.). As premier he was strongly criticized by radical economic reformers, who feared that his actions were increasing the danger of hyperinflation. Western economic institutions were more hesitant about granting financial aid to Russia during his premiership, as a result of his willingness to subsidize inefficient state enterprises. He has described the policies of Gaidar and Boris Fedorov (q.v.) as 'poorly thought-out experiments' and compared privatization to Stalin's forced collectivization in the 1930s. *Address:* Office of the Government, Russian Federation, Moscow, Staraya pl. 4.

CHORNOVIL, Vyacheslav Maksimovich: Ukrainian politician; b. 1937; m. *Education:* studied journalism at the University of Kiev. *Career:* from 1960 to 1965 he held various editorial jobs in television, radio and the press, all in Ukraine. He engaged in some dissident activity, was dismissed from his posts and was sentenced to prison and hard labour, in 1965. In 1968 he went on hunger strike, was pardoned and released. In 1972 he was again arrested for further dissident activity and, in 1975, despite many protests, he was sentenced to the Mordovian camp. He was subsequently released, after numerous petitions and complaints. In the late 1980s he became a leading figure in the radical wing of the Rukh nationalist opposition movement. He was elected as Chairman of Lvov Regional Council, Western Ukraine. In the presidential elections of December 1991 he came second to the victor, Leonid Kravchuk (q.v.), with 23% of the votes cast. According to preliminary figures, he was elected as deputy to the Ukrainian Supreme Council (Verkhovna Rada) on 27 March 1994, winning some 62.5% of the votes in his Ternopol constituency. *Address:* Verkhovna Rada, Ukraine, Kiev.

CHYNGYSHEV, Tursunbek: Kyrgyz politician and former premier. *Career:* an economist by training, he was appointed premier in February 1992, following the death of his predecessor, Nasirdin Isanov, in an automobile accident. However, the President, Askar Akayev (q.v.), was himself head of government until 1993. Charged with the reform of the economy, Prime Minister Chyngyshev did not have a basis of political support in parliament and probably received criticism which the opposition would rather have levelled at the popular President. His authority, if not his integrity, were compromised by the 'Seabeco affair' during 1993, when a naïve agreement with a Canadian brokerage company resulted in the apparent loss of a considerable part of the country's gold reserves. Although many of the accusations of corruption were politically motivated and the required two-thirds majority was not gained in the parliamentary vote of 'no confidence' in December 1993, Chyngyshev was dismissed. President Akayev was obliged to take this decision given his own quest for a stable political situation. However, Chyngyshev claimed that a Communist counter-revolution was being threatened and Akayev himself was under threat. *Address:* c/o Office of the President of the Republic, Kyrgyzstan, 720003 Bishkek, Government House.

CHZHEN, Viktor A.: Uzbekistan politician; b. 1944; ethnic Korean. *Career:* a Russian-speaker, he graduated in technical sciences. He was Minister of Local Industry until his appointment as one of the Deputy Chairmen of the Cabinet of Ministers and as Chairman of the State Committee for Property and Privatization in January 1994. His political value to the regime of President Islam Karimov (q.v.) was as a Russian-speaker holding high office in the newly independent Uzbek state. *Address:* Office of the Cabinet of Ministers, Uzbekistan, 700008 Tashkent, Government House.

CONSTANTINESCU, Emil: Romanian politician. *Career:* President of the opposition Democratic Convention of Romania (DCR) Alliance and the main rival to Ion Iliescu (q.v.) in the presidential election of September–October 1992. He received 38.57% of the votes cast in the second ballot. His party was centrist in policy, but favoured a more rapid introduction of market reforms. *Address:* Democratic Convention of Romania Alliance, Romania, 70001 Bucharest, Splaiul Unirii 5, ap. 1, sect. 3.

COPOSU, Corneliu: Romanian politician. *Career:* he was initially the leader of the National Peasants' Party, which merged with the Christian Democratic Party in 1990, to become the Christian Democratic National Peasants' Party, of which he became President. He was a prominent member of the Democratic Convention, the coalition opposed to the National Salvation Front. At the general election of 27 September 1992, his party was the most successful single party within the Democratic Convention of Romania (DCR) Alliance. *Address:* Christian Democratic National Peasants' Party, Romania, 70433 Bucharest, Bd. Carol 34.

ĆOSIĆ, Dobrica: Yugoslav (Serbian) politician and writer, former President of the Federal Republic of Yugoslavia; b. 29 Dec. 1921, in Velika Drenovina. *Education:* he studied at Belgrade University and Higher Party School. *Career:* he worked as a journalist and a freelance writer. He was expelled from the League of Communists of Yugoslavia and prosecuted, but became involved in politics once more in the 1980s. He was elected President of the newly formed Federal Republic of Yugoslavia (FRY—Serbia and Montenegro) on 15 June 1992 and re-elected, in a direct ballot, on 20 December 1992. He supported the candidature of federal premier Milan Panić (q.v.) in the Serbian presidential elections of December 1992 and openly criticized Serbian President Slobodan Milošević (q.v.). He participated in UN-EC negotiations on the former Yugoslavia in May 1993 and attempted to persuade Bosnian Serb leaders to accept the proposed peace plan. In June 1993 he was dismissed from office by the Federal Assembly after accusations that he had conspired with army generals to depose Milošević. *Address:* c/o Office of the Federal Government, Federal Republic of Yugoslavia, 11070 Belgrade, Lenjina 2.

CRVENKOVSKI, Branko: Chairman of the Cabinet of Ministers (Prime Minister) of Macedonia; b. 1962. *Career:* a member of the Macedonian League of Communists (which, after several name changes, became the Social Democratic Union of Macedonia), he succeeded Kiro Gligorov (q.v.) as leader when Gligorov became President of the Republic. As leader of one of the main parties he was appointed Chairman (Prime Minister) of a new coalition Government on 4 September 1992. *Address:* Office of the Prime Minister, Macedonia, 91000 Skopje, Dame Grueva 6.

CSURKA István: Hungarian politician. *Career:* the former Vice-Chairman of the Hungarian Democratic Forum (HDF), he was the target of particular criticism in September 1992 during a large demonstration in Budapest against the prevalence of right-wing movements. Having been expelled from the HDF, on 21 June 1993 he founded and became Co-Chairman of the Hungarian Justice and Life Party (HJP). *Address:* HJP, Hungary, c/o Office of Deputies, 1357 Budapest, Széchenyi rakpart 19.

DIMITROV, Filip: Bulgarian politician; b. 31 March 1955, in Sofia. *Education:* graduated in law, in Sofia. *Career:* from a professional, intellectual family, he became a lawyer and was not politically affiliated until the fall of Communism, in November 1989. He was a leader of the Greens and was elected leader of the main opposition coalition, the Union of Democratic Forces (UDF), as a compromise candidate, in December 1990. He was leader of the UDF—Movement, or Dark Blue, faction, which favoured more radical, right-wing policies. His success was confirmed by the departure of the liberal groups in mid-1991 and the main UDF victory in the elections of October 1991. Dimitrov therefore led Bulgaria's first Government without Communist membership since the Second World War. In December 1992, following a vote of censure by the National Assembly, he was replaced as Prime Minister. He continued, however, to exercise a leading role in Bulgarian politics, in his capacity as Chairman of the UDF. *Address:* Bulgaria, 1000 Sofia, Blvd Rakovski 134.

DJUKANOVIĆ, Milo: Yugoslav politician, Prime Minister of Montenegro; b. 15 Feb. 1962, in Nikšić, Montenegro. *Education:* he is a graduate in economics. *Career:* he joined the League of Communists of Yugoslavia in 1979. In early 1989 the Montenegrin Communist leadership was forced to resign and was replaced by a relatively young group of Communists, of whom Djukanović was one. They favoured a Montenegrin renaissance, although they remained loyal allies of Serbia. The new leadership was among the first in Yugoslavia to agree to the holding of multi-party elections, which took place in December 1990 and were won by the League of Communists of Yugoslavia (subsequently renamed the Democratic Party of Socialists). This party which formed a Government, led by Djukanović, in January 1991. Following elections in December 1992, he formed a coalition Government. *Address:* Office of the Prime Minister of Montenegro, Federal Republic of Yugoslavia, Podgorica, Jovana Tomaševića bb.

DOĞAN, Ahmed: Bulgarian politician; b. 29 March 1954; ethnic Turk. *Education:* doctorate in philosophy. *Career:* under the Communist regime, he was prosecuted for his championing of ethnic Turkish rights and, in June 1989, he was arrested and sentenced to 10 years in prison for being a founder and leader of an 'anti-state organization', the Movement for Rights and Freedoms (MRF). He was amnestied in December of the same year. He was elected as a deputy in June 1990 and, after the October 1991 elections, his party was the third-largest in the National Assembly and agreed to support a Government of the Union of Democratic Forces. In December 1992 the MRF nominated Lyuben Berov (q.v.) as Prime Minister, and subsequently, with the majority of members of the Bulgarian Socialist Party and a schismatic section of the Union of Democratic Forces, provided him with a strong base of support in the National Assembly. *Address:* Bulgaria, 1408 Sofia, j.k. Ivan Vazov, Tzarigradsko Shosse 47/1.

DOMLJAN, Dr Žarko: Vice-President (deputy speaker) of the Croatian Assembly; b. 14 September 1932, at Imotski. *Education:* he graduated in English and history of art from the University of Zagreb and gained a doctorate in 1973. *Career:* he worked as a musician and a book editor, before becoming employed at the Institute of Historical Sciences (Zagreb) in 1987. Previously unaffiliated to any political organization, he joined the Croatian Democratic Union, in 1989, and was elected as a deputy to the Croatian Assembly, in 1990. In May he was elected to the post of parliamentary speaker (President of the Assembly). Following the elections to the Assembly on 2 August 1993 he assumed the role of Vice-President. *Address:* Croatia, 41000 Zagreb, Radićev trg. 6.

DRACH, Ivan Fedorovich: Ukrainian politician and writer; b. 1936, in Telizhentsy, Kiev district. *Education:* studied philology at University of Kiev, then theatre and drama at Moscow State University. *Career:* apart from writing novels and poetry (he has many published works), he has also worked on the *Literaturnaya Ukraina* newspaper, in the Kiev Aleksandr Dovenko Film Studio and on the Kiev newspaper, *Witczyna.* He joined the CPSU in 1959 but resigned his membership in 1990. A Ukrainian nationalist, he was a founding member of the People's Movement (Narodny Rukh) of the Ukraine for Perestroika and was elected leader of Rukh at its inaugural congress in September 1989. In 1990 he was elected to the Ukrainian Supreme Soviet (subsequently renamed the Supreme Council—Verkhovna Rada). He was re-elected as a deputy in the March–April 1994 elections. *Address:* Union of Ukrainian Writers, Ukraine, 252008 Kiev, ul. Ordzhonikidze 2.

DRAŠKOVIĆ, Vuk: Yugoslav (Serbian) politician; b. 29 Nov. 1946, in Media, in the Banat region of Vojvodina; m. (Danica). *Education:* he studied at Belgrade University. *Career:* an ardent nationalist, he was vociferous in demands for resistance to the Croats and the Albanians of Kosovo (now Kosovo-Metohija). His right-wing tendencies were said to have contributed to his poor showing in the presidential elections of 1990, when he gained only 20% of the votes cast. In March 1991, however, he emerged as the leading opposition figure, during the anti-government demonstrations in Belgrade. His party, the Serbian Renewal Movement, was the largest opposition group in the Serbian parliament, until 1992, when he formed an electoral coalition, the Democratic Movement of Serbia (DEPOS), which gained 49 seats in the December 1992 elections. Claiming electoral fraud, Drašković and other DEPOS deputies began a boycott of parliament from February 1993. During anti-government demonstrations in June, he was detained by police for five weeks and badly beaten. Charges of attempting to overthrow the constitutional order were eventually dropped. In December 1993 elections his DEPOS party gained 45 seats. *Address:* DEPOS, Federal Republic of Yugoslavia, Belgrade, Masarikova 5/VIII.

DRNOVSEK, Janez: Prime Minister of Slovenia; b. May 1950, in Izlake. *Education:* he has a doctorate in economics. *Career:* he worked variously as an industrialist, banker and diplomat. In May 1989 he was elected, in a direct popular ballot, as Slovenia's representative on the Yugoslavian federal State Presidency. Despite anxieties about his political inexperience, he was elected by the Presidency for Slovenia's turn as President of the federal head of state. He served in this capacity until May 1990. He then remained as a member of the State Presidency until 8 October 1991, when Slovenia formally recalled all its citizens from participation in federal institutions. He became President of the Liberal Democratic Party (LDP) and, following the resignation of Lojze Peterle in May 1992, he was appointed Prime Minister of Slovenia. His appointment was confirmed in January 1993, as a result of parliamentary elections held on 6 December 1992. *Address:* Office of the Prime Minister, Slovenia, 61000 Ljubljana, Gregorčičeva 20.

DRUC, Mircea: Moldovan politician. *Career:* a radical reformist, he was appointed Chairman of the Council of Ministers (Prime Minister) in May 1990; his administration was supported by the main anti-Communist opposition party, the Popular Front of Moldova (PFM), and undertook a series of political reforms, including revoking the Communists' constitutional monopoly of power and the assertion of the Republic's sovereignty. Although he was dismissed after a vote of 'no confidence' in the Supreme Soviet in May 1991, Druc's administration helped to advance Moldova's transition from a member state of the USSR to an independent country. He became leader of the PFM, which was renamed the Christian Democratic Popular Front in 1992. *Address:* Christian Democratic Popular Front, Moldova, 277014 Chişinău, str. Nicolae Iorga 5.

DUDAYEV, Gen. Jokhar Musayevich: Russian politician and President of the Chechen Republic-Ichkeria; b. April/May 1944; ethnic Chechen; m., with three c. *Education:* he graduated as a pilot from the Tambov Higher Military College and later attended Gagarin Air Force Academy. *Career:* his childhood was spent in Kazakhstan, following the deportation of many Chechens at the end of the Second World War. He served in the Air Force of the USSR, ending as commander of the Tartu (Estonia) base. In November 1990 he was elected Chairman of the Executive Committee of the All-National Congress of the Chechen People. This became an increasingly dominant force in the Chechen-Ingush Autonomous Republic (where the Chechen formed some 58% of the population, in 1989) and, following the discrediting of the conservative Supreme Soviet after the Moscow coup attempt of August 1991, it effectively replaced the Communist parliament in the territory. On 27 October 1991 he was elected President of the unilaterally proclaimed Chechen Republic. The Chechen Republic (Chechnya) was the only member of the Russian Federation not to recognize the Federation Treaty or to participate in the legislative elections of December 1993. In the same month, its population rejected the Russian Constitution. By the beginning of 1994 it had still not been recognized by the Russian authorities. He remained, however, one of the most prominent politicians of the Caucasus and, despite increasing opposition to his rule among some Chechen politicians. He had strong support among the Sufi orders of the region and in the Assembly of the Mountain Peoples of the Caucasus. *Address:* Russian Federation, Chechen Republic-Ichkeria, Grozny.

DZHUMAGULOV, Apas: Prime Minister of Kyrgyzstan—see under JUMAGULOV.

ELCHIBEY, Abulfaz Ali: former President of Azerbaijan; b. in Keleki, Nakhichevan. *Career:* as the leader of the Popular Front of Azerbaijan (PFA), the main democratic-nationalist opposition to the Communists, he was directly elected President of Azerbaijan on 7 June 1992. His regime became increasingly unpopular as a result of alleged corruption and of worsening economic conditions, which were, in turn, largely a result of the continuing struggle in Nagorny Karabakh. Moreover, he resorted to the use of force in a dispute with Col Surat Husseinov (q.v.), who retaliated by seizing the town of Gyanja, demanding the resignations of the Prime Minister, the Chairman of the Milli Majlis and of President Elchibey himself and ordering his forces to march on Baku. Having been told that the army would not defend him against Husseinov, Elchibey fled to Nakhichevan on the night of 17–18 June and presidential powers were assumed by the new Chairman of the Milli Majlis, Heydar Aliyev (q.v.). On 25 June the Milli Majlis voted to impeach Elchibey, who had refused to return to Baku, and when Husseinov arrived in the capital he recognized Aliyev as Acting President. On 29 June thousands of Elchibey's supporters protested against his impeachment, but two months later 97.5% of participants in a referendum on the issue voted in favour. The Milli Majlis endorsed this result on 1 September and Aliyev was elected President on 3 October. *Address:* c/o Popular Front of Azerbaijan, Azerbaijan, Nakhichevan, Keleki.

FEDOROV, Boris Grigorievich: Russian economist and politician; b. 1958, in Moscow. *Education:* Moscow Institute of Finance. *Career:* after graduating he worked for the State Bank of the USSR, where he was promoted to the position of Head of the Currency and Economics Department. In 1987–90 he worked as a researcher at the Institute of World Economics and International Relations, a section of the Academy of Sciences of the USSR. He entered politics in 1990, when he was appointed Minister of Finance of the Government of the Russian Federation. He resigned in protest at the denunciation of the '500-day programme' of economic reform, introduced by Boris Yeltsin (q.v.) on 3 September 1990, and subsequently acted as financial adviser to Yeltsin. In December 1992 he became a deputy premier and was re-appointed Minister of Finance in March 1993. He was elected as an independent candidate to the State Duma in the legislative elections of 12 December 1993. In January 1994, shortly after the resignation of Yegor Gaidar (q.v.) from the Russian Government, he too resigned, announcing that he could not remain finance minister in a Government dominated by conservatives in which he no longer occupied the post of deputy premier. A radical market reformer, he has consistently criticized the Chairman of the Central Bank, Viktor Geraschenko (q.v.), and the 'lifeless and illiterate state-planning ideology' of the so-called 'Red Directors'—the powerful industrialist lobby supported by the Russian premier, Viktor Chernomyrdin (q.v.). *Address:* State Duma, Russian Federation, Moscow, Novy Arbat 36.

FUNAR, Gheorghe: Romanian politician. *Career:* he was a rival to Ion Iliescu (q.v.) in the presidential election of September 1992, receiving 10.88% of the votes cast in the first ballot, which placed him in third position but excluded him from the second ballot. He was leader of the Romanian National Unity Party (RNUP), one of the most successful opposition parties not belonging to the Democratic Convention of Romania (DCR) Alliance. The RNUP was a nationalist party which favoured the more rapid introduction of market reforms. *Address:* Romanian National Unity Party, Romania, 4300 Tîrgu Mureş, Str. Bolyai F30.

FÜR, Lajos: Hungarian Minister of Defence; b. 21 Dec. 1930, in Egyházasrádóc. *Career:* an historian by training, he became a prominent member of the Hungarian Democratic Forum (HDF). On the centre-right of the movement, he became joint Chairman, with Jószef Antall (1932–93), in October 1990. He was nominated as the party's presidential candidate, in 1989, but the elections were postponed. In May 1990 he was made Minister of Defence. He was one of three possible candidates to succeed Antall as Prime Minister in December 1993, but, having come third in the first round of voting at the HDF leadership meeting, he withdrew his candidature. He remained Minister of Defence in the Government formed by Peter Boross (q.v.) and was elected leader of the HDF in February 1994. *Address:* Ministry of Defence, Hungary, 1055 Budapest, Balaton u. 7–11.

GAIDAR, Yegor Timurovich: Russian politician; b. 1956. *Education:* gained a doctorate of Economic Sciences at Moscow State University; speaks Serbo-Croat, English and Spanish. *Career:* he worked on the journal *Kommunist* and the newspaper *Pravda*, before being appointed director of the Institute of Economic Policy of the USSR Academy of Sciences. A Russian nationalist, he was the leading economist of the radical 'Young Turks' (*Mladoturki*) group of politicians. He was appointed to the Russian Federation's Government, in November 1991, becoming a Deputy Chairman and co-ordinator of the 13 ministries responsible for economic affairs. He was the primary co-ordinator of the harsh economic programme of reforms, including the removal of price controls at the beginning of 1992, which was the cause of increasing discontent. On 9 December the conservative Russian parliament rejected his nomination by President Boris Yeltsin (q.v.) to the post of Prime Minister and he left the Government shortly afterwards.

In 1993 he founded Russia's Choice, a coalition of democratic organizations, which won a total of 58 seats in the State Duma (the lower chamber of the new Federal Assembly) in December 1993. He returned to Yeltsin's administration for a brief period at the end of 1993, but, having been elected as a deputy to the State Duma, declined the offer of a new government post in January 1994, arguing that he could not work simultaneously as a member of the government and of the opposition. On 29 March it was announced that a party was to be formed from the Russia's Choice parliamentary faction, with himself as leader. *Address:* State Duma, Russian Federation, Moscow, Novy Arbat 36.

GAMBAROV, Isa Yunis ogly: Azerbaijani politician and historian; b. 1957, in Baku. *Education:* he studied at Baku State University. *Career:* a former researcher at the Institute of Oriental Studies of the Azerbaijan Academy of Sciences, he became involved in the democratic movement in the late 1980s. He was a member of the Supreme Soviet of Azerbaijan from 1990 and became Chairman of the Milli Majlis in 1992, but he resigned in June 1993 in accordance with the demands of the rebel warlord, Surat Husseinov (q.v.). He was Chairman of Musavat, the Muslim Democratic Party. *Address:* Musavat—'Equality' Muslim Democratic Party, Azerbaijan, Baku.

GAŠPAROVIČ, Ivan: Chairman of the National Council of the Slovak Republic (parliamentary speaker); b. 27 March 1941, in Poltár, in the Lučenec district. *Education:* he studied at Comenius University in Bratislava and gained a doctorate in law. *Career:* a former municipal Public Prosecutor in Bratislava and a teacher in the Faculty of Law at Comenius University, he was Procurator-General of Czechoslovakia in 1990–92. Having been a member of the Presidium of the Slovak National Council, he became Chairman in June 1992. He is a member of the Movement for a Democratic Slovakia. *Address:* National Council of the Slovak Republic, Októbrové nám. 12, Bratislava, Slovakia.

GEORGESCU, Florin: Romanian economist and politician; b. 25 Nov. 1953, in Bucharest. *Education:* he gained a doctorate from the Academy of Economic Studies in Bucharest. *Career:* having previously been a teacher at the Academy of Economic Studies in Bucharest, the author of numerous papers on economics and an employee of the Ministry of Finance, he was appointed Deputy Prime Minister and Minister of Finance in 1992. He was not associated with any political party. *Address:* Ministry of Finance, Romania, 70663 Bucharest, Str. Apolodor 17.

GERASCHENKO, Viktor Vladimirovich: Russian banker; b. 21 December 1937, in Moscow; m., with one s. and one d. *Education:* Moscow Financial Institute. *Career:* he held managerial posts in a variety of banks in Russia and abroad until his appointment as Chairman of the Board of the State Bank of the USSR in 1989. He continued in this office when the Bank became the Central Bank of the Russian Federation in 1992. His policies, in particular his printing of large numbers of roubles in order to subsidize inefficient state enterprises, came under increasing attack from his opponents, most notably the former finance minister, Boris Fedorov (q.v.). Some authorities reported that he had been termed 'the world's worst central banker'. However, his withdrawal from circulation of all pre-1993 (1961–92) rouble notes, in July 1993, was a serious attempt to control monetary emissions and inflation, particularly by ending the largely unregulated 'rouble zone' in other former Soviet countries. *Address:* Central Bank of the Russian Federation, Russian Federation, 103016 Moscow, ul. Neglinnaya 12.

GHERMAN, Oliviu: Speaker of the Senate of Romania. *Career:* he was President of the Democratic National Salvation Front (DNSF), the faction of the ruling National Salvation Front which supported President Ion Iliescu (q.v.) and split from the supporters of Petre Roman (q.v.) in March 1992. The DNSF gained a majority in the general election held in September of that year. He became Speaker of the Senate as a result of his party's victory. In July 1993, when the DNSF renamed itself the Party of Social Democracy of Romania, he remained its leader. *Address:* Party of Social Democracy of Romania, Romania, Bucharest, Str. Filioara 3, Sector 2.

GLEMP, Cardinal Archbishop Józef: Roman Catholic primate of Poland; b. 18 Dec. 1929, in Inowrocław. *Education:* in Polish literature at Warsaw and Toruń; he gained a double doctor's degree in canon law and civil law at the Lateran and Gregorianum Universities in Rome (Italy). *Career:* he was ordained in 1956 and studied in Rome, 1958–64. After joining the secretariat of the Polish Primate in 1967, he was appointed Archbishop-Metropolitan of Gniezno and Warsaw and Primate of Poland in 1981, and became a Cardinal in 1983. He has also worked on a government committees and been prominent in the political changes in Poland since the early 1980s. *Address:* Sekretariat Prymasa Polski, Poland, 00-246 Warsaw, ul. Miodowa 17/19.

GLIGOROV, Kiro: President of the Former Yugoslav Republic of Macedonia; b. 3 May 1917, in Štip. *Education:* graduated in law from Belgrade University (Yugoslavia) and is an economist. *Career:* he fought in the resistance struggle from 1941 and joined the Communist Party of Yugoslavia in 1944. He worked in various Party and government positions within the Socialist Federal Republic of Yugoslavia, most notably as deputy federal prime minister, 1967–69, as federal finance minister and, 1974–78, as President of the Federal Assembly. Following the Macedonian Assembly elections of 1990, the major parties decided to nominate him as State President, although they had failed to elect him on 19 January 1991, when he was only the Communist candidate. His experience of economic affairs and the support of the other parties eventually persuaded the largest party to vote for him, and he was elected President of Macedonia on 27 January. He remained President after Macedonia's secession from the Yugoslav federation. He was prominent in the campaign to secure international recognition for the new state. *Address:* Office of the President of the Republic, Macedonia, 91000 Skopje.

GÖNCZ, Árpád: President of Hungary; b. 10 Feb. 1922, in Budapest. *Education:* he studied law at the Pázmány Péter University of Budapest. *Career:* a playwright, he worked for one of the leaders of the Independent Smallholders' Party, until 1947, after which he worked as a welder. He was arrested and sentenced to life imprisonment in 1956, for his part in the anti-Communist Uprising. During the six years that he actually spent in prison, he taught himself English and used this skill to find work as a translator upon his release. In 1989 he was made president of the writers' union and in 1990 he gained a seat in the National Assembly, as a deputy for the Alliance of Free Democrats. He was named as interim President, on 2 May 1990, and was elected President by the National Assembly, on 3 August 1990. He was the only presidential candidate. *Address:* Office of the President, Hungary, 1055 Budapest, Kossuth Lajos tér. 1.

GORBACHEV, Mikhail Sergeyevich: Russian politician and last President of the USSR; b. 2 March 1931, in Privolnoye, Krasnogvardeisky district; m. (Raisa Gorbacheva, 1956), with one d. *Education:* in law at Moscow State University, and at Stavropol Agricultural Institute. *Career:* he began work as a machine operator, but soon moved to CPSU and Komsomol work. Although one of the youngest members of the Politburo, which he joined as a full member in October 1980, he became a likely successor to the Soviet leadership during the rule of Yury Andropov, who was also a native of the North Caucasus and advanced his prospects. However, the conservatives were not willing to elect him as Andropov's immediate successor, but, in March 1985, following the death of Konstantin Chernenko, he became General Secretary of the CPSU. He was elected to the position of titular head of state (Chairman of the Presidium of the Supreme Soviet of the USSR) in October 1988. In March 1990 he was elected to the new post of executive President of the USSR. He introduced a new style of leadership and dramatic reforms throughout the USSR, the key ideas being *glasnost* (openness), *perestroika* (restructuring) and 'new thinking' in foreign policy. He was credited with ending the Cold War and catalysing the massive changes in Soviet politics and society. However, he was discredited in his own country by the apparent failure of real reform, his continued faith in the use of the Communist Party and advocacy of a strong Union. Particularly following the unsuccessful coup attempt against him, in August 1991, he was unable to maintain the power of the Union in the face of the increasingly assertive republican leaderships. In December 1991 the formation of the Commonwealth of Independent States marked the end of the USSR and of his post; he resigned on 25 December and the USSR was deemed to have ceased to exist. He announced that he would remain involved in politics and, in January 1992, announced the formation of the Social and Political Research Foundation (Gorbachev Foundation), which also involved the Shevardnadze, Shatalin and Velikhov foundations. *Address:* International Foundation for Social, Economic and Political Research, Russian Federation, 125468 Moscow, Leningradsky pr. 49.

GORBUNOVS, Anatolijs: Chairman of the Supreme Council (parliamentary speaker) of Latvia; b. 1942, in Latvia. *Career:* a member of the Communist Party of Latvia, he had a career in the Party apparatus. However, he was also a Latvian nationalist and a supporter of full independence for the Republic. In October 1988 he spoke at the founding congress of the Latvian Popular Front and found favour even as the Communist Chairman of the Presidium of the Supreme Soviet from the same month. He was elected, with the support of the Front, in March 1990, and, although he remained with the Communists loyal to the CPSU after a split in April, the Front also supported his re-election as republican, *de facto*, head of state, now designated Chairman of the Supreme Council. He was prominent in the cautious development of Latvian independence, fully claimed on 21 August 1991, and in the efforts to secure the support of non-Latvian residents (only 52% of the population were ethnic Latvian, in 1989). He was re-elected speaker of the new parliament (renamed the Saeima), following the elections of 5 and 6 June 1993, but the head of state was now to be a President of the Republic. *Address:* Office of the Saeima, Jēkaba 11, Rīga 1811, Latvia.

GRANIĆ, Mate: Deputy Prime Minister of Croatia and Minister of Foreign Affairs. *Career:* a member of the ruling party, the Croatian Democratic Union, he was part of the coalition 'Government of Democratic Unity' appointed by President Tudjman (q.v.) and confirmed by the Croatian Assembly on 3 August 1991. He succeeded Zdenko Škrabako as foreign minister in 1993 and became a key figure in the negotiations to end the civil conflict in Croatia and in neighbouring Bosnia and Herzegovina. *Address:* Ministry of Foreign Affairs, Croatia, 41000 Zagreb, Visoka 22.

GREBENÍČEK, Miroslav: Czech politician. *Career:* prior to the dissolution of Czechoslovakia, he was Chairman of the Federal Council co-ordinating the two parties which had replaced the Communist Party of Czechoslovakia in 1991. In 1993 he became leader of one of those parties, the Communist Party of Bohemia and Moravia, which had been a major constituent of the opposition electoral alliance, Left Bloc. *Address:* Communist Party of Bohemia and Moravia, Politických Vězňů 9, 110 00 Prague 1.

GRYB, Myachyslav: Chairman of the Supreme Soviet (head of state) of Belarus—see under HRYB.

HAJIYEVA, Lala Shovket: Azerbaijani politician and diplomat; b. 1950. *Career:* formerly a surgeon in Moscow, in 1993 President Heydar Aliyev (q.v.) appointed her Secretary of State, a post which was abolished in January 1994, when she became Azerbaijan's Permanent Representative to the UN. *Address:* Office of the Secretary of State, Azerbaijan, 370016 Baku, Azadlyg Sq. 1, Government House.

HASSANOV, Hassan Aziz ogly: Minister of Foreign Affairs of Azerbaijan; b. 20 Oct. 1940. *Career:* a Communist since 1963 and senior Party official, he was a moderate reformist. He was appointed premier in January 1990, as part of the reorganization of government which was consequent upon the increase of nationalist sentiment and of ethnic violence. He was a contender for the leadership of the Communist Party, but was defeated by Ayaz Mutalibov (q.v.), who became President and whom he replaced as Chairman of the Council of Ministers. Hassanov was dismissed in early 1992, following the resignation of President Mutalibov, but was later nominated as Azerbaijan's ambassador to the UN. He was appointed Minister of Foreign Affairs in President Heydar Aliyev's (q.v.) administration in 1993. *Address:* Ministry of Foreign Affairs, Azerbaijan, 370004 Baku, Ghanjlar meydani 3.

HAVEL, Václav: President of the Czech Republic; b. 5 Oct. 1936, in Prague; m. Olga Šplíchalová, 1964. *Education:* studied drama at the Academy of Arts, Prague. He was excluded from further education in the 1950s because of his wealthy background and instead attended evening classes. *Career:* a playwright by profession, he worked at the Theatre on the Balustrade from 1959, and published his first play, *The Garden Party*, to great critical acclaim in 1963. In 1968 his political activities meant that his theatrical career was blocked and he could only find menial jobs thereafter. He was a co-founder of Charter 77 and its spokesman in 1977, 1978–79 and 1989. In the intervening years he was imprisoned on three separate occasions for his dissident activities. In 1978 he helped set up the Committee for the Defence of the Unjustly Persecuted. He was a co-founder of the samizdat publication *Lidové Noviny* in February 1988. In November 1989 he helped establish Civic Forum. The Federal Assembly elected him President of Czechoslovakia on 29 December 1989. He was re-elected on 5 July 1990, by a very large majority. He was active in attempting to resolve the constitutional negotiations between the federal and republican authorities. Havel resigned on 20 July 1992 (two months before his term of office was due to end), when a majority of Slovak deputies in the Federal Assembly refused to support his re-election as President. On 26 January 1993, soon after the dissolution of the Czech and Slovak Federative Republic, he was elected President of the independent Czech Republic. *Address:* Office of the President of the Republic, 119 08 Prague-Hradčany, Czech Republic.

HORN, Gyula: Hungarian politician and economist; b. 5 July 1932. *Education:* Rostow Institute of Economics and the Political Academy of Budapest. *Career:* he worked in government and the diplomatic service before spending 16 years at the international section of the Hungarian Socialist Workers' Party (now the Hungarian Socialist Party—HSP). He was State Secretary (1985–89) and Minister of Foreign Affairs (1989–90). He became Chairman of the HSP in May 1990. *Address:* Hungarian Socialist Party, Hungary, 1081 Budapest, Köztársaság tér. 26.

HRYB, Myacheslau: Chairman of the Supreme Soviet (head of state) of Belarus; b. 1937. *Career:* he was a colonel in the police force in the northern Vitebsk region during the Soviet era and was head of the security and defence committee of Belarus, part of the interior ministry, in the early 1990s and was a parliamentary deputy. He was elected to the post of Chairman of the Supreme Soviet on 28 January 1994 by 183 votes to 55, his candidacy supported by conservative factions in parliament. The dismissal of his predecessor, Stanislau Shushkevich (q.v.), and his appointment indicated a victory for the old-guard, 'Great Russian' Communists. He immediately proposed closer economic and political ties with Russia and was in favour of hastening re-entry to the 'rouble zone'. He announced that he would contest elections to the new executive presidency of the country (scheduled for June 1994) under the Constitution of March 1994. *Address:* Supreme Council of the Republic of Belarus, Belarus, 220016 Minsk, K. Marksa 38, Dom Urada.

HUSSEINOV, Col Surat D.: Prime Minister of Azerbaijan; b. 1959. *Career:* a former director of the state wool company, in June 1992 he was appointed as commander of Azerbaijan's forces in Nagorny Karabakh, where he met with considerable success. By employing his own wealth he was able to augment significantly the resources available to him from the official military budget. In early February 1993, however, he withdrew from northern Nagorny Karabakh to Gyanja, the second city of Azerbaijan. This strengthened the position of the Armenian militia. President Abulfaz Elchibey (q.v.) accused him of plotting a military coup against his Government and Husseinov was dismissed from his position and expelled from the Popular Front of Azerbaijan (PFA). The 709th Brigade, effectively a private army, remained loyal to him and it was believed that he received support from sections of the Russian military. On 4 June the Azerbaijani army attacked Husseinov's forces in Gyanja, but they were repelled and Husseinov gained control of the town. He demanded the resignation of the Prime Minister, the Chairman of the Milli Majlis and, later, the President himself, and ordered his forces to march on Baku. When they arrived, on 20 June, Husseinov claimed 'supreme power' in Azerbaijan, Elchibey having fled to Nakhichevan shortly before. However, four days later the Milli Majlis transferred the majority of presidential powers to its new Chairman, Heydar Aliyev (q.v.), and, when Husseinov himself arrived in Baku on 28 June, he recognized Aliyev as Acting President. He was nominated Prime Minister and Supreme Commander of the Armed Forces on 1 July 1993. In early 1994 there were rumours that he was about to resign. *Address:* Office of the Prime Minister, Azerbaijan, 370016 Baku, Azadlyg Sq. 1, Government House.

ILIESCU, Ion: President of Romania; b. 3 March 1930, in Oltenița, Ilfov district; m. Elena Iliescu. *Education:* studied at the Bucharest Polytechnic Institute, before going to Moscow to study water engineering at the Power Engineering Institute. *Career:* he was elected to the Communist Party Central Committee in 1968, after 22 years of Party membership. From 1971, however, his Party career was considered less promising, as he went from being the chief of propaganda in Timişoara and then First Secretary of the Iaşi local Party (1974). In 1979 he was made head of the National Water Council and, in 1984, director of a technical publishing house, which position he held until 1989. Following the overthrow of President Nicolae Ceauşescu, Iliescu, as head of the National Salvation Front (NSF), became interim President in December 1989. His presidency was confirmed by a direct popular vote in May 1990. In March 1992 the NSF split into two factions, those supporting Iliescu forming the Democratic National Salvation Front (DNSF), while the remainder supported Petre Roman (q.v.). In an election held on 27 September, Iliescu failed to secure the majority required for re-election as President, but, in a second ballot held on 11 October, he defeated his rival, Emil Constantinescu (q.v.), and was re-elected. The DNSF became the largest party in parliament and, in July 1993, renamed itself the Party of Social Democracy of Romania. *Address:* Romania, 71341 Bucharest, Piața Victorei 1.

IOSELIANI, Prof. Jaba: Georgian politician and playwright. *Career:* he gained a doctorate in philology and worked as an academic and playwright. An opponent of both the Communists and of President Zviad Gamsakhurdia, he was a paramilitary commander, the leader of the Mkhedrioni (Horsemen) group, which was established in 1989. He enjoyed significant popular support, but was barred from standing in the presidential elections of 1991 because he had been arrested, in February, and charged with the illegal possession of firearms. He was prominent in the opposition coalition and was released from detention by the anti-Gamsakhurdia forces in December. He and Tengiz Kitovani (q.v.) were joint heads of the Military Council, which the rebels announced had assumed power at the beginning of January 1992, declaring the President deposed and his office abolished. He was Deputy Chairman of the 50-member State Council formed on 10 March to replace the Military Council. A permanent Government was formed subsequent to the general election of 11 October, at which Ioseliani was elected as a deputy to the Georgian Supreme Soviet. Although he remained influential, his militia forces were incorporated into the official security-service structures and the Mkhedrioni were formally disbanded in February 1994. Ioseliani had lost office for a time in the previous year, however, after being implicated in an alleged plot to oust Georgian leader Eduard Shevardnadze (q.v.). *Address:* c/o Georgian Supreme Soviet, Georgia, Tbilisi.

ISĂRESCU, Mugur: Governor of the National Bank of Romania. *Career:* trained as an economist, he was appointed Governor of the Banca Națională (National Bank of Romania) in 1990. Formerly a Communist, a member of the old nomenklatura, he favoured the gradual implementation of reforms developing a free-market economy. *Address:* Banca Națională, Romania, 70421 Bucharest, Str. Lipscani 25.

IZETBEGOVIĆ, Dr Alija: President of the State Presidency of Bosnia and Herzegovina; b. 1925, in Bosanski Šamac, Bosnia and Herzegovina; ethnic Bosnian Muslim (Bosniak). *Education:* he studied law at the University of Sarajevo. *Career:* a legal adviser, he was a prominent dissident and political prisoner under the Communist regime. He was imprisoned for three years in 1946, for 'pan-Islamic activity', and again in 1983, for 14 years, although he was released in an amnesty of 1988. In 1970 he wrote the *Islamic Declaration,* on the all-inclusive nature of Islam. His book *Islam between East and West* (published in 1982), which attempts to define the unique position of Bosnian (Bosniak) Muslims, was the reason for his imprisonment in 1983. He is a strict Muslim, but claims not to be a fundamentalist; the party he founded, in May 1990, the Party of Democratic Action (PDA), is centrist politically. On 20 December 1990, as the leader of the largest party, he was elected President of the seven-member State Presidency of Bosnia and Herzegovina (*de facto* republican head of state). Having quit the leadership of the PDA in 1992, as head of state in a multi-ethnic state. However, he was re-elected on 27 March 1994, indicating that he envisaged conceding the presidency of the new Federation of Bosnia and Herzegovina, agreed by the Croats and Bosniaks and which was created in March 1994. *Address:* Office of the State Presidency of Bosnia and Herzegovina, Bosnia and Herzegovina, 71000 Sarajevo.

JAKOVČIĆ, Ivan: Croatian politician; b. 1957. *Career:* he became leader of the Istrian Democratic Assembly, a party which in the early 1990s made repeated claims for autonomy for the region of Istria, a peninsula situated in the north-west of Croatia, on the Slovenian border. His party achieved considerable popularity in Istria when Croatia gained independence, winning 51% of the votes cast in the region in elections to the Croatian Chamber of Deputies, on 2 August 1992, and 72% of the votes in elections to the upper chamber of the parliament, the Chamber of Counties, on 7 February 1993. Insisting that his party stood for a united Croatia, he initially argued that the granting of autonomous status to Istria, a relatively prosperous region (mainly as a result of tourism and trade) compared to other areas of Croatia, would benefit the country as a whole. However, the central Government's intransigence over the issue led him, in mid-1993, to abandon this stance, and to engage in increasingly outspoken confrontation with President Franjo Tudjman (q.v.). *Address:* Istrian Democratic Assembly, Croatia, Pula, Planajucka 29/I.

JANŠA, Janez: Slovenian politician; b. 17 Sept. 1958. *Education:* he is a graduate in defence studies. *Career:* he was a former adviser to the National Secretariat for National Defence. As a journalist, he was imprisoned in 1988 for criticizing the Jugoslavenska Narodna Armija (JNA—Yugoslav People's Army) in the youth newspaper, *Mladina.* This was a cause célèbre for Slovenian nationalism. After the electoral victory of the democratic opposition, in March 1990 he was appointed Minister of Defence of the Republic of Slovenia and remained in that post after Slovenia became independent. He was President of the Social Democratic Party of Slovenia from 1993. During 1993 he criticized the continued presence of former Communists in the Government and other positions of influence, and was alleged to have been involved in an arms-smuggling scandal in August of the same year. In March 1994 he was dismissed as Minister of Defence because of his alleged involvement in the beating by military police of a former Ministry of Defence employee, Milan Smolnikar, who had reportedly attempted to obtain military secrets. *Address:* Social Democratic Party of Slovenia, Slovenia, 61000 Ljubljana, Komenskega 11.

JESZENSZKY, Dr Géza: Hungarian Minister of Foreign Affairs; b. 10 Nov. 1941; m., with two c. *Education:* he studied history at the Loránd Eötvös University, Budapest. *Career:* having specialized in international relations, he worked on the foreign affairs committee of the anti-Communist opposition movement, the Hungarian Democratic Forum (HDF). He was made Minister of Foreign Affairs in May 1990, by his father-in-law, the then Prime Minister József Antall (1932–93). In December 1990 he was elected to the presidium of the HDF. He has been anxious to encourage NATO links with Hungary and to orientate Hungary, and the other Central European countries, towards the West. He remained Minister of Foreign Affairs in the Government formed by Peter Boross (q.v.) in December 1993. In April 1994 he presented Hungary's formal application to become a member of the European Union (known until November 1993 as the European Community), Hungary being the first former Communist country to do so. *Address:* Ministry of Foreign Affairs, Hungary, 1027 Budapest, Bem rkp. 47.

JUMAGULOV, Apas: Prime Minister of Kyrgyzstan; b. 1934. *Career:* a prominent Communist during the Soviet regime, he first became Chairman of the Council of Ministers (Prime Minister) in May 1986, as part of the anti-corruption campaign of the new republican Party leader, Absamat Masaliyev. Following Masaliyev's discrediting after ethnic riots in the Osh region in 1990, the liberal Askar Akayev (q.v.) was elected to the new post of executive President of the Republic. Although not opposed to Gorbachevite reforms, Jumagulov was not sympathetic to the new regime and, in January 1991, in a government reorganization by Akayev, was replaced as premier. He returned to office when Akayev was forced to make concessions to the turbulent and right-wing dominated legislature, the Jogorku Kenesh, and dismiss Prime Minister Tursunbek Chyngyshev (q.v.) in December 1993. His Government included prominent Communists, but pledged to continue a measure of reform, a decision necessarily reinforced by the overwhelming support for Akayev in a referendum at the end of January 1994. *Address:* Office of the Prime Minister, Kyrgyzstan, 720000 Bishkek, Government House.

KÁDÁR, Béla: Hungarian Minister of International Economic Relations; b. 21 March 1934, in Pécs. *Career:* an economist, he was director of the Hungarian World Economy Institute. He advised the Communist Government on economic issues and lectured abroad. An independent, he entered the Government as the Minister of International Economic Relations, in May 1990. He retained that post in the Government formed by Peter Boross (q.v.) in December 1993. *Address:* Ministry of International Economic Relations, Hungary, 1055 Budapest, Honvéd u. 13–15.

KALVODA, Jan: Deputy Prime Minister of the Czech Republic; b. 30 Oct. 1953, in Prague. *Education:* he gained a doctorate in law at Charles University, Prague. *Career:* he was a practising lawyer until 1990. In that year he became a Civic Forum deputy in the Czech National Council, of which he was Deputy Chairman in 1991–92. In March 1992 he became Chairman of the Civic Democratic Alliance (CDA), which was a constituent party in the Czech coalition Government formed by Václav Klaus (q.v.) in July of that year. He was appointed Deputy Prime Minister and remained in the position after the Czech Republic became independent. *Address:* Office of the Government of the Czech Republic, Lazarská 7, 113 48 Prague, Czech Republic.

KARADŽIĆ, Dr Radovan: Bosnian politician and President of the 'Serbian Republic of Bosnia and Herzegovina'; b. 1946, in Montenegro, Yugoslavia; ethnic Serb. *Career:* a trained psychiatrist, he was imprisoned in Yugoslavia during Communist rule, allegedly on charges of fraud. As the leader of the nationalist Serbian Democratic Party, he did not accept any government posts, but did agree to a coalition with the main Bosniak and Croat parties after the 1990 elections. However, as the Yugoslav crisis of 1991 escalated, he became less able to accept consensus decisions. He did not denounce the 'Serbian Autonomous Regions', which were proclaimed during the year, and helped organize the 'Assembly of the Serb Nation' (Serb Assembly), following the Republic's declaration of sovereignty in October. He articulated the Serb desire to remain in the Yugoslav federation, although he was accused of threatening the other ethnic groups of the heterogeneous Republic. Following the onset of civil war in Bosnia and Herzegovina, he pursued a policy of 'cantonization', envisaging the division of the Republic on ethnic grounds, and the eventual union of Serb-controlled territory with Serbia. He was named President of the 'Serbian Republic' at its proclamation on 27 March 1992. A champion of the interests of extreme nationalists, he is unpopular with many Bosnian Serbs, owing to his failure to compromise on the terms of a peace settlement. *Address:* Srpska Demokratska Stranka (BiH), Bosnia and Herzegovina, c/o Pale, 'Serb Assembly'.

KARIMOV, Islam (Islom) Abduganiyevich: President of Uzbekistan; b. 30 Jan. 1938. *Career:* he worked as a mechanical engineer before moving into economic planning in 1966. He became a regional Communist Party leader in 1986 and republican Party leader in 1989. He became the Chairman of the Supreme Soviet (President) of Uzbekistan in March 1990. Although he has a reputation as an old-style, conservative Communist (he did not condemn the Moscow coup attempt of August 1991 until it became clear that it had failed) and as the architect of a repressive regime, he did favour a greater degree of republican control over central government. After the failure of the attempted coup he banned the Communist Party, but it was succeeded by the People's Democratic Party of Uzbekistan, with the same personnel. In December he was elected President of the Republic in free elections. Until January 1992 he also performed the functions previously executed by the Chairman of the Council of Ministers, a position which he had abolished in November 1990. During 1992 and 1993 Karimov's leadership became increasingly absolutist as he consolidated his position of power. He extended his control over the mass media, precluded the spread of opposition movements from neighbouring Tajikistan by giving his full support to the restored Communist regime there and prevented domestic opposition movements from registering as political parties. There were also allegations that Karimov was implicated in the intimidation of opposition leaders. His stated concern was to ensure political stability during the transition to a free-market economy, and he particularly discouraged any religious or ethnic-based parties. *Address:* Office of the President, Uzbekistan, 700163 Tashkent, ul. Uzbekistanskaya 43.

KEBICH, Vyacheslau Frantsavich (Vyacheslav Frantsevich): Chairman of the Council of Ministers (Prime Minister) of Belarus; b. 10 June 1936. *Education:* he graduated in mechanical engineering from Minsk Polytechnic and the Higher Party School. *Career:* a member of the Communist Party from 1962, he worked as an engineer-technologist in Minsk from 1958, becoming director of the company. In 1980 he became Second Secretary of the Minsk Communists, and in 1983 was appointed head of the Heavy Industry Department of the Central Party Committee. In December 1985 Kebich was promoted to the post of deputy premier and Chairman of the State Planning Committee. In April 1990 he was elected Chairman of the Council of Ministers. He had acquired a reputation as an unorthodox, but successful, economic reformer. He stood as a candidate for the post of Chairman of the Supreme Soviet (president) of Belarus, but withdrew 'in the cause of unity', in favour of Stanislau Shushkevich (q.v.). He was strongly in favour of close relations with Russia and the establishment of a post-Soviet bloc, a stance which brought him into conflict with Shushkevich. In January 1994 Kebich survived a vote of 'no confidence' in the Belarusian assembly, at which time Shushkevich was dismissed. *Address:* Office of the Council of Ministers of the Republic of Belarus, Belarus, 220010 Minsk, pl. Nezavisimosti, Government House.

KELAM, Tunne: Estonian politician. *Career:* a prominent member of the Estonian National Independence Party, he favoured the election of an alternative assembly to the Supreme Soviet, based on the citizenship of independent Estonia. When this Congress of Estonia was elected, therefore, in March 1990, he was elected its leader. Although more right-of-centre and radical than the ruling Supreme Council (the renamed Supreme Soviet), the Congress and its executive Committee of Estonia were prepared to accept its interim authority. In August 1991, with Estonian independence fully established, it was agreed to form a Constituent Assembly, to which the Congress nominated one-half of the members. He was elected Deputy Speaker, following elections to the new legislature (Riigikogu), held on 20 September 1992. *Address:* Riigikogu, Endla 6-4, Tallinn 0001, Estonia.

KHASBULATOV, Ruslan Imranovich: Russian politician; ethnic Chechen. *Career:* a member of the parliament of the Russian Federation, he was elected for the constituency of Grozny, in the former Chechen-Ingush Autonomous Republic (which declared its independence in October 1991, and was subsequently renamed the Chechen Republic-Ichkeria). He was a member of the Democratic Russian group and a supporter of President Boris Yeltsin (q.v.). He replaced Yeltsin in the office of Chairman of the Supreme Soviet, in July 1991, after the elections for an executive President. He had previously been First Deputy Chairman (hence, deputy republican head of state) and was only Acting Chairman until October, when the deputies finally agreed on a permanent successor. From the beginning of 1992 he increasingly voiced his opposition to Yeltsin's policies and was one of the initiators of the so-called 'war of laws' between the President and the legislature, which culminated in the violent events of September–October 1993. He was arrested for his leading role in the anti-government uprising and was imprisoned at Lefortovo prison in Moscow. Following the amnesty granted by the State Duma on 23 February 1994 he was released, and returned to his native Chechen Republic-Ichkeria.

KITOVANI, Tengiz: Georgian politician, military leader, artist and sculptor. *Career:* the commander of Georgia's National Guard, he was formerly a nationalist supporter of President Zviad Gamsakhurdia (1939–93). In September 1991 he led a considerable number of his troops in refusing to acknowledge the attempted subordination of his command to the Ministry of Internal Affairs. By December he was heading the opposition military forces, which were now engaged in civil war with the presidential loyalists. He and Jaba Ioseliani (q.v.) were joint heads of the Military Council, which the rebels announced had assumed power, in January 1992, declaring the President deposed and his office abolished. Kitovani supported the return of Eduard Shevardnadze (q.v.), under whom he was defence minister. His intervention in Abkhazia in August 1992 provoked the resort to military conflict there and, in January and April 1993, there were reports that he was plotting against Shevardnadze. In May he was obliged to resign from the Government. *Address:* Georgia, Tbilisi.

KLAUS, Dr Václav: Prime Minister of the Czech Republic; b. 19 June 1941, in Prague. *Career:* he worked at the Economic Institute of the Czechoslovak Academy of Sciences during the 1960s, but was dismissed in 1970. In 1970–88 he was employed at the Czechoslovak State Bank, and then worked briefly for the Academy of Sciences again, at the Prognostic Institute. He was a leading member of Civic Forum and became Minister of Finance in the Federal Government in December 1989. He was reappointed in June 1990, after the elections. Previously the leader of Civic Forum, he became Chairman of the conservative Civic Democratic Party when the original organization split in 1991. He was made a Deputy Prime Minister in the federal Government in late 1991. Although it seemed likely that he would become federal premier, it had been decided that Czechoslovakia would be dissolved by the end of 1992 and, consequently, in early July he accepted the position of Prime Minister of the Czech Republic, leading a new coalition Government. He remained Prime Minister when the Czech Republic gained independence on 1 January 1993. *Address:* Office of the Government of the Czech Republic, Lazarská 7, 113 48 Prague 1, Czech Republic.

KLJUIĆ, Stjepan: Bosnian politician and member of the State Presidency of Bosnia and Herzegovina; ethnic Croat. *Career:* former leader of the Croatian Democratic Union in Bosnia and Herzegovina, which became the acknowledged representative of the Croats of the Republic at the elections of December 1990. He was directly elected to the seven-member State Presidency in the same month. Although in favour of retaining the ethnic balance in the Republic by consensus and the maintenance its identity, during 1991 he was forced to lead his community into closer alliance with the Bosnian Muslims (Bosniaks), against the Serb community. However, he was also accused of negotiating the cantonization or the division of the Republic between Serbia and Croatia. He resigned from the State Presidency in November 1992, allegedly under pressure, in favour of the Croat separatist, Miro Lazić, but was re-elected on 20 October 1993. The State Presidency was likely to be displaced under the new constitutional arrangements for the Croat–Bosniak Federation of Bosnia and Herzegovina, created in March 1994. *Address:* Bosnia and Herzegovina, 71000 Sarajevo, trg Dure Pucara bb.

KOČÁRNÍK, Ivan: Deputy Prime Minister and Minister of Finance of the Czech Republic; b. 29 Nov. 1944, in Trebon, in the Kutna Hora district. *Education:* he studied at the Prague Institute of Economics. *Career:* he was Director of the Research Department of the Czechoslovak Federal Ministry of Finance in 1985–89. In 1990 he was appointed Deputy Minister of Finance in the Federal Government and, from July 1992, he was a Deputy Prime Minister and Minister of Finance of the Czech Republic. He was a member of the Civic Democratic Party. *Address:* Office of the Government of the Czech Republic, Lazarská 7, 113 48 Prague 1, Czech Republic.

KONTIĆ, Radoje: Prime Minister of the Federal Republic of Yugoslavia; b. Montenegro. *Career:* his election to the post of premier followed the dismissal of Milan Panić (q.v.) in late December 1992, and he formed a Government which comprised the Serbian Socialist Party and the Montenegrin Party of Socialists in February 1993. *Address:* Office of the Federal Government, Federal Republic of Yugoslavia, 11070 Belgrade, Lenjina 2.

KOSTIĆ, Dr Branko: Yugoslav (Montenegrin) politician; b. 1939, in Rvaši, Montenegro. *Career:* he joined the Communist Party in 1957. He was a Party functionary until he was elected President of the Presidency of Montenegro, in March 1989. He failed to secure the Party's nomination for direct elections to the Presidency, in 1990, but, in March 1991, became the Republic's member on the federal State Presidency. He was considered strongly pro-Serb and, in May, he participated in blocking the election of the Croatian member to the State Presidency. In June, after the outbreak of civil war, Kostić was elected to the post of Vice-President of the collective body, which he held until 1992. In January 1993 he stood for election to the post of President of Montenegro, but was defeated. *Address:* c/o Office of the President of the Republic of Montenegro, Federal Republic of Yugoslavia, Podgorica.

KOVÁČ, Michal: President of Slovakia; b. 1 April 1936. *Career:* a former banker and Chairman of the Czechoslovak Federal Assembly, he was elected as President by the National Council of the Slovak Republic on 15 February 1993. He was deputy leader of the Movement for a Democratic Slovakia (MDS), but resigned this position on becoming head of state. During 1993, however, he was involved in repeated confrontations with the leader of his former party, Vladimír Mečiar (q.v.), the Prime Minister. Apart from vetoing various proposed ministerial appointments, he was also involved in the controversies surrounding Mečiar's dismissal, and the MDS leader demanded his resignation. Kováč was supported by the new Government formed in March 1994. *Address:* Office of the President of the Republic, Bratislava, Slovakia.

KOVÁČ, Roman: Deputy Prime Minister of Slovakia; b. 1940. *Career:* a former obstetrician, he was Chairman of the Czech and Slovak Confederation of Trade Unions between September 1990 and March 1992. In June 1992 he was elected a deputy in the House of Nations of the former Czechoslovak Federal Assembly and became Deputy Prime Minister (and Minister of Inspection, until September) in the Slovak Government. He remained deputy premier after Slovakia gained formal independence and, in January 1993, was an unsuccessful candidate for the Movement for a Democratic Slovakia (MDS) in the first round of voting by the National Council to elect a President. He resigned from the Government in February 1994, following his expulsion from the MDS and disagreements with Prime Minister Vladimír Mečiar (q.v.). However, in March he was reappointed to his former position by the new Prime Minister, Jozef Moravčík (q.v.). He was a leader of the Democratic Union of Slovakia, the party founded by himself and Moravčík in 1994. *Address:* Office of the Government of the Slovak Republic, nám. Slobody 1, 813 70 Bratislava, Slovakia.

KOZYREV, Andrey Vladimirovich: Russian Minister of Foreign Affairs; b. 1951, in Brussels, Belgium; ethnic Russian; m., with one d. *Education:* graduate of the Moscow State Institute of International Relations (1974); speaks English, French and Portuguese. *Career:* before studying for his degree, he worked at the Kommunar factory in Moscow. After graduating, he worked in the USSR Ministry of External Affairs and, in 1991, he was appointed head of the Dept of International Organizations. He was a member of the radical 'Young Turks' (*Mladoturki*) group of Russian politicians. In October 1990 Boris Yeltsin (q.v.) appointed him Foreign Minister of the newly assertive Russian Federation. Having previously adopted a conciliatory approach to the former Soviet states (the 'near abroad'), throughout 1993 and the beginning of 1994 his foreign policy became more aggressive, culminating in his assertion that the Russian Federation had the right to station troops on the territory of the former USSR. He was also more critical of Western organizations such as the North Atlantic Treaty Organisation (NATO). In April 1994 he criticized the West generally for giving too much credence to the Russian neo-Fascist Vladimir Zhirinovsky (q.v.), who he described as 'not a political but a medical phenomenon', demonstrating the limits of the Government's willingness to placate the nationalists. In December 1993, as a member of the Russia's Choice democratic election association, he was elected to the State Duma of the Federal Assembly. He agreed to be a member of the Russia's Choice party, which was formed on the basis of the parliamentary faction on 29 March 1994. *Address:* Ministry of Foreign Affairs, Russian Federation, 121200 Moscow, Smolenskaya-Sennaya pl. 32/34.

KRAJIŠNIK, Momčilo: Bosnian politician and President (speaker) of the 'Assembly of the Serb Nation'; ethnic Serb. *Career:* a member of the nationalist Serbian Democratic Party, he was elected as a deputy to the republican Assembly in December 1990. Following the coalition agreement between the three main parties, the SDP was allowed to nominate its candidate for parliamentary speaker, and Krajišnik was duly elected. On 14 October 1991 he attempted to prevent the Bosniak (Bosnian Muslim) and Croat deputies from declaring the Republic's sovereignty by ending the parliamentary session. He was subsequently elected speaker of the unilaterally proclaimed 'Assembly of the Serb Nation' (comprising Serb deputies of the Bosnian Assembly and constituted on 24 October), which declared its adherence to the Yugoslav federation. *Address:* Bosnia and Herzegovina, Pale, 'Serb Assembly'.

KRAVCHUK, Leonid Makarovich (Makarovych): President of Ukraine; b. 10 Jan. 1934. *Career:* a CPSU member since 1958, he was the Second Secretary of the Communist Party of the Ukraine when elected Chairman of the Ukrainian Supreme Soviet, in July 1990. Although a Communist, he won support from his Ukrainian nationalism and, against a divided opposition, he was elected President of Ukraine, with 63% of the votes cast, on 1 December 1991. On the same day overwhelming support for Ukrainian independence was expressed in a republican referendum. Kravchuk did agree to the formation of the Commonwealth of Independent States (originally with the Russian and Belarusian leaders), but maintained an independent stance against Russian domination of the new association. His relations with parliament were not always easy, particularly during 1993, notably when he made concessions to Russia over the Black Sea fleet or nuclear disarmament. *Address:* Office of the President of the Republic, Ukraine, Kiev.

KUČAN, Milan: President of Slovenia; b. 14 Jan. 1941, in Krizevci. *Education:* he graduated in law from Ljubljana University (1963). *Career:* he was president of the official Communist youth organization, the Slovene Socialist Youth League, 1968–69, and a member of its secretariat, 1969–73. He worked as secretary of the Socialist Alliance for Slovenia, 1973–78, and was President of the Slovene National Assembly, 1978–82. In 1986 he was made leader of the League of Communists of Slovenia. As with other Communists who espoused nationalist causes, he retained some popularity and, in the republican presidential elections of April 1990, he was elected President of the five-member State Presidency in a direct, popular ballot, despite the opposition parties winning the parliamentary contest. With the failure of attempts to reform the Yugoslav federation, he became head of state of an independent Slovenia, during 1991. On 6 December 1992 he was directly elected as President of the Republic. *Address:* Office of the President, Slovenia, 61000 Ljubljana, Erjavčeva 17.

KUCHMA, Leonid Maksimovich: Ukrainian politician and industrialist; b. 1938, in Chernigov obl. *Education:* Dnepropetrovsk State University. *Career:* he worked at Yuzmash, the largest missile factory in the country, from 1960 and eventually became its manager. A member of the CPSU in 1960–91, he was appointed to the Central Committee of the Communist Party of Ukraine in 1981, where he served for ten years. He was elected to the Ukrainian Supreme Soviet in October 1991. On 13 October 1992 his nomination as Prime Minister was approved by the Ukrainian parliament. Apparently reluctant to accept the post of premier, he nevertheless energetically pursued his policy of market reform, initially with the support of President Leonid Kravchuk (q.v.) and the influential parliamentary speaker, Ivan Plyushch (q.v.). In November he succeeded in persuading the parliament (renamed the Supreme Council—Verkhovna Rada) to grant him the power to rule by decree for a period of six months. At the end of this time, however, his powers were not renewed, and after consistent opposition to his economic reforms from the Verkhovna Rada and from the President himself, he eventually resigned. (His resignation was accepted by parliament on 9 September 1993, although he had offered to resign on two previous occasions.) *Address:* c/o Verkhovna Rada, Ukraine, Kiev.

KULIYEV, Rasul: Chairman of the Supreme Soviet of Azerbaijan (parliamentary speaker). *Career:* elected as a deputy to the Supreme Soviet in 1990, he was elected as one of the members of the smaller, standing parliament, the Milli Majlis (National Assembly) when it was established in May 1992. Eminent in the old Communist hierarchy, he was a supporter of Heydar Aliyev (q.v.), who was elected Chairman of the Supreme Soviet (and hence of the Milli Majlis) during the ousting of President Abulfaz Elchibey (q.v.) in June 1993. When Aliyev was elected President, Kuliyev replaced him in the chair of the legislature, a position which was again only a parliamentary speaker and not a head of state. *Address:* Milli Majlis, Azerbaijan, Baku.

KULOV, Feliks: Kyrgyz politician, administrator and former Vice-President. *Career:* he was a reformist Communist who was a strong supporter of the liberal President elected in 1990, Askar Akayev (q.v.). Minister of Internal Affairs in the Cabinet of Ministers, he resigned his Party membership after the August 1991 coup attempt in Moscow. In 1992 he replaced German Kuznetsov (q.v.) as Vice-President of the Republic. However, in March 1993 he was investigated for corruption, although it was also alleged that this was part of a right-wing parliamentary conspiracy to discredit prominent reformers, without directly attacking the popular President. With the scandals surrounding the 'Seabeco affair' (see under Chyngyshev above) increasing pressure on the administration, on 10 December 1993 Kulov resigned, for 'ethical reasons', and urged the Government to do likewise. For Akayev this was a gesture to the parliament, or Jogorku Kenesh, that he was willing to accommodate them in pursuit of stable government. However, he retained Kulov's services, and demonstrated his confidence in him, by appointing him to head the administration of the important Chu region (around the capital) later in December. *Address:* c/o Office of the President of the Republic, Kyrgyzstan, 720003 Bishkek, Government House.

KUZNETSOV, German Serapionovich: former Kyrgyz politician; b. 1948; ethnic Russian. *Career:* a Communist Party official, he rose to become Second Secretary of the Frunze (now Bishkek) City Committee. A reformist, he was an ally and deputy of President Askar Akayev (q.v.) and was himself elected Vice-President of the Republic (by direct popular election in October 1991). He resigned from the CPSU following the Moscow coup attempt of August 1991 and formed his own moderate, democratic party, called National Unity. In 1992 he resigned the vice-presidency, but joined the Cabinet of Ministers as the First Deputy Prime Minister. His support was important to Akayev, because he was the highest-ranking Slav in the country and was important in reassuring the ethnic Russians of their future in Kyrgyzstan. However, on 16 July, he announced that he was resigning all government posts and was emigrating to the Russian Federation. He complained that he was no longer involved sufficiently in the operation of government and despaired of the future of the Slavs in the newly renamed Kyrgyz Republic. *Address:* c/o Office of the President of the Republic, Kyrgyzstan, 720003 Bishkek, Government House.

KWASNIEWSKI, Aleksander: Polish politician; b. 15 Nov. 1954, in Białogard, Koszalin; m. with one d. *Education:* graduated from the Department of Transportation Economics of the University of Gdańsk. *Career:* an activist in the Socialist Union of Polish Students, he became editor-in-chief of *Itd* in 1981–84, and held the same post on *Sztandar Mlodych* in 1984–85. In 1985 he was appointed Minister without Portfolio (responsible for youth), until 1987. In the following year, he was appointed Chairman of the Polish Olympic Committee, a post which he retained until 1991. He was elected leader of Social Democracy of the Republic of Poland (SDRP) at its First Congress in January 1990 and re-elected in March 1993. Kwasniewski was also leader of the SDRP's electoral coalition with the All Poland Trade Unions Alliance, the Democratic Left Alliance (SLD). He gained a seat in the Sejm in 1991, which he retained in the 1993 elections. It was in this election that he gained the most number of votes of any parliamentary candidate and he was expected to lead the new Government. However, this post went to Waldemar Pawlak (q.v.), leader of the Polish Peasant Party, a coalition partner of the SLD. *Address:* Social Democracy of the Republic of Poland, Poland, 00-419 Warsaw, ul. Rozbrat 44A.

LAAR, Mart: Prime Minister of Estonia; b. 1960. *Education:* Tartu State University. *Career:* an historian and journalist, from 1983 to 1987 he taught in various schools in Tallinn, before embarking on a political career. As a member of the Christian Democratic Party, he was elected to the Supreme Soviet of Estonia in 1989. He became leader of the Isamaa (Fatherland) party, which was formed in 1992, following the merger of four of the five member parties of the Isamaa electoral alliance. The alliance had won a total of 29 seats in the elections to the new parliament, the Riigikogu, in September 1992. The following month he became head of a coalition Government, which was dominated by members of Isamaa. His administration came under increasing criticism by parliamentary deputies and by the Estonian President, Lennart Meri (q.v.), concerning foreign policy, particularly relations with Russia over the Slav population in Estonia and the withdrawal of ex-Soviet troops from its territory. He survived a vote of 'no confidence' in the Riigikogu on 15 November 1993. *Address:* Office of the Prime Minister, Lossi 1A, Tallinn 0100, Estonia.

LAZOVIĆ, Miro: Bosnian politician and President (speaker) of the Assembly of Bosnia and Herzegovina; ethnic Serb. *Career:* a former Communist, he was elected President of the bicameral Assembly to replace Momčilo Krajisnik (q.v.), who left his post in October 1991 to form a 'Serb Assembly'. Despite his ethnicity, he remained opposed to the idea of a Bosnian confederation, supporting the ideal of the multi-ethnic unitary state. However, he agreed to the formation of the predominantly Croat–Bosniak Federation of Bosnia and Herzegovina in early 1994, under an accord signed in Washington, DC (USA). *Address:* National Assembly, Bosnia and Herzegovina, 71000 Sarajevo, trg Dure Pucara.

LILIĆ, Zoran: President of the Federal Republic of Yugoslavia (FRY); b. 1953, in Serbia. *Career:* a member of the Serbian League of Communists, subsequently the Serbian Socialist Party, he was President (speaker) of the National Assembly of Serbia in 1992–93, before being elected by the Federal Assembly as federal President on 25 June 1993. He was a supporter of the Serbian President, Slobodan Milošević (q.v.). *Address:* Office of the Federal Government, Federal Republic of Yugoslavia, 11070 Belgrade, Lenjina 2.

LUBACHIVSKY, Cardinal Myroslav Ivan: Ukrainian religious leader. *Career:* a Uniate or 'Greek' Catholic, he fled Ukraine in 1939, living in exile in Rome (Italy) and the USA, of which he became a citizen. The leader of the Roman Catholic Church, Pope John Paul II, made him a Cardinal and the head of the Ukrainian Uniates (the most numerous of the Roman Catholics of the former USSR). In March 1991, as the Cardinal Archbishop-Major of Lvov, in Western Ukraine, he returned to his homeland and, in June, announced that he would take up permanent residence in Lvov. Soon after this, the authorities granted legal recognition to the Uniates. *Address:* St George's Cathedral, Ukraine, Lvov.

LUCINSCHI, Petru: Moldovan politician. *Career:* an ethnic Romanian, he was a member of the Communist Party Politburo and was the penultimate First Secretary of the Communist Party of Moldova, taking over from Kuzmich Grossu in November 1989. Following the country's independence, in 1991, he became Moldova's first ambassador to Russia. He was leader of the Agrarian bloc, which came to prominence in the early 1990s, and supported Moldovan independence (i.e. he opposed union with Romania), membership of the Commonwealth of Independent States and agricultural reform. In January 1993 he became Chairman (speaker) of the Moldovan Parliament, forming a 'triumvirate' with Prime Minister Andrei Sangheli (q.v.) and President Mircea Snegur (q.v.), which attempted to negotiate directly with the Transdnestrian separatists. In February 1994 Lucinschi's bloc contested the legislative elections as the Agrarian Democratic Party and gained a majority (56 seats) in the Moldovan Parliament. *Address:* Agrarian Democratic Party, Moldova, Chişinău.

LUIK, Juri: Estonian Minister of Foreign Affairs; b. 1966. *Career:* He joined the Government in 1992 as Minister without Portfolio. He was subsequently appointed Minister of Defence in the second half of 1993 and replaced Trivime Velliste as Minister of Foreign Affairs in a government reorganization in January 1994. His rapid promotion to a prominent ministerial position was, in part, due to the role he played as representative in the Estonian–Russian negotiations on the highly sensitive issue of the withdrawal of ex-Soviet troops from Estonia. *Address:* Ministry of Foreign Affairs, Rävala 9, Tallinn 0100, Estonia.

LUX, Josef: Deputy Prime Minister and Minister of Agriculture of the Czech Republic; b. 1 Feb. 1956, in Ustí nad Orlicí. *Education:* he studied at the Agricultural College in Brno. *Career:* he became Chairman of the Czechoslovak People's Party in 1990. In 1990–92 he was Vice-Chairman for the Environment in the House of Nations of the Czechoslovak Federal Assembly. From 1992 he was Chairman of the Christian Democratic Union—Czechoslovak People's Party, which became a member of the coalition Czech Government formed by Václav Klaus (q.v.) in July of that year. He was appointed Deputy Prime Minister and Minister of Agriculture and retained those posts after the Czech Republic became independent. *Address:* Office of the Government of the Czech Republic, Lazarská 7, 113 48 Prague, Czech Republic.

MAKSIM, His Holiness Patriarch: Head of the Bulgarian Orthodox Church, Chairman of the Bulgarian Patriarchy; b. 29 April 1914, in Oreshak village, Lovech region. *Education:* graduate of Sofia Academy of Theology. *Career:* originally Marin Naydenov Minkov, he graduated in 1935 and served the Church in Ruse and Lovech. He became a monk in 1941, when he took the name of Maksim; in 1947 he was appointed Archimandrite and Coadjutor in the Ruse diocese; in 1950–55 he represented the Bulgarian Church in Moscow; in 1955 he became Secretary-General of the Holy Synod and was ordained bishop in 1956; he became Bishop of Lovech in 1960; in 1971 he was elected Bishop of Sofia and Patriarch of Bulgaria. In

1992 his authority was challenged when a schism emerged in the Bulgarian Church—several bishops rejected the authority of the Patriarchy, even after a visit by the Ecumenical Patriarch of Constantinople during 1993. *Address:* Bulgaria, 1090 Sofia, Oborishte str. 4, Synod Palace.

MAMEDOV, Etibar: Azerbaijani politician. *Career:* Chairman of Istiklal—National Independence, the party founded in opposition to the Popular Front of Azerbaijan in 1992. He was in favour of links with Russia and was an ally of Heydar Aliyev (q.v.), until he was estranged by the appointment of Surat Husseinov (q.v.) as Prime Minister in June 1993. He therefore decided to remain in opposition. *Address:* Istiklal—National Independence, Azerbaijan, Baku.

MANOLESCU, Nicolae: Romanian politician and author; b. 27 Nov. 1939, in Rîmnicu Vîlcea. *Education:* graduated in philosophy from Bucharest University. *Career:* he worked as a journalist, historian and academic. He became a politician and a leader of the Civic Alliance, a grouping of opposition movements not represented in the legislature. In 1991 he founded a parallel political group, the Party of the Civic Alliance (PCA), and was elected President of the electoral coalition, the Democratic Convention, which opposed the ruling National Salvation Front. He was replaced as leader of the Democratic Convention in 1992, but remained President of the PCA. *Address:* Party of the Civic Alliance, Romania, 73311 Bucharest, Bd. Matiunilor Unite 5, block 110.

MANUKYAN, Vazgen: Armenian politician. *Career:* a leader of the Armenian Pan-national Movement (APM), he became Chairman of the Council of Ministers (head of government) when the APM, the largest single party, gained some 35% of the votes cast in elections to the Armenian Supreme Soviet in May–July 1990. He was replaced as premier in November 1991 and became the leader of the National Democratic Union, a splinter party of the APM founded in the same year. He was appointed Minister of Defence during the latter half of 1992, but resigned in mid-1993. *Address:* National Democratic Union, Armenia, Yerevan.

MARJANOVIĆ, Mirko: Yugoslav politician and Prime Minister of Serbia. *Education:* he is a graduate in economics. *Career:* he was a former Communist and a supporter of the Serbian President, Slobodan Milošević (q.v.). Before being appointed Serbian premier in March 1994, he was director-general of the Belgrade company, Progres. *Address:* Office of the Prime Minister of the Republic of Serbia, Federal Republic of Yugoslavia, 11000 Belgrade, Nemanjina 11.

MARTIĆ, Milan: Croatian ('Serbian Krajina') politician and President of the 'Republic of Serbian Krajina'; ethnic Serb. *Career:* a former police officer in rural Croatia and a Serb extremist, following a referendum on autonomy for the Serb population of the Krajina region, he organized a military force to protect their interests. In May 1991 he was appointed Minister of Internal Affairs in the Krajina administration. Having been a close ally of Milan Babić (q.v.), the head of the Government of Krajina at that time, he became the preferred representative of President Slobodan Milošević (q.v.) of Serbia as Milošević attempted to bring about a peace settlement in the former Yugoslavia and Babić opposed him. Martić stood against Babić in the elections to the presidency of the RSK in December 1993 and January 1994. He was not affiliated to a political party, but was supported in his candidacy by Miloševič. Amidst widespread expectation that he would be defeated by Babić, owing to the decreasing influence of the Serbian Government in the RSK, he was elected to succeed Goran Hadzić as President after a second round of voting, winning 51.7% of the votes cast. He took office in January 1994 and agreed to the 'permanent' cease-fire arranged with the Croatian Government in April 1994. *Address:* Office of the Government of Serbian Krajina, Croatia, Krajina, Knin.

MAZOWIECKI, Tadeusz: Polish politician and lawyer; b. 18 April 1927, in Płock. *Education:* he graduated in law. *Career:* Chairman of the Academy Publishing Co-operative, in Warsaw (1947–48), he wrote for *PAX* until his suspension in 1955. He was co-founder and editor-in-chief of the Roman Catholic monthly, *Więź* (1968–). As a deputy in the Sejm (1961–72) he fought for democratization. An adviser to Solidarity, from 1980, he was also editor of the Solidarity weekly *Tygodnik Solidarność*. He was interned in 1981–82. In August 1989 he became the first non-Communist Prime Minister in the Soviet bloc, governing until November 1990. He was leader of the Democratic Union, which, it was announced in March 1994, was to merge with the Liberal Democratic Congress. He is known as an intellectual and a member of the liberal centre of the political spectrum. *Address:* Democratic Union, Poland, 00-024 Warsaw, Al. Jerozolimskie 30.

MEČIAR, Vladimír: Slovak politician and former premier; b. 26 July 1942, in Zvolen. *Education:* graduated in law from Comenius University, Bratislava (1973). *Career:* a former pugilist, from 1959 he spent several years working in the Communist youth movement. In 1969 he was accused of supporting the reformists. He was expelled from the Communist Party of Czechoslovakia in 1970. While studying law he worked as a welder in Dubnica. He then worked as an enterprise lawyer, until November 1989, when he became Minister of the Interior and the Environment in the new Government of Slovakia. He became Premier after the elections of June 1990, but split from the ruling Public Against Violence movement (Slovakia's counterpart to the Czech Civic Forum) to found the Movement for a Democratic Slovakia (MDS), in March 1991. On 23 April 1991, therefore, he was dismissed as Premier by the Slovak National Council (republican assembly). However, following elections in June 1992, in which the MDS emerged as the dominant Slovak party, the Slovak National Council elected Mečiar as Premier, leading a Government composed primarily of MDS members. After Slovakia gained independence, the Government became increasingly divided, as Mečiar indulged in nationalistic politics rather than encouraging economic reform. However, Mečiar remained in office when a new, short-lived coalition was formed in November 1993. On 12 March 1994 this Government received a vote of 'no confidence' in the National Council and Mečiar was dismissed two days later. He was Chairman of the MDS until early 1994, by which time his successor as Premier, Jozef Moravčík (q.v.), and Deputy Prime Minister Roman Kováč (q.v.) had left the party and formed the Democratic Union of Slovakia (DUS). *Address:* Movement for a Democratic Slovakia, Tomašíkova 32, 823 69 Bratislava, Slovakia.

MEKSI, Dr Aleksander: Chairman of the Council of Ministers (Prime Minister) of Albania. *Career:* a member of the main anti-Communist Democratic Party of Albania (DPA), he was Deputy Chairman of the Kuvendi Popullor (People's Assembly) in 1991–92. Following the electoral defeat of the Communists in April 1992, Meksi was appointed Chairman of the Council of Ministers by the new President, and DPA leader, Sali Berisha (q.v.). *Address:* Office of the Council of Ministers, Këshilli i Ministrave, Tirana, Albania.

MELESCANU, Teodor Viorel: Romanian Deputy Prime Minister and Minister of Foreign Affairs; b. 1 March 1941, in Brad, Hunedoara county. *Education:* he studied at Bucharest University and the Graduate Institute of International Studies of the University of Geneva, Switzerland. *Career:* he joined the Ministry of Foreign Affairs in 1966 and his posts included First Secretary at the Romanian Permanent Mission to the UN in Geneva (Switzerland). He was appointed Deputy Prime Minister and Minister of Foreign Affairs in 1992. A professional diplomat, he was not associated with any political party, but was considered to be a member of the old Communist nomenklatura. *Address:* Ministry of Foreign Affairs, Romania, 71274 Bucharest, Al. Modrogan 14.

MERI, Lennart: President of Estonia; b. 29 March 1929, in Tallinn; m. with two s. and one d. *Education:* Tartu University. *Career:* a former script writer and film director, he entered politics in 1990, when he was appointed Minister of Foreign Affairs. In April–October 1992 he worked as ambassador to Finland, and was one of four candidates for the presidency in the nation-wide elections held on 20 September 1992. Owing to the lack of an overall majority in the elections, the Riigikogu subsequently voted on the two most popular candidates. He was elected President on 5 October, beating his opponent, Arnold Rüütel, by 59 votes to 31. *Address:* Office of the President, Tallinn, Estonia.

MESHKOV, Yury: Ukrainian politician and President of the Crimean Republic; b. 1940, in Crimea; ethnic Russian. *Career:* he worked as a border guard for the Soviet Committee of State Security (KGB) before embarking on a legal career. He entered politics as a Russian nationalist in a Crimea unhappy at the dissolution of the USSR and the Ukrainian economy. He was elected President of the Crimean Republic (the autonomy of which had recently been conceded by the Ukrainian parliament in October 1993), following a campaign of 'Great Russian' nationalist rhetoric and appeals for reunification with Russia. However, following his election he was more conciliatory towards the Ukrainian authorities, although he did continue to advocate the adoption by the Crimea of the Russian rouble, instead of the beleaguered Ukrainian currency. Furthermore, he urged a boycott of the national parliamentary elections, held on 27 March 1994, and supported a referendum on several controversial issues, including the status of the Republic in relation to mainland Ukraine. He was supported in his policies by some 70% of participants. On the same day as the elections, in a further act of mild rebellion against President Leonid Kravchuk (q.v.), he decreed that the Crimea change time zones, to coincide with Moscow (Russia), rather than Ukrainian, time. *Address:* Office of the President, Ukraine, Crimea, Simferopol.

MESIĆ, Stjepan ('Stipe'): President of the Croatian Sabor (parliamentary speaker) and former President of the Yugoslav federal State Presidency; *Career:* a member of the Croatian Democratic Union, which won the republican elections in Croatia, he was then made Premier (Prime Minister) of the Republic, in May 1990. In August he was elected as the Croatian member of the federal State Presidency and, consequently, its Vice-President. An anti-Communist and Croat nationalist, he was also one of the Presidency members who refused to vote for the Serbian request for a state of emergency, in March 1991. The Serbian-dominated establishment, therefore, refused to countenance what should have been the automatic election of the Croatian member as President of the federal Presidency, in May. Following the declarations of 'dissociation' by Croatia and Slovenia, and an EC-negotiated cease-fire at the start of the civil war, he was elected Yugoslav President, at the end of June 1991 (the first non-Communist President). However, the Presidency was increasingly revealed as too divided to function effectively, and the armed forces were reluctant to obey the orders of a Croat who supported his Republic's attempted secession. In October the 'Serbian bloc' of Presidency members began to meet without Mesić or the members for Bosnia and Herzegovina, Macedonia or Slovenia. Mesić's position was rendered more ambiguous by Croatia's recall of its citizens from federal institutions. On 5 December he formally resigned his federal post but pursued a political career in Croatia, where he was one of the most popular politicians. Following the parliamentary elections held on 2 August 1992 he was elected President of the Croatian Assembly (Sabor). *Address:* Croatian Assembly, Croatia, 41000 Zagreb, Radićev trg 6.

MILOŠEVIĆ, Slobodan: Yugoslav politician, President of Serbia; b. 20 August 1941, in Požarevac, Serbia; m. (Mirjana Marković), with one d. and one s. *Education:* he graduated in law, from Belgrade University (1964). *Career:* a conservative Communist, he worked in local government until 1969, when he became deputy director and then, in 1973, director-general of Tehnogas Enterprises. He was leader of the Belgrade Communists, until 1986, when he was made leader of the League of Communists of Serbia. He initiated an 'anti-bureaucratic revolution' and espoused nationalist rhetoric, which maintained the popularity of the ruling party (subsequently renamed the Socialist Party of Serbia—SPS). In May 1989 he was made President of the republican State Presidency. In December 1990 he was elected, by direct ballot, to the new post of sole, executive President, and was re-elected in December 1992 and in December 1993. His centralizing and pan-Serbian policies were important in provoking the dissolution of the old federation, but consistently secured him a parliamentary majority (at both federal and republican levels). This was no doubt helped by his control of the mass media and by the divisions in the opposition. His administration was condemned for its involvement in the wars in Croatia and Bosnia and Herzegovina. He was instrumental in establishing the Federal Republic of Yugoslavia (FRY), comprising Serbia and Montenegro, in April 1992, following the secession of the other four Republics. After sanctions were imposed on the FRY, in May 1992, he made efforts, in 1993, to persuade the Bosnian Serb leaders to accept the internationally mediated peace proposals. In 1993 he sought further to increase his power within the FRY by replacing many members of federal institutions with those thought to be more loyal to him, including the FRY President, Dobrica Ćosić (q.v.). Threatened by other parliamentary parties in October, he dissolved the Serbian legislature and managed to secure an increased majority for the SPS in December elections. *Address:* Office of the President of the Republic of Serbia, Federal Republic of Yugoslavia, 11000 Belgrade, Andrićev venac 1, Belgrade, Dedinje, Tolstoy 33.

MIRSAIDOV, Shukurulla Rakhmatovich: Uzbekistan politician; b. 1938. *Career:* a Communist official, he worked as an economic planner in Uzbekistan, for 25 years, but retained a reputation for integrity, despite the widespread corruption. In the 1980s he was Chairman of the Soviet (mayor) of Tashkent for five years, and was made a deputy premier of the republican Government in 1989. He became Chairman of the Council of Ministers in March 1990 and, in November, when that position was abolished, Vice-President of the Republic. In January 1992, when the position of Vice-President was also abolished, he was appointed as State Secretary, in an advisory role to President Islam Karimov (q.v.). However, Mirsaidov disagreed with Karimov on the question of economic reforms and resigned shortly after, citing the slowness of Uzbekistan's progress towards democracy. During the same year Karimov accused him of instigating riots by students in Tashkent, which seemed to suggest that the President perceived him as a potential threat. In June 1993 Mirsaidov was charged with corruption, namely of authorizing the sale of cotton to insolvent companies outside Uzbekistan, at a cost to the state of several million US dollars. He was sentenced to three years in prison, but immediately pardoned by Karimov. In August Mirsaidov survived a car bomb detonated near his home and, in the following month, he was attacked by anonymous assailants in Tashkent. Despite these incidences of what might be interpreted as intimidation, he declared his intention to rally Karimov's opponents. *Address:* c/o Union of Writers of Uzbekistan, Uzbekistan, 700000 Tashkent, ul. Pushkina 1.

MLADIĆ, Gen. Ratko: Bosnian military leader—Commander of the Bosnian Serb Army; b. Kalinovik, eastern Herzegovina; ethnic Serb. *Career:* a radical Serb nationalist, his father was killed by the German army during the Second World War. He became a tank officer in the Jugoslavenska Narodna Armija (JNA, Yugoslav People's Army) and, during the civil war in Croatia in 1991, he gained popularity among the Serbs for his support of their claim to the enclave of Krajina. In 1992 he was appointed commanding officer of the JNA and subsequently commanded the siege of Sarajevo and the 'ethnic cleansing' of countless Bosnian Muslim (Bosniak) communities. Aiming to bring about the 'total miliatary defeat of the Muslims' and the formation of a 'Greater Serbia', he strongly opposed any peace settlement to the Bosnian civil war, and reiterated this in March 1994. *Address:* Bosnia and Herzegovina, Pale, 'Serb Assembly'.

MORAVČÍK, Jozef: Prime Minister of Slovakia; b. 19 March 1945. *Education:* he studied law at the Charles University in Prague and the Comenius University in Bratislava. *Career:* he was elected Dean of the Faculty of Law at the Comenius University in 1990. In February of the following year, as a member of Public Against Violence (PAV), he became a deputy in the Slovak National Council and, in June 1992, he was elected to the Czechoslovak Federal Assembly as a member of the recently established Movement for a Democratic Slovakia

(MDS). Between July and December of that year he was Minister of Foreign Affairs in the Federal Government and Chairman of the CSCE Council of Ministers. In March 1993 Moravčík was appointed Minister of Foreign Affairs of the newly independent Slovak Republic, but he resigned from that position in February 1994, having been expelled from the MDS. In March he was invited to form a new coalition Government, which included his own newly founded party, the Democratic Union of Slovakia, and several former opposition groupings. *Address:* Office of the Government of the Slovak Republic, nám. Slobody 1, 813 70 Bratislava, Slovakia.

MURADOV, Sakhat Nepesovich: Chairman of the Majlis of Turkmenistan (parliamentary speaker); b. 7 May 1932, in Ivanovo, Russian Federation. *Career:* a conservative Communist, he was head of the department responsible for science and education in the Central Committee of the Turkmen Communist Party, 1968–71. He was a minister for education from 1979 and a full member of the Central Committee from 1981. As deputy to Saparmurat Niyazov (q.v.), he replaced him as Chairman of the Supreme Soviet, in November 1990, when the latter was elected to the post of executive President of the Republic. In May 1992, when the new Turkmen Constitution replaced the Supreme Soviet with the Majlis, Muradov remained Chairman of the renamed legislature. *Address:* Majlis, Turkmenistan, Ashgabat.

MUTALIBOV, Ayaz Niyazi ogly: former President of Azerbaijan; b. 12 May 1938. *Career:* a member of the CPSU since 1963, in January 1990 he was appointed First Secretary of the Azerbaijan Communist Party Central Committee, in July 1990 a member of the CPSU Politburo and, in May 1990, Chairman of the Supreme Soviet (President) of Azerbaijan. He resigned as Communist First Secretary following the Moscow coup attempt of August 1991, although there were reports that he had initially reacted favourably to the news of President Mikhail Gorbachev's (q.v.) deposition. In September 1991 there were direct elections to the post of President of the Republic, and Mutalibov was elected unopposed. In March 1992 he was forced to resign over the progress of the war in Nagorny Karabakh. The Supreme Soviet voted to reinstate him in May, but he was deposed by the Popular Front of Azerbaijan (PFA) after one day in office. He was thereafter resident in Moscow (Russian Federation) and was believed to be the favoured Russian candidate for leadership in Azerbaijan. However, in June 1993 Heydar Aliyev (q.v.) achieved office and, as he was pro-Russian also, the prospect of a return to power for Mutalibov receded.

MUTALOV, Abdulkhashim: Chairman of the Cabinet of Ministers (Prime Minister) of Uzbekistan; b. 1947. *Career:* a Communist Party official, he was Minister of Grain and a Deputy Chairman of the Council of Ministers, under the President. On 13 January 1992 the Supreme Soviet elected him to the restored post of premier (Chairman of the Cabinet of Ministers). He was one of President Islam Karimov's (q.v.) most loyal supporters. *Address:* Office of the Cabinet of Ministers, Uzbekistan, 700008 Tashkent, Government House.

NANO, Fatos: Albanian politician and former premier; b. 1951. *Career:* an economist and a reformist Communist, he became a member of the Government in January 1991, when the ruling Party was under pressure to satisfy popular demands. In March he was appointed to lead a provisional Council of Ministers, which was confirmed in office by the Communist-dominated Assembly. He was forced to resign in June, but, in the same month, became President of the newly renamed Socialist Party of Albania (the former Communists), which remained the largest party. In July 1993 he was arrested, along with other former Communist leaders, on charges financial impropriety. He went on trial for these charges in March 1994. The Socialist Party refused to replace him as leader, claiming that the trial was politically motivated. *Address:* Socialist Party of Albania, Tirana, Albania.

NAŠTASE, Adrian: President of the Assembly of Deputies (parliamentary speaker) of Romania; b. 22 June 1950, in Bucharest. *Education:* graduated in law from Bucharest University (1973) and then studied for a doctorate in international law (1978). *Career:* he expressed some dissent under President Nicolae Ceauşescu, in December 1989 becoming a member of the National Salvation Front, for whom he was elected to parliament. He was Vice-President of the Romanian Association of International Law and International Relations from 1977 and held associate membership of the International Institute for Human Rights (Strasbourg, France). He was appointed Minister of Foreign Affairs in May 1990 and remained in that post until late 1992. He became President of the Assembly of Deputies after the general election held in September 1992 and was also Executive President of the ruling Party of Social Democracy of Romania (formerly the Democratic National Salvation Front). *Address:* Party of Social Democracy of Romania, Romania, Bucharest, Str. Filioara 3, Sector 2.

NAZARBAYEV, Nursultan Abishevich: President of Kazakhstan; b. 6 July 1940. *Career:* he joined the CPSU in 1962, while working at the Karaganda Metallurgical Combine and, in 1969, began work with the Komsomol in Temirtau. He rose rapidly in the republican Party and state apparatus, becoming the Chairman of the Kazakh Council of Ministers in 1984. In June 1989 he became First Secretary of the Kazakh Communist Party. In April 1990 the Kazakh Supreme Soviet elected him to the new post of executive President. In July 1990 he became a member of the all-Union Party Politburo and an increasingly important politician outside Kazakhstan. He was known as an astute negotiator. He was a supporter of the Union and, after independence, was in favour of close links within the Commonwealth of Independent States (which was founded in Almaty in December 1991). Much of the rhetoric on this subject was dictated by the need to assuage the anxieties of the large ethnic Russian community in Kazakhstan, whose trust he seemed to have retained in the early years of independence. There were allegations of electoral malpractice and official discrimination against ethnic Russians in the general election of March 1994, but the overwhelming majority in parliament was comprised of supporters of Nazarbayev, who continued to advocate close links with Russia. In reality, the transfer to a free-market economy (Nazarbayev had favoured economic reform and republican autonomy in the economy even before the dissolution of the USSR) inevitably resulted in some weakening of links, although the process of change was fairly gradual. His main concern was political stability, which resulted in a limit on democratic development, although some of this could be attributed to a general cultural preference for consensus. The political party which he agreed to lead, the People's Unity Party of Kazakhstan (SNEK), indicated his concerns in its title—not only did he have to reassure the non-Kazakh ethnic groups in the country, but also many of the Kazakhs, who accused him of favouring his own Great Horde kin in official appointments. He enjoyed good relations with the West, as his authoritarian but benign regime provided stability in a potentially wealthy country and in the region as a whole. *Address:* Office of the President, Kazakhstan, 480091 Almaty, Respubliki 4.

NIYAZOV, Saparmurat Atayevich: President and Prime Minister of Turkmenistan; b. 19 Feb. 1940. *Career:* he joined the Communist Party in 1962, heading the Ashgabat organization until 1984, when he went to the central CPSU headquarters in Moscow. In 1985 he returned to Turkmenia (now Turkmenistan) as premier and, subsequently, Party leader. He was elected Chairman of the Supreme Soviet (*de facto* head of state), in January 1990, and was returned unopposed as a directly elected President in October. A conservative Communist, he did not condemn or condone the coup attempt of August 1991 and retained the Communists as the ruling party (although the name was changed to the Democratic Party of Turkmenistan). No opposition parties were permitted to register in Turkmenistan, which remained the least reformed of the former Soviet Republics and had been the one least interested in independence. Niyazov also became Prime Minister (head of government) and Supreme Commander of the Armed Forces in May 1992, in accordance with the new Turkmen Constitution. In June he was unopposed in presidential elections and thus re-elected as President and, in a referendum in

January 1994, 99.9% of the electorate voted to exempt him from the obligation to seek re-election in 1997. This indicated the extent to which Niyazov had consolidated his power since Turkmenistan became independent. The natural gas resources of the country meant that it had the potential wealth necessary to secure Niyazov's aim of achieving true independence for Turkmenistan. He favoured regional economic co-operation, but avoided political or military involvements, such as in Tajikistan. *Address:* Office of the President, Turkmenistan, Ashgabat.

OLECHOWSKI, Andrzej: Polish Minister of Foreign Affairs. *Career:* after resigning from the post of finance minister in the Olszewski Government in May 1992, he was appointed by President Lech Wałęsa (q.v.) in December 1992 to lead a controversial 47-strong Committee on Economic Development. He was also leader of the President's Non-Party Bloc for Political Reform, founded in 1993. He became foreign minister in the new Government of October 1992. *Address:* Ministry of Foreign Affairs, Poland, 00-580 Warsaw, Al. Szucha 23.

OLEKSY, Jozef: Marshal (speaker) of the Polish Sejm. *Career:* he joined the Polish United Workers' Party (PZPR) in 1968 and was prominent in local government in 1987–89. He was a minister in Mieczysław Rakowski's short-lived Government in 1988–89 and became Deputy Chairman of Social Democracy of the Republic of Poland, the party which replaced the Communist PZPR in 1990. He was elected Marshal (speaker) of the lower house of the Polish parliament, the Sejm, on 14 October 1993, after the left's electoral victory. *Address:* Sejm, Poland, Warsaw.

OTCHERTSEV, Valery: Deputy Prime Minister of Turkmenistan. *Career:* he was Minister of Trade in 1992–93. In late 1993–early 1994 he was appointed Deputy Prime Minister (replacing Ata Charyev) and Minister of the Economy and Finance, although the appointment was not immediately publicized by President Niyazov (q.v.). *Address:* Ministry of the Economy and Finance, Turkmenistan, Ashgabat.

PANIĆ, Milan: Yugoslav politician and former federal premier; US citizen of Serbian origin. *Career:* before becoming premier of the Federal Republic of Yugoslavia (FRY), on 14 July 1992, he was director of a pharmaceuticals company in California (USA). Whilst in office he was openly critical of the Serb leaders in Croatia and in Bosnia and Herzegovina, and offered appeasement to ethnic Albanians in Kosovo-Metohija. He stood against Slobodan Milošević (q.v.) in the December 1992 Serbian presidential elections, but failed to be elected to the post, and on 29 December was removed from office following a vote of 'no confidence' in the Federal Assembly. He was forced to leave the country. *Address:* c/o Office of the Federal Government, Federal Republic of Yugoslavia, 11070 Belgrade, Lenjina 2.

PASHKO, Gramoz: Albanian politician. *Career:* the son of a Communist government minister, he was Professor of Economics at Tirana University. As a leader of the main opposition Democratic Party of Albania (DPA), he was the author of their economic policy proposals. He was a Deputy Prime Minister in the coalition Bufi Government of 1991 and opposed the DPA's withdrawal from it, in December. In September 1992, following a division in the DPA, he co-founded a new political grouping, the Albanian Democratic Alliance. He was a vociferous opponent of the administration of Sali Berisha (q.v.), accusing it of 'right-wing extremism'. *Address:* Albanian Democratic Alliance, Tirana, Albania.

PATSATSIA, Otar: Georgian Prime Minister; b. 1929, in Zugdidi. *Education:* he graduated from the Leningrad Technological Institute and in 1970 gained a further degree at the Forestry Academy, Leningrad (now St Petersburg, Russian Federation). *Career:* in 1965 he was appointed director of a major cellulose and paper plant in Zugdidi. During the 1980s he was repeatedly praised by the Georgian Communist Party for his innovations in improving the living conditions of workers at the plant. Having previously been the leader of the local administration in Zugdidi, he was nominated by President Eduard Shevardnadze (q.v.) as the next Prime Minister and his appointment was approved by the Supreme Soviet on 20 August 1993. He was praised by President Shevardnadze for his honesty, and had a reputation for good personal relations and for solving economic problems. *Address:* Office of the Prime Minister, Georgia, 380034 Tbilisi, Ingorokva.

PAWLAK, Waldemar: Polish Prime Minister; b. 5 September 1959, in Pacyna, Płock. *Education:* graduated from Warsaw Technical University with a degree in automotive and agricultural machinery. *Career:* he was a member of the United Peasant Party (which was replaced in 1990 by the Polish Peasant Party—PPP) from 1984, and became leader of the party's voivodship committee in Płock in 1988–89. In the 1989 election Pawlak was elected to the Sejm, the then unicameral parliament. Supported by Rural Solidarity, he was part of the reformist movement which led the PPP to join the Solidarity-led coalition government in 1989 and to oust its discredited leadership. In June 1991 he was appointed leader of the PPP. Following the 1991 elections, he became parliamentary faction leader of the PPP. In June 1992 Pawlak was invited to form a government but failed to do so and was replaced by Hanna Suchocka as Prime Minister. However, in October 1993, following the success of the PPP in the September parliamentary elections, Pawlak became Prime Minister of a coalition Government, comprising the PPP, the Democratic Left Alliance (former Communists) and the Union of Labour. *Address:* Office of the Prime Minister, Poland, 00-567 Warsaw, Al. Ujazdowskie 1/3.

PAZNIAK, Zianon: Belarusian politician; b. 1944, in western Belarus. *Education:* he was educated as an archaeologist and art historian. *Career:* an anti-Communist dissident, who spent the Soviet era leading resistance movements in Minsk (Miensk) and exposing Stalinist crimes in Belarus, he was a founder member of the Belarusian Popular Front 'Revival' (BPF), formed in October 1988. He was formally elected its leader at the founding congress, in Vilnius (Lithuania), in June 1989. The BPF was forbidden to participate in elections to the republican Supreme Soviet, in March 1990, but sponsored candidates in coalition with other groups, known as the Belarusian Democratic Bloc. Paznyak was elected as a deputy in the Belarusian parliament and became one of the leaders of the small democratic opposition. He was considered a likely contender in the presidential elections scheduled for June 1994. *Address:* Belarusian Popular Front 'Revival'—BPF, Belarus, 220040 Minsk, POB 208.

PERIŠIĆ, Col-Gen. Momčilo: Yugoslav Army Chief of Staff; b. 22 May 1944 in Kostunici, near Gornji Milanovać, Serbia. *Education:* he attended a Military Academy for Ground Forces, where he trained as an artillery officer and then graduated in psychology at the Higher Military-Political School of the Yugoslav People's Army. *Career:* at the outbreak of the civil war in the former Yugoslavia he was a colonel and commandant of the military school in Zadar (Croatia), where he successfully broke a Croatian blockade. He was then transferred to eastern Herzegovina (Bosnia and Herzegovina), where he became corps commander, and later participated in the bombardment of Dubrovnik (Croatia). He was active in battles in Foca and Mostar (both Bosnia and Herzegovina), and it was such victories against Croat forces that earned him the sobriquet the 'Knight of Mostar'. Perišić was Commander of the Third Army, at Niš, before becoming Chief of Staff in August 1993, supposedly because of his loyalty to Serbian President Milošević (q.v.). *Address:* c/o Federal Ministry of National Defence, Federal Republic of Yugoslavia, 11000 Belgrade, Kneza Miloša 29.

PETERLE, Lojze: Slovenian politician; b. 5 July 1948. *Education:* he graduated in economics and geography. *Career:* He was an advisor on environmental protection at the Institute for Social Planning. As leader of the Slovenian Christian Democrats, which emerged as the largest party in the victorious DEMOS coalition after the republican general elections of April 1990, he became Premier or Prime Minister of the Government. He co-ordinated the policy of gradual secession, or 'dissociation', of Slovenia from the Yugoslav federation. In May 1992 he resigned as Prime Minister following a vote of 'no confidence' by the National Assembly. He became Minister of Foreign Affairs after the elections of December 1992. He was Deputy President of the European Union of Christian Democrats. *Address:* Ministry of Foreign Affairs, Slovenia, 61000 Ljubljana, Gregorčičeva st. 25.

PETKOV, Prof. Dr Krustyu: Bulgarian trade union leader; b. 18 November 1943, in Dimovo, Vidin region; m., with two c. *Education:* educated as an economist, he has a doctorate. *Career:* an academic, who was a professor of labour sociology, he was involved in the official trade union movement of Communist Bulgaria. He led the Communist-dominated Bulgarian Professional Union in its renunciation of any political affiliations and, in February 1990, its transformation into the Confederation of Independent Trade Unions in Bulgaria, of which he became Chairman. It remained the largest trade union body in the country. *Address:* Bulgaria, Sofia, pl. D. Blagoev.

PLYUSHCH, Ivan: Chairman of the Supreme Council (Verkhovna Rada) of Ukraine. *Career:* previously the First Deputy Chairman of the Supreme Soviet (subsequently renamed the Supreme Council—Verkhovna Rada), he was elected Chairman on 5 December 1991. This post, which was previously the *de facto* republican head of state, had been vacated by Leonid Kravchuk (q.v.), who had been elected executive President of the now-independent country. Plyushch succeeded to the functions of a parliamentary speaker. He remained an influential politician and was re-elected to the new Verkhovna Rada in March–April 1994. *Address:* Verkhovna Rada, Ukraine, 252019 Kiev, vul. M. Hrushevskoho 5.

POPESCU, Dan Mircea: Romanian Deputy Prime Minister and Minister of Employment and Social Protection; b. 6 Oct. 1950, in Bucharest. *Education:* he studied at the Faculty of Law of Bucharest University. *Career:* having previously been an academic and a presidential advisor on domestic policy, in early 1991 he was appointed Minister of State in charge of the Quality of Life and Social Security. From 1991 he was Minister of Employment and Social Protection, also becoming a Deputy Prime Minister in November 1992. He was Vice-President of the ruling Democratic National Salvation Front, which was renamed the Party of Social Democracy of Romania in 1993. *Address:* Ministry of Employment and Social Protection, Romania, 70119 Bucharest 1, Str. Demetru I. Dobrescu 2–4.

POPOV, Gavriil Kharitonovich: Russian politician and economist; b. 1936, in Moscow; ethnic Greek. *Education:* he studied economics at Moscow State University. *Career:* he joined the CPSU in 1959 and was an economist and academic. In 1988 he also served as editor-in-chief of *Voprosy Ekonomiki.* He acted as Chairman of the Soviet Greek Society. In 1989 he was elected to the Congress of People's Deputies and to the Moscow City Soviet (Council), of which he became Chairman (that is, mayor of Moscow). A radical reformer and a prominent member of the democratic movement, he resigned from the CPSU in July 1990 and was a strong supporter of Boris Yeltsin (q.v.). In December 1991 he threatened to resign, in protest at obstacles to his reforms, but he was persuaded to remain in office. He eventually left in 1992, but continued to play an active role in politics. He chaired the Russian Movement for Democratic Reforms, a union of several democratic forces founded in 1991, which won 4 seats in the State Duma in the elections of December 1993. *Address:* State Duma, Russian Federation, Moscow, Novy Arbat 36.

PUČNIK, Dr Jože: Slovenian politician. *Career:* he spent some 20 years in exile in the Federal Republic of Germany, because of his political views. With the disintegration of the Communist system, opposition parties began to be formed in Slovenia, in 1989. In February the Social Democratic Party of Slovenia (SDPS), of which he was elected leader, was formed by protesting workers. Later in the year the SDPS and five other opposition parties formed a coalition, the Democratic Opposition of Slovenia (DEMOS). Pučnik was elected leader of DEMOS, but he failed to win the presidential elections of April 1990 and did not immediately hold any state or government office. This partly accounted for the weak presence of the SDPS in the ruling coalition, but he became important in easing the increasingly strained relations between the coalition partners. Pučnik remained President of the SDPS after the dissolution of the DEMOS coalition in February 1992. He was Deputy Prime Minister responsible for General Affairs from May 1992 until early 1993, when the National Assembly passed a law which reduced the number of members of the Council of Ministers. During 1993 he became Parliamentary Group Leader of the SDPS, ceding the presidency of the party to Janez Janša (q.v.). *Address:* Social Democratic Party of Slovenia, Slovenia, Komenskega 11.

PULATOV, Abdurakhim: Uzbekistan politician. *Career:* an academic and a nationalist, he was a founder and co-Chairman of one of the main opposition groups in Uzbekistan, the Popular Front, Birlik (Unity). The Government would only allow his organization to register as a movement and not as a political party, to limit its ability to participate in elections. In July 1992 he was attacked in the street in Tashkent by unknown assailants, who were suspected of acting on behalf of the Government. His brother, Abdumannob, was also an opposition activist, the head of the Human Rights Association in Uzbekistan. *Address:* c/o Union of Writers, Uzbekistan, 700000 Tashkent, ul. Pushkina 1.

RAHMONOV, Imamali Sharipovich: Chairman of the Supreme Soviet (head of state) of Tajikistan; b. 1953 in Dangar rayon, Kulyab Oblast (now Hatlon Oblast). *Education:* he studied economics at Dushanbe's Lenin University. *Career:* worked, variously, in positions ranging from an electrician to the director of a collective farm in his native district. He was reportedly a protégé of the main Kulyabi militia leader in the 1992–93 civil war, Sangak Safarov. He became head of the Kulyab Oblast administration on 2 November 1992, but within a few weeks, on 19 November, he was elected Chairman of the Supreme Soviet (with the abolition of the presidency, therefore head of state). This was a mark of the importance of the Kulyabi militias to the victory of the Communist reactionaries, although the traditional ruling élite from Khojand provided the premier. Rahmonov appointed many fellow Kulyabis to high office, although he could not afford to alienate the wealthy Khojandis completely. Their main demand was for him to disarm the militias, but he had limited success in this at first. Eventually it was decided to achieve this by incorporating the militias into national security services, although the Khojand families were dubious about thus institutionalizing the Kulyab military advantage. Progress was made in this process mainly after Safarov's mysterious death in a shooting incident in March 1993. The main military assistance for the Rahmonov administration, however, came from Russia and Uzbekistan, which favoured a conservative Communist regime rather than 'Islamic fundamentalists', as the Islamic-democratic opposition was dubbed. The opposition forces, defeated in the civil war, caused considerable concern to Russia and Tajikistan's Central Asian neighbours with their *mujahidin*-style border raids from Afghanistan. By March 1994 Russian pressure had persuaded Rahmonov that negotiations with the exiled opposition, armed and unarmed, could take place. Kulyabi interests had favoured a continuation of the crisis situation, because this justified their military presence as well as continued foreign support. However, Russia (fearing a lengthy involvement in the area) and Khojand (which was anxious for economic recovery) were not prepared to countenance this indefinitely, and Rahmonov wished to consolidate his position on a more secure basis. *Address:* Office of the Chairman of the Supreme Soviet, Tajikistan, Dushanbe.

RAZNJATIVIĆ, Zelkjo ('Arkan'): Yugoslav politician and former militia leader; b. 1952, in Serbia; m. *Career:* he was supposedly an assassin in the Yugoslav secret service. In 1990 he became president of the Belgrade Red Star Supporters' Club. Following the outbreak of war in Croatia, he was leader of the paramilitary group, the Tigers, which allegedly committed atrocities in villages around Vukovar in 1991, and later, in Bosnia and Herzegovina, in particular in Bijeljina. The US Government proposed that he be tried for war crimes. He formed the nationalist Serbian Unity Party in 1993. In the Serbian election campaign in 1993 his party's manifesto included the expulsion of ethnic Albanians who refused to acknowledge Serbian rule in Kosovo. He was also accused of being involved in organized crime in Serbia, including the smuggling of petroleum and cigarettes. He was wanted for bank robberies in several countries, including Sweden where, it was reported, he shot his way out of a courtroom, and the Netherlands where he escaped from prison. *Address:* Serbian Unity Party, Federal Republic of Yugoslavia, Belgrade.

REPSE, Einars: President of the Bank of Latvia; b. 1961. *Career:* having graduated in physics he became involved in politics, helping to form the Latvian independence movement in the late 1980s. He was elected to the Supreme Council in 1990 and became a close political ally of the then premier, Ivars Godmanis. He taught himself economics and subsequently became a member of the parliamentary Economics Commission. In September 1991 he was appointed President of the Bank of Latvia. He has been credited with the smooth transition of the Latvian economy from a Soviet centrally planned structure to a successful product of monetary reform. He stressed the need for an independent central bank and the introduction of a new currency (the transitionary Latvian rouble in May 1992, followed by the lats). In spite of opposition from bureaucrats and heads of state-owned companies, who resented the high interest rates, he remained committed to a tight credit policy and by the beginning of 1994 had achieved relative economic stability in Latvia. *Address:* Bank of Latvia, K. Valdemāra 2A, Rīga, Latvia.

RIGELNIK, Herman: President of the Slovenian National Assembly (parliamentary speaker); b. 29 March 1942. *Education:* master of economic science. *Career:* worked for Metalna Maribor and Kovinotehna Celje. He was Minister of Industry and Construction of the Socialist Republic of Slovenia in 1982–83, head of the Gorenje manufacturing group in Velenje from 1983 to 1991 and the representative of the Ljubljanska Banka in Munich in 1991–92. Rigelnik served as Deputy Prime Minister responsible for Economic Affairs in Janez Drnovšek's first coalition Government from May 1992 until early 1993, when the National Assembly passed a law which reduced the number of members of the Council of Ministers. During 1993 he became President of the National Assembly (Drzavni Zbor). He was a member of the Liberal Democratic Party. *Address:* National Assembly, Slovenia, 61000 Ljubljana, Šubičeva st. 4.

ROMAN, Petre: Romanian politician; b. 22 July 1946, in Bucharest; m., with two c. *Education:* at Bucharest Polytechnic, and then in Toulouse (France), where he completed his doctorate in 1974. *Career:* the son of prominent members of the Communist nomenklatura, he became a professor and head of the Department of Hydraulics at Bucharest Polytechnic. He became involved in the 1989 Revolution, despite his membership of the Romanian Communist Party. He was nominated as Prime Minister by the National Salvation Front (NSF), on 26 December 1989. He resigned on 26 September 1991, following protests from striking coal-miners, but remained the leader of the ruling NSF, which supported the Government of Prime Minister Theodor Stolojan (q.v.). In March 1992 the NSF split into two factions, with supporters of Ion Iliescu (q.v.) forming the Democratic National Salvation Front (later renamed the Party of Social Democracy of Romania), while Roman's supporters remained within the NSF. The decreasing importance of the 'rump' NSF was indicated by its relatively poor performance at the presidential and legislative elections held in September 1992. The NSF was not represented in the new Government formed in November. Roman remained President of the party when the NSF changed its name to the Democratic Party—NSF in May 1993. *Address:* Democratic Party—NSF, Romania, 70024 Bucharest, Al. Modrogan 1.

RUGOVA, Dr Ibrahim: Yugoslav (Kosovo-Metohija/Serbian) politician, 'President of the Republic of Kosovo' and writer; b. in Kosovo (now Kosovo-Metohija), Serbia; ethnic Albanian. *Career:* a prominent dissident writer, who consistently championed the rights of the Kosovar (Albanian) population, in 1990 he founded and became leader of the Democratic Alliance of Kosovo. This became the mass party of the ethnic Albanians after its effective take-over of the provincial Socialist Alliance of Working People. He led the boycott of the 1990 constitutional referendum and elections. He supported the creation of Kosovo as the ethnic Albanian 'home' Republic, in the Yugoslav federation, although union with Albania had considerable support in the province. On 24 May 1992 he was elected President of the self-proclaimed 'Republic of Kosovo' and his party gained the most seats in an Assembly declared illegitimate by the Serbian authorities. *Address:* Democratic Alliance of Kosovo, Federal Republic of Yugoslavia, Kosovo-Metohija, 38000 Priština.

RUTSKOY, Col Aleksandr Vladimirovich: Russian politician; b. 1947. *Career:* a soldier by profession, he was a fighter-bomber commander and fought in the Afghan war. A moderate Communist, Boris Yeltsin (q.v.) persuaded him to stand for election as the Vice-President of the Russian Federation, in the June 1991 presidential elections. This was to ensure some Communist support in the Supreme Soviet. He opposed the coup attempt of August 1991 and, in October, the party of which he was leader, Communists for Democracy, changed its name to the People's Party of Free Russia. As part of Yeltsin's reorganization of the Russian Government, in November 1991, Rutskoy was appointed head of a Centre for the Operational Supervision of the Progess of Reforms. From December, however, he came into increasing conflict with President Yeltsin, over political and economic policies. He was eventually dismissed by Yeltsin on 1 September 1993, ostensibly because a series of allegations, including that he owned a Swiss bank account, had made his position untenable. (These allegations were later withdrawn.) He commanded the defence of the parliament building throughout the political crisis of September–October. After the defeat of opponents to the Government, he was arrested and imprisoned. He was condemned by the People's Party of Free Russia for his active role in the uprising. He described his release from Lefortovo prison, following the amnesty granted by the State Duma on 23 February 1994, as 'a return to the people' and continued publicly to challenge Yeltsin's authority after his release. He was expected to stand as a candidate in the next presidential elections.

RYBKIN, Ivan Petrovich: Chairman (speaker) of the State Duma of the Russian Federation; b. 1946. *Career:* he formerly worked as deputy chief of the Main Directorate of Water Management of the Ministry of Agriculture. A member of the Agrarian Party, he won a seat in the State Duma in the legislative elections of 12 December 1993. His party controlled a total of 55 seats in the State Duma, and established a parliamentary bloc with the Democratic Party of Russia and the Communist Party of the Russian Federation on 13 January 1994. The following day he was elected Chairman of the State Duma, having won the support of members of his own party, the Communist Party and the right-wing nationalist Liberal Democratic Party. *Address:* State Duma, Russian Federation, Moscow, Novy Arbat 36.

ŠAINOVIĆ, Nikola: Yugoslav (Serbian) politician. *Career:* he rose through the ranks of the Socialist Party of Serbia (SPS—former Communists), and following the party's election victory in December 1992, was chosen as Serbian Prime Minister. He officially took office on 10 February 1993 and held the post until the end of 1993, when further legislative elections were held. In March 1994 federal premier Radoje Kontić (q.v.) appointed him as a deputy prime minister in his Government. *Address:* Office of the Federal Government, Federal Republic of Yugoslavia, 11070 Belgrade, Lenjina 2.

SAMADOV, Abdujalil Ahadovich: Chairman of the Council of Ministers (Prime Minister) of Tajikistan; b. in Khojand. *Career:* a member of the traditional ruling élite of Tajikistan, he was a Communist from Khojand (formerly Leninabad), and had risen through the ranks of the Party-state apparatus. A deputy premier in the first administration of Akbar Mirzoyev (who took office in January 1992), he was not included in the 'Government of National Reconciliation' of May, which had been joined by the Islamic-democratic parties. However, he was reinstated after the Communist victory in the civil war, although not until 1993, the year following the crucial Supreme

Soviet session of November 1992. Samadov succeeded Abdumalik Abdullojonov (q.v.) as Prime Minister in December 1993. President Imamali Rahmonov, a Kulyabi, still needed the support of the powerful clans of Khojand and so was prepared to reserve the premier's office for one of their number. Samadov stated that his priority was to deal with the economic crisis, and he committed himself to the continuation of free-market reforms. In March 1994 he was rumoured to be behind the creation of a new public and political organization, the Union of Progressive Forces, which was committed to national reconciliation, free-market economic reform (including the privatization of business and land) and close links with Russia and the Commonwealth of Independent States. *Address:* Office of the Council of Ministers, Tajikistan, Dushanbe.

SANGHELI, Andrei: Moldovan politician. *Career:* a former member of the Communist Party Politburo, he was the head of the parliamentary conciliation commissions which held negotiations with the Gagauz and Transdnestrian separatists in the early 1990s. He was appointed Prime Minister of Moldova in July 1992, heading a Government of 'national consensus', in which posts were reserved for representatives from the separatist regions. Sangheli, with President Mircea Snegur (q.v.) and parliamentary speaker Petru Lucinschi (q.v.) were the leading figures in an administration which favoured membership of the former Soviet countries' Commonwealth rather than union with Romania. Lucinschi's party emerged as the largest single parliamentary bloc following the March 1994 elections, and Sangheli formed a new Government in April. The electoral confirmation of his administration was considered likely to improve the prospects for a settlement with the Transdnestrian and Gagauz separatists. *Address:* c/o Ministry of the Interior, Moldova, Chişinău.

SAVISAAR, Edgar: Deputy Speaker of the Estonian Riigikogu and former premier; b. 1949, in Estonia. *Career:* an economist by training, he was a Communist (until January 1990), but also became a leader of the Estonian Popular Front, which was founded in April 1988. From July 1989 he was a deputy premier in the Estonian Government and, upon the 1990 electoral victory of the Front, he was appointed to lead the Council of Ministers. He enjoyed good relations with the rival Congress of Estonia, which rejected the validity of the existing institutions, but were prepared to accept the Government's interim authority. He supported the creation of the Constituent Assembly, upon the reclamation of full independence in August 1991. In January 1992, despite the hitherto relatively strong performance of the Estonian economy, he was obliged to ask for emergency powers because of the increasing shortage of supplies. Shortly afterwards he resigned as premier, but was elected to the post of Deputy Speaker of the Riigikogu (as the Constituent Assembly was renamed) following the parliamentary elections of 20 September. *Address:* Riigikogu, Endla 6-4, Tallinn 0001, Estonia.

SESELJ, Vojislav: Yugoslav (Serbian) politician; b. Bosnia and Herzegovina; ethnic Serb. *Career:* he spent time in prison in the 1970s, for accusing the Bosnian Government of corruption. It is claimed that, in prison, he suffered a series of serious sexual assaults by the Bosnian Muslim (Bosniak) policemen, an event which reportedly intensified his extreme nationalist views. He co-founded the Serbian Renewal Movement with Vuk Drašković (q.v.) in 1990, before forming his own party, the right-wing, nationalist Serbian Radical Party (SRS). Following the outbreak of civil war in the former Yugoslavia in 1991, he was closely associated with the nationalist paramilitary 'Chetnik' group, which allegedly committed atrocities in eastern Croatia and eastern Bosnia. In the December 1992 Serbian parliamentary elections his party took 73 seats and formed part of the coalition Government. During 1993, however, relations between him and President Slobodan Milošević (q.v.) deteriorated; a vote of 'no confidence' in the Government, which he proposed, led to an election campaign during which he was denounced as a war criminal. In the December elections the SRS retained 39 seats. *Address:* Serbian Radical Party, Federal Republic of Yugoslavia, 11000 Belgrade, Ohridska 1.

SHAKHRAY, Sergey Mikhailovich: Russian politician; b. 30 April 1951, in Simferopol, Crimea, Ukraine. *Education:* Rostov State University. *Career:* he was elected a People's Deputy in 1990 and was Chairman of the Legislative Committee of the Russian Supreme Soviet in 1990–91. He was appointed to the cabinet in December 1991, as deputy premier, and was elected to the Supreme Soviet in April 1992. He rejoined the Government in November that year, as Chairman of the State Committee for Nationalities Policy, an office which was upgraded to a ministerial post at the end of 1993. In 1993 he established the Party of Russian Unity and Concord, a rival democratic bloc to Yegor Gaidar's (q.v.) Russia's Choice. His party won a total of 19 seats in the elections to the State Duma of 12 December 1993, and Shakhray himself was elected. A future contender for the presidency, in the election campaign he stated that his party stood for conservative values, and stressed the need to preserve the Russian Federation as a unified state. *Address:* State Duma, Russian Federation, Moscow, Novy Arbat 36.

SHERIMKULOV, Medetkan: Chairman of the Jogorku Kenesh of Kyrgyzstan. *Career:* he was elected to be the republican parliamentary speaker in December 1990, following the resignation of Absamat Masaliyev. Sherimkulov contested the elections to the new post of executive President, but these were won by the reformist Askar Akayev (q.v.). Sherimkulov resigned from the CPSU following the Moscow coup attempt of August 1991, but was not considered to be a supporter of the Government. However, the Supreme Soviet, renamed the Jogorku Kenesh, was vigorous in maintaining parliamentary independence and Sherimkulov seemed likely to remain in office until the next general election (due by 1995). *Address:* Office of the Jogorku Kenesh, Kyrgyzstan, 720000 Bishkek.

SHEVARDNADZE, Eduard Amvrosis dze: Chairman of the Georgian Supreme Soviet (head of state) and former Soviet foreign minister; b. 1928. *Career:* he was a member of Komsomol, becoming its leader in 1957. In 1961 he joined the hierarchy of the Communist Party. He soon became a minister of the republican government and, in 1971, Georgian Party leader. He campaigned against corruption, but also gained a reputation for being harsh with dissidents and nationalists. In 1978 he became a candidate member of the CPSU Politburo and, in July 1985, a full member (the first Georgian to be so since the death of Stalin). At the same time, as a close colleague of Mikhail Gorbachev (q.v.), he was appointed Soviet foreign minister. His and Gorbachev's 'new thinking' in foreign policy caused dramatic changes in international politics, but, in December 1990, he resigned, warning of the approach of 'dictatorship'. In 1991 he was a founder and leader of an all-Union democratic opposition party and was briefly Soviet foreign minister again at the end of the year. His political future was uncertain with the demise of the USSR in December, but, in March 1992 he was invited to return to Georgia by the new regime, to which he gave international respectability, and he became Chairman of a State Council. Despite increasing civil unrest, he arranged for elections to a new Supreme Soviet (legislature) and was himself elected its Chairman (head of state) in direct popular elections in October 1992. In 1993 his regime seemed in danger of disintegrating with the country, particularly after the fall of Sukhumi (which he had personally committed himself to defend) to Abkhazian rebel forces in September. However, by joining the Commonwealth of Independent States before the end of that year (thus securing Russian aid), despite nationalist opposition, and with the death of ex-President Zviad Gamsakhurdia (1939–93) on the last day of the year, by the beginning of 1994 his administration seemed more secure. *Address:* Georgian Supreme Soviet, Georgia, Tbilisi.

SHOKHIN, Aleksandr Nikolayevich: Russian Minister of the Economy. b. 1951. *Career:* he was appointed a Deputy Chairman of the Russian Government and Minister of Labour and Employment, under Boris Yeltsin (q.v.), in November 1991, and made responsible for the co-ordination of five ministries involved in social welfare. A centrist economist, who advocated a slow pace of reform, he was appointed Minister of the Economy in 1993. In the parliamentary elections held in

December that year he was elected to the State Duma, the lower chamber of the Federal Assembly, as a member of the democratic bloc, the Party of Russian Unity and Concord. *Address:* Ministry of the Economy, Russian Federation, 103009 Moscow, Okhotny ryad 6.

SHUMEYKO, Vladimir Filippovich: Russian economist, manager and politician; b. 10 February 1945, in Rostov-on-Don; m., with two d. *Education:* Rostov Polytechnic Institute. *Career:* he worked as foreman, engineer and chief engineer before being appointed director-general of the Krasnoyarsk Factory of Measuring Instruments, a post he held until 1991. In 1990–92 he was a People's Deputy of Russia and was elected Vice-Chairman of the Russian Supreme Soviet, as Ruslan Khasbulatov's (q.v.) deputy in 1991. A close ally of Boris Yeltsin (q.v.), he was appointed to the Russian Government in 1992 as first deputy premier. He was elected as an independent candidate to the Federation Council, the upper chamber of the Federal Assembly, in the legislative elections of December 1993. On 13 January 1993 the chamber elected him Chairman. On 8 February he was chosen as Chairman of the Council of the Commonwealth of Independent States Interparliamentary Assembly. *Address:* Federation Council, Russian Federation, Moscow, 26 Bolshaya Dmitrovka ul.

SHUSHKEVICH, Stanislau Stanislavavich: former Chairman of the Supreme Soviet (head of state) of Belarus; b. 1934, in Minsk. *Education:* he graduated in physics from Belarusian State University. *Career:* he was the son of a poet, who died in Stalin's camps. In 1969 he became a lecturer at the State University, and, later, doctor of sciences and professor. He is the author of several textbooks and a member of the Belarusian Academy of Sciences. Although he was a Communist Party member, he only became involved in politics after 1986, in response to the aftermath of the Chernobyl (Ukraine) nuclear accident. He was elected to the republican Supreme Soviet with the support of the opposition Belarusian Popular Front in March 1990. After his election as the First Deputy Chairman of the Supreme Soviet, he was revealed as a more cautious reformist than initially thought, and resigned from the Party only after the failure of the Moscow coup attempt in August 1991. However, he gained credit as a nationalist and a supporter of attempts to revive the Belarusian language. On 19 September 1991 he was elected to be the Belarusian head of state (Chairman of the Supreme Soviet). He was one of the original signatories of the Commonwealth of Independent States (CIS), which was based in Minsk. His refusal to sign the CIS Collective Security Treaty, on the grounds that its terms violated Belarusian neutrality and sovereignty, earned him the enmity of the pro-Russian, former Communist majority in the Supreme Soviet, although he survived a vote of 'no confidence' in the parliament in July 1993. However, in January 1994 he was dismissed by parliament, following allegations of misappropriating state funds. He denied the accusations, which appeared to be politically motivated. Crucially, he had lost the support of the opposition by signing the CIS military agreement, after the continuing insistence of the legislature. He remained widely trusted in the country and was likely to be a candidate in the presidential elections (scheduled for June 1994), as the candidate of the Association of Democratic Forces 'Spring 94'. *Address:* c/o Supreme Council of the Republic of Belarus, Belarus, 220016 Minsk, K. Marksa 38, Dom Urada.

SIGUA, Tengiz Ippolitovich: Georgian politician; b. 9 Nov. 1939. *Career:* an engineer and director of the Metallurgy Institute of the Georgian Academy of Sciences, he was a leading member of the Round Table-Free Georgia alliance, which won the 1990 elections. His nationalist sympathies were attested by his chairmanship of the All-Georgia Rusteveli Society. He was appointed head of government by Zviad Gamsakhurdia (1939–93), Chairman of the Supreme Soviet (later President) of Georgia, in November 1990. He resigned from the Government in August 1991, joining the opposition, which was soon involved in armed rebellion. By December there was civil war and Sigua was prominent in the coalition of opposition forces. At the beginning of January 1992 the opposition declared the President deposed, his office abolished and the parliament dissolved. Power was assumed by a Military Council, which appointed Sigua Prime Minister. He continued as premier under Eduard Shevardnadze's (q.v.) State Council and after the parliamentary elections of October. However, with the legislature's rejection of the budget in August 1993, Sigua and his Government resigned, although the new administration was not confirmed in office until September. *Address:* Georgian Supreme Soviet, Georgia, Tbilisi.

SILADŽIĆ, Haris: Prime Minister of Bosnia and Herzegovina. *Career:* he was appointed Bosnian Minister of Foreign Affairs on the creation of the Ministry in 1992. A close political ally of Izetbegović (q.v.), he was appointed premier following the dismissal of Mile Akmadžić. He subsequently represented the Bosnian Government at a series of peace negotiations, including the talks in Washington, DC (USA), in February–March 1994, where a Croat–Muslim federation was agreed. *Address:* Office of the Prime Minister, Bosnia and Herzegovina, 71000 Sarajevo, Vojvode Putnika 3.

SKUBISZEWSKI, Prof. Krzysztof: Polish politician; b. 8 October 1926, in Poznań. *Education:* he studied at Poznań University, at the University of Nancy (France) and at Harvard University (USA). *Career:* a lawyer by training, he was a staff member at Poznań University, 1948–73, and was then at the Polish Academy of Sciences, Warsaw. He taught at many universities in the West, as a visiting lecturer. He was appointed Minister of Foreign Affairs in 1989 and was considered popular, because of his efforts to maintain Polish independence and to promote good relations with Germany and the USSR and its successor states. His appointment was again confirmed for the new Government formed in December 1991 and he continued in the post under various prime ministers until May 1993, when a vote of 'no confidence' was passed in the Suchocka Government. *Address:* c/o Ministry of Foreign Affairs, 00-580 Warsaw, Poland, Al. Szucha 23.

ŠLEŽEVIČIUS, Adolfas: Prime Minister of Lithuania. *Career:* a member of the Lithuanian Democratic Labour Party (LDLP—formerly the Communist Party of Lithuania) he was appointed head of a new administration in March 1993 by President Brazauskas (q.v.), also a member of the LDLP. This party had secured a significant majority in the elections to the Lithuanian parliament (Seimas) at the end of 1992 by promising vast improvements in the Lithuanian economy, particularly the agricultural sector. As premier he was forced to fulfil the LDLP's commitments to the electorate, while implementing the austerity measures imposed by the West as a condition for financial aid. Despite a deterioration in the economy throughout 1993, support for his Government remained relatively solid. *Address:* Office of the Prime Minister, Gedimino 11, Vilnius 2039, Lithuania.

SNEGUR, Mircea Ion: President of Moldova; b. 1939. *Career:* an agronomist by profession, he became a Communist official in the 1980s, but was also a nationalist, strongly supported by the Popular Front of Moldova. He was elected the republican leader, Chairman of the Presidium of the Supreme Soviet, in July 1989, and re-elected, as Chairman of the Supreme Soviet, in April 1990. In September he was elected unopposed to the new post of executive President and, in the first popular presidential elections, held in December 1991, Snegur, the sole candidate, won more than 98% of the votes cast and was therefore re-elected to the post. He advocated the sovereignty and economic independence of Moldova, but repudiated any unification with Romania, particularly in attempting to allay the fears of the secessionist Transdnestrians and Gagauz. In 1993 direct negotiations were opened with the Transdnestrian separatist leadership. He was in favour of full membership of the Commonwealth of Independent States (CIS) and continued to attend meetings of CIS leaders, despite parliament's failure to ratify Moldova's membership in August 1993. This anomaly was likely to be resolved following the electoral victory of his close political associate Petru Lucinschi's (q.v.) Agrarian Democratic Party in February 1994. *Address:* Office of the President, Moldova, Chişinău.

SOBCHAK, Anatoly Aleksandrovich: Russian politician; b. 1937, in Leningrad (now St Petersburg). *Education:* graduated as a lawyer from Leningrad University. *Career:* a former law professor, in 1989 he was elected as a radical People's Deputy to the Soviet parliament. His intellect and political style gained him one of the most formidable reputations among the reformists in the Supreme Soviet of the USSR. He was a founder member of the Inter-Regional Group of Soviet deputies and a prominent member of the democratic movement. In May 1990 he was elected head of the Leningrad City Soviet or Council (mayor); in 1991 a referendum in the city endorsed a proposal, which he supported, to change the name from Leningrad back to St Petersburg. During the coup attempt of August 1991 he was prominent in rallying his city against the putschists. Late in 1992 he succeeded in persuading the Russian central authorities that St Petersburg City (like Moscow) should be granted the status of a Federal City and be an equal partner in the Russian Federation. He subsequently signed the Federation Treaty. *Address:* St Petersburg City Council, Russian Federation, St Petersburg.

SOLIKH, Muhammad: Uzbekistan politician. *Career:* he was a writer and former deputy of the Supreme Soviet. Having been a founding member of the opposition movement, Birlik (Unity), in 1989, he left following disagreements with other members and in 1990 established the democratic party, Erk (Freedom), of which he became the Chairman. As the only opponent to Islam Karimov (q.v.) in the presidential elections held in December 1991, he obtained 12% of the votes cast. Solikh was one of a number of opposition leaders prevented from attending a human rights conference held in Bishkek (Kyrgyzstan), in December 1992. In April 1993 he was arrested and interrogated by the Ministry of Internal Affairs about a history of his party published in Turkey. Solikh was also instructed to remain in Tashkent and charged with involvement in a plot to establish an alternative legislature, or Melli Majlis. However, he left Uzbekistan in May–June, shortly before the Melli Majlis trial began. *Address:* n/a (the Erk party was twice deprived of its headquarters during 1993).

SPIROIU, Lt-Gen. Constantin Nicolae: Romanian politician; b. 6 July 1936, in Bucharest. *Career:* a career officer, he joined the National Salvation Front at the time of the 1989 Revolution, and was appointed as Minister of National Defence in June 1990. He remained at that post in successive Governments until 6 March 1994, when he was appointed as the national representative to the North Atlantic Treaty Organisation (NATO) in Brussels (Belgium), where he was responsible for ensuring Romania's compliance with the requirements of the 'Partnership for Peace'. *Address:* c/o Ministry of Foreign Affairs, Romania, 71274 Bucharest, Al. Modrogan 14.

STANKEVICH, Sergey Borisovich: Russian politician and historian; b. 1954, in Moscow district. *Education:* he was educated at the Lenin Pedagogical Institute, Moscow. *Career:* before entering politics he was a senior researcher at the Institute of World History, in Moscow, where he studied foreign political systems and parliaments. In 1989 he was elected to the Congress of People's Deputies and to the Supreme Soviet, where he was to become co-chairman of the radical Inter-Regional Group of deputies. He made himself known in the Supreme Soviet for his reformist views and for his criticism of President Mikhail Gorbachev's (q.v.) increasing powers. In March 1990 he was elected to the Moscow City Soviet (Council) and was quickly elevated to the office of deputy mayor, a post which he held until the suspension of the City Soviet by President Boris Yeltsin (q.v.) on 7 October 1993. He left the CPSU at the Congress of July 1990, together with Yeltsin. He became a leading member of the Democratic Russia coalition and an adviser to President Yeltsin. In December 1993 he was elected, as a member of the Party of Russian Unity and Concord electoral association, to the State Duma. *Address:* State Duma, Russian Federation, Moscow, Novy Arbat 36.

STOLOJAN, Theodor: Romanian economist and politician and former premier; b. 24 Oct. 1943, in Tîrgoviste; m., with two c. *Education:* graduate (1966) and doctor (1980) of the Bucharest Institute of Economics. *Career:* he worked as an economist in the food industry and then, for almost 20 years, in the state administration. After the Revolution of December 1989 he was appointed First Deputy Minister of Finance. He remained a financial minister under Petre Roman (q.v.) until April 1991, when he resigned, reportedly because he considered that economic reform was being implemented too slowly. Between May and October he was President of the National Agency for Privatization. On 3 October 1991 President Iliescu (q.v.) designated him for the office of Prime Minister and he formed a coalition Government, which was supported by the National Salvation Front (NSF). In November 1992, however, following legislative elections in which the NSF performed poorly, he was dismissed by President Iliescu and a new Government was formed. He was subsequently an economist with the International Bank for Reconstruction and Development (IBRD—World Bank) in the USA. *Address:* c/o IBRD, 1818 H St, NW, Washington, DC 20433, USA.

STRŠKÝ, Jan: Czech politician and former federal premier. *Career:* previously a Deputy Prime Minister of the Czech Republic, he was appointed as the head of a transitional federal Government in July 1992. His premiership ended with the dissolution of the Czech and Slovak Federative Republic on 1 January 1993. He was subsequently appointed Minister of Transport of the Czech Republic. *Address:* Ministry of Transport, Nábř. L. Svobody 12, 125 11 Prague 1, Czech Republic.

STRUZIK, Adam: Marshal (speaker) of the Polish Senat; b. 1957. *Career:* a physician who ran a hospital in Płoc , he was elected Marshal (speaker) of the Senat (Senate—the upper chamber of the National Assembly) on 15 October 1993. He was a member of Solidarity and the Polish Peasant Party. *Address:* Senat, Warsaw, Poland.

SULEYMENOV, Olzhas: Kazakh politician, environmentalist and poet. *Career:* a noted poet, he effectively founded a mass, organized environmental movement in Kazakhstan with an unexpected and unheralded speech on republican television in 1989. His Nevada-Semipalatinsk movement was opposed to the testing of nuclear weapons at the Semipalatinsk test site (its US counterpart was in Nevada—hence the name of the organization) and became a rallying force for ethnic Kazakhs particularly. Nevada-Semipalatinsk was never truly an opposition movement and, indeed, eventually became a Party cause, once its popularity was apparent. In 1990 and 1991 President Nursultan Nazarbayev (q.v.) urged the cessation of nuclear tests and, after August 1991, was able to implement a ban. This removed much of the movement's focus and in the early years of independence it laboured under charges of corruption and with problems of internal strife. Nevertheless, it had provided Suleymenov with the platform for his formation of the People's Congress of Kazakhstan (NKK) in 1991. This was a centrist popular front, which began by enjoying Nazarbayev's endorsement, but proved too much Suleymenov's creation to become the main official party. In the March 1994 elections, Suleymenov won one of the party's nine seats in the Supreme Kenges, where it was the third largest single group. *Address:* Office of the Supreme Kenges, Kazakhstan, 480091 Almaty, Dom pravitelstva.

SULTANOV, Kuanysh: Kazakh politician. *Career:* he was a member of the Communist Party, but only joined the Government after independence, when, in 1992, he was appointed Minister of the Press and Mass Information. He was a trusted supporter of President Nursultan Nazarbayev (q.v.) and a member of the same kinship group, the Great Horde. On 9 October 1993, as a mark of presidential endorsement for the new People's Unity movement, he was elected its Chairman. By now a deputy premier and presidential adviser, his association with the movement helped ensure that it became the main pro-government party in the elections of 7 March 1994. Sultanov was one of the 30 deputies elected, although as a result of his election as a legislator, he had to give up his government posts, of which he was relieved on 18 March. *Address:* Office of the Supreme Kenges, Kazakhstan, 480091 Almaty, Dom pravitelstva.

SWIATEK, Archbishop Kazimierz: Roman Catholic Archbishop of Minsk and Mogilev; b. 21 October 1914. *Education:*

he graduated from the Higher Theological Seminary in Pinsk, in 1939. *Career:* he was elevated to the rank of metropolitan-archbishop in January 1992. He was supporter of the revival of the Belarusian language and favoured its introduction into religious services. He prohibited the display of Polish symbols in Belarus's Roman Catholic churches. As well as being Archbishop of Minsk and Mogilev, he was also apostolic administrator of the Pinsk diocese and head of Belarus's Roman Catholics. *Address:* Archdiocese of Minsk and Mogilev, Belarus, 231011 Grodno, Krasnopartizanskaya 1, kv. 2.

SZABAD, Dr György: President of the Hungarian National Assembly (parliamentary speaker); b. Aug. 1924, in Arad, Romania; ethnic Hungarian; m., with one d. *Education:* studied at the Loránd Eötvös University, Budapest. *Career:* an historian, he worked in a forced labour camp (1944) before returning to an academic career. He became a professor in 1970, his career having been impeded by his involvement in the 1956 Uprising. In 1989 he was a founding member of the Hungarian Democratic Forum and was elected to be President (speaker) of the National Assembly in April 1990. *Address:* National Assembly, Hungary, 1055 Budapest, Kossuth Lájos tér. 1–3.

TEOCTIST, His Holiness Patriarch: Head of the Romanian Orthodox Church, Patriarch of the Metropolitan of Muntnia and Dobrogea and Archbishop of Bucharest; b. 1915. *Career:* born Teoctist Arăpaşu, he was made Bishop of the Romanian Missionary Diocese in the USA, in 1963, but failed to attain a residency permit. In March 1973 he was made Archbishop of Craiova, Metropolitan of Oltenia-Craiova, and later Metropolitan of Moldavia and Suceava. In October 1977 he was appointed Archbishop of Iaşi. In 1986 he was elected Patriarch of the Romanian Orthodox Church. After the Revolution of December 1989 he offered his resignation, but any likely successor was considered as tainted by association with the previous regime as he was, and he was reinstated. *Address:* Holy Synod, Romania, 70666 Bucharest, Str. Antim 29.

TER-PETROSYAN, Levon Akopovich: President of Armenia; b. 9 Jan. 1945. *Career:* he worked at the Armenian Institute of Literature in the mid-1970s and at the Matenadazan Archive intermittently from 1978 to 1990. A radical nationalist, he was a member of the Karabakh Committee and was in prison, December 1988–May 1989. He was leader of the Armenian Pan-national Movement and, in August 1990, was elected Chairman of the Supreme Soviet (*de facto* head of state). He was confirmed in office by an overwhelming victory in direct elections for the post of executive President of the Republic, in October 1991. The popularity of his regime decreased gradually over the following years, as a result of the protracted civil war in Armenia and consequent economic conditions. One major problem in 1992–93 was the conflict between pragmatic Armenians like Ter-Petrosyan himself, who favoured the development of closer links with Turkey, and more extreme, nationalist groups, such as the Union for National Self-determination and the Armenian Revolutionary Federation (Dashnaktsutyun), which were strongly opposed to such links. The radical nationalists enjoyed close links with the Armenian diaspora, the financial support of which was vital to the Armenian state. *Address:* Office of the President of the Republic, Armenia, Yerevan.

TERESHCHENKO, Sergey Aleksandrovich: Prime Minister of Kazakhstan; b. 30 March 1951, in Chimkent (Shymkent) region; ethnic Ukrainian. *Education* Almaty Institute of Agriculture. *Career:* he became involved in the Party and state apparatus of his native Chimkent region from 1986. In 1989 he was appointed First Deputy Chairman of the Kazakh Council of Ministers, at the time of the accession to power of Nursultan Nazarbayev (q.v.). In 1990 Tereshchenko returned to Chimkent as head of the regional administration, but he was reappointed to republican government in the following year. Briefly Vice-President, he became Chairman of the Council of Ministers (Prime Minister). Like President Nazarbayev, of whom he was one of the principal supporters, he had resigned his Party membership following the attempted coup in Moscow in August 1991. At the beginning of 1994 he remained the highest-ranking ethnic Slav in Kazakhstan and his support was important to Nazarbayev for that reason alone. *Address:* Office of the Cabinet of Ministers, Kazakhstan, 480091 Almaty, Respubliki 4.

TŐKES, László: Romanian religious leader; b. 1 April 1952, in Transylvania; ethnic Hungarian. *Education:* he studied at the Protestant Theological Institute in Cluj. *Career:* the son of a minister in the Calvinist Reformed Church, he too became a pastor. He was a vociferous critic of the Ceauşescu regime, and championed the rights of the ethnic Hungarian minority and human rights generally. It was the authorities' attempt to arrest him that was the catalyst for the December Revolution of 1989. He was subsequently made Bishop of Oradea for the Reformed Church. Although he was appointed as a member of the Provisional National Unity Council, he became increasingly critical of the ruling National Salvation Front. By January 1992, however, there was serious concern for his life, following a series of death threats. He was Honorary President of the Hungarian Democratic Union of Romania, a party which supported the rights of Hungarians in Romania. *Address:* Romania, 3700 Oradea, Str. Craiovei 1.

TOLGYESSY, Peter: Hungarian politician; b. 1956. *Career:* a lawyer who specialized in constitutional law, he had a major role in the round-table negotiations, in 1989. On 24 November 1991 he was elected Chairman of the Alliance of Free Democrats, the main opposition party, in succession to János Kis. *Address:* Alliance of Free Democrats, Hungary, 1051 Budapest, Mérleg u. 5.

TÖRGYÁN, Dr József: Hungarian politician. *Career:* Chairman of the Independent Smallholders' and Peasants' Party (ISP), the third most successful party in the general election of March–April 1990 and a member of the ruling coalition. *Address:* FKgP, Hungary, 1056 Budapest, Belgrád rkp. 24.

TOŠOVSKÝ, Josef: Governor of the Czech National Bank; b. 28 Sept. 1950, in Náchod. *Education:* he studied at the School of Economics in Prague. *Career:* having worked for the State Bank of Czechoslovakia in various capacities since 1973, he was appointed director of the reorganized bank in 1990. He was also Chief Economist and, briefly, Deputy Director of Živnobanka in London, United Kingdom, during the 1980s. He became Governor of the Czech National Bank when it was established in 1993. *Address:* Czech National Bank, Na příkopě 28, 110 03 Prague 1, Czech Republic.

TRAVKIN, Nikolay Ilyich: Russian politician; b. 19 March 1946, in Novo-Nikolskoye, Moscow obl. *Education:* Kolomna Pedagogical Institute. *Career:* having joined the Communist Party of the Soviet Union in 1970, he became a member of the Democratic Russia movement in 1988. He was elected as a People's Deputy of Russia in 1989, and in 1990 he founded the Democratic Party of Russia, a liberal-conservative party which, after the disintegration of the USSR, advocated a centralized Russian state and stressed the importance of strengthening the structures of the Commonwealth of Independent States. He was elected to the State Duma in December 1993, where his party won a total of 15 seats. *Address:* Democratic Party of Russia, Russian Federation, Moscow, ul. Shabolovka 8.

TUDJMAN, Dr Franjo: President of Croatia; b. 14 May 1922, in Veliko Trgovišće, northern Croatia. *Education:* he studied at the Higher Military Academy in Belgrade, after the Second World War, and, in 1965, he gained a doctorate in history, at the University of Zagreb. *Career:* he joined Tito's Partisans, in 1941, and, after attending the military academy, he worked in the Ministry of Defence and for the Jugoslavenska Narodna Armija (JNA—Yugoslav People's Army). He attained the rank of major-general and then left the military to pursue his academic interests in history. He was a professor of history at Zagreb University, from 1963, but was dismissed for his nationalist tendencies, in 1967, and expelled from the League of Communists. An adherent of the *Maspok* movement, he was imprisoned in 1972–74. His dissident activities earned him a prison sentence again, in 1981–84. In 1989 he founded the Croatian Democratic Union (CDU), which won the elections to the Croatian Assembly in 1990. On 30 May the Assembly elected him President of Croatia. He led Croatia towards independence, the moves towards which were formally begun on 25 June 1991, and in the civil war which began that year. Sometimes accused of being too right-wing, he was under pressure from both the moderates and the extreme nationalists, with a policy dependent upon foreign support, which was slow in being realized. He was re-elected to the presidency on 2 August 1992, winning a total of 56% of the votes cast. Subsequently, however, his administration came under increasing criticism by his political opponents and the international community. This was mainly a result of his policy of intervention, in support of the Bosnian Croats, in the civil war in neighbouring Bosnia and Herzegovina. His regime was also accused of being intolerant of opposition and criticism, but, in April 1994, following his support of the Croat–Bosniak federation in neighbouring Bosnia and Herzegovina, he signed a 'permanent' cease-fire with the secessionist Serbs of Krajina. *Address:* Office of the President, Croatia, 41000 Zagreb, Banski Dvori.

TURAJONZODA, Hajji Akbar: Tajikistan religious and opposition leader; b. in Orjonikidzeabad, near Dushanbe. *Education:* his religious training was done in Uzbekistan, at the *madrassa* in Bukhara, then at the Tashkent centre of official Central Asian Islam, before he went to Jordan, the University of Amman. *Career:* he was appointed the Chief Kazi of Tajikistan at the beginning of 1990. He immediately gained some prominence with his appeals for reconciliation following the February 1990 riots in Dushanbe. He also began the process of bringing 'official' Islam closer to the parallel Muslim mullahs blamed for the riots. He soon gained the confidence of many of the Sufi spiritualists, who were fiercely opposed to Communism and were inspired by the Afghan *mujahidin*. However, he initially concentrated on orthodox channels and was elected to the republican Supreme Soviet (legislature) later in 1990. He did succeed in having the major Muslim feast days adopted as public holidays, but failed in his enthusiastic campaigns for such measures as a change in the weekly day off work or Islamic regulations to be introduced into slaughter houses. This led him to align himself with the opposition, although he was careful to reject 'Islamic fundamentalism' or the imposition of any policy against the popular will. The extent of his involvement is indicated by the fact that the headquarters of the united opposition (principally the Islamic Renaissance Party and the Democratic Party of Tajikistan) was based in the kaziate buildings. Previously stating that the Chief Kazi should be apolitical, the fierce opposition to him in the Supreme Soviet and his role as the focus of increasing anticlericalism in the establishment, led him to his position as effective head of the Islamic-democratic coalition. The authorities' attitude was reflected in the opposition of his technical subordinates in the official hierarchy: the mullah of Kulyab (Fatkhullo Sharifov, later appointed Chief Mufti of Tajikistan) rejected his authority as early as 1990; the mullah of Leninabad in 1992. Following the Communist reaction to Islamic-democratic gains and the capture of Dushanbe in December 1992 by militias loyal to the new, Communist Government, Turajonzoda was obliged to flee into exile in Afghanistan. There he was believed to be organizing the resistance and his continued prominence was indicated by continuing official vilification of him. The new Government replaced him as religious leader of Tajikistan on 12 February 1993, by abolishing the kaziate and instituting an independent muftiate. In early 1994 it was believed that Turajonzoda would head the opposition delegation to negotiations with the Government, which had been agreed after Russian mediation. *Address:* c/o Government of Afghanistan, Shar Rahi Sederat, Kabul, Afghanistan.

UHDE, Milan: Chairman of the Czech Chamber of Deputies; b. 28 July 1936, in Brno. *Education:* he studied at Masaryk University in Brno. *Career:* having previously been a literary editor and a reader in the Faculty of Philosophy at Masasyk University, he was also a noted journalist and playwright. He was Minister of Culture in the Czech Government from 1990 to 1992, Chairman of the Czech National Council from June 1992 and, after the Czech Republic gained independence, he became Chairman of the Chamber of Deputies, the lower house of the new parliament. He was a member of the Civic Democratic Party. *Address:* Chamber of Deputies, Prague, Czech Republic.

ULMANIS, Guntis: President of Latvia; b. 13 September 1939, in Rīga. *Education:* University of Latvia. *Career:* having been deported to Siberia in 1941, his family was only allowed to return to Latvia in 1946. Although he joined the Latvian Communist Party in 1965, he did so merely to enable himself to find employment as an economist. In spite of his party membership, however, Soviet resentment of his family background (his great-uncle, Kārlis Ulmanis, was President of an independent Latvia immediately before the Soviet occupation of 1940) ensured that he did not advance far in his profession. He was a member of the board of the Bank of Latvia for a time and, in 1992, he joined the Latvian Farmers' Union (a nationalist party established in 1917 and refounded in 1990) and soon became an important figure in the party. He was elected President by the Saeima on 7 July 1993, after a third round of balloting in which he was the only candidate. He was inaugurated the following day, replacing the parliamentary speaker, Anatolijs Gorbunovs (q.v.) as head of state, according to the provisions of the new Constitution. *Address:* Office of the President, Rīga, Latvia.

UTAH, Abdullah: Uzbekistan politician. *Career:* he was leader of the Islamic Renaissance Party (originally an all-Union party) in Uzbekistan. It held a founding congress in Tashkent in January 1991, but was subsequently declared outlawed. It was, however, believed to be one of the more significant opposition groups in the country. Utah was reportedly imprisoned with 20 other members of his party on 6 December 1992, but in June 1993 the Uzbek authorities denied any knowledge of his location. In early 1994 he was still missing.

VACAROIU, Nicolae: Prime Minister of Romania; b. 5 Dec. 1943, in Bolgrad, Ukraine. *Education:* he studied at Bucharest Academy of Economic Studies. *Career:* an economist nominally unaffiliated to any political party, he was appointed Deputy Minister of National Economy in 1990. In November 1992 he formed a Council of Ministers comprising equal numbers of independents and members of the Democratic National Salvation Front (DNSF—renamed the Party of Social Democracy of Romania in 1993). *Address:* Office of the Prime Minister, Romania, 71201 Bucharest, Piața Victoriei 1.

VALENTIĆ, Nikica: Prime Minister of Croatia. *Career:* a businessman, he was formerly head of INA, a state petroleum company in Croatia. In March 1993 he was appointed Prime Minister of Croatia, following the resignation of Hrvoje Sarinić, whose administration had been discredited by financial scandals and a worsening economic situation. *Address:* Government of the Republic of Croatia, Croatia, 41000 Zagreb, Radićev trg 7.

VAZGEN I, His Holiness Supreme Patriarch: Catholicos of All Armenians, Head of the Armenian Apostolic Church; b. 1908, in Romania. *Career:* born L. K. Baljian, he was ordained a priest in Romania and later appointed head of the Armenian Church in Romania and Bulgaria. He was elected Catholicos of All Armenia in 1955. From the mid-1980s he became active in attempting to find a peaceful solution to the dispute over Nagorny Karabakh. *Address:* Residence of the Catholicos of Armenia, Armenia, Echmiadzin.

VIDENOV, Zhan: Bulgarian politician; b. 1959; m. *Education:* graduate of the Moscow Institute of International Relations (speaks Russian, English and Arabic). *Career:* he began his Communist Party career as a Young Communist and worked as a specialist in foreign economic relations. A known conservative of the Bulgarian Socialist Party (BSP—former Communists), he was first elected as a deputy in June 1990, in Plovdiv city. In December 1991 he was elected Chairman of the Supreme Council (leader) of the BSP, as the favoured successor of Aleksandur Lilov. He continued to play an active role in Bulgarian politics, in his capacity as leader of the BSP, which emerged as the second largest party in the National Assembly (with a total of 106 seats), following the parliamentary elections of October 1991. The BSP supported the coalition Government of Lyuben Berov (q.v.), which was formed in December 1992, and continued to do so through 1993. *Address:* Bulgaria, 1000 Sofia, pl. Aleksandur Battenberg.

VULCHEV, Prof. Todor: Pres. of the National Bank of Bulgaria; b. 28 October 1922; m., with two c. *Education:* graduated from the National and World Economy Institute of Sofia University. *Career:* he worked mainly at the Bulgarian Academy of Sciences, until being appointed head of the National Bank in 1990. *Address:* Bulgaria, 1000 Sofia, pl. Aleksandur Battenberg 2.

WAŁĘSA, Lech: President of Poland; b. 29 September 1943, in Popowo, in the Włocławek district; m. (Danuta Wałęsa, 1969), with four s. and four d. *Career:* worked as an electrician for a collective farm, fulfilling his two years military service in 1963–65. In 1967 he began work at the Lenin Shipyard, in Gdańsk. By December 1970 he was the head of a strike committee; six years later he was dismissed for his protests about working conditions, voiced at a union meeting. Having then found work repairing machinery, in 1979 he again lost his job, for commemorating the 1970 strike. In August 1980 he joined strikers at the Lenin Shipyard and became head of their 'inter-factory' committee. His success in negotiations with the Government led to the signing of the 'Gdańsk accords', which permitted free trade unions and the right to strike. By 1981 Wałęsa was Chairman of the Solidarity union and movement, which was banned under the martial law introduced in December. He was arrested and interned, in 1981–82, but was involved in subsequent negotiations with the Government, in 1988, which resulted in the lifting of the ban on Solidarity and the prospect of democratic reform. He headed the coalition which defeated Communist rule in the legislative elections of 1989, and was elected President in December 1990. He resigned as leader of Solidarity. As President he acquired a reputation for attempting to dominate government policy, which was more popular when there was still a Communist-dominated parliament. Throughout the early 1990s he became involved in disputes with succeeding Governments over his presidential role. In 1993 these conflicts increased and Wałęsa was frequently accused of authoritarianism, exacerbated by his creation of presidential councils which were involved in policy-making decisions. Wałęsa formed the Non-Party Bloc for Political Reform which participated in the 1993 legislative elections. However, these were won by former Communist and other left-wing parties and, at the beginning of 1994, President Wałęsa was again involved in disagreements with parliament over the extent of his powers. *Address:* Office of the President, Warsaw, Poland, Belvedere Palace.

WEISS, Peter: Slovak politician. *Career:* First Deputy Chairman of the National Council of Slovakia and Chairman of the Party of the Democratic Left (PDL). The PDL, founded in 1991 to replace the Communist Party of Slovakia, was the second most successful party in the Slovak legislative elections of June 1992. He was an important opposition leader until March 1994, when his party was included in the new coalition formed by Jozef Moravčík (q.v.). *Address:* Party of the Democratic Left, Gundulovičova 12, 816 10 Bratislava, Slovakia.

YAVLINSKY, Grigory Alekseyevich: Russian economist and politician; b. 10 April 1952, in Lvov, Ukraine; m., with two s. *Education:* Plekhanov Institute of National Economics. *Career:* he originally worked as an electrician and became involved in economics in the early 1980s. He was the author of the radical '500-day programme' of economic reform, introduced on 3 September 1990, and served as deputy premier in June–November 1990. In 1991 he worked as economic advisor to the Russian Government and to the Soviet leader, Mikhail Gorbachev (q.v.). In December that year he became a member of the Economic Council of the President of Kazakhstan. In 1993 he founded a Russian electoral bloc with Yury Boldyrev and Vladimir Lukin, a liberal alliance, which campaigned for more 'conceptual reform' in the Russian parliament and won a total of 22 seats in the State Duma in December. He was himself elected as a parliamentary deputy. At this time he also announced his intention to stand in the presidential elections, and was perceived by many democrats as a strong liberal alternative to President Boris Yeltsin (q.v.). *Address:* State Duma, Russian Federation, Moscow, Novy Arbat 36.

YELTSIN, Boris Nikolayevich: President of the Russian Federation; b. 1 Feb. 1931, in Sverdlovsk (now Yekaterinburg). *Education:* he graduated from the Urals Polytechnic Institute. *Career:* after several years spent working for construction companies, he began full-time Communist Party work in 1968. He gained a reputation outside Sverdlovsk Oblast (region), where he was appointed First Secretary in 1976. When Mikhail Gorbachev (q.v.) came to power, in 1985, he was appointed First Secretary of the Moscow Party Committee. He became outspoken in his commitment to reform and an end to corruption in the Party. His criticism of the slow pace of reform led, in 1987, to his dismissal from his post and from the Politburo and a demotion to a post in the State Construction Committee. In 1989, however, he stood in the elections to the Congress of People's Deputies and won over 90% of the vote in the Moscow constituency. He continued to demand more radical reforms and the dismissal of conservative Communists, such as Yegor Ligachev. In 1990 he was elected to the Russian Supreme Soviet and, by a narrow margin, was elected its Chairman. In early 1991 he was granted executive powers by the Supreme Soviet, pending direct elections to an executive presidency of the Russian Federation in June. He won these elections with a convincing mandate and further secured his authority by his leadership against the coup attempt of August 1991. He was an original signatory of the Minsk Agreement of December, which established the Commonwealth of Independent States and ensured the demise of the USSR. As President of a newly independent Russian Federation (the recognized successor state to the USSR), he introduced a radical economic reform programme (termed 'shock therapy') under Yegor Gaidar (q.v.). This policy alienated both extremists and the centre, who continued to hinder the implementation of this and other reforms in parliament. On 20 March 1993, his emergency powers having been suspended by parliament, he introduced a period of emergency rule and scheduled a referendum of confidence for 25 April, in which he gained 57.4% of the votes cast. His position appeared to be further strengthened after his suppression of the rebellion by parliament of September–October 1993 and the endorsement of a new Constitution, which provided for a more powerful presidency, by 58.4% of participants in a nation-wide plebiscite on 12 December. However, the elections to the new legislature, held on the same day, resulted in a far larger victory for the extreme right-wing Liberal Democratic Party than anticipated, and many fewer seats being won by his potential supporters in parliament, Russia's Choice. The anti-reform bloc in the lower chamber of parliament, the State Duma, was large enough to continue to hinder reforms, and to challenge his authority, as was demonstrated by the amnesty granted to his political enemies in February 1994. *Address:* Office of the President, Russian Federation, Moscow, Kremlin.

YULDASHEV, Shavkat Mukhitdinovich: Chairman of the Supreme Soviet (parliamentary speaker) of Uzbekistan; b. 20 Sept. 1943, in Namangan. *Education:* he studied at the Moscow Energy Institute. *Career:* he began working as an engineer at the Institute of Electronics of the Uzbek Academy of Sciences in 1968 and had become its Director by 1974. He later became an official of the Communist Party of the Soviet Union and was Chairman of the Central Controlling Committee of the Communist Party of Uzbekistan in 1990–91. He became Chairman of the Supreme Soviet of Uzbekistan in June 1991. It was to be replaced by a new legislative body, the Oly Majlis, following elections scheduled for 1994. *Address:* Office of the Supreme Soviet, Uzbekistan, 700008 Tashkent, Government House.

ZHELEV, Dr Zheliu: President of Bulgaria; b. 3 March 1935, in Vesselinovo village, Shumen district; m., with two c. *Education:* doctorate in philosophy from the University of Sofia. *Career:* in 1965 he was expelled from the Communist Party for an anti-Leninist doctoral thesis (the thesis was not accepted until 1975), after which he was unemployed until 1972, when he began work as a sociologist. He achieved further notoriety in 1982, when his book, *Fascism,* on the nature of totalitarianism, was banned. In the late 1980s, as a prominent dissident, he was one of the founders of the Club for the Support of *Glasnost* and *Perestroika*. In December 1989 he became leader of the opposition coalition, the Union of Democratic Forces (UDF). He resigned form this post in August 1990, when he was elected President of the Republic by parliament. In January 1992 he became the first democratically elected head of state, after a second round of voting in nationwide presidential elections. His relationship with the UDF deteriorated in 1992 and 1993: in August 1992 he publicly voiced his serious disagreement over several issues with the UDF-backed premier, Filip Dimitrov (q.v.), who left office in December. Furthermore, in mid-1993 participants in mass demonstrations, organized by the UDF, demanded his resignation. The political crisis intensified in July, when his deputy, Vice-President Blaga Dimitrova, resigned. During the conflict in the former Yugoslavia he persistently referred to the economic damage suffered by Bulgaria as a result of the sanctions imposed on Serbia and Montenegro (Yugoslavia) and stressed the need for a solution to the crisis. *Address:* Bulgaria, 1000 Sofia, 2 Blvd Dondukov.

ZHIRINOVSKY, Vladimir Volfovich: Russian politician; b. 25 April 1946, in Almaty, Kazakhstan; m., with two s. *Education:* Moscow State University. *Career:* until 1983 he worked with the Ministry of Defence of the USSR, with the General Staff of the Transcaucasian command and with the Soviet Society of Friendship and Cultural Relations. In 1983–89 he worked as a legal consultant to Mir Publications. In 1989 he founded the Liberal Democratic Party (LDP), an ultranationalist, neo-Fascist organization, of which he was Chairman. In the presidential elections of 12 June 1991, which were won by Boris Yeltsin (q.v.), he came third out of six candidates, winning over 6m. votes. He was described as a demagogue and an anti-Semite, although there were also numerous suggestions concerning his own Jewish background, including one, made in April 1994, that until the age of 18 years his surname was Edelshtein. However, his relentless campaigning before the elections to the Federal Assembly of December 1993 resulted in unexpectedly high gains for the LDP, particularly in the provinces. His political ideas, which included the annexation of the Baltic states, Afghanistan and parts of Alaska, Finland and Poland, provoked anger and suspicion in other countries. In Russia, however, his simplistic solutions to the nation's problems ensured him the support of a large section of the population, who were disenchanted with the deterioration in their standard of living and the decline of Russia's status in the international community. In April 1994, however, the Russian foreign minister, Andrey Kozyrev (q.v.), criticized the West and its media for satisfying Zhirinovsky's manipulation of publicity. A future presidential candidate, rather than a parliamentarian, at the beginning of 1994 his actions led to the dissociation from the LDP of four of its senior deputies. *Address:* State Duma, Russian Federation, Moscow, Novy Arbat 36.

ZYUGANOV, Gennady Andreyevich: Russian politician; b. 1944. *Career:* as Chairman of the Central Committee of the Communist Party of the Russian Federation, he was elected to the State Duma in December 1993, in which his party won a total of 48 seats. On 13 January 1994 representatives of the Communist Party in the State Duma formed a conservative parliamentary bloc with the Agrarian Party and the Democratic Party of Russia, which controlled 115 seats out of a total of 450 in the chamber. *Address:* State Duma, Russian Federation, Moscow, Novy Arbat 36.